The **Shelly Cashman** Series®

Technology for Success

Microsoft® 365® & Office®

First Edition

Concepts & Office Introductory

AF901357

Jennifer T. Campbell • Mark Ciampa
Barbara Clemens • Steven M. Freund
Mark Frydenberg • Ralph E. Hooper
Victoria Kaye • Lisa Ruffolo
Susan L. Sebok • Misty E. Vermaat
Jill West

Cengage

Australia • Brazil • Canada • Mexico • Singapore • United Kingdom • United States

Cengage

Technology For Success & The Shelly Cashman Series® Microsoft® 365® & Office® Introductory,
First Edition

Jennifer T. Campbell, Mark Ciampa, Barbara Clemens, Steven M. Freund, Mark Frydenberg, Ralph E. Hooper, Victoria Kaye, Lisa Ruffolo, Susan L. Sebok, Misty E. Vermaat, Jill West

SVP, Product Management: Cheryl Costantini

VP, Product Management & Marketing: Thais Alencar

Senior Product Director, Portfolio Product Management: Mark Santee

Portfolio Product Director: Rita Lombard

Senior Portfolio Product Manager: Amy Savino

Senior Product Assistant: Ciara Boynton

Learning Designer: Zenya Molnar

Senior Content Managers: Anne Orgren, Michelle Ruelos Cannistraci

Digital Project Manager: Jim Vaughey

Technical Editor: Mary-Terese Cozzola

Developmental Editor: Mary-Terese Cozzola, Barbara Clemens, Deb Kaufmann, Lyn Markowicz

Senior Director, Product Marketing: Danae April

Senior Marketing Manager: Mackenzie Paine

Portfolio Specialist: Matt Schiesl

Content Acquisition Analyst: Callum Panno

Production Service: Lumina Datamatics Ltd.

Senior Designer: Erin Griffin

Cover Image Source: shunli zhao/Moment/Getty Images

Copyright © 2025 Cengage Learning, Inc. ALL RIGHTS RESERVED.

WCN: 01-100-393

No part of this work covered by the copyright herein may be reproduced or distributed in any form or by any means, except as permitted by U.S. copyright law, without the prior written permission of the copyright owner.

Unless otherwise noted, all content is Copyright © Cengage Learning, Inc.

Mac Users: If you're working through this product using a Mac, some of the steps may vary. Additional information for Mac users is included with the Data files for this product.

Disclaimer: This text is intended for instructional purposes only; data is fictional and does not belong to any real persons or companies.

Disclaimer: The material in this text was written using Microsoft Windows 11 and Office 365 Professional Plus and was Quality Assurance tested before the publication date. As Microsoft continually updates the Windows operating system and Office 365, your software experience may vary slightly from what is presented in the printed text.

Windows, Access, Excel, and PowerPoint are registered trademarks of Microsoft Corporation. Microsoft and the Office logo are either registered trademarks or trademarks of Microsoft Corporation in the United States and/or other countries. This product is an independent publication and is neither affiliated with, nor authorized, sponsored, or approved by, Microsoft Corporation.

The names of all products mentioned herein are used for identification purposes only and may be trademarks or registered trademarks of their respective owners. Cengage Learning disclaims any affiliation, association, connection with, sponsorship, or endorsement by such owners.

Previous edition(s): © 2023, © 2020

For product information and technology assistance, contact us at **Cengage Customer & Sales Support, 1-800-354-9706 or support.cengage.com.**

For permission to use material from this text or product, submit all requests online at **www.copyright.com.**

Library of Congress Control Number: 2024921269

Student Edition ISBN: 978-0-357-88151-4
Loose-Leaf Edition ISBN: 978-0-357-88152-1
K12 Edition ISBN: 978-0-357-88153-8

Cengage
5191 Natorp Boulevard
Mason, OH 45040
USA

Cengage is a leading provider of customized learning solutions. Our employees reside in nearly 40 different countries and serve digital learners in 165 countries around the world. Find your local representative at **www.cengage.com.**

To learn more about Cengage platforms and services, register or access your online learning solution, or purchase materials for your course, visit **www.cengage.com.**

Notice to the Reader

Publisher does not warrant or guarantee any of the products described herein or perform any independent analysis in connection with any of the product information contained herein. Publisher does not assume, and expressly disclaims, any obligation to obtain and include information other than that provided to it by the manufacturer. The reader is expressly warned to consider and adopt all safety precautions that might be indicated by the activities described herein and to avoid all potential hazards. By following the instructions contained herein, the reader willingly assumes all risks in connection with such instructions. The publisher makes no representations or warranties of any kind, including but not limited to, the warranties of fitness for particular purpose or merchantability, nor are any such representations implied with respect to the material set forth herein, and the publisher takes no responsibility with respect to such material. The publisher shall not be liable for any special, consequential, or exemplary damages resulting, in whole or part, from the readers' use of, or reliance upon, this material.

Printed at CLDPC, USA, 01-25

Brief Contents

Contents

Word

PowerPoint

Module 1: Creating and Editing Presentations with Pictures .... PPT 1-1

Module 2: Enhancing Presentations with Shapes and SmartArt .... PPT 2-1

Module 3: Inserting WordArt, Charts, and Tables .... PPT 3-1

Excel

Access

Preface: Technology for Success and The Shelly Cashman Series® Collection: Microsoft® 365® & Office®, First Edition

About the Authors

Technology for Success

Jennifer T. Campbell has written and co-authored several leading technology texts, including *Technology for Success*; *Discovering Computers: Digital Technology, Data, and Devices*; *Discovering the Internet*; *Web Design: Introductory*; *Microsoft Expression Web Introductory Concepts and Techniques*; *Computer Literacy Basics: Microsoft Office 2007 Companion*; and *Microsoft Office Quick Reference Pocket Guide*. For almost 30 years, she has served integral roles in computer educational publishing as an editor, author, and marketing manager. She holds a B.A. in English from The College of William and Mary.

Jill West authors Cengage courses for CompTIA Cloud+, CompTIA Network+, Data Communications, the Shelly Cashman Series, and the popular *Technology for Success*. She has taught kindergarten through college and currently teaches computer technology courses at Georgia Northwestern Technical College. With degrees in psychology, education, and IT, Jill innovates at the crossroads of IT and education, specializing in designing courses for popular IT certifications, presenting at conferences on IT education, and mentoring lifelong student learners in IT. Jill also teaches edutainment AWS courses with ACI Learning (formerly ITProTV) and is an AWS Academy Accredited Educator. Jill and her husband, Mike, live in northwest Georgia with their four children.

Dr. Mark Ciampa is a Professor of Analytics and Information Systems and Program Director of the graduate Cybersecurity Data Analytics program in the Gordon Ford College of Business at Western Kentucky University in Bowling Green, Kentucky. Before this, he was an associate professor and served as the Director of Academic Computing at Volunteer State Community College in Gallatin, Tennessee, for 20 years. Dr. Ciampa has worked in the IT industry as a computer consultant for businesses, government agencies, and educational institutions. He has published over 25 articles in peer-reviewed journals and books. He is also the author of over 30 technology textbooks from Cengage, including *CompTIA Security+ Guide to Network Security Fundamentals, Eighth Edition*; *CompTIA CySA+ Guide to Cybersecurity Analyst, Third Edition*; *CWNA Guide to Wireless LANs, Third Edition*; *Guide to Wireless Communications*; *Security Awareness: Applying Practical Cybersecurity in Your World, Sixth Edition*; and *Networking BASICS*. Dr. Ciampa holds a PhD in technology management with a specialization in digital communication systems from Indiana State University and has certifications in security and healthcare.

Shelly Cashman Series

The Shelly Cashman Series® offers application-specific comprehensive print titles for Word®, Excel®, PowerPoint®, Access®, Publisher®, Outlook®, and Windows®. The modules (chapters) of the four main Microsoft® applications (Word®, Excel®, PowerPoint®, and Access®) are also offered together in each of three print titles organized by level: introductory, intermediate, and advanced. The MindTap Collection includes all of the preceding content, plus additional digital-only content for Teams®, the Mac operating system, and more.

Word: Misty E. Vermaat has more than 30 years of experience in the field of computer and information technology. In addition to consulting in the field, she was an Associate Professor at Purdue University Calumet, teaching or developing courses in Microsoft® Office, computer concepts, database management, systems analysis and design, and programming. Since 1990, she has led the development of the Shelly Cashman Series and has authored and co-authored numerous series textbooks, including many editions of Discovering Computers, Discovering Computers Fundamentals, Microsoft® Publisher®, and Microsoft® Word® books.

PowerPoint: Susan L. Sebok is a retired professor at South Suburban College in South Holland, Illinois, and is also a licensed attorney. Working with the leading Shelly Cashman Series® since 1993, she has co-authored several successful textbooks, including multiple versions of Discovering Computers and Microsoft® PowerPoint®. She holds both Master of Arts and Juris Doctor degrees.

Excel: Victoria Kaye brings her industry knowledge and instructor experience to Cengage Group for the Shelly Cashman Series. As an avid Excel user with Microsoft teaching experience ranging from secondary to undergraduate levels, she is thrilled to be part of the esteemed Shelly Cashman Excel Series legacy.

Dr. Mark Shellman is an instructor and Chair of the Information Technology Department at Gaston College in Dallas, North Carolina. Dr. Mark, as his students call him, prides himself on being student-centered and loves learning himself. His favorite subjects in the information technology realm include databases and programming languages. Dr. Mark has been teaching for more than 30 years and has co-authored several texts in the New Perspective series on Microsoft® Office 365 & Access®, along with a textbook on Structured Query Language.

Access: Jill West authors Cengage courses for CompTIA Cloud+, CompTIA Network+, Data Communications, Technology for Success, and the popular Shelly Cashman Series. She has taught kindergarten through college and currently teaches computer technology courses at Georgia Northwestern Technical College. Jill specializes in designing innovative, critical-thinking activities and building courses that teach popular IT certifications. She regularly presents at conferences and webinars on preparing for CompTIA certifications, teaching cloud computing and computer networking, and mentoring lifelong student learners in IT. She's a member of the 2019 inaugural cohort of Faculty Ambassadors for AWS Educate and is currently an AWS Academy Accredited Educator. Jill and her husband, Mike, live in northwest Georgia with their four children.

Windows 11: Steven M. Freund serves as a lead instructor of various Microsoft® Office, computer concepts, programming, and Internet technology courses throughout central Florida. An integral author for the successful Shelly Cashman Series since 2001, he has presented at the annual customer conference, the Shelly Cashman Series Institute, and other customer events. Freund has co-authored multiple editions of Discovering Computers, Mozilla Firefox, Windows® Internet Explorer, Windows® Office, and Dreamweaver books. In addition, he has written numerous successful instructor supplements. He attended the University of Central Florida.

Introduction

Technology for Success

People use technology dozens of times a day on their phones, computers, and other digital devices to keep in touch with friends and family, research and complete school assignments, shop, and entertain themselves. Even though we use technology every day, understanding how that technology works and how it can work for us will give students the edge they want as they pursue their education and careers. The concepts in this book help students become digitally literate and strong digital citizens who not only understand technological concepts but recognize the right ways to use technology.

Technology for Success: Computer Concepts 2e will explain the What, Why, and How of technology as it relates to everyday life so that students can unlock the door to success in the workplace, at home, and at school. It also provides guidance on how to safely use digital devices. *Technology for Success: Computer Concepts* will help students master the computer concepts they need to impress at their dream job interview in this age of digital transformation. With new and expanded coverage of cutting-edge technologies like cloud computing, e-commerce, databases, digital ethics, and artificial intelligence, students will be ready to put technology to work as they pursue their goals and live their lives.

The book assumes no prior computer experience and uses clear, familiar language and brief lessons in order to provide a solid foundation of computer concepts. The real-life applications prepare students to continue building their skills, in future courses and beyond.

Shelly Cashman Series

Shelly Cashman's trademark step-by-step, screen-by-screen, project-based approach encourages students to expand their understanding of Office applications through hands-on experimentation and critical thinking. Module learning objectives are mapped to Microsoft Office Specialist certification objectives, reinforcing the critical skills needed for success in college and career. Other Ways boxes help users identify alternate click paths to achieve a step, while BTW sidebars offer helpful hints as readers work through projects, enabling them to make the most of Microsoft Office tools. MindTap and updated SAM (Skills Assessment Manager) online resources are also available to guide additional study to maximize results.

Shelly Cashman prepares students for success in the real world by using current and relevant scenarios that apply to everyday life and careers. It also prepares students to take the Microsoft Office Specialist (MOS) exam, which they can leverage in their careers.

Shelly Cashman is designed for students at two- and four-year schools as well as in continuing education programs. Skill levels can range from experienced—for those with a foundational understanding from prior exposure to technology—to introductory—for those using a computer or technology device for the first time.

The Shelly Cashman Series® offers application-specific comprehensive print titles for Word®, Excel®, PowerPoint®, Access®, Publisher®, Outlook®, and Windows®. The modules (chapters) of the four main Microsoft® applications (Word®, Excel®, PowerPoint®, and Access®) are also offered together in each of three print titles organized by level: introductory, intermediate, and advanced. The MindTap Collection includes all of the preceding content, plus additional digital-only content for Teams®, the Mac operating system, and more.

Market research is conducted semi-annually with both current Cengage users and those who use other learning materials. The focus of the market research is to gain insights into the user experience and overall learner needs so we can continuously evolve our content to exceed user expectations. We survey hundreds of instructors to ensure we gather information from a large and varied demographic.

New to This Edition

Technology for Success

- At least half of the End-of-Module questions have been updated. In addition, the number of questions by type has been standardized across all modules. Each module includes 12 Review Questions (with two True/False and 10 Multiple Choice), four Discussion Questions, four Critical Thinking Questions, and one Apply Your Skills exercise, a new feature that maps to the introductory case scenario and includes questions relating to each Learning Objective.
- Instructor supplements have been updated to reflect content changes. The PowerPoint presentations now include metacognitive opportunities and interactive activities.

- Throughout the text, key terms and figures have been updated and added to reflect important technological developments and our use of technology.

The following lists and describes all modules, including additional, changed, or expanded topics from the previous edition.

Module 1: Impact of Digital Technology (Technology use in society, both personal and professional)

- Key terms that students need for understanding later modules are introduced, including cloud computing, Bluetooth, and network.

Module 2: The Web (The role of the web, accessing websites and webpages, e-commerce, and searching and conducting online research)

- New section on connecting to the Internet, which includes discussion of ISPs, Wi-Fi, and hotspots.
- New section on Net Neutrality (moved up from Module 10 in the previous edition).

Module 3: Hardware and Processors (Types of hardware and processors, input and output devices, and hardware maintenance)

- Added figures that visually differentiate between how computers interact with data and information as well as differentiate between ROM and RAM.
- New section on the use of QR codes as input methods.
- Rearranged content to group hardware devices with similar functions together.

Module 4: Operating Systems and File Management (Types and uses of operating systems, customizing an operating system, and managing files and folders)

- User interface coverage now includes NUIs (natural user interfaces).
- Expanded section on Selecting an Operating System.
- Presented content in a more device-diagnostic manner to ensure coverage goes beyond Windows and PCs and includes mobile devices.

Module 5: App Use (Types and purposes of apps, using productivity and graphics apps)

- Added content to clearly differentiate between "software" and "apps and programs."
- Added information to the Presentation app section about presenting over the web.

Module 6: Cybersecurity and Safety (Cybersecurity risks, hazards of technology use, repelling cyber-attacks, and protecting against hazards)

- New coverage of the importance of cybersecurity.
- Expanded information about authentication.
- Additional coverage on the risks of data collection.

Module 7: Digital Media (Uses of and creating digital media)

- New section on using digital media for business.
- New section on protecting your digital media creations with copyrights.
- Added coverage of emerging technologies, such as meme, NFT, and blockchain.

Module 8: App Development (Development roles, methods, phases, tools, and strategies, and how to sell apps)

- Focus changed from app use and development to just development.
- Added coverage on change management, including dealing with scope creep.
- New section on vendor proposals: types, evaluating, and making decisions.
- New section on project management techniques and tools.

Module 9: Web Development (Comparing HTML5, CSS, and JavaScript, strategies for creating and publishing websites, using data tools and analytics, and coding a website)

- New section on dashboards and website data analytics.
- Replaced and updated Case Study scenario.

Module 10: Networking (Connected network features, connecting to a network, and network security)

- Added comparison of 2.4 GHz Wi-Fi and 5 GHz Wi-Fi.
- Added content on networking with IoT devices.
- Updated information on wireless standards.

Module 11: Digital Communication (Comparing and using digital communication tools and evaluating their impact)

- Updated market statistics.
- Added coverage of new, popular social media sites.

Module 12: Digital Transformation (Cloud computing, doing business on the Internet, and AI and other new technologies)

- Added coverage of distributed computing.
- Added content on virtual reality and robotics.
- Expanded AI content to include generative AI tools and examples, plus coverage of prompt engineering.

Module 13: Databases (The importance of databases, using a database management system, and using data to make business decisions)

- Added coverage of ACID and BASE models.
- Added content on read replicas.
- Expanded coverage of cloud database services.
- Expanded coverage of how database types are selected for websites.

Module 14: Digital Ethics and Lifestyle (Responsibilities of a digital citizen, information accuracy, content accessibility, and promoting a healthy digital lifestyle)

- Expanded coverage of technology laws to include AI regulations and the Right to Be Forgotten.
- New coverage of deceptive technology practices: catfishing, deep fakes, AI misuse, and deceptive design.
- New coverage of ethical SEO practices and accessibility in web and app development.
- New coverage of content biases, including speech recognition and data pools.

Shelly Cashman Series

Shelly Cashman provides thoroughly updated coverage that reflects current Microsoft® 365® features. Narrative content has been authored using Microsoft® 365 Business Standard. Module projects incorporate career topics that apply diversity, equity, and inclusion principles and ensure accessibility. All projects, assignments, and lessons have been refreshed with authentic case scenarios that focus on practical skills and employability.

Word: New features in the Word content include the enhanced Accessibility Checker, which identifies potential accessibility issues and presents suggestions to make documents more inclusive. The Word coverage also introduces Focus mode, the updated collaboration experience, Microsoft's expanded search tool, and voice options. The Immersive Reader is covered, as is the ability to create a private document copy and use Word's screen reader.

PowerPoint: The PowerPoint content introduces the new commenting experience, which lets users display comments in contextual view or the Comments pane. The comment anchor helps reviewers identify specific slide elements with comments and place the comment bubble anywhere on the slide. With the revised search feature, users can enter a word or phrase in the Search box to find the definition. Microsoft Search also provides support articles to help perform tasks. Users can record and save a presentation that includes digital inking to capture text, drawings, and annotations, and then play back animated drawings. The Speaker Coach uses artificial intelligence (AI) to improve presentation skills by giving feedback on body language, the use of sensitive and filler words, and perceived mispronounced words.

Excel: With the Excel modules, students learn both long-standing Excel functions and tools as well as the most recent innovations. Updates to the Excel content include the new XLOOKUP and LET functions, dynamic arrays, and the Analyze Data feature. Also covered is the Accessibility Checker, which identifies issues and offers solutions to produce an accessible workbook.

Access: New features in the Access coverage include updated, real-world scenarios from a variety of industries that illustrate the relevance of Access databases in today's businesses. Completely updated projects use gapped Start and Solution files to ensure students use new, authentic files for each project from one module to the next. Module projects alternate between two sets of scenarios for expanded relevance and practicality. Further, an off-module scenario database receives updates comparable to the on-module scenario so that students see similar progression in all databases. A Solutions to Critical Thinking Questions document for each module guides instructors on what to look for in student work. Critical Thinking Questions invite students to engage with the module's skills and information at a conceptual level, and to reflect on their learning, thinking processes, and the relevance of learned skills to their chosen careers.

Windows: The updates to the Windows modules reflect the changes from Windows 10 to Windows 11. New end-of-module exercises incorporate current terminology and features. Module projects have been updated with the latest Windows 11 features, including widgets, the revised Start and Search menus, and the Immersive Reader.

Organization of the Text

Technology for Success

Technology for Success: Computer Concepts has the following components: a student text; activities and resources online in the MindTap platform; and a suite of instructor supplements. The textbook contains 14 modules, each with 3–5 learning objectives to which the text, activities, and assessments are aligned.

The book starts and ends with topics relating to being a digital citizen. Modules have been organized to be standalone topics, although the intent is to first introduce basic topics, such as apps and hardware, then delve into more specific ones such as digital media, databases, and cyber security. Module 1 includes an introduction and explanation of what it means to be a digital citizen, and the last module wraps up several concepts discussed in the book by framing them within an ethical standpoint.

Shelly Cashman Series

The *Shelly Cashman Series: Microsoft 365 & Office, First Edition* is a comprehensive introduction to Microsoft applications and is intended for students in introductory computing courses. Each application is divided into modules within the three levels—introductory, intermediate, and advanced. Each module introduces a topic through a real-world project and presents content that aligns directly with the learning objectives listed at the beginning of the module. To enable students to practice and apply skills learned, each module ends with a summary and a Consider This: Plan Ahead master planning guide that students use as they complete assignments and create projects on their own. Lastly, the end-of-module assignments are related to the top 25 industries for each application and include critical thinking questions. To increase students' confidence in their abilities, the assignments build from applying skills to experimenting beyond the module content to implementing a solution using creative thinking and problem-solving approaches.

Features of the Text

Technology for Success

Based on extensive research and feedback from students today, we've learned that students absorb information more easily if topics are broken down into smaller lessons that are authentic to everyday life. With this in mind, and to ensure a deeper understanding of technology in the real world, *Technology for Success: Computer Concepts* uses the following approach to helping users understand and apply its contents:

Module Objectives establish the goals of the module and what students should be able to achieve by the end.

In This Module

- Explain the evolution of society's reliance on technology
- Develop personal uses for technology to help with productivity, learning, and future career growth
- Explain the role of technology in the professional world

baranq/Shutterstock.com

Shea Foley is finishing her degree in social media marketing. During her time at school, she has learned about how to use technology for productivity, and specifically how to use technology in social media marketing. Shea recently visited her school's career advisory center and received a list of tips to use technology to find an entry-level job in her field. She will use the technology with which she is familiar to search for openings, research the companies, schedule and keep track of interviews, and create a professional online presence.

Headings distill key takeaways to help students understand the big picture and serve as the building blocks of the module, designed to help achieve mastery. Each module has 3–5 learning objectives. Each objective is a content heading in the module and is further broken down by subheadings that describe the technologies and how they are used.

Explain the Role of Technology in the Professional World

Nearly every job requires you to interact with technology to complete projects, exchange information with coworkers, and meet customers' needs. Technology careers span a range of specialities from software development to IT consulting to web marketing. And, no matter what business they're in, people interact with technology in almost every field, including business, education, and manufacturing. Whether you are looking for a job in a technology field or other area, you can use technology to prepare for and search for a job.

Explain Enterprise Computing

A large business with many employees is known as an enterprise. **Enterprise computing** refers to the use of technology by a company's employees to meet the needs of a large business. Each department of a company uses technology specific to its function. **Table 1-1** lists some of the uses of technology for different functional units.

Module Summary recaps the concepts covered in the module to help students organize their learning experience.

Module 3 Summary

The hardware you use depends on what you are trying to accomplish, such as receive input, produce output, store data, play games, or connect to the Internet. Many hardware devices have more than one use. Input devices communicate instructions that the computer or device translates into data that the computer can read and use to produce information. Output devices convey information produced by a computer or device. Computers use the binary system to interpret data and produce information using a coding scheme, such as ASCII or Unicode.

Laptops, desktops, and all-in-ones are types of computers, as are mobile devices such as tablets and smartphones. Laptops are more common than desktops and all-in-ones because they are more portable. Smartphones are so prevalent that not having access to one is a factor in the digital divide. Peripheral devices extend the capability of a computer or device. Examples of peripheral devices include printers, keyboards, and speakers. You can connect a peripheral device wirelessly or using a port or USB hub.

Storage solutions include cloud storage and internal or external hard drives, as well as USB flash drives and optical media. All computers and devices come with an internal hard drive for storage. Solid state drives are common in mobile devices and laptops. An external hard drive can be used to extend the storage capacity of your computer. Cloud storage is popular because it allows for easier sharing and collaboration among multiple users in different physical locations. Flash memory devices and optical media are no longer widely used as more users rely on the cloud.

Review Questions help students test their understanding of each topic. These questions have been standardized to include 12 questions, which are a mix of True/False and Multiple Choice.

Review Questions

1. Data is ________.
   a. raw facts, such as text or numbers
   b. processed output
   c. the result of a calculation
   d. another term for software
2. The second generation of computers replaced vacuum tubes with ________.
   a. display devices
   b. glass crystals
   c. transformers
   d. transistors

6. (True or False) Green computing involves reducing electricity consumed and environmental waste generated when using computers, mobile devices, and related technologies.
7. A company's ________ department oversees the centralized computer equipment and administers the network.
   a. management
   b. technical support
   c. operations
   d. information security

Discussion Questions and **Critical Thinking Activities** help students relate their understanding of the module to the real world and reflect on their own experiences with technology.

Discussion Questions

1. How have embedded computers and the IoT impacted your daily life? What additional uses can you see yourself using? What security or other risks might you encounter with IoT?
2. How do the following technologies help you in your quest to become a digital citizen: kiosks, enterprise computing, and green computing?
3. What additional uses of technology can you see in the workplace? List ways technology impacts other careers not discussed in this module, such as finance, government, non-profits, and agriculture.
4. List guidelines for creating a professional online presence. View your own online presence and make a list of changes you should make in order to enhance how potential employers might view you. How should you go about making these changes? What additional advice would you give to others seeking jobs?

Critical Thinking Activities

1. You work in the educational software industry. Your boss asks you to give a brief lecture to other employees about the digital divide. Create a one-page document in which you define in your own words and give examples of the impact of the digital divide, and list ways your company can work to narrow the gap between students without reliable access to educational software, the Internet, and the hardware on which to run both. What is your role as a company and employee to address the digital divide? What aspects of the digital divide do you find most troubling or confusing?
2. You decide to reduce your environmental impact by recycling more, going paperless, and using environmentally safe cleaning products. List one or two reasons why you should add green computing to your efforts. Research five ways you can apply green computing to your daily life and rank them in order of importance. The next time you think about replacing a device, do you think this information will impact your decision? In what ways can you encourage others to do the same?

Apply Your Skills exercise ties in what students have learned in the module with the character introduced at the beginning of the module and supports them in applying what they've learned to an in-depth case scenario.

Apply Your Skills

Shea Foley is finishing her degree in social media marketing. During her time at school, she has learned about how to use technology for productivity, and specifically how to use technology in social media marketing. Shea recently visited her school's career advisory center and received a list of tips to use technology to find an entry-level job in her field.

Working in a small group or by yourself, complete the following:

1. How have past technological developments helped provide the basis for Shea's job and her ability to do her assigned tasks? If you could come up with an additional technological development that might occur in the future, what would it be, and what would Shea use it for? How might you apply the technologies you have learned about in this module to your current job or schoolwork, or to a job you have held in the past?
2. List three ways in which Shea will use technology to perform her daily tasks. Which technologies do you think will be most effective, and why?
3. What other departments might Shea interact with at work, and in what ways? List three. Which would be most important? Why? Which department interests you most? What skills might you need to be able to find a career in that department or field?

Shelly Cashman Series

The features of the text, which are found consistently throughout all modules, are designed to aid the student in a specific way.

The projects are focused on employability based on current research and data. They use authentic case scenarios and a step-by-step approach to be as engaging, comprehensive, and easy to use as possible.

Heading levels organize topics within a module. Unique to the Shelly Cashman Series are "To-Do" heading levels for step-by-step task sequences. A To-Do head lead-in paragraph may include a **Why?** element to clarify why students are performing the steps.

To Display a Different Tab on the Ribbon

When you start Word, the ribbon displays 11 main tabs: File, Home, Insert, Draw, Design, Layout, References, Mailings, Review, View, and Help. (Note that depending on the type of computer or device you are using, the Draw tab may not appear.) The tab currently displayed is called the active tab. To display a different tab on the ribbon, you click the tab. The following step displays the View tab, that is, makes it the active tab. **Why?** When working with Word, you may need to switch tabs to access other options for working with a document or to verify settings.

Step-by-step sequences include the following features:

Q&A boxes provide troubleshooting information, equivalent touch instructions, or an additional explanation for a step.

Experiment steps encourage students to explore a feature such as the Themes gallery.

2

- If necessary, scroll to and then point to Facet in the Themes gallery to display a Live Preview of that theme applied to the document (Figure 1-37).
- **Experiment:** Point to various themes in the Themes gallery to display a Live Preview of the various themes applied to the document in the document window.

Q&A What is Live Preview?
Recall from the discussion earlier in this module that Live Preview is a feature that allows you to point to a gallery choice and see its effect in the document — without actually selecting the choice.

Can I use Live Preview on a touch screen?
Live Preview may not be available on all touch screens.

Other Ways provide additional methods to accomplish the tasks covered in specific To-Do steps.

Other Ways

1. Right-click paragraph (or if using touch, tap 'Show Context Menu' button on Mini toolbar), click Paragraph on shortcut menu, click Indents and Spacing tab (Paragraph dialog box), click Alignment arrow, click Centered, click OK
2. Click Paragraph Dialog Box Launcher (Home tab or Layout tab | Paragraph group), click Indents and Spacing tab (Paragraph dialog box), click Alignment arrow, click Centered, click OK
3. Press CTRL+E

By the Way (BTW) boxes are short marginal elements that add value for students by expanding on information in the module.

> BTW
> **Printing Document Properties**
> To print document properties, click File on the ribbon to open Backstage view, click Print in Backstage view to display the Print screen, click the first button in the Settings area to display a list of options specifying what you can print, click Document Info in the list to specify you want to print the document properties instead of the actual document, and then click the Print button in the Print screen to print the document properties on the currently selected printer.

Other in-text pedagogical elements include the following:

Key terms are bold and blue in the running text. In the MindTap, each bolded key term is linked to its definition in the Master Glossary.

> Calibri and Calibri Light are **sans serif fonts**, which are fonts that do not ends of their characters. Other fonts such as Calisto MT are **serif fonts**,

Consider This is a pedagogical sidebar in the form of a question and answer that appears within the module and in the end-of-module student assignments. The question addresses conceptual or critical thinking topics, general information about the app, or other important information students should know.

> **Consider This**
> **How do you use the touch keyboard with a touch screen?**
> To display the on-screen touch keyboard, tap the Touch Keyboard button on the Windows taskbar. When finished using the touch keyboard, tap the X button on the touch keyboard to close the keyboard.

Break Point is a note to students that indicates a good place to take a break. Every module includes at least one break point.

> **Break Point:** If you want to take a break, this is a good place to do so. You can exit Word now. To resume later, start Word and continue following the steps from this location forward.

SAM Upload and Download icons are for SAM users. A SAM download icon appears next to any step where students download a data file to begin a SAM Project.

> 1
> • sam Click the Start button on the Windows taskbar to display the Start

A SAM upload icon appears next to any step where students submit a file to SAM for a completed SAM Project.

> **3**
>
> - Click the 'Clear Search String' button to remove the search string and redisplay all objects.
>
> **Q&A** Did I have to click the button to redisplay all objects? Could I simply have erased the current string to achieve the same result?
> You did not have to click the button. You could have used DEL or BACKSPACE to erase the current search string.
>
> - If desired, sign out of your Microsoft account.
> - sam Exit Access.

Figure callouts point to important parts of a screen and include two types:

Action/navigation callouts point to commands or buttons used in the step. Action/navigation callout boxes are a different color from explanatory callouts to help students easily locate screen elements referenced in step instructions.

Explanatory callouts direct students to other significant screen elements in the figure.

1. With the text selected (shown in Figure 1–55), click the Font Size arrow (Home tab | Font group) to display the Font Size gallery.
2. Click 20 in the Font Size gallery to increase the font size of the selected text.
3. Click anywhere in the document window to remove the selection from the text (Figure 1–56).

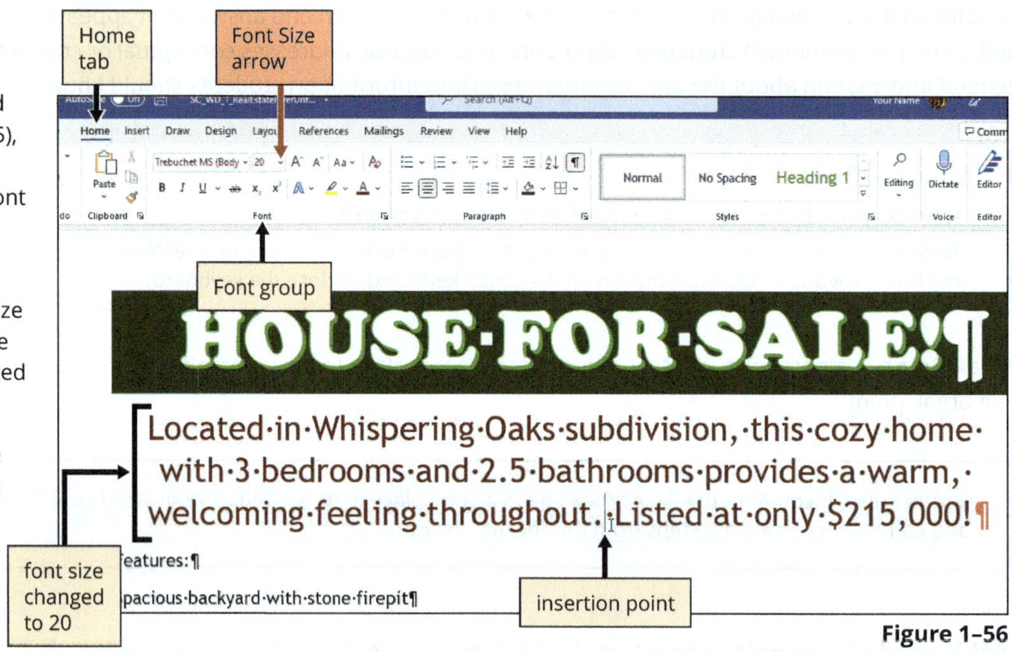

Figure 1–56

Course Solutions

Technology for Success

Online Learning Platform: MindTap

Today's leading online learning platform, MindTap for Technology for Success, Second Edition, gives instructors complete control of a course to craft a personalized, engaging learning experience that challenges students, builds confidence, and elevates performance.

MindTap introduces students to core concepts from the beginning of the course using a simplified learning path that progresses from understanding to application and delivers access to eTextbooks, study tools, interactive media, auto-graded assessments, and performance analytics.

Instructors can use MindTap for Technology for Success, Second Edition as is, or personalize it to meet specific course needs. Instructors can also easily integrate MindTap into a Learning Management System (LMS).

The online learning experience includes hands-on trainings and critical thinking challenges that encourage students to problem-solve in a real-world scenario. *Technology for Success: Computer Concepts* is designed to help students build foundational knowledge and integrate it into their daily lives with interactive experiences in the MindTap and SAM platforms.

- **Readings** cover focused, concrete content designed to reinforce learning objectives.
- **Skills Trainings** are comprised of brief, skills-based videos which are each followed by a multiple-choice question. SAM trainings are designed to give students concrete experience with specific technology skills.
- **Critical Thinking Challenges** place students in real-world scenarios to practice their problem-solving and decision-making skills.
- **Module Exams** assess students' understanding of how the learning objectives connect and build on one another.
- **In The News activities** offer an opportunity to explore the latest technology news through various mediums to help students understand its impact on our daily lives, the economy, and society and to build lifelong learning habits.

To learn more, visit:

- MindTap—https://www.cengage.com/mindtap
- Introductory Computing—https://www.cengage.com/mindtap-collections/

Shelly Cashman Series

Online Learning Platform: MindTap with SAM

The Shelly Cashman Series MindTap Collection, powered by SAM (Skills Assessment Manager), enables proficiency in Microsoft Office and computing concepts for Introductory Computing courses. With a library of renowned course materials, including ready-to-assign, auto-graded learning modules, instructors can easily adapt their courses to best prepare students for the evolving job market. In addition to an eReader that includes the full content of the printed book, The Shelly Cashman Series, First Edition MindTap course includes the following:

- **SAM Textbook Projects:** Follow the steps and scenarios outlined in the textbook readings; enable students to complete projects based on a real-world scenario live in Microsoft Office applications and submit them in SAM for automatic grading and feedback.
- **SAM Training and Exam:** Trainings teach students to complete specific skills in a simulated Microsoft application environment while exams allow students to demonstrate their proficiency (also in a simulated environment).
- **SAM Projects:** Students complete projects based on real-world scenarios live in Microsoft applications and submit the projects in SAM for automatic grading and feedback. SAM offers several types of projects, each with a unique purpose: 1A and 1B, critical thinking, end of module, capstone, and integration.
- **Microsoft Office Specialist (MOS) resources:** Training and exams are based on the Microsoft Office 365 Objective Domains for the MOS Exam and exam simulation that replicates the test-taking environment of the MOS exam for Word, Excel, Access, PowerPoint, and Outlook.

To learn more, go to: https://www.cengage.com/mindtap-collections/

Ancillary Packages

Technology for Success

Instructor Resources

Additional instructor resources for this product are available online. Instructor assets include an Instructor's Manual, Educator Guide, PowerPoint® slides, and a test bank powered by Cognero®. Sign up or sign in at www.cengage.com to search for and access this product and its online resources.

Test Banks: Questions written by the author are aligned with each module's learning objectives.

Instructor Manual: The module outline corresponds directly with the content in each module and additional discussion questions and activities are aligned to headings in the book.

Educator Guide: The guide provides a detailed outline of the corresponding MindTap course.

PowerPoints: The icebreaker activity relates to the module topic, and the learning objectives and content slides align with the book. Activities and the self-assessment align with learning objectives and supplement the content of the book.

Solution and Answer Guide: The answers provided are written by the authors and correspond to the end-of-module activities.

Transition Guide: The guide is written by the authors and provides information on what has changed in this edition so that instructors know what to expect.

Shelly Cashman Series

Instructor and Student Resources

Additional instructor and student resources for this product are available online. Instructor assets include an Instructor Manual, an Educator Guide, PowerPoint® slides, a Guide to Teaching Online, Solution Files, a test bank powered by Cognero®, and a Transition Guide. Student assets include data files and a glossary. Sign up or sign in at www.cengage.com to search for and access this product and its online resources. The instructor and student companion sites contain ancillary material for the full Shelly Cashman Series Collection, along with instructions on how to find specific content within the companion site.

Instructor Manual: This guide provides additional instructional material to assist in class preparation, including module objectives, module outlines, discussion questions, and additional activities and assignments. Each outline corresponds directly with the content in the module and additional discussion questions and activities are aligned to headings in the book.

Educator Guide: The MindTap Educator Guide contains a detailed outline of the corresponding MindTap course, including activity types and time on task. The SAM Educator Guide explains how to use SAM functionality to maximize a course.

PowerPoint slides: The slides may be used to guide classroom presentations, to provide to students for module review, or to print as classroom handouts. The slides align closely with the book while activities and the self-assessment align with module learning objectives and supplement the content in the book.

Guide to Teaching Online: This guide presents technological and pedagogical considerations and suggestions for teaching the Introductory Computing course when instructors can't be in the same room with students.

Solution and Answer Guide: The answers to the critical thinking questions are written by the author and correspond to critical thinking questions in the end-of-module activities.

Solution files: These files provide solutions to all textbook projects for instructors to use to grade student work.

- Instructors using SAM do not need solution files since projects are auto-graded within SAM.
- Solution files are provided on the instructor companion site for instructors *not* using SAM.

Data files: These files are provided for students to complete the projects in each module.

- Students using SAM to complete the projects download the required data files directly from SAM.
- Students who are *not* using SAM to complete the projects can find data files on the student companion site and within MindTap.

Test banks: A comprehensive test bank, offered in Cognero, Word, Blackboard, Moodle, Desire2Learn, Canvas, and SAM formats, contains questions aligned with each module's learning objectives and is written by subject matter experts. Powered by Cognero, Cengage Testing is a flexible, online system that allows instructors to author, edit, and manage test bank content from multiple Cengage solutions and to create multiple test versions that instructors can deliver from an LMS, classroom, or wherever they want.

Transition Guide: This guide highlights all of the changes in the text and the digital offerings from the previous edition to the current one so that instructors know what to expect.

Acknowledgments

Technology for Success

Jennifer T. Campbell: I would like to thank MT Cozzola for her expert editorial guidance, my co-authors Jill and Mark for their collaboration, and Michelle, Zenya, Amy, Anne, and Ciara at Cengage for their contributions to the process. I couldn't do this without the inspiration from my two amazing children, Emma and Lucy, to whom I dedicate this book.

Jill West: Teaching is one of the greatest privileges of my life. I'm grateful to every one of my students that you allow me to accompany you on part of your educational and career journey. You inspire me to always do better. Thanks to all the Cengage folks who make these projects not only possible but truly an evolution of academic progress. To our team members—MT, Zenya, Michelle, Anne, Ciara, and Amy—I have so enjoyed working with you again and getting to know you better. To my co-authors, Jennifer and Mark, it's been an honor to write alongside you. A special thank you to my husband for supporting me through the long months of intense deadlines. And thank you to my kiddos—Winn, Sarah, Daniel, and Zack—for your hugs, help, and encouragement.

Mark Ciampa: It is a privilege to be a part of the team that worked so diligently on this project. Thanks to Amy, MT, Zenya, Michelle, and Anne, along with co-authors Jennifer and Jill.

Shelly Cashman Series

Jill West: It's always a privilege to work with the incredible teams Cengage puts together, and this course is no exception. I've worked on many projects under the energetic and resourceful leadership of Amy Savino, whom I greatly admire and will forever be thankful for her vote of confidence in me when I needed it most. I've thoroughly enjoyed getting to know Anne Orgren, who has been our attentive and supportive content manager, providing just enough guidance exactly when needed. I can't say enough good things about MT Cozzola, developmental editor for this project. With her diversity of talents and skills, she has been a learner advocate, bringing the student's perspective to every conversation and providing synergistic insight. And I'm grateful for another opportunity to work with learning designer Zenya Molnar, who brings creative solutions to design challenges. Many other folks worked diligently behind the scenes to ensure consistency of quality, design, and innovation—their efforts are enthusiastically noted and greatly appreciated.

I owe a special thanks to my husband, Mike, for his tireless support and encouragement. And thanks to my kiddos: Winn, Sarah, Daniel, and Zack.

Victoria Kaye: Thank you for the many individuals who have made this edition possible. A text like this is not done without great effort, teamwork, and planning. Thank you to those individuals who contributed their expertise to this text, and an extra special thank you to developmental editors Barbara Clemens and MT Cozzola. Without your vast knowledge and careful consideration, this edition would not be possible. Thank you to the editorial team and their staff: Amy Savino, Senior Portfolio Product Manager; Anne Orgren, Senior Content Manager; and Zenya Molnar, Learning Designer. It is simply not possible to sum up the value of your contributions.

Getting to Know Microsoft Office Versions

Cengage is proud to bring you the next edition of Microsoft Office. This edition was designed to provide a robust learning experience that is not dependent upon a specific version of Office.

Microsoft supports several versions and editions of Office: (Refer to Table 1 below for more information)

- **Microsoft 365 (formerly known as Office 365):** A service that delivers the most up-to-date, feature-rich, modern Microsoft productivity applications direct to your device. There are several combinations of Microsoft 365 programs for business, educational, and personal use. Microsoft 365 is cloud-based, meaning it is stored, managed, and processed on a network of remote servers hosted on the Internet, rather than on local servers or personal computers. Microsoft 365 offers extra online storage and cloud-connected features, as well as updates with the latest features, fixes, and security updates. Microsoft 365 is purchased for a monthly subscription fee that keeps your software up to date with the latest features.
- **Office 2021:** The Microsoft "on-premises" version of the Office apps, available for both PCs and Macintosh computers, offered as a static, one-time purchase and outside of the subscription model. Unlike Microsoft 365, Office 2021 does not include online product updates with new features.
- **Microsoft 365 Online (formerly known as Office Online):** A free, simplified version of Microsoft web applications (Teams, Access, Word, Excel, PowerPoint, and OneNote) that lets users create and edit files collaboratively.
- **Office 365 Education:** A free subscription including Word, Excel, PowerPoint, OneNote, and now Microsoft Teams, plus additional classroom tools. Only available for students and educators at select institutions.

Table 1 Microsoft Office applications — uses and availability

Application	Use	Availability/Editions
Word	Create documents and improve your writing with intelligent assistance features.	Microsoft 365 Family, Home, Business, Office 2021, Office 365 Education
Excel	Simplify complex data into easy-to-read spreadsheets.	Microsoft 365 Personal, Home, Business, Office 2021, Office 365 Education
PowerPoint	Create presentations that stand out.	Home, Business, Office 2021, Office 365 Education
OneNote	A digital notebook for all your note-taking needs.	Home, Office 365 Education
OneDrive	Save and share your files and photos wherever you are.	Home, Business
Outlook	Manage your email, calendar, tasks, and contacts all in one place.	Home, Business
SharePoint	Create team sites to share information, files, and resources.	Business
Publisher	Create polished, professional layouts without the hassle.	Home, Business, Office 2021 (PC only)
Access	Create your own database apps easily in formats that serve your business best.	Home, Business, Office 2021 (PC only)
Teams	Bring everyone together in one place to meet, chat, call, and collaborate.	Business, Office 365 Education
Exchange	Business-class email and calendaring.	Business

Over time, the Microsoft 365 cloud interface will continuously update using its web connection, offering new application features and functions, while Office 2021 will remain static.

Because Microsoft 365 releases updates continuously, your onscreen experience may differ from what you see in this product. For example, the more advanced features and functionalities covered in this product may not be available in Microsoft 365 Online, may have updated from what you see in Office 2021, or may be from a post-publication update of Microsoft 365.

For up-to-date information on the differences between Microsoft 365, Office 2021, and Microsoft 365 Online, please visit the Microsoft Support website.

Cengage is committed to providing high-quality learning solutions for you to gain the knowledge and skills that will empower you throughout your educational and professional careers.

Thank you for using our product, and we look forward to exploring the future of Microsoft Office with you!

Using SAM Projects and Textbook Projects

SAM (Skills Assessment Manager) **Projects** allow you to actively apply the skills you learned in Microsoft Word, Excel, PowerPoint, or Access. You can also submit your work to SAM for online grading. You can use SAM Projects to become a more productive student and use these skills throughout your career.

To complete SAM Textbook Projects, please follow these steps:

SAM Textbook Projects allow you to complete a project as you follow along with the steps in the textbook. As you read the module, look for icons that indicate when you should download your SAM Start file(s) and when to upload your solution file to SAM for grading.

Everything you need to complete this project is provided within SAM. You can launch the eBook directly from SAM, which will allow you to take notes, highlight, and create a custom study guide, or you can use a print textbook or your mobile app. Download IOS or Download Android.

To get started, launch your SAM Project assignment from SAM, MindTap, or a link within your learning management system.

1. Step 1:
   Download Files
   - Click the "Download All" button or the individual links to download your **Start File** and **Support File(s)** (when available). You must use the SAM Start file.
   - Click the Instructions link to launch the eBook (or use the print textbook or mobile app).
   - Disregard any steps in the textbook that ask you to create a new file or to use a file from a location outside of SAM.
   - Look for the SAM Download icon to begin working with your start file.
   - Follow the module's step-by-step instructions until you reach the SAM Upload icon.
   - Save and close the file.

2. Step 2:
   Save Work to SAM
   - Ensure you rename your project file to match the Expected File Name.
   - Upload your in-progress or completed file to SAM. You can download the file to continue working or submit it for grading in the next step.
3. Step 3:
   Submit for Grading
   - Upload your completed solution file to SAM for immediate feedback and to view the available Reports.
     - The **Graded Summary Report** provides a detailed list of project steps, your score, and feedback to aid you in revising and resubmitting the project.
     - The **Study Guide** provides your score for each project step and links to the associated training and textbook pages.
   - If additional attempts are allowed, use your reports to assist with revising and resubmitting your project.
   - To re-submit your project, download the file you saved in step 2.
   - Edit, save, and close the file, then re-upload and submit it again.

For all other SAM Projects, please follow these steps:

To get started, launch your SAM Project assignment from SAM, MindTap, or a link within your learning management system.

1. Step 1:
   Download Files
   - Click the "Download All" button or the individual links to download your **Instruction File**, **Start File**, and **Support File(s)** (when available). You must use the SAM Start file.
   - Open the Instruction file and follow the step-by-step instructions. Ensure you rename your project file to match the Expected File Name (change _1 to _2 at the end of the file name).

2. Step 2:
   Save Work to SAM
   - Upload your in-progress or completed file to SAM. You can download the file to continue working or submit it for grading in the next step.
3. Step 3:
   Submit for Grading
   - Upload the completed file to SAM for immediate feedback and to view available Reports.
     - The **Graded Summary Report** provides a detailed list of project steps, your score, and feedback to aid you in revising and resubmitting the project.
     - The **Study Guide** provides your score for each project step and links to the associated training and textbook pages.
   - If additional attempts are allowed, use your reports to assist with revising and resubmitting your project.
   - To re-submit the project, download the file saved in step 2.
   - Edit, save, and close the file, then re-upload and submit it again.

For additional tips to successfully complete your SAM Projects, please view our SAM Video Tutorials.

Module 1

Impact of Digital Technology

In This Module

- Explain the evolution of society's reliance on technology
- Develop personal uses for technology to help with productivity, learning, and future career growth
- Explain the role of technology in the professional world

baranq/Shutterstock.com

Shea Foley is finishing her degree in social media marketing. During her time at school, she has learned about how to use technology for productivity, and specifically how to use technology in social media marketing. Shea recently visited her school's career advisory center and received a list of tips to use technology to find an entry-level job in her field. She will use the technology with which she is familiar to search for openings, research the companies, schedule and keep track of interviews, and create a professional online presence.

In the course of a day, you might use technology to complete assignments, watch an online streaming video, flip through news headlines, search for map directions, make a dinner reservation, scroll through social media, or buy something online. At school, at home, and at work, technology plays a vital role in your activities.

In this module, you will learn how technology has developed over time, explore the ways technology impacts our daily home and work lives, and discover how to choose and prepare for a career in technology. As you reflect on what you learn in this module, ask yourself: How has your use of technology changed in your lifetime? How can you use technology to keep learning? What types of technology will be necessary for you to learn to help you in your career?

Explain the Evolution of Society's Reliance on Technology

Over the last quarter century, technology has revolutionized our lives. Because of advances in technology, you can access, search for, and share information more quickly and effectively than ever before. You can manage your finances, calendars, and tasks. You can play games and watch videos on your phone or computer for entertainment and relaxation. **Digital literacy** (also called **computer literacy**) involves having a current knowledge and understanding of computers, mobile devices, the web, and related technologies. Being digitally literate is essential for acquiring a job, using and contributing to global communications, and participating effectively in society and the international community.

A **computer** is an electronic device, operating under the control of instructions stored in its own memory, that can accept data, process the data to produce information, and store the information for future use. **Data** is raw facts, such as text or numbers. A computer includes hardware and software. **Hardware** is the device itself and its components, such as wires, cases, switches, and electronic circuits. **Software** consists of the programs and apps that instruct the computer to perform tasks. **Programs** and **apps** include a set of coded instructions written for a computer, such as an operating system program or an application program. The two terms are often used interchangeably, though "app" is a more accurate term for software applications while "program" may refer more broadly to instructions for operating systems as well. Software processes data into meaningful **information**.

Outline the History of Computers

People have relied on tools and machines to count and manipulate numbers for thousands of years. These tools and technologies have evolved from the abacus, a calculation tool that used a series of beads in ancient times, to the first computing machines in the nineteenth century, to today's powerful handheld devices such as smartphones and tablets and technologies that enable voice and motion interaction.

The first generation of computers used **vacuum tubes** (**Figure 1-1**), cylindrical glass tubes that controlled the flow of subatomic particles called electrons. The ENIAC and UNIVAC are examples of these expensive machines. Their use and availability were limited due to their large size, the amount of power they consumed, the heat they generated, and how quickly they wore out.

The second generation of computers replaced vacuum tubes with **transistors**, which were smaller, cheaper, and more reliable replacements for vacuum tubes. These computers contained many components still in use today, including tape and disk storage, memory, operating systems, and stored programs.

Figure 1-1: Electronic digital computer with vacuum tubes

Emkaplin/Shutterstock.com

In the 1960s, computer engineers developed **integrated circuits**, which packed the equivalent of thousands of vacuum tubes or transistors into a silicon chip about the size of your thumb. In 1971, Ted Hoff and a team of engineers at the companies Intel and IBM introduced the microprocessor. A **microprocessor** is the "brains" of a computer, a chip that contains a central processing unit. Microprocessors were even faster, smaller, and less expensive than integrated circuits. Microprocessors often are called processors for short.

In the 1970s and 1980s, computers meant for personal use started to gain popularity. In 1978, Steve Jobs and Steve Wozniak of Apple Computer Corporation introduced the Apple II (**Figure 1-2**), a preassembled computer with color graphics and popular spreadsheet software called VisiCalc.

IBM followed Apple's lead in 1981, introducing its **personal computer (PC)**, which was designed for personal use, as opposed to commercial or industrial use. Other manufacturers also started making similar machines, and the market grew. Since 1981, the number of PCs in use has grown to the billions. However, many people today use tablets and smartphones in addition to or instead of PCs.

Computers have evolved into connected devices that can share data using the Internet or wireless networks. One of the many ways users communicate with each other is **email**, a system used to send and receive messages and files using the Internet. A **network** is a collection of two or more computers connected together to share resources. Wireless networks use **Wi-Fi** (short for wireless fidelity), a wireless data network technology that provides high-speed data connections that do not require a physical connection. You can save and share files over the cloud. **Cloud computing** is an Internet-based delivery of computing services, including data storage and apps. **Bluetooth** technology is wireless short-range radio connection that simplifies communications among Internet devices and between devices and the Internet.

Today's computers are smaller, faster, and have far greater capabilities than previous computers. In fact, your smartphone probably has more computing power than the computer that guided the U.S. Apollo mission to the moon in 1969! And while you might think of a PC when you think of a computer, a computer is any electronic device that includes instructions and processing power, including smartphones, tablets, and more.

Figure 1-2: Apple II computer

Trong Nguyen/Shutterstock.com

Explain the Impact of the Internet of Things and Embedded Computers

The **Internet of Things (IoT)** is an environment where processors are embedded in every product imaginable (things), and these things communicate with one another via the Internet or wireless networks. Alarm clocks, coffeemakers, thermostats, streetlights, navigation systems, in-vehicle controls, and much more are enhanced by the growth of IoT. IoT-enabled

Figure 1-3: Smart devices use IoT to control home functions, such as a thermostat

Saklakova/Shutterstock.com

devices often are referred to as **smart devices** (**Figure 1-3**) because of their ability to communicate, locate, and predict. Smart devices often have associated apps to control and interact with them directly or by using another device or control.

The basic premise of IoT is that objects can be tagged, tracked, and monitored through a local network or across the Internet. Communication technologies such as Bluetooth, RFID tags, near-field communications (NFC), and sensors have become readily available, more powerful, and less expensive. Sensors and tags can transmit data to a server on the Internet over a wireless network at frequent intervals for analysis and storage.

Recent technological developments have made it possible to efficiently access, store, and process the mountain of data reported by sensors. Mobile service providers offer connectivity to a variety of devices so that transmitting and receiving data can take place quickly.

An **embedded computer** is a computer that functions as one component in a larger product, and which has a specific purpose. Embedded computers usually are small and have limited hardware on their own but enhance the capabilities of everyday devices. Embedded computers perform a specific function based on the requirements of the product in which they reside. For example, an embedded computer in a printer monitors the ink levels, detects paper jams, and determines if the printer is out of paper.

Embedded computers are everywhere. This technology enables computers and devices to connect with one another over the Internet using IoT. You encounter examples of embedded computers multiple times a day, perhaps without being aware of it.

Today's vehicles have many embedded computers. These enable you to use a camera to guide you when backing up, warn you if a vehicle or object is in your blind spot, or alert you to unsafe road conditions. Some newer cars include screens that determine and guide your route, or that enable you to use touch or voice commands to control the temperature, car lights, and more. Recently, all new cars were required to include backup cameras and electronic stability control, which can assist with steering the car in case of skidding. All of this technology is intended to make driving safer (**Figure 1-4**).

Critics of in-vehicle technology claim that it can provide drivers with a false sense of security. If you rely on a sensor while backing up, parking, or changing lanes, you may miss other obstructions that can cause a crash. Reliance on electronic stability control may cause you to drive faster than conditions allow, or to pay less attention to the distance between your vehicle and others.

Figure 1-4: Some of the embedded computers designed to improve safety, security, and performance in today's vehicles

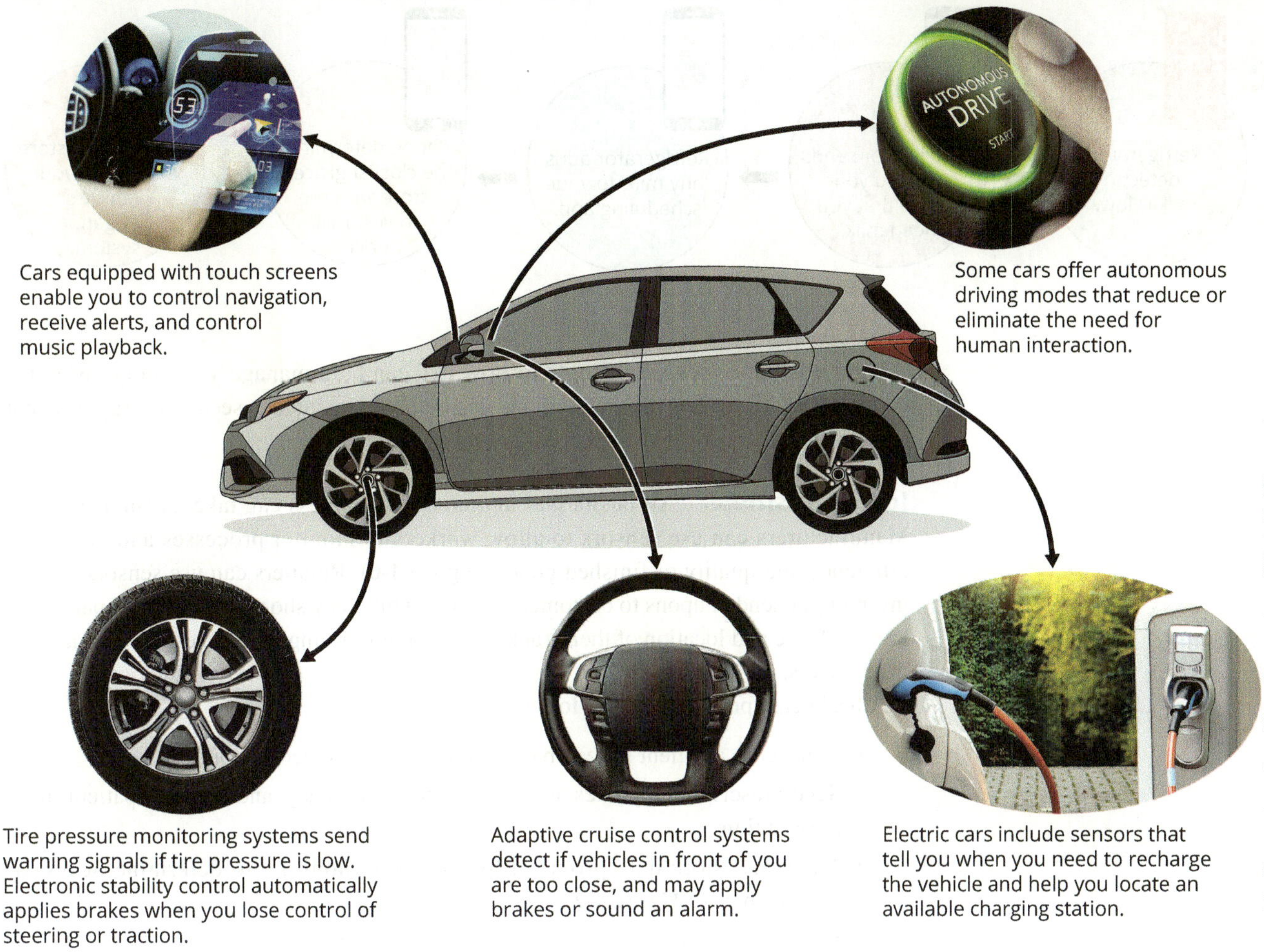

vectorhebat/Shutterstock.com; Ground Picture/Shutterstock.com; Olivier Le Moal/Shutterstock.com; Scharfsinn/Shutterstock.com; photobeps/Shutterstock.com; Evannovostro/Shutterstock.com

ATMs and Kiosks Automated teller machines (ATMs) are one of the more familiar uses of IoT. You can use your ATM card to withdraw cash, deposit checks, and interact with your bank accounts. Recent innovations are improving card security, such as **chip-and-pin technology** that stores data on an embedded chip instead of a magnetic stripe.

ATMs are a type of kiosk. A **kiosk** is a freestanding booth usually placed in a public area that can contain a display device used to present information to the public or event attendees. Kiosks enable self-service transactions in hotels and airports, for example, to enable users to check in for a flight or room. Healthcare providers also use kiosks for patients to check in and enter information, such as their insurance card number.

IoT at Home IoT enables you to manage devices remotely in your home, such as to start the washing machine at a certain time, view potential intruders via a webcam, or adjust the room temperature. Personal IoT uses include wearable fitness trackers that record and send data to your smartphone or computer about your exercise activity, the number of steps you take in a day, and your heart rate.

Figure 1-5: IoT-enabled devices can help you with daily tasks such as grocery shopping

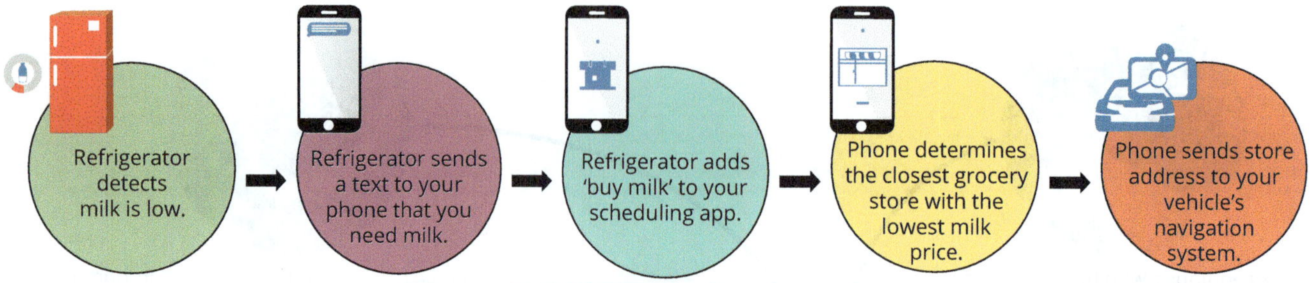

Figure 1-5 provides an example of how IoT can help manage your daily tasks. IoT continues to advance its capabilities, and can help you maintain a secure, energy-efficient, connected, voice-activated, remotely accessible home.

IoT in Business All businesses and areas of business can take advantage of IoT. Manufacturers can use sensors to allow workers to monitor processes and ensure the efficiency and quality of finished goods (**Figure 1-6**). Retailers can use sensors to track inventory or send coupons to customers' phones while they shop. Shipping companies can track mileage and location of their trucks and monitor driving times to ensure the safety of their drivers.

A healthcare provider can use IoT to:

- Connect to a patient's wearable blood pressure or glucose monitor
- Send prescription updates and changes to a pharmacy, and alert the patient of the prescription
- Track and store data provided by wearable monitors to determine necessary follow-up care (**Figure 1-7**)
- Send the patient reminders about upcoming appointments or tests

The uses of IoT are expanding rapidly, and connected devices continue to impact and enhance business practices at all levels.

Figure 1-6: Manufacturing technology enables oversight of quality, safety, and procedures

Blue Planet Studio/Shutterstock.com

Figure 1-7: Wearable monitors enable users to monitor glucose levels and administer insulin

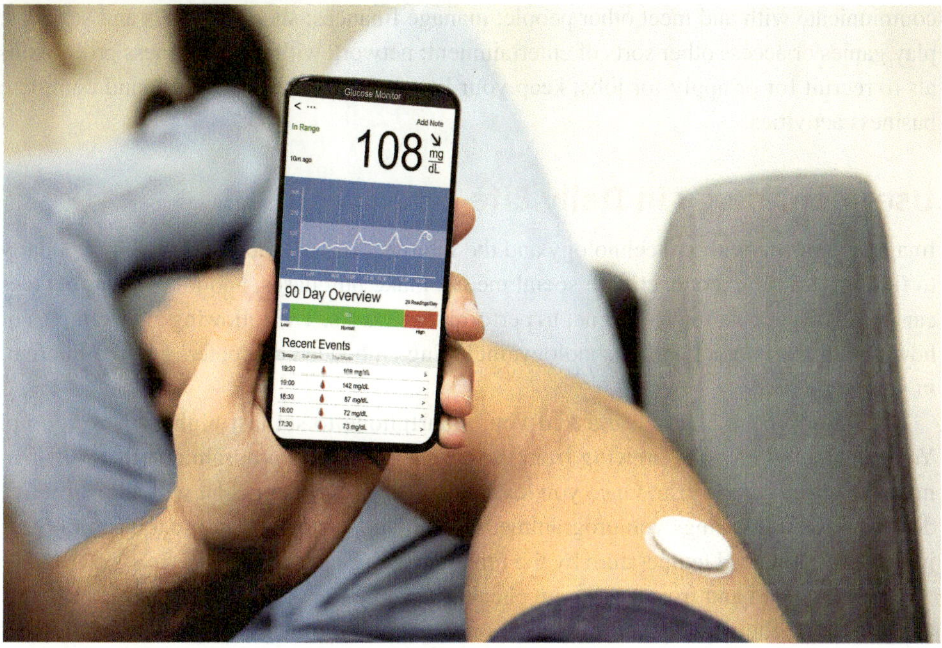

Andrey_Popov/Shutterstock.com

Recognize the Impact of the Digital Divide

All of this technology has many uses for both personal and business needs. However, it is not available to everyone. The **digital divide** is the gap between those who have access to technology and its resources and information, especially on the Internet, and those who do not. Socioeconomic (relative position in society), geographic (location), and demographic (population indicators, such as age or ethnicity) factors contribute to the digital divide, which can impact individuals, households, businesses, or geographic areas.

Imagine the educational opportunities when you have access to high-speed, unfiltered Internet content; your own laptop, tablet, or smart device; and software to create, track, and process data and information. Then compare these opportunities with the opportunities available to students who live in countries where the government restricts access to Internet content, and economics prevent them from owning their own devices and the software or apps used on them. Inequalities such as limited or no access to unfiltered information at a high speed can affect learning, knowledge, and opportunities and can have a lasting impact on the future of those affected.

Corporations, non-profits, educational institutions, and governments are working on solutions to narrow the digital divide so that all learners can become digitally literate.

Develop Personal Uses for Technology to Help with Productivity, Learning, and Future Career Growth

You can use technology to help with productivity, learning, and future career growth. In your daily life you interact with embedded computers in stores, public transportation, your car or truck, and more. Assistive technologies help people with disabilities to use technology. Green computing practices reduce the impact of electronic waste on the planet.

Just as any society has rules and regulations to guide its citizens, so does the digital world. As a **digital citizen**, you should be familiar with how to use technology to become an educated and productive member of the digital world.

Technology can enable you to more efficiently and effectively access and search for information; share personal ideas, photos, and videos with friends, family, and others; communicate with and meet other people; manage finances; shop for goods and services; play games or access other sorts of entertainment; network with other business professionals to recruit for or apply for jobs; keep your life and activities organized; and complete business activities.

Use Technology in Daily Life

Imagine your life without technology and the Internet. You probably use the Internet daily to find information, connect with social media, make purchases, and more. Your devices can help you connect to the Internet to perform these tasks. The following are examples of how you might interact with technology, including embedded computers and the Internet, in your daily life.

The sound of the alarm you asked your smartphone to set last night wakes you up. You can smell the coffee brewing from the coffee maker you programmed to go off five minutes before your alarm. Once you leave for work, your thermostat will adjust by five degrees based on settings you programmed into an app; later you can use the app to readjust to your preferred temperature by the time you arrive home.

On your way to and from work, you check the public transportation app on your phone to navigate to the subway station and check how much time you have before the next train arrives. Once there, you scan your phone to pay your fare and access the terminal (**Figure 1-8**). A screen in the station displays an alert when the train is incoming. As the subway speeds toward the next station, it relies on sensors to determine any oncoming traffic and report delays, changes in routes, and the next available stop.

After work, you need to pick up a new printer you previously researched using a technology review website, purchased using the store's app, and scheduled for a 5:30 PM pickup time. You go home and get in your car, which adjusts the seats and mirrors to your settings, and uses Bluetooth to start playing your favorite playlist (**Figure 1-9**). You program your vehicle's GPS to take you to the store. As you drive, your car senses the space between

Figure 1-8: Public transit apps enable you to pay electronically and monitor train arrivals

Zephyr_p/Shutterstock.com

Figure 1-9: Bluetooth enables your car stereo to play music from your smartphone

Capix Denan/Shutterstock.com

you and the car ahead and slows your speed to keep a safe distance. Outside the store, you use your car's cameras to safely navigate into an open spot and use the store's app to let them know you have arrived.

At your next stop, you need to pick up a new top to wear to a friend's birthday party. Before heading into the store, you decide to check your balance on your debit card. Your banking app tells you how much money is in your checking account. You tap to transfer $40 to your smartphone's payment app, then you head to the store.

You walk into a bookstore, searching for a new book to read. You talk to a sales associate, who uses her tablet to look up your personal profile, including past purchases, based on your phone number. The sales associate tells you what genres you like to read, and what authors you have bought books by in the past few years. Together, you find a book by a new author that looks appealing to you. Before using the store's self-checkout, you check your store loyalty app on your smartphone to access available coupons.

Later, back at home, you log onto your school's network to access your assignments. You use video conferencing to discuss a group project with your classmates and complete a research paper using credible online sources and giving proper citations to the facts and quotes you find. You turn in your paper using the school's plagiarism checker and shut down your laptop for the night. You make sure your alarm is set for tomorrow and call it a night.

Use Technology to Assist Users with Disabilities

The ever-increasing presence of computers in everyone's lives has generated an awareness of the need to address computing requirements for individuals with certain disabilities, such as learning disabilities, mobility issues, and hearing and visual disabilities. **Accessibility** is the practice of removing barriers that may prevent individuals with disabilities from interacting with data or an app.

The **Americans with Disabilities Act (ADA)** requires any company with 15 or more employees to make reasonable attempts to accommodate the needs of workers with disabilities. The **Individuals with Disabilities Education Act (IDEA)** requires that public schools purchase or acquire funding for adaptive technologies. These laws were put in place to ensure that people with disabilities can access the same resources, information, and services as able-bodied individuals using the appropriate technology.

Figure 1-10: A Braille printer

Andy Shell/Shutterstock.com

Users with visual disabilities can change screen settings, such as increasing the size or changing the color of the text to make the words easier to read. Changing the color of text also can address the needs of users with certain types of color blindness. Instead of using a monitor, blind users can work with voice output. That is, the computer speaks out loud the information that appears on a screen. A Braille printer prints information on paper in Braille (**Figure 1-10**).

Screen reader technology uses audio output to describe the contents of the screen. Screen readers can read aloud webpages and documents or provide narration of the computer or device's actions. **Alternative text (alt text)** is descriptive text added to an object, such as a picture or drawing (**Figure 1-11**). A screen reader will read the alt text aloud so that the user understands the image and its purpose. Webpages and documents should include alt text for all images. Alt text can be as simple as the name of a famous individual shown in a photograph, or more complex, such as interpreting the results of a chart or graph. Productivity applications such as Microsoft Office and webpage creation apps prompt users to add alt text, and sometimes provide suggested alt text content.

Figure 1-11: Screen readers use alt text to describe an image

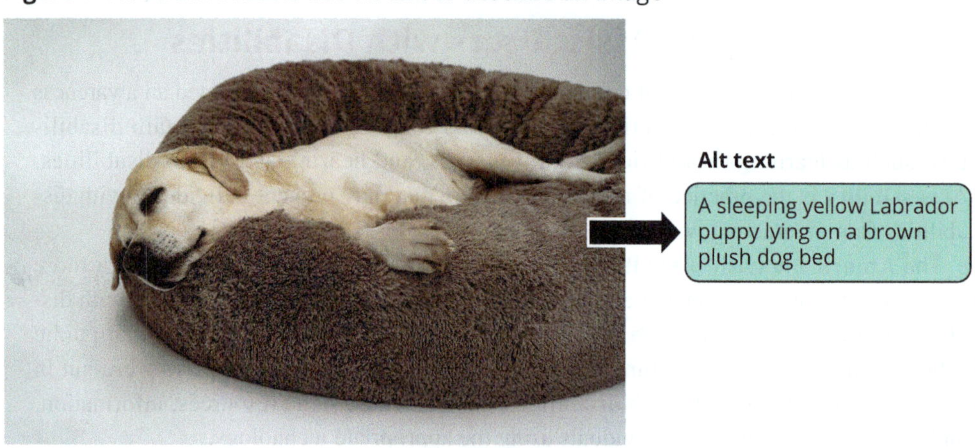

Lily Chernysheva/Shutterstock.com

Figure 1-12: Specialized keyboard for users with mobility issues

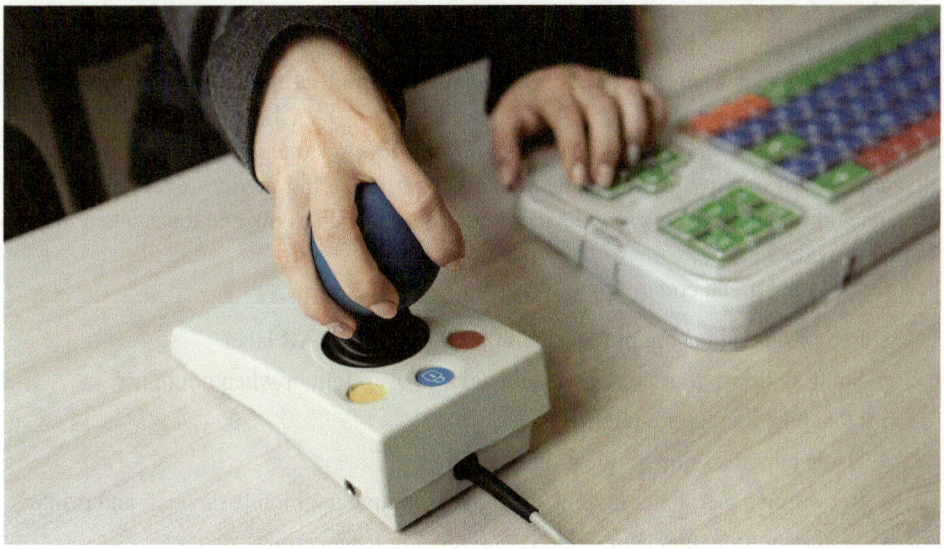

Reshetnikov_art/Shutterstock.com

Deaf or Deaf-Blind individuals can instruct programs or apps to display words or other visual clues instead of sounds, such as for a notification from an app. Captioning software displays scrolling text for dialogue in a video. Cameras can interpret sign language gestures into text.

Mobility issues can impact a user's ability to interact with hardware, such as a keyboard or a mouse (**Figure 1-12**). Users with limited hand mobility can use an on-screen keyboard, a keyboard with larger keys, or a hand-mounted pointer to control the pointer or insertion point. Alternatives to mouse buttons include a hand pad, a foot pedal, a receptor that detects facial motions, or a pneumatic instrument controlled by puffs of air. Users with a physical disability that causes hands to move involuntarily can purchase input devices such as a keyboard or mouse that are less sensitive to accidental interaction due to trembling or spasms.

Users with learning disabilities might struggle with reading words on a screen, handwriting, or retaining information. Technologies that help these users learn or perform tasks include:

- **Audio books** to read information aloud to the user instead of reading on a printed page or on the screen
- **Speech recognition programs** so the user can input data or information verbally
- **Graphic organizers** to enable a user to create an outline or structure of information

The basic premise of assisted technology is to improve accessibility for all users and provide the same opportunities to learn, work, and play as able-bodied users, no matter what disabilities a user has.

Apply Green Computing Concepts to Daily Life

People use, and often waste, resources such as electricity and paper while using technology. The practice of **green computing** involves reducing electricity consumed and environmental waste generated when using computers, mobile devices, and related technologies.

Personal computers, displays, printers, and other devices should comply with guidelines of the ENERGY STAR program (**Figure 1-13**). The United States Department of Energy (DOE) and the United States

Figure 1-13: Look for the Energy Star logo when purchasing appliances or devices

US Environmental Protection Agency, ENERGY STAR program

Environmental Protection Agency (EPA) developed the ENERGY STAR program to help reduce the amount of electricity used by computers and related devices. This program encourages manufacturers to create energy-efficient devices. For example, many devices switch to sleep or power save mode after a specified amount of inactive time.

Electronic waste and trash have a negative effect on the environment where it is discarded. You can avoid electronic waste by not replacing devices every time a new version comes out, and recycling devices and products such as ink and toner when they no longer provide value.

Your personal green computing efforts should include:

- Purchasing and using products with an ENERGY STAR label
- Shutting down your computers and devices overnight or when not in use
- Donating computer equipment
- Using paperless communication
- Recycling paper, toner and ink cartridges, computers, mobile devices, and printers
- Telecommuting and using video conferencing for meetings

Organizations can implement a variety of measures to reduce electrical waste, such as:

- Consolidating servers
- Purchasing high-efficiency equipment
- Using sleep modes and other power management features for computers and devices
- Buying computers and devices with lower power consumption processors and power supplies
- Using outside air, when possible, to cool the data center or computer facility
- Allowing employees to telecommute to save gas and reduce emissions from vehicles

Green computing practices are usually easy to implement and can make a huge impact on the environment.

Explain the Role of Technology in the Professional World

Nearly every job requires you to interact with technology to complete projects, exchange information with coworkers, and meet customers' needs. Technology careers span a range of specialities from software development to IT consulting to web marketing. And, no matter what business they're in, people interact with technology in almost every field, including business, education, and manufacturing. Whether you are looking for a job in a technology field or other area, you can use technology to prepare for and search for a job.

Explain Enterprise Computing

A large business with many employees is known as an enterprise. **Enterprise computing** refers to the use of technology by a company's employees to meet the needs of a large business. Each department of a company uses technology specific to its function. **Table 1-1** lists some of the uses of technology for different functional units.

Table 1-1: Enterprise functional units

Functional unit	Technology uses
Human resources	Track employees' personal data, including pay rates, benefits, and vacation time
Accounting	Keep track of income and spending
Sales	Manage contacts, schedule meetings, log customer interactions, and process orders
Information technology	Maintain and secure hardware and software
Engineering and product development	Develop plans for and test new products
Manufacturing	Monitor assembly of products and manage inventory of parts and products
Marketing	Create and track success of marketing campaigns that target specific demographics
Distribution	Analyze and track inventory and manage shipping
Customer service	Manage customer interactions

Identify Uses of Technology in the Workplace

Technological advances, such as the PC, enabled workers to do their jobs more efficiently while at their desks. Today's workers can use smartphones, the Internet, the cloud, and more to work remotely, whether they are **telecommuting** (working from home), or traveling halfway around the world.

An **intelligent workplace** uses technology to enable workers to connect to the company's network, communicate with each other, use productivity software and apps, meet via web conferencing, and more. Some companies provide employees with computers and devices that come with the necessary software and apps, network connectivity, and security. Other workplaces have a **BYOD (bring your own device)** policy, enabling employees to use their personal devices to conduct business. Companies use online collaborative productivity software to allow employees to share documents such as reports or spreadsheets and to make edits or comments.

Outline Technology Careers

The technology field provides opportunities for people of all skill levels and interests, and demand for computer professionals continues to grow. The following sections describe general technology career areas.

Software and Apps The software and apps field consists of companies that develop, manufacture, and support programs for computers, the web, and mobile devices. Some companies specialize in a certain area, such as productivity software or gaming. Other companies sell many types of software that work with both computers and mobile devices and may use the Internet to sync data and use collaborative features.

Technology Equipment The technology equipment field consists of manufacturers and distributors of computers, mobile devices, and other hardware. In addition to the companies that make the finished products, this field includes companies that manufacture the internal components such as chips, cables, and power supplies.

Table 1-2: IT responsibilities

IT area	Responsibilities
Management	Directs the planning, research, development, evaluation, and integration of technology
Research and software development	Analyzes, designs, develops, and implements new information technology and maintains existing systems
Technical support	Evaluates and integrates new technologies, administers the organization's data resources, and supports the centralized computer operating system and servers
Operations	Oversees the centralized computer equipment and administers the network
Training and support	Teaches employees how to use the information system and answers user questions
Information security	Develops and enforces policies that are designed to safeguard an organization's data and information from unauthorized users

IT Departments Most medium and large businesses and organizations have an **Information Technology (IT) department**. IT staff are responsible for ensuring that all the computer operations, mobile devices, and networks run smoothly. They also determine when and if the organization requires new hardware, mobile devices, or software. IT jobs typically are divided into the areas described in **Table 1-2**.

Technology Service and Repair The technology service and repair field provides preventative maintenance, component installations, and repair services to customers. Some technicians receive training and certifications from manufacturers to become specialists in devices from that manufacturer. Many technology equipment manufacturers include diagnostic software with their computers and devices that assist technicians in identifying problems. Technicians can use the Internet to diagnose and repair software remotely, by accessing the user's computer or device from a different location.

Technology Sales Technology salespeople must possess a general understanding of technology, as well as specific knowledge of the product they are selling. Strong people skills, including listening and communicating, are important. Some salespeople work directly for a technology equipment or software manufacturer, while others work for resellers of technology, including retail stores.

Technology Education, Training, and Support Schools, colleges, universities, and companies all need qualified educators to provide technology-related education and training. Instructors at an educational institution typically have a background and degree related to the technology they are teaching. Corporate trainers teach employees how to use the technology specific to the business or industry. Help desk specialists provide support by answering questions from employees to help them troubleshoot problems.

IT Consulting An IT consultant typically has gained experience in one or more areas, such as software development, social media, or network configuration. IT consultants provide technology services to clients based on their specific areas of expertise. Sometimes a company will hire a large group of IT consultants to work together on a specific task, such as building a new network infrastructure or database.

System Development System developers analyze and create software, apps, databases, websites and web-based development platforms, cloud services, and networks. Developers identify the business requirements and desired outcomes for the system, specify the structure and security needed, and design and program the system.

Web Marketing and Social Media Careers in web marketing require you to be familiar not only with marketing strategies, but also with web-based platforms and social media apps. Web marketers create social media plans, including the content and timing of marketing campaigns, posts, and emails. Search engine optimization (SEO) knowledge helps to create web content and layout that enhances the content's results when users search for content.

Data Storage, Retrieval, and Analysis Employees in this field must be knowledgeable about collecting, analyzing, storing, and reporting data from databases or the web. Data scientists use analytics to compile statistics on data to create strategies or analyze business practices. Web analytics experts measure Internet data, such as website traffic patterns and ads (**Figure 1-14**). Digital forensics examiners use evidence found on computers, networks, and devices to help solve crimes.

Information and Systems Security Careers in information and systems security require you to be informed about how to address and prevent potential threats to a device or network, including viruses and hacking. Security specialists need to know tools and techniques to prevent against and recover from digital attacks.

Figure 1-14: Web analytic data measures website traffic patterns

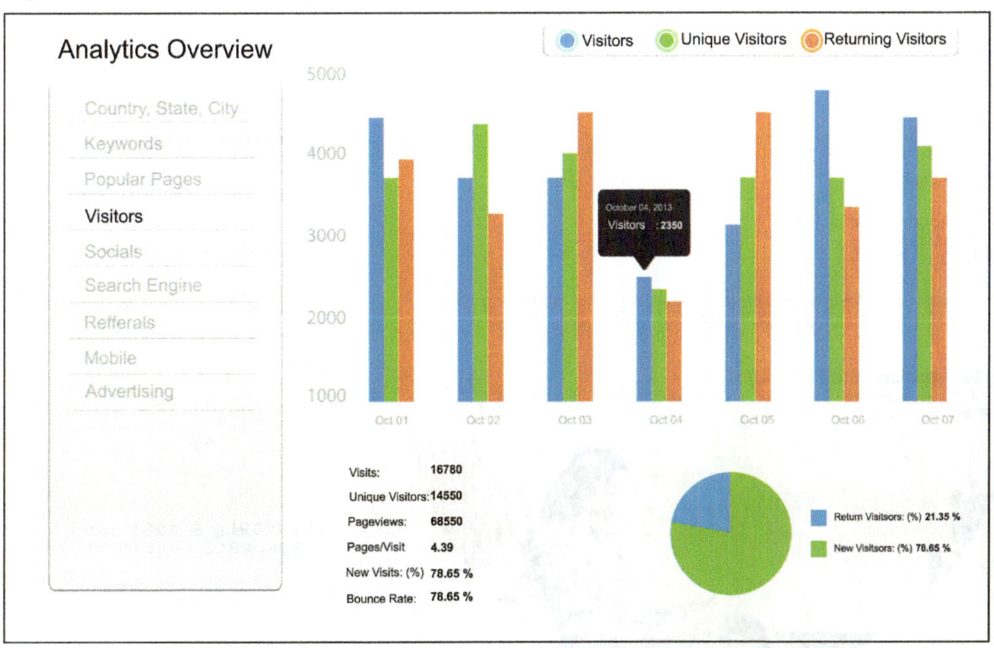

Artgraphixel/Shutterstock.com

Explain How You Might Prepare for a Career in Technology

You can use both social media and job search websites to learn about technology careers and to promote yourself to potential employers. By creating a profile on a career networking site or creating a personal website or blog that showcases your talents, hiring managers can learn more about you beyond what you can convey in a traditional, one-page paper resume.

Professional Online Presence Recommended strategies for creating a professional online presence include:

- Do not use humorous or informal names for your account profiles, blog, or domain name.
- Include a photo that represents you in a confident, professional manner.
- Upload an electronic copy of your resume.
- Include links to videos, publications, or digital content you have created.
- Proofread your resume, blog, website, or profile carefully to avoid spelling and grammar mistakes.
- Enable privacy settings on your personal social media accounts, and never post anything online that you would not want a potential employer to access.

Online social networks for professionals can help you keep up with past coworkers, instructors, potential employers, and others with whom you have a professional connection. You can use these networks to search for jobs, learn about a company before interviewing, join groups of people with similar interests or experiences, share information about your career, and communicate with contacts. LinkedIn (**Figure 1-15**) and other professional networking websites also offer online training courses to keep your skills up-to-date.

Certifications Some technology careers require you to have certain certifications. A certification demonstrates your knowledge in a specific area to employers and potential employers. Online materials and print books exist to help you prepare for a certification

Figure 1-15: LinkedIn is a career-based social networking site

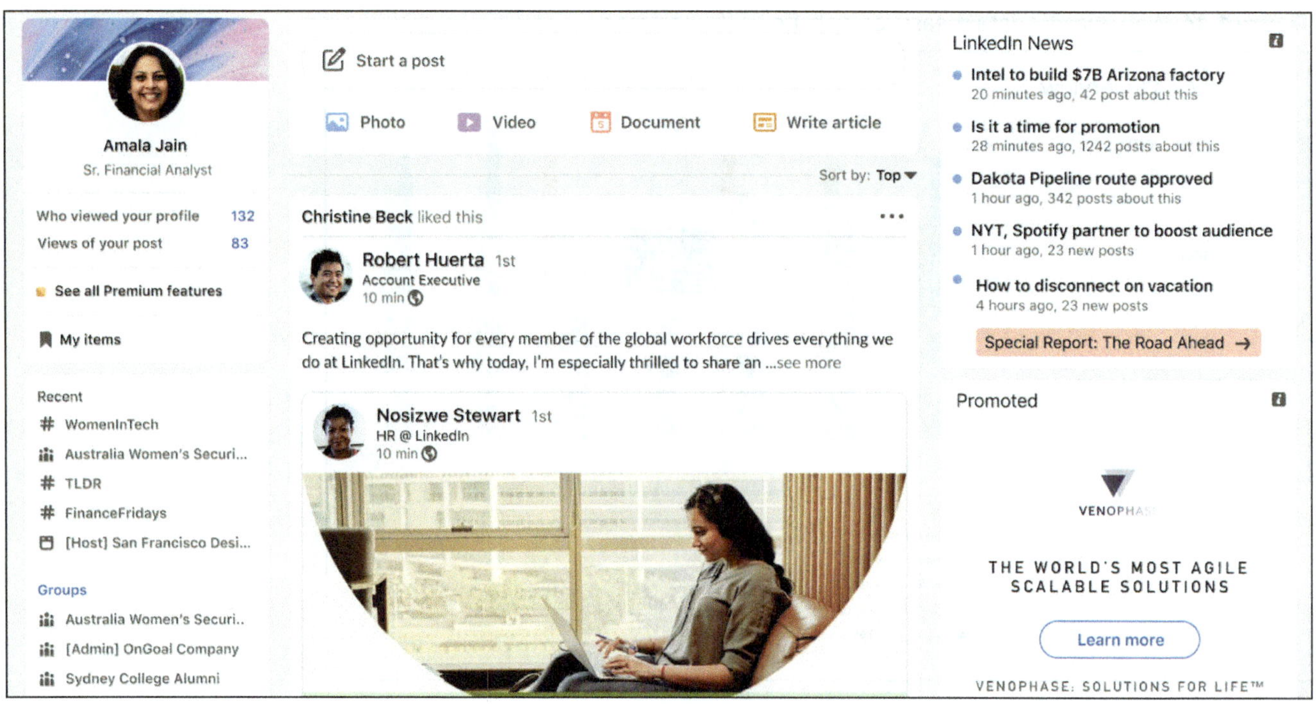

LinkedIn Corporation

exam. Most certifications do not require coursework assignments, but instead require you to pass an exam that demonstrates your proficiency in the area. Tests typically are taken at an authorized testing center. Some tests are multiple choice, while others are skills-based. You likely will have to pay a fee to take the exam. Some areas that offer certifications include:

- Application software
- Data analytics, database, and web design
- Hardware
- Networking
- Operating systems
- Programming
- Cybersecurity

Obtaining a certification requires you to spend time and money. Certifications demonstrate your commitment to your chosen area and can help you land a job.

Technology in K-12 Education Schools use social networking tools to promote school events, work cooperatively on group projects, and teach concepts such as anti-bullying. Online productivity software enables students to work collaboratively on projects and send the finished assignment to the teacher using email, reducing the need for paper printouts. These factors and more create an **intelligent classroom**, in which technology is used to facilitate learning and communication.

Technology in Higher Education A college or university might use a **learning management system (LMS)** to set up web-based training sites where students can check their progress in a course, take practice tests, and exchange messages with the instructor or other students. Students also can view instructor lectures online and take classes or earn a degree online. Ebooks let students read and access content from their tablet or device, and access digital assets like videos associated with the content.

Technology in Healthcare Physicians use computers to monitor patients' vital signs and research symptoms and diagnoses. The **mobile health (mHealth)** trend refers to healthcare professionals using smartphones or tablets to access health records stored in the cloud, and to patients using digital devices to monitor their conditions and treatments, reducing the need for visits to the doctor's office. For example, mHealth apps can track prescription information and text reminders to take medication, or even contact the pharmacy to refill the prescription. Medical monitoring devices, such as electronic bracelets, collect vital signs and send the data to a specialist. Patients can ingest smart pills that contain sensors to monitor medication or tiny cameras to enable a physician to view the patient's internal organs without invasive procedures. Healthcare also uses 3-D printers to manufacture skin for burn patients, and prosthetic devices and casts.

Figure 1-16: Codes on packages can be scanned to determine their location

DC Studio/Shutterstock.com

Technology in the Transportation Industry Transportation workers use handheld computers to scan codes on packages or containers of products before loading them on a vehicle, train, ship, or plane (**Figure 1-16**). You then can track the progress of your package as it makes its way to you. Computers find an efficient route for

Figure 1-17: Robots often are used in computer manufacturing

Gorodenkoff/Shutterstock.com

the packages and track their progress. Drivers use GPS to navigate quickly and safely, avoiding traffic and hazardous conditions. Soon, self-driving trucks will use robotics for mechanical control. Automated vehicles increase independent transportation options for people with disabilities.

Technology in Manufacturing Manufacturers use **computer-aided manufacturing (CAM)** to streamline production and ship products more quickly. With CAM, robots perform work that is too dangerous, detailed, or monotonous for people (**Figure 1-17**). In particular, they play a major role in automotive, metal and plastics, and electrical and electronics manufacturing. In the automotive industry, for example, robots typically paint the bodies of cars because painting is complex, difficult, and hazardous. Pairing robotic systems with human workers also improves quality, cost efficiency, and competitiveness. Computers and mobile devices make it possible to order parts and materials from the warehouse to assemble custom products. A company's computers monitor assembly lines and equipment using **machine-to-machine (M2M)** communications.

Module 1 Summary

Computers have evolved from large, inefficient, and expensive devices that used technology such as vacuum tubes to smaller, more powerful connected devices such as PCs, smartphones, and more.

Computers impact your daily life in many ways, including the use of embedded computers in vehicles, ATMs, and stores, and the Internet of Things (IoT) that allows smart home appliances and other devices to communicate over the Internet or a wireless network. IoT has many applications within both the personal realm (such as wearable fitness trackers and managing appliances) and the business world (such as manufacturing sensors or retail inventory tracking). Differences in access to technology, especially the Internet, have led to a digital divide that limits opportunities for many.

Users with disabilities can use many different devices and software that enable them to access and use technology. These are crucial in providing everyone with the same opportunities to learn, work, and play. Many technologies exist to help provide accessibility to all users, and laws such as the Americans with Disabilities Act (ADA) require workplaces to provide accessible products.

There are many ways you can employ green computing practices to help reduce your impact on the environment, including donating old computer equipment, telecommuting, and purchasing ENERGY STAR products.

Technology has had a large impact on the professional world. Enterprise computing refers to the needs of large companies to provide technology for their different functional units, such as customer service and accounting. Intelligent workplaces enable employees to communicate and perform tasks efficiently. Education, transportation, healthcare, and manufacturing all use technology to reduce costs and increase safety and efficiency.

There are many careers available to you in the technology field, including software development, technology equipment, IT, service and repair, education and training, consulting, system development, marketing and social media, data storage and analysis, and security. To prepare for a career in technology, you should create a professional online presence and take advantage of certification options.

Review Questions

1. Data is ________.

a. raw facts, such as text or numbers
b. processed output
c. the result of a calculation
d. another term for software

2. The second generation of computers replaced vacuum tubes with ________.

a. display devices
b. glass crystals
c. transformers
d. transistors

3. The premise that objects can be tagged, tracked, and monitored through a local network or across the Internet refers to ________.

a. intelligent workspaces
b. the digital divide
c. the Internet of Things
d. networking

4. The gap between those who have access to technology and its resources and information, especially on the Internet, and those who do not, is known as the ________.

a. Internet of Things
b. digital divide
c. information abyss
d. accessibility factor

5. Descriptive text added to an object is called ________ text.

a. associative
b. alternative
c. accessible
d. assistive

6. (True or False) Green computing involves reducing electricity consumed and environmental waste generated when using computers, mobile devices, and related technologies.

7. A company's ________ department oversees the centralized computer equipment and administers the network.

a. management
b. technical support
c. operations
d. information security

8. The use of technology by a company's employees to meet the needs of a large business is called ________ computing.

a. enterprise
b. macro
c. ultra
d. resourceful

9. A company's BYOD policy refers to allowing employees to bring their own ________.

a. dogs
b. data
c. documents
d. devices

10. Colleges set up web-based training sites where students can check their progress in a course, take practice tests, and exchange messages with the instructor or other students using a ________ management system (LMS).

a. learning
b. linked
c. locational
d. live

11. A company's computers monitor assembly lines and equipment using _________ communications.
    a. CAM
    b. AI
    c. IT
    d. M2M

12. (True or False) When looking for a job, you should use humorous or informal names for your account profiles, blog, or domain name to make yourself stand out.

Discussion Questions

1. How have embedded computers and the IoT impacted your daily life? What additional uses can you see yourself using? What security or other risks might you encounter with IoT?
2. How do the following technologies help you in your quest to become a digital citizen: kiosks, enterprise computing, and green computing?
3. What additional uses of technology can you see in the workplace? List ways technology impacts other careers not discussed in this module, such as finance, government, non-profits, and agriculture.
4. List guidelines for creating a professional online presence. View your own online presence and make a list of changes you should make in order to enhance how potential employers might view you. How should you go about making these changes? What additional advice would you give to others seeking jobs?

Critical Thinking Activities

1. You work in the educational software industry. Your boss asks you to give a brief lecture to other employees about the digital divide. Create a one-page document in which you define in your own words and give examples of the impact of the digital divide, and list ways your company can work to narrow the gap between students without reliable access to educational software, the Internet, and the hardware on which to run both. What is your role as a company and employee to address the digital divide? What aspects of the digital divide do you find most troubling or confusing?
2. You decide to reduce your environmental impact by recycling more, going paperless, and using environmentally safe cleaning products. List one or two reasons why you should add green computing to your efforts. Research five ways you can apply green computing to your daily life and rank them in order of importance. The next time you think about replacing a device, do you think this information will impact your decision? In what ways can you encourage others to do the same?
3. Research the history of the IDEA and the ADA. List achievements and developments of both, and compare how they impact both students and employees. What examples of the impact of both have you seen in your school or workplace?
4. In addition to the developments outlined in this module, list and describe other technological advances of which you are aware that occurred before you were born and after. Which advancement has had the most impact on you, personally? Why?

Apply Your Skills

Shea Foley is finishing her degree in social media marketing. During her time at school, she has learned about how to use technology for productivity, and specifically how to use technology in social media marketing. Shea recently visited her school's career advisory center and received a list of tips to use technology to find an entry-level job in her field.

Working in a small group or by yourself, complete the following:

1. How have past technological developments helped provide the basis for Shea's job and her ability to do her assigned tasks? If you could come up with an additional technological development that might occur in the future, what would it be, and what would Shea use it for? How might you apply the technologies you have learned about in this module to your current job or schoolwork, or to a job you have held in the past?
2. List three ways in which Shea will use technology to perform her daily tasks. Which technologies do you think will be most effective, and why?
3. What other departments might Shea interact with at work, and in what ways? List three. Which would be most important? Why? Which department interests you most? What skills might you need to be able to find a career in that department or field?

Module 2

The Web

In This Module

- Explain the role of the web in daily life
- Describe websites and webpages
- Use e-commerce
- Explain how information literacy applies to web searches and research
- Conduct online research

VAKS-Stock Agency/Shutterstock.com

Unathi Mwange uses the web in every aspect of his life, even as he commutes to school. Connecting to the cloud with his mobile phone, he stores, retrieves, and shares files. He uses his browser to log onto his school's LMS to check his grades, participate in web-based lectures, and gather content for class projects from reliable online resources. He completes assignments using web apps, compares deals on headphones at e-commerce websites, and uses an online auction website to buy and sell sports memorabilia.

You probably use the web dozens or hundreds of times a day to do things such as locate and reserve a place for lunch, keep track of your budget, shop for new clothes, post a comment on a blog or message board, or search for photos or facts you need to complete a project at school or work. As a vast library of content, the web is where you go for entertainment, bargains, news, and information of all kinds. To find what you need on the web, you should understand the types of resources the web provides.

In this module, you will examine the role of the web in daily life. You will explore the components of websites, webpages, and e-commerce, determine how to connect to the Internet, gain an understanding of information literacy, and learn about tools for trustworthy web searches and online research. As you reflect on what you learn in this module, ask yourself: How would your life be different if you didn't have access to the web? What types of websites are most useful to you? How can you ensure you are participating in e-commerce safely? What impact does net neutrality have on how you access the Internet? How do you ensure that the information you find online is accurate?

Explain the Role of the Web in Daily Life

While sometimes used interchangeably, the Internet and the web are two different things. The **Internet** is a global collection of millions of *computers* linked together to share information worldwide. The **web**, originally known as the **World Wide Web**, is a collection of *webpages* located on computers around the world, connected through the Internet. The web has changed the way people access information, conduct business transactions, and communicate (**Figure 2-1**). Almost everyone can use the web because it is part of the Internet. Today, billions of people use the Internet and the web. The more you know about the web and how to access its contents, the more you can benefit from using it.

Figure 2-1: The web can be used to communicate, shop, share information, travel, and more

Viewvie/Shutterstock.com

Define Web Browsing Terms

When you use a mobile phone or other device to access the web, you are accessing a collection of webpages located on computers around the world, connected through the Internet. A **webpage** (**Figure 2-2**) is an electronic document that can contain text, graphics, sound, video, and links to other webpages. The main page in a website is called the **home page**. Webpages can be either static or dynamic, depending on how the content is presented. A webpage that is **static** is one where the content does not change very often. A webpage that

Figure 2-2: Webpage

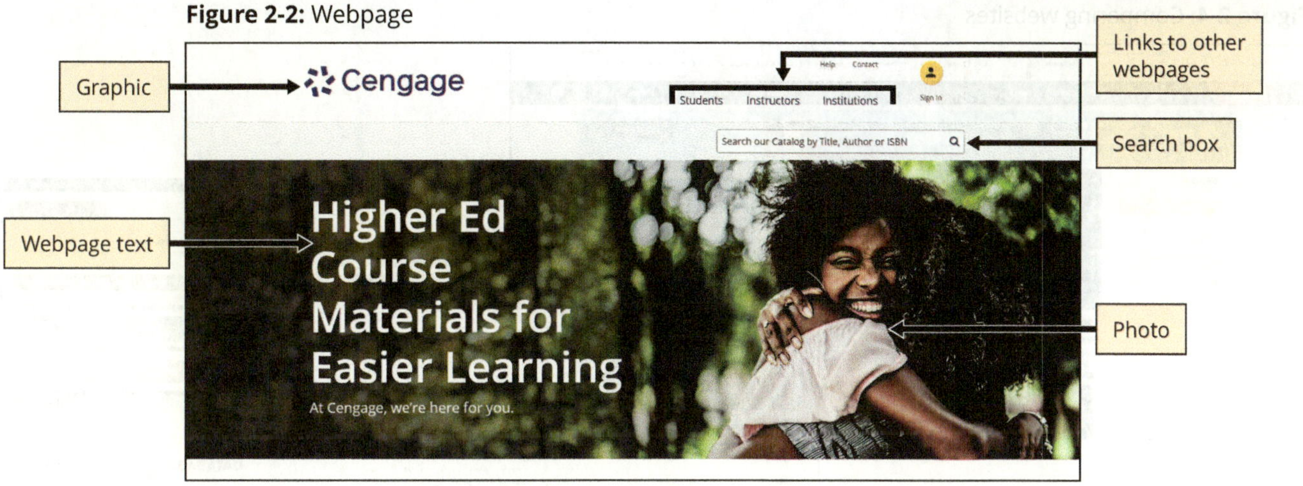

is **dynamic** is one with content that changes as you interact with it, such as a news site that updates based on breaking news, or for a weather website that displays content based on the visitor's location or preferences.

Successful websites are designed to be visually appealing, and to present the content in a logical format. Most web designers use the concept of **responsive web design**, which is a way to provide content so that it adapts appropriately to the size of the display on any device, such as on a laptop or a smartphone (**Figure 2-3**).

A collection of webpages (often shortened to "pages") makes up a **website** (often shortened to "site"). A company, organization, institution, group, or person creates and maintains a website. In general, websites focus on a specific topic, business, or service.

Figure 2-3: Responsive web design adapts content to fit different devices

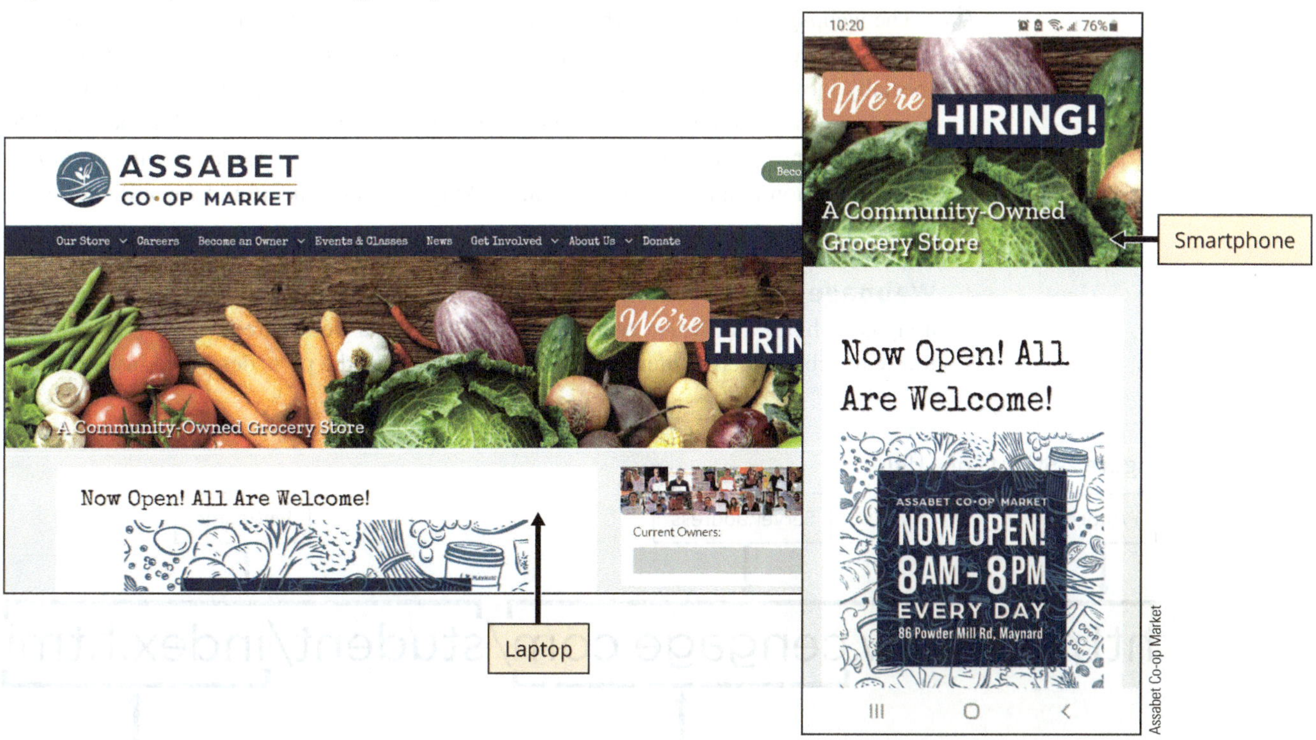

Figure 2-4: Comparing websites

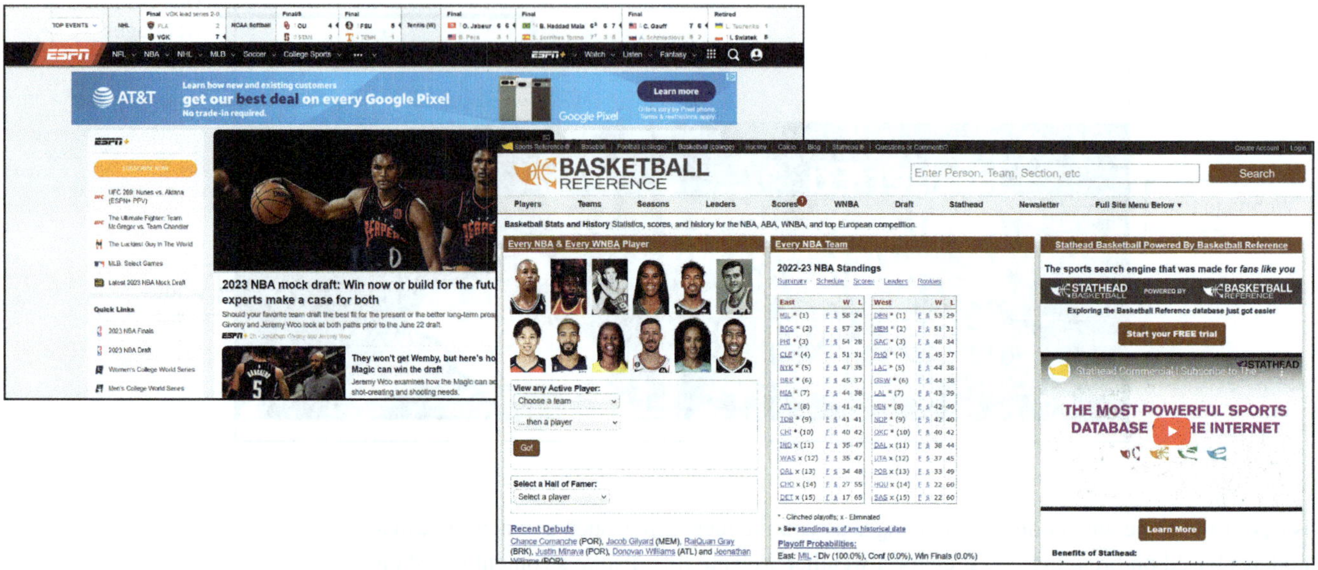

ESPN Sports Media Ltd; Basketball Reference

When you visit a website for the first time, figure out its purpose so you know what type of content to expect and which actions are appropriate. For example, the purpose of the ESPN website is to provide sports news and entertainment for free, while the Basketball Reference website provides statistics only, and has additional information for subscribers. Both websites are dedicated to sports, but each has a different purpose (**Figure 2-4**).

Browsers To access the web, you open a **browser**, which is an app designed to display webpages. Google Chrome, Apple Safari, Mozilla Firefox, and Microsoft Edge are examples of popular browsers. You use the tools in a browser to **navigate** the web, or move from one webpage to another.

The webpage that appears when you open a browser is called the **home page** or **start page**. To display a different webpage, you use a link, short for **hyperlink**, which is a specially formatted word, phrase, or graphic that, when clicked or tapped, lets you display a webpage on the Internet, another file, an email, or another location within the same file, or perform another action, such as sending an email message. Links enable you to pursue information in a nonlinear fashion, clicking relevant links if and when their content appeals to you.

Webpage Identification To keep track of billions of webpages, the Internet assigns each one a **uniform resource locator (URL)**, a web address used by a browser to locate a website on the Internet. A URL can consist of the parts described in **Figure 2-5**.

Figure 2-5: Parts of a URL

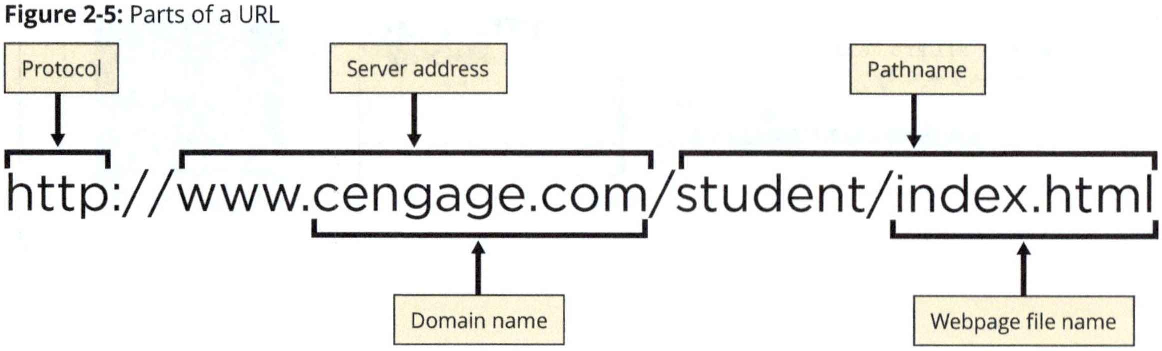

Table 2-1: URL parts

URL part	Definition
Protocol	A standardized procedure computers use to exchange information
Server address	The address of the server storing the webpage
Pathname	The address to the folder containing the webpage
File name	The name of the webpage file

If you can interpret a URL, you can learn about the sponsor, origin, and location of the webpage and catch a glimpse of how the web works. **Table 2-1** defines each part of a URL.

When the URL for a webpage starts with http://, the browser uses the **Hypertext Transfer Protocol (HTTP)**, the most common way to transfer information around the web, to retrieve the page. Often when giving a URL, the http:// prefix is omitted, but the browser knows to fill it in.

A server is a powerful networked computer that provides resources to other computers. A **web server** stores webpages and delivers them to computers requesting the pages through a browser. In the server address www.cengage.com, the www indicates that the server is a web server, cengage is the name the Cengage company chose for this website, and .com means that a commercial entity runs the web server.

The server address in a URL corresponds to an Internet Protocol (IP) address, which identifies every computer on the Internet. An **Internet Protocol (IP) address** is a unique number that consists of four to six sets of numbers from 0 to 255 separated by periods, or dots, as in 69.32.132.255. Although computers can use IP addresses easily, they are difficult for people to remember, so domain names were created. A **domain name** identifies one or more IP addresses, such as cengage.com. URLs use the domain name in the server address part of the URL to identify a particular website.

In addition, each file stored on a web server has a unique pathname. The pathname in a URL includes the names of the folders containing the file, the file name, and its extension. A common file name extension for webpages is .html, sometimes shortened to .htm. For example, the pathname might be student/index.html, which specifies a file named index, saved in the .html format, and stored in a folder named student.

Not all URLs include a pathname. If you don't specify a pathname or file name in a URL, most web browsers open a file named index.html or index.htm, which is the default name for a website's main page.

Web Navigation The **address bar** is the part of a browser window that displays the location of the current webpage (**Figure 2-6**). You can also use the address bar to type the URL of the webpage you want to display, or enter terms for which you want to search.

Figure 2-6: Navigating the web with a browser

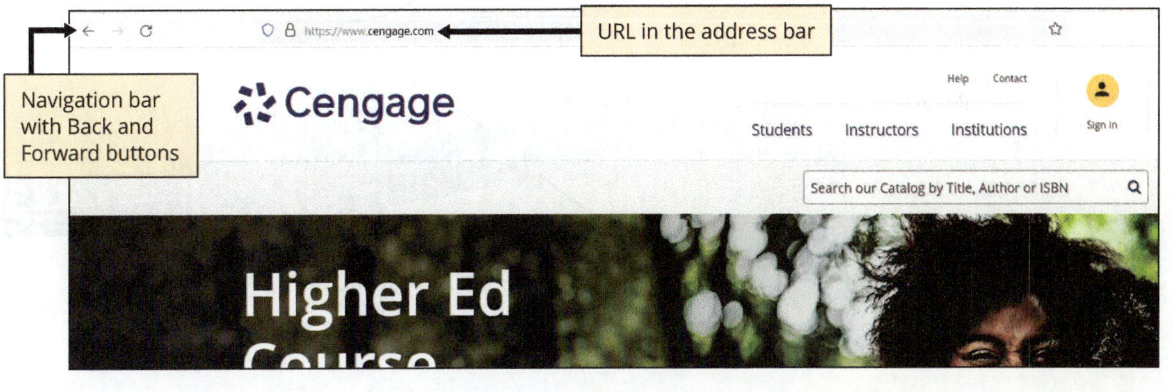

As you navigate websites, your browser keeps a copy of each page you view in a **cache**, so that the next time you go to a webpage, it loads more quickly. The browser also keeps track of pages you have viewed in sequence by tracking **breadcrumbs**—the path you followed to display a webpage. The **navigation bar** in a browser includes buttons such as Back and Forward that you can use to revisit webpages along the breadcrumb path.

Connect to the Internet

In order to access the Internet, you first must create a connection between the Internet and your device. You can connect your computers or devices to the Internet using wired or wireless technology. With a wired connection, a computer or device physically attaches via a cable or wire to a communications device that transmits data and other items over transmission media to the Internet. A **modem**, a device that sends and receives data over telephone or cable lines and is connected to your computer, is an example of a communications device. Wireless communications can use technologies including cellular radio, satellite, or Wi-Fi to connect to the Internet. **Wi-Fi** is a wireless data network technology that provides high-speed data connections that do not require a physical connection. It is used for mobile devices.

Before you can connect to the Internet, you need to select an Internet Service Provider. An **Internet Service Provider (ISP)** is a company that sells Internet access. Methods to connect to the Internet include cellular networks, Wi-Fi hot spots, and mobile hot spots. A **hot spot** is a wireless network device that provides Internet connections to mobile computers and devices. A **mobile hot spot** enables you to connect a phone, computer, or other device to the Internet through the cellular network. Various types of cellular networks, including 4G and 5G ("G" stands for "generation") can provide Internet services in most locations where cellular service is offered (**Figure 2-7**). 5G networks provide higher-speed data transmission.

Figure 2-7: How a cellular network might work

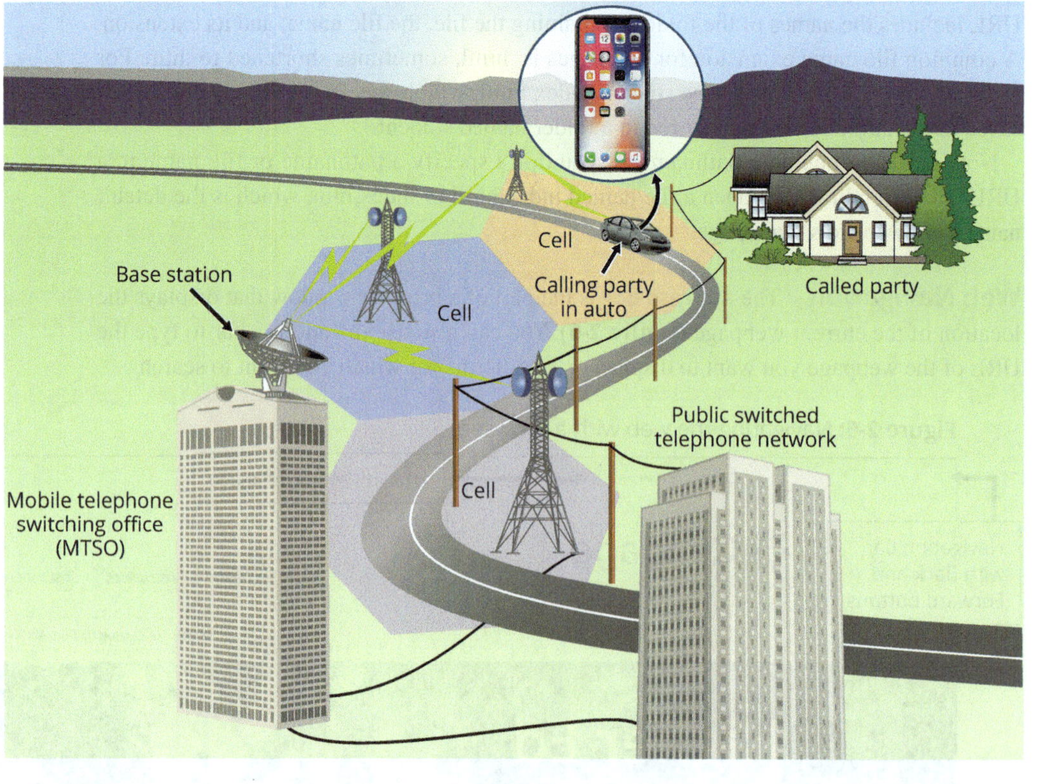

Table 2-2: Popular TLDs in the United States

TLD	Generally used for
.biz	Unrestricted use, but usually identifies businesses
.com	Most commercial sites that sell products and services
.edu	Academic and research sites such as schools and universities
.gov	U.S. government organizations
.int	International treaty organizations
.mil	Military organizations
.mobi	Sites optimized for mobile devices
.net	Network providers, ISPs, and other Internet administrative organizations
.org	Organizations such as political or not for profit (any website can have the .org TLD but, traditionally, only professional and nonprofit organizations such as churches and humanitarian groups use it)
.pro	Licensed professionals

Explain the Purpose of a Top-Level Domain

In a web address, the three-letter extension after the period in a domain name indicates a **top-level domain (TLD)**, such as the "com" in "cengage.com". The TLD identifies the type of organization associated with the domain. As you visit websites, you might notice some that have TLDs other than .com, such as .edu for educational institutions and .gov for U.S. government agencies. The TLD provides a clue about the content of the website.

An organization called Public Technical Identifiers (PTI) approves and controls TLDs, such as those in **Table 2-2**, which lists popular TLDs in the United States. For websites outside the United States, the suffix of the domain name often includes a two-letter country code TLD, such as .au for Australia and .uk for the United Kingdom.

Describe Internet Standards

Have you ever wondered who is in charge of the web? Who maintains the webpages? Who makes sure all the parts of the complex system work together? One organization is the **Internet Engineering Task Force (IETF)**. This group sets standards that allow devices, services, and applications to work together across the Internet. For example, the IETF sets standards for IP addresses, as well as rules for routing data, securing websites, and developing guidelines for responsible Internet use.

Another leading organization is the **World Wide Web Consortium (W3C)**, which consists of hundreds of organizations and experts that work together to write web standards. The W3C publishes standards on topics including building webpages, technologies for enabling web access from any device, and browser and search engine design.

Describe Websites and Webpages

People around the world visit websites and webpages to accomplish the types of online tasks (**Figure 2-8**). In addition, you can use websites to play games; access news, weather, and sports information; download or read books; participate in online training; attend classes; and more.

Identify Types of Websites

Chances are, a certain type of website provides whatever service or content you're looking for. Most websites fall into one or more of the following categories:

banking and finance	entertainment	portals
blogs	government or organization	retail and auctions
bookmarking	health and fitness	science
business	information and research	search sites
careers and employment	mapping	travel and tourism
content aggregation	media sharing	website creation and management
e-commerce	news, weather, sports, and other mass media	web apps and software as a service (SaaS)
educational	online social networks	wikis and collaboration

Besides displaying information and other content, some websites provide ways to interact with them. You can contribute ideas, comments, images, and videos to an online conversation through interactive community pages, social media sites, and **blogs**, which are informal websites with time-stamped articles, or posts, in a diary or journal format.

A **content aggregator** site gathers, organizes, and then distributes web content. As a subscriber, you choose the type of content you want and receive updates when new content is available.

Figure 2-8: Tasks you can accomplish using websites

photosince/Shutterstock.com; Rawpixel.com/Shutterstock.com; fizkes/Shutterstock.com

Figure 2-9: Educational website

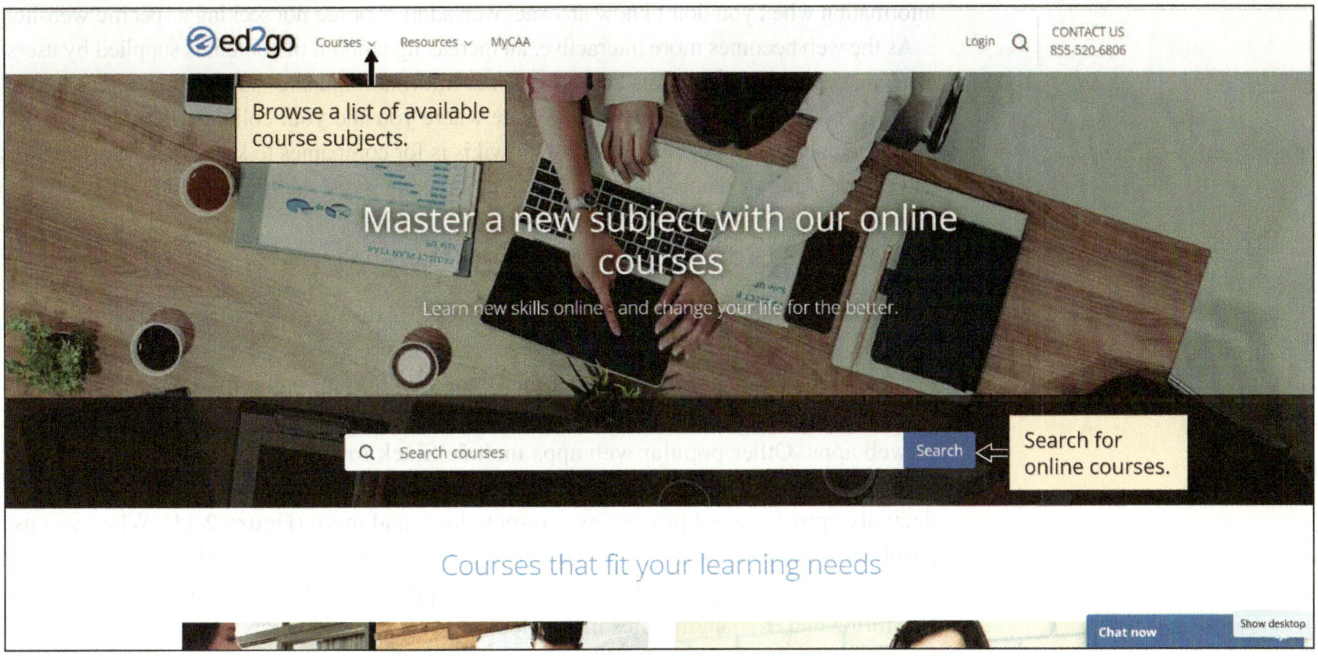

Education To Go

An educational website such as ed2go (**Figure 2-9**) offers formal and informal teaching and learning. The web contains thousands of tutorials where you can learn how to build a website or cook a meal. For a more structured learning experience, companies provide online training to employees, and colleges offer online classes and degrees.

On entertainment websites, you can view or discuss activities ranging from sports to videos. For example, you can cast a vote on a topic for a television show.

With a **media sharing site**, such as YouTube or TikTok, you can display and view various types of media, such as photos, videos, and music, share it with other site members, and manage it. Use a media sharing site to post, organize, store, and download media.

An **online social network**, also called a **social network** or **social media** site, is an online community where users can share their interests, ideas, stories, photos, music, and videos online with other registered users. In many online social networks, you can communicate through text, voice, and video chat, and play games with other members. Facebook, X (formerly known as Twitter), WhatsApp, Instagram, Pinterest, and Tumblr are some websites classified as online social networks. You interact with an online social network through a website or mobile app on your computer or mobile device (**Figure 2-10**).

Figure 2-10: Online social networking websites

xlaura/Shutterstock.com

A **web portal**, or **portal**, is a website that combines pages from many sources and provides access to those pages. Most web portals are customized to meet your needs and interests. For example, your bank might create a web portal that includes snapshots of your accounts and access to financial information.

Using a search site such as Google, you can find websites, webpages, images, videos, news, maps, and other information related to a specific topic. A **search engine** is software used by search sites to locate relevant webpages by creating a simple query based on your search criteria and storing the collected data in a search database. You also can use a search engine to solve mathematical equations, define words, find flights, and more.

General-purpose search sites such as Google, Yahoo!, and Bing help you locate web information when you don't know an exact web address or are not seeking a specific website.

As the web becomes more interactive, an increasing amount of content is supplied by users. You can contribute comments and opinions to informational sites such as news sites, blogs, and wikis. A **wiki** is a collaborative website where you and your colleagues can modify and publish content on a webpage. One use of wikis is for companies to keep track of procedures and policies, and to enable employees to contribute notes and additional information.

Explain the Pros and Cons of Web Apps

In addition to using a browser to visit websites and display webpages, you can use it to access a **web app**, which is an app stored on an Internet server that you can run entirely in a browser. A web app resides on a server on the Internet, rather than on your computer or mobile device. For example, Microsoft Office provides Excel, PowerPoint, and Word as web apps. Other popular web apps include Slack for group collaboration, Trello for project management, and Google Docs, which, like Microsoft Office, offers a suite of productivity apps for word processing, presentations, and more (**Figure 2-11**). When you use a web app, you usually store your data on the web app's server using cloud computing.

You can run many apps as traditional installed apps or as web apps. Examples include Box, for storing and exchanging files in the cloud, and Skype, which lets you communicate with others using video and voice. **Table 2-3** summarizes the pros and cons of using web apps.

Figure 2-11: Web apps running in a browser

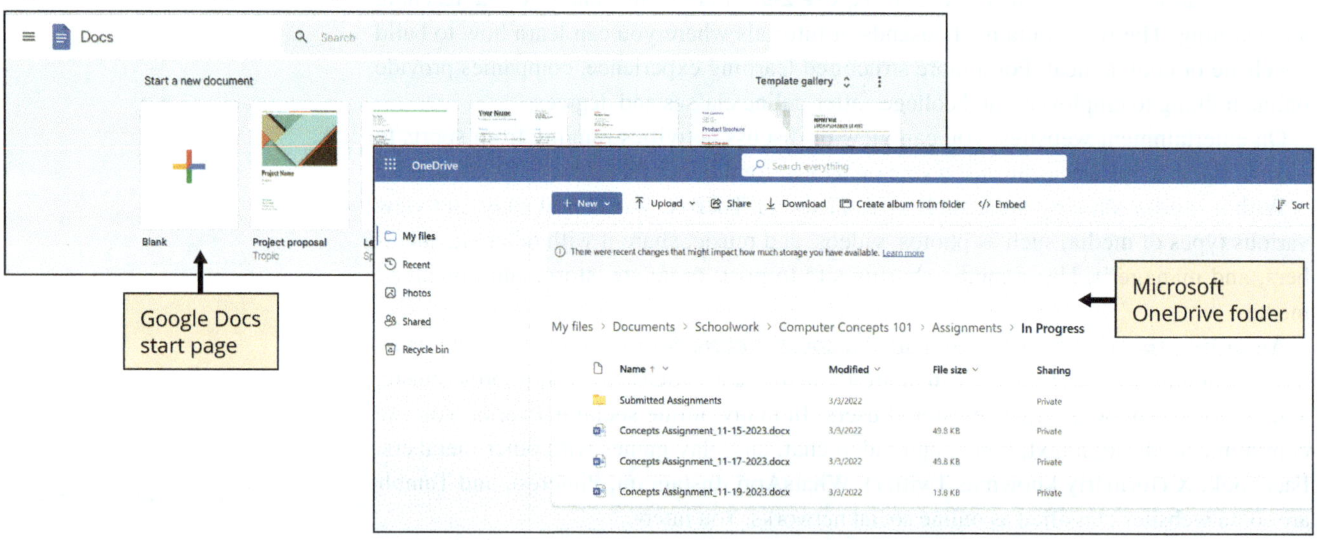

Google LLC

Table 2-3: Pros and cons of web apps

Pros	Cons
Access web apps from any device with a browser and Internet connection.	You must be online to use web apps.
Collaborate with others no matter their location.	Your files are more vulnerable to security and privacy violations.
Store your work on the app's website so you can access it anytime and anywhere.	If the web app provider has technical problems, you might not be able to access your work.
Save storage space on your device.	If the web app provider goes out of business, you can lose your files.
Access the latest version of the app without installing updates.	Web apps often offer fewer features and may run more slowly than installed apps.

Identify the Major Components of a Webpage

Although web design is constantly evolving, webpages typically include five major areas: header or banner, navigation bar or menu, body, social media links, and footer (**Figure 2-12**). Each area can include text, graphics, links, and media such as audio and video.

- **Header**: Located at the top of a webpage, the header or banner usually includes a logo to identify the organization sponsoring the webpage and a title to indicate the topic or purpose of the webpage. Headers and navigation bars can also provide a Search tool for searching the website.
- **Navigation bar**: A bar or menu lists links to other major parts of the website.
- **Body**: The body is the main content area of the webpage, and can provide text, images, audio, and video.
- **Social media links**: An area that includes links to social networking accounts and platforms. These often appear in a sidebar on the webpage, near the navigation bar, or in the footer.
- **Footer**: Located at the bottom of a webpage, the footer contains links to other parts of the website and lists information about the webpage, such as who owns the content.

Figure 2-12: Parts of a webpage

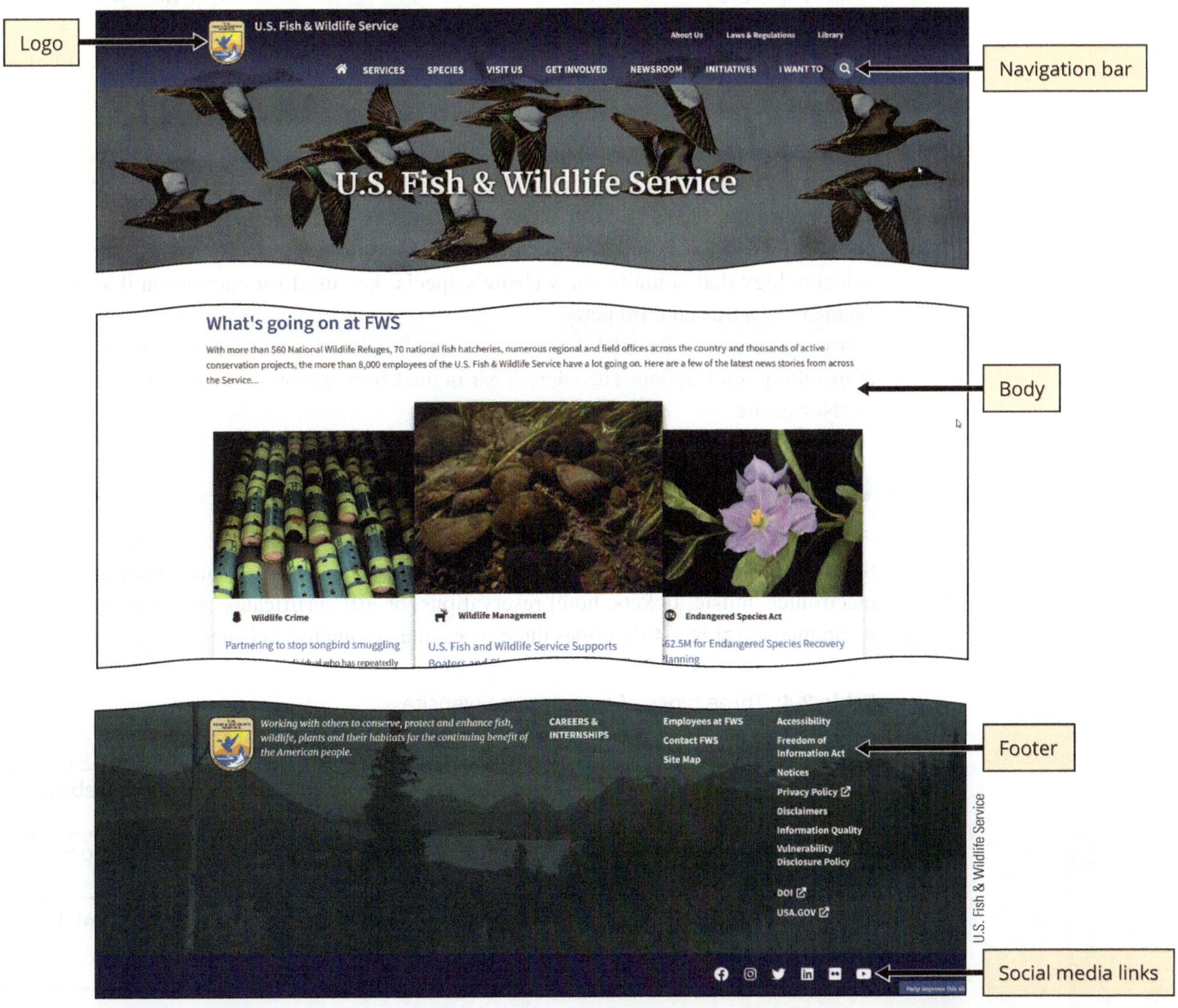

Figure 2-13: Secure website

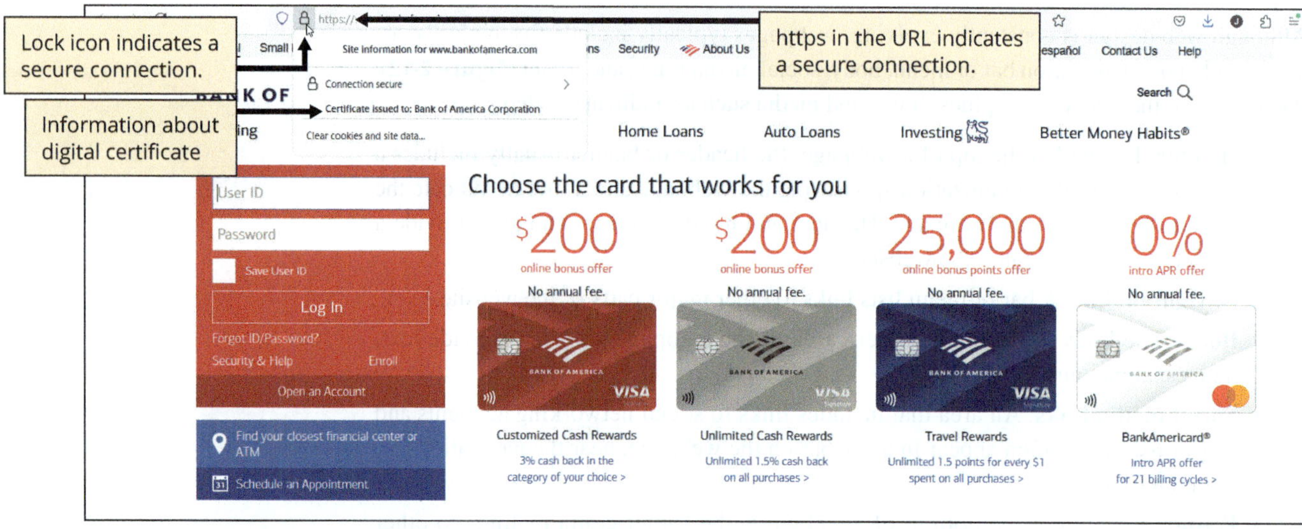

Bank of America Corporation

Identify Secure and Insecure Websites

Before you make a payment on a website or provide sensitive information such as a credit card number, make sure the website is secure. Otherwise, an unauthorized web user could intercept the payment or information and steal your funds or identity. **Figure 2-13** demonstrates how you can identify a secure website.

A secure website uses encryption to safeguard transmitted information. **Encryption** is a security method that scrambles or codes data so it is not readable while being transmitted until it is decrypted.

A secure website connection displays https instead of http in the URL. The "s" in https stands for "secure," so https means **Hypertext Transfer Protocol Secure**. Most websites, especially banks and online retail stores, use the https protocol to make a secure connection to your computer. Secure websites often use a **digital certificate**, which is technology that contains the website's special key used for encryption that has been "signed" by a trusted third party.

An insecure website URL starts with "http," indicating an unprotected protocol for transmitting information. The address bar in the Chrome browser identifies such websites as "Not secure."

Use E-commerce

E-commerce, short for electronic commerce, refers to business transactions on an electronic network such as the Internet. If you have bought or sold products such as clothing, electronics, music, tickets, hotel reservations, or gift certificates, you have engaged in e-commerce. **Table 2-4** describes three types of e-commerce websites.

Table 2-4: Three types of e-commerce websites

Type of E-commerce	Description	Example
Business-to-consumer (B2C)	Involves the sale of goods and services to the general public	Shopping websites
Consumer-to-consumer (C2C)	Occurs when one consumer sells directly to another	Online auctions
Business-to-business (B2B)	Consists of businesses providing goods and services to other businesses	Market research websites

Table 2-5: E-commerce pros and cons for consumers

Pros	Explanation
Variety	You can choose goods from any vendor in the world. Websites have more models, sizes, and colors, for example, than a physical store.
Convenience	You can shop no matter your location, time of day, or conditions, such as bad weather. You save time by visiting websites instead of stores.
Communication	Chat features, contact forms, frequently asked question pages, and other tools enable you to ask or find additional information relevant to your purchase.
Budget	By searching effectively and comparing prices online, you can find products that meet your budget.
Cons	**Explanation**
Security	At insecure e-commerce sites, you risk unauthorized users intercepting your credit card information and other personal data.
Fraud	Some shopping websites are fraudulent, designed to look legitimate while accessing your account information.
Indirect experience	You cannot experience a product directly to verify its color, quality, or texture. You lose the social interaction that is a natural part of shopping at a physical retailer.

Explain the Role of E-commerce in Daily Life

Consumers use e-commerce to access products and services without stepping foot in a store. Businesses use e-commerce to generate revenue and communicate with customers. You should understand the advantages and risks of using e-commerce to make your online transactions satisfying and safe. **Table 2-5** outlines the pros and cons of e-commerce for consumers.

Use E-commerce in Business Transactions

B2B e-commerce involves transferring goods, services, or information between businesses. In fact, most e-commerce is actually between businesses. B2B services include advertising, technical support, and training. B2B products include raw materials, tools and machinery, and electronics. The Shiply website is a B2B site that helps businesses ship goods (**Figure 2-14**).

Figure 2-14: B2B website

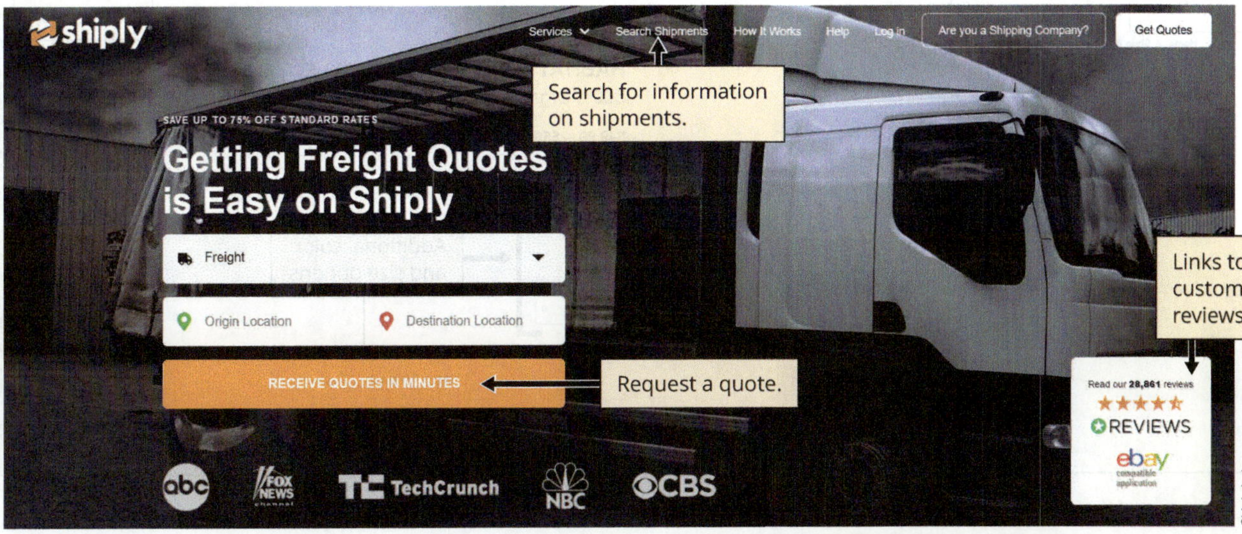

Shiply Ltd.

The more you know about B2B websites, the more valuable you can be to your employer. B2B websites are different from B2C websites. For example, consumer-focused shopping websites offer fixed, consistent pricing; for B2B purchases, pricing can vary based on the level of service provided, negotiated terms, and other factors.

At B2C websites, the consumer is the decision maker. In a B2B transaction, a team of people often need to review and make a purchasing decision. They usually have to follow company procedures, which can lengthen or complicate the transaction.

Use E-commerce in Personal Transactions

You can purchase just about any product or service at a B2C e-commerce website. Doing so is sometimes called e-retail or e-tail (short for electronic retail). To make a purchase online, you visit an **electronic storefront**, an e-commerce website that sells products or services. This type of storefront usually contains product descriptions, images, and a shopping cart to collect items you want to purchase. When you're ready to complete the sale, you enter personal data and the method of payment, which should be through a secure Internet connection.

A B2C website tracks your selected items using **cookies**, small text files created by the website that store information on your computer. These cookies act like a storage bin for the items you place in your shopping cart. Cookies store shopping cart item numbers, saved website preferences, and other information.

B2C websites are usually designed to be easy to use so you can find what you want fast (**Figure 2-15**). They include reviews from other customers to help you make purchasing decisions, special offers for web customers only, and wish lists to encourage you to return to the site. Many B2C websites let you research online and then pick up the purchased item in a physical store.

Figure 2-15: B2C website

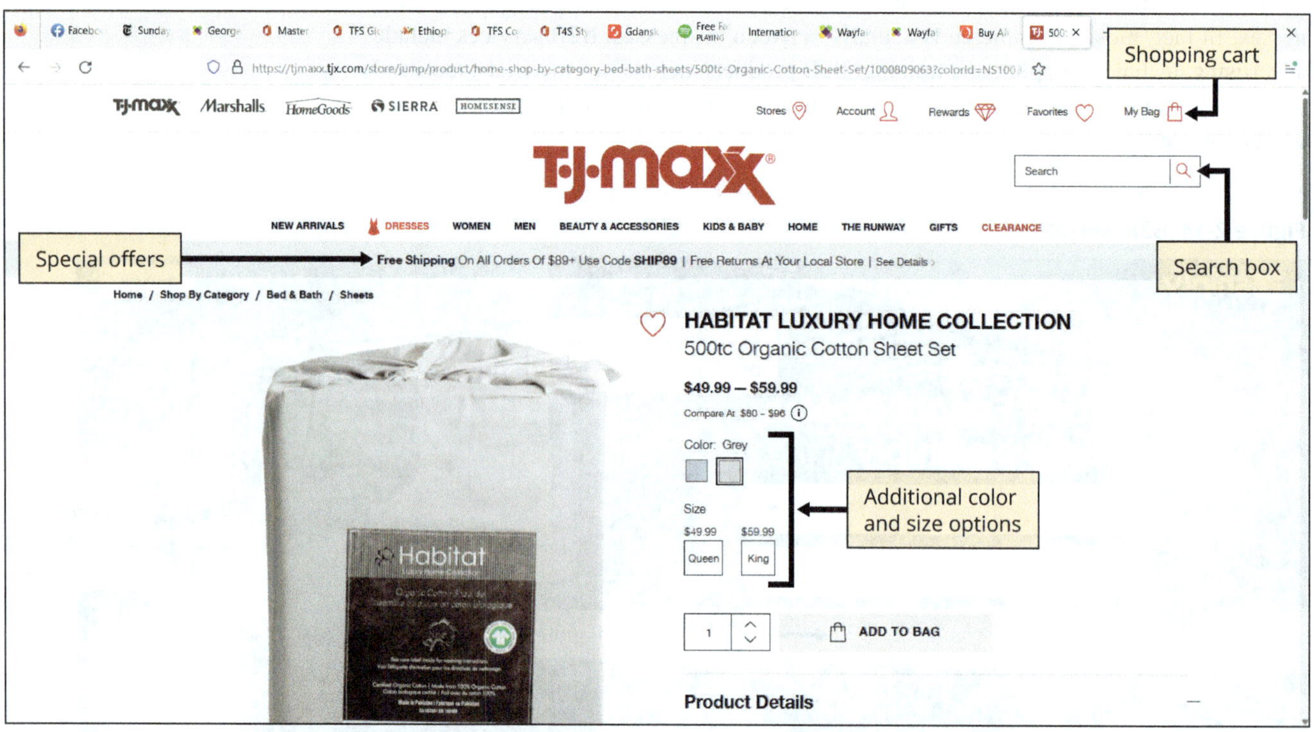

T.J. Maxx

Online classified ads and online auctions are examples of C2C e-commerce websites. An online auction works much like a real-life auction or yard sale. You bid on an item being sold by someone else. The highest bidder at the end of the bidding period purchases the item. eBay is one of the more popular online auction websites.

C2C sites have many sellers promoting the goods, rather than a single merchant hosting a B2C site. Many C2C sites use email forwarding, which hides real email identities, to connect buyer with seller and still protect everyone's privacy. You pay a small fee to the site if you sell an item.

E-commerce Security To make e-commerce payments in a B2C transaction, you can provide a credit card number. **3D Secure** is a standard protocol for securing credit card transactions over the Internet, and is used by online merchants. Using both encryption and digital certificates, 3D Secure provides an extra layer of security on a website.

Besides the https protocol, e-commerce sites also use **Transport Layer Security (TLS)** to encrypt data and provide other services. This technology helps protect consumers and businesses from fraud and identity theft when conducting commerce on the Internet.

To provide an alternative to entering credit card information online, some shopping and auction websites let you use an online payment service, such as PayPal, Venmo, and Zelle. To use an online payment service, you create an account that is linked to your credit card or funds at a financial institution. When you make a purchase, you use your online payment service account, which manages the payment transaction without revealing your financial information.

You can also use smartwatches and smartphones to make e-commerce payments. ApplePay and Google Wallet are two of several mobile payment and digital wallet services available on smartphones and smartwatches. Scan the watch or phone over a reader, often available in stores, to make the electronic payment.

Another payment method is to use a one-time or virtual account number, which lets you make a single online payment without revealing your actual account number. These numbers are good only at the time of the transaction; if they are stolen, they are worthless to thieves.

Explain How to Find E-commerce Deals

You can find online deals in at least two ways: visiting comparison shopping sites and using digital deals.

Websites such as BizRate and PriceGrabber are comparison shopping websites that save you time and money by letting you compare prices from multiple vendors, as well as read industry and user reviews to find product.

Digital deals can be gift certificates, gift cards, or coupons. Groupon and NewEgg are examples of deal-of-the-day websites, which help you save money on restaurant meals, retail products, travel, and personal services. Digital coupons consist of promotional codes that you enter when you check out and pay for online purchases. Sites and apps such as RetailMeNot and browser extensions such as PayPal Honey provide coupon codes and offer alerts for e-commerce discounts (**Figure 2-16**).

Figure 2-16: Some websites and shopping apps offer deals and coupons

Explain How Information Literacy Applies to Web Searches and Research

You can search for and find virtually any information you want on the Internet. Search engines let you enter search criteria and then compile a list of webpages that match your criteria. Of the billions of webpages you can access using Google or another search site, some are valuable and some are not.

Define Information Literacy

Information literacy is the ability to find, evaluate, use, and communicate online information. Being able to distinguish legitimate websites and information sources is part of being a digital citizen. If you have information literacy, you can do the following:

- Navigate many sources of information, including the Internet, online libraries, and popular media sites.
- Select the right tool for finding the information you need.
- Recognize that not all information is created equal.
- Evaluate whether information is misleading, biased, or out of date.
- Manage information to become a knowledgeable decision maker.

Information literacy is gained by understanding and selecting the tools, techniques, and strategies for locating and evaluating information (**Figure 2-17**).

Explain How Search Engines Work

Suppose you're working on a presentation about mobile phone technology and need to know about current innovations.

To find information quickly, you could start a **general search engine** such as Google, Bing, or Yahoo!, which is designed to find general results, and enter a search term or phrase such as *net neutrality*. Within seconds, the first page of search results lists a dozen webpages that might contain the information you need.

Figure 2-17: Viewing and evaluating search results

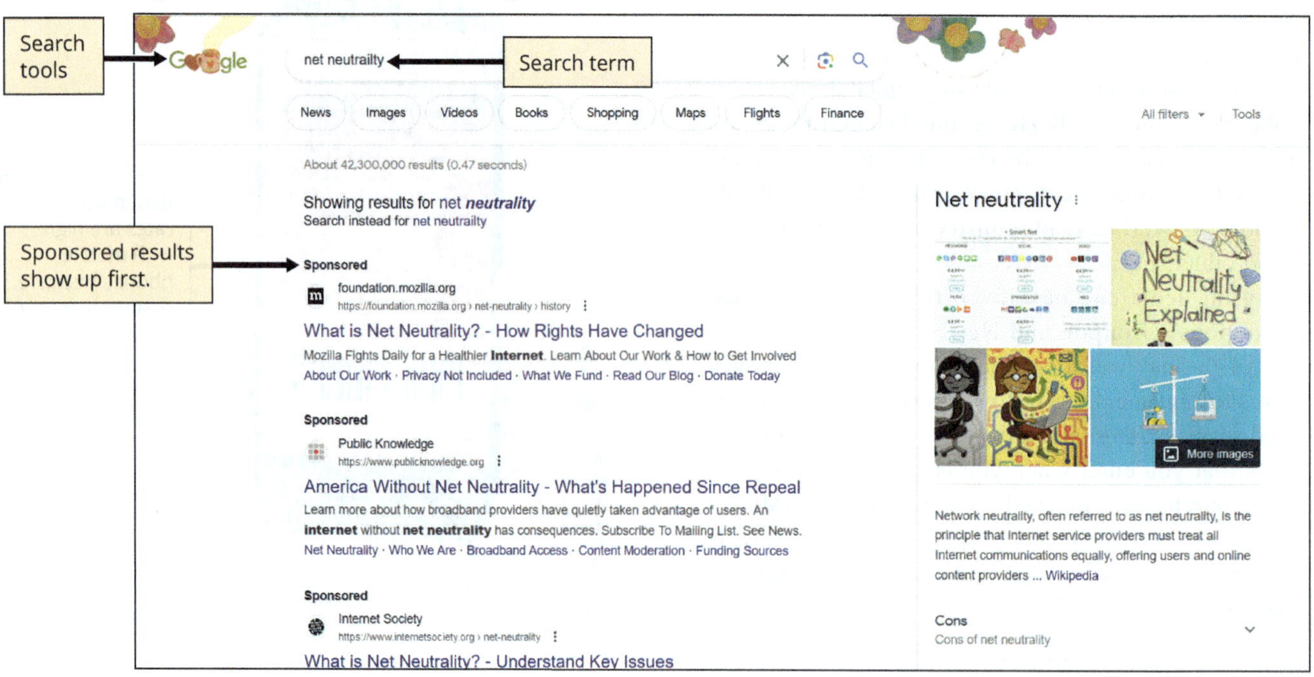

Google, LLC.

When you perform a search, a general search engine does not search the entire Internet. Instead, it accesses a database of information about webpages. It uses programs called **spiders** or **crawlers**, software that combs the web to find webpages and add new data about them to the database. These programs build an **index** of terms and their locations.

When you enter a search term, or **query**, a general search engine refers to its database index and then lists results that match your search term, ranked by how closely they answer your query.

Each search engine uses a different method to retrieve webpage information from an index and create a ranked list of results. The ranking depends on how often and where a search term appears on the webpage, how long the webpage has been published, and the number of other webpages that link to it. Website creators and content writers use **search engine optimization (SEO)**, which includes tools to allow search engines to better find or index your website. SEO strategies include arranging content order, including keywords, and ensuring other content is linked to yours.

Use Search Tools and Strategies

A **search tool** finds online information based on criteria you specify or selections you make. Search tools include search engines and search boxes on webpages. The more effectively you use search tools, the more quickly you can find information and the more relevant that information will be.

Another type of search tool is a **web directory**, or **subject directory**, an online guide to subjects or websites, usually arranged in alphabetic order.

Search engines and web directories take different approaches to searching for information. Instead of using an index created by digital spiders, a human editor creates the index for a web directory, selecting categories that make sense for the information the web directory provides. The editor usually reviews sites that are submitted to the directory and can exclude those that do not seem credible or reliable. For this reason, a web directory is often a better choice than a search engine if you are conducting research online.

A **specialized search tool** concentrates on specific resources, such as scholarly journals or the United States Congress. Examples include the Directory of Open Access Journals, Congress.gov Legislative Search (**Figure 2-18**), and Google Books. If you need to research the latest academic studies or look up the status of a bill, using a specialized search tool is more efficient than using a general search engine such as Google.

Figure 2-18: Specialized search tool

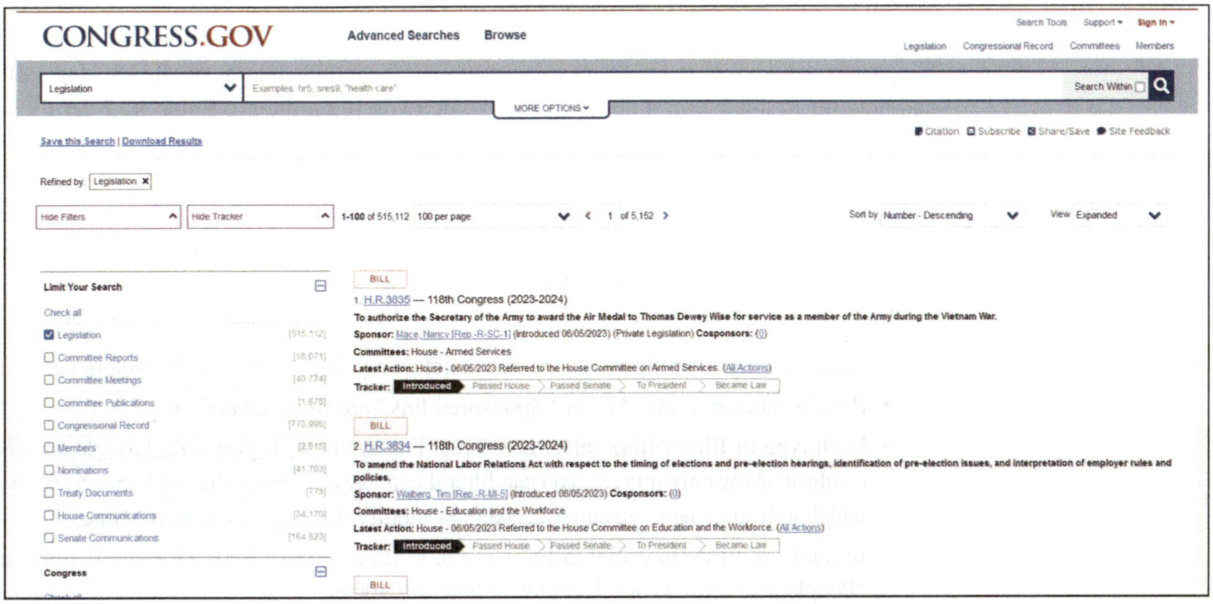

Library of Congress

Figure 2-19: Search strategy

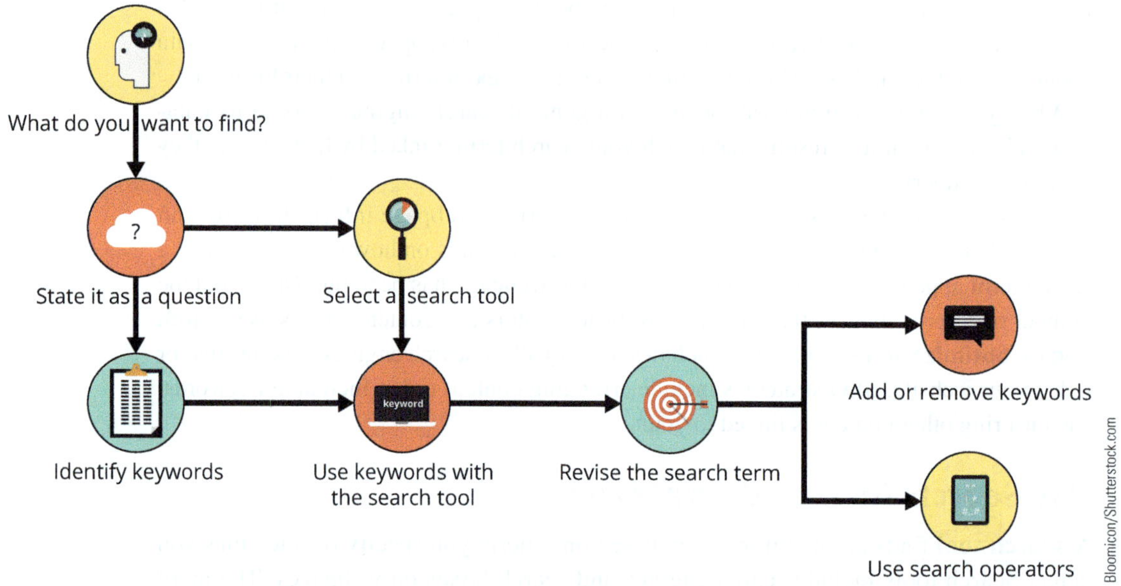

To get the most out of a web search, develop a search strategy, which involves performing the following tasks before you start searching:

- State what kind of information you are seeking, as specifically as possible.
- Phrase the search term as a question, as in "How do businesses use augmented reality?"
- Identify the keywords or phrases that could answer the question.
- Select an appropriate search tool.

Next, perform the search. For example, if you want to know about how website designers use SEO, you could search using *search engine optimization strategies* as the **keywords**, the descriptive words you enter to obtain a list of results that include the words or phrase. If you find the results you need, you can stop searching.

If the term you use is too general, you are likely to find millions of webpages that mention the term. If the term you use is too specific, you might miss useful webpages related to your term. In either case, you need to refine the web search to narrow or broaden the results. **Figure 2-19** summarizes an online search strategy.

Refine Web Searches

Suppose you are interested in the next generation of the mobile Internet, called 5G Internet, and how it can make you more productive when you're on the go. Enter *5G internet* in a search engine, and the results could include millions of webpages about 5G products, news, definitions, and research.

To find the information you're seeking, learn from the search engine results page (SERP) by using the features your search tool provides, including filters for subject or time, or questions others may have asked about the same topic.

Other practices search engines follow practices when listing search results include:

- Search engines list the most relevant matched results, or **hits**, on the first page.
- Results labeled as an "Ad" or "Sponsored link" are from advertisers.
- Each type of filter offers related features. For example, if you filter Google search results to show only images, you can filter the images by size, color, and **usage rights**, which indicate when you can use, share, or modify the images you find online.
- In addition to listing related links at the bottom of the SERP, Google displays a "People also search for" list below a link you visited.

Table 2-6: Common search operators

Operator	Means	Example
" " (quotation marks)	Find webpages with the exact words in the same order	"augmented reality" in business
| (vertical bar)	OR	augmented | virtual
- (hyphen)	NOT	augmented reality -virtual
*	**Wildcard** (placeholder for any number of characters)	augment* reality
#..#	Find webpages within a range of numbers	augmented reality 2017..2022

Table 2-7: Examples of web searches

Keywords	Possible results	Suggested change
Looking for a used smartphone	A list of all used phones; returns too many hits	Add the word "Android."
Looking for a used Android smartphone	Still too many hits	Remove common words such as "the" and "an"; remove verb.
Used Android smartphone	Results still include other smartphones	Search for an exact phrase by entering it in quotation marks.
Used "Android smartphone"	List of used Android smartphones	Results are targeted; no changes are needed.

You can also refine a web search by using one or more **search operators**, also called **Boolean operators**, which are characters, words, or symbols that focus the search. **Table 2-6** lists common search operators.

Now you're ready to try a new search. **Table 2-7** lists examples of keywords you might use to find information on buying used Android smartphones.

Many search sites have advanced search operators, which are special terms followed by a colon (:). For example, *site:* means to search only the specified site, as in *site: www.cengage.com sam*, which finds information about SAM on the cengage.com website. You can find the advanced search operators by referring to the site's help pages.

To broaden a search, you can use a **word stem**, which is the base of a word. For example, instead of using *businesses* as a keyword, use *business*. You can also combine the word stem with an asterisk (*), as in *tech** to find technology, technician, and technique.

Evaluate the Pros and Cons of Net Neutrality

The concept of **net neutrality** is that one website has the same value or priority as other websites, resulting in equal, unrestricted access to each site. When net neutrality is enforced, ISPs must provide the same level of service to all websites, regardless of their content or purpose. Net neutrality supports the concept that the Internet should be neutral and all traffic should be treated equally.

Networks transmit data over a communication channel, which can be a wire or over the air (wireless). Each type of communication channel can support a certain amount of data being transferred at a given time. **Bandwidth** is a term commonly used to describe the capacity of a communication channel. When a communication medium or connection supports transferring a large amount of data at one time, it is said to be a high-bandwidth connection. High-bandwidth connections (also called broadband connections) support capacity for transferring content such as videos, music, and other large files, and can support online gaming. Low-bandwidth connections (also called narrowband connections) support only slower transfer speeds as they have less capacity. These connections are suitable for performing functions such as sending and receiving email, transferring small files, and viewing basic websites.

Supporters of net neutrality like the fact that access to websites and other Internet services cannot be restricted based on factors such as content or bandwidth requirements. Those who oppose net neutrality argue that the ability for users to access certain types of high-bandwidth content such as music and movies might result in slower Internet speeds for others who are also connecting to the Internet using the same ISPs. Without net neutrality, Internet Service Providers could charge more money for those wanting access to content requiring more resources (such as streaming music and movies) and charge less money to those who require access to less resource-intensive services.

Although the Internet is a global resource, the U.S. Federal Communication Commission (FCC) is responsible for releasing rules surrounding Internet access for U.S. users. Other countries or areas have different governing bodies and rules. Some individuals feel the government should not control Internet access and its content, but one primary goal of the FCC is to guarantee accessibility to all Internet users.

Conduct Online Research

When you need to conduct online research for an assignment or project, using search engines designed for research yields more reliable results, saving you time and effort and ensuring the validity of the content you find.

Use Specialty Search Engines

Where do you go to find academic information for your research? Try using a **specialty search engine**, which lets you search databases, news providers, podcasts, and other online information sources that general search engines do not always access.

Much of the information on the web is stored in databases. To access this database information, you need to use a special search form and may need to enter a user name and password. For example, Google Scholar searches scholarly literature from many disciplines and includes articles, books, theses, and abstracts.

Other specialty search tools let you find information published on certain types of sites. For example, use Google News or Alltop to find news stories and Listen Notes to search podcasts.

Figure 2-20: CARS checklist

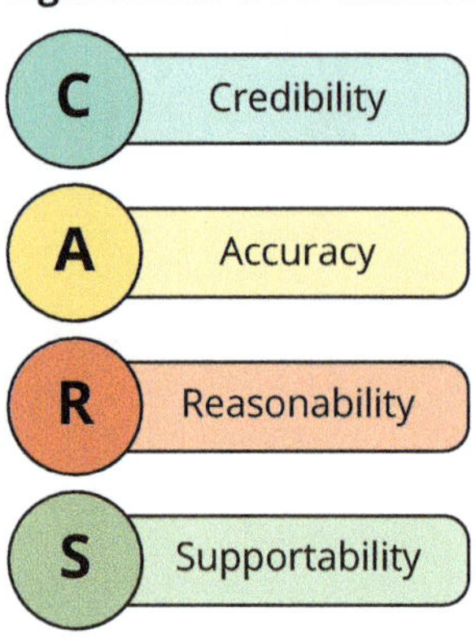

Evaluate Online Information

On the Internet, anyone can publish anything to a website, a blog, or a social media site, regardless of whether the information is true. How can you tell if a website is worth your time? In general, look for sites from trusted, expert institutions or authors. Avoid sites that show bias or contain outdated information.

When you use the Internet for research, be skeptical about the information you find online. Evaluate a webpage before you use it as an information source. One way to evaluate a webpage is to use the CARS checklist (**Figure 2-20**) to determine whether the online information is credible, accurate, reasonable, and supportable.

Credibility: When someone is providing you information face to face, you pay attention to clues such as body language and voice tone to determine whether that information is credible, or believable. Obviously, you can't use that same technique to evaluate the credibility of a webpage.

To determine the credibility of a website:

- Identify the author of the webpage and check their credentials. This information is often listed on the Contact Us page or the About page.
- If you find biographical information, read it to learn whether the author has a degree in a field related to the topic.
- Use a search engine such as Google or the professional networking site LinkedIn to search for the author's name and see whether the author is an expert on the subject.

Accuracy: You're attending a classmate's presentation on the history of the personal computer, and he mentions that Bill Gates invented the first PC for home use in 1980, citing an online resource. You know it was actually Steve Wozniak and Steve Jobs in 1976. That inaccuracy makes you doubt the accuracy of the rest of the presentation.

To check the accuracy of a website:

- Verify its facts and claims. Consult an expert or use fact-checking sites such as snopes.com and factcheck.org to find professionally researched information.
- Evaluate the information source. Be wary of web addresses that contain slight modifications of legitimate sites, use unusual domain names, or have long URLs.
- Find out more about an organization that has no history, physical location, or staff.
- Check to see if the source has a bias and evaluate the information with the bias in mind.
- Check the webpage footer for the date the information was published or updated. For many topics, especially technology, you need current information.

Reasonableness: Along with credibility and accuracy, consider how reasonable an online information source is. Reasonable means fair and sensible, not extreme or excessive.

To check how reasonable a website is:

- Identify the purpose of the webpage. Is the page designed to provide facts and other information, sell a product or service, or express opinions?
- Evaluate whether the webpage offers more than one point of view.
- Emotional, persuasive, or biased language is often a sign that the author is not being fair or moderate. Even opinions should be expressed in a moderate tone.
- Look for a conflict of interest. For example, if the page reviews a certain brand of smartphone and the author sells those types of phones, he or she has a conflict of interest.

Support: Suppose a webpage refers to a study concluding that most people consider computer professionals to be highly ethical. But the page doesn't link to the study itself or mention other sources that support this claim. The page is failing the final criterion in the CARS checklist: support.

To evaluate a webpage's support:

- Look for links or citations to reputable sources or authorities. Test the links to make sure they work.
- Check other webpages and print material on the topic to see if they cite the same sources.
- Look for quotations from experts.
- For photos or other reproduced content, a credit line should appear somewhere on the page that states the source and any necessary copyright information.

Gather Content from Online Sources

As you conduct research online, you gather content from webpages, including text, photos, and links to resources. Follow ethical guidelines and be aware of ownership rights to avoid legal, academic, and professional sanctions and be a responsible member of the online community.

Intellectual property is unique and original works, such as ideas, inventions, art, writings, processes, company and product names, and logos. If you copy a photo from the Internet and use it in a report, you might be violating the photographer's **intellectual property rights**, which are legal rights protecting those who create works such as photos, art, writing, inventions, and music.

A **copyright** gives authors and artists the legal right to sell, publish, or distribute an original work. A copyright goes into effect as soon as the work exists in physical or digital form.

If you want to use a photo in your report, you need to get permission from the photo's owner. Contact the photographer by email, and explain what you want to use and how you plan to use it. If a copyright holder gives you permission, keep a copy of the message or document for your records. The holder may also tell you how a credit line should appear. Acquiring permission protects you from potential concerns over your usage and protects the copyright holder's intellectual property rights.

Some online resources, such as e-books, newspapers, magazines, and journals, are protected by **digital rights management (DRM)**, which refers to a collection of technologies used by software publishers and trade groups to fight software piracy and prevent unauthorized copying of digital content. It is a violation of copyright law to circumvent these protections to obtain and then use the materials. To avoid legal trouble, only use materials to which you have legal access, and then follow accepted usage laws for any information you obtain.

Some work is in the **public domain**, which means that the item, such as a photo, is available and accessible to the public without requiring permission to use, and therefore not subject to copyright. This applies to material for which the copyright has expired and to work that has been explicitly released to the public domain by its owner. Many websites provide public domain files free for you to download. Much information on U.S. government sites is in the public domain (**Figure 2-21**), although you must attribute the information and be aware that the sites might contain other copyrighted information.

For any online source, if you don't see a copyright symbol, look for a statement that specifically defines the work as being in the public domain. For quotations and other cited material, the United States **fair use doctrine** allows you to use a sentence or paragraph of text without permission if you include a citation to the original source.

Figure 2-21: Copyright information from the U.S. Department of Agriculture site

Digital Rights and Copyright

Most information presented on the USDA Web site is considered public domain information. Public domain information may be freely distributed or copied, but use of appropriate byline/photo/image credits is requested. Attribution may be cited as follows: "U.S. Department of Agriculture."

Some materials on the USDA Web site are protected by copyright, trademark, or patent, and/or are provided for personal use only. Such materials are used by USDA with permission, and USDA has made every attempt to identify and clearly label them. You may need to obtain permission from the copyright, trademark, or patent holder to acquire, use, reproduce, or distribute these materials.

U.S. Department of Agriculture

Figure 2-22: Creative Commons site

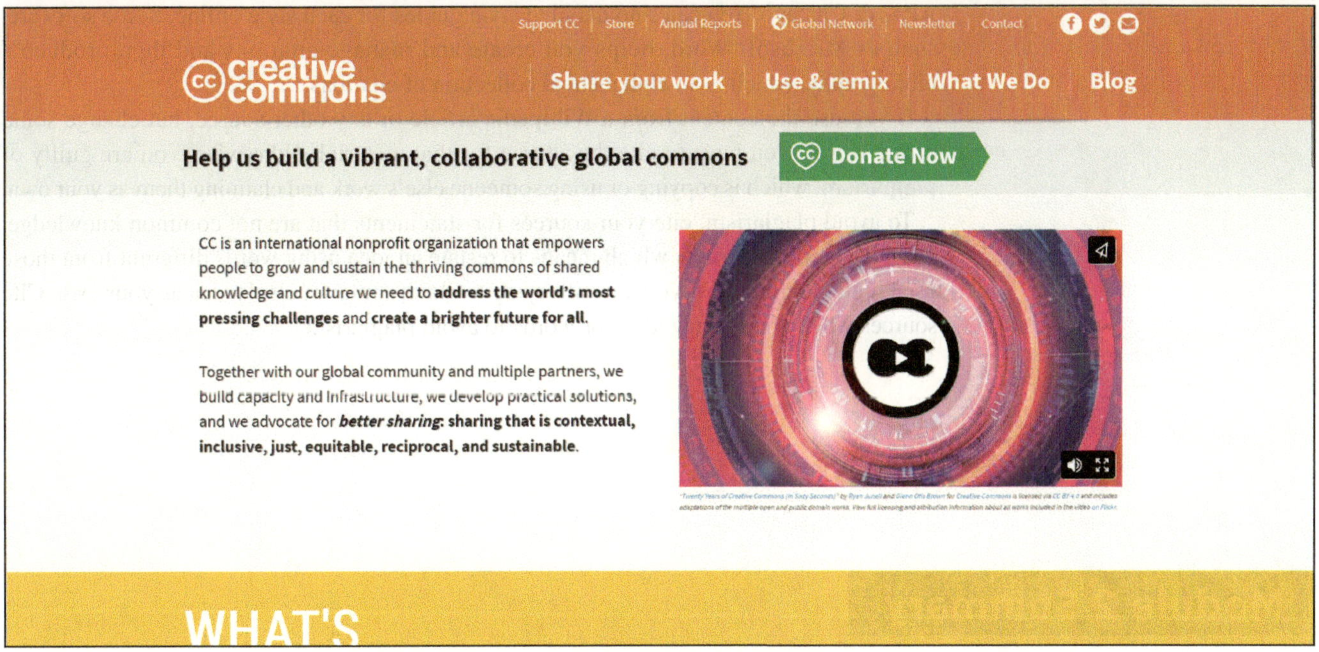

Creative Commons

If the discussion about rights and legal trouble makes you nervous, you're not alone. Clearly, it can be hard to know what is acceptable to use and what's not. Most people are not legal experts, so how can you know what you can use and how you can use it? If you make your writing, photographs, or artwork available online, how do you specify to others how they can use that content?

Creative Commons **Creative Commons (CC)** is a U.S. nonprofit organization that makes it easy for content creators to license and share their work by supplying easy-to-understand copyright licenses; the creator chooses the conditions under which the work can be used. As a creator, set these conditions by you selecting a CC license that explains how others can use your work. For example, you can choose whether to allow commercial use of your poem, or allow derivative works, such as translations or adaptations. People who use content that carries a Creative Commons license must follow CC license rules on giving credit for works they use and displaying copyright notices.

CC licenses are based on copyright law and are legal around the world. The CC organization is helping to build a large and ever-growing digital commons (**Figure 2-22**), a collection of content that users can legally copy, distribute, and expand.

Apply Information Literacy Standards

Part of information literacy involves the ethical use of the information you find on the web. When you use the Internet for research, you face ethical decisions. **Ethics** refers to the moral principles that govern people's behavior. Many schools and other organizations post codes of conduct for computer use, which can help you make ethical decisions while using a computer.

Ethically and legally, you can use other people's ideas in your research papers and presentations as long as you cite the source for any information that is not common knowledge. A **citation** is a reference to a source, such as a published work.

Thorough research on technology and other topics usually involves books, journals, magazines, and websites. Each type of information source uses a different **citation style**, or sequence of elements, such publication name and author name, and the punctuation between them. Instructors often direct you to use a particular citation style, such as MLA, APA, or Chicago. You can find detailed style guides for each style online. Some software, such as Microsoft Word, helps you create and manage citations and then produce a bibliography, which is an alphabetical collection of citations.

If you use the content from a Wikipedia article or any other source, but change some of the words, you have to cite the source for that material. Otherwise, you are guilty of **plagiarism**, which is copying or using someone else's work and claiming them as your own.

To avoid plagiarism, cite your sources for statements that are not common knowledge. Even if you **paraphrase**, which means to restate an idea using words different from those used in the original text, you are still trying to claim someone else's idea as your own. Cite sources when you borrow ideas or words to avoid plagiarism.

Module 2 Summary

The Internet is a global collection of millions of computers linked together to share information worldwide, and the web is one part of the Internet. A webpage is an electronic document that can contain text, graphics, sound, video, and links to other webpages, while a website is a collection of webpages. You use a browser to display webpages and enter web addresses, or URLs, which identify the location of webpages on the Internet. Webpages can be static or dynamic. Web designers use responsive web design to optimize how webpages appear on different devices.

You connect to the Internet using wired or wireless technology, and connect through an ISP using devices such as a modem or hotspot.

Nonprofit organizations set the rules for the Internet, such as the names of top-level domains. The IETF sets standards for IP addresses. The W3C publishes standards for websites and webpages.

Websites can be classified into one or more categories, such as blogs, content aggregators, or entertainment sites. A web portal combines pages from many sources and provides access to those pages. Search sites use search engines, software designed to find webpages based on your search criteria.

In addition to using a browser to visit websites and display webpages, you can use it to access web apps, which are apps you run in a browser. A web app offers the advantages of convenience and portability, but involves risks to security and privacy. Webpages typically include the following areas: header or banner, navigation bar or menu, body, social media links, and footer.

A secure website uses encryption to safeguard transmitted information. Signs of a secure website are a lock icon and the https protocol in the address bar. In an insecure website, the URL starts with "http," indicating an unprotected protocol for transmitting information.

E-commerce refers to business transactions on an electronic network such as the Internet. The three types of e-commerce are business-to-business (B2B), business-to-consumer (B2C), and consumer-to-consumer (C2C). For consumers, e-commerce websites provide the benefits of variety, convenience, and cost, but have the drawbacks of reduced security, fraud, and indirect experience.

B2B e-commerce involves transferring goods, services, or information between businesses. Most e-commerce is actually between businesses. To make a purchase at a B2C website, you visit an electronic storefront, collect items in a shopping cart, and then enter personal data and the method of payment to complete the purchase.

To make secure online payments, use e-commerce websites with the 3D Secure or TLS protocol. You can also use an online payment service to scan your mobile phone or smartwatch, or a virtual account number.

To find deals for goods and services online, visit comparison shopping sites and use digital deals. Comparison websites let you compare prices from multiple vendors. Digital deals come in the form of gift certificates, gift cards, and coupons.

How you find, evaluate, use, and communicate online information depends on your information literacy. You become information literate by understanding and selecting the tools, techniques, and strategies for locating and evaluating information.

When you perform an online search, a general search engine compiles a database of information about webpages. The search engine refers to its database index when you enter a search term and then lists pages that match the term, ranked by how closely they answer your query.

A search tool finds online information based on criteria you specify or selections you make. Search tools include search engines, search boxes on webpages, and web directories, which are online guides to subjects or websites, usually arranged in alphabetic order. Net neutrality refers to the concept of equal, unrestricted access to all websites for all users.

To find academic information for research, you can use a specialty search engine, which lets you search databases, news providers, podcasts, and other online information sources that general search engines do not always access.

When evaluating online information, look for sites from trusted, expert institutions or authors. Avoid sites that show bias or contain outdated information. Evaluate a website using the CARS (credibility, accuracy, reliability, supportability) checklist.

As you gather content from webpages, follow ethical guidelines and be aware of ownership rights to avoid legal, academic, and professional sanctions. Observe intellectual property rights and copyrights to be a responsible member of the online community.

When you use the Internet for research, you face ethical decisions. Ethically and legally, you can use other people's ideas in your research papers and presentations as long as you cite the source for any information that is not common knowledge.

Review Questions

1. (True or False) The web is a global collection of millions of computers linked together to share information worldwide.

2. Most web designers provide content so that it adapts appropriately to the size of the display on any device using __________ web design.
   - **a.** adaptive
   - **b.** responsive
   - **c.** alternative
   - **d.** reactive

3. Each webpage is assigned an address that identifies the location of the page on the Internet, called a(n) __________.
   - **a.** Internet Protocol (IP)
   - **b.** uniform resource locator (URL)
   - **c.** top-level domain (TLD)
   - **d.** Hypertext Transfer Protocol (HTTP)

4. An ISP is a company that __________.
   - **a.** manages and assigns top-level domains
   - **b.** promotes net neutrality
   - **c.** manages C2C e-commerce
   - **d.** sells Internet access

5. A(n) __________ website gathers, organizes, and then distributes web content.
   - **a.** content aggregator
   - **b.** media sharing
   - **c.** entertainment
   - **d.** search engine

6. Which of the following indicates an encrypted website connection?
   - **a.** https in the URL
   - **b.** http in the URL
   - **c.** The message "secure website" in the address bar
   - **d.** A shield icon in the address bar

7. Which of the following best describes business-to-business (B2B) e-commerce purchases?
   - **a.** The consumer is the decision maker.
   - **b.** Pricing can vary based on level of service.
   - **c.** Customers bid on items being sold by other customers.
   - **d.** Customers can pick up the purchased item in a physical store.

8. A business-to-consumer (B2C) website tracks the items you place in a shopping cart using __________.
   - **a.** a digital wallet
   - **b.** the Transport Layer Security (TLS) protocol
   - **c.** crawlers
   - **d.** cookies

9. Who or what creates the index for a web directory?
   - **a.** A digital spider
   - **b.** A human editor
   - **c.** A wiki
   - **d.** A search operator

10. Bandwidth refers to the ________.
    a. capacity of a communication channel
    b. speed of an Internet search
    c. size of a search directory
    d. security of a website

11. In the CARS checklist, the A stands for ________.
    a. accessibility
    b. adaptability
    c. accuracy
    d. authority

12. (True or False) Creative Commons licenses are legal only in the United States.

Discussion Questions

1. What is the difference between the Internet and the web? How does each affect your daily life?
2. Media sharing websites let you post photos and videos to share with other people. Social media websites enable you to share thoughts, follow others, and post content. What are the benefits and drawbacks of using these websites?
3. Explain the concept of net neutrality. Why is it important? What drawbacks might there be to enforcing it? Has it impacted you? If so, how?
4. On the Internet, anyone can publish anything to a website, a blog, or a social media site, regardless of whether the information is true. Recent years have seen a spike in misleading or false "news" and hoaxes that are shared as fact on social media. How can you tell fake news stories from real ones?

Critical Thinking Activities

1. You are a part time student going back to school to finish your degree. Knowing you will often research topics using your mobile phone and laptop, you want a fast, secure browser that is also easy to use. Evaluate and compare reviews of three browsers, at least one of them a mobile browser. Consider Google Chrome, Microsoft Edge, Apple Safari, Mozilla Firefox, Opera, and others you might find in your research. Recommend two browsers: one for when you use your laptop, and one for when you use your mobile phone. What factors did you use to make your recommendation? Which is more important to you: speed or security? Why?
2. You are starting a new job in the Sales and Marketing Department of a financial services company and are part of a team redesigning the company's website. You want to become better acquainted with current website design principles, including SEO and responsive web design. Search for tips on how to incorporate both strategies into your website. List three that you find most important. Why did you select these strategies? What might be the downside of not following either principle? What other current trends in website design did you find?
3. You want to purchase a new bicycle that you can use to get from school to home and your job. You know you can use the web to find reviews of bikes, help you find the type of bike you need, purchase accessories, and connect with people selling bikes on social media or a local online marketplace. Outline your strategy for researching, selecting, and purchasing a bike. What websites will you use? How can you ensure your purchase is secure?
4. You have been putting off writing a research paper, and now it's due in two days. You have gathered a few notes, but forgot to write down your sources, and aren't sure if your notes are paraphrased or in your own words. You decide it's best to start your research over. What strategies should you use to verify your sources and cite them properly? Why is this important? What consequences might there be if you fail to follow good practices?

Apply Your Skills

Unathi Mwange uses the web in every aspect of his life, even as he commutes to school. Connecting to the cloud with his mobile phone, he stores, retrieves, and shares files. He uses his browser to log onto his school's learning management system to check his grades, participate in web-based lectures, and gather content for class projects from reliable online resources. He completes assignments using web apps, compares deals on headphones at e-commerce websites, and uses an online auction website to buy and sells sports memorabilia.

Working in a small group or by yourself, complete the following:

1. Describe how Unathi can connect to the Internet. List the parts of a URL. What additional ways can you think of that Unathi can benefit from using the web? Imagine your life without the Internet. What would be the biggest change?
2. Identify the main parts of a webpage. How can this knowledge help you navigate a webpage or website? What types of webpages do you visit most frequently?
3. Explain how Unathi can keep safe while shopping online. What tools can he use to find online deals or coupons? Do you use digital coupons or deals? How does this impact you?
4. Come up with an example of something Unathi might have to research for his job or school. What search tools and terms should he use? How can he evaluate the content for accuracy and relevance? What strategies for refining searches and verifying results did you learn from this module? How will you use those going forward?
5. Imagine an example of how Unathi might use the Creative Commons. Describe the responsibility of Unathi to properly cite his sources. If you were an artist or writer and found your content being used without attribution, what impact would that have on you?

Hardware and Processors

In This Module

- Categorize the various types of hardware and processors
- Demonstrate familiarity with input and output devices
- Maintain hardware components

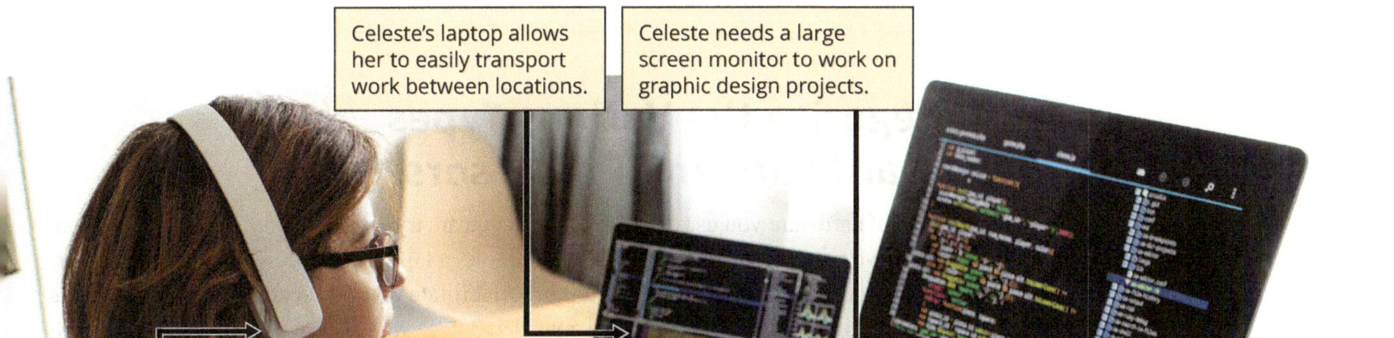

Pressmaster/Shutterstock.com

Celeste Rosa is an office manager at a small graphic design firm with ten employees in Denver, Colorado. In addition to supporting the designers who create professional graphics for large corporations worldwide, Celeste is responsible for maintaining the staff's computers and mobile devices. Each employee is issued a laptop they can bring home to use in telecommuting and a tablet they can use in presenting work to potential and current customers, and all share a variety of printers and projectors.

When you perform activities on a smartphone, tablet, or computer, you are using hardware, the physical components that allow your device to operate properly. Hardware can include externally connected devices, and also can include internal components that you can't see, such as the processor. Hardware is used to accept data and transmit information. Like any equipment, hardware and its components must be maintained.

In this module you will learn about the many different types of hardware, how to choose hardware that will best meet your needs, and methods for maintaining and troubleshooting hardware problems. As you reflect on what you learn in this module, ask yourself: How can you use different types of hardware effectively? What methods of input and output are most relevant to your school or work? How can you address hardware maintenance needs and prevent or minimize problems?

Categorize the Various Types of Hardware and Processors

The type of hardware you use depends on what you are trying to accomplish. Most hardware devices have more than one purpose. For example, a laptop can receive input, display output, store data, and connect to the Internet to facilitate communication. The components residing within your computer are also considered hardware. These components help translate data into information, provide storage, and control the device's memory.

Differentiate between Input and Output Devices

An **input device** communicates instructions and commands to a computer, which then translates the input into data that the computer can interpret. On a computer, the most common input device might be a keyboard, which can communicate text and instructions. On a mobile phone, the most common input device is its touchscreen. A **touchscreen** is a display that lets you touch areas of the screen to interact with software. Additional types of input devices include, but are not limited to, a mouse, stylus, scanner, webcam, microphone, and game controller (**Figure 3-1**).

Figure 3-1: Input devices send data to a computer or device

valiantsin suprunovich/Shutterstock.com; Koloj/Shutterstock.com; guteksk7/Shutterstock.com; Evgeny Karandaev/Shutterstock.com

Figure 3-2: Output devices produce or display information from a computer or device

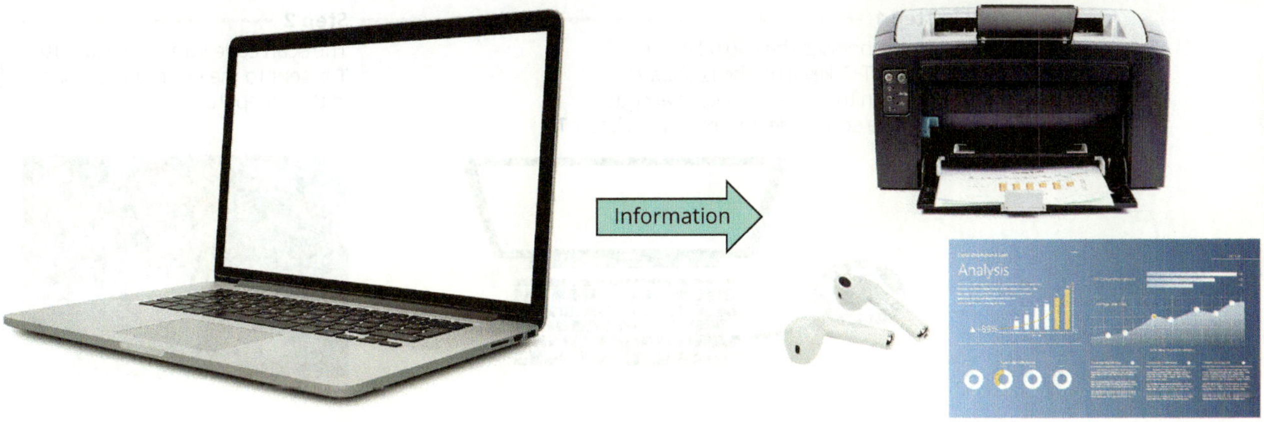

Anan Chincho/Shutterstock.com; Gorodenkoff/Shutterstock.com; Sergiy Kuzmin/Shutterstock.com; guteksk7/Shutterstock.com

An **output device** conveys information from the computer to the user, based on the data and instructions that are input by the user. On a computer or mobile device, the most common output device might be its display device. Other types of output devices include speakers, headphones, projectors, and printers (**Figure 3-2**).

Explain How Computers Represent Data

Most computers are digital and use a binary system to operate. The **binary system** is a number system that has two digits, 0 and 1. The digit 0 indicates the absence of an electronic charge, and a 1 indicates the presence of an electronic charge. These electronic charges (or absence thereof), when grouped together, represent data. Each 0 or 1 is called a bit. A **bit** (short for binary digit) is the smallest unit of data a computer can process. When 8 bits are grouped together, they form a **byte**. A byte can represent a single character in the computer or mobile device (**Figure 3-3**).

When you enter numbers, letters, and special characters using an input device such as a keyboard, microphone, or stylus, the computer translates them into the corresponding bits and bytes that it can understand. This translation spares you from having to manually enter or translate the bits for each number, letter, or special character. When you display text on an output device such as a screen, the computer translates the various bits back to numbers, letters, and special characters that you can understand (**Figure 3-4**).

When a computer translates a character into bits and bytes, it uses a text coding scheme. Two popular text coding schemes are ASCII and Unicode. **ASCII** is an 8-bit coding scheme, which means that 8 bits are used to represent uppercase and lowercase letters,

Figure 3-3: Eight bits grouped together as a unit are called a byte

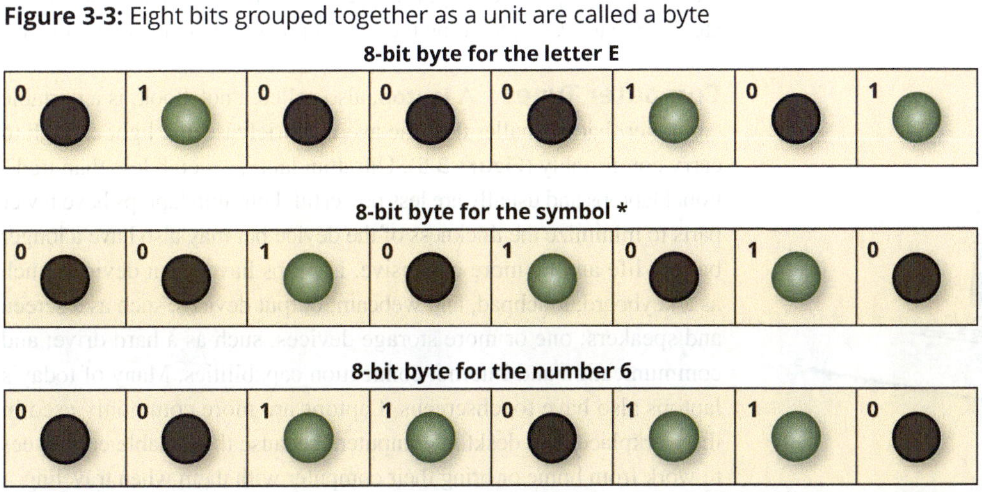

Figure 3-4: Converting a letter to binary form and back

Wirestock Creators/Shutterstock.com; Pixfiction/Shutterstock.com; raigvi/Shutterstock.com; Artjazz/Shutterstock.com

mathematical operators, and logical operations. **Unicode** is a 16-bit coding scheme that is an extension of ASCII and can support more than 65,000 symbols and characters, including Chinese, Japanese, Arabic, and other pictorial characters.

Identify Types of Computers and Processing Components

Various types of computers exist, including laptop computers, desktop computers, and all-in-one computers. Mobile devices, such as tablets and smartphones, also are computers. A **mobile device** is a portable or handheld computing device, such as a smartphone or a tablet, with a screen size of 10.1 inches or smaller. Peripheral and storage devices are other types of hardware for input and output. Processing components are also associated with hardware, including the central processing unit, and memory.

Figure 3-5: Typical laptop

ifong/Shutterstock.com

Computer Types

A **laptop**, also called a notebook, is a portable computer that is smaller than the average briefcase and light enough to carry comfortably (**Figure 3-5**). Ultrathin laptops weigh less than traditional laptops and usually are less powerful. Ultrathin laptops have fewer parts to minimize the thickness of the device but may also have a longer battery life and be more expensive. Laptops have input devices, such as a keyboard, touchpad, and webcam; output devices, such as a screen and speakers; one or more storage devices, such as a hard drive; and communication and Internet connection capabilities. Many of today's laptops also have touchscreens. Laptops are more commonly used in the workplace than desktop computers because they enable employees to work from home or bring their computer with them when traveling.

Figure 3-6: Typical desktop computer

Den Rozhnovsky/Shutterstock.com

Figure 3-7: Typical all-in-one computer

Krisda/Shutterstock.com

A **desktop computer** typically consists of the system unit, monitor, keyboard, and mouse (**Figure 3-6**). Because desktop computers consist of multiple separate components, they are not very portable. However, these computers often can be more powerful and contain more storage than mobile equivalents such as laptops and tablets. Hardware components such as hard drive and memory can be more easily upgraded in desktop computers than in other types of computers. You might use a desktop computer in a location where you do not need the ability to frequently move the device from place to place.

An **all-in-one computer** is similar to a desktop computer, but the monitor and system unit are housed together (**Figure 3-7**). All-in-one computers take up less space than desktop computers and are easier to transport but typically are more difficult to service or upgrade because the components are housed in a very limited space. All-in-one computers sometimes are more expensive than a desktop computer with equivalent hardware specifications. Because of their expense and limited portability, they are not as common as laptops. Unlike a desktop computer, with an all-in-one you cannot choose a monitor that meets your needs, such as one with a large screen or touchscreen capabilities.

A **tablet** is a small, flat computer with a touch-sensitive screen that accepts input from your fingertip, your voice, a digital pen, or a stylus (**Figure 3-8**). Tablets often are less powerful than other types of computers, but provide an easy, convenient way to browse the web, read

Figure 3-8: Typical tablet

Andrey_Popov/Shutterstock.com

Figure 3-9: Typical smartphone

Kaspars Grinvalds/Shutterstock.com

and respond to emails, and create simple documents. Tablets are also easy to transport, making them ideal to take to classes and meetings for accessing information and taking notes. Tablets are used in a variety of professions, such as the medical profession, to easily collect data from patients for storage in their permanent medical records. While the primary method of input on a tablet is by using a fingertip, digital pen, microphone, or stylus, you also may be able to connect a wireless Bluetooth keyboard to make it easier to type. It often is not possible to upgrade a tablet; if your tablet's performance begins to deteriorate or cannot keep up with the latest operating systems and apps, it may be necessary to replace the device.

Two popular types of tablets are slate and convertible. A slate tablet resembles a letter-sized pad and does not contain a physical keyboard. A convertible tablet is a tablet that has a screen in its lid and a keyboard in its base, with the lid and base connected by a swivel-type hinge. You can use a convertible tablet like a traditional laptop, or you can rotate the display and fold it down over the keyboard so that it looks like a slate tablet.

A **smartphone** is an Internet-capable phone that usually also includes a calendar, an address book, and games, in addition to apps (**Figure 3-9**). Because many companies and organizations assume everyone has a smartphone these days, providing things like boarding passes and transit cards through apps instead of in physical form, those who do not have use of a smartphone find themselves on the wrong side of the digital divide. If you have a smartphone you likely use it to communicate, look up information, and use apps and games.

Peripheral Devices An add-on device, also referred to as a **peripheral device**, is a device such as a keyboard, mouse, printer, or speakers that can connect to and extend the capability of a computer or mobile device. For example, if you need to share hard copies of documents you create, you can send the document to a printer. If you plan to work in a quiet location while listening to a podcast or music, you should consider using a headset or earbuds. If you will need to regularly bring files from one computer to another, and do not want to rely on the cloud, you could purchase an external storage device that you can connect to various computers. Peripheral devices can be used for input, output, or a combination of both.

When purchasing a peripheral device for your computer, you should make sure that the device is compatible. A peripheral device may only be compatible with a device- or platform-specific operating system such as those made by Microsoft, Apple, or Android. In addition to making sure that the device is compatible with the software on your computer, you also should make sure you have the necessary ports to connect the device or have the capability to attach the shared device wirelessly to a network. Most peripherals have the capability to connect wirelessly. To connect to a device physically, you might use a port or hub. A **port** is a slot on the computer where you can attach a peripheral device. For example, if a peripheral device is designed to connect to a USB port on the computer, you should make sure that you have an available USB port. If all USB ports on your computer are in use, you might consider purchasing a USB hub. A **USB hub** is an external device that contains many USB ports (**Figure 3-10**).

Figure 3-10: USB hub

Willem Marnix Boer/Shutterstock.com

Storage Solutions One of the benefits of using a computer or mobile device is the ability to store files that you download or create. Various storage solutions exist, each with its own set of strengths

Figure 3-11: Internal magnetic hard drives have a disk and other moving parts

hadescom/Shutterstock.com

Figure 3-12: Solid state drives have no moving parts

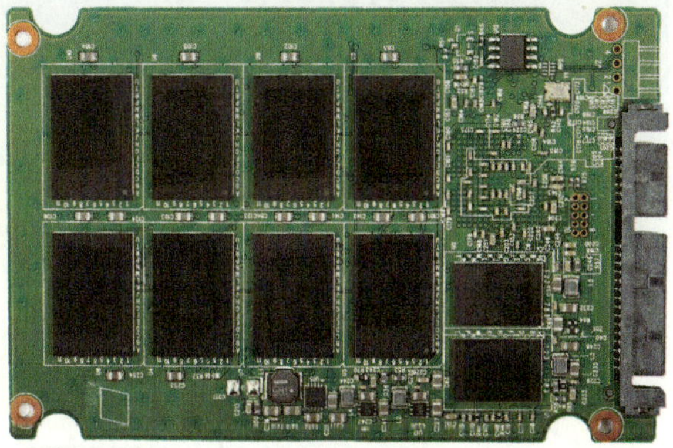

Peter Gudella/Shutterstock.com

and weaknesses. For example, if you want to completely back up the contents of your computer, you might store those contents on an external hard drive or in cloud storage. However, your internal hard drive might store your operating system and apps you currently are using. If you want to move several files from one computer to another, consider using a USB flash drive. Finally, you might use a DVD or other type of optical disc to store a movie.

All computers, including smartphones and tablets, come with internal storage, such as one or more internal hard drives (**Figure 3-11**). A **hard drive** is the most computer common storage medium, and can be magnetic or solid state. Internal hard drives are installed in the computer or device you are using. For example, if you are creating a file on your work computer and store it on an internal hard drive, you will not be able to access the file from a different computer unless you send it electronically, or copy the file to a location on the cloud, an external hard drive, or a USB flash drive. Magnetic hard disk drives (HDDs) typically have greater storage capacity and are less expensive than their solid state equivalents, but have several moving parts, making it inadvisable to move the computer while they are running. A **solid state drive (SSD)** is a hard drive without moving parts, and is faster and more durable than a magnetic drive (**Figure 3-12**). Solid state drives often are used on mobile devices such as laptops and tablets and come in various physical sizes.

In addition to storing data and information on an internal hard drive, you also can store it on an external hard drive. **External hard drives** are housed in a separate case, and typically connect to your computer using a USB cable (**Figure 3-13**), instantly adding storage capacity to your computer. Similar to internal hard drives, external hard drives can use either magnetic or solid state technology. External hard drives also can be transported from one computer to another, so if you are working on a file and save it to the external hard drive, you can connect the drive to a different computer to continue working on that same file. An external hard drive can enable you to store large files and can be a good solution if you are unsure of access to the cloud, but only enable you to access the stored files if you can transport and connect the external hard drive to a computer or mobile device.

Figure 3-13: External hard drive

Anton Starikov/Shutterstock.com

Cloud storage involves storing electronic files on the Internet, not on a local computer, a practice called storing data "in the cloud." Cloud storage enables you to store your files remotely on servers that could be in a different city, state, or part of the world. Storing files

Figure 3-14: Cloud storage

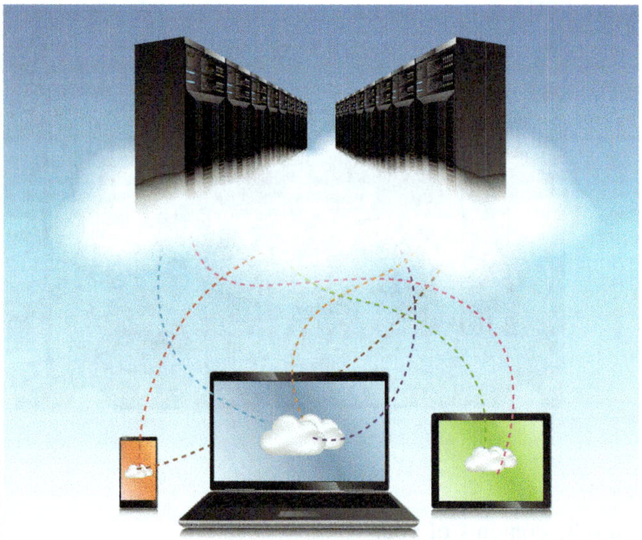

iStock.com/Lvcandy

to and retrieving files from cloud storage typically requires only a computer or mobile device with an Internet connection (**Figure 3-14**). With cloud storage, you might not require as much storage on your computer because you can store your files remotely. Examples of cloud storage include Google Drive, Microsoft OneDrive, and Box. Disadvantages to cloud storage include that you must be connected to the Internet, may be limited to the amount of free storage available, and could have concerns about security. However, the ease of access to files stored on the cloud, and the ability to share and collaborate with others, makes cloud storage a popular storage method.

Flash memory is a type of nonvolatile memory that can be erased electronically and rewritten. This type of memory typically is less expensive than most types of RAM, and can retain its contents in the absence of power. SSDs are a type of flash memory. Two other widely used types of flash memory storage include memory cards and USB flash drives. A **memory card** is a removable flash memory storage device, usually no bigger than 1.5 inches in height or width, that you insert and remove from a slot in a computer, digital camera, mobile device, or card reader/writer. Memory cards enable mobile uses to easily transport files to and from devices. A **USB flash drive**, also known as a flash drive, pen drive, jump drive, or thumb drive, is a removable storage device that you plug into a USB port on your computer, making it easy to transport files and folders to other computers or devices (**Figure 3-15**). Storage capacities of USB flash drives and memory cards vary. They are easily portable, but also easy to lose because of their small size. Like most physical storage, their uses are being phased out because of the reliance on cloud storage.

Figure 3-15: USB flash drive

IB Photography/Shutterstock.com

Optical media include CDs, DVDs, and Blu-ray discs (BDs) and use laser technology for storage and playback. Optical media were once widely used to distribute installation files for programs and apps, but saving files to optical media required special software or capabilities within the operating system. While optical media is easy to transport, if the discs get damaged, you might not be able to access your stored files. Because of the rise in availability of streaming services for music or video, and the cloud for storage, optical media's use as storage is declining.

The CPU The **central processing unit (CPU)** is a complex integrated circuit consisting of millions of electronic parts and is primarily responsible for converting input (data) into meaningful output (information). Data travels in and out of the CPU on embedded wires collectively called a **bus**. The location of the CPUs in varies, depending on the type of computer or mobile device (**Figure 3-16**).

When you purchase a device, you might notice that processors can be advertised as having one or more cores. A processor core is a unit on the processor with the circuitry necessary to execute instructions. Processors with more cores typically perform better and are more expensive than processors with fewer cores. A processor with multiple cores is referred to as a **multi-core processor**. Computers and devices rely more on multi-core processors today than in the past, as the performance requirements for the devices have increased.

If a processor uses specific data frequently it can store that data in a processor cache. A **processor cache** stores frequently used data next to the processor so that it can easily and quickly be retrieved.

Figure 3-16: Central processing units

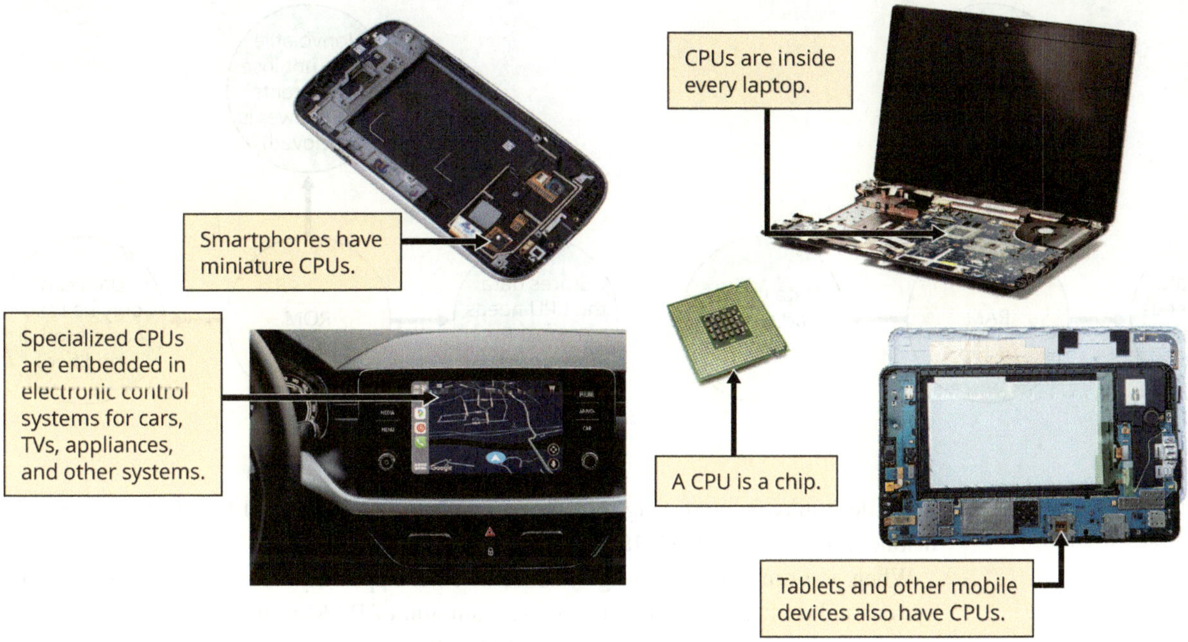

shahreen/Shutterstock.com; Raw Group/Shutterstock.com; Vladimka production/Shutterstock.com; aarrows/Shutterstock.com; Vervaridis Vasilis/Shutterstock.com

When a CPU executes instructions as it converts input into output, it does so with the control unit and the arithmetic logic unit (ALU). The **arithmetic logic unit (ALU)** is responsible for performing arithmetic operations in the CPU. The **control unit** manages the flow of instructions within the processor. Instructions executed by the CPU go through a series of four steps, often referred to as a machine cycle or an instruction cycle. This cycle includes the steps the CPU completes to run programmed instructions, make calculations, and make decisions. The four steps in the machine cycle include fetching, decoding, executing, and storing. The fetching and decoding instructions are performed by the control unit, while the executing and storing instructions are performed by the ALU (**Figure 3-17**).

Figure 3-17: Machine cycle

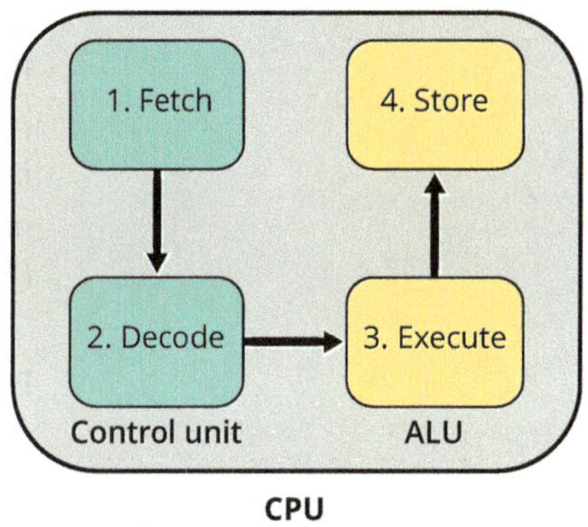

Memory Memory is responsible for holding data and programs as they are being processed by the CPU. Different types of memory exist, including random access memory (RAM), read-only memory (ROM), and virtual memory.

Random access memory (RAM) is the storage location that is part of every computer and that temporarily stores open apps and document data while a computer is on. On a computer, RAM is stored on one or more chips connected to the main circuit board, also referred to as the motherboard. The **motherboard** contains the microprocessor, the computer memory, and other internal devices. RAM temporarily stores data needed by the operating system and apps you use. When you start an app, the app's instructions are transferred from the hard drive to RAM. Although accessing an app's instructions from RAM results in increased performance, the contents of RAM are lost when power is removed. Memory that loses its contents when power is removed is said to be **volatile memory**. **Nonvolatile memory** does not lose its contents when power is removed.

Read-only memory (ROM) is permanently installed on your computer and is attached to the motherboard. The ROM chip contains the BIOS (basic input/output system), which tells your computer or device how to start. At startup, the BIOS also performs a **power-on self test (POST)**, which tests all components for proper operation. The ROM also provides the means of communication between the operating system and hardware devices. Manufacturers often update the instructions on the ROM chip, which are referred to as **firmware**. These updated instructions, or firmware version, can enable your computer to perform additional tasks or fine-tune how your computer communicates with other devices.

Figure 3-18: Differences between ROM and RAM

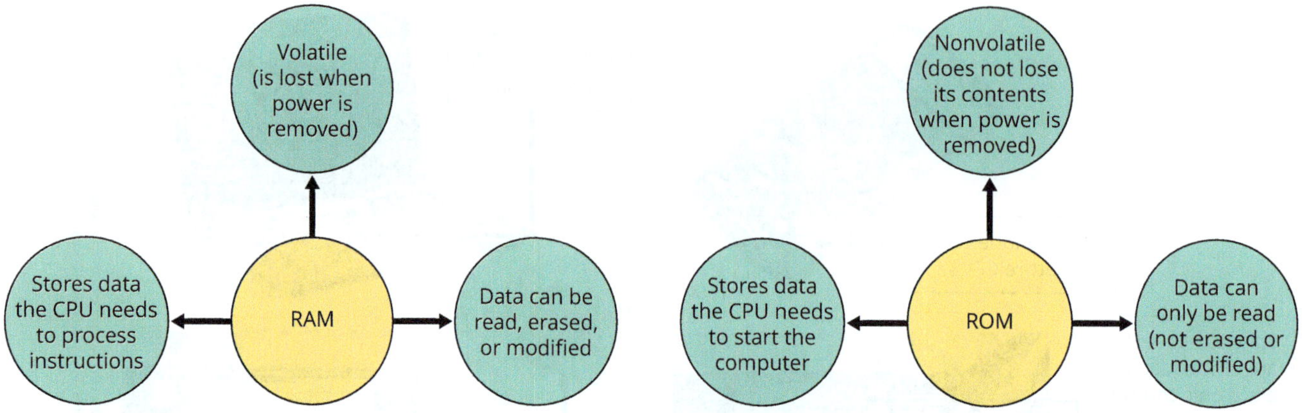

While it may be confusing to differentiate between RAM and ROM, they each have distinct functions (**Figure 3-18**).

When you run your operating system and other apps on your computer, the operating system and each app will require a certain amount of RAM to function properly. As you run more apps simultaneously, more RAM will be required. If your computer runs low on RAM, it may need to swap the contents of RAM to and from the hard drive. When this takes place, your operating system uses its **virtual memory** capability, temporarily storing data on a storage medium until it can be swapped into RAM. A **swap file** or **paging file** is a file that contains the area of the hard that cannot fit in RAM, and which is stored in the hard disk's virtual memory. Depending on the type of hard drive installed on your computer, using virtual memory may decrease your computer's performance (**Figure 3-19**).

Various types of random access memory exist, and the different types vary in cost, performance, and whether or not they are volatile. **Table 3-1** lists common types of RAM.

Figure 3-19: How a computer might use virtual memory

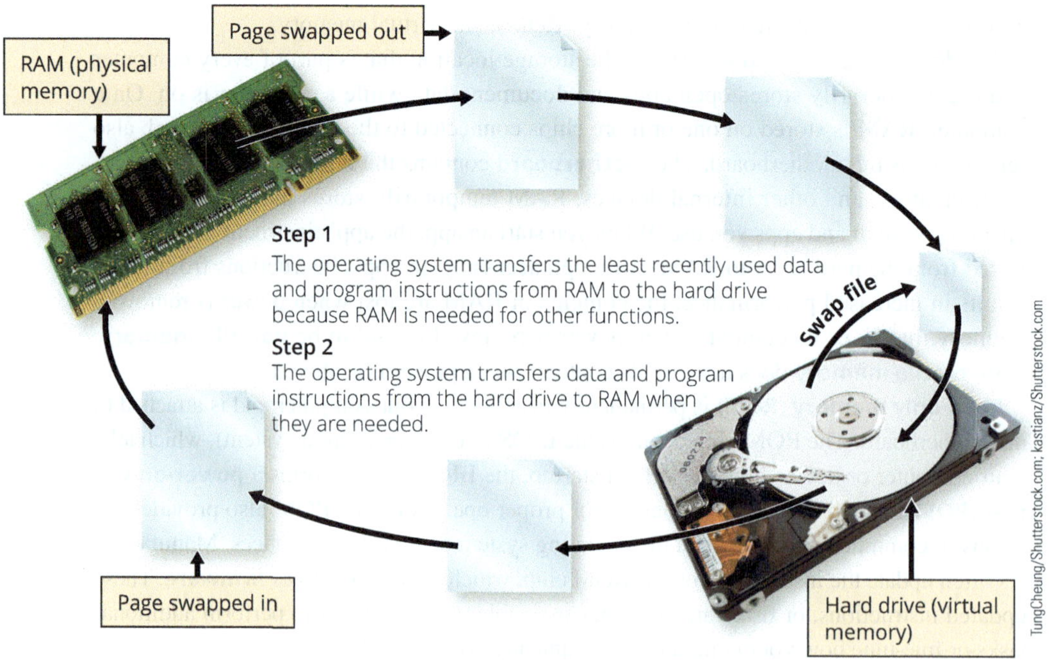

Table 3-1: Types of RAM

Type of RAM	Description	Volatile or nonvolatile
Dynamic RAM (DRAM)	Memory needs to be constantly recharged or contents will be erased	Volatile
Static RAM (SRAM)	Memory can be recharged less frequently than DRAM, but can be more expensive than DRAM	Volatile
Magnetoresistive RAM (MRAM)	Memory uses magnetic charges to store contents, and can retain its contents in the absence of power	Nonvolatile
Flash memory	Fast, inexpensive memory that can retain its contents in the absence of power	Nonvolatile

While RAM is used to temporarily store instructions used by apps, storage devices are designed to store data and information for extended periods of time. The type and amount of data you want to store will help you determine the most appropriate storage device to use.

Explain Considerations When Purchasing a Computer

With the powerful capabilities of tablets and smartphones, you may not need to purchase a laptop or desktop of your own. However, many feel that the larger screen, built-in keyboard, and pointing device make a personal laptop or desktop computer still necessary. Your employer may also place restrictions on personal uses of company-issued computers. When purchasing a computer, understanding your needs will help you to select the most appropriate device.

If your primary needs are to do activities such as check your email, use social media, do online banking, and browse the web, your hardware and software needs will be different than if you will be creating and editing video content or other multimedia and graphics, which require more processing power and a larger monitor. When choosing a computer, you should select one with the platform, hardware, form factor, and add-on devices that best meet your needs. **Table 3-2** identifies factors to consider when buying a computer, as well as questions that will help you in making the most appropriate choices.

Platform refers to the software, or operating system, a computer or device uses. It typically is easier to transfer files between computers and devices that use the same platform. If you are purchasing a computer to do schoolwork, for example, consider purchasing one that uses the same operating system as the computers at your school. If you have a job

Table 3-2: Factors to consider in buying a computer

Consideration	Questions
Platform	• Do I need to use software that requires a specific platform? • Does the computer need to be compatible with other devices I own that use a particular platform?
Hardware	• Do I require specific hardware to perform intended tasks? • How much data and information do I plan to store on the computer?
Hardware specifications	• Will the tasks I perform or software I want to run require certain hardware specifications?
Form factor	• Will I be using this computer in one location, or will I need it to be mobile?
Add-on devices	• What additional devices will I need to perform my intended tasks?

and want the ability to do some work both on your office and home computer, consider purchasing a computer that uses the same operating system as your work computer. The operating systems used elsewhere in your home, both on computers and mobile devices, also might play a role in the selection. For example, if you own an iPhone or iPad, you might choose to purchase an Apple computer for maximum compatibility between the devices. A Chromebook is a type of laptop that runs the ChromeOS operating system. While these are budget friendly, they often do not have as many advanced features or support as many apps as computers running Windows or macOS, which are the leading desktop operating systems.

When you buy a computer, you should review the computer's hardware specifications so that you purchase one that meets your needs. Computers are available in a variety of brands. Each brand might include models that have varying types of processors, amounts of memory, storage devices, and form factors. You can find specifications about a computer on the computer's packaging, on signage next to the computer's display in a store, or on the manufacturer's or retailer's website (**Figure 3-20**).

Your budget will play a big role in the computer you purchase, and there may be many computers available in the same price range. For example, one computer available for $1,000 might have a great processor and a mediocre hard drive, but another computer at the same price might have a mediocre processor and a great hard drive. It is important to evaluate what each computer has to offer so that you can select the device that best meets your needs.

A common way to determine the required hardware specifications for your computer is to evaluate the minimum hardware requirements, also called system requirements, for the software you plan to use. Each program or app you plan to use has its own system requirements. The system requirements for one program or app might conflict with the system requirements of the other(s), so you will need to select the computer with the hardware specifications that can accommodate a variety of programs or apps. **Table 3-3** describes how to evaluate conflicting system requirements.

Figure 3-20: Detailed hardware specifications

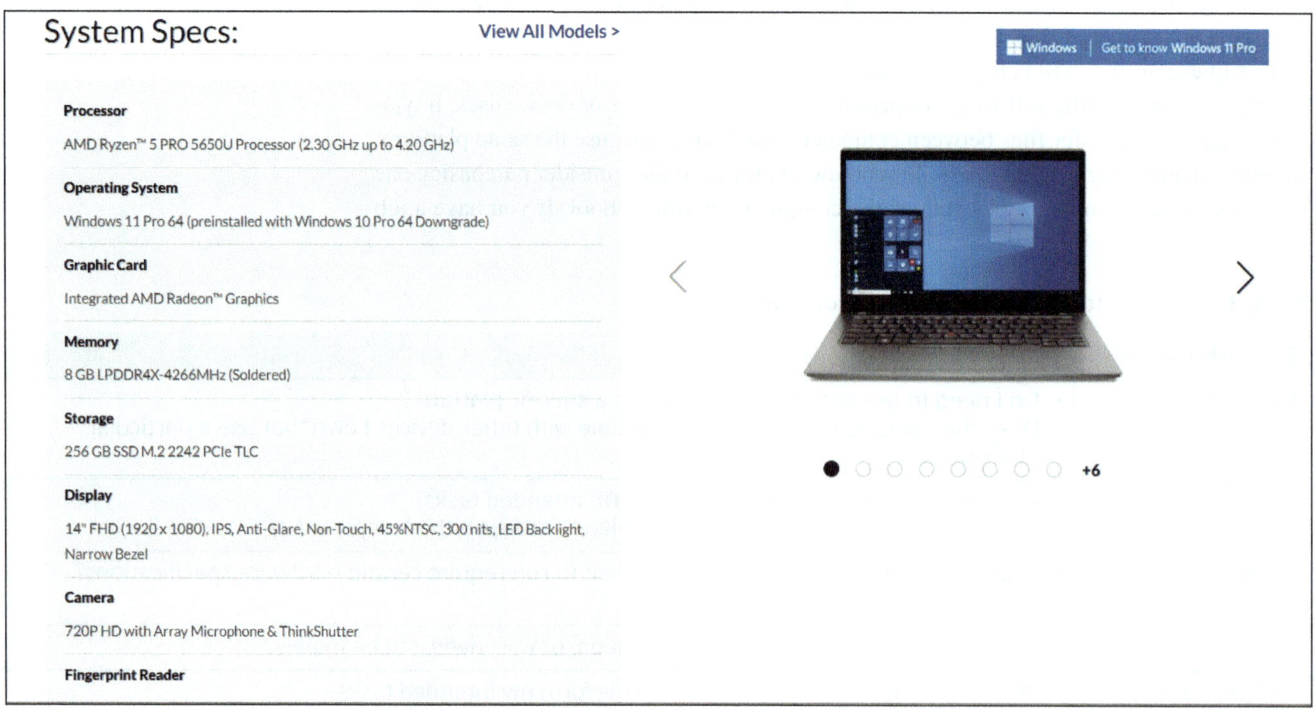

Lenovo

Table 3-3: Evaluating system requirements

Specification	Recommended solution
Different processor requirements	Identify the program or app with the greatest processor requirement and select a computer with a processor that meets or exceeds the requirement.
Different memory requirements	Identify the program or app with the greatest memory requirement and select a computer with a memory type and capacity that meets or exceeds this requirement. Computers with as little as 4 GB of RAM are adequate for basic web browsing and very basic productivity tasks, while virtual reality applications, high-end gaming, and other intensive tasks often require as much as 32 GB.
Different storage requirements	Add the storage requirements for each program or app you want to use, and select a computer with the storage capacity that exceeds the sum of all storage requirements.
Other differing hardware requirements	In most cases, identify the program or app with the greatest requirement and select a computer that at least meets or exceeds this requirement.

Although following these guidelines will help you select an appropriate computer, keep in mind that you likely want the computer to meet your needs for the next three to five years. If you select a computer that exactly meets the system requirements for the present software you intend to use, you might not be able to install or use additional programs or apps in the future. In addition, you should purchase a computer that has enough storage capacity not only for the programs and apps you want to use, but also for the files you intend to store on the computer (homework, photos, videos, important documents, etc.). Cloud storage can extend the capabilities of your computer, so consider your access and storage limits to cloud storage drives when evaluating storage needs. While purchasing the most expensive computer you can afford might meet your needs, you might not ever use all available resources. For example, if the system requirements for the programs and apps you want to use call for 12 gigabytes (GB) of memory, it might be reasonable to select a computer with 16 GB of memory, but it could be a waste of money to purchase a computer with 32 GB of memory. If you intend to use a computer to play games, you might consider a computer built specifically for gaming applications. These computers typically have a large amount of RAM, as well as other supporting hardware to support an immersive gaming experience. Evaluate your options carefully and seek advice from professionals if you are unsure of your exact needs.

After you have determined the platform and hardware requirements for the computer you want to purchase, you will select a form factor. The **form factor** refers to the shape and size of the computer. Not all form factors may support the hardware you need. For example, a tablet might not contain adequate hardware specifications for editing videos. Choosing between a desktop and laptop usually comes down to whether you need to be able to easily transport your computer. You also should consider the need for peripheral devices such as a keyboard, mouse, webcam, speakers, and printer. Depending on your needs, it may also be necessary to use two monitors that can display different documents or apps (**Figure 3-21**).

Figure 3-21: Two monitor setup

Gorodenkoff/Shutterstock.com

Demonstrate Familiarity with Input and Output Devices

Input and output devices are necessary to provide information to and receive information from a computer. Manual input devices include keyboards. Touchscreens are another common method of input used by mobile devices, and increasingly on computer monitors. Audio, visual, and gaming are other types of input. Output can be display, audio, or print.

Investigate Input Devices

Various types of input devices are available, such as keyboards, pointing devices, touchscreens, microphones, webcams, digital cameras, scanners, and game controllers. Some input devices are peripheral devices, such as printers, which are shared by multiple devices or users on a network. Others are built into the computer or device. For example, most laptop computers today come with a keyboard, pointing device, touchscreen, microphone, and webcam, and smartphones also include a microphone, digital camera, and webcam.

Manual Input A **keyboard** is an input device that contains keys for entering letters, numbers, punctuation, and symbols, and issuing commands (**Figure 3-22**). Desktop computers have keyboards connected either wired or wirelessly, and laptop computers have a keyboard built-in. Mobile devices such as tablets and smartphones typically have an on-screen keyboard; that is, an image of a keyboard displays on the screen, and you touch the appropriate keys to enter letters, numbers, and symbols.

A **pointing device** is used to point to and select specific objects on the computer screen. Pointing devices can be used to select objects, move objects, and position or draw items on the screen. Examples of pointing devices include a mouse, touchpad, and trackball (**Figure 3-23**).

- A **mouse** is the most common type of pointing device used with computers. A mouse fits under your hand and can connect to your computer either with a wire or wirelessly. Moving the mouse on a flat surface, such as a desk, moves a pointer on the screen. When the pointer is positioned over an object you want to select, you can press a button on the mouse to select the object. This action is referred to as clicking the mouse.

Figure 3-22: Typical computer keyboard

Volodymyr Krasyuk/Shutterstock.com

Figure 3-23: Typical pointing devices

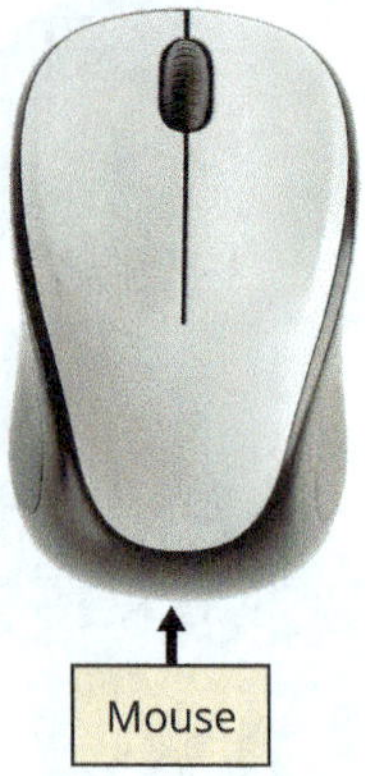

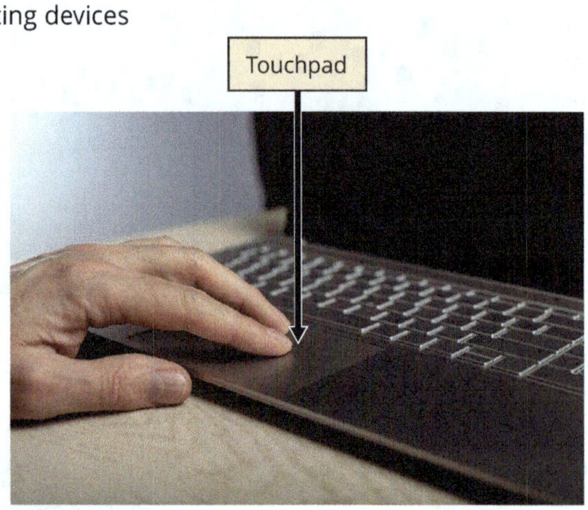

New Africa/Shutterstock.com; valiantsin suprunovich/Shutterstock.com; Mikhail Gorshenin/Shutterstock.com

- A touchpad is a pointing device that is commonly used on laptops. A **touchpad** is a flat surface that is touch-sensitive, and you move your finger around the touchpad to move the pointer on the screen. When the pointer is over an item on the screen you wish to select, you can tap the touchpad with your finger to select the object.
- A **trackball** is a stationary pointing device with a ball anchored inside a casing, as well as two or more buttons. Moving the ball moves the pointer on the screen, and pressing the buttons issues the commands to the computer.

Figure 3-24: Digital pen

Mak3t/Shutterstock.com

Touchscreen Input In addition to responding to the touch of your fingers, touchscreens also may be able to respond to a stylus or digital pen to enter commands. **Multitouch screens** can respond to multiple fingers touching the screen simultaneously. This is useful when you are performing a gesture such as pinching or stretching an object to resize it. Other touchscreen input methods include tapping (to select an object or command), and swiping (to move the screen).

Pen input is used to make selections or draw on a touchscreen with more precision than a finger. Common pen input devices include a stylus and a digital pen. A **stylus** is a pen-shaped digital tool that you can use to make selections or enter information on a touchscreen, as well as draw, tap icons, or tap keys on an on-screen keyboard. A **digital pen** is similar to a stylus, but is more capable because it has programmable buttons. Some digital pens can also capture your handwriting as you write on paper or on the screen (**Figure 3-24**).

Audio and Visual Input An option for issuing instructions to your computer without using your hands is using your voice. A **microphone** is used to enter voice or sound data into a computer. Examples of activities that might require a microphone include video conferencing, voice recognition, and recording live music. Many laptops and tablets have built-in microphones, but you can connect a microphone to other types of computers either using a wire or wirelessly. Using a microphone, you can record audio, issue commands to the computer, or speak while the computer translates your words to text in a document. Microphones are also essential if you are using the computer to have an audio or video conversation with one or more other people.

A **digital camera** creates a digital image of an object, person, or scene, and allows you to download or send pictures or videos to a computer. Most computers come with a built-in camera called a **webcam**, a type of digital video camera that captures video and still images as well as audio input, primarily for use in videoconferencing, chatting, or online gaming (**Figure 3-25**). If the computer does not have a built-in webcam, or you would like to connect a different type of camera to your computer, you can do so either via a wired or wireless connection.

A **scanner** is an input device that converts an existing paper image into an electronic file that you can open and work with on your computer. For example, if you want to convert a printed logo to digital form so that you can edit and duplicate it, you could use a scanner to convert the printed logo to a format a computer can understand. In addition to scanning printed materials such as logos and documents, 3D scanners can scan three-dimensional objects, which then can be manipulated and possibly printed. You can also use a scanner to scan a printed document so that you can edit it using an app on your computer.

Figure 3-25: Webcam

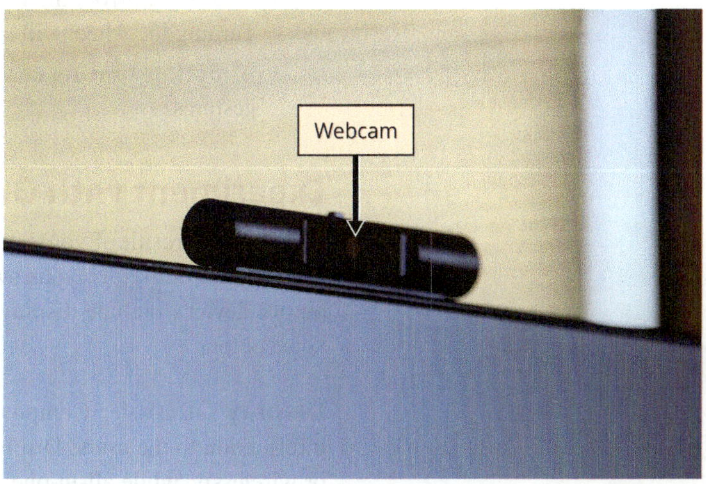

Emre Unluturk/Shutterstock.com

Figure 3-26: QR code

Figure 3-27: Gaming wheel

Tinxi/Shutterstock.com

Another common type of visual input is QR codes. A **QR code** is a square-shaped graphic that corresponds to a web address or other information (**Figure 3-26**). QR is short for quick response. QR codes often appear on flyers, menus, or other printed materials, including books and signs. The advantage of a QR code is that they are easy and free to generate, and can enable users to use their smartphone's camera to easily navigate to a specific website.

Gaming Input A **game controller** is an input device you use when playing a video game. Various types of game controllers exist such as joysticks, gamepads, dance pads, wheels, and motion-sensing controllers.

- A **joystick** includes a handheld vertical lever, mounted on a base, that you move in different directions to control the actions of the simulated vehicle or player.
- A **gamepad** is held in both hands and controls the movement and actions of players or objects. On gamepads, users press buttons with their thumbs or move sticks in various directions to trigger events.
- A **dance pad** is a flat, electronic device divided into panels that users press with their feet in response to instructions from the video game.
- A **wheel** mirrors the functionality of a steering wheel in a vehicle (**Figure 3-27**). Turning the wheel will turn the vehicle you are driving in the game.
- A **motion-sensing controller** allows users to guide on-screen elements with air gestures.

Experiment with Output Devices

Output is the result of your actions, creations, or commands, and can be print or digital. You can use output for your own purposes or share output with others. Commonly used output devices include display devices, speakers, headphones, printers, projectors, and voice output.

Display Output Computers use display devices as output devices to communicate information to the users. Display devices are connected to desktop computers via a cable or wirelessly, while all-in-one computers, laptops, tablets, and smartphones have built-in display devices. Display devices come in a variety of sizes. If you are simply using a computer to browse the web and check your email, you might consider a smaller display device. However, if you are working with graphics or large spreadsheets, you might use a larger display device, and/or multiple display devices, which allow you to display one app or document window on one screen and another app or document on another.

To present onscreen information to a group, you might consider using a projector. **Projectors** can display output from a computer on a large surface such as a wall or screen (**Figure 3-28**). Projectors are often used in classroom or conference room environments where individuals give presentations. Projectors are connected to computers or device using a cable or wirelessly and can either duplicate what is on your monitor or screen or act as an extension of the monitor (your monitor might display one thing while the projector displays another). Some projectors are small and easy to transport, while others are larger and may be permanently mounted in a room. Many conference rooms and classrooms now have screens that connect directly to a computer or device, eliminating the need for a projector.

Figure 3-28: Ceiling mounted projector

v74/Shutterstock.com

Audio Output **Speakers** are used to convey audio output, such as music, voice, sound effects, or other sounds. While speakers often are built into computers, tablets, and smartphones, you can also connect speakers via a wired or wireless connection. For example, if you want to play music in a small office setting and would like others to hear it, you might connect a separate speaker to your computer so that it can play more loudly. If you prefer to listen to audio in a public space without disturbing others, consider using headphones. **Headphones** consist of a pair of small listening devices that fit into a band placed over your ears. As an alternative to headphones, **earbuds** are speakers that are small enough to place in your ears (**Figure 3-29**). If you prefer a device that provides audio output while being able to accept voice input, consider a headset. **Headsets** include one or more headphones for output, and a microphone for input.

Figure 3-29: Earbuds

Anton Starikov/Shutterstock.com

In addition to output being displayed or printed, computers can also provide voice output. A **voice synthesizer** converts text to speech. Some apps and operating systems have a built-in voice synthesizer. In addition to this form of output being convenient for some, it is also helpful for those with visual impairments.

Print Output A **printer** creates hard copy output on paper, film, and other media. A printer can be connected to a computer via a cable, a network, or wirelessly. **Table 3-4** describes the various types of printers.

Table 3-4: Types of printers

Type of printer	Description
Ink-jet printer	Prints by spraying small dots of colored ink onto paper
Laser printer	Uses a laser beam and toner to print on paper
Multifunction device (MFD)	Also called an all-in-one printer; can serve as an input device by copying and scanning, as well as an output device by faxing and printing
Mobile printer	Small, lightweight printer that is built into or attached to a mobile device for mobile printing
Plotter	Large-format printer that uses charged wires to produce high-quality drawings for professional applications such as architectural blueprints; plotters draw continuous lines on large rolls of paper
3D printer	Creates objects based on computer models using special plastics and other materials

Figure 3-30: 3D printer

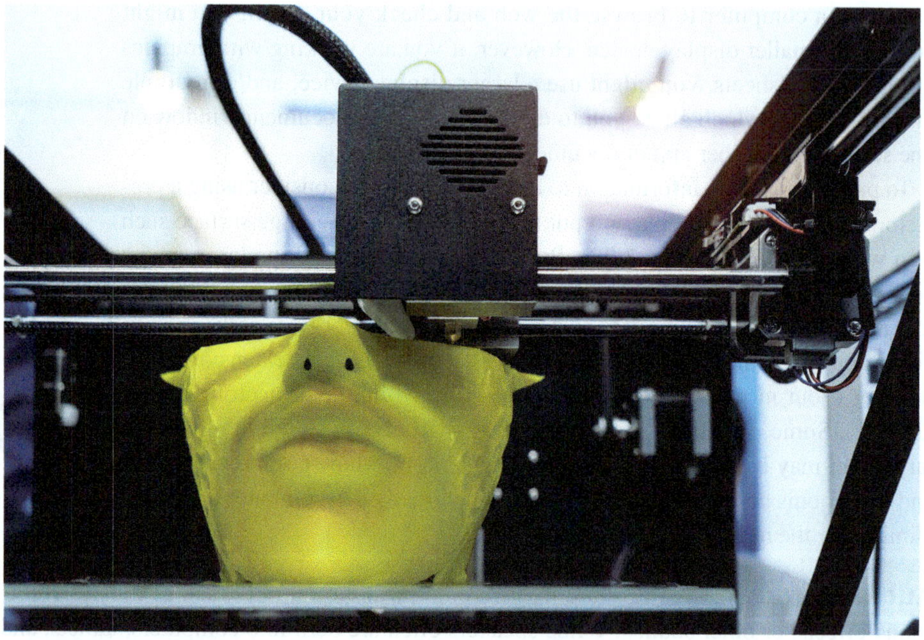

A **3D printer** uses a process called additive manufacturing to create an object by adding material one horizontal layer at a time to print solid objects, such as clothing, prosthetics, eyewear, implants, toys, parts, prototypes, and more (**Figure 3-30**). 3D printers and the materials required to use them are expensive, limiting their use. While some personal users have 3D printers, they often are associated with manufacturing, scientific and medical, and other industrial uses. For example, in manufacturing, 3D printers can produce parts quickly and efficiently. Medical professionals can create organ models that can be used in training or preparation for complex surgeries.

Explain How to Install Computer Hardware

When you purchase a desktop or laptop computer, you should determine an ideal location to use the computer. Select an area that is free from clutter, is not subject to extreme temperatures or water, and is comfortable for you to work. Before you turn on your computer or device for the first time, you should make sure that all necessary components are included and that the device is charged or connected to a power source. You should also inspect the computer or device to make sure it is free from damage.

If you are installing a desktop or all-in-one computer, carefully unpack all components from the box and place them in their desired locations. Connect all components and accessories, such as your keyboard and mouse, and then connect the power. Finally, you can turn on the computer and follow all remaining steps on the screen. Most computer manufacturers include installation instructions with their computers, so be sure to follow any additional steps included in those instructions.

If you are installing a laptop, carefully unpack the laptop and place it in a location next to a power source. It is a good idea to fully charge the laptop's battery before using the device for the first time.

In addition to installing a computer, you might buy peripheral devices, such as a printer or scanner, to connect to the computer. These peripheral devices communicate with the computer through a port. Some devices, called **plug-and-play** devices, will begin functioning properly as soon as you connect them to your computer. Other devices might require that you manually install special software, called a device driver, to work properly. A **device driver** is a program that controls a device attached to your computer, such as a printer, monitor, or video card. If you have to install a program or app for your device to work, make sure you are signed in to the computer with a user account that has the necessary permission to install programs and apps. Some components must be installed inside your computer. If you are uncomfortable or inexperienced in opening a computer and installing or replacing components, contact a professional.

Devices can also connect to a computer wirelessly. To connect a wireless device to your computer, follow the installation instructions that come with the device.

Maintain Hardware Components

After purchasing a computer or device, you will want to make sure it runs optimally and is well maintained to guarantee proper performance. Some methods for ensuring performance include measuring the performance of computer hardware, troubleshooting problems with hardware and peripherals, and maintaining hardware and software.

Measure Hardware Performance

When searching for a computer or device to purchase, you should be able to evaluate the hardware specifications so that you can select one that best meets your needs. The following methods evaluate the processor and other factors that impact efficiency.

- A processor's **clock speed** measures the speed at which it can execute instructions. Clock speed can be measured in either megahertz (MHz) or gigahertz (GHz). Megahertz specifies millions of cycles per second, while gigahertz specifies billions of cycles per second.
- A **cycle** is the smallest unit of time a process can measure. The efficiency of a CPU is measured by instructions per cycle (IPC).
- The **bus width** determines the speed at which data in a computer travels, and is also referred to as the **word size**. The wider the bus, the more data that can travel on it. A 64-bit bus, for example, transfers data faster than a 32-bit bus. If you have a fast CPU but the bus speed is slow, that can cause a condition called bottlenecking.

While manufacturers advertise performance factors such as clock speed and bus speed, there are other factors that can affect processor performance. For this reason, you should research benchmark test results for the processor(s) you are considering. A **benchmark** is a test run by a laboratory or other organization to determine processor speed and other performance factors. Benchmarking tests compare similar systems performing identical tasks. You typically can find benchmarking information online.

Troubleshoot Hardware Problems

At some point you probably will experience a technology problem with your computer or device that requires troubleshooting. Technology problems that remain unresolved may impact your ability to use your device. Often issues with powering on or holding a battery charge stem from a faulty device used to plug in the device, such as the adapter. Laptops often come with **adapters**, which are external batteries that provide power to the laptop and help its battery recharge.

Table 3-5 outlines some common problems you might experience with a computer or device, as well as some recommended solutions. Before troubleshooting, you should properly turn off the computer or device and remove it from its power source, and make sure your files are backed up to the cloud or external storage. Failure to do so might result in damaging the computer's physical components.

Table 3-5: Troubleshooting hardware problems

Problem	Recommended solution(s)
Computer or device does not turn on	It might be in sleep or hibernate mode; to wake it up, try pressing a key on the keyboard, pressing the power button, or tapping the touchscreen. Make sure power or charging cables are plugged securely into both the external or wall outlet and the device itself. Make sure the battery is charged if not connected to an external power source. If the battery is charged, connect the adapter or charging cord and attempt to turn on the computer or device. If it still does not turn on, the problem may be with the computer or device.
Computer or device gets wet	Turn off the computer or device, remove the battery, and dry off visible water with a cloth. Fill a plastic bag or box with uncooked rice, submerge the computer or device and battery into the rice so that it is surrounded completely, and then do not turn on the computer or device for at least 24 hours. If the computer or device does not work after it is dry, contact a professional for your options.
Battery does not hold a charge or drains very quickly	Verify that the adapter, cable, and/or charging cord used to charge the battery are all working properly. If the computer or device can run from the adapter or charging cord without a battery installed, you may need to replace the battery.
The device issues a series of beeps	Refer to your user manual to determine what the beeps indicate, as different sequences of beeps may indicate different hardware problems specific to your model of computer.
Device turns on, but operating system does not run	Disconnect all nonessential peripheral devices, remove all storage media, and then restart the computer or device. If the problem persists, the operating system might need to be restored or the device reset. If these measures do not work, the hard drive might be failing.
Display device does not display anything	On a desktop, verify that the monitor is turned on and set to the right input, and that the video cable is connected securely to the computer and monitor and plugged in to an outlet. Restart the computer or device. There might be a problem with the video card, requiring it to be replaced. The **video card** is a circuit board that processes image signals. If you have access to a spare monitor, see if that monitor will work. If so, your original monitor might be faulty. If not, the problem may be with the hardware or software configuration.
Peripheral device does not work	Verify that the peripheral device is connected properly. If it is wireless, make sure it is turned on and is charged or has working batteries, and then attempt to pair it again with the computer or wireless receiver. If you have access to a spare device, see if it will work. If so, your original peripheral device might be faulty. If not, the problem may be with the hardware or software configuration.
Sound does not work	Verify that speakers, headphones, or earbuds are connected, charged, and turned on. Make sure the volume is not muted and is turned up on the computer or mobile device.
Hard drive makes noise	If the computer is not positioned on a flat surface, move it to a flat surface. If something has impacted the hard drive, it might have caused the hard drive to fail. If the problem persists, contact a professional.

Problem	Recommended solution(s)
Program or app does not run	Restart the computer or device and try running the program or app again. If feasible, uninstall the program or app, reinstall it, and then try running it again. If the problem persists, the problem may be with the operating system's configuration.
Computer or device displays symptoms of a virus or other malware	Make sure your antivirus software is up to date, and then disconnect the computer or device from the network and run antivirus software to attempt to remove the malware. Continue running scans until no threats are detected and then reconnect the computer to the network. If you do not have antivirus software installed, obtain and install a reputable antivirus program or app and then scan your computer in an attempt to remove the malware. You should have only one antivirus program or app installed on your computer or mobile device at one time. If you are unable to remove the malware, take your computer to a professional who may be able to remove the malicious program or app.
Screen is damaged physically	Contact a professional to replace the screen; if the computer or device is covered under a warranty, the repair may be free. Replacing a broken screen on a computer or device might be more costly than replacing the computer or device.
Touchscreen does not respond	Clean the touchscreen. Restart the computer or device.
Computer or device does not connect to a wireless network	Verify that you are within range of a wireless access point. Make sure the information to connect to the wireless network is configured properly on the computer or device. Make sure the wireless capability on the computer or device is turned on. Make sure your router or modem is turned on properly.
Computer or device cannot synchronize with Bluetooth accessories	Verify that the Bluetooth device is turned on. Verify that the Bluetooth functionality on your computer or device is enabled. Verify that the computer or device has been paired properly with the accessory. Make sure the Bluetooth device is charged.
Device continuously has poor mobile phone reception	Restart the device. If you have a protective case, remove the case to see if reception improves. If you are using the device inside a building, try moving closer to a window or open doorway. Contact your wireless carrier for additional suggestions.
Printer does not print	Verify that the printer is plugged in and turned on. Verify that the printer is properly connected to the computer either via a wired or wireless connection. Verify that there is paper in the paper tray. Verify that there is sufficient ink or toner.

If you are uncomfortable performing any of the recommended solutions or the solutions are not solving the problem(s), you should consult a professional (independent computer repair company, technical support department, or computer or mobile device manufacturer) for further assessment and resolution. If the problem you are experiencing is not listed, you can perform a search on the Internet to identify potential solutions.

Before attempting to resolve computer or mobile device problems on your own, be sure to follow all necessary safety precautions. Contact a professional if you require additional information.

Maintain Computer Hardware

You should perform tasks periodically to keep your hardware in good condition and the software functioning properly. Failure to properly maintain hardware can result in decreasing its lifespan and/or its performance.

Table 3-6: Maintaining hardware

Recommendation	Proactive steps
Keep it clean	Keep your computer and device away from dusty or cluttered areas. Use a damp cloth to clean the screen or monitor gently. Do not use any special cleaners to clean the display. Periodically use a can of compressed air to free your keyboard from any dirt and debris. Always hold the can of compressed air upright to avoid damaging the keyboard. If the computer has an air vent where a fan removes heat, make sure the vent is free of dust and debris. If the air vent is dirty, contact a trained professional to have it cleaned properly. Do not attempt to clean the air vent yourself, as it is possible that dirt and debris can enter the computer.
Avoid water and moisture	Avoid exposure to water and moist air by keeping liquids away and keeping the computer or device in a climate-controlled space when possible.
Monitor available storage to ensure the computer or device runs efficiently	Make sure you have enough free space on your hard drive. When computers or devices run low on available hard drive space, performance can quickly deteriorate. If you are unable to free enough space on your hard drive to run properly, consider archiving or moving files to the cloud, deleting files, or purchasing additional internal or external storage hardware.
Don't allow overheating	Extreme temperatures or humidity can damage the electronics. Many devices will alert you when the temperature is too high or will automatically shut down. For a laptop, consider purchasing a cooling pad that protects it from overheating.

Hardware maintenance involves performing tasks to keep the computer's physical components in good working order. **Table 3-6** lists maintenance recommendations that will help keep your computer functioning properly.

Following these maintenance recommendations will enable you to prevent many common problems from occurring in the first place. Another proactive step you can take to protect desktop and laptop computers is to avoid power fluctuations such as power spikes or power surges. To do so, consider purchasing and connecting an uninterruptable power supply (UPS) or a surge suppressor. An **uninterruptable power supply (UPS)** maintains power to computer equipment in case of an interruption in the primary electrical source, usually in the form of a short-term battery backup that comes on automatically in case of power loss (**Figure 3-31**). A **surge suppressor** is a device that prevents power fluctuations from damaging electronic components.

Figure 3-31: Uninterruptible power supply

Nor Gal/Shutterstock.com

Restore a Device

If you are experiencing a problem with your computer or device, you might need to take corrective actions such as restoring the operating system, correcting display problems, or updating device drivers.

If you are experiencing a problem with your operating system, often characterized by programs and apps not properly starting, persistent error messages, or slow performance, you should consider restoring the operating system. Before you attempt to restore the operating system, you should copy all personal files to a separate storage device such as a USB flash drive or external hard drive. When you **restore** an operating system, you are reverting all settings back to their default, or migrating back to the operating system's previous version. To restore your operating system, review the help documentation and follow the specified steps (**Figure 3-32**). You should always regularly back up your files to the cloud or to an external hard drive as a preventative measure.

Figure 3-32: Windows includes a feature to restore your operating system

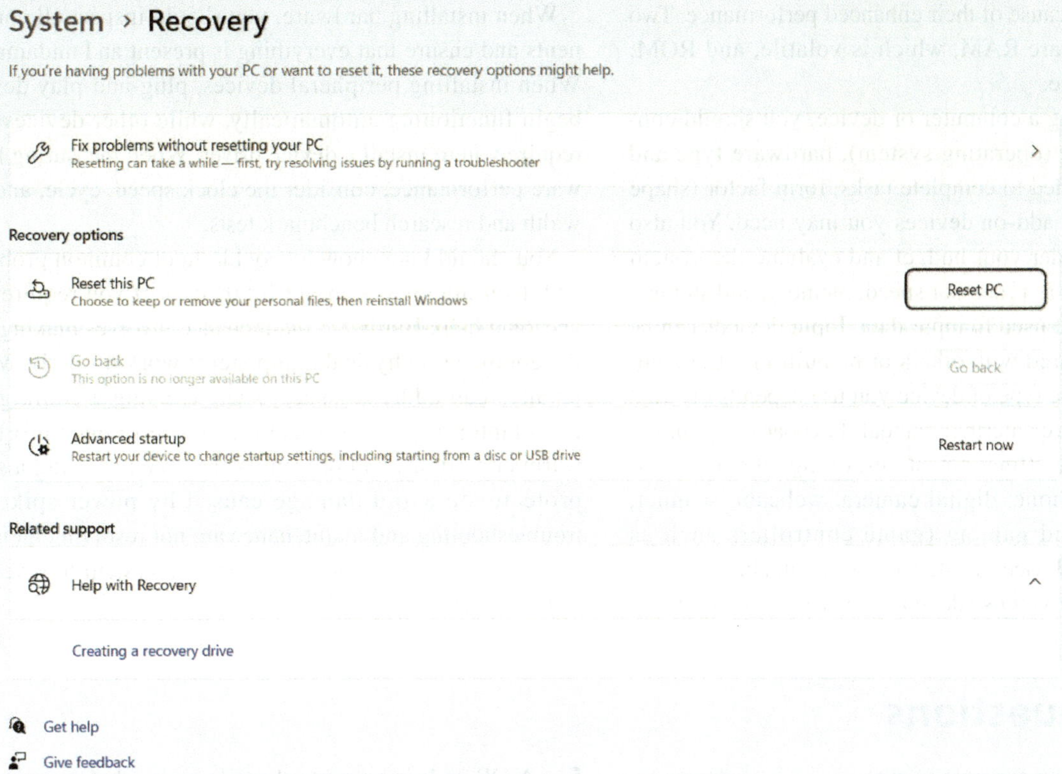

Module 3 Summary

The hardware you use depends on what you are trying to accomplish, such as receive input, produce output, store data, play games, or connect to the Internet. Many hardware devices have more than one use. Input devices communicate instructions that the computer or device translates into data that the computer can read and use to produce information. Output devices convey information produced by a computer or device. Computers use the binary system to interpret data and produce information using a coding scheme, such as ASCII or Unicode.

Laptops, desktops, and all-in-ones are types of computers, as are mobile devices such as tablets and smartphones. Laptops are more common than desktops and all-in-ones because they are more portable. Smartphones are so prevalent that not having access to one is a factor in the digital divide. Peripheral devices extend the capability of a computer or device. Examples of peripheral devices include printers, keyboards, and speakers. You can connect a peripheral device wirelessly or using a port or USB hub.

Storage solutions include cloud storage and internal or external hard drives, as well as USB flash drives and optical media. All computers and devices come with an internal hard drive for storage. Solid state drives are common in mobile devices and laptops. An external hard drive can be used to extend the storage capacity of your computer. Cloud storage is popular because it allows for easier sharing and collaboration among multiple users in different physical locations. Flash memory devices and optical media are no longer widely used as more users rely on the cloud.

Processing components include the CPU and memory. The CPU converts input into output using the control unit and the ALU. More computers and devices rely on multi-core processors because of their enhanced performance. Two types of memory are RAM, which is volatile, and ROM, which is nonvolatile.

When purchasing a computer or device, you should consider the platform (operating system), hardware type and specifications needed to complete tasks, form factor (shape and size), and any add-on devices you may need. You also will need to consider your budget and evaluate the system requirements, such as processor speed, memory, and storage.

Input devices are used to input data. Input devices can be peripheral and shared with others or be built into the computer or device. The type of device you use depends on what type of input you are entering: manual (keyboard or pointing device), touchscreen (fingertip, stylus, or digital pen), audio or visual (microphone, digital camera, webcam, scanner, or QR codes), and gaming (game controllers such as joysticks). Output devices display print or digital information. The type of device you use depends on what type of output you want to present or distribute: display (monitor, screen, or projector), audio (speakers, headsets, or earbuds), or print (printers that produce paper or 3D output).

When installing hardware, you should inspect all components and ensure that everything is present and undamaged. When installing peripheral devices, plug-and-play devices begin functioning automatically, while other devices may require you to install a device driver. When measuring hardware performance, consider the clock speed, cycle, and bus width and research benchmark tests.

You should know how to troubleshoot common problems and determine if you might fix them or if you require professional help. Hardware maintenance involves making sure the computer's physical components work properly. Maintenance can address issues, such as using a cooling pad for a laptop if you must use the device in uncomfortably warm conditions, and prevent issues, such as using a surge protector to avoid damage caused by power spikes. If troubleshooting and maintenance are not resolving an issue, you may need to restore the operating system to revert all settings back to their default.

Review Questions

1. A keyboard is an example of a(n) ________ device.
   a. output
   b. input
   c. pointing
   d. processing
2. The binary system is a number system that has two digits, ________.
   a. a and b
   b. 0 and 1
   c. positive and negative
   d. small and large
3. A slot on the computer where you can attach a peripheral device is called a(n) ________.
   a. port
   b. bus
   c. outlet
   d. node
4. The form factor refers to the ________ of a computer.
   a. operating system
   b. bandwidth
   c. purpose
   d. shape and size
5. A QR code is a square-shaped graphic that corresponds to a ________.
   a. web address
   b. byte
   c. peripheral device
   d. binary code
6. A 3D printer uses a process called ________ manufacturing to create an object.
   a. predictive
   b. incremental
   c. additive
   d. virtual
7. (True or False) A plug-and-play device will begin functioning properly as soon as you connect it to your computer.
8. The smallest unit of time a process can measure is a ________.
   a. cycle
   b. clock speed
   c. bit
   d. byte
9. (True or False) The clock speed determines the speed at which data travels.

10. A circuit board that processes image signals is called a(n) __________.

   a. ALU
   b. video card
   c. scanner
   d. USB flash drive

11. To prevent power fluctuations from damaging electronic components, you should use a(n) __________.

   a. surge suppressor
   b. UPS
   c. ALU
   d. adapter

12. When you __________ an operating system, you are reverting all settings back to their default.

   a. rewind
   b. reverse
   c. restore
   d. reconnect

Discussion Questions

1. When you are purchasing a computer or device, you might be tempted to get the most expensive one you can afford. Why might this not be a good idea? What questions should you ask that can help you determine what type of computer or device to purchase? Does your current computer or device meet your needs? If not, what would you consider if you were able to replace it?
2. What is the difference between input and output devices? What types of input and output devices are necessary for a college student? Why? What types of input and output devices are necessary for an employee in the field in which you work or plan to work? What types of input and output devices do you rely on? Why are they important?
3. Despite how well you might take care of your computer or device, problems can always arise. When troubleshooting problems you encounter, at what point should you engage a professional for assistance? Why? At what point might you consider purchasing a new computer or device? Have you ever had a situation in which you were able to troubleshoot a problem?
4. List and describe three types of storage solutions available for use. What should you do if you run out of space on your device? What type of storage is available with your device? Which do you prefer? Why?

Critical Thinking Activities

1. You are pursuing a degree in graphic design. What hardware specifications should you look for if you were to purchase a new computer to help with your studies? Why did you choose the central processing unit? Why did you choose the amount of RAM? Why did you choose the storage solution? How does the computer you chose compare with your current device?
2. You are a financial advisor who works in an open office with coworkers nearby. You advise clients in person, over the phone, and using video calls. What types of input and output devices might you require to do your job? If you were working in this role, are there other input or output devices you feel might make your work easier or more enjoyable?
3. You are working part time providing computer support for a veterinarian's office. When you arrive to work one morning, the receptionist informs you that the computer monitor is not displaying anything. List at least three steps you will perform to troubleshoot the problem, and list three possible causes.

4. Explain how a computer represents data. What is the role of an input device? What is the role of an output device? Do you think it is important for the average user to understand how computers represent data? Why or why not?

Apply Your Skills

Celeste Rosa is an office manager at a small graphic design firm with ten employees in Denver, Colorado. In addition to supporting the designers who create professional graphics for large corporations worldwide, Celeste is responsible for maintaining the staff's computers and mobile devices. Each employee is issued a laptop they can bring home to use in telecommuting and a tablet they can use in presenting work to potential and current customers, and all share a variety of printers and projectors.

Working in a small group or by yourself, complete the following:

1. List three types of storage solutions that Celeste should ensure her employees can access. What are the benefits and drawbacks of each? Have you ever run out of storage? How did/could you solve the problem?
2. In addition to a laptop and tablet, and shared printers and projectors, name one input and one output device Celeste should consider for employees to have access. What would be the purpose of these additional devices? How might it benefit employees to have access to them? Which of the ones that you chose would you consider the most important? Why?
3. Celeste wants to help her employees know how to troubleshoot various common issues, but also know how to do so safely and when they should instead call on someone in the technical support department. Describe a common problem and how the employee might solve it on their own. Have you ever had to rely on a professional technical support person to help you with a problem? Did you learn anything useful about your device during the experience?

Module 4

Operating Systems and File Management

In This Module

- Examine the types of operating systems
- Explain how an operating system works
- Personalize an operating system to increase productivity
- Manage files and folders

Art_Photo/Shutterstock.com

Qing Chan has an internship with an accounting firm, which has provided them with a laptop and a smartphone. The laptop runs Microsoft Windows as its operating system and the phone uses the Apple iOS operating system. Qing uses the apps and utilities provided with their devices to share and collaborate on files, send communications, and participate in web conferences. Qing recently made modifications to the operating systems' settings to personalize them so that they can work more efficiently.

The system software on your computer or device, including the operating system, determines how your device runs and how you interact with it. Most computers and devices come preloaded with system software. Some factors that affect an operating system's capabilities include the time in which it responds to your instructions, its reliability, the tools available to enable you to work productively and efficiently, and how and where you store your files.

In this module, you will learn about different types of operating systems and compare options of each type. You will begin to understand how an operating system works to help your computer or device function. You will explore methods to personalize your operating system and program settings to increase your productivity. Lastly, you will learn how to manage the files and folders you store on your computer or device so that you can access them easily. As you reflect on what you learn in this module, ask yourself: What type of operating system best suits your needs? How does knowing how an operating system works impact your ability to use it efficiently? In what ways can you customize your operating system experience to support the way you like to work? What tools can you use to better manage your files and folders?

Examine the Types of Operating Systems

System software is the software that runs a computer, including the operating system and utilities. The operating system and utility programs control the behind-the-scenes operations of a computer or mobile device. An **operating system (OS)** is a program that manages the complete operation of your computer or mobile device and lets you interact with it. An operating system also is called a platform. Every computer or device has an operating system, even embedded computers such as those found in ATMs or digital cameras. Embedded computers use operating systems specifically built for embedded computers.

Explain How You Interact with an Operating System

When you start your computer or device, the operating system and other system software starts running in the background. The operating system enables you to keep track of files, print documents, connect to networks, and manage hardware and other programs. The operating system is critical to using your computer or device; without the operating system, the computer or device cannot function. Most programs and apps you run on your computer come in versions specific to your operating system and are optimized to take advantage of the operating system's features.

Suppose you are writing a report and want to save the document to your hard drive. **Figure 4-1** lists the steps the operating system takes to enable you to perform this task.

Figure 4-1: Interacting with the operating system

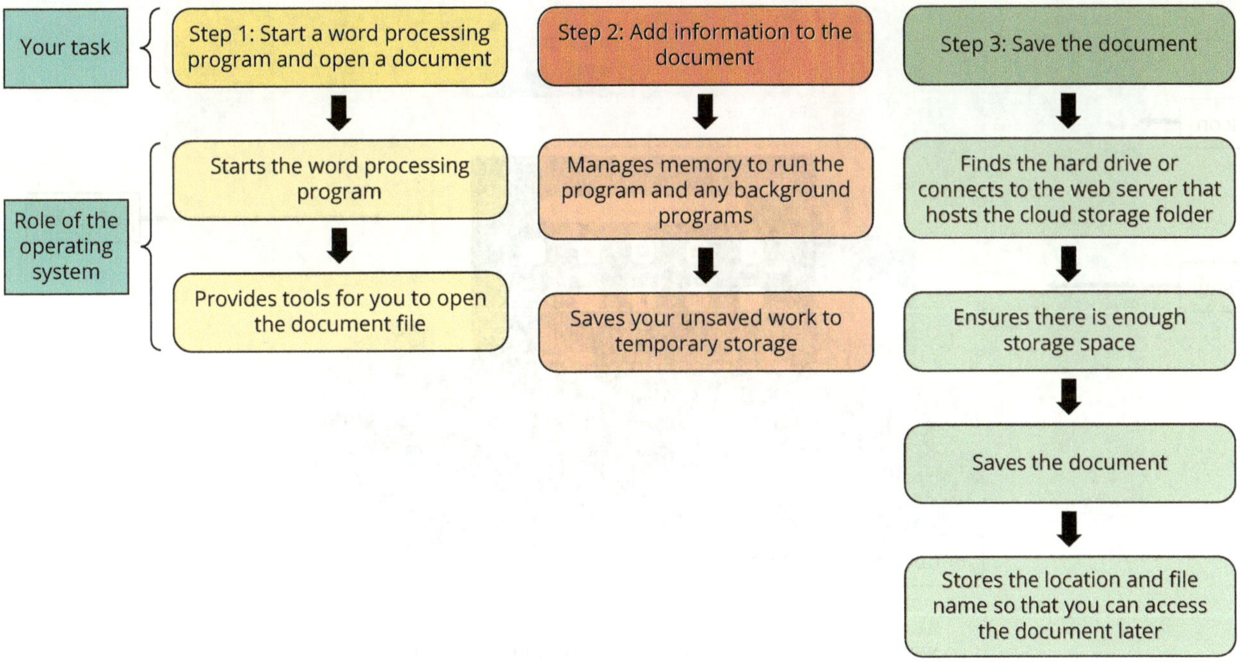

Operating System Features One of the main roles of an operating system is to provide a way for you to interact with your computer. An operating system provides a **graphical user interface (GUI)**, which is a collective term for all the ways you interact with the device; a GUI controls how you interact with menus, programs and apps, and visual images such as icons by touching, pointing, tapping, or clicking buttons and other objects to issue commands.

A **natural user interface (NUI)** is a GUI interface that enables you to train it to respond to your gestures and voice commands. As you continue to work with a NUI, it learns more about you and enables you to improve efficiency and perform more complex tasks. NUIs are especially helpful to those who require assistive technologies that do not require either a pointing device and/or a keyboard.

The main workspace of an operating system is called the **desktop** or, for mobile devices, **home screen** (**Figure 4-2**). This area contains icons for programs and files, as

Figure 4-2: The main workspace of an operating system

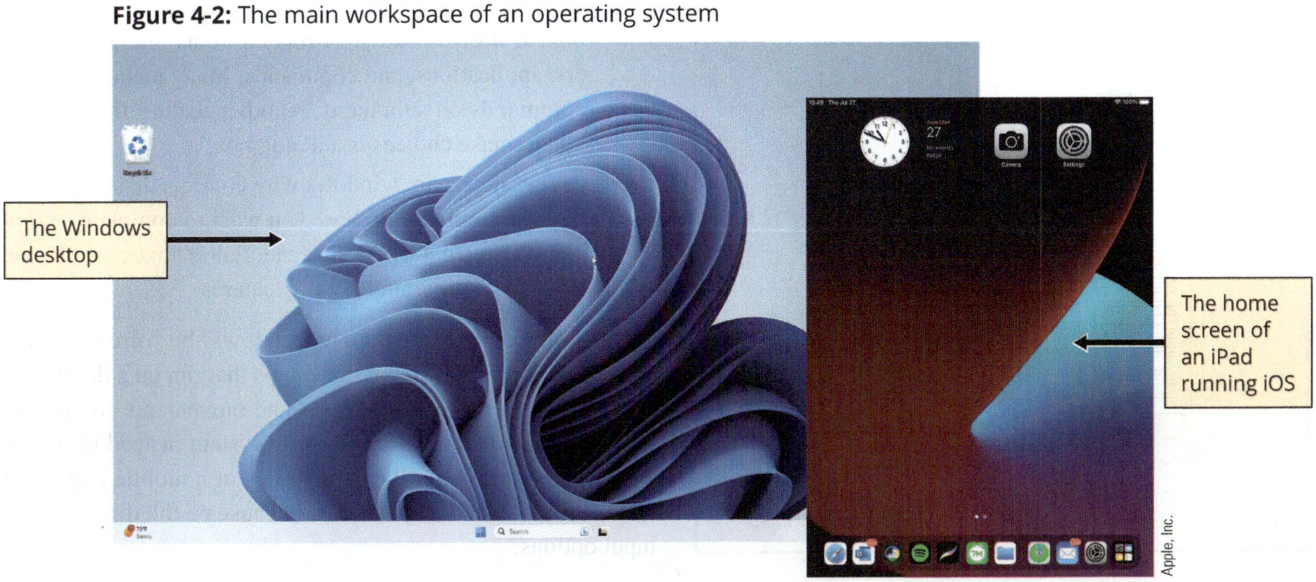

Apple, Inc.

Figure 4-3: GUI objects

well as toolbars, taskbars, menus, and buttons you can use to start programs and apps. A notification area displays the date and time, as well as shortcuts to utilities such as audio controls and network connections.

GUIs use visual objects that you can select by tapping, clicking, or double-clicking to perform tasks or issue commands (**Figure 4-3**). These objects include:

- **Icons**, which are small pictures that represents an app, file, or peripheral device.
- **Buttons**, which are icons you tap or click to execute commands you need to work with an app.
- **Windows**, which are rectangular-shaped work areas that display an app or a collection of files, folders, and tools. Every time you open a new program or file, a new window opens. You can switch between windows to access different information or resources.
- To perform tasks, make selections, or execute commands on a desktop you might use a menu or a dialog box. A **menu** is a list of related items, including folders, applications, and commands. Many menus organize commands on submenus. Another feature that enables you to make choices is a dialog box.
- **Dialog boxes** are windows with controls that let you tell the operating system how you want to complete a command (**Figure 4-4**). Menus and dialog boxes enable you to access a program or app's features.

Figure 4-4: A dialog box

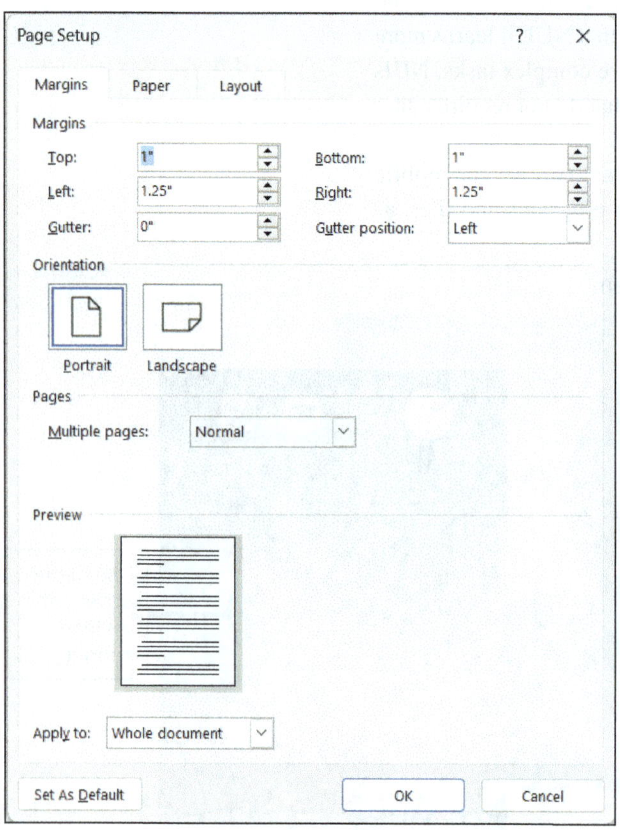

Mobile operating systems use windows, but often provide scaled down versions of the same apps that run on a desktop or laptop computer. Simple gestures and movements are used to perform tasks on a mobile operating system instead of menus or dialog boxes. Often the capabilities of a mobile app differ from those of a desktop version because of the difference in input options.

Classify Operating System Types

Operating systems differ based on the purpose, manufacturer, development method, and form factor of the computer or device. The type of operating system you select or have access to will depend on several factors, including whether it is one you select or if it comes with a computer or device issued by your job or school.

Operating System Models Operating system names identify the manufacturer and program name, and sometimes specify the purpose, year, or release number. For example, Microsoft Windows is a popular operating system. Microsoft Windows 11 indicates the number assigned to the release of the program, whereas Microsoft Windows Server indicates that the purpose of the version is to provide system software for a server.

Some software manufacturers are doing away with version numbers, and instead offering Software as a Service. **Software as a Service (SaaS)** is software that is distributed online for a monthly subscription or an annual fee (**Figure 4-5**). Instead of releasing a new complete version of the program to purchase, the company will provide updates to its subscribers that include fixes for issues or additional functionality. Your tablet or smartphone's operating system likely will update automatically with any changes or fixes, or to the latest version of the operating system compatible with your device.

Closed vs. Open Source Another classification when choosing an operating system is open vs. closed source. **Closed source** programs keep all or some of the code hidden, enabling developers to control and profit from the program they create. Closed

Figure 4-5: SaaS subscription information

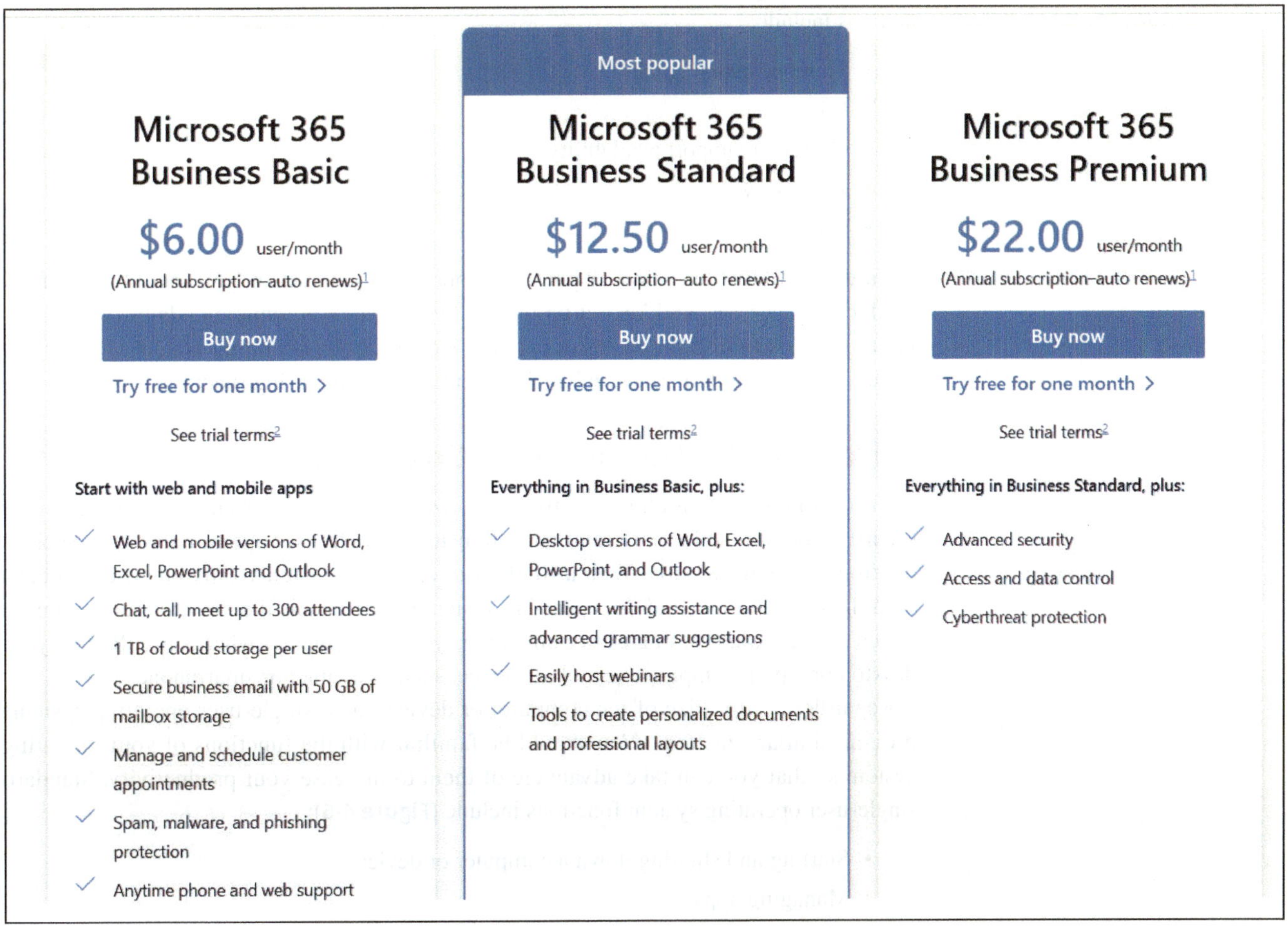

source programs have standard features and can only be customized using the operating system's tools. Microsoft Windows and macOS are examples of closed source operating systems.

Open source programs and apps (including operating systems) have no restrictions from the copyright holder regarding modification and redistribution. Users can add functionality and sell or give away their versions to others. Proponents of open source programs state that because the code is public, coders can examine, correct, and enhance programs. Some have concerns about unscrupulous programmers adding malicious code that can damage a user's system or be used to gather data without the user's knowledge. Unix is an example of an open source operating system.

Select an Operating System

Whether you are choosing an open or closed source operating system, program, or app, be sure to research carefully and read reviews to ensure you are getting the highest quality program.

If you receive a laptop or have access to a computer through your school or workplace, you likely will not have a choice in operating system. If you purchase a computer or device for yourself, you may not have a choice as certain computers and devices only run operating systems designed specifically for the computer or device. You also might want to choose a computer or device because of its operating system.

If you do have a choice when selecting an operating system, compare factors such as available programs and apps, hardware and software support, and security. Determine your needs and priorities to choose the operating system that will help you be productive. Always choose the most updated version of an operating system, or choose a SaaS model, to take advantage of any new features as well as security settings and fixes. Other considerations include:

- Memory management
- Price
- Customer support availability
- Reliability
- Security

Regardless of how you select or purchase your operating system, you should register the product if necessary, and keep it up to date by accepting automatic updates or responding to requests to install updates or patches. Updates to an operating system or other app include fixing program errors, enhancing security, and improving functionality.

Differentiate Among Operating Systems

Some operating systems allow specific, authorized users to control a network or administer security. You are likely more familiar with using a single-user operating system, such as desktop or mobile version. With a single-user operating systems, only one user interacts with the OS at a time, and the operating system only controls the device or computer on which it is installed. A single-user operating system is typically what is installed on your desktop or laptop computer, or mobile device, such as a tablet or smartphone.

Regardless of the size of the computer or device, most single-user operating systems provide similar functions. You should be familiar with the functions of your operating system so that you can take advantage of them to increase your productivity. Standard single-user operating system functions include (**Figure 4-6**):

- Starting and shutting down a computer or device
- Managing apps
- Managing memory

Figure 4-6: Common operating system functions

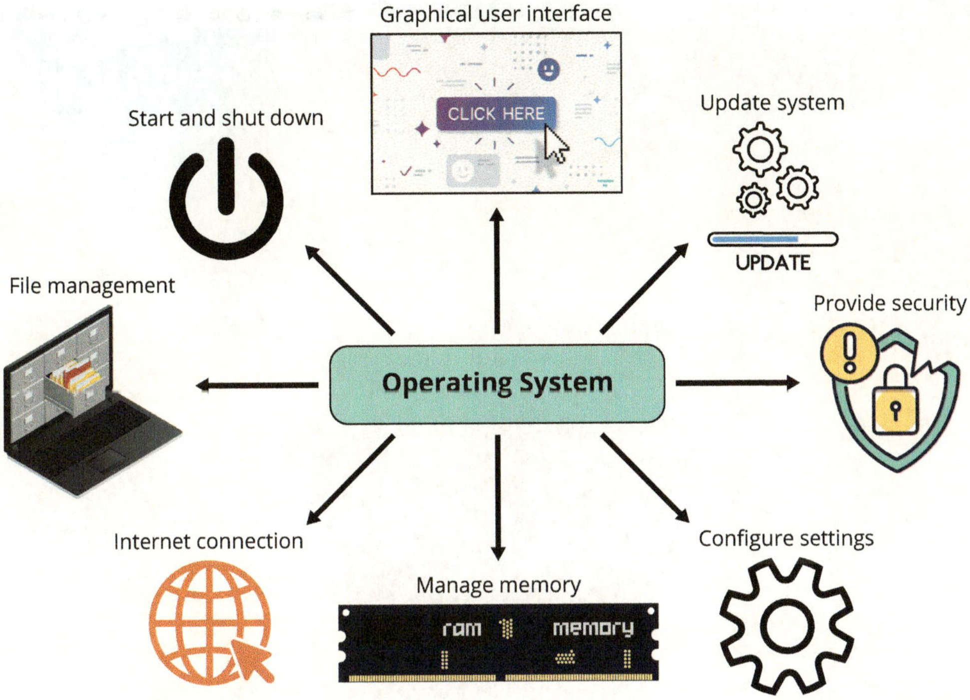

- Coordinating tasks
- Configuring peripheral devices
- Establishing an Internet connection
- Monitoring performance
- Providing file management
- Updating operating system software
- Monitoring security
- Controlling network access

Operating systems also provide **utilities**, apps or programs that enable you to perform maintenance-type tasks related to managing the computer or device (**Figure 4-7**). The tools you use to manage files, search for content or programs, view images, install and uninstall programs and apps, compress and back up files, secure your device, and maintain the computer or device are all utilities.

Desktop Operating Systems An operating system installed on a single laptop or desktop computer is called a **desktop operating system** or a **PC (personal computer) operating system**. Most are single-user operating systems. Examples include Microsoft Windows and Apple's macOS (**Figure 4-8**). Other operating systems include:

- UNIX, a multitasking operating system with many versions, as the code is licensed to different developers.

Figure 4-7: Utilities can help manage storage and other functions

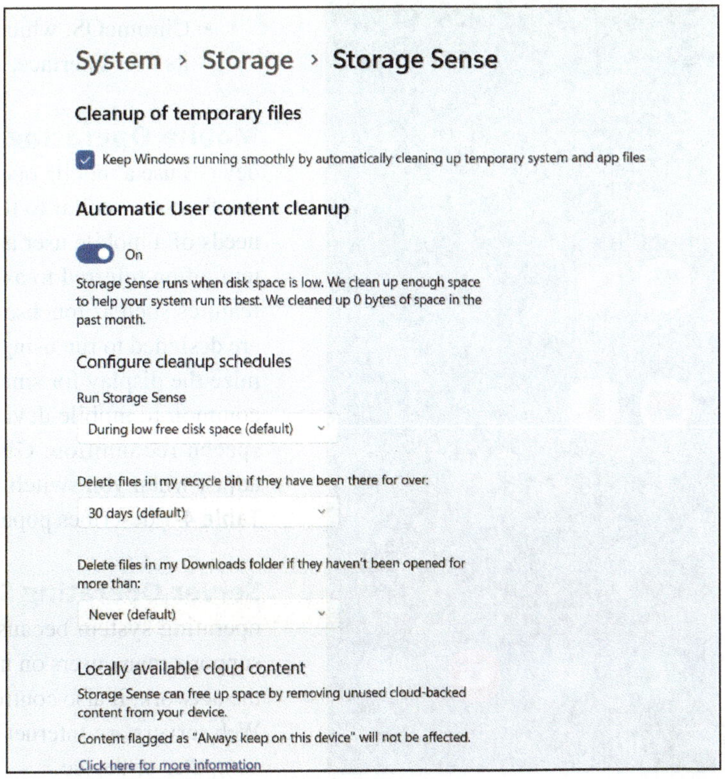

Figure 4-8: macOS desktop operating system

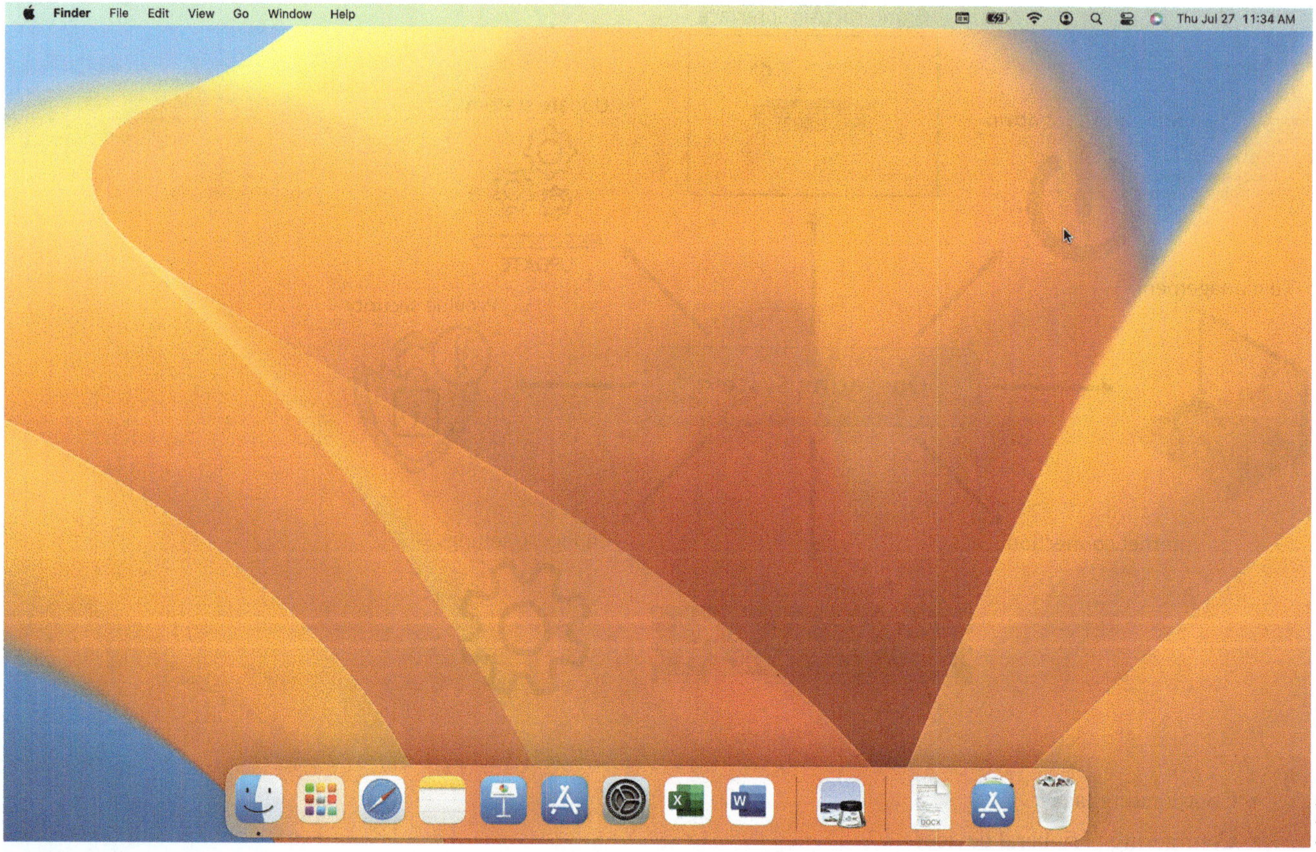

Apple, Inc.

Figure 4-9: Android mobile operating system

Google LLC

- Linux, which is distributed under the terms of a General Public License (GPL), which allows you to copy the OS for your own use, to give to others, or to sell.
- ChromeOS, which is based on Linux, uses the Google Chrome browser as its user interface, and primarily runs web apps.

Mobile Operating Systems Smartphones, tablets, and other mobile devices use a mobile operating system (**Figure 4-9**). A **mobile operating system** has features similar to those of a desktop operating system but is focused on the needs of a mobile user and the capabilities of the device. A mobile operating system, often referred to as a mobile OS, works especially well with mobile device features such as touchscreens, voice recognition, and Wi-Fi networks. They also are designed to run using the limited memory of most mobile devices, and to optimize the display for smaller screen sizes. They are programmed to manage tools common to mobile devices, including video and photo cameras, media players, speech recognition, GPS, wireless capabilities, rotating screen displays that adjust when you switch orientation of your device's screen, and text messaging. **Table 4-1** describes popular mobile operating systems.

Server Operating Systems A **server operating system** is a multiuser operating system because it controls a single, centralized server computer that supports many users on networked computers. A server operating system manages the network. It also controls access to network resources, such as network printers. Web servers are Internet computers that store webpages and deliver them to your computer or device.

Table 4-1: Mobile operating systems

OS	Notable features
Android	Developed by Google based on Linux, and designed to be run on many types of smartphones and tablets.
iOS	Runs only on Apple devices, including the iPhone and iPad; derived from macOS. Apple watches run ApplewatchOS.

Table 4-2: Server operating systems

OS	Notable features
Windows Server	The server version of Windows. It includes advanced security tools and a set of programs called Internet Information Services that manage web apps and services.
macOS Server	Supports all sizes of networks and servers. One unique feature is that it lets authorized users access servers using their iPhones or other Apple devices.
UNIX	A multipurpose operating system that can run on a desktop PC or a server. Many web servers use UNIX because it is a powerful, flexible operating system

Although desktop operating systems include network capability, server operating systems are designed specifically to support all sizes of networks. Many also enable virtualization. **Virtualization** is the practice of sharing computing resources, such as servers or storage devices, among computers and devices on a network. Virtualization supports green computing initiatives because it limits the number of machines required, thereby reducing e-waste, emissions, and the environmental impacts of producing multiple machines.

Although you may not realize it, you take advantage of a server operating system whenever you download mail or files, access networked resources such as a printer or database, or access information on the web. When you instruct your computer or device to do those tasks, the computer or device interacts with a server and its operating system to complete the request. Unless you are a network administrator, you likely will not directly interact with a server operating system, but you should be familiar with its capabilities. **Table 4-2** lists popular server operating systems.

Explain How an Operating System Works

An operating system takes care of the technical tasks of running the computer or device so that you can work on school or professional projects, watch videos, connect with friends, or play games. Operating systems process data, manage memory, control hardware, and provide a user interface. You interact with the operating system to start programs, manage files and folders, get help, and customize the user interface. The operating system is critical to the start process of the computer or device.

Explain the Role of an Operating System

When you enter instructions and data, your computer or device coordinates the resources and activities to process them and then provides information from the system back to you. The operating system also manages interactions between hardware and software. For example, if you want to print a flyer you created in your word processing program, the operating system establishes a connection to the printer, sends the flyer document to the printer, and lets other software know the printer is busy until it finishes printing the flyer. During this process, the operating system directs internal components such as the processor, RAM, and storage space to manage and complete its task.

Files and Folders A **file** is a collection of information stored on your computer, such as a text document, spreadsheet, photo, or song. You use an operating system to manage files. Files can be divided into two categories: data and executable. A **data file** contains words, numbers, and pictures that you can manipulate. For example, a spreadsheet, a database, a presentation, and a word processing document all are data files. Graphic and media files also are data files. An **executable file** contains the instructions your computer or device needs to run programs and apps. Unlike a data file, you cannot open and read an executable file. You run it to perform a task, such as opening a program or app.

Files are stored in folders. A **folder** is a named location on a storage medium that usually contains related documents. You name the folder so that you know what it contains, and in the folder you store related files. An operating system comes with tools to manage files and folders. These tools allow you to create new, named folders; choose the location of folders; move files between folders; and create a folder hierarchy that includes subfolders (**Figure 4-10**). The term subfolder refers to a folder that is inside another folder. Every file you save will have a destination folder—by choosing the correct folder, or adding new folders, you can help keep your files accessible and organized.

A **library** is a special folder that catalogs specific files and folders in a central location, regardless of where the items are actually stored on your device. Library files might include pictures, music, documents, and videos. Your operating system most likely comes with a few libraries. You can customize your libraries to add additional folders, and include

Figure 4-10: Creating a folder hierarchy helps keep files organized

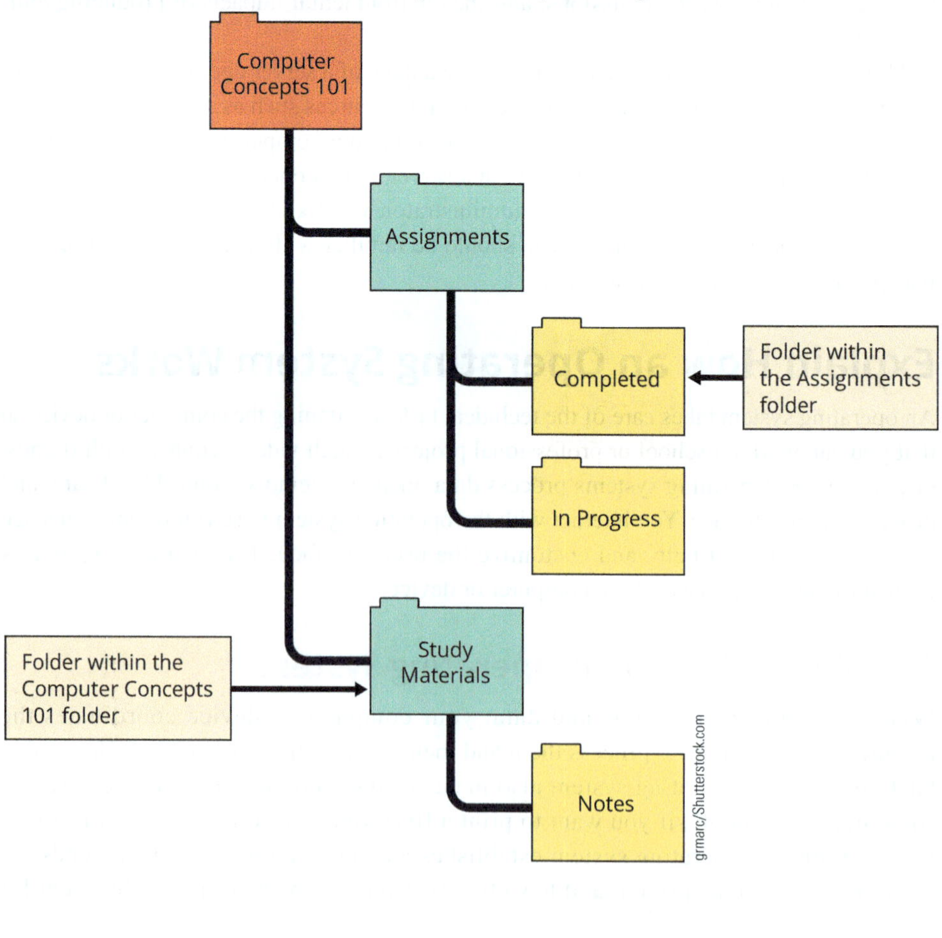

Table 4-3: Common file extensions

File type	Extensions
Microsoft Office	.docx (Word), .xlsx (Excel), .pptx (PowerPoint)
Text file	.txt, .rtf
Webpage	.htm or .html, .xml, .asp or .aspx, .css
Graphics	.jpg, .png, .tif

files from the Internet or a network. Libraries are helpful to find all files of a certain type, no matter where they are located on your computer or device. Windows computers use libraries, but mobile devices typically do not.

File format refers to the organization and layout of data in a file. The file format determines the type or types of programs and apps that you can use to open and display or work with a file. Some files only can be opened in the program with which they were created. Others, such as graphics files, can be opened in multiple programs or apps. A file extension is three- or four-letter sequence, preceded by a period, at the end of a file name that identifies the file as a particular type of document, such as .docx (Microsoft Word document), or .jpg (a type of graphic file). When you save a file, the program or app assigns the file extension. **Table 4-3** shows some common file extensions by file type.

Describe How an Operating System Manages Memory

The purpose of memory management is to optimize the use of a computer or device's internal memory to allow the computer or device to run more efficiently. Memory consists of electronic components that store instructions waiting to be executed by the processor, data needed by those instructions, and the results of processing the data into information.

The operating system uses RAM to temporarily store open apps and document data while they are being processed. It carefully monitors the contents of memory, and releases items when the processor no longer requires them. Frequently used instructions and data are stored in the temporary storage area designed to help speed up processing time, called a cache.

Every program or app, including the operating system, requires RAM. The more RAM a device has, the more efficiently it runs. If several programs or apps are running simultaneously, your computer or device might use up its available RAM. When this happens, the computer or device may run slowly.

The operating system can allocate a portion of a storage medium, such as a hard disk, to become virtual memory to function as additional RAM. Virtual memory temporarily stores data in an area of the hard drive called the swap file until it can be swapped into RAM. Because a page is the amount of data and program instructions the operating system can swap at a given time, the technique of swapping items between memory and storage is called paging. Paging is time consuming. When an operating system spends more of its time paging instead of executing apps, the whole system slows down and it is said to be thrashing. You may be able to adjust the settings on your operating system to free up virtual memory in order to enable your computer or device to run more quickly.

List Steps in the Boot Process

To start an operating system, you simply turn on the computer or device. Before you can interact with the operating system, the computer or device goes through the **boot process**, which triggers a series of steps and checks as the computer loads the operating system. The boot process includes the following steps:

1. The computer or device receives power from the power supply or battery and sends it to the circuitry.
2. The processor begins to run the bootstrap program, which is a special built-in startup program.
3. The **bootstrap program** executes a series of tests to check the components, including the RAM, input devices, and storage, and identifies connected devices and networks and checks their settings.
4. Once the tests are completed successfully, the computer or device loads the operating system files into RAM, including the kernel. The **kernel** is the core of an operating system, which manages memory, runs programs, and assigns resources.
5. The computer or device loads the system configuration information, prompts you for user verification if necessary, establishes connections with networks and peripheral devices, and loads all startup programs, such as antivirus programs or apps.

The boot process starts automatically when you turn on your computer or device. You cannot use the computer or device until the boot process is complete. Depending on your operating system, you may be able to customize your settings to instruct that certain programs or apps you frequently use be started at the same time as your operating system.

If a computer or device is slow in accepting or providing input or output, the operating system uses buffers. A **buffer** is an area of memory that stores data and information waiting to be sent to an input or output device. Placing data into a buffer is called **spooling**. An example of spooling is when a document is sent to the buffer while it waits for the printer to be available. By sending data to a buffer, the operating system frees up resources to perform other tasks while the data waits to be processed. While the buffer and cache may both serve the purpose of freeing up RAM, a buffer typically is used for input and output processes, while a cache is used when reading and writing from the disk.

Personalize an Operating System to Increase Productivity

When you start using a computer or device, the operating system and related software and hardware have default settings. **Default settings** are standard settings that control how the screen is set up and how a document looks when you first start typing. As you continue to work with your computer or device, you may decide to customize the settings to be more productive.

Customize an Operating System

Every operating system has its own tools for customization. Operating systems allow you to make adjustments such as:

- Changing the brightness of the screen
- Adding a desktop theme, which is a predefined set of elements such as background images and colors
- Adjusting the screen resolution, which controls how much content you can see on a screen without scrolling
- Adding a sound scheme, which associates sounds such as a bell chime with an event, such as closing a window or receiving a message

Figure 4-11: Windows Settings dialog box

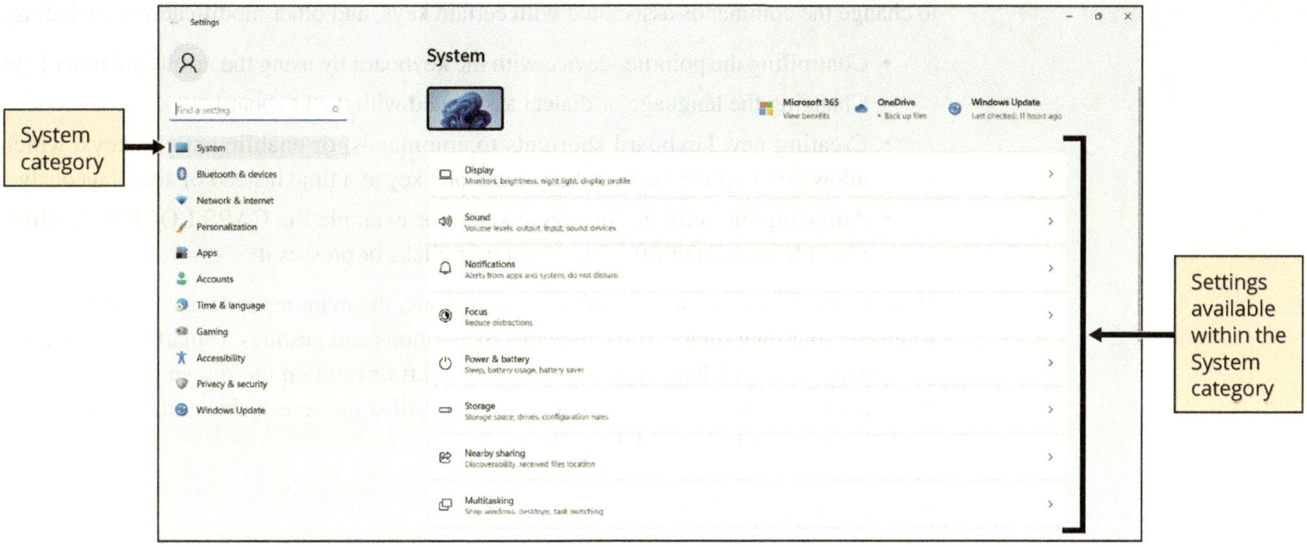

- Adjusting or silencing the volume of media playback and/or notifications
- Pinning frequently used apps to the taskbar or home screen for easy access
- Selecting items to appear in the Notification area

You also can use these tools to link your devices and computers to each other and to networks and peripheral devices, uninstall apps, add accounts, manage your network connections, and adjust privacy settings.

On a Windows computer, you use the Settings dialog box. To open the Settings dialog box, click the Start button on the Windows taskbar, and then click the Settings icon. In the Windows Settings dialog box (**Figure 4-11**), click an option to access further options. For example, if you click System, you can adjust settings such as the display, sounds, power, battery, storage, and more.

You also can customize the desktop on a computer by moving the taskbar or other items, creating and organizing icons and folders for apps and files, and more. In addition, you can create links to files and apps called **shortcuts**. Shortcuts do not place the actual file, folder, or app on the desktop—the object remains in the location where it is saved on your computer or device. A shortcut merely allows you to access the object from the desktop without going through a file manager or a program menu such as the Start menu.

Access to settings on a mobile device differs depending on the device. For instance, on an Android smartphone, you swipe down from the top of the screen, then tap the Settings button to open the Settings screen (**Figure 4-12**).

Figure 4-12: Settings window on an Android smartphone

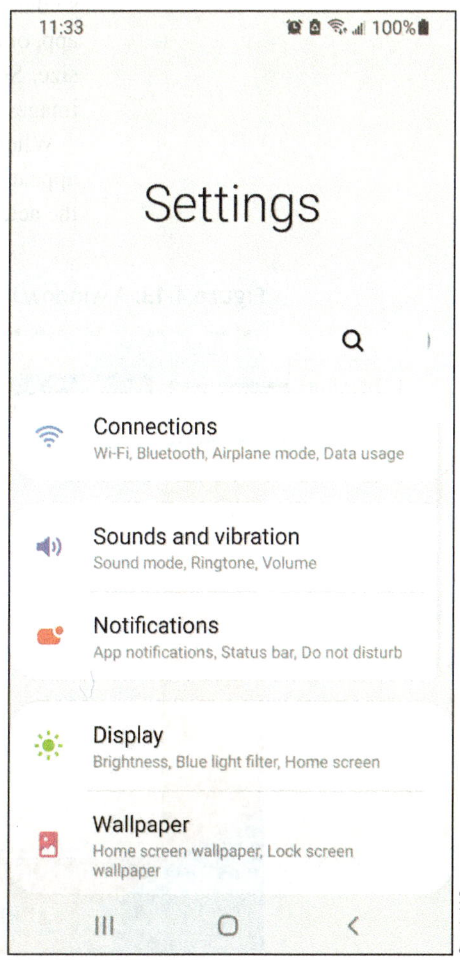

Google LLC

Customize Hardware Using System Software

Pointing devices let you interact with your computer by controlling the movement of the pointer on your screen; examples include a mouse, trackball, touchpad, or for touch-enabled devices, a stylus or your finger. You can change the settings of your pointing device. For example, you can switch the mouse buttons if you are left-handed, or adjust the sensitivity of your touchpad.

On a desktop computer or laptop, the keyboard is the main input device. The keyboard contains not only characters such as letters, numbers, and punctuation, but also keys that can issue commands. You can adjust the keyboard settings to change the commands associated with certain keys, and other modifications, including:

- Controlling the pointing device with the keyboard by using the arrow and other keys
- Changing the language or dialect associated with the keyboard
- Creating new keyboard shortcuts to commands, or enabling sticky keys, which allow you to press keyboard shortcuts one key at a time instead of simultaneously
- Adjusting the settings for toggle keys, for example the CAPS LOCK key, which turn a feature on or off each time a user clicks or presses it

On a mobile device, such as a tablet or smartphone, the main input device is a digital pen, stylus, or your own finger. You can adjust the motions and gestures a smartphone or tablet recognizes, such as what happens if you swipe left or right on the screen, using a fingerprint sensor to open or close apps, and you can adjust the screen size and layout to more easily operate the device with just one hand.

Manage Windows

When you open an app, file, or folder, it appears in a window. Most windows share common elements: the center area of the window displays its contents, and a title bar at the top displays the name of the app, file, or folder (**Figure 4-13**). When there is more information than fits on the screen, vertical and horizontal scroll bars appear that you drag to display contents currently out of view.

On a desktop or laptop computer, a **Maximize button** and **Minimize button** on the title bar enables you to expand a window so that it fills the entire screen or reduce a window so that it only appears as an icon on the taskbar. A **Close button** closes the open window, app, or document. The **Restore Down button** reduces a window to its last non-maximized size. Some windows include a ribbon, toolbar, or menu bar that contains text, icons, or images you select to perform actions and make selections.

When you have multiple windows, files, and apps open at a time, the windows can appear side-by-side or stacked. Most mobile devices only display stacked windows, with the active window in the foreground and maximized to fit the screen. The **active window**

Figure 4-13: A window in macOS

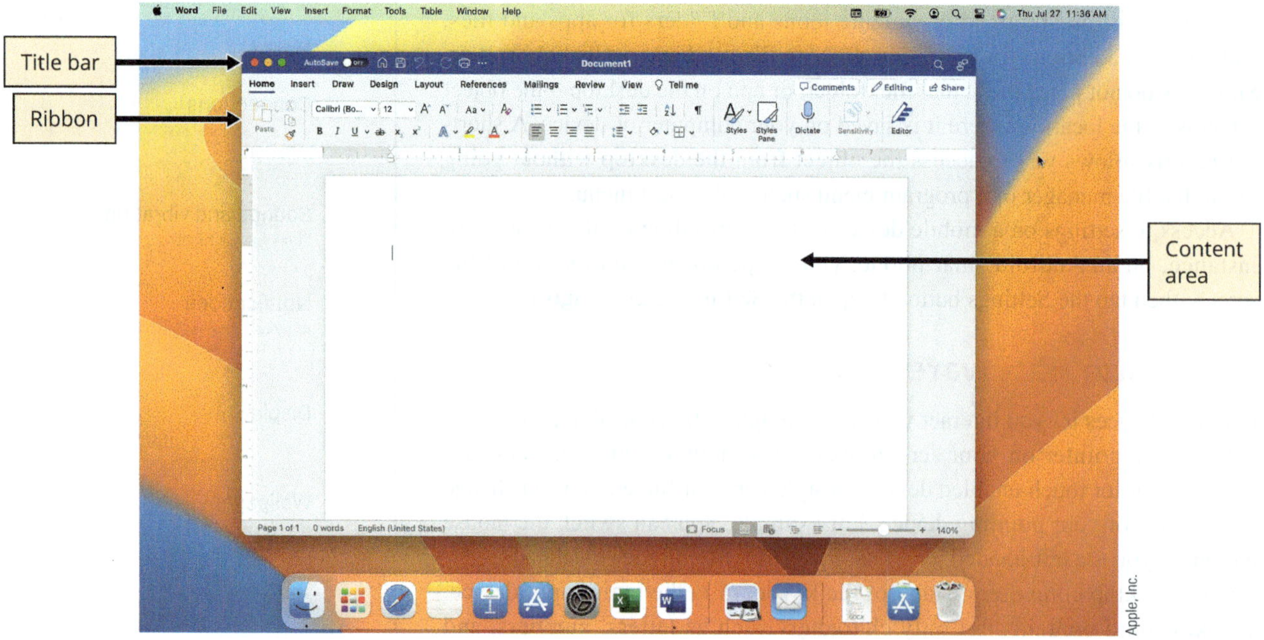

Apple, Inc.

Figure 4-14: Apple Dock

Apple, Inc.

is the window you are currently using, which appears in front of any other open windows. The steps to switch between windows depends on the type of device or operating system you are running.

- On a mobile device, you might have a button near the Home button that displays all open windows in a stack. When you select it, it displays the stack of open windows and apps. You can select a window to make it the active window, close individual windows, or close all open windows.
- On a computer, you can click an icon on the Windows taskbar or the Dock on the macOS desktop (**Figure 4-14**). You also can use keyboard shortcuts to cycle through thumbnails of open windows. If multiple windows are open and visible on the screen, you can click in each desired window as needed to switch or toggle between one and another.

There are two types of windows: a **program window** displays a running program; a **folder window** displays the contents of a folder, drive, or device. To start a Windows program, you click the Start button on the taskbar, and then click the program name. To start a Mac program, click the Launchpad (rocket) icon on the dock, then click the app icon. Or, for either Mac or Windows, you can click a shortcut to the app on the desktop. To open a folder window, open your system's folder management tool, such as File Explorer or Finder, and then navigate to the folder you want. To close any type of window, tap or click its Close button. To open a window on a mobile device, you click its icon on the screen. You can arrange your apps on a mobile device into folders by category so that you can easily find your games, travel apps, and other app types.

You can rearrange windows on a computer's desktop to work effectively and to access other items on the desktop. To move a window, point to its title bar, and then drag the window to its new location. To resize a window to display more or less of its content, point to a border or corner of the window, then drag the resizing pointer to make it smaller or larger. Windows and other desktop operating systems allow you to drag a window to the left or right side of the screen, where it "snaps" to fill that half of the screen and displays remaining open windows as thumbnails you can click to fill the other half of the screen. Mobile device windows tend to take up the full screen.

Use Administrative Tools

An operating system controls the **resources** of a device, which are the components required to perform work, such as the processor, RAM, storage space, and connections to other devices and networks. The operating system tracks the names and locations of files, as well as empty storage areas where you can save new files. It alerts you if it detects a resource problem, such as too many programs or apps are open for the memory to handle, or the printer is not turned on, or if your hard drive is out of space. To manage RAM resources, an operating system keeps track of the apps, processes, and other tasks the system performs. Microsoft Windows, for example, displays this information

Figure 4-15: Windows Task Manager dialog box

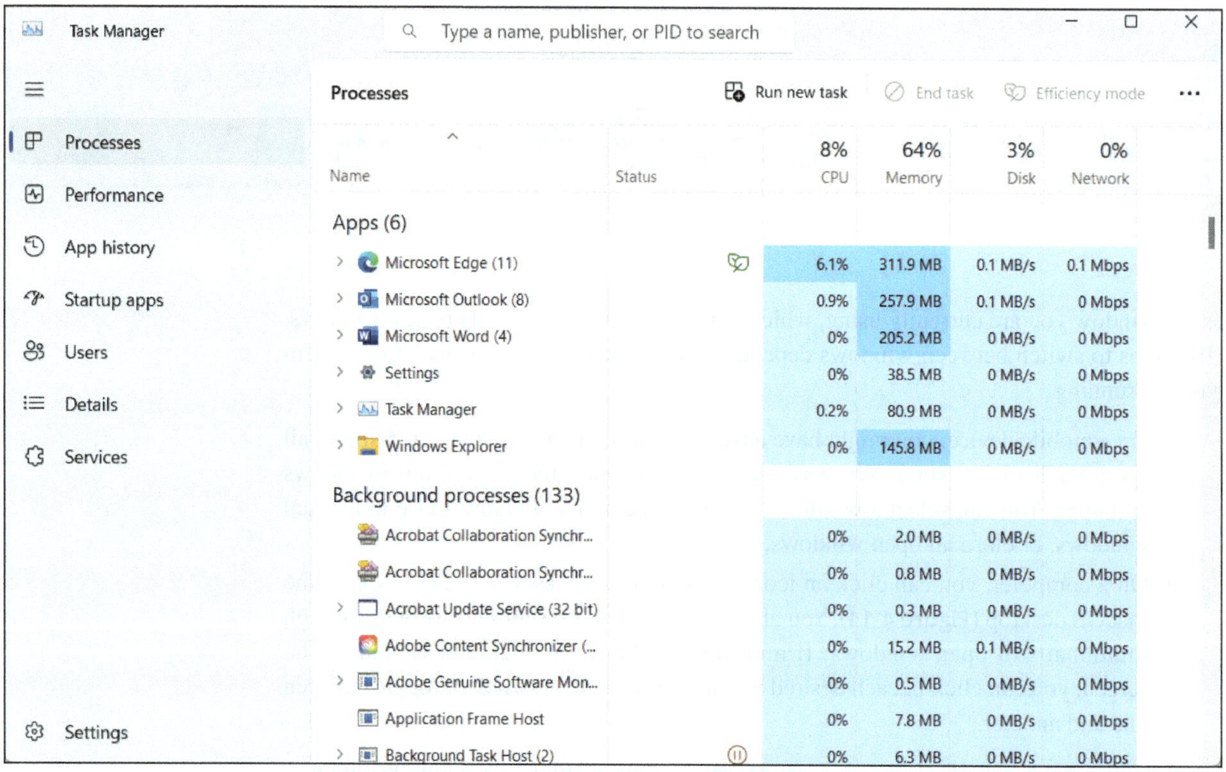

in the Windows Task Manager dialog box (**Figure 4-15**). You can open your computer or device's version of the task manager to view running programs and see the percentage of RAM being used. You can shut down programs and apps in the task manager to free up RAM.

Utilities Regardless of the operating system you're using, if your computer starts to slow down or act erratically, you can use a utility to diagnose and repair the problem. A common solution is to use a cleanup utility that archives files by backing up infrequently used or older files to the cloud, and then deletes them from the computer or device. Some cleanup utilities will remove files that the system determines are no longer needed, such as old website cookies or files related to the operation of an uninstalled program.

The Recycle Bin, or Trash folder, is another type of disk utility. This folder stores files you designate to be deleted. When you move a file to the Recycle Bin or Trash, it still takes up storage space, but no longer appears in the folder or location where it was created. The file only is permanently deleted when you empty the folder or run a cleanup utility. To avoid wasting time searching for files you have saved, or to manage file locations and sizes, you can use file utilities. A file management tool gives you an overview of stored files and lets you open, rename, delete, move, and copy files and folders. A search tool finds files that meet criteria you specify, such as characters in a file name, or the saved date.

Adjust Power Settings

You may keep your computer or device running constantly, or you may choose to shut it down, either to save power or prevent it from being shut down suddenly and unexpectedly, such as by a thunderstorm (if connected to a power source that uses an electrical outlet) or battery issue. Operating systems provide shut-down options so that you can close programs and processes properly. You can instruct the device to completely shut down, which turns off the power, and may close any open files or apps. Some operating systems have a Sleep option to use low power instead of shutting down. Sleep stores the current state of open programs and files, saving you time when you resume using your device.

Since you tend to keep your desktop computer or laptop plugged in while in use, battery life is a bigger concern with mobile devices. You can switch to a low power mode, which limits data usage, dims the screen brightness, and makes other adjustments to slow down battery usage. You also can purchase a portable charger you can plug in with a USB cord to charge your device, use a wireless charging station, or use a replacement battery to switch when your battery power gets low.

Run More than One Operating System

A **virtual machine (VM)** enables a computer or device to run another operating system in addition to the one installed. You might want to enable a virtual machine if you have an app that is incompatible with your current operating system, or to run multiple operating systems on one computer. To run a virtual machine, you need a program or app that is specifically designed to set up and manage virtual machines (**Figure 4-16**). You also will need access to installation files for the operating system you want to run on the virtual machine.

The virtual machine runs separately in a section of the hard disk that functions like a separate disk, called a **partition** or a **volume**. You can only access one partition of a hard disk at a time. To use the virtual machine, you need to perform the following steps:

1. Run the virtual machine software.
2. Select the virtual machine you want to run.
3. Click the button to run the virtual machine.
4. When you are finished using the virtual machine, shut down the operating system similarly to how you would shut down your computer.
5. Exit the virtual machine software.

With many companies allowing or requiring employees to work remotely, virtualization, such as use of VMs, has increased dramatically. Companies may enable temporary or contract employees to set up a VM on their own device, which incorporates greater security than the user's device might normally use. In addition, if VMs are set up for a specific

Figure 4-16: Windows VM running on macOS

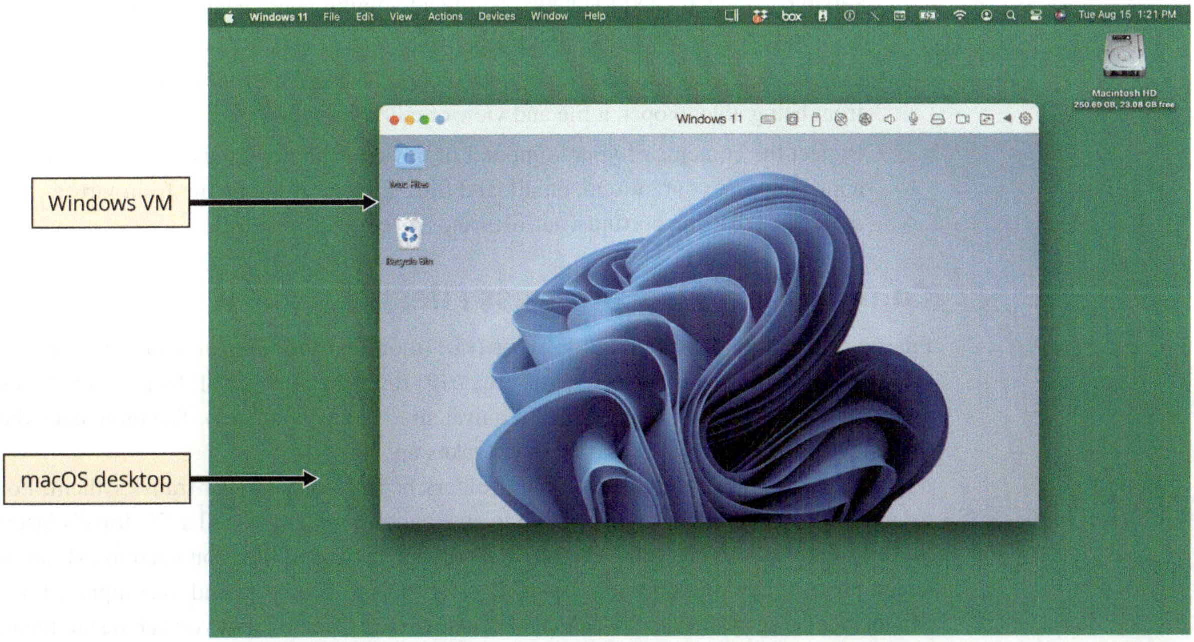

Apple, Inc.

purpose, such as a project, and then abandoned, the VM should be removed so as not to crowd the servers with unnecessary resources. VM management software can track access, permissions, and activity on a VM.

Manage User Accounts

User accounts identify the resources, such as apps and storage locations, a user can access when working with the computer. User accounts protect your computer against unauthorized access. A user account includes information such as the user name or ID, and a password. You can set preferences for each user account on your computer or device, as well as set permissions to certain folders or files. A standard user account is designed for the everyday user, who will be using the computer or device for work or recreation. An **administrator account** provides full access to the computer. Additional responsibilities associated with an administrator account include installing programs and apps, adjusting security settings, and managing network access. On a computer you use at your home, you likely will not have a separate administrator account—the main user account will have administrator capabilities. On a networked computer, such as at your school or workplace, you will not have access to the administrator account.

Manage Files and Folders

There are many ways to manage files and folders on your computer or device. You can change or view the properties of a file, compress a file to save storage space, move or rename a file or folder, and more.

Protect Files

Whether you are working on a presentation for a school assignment, keeping a journal, or tracking your budget in a spreadsheet, you do not want to lose the information in your files. Guidelines for protecting your files and folders include:

- Saving them to a cloud folder and regularly backing up. A cloud folder likely has regular backup and encryption, and, unlike your hard drive, is not as susceptible to loss due to physical damage.
- When you are planning to make major changes to a file, consider saving it as a new version, using a related file name, before attempting your changes. This preserves a version to which you can revisit if necessary.
- Encrypt or password-protect files and folders. This will prevent unauthorized others from being able to open a file and view or edit its contents.
- Protect the contents of your computer or device from malicious code by installing apps that scan your system, email, and files you receive or create from viruses and other apps that can corrupt your files and system.

Compress and Uncompress Files

File size is usually measured in **kilobytes (KB)** (thousands of bytes of data), **megabytes (MB)** (millions of bytes of data), **gigabytes (GB)** (billions of bytes of data), or terabytes (trillions of bytes of data; a **terabyte** is equivalent to 1,000 gigabytes). The more data, the larger the file and the more storage space it takes up.

You often need to compress files and folders before you share or transfer them. For example, by attaching a compressed file to an email message the smaller file travels faster to its destination. Before you can open and edit a compressed file, you need to extract or uncompress it. Desktop operating systems offer tools to compress and uncompress files. Mobile operating systems do not always include these by default, but you can install them.

To compress a file or folder, select it in your operating system's file management tool, and then instruct the tool to zip or compress the file. To uncompress, double-click the file in the file management tool, and either drag selected files to another folder, or instruct the tool to extract all files into a new folder.

Save Files and Folders to File Systems

The first time you save a file, you need to name it. On a computer running a locally installed version of an app, instructing the computer to save a new file opens a Save As dialog box or screen, depending on the program or app. Save As includes controls that let you specify where to store the file, and what file name to use. Navigate to the correct folder on your computer or device, or to another location such as a flash drive or cloud folder. Type the file name, select the file extension if necessary, and then click Save. You then should frequently use the save command to save any changes, or enable the AutoSave feature. If using a web app, such as Microsoft Office 365 or Google Docs, your file is automatically saved once you start it, but you still will need to name it. Any changes you make as you work on a file using a web app automatically are saved.

Besides saving files to your hard drive or on a flash drive, you can save them in the cloud. The cloud is a storage area located on a server that you access through the Internet or a network. You can upload files to cloud storage to share them with others or to back up your files to a secure, offsite location. You can access files stored on the cloud from any device connected to the Internet. To access a cloud storage location, you may need to download an app, or create an account. Popular cloud storage apps include Dropbox, Microsoft OneDrive, Google Drive, and iCloud. You can save a file to OneDrive from within any Microsoft Office program if you have the required permissions.

Determine File Properties

Every file has properties such as its name, type, location, and size (**Figure 4-17**). File properties also include the dates when the file was created, modified, and last accessed. The modified date is useful if you have several versions of a file and want to identify

Figure 4-17: File properties

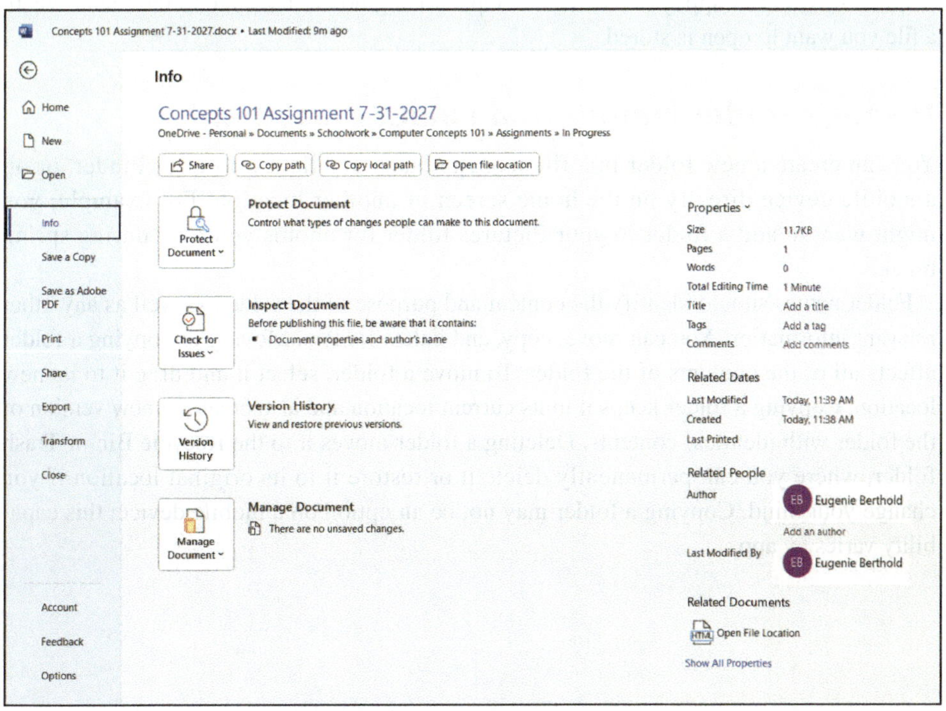

the most recent version. The operating system assigns some properties to files, such as type or format, and updates other properties, such as date, size, and location. Some file types have unique properties. For example, an image might contain information about the dimensions (size) of the image, while a song or media file might include the artist(s) names.

You can view a file's properties to determine information not shown in the file manager, such as the original creation date, the program used to create the file, and more.

Manage File Names and File Placement

Every file has a name. Most file names contain an extension that tells something about its contents, such as the type of platform or app on which the file can be used. File name extensions are added automatically when you save a file, but you can change the extension in some cases.

While you can have many files on your computer or device that have the same name, each folder can only include one file with the same name of the same type. To differentiate a version of a file without overwriting the original, you could add additional characters such as numbers, the date, or the initials of the person who modified the file.

You should be specific when naming files to clearly identify the contents of each, to make them easier to find and organize. A file name should identify the content and purpose of the file, as well as any other information, such as whether the file is a draft or final. For instance, a specific file name such as Q1_Budget_For_Review_Draft-1 is more specific than Budget.

If you want to copy or move files from one location to another, you must first select the files. You can select them from a file management tool, the desktop, or another location. You can select multiple files at once, or just a single file. You also can drag files and folders between or within file management tool windows.

You open a saved file using the same techniques as when saving the file, except you use a different dialog box or window. To open a file, you must first find its location. You can locate a file in Windows using File Explorer, or the Finder in macOS. On a mobile device, you can use the search tool if you are unsure of in which folder the file is stored. From within a program or app, you can use the Open dialog box to navigate to the folder where a file you want to open is stored.

Manage Folder Names and Folder Placement

You can create a new folder in a file manager such as File Explorer or Finder, or on a mobile device directly on the home screen or another location. For example, you might want to add a folder to your Pictures folder for photos you took during spring break.

Folder names should identify the content and purpose of the folder, as well as any other relevant information. You can move, copy, and delete folders. Moving or copying a folder affects all of the contents of the folder. To move a folder, select it and drag it to its new location. Copying a folder keeps it in its current location and also creates a new version of the folder with identical contents. Deleting a folder moves it to the Recycle Bin or Trash folder, where you can permanently delete it or restore it to its original location if you change your mind. Copying a folder may not be an option on a mobile device; this capability varies by app.

Module 4 Summary

The system software on your computer or device, which includes the operating system, determines how your device runs and how you interact with it. Every computer has an operating system, also called a platform, that manages its operations and allows you to interact with it. Your operating system will have a GUI (or possibly a NUI) that includes visual objects, such as buttons or icons, that you click or tap to select options, or issue commands.

Operating systems often are offered using SaaS subscription models that automatically provide access to updates and fixes. An operating system's code may be closed or open, depending on whether the manufacturer enables others to access, modify, and distribute versions of the system. Windows and macOS are examples of closed source operating systems. Desktop and mobile operating systems are single-user systems that enable the computer or device's user to start and shut down the computer or device, manage apps and memory, coordinate tasks, configure peripheral devices, establish an Internet connection, monitor performance, manage files, update system software, monitor security, and control network access. A server operating system is a multiuser system that controls a single computer that supports others on a network. Some server operating systems enable virtualization, which is the practice of sharing computing resources.

The operating system coordinates interactions between hardware and software. Files include data files such as text documents and photos, as well as executable files. The operating system can manage your files and help you store them in folders or libraries to keep them organized so that you can find them. Every program or app, including the operating system, requires RAM. The operating system manages memory and uses RAM to temporarily store open apps and data while they are being processed. It also uses processes such as buffering, spooling, and swapping to efficiently use memory. When you start your computer or device, it goes through a boot process that loads the operating system using the bootstrap program to load the kernel and other operating system files.

You can customize your operating system to meet your needs by changing how the screen is set up, adjusting the screen brightness or resolution, adding a theme or sound scheme, and pinning or creating shortcuts to items to the taskbar or home screen. You also can configure input devices to change commands for keys on a keyboard, or to use a mobile device with one hand.

Administrative tools help you manage resources. Adjusting your power settings can help you manage the power and battery charge efficiently. Utilities help you with a variety of maintenance-type tasks, such as diagnosing and repairing problems, cleaning up your disk, and restoring deleted files or folders. Using a virtual machine enables you to run more than one operating system on a computer or device. You also can use the operating system to set up and manage user accounts for multiple users on a device.

You can manage files and folders using your operating system. Protecting files by storing them safely and using password protection can help prevent loss or unauthorized access. Compressing the file size reduces the storage space that it takes up, making it easier to store, share, or transfer. You can save your files to folders and file systems in order to keep them organized. Determining the file properties helps you identify the name, type, location, and size, as well as when the file was created, modified, or accessed. A file name contains an extension that tells the platform or app on which the file can be used. File and folder names should be specific to the contents and purpose of the item. Folders and files can be copied or moved or placed in the Recycle Bin or Trash folder.

Review Questions

1. A GUI controls the ________ of an operating system.
   - **a.** memory
   - **b.** interface
   - **c.** boot process
   - **d.** type
2. The practice of sharing computing resources among multiple computers or devices is called ________.
   - **a.** virtualization
   - **b.** spooling
   - **c.** utilizing
   - **d.** buffering
3. (True or False) A data file contains the instructions your computer or device needs to run programs and apps.
4. The core of an operating system is its ________ .
   - **a.** source code
   - **b.** kernel
   - **c.** nugget
   - **d.** executable file

5. Standard settings that control how the screen is set up are called ________ settings.
   a. typical
   b. average
   c. normal
   d. default

6. An operating system controls the components required to perform work, called the ________.
   a. resources
   b. functions
   c. settings
   d. devices

7. (True or False) When you move a file to the Recycle Bin or Trash, it still takes up storage space, but no longer appears in the folder or location where it was created.

8. The separate hard disk space on which a virtual machine functions is called a(n) ________.
   a. buffer
   b. partition
   c. external hard disk
   d. cloud folder

9. The user account that provides full access to the computer is called a(n) ________ account.
   a. standard user
   b. administrator
   c. controller
   d. default

10. Which of the following units measure billions of bytes of data?
    a. Kilobytes
    b. Megabytes
    c. Gigabytes
    d. Terabytes

11. Microsoft Office 365 and Google Docs are examples of ________.
    a. file management tools
    b. multiuser operating systems
    c. web apps
    d. desktop operating systems

12. You can locate a file in the macOS using the ________.
    a. File Explorer
    b. search engine
    c. source code
    d. Finder

Discussion Questions

1. What characteristics are common among operating systems? List types of operating systems, and examples of each. How does the device affect the functionality of an operating system? Explain the benefits of a SaaS model. What operating system is installed on your computer or device? If you had the choice, would you change it? Why or why not?
2. Discuss how an operating system manages the computer's memory. What is virtual memory, and why is it important? Have you ever had issues with the memory on your computer or device? What steps can you take to make sure you have ample memory?
3. List three administrative tools and utilities and explain how they are used. What utilities have you used, and for what purpose?
4. Explain what you can determine about a file by looking at its properties. List two types of information a file name should include. Have you ever been unable to find a file that you created? How can you be sure to avoid this problem?

Critical Thinking Activities

1. You are a coder who is working with a team to create a new mobile operating system. At your last meeting, the team discussed whether to make the code open source or closed source. What are benefits to each for the developer and for the user? What concerns might a developer have to ensure the quality of an open source program? Would you use an open source operating system? Why or why not?
2. You are a teaching assistant for an introductory computer concepts course at your local community college. The instructor asks you to prepare a lecture explaining the boot process and the role of the operating system. List four important steps in the boot process. How could learning about the boot process help you if you had any issues with starting your computer or device?
3. You have purchased a new laptop and want to customize the operating system to meet your needs. List three ways you might customize your operating system, and explain why and what tools or types of tools you might need. Have you ever customized your operating system? How did/might you do this to improve your user experience?
4. You work with a lot of different documents in your internship with a software development company. What kinds of actions can you take to keep your files and folders organized? Discuss the importance of file naming, folder names, and folder structure in keeping yourself organized.

Apply Your Skills

Qing Chan has an internship with an accounting firm, which has provided them with a laptop and a smartphone. The laptop runs Microsoft Windows as its operating system, and the phone uses the Apple iOS operating system. Qing uses the apps and utilities provided with their devices to share and collaborate on files, send communications, and participate in web conferences. Qing recently made modifications to the operating systems' settings to personalize them so that they can work more efficiently.

Working in a small group or by yourself, complete the following:

1. List common operating system functions. What differences are there between single-user and multiuser operating systems? What differences are there between desktop and mobile operating systems? List three factors Qing might use when selecting an operating system. Have you ever interacted directly with a server operating system? How might you have indirectly interacted with a server operating system without realizing it?
2. Differentiate between a data file and an executable file. In what circumstances might Qing use each? Differentiate between a folder and a library. Have you ever used a library? How did/might you benefit from using one?
3. For a project Qing is working on, they need to run two operating systems on their laptop. Explain how they can accomplish this. Have you ever used a virtual machine? Why might you use a virtual machine over using two computers running different operating systems?
4. Explain why Qing may want to compress and uncompress files and folders, and how they might accomplish this. Have you ever compressed a file or folder or received one?

Module 5

App Use

In This Module

- Explain apps and their purposes
- Use common features of productivity apps
- Recognize graphics apps

Foxy burrow/Shutterstock.com

Sara Jackson is starting her own interior design consulting firm. While she is based in the United Kingdom, her customers will be from all over the world. She will need to use a variety of apps to create presentations and drawings for customers and graphics for her firm's website. She will write work proposals and contracts using a word processing app, manage her firm's income and expenses in a spreadsheet, and track her customers in a database. Sara uses graphic software to adapt customers' photos and videos of their space to demonstrate how it would look with different furnishings.

Everything you do with your smartphone, computer, or tablet requires an app. Whether you are sending messages, watching videos, browsing the web, or checking the news, apps help you accomplish these tasks. Businesses and home users use apps to manage documents, spreadsheets, presentations, and databases. With graphics apps, you can edit and enhance digital images and videos.

In this module, you will learn about different types of apps and how they are used in your personal and work life. You will learn about different kinds of productivity apps. You will explore how digital artists use drawing, paint, video, and photo editing apps. As you reflect on what you learn in this module, ask yourself: What are the benefits and drawbacks to using mobile apps? How can you use productivity software to do your job? What can a graphic artist accomplish using graphics apps?

Explain Apps and Their Purposes

The terms software, program, and apps often are used interchangeably. Software is any set of instructions that tell the computer or device how to operate. Apps (also called programs or application software) are programs that help you perform specific tasks when using your computer or smartphone. All apps are software, but not all software is an app; the main difference is that if end-user interaction is required, the software is an app. With apps, you can create documents, edit photos, record videos, read the news, get travel directions, go shopping, make online calls, manage your device, and more (**Figure 5-1**).

Figure 5-1: People use a variety of apps

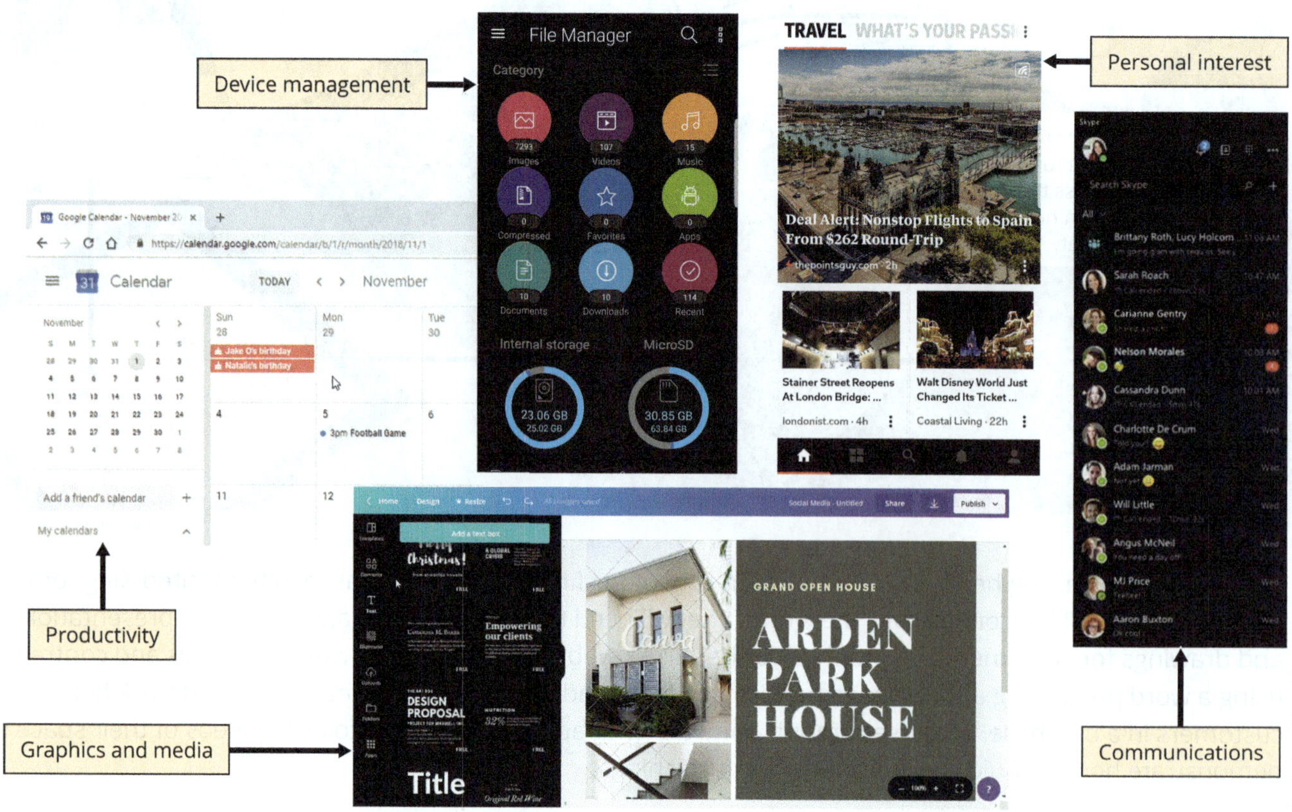

Google, Inc.; Flipboard; Canva

Describe Types of Apps

While all apps allow you to accomplish a task, the device on which you access them and the way you obtain the app can determine its capabilities. Desktop- or laptop-installed native versions of the apps generally provide the most complete and advanced capabilities. Web, mobile, and portable versions are often simpler, or lightweight, and contain the most basic and most popular basic features.

- A **native app**, also called a local app, is an app written for a specific operating system and installed on a computer or mobile device. Native apps can take advantage of specific features of the devices on which they are installed, such as a smartphone's camera, microphone, or contacts list. You may install native mobile apps by downloading them from an app store. Many native apps require an Internet connection to provide full functionality. Some apps can run offline and will store information on your device until they can synchronize with the cloud.
- **Mobile apps** are native apps that you access on a smartphone or tablet. Usually you download and install these from your device's app store. Because screens on mobile devices tend to be small, mobile apps might focus on a single task, such as checking email, searching the web, or sending a text message. **Figure 5-2** compares mobile and web apps.
- Web apps are stored on an Internet server that can be run entirely in a web browser. Because these programs run over the Internet, web apps often offer collaboration features, and store the files or documents you create in the cloud.
- **Mobile web apps** are stored on an Internet server and can be run entirely in a web browser using a smartphone or tablet. Like all web apps, they do not require device storage space or updates, as they run from a browser.
- **Portable apps** run from a removable storage device such as an external hard drive or flash drive, or from the cloud. When using an external hard drive or flash drive, you connect the storage device to your computer and then run the application. When installed in the cloud, you can access portable apps from a folder in your cloud storage. Portable apps are useful when you have limited storage space on your computer, or if you are using a very specific type of app that you need to be able to use on multiple devices.

Figure 5-2: Mobile and web apps

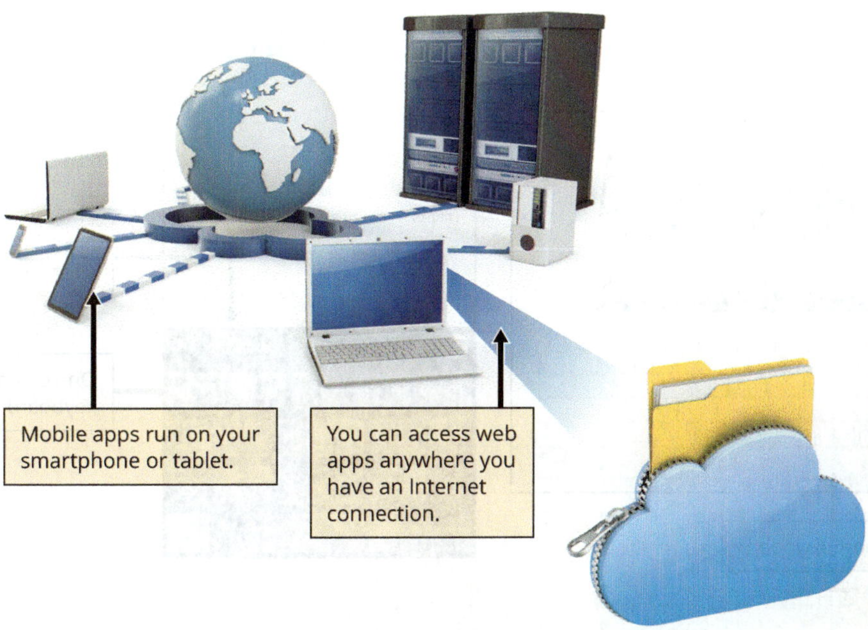

dny3d/Shutterstock.com; mipan/Shutterstock.com

Figure 5-3: Mobile and web apps can synchronize data

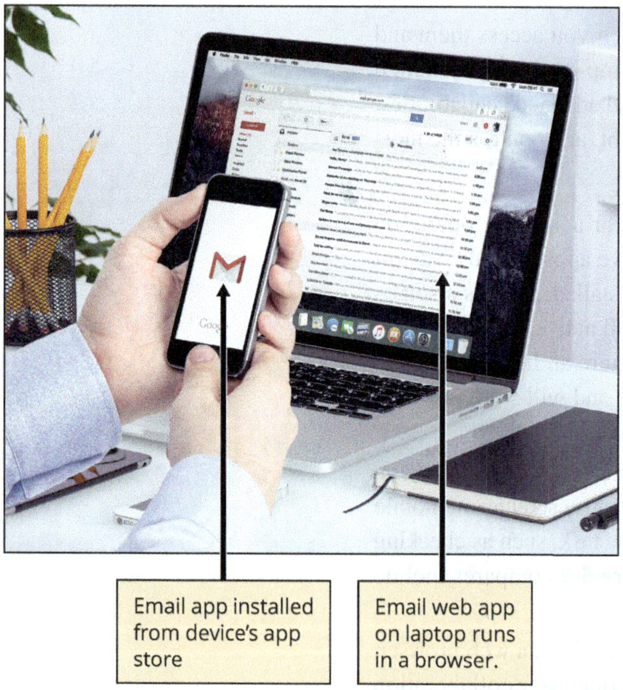

Alexey Boldin/Shutterstock.com

Identify Common Features of Apps

Apps have many common features, regardless of whether they run on a computer or mobile device. They:

- Usually are represented on your computer's desktop or smartphone's home screen by an icon
- Can be run by double-clicking or tapping the icon
- Open in a window that has buttons, icons, menus, and a workspace
- Have menus that give you options to access different features of the program or app
- Have buttons to click or tap to give commands or perform actions

Some apps are available as both a web app and a native app. In this case, you typically can **synchronize** the data, settings, preferences, and apps so they are set up the same way on all your devices. For example, you might look at your Gmail account on your smartphone or tablet, and access Gmail on your computer via its website (**Figure 5-3**). In both cases, the email messages displayed in your inbox are the same. If you delete an email message using the email app on your mobile device, it will not appear when you check email using the email application on your laptop later.

Use Mobile Apps

To interact with a mobile app, you touch or tap the screen. To enter text, you can use a keyboard (**Figure 5-4**). An **on-screen keyboard** is displayed on the screen and includes keys for typing text, numbers, and symbols. Many on-screen keyboards assist you by predicting words and phrases you might want to type based on context, or by providing automatic

Figure 5-4: Sample Bluetooth and on-screen keyboards

Sorapop Udomsri/Shutterstock.com

corrections. Some on-screen keyboards include voice recognition capabilities, so you can speak the words to be typed. Users who need to type significant amounts of information may opt for a portable keyboard that they can connect to their smartphones using Bluetooth.

Many mobile devices come pre-installed with apps for managing email, contacts, calendars, a photo gallery, a web browser, sending and receiving text messages, a camera, a voice recorder, mobile payments, and more. You can organize apps into groups by category, such as Games or Social Media, to make them easier to find.

Figure 5-5 shows how you might interact with mobile apps throughout your day.

Figure 5-5: Using mobile apps throughout the day

GaudiLab/Shutterstock.com; vasabi/Shutterstock.com

Table 5-1 lists common mobile apps and the tasks they can help you accomplish.

Describe the Pros and Cons of Mobile Apps

Although mobile apps are popular and convenient, they have limitations, as described in **Table 5-2**.

Apps are represented by icons on your screen (**Figure 5-6**). Many mobile apps require the ability to connect to the Internet, either over Wi-Fi, or using your carrier's mobile network. Connectivity is crucial to today's mobile user; people want to stay connected to

Table 5-1: Popular types of mobile apps

Type of app	Helps you to	Examples
Banking and payment	Manage bank accounts, pay bills, deposit checks, transfer money, make payments	Your bank's mobile app, Venmo, PayPal
Calendar	Maintain your online calendar, schedule appointments	Google Calendar, Outlook Calendar
Cloud storage	Store your files in the cloud	Box, OneDrive, Google Drive, iCloud, Amazon Drive
Contact management	Organize your address book	Contacts
Device maintenance	Optimize storage, delete unused or duplicate files, optimize device performance	CCleaner, PhoneClean
Email	Send and receive email messages from your mobile device	Outlook, Gmail
Fitness	Track workouts; set weight-loss goals, review stats from fitness tracking devices	Fitbit, MyFitnessPal
Games	Play games on your mobile device	Candy Crush
Location sharing	Share your location with friends	Find My Friends, Find My Family, Google Maps
Mapping/GPS	View maps; obtain travel directions based on your location	Google Maps, Waze
Messaging	Send text messages, photos, or short videos, or make voice or video calls to your friends	Facebook Messenger, FaceTime, WhatsApp, GroupMe
News and information	Stay up to date on current affairs of interest to you	Flipboard, Google News, Weather Channel, CNN
Personal assistant	Search the Internet, set timers, add appointments to your calendar, make hands-free calls by speaking commands	Siri, Cortana, Google Home, Amazon Alexa
Personal productivity	View and make minor edits to documents received by email, or stored on your device or in the cloud	Microsoft Word, PowerPoint, Outlook, Excel, Gmail, Google Docs, Spreadsheets, Slides
Photo and video editing and sharing	Modify photos and videos by cropping, adding filters, adjusting brightness and contrast	Fotor, Canva, Adobe Lightroom
Shopping	Make online retail purchases	Amazon.com
Social media	Share status updates, photos, or videos on social networking sites or view friends' posts	Facebook, Instagram, LinkedIn
Travel	Make airline, hotel, and restaurant reservations; read and post reviews	Airbnb, Kayak, Priceline, Yelp, TripAdvisor
Web browsing	View websites on your mobile devices	Chrome, Edge, Firefox, Safari

Table 5-2: Pros and cons of mobile apps

Pros	Cons
Can be created quickly compared to native apps	Not as fast as and have fewer features than native web apps or desktop apps
You can access your information on the go	Poorly designed apps can turn people away
Voice input, touch screens, and smart on-screen keyboard simplify interactions	Typing using a small on-screen keyboard can be cumbersome

their office, home, and friends all the time, no matter where they are. Files that the apps use or create often are compatible between your desktop or laptop computer and your mobile device.

Most mobile apps are **platform-specific**, that is, designed for a specific operating system like Android OS or iOS. If you have an Android phone, you need to install the Android version of your app; if you have an iPhone, you need to download the iPhone version of your app. In most cases, the capabilities of different versions of the same app are comparable; each device's app has a consistent look and feel with that device's user interface and is built to run with that device's mobile operating system.

Figure 5-6: App icons and grouped apps

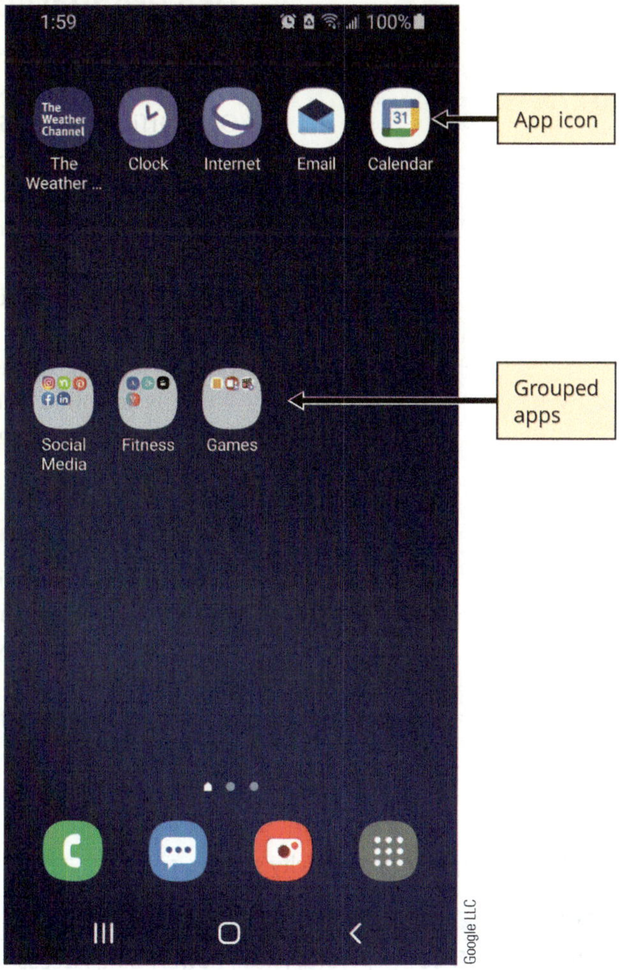

List Additional App Categories

In addition to productivity and graphics apps, which are covered in the next sections, there are many other types of apps that you can use.

Personal interest apps give you tools to pursue your interests. You might use travel, mapping, and navigation apps to view maps, obtain route directions, or locate points of interest. News apps gather the day's news from several online sources in one place, based on your preferences. Reference apps provide access to information from online encyclopedias, dictionaries, and databases. Educational apps provide training on a variety of subjects and topics. Entertainment apps include games, movie times, and reviews. Social media apps enable you to share messages, photos, and videos with your friends and colleagues. Shopping apps allow you to make purchases online.

Communications apps provide tools for sharing or receiving information. Using a browser, you can access webpages; with email apps you can send and receive electronic mail messages. Messaging apps share short messages, videos, and images, usually between mobile phone users. Video conferencing apps provide the ability to have voice and video conversations over the Internet. Other communications apps allow you to transfer files between your computer and a server on the Internet.

Device management apps provide tools for maintaining your computer or mobile device. With a file manager app, you can store, locate, and organize files in your device's storage or in the cloud. A screen saver shows a moving image after a period of no keyboard or mouse activity. Security apps will keep your computer or mobile device safe from malicious activity.

Use Common Features of Productivity Apps

Productivity apps are apps for personal use that you may use to create documents, develop presentations, track appointments, or stay organized. You use productivity apps when you are writing a letter or report, maintaining a budget, creating slides for a presentation, or managing the membership list for an organization. Productivity apps include word processing apps for creating documents, spreadsheet apps for creating worksheets, presentation apps for creating slides, and may include email, database, note-taking, and other apps for creating a variety of documents.

Use Productivity Suites

Many vendors bundle their individual apps into a **productivity suite**, or collection of productivity apps such as Microsoft Office 365, Apple iWork, G Suite, or Apache OpenOffice (**Table 5-3**). You can share text, graphics, charts, and other content among projects you create with individual apps and download additional templates for creating specialized projects. For example, you could include a chart created in a spreadsheet app as part of a slide in a presentation, or as a figure in a word processing document.

In addition to productivity apps that are part of a productivity suite, individual productivity apps are popular as well. For example, Prezi is an online presentation app that you can use to zoom in and out of parts of a canvas to create an online presentation. Zoho Writer is an online word processing app with additional features such as posting directly to popular online blogging platforms.

Use Collaboration Tools

By storing documents in the cloud, you can share documents with several people who can read, edit, and comment on the same document at the same time (**Figure 5-7**). If they are unsure of the edits, they can discuss the changes in comments and tracked changes to compare versions, without creating multiple copies of the same file. This process of collaboration is often more efficient than exchanging multiple versions of the same file by email, and then merging each person's changes together.

Table 5-3: Popular productivity suites

Suite	Available programs	Versions	Cloud storage
Microsoft Office	Word, Excel, PowerPoint, Access (database) Outlook (email), and OneNote (note taking)	Microsoft Windows and macOS, and as Office Online, a collection of web apps in a browser	Microsoft OneDrive
Apple iWork	iWork (word processing, spreadsheet, and presentations), Apple Pencil (drawing)	macOS and iOS	iCloud
G Suite	Docs, Sheets, Slides, Google Calendar, Gmail (email), SketchUp (drawing)	ChromeOS and as a web app, as well as mobile app for Android and iOS	Google Drive
Apache OpenOffice	Writer, Calc, Impress (presentations), Draw and Base (database)	Open source app downloaded from a website for free	

Figure 5-7: Creating, collaborating, and commenting on a shared document

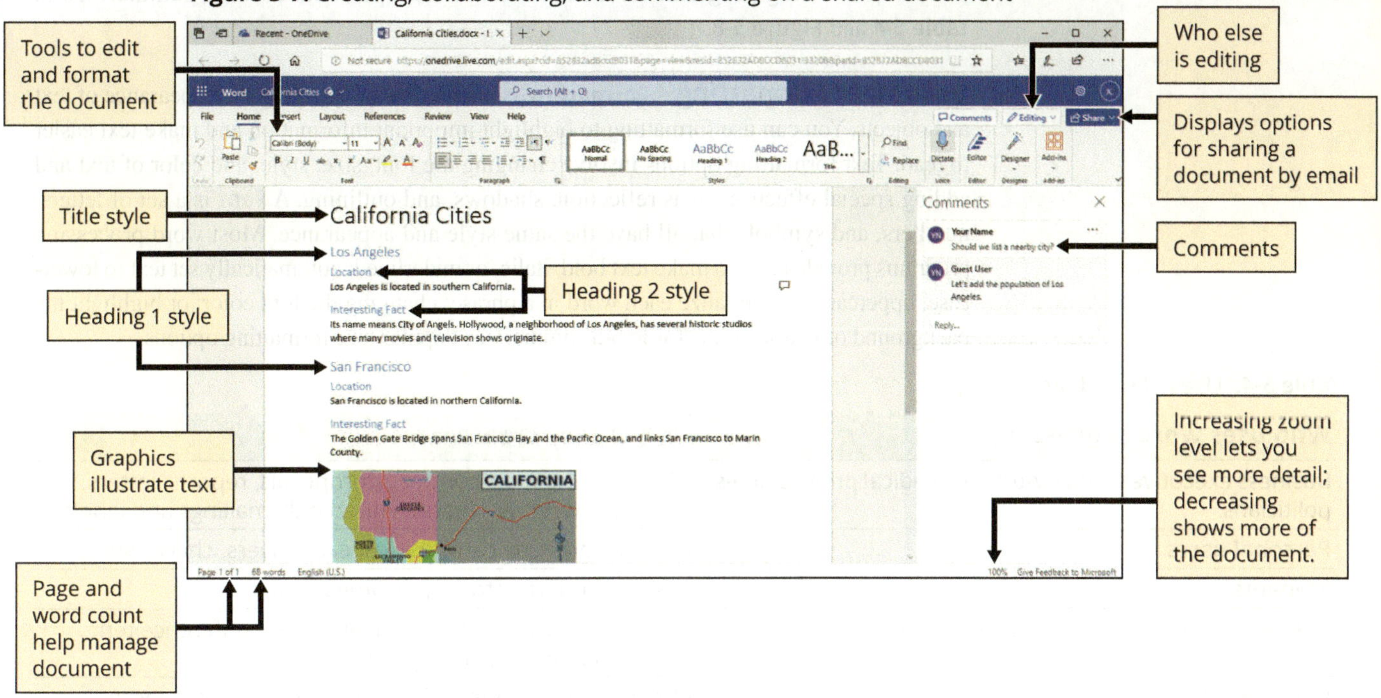

Messaging apps such as Slack and Microsoft Teams are used to send messages regarding work projects among colleagues. While they can have personal uses, they are widely used in business. Within these apps you can participate in video conferencing, store and share files, and chat with others. Microsoft Teams can be used with cloud-based versions of Microsoft Office to enable collaboration.

Use Word Processing Apps

Word processing is one of the most widely used types of apps. A **word processing app** includes tools for entering, editing, and formatting text and graphics. You can create documents and reports, mailing labels, flyers, brochures, newsletters, resumes, letters, and more. You can enhance your documents to look more professional, as well as share and collaborate with others.

Word Processing Features All word processors share some common key features. The electronic files you create are called **documents**. A document can contain only one page or an unlimited number of pages. When you open a word processing program, a blank document opens on the screen. The screen displays an **insertion point**, a blinking vertical line that appears when you click the screen, indicating where new text or an object will be inserted. **Scroll bars** appear on the right edge (vertical scroll bar) and bottom edge (horizontal scroll bar) of a document window to let you view a document that is too large to fit on the screen at once. You can use scroll bars to navigate to view parts of a document that are too large to fit on the screen all at once.

With some word processing programs, you can speak the text into a microphone connected to your computer or mobile device, and the program will convert your speech to text and type it for you. As you type or speak text, when you reach the end of one line, the word processing software automatically "wraps" the words onto the next line. When the text fills the page, the new text automatically flows onto a new page.

Word processing programs have both business and personal uses, as summarized in **Table 5-4** and **Figure 5-8**.

Document Formatting **Formatting** is the process of changing the appearance of text and objects. You can use formatting to highlight important information and make text easier to read. Text formatting options involve changing the font, size, style, and color of text and adding special effects such as reflection, shadows, and outlining. A **font** is a set of letters, numbers, and symbols that all have the same style and appearance. Most word processing programs provide tools to make text bold, italic, or underlined; automatically set text to lowercase, uppercase, or capitalize each word in a phrase; changing the font color; or highlight the background of text in color. **Table 5-5** summarizes popular text-formatting options.

Table 5-4: Uses of word processing

Who uses word processing	What they create
Business executives, office workers, medical professionals, politicians	Agendas, memos, contracts, proposals, reports, letters, email, newsletters, personalized bulk mailings and labels
Personal users	Letters, greeting cards, notes, event flyers, check lists
Students	Essays, reports, stories, resumes, notes
Conference promoters and event planners	Business cards, postcards, invitations, conference tent cards, name tags, gift tags, stickers
Web designers	Documents for publishing to the web after converting them to HTML

Figure 5-8: Word processing programs have both personal and business uses

Table 5-5: Text formatting options

Format option	Description and use	Examples
Font type	Defines what characters look like. Some fonts have rounded letters; others are more angular. Some are formal; others are more casual.	Times New Roman Arial **Arial Black**
Font size	Determines the size of the character, measured in *points*; each point is 1/72 of an inch; change the title font to be bigger than the rest of your text or use smaller fonts for footnotes or endnotes.	This text is 12 points This text is 18 points
Font style	Adds visual effects features to text; bolding text makes it stand out on the page, shadow gives it depth, underlining, italicizing, and highlighting text provide emphasis.	**bold** shadow underline *italics* highlighting

You can format the layout of a document to improve its appearance and readability. Document formatting features include formatting in multiple columns, adding borders around text, adding a page break to specify a location for a new page to begin, and changing spacing between lines of text. You also can specify a document's margins and the **page orientation**, which is the direction in which content is printed on the page. **Portrait orientation** prints a page so that it is taller than it is wide. **Landscape orientation** prints a page so that it is wider than it is tall.

To give a document a professional appearance, you can specify styles for a document's title, headings, paragraphs, quotes, and more. A **style** is a named collection of formats that are stored together and can be applied to text or objects. For example, the Heading 1 style for a document might format text using Calibri font, size 16, blue text color, left justified. Any text in the document formatted with the Heading 1 style will have those characteristics. If you modify the characteristics of a style, all the format of text in that style will update to reflect the new characteristics.

Many productivity suites offer built-in templates for creating different kinds of documents. A **template** is a document that has been preformatted for a specific purpose (such as an invitation, a brochure, a flyer, a cover letter, or a resume). You can specify the content of your documents, but you do not have to develop a color scheme or design a layout.

In addition, you might make use of the features shown in **Table 5-6** when creating or editing a document.

Other tools include mail merge, which you can use to create and send customized letters or email messages that are personalized with the recipient's name and other information, and reference tools which you can use to create a bibliography containing citations to reference articles in a research paper.

Some word processing features are included in programs and apps for creating different types of documents. **Table 5-7** lists several examples.

Table 5-6: Additional document formatting options

Use this feature	When you want to
Alignment	Align paragraphs or lines of text at the left margin, right margin, or center of the page
Graphics	Add photos, pictures, logos, charts, or screenshots to your document to add visual appeal
Headers and Footers	Display information such as a document title, author's name, or page number at the top or bottom of each page
Hyperlinks	Direct readers to related documents, email addresses, or websites online
Line Spacing	Specify how much "white space" appears before, between, or after each line of text (measured in points)
Lists	Display a list of items preceded by numbers or a symbol called a bullet
Margins	Specify the region of the page where text will appear, measured from the left, right, top, and bottom edges of the page
Tables	Organize text in rows and columns

Table 5-7: Programs and apps for creating different types of documents

Related program	Function	Use to create
Desktop publishing	Combines word processing with graphics and advanced layout capabilities	Newsletters, brochures, flyers
Text / code editor	Creates webpages using HTML tags	Webpages
Note taking	Stores and accesses thoughts, ideas, and lists	Notes
Speech recognition	Enters text that you speak, rather than type	Documents

Document Management **Document management tools** protect and organize files and let you share your document with others. Collaboration tools are an example of document management tools. You also can copy elements of a document, such as text and graphics from a word processing document or a chart from a spreadsheet, from one to another.

When sharing a document, you can restrict access to a document by providing view-only or read-only access. A **view-only link** is a link to content on a OneDrive or other online location that can be viewed by users. **Read-only access** offers a way to share files so others may read the file but cannot change it.

Use Spreadsheet Apps

You can use spreadsheet apps to manipulate numbers or display numerical data. Keeping to-do lists, creating a budget, tracking your personal finances, following the performance of your favorite sports teams, and calculating payments on a loan are all tasks you can accomplish using a spreadsheet. Businesses often use spreadsheets to calculate taxes or payroll.

A **spreadsheet** is a grid of cells that contain numbers and text (**Figure 5-9**). In Microsoft Excel, a spreadsheet is called a worksheet. You use spreadsheet software to create, edit, and format worksheets. A **worksheet** is a single sheet in a workbook file that is laid out in in a grid of rows and columns. A **workbook** is collection of related worksheets contained within a single file.

You can use spreadsheet apps to enter, create, and interact with numbers, charts, graphics, text, and data. Using a spreadsheet you can perform calculations on data stored in a grid of cells. If you enter new data that is used in a calculation, the spreadsheet recalculate values automatically.

Figure 5-9: Using spreadsheet software

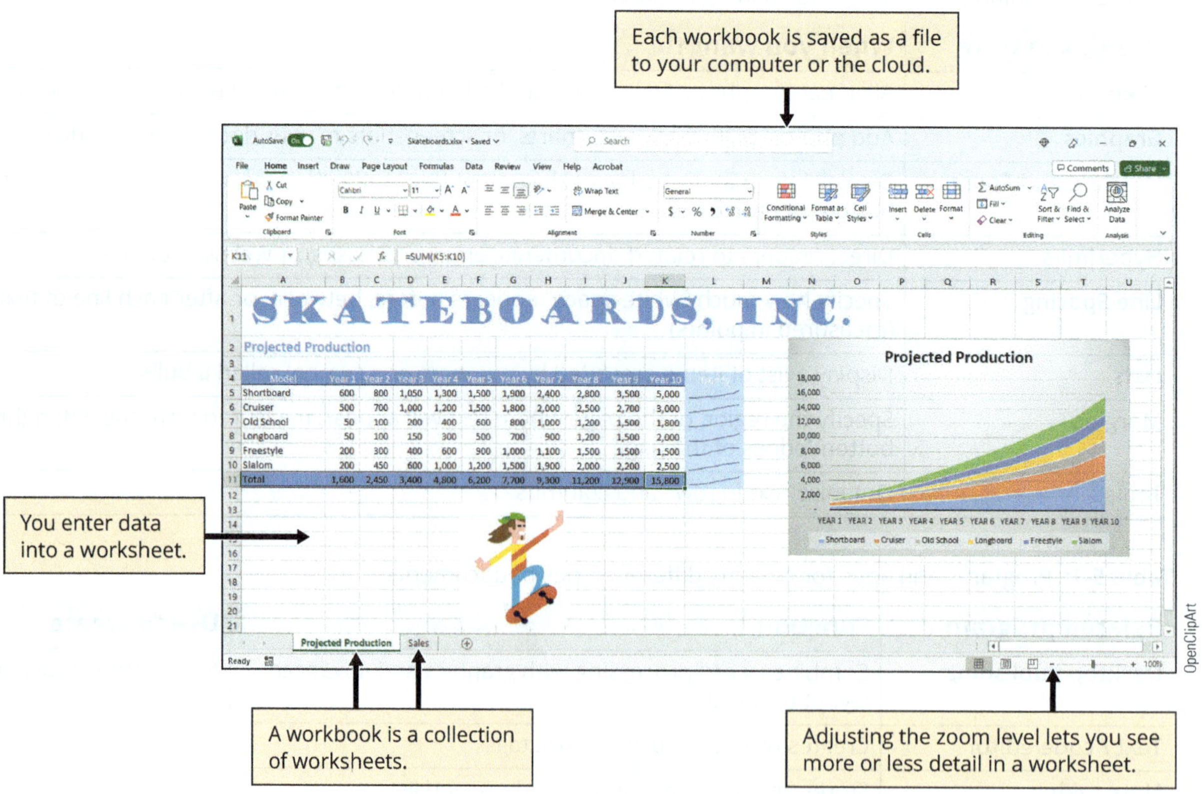

A **cell** is the box formed by the intersection of a column and a row. Worksheets use letters or pairs of letters, such as A or AB, to identify each column and consecutive numbers to identify each row. You can refer to a cell by its **cell address**, or location in the worksheet. For example, cell K11 is located at the intersection of column K and row 11. In **Figure 5-10**, cell K11 contains the number 11,800, which represents the number of total projected production of skateboards in Year 10.

Spreadsheets Features Spreadsheet software often includes many additional features (**Table 5-8**).

You can automate your worksheets with **macros**, small programs you can create to perform repetitive tasks. For example, if your worksheet contains information for a sales invoice, you can create a macro to save it as a PDF file, centered on the page. By assigning these steps to a macro, you can perform this task with one button click.

Spreadsheet Formatting You can change how a worksheet looks by using formatting features as well as by inserting elements such as graphics. Formatting highlights important data and makes worksheets easier to read; graphic elements enhance a worksheet. When you format a number, the value remains the same, even if the way it appears in a cell changes.

Figure 5-10: Basic features of spreadsheet software

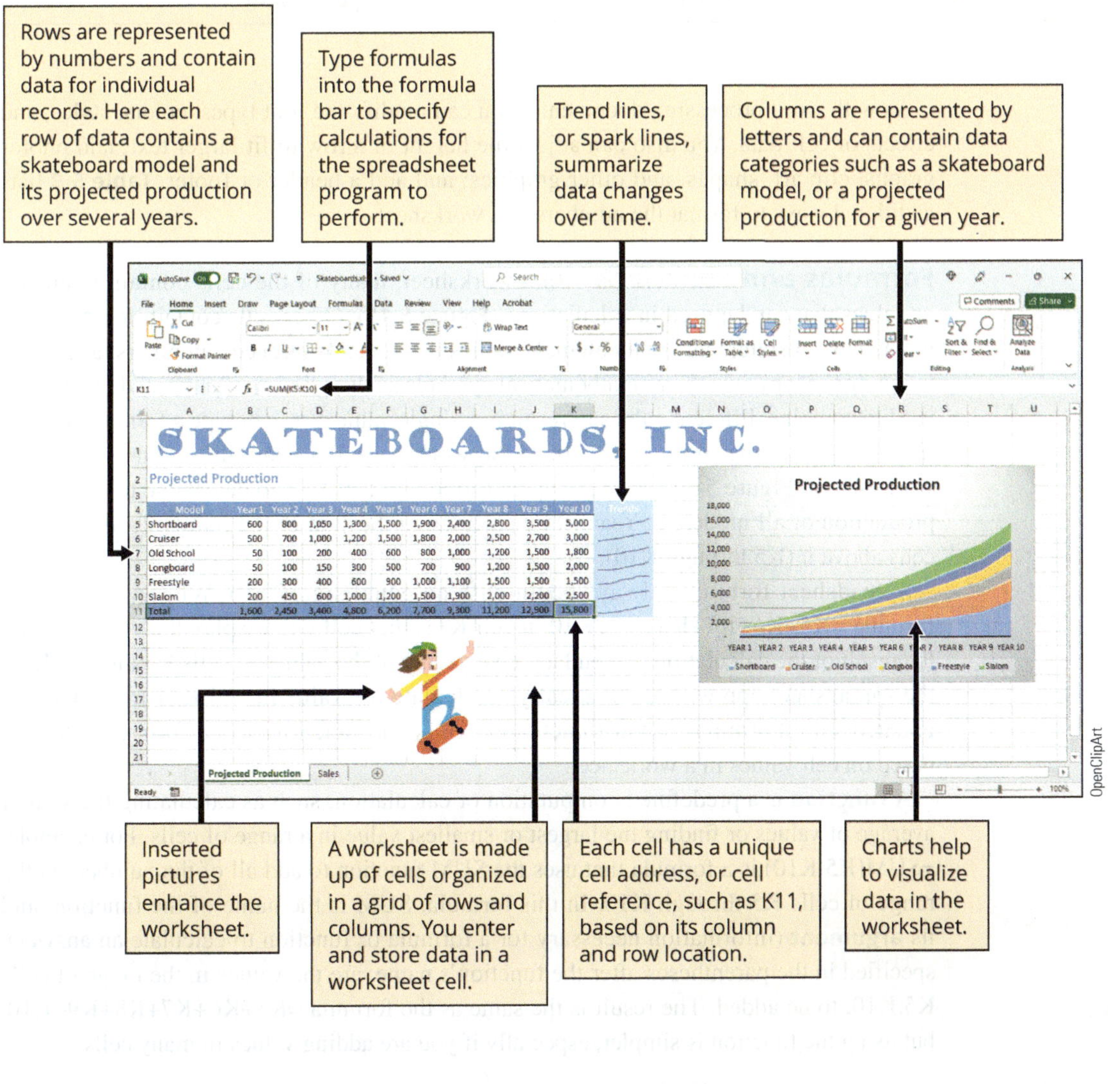

Table 5-8: Spreadsheet features

Feature	Use to
Formatting tools	Change a worksheet's appearance
Page layout and view features	Change the zoom level, divide a worksheet into panes, or freeze rows or columns, to make large worksheets easier to read
Printing features	Control whether you want to print entire worksheets or only selected areas
Web capabilities	Share workbooks online, add hyperlinks, and save worksheets as webpages
Developer tools	Add customized functions
Charts and graphs	Analyze data in a spreadsheet

Table 5-9: Formatting worksheet data

Formatting option	Use to	Examples
Currency	Identify currency value such as dollars, pounds, or euros	$4.50 or £4.50 or €4.50
Decimal places	Display additional level of accuracy	4.50, 4.500, 4.5003
Date or Time	Display dates or times while enabling them to be used in calculations	3/4/2027 or March 4, 2027 12:31:00 or 12:31 PM
Percentage or fraction	Display the results of a calculation	80% or 4/5

As with word processing documents, you can modify the font types, colors, styles, and effects of cell data. You also can adjust the height of a row to fit larger text; add photographs, clip art, shapes, and other graphics; and add a header or footer. **Table 5-9** lists additional ways to format the numbers in a worksheet.

Formulas and Functions In a worksheet, many of the cells contain numbers, or values that can be used in calculations (**Figure 5-11**). Other cells contain **formulas**, or mathematical statements that calculate values using cell references, numbers, and arithmetic **operators**, which are mathematical symbols such as "+", "−", "*", and "/" that are used to combine different values to result in a single value. You can type a formula directly into a cell or in the formula bar above the worksheet. For example, when creating the worksheet in Figure 5-11, you can type a formula in cell K11 to determine the projected production of all models in Year 10 by calculating the sum of the numeric values in the cells above it (K5 through K10).

Spreadsheet formulas always begin with an equal sign ("="). When you type the formula =K5+K6+K7+K8+K9+K10 in cell K11, that cell will display the value 15,800, the result of the calculation. If you later change any of the values in cells K5 through K10, the spreadsheet app will automatically recalculate the value in cell K11 to display the updated sum. Formulas use arithmetic operators and functions to perform calculations based on cell values in a worksheet.

A **function** is a predefined computation or calculation, such as calculating the sum or average of values or finding the largest or smallest value in a range of cells. For example, =SUM(K5:K10) is a formula that uses the SUM function to add all of the numbers in the range of cells K5 through K10. In this formula, SUM is the name of the function, and its **argument** (information necessary for a formula or function to calculate an answer), specified in the parentheses after the function's name, are the values in the range of cells K5:K10, to be added. The result is the same as the formula =K5+K6+K7+K8+K9+K10, but using the function is simpler, especially if you are adding values in many cells.

Figure 5-11: Working with charts

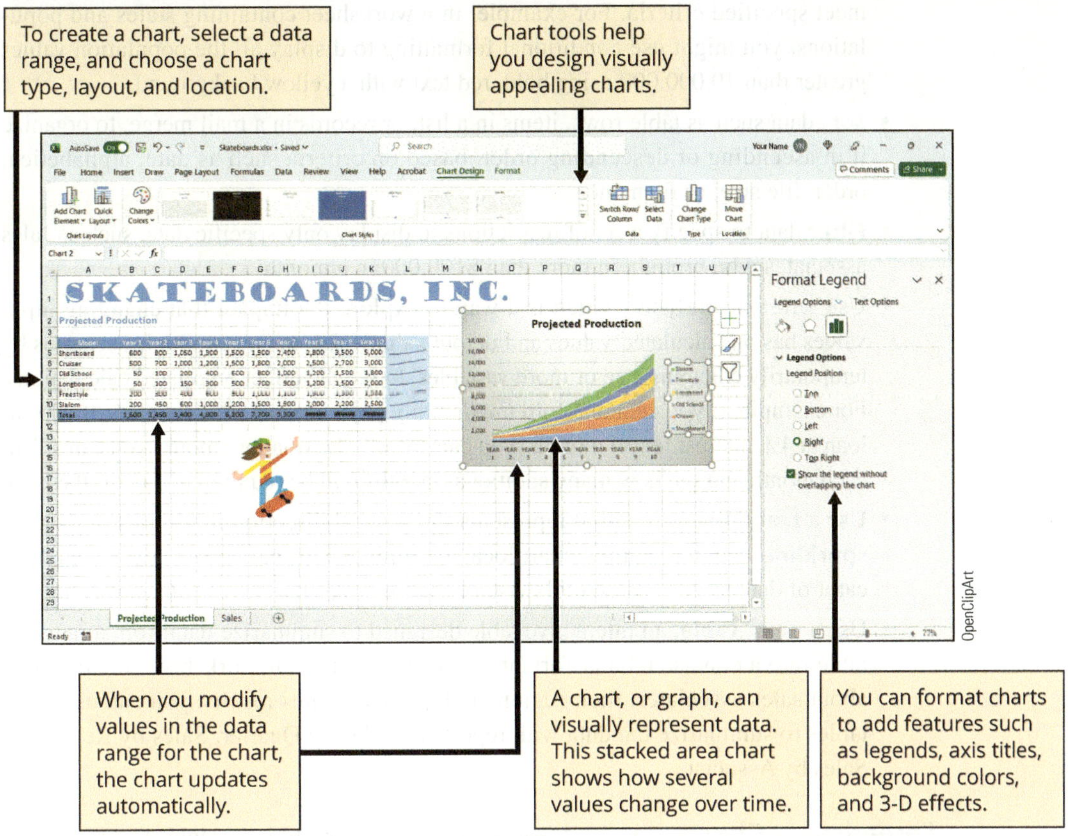

Formula arguments can be values or cell references. An **absolute cell reference** is a cell reference refers to a specific cell and does not change when you copy the formula and paste it in a new location. A **relative cell reference** is cell address that automatically changes to reflect the new location when the formula is copied or moved. Relative references are the default type of referencing used in Excel worksheets.

Spreadsheet apps contain **built-in functions** to perform financial, mathematical, logical, date and time, and other calculations (**Table 5-10**). Many spreadsheet apps allow users to write their own custom functions to perform special purpose calculations.

Spreadsheet Data Organization and Analysis Once you enter data into a worksheet, you can use several tools to make the data more meaningful.

Table 5-10: Common spreadsheet functions

Use these functions	To do this
SUM, AVERAGE, COUNT	Calculate the sum, average, or count of cells in a range
RATE, PMT	Calculate interest rates and loan payments
DATE, TIME, NOW	Obtain the current date, time, or date and time
IF, AND, OR, NOT	Perform calculations based on logical conditions
MAX, MIN	Calculate largest and smallest values in a group of cells
VLOOKUP	Look up values in a table

- Use **conditional formatting**, which is special formatting that is applied if values meet specified criteria. For example, in a worksheet containing states and populations, you might use conditional formatting to display all the population values greater than 10,000,000 using bold, red text with a yellow background.
- **Sort** data such as table rows, items in a list, or records in a mail merge, to organize it in ascending or descending order, based on criteria such as date, alphabetical order, file size, or filename.
- **Filter** data to specify a set of restrictions to display only specific data, such as sales associates who brought in more than $100,000 in a month.
- Use **what-if analysis**, which is a way to explore the impact that changing input values has on calculated values and output values. You can test multiple scenarios by temporarily changing one or more variables, to see the effect on related calculations. For example, if you cannot afford the monthly payment of $590.48 on a $20,000 car loan at 4% interest for 36 months, you can specify the smaller amount you can afford each month and see how many additional months will be required to pay off the loan.
- Use a **trendline**, a line that represents the general direction in a series of data, or **sparkline**, a quick, simple chart located within a cell that serves as a visual indicator of data trends. These tools visually summarize changes in values over time.
- Use a **pivot table**, an interactive table designed to summarize data from a range or table into a concise tabular format. For example, if your worksheet contains data about sales associates, their region, and quarterly sales results, you can use pivot tables to summarize the data with reports of Sales by Quarter, Sales by Region, or Sales by Associate.

Spreadsheet Charts A **chart** (sometimes called a graph) is a graphic that represents data using bars, columns, dots, lines, or other symbols to make the data easier to understand and to make it easier to see the relationships among the data. You can visualize data using pie charts, bar graphs, line graphs, and other chart types. A line chart tracks trends over time. A column chart compares categories of data to one another, and a pie chart compares parts (or slices) to the whole. A stacked area chart illustrates how several values (projected production of various models of skateboards) change over time in the same graphic.

Use Presentation Apps

A **presentation app** lets you create visual aids for presentations to communicate ideas, messages, and other information to a group. You might create a presentation for work or school, show slides of photos from your vacation to friends, or create digital signs. Presentations can be printed; viewed on a laptop, desktop, or mobile device; projected on a wall using a multimedia projector connected to a computer; or displayed on large monitors or information kiosks.

With presentation apps you can create slides that visually communicate ideas, messages, and other information. A **presentation**, also called a **slide show**, is a document that lets you create and deliver a dynamic, professional-looking message to an audience in the form of a slide show. Each slide has a specific layout based on its content (such as titles, headings, text, graphics, videos, and charts), and each layout has predefined placeholders for these content items (such as title layout, two-column layout, and image with a caption layout).

As you work, you can display presentations in different views. Normal view shows thumbnails, or small images of slides, and an editing pane, where you can add or modify content. In Notes view, you can add speaker's notes with talking points for each slide when giving the presentation. You can insert, delete, duplicate, hide, and move slides within your presentation.

Figure 5-12: Creating a presentation

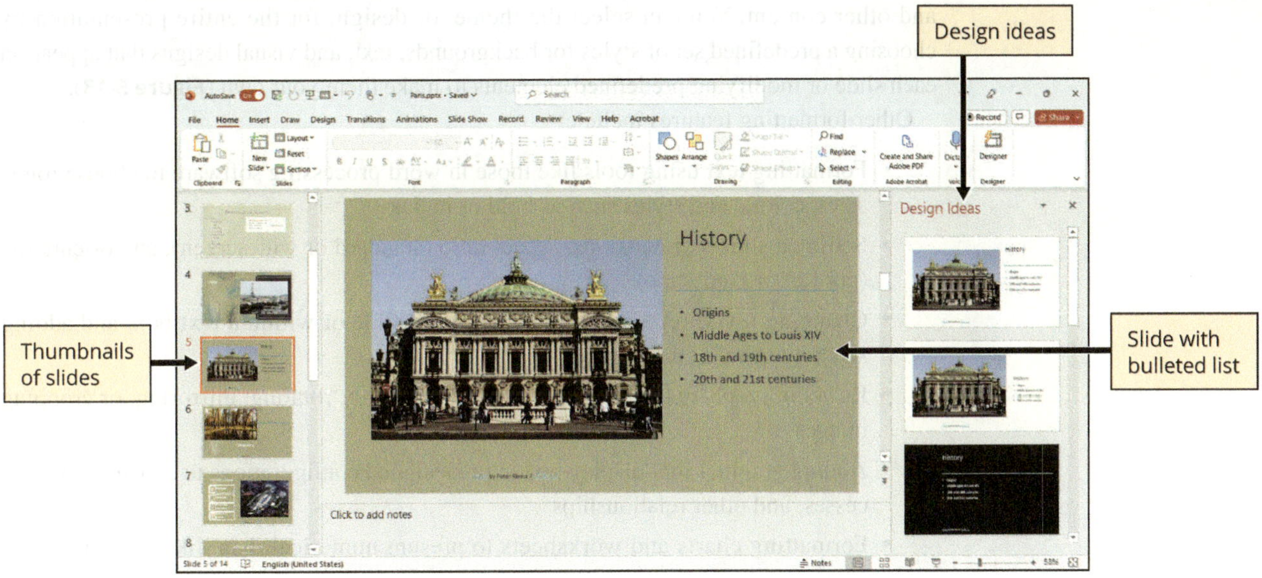

Presentation apps sometimes include a gallery that provides images, photos, video clips, and audio clips to give presentations greater impact. Some presentation apps offer a search tool to help you locate online images or videos to include in your slides. Some presentation apps even offer design ideas to give your slides a more professional appearance (**Figure 5-12**).

You can add main points to a slide as a bulleted list by typing them into a text box on the slide. You also can add graphics or images to illustrate your talking points. Presentation apps may also incorporate features such as checking spelling, formatting, researching, sharing, and publishing presentations online. Adding headers and footers lets you display the presentation title, slide number, date, logos, or other information on a single slide, or on all slides automatically.

There are many ways to present slide content so it appears in the clearest way for your audience (**Table 5-11**).

Table 5-11: Adding content to slides

Slide content	How to enter	Provides
Text in a paragraph or bulleted list	Click a placeholder and type, or copy and paste text from another file, or insert text from a document file.	Content; most programs offer a variety of bullet styles, including number and picture bullets
Graphics such as line art, photographs, clip art, drawn objects, diagrams, data tables, and screenshots	Click a content placeholder, draw directly on the slide, or copy and paste a graphic from another file.	Illustrations to convey meaning and information for the slide content
Media clips, such as video and audio, including recorded narrations	Click a content placeholder and choose a file, or insert the file directly onto a slide by recording it.	Media content to enhance a slide show
Links	Click content placeholder, copy and paste links from a website or type the link directly.	Links to another slide, another document, or a webpage
Embedded objects	Click menu commands or a content placeholder.	External files in a slide
Charts	Link or embed a worksheet or chart from a spreadsheet or create a chart directly within the presentation.	Graphic display of data to support your presentation

Presentation Formatting Slides can contain text, graphics, audio, video, links, and other content. You can select the theme, or design, for the entire presentation by choosing a predefined set of styles for backgrounds, text, and visual designs that appear on each slide or modifying predefined elements to make them your own (**Figure 5-13**).

Other formatting features include:

- Formatting text using tools like those in word processing software to choose fonts, sizes, colors, and styles such as bold or italics
- Setting a slide's dimensions, aspect ratio (standard or widescreen), and orientation (portrait or landscape)
- Changing text direction, aligning text on a slide or within a text box, and adding shadows or reflection effects
- Resizing graphics to make them larger or smaller; rotating, mirroring, or cropping images
- Adding graphics that display text in predesigned configurations to convey lists, processes, and other relationships
- Formatting charts and worksheets to present numerical data, like those found in spreadsheets
- Moving objects to different locations on a slide, aligning objects, and grouping objects

Transitions, Animations, and Templates A **transition** refers to the manner in which a slide appears on the screen in place of the previous slide in a slide show. For example, you can apply a push transition to "push" an existing slide off the right edge of the screen as a new one slides in from the left, or apply a cube transition that will make the new slide appear as if it was on the side of a rotating cube. You can set many options for transitions, such as sound effects, direction, and duration. You can set transitions for individual slides or for the entire presentation, to begin automatically after a preset amount of time, or manually with a screen tap or mouse click.

Figure 5-13: Formatting a presentation

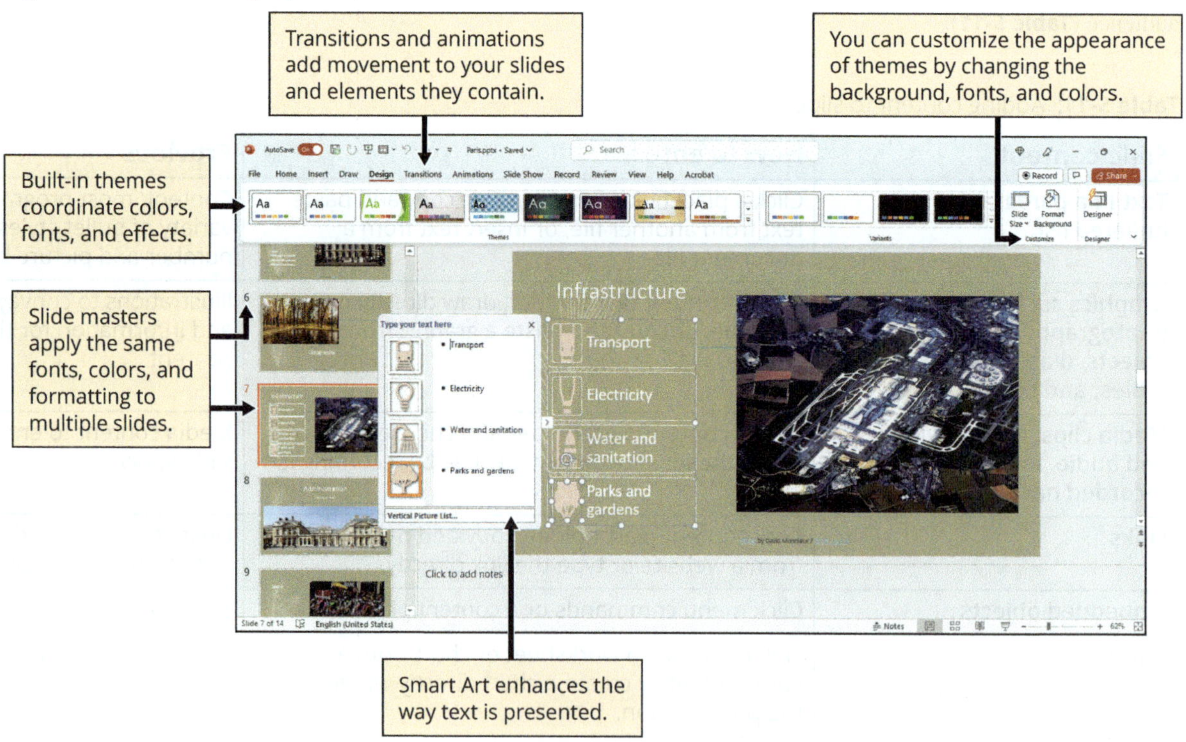

Animations are effects you apply to an object that make the object appear, disappear, or move. Presentation apps offer a variety of animations, such as entrance, exit, and emphasis, each with a variety of options. A photo can fade in as you display a slide, or an object can fly in from the edge of the slide. You can set animations to begin automatically when you advance a slide, or to start when you click or tap. Animations can move horizontally, vertically, or diagonally across the slide. You can set the order for multiple animations, such as displaying a bulleted list one item at a time, and then float in a graphic from the bottom edge of the slide.

Using a presentation template, you can add your content to a predefined design to create common presentations such as calendars, diagrams, and infographics. A **slide master** is the template for the slides in a presentation that contains theme elements and styles, text formatting, the slide background, and other objects that appear on all the slides in the presentation.

Share and Display Presentations When giving a presentation to a large group, you often display the slides on a large monitor or project them to a screen as a slide show, so everyone can see them (**Figure 5-14**). You might print handouts from your slides so audience members can take notes or send a link to your slides by email so audience members can follow along during the presentation on their own devices. When presentations are stored in the cloud, others can access them online. You also can share them on a blog or website by a code provided by the presentation app's share option and pasting it into a blogpost or webpage.

Presentation Design and Delivery When creating a presentation, it is important to communicate the content as clearly as possible. By following these tips, you can design effective presentations.

- Organize your presentation to have a beginning, a middle, and an end. Figure out how to visualize each of your topics.
- Your audience can read a slide faster than you can talk about it. Plan your presentation so you focus on one topic or item at a time. Be careful not to cram too much information on one slide. When including text on a slide, many people follow the 6 × 6 rule: no more than six bullets or lines of text with no more than six words per line. However, the clarity of your message is more important than word count on a slide.

Figure 5-14: Giving a presentation

- Choose appropriate backgrounds, colors, and fonts. Use large fonts (at least 20 point) so the audience can see your text from across the room. Be careful with your choice of font color: many people with color blindness cannot see the difference between red or green, so do not use these colors when formatting text to categorize items.
- Use graphics wisely, so they enhance the story your presentation is trying to convey. When searching online for graphics or images, look for public domain or Creative Commons-licensed content that you can modify, adapt, or build upon for use in your presentations. Verify that you have permission to use any image or photo you did not create yourself and provide attribution as necessary.
- Use animations carefully to enhance the presentation; too many transitions or animations can be a distraction. Pick one or two transitions and apply them to the entire presentation. You want your audience to focus on the slide's message, not the elaborate screen effects.
- Use the spelling and grammar features built into your presentation software. If your slides have spelling or grammatical errors, your content will lose credibility.

When delivering a presentation, follow these tips to keep your audience interested and engaged:

- Check your equipment in advance. If presenting to an in-person audience, be sure your laptop or mobile device is connected to the projector and perform a sound check if your presentation includes music or other audio, and make sure you can hear the audio through any connected speakers. If presenting over a web conferencing tool, make sure you have a steady Internet connection.
- Speak loudly and clearly, as if you are having a conversation with the audience. If the room is large, use a microphone so everyone can hear you. Consider muting the audience members in a web presentation to eliminate unnecessary noise.
- Don't read your slides when giving a presentation. Use as few words on your slides as possible. Instead, let the slides be reminders for you about what to talk about, and the images on the slide a backdrop as you tell your story and look at the audience.
- If in person, try not to stand behind a podium or only in one place. Moving around the stage or the room and interacting with audience members will keep their attention.
- Consider using technology to enhance your presentation. Use a laser pointer or other pointing device when explaining figures on your slides. Use a wireless remote control to advance your slides so you do not have to stand behind a podium computer. Use a tablet computer so you can write on slides with a stylus.
- To ensure accessibility for audience members with visual impairments, send an electronic version to them ahead of time so that they can follow along on a tablet or e-reader.
- Involve your audience. Ask a question and use an interactive polling tool or your web conferencing tool's chat or polling feature (**Figure 5-15**) to invite the audience to respond. Consider having a colleague monitor responses and other comments.

Figure 5-15: Collecting and displaying poll results during a conference

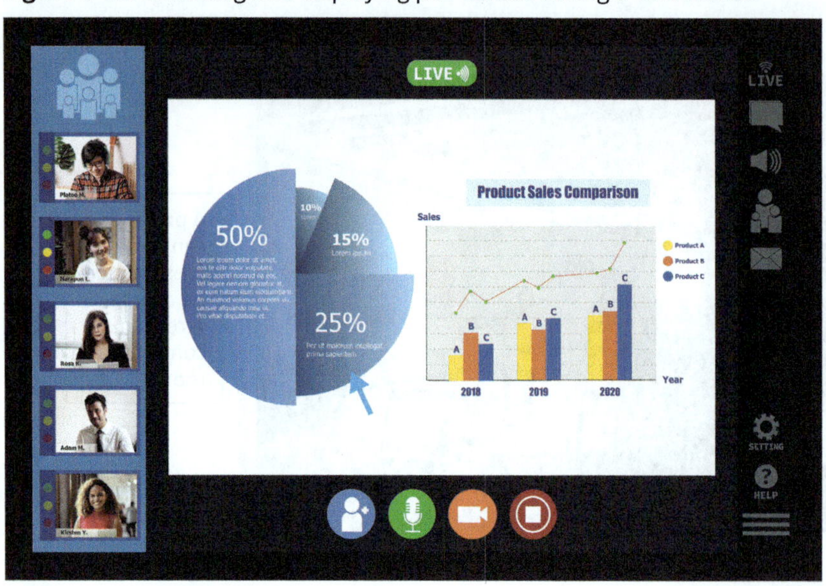

Platoo Studio/Shutterstock.com

- Practice beforehand to get a sense of how much time the presentation will take. If you give a short presentation, such as 5 minutes, you might consider creating a presentation with 20 slides and setting the timing so that slides advance automatically at preset intervals, such as 15 seconds apart. This technique allows the speaker to talk to the audience without having to advance the slides manually. It ensures the presentation will end on time, and the slides become a visual backdrop for engaging the audience with your message.

Use Database Apps

You can use database software to keep track of contacts, addresses, collections, and more. Large enterprises use databases to store vast quantities of data that enable us to shop online, execute web searches, or find friends on social media.

A **database** is a collection of data organized in a manner that allows access, retrieval, and reporting of that data. With database software, you can create, access, and manage a database by adding, updating, and deleting data; filter, sort and retrieve data from the database; and create forms and reports using the data in the database. To create reports from a database, you specify queries, or requests for information from the database.

Databases are used for many purposes. For example:

- Individuals use database software on a personal computer to track contacts, schedules, possessions, or collections.
- Small businesses use database software to process orders, track inventory, maintain customer lists, or manage employee records.
- Companies use databases to store customer relationship management data, such as interactions with customers and their purchases.

Database software provides visual tools to create queries. The database software represents a query in **SQL (Structured Query Language)**, a language that provides a standardized way to request information from a relational database system. Advanced users may type SQL commands directly to interact with a database.

Database software is available as a desktop, server, or web-enabled application. Desktop applications are designed for individual users to run on desktop or laptop computers. When a database has multiple users accessing it simultaneously, a server solution is usually the best. Products such as Oracle, Microsoft SQL Server, and MySQL allow you to organize large amounts of data, and have many users update it simultaneously.

Databases can be stored in a file on a hard disk, a solid-state drive, an external drive, or in cloud storage. Because many users may need to access a database at the same time, and databases can be quite large, enterprise databases generally run on a shared computer called a server. Data can be exported from a database into other programs, such as a spreadsheet program, where you can create charts to visualize data that results from a query. You also can export data from a database to other formats, including HTML, to publish it to the web.

A **relational database management system (RDBMS)**, or **relational database**, is a database that consists of a collection of tables where items are organized in columns and rows. A unique key identifies the value in each row. Common values in different tables can be related, or linked, to each other, so that data does not have to be repeated, making it less prone to error.

Microsoft Access is a popular relational database for personal computers. While Microsoft Access is geared toward consumers and small businesses, SQL Server and Oracle provide advanced database solutions for enterprise use.

Databases and spreadsheets both are used to store data. Database tables are similar to spreadsheets in that the data is stored in rows and columns and can be used in formulas and calculations. However, unlike a spreadsheet, you can establish relationships between data using a database. For example, you can use data from the same table in both a query and a report. If you update the data in the table, the query and report data are updated. Databases are better for storing large quantities of data in order to analyze it. **Big Data** refers to large and complex data sources that defy easy handling with traditional data processing methods.

After opening a database, you choose options to view tables, create queries, and perform other tasks. The software displays commands and work areas appropriate to the view for your task. You enter and edit data in some views. You design, modify, and format layouts of database objects such as tables, queries, reports, and forms in others. You can retrieve data using queries and print reports to see the results.

Database Tables In a relational database, such as Microsoft Access, data is organized into tables and stored electronically in a database. A **table** is a collection of records for a single subject, such as all the customer records, organized in grids of rows and columns, much like worksheets in spreadsheet applications. Tables store data for the database. Columns contain fields; rows contain records. A database can contain one or more tables.

Records are rows of data in a table, representing a complete set of field values for a specific person, place, object, event, or idea. Each piece of data in a database is entered and stored in an area called a **field**, a column containing a specific property for each record, such as a person, place, object, event, or idea. Each field is assigned a **field name**, a column label that describes the field. Fields are defined by their data type, such as text, date, or number. The text data type stores characters that cannot be used in mathematical calculations. Logical data types store yes/no or true/false values. Hyperlinks store data as web addresses.

You can sort table data by one or more fields to create meaningful lists. For example, you might sort customer data by the amounts of their purchases in decreasing order, to see the customers with the largest purchases first. Filters let you see only the records that contain criteria you specify, such as purchases over $1,000. **Figure 5-16** shows a table in an Access database for an animal care center.

Database Queries A **query** is an object that provides a spreadsheet-like view of data, similar to that in tables; it may provide the user with a subset of fields and/or records from one or more tables. Queries extract data from a database based on specified criteria, or conditions, for one or more fields. For example, you might query a sales database to find all the customers in Connecticut who made purchases of more than $1,000 in January and sort the results in decreasing order by the purchase amount. **Figure 5-17** shows a query on the animal care center database that returns the animal names in alphabetical order, with their owner's first and last names.

A query contains the tables and fields you want to search along with the parameters, or pieces of information, you want to find. You can use text criteria or logical operators to specify parameters. The query displays results in a datasheet, which you can view on-screen or print. You can save queries to run later; query results are updated using the current data in the tables each time you run the query.

You can build queries using a visual query builder tool, which converts your query specifications to SQL. SQL provides a series of keywords and commands that advanced users might type directly to create and run queries.

Database Forms A **form** is an object that provides an easy-to-use data entry screen that generally shows only one record at a time. Like paper forms, database forms guide users to fill in information in specified formats. A form is made up of **controls**, which are elements such as labels, text boxes, or combo boxes. Controls specify where content is placed and how it is formatted.

You can use controls to reduce data entry errors. For example, a form might contain a text box in which a database user can type an email address. The form only would accept data that is in the format of a valid email address.

Figure 5-16: Tables, fields, records, and relationships in a database

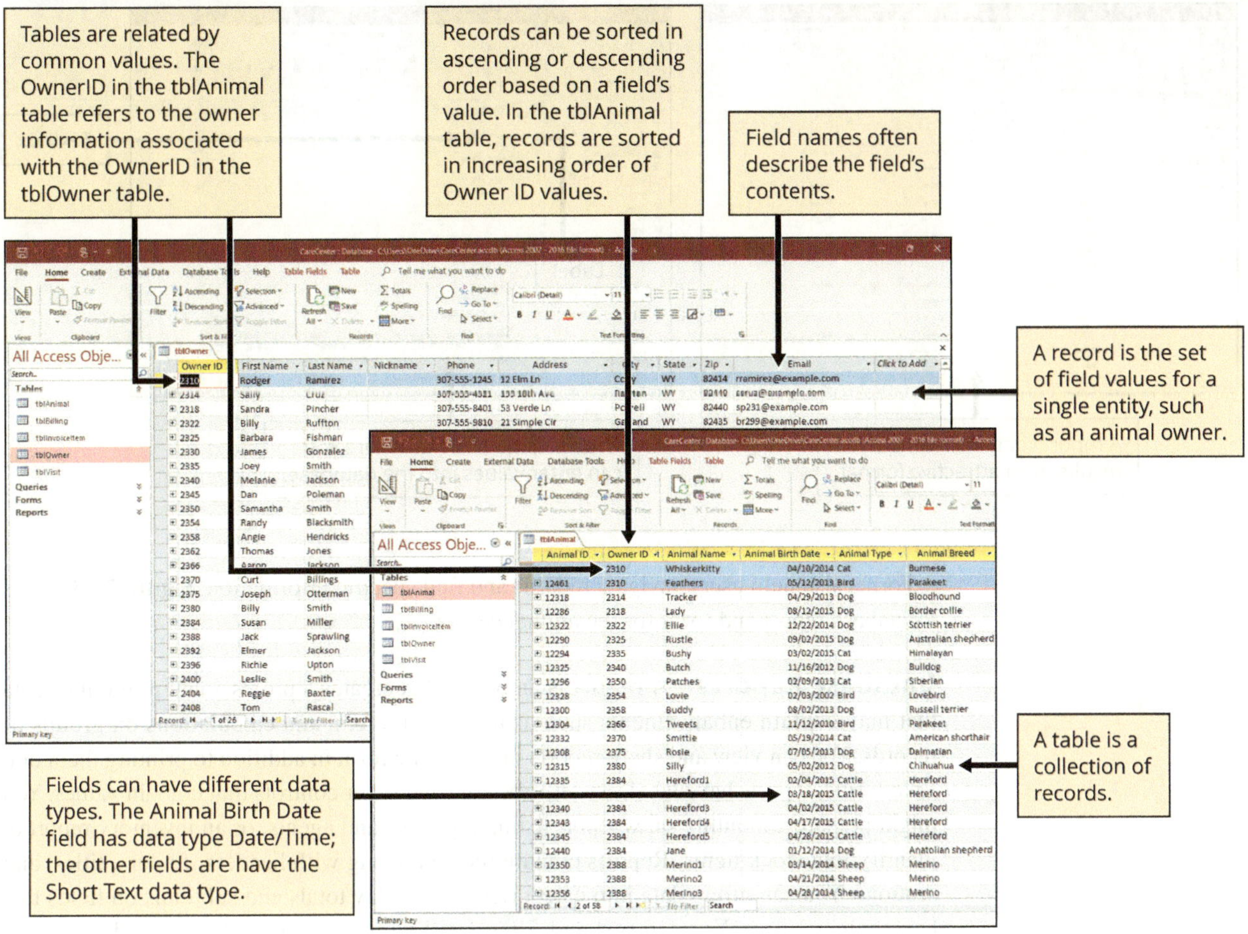

Figure 5-17: Creating and running a database query

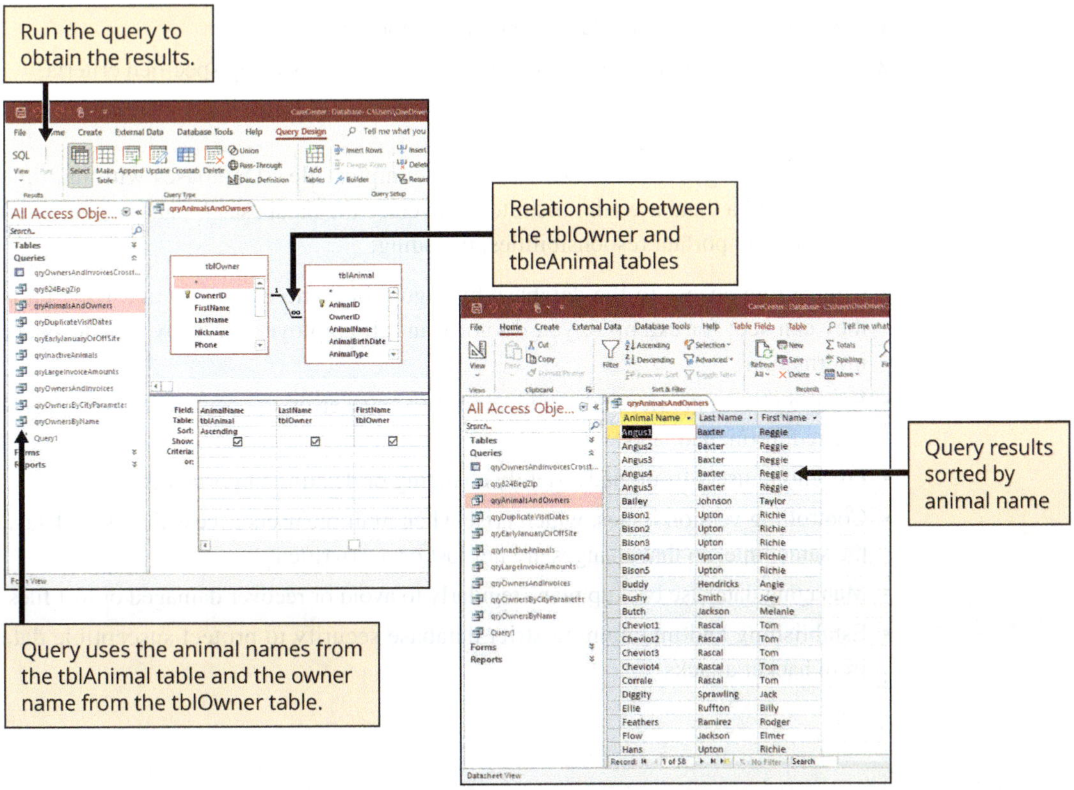

Figure 5-18: Creating and running a database query

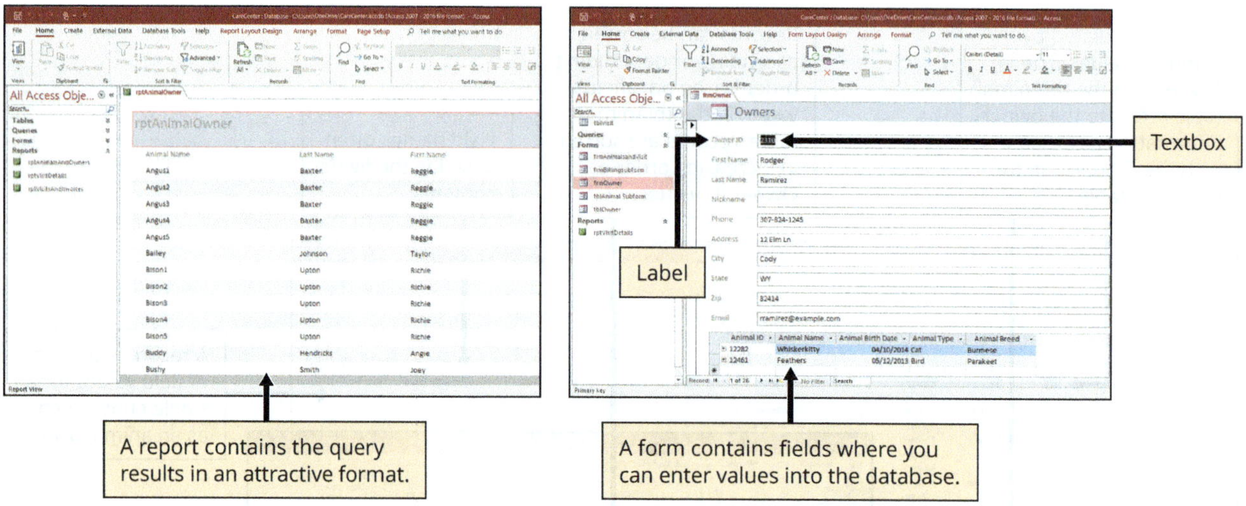

Forms also help users navigate records and find specific information. **Figure 5-18** shows a database report and form for the animal center.

Database Reports A **report** is an object that creates a professional printout of data that may contain enhancements such as headers, footers, and calculations on groups of records. You can view and share reports in electronic form in addition to printing them out. Like forms, reports have labels to describe data and other controls that contain values. You might prepare a monthly sales report listing top deals and agents, or an inventory report to identify low-stock items. Reports contain the data along with headers, footers, titles, and sections. You can group data into categories and display totals and subtotals on fields that have numeric data. You can sort and filter data by one or more fields, and add graphics such as charts, diagrams, or a company's logo.

Follow these steps to create a report:

1. Specify the format and layout options for the report.
2. Identify data to include based on a data set or queries using specified criteria.
3. Run the report to populate it with data from the database.

Database Management Databases are complex files. Databases with multiple users usually need a database administrator to oversee the database. A database administrator has several important responsibilities, including:

- Controlling access to the database by regulating who can use it and what parts they can see; for example, you do not want all employees to view private salary information
- Ensuring data integrity and minimizing data entry errors by controlling how data is entered, formatted, and stored
- Preventing users from inadvertently changing or deleting important data
- Controlling version issues, which arise when multiple users access the same data at the same time, so that changes are not lost or overwritten
- Managing database backup plans regularly to avoid or recover damaged or lost files
- Establishing and maintaining strict database security to protect susceptible data from hacker attacks

Recognize Graphics Apps

To create digital sketches, resize or add special effects to digital photos, or add titles and credits to a video, you will want to use graphics apps. Graphics apps include tools for creating drawings and three-dimensional objects and editing photos and videos. Graphics apps let you create multimedia to include in letters and reports, presentations, spreadsheets, and other documents.

Graphics and media apps allow you to interact with digital media. With photo editing apps, you can modify digital images, performing actions such as cropping, applying filters, and adding or removing backgrounds and shapes. With video and audio editing apps, you can arrange recorded movie clips, and add music, titles, or credits to videos. With media player apps, you can listen to audio or music, look at photos, and watch videos.

When you need a new banner image for your website, or you want to edit a digital photo, or create a logo for your business, you can use graphics software to accomplish the task. You can create, view, manipulate, and print many types of digital images using graphics programs and apps.

Digital images are stored either in bitmap, sometimes called raster, or vector format. **Bitmap** images, also called **raster** images, are based on a grid of square colored dots, called **pixels** (picture elements). A bitmap assigns a color to each pixel in a graphic. The large number and small size of pixels gives your eye the illusion of continuity, and results in a realistic looking image (see **Figure 5-19**). A high-resolution photo can contain thousands of pixels, so bitmap files can be large and difficult to modify. Resizing the bitmap image can distort it and decrease its resolution.

Vector graphics consist of shapes, curves, lines, and text created by mathematical formulas. Vector graphics are useful for images that can be shrunk or enlarged and still maintain their crisp outlines and clarity. Many company logos are designed as vector graphics because they need to scale to different sizes. They must look sharp when shrunk to fit on business cards as well as when they are enlarged to display on webpages or print on large signs.

Figure 5-19: Comparing vector and bitmap images

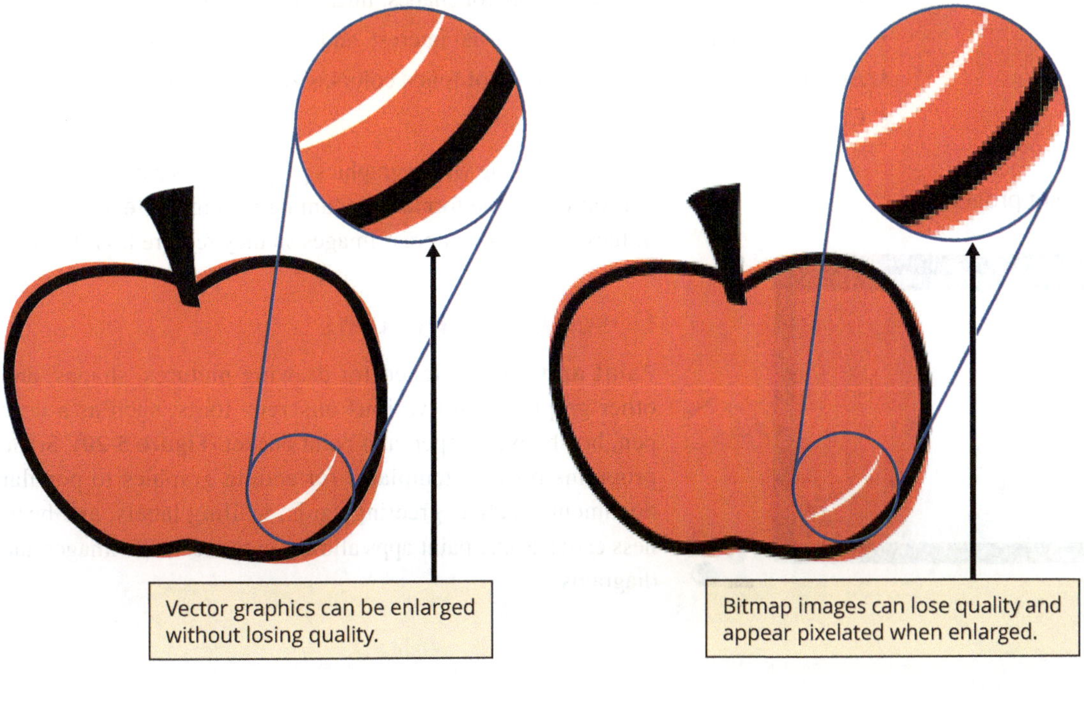

Table 5-12: Popular graphics formats

Name	Extension	Description
Bitmap	.bmp	Uncompressed file format that codes a value for each pixel. Files can be large.
TIFF (Tagged Image File Format)	.tiff	Large image format commonly used for print publishing because it maintains quality. Avoid using on webpages because of the large file sizes.
JPEG (Joint Photographic Experts Group)	.jpg	A compressed image file format usually used to save photos taken with digital cameras. Useful for images on webpages and in documents, because they have high quality and small file sizes.
GIF (Graphics Interchange Format)	.gif	A proprietary compressed graphics format that supports images with animation and transparent backgrounds.
PNG (Portable Networks Graphics)	.png	An open compressed format that has replaced GIF in many cases. Supports images with transparent backgrounds. Low resolution images that you can edit without losing quality. Great for use on webpages.
Raw data	.raw	Uncompressed and unprocessed data from a digital camera, usually used by professional photographers.

Most clip art images are stored as vector graphics. **Clip art** is a collective term for pre-made pictures and symbols you can use in electronic documents. Clip art libraries include images that are available sometimes for free, or for a small fee. Clip art is a quick way to add simple graphics to your work.

Graphics software programs use a variety of drawing and editing tools to create, modify, and enhance images. You can use tools to change the size, crop, rotate, and flip an image. Many programs have features to adjust the brightness, color saturation, and contrast of photos. Many graphics programs allow you to:

- Use a mouse or stylus to draw on the screen using a crayon, pencil, paintbrush, or calligraphy pen, and set the color and thickness
- Use shape tools to create lines, circles, rectangles, arrows, and callouts
- Use color palettes to specify colors for shapes, lines, and borders
- Add filters and effects to provide visual interest, and adjust brightness and contrast
- Add text to graphics using a variety of fonts, colors, sizes, and styles
- Crop or resize an image

When working with a graphics program, you can save images in a variety of file formats, as summarized in **Table 5-12**. Some of these formats compress images so they require less storage.

Figure 5-20: Using a paint program

Describe Paint Apps

Paint apps are designed for drawing pictures, shapes, and other graphics with various onscreen tools, such as a text, pen, brush, eyedropper, and paint bucket (**Figure 5-20**). Some programs provide templates for adding graphics to popular documents such as greeting cards, mailing labels, and business cards. Some paint apps allow you to create 3D images and diagrams.

Microsoft Paint and Paint 3D are easy-to-use paint programs. GIMP is a free paint program you can download, and SumoPaint is a free web-based paint app with many features.

Describe Photo Editing Apps

Photo and image editing apps provide the capabilities of paint apps and let you enhance and modify existing photos and images. Modifications can include adjusting or enhancing brightness, contrast, saturation, sharpness, or tint (**Figure 5-21**).

Image editing software for the home or small business user provides an easy-to-use interface; includes tools to draw pictures, shapes, and other images; and provides the capability of modifying existing graphics and photos. Lightroom and Adobe Photoshop are popular image and photo editing apps. Word processing, presentation, and other productivity applications usually include basic image editing capabilities.

Before copying or downloading any image or photo you did not create, you need to find out its copyright status. You many need to purchase the image, or simply give credit to the owner. An image owner or creator may provide you with a license that specifies how you can use the image. Some images can be edited or manipulated, but others cannot. Before manipulating any image, even ones that you create or own, consider any ethical implications. If your edits make the image misleading or inaccurate and you are using it to support an argument, that may not be ethical. Also be aware of how any appearance changes to a person in your photo may be viewed by that person.

With photo management apps you can view, organize, sort, search, print, and share digital photos. Some photo management app services such as Google Photos will organize your photos for you based on the date, time, or location where they were taken. They use advanced image recognition techniques to search your photos for particular items, colors, people, or scenes.

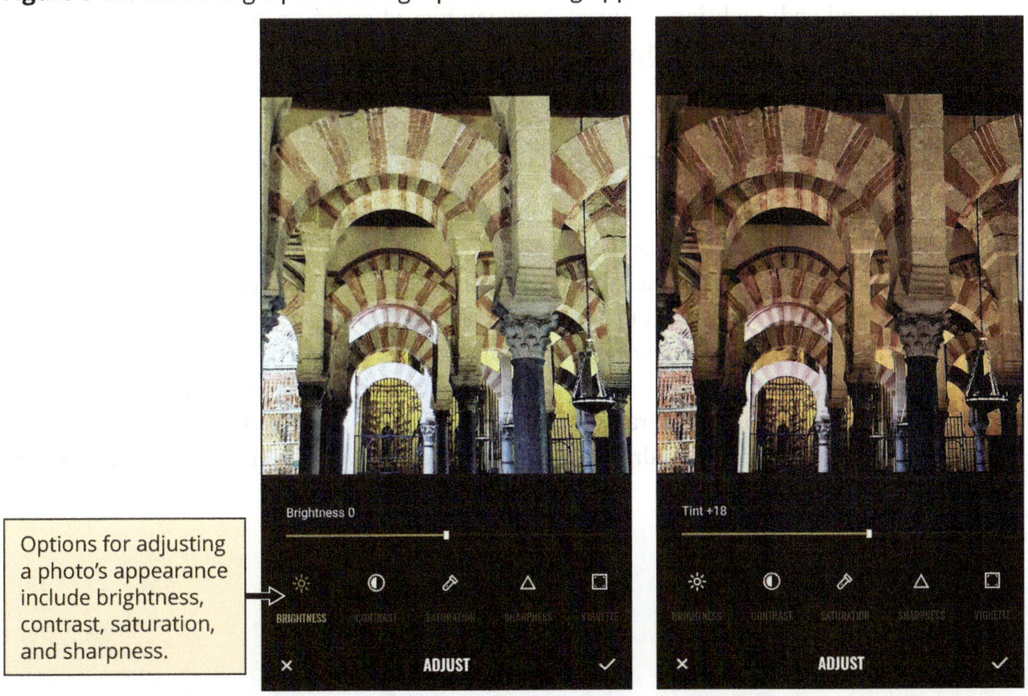

Figure 5-21: Enhancing a photo using a photo editing app

Fotor app

Figure 5-22: Editing a video using a video editing app

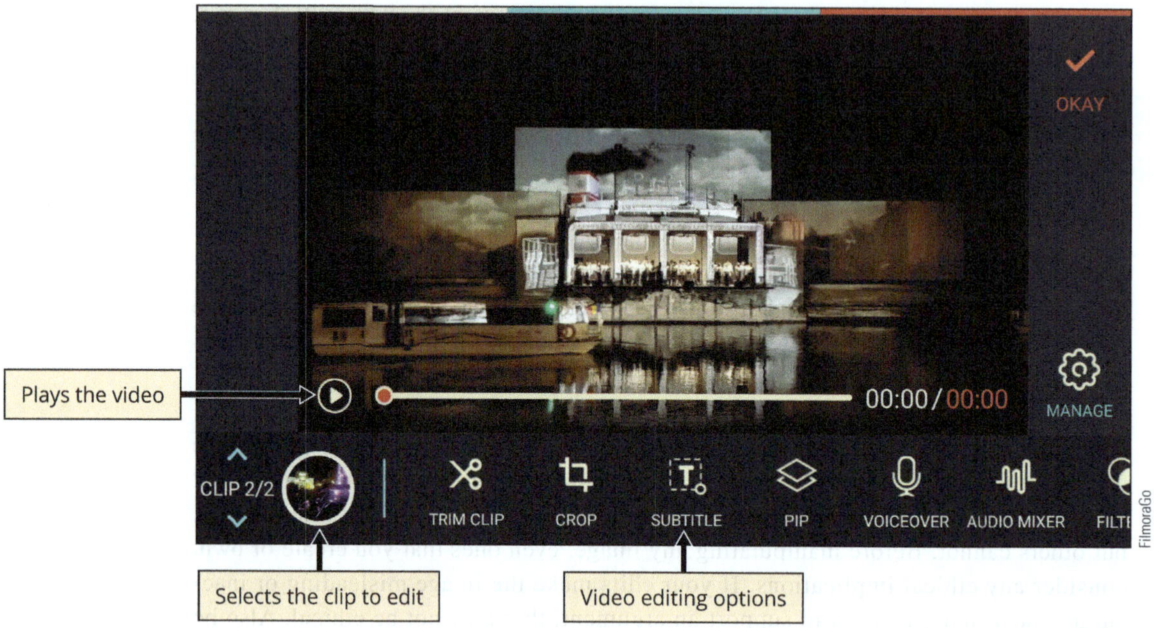

Video editing apps, such as FilmoraGo, allow you to modify a segment of a video, called a clip. For example, you can reduce the length of a video clip, reorder a series of clips, or add special effects, such as a title at the beginning of the video, or credits that scroll up at the end (**Figure 5-22**). Video editing software typically includes audio editing capabilities. With audio editing apps, such as Audacity, you can modify audio clips, produce studio-quality soundtracks, and change the playback speed. Most television shows and movies and many online videos are created or enhanced using video and audio editing software. You can record audio or video using your mobile device, and use audio and video editing apps on your phone, tablet, or computer to edit these files.

Describe Drawing Apps

Drawing apps let you create simple, two-dimensional images. In contrast to paint apps, drawing apps generally create vector graphics. You can modify and resize vector graphics without changing image quality. Some drawing programs can layer graphics one on top of another to create a unique complex graphic or collage of images.

Drawing programs feature freehand drawing tools such as pens or brushes, as well as tools for drawing lines and shapes, and specifying their colors. You can use drawing programs to create logos, diagrams, blueprints, business cards, flyers, and banner graphics for your website. Popular drawing programs include Adobe Illustrator, CorelDraw, and OpenOffice Draw.

Module 5 Summary

The term software is often used interchangeably with apps and programs. While apps and programs mean the same thing, software is any set of instructions that tell the computer or device how to operate. Apps require end-user interaction.

Types of apps include native, web, mobile, and portable. Native apps are written for a specific operating system and installed on a computer or mobile device. Web apps are stored on the Internet and run from within a browser. Mobile apps are native apps that are downloaded and installed on a mobile device. Mobile web apps are stored on an Internet server and can be run entirely in a web browser using a smartphone or tablet. Portable apps run from a removable storage device. Some benefits of mobile apps include that they are easy to create, information can be accessed on the go, and the input methods simplify interactions. Downsides include a slower speed than native apps, and the challenges of typing on a small on-screen keyboard.

Other app categories include: personal interest (travel, news, reference, educational, entertainment, social media, and shopping); communications (browsers, messaging, and video conferencing); and device management (maintenance, file management, screen saver, and security).

Productivity apps are used for personal use to create documents, develop presentations, and stay organized. Many share features in common such as icons on a desktop you can use to open the app, and a window with menus and buttons you can use to access features or issue commands. Some vendors bundle apps into productivity suites you can use to share information between apps. Microsoft Office, Apple iWork, G Suite, and Apache Open Office are examples of productivity suites. You can use collaboration tools to share documents and communicate with colleagues.

Word processing apps enable you to create documents by adding and formatting text and graphics. Spreadsheet apps enable you to manipulate numbers or display numerical data.

You can use presentation apps to create visual aids for presentations, called a presentation or a slide show. When delivering a presentation, always prepare your equipment ahead of time, speak clearly, use technology, and involve the audience. Database apps enable you to store and work with large collections of data. A database can be quite large; enterprise databases generally run on a server. Big data refers to very large data sources that cannot be handled with traditional data processing methods.

In addition to productivity apps, you should be familiar with graphics apps, which allow you to interact with digital media, and include photo editing apps, video and audio editing apps, and media player apps. With graphic programs you can draw, use shape tools, apply color palettes, add filters and effects, add text, and modify images. Paint apps enable you to draw pictures, shapes and other graphics, and possibly 3D graphics. Photo and image editing apps are used to enhance and modify existing photos and images. You can use video editing apps to reduce the length of a video, reorder clips, or add effects. Drawing apps let you create simple, two-dimensional images.

Review Questions

1. A native app runs from ________.
   - **a.** a web browser
   - **b.** a USB flash drive
   - **c.** the cloud
   - **d.** the device upon which it is installed

2. When an app is available as both a web app and a native app, you can ________ the data and settings so that the app is set up the same way on all of your devices.
   - **a.** synchronize
   - **b.** paste
   - **c.** analyze
   - **d.** report

3. Canva is an example of a ________ app.
   - **a.** personal productivity
   - **b.** photo editing
   - **c.** shopping
   - **d.** messaging

4. (True or False) Mobile apps are not as fast as and have fewer features than desktop apps.

5. A screen saver appears ________.
   - **a.** after a period of no keyboard or mouse activity
   - **b.** when you restart the computer or device
   - **c.** when you receive a notification from a messaging app
   - **d.** during a transition between slides in a presentation

6. A named collection of formats that are stored together and can be applied to text or objects is called a _________.
   a. font type
   b. template
   c. style
   d. format

7. In a spreadsheet formula, characters such as "+", "−", "*", and "/" are called _________.
   a. operators
   b. functions
   c. arguments
   d. values

8. In a presentation, an effect that you apply to an object that makes the object appear, disappear, or move is called a(n) _________.
   a. animation
   b. transition
   c. format
   d. 3D image

9. In a database table, a row of data in a table is called a _________.
   a. field
   b. query
   c. form
   d. record

10. Most paint programs produce _________ images.
    a. bitmap
    b. vector
    c. photographic
    d. video still

11. Adobe Illustrator is an example of a _________ app.
    a. photo editing
    b. word processing
    c. drawing
    d. video editing

12. (True or False) Google Photos is an example of a photo management app.

Discussion Questions

1. Explain the differences between native apps and web apps. How can you ensure your settings and data from both types of apps will transfer between devices? Name one reason you would use a portable app. Have you ever had trouble getting your data to appear in both a web and native app? Do you prefer mobile apps or desktop apps? Why?
2. Define the terms read-only access and view-only link in terms of document management. In what other ways can you take advantage of document management tools? Have you ever collaborated on a document with others? For what purpose did/might you use collaboration tools?
3. Define the following database objects: tables, queries, forms, and reports. Come up with an example of a database, and explain how you might use each object within the database. Why is using a form important for data entry? Have you ever used a form on a website or other format to enter data?
4. Differentiate between vector and bitmap graphics. Why might you choose to create a vector graphic? Why might you choose to create a bitmap graphic?

Critical Thinking Activities

1. You teach a class at a community center in your city about technology. A common question you get from attendees of your classes is whether mobile apps are reliable and how to use them. List two pros and cons for using mobile apps. What is your experience with using mobile apps? Why did you choose a mobile app over a native app?
2. You have been asked to give a presentation at your company's annual meeting about the company's finances from the previous year. Name three features of presentation apps you will use for your presentation and why you would choose each. List three pieces of advice for delivering your presentation. As an audience member, what factors do you feel make a presentation successful?

3. You run a pet day care center. You need to keep track of contact information for your customers, their animals, the services provided (such as walking and grooming), and the staff who are assigned to care for them. You also must send out invoices for payment each month. What features of spreadsheet and/or database software might you use to facilitate your business? Explain your choices. Why might you choose a spreadsheet over a database? Do you prefer filling out paper forms over digital? Why or why not?
4. You are taking a class in graphic design and must select a graphics app to create your own project for your final project. Explain the differences between paint, photo editing, and drawing apps, and give an example of each. What ethical concerns do you have about enhancing or modifying graphics?

Apply Your Skills

Sara Jackson is starting her own interior design consulting firm. While she is based in the United Kingdom, her customers will be from all over the world. She will need to use a variety of apps to create presentations and drawings for customers and graphics for her firm's website. She will write work proposals and contracts using a word processing app, manage her firm's income and expenses in a spreadsheet, and track her customers in a database. Sara uses graphic software to adapt customers' photos and videos of their space to demonstrate how it would look with different furnishings.

Working in a small group or by yourself, complete the following:

1. Explain what additional app categories Sara might want to use for her business or personal use, and give an example of how she would use each. Have you used a tool to manage your device? For what purpose?
2. List two examples of how Sara would use each of the following app types for her business: word processing, spreadsheet, presentation, and database. Which of those have you used? For what purpose?
3. Explain what types of tools Sara may have used to create a logo for her business. Give an example of each. In what other ways could she use graphics apps? Why is it important to make sure to use Creative Commons content?

Module 6

Cybersecurity and Safety

In This Module

- Determine the risks associated with cybersecurity attacks
- Describe the hazards associated with using technology
- Apply defenses to repel cyber attacks
- Use protective measures against technology hazards

iStock.com/Giulio Fornasar

Tony Blanco has been hired as an intern at a company that installs solar panels. Because he is completing his degree in cybersecurity at the local college, he works in the company's security operations center (SOC) assisting security managers and technicians who protect the company's computers and networks from cyberattacks. One of Tony's recent assignments was helping the technicians who monitor for signs of attacks and then take action to prevent the attacks from quickly spreading. Tony has begun offering Lunch-and-Learn sessions for employees with hands-on training on how to keep their devices safe.

Consider all the technology devices that you use every day: smartphone, laptop computer, smart watch, tablet, and voice assistant, just to name a few. You use these devices to exchange messages with friends and coworkers, search for a new restaurant, work on school assignments, play games, shop for clothes, and stream movies, among many other activities. But each of our devices has a darker side: as a pathway for attackers to steal our data, invade our privacy, empty our bank accounts, and turn our entire lives upside down in a matter of moments. These attackers, who may be in a coffee shop down the street or a basement halfway across the world, are constantly probing for the tiniest opening to invade our devices and wreak havoc.

In this module, you will examine the risks that come from cybersecurity attacks and the potential dangers associated with using technology. You'll discover strategies for protecting your devices and your personal information from attackers. You will also learn how to use protective measures against additional technology hazards, such as the risks associated with data collection and physical, behavioral, and environmental risks. As you reflect on what you learn in this module, ask yourself: Do you know the cyberattacks that your devices face daily? Have you ever suffered neck or arm pain from using your computer? Are you aware of how to harden your devices, to defend them from attackers? Do you want to lessen the environmental impact when disposing of old technology?

Determine the Risks Associated with Cybersecurity Attacks

Cybersecurity events have become commonplace, with stories such as "Hackers Exploit Gaping Loophole to Give Their Malware Access," "U.S. Government Agencies Earn a Grade of D For Cybersecurity," and "EV Charging Stations Are the Latest Targets of Attackers" hitting newsfeeds every day. What exactly is cybersecurity? Who are the attackers? By understanding the different types of attacks that can occur, you can begin to understand the importance of actively following proactive security recommendations.

Define Cybersecurity

The word "security," which comes from the Latin meaning freedom from care, means something that makes us safe. You take steps every day to stay safe: you press a button on a key fob to lock your car, you stay aware of your surroundings when walking at night, and you use a shredder to destroy documents that contain personal information.

Cybersecurity refers to the practices, processes, and technologies used to protect devices, networks, and programs that process and store data in an electronic form. In short, cybersecurity includes everything you do to keep your electronic devices and the data stored on them safe.

Figure 6-1: Attacker wants to steal your money

Sasun Bughdaryan/Shutterstock.com

Describe the Importance of Cybersecurity

Cybersecurity is important because the primary goal of cyber attackers is to make money from their attacks, often leaving us responsible to repay the stolen funds and spend hundreds of hours trying to resolve the situation (**Figure 6-1**). While at one time banks and financial institutions would absorb any financial losses that occurred due to a cyber event so that a customer would not be responsible, that is no longer the case.

One type of data that cyber attackers want to steal is your payment card numbers, such as debit cards, credit cards, or gift cards. Once the attacker has these numbers, they can use them to purchase thousands of dollars of merchandise online—without having the actual card—before you or your bank is even aware the number has been stolen.

Another type of data that attackers steal is your personal information, such as a Social Security number, which they then use to impersonate you for financial gain. The thieves may create new bank or credit card accounts under your name and then charge large purchases to these accounts, leaving you responsible for the debts and ruining your credit rating. This type of criminal activity is known as **identity theft**, using someone's personal information, such as their name, Social Security number, or credit card number, to commit financial fraud. A new victim of identity theft occurs every two seconds. Each year, losses from reported identity theft exceeds $3 billion. In one year, 47 percent of Americans experienced financial identity theft, and 30 percent have experienced identity theft more than once.

Explain the Difficulties of Cybersecurity

Why is it so hard to prevent attacks? Can't we just install a software program to thwart all attacks or add a hardware device to block any intruders? Unfortunately, there is no one-size-fits-all cybersecurity solution. Preventing attacks involves addressing a constantly evolving host of difficulties, which include:

- **Universally connected devices**. It is unthinkable today for any technology device—not only a laptop computer or tablet but also a smartphone, door lock, or doorbell camera—not to be connected to the Internet. Although this connectivity provides enormous benefits, it also makes it easy for an attacker halfway around world to silently launch an attack against any connected device.

Figure 6-2: Cybersecurity can be confusing

fizkes/Shutterstock.com

- **Increased speed of attacks**. Attackers can quickly scan millions and millions of devices to find weaknesses and then immediately launch attacks with unprecedented speed. And these attack tools will "scan and attack" completely on their own without any human help, thus increasing the speed at which users are attacked.
- **Greater sophistication of attacks**. Attacks are becoming more complex, making it difficult to detect and defend against them. Attackers today use common Internet communications and web applications to hide their attacks, making it more difficult to distinguish an attack from legitimate network traffic. Other attack tools even vary their behavior, so the same attack appears differently each time, further complicating detection.
- **User confusion**. The one factor that accounts for the greatest difficulty in preventing attacks is user confusion (**Figure 6-2**). For many years, end users have been called upon to make often difficult security decisions and then perform complicated procedures on their devices—often with little information to guide them. This is compounded even more by cybersecurity information circulated through consumer news outlets and websites that is often contradictory, inaccurate, or misleading, resulting in even more user confusion.

Catalog Types of Attackers

At one time the word "hacker" was used to refer to a person who had advanced computer skills that were used to attack computers. However, as cybersecurity attacks have changed, so too have the terms used to refer to attackers. Today, **threat actor** is the formal term used to describe an individual or entity responsible for launching cyberattacks. The informal or generic term is simply *attacker*.

Attackers are classified in distinct categories:

- **Cybercriminals**. The very first cyberattacks that occurred were mainly for the attackers to show off their technology skills (fame). However, that soon gave way to attackers with the focused goal of financial gain (fortune). A person who conducts cyber-related attacks for financial gain is a **cybercriminal**. Cybercriminals seek out not only individual users but also businesses and even government computers to steal data and make money.
- **Script kiddies**. **Script kiddies** are typically younger individuals who want to attack computers but lack the knowledge of computers and networks needed to do so. Script kiddies instead do their work by downloading automated attack software (scripts) from websites and using it to perform attacks acts (**Figure 6-3**).
- **Brokers**. Many software companies offer money to individuals who uncover vulnerabilities in their software and then privately report it so that they can be fixed. However, some individuals who uncover vulnerabilities do not report it to the software company but instead sell them to the highest bidder. Known as **brokers**, these individuals are willing to sell their knowledge of a hardware or software vulnerability to other attackers or even governments. The buyers are willing to pay a high price because this vulnerability is unknown to anyone else and thus is unlikely to be fixed until after new attacks based on it are already widespread.

Figure 6-3: Script kiddie web site

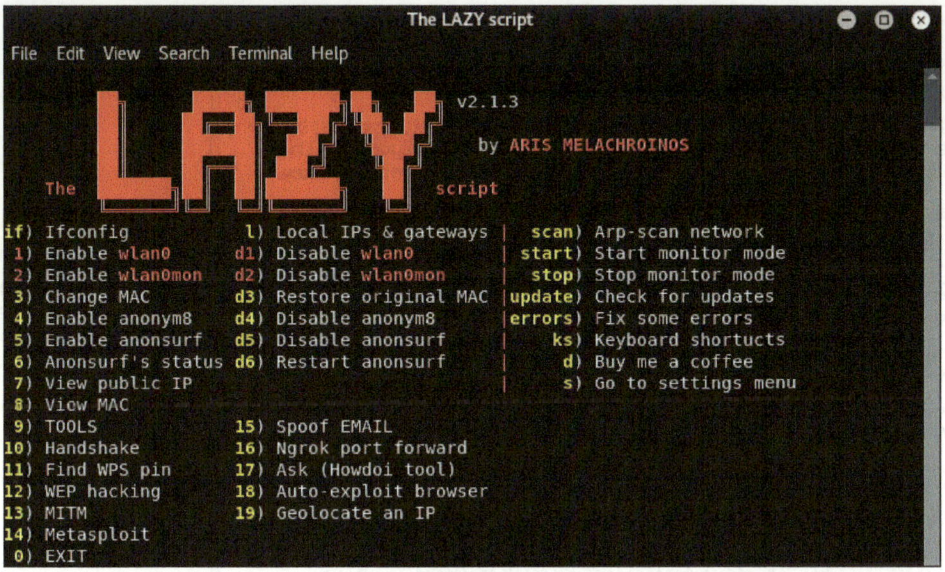

- **Cyberterrorists.** Terrorism today has expanded from planting bombs or other acts of violence against innocent civilians to cyberattacks on a nation's network and computer infrastructure, such as bringing down a power grid or crippling a water treatment plant. Known as **cyberterrorists**, the goal of these attackers are to cause disruption and panic among citizens and their motivation is ideological (relating to their principles or beliefs). Cyberterrorists are the attackers that are most feared, for it is almost impossible to predict when or where an attack may occur.
- **Hacktivists.** Another type of attacker who is strongly motivated by principles or beliefs is a **hacktivist** (a combination of the words *hack* and *activism*) who typically acts alone or in small groups and targets businesses or government agencies with which they disagree. For example, one hacktivist group disabled the website belonging to a bank because that bank had stopped accepting online payments that were deposited into accounts belonging to groups supported by hacktivists. Today many hacktivists work through "disinformation campaigns" by spreading fake news and supporting conspiracy theories.
- **State actors.** Instead of using an army to march across the battlefield to strike an adversary, governments are increasingly employing cyber attackers known as **state actors** to launch cyberattacks against the government's foes. Their foes may be foreign governments or even citizens of their own nation that the government considers hostile or threatening.

Contrast Different Cybersecurity Attacks

There are two types of cyberattacks, malware attacks and social engineering attacks.

Malware Attacks

Most successful attacks use **malware**, software that enters a device without the user's knowledge or permission and then performs a harmful action. The term combines two words, *mal*icious and soft*ware*, and refers to a wide variety of damaging programs.

Kidnapping is a crime that involves capturing a person and then holding them as a captive until a ransom is paid for their release. In a similar fashion, cyber attackers can perform a "kidnapping" of a user's device and hold it "hostage" until a ransom is paid. **Ransomware** is a type of malware that prevents a user's device from properly and fully

Figure 6-4: Ransomware message

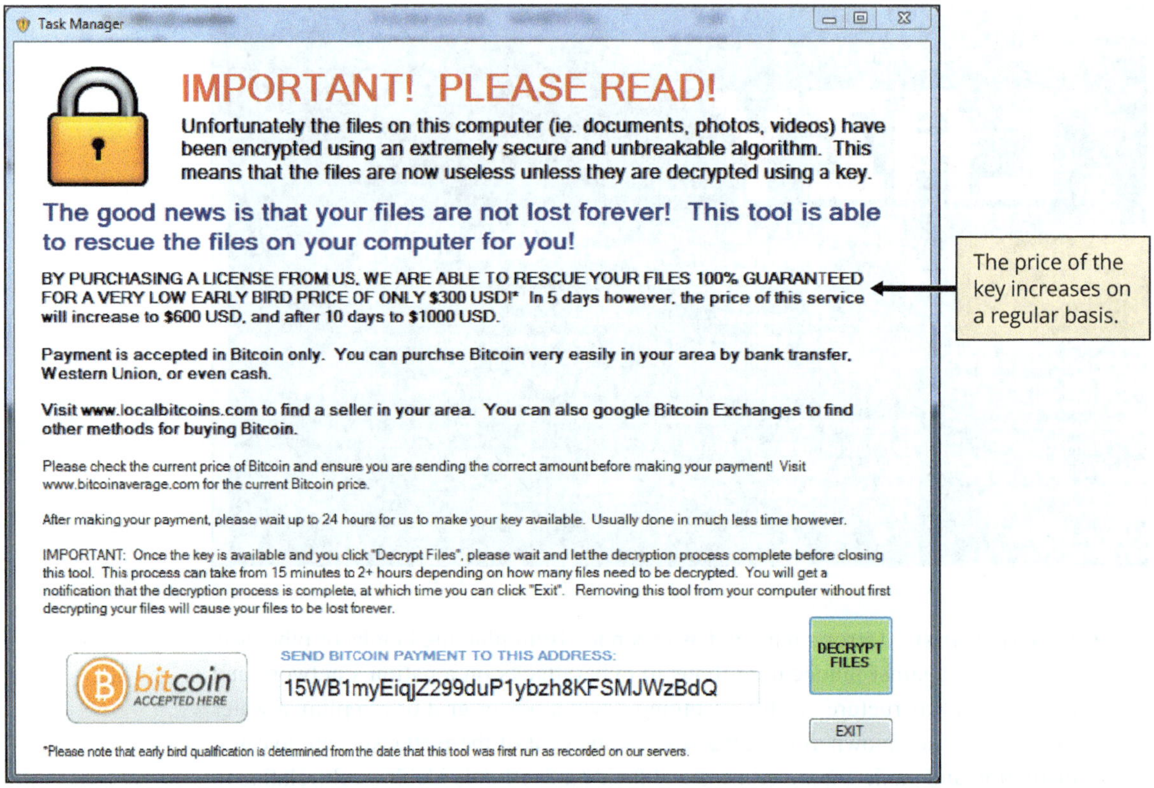

functioning until the user pays a fee. The ransomware embeds itself onto the computer in such a way that it cannot be bypassed, even by rebooting. For instance, a ransomware attack could lock a spreadsheet containing important financial data or a document of a research paper. After the files have been locked, a message appears on the screen telling the victim what has occurred and that money must be paid to receive a key to unlock the files (**Figure 6-4**). Usually, the message contains a warning claiming that the cost for the key increases every few hours, the goal being to increase the victim's sense of urgency and spur them to action. On some occasions, attackers will start deleting locked files and increase the number deleted each hour until they receive payment. And, if the ransom is not paid by a specific deadline, the key to unlock the files can never be purchased.

Another type of malware is a **keylogger**, which captures a user's keystrokes and may also capture screen images and other information without the user's knowledge. The attacker can then search the captured text for any useful information such as passwords, credit card numbers, or personal information. Keyloggers can go far beyond just capturing a user's keystrokes. These programs can also make screen captures of everything that is on the user's screen and silently turn on the computer's web camera to record images of the user (**Figure 6-5**).

According to ancient legend, the Greeks won the Trojan War by hiding soldiers in a large hollow wooden horse that was presented as a gift to the city of Troy. Once the horse was wheeled into the fortified city, the soldiers crept out of the horse during the night and attacked the unsuspecting defenders. A computer **Trojan** is malware that pretends to be a program performing a normal activity but also does something malicious. For example, a user might download what is advertised as a calendar program, yet when it is installed, in

Figure 6-5: Keylogger

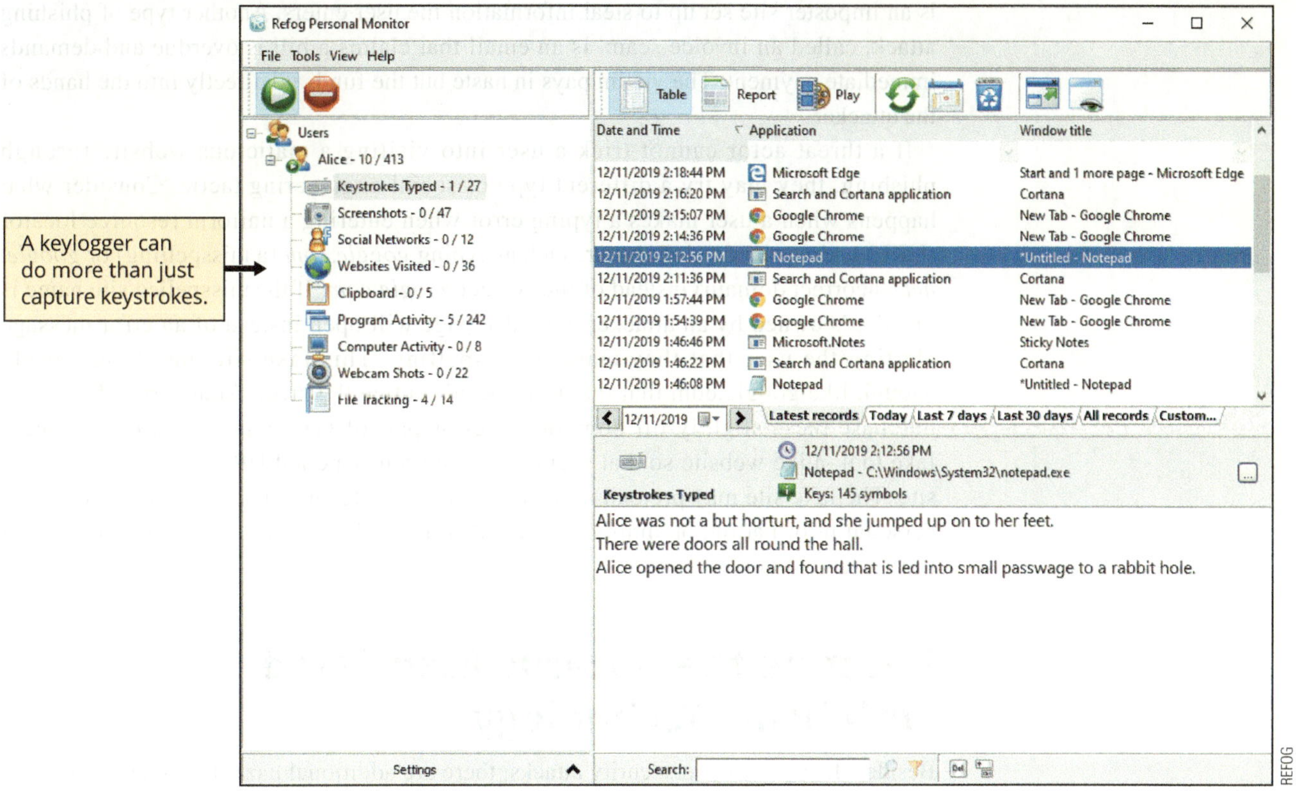

addition to providing a calendar, it also installs malware that scans the system for credit card numbers and passwords, connects through the network to a remote system, and then transmits that information to the attacker.

A computer **virus** is a computer program designed to copy itself into other programs with the intention of causing mischief or harm, usually without the user's knowledge or permission. Each time the infected program is launched, or the data file is opened, the virus first unloads its payload to perform a malicious action (delete files, prevent programs from launching, steal data to be sent to another computer, cause a computer to crash repeatedly, turn off the computer's security settings, etc.). Then the virus reproduces itself by inserting its code into another file. When a user copies or emails an infected file to another computer, that device then becomes infected with the virus.

Social Engineering Attacks Not all attacks rely on malware; in fact, many cyberattacks use little if any technology to achieve their goals. **Social engineering** is a category of cyberattack that attempts to trick the victim into giving valuable information to the attacker.

One of the most common attacks based on social engineering is **phishing**, which is sending an email or displaying a web announcement that falsely claims to be from a legitimate enterprise in an attempt to trick the user into giving private information. The word phishing is a variation on the word "fishing," with the idea being that bait is thrown out knowing that while most will ignore it, some will "bite." For example, a user may receive an email that looks like it came from their bank. They are directed to a website that looks like it is their bank's website where they must update personal information, such as passwords, credit card numbers, Social Security numbers, bank account numbers, or other information. However, the email is from an attacker and the website is an imposter site set up to steal information the user enters. Another type of phishing attack, called an invoice scam, is an email that claims a bill is overdue and demands immediate payment. The victim pays in haste but the funds go directly into the hands of the attacker.

If a threat actor cannot trick a user into visiting a malicious website through phishing, they may try a different type of social engineering tactic. Consider what happens when a user makes a typing error when entering a uniform resource locator (URL) address in a web browser, such as typing *goggle.com* (a misspelling) or *google.net* (incorrect domain) instead of the correct *google.com*. If the misspelled site name is one that's owned by an attacker, the false page will open instead of an error message alerting the user that they made a misspelling. This fake site may look closely enough like google.com that the user doesn't notice the error. Attackers deliberately purchase these slightly-off domain names as part of **typo squatting**, registering a fake look-alike website so that users who enter a misspelled URL are directed to that site. The fake site may pretend to be the legitimate site and trick the user into entering personal information, or simply display ads for which the attacker receives money for traffic generated to the site.

Describe the Hazards Associated with Using Technology

Besides the risk of cybersecurity attacks, there are additional hazards that are associated with using technology. These include the risk of data collection, as well as physical, behavioral, and environmental hazards.

Narrate the Risks of Data Collection

You and everyone else have a large amount of personal data: your name, where you live, your Social Security number, your school records, your health information, and on and on. Sometimes you are asked to give some of that personal data to another person or entity. For example, your physician may ask you to provide your address and mobile phone number because they have a legitimate business need for that information, and they openly ask you for that information.

However, increasingly your personal data is collected in a concealed and questionable way—concealed when it's done without your knowledge and express permission; and questionable when there is not a clear business case for gathering it.

Many organizations today take advantage of the fact that every time you use technology you leave behind a "data trail," which is a digital record of your activity. This includes obvious activities such as sending an email, browsing the Internet, and making a purchase. Yet it also includes any activity using technology.

Merchants collect digital data using tracking features, often known simply as trackers, that are embedded in virtually every app on your smartphone; in fact, the average app has six trackers. Trackers allow third parties to collect data from your interaction with the app along with exactly where you are located throughout the day. As people perform more and more everyday activities electronically, using more and more interconnected devices, the volume of data compiled on you grows exponentially.

Table 6-1: Risks of data collection

Risk	Explanation
The data is gathered and kept in secret.	You have no formal rights to find out what private information is being gathered, who gathers it, or how it is being used.
The accuracy of the data cannot be verified.	Because you do not have the right to correct or control what personal information is gathered, if it contains errors you cannot check and correct it.
Identity theft can impact the accuracy of data.	Victims of identity theft will often have information added to their profile that was the result of actions by the identity thieves with no right to see or correct the information.
Data is being used for important decisions.	Private data is being used on an ever-increasing basis to determine eligibility in significant life opportunities, such as jobs, consumer credit, insurance, and identity verification.

This data collection results in advertisements appearing in our web browsers and through email messages that we receive and is called **adware**. Adware itself is not considered harmful. Although some users find it annoying, other users like that the ads they receive are tailored to their interests. However, beyond adware there are serious risks with this secret collection and use of your private data, as described in **Table 6-1**.

Define Other Technology Hazards

"Warning: Using This Device Could Be Hazardous to Your Safety and Health" is a label you may never see on a computer. But using a computer can carry hazards that are more tangible than that of data collection, including physical, behavioral, and environmental.

Physical Hazards Many users of technology devices report aches and pains associated with repeated and long-term usage of the devices, a hazard known collectively as **repetitive strain injury (RSI)**. Also called repetitive stress injury, RSI impacts your muscles, nerves, tendons, and ligaments, and most often affects the upper parts of the body, including elbows, forearms, hands, neck, shoulders, and wrists. It is usually caused by one or more of three factors, listed in **Table 6-2**.

Table 6-2: Causes and examples of RSI

Cause	Description	Example
Repetitive activity	Repeating the same activity over a lengthy time period	Typing on a keyboard for multiple hours every day over several years
Improper technique	Using the wrong procedure or posture	Slouching in a chair
Uninterrupted intensity	Performing the same high-level activity without frequent periods of rest	Working at a computer all day with no breaks

Figure 6-6: Incorrect posture while working on a computer

Many computer users suffer from RSI that is brought about through using an improper technique for sitting at a computer. Examples of incorrect posture while working on a computer include: the user is not sitting up straight in the chair, he is too close to the computer screen, and glare from the window behind him is reflecting off the screen (**Figure 6-6**). Being too close to a screen or looking at screens without regular breaks can cause eyestrain.

Behavioral Hazards Just as there are hazards to physical health from using digital devices, there also are behavioral health hazards. These hazards are sometimes more difficult to observe but every bit as serious as RSI and other physical hazards.

One behavioral hazard is **technology addiction**, which occurs when a user is obsessed with using a technology device and cannot walk away from it without feeling extreme anxiety. Because near-constant use of technology has become the norm, technology addiction can be difficult to identify in a friend or companion, and in yourself. Some symptoms may include having significant mood swings, focusing exclusively on the Internet and digital media, being unable to control how much time they spend on technology, and showing withdrawal symptoms when not using the Internet or technology.

In addition to technology addiction, there are other behavioral risks associated with using technology, including:

- **Sedentary lifestyle**. Too much time spent using a technology device often results in too little time for physical activity and can contribute to an overall sedentary lifestyle.
- **Psychological concerns**. Excessive use of technology has been associated with several psychological mental health concerns such as poor self-confidence, anxiety, depression, lower emotional stability, and even lower life satisfaction.
- **Hindered social interaction**. Users who spend excessive amounts of time using technology often resist face-to-face interaction with others, and this may hinder social skill development or even cause social withdrawal.

Another risk that can result in serious emotional harm is a type of bullying, which is the act of using strength or influence to intimidate someone else. **Cyberbullying** is bullying that takes place on technology devices like smartphones, computers, and tablets using online social media platforms, public online forums, gaming sites, text messaging, or email. Cyberbullying includes sending, posting, or sharing negative, harmful, mean-spirited, and

Table 6-3: Harmful features of cyberbullying

Feature	Bullying	Cyberbullying
Seems to never end	A person may be bullied at school or work, but once the person goes home the bullying ceases.	Because cyberbullying comments posted online are visible all the time, to the victim the bullying never ends.
Everyone knows about it	Mean-spirited words spoken to a victim may be witnessed only by those who are nearby.	A cyberbully can post comments online that everyone can read.
May follow for a lifetime	Bullying usually stops when the person or victim leaves the school or organization.	Posted cyberbullying comments may remain visible online for years and even follow the victim through life, impacting college admissions and employment.

usually false content about another person. It can even include sharing personal or private information to cause embarrassment or humiliation to that person before others. Cyberbullying, once it begins, is difficult to control because it is done online and many web sites consider it as "free speech" that should not be censored. **Table 6-3** compares features of bullying to cyberbullying.

Figure 6-7: E-waste

Environmental Hazards What happens to an electronic device when it reaches the end of its useful life? It's estimated that only 12 percent of these unwanted devices are taken to an approved recycling center to be dismantled and the components reused, while the rest are thrown away. This results in large amounts of **e-waste**, or electronic waste, which is electrical or electronic equipment that no longer works or is no longer being used. Some of this equipment may be broken and cannot be repaired so it is thrown away as garbage. Other equipment may still work but the owner no longer wants it and just throws it away. About 40 million tons of e-waste are generated each year worldwide, through people throwing out devices (**Figure 6-7**). That's the equivalent of disposing of 800 laptop computers every second.

E-waste is a hazard to humans. Computer parts contain harmful toxins including mercury, lead, cadmium, polybrominated flame retardants, barium, and lithium. Most e-waste is incinerated, which releases these toxins into the air. E-waste that is buried in landfills can eventually contaminate the ground and water supply, causing harm to the environment and all living beings.

Apply Defenses to Repel Cyber Attacks

As an informed computer user, you can apply defenses to block cyberattacks. To do so effectively, it's important to acknowledge a basic principle about the relationship between security and convenience: it is not directly proportional. That is, as security around your data and devices increases, convenience does not increase. Instead, this relationship is inversely proportional: as security increases, convenience actually decreases. In other words, the more secure something becomes, the less convenient it may become to use. In addition, increasing its convenience usually decreases its security (**Figure 6-8**).

Figure 6-8: Relationship of security to convenience

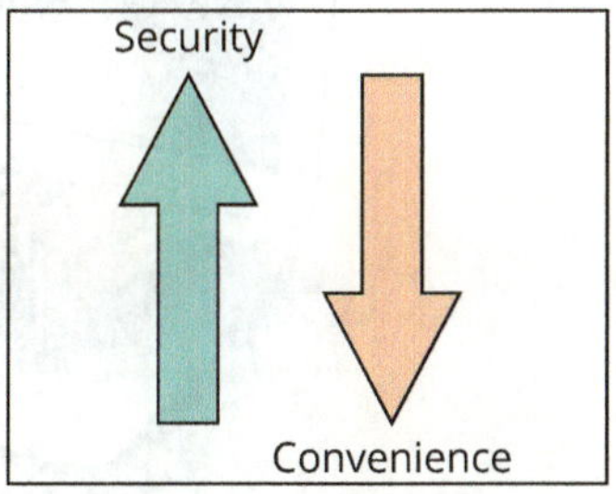

Consider accessing your bank's online website. While it would be quicker and easier for you not to enter a username and password, that extra protection is well worth the cost of the extra security that it gives. Security is often described as sacrificing some convenience for the sake of safety. When considering whether an extra security measure is worth the time or trouble, remember the consequences of not protecting your device. You can have money taken from your bank account, an imposter taking out a loan in your name, or any number of serious issues.

Use Strong Authentication

Authentication is the process of ensuring that the person requesting access to a computer or other resources is authentic, and not an imposter. There are different types of authentications or "proof of genuineness" that can be presented.

Passwords Virtually all user technology devices rely on something that only the "real" user knows and an imposter does not know for authentication. This is done by entering a **password**, a string of uppercase and lowercase letters, numbers, and symbols that when entered correctly, allow you to open a password-protected device or account. A secret password serves as the key to unlock access to a device by proving you are the authentic user (**Figure 6-9**).

Despite their widespread use, passwords provide only weak protection. The weakness is due not to technology but to the frailties of human memory. First, the best passwords are long and complex, but these are difficult to memorize and then accurately recall. Second, because passwords should be unique for each device, users must remember multiple passwords for all their devices and accounts. These can include different computers and mobile devices at work, school, and home; multiple email accounts; online banking; Internet site accounts; social media accounts, and so on.

To make signing on easier, many users instead take shortcuts that make the process more convenient but much less secure. They may use a **weak password**, which is one that is short in length (less than 15 characters), and/or uses a common word as a password (princess), a predictable sequence of characters (abc123), or personal information (Braden). Another common shortcut is to repeat the same password on more than on device or account, which, if the password were discovered, would compromise not just one account but all accounts that use that same password. Weak and duplicate passwords make your devices and accounts vulnerable to an attacker.

Figure 6-9: Password

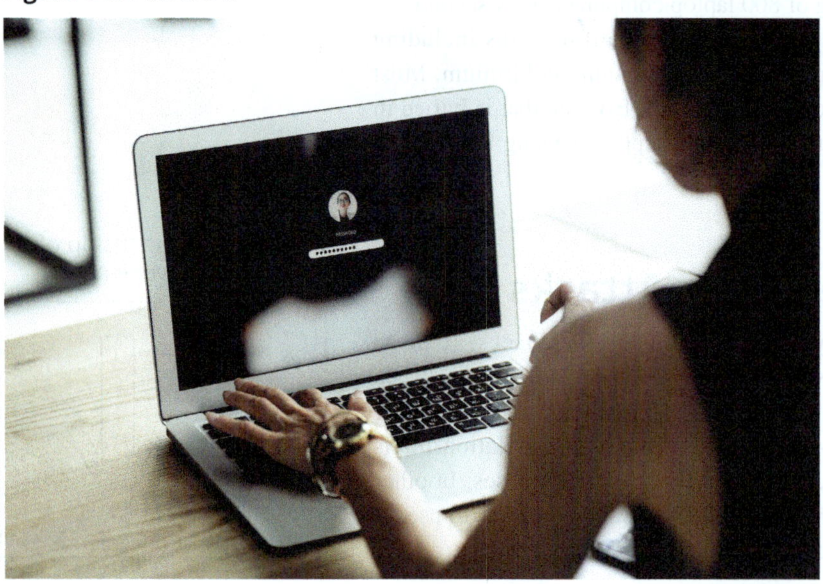

Thomas Andreas/Shutterstock.com

The most important characteristic of a password that makes it resistant to attacks is its length and not its complexity. A longer password is always more secure than a shorter password, regardless of complexity. An easy way to remember this is "Long is strong." Most security experts recommend that a secure password should be a minimum of 20 characters in length.

A **strong password** is a password that is long and contains a mix of letters (both uppercase and lowercase), numbers, and symbols. Strong passwords should not use dictionary words or phonetic words; it should not repeat characters (xxx) or use sequences (abc, 123, qwerty); and it should not contain birthdays, family member names, pet names, addresses, or any personal information.

Figure 6-10: Password manager

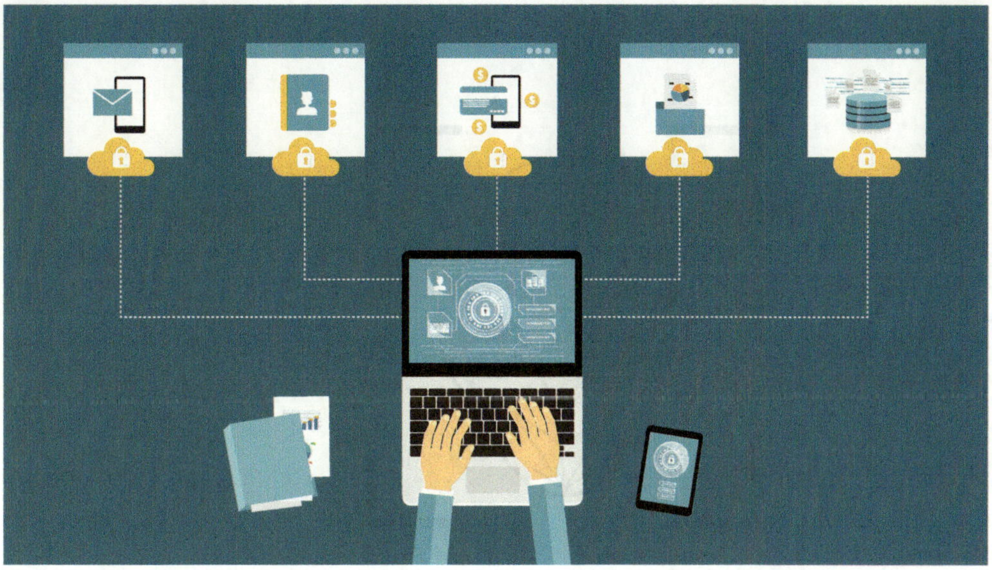

Graphic farm/Shutterstock.com

You may wonder, how can I possibly apply all these recommendations and memorize long, complex, and unique passwords for all my accounts? The simple answer is that you cannot. But instead of relying on your memory for passwords, you should use a **password manager**, which is a program or secure website in which you can create and store all your strong passwords in single user "vault" file that is protected by one strong master password. You can then retrieve individual passwords as needed from the vault file, thus freeing you from the need to memorize multiple passwords (**Figure 6-10**). The value of using a password manager is that unique strong passwords such as *WUuAôxB$2aWøBnd&Tf7MfEtm* can be easily created and used for any of your accounts.

Multifactor Authentication (MFA) Combining multiple types of authentication, known as **multifactor authentication (MFA)**, is a way to increase security when using passwords. The combination most often used is a password (something you know) and a smartphone (something you have). After correctly entering your password, a four- to six-digit code is sent to your smartphone. The code must then be entered as the second authentication method, proving that you are the genuine user (**Figure 6-11**).

Figure 6-11: Multifactor authentication (MFA)

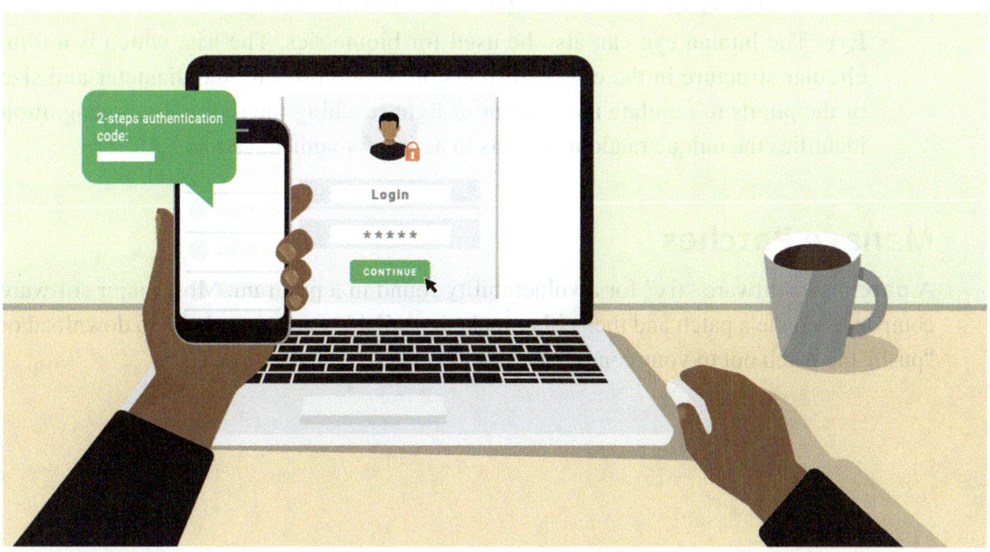

Julia Tim/Shutterstock.com

Figure 6-12: Face recognition

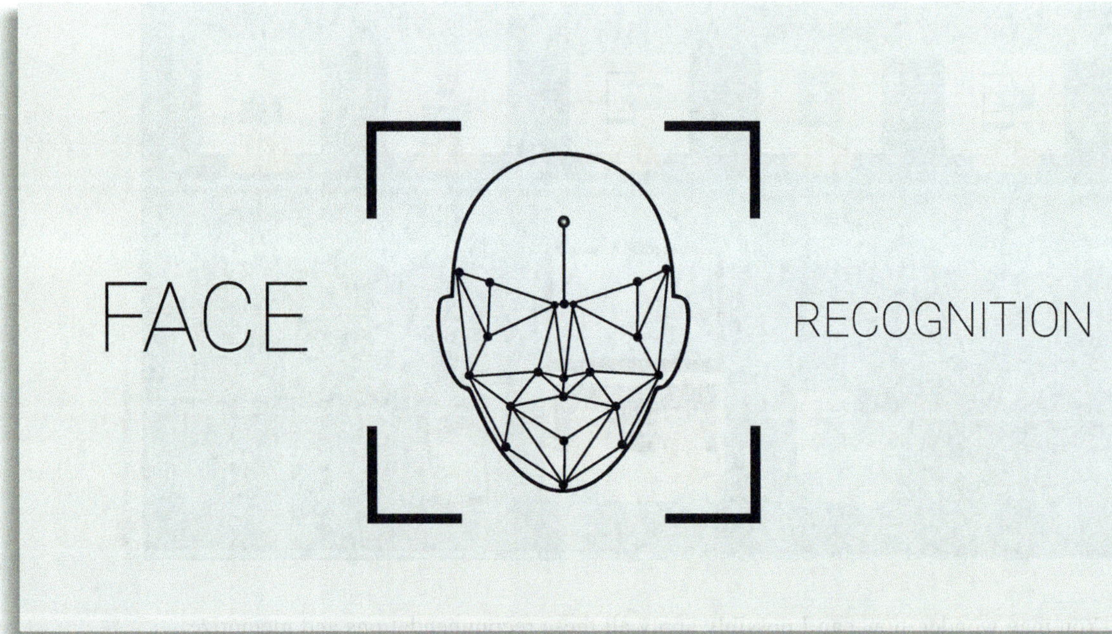

Spiffy Digital Creative/Shutterstock.com

Biometrics Another increasingly common type of authentication uses **biometrics**, the unique characteristics of a body part for authentication. Compared to things that you *know*, such as entering a password or using two-factor authentication, biometrics rely on something you *are*—your unique fingerprint or face, for instance. The most common biometrics in use today are:

- **Fingerprint**. Your fingerprint consists of a unique pattern of ridges and valleys. A static fingerprint scanner requires you to place your entire thumb or finger on a window or button that takes an optical "picture" of the fingerprint and compares it with the fingerprint image on file.
- **Face**. A biometric authentication that is becoming increasingly popular on smartphones is facial recognition. Every person's face has several distinguishable "landmarks" called nodal points (**Figure 6-12**). Facial recognition software can measure these nodal points and create a numerical code (faceprint) that represents the face to compare it with the original code faceprint created.
- **Eye**. The human eye can also be used for biometrics. The iris, which is a thin, circular structure in the eye, is responsible for controlling the diameter and size of the pupils to regulate the amount of light reaching the retina. Eye recognition identifies the unique random patterns in an iris for authentication.

Manage Patches

A **patch** is a software "fix" for a vulnerability found in a program. Most major software companies create a patch and then either make it available on their website to download or "push" the patch out to your computer.

Both Microsoft Windows and Apple macOS distribute, or "push," patches out to your computer. Depending on how your computer is configured, you may receive a notification that a patch is available or has already been downloaded and installed on your computer or will be installed at a later time.

Promptly installing patches once they are available is the most important step to protecting your device. You can facilitate this by configuring your devices to automatically download and install patches when they become available. You may still have to confirm the installation or restart your computer, but the process is more streamlined than having to manually check for updates and hope that you don't forget.

Back Up Your Data

One of the most important defenses against ransomware and malware attacks, as well as a wide range of other threats, is frequently overlooked. A **data backup** is a copy of a file or message that is stored in another location for safekeeping. Data backups should be conducted on a regular basis. Data backups protect against cyberattacks because they can restore infected computers to their properly functioning state, and they can also protect against hardware malfunctions, user error, software corruption, and natural disasters.

The most comprehensive solution for most users is a continuous cloud backup. This type of backup occurs continually, without the user needing to intervene. Instead, software monitors which files have changed and automatically updates the backed-up files with the most recent versions. These backups are stored online in the cloud. There are several cloud-based services available that provide features such as:

- **Automatic continuous backup**. Once the initial backup is completed, any new or modified files are also backed up. Usually the backup software will "sleep" while the computer is being used and perform backups only when there is no user activity. This helps to lessen any impact on the computer's performance or Internet speed.
- **Universal access**. Files backed up through online services can be made available to another computer.
- **Optional program file backup**. In addition to user data files, these services have an option also to back up all program and operating system files.
- **Delayed deletion**. Files that are copied to the online server will remain accessible for up to 30 days before they are deleted. This allows a user to have a longer window of opportunity to restore a deleted file.

Recognize Social Engineering Attacks

There are two basic principles when combating social engineering attacks. The first principle is that attacks based on social engineering can come at any time without any advanced warning. The second principle is that the attacker presents themself as someone who can be trusted. This means that both of these principles must be counteracted: you must always be aware, and you must not automatically trust everything that you receive.

Table 6-4: Social engineering defenses

Social engineering attack	Secure action	Explanation
An email stating you have won a prize and you must send your bank account number for the money to be deposited.	Recognize scams.	Any offer for "easy money" that requires you to provide something should be rejected.
A text message that a friend vacationing overseas has lost her purse and needs you to immediately purchase gift cards or a money wire transfer to send funds to a foreign bank account.	Think before you click.	Attackers employ a sense of urgency to make you act now and think later, so action on any highly urgent or high-pressure messages should be paused until it can be verified through another method of communication different from the message itself (like calling the person if a text message was received).
An email from a company that says your credit card will be charged for a recent purchase, but you did not make the purchase; you are asked to open the email attachment for proof.	Research sources.	Always be careful of any unsolicited messages, and instead of responding through email or text call about it.
You receive an email from a friend that has an attachment with the subject line "I can't believe this is a picture of you doing this!"	Never download unexpected file attachments.	Always verify through a different channel (phone, text message, etc.) with the sender that the attachment is legitimate, especially if there is a sense of urgency with the message.
A text message asks you to make a donation to a disaster recovery effort due to a tornado that occurred last night.	Reject requests for help.	Perform research into the organization asking for funds.
An email says that you are eligible to apply for federal disaster relief and this company will assist you.	Deny unsolicited offers of assistance.	Go directly to the website that provides assistance and never give personal information through an email to an unknown sender.

Table 6-4 list several social engineering defenses.

Configure Your Web Browser Settings

Modern web browsers allow you to tailor settings based on your personal preferences. Beyond basic settings such as preferred home page and the size of displayed characters, browsers also allow you to customize cybersecurity settings.

However, the number of different options for customizing a secure web browser can quickly become overwhelming and even confusing. To address this, modern browsers now implement "modes" of cybersecurity that encompass multiple settings. This requires a user only to select an appropriate mode, such as Balanced or Strict, rather than sorting through multiple individual settings (**Figure 6-13**).

It is recommended that the highest level of security mode be turned on in a web browser. If this proves to be too restrictive, then exceptions can be made to this highest level. For example, in Microsoft Edge, an exception list can be made for accessing certain websites that are known to be trustworthy. If creating exceptions still impact the browsing experience, then the lower-level mode can be implemented.

Figure 6-13: Microsoft Edge security modes

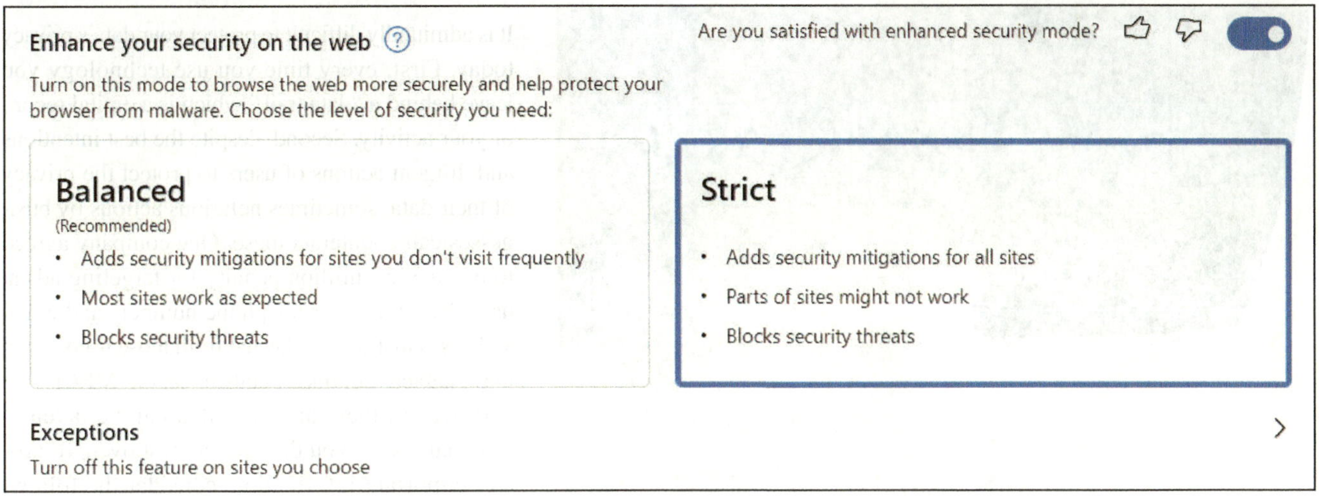

Use Antimalware Software

Antimalware software is software that can combat various malware attacks to protect files. One of the earliest antimalware software security applications was antivirus (AV) software. This software can examine a computer for any infections as well as monitor computer activity and scan new documents that might contain a virus. (This scanning is typically performed when files are opened, created, or closed.) If a virus is detected, options generally include cleaning the file of the virus, quarantining the infected file, or deleting the file.

At one time, running AV software was considered to be the primary—and often the only required—defense against attacks. However, it was later recognized that due to the many different types of malware, AV software, despite many user's perceptions, is not a complete security solution.

In addition to AV protection, modern antimalware software often includes the following:

- **Intrusion prevention**. The software analyzes information arriving from a network and blocks potential threats before they enter a computer.
- **Reputation protection**. Using information gathered from a global network, it is able to classify software application files as "dangerous," "risky," or "safe" based on their attributes.
- **Behavioral protection**. This monitors applications for suspicious behavior and automatically blocks the software if necessary.

Both Microsoft Windows and Apple macOS have built-in comprehensive antimalware software, Microsoft Defender Antivirus and Apple XProtect. Despite that fact that antimalware software is not perfect and does not provide absolute protection, it does provide a degree of protection that would be lacking if this software was not running. Without a valid reason, you should not turn off built-in comprehensive antimalware protection. However, antimalware software should be recognized as one tool but not the only tool that can be deployed to protect the integrity of files.

Use Protective Measures against Technology Hazards

There are several steps that can be taken to protect against technology hazards. These including securing your privacy, practicing good ergonomics, and protecting the environment.

Figure 6-14: Micro-cut shredder

Sarah Biesinger/Shutterstock.com

Secure Your Privacy

It is admittedly difficult to protect your data's privacy today. First, every time you use technology you leave behind a "data trail," which is a digital record of your activity. Second, despite the best intentions and diligent actions of users to protect the privacy of their data, sometimes nefarious actions by businesses can counteract these. One company agreed to pay a $150 million penalty for targeting ads at users by using their telephone numbers and email addresses that were collected from those users when they enabled multifactor authentication (MFA).

However, there are steps that can be taken to safeguard what you do have control over. To protect important information, consider the following privacy best practices:

- Do not provide personal information either over the phone or through an email or text message.
- Be cautious about what information you post on social networking sites and who can view your information. Show a reduced version of a profile to "limited friends," such as casual acquaintances or business associates.
- Use common sense: websites that request more personal information than would normally be expected, such as a username and password to another account, should be avoided.
- Be sure that strong passwords are used on all accounts and use multifactor authentication (MFA) when available.
- Shred financial documents and other paperwork that contains personal information before discarding it. There are three common types of shredders. The most secure is a micro-cut shredder device will shred documents into tiny pieces (**Figure 6-14**).
- Give cautious consideration before giving permission to a website or app request to collect data.
- Be sure that "https" appears at the beginning of a web address that asks for credit card numbers or other sensitive information. Do not provide any information if that is not present.
- Be cautious about surrendering personal information in exchange for a coupon or to enter a contest. Today brands are deploying an array of tactics to persuade users to surrender data to the brand itself through loyalty programs, sweepstakes, newsletters, quizzes, and polls. Resist the temptation to trade your personal information to enter a contest.
- Advocate for state and federal regulations that limit the collection and usage of private data.

Practice Good Ergonomics

To prevent RSI, you should arrange your workplace so that you are positioned ergonomically. **Ergonomics** is an applied science that specifies the design and arrangement of items that you use so that you and the items interact efficiently and safely. There are correct ergonomic posture and techniques for working on a computer (**Figure 6-15**). These include:

- **Arms**. The arms are parallel to the floor at approximately a 90-degree angle.
- **Eyes**. The distance to the screen is 18–28 inches (45–61 centimeters) from the eyes, and the viewing angle is downward at about 20 degrees to the center of the screen.

Figure 6-15: Correct ergonomics

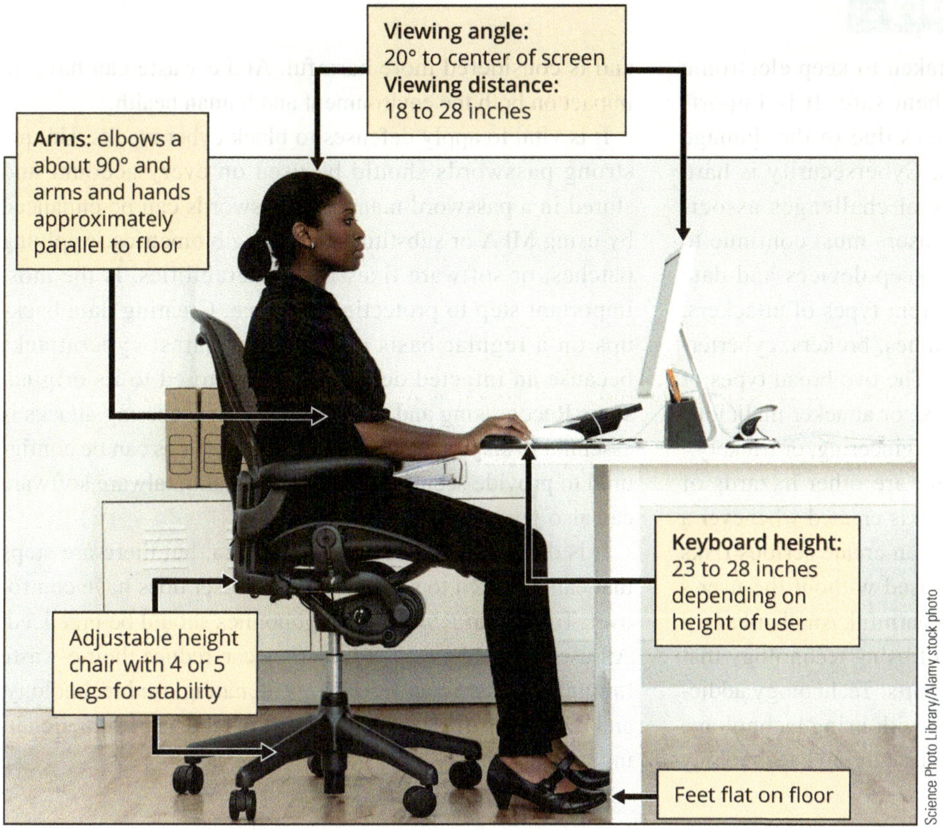

- **Feet**. The feet are flat on the floor. Use a proper chair with adjustable height and multiple legs for stability.
- **Back**. A lumbar support pillow for an office chair can provide back support.
- **Lighting**. The easiest way to reduce glare and screen reflections is to adjust the display's tilt and swivel mechanisms. You can also change the monitor's background and adjust the text colors. Light characters on a dark background will produce the minimal amount of screen glare, while dark characters on a light background can increase screen glare.

Reduce E-Waste

All users should consider how they can reduce their e-waste. An initiative called Sustainable Electronics Management (SEM) promotes the reduction of e-waste. **Table 6-5** outlines the action steps of SEM. As a security best practice, always remove any personal data before donating or recycling any device.

Table 6-5: Sustainable Electronics Management

Step	Action	Description
1	Buy green	When purchasing new electronic equipment, buy only products that have been designed with environmentally preferable attributes.
2	Donate	Donate used but still functional equipment to a school, charity, or non-profit organization.
3	Recycle	Send equipment to a verified used electronics recycling center.

Module 6 Summary

Cybersecurity involves the steps taken to keep electronic devices and the data stored on them safe. It is important for users to secure their devices due to the damage that can be inflicted by attackers. Cybersecurity is hard to achieve because there are several challenges associated with countering attacks, and users must continue to meet those challenges in order to keep devices and data safe. Potential threats include different types of attackers, including cybercriminals, script kiddies, brokers, cyberterrorists, hacktivists, and state actors. The two broad types of cyberattacks are those using malware, or attacker malicious software, and those based on social engineering, or trickery.

Besides attacks on devices, there are other hazards of using technology. Because a data trail is created whenever a user interacts with technology, this can create serious risks of private data being exposed and used without the user's permission and in ways that could be harmful. Another hazard is RSI, which is a physical hazard of using technology that causes physical discomfort in body parts. Technology addiction occurs when a user is obsessed with using technology. Cyberbullying is bullying that takes place through technology and is considered more harmful. And e-waste can have an impact on both the environment and human health.

It is vital to apply defenses to block cyberattacks. Unique strong passwords should be used on every account and stored in a password manager. Passwords can be enhanced by using MFA or substituted by using biometrics. Applying patches, or software fixes for vulnerabilities, is the most important step to protecting a device. Creating data backups on a regular basis can protect against cyberattacks because an infected device can be restored to its original state. Recognizing and resisting social engineering attacks is essential to staying safe. Web browser settings can be configured to provide security, and installing antimalware software can also give a degree of protection.

It is difficult to protect personal data, but there are steps that can be taken to safeguard what a user does have control over. To prevent RSI proper ergonomics should be practiced. All users should consider how they can reduce their e-waste through buying green technology, donating used technology, and recycling (always removing personal data prior to donating or recycling).

Review Questions

1. Cybersecurity refers to protecting devices, networks, and programs with practices, processes, and ________.

- **a.** technologies
- **b.** people
- **c.** malware
- **d.** policies

2. An attack that occurs when an attacker steals your Social Security number and then uses that to impersonate you is called ________.

- **a.** data theft
- **b.** identity theft
- **c.** personal heist
- **d.** data scraping

3. The one factor that undoubtedly accounts for the greatest difficulty in preventing attacks is ________.

- **a.** universally connected devices
- **b.** increased speed of attacks
- **c.** user confusion
- **d.** decreased law enforcement

4. What category of cyber attacker sells software vulnerabilities to the highest bidder?

- **a.** Brokers
- **b.** Cyberterrorists
- **c.** Hacktivists
- **d.** State actors

5. Which of the following attacks locks down a user's device until a fee is paid?

- **a.** Kidnapping
- **b.** Keylogging
- **c.** Virus control
- **d.** Ransomware

6. A risk of data collection is that ________.

- **a.** the accuracy of the data cannot be verified
- **b.** it takes time for merchants to collect the data
- **c.** there may not be enough data collected for it to be worth the effort
- **d.** data can only be collected when a smartphone is in sleep mode

7. What is the name of the technology hazard that impacts your muscles, nerves, tendons, and ligaments?

- **a.** CSI
- **b.** SISI
- **c.** RSI
- **d.** KTI

8. (True or False) Data backups can protect you from more than just cybersecurity attacks.

9. The most important characteristic of a password that makes it resistant to attacks is ________.

- **a.** complexity
- **b.** length
- **c.** native language
- **d.** how quickly it can be memorized

10. What is the most important step to protecting a device?

- **a.** Using antimalware software
- **b.** Keeping your device turned off when not being used
- **c.** Backing up your data once per month
- **d.** Promptly installing patches

11. Which of the following is correct about antimalware software?

- **a.** You should always turn off built-in antimalware software because it can slow down your computer.
- **b.** Antimalware software is the only defense that you need on your computer to protect against cyberattacks.
- **c.** Antimalware software should be recognized as one tool for protection.
- **d.** Antimalware software should only be manually turned on when you are under attack.

12. (True or False) A recommended ergonomic practice is to have your arms parallel to the floor at approximately a 90-degree angle.

Discussion Questions

1. Why is it unrealistic to seek a one-size-fits-all cybersecurity solution to prevent all attacks? Identify at least three difficulties associated with cybersecurity.
2. What is the difference between bullying and cyberbullying? What forms does cyberbullying commonly take, and how do these types of actions intimidate the person they target? Why is cyberbullying difficult to control? Identify at least two differences between bullying and cyberbullying that make cyberbullying such a serious hazard.
3. Describe two or three shortcuts users commonly take when creating passwords and explain how these shortcuts result in weak passwords. Describe the most important characteristic of a strong password, especially as compared to a weak one.
4. What are the risks associated with data collection? What common activities leave a data trail for organizations who are seeking your personal data? How can this activity harm you?

Critical Thinking Activities

1. After the bank account of a friend was compromised by attackers, you learn that it was because of a weak password that your friend used on the account, a password they also used on several other of their accounts. You decide to review the passwords for your accounts to prevent any future vulnerabilities. List three items you would look for to identify weak passwords. Give each item a negative numeric value from –1 to –10 based on your estimate of the relative negative impact of this item to creating a weak password; that is, if X is the item that would have the greatest negative impact on a password, then you might assign it the value –10. Next, list three items that would make for a strong password. Rate those with a positive numeric value from +1 to +10, assigning the value +10 to the item you think would have the highest relative value in making a strong password. When you reflect on this list and think of the passwords you use for you own accounts, do you feel your passwords are strong enough, or do you think you may need to make some changes?

2. You are starting as an intern in the Marketing Department of a local bank. After several days on the job, you realize that the bank has been using personal information about its customers without their permission for advertising. At a meeting the director of the department has announced that they are finalizing a new smartphone app that will have six trackers installed to monitor the users' smartphone activity and will also start using this data in their marketing campaigns. None of the users will be asked for their permission to gather and use their personal data. What should you do? Should you speak up about the risks of using personal data? Or should you remain silent since many companies use this technique? If you were in this situation, would you speak out?

3. One evening your roommate is working on their laptop computer while sitting on the floor. They begin to complain about the chronic pain in their neck and how tired their eyes are. You suggest that the discomforts could be a result of where they are sitting and the lighting of the room. Your roommate asks if you could help them create a workspace that could prevent these pains. Create a checklist of correct ergonomic postures and techniques that could help your roommate work in a pain-free environment. As you consider your own computer use, do you experience any of these issues? If so, how do they impact your overall well-being?

4. While you are away on vacation you wake up to an unsettling email. The email is from your bank that says several days ago you used your credit card multiple times and one of the charges was for purchasing clothing that cost several hundreds of dollars. That now makes your balance above your credit limit and any future charges will be declined. Because your spending pattern while away on vacation has been very different, you cannot remember whether you made this purchase. You are depending on using your credit card to pay for your hotel room and to get back home, but if your card is now "frozen" you are unable to use it. The email from the bank includes an attachment for you to open that lists details about the charge. You are tempted to immediately open the attachment but are unsure if it may be a phishing attack. What process should you go through to determine if the email is legitimate? Have you ever been the victim of a phishing attack? How did you cope with it?

Apply Your Skills

Tony Blanco has been hired as an intern at a company that installs solar panels. Because he is completing his degree in cybersecurity at the local college, he works in the company's security operations center (SOC) assisting security managers and technicians who protect the company's computers and networks from cyberattacks. One of Tony's recent assignments was helping the technicians who monitor for signs of attacks and then take action to prevent the attacks from quickly spreading. Tony has begun offering Lunch-and-Learn sessions for employees with hands-on training on how to keep their devices safe.

Working in a small group or by yourself, complete the following:

1. Tony has been asked to give a Lunch-and-Learn session to new interns who are unfamiliar with social engineering attacks. What types of social engineering attacks should Tony discuss? Provide at least three examples he should cover.

2. Tony receives a text message from a new intern that says they are very concerned that their supervisor is exhibiting behaviors that shows they have technology addiction. The reasons given are the supervisor is always working on their computer throughout the day, they rarely leave their desk, the only conversations they have seem to be about the latest technology, and they constantly look at their smartphone while eating lunch. Is this technology addiction or is it the normal use of technology by a busy supervisor? Have you ever been concerned that you or someone close to you may be addicted to technology? How did you address the concern?

3. A recent data breach occurred in the company, and it was tracked down to an accountant who reused the same password on all their accounts, including social media and their work accounts. What are two solutions that Tony can give this accountant to help prevent this occurring again? In acknowledging that these solutions may decrease convenience around accessing accounts, do you feel that using them would be worth your time?

4. Several new interns have complained to Tony about their working conditions. The interns all share a cramped office that used to be a storage area and has very poor lighting. Instead of desks there are only two tables that all the interns must share as their workspaces, and because the chairs are not office chairs, they lack armrests and adequate back support. Use the Internet to research potential ergonomic products that Tony could recommend to create a better environment for the interns. For example, you might research ergonomic products such as desks, standing desks, office chairs, indirect lighting, copyholders, keyboard trays, elevated mouse pads, antiglare screen covers, footrests, and wrist rests, among other ergonomic tools. Based on your research, create a list of at least five potential products. Rank the five products from 1 to 5 in terms of their importance for creating an ergonomic environment, with 5 being the most important and 1 being the least.

Creating and Modifying a Flyer

Objectives

After completing this module, you will be able to:

- Start and exit Word
- Create a blank document and insert text in it
- Change how a Word document appears in the Word window
- Modify page setup in a Word document
- Check spelling and grammar
- Save a document
- Check accessibility issues
- Format text, paragraph, page, and document elements
- Undo and redo commands or actions
- Insert and format a picture
- View and change document properties
- Open and close a document
- Cut, copy, and paste text
- Print a document
- Use Word Help

What Is Word?

Microsoft Word, or Word, is a full-featured word processing app that allows you to create professional-looking documents and revise them easily. With Word, you can create business, academic, and personal documents, including flyers, research papers, letters, memos, resumes, reports, mailing labels, and newsletters.

Word has many features designed to simplify the production of documents and add visual appeal. Using Word, you easily can change the shape, size, and color of text. You also can include borders, shading, tables, pictures, charts, and other objects in documents. While you are typing, Word performs many tasks automatically. For example, Word detects and corrects spelling and grammar errors in several languages. Word's thesaurus allows you to add variety and precision to your writing. In addition to formatting text as you type, such as headings, lists, fractions, borders, and web addresses, Word includes a great deal of predefined text and many predefined objects and document types. Word also provides tools that enable you to create webpages and save the webpages directly on a web server.

To illustrate the features of Word, this book presents a series of projects that use Microsoft Word 365 to create documents similar to those you will encounter in business and academic environments.

Introduction

To convey a message or announcement to employees or staff members, campus or school students, or the community or public, you may want to create a flyer. You then can post the flyer in a location targeted to your intended audience, such as on an employee bulletin board or in an office cubicle, at a kiosk, or on a hallway wall. You may also see flyers on webpages, on social media, or in email messages.

Project: Flyer with a Picture

Businesses create flyers to gain attention for a message or an announcement. Flyers, which usually are a single page in length, are an inexpensive means of reaching an audience. Many flyers, however, go unnoticed because they are designed poorly.

The project in this module follows generally accepted design guidelines and uses Word to create the flyer shown in Figure 1–1. This colorful, eye-catching flyer, created by an administrative assistant at the real estate agency, presents details about a house the agency just listed for sale. The flyer, which will be displayed at local businesses and on library bulletin boards, contains a digital picture of the house for sale. The headline on the flyer is large and colorful to draw attention into the text. The body copy below the headline briefly describes the location, size, and price of the home, along with a bulleted list that highlights features of the house and a numbered list that identifies recent updates made to the interior and exterior of the house. The signature line of the flyer identifies contact information for interested parties. Some words in the flyer are in a different color or further emphasized so that they stand apart from the rest of the text on the flyer. Finally, the page border nicely frames and complements the contents of the flyer.

BTW
Microsoft Updates
The material in this book was written using Microsoft 365 and was quality-assurance tested before the publication date. As Microsoft continually updates Microsoft 365, your software experience may vary slightly from what is seen in the printed text.

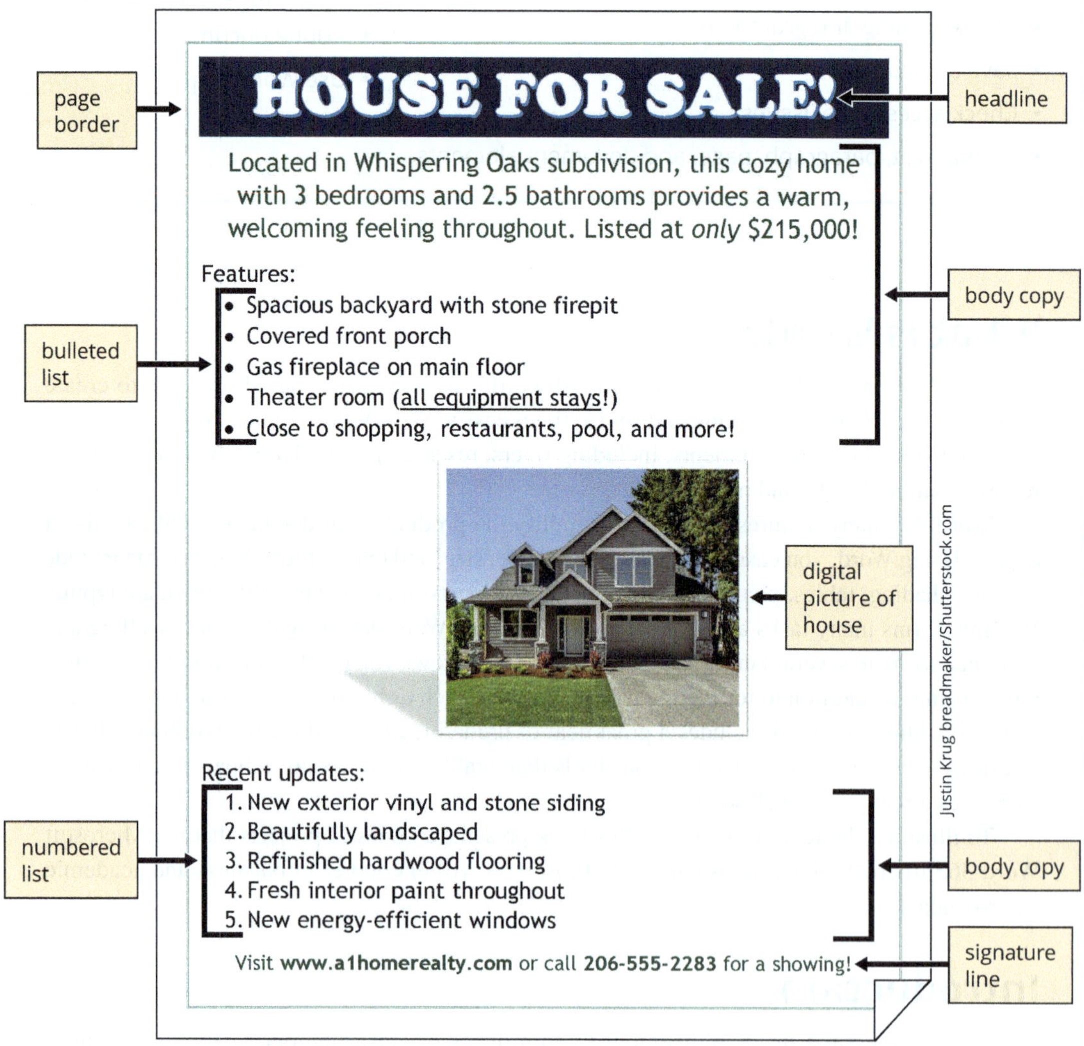

Figure 1–1

In this module, you will learn how to create the flyer shown in Figure 1–1. You will perform the following general tasks as you progress through this module:

1. Start and use Word.
2. Enter text in a document.
3. Format the text in the flyer.
4. Insert and format a picture in the flyer.
5. Enhance the layout of the flyer on the page.
6. Correct errors and revise text in the flyer.

Starting and Using Word

To use Word, you must instruct the operating system (i.e., Windows) to start the app. The following sections start Word, discuss some elements of the Word window, and perform tasks to specify Word settings.

If you are using a computer or device to step through the project in this module and you want your screen to match the figures in this book, you should change your screen's resolution to 1366 × 768.

BTW
Resolution
For information about how to change a computer's resolution, search for 'change resolution' in your operating system's Help files.

To Start Word and Create a Blank Document

The following steps, which assume Windows is running, start Word and create a blank document based on a typical installation. **Why?** You will use Word to create the flyer in this module. You may need to ask your instructor how to start Word on your computer or device.

1

- **sam** Click the Start button on the Windows taskbar to display the Start menu.

Q&A What is a menu?
A **menu** contains a list of related items, including commands, apps, programs, and folders. Each **command** is a menu item that performs a specific action, such as saving a file or obtaining help. A **folder** is a named location on a storage medium that usually contains related documents.

- If necessary, click the All apps button on the Start menu and then scroll through the list of apps on the Start menu until the Word app name appears (Figure 1–2).

Q&A What if my Word app is in a folder?
Click the appropriate folder name to display the contents of the folder.

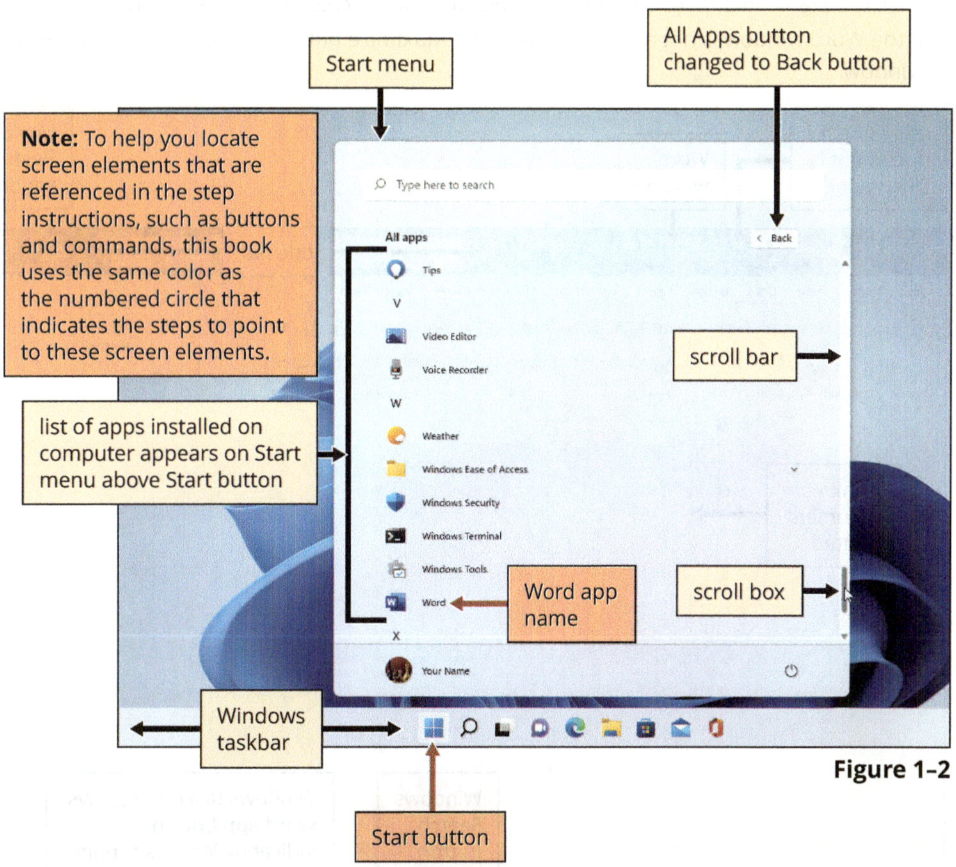

Figure 1–2

2

- Click Word on the Start menu to start Word and display the Word start screen (Figure 1–3).

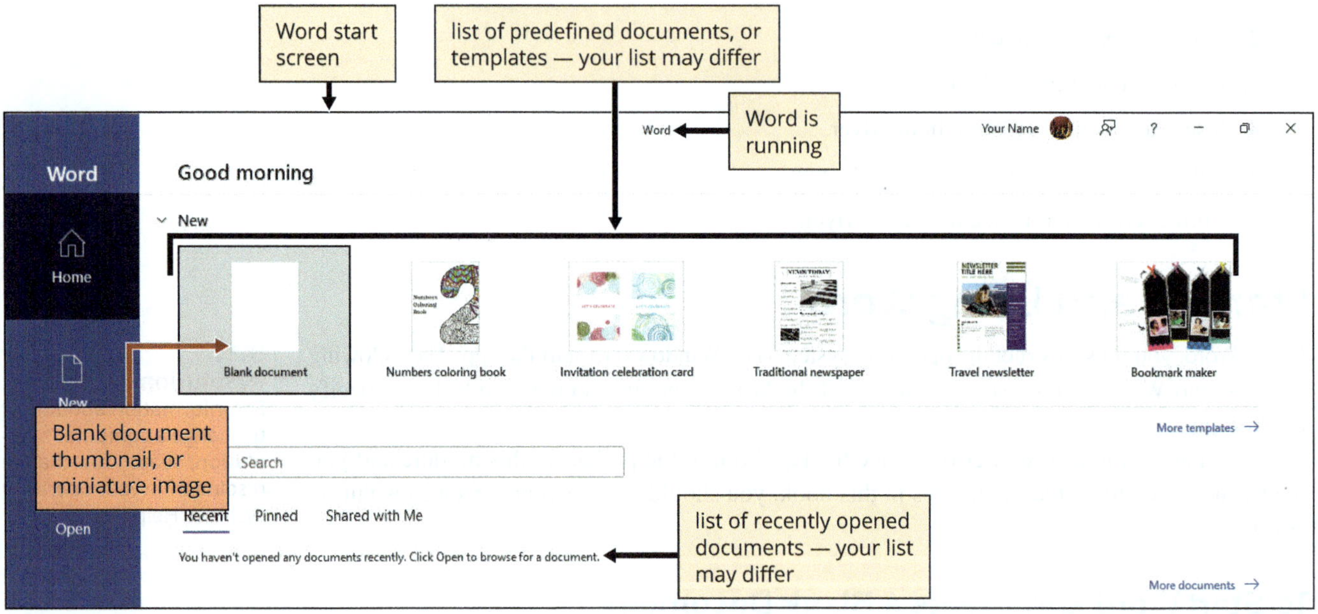

Figure 1–3

3

- Click the Blank document thumbnail on the Word start screen to create a blank document in the Word window (Figure 1–4).
- If the Word window is not maximized, click the Maximize button next to the Close button on the title bar to maximize the window.

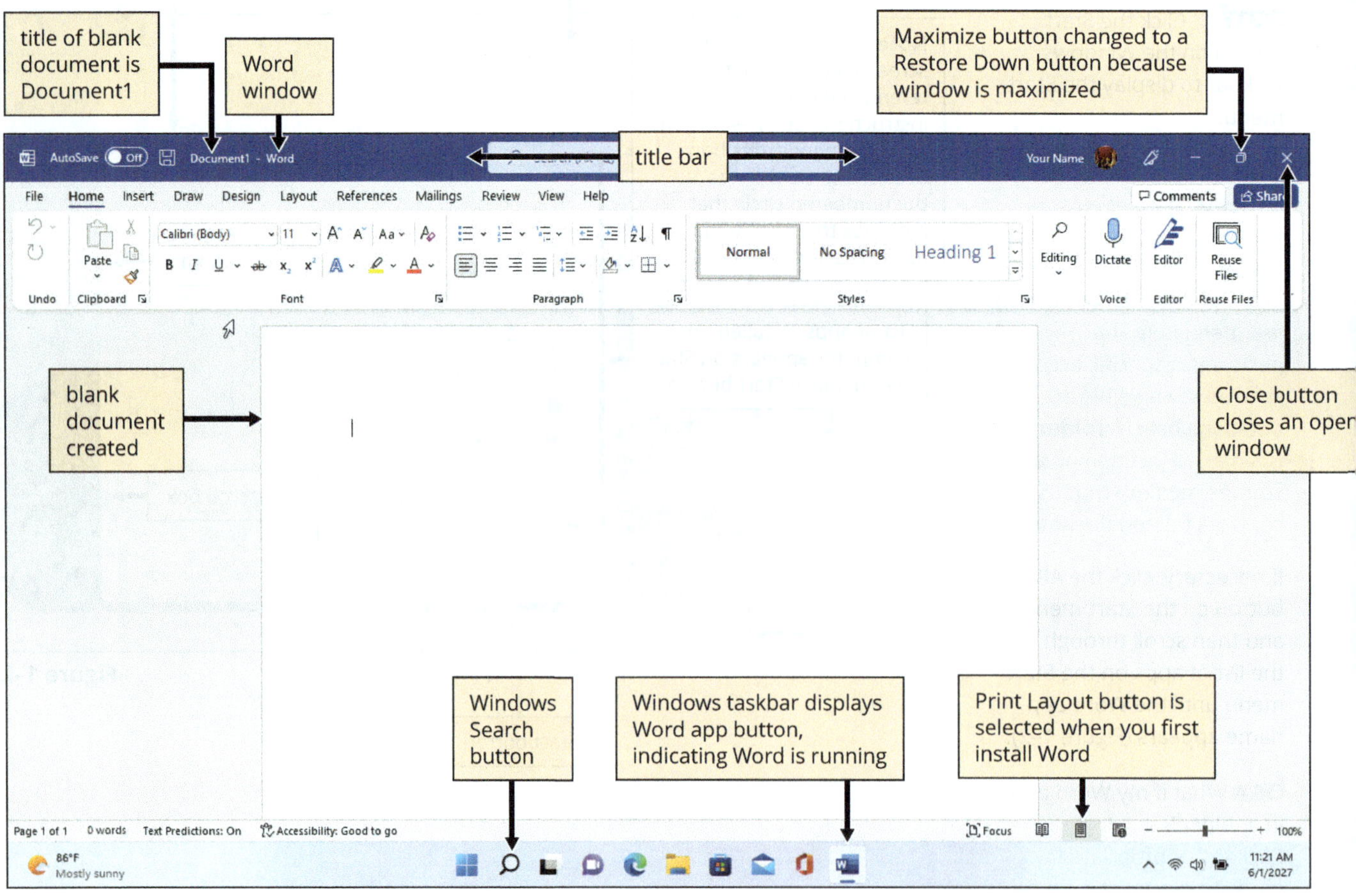

Figure 1–4

Q&A What is a maximized window?

A maximized window fills the entire screen. When you maximize a window, the Maximize button changes to a Restore Down button.

4

- If the Print Layout button is not selected, click it so that your screen layout matches Figure 1–4.

Q&A What is Print Layout view?

The default (preset) view in Word is **Print Layout view**, which shows the document on an image of a sheet of paper in the document window.

Other Ways

1. Click Windows Search button on taskbar, type app name in Windows Search box, click app name in results list
2. Double-click Word icon on desktop, if one is present
3. Click Office button on taskbar, if one is present, click app name in Office window

The Word Window

The Word window consists of a variety of components to make your work more efficient and documents more professional. These include the document window and several other elements, depending on the task you are performing: scroll bar(s), status bar, ribbon, Search box, Quick Access Toolbar, Mini toolbar, shortcut menus, KeyTips, and the account manager. Most of these are common to other Microsoft 365 apps; others are unique to Word. The following sections briefly describe these elements; others are discussed as they appear in the Word window.

You view or work with a document on the screen through a **document window**, which is a window within Word that displays all or part of an open document (Figure 1–5). In the document, the **insertion point** is a blinking vertical line that appears when you click in the document and indicates where new text, images, and other objects will be inserted. As you type, the insertion point moves to the right, and when you reach the end of a line, it moves down to the beginning of the next line. The **pointer** is a small symbol on the screen that becomes different shapes depending on the task you are performing in Word and the pointer's location on the screen. You move the pointer with a pointing device, such as a mouse or touchpad. The pointer in Figure 1–5 is the shape of an I-beam.

BTW
The Word Window
The modules in this book begin with the Word window appearing as it did at the initial installation of the software. Your Word window may look different depending on your screen resolution and other Word settings.

BTW
Pointer
If you are using a touch screen, the pointer may not appear on the screen as you perform touch gestures. The pointer will reappear when you begin using the mouse.

Scroll Bar You use **scroll bars**, which appear at the right and bottom edges of the document window, to view documents that are too large to fit on the screen at once. At the right edge of the document window is a vertical scroll bar. If a document is too wide to fit in the document window, a horizontal scroll bar also appears at the bottom of the document window. On a scroll bar, the position of the **scroll box** reflects the location of the portion of the document that is displayed in the document window; you can drag the scroll box, or click above or below it, to scroll through or display different parts of the document in the document window. A **scroll arrow** is a small triangular up or down arrow that is located at each end of a scroll bar; you can click the scroll arrows to scroll through the document in small increments.

Status Bar The **status bar**, located at the bottom of the document window above the Windows taskbar, presents information about the document, the progress of current tasks, and the status of certain commands and keys; it also provides controls for viewing the document, such as zoom controls. As you type text or perform certain commands, various indicators and buttons may appear on the status bar.

The left side of the status bar in Figure 1–5 shows the current page followed by the total number of pages in the document, the number of words in the document, along with the status of the document's spelling and grammar, text prediction, and accessibility. The right side of the status bar includes buttons and controls you can use to change the view of a document and adjust the size of the displayed document.

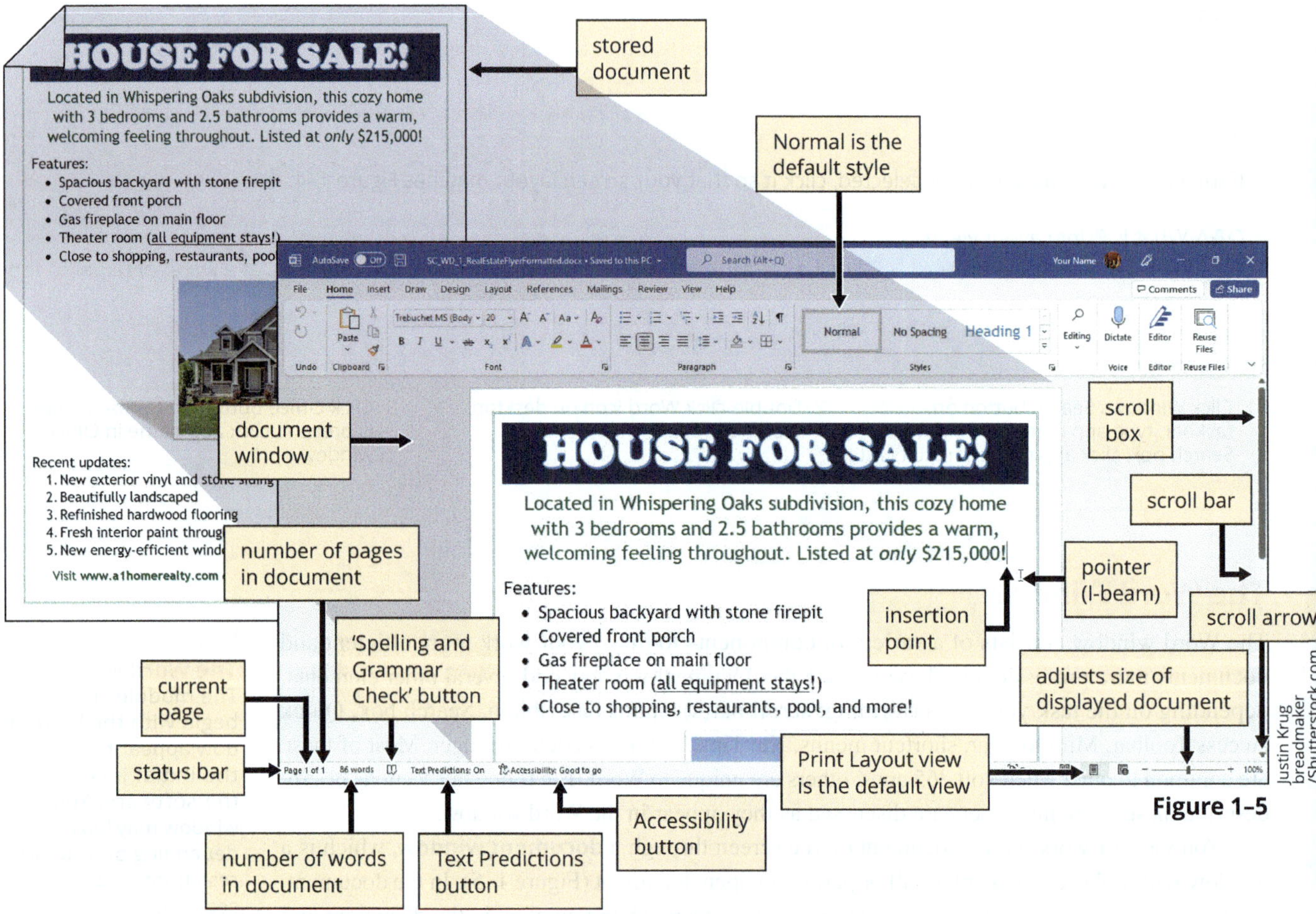

Figure 1–5

Ribbon The **ribbon**, which is a horizontal strip located near the top of the Word window below the title bar, is the control center in Word that contains tabs of grouped commands that you click to interact with Word (Figure 1–6a). Each **tab** contains a collection of groups, and each **group** contains related commands. The ribbon provides easy, central access to the tasks you perform while creating a document.

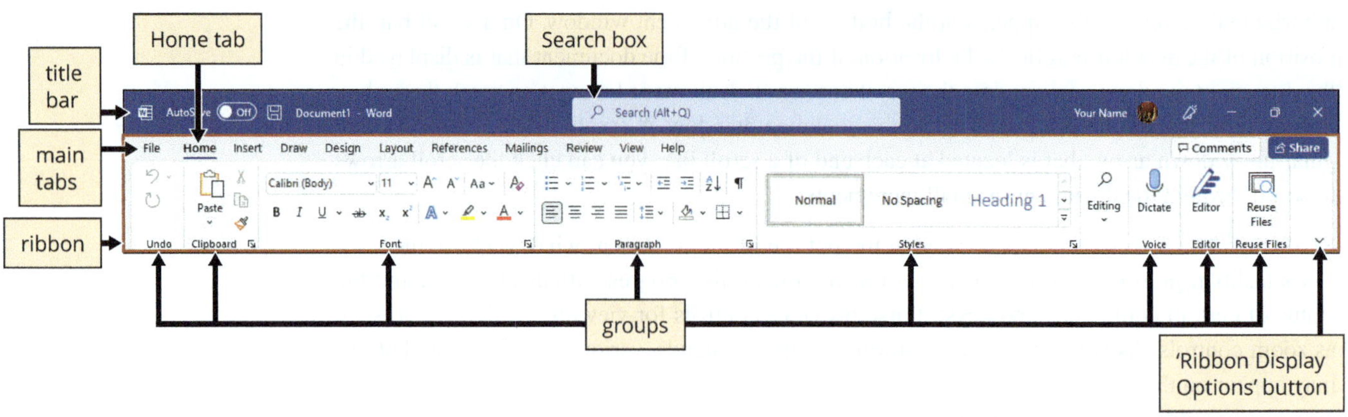

Figure 1–6a

When you start Word, the ribbon displays several main tabs, also called default or top-level tabs (i.e., File, Home, Insert, Draw, Design, Layout, References, Mailings, Review, View, and Help). (Note that depending on the type of computer or device you are using, the Draw tab may not appear.) The **Home tab**, also called the primary tab, contains the more frequently used commands. The tab currently displayed is called the **active tab**.

To display more of the document in the document window, some users prefer to collapse the ribbon, which hides the groups on the ribbon and displays only the main tabs (Figure 1–6b). To collapse the ribbon, click the 'Ribbon Display Options' button at the right edge of the ribbon and then click 'Show tabs only' on the menu; right-click any of the main tabs and then click 'Collapse the Ribbon' on the menu; or press CTRL+F1. To use commands on a collapsed ribbon, click the tab that you wish to expand. To expand the ribbon, double-click any of the main tabs; click the 'Ribbon Display Options' button on the right edge of the ribbon and then click 'Always show Ribbon' on the menu; right-click any of the main tabs and then click 'Collapse the Ribbon' on the menu to deselect the command; or press CTRL+F1.

BTW
The Ribbon and Screen Resolution
Word may change how the groups and buttons within the groups appear on the ribbon, depending on the computer or mobile device's screen resolution. Thus, your ribbon may look different from the ones in this book if you are using a screen resolution other than 1366 × 768.

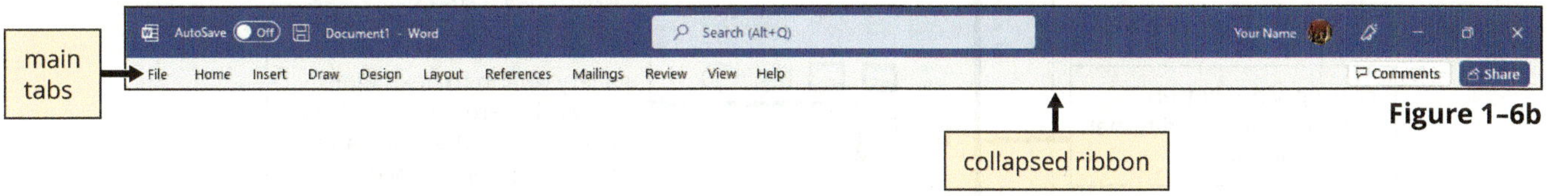

Figure 1–6b

Each time you start Word, the ribbon appears the same way it did the last time you used Word. The modules in this book, however, begin with the ribbon appearing as it did at the initial installation of the software.

In addition to the main tabs, Word displays other tabs, called **contextual tabs**, when you perform certain tasks or work with objects such as pictures or tables. If you insert a picture in the document, for example, the Picture Format tab appears (Figure 1–6c). When you are finished working with the picture, the Picture Format tab disappears from the ribbon. Word determines when contextual tabs should appear and disappear based on tasks you perform. Some tasks involve more than one contextual tab. For example, when you work with tables, the Table Design tab and the Layout tab appear.

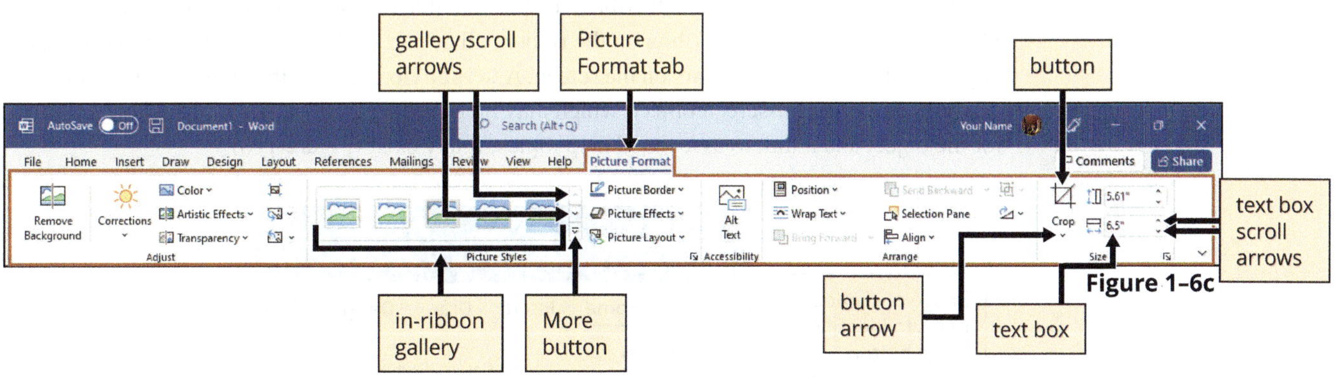

Figure 1–6c

Items on the ribbon include buttons, boxes (text boxes, check boxes, etc.), and galleries (shown in Figure 1–6c). A **gallery** is a set of choices, often graphical, arranged in a grid or in a list that you can browse through before making a selection. You can scroll through choices in an in-ribbon gallery by clicking the gallery's scroll arrows. Or, you can click a gallery's More button to view more gallery options on the screen at a time.

Some buttons and boxes have arrows that, when clicked, also display a gallery; others always cause a gallery to be displayed when clicked. Most galleries support **Live Preview**, which is a feature that allows you to point to a gallery choice and see its effect in the document — without actually selecting the choice (Figure 1–7).

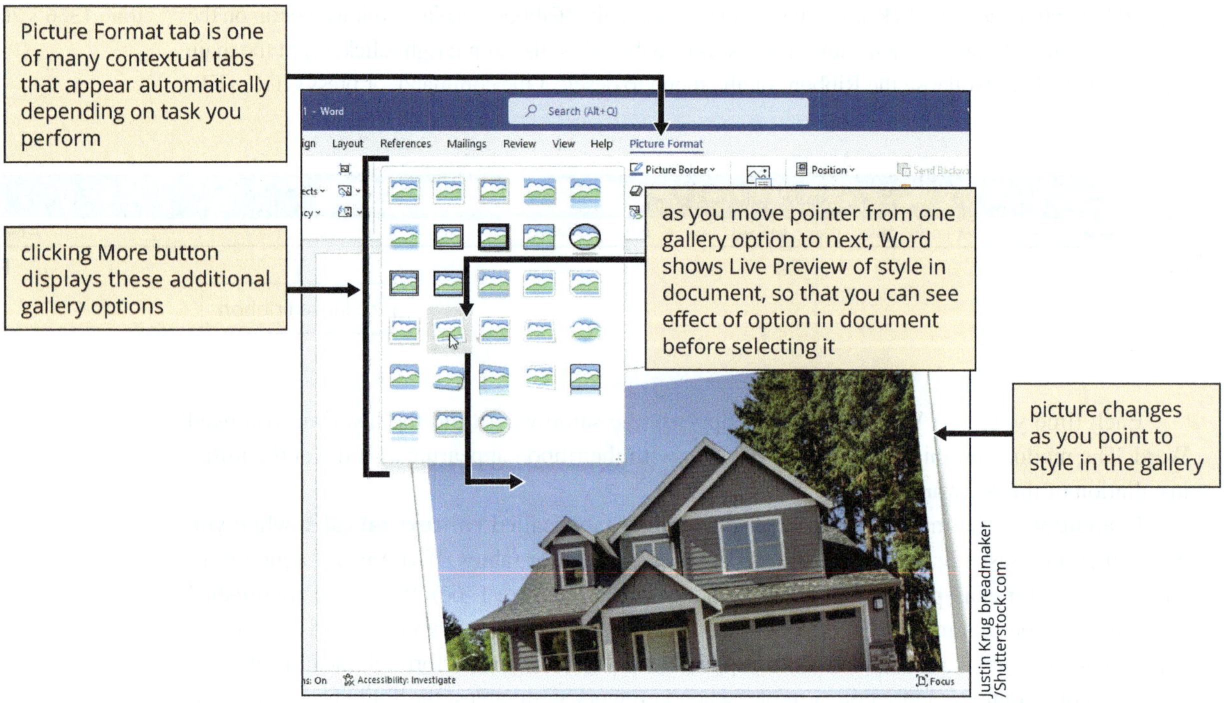

Figure 1–7

Some buttons and boxes on the ribbon display an image to help you remember their function. When you point to a button or box on the ribbon, all or part of the button or box glows in shades of gray, and a ScreenTip appears on the screen. A **ScreenTip** is a label that appears when you point to a button or other on-screen object, which may include the name, purpose, or keyboard shortcut for the object and a link to associated help topics, if any exist (Figure 1–8).

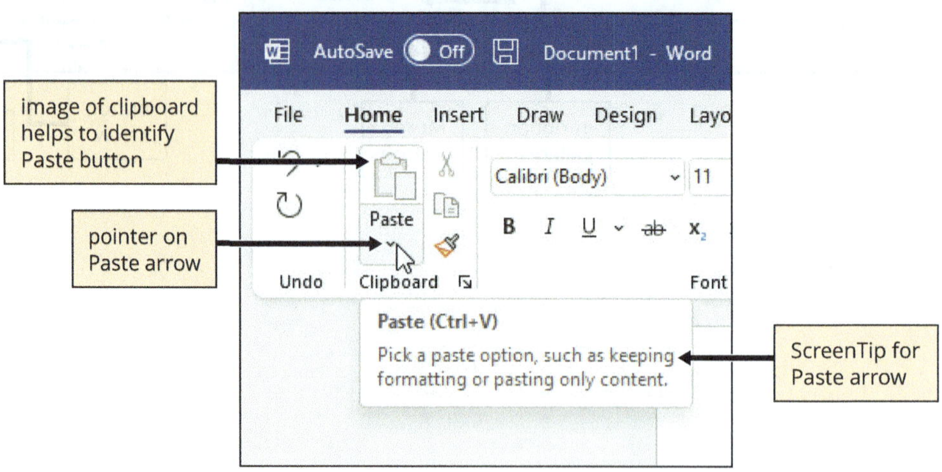

Figure 1–8

Some groups on the ribbon have a small arrow in the lower-right corner, called a **Dialog Box Launcher**, that when clicked, displays a dialog box or opens a pane with additional options for the group (Figure 1–9). When presented with a dialog box, you make selections and must close the dialog box before returning to the document. A **pane**, in contrast to a dialog box, is a window that can remain open and visible while you work in the document and provides additional options.

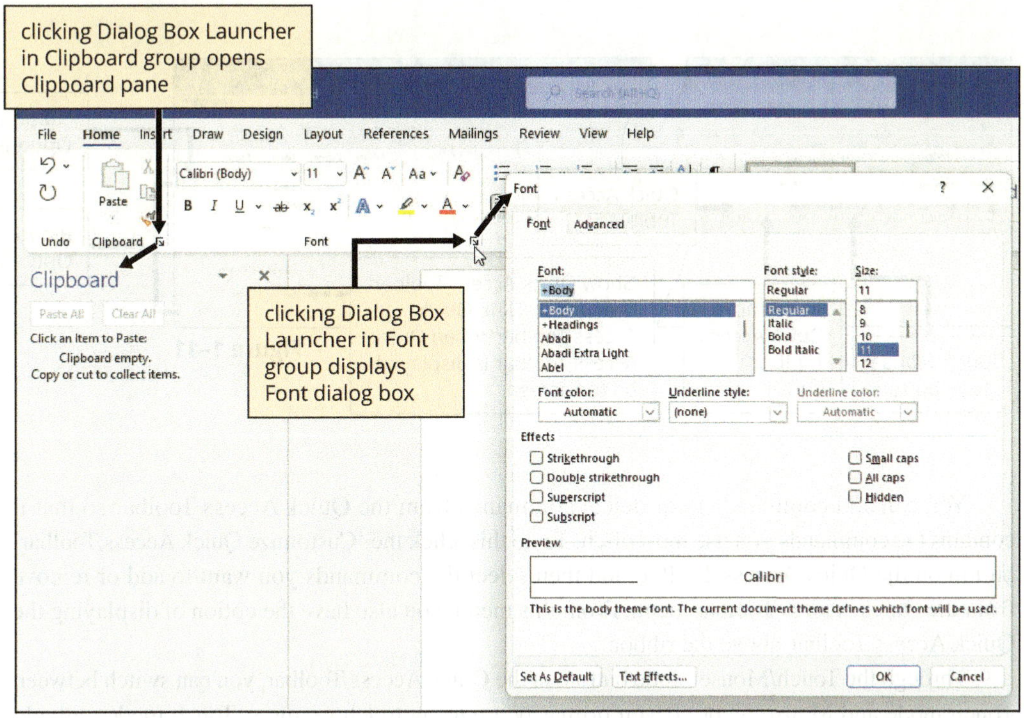

Figure 1–9

Search Box The **Search box**, which appears on the title bar, is a text box that helps you to find a command in Word or access the Word Help system (Figure 1–10). As you enter text in the Search box, the word-wheeling feature displays search results that are refined as you type. For example, if you want to insert an image in a document, you can type the text "insert image" in the Search box and then select the appropriate command.

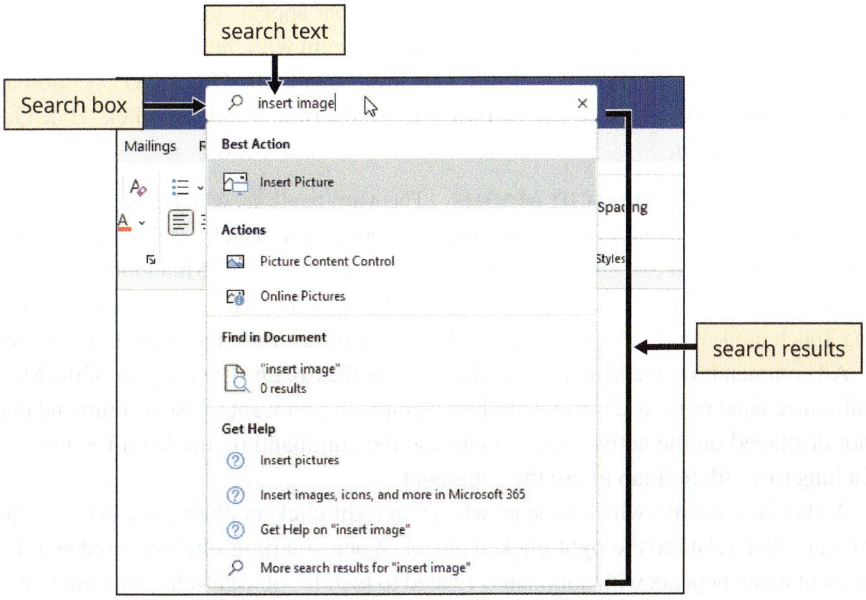

Figure 1–10

Quick Access Toolbar The **Quick Access Toolbar**, which initially is hidden by default, is a customizable toolbar that contains buttons you can click to perform frequently used commands (Figure 1–11). To display the Quick Access Toolbar, click the 'Ribbon Display Options' button at the right edge of the ribbon and then click 'Show Quick Access Toolbar' on the menu. When the Quick Access Toolbar is displayed on the screen, its commands always are available, regardless of the task you are performing.

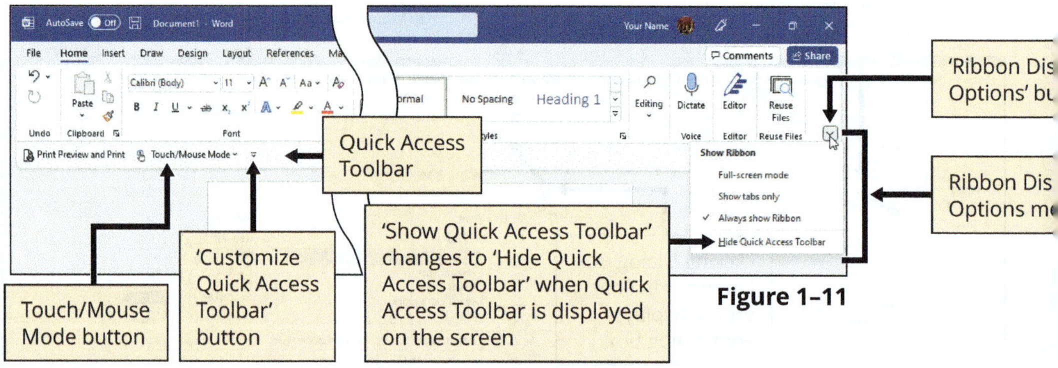

Figure 1–11

BTW
Mouse Mode
The figures in this book use Mouse mode. To switch to Mouse mode, click the 'Touch/Mouse Mode' button on the Quick Access Toolbar and then click Mouse on the Touch/Mouse Mode menu. If you are using Touch mode, you might notice that the function or appearance of your touch screen in Word differs slightly from this module's presentation.

You can add commands to or delete commands from the Quick Access Toolbar so that it contains the commands you use most often. To do this, click the 'Customize Quick Access Toolbar' button on the Quick Access Toolbar and then select the commands you want to add or remove from the Quick Access Toolbar menu. From this menu, you also have the option of displaying the Quick Access Toolbar above the ribbon.

Through the Touch/Mouse Mode button on the Quick Access Toolbar, you can switch between Touch mode and Mouse mode. If you primarily are using touch gestures, Touch mode will add more space between commands on menus and on the ribbon so that they are easier to tap. While touch gestures are convenient ways to interact with Word, not all features are supported when you are using Touch mode. If you are using a mouse, Mouse mode will not add the extra space between buttons and commands. The modules in this book show the screens in Mouse mode.

If you are using a mouse, verify that you are using Mouse mode so that your screens match the figures in this book by clicking the Touch/Mouse Mode button on the Quick Access Toolbar (shown in Figure 1–11) and then, if necessary, clicking Mouse on the menu.

Each time you start Word, the Quick Access Toolbar appears the same way it did the last time you used Word. The modules in this book, however, begin with the Quick Access Toolbar hidden, as it is with the initial installation of the software. To hide the Quick Access Toolbar, click the 'Ribbon Display Options' button at the right edge of the ribbon and then click 'Hide Quick Access Toolbar' on the menu.

BTW
Turning Off the Mini Toolbar
If you do not want the Mini toolbar to appear, click File on the ribbon to open Backstage view, click Options in Backstage view, if necessary, click General (Options dialog box), remove the check mark from the 'Show Mini Toolbar on selection' check box, and then click OK.

Mini Toolbar and Shortcut Menus The **Mini toolbar**, which appears near selected text, contains the most frequently used text formatting commands (which are those commands related to changing the appearance of text in a document). If you do not use the Mini toolbar, it disappears from the screen. The buttons, arrows, and boxes on the Mini toolbar vary, depending on whether you are using Touch mode or Mouse mode. To use the Mini toolbar, move the pointer into the Mini toolbar.

All commands on the Mini toolbar also exist on the ribbon. The purpose of the Mini toolbar is to minimize hand or mouse movement. For example, if you want to use a command that currently is not displayed on the active tab, you can use the command on the Mini toolbar — instead of switching to a different tab to use the command.

A **shortcut menu**, which appears when you right-click an object, is a list of frequently used commands that relate to the right-clicked object. When you right-click selected text, for example, a shortcut menu appears with commands related to text. If you right-click an item in the document window, Word displays both the Mini toolbar and a shortcut menu (Figure 1–12).

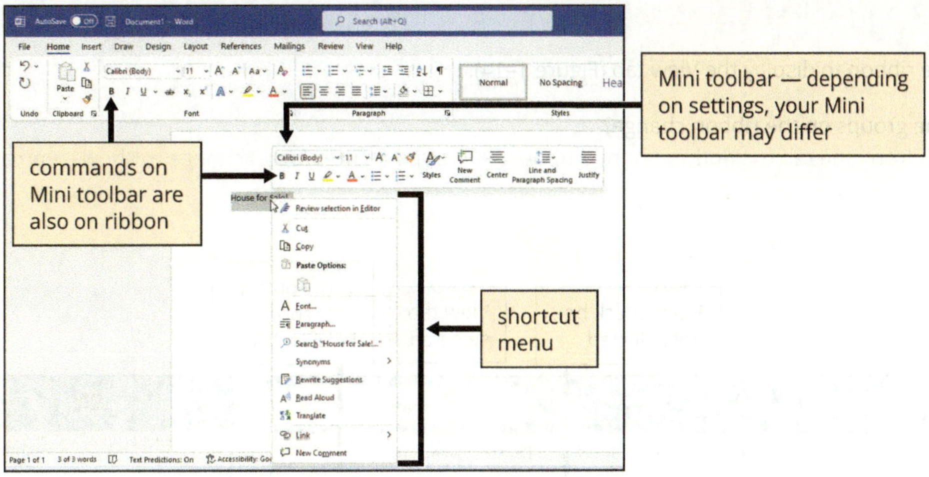

Figure 1–12

KeyTips If you prefer using the keyboard instead of the mouse, you can press ALT on the keyboard to display **KeyTips**, which are labels that appear over each tab and command on the ribbon (Figure 1–13). To select a tab or command using the keyboard, press the letter or number displayed in the KeyTip, which may cause additional KeyTips related to the selected command to appear. For example, to select the Bold button on the Home tab, press ALT, then press H, and then press 1. To remove the KeyTips from the screen, press ALT or ESC until all KeyTips disappear, or click anywhere in the Word window.

Figure 1–13

Account Manager You easily can switch or sign out of a Microsoft account by clicking the button that shows your profile photo or name on the right edge of the title bar (shown in Figure 1–13) to display the account manager menu. From this menu, you can view your Microsoft account and Office user info, or you can switch to a different account or sign out of an account.

To Display a Different Tab on the Ribbon

When you start Word, the ribbon displays 11 main tabs: File, Home, Insert, Draw, Design, Layout, References, Mailings, Review, View, and Help. (Note that depending on the type of computer or device you are using, the Draw tab may not appear.) The tab currently displayed is called the active tab. To display a different tab on the ribbon, you click the tab. The following step displays the View tab, that is, makes it the active tab. **Why?** When working with Word, you may need to switch tabs to access other options for working with a document or to verify settings.

1

- Click View on the ribbon to display the View tab (Figure 1–14).

Q&A Why did the groups on the ribbon change?
When you switch from one tab to another on the ribbon, the groups on the ribbon change to show commands related to the selected tab.

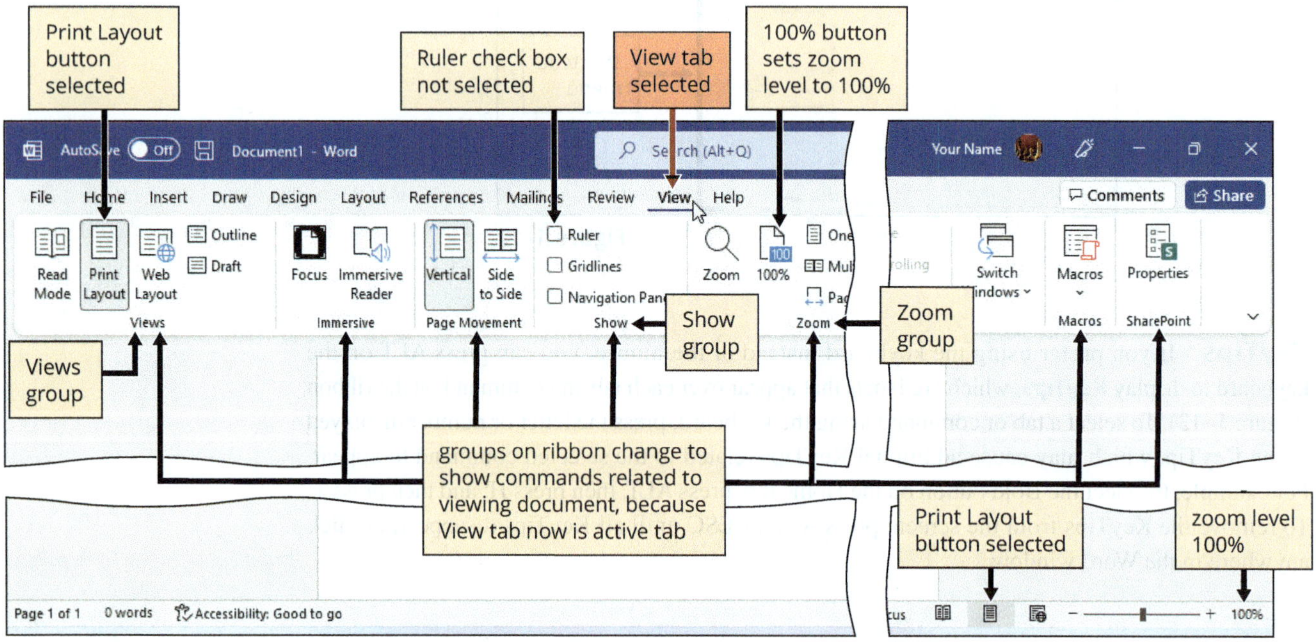

Figure 1–14

2

- Verify that the Print Layout button (View tab | Views group) is selected. (If it is not selected, click it to ensure the screen is in Print Layout view.)
- Verify that the zoom level is 100% on the status bar. (If it is not, click the 100% button (View tab | Zoom group) to set the zoom level to 100%.)
- Verify that the Ruler check box (View tab | Show group) is not selected. (If it is selected, click it to remove the selection because you do not want the rulers to appear on the screen.)
- **Experiment:** Click the other tabs on the ribbon to view their contents. When you are finished, click Home on the ribbon to display the Home tab.
- Verify that Normal (Home tab | Styles group) is selected in the Styles gallery (shown in Figure 1–5). (If it is not selected, click it so that your document uses the Normal style.)

Q&A What is the Normal style?
When you create a document, Word formats the text using a particular style. The **Normal style** is the default style that is applied to all text when you start Word.

To Adjust the Margins

Word is preset to use standard 8.5-by-11-inch paper, with 1-inch top, bottom, left, and right margins. The flyer in this module uses .5-inch top, bottom, left, and right margins. **Why?** You would like more text to fit from left to right and top to bottom on the page.

When you change the default (preset) margin settings, the new margin settings affect every page in the document. If you wanted the margins to affect just a portion of the document, you would divide the document into sections (discussed in a later module), which enables you to specify different margin settings for each section. The following steps change margin settings.

1

- Click Layout on the ribbon to display the Layout tab.
- Click the Margins button (Layout tab | Page Setup group) to display the Margins gallery (Figure 1–15).

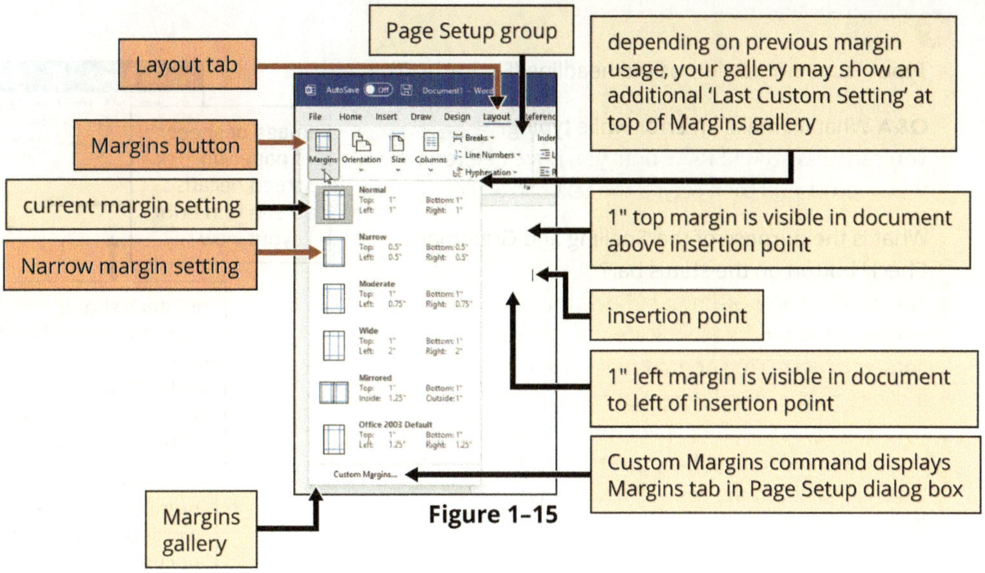

Figure 1–15

2

- Click Narrow in the Margins gallery to change the margins to the specified settings (Figure 1–16).

Q&A What if the margin settings I want are not in the Margins gallery?
You can click Custom Margins in the Margins gallery and then enter your desired margin values in the top, bottom, left, and right boxes in the Page Setup dialog box.

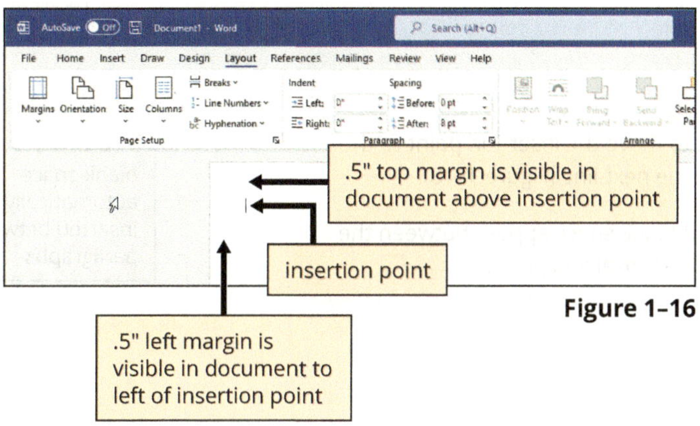

Figure 1–16

Other Ways

1. Position pointer on margin boundary on ruler; when pointer changes to two-headed arrow, drag margin boundary on ruler

Entering Text in a Document

The first step in creating a document is to enter its text. With the projects in this book, you enter text by typing on the keyboard. By default, Word positions text you type at the left margin. In a later section of this module, you will learn how to format, or change the appearance of, the entered text.

BTW
Character Widths
Many word processing documents use variable character fonts, where some characters are wider than others; for example, the letter w is wider than the letter i.

To Type Text

To begin creating the flyer in this module, type the headline in the document window. **Why?** The headline is the first line of text in the flyer. The following steps type the first line of text in the document.

1

- Type **House for Sale!** as the headline (Figure 1–17).

Q&A What if I make an error while typing?
You can press BACKSPACE until you have deleted the text in error and then retype the text correctly.

What is the purpose of the 'Spelling and Grammar Check' button on the status bar?
The 'Spelling and Grammar Check' button displays either a check mark to indicate the entered text contains no spelling or grammar errors, or an X to indicate that it found potential errors. Word flags potential errors in the document with squiggly, dotted, or double underlines that appear in a variety of colors. Later in this module, you will learn how to fix or ignore flagged errors.

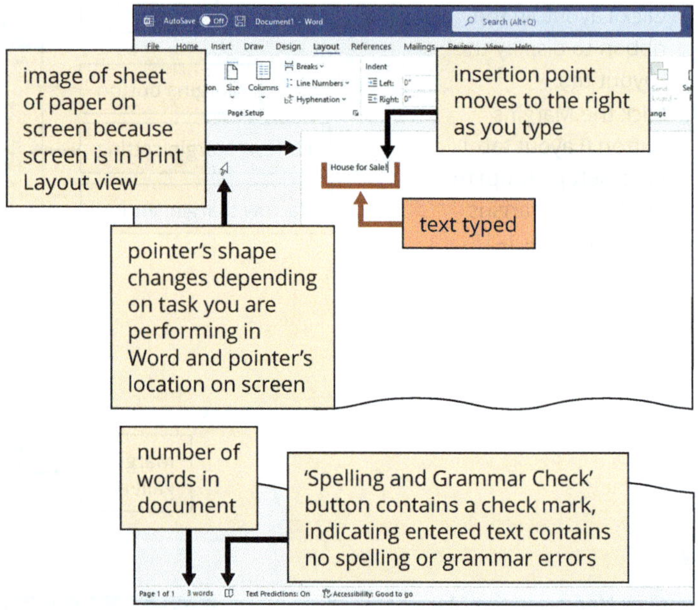

Figure 1–17

2

- Press ENTER to move the insertion point to the beginning of the next line (Figure 1–18).

Q&A Why did blank space appear between the headline and the insertion point?
Each time you press ENTER, Word creates a new paragraph and inserts blank space between the two paragraphs. Later in this module, you will learn how to increase and decrease the spacing between paragraphs.

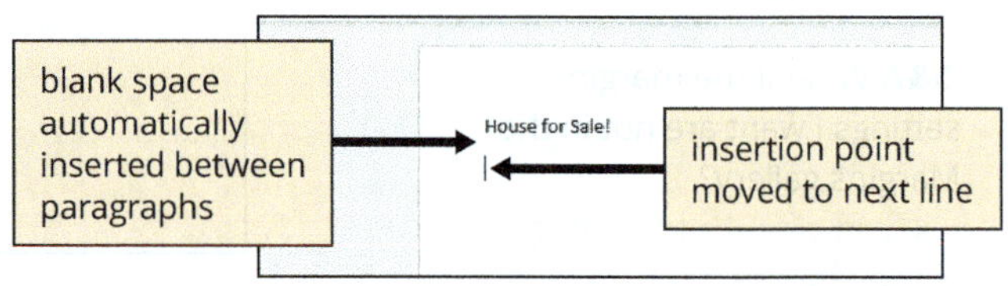

Figure 1–18

Consider This

How do you use the touch keyboard with a touch screen?
To display the on-screen touch keyboard, tap the Touch Keyboard button on the Windows taskbar. When finished using the touch keyboard, tap the X button on the touch keyboard to close the keyboard.

To Change the Zoom to Page Width

The next step in creating this flyer is to enlarge the contents that appear on the screen. **Why?** You would like the text on the screen to be larger so that it is easier to read. The document currently displays at a zoom level of 100% (shown in Figure 1–14). With Word, you can change the zoom to page width, which zooms (enlarges or shrinks) the image of the sheet of paper on the screen so that it is the width of the Word window. The following step changes the zoom to page width.

1

- Click View on the ribbon to display the View tab.
- Click the Page Width button (View tab | Zoom group) to display the page the same width as the document window (Figure 1–19).

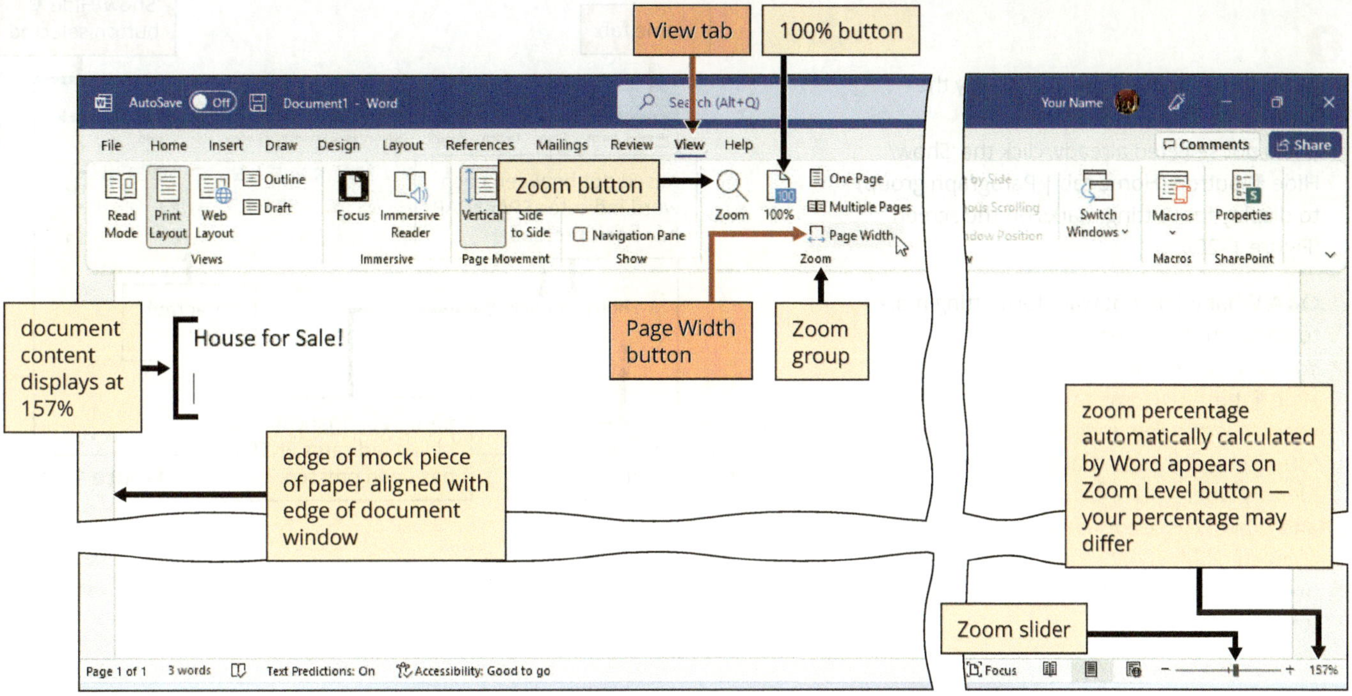

Figure 1–19

Q&A If I change the zoom, will the document print differently?

Changing the zoom has no effect on the printed document.

What are the other predefined zoom options?

Through the View tab | Zoom group or the Zoom dialog box (Zoom button in Zoom group), you can zoom to one page (an entire single page appears in the document window), many pages (multiple pages appear at once in the document window), page width, text width, and a variety of set percentages. Whereas changing the zoom to page width places the edges of the page at the edges of the document window, changing the zoom to text width places the document contents at the edges of the document window.

What if I wanted to change the Zoom back to 100%?

You could click the 100% button (View tab | Zoom group) or drag the zoom slider until 100% appears on Zoom level button.

Other Ways

1. Click Zoom button (View tab | Zoom group), click Whole page (Zoom dialog box), click OK

To Display Formatting Marks

You may find it helpful to display formatting marks while working in a document. **Why?** Formatting marks indicate where in a document you pressed ENTER, SPACEBAR, and other nonprinting characters. A **formatting mark** is a nonprinting character that appears on the screen to indicate the ends of paragraphs, tabs, and other formatting elements. For example, the paragraph mark (¶) is a formatting mark that indicates where you pressed ENTER. A raised dot (·) shows where you pressed SPACEBAR. Formatting marks are discussed as they appear on the screen.

Depending on settings made during previous Word sessions, your Word screen already may display formatting marks (shown in Figure 1–20). The following step displays formatting marks, if they do not show already on the screen.

1

- Click Home on the ribbon to display the Home tab.
- If it is not selected already, click the 'Show/Hide ¶' button (Home tab | Paragraph group) to display formatting marks on the screen (Figure 1–20).

Q&A What if I do not want formatting marks to show on the screen?
You can hide them by clicking the 'Show/Hide ¶' button (Home tab | Paragraph group) again. It is recommended that you display formatting marks so that you visually can identify when you press ENTER, SPACEBAR, and other keys associated with nonprinting characters. Most of the document windows presented in this book, therefore, show formatting marks.

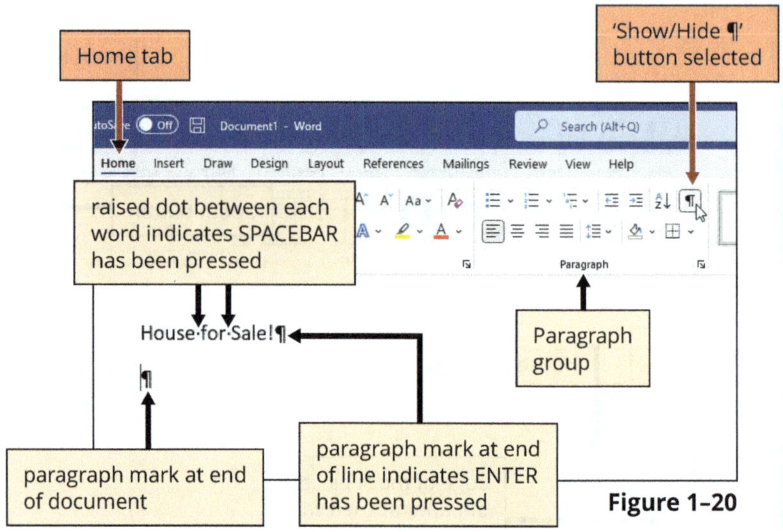

Figure 1–20

Other Ways

1. Press CTRL+SHIFT+*

BTW
Formatting Marks
With some fonts, the formatting marks will not be displayed properly on the screen. For example, the raised dot that signifies a blank space between words may be displayed behind a character instead of in the blank space, causing the characters to look incorrect. Even if they look incorrect, they still will print correctly.

BTW
Text Predictions
While entering text for any project in this book, even when the instructions state to type the text, you may use the text predictions to save typing time.

Wordwrap

Wordwrap allows you to type words in a paragraph continually without pressing ENTER at the end of each line. As you type, if a word extends beyond the right margin, Word also automatically positions that word on the next line along with the insertion point.

Word creates a new paragraph each time you press ENTER. Thus, as you type text in the document window, do not press ENTER when the insertion point reaches the right margin. Instead, press ENTER only in these circumstances:

1. To insert a blank line(s) in a document (as shown in a later set of steps)
2. To begin a new paragraph
3. To terminate a short line of text and advance to the next line
4. To respond to questions or prompts in Word dialog boxes, panes, and other on-screen objects

To Wordwrap Text as You Type

The next step in creating the flyer is to type the body copy. **Why?** In many flyers, the body copy text appears below the headline. The following steps illustrate how the body copy text wordwraps as you enter it in the document, which means you will not have to press ENTER at the end of the line.

1

- Begin typing the first sentence of the body copy up to the e in the word, bedrooms, and notice that Word displays the rest of the word, bedrooms, in a light gray color (Figure 1–21): **Located in Whispering Oaks subdivision, this cozy home with 3 be**

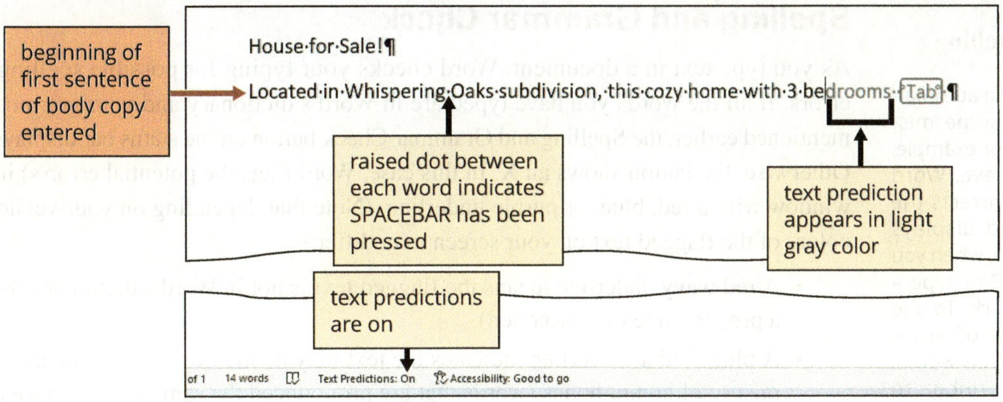

Figure 1–21

Q&A Why does Word display the rest of the word in a light gray color, even though I have not typed the rest of the word?
To help you type text more quickly and efficiently, Word may provide **text predictions**, where it anticipates text as you type and presents suggested words or phrases in a light gray color. To accept the suggestion, press TAB or RIGHT ARROW; to ignore a suggestion, simply continue typing and the suggestion will disappear.

Can I turn text predictions off?
Yes. The status bar displays whether text predictions are on or off. To turn off text predictions, click the Text Predictions button on the status bar to display the options in the Advanced tab of the Word Options dialog box, remove the check mark from the 'Show text predictions while typing' check box, and then click OK to close the dialog box. Conversely, be sure the 'Show text predictions while typing' check box contains a check mark to turn text predictions on.

2

- Press TAB to accept the suggestion.

Q&A What if the text prediction does not appear or it disappears before I can press TAB?
Type **drooms** to enter the rest of the word.

3

- Press SPACEBAR and then continue typing the paragraph of the body copy: **and 2.5 bathrooms provides a warm, welcoming feeling throughout. Listed at only $215,000!**

Q&A Why does my document wrap on different words?
The printer connected to a computer or device is one factor that can control where wordwrap occurs for each line in a document. Thus, it is possible that the same document could wordwrap differently if printed on different printers.

4

- Press ENTER to position the insertion point on the next line in the document (Figure 1–22).

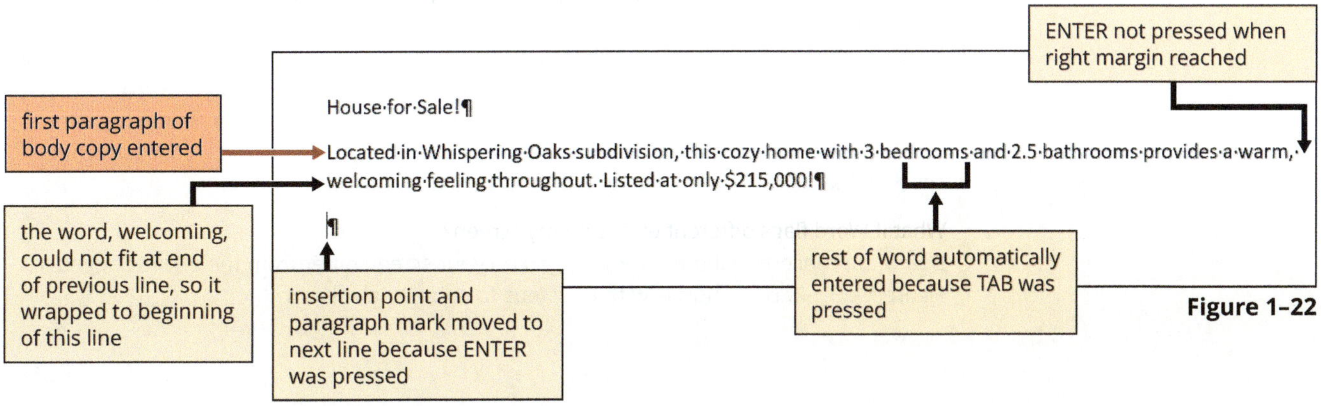

Figure 1–22

BTW
Automatic Spelling Correction
As you type, Word automatically corrects some misspelled words. For example, if you type recieve, Word automatically corrects the misspelling and displays the word, receive, when you press SPACEBAR or type a punctuation mark. To see a complete list of automatically corrected words, click File on the ribbon to open Backstage view, click Options in Backstage view, click Proofing in the left pane (Word Options dialog box), click the AutoCorrect Options button, and then scroll through the list near the bottom of the dialog box.

Spelling and Grammar Check

As you type text in a document, Word checks your typing for possible spelling and grammar errors. If all the words you have typed are in Word's dictionary and your grammar is correct, as mentioned earlier, the Spelling and Grammar Check button on the status bar displays a check mark. Otherwise, the button shows an X. In this case, Word flags the potential error(s) in the document window with a red, blue, or purple underline. (Note that depending on your version of Word, the colors of the flagged text on your screen may differ.)

- A red wavy underline means the flagged text is not in Word's dictionary (because it is a proper name or misspelled).
- A blue double underline indicates the text may be incorrect grammatically, such as a misuse of homophones (words that are pronounced the same but that have different spellings or meanings, such as one and won).
- A purple dotted underline indicates that Word can present a suggestion for more concise writing or different word usage.

A flagged word is not necessarily misspelled or grammatically incorrect. For example, many names, abbreviations, and specialized terms are not in Word's main dictionary. In these cases, you can instruct Word to ignore the flagged word. As you type, Word also detects duplicate words while checking for spelling errors. For example, if your document contains the phrase, to the the store, Word places a red wavy underline below the second occurrence of the word, the.

To Enter More Text with Spelling and Grammar Errors

BTW
Zooming
If text is too small for you to read on the screen, you can zoom the document by dragging the Zoom slider on the status bar or by clicking the Zoom Out or Zoom In buttons on the status bar. Changing the zoom has no effect on the printed document.

When entering the following text in the flyer, you will intentionally make some spelling and grammar errors, because the next set of steps illustrates checking spelling and grammar as you work in a document. The following steps enter text in the flyer that contains spelling and grammar errors. Later in this module, the text you enter here will be formatted as a bulleted list.

1. With the insertion point positioned as shown in Figure 1–22, type **Features:**
2. Press ENTER and then type **Spasius backyard with stone firepit**
3. Press ENTER and then type **Covered front porch**
4. Press ENTER and then type **Gas fireplace on mane floor**
5. Press ENTER and then type **Theater room (all equipment stays!)**
6. Press ENTER and then type **Close to shopping, restaurants, pool, and also more more!** and then press ENTER (as shown in Figure 1–23).

Q&A What if Word does not flag my spelling and grammar errors with wavy, dotted, or double underlines?
To verify that the features to check spelling and grammar as you type are enabled, click File on the ribbon to open Backstage view and then click Options in Backstage view. When the Word Options dialog box is displayed, click Proofing in the left pane and then ensure the 'Check spelling as you type' and 'Mark grammar errors as you type' check boxes contain check marks. Click OK to close the Word Options dialog box.

What if Word flags different errors on my screen?
Do not be concerned if the errors flagged on your screen differ from the errors flagged in Figure 1–23. Simply continue with the steps to correct any errors.

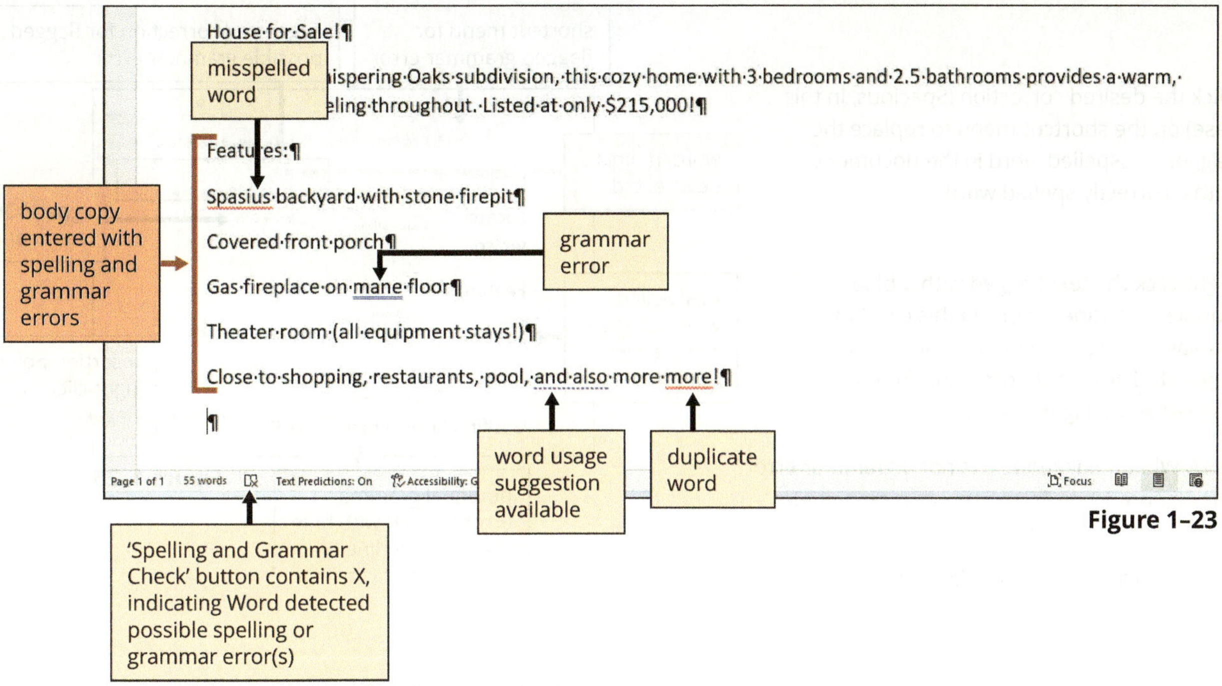

Figure 1–23

To Check Spelling and Grammar as You Work in a Document

Although you can check an entire document for spelling and grammar errors at once, you also can check flagged errors as they appear on the screen while you work in a document. The following steps correct the spelling and grammar errors entered in the previous steps. **Why?** These steps illustrate Word's features that check spelling and grammar as you type. If you are completing this project on a computer or device, your flyer may contain additional or different flagged words, depending on the accuracy of your typing. If your screen does not flag the text shown here, correct the errors without performing these steps.

1

- Right-click the word flagged with a red wavy underline (Spasius, in this case) to display a shortcut menu that presents a list of suggested spelling corrections for the flagged word (Figure 1–24).

Q&A What if, when I right-click the misspelled word, my desired correction is not in the list on the shortcut menu?
You can click outside the shortcut menu to close the shortcut menu and then retype the correct word.

What if a flagged word actually is, for example, a proper name and spelled correctly?
Click Ignore All on the shortcut menu to instruct Word not to flag future occurrences of the same word in this document. Or, click 'Add to Dictionary' to add it to Word's dictionary so that it is not flagged in the future.

What happens if I click in the flagged word instead of right-clicking it?
An abbreviated menu is displayed that shows only the list of suggested alternatives for the flagged text along with the Ignore command. If you only want these options, click the flagged word instead of right-clicking it.

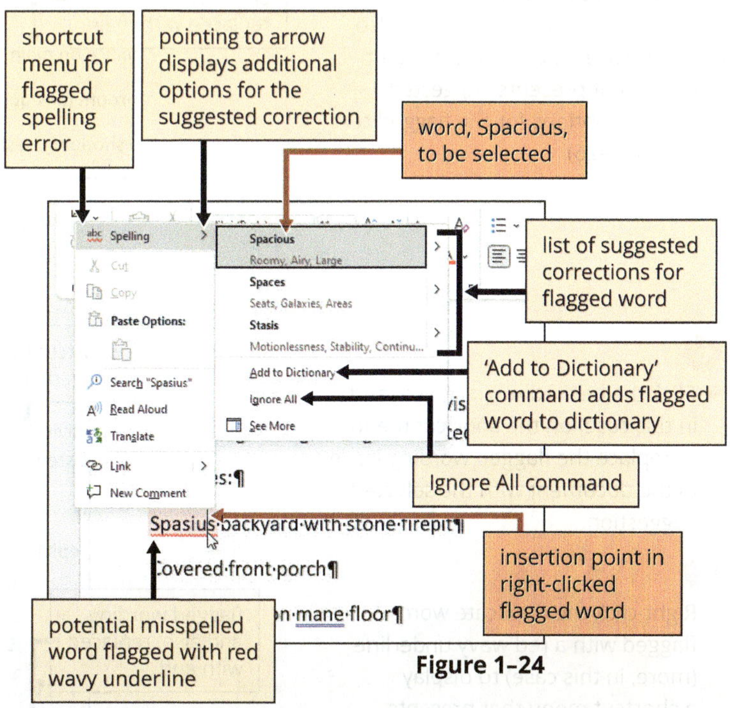

Figure 1–24

2

- Click the desired correction (Spacious, in this case) on the shortcut menu to replace the flagged misspelled word in the document with a correctly spelled word.

3

- Right-click the text flagged with a blue double underline (mane, in this case) to display a shortcut menu that presents a suggested grammar correction for the flagged word (Figure 1–25).

Q&A What if flagged text is not a grammar error?
Click Ignore Once on the shortcut menu to instruct Word to ignore flagged text.

What if a true error is not flagged?
Simply correct the error yourself by adding or deleting the appropriate text.

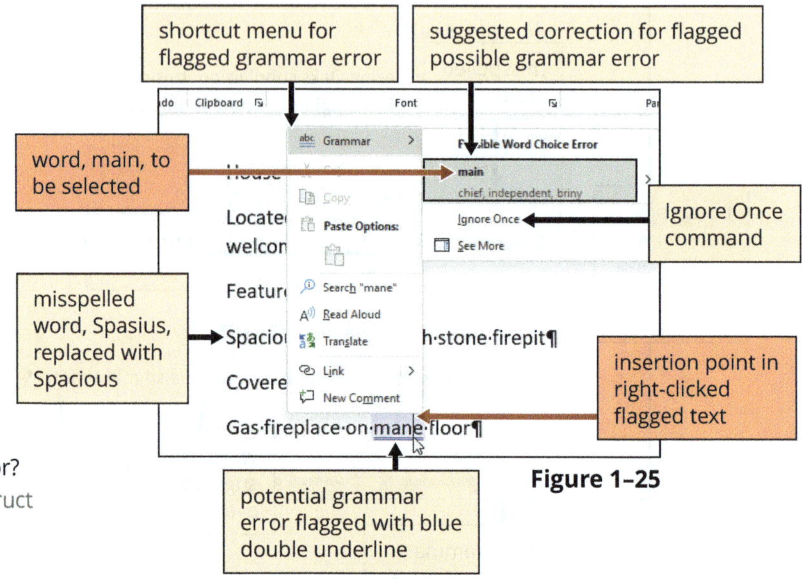

Figure 1–25

4

- Click the desired correction (main, in this case) on the shortcut menu to replace the flagged grammar error in the document with the selected suggestion.

5

- Right-click the text flagged with a purple dotted underline (and also, in this case) to display a shortcut menu that presents suggested wording options for the flagged text (Figure 1–26).

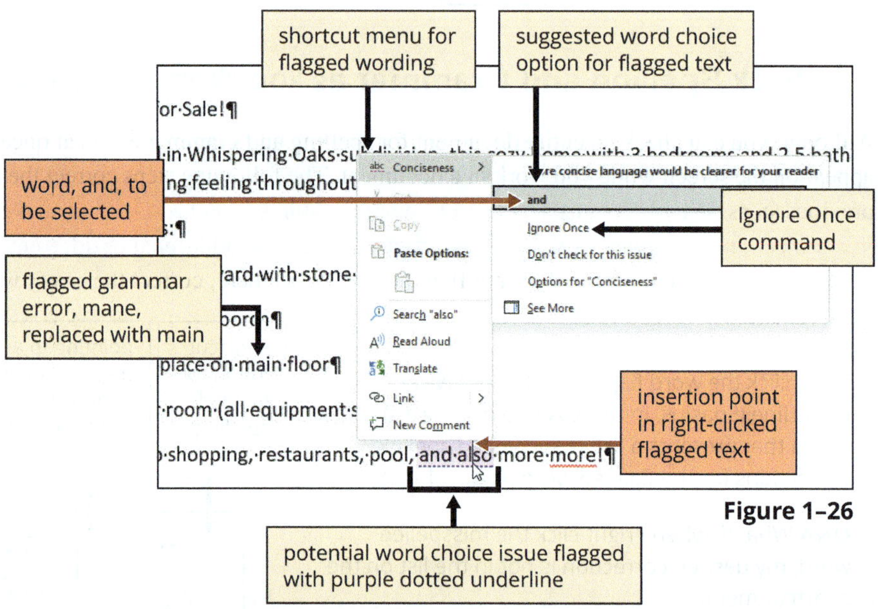

Figure 1–26

6

- Click the desired word choice (and, in this case) on the shortcut menu to replace the flagged wording issue in the document with the selected suggestion.

7

- Right-click the duplicate word flagged with a red wavy underline (more, in this case) to display a shortcut menu that presents a menu option for deleting the repeated word (Figure 1–27).

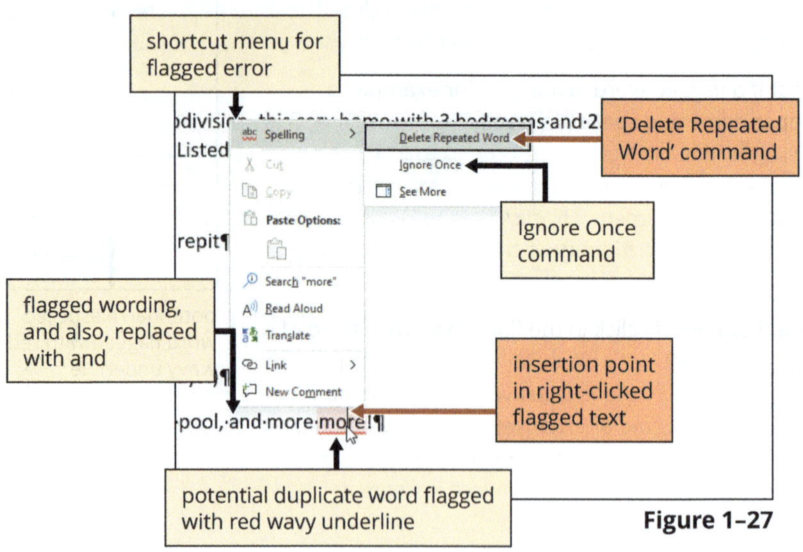

Figure 1–27

8

- Click 'Delete Repeated Word' on the shortcut menu to delete the repeated flagged wording (shown in Figure 1–28).

Other Ways

1. Click flagged text, click desired correction or command in menu	2. Click 'Spelling and Grammar Check' button on status bar, click desired correction or commands in Editor pane, close Editor pane	3. Click 'Editor' button (Review tab | Proofing group), click desired correction or commands in Editor pane, close Editor pane	4. Press F7, click desired correction or commands in Editor pane, close Editor pane

To Insert a Blank Line

In the flyer, the digital picture showing the house for sale appears between the two lists in the body copy. You will not insert this picture, however, until after you enter and format all text. **Why?** Although you can format text and insert pictures in any order, for illustration purposes, this module formats all text first before inserting the picture. Thus, you leave a blank line in the document as a placeholder for the picture.

To enter a blank line in a document, press ENTER without typing any text on the line. The following steps insert a blank line in the document.

1

- Position the insertion point on the paragraph mark at the left margin on the line below the entered text (Figure 1–28).

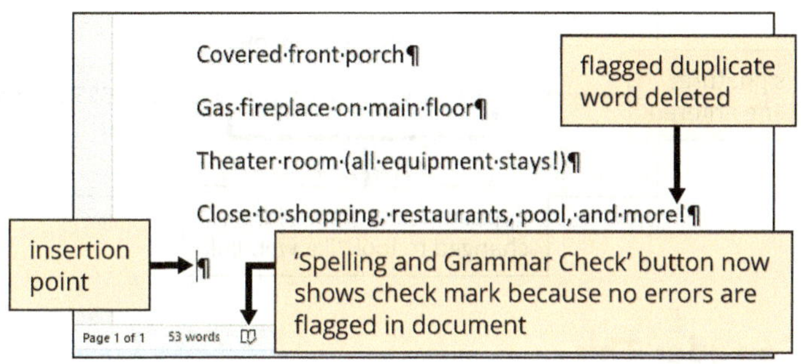

Figure 1–28

2

- Press ENTER to insert a blank line in the document above the insertion point (Figure 1–29).

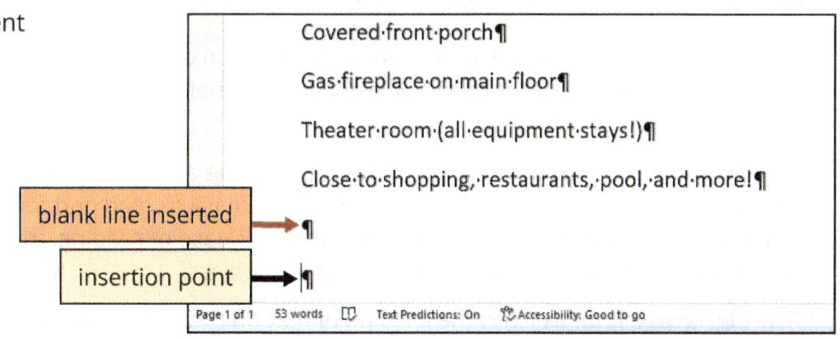

Figure 1–29

To Enter More Text

In the flyer, the text yet to be entered includes the remainder of the body copy, some of which will be formatted as a numbered list, and the signature line. The following steps enter the remainder of text in the flyer.

1. With the insertion point positioned as shown in Figure 1–29, type **Recent updates:** and then press ENTER.
2. Type **New exterior vinyl and stone siding** and then press ENTER.
3. Type **Refinished hardwood flooring** and then press ENTER.
4. Type **Beautifully landscaped** and then press ENTER.

5. Type **Fresh interior paint** and then press ENTER.

6. Type **New energy-efficient windows** and then press ENTER.

7. Type the signature line in the flyer (Figure 1–30): **Visit www.a1homerealty.com or call 206-555-2283 for a showing!**

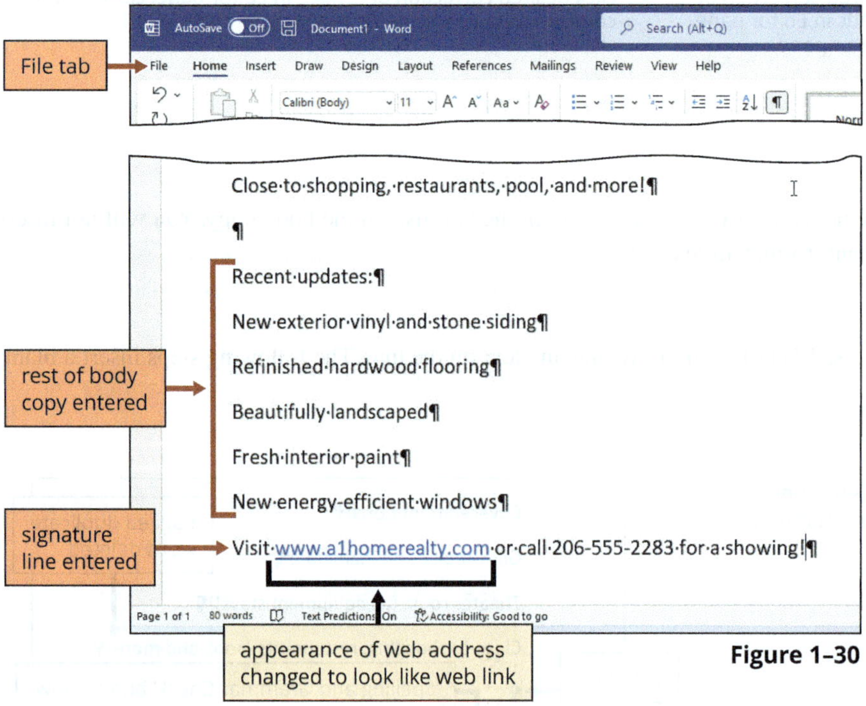

Figure 1–30

Q&A Why is the text, www.a1homerealty.com, the color blue and underlined?

Word recognized the text as a web address and automatically changed its appearance to look and function like a web link. Later in this project, you will change its appearance and function back to regular text.

Consider This

How should you organize text in a flyer?

The text in a flyer typically is organized into three areas: headline, body copy, and signature line.

- The **headline** is the first line of text on the flyer. It can contain a message (i.e., house for sale), name the product or service being offered (i.e., job fair), or identify the benefit that will be gained (such as a convenience, better performance, greater security, or higher earnings).
- The **body copy** consists of text between the headline and the signature line. This text highlights the key points of the message in as few words as possible. It should be easy to read and follow. While emphasizing the positive, the body copy must be realistic, truthful, and believable. For ease of reading, the body copy often contains a bulleted list and/or a numbered list and a picture or other graphical object.
- The **signature line**, which is the last line of text on the flyer, may contain contact information, reference additional information, or identify a call to action.

BTW

Minimize Wrist Injury

Computer users frequently switch among the keyboard, the mouse, and touch gestures during a word processing session; such switching strains the wrist. To help prevent wrist injury, minimize switching. For instance, if your fingers already are on the keyboard, use keyboard keys to scroll. If your hand already is on the mouse, use the mouse to scroll. If your fingertips already are on the touch screen, use your finger to slide the document to a new location (or use touch gestures to scroll).

Navigating a Document

You view only a portion of a document on the screen through the document window. At some point when you type text or insert objects (such as pictures), Word probably will scroll the top or bottom portion of the document off the screen. Although you cannot see the text and objects once they scroll off the screen, they remain in the document.

You can use touch gestures, the keyboard, or a mouse to scroll to a different location in a document and/or move the insertion point around a document. If you are using a touch screen, simply use your finger to slide the document up or down to display a different location in the document and then tap to move the insertion point to a new location. When you use the keyboard, the insertion point automatically moves when you press the desired keys. Table 1–1 outlines various techniques to navigate a document using the keyboard.

Table 1-1: Moving the Insertion Point with the Keyboard

Insertion Point Direction	Key(s) to Press	Insertion Point Direction	Key(s) to Press
Left one character	LEFT ARROW	Up one paragraph	CTRL+UP ARROW
Right one character	RIGHT ARROW	Down one paragraph	CTRL+DOWN ARROW
Left one word	CTRL+LEFT ARROW	Up one screen	PAGE UP
Right one word	CTRL+RIGHT ARROW	Down one screen	PAGE DOWN
Up one line	UP ARROW	To top of document window	ALT+CTRL+PAGE UP
Down one line	DOWN ARROW	To bottom of document window	ALT+CTRL+PAGE DOWN
To end of line	END	To beginning of document	CTRL+HOME
To beginning of line	HOME	To end of document	CTRL+END

With the mouse, you can use the scroll arrows or the scroll box on the scroll bar to display a different portion of the document in the document window and then click the mouse to move the insertion point to that location. Table 1–2 explains various techniques for using the scroll bar to scroll vertically with the mouse.

Table 1-2: Using the Scroll Bar to Scroll Vertically with the Mouse

Scroll Direction	Mouse Action	Scroll Direction	Mouse Action
Up	Drag the scroll box upward.	Down one screen	Click anywhere below the scroll box on the vertical scroll bar.
Down	Drag the scroll box downward.	Up one line	Click the scroll arrow at the top of the vertical scroll bar.
Up one screen	Click anywhere above the scroll box on the vertical scroll bar.	Down one line	Click the scroll arrow at the bottom of the vertical scroll bar.

To Save a Document for the First Time

While you are creating a document, the computer or mobile device stores it in memory. When you **save** a document, the computer or mobile device places it on a storage medium such as a hard drive, USB flash drive, or online using a cloud storage service, such as OneDrive, so that you can retrieve it later. A saved document is referred to as a **file**, which contains a collection of information stored on a computer, such as a document, photo, or song. A **file name** is a unique, descriptive name that identifies the file's content and is assigned to a file when it is saved.

When saving a document, you must decide which storage medium to use:

- If you always work on the same computer and have no need to transport your projects to a different location, then your computer's hard drive will suffice as a storage location. It is a good idea, however, to save a backup copy of your projects on a separate medium in case the file becomes corrupted or the computer's hard drive fails. The documents created in this book are saved to the computer's hard drive.
- If you plan to work on your documents in various locations or on multiple computers or mobile devices, then you should save your documents to an online cloud storage service, such as OneDrive, or on a portable medium, such as a USB flash drive.

The following steps save a document in the Documents library on your computer's hard drive. **Why?** You have performed many tasks while creating this project and do not want to risk losing the work completed thus far. Accordingly, you should save the file.

1

- Click File on the ribbon (shown in Figure 1–30) to open Backstage view (Figure 1–31).

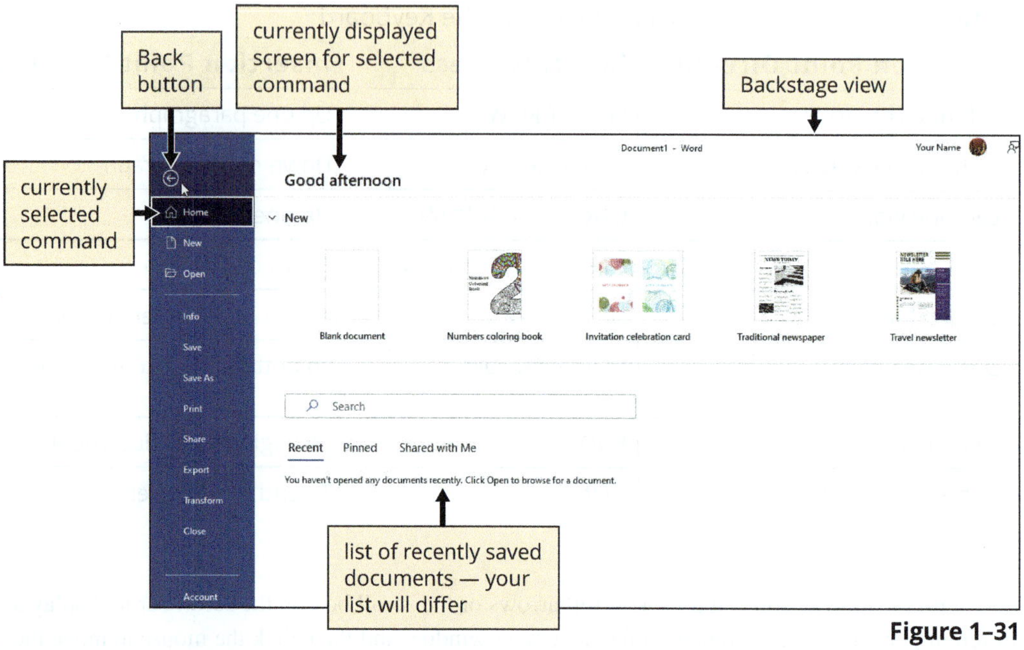

Figure 1–31

Q&A What is the purpose of the File tab on the ribbon, and what is Backstage view?
The File tab opens **Backstage view**, which contains a set of commands that enable you to manage documents and options for Word. As you click different commands along the left side of Backstage view, the associated screen is displayed on the right side of Backstage view.

What if I accidentally click the File tab on the ribbon?
Click the Back button in Backstage view to return to the document window.

2

- Click Save As in Backstage view to display the Save As screen.
- Click This PC in the Save As screen to display the default save location on the computer or mobile device (Figure 1–32).

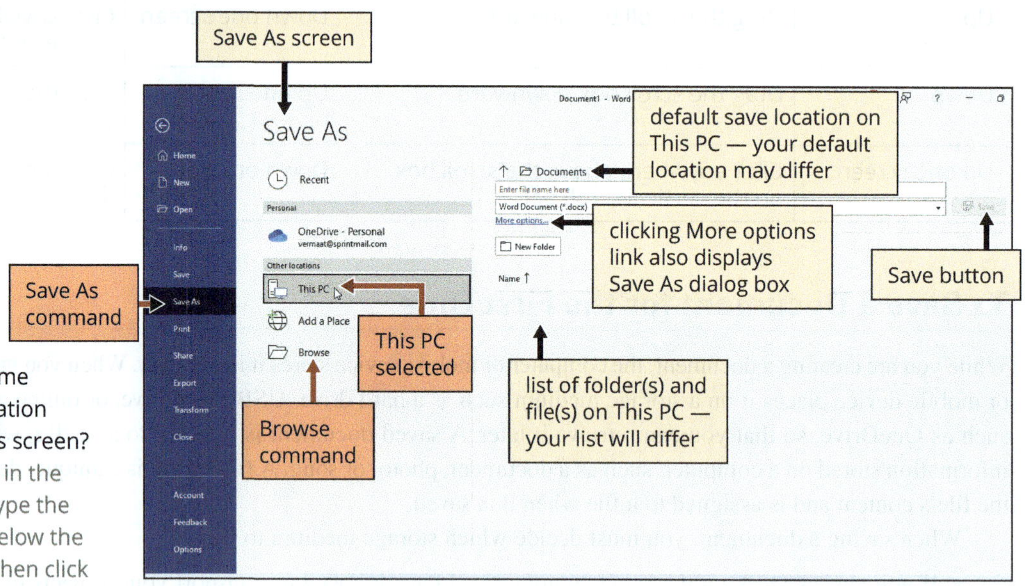

Figure 1–32

Q&A Can I type the file name below the default save location that displays in the Save As screen?
If you want to save the file in the default location, you can type the file name in the text box below the default save location and then click the Save button to the right of the default save location. These steps show how to display the Browse dialog box, in case you wanted to change the save location.

What if I wanted to save on OneDrive instead?
You would click OneDrive in the Save As screen.

3

- Click Browse in the Save As screen to display the Save As dialog box.

Q&A Why does a file name already appear in the File name box in the Save As dialog box?
Word automatically suggests a file name the first time you save a document. The suggested name usually consists of the first few words contained in the document. Because the suggested file name is selected in the File Name box, you do not need to delete it; as soon as you begin typing, the new file name replaces the selected text.

- Type **SC_WD_1_RealEstateFlyerUnformatted** in the File name text box (Save As dialog box) to specify the file name for the flyer (Figure 1–33).

Q&A Why is my list of files, folders, and drives arranged and named differently from those shown in the figure?
Your computer or mobile device's configuration determines how the list of files and folders is displayed and how drives are named. You can change the save location by clicking locations in the Navigation pane.

Do I have to save to the Documents library?
No. You can save to any device or folder. You also can create your own folders by clicking the New folder button shown in Figure 1–33.

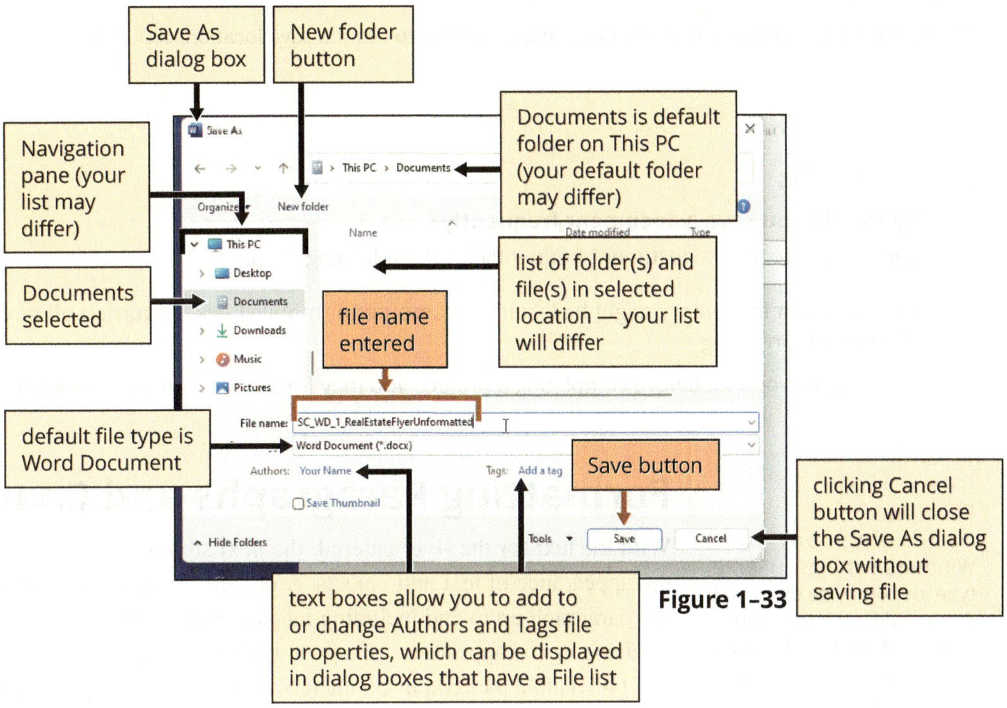

Figure 1–33

What characters can I use in a file name?
The only invalid characters are the backslash (\), slash (/), colon (:), asterisk (*), question mark (?), quotation mark ("), less than symbol (<), greater than symbol (>), and vertical bar (|).

What are all those characters in the file name in this project?
Some companies require certain rules be followed when creating file names; others allow you to choose your own. While you could have used the file name 'Real Estate Flyer Unformatted' with spaces inserted for readability, the file names in this book do not use spaces and all begin with SC (for Shelly Cashman) and WD (for Word) followed by the module number and then a descriptor of the file contents, so that they work with SAM, if you are using that platform as well.

4

- Click Save to save the flyer with the file name, SC_WD_1_RealEstateFlyerUnformatted, to the default save location (Figure 1–34).

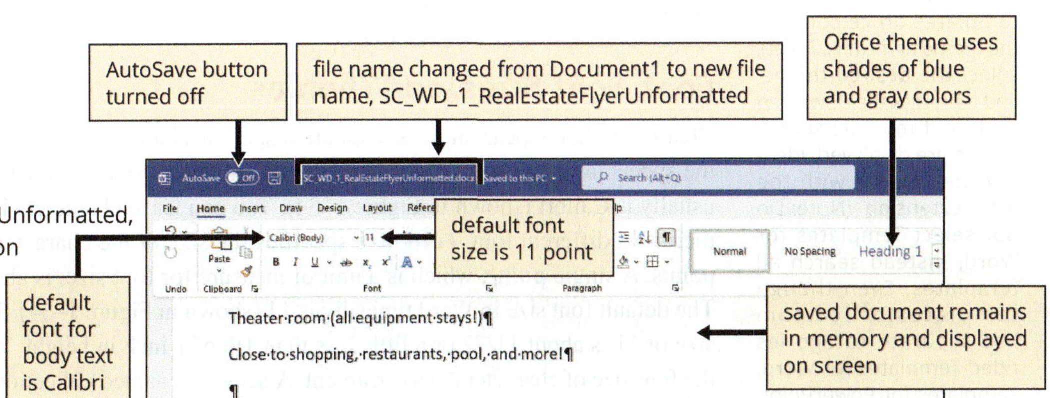

Figure 1–34

Q&A How do I know that Word saved the document?

While Word is saving your file, it briefly displays a message on the status bar indicating the amount of the file saved. When the document appears after saving, the new file name will be displayed in the title bar.

Why is the AutoSave button turned off on the title bar?

If you are saving the file on a computer or mobile device, the AutoSave button on the title bar is turned off. If you are saving the file on OneDrive, the AutoSave button is turned on, allowing Word to save the document as you make changes to it. If AutoSave is turned off, you will need to continue saving changes manually.

Other Ways

1. Press F12, type file name (Save As dialog box), navigate to desired save location, click Save

Consider This

Why should you save a document frequently?

It is important to save a document frequently for the following reasons:

- The document in memory might be lost if the computer or mobile device is turned off or you lose electrical power while Word is running.
- If you run out of time before completing a project, you may finish it at a future time without starting over.

BTW
File Type
Depending on your Windows settings, the file type .docx may be displayed on the title bar immediately to the right of the file name after you save the file. The file type .docx identifies the most recent type of Word document.

BTW
Office Themes
If a theme, such as the Facet theme used in this project, is not installed on your computer, follow these steps to locate and download it. Search templates.office.com for the theme name (i.e., Facet), select the desired theme, and then click the Download button. If multiple search results are displayed, identify the version with the .potx extension. (Note: Do not select Templates for Word; instead search all templates. Even though templates.office.com has separate categories titled Templates for Word, Templates for PowerPoint, etc., all applications use the same theme files.)

Formatting Paragraphs and Characters

With the text for the flyer entered, the next step is to **format**, which is the process of changing the appearance of text and objects. A paragraph encompasses the text from the first character in the paragraph up to and including its paragraph mark (¶). **Paragraph formatting** is the process of changing the appearance of a paragraph on-screen and in print. For example, you can center or add bullets to a paragraph. Characters include letters, numbers, punctuation marks, and symbols. **Character formatting** is the process of changing the way characters appear on the screen and in print. You use character formatting to emphasize certain words and improve readability of a document. For example, you can color, italicize, or underline characters. Often, you apply both paragraph and character formatting to the same text. For example, you may center a paragraph (paragraph formatting) and underline some of the characters in the same paragraph (character formatting).

Although you can format paragraphs and characters before you type, many Word users enter text first and then format the existing text. Figure 1–35a shows the flyer in this module before formatting its paragraphs and characters. Figure 1–35b shows the flyer after formatting its paragraphs and characters. As you can see from the two figures, a document that is formatted is easier to read and looks more professional. The following sections discuss how to format the flyer so that it looks like Figure 1–35b.

Font, Font Sizes, and Themes

Characters that appear on the screen are a specific shape and size. The **font**, or typeface, defines the appearance and shape of the letters, numbers, and special characters. In Word, the default font usually is Calibri (shown in Figure 1–34). You can leave characters in the default font or change them to a different font. **Font size** specifies the size of the characters, measured in units called points. A single **point**, which is a unit of measure for font size, is about 1/72 of 1 inch in height. The default font size in Word typically is 11 (shown in Figure 1–34). Thus, a character with a font size of 11 is about 11/72 or a little less than 1/6 of 1 inch in height. You can increase or decrease the font size of characters in a document. A **style** is a named collection of character and paragraph formats, including font, font size, font styles, font color, and alignment, that are stored together and can be applied to text to format it quickly, such as Heading 1 or Title.

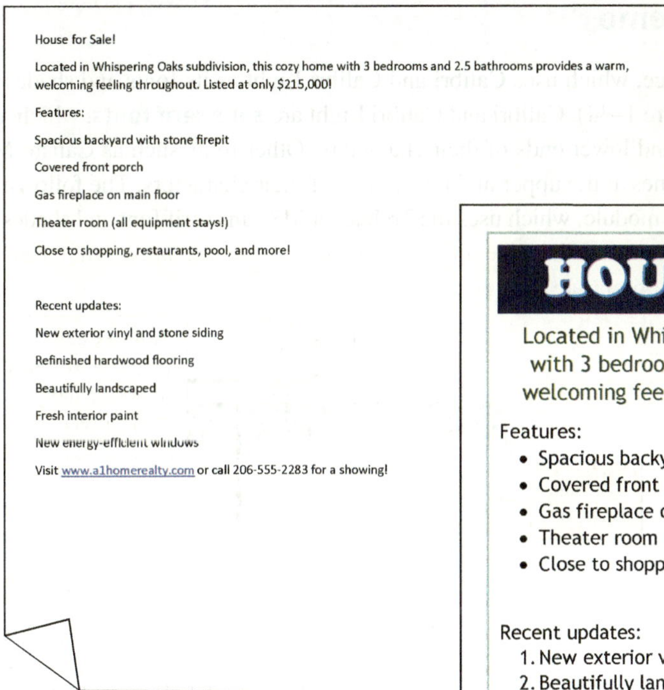

House for Sale!

Located in Whispering Oaks subdivision, this cozy home with 3 bedrooms and 2.5 bathrooms provides a warm, welcoming feeling throughout. Listed at only $215,000!

Features:

Spacious backyard with stone firepit

Covered front porch

Gas fireplace on main floor

Theater room (all equipment stays!)

Close to shopping, restaurants, pool, and more!

Recent updates:

New exterior vinyl and stone siding

Refinished hardwood flooring

Beautifully landscaped

Fresh interior paint

New energy-efficient windows

Visit www.a1homerealty.com or call 206-555-2283 for a showing!

Figure 1-35(a): Unformatted Flyer

HOUSE FOR SALE!

Located in Whispering Oaks subdivision, this cozy home with 3 bedrooms and 2.5 bathrooms provides a warm, welcoming feeling throughout. Listed at *only* $215,000!

Features:

- Spacious backyard with stone firepit
- Covered front porch
- Gas fireplace on main floor
- Theater room (all equipment stays!)
- Close to shopping, restaurants, pool, and more!

Recent updates:

1. New exterior vinyl and stone siding
2. Beautifully landscaped
3. Refinished hardwood flooring
4. Fresh interior paint throughout
5. New energy-efficient windows

Visit **www.a1homerealty.com** or call **206-555-2283** for a showing!

Figure 1-35(b): Formatted Flyer

A **document theme** is a coordinated combination of formats for fonts, colors, pictures, and other objects. Word includes a variety of document themes to assist you with coordinating these visual elements in a document. The default theme fonts are Calibri Light for headings and Calibri for body text. By changing the document theme, you quickly can give your document a new look. You also can define your own document themes.

Consider This

How do you know which formats to use in a flyer?

In a flyer, consider the following formatting suggestions.

- **Increase the font size of characters.** Flyers usually are posted on a bulletin board, on a wall, or in a window. Thus, the font size should be as large as possible so that your audience easily can read the flyer. To give the headline more impact, its font size should be larger than the font size of the text in the body copy.
- **Change the font of characters.** Use fonts that are easy to read. Try to use only two different fonts in a flyer; for example, use one for the headline and the other for all other text. Too many fonts can make the flyer visually confusing.
- **Change the paragraph alignment.** The default alignment for paragraphs in a document is **left-aligned**, that is, flush at the left margin of the document with uneven right edges. Consider changing the alignment of some of the paragraphs to add interest and variety to the flyer.
- **Highlight key paragraphs with bullets or numbers.** A bulleted paragraph is a paragraph that begins with a dot or other symbol. Use bulleted paragraphs to highlight important points in a flyer. A numbered paragraph is a paragraph that begins with a number. Use numbered paragraphs (lists) to organize a sequence.
- **Emphasize important words.** To call attention to certain words or lines, you can underline them, italicize them, or bold them. Use these formats sparingly, however, because overuse will minimize their effect and make the flyer look too busy.
- **Use color.** Use colors that complement one another and convey the meaning of the flyer. Vary colors in terms of hue and brightness. Headline colors, for example, can be bold and bright. Signature lines should stand out but less than headlines. Keep in mind that too many colors can detract from the flyer and make it difficult to read.

To Change the Document Theme

The current default document theme is Office, which uses Calibri and Calibri Light as its fonts and shades of grays and blues primarily (shown in the Styles group in Figure 1–34). Calibri and Calibri Light are **sans serif fonts**, which are fonts that do not include short decorative lines at the upper and lower ends of their characters. Other fonts such as Calisto MT are **serif fonts**, which are fonts that have short decorative lines at the upper and lower ends of their characters. The following steps change the document theme to Facet for the flyer in this module, which uses the Trebuchet MS sans serif font and shades of green primarily. **Why?** Some organizations specify document themes that all employees should use when creating printed and online documents. The Facet theme provides colors and fonts appropriate for a flyer.

1

- Press CTRL+HOME to display the top of the flyer in the document window.
- Click Design on the ribbon to display the Design tab.
- Click the Themes button (Design tab | Document Formatting group) to display the Themes gallery (Figure 1–36).

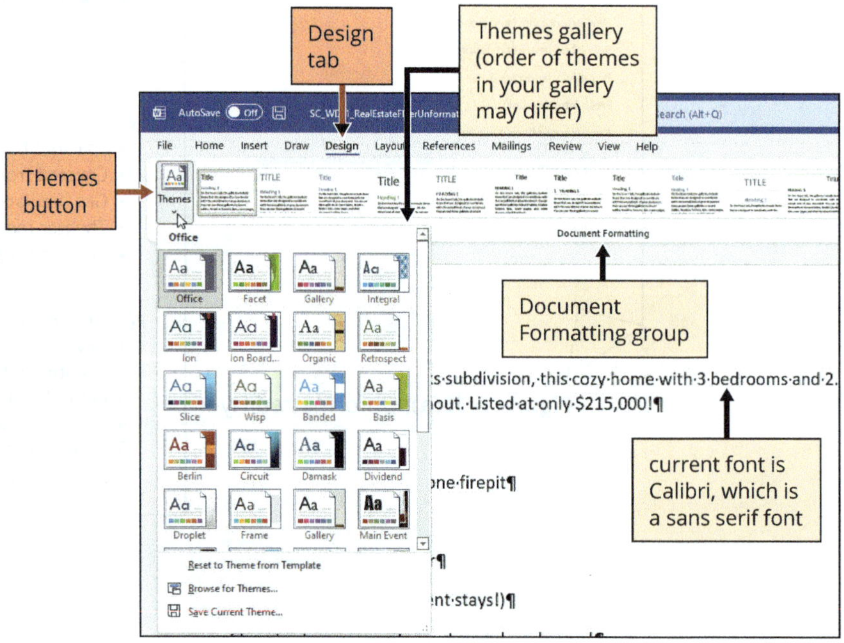

Figure 1–36

2

- If necessary, scroll to and then point to Facet in the Themes gallery to display a Live Preview of that theme applied to the document (Figure 1–37).
- **Experiment:** Point to various themes in the Themes gallery to display a Live Preview of the various themes applied to the document in the document window.

Q&A What is Live Preview?
Recall from the discussion earlier in this module that Live Preview is a feature that allows you to point to a gallery choice and see its effect in the document — without actually selecting the choice.

Can I use Live Preview on a touch screen?
Live Preview may not be available on all touch screens.

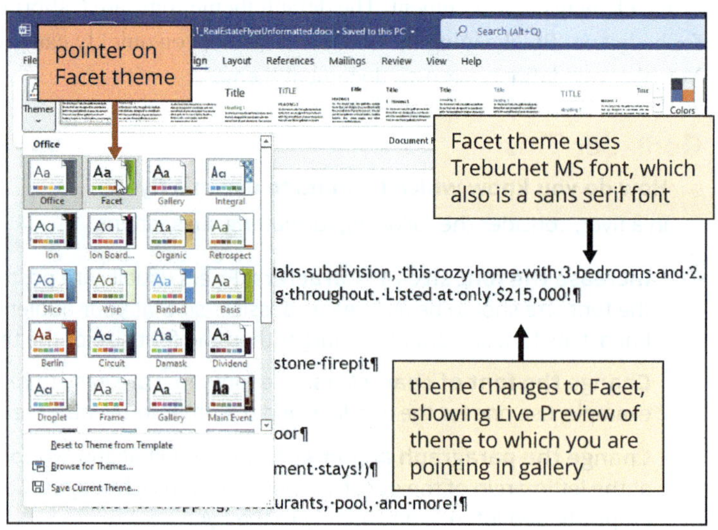

Figure 1–37

3

- Click Facet in the Themes gallery to change the document theme.

To Center a Paragraph

The headline in the flyer currently is left-aligned. **Why?** Word, by default, left-aligns text, unless you specifically change the alignment. You want the headline to be **centered**, that is, positioned evenly between the left and right margins, or placeholder edges, on the page. Recall that Word considers a single short line of text, such as the one-word headline, a paragraph. Thus, you will center the paragraph containing the headline. The following steps center a paragraph.

1

- Click Home on the ribbon to display the Home tab.
- Click somewhere in the paragraph to be centered (in this case, the headline) to position the insertion point in the paragraph to be centered (Figure 1–38).

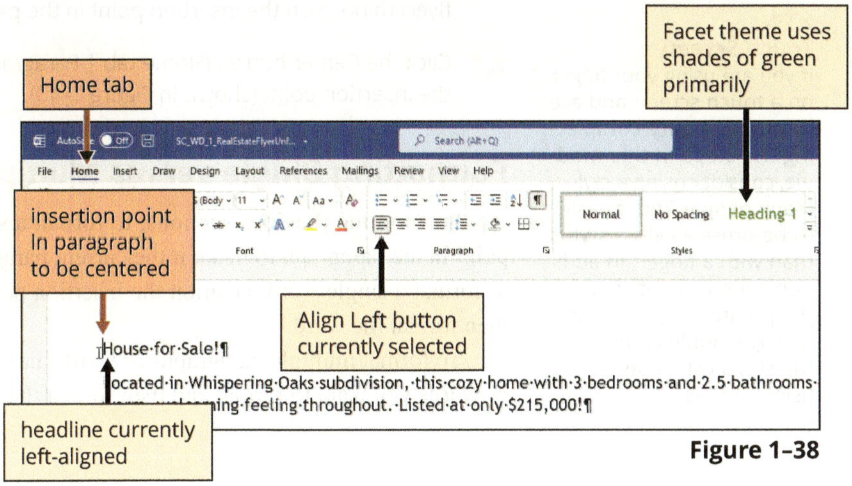

Figure 1–38

2

- Click the Center button (Home tab | Paragraph group) to center the paragraph containing the insertion point (Figure 1–39).

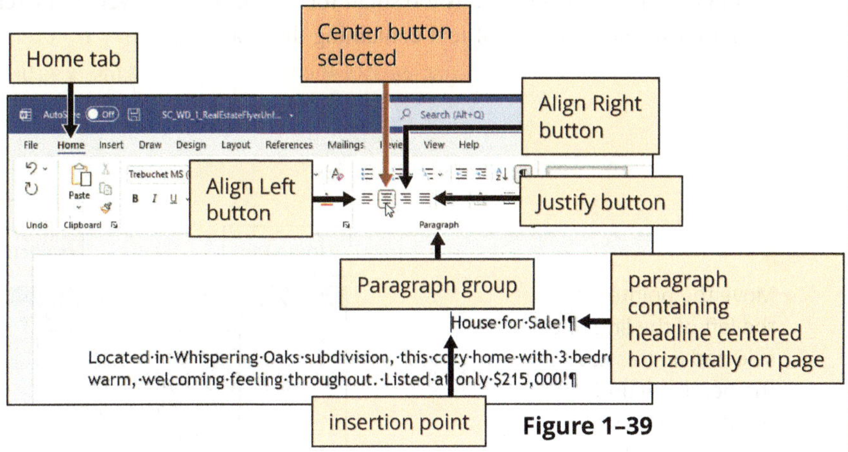

Figure 1–39

Q&A What if I want to return the paragraph to left-aligned?
You would click the Center button again or click the Align Left button (Home tab | Paragraph group).

What are other ways to align a paragraph?
A **right-aligned** paragraph appears flush at the right margin of the document with uneven left edges. You right-align a paragraph by clicking the Align Right button (Home tab | Paragraph group). A **justified** paragraph means that full lines of text are evenly spaced between both the left and right margins, like the edges of newspaper columns, with extra space placed between words. You justify a paragraph by clicking the Justify button (Home tab | Paragraph group).

Other Ways

1. Right-click paragraph (or if using touch, tap 'Show Context Menu' button on Mini toolbar), click Paragraph on shortcut menu, click Indents and Spacing tab (Paragraph dialog box), click Alignment arrow, click Centered, click OK
2. Click Paragraph Dialog Box Launcher (Home tab or Layout tab | Paragraph group), click Indents and Spacing tab (Paragraph dialog box), click Alignment arrow, click Centered, click OK
3. Press CTRL+E

To Center Another Paragraph

The second paragraph in the flyer (the first paragraph of body copy) also is centered. The following steps center the first paragraph of body copy.

1. Click somewhere in the paragraph to be centered (in this case, the second paragraph on the flyer) to position the insertion point in the paragraph to be formatted.

2. Click the Center button (Home tab | Paragraph group) to center the paragraph containing the insertion point (shown in Figure 1–40).

BTW

Touch Screen

If you are using your finger on a touch screen and are having difficulty completing the steps in this module, consider using a stylus. Many people find it easier to be precise with a stylus than with a finger. In addition, with a stylus you see the pointer. If you still are having trouble completing the steps with a stylus, try using a mouse.

Formatting Single versus Multiple Paragraphs and Characters

As shown in the previous sections, to format a single paragraph, simply position the insertion point in the paragraph to make it the current paragraph and then format the paragraph. Similarly, to format a single word, position the insertion point in the word to make it the current word and then format the word.

To format multiple paragraphs or words, however, you first must select the paragraphs, lines, or words you want to format and then format the selection.

To Select a Line

The default font size of 11 point is too small for a headline in a flyer. To increase the font size of the characters in the headline, you first must select the line of text containing the headline. **Why?** If you increase the font size of text without selecting any text, Word will increase the font size only of the word containing the insertion point. The following steps select a line.

1.
- Move the pointer to the left of the line to be selected (in this case, the headline) until the pointer changes to a right-pointing block arrow (Figure 1–40).

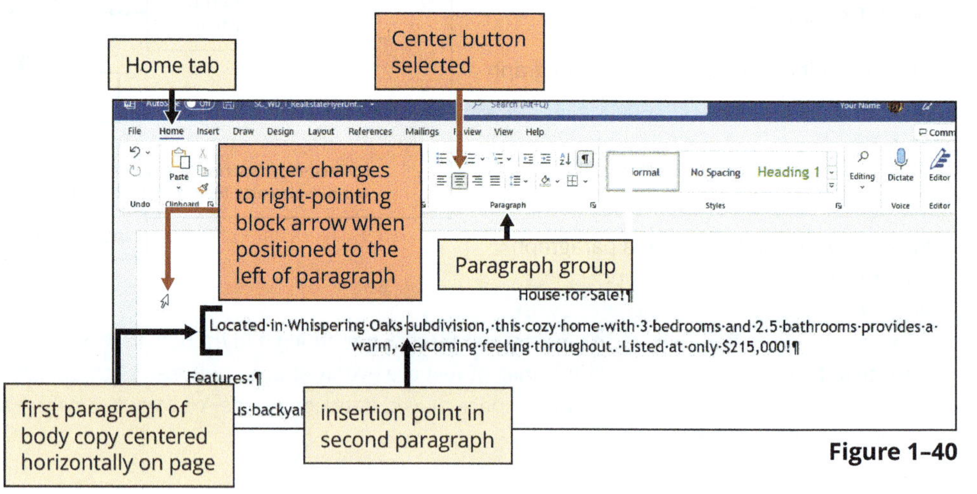

Figure 1–40

2.
- While the pointer is a right-pointing block arrow, click the mouse button to select the entire line to the right of the pointer (Figure 1–41).

Figure 1–41

Q&A What if I am using a touch screen?
You would double-tap to the left of the line to be selected to select the line.

Why is the selected text shaded gray?
If your screen normally displays dark letters on a light background, which is the default setting in Word, then selected text is displayed with a light shading color, such as gray, on the dark letters. Note that the selection that appears on the text does not print.

Why do the buttons on my Mini toolbar differ from the figure?
Depending on your version of Word, your Mini toolbar may be adaptive, meaning the buttons and commands on the Mini toolbar can change based on how you use Word. Buttons and commands on the left side of the Mini toolbar generally are the same across versions, but the ones toward the right of the Mini toolbar may change as you use Word.

Other Ways

1. Drag pointer through line
2. With insertion point at beginning of desired line, press CTRL+SHIFT+DOWN ARROW

To Change the Font Size of Selected Text

The next step is to increase the font size of the characters in the selected headline. **Why?** You would like the headline to be as large as possible and still fit on a single line, which in this case is 48 point. The following steps increase the font size of the headline from 11 to 48 point.

1

- With the text selected, click the Font Size arrow (Home tab | Font group) to display the Font Size gallery (Figure 1–42).

Q&A What is the Font Size arrow?
The Font Size arrow is the arrow to the right of the Font Size box, which is the text box that displays the current font size.

Why are the font sizes in my Font Size gallery different from those in Figure 1–42?
Font sizes may vary depending on the current font and your printer driver.

What happened to the Mini toolbar?
Recall that the Mini toolbar disappears if you do not use it. These steps use the Font Size arrow on the Home tab instead of the Font Size arrow on the Mini toolbar.

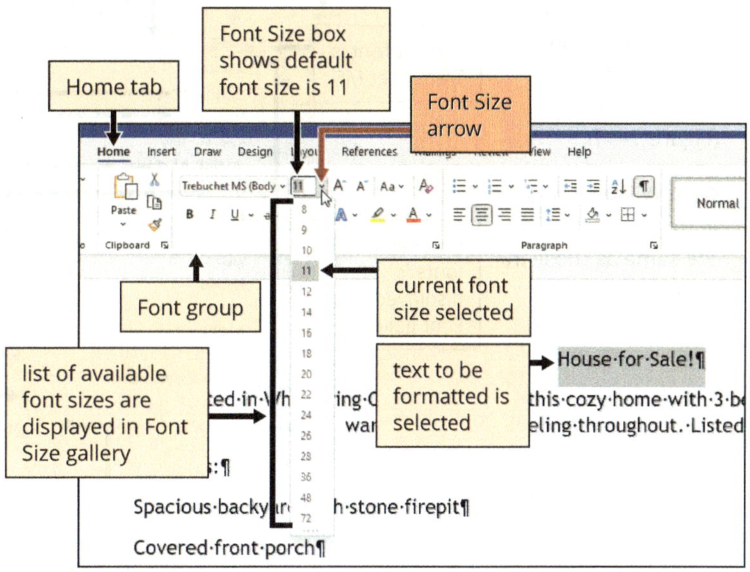

Figure 1–42

2

- Point to 48 in the Font Size gallery to display a Live Preview of the selected text at the selected point size (Figure 1–43).
- **Experiment:** Point to various font sizes in the Font Size gallery and watch the font size of the selected text change in the document window.

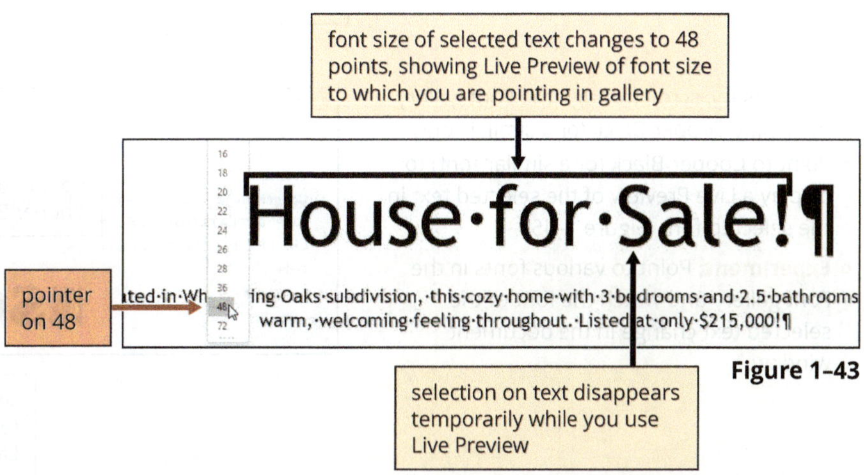

Figure 1–43

3

- Click 48 in the Font Size gallery to increase the font size of the selected text.

Other Ways

1. Click Font Size arrow on Mini toolbar, click desired font size in Font Size gallery	2. Right-click selected text (or, if using touch, tap 'Show Context Menu' button on Mini toolbar), click Font on shortcut menu, click Font tab (Font dialog box), select desired font size in Size list, click OK	3. Click Font Dialog Box Launcher (Home tab | Font group), click Font tab (Font dialog box), select desired font size in Size list, click OK	4. Press CTRL+D or CTRL+SHIFT+F, click Font tab (Font dialog box), select desired font size in Size list, click OK

To Change the Font of Selected Text

The default font when you install Word is Calibri. The font for characters in this document is Trebuchet MS because earlier you changed the theme to Facet. Many other fonts are available, however, so that you can add variety to documents.

The following steps change the font of the headline from Trebuchet MS to Cooper Black. **Why?** To draw more attention to the headline, you change its font so that it differs from the font of other text in the flyer.

1

- With the text selected, click the Font arrow (Home tab | Font group) to display the Font gallery (Figure 1–44).

Q&A Will the fonts in my Font gallery be the same as those in Figure 1–44?
Your list of available fonts may differ, depending on the type of printer you are using and other settings.

What if the text no longer is selected?
Follow the steps described earlier to select a line and then perform Step 1.

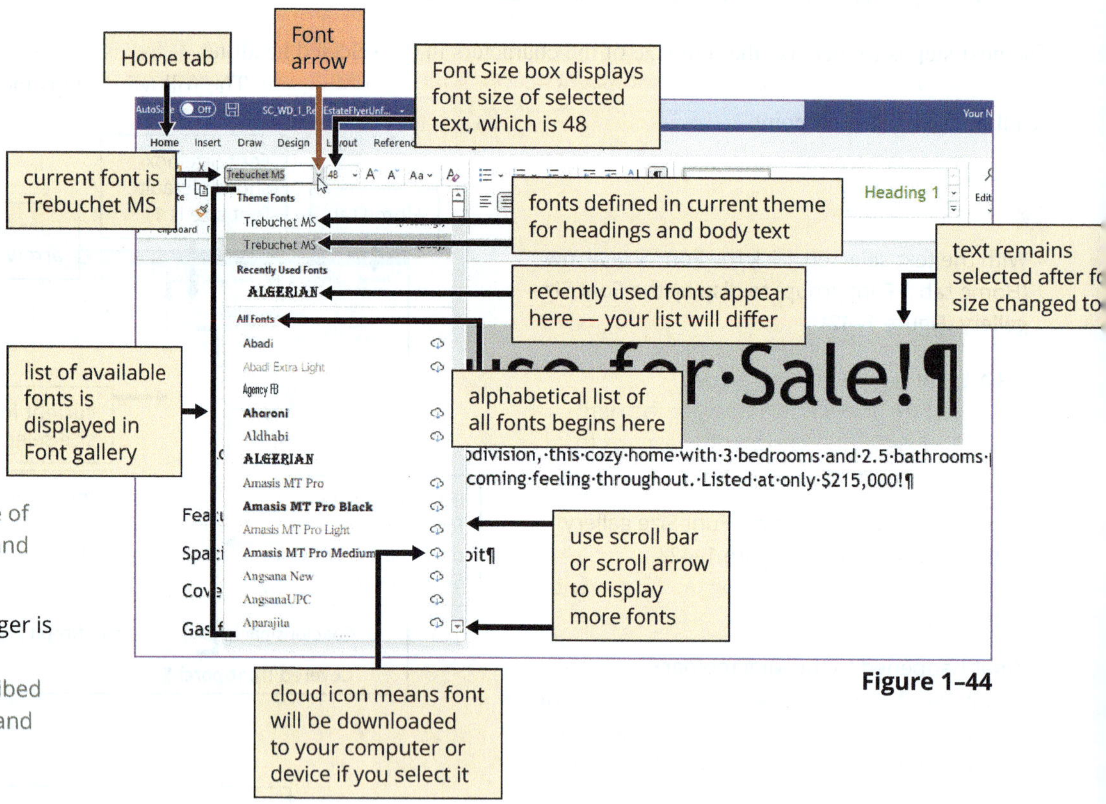

Figure 1–44

2

- If necessary, scroll through the Font gallery to display Cooper Black (or a similar font).
- Point to Cooper Black (or a similar font) to display a Live Preview of the selected text in the selected font (Figure 1–45).
- **Experiment:** Point to various fonts in the Font gallery and watch the font of the selected text change in the document window.

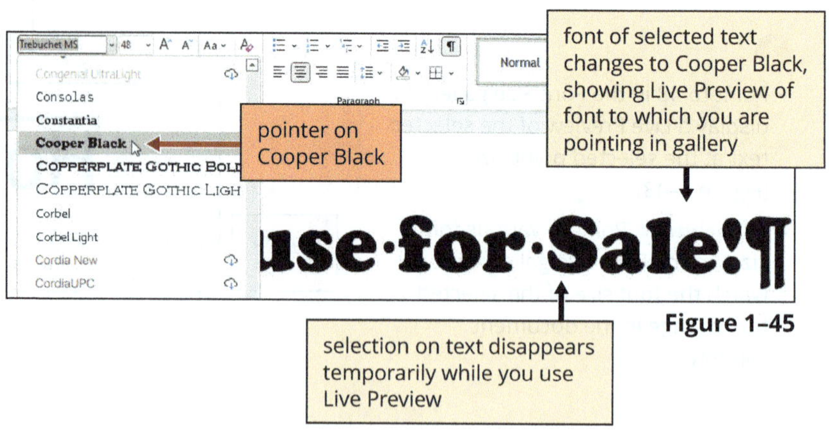

Figure 1–45

3

- Click Cooper Black (or a similar font) in the Font gallery to change the font of the selected text.

Q&A If the font I want to use appears in the Recently Used Fonts list at the top of the Font gallery, could I click it there instead?
Yes.

Other Ways

1. Click Font arrow on Mini toolbar, click desired font in Font gallery
2. Right-click selected text (or, if using touch, tap 'Show Context Menu' button on Mini toolbar), click Font on shortcut menu, click Font tab (Font dialog box), select desired font in Font list, click OK
3. Click Font Dialog Box Launcher (Home tab | Font group), click Font tab (Font dialog box), select desired font in Font list, click OK
4. Press CTRL+D or CTRL+SHIFT+F, click Font tab (Font dialog box), select desired font in Font list, click OK

To Change the Case of Selected Text

The headline currently shows the first letter in each word capitalized, which sometimes is referred to as title case. The following steps change the headline to uppercase. **Why?** To draw more attention to the headline, you would like the entire line of text to be capitalized, or in uppercase letters.

1

- With the text selected, click the Change Case button (Home tab | Font group) to display the Change Case gallery (Figure 1–46).

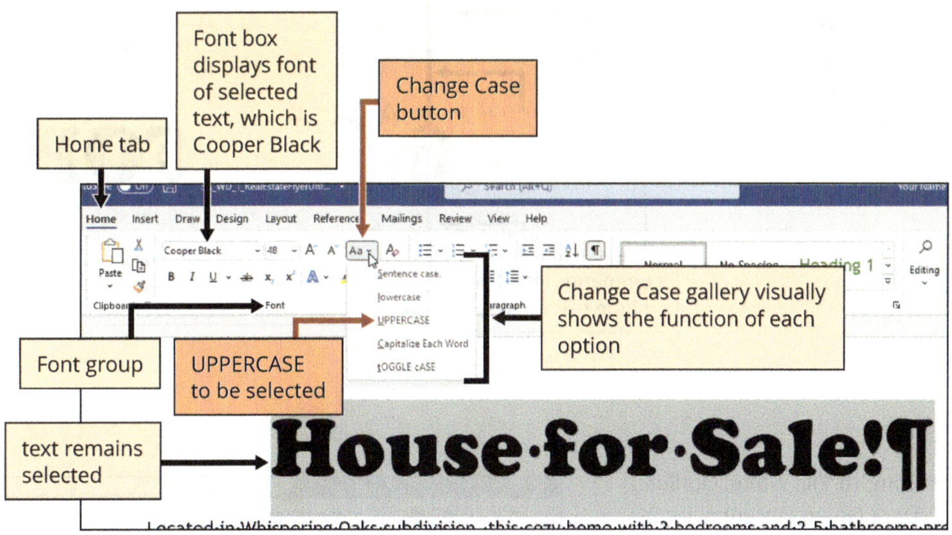

Figure 1–46

2

- Click UPPERCASE in the Change Case gallery to change the case of the selected text (Figure 1–47).

Figure 1–47

Q&A What if a ruler appears on the screen or the pointer shape changes?

If you are using a mouse, depending on the position of your pointer and locations you click on the screen, a ruler may appear automatically or the pointer's shape may change. Simply move the mouse and the ruler should disappear and/or the pointer shape will change. If you wanted to show the rulers, you would select the Ruler check box (View tab | Show group). To hide the rulers, deselect the Ruler check box (View tab | Show group).

Other Ways

1. Right-click selected text (or, if using touch, tap 'Show Context Menu' button on Mini toolbar), click Font on shortcut menu, click Font tab (Font dialog box), select All caps in Effects area, click OK
2. Click Font Dialog Box Launcher (Home tab | Font group), click Font tab (Font dialog box), select All caps in Effects area, click OK
3. Press SHIFT+F3 repeatedly until text is desired case

To Apply a Preset Text Effect to Selected Text

Word provides many text effects to add interest and variety to text. The following steps apply a preset text effect to the headline. **Why?** You would like the text in the headline to be even more noticeable.

1

- With the text selected, click the 'Text Effects and Typography' button (Home tab | Font group) to display the Text Effects and Typography gallery (Figure 1–48).

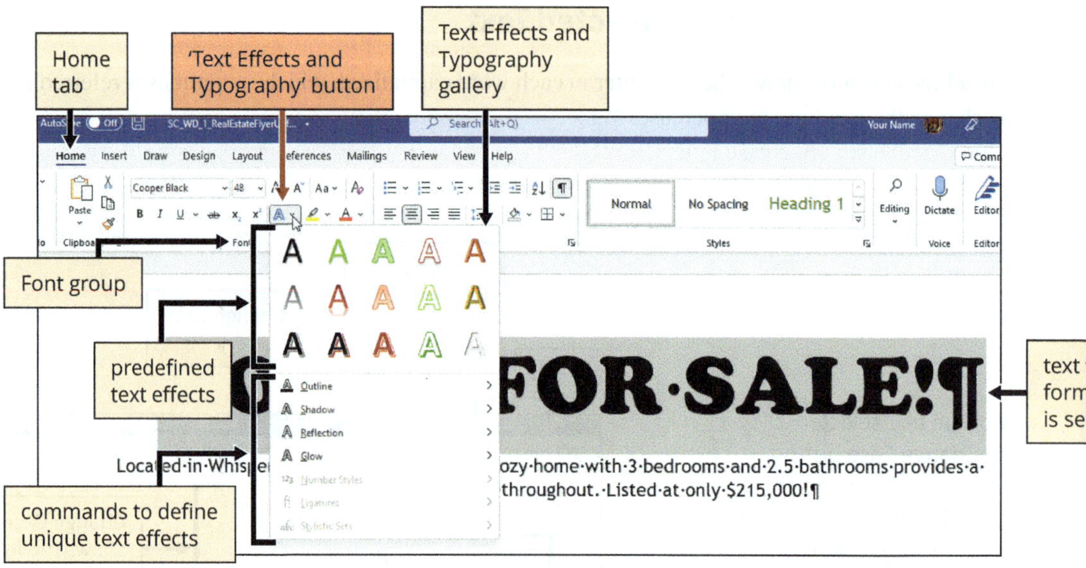

Figure 1–48

2

- Point to 'Fill: White; Outline: Dark Green, Accent color 2; Hard Shadow: Dark Green, Accent color 2' (fourth text effect in last row) to display a Live Preview of the selected text with the selected text effect (Figure 1–49).
- **Experiment:** Point to various text effects in the Text Effects and Typography gallery and watch the text effects of the selected text change in the document window.

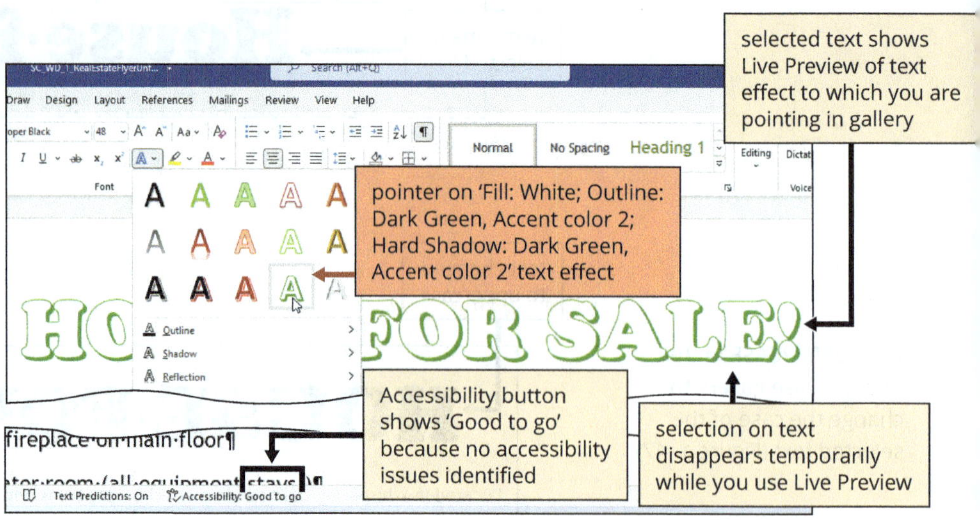

Figure 1–49

3

- Click 'Fill: White; Outline: Dark Green, Accent color 2; Hard Shadow: Dark Green, Accent color 2' to change the text effect of the selected text.

4

- Click anywhere in the document window to remove the selection from the selected text.

Q&A What happened to the formatting marks in the headline?
The formatting marks may disappear or change colors when you apply a text effect.

Other Ways

1. Right-click selected text (or, if using touch, tap 'Show Context Menu' button on Mini toolbar), click Font on shortcut menu, click Font tab (Font dialog box), click Text Effects button, expand Text Fill or Text Outline section and then select the desired text effect(s) (Format Text Effects dialog box), click OK, click OK
2. Click Font Dialog Box Launcher (Home tab | Font group), click Font tab (Font dialog box), click Text Effects button, expand Text Fill or Text Outline section and then select desired text effect (Format Text Effects dialog box), click OK, click OK
3. Press CTRL+D, click Font tab (Font dialog box), click Text Effects button, expand Text Fill or Text Outline section and then select desired text effect (Format Text Effects dialog box), click OK, click OK

To Check Accessibility and Identify Issue(s)

It is important that everyone easily can read and work with a document you create. For this reason, Word includes an **Accessibility Checker** that identifies potential accessibility issues and presents suggestions to make your document more inclusive.

The next step is to check accessibility of the document you have created thus far. **Why?** You notice that instead of the phrase, Good to go (shown in Figure 1–49), the Accessibility button on the status bar now shows the word, Investigate (shown in Figure 1–50). The following steps use the Accessibility Checker to identify the potential accessibility issues in the document.

1

- Click the Accessibility button on the status bar to open the Accessibility pane.
- Click the arrow to the left of 'Hard-to-read text contrast' to expand the description, which identifies the contrast of the colors in the headline are difficult to read (Figure 1–50).

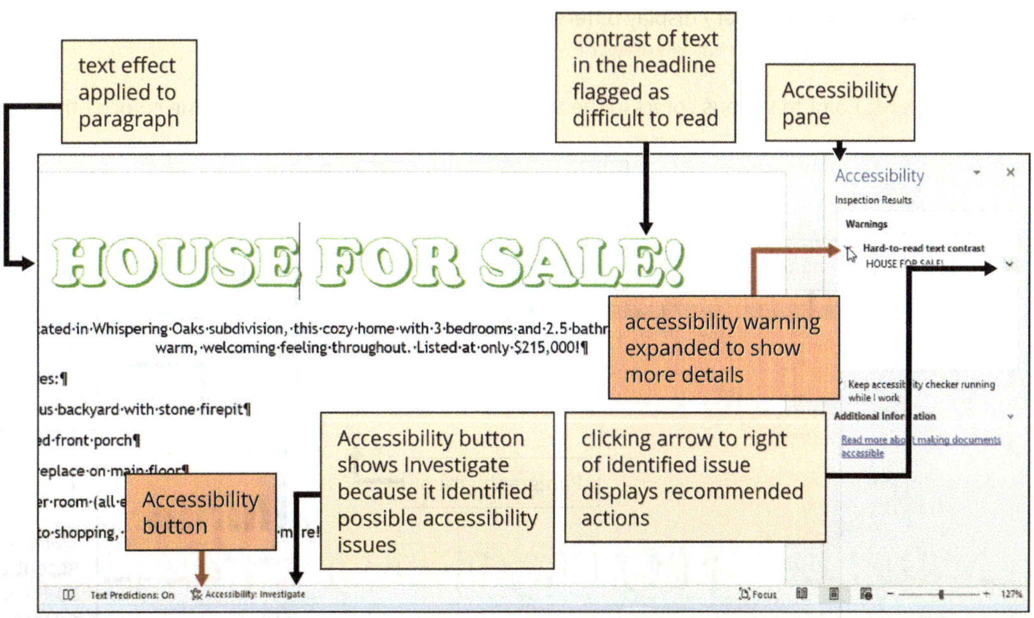

Figure 1–50

Q&A How do I fix the identified accessibility issue?
You can click the arrow to the right of the identified issue to display a menu of recommended actions, or you can apply different formats in the document to see if the accessibility returns to 'Good to go'.

2

- Leave the Accessibility pane open for the next set of steps so that you can see if changing the shading color of paragraph containing the headline fixes the issue.

Other Ways

1. Click Check Accessibility button (Review tab | Accessibility group), fix issue(s), click Close button in task pane
2. Click File tab, click Info in Backstage view, click 'Check for Issues' button, click Check Accessibility, fix issue(s), click Close button in task pane

To Shade a Paragraph

Shading is the process of applying a background color or pattern to a page, text, table, or other object. When you shade a paragraph, Word shades the area from the left margin to the right margin of the current paragraph. To shade a paragraph, place the insertion point in the paragraph. To shade any other text, you must first select the text to be shaded. For example, to shade a word, you would select the word before performing these steps.

This flyer uses a shading color for the headline. **Why?** To make the headline of the flyer more eye-catching, you shade it. At the same time, you want to check that the shading color fixes the accessibility issue identified in the previous steps. The following steps shade a paragraph.

1

- Click somewhere in the paragraph to be shaded (in this case, the headline) to position the insertion point in the paragraph to be formatted.
- Click the Shading arrow (Home tab | Paragraph group) to display the Shading gallery (Figure 1–51).

Q&A What if I click the Shading button by mistake?
Click the Shading arrow and proceed with Step 2. Note that if you are using a touch screen, you may not have a separate Shading button.

Why does my Shading gallery display different colors?
Your theme colors setting may display colors in a different order.

- **Experiment:** Point to various colors in the Shading gallery and watch the shading color of the current paragraph change.

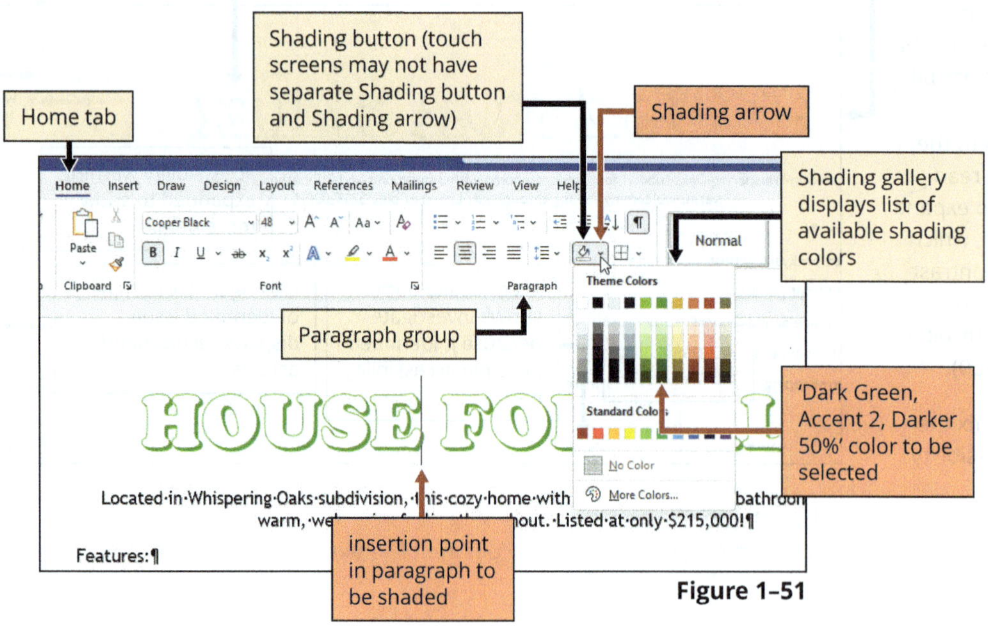

Figure 1–51

2

- Click 'Dark Green, Accent 2, Darker 50%' (sixth color in bottom row) to shade the current paragraph (Figure 1–52).

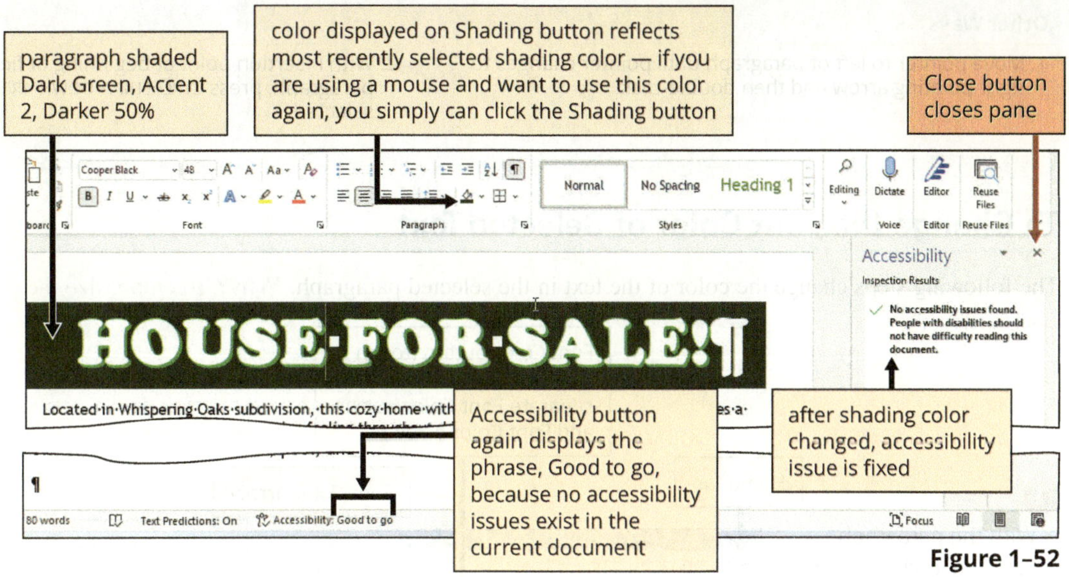

Figure 1–52

Q&A What if I apply a dark shading color to dark text?
When the font color of text is Automatic, the color usually is black. If you select a dark shading color, Word automatically may change the text color to white so that the shaded text is easier to read and does not create an accessibility issue.

Other Ways

1. Click Borders arrow (Home tab | Paragraph group), click 'Borders and Shading', click Shading tab (Borders and Shading dialog box), click Fill arrow, select desired color, click OK

To Close the Accessibility Pane

The accessibility issue is corrected. Thus, the following step closes the Accessibility pane.

1 Click the Close button on the Accessibility pane (shown in Figure 1–52) to close the pane.

Q&A Can I check accessibility issues at any time?
Yes. You can check and fix them as you create a document, or you can check the entire document at once when you are finished creating it.

To Select a Paragraph

The next step is to change the color of the text in the paragraph below the headline. To format all the characters in a paragraph, you first must select the text in the paragraph. **Why?** If you change the font color without selecting any text, Word will change the font color only of the word containing the insertion point. The following step selects a paragraph.

1

- Move the pointer into the paragraph to be selected and then triple-click to select the entire paragraph (Figure 1–53).

Q&A What if I am using a touch screen?
You would triple-tap the paragraph to be selected to select the paragraph.

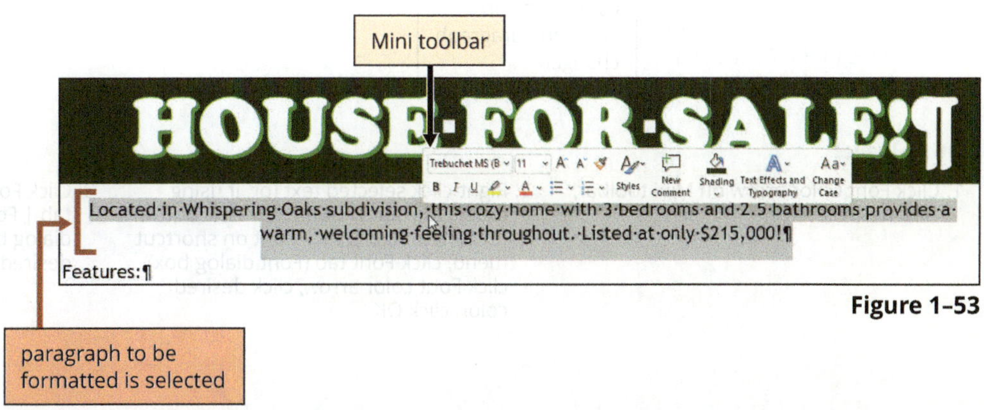

Figure 1–53

Other Ways

1. Move pointer to left of paragraph until pointer changes to right-pointing arrow and then double-click
2. With insertion point at beginning of first character in paragraph, press CTRL+SHIFT+DOWN ARROW until paragraph is selected

To Change the Font Color of Selected Text

The following steps change the color of the text in the selected paragraph. **Why?** To emphasize the paragraph, you change its font color.

1

- With the paragraph selected, click the Font Color arrow (Home tab | Font group) to display the Font Color gallery (Figure 1–54).

Q&A What if I click the Font Color button by mistake?
Click the Font Color arrow and then proceed with Step 2. Note that you may not have a separate Font Color button if you are using a touch screen.

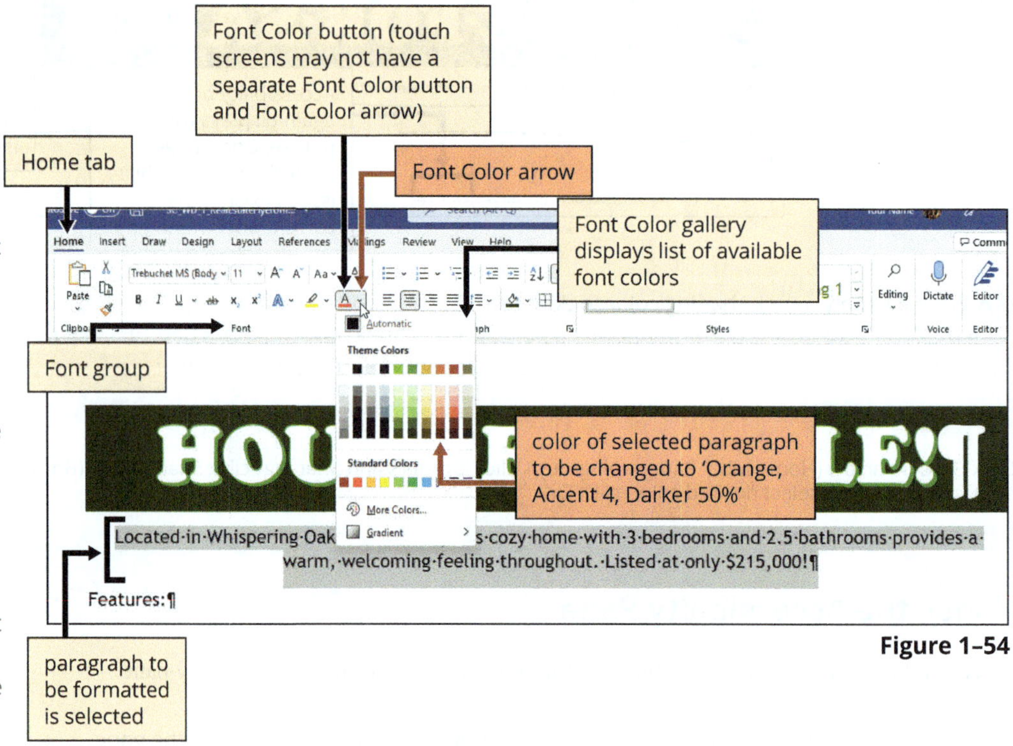

Figure 1–54

- **Experiment:** If you are using a mouse, point to various colors in the Font Color gallery and watch the color of the current word change.

2

- Click 'Orange, Accent 4, Darker 50%' (eighth color in bottom row) to change the color of the selected text (Figure 1–55).

Q&A How would I change the text color back to black?
You would select the text or position the insertion point in the text to format, click the Font Color arrow (Home tab | Font group), and then click Automatic in the Font Color gallery.

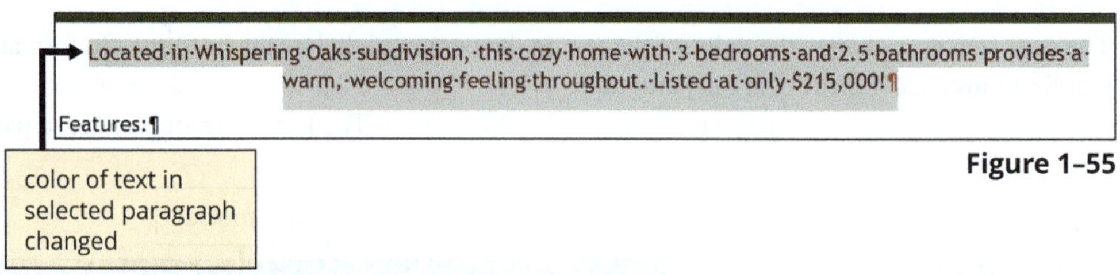

Figure 1–55

Other Ways

1. Click Font Color arrow on Mini toolbar, click desired color
2. Right-click selected text (or, if using touch, tap 'Show Context Menu' button on Mini toolbar), click Font on shortcut menu, click Font tab (Font dialog box), click Font color arrow, click desired color, click OK
3. Click Font Dialog Box Launcher (Home tab | Font group), click Font tab (Font dialog box), click Font color arrow, click desired color, click OK

To Change the Font Size of Selected Text

The font size of characters in the currently selected paragraph is 11 point. To make them easier to read from a distance, this flyer uses a 20-point font size for these characters. The following steps change the font size of the selected text.

1. With the text selected (shown in Figure 1-55), click the Font Size arrow (Home tab | Font group) to display the Font Size gallery.
2. Click 20 in the Font Size gallery to increase the font size of the selected text.
3. Click anywhere in the document window to remove the selection from the text (Figure 1-56).

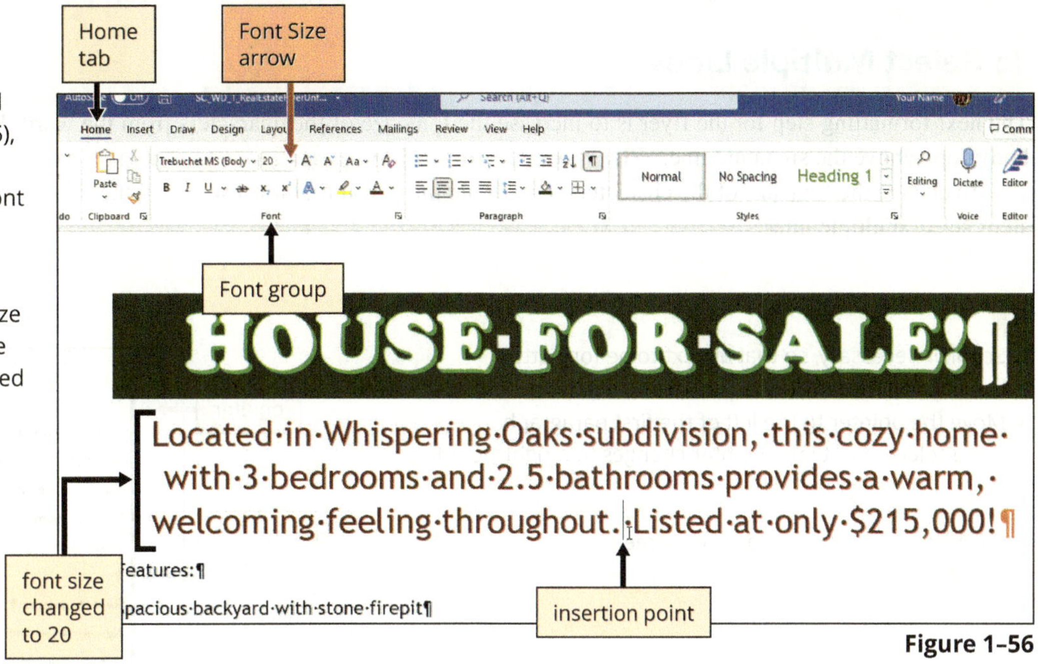

Figure 1-56

To Change the Zoom Percentage

In the steps in the following sections, you will format multiple paragraphs of text at once that currently cannot all be displayed in the document window at the same time. The next task is to adjust the zoom percentage. **Why?** You want to be able to see all the text to be formatted in the document window. The following step zooms the document.

1.

- **Experiment:** Repeatedly click the Zoom Out and Zoom In buttons on the status bar and watch the size of the document change in the document window.

Q&A What if I am using a touch screen?
Repeatedly pinch (move two fingers together on the screen) and stretch (move two fingers apart on the screen) and watch the size of the document change in the document window.

- Click the Zoom Out or Zoom In button as many times as necessary until the Zoom level button on the status bar displays 120% on its face.
- Scroll if necessary to display all text beginning with the word, Features:, to the signature line (Figure 1-57).

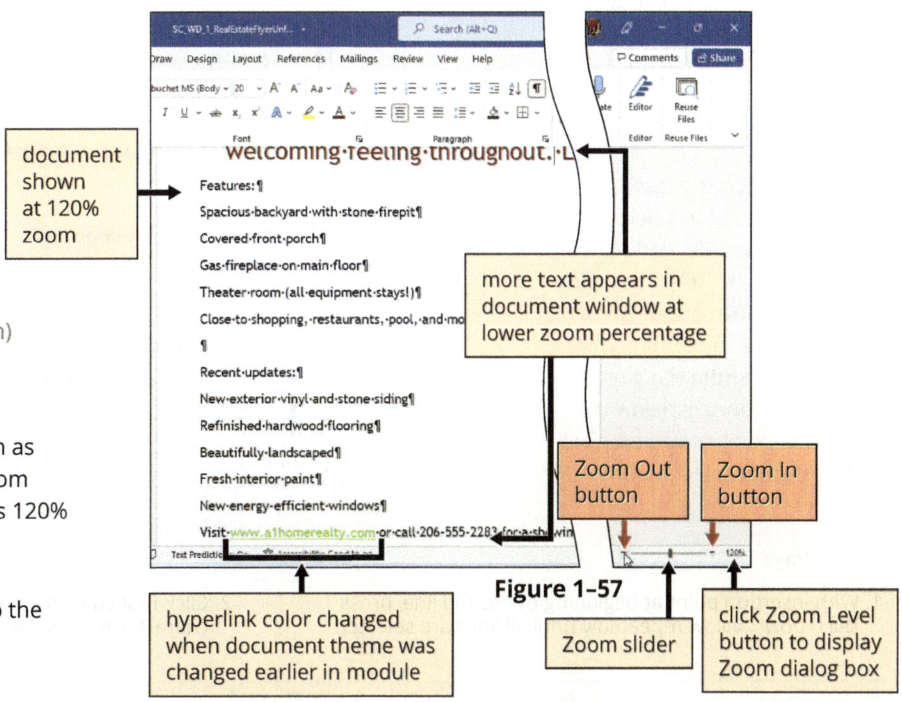

Figure 1-57

Other Ways

1. Drag Zoom slider on status bar
2. Click Zoom level button on status bar, select desired zoom percent or zoom type (Zoom dialog box), click OK
3. Click Zoom button (View tab | Zoom group), select desired zoom percent or zoom type (Zoom dialog box), click OK

To Select Multiple Lines

The next formatting step for the flyer is to increase the font size of the characters from the word, Features:, to the last line of body copy above the signature line. **Why?** You want this text to be easier to read from a distance.

To change the font size of the characters in multiple lines, you first must select all the lines to be formatted. The following steps select multiple lines.

1

- Scroll, if necessary, so that all text to be formatted is displayed on the screen.
- Move the pointer to the left of the first paragraph to be selected until the pointer changes to a right-pointing block arrow (Figure 1–58).

Q&A What if I am using a touch screen?
You would tap to position the insertion point in the text to select.

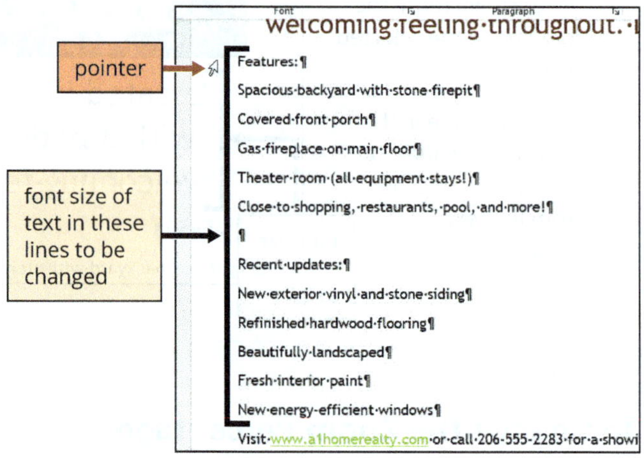

Figure 1–58

2

- While the pointer is a right-pointing block arrow, drag downward to select all lines that will be formatted (Figure 1–59).

Q&A What if I am using a touch screen?
Tap to position the insertion point in the text to select and then drag the selection handle(s) as necessary to select the text that will be formatted. When working on a touch screen, a **selection handle** is a small circle that appears below the insertion point as you drag with a fingertip to select text.

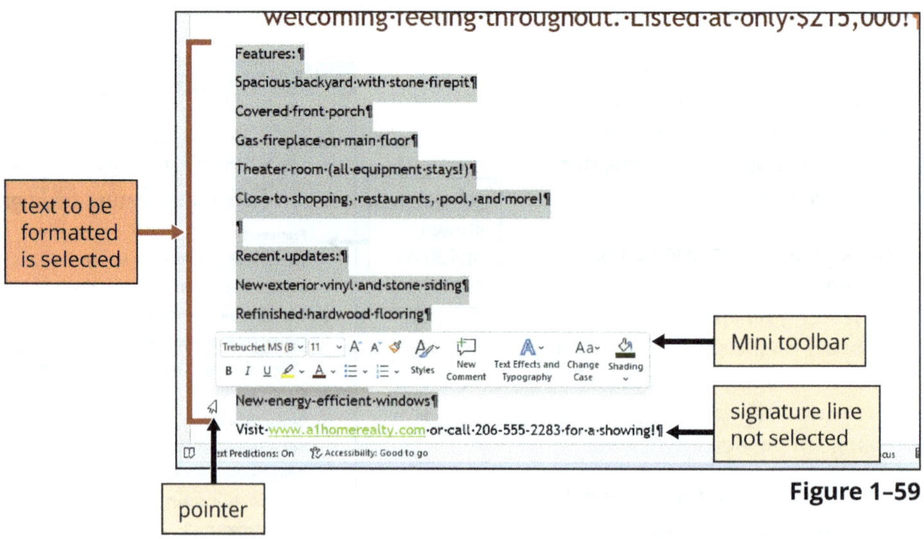

Figure 1–59

Other Ways

1. With insertion point at beginning of desired line, press SHIFT+DOWN ARROW repeatedly until all lines are selected
2. Click first character to be selected and then SHIFT+click last character to be selected

To Change the Font Size of Selected Text

The characters in the selected text currently are 11 point. To make them easier to read from a distance, this flyer uses an 18-point font size for these characters. The following steps change the font size of the selected text.

1. With the text selected, click the Font Size arrow (Home tab | Font group) to display the Font Size gallery.
2. Click 18 in the Font Size gallery to increase the font size of the selected text (Figure 1–60).
3. Click anywhere in the document window to remove the selection from the text.

Q&A How do I see the format for the text that scrolled off the screen?
Use one of the techniques described in Table 1–1 or Table 1–2 earlier in this module to scroll through the document.

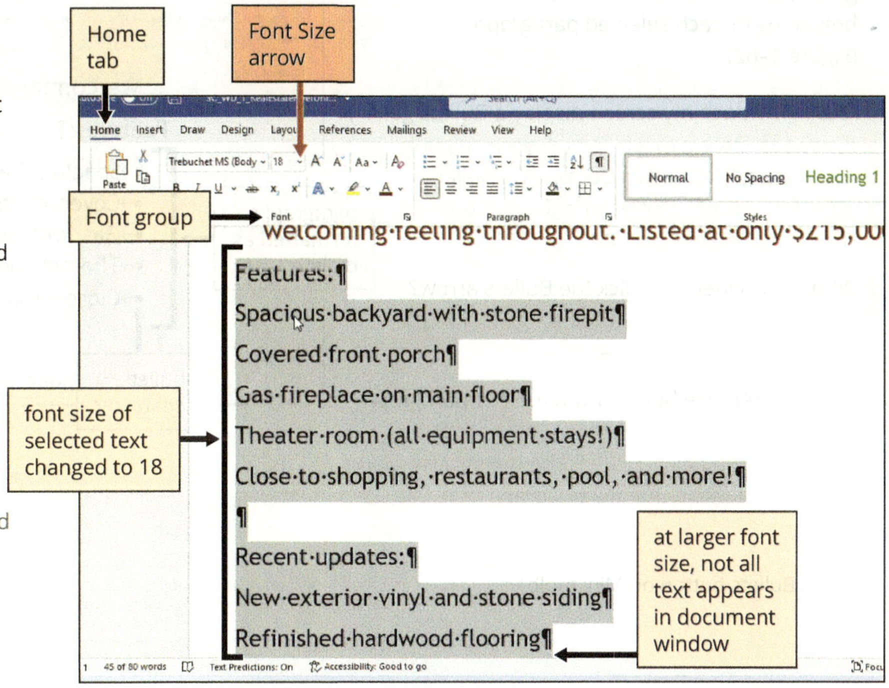

Figure 1–60

To Bullet a List of Paragraphs

A **bulleted list** is a series of paragraphs, each beginning with a bullet character, such as a dot or check mark. The next step is to format the five paragraphs that identify features of the home for sale as a bulleted list.

To format a list of paragraphs as a bulleted list, you first must select all the lines in the paragraphs. **Why?** If you do not select all paragraphs, Word will place a bullet only in the paragraph containing the insertion point. The following steps bullet a list of paragraphs.

1.
- If necessary, scroll to position the text to be formatted in the document window.
- Move the pointer to the left of the first paragraph to be selected until the pointer changes to a right-pointing block arrow.
- Drag downward until all paragraphs that will be formatted with a bullet character are selected (Figure 1–61).

Q&A What if I am using a touch screen?
Tap to position the insertion point in the text to select and then drag the selection handle(s) as necessary to select the text that will be formatted.

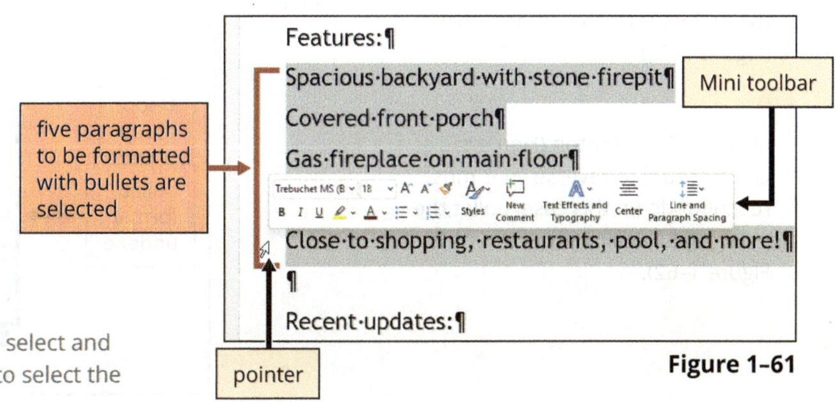

Figure 1–61

2

- Click the Bullets button (Home tab | Paragraph group) to place a bullet character at the beginning of each selected paragraph (Figure 1–62).

Q&A Why does my screen display a Bullets gallery? If you are using a touch screen, you may not have a separate Bullets button and Bullets arrow. In this case, select the desired bullet style in the Bullets gallery.

What if I accidentally click the Bullets arrow? Press ESC to remove the Bullets gallery from the screen and then repeat Step 2.

How do I remove bullets from a list or paragraph? Select the list or paragraph and then click the Bullets button again, or click the Bullets arrow and then click None in the Bullet Library.

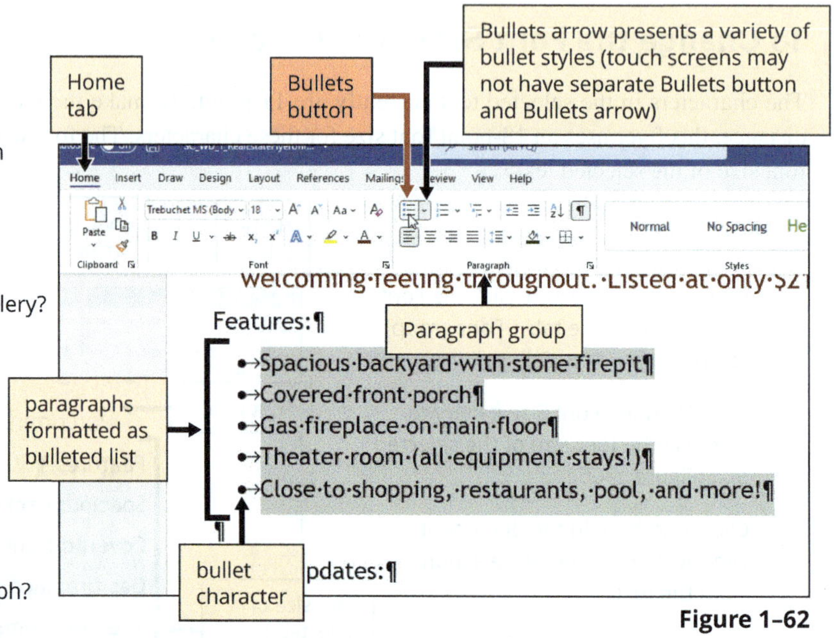

Figure 1–62

Other Ways

1. Click Bullets button on Mini toolbar

To Undo and Redo an Action

Word provides a means of canceling your recent command(s) or action(s). For example, if you format text incorrectly, you can undo the format and try it again. When you point to the Undo button, Word displays the action you can undo as part of a ScreenTip.

If, after you undo an action, you decide you did not want to perform the undo, you can redo the undone action. Word does not allow you to undo or redo some actions, such as saving or printing a document. The following steps undo the bullet format just applied and then redo the bullet format. **Why?** These steps illustrate the undo and redo actions.

1

- Click the Undo button (Home tab | Undo group) to reverse your most recent action (in this case, remove the bullets from the paragraphs) (Figure 1–63).

2

- Click the Redo button (Home tab | Undo group) to reverse your most recent undo (in this case, bullet the paragraphs again) (shown in Figure 1–62).

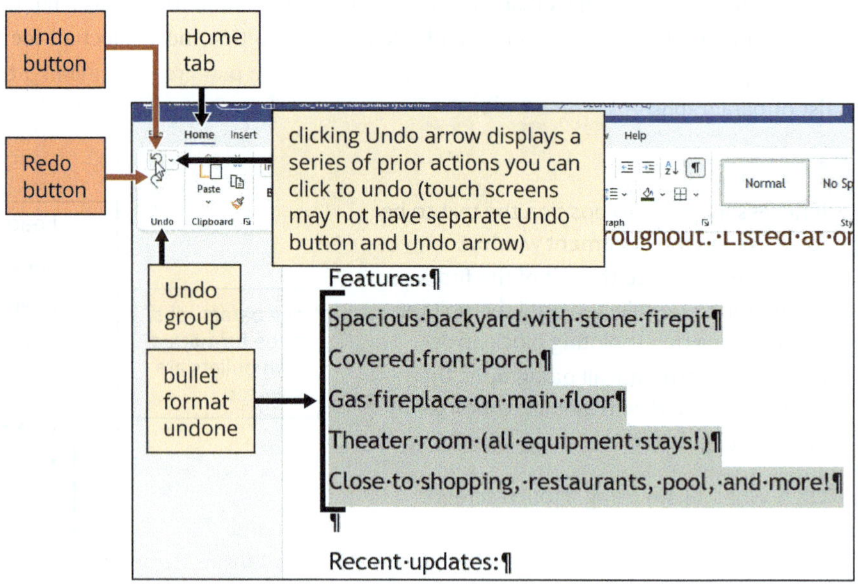

Figure 1–63

Other Ways

1. Press CTRL+Z to undo; press CTRL+Y to redo

To Number a List of Paragraphs

A **numbered list** is a series of paragraphs, each beginning with a sequential number that may or may not be followed by a separator character, such as a period or parenthesis. The next step is to format the five paragraphs that describe the recent updates to the home for sale as a numbered list.

To format an existing list of paragraphs in a document as a numbered list, you first must select all the lines in the paragraphs. **Why?** If you do not select all paragraphs, Word will place a number only in the paragraph containing the insertion point. The following steps number a list of paragraphs.

1

- If necessary, scroll to position the text to be formatted in the document window.
- Move the pointer to the left of the first paragraph to be selected until the pointer changes to a right-pointing block arrow.
- Drag downward until all paragraphs that will be formatted as a numbered list are selected (Figure 1–64).

Q&A What if I am using a touch screen?
Tap to position the insertion point in the text to select and then drag the selection handle(s) as necessary to select the text that will be formatted.

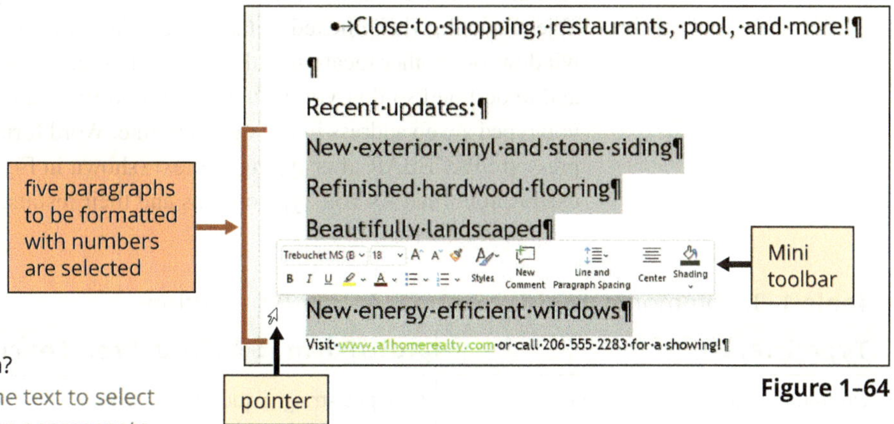

Figure 1–64

2

- Click the Numbering button (Home tab | Paragraph group) to place a number followed by a period at the beginning of each selected paragraph.

Q&A Why does my screen display a Numbering gallery?
If you are using a touch screen, you may not have a separate Numbering button and Numbering arrow. In this case, select the desired numbering style in the Numbering gallery.

What if I accidentally click the Numbering arrow?
Press ESC to remove the Numbering gallery from the screen and then repeat Step 2.

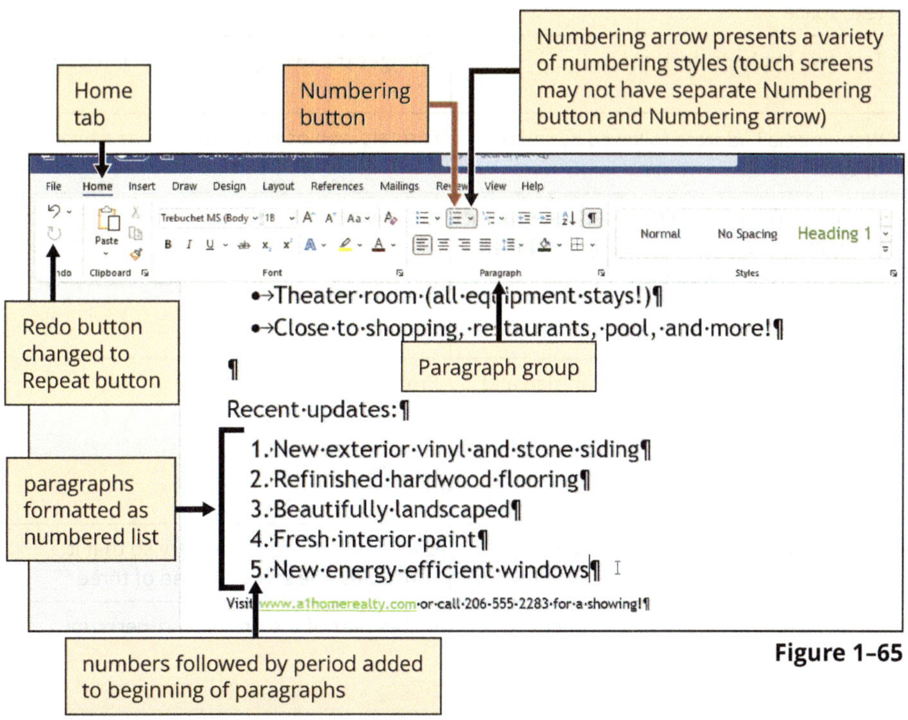

Figure 1–65

3

- Click anywhere in the document window to remove the selection from the text (Figure 1–65).

Q&A How do I remove numbering from a list or paragraph?
Select the list or paragraph and then click the Numbering button again, or click the Numbering arrow and then click None in the Numbering Library.

Why did the appearance of the Redo button change?
It changed to a Repeat button. When it is a Repeat button, you can click it to repeat your last action. For example, you can select different text and then click the Repeat button to apply (repeat) the number format to the selected text.

Other Ways

1. Click Numbering button on Mini toolbar

AutoFormat As You Type

As you type text in a document, Word automatically formats some of it for you. For example, when you press ENTER or SPACEBAR after typing an email address or web address, Word automatically formats the address as a hyperlink. A **hyperlink**, or link, is a specially formatted word, phrase, or object, which, when clicked or tapped, displays a webpage on the Internet, another file, an email window, or another location within the same file. Links usually are formatted in a different color and underlined so that you visually can identify them. Recall that earlier in this module, when you typed a web address in the signature line, Word formatted the text as a hyperlink because you pressed SPACEBAR after typing the text (shown in Figure 1–66). Table 1–3 outlines commonly used AutoFormat As You Type options and their results.

Table 1-3: Commonly Used AutoFormat As You Type Options

Typed Text	AutoFormat As You Type Feature	Example
Quotation marks or apostrophes	Changes straight quotation marks or apostrophes to curly ones	"the" becomes “the”
Text, a space, one hyphen, one or no spaces, text, space	Changes the hyphen to an en dash	ages 20-45 becomes ages 20–45
Text, two hyphens, text, space	Changes the two hyphens to an em dash	Two types-yellow and red becomes Two types—yellow and red
Web or email address followed by SPACEBAR or ENTER	Formats web or email address as a hyperlink	www.cengage.com becomes www.cengage.com
Number followed by a period, hyphen, right parenthesis, or greater than sign and then a space or tab followed by text	Creates a numbered list	1. Word 2. PowerPoint becomes 1. Word 2. PowerPoint
Asterisk, hyphen, or greater than sign and then a space or tab followed by text	Creates a bulleted list	* Home tab * Insert tab becomes • Home tab • Insert tab
Fraction and then a space or hyphen	Condenses the fraction entry so that it consumes one space instead of three	1/2 becomes ½
Ordinal and then a space or hyphen	Makes part of the ordinal a superscript	3rd becomes 3rd

To Remove a Hyperlink

The web address in the signature line of the flyer should be formatted as regular text; that is, it should not be a different color or underlined. **Why?** Hyperlinks are useful only in online documents, and this flyer will be printed instead of distributed electronically. The following steps remove a hyperlink format.

1

- Right-click the hyperlink (in this case, the web address) to display a shortcut menu (Figure 1–66).

Q&A What if I am using a touch screen?
Press and hold the hyperlink and then tap the 'Show Context Menu' button on the Mini toolbar.

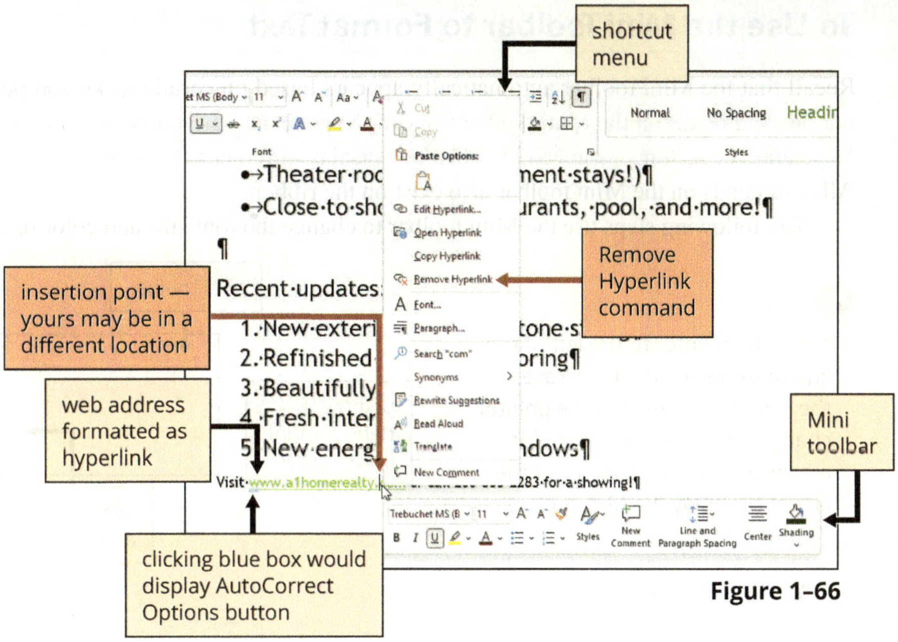

Figure 1–66

2

- Click Remove Hyperlink on the shortcut menu to remove the hyperlink format from the text; if the text remains colored and underlined, change the color to Automatic and remove the underline by clicking the Underline button (Home tab | Font group) (Figure 1–67).

Q&A Could I have used the AutoCorrect Options button instead of the Remove Hyperlink command?
Yes. Alternatively, you could have pointed to the small blue box at the beginning of the hyperlink (if it is visible), clicked the AutoCorrect Options button, and then clicked Undo Hyperlink on the AutoCorrect Options menu.

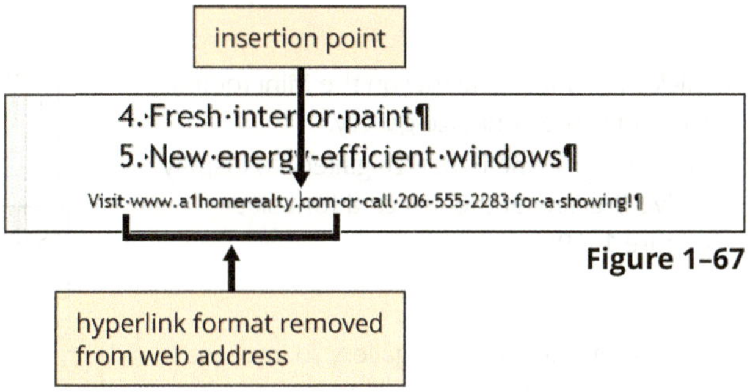

Figure 1–67

Other Ways

1. With insertion point in hyperlink, click Links button (Insert tab | Links group), click Link button, click Remove Link button (Edit Hyperlink dialog box)

To Center Another Paragraph

In the flyer, the signature line is to be centered to match the paragraph alignment of the headline. The following steps center the signature line.

1 If necessary, click somewhere in the paragraph to be centered (in this case, the signature line) to position the insertion point in the paragraph to be formatted.

2 Click the Center button (Home tab | Paragraph group) to center the paragraph containing the insertion point (shown in Figure 1–68).

To Use the Mini Toolbar to Format Text

Recall that the Mini toolbar automatically appears based on certain tasks you perform. **Why?** Word places commonly used buttons and boxes on the Mini toolbar for your convenience. If you do not use the Mini toolbar, it disappears from the screen. Depending on settings, your Mini toolbar may display different buttons and commands than the Mini toolbar shown in this book. All commands on the Mini toolbar also exist on the ribbon.

The following steps use the Mini toolbar to change the font size and color of text in the signature line of the flyer.

1

- Move the pointer to the left of the line to be selected (in this case, the signature line) until the pointer changes to a right-pointing block arrow and then click to select the line and display the Mini toolbar (Figure 1–68).

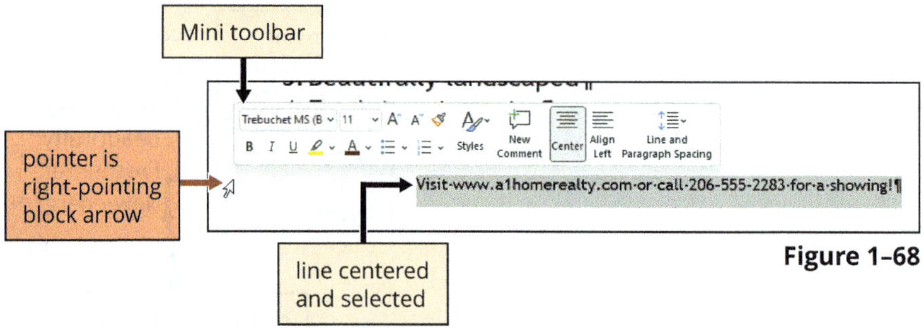

Figure 1–68

Q&A What if I am using a touch screen?
Double-tap to the left of the line to be selected to select the line and then tap the selection to display the Mini toolbar. If you are using a touch screen, the buttons and boxes on the Mini toolbar differ. For example, it contains a 'Show Context Menu' button at the far-right edge, which you tap to display a shortcut menu.

2

- Click the Font Size arrow on the Mini toolbar to display the Font Size gallery.
- Point to 16 in the Font Size gallery to display a Live Preview of the selected font size (Figure 1–69).

3

- Click 16 in the Font Size gallery to increase the font size of the selected text.

4

- With the text still selected and the Mini toolbar still displayed, click the Font Color arrow on the Mini toolbar to display the Font Color gallery.
- Point to 'Orange, Accent 4, Darker 50%' (eighth color in the bottom row) to display a Live Preview of the selected font color (Figure 1–70).

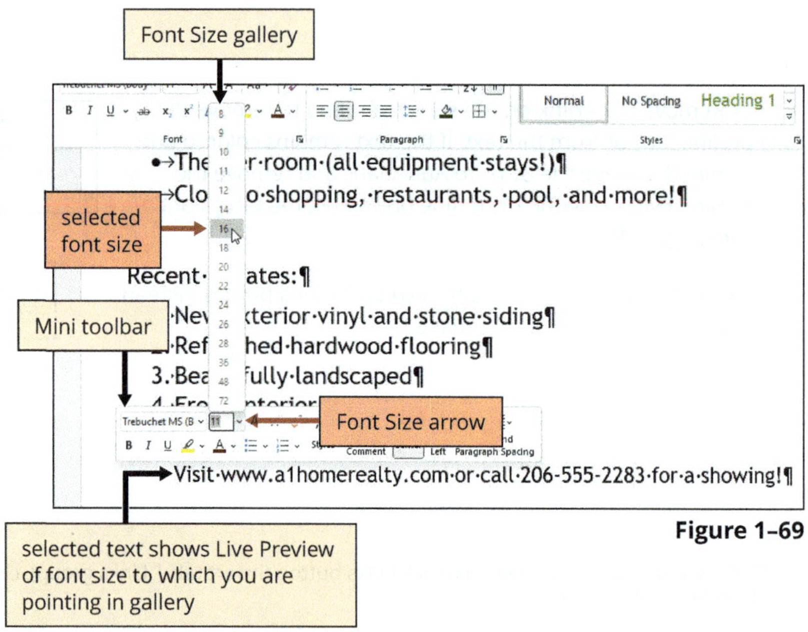

Figure 1–69

5

- Click 'Orange, Accent 4, Darker 50%' to change the color of the selected text.
- Click anywhere in the document window to remove the selection from the text.

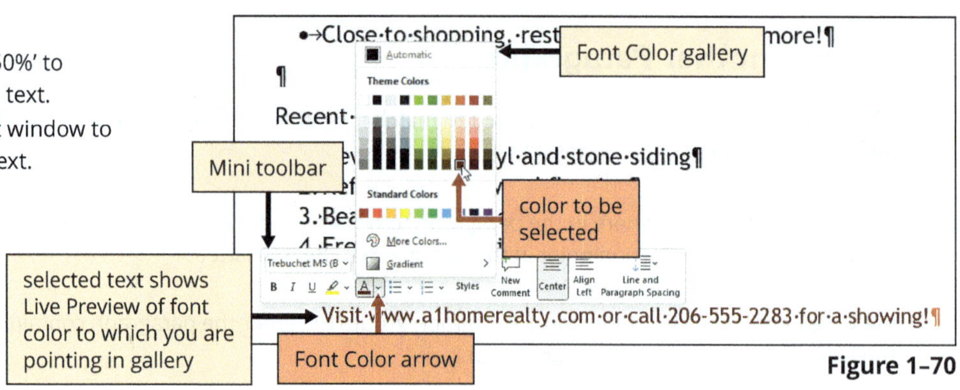

Figure 1–70

To Select a Group of Words

The words, all equipment stays, in the bulleted list of the flyer, are underlined to further emphasize them. To format a group of words, you first must select them. **Why?** If you underline text without selecting any text first, Word will underline only the word containing the insertion point. The following steps select a group of words.

1

- If necessary, scroll to display the entire bulleted list in the document window.
- Position the pointer immediately to the left of the first character of the text to be selected, in this case, the a in the word, all (Figure 1–71).

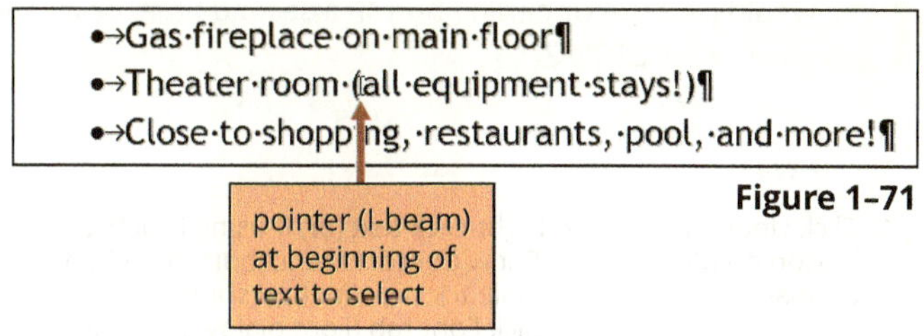

Figure 1–71

Q&A Why did the shape of the pointer change?
The pointer's shape is an I-beam when positioned in unselected text in the document window.

2

- Drag the pointer through the last character of the text to be selected, in this case, the last s in the word, stays (Figure 1–72).

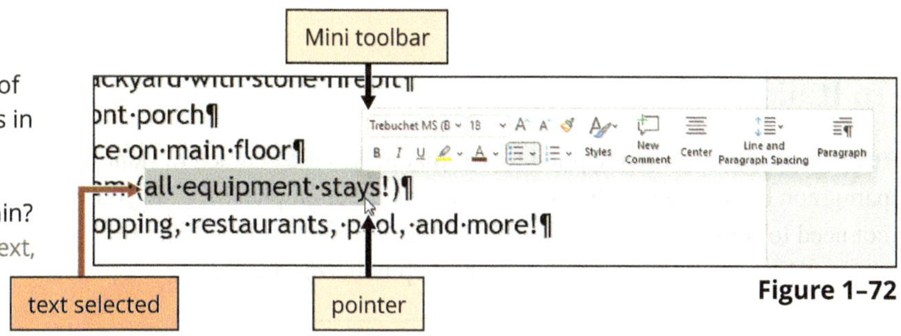

Figure 1–72

Q&A Why did the pointer shape change again?
When the pointer is positioned in selected text, its shape is a left-pointing block arrow.

Other Ways

1. With insertion point at beginning of first word in group, press CTRL+SHIFT+RIGHT ARROW repeatedly until all words are selected

To Underline Text

Underlined text displays with an underscore (_) below each character, including spaces. In the flyer, the text, all equipment stays, in the bulleted list is underlined. **Why?** Underlines are used to emphasize or draw attention to specific text. The following step formats selected text with an underline.

1

- With the text selected, click the Underline button (Home tab | Font group) to underline the selected text (Figure 1–73).

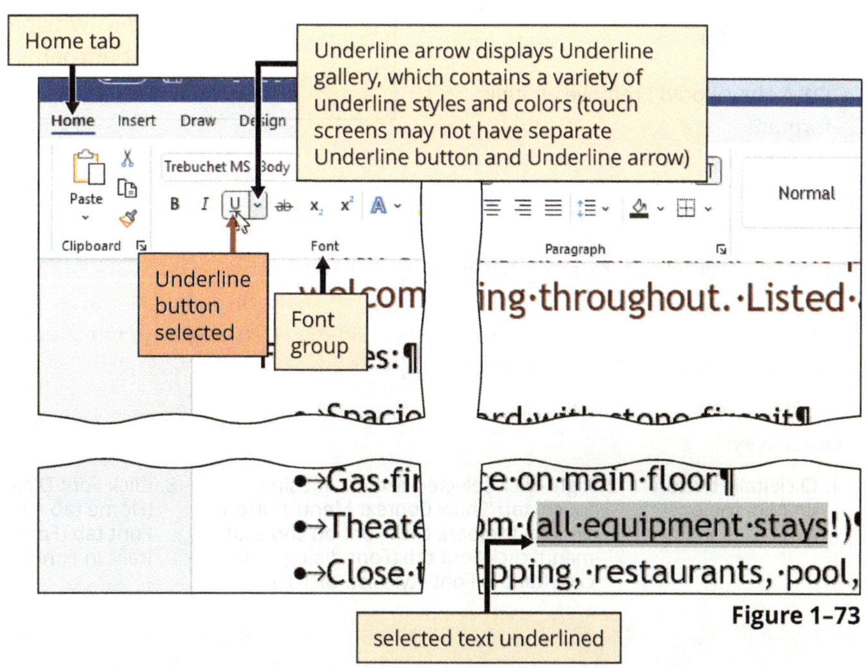

Figure 1–73

Q&A What if my screen displays an Underline gallery?
If you are using a touch screen, you may not have a separate Underline button and Underline arrow. In this case, select the desired underline style in the Underline gallery.

If a button exists on the Mini toolbar, can I click that instead of using the ribbon?
Yes.

How would I remove an underline?
You would click the Underline button a second time, or you immediately could click the Undo button (Home tab | Undo group) or press CTRL+Z.

Other Ways

1. Click Underline button on Mini toolbar
2. Right-click text (or, if using touch, tap 'Show Context Menu' button on Mini toolbar), click Font on shortcut menu, click Font tab (Font dialog box), click Underline style box arrow, click desired underline style, click OK
3. Click Font Dialog Box Launcher (Home tab | Font group), click Font tab (Font dialog box), click Underline style arrow, click desired underline style, click OK
4. Press CTRL+U

To Italicize Text

Italic is a type of format applied to text that makes the characters slant to the right. The next step is to italicize the word, only, paragraph below the headline in the flyer to further emphasize it. If you want to format the characters in a single word, you do not need to select the word. **Why?** To format a single word, you simply position the insertion point somewhere in the word and apply the desired format. The following step italicizes a word.

1

- If necessary, scroll to the top of the document in the document window.
- Click somewhere in the word to be italicized (only, in this case) to position the insertion point in the word to be formatted.
- Click the Italic button (Home tab | Font group) to italicize the word containing the insertion point (Figure 1–74).

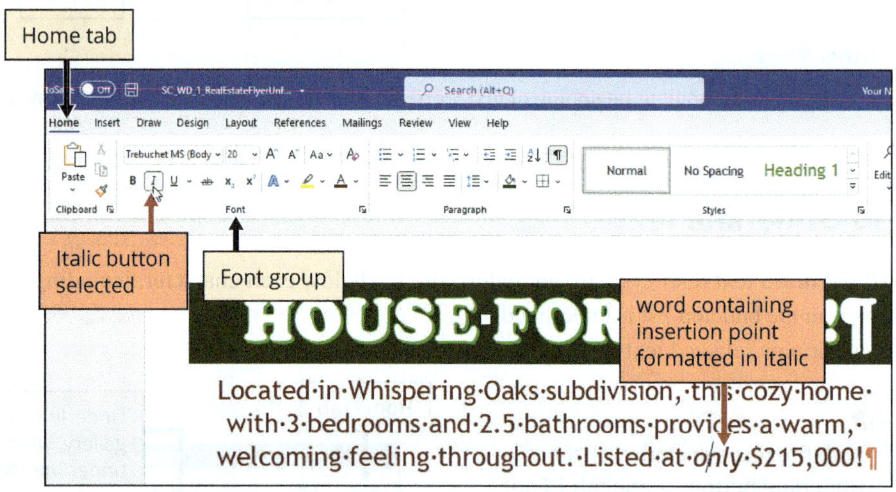

Figure 1–74

Q&A How would I remove an italic format?
You would click the Italic button a second time, or you immediately could click the Undo button (Home tab | Undo group) or press CTRL+Z.

How can I tell what formatting has been applied to text?
The selected buttons and boxes on the Home tab show formatting characteristics of the location of the insertion point. With the insertion point in the word, only, the Home tab shows these formats: 20-point Trebuchet MS italic font.

Other Ways

1. Click Italic button on Mini toolbar
2. Right-click selected text (or, if using touch, tap 'Show Context Menu' button on Mini toolbar), click Font on shortcut menu, click Font tab (Font dialog box), click Italic in Font style list, click OK
3. Click Font Dialog Box Launcher (Home tab | Font group), click Font tab (Font dialog box), click Italic in Font style list, click OK
4. Press CTRL+I

To Select Nonadjacent Text

The next step is to select the web address and phone number in the signature line and bold them. **Why?** You want to emphasize these items further. Word provides a method of selecting nonadjacent items, which are items such as text, pictures, or other objects that are not immediately beside one another. When you select nonadjacent items, you can format all occurrences of the selected items at once. The following steps select nonadjacent text.

1

- If necessary, scroll to display the bottom of the document in the document window.
- Select the first text to format (in this case, drag through the web address) (Figure 1–75).

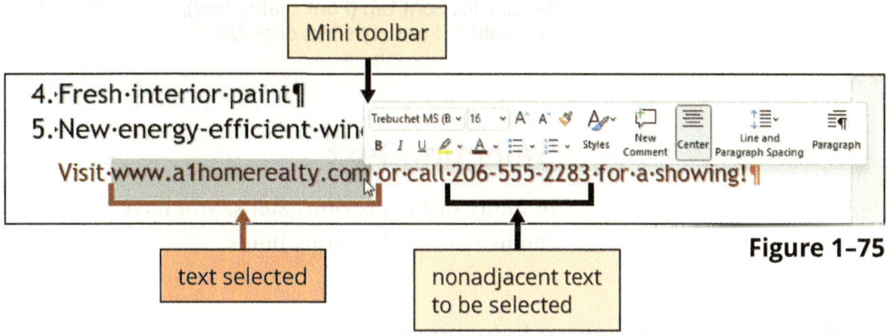

Figure 1–75

2

- While holding down CTRL, select the next text to format (in this case, drag through the phone number), which selects the nonadjacent text (Figure 1–76).

Q&A Do I follow the same procedure to select any nonadjacent item?
Yes. Select the first item and then hold down CTRL while selecting the remaining items.

What if my keyboard does not have a key labeled CTRL?
You will need to format each item individually, one at a time.

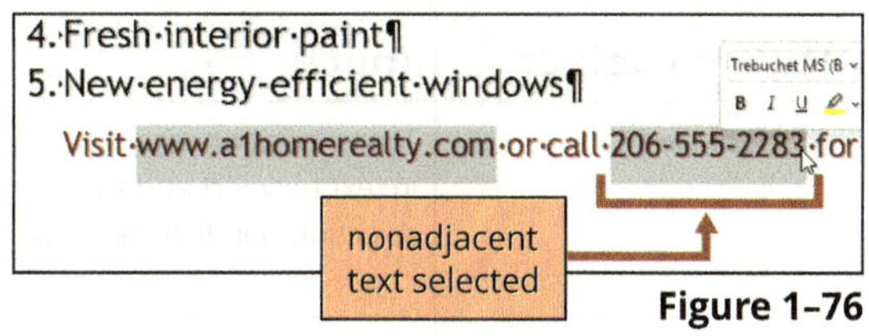

Figure 1–76

To Bold Text

Bold is a type of format applied to text that makes the characters appear somewhat thicker and darker than those that are not bold. The following steps format the selected text in bold characters. **Why?** To further emphasize this text, it is bold in the flyer. Recall that if you want to format a single word, you simply position the insertion point in the word and then format the word. To format text that consists of more than one word, as you have learned previously, you select the text first.

1

- With the text selected, click the Bold button (Home tab | Font group) to bold the selected text (Figure 1–77).

Q&A How would I remove a bold format?
You would click the Bold button a second time, or you immediately could click the Undo button (Home tab | Undo group) or press CTRL+Z.

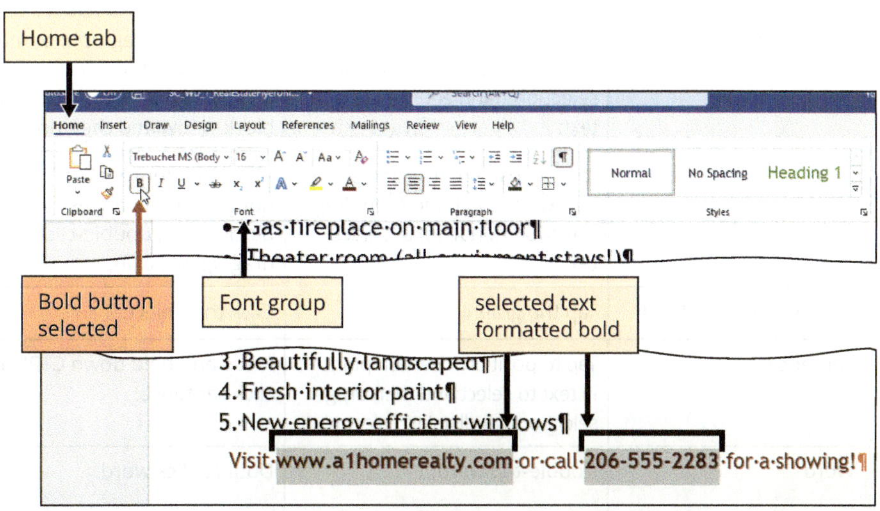

Figure 1–77

2

- Click anywhere in the document window to remove the selection from the screen.

Other Ways

1. Click Bold button on Mini toolbar
2. Right-click selected text (or, if using touch, tap 'Show Context Menu' button on Mini toolbar), click Font on shortcut menu, click Font tab (Font dialog box), click Bold in Font style list, click OK
3. Click Font Dialog Box Launcher (Home tab | Font group), click Font tab (Font dialog box), click Bold in Font style list, click OK
4. Press CTRL+B

Selecting Text

In many of the previous steps, you have selected text. Table 1–4 summarizes the techniques you can use to select various items.

Table 1–4: Techniques for Selecting Text

Item to Select	Touch	Mouse	Keyboard (where applicable)
Block of text	Tap to position insertion point in text to select and then drag selection handle(s) to select text.	Click at beginning of selection, scroll to end of selection, position pointer at end of selection, hold down SHIFT, and then click; or drag through the text.	
Character(s)	Tap to position insertion point in text to select and then drag selection handle(s) to select text.	Drag through character(s).	SHIFT+RIGHT ARROW or SHIFT+LEFT ARROW
Entire Document		Move pointer to left of text until pointer changes to right-pointing block arrow and then triple-click.	CTRL+A
Line	Double-tap to left of line to be selected.	Move pointer to left of line until pointer changes to right-pointing block arrow and then click.	HOME, then SHIFT+END or END, then SHIFT+HOME
Lines	Tap to position insertion point in text to select and then drag selection handle(s) to select text.	Move pointer to left of first line until pointer changes to right-pointing block arrow and then drag up or down.	HOME, then SHIFT+DOWN ARROW or END, then SHIFT+UP ARROW
Paragraph	Tap to position insertion point in text to select and then drag selection handle(s) to select text.	Triple-click paragraph; or move pointer to left of paragraph until pointer changes to right-pointing block arrow and then double-click.	CTRL+SHIFT+DOWN ARROW or CTRL+SHIFT+UP ARROW
Paragraphs	Tap to position insertion point in text to select and then drag selection handle(s) to select text.	Move pointer to left of paragraph until pointer changes to right-pointing block arrow, double-click, and then drag up or down.	CTRL+SHIFT+DOWN ARROW or CTRL+SHIFT+UP ARROW repeatedly
Picture or other object	Tap the graphic.	Click the object.	
Sentence	Tap to position insertion point in text to select and then drag selection handle(s) to select text.	Press and hold down CTRL and then click sentence.	
Word	Double-tap word.	Double-click word.	CTRL+SHIFT+RIGHT ARROW or CTRL+SHIFT+LEFT ARROW
Words	Tap to position insertion point in text to select and then drag selection handle(s) to select text.	Drag through words.	CTRL+SHIFT+RIGHT ARROW or CTRL+SHIFT+LEFT ARROW repeatedly

To Save an Existing Document with a Different File Name

You might want to save a file with a different file name. For example, you might start a homework assignment with a data file and then save it with a final file name for submission to your instructor, saving it to a location designated by your instructor.

The following steps save the SC_WD_1_RealEstateFlyerUnformatted file with a different file name.

1. Click File on the ribbon to open Backstage view.

2. Click Save As in Backstage view to display the Save As screen.

3. Type **SC_WD_1_RealEstateFlyerFormatted** in the File name box, replacing the existing file name (Figure 1–78).

4. Click the Save button in the Save As screen to save the flyer with the new name in the same save location.

Q&A What if I wanted to save the file to a different location?
You would click the Browse button or click the More options link in the Save As screen to display the Save As dialog box, navigate to the desired save location, and then click Save in the dialog box.

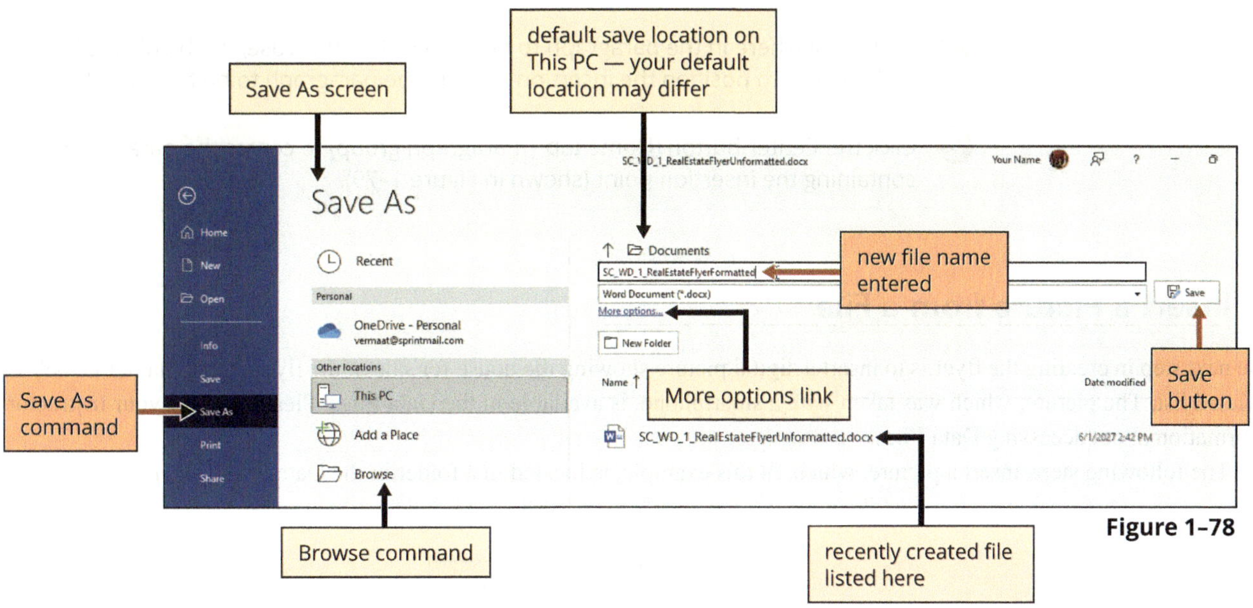

Figure 1–78

BTW
Organizing Files and Folders
You should organize and store files in folders so that you easily can find the files later. For example, if you are taking an introductory technology class called CIS 101, a good practice would be to save all Word files in a Word folder in a CIS 101 folder.

Break Point: If you want to take a break, this is a good place to do so. To resume later, start Word and continue following the steps from this location forward.

Inserting and Formatting a Picture in a Word Document

With the text formatted in the flyer, the next step is to insert a digital picture in the flyer and format the picture. Flyers usually contain a picture or other object to attract the attention of passersby. In the following sections, you will perform these tasks:

1. Insert a digital picture into the flyer.
2. Reduce the size of the picture.
3. Change the look of the picture.

Consider This

How do you locate a picture to use in a document?

To use a picture in a Word document, the image must be stored digitally in a file. Files containing pictures are available from a variety of sources:

- The web has pictures available, some of which are free, while others require a fee.
- You can take a picture with a smartphone or digital camera and **download** it, which is the process of transferring (copying) a file (such as a picture) from a server, computer, or device (such as a phone or camera) to another computer or device.
- With a scanner, you can convert a printed picture, drawing, diagram, or other object to a digital file.

If you receive a picture from a source other than yourself, do not use the file until you are certain it does not contain a virus. A **virus** is a potentially damaging program that affects a computer or device negatively by altering the way it works, usually without the user's knowledge or permission. Use an antivirus program or app to verify that any files you use are virus free.

To Center a Paragraph

In the flyer, the digital picture showing the house for sale should be centered on the blank line between the numbered list and the bulleted list. The blank paragraph below the bulleted list currently is left-aligned. The following steps center this paragraph.

1. Click somewhere in the paragraph to be centered (in this case, the blank line below the bulleted list) to position the insertion point in the paragraph to be formatted.

2. Click the Center button (Home tab | Paragraph group) to center the paragraph containing the insertion point (shown in Figure 1–79).

To Insert a Picture from a File

The next step in creating the flyer is to insert a digital picture showing the house for sale in the flyer on the blank line below the bulleted list. The picture, which was taken with a smartphone, is available in the Data Files. Please contact your instructor for information about accessing Data Files.

The following steps insert a picture, which, in this example, is located in a folder in the Data Files folder. **Why?** It is good practice to organize and store files in folders so that you easily can find the files at a later date.

1

- If necessary, position the insertion point at the location where you want to insert the picture (in this case, on the centered blank paragraph below the bulleted list).
- Click Insert on the ribbon to display the Insert tab.
- Click the Insert Pictures button (Insert tab | Illustrations group) to display the Insert Picture From menu (Figure 1–79).

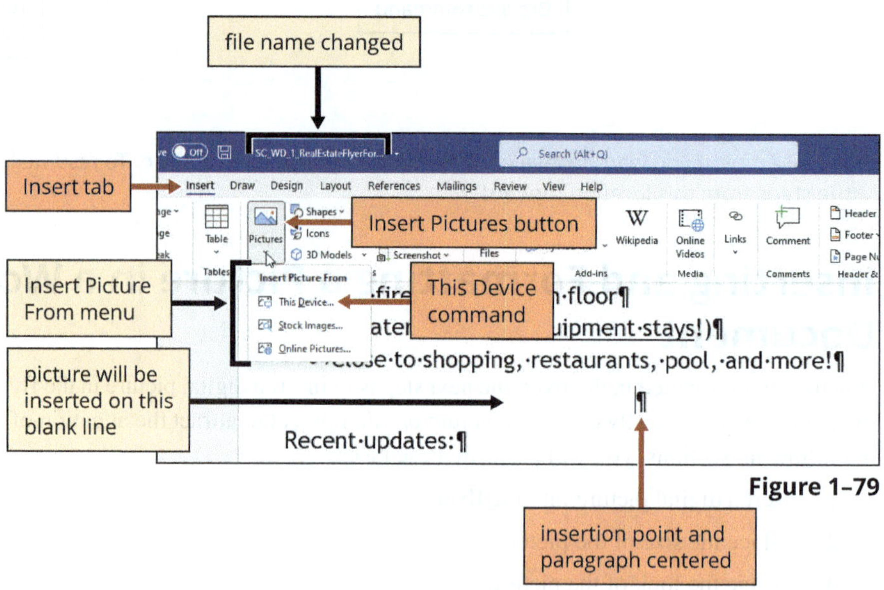

Figure 1–79

2

- Click This Device on the Insert Picture From menu to display the Insert Picture dialog box.
- In the Insert Picture dialog box, navigate to the location of the digital picture (in this case, the Module folder in the Data Files folder).
- Click Support_WD_1_House to select the file (Figure 1–80).

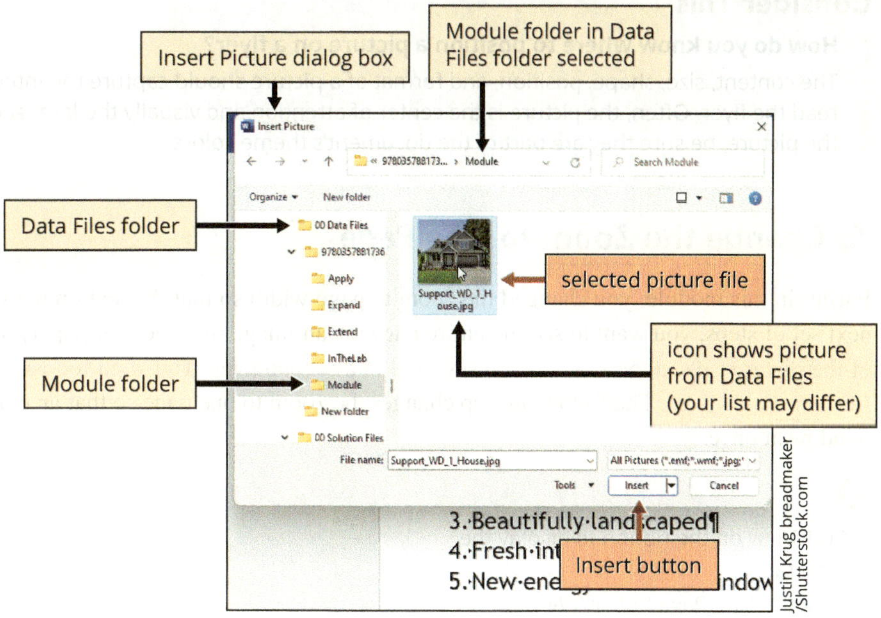

Figure 1–80

3

- Click the Insert button (Insert Picture dialog box) to insert the picture at the location of the insertion point in the document (Figure 1–81).

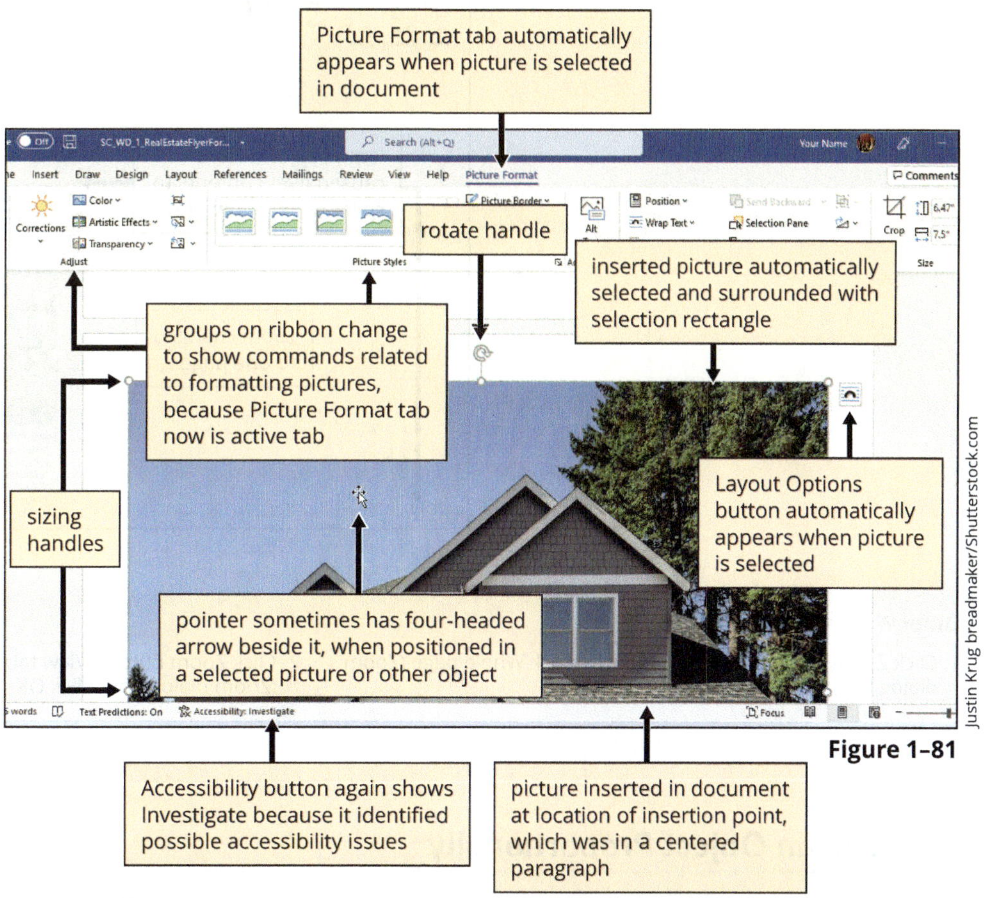

Figure 1–81

Q&A What are the symbols around the picture?
A selected object, such as a picture, appears surrounded by a **selection rectangle**, which is a box that has small circles, called **sizing handles**, at each corner and middle location, and a rotate handle; you drag the sizing handles to resize the selected object. When you drag a picture or other object's **rotate handle**, which is the small circular arrow at the top of the selected object, the object moves in either a clockwise or counterclockwise direction.

What is the purpose of the Layout Options button?
When you click the Layout Options button, Word provides options for changing how the selected picture or other object is positioned with text in the document.

Should I check accessibility now?
Notice that the Accessibility button on the taskbar again displays Investigate, meaning potential accessibility issues again exist in the document. You will address all accessibility issues later in this project.

Consider This

How do you know where to position a picture on a flyer?

The content, size, shape, position, and format of a picture should capture the interest of your audience, enticing them to read the flyer. Often, the picture is the center of attention and visually the largest element on a flyer. If you use colors in the picture, be sure they are part of the document's theme colors.

To Change the Zoom to One Page

Earlier in this module, you changed the zoom to page width so that the text on the screen was larger and easier to read. In the next set of steps, you want to see the entire page (as an image of a sheet of paper) on the screen at once. **Why?** The large size of the picture caused the flyer contents to spill to a second page. You want to resize the picture enough so that the entire flyer fits on a single page. The following step changes the zoom to one page so that an entire page can be displayed in the document window at once.

1

- Click View on the ribbon to display the View tab.
- Click the One Page button (View tab | Zoom group) to change the zoom to one page (Figure 1-82).

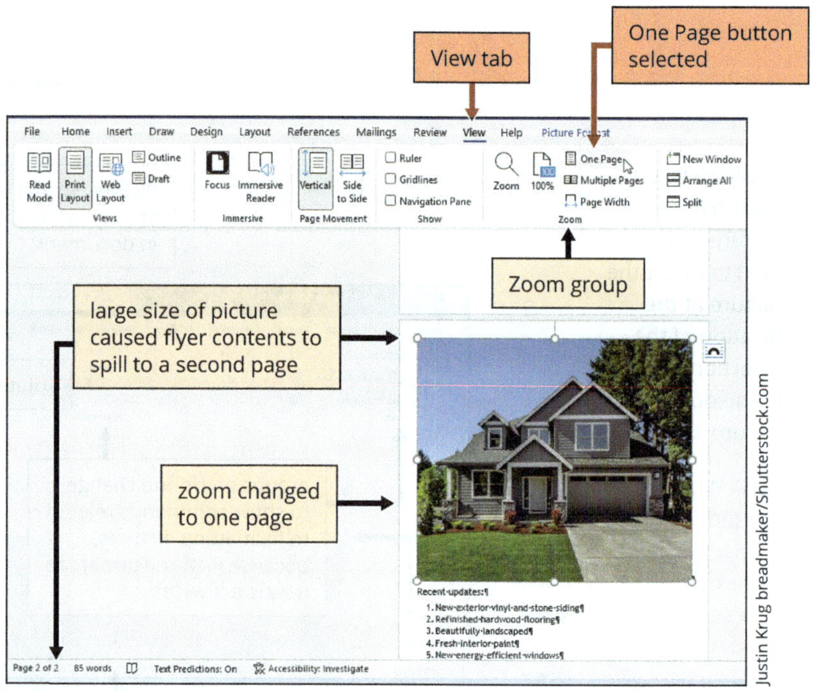

Figure 1-82

Other Ways

1. Click Zoom level button on status bar, click Whole page (Zoom dialog box), click OK
2. Click Zoom button (View tab | Zoom group), click Whole page (Zoom dialog box), click OK

To Resize an Object Proportionally

When you **resize** an object, such as a picture, you increase or decrease its size. The next step is to resize the picture so that it is smaller in the flyer. **Why?** You want the picture and all the text on the flyer to fit on a single sheet of paper. The following steps resize a selected object (picture).

1

- Be sure the picture still is selected.

Q&A What if the object (picture) is not selected?

To select a picture, click it.

- If necessary, click Picture Format on the ribbon to display the Picture Format tab.
- Point to the lower-left corner sizing handle on the picture so that the pointer shape changes to a two-headed arrow (Figure 1–83).

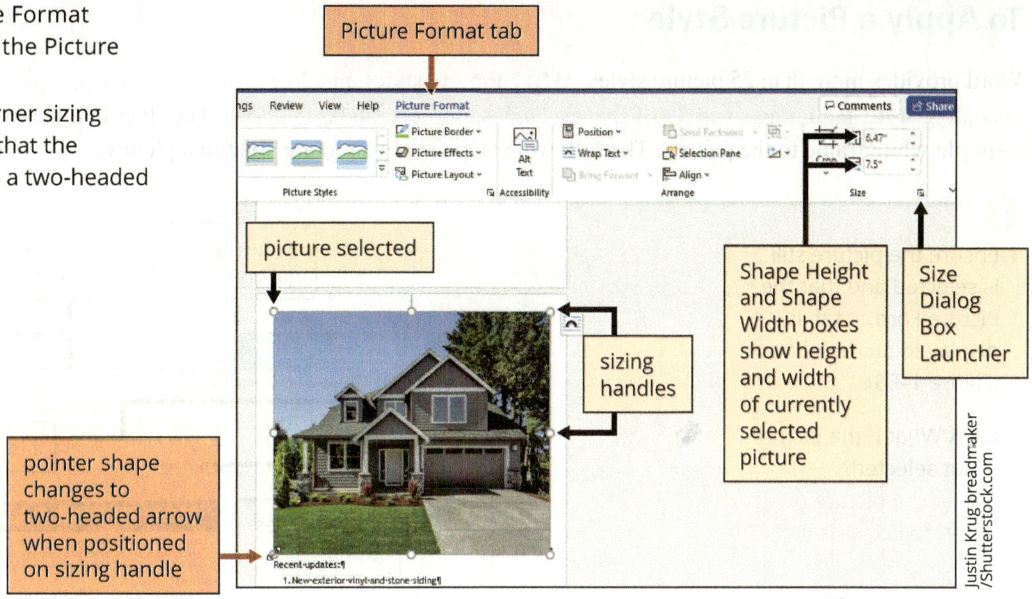

Figure 1–83

Justin Krug breadmaker/Shutterstock.com

2

- Drag the sizing handle diagonally inward until the lower-left corner of the picture is positioned approximately as shown in Figure 1–84. Do not release the mouse button at this point.

Q&A What if I am using a touch screen?

Drag a corner of the picture, without lifting your finger, until the picture is the desired size.

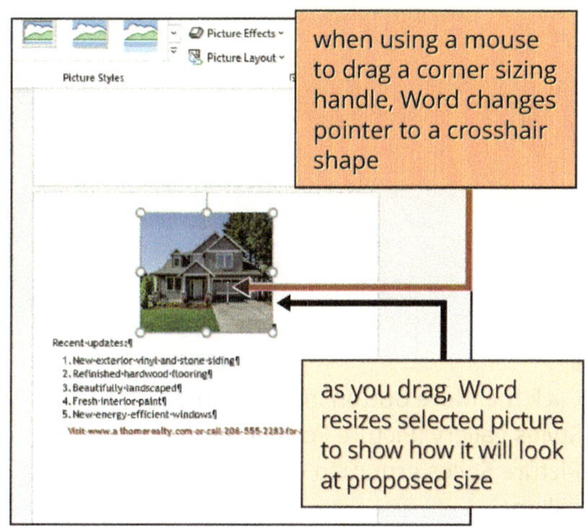

Figure 1–84

Justin Krug breadmaker/Shutterstock.com

3

- Release the mouse button to resize the picture, so that the entire flyer contents fit on a single page, as shown in Figure 1–85; the resized picture should have a height of about 2.85" and a width of about 3.3" (shown in Figure 1–85).

Q&A How can I see the height and width measurements?

Look in the Size group on the Picture Format tab to see the height and width measurements of a currently selected graphic (shown in Figure 1–85). If necessary, click the Picture Format tab on the ribbon to display the tab.

What if the object (picture) is the wrong size?

Repeat Steps 1, 2, and 3, or enter the desired height and width values in the Shape Height and Shape Width boxes (Picture Format tab | Size group).

What if I want to return an object (picture) to its original size and start again?

With the object (picture) selected, click the Size Dialog Box Launcher (Picture Format tab | Size group), click the Size tab (Layout dialog box), click the Reset button, and then click OK.

Other Ways

1. Enter height and width of selected object in Shape Height and Shape Width boxes (Picture Format tab | Size group)
2. Click Size Dialog Box Launcher (Picture Format tab | Size group), click Size tab (Layout dialog box), enter desired height and width values in boxes, click OK

To Apply a Picture Style

Word provides more than 25 picture styles. **Why?** Picture styles enable you easily to change a picture's look to a more visually appealing style, including a variety of shapes, angles, borders, and reflections. The flyer in this module uses a style that applies a simple white frame to the picture. The following steps apply a picture style to a picture.

1

- Ensure the picture still is selected and that the Picture Format tab is displayed on the ribbon (Figure 1–85).

Q&A What if the picture is not selected?
To select a picture or other object, click it.

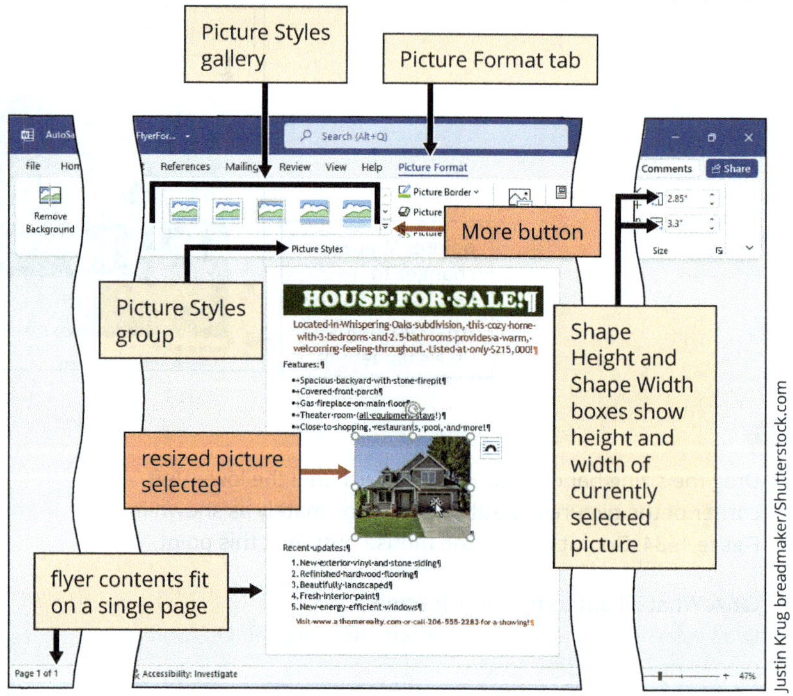

Figure 1–85

2

- Click the More button in the Picture Styles gallery (Picture Format tab | Picture Styles group) to expand the gallery.
- Point to 'Simple Frame, White' in the Picture Styles gallery (first style in first row) to display a Live Preview of that style applied to the picture in the document (Figure 1–86).
- **Experiment:** Point to various picture styles in the Picture Styles gallery and watch the style of the picture change in the document window.

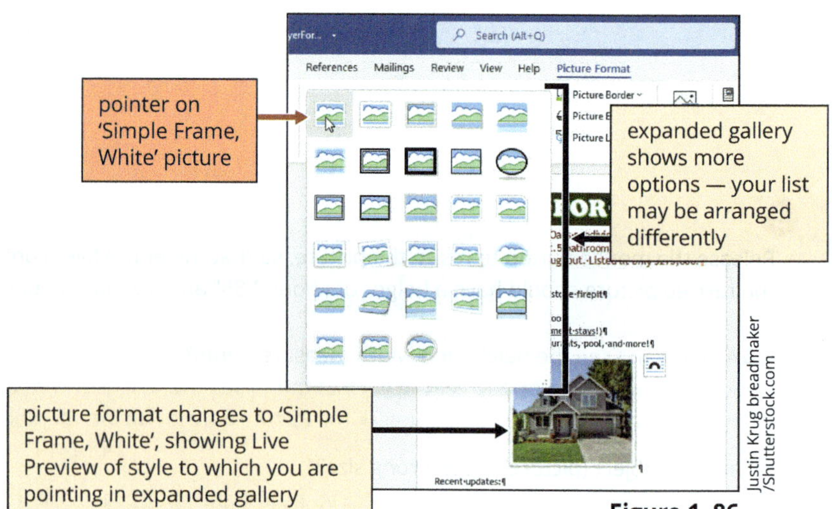

Figure 1–86

3

- Click 'Simple Frame, White' in the Picture Styles gallery to apply the style to the selected picture.

Q&A What if the flyer contents spill to a second page?
Reduce the size of the picture.

Other Ways

1. Right-click picture, click Picture Styles button on Mini toolbar, select desired style

To Apply a Picture Effect

Word provides a variety of picture effects, such as shadows, reflections, glows, soft edges, bevels, and 3-D rotations. The difference between the effects and the styles is that each effect has several options, providing you with more control over the exact look of the image.

In this flyer, the picture has a shadow. The following steps apply a picture effect to the selected picture. **Why?** Picture effects enable you to further customize a picture.

1

- With the picture still selected, click the Picture Effects button (Picture Format tab | Picture Styles group) to display the Picture Effects menu.
- Point to Shadow on the Picture Effects menu to display the Shadow gallery.
- Point to 'Perspective: Upper Left' in the Shadow gallery to display a Live Preview of the selected shadow effect applied to the picture in the document window (Figure 1–87). (Note that depending on your version of Word, your screen may display the text 'Perspective: Top Left' instead of 'Perspective: Upper Left' when you point to the shadow effect.)
- **Experiment:** If you are using a mouse, point to various shadow effects in the Shadow gallery and watch the picture change in the document window.

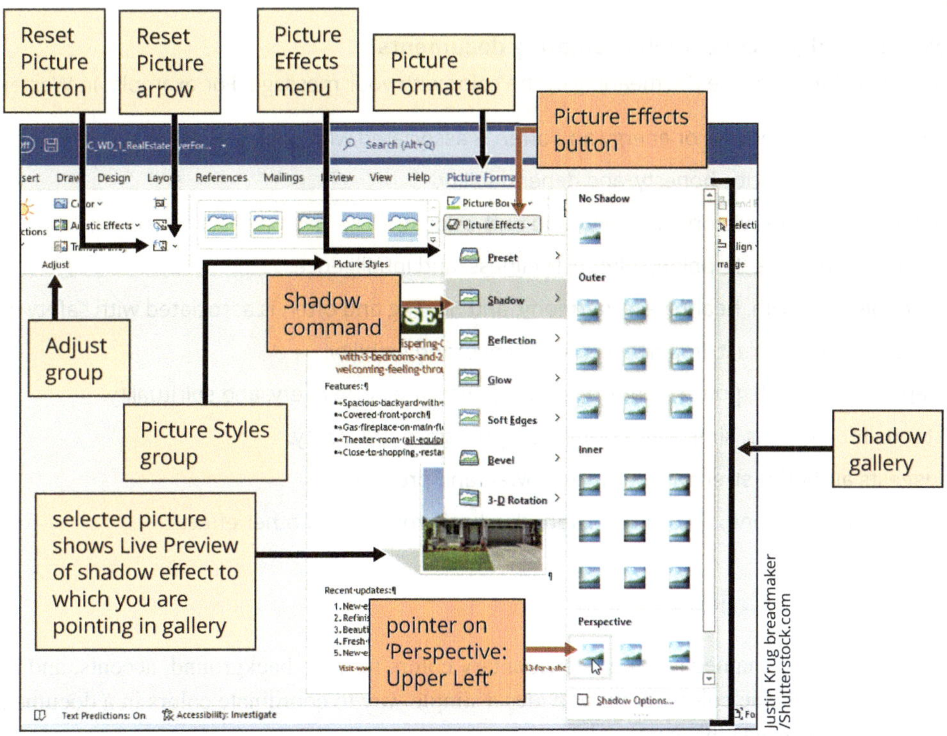

Figure 1–87

2

- Click 'Perspective: Upper Left' in the Shadow gallery to apply the selected picture effect.

Q&A What if I wanted to discard formatting applied to a picture?
You would click the Reset Picture button (Picture Format tab | Adjust group). To reset formatting and size, you would click the Reset Picture arrow (Picture Format tab | Adjust group) and then click 'Reset Picture & Size' on the Reset Picture menu.

Other Ways

1. Right-click picture (or, if using touch, tap 'Show Context Menu' button on Mini toolbar), click Format Picture on shortcut menu, click Effects button (Format Picture pane), select desired options, click Close button
2. Click Picture Styles Dialog Box Launcher (Picture Format tab | Picture Styles group), click Effects button (Format Picture pane), select desired options, click Close button

BTW
Color Palettes and Theme Colors
If your color palettes display differently than those shown in this book due to screen resolution or other settings, you can identify the locations of colors by identifying the location of the theme colors. The first row of colors that appear in any of the color palettes in this book (such as the one shown in Figure 1–90) are the theme colors (identified in the Colors gallery shown in Figure 1–88). The remaining rows that appear in a color palette are various shades of the theme colors.

Enhancing the Page

With the text and picture entered and formatted, the next step is to look at the page as a whole and determine if it looks finished in its current state. As you review the page, answer these questions:

- Are the colors appropriate for the message?
- Does it need a page border to frame its contents, or would a page border make it look too busy?
- Is the spacing between paragraphs and the picture on the page adequate? Do any sections look as if they are positioned too closely to the items above or below them?

You determine that you would like to change the text and shading colors and that a graphical, color-coordinated border would enhance the flyer. You also notice that the flyer would look more balanced if the headings of the bulleted and numbered list were spaced more closely to the lists themselves. The following sections make these enhancements to the flyer.

Consider This

What colors should you choose when creating documents?

When choosing color, associate the meaning of the color with your message. For example, in Western culture:

- Red expresses danger, power, or energy and often is associated with sports or physical exertion.
- Brown represents simplicity, honesty, and dependability.
- Orange denotes success, victory, creativity, and enthusiasm.
- Yellow suggests sunshine, happiness, hope, liveliness, and intelligence.
- Green symbolizes growth, healthiness, harmony, and healing and often is associated with safety or money.
- Blue indicates integrity, trust, importance, confidence, and stability.
- Purple represents wealth, power, comfort, extravagance, magic, mystery, and spirituality.
- White stands for newness, simplicity, cleanliness, precision, and clarity.
- Black suggests authority, strength, elegance, power, and prestige.
- Gray conveys neutrality and, thus, often is found in backgrounds and other effects.

To Change Theme Colors

A **theme color** in Word is a named set of complementary colors for text, background, accents, and links in a document. With more than 20 predefined theme colors, Word provides a simple way to coordinate colors in a document.

In the flyer, you will change the theme colors. **Why?** You want the colors in the flyer to represent integrity, trust, importance, confidence, and stability, which are conveyed by shades of blues. In Word, the Blue II theme color uses these colors. The following steps change theme colors.

1

- Click Design on the ribbon to display the Design tab.
- Click the Colors button (Design tab | Document Formatting group) to display the Colors gallery.
- Point to Blue II in the Colors gallery to display a Live Preview of the selected theme color (Figure 1–88).
- **Experiment:** Point to various theme colors in the Colors gallery and watch the colors change in the document.

2

- Click Blue II in the Colors gallery to change the document theme colors.

Q&A What if I want to return to the default theme colors?
You would click the Colors button again and then click Office in the Colors gallery.

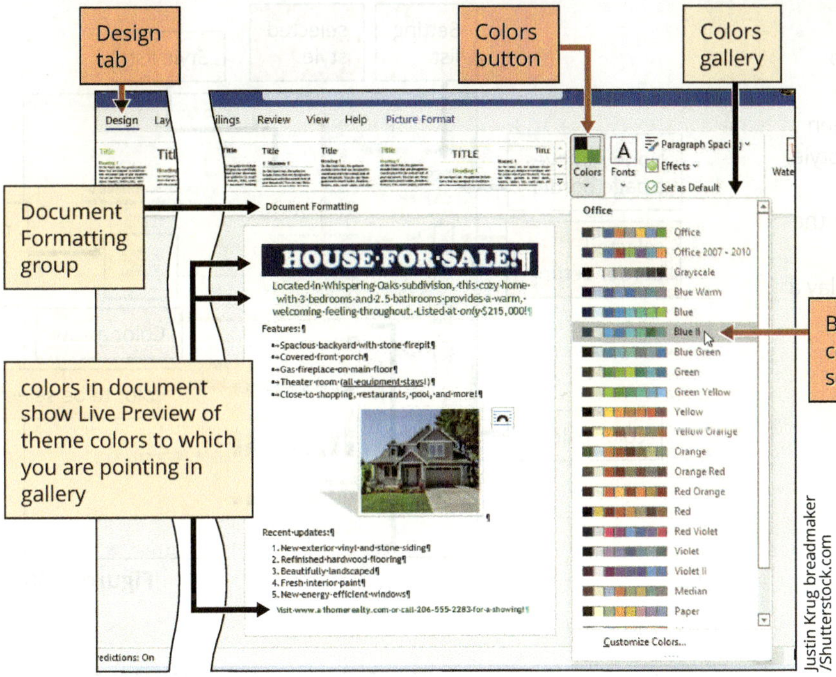

Figure 1–88

To Add a Page Border

In Word, you can add a border around the perimeter of an entire page. The flyer in this module has a blue-green border. **Why?** This border color complements the color of the flyer contents. The following steps add a page border.

1

- Click the Page Borders button (Design tab | Page Background group) to display the Borders and Shading dialog box (Figure 1–89).

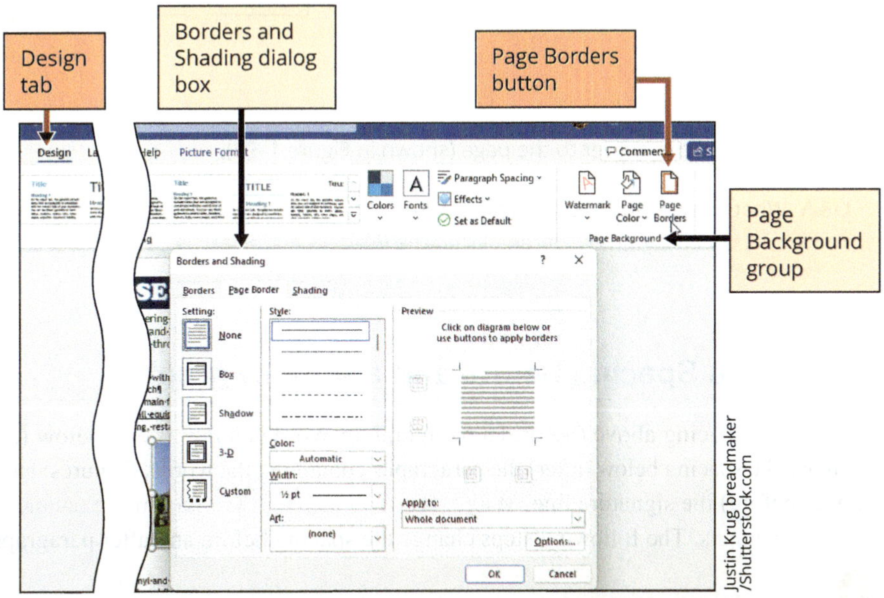

Figure 1–89

2

- Click Box in the Setting list to select the border setting.
- Scroll to, if necessary, and then click the double line border style in the Style list (Borders and Shading dialog box) to select the border style.
- Click the Color arrow to display a color palette (Figure 1–90).

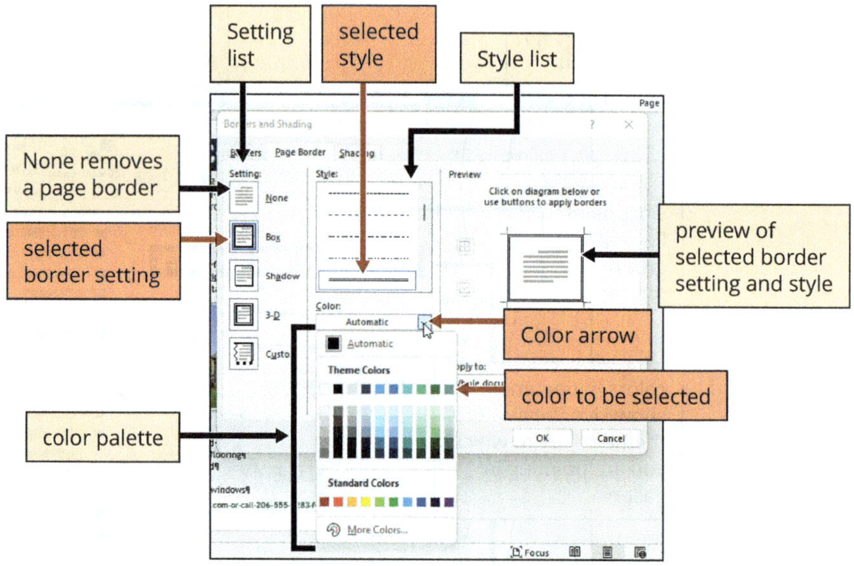

Figure 1–90

3

- Click 'Teal, Accent 6' (last color in first row) in the color palette to select the color for the page border (Figure 1–91).

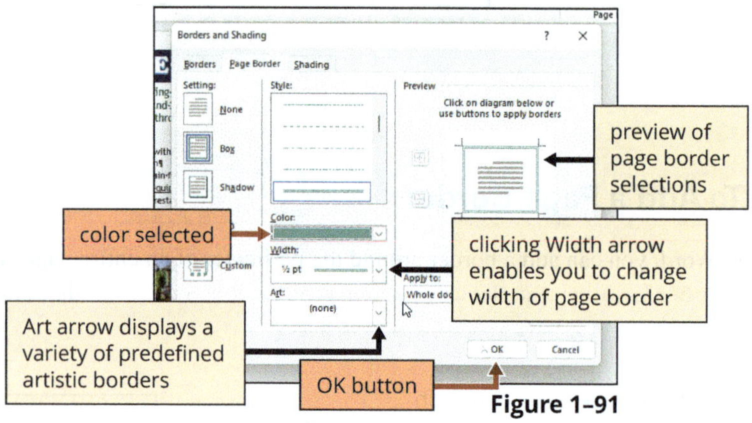

Figure 1–91

4

- Click OK to add the border to the page (shown in Figure 1–92).

Q&A What if I wanted to remove the border?
You would click None in the Setting list in the Borders and Shading dialog box.

To Change Spacing before and after Paragraphs

The default spacing above (before) a paragraph in Word is 0 points and below (after) is 8 points. In the flyer, you want to decrease the spacing below (after) the paragraphs containing the words, Features: and Recent updates:, and increase the spacing above (before) the signature line. **Why?** The flyer spacing will look more balanced with spacing adjusted above and below these paragraphs. The following steps change the spacing before and after paragraphs.

1

- Position the insertion point in the paragraph to be adjusted, in this case, the paragraph containing the word, Features:.
- Click Layout on the ribbon to display the Layout tab.
- Click the Spacing Before up arrow (Layout tab | Paragraph group) as many times as necessary so that 12 pt is displayed in the Spacing Before box to increase the space above the current paragraph.

- Click the Spacing After down arrow (Layout tab | Paragraph group) as many times as necessary so that 0 pt is displayed in the Spacing After box to decrease the space below the current paragraph (Figure 1–92).

Q&A What happened to the Picture Format tab?
The Picture Format tab disappears from the screen when the picture is not selected.

How would I redisplay the Picture Format tab?
Click the picture to select it and the Picture Format tab will reappear.

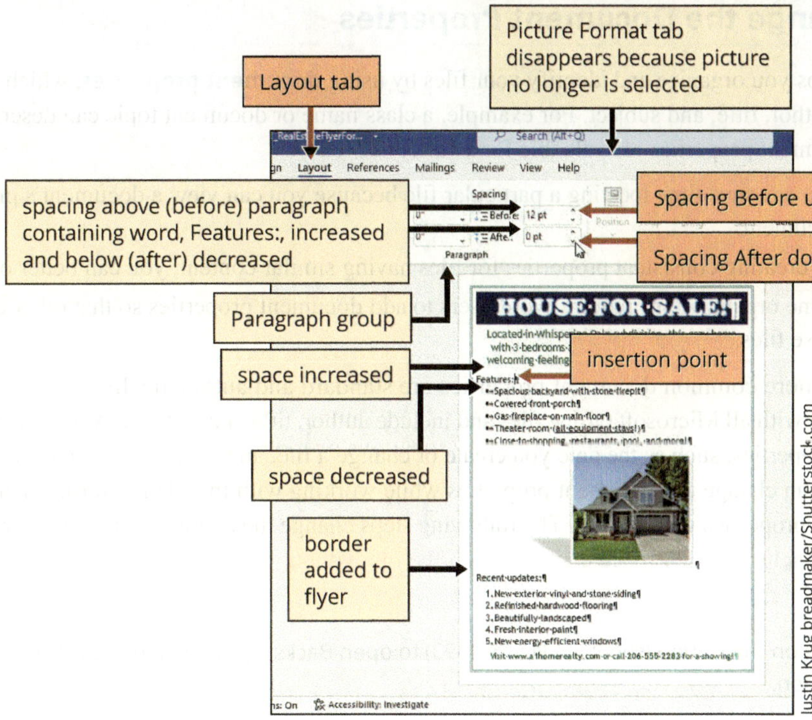

Figure 1–92

2

- Position the insertion point in the next paragraph to be adjusted, in this case, the paragraph containing the word, Recent updates:.
- Click the Spacing After down arrow (Layout tab | Paragraph group) as many times as necessary so that 0 pt is displayed in the Spacing After box to decrease the space below the current paragraph.
- Position the insertion point in the paragraph to be adjusted, in this case, the paragraph containing the signature line.
- Click the Spacing Before up arrow (Layout tab | Paragraph group) as many times as necessary so that 12 pt is displayed in the Spacing Before box to increase the space above the current paragraph (Figure 1–93).
- If the text flows to two pages, reduce the spacing above and below paragraphs as necessary so that the entire flyer fits on a single page.

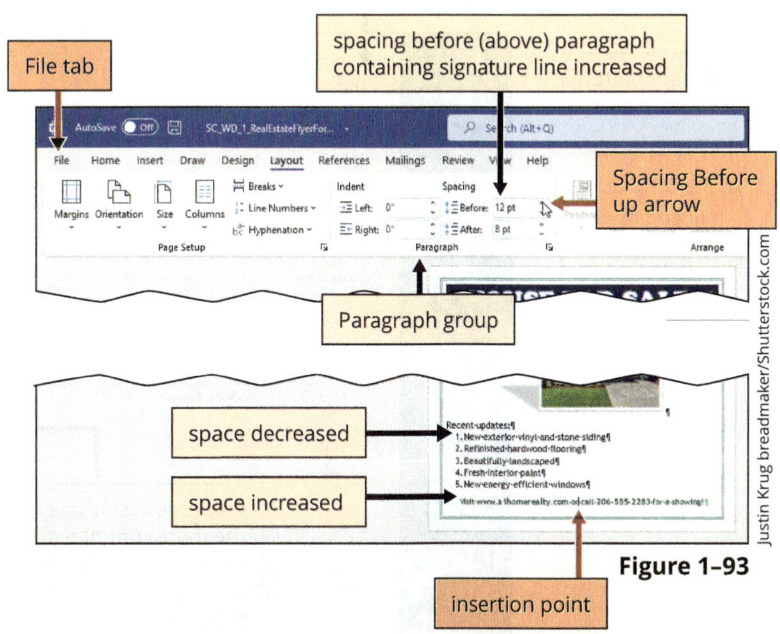

Figure 1–93

Other Ways

1. Right-click paragraph (or, if using touch, tap 'Show Context Menu' button on Mini toolbar), click Paragraph on shortcut menu, click Indents and Spacing tab (Paragraph dialog box), enter spacing before and after values, click OK
2. Click Paragraph Dialog Box Launcher (Home tab or Layout tab | Paragraph group), click Indents and Spacing tab (Paragraph dialog box), enter spacing before and after values, click OK

To Change the Document Properties

Word helps you organize and identify your files by using **document properties**, which are the details about a file, such as the project author, title, and subject. For example, a class name or document topic can describe the file's purpose or content.

Document properties are valuable for a variety of reasons:

- You can save time locating a particular file because you can view a document's properties without opening the document.
- By creating consistent properties for files having similar content, you can better organize your documents.
- Some organizations require Word users to add document properties so that other employees can view details about these files.

The more common document properties are standard and automatically updated properties. **Standard properties** are associated with all Microsoft Office files and include author, title, and subject. **Automatically updated properties** include file system properties, such as the date you create or change a file, and statistics, such as the file size.

You can change the document properties while working with the file in Word. When you save the file, Word will save the document properties with the file. The following steps change the comment document property. **Why?** Adding document properties will help you identify characteristics of the file without opening it.

1

- Click File on the ribbon (shown in Figure 1–93) to open Backstage view and then click Info in Backstage view to display the Info screen.

Q&A What is the purpose of the Info screen in Backstage view?
The Info screen contains commands that enable you to protect a document, inspect a document, and manage versions of a document, as well as view and change document properties.

- Click to the right of the Comments property in the Properties list and then type **CIS 101 Assignment** in the Comments text box (Figure 1–94).

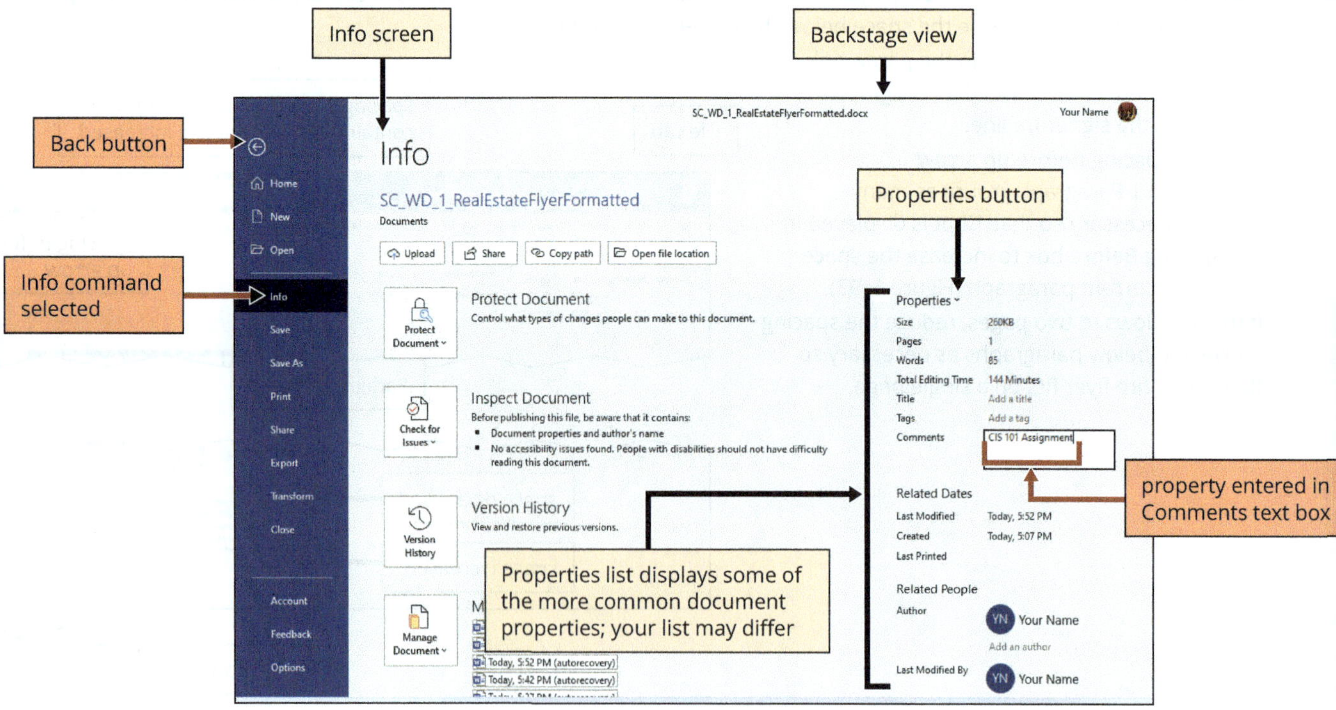

Figure 1–94

Q&A Why are some of the document properties already filled in?
Depending on previous Word settings and where you are using Word, your school, university, or place of employment may have customized the properties.

2

- Click the Back button in the upper-left corner of Backstage view to return to the document window.

Q&A What if the property I want to change is not displayed in the Properties list?
Scroll to the bottom of the Info screen and then click the 'Show All Properties' link to display more properties in the Properties list, or click the Properties button to display the Properties menu, and then click Advanced Properties on the Properties menu to display the Summary tab in the Properties dialog box. Type your desired text in the appropriate property text boxes. Click OK (Properties dialog box) to close the dialog box and then click the Back button in the upper-left corner of Backstage view to return to the document window.

To Save an Existing Document with the Same File Name

Saving frequently cannot be overemphasized. **Why?** You have made modifications to the document since you last saved it. Thus, you should save it again. Similarly, you should continue saving files frequently so that you do not lose the changes you have made since the time you last saved the file. You can use the same file name, such as SC_WD_1_RealEstateFlyerFormatted, to save the changes made to the document. The following step saves a file again with the same file name in the same save location.

1

- Click the Save button on the title bar to overwrite the previously saved file (SC_WD_1_RealEstateFlyerFormatted, in this case) in the same location it was saved previously (Documents library) (Figure 1–95).

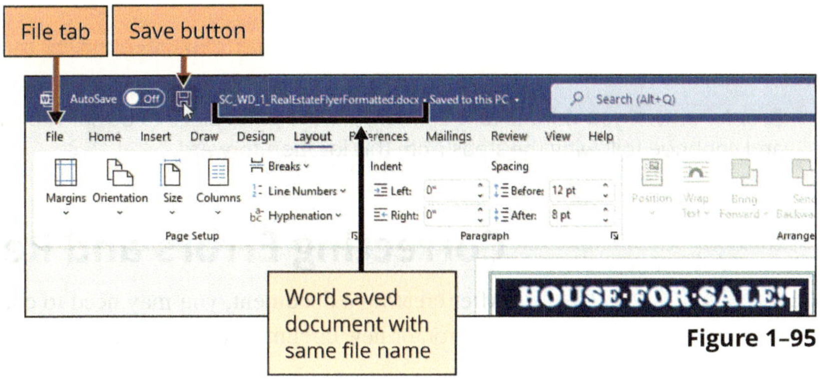

Figure 1–95

Other Ways

1. Press CTRL+S
2. Press SHIFT+F12

To Close a Document

Although you still need to make some edits to this document, you want to close the document at this time. **Why?** You should close a file when you are done working with it or wish to take a break so that you do not make inadvertent changes to it. The following steps close the current active Word document, SC_WD_1_RealEstateFlyerFormatted.docx, without exiting Word.

1

- Click File on the ribbon (shown in Figure 1–95) to open Backstage view (Figure 1–96).

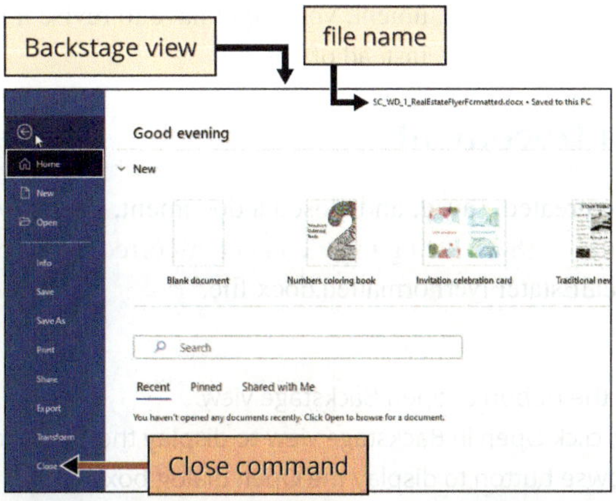

Figure 1–96

2

- Click Close in Backstage view to close the currently open document (SC_WD_1_RealEstateFlyerFormatted.docx, in this case) without exiting Word (Figure 1–97).

Q&A What if Word displays a dialog box about saving?
Click Save if you want to save the changes, click Don't Save if you want to ignore the changes since the last time you saved, and click Cancel if you do not want to close the document.

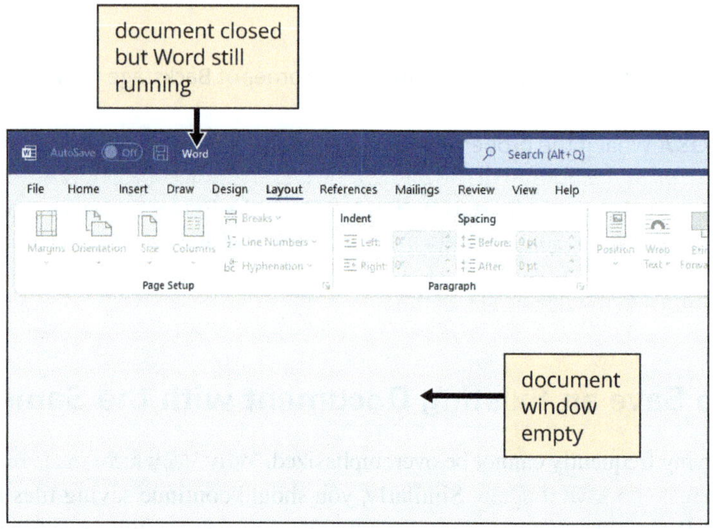

Figure 1–97

Other Ways

1. Press CTRL+F4

Break Point: If you want to take a break, this is a good place to do so. You can exit Word now. To resume later, start Word and continue following the steps from this location forward.

Correcting Errors and Revising a Document

After creating a document, you may need to change it. For example, the document may contain an error, or new circumstances may require you to add text to the document.

Types of Changes Made to Documents

The types of changes made to documents normally fall into one of the three following categories: additions, deletions, or modifications.

Additions Additional words, sentences, or paragraphs may be required in a document. Additions occur when you omit text from a document and want to insert it later. For example, you may want to add an email address to the flyer.

Deletions Sometimes, text in a document is incorrect or no longer is needed. For example, you may discover that the firepit is not made of stone. In this case, you would delete the word, stone, from the flyer.

Modifications If an error is made in a document or changes take place that affect the document, you might have to revise a word(s) in the text. For example, the fireplace may be electric instead of gas.

To Open a Document

Once you have created, saved, and closed a document, you may need to retrieve it from storage. **Why?** You may have more changes to make, such as adding more content or correcting errors, or you may want to print it. The following steps open the SC_WD_1_RealEstateFlyerFormatted.docx file.

1

- Click File on the ribbon to open Backstage view.
- If necessary, click Open in Backstage view to display the Open screen.
- Click the Browse button to display the Open dialog box.

Q&A Why is the Open dialog box in a different location from my screen?
You can move a dialog box anywhere on the screen by dragging its title bar.

- If necessary, navigate to the location of the file to open (in this case, SC_WD_1_RealEstateFlyerFormatted.docx in the Documents folder).
- Click the file name, SC_WD_1_RealEstateFlyerFormatted, to select the file (Figure 1–98).

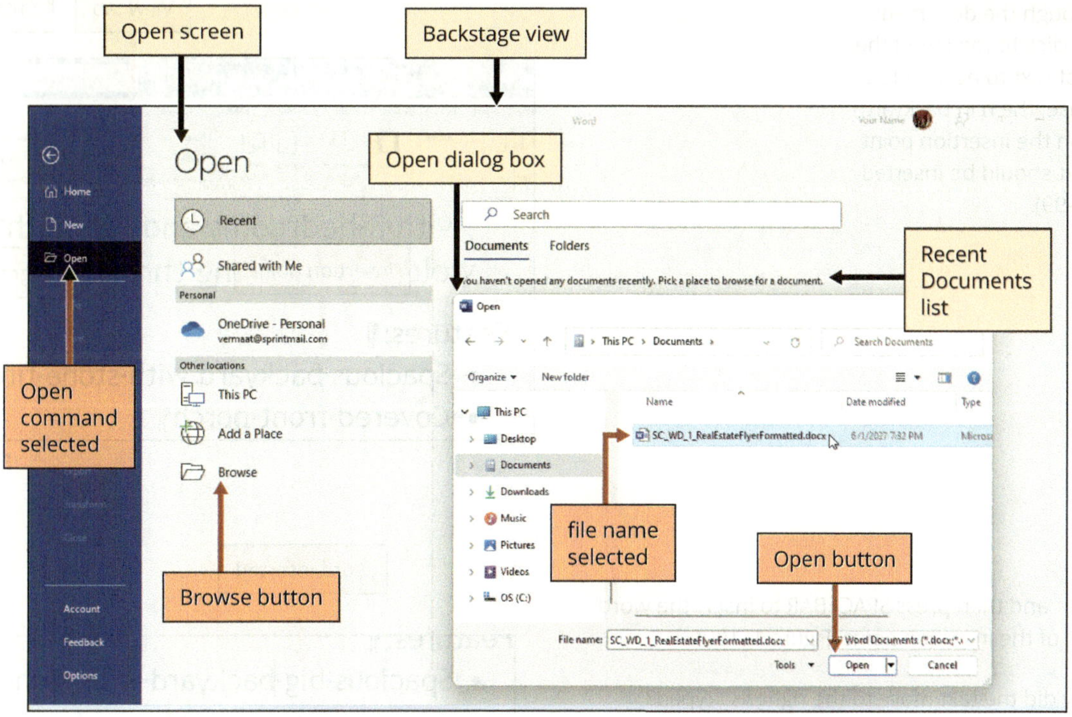

Figure 1–98

Q&A If the file name I want to open is listed in the Recent Documents list, can I click the file name to open the document without using the Open dialog box?
Yes.

2

- Click the Open button (Open dialog box) to open the selected file and display its contents in the document window (shown in Figure 1–99). If necessary, click the Enable Content button.

Other Ways

1. If file appears in Recent Documents list, click file name	2. Press CTRL+O	3. Navigate to file in File Explorer window, double-click file name

To Change the Zoom to Page Width

Because the document contents are small when displayed on one page, the following steps zoom page width again.

1 Click View on the ribbon to display the View tab.

2 Click the Page Width button (View tab | Zoom group) to display the page the same width as the document window.

To Insert Text in an Existing Document

Word inserts text to the left of the insertion point. The text to the right of the insertion point moves to the right and downward to fit the new text. The following steps insert the word, big, to the left of the word, backyard, in the bulleted list in the flyer. **Why?** These steps illustrate the process of inserting text.

1

- Scroll through the document and then click to the left of the location of text to be inserted (in this case, the b in backyard) to position the insertion point where text should be inserted (Figure 1–99).

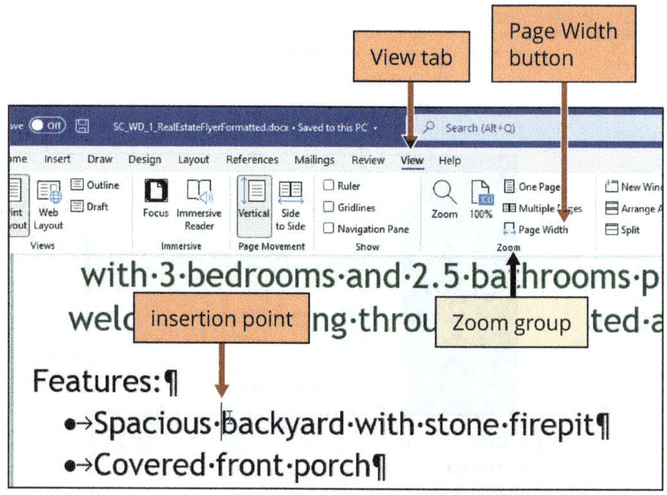

Figure 1–99

2

- Type **big** and then press SPACEBAR to insert the word to the left of the insertion point (Figure 1–100).

Q&A Why did the text move to the right as I typed?
In Word, the default typing mode is **Insert mode**, which means as you type a character, Word moves all the characters to the right of the typed character one position to the right.

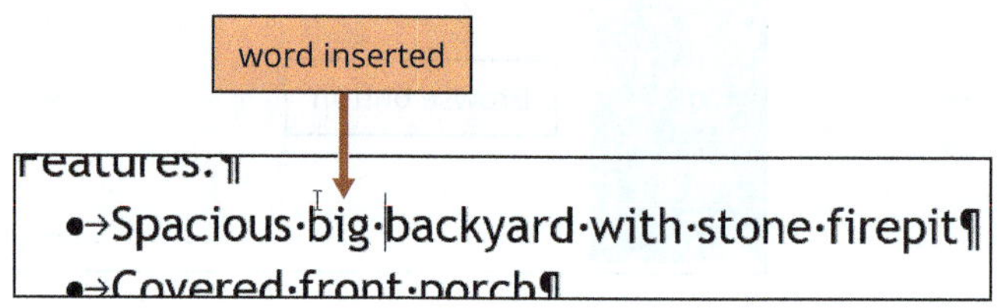

Figure 1–100

BTW
Delete versus Cut
When you press DELETE, the deleted text is not placed on the Office Clipboard. If you want deleted text to be placed on the Office Clipboard, use the Cut button (Home tab | Clipboard group).

Cutting, Copying, and Pasting

The **Office Clipboard** is a temporary storage area in a computer's memory that lets you collect up to 24 items (text or objects) from any Office document and then paste these items into almost any other type of document. The Office Clipboard works with the copy, cut, and paste commands:

- To **copy** is the process of selecting text or an object and placing a copy of the selected items on the Office Clipboard, leaving the item in its original location in the document.
- To **cut** is the process of removing text or an object from a document and placing it on the Office Clipboard.
- To **paste** is the process of placing an item stored on the Office Clipboard in the document at the location of the insertion point.

To Delete or Cut Text

It is not unusual to type incorrect characters or words in a document. As discussed earlier in this module, you can click the Undo button (Home tab | Undo group) or press CTRL+Z to undo a command or action immediately — this includes typing. Word also provides other methods of correcting typing errors.

To delete an incorrect character in a document, simply click next to the incorrect character and then press BACKSPACE to erase to the left of the insertion point, or press DELETE to erase to the right of the insertion point.

To cut a word or phrase, you first must select the word or phrase. The following steps select the word, big, which was just added in the previous steps, and then cuts the selection. **Why?** These steps illustrate the process of selecting a word and then cutting selected text.

1

- Click Home on the ribbon to display the Home tab.
- Double-click the word to be selected (in this case, big) to select the word (Figure 1–101).

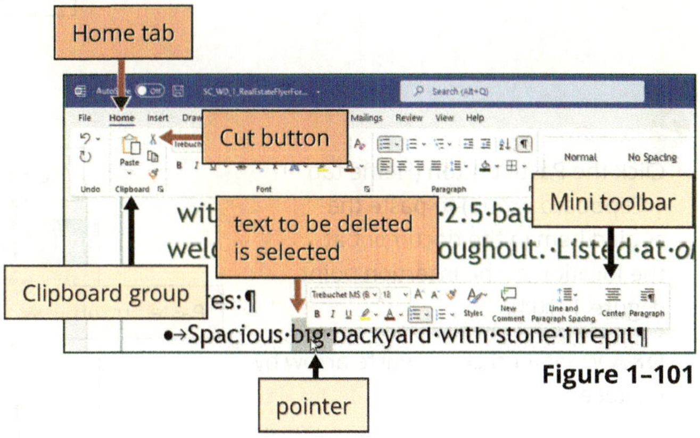

Figure 1–101

2

- Click the Cut button (Home tab | Clipboard group) to cut the selected text (shown in Figure 1–102).

Q&A What if I am using a touch screen?
Tap the selected text to display the Mini toolbar and then tap the Cut button on the Mini toolbar to delete the selected text.

Other Ways

1. Right-click selected item, click Cut on shortcut menu
2. Select item, press BACKSPACE to delete to left of insertion point or press DELETE to delete to right of insertion point
3. Select item, press CTRL+X or DELETE

To Copy and Paste

In the flyer, you copy a word from one location (the word, throughout, in the paragraph below the headline) to another location (the fourth numbered list item). **Why?** The fourth numbered item is clearer with the word, throughout, after the word, paint. Instead of typing the word again, you copy it from one location to another. The following steps copy and paste a word.

1

- If necessary, scroll to display the paragraph below the headline in the document window.
- Select the item to be copied (the word, throughout, in this case).
- Click the Copy button (Home tab | Clipboard group) to copy the selected item in the document to the Office Clipboard (Figure 1–102).

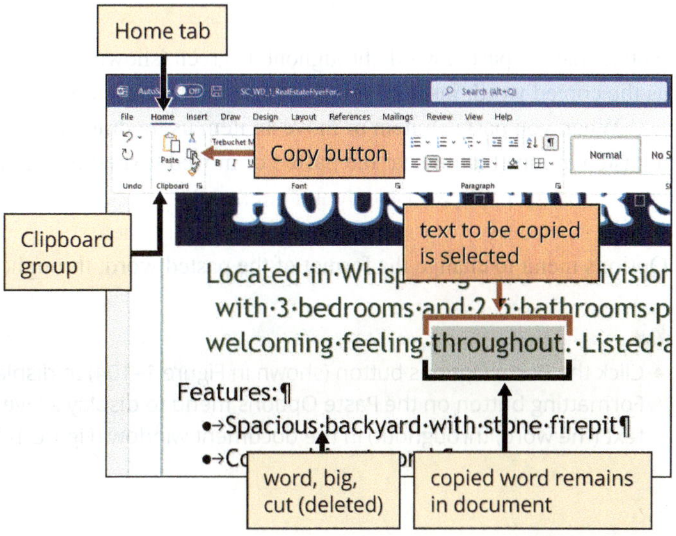

Figure 1–102

2

- Scroll to and then position the insertion point at the location where the item should be pasted (immediately to the right of the word, paint, in the fourth numbered list item) (Figure 1–103).

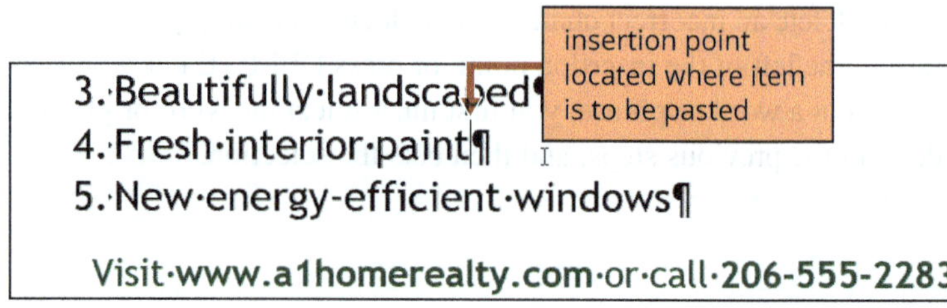

Figure 1–103

3

- Click the Paste button (Home tab | Clipboard group) to paste the copied item in the document at the location of the insertion point (Figure 1–104).

Q&A What if I click the Paste arrow by mistake?
Click the Paste arrow again to remove the Paste menu and repeat Step 3.

Why is the pasted word green?
Word, by default, pastes using the same format as the copied item; in this case, the pasted word is the same color (green) as the copied word. The next steps instruct Word to format the pasted item using the same format as the location to where it was pasted.

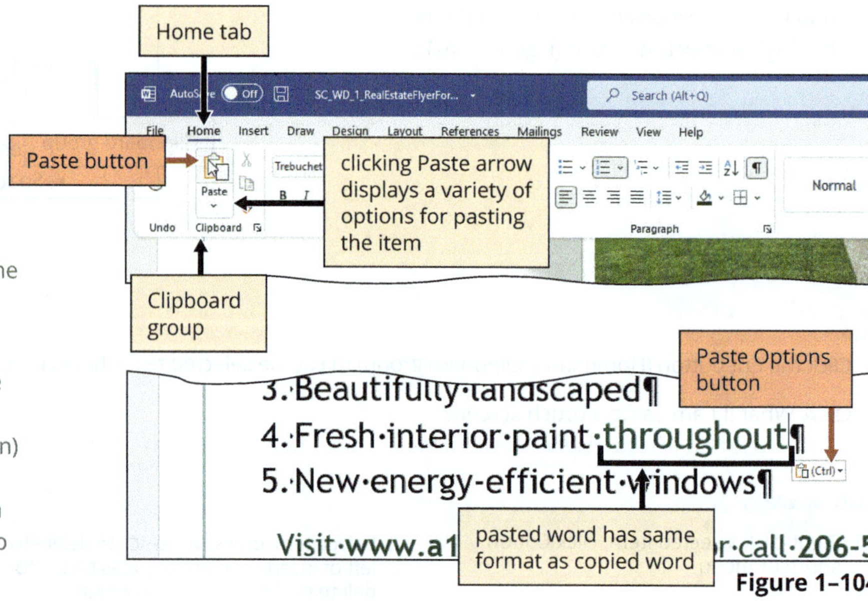

Figure 1–104

Other Ways

1. Right-click selected text (or, if using touch, tap 'Show Context Menu' button on Mini toolbar), click Copy on shortcut menu (or, if using touch, tap Copy on Mini toolbar), right-click where item is to be pasted, click 'Keep Source Formatting' in Paste Options area on shortcut menu (or, if using touch, tap Paste on Mini toolbar)
2. Select item, press CTRL+C, position insertion point at paste location, press CTRL+V

To Use the Paste Options Menu

Notice that the pasted word, throughout, is green (shown in Figure 1–104). You do not want the pasted word to be the same color as the copied word; instead, you want it to be the same color as the rest of the text in the numbered list.

When you paste an item or move an item using drag and drop (discussed in the next section), Word automatically displays a Paste Options button near the pasted or moved text (shown in Figure 1–104). **Why?** The Paste Options button allows you to change the format of a pasted item. For example, you can instruct Word to format the pasted item the same way as where it was copied (the source) or format it the same way as where it is being pasted (the destination). The following steps use the Paste Options menu to change the format of the pasted word, throughout, to match the destination format.

1

- Click the Paste Options button (shown in Figure 1–104) to display the Paste Options menu and then point to the Merge Formatting button on the Paste Options menu to display a Live Preview of the selected paste option applied to the pasted text (the word, throughout) in the document window (Figure 1–105).

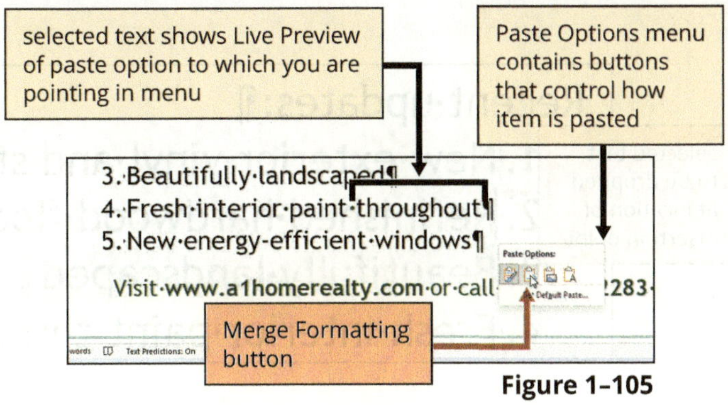

Figure 1–105

Q&A What happened to the Paste Options button?

It may disappear when you point to the buttons in the Paste Options menu.

What are the functions of the buttons on the Paste Options menu?

In general, the left button ('Keep Source Formatting' button) indicates the pasted item should look the same as it did in its original location (the source). The second button (Merge Formatting button) formats the pasted text to match the rest of the item where it was pasted (the destination). The third button (Picture button) pastes the item as a picture, and the fourth button (Keep Text Only button) removes all formatting from the pasted item. The 'Set Default Paste' command displays the Word Options dialog box. Keep in mind that the buttons shown on a Paste Options menu will vary, depending on the item being pasted.

2

- Click the Merge Formatting button on the Paste Options menu to format the pasted text (the word, throughout) to match the formatting in the rest of the numbered list (the destination).
- Press ESC to remove the Paste Options button from the document window.

To Move Text

If you are moving text a short distance, instead of using cut and paste, you could use drag and drop. With **drag and drop**, you move an item by selecting it, dragging the selected item to a new location, and then dropping, or inserting, it in the new location.

The following steps use drag and drop to move text. **Why?** While proofreading the flyer, you realize that the body copy would read better if the second and third numbered paragraphs were reversed.

1

- Select the text to be moved (in this case, the third numbered item).
- Position the pointer in the selected text and then press and hold down the mouse button, which displays a small dotted box with the pointer (Figure 1–106).

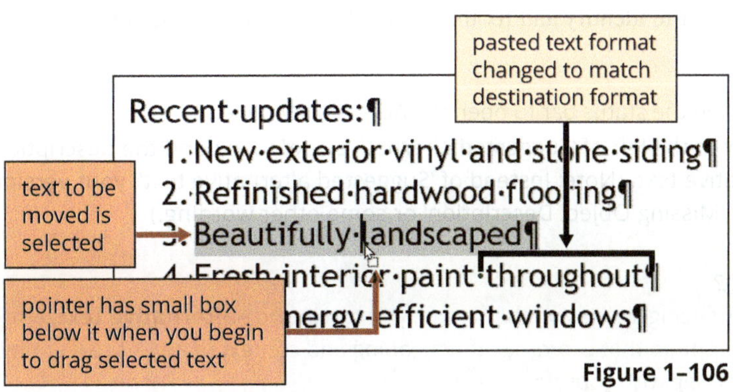

Figure 1–106

2

- Drag the insertion point to the location where the selected text is to be moved, as shown in Figure 1–107.

Figure 1–107

3

- Release the mouse button to move the selected text to the location of the dotted insertion point (Figure 1–108).

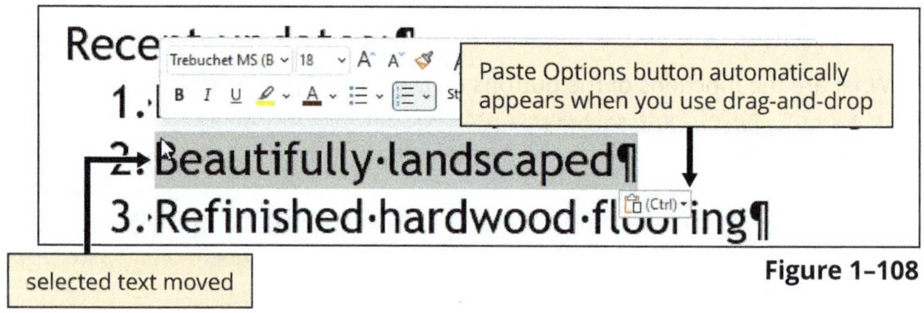

Figure 1–108

Q&A What if I accidentally drag text to the wrong location?
Click the Undo button (Home tab | Undo group) or press CTRL+Z and try again.

Can I use drag and drop to move any selected item?
Yes, you can select words, sentences, phrases, pictures, or any object and then use drag and drop to move them.

- Press ESC to remove the Paste Options button from the window.
- Click anywhere in the document window to remove the selection from the numbered item.

Q&A What if I am using a touch screen?
If you have a stylus, you can follow Steps 1 through 3 using the stylus. If you are using your finger, you will need to use cut and paste, which was described earlier in this section.

To Check and Fix an Image Accessibility Issue

Recall that Word includes an Accessibility Checker that identifies potential accessibility issues and presents suggestions to make your document more inclusive. Earlier in this module, you identified the 'Hard-to-read text contrast' issue and fixed it by applying shading behind the text. This time, you would like to fix the identified issue using the recommendations from the Accessibility Checker. **Why?** You notice that instead of the phrase, Good to go, the Accessibility button on the status bar once again shows the word, Investigate (shown in Figure 1–109). These steps illustrate using the Accessibility Checker to fix the issue. The following steps use the Accessibility Checker to identify and fix the potential accessibility issues in the document.

1

- Click the Accessibility button on the status bar to open the Accessibility pane.
- If necessary, click the arrow to the left of 'Suggested alternative text' to expand the description, which suggests the picture should have alternative text. (Note: Instead of 'Suggested alternative text', your version of Word may display 'Missing alternative text' or 'Missing Object Description' or some other wording.)

Q&A What is alternative text?
For users who have difficulty seeing images on the screen, you can include **alternative text**, also called **alt text**, to your images, which is a short description that expresses the meaning and context of an image so that these users can see or hear the alternative text when working with your document.

2

- Click the arrow to the right of Picture 1 to display the Recommended Actions menu (Figure 1–109).

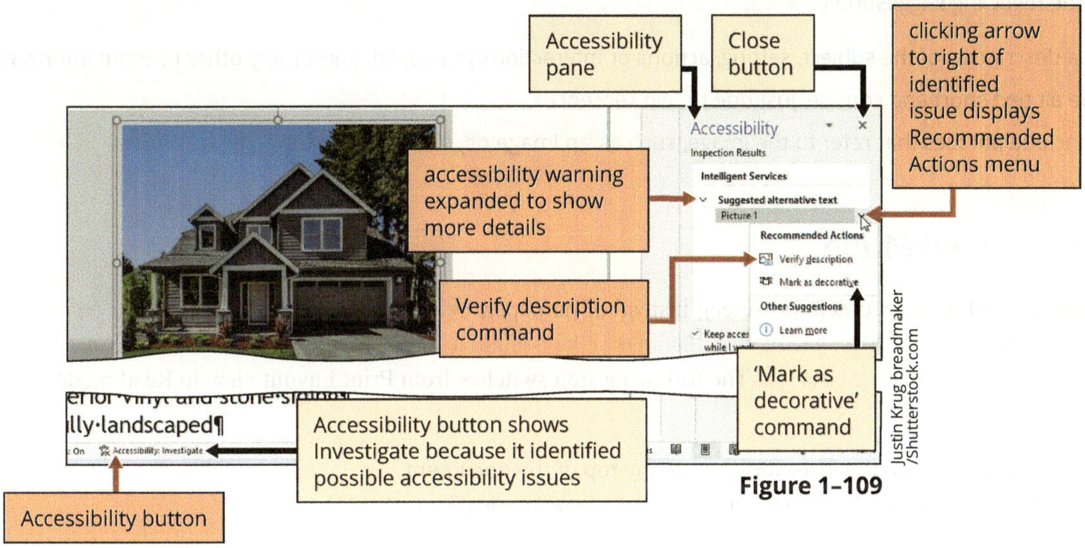

Figure 1–109

3

- Click Verify description on the Recommended Actions menu to display the automatically generated alternate text description in a text box in the Alt Text pane. (Note: Instead of Verify description, your version of Word may display an 'Add a description' command.)
- If necessary, delete the automatically generated description in the text box (A house with a garage) and then type this new description (Figure 1–110): **Beautifully landscaped home with medium-gray vinyl and stone siding, a covered porch, and a two-car garage.**

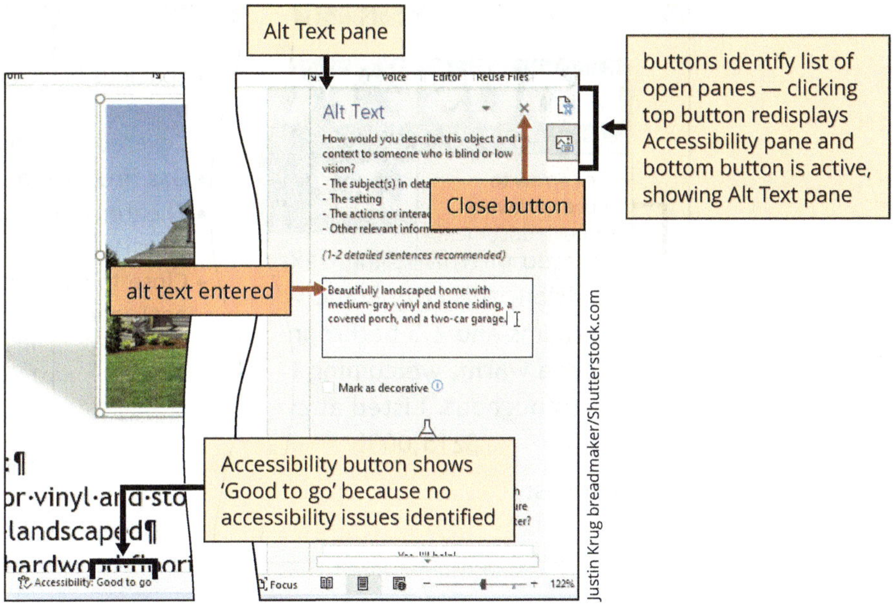

Figure 1–110

Q&A When would I choose the 'Mark as decorative' command on the Recommended Actions menu?
A decorative object adds visual appeal but does not convey any meaning, such as an art border.

4

- If necessary, click the Close button in the Alt Text pane (shown in Figure 1–110) to close the pane.
- Click the Close button in the Accessibility pane (shown in Figure 1–109) to close the pane.

Other Ways

1. Click Check Accessibility button (Review tab | Accessibility group), fix issue(s), click Close button in pane
2. Click File tab, click Info in Backstage view, click Check for Issues button, click Check Accessibility, fix issue(s), click Close button in pane

Consider This

What should you consider when writing alt text for an image?

Alt text that is well written increases the likelihood users will understand the content of the image. When writing alt text, consider the following suggestions.

- Include a description of the subject, setting, actions or interactions portrayed, and/or any other relevant information.
- Keep the alt text short and concise, just one to two sentences.
- Do not include phrases that refer to the image, such as 'an image of', in the alt text.

To Switch to Read Mode

Some users prefer reading a document on-screen instead of on paper. **Why?** If you are not composing a document, you can switch to **Read mode**, which is a document view that makes the document easier to read by hiding the ribbon and other writing tools so that more content fits on the screen. The following step switches from Print Layout view to Read mode.

1

- Press CTRL+HOME to position the insertion point at the top of the document.
- Click the Read Mode button on the status bar to switch to Read mode (Figure 1–111).

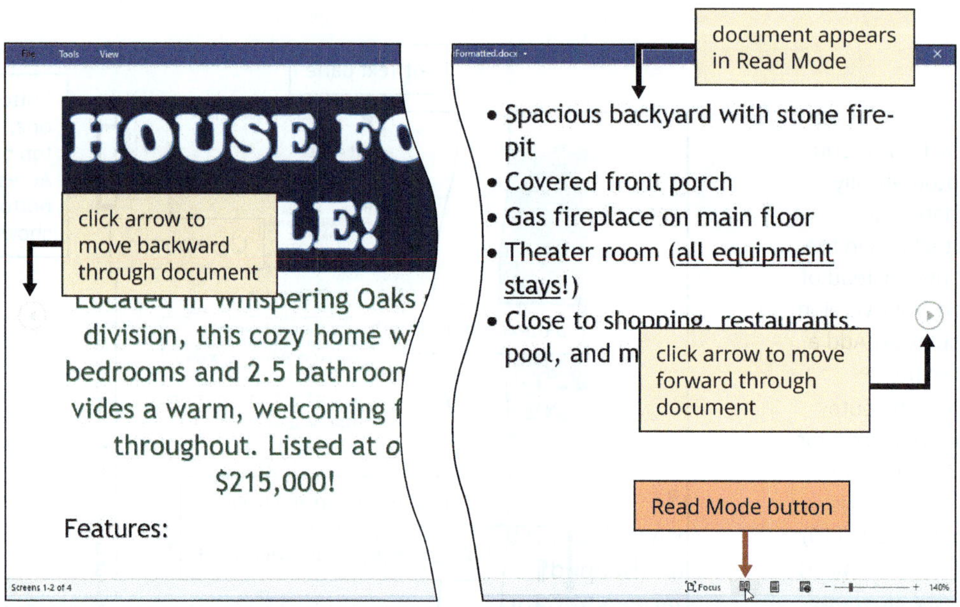

Figure 1–111

- **Experiment:** Click the arrows to advance forward and then move backward through the document. (Note that the arrows on your screen may be dimmed because all text fits in the document window due to screen resolution or other settings.)

Q&A Besides reading, what can I do in Read mode?
You can zoom, copy text, highlight text, search, add comments, and more.

Other Ways

1. Click Read Mode button (View tab | Views group)

To Switch to Print Layout View

Why? If you want to show the document on an image of a sheet of paper in the document window, along with the ribbon and other writing tools, you should switch to Print Layout view. The following step switches to Print Layout view.

1

- Click the Print Layout button on the status bar to switch to Print Layout view (Figure 1–112).

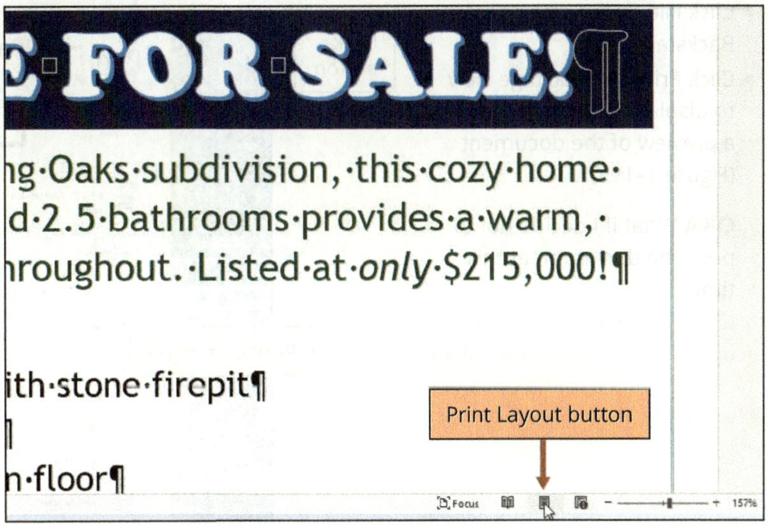

Figure 1–112

Other Ways

1. Click Print Layout button (View tab | Views group)
2. In Read Mode, click View on the ribbon, click Edit Document

To Save a Document with the Same File Name

It is a good practice to save a document before printing it, in the event you experience difficulties printing. The following step saves the document again on the same storage location with the same file name.

1 Click the Save button on the title bar to overwrite the previously saved file (SC_WD_1_RealEstateFlyerFormatted, in this case) in the same location it was saved previously (Documents library).

Q&A Why should I save the flyer again?
You have made several modifications to the flyer since you last saved it; thus, you should save it again.

BTW
Conserving Ink and Toner
If you want to conserve ink or toner, you can instruct Word to print draft quality documents by clicking File on the ribbon to open Backstage view, clicking Options in Backstage view to display the Word Options dialog box, clicking Advanced in the left pane (Word Options dialog box), scrolling to the Print area in the right pane, placing a check mark in the 'Use draft quality' check box, and then clicking OK. Then, use Backstage view to print the document as usual.

To Print a Document

After creating a document, you may want to print it. **Why?** You want to see how the flyer will appear on a printed piece of paper. The following steps print the contents of the document on a printer.

1

- Click File on the ribbon to open Backstage view.
- Click Print in Backstage view to display the Print screen and a preview of the document (Figure 1–113).

Q&A What if I decide not to print the document at this time?
Click the Back button in the upper-left corner of Backstage view to return to the document window.

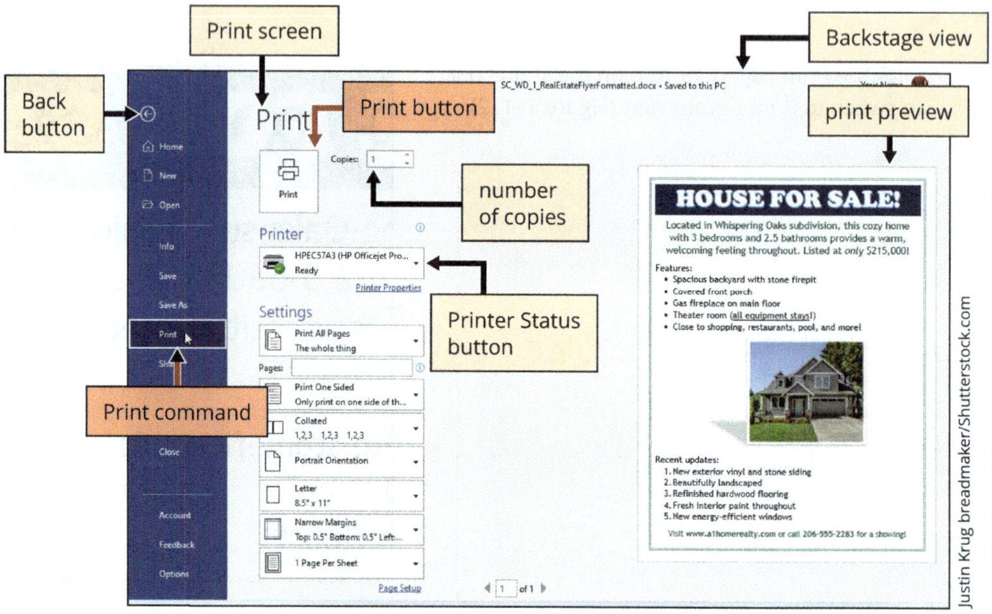

Figure 1–113

2

- Verify that the selected printer will print the document. If necessary, click the Printer Status button to display a list of available printer options and then click the desired printer to change the currently selected printer.

Q&A How can I print multiple copies of my document?
Increase the number in the Copies box in the Print screen.

3

- Click the Print button in the Print screen to print the document on the currently selected printer.
- When the printer stops, retrieve the printed document (shown in Figure 1–1).

Q&A What if one or more of my borders do not print?
Click the Page Borders button (Design tab | Page Background group), click the Options button (Borders and Shading dialog box), click the Measure from arrow and click Text, change the four text boxes to 15 pt, and then click OK in each dialog box. Try printing the document again. If the borders still do not print, adjust the boxes in the dialog box to a number smaller than 15 point.

Do I have to wait until my document is complete to print it?
No, you can print a document at any time while you are creating it.

Other Ways

1. Press CTRL+P

BTW
Printing Document Properties
To print document properties, click File on the ribbon to open Backstage view, click Print in Backstage view to display the Print screen, click the first button in the Settings area to display a list of options specifying what you can print, click Document Info in the list to specify you want to print the document properties instead of the actual document, and then click the Print button in the Print screen to print the document properties on the currently selected printer.

Using Word Help

At any time while you are using Word, you can use Word Help to display information about all topics associated with Word. You can search for help by using the Search box or the Help pane.

To Use the Search Box

If you are having trouble finding a button, box, or other command in Word, you can use the Search box to search for the task you are trying to perform. As you type, the Search box will suggest commands that match the search text you are entering. **Why?** You can use the Search box to access commands quickly that you otherwise may be unable to find on the ribbon or to display help about a command. The following steps find information about margins.

1

- Type **margins** in the Search box and watch the search results appear.
- Point to (or click, if necessary) Adjust Margins on the Search menu to display the Margins gallery (Figure 1–114).

Q&A Does this Margins gallery work the same as the one I used earlier in this module to change the margins?
Yes, it is the exact same Margins gallery. You can select an option in the gallery to apply that command to the document.

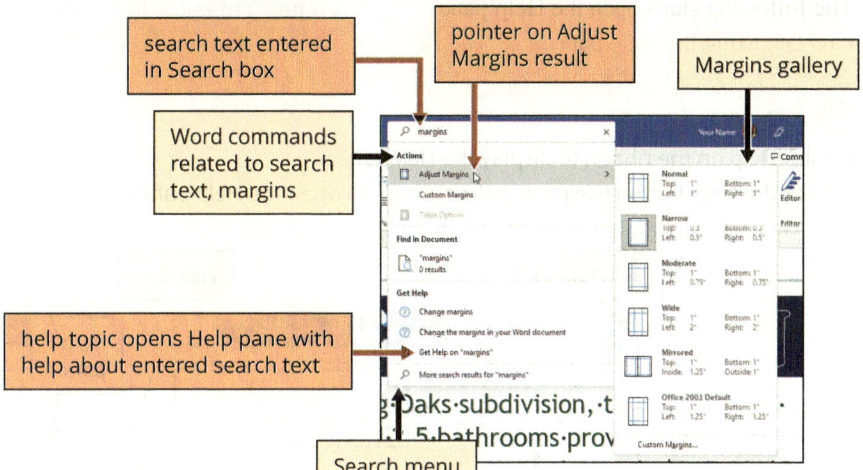

Figure 1–114

2

- Click 'Get Help on "margins"' on the Search menu to open the Help pane, which displays a help topic for the search text, margins (Figure 1–115).

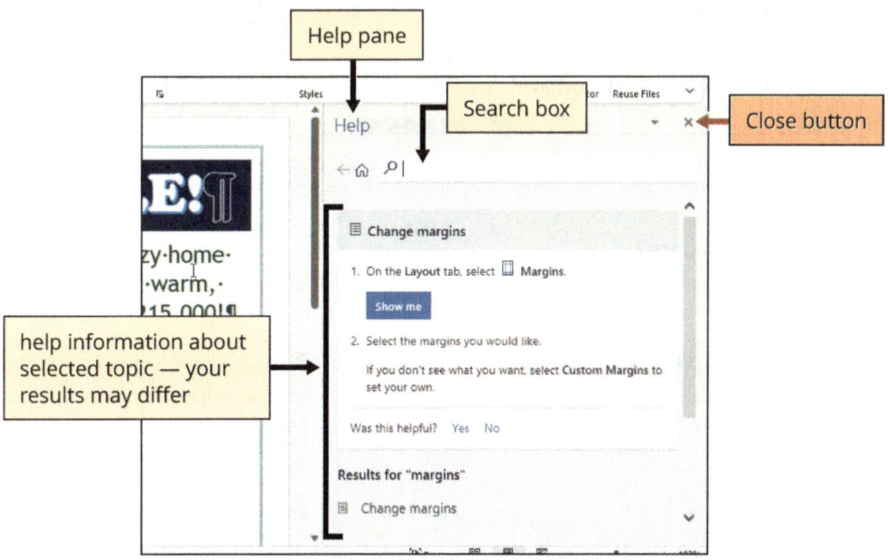

Figure 1–115

Q&A Why do my search results differ?
If you do not have an Internet connection, your results will reflect only the content of the Help files on your computer. When searching for help online, results also can change as content is added, deleted, and updated on the online Help webpages maintained by Microsoft.

Can I search for additional help topics by entering search text in the Search box in the Help pane?
Yes.

3

- After you have finished reading the help information, click the Close button in the Help pane to close the pane.

To Use the Help Pane

The following steps open the Help pane. **Why?** You may not know the exact help topic you are trying to find, so you want to navigate using the Help pane.

1

- Click Help on the ribbon to display the Help tab.
- Click the Help button (Help tab | Help group) to open the Help pane (Figure 1–116).

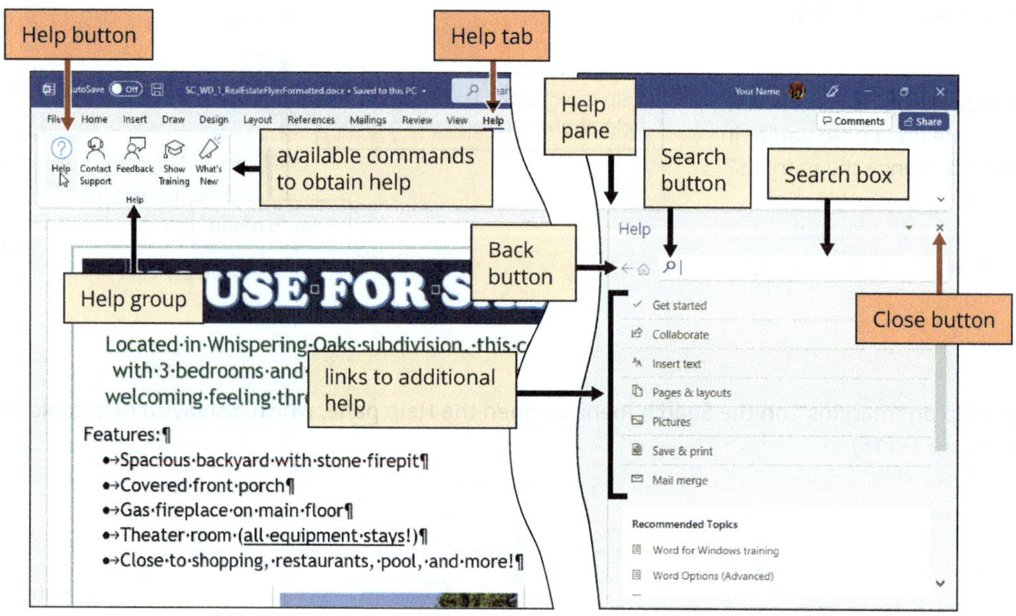

Figure 1–116

Q&A How do I navigate the Help pane?
You can scroll through the displayed information in the Help pane, click any of the links to additional help, click the Back button in the Help pane to return to a previously displayed screen, or enter search text in the Search box.

Does the Search box in the Help pane work the same as the Search box?
Yes. In the same way that you entered search text in the Search box, you would enter search text in the Search box in the Help pane and then press ENTER or click the Search button to display a list of Help topics that match the entered search text.

2

- When you are finished with the Help pane, click its Close button to close the pane.

Other Ways

1. Press F1

Obtaining Help while Working in Word

You also can access Help without first using the Search box or opening the Help pane and initiating a search. For example, you may be unsure about how a particular command works, or you may be presented with a dialog box that you are not sure how to use.

If you want to learn more about a command, point to its button and wait for the ScreenTip to appear, as shown in Figure 1–117. If the Help icon and 'Tell me more' link appear in the ScreenTip, click the 'Tell me more' link (or press F1 while pointing to the button) to open the Help pane and display a help topic associated with that command.

Dialog boxes also contain Help buttons, as shown in Figure 1–118. Clicking the Help button or pressing F1 while the dialog box is displayed opens a help window in your browser, which will display help contents specific to that dialog box, if available.

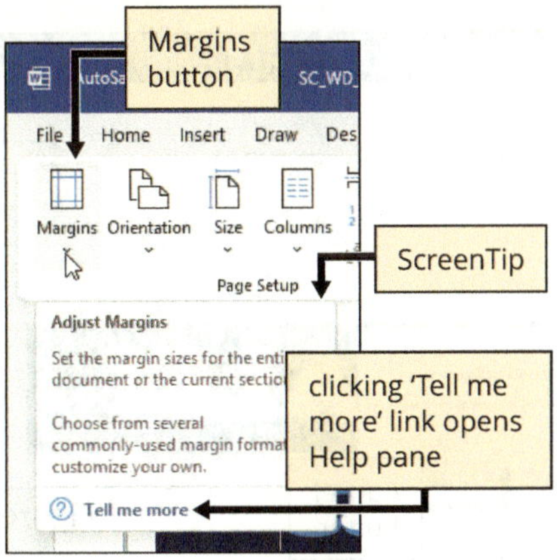

Figure 1–117

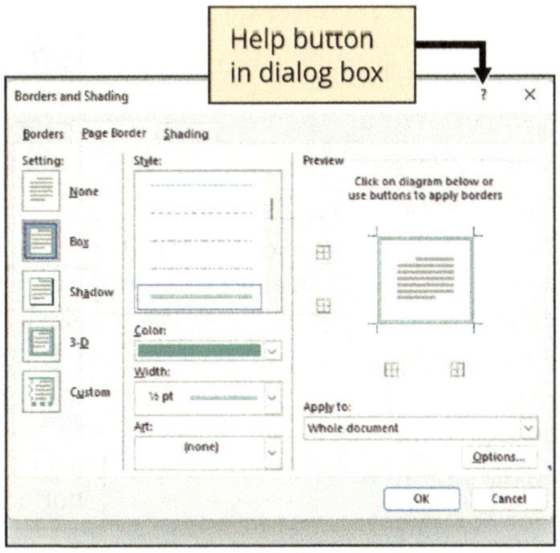

Figure 1–118

To Sign Out of a Microsoft Account If you are using a public computer or otherwise wish to sign out of your Microsoft account, you should sign out of the account. Signing out of the account is the safest way to ensure that no one else can access online files or settings stored in your Microsoft account. If you wanted to sign out of a Microsoft account from Word, you would perform the following steps.

1. Click File on the ribbon to open Backstage view and then click Account to display the Account screen, or click the button that shows your profile photo or name on the right edge of the title bar to display the account manager menu.
2. Click the Sign out link or button, which displays the Sign out of Office dialog box. If a Can't remove Windows accounts dialog box appears instead of the Sign out of Office Account dialog box, click OK and skip the remaining steps.

   Q&A Why does a Can't remove Windows accounts dialog box appear?
   If you signed in to Windows using your Microsoft account, then you also must sign out from Windows, rather than signing out from within Word. When you are finished using Windows, be sure to sign out at that time.

3. Click the Sign out button (Sign out of Office dialog box) to sign out of your Microsoft account on this computer.

   Q&A Should I sign out of Windows after signing out of my Microsoft account?
   When you are finished using the computer, you should sign out of Windows for maximum security.

4. If necessary, click the Back button in the upper-left corner of Backstage view to return to the document window.

BTW
Office 365 Apps
Word is part of Microsoft 365 apps; other Premium Office apps include Microsoft PowerPoint, Microsoft Excel, Microsoft Access, and Microsoft Outlook. The Microsoft 365 apps typically use a similar interface and share features.

To Exit Word

You saved the document prior to printing and did not make any changes to the project. The following step exits Word. **Why?** The SC_WD_1_RealEstateFlyerFormatted.docx project now is complete, and you are ready to exit Word.

1

- Click the Close button in the upper-right corner of the Word window to exit Word.
- **sam** If a Microsoft Word dialog box is displayed (Figure 1–119), click Save to save changes before exiting.

Q&A When I exited Word, a dialog box did not appear. Why not?

If you made changes to your document since you last saved it, the dialog box shown in Figure 1–119 will appear when you exit Word. If you want to save changes before exiting, click Save; if you do not want to save changes, click Don't Save; if you change your mind and do not want to exit Word, click Cancel to return to the document in the document window. If you did not make changes to your document since you last saved it, this dialog box will not appear.

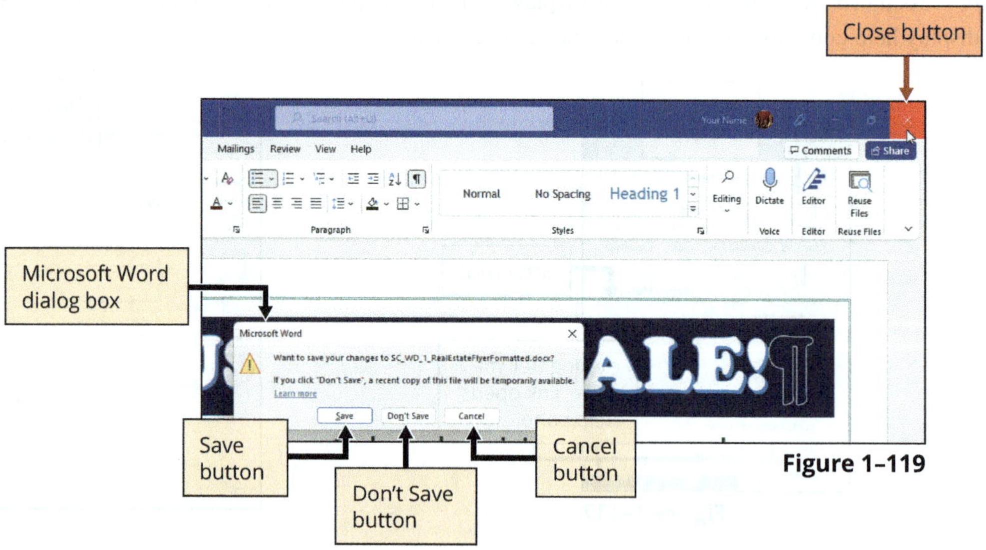

Figure 1–119

Other Ways

1. Right-click Microsoft Word button on Windows taskbar, click 'Close all windows' on shortcut menu

Summary

In this module, you learned how to start and use Word, enter text in a document, correct spelling and grammar errors as you work in a document, format paragraphs and characters, insert and format a picture, add a page border, adjust paragraph and page spacing, check and fix accessibility issues, revise a document, print a document, and use Word Help.

Consider This: Plan Ahead

What decisions will you need to make when creating your next flyer?

Use these guidelines as you complete the assignments in this module and create your own flyers outside of this class.

1. Choose the text for the headline, body copy, and signature line, using as few words as possible to make a point.
2. Format various elements of the text.
   a) Select appropriate font sizes for text in the headline, body copy, and signature line.
   b) Select appropriate fonts for text in the headline, body copy, and signature line.
   c) Adjust paragraph alignment, as appropriate.
   d) Highlight key paragraphs with bullets or numbers.
   e) Emphasize important words.
   f) Use color to convey meaning and add appeal.
3. Find an eye catching picture(s) that conveys the overall message and meaning of the flyer.
4. Establish where to position and how to format the picture(s) so that it grabs the attention of passersby and draws them into reading the flyer.
5. Determine whether the flyer needs enhancements, such as a graphical, color-coordinated border, or spacing adjustments to improve readability or overall appearance.
6. Correct errors and revise the document as necessary.
   a) Place the flyer on a wall and make sure all text and images are legible from a distance.
   b) Check that all accessibility issues have been addressed.
   c) Ask someone else to read the flyer and give you suggestions for improvements.
7. Determine the best method for distributing the document, such as printing, sending via email, or posting on the web or social media.

BTW

Distributing a Document

Instead of printing and distributing a hard copy of a document, you can distribute the document electronically. Options include sending the document via email; posting it on cloud storage (such as OneDrive) and sharing the file with others; posting it on social media, a blog, or other website; and sharing a link associated with an online location of the document. You also can create and share a PDF or XPS image of the document, so that users can view the file in Adobe Acrobat Reader or XPS Viewer instead of in Word.

Student Assignments

Apply Your Knowledge

Reinforce the skills and apply the concepts you learned in this module.

Modifying Text and Formatting a Document

Note: To complete this assignment, you will be required to use the Data Files. Please contact your instructor for information about accessing the Data Files.

Instructions: Start Word. Open the document, SC_WD_1-1.docx, which is located in the Data Files. The file you open contains an unformatted flyer that announces a financial planning seminar for Greenway Investments. The asset manager, who created the text in the unformatted flyer, has asked you (his administrative assistant) to modify the text in the flyer, format its paragraphs and characters, and insert a picture to create the formatted flyer shown in Figure 1–120.

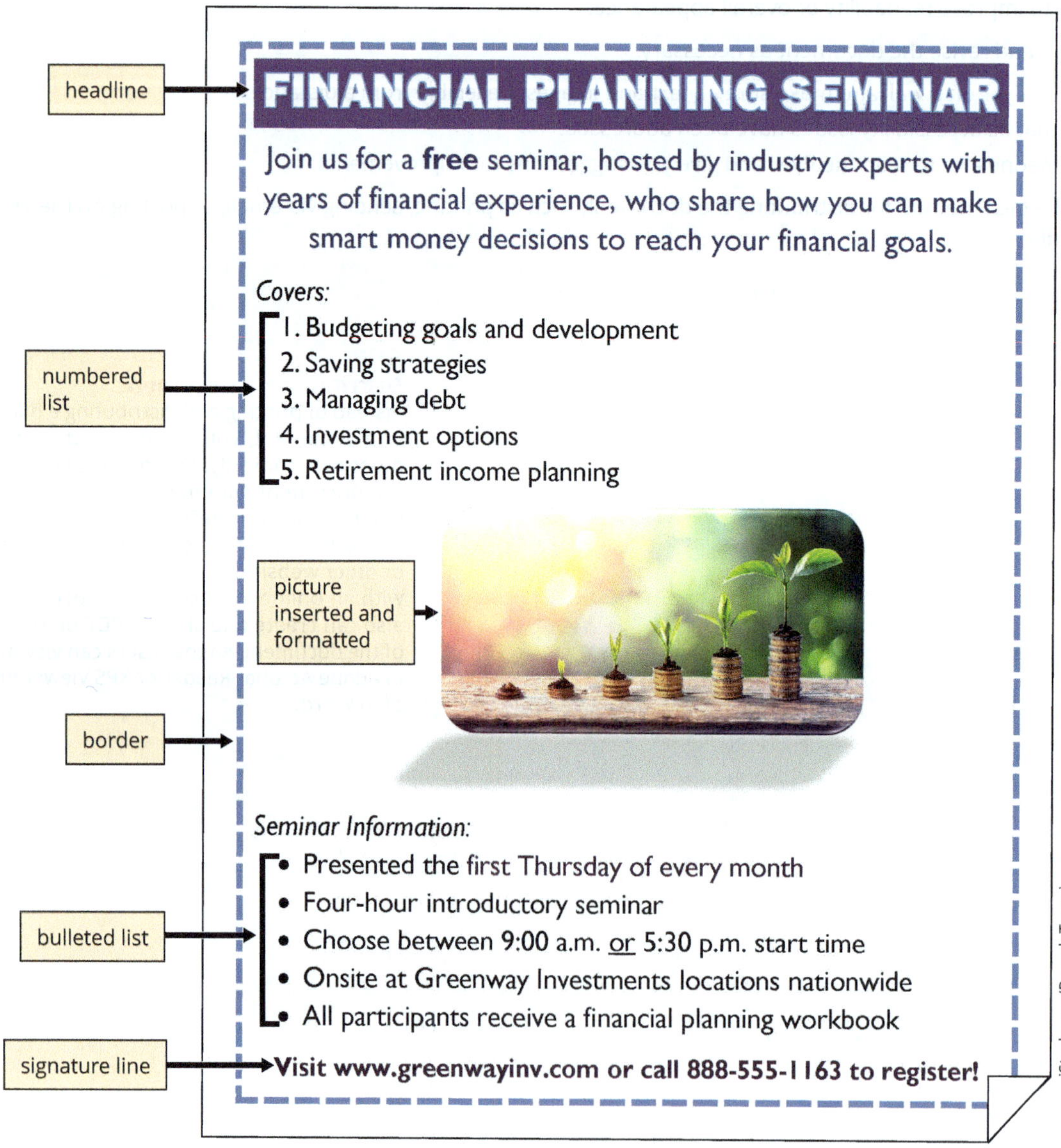

iStock.com/RomoloTavani

Figure 1–120

Perform the following tasks:

1. If necessary, change the zoom to Page Width, and display formatting marks on the screen.
2. Click File on the ribbon, click Save As, and then save the document using the new file name, SC_WD_1_FinancialPlanningSeminarFlyer.
3. Review each spelling and duplicate word (red wavy underline), grammar (blue double underline), and word choice (purple dotted underline) suggestion in the document by right-clicking the flagged text and then clicking the appropriate correction on the shortcut menu. Use the Ignore All command if the company name, Greenway, is flagged because it is a proper name and spelled correctly.
4. Delete the second exclamation point following the word, register, in the signature line, so that only one exclamation point ends the sentence.
5. Delete the word, very, in the paragraph of text below the headline.
6. Insert the word, call, to the left of the phone number in the signature line (so that it reads: …or call 888-555-1163).
7. Change the word, Wednesday, to the word, Thursday, in the first paragraph below the paragraph with the text, Seminar Information.
8. If requested by your instructor, change the phone number in the flyer to your phone number.
9. Change the document theme to Gallery.
10. Change the margins to Narrow (that is, .5" top, bottom, left, and right margins).
11. Center the headline, the first paragraph of body copy below the headline, and the signature line in the flyer.
12. Change the font size of all the body copy text between the headline and signature line to 20 point.
13. Select the five paragraphs of body copy below the word, Covers:, in the flyer and format the selected paragraphs as a numbered list.
14. Select the five paragraphs of body copy below the words, Seminar Information, and format the selected paragraphs as a bulleted list.
15. Change the font and font size of the headline to 36-point Franklin Gothic Heavy, or a similar font. Change the case of the text in the headline to uppercase letters. Apply the preset text effect called 'Fill: White; Outline: Indigo, Accent color 5; Shadow' (fourth text effect in first row) to the entire headline. Shade the paragraph containing the headline 'Pink, Accent 2, Darker 25%' (sixth color in fifth row).
16. Change the theme colors to Violet II.
17. Change the font color of the paragraph of body copy below the headline to 'Blue, Accent 6, Darker 50%' (last color in last row). Change the font size of text in this paragraph to 22 points.
18. Cut the word, Investments, in the fourth bulleted paragraph. Paste the cut word in the same paragraph before the word, locations, so the line reads: Onsite at Greenway Investments locations nationwide
19. Copy the word, financial, before the word, experience, in the paragraph below the headline. Paste the copied word before the word, planning, in the last bulleted paragraph, so that it reads: All participants receive a financial planning workbook. Click the Paste Options button that appears at the end of the pasted text and then click Merge Formatting on the Paste Options menu so that the pasted text has the same formats as the destination location.
20. Remove the hyperlink format from the web address in the signature line. If the text is still colored and underlined, change the color to Automatic and remove the underline.
21. Select the last paragraph on the page (the signature line) and then use the Mini toolbar to change the font size of the text in this paragraph to 18 point and its font color to 'Dark Purple, Text 2, Darker 25%' (fourth color in fifth row). Bold the text in this line.
22. Switch the second and third paragraphs in the numbered list. That is, select the Saving strategies numbered paragraph and use drag and drop to move it so that it is the second numbered paragraph (which then makes the Managing debt entry the third numbered paragraph).

Continued on next page

23. Select the words, first Thursday of every month, in the first bulleted paragraph and change its font color to 'Dark Purple, Text 2, Darker 25%' (fourth color in fifth row). Undo this change and then redo the change.
24. Select the paragraph, Covers:, above the numbered list and then select the nonadjacent paragraph, Seminar Information:, above the bulleted list. (Be sure to include the colon characters (:) in your selections.) Italicize the selected text.
25. Bold the word, free, in the paragraph below the headline.
26. Underline the word, or, in the bulleted list.
27. Change the zoom to One Page, so that the entire page is visible in the document window.
28. Insert the money growth concept picture so that it is centered on the blank line below the numbered list. The picture is called Support_WD_1_MoneyGrowthConcept.jpg and is available in the Data Files. Resize the picture proportionally so that it is approximately 2.2" × 4.22". Apply the Bevel Rectangle picture style to the inserted picture. Add the 'Perspective: Lower Left' shadow picture effect to the inserted picture.
29. Change the spacing before the paragraph containing the word, Covers:, to 12 points and the spacing after this paragraph to 0 points. Change the spacing after the paragraph containing the words, Seminar Information:, to 0 points. Change the spacing before the signature line to 12 points.
30. The entire flyer should fit on a single page. If it flows to two pages, resize the picture or decrease spacing before and after paragraphs until the entire flyer text fits on a single page.
31. Add a page border to the flyer using these formats: Setting: Box; Style: third style in list (medium-sized dashes); Color: 'Blue, Accent 6' (last color in first row); Width: 4 ½ pt.
32. Change the zoom to text width, then page width, then 25%, then 100% and notice the differences.
33. If requested by your instructor, enter the text, Financial Planning Seminar Flyer, as the comments in the document properties. Change the other document properties, as specified by your instructor.
34. Check accessibility. Add the following alt text to Picture 1: Six stacks of coins showing the concept of money growing. Arranged from the smallest coin stack to the largest, the first is topped with a seed and the remaining stacks each hold a larger plant.
35. Proofread your flyer, compare it to Figure 1–120, and correct any spelling, grammar, or punctuation errors. Save the document again with the same file name.
36. Print the document. Switch to Read Mode and browse pages through the document. Switch to Print Layout view.
37. Close the document. Exit Word.
38. Submit the revised document, shown in Figure 1–120, in the format specified by your instructor.
39. **Consider This:** If this flyer were announcing a company retreat instead of a financial planning seminar, which theme colors would you apply and why?

Extend Your Knowledge

Extend the skills you learned in this module and experiment with new skills. You may need to use Help to complete the assignment.

Modifying Text, Lists, and Picture Formats and Adding Page Borders

Note: To complete this assignment, you will be required to use the Data Files. Please contact your instructor for information about accessing the Data Files.

Instructions: Start Word. Open the document called SC_WD_1-2.docx, which is located in the Data Files. The document contains a flyer, drafted by members of the Student Government Association at Coastline College, that communicates information about its upcoming food drive. You will enhance the look of the flyer shown in Figure 1–121.

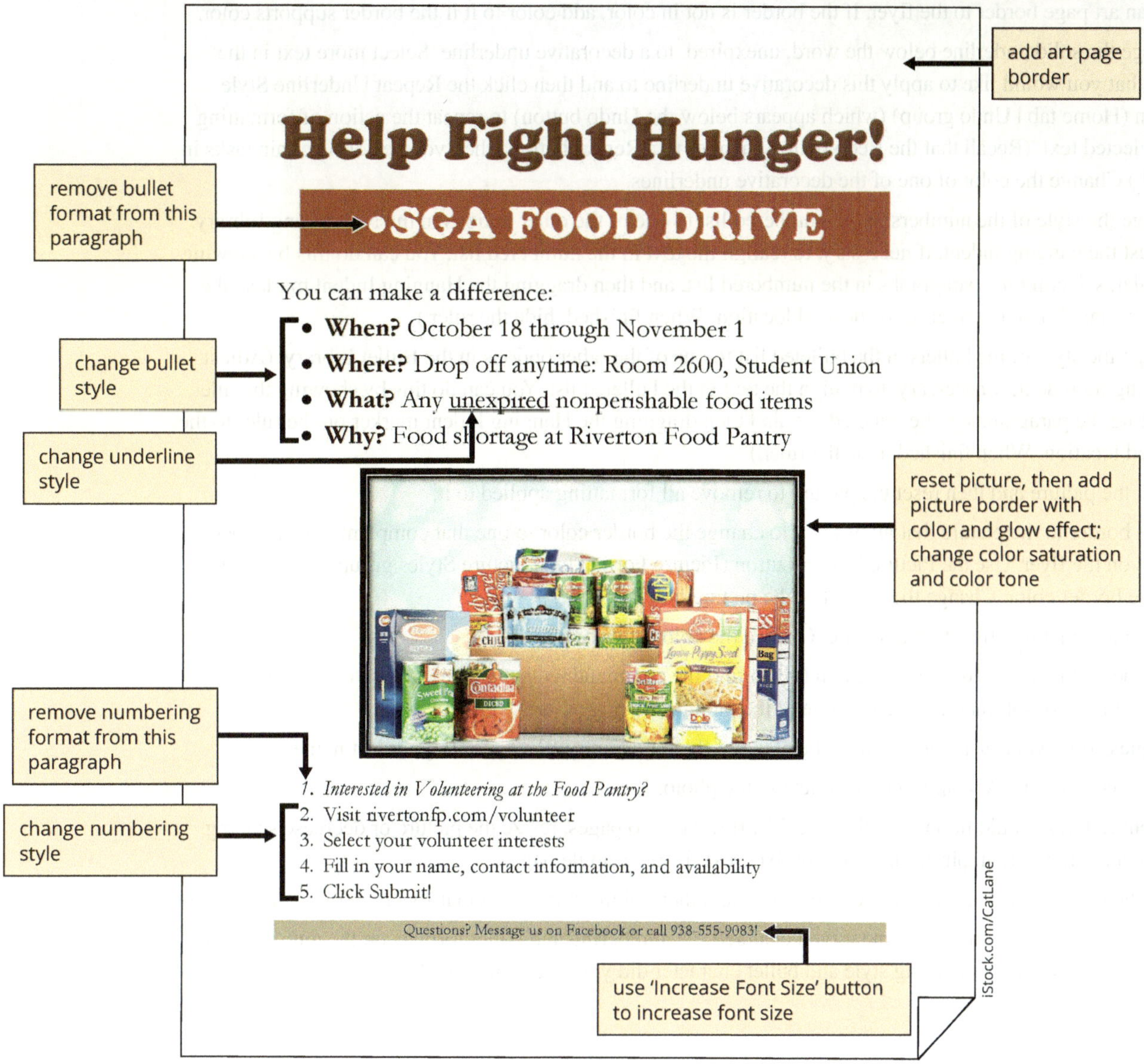

Figure 1–121

Perform the following tasks:

1. Use Help and the Search box to learn about the following: remove bullets from a paragraph, remove numbers from a paragraph, grow font, shrink font, art page borders, decorative underlines, bulleted list formats, numbering formats, hanging indent, picture border shading, picture border color, shadow picture effects, increase and decrease indents, and color saturation and tone.
2. Click File on the ribbon, click Save As, and then save the document using the new file name, SC_WD_1_FoodDriveFlyer.
3. Remove the bullet format from the paragraph immediately below the headline, so that it reads: SGA FOOD DRIVE.
4. Remove the numbering format from the first numbered list item, so that the first list item is: Visit rivertonfp.com/volunteer. In this same paragraph, use the Decrease Indent button (Home tab | Paragraph group) to decrease the left indent so that the paragraph does not have any indent.
5. Select the paragraph containing the signature line, Questions? Message us on Facebook or call 938-555-9083!, and use the 'Increase Font Size' button (Home tab | Font group) to increase its font size.

Continued on next page

6. Add an art page border to the flyer. If the border is not in color, add color to it if the border supports color.
7. Change the solid underline below the word, unexpired, to a decorative underline. Select more text in the flyer that you would like to apply this decorative underline to and then click the Repeat Underline Style button (Home tab | Undo group) (which appears below the Undo button) to repeat the action of formatting the selected text. (Recall that the Redo button changes to a Repeat button when you perform certain tasks in Word.) Change the color of one of the decorative underlines.
8. Change the style of the numbers in the numbered list to one of the other options in the Numbering Library. (Adjust the hanging indent, if necessary, to realign the text in the numbered list. You can do this by showing the ruler, selecting the paragraphs in the numbered list, and then dragging the Hanging Indent marker (the bottom triangle) on the ruler to the desired location. When finished, hide the ruler.)
9. Change the style of the bullets in the bulleted list to one of the other options in the Bullet Library. (Adjust the hanging indent, if necessary, to realign the text in the bulleted list. You can do this by showing the ruler, selecting the paragraphs in the bulleted list, and then dragging the Hanging Indent marker on the ruler to the desired location. When finished, hide the ruler.)
10. Select the picture and then reset the picture to remove all formatting applied to it.
11. Add a border to the picture that allows you to change the border color to one that complements the other colors on the flyer. Use the Picture Border button (Picture Format tab | Picture Styles group) to change the picture border color. Change the weight of the picture border.
12. Add a glow picture effect to the picture. Change the color of the glow.
13. With the picture selected, use the Search box to find the command to change the color saturation. Then, change the color saturation and color tone of the picture.
14. If requested by your instructor, change the name of the food pantry (Riverton) to your last name.
15. Check accessibility. Add appropriate alt text to the photo.
16. The entire flyer should fit on a single page. If it flows to two pages, resize the picture or decrease spacing before and after paragraphs until the entire flyer text fits on a single page.
17. Save the revised flyer again with the same name and then submit it in the format specified by your instructor.
18. **Consider This:** In this assignment, you changed the numbering and bullet formats on the numbered and bulleted lists. Which numbering style and bullet character did you select and why?

Expand Your World

Create a solution that uses cloud or web technologies by learning and investigating on your own from general guidance.

Using Word Online to Create a Flyer with a Picture

Note: To complete this assignment, you will be required to use the Data Files. Please contact your instructor for information about accessing the Data Files.

Instructions: You will use Word Online to prepare a flyer. As assistant to the marketing director at Triton Memorial Hospital, you will create a flyer announcing an upcoming community wellness day to be held at the local community center. Figure 1–122 shows the unformatted flyer. You will enter the text and insert the picture in Word Online and then use its tools to enhance the look of the flyer.

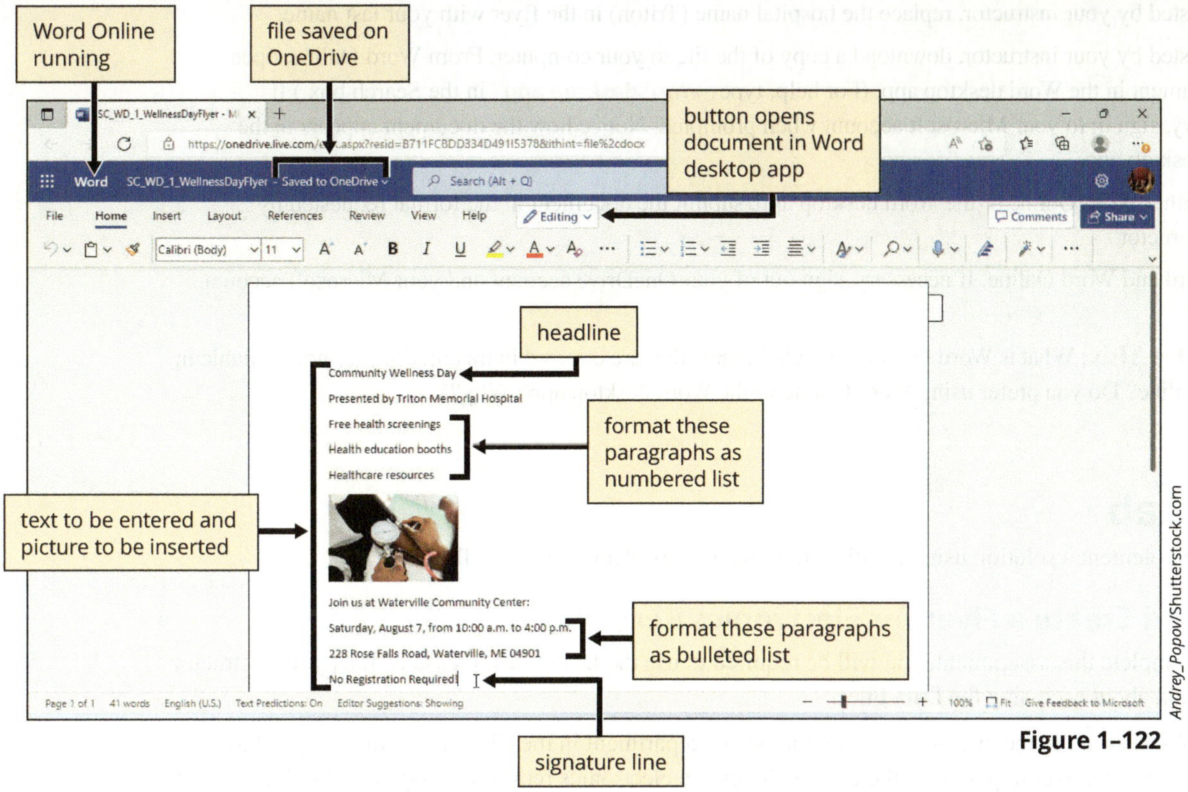

Figure 1–122

Perform the following tasks:

1. Start a browser. Search for the text, Word Online, using a search engine. Visit several websites to learn about Word Online. Navigate to the Word Online website. You will need to sign in to your OneDrive account.
2. Create a new blank Word document using Word Online. Rename the document from the default (i.e., Document 1) to the name SC_WD_1_WellnessDayFlyer.
3. Notice the differences between Word Online and the Word desktop app you used to create the project in this module.
4. Enter the following text in the flyer, as shown in Figure 1–122, checking spelling and grammar as you work in the document:
   Community Wellness Day
   Presented by Triton Memorial Hospital
   Free health screenings
   Health education booths
   Healthcare resources
   Join us at Waterville Community Center:
   Saturday, August 7, from 10:00 a.m. to 4:00 p.m.
   228 Rose Falls Road, Waterville, ME 04901
   No Registration Required!
5. Insert the picture called Support_WD_1_BloodPressure.jpg, which is located in the Data Files, below the numbered list, as shown in the figure.
6. Use the features available in Word Online, along with the concepts and techniques presented in this module, to format this flyer. Be sure to change the document margins, font and font size of text, center a paragraph(s), bold text, italicize text, color text, and underline text. Apply bullets and numbering to paragraphs as indicated in the figure. Practice using the Increase Indent and Decrease Indent buttons (Home tab | Paragraph group) with the numbered list. Resize the picture and apply a picture style. Adjust spacing above and below paragraphs as necessary. The flyer should fit on a single page.

Continued on next page

7. If requested by your instructor, replace the hospital name (Triton) in the flyer with your last name.
8. If requested by your instructor, download a copy of the file to your computer. From Word Online, open the document in the Word desktop app. (For help, type **Word desktop app** in the Search box.) If necessary, sign in to your Microsoft account when prompted. Notice how the document appears in the Word desktop app.
9. Using either Word Online or the Word desktop app, submit the document in the format requested by your instructor.
10. Exit Word and Word Online. If necessary, sign out of your OneDrive account and your Microsoft account in Word.
11. **Consider This:** What is Word Online? Which features that are covered in this module are not available in Word Online? Do you prefer using Word Online or the Word desktop app? Why?

In the Lab

Design and implement a solution using creative thinking and problem-solving skills.

Design and Create a Flyer for Electronics Recycling

Note: To complete this assignment, you will be required to use the Data Files. Please contact your instructor for information about accessing the Data Files.

Problem: As assistant to the director of the public works department in the City of Northridge, you have been asked to create a flyer to publicize the city's self-service electronics recycling program. The flyer should identify the location of the electronics recycling center, along with items that can be recycled at that location.

Perform the following tasks:

Part 1: The flyer should contain a digital picture appropriately resized; the Data Files contain a picture reflecting electronics recycling called Support_WD_1_ElectronicsRecycling.jpg, or you can use your own digital picture if it is appropriate for the topic of the flyer.

The flyer should contain the headline, Self-Service Electronics Recycling, and this signature line: Visit www.northridgepw.com/electronics-recycling for more information. The body copy consists of the two lists (formatted as bulleted or numbered lists), the contents of which can appear in any order: accepted items and location information.

Following is the list of accepted items: all sizes of desktop, laptop, and tablet computers; computer monitors and displays; keyboards, disk drives, and mouse devices; printers, fax machines, and scanners; televisions, DVD players/recorders, and VCRs; video game consoles; and portable digital music players.

Following is the location information: City of Northridge Public Works Facility; Self-Serve Electronics Recycling building; 1302 Front Street in Northridge; Open Monday through Friday from 6:00 a.m. to 3:30 p.m. and Saturdays from 8:00 a.m. to 11:00 a.m.

Use the concepts and techniques presented in this module to create a new blank document and format this flyer. Be sure to check spelling and grammar, accepting and ignoring suggested spelling and grammar changes as appropriate. Check and fix any accessibility issues. When finished, save the flyer with the file name, SC_WD_1_ElectronicsRecyclingFlyer. Submit your assignment and answers to the Part 2 critical thinking questions in the format specified by your instructor.

Part 2: **Consider This:** You made several decisions while creating the flyer in this assignment: where to place text, which margin settings and document themes to use, how to format the text (i.e., font, font size, paragraph alignment, bulleted paragraphs, numbered paragraphs, underlines, italics, bold, and color), which picture to use, where to position the picture, how to format the picture, and which page enhancements to add (i.e., theme colors, borders, and spacing before/after paragraphs). What was the rationale behind each of these decisions? When you proofread the document, what further revisions did you make and why?

Creating a Research Paper

Objectives

After completing this module, you will be able to:

- Describe the MLA documentation style for research papers
- Modify and apply styles
- Modify text, paragraph, and page formatting
- Use a header to number pages in a document
- Change how a Word document appears in the Word window
- Use the AutoCorrect Options button and create an AutoCorrect entry
- Insert and edit citations and their sources
- Add and edit footnotes
- Check document stats using the Word Count dialog box
- Create and update a bibliographical list of sources
- Navigate to a specific location in a document
- Find and replace text or formatting
- Use the thesaurus
- Check spelling and grammar
- Use Smart Lookup and Researcher
- Insert, edit, delete, and view comments in a document

Introduction

In both business and academic environments, you will be asked to write reports. Business reports range from proposals to cost justifications to five-year plans to research findings. Academic reports focus mostly on research findings.

A **research paper** is a document you can use to communicate the results of research findings. To write a research paper, you learn about a particular topic from a variety of sources (research), organize your ideas from the research results, and then present relevant facts and/or opinions that support the topic. Your final research paper combines properly credited outside information along with personal insights. Thus, no two research papers — even if they are about the same topic — will or should be the same.

Project: Research Paper

When preparing a research paper, you should follow a standard documentation style that defines the rules for creating the paper and crediting sources. A variety of documentation styles exists, depending on the nature of the research paper. Each style requires the same basic information; the differences in styles relate to requirements for presenting the information. For example, one documentation style uses the term, bibliography, for the list of sources, whereas another uses the term, references, and yet a third prefers the term, works cited. Two popular documentation styles

BTW
APA Documentation Style
In the APA style, a separate title page is required instead of placing the name and course information on the paper's first page. Double-space all pages of the paper with one-inch top, bottom, left, and right margins. Indent the first word of each paragraph one-half inch from the left margin. In the upper-right margin of each page, including the title page, place a running head that consists of the page number preceded by a brief summary of the paper title.

for research papers are the MLA and APA styles. The **MLA (Modern Language Association of America)** style defines a set of formatting and content guidelines for publications and student research papers in the humanities and other fields, whereas the **APA (American Psychological Association)** style defines a set of formatting and content guidelines for publications and student research papers in the social and behavioral sciences. This module uses the MLA documentation style because it is used in a wider range of disciplines.

The project in this module follows research paper guidelines and uses Word to create the short research paper shown in Figure 2–1. As an associate sales representative at a mobile phone retailer, you communicate with and educate customers. You also are a part-time student who has been assigned a short research paper. The purpose of this short paper (only 250 to 325 words) is to acquaint you with the features in Word that are useful for creating papers of any length, regardless of whether it is a short essay or a lengthy dissertation. You decide to combine your work and school interests and compose a short research paper about smartphone biometrics. Your supervisor has expressed interest in incorporating the information in your paper on the company website.

This paper, which discusses smartphone biometrics, follows the MLA documentation style. Each page contains a page number. The first two pages present the name and course information (student name, instructor name, course name, and paper due date), paper title, an introduction with a thesis statement, details that support the thesis, and a conclusion. This section of the paper also includes references to research sources and a footnote. The third page contains a detailed, alphabetical list of the sources referenced in the research paper. All pages include a header at the upper-right edge of the page.

In this module, you will learn how to create the research paper shown in Figure 2–1. You will perform the following general tasks as you progress through this module:

1. Change the document settings.
2. Create the header, which will appear on each page of the research paper.
3. Type the research paper text with citations.
4. Create an alphabetical works cited page.
5. Proofread and revise the research paper.
6. Work with comments in the research paper.

MLA Documentation Style

The research paper in this project follows the guidelines presented by the MLA. To follow the MLA documentation style, use an 11- to 13-point font size in an easily discernible font, such as Times New Roman. Double-space text on all pages of the paper using one-inch top, bottom, left, and right margins. Indent the first word of each paragraph one-half inch from the left margin. At the right margin of each page, place a page number one-half inch from the top margin. On each page, precede the page number with your last name.

The MLA documentation style does not require a title page. Instead, place your name and course information in a block at the left margin beginning one inch from the top of the page. Center the title one double-spaced line below your name, course, and date information.

In the text of the paper, place author references in parentheses, called **in-text citations**, along with the page number(s) of the referenced information, if applicable. The MLA documentation style uses these in-text citations to reference sources used in a research paper instead of noting each reference at the bottom of the page or at the end of the paper. In the MLA documentation style, notes are used only for optional content or bibliographic notes.

If used, content notes elaborate on points discussed in the paper, and bibliographic notes direct the reader to evaluations of statements in a source or provide a means for identifying multiple sources. Use a superscript (raised number) both to signal that a note exists and to sequence the notes. Position notes at the bottom of the page as footnotes or at the end of the paper as endnotes. Indent the first line of each note one-half inch from the left margin. Place one space following the superscripted number before beginning the note text. Double-space the note text. These formats are shown in Figure 2–1.

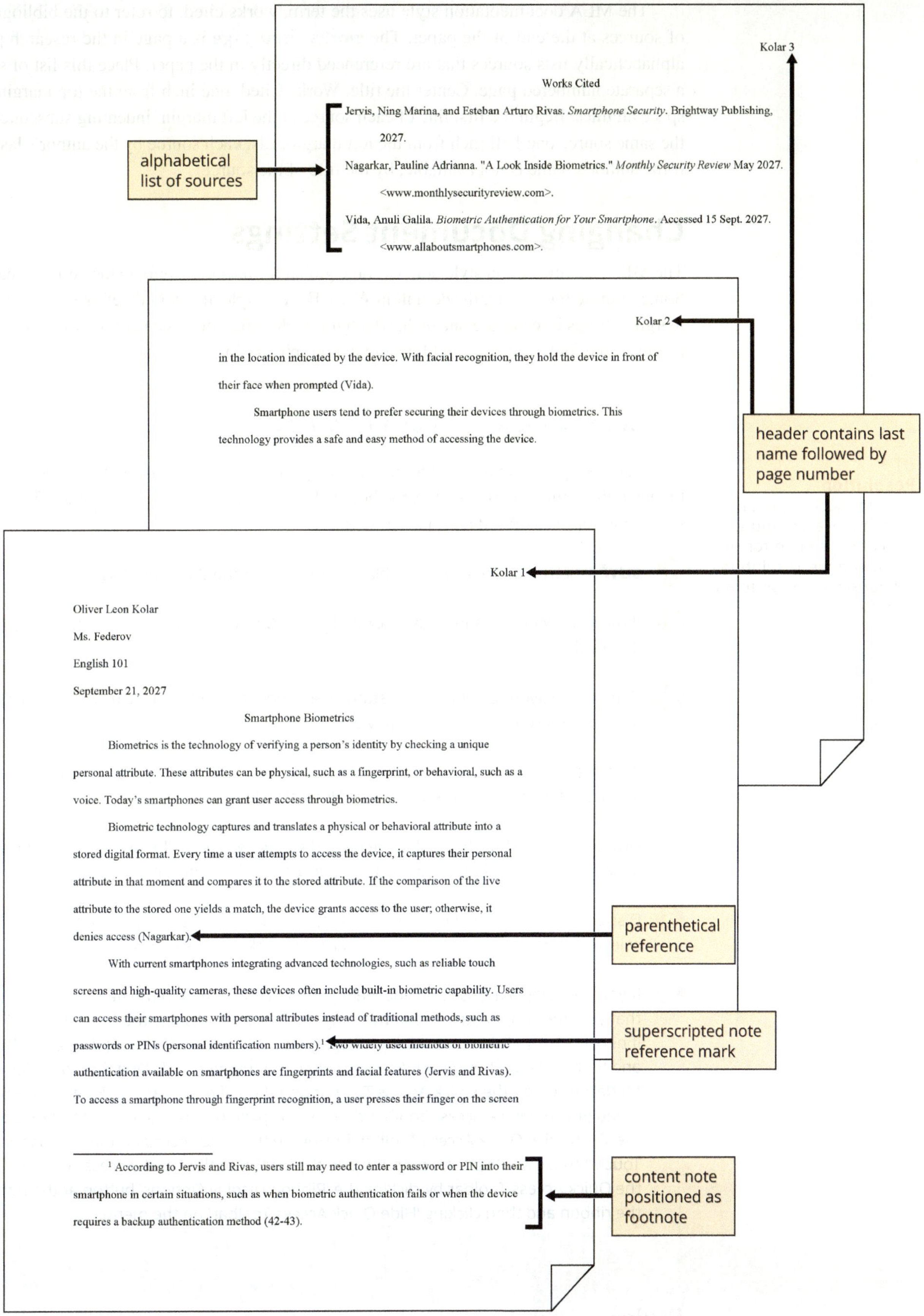
Kolar 3
Works Cited
Jervis, Ning Marina, and Esteban Arturo Rivas. *Smartphone Security*. Brightway Publishing, 2027.
Nagarkar, Pauline Adrianna. "A Look Inside Biometrics." *Monthly Security Review* May 2027. <www.monthlysecurityreview.com>.
Vida, Anuli Galila. *Biometric Authentication for Your Smartphone*. Accessed 15 Sept. 2027. <www.allaboutsmartphones.com>.
alphabetical list of sources
Kolar 2
in the location indicated by the device. With facial recognition, they hold the device in front of their face when prompted (Vida).
Smartphone users tend to prefer securing their devices through biometrics. This technology provides a safe and easy method of accessing the device.
header contains last name followed by page number
Kolar 1
Oliver Leon Kolar
Ms. Federov
English 101
September 21, 2027
Smartphone Biometrics
Biometrics is the technology of verifying a person's identity by checking a unique personal attribute. These attributes can be physical, such as a fingerprint, or behavioral, such as a voice. Today's smartphones can grant user access through biometrics.
Biometric technology captures and translates a physical or behavioral attribute into a stored digital format. Every time a user attempts to access the device, it captures their personal attribute in that moment and compares it to the stored attribute. If the comparison of the live attribute to the stored one yields a match, the device grants access to the user; otherwise, it denies access (Nagarkar).
parenthetical reference
With current smartphones integrating advanced technologies, such as reliable touch screens and high-quality cameras, these devices often include built-in biometric capability. Users can access their smartphones with personal attributes instead of traditional methods, such as passwords or PINs (personal identification numbers).[1]
authentication available on smartphones are fingerprints and facial features (Jervis and Rivas). To access a smartphone through fingerprint recognition, a user presses their finger on the screen
superscripted note reference mark
[1] According to Jervis and Rivas, users still may need to enter a password or PIN into their smartphone in certain situations, such as when biometric authentication fails or when the device requires a backup authentication method (42-43).
content note positioned as footnote

Figure 2–1

The MLA documentation style uses the term, works cited, to refer to the bibliographic list of sources at the end of the paper. The **works cited page** is a page in the research paper that alphabetically lists sources that are referenced directly in the paper. Place this list of sources on a separate numbered page. Center the title, Works Cited, one inch from the top margin. Double-space all lines. Begin the first line of each source at the left margin, indenting subsequent lines of the same source one-half inch from the left margin. List each source by the author's last name or, if the author's name is not available, by the title of the source.

Changing Document Settings

The MLA documentation style defines some global formats that apply to the entire research paper. Some of these formats are the default in Word. For example, the default left, right, top, and bottom margin settings in Word are one inch, which meets the MLA documentation style. You will modify, however, the font, font size, and line and paragraph spacing.

To Start Word and Specify Settings

BTW
Resolution
For information about how to change a computer's resolution, search for the term, change resolution, in your operating system's Help files.

If you are using a computer to step through the project in this module and you want your screens to match the figures in this book, you should change your screen's resolution to 1366 × 768. The following steps start Word and specify settings.

1. sam Start Word and create a blank document in the Word window.
2. If the Word window is not maximized, click the Maximize button on its title bar to maximize the window.
3. If the Print Layout button on the status bar is not selected (shown in Figure 2-2), click it so that your screen is in Print Layout view.
4. If Normal (Home tab | Styles group) is not selected in the Styles gallery (shown in Figure 2-2), click it so that your document uses the Normal style.
5. Display the View tab. To display the page the same width as the document window, if necessary, click the Page Width button (View tab | Zoom group).
6. Display the Home tab. If the 'Show/Hide ¶' button (Home tab | Paragraph group) is not selected already, click it to display formatting marks on the screen.
7. If you are using a mouse and you want your screens to match the figures in the book, verify that you are using Mouse mode by doing the following: display the Quick Access Toolbar, if necessary, by clicking the 'Ribbon Display Options' button at the right edge of the ribbon and then clicking 'Show Quick Access Toolbar' on the menu; clicking the 'Touch/Mouse Mode' button on the Quick Access Toolbar and then, if necessary, clicking Mouse on the menu (if your Quick Access Toolbar does not display the 'Touch/Mouse Mode' button, click the 'Customize Quick Access Toolbar' button on the Quick Access Toolbar and then click Touch/Mouse Mode on the menu to add the button to the Quick Access Toolbar); then hide the Quick Access Toolbar by clicking the 'Ribbon Display Options' button at the right edge of the ribbon and then clicking 'Hide Quick Access Toolbar' on the menu.

Styles

When you create a document, Word formats the text using a particular style. A **style** is a named collection of character and paragraph formats, including font, font size, font styles, font color, and alignment, that are stored together and can be applied to text or objects to format them quickly. The default style that is applied to all text in Word is called the **Normal style**, which based on default Word installation settings uses an 11-point Calibri font. If you do not specify a style for text you type, Word applies the Normal style to the text. In addition to the Normal style, Word has many other built-in, or predefined, styles that you can use to format text. Styles make it easy to apply many formats at once to text. You can modify existing styles and create your own styles. Styles are discussed as they are used in this book.

BTW
The Word Window
The modules in this book begin with the Word window appearing as it did at the initial installation of the software. Your Word window may look different depending on your screen resolution and other Word settings.

To Modify a Style

The MLA documentation style requires that all text in the research paper use an 11- to 13-point font size and an easily discernible font, such as Times New Roman. If you change the font and font size using buttons on the ribbon, you will need to make the change many times while creating the paper. **Why?** Word formats various areas of a document based on the Normal style, which, by default, uses an 11-point Calibri font. For example, body text, headers, and bibliographies all display text based on the Normal style.

Thus, instead of changing the font and font size for various document elements, a more efficient technique is to change the Normal style for this document to use the font and font size you will use for this paper. **Why?** By changing the Normal style, you ensure that all text in the document will use the format required by the MLA. You will use 12-point Times New Roman in this paper. The following steps change the Normal style to this font and font size.

1

- Right-click Normal in the Styles gallery (Home tab | Styles group) to display a shortcut menu related to styles (Figure 2–2).

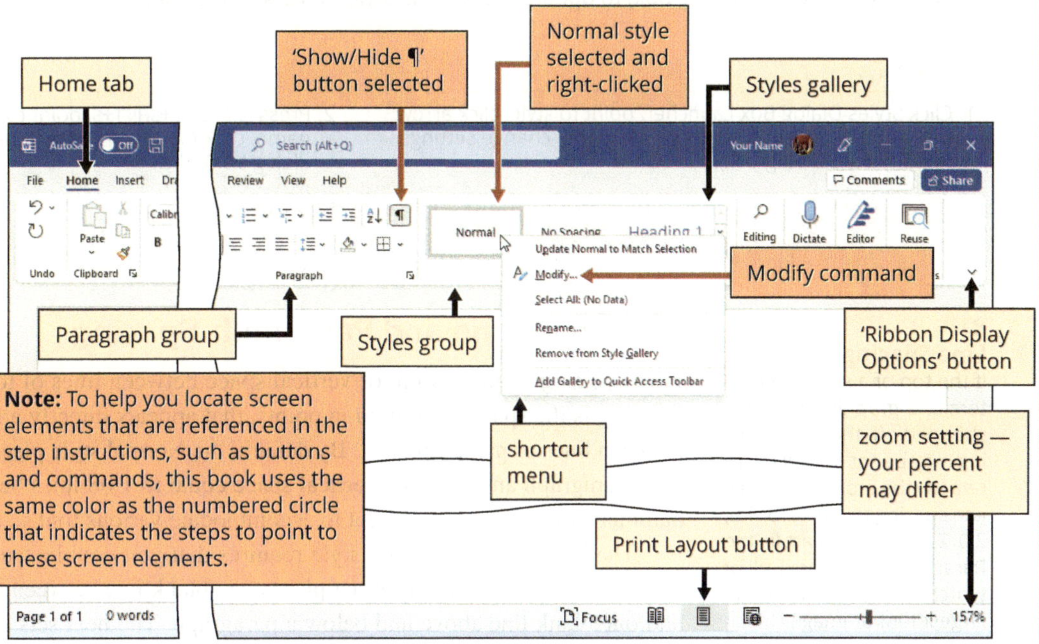

Figure 2–2

2

- Click Modify on the shortcut menu to display the Modify Style dialog box (Figure 2–3).

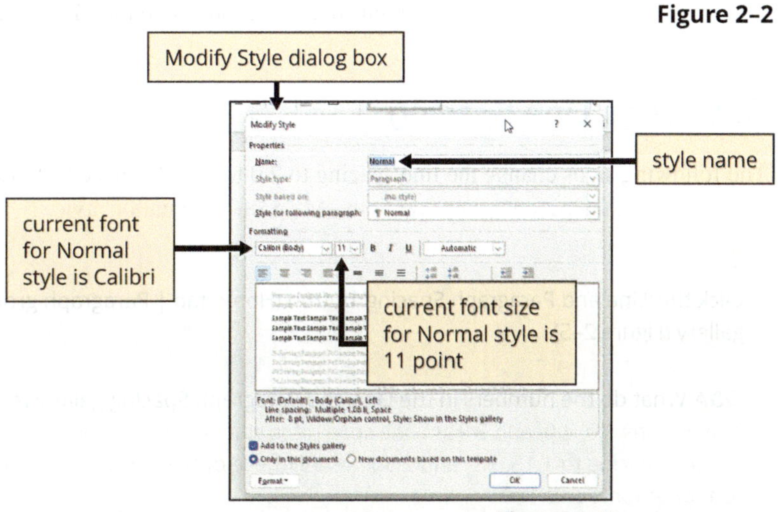

Figure 2–3

3

- Click the Font arrow (Modify Style dialog box) to display the Font list. Scroll to and then click 'Times New Roman' in the list to change the font for the style being modified.
- Click the Font Size arrow (Modify Style dialog box) and then click 12 in the Font Size list to change the font size for the style being modified.
- Ensure that the 'Only in this document' option button is selected (Figure 2–4).

Q&A Will all future documents use the new font and font size?
No, because the 'Only in this document' option button is selected, only this document will use the modified settings for the Normal style. If you wanted all future documents to use a new setting, you would select the 'New documents based on this template' option button.

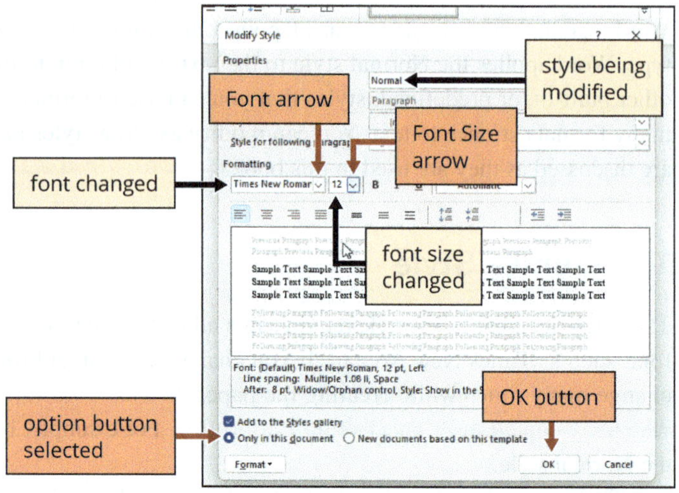

Figure 2–4

4

- Click OK (Modify Style dialog box) to update the Normal style to the specified settings.

Other Ways

1. Click Styles Dialog Box Launcher, point to style, click arrow next to style name, click Modify on menu, change settings (Modify Style dialog box), click OK
2. Press ALT+CTRL+SHIFT+S, point to style, click arrow next to style name, click Modify on menu, change settings (Modify Style dialog box), click OK

BTW
Line Spacing
If the top of a set of characters or a graphical image is chopped off, then line spacing may be set to Exactly. To remedy the problem, change line spacing to 1.0, 1.15, 1.5, 2.0, 2.5, 3.0, or At least (in the Paragraph dialog box), all of which accommodate the largest font or image.

Adjusting Line and Paragraph Spacing

Line spacing is the amount of vertical space between lines of text in a paragraph. **Paragraph spacing** is the space, measured in points, that appears directly above and below a paragraph, or between lines of paragraph text. By default, the Normal style places 8 points of blank space after each paragraph and inserts a vertical space equal to 1.08 lines between each line of text. It also automatically adjusts line height to accommodate various font sizes and graphics.

The MLA documentation style requires that you double-space the entire research paper. A **double-spaced** paragraph format places one blank line between each line of text in a paragraph and one blank line above and below a paragraph. The next sets of steps adjust line spacing and paragraph spacing according to the MLA documentation style.

To Change Line Spacing

The following steps change the line spacing to 2.0 to double-space lines in a paragraph. **Why?** The lines of the research paper should be double-spaced, according to the MLA documentation style.

1

- Click the 'Line and Paragraph Spacing' button (Home tab | Paragraph group) to display the Line and Paragraph Spacing gallery (Figure 2–5).

Q&A What do the numbers in the Line and Paragraph Spacing gallery represent?
The options 1.0, 2.0, and 3.0 set line spacing to single, double, and triple, respectively. Similarly, the 1.15, 1.5, and 2.5 options set line spacing to 1.15, 1.5, and 2.5 lines. All these options will adjust line spacing automatically to accommodate the largest font or graphic on a line.

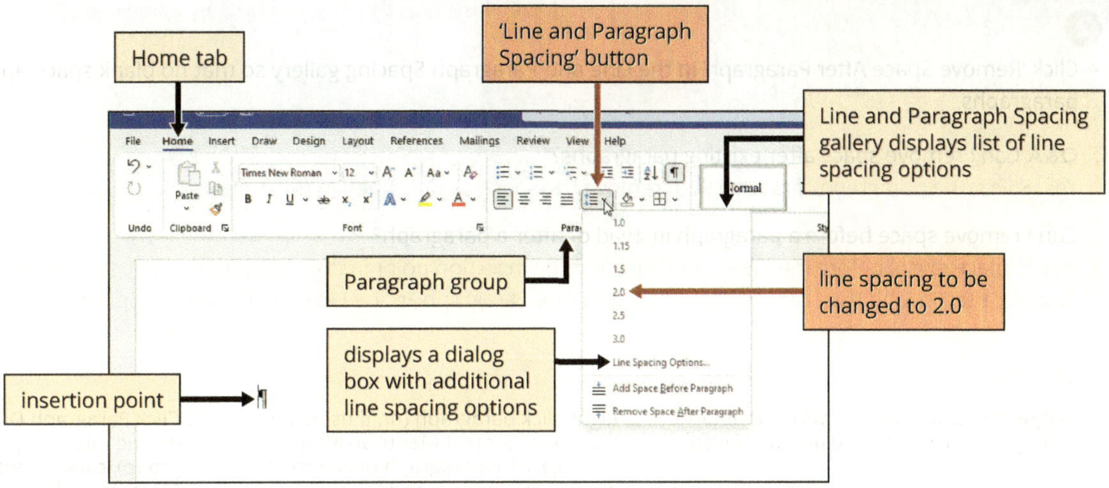

Figure 2-5

2

- Click 2.0 in the Line and Paragraph Spacing gallery to change the line spacing at the location of the insertion point.

Q&A Can I change the line spacing of existing text or the entire document?
Yes. Select the text first or select the entire document and then change the line spacing as described in these steps. To select the entire document, click the Editing group button (Home tab), if necessary, to display the Editing group, click the Select button on the Editing group (Home tab | Editing group), and then click Select All on the Select menu; or press CTRL+A.

Other Ways

1. Right-click paragraph (or, if using touch, tap 'Show Context Menu' on Mini toolbar), click Paragraph on shortcut menu, click Indents and Spacing tab (Paragraph dialog box), click Line spacing arrow, select desired spacing, click OK
2. Click Paragraph Dialog Box Launcher (Home tab or Layout tab | Paragraph group), click Indents and Spacing tab (Paragraph dialog box), click Line spacing arrow, select desired spacing, click OK
3. Press CTRL+2 for double-spacing

To Remove Space after a Paragraph

The following steps remove space after a paragraph. **Why?** The research paper should not have additional blank space after each paragraph, according to the MLA documentation style.

1

- Click the 'Line and Paragraph Spacing' button (Home tab | Paragraph group) to display the Line and Paragraph Spacing gallery (Figure 2–6).

Q&A Why does a check mark appear to the left of 2.0 in the gallery?
The check mark indicates the currently selected line spacing.

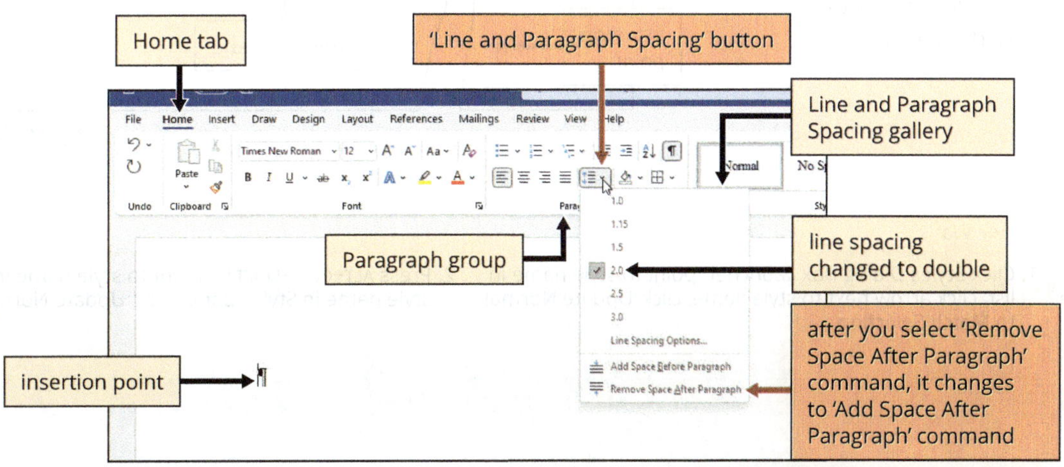

Figure 2–6

2

- Click 'Remove Space After Paragraph' in the Line and Paragraph Spacing gallery so that no blank space appears after paragraphs.

Q&A Can I remove space after existing paragraphs?
Yes. Select the paragraphs first and then remove the space as described in these steps.

Can I remove space before a paragraph instead of after a paragraph?
Yes. If space exists before the paragraph, position the insertion point in the paragraph to adjust, click the 'Line and Paragraph Spacing' button, and then click 'Remove Space Before Paragraph' in the Line and Paragraph Spacing gallery.

Other Ways

1. Adjust Spacing After arrows (Layout tab | Paragraph group) until 0 pt is displayed
2. Right-click paragraph (or, if using touch, tap 'Show Context Menu' on Mini toolbar), click Paragraph on shortcut menu, click Indents and Spacing tab (Paragraph dialog box), adjust After arrows until 0 pt is displayed, click OK
3. Click Paragraph Dialog Box Launcher (Home tab or Layout tab | Paragraph group), click Indents and Spacing tab (Paragraph dialog box), adjust After arrows until 0 pt is displayed, click OK

To Update a Style to Match a Selection

To ensure that all paragraphs in the paper will be double-spaced and do not have space after the paragraphs, you want the Normal style to include the line and paragraph spacing changes made in the previous two sets of steps. The following steps update the Normal style. **Why?** You can update a style to reflect the settings of the location of the insertion point or selected text. Because no text has been typed in the research paper yet, you do not need to select text prior to updating the Normal style.

1

- Right-click Normal in the Styles gallery (Home tab | Styles group) to display a shortcut menu (Figure 2–7).

2

- Click 'Update Normal to Match Selection' on the shortcut menu to update the selected (or current) style to reflect the settings at the location of the insertion point.

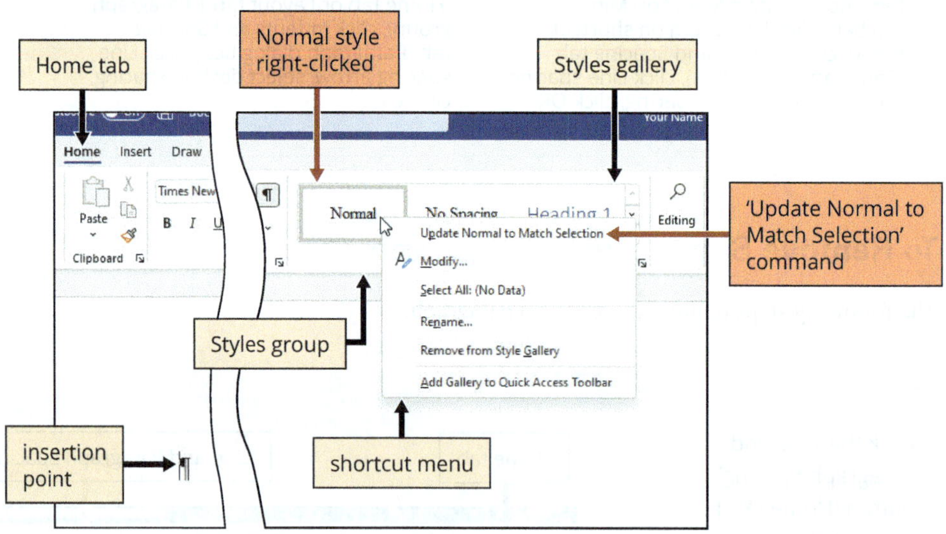

Figure 2–7

Other Ways

1. Click Styles Dialog Box Launcher, point to style name in list, click arrow next to style name, click 'Update Normal to Match Selection'
2. Press ALT+CTRL+SHIFT+S, point to style name in list, click arrow next to style name in Styles pane, click 'Update Normal to Match Selection'

Creating a Header

A **header** is text, information, pictures, and other objects that appear in an area above the top margin on one or more page(s) in a document. Similarly, a **footer** is text, information, pictures, and other objects that appear in an area below the bottom margin on one or more page(s) in a document. Unless otherwise specified in Word, headers appear one-half inch from the top of every page, and footers appear one-half inch from the bottom of each page, which meets the MLA documentation style. In addition to text, pictures, and objects, headers and footers can include document information, such as the page number, current date, current time, and author's name.

In this research paper, you are to precede the page number with your last name placed one-half inch from the upper-right edge of each page. The procedures in the following sections enter your name and the page number in the header, as specified by the MLA documentation style.

BTW
Footers
If you wanted to create a footer, you would click the Footer button (Insert tab | Header & Footer group) and then select the desired built-in footer. If you wanted to edit a footer, you would click the Footer button (Insert tab | Header & Footer group) and then click Edit Footer in the Footer gallery, or you could double-click the dimmed footer.

To Insert a Header

The following steps insert a blank built-in header. **Why?** To enter text in the header, you instruct Word to insert a header, which you will edit.

1

- Click Insert on the ribbon to display the Insert tab.
- Click the Header button (Insert tab | Header & Footer group) to display the Header gallery (Figure 2–8).
- **Experiment:** Click the down scroll arrow in the Header gallery to see the available built-in headers.

Q&A How would I enter a footer in a document?
You would click the Footer button (Insert tab | Header & Footer group) and select the desired footer in the list. To edit a footer, you would click the Footer button (Insert tab | Header & Footer group) and the click Edit Footer in the Footer gallery.

How would I remove a header (or footer) from a document?
You would click Remove Header in the Header gallery. Similarly, to remove a footer, you would click Remove Footer in the Footer gallery.

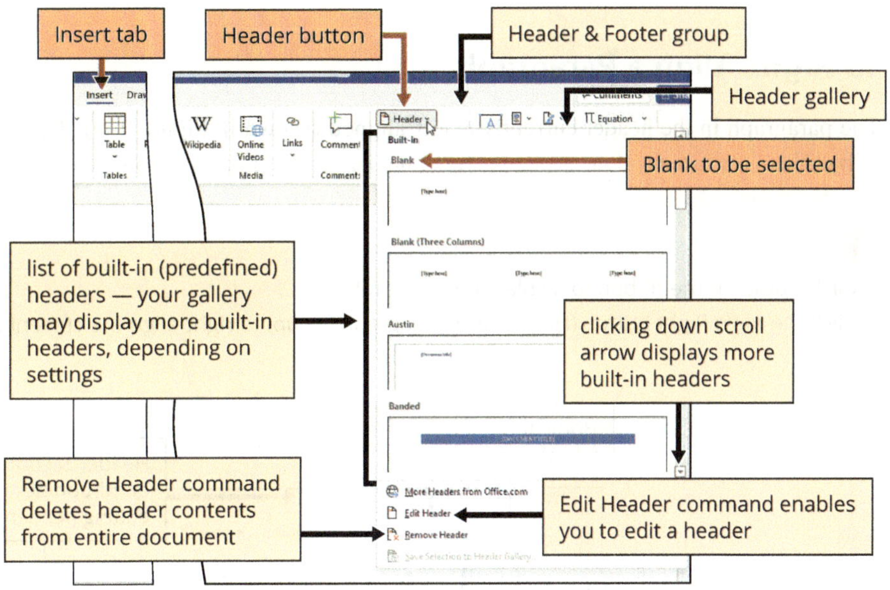

Figure 2–8

2

- Click Blank in the Header gallery to switch from the document text to the header and insert placeholder text in the header (Figure 2–9).

Q&A What is placeholder text?
Placeholder text is default text that indicates where text can be typed.

How do I remove the Header & Footer tab from the ribbon?
When you are finished editing the header, you will close the header, which removes the Header & Footer tab.

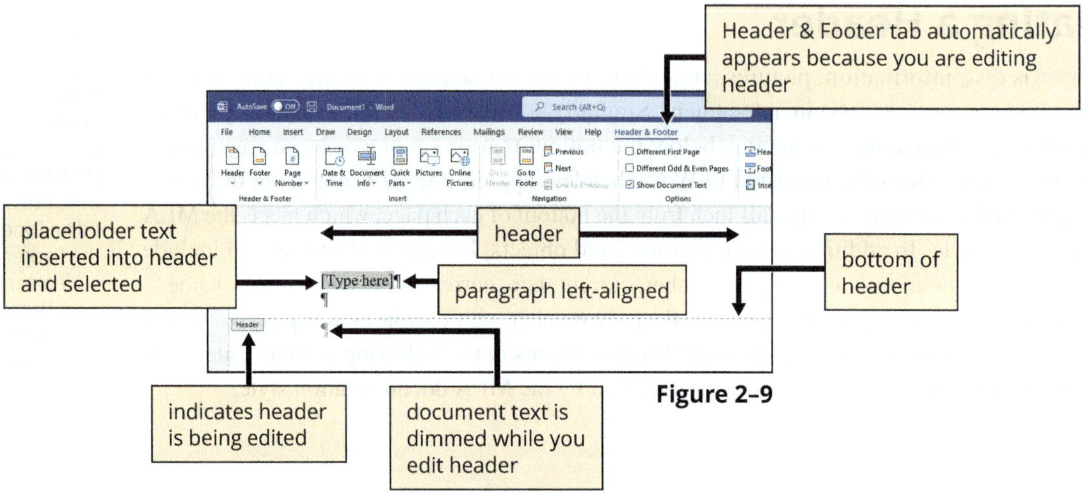

Figure 2–9

Other Ways

1. Double-click dimmed header
2. Right-click header in document, click Edit Header button that appears

To Right-Align a Paragraph

The paragraph in the header currently is left-aligned (shown in Figure 2–9). The following step right-aligns this paragraph. **Why?** Your last name and the page number in the header should be **right-aligned**, that is, they should appear at the right margin, according to the MLA documentation style.

1

- Click Home on the ribbon to display the Home tab.
- Click the Align Right button (Home tab | Paragraph group) to right-align the current paragraph (Figure 2–10).

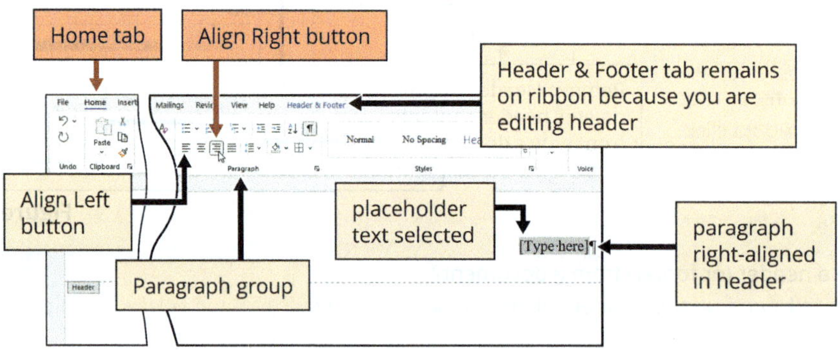

Figure 2–10

Q&A What if I wanted to return the paragraph to left-aligned?

You would click the Align Right button again, or click the Align Left button (Home tab | Paragraph group).

Other Ways

1. Right-click paragraph (or, if using touch, tap 'Show Context Menu' button on Mini toolbar), click Paragraph on shortcut menu, click Indents and Spacing tab (Paragraph dialog box), click Alignment arrow, click Right, click OK
2. Click Paragraph Dialog Box Launcher (Home tab or Layout tab | Paragraph group), click Indents and Spacing tab (Paragraph dialog box), click Alignment arrow, click Right, click OK
3. Press CTRL+R

To Enter Text in a Header

The following step enters the last name right-aligned in the header area.

1 With the [Type here] placeholder text selected (as shown in Figure 2–10), type **Kolar** and then press SPACEBAR to enter the last name in the header.

Q&A What if my placeholder text is not selected?
Drag through the placeholder text to select it and then perform Step 1.

To Insert Page Numbers

The following steps insert a page number at the location of the insertion point and in the same location on all subsequent pages in the document. **Why?** The MLA documentation style requires a page number following the last name in the header.

1

- Click Header & Footer on the ribbon to display the Header & Footer tab.
- Click the Page Number button (Header & Footer tab | Header & Footer group) to display the Page Number menu.
- Point to Current Position on the Page Number menu to display the Current Position gallery (Figure 2–11).
- **Experiment:** Click the down scroll arrow in the Current Position gallery to see the available page number formats.

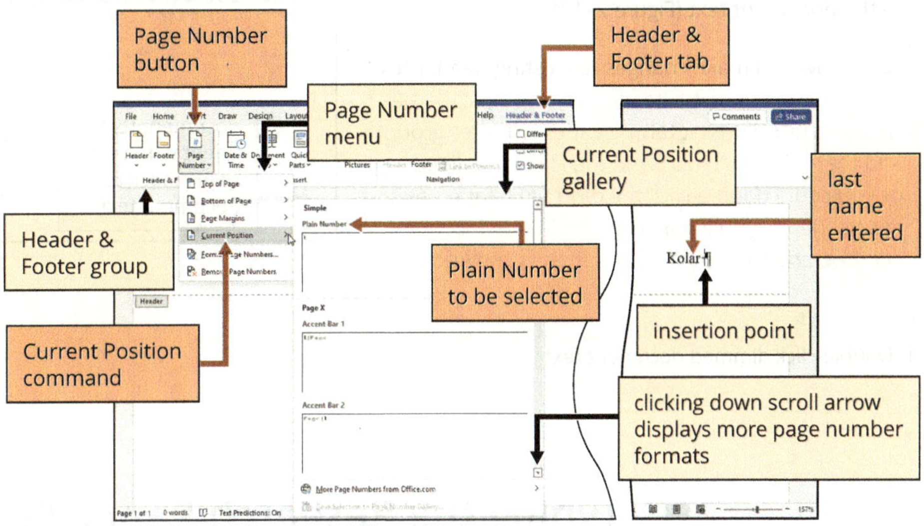

Figure 2–11

Q&A Why does my button name differ from the name on the face of the button in the figure?
The text that appears on the face of the button may vary, depending on screen resolution.

2

- If necessary, scroll to the top of the Current Position gallery.
- Click Plain Number in the Current Position gallery to insert an unformatted page number at the location of the insertion point (Figure 2–12).

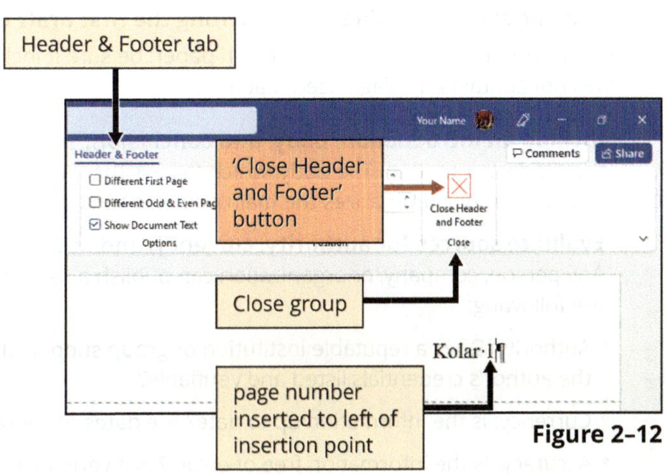

Figure 2–12

Other Ways

1. Click Page Number button (Insert tab | Header & Footer group)
2. Click 'Explore Quick Parts' button (Insert tab | Text group) or Quick Parts button (Header & Footer tab | Insert group), click Field on Explore Quick Parts menu or Quick Parts menu, select Page in Field names list (Field dialog box), select desired format in Format list, click OK

To Close the Header

The next task is to close the header and switch back to the document text. **Why?** You are finished entering text in the header. The following step closes the header.

1

- Click the 'Close Header and Footer' button (Header & Footer tab | Close group) (shown in Figure 2–12) to close the header and switch back to the document text (Figure 2–13).

Q&A How do I make changes to existing header text?
If you wanted to edit a header, you would click the Header button (Insert tab | Header & Footer group) and then click Edit Header in the Header gallery, or you could double-click the dimmed header, edit the header as you would edit text in the document window, and then close the header as shown here.

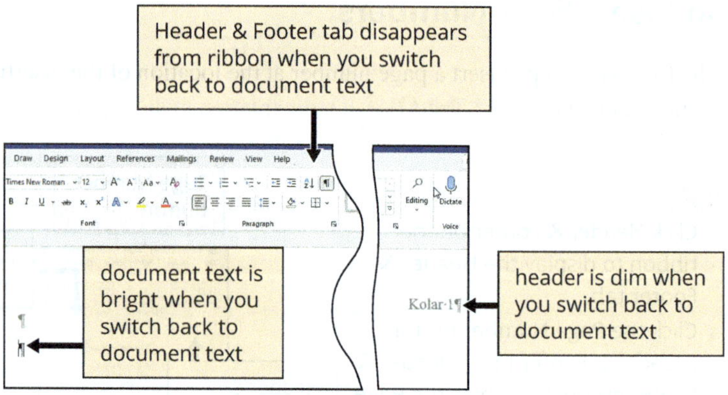

Figure 2–13

Other Ways

1. Double-click dimmed document text

Typing the Research Paper Text

The text of the research paper in this module encompasses the first two pages of the paper. You will type the text of the research paper and then modify it later in the module, so that it matches Figure 2–1 shown at the beginning of this module.

Consider This

What should you consider when writing the first draft of a research paper?

As you write the first draft of a research paper, be sure it includes the proper components, uses credible sources, and does not contain any plagiarized material.

- **Include an introduction, body, and conclusion.** The first paragraph of the paper introduces the topic and captures the reader's attention. The body, which follows the introduction, consists of several paragraphs that support the topic. The conclusion summarizes the main points in the body and restates the topic.
- **Evaluate sources for authority, currency, and accuracy.** Be especially wary of information obtained on the web. Any person, company, or organization can publish a webpage on the Internet. When evaluating the source, consider the following:
  - Authority: Does a reputable institution or group support the source? Is the information presented without bias? Are the author's credentials listed and verifiable?
  - Currency: Is the information up to date? Are dates of sources listed? What is the last date revised or updated?
  - Accuracy: Is the information free of errors? Is it verifiable? Are the sources clearly identified?

- **Acknowledge all sources of information; do not plagiarize.** Sources of research include books, magazines, newspapers, the Internet, and more. As you record facts and ideas, list details about the source: title, author, place of publication, publisher, date of publication, etc. When taking notes, be careful not to plagiarize, that is, do not copy or use someone else's work and claim it to be your own. If you copy information directly, place it in quotation marks and identify its source. Not only is plagiarism unethical, but it is considered an academic crime that can have severe punishments, such as failing a course or being expelled from school.

When you summarize, paraphrase (rewrite information in your own words), present facts, give statistics, quote exact words, or show a map, chart, or other object, you must acknowledge the source. Information that commonly is known or accessible to the audience constitutes common knowledge and does not need to be acknowledged. If, however, you question whether certain information is common knowledge, you should acknowledge it — just to be safe.

To Enter Name and Course Information

As discussed earlier in this module, the MLA documentation style does not require a separate title page for research papers. Instead, place your name and course information in a block at the top of the page, below the header, at the left margin. The following steps enter the name and course information in the research paper.

1. With the insertion point positioned as shown in Figure 2–13, type **Oliver Leon Kolar** as the student name and then press ENTER.
2. Type **Ms. Federov** as the instructor name and then press ENTER.
3. Type **English 101** as the course name and then press ENTER.
4. Type **September 21, 2027** as the paper's due date and then press ENTER (Figure 2–14).

BTW
Date Formats
The MLA style prefers the day-month-year (6 October 2021) or month-day-year (October 6, 2021) format.

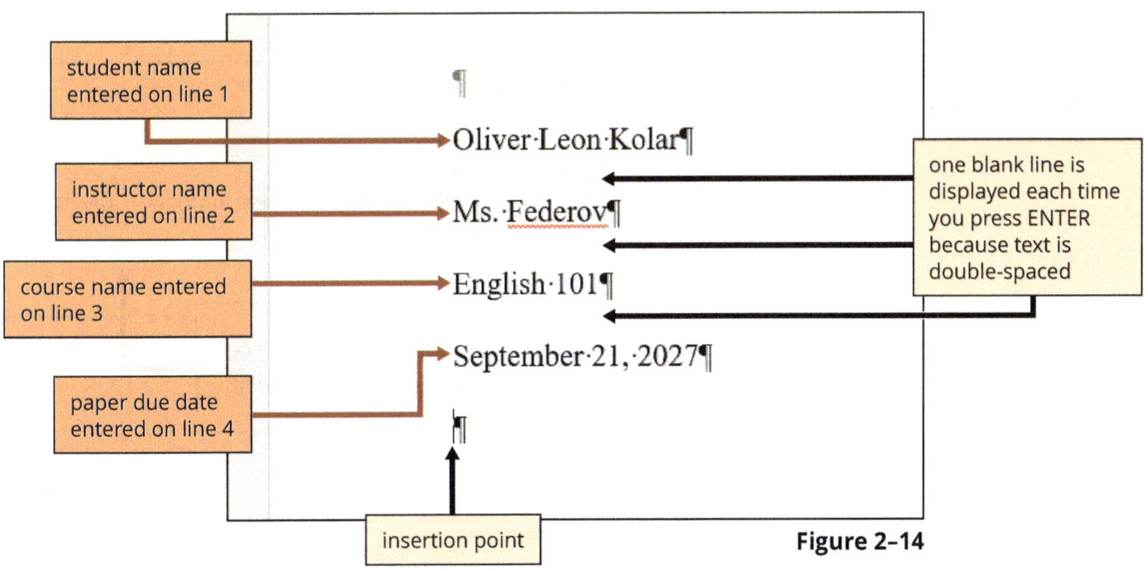

Figure 2–14

To Click and Type

The next task is to enter the title of the research paper centered between the page margins. In Module 1, you used the Center button (Home tab | Paragraph group) to center text and pictures. As an alternative, if you are using a mouse, you can use Word's Click and Type feature to format and enter text, pictures, and other objects. *Why? With* ***Click and Type****, you can double-click a blank area of the document and Word automatically formats the item you type or insert based on the location where you double-clicked.* The following steps use Click and Type to center and then type the title of the research paper.

1

- **Experiment:** Move the pointer around the document below the entered name and course information and observe the various icons that appear with the I-beam.
- Position the pointer in the center of the document at the approximate location for the research paper title until a center icon appears below the I-beam (Figure 2–15).

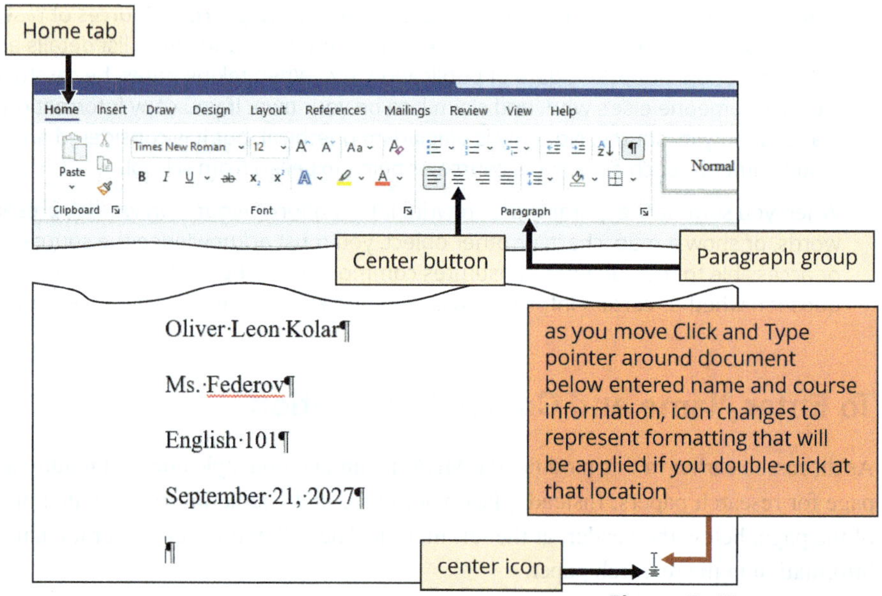

Figure 2–15

Q&A What are the other icons that appear in the Click and Type pointer?
A left-align icon appears to the right of the I-beam when the Click and Type pointer is in certain locations on the left side of the document window. A right-align icon appears to the left of the I-beam when the Click and Type pointer is in certain locations on the right side of the document window.

What if I am using a touch screen?
Tap the Center button (Home tab | Paragraph group) and then proceed to Step 3 because the Click and Type feature does not work with a touch screen.

2

- Double-click to center the paragraph mark and insertion point between the left and right margins.

3

- Type **Smartphone Biometrics** as the paper title and then press ENTER to position the insertion point on the next line (Figure 2–16).

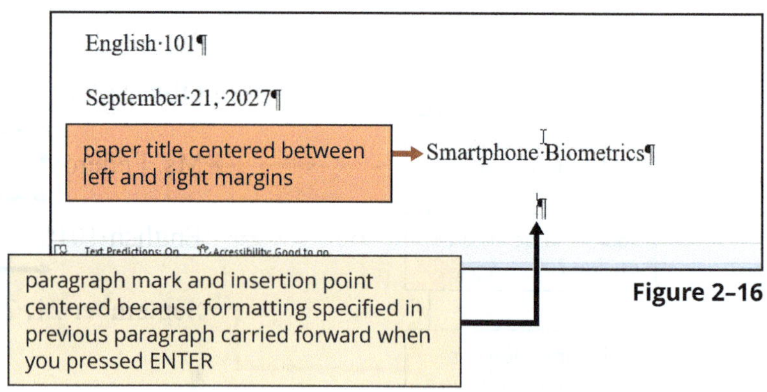

Figure 2–16

Keyboard Shortcuts for Formatting Text

Word has many **keyboard shortcuts**, sometimes called shortcut keys or keyboard key combinations, which are a key or combination of keys you press to access a feature or perform a command, instead of using a mouse or touch gestures. Many users find keyboard shortcuts a convenience while typing. Table 2–1 lists the common keyboard shortcuts for formatting characters. Table 2–2 lists common keyboard shortcuts for formatting paragraphs.

Table 2–1: Keyboard Shortcuts for Formatting Characters

Character Formatting Task	Keyboard Shortcut
All capital letters	CTRL+SHIFT+A
Bold	CTRL+B
Case of letters	SHIFT+F3
Decrease font size	CTRL+SHIFT+<
Decrease font size 1 point	CTRL+[
Double-underline	CTRL+SHIFT+D
Increase font size	CTRL+SHIFT+>
Increase font size 1 point	CTRL+]
Italic	CTRL+I
Remove character formatting (plain text)	CTRL+SPACEBAR
Small uppercase letters	CTRL+SHIFT+K
Subscript	CTRL+EQUAL SIGN
Superscript	CTRL+SHIFT+PLUS SIGN
Underline	CTRL+U
Underline words, not spaces	CTRL+SHIFT+W

Table 2–2: Keyboard Shortcuts for Formatting Paragraphs

Paragraph Formatting Task	Keyboard Shortcut
1.5 line spacing	CTRL+5
Add/remove one line above paragraph	CTRL+0 (ZERO)
Center paragraph	CTRL+E
Decrease paragraph indent	CTRL+SHIFT+M
Double-space lines	CTRL+2
Hanging indent	CTRL+T
Increase paragraph indent	CTRL+M
Justify paragraph	CTRL+J
Left-align paragraph	CTRL+L
Remove hanging indent	CTRL+SHIFT+T
Remove paragraph formatting	CTRL+Q
Right-align paragraph	CTRL+R
Single-space lines	CTRL+1

To Format Text Using a Keyboard Shortcut

The paragraphs below the paper title should be left-aligned instead of centered. Thus, the next step is to left-align the paragraph below the paper title. When your fingers already are on the keyboard, you may prefer using keyboard shortcuts to format text as you type it.

The following steps left-align a paragraph using the keyboard shortcut CTRL+L. (A notation such as CTRL+L means to press the letter L on the keyboard while holding down CTRL.)

1. Press CTRL+L to left-align the current paragraph, that is, the paragraph containing the insertion point (shown in Figure 2–17).

Q&A Why would I use a keyboard shortcut instead of the ribbon to format text?
Switching between the mouse and the keyboard takes time. If your hands are already on the keyboard, use a keyboard shortcut. If your hand is on the mouse, use the ribbon.

2. Save the research paper on your hard drive, OneDrive, or other storage location using the file name, SC_WD_2_SmartphoneBiometricsPaper.

BTW
Keyboard Shortcuts
To see a complete list of keyboard shortcuts in Word, press F1 to open the Help pane, type **keyboard shortcuts** in the Search box in the Word Help pane, press ENTER, and then click the 'Keyboard shortcuts in Word' link. To create a Word document with all keyboard shortcuts, click the 'Word 2016 for Windows keyboard shortcuts' link in the Help pane to open a Downloads window. Click the Download button or link in the Downloads window, click the link to open a Word document with all keyboard shortcuts, and then, if necessary, click the Enable Editing button. You can print or save the Word document. When finished, exit Word and then close the Help pane.

Q&A Why should I save the research paper at this time?
You have performed many tasks while creating this research paper and do not want to risk losing work completed thus far.

To Display the Rulers

According to the MLA documentation style, the first line of each paragraph in the research paper is to be indented one-half inch from the left margin. Although you can use a dialog box to indent paragraphs, Word provides a quicker way through the **horizontal ruler**, which is a ruler that appears below the ribbon in the document window in Print Layout and other views. Word also provides a **vertical ruler** that appears along the left edge of the document window in Print Layout view. The following step displays the rulers. **Why?** You want to use the horizontal ruler to indent paragraphs.

1

- If necessary, scroll the document so that the research paper title is at the top of the document window.
- Click View on the ribbon to display the View tab.
- If the rulers are not displayed, click the Ruler check box (View tab | Show group) to place a check mark in the check box and display the horizontal and vertical rulers on the screen (Figure 2–17).

Q&A What tasks can I accomplish using the rulers?
You can use the horizontal and vertical rulers, usually simply called **rulers**, to indent paragraphs, set tab stops, change page margins, adjust column widths, and measure or place objects.

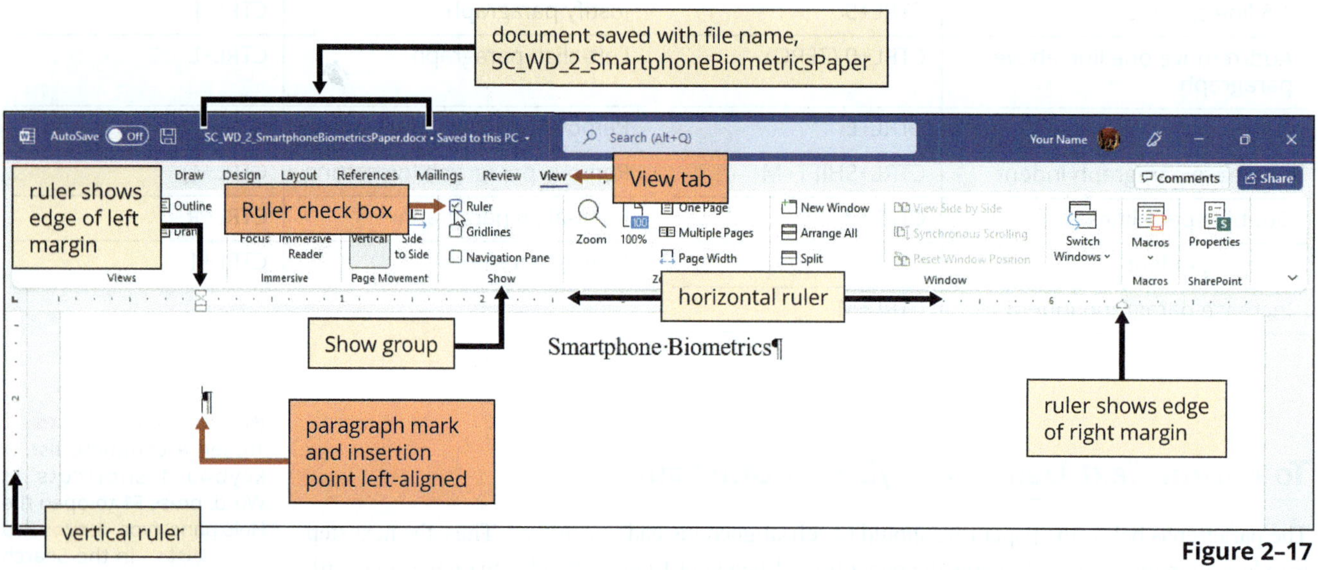

Figure 2–17

To First-Line Indent Paragraphs

If you are using a mouse, you can use the horizontal ruler to indent just the first line of a paragraph, which is called a **first-line indent**. The left margin on the ruler contains two triangles above a square. The 'First Line Indent' marker is the top triangle at the 0" mark on the ruler (shown in Figure 2–18). The bottom triangle, which is the Hanging Indent marker, is discussed later in this module. The small square at the 0" mark is the Left Indent marker. The Left Indent marker allows you to change the entire left margin, whereas the 'First Line Indent' marker indents only the first line of the paragraph.

The following steps first-line indent paragraphs in the research paper. **Why?** The first line of each paragraph in the research paper is to be indented one-half inch from the left margin, according to the MLA documentation style.

1

- With the insertion point on the paragraph mark below the research paper title, point to the 'First Line Indent' marker on the ruler (Figure 2–18).

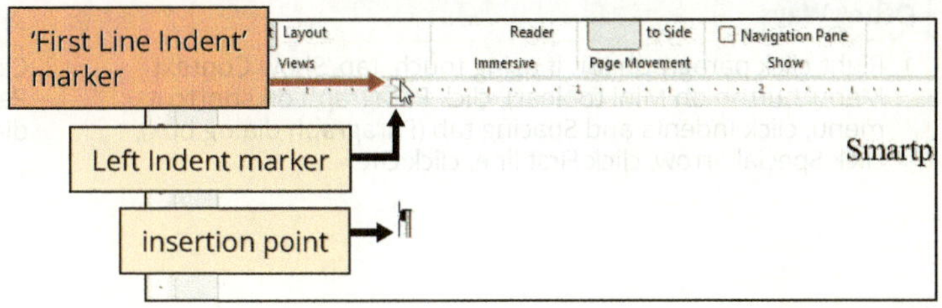

Figure 2–18

2

- Drag the 'First Line Indent' marker to the .5" mark on the ruler to display a vertical dotted line in the document window, which indicates the proposed indent location of the first line of the paragraph (Figure 2–19).

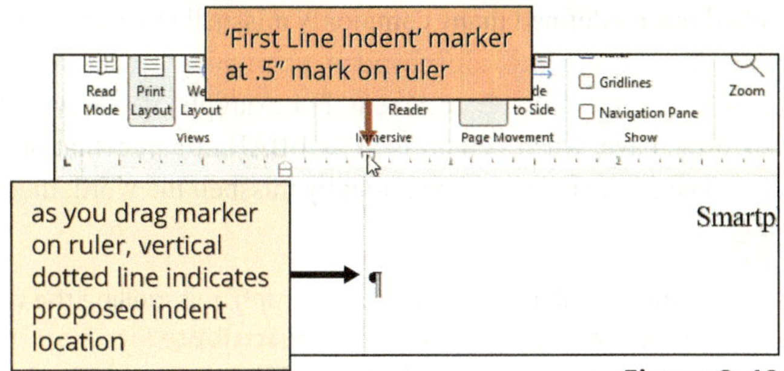

Figure 2–19

3

- Release the mouse button to place the 'First Line Indent' marker at the .5" mark on the ruler, or one-half inch from the left margin (Figure 2–20).

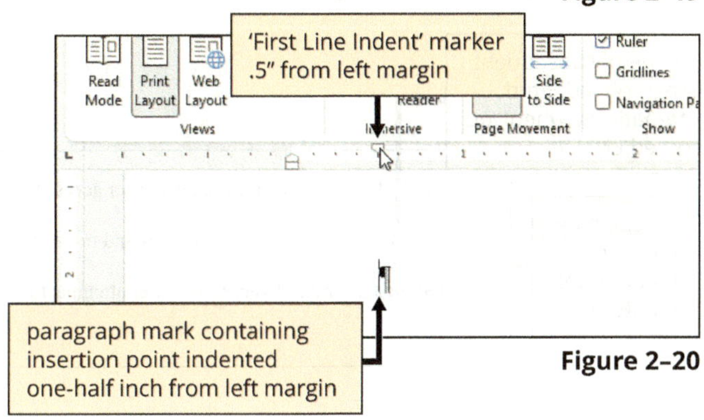

Figure 2–20

Q&A What if I am using a touch screen?
If you are using a touch screen, you cannot drag the 'First Line Indent' marker and must follow these steps instead: tap the Paragraph Dialog Box Launcher (Home tab or Layout tab | Paragraph group) to display the Paragraph dialog box, tap the Indents and Spacing tab (Paragraph dialog box), tap the Special arrow, tap First line, and then tap OK.

4

- Type **Biometrics is the technology of checking a person's identity by checking a unique personal attribute. These attributes can be physical, such as a fingerprint, or behavioral, such as a voice. Today's smartphones can give user access through biometrics.** and notice that Word automatically indents the first line of the paragraph by one-half inch.

5

- Press ENTER and notice that Word automatically indents the first line of the next paragraph by one-half inch (Figure 2–21).

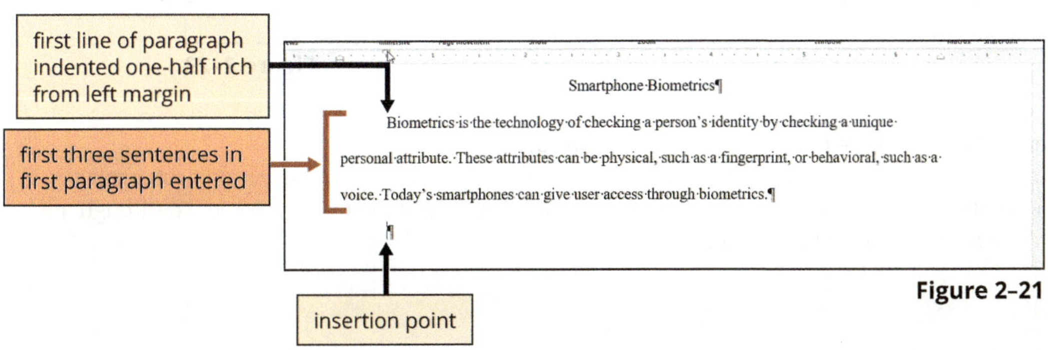

Figure 2–21

Q&A Will I have to set a first-line indent for each paragraph in the paper?
No. Each time you press ENTER, paragraph formatting in the previous paragraph carries forward to the next paragraph. Thus, once you set the first-line indent, its format carries forward automatically to each subsequent paragraph you type.

Other Ways

1. Right-click paragraph (or, if using touch, tap 'Show Context Menu' button on Mini toolbar), click Paragraph on shortcut menu, click Indents and Spacing tab (Paragraph dialog box), click Special arrow, click First line, click OK
2. Click Paragraph Dialog Box Launcher (Home tab or Layout tab | Paragraph group), click Indents and Spacing tab (Paragraph dialog box), click Special arrow, click First line, click OK

To AutoCorrect as You Type

Word has predefined many commonly misspelled words, which it automatically corrects for you. **Why?** As you type, you may make typing, spelling, capitalization, or grammar errors. Word's AutoCorrect feature automatically corrects these kinds of errors as you type them in the document. For example, if you type the characters, ahve, Word automatically changes it to the correct spelling, have, when you press SPACEBAR or a punctuation mark key, such as a period or comma.

The following steps intentionally misspell the word, their, as thier, to illustrate the AutoCorrect feature.

1

- Type the beginning of the next paragraph, misspelling the word, their, as follows: **Biometric technology captures and translates a physical or behavioral attribute into a stored digital format. Every time a user attempts to access the device, it captures thier** (Figure 2–22).

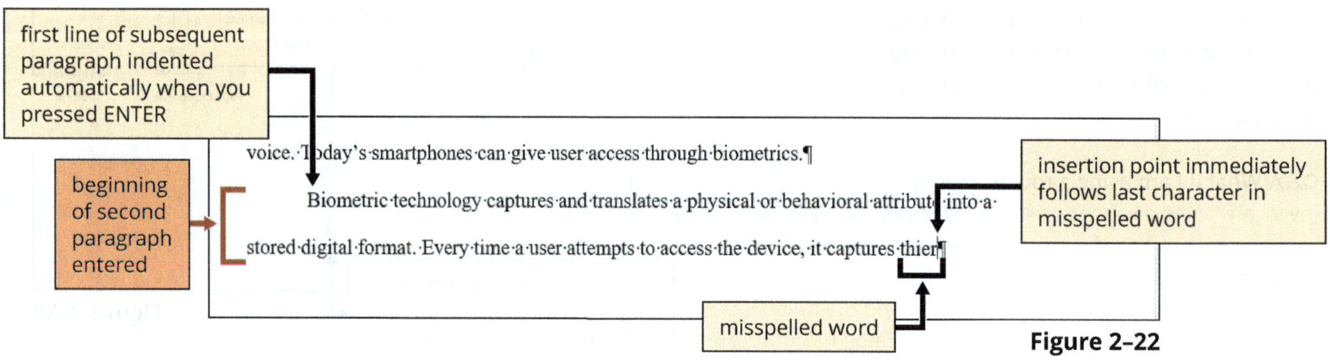

Figure 2–22

2

- Press SPACEBAR and watch Word automatically correct the misspelled word.
- Type the rest of the sentence (Figure 2–23): **personal attribute in that moment and compares it to the stored attribute.**

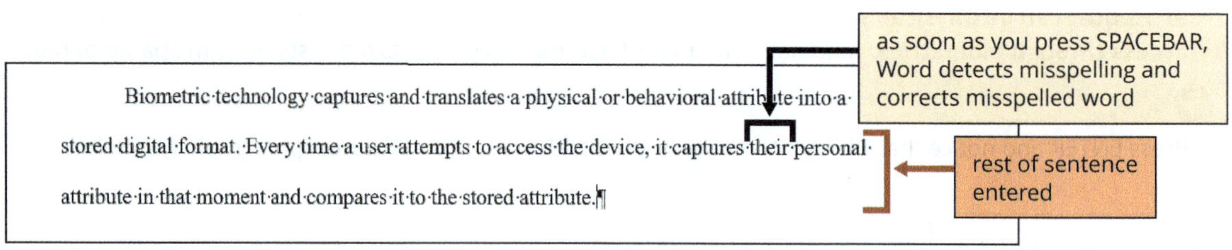

Figure 2–23

Q&A What if I do not want to keep a change made automatically by Word?
If you notice the automatically corrected text immediately, you can press CTRL+Z or click the Undo button (Home tab | Undo group) to undo the automatic correction. If you do not notice it immediately, you can undo a correction through the AutoCorrect Options button shown in the next set of steps.

To Use the AutoCorrect Options Button

The following steps illustrate the AutoCorrect Options button and menu. **Why?** If you are using a mouse, when you position the pointer on text that Word automatically corrected, a small blue box appears below the text. If you point to the small blue box, Word displays the AutoCorrect Options button. When you click the **AutoCorrect Options button**, which appears below the automatically corrected text, Word displays a menu that allows you to undo a correction or change how Word handles future automatic corrections of this type.

1

- Position the pointer in the text automatically corrected by Word (the word, their, in this case) to display a small blue box below the automatically corrected word (Figure 2–24).

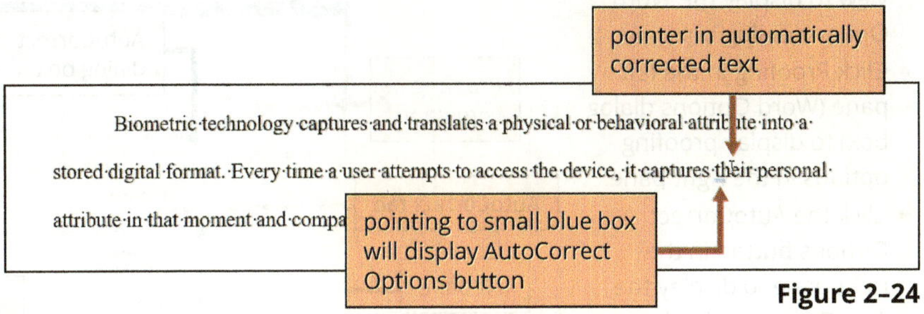

Figure 2–24

2

- Point to the small blue box to display the AutoCorrect Options button.
- Click the AutoCorrect Options button to display the AutoCorrect Options menu (Figure 2–25).

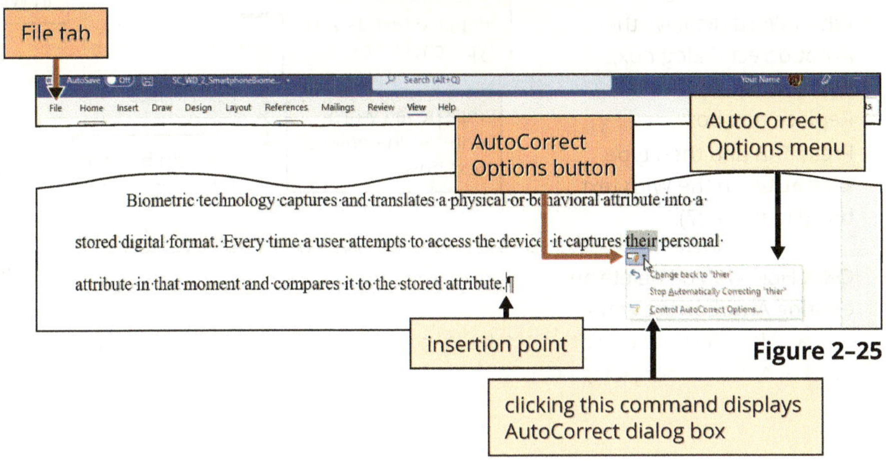

Figure 2–25

3

- Press ESC to remove the AutoCorrect Options menu from the screen.

Q&A Do I need to remove the AutoCorrect Options button from the screen?
No. When you move the pointer, the AutoCorrect Options button will disappear from the screen. If, for some reason, you wanted to remove the AutoCorrect Options button from the screen, you could press ESC a second time.

To Create an AutoCorrect Entry

The next steps create an AutoCorrect entry. **Why?** In addition to the predefined list of AutoCorrect spelling, capitalization, and grammar errors, you can create your own AutoCorrect entries to add to the list. For example, if you tend to mistype the word attribute as atribute, you should create an AutoCorrect entry for it.

1

- Click File on the ribbon (shown in Figure 2–25) to open Backstage view (Figure 2–26).

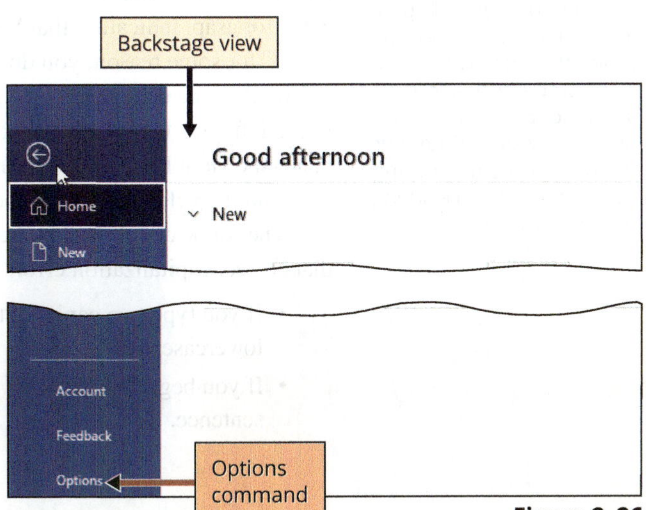

Figure 2–26

2

- Click Options in Backstage view to display the Word Options dialog box.
- Click Proofing in the left pane (Word Options dialog box) to display proofing options in the right pane.
- Click the AutoCorrect Options button in the right pane to display the AutoCorrect dialog box.
- When Word displays the AutoCorrect dialog box, type **atribute** in the Replace text box.
- Press TAB and then type **attribute** in the With text box (Figure 2–27).

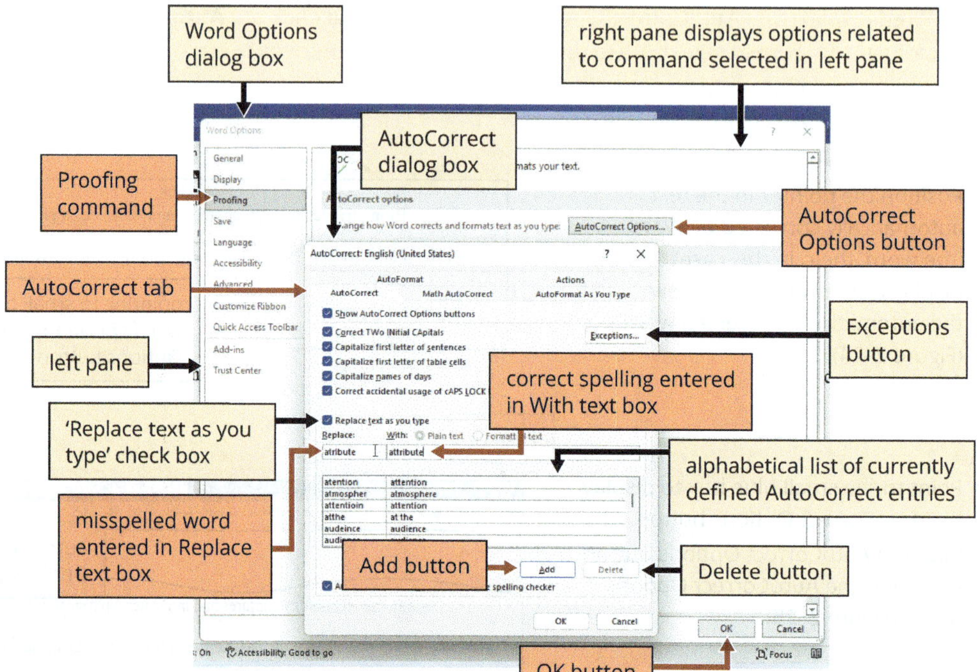

Figure 2–27

Q&A How would I delete an existing AutoCorrect entry?
You would select the entry to be deleted in the list of defined entries in the AutoCorrect dialog box and then click the Delete button (AutoCorrect dialog box).

3

- Click the Add button (AutoCorrect dialog box) to add the entry alphabetically to the list of words to correct automatically as you type. (If your dialog box displays a Replace button instead, click it and then click the Yes button in the Microsoft Word dialog box to replace the previously defined entry.)
- Click OK (AutoCorrect dialog box) to close the dialog box.
- Click OK (Word Options dialog box) to close the dialog box.

BTW
Word Help
At any time while using Word, you can find answers to questions and display information about various topics through Word Help. Used properly, this form of assistance can increase your productivity and reduce your frustrations by minimizing the time you spend learning how to use Word.

The AutoCorrect Dialog Box

In addition to creating AutoCorrect entries for words you commonly misspell or mistype, you can create entries for abbreviations, codes, and so on. For example, you could create an AutoCorrect entry for asap, indicating that Word should replace this text with the phrase, as soon as possible.

If, for some reason, you do not want Word to correct automatically as you type, you can turn off the Replace text as you type feature by clicking Options in Backstage view, clicking Proofing in the left pane (Word Options dialog box), clicking the AutoCorrect Options button in the right pane (shown in Figure 2–27), removing the check mark from the 'Replace text as you type' check box, and then clicking OK in each open dialog box.

The AutoCorrect sheet in the AutoCorrect dialog box (Figure 2–27) contains other check boxes that correct capitalization errors if the check boxes are selected:

- If you type two capital letters in a row, such as TH, Word makes the second letter lowercase, Th.
- If you begin a sentence with a lowercase letter, Word capitalizes the first letter of the sentence.

- If you begin text in a table cell with a lowercase letter, Word capitalizes the first letter in the cell. (Tables are discussed in Module 3.)
- If you type the name of a day in lowercase letters, such as tuesday, Word capitalizes the first letter in the name of the day, Tuesday.
- If you leave CAPS LOCK on and begin a new sentence, Word corrects the typing and turns off CAPS LOCK.

If you do not want Word to perform any of these corrections automatically, simply remove the check mark from the appropriate check box in the AutoCorrect dialog box.

Sometimes, you do not want Word to AutoCorrect a particular word or phrase. For example, you may use WD. as a code in your documents. Because Word automatically capitalizes the first letter of a sentence, the character you enter following the period will be capitalized (in the previous sentence, it would capitalize the letter a in the word, as). To allow the code, WD., to be entered into a document and still leave the AutoCorrect feature turned on, you would set an exception. To set an exception to an AutoCorrect rule, click Options in Backstage view, click Proofing in the left pane (Word Options dialog box), click the AutoCorrect Options button in the right pane, click the Exceptions button (shown in Figure 2–27), click the appropriate tab in the AutoCorrect Exceptions dialog box, type the exception entry in the text box, click the Add button, click the Close button (AutoCorrect Exceptions dialog box), and then click OK in each of the remaining dialog boxes.

BTW
Spacing after Punctuation
Because word processing documents use variable character fonts, it often is difficult to determine in a printed document how many times someone has pressed the SPACEBAR between sentences. Thus, the rule is to press the SPACEBAR only once after periods, colons, and other punctuation marks.

Citations

Both the MLA and APA guidelines suggest the use of in-text citations (placed at the end of a sentence) instead of footnoting each source of material in a paper. These in-text citations (sometimes called parenthetical references) guide the reader to the end of the paper for complete information about the source.

Word provides tools to assist you with inserting citations in a paper and later generating a list of sources from the citations. With a documentation style selected, Word automatically formats the citations and list of sources according to that style. The process for adding citations in Word is as follows:

1. Change the documentation style, if necessary.
2. Insert a citation placeholder.
3. Enter the source information for the citation.

You can combine Steps 2 and 3, where you insert the citation placeholder and enter the source information at once. Or, you can insert the citation placeholder as you write and then enter the source information for the citation at a later time. While creating the research paper in this module, you will use both methods.

BTW
The Ribbon and Screen Resolution
Word may change how the groups and buttons within the groups appear on the ribbon, depending on the computer or mobile device's screen resolution. Thus, your ribbon may look different from the ones in this book if you are using a screen resolution other than 1366 × 768.

To Change the Bibliography Style

The first step in inserting a citation is to be sure the citations and sources will be formatted using the correct documentation style, called the bibliography style in Word. **Why?** You want to ensure that Word is using the MLA documentation style for this paper. The following steps change the specified documentation style.

1

- Click References on the ribbon to display the References tab.
- Click the Style arrow (References tab | Citations & Bibliography group) to display the Style gallery, which lists predefined documentation styles (Figure 2–28).

2

- Click 'MLA Seventh Edition' in the Style gallery to change the documentation style to MLA.

Q&A What if I am using a different edition of a documentation style shown in the Bibliography Style gallery?

Select the closest one and then, if necessary, perform necessary edits before submitting the paper. As of this writing, for example, the MLA documentation style is in its tenth edition. Later in this module, you will edit two of the works to meet requirements of this later edition.

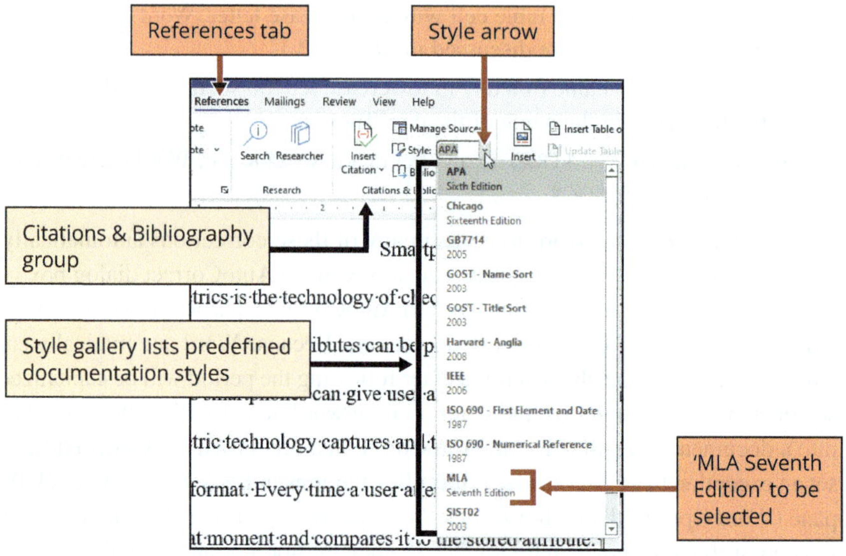

Figure 2–28

Consider This

What details are required for sources?

During your research, be sure to record essential publication information about each of your sources. Following is a sample list of types of required information for the MLA documentation style:

- Book: full name of author(s), complete title of book, edition (if available), volume (if available), publication city (for a pre-1900 work), publisher name, and publication year
- Magazine: full name of author(s), complete title of article, magazine title, issue number (if available), date of magazine, and page numbers of article, if applicable
- Website: full name of author(s), title of website, publication date, if applicable, and date viewed

To Insert a Citation for a New Source

With the documentation style selected, the next task is to insert a citation at the location of the insertion point and enter the source information for the citation. You can accomplish these steps at once by instructing Word to add a new source. The following steps add a new source for a magazine (periodical) article on the web. **Why?** The material preceding the insertion point was summarized from an online magazine article.

1

- Press SPACEBAR. Type the next sentence in the paper up to the location of the in-text citation: **If the comparison of the live attribute to the stored one yields a match, the device gives access to the user; otherwise, it denies access** (as shown in Figure 2–29).

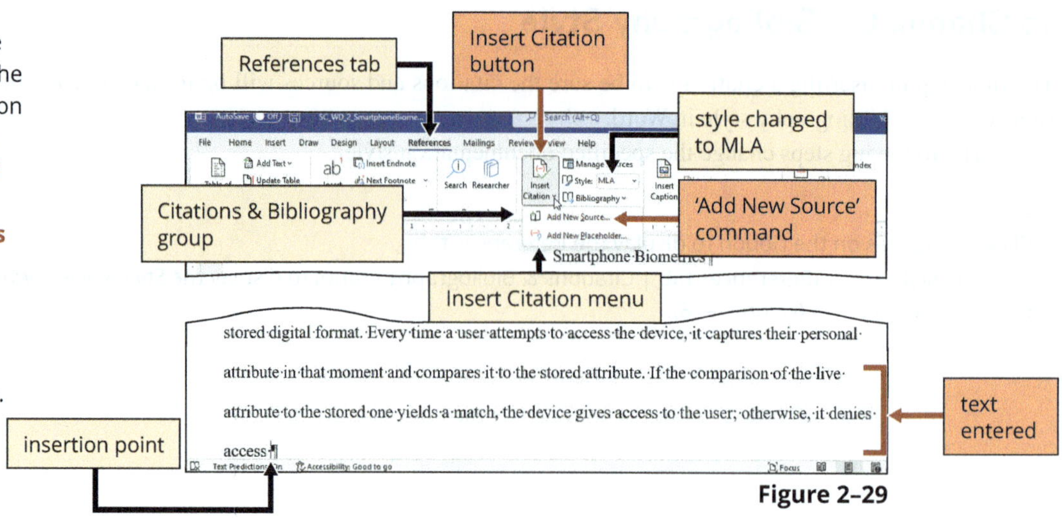

Figure 2–29

- Press SPACEBAR and then click the Insert Citation button (References tab | Citations & Bibliography group) to display the Insert Citation menu (Figure 2–29).

2

- Click 'Add New Source' on the Insert Citation menu to display the Create Source dialog box (Figure 2–30).

Q&A What are the Bibliography Fields in the Create Source dialog box?
A **field** is a code that serves as a placeholder for data whose contents can change. You enter data in some fields; Word supplies data for others. In this case, you enter the contents of the fields for a particular source, for example, the author name in the Author field.

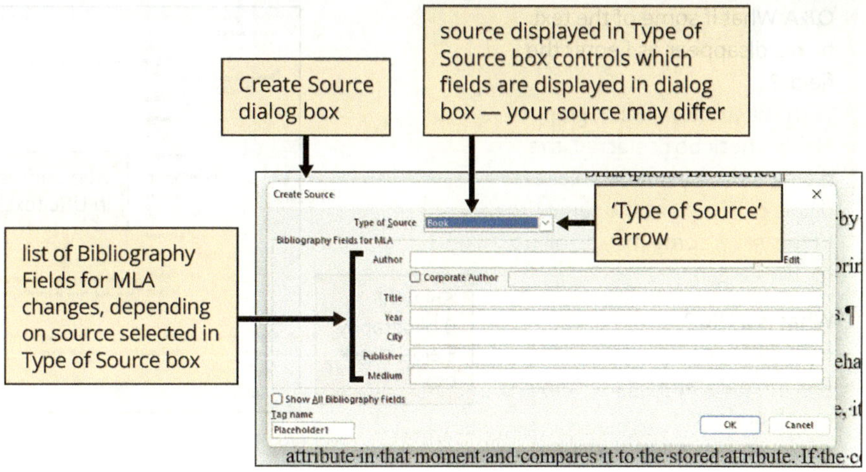

Figure 2–30

- **Experiment:** Click the 'Type of Source' arrow and then click one of the source types in the list, so that you can see how the list of fields changes to reflect the type of source you selected.

3

- If necessary, click the 'Type of Source' arrow (Create Source dialog box) and then click 'Article in a Periodical', so that the list shows fields required for a magazine (periodical).
- Click the Author text box. Type **Nagarkar, Pauline Adrianna** as the author.
- Click the Title text box. Type **A Look Inside the Biometrics** as the article title.
- Press TAB and then type **Monthly Security Review** as the periodical title.
- Press TAB and then type **2027** as the year.
- Press TAB and then type **May** as the month (Figure 2–31).

Q&A Should the month names ever be abbreviated?
The MLA documentation style abbreviates all months, except May, June, and July, when they appear in a source.

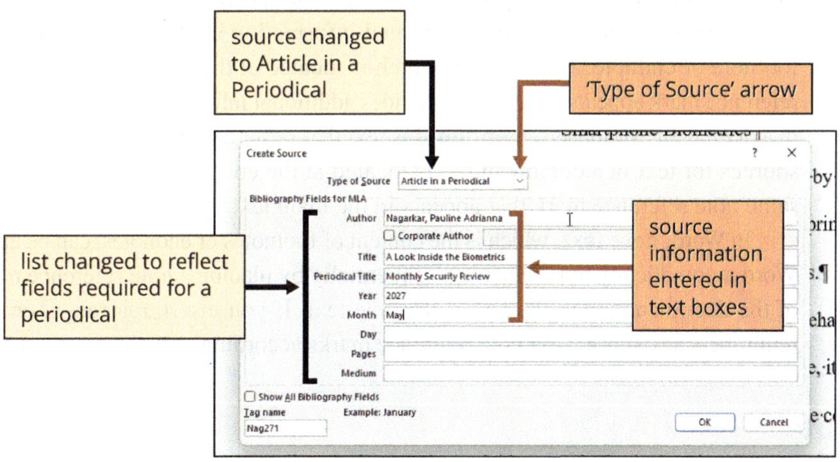

Figure 2–31

4

- Place a check mark in the 'Show All Bibliography Fields' check box so that Word displays all fields available for the selected source, including the URL field.
- If necessary, scroll to the bottom of the Bibliography Fields list to the URL field.
- Click the URL text box and then type **www.monthlysecurityreview.com** as the web address (Figure 2–32).

Q&A What if some of the text boxes disappear as I enter the fields?

With the 'Show All Bibliography Fields' check box selected, the dialog box may not be able to display all fields at the same time. In this case, some may scroll up off the screen.

What is a URL?

URL, which stands for Uniform Resource Locator, is the same as a web address.

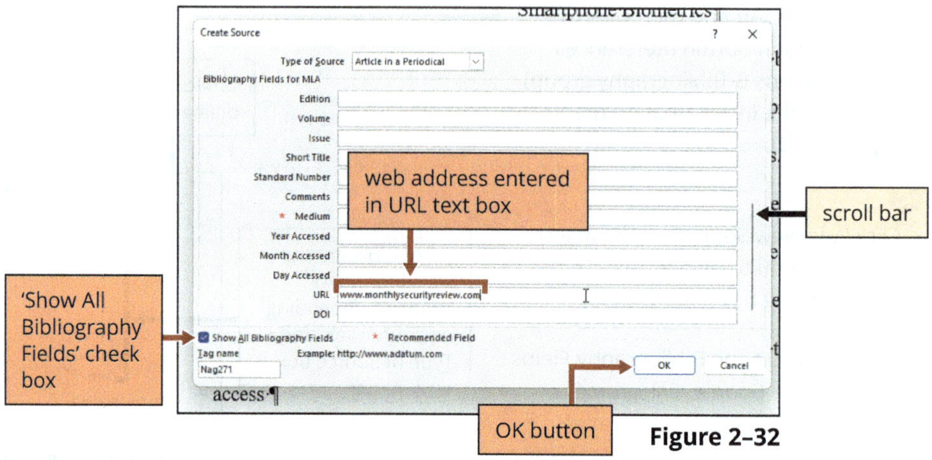

Figure 2–32

5

- Click OK to close the dialog box, create the source, and insert the citation in the document at the location of the insertion point.
- If necessary, press END to move the insertion point to the end of the line, which also will deselect the citation.
- Press the PERIOD key to end the sentence (Figure 2–33).

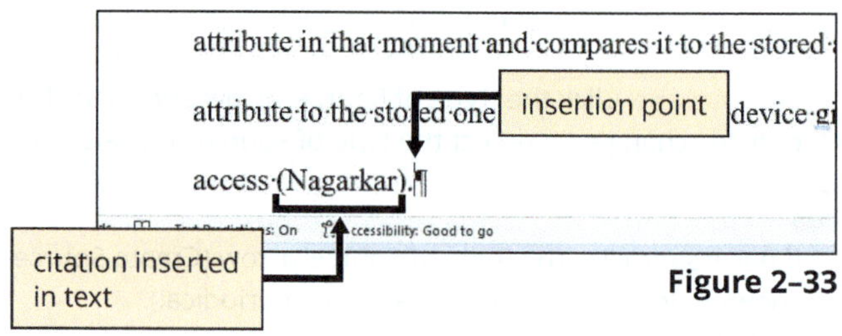

Figure 2–33

BTW

Organizing Files and Folders

You should organize and store files in folders so that you easily can find the files later. For example, if you are taking an introductory technology class called CIS 101, a good practice would be to save all Word files in a Word folder in a CIS 101 folder.

Footnotes

As discussed earlier in this module, notes are optional in the MLA documentation style. If used, content notes elaborate on points discussed in the paper, and bibliographic notes direct the reader to evaluations of statements in a source or provide a means for identifying multiple sources. The MLA documentation style specifies that a superscript (raised number or letter) be used for a **note reference mark** to signal that additional information is offered in a note that exists either as a footnote or endnote. A **footnote**, which is located at the bottom of the page on which the note reference mark appears, is text that provides additional information or acknowledges sources for text in a document. Similarly, an **endnote** is text that provides additional information or acknowledges sources for text in a document but is located at the end of a document (or section) and uses the same note reference mark that appears in the main text.

In Word, **note text**, which is the content of footnotes or endnotes, can be any length and format. Word automatically numbers notes sequentially by placing a note reference mark both in the body of the document and to the left of the note text. If you insert, rearrange, or remove notes, Word renumbers any subsequent note reference marks according to their new sequence in the document.

To Insert a Footnote

The following steps insert a note reference mark in the document at the location of the insertion point and at the location where the footnote text will be typed. **Why?** You will insert a content note about the possible continued need for a password, which you want to position as a footnote.

1

- With the insertion point at the end of the second paragraph (as shown in Figure 2–33), press ENTER and then type the first sentence in the third paragraph of the paper (shown in Figure 2–34): **With current smartphones integrating advanced technologies, such as reliable touch screens and high-quality cameras, these devices often include built-in biometric capability.**

- Press SPACEBAR and then type the second sentence in the third paragraph of the paper, up to the location for the footnote (Figure 2–34): **Users can access their smartphones with personal attributes instead of traditional methods, such as passwords or PINs (personal identification numbers).**

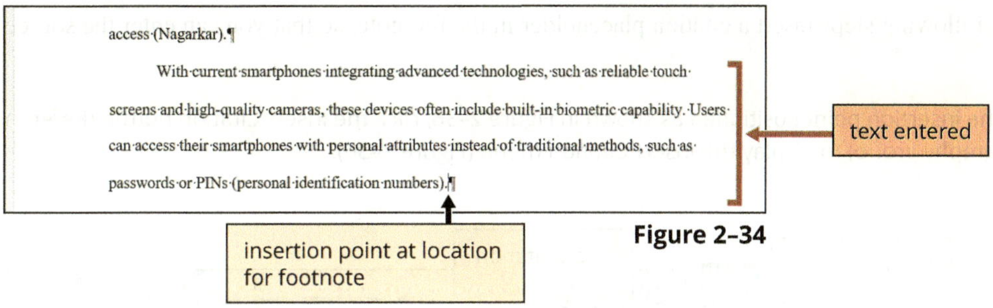

Figure 2–34

2

- With the insertion point positioned at the location for the footnote (as shown in Figure 2–34), click the Insert Footnote button (References tab | Footnotes group) to display a note reference mark (a superscripted 1) in two places: (1) in the document window at the location of the insertion point and (2) at the bottom of the page where the footnote text will be positioned, just below a separator line (Figure 2–35).

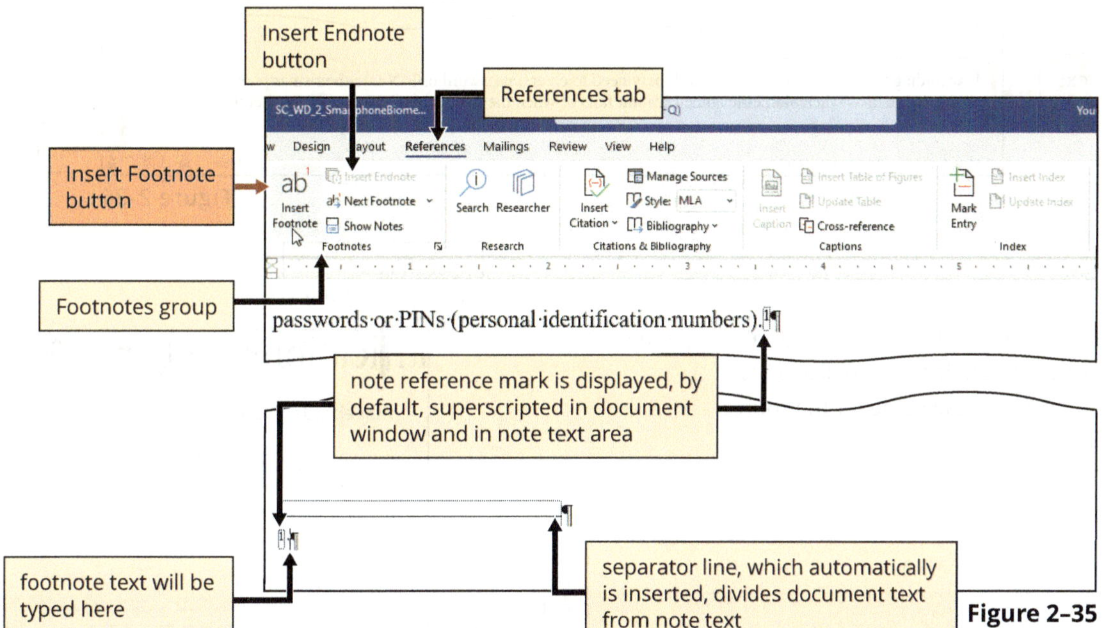

Figure 2–35

Q&A What if I wanted notes to be positioned as endnotes instead of as footnotes?
You would click the Insert Endnote button (References tab | Footnotes group), which places the separator line and the endnote text at the end of the document, instead of the bottom of the page containing the reference.

3

- Type the footnote text up to the citation (shown in Figure 2–36): **According to Jervis and Rivas, users still may need to enter a password or PIN into their smartphone in certain situations, such as when biometric authentication fails or when the device requires a backup authentication method** and then press SPACEBAR.

Other Ways

1. Press ALT+CTRL+F

To Insert a Citation Placeholder

Earlier in this module, you inserted a citation and its source at once. In Word, you also can insert a citation without entering the source information. **Why?** Sometimes, you may not have the source information readily available and would prefer to enter it at a later time.

The following steps insert a citation placeholder in the footnote, so that you can enter the source information later.

1

- With the insertion point positioned as shown in Figure 2–36, click the Insert Citation button (References tab | Citations & Bibliography group) to display the Insert Citation menu (Figure 2–36).

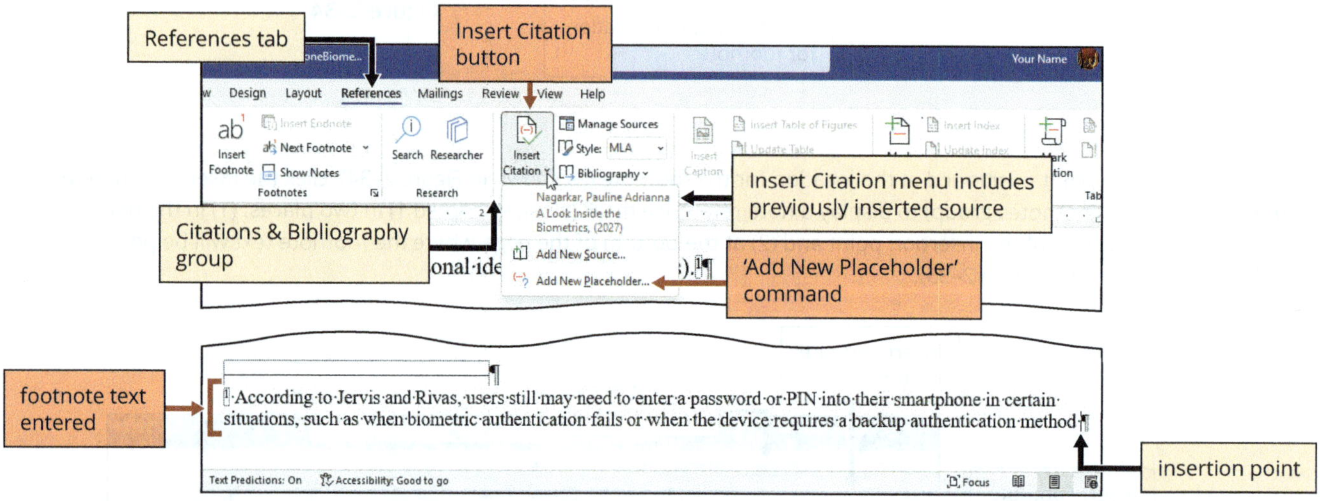

Figure 2–36

2

- Click 'Add New Placeholder' on the Insert Citation menu to display the Placeholder Name dialog box.
- Type **Jervis** as the tag name for the source (Figure 2–37).

Q&A What is a tag name?

A tag name is an identifier that links a citation to a source. Word automatically creates a tag name when you enter a source. When you create a citation placeholder, enter a meaningful tag name, which will appear in the citation placeholder until you edit the source.

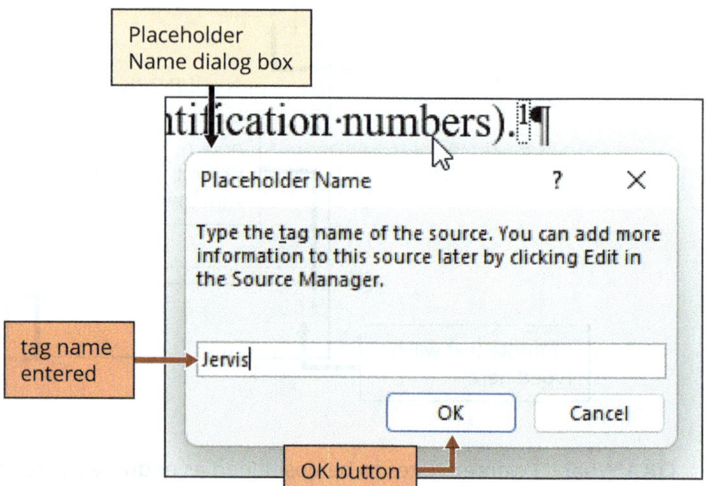

Figure 2–37

3

- Click OK (Placeholder Name dialog box) to close the dialog box and insert the entered tag name in the citation placeholder in the document (shown in Figure 2–38).
- Press the PERIOD key to end the sentence.

Q&A What if the citation is in the wrong location?

Click the citation to select it and then drag the citation tab (on the upper-left corner of the selected citation) to any location in the document.

Footnote Text Style

When you insert a footnote, Word formats it using the Footnote Text style, which does not adhere to the MLA documentation style. For example, notice in Figure 2–36 that the footnote text is single-spaced, left-aligned, and a smaller font size than the text in the body of the research paper. According to the MLA documentation style, notes should be formatted like all other paragraphs in the paper.

You could change the paragraph formatting of the footnote text to first-line indent and double-spaced and then change the font size from 10 to 12 point. If you use this technique, however, you will need to change the format of the footnote text for each footnote you enter in the document.

A more efficient technique is to modify the format of the Footnote Text style so that every footnote you enter in the document will use the formats defined in this style.

BTW

Style Formats

To see the formats assigned to a particular style in a document, click the Styles Dialog Box Launcher (Home tab | Styles group) and then click the Style Inspector button in the Styles pane. Position the insertion point in the style in the document and then point to the Paragraph formatting or Text level formatting areas in the Style Inspector pane to display a ScreenTip describing formats assigned to the location of the insertion point. You also can click the Reveal Formatting button in the Style Inspector pane or press SHIFT+F1 to open the Reveal Formatting pane.

To Modify a Style Using a Shortcut Menu

The Footnote Text style specifies left-aligned single-spaced paragraphs with a 10-point font size for text. The following steps modify the Footnote Text style. **Why?** To meet MLA documentation style, the footnotes will be double-spaced with a first-line indent and a 12-point font size for text.

1

- Right-click the note text in the footnote to display a shortcut menu related to footnotes (Figure 2–38).

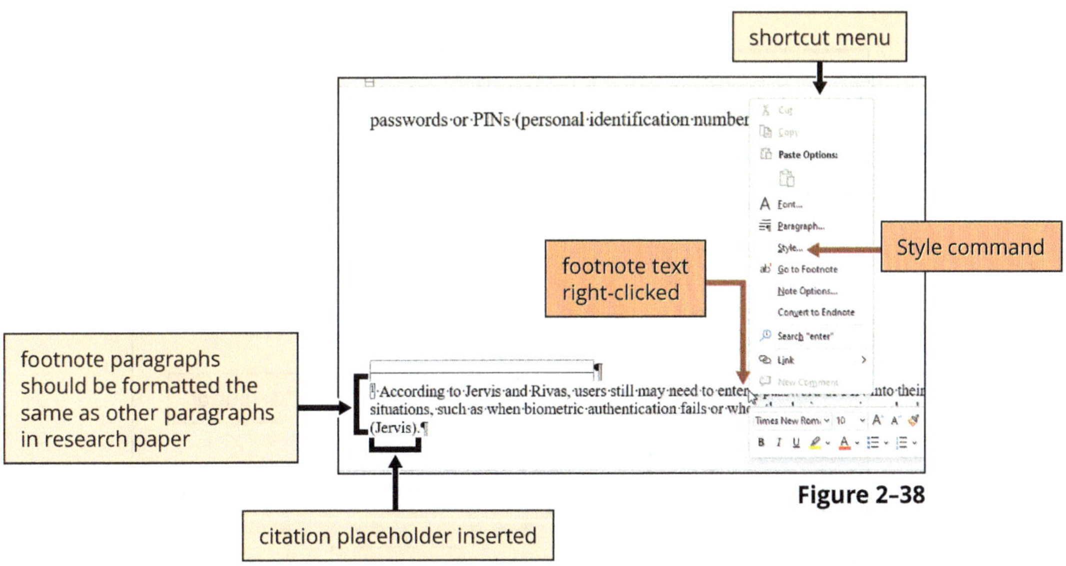

Figure 2–38

2

- Click Style on the shortcut menu to display the Style dialog box. If necessary, click the Category arrow, click All styles in the Category list, and then click Footnote Text in the Styles list to select the style to modify.
- Click the Modify button (Style dialog box) to display the Modify Style dialog box.
- Click the Font Size arrow (Modify Style dialog box) to display the Font Size list and then click 12 in the Font Size list to change the font size.

- Click the Double Space button to change the line spacing.
- Click the Format button to display the Format menu (Figure 2–39).

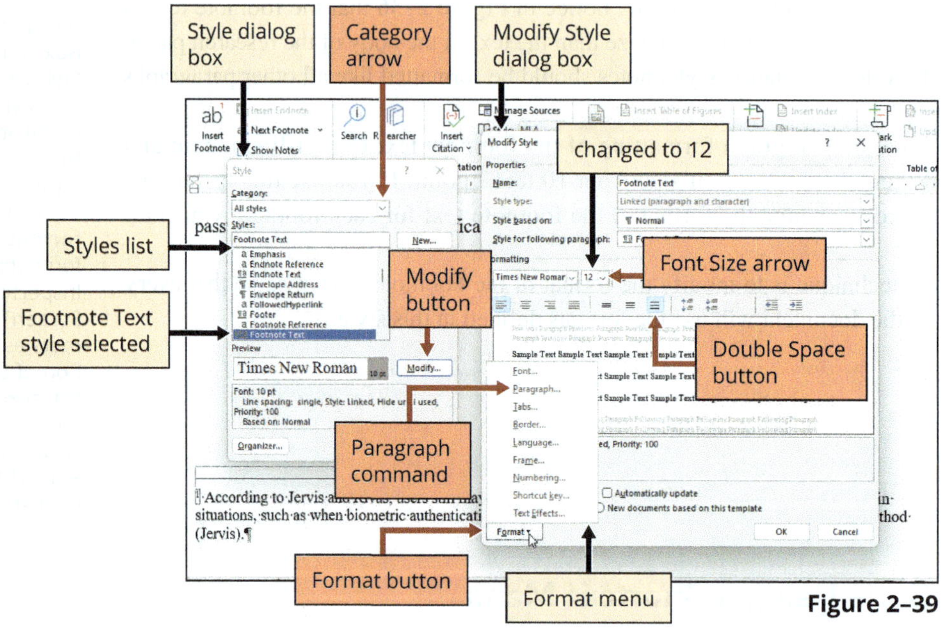

Figure 2–39

3

- Click Paragraph on the Format menu (Modify Style dialog box) to display the Paragraph dialog box.
- Click the Special arrow in the Indentation area (Paragraph dialog box) and then click First line (Figure 2–40).

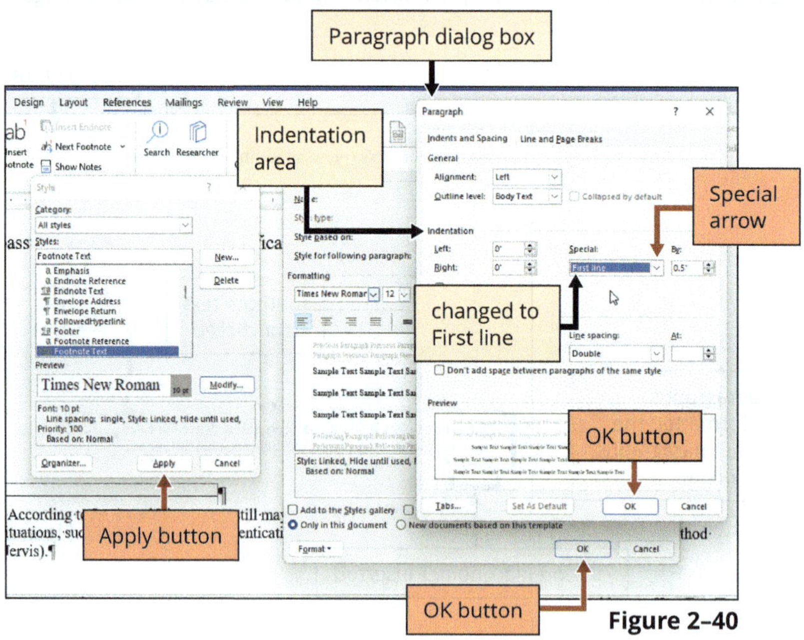

Figure 2–40

4

- Click OK (Paragraph dialog box) to close the dialog box.
- Click OK (Modify Style dialog box) to close the dialog box.
- Click the Apply button (Style dialog box) to apply the style changes to the footnote text (Figure 2–41).

Q&A Will all footnotes use this modified style?

Yes. Any future footnotes entered in the document will use a 12-point font with the paragraphs first-line indented and double-spaced.

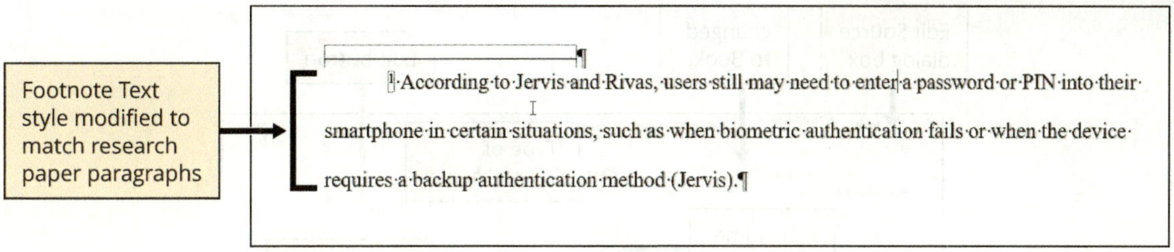

Figure 2–41

Other Ways

1. Click Styles Dialog Box Launcher (Home tab | Styles group), point to style name in list, click style name arrow, click Modify, change settings (Modify Style dialog box), click OK
2. Click Styles Dialog Box Launcher (Home tab | Styles group), click Manage Styles button in pane, select style name in list, click Modify button (Manage Styles dialog box), change settings (Modify Style dialog box), click OK in each dialog box

To Edit a Source

When you typed the footnote text for this research paper, you inserted a citation placeholder for the source. The following steps edit a source. **Why?** Assume you now have the source information and are ready to enter it.

1

- Click somewhere in the citation placeholder to be edited, in this case (Jervis), to select the citation placeholder.
- Click the Citation Options arrow to display the Citation Options menu (Figure 2–42).

Q&A What is the purpose of the tab to the left of the selected citation?
If, for some reason, you wanted to move a citation to a different location in the document, you would select the citation and then drag the citation tab to the desired location.

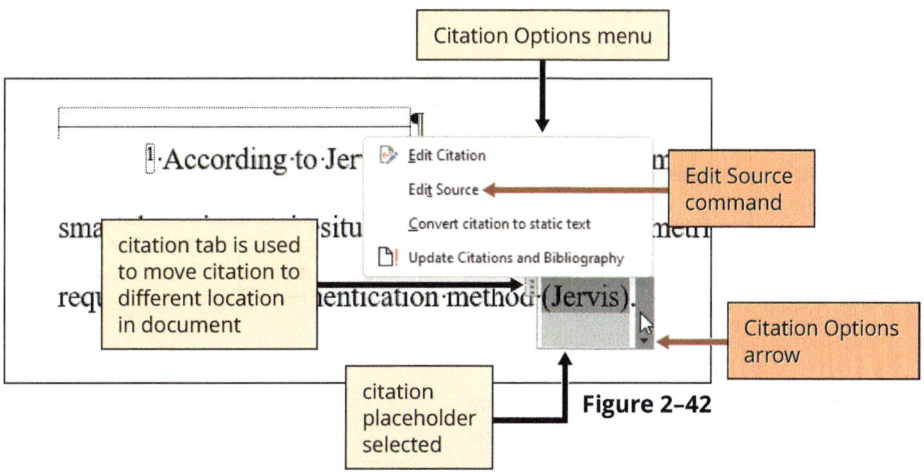

Figure 2–42

2

- Click Edit Source on the Citation Options menu to display the Edit Source dialog box.
- If necessary, click the 'Type of Source' arrow (Edit Source dialog box) and then click Book, so that the list shows fields required for a book.
- Because this source has two authors, click the Edit button to display the Edit Name dialog box, which assists you with entering multiple author names.
- Type **Jervis** as the first author's last name; press TAB and then type **Ning** as the first name; press TAB and then type **Marina** as the middle name (Figure 2–43).

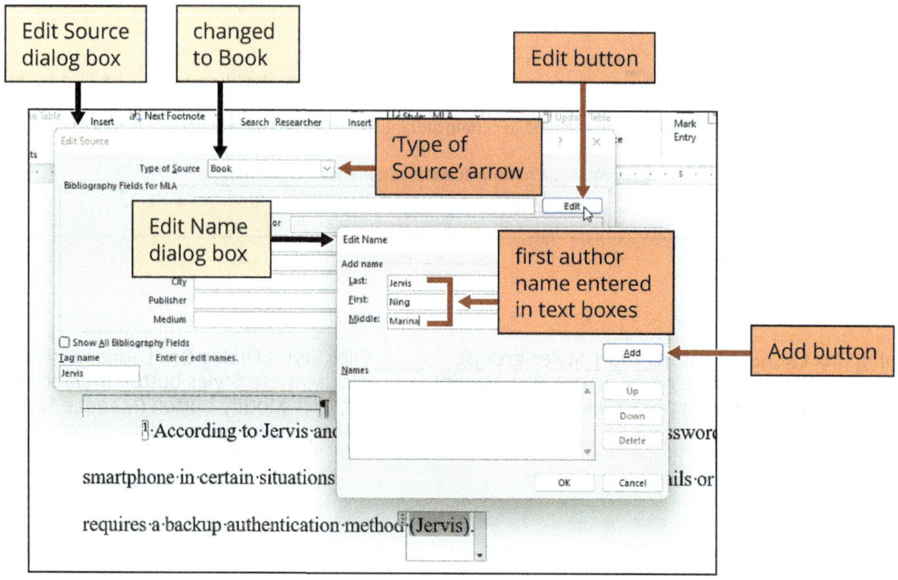

Figure 2–43

Q&A What if I already know how to punctuate the author entry properly?
You can enter the name directly in the Author box.

3

- Click the Add button (Edit Name dialog box) to add the first author's name to the Names list.
- Type **Rivas** as the second author's last name; press TAB and then type **Esteban** as the first name; press TAB and then type **Arturo** as the middle name.
- Click the Add button (Edit Name dialog box) to add the second author's name to the Names list (Figure 2–44).

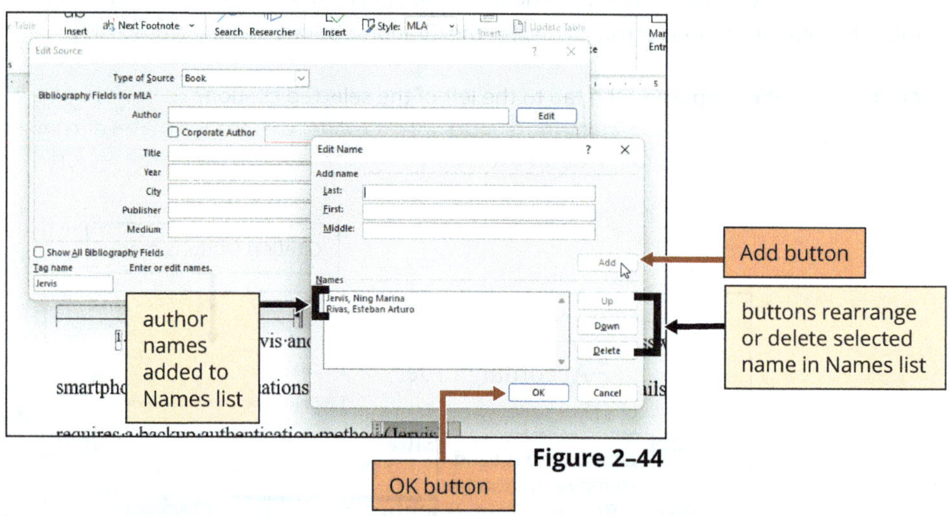

Figure 2–44

4

- Click OK (Edit Name dialog box) to add the author names that appear in the Names list to the Author box in the Edit Source dialog box.
- Click the Title text box (Edit Source dialog box). Type **Smartphone Security** as the book title.
- Press TAB and then type **2027** as the year.
- Press TAB twice and then type **Brightway Publishing** as the publisher (Figure 2–45).

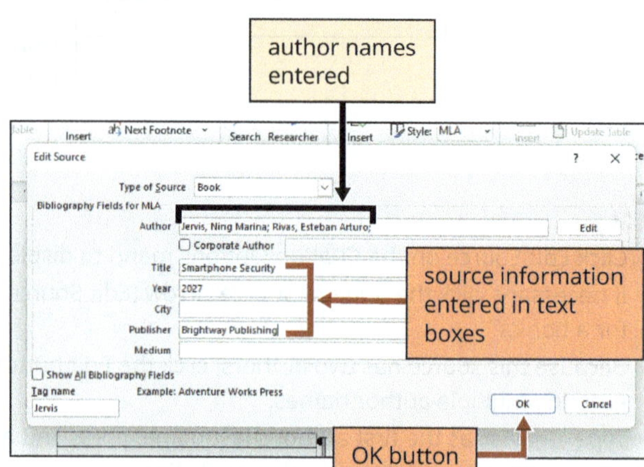

Figure 2–45

5

- Click OK to close the dialog box, create the source, and update the citation to display both author last names (shown in Figure 2–46).

Other Ways

1. Click Manage Sources button (References tab | Citations & Bibliography group), click placeholder source in Current List, click Edit button (Source Manager dialog box), make desired edits, click OK (Edit Source dialog box), click Close (Source Manager dialog box)

To Edit a Citation

In the MLA documentation style, if a source has page numbers, you should include them in the citation. Thus, Word provides a means to enter the page numbers to be displayed in the citation. Also, if you reference the author's name in the text, you should not list it again in the parenthetical citation. Instead, just list the page number(s) in the citation. To do this, you instruct Word to suppress author and title. **Why?** If you suppress the author, Word automatically displays the title, so you need to suppress both the author and title if you want just the page number(s) to be displayed. The following steps edit the citation, suppressing the author and title but displaying the page numbers.

1

- If necessary, click somewhere in the citation to be edited, in this case somewhere in (Jervis and Rivas), which selects the citation and displays the Citation Options arrow.
- Click the Citation Options arrow to display the Citation Options menu (Figure 2–46).

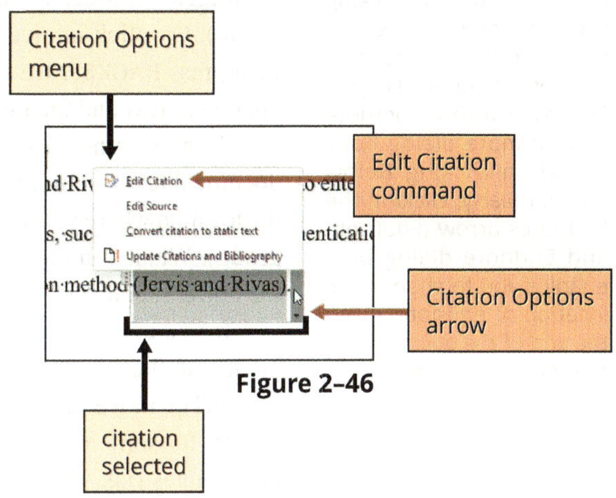

Figure 2–46

2

- Click Edit Citation on the Citation Options menu to display the Edit Citation dialog box.
- Type **42–43** in the Pages text box (Edit Citation dialog box).
- Click the Author check box to place a check mark in it.
- Click the Title check box to place a check mark in it (Figure 2–47).

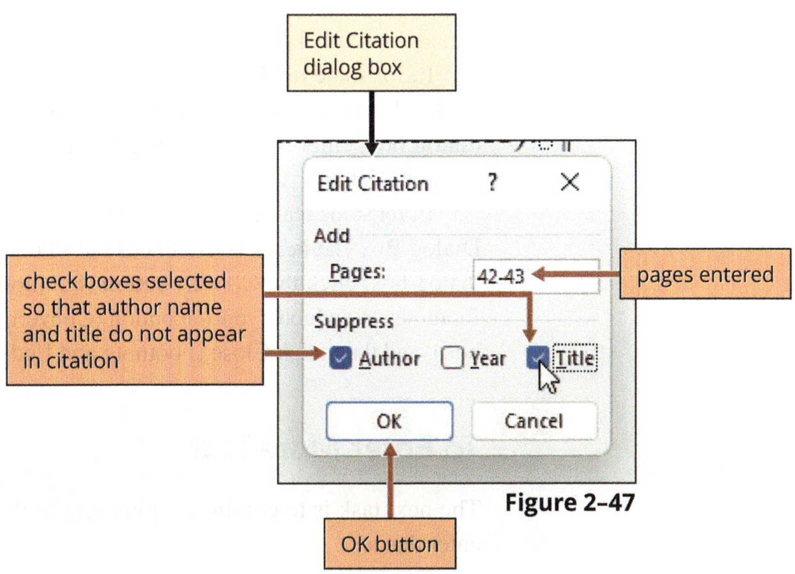

Figure 2–47

3

- Click OK to close the dialog box, remove the author names from the citation in the footnote, suppress the title from showing, and add page numbers to the citation.
- Press END to move the insertion point to the end of the line, which also deselects the citation (Figure 2–48).

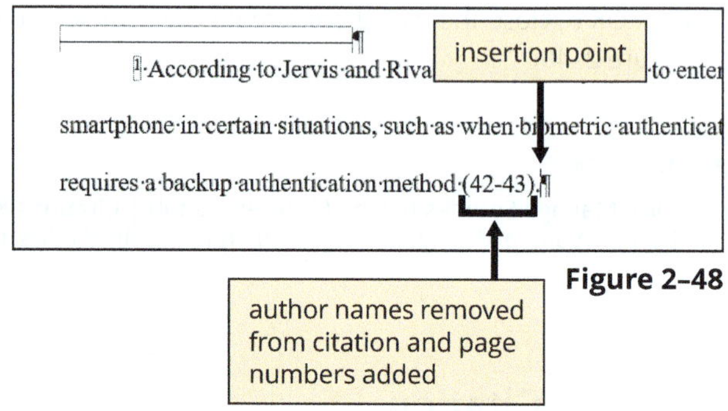

Figure 2–48

BTW
Footnote and Endnote Location
You can change the location of footnotes from the bottom of the page to the end of the text by clicking the Footnotes Dialog Box Launcher (References tab | Footnotes group), clicking the Footnotes arrow (Footnote and Endnote dialog box), and then clicking Below text. Similarly, clicking the Endnotes arrow (Footnote and Endnote dialog box) enables you to change the location of endnotes from the end of the document to the end of a section.

Working with Footnotes and Endnotes

You edit footnote text just as you edit any other text in the document. To delete or move a note reference mark, however, the insertion point must be in the document text (not in the footnote text).

To delete a note, select the note reference mark in the document text (not in the footnote text) by dragging through the note reference mark and then click the Cut button (Home tab | Clipboard group). Or, click immediately to the right of the note reference mark in the document text and then press BACKSPACE twice, or click immediately to the left of the note reference mark in the document text and then press DELETE twice.

To move a note to a different location in a document, select the note reference mark in the document text (not in the footnote text), click the Cut button (Home tab | Clipboard group), click the location where you want to move the note, and then click the Paste button (Home tab | Clipboard group). When you move or delete notes, Word automatically renumbers any remaining notes in the correct sequence.

If you are using a mouse and position the pointer on the note reference mark in the document text, the note text is displayed above the note reference mark as a ScreenTip. To remove the ScreenTip, move the pointer.

If, for some reason, you wanted to change the format of note reference marks in footnotes or endnotes (i.e., from 1, 2, 3 to A, B, C), you would click the Footnotes Dialog Box Launcher (References tab | Footnotes group) to display the Footnote and Endnote dialog box, click the Number format button (Footnote and Endnote dialog box), click the desired number format in the list, and then click the Apply button.

If, for some reason, you wanted to change a footnote number, you would click the Footnotes Dialog Box Launcher (References tab | Footnotes group) to display the Footnote and Endnote dialog box, enter the desired number in the Start at box, and then click Apply (Footnote and Endnote dialog box).

If, for some reason, you wanted to convert footnotes to endnotes, you would click the Footnotes Dialog Box Launcher (References tab | Footnotes group) to display the Footnote and Endnote dialog box, click the Convert button (Footnote and Endnote dialog box), select the 'Convert all footnotes to endnotes' option button (Convert Notes dialog box), click OK (Convert Notes dialog box), and then click Close (Footnote and Endnote dialog box).

To Enter More Text

The next task is to continue typing text in the body of the research paper. The following steps enter this text.

1 Position the insertion point after the note reference mark in the document and then press SPACEBAR.

2 Type the next sentence in the third paragraph of the research paper (shown in Figure 2–49): **Two widely used methods of biometric authentication available on smartphones are fingerprints and facial features.**

3 Press SPACEBAR.

To Count Words

Often when you write papers, you are required to compose the papers with a minimum number of words. The minimum requirement for the research paper in this module is 250 words. You can look on the status bar and see the total number of words thus far in a document. For example, Figure 2–49 shows the research paper has 208 words, but you are not sure if that count includes the words in your footnote. The following steps display the Word Count dialog box. **Why?** You want to verify that the footnote text is included in the count.

1

- Click the Word Count button on the status bar to display the Word Count dialog box.
- If necessary, place a check mark in the 'Include textboxes, footnotes and endnotes' check box (Word Count dialog box) (Figure 2–49).

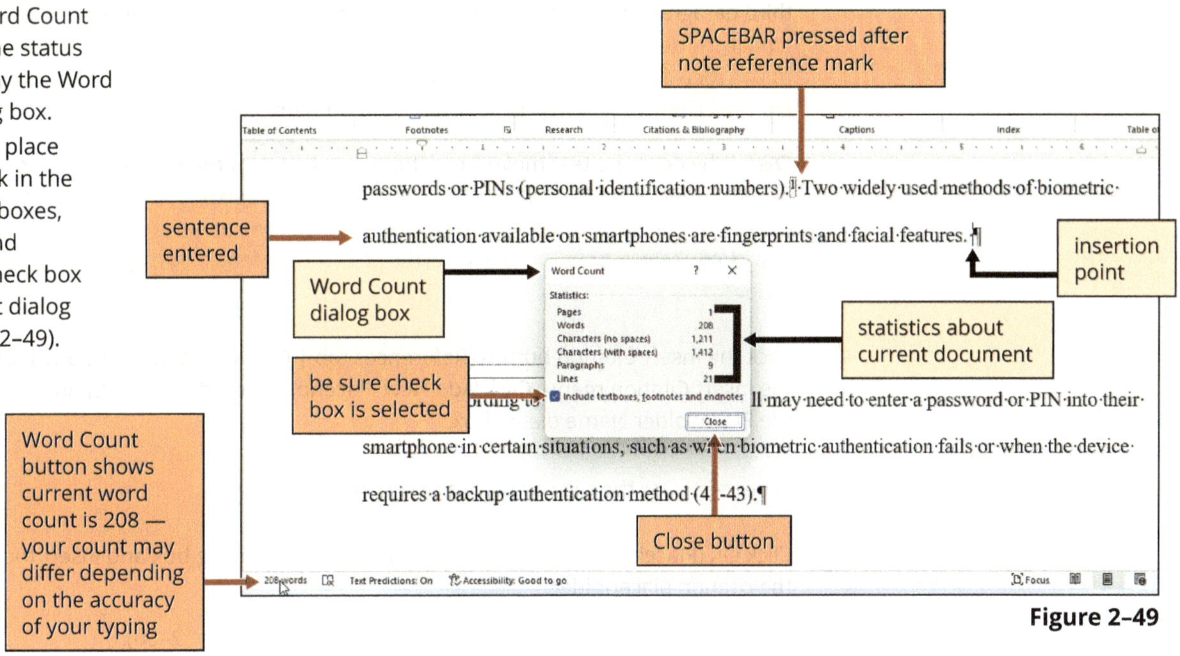

Figure 2–49

Q&A Why do the statistics in my Word Count dialog box differ from those in Figure 2–49?
Depending on the accuracy of your typing, your statistics may differ.

2

- Click the Close button (Word Count dialog box) to close the dialog box.

Q&A Can I display statistics for just a section of the document?
Yes. Select the section and then click the Word Count button on the status bar to display statistics about the selected text.

Other Ways

1. Click Word Count button (Review tab | Proofing group)
2. Press CTRL+SHIFT+G

Automatic Page Breaks

As you type documents that exceed one page, Word automatically inserts page breaks at the bottom of a page, called **automatic page breaks** or **soft page breaks**, when it determines the text has filled one page according to paper size, margin settings, line spacing, and other settings. If you add text, delete text, or modify text on a page, Word recalculates the location of automatic page breaks and adjusts them accordingly.

Word performs page recalculation between the keystrokes, that is, in between the pauses in your typing. Thus, Word refers to the automatic page break task as **background repagination**. An automatic page break will occur in the next set of steps.

BTW
Page Break Locations
As you type, your page break may occur at different locations, depending on Word settings and the type of printer connected to the computer.

To Enter More Text and Insert a Citation Placeholder

The next task is to type the remainder of the third paragraph in the body of the research paper. The following steps enter this text and a citation placeholder at the end of the paragraph.

1. With the insertion point positioned as shown in Figure 2–49, type the last sentence in the third paragraph up to the location of the in-text parenthetical reference: **To access a smartphone through fingerprint recognition, a user presses their finger on the screen in the location indicated by the device. With facial recognition, they hold the device in front of their face when prompted** and then press SPACEBAR.

   Q&A Why does the text move from the second page to the first page as I am typing?
   Word, by default, will not allow the first line of a paragraph to appear by itself at the bottom of a page (an **orphan**) or the last line of a paragraph to appear by itself at the top of a page (a **widow**). As you type, Word adjusts the placement of the paragraph to avoid orphans and widows.

2. Click the Insert Citation button (References tab | Citations & Bibliography group) to display the Insert Citation menu. Click 'Add New Placeholder' on the Insert Citation menu to display the Placeholder Name dialog box.

3. Type **Vida** as the tag name for the source.

4. Click OK (Placeholder Name dialog box) to close the dialog box and insert the tag name in the citation placeholder.

5. Press the PERIOD key to end the sentence (shown in Figure 2–50).

To Hide and Show White Space

With the footnote, page break, and header, it is difficult to see the entire third paragraph at once on the screen. With the screen in Print Layout view, you can hide white space, which is the space that is displayed at the top and bottom of pages (including headers and footers) and also the space between pages. The following steps hide white space, if your screen displays it, and then shows white space. **Why?** You want to see as much of the third paragraph as possible at once, which spans the bottom of the first page and the top of the second page.

1

- Position the pointer in the document window in the space between pages so that the pointer changes to a 'Hide White Space' button (Figure 2–50).

Q&A What if I am using a touch screen?
Proceed to Step 2.

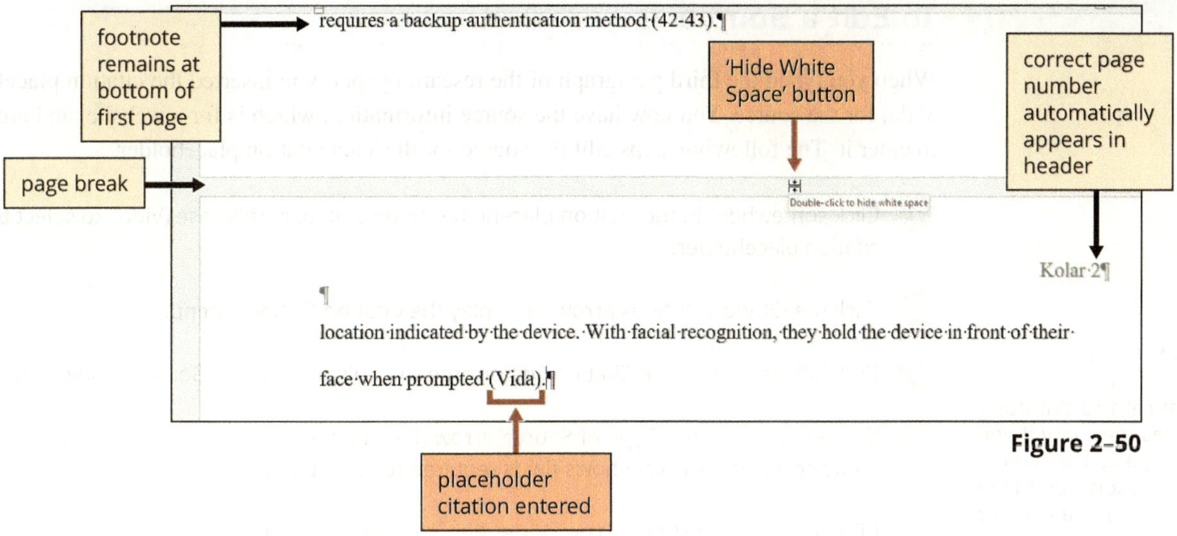

Figure 2–50

2

- Double-click while the pointer is a 'Hide White Space' button to hide white space.
- If necessary, scroll so that both pages appear in the document window at once.

Q&A What if I am using a touch screen?
Double-tap in the space between pages.

Does hiding white space have any effect on the printed document?
No.

3

- Position the pointer in the document window on the page break between pages so that the pointer changes to a 'Show White Space' button (Figure 2–51).

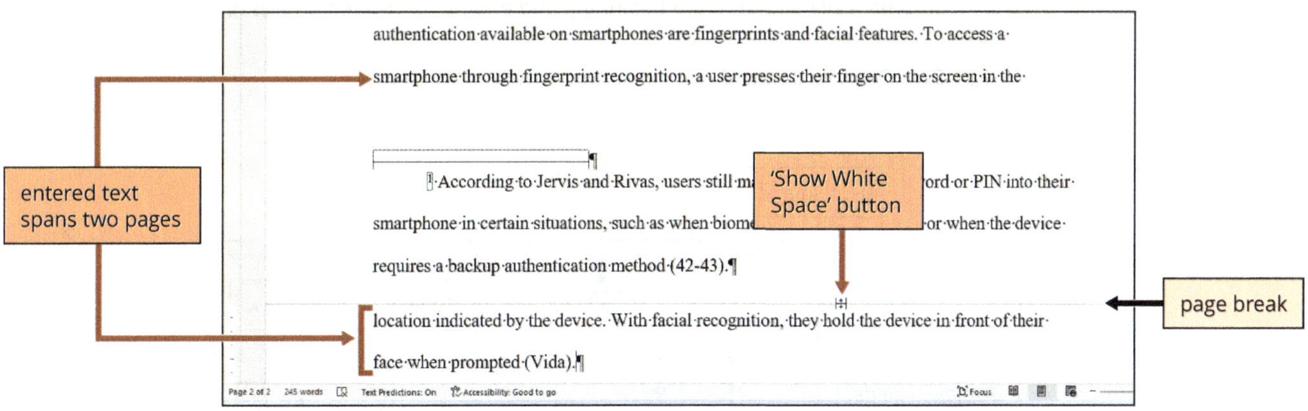

Figure 2–51

4

- Double-click while the pointer is a 'Show White Space' button to show white space.

Q&A What if I am using a touch screen?
Double-tap the page break.

Other Ways

1. Click File on ribbon, click Options in Backstage view, click Display in left pane (Word Options dialog box), remove or select check mark from 'Show white space between pages in Print Layout view' check box, click OK

To Edit a Source

When you typed the third paragraph of the research paper, you inserted the citation placeholder, Vida, for the source. You now have the source information, which is for a website, and are ready to enter it. The following steps edit the source for the Vida citation placeholder.

1. Click somewhere in the citation placeholder to be edited, in this case (Vida), to select the citation placeholder.
2. Click the Citation Options arrow to display the Citation Options menu.
3. Click Edit Source on the Citation Options menu to display the Edit Source dialog box.
4. If necessary, click the 'Type of Source' arrow (Edit Source dialog box); scroll to and then click Web site, so that the list shows fields required for a Web site.
5. Click the Author text box. Type **Vida, Anuli Galila** as the author.
6. Click the 'Name of Web Page' text box. Type **Biometric Authentication for Your Smartphone** as the webpage name.
7. Click the Year Accessed text box. Type **2027** as the year accessed.
8. Press TAB and then type **Sept.** as the month accessed.
9. Press TAB and then type **15** as the day accessed (Figure 2-52).
10. Place a check mark in the 'Show All Bibliography Fields' check box so that Word displays all fields available for the selected source, including the URL fields.
11. Scroll to, if necessary, and then click the URL field to position the insertion point in it. Type **www.allaboutsmartphones.com** as the URL (shown in Figure 2-57 with angle brackets automatically added to the beginning and ending of the web address).
12. Click OK to close the dialog box and create the source.

BTW
Touch Screen Differences
The Office and Windows interfaces may vary if you are using a touch screen. For this reason, you might notice that the function or appearance of your touch screen differs slightly from this module's presentation.

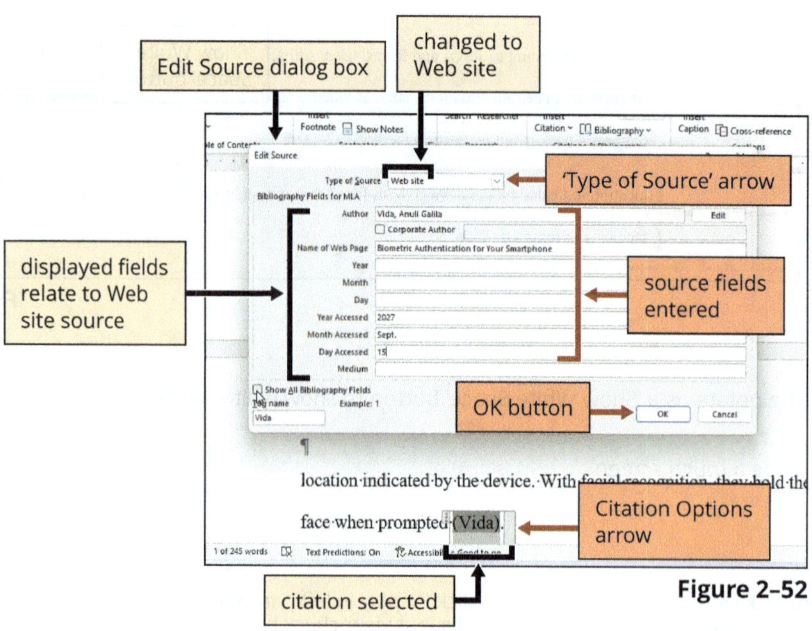

Figure 2-52

To Enter More Text

The next task is to type the last paragraph of text in the research paper. The following steps enter this text that contains spelling and grammar errors you will correct later in this module.

1. Press END to position the insertion point at the end of the third paragraph and then press ENTER.

2. Type the last paragraph of the research paper, entering the spelling and grammar errors as follows (Figure 2–53): **Smartphone users tend to prefer scuring their devices through biometrics. This technology provides an safe and easy method of accessing the device.**

> **Q&A** Why is the word, securing, misspelled?
> Later in this module, you will use Word's check spelling and grammar at once feature to check the entire document for errors.
>
> Why does the word, an, have a double blue underline below it?
> The double blue underline indicates that Word detected a potential grammar error. Later in this module, you will use Word's check spelling and grammar at once feature to check the entire document for flagged text.

3. Save the research paper again on the same storage location with the same file name.

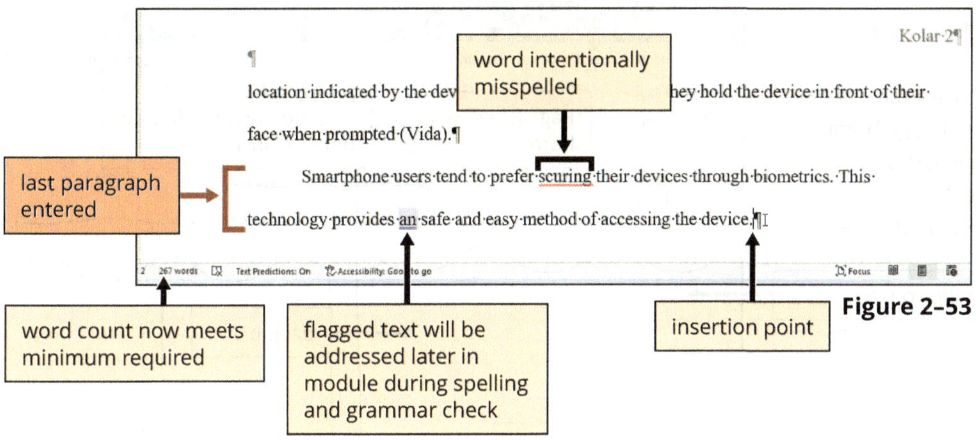

Figure 2–53

Break Point: If you want to take a break, this is a good place to do so. You can exit Word now. To resume later, start Word, open the file called SC_WD_2_SmartphoneBiometricsPaper.docx, and continue following the steps from this location forward.

Creating an Alphabetical Works Cited Page

According to the MLA documentation style, the works cited page is a page in a research paper that alphabetically lists sources that are referenced directly in the paper. You place the list on a separate numbered page with the title, Works Cited, centered one inch from the top margin. The works are to be alphabetized by the author's last name or, if the work has no author, by the work's title. The first line of each entry begins at the left margin. Indent subsequent lines of the same entry one-half inch from the left margin.

Consider This

What is a bibliography?

A **bibliography**, also called a bibliographical list, is an alphabetical list of sources referenced in a paper. Whereas the text of the research paper contains brief references to the source (the citations), the bibliography lists all publication information about the source. Documentation styles differ significantly in their guidelines for preparing a bibliography. Each style identifies formats for various sources, including books, magazines, pamphlets, newspapers, websites, television programs, paintings, maps, advertisements, letters, memos, and much more. You can find information about various styles and their guidelines in style guides and on the web.

To Insert a Page Break

The next step is to insert a manual page break following the body of the research paper. **Why?** According to the MLA documentation style, the works cited are to be displayed on a separate numbered page.

A **manual page break**, or **hard page break**, is a page break that you force into the document at a specific location so that the text following the break begins at the top of the next page, whether or not the previous page is full. Word never moves or adjusts manual page breaks. Word, however, does adjust any automatic page breaks that follow a manual page break. Word inserts manual page breaks immediately above or to the left of the location of the insertion point. The following step inserts a manual page break after the text of the research paper.

1

- Verify that the insertion point is positioned at the end of the text of the research paper, as shown in Figure 2-53.
- Click Insert on the ribbon to display the Insert tab.
- Click the Page Break button (Insert tab | Pages group) to insert a manual page break immediately to the left of the insertion point and position the insertion point immediately below the manual page break (Figure 2-54).

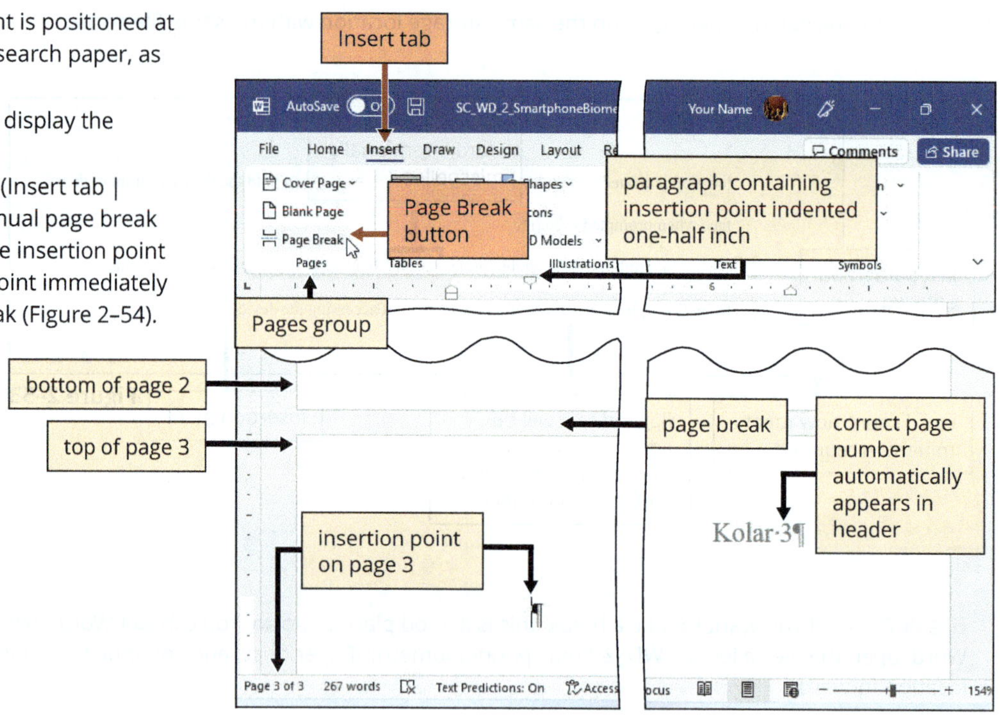

Figure 2-54

Other Ways

1. Press CTRL+ENTER

To Apply a Style

The works cited title is to be centered between the margins of the paper. If you simply issue the Center command, the title will not be centered properly. **Why?** It will be to the right of the center point because earlier you set the first-line indent for paragraphs to one-half inch.

To properly center the title of the works cited page, you could drag the 'First Line Indent' marker back to the left margin before centering the paragraph, or you could apply the Normal style to the location of the insertion point. Recall that you modified the Normal style for this document to 12-point Times New Roman with double-spaced, left-aligned paragraphs that have no space after the paragraphs.

To apply a style to a paragraph, first position the insertion point in the paragraph and then apply the style. The following step applies the modified Normal style to the location of the insertion point.

1

- Click Home on the ribbon to display the Home tab.
- With the insertion point on the paragraph mark at the top of page 3 (as shown in Figure 2–54) even if Normal is selected, click Normal in the Styles gallery (Home tab | Styles group) to apply the Normal style to the paragraph containing the insertion point (Figure 2–55).

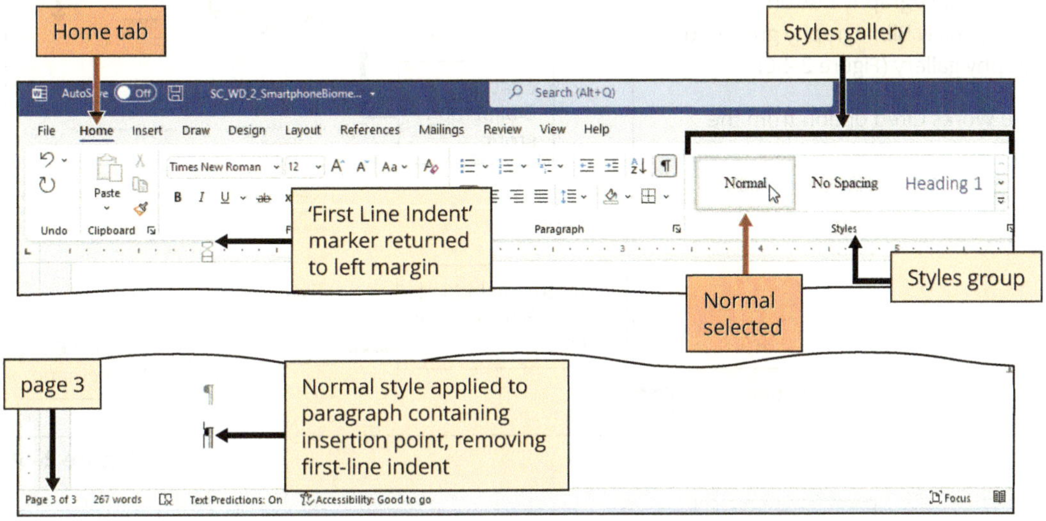

Figure 2–55

Q&A What if I wanted to apply a different style (besides Normal) to the paragraph?
You would click desired style in the Styles gallery (Home tab | Styles group) to apply a style to the current paragraph.

Other Ways

1. Click Styles Dialog Box Launcher (Home tab | Styles group), select desired style in Styles pane
2. Press CTRL+SHIFT+S, click Style Name arrow in Apply Styles pane, select desired style in list

To Center Text

The next task is to enter the title, Works Cited, centered between the margins of the paper. The following steps use a keyboard shortcut to format the title.

1. Press CTRL+E to center the paragraph mark.
2. Type **Works Cited** as the title (shown in Figure 2–57).
3. Press ENTER.
4. Press CTRL+L to left-align the paragraph mark (shown in Figure 2–56).

To Create a Bibliographical Reference List

While typing the research paper, you created several citations and their sources. The next task is to use Word to format the list of sources and alphabetize them in a bibliographical list. **Why?** Word can create a bibliographical list with each element of the source placed in its correct position with proper punctuation, according to the specified style, saving you time looking up style guidelines. For example, in this research paper, the book source will list, in this order, the author name(s), book title, publishing company name, and publication year with the correct punctuation between each element according to the MLA documentation style. The following steps create an MLA-styled bibliographical list from the sources previously entered.

1

- Click References on the ribbon to display the References tab.
- With the insertion point positioned as shown in Figure 2–56, click the Bibliography button (References tab | Citations & Bibliography group) to display the Bibliography gallery (Figure 2–56).

Q&A Will I select the Works Cited option from the Bibliography gallery?

No. The title it inserts is not formatted according to the MLA documentation style. Thus, you will use the Insert Bibliography command instead.

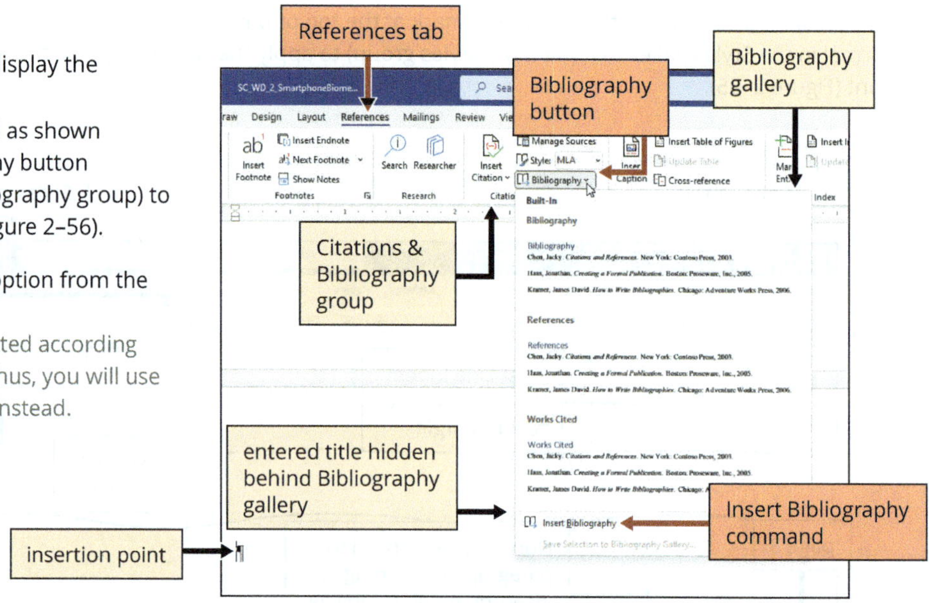

Figure 2–56

2

- Click Insert Bibliography in the Bibliography gallery to insert a list of sources at the location of the insertion point.
- If necessary, scroll to display the entire list of sources in the document window (Figure 2–57).

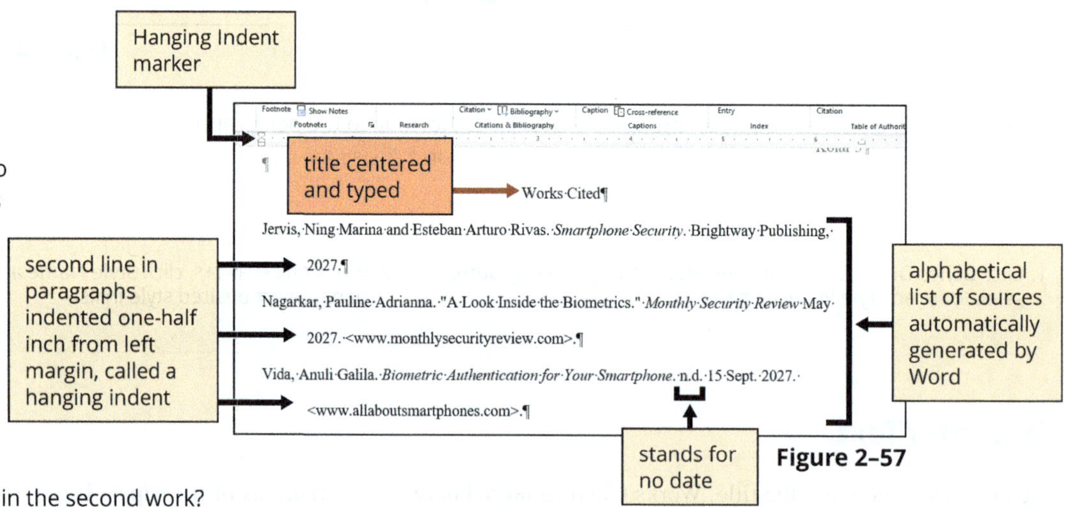

Figure 2–57

Q&A What is the n.d. in the second work?

It is an abbreviation n.d. for no date (for example, no date appears on the webpage). The current MLA documentation style does not require a publication date for webpage sources, but it does require the word, Accessed, to appear before the date accessed. Later in this module, you will edit two of the works cited to match guidelines in the current MLA edition.

What if my list is not double-spaced and has extra spacing after each paragraph?

You skipped a step earlier in this module. Select the entire bibliography, change line spacing to double, and remove space after the paragraph.

3

- Save the research paper again on the same storage location with the same file name.

To Format Paragraphs with a Hanging Indent Notice in Figure 2–57 that the first line of each source entry hangs to the left of the rest of the paragraph; this type of paragraph formatting is called a **hanging indent** because the first line of the paragraph begins at the left margin and subsequent lines in the same paragraph are indented from the left margin. The Bibliography style in Word automatically formats the works cited paragraphs with a hanging indent.

If you wanted to format paragraphs with a hanging indent, you would use one of the following techniques.

- With the insertion point in the paragraph to format, drag the Hanging Indent marker (the bottom triangle) on the ruler to the desired mark on the ruler (i.e., .5") to set the hanging indent at that location from the left margin.
  or
- Right-click the paragraph to format (or, if using a touch screen, tap the 'Show Context Menu' button on the Mini toolbar), click Paragraph on the shortcut menu, click the Indents and Spacing tab (Paragraph dialog box), click the Special arrow, click Hanging, and then click OK.
  or
- Click the Paragraph Dialog Box Launcher (Home tab or Layout tab | Paragraph group), click the Indents and Spacing tab (Paragraph dialog box), click the Special arrow, click Hanging, and then click OK.
  or
- With the insertion point in the paragraph to format, press CTRL+T.

Proofreading and Revising the Research Paper

As discussed in Module 1, once you complete a document, you might find it necessary to make changes to it. Before submitting a paper to be graded, you should proofread it. While **proofreading**, ensure all the information is correct and look for grammatical, typographical, and spelling errors. Also ensure that transitions between sentences flow smoothly and the sentences themselves make sense.

To assist you with the proofreading effort, Word provides several tools. You can go to a page, find text, replace text, insert a synonym, check spelling and grammar, and look up information. The following pages discuss these tools.

BTW
Rewrite Suggestions Feature
To find suggestions for revising text, use the Rewrite Suggestions feature. Select a phrase, right-click the selection, and then click Rewrite Suggestions on the shortcut menu. The Editor pane opens, listing suggestions for improving the text. Click a suggestion to replace the selected text with the revision.

Consider This

What should you consider when proofreading and revising a paper?

As you proofread the paper, look for ways to improve it. Check all grammar, spelling, and punctuation. Be sure the text is logical and transitions are smooth. Where necessary, add text, delete text, reword text, and move text to different locations. Ask yourself these questions:

- Does the title suggest the topic?
- Is the thesis clear?
- Is the purpose of the paper clear?
- Does the paper have an introduction, body, and conclusion?
- Does each paragraph in the body relate to the thesis?
- Is the conclusion effective?
- Are sources acknowledged correctly?

To Edit a Source Using the Source Manager Dialog Box

While proofreading the paper, you notice an error in the magazine title; specifically, the word, the, should be removed. Then, you will instruct Word to update the bibliography so that the change is reflected in the paper. **Why?** The bibliography is a field, and depending on settings, it may not update automatically after you edit the source. The following steps delete a word from the title of the magazine article.

1

- Click the Manage Sources button (References tab | Citations & Bibliography group) to display the Source Manager dialog box.
- Click the source you wish to edit in the Current List, in this case the article by Nagarkar, to select the source.
- Click the Edit button (Source Manager dialog box) to display the Edit Source dialog box.
- In the Title text box (Edit Source dialog box), delete the word, the, from the title (Figure 2–58).

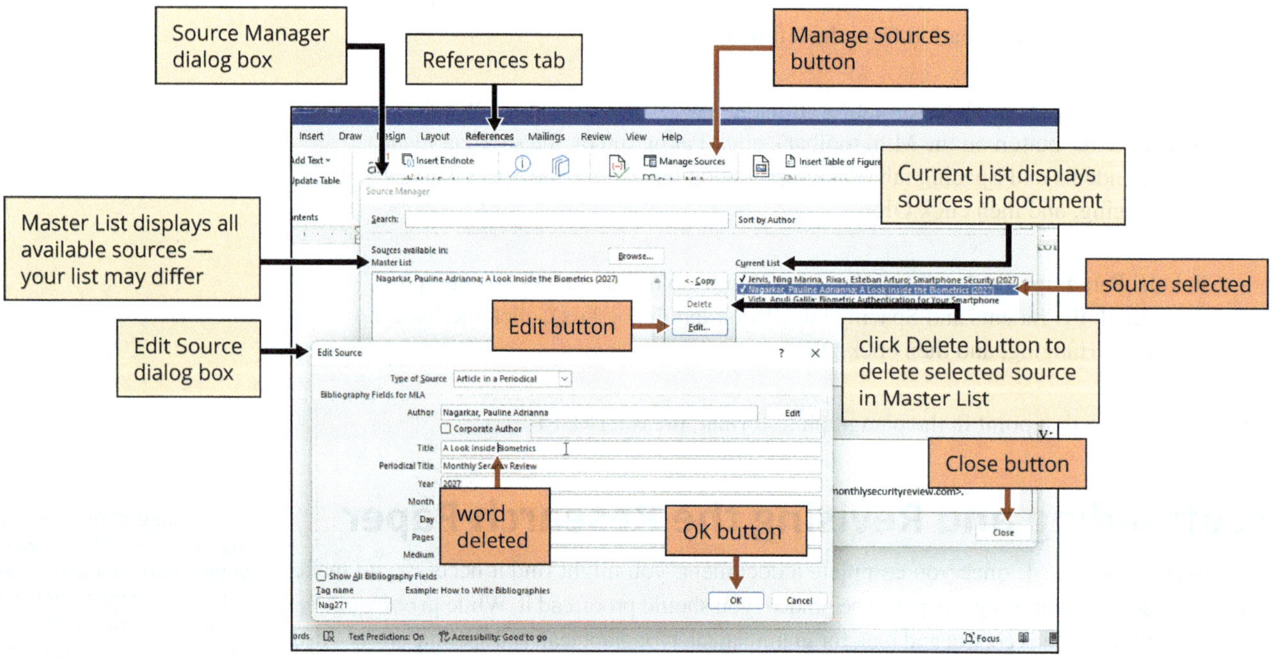

Figure 2–58

2

- Click OK (Edit Source dialog box) to close the dialog box.
- If a Microsoft Word dialog box appears, click Yes to update all occurrences of the source.
- Click the Close button (Source Manager dialog box) to update the list of sources and close the dialog box.

Q&A How would I delete an existing source?
You would select the source in the Master List and then click Delete (Source Manager dialog box). If the source is not listed in the Master List, click the source in the Current List and then click Copy (Source Manager dialog box) to copy the source from the Current List to the Master List.

To Update a Field (the Bibliography)

Depending on settings, the bibliography field may not automatically reflect the edited magazine title. Thus, the following steps update the bibliography field. **Why?** Because the bibliography is a field, you may need to instruct Word to update its contents.

1

- Right-click anywhere in the bibliography text to display a shortcut menu related to fields (Figure 2–59).

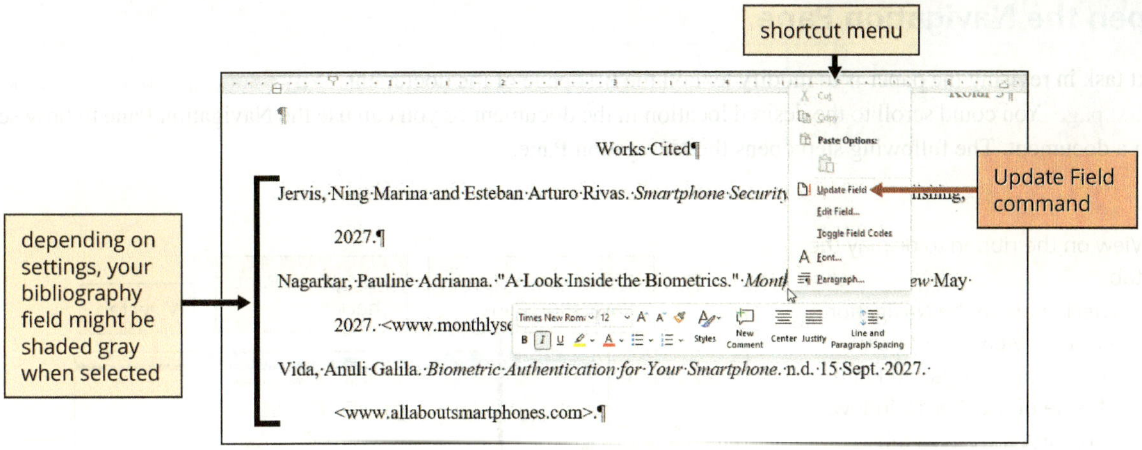

Figure 2–59

Q&A What if I am using a touch screen?

Press and hold anywhere in the bibliography text and then tap the 'Show Context Menu' button on the Mini toolbar.

Why are all the words in my bibliography shaded gray?

Depending on settings, selected fields may appear shaded gray on your screen.

How would I shade selected fields in gray?

Click File on the ribbon to open Backstage view, click Options in Backstage view, click Advanced in the left pane (Word Options dialog box), scroll to the 'Show document content' area, click the Field shading arrow, click When selected, and then click OK.

2

- Click Update Field on the shortcut menu to update the selected field.
- If necessary, press ESC to remove the selection from the bibliography field (Figure 2–60).

Q&A What if pressing ESC does not remove the selection from the bibliography field?

Press CTRL+A to select the entire document and then click the paragraph mark below the bibliography to remove the selection from the bibliography field.

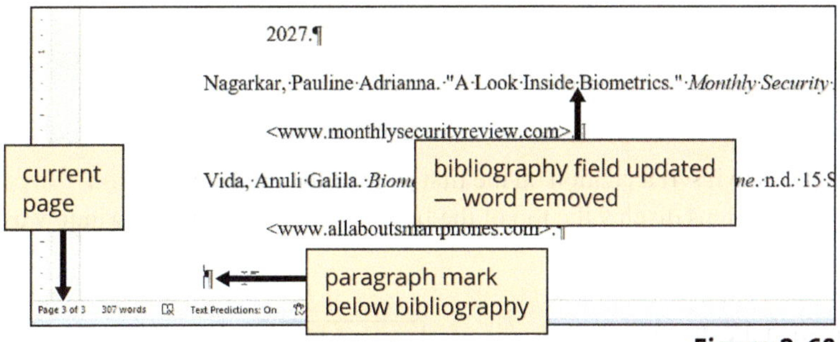

Figure 2–60

Q&A Can I update all fields in a document at once?

Yes. Select the entire document and then follow these steps.

Other Ways

1. Select the field, press F9

To Convert a Field to Regular Text If, for some reason, you wanted to convert a field, such as the bibliography field, to regular text, you would perform the following steps. Keep in mind, though, once you convert the field to regular text, it no longer is a field that can be updated.

1. Click somewhere in the field to select it, in this case, somewhere in the bibliography.
2. Press CTRL+SHIFT+F9 to convert the selected field to regular text.

To Open the Navigation Pane

The next task in revising the paper is to modify text on the first page of the document. **Why?** You want to insert another citation on the first page. You could scroll to the desired location in the document or you can use the Navigation Pane to browse through pages in a document. The following step opens the Navigation Pane.

1

- Click View on the ribbon to display the View tab.
- Place a check mark in the Navigation Pane check box (View tab | Show group) to open the Navigation Pane on the left side of the Word window.
- If necessary, click the Pages tab in the Navigation Pane to display thumbnails of the pages in the document (Figure 2–61).

Q&A What is the Navigation Pane?
The Navigation Pane is a task pane that enables you to browse through headings in a document, browse through pages in a document, or search for text in a document.

How do I close the Navigation Pane?
You click the Close button in the upper-right corner of the pane, or remove the check mark from the Navigation Pane check box (View tab | Show group).

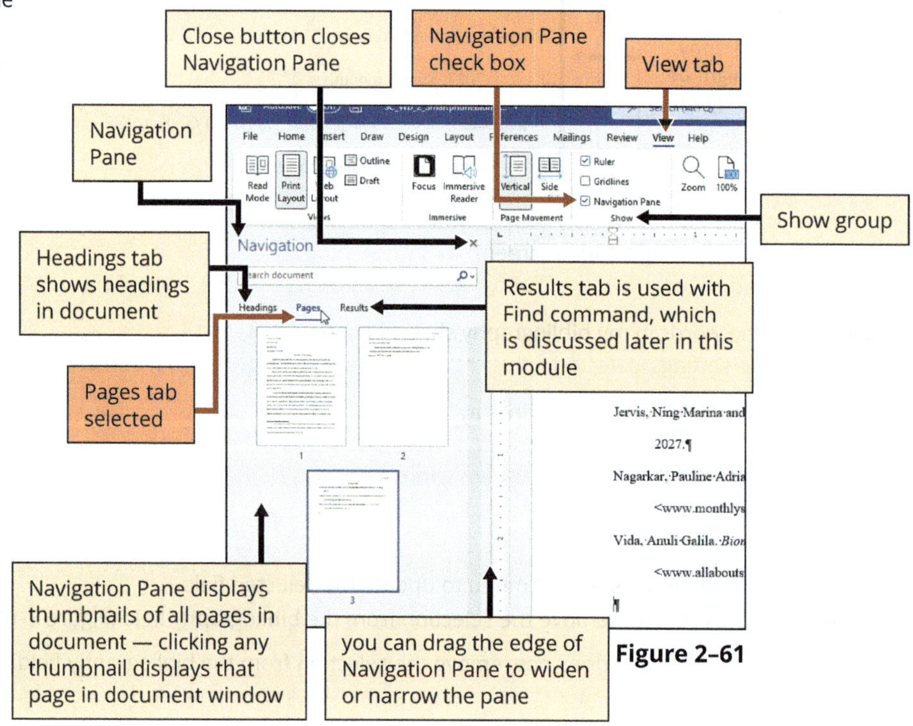

Figure 2–61

To Go to a Page

The next task in revising the paper is to insert a citation on the first page of the document. **Why?** You overlooked a citation when you created the paper. The following steps display the top of the first page in the document window using the Navigation Pane.

1

- With the Navigation Pane open in the document window, if the Pages tab is not selected, click it to select it.

Q&A What if the Navigation Pane is not open?
Repeat the previous set of steps.

- Scroll to, if necessary, and then click the thumbnail of the first page in the Navigation Pane to display the top of the selected page in the top of the document window (Figure 2–62).

2

- Click the Close button in the Navigation Pane to close the pane.

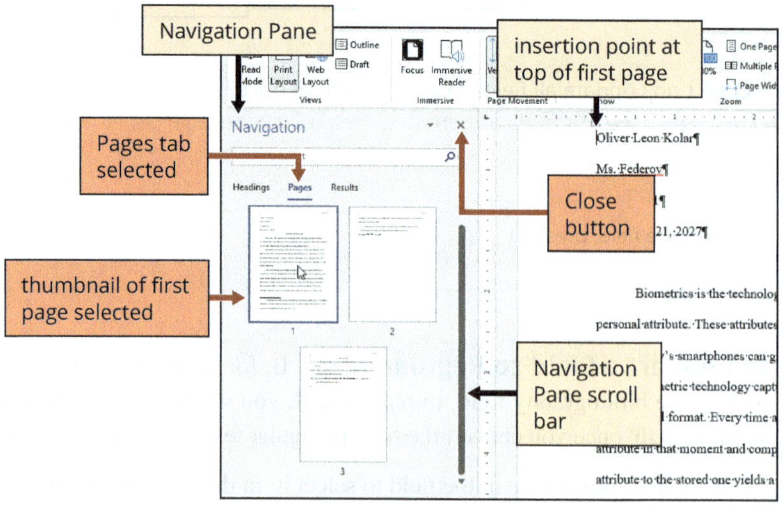

Figure 2–62

Other Ways

1. Click Editing group button (Home tab) if necessary, click Find arrow (Home tab | Editing group), click Go To on Find menu, click Go To tab (Find and Replace dialog box), enter page number, click Go To button
2. Click Page Number button on status bar, click Pages tab in Navigation Pane, click thumbnail of desired page (Navigation Pane)
3. Press CTRL+G, enter page number (Find and Replace dialog box), click Go To button

To Insert a Citation Using an Existing Source

While proofreading the paper, you notice that you omitted a citation that should appear in the second paragraph of the research paper. The source already exists because you referenced it in the footnote. The following steps insert a citation for an existing source. **Why?** You want to insert a citation for an existing source in a second location in the document.

1

- Scroll to, if necessary, and position the insertion point at the location for the citation (on the first page, at the end of the first sentence in the third paragraph before the period, as shown in Figure 2–63).
- Click References on the ribbon to display the References tab.
- Click the Insert Citation button (References tab | Citations & Bibliography group) to display the Insert Citation menu (Figure 2–63).

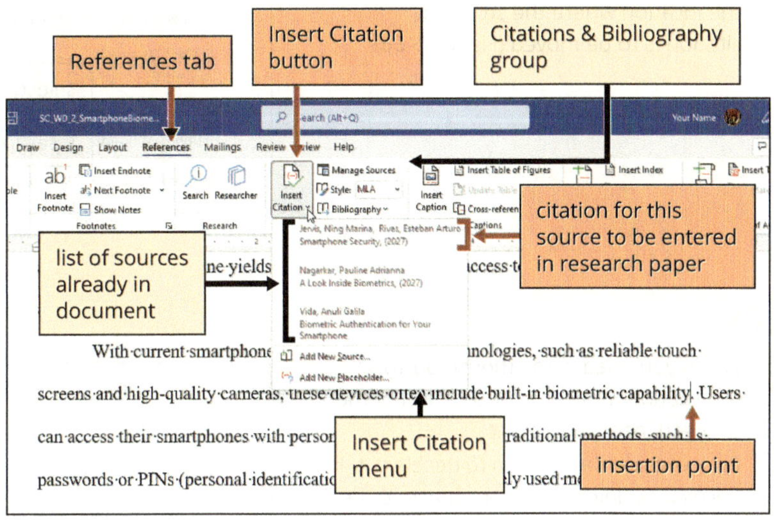

Figure 2–63

2

- Click the first source listed (for Jervis and Rivas) on the Insert Citation menu to insert a citation for the existing source at the location of the insertion point (Figure 2–64).

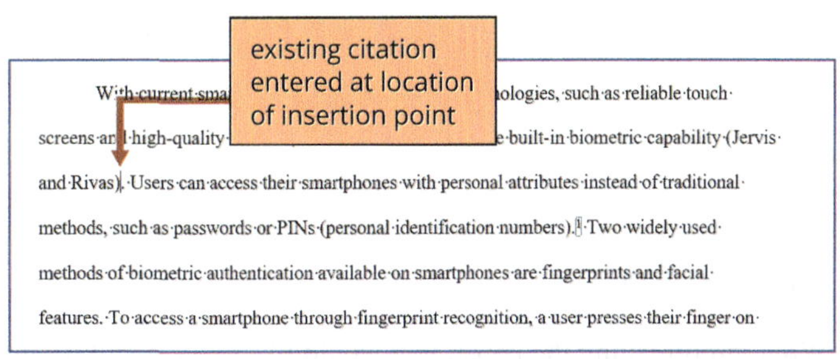

Figure 2–64

To Move a Citation

The citation just entered is not in the correct location. The following steps move a citation in a document. **Why?** You want to move the citation to the end of the next sentence.

1

- Click somewhere in the citation to be moved to select it.
- Position the pointer on the citation tab until the pointer changes to a left-pointing block arrow (Figure 2–65).

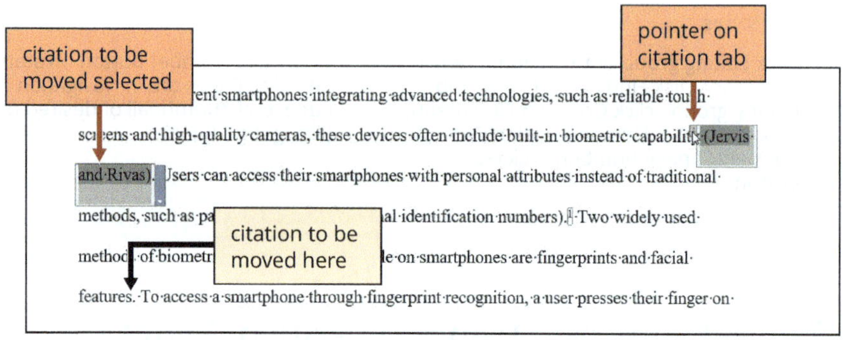

Figure 2–65

2

- Drag the citation tab, which changes to an insertion point as you drag, to the location where the selected citation is to be moved (Figure 2–66).

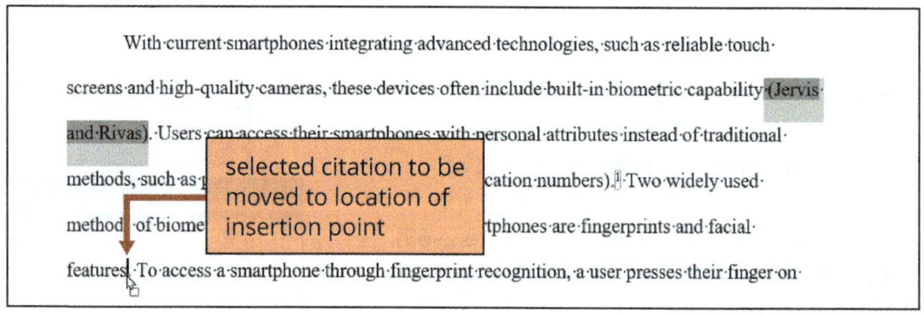

Figure 2–66

3

- When you release the mouse button, the citation moves to the location of the dragged insertion point.
- Click outside the citation to deselect it. If necessary, delete the extra space to the left of the moved citation (Figure 2–67).

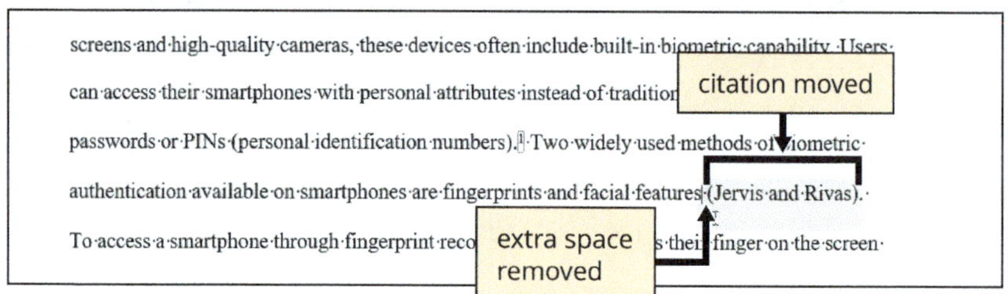

Figure 2–67

To Find Text

While proofreading the paper, you would like to locate all occurrences of the word, method. **Why?** Your instructor required at least one occurrence of the word, method, in your paper. The following steps find all occurrences of specific text in a document.

1

- Click Home on the ribbon to display the Home tab.
- Click the Editing group button (Home tab) to the right of the Styles group to display the Editing group (Figure 2–68).

Q&A What if my screen shows an Editing group instead of an Editing group button?
Skip this step and proceed to Step 2.

What if I am using a touch screen?
Tap the Editing group button (Home tab).

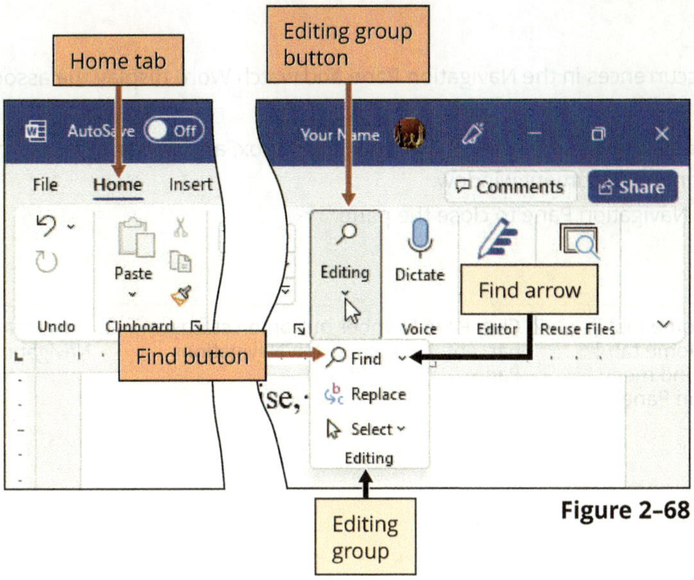

Figure 2–68

2

- Click the Find button (Home tab | Editing group) to open the Navigation Pane.

Q&A Why did the Find menu appear?
You clicked the Find arrow. Press ESC and repeat Steps 1 and 2.

What if I am using a touch screen?
Tap the Find button (Home tab | Editing group) and then tap Find on the menu.

- If necessary, click the Results tab in the Navigation Pane, which displays a Search box where you can type text for which you want to search (Figure 2–69).

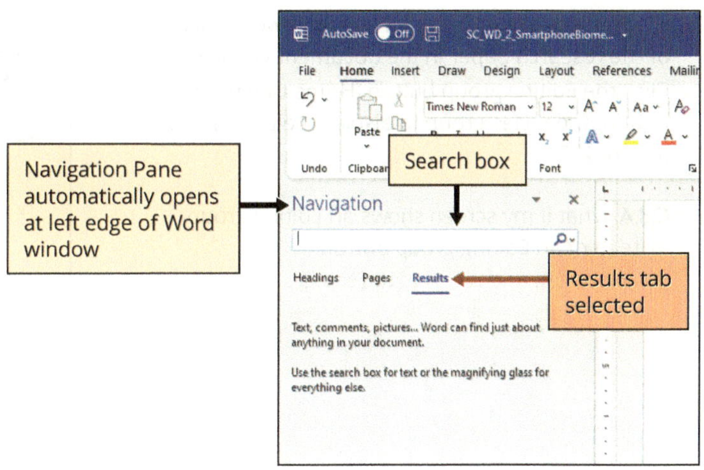

Figure 2–69

3

- Type **method** in the Navigation Pane Search box to display all occurrences of the typed text, called the search text, in the Navigation Pane and to highlight the occurrences of the search text in the document window (Figure 2–70).

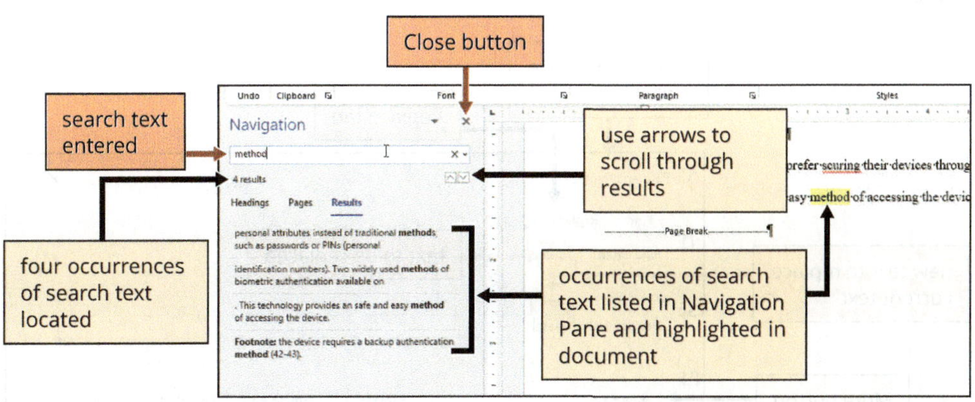

Figure 2–70

4

- **Experiment:** Click all four occurrences in the Navigation Pane and watch Word display the associated text in the document window.
- **Experiment:** Type various search text in the Navigation Pane Search box, and watch Word list matches in the Navigation Pane and highlight matches in the document window.
- Click the Close button in the Navigation Pane to close the pane.

Other Ways

1. Click Editing group button (Home tab) if necessary, click Find arrow (Home tab | Editing group), click Find on Find menu, enter search text in Navigation Pane
2. Click Page Number button on status bar, enter search text in Navigation Pane
3. Press CTRL+F, enter search text in Navigation Pane

To Replace Text

You decide to change all occurrences of the word, give, to the word, grant. **Why?** The term, grant, is a more appropriate term when discussing security access. Word's find and replace feature locates each occurrence of a word or phrase and then replaces it with text you specify. The following steps find and replace text.

1

- If necessary, scroll to display the first two paragraphs of the research paper in the document window.
- Click the Editing group button (Home tab) to the right of the Styles group to display the Editing group (Figure 2–71).

Q&A What if my screen shows an Editing group instead of an Editing group button?

Skip this step and proceed to Step 2.

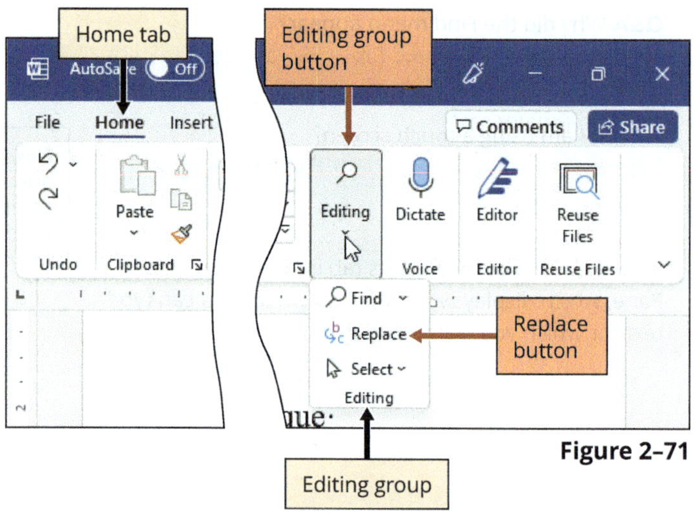

Figure 2–71

2

- Click the Replace button (Home tab | Editing group) to display the Replace sheet in the Find and Replace dialog box.
- If necessary, type **give** in the Find what box (Find and Replace dialog box).
- Type **grant** in the Replace with box (Figure 2–72).

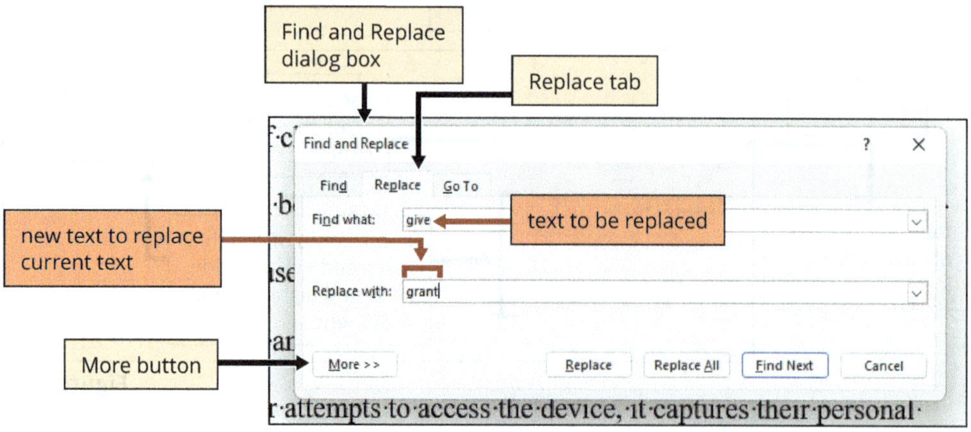

Figure 2–72

3

- Click the Replace All button to instruct Word to replace all occurrences of the Find what text with the Replace with text (Figure 2–73). If Word displays a dialog box asking if you want to continue searching from the beginning of the document, click Yes.

Q&A Does Word search the entire document?
If the insertion point is at the beginning of the document, Word searches the entire document; otherwise, Word may search from the location of the insertion point to the end of the document and then display a dialog box asking if you want to continue searching from the beginning. You also can search a section of text by selecting the text before clicking the Replace or Replace All button.

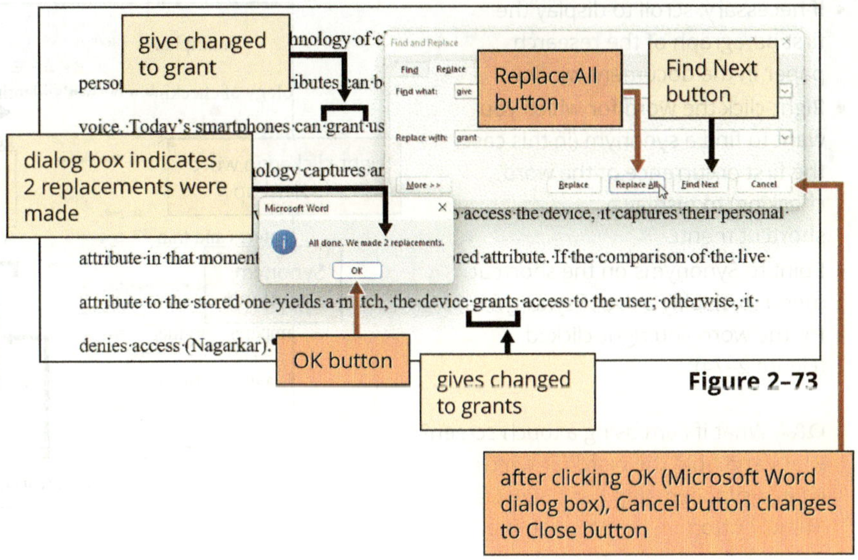

Figure 2–73

4

- Click OK (Microsoft Word dialog box) to close the dialog box.
- Click the Close button (Find and Replace dialog box) to close the dialog box.

Other Ways

1. Press CTRL+H

Find and Replace Dialog Box

The Replace All button (Find and Replace dialog box) replaces all occurrences of the Find what text with the Replace with text. In some cases, you may want to replace only certain occurrences of a word or phrase, not all of them. To instruct Word to confirm each change, click the Find Next button (Find and Replace dialog box) (shown in Figure 2–73) instead of the Replace All button. When Word locates an occurrence of the text, it pauses and waits for you to click either the Replace button or the Find Next button. Clicking the Replace button changes the text; clicking the Find Next button instructs Word to disregard the replacement and look for the next occurrence of the Find what text.

If you accidentally replace the wrong text, you can undo a replacement by clicking the Undo button (Home tab | Undo group) or by pressing CTRL+Z. If you used the Replace All button, Word undoes all replacements. If you used the Replace button, Word undoes only the most recent replacement.

BTW
Finding Formatting and Special Characters
To search for formatting or a special character, click the Find tab or Replace tab in the Find and Replace dialog box and then click the More button (Find and Replace dialog box) (shown in Figure 2–72). To find formatting, use the Format button in the Find dialog box. To find a special character, use the Special button. To specify search options, place a check mark in the desired option in the Search Options area.

To Use the Thesaurus

In this project, you would like a synonym for the first use of the word, checking, in the first sentence of the research paper. **Why?** When writing, you may discover that you used the same word in multiple locations or that a word you used was not quite appropriate, the former of which is the case here. In these instances, you will want to look up a **synonym**, or a word similar in meaning, to the duplicate or inappropriate word. A **thesaurus** is list of alternate word choices. Word provides synonyms and a Thesaurus pane for your convenience. The following steps find a suitable synonym.

1

- If necessary, scroll to display the first paragraph of the research paper in the document window.
- Right-click the word for which you want to find a synonym (in this case, the first occurrence of the word, checking) to display a shortcut menu.
- Point to Synonyms on the shortcut menu to display a list of synonyms for the word you right-clicked (Figure 2–74).

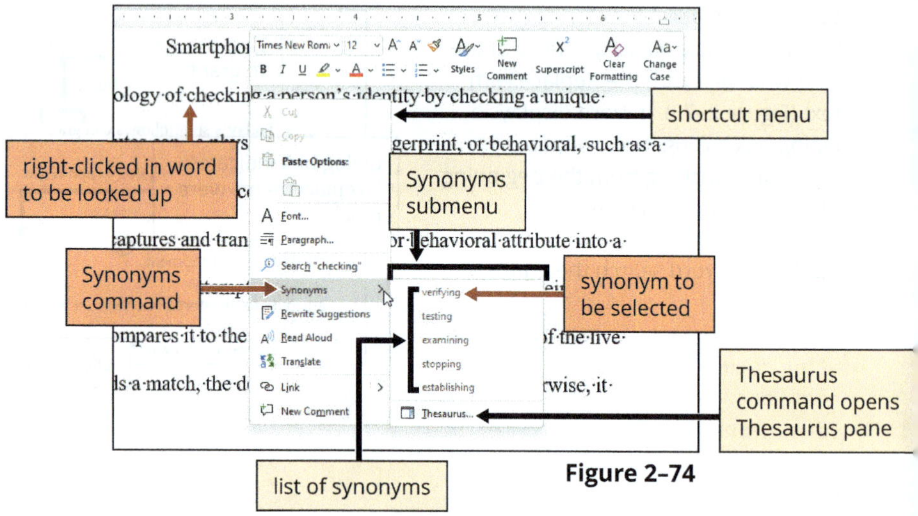

Figure 2–74

Q&A What if I am using a touch screen?
Press and hold the word for which you want a synonym, tap the 'Show Context Menu' button on the Mini toolbar, and then tap Synonyms on the shortcut menu.

What if my list differs from Figure 2–74 or the synonyms list on the shortcut menu does not display a suitable word?
You can display the thesaurus in the Thesaurus pane by clicking Thesaurus on the Synonyms submenu. The Thesaurus pane displays a complete thesaurus, in which you can look up synonyms for various meanings of a word. To select a word in the Thesaurus pane, point to the desired alternative word, click the arrow to the right of the desired alternative word, and then click Insert on the menu.

2

- Click the synonym you want (in this case, verifying) on the Synonyms submenu to replace the selected word in the document with the selected synonym (Figure 2–75).

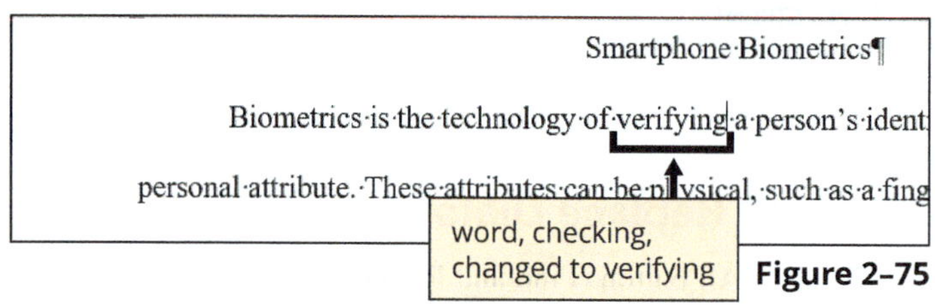

Figure 2–75

Other Ways

1. Click Thesaurus button (Review tab | Proofing group)
2. Press SHIFT+F7

To Check Spelling and Grammar at Once

As discussed previously, Word checks spelling and grammar as you type and flags possible spelling or grammar errors with different types of underlines, depending on the potential error type. The following steps check spelling and grammar in the entire document at once. **Why?** Some users prefer to wait and check their entire document for spelling and grammar errors at once rather than checking as they type.

Previously in this module, you typed the word, securing, misspelled intentionally as scuring and typed the word, an, instead of the word, a, to illustrate the use of Word's check spelling and grammar at once feature. If you are completing this project on a computer or mobile device, your research paper may contain different misspelled words, depending on the accuracy of your typing.

1

- Press CTRL+HOME because you want the spelling and grammar check to begin from the top of the document.
- Click Review on the ribbon to display the Review tab.
- Click the 'Spelling and Grammar' button (Review tab | Proofing group) to begin the spelling and grammar check at the location of the insertion point, which, in this case, is at the beginning of the document; when Word identifies a potential spelling error, it opens the Editor pane (Figure 2–76).

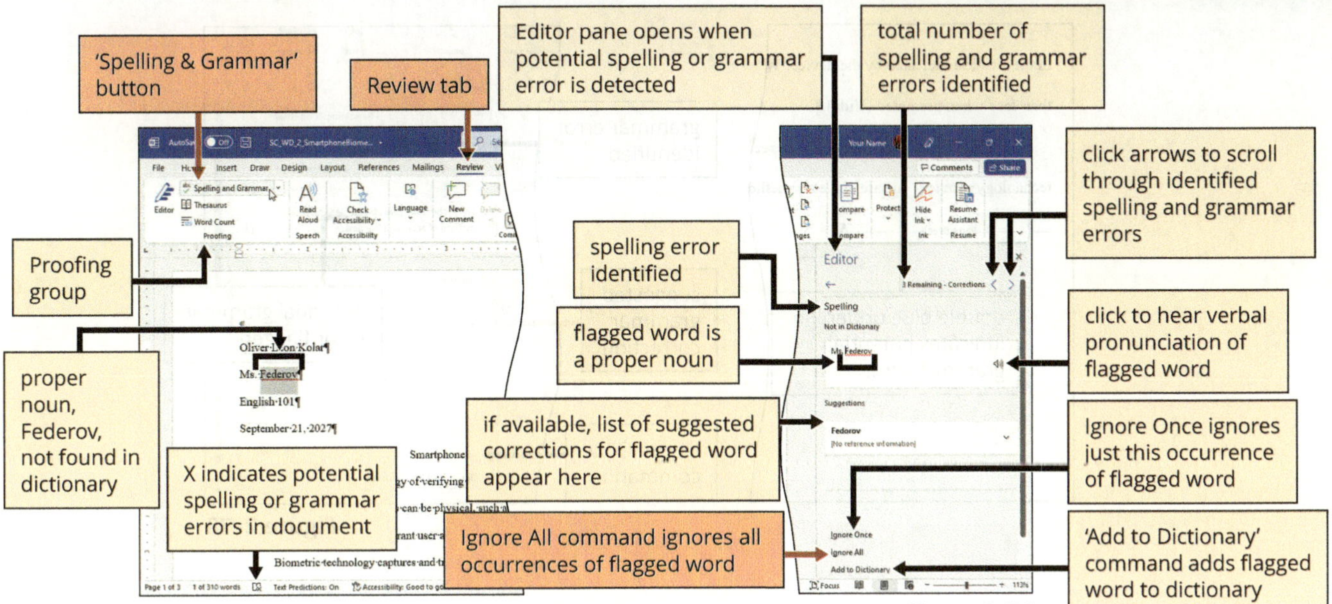

Figure 2–76

Q&A Why did the Spelling and Grammar menu appear?
You clicked the Spelling and Grammar arrow. Press ESC and then click the Spelling and Grammar button.

What if my screen does not have a 'Spelling and Grammar' button?
Depending on your screen resolution, you may have an Editor button instead of a 'Spelling and Grammar' button. In this case, click the Editor button (Review tab | Proofing group) to open the Editor pane and begin the spelling and grammar check.

2

- Because the first occurrence of flagged text is a proper noun and spelled correctly (Federov), click Ignore All in the Editor pane to ignore this and future occurrences of the flagged proper noun and then continue the spelling and grammar check until the next potential error is identified or the end of the document is reached; in this case, it identifies the potential misspelled word, scuring.

Q&A What if the proper noun is not the first flagged item?
Click the right or left scroll arrow in the Editor pane until the flagged proper noun is displayed and then repeat Step 2.

3

- Click the arrow to the right of the desired suggestion (securing) to display a suggestion menu for the desired suggestion (Figure 2–77).

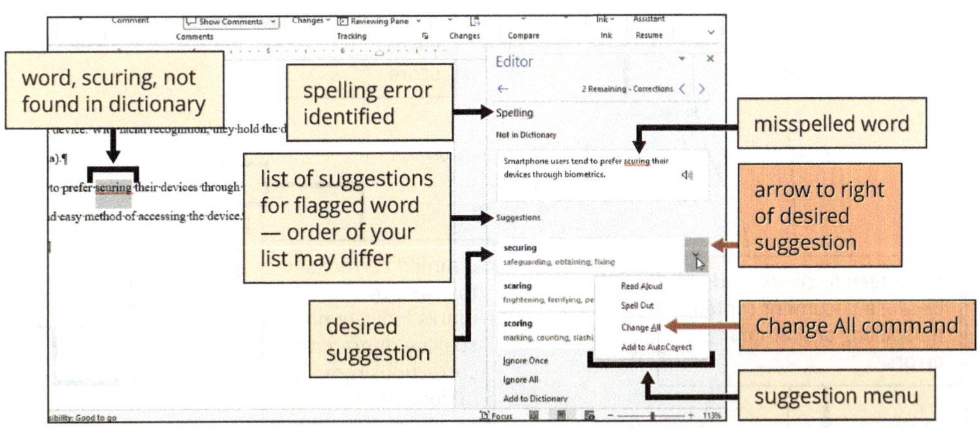

Figure 2–77

4

- Click Change All on the suggestion menu to change the flagged word, and any other exact misspellings of this word, to the selected suggestion and then continue the spelling and grammar check until the next error is identified or the end of the document is reached, which in this case is a suggestion in the Grammar category (Figure 2–78).

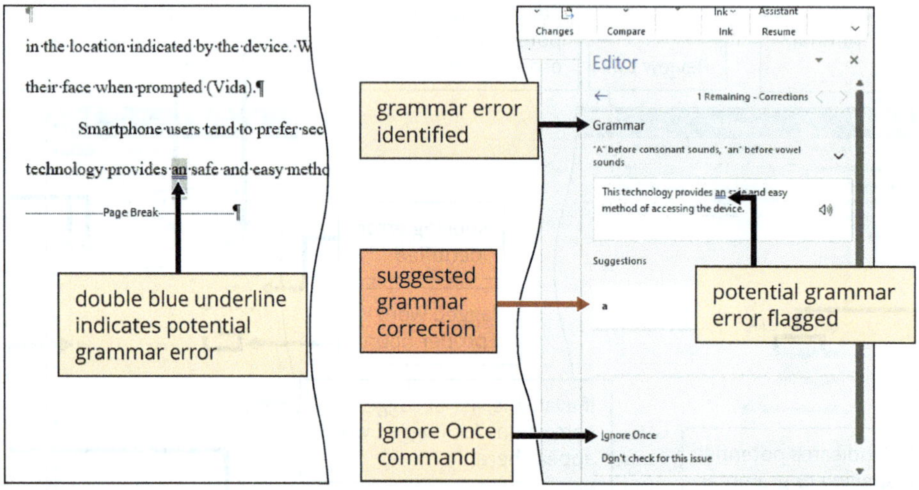

Figure 2–78

Q&A How would I change just the flagged text (and not all occurrences of the misspelled word)?
You would click the desired suggestion instead of the arrow to the right of the suggestion.

5

- Click the desired grammar correction in the list of suggestions in the Editor pane (a, in this case).

Q&A What if I did not want to change the flagged text to any of the suggestions?
You would click Ignore Once at the bottom of the Editor pane.

- When the spelling and grammar check is finished, the Editor displays a score and Word displays a dialog box (Figure 2–79).
- If Word displays a Readability Statistics dialog box, click OK.

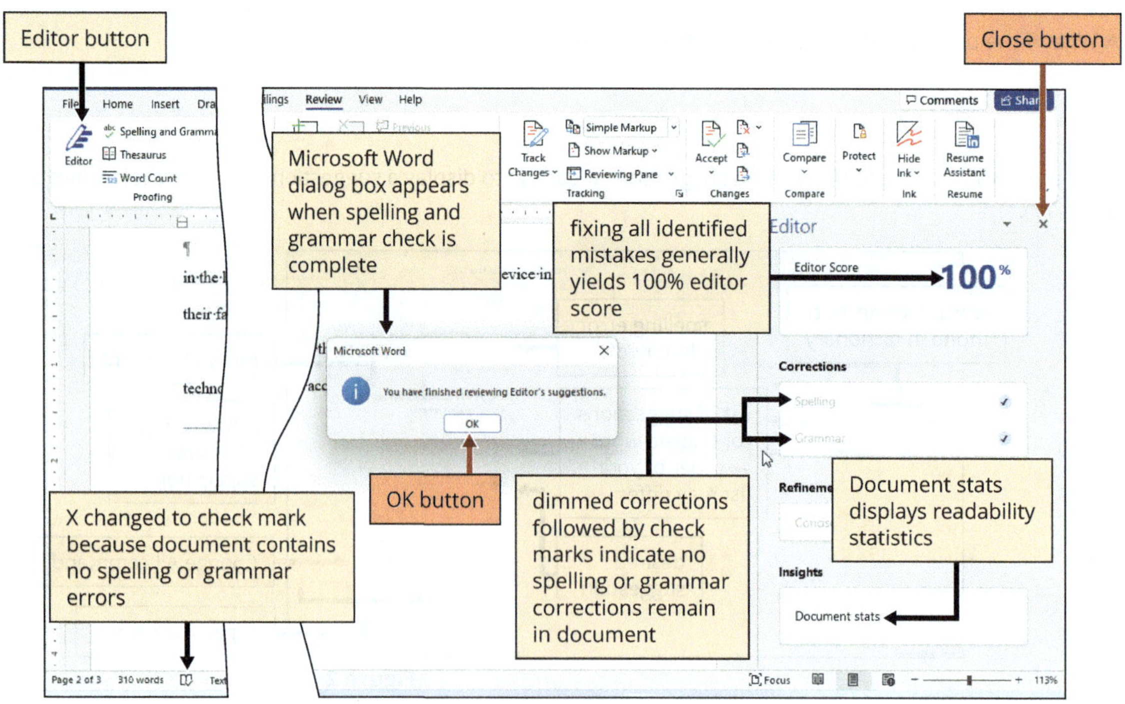

Figure 2–79

Q&A What is the purpose of the Editor button (Review tab | Proofing group)?

The Editor button opens the Editor pane and uses **Editor**, which is an intelligent writing assistant included with recent versions of Word. In addition to checking spelling and grammar, if desired, Editor also can check a document's formality and can provide suggestions to refine your writing by checking areas such as clarity and conciseness or readability statistics.

Can I check selected text instead of the entire document or a flagged word?

Yes. Select the text you would like checked, right-click the selected text, and then click 'Review selection in Editor' on the shortcut menu.

6

- Click OK to close the dialog box.
- Click the Close button (shown in Figure 2–79) to close the Editor pane.

Other Ways

1. Click 'Spelling and Grammar Check' button on status bar
2. Press F7

The Main and Custom Dictionaries

As shown in the previous steps, Word may flag a proper noun as an error because the proper noun is not in its main dictionary. You may want to add some proper nouns that you use repeatedly, such as a company name or employee names, to Word's dictionary. To prevent Word from flagging proper nouns as errors, you can add the proper nouns to the custom dictionary. To add a correctly spelled word to the custom dictionary, click 'Add to Dictionary' at the bottom of the Editor pane when the flagged word is displayed or right-click the flagged word (or, if using touch, press and hold and then tap 'Show Context Menu' button on the mini toolbar), point to Spelling on the shortcut menu, and then click 'Add to Dictionary' on the submenu. Once you have added a word to the custom dictionary, Word no longer will flag it as an error.

BTW

Readability Statistics

Three readability statistics Word checks are the percent of passive sentences, the Flesch Reading Ease score, and the Flesch-Kincaid Grade Level score. The Flesch Reading Ease score uses a 100-point scale to rate the ease with which a reader can understand the text in a document. A higher score means the document is easier to understand. The Flesch-Kincaid Grade Level score rates the text in a document on a U.S. school grade level. For example, a score of 10.0 indicates a student in the tenth grade can understand the material. To display readability statistics on demand, open the Editor pane (Home tab or Review tab) and then click Document stats. To show readability statistics every time the spelling check is complete, open Backstage view, click Options in Backstage view, click Proofing in the left pane (Word Options dialog box), place a check mark in the 'Show readability statistics' check box, and then click OK. Readability statistics will be displayed the next time you check spelling and grammar at once in the document.

To View or Modify Entries in a Custom Dictionary To view or modify the list of words in a custom dictionary, you would follow these steps.

1. Click File on the ribbon and then click Options in Backstage view.
2. Click Proofing in the left pane (Word Options dialog box).
3. Click the Custom Dictionaries button.
4. When Word displays the Custom Dictionaries dialog box, if necessary, place a check mark next to the dictionary name to view or modify and then click the 'Edit Word List' button (Custom Dictionaries dialog box). (In this dialog box, you can add or delete entries to and from the selected custom dictionary.)
5. When finished viewing and/or modifying the list, click OK in the dialog box.
6. Click OK (Custom Dictionaries dialog box).
7. If the 'Suggest from main dictionary only' check box is selected in the Word Options dialog box, remove the check mark. Click OK (Word Options dialog box).

To Set the Default Custom Dictionary If you have multiple custom dictionaries, you can specify which one Word should use when checking spelling. To set the default custom dictionary, you would follow these steps.

1. Click File on the ribbon and then click Options in Backstage view.
2. Click Proofing in the left pane (Word Options dialog box).
3. Click the Custom Dictionaries button.
4. When the Custom Dictionaries dialog box is displayed, place a check mark next to the desired new dictionary name and then select the dictionary name in the list. Click the Change Default button (Custom Dictionaries dialog box).

5. Click OK (Custom Dictionaries dialog box).
6. If the 'Suggest from main dictionary only' check box is selected in the Word Options dialog box, remove the check mark. Click OK (Word Options dialog box).

To Edit the Works Cited to Match Current MLA Guidelines

Specifications for the punctuation and verbiage for works in current edition of the MLA documentation style differ slightly from the edition used by this version of Word. For example, in a multiauthor work, a comma should precede the word, and. As mentioned earlier in this project, the n.d. notation is not required in works from the web, and the word, Accessed, should precede the date accessed data. The following steps make these adjustments to the works on the Works Cited page.

1. Scroll to display the works cited in the document window.
2. Insert a comma after the name, Marina, in the first work.
3. Delete the notation, n.d., in the third work.
4. Insert the text, Accessed, before the date in the third work and then, if necessary, press SPACEBAR (Figure 2–80).

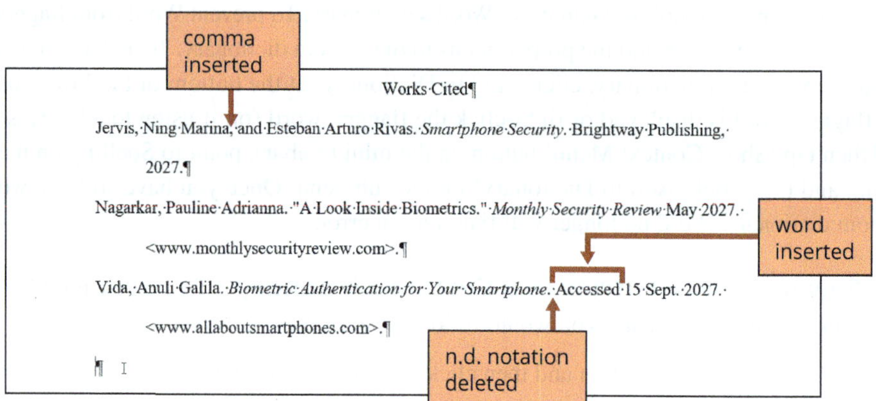

Figure 2–80

Q&A How would I go back to the bibliography created by Word?
You would update the bibliography field by right-clicking the bibliography text and then clicking Update Field on the shortcut menu.

How would I make these changes permanent so that the bibliography field could not be updated?
You would convert the field to regular text by clicking anywhere in the bibliography field and then pressing CTRL+SHIFT+F9.

To Save and Print the Document

The following steps save and print the document.

1. **sam** Save the research paper again on the same storage location with the same file name.
2. If requested by your instructor, print the research paper.

BTW
Printing Document Properties
To print document properties, click File on the ribbon to open Backstage view, click Print in Backstage view to display the Print screen, click the first button in the Settings area to display a list of options specifying what you can print, click Document Info in the list to specify you want to print the document properties instead of the actual document, and then click the Print button on the Print screen to print the document properties on the currently selected printer.

BTW
Conserving Ink and Toner
If you want to conserve ink or toner, you can instruct Word to print draft quality documents by clicking File on the ribbon to open Backstage view, clicking Options in Backstage view to display the Word Options dialog box, clicking Advanced in the left pane (Word Options dialog box), scrolling to the Print area in the right pane, placing a check mark in the 'Use draft quality' check box, and then clicking OK. Then, use Backstage view to print the document as usual.

To Recover Unsaved Documents If you accidently exit Word without saving a document, you may be able to recover the unsaved document in Word. If you wanted to recover an unsaved document, you would perform these steps.

1. Start Word and create a blank document in the Word window.
2. Open Backstage view and then, if necessary, click Info to display the Info screen. If the autorecovery file name appears below the Manage Document list, click the file name to display the unsaved file in the Word window.

   or

   Open Backstage view and then, if necessary, click Open to display the Open screen. At the bottom of the right pane, click the 'Recover Unsaved Documents' button to display an Open dialog box that lists unsaved files retained by Word. Select the file to recover and then click Open to display the unsaved file in the Word window.

   or

   Open Backstage view and then, if necessary, click Info to display the Info screen. Click the Manage Document button to display the Manage Document menu. Click 'Recover Unsaved Documents' on the Manage Document menu to display an Open dialog box that lists unsaved files retained by Word. Select the file to recover and then click Open to display the unsaved file in the Word window.
3. To save the document, click the Save As button on the Message Bar.

BTW
Versions
If you are using OneDrive to save your Word documents, you can view previous versions of an open document. Click File on the ribbon to open Backstage view, click Info in Backstage view to display the Info screen, and then click the Version History button to open the Version History pane. To view a previous version, click the Open version link in the Version History pane to open the previous version in a separate window. To restore the previous version, click the Restore button that appears below the ribbon.

To Delete All Unsaved Documents If you wanted to delete all unsaved documents, you would perform these steps.

1. Start Word and create a blank document in the Word window.
2. Open Backstage view and then, if necessary, click Info to display the Info screen.
3. Click the Manage Document button to display the Manage Document menu.
4. If available, click 'Delete All Unsaved Documents' on the Manage Document menu.
5. When Word displays a dialog box asking if you are sure you want to delete all copies of unsaved files, click Yes to delete all unsaved documents.

To Use Smart Lookup

If you are connected to the Internet, you can use Smart Lookup, which displays the Search pane that provides you with various forms of reference information from the web, possibly including images and a definition. The following steps use Smart Lookup to display information about a series of words. **Why?** Assume you want to know more about fingerprint recognition.

1

- Select the words you want to look up (in this case, fingerprint recognition).
- Click References on the ribbon to display the References tab.

Q&A What if I wanted to look up a single word?
You would position the insertion point in the word you want to look up.

- Click the Search button (References tab | Research group) to open the Search pane (Figure 2–81).

Q&A What if Word asks if I want to turn on intelligent services?
Select the option to turn on intelligent services.

Why does my Search pane look different?
Depending on your settings, your Search pane may appear different from the figure shown here.

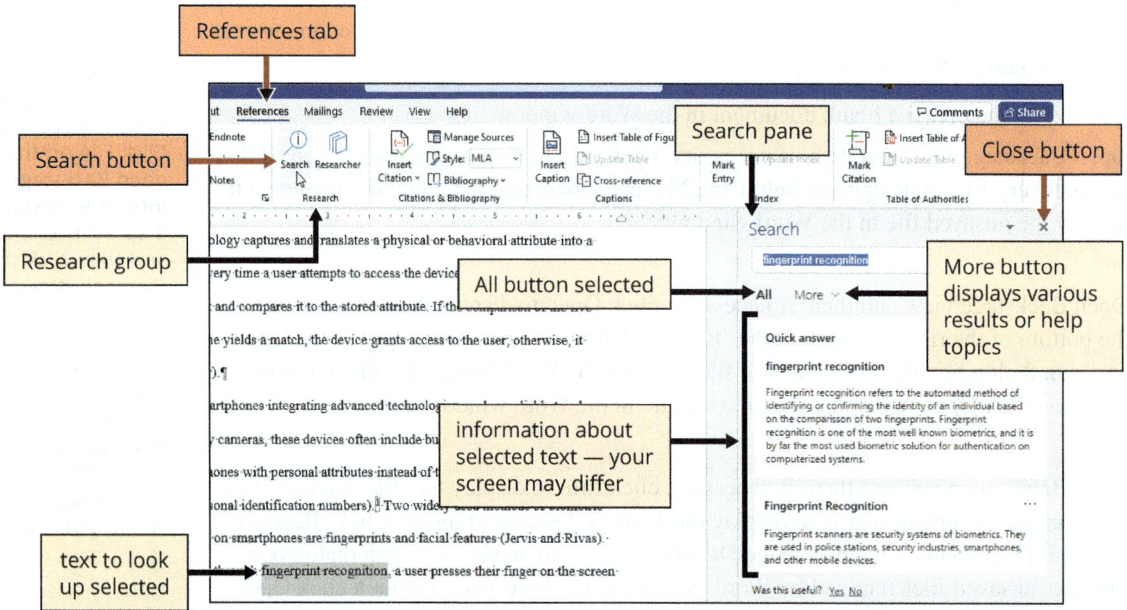

Figure 2–81

- **Experiment:** With the All button selected in the Search pane, scroll through the information that appears in the Search pane. Click the More button in the Search pane and then click an option to see other types of information. Click the All button to redisplay information from the web about the selected text. Click a link in the Search pane to view additional information. If a Back button appears at the top of the Search pane, click it to return to the previous display.

2

- Click the Close button in the Search pane to close the pane.
- Click anywhere in the document window to deselect the text.

Other Ways

1. Right-click selected text and then click Search "[selected text]" on shortcut menu

To Use Researcher

If you are connected to the Internet, you can use the Researcher pane to search through various forms of reference information on the web and locate sources for research papers from within Word. The following steps use the Researcher pane to look up information about fingerprint recognition. **Why?** Assume you want to see additional sources for this topic. Note that the Researcher is only available to Microsoft 365 installations. If you do not have Microsoft 365, read these steps without performing them.

1

- Click the Researcher button (References tab | Research group) to open the Researcher pane (Figure 2–82).

Q&A Why does my Researcher pane look different?
Depending on your settings, your Researcher pane may appear different from the figure shown here.

2

- Type **fingerprint recognition** in the Search box in the Researcher pane and then press ENTER to display topics and sources related to the search text (Figure 2–83).

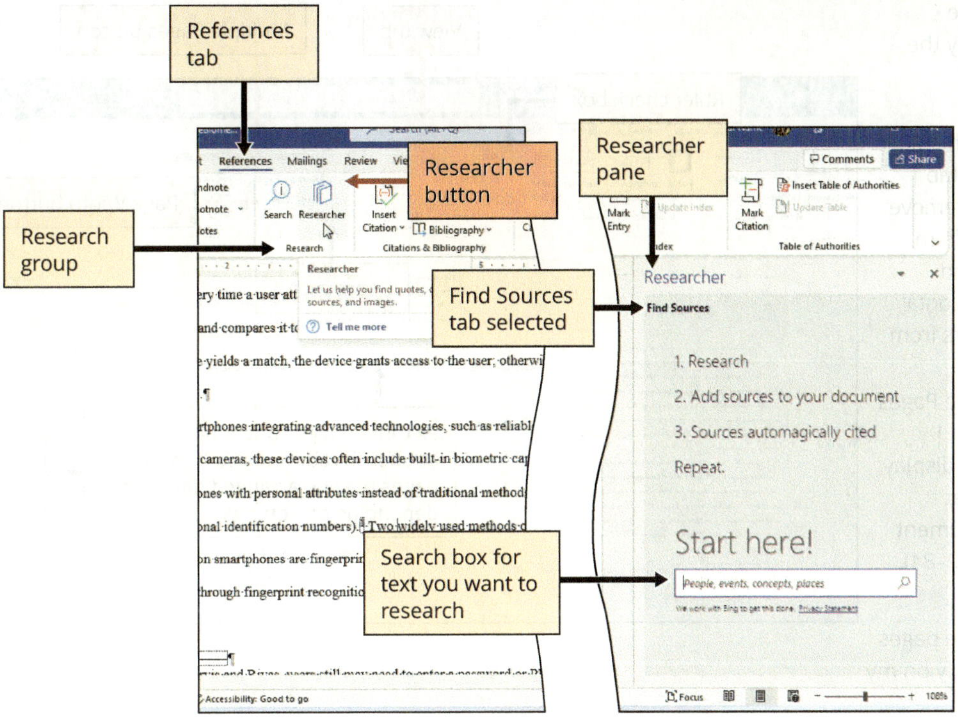

Figure 2–82

- **Experiment:** Scroll through the topics and sources that appear in the Researcher pane. Point to the + symbols on the right edge of the topics and sources and read their function (be careful not to click the + symbols; clicking these symbols will add content to your paper). Click one of the topics and read its information. Drag through text in the topic and notice the submenu with the 'Add and Cite' command, which allows you to add the text in your document at the location of the insertion point and cite its source. Click the Back button at the top of the Researcher pane to return to the previous display. Click one of the sources and read its information. Click the Back button to return to the previous display.
- Click the Close button in the Researcher pane to close the pane.

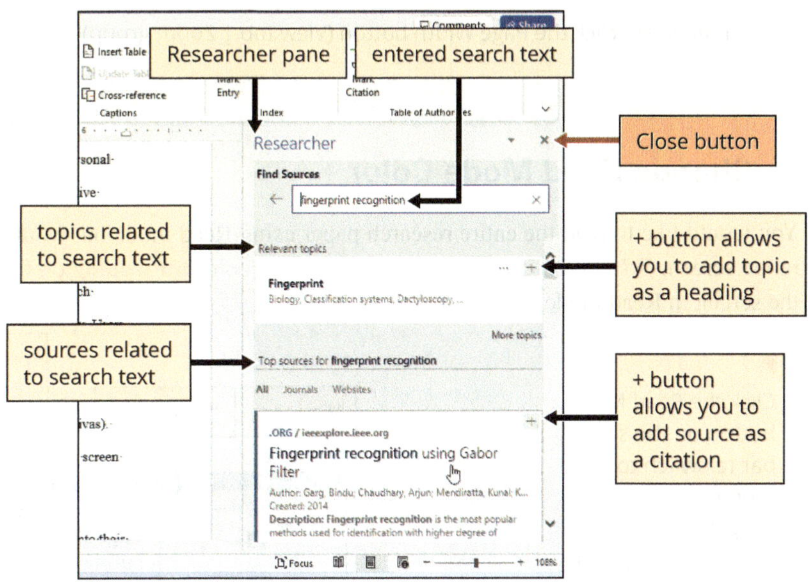

Figure 2–83

Q&A Can I use the information in my paper that I add from the Researcher pane?
Yes, you can use the information, but be sure not to plagiarize.

To Change the Zoom to Multiple Pages

The following steps display multiple pages in the document window at once. **Why?** You want to be able to see all pages in the research paper on the screen at the same time. You also hide formatting marks and the rulers so that the display is easier to view.

1

- Click Home on the ribbon to display the Home tab.
- If the 'Show/Hide ¶' button (Home tab | Paragraph group) is selected, click it to hide formatting marks.

- Click View on the ribbon to display the View tab.
- If the rulers are displayed, click the Ruler check box (View tab | Show group) to remove the check mark from the check box and remove the horizontal and vertical rulers from the screen.
- Click the Multiple Pages button (View tab | Zoom group) to display all three pages at once in the document window (Figure 2–84).

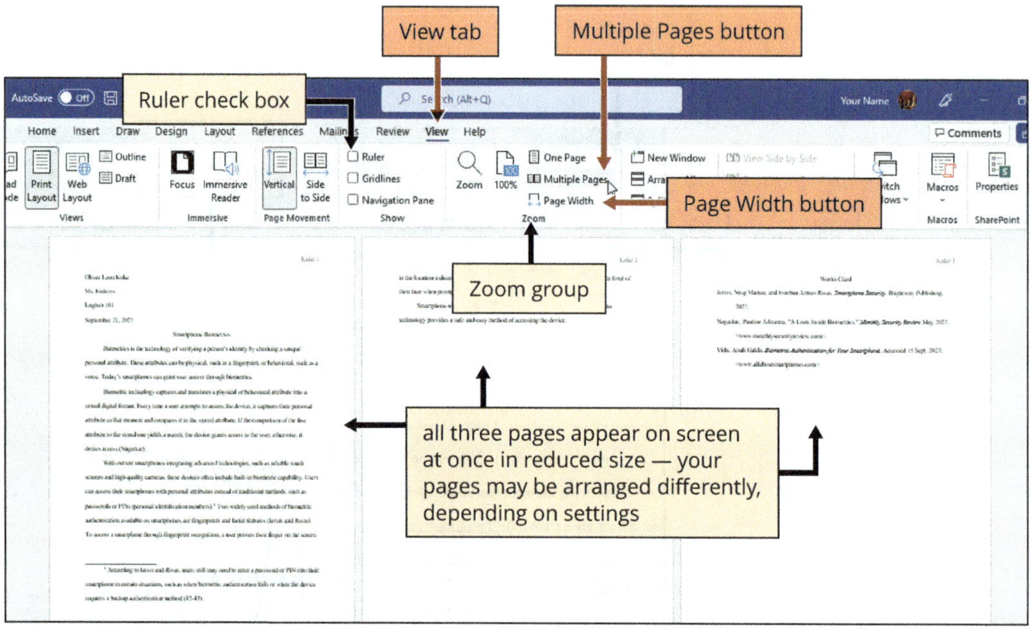

Figure 2–84

Q&A Why do the pages appear differently on my screen?

Depending on settings, Word may display all the pages as shown in Figure 2–84 or may show the pages differently.

2

- When finished, click the Page Width button (View tab | Zoom group) to return to the page width zoom.

To Change Read Mode Color

You would like to read the entire research paper using Read mode but would like to change the background color of the Read mode screen. **Why?** You prefer a softer background color for reading on the screen. The following steps change the color of the screen in Read mode.

1

- Click the Read Mode button on the status bar to switch to Read mode.
- Click the View on the toolbar to display the View menu.
- Point to Page Color on the View menu to display the Page Color submenu (Figure 2–85).

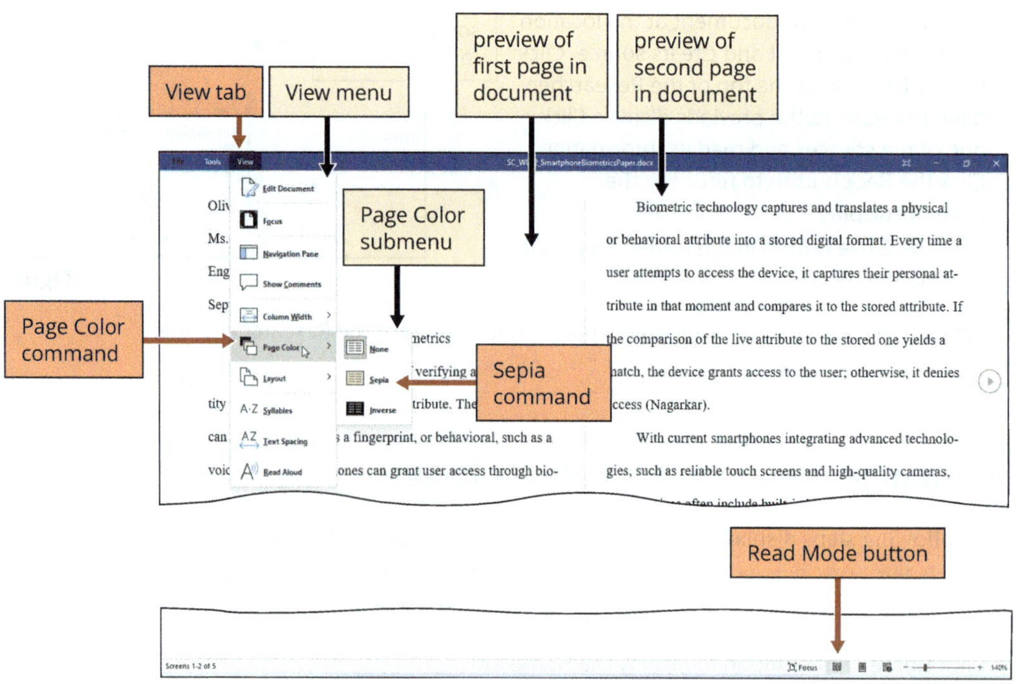

Figure 2–85

2

- Click Sepia on the Page Color submenu to change the color of the Read mode screen to sepia (Figure 2-86).

3

- When finished, remove the page color by clicking the View on the toolbar to display the View menu, pointing to Page Color on the View menu to display the Page Color submenu, and then clicking None on the Page Color submenu.
- Click the Print Layout button (shown in Figure 2-86) on the status bar to return to Print Layout view.

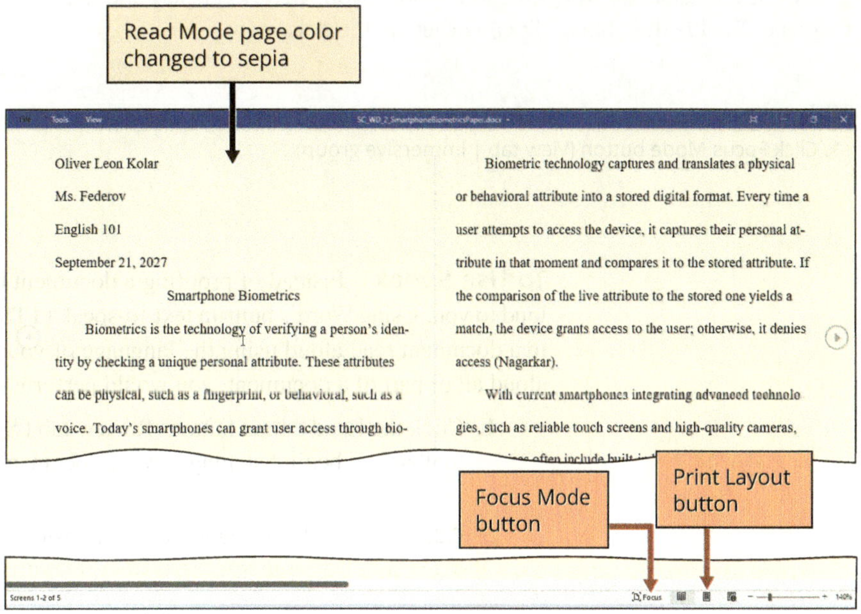

Figure 2-86

To Use Focus Mode

Instead of Read mode, you would like to read the research paper using Focus mode. **Why?** You would like to hide everything in the Word window, except for the document, so you have a clutter-free screen while reading. The following steps switch from Print Layout view to Focus mode.

1

- Click the Focus Mode button on the status bar (shown in Figure 2-86) to switch to Focus mode (Figure 2-87).
- **Experiment:** Use the mouse to scroll through the research paper.

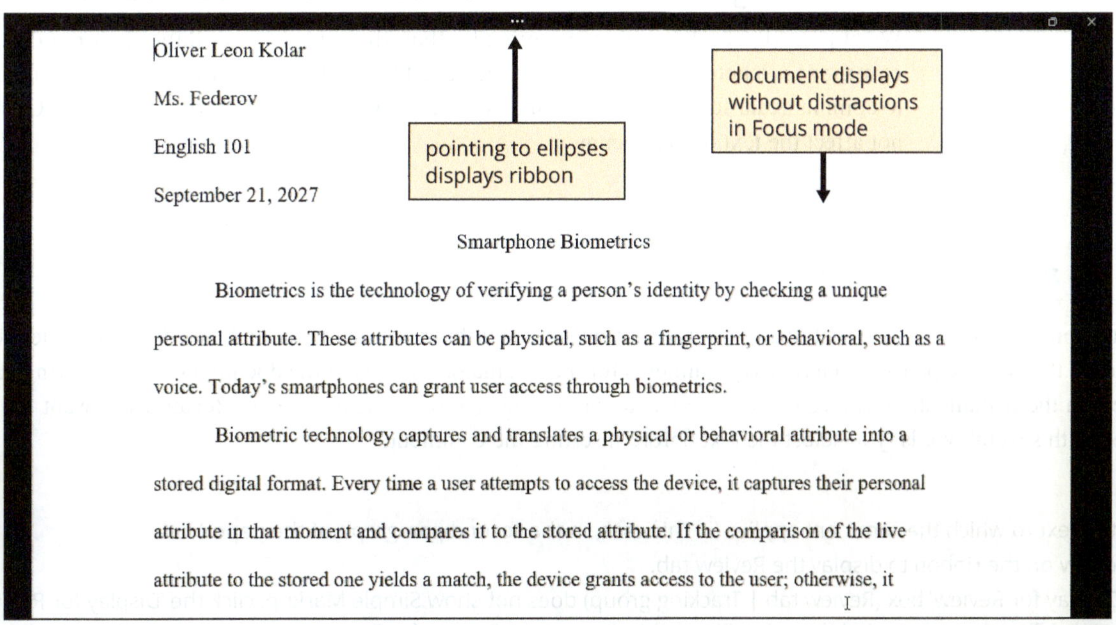

Figure 2-87

2

- Press ESC to exit Focus mode and redisplay the document window.

Q&A Can I edit the document in Focus mode?

Yes. Click or select text the same as in Print Layout view. To display and use the ribbon, point to the ellipses at the top of the screen. To hide the ribbon, click anywhere in the document.

Other Ways

1. Click Focus Mode button (View tab | Immersive group)

To Use Speak Instead of proofing a document by reading it, you can have Word read it out loud to you. Using Word's built-in text-to-speak (TTS) feature, called Speak, you can have the text in a document read aloud using the language of your Office version. If you wanted Word to read aloud all or part of a document, you would perform these steps.

1. Click the Read Aloud button (Review tab | Speech group) to display the Read Aloud toolbar and begin listening to your document from the location of the insertion point.

Q&A What if I do not hear a voice speaking?

Make sure that your speakers are turned on and the volume is up.

Can I change the reading speed?

Yes. Click the Settings button on the Read Aloud toolbar and drag the Reading speed slider to the desired speed.

2. To pause the reading aloud, click the Pause button on the Read Aloud toolbar. To continue reading aloud, click the Play button.
3. When you are finished listening to the reading of your document, close the Read Aloud toolbar by clicking its Stop button.

Q&A Can I listen to a section of the document?

Yes. Select the section you wish to be read aloud and then repeat these steps.

Working with Comments in a Document

Word provides tools, such as comments, that allow users to collaborate on a document. A **comment** is a note that an author or reviewer adds to a document. Reviewers often use comments to communicate suggestions, tips, and other messages to the author of a document. Comments do not affect the text of the document.

To Insert a Comment

For illustration purposes, assume that one of your classmates created this research paper and asked you to review the paper. After reading through the paper, you have two comments for the originator (author) of the document. The following steps insert a comment in the document. **Why?** You want to create a note for the author of the document. Because you want the comment associated with several words, you select the text before inserting the comment.

1

- Select the text to which the comment applies (in this case, in the second paragraph of the paper).
- Click Review on the ribbon to display the Review tab.
- If the 'Display for Review' box (Review tab | Tracking group) does not show Simple Markup, click the 'Display for Review' arrow (Review tab | Tracking group) and then click Simple Markup on the Display for Review menu to instruct Word to display a simple markup.

Q&A What is Simple Markup?
Simple Markup is a less cluttered view of comments and other collaboration elements than All Markup.

- If the Show Comments button (Review tab | Comments group) is not selected, click it to select it (Figure 2–88).

Q&A What is the purpose of the Show Comments button?
When the Show Comments button is selected, the comments appear in the markup area to the right of the document, or in the Comments pane (which opens when you click the Comments button on the upper-right edge of the ribbon). When it is not selected, comments appear as icons in the document.

Do I have to select text before inserting a comment?
No, you can position the insertion point at the location where the comment should be located. If you do not select text on which you wish to comment, Word automatically selects the text to the right or left of the insertion point for the comment.

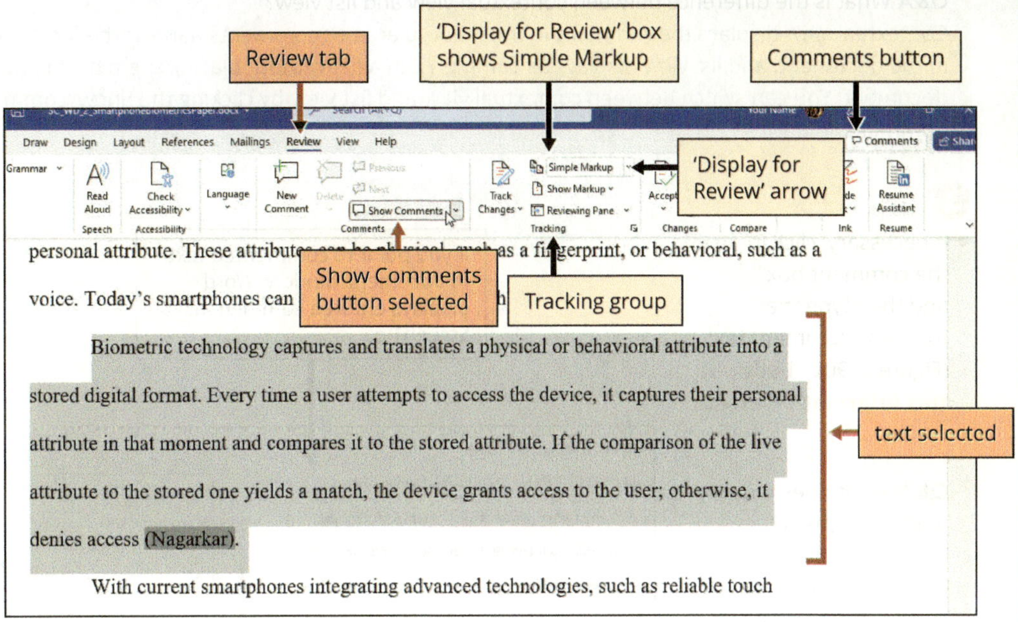

Figure 2–88

2

- Click the New Comment button (Review tab | Comments group) to display a comment box in the markup area in the document window.
- If necessary, change the zoom so that the entire document and markup area are visible in the document window (Figure 2–89).

Q&A What should I do if the comment box appears in the Comments pane?
Click the Show Comments arrow (Review tab | Comments group) and then click Contextual to display the comment box in the markup area next to the page content.

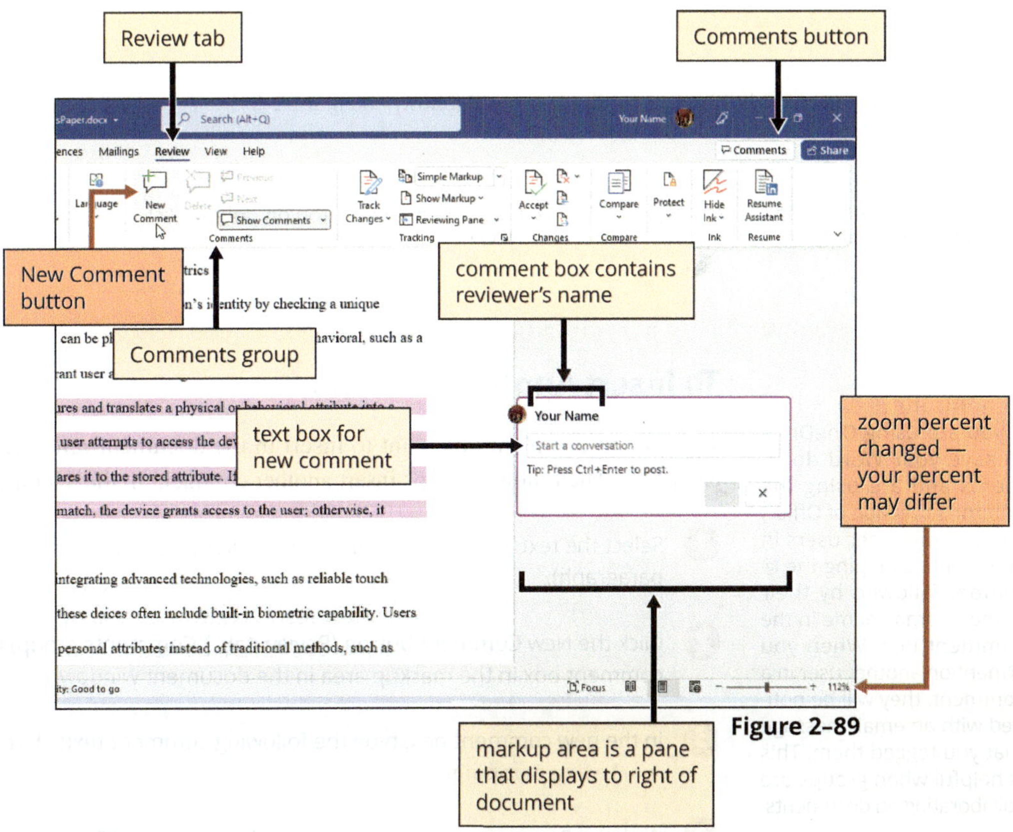

Figure 2–89

Q&A What is the difference between contextual view and list view?

Contextual view displays the comment in the markup area or comments pane at the location of the commented content in the document, and list view displays all comments in a list without placing them beside the commented content in the document. You can switch between contextual view and list view by clicking the Show Comments arrow (Review tab | Comments group).

3

- If necessary, click in the comment box and then type the following comment text (Figure 2–90): **Let's put this information on our website.**

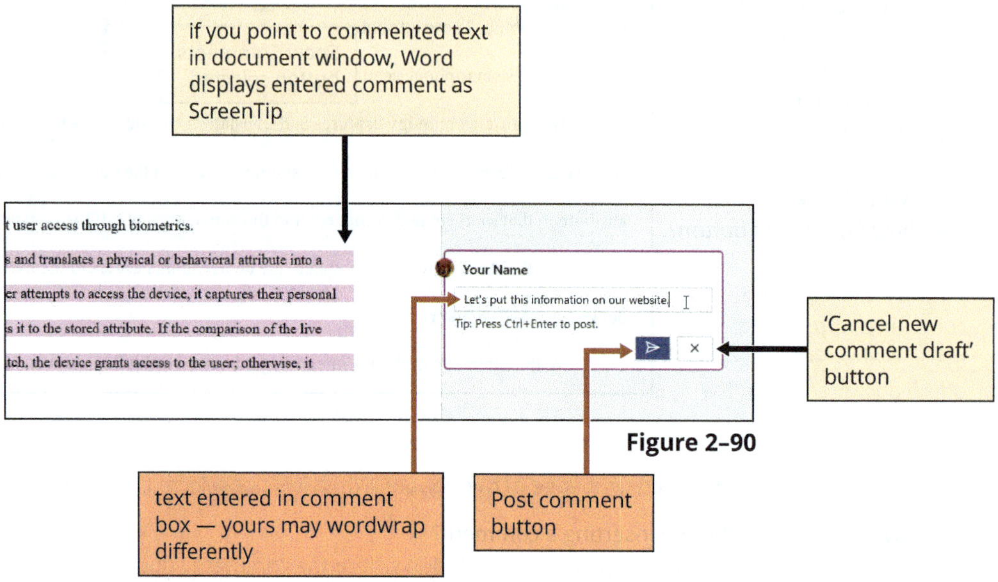

Figure 2–90

Q&A What does it mean to post a comment?

Posting a new comment creates a **thread**, or a collection of related comments. Replies appear with the original comment to help you follow the discussion.

What if I decide to not post a comment?

Click the 'Cancel new draft comment' button in the comment box to delete the comment box before it is posted.

What if I do not have a Post comment button in a comment box?

Press CTRL+ ENTER or click outside a comment box to post a comment

4

- Click the Post comment button to post the comment (shown in Figure 2–91).

Other Ways

1. Click Comment button (Insert tab | Comments group)
2. Click Comments button on ribbon, click New button in Comments pane
3. Press CTRL+ALT+M

BTW
@mentions
If you are using OneDrive to save your Word documents and are using the Enterprise version of Office, you can tag other users in comments by typing the @ symbol followed by their name or email name in the comment box. When you @mention another user in a comment, they will be notified with an email message that you tagged them. This is helpful when groups are collaborating on documents.

To Insert Another Comment

The second comment you want to insert in the document refers to a point for the marketing campaign. The following steps insert another comment in the document.

1. Select the text to which the comment applies (in this case, the third sentence of the third paragraph).
2. Click the New Comment button (Review tab | Comments group) to display another comment box in the markup area in the document window.
3. In the new comment box, type the following comment text: **Let's stress this point in our marketing campaigns.**
4. Click the Post comment button to post the comment (Figure 2–91).

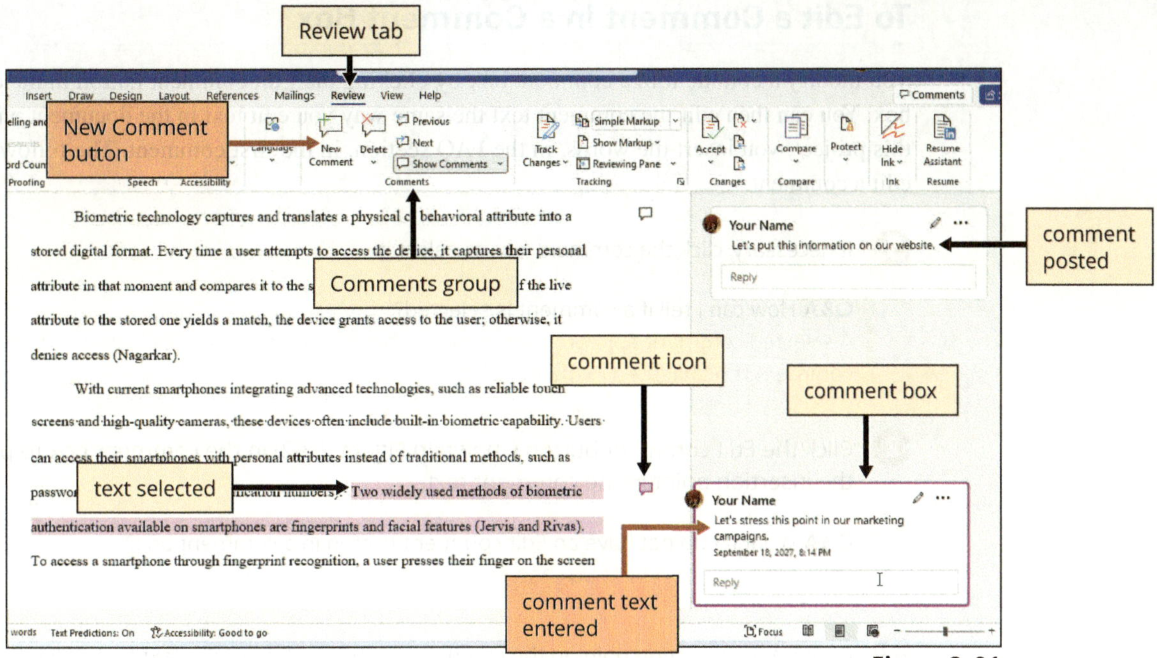

Figure 2–91

To Go to a Comment

The next step is to display the previous comment. **Why?** You could scroll through the document to locate a comment by reading them as they appear in the markup area, but it is more efficient to use the Review tab. The following step displays the previous comment in the document.

1

- Click the Previous button (Review tab | Comments group), which causes Word to locate and select the previous comment in the document (Figure 2–92).

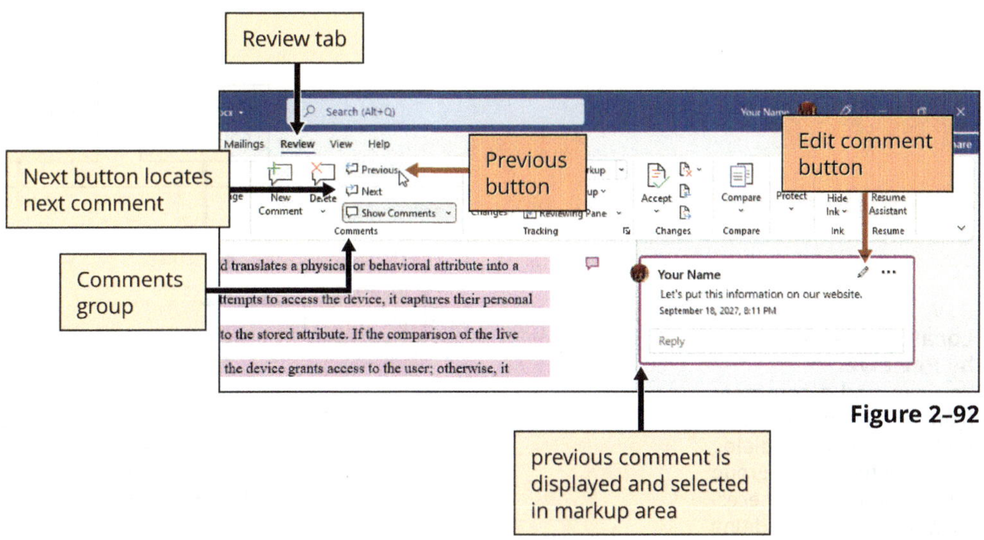

Figure 2–92

Q&A What if I wanted to see the next comment, instead of the previous comment, in a document?
You would click the Next button (Review tab | Comments group) instead of the Previous button.

What if I wanted to move from one comment to the next in a document from the beginning of the document?
You would position the insertion point at the top of the document and then click the Next button (Review tab | Comments group) repeatedly until you have seen all comments in the document.

Other Ways

1. Click Editing group button (Home tab) if necessary, click Find arrow (Home tab | Editing group), click Find arrow (Home tab | Editing group), click Go To, click Comment in Go to what area (Find and Replace dialog box), click Next button
2. Press CTRL+G, click Comment in Go to what area (Find and Replace dialog box), click Next button

To Edit a Comment in a Comment Box

You modify a comment in a comment box by clicking the Edit comment button in the comment box. You can then edit the comment text the same way you edit text in the document window. In this project, you insert the words, in the FAQ section, in the first comment. The following steps edit a comment.

1. If necessary, click the comment box to select it.

   Q&A How can I tell if a comment is selected?
   A selected comment appears with a colored border and the text associated with the comment is highlighted in the document.

2. Click the Edit comment button (shown in Figure 2–92) in the comment box to position the insertion point in the comment text.

   Q&A What if I do not have an Edit comment button in a comment box?
   Click inside the comment box and edit the same way you edit text in the document window.

3. Position the insertion point in the comment at the location of the text to edit (in this case, to the left of the o in the word, on, in the first comment).

4. Type **in the FAQ section** and then press SPACEBAR to edit the comment (Figure 2–93).

   Q&A What is an FAQ?
   An FAQ is a list that helps a user find answers to frequently asked questions.

5. Click the Post comment button in the comment box to save the change to the comment.

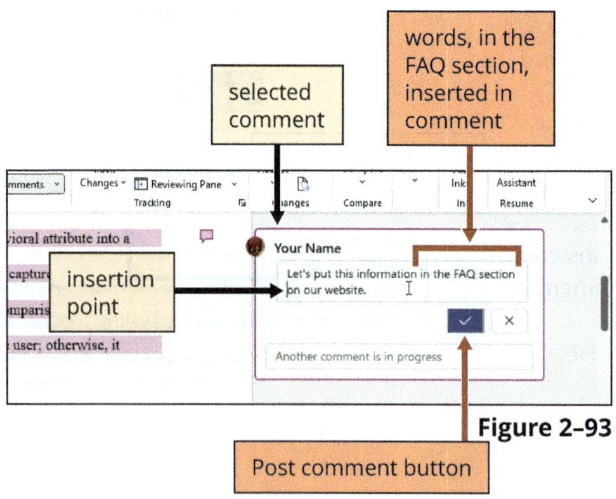

Figure 2–93

BTW
Locating Comments by Reviewer
You can find a comment from a specific reviewer through the Go To dialog box. Click the Editing group button (Home tab), if necessary, to display the Editing group, click the Find arrow (Home tab | Editing group), and then click Go To, or press CTRL+G to display the Go To sheet in the Find and Replace dialog box. Click Comment in the Go to what list (Find and Replace dialog box). Select the reviewer whose comments you wish to find and then click the Next button.

To Go to a Comment

The next step is to display the next comment because you want to reply to it. The following step displays the next comment in the document.

1. Click the Next button (Review tab | Comments group), which causes Word to locate and select the next comment in the document (shown in Figure 2–94).

Q&A What if I reach the last comment in a document?
When you click the Next button (Review tab | Comments group), Word moves to the top of the document and displays the first comment in the document.

To Reply to a Comment

Sometimes, you want to reply to an existing comment. **Why?** You may want to respond to a question by another reviewer or provide additional information to a previous comment you inserted. The following steps reply to the comment you inserted on the second page of the document.

1

- If necessary, click the comment box to which you wish to reply to select it (in this case, the second comment).
- Click the Reply box in the selected comment to position the insertion point in the box.

2

- Type the following comment text: **Excellent idea!** (Figure 2–94).

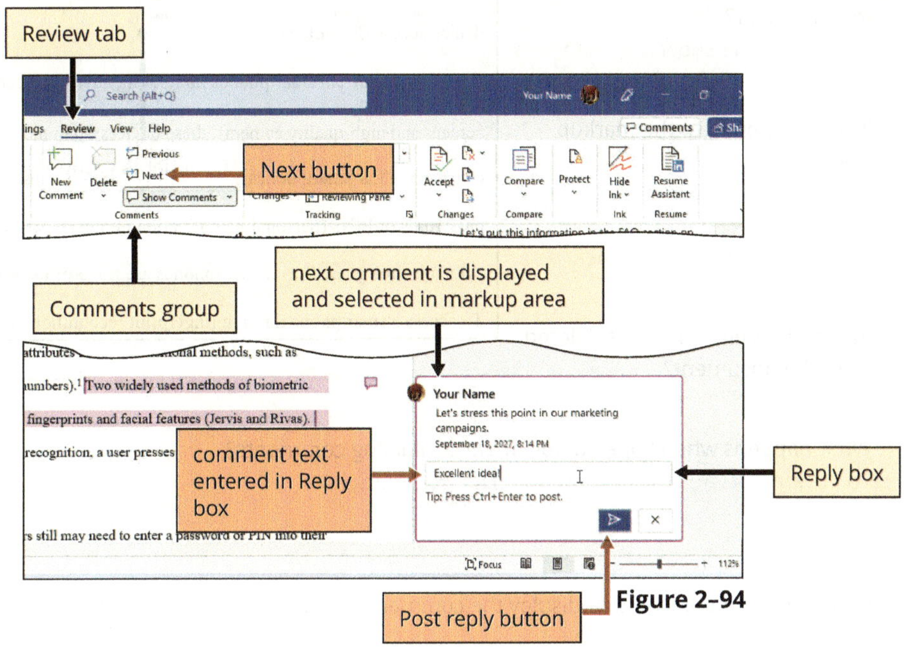

Figure 2–94

3

- Click the Post reply button to add the reply to the thread (Figure 2–95).

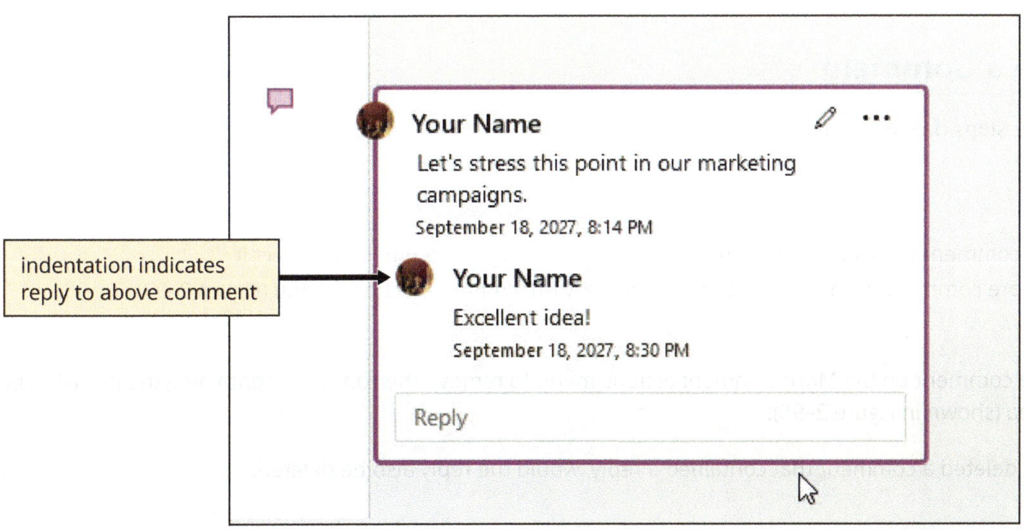

Figure 2–95

To Hide and Show Comments

The next step is to hide all comments in the document. **Why?** You would like to view the document without the markup area on the screen but do not want to delete the comments at this time. The following steps hide comments and then show them.

1

- If the Show Comments button (Review tab | Comments group) is selected, click it to deselect it, which hides comments in the document (Figure 2–96).

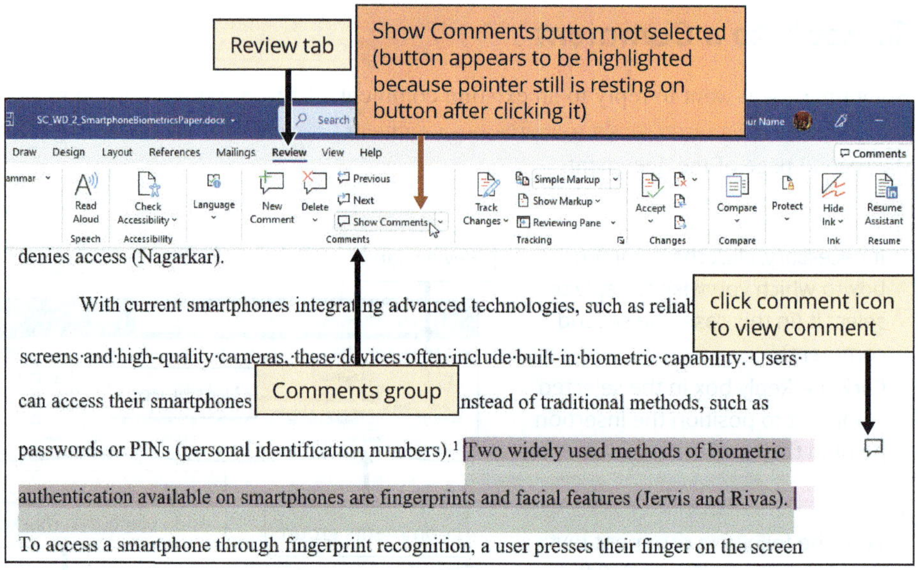

Figure 2–96

Q&A Why did the Show Comments menu appear?
You clicked the Show Comments arrow. Press ESC and repeat Step 1.

What happened to the markup area?
When the Show Comments button is not selected, the markup area is hidden and comments appear as icons in the document.

Are the hidden comments deleted from the document?
No.

What happens when I open a document containing comments?
The comments appear in the markup area by default.

2

- Click the comment icon to redisplay the comments in the markup area (shown in Figure 2–97).

Other Ways

1. Click comment icon again to hide comment

To Delete a Comment

The following steps delete a comment. **Why?** You have read the reply to the second comment and want to remove it from the document.

1

- Click in the comment to delete, in this case, the reply to the second comment, to select it.
- Click the 'More comment actions' button to display the More comment actions menu (Figure 2–97).

2

- Click Delete comment on the More comment actions menu to remove the comment containing the insertion point from the markup area (shown in Figure 2–98).

Q&A If you deleted a comment that contained a reply, would the reply also be deleted?
Yes.

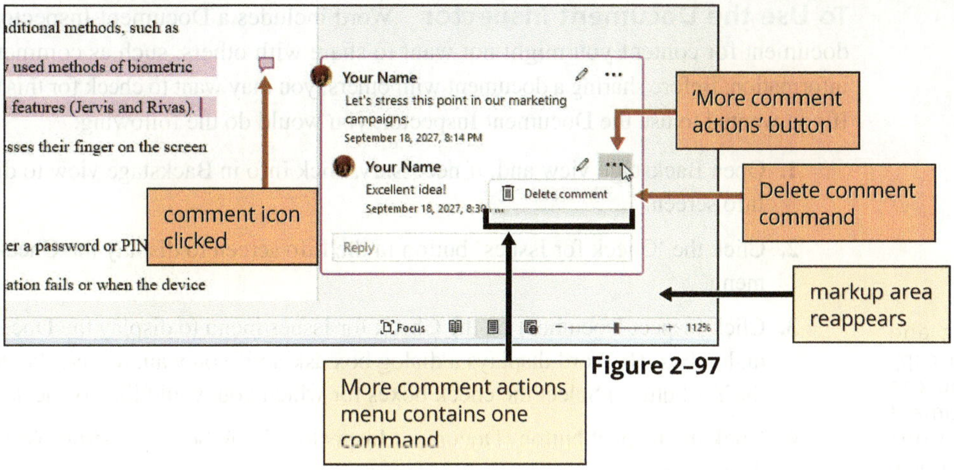

Figure 2–97

Other Ways

1. Click Delete button (Review tab | Comments group) to remove selected comment

To Resolve a Comment Instead of deleting comments, some users prefer to leave them in the document but mark them as resolved. This is especially useful when multiple users are collaborating on the same document. When you resolve a comment, Word removes it from the markup area and displays a check mark in the comment icon. To view a resolved comment, you would click the check mark in the comment icon or display the Comments pane by clicking the Comments button on the ribbon. If you wanted to resolve a comment, you would perform the following step.

1. Click the 'More thread actions' button in the comment box and then click Resolve thread.

To Delete All Comments

The following steps delete all comments at once. **Why?** Assume you now want to delete all the comments in the document at once because you have addressed them all.

1

- Click the Delete arrow (Review tab | Comments group) to display the Delete menu (Figure 2–98).

2

- Click 'Delete All Comments in Document' on the Delete menu to remove all comments from the document, which also closes the markup area.
- If the Comments pane remains open, click its Close button to close the pane.

Q&A What if I accidentally click the Delete button?
You will delete only the current comment. Repeat Steps 1 and 2 to delete all comments in the document.

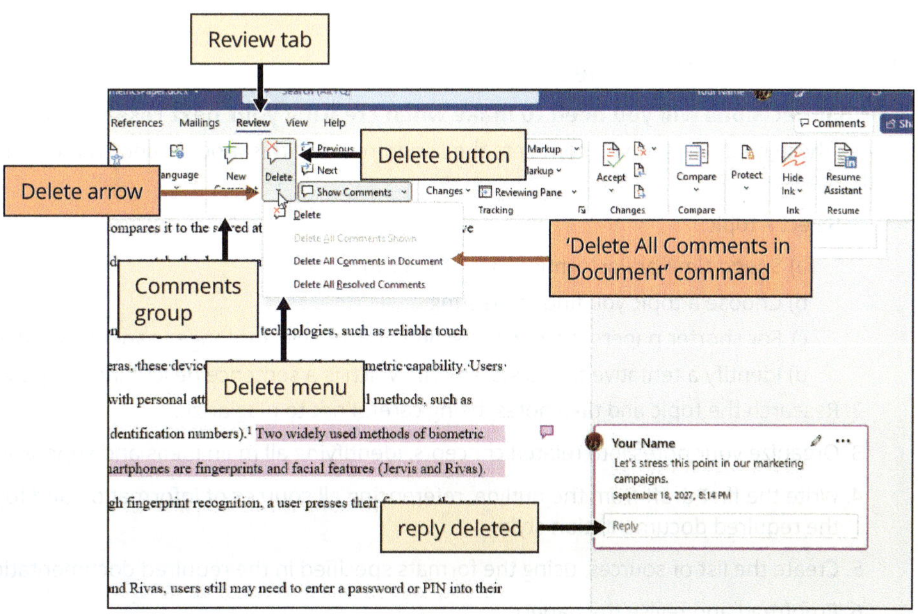

Figure 2–98

To Use the Document Inspector Word includes a Document Inspector that checks a document for content you might not want to share with others, such as comments or personal information. Before sharing a document with others, you may want to check for this type of content. If you wanted to use the Document Inspector, you would do the following:

1. Open Backstage view and, if necessary, click Info in Backstage view to display the Info screen.
2. Click the 'Check for Issues' button in the Info screen to display the Check for Issues menu.
3. Click Inspect Document on the Check for Issues menu to display the Document Inspector dialog box. (If Word displays a dialog box asking if you want to save the document, click the Yes button.) Select the check boxes for which you would like to check the document.
4. Click the Inspect button (Document Inspector dialog box) to instruct Word to inspect the document.
5. Review the results (Document Inspector dialog box) and then click the Remove All button(s) for any item that you do not want to be saved with the document.
6. When finished removing information, click the Close button to close the dialog box.

BTW
Distributing a Document
Instead of printing and distributing a hard copy of a document, you can distribute the document electronically. Options include sending the document via email; posting it on cloud storage (such as OneDrive) and sharing the file with others; posting it on social media, a blog, or other website; and sharing a link associated with an online location of the document. You also can create and share a PDF or XPS image of the document, so that users can view the file in Acrobat Reader or XPS Viewer instead of in Word.

To Exit Word

You are finished with this project. The following step exits Word.

1 Exit Word.

Summary

In this module, you learned how to modify styles, adjust line and paragraph spacing, use headers to number pages, insert and edit citations and their sources, add footnotes, create a bibliographical list of sources, update a field, go to a page, find and replace text, check spelling and grammar, look up information, and work with comments.

Consider This: Plan Ahead

What decisions will you need to make when creating your next research paper?

Use these guidelines as you complete the assignments in this module and create your own research papers outside of this class.

1. Select a topic.
   a) Spend time brainstorming ideas for a topic.
   b) Choose a topic you find interesting.
   c) For shorter papers, narrow the scope of the topic; for longer papers, broaden the scope.
   d) Identify a tentative thesis statement, which is a sentence describing the paper's subject matter.
2. Research the topic and take notes, being careful not to plagiarize.
3. Organize your notes into related concepts, identifying all main ideas and supporting details in an outline.
4. Write the first draft from the outline, referencing all sources of information and following the guidelines identified in the required documentation style.
5. Create the list of sources, using the formats specified in the required documentation style.
6. Proofread and revise the paper.

Student Assignments

Apply Your Knowledge

Reinforce the skills and apply the concepts you learned in this module.

Revising Content and Working with Citations and Sources in a Document

Note: To complete this assignment, you will be required to use the Data Files. Please contact your instructor for information about accessing the Data Files.

Instructions: Start Word. Open the document, SC_WD_2-1.docx, which is located in the Data Files. The document you open contains two paragraphs of text that are notes about global positioning system (GPS) technology. The manager of Clear Signal Manufacturing, who created the GPS notes, has asked you to revise the document as follows: check spelling and grammar, change paragraph indentation, change line spacing, remove space before and after paragraphs, find all occurrences of a word, replace all occurrences of a word with another word, locate a synonym, edit the header, add a sentence, insert and edit citations and sources, delete a source, and insert a reference list. The modified document is shown in Figure 2–99.

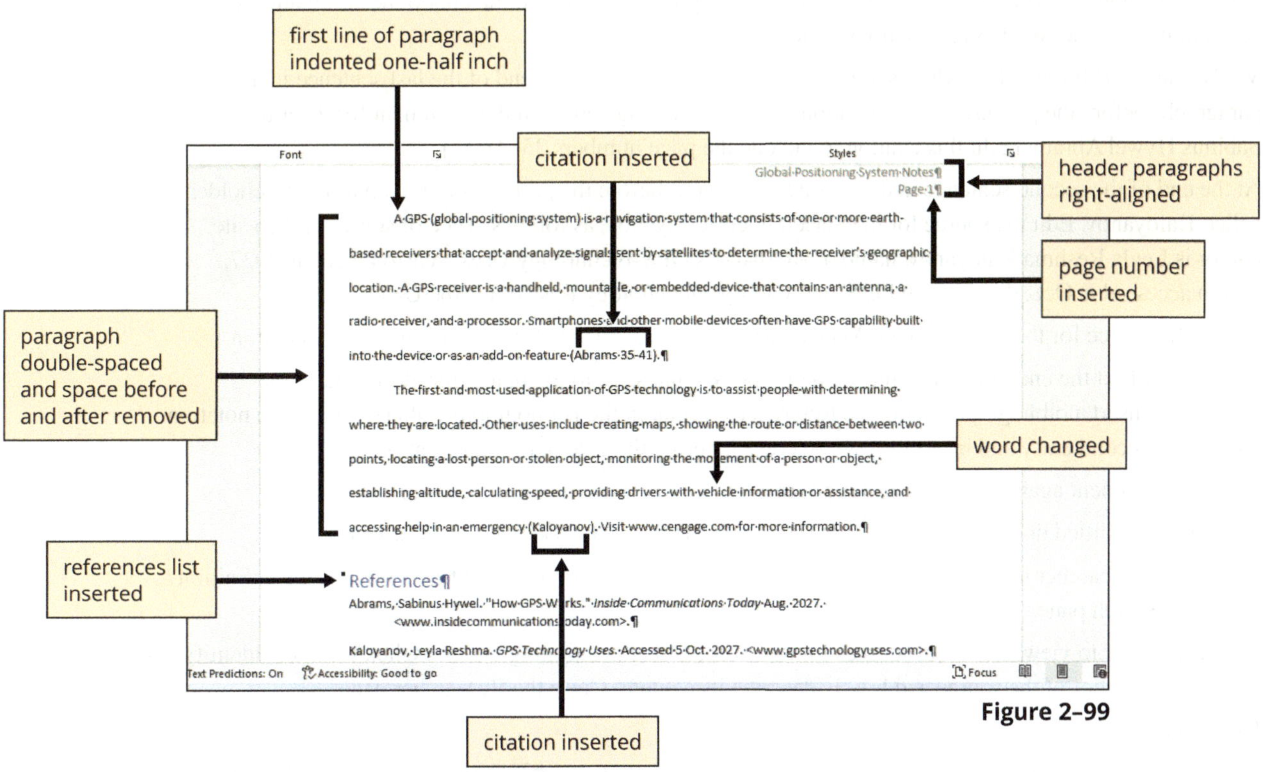

Figure 2–99

Perform the following tasks:

1. Click File on the ribbon, click Save As, and then save the document using the new file name, SC_WD_2_GPSNotes.
2. Check spelling and grammar at once. Correct the spelling and grammar mistakes in the document. Change all instances of the suggested spelling change, person, for the misspelled word, persone.
3. Display the ruler, if necessary. Use the ruler to indent the first line of the first paragraph one-half inch. (If you are using a touch screen, use the Paragraph dialog box.) Hide the ruler.
4. Select the entire document and change the line spacing to double. With the entire document selected, remove space before and after paragraphs. (**Hint:** Use the 'Line and Paragraph Spacing' button for each command.)

Continued on next page

5. Find all occurrences of the word, GPS. How many are there?
6. Use the Find and Replace dialog box to replace all occurrences of the word, unit, with the words, device. How many replacements were made?
7. Show the Navigation Pane. Use the Navigation Pane to find the word, automobile. Close the Navigation Pane. Use Word's thesaurus to change the word, automobile, to the word, vehicle. What other words are in the list of synonyms?
8. Switch to the header so that you can edit it. In the first line of the header, insert the word, System, after the word, Positioning, so that it reads: Global Positioning System Notes.
9. In the second line of the header, insert a page number (a plain number with no formatting) one space after the word, Page.
10. If requested by your instructor, enter your first and last name on a separate line below the page number in the header.
11. Change the alignment of all lines of text in the header from left-aligned to right-aligned. Close the header and footer.
12. At the end of the second paragraph, type **Visit www.cengage.com for more information.** After you type the web address, continue typing to accept the automatic correction of the web address to a hyperlink format. Use the AutoCorrect Options button (point to the web address to display the small blue underline and then point to the blue underline to display the AutoCorrect Options button) and then undo the automatic hyperlink correction using the AutoCorrect Options button.
13. Verify that the Bibliography style is set to MLA Seventh Edition. At the end of the last sentence in the first paragraph (before the period), insert a citation using the existing source in the document for the article by Sabinus Hywel Abrams. Edit this citation to include the page numbers 35–41.
14. At the end of the second sentence in the second paragraph (before the period), insert a citation placeholder called Kaloyanov. Edit the source for the placeholder, Kaloyanov, as follows: Type of source is Web site, author is Leyla Reshma Kaloyanov, name of webpage is GPS Technology Uses, year accessed is 2027, month accessed is Oct., day accessed is 5, and www.gpstechnologyuses.com is the URL.
15. Delete the source for the author named Matteus Ralf O'Toole. (**Hint:** Use the Manage Sources button.)
16. Press ENTER at the end of the document. Apply the Normal style to the blank line at the end of the document. Insert a bibliography using the References format in the Bibliography gallery. Delete the notation, n.d., in the second entry and insert the text, Accessed, before the date in the same entry.
17. Save the document again with the same file name.
18. Submit the modified document, shown in Figure 2–99, in the format specified by your instructor.
19. Use Smart Researcher to look up the word, altitude. (Be sure to select the word first.) What is the definition? Close the Search pane.
20. Use Researcher to view additional sources for the word, global positioning system. Click a source; identify the title and author of the source and briefly describe its content. Close the Researcher pane.
21. Exit Word.
22. **Consider This:** Answer the questions posed in #5, #6, #7, #19, and #20. How would you find and replace a special character, such as a paragraph mark?

Extend Your Knowledge

Extend the skills you learned in this module and experiment with new skills. You may need to use Help to complete the assignment.

Working with References and Proofing Tools

Note: To complete this assignment, you will be required to use the Data Files. Please contact your instructor for information about accessing the Data Files.

Instructions: As a customer relationship coordinator at Riverton Internet Services, you communicate technology tips to customers. You also are a part-time student who has been assigned a research paper. You decide to combine your work and school interests and compose a short research paper about computer viruses. You will communicate your findings with customers.

Start Word. Open the document, SC_WD_2-2.docx, which is located in the Data Files. The document is your draft research paper. You will do the following to finish the paper: find formats and special characters, delete a footer, add another footnote to the paper, change the format of the note reference marks, convert the footnotes to endnotes, modify a style, use Word's readability statistics, work with comments, and translate the document to another language (Figure 2–100).

Perform the following tasks:

1. Use Help to learn more about finding formats and special characters, footers, footnotes and endnotes, readability statistics, bibliography styles, AutoCorrect, and Word's translation features.
2. Click File on the ribbon, click Save As, and then save the revised document using the new file name, SC_WD_2_ComputerViruses. Verify that the Citations and Bibliography style is set to MLA Seventh Edition.
3. Use the Advanced Find command on the Find menu and the Replace tab in the Find and Replace dialog box to find the Bold font format in the body of the research paper and replace it with the Not Bold format.
4. Use the Advanced Find command on the Find menu to find a footnote mark in the paper (which is a special character). (**Hint:** You may need to click the No Formatting button in the dialog box to remove the Bold format search from the previous step.) What characters did Word place in the Find what box to search for the footnote mark? What number in the research paper is the footnote reference mark?
5. Edit the footer so that it reads: Delete this footer from the research paper. Delete the footer from the document.

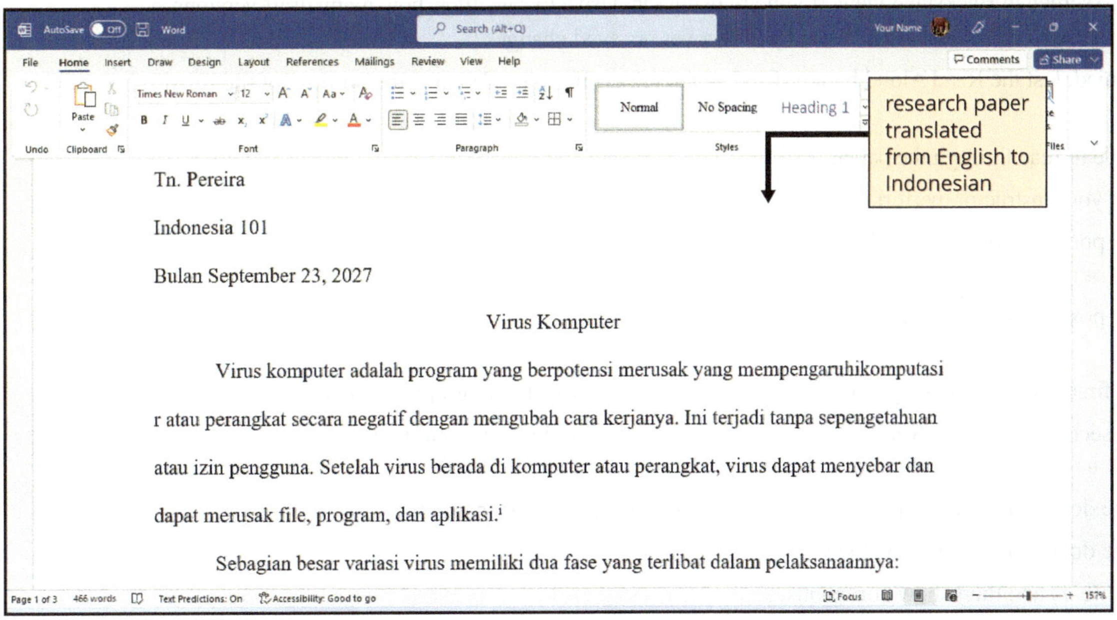

Figure 2–100

6. Insert a second footnote at an appropriate place in the research paper. Use the following footnote text: **When you purchase a new computer, it may include a trial version of antivirus software. Many email servers also have antivirus software installed to check incoming and outgoing email messages for viruses.**
7. Change the location of the footnotes from bottom of page to below text. How did the placement of the footnotes change?
8. Change the format of the note reference marks to capital letters (A, B, etc.). (**Hint:** Change the footnote number format using the Footnote and Endnote dialog box.)

Continued on next page

9. Convert the footnotes to endnotes. Use the Navigation Pane to display each page in the document. Where are the endnotes positioned? What is the format of the note reference marks when they are endnotes?
10. Modify the Endnote Text style to 12-point (if necessary), double-spaced text with a hanging indent by clicking Style on the shortcut menu, clicking Endnote Text (Style dialog box), clicking the Modify button, and then selecting appropriate options in the Modify Style dialog box. If necessary, close the Navigation Pane.
11. Insert this endnote for the first paragraph in the paper: **Viruses do not generate by chance. The programmer of a virus, known as a virus author, intentionally writes a virus program. Writing a virus program usually requires significant programming skills.**
12. Add an AutoCorrect entry that replaces the word, comptuers, with the word, computers. Type the following sentence as the last sentence in the last paragraph of the paper, misspelling the word, computers, as comptuers, to test the AutoCorrect entry: **Due to the increasing threat of viruses attacking comptuers and devices, it is more important than ever to use antivirus software.** Delete the AutoCorrect entry that replaces comptuers with the word, computers.
13. Display the Word Count dialog box. How many words, characters without spaces, characters with spaces, paragraphs, and lines are in the document? Be sure to include footnote and endnote text in the statistics.
14. Check spelling of the document, displaying readability statistics. What is the Flesch Reading Ease score and the Flesch-Kincaid Grade Level? How could you modify the paper to increase the reading ease score and lower the grade level?
15. If requested by your instructor, change the student name at the top of the paper to your name, including the last name in the header.
16. Change the zoom to multiple pages. How many pages are in the document?
17. Save the revised document paper again with the same name and then submit it in the format specified by your instructor.
18. Display the Info screen in Backstage view. If you are using OneDrive to save files, how many draft versions of this document have been saved? How would you recover unsaved changes?
19. If it is not dimmed, test the Read Aloud button (Review tab | Speech group). What is the purpose of the Read Aloud button?
20. Use Focus mode to read through the paper.
21. If requested by your instructor, perform these tasks:
    a. Insert and post this comment in the second paragraph: **Add a discussion about types of viruses after this paragraph.**
    b. Insert and post another comment in the third paragraph: **Add a paragraph about signs of virus infection.**
    c. Go to the first comment. Change the word, discussion, to the word, paragraph, in the first comment.
    d. Go to the second comment. Reply to the second comment with this comment text: **Also discuss virus hoaxes.**
    e. Submit the document with comments in the format specified by your instructor.
    f. Inspect the document and review the results.
    g. Hide comments and then show comments.
    h. Delete the first comment. Resolve the second comment.
    i. Delete all comments.
22. If you have an Internet connection, translate the research paper into a language of your choice using the Translate button (Review tab | Language group), as shown in Figure 2–100. If requested by your instructor, submit the translated document in the format specified by your instructor.
23. **Consider This:** Answer the questions posed in #4, #7, #9, #13, #14, #16, #18, and #19. Where did you insert the footnote specified in instruction #6 and why?

Expand Your World

Create a solution that uses cloud or web technologies by learning and investigating on your own from general guidance.

Using an Online Bibliography Tool to Create a List of Sources

Note: You may need to watch advertisements or view sponsored messages in order to use the free version of an online bibliography tool.

Instructions: Assume you are attending a conference about food safety and the computer or mobile device you have available at the conference does not have Word but has Internet access. As a human resources specialist for Midwest Markets, you are responsible for providing up-to-date reference material for company employees. You decide to use an online bibliography tool to create a list of sources that you can copy and paste into the Works Cited pages of a paper you will create when you return to the office.

Perform the following tasks:

1. Start a browser. Search for the text, online bibliography tool, using a search engine. Visit several of the online bibliography tools and determine which you would like to use to create a list of sources. Navigate to the desired online bibliography tool. If available, select MLA as the documentation style.
2. Use the online bibliography tool to enter the list of sources shown below (Figure 2–101):

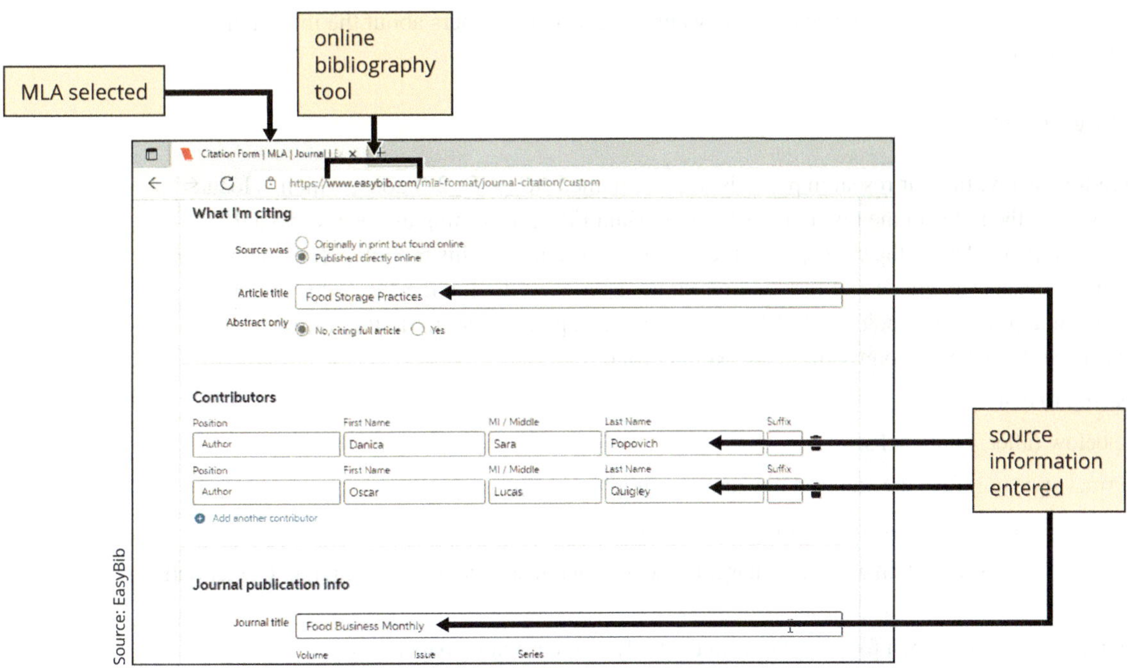

Figure 2–101

Book: Forester, Emilie Renee, and Amir Hemera Nozawa. *Managing Food Safety*. Rolling City Press, 2027.

Article in a journal/periodical: Hersch, Carla Marcel. "Food Sanitation Principles." *Food Practices Journal*. Sept. 2027. <www.foodpracticesjournal.com>.

Website: Estrada, Flora Alexandra. *Wisely Approaching Food Safety.* **Accessed** 9 Sept. 2027. <www.wafs.com>.

Book: Nguyen, Nhung Quang. *The Food Safety Handbook.* Sunrise Publishing, 2027.

Book: Tawfiq, Leila Noura. *Food Science*. East Coast Publications, 2025.

Article in a journal/periodical: Popovich, Danica Sara, and Oscar Lucas Quigley. "Food Storage Practices." *Food Business Monthly*. June 2027. <www.foodbusinessmonthly.com>.

Continued on next page

3. If requested by your instructor, replace the name in one of the sources above with your name.
4. If requested by your instructor, search for another source that discusses food safety. Add that source.
5. Use the Export/Save option in the online bibliography tool or copy and paste the list of sources into a Word document.
6. Save the document with the file name, SC_WD_2_FoodSafetySources. Submit the document in the format specified by your instructor.
7. **Consider This:** Which online bibliography tools did you evaluate? Which one did you select to use and why? Do you prefer using the online bibliography tool or Word to create sources? Why? What differences, if any, did you notice between the list of sources created with the online bibliography tool and the lists created when you use Word?

In the Lab

Design and implement a solution using creative thinking and problem-solving skills.

Create a Research Paper about Two-Step Verification

Note: To complete this assignment, you will be required to use the Data Files. Please contact your instructor for information about accessing the Data Files.

Problem: As the administrative assistant for the marketing director at Carlton Bank and Trust, you create a research paper about two-step authentication because you want to educate customers about the importance of securing access to their accounts.

Perform the following tasks:

Part 1: The source for the text in your research paper is in a file named SC_WD_2-3.docx, which is located in the Data Files. Organize the notes in the text in the file in the Data Files, rewording as necessary so that you can create a research paper. Using the concepts and techniques presented in this module, along with your organized notes from the Data File, create and format a research paper according to the MLA documentation style (be sure to write an appropriate conclusion). While creating the paper, be sure to do the following:

1. Modify the Normal style to the 12-point Times New Roman font.
2. Adjust line spacing to double.
3. Remove space below (after) paragraphs.
4. Update the Normal style to reflect the adjusted line and paragraph spacing.
5. Insert an MLA-style header, and insert page numbers in the header.
6. Type the name and course information at the left margin. Use your name and course information. Center and type the title.
7. Set a first-line indent to one-half inch for paragraphs in the body of the research paper.
8. Add an AutoCorrect entry to correct a word you commonly mistype.
9. Type the body of the research paper from the notes. If necessary, change the bibliography style to MLA. As you insert citations, enter their source information. Edit the citations so that they are displayed according to the MLA documentation style. Enter at least one footnote using the notes. Use the Rewrite Suggestions feature to rewrite some of the notes in the paper.
10. At the end of the research paper text, press ENTER and then insert a page break so that the Works Cited page begins on a new page. Enter and format the works cited title and then use Word to insert the bibliographical list (bibliography).
11. If your instructor requests, use Smart Lookup to obtain the definition of a word or phrase in the paper and enter the definition as a note positioned as a footnote in the paper with the appropriate citation and source added. Then, use Researcher to obtain information from another source about a topic in the paper and include that information as another note also positioned as a footnote in the paper, and enter its corresponding citation and source information as appropriate. Update the bibliography.

12. Edit the citations and works cited so that they are displayed according to the current MLA documentation style.
13. Check the spelling and grammar of the paper at once. Add one of the source last names to the dictionary. Ignore all instances of one of the source last names. If necessary, set the default dictionary.
14. Use the Editor button to check, and fix if necessary, the clarity, conciseness, formality, and other aspects of your writing.

When you are finished with the research paper, save it with the file name, SC_WD_2_TwoStepVerificationPaper. Submit your assignment and answers to the Part 2 critical thinking questions in the format specified by your instructor.

Part 2: **Consider This:** You made several decisions while creating the research paper in this assignment: how to organize and rewrite the notes, what text to use for the conclusion, where to place citations, how to format sources, which of the notes to use as a footnote, and which source on the web to use for a second footnote (if requested by your instructor). What was the rationale behind each of these decisions? When you proofread the document, what further revisions did you make and why?

Creating a Business Letter

Objectives

After completing this module, you will be able to:

- Insert and format a shape
- Arrange and format objects
- Modify text and paragraph formatting
- Insert an online picture and format the picture
- Copy and paste objects
- Insert a symbol
- Add and format paragraph borders
- Clear formatting
- Apply a style
- Set and use tab stops
- Insert the current date
- Insert, edit, and format a Word table
- Use the format painter
- Insert, edit, and format a SmartArt graphic
- Address and print an envelope

Introduction

In a business environment, people use documents to communicate with others. Business documents can include letters, memos, newsletters, proposals, and resumes. An effective business document clearly and concisely conveys its message and has a professional, organized appearance. You can use your own creative skills to design and compose business documents. Using Word, for example, you can develop the content and decide on the location of each item in a business document.

Project: Business Letter

At some time, you more than likely will prepare a business letter. Contents of business letters include requests, inquiries, confirmations, acceptances, applications, acknowledgments, recommendations, notifications, responses, thank you letters, invitations, offers, referrals, references, commendations, complaints, and more.

The project in this module follows generally accepted guidelines for writing letters and uses Word to create the business letter shown in Figure 3–1. This letter, written by the coordinator at the We Care Food Pantry, is a response letter that outlines volunteer and donation opportunities available to community members who have expressed interest in helping the organization. The letter includes a custom letterhead, as well as all essential business letter components: date line, inside address, salutation, body, complimentary close, and signature block. To easily present the mobile food pantry schedule, the letter shows this information in a table. The volunteer age restrictions appear in a bulleted list. The second page contains a visual representation of the volunteer and donation opportunities.

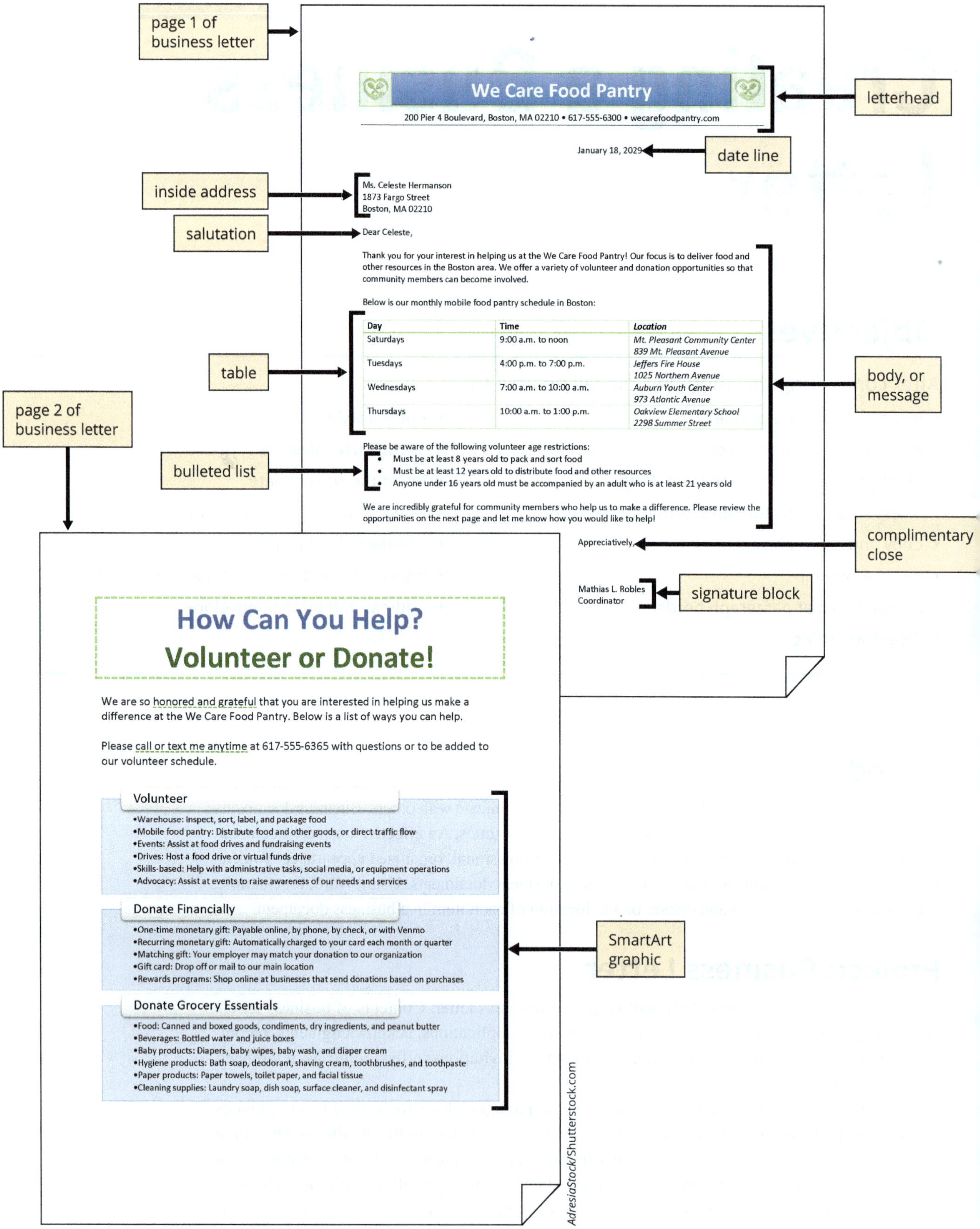

We Care Food Pantry

200 Pier 4 Boulevard, Boston, MA 02210 • 617-555-6300 • wecarefoodpantry.com

January 18, 2029

Ms. Celeste Hermanson
1873 Fargo Street
Boston, MA 02210

Dear Celeste,

Thank you for your interest in helping us at the We Care Food Pantry! Our focus is to deliver food and other resources in the Boston area. We offer a variety of volunteer and donation opportunities so that community members can become involved.

Below is our monthly mobile food pantry schedule in Boston:

Day	Time	*Location*
Saturdays	9:00 a.m. to noon	*Mt. Pleasant Community Center 839 Mt. Pleasant Avenue*
Tuesdays	4:00 p.m. to 7:00 p.m.	*Jeffers Fire House 1025 Northern Avenue*
Wednesdays	7:00 a.m. to 10:00 a.m.	*Auburn Youth Center 973 Atlantic Avenue*
Thursdays	10:00 a.m. to 1:00 p.m.	*Oakview Elementary School 2298 Summer Street*

Please be aware of the following volunteer age restrictions:

- Must be at least 8 years old to pack and sort food
- Must be at least 12 years old to distribute food and other resources
- Anyone under 16 years old must be accompanied by an adult who is at least 21 years old

We are incredibly grateful for community members who help us to make a difference. Please review the opportunities on the next page and let me know how you would like to help!

Appreciatively,

Mathias L. Robles
Coordinator

How Can You Help?
Volunteer or Donate!

We are so honored and grateful that you are interested in helping us make a difference at the We Care Food Pantry. Below is a list of ways you can help.

Please call or text me anytime at 617-555-6365 with questions or to be added to our volunteer schedule.

Volunteer
- Warehouse: Inspect, sort, label, and package food
- Mobile food pantry: Distribute food and other goods, or direct traffic flow
- Events: Assist at food drives and fundraising events
- Drives: Host a food drive or virtual funds drive
- Skills-based: Help with administrative tasks, social media, or equipment operations
- Advocacy: Assist at events to raise awareness of our needs and services

Donate Financially
- One-time monetary gift: Payable online, by phone, by check, or with Venmo
- Recurring monetary gift: Automatically charged to your card each month or quarter
- Matching gift: Your employer may match your donation to our organization
- Gift card: Drop off or mail to our main location
- Rewards programs: Shop online at businesses that send donations based on purchases

Donate Grocery Essentials
- Food: Canned and boxed goods, condiments, dry ingredients, and peanut butter
- Beverages: Bottled water and juice boxes
- Baby products: Diapers, baby wipes, baby wash, and diaper cream
- Hygiene products: Bath soap, deodorant, shaving cream, toothbrushes, and toothpaste
- Paper products: Paper towels, toilet paper, and facial tissue
- Cleaning supplies: Laundry soap, dish soap, surface cleaner, and disinfectant spray

AdresiaStock/Shutterstock.com

Figure 3–1

In this module, you will learn how to create the letter shown in Figure 3–1. You will perform the following general tasks as you progress through this module:

1. Create and format a letterhead with graphics.
2. Specify the letter formats according to business letter guidelines.
3. Insert a table in the letter.
4. Format the table in the letter.
5. Insert a bulleted list in the letter.
6. On a second page, insert and format a SmartArt graphic.
7. Address an envelope for the letter.

To Start Word and Specify Settings

If you are using a computer to step through the project in this module and you want your screens to match the figures in this book, you should change your screen's resolution to 1366 × 768. The following steps start Word and specify settings.

1. sam Start Word and create a blank document in the Word window. If necessary, maximize the Word window.
2. If the Print Layout button on the status bar is not selected (shown in Figure 3–2), click it so that your screen is in Print Layout view.
3. If the 'Show/Hide ¶' button (Home tab | Paragraph group) is not selected already, click it to display formatting marks on the screen.
4. To display the page the same width as the document window, if necessary, click the Page Width button (View tab | Zoom group).
5. If you are using a mouse and you want your screens to match the figures in the book, verify that you are using Mouse mode by doing the following: display the Quick Access Toolbar, if necessary, by clicking the 'Ribbon Display Options' button at the right edge of the ribbon and then clicking 'Show Quick Access Toolbar' on the menu; clicking the 'Touch/Mouse Mode' button on the Quick Access Toolbar and then, if necessary, clicking Mouse on the menu (if your Quick Access Toolbar does not display the 'Touch/Mouse Mode' button, click the 'Customize Quick Access Toolbar' button on the Quick Access Toolbar and then click Touch/Mouse Mode on the menu to add the button to the Quick Access Toolbar). Then, hide the Quick Access Toolbar by clicking the 'Ribbon Display Options' button at the right edge of the ribbon and then clicking 'Hide Quick Access Toolbar' on the menu.

BTW
Touch Mode Differences
The Office and Windows interfaces may vary if you are using Touch mode. For this reason, you might notice that the function or appearance of your touch screen differs slightly from this module's presentation.

Creating a Letterhead

The cost of preprinted letterhead can be high; thus, some organizations and individuals create their own letterhead and save it in a file. Then, when you want to create a letter at a later time, you can start by using the letterhead file. The following sections create a letterhead and then save it in a file for future use.

Consider This

What is a letterhead?

A **letterhead**, which often appears at the top of a letter, is the section of a letter that identifies an organization or individual. Although you can design and print a letterhead yourself, many businesses pay an outside firm to design and print their letterhead, usually on higher-quality paper. They then use the professionally preprinted paper for external business communications.

If you do not have preprinted letterhead paper, you can design a creative letterhead. It is important the letterhead appropriately represents the essence of the organization or individual (i.e., formal, technical, creative, etc.). That is, it should use text, graphics, formats, and colors that reflect the organization or individual. The letterhead should leave ample room for the contents of the letter.

When designing a letterhead, consider its contents, placement, and appearance.

- **Contents of letterhead.** A letterhead should contain these elements:
  - Complete name of the individual, group, or company
  - Complete mailing address: street address including building, room, suite number, or post office box, along with city, state, and postal code
  - Phone number(s) and fax number, if applicable
  - Email address, if applicable
  - Web address, if applicable
  - Many letterheads also include a logo or other image; if an image is used, it should express the organization or individual's personality or goals
- **Placement of elements in the letterhead.** Many letterheads center their elements across the top of the page. Others align some or all of the elements with the left or right margins. Sometimes, the elements are split between the top and bottom of the page. For example, a name and logo may be at the top of the page with the address at the bottom of the page.
- **Appearance of letterhead elements.** Use fonts that are easy to read. Give the organization or individual name impact by making its font size larger than the rest of the text in the letterhead. For additional emphasis, consider formatting the name in bold, italic, or a different color. Choose colors that complement one another, meet accessibility guidelines, and convey the goals of the organization or individual.

When finished designing the letterhead, determine if a divider line would help to visually separate the letterhead from the remainder of the letter.

The letterhead for the letter in this module consists of the food pantry name, postal address, phone number, web address, and images of a fork and spoon surrounded by a heart and hand. The name and images are enclosed in a rectangular shape (shown in Figure 3–1), and the contact information is below the shape. You will follow these general steps to create the letterhead in this module:

1. Insert and format a shape.
2. Enter and format the food pantry name in the shape.
3. Insert, format, and position the images with the shape.
4. Enter the contact information below the shape.
5. Add a border below the contact information.

BTW

Save a Shape as a Picture

You can save a shape you have inserted, edited, and formatted as a picture file so that you easily can reuse it elsewhere. To save a shape you have created, right-click the shape, click 'Save as Picture' on the shortcut menu, type the file name in the Save As Picture dialog box, navigate to the desired save location (Save As Picture dialog box), and then click the Save button.

To Insert a Shape

Word has a variety of predefined shapes, which are a type of drawing object, that you can insert in documents. A **drawing object** is a graphic that you create using Word. Examples of shape drawing objects include rectangles, circles, triangles, arrows, flowcharting symbols, stars, banners, and callouts. The following steps insert a rectangle shape in the letterhead. **Why?** The food pantry name is placed in a rectangle for emphasis and visual appeal.

1

- Display the Insert tab.
- Click the Shapes button (Insert tab | Illustrations group) to display the Shapes gallery (Figure 3–2).

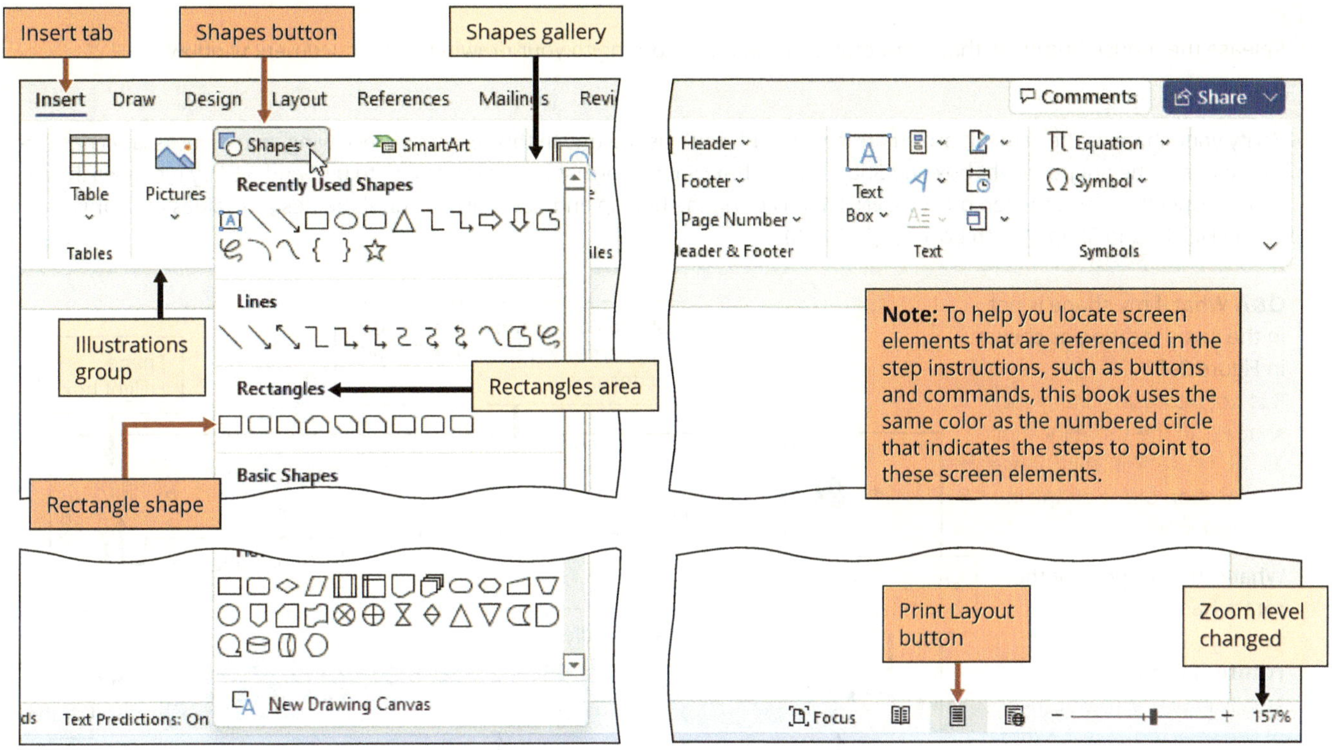

Figure 3–2

2

- Click the Rectangle shape in the Rectangles area in the Shapes gallery, which removes the gallery.

Q&A What if I am using a touch screen?
The shape is inserted in the document window. Skip Steps 3 and 4, and proceed to Step 5.

- Position the pointer (a crosshair) in the approximate location for the upper-left corner of the desired shape (Figure 3–3).

Q&A What is the purpose of the crosshair pointer?
You drag the crosshair pointer from the upper-left corner to the lower-right corner to form the desired location and size of the shape.

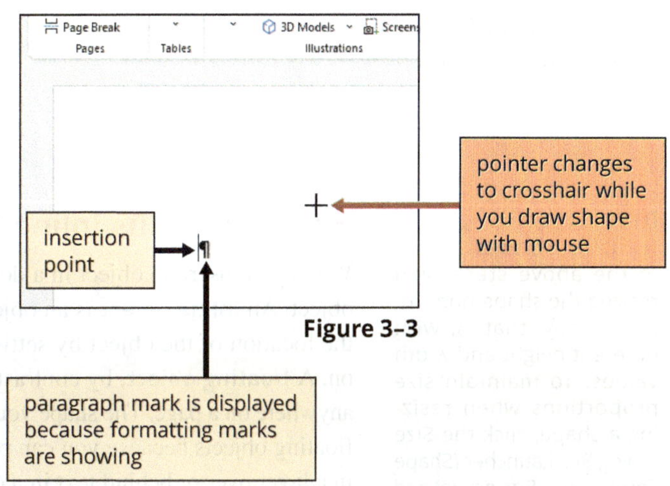

Figure 3–3

3

- Drag the mouse to the right and downward to form the approximate boundaries of the shape, as shown in Figure 3-4. Do not release the mouse button.

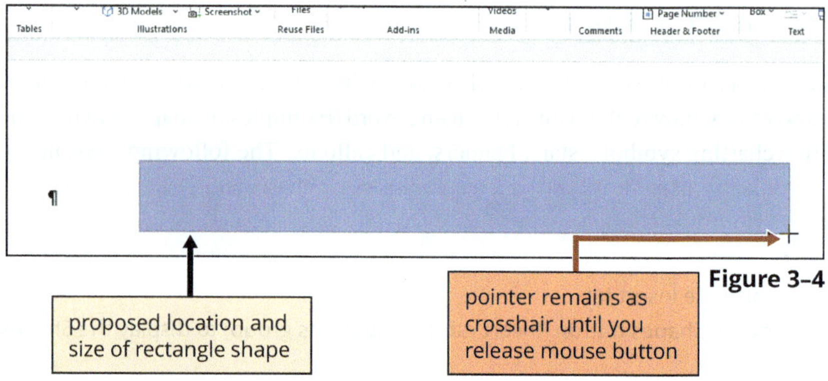

Figure 3-4

4

- Release the mouse button so that Word draws the shape according to your drawing in the document window.

5

- Verify your shape is the same approximate height and width as the one in this project by reviewing, and if necessary changing, the values in the Shape Height box and Shape Width box (Shape Format tab | Size group) to 0.5" and 5.5" by typing each value in the respective box and then pressing ENTER or clicking the box up and down arrows until the desired values appear in the Shape Height and Shape Width boxes (Figure 3-5).

Q&A What if my shape is not in the same location as shown in Figure 3-5?
It is not necessary that your shape is in the same location as the figure. You will change the location of the shape in the next steps.

What is the purpose of the rotate handle?
When you drag an object's **rotate handle**, which is the small circular arrow at the top of the selected object, Word turns the selected object in a clockwise or counterclockwise direction, depending on the direction you drag the mouse.

What if I wanted to delete a shape and start over?
With the shape selected, you would press DELETE.

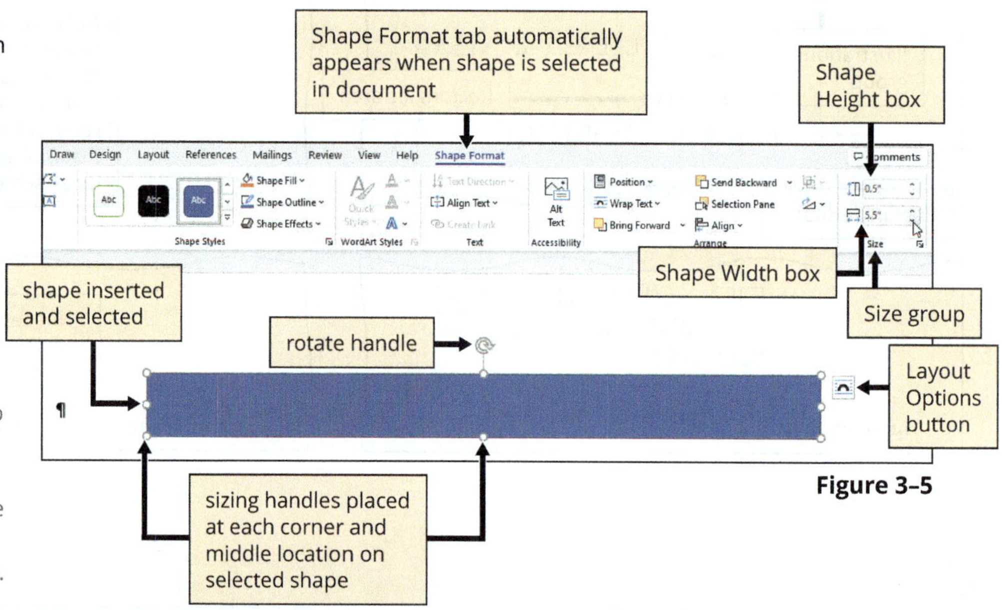

Figure 3-5

BTW
Resizing Shapes
In the above steps, you resized the shape nonproportionally, that is, with different height and width values. To maintain size proportions when resizing a shape, click the Size Dialog Box Launcher (Shape Format tab | Size group) and then place a check mark in the 'Lock aspect ratio' check box (Layout dialog box).

Floating versus Inline Objects

When you insert an object in a document, Word inserts it as either an inline object or a floating object. An **inline object** is an object that is part of a paragraph. With inline objects, you change the location of the object by setting paragraph options, such as centered, right-aligned, and so on. A **floating object**, by contrast, is an object that is independent of text and able to be moved anywhere on a page. The shape you just inserted is a floating object. You have more flexibility with floating objects because you can position a floating object at a specific location in a document or in a layer over or behind text in a document.

In addition to changing an object from inline to floating and vice versa, Word provides several floating options, which (along with inline) are called text wrapping options because they affect how text wraps with or around the object. Table 3-1 presents the various text wrapping options.

Table 3-1: Text Wrapping Options

Text Wrapping Option	Object Type	How It Works
In Line with Text	Inline	Object positioned according to paragraph formatting; for example, if the paragraph is centered, the object will be centered with any text in the paragraph.
Square	Floating	Text wraps around the object, with the text forming a box around the object.
Tight	Floating	Text wraps around the object, with the text forming to the shape of the object.
Through	Floating	Object appears at the beginning, middle, or end of text. Moving the object changes location of the text.
Top and Bottom	Floating	Object appears above or below text. Moving the object changes location of the text.
Behind Text	Floating	Object appears behind the text.
In Front of Text	Floating	Object appears in front of the text and may cover the text.

To Change an Object's Position

You can specify an object's vertical position within the margins on a page (top, middle, bottom) and its horizontal position (left, center, right). The following steps change the position of an object, specifically, the rectangle shape. **Why?** You want the shape to be centered at the top of the page in the letterhead.

1

- With the shape still selected, click the Position button (Shape Format tab | Arrange group) to display the Position gallery (Figure 3-6).

Q&A What if the shape is not still selected?
Click the shape to select it.

- **Experiment:** Point to various options in the Position gallery and watch the shape move to the selected position option.

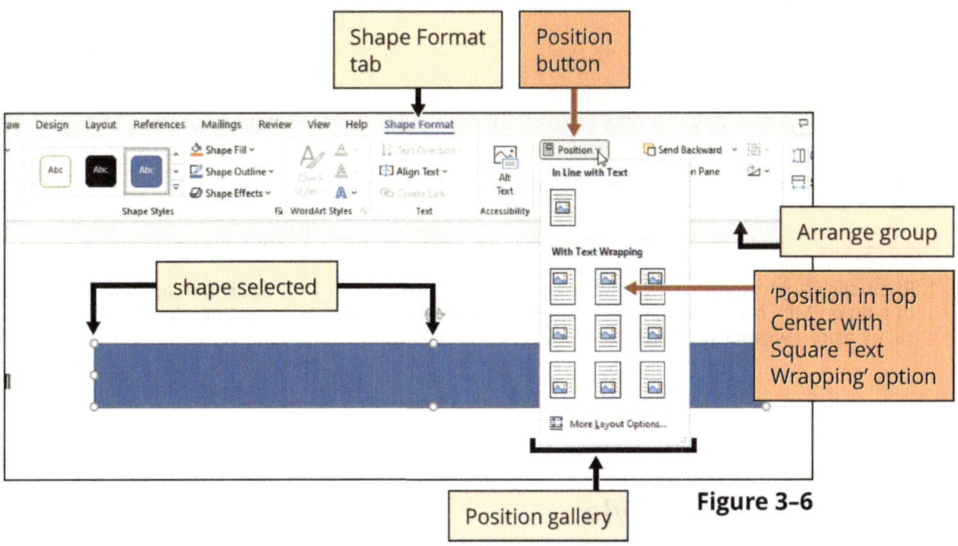

Figure 3-6

2

- Click 'Position in Top Center with Square Text Wrapping' in the Position gallery so that the object does not cover the document and is centered at the top margin of the document.

Q&A What if I wanted to center the object in its current vertical location (and not at the top, center, or bottom of the page)?
You would click the Align button (Shape Format tab | Arrange group) (shown in Figure 3-7) and then click the desired alignment in the list.

Other Ways

1. Click Layout Options button attached to object (shown in Figure 3-5), click See more link in Layout Options gallery, click Horizontal Alignment arrow and select alignment (Layout dialog box), click Vertical Alignment arrow and select alignment, click OK
2. Click a Size Dialog Box Launcher (Shape Format tab | Size group), click Position tab (Layout dialog box), click Horizontal Alignment arrow and select alignment, click Vertical Alignment arrow and select alignment, click OK

To Change an Object's Text Wrapping

When you insert a shape in a Word document, the default text wrapping is In Front of Text, which means the object will cover any text behind it. The previous steps, which changed the shape's position, changed the text wrapping to Square. In the letterhead, you want the shape's text wrapping to be Top and Bottom. **Why?** You want the letterhead above the contents of the letter when you type it, instead of covering the contents of the letter. The following steps change an object's text wrapping, specifically, the shape.

1

- With the shape still selected, click the Layout Options button attached to the object to display the Layout Options gallery (Figure 3–7).

2

- Click 'Top and Bottom' in the Layout Options gallery so that the object does not cover the document text.

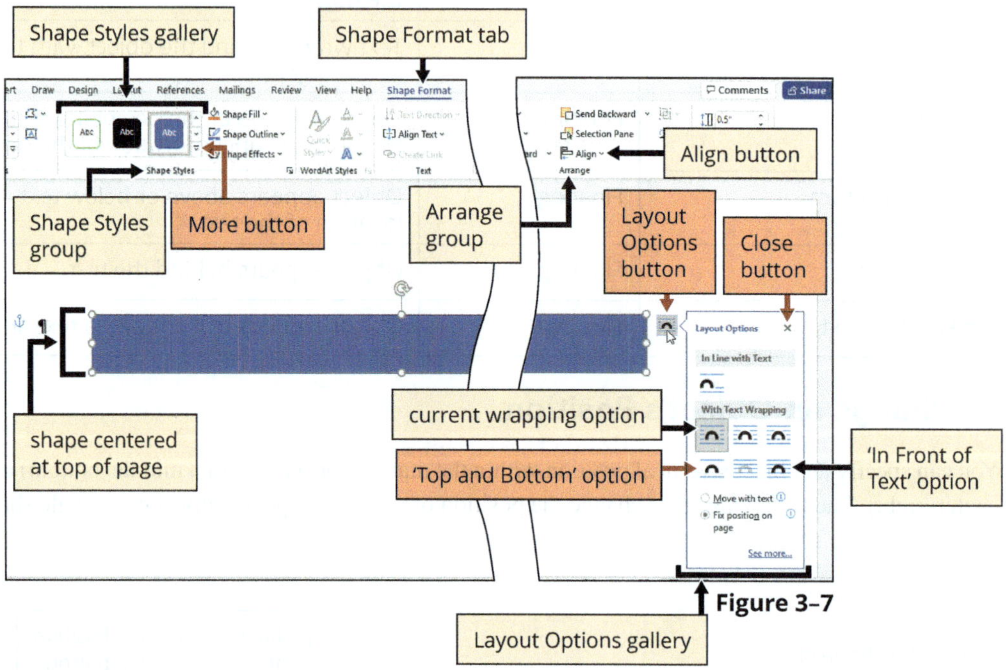

Figure 3–7

Q&A How can I tell that the text wrapping has changed?
Because the letter has no text, you need to look at the paragraph mark, which now is positioned below the shape instead of to its left (shown in Figure 3–8).

- Click the Close button in the Layout Options gallery to close the gallery.

Other Ways

1. Right-click object (or, if using touch, tap 'Show Context Menu' button on Mini toolbar), point to Wrap Text on shortcut menu, click desired wrapping option
2. Click Wrap Text button (Shape Format tab | Arrange group), select desired wrapping option

To Apply a Shape Style

Why apply a shape style? Word provides a Shape Styles gallery so that you easily can change the appearance of the shape. The following steps apply a shape style to the rectangle shape.

1

- With the shape still selected, click the More button (shown in Figure 3–7) in the Shape Styles gallery (Shape Format tab | Shape Styles group) to expand the gallery.

Q&A What if the shape no longer is selected?
Click the shape to select it.

- Point to 'Moderate Effect - Blue, Accent 5' (sixth style in fifth row) in the Shape Styles gallery to display a Live Preview of that style applied to the shape in the document (Figure 3–8).

- **Experiment:** Point to various styles in the Shape Styles gallery and watch the style of the shape change in the document.

2

- Click 'Moderate Effect - Blue, Accent 5' in the Shape Styles gallery to apply the selected style to the shape.

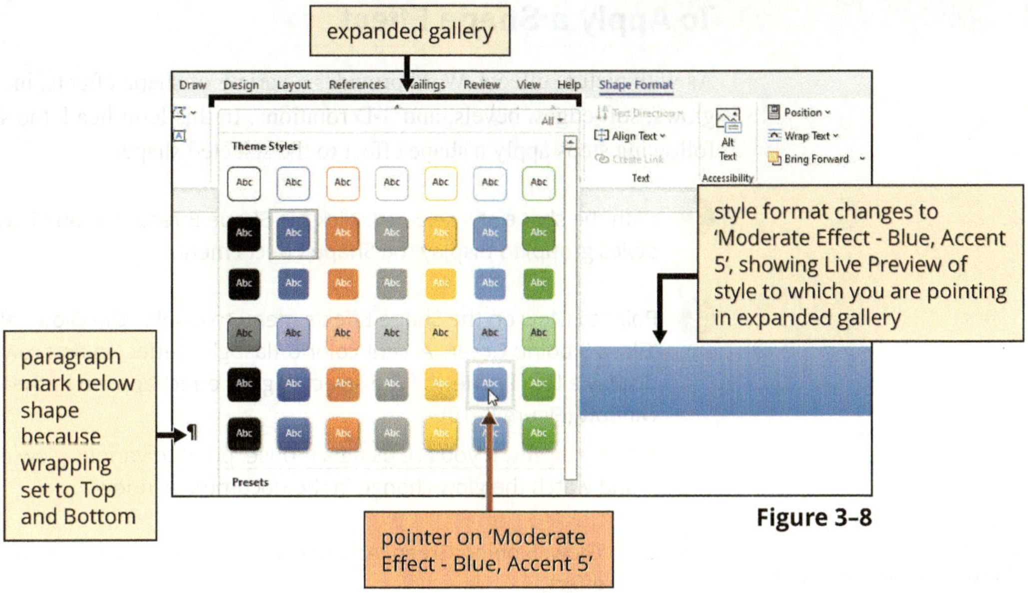

Figure 3–8

Other Ways

1. Right-click shape, click Style button on Mini toolbar, select desired style
2. Click Shape Styles Dialog Box Launcher (Shape Format tab | Shape Styles group), click 'Fill & Line' button (Format Shape pane), expand Fill section, select desired colors, click Close button

To Change the Shape Outline

The rectangle shape currently has a blue outline that matches the fill color inside the shape. The following steps change the outline color on the shape. **Why?** You would like a darker shade of blue for the outline to differentiate it from the fill color on the shape.

1

- Click the Shape Outline arrow (Shape Format tab | Shape Styles group) to display the Shape Outline gallery.
- Point to 'Blue, Accent 5, Darker 50%' (ninth color in last row) in the Shape Outline gallery to display a Live Preview of that outline color around the shape (Figure 3–9).
- **Experiment:** Point to various colors in the Shape Outline gallery and watch the outline color on the shape change in the document window.

2

- Click 'Blue, Accent 5, Darker 50%' in the Shape Outline gallery to change the shape outline color.

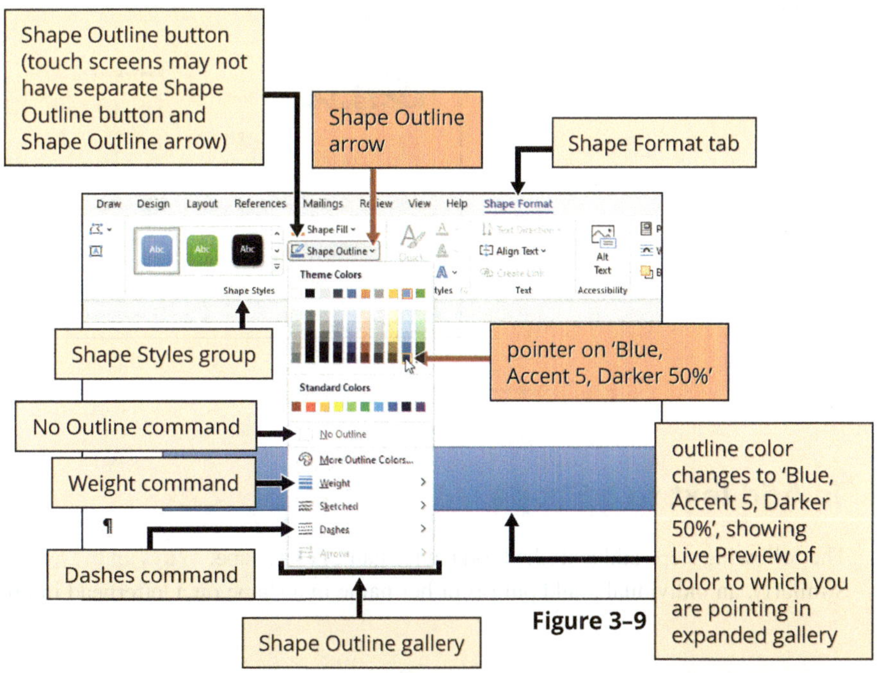

Figure 3–9

Q&A How would I remove an outline color from a shape?
With the graphic selected, you would click No Outline in the Shape Outline gallery.

When would I use the Weight and Dashes commands in the Shape Outline gallery?
The Weight command enables you to change the thickness of the outline, and the Dashes command provides a variety of dashed outline options.

To Apply a Shape Effect

As with picture effects, Word provides a variety of shape effects, including shadows, reflections, glows, soft edges, bevels, and 3-D rotations. In this letterhead, the shape has a glow effect. The following steps apply a shape effect to the selected shape.

1. With the shape still selected, click the Shape Effects button (Shape Format tab | Shape Styles group) to display the Shape Effects menu.

2. Point to Glow on the Shape Effects menu to display the Glow gallery and then point to 'Glow: 5 point; Green, Accent color 6' (last glow effect in first row) in the Glow gallery to display a Live Preview of the selected glow effect applied to the picture in the document window (Figure 3–10).
   - **Experiment:** If you are using a mouse, point to various glow effects in the Glow gallery and watch the glow change in the document window.

3. Click 'Glow: 5 point; Green, Accent color 6' in the Glow gallery to apply the selected glow effect.

BTW
The Ribbon and Screen Resolution
Word may change how the groups and buttons within the groups appear on the ribbon, depending on the computer or mobile device's screen resolution. Thus, your ribbon may look different from the ones in this book if you are using a screen resolution other than 1366 × 768. For information about how to change a computer's resolution, use the search text, change resolution, in your operating system's Help files.

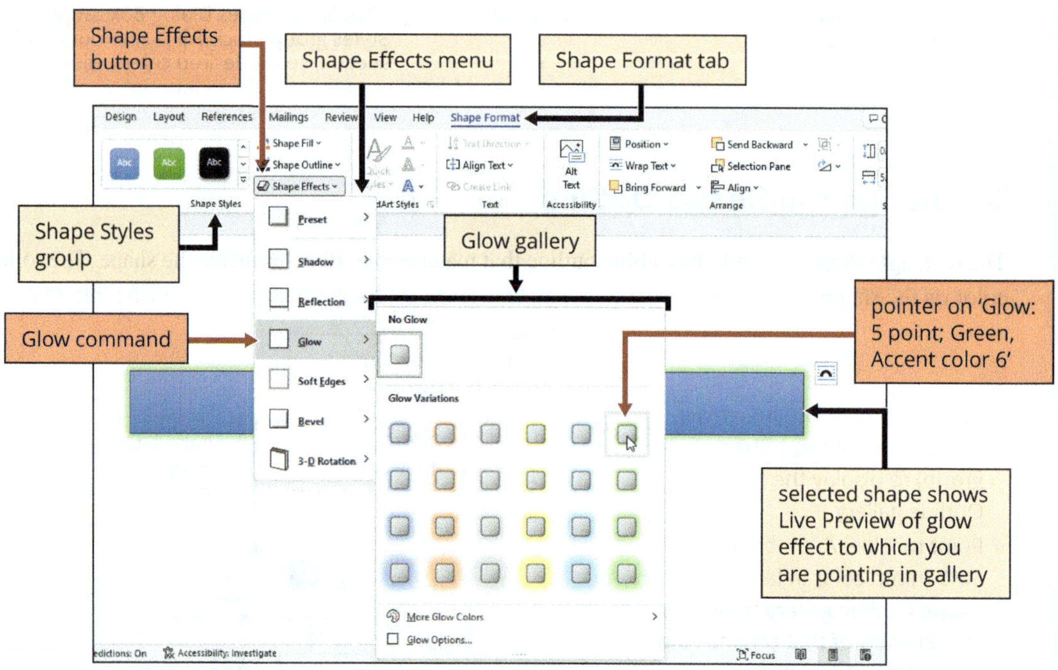

Figure 3–10

To Add Text to a Shape

The following steps add text (the food pantry name) to a shape. **Why?** In the letterhead for this module, the name is in the shape. Similarly, an individual could put his or her name in a shape on a letterhead in order to create personalized letterhead.

1

- Right-click the shape to display a Mini toolbar and/or shortcut menu (Figure 3–11).

2

- Click Add Text on the shortcut menu to place an insertion point in the shape.

Q&A What if I am using a touch screen?
Tap the Edit Text button on the Mini toolbar.

Why do the buttons on my Mini toolbar differ?
If you are using a mouse in Mouse mode, the buttons on your Mini toolbar will differ from those that appear when you use a touch screen in Touch mode.

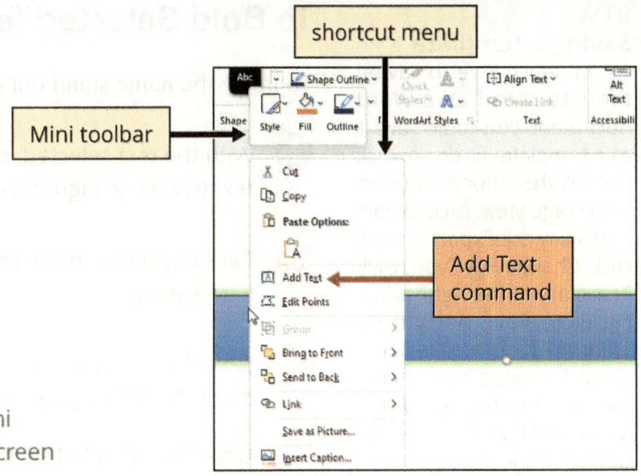

Figure 3–11

- If the insertion point and paragraph mark are not centered in the shape, click the Center button (Home tab | Paragraph group) to center them.

- Type **We Care Food Pantry** as the name in the shape (Figure 3–12).

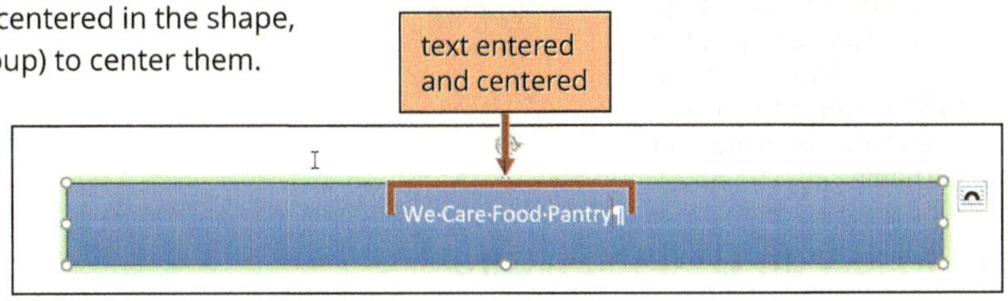

Figure 3–12

To Use the 'Increase Font Size' Button

While you can use the Font Size arrow (Home tab | Font group) to change the font size of text, Word also provides an 'Increase Font Size' button (Home tab | Font group) that increases the font size of selected text each time you click the button. The following steps use the 'Increase Font Size' button to increase the font size of the name in the shape to 24 point. **Why?** You want the name to be larger in the shape.

1

- Drag through the text to be formatted (in this case, the name in the shape).

2

- If necessary, display the Home tab.
- Repeatedly click the 'Increase Font Size' button (Home tab | Font group) until the Font Size box displays 24 to increase the font size of the selected text (Figure 3–13).

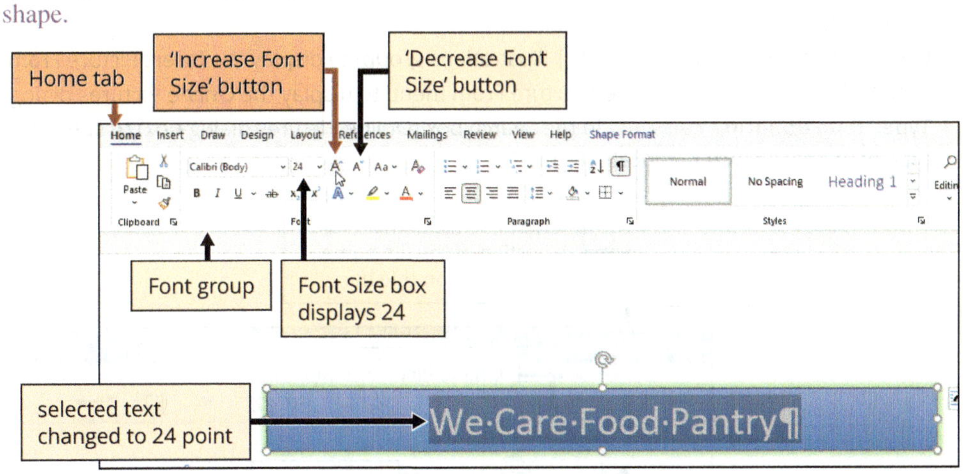

Figure 3–13

Q&A What if I click the 'Increase Font Size' button (Home tab | Font group) too many times, causing the font size to be too big?
Click the 'Decrease Font Size' button (Home tab | Font group) until the desired font size is displayed.

- **Experiment:** Repeatedly click the 'Increase Font Size' and 'Decrease Font Size' buttons (Home tab | Font group) and watch the font size of the selected text change in the document window. When you are finished experimenting with these two buttons, set the font size to 24.

Other Ways

1. Press CTRL+SHIFT+>

BTW
Saving a Template
As an alternative to saving the letterhead as a Word document, you could save it as a template. To do so, click File on the ribbon to open Backstage view, click Export to display the Export screen, click 'Change File Type', click Template in the right pane, click the Save As button, enter the template file name (Save As dialog box), if necessary select the Templates folder, and then click the Save button in the dialog box. To use the template, click File on the ribbon to open Backstage view, click New to display the New gallery, click the Personal tab in the New screen, and then click the template icon or file name.

To Bold Selected Text and Save the Letterhead Document

To make the name stand out even more, bold it. The following steps bold the selected text.

1. With the text selected, click the Bold button (Home tab | Font group) to bold the selected text (shown in Figure 3–16).

2. Click anywhere in the text in the shape to remove the selection and place the insertion point in the shape.

3. Save the letterhead on your hard drive, OneDrive, or other storage location using the file name, SC_WD_3_WeCareFoodPantryLetterhead.

Q&A Why should I save the letterhead at this time?
You have performed many tasks while creating this letterhead and do not want to risk losing work completed thus far.

To Insert an Online Picture

Files containing pictures and other images are available from a variety of sources. In this project, you insert a picture from the web. Microsoft 365 applications can access a collection of royalty-free photos and animations.

The letterhead in this project contains an image of a fork and spoon surrounded by a heart and hand (shown in Figure 3–1). **Why?** The food bank uses an image that shows the concept of food donation. The following steps insert an online picture in the document.

1.
- If necessary, click the paragraph mark below the shape to position the insertion point where you want to insert the picture.
- Display the Insert tab.
- Click the Pictures button (Insert tab | Illustrations group) to display the Insert Picture From menu.
- Click Online Pictures on the Insert Picture From menu to display the Online Pictures dialog box.
- Type **food donation concept** in the Search box (Online Pictures dialog box) to specify the search text, which indicates the type of image you want to locate (Figure 3–14).

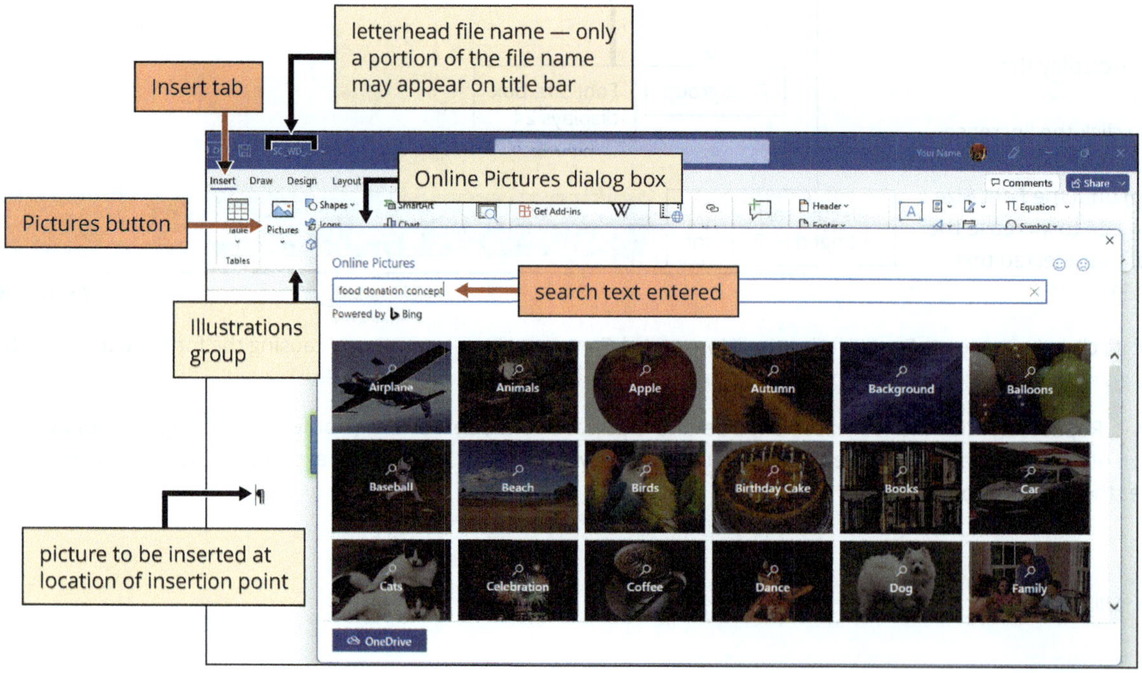

Figure 3–14

2

- Press ENTER to display a list of online pictures that matches the entered search text.
- Scroll through the list of pictures to locate the one shown in Figure 3–15, or a similar square-shaped image.

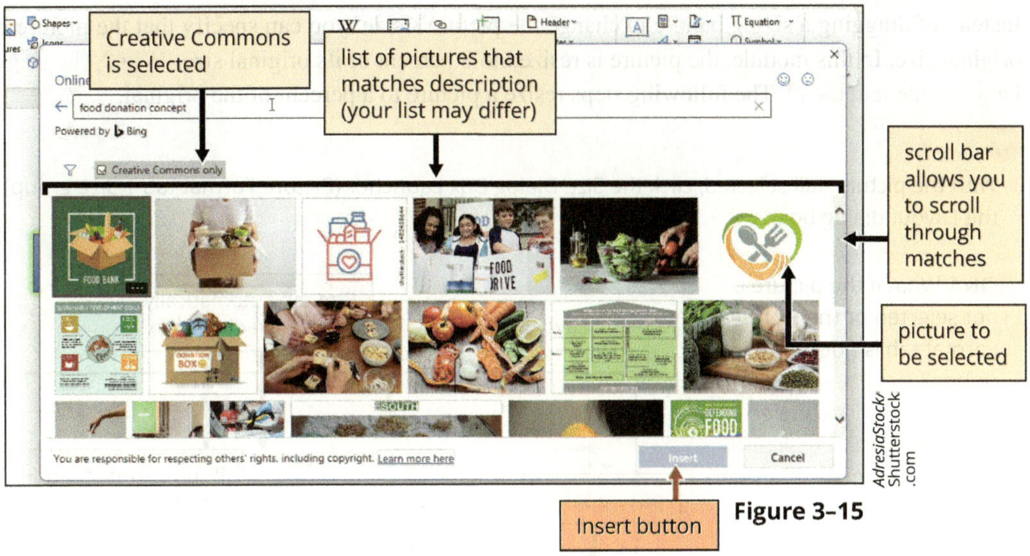

Figure 3–15

Q&A Why is my list of pictures different from Figure 3–15?
The online images are updated continually.

What is Creative Commons?
Creative Commons is a nonprofit organization that makes it easy for content creators to license and share their work by supplying easy-to-understand copyright licenses; the creator chooses the conditions under which the work can be used. Be sure to follow an image's guidelines when using it in a document.

Can I access other types of online pictures from within Word?
Yes. If you use Word 365, you can access a library of stock photos by clicking the Pictures button (Insert tab | Illustrations group) and then clicking Stock Images.

What if I cannot locate the image in Figure 3–15, and I would like to use that exact image?
The image is located in the Data Files. You can click the Cancel button (Online Pictures dialog box) and then click the Pictures button (Insert tab | Illustrations group), click This Device, navigate to and select the file called Support_WD_3_FoodDonationConcept.jpg in the Data Files, and then click the Insert button (Insert Picture dialog box).

3

- Click the desired picture to select it.
- Click the Insert button (Online Pictures dialog box) to insert the selected image in the document at the location of the insertion point. If necessary, scroll to display the image (picture) in the document window (Figure 3–16).

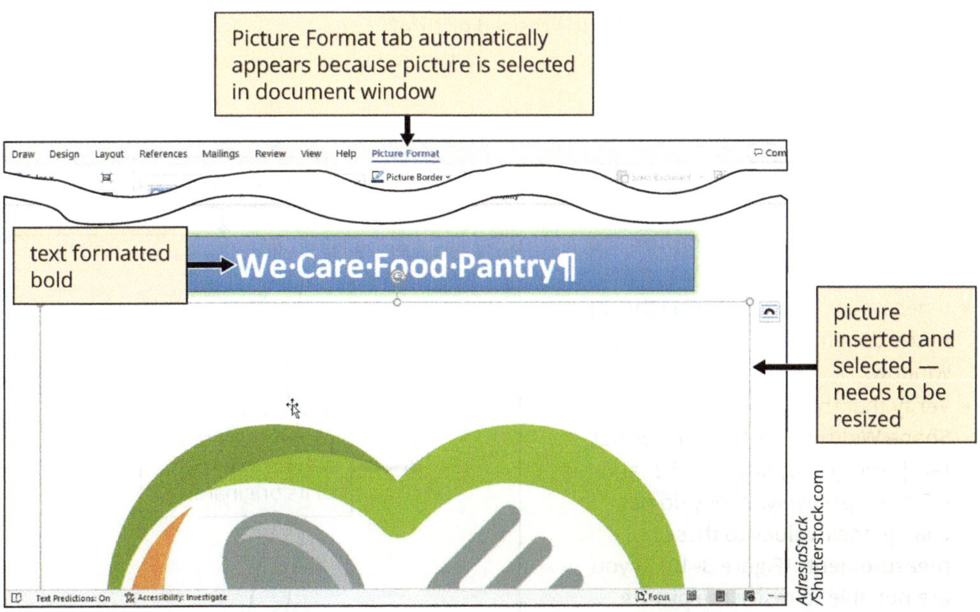

Figure 3–16

To Resize a Picture to a Percent of the Original Size

Instead of dragging a sizing handle to change the picture's size, you can specify that the picture be resized to a percent of its original size. In this module, the picture is resized to 8 percent of its original size. **Why?** The original size of the picture is too large for the letterhead. The following steps resize a picture to a percent of the original.

1

- With the picture still selected, click the Size Dialog Box Launcher (Picture Format tab | Size group) to display the Size sheet in the Layout dialog box.

Q&A What if the picture is not selected or the Picture Format tab is not on the ribbon?
Click the picture to select it or double-click the picture to make the Picture Format tab the active tab.

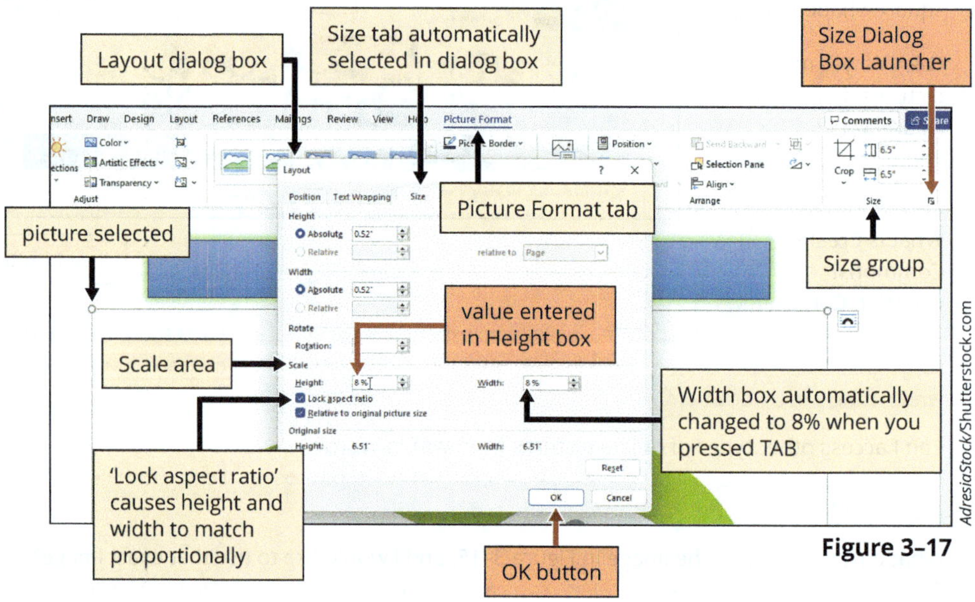

Figure 3–17

2

- In the Scale area (Layout dialog box), double-click the current value in the Height box to select it.
- Type **8** in the Height box and then press TAB to display the same percent value in the Width box (Figure 3–17).

Q&A Why did Word automatically fill in the value in the Width box?
When the 'Lock aspect ratio' check box (Layout dialog box) is selected, Word automatically maintains the size proportions of the selected picture. If you wanted to resize the picture nonproportionally, you would remove the check mark from this check box.

How do I know to use 8 percent for the resized picture?
The larger picture consumed too much room on the page. Try various percentages to determine the size that works best in the letterhead design.

3

- Click OK to close the dialog box and resize the selected picture.
- If necessary, scroll to display the top of the document in the document window.
- Verify that the Shape Height and Shape Width boxes (Picture Format tab | Size group) display 0.52" and 0.52", respectively. If they do not, change their values to these measurements (Figure 3–18). If you are not able to resize the picture exactly, remove the check mark from the 'Lock aspect ratio' check box (Layout dialog box) and then try again.

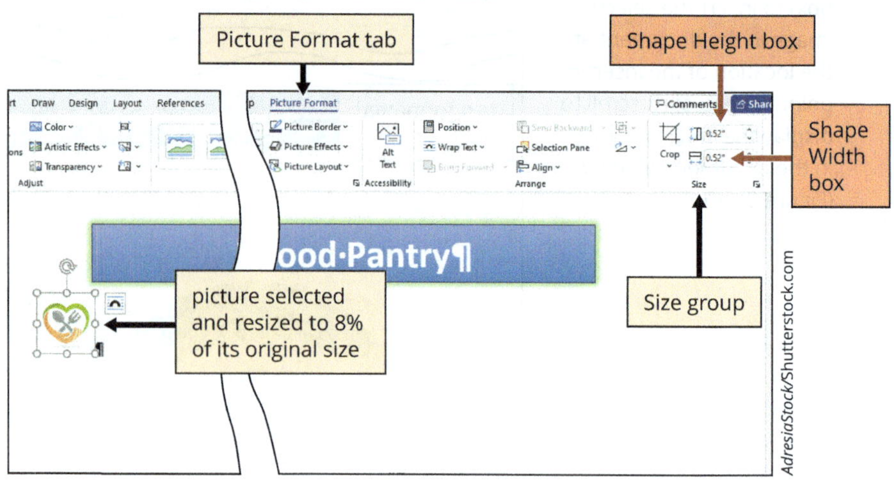

Figure 3–18

Other Ways

1. Click Layout Options button attached to picture, click See more link in the Layout Options gallery, click Size tab (Layout dialog box), enter height and width values, click OK
2. Right-click picture, click 'Size and Position' on shortcut menu, enter height and width values (Layout dialog box), click OK

To Change the Color of a Picture

In Word, you can change the color of a picture. The food donation concepts picture currently is bright orange and green colors. The following steps change the color of the picture. **Why?** Because the image in this project will be placed beside the rectangle shape, you prefer to use colors that will match the shape.

1

- With the picture still selected (shown in Figure 3–18), click the Color button (Picture Format tab | Adjust group) to display the Color gallery.
- Point to 'Green, Accent color 6 Light' (last color in last row) in the Recolor area in the Color gallery, which would display a Live Preview of that color applied to the selected picture in the document if the picture was not hidden by the Color gallery (Figure 3–19).

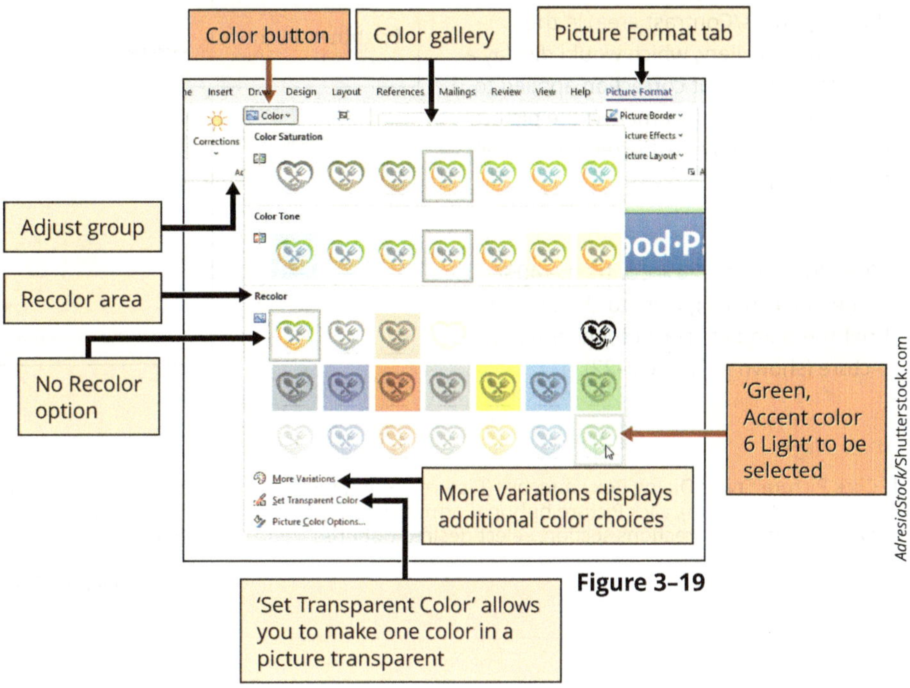

Figure 3–19

2

- Click 'Green, Accent color 6 Light' in the Color gallery to change the color of the selected picture (Figure 3–20).

Q&A How would I change a picture back to its original colors?

With the picture selected, you would click No Recolor, which is the upper-left color in the Recolor area in the Color gallery.

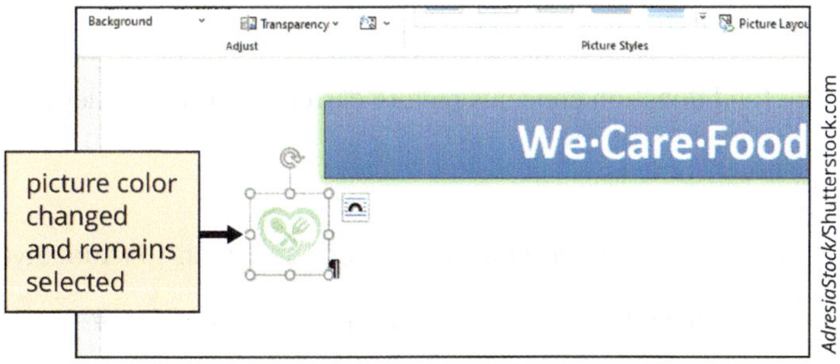

Figure 3–20

Other Ways

1. Click Picture Styles Dialog Box Launcher (Picture Format tab | Picture Styles group), click Picture button (Format Picture pane), expand Picture Color section, select desired options
2. Right-click picture (or, if using touch, tap 'Show Context Menu' button on Mini toolbar), click Format Picture on shortcut menu (or, if using touch, tap Format Object), click Picture button (Format Picture pane), expand Picture Color section, select desired options

To Adjust the Brightness and Contrast of a Picture

In Word, you can adjust the brightness, or lightness, of a picture and also the **contrast**, or the difference between the lightest and darkest areas of the picture. The following steps decrease the brightness of the food donation concept picture by 20% and increase the contrast by 40%. **Why?** You want to darken the picture slightly and, at the same time, increase the difference between the light and dark areas of the picture.

1

- If necessary, display the Picture Format tab.
- With the picture still selected (shown in Figure 3–20), click the Corrections button (Picture Format tab | Adjust group) to display the Corrections gallery.
- Point to 'Brightness: −20% Contrast: +40%' (second image in bottom row in the Brightness/Contrast area) in the Corrections gallery, which would display a Live Preview of that correction applied to the picture in the document if the picture was not hidden by the Corrections gallery (Figure 3–21).

2

- Click 'Brightness: −20% Contrast: +40%' in the Corrections gallery to change the brightness and contrast of the selected picture (shown in Figure 3–22).

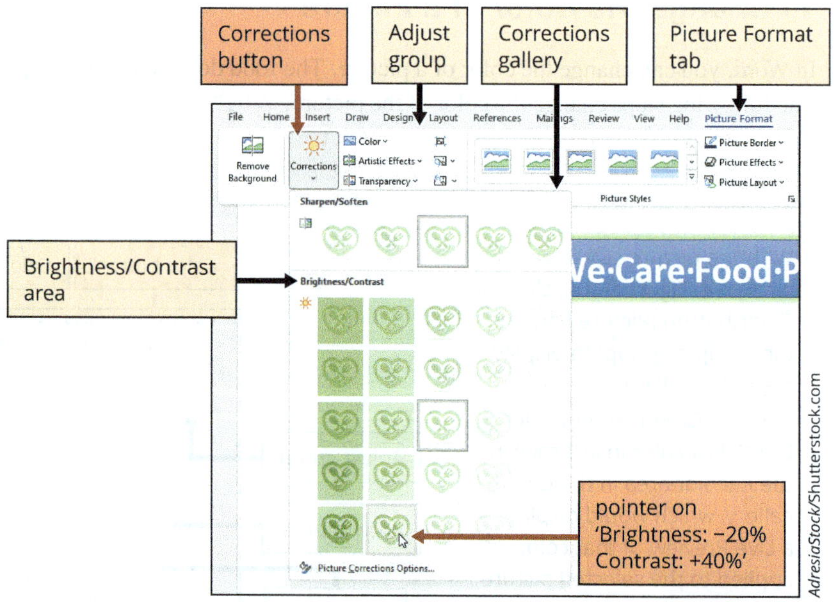

AdresiaStock/Shutterstock.com

Figure 3–21

Other Ways

1. Click Picture Styles Dialog Box Launcher (Picture Format tab | Picture Styles group), click Picture button (Format Picture pane), expand Picture Corrections section, select desired options
2. Right-click picture (or, if using touch, tap 'Show Context Menu' button on Mini toolbar), click Format Picture on shortcut menu (or, if using touch, tap Format Object on shortcut menu), click Picture button (Format Picture pane), expand Picture Corrections section, select desired options

To Add a Picture Border

The food donation concepts picture currently has no border (outline). The following steps add a border to the picture. **Why?** You would like the picture to have a green border so that it matches the glow on the rectangle shape.

1

- Click the Picture Border arrow (Picture Format tab | Picture Styles group) to display the Picture Border gallery.

Q&A What if I click the Picture Border button by mistake?
Click the Picture Border arrow and proceed with Step 2.

- Point to 'Green, Accent 6, Lighter 40%' (last theme color in fourth row) in the Picture Border gallery to display a Live Preview of that border color around the picture (Figure 3–22).
- **Experiment:** Point to various colors in the Picture Border gallery and watch the border color on the picture change in the document window.

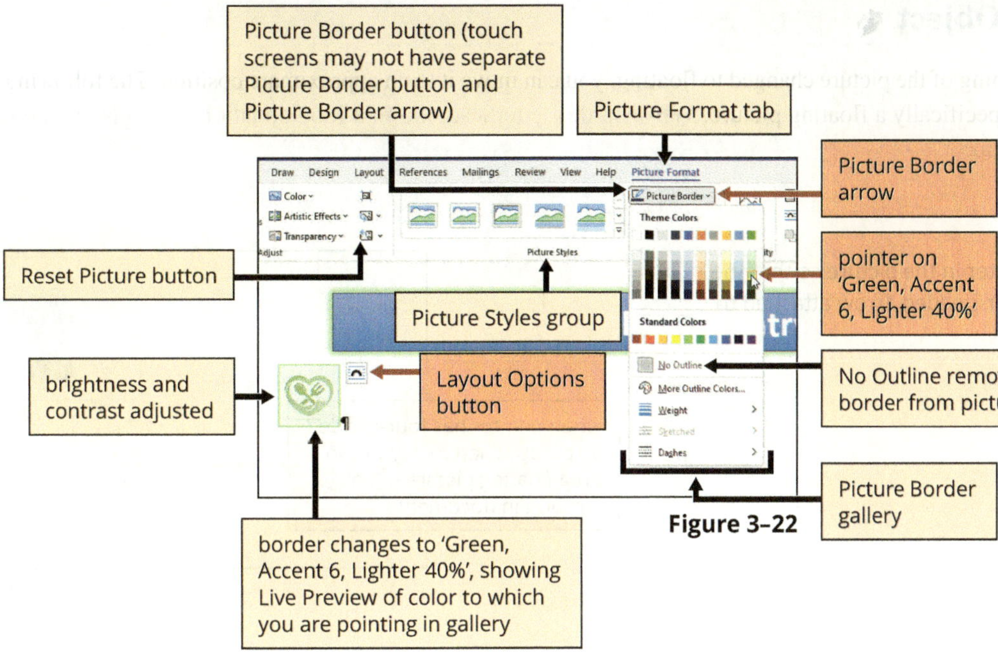

Figure 3-22

AdresizStock/Shutterstock.com

2

- Click 'Green, Accent 6, Lighter 40%' in the Picture Border gallery to change the picture border color.

Q&A How would I remove a border from a picture?
With the picture selected, you would click No Outline in the Picture Border gallery.

Can I remove all formatting applied to a picture and start over?
Yes. With the picture selected, you would click the Reset Picture button (Picture Format tab | Adjust group).

To Change an Object's Text Wrapping

The food donation concepts picture is to be positioned to the left of the rectangle shape. By default, when you insert a picture, it is formatted as an inline graphic. Inline graphics cannot be moved to a precise location on a page. Recall that inline graphics are part of a paragraph and, thus, can be positioned according to paragraph formatting, such as centered or left-aligned. To move the picture to the left of the shape, you format it as a floating object with In Front of Text wrapping. The following steps change a picture's text wrapping.

1. If necessary, click the picture to select it.
2. Click the Layout Options button attached to the picture (shown in Figure 3–22) to display the Layout Options gallery.
3. Click 'In Front of Text' in the Layout Options gallery (shown in Figure 3–7) so that you can position the object on top of any item in the document, in this case, on top of the rectangular shape.
4. Click the Close button to close the Layout Options gallery.

To Move an Object

With the text wrapping of the picture changed to floating, you can move it to an approximate position. The following steps move a floating object, specifically a floating picture. **Why?** In this letterhead, the first food donation concepts picture is positioned to the left of the shape.

1

- Position the pointer in the picture so that the pointer has a four-headed arrow attached to it (Figure 3–23).

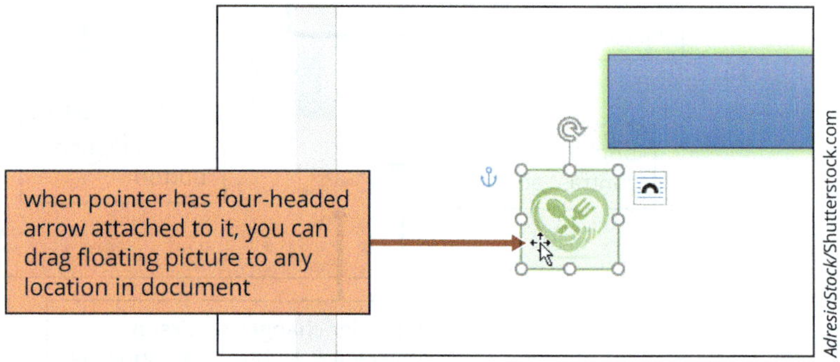

Figure 3–23

2

- Drag the picture to the left of the shape, as shown in Figure 3–24. Scroll, if necessary, to see the entire picture.

Q&A What if I moved the picture to the wrong location?
Repeat these steps. You can drag a floating picture to any location in a document. You also can use the arrow keys on the keyboard to move the floating picture incrementally.

Why do green lines appear on my screen as I drag a picture?
You have alignment guides set, which help you line up objects. To set alignment guides, click the Align button (Picture Format tab | Arrange group) and then click 'Use Alignment Guides'.

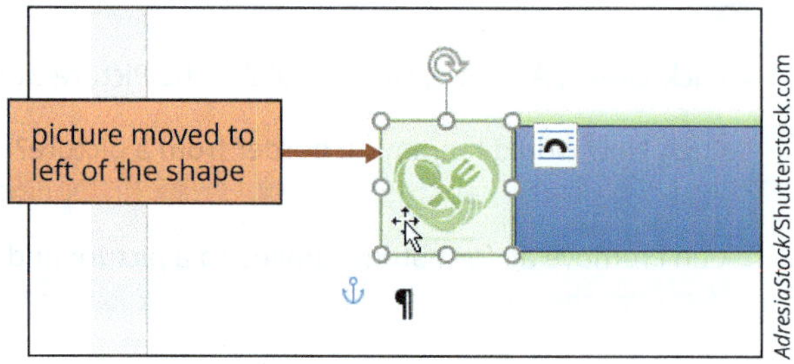

Figure 3–24

To Copy an Object

In this project, the same food donation concepts picture is to be placed to the right of the shape. Instead of performing the same steps to insert and format a second identical food donation concepts picture, you can copy the picture to the Office Clipboard, paste it from the Office Clipboard, and then move it to the desired location.

You use the same steps to copy a picture as to copy text. The following steps copy a picture.

1 If necessary, click the picture to select it.

2 Display the Home tab and then click the Copy button, shown in Figure 3–25 (Home tab | Clipboard group), or press CTRL+C to copy the selected item to the Office Clipboard.

To Use Paste Options to Paste an Object

The following steps paste a picture using the Paste Options gallery. **Why?** You can specify the format of a pasted item using Paste Options.

1

- If necessary, display the Home tab.
- Click the Paste arrow (Home tab | Clipboard group) to display the Paste gallery.

Q&A What if I accidentally click the Paste button?
Click the Paste Options button below the picture pasted in the document to display a Paste Options gallery.

- Point to the 'Keep Source Formatting' button in the Paste gallery to display a Live Preview of that paste option (Figure 3–25).
- **Experiment:** Point to the two buttons in the Paste gallery and watch the appearance of the pasted picture change.

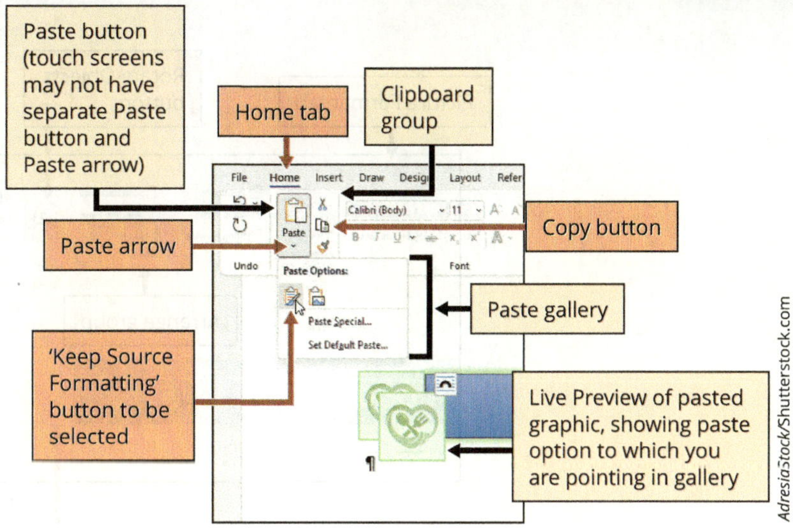

Figure 3–25

Q&A What do the buttons in the Paste gallery mean?
The 'Keep Source Formatting' button indicates the pasted object should have the same formats as it did in its original location. The Picture button removes some formatting from the object.

Why are these paste buttons different from when you paste text?
The buttons that appear in the Paste gallery differ depending on the item you are pasting. Use Live Preview to see how the pasted object will look in the document.

2
- Click the 'Keep Source Formatting' button in the Paste gallery to paste the picture using the same formatting as the copied picture.

To Move an Object

The next step is to move the second food donation concepts picture so that it is positioned to the right of the rectangle shape. The following steps move an object.

1 If you are using a mouse, position the pointer in the picture so that the pointer has a four-headed arrow attached to it.

2 Drag the picture to the location shown in Figure 3–26.

To Flip an Object

The following steps flip a selected object horizontally. **Why?** In this letterhead, you want the spoon in each food donation concepts picture to be on the outside edge of the picture.

1
- If necessary, display the Picture Format tab.
- With the picture still selected, click the Rotate Objects button (Picture Format tab | Arrange group) to display the Rotate Objects gallery (Figure 3–26).
- **Experiment:** Point to the various rotate options in the Rotate Objects gallery and watch the picture rotate in the document window.

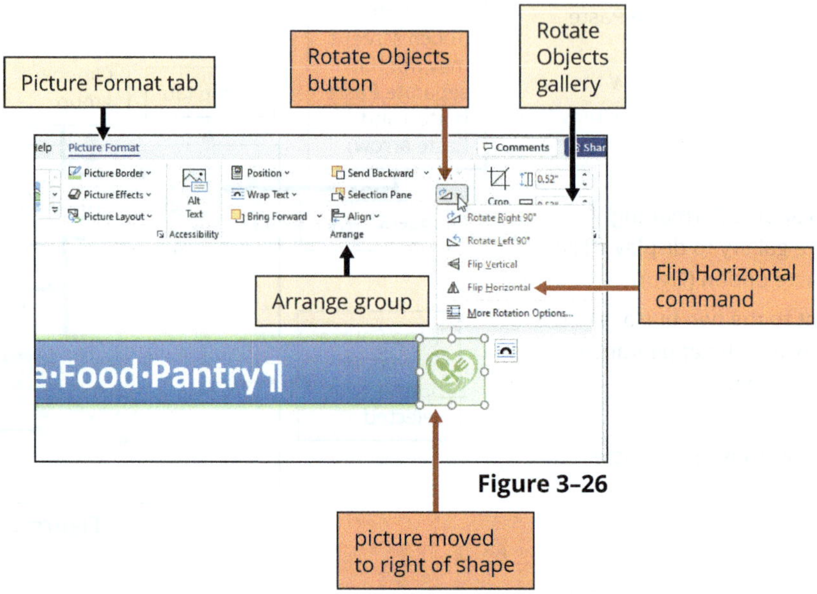

AdresiaStock/Shutterstock.com

Figure 3–26

2

- Click Flip Horizontal in the Rotate Objects gallery, so that Word flips the picture to display its mirror image (shown in Figure 3–27).

Q&A Can I flip an object vertically?
Yes, you would click Flip Vertical in the Rotate Objects gallery. You also can rotate an object clockwise or counterclockwise by clicking 'Rotate Right 90°' and 'Rotate Left 90°', respectively, in the Rotate Objects gallery.

BTW
Grouping Objects
You can group objects together if you want to move or format them together as a group. To group multiple objects, you select the first object and then SHIFT+click each additional object until all objects are selected. Then, click the Group button (Format tab | Arrange group) and click Group on the Group menu to group the selected objects into a single selected object.

To Format and Enter Text

The contact information for the letterhead in this project is located on the line below the shape containing the name. The following steps enter the mailing address in the letterhead.

1 Position the insertion point on the line below the shape containing the name.

2 If necessary, display the Home tab. Click the Center button (Home tab | Paragraph group) or press CTRL+E to center the paragraph.

3 Type **200 Pier 4 Boulevard, Boston, MA 02210** and then press SPACEBAR (shown in Figure 3–27).

To Insert a Symbol from the Symbol Gallery

Word provides a method of inserting bullets and other symbols, such as letters in the Greek alphabet and mathematical characters, that are not on the keyboard. In the letterhead, a bullet symbol separates the postal code from the phone number. The following steps use the Symbol gallery to insert a bullet symbol in the letterhead. **Why?** You want a visual separator between the mailing address and the phone number.

1

- Display the Insert tab.

2

- Click the Symbol button (Insert tab | Symbols group) to display the Symbol gallery (Figure 3–27).

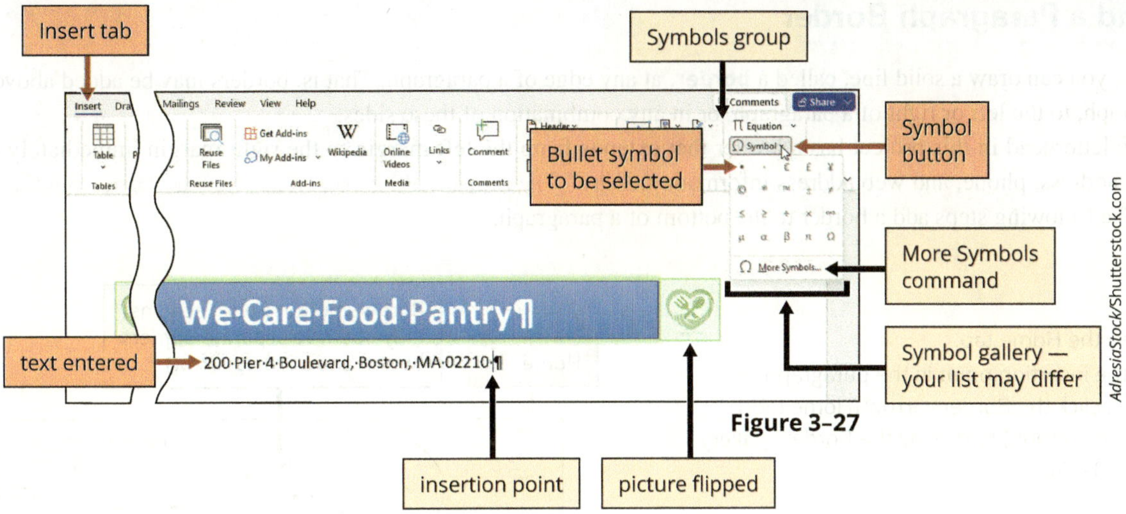

Figure 3–27

3

- Click the Bullet symbol in the Symbol gallery to insert the symbol at the location of the insertion point (shown in Figure 3–28).

Q&A What if the Bullet symbol is not in my Symbol gallery?
Click the More Symbols command in the Symbol gallery to display the Symbol dialog box, scroll through the symbols in the dialog box to locate the desired symbol, click the desired symbol to select it (in this case, the Bullet symbol is in the (normal text) Font and the General Punctuation subset), click the Insert button in the dialog box to insert the symbol in the document, and then click the Close button to close the dialog box.

To Enter Text

The following steps finish the text in the letterhead.

1 Press SPACEBAR. Type **617-555-6300** and then press SPACEBAR.

2 Click the Symbol button (Insert tab | Symbols group) to display the Symbol gallery and then click the Bullet symbol to insert another bullet symbol in the letterhead at the location of the insertion point.

3 Press SPACEBAR and then type **wecarefoodpantry.com** to finish the text in the letterhead (Figure 3–28).

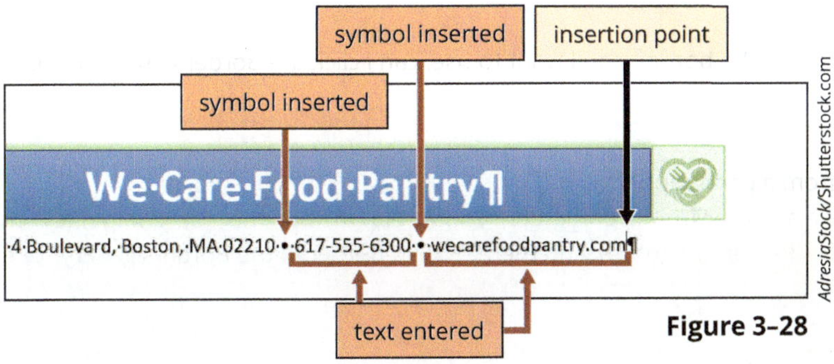

Figure 3–28

BTW
Inserting Special Characters
In addition to symbols, you can insert a variety of special characters, including dashes, hyphens, spaces, apostrophes, and quotation marks. Click More Symbols in the Symbol gallery (shown in Figure 3–27), click the Special Characters tab in the Symbol dialog box, click the desired character in the Character list, click the Insert button, and then click the Close button (Symbol dialog box).

To Add a Paragraph Border

In Word, you can draw a solid line, called a **border**, at any edge of a paragraph. That is, borders may be added above or below a paragraph, to the left or right of a paragraph, or in any combination of these sides.

The letterhead in this project has a border that extends from the left margin to the right margin immediately below the mailing address, phone, and web address information. **Why?** The horizontal line separates the letterhead from the rest of the letter. The following steps add a border to the bottom of a paragraph.

1

- Display the Home tab.
- With the insertion point in the paragraph to border, click the Borders arrow (Home tab | Paragraph group) to display the Borders gallery (Figure 3–29).

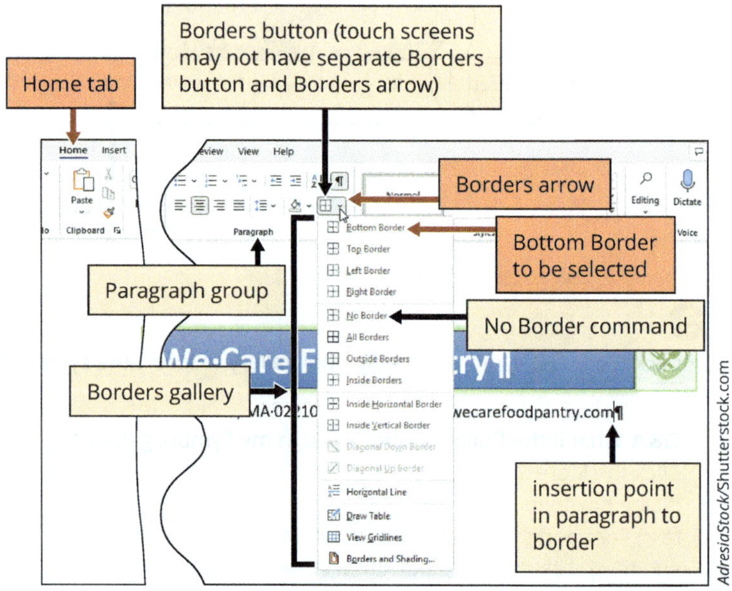

Figure 3–29

2

- Click Bottom Border in the Borders gallery to place a border below the paragraph containing the insertion point (Figure 3–30).

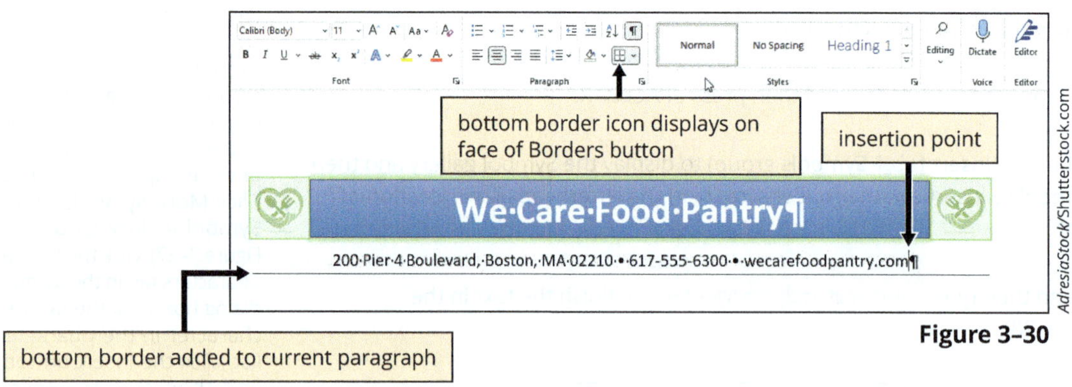

Figure 3–30

Q&A If the face of the Borders button displays the border icon I want to use, can I click the Borders button instead of using the Borders arrow?
Yes.

How would I remove an existing border from a paragraph?
If, for some reason, you wanted to remove a border from a paragraph, you would position the insertion point in the paragraph, click the Borders arrow (Home tab | Paragraph group), and then click No Border in the Borders gallery.

Other Ways

1. Click Page Borders button (Design tab | Page Background group), click Borders tab (Borders and Shading dialog box), select desired border options, click OK

To Clear Formatting

The next step is to position the insertion point below the letterhead, so that you can type the contents of the letter. When you press ENTER at the end of a paragraph containing a border, Word moves the border forward to the next paragraph. The paragraph also retains all current settings, such as the center format. Instead, you want the paragraph and characters on the new line to use the Normal style: black font with no border.

Word uses the term, **clear formatting**, to refer to returning the formats to the Normal style. The following steps clear formatting at the location of the insertion point. **Why?** You do not want to retain the current formatting in the new paragraph.

1

- With the insertion point between the web address and paragraph mark at the end of the contact information line (as shown in Figure 3–30), press ENTER to move the insertion point and paragraph to the next line (Figure 3–31).

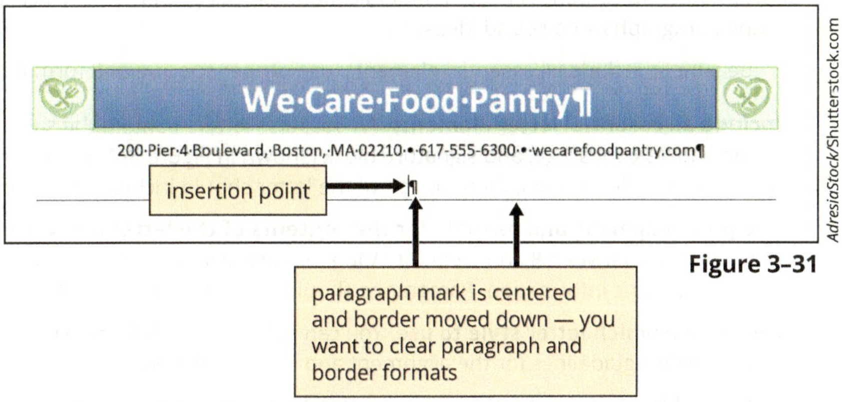

Figure 3–31

2

- Click the 'Clear All Formatting' button (Home tab | Font group) to apply the Normal style to the location of the insertion point (Figure 3–32).

3

- Save the letterhead again on the same storage location with the same file name.

Q&A Why should I save the letterhead at this time?
You are finished editing the letterhead.

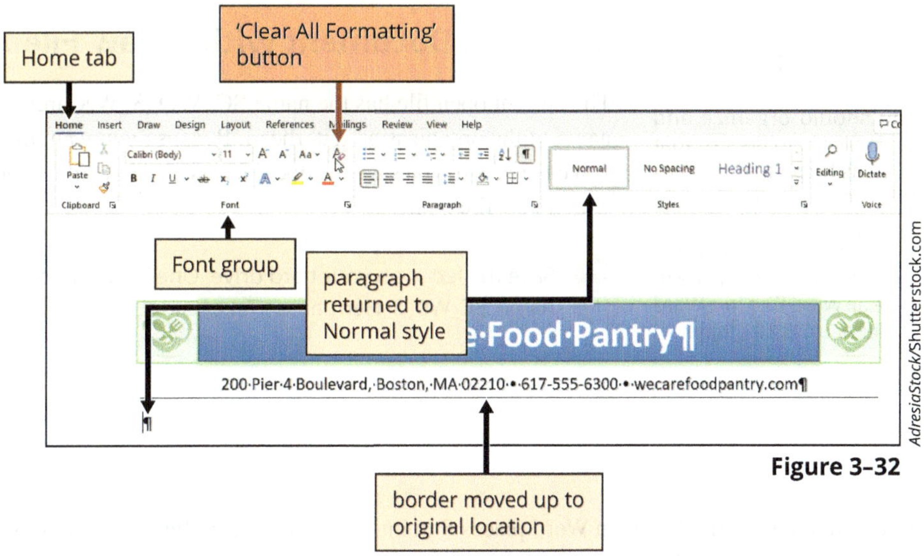

Figure 3–32

Other Ways

1. Click More button in Styles gallery (Home tab | Styles group), click Clear Formatting
2. Click Styles Dialog Box Launcher (Home tab | Styles group), click Clear All in Styles pane
3. Position insertion point in text, press CTRL+SPACEBAR, press CTRL+Q

Break Point: If you want to take a break, this is a good place to do so. You can exit Word now. To resume later, start Word, open the file called SC_WD_3_WeCareFoodPantryLetterhead.docx, and continue following the steps from this location forward.

Creating a Business Letter

With the letterhead for the business letter complete, the next task is to create the remainder of the content in the letter. The following sections use Word to create a business letter that contains a table and a bulleted list.

Consider This

What should you consider when writing a business letter?

A finished business letter should look like a symmetrically framed picture with evenly spaced margins, all balanced below an attractive letterhead. The letter should be well written, properly formatted, logically organized, and use visuals where appropriate. The content of a letter should contain proper grammar, correct spelling, logically constructed sentences, flowing paragraphs, and sound ideas.

Be sure to include all essential elements, use proper spacing and formats, and determine which letter style to use.

- **Include all essential letter elements.** All business letters contain the same basic elements, including the date line, inside address, message, and signature block (shown in Figure 3-1 at the beginning of this module). If a business letter does not use a letterhead, then the top of the letter should include return address information in a heading.
- **Use proper spacing and formats for the contents of the letter below the letterhead.** Use a font that is easy to read, in a size between 8 and 12 point. Add emphasis with bold, italic, and lists where appropriate, and use tables to present numeric information. Paragraphs should be single-spaced, with double-spacing between paragraphs.
- **Determine which letter style to use.** You can follow many different styles when creating business letters. A letter style specifies guidelines for the alignment and spacing of elements in the business letter.

If possible, keep the length of a business letter to one page. Be sure to proofread the finished letter carefully.

BTW
Organizing Files and Folders
You should organize and store files in folders so that you easily can find the files later. For example, if you are taking an introductory technology class called CIS 101, a good practice would be to save all Word files in a Word folder in a CIS 101 folder.

To Save a Document with a New File Name

The current open file has the name SC_WD_3_WeCareFoodPantryLetterhead.docx, which is the name of the organization letterhead. Because you want the letterhead file to remain intact so that you can reuse it, you save the document with a new file name. The following step saves a document with a new file name.

1. Save the letter on your hard drive, OneDrive, or other storage location using a new file name, SC_WD_3_HermansonTakeActionLetter.

To Apply a Style

Recall that the Normal style in Word places 8 points of blank space after each paragraph and inserts a vertical space equal to 1.08 lines between each line of text. You will need to modify the spacing used for the paragraphs in the business letter. **Why?** Business letters should use single spacing for paragraphs and double spacing between paragraphs.

Word has many built-in, or predefined, styles that you can use to format text. The No Spacing style, for example, defines line spacing as single and does not insert any additional blank space between lines when you press ENTER. To apply a style to a paragraph, you first position the insertion point in the paragraph. The following step applies the No Spacing style to a paragraph.

1

- With the insertion point positioned in the paragraph to be formatted, click No Spacing in the Styles gallery (Home tab | Styles group) to apply the selected style to the current paragraph (Figure 3-33).

Q&A Will this style be used in the rest of the document?
Yes. The paragraph formatting, which includes the style, will carry forward to subsequent paragraphs each time you press ENTER.

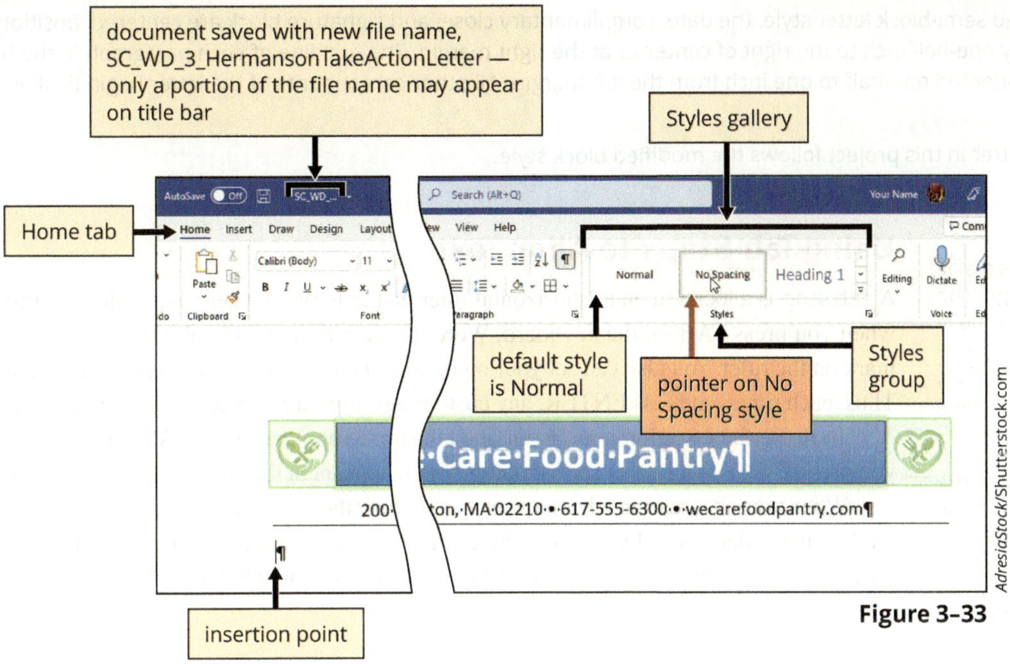

Figure 3–33

Other Ways

1. Click Styles Dialog Box Launcher (Home tab | Styles group), click desired style in Styles pane
2. Press CTRL+SHIFT+S, click Style Name arrow in Apply Styles pane, click desired style in list

Consider This

What elements should a business letter contain?

Be sure to include all essential business letter elements, properly spaced, in your letter:

- The **date line**, which consists of the month, day, and year, is positioned two to six lines below the letterhead.
- The **inside address**, placed three to eight lines below the date line, usually contains the addressee's courtesy title plus full name, job title, business affiliation, and full geographical address.
- The **salutation**, if present, is the greeting in the letter that begins two lines below the last line of the inside address. If you do not know the recipient's name, avoid using the salutation "To whom it may concern" — it is impersonal. Instead, use the recipient's title in the salutation, for example, Dear Personnel Director. In a formal business letter, use a colon (:) at the end of the salutation; in a casual business letter or personal letter, use a comma.
- The body of the letter, the **message**, begins two lines below the salutation. Within the message, paragraphs are single-spaced with one blank line between paragraphs.
- Two lines below the last line of the message, the closing line or **complimentary close** is displayed. Capitalize only the first word in a complimentary close.
- Type the **signature block** at least four blank lines below the complimentary close, allowing room for the author to sign their name.

Consider This

What are the common styles of business letters?

Three common business letter styles are the block, the modified block, and the modified semi-block. Each style specifies different alignments and indentations.

- In the block letter style, all components of the letter begin flush with the left margin.
- In the modified block letter style, the date, complimentary close, and signature block are positioned approximately one-half inch to the right of center or at the right margin. All other components of the letter begin flush with the left margin.

- In the modified semi-block letter style, the date, complimentary close, and signature block are centered, positioned approximately one-half inch to the right of center or at the right margin. The first line of each paragraph in the body of the letter is indented one-half to one inch from the left margin. All other components of the letter begin flush with the left margin.

The business letter in this project follows the modified block style.

BTW
Tabs Dialog Box
You can use the Tabs dialog box to set, change the alignment of, and remove custom tab stops. To display the Tabs dialog box, click the Paragraph Dialog Box Launcher (Home tab or Layout tab | Paragraph group) and then click the Tabs button (Paragraph dialog box). To set a custom tab stop, enter the desired tab position (Tabs dialog box) and then click the Set button. To change the alignment of a custom tab stop, click the tab stop position to be changed, click the new alignment, and then click the Set button. To remove an existing tab stop, click the tab stop position to be removed and then click the Clear button. To remove all tab stops, click the Clear All button in the Tabs dialog box.

Using Tab Stops to Align Text

A **tab stop** is a location on the horizontal ruler that tells Word where to position the insertion point when you press TAB on the keyboard. Word, by default, places a tab stop at every one-half inch mark on the ruler. You also can set your own custom tab stops. Tab settings are a paragraph format. Thus, each time you press ENTER, any custom tab stops are carried forward to the next paragraph.

To move the insertion point from one tab stop to another, press TAB on the keyboard. When you press TAB, a **tab character** formatting mark appears in the empty space between the tab stops.

When you set a custom tab stop, you specify how the text will align at a tab stop. The tab marker on the ruler reflects the alignment of the characters at the location of the tab stop. Table 3–2 shows types of tab stop alignments in Word and their corresponding tab markers.

Table 3–2: Types of Tab Stop Alignments

Tab Stop Alignment	Tab Marker	Result of Pressing TAB	Example
Left Tab		Left-aligns text at the location of the tab stop	toolbar ruler
Center Tab		Centers text at the location of the tab stop	toolbar ruler
Right Tab		Right-aligns text at the location of the tab stop	toolbar ruler
Decimal Tab		Aligns text on decimal point at the location of the tab stop	45.72 223.75
Bar Tab		Aligns text at a bar character at the location of the tab stop	| toolbar | ruler

To Display the Ruler

One way to set custom tab stops is by using the horizontal ruler. Thus, the following steps display the ruler in the document window.

1. If the rulers are not showing, display the View tab.
2. Click the Ruler check box (View tab | Show group) to place a check mark in the check box and display the horizontal and vertical rulers on the screen (shown in Figure 3–34).

To Set Custom Tab Stops

The first required element of the business letter is the date line, which in this letter is positioned two lines below the letterhead. The date line contains the month, day, and year, and begins 3½ inches from the left margin. **Why?** Business letter guidelines specify to begin the date line approximately one-half inch to the right of center. Thus, you should set a custom tab stop at the 3.5" mark on the ruler. The following steps set a left-aligned tab stop.

1

- With the insertion point on the paragraph mark below the border (shown in Figure 3–33), press ENTER so that a blank line appears above the insertion point.
- If necessary, click the tab selector at the left edge of the horizontal ruler until it displays the type of tab you wish to use, which is the Left Tab icon in this case.
- Position the pointer on the 3.5" mark on the ruler, which is the location of the desired custom tab stop (Figure 3–34).

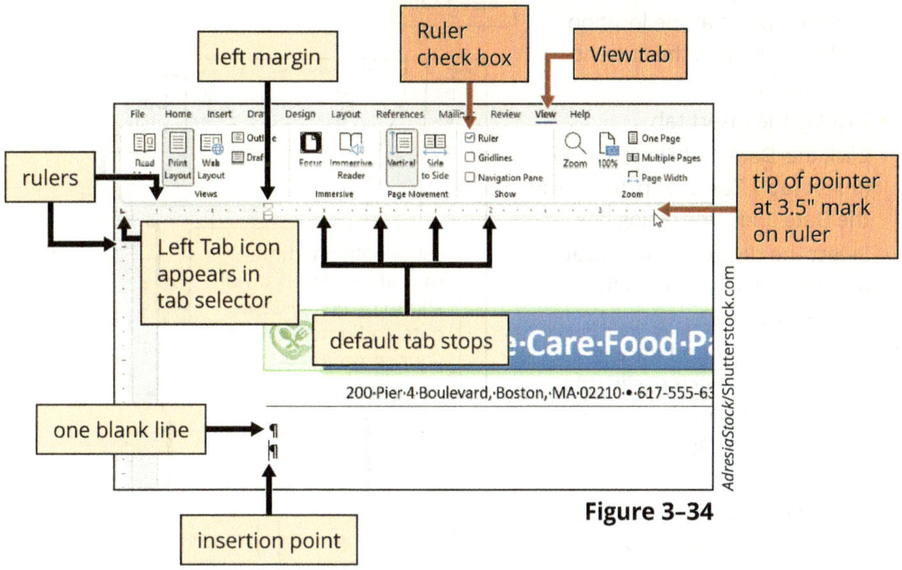

Figure 3–34

Q&A What is the purpose of the tab selector?
Before using the ruler to set a tab stop, ensure the correct tab stop icon appears in the tab selector. Each time you click the tab selector, its icon changes. The Left Tab icon is the default. For a list of the types of tab stops, refer to Table 3–2.

2

- Click the 3.5" mark on the ruler to place a tab marker at that location (Figure 3–35).

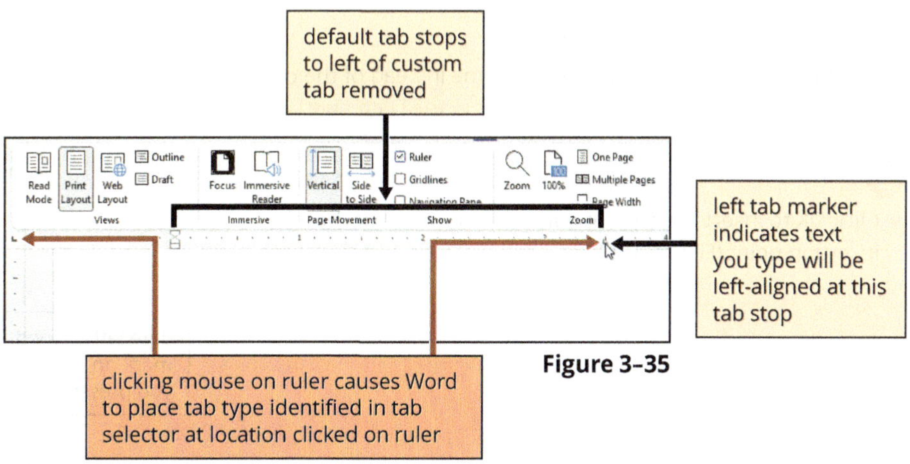

Figure 3–35

Q&A What if I click the wrong location on the ruler?
You can move a custom tab stop by dragging the tab marker to the desired location on the ruler. Or, you can remove an existing custom tab stop by pointing to the tab marker on the ruler and then dragging the tab marker down and out of the ruler.

What if I am using a touch screen?
Display the Home tab, tap the Paragraph Dialog Box Launcher (Home tab | Paragraph group), tap the Tabs button (Paragraph dialog box), type **3.5** in the Tab stop position box (Tabs dialog box), tap the Set button, and then tap OK to set a custom tab stop and place a corresponding tab marker on the ruler.

Other Ways

1. Click Paragraph Dialog Box Launcher (Home tab or Layout tab | Paragraph group), click Tabs button (Paragraph dialog box), type tab stop position (Tabs dialog box), click Set button, click OK

To Insert the Current Date in a Document

The next step is to enter the current date at the 3.5" tab stop in the document. **Why?** The date in this letter will be positioned according to the guidelines for a modified block style letter. In Word, you can insert a computer's system date in a document. The following steps insert the current date in the letter.

1

- Press TAB to position the insertion point at the location of the tab stop in the current paragraph.
- Display the Insert tab.
- Click the 'Date and Time' button (Insert tab | Text group) to display the Date and Time dialog box.
- Select the desired format (Date and Time dialog box), in this case January 18, 2029.
- If the Update automatically check box is selected, click the check box to remove the check mark (Figure 3–36).

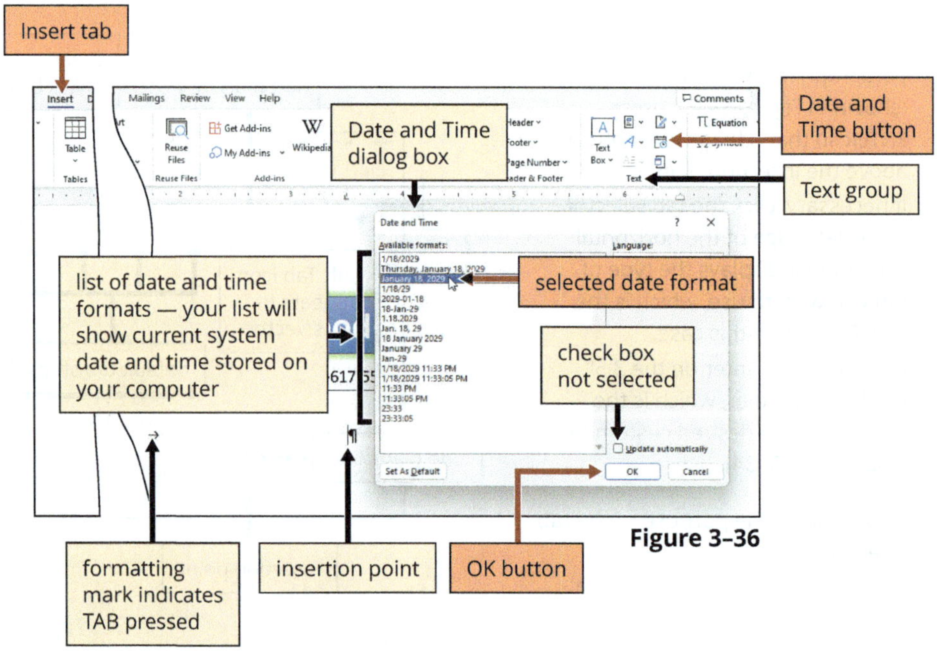

Figure 3–36

Q&A Why should the Update automatically check box not be selected?
In this project, the date at the top of the letter always should show today's date (for example, January 18, 2029). If, however, you wanted the date always to change to reflect the current computer date (for example, showing the date you open or print the letter), then you would place a check mark in this check box.

What if I wanted to insert the current time instead of the current date?
You would click one of the time formats in the Date and Time dialog box.

2

- Click OK to insert the current date at the location of the insertion point (Figure 3–37).

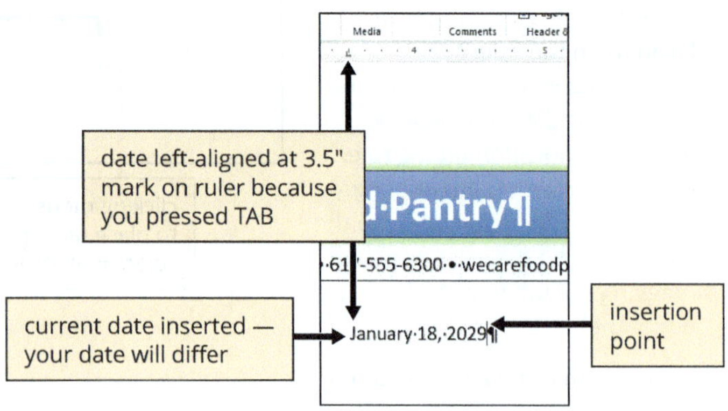

Figure 3–37

To Enter the Inside Address and Salutation

The next step in composing the business letter is to type the inside address and salutation. The following steps enter this text.

1 With the insertion point at the end of the date (shown in Figure 3–37), press ENTER three times.

2. Type **Ms. Celeste Hermanson** and then press ENTER.

3. Type **1873 Fargo Street** and then press ENTER.

4. Type **Boston, MA 02210** and then press ENTER twice.

5. Type **Dear Celeste,** and then press ENTER twice to complete the inside address and salutation entries.

6. Type the first paragraph of body copy: **Thank you for your interest in helping us at the We Care Food Pantry! Our focus is to deliver food and other resources in the Boston area. We offer a variety of volunteer and donation opportunities so that community members can become involved.**

7. Press ENTER twice.

8. Type **Below is our monthly mobile food pantry schedule in Boston:** and then press ENTER twice (Figure 3–38).

> **Q&A** Why does my document wrap on different words?
> Differences in wordwrap may relate to the printer connected to your computer. Thus, it is possible that the same document could wordwrap differently if associated with a different printer.

9. Save the letter again on the same storage location with the same file name.

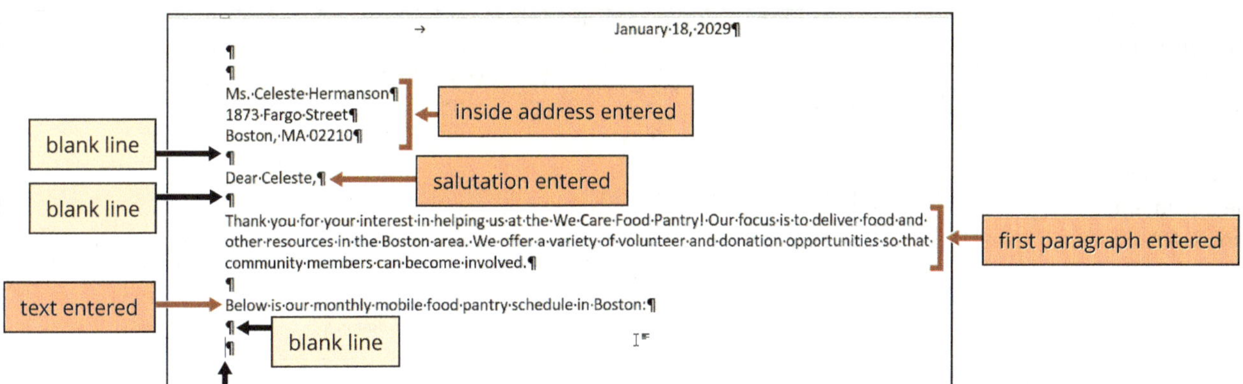

Figure 3–38

BTW
Voice Dictation and Search
Using a microphone, you can dictate document content and commands into a Word document. To use Word's speech-to-text tool, click the Dictate button (Home tab | Voice group). More recent versions of Word also include voice search, where you can click the Microphone button at the right edge of the Search box and then speak your query.

Tables

The next step in composing the business letter is to place a table listing the monthly mobile food pantry schedule (shown in Figure 3–1). A Word **table** is a grid of rows and columns that can contain text and graphics. The intersection of a row and a column is called a **cell** (which looks like a box), and cells are filled with data.

The first step in creating a table is to insert an empty table in the document. When inserting a table, you must specify the total number of rows and columns required, which is called the **dimension** of the table. The table in this project has three columns. You often do not know the total number of rows in a table. Thus, many Word users create one row initially and then add more rows as needed. In Word, the first number in a dimension is the number of columns, and the second is the number of rows. For example, in Word, a 3 × 1 (pronounced "three by one") table consists of three columns and one row.

BTW
Word Help
At any time while using Word, you can find answers to questions and display information about various topics through Word Help. Used properly, this form of assistance can increase your productivity and reduce your frustrations by minimizing the time you spend learning how to use Word.

To Insert an Empty Table

The next step is to insert an empty table in the letter. The following steps insert a table with three columns and one row at the location of the insertion point. **Why?** The first column will identify the day, the second will identify the time, and the third will identify the location. You will start with one row and add more rows as needed.

1

- Scroll the document so that you will be able to see the table in the document window.
- If necessary, display the Insert tab.
- With the insertion point positioned as shown in Figure 3–39, click the Table button (Insert tab | Tables group) to display the Table gallery (Figure 3–39).
- **Experiment:** Point to various cells on the grid to see a preview of various table dimensions in the document window.

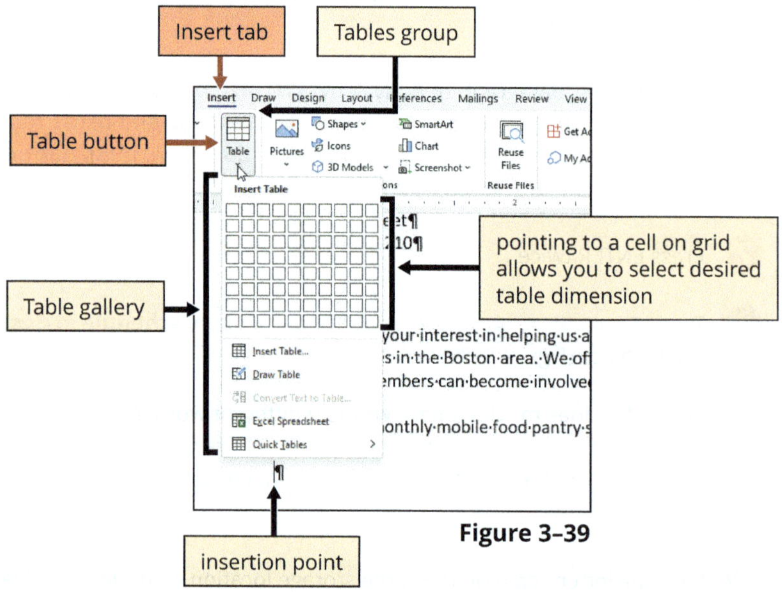

Figure 3–39

2

- Position the pointer on the cell in the first row and third column of the grid to preview the desired table dimension in the document (Figure 3–40).

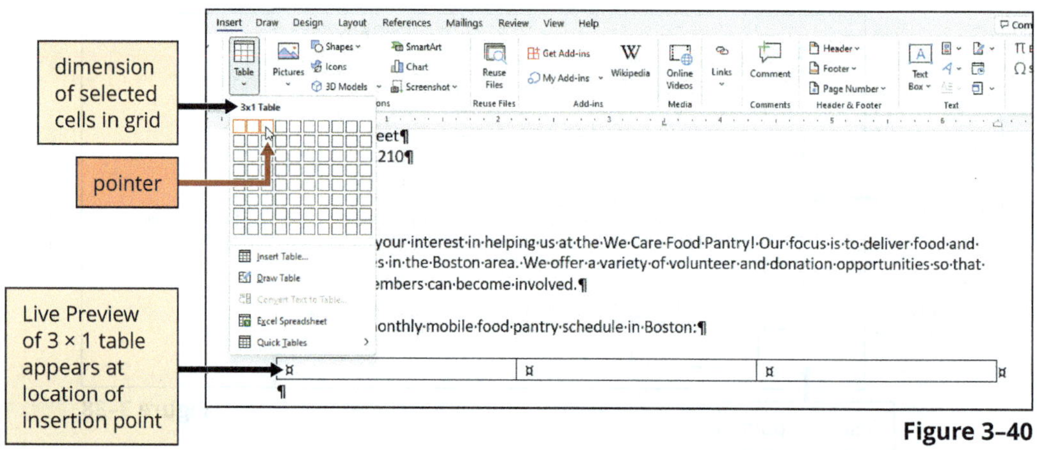

Figure 3–40

3

- Click the cell in the first row and third column of the grid to insert an empty table with one row and three columns in the document.
- If necessary, scroll the document so that the table is visible (Figure 3–41).

Q&A What are the small circles in the table cells?

Each table cell has an **end-of-cell mark**, which is a formatting mark that assists you with selecting and formatting cells. Similarly, each row has an **end-of-row mark**, which is a formatting mark that you can use to add columns to the right of a table. Recall that formatting marks do not print on a hard copy. The end-of-cell marks currently are left-aligned, that is, positioned at the left edge of each cell.

Is the contextual Layout tab different from the main Layout tab?

Yes. The main Layout tab, which always appears on the ribbon, is used to change page setup, format paragraphs, and arrange objects in a document. The contextual Layout tab appears only when you are working in a table and is used to change the properties and organization of a table and its rows, columns, and cells.

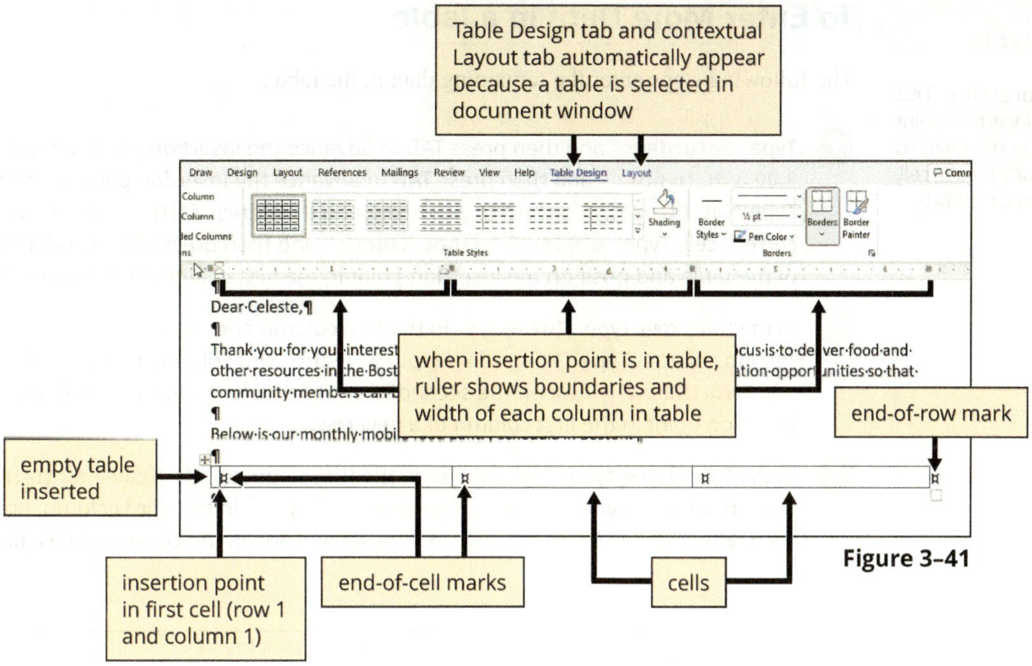

Figure 3–41

Other Ways

1. Click Table button (Insert tab | Tables group), click Insert Table in Table gallery, enter number of columns and rows (Insert Table dialog box), click OK

To Enter Data in a Table

The next step is to enter data in the cells of the empty table. The data you enter in a cell wordwraps just as text wordwraps between the margins of a document. To place data in a cell, you click the cell and then type.

To advance rightward from one cell to the next, press TAB. When you are at the rightmost cell in a row, press TAB to move to the first cell in the next row; do not press ENTER. **Why?** You press ENTER only if you want to begin a new paragraph within a cell. One way to add new rows to a table is to press TAB when the insertion point is positioned in the bottom-right corner cell of the table. The following step enters data in the first row of the table and then inserts a blank second row.

1

- With the insertion point in the left cell of the table, type **Day** and then press TAB to advance the insertion point to the next cell.
- Type **Time** and then press TAB to advance the insertion point to the next cell.
- Type **Location** and then press TAB to add a second row at the end of the table and position the insertion point in the first column of the new row (Figure 3–42).

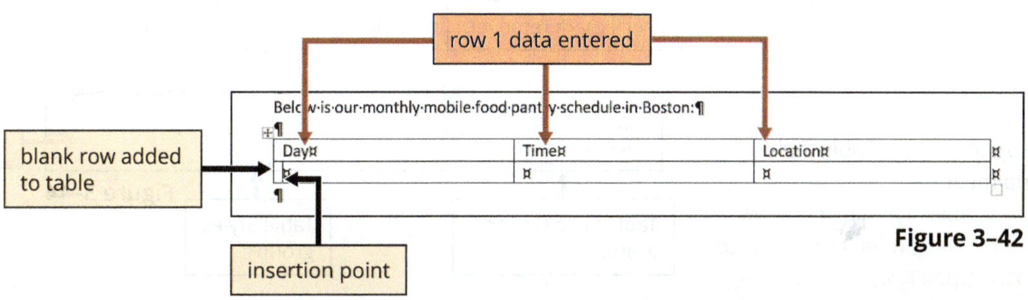

Figure 3–42

Q&A How do I edit cell contents if I make a mistake?
Click in the cell and then correct the entry.

BTW
Tab Character in Tables
In a table, pressing TAB advances the insertion point from one cell to the next. To insert a tab character in a cell, you must press CTRL+TAB.

To Enter More Data in a Table

The following steps enter the remaining data in the table.

1. Type **Saturdays** and then press TAB to advance the insertion point to the next cell. Type **9:00 a.m. to noon** and then press TAB to advance the insertion point to the next cell. Type **Mt. Pleasant Community Center** and then press ENTER to create a new line in the current cell. Type **839 Mt. Pleasant Avenue** and then press TAB to add a row at the end of the table and position the insertion point in the first column of the new row.

2. In the third row, type **Tuesdays** in the first column and **4:00 p.m. to 7:00 p.m.** in the second column. Type **Jeffers Fire House** in the third column, press ENTER, and then type **1025 Northern Avenue** on the second line in the current cell. Press TAB to position the insertion point in the first column of a new row.

3. In the fourth row, type **Thursdays** in the first column and **10:00 a.m. to 1:00 p.m.** in the second column. Type **Oakview Elementary School** in the third column, press ENTER, and then type **2298 Summer Street** on the second line in the current cell (Figure 3–43).

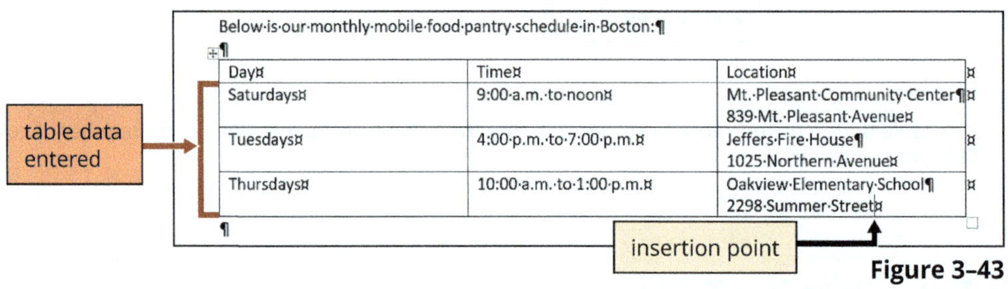

Figure 3–43

To Apply a Table Style

Word provides a gallery of more than 90 table styles, which include a variety of colors and shading. **Why?** Table styles allow you to change the basic table format to a more visually appealing style. The following steps apply a table style to the table in the letter.

1.
- If necessary, display the Table Design tab.
- If the First Column check box in the Table Style Options group (Table Design tab) contains a check mark, click the check box to remove the check mark because you do not want the first column in the table formatted differently from the rest of the table. Be sure the remaining check marks match those in the Table Style Options group (Table Design tab) (Figure 3–44).

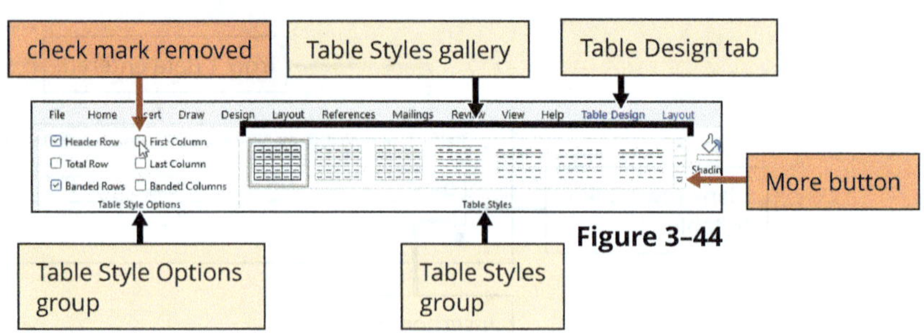

Figure 3–44

Q&A What if the Table Design tab no longer is the active tab?
Click in the table and then display the Table Design tab.

What do the options in the Table Style Options group mean?
When you apply table styles, if you want the top row of the table (header row), a row containing totals (total row), first column, or last column to be formatted differently, select those check boxes. If you want the rows or columns to alternate with colors, select Banded Rows or Banded Columns, respectively.

2

- With the insertion point in the table, click the More button in the Table Styles gallery (Table Design tab | Table Styles group), shown in Figure 3–44, to expand the gallery.
- Point to 'Grid Table 1 Light - Accent 6' (seventh style in first row in Grid Tables section) in the Table Styles gallery to display a Live Preview of that style applied to the table in the document (Figure 3–45).

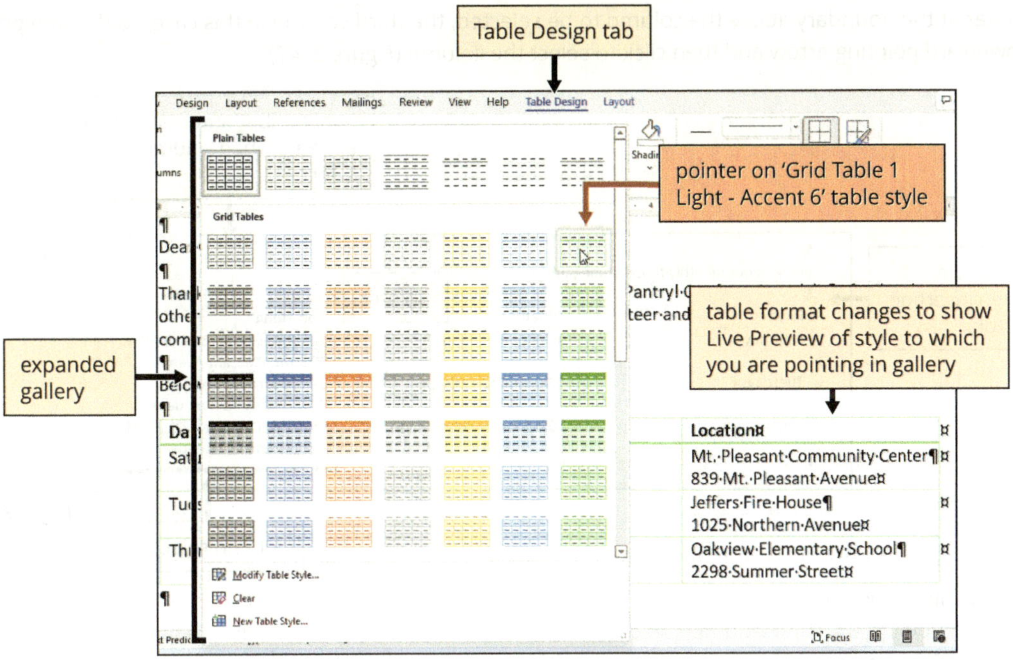

Figure 3–45

- **Experiment:** Point to various styles in the Table Styles gallery and watch the format of the table change in the document window.

3

- Click 'Grid Table 1 Light - Accent 6' in the Table Styles gallery to apply the selected style to the table. Scroll up, if necessary, to display the entire table (Figure 3–46).
- **Experiment:** Select and remove check marks from various check boxes in the Table Style Options group and watch the format of the table change in the document window. When finished experimenting, be sure the check marks match those shown in Figure 3–46.

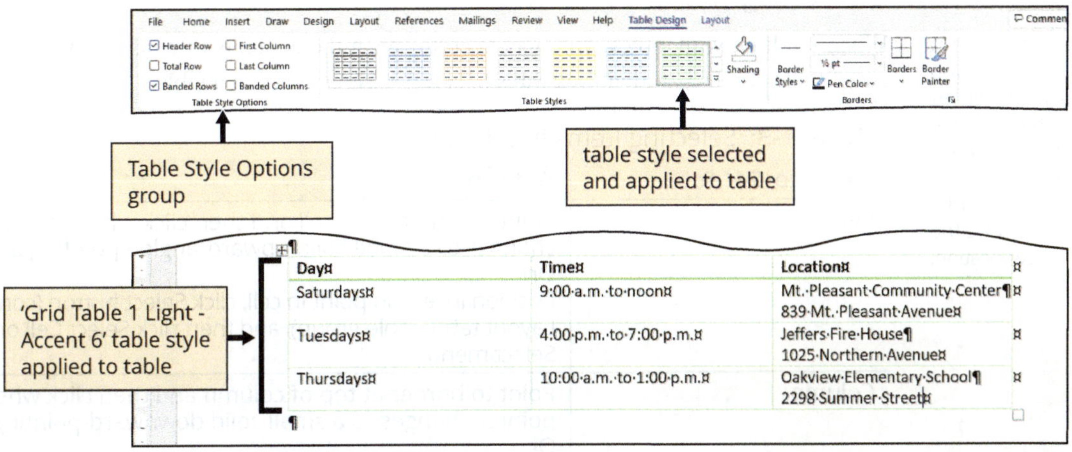

Figure 3–46

To Select a Column in a Table

The next task is to italicize the data in cells in the third column of the table. To do this, you first must select the column. **Why?** If you want to format the contents of a single cell, simply position the insertion point in the cell. To format a series of cells, you first must select them. The following steps select a column.

1

- Position the pointer at the boundary above the column to be selected, the third column in this case, so that the pointer changes to a downward pointing arrow and then click to select the column (Figure 3–47).

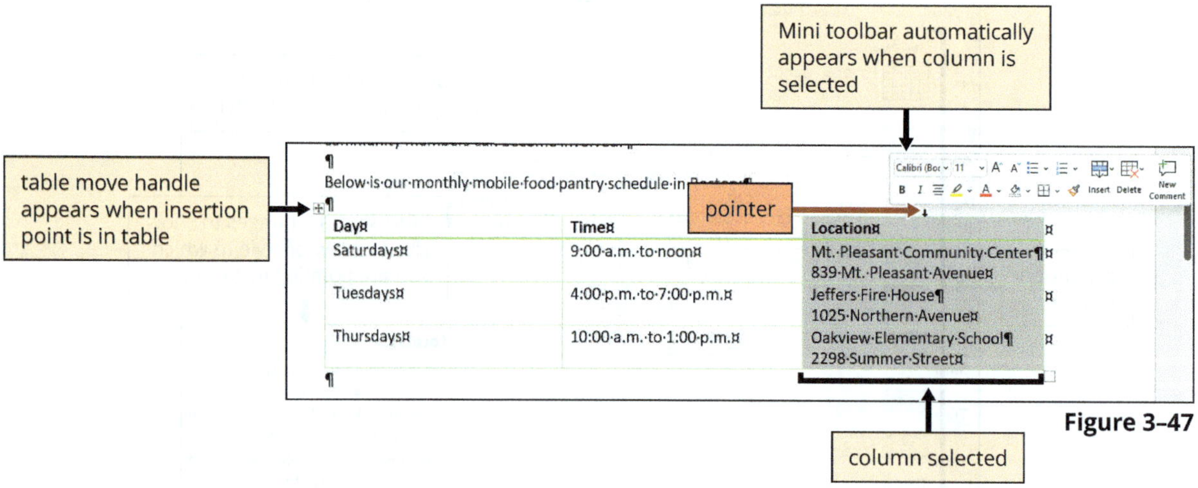

Figure 3–47

Q&A What if I am using a touch screen?
Position the insertion point in the third column, tap the Select button (contextual Layout tab | Table group), and then tap Select Column on the Select menu.

2

- Press CTRL+I to italicize the selected text.
- Click anywhere to remove the selection from the table.

Other Ways

1. Position insertion point in column to be selected, click Select button (contextual Layout tab | Table group), click Select Column on Select menu

BTW
Moving Tables
If you wanted to move a table to a new location, you would point to the upper-left corner of the table until the table move handle appears (shown in Figure 3–47), point to the table move handle, and then drag it to move the entire table to a new location.

Selecting Table Contents

When working with tables, you may need to select the contents of cells, rows, columns, or the entire table. Table 3–3 identifies ways to select various items in a table.

Table 3-3: Selecting Items in a Table

Item to Select	Action
Cell	Point to left edge of cell and then click when the pointer changes to a small solid upward-angled pointing arrow. Or Position insertion point in cell, click Select button (contextual Layout tab | Table group), and then click Select Cell on the Select menu.
Column	Point to border at top of column and then click when the pointer changes to a small solid downward-pointing arrow. Or Position insertion point in column, click Select button (contextual Layout tab | Table group), and then click Select Column on the Select menu.

Item to Select	Action
Row	Point to the left of the row and then click when pointer changes to a right-pointing block arrow. Or Position insertion point in row, click Select button (contextual Layout tab | Table group), and then click Select Row on the Select menu.
Multiple cells, rows, or columns adjacent to one another	Drag through cells, rows, or columns.
Multiple cells, rows, or columns not adjacent to one another	Select first cell, row, or column (as described above) and then hold down CTRL while selecting next cell, row, or column.
Next cell	Press TAB.
Previous cell	Press SHIFT+TAB.
Table	Point somewhere in table and then click table move handle that appears in upper-left corner of table (shown in Figure 3–47). Or Position insertion point in table, click Select button (contextual Layout tab | Table group), and then click Select Table on the Select menu.

BTW
Tables
For simple tables, such as the one just created, Word users often select the table dimension in the Table gallery to create the table. For a more complex table, such as one with a varying number of columns per row, Word has a Draw Table feature that allows users to draw a table in the document using a pencil pointer. To use this feature, click the Table button (Insert tab | Tables group) and then click Draw Table on the Table menu.

To Insert a Row in a Table

The next step is to insert a row in the table. **Why?** You inadvertently omitted the Wednesday schedule from the table. As discussed earlier, you can insert a row at the end of a table by positioning the insertion point in the bottom-right corner cell and then pressing TAB. You cannot use TAB to insert a row at the beginning or middle of a table. Instead, you use the Insert Above or Insert Below command (contextual Layout tab | Rows & Columns group) or the Insert Control. The **Insert Control**, which allows you to insert rows or columns in a table, is a circle containing a plus sign that appears when you use a mouse to point immediately above or to the left of columns or rows in a table. The following steps insert a row in the middle of a table.

1

- Position the pointer to the left of the table between the rows where you want the row to be inserted to display the Insert Control, in this case, above the Thursdays row (Figure 3–48).

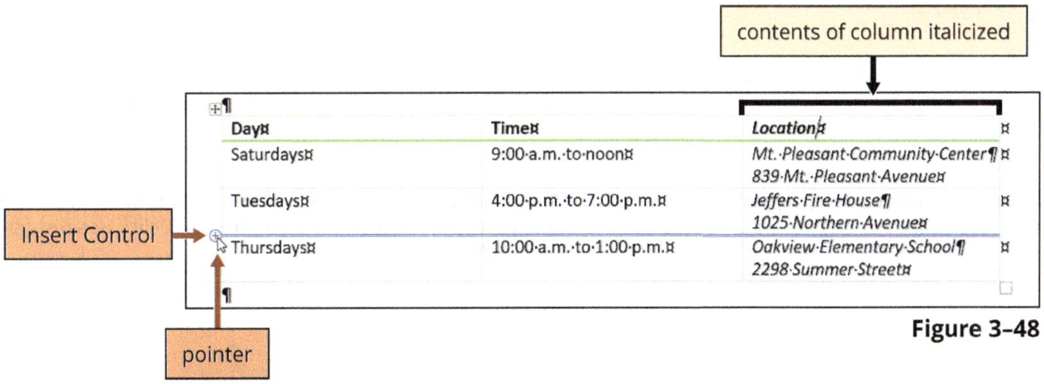

Figure 3–48

2

- Click the Insert Control to insert a row at the location of the pointer and then select the newly inserted row (Figure 3–49).
- **Experiment:** Click the contextual Layout tab to see the options available on this tab (shown in Figure 3–49).

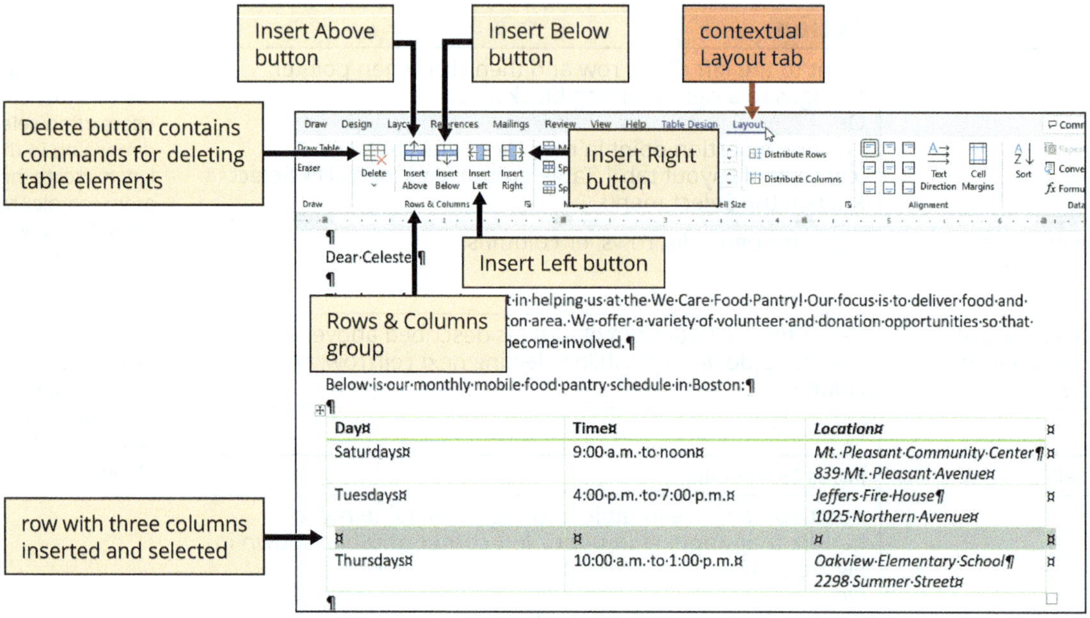

Figure 3–49

3

- If necessary, click the first cell in the newly added blank row to position the insertion point in the cell.
- Type **Wednesdays** and then press TAB.
- Type **7:00 a.m. to 10:00 a.m.** and then press TAB.
- Type **Auburn Youth Center** on the first line, press ENTER, and then type **973 Atlantic Avenue** in the last cell. Scroll, if necessary, to display the entire table in the document window (Figure 3–50).

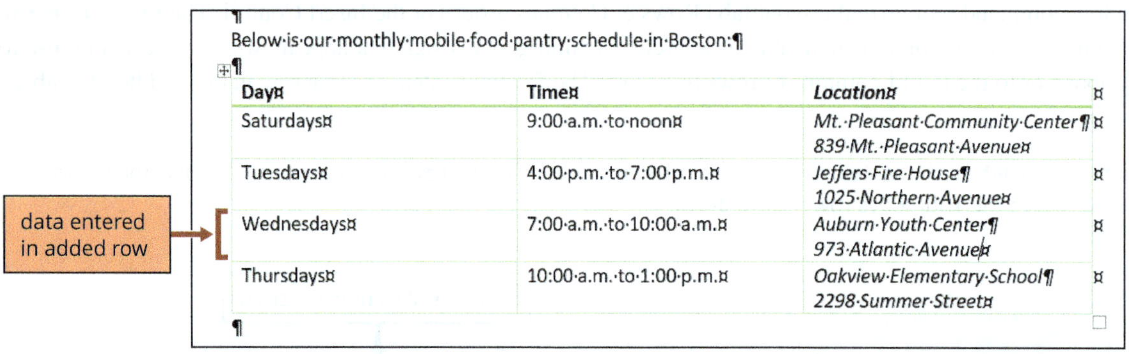

Figure 3–50

Other Ways

1. Click Insert Above or Insert Below button (Layout tab | Rows & Columns group)
2. Right-click row, point to Insert on shortcut menu (or, if using touch, tap Insert button on Mini toolbar), click desired option on Insert submenu

To Insert a Column in a Table If you wanted to insert a column in a table, instead of inserting rows, you would perform the following steps.

1. Point above the table and then click the desired Insert Control.

or

1. Position the insertion point in the column to the left or right of where you want to insert the column.

2. Click the Insert Left button (contextual Layout tab | Rows & Columns group) to insert a column to the left of the current column, or click the Insert Right button (contextual Layout tab | Rows & Columns group) to insert a column to the right of the current column.

or

1. Right-click the table, point to Insert on the shortcut menu (or, if using touch, tap Insert button on the Mini toolbar), and then click 'Insert Columns to the Left' or 'Insert Columns to the Right' on the Insert submenu (or, if using touch, tap 'Insert Columns to the Left' or 'Insert Columns to the Right').

BTW
Resizing Table Columns and Rows
To change the width of a column or height of a row to an exact measurement, hold down ALT while dragging markers on the ruler. Or, enter values in the Width or Height boxes (contextual Layout tab | Cell Size group).

Deleting Table Data

If you want to delete row(s) or delete column(s) from a table, position the insertion point in the row(s) or column(s) to delete, click the Delete button (contextual Layout tab | Rows & Columns group) (shown in Figure 3–49), and then click Delete Rows or Delete Columns on the Delete menu. Or, select the row or column to delete, right-click the selection, and then click Delete Rows or Delete Columns on the Mini toolbar or shortcut menu.

To delete the contents of a cell, select the cell contents and then press DELETE or BACKSPACE. You also can drag and drop or cut and paste the contents of cells. To delete an entire table, position the insertion point in the table, click the Delete button (contextual Layout tab | Rows & Columns group), and then click Delete Table on the Delete menu. To delete the contents of a table and leave an empty table, you would select the table and then press DELETE.

To Add More Text

The table now is complete. The next step is to enter text below the table. The following steps enter text.

1. Scroll, if necessary, to see the space below the table on the letter.
2. Position the insertion point on the paragraph mark below the table and then press ENTER.
3. Type **Please be aware of the following volunteer age restrictions:** and then press ENTER (shown in Figure 3-51).

BTW
Aligning Tables
To align an entire table, such as centering it between the margins on the page, select the table and then press CTRL+E or click the Center button (Home tab | Paragraph group). To align contents of cells, select the cells and then click the desired alignment button in the Alignment group on the contextual Layout tab.

To Bullet a List as You Type

If you know before you type that a list should be bulleted, you can use Word's AutoFormat As You Type feature to bullet the paragraphs as you type them instead of formatting the paragraphs with bullets after you enter them. **Why?** The AutoFormat As You Type feature saves you time because it applies formats automatically. The following steps add bullets to a list as you type.

1
- Press the ASTERISK key (*) as the first character on the line (Figure 3-51).

2
- Press SPACEBAR to convert the asterisk to a bullet character.

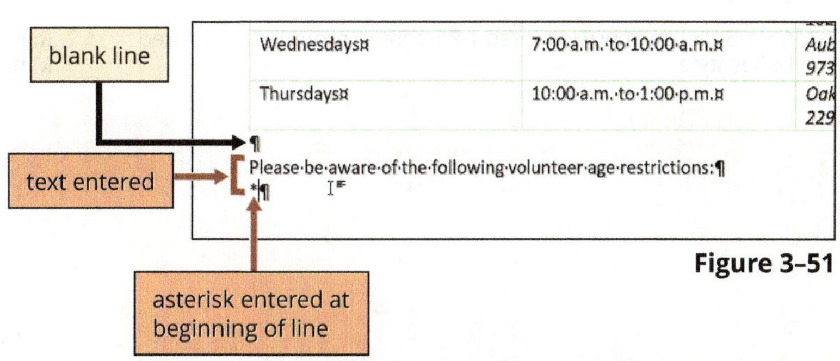

Figure 3-51

Q&A What if I did not want the asterisk converted to a bullet character?

You could undo the AutoFormat by clicking the Undo button (Home tab | Undo group); pressing CTRL+Z; clicking the AutoCorrect Options button that appears to the left of the bullet character as soon as you press SPACEBAR and then clicking 'Undo Automatic Bullets' on the AutoCorrect Options menu; or clicking the Bullets button (Home tab | Paragraph group).

3

- Type **Must be at least 8 years old to pack and sort food** as the first bulleted item.
- Press ENTER to place another bullet character at the beginning of the next line (Figure 3–52).

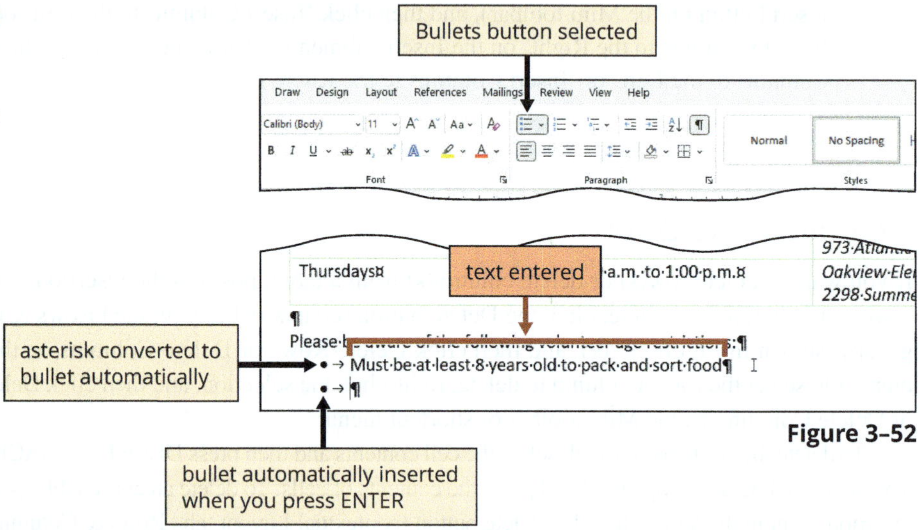

Figure 3–52

4

- Type **Must be at least 12 years old to distribute food and other resources** and then press ENTER.
- Type **Anyone under 16 years old must be accompanied by an adult who is at least 21 years old** and then press ENTER.
- Press ENTER again to turn off automatic bullets as you type (Figure 3–53).

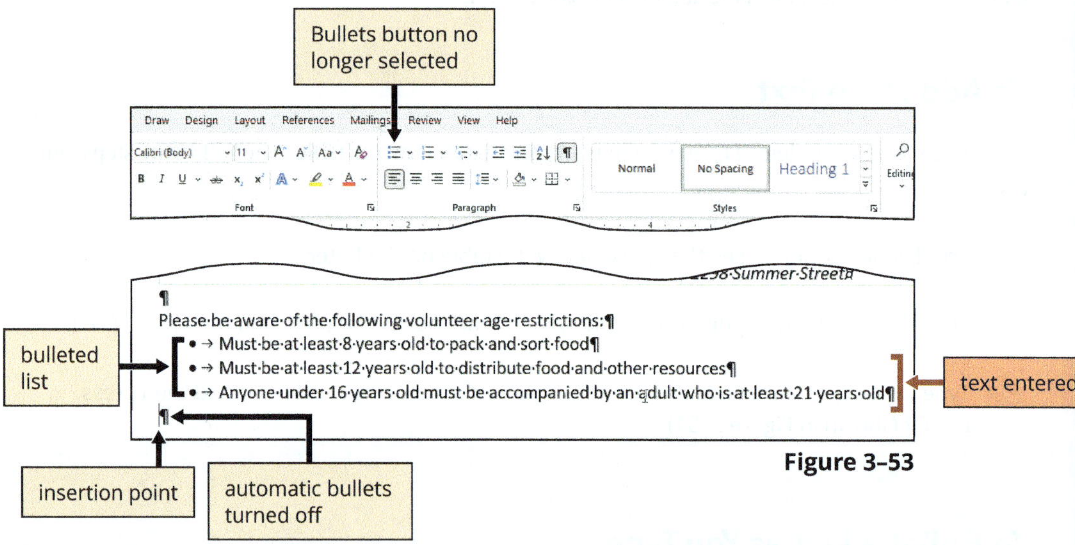

Figure 3–53

Q&A Why did automatic bullets stop?

When you press ENTER without entering any text after the automatic bullet character, Word turns off the automatic bullets feature.

Other Ways

1. Click Bullets arrow (Home tab | Paragraph group), click desired bullet style
2. Right-click paragraph to be bulleted, click Bullets arrow on Mini toolbar, click desired bullet style, if necessary

To Enter More Text and Then Save the Letter

The following steps enter the remainder of the letter content.

1. With the insertion point positioned on the paragraph below the bulleted list, press ENTER and then type the sentence: **We are incredibly grateful for community members who help us to make a difference. Please review the opportunities on the next page and let me know how you would like to help!**

2. Press ENTER twice. Press TAB to position the insertion point at the tab stop set at the 3.5" mark on the ruler. Type **Appreciatively,** and then press ENTER four times.

3. Press TAB to position the insertion point at the tab stop set at the 3.5" mark on the ruler. Type **Mathias L. Robles** and then press ENTER.

4. Press TAB to position the insertion point at the tab stop set at the 3.5" mark on the ruler. Type **Coordinator** to finish the letter. Scroll up, if necessary (Figure 3–54).

5. Save the letter again on the same storage location with the same file name.

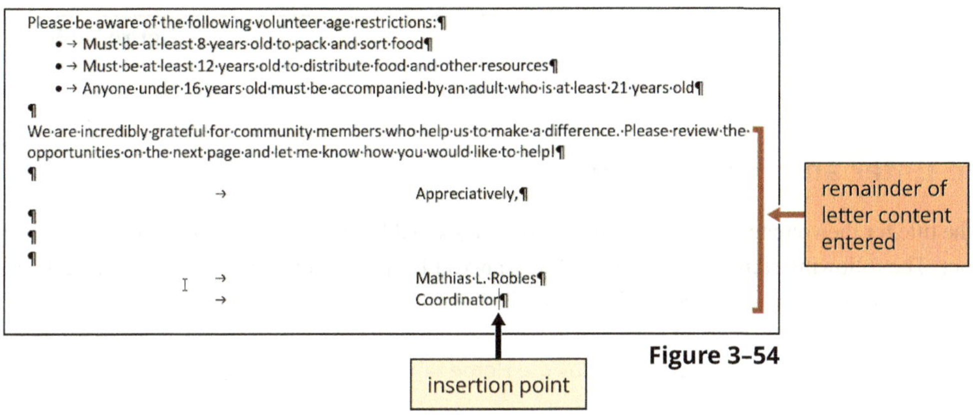

Figure 3–54

BTW

Nonbreaking Spaces and Hyphens

If you do not want a compound word, such as a proper noun, date, unit of time and measure, abbreviations, or geographic destinations, to be split, where part of the compound word appears at the end of one line and the other part appears at the beginning of the next line, you can insert a nonbreaking space or a nonbreaking hyphen. To insert a nonbreaking space, you would press CTRL+SHIFT+SPACEBAR instead of SPACEBAR in the middle of the compound word. To insert a nonbreaking hyphen, you would press CTRL+SHIFT+HYPHEN instead of a hyphen in the middle of the compound word.

Working with SmartArt Graphics

The response letter to the community member referenced opportunities for volunteering and donating. These opportunities are to appear on a separate page after the content of the letter. The following sections insert a page break and then create the content for the volunteer and donation opportunities.

To Insert a Page Break

The first step in creating the page that will contain the volunteer and donation opportunities is to insert a page break at the end of the response letter. The following steps insert a page break.

1. Verify that the insertion point is positioned at the end of text in the letter, as shown in Figure 3–54.

2. Click Insert on the ribbon to display the Insert tab.

3. Click the Page Break button (Insert tab | Pages group) to insert a page break immediately to the left of the insertion point and position the insertion point at the beginning of a new blank page (Figure 3–55).

BTW

Sections and Section Breaks

Every document has at least one section. You can create multiple sections if you need to change page formatting in a portion of a document. A section break divides one section from another. To insert a next page section break, click the Breaks button (Layout tab | Page Setup group) and then click Next Page in the Section Breaks area of the Breaks gallery. Other section break options are in the Breaks gallery, as well.

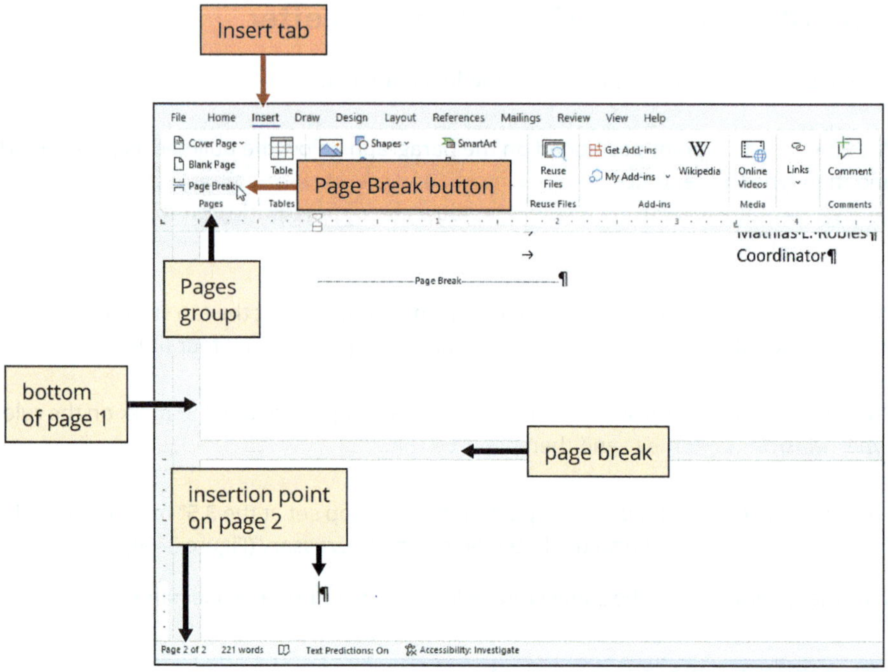

Figure 3–55

To Enter and Format Text

The title for the volunteer and donation opportunities should use a large font size and an easy-to-read font. The following steps enter the text, How Can You Help?, centered on the first line and the text, Volunteer or Donate!, centered on the second line.

1. Click Home on the ribbon to display the Home tab.
2. Click the Center button (Home tab | Paragraph group) to center the paragraph that will contain the title.
3. Click the Bold button (Home tab | Font group), so that the text you type will be formatted with bold characters.
4. Click the Font Size arrow (Home tab | Font group) and then click 36 in the Font Size gallery, so that the text you type will use the selected font size.
5. Click the Font Color arrow (Home tab | Font group) and then click 'Blue, Accent 1' (fifth color in first row) in the Font Color gallery, so that the text you type will use the selected font color.
6. Scroll, if necessary, to see the insertion point and paragraph mark. Type **How Can You Help?** and then press ENTER to enter the first line of the title.
7. Click the Font Color arrow (Home tab | Font group) and then click 'Green, Accent 6, Darker 25%' (last color in fifth row) in the Font Color gallery, so that the text you type will use the selected font color.
8. Type **Volunteer or Donate!** as the second line of the title (Figure 3–56).

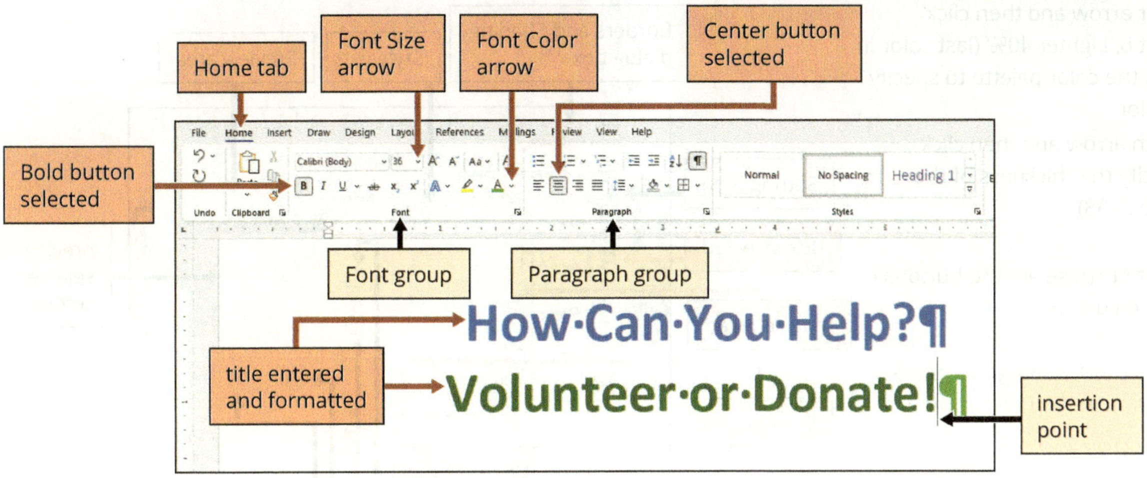

Figure 3–56

To Add and Format a Paragraph Border

If you click the Borders button (Home tab | Paragraph group), Word applies the most recently defined border, or, if one has not been defined, it applies the default border to the current paragraph. To specify a border different from the most recently defined border, you click the Borders arrow (Home tab | Paragraph group).

In this project, the title for the volunteer and donation opportunities has a 2¼-point green dashed border around it. **Why?** You want the title to stand out on the page. The following steps add a border to all edges of the selected paragraphs.

1

- Select the paragraphs to border, in this case, the first two lines of the page.
- Click the Borders arrow (Home tab | Paragraph group) to display the Borders gallery (Figure 3–57).

Q&A What if I wanted to border just a single paragraph?
You would position the insertion point in the paragraph before clicking the Borders arrow.

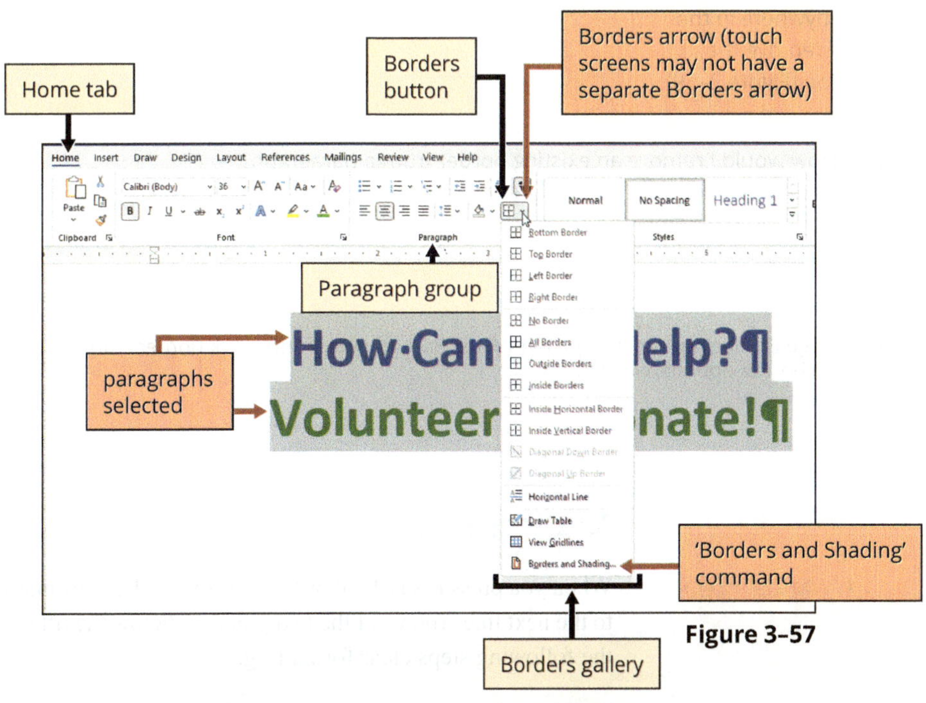

Figure 3–57

2

- Click 'Borders and Shading' in the Borders gallery to display the Borders and Shading dialog box.
- Click Box in the Setting area (Borders and Shading dialog box), which will place a border on each edge of the selected paragraphs.
- Click the fourth style in the Style list to specify the border style.

- Click the Color arrow and then click 'Green, Accent 6, Lighter 40%' (last color in fourth row) in the color palette to specify the border color.
- Click the Width arrow and then click 2 ¼ pt to specify the thickness of the border (Figure 3–58).

Q&A For what purpose are the buttons in the Preview area used?
They are toggles that display and remove the top, bottom, left, and right borders from the diagram in the Preview area.

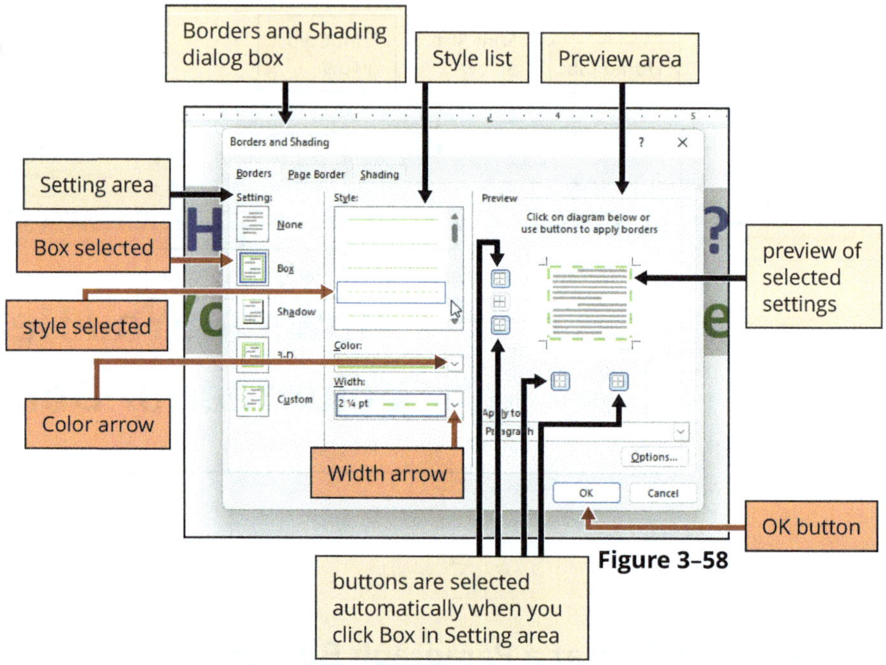

Figure 3–58

3

- Click OK (Borders and Shading dialog box) to place the border shown in the preview area of the dialog box around the selected paragraphs in the document.
- Click anywhere in the title to remove the selection (Figure 3–59).

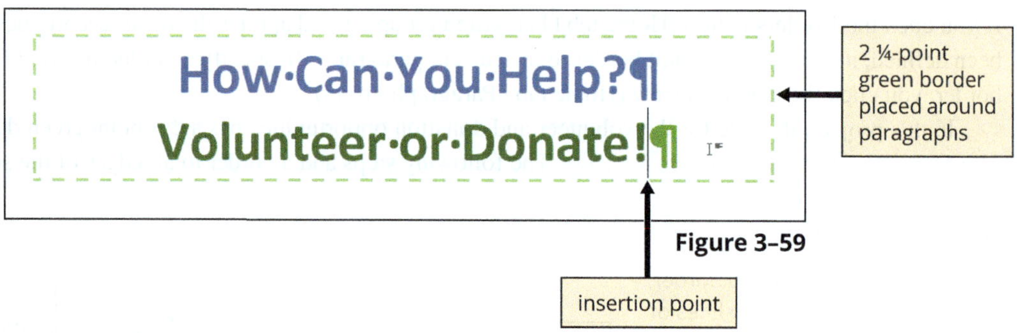

Figure 3–59

Q&A How would I remove an existing border from a paragraph?
Click the Borders arrow (Home tab | Paragraph group) and then click the border in the Borders gallery that identifies the border you wish to remove, or click No Border to remove all borders.

Other Ways

1. Click Page Borders button (Design tab | Page Background group), click Borders tab (Borders and Shading dialog box), select desired border options, click OK

To Clear Formatting

When you press ENTER, Word carries forward any formatting at the location of the insertion point to the next line. You want the text you type below the title to be returned to the Normal style. Thus, the following steps clear formatting.

1 Position the insertion point at the end of the second line of the title, as shown in Figure 3–59, and then press ENTER.

2 Click the 'Clear All Formatting' button (Home tab | Font group) to apply the Normal style to the location of the insertion point (Figure 3–60).

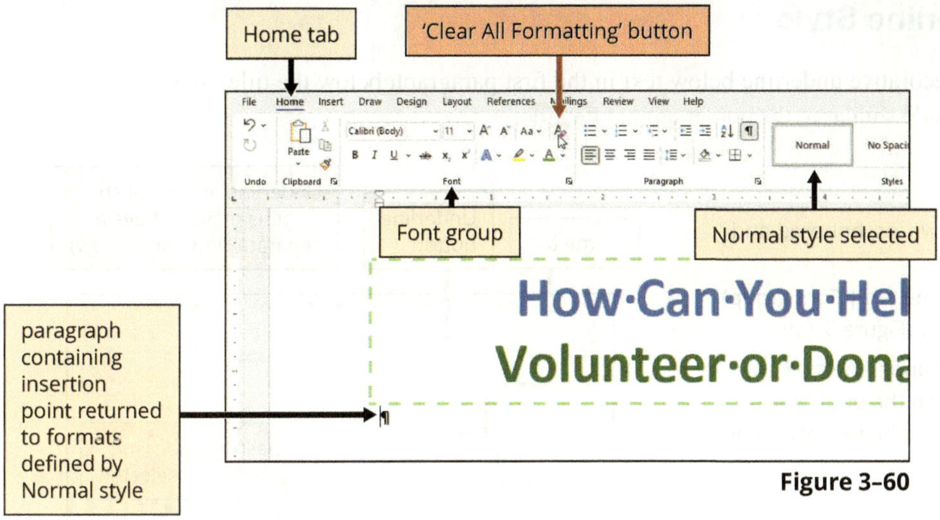

Figure 3–60

To Apply a Style and Enter More Text

The text below the title should use single spacing with double spacing between paragraphs. Thus, the following steps apply the No Spacing style and then enter two paragraphs of text.

1. With the insertion point positioned below the title, click No Spacing in the Styles gallery (Home tab | Styles group) to apply the selected style to the current paragraph.

2. Click the Font Size arrow (Home tab | Font group) and then click 14 in the Font Size gallery, so that the text you type will use the selected font size.

3. Press ENTER and then type **We are so honored and grateful that you are interested in helping us make a difference at the We Care Food Pantry. Below is a list of ways you can help.**

4. Press ENTER twice and then type **Please call or text me anytime at 617-555-6365 with questions or to be added to our volunteer schedule.** (Figure 3–61).

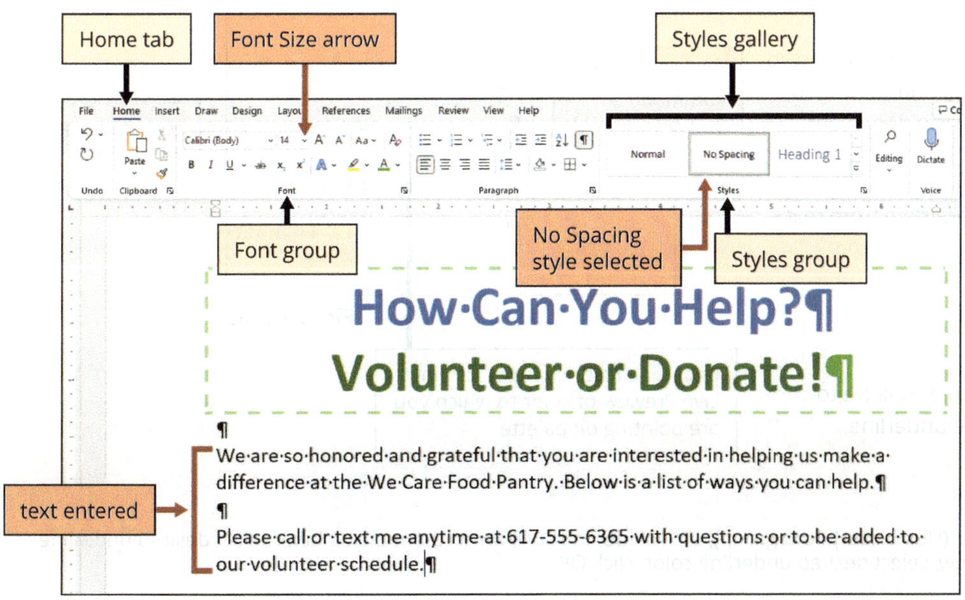

Figure 3–61

To Change the Underline Style

The following steps place a decorative underline below text in the first paragraph below the title. **Why?** You would like to emphasize text and use a line style similar to the border around the title.

1

- Select the text to format (the words, honored and grateful, in this case).
- Click the Underline arrow (Home tab | Font group) to display the Underline gallery (Figure 3–62).
- **Experiment:** Point to various underline styles in the Underline gallery and watch the underline style on the selected text change in the document window.

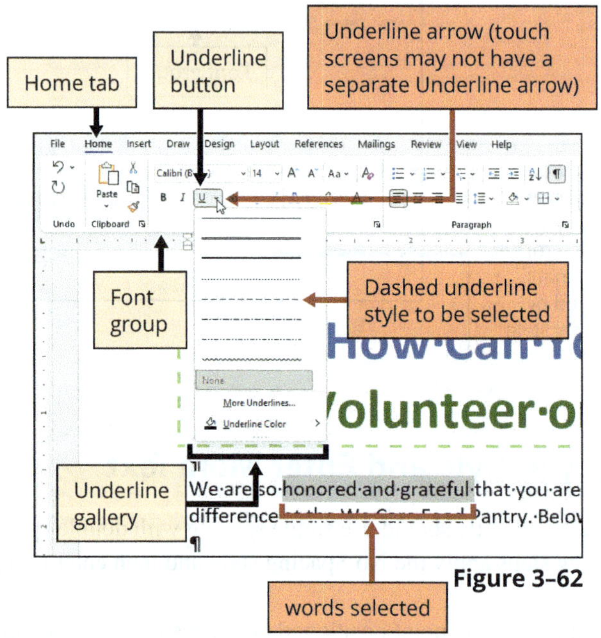

Figure 3–62

2

- Click the fifth underline style (Dashed underline) in the Underline gallery to apply the selected underline style to the selected text.
- Click the Underline arrow (Home tab | Font group) to display the Underline gallery again.
- Point to Underline Color in the Underline gallery to display a color palette.
- Point to 'Green, Accent 6' (last color in first row) in the color palette to display a Live Preview of that underline color on the selected text (Figure 3–63).
- **Experiment:** Point to various underline colors in the color palette and watch the underline color on the selected text change in the document window.

Q&A How would I remove underline from text?
With the text selected, you would click the Underline button (Home tab | Font group).

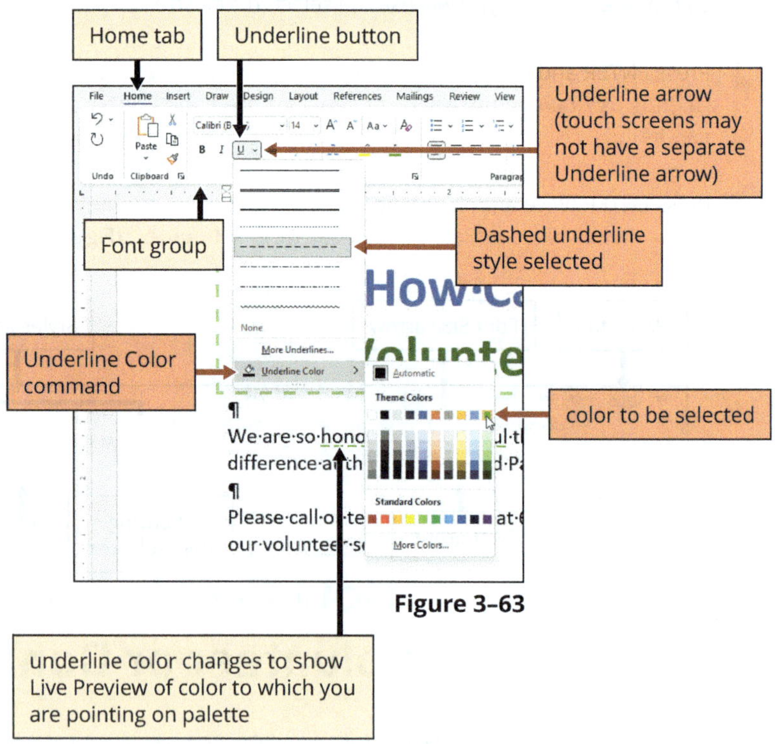

Figure 3–63

3

- Click 'Green, Accent 6' in the color palette to apply the selected color to the underline.

Other Ways

1. Click Font Dialog Box Launcher (Home tab | Font group), click Underline style arrow (Font dialog box), select desired underline style, click Underline color arrow, select desired underline color, click OK

To Use the Format Painter Button

The words, call or text me anytime, in the next paragraph are to use the same decorative underline as the words, honored and grateful, that you just formatted. **Why?** You would like the underline format to be consistent. Instead of selecting the words, call or text me anytime, and following the steps to apply the same underline format, you will copy the format from the currently selected text. The following steps copy formatting using the Format Painter button.

1

- With the text selected that contains the formatting you wish to copy (the text, honored and grateful, in this case), click the Format Painter button (Home tab | Clipboard group) to turn on the format painter.

Q&A What if I wanted to copy a format to multiple locations?
To copy formats to only one other location, click the Format Painter button (Home tab | Clipboard group) once. If you want to copy formatting to multiple locations, double-click the Format Painter button so that the format painter remains active until you turn it off, or click it again.

- Move the pointer to where you want to copy the formatting (the text, call or text me anytime, in this case) and notice that the format painter is active (Figure 3–64).

Q&A How can I tell if the format painter is active?
The pointer has a paintbrush attached to it when the format painter is active.

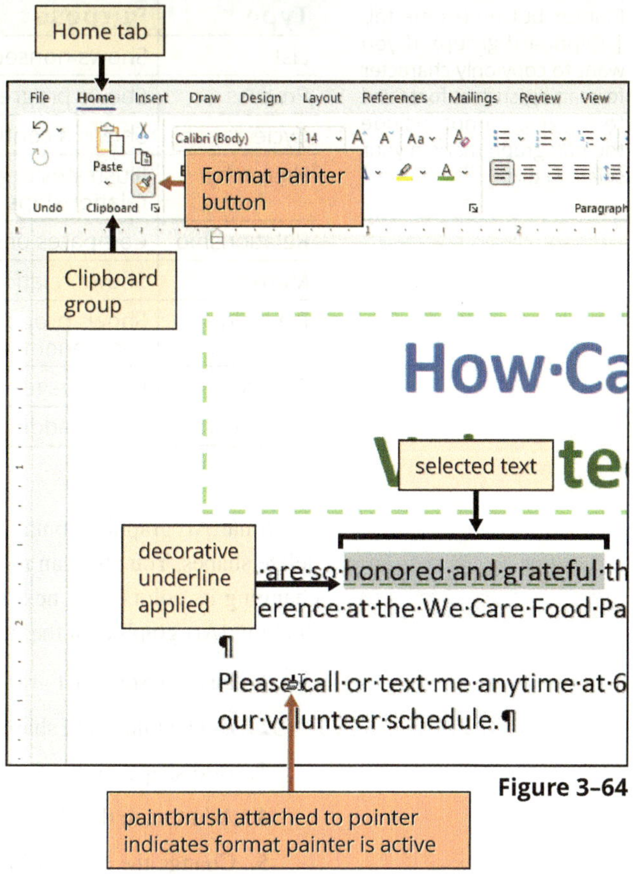

Figure 3–64

2

- Select the text that should have the same underline format (the text, call or text me anytime, in this case) to paste the copied format to the selected text (Figure 3–65).

Q&A What if I wanted to copy formats from one object to another, such as a picture or table cell?
You would follow these same steps, except select the object instead of text.

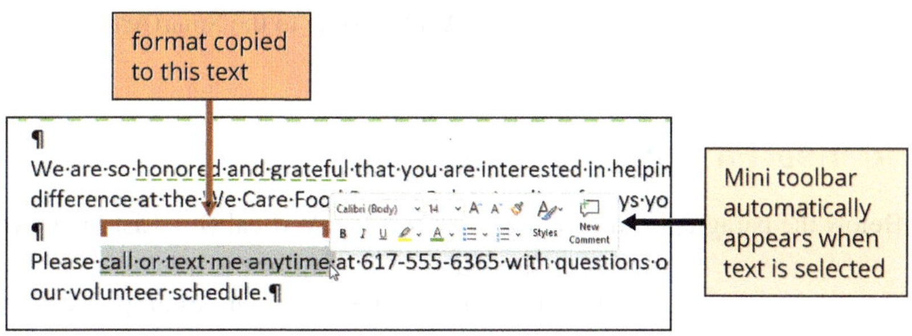

Figure 3–65

3

- Press CTRL+END to position the insertion point at the end of the last line of text on the current page and then press ENTER twice to position the insertion point two lines below the last line of text on the page.
- Save the letter again on the same storage location with the same file name.

SmartArt Graphics

Microsoft Office includes **SmartArt graphics**, which are customizable diagrams that you use to pictorially present lists, processes, and relationships. Many different types of SmartArt graphics

BTW
Format Painter
If you also want to copy paragraph formatting, such as alignment and line spacing, select the paragraph mark at the end of the paragraph prior to clicking the Format Painter button (Home tab | Clipboard group). If you want to copy only character formatting, such as fonts and font sizes, do not include the paragraph mark in your selected text.

are available, allowing you to choose one that illustrates your message best. Table 3–4 identifies the purpose of some of the more popular types of SmartArt graphics. Within each type, Office provides numerous layouts. For example, you can select from 40 different layouts of the list type.

Table 3-4: SmartArt Graphic Types

Type	Purpose
List	Shows nonsequential or grouped blocks of information.
Process	Shows progression, timeline, or sequential steps in a process or workflow.
Cycle	Shows a continuous sequence of steps or events.
Hierarchy	Illustrates organization charts, decision trees, and hierarchical relationships.
Relationship	Compares or contrasts connections between concepts.
Matrix	Shows relationships of parts to a whole.
Pyramid	Shows proportional or interconnected relationships with the largest component at the top or bottom.
Picture	Uses images to present a message.
Office.com	Shows additional layouts available at Office.com.

SmartArt graphics contain shapes. You can add text or pictures to shapes, add more shapes, or delete shapes. You also can modify the appearance of a SmartArt graphic by applying styles and changing its colors. The next several sections demonstrate the following general tasks to create the SmartArt graphic on the title page in this project:

1. Insert a SmartArt graphic.
2. Delete unneeded shapes from the SmartArt graphic.
3. Add shapes to the SmartArt graphic.
4. Add text to the shapes in the SmartArt graphic.
5. Change the colors of the SmartArt graphic.
6. Apply a style to the SmartArt graphic.

To Insert a SmartArt Graphic

Below the paragraphs of text, you wish to add a Vertical Box List SmartArt graphic. **Why?** The Vertical Box List SmartArt graphic allows you to place multiple lists one above the next in the document, which works well for the list of the volunteer and donation opportunities. The following steps insert a SmartArt graphic centered at the location of the insertion point.

1

- With the insertion point on the blank paragraph, click the Center button (Home tab | Paragraph group) so that the inserted SmartArt graphic will be centered at the location of the insertion point.
- Display the Insert tab.
- Click the SmartArt button (Insert tab | Illustrations group) to display the Choose a SmartArt Graphic dialog box (Figure 3-66).
- **Experiment:** Click various SmartArt graphic types in the left pane of the dialog box and watch the related layout choices appear in the middle pane.
- Click various layouts in the list of layouts in the middle pane to see the preview and description of the layout appear in the right pane of the dialog box.

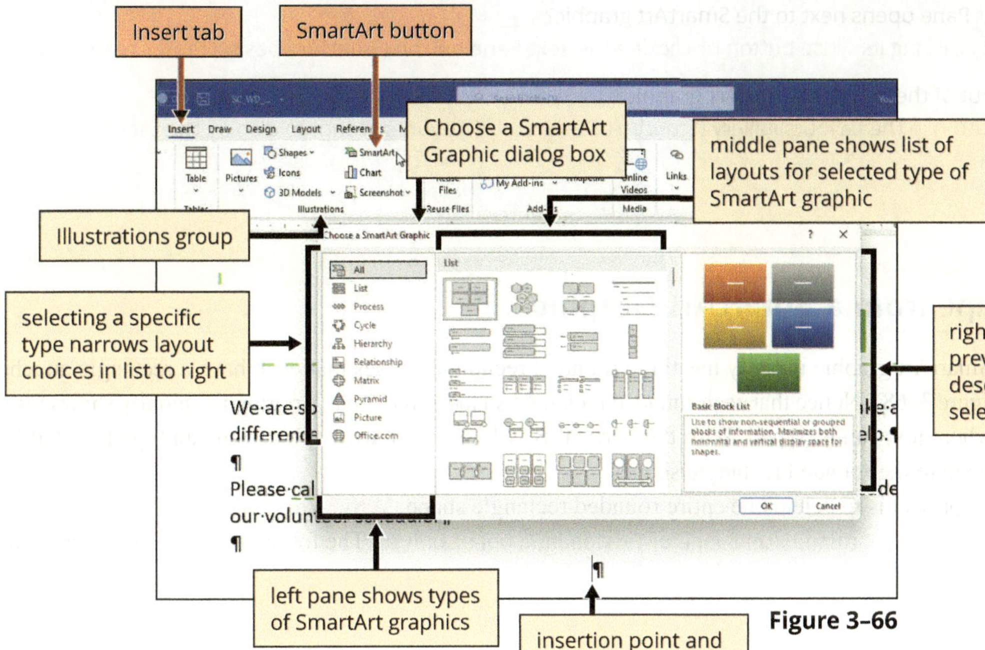

Figure 3–66

2

- Click List in the left pane (Choose a SmartArt Graphic dialog box) to display the layout choices related to the selected SmartArt graphic type.
- Click 'Vertical Box List' in the middle pane, which displays a preview and description of the selected layout in the right pane (Figure 3–67).

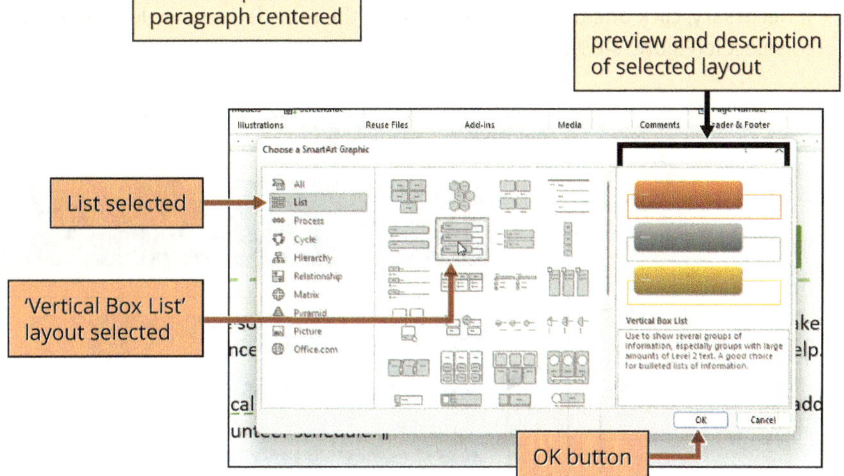

Figure 3–67

3

- Click OK to insert the selected SmartArt graphic in the document at the location of the insertion point (Figure 3–68). Scroll, if necessary, to see the SmartArt graphic.

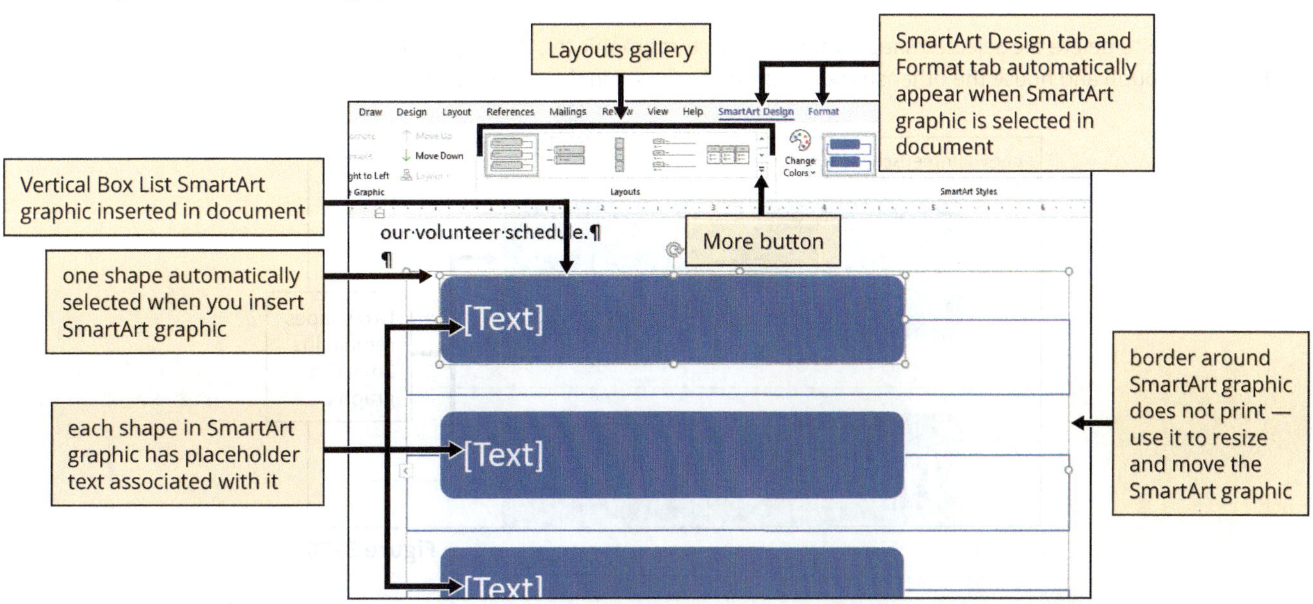

Figure 3–68

Q&A What if the Text Pane opens next to the SmartArt graphic?
Close the Text Pane by clicking its Close button or clicking the Text Pane button (SmartArt Design tab | Create Graphic group).

Can I change the layout of the inserted SmartArt graphic?
Yes. Click the More button in the Layouts gallery (SmartArt Design tab | Layouts group) to display the list of layouts and then select the desired layout.

To Delete a Shape from a SmartArt Graphic

The Vertical Box List SmartArt graphic initially has three rounded rectangle shapes that each have a rectangle attached below each shape (shown in Figure 3–68). Notice that each rounded rectangle shape in the SmartArt graphic initially shows **placeholder text**, which indicates where text can be typed. With the Vertical Box List SmartArt graphic, you can type bulleted lists in the rectangles that are attached to the rounded rectangle shapes.

The next step in this project is to delete one entire rounded rectangle shape. **Why?** You initially believe you will need only two lists: one for the volunteer opportunities and another for donation opportunities. The following steps delete one of the shapes in the SmartArt graphic.

1

- If necessary, click one of the edges of one of the rounded rectangle shapes that says the word, [Text], in the SmartArt graphic to select it (Figure 3–69).

Figure 3–69

2

- Press DELETE to delete the selected shape from the SmartArt graphic (or, if using touch, tap the Cut button (Home tab | Clipboard group)) and notice the other shapes resize and relocate in the graphic (Figure 3–70).

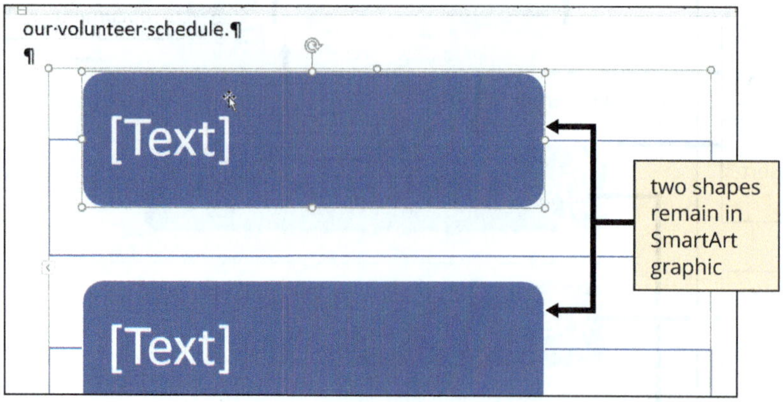

Figure 3–70

Q&A What if the text inside the shape is selected instead of the shape itself?
Click the shape again, ensuring you click the edge of the shape.

Other Ways

1. Click Cut button (Home tab | Clipboard group)	2. Right-click selected shape, click Cut on shortcut menu	3. Press BACKSPACE with shape selected

To Add Text to Shapes in a SmartArt Graphic

The following steps add text to the first shape. **Why?** The first shape will identify the volunteer opportunities.

1

- If necessary, click placeholder text, [Text], in the top rounded rectangle shape to select and delete the placeholder text. Type **Volunteer** to replace placeholder text with the entered text (Figure 3–71).

Figure 3–71

Q&A How do I edit placeholder text if I make a mistake?
Click the placeholder text to select it and then correct the entry.

What if my typed text is longer than the shape?
The font size of the text in the shape may be adjusted or the text may wordwrap within the shape.

2

- Click the rectangle attached to the bottom of the Volunteer shape to select the rectangle (Figure 3–72).

Figure 3–72

3

- With the rectangle selected, type **Warehouse: Inspect, sort, label, and package food** as the first bulleted item below the Volunteer heading and notice that Word automatically adjusts the font size to accommodate the text and also places a bullet character at the beginning of the typed text (Figure 3–73).

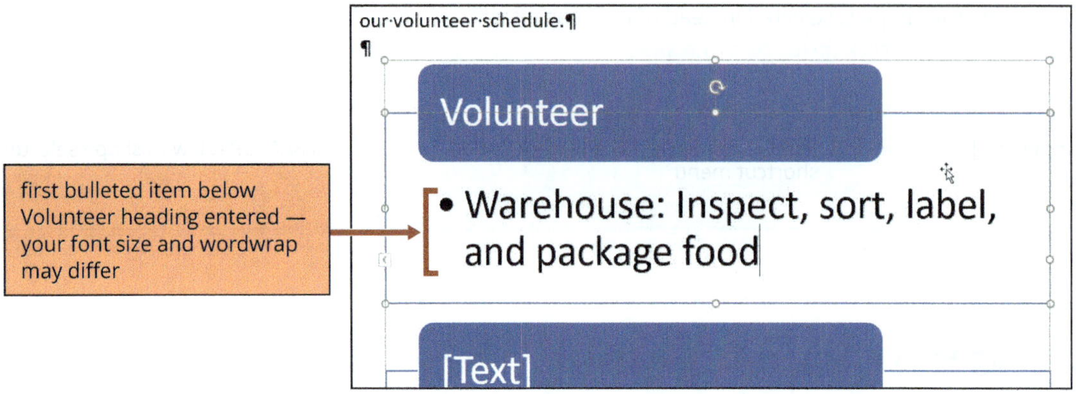

Figure 3–73

4

- Press ENTER and then type **Mobile food pantry: Distribute food and other goods, or direct traffic flow** as the second bulleted volunteer item.
- Press ENTER and then type **Events: Assist at food drives and fundraising events** as the third bulleted volunteer item.
- Press ENTER and then type **Drives: Host a food drive or virtual funds drive** as the fourth bulleted volunteer item.
- Press ENTER and then type **Skills-based: Help with administrative tasks, social media, or equipment operations** as the fifth bulleted volunteer item.
- Press ENTER and then type **Advocacy: Assist at events to raise awareness of our needs and services** as the sixth bulleted volunteer item.
- Scroll, if necessary, to see the entire completed shape identifying volunteer opportunities (Figure 3–74).

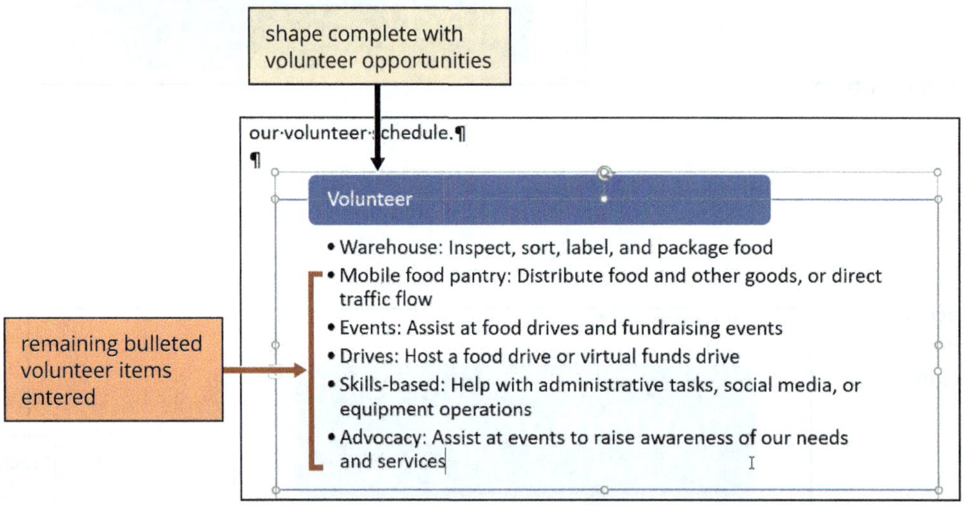

Figure 3–74

Q&A Word is not checking spelling in the shapes. Why not?
Word does not check spelling in objects, so be sure to proofread your entered text in any objects.

Other Ways

1. Click Text Pane control, enter text in Text Pane, close Text Pane
2. Click Text Pane button (SmartArt Design tab | Create Graphic group), enter text in Text Pane, click Text Pane button again
3. Right-click shape and click Edit Text (or, if using touch, tap Edit Text button on Mini toolbar), click 'Exit Edit Text' on shortcut menu, enter text

To Add More Text to a Shape in a SmartArt Graphic

The following steps add text to the next shape in the SmartArt graphic.

1. Scroll to display the next rounded rectangle shape. Click placeholder text, [Text], in the second rounded rectangle shape to select and delete the placeholder text. Type **Donate Financially** to replace placeholder text with the entered text.

2. Click the rectangle attached to the bottom of the Donate Financially shape to select the rectangle and then type **One-time monetary gift: Payable online, by phone, by check, or with Venmo** as the first bulleted item below the Donate Financially heading and notice that Word automatically adjusts the font size to accommodate the text and also places a bullet character at the beginning of the typed text.

3. Press ENTER and then type **Recurring monetary gift: Automatically charged to your card each month or quarter** as the second bulleted donate financially item.

4. Press ENTER and then type **Matching gift: Your employer may match your donation to our organization** as the third bulleted donate financially item.

5. Press ENTER and then type **Gift card: Drop off or mail to our main location** as the fourth bulleted donate financially item.

6. Press ENTER and then type **Rewards programs: Shop online at businesses that send donations based on purchases** as the fifth bulleted donate financially item (Figure 3–75).

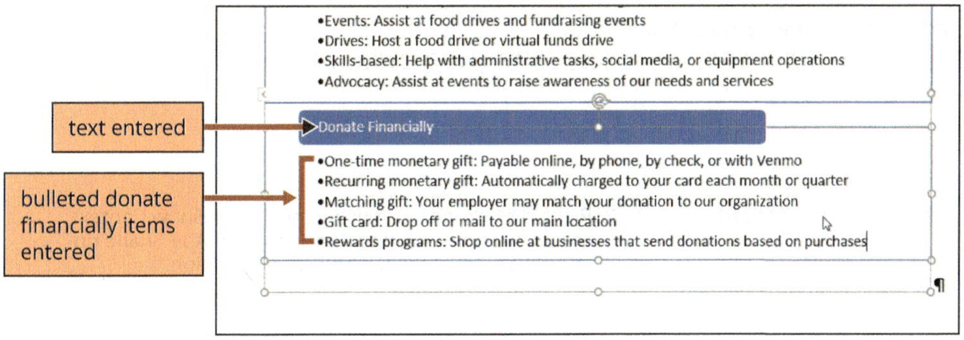

Figure 3–75

To Add a Shape to a SmartArt Graphic

The following step adds a shape to the SmartArt graphic. **Why?** You decided to split the donation opportunities into two separate lists: Donate Financially and Donate Grocery Essentials. Thus, you will need to add a shape for the Donate Grocery Essentials list.

1.

- If necessary, click SmartArt Design on the ribbon to display the SmartArt Design tab.
- Click the Donate Financially rounded rectangle shape to select it and then click the Add Shape button (SmartArt Design tab | Create Graphic group) to add a shape to the SmartArt graphic below the currently selected shape (or, if using touch, tap the Add Shape button (SmartArt Design tab | Create Graphic group) and then tap 'Add Shape After') (Figure 3–76).

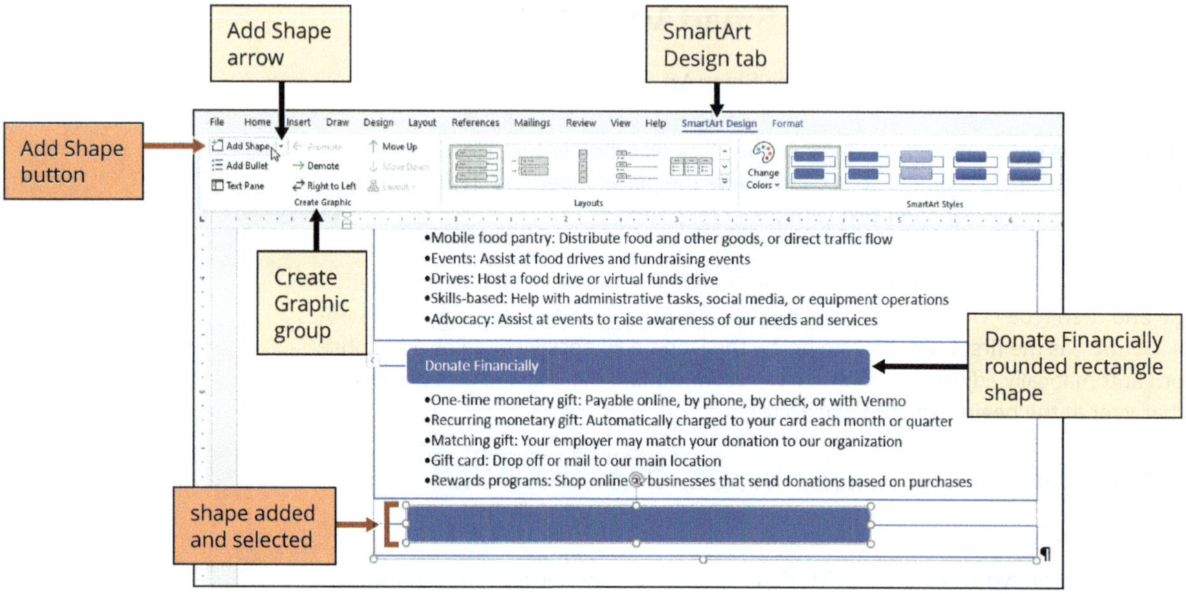

Figure 3–76

Q&A Why is the Add Shape button dimmed?
A shape is not selected in the SmartArt graphic. For example, the insertion point could be in the bulleted list below the rounded rectangle shape. Click the rounded rectangle shape to select it.

What if a menu appears?
You clicked the Add Shape arrow instead of the Add Shape button. Click 'Add Shape After' on the Add Shape menu to add the shape to the SmartArt graphic below the currently selected shape.

What if I wanted the shape to be added above the current shape?
You would click the Add Shape arrow and then click 'Add Shape Before' on the Add Shape menu to add the shape to the SmartArt graphic above the currently selected shape.

Other Ways

1. Click Add Shape arrow (SmartArt Design tab), click desired shape position
2. Right-click shape (or, if using touch, tap 'Show Context Menu' button on Mini toolbar), point to Add Shape on shortcut menu, click desired shape position

To Add More Text to a Shape in a SmartArt Graphic

The following steps add text to the next shape in the SmartArt graphic.

1. Click in the third rounded rectangle shape and then type **Donate Grocery Essentials** to enter text in the third shape.
2. Click the rectangle attached to the bottom of the Donate Grocery Essentials shape to select the rectangle and then type **Food: Canned and boxed goods, condiments, dry ingredients, and peanut butter** as the first bulleted item below the Donate Grocery Essentials heading and notice that Word automatically adjusts the font size to accommodate the text and also places a bullet character at the beginning of the typed text.
3. Press ENTER and then type **Beverages: Bottled water and juice boxes** as the second bulleted donate grocery essentials item.
4. Press ENTER and then type **Baby products: Diapers, baby wipes, baby wash, and diaper cream** as the third bulleted donate grocery essentials item.

5 Press ENTER and then type **Hygiene products: Bath soap, deodorant, shaving cream, toothbrushes, and toothpaste** as the fourth bulleted donate grocery essentials item.

6 Press ENTER and then type **Paper products: Paper towels, toilet paper, and facial tissue** as the fifth bulleted donate grocery essentials item.

7 Press ENTER and then type **Cleaning supplies: Laundry soap, dish soap, surface cleaner, and disinfectant spray** as the sixth bulleted donate grocery essentials item (Figure 3–77).

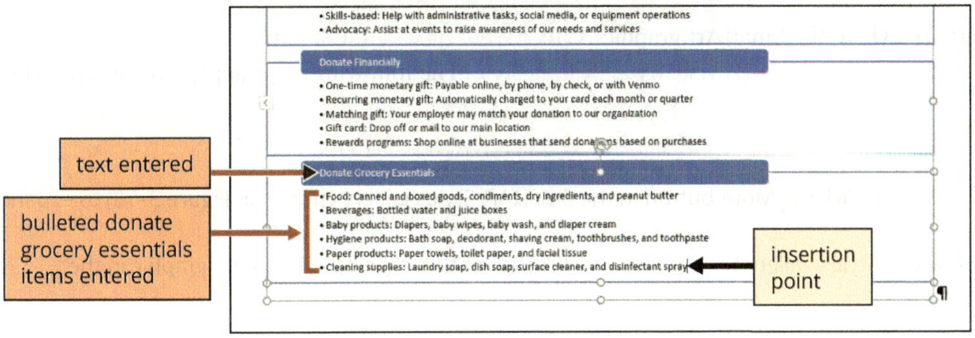

Figure 3–77

To Change Colors of a SmartArt Graphic

Word provides a variety of colors for a SmartArt graphic and the shapes in the graphic. In this project, you would like the bulleted list to have a blue shading behind the text. **Why?** You would like to draw more attention to the bulleted items. The following steps change the colors of a SmartArt graphic.

1

- If necessary, scroll to display the SmartArt graphic. With the insertion point in the SmartArt graphic (shown in Figure 3–77), click the Change Colors button (SmartArt Design tab | SmartArt Styles group) to display the Change Colors gallery.

Q&A What if the SmartArt graphic is not selected?
Click the SmartArt graphic to select it.

- Scroll to and then point to 'Colored Outline - Accent 5' in the Change Colors gallery to display a Live Preview of the selected color applied to the SmartArt graphic in the document (Figure 3–78).

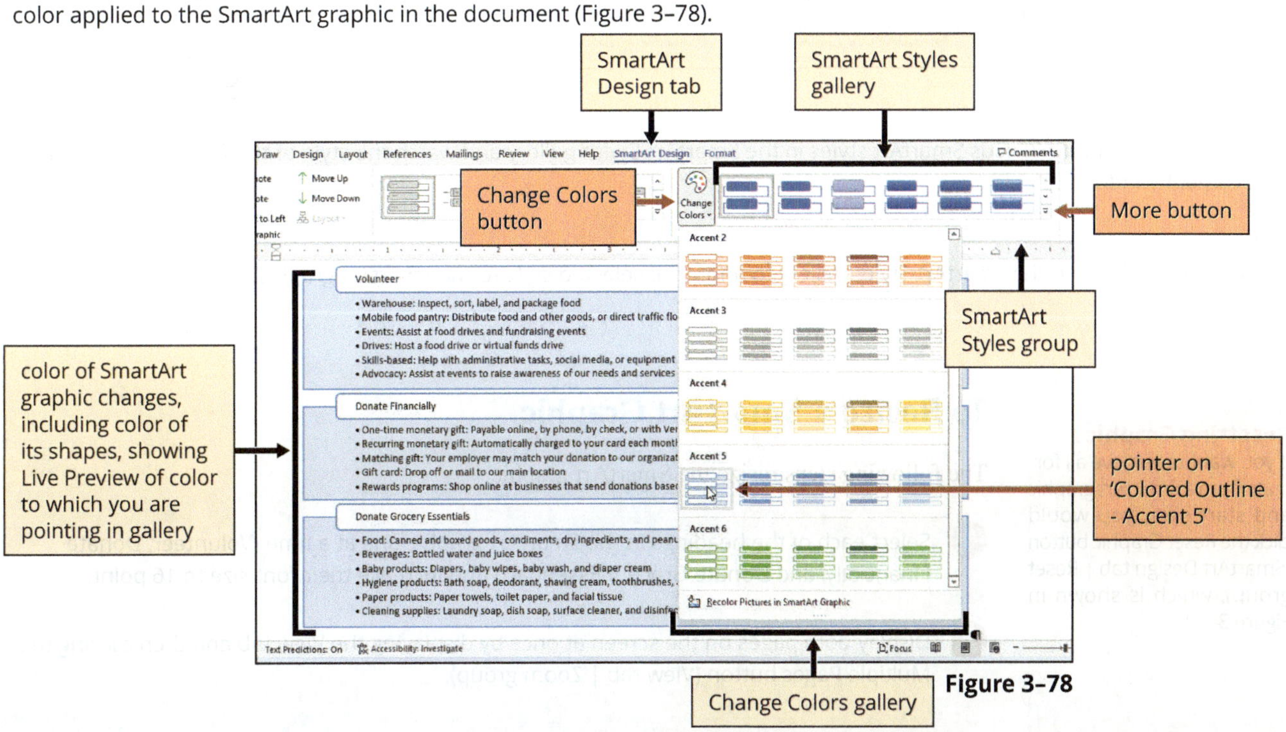

Figure 3–78

- **Experiment:** Point to various colors in the Change Colors gallery and watch the colors of the graphic change in the document window.

2

- Click 'Colored Outline - Accent 5' in the Change Colors gallery to apply the selected color to the SmartArt graphic.

To Apply a SmartArt Style

The next step is to apply a SmartArt style to the SmartArt graphic. **Why?** Word provides a SmartArt Styles gallery, allowing you to change the SmartArt graphic's format to a more visually appealing style. The following steps apply a SmartArt style to a SmartArt graphic.

1

- With the SmartArt graphic still selected, click the More button in the SmartArt Styles gallery (shown in Figure 3–78) to expand the SmartArt Styles gallery.
- Point to Intense Effect in the SmartArt Styles gallery to display a Live Preview of that style applied to the graphic in the document (Figure 3–79).

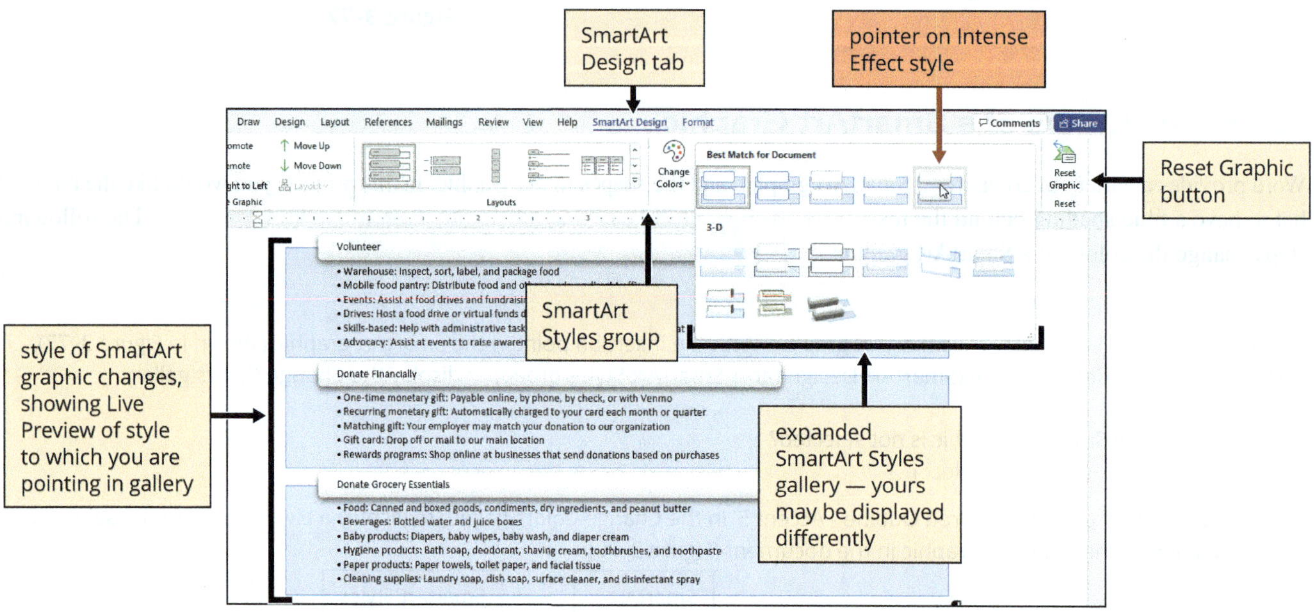

Figure 3–79

- **Experiment:** Point to various SmartArt styles in the SmartArt Styles gallery and watch the style of the graphic change in the document window.

2

- Click Intense Effect in the SmartArt Styles gallery to apply the selected style to the SmartArt graphic.

BTW
Resetting Graphics
If you want to remove all formats from a SmartArt graphic and start over, you would click the Reset Graphic button (SmartArt Design tab | Reset group), which is shown in Figure 3–79.

To Resize a SmartArt Graphic

The following steps resize the SmartArt graphic.

1 Select each of the headings in the SmartArt graphic one at a time (Volunteer, Donate Financially, and Donate Grocery Essentials) and increase their font size to 16 point.

2 Display both pages on the screen at once by displaying the View tab and then clicking the Multiple Pages button (View tab | Zoom group).

3 Click the outer edge of the SmartArt graphic to select the entire graphic.

4 Click Format on the ribbon to display the Format tab.

5 Click the Size group button (Format tab) and then click the Height box up and down arrow keys and the Width box up and down arrow keys to change the height of the SmartArt graphic to 5" and width to 6.5" (Figure 3–80).

6 Change the zoom to page width by clicking the Page Width button (View tab | Zoom group).

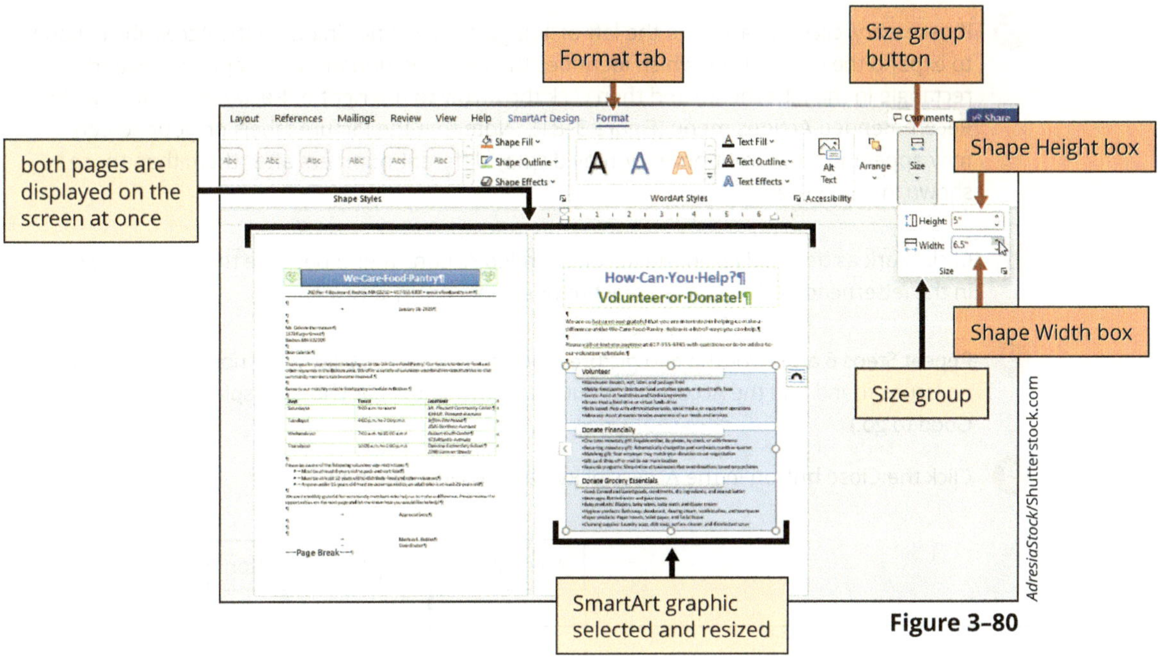

Figure 3–80

Enhancing a Document's Accessibility

Word provides several options for enhancing the accessibility of documents so that everyone easily can read and work with documents you create. Some tasks you can perform to assist users include increasing zoom and font size, ensuring tab/reading order in tables is logical, and using Read mode. You also can use the accessibility checker to locate and address problematic issues, and you can add alternative text to graphics and tables.

To Check and Fix Accessibility Issues

Recall that Word includes an Accessibility Checker that identifies potential accessibility issues and presents suggestions to make your documents more inclusive. Notice that instead of the phrase, Good to go, the Accessibility button on the status bar shows the word, Investigate. The following steps use the Accessibility Checker to fix the accessibility issues.

1 Click the Accessibility button on the status bar to open the Accessibility pane.

2 If necessary, click the arrow to the left of 'Missing alternative text' in the Accessibility pane to expand the description, which suggests the diagram (SmartArt) should have alternative text. (Note: Instead of 'Missing alternative text', your version of Word may display 'Suggested alternative text'.)

3. Click the arrow to the right of Diagram to display the Recommended Actions menu. (Note that the word, Diagram, on your screen may display a number after it.)

4. Click 'Add a description' on the Recommended Actions menu to display the Alt Text pane and then type this description in the text box: **Diagram outlining the ways people can help by volunteering, donating financially, or donating grocery essentials.**

5. Click the Close button in the Alt Text pane to close the pane. (The Accessibility pane reappears.)

6. If necessary, click the arrow to the left of 'Image or object not inline' in the Accessibility pane to expand the description (which identifies the two food donation concept images and the rectangle in the letterhead) and then click the arrow to the right of Rectangle to display the Recommended Actions menu (Figure 3–81). (Note that the Picture labels on your screen may appear in a different order or may display different numbers after them than those shown in the figure.)

7. Click 'Mark as decorative' on the Recommended Actions menu because the rectangle object in the letterhead adds visual appeal but does not convey any meaning.

8. Repeat Steps 6 and 7 for the two picture objects. (The Accessibility pane now should indicate no issues found and the Accessibility button on the status bar should display the phrase, Good to go.)

9. Click the Close button in the Accessibility pane to close the pane.

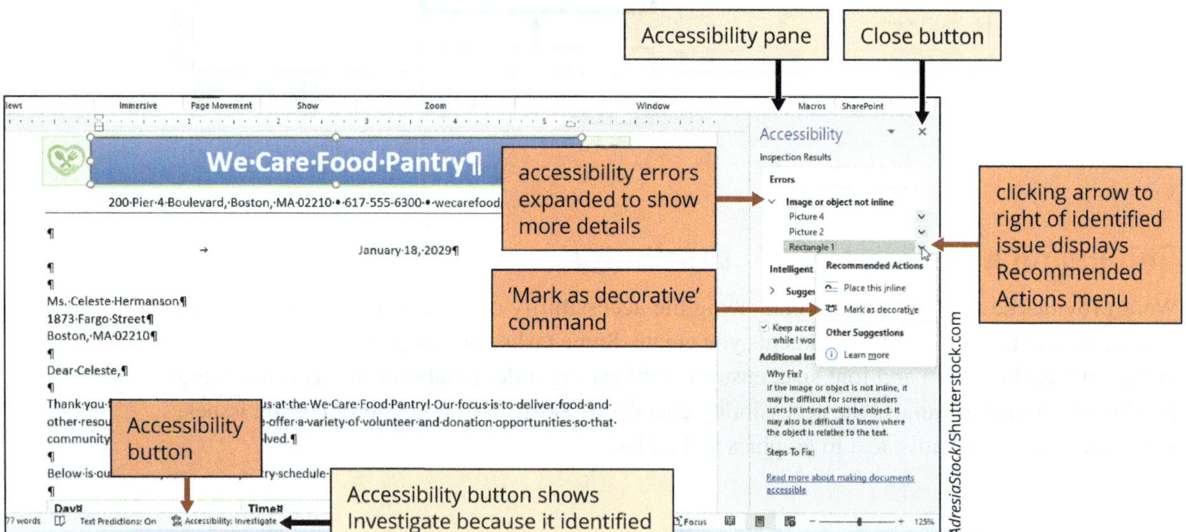

Figure 3–81

To Add Alternative Text to Tables If you wanted to add alternative text to a table, you would perform the following steps.

1. Click the Properties button (contextual Layout tab | Table group), or right-click the table and then click Table Properties on the shortcut menu to display the Table Properties dialog box.
2. Click the Alt Text tab (Table Properties dialog box) to display the Alt Text sheet.

3. Type a brief title and then type a narrative description of the table in the respective text boxes.
4. Click OK to close the dialog box.

To Save and Print a Letter

The following steps save and print the letter.

1. Save the letter again on the same storage location with the same file name.
2. If requested by your instructor, print the letter.

BTW
Conserving Ink and Toner
If you want to conserve ink or toner, you can instruct Word to print draft quality documents by clicking File on the ribbon to open Backstage view, clicking Options in Backstage view to display the Word Options dialog box, clicking Advanced in the left pane (Word Options dialog box), scrolling to the Print area in the right pane, placing a check mark in the 'Use draft quality' check box, and then clicking OK. Then, use Backstage view to print the document as usual.

Addressing and Printing Envelopes and Mailing Labels

With Word, you can print mailing address information on an envelope or on a mailing label. Computer-printed addresses look more professional than handwritten ones.

To Address and Print an Envelope

The following steps address and print an envelope. If you are in a lab environment, check with your instructor before performing these steps. **Why?** Some printers may not accommodate printing envelopes; others may stop printing until an envelope is inserted.

1
- Scroll through the letter to display the inside address in the document window.
- Drag through the inside address to select it (Figure 3-82).

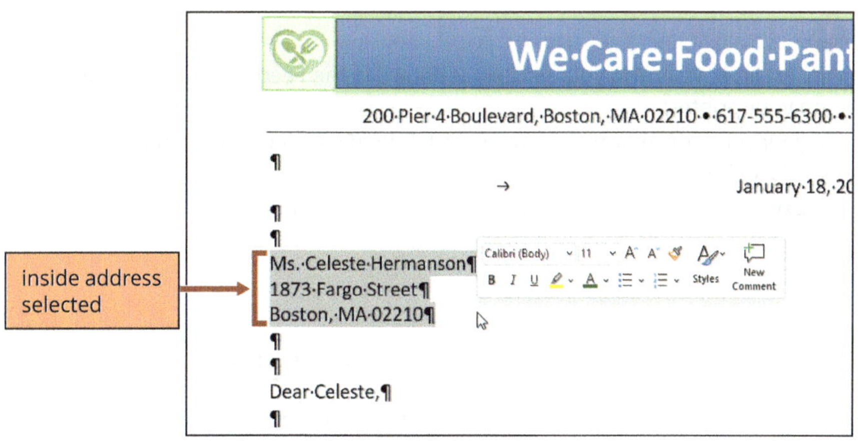

AdresiaStock/Shutterstock.com

Figure 3-82

2
- Display the Mailings tab.
- Click the Envelopes button (Mailings tab | Create group) to display the Envelopes and Labels dialog box.
- If necessary, click the Envelopes tab (Envelopes and Labels dialog box), which automatically displays the selected delivery address in the dialog box.
- Type the return address as shown in Figure 3-83.

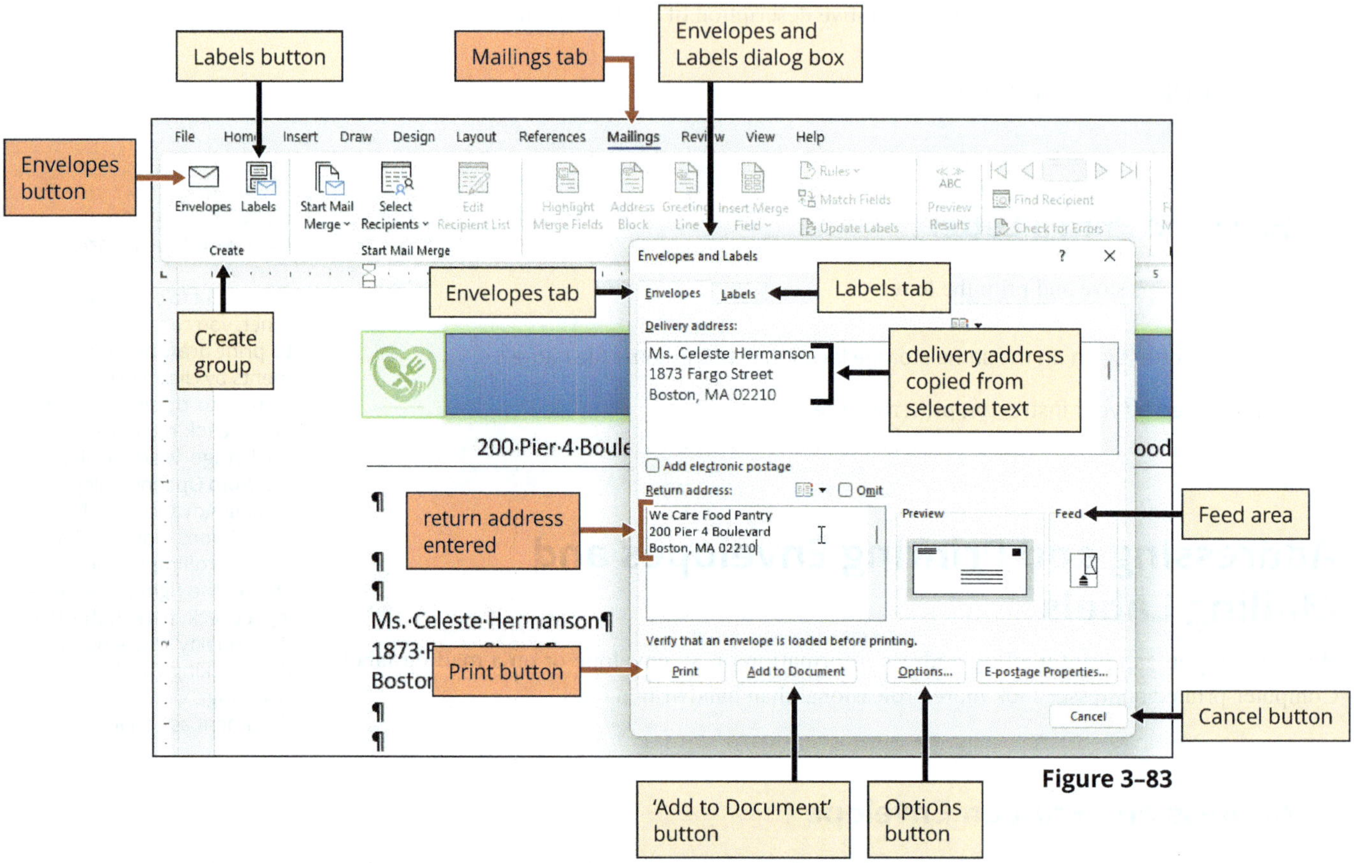

AdresiaStock/Shutterstock.com

Figure 3–83

3

- Insert an envelope in your printer, as shown in the Feed area of the dialog box (your Feed area may be different, depending on your printer).
- If your printer can print envelopes, click Print (Envelopes and Labels dialog box) to print the envelope; otherwise, click Cancel to close the dialog box.
- sam Because the project now is complete, you can exit Word.

Envelopes and Labels

Instead of printing the envelope immediately, you can add it to the document by clicking the 'Add to Document' button (Envelopes and Labels dialog box) (shown in Figure 3–83). To specify a different envelope or label type (identified by a number on the box of envelopes or labels), click the Options button (Envelopes and Labels dialog box) (shown in Figure 3–83).

Instead of printing an envelope, you can print a mailing label. To do this, click the Labels button (Mailings tab | Create group) (shown in Figure 3–83) and then type the delivery address in the Address box. To print the same address on all labels on the page, select the 'Full page of the same label' option button in the Print area. Click the Print button (Envelopes and Labels dialog box) to print the label(s).

Summary

In this module, you have learned how to use Word to insert and format a shape, change text wrapping, insert and format a picture, move and copy objects, insert symbols, add a border, clear formatting, set and use tab stops, insert the current date, insert and format tables, use the format painter, insert and format a SmartArt graphic, and address and print envelopes and mailing labels.

Consider This: Plan Ahead

What decisions will you need to make when creating your next business letter?

Use these guidelines as you complete the assignments in this module and create your own business letters outside of this class.

1. Create a letterhead.
   a) Ensure that the letterhead contains a complete name, mailing address, phone number, and, if applicable, fax number, email address, web address, logo, or other image.
   b) Place elements in the letterhead in a visually appealing location.
   c) Format the letterhead with appropriate fonts, font sizes, font styles, and color.
2. Compose an effective business letter.
   a) Include a date line, inside address, message, and signature block.
   b) Use proper spacing and formats for letter contents.
   c) Follow the alignment and spacing guidelines based on the letter style used (i.e., block, modified block, or modified semi-block).
   d) Ensure the message is well written, properly formatted, and logically organized.

BTW

Distributing a Document

Instead of printing and distributing a hard copy of a document, you can distribute the document electronically. Options include sending the document via email; posting it on cloud storage (such as OneDrive) and sharing the file with others; posting it on social media, a blog, or other website; and sharing a link associated with an online location of the document. You also can create and share a PDF or XPS image of the document, so that users can view the file in Acrobat Reader or XPS Viewer instead of in Word.

Student Assignments

Apply Your Knowledge

Reinforce the skills and apply the concepts you learned in this module.

Working with Tabs, Tables, and SmartArt Graphics

Note: To complete this assignment, you will be required to use the Data Files. Please contact your instructor for information about accessing the Data Files.

Instructions: Start Word. Open the document called SC_WD_3-1.docx, which is located in the Data Files. The document you open contains a Word table. As administrative assistant to the marketing director at Sunrise Health and Fitness Centers, you send mailers promoting the centers to residents within 30 miles of all facilities nationwide. Although the letters will not go out for several weeks, you want to create some of the letter components at this time. You began composing a Word table of membership plans that you need to edit and format. You also want to create a SmartArt graphic for the letter that identifies types of group fitness classes. The revised table, along with the SmartArt graphic you create, is shown in Figure 3–84.

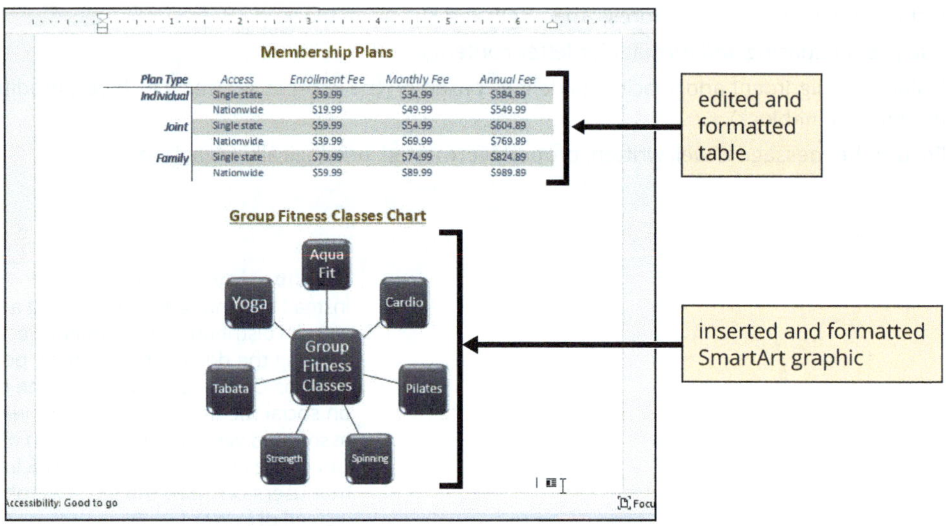

Figure 3–84

Perform the following tasks:

1. Click File on the ribbon, click Save As, and then save the document using the new file name, SC_WD_3_MembershipPlansTableAndClassesSmartArt.
2. In the line containing the table title, Membership Plans, remove the tab stop at the 1" mark on the ruler.
3. Set a centered tab at the 3" mark on the ruler. Move the centered tab stop to the 3.25" mark on the ruler.
4. In the line containing the SmartArt graphic title, Group Fitness Classes Chart, remove (clear) all tab stops.
5. Bold the characters in the Membership Plans title. Use the 'Increase Font Size' button to increase their font size to 20. Use the 'Decrease Font Size' button to decrease their font size to 18. Change their color to 'Gold, Accent 4, Darker 50%' (eight color in last row).
6. Use the format painter to copy the formatting from the table title paragraph to the SmartArt graphic title paragraph (so that the SmartArt graphic title has a centered tab stop at the 3.25" mark on the ruler and has the same text formats).
7. Apply the underline style called Thick underline below the characters in the Group Fitness Classes Chart title. Change the underline color to 'Gray, Accent 3' (seventh color in first row).

8. In the table, select one of the duplicate rows containing the plan type of joint and category of single state and then delete the duplicate row.
9. Insert a column between the Enrollment Fee and Annual Fee columns. Fill in the column as follows:
   Column Title – Monthly Fee
   Individual single state – $34.99
   Joint single state – $54.99
   Joint nationwide – $69.99
   Family single state – $74.99
   Family nationwide – $89.99
10. Insert a new row above the joint single state row. Leave the first cell of the new row blank and fill in the cells in the remainder of the row as follows:
    Access – Nationwide
    Enrollment Fee – $19.99
    Monthly Fee – $49.99
    Annual Fee – $549.99
11. In the Table Style Options group (Table Design tab), ensure that these check boxes have check marks: Header Row, Banded Rows, and First Column. The Total Row, Last Column, and Banded Columns check boxes should not have check marks.
12. Apply the 'List Table 7 Colorful' style to the table.
13. Select the entire table. Change the font color of all text in the selected table to 'Blue, Accent 5, Darker 50%' (ninth color in last row).
14. If necessary, use the View Gridlines button (contextual Layout tab | Table group) to display table gridlines so that you can see the boundaries of the table cells, columns, and rows. Select the first column and bold its contents. Select the second, third, fourth, and fifth columns and center them. Hide table gridlines.
15. Position the insertion point at the end of the Group Fitness Classes Chart title and then press ENTER. Clear formatting on this new line and then center the insertion point on the line.
16. On the blank line below the title Group Fitness Classes Chart, insert a Radial Cluster SmartArt graphic (in the Cycle category). Add four shapes to the inserted SmartArt graphic.
17. In the SmartArt graphic, enter the text, Group Fitness Classes, in the center shape. In the exterior shapes, starting with the top and moving clockwise, enter this text: Aqua Fit, Cardio, Pilates, Spinning, Strength, Tabata, and Yoga. (Note: if the placeholder text does not appear, open the Text Pane to add the text.)
18. Change the SmartArt colors to 'Dark 2 Fill', and apply the SmartArt Style called Polished.
19. If requested by your instructor, enter your name on the line below the table.
20. Check accessibility. Add appropriate alt text to the SmartArt graphic.
21. Save the document again with the same file name. Submit the modified document, shown in Figure 3–84, in the format specified by your instructor.
22. Exit Word.
23. **Consider This:** If you wanted to add a row to the end of the table, how would you add the row?

Extend Your Knowledge

Extend the skills you learned in this module and experiment with new skills. You may need to use Help to complete the assignment.

Working with Shapes and Pictures

Note: To complete this assignment, you will be required to use the Data Files. Please contact your instructor for information about accessing the Data Files.

Continued on next page

Instructions: Start Word. Open the document, SC_WD_3-2.docx, which is located in the Data Files. The document is a draft of a letter started earlier this week. The department chair and professor at Eagle Ridge College has drafted a reference letter to a student's prospective employer. As the administrative assistant, you have been tasked with designing a letterhead using the school logo and finalizing the table in the letter. You will work with shapes and pictures to design the letterhead in the letter and will complete the table so that the letter is ready to send.

Perform the following tasks:

1. Use Help to learn about grouping objects and formatting pictures and shapes.
2. Click File on the ribbon, click Save As, and then save the document using the new file name, SC_WD_3_ReferenceLetter.
3. Select the oval shape at the top of the letter. Drag the rotate handle on top of the selected shape clockwise and watch the shape rotate. Delete the selected shape.
4. Insert a Rectangle: Diagonal Corners Snipped shape at the top of the letter, sizing it across the top of the page. Drag the edges to form a rectangle. After drawing the shape, specify the exact dimensions of a height of 0.7" and a width of 6.5".
5. Position the rectangular shape in the 'Position in Top Center with Square Text Wrapping' using the Position button (Shape Format tab | Arrange group). Then, change the text wrapping to 'Top and Bottom'.
6. Apply a shape style of your choosing to the shape. Enter the text, Eagle Ridge College, in the shape. Format the text as you deem appropriate. Apply an appropriate shape outline to the shape. Apply a shape effect of your choosing to the shape.
7. Resize the eagle picture to 50 percent of its current size. With the picture inline, click the paragraph mark to the right of the picture and then click the Center button (Home tab | Paragraph group). Then, click the Align Right button (Home tab | Paragraph group). How do you move inline pictures?
8. Resize the picture so its height is exactly 0.6" and its width is 0.88". Change the text wrapping of the picture to 'In Front of Text'. Click the Position button (Picture Format tab | Arrange group) and select different options. Click the Align button (Picture Format tab | Arrange group) and select different alignments. Drag the picture into the shape in an appropriate location (Figure 3–85). How do you move floating pictures?

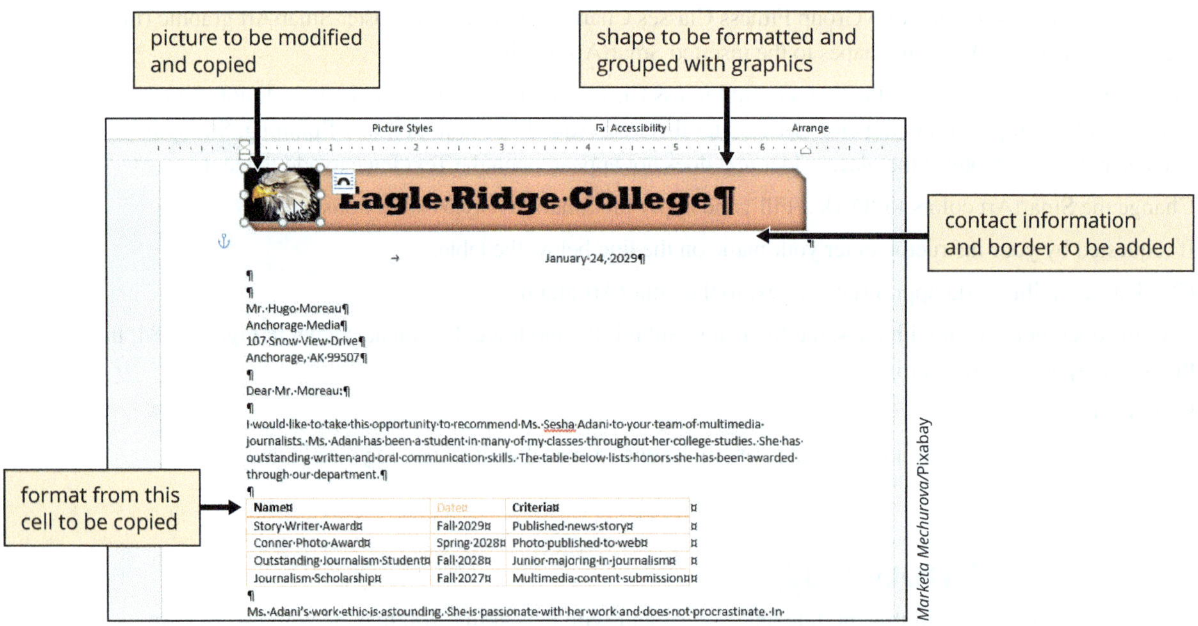

Figure 3–85

9. Change the brightness and contrast of the picture as you deem appropriate. Copy the picture. Use Paste arrow to paste as a Picture. Is the pasted picture an inline or floating object? Delete the pasted picture. Use the Paste Options arrow to paste with source formatting. Why did it paste the picture as a floating object this time? Drag the pasted picture to an appropriate location in the shape.

10. Rotate one of the pictures 90 degrees to the right. Rotate the same picture 90 degrees to the right again. Flip the same picture vertically. Flip the same picture horizontally. Flip it in the direction that you feel looks best in the letterhead.
11. Recolor one of the pictures to a color of your choice. Add a border color of your choice to the same picture. Use the Reset Picture button (Picture Format tab | Adjust group) to clear the formatting of this picture. Readjust the brightness and contrast of this picture, if appropriate. How would you reset the formatting and the size of the picture?
12. Select the shape around the Eagle Ridge College title and then use the Edit Shape button (Shape Format tab | Insert Shapes group) to change the shape to a shape of your preference.
13. Move the two eagle pictures to desired locations in the rectangular shape. Group the two eagle pictures with the shape. Change the text wrapping of the grouped shape to Top and Bottom.
14. Add the contact information centered below the shape, using a symbol of your choice from the Symbol gallery between the mailing address (223 Bartlett Drive, Anchorage, AK 99507), the phone number (907-555-9400), and the web address (eagleridgecollege.edu). If necessary, insert a blank line between the contact information and the date in the letter.
15. Add a bottom border to the paragraph containing the contact information.
16. Select the table in the letter and center it between the margins.
17. Select the upper-left cell in the table that contains the text, Name. Use the format painter to copy the formats of the selected cell to the cell immediately to the right with the text, Date.
18. Position the insertion point in the table and, one at a time, select and deselect each check box in the Table Style Options group. What are the functions of each check box: Header Row, Total Row, Banded Rows, First Column, Last Column, and Banded Columns? Select the check boxes you prefer for the table.
19. If requested by your instructor, change the name in the signature block to your name.
20. Check accessibility. Mark the group containing the shape and pictures in the letterhead as decorative. Fix any other accessibility issues in the document.
21. Save the document again with the same file name. Submit the modified document in the format specified by your instructor.
22. If requested by your instructor, create an envelope for the letter.
23. If requested by your instructor, print a single mailing label for the letter and then a full page of mailing labels, each containing the address shown in Figure 3–85.
24. **Consider This:** Answer the questions posed in #7, #8, #9, #11, and #18. Why would you group objects? (If requested by your instructor, insert a next page section break at the end of the letter and write your responses on the inserted blank page and insert the current time.)

Expand Your World

Create a solution that uses cloud or web technologies by learning and investigating on your own from general guidance.

Using Google Docs to Upload and Edit Files

Notes:

- To complete this assignment, you will be required to use the Data Files. Please contact your instructor for information about accessing the Data Files.
- To complete this assignment, you will use a Google account, which you can create at no cost. If you do not have a Google account and do not want to create one, perform Steps 1 through 3 and then read the remainder of his assignment without performing the instructions.

Instructions: Assume you are composing a commendation letter to send to the general manager at Plateau Hotel and Conference Center for the excellent service you received for your daughter's quinceanera. You will

Continued on next page

finish creating the letter in Word at your office and then will proofread and edit it at home before sending it to the general manager. The problem is that you do not have Word at home. You do, however, have an Internet connection at home. Because you have a Google account, you upload your Word document to Google Drive so that you can view and edit it later from a computer that does not have Word installed.

Perform the following tasks:

1. In Word, open the document, SC_WD_3-3.docx, from the Data Files. Click File on the ribbon, click Save As, and then save the document using the new file name, SC_WD_3_CommendationLetter.
2. Add a box border around the two paragraphs containing the name, Isabel Valeria Lozano, and the contact information in the letterhead. Select style, width, and color for the box border other than the default. Apply a shading color to the paragraph containing the name.
3. Look through the letter so that you are familiar with its contents and formats. If desired, print the letter so that you easily can compare it to the Google Docs converted file. Save and close the document.
4. Start a browser. Search for the text, google docs, using a search engine. Visit several websites to learn about Google Docs and Google Drive. Navigate to the Google website. Read about how to create files in Google Docs and upload files to Google Drive. If you do not have a Google account and you want to create one, follow the instructions to create an account. If you do not have a Google account and you do not want to create one, read the remaining instructions without performing them. If you have a Google account, sign in to your account.
5. If necessary, display Google Drive. Upload the file, SC_WD_3_CommendationLetter.docx, to Google Drive.
6. Rename the file on Google Drive to SC_WD_3_CommendationLetter_inGoogle. Open the file in Google Docs (Figure 3–86). What differences did you notice between the Word document and the Google Docs converted document?

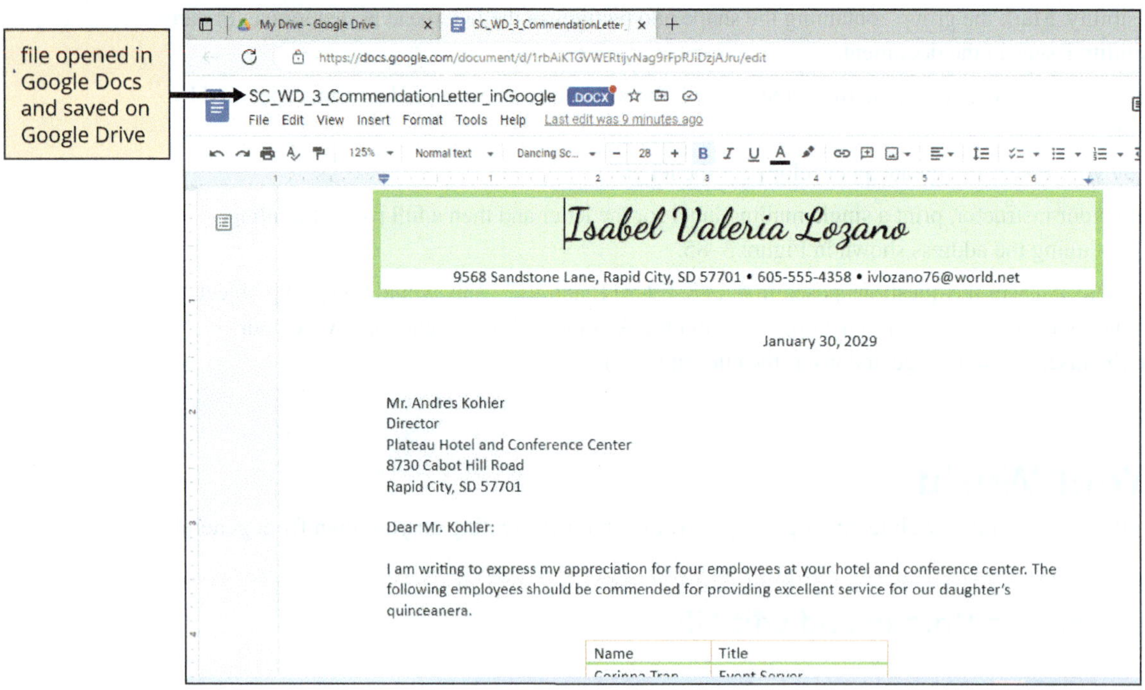

Figure 3–86

7. Modify the document in Google Docs as follows: change the font and font size of the name in the letterhead, bold the name in the letterhead, change the font color of the name in the letterhead, change the background color for the paragraph containing the name, change the border color and width around the two paragraphs in the letterhead, change the job title in the inside address from Director to General Manager, and then display the document at various zoom levels. (Note that you may need to use the menus to accomplish some of these tasks.)

8. If requested by your instructor, change the name in the letterhead and signature block to your name.
9. Download the revised document to your local storage media, changing its format to Microsoft Word. (Note that Word may display a message asking if you trust the source when you download the document.) Submit the document in the format requested by your instructor.
10. **Consider This:** What is Google Drive? What is Google Docs? Answer the question posed in #6. Do you prefer using Google Docs or Word? Why?

In the Lab

Design and implement a solution using creative thinking and problem-solving skills.

Create a Letter to a Potential Employer

Problem: As an assistant in the Office of Career Development at your school, you have been asked to prepare a sample letter to a potential employer as a sales representative in the healthcare industry. Students on campus seeking employment will use this letter as a reference document when creating their own letters.

Perform the following tasks:

Part 1: Using your name, mailing address, phone number, and email address, create a letterhead for the letter. Be sure to include an image in the letterhead and appropriate separator lines and marks. Once the letterhead is designed, write the letter to this potential employer: Ms. Valeria Chen, Human Resources Director, Tulsa Pharmaceuticals, 90987 South Phoenix Avenue, P.O. Box 5465, Tulsa, OK 74008.

The draft wording for the letter is as follows:

First paragraph: I am responding to your online advertisement for the sales representative position. I have the credentials you are seeking and believe I can be a valuable asset to Tulsa Pharmaceuticals.

Second paragraph: In May, I will be earning my bachelor's degree in Public Health from Tulsa College. My relevant coursework includes the following:

Below the second paragraph, insert the following in table form:

Biology and chemistry, 18 hours

Environment and health, 12 hours

General public health, 12 hours

Health administration, 12 hours

Health promotion, 18 hours

Third paragraph: In addition to my college coursework, I have the following experience:

Below the third paragraph, insert the following items as a bulleted list: Intern at Oak Road Pharmacy; Sales clerk at Oswego Nutrition; Volunteer at Tulsa Hospital free clinics.

Last paragraph: I look forward to hearing from you to schedule an interview and to discuss my career opportunities at Tulsa Pharmaceuticals.

Use the concepts and techniques presented in this module to create and format a letter according to a letter style and creating appropriate paragraph breaks. The letter should contain a letterhead that includes a shape and an online picture(s); a table with an appropriate table title, column headings, and table style applied (unformatted table contents listed above); and a bulleted list (unformatted experience list items above). If requested by your instructor, insert nonbreaking spaces in the company name, Tulsa Pharmaceuticals. If requested by your instructor, set a transparent color in the picture.

Continued on next page

While creating the letter, be sure to do the following:

1. Create a letterhead: insert and format a shape, insert and format at least one online picture, insert symbols from the Symbol gallery in the contact line, and add a paragraph border.
2. Create the letter contents: apply the No Spacing style, set left-aligned tab stops where appropriate, insert the current date, insert the table and format it, center the table, bullet the list as you type it, and use your name in the signature line in the letter.
3. Be sure to check the spelling and grammar of the finished letter.
4. Add alt text to the table and to the picture(s) in the document. Check the document accessibility of the finished letter and fix any issues.

When you are finished with the letter, save it with the file name, SC_WD_3_LetterToEmployer. Submit your assignment and answers to the Part 2 critical thinking questions in the format specified by your instructor.

Part 2: **Consider This:** You made several decisions while creating the letter in this assignment: where to position elements in the letterhead, how to format elements in the letterhead, which shape and picture(s) to use in the letterhead, which font size to use for the letter text, which table style to use, and which letter style to use. What was the rationale behind each of these decisions?

Creating and Editing Presentations with Pictures

Objectives

After completing this module, you will be able to:

- Create a blank presentation
- Select and change a document theme
- Create a title slide and a text slide with a multilevel bulleted list
- Add new slides and change slide layouts
- Change font size and color
- Bold, italicize, and underline text
- Insert pictures into slides with and without content placeholders
- Move and resize pictures
- Arrange slides
- Change theme colors
- Check spelling
- Review a presentation in different views
- Enter slide notes
- Save a presentation
- Print a presentation

What Is PowerPoint?

Microsoft PowerPoint, or PowerPoint, is a full-featured presentation app that allows you to produce compelling presentations to deliver and share with an audience. A PowerPoint **presentation** also is called a **slide show**. The collection of slides in a presentation is called a **deck**, resembling a deck of cards that are stacked on top of each other. A common use of slide decks is to enhance an oral presentation. A speaker might desire to convey information, such as urging students to volunteer at a fund-raising event, explaining changes in employee compensation packages, or describing a new laboratory procedure. The PowerPoint slides should reinforce the speaker's message and help the audience retain the information presented. PowerPoint contains many features to plan, develop, and organize slides, including providing design ideas, formatting text, adding and editing video and audio clips, creating tables and charts, applying artistic effects to pictures, animating graphics, and collaborating with friends and colleagues. An accompanying handout gives audience members reference notes and review material for your presentation.

A PowerPoint presentation can help you deliver a dynamic, professional-looking message to an audience. PowerPoint allows you to produce slides to use in academic, business, or other environments. Custom slides can fit your specific needs and contain diagrams, charts, tables, pictures, shapes, video, sound, and animation effects to make your presentation more effective. You then can print a handout, turn your presentation into a video, broadcast your slide show on the web, or create a photo album.

BTW
Microsoft 365 Suite
PowerPoint is part of the Microsoft 365 suite; other apps in the suite include Word, Excel, Outlook, OneNote, and OneDrive, and on your PC, Access and Publisher. Apps in a suite, such as Microsoft 365, typically use a similar interface and share features.

BTW
The PowerPoint Window
The modules in this book begin with the PowerPoint window appearing as it did at the initial installation of the software. Your PowerPoint window may look different depending on your screen resolution and other PowerPoint settings.

To illustrate the features of PowerPoint, this book presents a series of projects that use PowerPoint to create presentations like those you will encounter in business environments.

Project: Presentation with a Bulleted List and Pictures

In this module's project, you will follow proper design guidelines and learn to use PowerPoint to create, save, and view the slides shown in Figures 1–1a through 1–1d. The objective is to produce a presentation, titled Security, that discusses managing passwords to help prevent online thieves from accessing private information. This slide show has a variety of pictures and visual elements to add interest and give facts about password creation and security threats. Some of the text has formatting and color enhancements, and the slides have a variety of layouts.

Figure 1–1(a): Slide 1 (Title Slide with Picture)

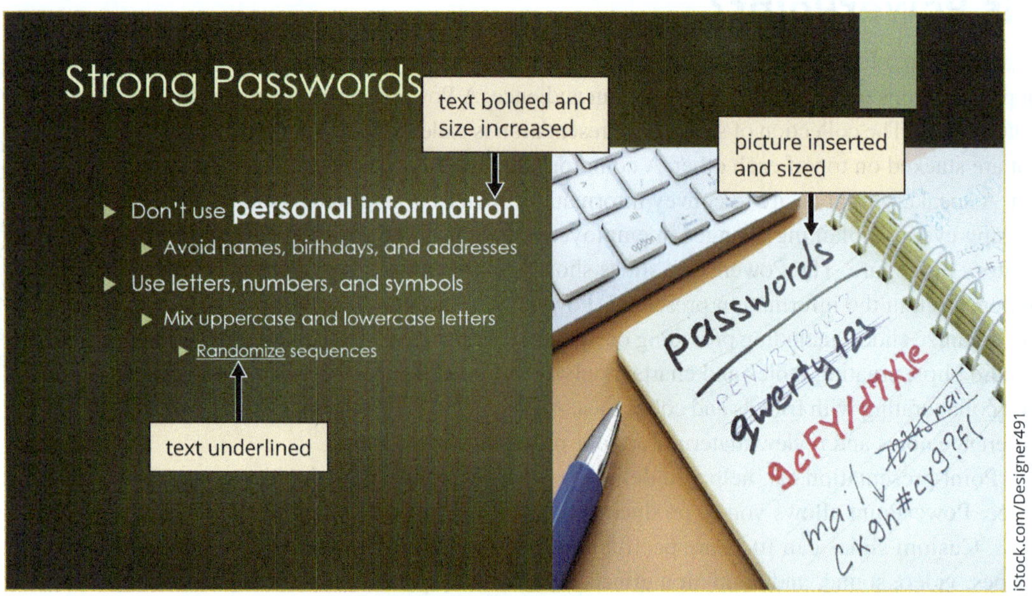

Figure 1–1(b): Slide 2 (Multilevel Bulleted List with Picture)

Figure 1-1(c): Slide 3 (Title and Picture)

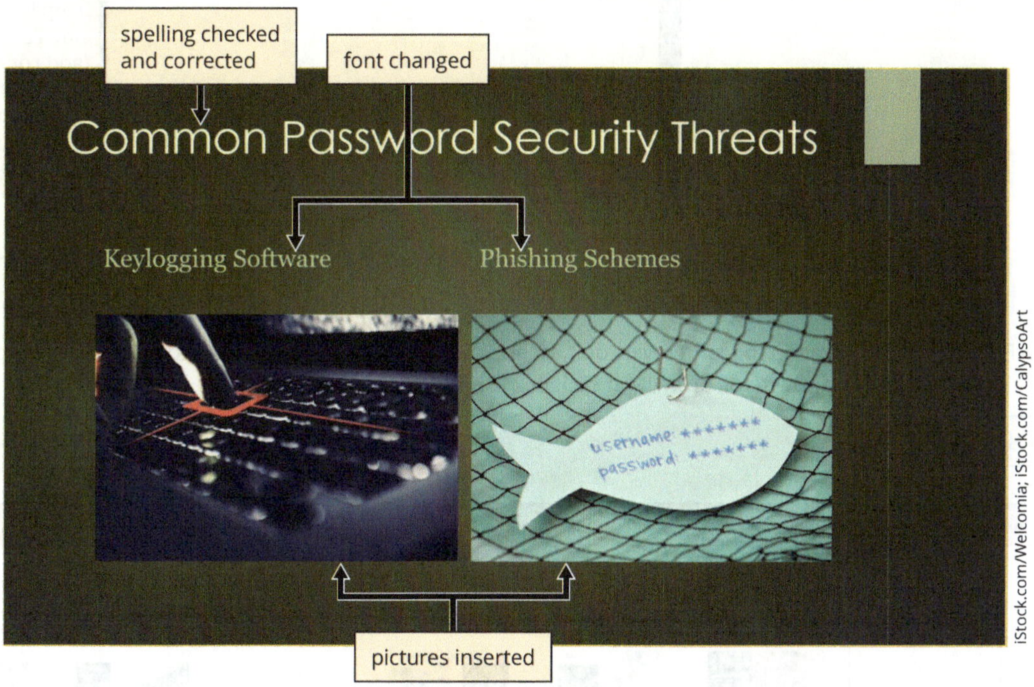

Figure 1-1(d): Slide 4 (Comparison Layout and Pictures)

In this module, you will learn how to perform basic tasks using PowerPoint. You will perform the following general tasks as you progress through this module:

1. Start and use PowerPoint.
2. Insert four presentation slides, using various layouts.
3. Enter and format the text on each slide.
4. Insert, size, and position pictures.
5. Display the slides.
6. Correct errors and print the slides.

BTW
Ribbon and Screen Resolution
PowerPoint may change how the groups and buttons within the groups appear on the ribbon, depending on the screen resolution of your computer. Thus, your ribbon may look different from the ones in this book if you are using a screen resolution other than 1920 × 1080.

Starting and Using PowerPoint

To use PowerPoint, you must instruct the operating system (such as Windows or Mac) to start the app. The following sections start PowerPoint and discuss some elements of PowerPoint.

To Start PowerPoint and Create a Blank Presentation

The following steps, which assume Windows is running, start PowerPoint and create a blank presentation based on a typical installation. You may need to ask your instructor how to start PowerPoint on your computer or device.

1

- **sam** Click Start on the Windows taskbar to display the Start menu.
- If necessary, scroll through the list of apps on the Start menu until the PowerPoint app name appears (Figure 1–2).

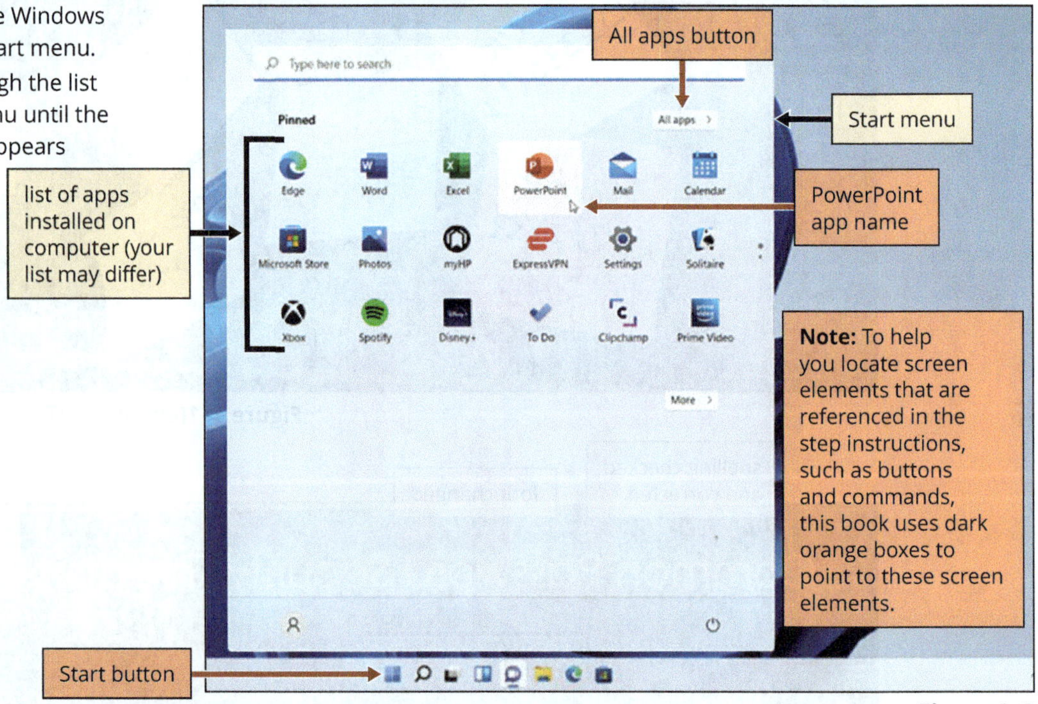

Figure 1–2

2

- Click PowerPoint on the Start menu to start PowerPoint. If the PowerPoint app is not displayed, click the All apps button to display an alphabetical list of apps, scroll down, and click PowerPoint (Figure 1–3).

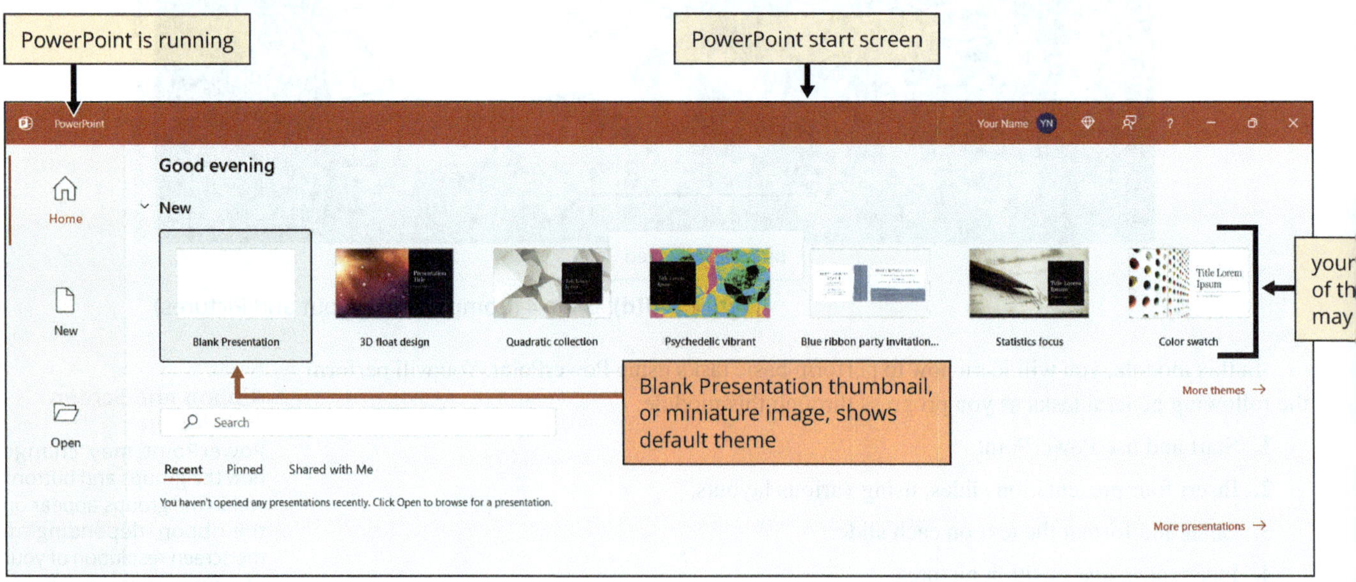

Figure 1–3

BTW
Resolution
For information about how to change a computer's resolution, search for 'change resolution' in your operating system's help files.

Other Ways

1. Click Windows search tool in taskbar, type app name in search box, click app name in results list
2. Double-click PowerPoint icon on desktop or in taskbar, if one is present

3

- Click the Blank Presentation thumbnail on the PowerPoint start screen to create a blank PowerPoint presentation in the PowerPoint window (Figure 1–4).
- If the Design Ideas pane is open, click Stop showing ideas for new presentations or click its Close button to close it.

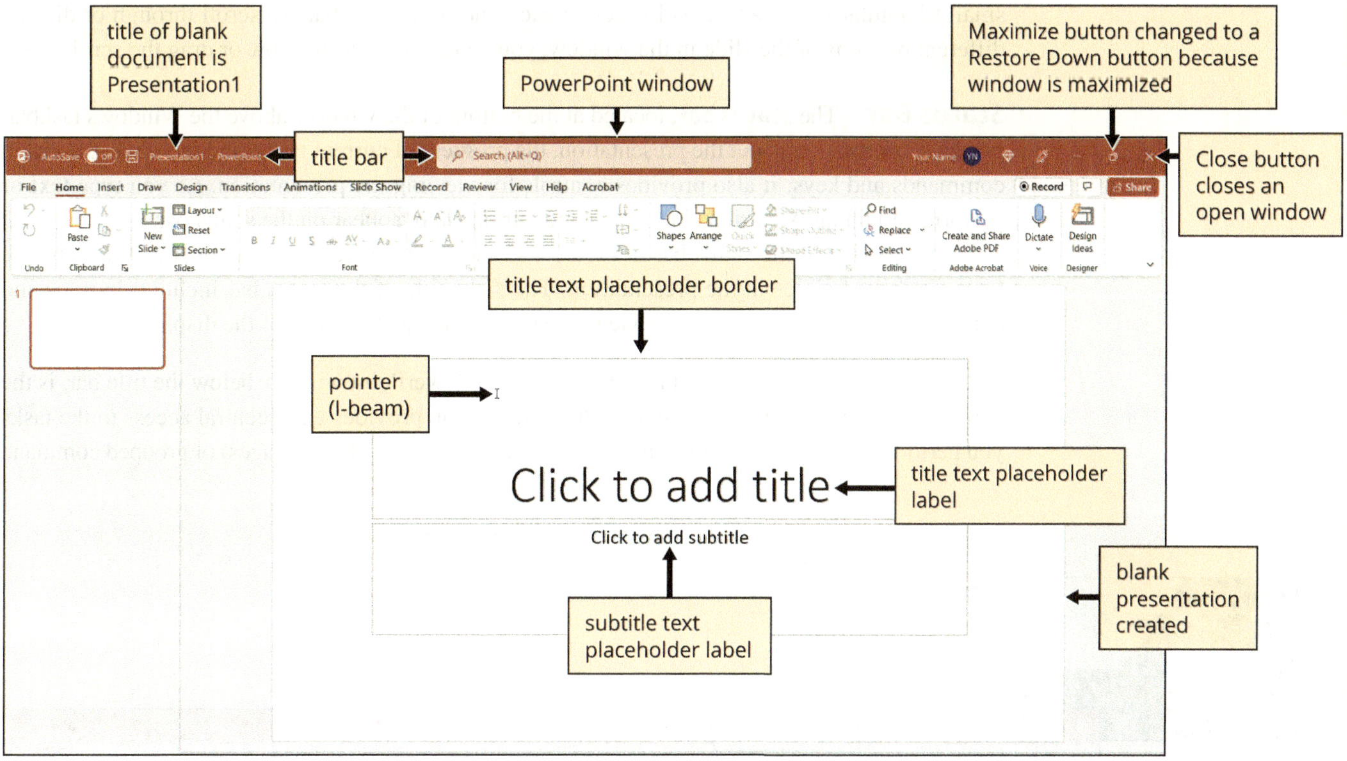

Figure 1–4

4

- If the PowerPoint window is not maximized, click the Maximize button next to the Close button on the title bar to maximize the window.

Q&A How do I know whether a window is maximized?
A window is maximized if it fills the entire display area and the Restore Down button is displayed on the title bar.

The PowerPoint Window

The PowerPoint window consists of a variety of components to make your work more efficient and presentations more professional: the window, ribbon, AutoSave button, Search box, Mini toolbar, shortcut menus, Quick Access Toolbar, and Microsoft Account area. Most of these elements are common to other Microsoft 365 apps; others are unique to PowerPoint.

The basic unit of a PowerPoint presentation is a **slide**. A slide may contain text and objects, such as graphics, tables, charts, and drawings. When you create a new presentation, the default **Title Slide** layout appears (shown in Figure 1–4). PowerPoint includes several other built-in standard layouts. All layouts except the Blank slide layout contain placeholders for text or other content such as pictures, charts, or videos. The title slide in Figure 1–4 has two text placeholders for the main heading (title) and the subtitle.

In the slide, the **insertion point** is a blinking vertical line that indicates where text, pictures, and other objects will be inserted. When you type, the insertion point moves to the right, and when you reach the end of a placeholder, it moves down to the beginning of the next line. The **pointer** is a small screen icon that moves as you move a mouse or pointing device on a surface and becomes different shapes depending on the task you are performing in PowerPoint. You move the pointer with a pointing device, such as a mouse or touchpad. The pointer in Figure 1–4 is the shape of an I-beam.

Scroll Bar You use a **scroll bar** to display different portions of a presentation in the window. At the right edge of the window is a vertical scroll bar. If a slide is too wide to fit in the window, a horizontal scroll bar also appears at the bottom of the window. On a scroll bar, the position of the **scroll box** reflects the location of the portion of the slide that is displayed in the window. A small triangular **scroll arrow** is located at each end of a scroll bar. To scroll through or display different portions of the slide in the window, you can click a scroll arrow or drag the scroll box.

Status Bar The **status bar**, located at the bottom of the window above the Windows taskbar, presents information about the presentation, the progress of current tasks, and the status of certain commands and keys; it also provides controls for viewing the presentation. As you type text or perform certain tasks, various indicators and buttons may appear on the status bar.

The left side of the status bar in Figure 1–5 shows the current slide number followed by the total number of slides in the presentation. The right side of the status bar includes buttons and controls you can use to change the view of a slide and adjust the size of the displayed slide.

Ribbon The **ribbon**, located near the top of the PowerPoint window below the title bar, is the control center in PowerPoint (Figure 1–6a). The ribbon provides easy, central access to the tasks you perform while creating a presentation. The ribbon consists of tabs (pages) of grouped command

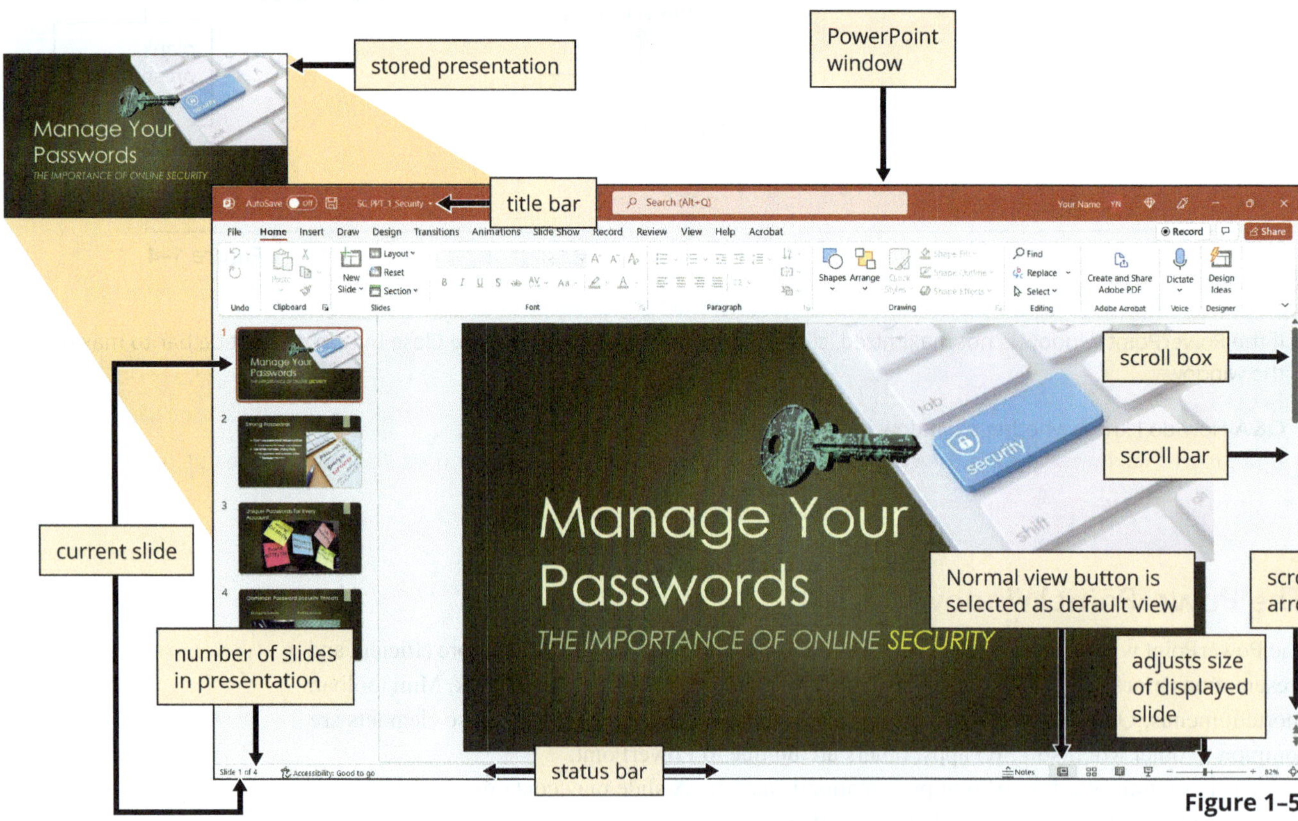

Figure 1–5

iStock.com/MicroStockHub; iStock.com/The-lightwriter

buttons that you click to interact with PowerPoint. Each **tab** contains a collection of groups, and each **group** contains related command buttons and boxes.

When you start PowerPoint, the ribbon initially displays several main tabs, also called default or top-level tabs. The **Home tab**, also called the primary tab, contains the more frequently used commands. The ribbon tab currently displayed is called the **active tab**.

To display more of the slide in the window, some users prefer to collapse the ribbon, which hides the groups on the ribbon and displays only the main tabs (Figure 1–6b). To collapse the ribbon when it is visible, double-click any ribbon tab, right-click any ribbon tab, and then click 'Collapse the Ribbon' on the menu, right-click the 'Ribbon Display Options' icon and then click 'Collapse the Ribbon' on the menu, or press CTRL+F1. To use commands on a collapsed ribbon, click the tab that you wish to expand. To expand the ribbon when it is collapsed, double-click any tab, right-click any tab, and then click to uncheck 'Collapse the Ribbon' on the menu or press CTRL+F1. To always display the ribbon, click the 'Ribbon Display Options' button when the ribbon is visible and then click 'Always show Ribbon' on the menu.

BTW
Ribbon Icons
Three icons are displayed on the right side of the ribbon: Record, Comment, and Share. These PowerPoint features allow you to rehearse and save a presentation, view and respond to comments other people have made about your slides, and distribute your presentation with others.

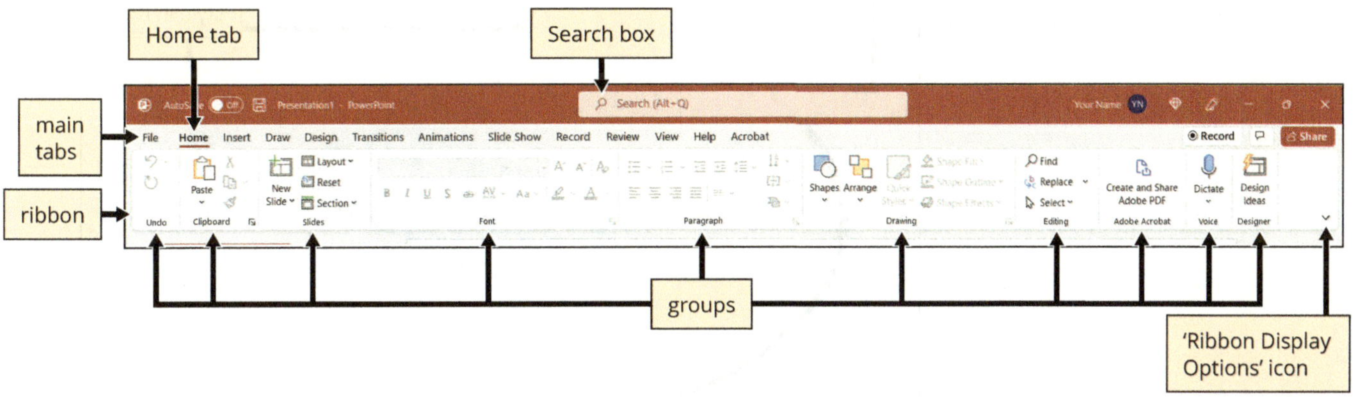

Figure 1–6a

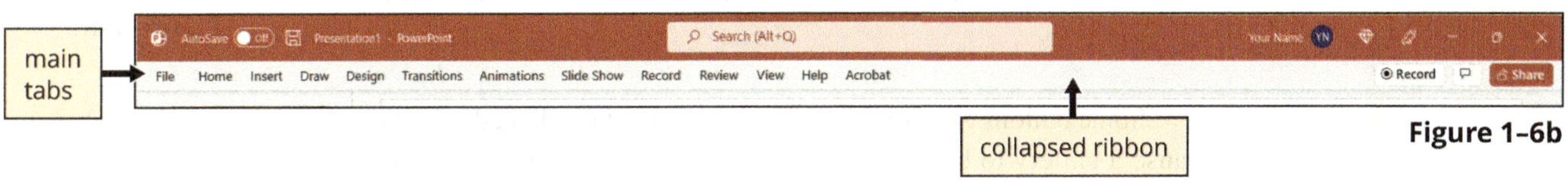

Figure 1–6b

Each time you start PowerPoint, the ribbon appears the same way it did the last time you used PowerPoint. The modules in this book begin with the ribbon always displayed.

In addition to the main tabs, PowerPoint displays **contextual tabs** when you perform certain tasks or work with objects such as pictures or tables. If you insert a picture in a PowerPoint presentation, for example, the Picture Format tab appears (Figure 1–7). When you are finished working with the picture, the Picture Format tab disappears from the ribbon. PowerPoint determines when contextual tabs should appear and disappear based on tasks you perform. Some tasks involve more than one contextual tab. For example, when you work with tables, the Table Design tab and the Layout tab appear.

BTW
Adobe Acrobat
If Adobe Acrobat is installed on your system, you might have a 'Create and Share Adobe PDF' button on the Home tab and an Acrobat tab on the ribbon, as shown in Figure 1-6a and throughout this project.

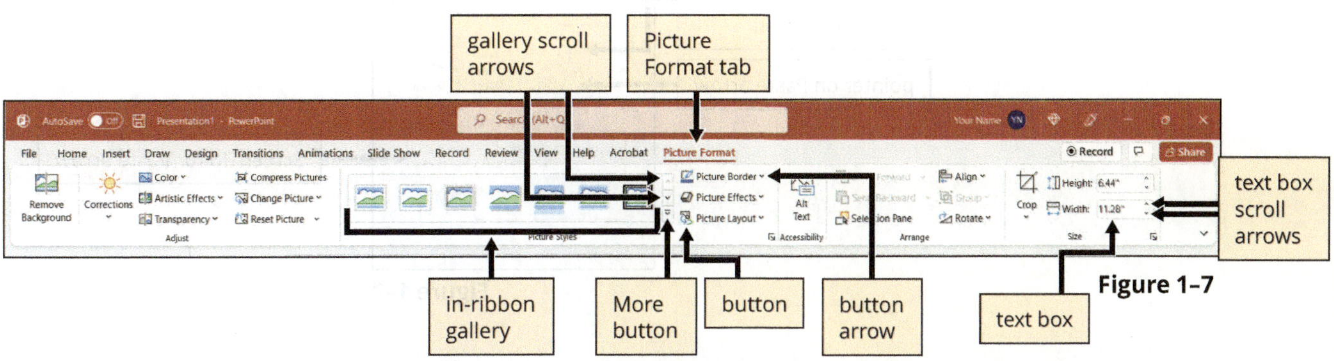

Figure 1–7

Groups on the ribbon include buttons, boxes (text boxes, check boxes, etc.), and galleries (Figure 1–8). A **gallery** is a collection of choices, often graphical, arranged in a grid or in a list that you can browse through before making a selection. You can scroll through choices in an in-ribbon gallery by clicking the gallery's scroll arrows. Or, you can click a gallery's More button to view more gallery options on the screen at a time.

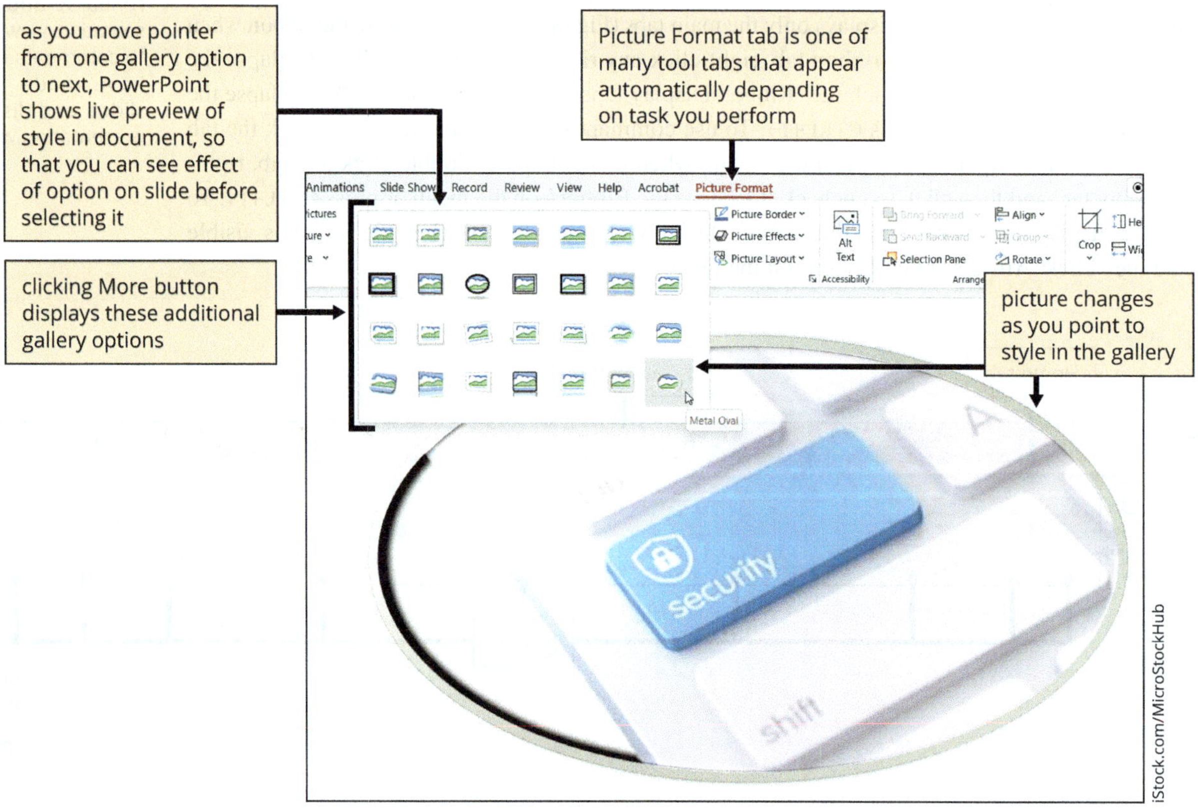

Figure 1–8

Some buttons and boxes have arrows that, when clicked, also display a gallery; others always cause a gallery to be displayed when clicked. Most galleries support **Live Preview**, a feature that allows you to point to a gallery choice and see its effect in the presentation without actually selecting the choice.

Some commands on the ribbon display an image to help you remember their function. When you point to a command on the ribbon, all or part of the command glows in a shade of gray, and a ScreenTip appears on the screen. A **ScreenTip** is a label that appears when you point to a button or object that provides the name of the command, its purpose, available keyboard shortcut(s), and sometimes instructions for how to obtain help about the command (Figure 1–9).

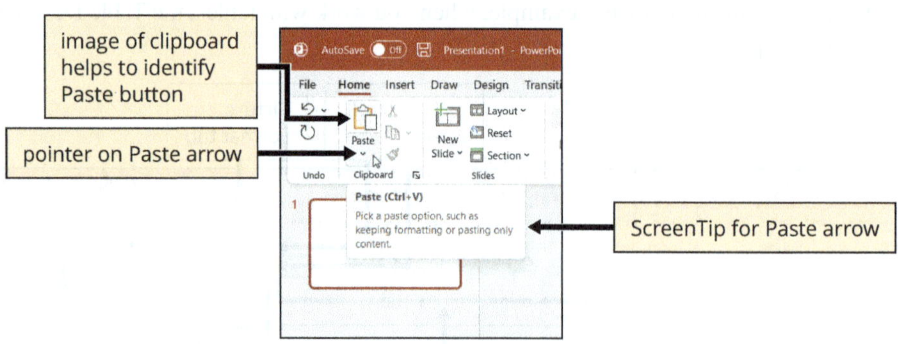

Figure 1–9

Some groups on the ribbon have a small arrow in the lower-right corner, called a **Dialog Box Launcher**, that when clicked, displays a dialog box or a pane with additional options for the group (Figure 1–10). When presented with a dialog box, you make selections and must close the dialog box before returning to the presentation. A **pane**, in contrast to a dialog box, is a window that can remain open and visible while you work in the presentation and provides additional options.

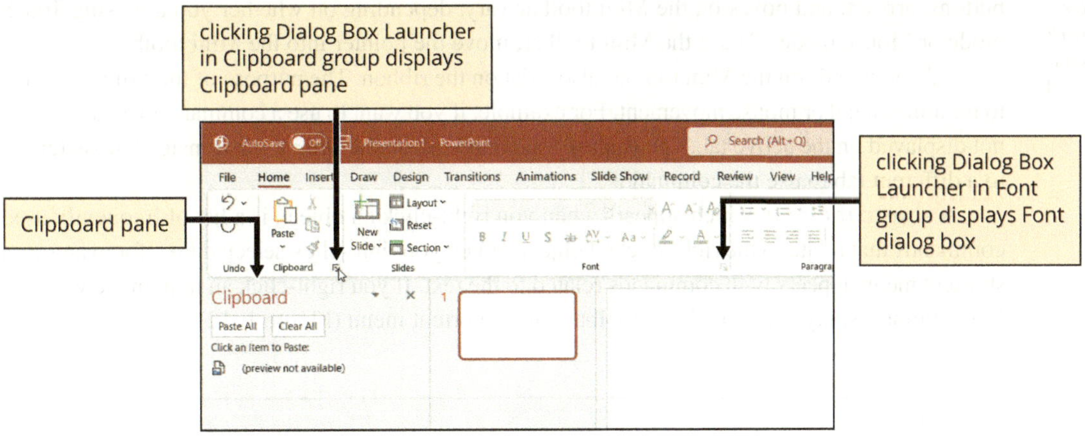

Figure 1–10

Search Box The **Search box**, which appears on the title bar, is used to find a command, perform specific tasks in PowerPoint, or access the PowerPoint Help system (Figure 1–11). As you type in the Search box, the word-wheeling feature displays search results that are refined as you type. For example, if you want to align objects on a slide, you can type "align" in the Search box and then select the appropriate command.

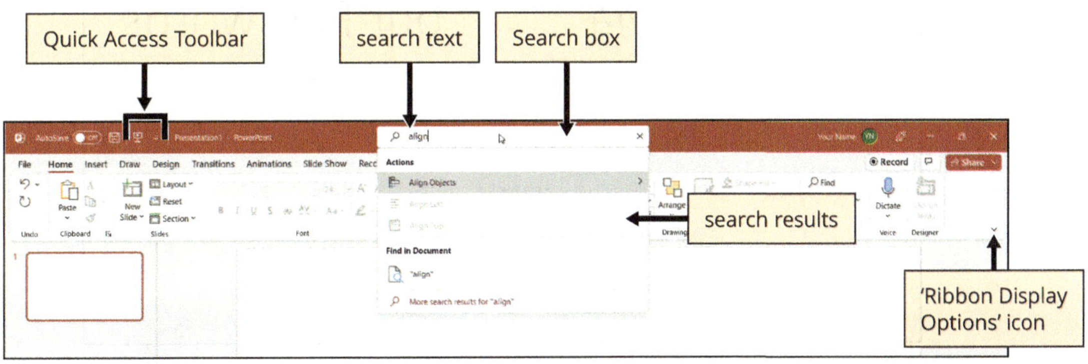

Figure 1–11

Quick Access Toolbar The **Quick Access Toolbar**, located initially (by default) above the ribbon at the left edge of the title bar, provides convenient one-click access to frequently used commands (shown in Figure 1–11). If the Quick Access Toolbar is not displayed, click the 'Ribbon Display Options' icon and then click 'Show Quick Access Toolbar' in the menu. The commands on the Quick Access Toolbar always are available, regardless of the task you are performing.

You can add commands to or delete commands from the Quick Access Toolbar so that it contains the commands you use most often. To do this, click the 'Customize Quick Access Toolbar' button on the Quick Access Toolbar and then select the commands you want to add or remove. As you add commands to the Quick Access Toolbar, its length may interfere with the document title on the title bar. For this reason, PowerPoint provides an option of displaying the Quick Access Toolbar below the ribbon on the Customize Quick Access Toolbar menu.

> **BTW**
> **Turning Off the Mini Toolbar**
> If you do not want the Mini toolbar to appear, click File on the ribbon to open Backstage view, click Options in Backstage view, if necessary click General (Options dialog box), remove the check mark from the 'Show Mini Toolbar on selection' check box, and then click OK.

Each time you start PowerPoint, the Quick Access Toolbar appears the same way it did the last time you used PowerPoint. The modules in this book show the Quick Access Toolbar displayed.

Mini Toolbar and Shortcut Menus The **Mini toolbar** is a small toolbar that appears next to selected text and contains the most frequently used text formatting commands such as bold, italic, font color, and font size. If you do not use the Mini toolbar, it disappears from the screen. The buttons, arrows, and boxes on the Mini toolbar vary, depending on whether you are using Touch mode or Mouse mode. To use the Mini toolbar, move the pointer into the Mini toolbar.

All commands on the Mini toolbar also exist on the ribbon. The purpose of the Mini toolbar is to minimize hand or mouse movement. For example, if you want to use a command that currently is not displayed on the active tab, you can use the command on the Mini toolbar instead of switching to a different tab to use the command.

A **shortcut menu**, which appears when you right-click an object, is a list of frequently used commands that relate to the right-clicked object. When you right-click selected text, for example, a shortcut menu appears with commands related to the text. If you right-click an item in the window, PowerPoint displays both the Mini toolbar and a shortcut menu (Figure 1–12).

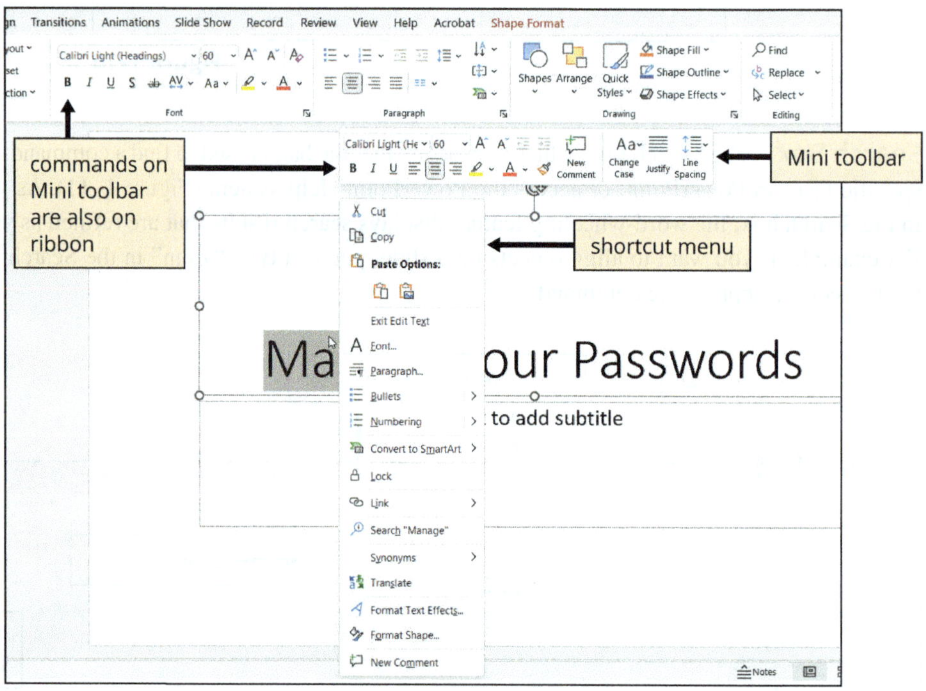

Figure 1–12

KeyTips If you prefer using the keyboard instead of the mouse, you can press ALT on the keyboard to display **KeyTips**, or keyboard code labels, for certain commands (Figure 1–13). To select a command using the keyboard, press the letter or number displayed in the KeyTip, which may cause additional KeyTips related to the selected command to appear. For example, to select the Bold button on the Home tab, press ALT, then press H, and then press 1. To remove KeyTips from the screen, press ALT or ESC until all KeyTips disappear, or click anywhere in the PowerPoint window.

Microsoft Account Area In the **Microsoft account area** (shown in Figure 1–13), you can use the Sign in link to sign in to your Microsoft account. Once signed in, you will see your account information.

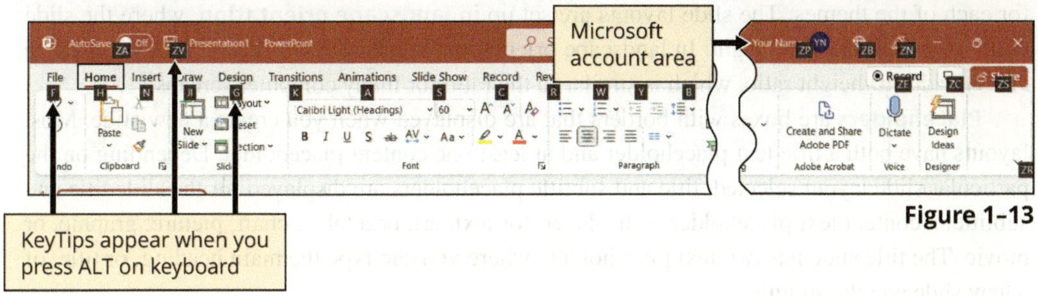

Figure 1-13

To Display a Different Tab on the Ribbon

When you start PowerPoint, the ribbon displays 12 main tabs: File, Home, Insert, Draw, Design, Transitions, Animations, Slide Show, Record, Review, View, and Help. You might have additional tabs, such as Acrobat, depending on the software installed on your system. The tab currently displayed is the active tab. To display a different tab on the ribbon, you click the tab. The following step displays the Design tab, that is, makes it the active tab. **Why?** You are going to change the slide design, so you need to switch tabs to access options for completing this task.

1

- Click Design on the ribbon to display the Design tab (Figure 1-14).
- **Experiment:** Click the other tabs on the ribbon to view their contents. When you are finished, click Design on the ribbon to redisplay the Design tab.

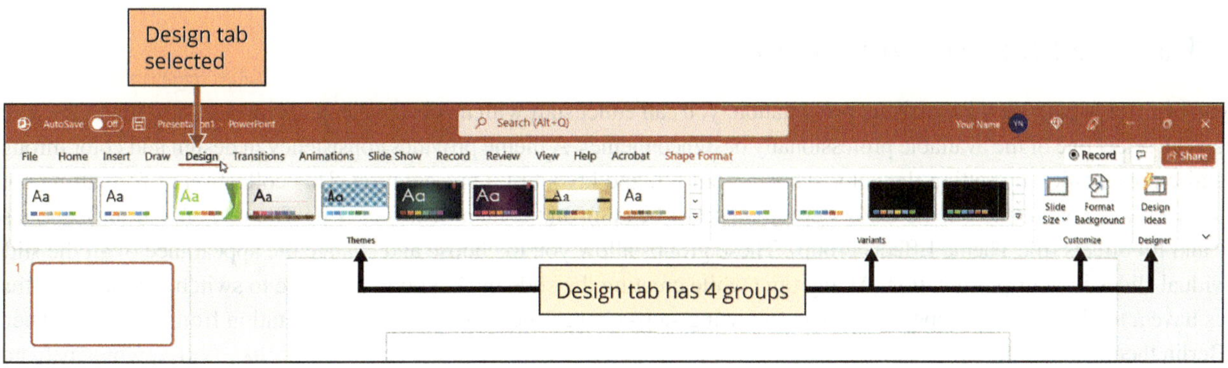

Figure 1-14

Other Ways

1. Press ALT, press letter corresponding to tab to display
2. Press ALT, press LEFT ARROW or RIGHT ARROW until desired tab is displayed

Creating a Title Slide

You easily can give the slides in a presentation a professional and integrated appearance by using a theme. A **theme** is a predefined design with coordinating colors, fonts, and graphical effects such as shadows and reflections that can be applied to presentations to give them a consistent, professional look. Themes are also sometimes called **templates**. Several themes are available when you start PowerPoint, each with a specific name. You also can add or change a theme while you are creating slides. Using one of the formatted themes makes creating a professional-looking presentation easier and quicker than using the Blank Presentation template, where you would need to make all design decisions.

When you open a new presentation, the default Title Slide layout appears. The purpose of this layout is to introduce the presentation to the audience. PowerPoint includes other standard layouts

BTW
Customizing a Slide Layout
PowerPoint provides a wide variety of slide layouts for each theme, but you can customize the layouts to make your deck unique. Display the View tab, click Slide Master (View tab | Master Views group), select the thumbnail below the slide master in the left pane that you would like to customize, and then make the desired modifications.

for each of the themes. The slide layouts are set up in **landscape orientation**, where the slide width is greater than its height. In landscape orientation, the slide size is preset to a Widescreen (16:9) width-to-height ratio, which is similar to the ratio for many computer screens.

Placeholders are boxes with borders that are displayed when you create a new slide. Most layouts have both a title text placeholder and at least one content placeholder. Depending on the particular slide layout selected, title and subtitle placeholders are displayed for the slide title and subtitle; a content text placeholder is displayed for text, art, or a table, chart, picture, graphic, or movie. The title slide has two text placeholders where you can type the main heading, or title, of a new slide and the subtitle.

With the exception of the Blank slide layout, PowerPoint assumes every new slide has a title. Any text you type after a new slide appears becomes title text in the title text placeholder. The following steps change the theme and then create the title slide for this presentation.

Consider This

How do I choose the words for the slide?

All presentations should follow the 7 × 7 rule, which states that each slide should have a maximum of seven paragraphs, and each paragraph should have a maximum of seven words. In most cases, you should use the fewest words possible. PowerPoint designers choose their words carefully and, in turn, help viewers read the slides easily.

In most cases, avoid line wraps. Your audience's eyes want to stop at the end of a line. Thus, plan your words carefully or adjust the font size so that each point displays on only one line.

To Choose a Presentation Theme

As you begin creating a new PowerPoint presentation, you can either start with no design elements by choosing Blank Presentation or you can select one of the available professionally designed themes. A theme provides consistency in design and color throughout the entire presentation by setting the color scheme, font set, and layout of a presentation. This collection of formatting choices includes a set of colors (the Theme Colors group), a set of heading and content text fonts (the Theme Fonts group), and a set of lines and fill effects (the Theme Effects group). These groups allow you to choose and change the appearance of all the slides or individual slides in your presentation. At any time while creating the slide deck, you may decide to switch the theme so that the slides have a totally different appearance. The following steps change the theme for this presentation from the Office Theme to the Berlin theme. **Why?** The title slide will have text and a picture, so you want to select a theme, like Berlin, with a background that attracts attention but does not distract from the picture.

1

- With the Design tab displayed and the slide selected, point to the More button (Design tab | Themes group) (Figure 1–15).

Q&A Why does a gray border display around the first theme thumbnail?
The gray border indicates the current theme. PowerPoint applied the default Office Theme when you chose the Blank Presentation theme.

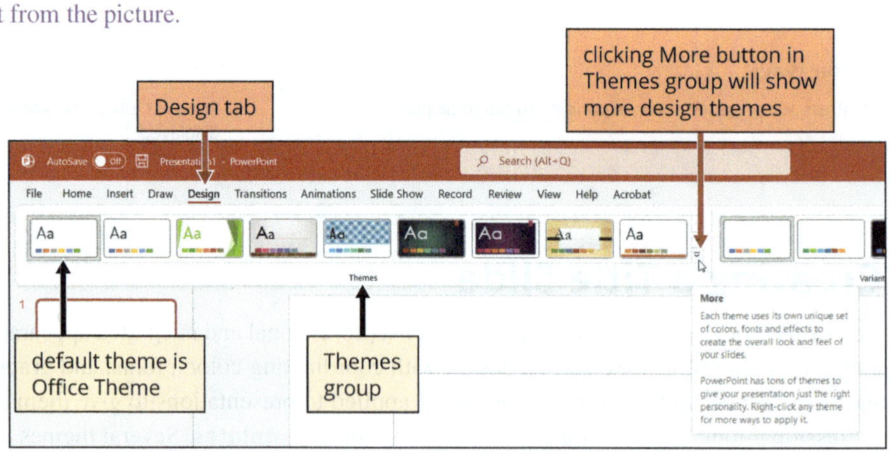

Figure 1–15

2

- Click the More button (Design tab | Themes group) to expand the gallery, which shows more theme gallery options. If necessary, scroll down and then point to the Berlin thumbnail to see a preview of that theme on Slide 1 (Figure 1–16).
- **Experiment:** Point to various themes in the Themes gallery and watch the designs change on Slide 1.

Q&A Are the themes displayed in a specific order?
No. Your themes might be in a different order than shown here.

How can I determine the theme names?
If you point to a theme, a ScreenTip with the theme's name appears on the screen.

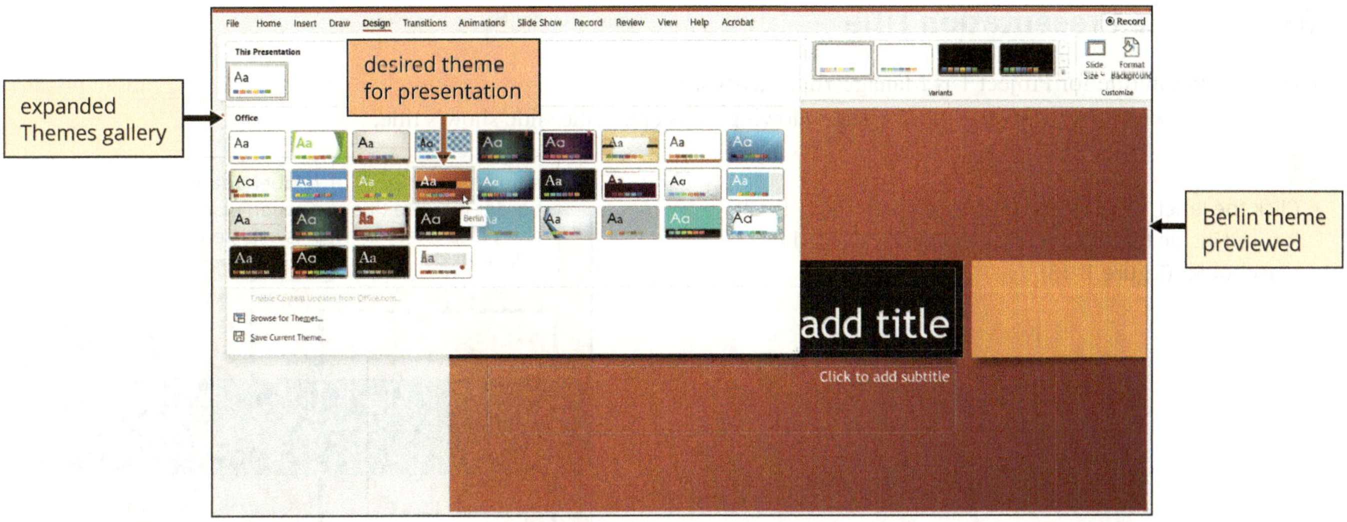

Figure 1–16

3

- Click the Berlin theme to apply this theme to the presentation (Figure 1–17).

Q&A If I decide at some future time that this design does not fit the theme of my presentation, can I apply a different design?
Yes. You can repeat these steps at any time while creating your presentation.

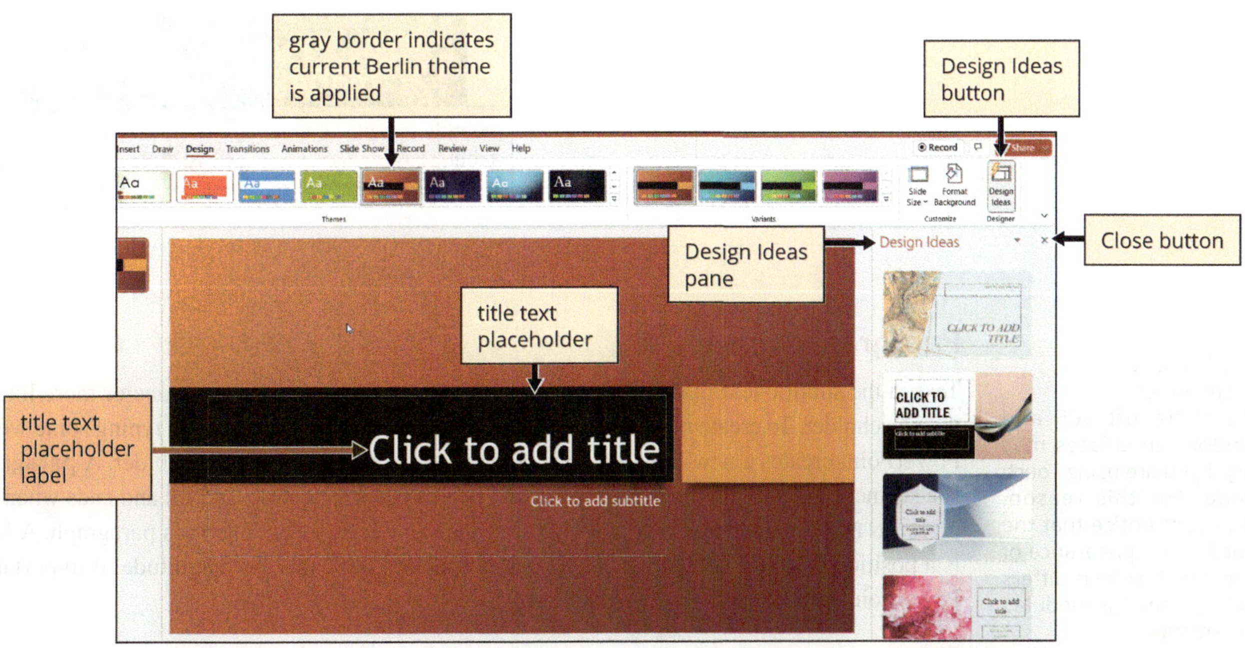

Figure 1–17

4
- If the Design Ideas pane is displayed, click the Close button to close this pane.

Q&A What is the Design Ideas pane?
PowerPoint generates suggestions automatically for arranging pictures, charts, tables, and other content on slides. You can scroll through these ideas and click one that meets your needs. PowerPoint then will arrange your slide content.

How can I view the Design Ideas pane if it is not displayed?
Click the Design Ideas button (Design tab | Designer group) to open the pane.

To Enter the Presentation Title

The presentation title for Project 1 is Manage Your Passwords. **Why?** The presentation focuses on protecting online private information by creating quality passwords. The following steps create the slide show's title.

1
- Click the label, 'Click to add title', (shown in Figure 1–17) located inside the title text placeholder to select the placeholder (Figure 1–18).

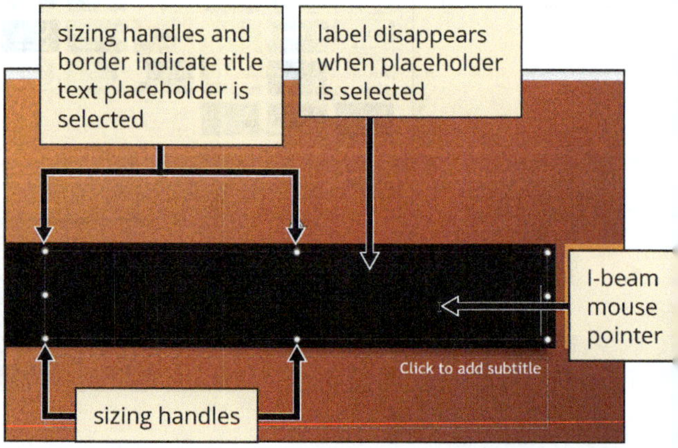

Figure 1–18

2
- Type **Manage Your Passwords** in the title text placeholder. Do not press ENTER (Figure 1–19).

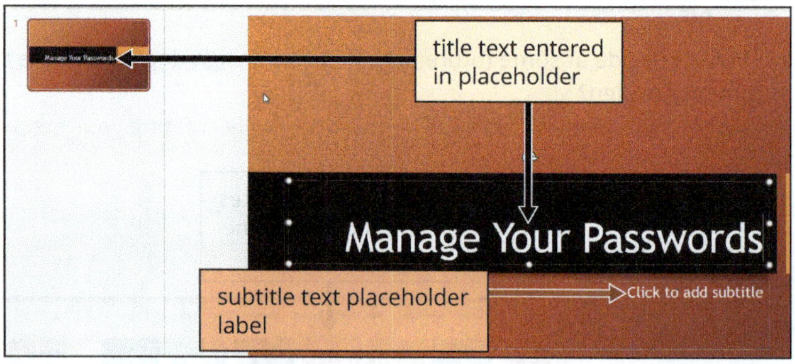

Figure 1–19

BTW
Touch Mode Differences
The Microsoft 365 and Windows interfaces may vary if you are using Touch mode. For this reason, you might notice that the function or appearance of your touch screen differs slightly from this module's presentation.

Paragraphs

Text in the subtitle text placeholder supports the title text. It can appear on one or more lines in the placeholder. To create more than one subtitle line, you press ENTER after typing some words. PowerPoint creates a new line, which is the second paragraph in the placeholder. A **paragraph** is a segment of text with the same format that begins when you press ENTER and ends when you press ENTER again. This new paragraph is at the same level as the previous paragraph. A **level** is a position within a structure, such as an outline, that indicates the magnitude of importance. PowerPoint allows for five paragraph levels.

To Enter the Presentation Subtitle Paragraph

The first subtitle paragraph is related to the title. **Why?** The subtitle emphasizes that strong passwords can offer security when working online. The following steps enter the presentation subtitle.

1

- Click the label, 'Click to add subtitle', located inside the subtitle text placeholder to select the placeholder (Figure 1-20).

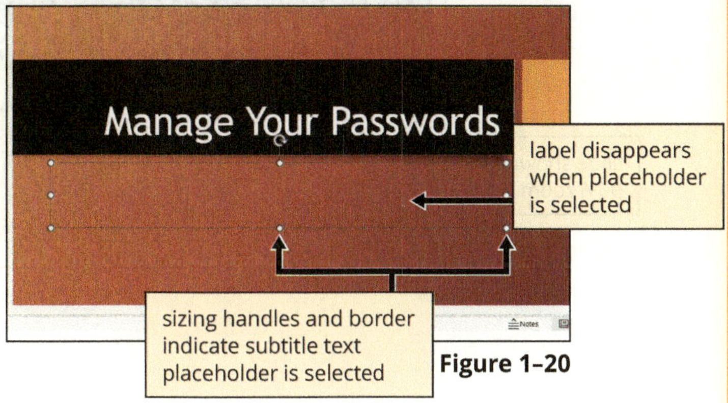

Figure 1-20

2

- Type **The Importance of Online Security** but do not press ENTER (Figure 1-21).

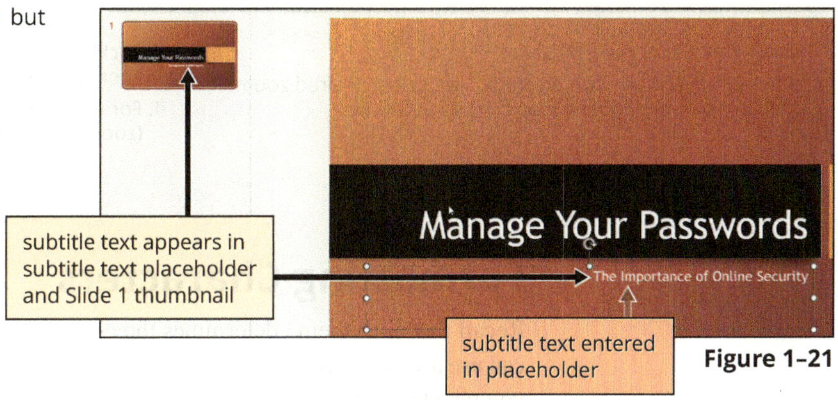

Figure 1-21

To Zoom a Slide

You can **zoom** the view of the slide on the screen so that the text or other content is enlarged or shrunk. When you zoom in, you get a close-up view of your slide; when you zoom out, you see more of the slide at a reduced size. You will be modifying the text and other slide components as you create the presentation, so you can enlarge the slide on the screen. **Why?** Zooming the slide can help you see slide elements more clearly so that you can position them precisely where desired. The following step changes the zoom to 90 percent.

1

- Click the Zoom In or Zoom Out button as many times as necessary until the Zoom button on the status bar displays 90% on its face (Figure 1-22).
- **Experiment:** Repeatedly click the Zoom In and Zoom Out buttons on the status bar and watch the size of the slide change in the Slide pane.

Q&A If I change the zoom percentage, will the slide display differently when I run the presentation?
No. Changing the zoom helps you develop the slide content and does not affect the slide show.

Figure 1–22

Other Ways

1. Drag Zoom slider on status bar
2. Click Zoom level button on status bar, select desired zoom percent or type (Zoom dialog box), click OK
3. Click Zoom button (View tab | Zoom group), select desired zoom percent or type (Zoom dialog box), click OK
4. For touch screens: Pinch two fingers together in Slide pane (zoom out) or stretch two fingers apart (zoom in)

Formatting Characters

Recall that each theme determines the color scheme, font set, and layout of a presentation. You can use a specific theme and then change the characters' formats any time before, during, or after you type the text.

Fonts and Font Styles

Characters that appear on the screen are a specific shape and size. Examples of how you can modify the appearance, or **formatting**, of these typed characters on the screen and in print include changing the font, style, size, color, and alignment. The **font**, or typeface, defines the appearance and shape of the letters, numbers, and special characters. A **font style** indicates how the characters are formatted. PowerPoint's text font styles include regular, italic, bold, and bold italic. **Font size** specifies the height of the characters measured in units called points. A **point** is 1/72 of an inch in height. Thus, a character with a font size of 36 is 36/72 (or 1/2) of an inch in height. **Font color** defines the hue of the characters.

This presentation uses the Berlin document theme, which has particular font styles and font sizes. The Berlin document theme default title text font is named Trebuchet MS. It has no special effects, and its size is 54 point. The Berlin default subtitle text font also is Trebuchet MS with a font size of 20 point.

To Select a Paragraph

You can use many techniques to format characters. When you want to apply the same formats to multiple words or paragraphs, it is helpful to select these words. **Why?** It is efficient to select the desired text and then make the desired changes to all the characters simultaneously. The first formatting change you will make will apply to the title slide subtitle. The following step selects this paragraph.

1

- Triple-click the paragraph, The Importance of Online Security, in the subtitle text placeholder to select the paragraph (Figure 1–23).

Figure 1–23

Other Ways

1. Position pointer to left of first paragraph and drag to end of line

To Italicize Text

Different font styles often are used on slides. **Why?** These style changes make the words more appealing to the reader and emphasize particular text. **Italic** text has a slanted appearance. Used sparingly, it draws the readers' eyes to these characters. The following step adds emphasis to the line of the subtitle text by changing regular text to italic text.

1

- With the subtitle text still selected, click the Italic button on the Mini toolbar to italicize that text on the slide (Figure 1–24).

Q&A If I change my mind and decide not to italicize the text, how can I remove this style?
Immediately click the Undo button on the Home tab in the Undo group, click the Italic button a second time, or press CTRL+Z. Your Quick Access Toolbar also may include the Undo button.

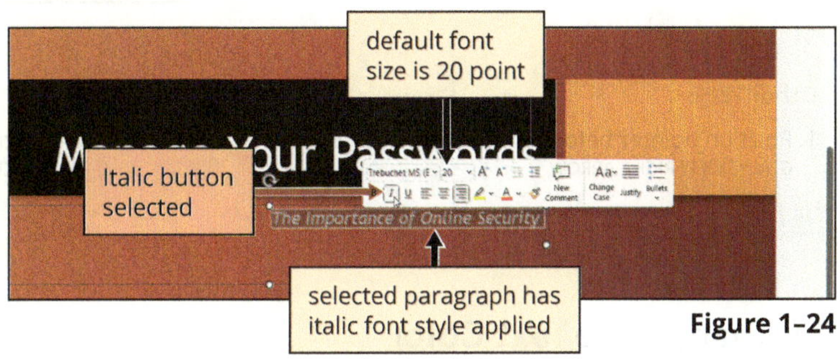

Figure 1–24

Other Ways

1. Right-click selected text, click Italic button in Mini toolbar near shortcut menu
2. Select text, click Italic button (Home tab | Font group)
3. Click Font dialog box launcher (Home tab | Font group), click Font tab (Font dialog box), click Italic in Font style list, click OK
4. Select text, press CTRL+I

To Increase Font Size

Why? To add emphasis, you increase the font size for the subtitle text. The 'Increase Font Size' button on the Mini toolbar increases the font size in preset increments. The following step uses this button to increase the font size.

1

- With the text, The Importance of Online Security, selected, click the 'Increase Font Size' button on the Mini toolbar three times to increase the font size of the selected text from 20 to 32 point (Figure 1–25).

Q&A If the Mini toolbar disappears from the screen, how can I display it again?
Right-click the selected text, and the Mini toolbar should appear below a shortcut menu.

Figure 1–25

Other Ways

1. Click Font Size arrow on Mini toolbar, click desired font size in Font Size gallery
2. Click 'Increase Font Size' button (Home tab | Font group)
3. Click Font Size arrow (Home tab | Font group), click desired font size in Font size gallery
4. Press CTRL+SHIFT+>

To Select a Word

PowerPoint designers use many techniques to emphasize words and characters on a slide. To accentuate the word, Security, on your slide, you want to increase the font size and change the font color to yellow for this word in the title text. To make these changes, you should begin by selecting the word, Security. **Why?** You could perform these actions separately, but it is more efficient to select the word and then change the font attributes. The following step selects a word.

1

- Position the pointer somewhere in the word to be selected (in this case, in the word, Security).
- Double-click the word to select it (Figure 1–26).

Figure 1–26

Other Ways

1. Position pointer before first character, press CTRL+SHIFT+RIGHT ARROW
2. Position pointer before first character, drag right to select word

To Change the Text Color

PowerPoint allows you to use one or more text colors in a presentation. You decide to change the color of the word you selected, Security. **Why?** The color, yellow, adds subtle emphasis to this word in your subtitle slide text. The following steps change the font color from white to yellow.

1

- With the word, Security, selected, click the Font Color arrow on the Mini toolbar to display the Font Color gallery, which includes Theme Colors and Standard Colors (Figure 1–27).
- **Experiment:** Point to various colors in the gallery and watch the word's font color change.

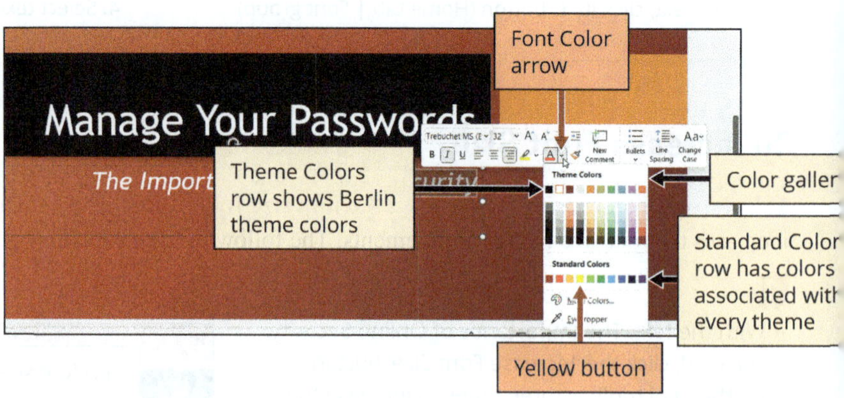

Figure 1–27

2

- Click Yellow in the Standard Colors row on the Mini toolbar (fourth color from left) to change the font color to Yellow (Figure 1–28).

Q&A What is the difference between the colors shown in the Theme Colors area and the Standard Colors?
The 10 colors in the top row of the Theme Colors area are two text, two background, and six accent colors in the Berlin theme; the five colors in each column under the top row display different transparencies. The Standard Colors are available in every document theme.

Figure 1–28

3

- Click outside the selected area to deselect the word.

Other Ways

1. Right-click selected text, click Font on shortcut menu, click Font Color button, click desired color
2. Click Font Color arrow (Home tab | Font group), click desired color

To Zoom a Slide

You have modified the subtitle text on Slide 1, so you now can zoom out to see more of the slide. The following step changes the zoom to 70 percent.

1 Click the Zoom Out button as many times as necessary until the Zoom button on the status bar displays 70% on its face (Figure 1–29).

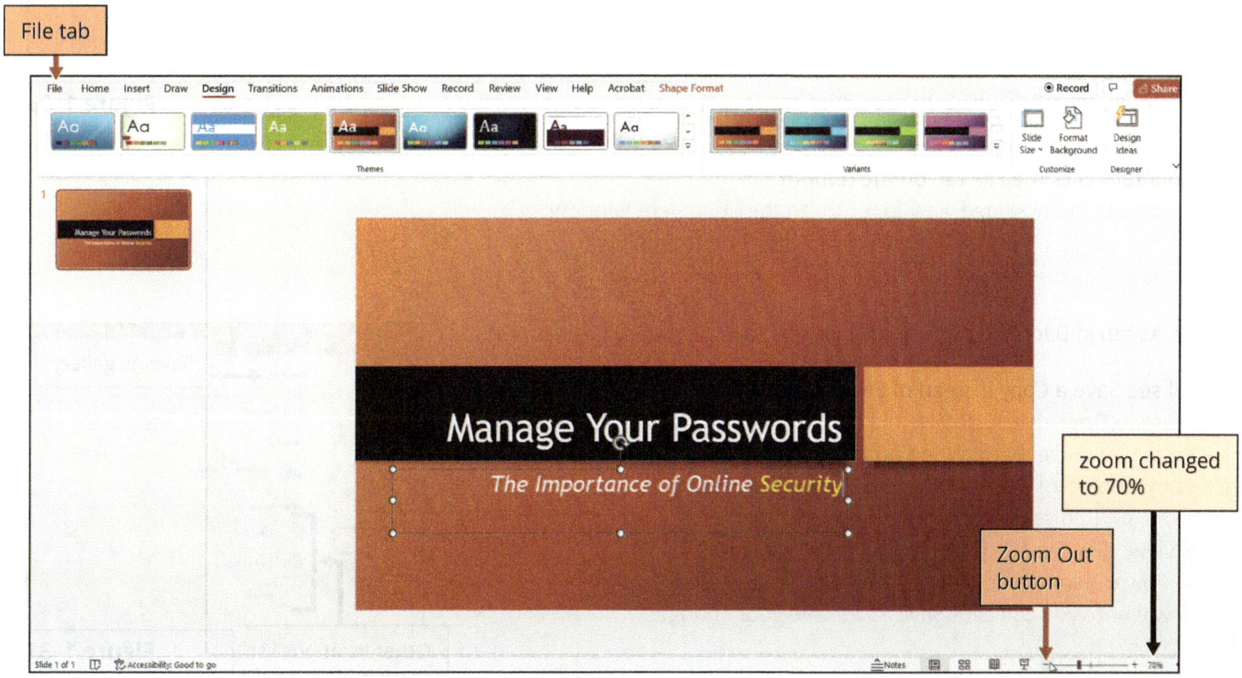

Figure 1–29

To Save a Presentation for the First Time

While you are building slides in a presentation, the computer or device stores it in memory. When you **save** a presentation, it is stored permanently on a storage medium such as a hard disk, USB flash drive, or online using a cloud storage service such as OneDrive so that you can retrieve it later. Once information is saved, it is referred to as a **file**. A **file name** is a unique, descriptive name assigned to a file when it is saved.

When saving a presentation, you must decide which storage medium to use:

- If you always work on the same computer and have no need to transport your projects to a different location, then your computer's hard drive will suffice as a storage location. It is a good idea, however, to save a backup copy of your projects on a separate medium in case the file becomes corrupted or the computer's hard drive fails. The documents created in this book are saved to the computer's hard drive.
- If you plan to work on your documents in various locations or on multiple computers or mobile devices, then you should save your documents on a portable medium, such as a USB flash drive. Alternatively, you can save your documents to an online cloud storage service such as OneDrive.

BTW
Organizing Files and Folders
You should organize and store files in folders so that you easily can find the files later. For example, if you are taking an introductory technology class called CIS 101, a good practice would be to save all PowerPoint files in a PowerPoint folder in a CIS 101 folder.

The following steps save a presentation in the Documents library on your computer's hard drive using the file name, Passwords. **Why?** You have performed many tasks while creating this project and do not want to risk losing the work completed thus far. Accordingly, you should save the presentation.

1

- Click File on the ribbon (shown in Figure 1–29) to display Backstage view (Figure 1–30).

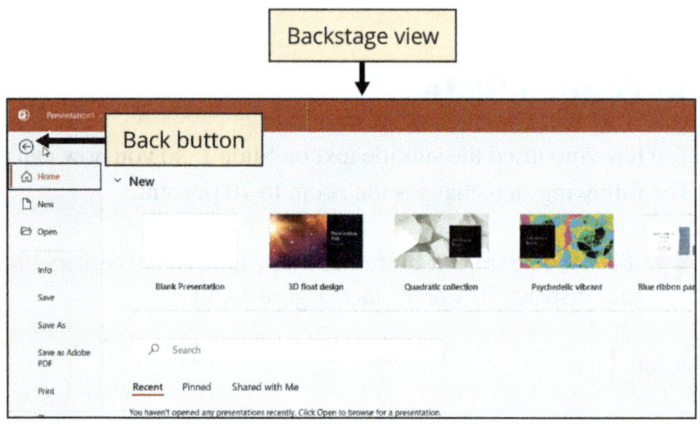

Figure 1–30

Q&A What is the purpose of the File tab on the ribbon, and what is Backstage view?
The File tab opens Backstage view in PowerPoint. **Backstage view** contains commands that allow you to manage files and options for PowerPoint. As you click different tabs along the left side of Backstage view, the associated gallery displays on the right side of Backstage view.

What if I accidentally click the File tab on the ribbon?
Click the Back button in Backstage view to return to the document window.

2

- Click the Save As tab in Backstage view to display the Save As gallery (Figure 1–31).

Q&A What if I see Save a Copy instead of Save As?
If you are saving to OneDrive, AutoSave may be enabled to save your changes as you make them. When AutoSave is enabled, you see Save a Copy instead of Save As. You can use Save a Copy in place of Save As, or, to disable AutoSave, click the Back button in Backstage view, click the AutoSave On button in the upper-left corner of the PowerPoint window to turn it to Off, and return to Backstage view where you can click Save As to save your changes manually.

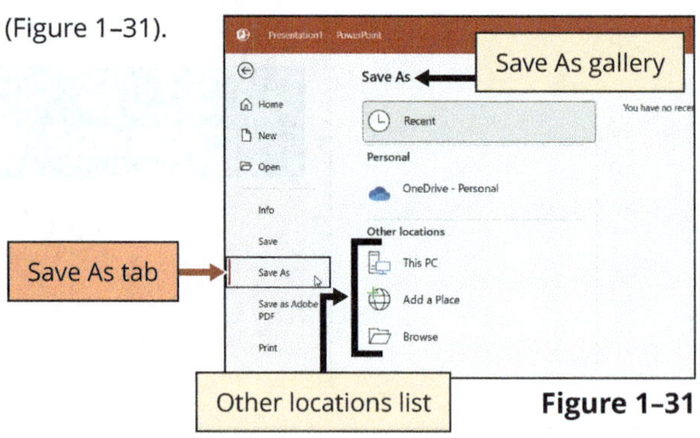

Figure 1–31

3

- If you are saving to OneDrive, click OneDrive in the Save As gallery, or if AutoSave is enabled, click Save a Copy to save to OneDrive. Otherwise, click This PC in the Other locations list to display the default save location on the computer or mobile device (Figure 1–32).

Q&A Can I type the file name below the default save location that displays in the Save As gallery?
If you want to save the file in the default location, you can type the file name in the text box below the default save location and then click the Save button to the right of the default save location. These steps show how to change to a different location on This PC.

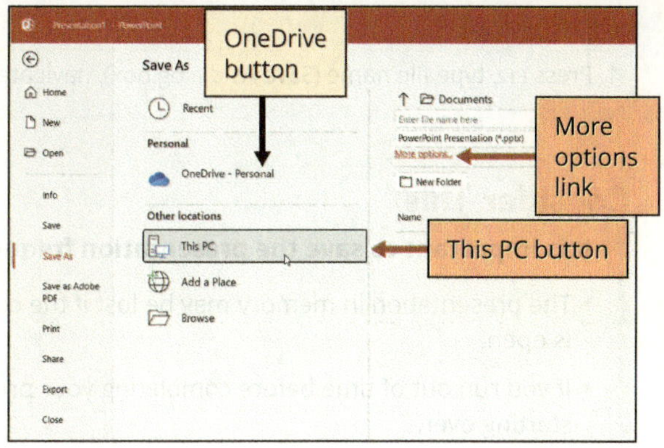

Figure 1–32

4

- Click the More options link to display the Save As dialog box.
- If necessary, click Documents in the Navigation pane to select the Documents library as the save location or navigate to the location specified by your instructor to save your presentation.
- Type **Passwords** in the File name box to specify the file name for the presentation (Figure 1–33).

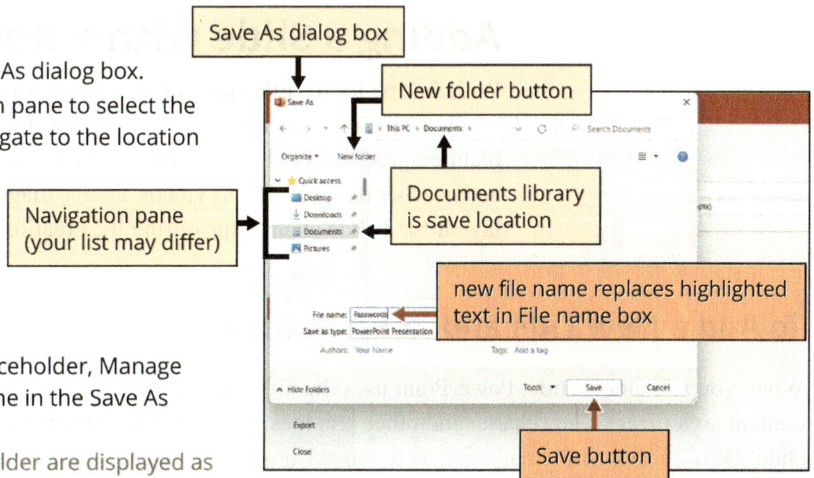

Figure 1–33

Q&A Why did the words from the title text placeholder, Manage Your Passwords, display as the default file name in the Save As dialog box?
Words from the presentation title text placeholder are displayed as the default file name. Because the suggested file name is selected in the File Name box, you do not need to delete it; as soon as you begin typing, the new file name replaces the selected text.

Do I have to save to the Documents library?
No. You can save to any device, default folder, or a different folder. You also can create your own folders by clicking the New folder button shown in Figure 1–33. To save to a different location, navigate to that location in the Navigation pane instead of clicking Documents.

What characters can I use in a file name?
The only invalid characters are the backslash (\), slash (/), colon (:), asterisk (*), question mark (?), quotation mark ("), less than symbol (<), greater than symbol (>), and vertical bar (|).

Why is my list of files, folders, and drives arranged and named differently from those shown in the figure?
Your computer or mobile device's configuration determines how the list of files and folders is displayed and how drives are named. You can change the save location by clicking links in the Navigation pane.

5

- Click the Save button to save the presentation with the file name, Passwords, to the save location (Figure 1–34).

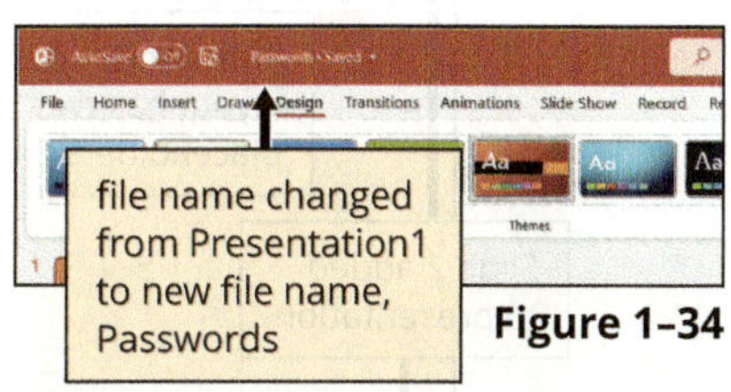

Figure 1–34

Q&A How do I know that PowerPoint saved the presentation?
While PowerPoint is saving your file, it briefly displays a message on the status bar indicating the amount of the file saved. When the presentation appears after saving, the new file name will be displayed in the title bar.

BTW
File Type
Depending on your Windows settings, the file type .pptx may be displayed on the title bar immediately to the right of the file name after you save the file. The file type .pptx identifies a PowerPoint presentation.

Other Ways

1. Press F12, type file name (Save As dialog box), navigate to desired save location, click Save

Consider This

It is important to save the presentation frequently for the following reasons:

- The presentation in memory may be lost if the computer is turned off or you lose electrical power while PowerPoint is open.
- If you run out of time before completing your presentation, you may finish your project at a future time without starting over.

Adding a Slide with a Bulleted List

With the text for the title slide for the presentation created, the next step is to add the first text slide immediately after the title slide. Usually, when you create a presentation, you add slides with text, pictures, graphics, or charts. Some placeholders allow you to double-click the placeholder and then access other objects, such as videos, charts, diagrams, and organization charts. You can change the layout for a slide at any time during the creation of a presentation.

To Add a New Title and Content Slide

When you add a new slide, PowerPoint uses the Title and Content slide layout. This layout provides a title placeholder and a content area for text, art, charts, and other graphics. A vertical scroll bar appears in the Slide pane when you add the second slide. **Why?** The scroll bar allows you to move from slide to slide easily. A small thumbnail image of this slide also appears in the Slides tab. The following step adds a new slide with the Title and Content slide layout.

1

- Click Home on the ribbon to display the Home tab.
- Click the New Slide button (Home tab | Slides group) to insert a new slide with the Title and Content layout (Figure 1–35).

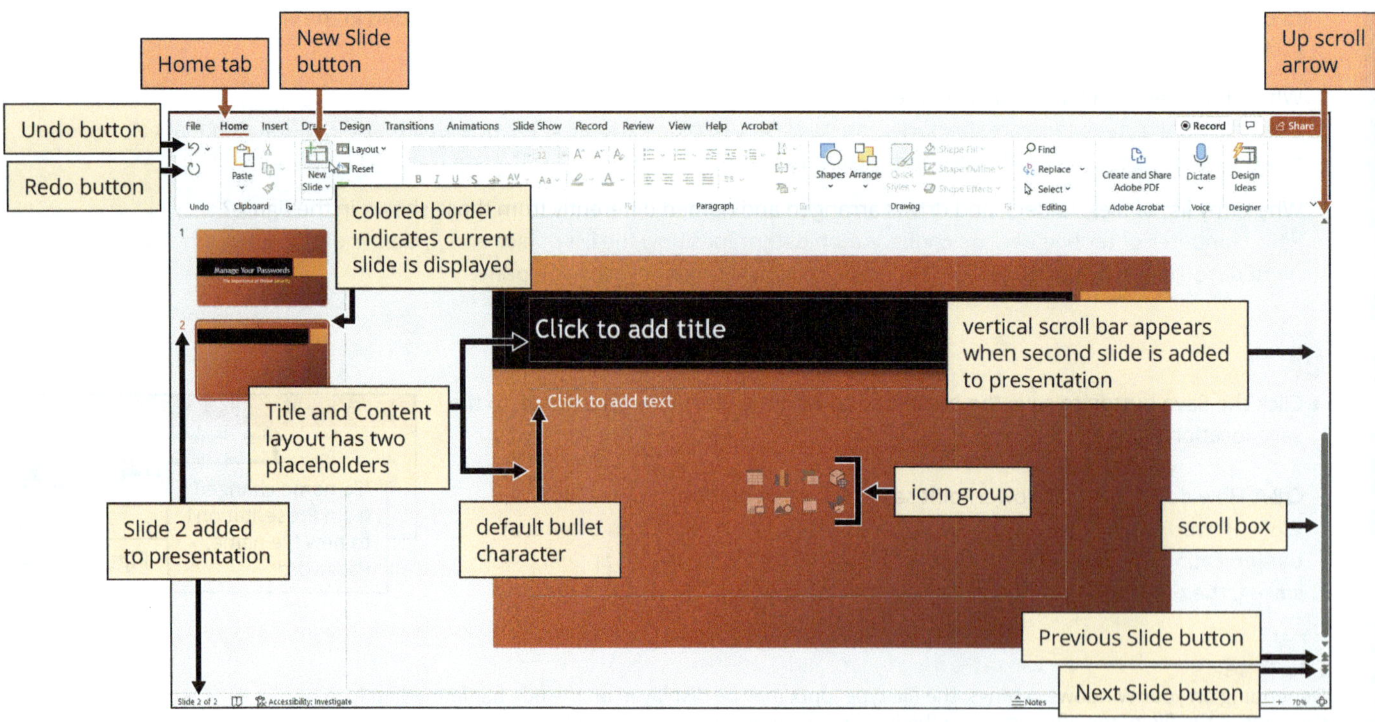

Figure 1–35

Q&A Why does the bullet character display a white dot?
The Berlin document theme determines the bullet characters. Each paragraph level has an associated bullet character.

I clicked the New Slide arrow instead of the New Slide button. What should I do?
Click the Title and Content slide thumbnail in the Berlin layout gallery.

How do I know which slide number I am viewing?
The left edge of the status bar shows the current slide number followed by the total number of slides in the document. In addition, the slide number is displayed to the left of the slide thumbnail.

What are the icons grouped in the middle of the Slide pane?
You can click one of the icons to insert a specific type of content: table, chart, SmartArt graphic, 3D model, picture, online picture, video, or icon.

Other Ways

1. Click New Slide button (Insert tab | Slides group)
2. Press CTRL+M

Correcting a Mistake When Typing

If you type the wrong letter, press BACKSPACE to erase all the characters back to and including the one that is incorrect. If you mistakenly press ENTER after typing the title and the insertion point is on the new line, simply press BACKSPACE to return the insertion point to the right of the last letter in the previous line.

By default, PowerPoint allows you to reverse up to the last 20 changes by clicking the Undo button (Home tab | Undo group), shown in Figure 1–35. The ScreenTip that appears when you point to the Undo button changes to indicate the type of change just made. For example, if you type text in the title text placeholder and then point to the Undo button, the ScreenTip that appears is Undo Typing. For clarity, when referencing the Undo button in this project, the name displaying in the ScreenTip is used. You can reapply a change that you reversed with the Undo button by clicking the Redo button (Home tab | Undo group). Clicking the Redo button reverses the last undo action. The ScreenTip name reflects the type of reversal last performed.

Creating a Multilevel Bulleted List

The information in the Slide 2 text placeholder is presented in a bulleted list with three levels. A **bulleted list** is a series of paragraphs, each of which may be preceded by a bullet character, such as a dot, arrow, or checkmark. Most themes display a bullet character at the start of a paragraph by default. Some slides show more than one level of bulleted text, called a **multilevel bulleted list**. In a multilevel bulleted list, a lower-level paragraph is a subset of a higher-level paragraph. It usually contains information that supports the topic in the paragraph immediately above it.

Looking back at Figure 1–1b, you can see that two of the Slide 2 paragraphs appear at the same level, called the first level: Don't use personal information, and Use letters, numbers, and symbols. Beginning with the second level, each paragraph indents to the right of the preceding level and is pushed down to a lower level. For example, if you increase the indent of a first-level paragraph, it becomes a second-level paragraph. The second and fourth paragraphs on Slide 2 are second-level paragraphs. The last paragraph, Randomize sequences, is a third-level paragraph.

Creating a text slide with a multilevel bulleted list requires several steps. Initially, you enter a slide title in the title text placeholder. Next, you select the content text placeholder. Then, you type the text for the multilevel bulleted list, increasing and decreasing the indents as needed. The next several sections enter the slide title and slide text with a multilevel bulleted list.

To Enter a Slide Title

PowerPoint assumes every new slide has a title. **Why?** The audience members read the title and then can begin to focus their attention on the information being presented on that slide. The title for Slide 2 is Strong Passwords. The following step enters this title.

1

- Click the label, 'Click to add title', to select it and then type **Strong Passwords** in the title text placeholder. Do not press ENTER (Figure 1–36).

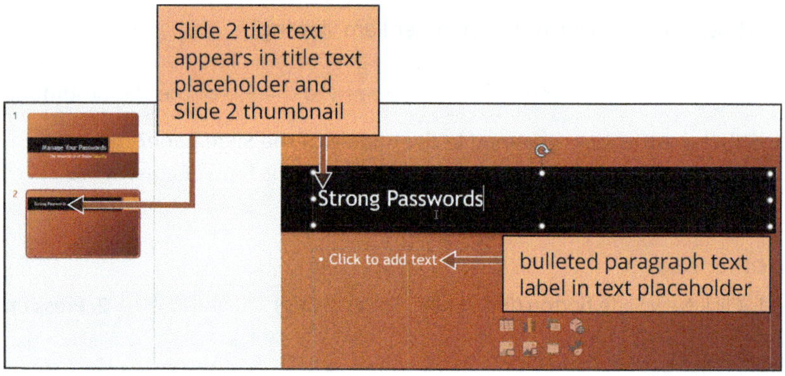

Figure 1–36

To Select a Text Placeholder

Why? Before you can type text into a content placeholder, you first must select it. The following step selects the text placeholder on Slide 2.

1

- Click the label, 'Click to add text', to select the content placeholder (Figure 1–37).

Q&A Why does my pointer have a different shape?
If you move the pointer away from the bullet, it will change shape.

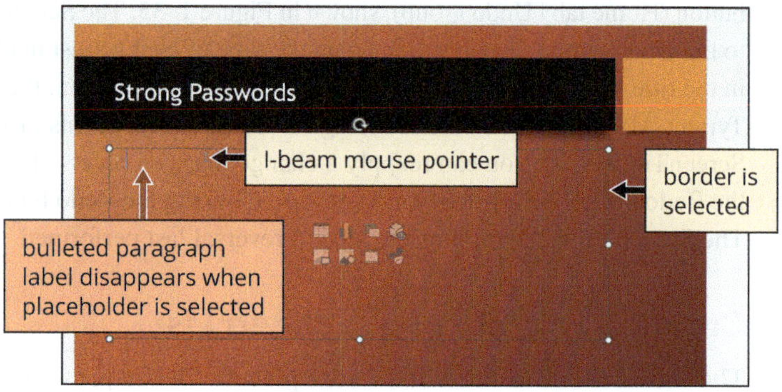

Figure 1–37

Other Ways

1. Press CTRL+ENTER

To Type a Multilevel Bulleted List

The content placeholder provides an area for the text characters. When you click inside a placeholder, you then can type or paste text. As discussed previously, a bulleted list is a list of paragraphs, each of which is preceded by a bullet. A paragraph is a segment of text ended by pressing ENTER. The theme determines the bullets for each level. **Why?** The bullet variations are determined by the specific paragraph levels, and they generally vary in size, shape, and color.

The content text placeholder is selected, so the next step is to type the multilevel bulleted list that consists of six paragraphs, as shown in Figure 1–1b. When you create a lower-level paragraph, you **demote** text (increase the list level); when you create a higher-level paragraph you **promote** text (decrease the list level). The following steps create a multilevel bulleted list consisting of three levels.

1

- Type **Don't use personal information** and then press ENTER (Figure 1-38).

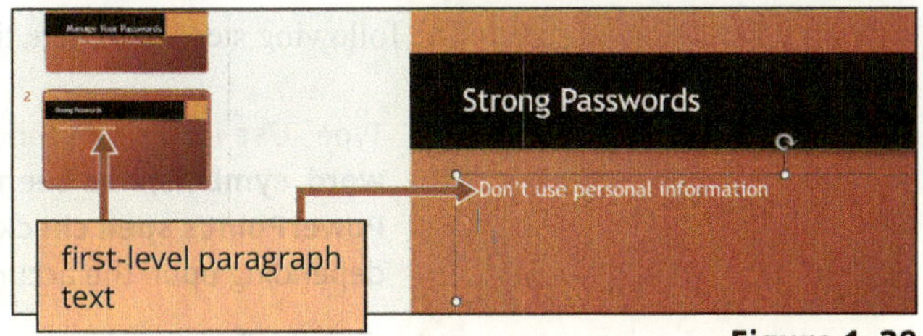

Figure 1-38

2

- Click the 'Increase List Level' button (Home tab | Paragraph group) to indent the second paragraph below the first and create a second-level paragraph (Figure 1-39).

Q&A Why does the bullet for this paragraph have a different size?
A different bullet is assigned to each paragraph level.

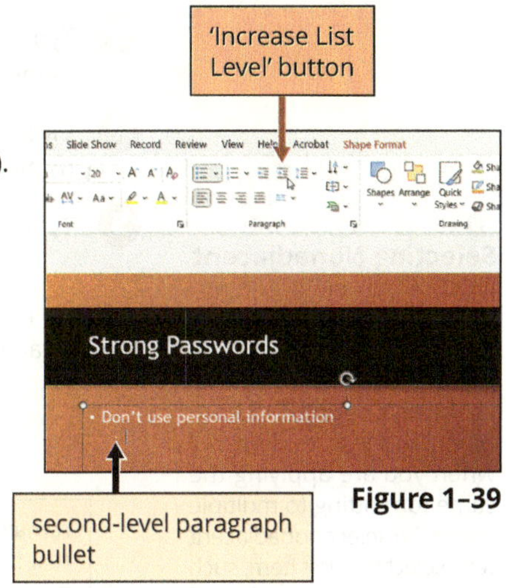

Figure 1-39

3

- Type **Avoid names, birthdays, and addresses** and then press ENTER (Figure 1-40).

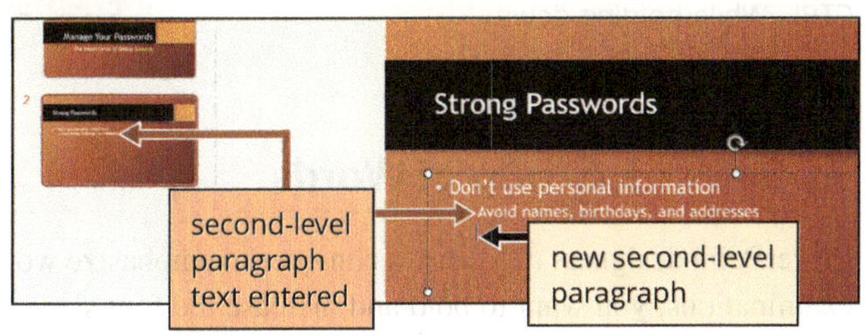

Figure 1-40

4

- Click the 'Decrease List Level' button (Home tab | Paragraph group) so that the second-level paragraph becomes a first-level paragraph (Figure 1-41).

Q&A Can I delete bullets on a slide?
Yes. If you do not want bullets to display in a particular paragraph, click the Bullets button (Home tab | Paragraph group) to toggle them off, or right-click the paragraph and then click the Bullets button on the shortcut menu. You can also position the insertion point at the beginning of the line and press BACKSPACE.

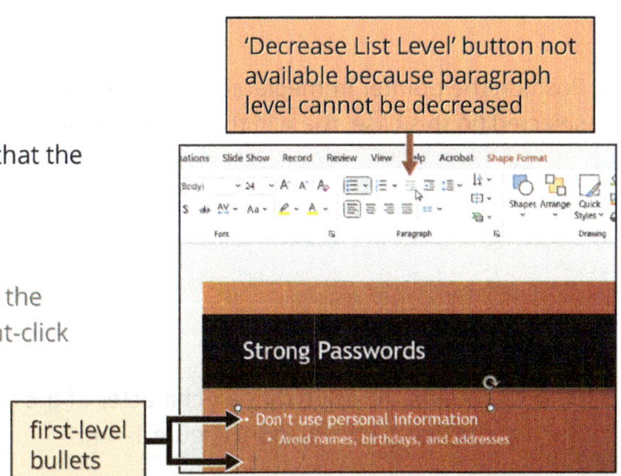

Figure 1-41

Other Ways

1. Press TAB to increase list level; press SHIFT+TAB to decrease list level

To Type the Remaining Text

The following steps complete the text for Slide 2.

1. Type **Use letters, numbers, and simbols** and then press ENTER. **Note: In this step, the word, symbols, has been misspelled intentionally as simbols to illustrate the use of PowerPoint's spell check feature.** Your slides may contain different misspelled words, depending upon the accuracy of your typing.
2. Click the 'Increase List Level' button (Home tab | Paragraph group) to demote the paragraph to the second level.
3. Type **Mix uppercase and lowercase letters** and then press ENTER to add a new paragraph at the same level as the previous paragraph.
4. Click the 'Increase List Level' button (Home tab | Paragraph group) to demote the paragraph to the third level.
5. Type **Randomize sequences** but do not press ENTER (Figure 1–42).

BTW
Selecting Nonadjacent Text
In PowerPoint, you can use keyboard keys to select letters, numbers, or special characters not next to each other. This feature is helpful when you are applying the same formatting to multiple words. To select nonadjacent text, select the first item, such as a word or paragraph, and then press and hold down CTRL. While holding down CTRL, select additional items.

Q&A I pressed ENTER in error, and now a new bullet appears after the last entry on this slide. How can I remove this extra bullet?

Press BACKSPACE twice.

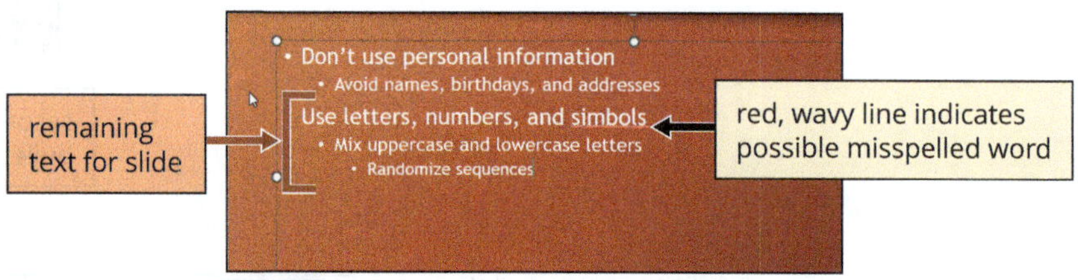

Figure 1–42

To Select a Group of Words

PowerPoint designers use many techniques to emphasize words and characters on a slide. To highlight the availability of regular examinations, you want to bold and increase the font size of the words, personal information, in the body text. The following steps select two words. **Why?** You could perform these actions separately, but it is more efficient to select the words and then change the font attributes.

1

- Position the pointer immediately to the left of the first character of the text to be selected (in this case, the p in the word, personal) (Figure 1–43).

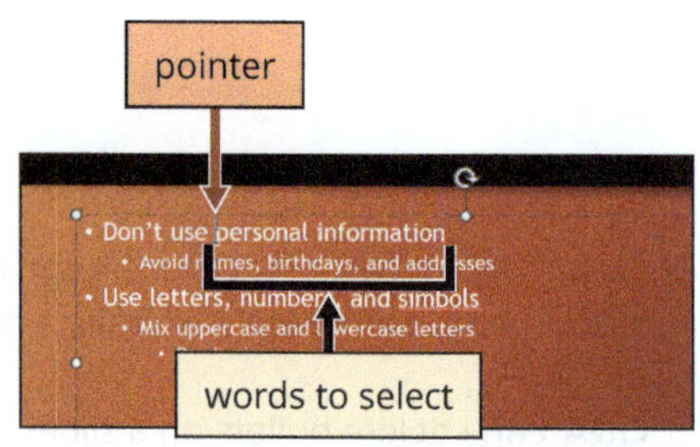

Figure 1–43

2

- Drag the pointer through the last character of the text to be selected (in this case, the n in the word, information) (Figure 1–44).

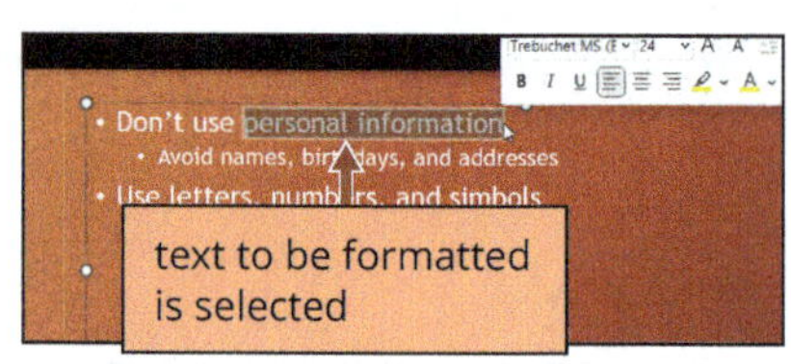

Figure 1–44

Other Ways

1. Press CTRL+SHIFT+RIGHT ARROW repeatedly until desired words are selected

To Bold Text

Why? To add more emphasis to the fact that a person's private details should be avoided, you want to bold the words, personal information. **Bold** characters display somewhat thicker and darker than those that display in a regular font style. Clicking the Bold button on the Mini toolbar is an efficient method of bolding text. The following step bolds this text.

1

- With the words, personal information, selected, click the Bold button on the Mini toolbar to bold the two words (Figure 1–45).

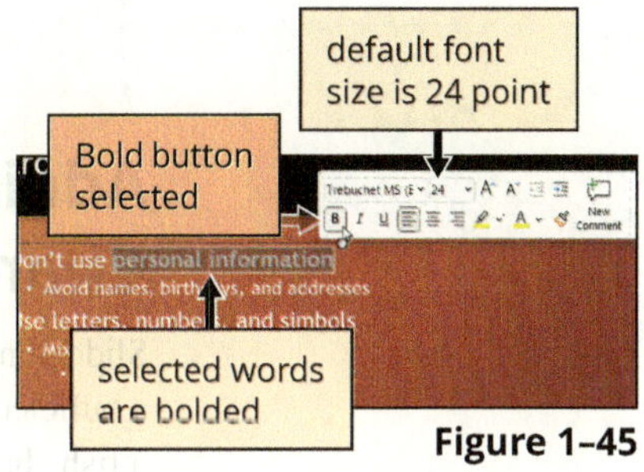

Figure 1–45

Other Ways

1. Right-click selected text, click Font on shortcut menu, click Font tab (Font dialog box), click Bold in Font style list, click OK
2. Select text, click Bold button (Home tab | Font group)
3. Click Font dialog box launcher (Home tab | Font group), click Font tab (Font dialog box), click Bold in Font style list, click OK
4. Select text, press CTRL+B

To Increase Font Size

The following steps increase the font size from 24 to 28 point. **Why?** To add emphasis, you increase the font size for the words, personal information.

1 With the words, personal information, still selected, click the 'Increase Font Size' button on the Mini toolbar once (Figure 1–46).

2 Click outside the selected area to deselect the two words.

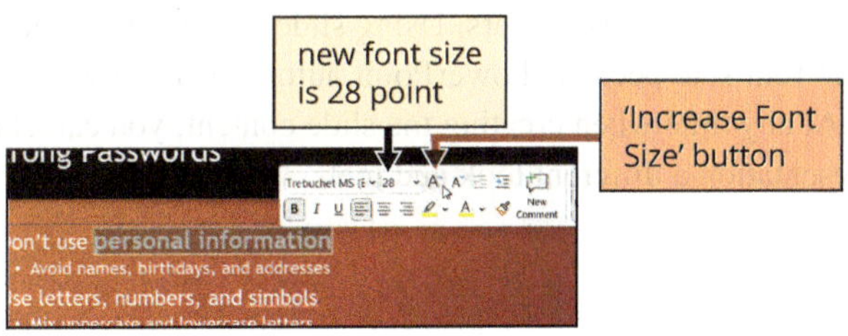

Figure 1–46

To Underline Text

Why? Underlined characters draw the audience's attention to that area of the slide and emphasize important information. Clicking the Underline button on the Mini toolbar is an efficient method of underlining text. To add more emphasis to the fact that the password characters should be arbitrary, you want to underline the word, Randomize. The following steps underline this text.

1

- Select the word, Randomize, on the slide.
- Click the Underline button on the Mini toolbar to underline the word (Figure 1–47).

2

- Click outside the selected area to deselect the word.

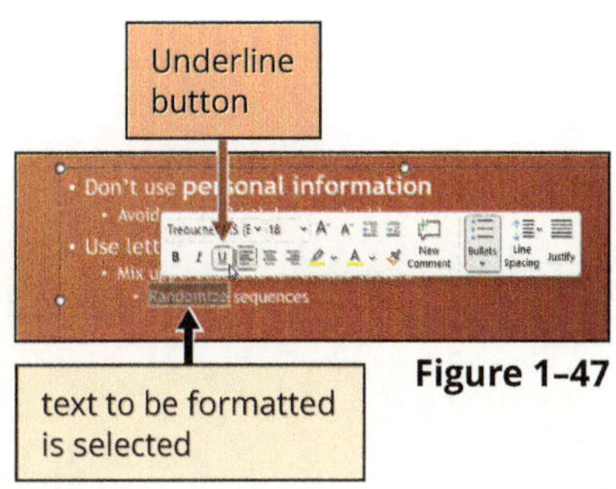

Figure 1–47

Other Ways

1. Right-click selected text, click Font on shortcut menu, click Font tab (Font dialog box), click Underline style arrow, click Single line in Underline style list, click OK
2. Select text, click Underline button (Home tab | Font group)
3. Click Font dialog box launcher (Home tab | Font group), click Font tab (Font dialog box), click Underline style arrow, click Single line in Underline style list, click OK
4. Select text, press CTRL+U

Adding Slides, Changing Slide Layouts, and Changing the Theme

Slide 3 in Figure 1–1c contains a picture of a monitor with several sticky notes and does not contain a bulleted list. Slide 4 in Figure 1–1d contains two pictures: a keyboard with one key selected and a fish shape caught in a net. When you add a new slide, PowerPoint applies the Title and Content layout. This layout and the Title Slide layout for Slide 1 are the default styles. A **layout** specifies the arrangement of placeholders on a slide. These placeholders are arranged in various configurations and can contain text, such as the slide title or a bulleted list, or they can contain content, such as SmartArt graphics, pictures, charts, tables, and shapes. The placement of the text in relationship to the content depends on the slide layout. You can specify a particular slide layout when you add a new slide to a presentation or after you have created the slide.

Using the **layout gallery**, you can choose a slide layout. The nine layouts in this gallery have a variety of placeholders to define text and content positioning and formatting. Three layouts are for text: Title Slide, Section Header, and Title Only. Five are for text and content: Title and Content, Two Content, Comparison, Content with Caption, and Picture with Caption. The Blank layout has no placeholders. If none of these standard layouts meets your design needs, you can create a **custom layout**. A custom layout specifies the number, size, and location of placeholders, background content, and optional slide and placeholder-level properties.

When you change the layout of a slide, PowerPoint retains the text and objects and repositions them into the appropriate placeholders. Using slide layouts eliminates the need to resize objects and change the font size because PowerPoint automatically sizes the objects and text to fit the placeholders. At any time when creating the slide content, you can change the theme and variant to give the presentation a different look and feel.

To Add a New Slide and Enter a Slide Title and Headings

The text on Slide 3 in Figure 1–1c consists of a title and two headings. The appropriate layout for this slide is named Comparison. **Why?** The Comparison layout has two headings and two text placeholders adjacent to each other, so an audience member easily can compare and contrast the items shown side by side. The following steps add Slide 3 to the presentation with the Comparison layout and then enter the title and heading text for this slide.

1

- Click the New Slide arrow in the Slides group to display the Berlin layout gallery (Figure 1–48).

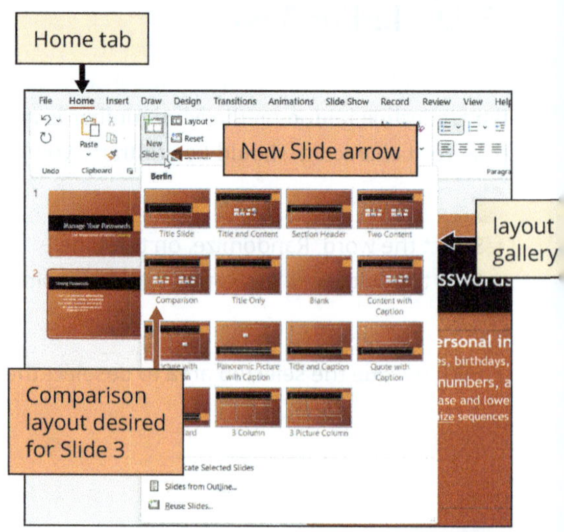

Figure 1–48

2

- Click Comparison to add Slide 3 and apply that layout (Figure 1–49).

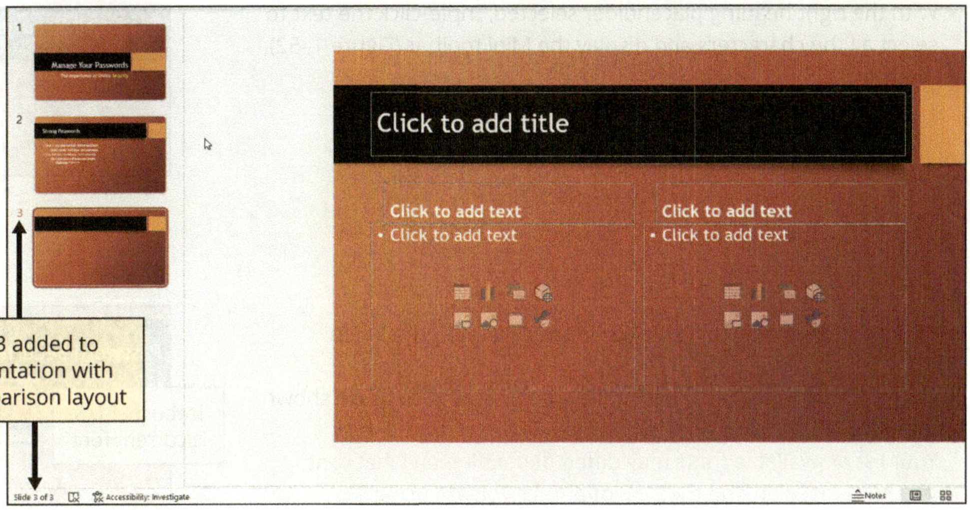

Figure 1–49

3

- Type **Comon Password Security Threats** in the title text placeholder. **Note: In this step, the word, Common, has been misspelled intentionally as Comon to illustrate the use of PowerPoint's spell check feature.** Your slides may contain different misspelled words, depending upon the accuracy of your typing.

Figure 1–50

- Click the left heading placeholder with the label, 'Click to add text', to select this placeholder (Figure 1–50).

4

- Type **Keylogging Software** in the placeholder.
- Select the right heading placeholder and then type **Phishing Schemes** but do not press ENTER (Figure 1–51).

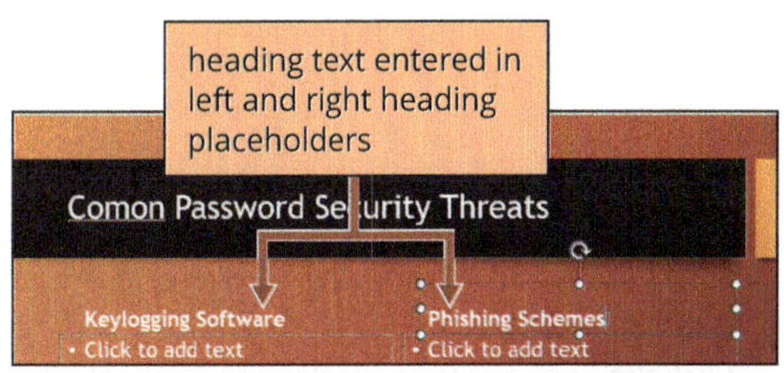

Figure 1–51

To Change the Font

The default theme font is Trebuchet MS, which is shown in the Font box. To draw more attention to two common cybercriminal activities, you want to change the font to Georgia. **Why?** Georgia is a serif typeface, meaning the ends of some of the letters are adorned with small decorations, called serifs. These adornments slow down the viewer's reading speed, which might help them retain the information they saw. To change the font, you must select the text you want to format. Earlier in this module you selected a paragraph and then formatted the characters, and you follow the same procedure to change the font. The following steps change the text font in the two Slide 3 heading placeholders.

1

- With the right heading placeholder selected, triple-click the text to select all the characters and display the Mini toolbar (Figure 1–52).

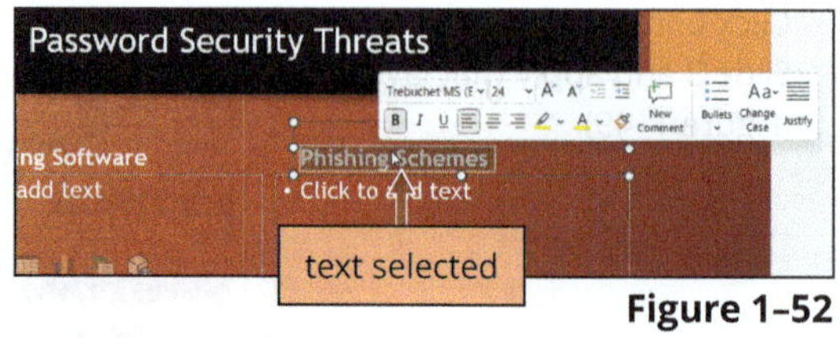

Figure 1–52

2

- Click the Font arrow to display the Font gallery (Figure 1–53).

Q&A Will the fonts in my Font gallery be the same as those shown in Figure 1–53?
Your list of available fonts may differ, depending on what fonts you have installed and the type of printer you are using.

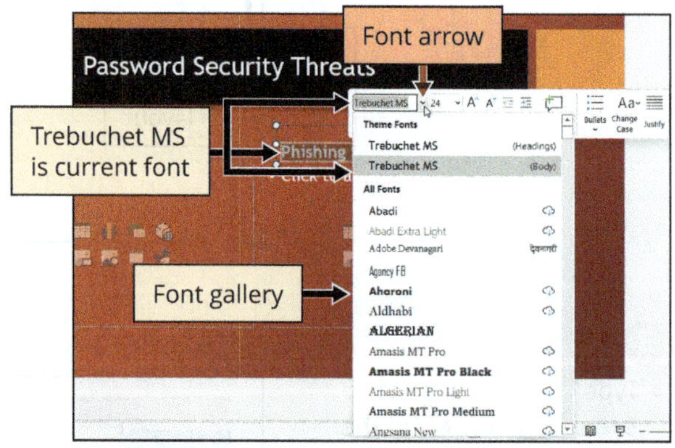

Figure 1–53

3

- Scroll through the Font gallery and then point to Georgia (or a similar font) to display a live preview of the title text in the Georgia font (Figure 1–54).
- **Experiment:** Point to various fonts in the Font gallery and watch the subtitle text font change in the slide.
- Click Georgia (or a similar font) to change the font of the selected text to Georgia.

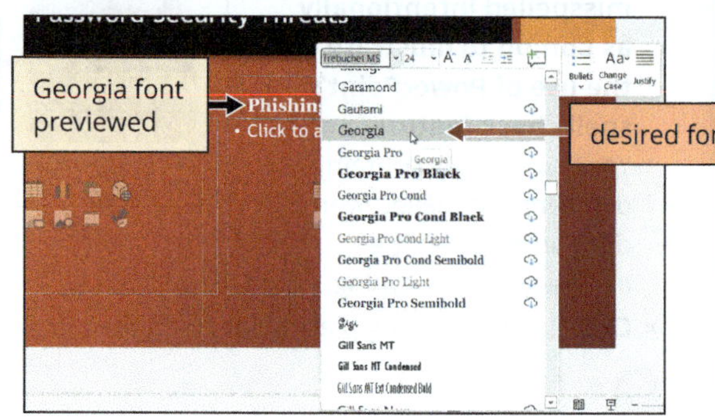

Figure 1–54

4

- Select the words, Keylogging Software, in the left placeholder to display the Mini toolbar.
- Click the Font arrow to display the Font gallery. Note that Georgia is now displayed under Recently Used Fonts.
- Click Georgia (or a similar font) to change the font of the selected text to Georgia (Figure 1–55).

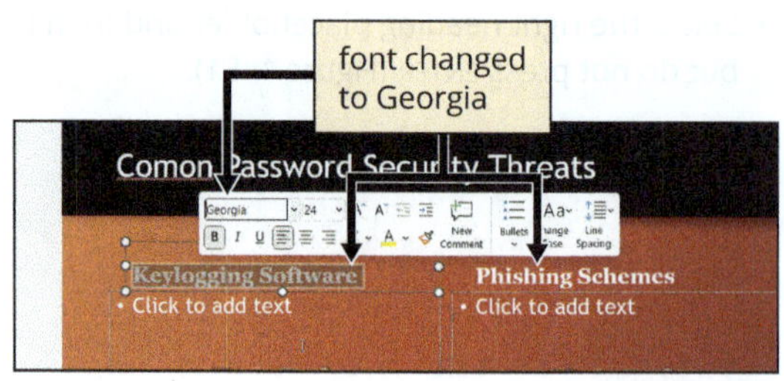

Figure 1–55

Other Ways

1. Click Font arrow (Home tab | Font group), click desired font in Font gallery
2. Right-click selected text, click Font on shortcut menu (Font dialog box), click Font tab, select desired font in Font list, click OK
3. Click Font dialog box launcher (Home tab | Font group), click Font tab (Font dialog box), select desired font in Font list, click OK
4. Press CTRL+SHIFT+F, click Font tab (Font dialog box), select desired font in the Font list, click OK
5. Right-click selected text, click Font arrow on Mini toolbar, select desired font

To Add a Slide with the Title Only Layout

The following steps add Slide 4 to the presentation with the Title Only slide layout style. **Why?** The only text on the slide is the title, and the majority of the slide content is the picture.

1

- If necessary, click Home on the ribbon to display the Home tab.
- Click the New Slide arrow (Home tab | Slides group) to display the Berlin layout gallery (Figure 1-56).

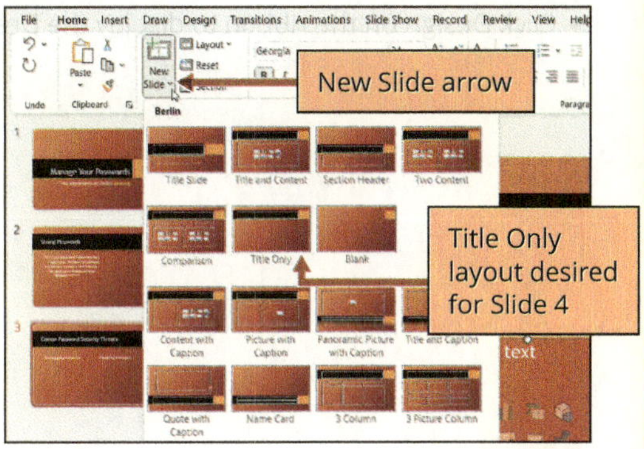

Figure 1-56

2

- Click Title Only to add a new slide and apply that layout to Slide 4 (Figure 1-57).

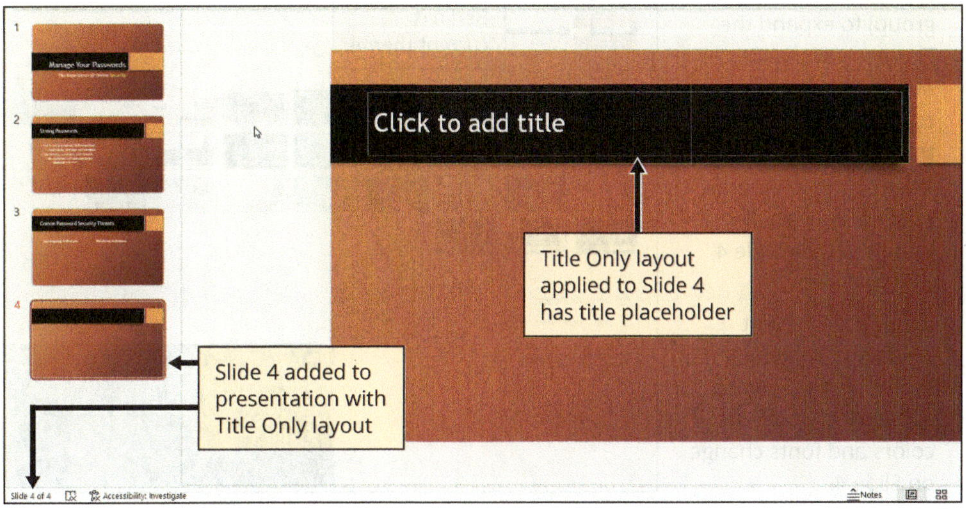

Figure 1-57

To Enter a Slide Title

The only text on Slide 4 is the title. The following step enters the title text for this slide. **Why?** Most slides include a title to identify the main topic of the slide.

1 Type **Different Passwords for Every Account** as the title text but do not press ENTER (Figure 1-58).

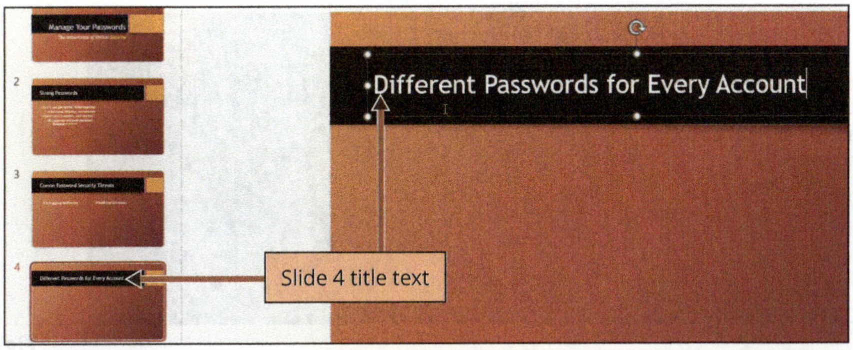

Figure 1-58

To Change the Theme

The Berlin theme applied to the presentation is simple and does not have many design elements. The following steps change the theme for the presentation. **Why?** You want a subtle design that calls attention to the important guidelines provided on the slides.

1

- Click Design on the ribbon to display the Design tab (Figure 1–59).

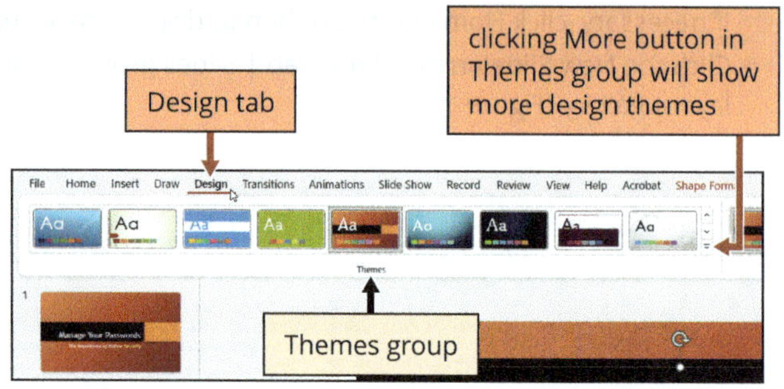

Figure 1–59

2

- Click the More button (Design tab | Themes group) to expand the Themes gallery. If necessary, scroll down to view the Ion theme thumbnail.
- Point to the Ion theme to see a preview of that theme on Slide 4 (Figure 1–60).
- **Experiment:** Point to various document themes in the Themes gallery and watch the colors and fonts change on Slide 4.

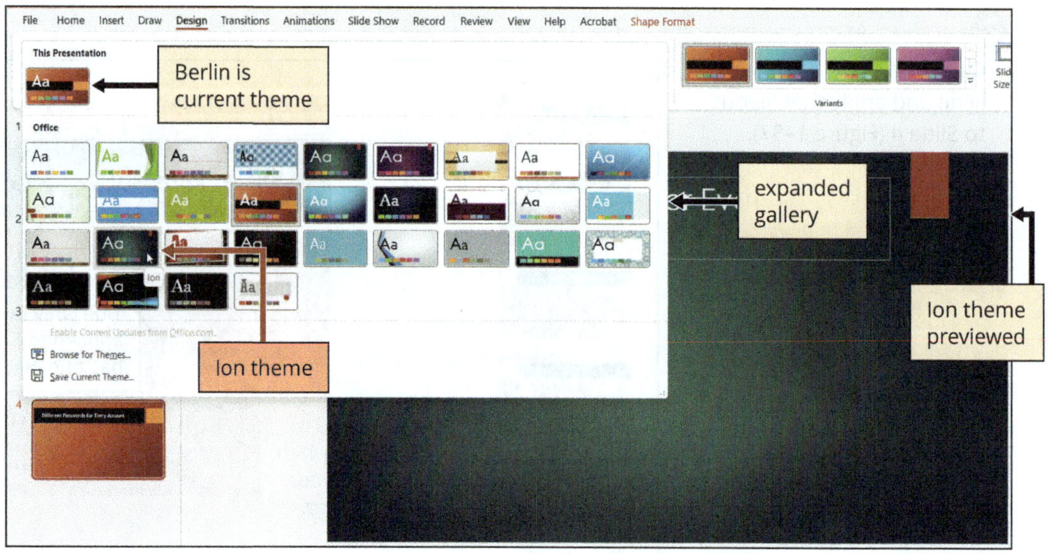

Figure 1–60

3

- Click the Ion theme to apply this theme to all four slides (Figure 1–61).
- If the Design Ideas pane is displayed, close it.

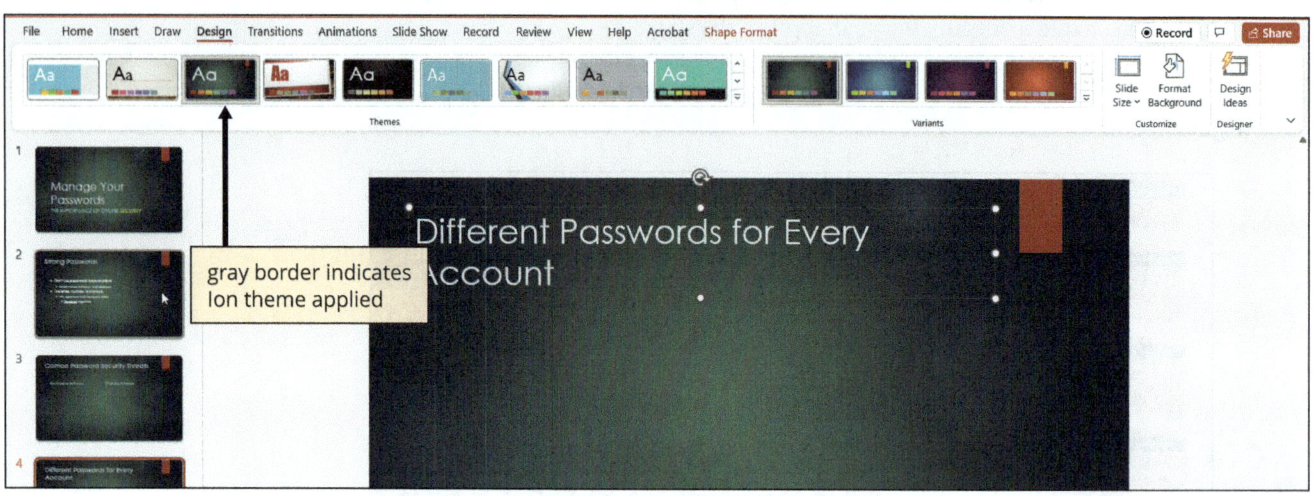

Figure 1–61

PowerPoint Views

The PowerPoint window display varies depending on the view. A **view** is the mode in which the presentation appears on the screen. You will use some views when you are developing slides and others when you are delivering your presentation. When creating a presentation, you most likely will use Normal, Slide Sorter, Notes Pane, and Outline views. When presenting your slides to an audience, you most likely will use Slide Sorter, Presenter, and Reading views.

The default view is **Normal view**, which is composed of three areas that allow you to work on various aspects of a presentation simultaneously. The large area in the middle, called the **Slide pane**, displays the slide you currently are developing and allows you to enter text, tables, charts, graphics, pictures, video, and other elements. As you create the slides, miniature views of the individual slides, called thumbnails, are displayed in the **Slides tab** on the left of the screen. You can rearrange the thumbnails in this pane. The **Notes pane**, by default, is hidden at the bottom of the window. If you want to type notes to yourself or remarks to share with your audience, you can click the **Notes button** in the status bar to open the Notes pane. After you have created at least two slides, a scroll bar containing scroll arrows and scroll boxes will appear on the right edge of the window.

BTW
Pointer
If you are using a touch screen, the pointer may not appear on the screen as you perform touch gestures. The pointer will reappear when you begin using the mouse.

BTW
Touch Screen
If you are using your finger on a touch screen and are having difficulty completing the steps in this module, consider using a stylus. Many people find it easier to be precise with a stylus than with a finger. In addition, with a stylus you see the pointer. If you still are having trouble completing the steps with a stylus, try using a mouse.

To Move to Another Slide in Normal View

Why? When creating or editing a presentation in Normal view (the view you are currently using), you often want to display a slide other than the current one. Before continuing with developing this project, you want to display the title slide. You can click the desired slide in the Slides tab or drag the scroll box on the vertical scroll bar; if you are using a touch screen, you can tap the desired slide in the Slides tab. When you drag the scroll box, the **slide indicator** shows the number and title of the slide you are about to display. Releasing shows the slide. The following steps move from Slide 4 to Slide 1 using the scroll box in the Slide pane.

1

- With Slide 4 displayed, position the pointer on the scroll box.
- Press and hold down the mouse button so that Slide: 4 of 4 Different Passwords for Each Acc... appears in the slide indicator (Figure 1–62).

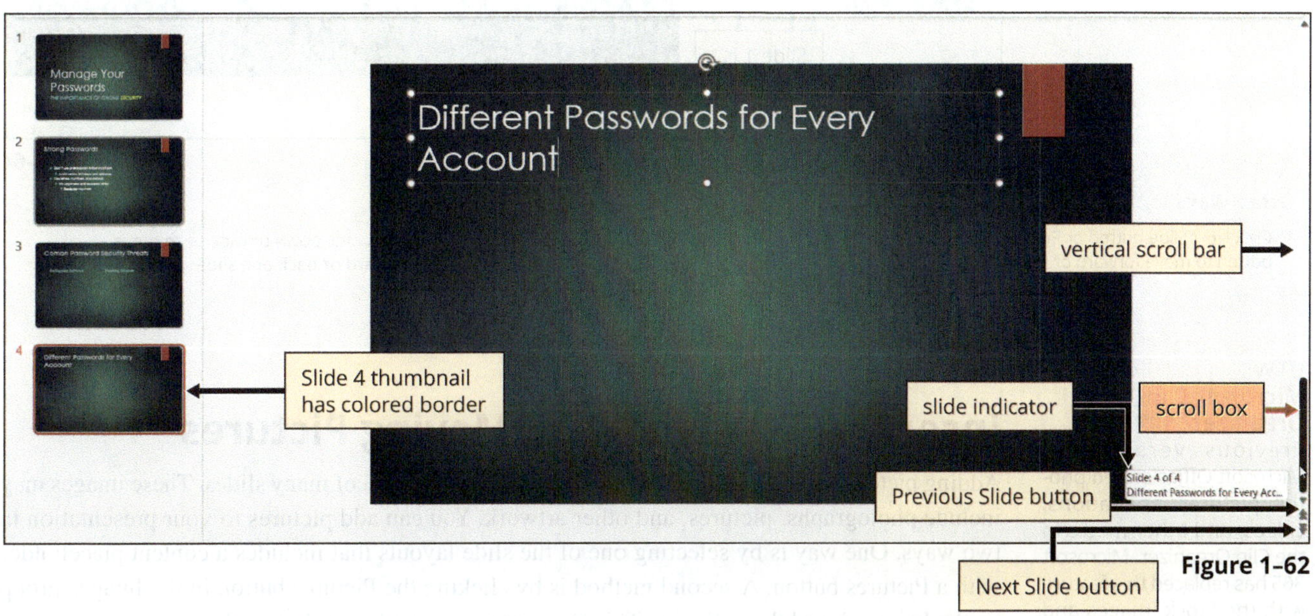

Figure 1–62

2

- Drag the scroll box up the vertical scroll bar until Slide: 1 of 4 Manage Your Passwords appears in the slide indicator (Figure 1-63).

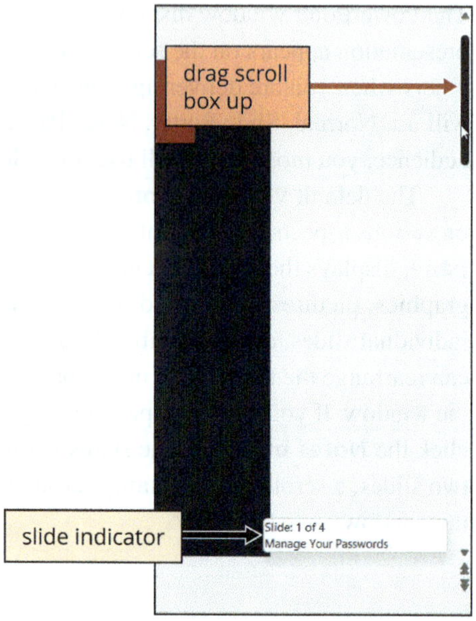

Figure 1-63

3

- Release so that Slide 1 appears in the Slide pane and the Slide 1 thumbnail has a colored border in the Slides tab (Figure 1-64).

Figure 1-64

Other Ways

1. Click Next Slide button or Previous Slide button to move forward or back one slide
2. Click slide in Slides tab
3. Press PAGE DOWN or PAGE UP to move forward or back one slide

BTW
Microsoft Clip Organizer
Previous versions of Microsoft Office stored photos, pictures, animations, videos, and other media in the Clip Organizer. Microsoft 365 has replaced this feature with the Stock Images and Online Pictures options in the Insert Picture From gallery. Both options provide windows where you can search for and insert files.

Inserting, Resizing, and Moving Pictures

Adding pictures can help increase the visual and audio appeal of many slides. These images may include photographs, pictures, and other artwork. You can add pictures to your presentation in two ways. One way is by selecting one of the slide layouts that includes a content placeholder with a Pictures button. A second method is by clicking the Pictures button in the Images group on the Insert tab and then clicking This Device to open the Insert Picture dialog box. The **Insert Picture dialog box** allows you to search for picture files that are stored on your computer or a storage device. Contact your instructor if you need the pictures used in the following steps.

Consider This

How can you design a title slide that holds your audience's attention?

Develop a slide that reflects the content of your presentation but does so in a thought-provoking way. A title, at the very least, should prepare your audience for the material they are about to see and hear. Look for ways to focus attention on your theme and the method in which you plan to present this theme. A unique photograph or graphic can help generate interest. You may decide to introduce your topic with a startling fact, a rhetorical question, or a quotation. The device you choose depends upon your audience, the occasion, and the presentation's purpose.

To Insert a Picture into a Slide without a Content Placeholder

Slide 1 uses the Title Slide layout, which has two placeholders for text but none for graphical content. If the layout does not have a content placeholder, an inserted image generally displays in the center of the slide. You want to place a graphic on Slide 1. **Why?** It is likely that your viewers will see an image on this slide before they read any text, so you want to include a picture to create interest in the presentation and introduce your audience to the topic. For this presentation, you will insert a partial keyboard with the word, security, printed on one key. Later in this module, you will resize and position the picture in an appropriate location. The following steps add a picture to Slide 1.

Note: To complete this assignment, you will be required to use the Data Files. Please contact your instructor for information about accessing the Data Files.

1

- With Slide 1 displayed, click Insert on the ribbon to display the Insert tab (Figure 1–65).

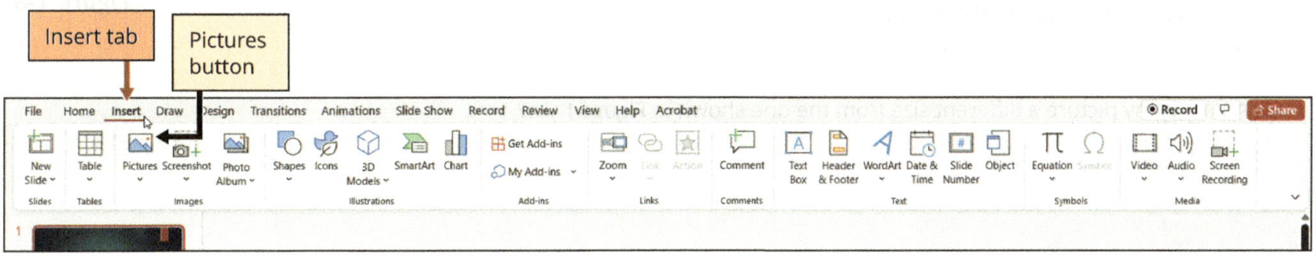

Figure 1–65

2

- Click the Pictures button (Insert tab | Images group) to display the Insert Picture From gallery.
- Click This Device in the Insert Picture From gallery to display the Insert Picture dialog box.

Q&A What should I do if no pictures are displayed when I click the Pictures button?
You may need to click the Online Pictures button instead of the Pictures button.

- Navigate to the PowerPoint1 folder. If necessary, scroll down and then click the picture called Support_PPT_1_Security.png, which is located in the Data Files (Figure 1–66).

Q&A Why do I see only a list of file names and not thumbnails of the pictures in my folder?
Your view is different from the view shown in Figure 1–66.

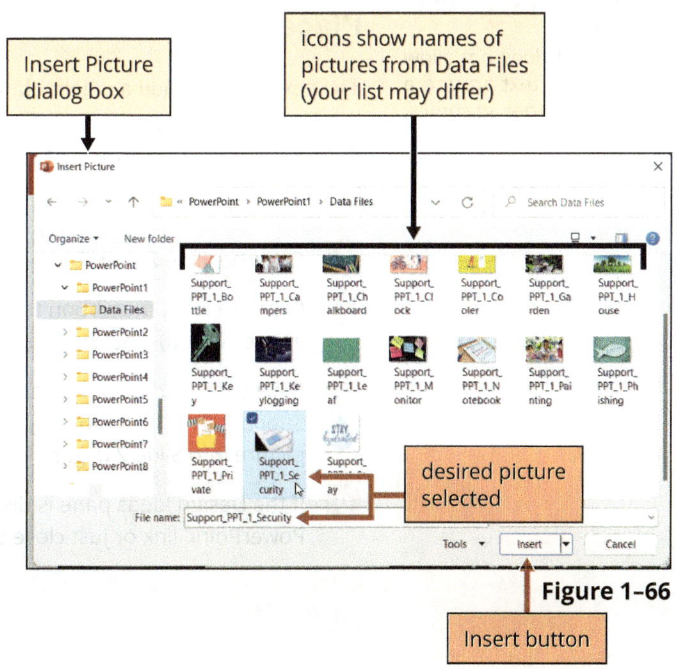

Figure 1–66

3

- Click the Insert button (Insert Picture dialog box) to insert the picture into Slide 1 (Figure 1–67).

Q&A Can I double-click the picture or file name instead of selecting it and clicking the Insert button?
Yes. Either method inserts the picture.

Why is this picture displayed in this location on the slide?
The slide layout does not have a content placeholder, so PowerPoint inserts the file in an area of the slide. You will move and resize the picture later in this module.

What is the Alt Text shown at the bottom of the picture?
Alternative text (Alt text) descriptions help visually impaired people who use screen readers understand the content of pictures.

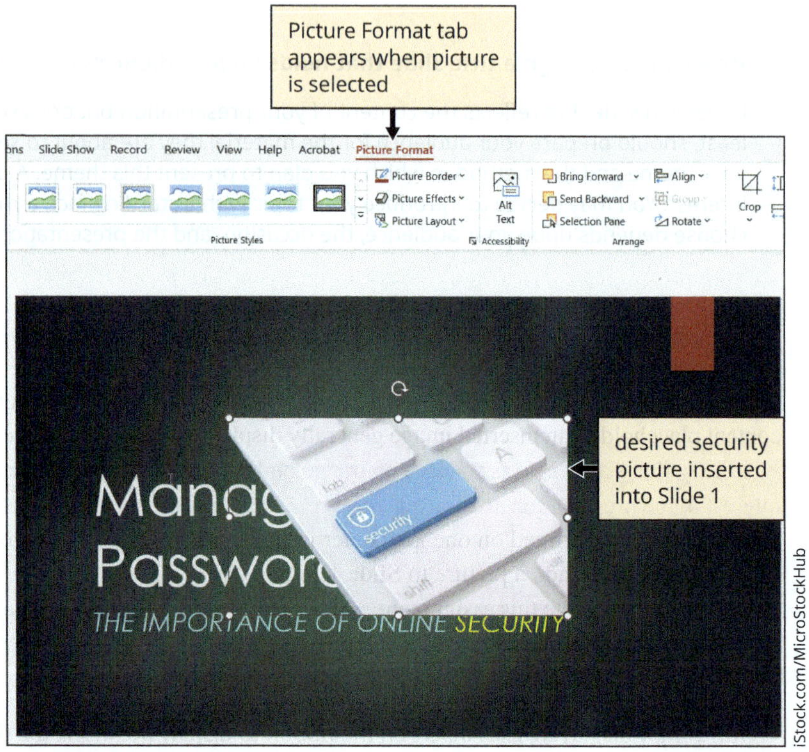

Figure 1–67

4

- If the Design Ideas pane is displayed, click the 'Stop suggesting ideas until I restart PowerPoint' link or just close the pane.

Q&A Why is my picture a different size from the one shown in Figure 1–1b?
The clip was inserted into the slide and not into a content placeholder. You will resize the picture later in this module.

BTW
Wrapping Text around a Photo
PowerPoint does not allow you to wrap text around a picture or other graphics, such as tables, shapes, and charts. This feature, however, is available in Word.

To Insert another Picture into a Slide without a Content Placeholder

The next step is to add a notebook with hand-written passwords to Slide 2. This slide has a bulleted list in the text placeholder, so the icon group does not display in the center of the placeholder. Later in this module, you will resize this inserted picture. The following steps add one picture to Slide 2.

1. Click the Slide 2 thumbnail in the Slides tab to display Slide 2.
2. Click Insert on the ribbon to display the Insert tab, click the Pictures button (Insert tab | Images group), and then click This Device to display the Insert Picture dialog box.
3. If necessary, scroll down the list of files and then open the picture called Support_PPT_1_Notebook.jpg, which is located in the Data Files, to insert the picture into Slide 2 (Figure 1–68).
4. If the Design Ideas pane is displayed, click the 'Stop suggesting ideas until I restart PowerPoint' link or just close the pane.

Figure 1-68

To Insert Another Picture into a Slide without a Content Placeholder

Next, you will add a picture to Slide 4. Later in this module, you will resize this picture. The following steps add a picture to Slide 4.

1. Click the Slide 4 thumbnail in the Slides tab.
2. Display the Insert tab, click the Pictures button, click This Device, and then insert the Support_PPT_1_Monitor.jpg file into Slide 4 (Figure 1-69).
3. If the Design Ideas pane is displayed, click the 'Stop suggesting ideas until I restart PowerPoint' link or just close the pane.

Figure 1-69

To Insert a Picture into a Content Placeholder

Slide 3 uses the Comparison layout, which has a content placeholder below each of the two headings. You desire to insert pictures into both content placeholders. **Why?** You want to display two images depicting two common cybercriminal activities: keylogging and phishing. The following steps insert a keyboard with one key selected into the left content placeholder and a fish shape caught in a net into the right content placeholder on Slide 3.

1

- Click the Slide 3 thumbnail in the Slides tab to display Slide 3 (Figure 1–70).

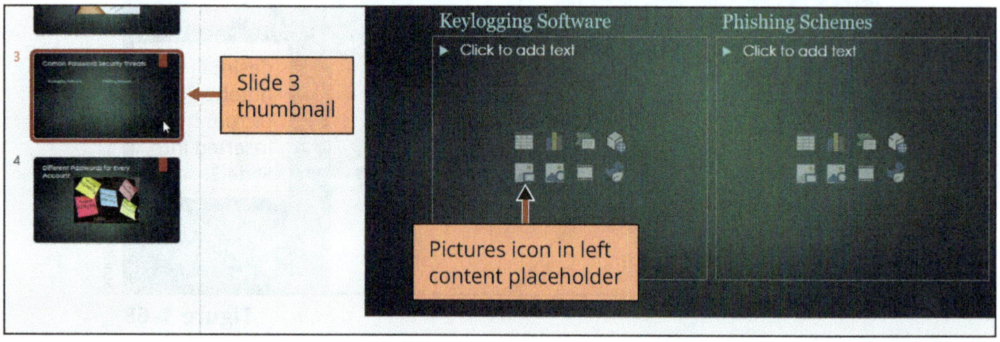

Figure 1–70

2

- Click the Pictures icon in the left content placeholder to select that placeholder and to open the Insert Picture dialog box.
- If necessary, scroll down the list of files, click Support_PPT_1_Keylogging.jpg to select the file, and then double-click to insert the picture into the left content placeholder (Figure 1–71).

Q&A Do I need to select the file name before double-clicking to insert the picture?
No. You just can double-click the file name.

Figure 1–71

3

- Click the Pictures icon in the right content placeholder to select that placeholder and to open the Insert Picture dialog box.
- If necessary, scroll down the list to display the Support_PPT_1_Phishing.jpg file name and then insert this picture into the right content placeholder (Figure 1–72).

Figure 1–72

Resizing Photos and Illustrations

Sometimes it is necessary to change the size of pictures. **Resizing** includes enlarging or reducing the size of a graphic. You can resize these images using a variety of techniques. One method involves changing the size of a picture by specifying exact dimensions in a dialog box or in the Height and Width boxes in the Size group on the Picture Format tab. Another method involves sliding or dragging one of the graphic's sizing handles to the desired location. A selected graphic appears surrounded by a **selection rectangle** which has small circles, called **sizing handles** or move handles, at each corner and middle location.

To Proportionally Resize Pictures

Why? On Slides 1, 2, and 4, the picture sizes are too small to display aesthetically on the slides. At times it is important to maintain the proportions of a picture, such as when a person is featured prominently. To change the size of a picture and keep the width and height in proportion to each other, drag the corner sizing handles to view how the image will look on the slide. Using these corner handles maintains the graphic's original proportions. If, however, the proportions do not need to be maintained precisely, as with the passwords picture you inserted in Slide 2, you can drag the side sizing handles to alter the proportions so that the graphic's height and width become larger or smaller. The following steps proportionally increase the size of the Slide 1 picture using a corner sizing handle.

1

- Click the Slide 1 thumbnail in the Slides tab to display Slide 1.
- Click the security picture to select it and display the selection rectangle.
- Point to the upper-right corner sizing handle on the picture so that the pointer changes to a two-headed arrow (Figure 1–73).

Q&A I am using a touch screen and do not see a two-headed arrow when I press and hold the lower-right sizing handle. Why?
Touch screens may not display pointers; you can just press and slide sizing handles to resize.

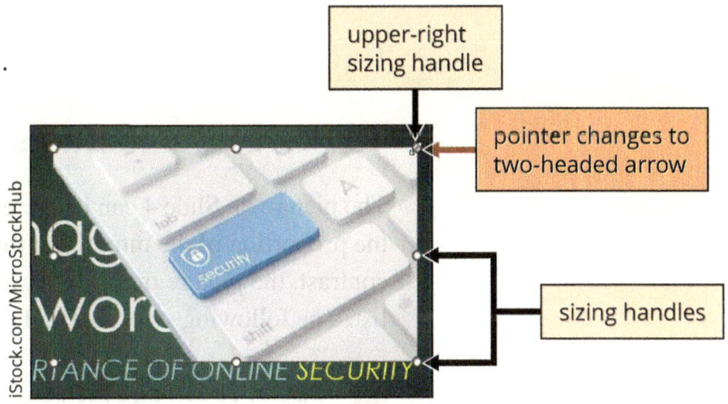

Figure 1–73

2

- Drag the upper-right sizing handle diagonally toward the upper-right corner of the slide until it is positioned approximately as shown in Figure 1–74.

Q&A What if the picture is not the same size as the one shown in Figure 1–74?
Repeat Steps 1 and 2.

Can I drag any corner sizing handle diagonally outward toward the opposite corner to resize the picture?
Yes.

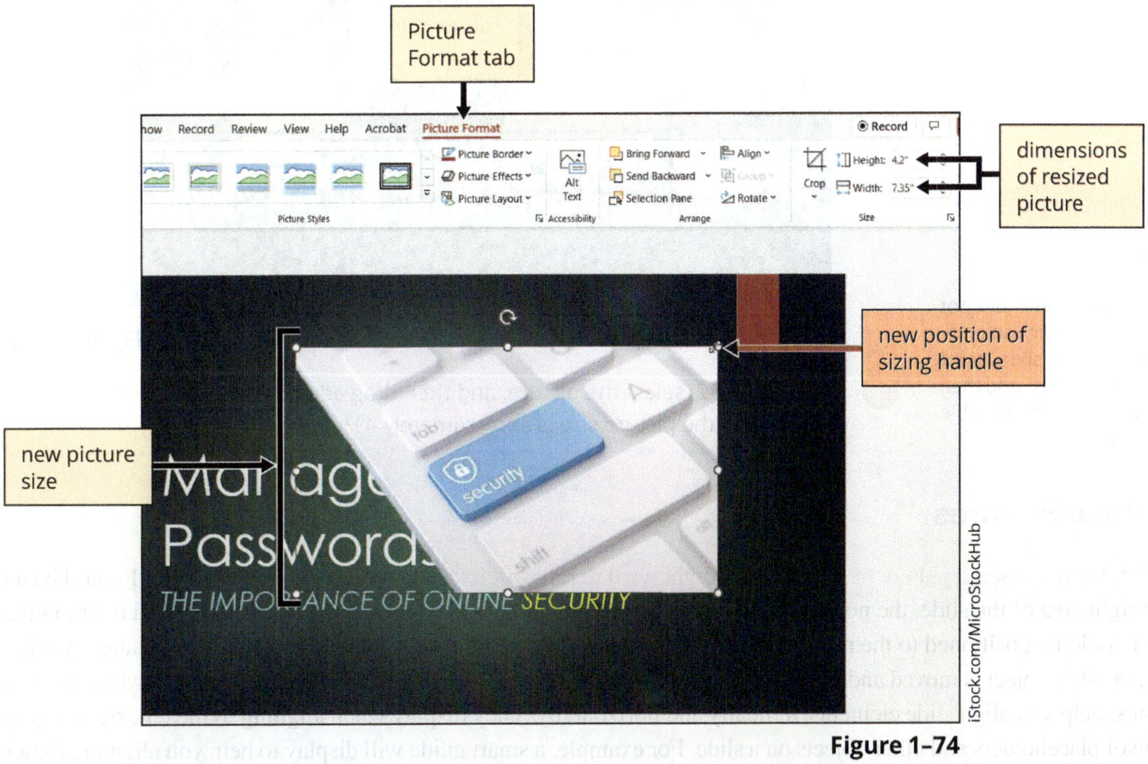

Figure 1–74

3

- Release to resize the picture.
- View the Height and Width boxes (Picture Format tab | Size group) to verify that the picture size is approximately 4.2" x 7.35".

Q&A What if I want to return the picture to its original size and start again?
With the picture selected, click the Reset Picture arrow (Picture Format tab | Adjust group) and then click Reset Picture & Size in the Reset Picture gallery.

Can I resize the picture to exact measurements?
Yes. Click the Height and Width arrows (Picture Format tab | Size group) or manually enter the dimensions to adjust the picture size.

To Resize the Pictures on Slides 4 and 2

The picture on Slide 4 can be increased to fit much of the space on the slide. You want to maintain the proportion of the monitor in this picture, so you will drag one of the corner sizing handles. In contrast, the picture on Slide 2 can be decreased to fill the space on the right side of the bulleted list. The following steps resize these pictures using a corner sizing handle.

1 Display Slide 4 and then click the picture to select it.

2 Drag any corner sizing handle on the picture diagonally outward until the picture is resized approximately as shown in Figure 1–75. The picture size should be approximately 5.6" x 8.4".

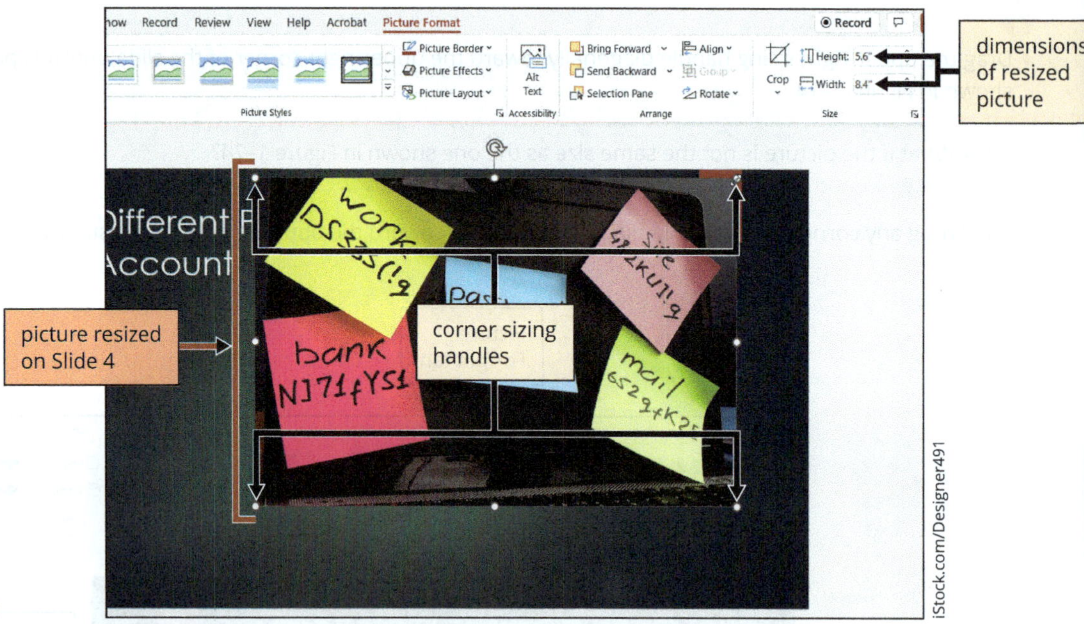

Figure 1–75

3 Display Slide 2, select the picture, and then drag any sizing handle on the picture diagonally inward until the picture size is approximately 4" x 6".

BTW
Displaying Smart Guides
If your smart guides are not displaying, right-click an empty space on your slide, point to 'Grid and Guides', and then click Smart Guides to enable this option.

To Move Pictures

Why? After you insert a picture on a slide, you might want to reposition it. The security picture on Slide 1 could be moved to the upper-right area of the slide, the notebook picture on Slide 2 could be moved beside the bulleted list, and the monitor picture on Slide 4 could be positioned to the right of the word, Account. PowerPoint displays **smart guides** automatically when a picture, shape, or other object is moved and is close to lining up with another slide element. These layout guides, which display as dashed red lines, help you align slide elements vertically and horizontally. They display when aligning to the left, right, top, bottom, and middle of placeholders and other objects on a slide. For example, a smart guide will display to help you align the right or left edge of a picture in relation to a text placeholder or to another picture. The following steps move the pictures on Slides 4, 2, and 1.

1

- If necessary, click the picture on Slide 4 to select it.
- With the four-headed arrow displayed, drag the picture downward until the vertical smart guide is displayed through the center of the picture and the horizontal smart guide is displayed along the bottom of the slide, as shown in Figure 1–76, and then release.
- If necessary, select the picture and then use the ARROW keys to position it precisely as shown in Figure 1–76.

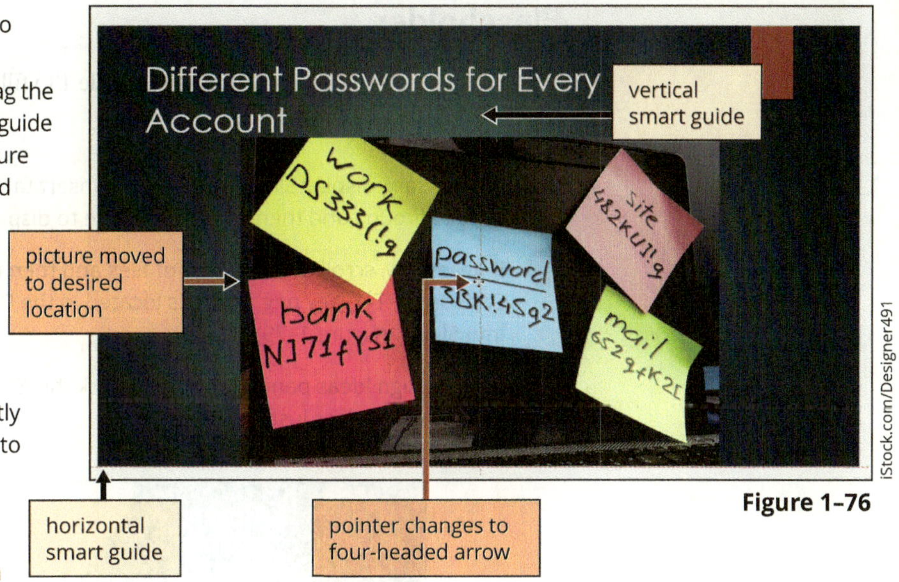

Figure 1–76

Q&A The picture still is not located exactly where I want it to display. What can I do to align the image?

Press CTRL while you press the ARROW keys. This key combination moves the picture in smaller increments than when you press only an ARROW key.

I cannot see the vertical smart guide. What should I do?

Decrease the zoom to less than 100 percent.

2

- Display Slide 2 and then click the picture to select it.
- Drag the picture until the vertical smart guide is displayed on the right side of the picture and the horizontal smart guide is displayed through the center of the picture (Figure 1–77).

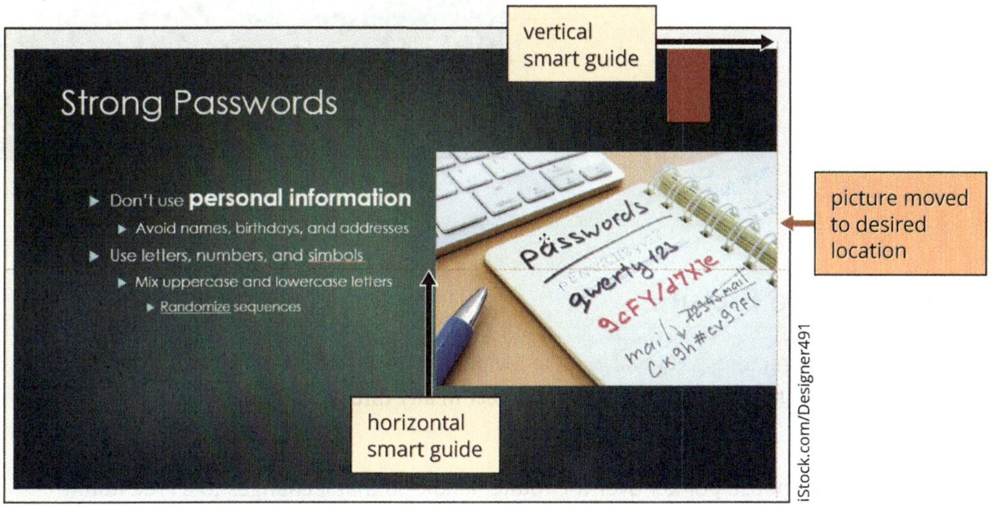

Figure 1–77

3

- Display Slide 1 and then click the picture to select it.
- Drag the picture upward and to the right corner of the slide. The vertical smart guide is displayed along the right edge of the picture and the horizontal smart guide is displayed along the top side of the slide (Figure 1–78).

Figure 1–78

To Insert Another Picture into a Slide without a Content Placeholder

The next step is to add a picture of a key to Slide 1 to fill the space above the title text. The following steps add another picture to Slide 1.

1. If necessary, display Slide 1, display the Insert tab, click the Pictures button (Insert tab | Images group), and then click This Device to display the Insert Picture dialog box.
2. If necessary, scroll down the list of files and then open the picture called Support_PPT_1_Key.png, which is located in the Data Files, to insert the picture into Slide 1 (Figure 1–79).
3. If the Design Ideas pane is displayed, click the 'Stop suggesting ideas until I restart PowerPoint' link or just close the pane.

Figure 1–79

To Rotate a Picture

Why? The key picture is vertical, and you want to turn it so that it is parallel to the title text. Dragging the **rotate handle** above a selected object allows you to rotate an object in any direction. The following steps rotate the picture.

1

- Position the mouse pointer over the rotate handle so that it changes to a Free Rotate pointer (Figure 1–80).

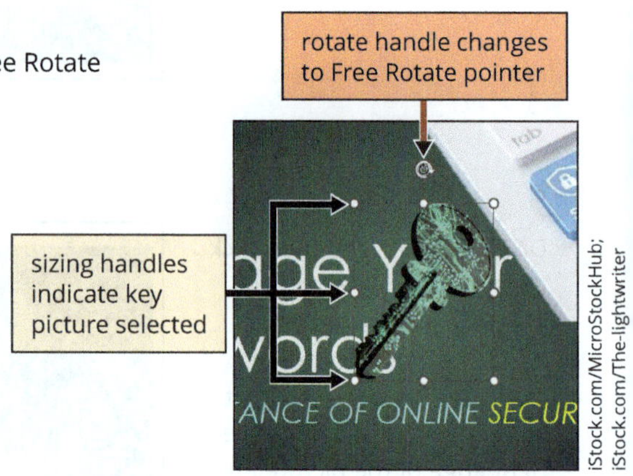

Figure 1–80

2

- Drag the rotate handle counterclockwise approximately 90 degrees so that it is parallel to the title text.
- Move the picture so that the vertical smart guide is displayed through the center of the picture and the horizontal smart guide is displayed in the center of the slide, as shown in Figure 1–81.

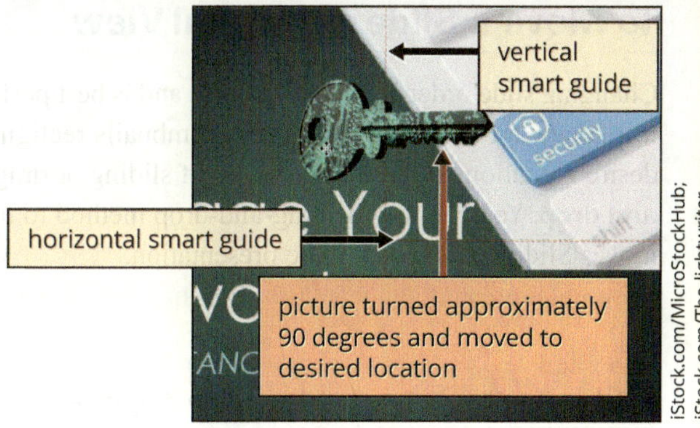

Figure 1–81

To Nonproportionally Resize the Picture on Slide 2

Why? The height of the notebook picture in Slide 2 can be increased to add to the viewers' interest and fill the space at the bottom of the slide. The height can be increased without negatively distorting the original image. You can change the height and width of a picture by dragging the sizing handles on the sides of the image. The following steps resize the height but not the width of the notebook picture using sizing handles along the sides of the image.

1

- Display Slide 2 and then select the notebook picture.
- With the selection rectangle displayed, point to the middle sizing handle on the bottom edge of the picture so that the pointer changes to a two-headed arrow (Figure 1–82).

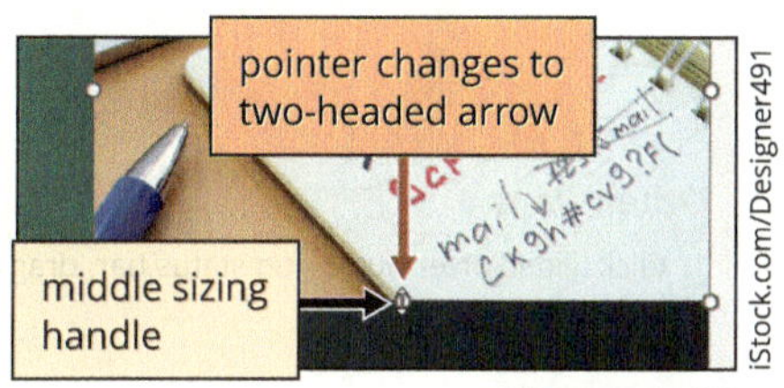

Figure 1–82

2

- Drag the sizing handle downward to the bottom edge of the slide until the horizontal smart guide is displayed and the sizing handle or crosshair is positioned as shown in Figure 1–83. The approximate picture size should be 5.75" x 6".

Q&A What if the picture is not the same size as the one shown in Figure 1–83?
Repeat Steps 1 and 2.

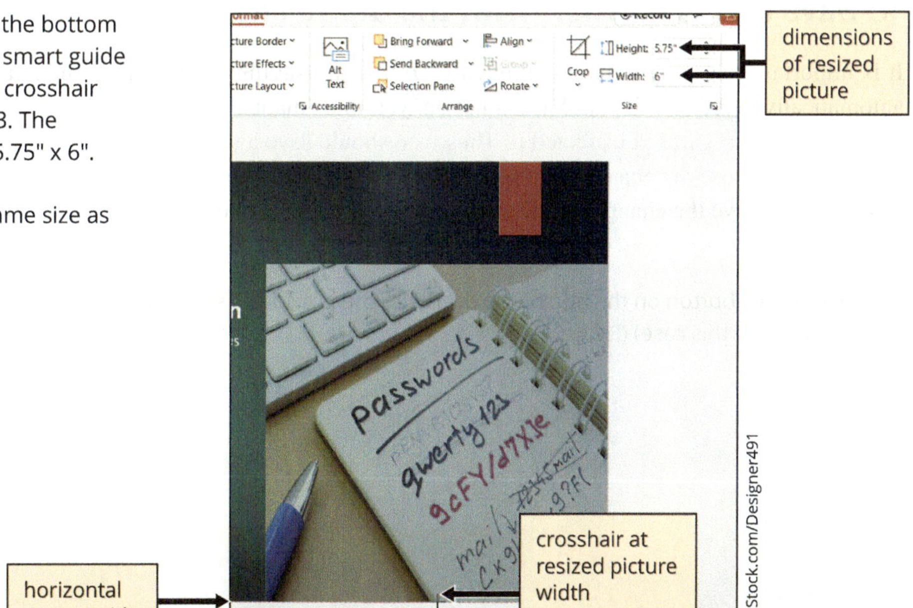

Figure 1–83

3

- Release to resize the picture.
- Click outside the picture to deselect it.

Q&A Can I move the picture in small increments?
Yes. To move or nudge the picture in very small increments, hold down CTRL with the picture selected while pressing the ARROW keys. You cannot perform this action using a touch screen.

To Move a Slide in Normal View

Changing slide order is an easy process and is best performed in the Slides tab. When you click the thumbnail and begin to drag it to a new location, the remaining thumbnails realign to show the new sequence. When you release, the slide drops into the desired location. Hence, this process of sliding or dragging and then dropping the thumbnail in a new location is called **drag and drop**. You can use the drag-and-drop method to move any selected item, including text and graphics. The following step moves Slide 3 to the end of the presentation. **Why?** Audience members often remember the final material they see and hear in a presentation, and you want to emphasize two of the cybersecurity threats that are prone to occur with weak passwords.

1

- Select the Slide 3 thumbnail and then drag it below the last slide in the Slides tab so that it becomes the new Slide 4 (Figure 1-84).

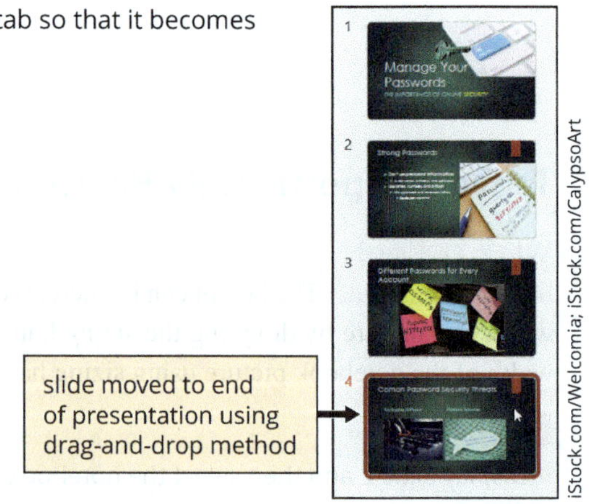

Figure 1-84

Other Ways

1. Click Slide Sorter button on status bar, drag thumbnail to new location
2. Click Slide Sorter button (View tab | Presentation Views group), click slide thumbnail, drag thumbnail to new location

To Save a Presentation with the Same File Name

It is important to save your work frequently. If you are saving to OneDrive and AutoSave is On, changes to your file are automatically saved. But if AutoSave is not on, you must manually save your file. **Why?** You have made modifications to the file (presentation) since you created it. Thus, you should save again. Similarly, you should continue saving files frequently so that you do not lose the changes you have made since the time you last saved the file. You can use the same file name, such as Passwords, to save the changes made to the presentation. The following step saves a file again with the same file name.

1

- Click the Save button on the title bar to overwrite the previously saved file (Passwords, in this case) (Figure 1-85).

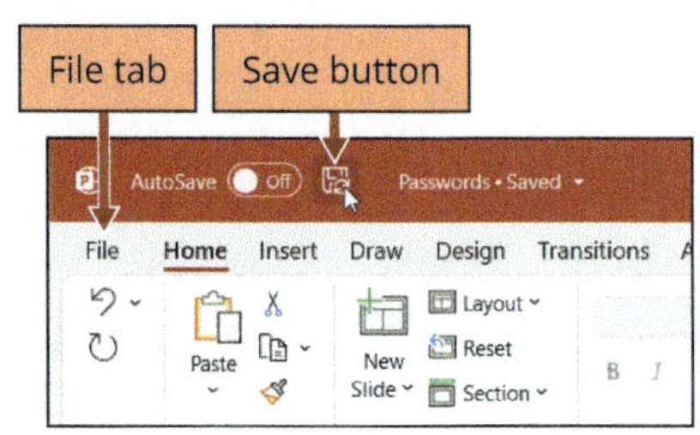

Figure 1-85

Other Ways

1. Press CTRL+S
2. Press SHIFT+F12

To Close a File Using Backstage View

Sometimes, you may want to close a Microsoft 365 file, such as a PowerPoint presentation, entirely and start over with a new file. You also may want to close a file when you are done working with it. **Why?** You should close a file when you are done working with it so that you do not make inadvertent changes to it. The following steps close the current active PowerPoint file, that is, the Passwords presentation, without exiting PowerPoint.

1

- Click File on the ribbon to open Backstage view (Figure 1–86).

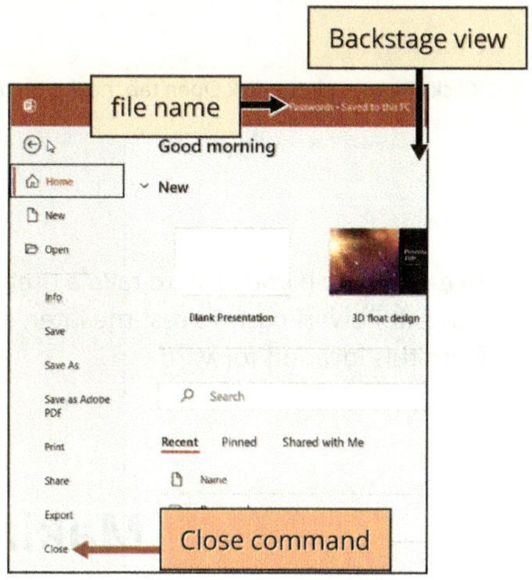

Figure 1–86

2

- Click Close in Backstage view to close the open file (Passwords, in this case) without closing PowerPoint.

Q&A What if PowerPoint displays a dialog box about saving?

Click the Save button if you want to save the changes, click the Don't Save button if you want to ignore the changes since the last time you saved, and click Cancel if you do not want to close the presentation.

Other Ways

1. Press CTRL+F4

To Open a Recent File Using Backstage View

You sometimes need to open a file that you recently modified. **Why?** You may have more changes to make, such as adding more content or correcting errors. Backstage view allows you to access recent files easily. The following steps reopen the Passwords file just closed.

BTW
Welcome Back!
If you are designing a slide in your deck other than Slide 1 and then save and close the document, PowerPoint's Welcome back! feature allows you to continue where you left off at the last save when you open the document. You may need to adjust the zoom if you are working at a different level than the default setting.

1

- Click File on the ribbon to open Backstage view.
- If necessary, click the Open tab in Backstage view to display the Open screen (Figure 1–87).

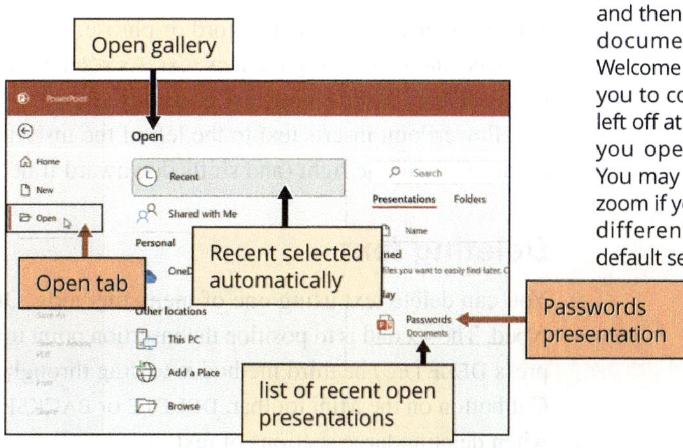

Figure 1–87

2

- Click the desired file name in the Recent list, Passwords in this case, to open the file.

Q&A Can I use Backstage view to open a recent file in other Microsoft 365 apps, such as Word and Excel?
Yes, as long as the file name appears in the list of recent files.

Other Ways

1. Click File on ribbon, click Open tab, navigate to file (Open dialog box), click Open button

Break Point: If you wish to take a break, this is a good place to do so. Be sure the file Passwords file is saved and then you can exit PowerPoint. To resume later, start PowerPoint, open the file called Passwords, and continue following the steps from this location forward.

Making Changes to Slide Text Content

After creating slides in a presentation, you may find that you want to make changes to the text. Changes may be required because a slide contains an error, the scope of the presentation shifts, or the style is inconsistent. This section explains the types of changes that commonly occur when creating a presentation.

You generally make three types of changes to text in a presentation: additions, replacements, and deletions.

- Additions are necessary when you omit text from a slide and need to add it later. You may need to insert text in the form of a sentence, word, or single character. For example, you may want to add the presenter's middle name on the title slide.
- Replacements are needed when you want to revise the text in a presentation. For example, you may want to substitute the word, their, for the word, there.
- Deletions are required when text on a slide is incorrect or no longer is relevant to the presentation. For example, a slide may look cluttered. Therefore, you may want to remove one of the bulleted paragraphs to add more space.

Editing text in PowerPoint basically is the same as editing text in a word processing program. The following sections illustrate the most common changes made to text in a presentation.

Replacing Text in an Existing Slide

When you need to correct a word or phrase, you can replace the text by selecting the text to be replaced and then typing the new text. As soon as you press any key on the keyboard, the selected text is deleted and the new text is displayed.

PowerPoint inserts text to the left of the insertion point. The text to the right of the insertion point moves to the right (and shifts downward if necessary) to accommodate the added text.

Deleting Text

You can delete text using one of many methods. One is to use BACKSPACE to remove text just typed. The second is to position the insertion point to the left of the text you want to delete and then press DELETE. The third method is to drag through the text you want to delete and then click the Cut button on the Mini toolbar, DELETE or BACKSPACE, or press CTRL+X. Use the third method when deleting large sections of text.

To Delete Text in a Placeholder

Why? You want to emphasize that passwords never should be repeated to avoid becoming at risk for cyberattacks. The following steps change Different to Unique in the Slide 3 title.

1

- Select Slide 3 and then position the pointer immediately to the left of the first character of the text to be selected in the title text placeholder (in this case, the D in the word, Different).
- Drag the pointer through the last character of the text to be selected (in this case, the t in the word, Different) (Figure 1–88).

Q&A Can I drag from left to right or right to left?
Yes. Either direction will select the letters.

Could I also have selected the word, Different, by double-clicking it?
Yes. Either method works to select a word.

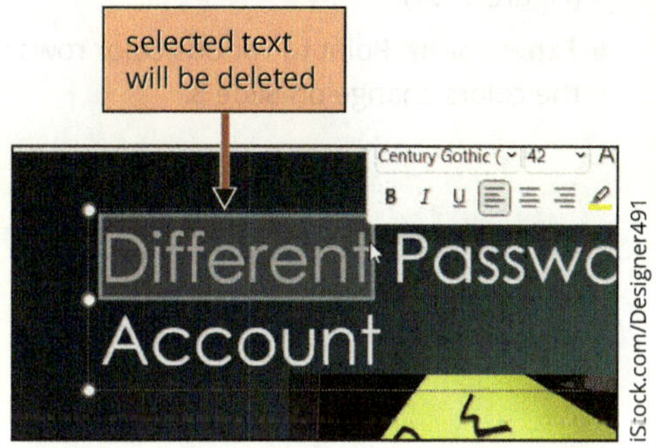

Figure 1–88

2

- Press DELETE to delete the selected text.
- Type **Unique** as the first word in the title text placeholder and then press SPACEBAR (Figure 1–89).

Q&A Could I have typed the word, Unique, while the word, Different, was selected without deleting the text first?
Yes. Either method works to replace words.

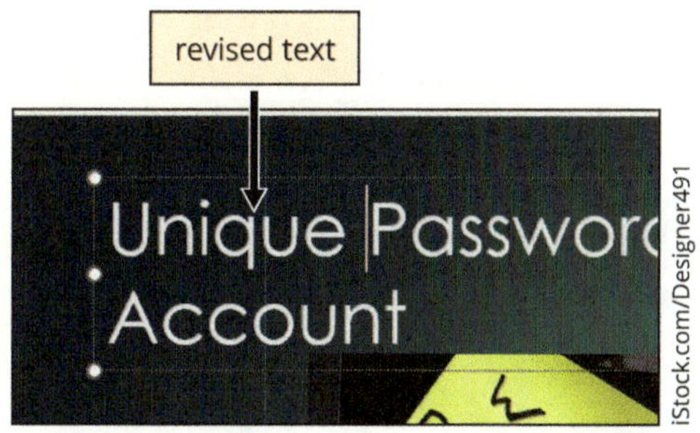

Figure 1–89

Other Ways

1. Right-click selected text, click Cut on shortcut menu
2. Select text, press DELETE or BACKSPACE
3. Select text, press CTRL+X

To Change the Theme Colors

Every theme has 10 standard colors: two for text, two for backgrounds, and six for accents. The following steps change the theme colors for the Passwords slides. **Why?** You can change the look of your presentation and add variety by applying the colors from one theme to another theme.

1

- Display the Design tab and then point to the More button in the Variants group (Design tab | Variants group) (Figure 1–90).

Figure 1–90

2

- Click the More button to expand the gallery.
- Point to Colors in the menu to display the Colors gallery (Figure 1–91).
- **Experiment:** Point to various color rows in the gallery and watch the colors change on Slide 3.

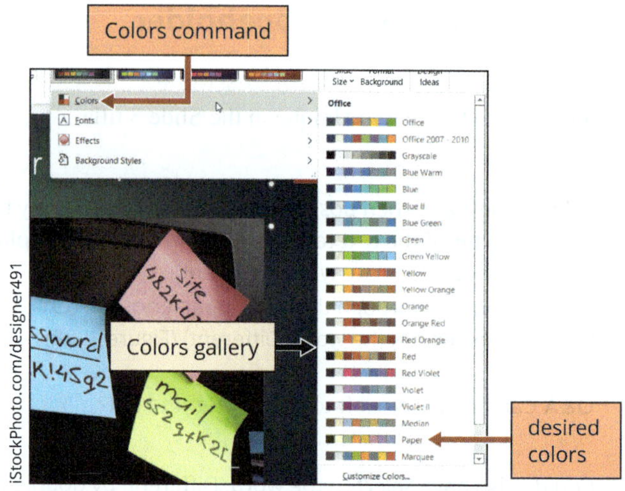

Figure 1–91

3

- Click Paper in the gallery to change the slides' theme colors (Figure 1–92).

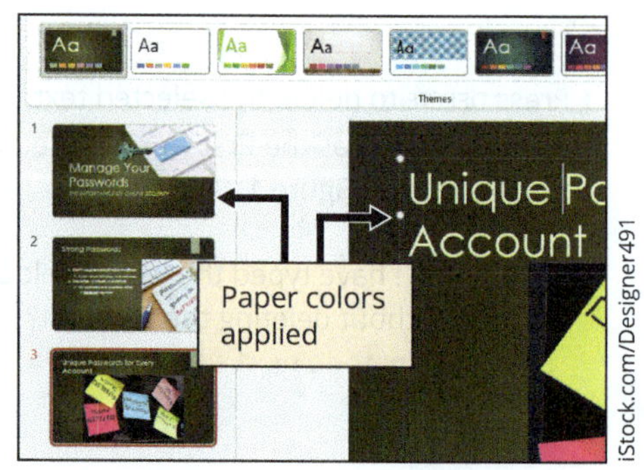

Figure 1–92

To Add Notes

Why? As you create slides, you may find material you want to state verbally and do not want to include on the slide. After adding these comments, you can print a set of speaker notes that will print below a small image of the slide. You can type and format comments in the Notes pane as you work in Normal view and then print this information as **notes pages**. Charts, tables, and pictures added to the Notes pane also print on these pages. The Notes pane is hidden until you click the Notes button on the status bar to open the pane. If you want to close the Notes pane, click the Notes button again. The following steps add text to the Notes pane on Slides 3 and 4.

1

- If necessary, click the Notes button on the status bar to display the Notes pane for Slide 3 (Figure 1–93).

Q&A Why might I need to click the Notes button?
By default, the Notes pane is closed when you begin a new presentation. Once you display the Notes pane for any slide, the Notes pane will remain open unless you click the Notes button to close it.

Can I make the Notes pane larger?
Yes. You can drag the splitter bar up to enlarge the Notes pane.

BTW
Formatting Notes Pane Text
You can format text in the Notes pane in the same manner you format text on a slide. To add emphasis, for example, you can italicize key words or change the font color and size.

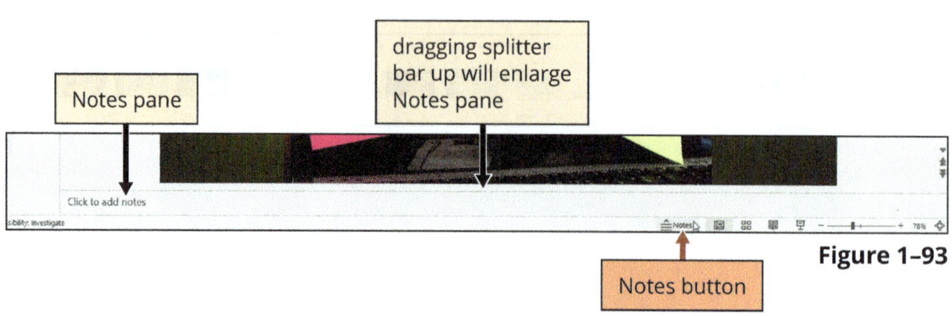

Figure 1–93

2

- Click the Notes pane and then type **Common passwords are 12345, qwerty, and password.** (Figure 1-94).

Figure 1-94

3

- Display Slide 4, click the Notes pane, and then type **Keylogging software stores every keystroke in a hidden file for later retrieval. Phishing is a scam in which a perpetrator tricks you into supplying your personal or financial information.** (Figure 1-95).

Q&A What if I cannot see all the lines I typed?
Clicking the Notes pane scroll arrows allows you to view the entire text.

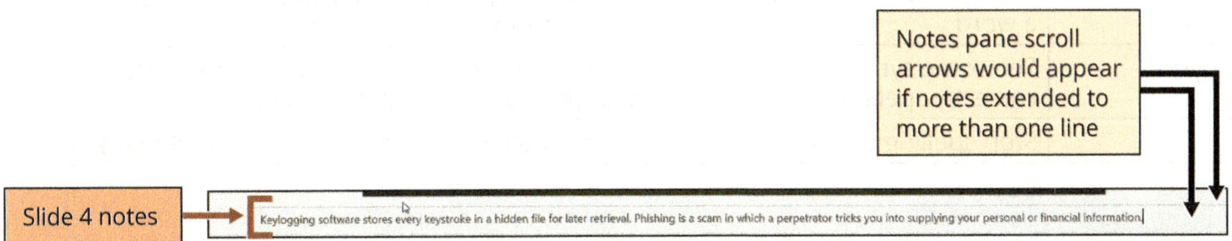

Figure 1-95

Checking Spelling

After you create a presentation, you should check it visually for spelling errors and style consistency. In addition, you can use PowerPoint's Spelling tool to identify possible misspellings on the slides and in the notes. You should proofread your presentation carefully by pointing to each word and saying it aloud as you point to it. Be mindful of commonly misused words such as its and it's, through and though, and to and too.

PowerPoint checks the entire presentation for spelling mistakes using a standard dictionary contained in the Microsoft 365 group. This dictionary is shared with the other Microsoft 365 applications such as Word and Excel. A custom dictionary is available if you want to add special words such as proper nouns, cities, and acronyms. When checking a presentation for spelling errors, PowerPoint opens the standard dictionary and the custom dictionary file, if one exists. When a word appears in the Spelling pane, you can perform one of several actions, as described in Table 1-1.

The standard dictionary contains commonly used English words. It does not, however, contain many proper nouns, abbreviations, technical terms, poetic contractions, or antiquated terms. PowerPoint treats words not found in the dictionaries as misspellings.

BTW
Automatic Spelling Correction
As you type, PowerPoint automatically corrects some misspelled words. For example, if you type overwieght, PowerPoint automatically corrects the misspelling and displays the word, overweight, when you press SPACEBAR or type a punctuation mark. To see a complete list of automatically corrected words, click File on the ribbon to open Backstage view, click the Options tab, click Proofing in the left pane (PowerPoint Options dialog box), click AutoCorrect Options, and then scroll through the list near the bottom of the dialog box.

BTW
Detecting Spelling Errors
The x in the Spell Check icon indicates PowerPoint detected a possible spelling error. A check mark in the icon indicates the entered text contains no spelling errors.

Table 1–1: Spelling Pane Buttons and Actions

Button Name/Action	When to Use	Action
Ignore Once	Word is spelled correctly but not found in dictionaries	Continues checking rest of the presentation but will flag word again if it appears later in document
Ignore All	Word is spelled correctly but not found in dictionaries	Ignores all occurrences of word and continues checking rest of presentation
Add	Add word to custom dictionary	Opens custom dictionary, adds word, and continues checking rest of presentation
Change	Word is misspelled	Click proper spelling of the word in Suggestions list; PowerPoint corrects word, continues checking rest of presentation, but will flag that word again if it appears later in document
Change All	Word is misspelled	Click proper spelling of word in Suggestions list; PowerPoint changes all occurrences of misspelled word and continues checking rest of presentation
Listen to the pronunciation	To hear the pronunciation of a word	Click audio speaker icon next to the properly spelled word near bottom of Spelling pane
View synonyms	See some synonyms for the correctly spelled word	View bullet list of synonyms below correctly spelled word near the bottom of Spelling pane
Close	Stop spelling checker	Closes spelling checker and returns to PowerPoint window

To Check Spelling

Why? Although PowerPoint's spelling checker is a valuable tool, it is not infallible. You should not rely on the spelling checker to catch all your mistakes. The following steps check the spelling on all slides in the Passwords presentation.

1

- Click Review on the ribbon to display the Review tab.
- Click the Spelling button (Review tab | Proofing group) to start the spelling checker and display the Spelling pane (Figure 1–96).

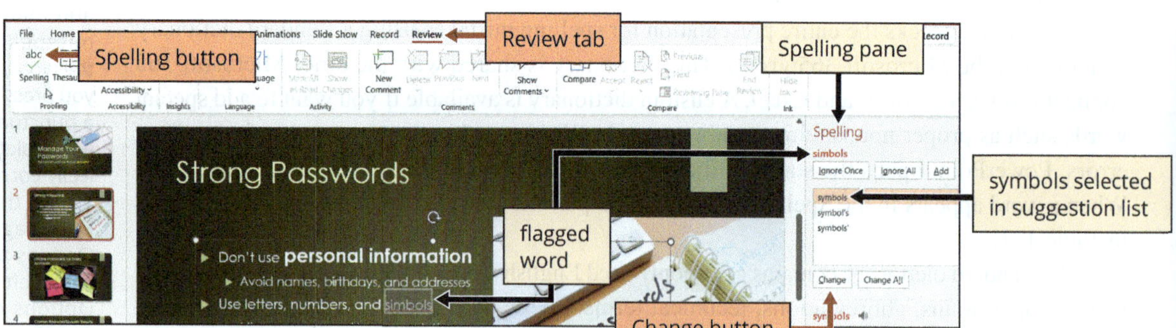

iStockPhoto.com/designer491

Figure 1–96

2

- With the word, simbols, selected in the slide and in the Spelling pane, click the Change button (Spelling pane) to replace the misspelled flagged word, simbols, with the selected correctly spelled word, symbols.

Q&A Could I have clicked the Change All button instead of the Change button?
Yes. When you click the Change All button, you change the current and future occurrences of the misspelled word. The misspelled word, simbols, appears only once in the presentation, so clicking the Change or the Change All button in this instance produces identical results.

Occasionally a correctly spelled word is flagged as a possible misspelled word. Why?
Your custom dictionary does not contain the word, so it is seen as spelled incorrectly. You can add this word to a custom dictionary to prevent the spelling checker from flagging it as a mistake.

3

- When Slide 4 is displayed, replace the misspelled word, Comon, with the word, Common (Figure 1–97).

iStockPhoto.com/welcomia; iStockPhoto.com/CalypsoArt

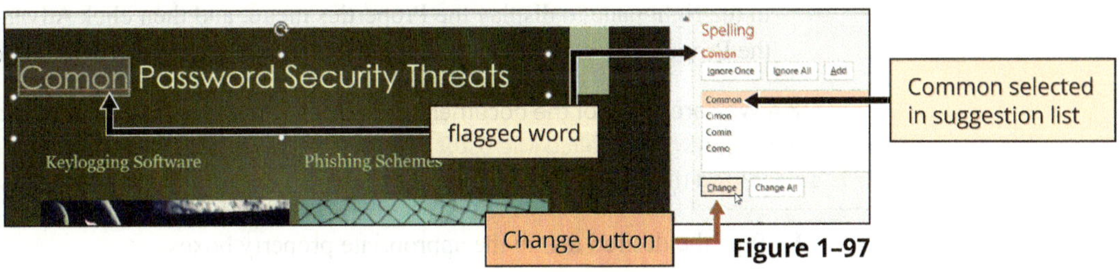

Figure 1–97

4

- Continue the spell check.
- When the Microsoft PowerPoint dialog box appears, click OK (Microsoft PowerPoint dialog box) to close the spelling checker and return to the slide where a possible misspelled word appeared (Figure 1–98).
- If necessary, close the Spelling pane.

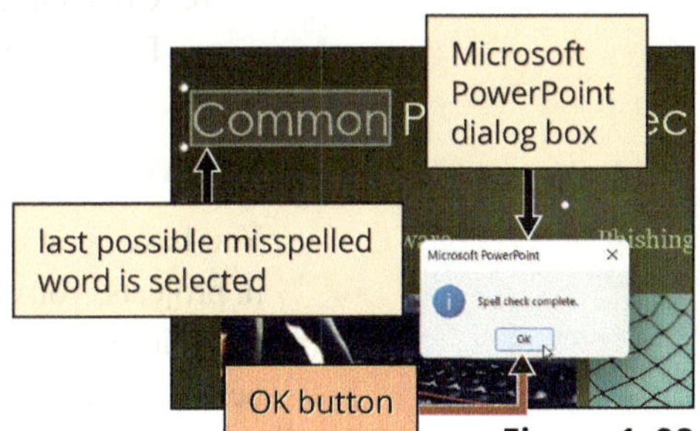

iStock.com/Welcomia; iStock.com/CalypsoArt

Figure 1–98

Other Ways

1. Click Spell Check icon on status bar
2. Right-click flagged word, click desired correct word
3. Press F7

Document Properties

PowerPoint helps you organize and identify your files by using **document properties**, which are the details about a file such as the project author, title, and subject. For example, a class name or presentation topic can describe the file's purpose or content.

Consider This

Why would you want to assign document properties to a presentation?

Document properties are valuable for a variety of reasons:

- Users can save time locating a particular file because they can view a file's document properties without opening the presentation.
- By creating consistent properties for files having similar content, users can better organize their presentations.
- Some organizations require PowerPoint users to add document properties so that other employees can view details about these files.

The more common document properties are standard and automatically updated properties. **Standard properties** are associated with all Microsoft 365 files and include author, title, and subject. **Automatically updated properties** include file system properties, such as the date you create or change a file, and statistics, such as the file size.

BTW
Printing Document Properties
PowerPoint does not allow you to print document properties. This feature, however, is available in Word.

To Change Document Properties

To change document properties, you would follow these steps.

1. Click File on the ribbon to open Backstage view and then, if necessary, click the Info tab in Backstage view to display the Info screen.
2. If the property you wish to change is displayed in the Properties list in the right pane of the Info screen, try to click that property. If a box with that property is displayed, type the text for the property in the box, and then click the Back button in the upper-left corner of Backstage view to return to the PowerPoint window. Skip the remaining steps.
3. If the property you wish to change is not displayed in the Properties list in the right pane of the Info screen or you cannot change it in the Info screen, click the Properties button in the right pane to display the Properties menu, and then click Advanced Properties on the Properties menu to display the Summary tab in the Properties dialog box.

Q&A Why are some of the document properties in my Properties List already filled in?
The person who installed Microsoft 365 on your computer or network may have set or customized the properties.

4. Type the desired text in the appropriate property boxes.
5. Click OK (Properties dialog box) to close the dialog box.
6. Click the Back button in the upper-left corner of Backstage view to return to the PowerPoint presentation window.

Changing Views

You have been using Normal view to create and edit your slides. Once you complete your slides in projects, you can review the final products by displaying each slide in **Slide Show view**, which occupies the full computer screen, to view how the slides will display in an actual presentation before an audience.

PowerPoint has other views to help review a presentation for content, organization, and overall appearance. **Slide Sorter view** allows you to look at several slides at one time. **Reading view** is similar to Slide Show view because each slide displays individually, but the slides do not fill the entire screen. Using this view, you easily can progress through the slides forward or backward with simple controls at the bottom of the window. Switching between Slide Sorter, Reading, and Normal views helps you review your presentation, assess whether the slides have an attractive design and adequate content, and make sure they are organized for the most impact. After reviewing the slides, you can change the view to Normal so that you may continue working on the presentation.

To Change Views

Why? You have made several modifications to the slides, so you should check for balance and consistency. The following steps change the view from Normal view to Slide Sorter view, then Reading view, and back to Normal view.

1

- Display Slide 1 and then click the Slide Sorter view button on the right side of the status bar to display the presentation in Slide Sorter view (Figure 1–99).

Q&A Why does a colored border display around Slide 1?
It is the current slide in the Slides tab.

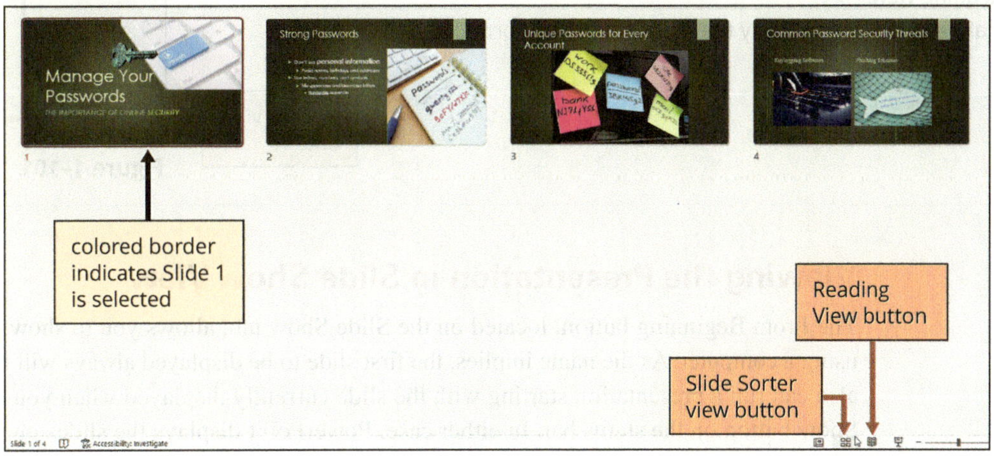

Figure 1–99

iStock.com/MicroStockHub; iStock.ccm/the-lightwriter; iStock.com/designer491; iStock.com/designer491; iStock.com/welcomia; iStock.com/CalypsoArt

2

- Click the Reading View button on the right side of the status bar to display Slide 1 of the presentation in Reading view (Figure 1–100).

Figure 1–100

iStock.com/MicroStockHub; iStock.com/the-lightwriter

3

- Click the Next button three times to advance through the presentation.
- Click the Previous button two times to display Slide 2.
- Click the Menu button to display commonly used commands (Figure 1–101).

4

- Click End Show to return to Slide Sorter view, which is the view you were using before Reading view.
- Click the Normal view button to display the presentation in Normal view.

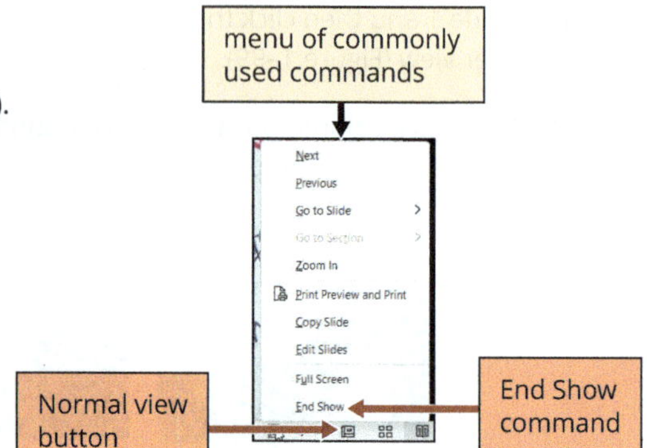

Figure 1–101

Viewing the Presentation in Slide Show View

The From Beginning button, located on the Slide Show tab, allows you to show a presentation using a computer. As the name implies, the first slide to be displayed always will be Slide 1. You also can run a presentation starting with the slide currently displayed when you click the Slide Show button on the status bar. In either case, PowerPoint displays the slides on the full screen without any of the PowerPoint window objects, such as the ribbon. The full-screen slide hides the toolbars, menus, and other PowerPoint window elements.

To Start Slide Show View

Why? You want to see your presentation as your audience would so you can see the slides in their entirety and view any transitions or other effects added to the slides. When making a presentation, you use Slide Show view to display slides so that they fill the entire screen. This is the view you use to show your presentation to an audience. You can start Slide Show view from Normal view or Slide Sorter view. Slide Show view begins when you click the From Beginning button or the Slide Show button. The following steps start Slide Show view starting with Slide 1.

1

- Click Slide Show on the ribbon to display the Slide Show tab.
- Point to the From Beginning button (Slide Show tab | Start Slide Show group) (Figure 1–102).

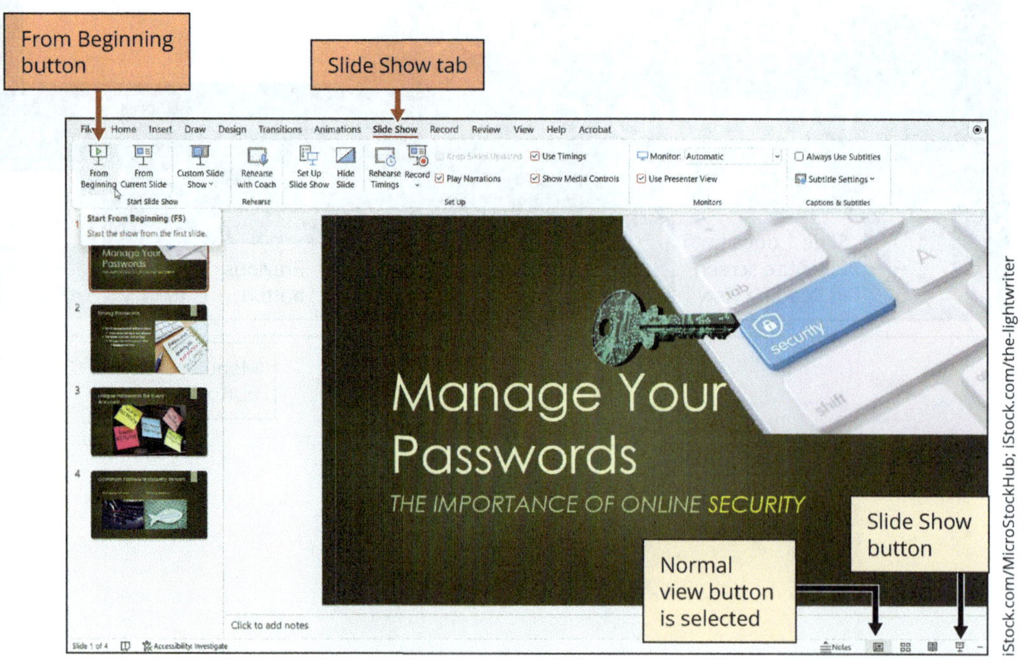

Figure 1–102

Q&A What would have displayed if I had clicked the Slide Show button on the status bar instead of the From Beginning button?

When you click the Slide Show button to start the presentation, PowerPoint begins the show with the currently displayed slide, which in this case is Slide 1. If, however, a different slide had been displayed, the slide show would have begun with that slide.

2

- Click the From Beginning button to display the title slide (Figure 1–103). The screen goes dark and then Slide 1 displays in the entire window.

Q&A Where is the PowerPoint window?

When you run a slide show, the PowerPoint window is hidden. It will reappear once you end your slide show.

I see a small toolbar in the lower-left corner of my slide. What is this toolbar?

You may see the Slide Show toolbar when you begin running a slide show and then move the pointer or click. The buttons on this toolbar allow you to navigate to the next slide or the previous slide, to mark up the current slide, or to change the current display. If you do not see the toolbar, hover the mouse near the lower-left corner of the screen.

iStock.com/MicroStockHub; iStock.com/the-lightwriter

Figure 1–103

Other Ways

1. Display Slide 1, click Slide Show button on status bar
2. Press F5
3. Click From Beginning button on Quick Access Toolbar, if available

To Move Manually through Slides in a Slide Show

After you begin Slide Show view, you can move forward or backward through the slides. PowerPoint allows you to advance through the slides manually or automatically. During a slide show, each slide in the presentation shows on the screen, one slide at a time. Each time you click the mouse, the next slide appears. The following steps move manually through the slides. **Why?** You can control the length of time each slide is displayed and change the preset order if you need to review a slide already shown or jump ahead to another slide designed to display later in the presentation.

1

- Click each slide until Slide 4 (Common Password Security Threats) is displayed (Figure 1–104).

Figure 1–104

2

- Click Slide 4 so that the black slide appears with a message announcing the end of the slide show (Figure 1–105).

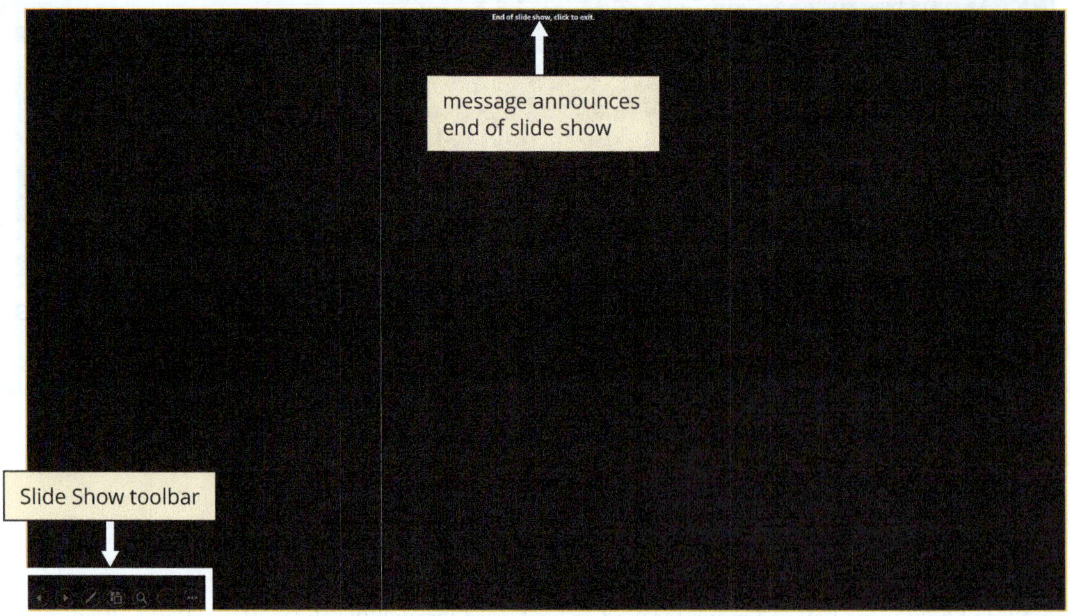

Figure 1–105

3

- Click the black slide to return to Normal view in the PowerPoint window.

Other Ways

1. Press PAGE DOWN to advance one slide at a time, or press PAGE UP to go back one slide at a time
2. Press RIGHT ARROW or DOWN ARROW to advance one slide at a time, or press LEFT ARROW or UP ARROW to go back one slide at a time
3. If Slide Show toolbar is displayed, click Next Slide or Previous Slide button on toolbar

Saving and Printing Files

While you are creating a presentation, the computer or mobile device stores it in memory. When you save a presentation, the computer or mobile device places it on a storage medium, such as a hard drive, solid state drive (SSD), USB flash drive, or cloud storage. The storage medium can be permanent in your computer, may be portable where you remove it from your computer, or may be on a web server you access through a network or the Internet.

To Save a File with a Different File Name

You might want to save a file with a different file name or to a different location. **Why?** You might start a homework assignment with a data file and then save it with a final file name for submission to your instructor, saving it to a different location designated by your instructor.

The following steps save the Passwords file with a different file name.

1. Click File on the ribbon to open Backstage view.
2. Click Save As (or Save a Copy if AutoSave is on) in Backstage view to display the Save As or Save a Copy screen.
3. Type **SC_PPT_1_Security** in the File name box, replacing the existing file name.

Q&A What are all those characters in the file name in this project?
Some companies require certain rules be followed when creating file names; others allow you to choose your own. The file names in this book do not use spaces and all begin with SC (for Shelly Cashman) and PPT (for PowerPoint) followed by the module number and then a descriptor of the file contents, and use underscores instead of spaces so that they work with SAM, if you are using that platform as well.

4. Click the Save button to save the presentation with the new name.

To Print Full Page Slides

With the presentation open, you may want to print it. **Why?** Because you want to see how the slides will appear on paper, you want to print a hard copy on a printer. The following steps print a hard copy of the contents of the presentation.

1

- Display Slide 1 and then click File on the ribbon to open Backstage view.
- Click the Print tab in Backstage view to display the Print screen and a preview of Slide 1 (Figure 1–106).

Q&A What if I decide not to print the presentation at this time?
Click the Back button in the upper-left corner of Backstage view to return to the document window.

Why does the preview of my slide appear in black and white?
Your printer determines how the preview appears. If your printer is not capable of printing color images, the preview may appear in black and white.

BTW
Conserving Ink and Toner
If you want to conserve ink or toner, you can instruct PowerPoint to print draft quality documents by clicking File on the ribbon to open Backstage view, clicking Options in Backstage view to display the PowerPoint Options dialog box, clicking Advanced in the left pane (PowerPoint Options dialog box), scrolling to the Print area in the right pane, verifying there is no check mark in the High quality check box, and then clicking OK. Then, use Backstage view to print the document as usual.

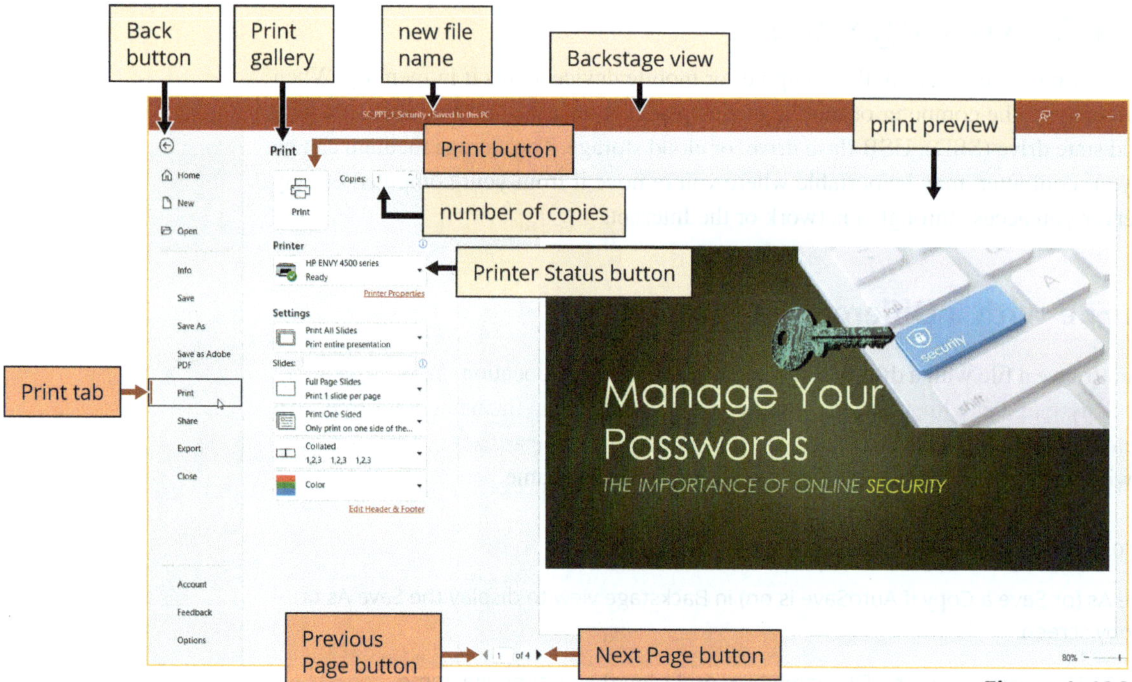

iStock.com/MicroStockHub; iStock.com/the-lightwriter

Figure 1–106

2

- Click the Next Page button to display Slide 2.

Q&A Do I need to change the display before I print?
No. You can print all the slides with any slide displaying in the preview window.

- Verify that the selected printer will print a hard copy of the presentation. If necessary, click the Printer Status button to display a list of available printer options and then click the desired printer to change the currently selected printer.

Q&A How can I print multiple copies of my presentation?
Increase the number in the Copies box in the Print screen.

3

- Click the Print button in the Print screen to print the presentation on the currently selected printer.
- When the printer stops, retrieve the hard copies (Figure 1–107).

Q&A What if I want to create a PDF of my presentation instead of printing a hard copy?
You would click the Printer Status button in the Print screen and then select Microsoft Print to PDF, Adobe PDF, or a similar option, which would create a PDF file.

Do I have to wait until my presentation is complete to print it?
No, you can print a presentation at any time while you are creating it.

BTW
Printing Background Images
If you do not use a color printer, background images display on the screen but may not display in the printouts. Graphics are displayed depending upon the settings in the Print gallery. For example, the background will print if Color is specified whereas it will not with a Grayscale or Pure Black and White setting.

iStock.com/MicroStockHub; iStock.com/the-lightwriter; iStock.com/welcomia; iStock.com/CalypsoArt

Figure 1–107

Other Ways

1. Press CTRL+P

To Preview and Print a Handout

Printing handouts is useful for reviewing a presentation. You can analyze several slides displayed simultaneously on one page. Additionally, many businesses distribute handouts of the slide show before or after a presentation so attendees can refer to a copy. Each page of the handout can contain reduced images of one, two, three, four, six, or nine slides. The three-slides-per-page handout includes lines beside each slide so that your audience can write notes conveniently. The following steps preview and print a presentation handout with two slides per page. **Why?** Two of the slides are predominantly pictures, so your audience does not need full pages of those images. The five bulleted paragraphs on Slide 2 can be read easily on one-half of a sheet of paper.

1

- If necessary, click File on the ribbon to open Backstage view and then click the Print tab.
- Click 'Full Page Slides' in the Settings area to display the Full Page Slides gallery (Figure 1–108).

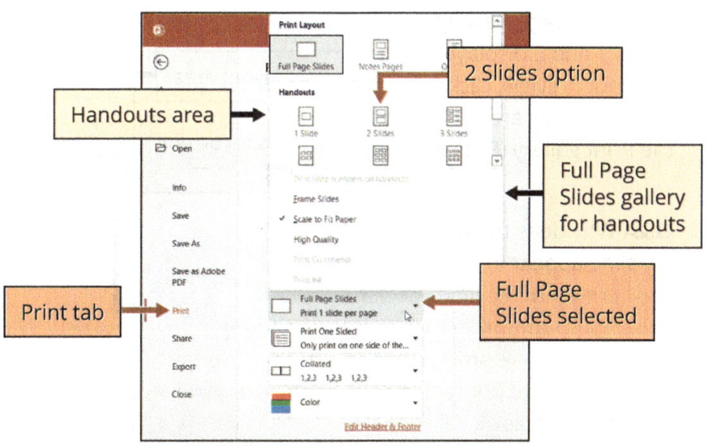

Figure 1–108

BTW

Distributing a Document

Instead of printing and distributing a hard copy of PowerPoint slides, you can distribute the slides electronically. Options include sending the slides via email; posting it on cloud storage (such as OneDrive) and sharing the link with others; posting it on social media, a blog, or other website; and sharing a link associated with an online location of the slides. You also can create and share a PDF or XPS image of the slides, so that users can view the file in Acrobat Reader or XPS Viewer instead of in PowerPoint.

2

- Click 2 Slides in the Handouts area to select this option and display a preview of the handout (Figure 1–109).

Q&A The current date displays in the upper-right corner of the handout, and the page number displays in the lower-right corner of the footer. Can I change their locations or add other information to the header and footer?
Yes. Click the 'Edit Header & Footer' link at the bottom of the Print screen, click the Notes and Handouts tab (Header and Footer dialog box), and then decide what content to include on the handout page.

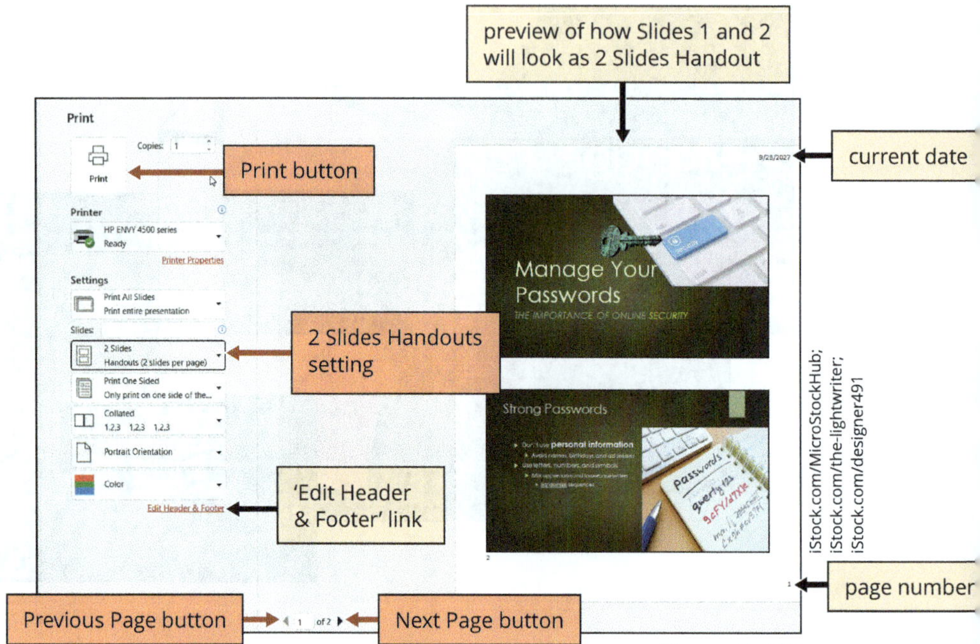

Figure 1–109

3

- Click the Next Page and Previous Page buttons to display previews of the two pages in the handout.
- Click the Print button in the Print screen to print the handout.
- When the printer stops, retrieve the printed handout.

To Print Speaker Notes

Why? Comments added to slides in the Notes pane give the speaker information that supplements the text on the slide. Notes will print with a small image of the slide at the top and the comments below the slide. The following steps print the speaker notes.

1

- With Backstage view open and Slides 1 and 2 displayed in the handout preview, click 2 Slides in the Settings area to display the Print gallery (Figure 1–110).

Q&A Why does the preview of my slide appear in color?
Your printer determines how the preview appears. If your printer is capable of printing color images, the preview appears in color. Some black-and-white printers also cause the preview to display in color.

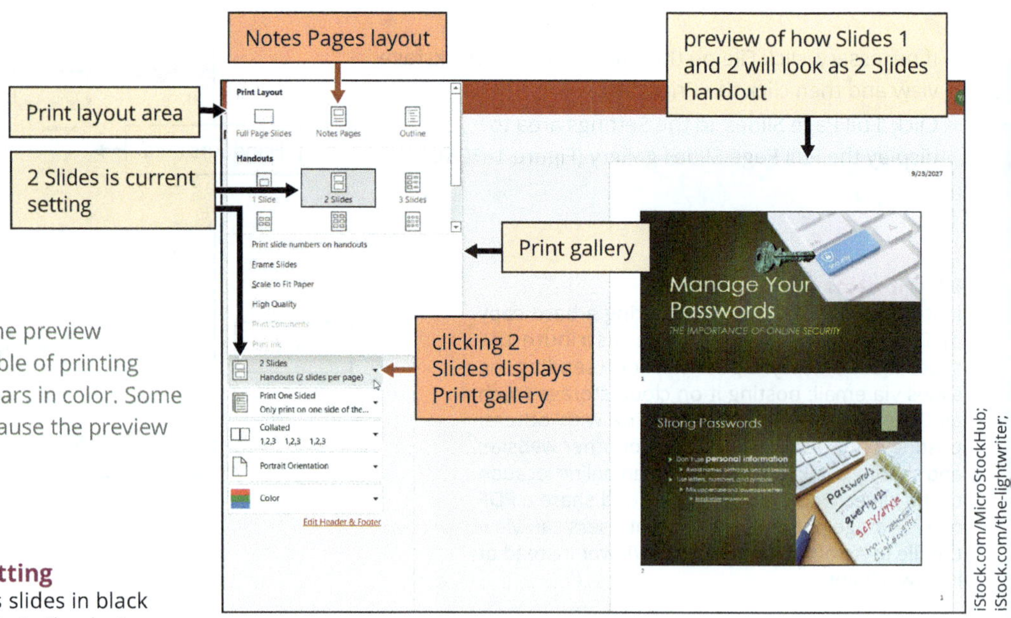

Figure 1–110

BTW
Using the Black and White Setting
The Black and White option prints slides in black and white. As a result, some objects in the design theme of the slide, such as embossing and drop shadows, will not print. Text will print as black even if you chose gray as the original color of the text.

2

- Click Notes Pages in the Print Layout area to select this option and then click the Next Page button two times to display a preview of Slide 3 and notes in a handout (Figure 1–111).

Q&A Can I preview other slides now?
Yes. Click the Next Page button or the Previous Page button to preview the other slides.

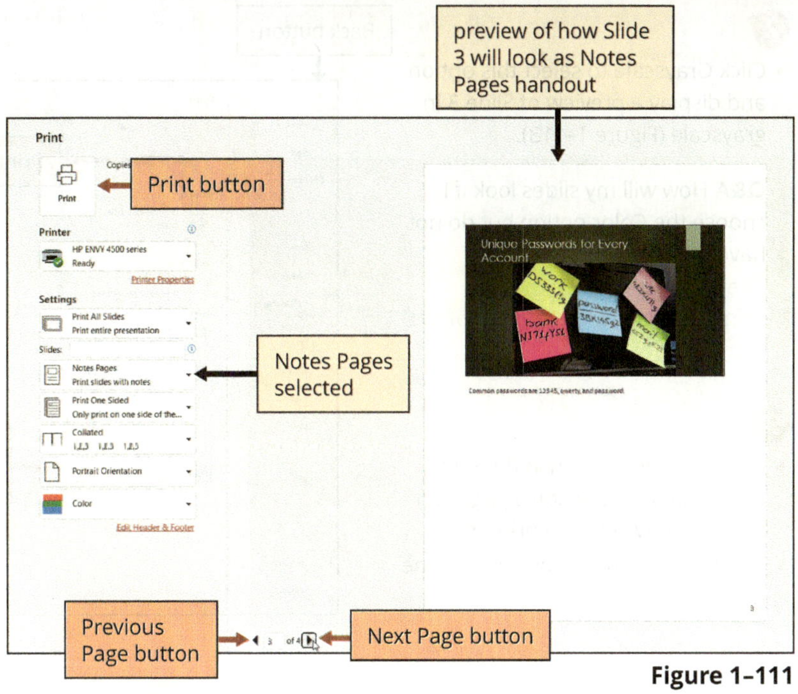

iStock.com/designer491

Figure 1–111

3

- Click the Print button in the Print gallery to print the notes pages on the currently selected printer.
- When the printer stops, retrieve the hard copy.

To Change the Print Color

Some printers are capable of printing in color, black and white, or grayscale. **Grayscale**, as the name implies, prints all objects on the page in black, white, and shades of gray. You can specify the print color by changing the setting in Backstage view. The following steps print the speaker notes in grayscale. **Why?** You are going to use a printer that does not have color printing capabilities.

1

- With Backstage view open and Slide 3 displayed in the handout preview, click Color in the Settings area to display the Color gallery (Figure 1–112).

Q&A How does the handout appear in Pure Black and White?
No shades of gray will print when the Pure Black and White setting is selected.

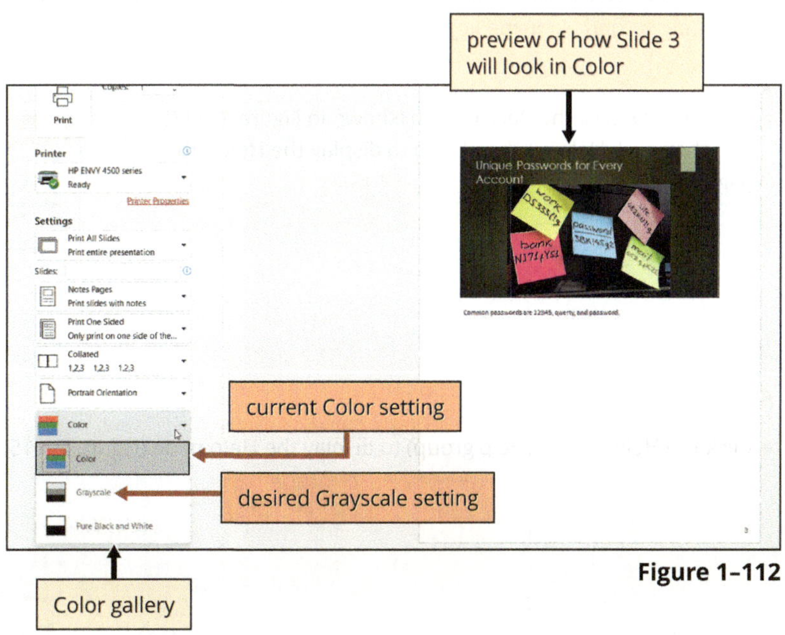

iStock.com/designer491

Figure 1–112

BTW
Using the Grayscale Setting
If you do not have a color printer or do not require a color printout, choosing Grayscale will print all pages in shades of gray. In grayscale, objects such as charts and tables will appear crisper and cleaner than if you chose the Color option on a non-color printer.

2

- Click Grayscale to select this option and display a preview of Slide 3 in grayscale (Figure 1–113).

Q&A How will my slides look if I choose the Color option but do not have a color printer?
The printout will be similar to printing in grayscale, but not of the same quality.

3

- Click the Print button in the Print gallery to print the notes pages on the currently selected printer.
- When the printer stops, retrieve the hard copy.

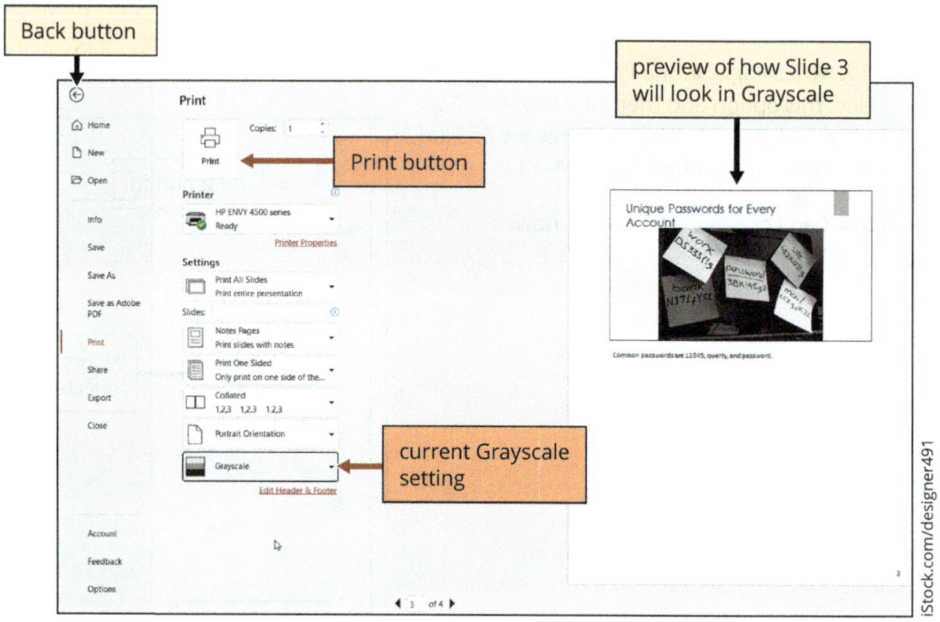

Figure 1–113

Using PowerPoint Help

At any time while you are using PowerPoint, you can use Help to display information about all topics associated with this app. Help is presented in a window that has browser-style navigation buttons. Once a Microsoft 365 app's Help window is open, several methods exist for navigating Help. You can search for help by using the Help pane or the Search box.

To Obtain Help Using the Help Pane

Assume for the following example that you want to know more about fonts. The following steps use the Help pane to obtain useful information about fonts by entering the word, fonts, as search text. **Why?** You may not know the exact help topic you are looking to find, so using keywords can help narrow your search.

1

- If necessary, click the Back button (shown in Figure 1–113) and then click Help on the ribbon to display the Help tab (Figure 1–114).

Figure 1–114

2

- Click the Help button (Help group) to display the Help pane (Figure 1–115).

Stock.com/MicroStockHub; Stock.com/the-lightwriter

Figure 1–115

3

- Type **fonts** in the Search help box at the top of the Help pane to enter the search text and display search suggestions.
- Point to change font in the search suggestions list (Figure 1–116).

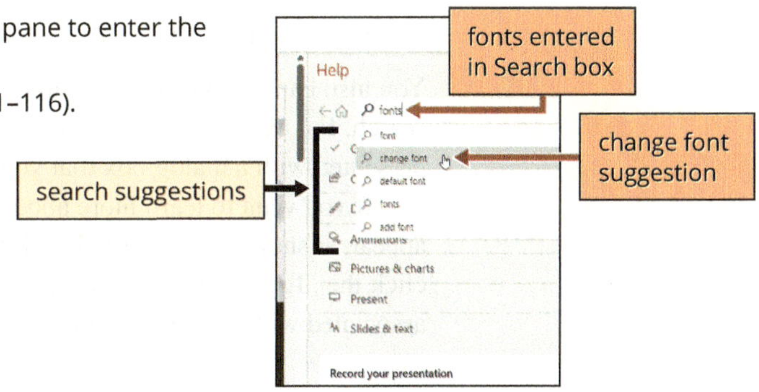

Figure 1–116

4

- Click change font and then scroll down and point to 'Change the fonts in a presentation' or a similar link (Figure 1–117).

Q&A Why do my search results differ?
If you do not have an Internet connection, your results will reflect only the content of the Help files on your computer. When searching for help online, results also can change as content is added, deleted, and updated on the online Help webpages maintained by Microsoft.

Why were my search results not very helpful?
When initiating a search, be sure to check the spelling of the search text; also, keep your search specific to return the most accurate results.

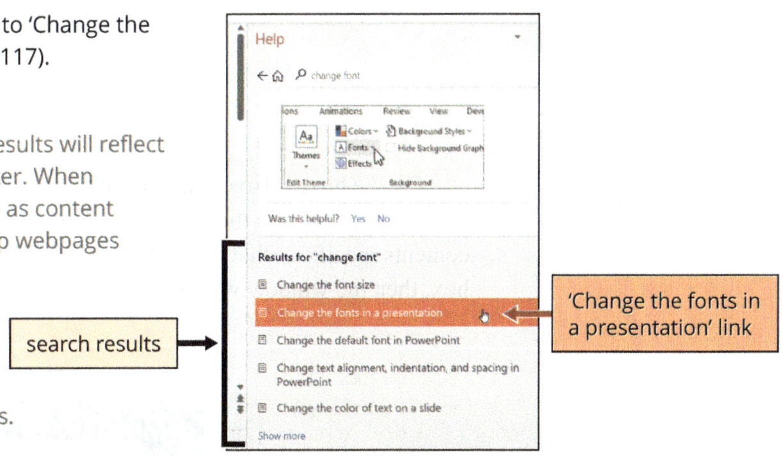

Figure 1–117

5

- Click 'Change the fonts in a presentation' or a similar link to display the Help information associated with the selected topic (Figure 1–118).

6

- Click the Close button in the Help pane to close the pane.
- Click Home on the ribbon to display the Home tab.

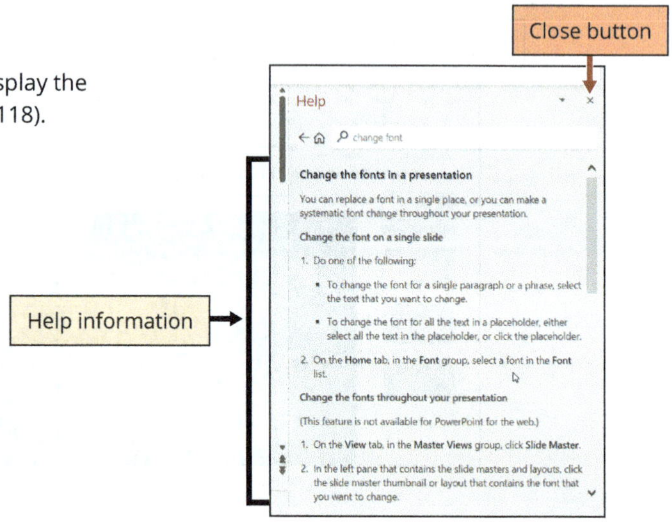

Figure 1–118

Obtaining Help while Working in PowerPoint

You also can access the Help functionality without first opening the Help pane and initiating a search. For example, you may be unsure about how a particular command works, or you may be presented with a dialog box that you are not sure how to use.

If you want to learn more about a command, point to its button and wait for the ScreenTip to appear, as shown in Figure 1–119. If the Help icon and 'Tell me more' link appear in the ScreenTip, click the 'Tell me more' link (or press F1 while pointing to the button) to open the Help window associated with that command.

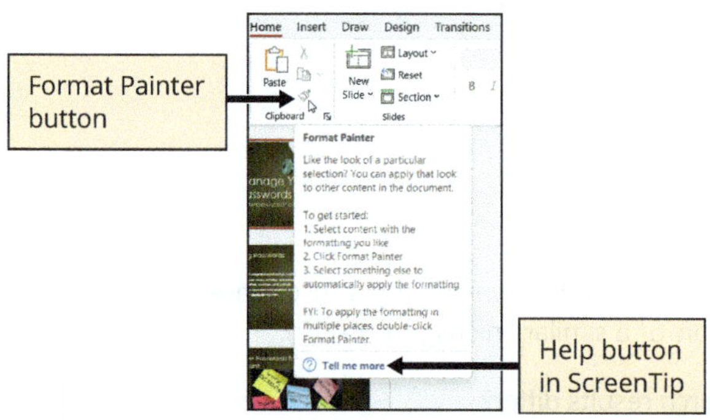

Figure 1–119

Dialog boxes also contain Help buttons, as shown in Figure 1–120. Clicking the Help button or pressing F1 while the dialog box is displayed opens a Help window, which will display help contents specific to that dialog box, if available. If no help file is available for that particular dialog box, then the window will display the Help home page.

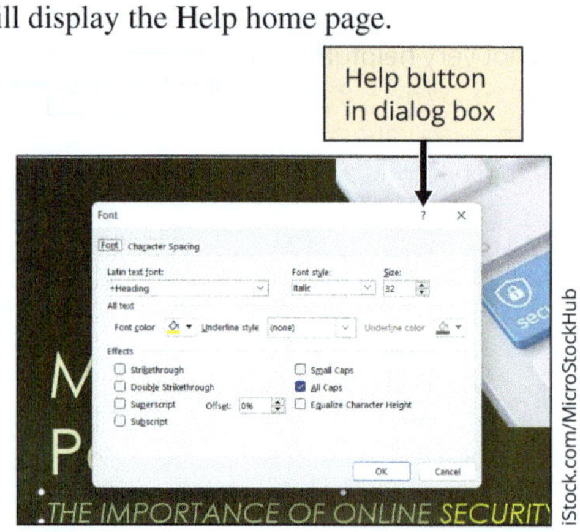

Figure 1–120

As mentioned previously, the Search box is integrated into the title bar in PowerPoint and most other Microsoft 365 apps and can perform a variety of functions. One of these functions is to provide easy access to commands and help content as you type.

To Obtain Help Using the Search Box

If you are having trouble finding a command in PowerPoint, you can use the Search box to search for the function you are trying to perform. As you type, the Search box will suggest commands that match the search text you are entering. **Why?** You can use the Search box to access commands quickly that you otherwise may be unable to find on the ribbon. The following steps find information about borders.

1

- Type **border** in the Search box and watch the search results appear.
- Point to Border Style to display a submenu showing the various border designs (Figure 1–121).

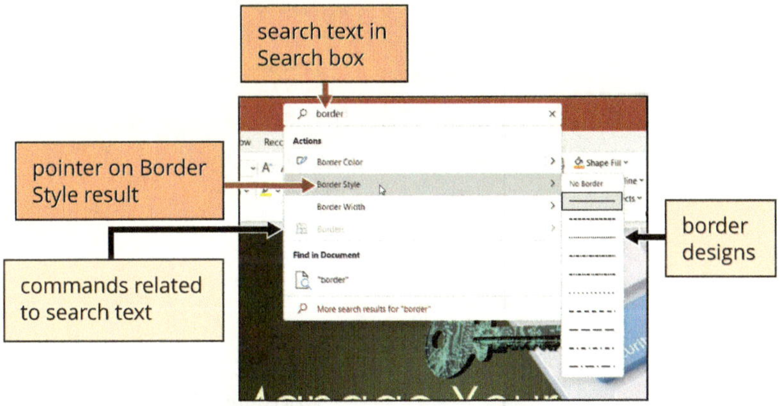

iStock.com/MicroStockHub; iStock.com/the-lightwriter

Figure 1–121

To Sign Out of a Microsoft Account

If you are using a public computer or otherwise wish to sign out of your Microsoft account, you should sign out of the account from the Accounts screen in Backstage view. Signing out of the account is the safest way to make sure that nobody else can access online files or settings stored in your Microsoft account. **Why?** For security reasons, you should sign out of your Microsoft account when you are finished using a public or shared computer. Staying signed in to your Microsoft account might enable others to access your files.

The following steps sign out of a Microsoft account from PowerPoint. If you do not wish to sign out of your Microsoft account, read these steps without performing them.

1. Click File on the ribbon to open Backstage view.
2. Click the Account tab to display the Account screen (Figure 1–122).
3. Click the Sign out link, which displays the Remove Account dialog box. If a Can't remove Windows accounts dialog box appears instead of the Remove Account dialog box, click OK and skip the remaining steps.

Q&A Why does a Can't remove Windows accounts dialog box appear?
If you signed in to Windows using your Microsoft account, then you also must sign out from Windows, rather than signing out from within PowerPoint. When you are finished using Windows, be sure to sign out at that time.

4. Click the Yes button (Remove Account dialog box) to sign out of your Microsoft account on this computer.

Q&A Should I sign out of Windows after removing my Microsoft account?
When you are finished using the computer, you should sign out of Windows for maximum security.

5. Click the Back button in the upper-left corner of Backstage view to return to the presentation.

6. sam Click the Close button to close the presentation and PowerPoint. If you are prompted to save changes, click Yes to save any changes made to the file since the last save.

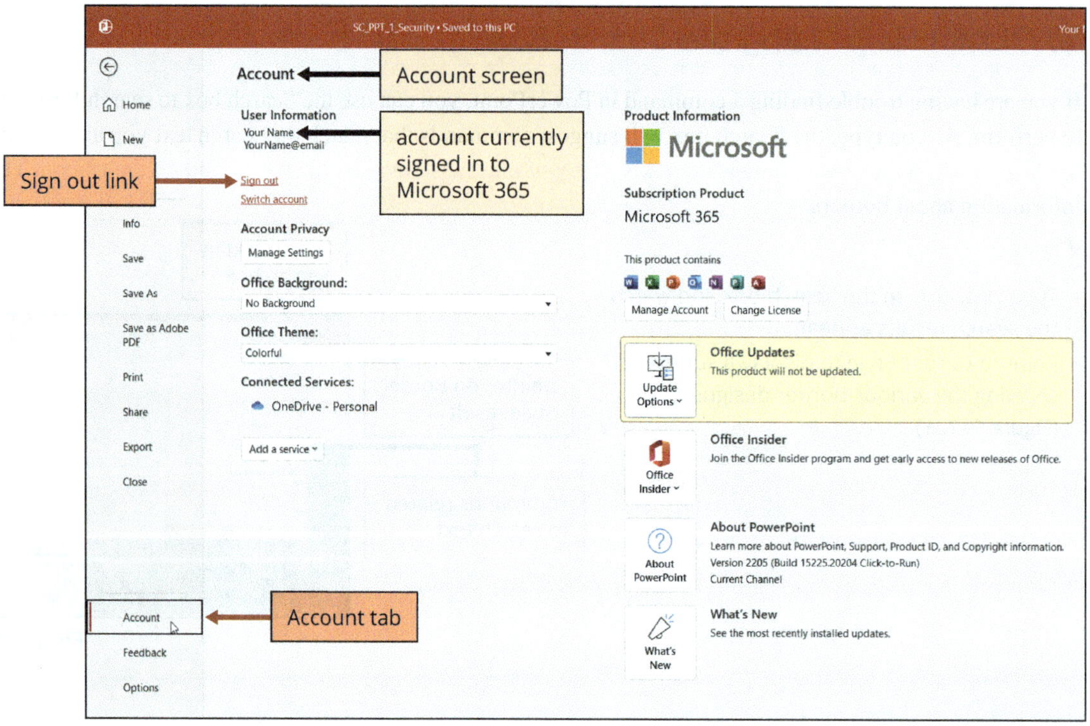

Figure 1-122

Summary

In this module, you learned how to use PowerPoint to create and enhance a presentation. Topics covered included starting PowerPoint, applying and changing a presentation theme and theme colors, creating a title slide and text slides with a multilevel bulleted list, inserting pictures and then resizing and moving them on a slide, formatting and editing text, adding notes, printing the presentation, and reviewing the presentation in several views.

Consider This: Plan Ahead

What decisions do you need to make when creating your next presentation?

Use these guidelines as you complete the assignments in this module and create your own slide show decks outside of this class.

1. Determine the content you want to include on your slides.
2. Determine which theme is appropriate.
3. Identify the slide layouts that best communicate your message.
4. Format various text elements to emphasize important points.
    a) Select appropriate font sizes.
    b) Emphasize important words with bold, italic, or underlined type and color.
5. Locate graphical elements, such as pictures, that reinforce your message.
    a) Size and position them aesthetically on slides.
6. Determine a storage location for the presentation.
7. Determine the best method for distributing the presentation.

Student Assignments

Apply Your Knowledge

Reinforce the skills and apply the concepts you learned in this module.

Modifying Character Formats and Paragraph Levels and Inserting and Moving a Picture

Note: To complete this assignment, you will be required to use the Data Files. Please contact your instructor for information about accessing the Data Files.

Instructions: Start PowerPoint. Open the presentation called SC_PPT_1-1.pptx, which is located in the Data Files. The marketing manager at your local bank has asked you to help develop a presentation for customers on the topic of avoiding identity theft. The manager has started by creating two unformatted slides. You open the presentation and then modify the theme and colors, indent the paragraphs, insert, resize and move a picture, and format the text so the slides look like Figure 1–123.

Perform the following tasks:

1. Change the document theme to Quotable. Change the theme colors to Blue.
2. On the title slide, use your name in place of Student Name and then italicize and underline your name.

   If requested by your instructor, change your first name to your childhood best friend's first name on the title slide.
3. Increase the title text font size to 72 point, change the font to Bookman Old Style, and then italicize this text.
4. Increase the subtitle text font size for both paragraphs to 36 point. Underline the word, Target, and change the color of this word to Red.
5. Insert the picture named Support_PPT_1_Private.jpg. Resize the picture to 4" × 4" and then position the picture using the smart guides to display the vertical guide along the right edge of the image and the horizontal smart guide in the center of the picture (Figure 1–123a).
6. On Slide 2, combine paragraphs two and three (Credit reports available and Three national credit bureaus) to read, **Reports available from three national credit bureaus**, as shown in Figure 1–123b. Increase the indent of this paragraph to second level. Then, increase the indent of the fourth and fifth paragraphs to second-level paragraphs and the sixth paragraph to a third-level paragraph.
7. On Slide 2 in the Notes pane, type **New account fraud is an extremely common form of identity theft. Thieves use personal information to open bank and credit card accounts.**
8. Click the 'Start From Beginning' button to start the show from the first slide. Then click to display the second slide and again to end the presentation.
9. Save the file with the file name, **SC_PPT_1_Identity**, and submit the revised presentation (shown in Figure 1–123) in the format specified by your instructor.
10. **Consider This:** In Step 6, you combined two paragraphs and indented paragraphs. How did these actions improve the slide content?

Continued on next page

Figure 1–123(a): Slide 1 (Title Slide with a Picture)

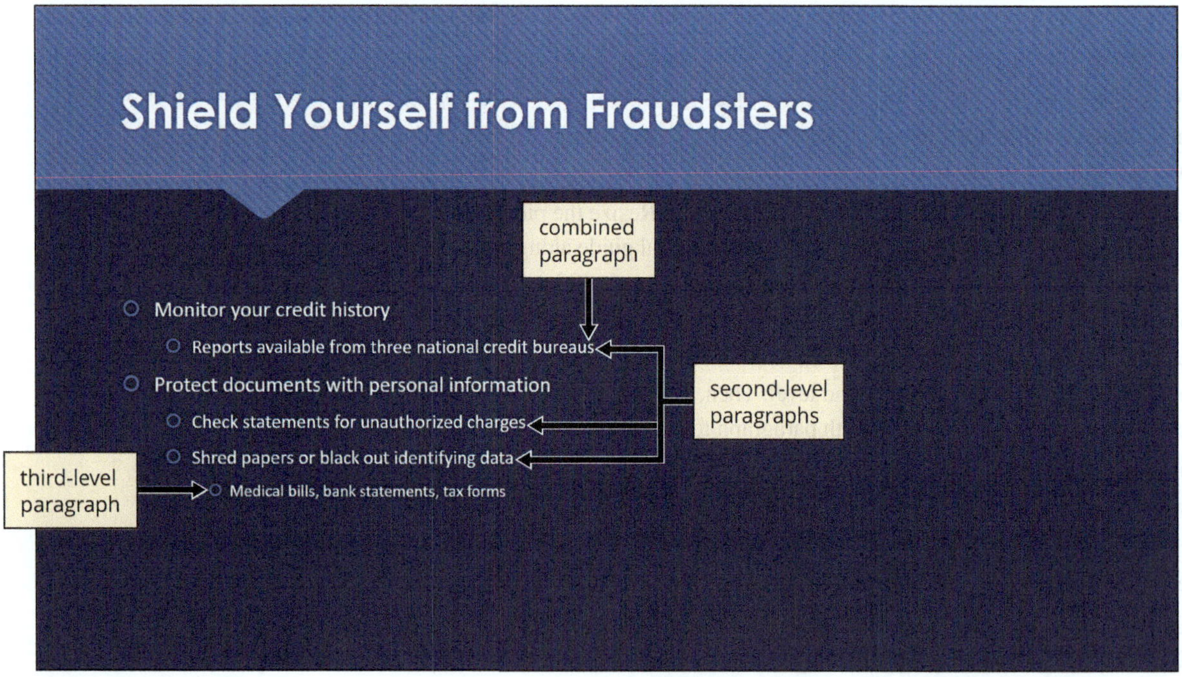

Figure 1–123(b): Slide 2 (Multilevel Bulleted List)

Extend Your Knowledge

Extend the skills you learned in this module and experiment with new skills. You may need to use Help to complete the assignment.

Changing the Slide Theme, Layout, and Text

Note: To complete this assignment, you will be required to use the Data Files. Please contact your instructor for information about accessing the Data Files.

Instructions: Start PowerPoint. Open the presentation called SC_PPT_1-2.pptx, which is located in the Data Files. Slide 1 is shown in Figure 1–124. The adult education instructors at your school offer a free program to educate community residents on how they can beautify their yards with environmentally friendly plants. They have developed three slides to accompany a speech they will be giving at your local garden center, and they have asked you to insert appropriate pictures, choose a theme, and format these slides.

Perform the following tasks:

1. Change the document theme to Organic and the theme colors to Green.
2. On Slide 1, format the title text using techniques you learned in this module, such as changing the font size and color and bolding, italicizing, and underlining words.
3. Replace the text, Student Name, with your name.
   If requested by your instructor, replace your last name on Slide 1 with the name of your hometown.
4. Delete the bullet preceding your name because, in most cases, a bullet is displayed as the first character in a list consisting of several paragraphs, not just one line of text.
5. Resize the picture and move it to an appropriate area on the slide.
6. On Slide 2, add bullets to the six paragraphs in the left content placeholder. To add bullets, select the paragraphs and then click the Bullets button (Home tab | Paragraph group). Insert the picture called Support_PPT_1_Garden.jpg, which is located in the Data Files, in the right content placeholder. Resize this picture and then move it to an appropriate area on the slide.
7. On Slide 3, add bullets to the three paragraphs in the left heading placeholder. Insert the picture called Support_PPT_1_Leaf.jpg, which is located in the Data Files. Resize this picture to approximately 2.5" × 4.0", rotate it 90 degrees, and then move it to the right side of the slide.
8. Duplicate the title slide. To duplicate this slide, select it, click the New Slide arrow (Home tab | Slides group) to display the layout gallery, and then click 'Duplicate Selected Slides' in the layout gallery.
9. Move the new slide to the end of the presentation. Change the title text to **Improve Your Environment** and then underline this text. Delete your name. Insert the two pictures, Support_PPT_1_Leaf.jpg and Support_PPT_1_Garden.jpg, and then size and move all three pictures to appropriate places on the slide.
10. Display Slide 1 and then click the Slide Show button to start the show from the first slide. Then click to display each slide and again to end the presentation.
11. Save the file with the file name, **SC_PPT_1_Yard**, and submit the revised presentation in the format specified by your instructor.
12. **Consider This:** How did you determine the appropriate size and location of the three pictures on the duplicated slide?

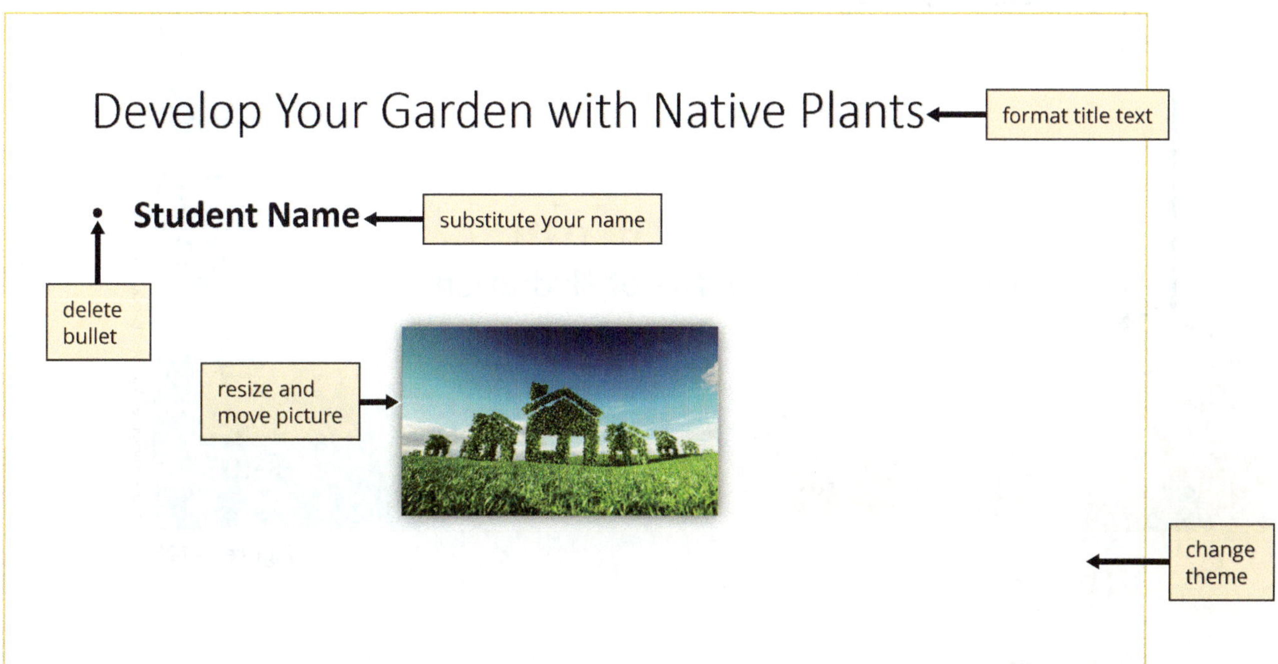

iStock.com/Petmal

Figure 1–124

Expand Your World

Create a solution that uses cloud and web technologies by learning and investigating on your own from general guidance.

Modifying and Exporting a Presentation

Note: To complete this assignment, you will be required to use the Data Files. Please contact your instructor for information about accessing the Data Files.

Instructions: Start PowerPoint. Open the presentation called SC_PPT_1-3.pptx, which is located in the Data Files. The presentation you open contains one title slide promoting drinking water regularly every day. The nutritionists at your community's fitness center want to emphasize the many benefits of drinking water, and they are planning to present a seminar on the topic of reasons to stay hydrated. You are part of a committee to publicize the event and want to share the title slide you developed. You have decided to store the file on OneDrive. You are going to modify the slide you have created, shown in Figure 1–125, and save it to OneDrive.

Perform the following tasks:

1. Insert the pictures called Support_PPT_1_Bottle.jpg and Support_PPT_1_Stay.jpg, which are located in the Data Files. Size and then move them to the areas indicated in Figure 1–125. Use the smart guides to help you position the pictures.

   If requested to do so by your instructor, change the words, Chicago, IL, to the town and state where you were born.
2. Save the file to your OneDrive account.
3. Save the file with the file name, **SC_PPT_1_Water**, and submit the presentation in the format specified by your instructor.
4. **Consider This:** When would you save one of your files for school or your job to OneDrive? Do you think using OneDrive enhances collaboration efforts? Why?

iStock.com/Semen Vasilyev; iStock.com/Mussbila; iStock.com/Nadia_bormotova

Figure 1–125

In the Lab

Apply your creative thinking and problem-solving skills to design and implement a solution.

Design and Create a Presentation about Summer Camp

Part 1: Your local park district is preparing to advertise its Kids Camp, and the public relations department employees have asked you to develop a PowerPoint presentation as part of your internship responsibilities. They inform you that this year's Camp will begin on July 1 and will run for 4 weeks. Popular activities include artistic workshops and field trips. Registration is being held now at the park district office, which is open from noon to 4 pm daily. The non-refundable Camp fee is $245, which includes lunch, and early registrants will receive a free t-shirt. Use the concepts and techniques presented in this module to prepare a presentation with a minimum of four slides that showcase the Kids Camp program. Research summer day camp programs held in previous years and in other communities for ideas about promoting the various activities. Select a suitable theme and include a title slide and bulleted lists. Use the pictures Support_PPT_1_Chalkboard.jpg, Support_PPT_1_Campers.jpg, Support_PPT_1_Painting.jpg, and Support_PPT_1_Clock.jpg, which are located in the Data Files. When finished, save your presentation with the file name, **SC_PPT_1_Camp**. Review and revise your presentation as needed. Submit your assignment in the format specified by your instructor.

Part 2: **Consider This:** You made several decisions while creating the presentation in this assignment: what theme to use, where to place text, how to format the text (font, font size, paragraph alignment, bulleted paragraphs, italics, bold, underline, color). What was the rationale behind each of these decisions? When you reviewed the slides, what further revisions did you make and why? Where would you recommend showing this slide show?

Enhancing Presentations with Shapes and SmartArt

Objectives

After completing this module, you will be able to:

- Search for and download an online theme
- Insert a symbol
- Convert text to SmartArt
- Edit and format SmartArt text
- Insert a hyperlink to a webpage
- Resize an inserted shape
- Apply effects to a shape
- Add text to a shape
- Apply a shape style
- Move an object smart guides
- Merge shapes
- Insert a picture as a shape fill
- Add a footer
- Add a slide transition and effect options

Introduction

In our visually oriented culture, audience members enjoy viewing effective graphics. Whether reading a document or viewing a PowerPoint presentation, people increasingly want to see photos, artwork, graphics, and a variety of typefaces. Researchers have known for decades that documents with visual elements are more effective than those that consist of only text because the illustrations motivate audiences to study the material. People remember at least one-third more information when the document they are seeing or reading contains visual elements. These graphics help clarify and emphasize details, so they appeal to audience members with differing backgrounds, reading levels, attention spans, and motivations.

BTW
Building Speaker Confidence
As you rehearse your speech, keep in mind that your audience will by studying the visual elements during your actual presentation and will not be focusing on you. Using graphics in a presentation should give you confidence as a presenter because they support your verbal message and help reinforce what you are trying to convey.

Project—Presentation with SmartArt and Shapes

In this module's project, you will follow proper design guidelines and learn to use PowerPoint to create the slides shown in Figures 2–1a through 2–1e. The objective is to produce a presentation for the Career Success Center that provides a variety of services to help students identify majors and find jobs that fit their interests, skills, and personality. The Center has an experienced staff with expertise in exploring careers, and they use the *Occupational Outlook Handbook* to provide information about the qualifications, salary, and work environment for hundreds of jobs. The Center's career coaches also give assessment tests and coordinate internships and networking opportunities. Students can begin their job search by using an online tool that allows them to search for and then apply for openings at a variety of organizations. The presentation shown in Figure 2–1 follows graphical guidelines and has a variety of visual elements that are clear and appealing to students exploring career options and searching for jobs. For example, the shapes have specific designs and effects. They are formatted using styles and SmartArt, which give the presentation a professional look. Transitions help one slide flow gracefully into the next during a slide show.

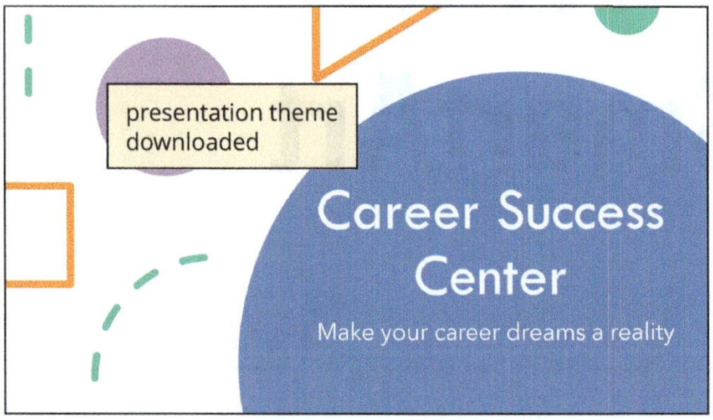

Figure 2–1(a): Slide 1 (Title Slide)

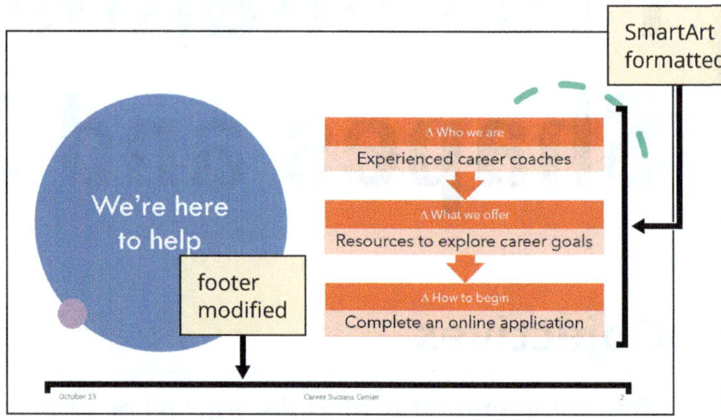

Figure 2–1(b): Slide 2 (Formatted SmartArt)

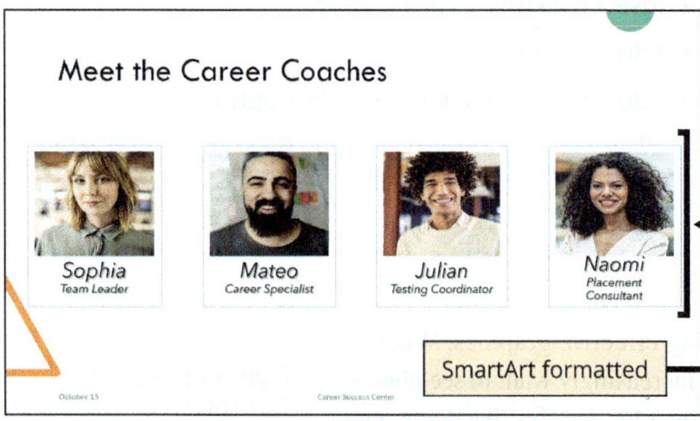

Figure 2–1(c): Slide 3 (Formatted SmartArt)

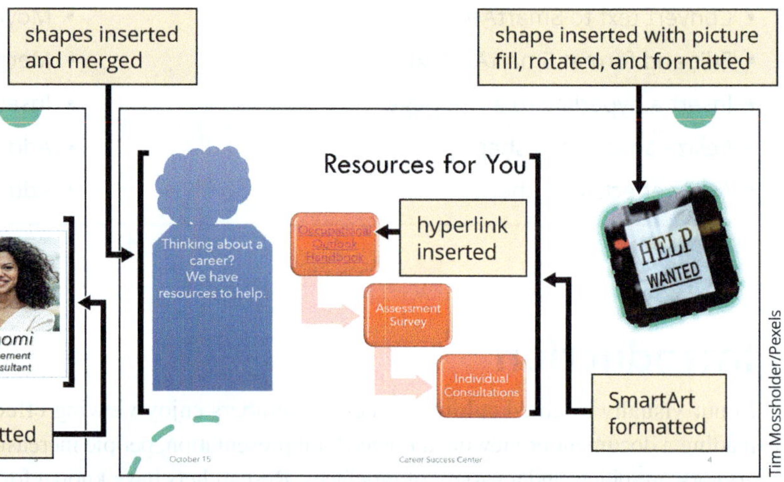

Tim Mossholder/Pexels

Figure 2–1(d): Slide 4 (Formatted SmartArt and Shape with Picture Fill)

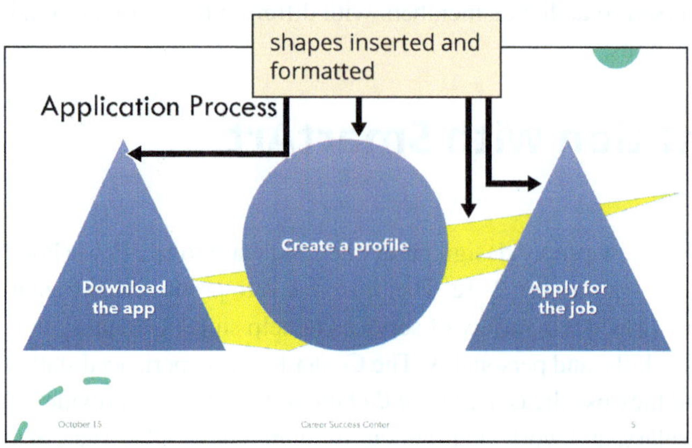

Figure 2–1(e): Slide 5 (Shapes Inserted and Formatted)

In this module, you will learn how to create the slides shown in Figure 2–1. You will perform the following general tasks as you progress through this module:

1. Download a theme and select slides for the presentation.
2. Create, edit, and format SmartArt.
3. Insert and format shapes.
4. Insert a symbol and a hyperlink.
5. Resize and merge shapes.
6. Move shapes using grids, guides, and the ruler.
7. Modify a footer and add a transition.

Downloading a Theme and Editing Slides

In Module 1, you selected a theme and then typed the content for the title and text slides. In this module, you will type the slide content for the title and text slides, insert and format SmartArt, and insert and format shapes. To begin creating the five slides in this presentation, you will download a theme, delete unneeded slides in this downloaded presentation, and then enter content in the slides.

BTW
Screen Resolution
If you are using a computer to step through the project in this module and you want your screens to match the figures in this book, you should change your screen's resolution to 1920 × 1080.

To Search for and Download an Online Theme

PowerPoint displays many themes that are varied and appealing and give you an excellent start at designing a presentation. At times, however, you may have a specific topic and design concept and could use some assistance in starting to develop the presentation. Microsoft offers thousands of predesigned themes and templates that could provide you with an excellent starting point. **Why?** You can search for one of these ready-made presentations, or you can browse one of the predefined categories, such as business or education. The themes and templates can save you time and help you develop content. The following steps search for a theme with a geometric concept.

1

- sam Run PowerPoint and then point to the More themes link (Figure 2–2).

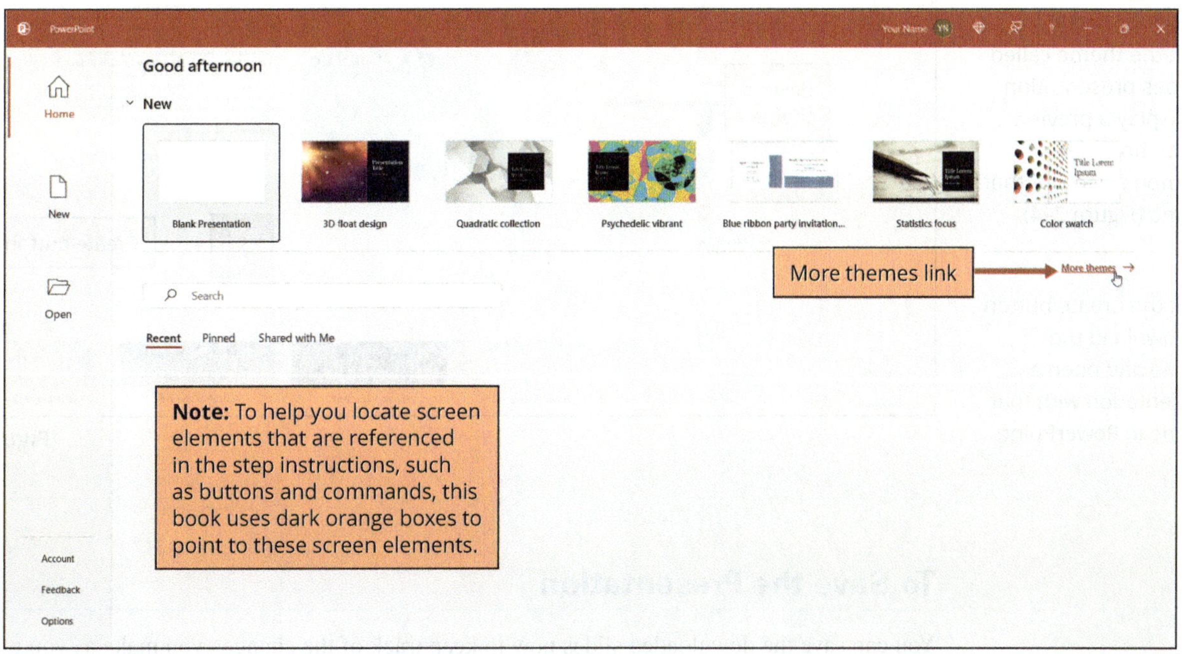

Figure 2–2

2

- Click the More themes link to display the New screen and then type **shapes** in the 'Search for online templates and themes' box (Figure 2–3).

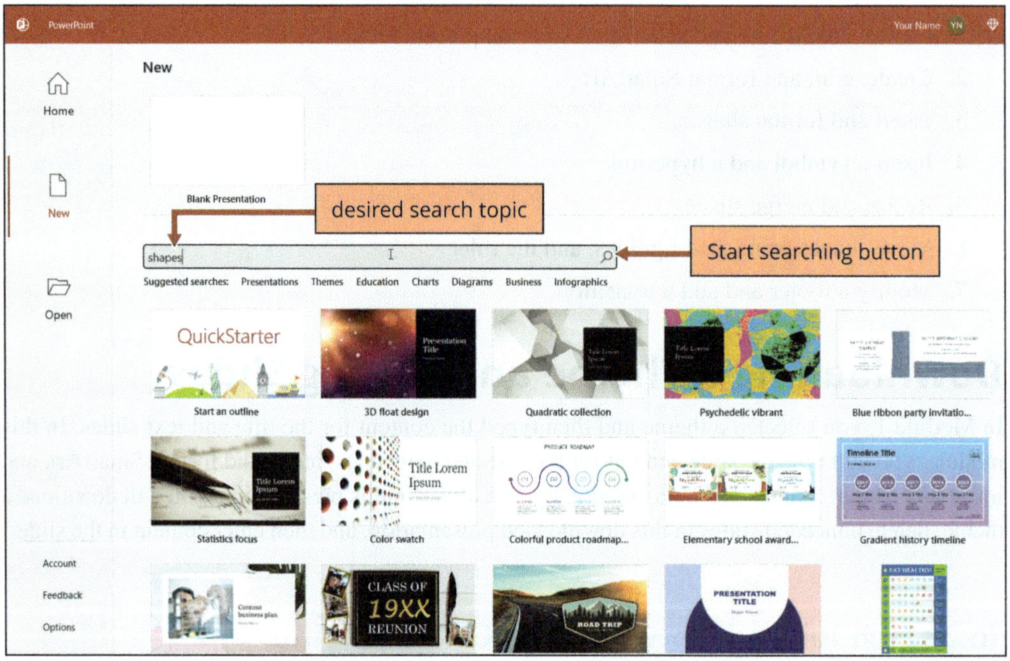

Figure 2–3

Q&A Why are my theme thumbnails displaying in a different order?
The order changes as you choose themes for presentations. In addition, Microsoft occasionally adds and modifies the themes, so the order may change.

Can I choose one of the keywords listed below the 'Search for online templates and themes' box?
Yes. Click one of the terms in the Suggested searches list to display a variety of templates and themes relating to those topics.

3

- Click the Start searching button (the magnifying glass) or press ENTER to search for and display all themes with the keyword, shapes.
- Click the theme called Shapes presentation to display a preview dialog box with a thumbnail view of that theme (Figure 2–4).

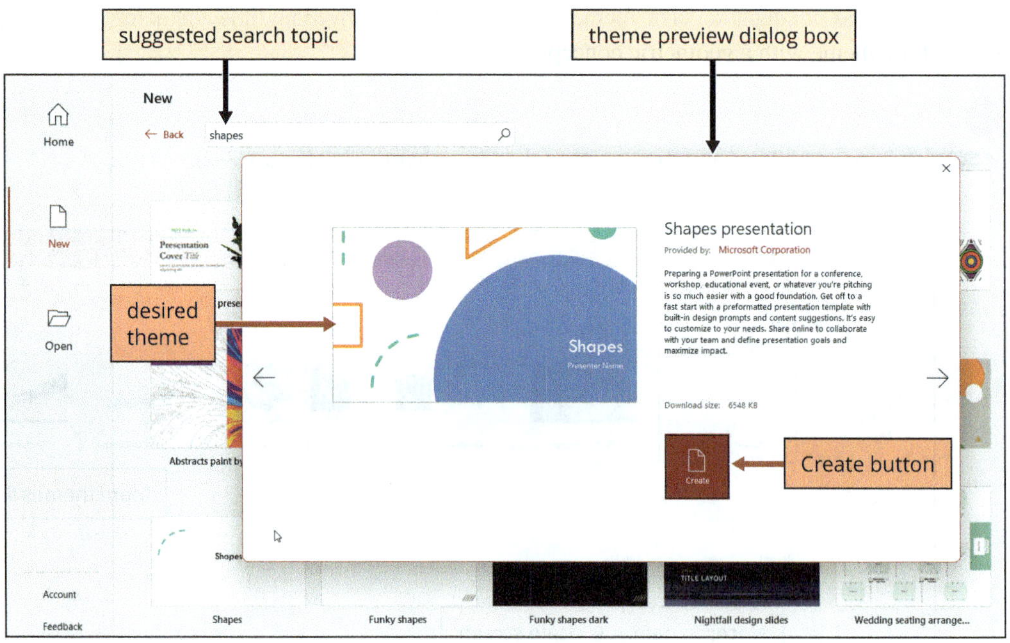

Figure 2–4

4

- Click the Create button to download the theme and open a presentation with that theme in PowerPoint.

To Save the Presentation

You can save the downloaded slides now to keep track of the changes you make as you progress through this module. The following steps save the file as a PowerPoint presentation.

1. Click the File tab to display the Backstage view, click the Save As tab to display the Save As gallery, and then click the default save location or the save location specified by your instructor to display the Save As dialog box.
2. Type **SC_PPT_2_Career** as the file name.
3. Click Save to save the presentation.

BTW
Organizing Files and Folders
You should organize and store files in folders so that you easily can find the files later. For example, if you are taking an introductory technology class called CIS 101, a good practice would be to save all PowerPoint files in a PowerPoint folder in a CIS 101 folder.

To Delete a Slide

The downloaded theme has 13 slides with a variety of layouts. You will use three of these different layouts in your Career presentation, so you can delete the slides you downloaded that you will not need. **Why?** Deleting the extra slides now helps reduce clutter and helps you focus on the layouts you will use. The following steps delete the extra slides.

1

- Click the Slide 3 thumbnail in the Slides tab to select this slide.
- Press and hold SHIFT, scroll down, and then click the thumbnail for Slide 7 to select slides 3 through 7 (Figure 2–5).

Q&A Do I need to select consecutive slides?
No. You can select an individual slide to delete. You also can select nonconsecutive slides by pressing and holding CTRL and then clicking the thumbnails of the slides you want to delete.

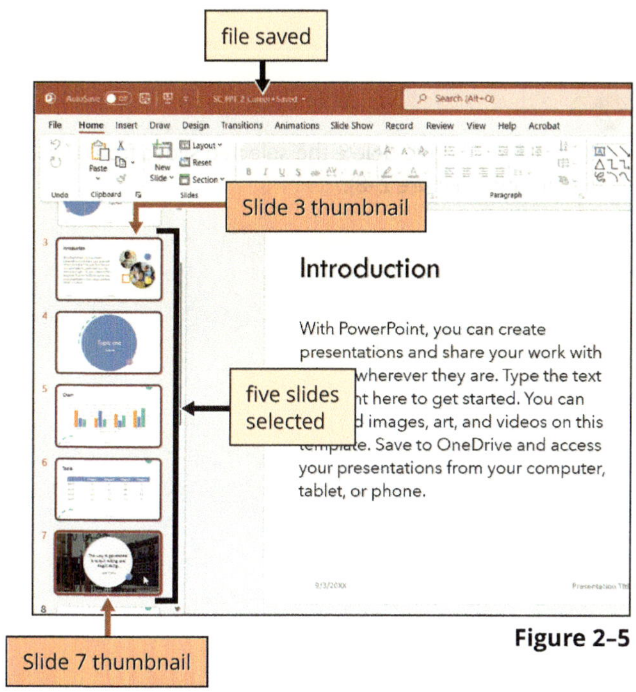

Figure 2–5

2

- Right-click any selected slide to display the shortcut menu (Figure 2–6).

3

- Click Delete Slide to delete the selected slides from the presentation.

4

- Click the Slide 4 thumbnail in the Slides tab to select this slide.
- Press and hold SHIFT, scroll down, and then click the thumbnail for Slide 8 to select slides 4 through 8.

Q&A How can I select nonconsecutive slides?
Hold CTRL and then click only the slides you want to select. In contrast, when you hold down SHIFT, you select consecutive slides between the first and last selected slides.

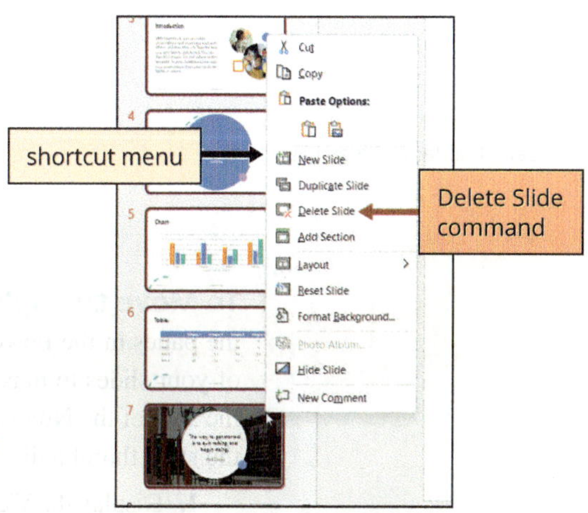

Figure 2–6

5

- Right-click any selected slide to display the shortcut menu (Figure 2–7).

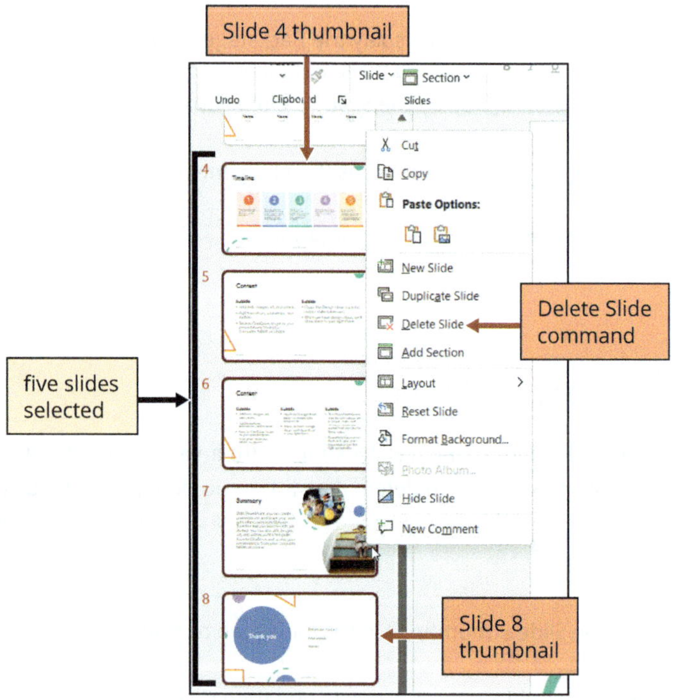

Figure 2–7

6

- Click Delete Slide to delete the selected slides from the presentation (Figure 2–8).

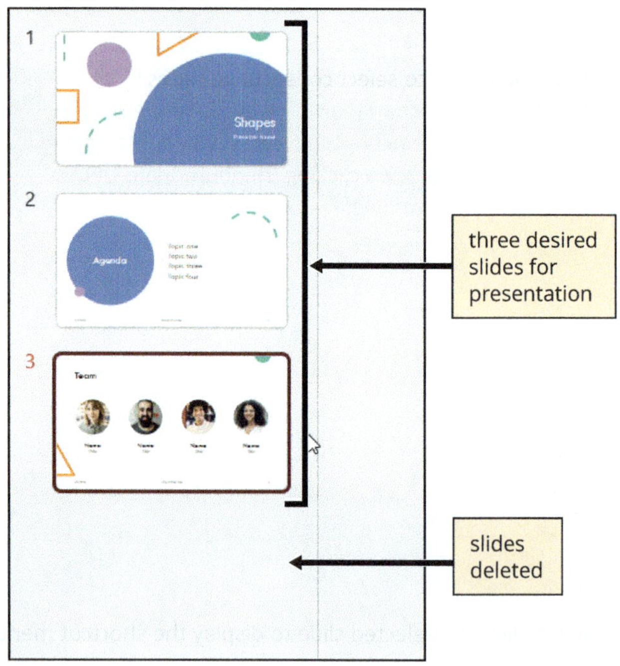

Figure 2–8

Other Ways

1. Select slide(s), press DELETE
2. Select slide(s), press BACKSPACE

To Move the Splitters in a Window You can maximize the working space of each of the panes in the PowerPoint window. You can, for example, hide or narrow the thumbnail views of your slides to maximize the editing space in the Slide pane. You also can increase or decrease the area of the Notes pane by dragging the splitter bar up or down. To hide or decrease the size of the slide thumbnails, you would perform the following steps.

1. Display the View tab and then click the Normal button (View tab | Presentation Views group).
2. Drag the splitter bar to the left until the slide thumbnails are the desired size or they are completely hidden.

To show or increase the size of the slide thumbnails, you would perform the following steps.

1. Display the View tab and then click the Normal button (View tab | Presentation Views group).
2. Point to the splitter bar between the Slide pane and the thumbnails, and then drag the splitter bar to the right.

If the thumbnails are hidden, you will see a collapsed Thumbnails menu. To show the thumbnails, you would perform the following step.

1. Click the collapsed menu button (a downward arrow) located to the right of the word, Thumbnails.

BTW

PowerPoint Help

At any time while using PowerPoint, you can find answers to questions and display information about various topics through PowerPoint Help. Used properly, this form of assistance can increase your productivity and reduce your frustrations by minimizing the time you spend learning how to use PowerPoint.

To Create a Title Slide

Recall from Module 1 that the title slide introduces the presentation to the audience. In addition to introducing the presentation, this project uses the title slide to capture the audience's attention by using title text. The following steps create the slide show's title slide.

1. Display Slide 1, select the title text (Shapes) in the title text placeholder, and then type **Career Success Center** as the title text.

2. Increase the font size of this title text to 80 point.

Q&A Why do I have to select the text in the placeholder before typing?
This downloaded template includes text in some of the placeholders that must be replaced with your own text.

3. Click the subtitle text placeholder, select the text (Presenter Name) in that placeholder, and then type **Make your career dreams a reality** as the subtitle text.

4. Increase the font size of this subtitle text to 32 point (Figure 2–9).

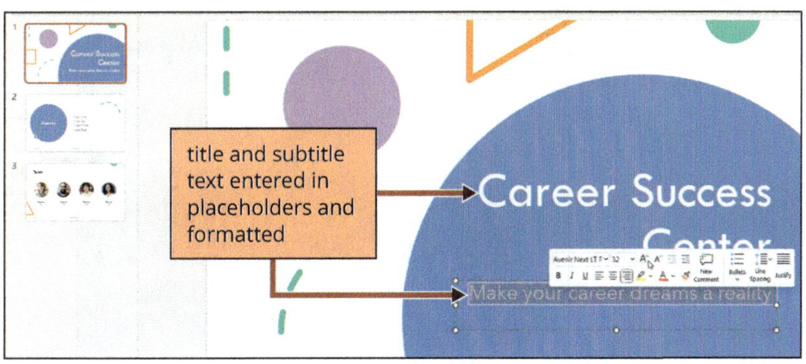

Figure 2–9

To Align a Paragraph

The PowerPoint design themes specify the default alignment of and spacing for text within a placeholder. For example, the text in most paragraphs is **left-aligned**, so the first character of each line is even with the left side of the placeholder. Text alignment also can be horizontally **centered** to position each line evenly between the left and right placeholder edges; **right-aligned**, so that the last character of each line is even with the last character of each line above or below it; and **justified**, where the first and last characters of each line are aligned and extra space is inserted between words to spread the characters evenly across the line.

By default, the title placeholder text in Slide 1 is right-aligned. You want the text to be centered in the blue circle. **Why?** You want the office name, Career Success Center, to display prominently in the center of the blue circle. The following steps center the text in the title placeholder on Slide 1.

1

- Place the insertion point anywhere in the Slide 1 title text (Figure 2–10).

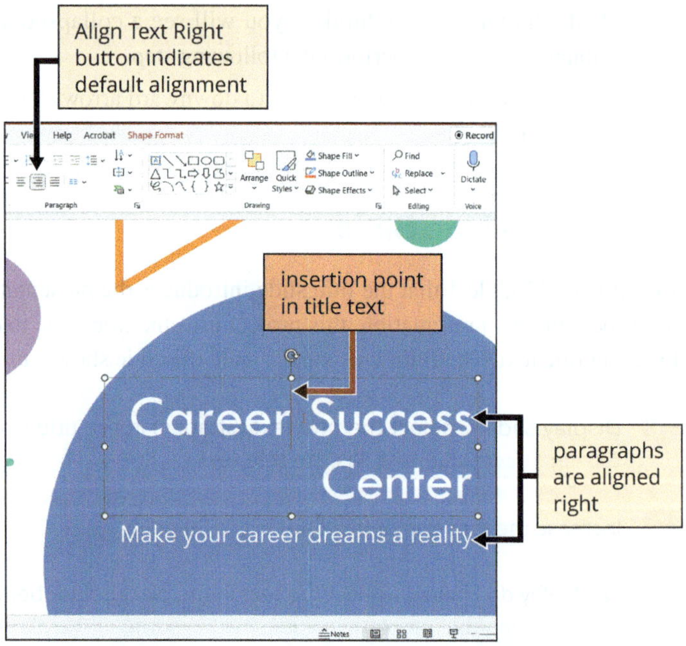

Figure 2–10

2

- Click the Center button (Home tab | Paragraph group) to center this paragraph (Figure 2–11).

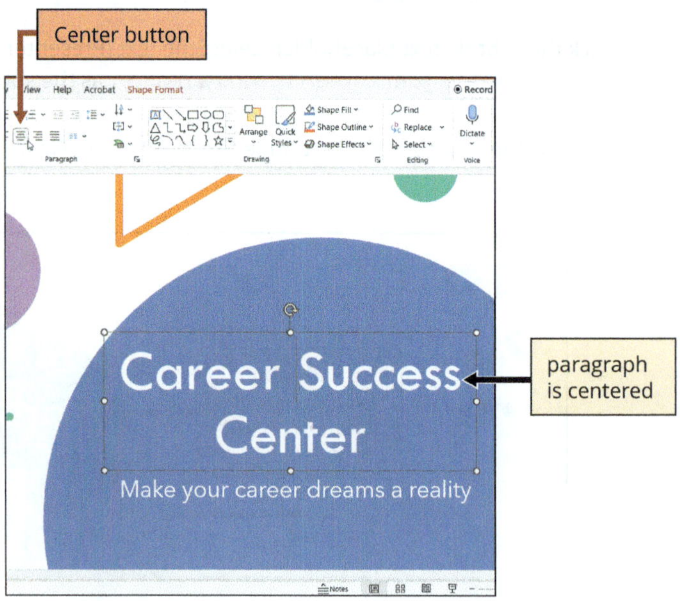

Figure 2–11

Other Ways

1. Click Center button on Mini toolbar
2. Right-click selected text, click Paragraph on shortcut menu, click Alignment arrow (Paragraph dialog box), click Center, click OK
3. Click Paragraph Dialog Box Launcher (Home tab | Paragraph group), click Alignment arrow (Paragraph dialog box), click Center, click OK
4. Press CTRL+E

To Create the First Text Slide

The first text slide you create in Module 2 emphasizes three Center aspects: the career coaches, the available resources, and the process to begin a career search. The following steps create the Slide 2 text slide using the Title and Content layout.

1. Display Slide 2, select the text (Agenda) in the title text placeholder, and then type **We're here to help** in the placeholder.
2. Select the first paragraph text (Topic one) in the content placeholder and then type **Who we are** as the first paragraph.
3. Press ENTER, click the 'Increase List Level' button to indent the second paragraph below the first, and then type **Experienced career coaches** as the first second-level paragraph.
4. Select the text in the next paragraph (Topic two) and then type **What we offer** as the second first-level paragraph.
5. Press ENTER, click the 'Increase List Level' button to indent the next paragraph, and then type **Resources to explore career goals** as the second second-level paragraph.
6. Select the text in the next paragraph (Topic three) and then type **How to begin** as the third first-level paragraph.
7. Press ENTER, click the 'Increase List Level' button, and then type **Complete an online application** as the third second-level paragraph.
8. Select the text in the last paragraph (Topic four) and then press DELETE to delete this paragraph (Figure 2–12).

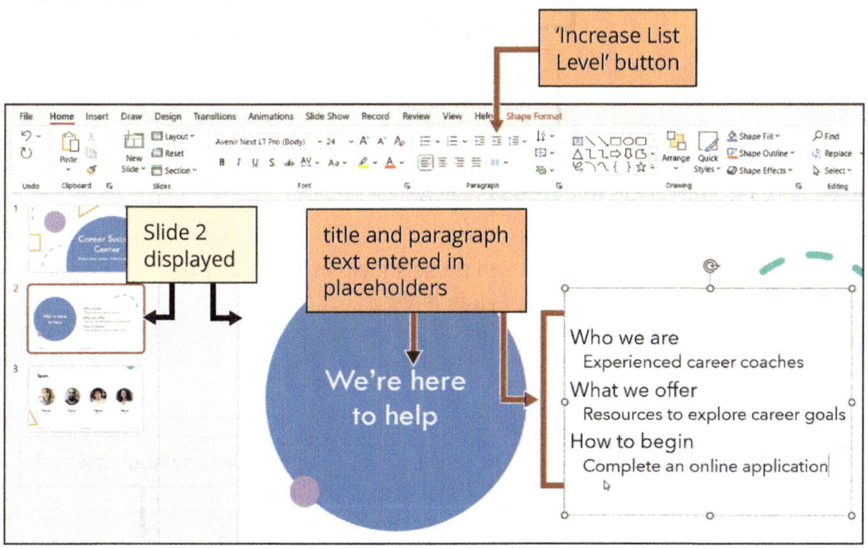

Figure 2–12

BTW
Ribbon and Screen Resolution
PowerPoint may change how the groups and buttons within the groups appear on the ribbon, depending on the screen resolution of your computer. Thus, your ribbon may look different from the ones in this book if you are using a screen resolution other than 1920 × 1080.

To Insert a Symbol

The Shapes presentation template has many geometric shapes on the slides. To add interest and coordinate with these shapes, you want to add a delta symbol (Δ) to the three first-level paragraphs. Many symbols are located in the Symbol, Webdings, and Wingdings fonts. The delta symbol is located in the Symbol font. **Why?** Many mathematical symbols, dots, and geometric shapes are found in this font. You insert symbols by changing the font. The following steps insert a delta symbol before the word, Who, in the first paragraph.

BTW
Delta Symbol
Delta is the fourth letter of the Greek alphabet and also has the value of four in the Greek numeral system. It commonly is used in mathematics, chemistry, and physics to represent change in a variable.

1

- Place the insertion point directly before the word, Who, in the first content paragraph.
- Display the Insert tab and then click the Symbol button (Insert tab | Symbols group) to display the Symbol dialog box (Figure 2–13).

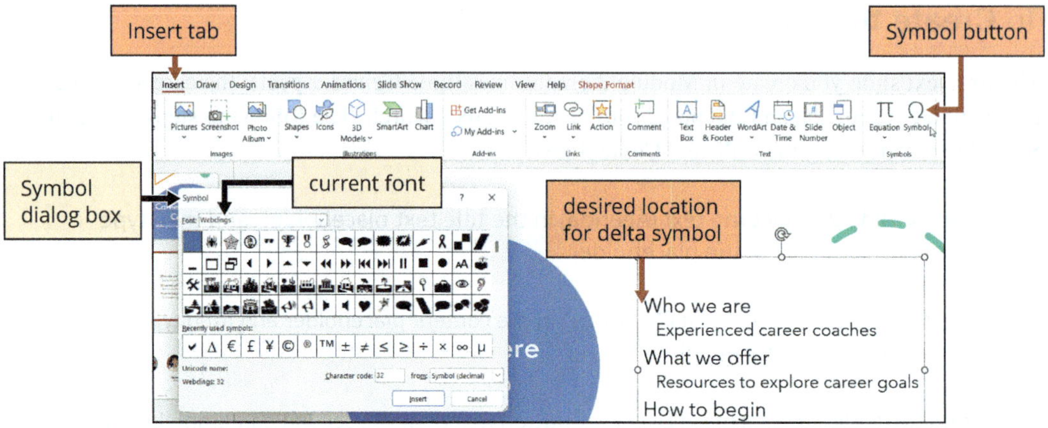

Figure 2–13

Q&A What if the Insert tab includes a Symbols button with an arrow?
Click the Symbols button to display the Symbols menu and then click the Symbol button.

2

- If necessary, click the Symbol dialog box title bar and then drag the dialog box near the left edge of the slide so that the content placeholder paragraphs are visible.

3

- If Symbol is not the font displayed in the Font box, click the Font arrow (Symbol dialog box) and then drag or scroll to Symbol and click this font.
- Click the delta symbol as shown in Figure 2–14. The symbol number and character code (68) appear at the bottom of the dialog box.

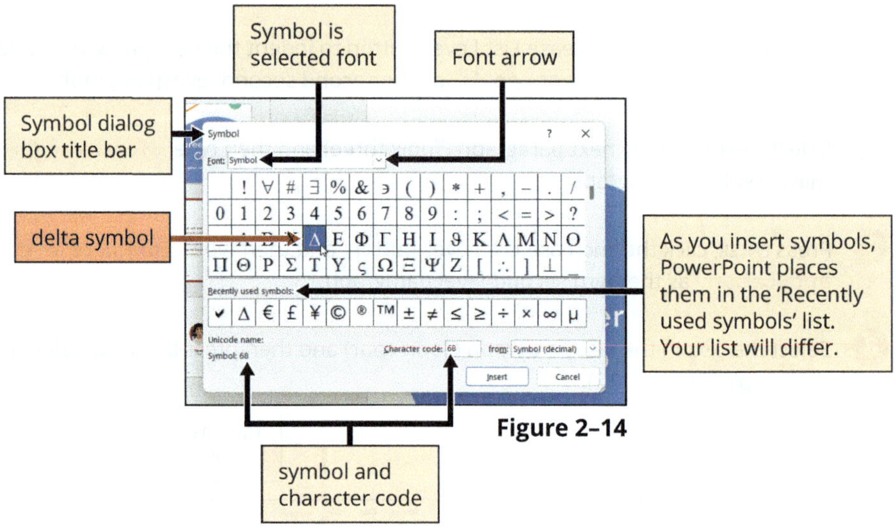

Figure 2–14

Q&A What if the symbol I want to insert already appears in the Symbol dialog box?
You can click any symbol shown in the dialog box to insert it into the slide.

Why does my 'Recently used symbols' list display different symbols from those shown in Figure 2–14?
As you insert symbols, PowerPoint places them in the 'Recently used symbols' list.

4

- Click the Insert button (Symbol dialog box) to place the delta symbol before the word, Who (Figure 2–15).

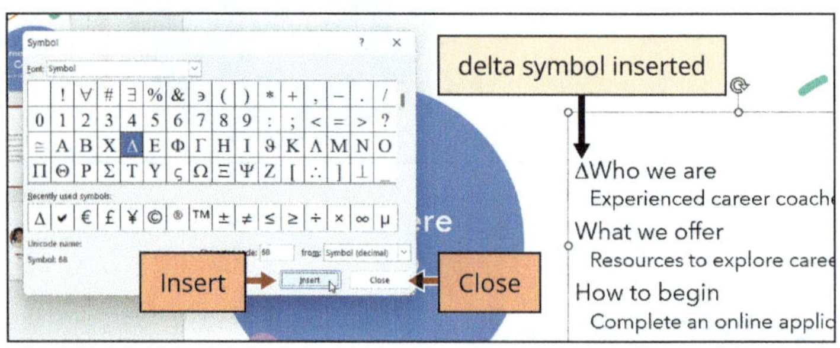

Figure 2–15

Q&A What is the delta symbol?
The uppercase Greek letter delta frequently is used in mathematics to denote "change" or "the change in."

Why is the Symbol dialog box still open?
The Symbol dialog box remains open, allowing you to insert additional symbols.

5

- Click the Close button (Symbol dialog box).

To Copy a Symbol

To add the delta symbol in the second first-level paragraph, you could repeat the process you used to insert the first symbol. Rather than inserting this symbol from the Symbol dialog box, you can copy the symbol and then paste it in the appropriate place. **Why?** This process can be accomplished more quickly with copy and paste when using the same symbol multiple times. The following steps copy the delta symbol before the word, What, in the second paragraph and before the word, How, in the third paragraph.

1

- Select the delta symbol in the first paragraph, display the Home tab, and then click the Copy button (Home tab | Clipboard group) to copy the delta symbol to the Office Clipboard (Figure 2–16).

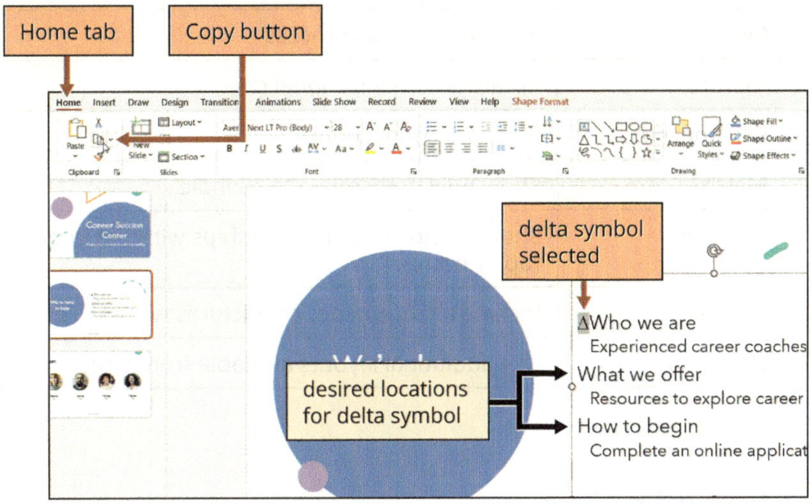

Figure 2–16

2

- Place the insertion point directly before the word, What, in the second first-level paragraph and then click the Paste button (Home tab | Clipboard group) to insert the delta symbol.

Q&A Why did PowerPoint add a space after the symbol when it was pasted?
Some AutoCorrect settings may cause this to occur. If a space is not added, press SPACEBAR to add a space between the symbol and the first word in the paragraph.

- Place the insertion point directly before the word, How, in the third first-level paragraph and then click the Paste button to insert the delta symbol.
- Place the insertion point between the delta symbol and the word, Who, in the first first-level paragraph and then press SPACEBAR to place a space between the symbol and the word (Figure 2–17).

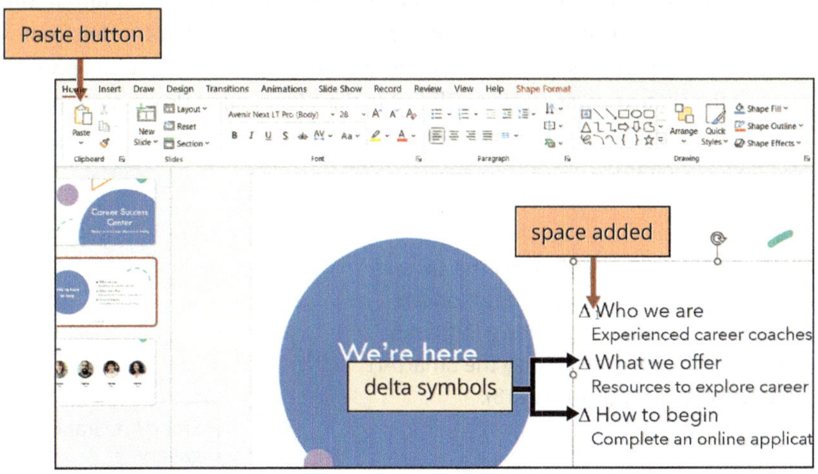

Figure 2–17

Creating and Formatting a SmartArt Graphic

An illustration often can help convey relationships between key points in your presentation. Microsoft 365 includes **SmartArt**, which consists of customizable diagrams that you can use to pictorially present lists, processes, and other relationships. The SmartArt layouts have a variety of shapes, arrows, and lines to correspond to the major points you want your audience to remember.

You can create a SmartArt graphic in two ways: Convert text or pictures already present on a slide to a SmartArt graphic, or select a SmartArt graphic type and then add text and pictures. Once the SmartArt graphic is present, you can customize its look. Table 2–1 lists the SmartArt types and their uses.

Table 2-1: SmartArt Graphic Layout Types and Purposes

Type	Purpose
List	Show nonsequential information
Process	Show steps in a process or timeline
Cycle	Show a continual process
Hierarchy	Create an organizational chart
Relationship	Illustrate connections
Matrix	Show how parts relate to a whole
Pyramid	Show proportional relationships with the largest component at the top or bottom
Picture	Include a placeholder for pictures within the graphic
Office.com	Use additional layouts available from Office.com

BTW
Updated Layouts
Some of the items in the SmartArt Styles gallery may be updates; Microsoft periodically adds layouts to Office.com and corresponding categories.

To Convert Text to a SmartArt Graphic

You quickly can convert small amounts of slide text and pictures into a SmartArt graphic. Once you determine the type of graphic, such as process or cycle, you then have a wide variety of styles from which to choose in the SmartArt Graphics gallery. As with other galleries, you can point to the samples and view a live preview if you are using a mouse. The following steps convert the six text paragraphs on Slide 2 to the 'Segmented Process' graphic, which is part of the Process category. **Why?** This SmartArt style is a good match for the content of Slide 2. It has three large areas for the titles and placeholders for the Level 2 text under each title.

1

- With Slide 2 displayed, select the six text paragraphs and then click the 'Convert to SmartArt Graphic' button (Home tab | Paragraph group) to display the SmartArt Graphics gallery (Figure 2-18).

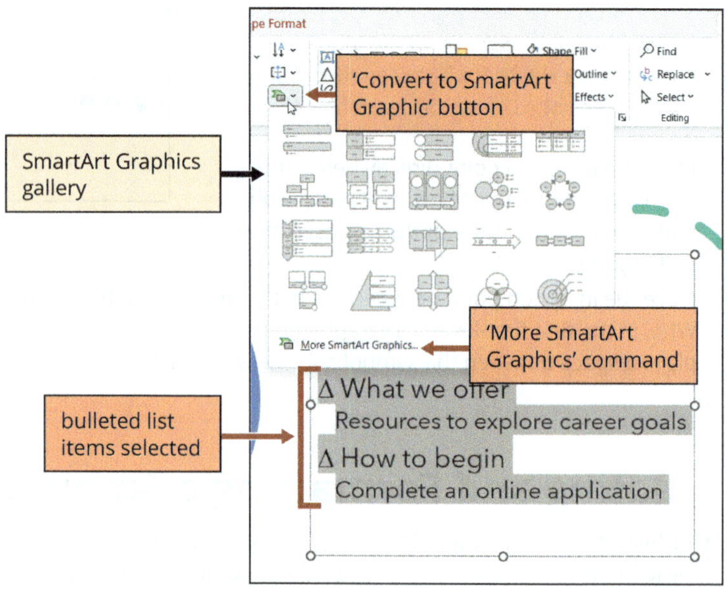

Figure 2-18

2

- Click 'More SmartArt Graphics' in the SmartArt Graphics gallery to display the Choose a SmartArt Graphic dialog box.
- Click Process in the left pane to display the Process gallery.
- Scroll down and then click the Segmented Process graphic (first graphic in the eighth row) to display a preview of this graphic in the right pane (Figure 2–19).
- **Experiment:** Click various categories and graphics in the SmartArt Styles gallery and view the various layouts.

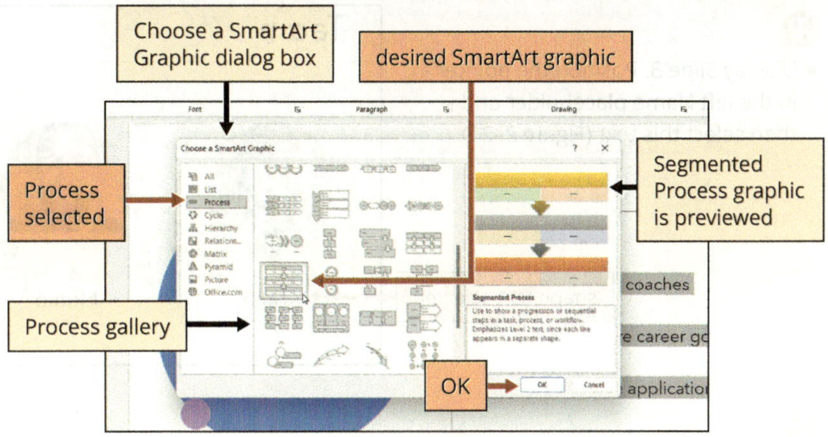

Figure 2–19

3

- Click OK (Choose a SmartArt Graphic dialog box) to apply this shape and convert the text (Figure 2–20).
- If the Text pane is displayed, click its Close button (the X in the upper-right corner) so that it no longer is displayed.

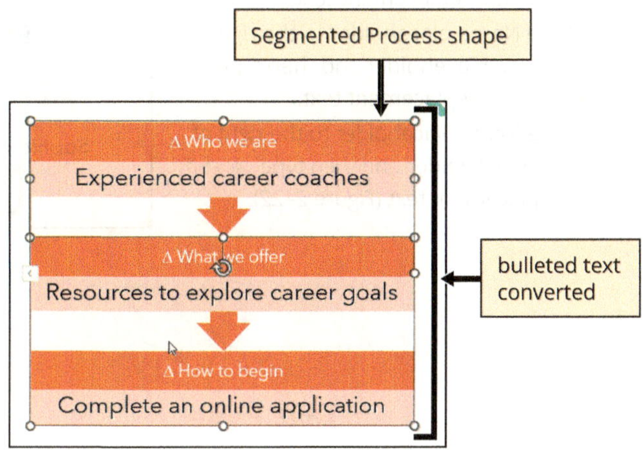

Figure 2–20

Other Ways

1. Select text, click 'Convert to SmartArt' on shortcut menu

To Edit SmartArt Shape Text

You may desire to change the text that appears in a SmartArt graphic. To do so, you can select the text and then make the desired changes. Also, if you display the Text Pane on the left side of the graphic, you can click the text you want to change and make your edits. The Shapes presentation theme included a slide with a People Portrait List SmartArt graphic, which is on Slide 3 of your slide deck. The following steps edit the sample text included in the graphic. First, you will edit the names below the four photos by selecting the text and then typing the replacement name. **Why?** Only first names are used, so it is easy to select the sample text and then type the replacement name.

1

- Display Slide 3. Position the pointer in the left Name placeholder and then select this text (Figure 2–21).

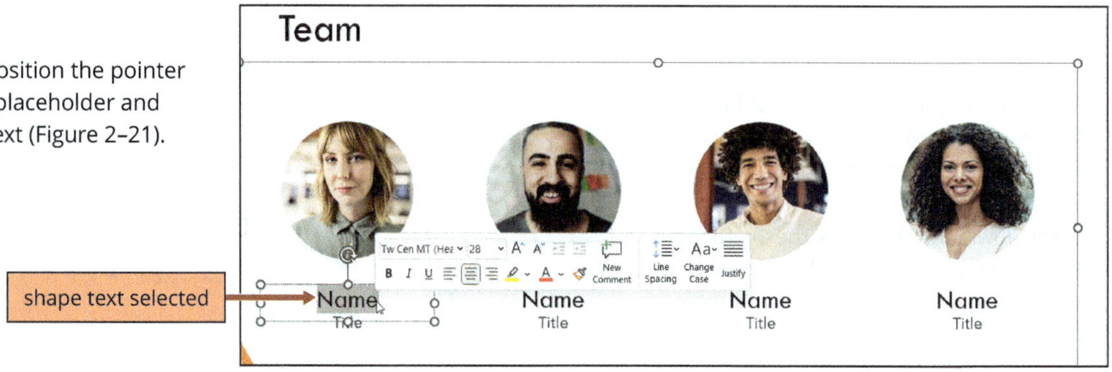

Figure 2–21

2

- Type **Sophia** as the replacement text.
- Select the Name placeholder to the right of the Sophia placeholder and then type **Mateo** as the replacement text.
- Select the Name placeholder to the right of the Mateo placeholder and then type **Julian** as the replacement text.
- Select the Name placeholder to the right of the Julian placeholder and then type **Naomi** as the replacement text (Figure 2–22).

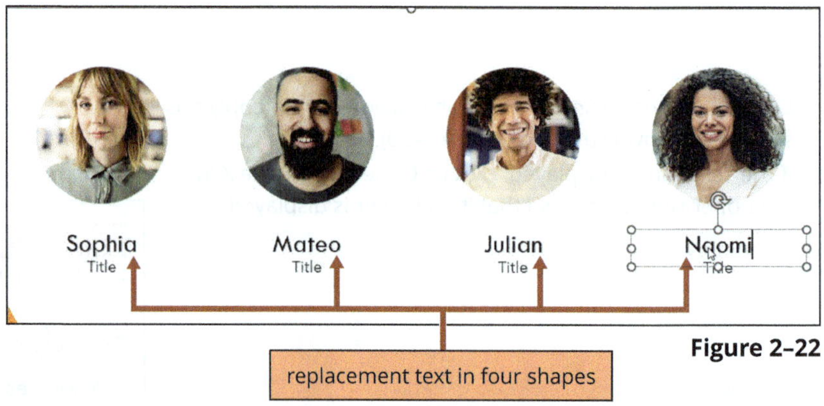

Figure 2–22

Text Pane

The **Text Pane** assists you in creating a graphic because you can direct your attention to developing and editing the message without being concerned with the actual graphic. The Text Pane consists of two areas: The top portion has the text that will appear in the SmartArt layout, and the bottom portion gives the name of the graphic and suggestions of what type of information is best suited for this type of visual. Each SmartArt graphic has an associated Text Pane with bullets that function as an outline and map directly to the image. You can create new lines of bulleted text and then indent and demote these lines. You also can check spelling. Table 2–2 shows the keyboard shortcuts you can use with the Text Pane.

Table 2–2: Text Pane Keyboard Shortcuts

Activity	Keyboard Shortcut
Indent text	TAB or ALT+SHIFT+RIGHT ARROW
Demote text	SHIFT+TAB or ALT+SHIFT+LEFT ARROW
Add a tab character	CTRL+TAB
Create a new line of text	ENTER
Check spelling	F7
Merge two lines of text	DELETE at the end of the first text line
Display the shortcut menu	SHIFT+F10
Switch between the SmartArt drawing canvas and the Text Pane	CTRL+SHIFT+F2
Close the Text Pane	ALT+F4
Switch the focus from the Text Pane to the SmartArt graphic border	ESC

To Edit SmartArt Text

Why? You want to add the titles of the Center's team. The graphic has four placeholders with the word, Title, for each of the four people shown. The following steps edit the paragraphs in the Slide 3 Text Pane.

1

- With the Slide 3 SmartArt selected, click the SmartArt Design tab and then click the Text Pane button (SmartArt Design tab | Create Graphic group) or the arrow icon on the left-center edge of the graphic to open the Text Pane.
- Select the text in the first Title second-level paragraph in the Text Pane (Figure 2–23).

2

- Type **Team Leader** as the replacement text for this second-level paragraph.
- Click the second bullet line or press the DOWN ARROW to move the insertion point to the next second-level paragraph. Select the text in this paragraph and then type **Career Specialist** as the replacement text.

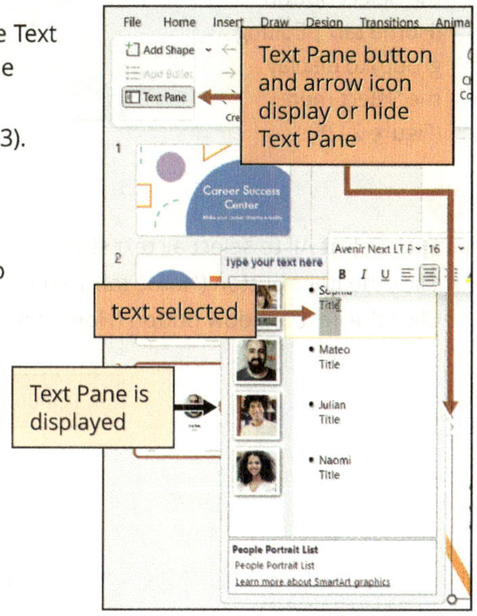

Figure 2–23

3

- Type **Testing Coordinator** as the replacement text for the next second-level paragraph.
- Type **Placement Consultant** as the replacement text for the rightmost second-level paragraph (Figure 2–24).

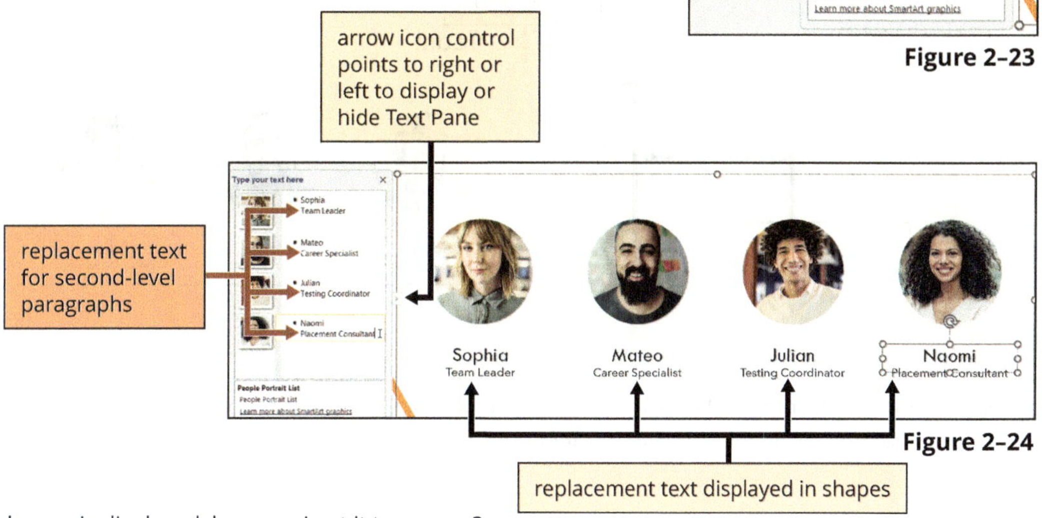

Figure 2–24

Q&A If my Text Pane no longer is displayed, how can I get it to appear?
Click the arrow icon control, which is the tab with a left-pointing arrow, on the left side of the SmartArt graphic.

I mistakenly pressed DOWN ARROW or ENTER. How can I delete the bullet paragraph I just added?
Press BACKSPACE to delete the paragraph.

I mistakenly pressed TAB to move to the next paragraph, and the current paragraph's level was changed. How can I fix it?
Press SHIFT+TAB to return to the previous level.

Other Ways

1. Right-click SmartArt graphic, click Show Text Pane on shortcut menu, enter text in Text Pane

To Format Text Pane Characters

Once the desired characters are entered in the Text Pane, you can change the font size and apply formatting features, such as bold, italic, and underlined text. **Why?** Changing the font and adding effects can help draw the audience members to the varied slide content and coordinate with the visual content. The following steps format the text by italicizing the letters and adding a shadow.

1

- With the Text Pane still displayed, display the Home tab and then click the Select button (Home tab | Editing group) to display the Select menu (Figure 2–25).

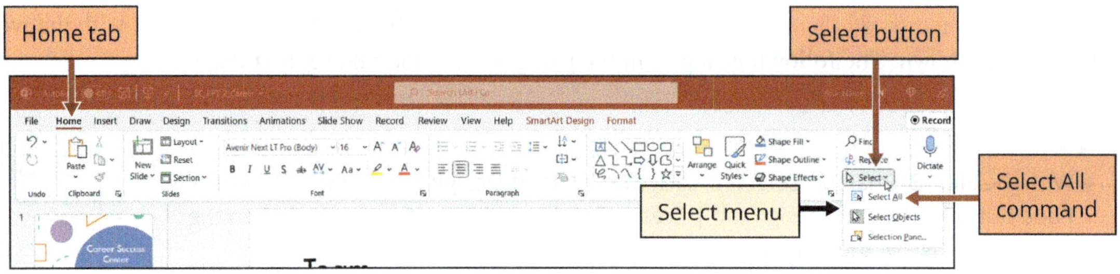

Figure 2–25

2

- Click Select All to select all text shapes in the SmartArt graphic.
- Click the Italic button (Home tab | Font group) to italicize all the text.
- Click the Text Shadow button (Home tab | Font group) to add a shadow to all the SmartArt text (Figure 2–26).

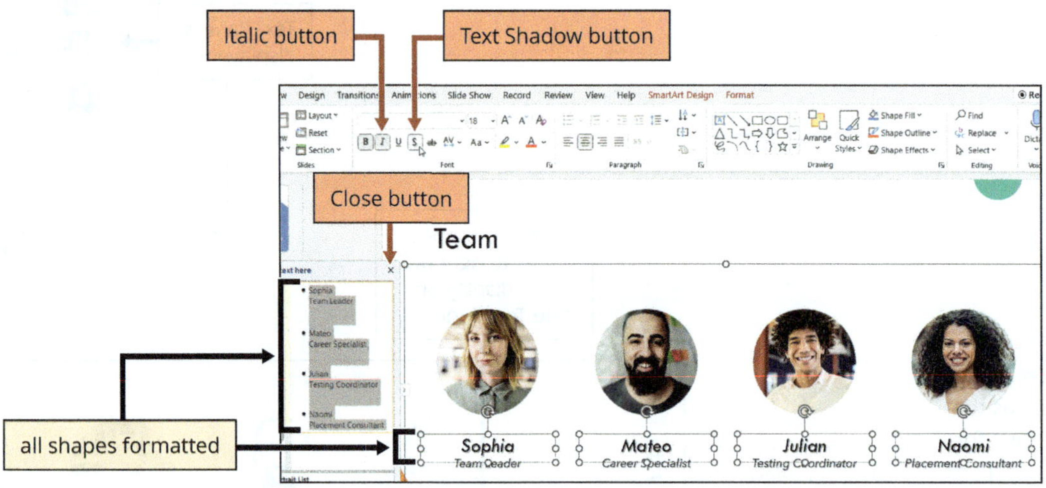

Figure 2–26

3

- Click the Close button in the Text Pane (shown in Figure 2–26) so that it no longer is displayed.
- Click a blank area inside the SmartArt border to deselect the shapes.

Other Ways

1. Drag through all text in Text pane, click Italic button and Text Shadow button on ribbon (Home tab | Font group)

To Change the SmartArt Layout

Once you begin formatting a SmartArt shape, you may decide that another layout better conveys the message you are communicating to an audience. PowerPoint allows you to change the layout easily. Any graphical changes that were made to the original SmartArt, such as changing and formatting text, are applied to the new SmartArt layout. The following steps change the SmartArt layout to Captioned Pictures. **Why?** It works well with the four photos and prominently displays the names and titles.

1

- With the Slide 3 SmartArt graphic still selected, display the SmartArt Design tab (Figure 2–27).

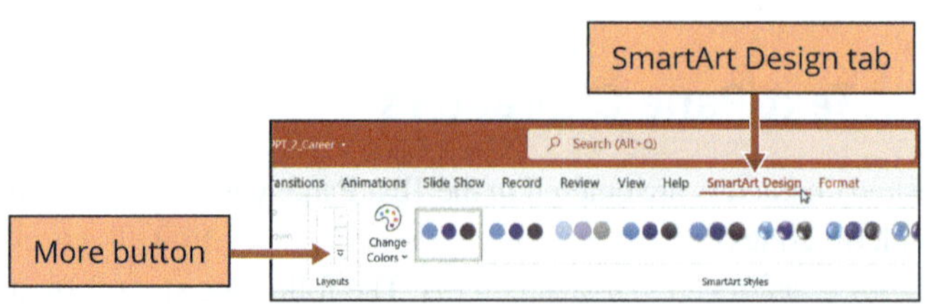

Figure 2–27

2

- Click the More button in the Layouts group (SmartArt Design tab) to display the Layouts menu (Figure 2–28).

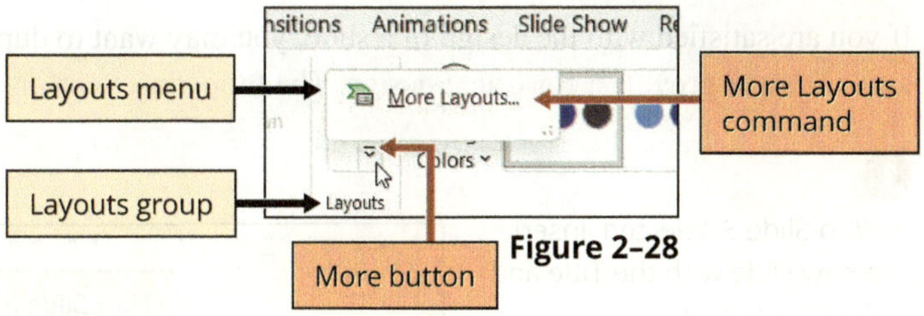

Figure 2–28

3

- Click More Layouts in the Layouts menu to display the Choose a SmartArt Graphic dialog box.
- Click Picture in the list of graphic categories and then click the Captioned Pictures layout (third layout in the second row) to display a picture and a description of this SmartArt layout (Figure 2–29).

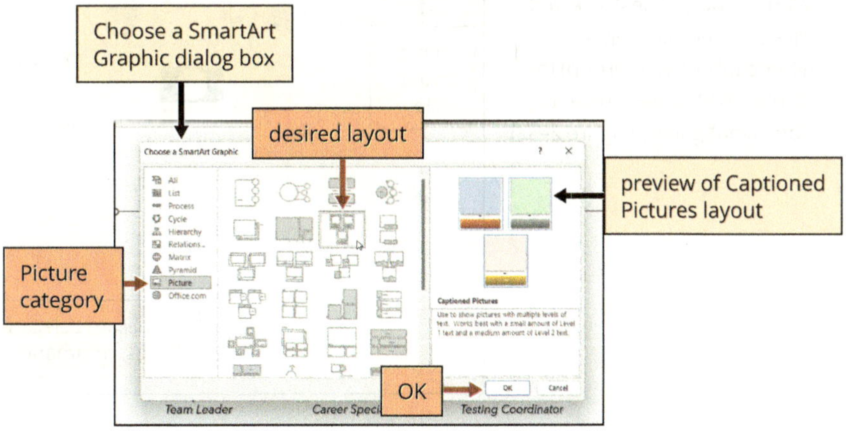

Figure 2–29

4

- Click OK (Choose a SmartArt Graphic dialog box) to change the layout (Figure 2–30).

Figure 2–30

To Edit the Title Text

The Slide 3 title text placeholder has the default wording from the online template. You need to change this text to reflect the current slide content. The following step edits the title text.

1 Select the current title text (Team) and then type **Meet the Career Coaches** as the replacement text (Figure 2–31).

Figure 2–31

To Duplicate a Slide

If you are satisfied with the design of a slide, you may want to duplicate it and then make slight modifications. **Why?** You can save time and provide a consistent design. The following steps insert a new slide and duplicate it.

1

- With Slide 3 selected, insert a new slide with the Title and Content layout.
- With the new Slide 4 selected, click the New Slide arrow (Home tab | Slides group) to display the Shapes presentation layout gallery (Figure 2–32).

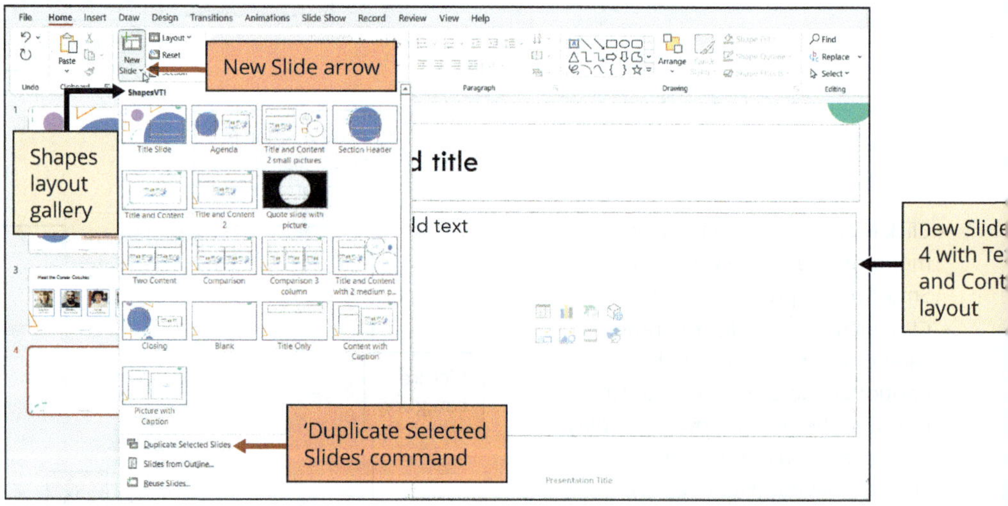

Figure 2–32

2

- Click 'Duplicate Selected Slides' in the Shapes presentation layout gallery to create a new Slide 5, which is a duplicate of Slide 4 (Figure 2–33).

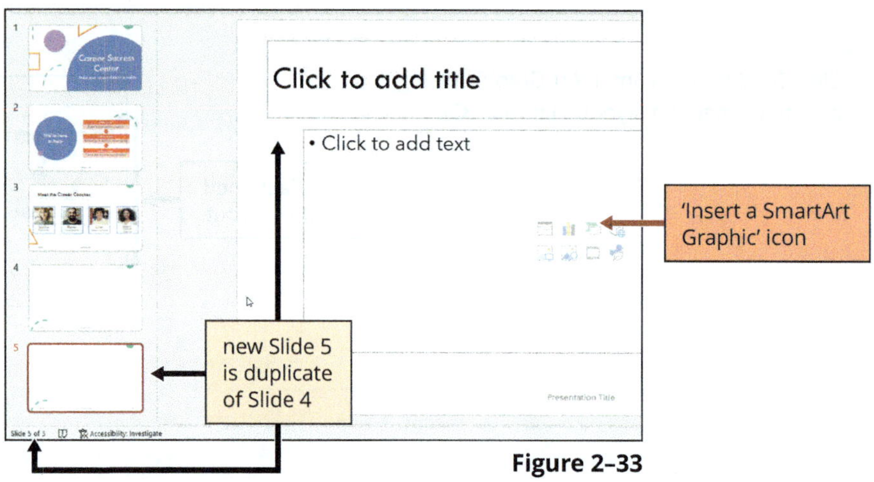

Figure 2–33

Other Ways

1. Right-click slide thumbnail in Slide pane, click Duplicate Slide

To Insert a SmartArt Graphic

Several SmartArt layouts have designs that reinforce concepts presented in a presentation. The Step Down Process graphic is appropriate for this presentation. **Why?** The student can begin by performing some independent research: checking the Occupational Outlook Handbook and then taking a survey to determine possible careers. Afterward, the student can meet with a coach. The following steps insert the Step Down Process SmartArt graphic.

1

- Display Slide 4 and then click the 'Insert a SmartArt Graphic' icon in the content placeholder (shown in Figure 2–33) to display the 'Choose a SmartArt Graphic' dialog box.

- Click Process in the left pane to display the Process gallery.
- Click the 'Step Down Process' graphic (third graphic in the first row) to display a preview of this layout in the right pane (Figure 2–34).
- **Experiment:** Click various categories and graphics in the SmartArt Styles gallery and view the various layouts.

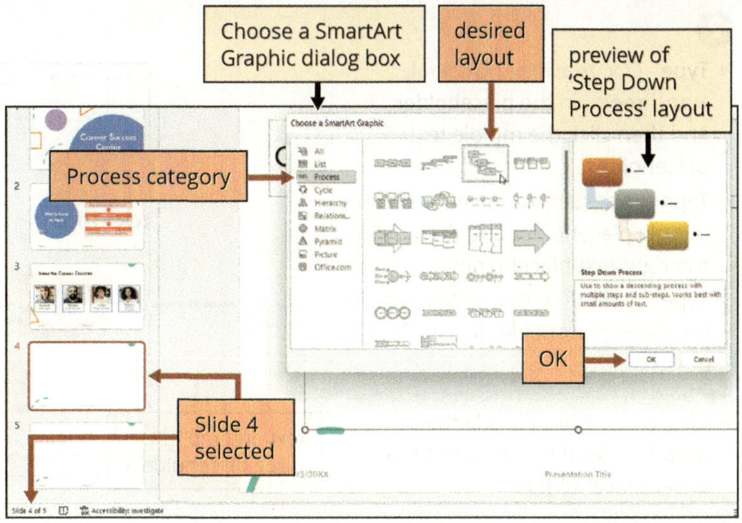

Figure 2–34

2

- Click OK (Choose a SmartArt Graphic dialog box) to insert the 'Step Down Process' SmartArt layout on Slide 4 (Figure 2–35).

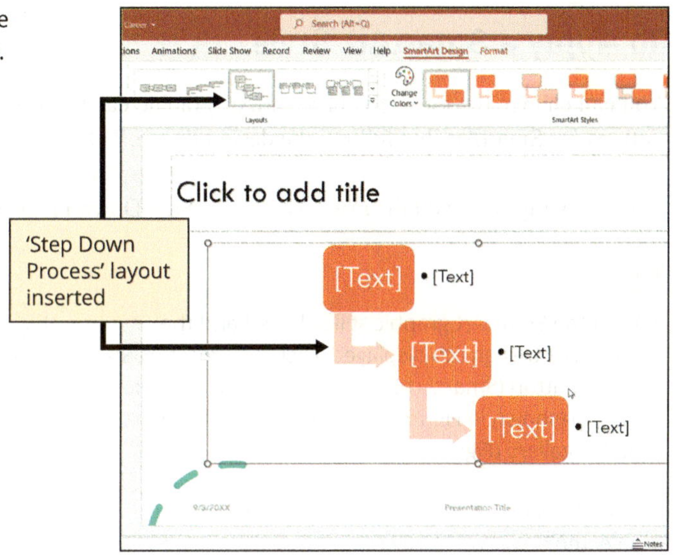

Figure 2–35

Other Ways

1. Click SmartArt button (Insert tab | Illustrations group)

To Add Text to the SmartArt Graphic

The Step Down Process SmartArt layout has three major orange placeholders for text. You can type a small amount of text, and PowerPoint assists with the graphic design. **Why?** PowerPoint automatically adjusts the font size for text in all the placeholders as you type. The following steps insert text into the three major SmartArt placeholders.

1

- Click the upper placeholder labeled [Text] to place the insertion point in that box (Figure 2–36).

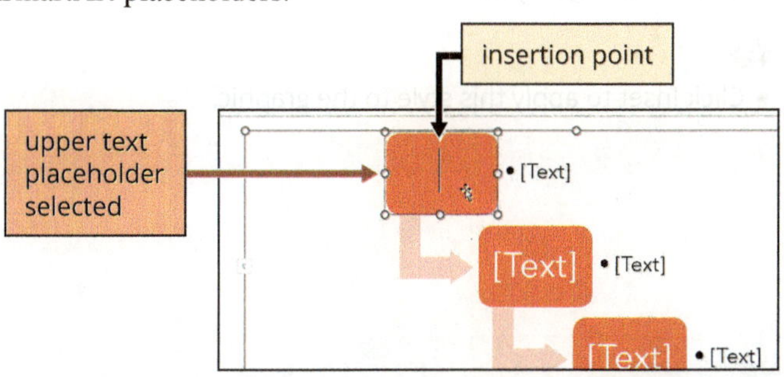

Figure 2–36

2

- Type **Occupational Outlook Handbook** in the placeholder and then click the middle text placeholder.
- Type **Assessment Survey** in the middle placeholder and then click the right text placeholder.
- Type **Individual Consultations** in the lower placeholder (Figure 2–37).

3

- Click a blank area inside the SmartArt border to deselect the lower placeholder.

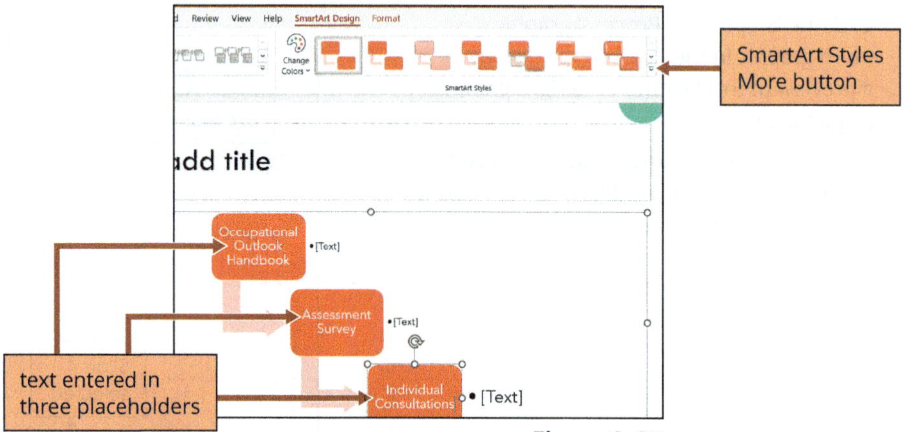

Figure 2–37

To Apply a SmartArt Style

You can change the look of your SmartArt graphic easily by applying a **SmartArt Style**, a pre-set combination of formatting options for SmartArt that follows the design theme. **Why?** You can use these professionally designed effects to customize the appearance of your presentation with a variety of shape fills, edges, shadows, line styles, gradients, and three-dimensional styles. The following steps add the Inset style to the Step Down Process SmartArt graphic.

1

- With the SmartArt graphic still selected and the SmartArt Design tab displayed, click the SmartArt Styles More button (SmartArt Design tab | SmartArt Styles group) (shown in Figure 2–37) to expand the SmartArt Styles gallery (Figure 2–38).

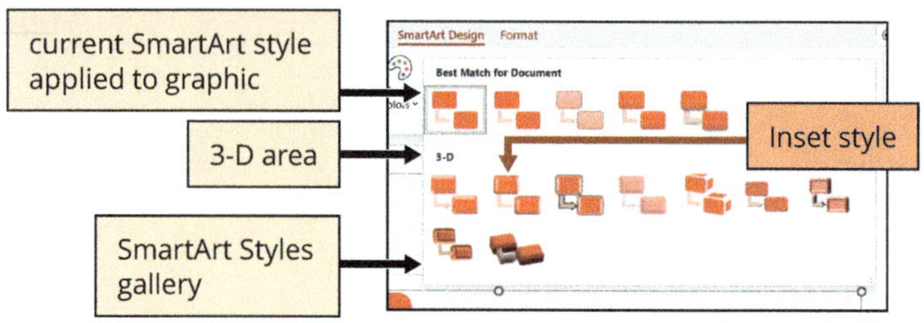

Figure 2–38

Q&A How do I select the graphic if it no longer is selected?
Click anywhere in the graphic.

Can I select one of the styles displayed in the SmartArt Styles group without expanding the SmartArt Styles gallery?
Yes. At times, however, you may want to display the gallery to view and preview the various styles.

2

- Point to the Inset style in the 3-D area (second style in the first 3-D row) in the SmartArt Styles gallery to display a live preview of this style (Figure 2–39).
- **Experiment:** Point to various styles in the SmartArt Styles gallery and watch the Step Down Process graphic change styles.

3

- Click Inset to apply this style to the graphic.

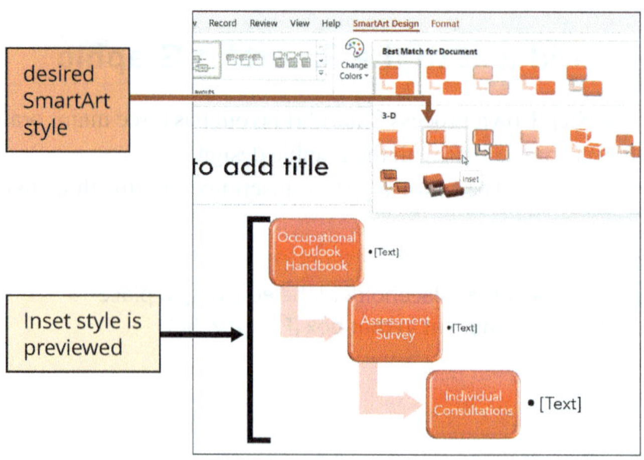

Figure 2–39

Other Ways

1. Right-click SmartArt graphic in an area other than a picture, click Style button

To Add a Hyperlink to a Paragraph

Speakers may desire to display a webpage during a slide show to add depth to the presented material and to enhance the overall message. When displaying Slide 4 of the Career slide show, for example, a speaker could access a website to show a specific resource. One method of accessing a webpage is by clicking a hyperlink on a slide. A **hyperlink**, also called a **link**, connects a slide or slide element to a webpage, another slide, a custom show consisting of specific slides in a presentation, an email address, or a file. A hyperlink can be any element of a slide. This includes a single letter, a word, a paragraph, or any graphical image such as a picture, shape, or graph.

If you are connected to the Internet when you run the presentation, you can click each hyperlinked paragraph, and your browser will open a new window and display the corresponding webpage for each hyperlink. By default, hyperlinked text is displayed with an underline and in a color that is part of the color scheme. The following steps create a hyperlink for the upper SmartArt rectangle on Slide 4. **Why?** The Occupational Outlook Handbook text will be a hyperlink to that website that gives career advice for hundreds of occupations.

1

- Display the Insert tab and then select the upper placeholder text, Occupational Outlook Handbook.
- Click the Link button (Insert tab | Links group) to display the Insert Hyperlink dialog box.
- If necessary, click the 'Existing File or Web Page' button in the Link to area (Figure 2–40).

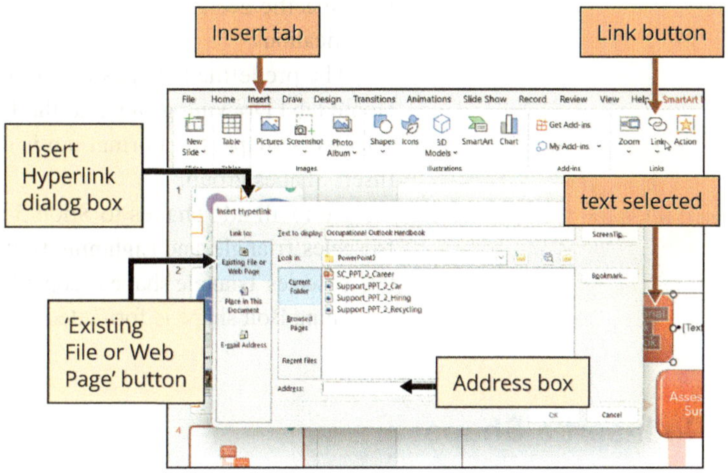

Figure 2–40

2

- If necessary, delete the text in the Address text box and then type **www.bls.gov/ooh** in the Address box (Figure 2–41).

Q&A Why does http:// appear before the address I typed?
PowerPoint automatically adds this protocol identifier before web addresses.

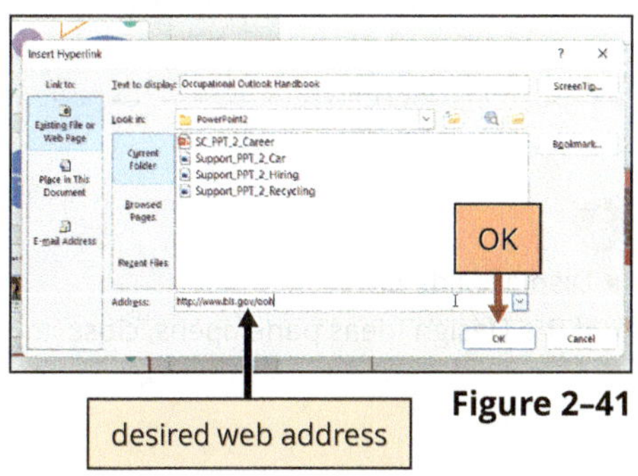

Figure 2–41

3

- Click OK to insert the hyperlink.

Q&A Why is this paragraph now underlined and displaying a new font color?
The default style for hypertlinks is underlined text. The Shapes presentation built-in theme hyperlink color is purple so PowerPoint formatted the paragraph to that color automatically.

- **Experiment:** Click outside the linked text, then press CTRL and click the link to access the website. Then, close the browser to return to PowerPoint.

Other Ways

1. Right-click selected text, click Hyperlink, click 'Existing File or Web Page,' type address, click OK
2. Select text, press CTRL+K, click 'Existing File or Web Page,' type address, press ENTER

Inserting and Formatting a Shape

One method of getting the audience's attention and reinforcing the major concepts being presented is to have graphical elements on the slide. PowerPoint provides a wide variety of predefined shapes that can add visual interest to a slide. Diagrams with labels often help audiences identify the parts of an object. Text boxes with clear, large type and an arrow pointing to a precise area of the object work well in showing relationships between components. You also can use shapes to create your own custom artwork.

Shape elements include lines, basic geometrical shapes, arrows, equation shapes, flowchart symbols, rectangles, banners, and callouts. After adding a shape to a slide, you can change its default characteristics by adding text, bullets, numbers, and styles. You also can combine multiple shapes to create a more complex graphic. At times, you may be unable to find a shape that fits your specific needs. In those instances, you might find a similar shape and then alter it to your specifications.

The predefined shapes are found in the Shapes gallery. This collection is found on the Home tab | Drawing group and the Insert tab | Illustrations group. Once you have inserted and selected a shape, the Format tab is displayed, and the Shapes gallery also is displayed in the Insert Shapes group.

You will add shapes to Slide 5 and then enhance them in a variety of ways. First, Oval, Isosceles Triangle, and Lightning Bolt shapes are inserted on the slide, sized, and formatted. Then, the Isosceles Triangle shape is copied. Then, text is added to the shapes and formatted. Finally, the Lightning Bolt shape is formatted and moved into position.

To Insert a Shape

Many of the shapes included in the Shapes gallery can direct the viewer to important aspects of the presentation. Ovals, squares, arrows, rectangles, and equation shapes are among the items included in the Shapes gallery. These shapes can be combined to show relationships among the elements, and they can help illustrate the basic concepts presented in your slide show. The following steps add Oval, Lightning Bolt, and Isosceles Triangle shapes to Slide 5. **Why?** The Shapes presentation slides have many geometric shapes, so the Oval and triangles complement these slide elements. The Lightning Bolt depicts the positive energy students will experience when they determine their career goals and apply for an appropriate job.

1

- Display Slide 5.
- If the Design Ideas pane opens, close it.

2

- Click the Shapes button (Insert tab | Illustrations group) to display the Shapes gallery (Figure 2–42).

Q&A I do not see a Shapes button shown in Figure 2–42. Instead, I have three rows of shapes and a Shapes More button. Why?
Monitor dimensions and resolution affect how buttons display on the ribbon. Click the Shapes More button to display the entire Shapes gallery.

My shapes are displayed in a different position. Why?
Monitor dimensions and resolution affect how the shapes display in the Shapes gallery.

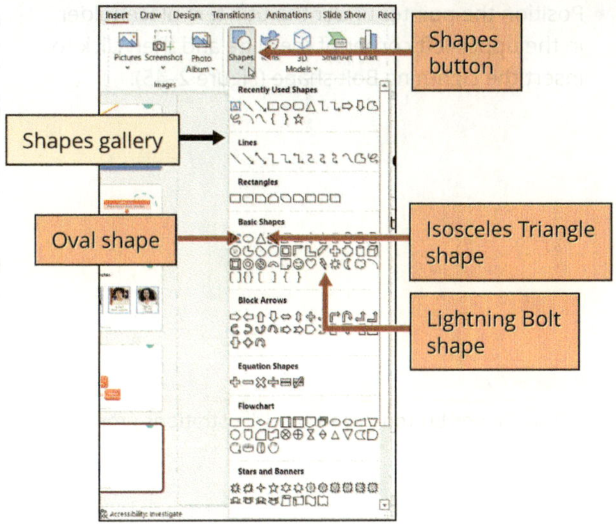

Figure 2–42

3

- Click the Oval shape (second shape in the first row of the Basic Shapes area) in the Shapes gallery.

Q&A Why did my pointer change shape?
The pointer changed to a plus shape to indicate the Oval shape has been added to the Clipboard.

- Position the pointer (a crosshair) near the center of the slide (Figure 2–43).

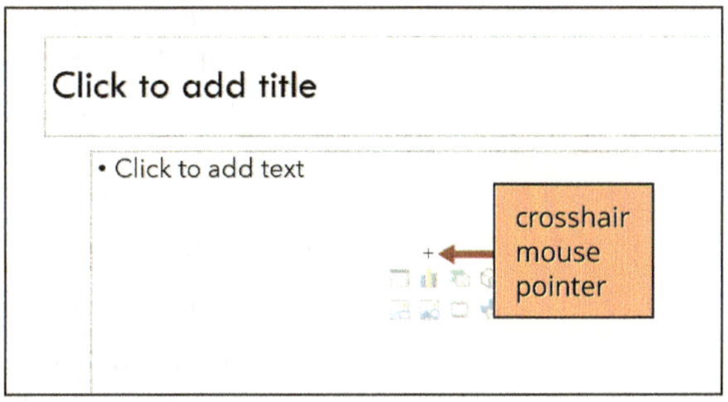

Figure 2–43

4

- Click Slide 5 to insert the Oval shape (Figure 2–44).

Q&A When I inserted the Oval shape, I selected it on the Home tab. Is the same Shapes gallery also displayed on the Shape Format tab?
Yes. The Shapes gallery is displayed on the Shape Format tab once an object is inserted and selected on the slide.

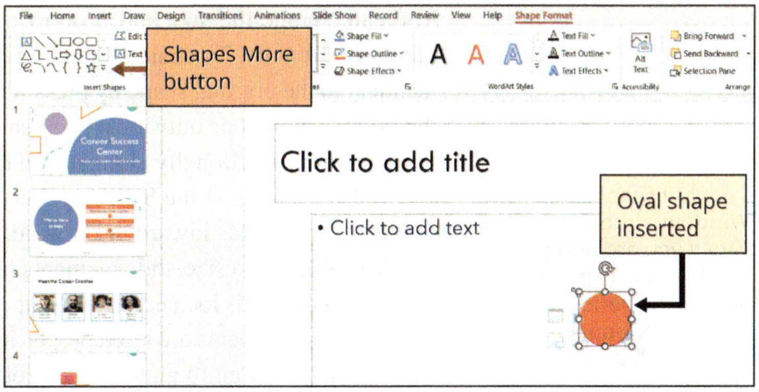

Figure 2–44

5

- Click the Shapes More button (Shape Format tab | Insert Shapes group) to display the Shapes gallery.
- Click the Isosceles Triangle shape (third shape in the first row of the Basic Shapes area) in the gallery (shown in Figure 2–42).
- Position the pointer toward the right side of the Oval and then click to insert the Isosceles Triangle shape.

6

- Display the Shapes gallery again and then click the Lightning Bolt shape (eighth shape in the third Basic Shapes row) in the gallery (shown in Figure 2–42).

- Position the pointer under the title text placeholder in the upper-left corner of the slide and then click to insert the Lightning Bolt shape (Figure 2–45).

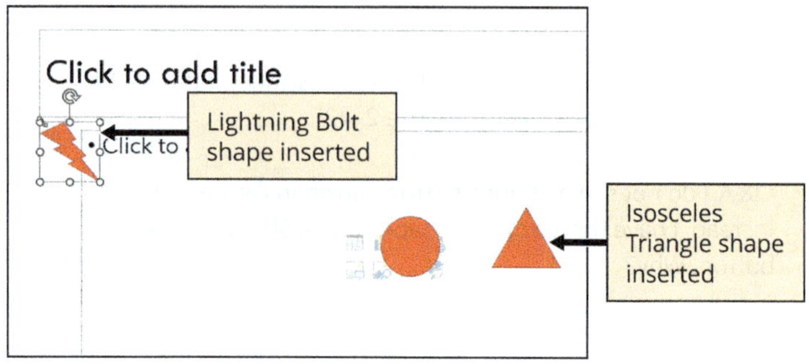

Figure 2–45

Other Ways

1. Click Shapes button (Insert tab | Illustrations group)

To Change a Shape Type Once you insert a shape, you can change it into another shape. To change the shape type, you would do the following.

1. Select the shape you want to change and then click the Edit Shape button (Shape Format tab | Insert Shapes group).
2. Point to Change Shape and then select the desired shape.

To Delete a Shape Once you insert a shape, you can delete it. To delete a shape, you would do the following.

1. Select the shape and then press DELETE.
2. If you want to delete multiple shapes, press CTRL while clicking the undesired shapes and then press DELETE.

Resizing Shapes

You can change the size and proportions of slide elements in two ways: proportionally and nonproportionally. To change them proportionally, you can keep the resized shape proportions identical to the original shape by pressing SHIFT while clicking a sizing handle and then dragging the pointer inward or outward to decrease or increase the size. If you do not hold down SHIFT, you can nonproportionally elongate the height or the width to draw an object that is not identical to the shape shown in the Shapes gallery. If you want to alter the shape's proportions, drag one of the sizing handles inward or outward.

You also can resize slide elements by entering exact height and width measurements in the Size group, which is located on the Shape Format tab and the Format contextual tab for SmartArt. Some graphic elements are sized proportionally, meaning the width changes in proportion to height changes. If you want to alter the slide object nonproportionally, you need to uncheck the 'Lock aspect ratio' check box in the Format Shape pane.

BTW
Touch Mode Differences
The Microsoft 365 and Windows interfaces may vary if you are using Touch mode. For this reason, you might notice that the function or appearance of your touch screen differs slightly from this module's presentation.

To Resize a Shape Proportionally

The three shapes on Slide 5 are the default sizes, and they need to be enlarged to be seen clearly and to allow text to be seen inside of them. The next step is to resize the Isosceles Triangle and Oval shapes. **Why?** *The Oval shape should be enlarged so that it is a focal point in the middle area of the slide, and the Isosceles Triangle shape needs to be large enough to contain text.* The following steps resize the Slide 5 Isosceles Triangle and Oval shapes.

1

- Select the Isosceles Triangle shape, press and hold down SHIFT, and then drag the lower-right corner sizing handle until the shape is resized approximately as shown in Figure 2–46.

Q&A Why did I need to press SHIFT while enlarging the shape?
Holding down SHIFT while dragging keeps the proportions of the original shape.

What if my shape is not selected?
To select a shape, click it.

If I am using a touch screen, how can I maintain the shape's original proportion?
If you drag one of the corner sizing handles, the object should stay in proportion.

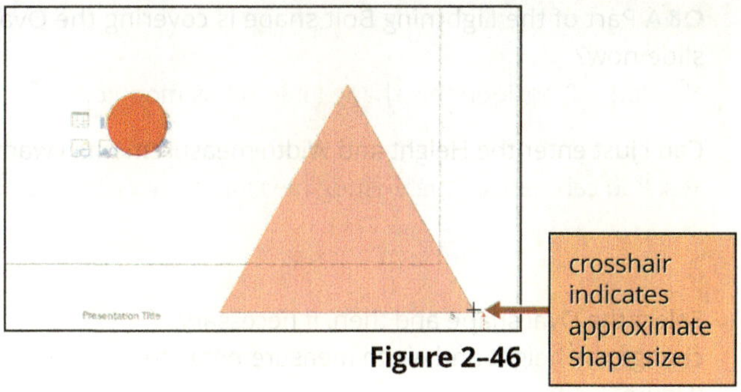

Figure 2–46

2

- Release the mouse button to resize the shape.

3

- Select the Oval shape, press and hold down SHIFT, and then drag the lower-left corner sizing handle until the shape is resized approximately as shown in Figure 2–47.

Q&A What if I want to move the shape to a precise location on the slide?
With the shape selected, press ARROW or CTRL+ARROW to move the shape to the desired location.

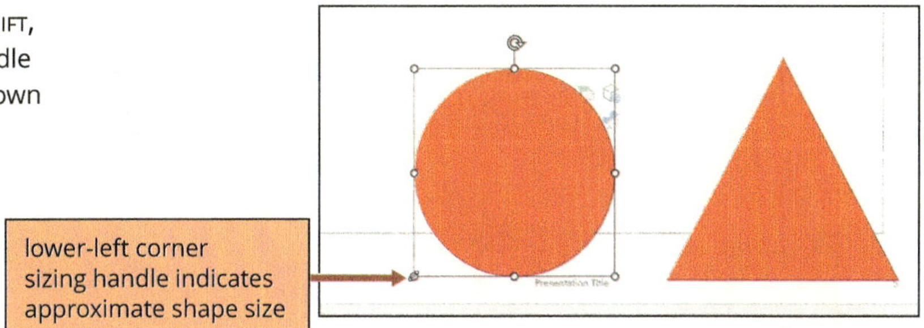

Figure 2–47

To Resize a Shape Nonproportionally by Entering an Exact Measurement

Why? Adequate space exists on the slide to increase all the SmartArt shapes. You can resize a slide element by dragging the sizing handles or by specifying exact measurements for the height and width. The following steps resize the Lightning Bolt shape by entering an exact measurement and then check the dimensions of the resized Oval and Isosceles Triangle.

1

- Select the Lightning Bolt shape and then, if necessary, display the Shape Format tab.

Q&A How will I know the Lightning Bolt shape is selected?
You will see the sizing handles around the outer edge of the shape.

- Click the Shape Height box up arrow (Shape Format tab | Size group) several times until the Height measurement is 3".
- Click the Shape Width box up arrow (Shape Format tab | Size group) several times until the Width measurement is 12.5" (Figure 2–48).

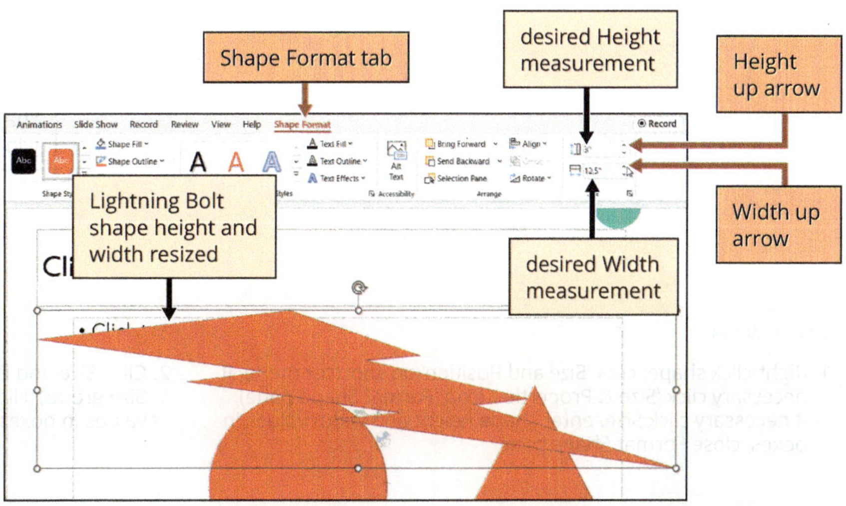

Figure 2–48

Q&A Part of the Lightning Bolt shape is covering the Oval and Isosceles Triangle shapes. Do I need to move it on the slide now?
No. You will position this shape later in this module.

Can I just enter the Height and Width measurements I want in the Height and Width boxes?
Yes. You can replace the existing measurements with your desired sizes.

2

- Select the Oval shape and then, if necessary, change the height and width measurements to 4" (Figure 2–49).

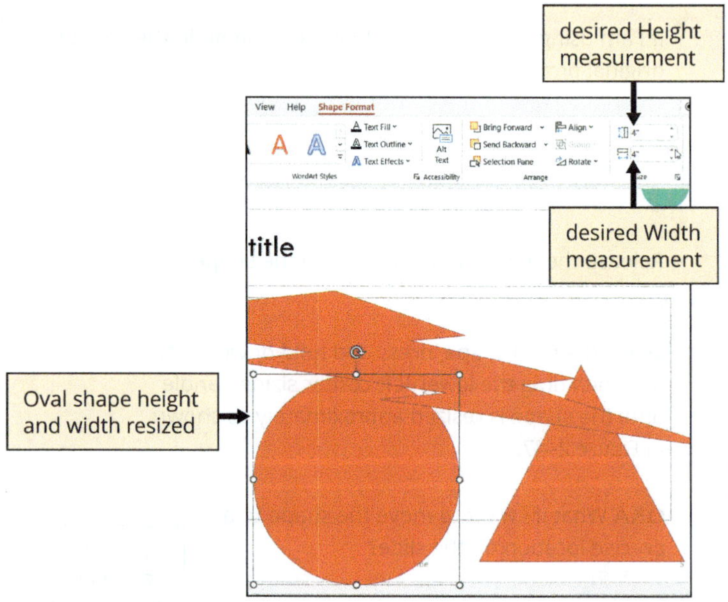

Figure 2–49

3

- Select the Isosceles Triangle shape and then, if necessary, change the height and width measurements to 4" (Figure 2–50).

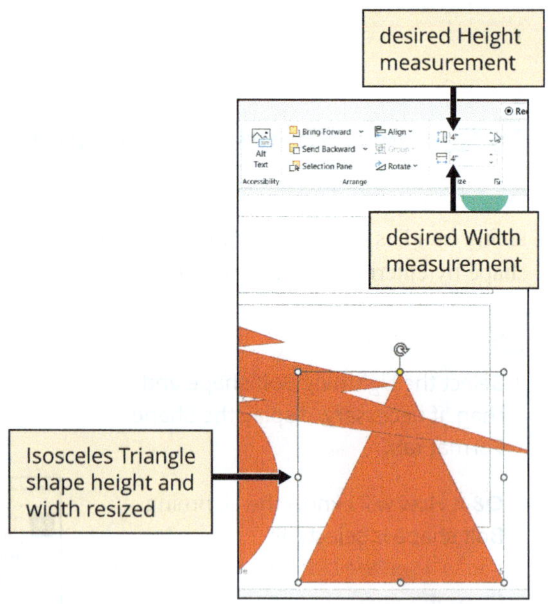

Figure 2–50

Other Ways

1. Right-click shape, click 'Size and Position' on shortcut menu, if necessary click 'Size & Properties' icon (Format Shape pane), if necessary click Size, enter shape height and width values in boxes, close Format Shape pane
2. Click Size and Position pane launcher (Shape Format tab | Size group), click Size tab, enter desired height and width values in boxes, click Close button

To Select Shapes

When you want to format multiple objects on a slide, one efficient method of performing this task is to select all these objects and then apply changes to them simultaneously. **Why?** You want to apply the same changes to all three shapes. Select these objects by selecting one shape, pressing and holding down SHIFT, and then selecting the second and third shapes. The following step selects three shapes on Slide 5.

1

- Select the Isosceles Triangle, if necessary.
- Press and hold down SHIFT and then click the Oval and the Lightning Bolt shapes (Figure 2–51).

Q&A Instead of selecting these three shapes individually, could I have clicked the Select button (Home tab | Editing group) and then chose Select All on the menu?

No. You also would have selected the footer text boxes because they are slide elements.

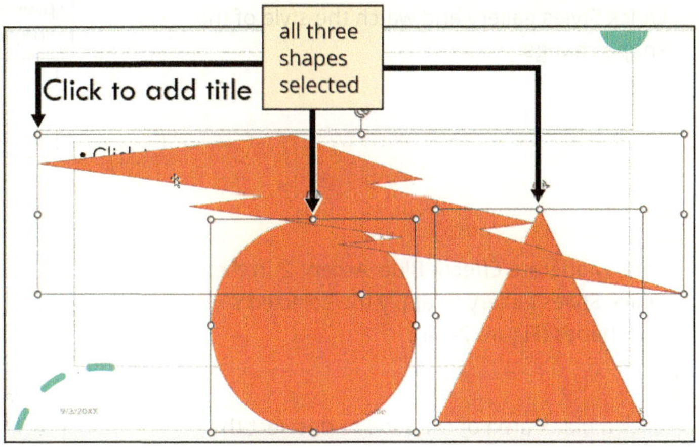

Figure 2–51

To Apply a Shape Style

The Quick Styles gallery has a variety of styles that change depending on the theme applied to the presentation. Formatting text in a shape follows the same techniques as formatting text in a placeholder. You can change the font, font color and size, and alignment. You later will add information to the Oval and Isosceles Triangle shapes, but first you want to apply a shape style. **Why?** The style will give depth and dimension to the object. The following steps apply a style to the three shapes on Slide 5.

1

- Display the Home tab and then click the Quick Styles button (Home tab | Drawing group) to display the Shape Quick Styles gallery (Figure 2–52).

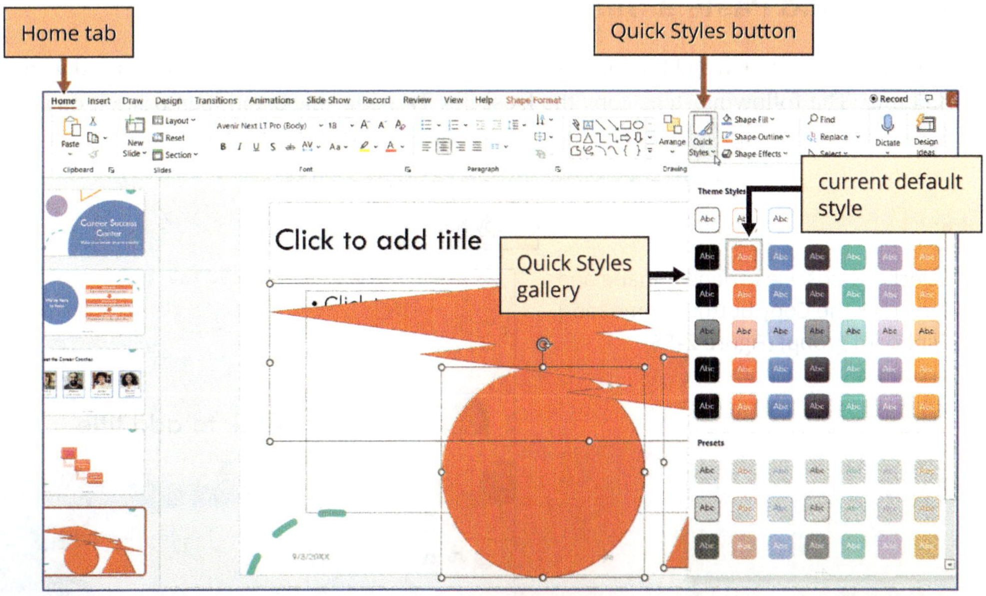

Figure 2–52

2

- Scroll down and then point to 'Moderate Effect - Blue, Accent 2' in the Quick Styles gallery (third shape in the fifth Theme Styles row) to display a live preview of that style applied to the shapes in the slide (Figure 2–53).
- **Experiment:** Point to various styles in the Quick Styles gallery and watch the style of the shape change.

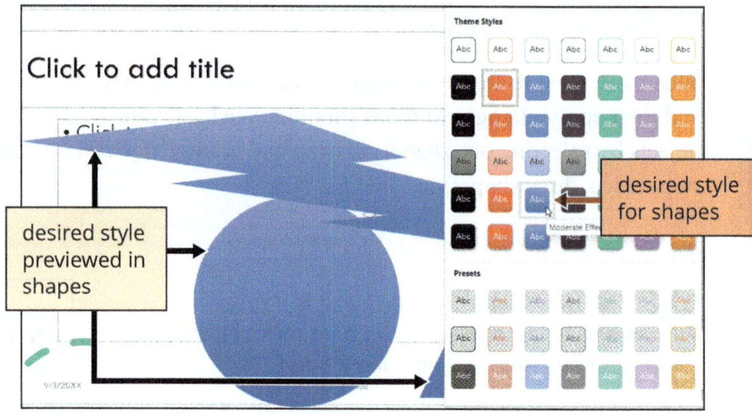

Figure 2–53

3

- Click 'Moderate Effect - Blue, Accent 2' in the Quick Styles gallery to apply the selected style to the shapes (Figure 2–54).

4

- Click a blank area of the slide to deselect the three objects.

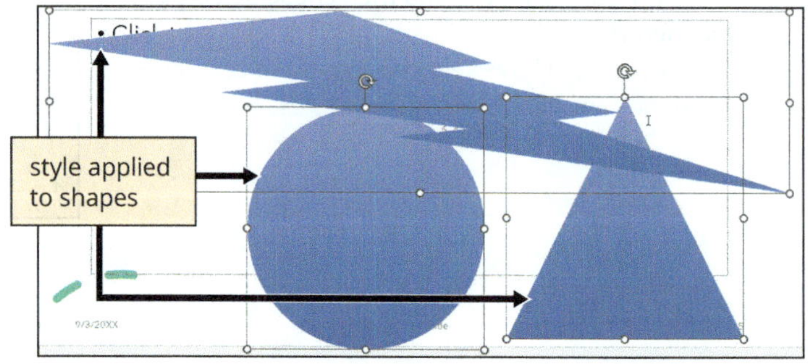

Figure 2–54

Other Ways

1. Click Shape Styles More button (Shape Format tab | Shape Styles group), select style
2. Right-click shape, click Style button on Mini toolbar, select desired style

To Copy and Paste a Shape

You already have created and formatted the Isosceles Triangle shape, and you now need to create a second shape with the same formatting. The following steps copy the Isosceles Triangle shape and then paste it on the left side of the slide. **Why?** You could repeat all the steps you performed to create the first Isosceles Triangle shape, but it is much more efficient to duplicate the formatted shape.

1

- Select the Isosceles Triangle shape and then click the Copy button (Home tab | Clipboard group) (Figure 2–55).

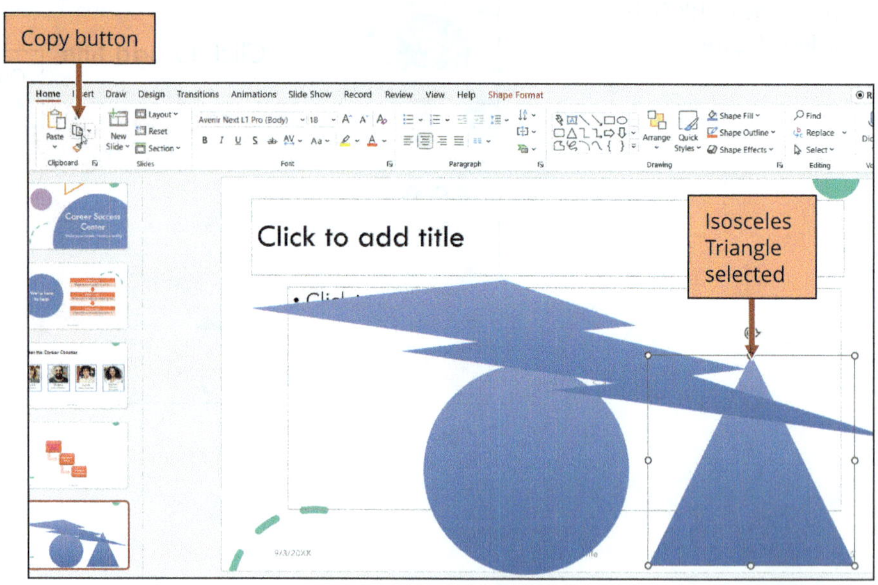

Figure 2–55

2

- Click the Paste button (Home tab | Clipboard group) to insert a duplicate Isosceles Triangle shape on Slide 5.

3

- Drag the new Isosceles Triangle shape to the left side of the slide (Figure 2–56).

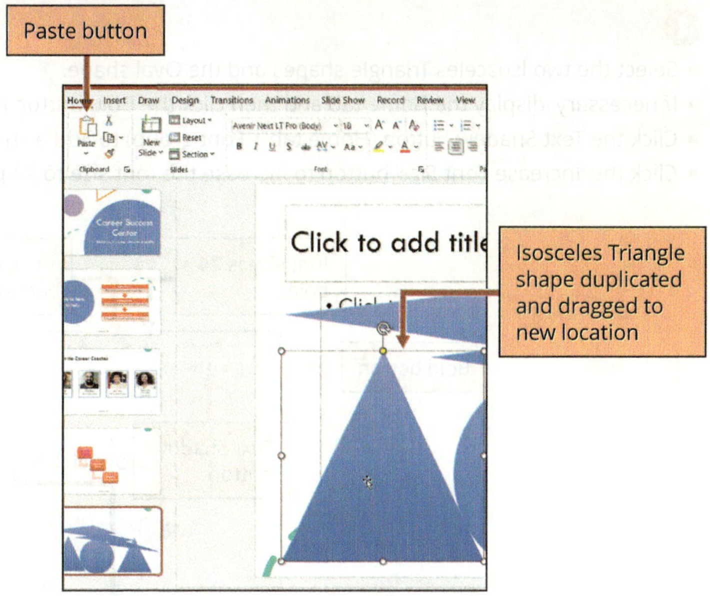

Figure 2–56

Other Ways

1. Right-click selected shape, click Copy on shortcut menu, right-click blank area, click Paste on shortcut menu
2. Select shape, press CTRL+C, press CTRL+V

To Add Text to a Shape

The shapes on Slide 5 help call attention to one of the key aspects of your presentation. **Why?** Your goal is to emphasize the simple process of using the app to create a profile and then apply for a job. The next step is to add this information to Slide 5. The following steps add text to the Isosceles Triangle and Oval shapes.

1

- With the left Isosceles Triangle shape selected, type **Download the app** to add the text in the shape.

2

- Click the Oval shape to select it and then type **Create a profile** to add the text in the shape.

3

- Click the right Isosceles Triangle shape to select it and then type **Apply for the job** to add the text in the shape (Figure 2–57).

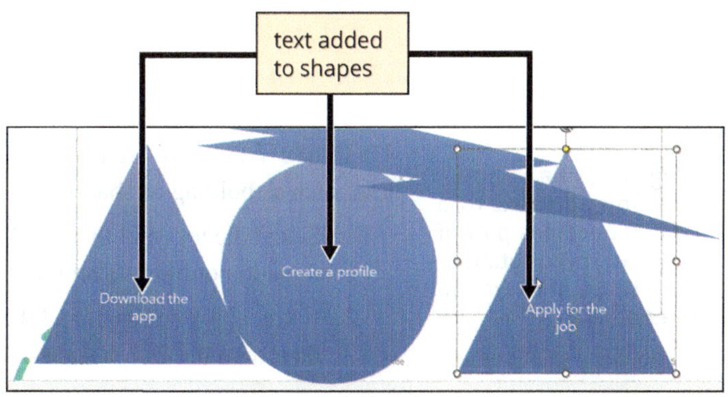

Figure 2–57

To Format Shape Text

The text in the three shapes has the default formatting, but you can enhance these letters. **Why?** The size, color, and other formatting aspects will make the text more readable. You can format shape text with the same features used to format slide placeholder text. The following step bolds the text, adds a shadow, and increases the font size on the text in all three shapes.

1

- Select the two Isosceles Triangle shapes and the Oval shape.
- If necessary, display the Home tab and then click the Bold button (Home tab | Font group).
- Click the Text Shadow button (Home tab | Font group) to add a shadow to the text.
- Click the 'Increase Font Size' button to increase the font size to 24 point (Figure 2–58).

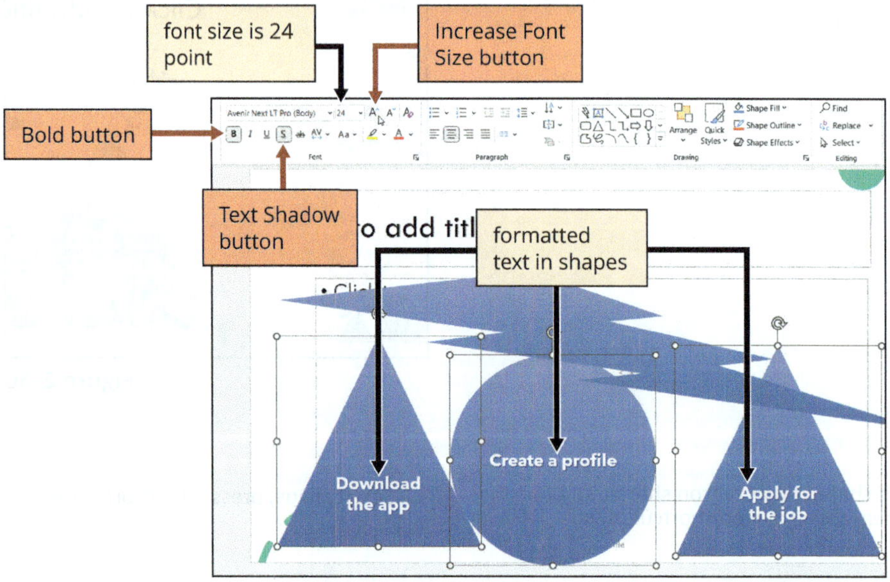

Figure 2–58

Q&A Can I make other formatting changes to the graphics' text?
Yes. You can format the text by making any of the modifications in the Font group.

If I am using a touch screen, can I modify all three rectangles simultaneously?
No. You need to repeat Step 1 for each of the shapes.

Other Ways

1. Right-click selected text, click desired text format button on Mini toolbar

BTW
Using Text in a Shape
When you add text to a shape, it becomes part of the shape. If you rotate or flip the shape, the text also rotates or flips.

To Undo Text Formatting Changes To remove a formatting change you have made to text, such as bolding or shadowing, you would do the following.

1. Select the text and then click the button that originally applied the format. For example, to undo bolding, select the text and then click the Bold button.
2. If you apply a format and then immediately decide to remove this effect, click the Undo button on the Quick Access Toolbar or press CTRL+Z.

To Change a Shape Fill Color

The Lightning Bolt shape has the same blue formatting as the three other slide shapes. You can change the Lightning Bolt shape's fill color to yellow. **Why?** The color yellow is associated with lightning and contrasts with the three blue shapes. The following steps change the fill color of the Lightning Bolt shape.

1

- Click the Lightning Bolt shape to select it and then click the Shape Fill arrow (Home tab | Drawing group) to display the Shape Fill gallery.

- Point to Yellow (fourth color in the Standard Colors row) to display a live preview of this fill color (Figure 2–59).
- **Experiment:** Point to various colors in the gallery and watch the fill color change.

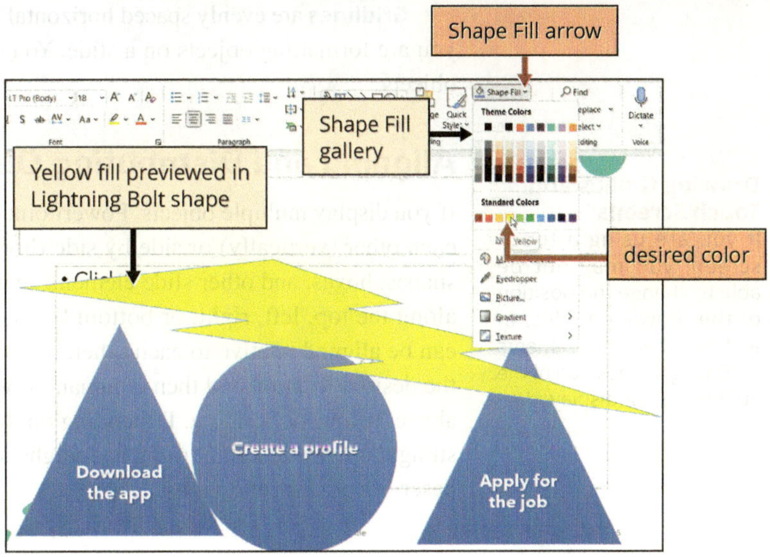

Figure 2–59

2

- Click Yellow to apply this color to the Lightning Bolt shape.
- Click a blank area of the slide outside of the Lightning Bolt shape to deselect this slide element (Figure 2–60).

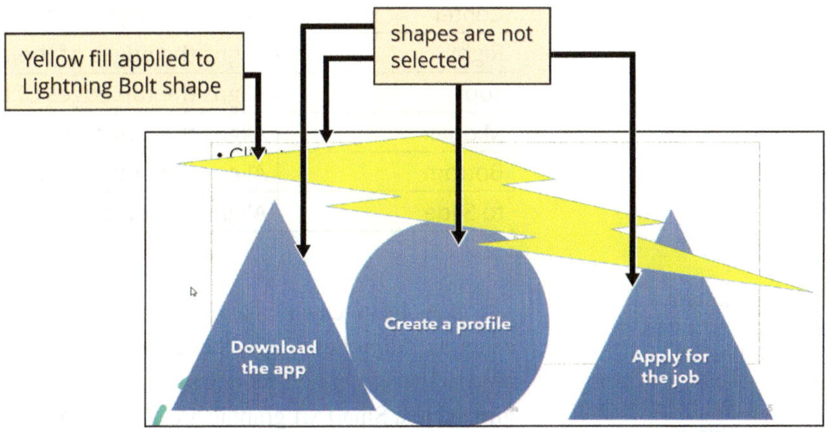

Figure 2–60

Other Ways

1. Click Shape Fill button (Shape Format tab | Shape Styles group)

Break Point: If you wish to take a break, this is a good place to do so. Be sure the Career file is saved and then you can exit PowerPoint. To resume later, start PowerPoint, open the file called SC_PPT_2_Career.pptx, and continue following the steps from this location forward.

Positioning Slide Elements

At times you may desire to arrange slide elements in precise locations. PowerPoint provides useful tools to help you position shapes and objects on slides. **Drawing guides** are two straight dotted lines, one horizontal and one vertical. When an object is close to a guide, its corner or its center (whichever is closer) will **snap**, or align precisely, on top of the guide. You can drag a guide to a new location to meet your alignment requirements. Guides can be added and deleted as you develop slide content. Another tool is the vertical or horizontal **ruler**, which can help you drag an object to a precise location on the slide. The center of a slide is 0.00 on both the vertical and the horizontal rulers.

Gridlines are evenly spaced horizontal and vertical lines that help give you visual cues when you are formatting objects on a slide. You can use gridlines to help you align shapes and other objects.

BTW
Drawing Guides and Touch Screens
If you are using a touch screen, you may not be able to change the position of the drawing guides. In addition, the measurements indicating the position of the guides are not displayed.

Aligning and Distributing Objects

If you display multiple objects, PowerPoint can **align** their center lines or edges above and below each other (vertically) or side by side (horizontally). The objects, such as SmartArt graphics, shapes, boxes, and other slide elements, can be aligned relative to the slide so that they display along the top, left, right, or bottom borders or in the center or middle of the slide. They also can be aligned relative to each other, meaning that you position either the first or last object in the desired location and then command PowerPoint to move the remaining objects in the series above, below, or beside it. Depending on the alignment option that you click, objects will move straight up, down, left, or right, and might cover an object already located on the slide. Table 2–3 describes alignment options.

Table 2-3: Alignment Options

Alignment	Action
Left	Aligns the edges of the objects to the left
Center	Aligns the objects vertically through the centers of the objects
Right	Aligns the edges of the objects to the right
Top	Aligns the top edges of the objects
Middle	Aligns the objects horizontally through the middle of the objects
Bottom	Aligns the bottom edges of the objects
to Slide	Aligns one object to the slide

BTW
Changing the Measurement Unit
The vertical and horizontal rulers display the units of measurement in inches by default. This measurement system is determined by the settings in Microsoft Windows. You can change the measurement unit to centimeters by customizing the numbers format in the 'Clock and Region' area of the Control Panel. Click Region, click Additional Settings, and then choose Metric.

One object remains stationary when you align objects relative to each other by their edges. For example, Align Left aligns the left edges of all selected objects with the left edge of the leftmost object. The leftmost object remains stationary, and the other objects are aligned relative to it. Objects aligned to a SmartArt graphic are aligned to the leftmost edge of the SmartArt graphic, not to the leftmost shape in the SmartArt graphic. Objects aligned relative to each other by their middles or centers are aligned along a horizontal or vertical line that represents the average of their original positions. All of the objects might move.

Smart Guides appear automatically when two or more shapes are in spatial alignment with each other, even if the shapes vary in size. To evenly space multiple objects horizontally or vertically, you **distribute** them. PowerPoint determines the total length between either the outermost edges of the first and last selected object or the edges of the entire slide. It then inserts equal spacing among the items in the series. You also can distribute spacing by using the Size and Position dialog box, but the Distribute command automates this task.

To Display the Drawing Guides

Why? Guides help you align objects on slides. Using a mouse, when you point to a guide and then press and hold the mouse button, PowerPoint displays a box containing the exact position of the guide on the slide in inches. An arrow is displayed below the guide position to indicate the vertical guide either left or right of the center. An arrow also is displayed to the right of the guide position to indicate the horizontal guide either above or below the center. The following step displays the guides.

1

- With Slide 5 displayed, display the View tab and then click the Guides check box (View tab | Show group) to place a checkmark in the box and display the horizontal and vertical guides (Figure 2–61).

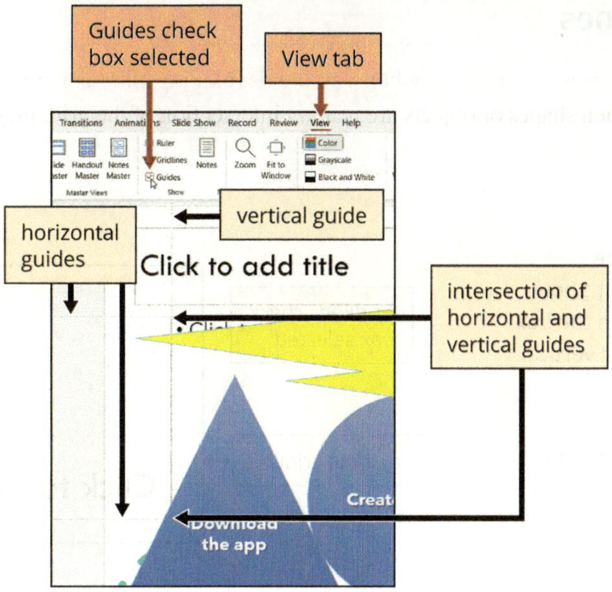

Figure 2-61

Other Ways

1. Right-click area of slide other than a placeholder or object, point to 'Grid and Guides' arrow on shortcut menu, click Guides
2. Press ALT+F9 to toggle guides on/off

To Display the Ruler

The ruler is another feature to use when positioning objects. **Why?** The ruler helps you align slide elements in a precise location on slides. One ruler is displayed horizontally at the top of the slide, and the other is displayed vertically along the left edge of the slide. The following step displays the ruler.

1

- With Slide 5 displayed, click the Ruler check box (View tab | Show group) to place a checkmark in the box and display the horizontal and vertical rulers (Figure 2–62).

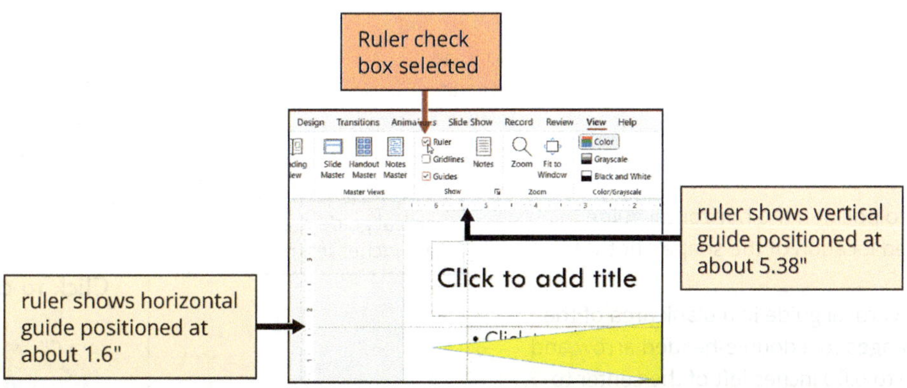

Figure 2-62

BTW
Displaying the Ruler
The ruler is not available in all views, such as Slide Sorter view. If the Ruler box is grayed out, try switching to Normal view.

BTW
Hiding the Vertical Ruler
To permanently hide the vertical ruler, click the File tab, click Options, click Advanced, scroll down to the Display section, and then clear the 'Show vertical ruler' box.

Other Ways

1. Right-click area of slide other than a placeholder or object, point to Ruler on shortcut menu, click Ruler

To Display the Gridlines

Why? The gridlines give you precise visual cues when you are developing slide content. The vertical and horizontal lines are spaced at one-inch intervals. When shapes or objects are near an intersection of the grid, they snap to this location. The following step displays the gridlines.

1

- With Slide 5 displayed, click the Gridlines check box (View tab | Show group) to place a checkmark in the box and display the horizontal and vertical gridlines (Figure 2–63).

Q&A What if I do not see the gridlines after checking the Gridlines box?
If you do not see any gridlines, try a higher zoom level (zoom in).

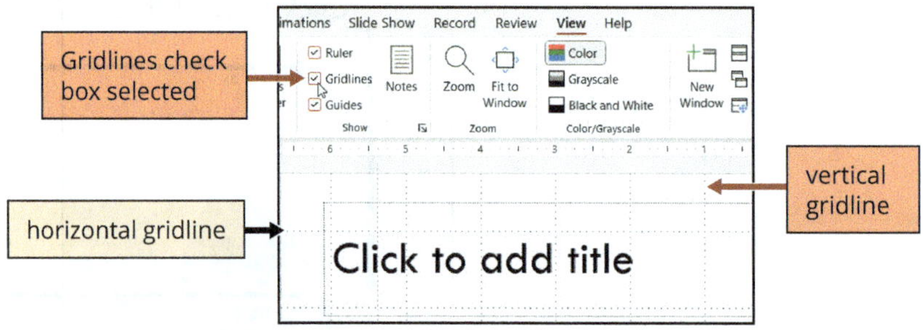

Figure 2–63

Other Ways

1. Right-click area of slide other than a placeholder or object, point to 'Grid and Guides' arrow on shortcut menu, click Gridlines

To Position a Shape Using Guides, Gridlines, and the Ruler

The lower edges of the Isosceles Triangle and the Oval shapes on Slide 5 should be displayed in the same horizontal location. **Why?** The design will look professional if they are aligned precisely near the bottom of the slide. You can use the rulers and gridlines to help you verify the desired guide locations and where to drag an object to an exact location on the slide. The center of a slide is 0.00 on both the vertical and the horizontal rulers. The following steps position the three shapes on Slide 5.

1

- Position the pointer on the lower horizontal guide in a blank area of the slide so that the pointer changes to a double-headed arrow and then drag the horizontal guide to 3.00 inches below the center. Do not release the mouse button (Figure 2–64).

Q&A Why does 3.00 display when I hold down the mouse button?
The ScreenTip displays the horizontal guide's position. A 0.00 setting means that the guide is precisely in the middle of the slide and is not above or below the center, so a 3.00 setting indicates the guide is 3 inches below the center line.

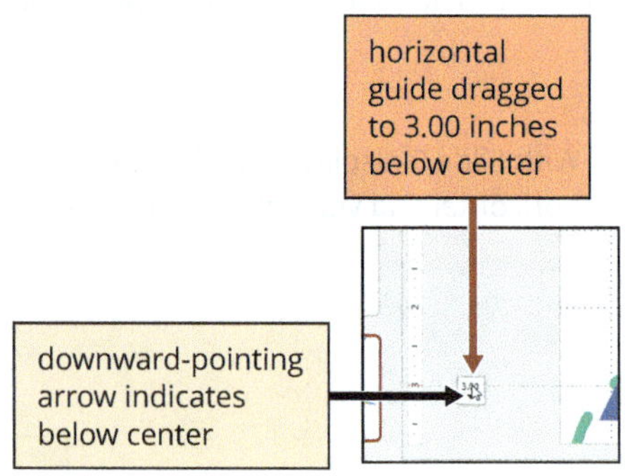

Figure 2–64

2

- Release the mouse button to position the horizontal guide at 3.00, which is the intended location of the shape's bottom border.
- Position the pointer on the vertical guide in a blank area of the slide so that the pointer changes to a double-headed arrow and then drag the vertical guide to 6.00 inches left of the center to position the vertical guide.
- Drag the left Isosceles Triangle shape so its lower-left corner touches the intersection of the vertical and horizontal guides to position the shape in the desired location (Figure 2–65).

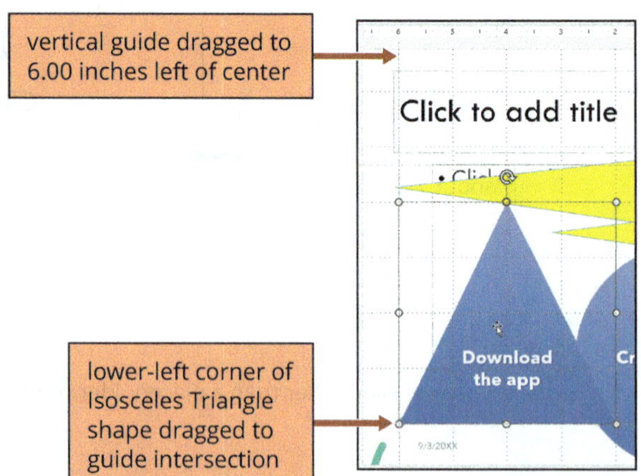

Figure 2–65

Q&A Can I add guides to help me align multiple objects?
Yes. Position the pointer over one guide and then press CTRL. When you drag your pointer, a second guide appears.

To Position the Remaining Shapes

The bottom edges of the Oval and right Isosceles Triangle shapes on Slide 5 should be positioned in the same location as the left Isosceles Triangle. The horizontal guide will display in the same location, but you can move the vertical guide to help you align these objects. The rulers and grid lines will help you verify the desired guide locations. The following steps position the Oval and right Isosceles Triangle shapes.

BTW
Overriding Snap-To Options
To temporarily override the snap-to options, hold down ALT while you drag the object, picture, or chart.

1. Drag the vertical guide to 2.00 left of the center. Select the Oval shape and then position it so its lower-left corner touches the intersection of the vertical and horizontal guides.

2. Drag the vertical guide to 6.00 right of the center. Select the right Isosceles Triangle shape and then position it so its lower-right corner touches the intersection of the vertical and horizontal guides (Figure 2-66).

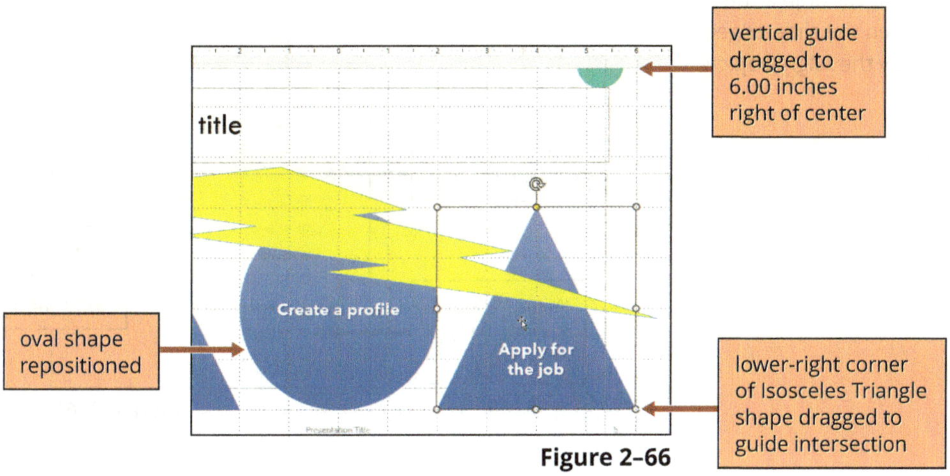

Figure 2-66

To Distribute Shapes

Now that the Isosceles Triangle and Oval shapes are aligned, you can have PowerPoint place the same amount of space between them. You have two distribution options: 'Align to Slide' spaces all the selected objects evenly across the entire width of the slide; 'Align Selected Objects' spaces only the middle objects between the fixed right and left objects. The following steps use the 'Align to Slide' option. **Why?** This option will distribute the three Slide 5 shapes horizontally to fill some of the space along the bottom of the slide.

1

- Select the left Isosceles Triangle, Oval, and right Isosceles Triangle shapes, display the Shape Format tab, and then click the Align button (Shape Format tab | Arrange group) to display the Align Objects menu (Figure 2–67).

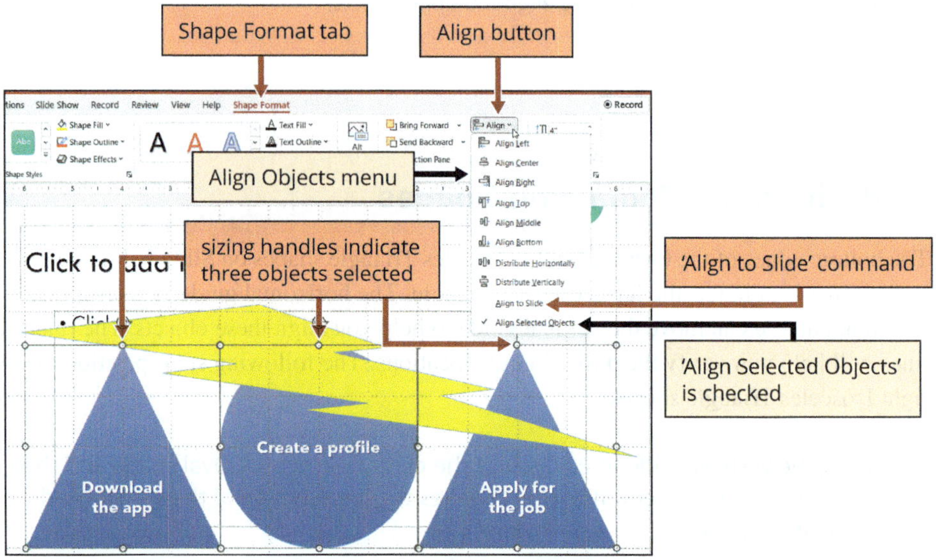

Figure 2–67

2

- Click 'Align to Slide' so that PowerPoint will adjust the spacing of the pictures evenly between the slide edges. Click the Align button again to display the Align Objects menu (Figure 2–68).

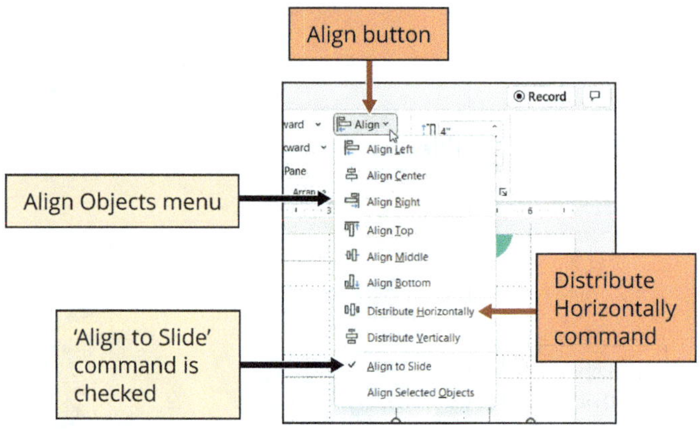

Figure 2–68

3

- Click Distribute Horizontally to adjust the spacing (Figure 2–69).

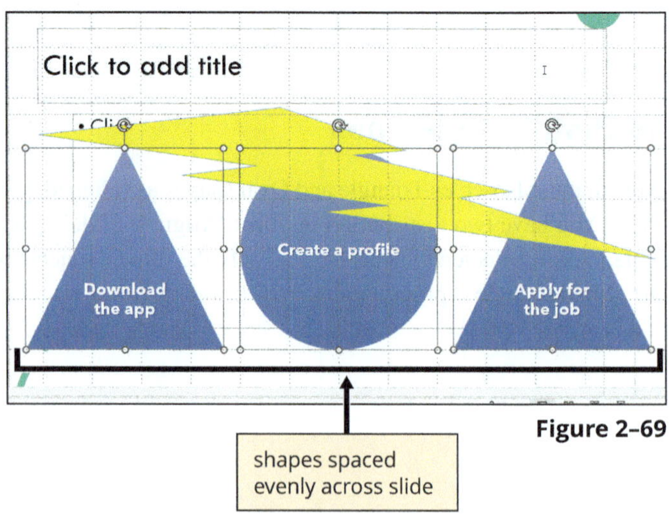

Figure 2–69

BTW

Changing Grid Measurements

You can change the increments of grid measurements, which allows you to adjust the precision of object alignment. In Normal view, right-click an empty area or margin of a slide (not a placeholder) and then click 'Grid and Guides'. Under Grid settings, enter the measurement that you want in the spacing list. If you want these settings to be the default settings for all your presentations, click 'Set as Default'.

To Align a Shape

Now that the Isosceles Triangle and Oval shapes are distributed evenly across the width of the slide, you can have PowerPoint center them vertically in the slide. The following steps use the Align Middle option. **Why?** This option will move the three Slide 5 shapes vertically to fill some of the space in the slide.

1

- With the three shapes still selected and the Shape Format tab displayed, click the Align button to display the Align Objects menu again (Figure 2–70).

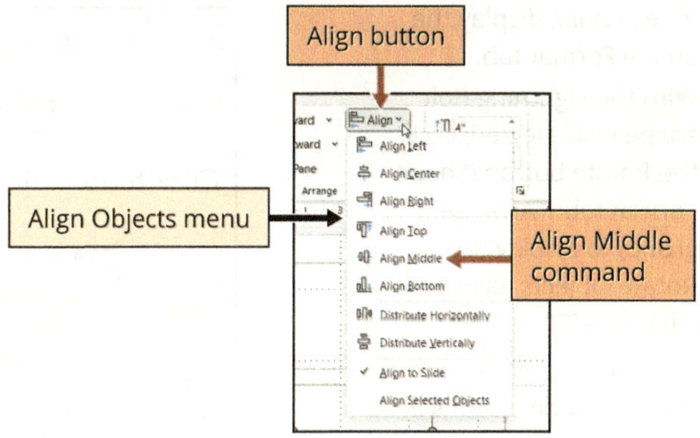

Figure 2–70

2

- Click Align Middle to move the three shapes to the middle of the slide (Figure 2–71).

Q&A What is the difference between the Align Middle and Align Center commands?
Align Middle places the center of each object vertically on the slide; Align Center places all the objects in the center of the slide.

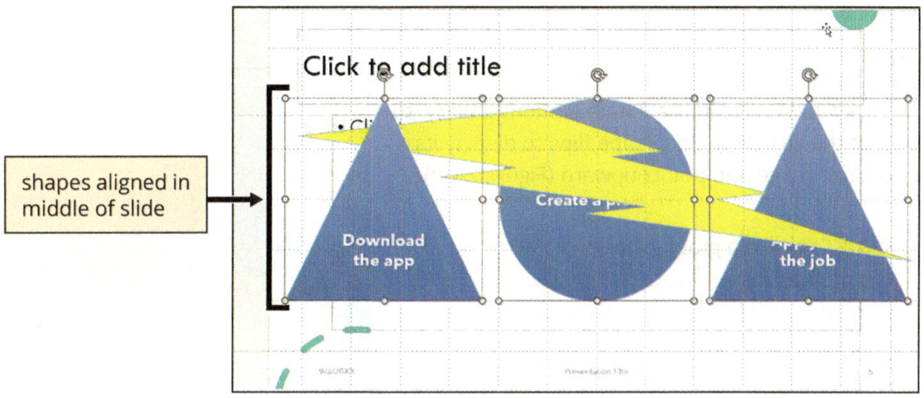

Figure 2–71

To Position the Lightning Bolt Shape

The Lightning Bolt shape represents the energy the students will feel when they pursue the application process, so you want it to display prominently flowing under the shapes and then pointing near the top of the slide. The following step positions the Lightning Bolt shape.

1 Drag the upper horizontal guide to 1.00 inch above the center and the vertical guide 6.00 inches left of the center. Select the Lightning Bolt shape and then drag it downward so the upper-left corner of the selection box touches the intersection of the vertical and horizontal guides (Figure 2–72).

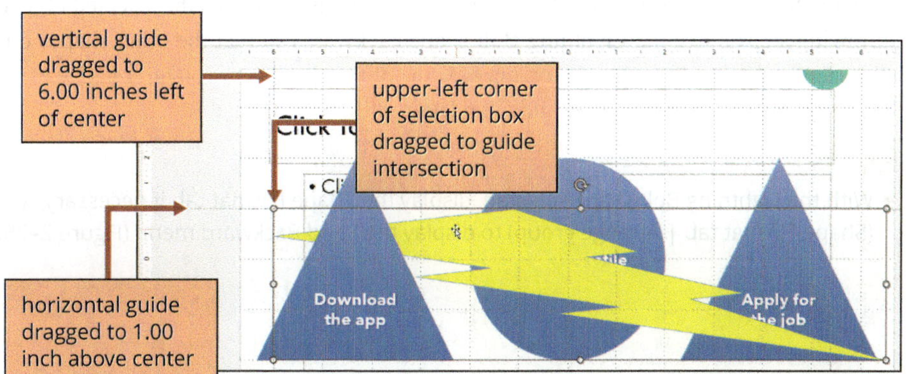

Figure 2–72

To Flip a Shape

The following steps flip the Lightning Bolt shape vertically. **Why?** You want the shape to point upward to indicate positive energy.

1

- If necessary, display the Shape Format tab.
- With the Lightning Bolt shape still selected, click the Rotate button (Shape Format tab | Arrange group) to display the Rotate Objects gallery (Figure 2–73).
- **Experiment:** Point to the various rotate options in the Rotate Options gallery and watch the shape rotate on the slide.

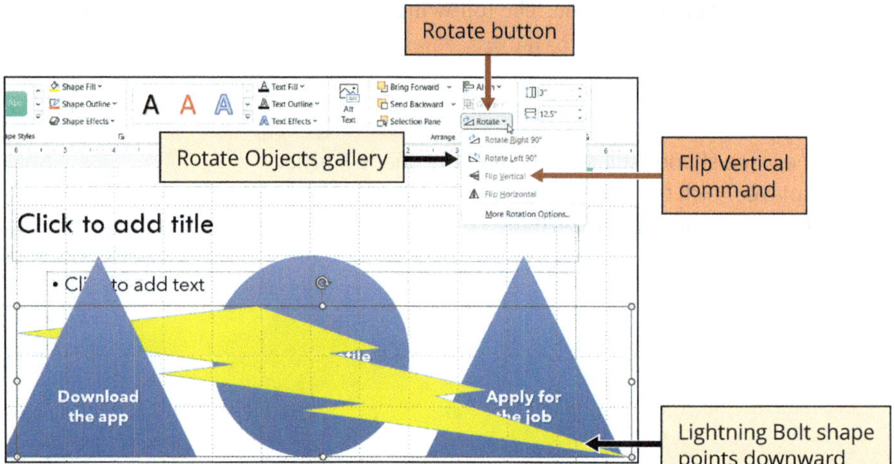

Figure 2–73

2

- Click Flip Vertical in the Rotate Options gallery, so that the Lightning Bolt shape flips to display its mirror image and points upward (Figure 2–74).

Q&A Can I flip a graphic horizontally?
Yes, you would click Flip Horizontal in the Rotate Options gallery. You also can rotate a graphic clockwise or counterclockwise by clicking 'Rotate Right 90°' and 'Rotate Left 90°'.

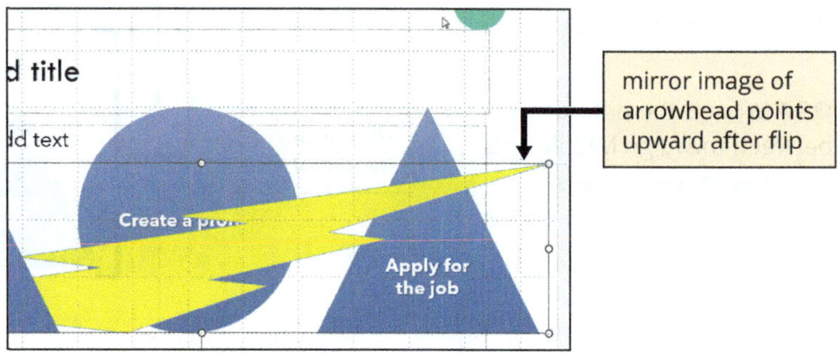

Figure 2–74

To Change the Stacking Order

The objects on a slide stack on top of each other, much like individual cards in a deck. To change the order of these objects, you use the Bring Forward and Send Backward commands. **Bring Forward** moves an object toward the top of the stack, and **Send Backward** moves an object underneath another object. When you click the Bring Forward arrow, PowerPoint displays a menu with an additional command, **Bring to Front**, which moves a selected object to the top of the stack. Likewise, when you click the Send Backward arrow, the **Send to Back** command moves the selected object underneath all objects on the slide. The following steps move the Lightning Bolt shape backwards so that the other shapes on the slide display over it. **Why?** On this slide, the Lightning Bolt shape is on top of some of the shapes, so you no longer can see some of the text. If you send the shape to the bottom of the stack on the slide, the letters will become visible.

1

- With the Lightning Bolt shape selected, display the Shape Format tab if necessary, and then click the Send Backward arrow (Shape Format tab | Arrange group) to display the Send Backward menu (Figure 2–75).

Q&A How can I see objects that are not on the top of the stack?
Press TAB or SHIFT+TAB to display each slide object.

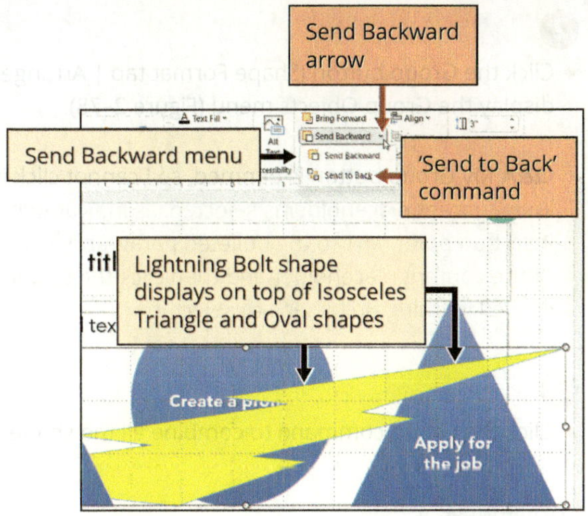

Figure 2–75

2

- Click 'Send to Back' to move the Lightning Bolt shape underneath the Isosceles Triangles and Oval shapes (Figure 2–76).

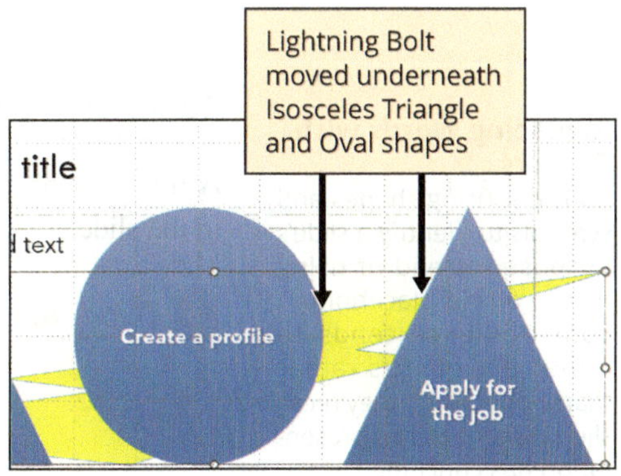

Figure 2–76

Other Ways

1. Click Send Backward arrow (Shape Format tab | Arrange group), press K
2. Right-click shape, point to 'Send to Back' on shortcut menu, click 'Send to Back'

To Group Objects

If you attempt to move or size the four shapes on Slide 5, you might encounter difficulties because the multiple objects are separate objects on the slide. Dragging or sizing affects only a selected object, not the entire collection of objects, so you must use caution when objects are not grouped. You can **group** the objects so they are assembled into a single unit. **Why?** When they are grouped, they cannot be accidentally moved or manipulated. The following steps group these four objects into one object.

1

- Select the two Isosceles Triangle and Oval shapes and then also select the Lightning Bolt shape by clicking the upper-right point that extends past the content placeholder (Figure 2–77).

Q&A Why do I need to click that part of the Lightning Bolt shape to select it?
If you click that shape inside of the content placeholder, the content placeholder also is selected.

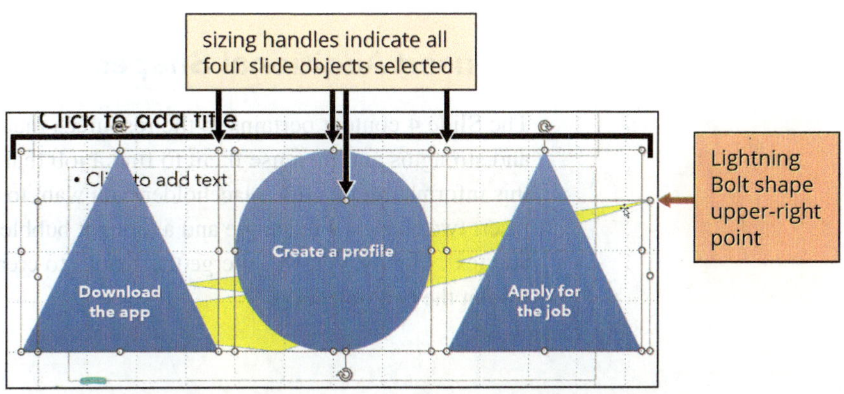

Figure 2–77

2

- Click the Group button (Shape Format tab | Arrange group) to display the Group Objects menu (Figure 2–78).

Q&A My Group button is dimmed, so I cannot click it. Why?
Your content placeholder is selected, as indicated by the insertion point next to the bulleted paragraph. Click outside of the content placeholder and then click the upper-right end of the Lightning Bolt shape to select it.

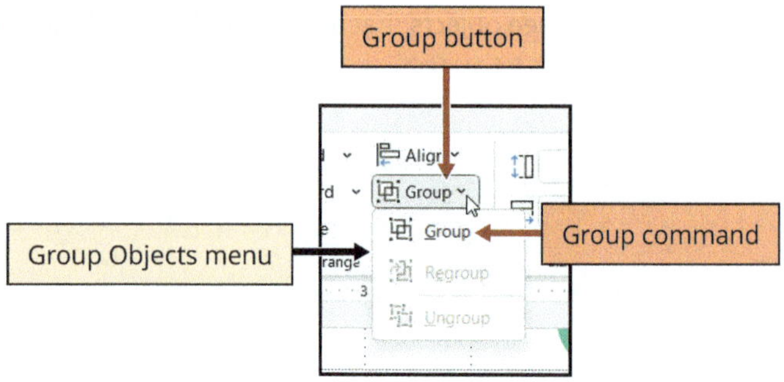

Figure 2–78

3

- Click the Group command to combine all the shapes.

Other Ways

1. Right-click selected shapes, point to Group on shortcut menu, click Group

BTW
Replacing Words with Objects
Consider using shapes and symbols to identify a slide's purpose instead of using text in a title placeholder. Your audience tends to remember objects rather than words when they recall slide content after a presentation has concluded.

To Add a Slide Title

A final enhancement you will make to Slide 5 is to add a title. The following steps add this title to the slide.

1 Type **Application Process** in the title text placeholder (Figure 2–79).

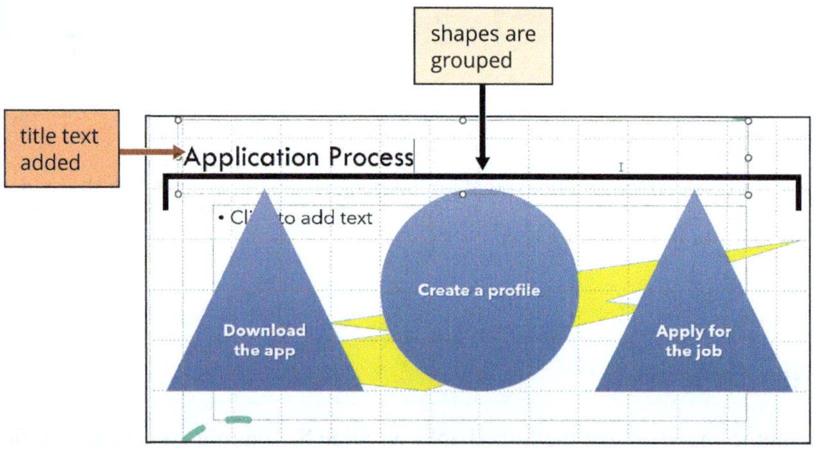

Figure 2–79

To Insert Additional Shapes

The Slide 4 content pertains to the resources that students can use to determine their interests and strengths and then use them to find a job that fits their career goals. Instead of identifying this information in a title placeholder, you want to create a unique shape with text. You first will insert two shapes: a rectangle and a thought bubble. Then, you will arrange and format them and add text. Finally, you will merge the shapes to create one object. The following steps insert and format the two objects.

1. Display Slide 4 and then click the Shapes More button (Home tab | Drawing group) to display the Shapes gallery.

2. Insert the Rectangle: Top Corners Snipped shape (fourth shape in the Rectangles row). Proportionally resize the Rectangle: Top Corners Snipped shape to approximately 3.4" × 2.5".

3. Align the Rectangle: Top Corners Snipped shape so that the left edge is 6 inches left of center (along the first vertical gridline from the left side of the slide) and the lower edge is 2.00 inches below center (along the sixth horizontal gridline).

4. Click the Shapes More button (Shape Format tab | Insert Shapes group) to display the Shapes gallery and then insert the Thought Bubble: Cloud shape (fourth shape in the Callouts row). Proportionally resize the Thought Bubble: Cloud shape to approximately 1.7" × 2".

5. Align the Thought Bubble: Cloud shape so that the left edge is 6 inches left of center (along the first vertical gridline from the left side of the slide) and the upper edge is 3.00 inches above center (along the first horizontal gridline).

6. With the Thought Bubble: Cloud shape selected, click the Shape Styles More button (Shape Format tab | Shape Styles group), and then apply the 'Moderate Effect - Blue, Accent 2' shape style (third style in the fifth Theme Styles row) (Figure 2–80).

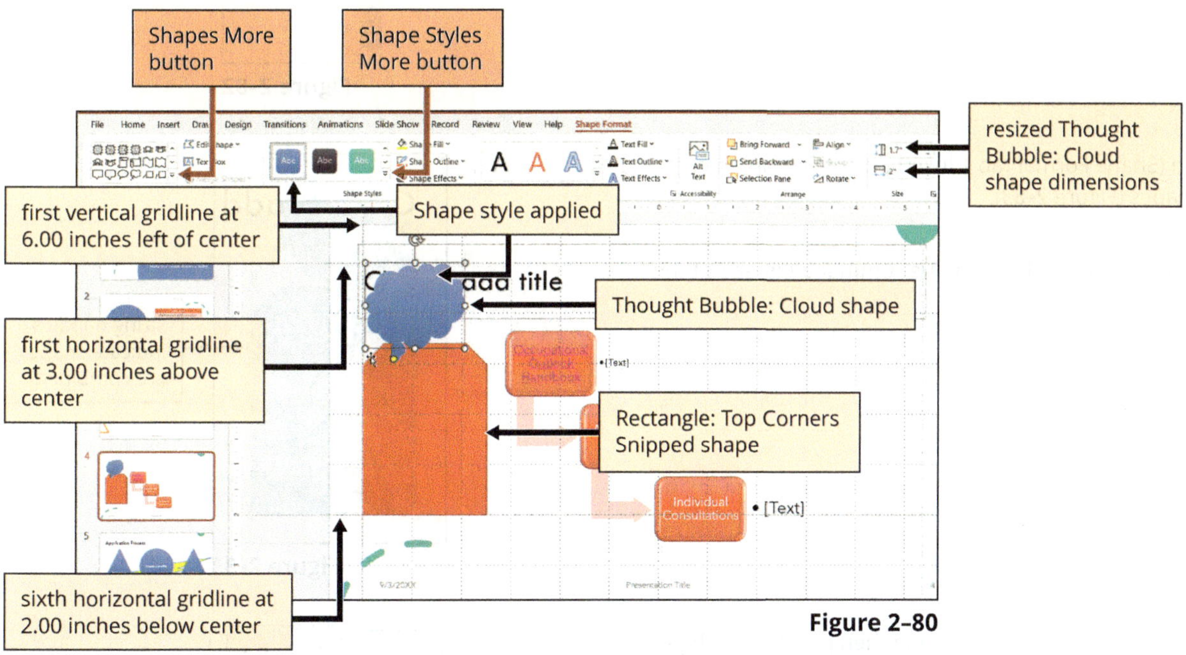

Figure 2–80

To Merge Shapes

The Thought Bubble: Cloud and Rectangle: Top Corners Snipped shapes appear as separate items. You can combine, or merge, them into one object. **Why?** The two elements will appear seamless as a unified graphical element. The following steps merge the two shapes.

1

- Select the Thought Bubble: Cloud and Rectangle: Top Corners Snipped shapes (Figure 2–81).

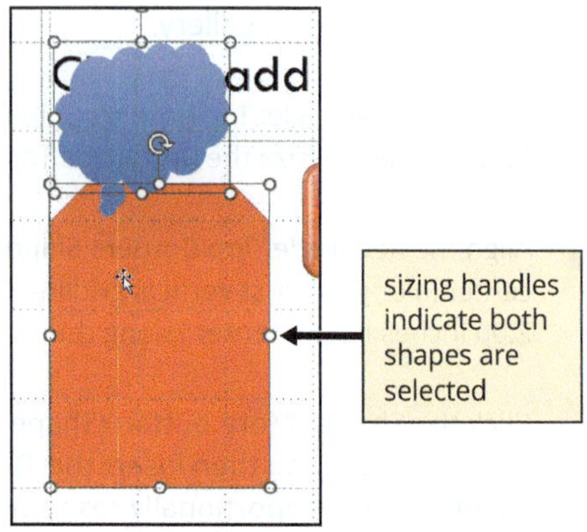

Figure 2–81

2

- With the Shape Format tab displayed, click the Merge Shapes button (Shape Format tab | Insert Shapes group) to display the Merge Shapes menu (Figure 2–82).

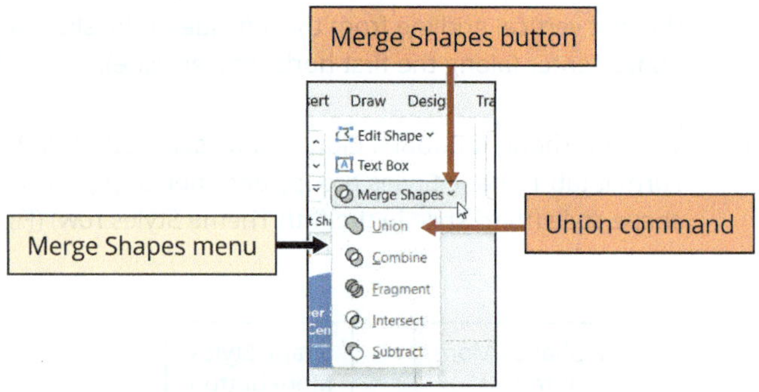

Figure 2–82

3

- Click Union (Shape Format tab | Insert Shapes group) to combine the two shapes (Figure 2–83).

Q&A When would I use the Combine command instead of the Union command?
The Combine command also joins shapes, but it deletes the area where two shapes overlap. The Union command joins the shapes using the formatting of the top shape. Thus, the united shape is now blue.

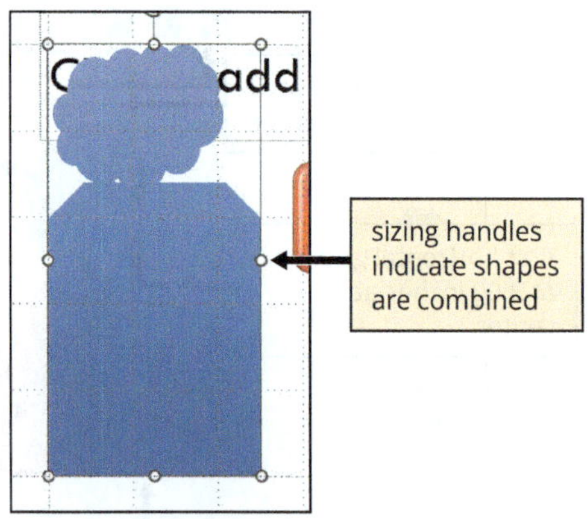

Figure 2–83

4

- Type **Thinking about a career?** and then press ENTER. Type **We have resources to help.** as the next sentence in the shape.
- Increase the font size of the text to 20 point (Figure 2–84).

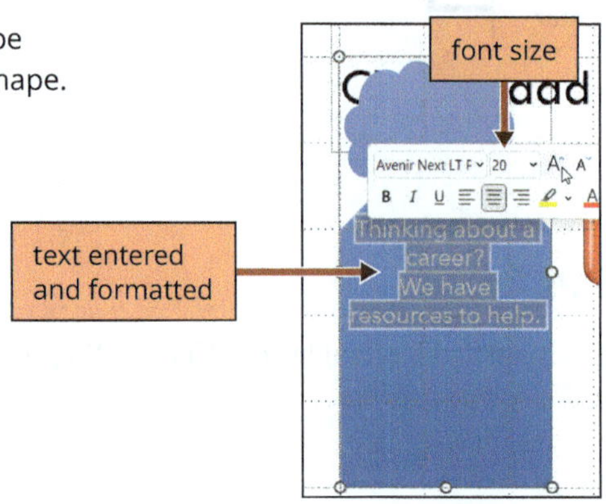

Figure 2–84

To Apply a Picture Fill to a Shape

Sufficient space exists on the right side of Slide 4 to insert a shape filled with a picture. **Why?** A shape and picture help to draw attention to the slide, reinforce the written message, and call attention to the career success theme. A picture with the words, HELP WANTED, coordinates with the resources shapes. You can insert a shape that has the default formatting and then add a picture. The following steps insert a shape and then insert a picture into the shape.

1

- With Slide 4 displayed, insert the Rectangle: Rounded Corners shape (second shape in the Rectangles row).
- Proportionally resize the Rectangle: Rounded Corners shape to 2.5" × 2.5".
- Align the Rectangle: Rounded Corners shape so that the right edge is 6 inches right of center (along the last vertical gridline from the right side of the slide) and the upper edge is 2 inches above center (along the second horizontal gridline) (Figure 2–85).

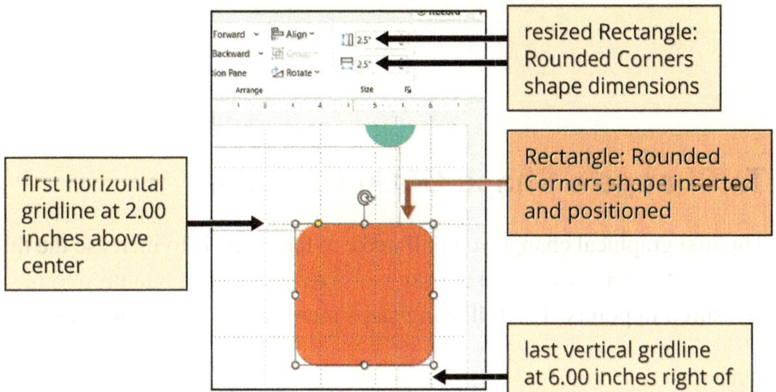

Figure 2–85

2

- With the Shape Format tab displayed, click the Shape Fill arrow (Shape Format tab | Shape Styles group) to display the Shape Fill gallery (Figure 2–86).

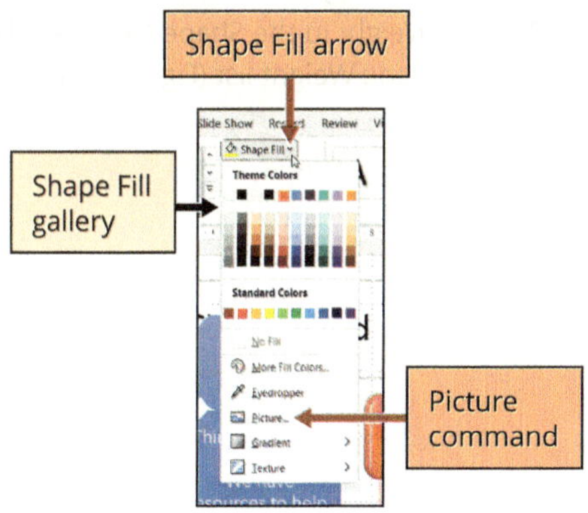

Figure 2–86

3

- Click Picture in the Shape Fill gallery to display the Insert Pictures dialog box, click From a File, and then navigate to the location where your Data Files are stored.
- Click Support_PPT_2_Hiring.jpg to select the file name (Figure 2–87).

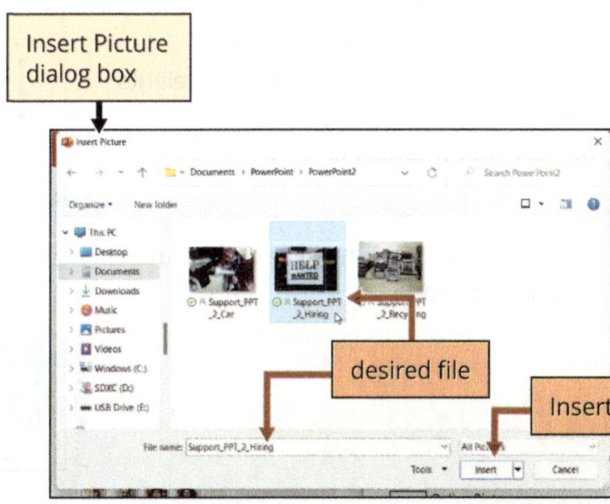

Figure 2–87

4

- Click the Insert button (Insert Picture dialog box) to insert the Hiring picture into the Rectangle: Rounded Corners shape (Figure 2–88).

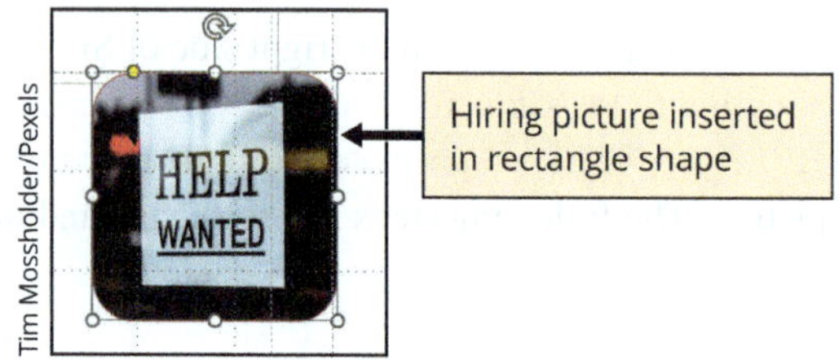

Figure 2–88

To Change a Shape Outline Weight

The first graphical change you will make to the shape is to increase the thickness of the border, which is called the outline. **Why?** This thicker line is a graphical element that helps to call attention to the shape. The weight, or thickness, of the shape border is measured in points. The following steps increase the outline weight.

1

- With the Rectangle: Rounded Corners shape still selected, click the Shape Outline arrow (Shape Format tab | Shapes Styles group) to display the Shape Outline gallery.
- Point to Weight in the Shape Outline gallery to display the Weight list (Figure 2–89).

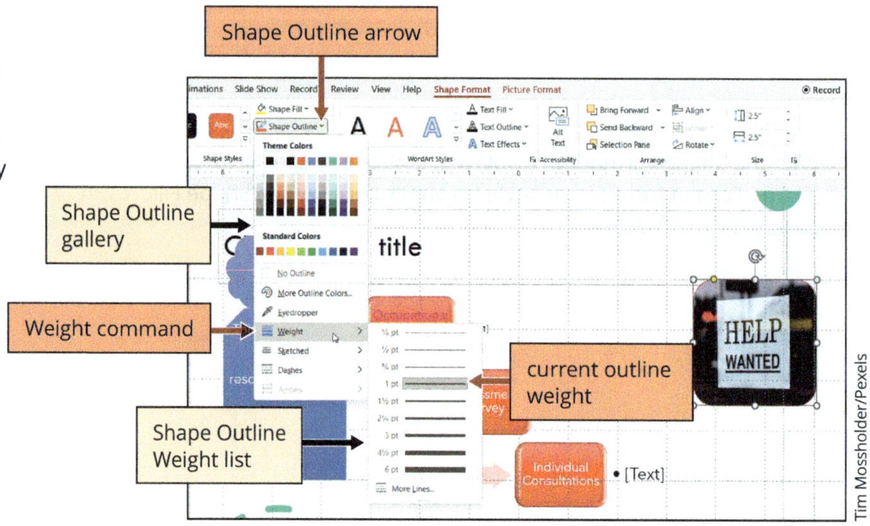

Figure 2–89

2

- Point to 6 pt to display a live preview of this outline line weight (Figure 2–90).
- **Experiment:** Point to various line weights on the Weight list and watch the border weights on the shape change.

3

- Click 6 pt to increase the size of the outline around the shape.

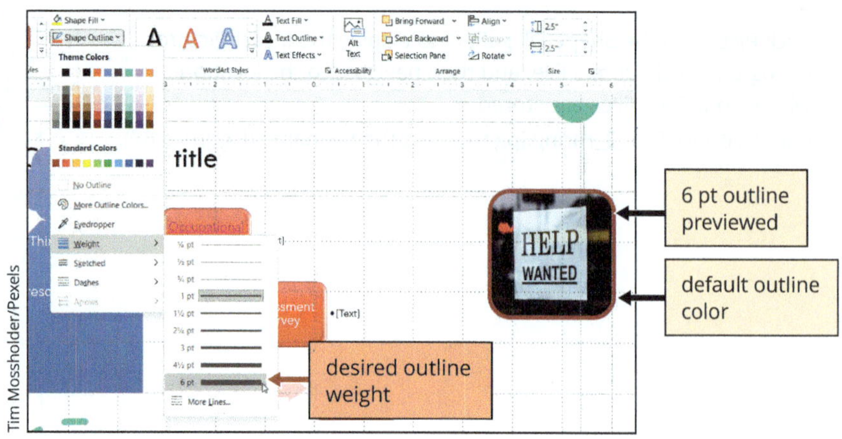

Figure 2–90

Other Ways

1. Click Shape Outline arrow (Home tab | Drawing group), click Weight
2. Right-click shape, click Outline below shortcut menu, click Weight

To Change a Shape Outline Color

The default outline color in the Shapes presentation theme is orange. In this project, you will change the outline color to teal. **Why?** The arc in the lower-left area of the slide and the dot in the upper-right area are teal, so the outline of the rectangle can repeat this color. The following steps change the shape outline color.

1

- With the Rectangle: Rounded Corners shape still selected, click the Shape Outline arrow again to display the Shape Outline gallery.
- Point to Teal, Accent 4 (eighth color in the first Theme Colors row) to display a live preview of that outline color on the shape (Figure 2–91).
- **Experiment:** Point to various colors in the Shape Outline gallery and watch the border colors on the shape change.

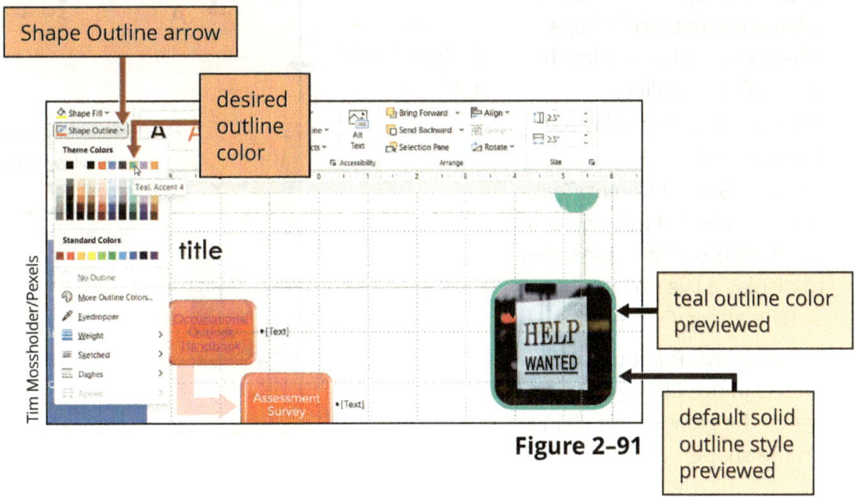

Figure 2–91

2

- Click Teal, Accent 4 to change the shape outline color.

To Change a Shape Outline Style

The default outline style is a solid line. You can add interest by changing the style to dashes, dots, or a combination of dashes and dots. The following steps change the shape outline style to Dash. **Why?** The dashes in this pattern coordinate with the arc in the lower-right corner of the slide.

1

- With the Rectangle: Rounded Corners shape still selected, display the Shape Outline gallery again and then point to Dashes to display the Dashes list.
- Point to 'Long Dash Dot' to display a live preview of this outline style (Figure 2–92).
- **Experiment:** Point to various styles in the Shape Outline gallery and watch the outlines on the shape change.

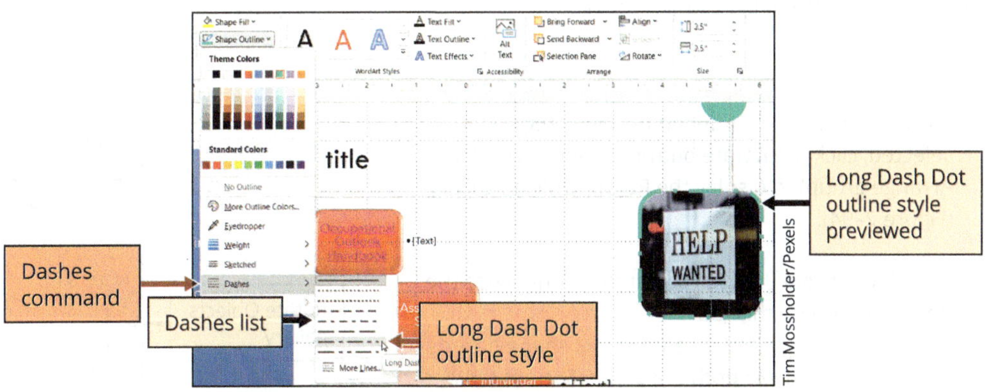

Figure 2–92

2

- Click 'Long Dash Dot' to change the shape outline style.

To Apply an Effect to a Shape

PowerPoint provides a variety of visual effects to add to the shape. They include shadow, glow, reflection, and 3-D rotation. The following steps apply a teal glow effect to the shape. **Why?** The outline color on the slide is teal.

1

- Click the Shape Effects button (Shape Format tab | Shape Objects group) to display the Shape Effects gallery.
- Point to Glow to display the Glow gallery.
- Point to 'Glow: 11 point; Teal, Accent color 4' (fourth color in the third Glow Variations row) to display a live preview of this outline effect (Figure 2–93).

◦ **Experiment:** Point to various effects in the Glow gallery and watch the glow effects change on the shape.

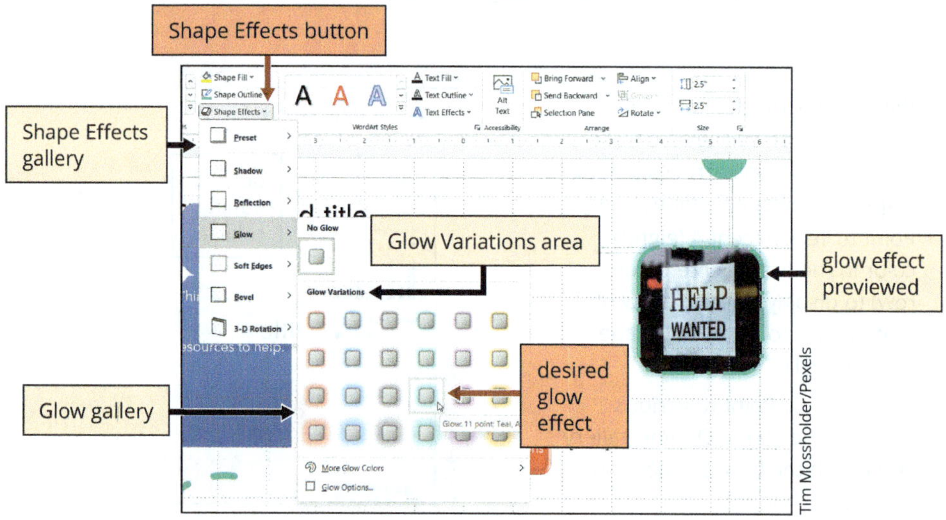

Figure 2–93

2

- Click the 'Glow: 11 point; Teal, Accent color 4' variation to apply the glow effect.

To Rotate a Shape to an Exact Value

In Module 1 you rotated a picture using the rotate handle. Similarly, you can rotate a shape using the rotate handle. You also can rotate a shape clockwise or counterclockwise in two preset values: Right 90° and Left 90°. In addition, you have the option of rotating the shape to any specific degree from 0 to 360. On Slide 4, you will rotate the Rectangle: Rounded Corners shape counterclockwise to the exact value of -15°. **Why?** You want to call attention to this slide element. The following steps rotate the Rectangle: Rounded Corners shape.

1

- With the Rectangle: Rounded Corners shape still selected, click the Rotate button (Shape Format tab | Arrange group) to display the Rotate Objects gallery (Figure 2–94).

Q&A I also see a Picture Format tab. Could I use the Rotate button on this tab?

Yes. The Rectangle: Rounded Corners shape includes a picture, so you see both the Shape Format tab and the Picture Format tab with similar commands in the Arrange group.

◦ **Experiment:** Point to the various rotate options in the Rotate Objects gallery and watch the shape rotate on the slide.

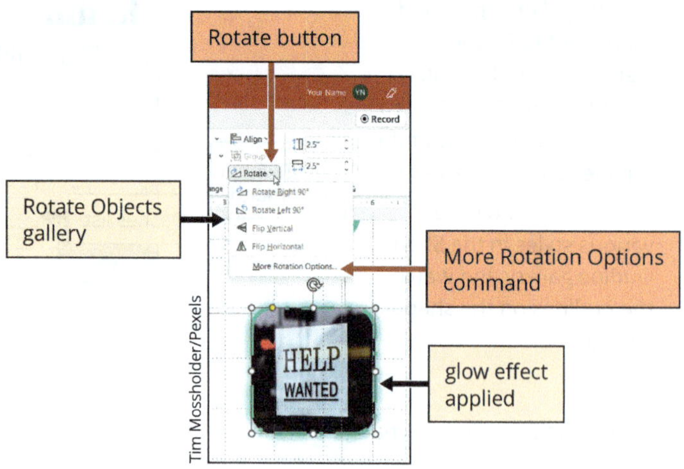

Figure 2–94

2

- Click 'More Rotation Options' in the Rotate Objects gallery to display the Format Picture pane.
- Click the Rotation down arrow several times until −15° is displayed (Figure 2–95).

Q&A Why is the rotation value negative?
When you rotate a shape counterclockwise, the degrees are expressed as a negative number.

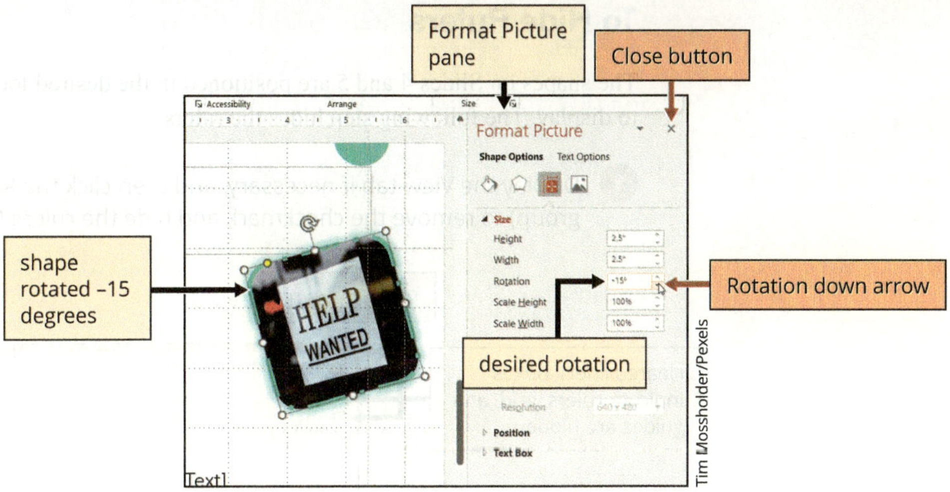

Figure 2–95

3

- Click the Close button (shown in Figure 2–95) to close the Format Picture pane.

To Enter the Title Text

You want to add a title to Slide 4. The following steps add the title text.

1. Type **Resources for You** in the title text placeholder.
2. Center the Slide 4 title text.
3. Click a blank area outside the title text placeholder to deselect this slide element.

To Hide the Grid and Guides

The shapes on Slides 4 and 5 are positioned in the desired locations, so the grid and guides no longer are needed. The following steps hide the grid and the guides.

1. Display the View tab and then click the Gridlines check box (View tab | Show group) to clear the checkmark and hide the grid.
2. Click the Guides check box to clear the checkmark and hide the guides.

Other Ways

1. Right-click area of slide other than a placeholder or object, click Grid and Guides on shortcut menu, click Gridlines to turn off Gridlines or Guides to turn off Guides
2. Press ALT+F9 to toggle guides on/off

To Hide Rulers

The shapes on Slides 4 and 5 are positioned in the desired locations, so the rulers no longer need to display. The following step hides the rulers.

1. Display the View tab if necessary, and then click the Ruler check box (View tab | Show group) to remove the checkmark and hide the rulers (Figure 2–96).

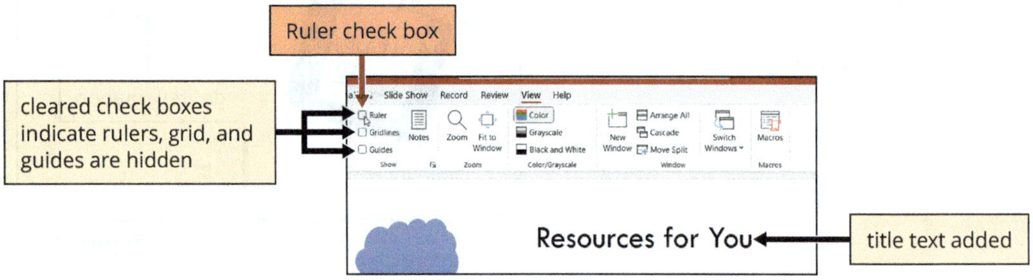

Figure 2–96

Other Ways

1. Right-click area of slide other than a placeholder or object, click Ruler
2. Press SHIFT+ALT+F9 to toggle ruler on/off

Consider This

How can I use handouts to organize my speech?

As you develop a lengthy presentation with many visuals, handouts can help you organize your material. Print handouts with the maximum number of slides per page. Use scissors to cut each thumbnail and then place these miniature slide images adjacent to each other on a flat surface. Any type on the thumbnails will be too small to read, so the images will need to work with only the support of the verbal message you provide. You can rearrange these thumbnails as you organize your speech. When you return to your computer, you can rearrange the slides on your screen to match the order of your thumbnail printouts. Begin speaking the actual words you want to incorporate in the body of the talk. This process of glancing at the thumbnails and hearing yourself say the key ideas of the speech is one of the best methods of organizing and preparing for the actual presentation. Ultimately, when you deliver your speech in front of an audience, the images on the slides or on your note cards should be sufficient to remind you of the accompanying verbal message.

BTW
Distributing a Document
Instead of printing and distributing a hard copy of PowerPoint slides, you can distribute the slides electronically. Options include sending the slides via email; posting it on cloud storage (such as OneDrive) and sharing the link with others; posting it on social media, a blog, or other website; and sharing a link associated with an online location of the slides. You also can create and share a PDF or XPS image of the slides, so that users can view the file in Acrobat Reader or XPS Viewer instead of in PowerPoint.

Adding and Modifying a Footer

Slides can contain information at the top or bottom. The area at the top of a slide is called a **header**, and the area at the bottom is called a **footer**. In general, footer content displays along the lower edge of a slide, but the theme determines where these elements are placed. As a default, no information is displayed in the header or footer. You can choose to apply only a header, only a footer, or both a header and footer. In addition, you can elect to have the header or footer display on single slides, all slides, or all slides except the title slide.

Slide numbers are one footer element. They help a presenter organize a talk. While few audience members are cognizant of this aspect of a slide, the presenter can glance at the number and know which slide contains particular information. If an audience member asks a question pertaining to information contained on a slide that had been displayed previously or is on a slide that has not yet been viewed, the presenter can jump to that slide in an effort to answer the question. In addition, the slide number helps pace the slide show. For example, a speaker could have the presentation timed so that Slide 4 is displayed three minutes into the talk.

PowerPoint gives the option of displaying the current date and time obtained from the system or a fixed date and time that you specify. In addition, you can add relevant information, such as your name, your school or business name, or the purpose of your presentation in the Footer area of the Header and Footer dialog box.

To Add a Footer with Fixed Information

The Shapes presentation theme you downloaded displays three footer placeholders for the date, text, and slide number. To reinforce the fact that the Career Success Center has created this presentation, you can modify this information by adding the Center's name and a date. The following steps add this text to all slides in the presentation except the title slide. **Why?** In general, the footer text should not display on the title slide.

1

- Display the Insert tab.
- Click the 'Header & Footer' button (Insert tab | Text group) to display the Header and Footer dialog box.
- If necessary, click the Slide tab to display the Slide sheet (Figure 2–97).

Q&A Can I use this dialog box to add a header?
The slide theme determines the location of the placeholders at the top or bottom of the slide. The footer elements generally are displayed along the lower edge of the slide. Some themes, however, have the footer elements along the top edge, so they are considered header text.

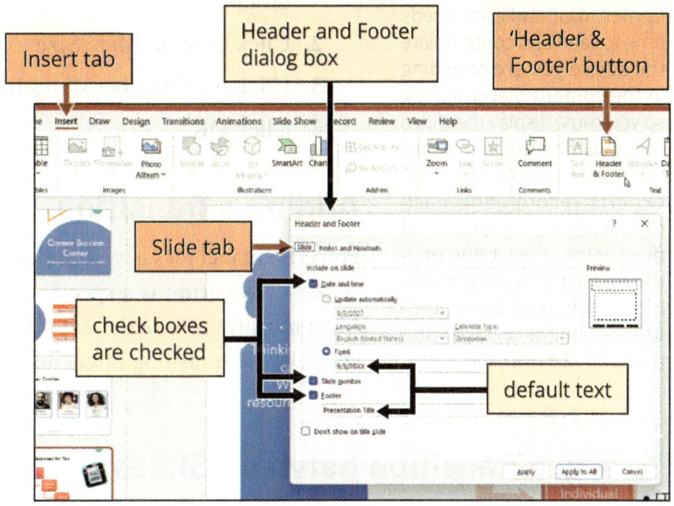

Figure 2–97

2

- With the Fixed option button selected, select the existing date (9/3/20XX) and then type **October 15** in the Fixed box.

Q&A Why is the date on my slide different from today's date?
The Shapes theme you downloaded uses the existing date instead of the current date in the Fixed box.

- Select the existing Footer text (Presentation Title) and then type **Career Success Center** in the Footer box.
- Click the 'Don't show on title slide' check box to place a checkmark in the box (Figure 2–98).

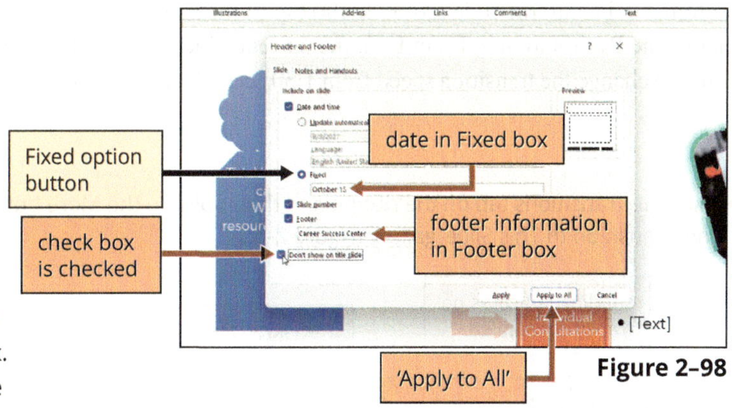

Tim Mossholder/Pexels

Figure 2–98

Q&A Can the footer information also appear on all the slides?
Yes. If the 'Don't show on title slide' check box is not selected, the footer will appear on all slides.

What if I want the current date and time to appear?
Click Update automatically in the 'Date and time' section.

3

- Click the 'Apply to All' button to display the date, footer text, and slide number on all slides except the title slide (Slide 1).

Q&A When would I click the Apply button instead of the 'Apply to All' button?
Click the Apply button when you want the header and footer information to appear only on the slide currently selected.

Other Ways

1. Click Insert Slide Number button (Insert tab | Text group), click Slide number check box (Header and Footer dialog box)
2. Click 'Date & Time' button (Insert tab | Text group), click 'Date and time' check box (Header and Footer dialog box)

To Edit a Footer The PowerPoint theme determines where the slide numbers, date, and footer text display on a slide. It also determines the font and font size. You can format the footer text in the same manner that you format slide text, such as changing the font, font size, and font color. In addition, you can change the slide numbering. By default, the starting slide number is 1. You can, however, change this footer character. To start your slide numbering with a specific number, you would follow these steps.

1. Display the Design tab and then click the Slide Size button (Design tab | Customize group).
2. Click Custom Slide Size to display the Slide Size dialog box.
3. Click the 'Number slides from' up or down arrow to change the slide number.
4. Click OK.

BTW
Displaying Slides
The slides in this presentation have important information about the Career Success Center. Your audience needs time to read and contemplate the advice you are providing in the content placeholders, so you must display the slides for a sufficient amount of time. Some public speaking experts recommend each slide in a presentation should display for at least one minute so that audience members can look at the material, focus on the speaker, and then refer to the slide again.

Adding a Transition

PowerPoint includes a wide variety of visual and sound effects that can be applied to text or content. A **slide transition** is a special effect used to progress from one slide to the next in a slide show. Most transitions have default rotations, but you can change the direction. You also can control the speed of the transition effect and add a sound.

To Add a Transition between Slides

Why? Transitions add interest when you advance the slides in a presentation and make a slide show presentation look professional. In this presentation, you apply the Pan transition in the Dynamic Content category to all slides. The default rotation is From Bottom, so the current slide moves to the top of the screen and a new slide appears from the bottom of the screen. When you change the Pan rotation to From Left, the current slide moves to the right of the screen and the new slide appears from the left. You also change the transition speed from 1.30 seconds to 3 seconds. The following steps apply this transition to the presentation.

1

- Click the Transitions tab on the ribbon and then point to the More button (Transitions tab | Transition to This Slide group) in the 'Transition to This Slide' gallery (Figure 2-99).

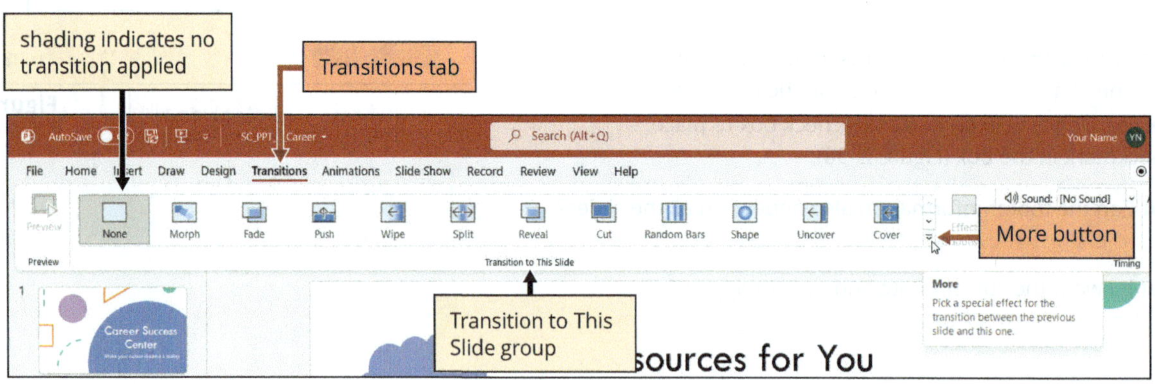

Figure 2-99

2

- Click the More button to expand the Transitions gallery.
- Point to the Pan transition in the Dynamic Content category in the Transitions gallery (Figure 2-100).

3

- Click Pan to view a preview of this transition and to apply this transition to the slide.

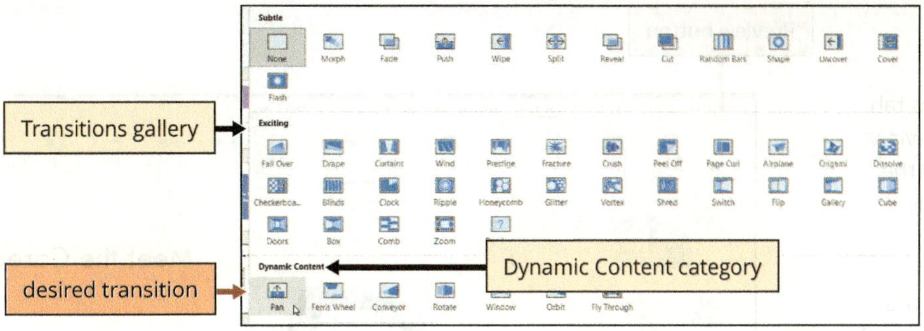

Figure 2–100

4

- Click the Effect Options button (Transitions tab | Transition to This Slide group) to display the Effect Options gallery (Figure 2–101).

Q&A Are the same four effects available for all transitions?
No. The transition effects vary depending upon the particular transition applied.

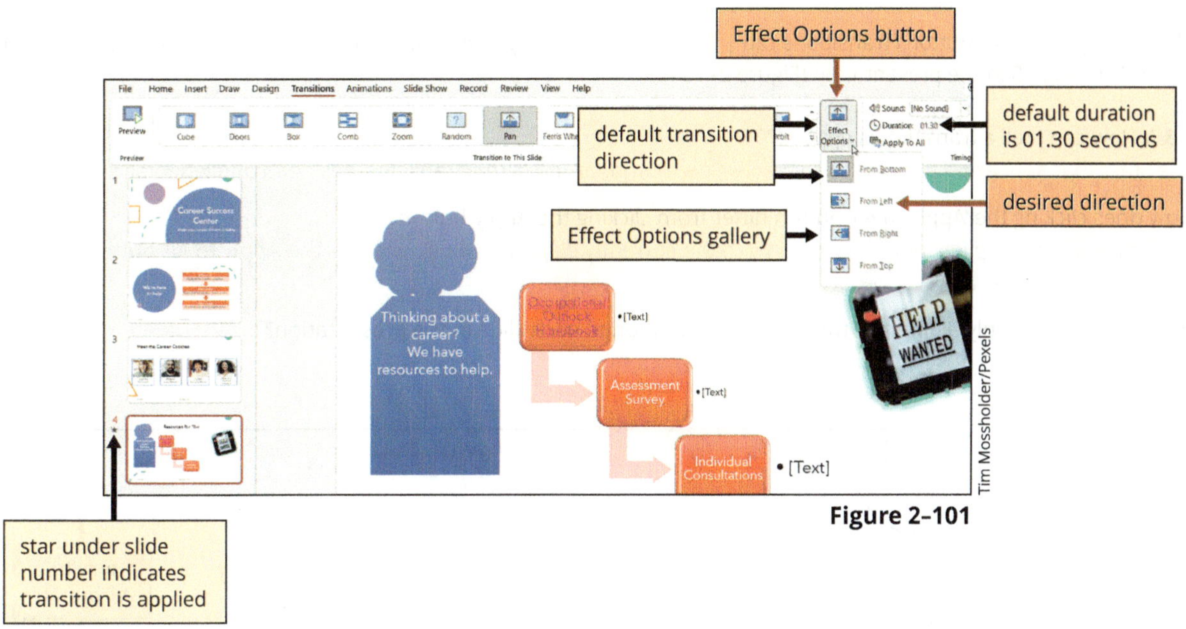

Figure 2–101

5

- Click the From Left effect to change the direction and preview the change.
- Click the Duration up arrow (Transitions tab | Timing group) several times to change the transition speed from 01.30 seconds to 03.00 seconds (Figure 2–102).

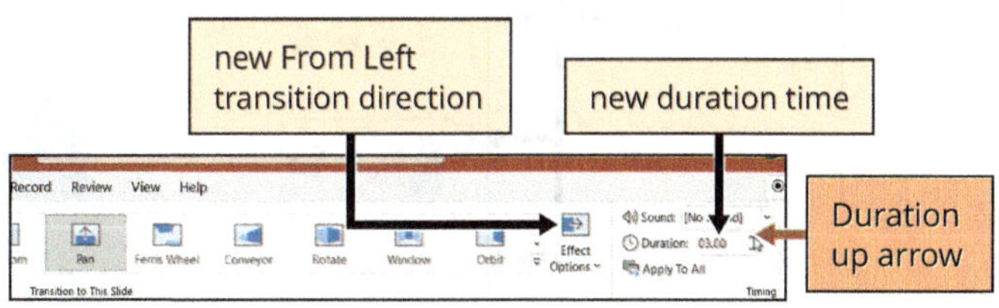

Figure 2–102

Q&A Does every transition have a default duration time of 01.00 seconds?
No. Each transition has its own default duration time.

6

- Click the Preview button (Transitions tab | Preview area) to view the transition and the new transition time (Figure 2–103).

Q&A Can I adjust the duration time I just set?
Yes. Click the Duration up or down arrows or type a speed in the Duration box and preview the transition until you find the time that best fits your presentation.

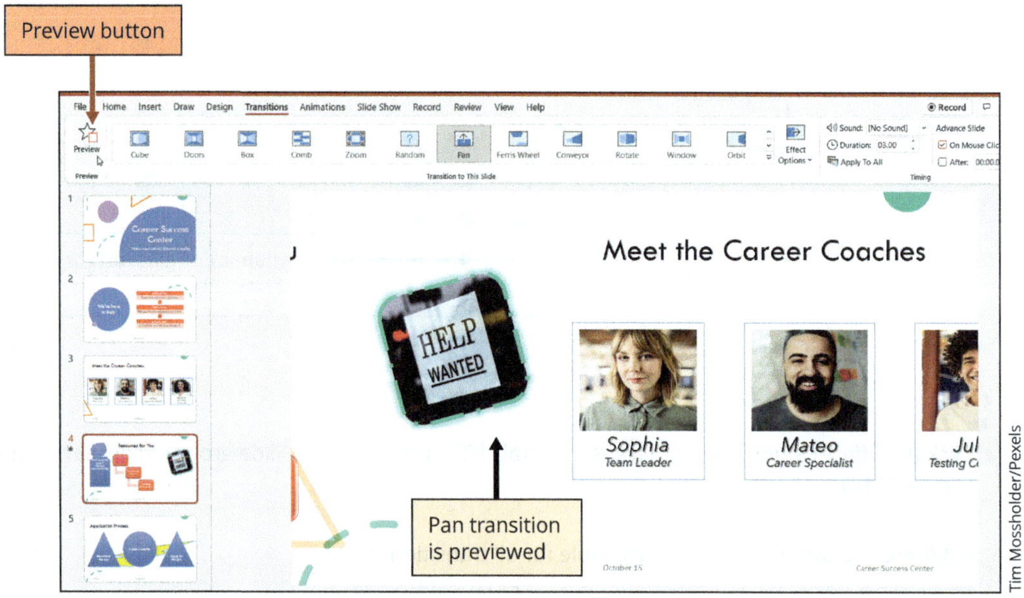

Figure 2–103

7

- Click the 'Apply To All' button (Transitions tab | Timing group) to apply the Pan transition and the increased transition time to Slides 1 through 5 in the presentation (Figure 2–104).

Q&A How can I tell a transition is applied?
The stars that appear on the left side of each slide thumbnail indicate a transition has been applied to all slides.

How does clicking the 'Apply to All' button differ from clicking the Apply button?
The Apply button applies the transition only to the currently displayed slide, whereas the 'Apply to All' button applies the transition to all slides.

What if I want to apply a different transition and duration to each slide in the presentation?
Repeat Steps 2 through 5 for each slide individually.

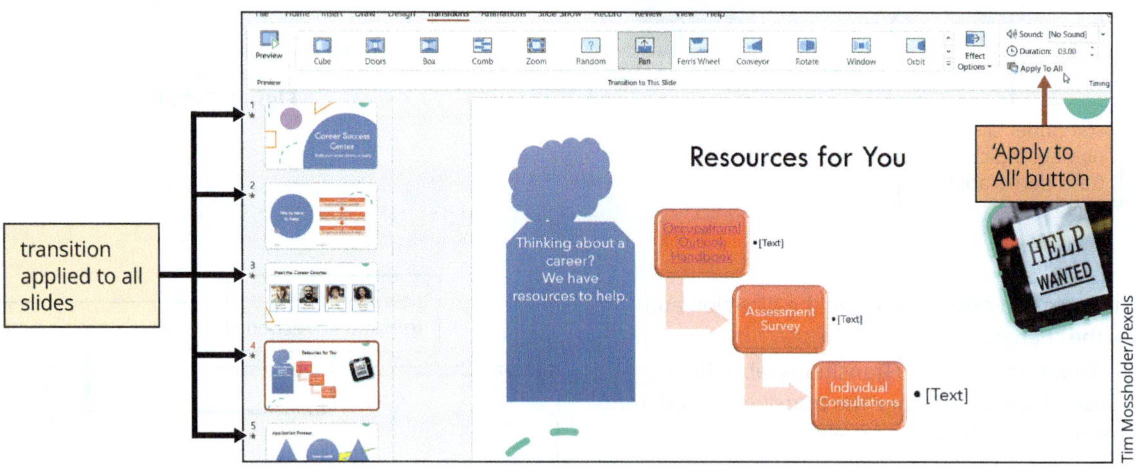

Figure 2–104

To Save and Print the Presentation

It is a good practice to save a presentation before printing it, in the event you experience difficulties printing. The following steps save and print the presentation.

1. Save the presentation again in the same storage location with the same file name.

2. Print the slides as a handout with two slides per page.

Q&A Do I have to wait until my presentation is complete to print it?
No, you can follow these steps to print a presentation at any time while you are creating it.

3. sam Because the project now is complete, you can close the presentation and exit PowerPoint.

BTW
Conserving Ink and Toner
If you want to conserve ink or toner, you can instruct PowerPoint to print draft quality documents by clicking File on the ribbon to open Backstage view, clicking Options in Backstage view to display the PowerPoint Options dialog box, clicking Advanced in the left pane (PowerPoint Options dialog box), scrolling to the Print area in the right pane, verifying there is no check mark in the High quality check box, and then clicking OK. Then, use Backstage view to print the document as usual.

BTW
Printing Document Properties
PowerPoint does not allow you to print document properties. This feature, however, is available in Word.

Summary

In this module, you learned how to use PowerPoint to enhance a presentation with SmartArt and formatted shapes. You searched for and downloaded an online theme; inserted a symbol and hyperlink; inserted, edited, and formatted SmartArt; resized and formatted shapes; moved objects using guides, gridlines, and the ruler; modified a footer; and added a transition.

Consider This: Plan Ahead

What decisions will you need to make when creating your next presentation?

Use these guidelines as you complete the assignments in this module and create your own slide show decks outside of this class.

1. Determine if an online theme can help you design and develop the presentation efficiently and effectively.
2. Identify symbols, shapes, and pictures that would create interest and promote the message being presented.
3. Develop SmartArt that emphasizes major presentation messages.
   a) Format text.
   b) Add styles.
   c) Add effects.
4. Locate shapes that supplement the verbal and written message.
   a) Size and position them aesthetically on slides.
   b) Add styles.
   c) Add and format outlines.
   d) Add a picture fill.
5. Use the guides, gridlines, and ruler to position slide elements.
6. Add a footer.
7. Add a transition.

Student Assignments

Apply Your Knowledge

Reinforce the skills and apply the concepts you learned in this module.

Adding Shapes and SmartArt

Note: To complete this assignment, you will be required to use the Data Files. Please contact your instructor for information about accessing the Data Files.

Instructions: Start PowerPoint. Open the presentation called SC_PPT_2-1.pptx, which is located in the Data Files. The presentation you open contains four unformatted slides. You work as a customer service representative at your local automotive repair facility, and many customers have been asking how they can improve their vehicles' fuel efficiency. You have decided to create a presentation with helpful answers to their questions and display it on monitors in the waiting area. You begin by modifying the unformatted slides by adding a theme, adding shapes and SmartArt, modifying a footer, and applying a transition so the slides look like Figure 2–105.

Perform the following tasks:

1. Add the Savon theme to the presentation. Apply the green color variant. If the Design Ideas pane opens, close it.
2. On the title slide, bold the subtitle text and then apply a text shadow.
3. With Slide 1 still displayed, insert the Rectangle: Top Corners Snipped shape located in the Rectangles area (fourth shape) and then resize it to a height of 2.2" and a width of 2". Insert the picture named Support_PPT_2_Fuel.png as a fill for this shape. Display the ruler, gridlines, and guides, and then align this shape so that the right edge is 1 inch right of the center and the top edge is at the top of the slide, as shown in Figure 2–105a.
4. On Slide 2 (Ways to Increase Gas Mileage), convert the numbered list into the Chevron List SmartArt graphic located in the Process category (first graphic in the sixth row). Change the SmartArt style to Metallic Scene (seventh style in the first 3-D row).
5. On Slide 2, insert a check mark symbol (symbol and character code 97) from the Webdings font before the words, Check, Reduce, and Avoid, in the first first-level paragraphs, as shown in Figure 2–105b.
6. Hide the ruler, gridlines, and guides.
7. On Slide 3 (Choose the Best Tire Type), change the fill color of the left circle (All Season) to Orange, the middle circle (All Terrain) to Dark Blue, and the right circle (Winter) to Light Blue. Resize each circle to a height of 3" and a width of 3" and then apply the 'Glow: 18 point; Green, Accent color 1' Glow Variation effect (first variation in last Glow Variations row) to the three shapes. Change the font of the text in these three circles to Rockwell and the font size to 40 point. Align these three circles to the slide and then distribute them horizontally.
8. Group the three circles.
9. With Slide 3 still displayed, insert the Arrow: Curved Right shape (first shape in the second Block Arrows row). Change the fill color to Dark Red and the outline weight to 3 point. Then add the 'Inside: Top Right' Shadow effect (last shadow in the first Inner row).
10. Resize the arrow shape to a height of 8" and a width of 3.3". Flip the shape vertical. Rotate this shape right 90 degrees. Use the smart guides to center the shape vertically at the top edge of the slide.
11. Send the arrow shape to the back (Figure 2–105c).
12. Delete Slide 4.
13. Add slide numbers and the fixed date of **October 21** to all slides except the title slide. Then use your name in place of Student Name as the footer text.

    If requested by your instructor, change your first name to your mother's first name in the footer text.

14. Apply the Peel Off transition in the Exciting category to all slides. Change the effect option to Right. Change the duration to 02.00 seconds.
15. Save the file with the file name, **SC_PPT_2_Fuel**, and submit the revised presentation in the format specified by your instructor. Slide Sorter view is shown in Figure 2–105d. Exit PowerPoint.
16. **Consider This:** In Steps 7 and 9 you applied many formatting styles to the circle and arrow shapes. How did these styles enhance the graphics?

Figure 2–105(a): Slide 1

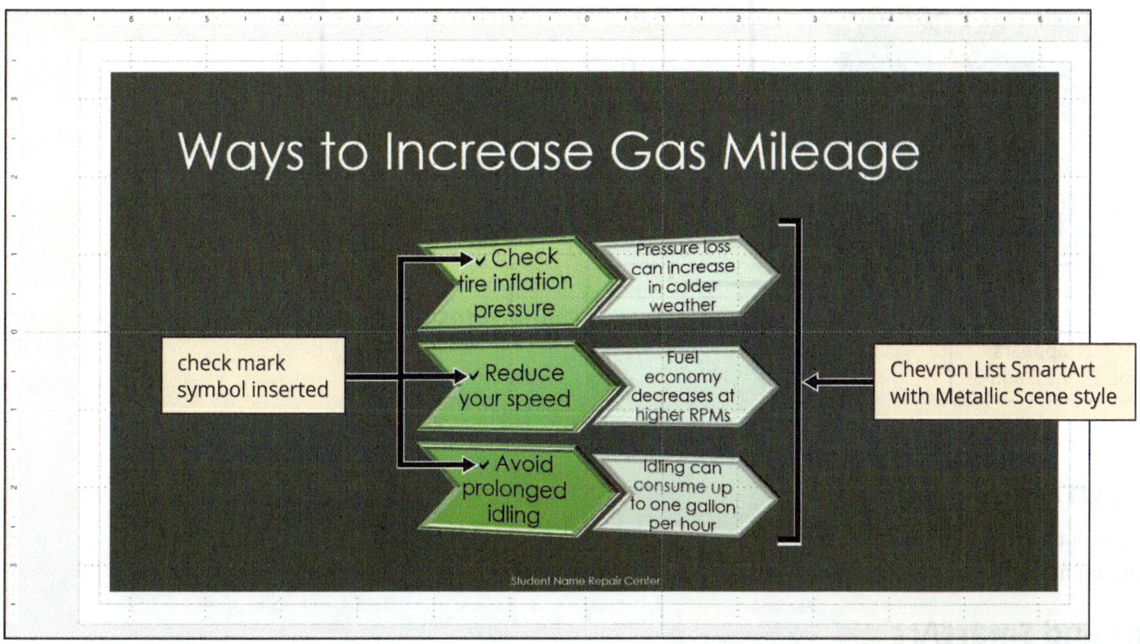

Figure 2–105(b): Slide 2

Continued on next page

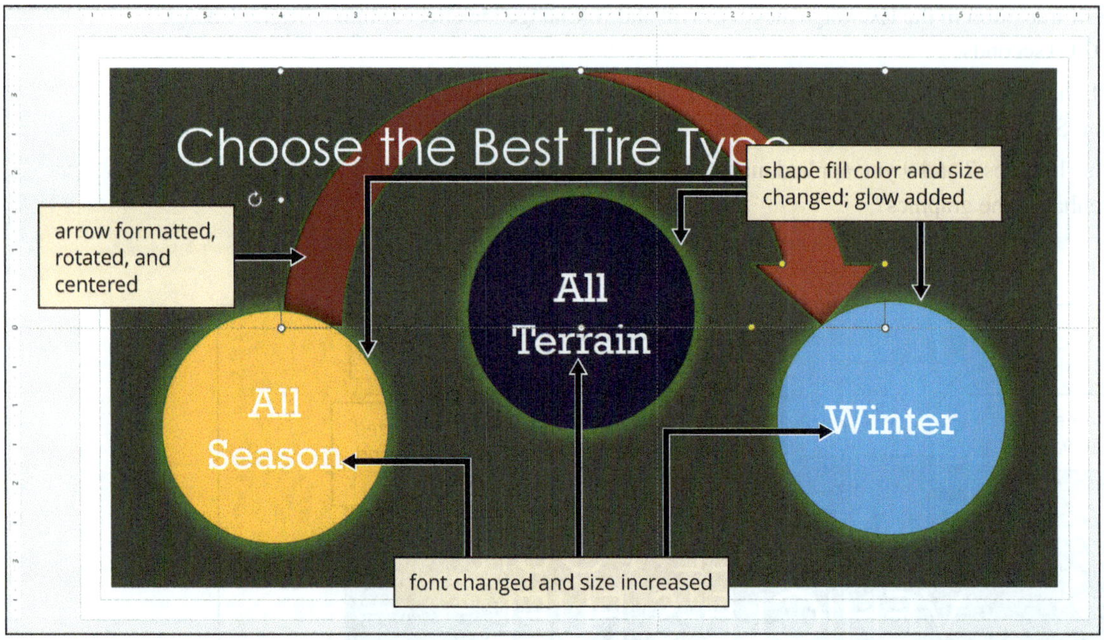

Figure 2–105(c): Slide 3

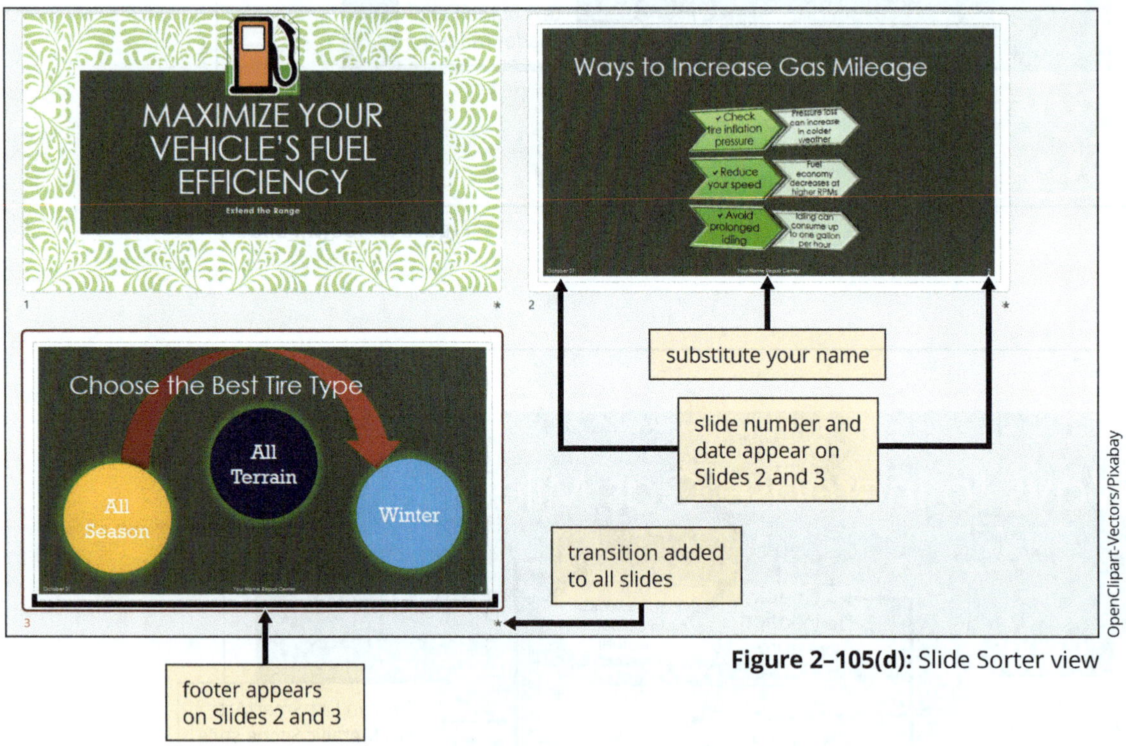

Figure 2–105(d): Slide Sorter view

Extend Your Knowledge

Extend the skills you learned in this module and experiment with new skills. You may need to use Help to complete the assignment.

Adding Icons and SmartArt

Note: To complete this assignment, you will be required to use the Data Files. Please contact your instructor for information about accessing the Data Files.

Instructions: Start PowerPoint. Open the presentation, SC_PPT_2-2.pptx, which is located in the Data Files. You will insert icons, apply a SmartArt Style and effect, and align the graphic to create the presentation.

Perform the following tasks:

1. On the title slide, insert the icon shown in Figure 2–106a in the hexagon shape. Inserting an icon is similar to inserting a picture from a file: you select the shape, click the Shape Fill button, and then click Picture in the Fill menu. When the Insert Pictures dialog box is displayed, click From Icons to display a dialog box with many categories of icons. Type **phone** in the search box to locate several icons with that description. Select the smartphone icon with a black border and then click Insert.
2. Center the title and subtitle paragraphs. Increase the subtitle paragraphs font size to 28 point.

   If requested by your instructor, add your current or previous pet's name in the Slide 1 subtitle text placeholder in place of Student Name.
3. On Slide 2, insert the Ascending Picture Accent Process SmartArt in the Picture category (second graphic in the sixth row). Type **Weather alerts** in the upper text placeholder and then type **Pedometer** in the lower text placeholder.
4. Add a third picture and caption by right-clicking the lower text placeholder, pointing to Add Shape in the shortcut menu, and then clicking 'Add Shape After'. Type **Document scanner** in the new text placeholder.
5. In the upper picture placeholder, insert a thunderstorm icon. In the middle picture placeholder, insert a scanner icon category. In the lower placeholder, insert a running icon, as shown in Figure 2–106b.
6. Change the SmartArt layout by clicking the More button in the Layouts group and then selecting 'Vertical Picture Accent List' in the Picture category (first graphic in the last row). Apply the Metallic Scene 3-D style.
7. Reverse each picture and text placeholder by clicking the 'Right to Left' button (SmartArt Design tab | Create Graphic category).
8. Align the SmartArt graphic in the middle of the slide.
9. On both slides, insert a footer with the text, **Available for iOS and Android** in the placeholder.
10. Apply an appropriate transition to all slides.
11. Save the presentation using the file name, **SC_PPT_2_Smartphone**, and submit the revised presentation in the format specified by your instructor.
12. **Consider This:** In this assignment, you used icons instead of shapes. How useful were these graphical elements in promoting the presentation's message? Did the new SmartArt layout and design in Step 6 enhance the presentation? Why or why not? Did reversing the picture and text placeholders in Step 7 add value to the design? Why or why not?

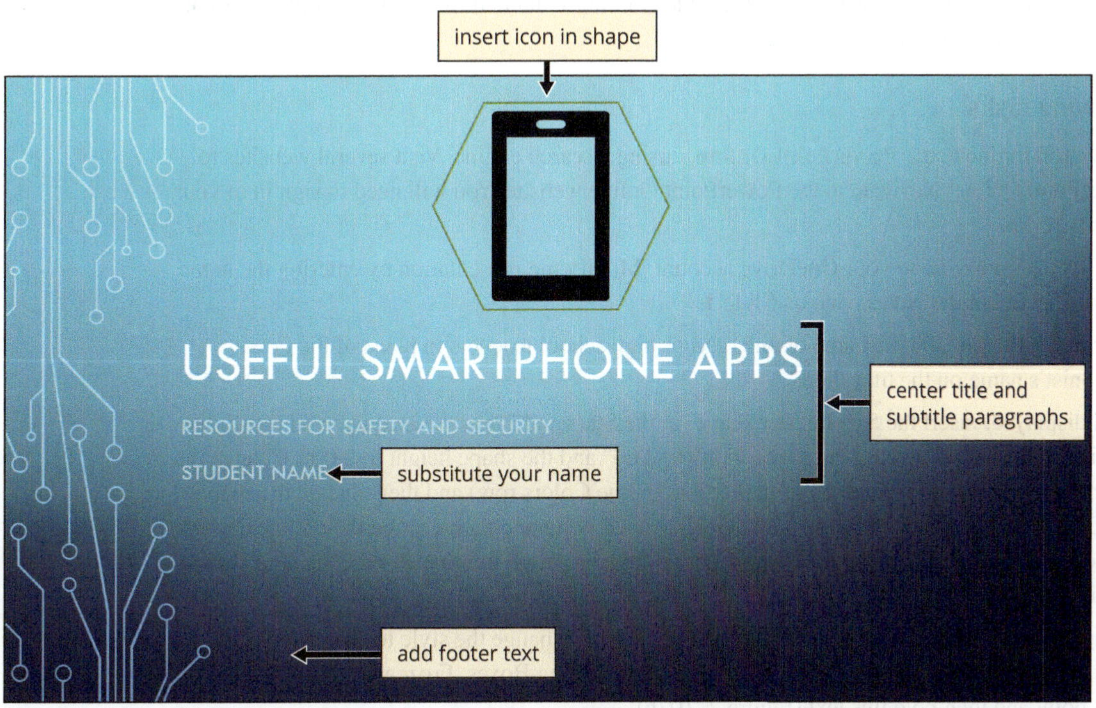

Figure 2–106(a): Slide 1

Continued on next page

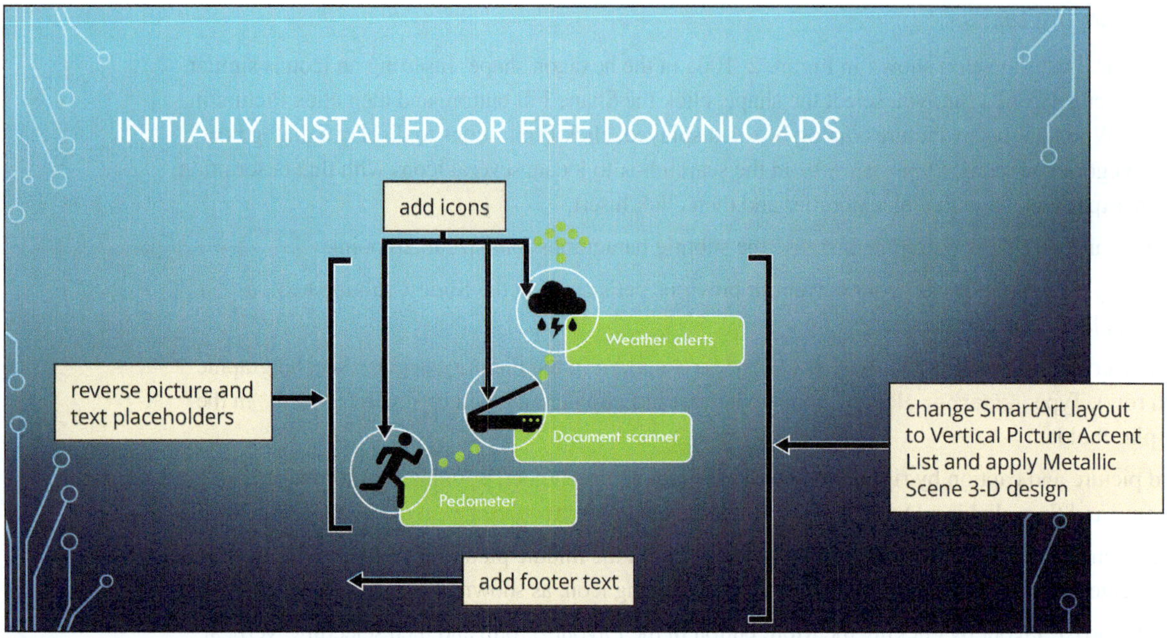

Figure 2–106(b): Slide 2

Expand Your World

Create a solution that uses cloud or web technologies by learning and investigating on your own from general guidance.

Modifying a Presentation Using PowerPoint Online

Note: To complete this assignment, you will be required to use the Data Files. Please contact your instructor for information about accessing the Data Files.

Instructions: As a receptionist in the food services department at your school, you are assisting the manager by developing slides for an upcoming presentation on recycling paper products. The presentation shows the paper products that can be recycled. You have created the slides in the file named SC_PPT_2-3.pptx, and you want to view and edit them using PowerPoint Online.

Perform the following tasks:

1. Run a browser. Search for the text, **PowerPoint Online**, using a search engine. Visit several websites to learn about PowerPoint Online. Navigate to the PowerPoint Online website. You will need to sign in to your OneDrive account.
2. Upload the SC_PPT_2-3.pptx file to your OneDrive account. Modify the presentation by entering the name and address of your school in the Notes pane on Slide 1.

   If requested by your instructor, add the name of one of your high school teachers in place of the Food Services Receptionist's name on the title slide.
3. With Slide 1 still displayed, insert the 5-Point Star shape (in the Stars and Banners category) and move it to the upper-right side of the slide. Increase the shape width to 2.00" and the shape height to 2.00". Change the shape fill color to Orange, Accent 5 (ninth color in the first Theme Colors row) and then change the shape outline color to Dark Red. Change the shape outline weight to 4½ point and then change the outline dashes to Round Dot. Rotate the shape 90° Right. Use the smart guides to position the shape in the location shown in Figure 2–107a.
4. On Slide 2, change the SmartArt layout to Vertical Box List and then change the style to Brick Scene. Increase the font size of the three paper products (Pizza boxes, Shipping Boxes, Frozen food and takeout containers) to 28 point and then bold this text (Figure 2–107b).

5. Add the Uncover transition and then change the effect option to From Top Right. Increase the duration to 2 seconds and then apply the transition to both slides.
6. Play the presentation from the beginning.
7. Rename the presentation using the file name, **SC_PPT_2_Paper**, and submit the presentation in the format requested by your instructor.
8. **Consider This:** How does modifying presentations using PowerPoint Online differ from modifying other presentations you have created in Module 2? Which tabs are not available when the simplified ribbon is used in PowerPoint Online? View the Home, Design, and Transitions tabs. Do you think the formatting functions, themes, and transitions are adequate to develop effective presentations? Why or why not?

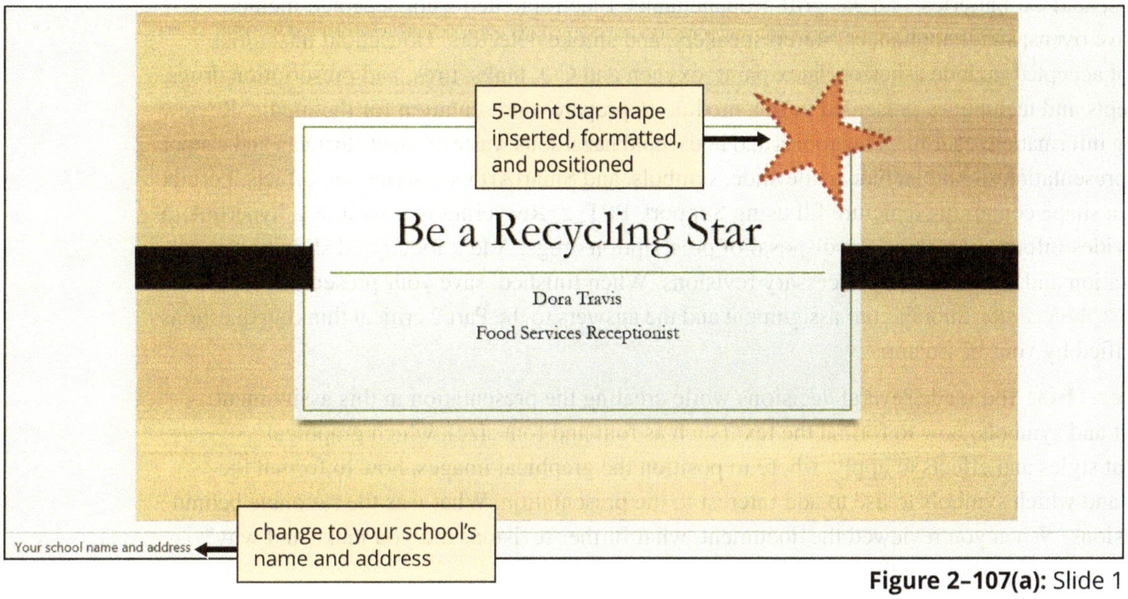

Figure 2–107(a): Slide 1

Figure 2–107(b): Slide 2

In the Lab

Apply your creative thinking and problem-solving skills to design and implement a solution.

Design and Create a Presentation about Your Town's Recycling Event

Part 1: Officials in the Public Works department in your town have scheduled a free electronics and household hazardous waste recycling event for the first Saturday of next month. They would like you to help prepare a presentation for the local media. Your town has been holding this event twice a year for the past five years and has collected thousands of pounds of waste. Residents who have participated in this program are helping to keep their neighborhood clean, which, in turn, helps improve the quality of life and protects the environment for future generations. Electronic items accepted include computers, monitors, printers, televisions, phones, and rechargeable batteries. Household hazardous waste materials include fire extinguishers, oil-based paints, household batteries, acid car batteries, and gas grill propane tanks. Electronic items not accepted include software, microwave ovens, small appliances, stereo speakers, and smoke detectors. Household hazardous waste materials not accepted include asbestos, latex paint, oxygen and CO_2 tanks, tires, and prescription drugs.

Use the concepts and techniques presented in this module to prepare a presentation for the media. Review websites containing information regarding electronics and household hazardous waste products that can and cannot be recycled. Your presentation should include a title slide, symbols, and SmartArt with styles and effects. Format the title slide with a shape containing a picture fill using Support_PPT_2_Recycling.jpg. Include a hyperlink to a website that provides information about the disposal of prescription drugs. Add a footer and slide transitions. View your presentation and then make any necessary revisions. When finished, save your presentation with the file name **SC_PPT_2_Recycling**. Submit your assignment and the answers to the Part 2 critical thinking questions in the format specified by your instructor.

Part 2: **Consider This:** You made several decisions while creating the presentation in this assignment: where to place text and symbols, how to format the text (such as font and font size), which graphical images to use, what styles and effects to apply, where to position the graphical images, how to format the graphical images, and which symbols to use to add interest to the presentation. What was the rationale behind each of these decisions? When you reviewed the document, what further revisions did you make and why? Where would you recommend showing this slide show?

Inserting WordArt, Charts, and Tables

Objectives

After completing this module, you will be able to:

- Insert a chart and enter data
- Change a chart style
- Insert a table and enter data
- Apply a table style
- Insert a text box
- Change text box defaults and apply preset effects
- Reuse slides from another presentation
- Insert a picture without using a content placeholder
- Crop a picture
- Change a picture color tone and softness
- Convert text to WordArt
- Change WordArt style, fill, and outline
- Animate text and change options
- Insert a video

Introduction

Audiences generally focus first on the visual elements displayed on a slide. Graphical elements increase **visual literacy**, which is the ability to examine and assess these images. Visual elements can be divided into two categories: images and information graphics. Images are the pictures you have used in Modules 1 and 2, and information graphics are tables, charts, graphs, and diagrams. Both sets of visuals help audience members interpret and retain material, so they should be designed and presented with care.

Project—Presentation with WordArt, a Chart, and a Table

In this module's project, you will follow proper design guidelines and learn to use PowerPoint to create the slides shown in Figures 3–1a through 3–1d. The objective is to produce a presentation for the Shelly Nature Center's annual tree sale. The Nature Center offers hundreds of carefully chosen resilient trees that are native to your area. These trees are resistant to disease and are customer favorites. Nature Center employees and volunteers will be present at the sale to help residents select the proper trees to enhance their landscapes and provide advice on tree growth rates and maximum heights. After community residents select their trees, they can enjoy the Nature Center's 1,500 acres of woodlands and hiking trails. The trees in this environment can boost mental and physical well-being and lift spirits with their beauty.

The PowerPoint presentation uses several visual elements to help audience members understand the benefits that trees provide and the species of trees that thrive in their climate. The title slide is enhanced with a WordArt graphic and formatted picture. The health and happiness benefits listed

BTW
Increasing Audience Retention
When audience members view graphics and listen to a speaker, they become engaged in the presentation. They tune out distractions and recall more material during a presentation when clear graphics, including WordArt, charts, and tables, are displayed visually and then explained verbally.

on Slide 2 are reinforced with a video clip. The three-dimensional pie chart on Slide 3 depicts the five popular trees in the region, and the three-column table on Slide 4 lists the tree names, their mature height, and the purchase price.

Figure 3–1(a): Slide 1 (Title Slide with WordArt and Enhanced Photo)

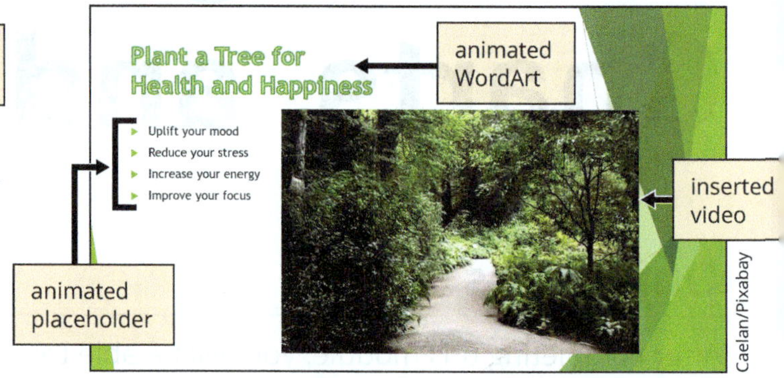

Figure 3–1(b): Slide 2 (WordArt and Video Clip)

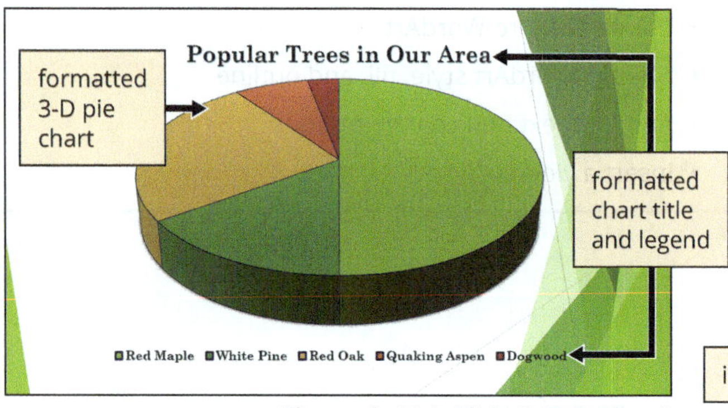

Figure 3–1(c): Slide 3 (3-D Chart)

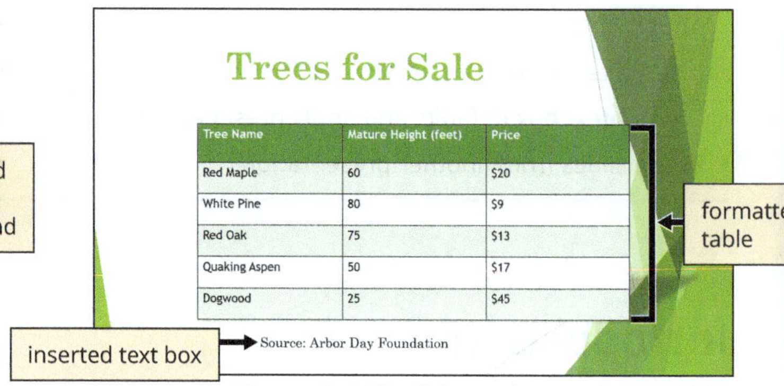

Figure 3–1(d): Slide 4 (Three-column Table)

> **BTW**
> **Preparation Time**
> Be certain to begin developing a presentation well in advance of assignment deadlines when incorporating information graphics. Create a schedule so that you have adequate time to prepare clear visuals. Developing a presentation incorporating charts and tables generally requires extra preparation time because you need to gather data from reputable and current sources to incorporate into these visual elements.

In this module, you will learn how to create the slides shown in Figure 3–1. You will perform the following general tasks as you progress through this module:

1. Create a chart to show proportions.
2. Format a chart by changing the chart style.
3. Create a table to compare and contrast data.
4. Change table format and content style.
5. Insert a text box.
6. Insert slides from another presentation.
7. Crop a picture and apply picture effects.
8. Insert and modify WordArt.
9. Add WordArt styles and effects.
10. Animate text.
11. Insert a video.

Adding a Chart to a Slide and Formatting

Many of the outstanding trees in your town thrive because the soil conditions and climate are optimal for their growth and health. Shade trees, such as maples, oaks, and aspens help conserve energy by providing summer shade. Ornamental trees, including dogwoods, provide interest during the growing season. Attractive evergreens, such as the white pine, provide color throughout the year and are ideal for most landscapes. The chart on Slide 3, shown earlier in Figure 3–1c, shows the proportion of the popular trees in your area.

When a slide contains a content placeholder, you can click the placeholder's Insert Chart button to start creating a chart. Alternatively, you can click the Chart button (Insert tab | Illustrations group) to add a chart to any slide. A sample **Clustered Column chart** displays in the Insert Chart dialog box. This default chart type is appropriate when comparing two or more items in specified intervals, such as comparing how inflation has risen during the past 10 years. Other popular chart types are line, bar, and pie. You will use a pie chart in Slide 3.

When you select a chart type and then click OK, the sample chart is inserted in the current slide and an associated Excel **worksheet** with sample data is displayed in a separate window. You enter data for the chart in this worksheet, which is a rectangular grid containing vertical columns and horizontal rows. Column letters display above the grid to identify each vertical **column**, and row numbers display on the left side of the grid to identify each horizontal **row**. A **cell** is the intersection of a row and a column. For example, cell A1 is the intersection of column A and row 1. Cells are the locations for chart data and text labels. Numeric and text data are entered in the **active cell**, which is the currently selected cell surrounded by a heavy border. You will replace the sample data in the worksheet by typing entries in the cells, but you also can import data from a text file, import an Excel worksheet or chart, or paste data obtained from another program. Once you have entered the data, you can modify the appearance of the chart using menus and commands.

In the following pages, you will perform these tasks:

1. Insert a chart and then replace the sample data.
2. Change the line and shape outline weights.
3. Resize the chart and then change the title and legend font size.

BTW
PowerPoint Help
At any time while using PowerPoint, you can find answers to questions and display information about various topics through PowerPoint Help. Used properly, this form of assistance can increase your productivity and reduce your frustrations by minimizing the time you spend learning how to use PowerPoint.

BTW
Screen Resolution
If you are using a computer to step through the project in this module and you want your screens to match the figures in this book, you should change your screen's resolution to 1920 × 1080.

To Run PowerPoint, Apply a Theme, and Save the Presentation

You can keep track of the changes you make as you progress through this module. The following steps open PowerPoint, apply a theme and a slide layout, and save the file as a PowerPoint presentation.

1. sam Run PowerPoint. Create a blank presentation. If necessary, maximize the PowerPoint window.
2. Apply the Facet theme.
3. Apply the Title and Content layout. Close the Design Ideas pane if it opens (Figure 3–2).
4. Save the presentation using **SC_PPT_3_Trees** as the file name.

BTW
Organizing Files and Folders
You should organize and store files in folders so that you easily can find the files later. For example, if you are taking an introductory technology class called CIS 101, a good practice would be to save all PowerPoint files in a PowerPoint folder in a CIS 101 folder.

BTW
Ribbon and Screen Resolution
PowerPoint may change how the groups and buttons within the groups appear on the ribbon, depending on the screen resolution of your computer. Thus, your ribbon may look different from the ones in this book if you are using a screen resolution other than 1920 × 1080.

Figure 3–2

To Delete a Placeholder

When you run a slide show, empty placeholders do not display. You may desire to delete unused placeholders from a slide. **Why?** Empty placeholders can be a distraction when you are designing slide content because they cover an area of the slide that can display other slide content. The title text placeholder on Slide 1 is not required for this presentation, so you can remove it. The following steps remove the Slide 1 title text placeholder.

1

- Click a border of the title text placeholder so that it appears as a solid or finely dotted line (Figure 3–3). The words, Click to add title, still will be displayed.

2

- Press DELETE to remove the title text placeholder.

Q&A Can I also click the Cut button (Home tab | Clipboard group) to delete the placeholder?
Yes. Generally, however, Cut is used when you desire to remove a selected slide element, place it on the Clipboard, and then paste it in another area. DELETE is used when you do not want to reuse that particular slide element.

If I am using a touch screen, how do I delete the placeholder?
Press and hold on a border of the title text placeholder and then tap DELETE on the shortcut menu to remove the placeholder.

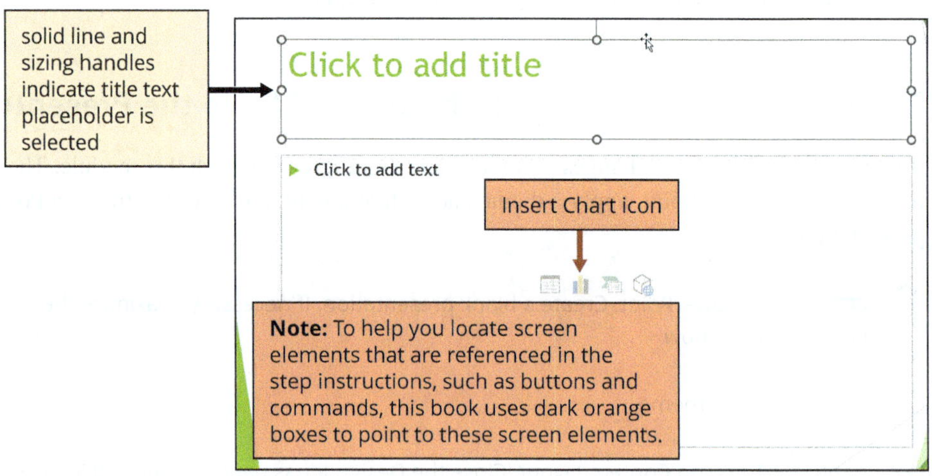

Figure 3–3

Other Ways

1. Select placeholder, press BACKSPACE

Consider This

How can I choose an appropriate chart type?

General adult audiences are familiar with bar and pie charts, so those chart types are good choices. Specialized audiences, such as engineers and architects, are comfortable reading scatter and bubble charts. Common chart types and their purposes are as follows:

- Column—Vertical bars compare values over a period of time.
- Bar—Horizontal bars compare two or more values to show how the proportions relate to each other.
- Line—A line or lines show trends, increases and decreases, levels, and costs during a continuous period of time.
- Pie—A pie chart divides a single total into parts to illustrate how the segments differ from each other and the whole.
- Scatter—A scatterplot displays the effect on one variable when another variable changes.

In general, three-dimensional charts are more difficult to comprehend than two-dimensional charts. The added design elements in a three-dimensional chart add clutter and take up space. A chart may include a **legend**, which is information that identifies parts of the chart and coordinates with the colors assigned to the chart categories. A legend may help to unclutter the chart, so consider using one prominently on the slide.

To Insert a Chart

The first step in developing slide content for this presentation is to insert a pie chart. **Why?** The pie chart is a useful tool to show proportional amounts. In this presentation, you want to show the proportion of popular trees in your region. The following steps insert a chart with sample data into a content placeholder on Slide 1.

1

- Click the Insert Chart icon in the content placeholder to display the Insert Chart dialog box.
- Click Pie in the left pane to display the Pie gallery and then click the 3-D Pie button (second chart) to select that chart type (Figure 3–4).
- **Experiment:** Point to the 3-D Pie chart to see a large preview of this type.

Q&A Can I change the chart type after I have inserted a chart?
Yes. Click the 'Change Chart Type' button in the Type group on the Chart Design tab to display the Change Chart Type dialog box and then make another selection.

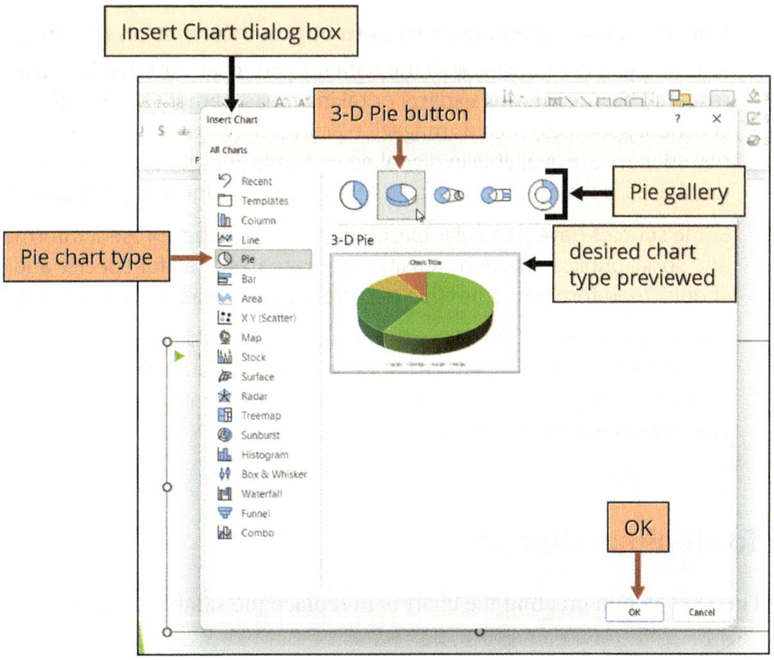

Figure 3–4

2

- Click OK (Insert Chart dialog box) to start the Excel program and open a worksheet on the top of the Trees presentation (Figure 3–5).

Q&A What do the numbers in the worksheet and the chart represent?
Excel places sample data in the worksheet and charts the sample data in the default chart type.

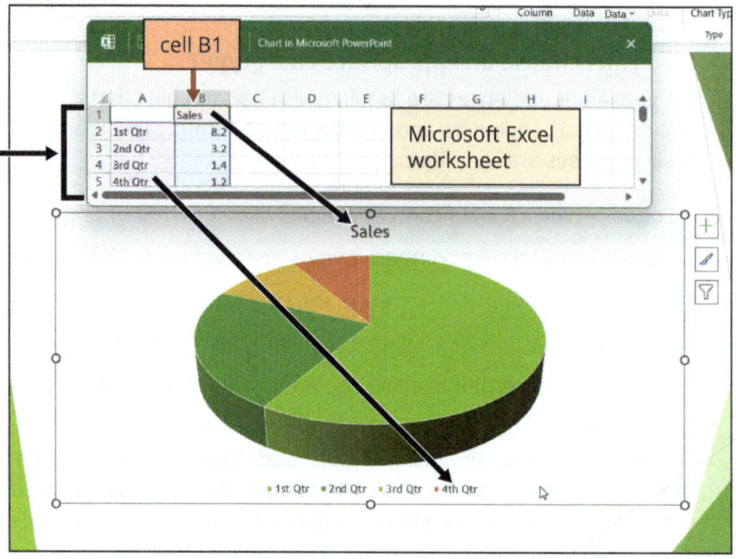

Figure 3–5

Other Ways

1. Click Chart (Insert tab | Illustrations group)

Consider This

How do I locate credible sources to obtain information for the graphic?

At times, you are familiar with the data for your chart or table because you have conducted in-the-field, or primary, research by interviewing experts or taking measurements. Other times, however, you must gather the data from secondary sources, such as magazine articles, newspaper articles, or websites. Digital and print magazines and newspapers are available in digital newsstands and have features that provide in-depth information. Also, online databases, such as EBSCOhost, FirstSearch, Nexis Uni, and NewsBank contain articles from credible sources.

Some sources have particular biases, however, and they present information that supports their causes. Political, religious, and social publications and websites often are designed for specific audiences who share a common point of view. You should, therefore, recognize that data from these sources can be skewed.

If you did not conduct the research yourself, you should give credit to the source of your information. You are acknowledging that someone else provided the data and giving your audience the opportunity to obtain the same materials you used. Type the source at the bottom of your chart or table, especially if you are distributing handouts of your slides. At the very least, state the source during the body of your speech.

To Replace Sample Data

The next step in creating the chart is to replace the sample data, which will redraw the chart. **Why?** The worksheet displays sample data in two columns and five rows, but you want to change this data to show the specific trees and the numbers of each tree in your area. The first row and left column contain text labels and will be used to create the chart title and legend. The other cells contain numbers that are used to determine the size of the pie slices. The following steps replace the sample data in the worksheet.

1

- If necessary, click cell B1, which is the intersection of column B and row 1, to select it.
- Type **Popular Trees in Our Area** in cell B1 (Figure 3–6).

Q&A Why did my pointer change shape?
The pointer changes to a block plus sign to indicate a cell is selected.

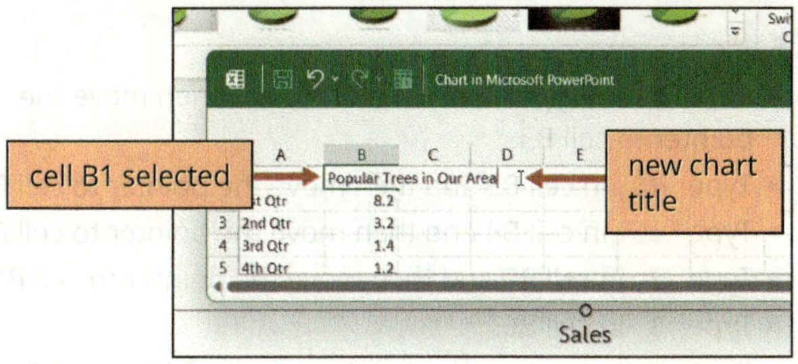

Figure 3–6

2

- Click cell A2 to select that cell and to replace the sample chart title.
- Type **Red Maple** in cell A2 (Figure 3–7).

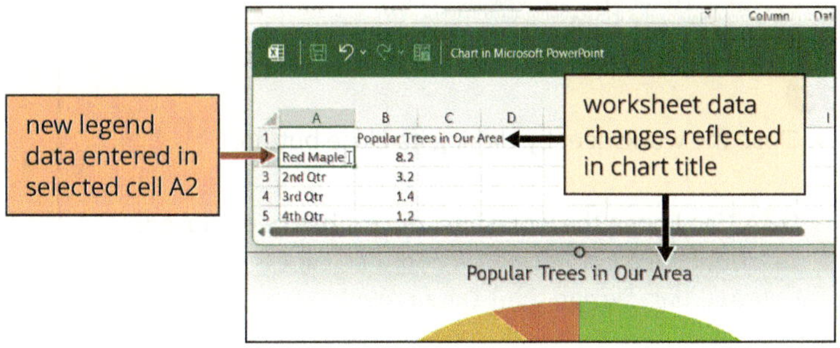

Figure 3–7

3

- Move the pointer to cell A3.
- Type **White Pine** in cell A3 and then move the pointer to cell A4.
- Type **Red Oak** in cell A4 and then move the pointer to cell A5.
- Type **Quaking Aspen** in cell A5 and then press ENTER to move the pointer to cell A6.
- Type **Dogwood** in cell A6 (Figure 3–8).

Q&A Dogwood is displayed in cell A6 but not in the chart legend. Why?
Dogwood will appear in the chart legend once the cell pointer moves away from cell A6.

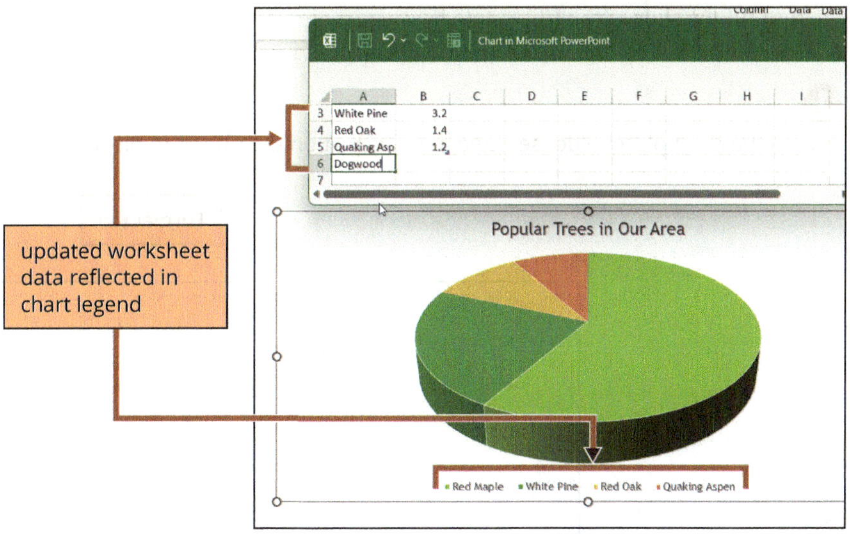

Figure 3–8

4

- Click cell B2, type **50** in that cell, and then move the pointer to cell B3.
- Type **15** in cell B3 and then move the pointer to cell B4.
- Type **25** in cell B4 and then move the pointer to cell B5.
- Type **7** in cell B5 and then move the pointer to cell B6.
- Type **3** in cell B6.
- Press ENTER to move the pointer to cell B7 (Figure 3–9).

Q&A Why do the slices in the PowerPoint pie chart change locations?

As you enter data in the worksheet, the chart slices rotate to reflect these new figures.

5

- Close the worksheet by clicking its Close button.

Q&A Can I open the worksheet once it has been closed?

Yes. Click the chart to select it and then click the Edit Data button (Chart Design tab | Data group).

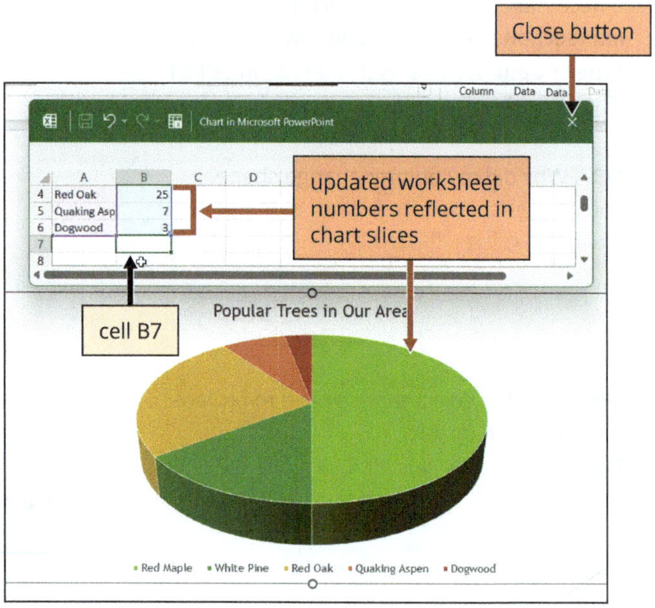

Figure 3–9

To Resize a Chart

You resize a chart the same way you resize a SmartArt graphic or any other graphical object. The following steps resize the chart to fill the slide. **Why?** The slide has a large area of white space, so you are able to enlarge the chart to aid readability. In addition, the chart layout displays a title that provides sufficient information to describe the chart's purpose.

1

- With the chart placeholder selected, click Format on the ribbon to display the Format tab (Figure 3–10).

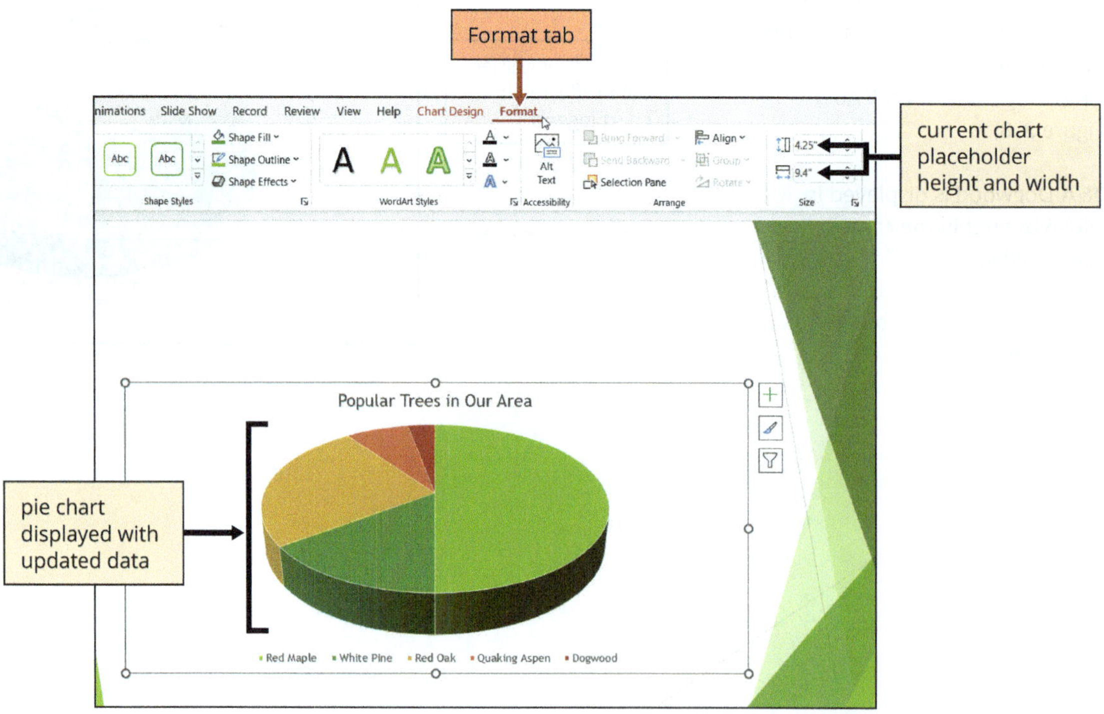

Figure 3–10

2

- Click the Shape Height up arrow repeatedly until 6.5" is displayed in the box.
- Click the Shape Width up arrow repeatedly until 10.5" is displayed in the box (Figure 3–11).

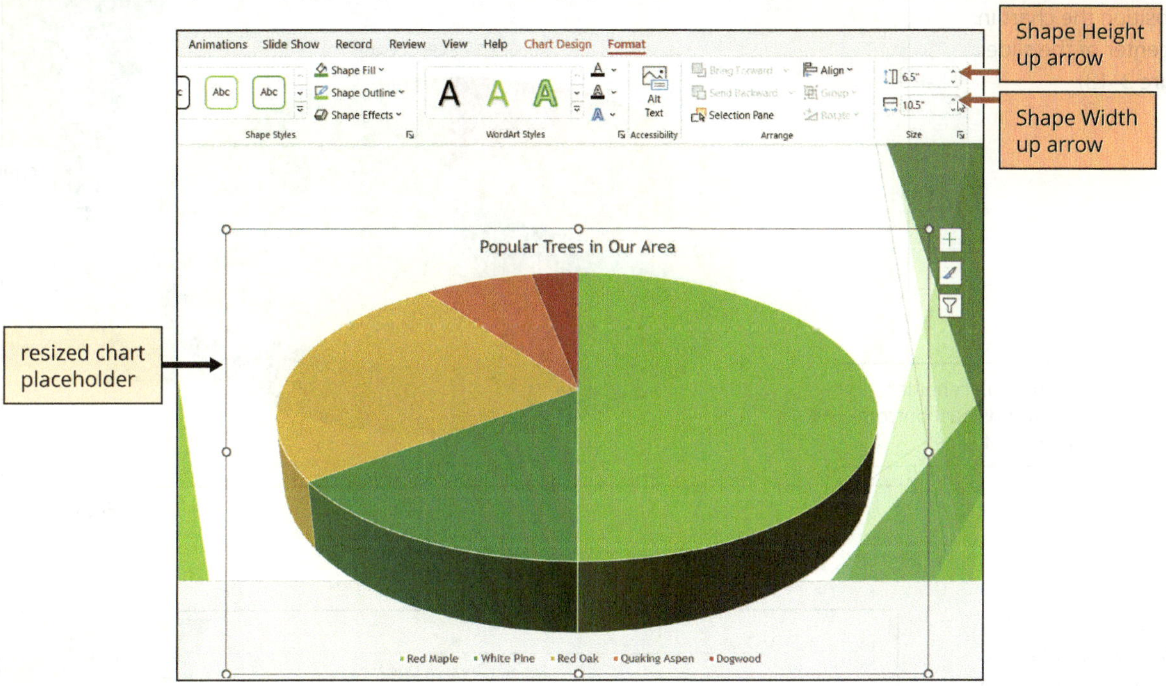

Figure 3–11

To Align a Chart

Part of the resized chart placeholder is located below the slide, so you need to reposition it. **Why?** You can move the placeholder to the center and middle of the slide so that the entire chart and legend can be seen. The following steps align the chart.

1

- With the chart selected and the Format tab displayed, click the Align button (Format tab | Arrange group) to display the Align Objects menu (Figure 3–12).

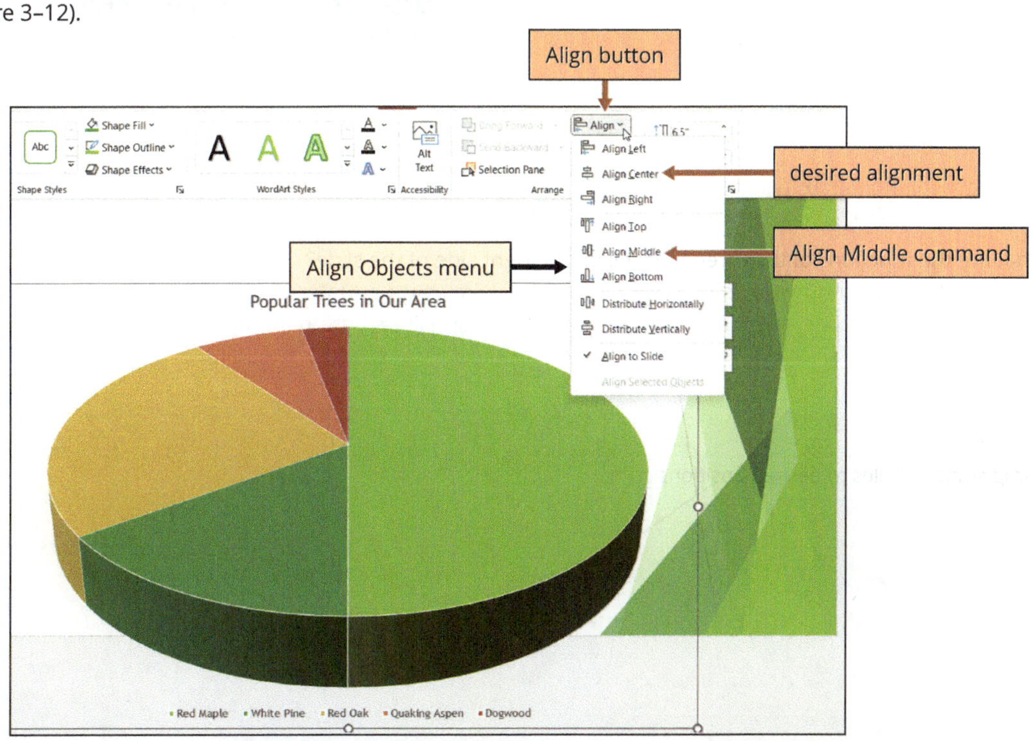

Figure 3–12

2

- Click Align Center on the Align Objects menu to position the chart in the center of the slide (Figure 3–13).

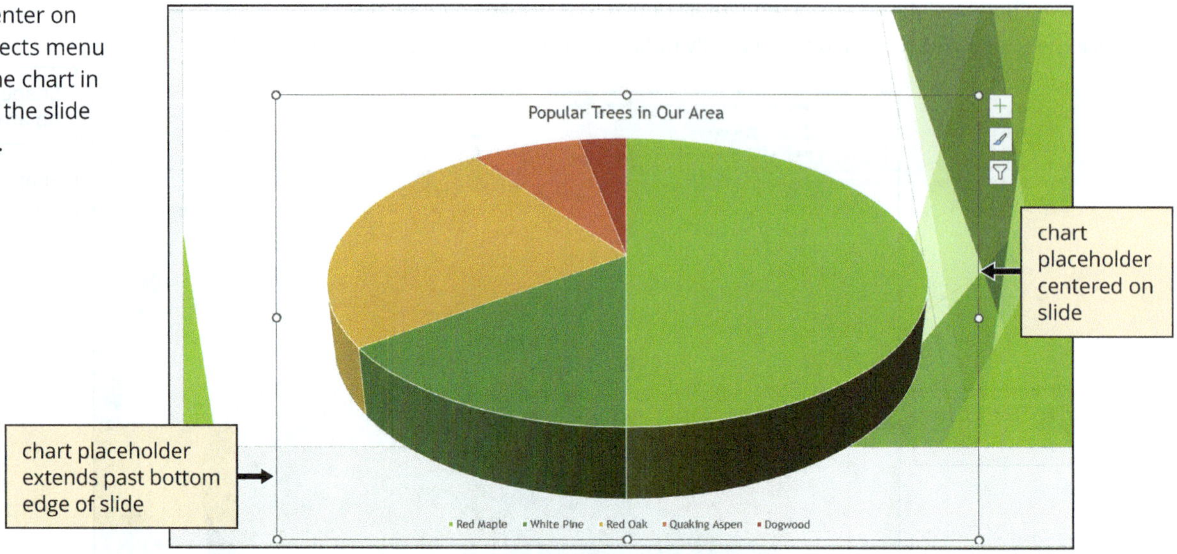

Figure 3–13

3

- Click Align again and then click Align Middle (shown in Figure 3–12) to position the chart in the middle of the slide (Figure 3–14).

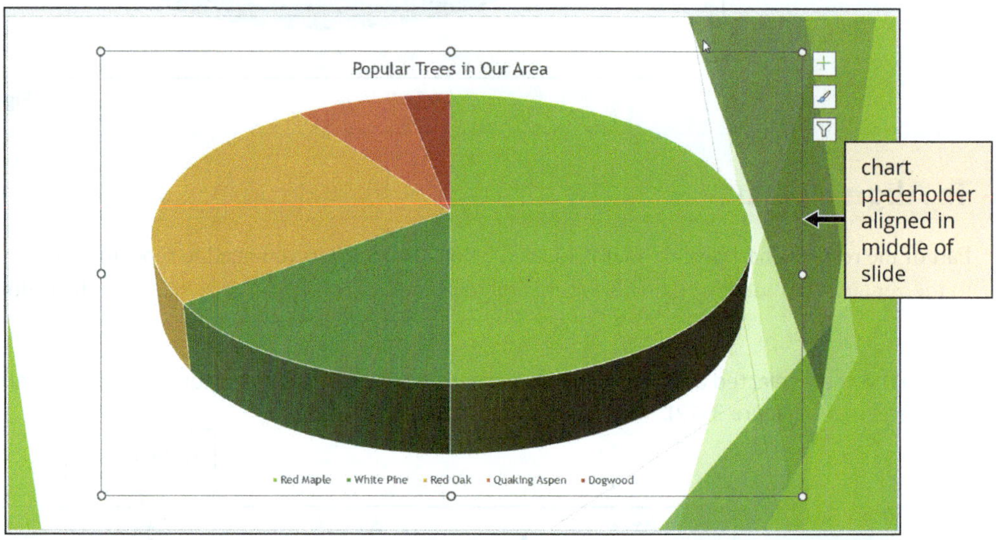

Figure 3–14

Q&A Can I specify a precise position where the chart will display on the slide?

Yes. Right-click the edge of the chart, click 'Format Chart Area' on the shortcut menu, click 'Size & Properties' in the Format Chart Area pane, enter measurements in the Position section, and then specify from the Top Left Corner or the Center of the slide.

What are the functions of the three buttons on the right side of the slide?

The Chart Elements button (plus sign) allows you to display the chart title, data labels, and legends; the Chart Styles button (paintbrush) shows chart styles and color options; the Chart Filters button (funnel) allows you to show, hide, edit, or rearrange data.

Other Ways

1. Drag sizing handles to desired positions

To Change a Chart Style

Once you have selected a chart type, you can modify the look of the chart elements by changing its style. The various layouts move the legend above or below the chart, or they move some or all of the legend data directly onto the individual chart pieces. For example, in the pie chart type, seven different layouts display various combinations of percentages and identifying information on the chart, and they show or do not show the chart title. The following steps apply a chart style with a title and legend that displays below the pie slices. **Why?** Your data consists of tree names and percentages, so you need a layout that shows the proportion of each category along with a corresponding legend.

1

- With the chart still selected, click the Chart Styles button (paintbrush icon) on the right side of the chart area to display the Chart Styles gallery with the Style tab displayed.
- Scroll down until the fifth style (Style 5) in the Chart Styles gallery is displayed and then point to this style to see a live preview on the slide (Figure 3–15).
- **Experiment:** Point to various chart styles and watch the layouts on the chart change.

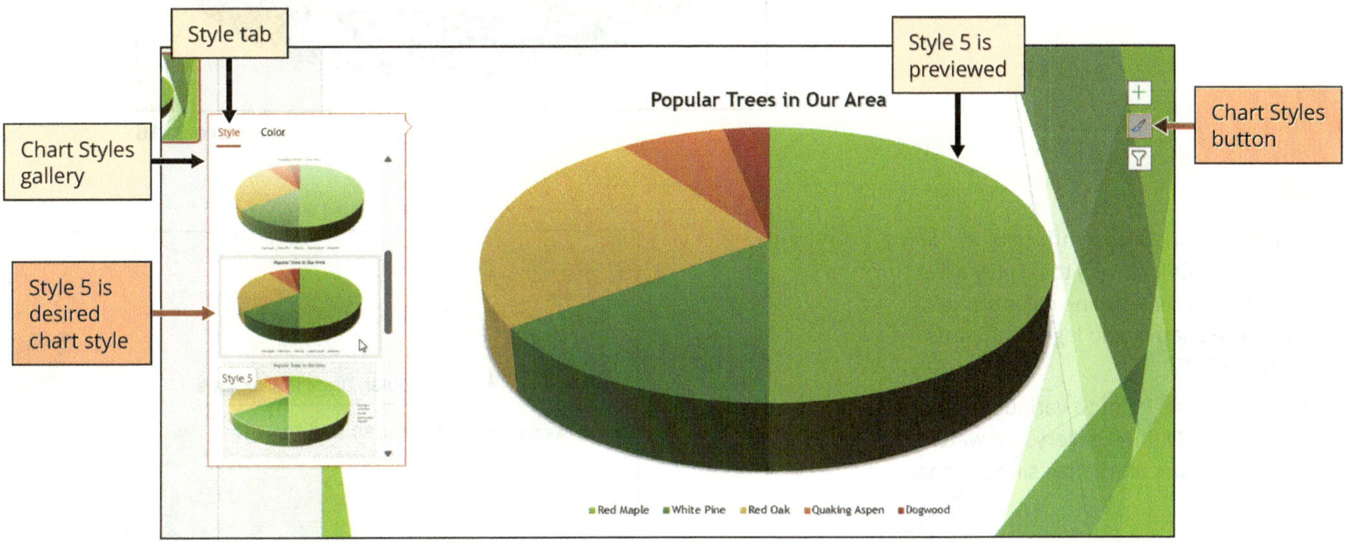

Figure 3–15

2

- Click Style 5 in the Chart Styles gallery to apply the selected chart style to the chart.

3

- Click the Chart Styles button to hide the Chart Styles gallery.

To Change the Shape Outline Color

You can change the outline color to add contrast to each slice and legend color square. The following steps change the shape outline color to Dark Blue. **Why?** At this point, it is difficult to see the borders around the legend squares and around each pie slice. The chart colors resemble colors found in nature, and the color blue also is seen in natural settings such as in the sky or lakes.

1

- Click the center of the pie chart to select it and to display the sizing handles around each slice.

2

- Click the Shape Outline arrow (Format tab | Shape Styles group) to display the Shape Outline gallery (Figure 3–16).

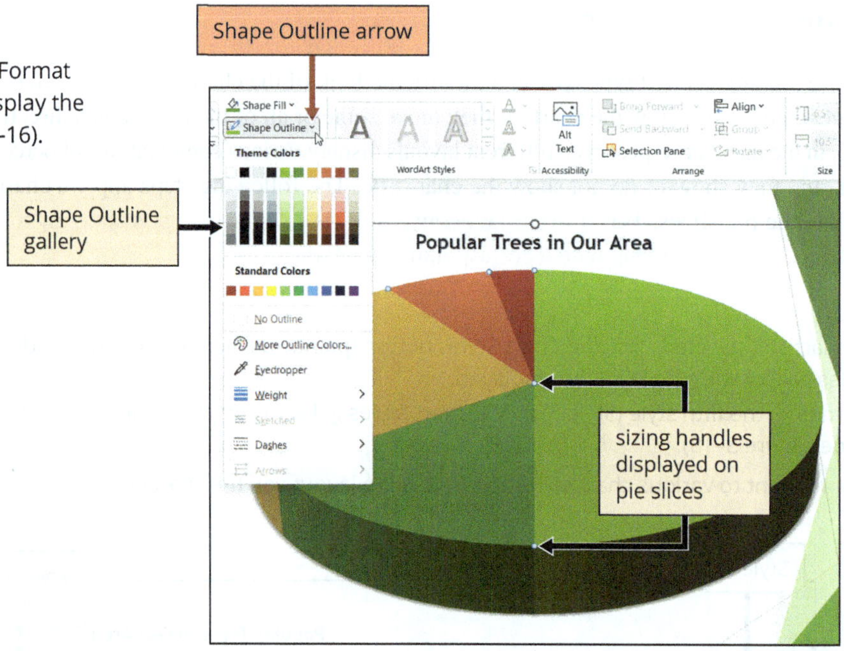

Figure 3–16

3

- Point to Dark Blue (ninth color in the Standard Colors row) to display a live preview of that outline color on the pie slice shapes and legend squares (Figure 3–17).
- **Experiment:** Point to various colors in the Shape Outline gallery and watch the outline colors on the pie slices change.

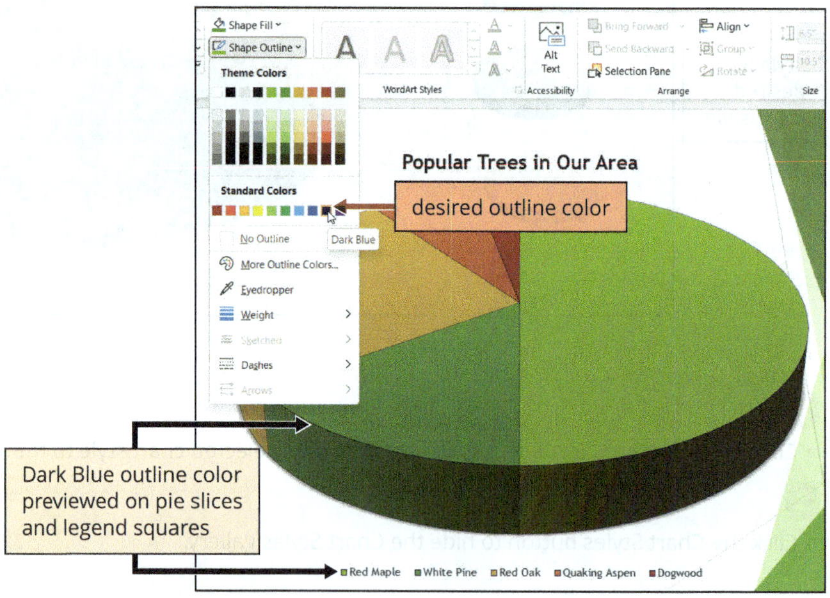

Figure 3–17

4

- Click Dark Blue to add dark blue outlines around each slice and also around the color squares in the legend.

Other Ways

1. Right-click chart, Outline, click desired color

To Change the Shape Outline Weight

The chart has a thin outline around each pie slice and around each color square in the legend. You can change the weight of these lines. **Why?** A thicker line can accentuate each slice and add another strong visual element to the slide. The following steps change the outline weight.

1

- If necessary, click the center of the pie chart to select it and to display the sizing handles around each slice.
- Click the Shape Outline arrow (Format tab | Shape Styles group) again to display the Shape Outline gallery.
- Point to Weight in the Shape Outline gallery to display the Weight gallery.
- Point to 3 pt to display a live preview of this outline line weight (Figure 3–18).
- **Experiment:** Point to various weights on the submenu and watch the border weights on the pie slices change.

2

- Click 3 pt to increase the border around each slice to that width.

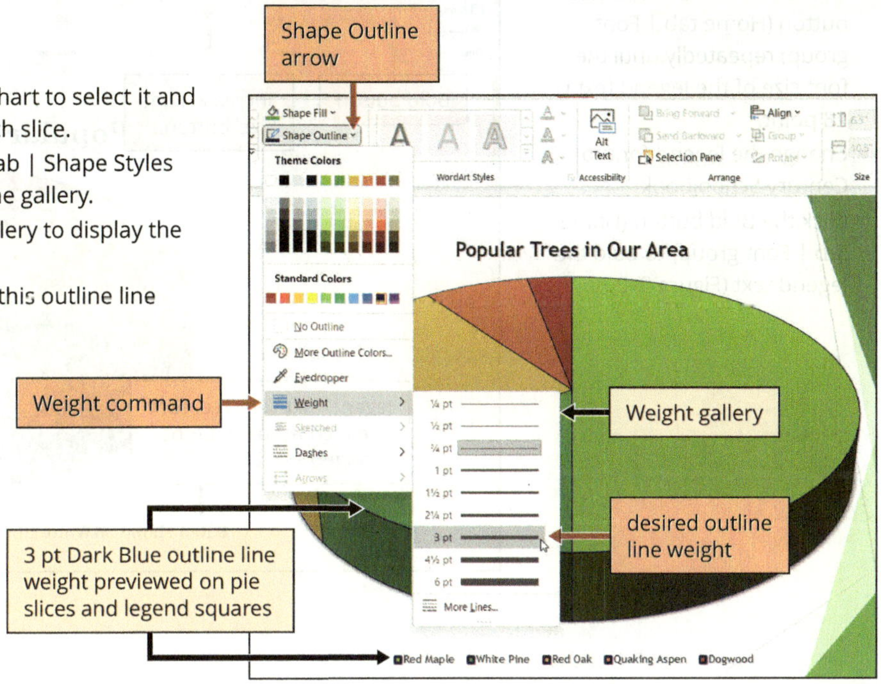

Figure 3–18

Other Ways

1. Right-click chart, click Outline button, click Weight

To Change the Title and Legend Font and Font Size

Depending upon the complexity of the chart and the overall slide, you may want to increase the font size of the chart title and legend. **Why?** The larger font size increases readability. The following steps change the font size of both of these chart elements.

1

- Click the chart title, Popular Trees in Our Area, to select the text box.
- Display the Home tab and then click the 'Increase Font Size' button (Home tab | Font group) repeatedly until the font size is 32 point.
- Change the font of the chart title to Century Schoolbook (Figure 3–19).

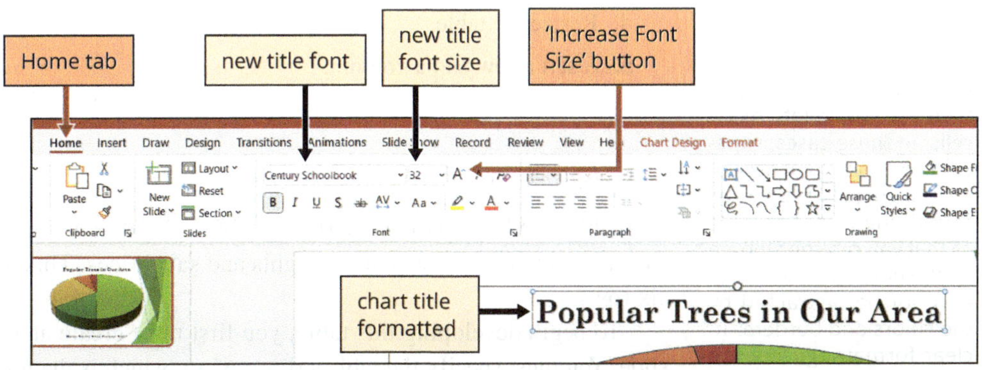

Figure 3–19

2

- Click one of the legends to select the legends text box.
- Click the 'Increase Font Size' button (Home tab | Font group) repeatedly until the font size of the legend text is 18 point.
- Change the legend font to Century Schoolbook.
- Click the Bold button (Home tab | Font group) to bold the legend text (Figure 3–20).

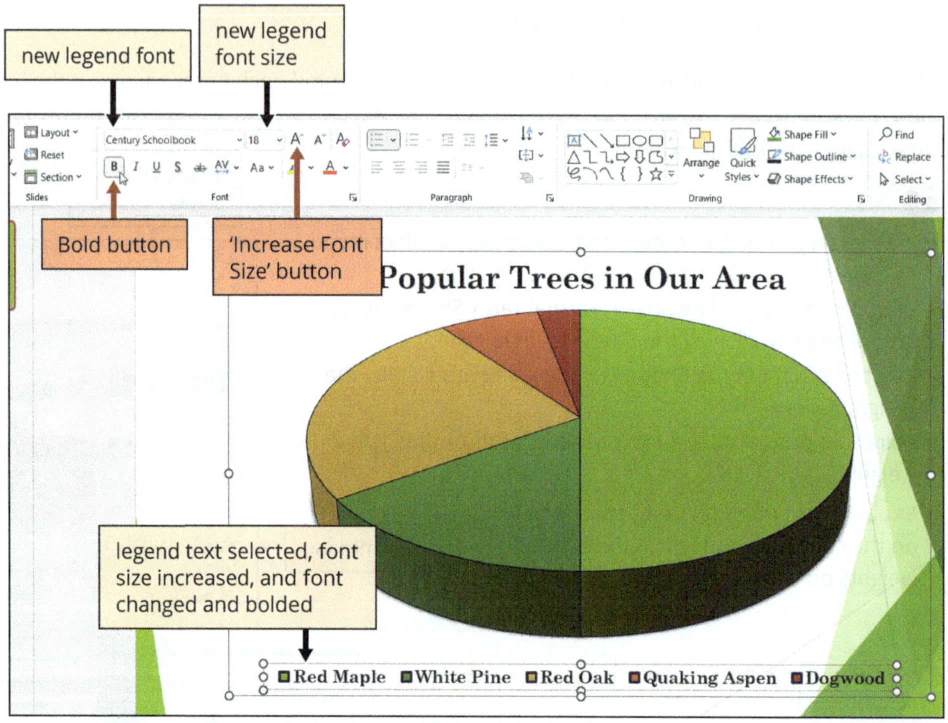

Figure 3–20

Adding a Table to a Slide and Formatting

One effective method of organizing information on a slide is to use a **table**, which is a grid consisting of rows and columns that can contain text and graphics. You can enhance a table with formatting, including adding colors, lines, and backgrounds, and changing fonts.

In the following pages, you will perform these tasks:

1. Insert a table and then enter data.
2. Apply a table style.
3. Add table borders and an effect.
4. Resize the table.
5. Insert a row and a column.

BTW
Clearing Table Formatting
Many times you may need to create large tables and then enter data into many cells. In these cases, experienced PowerPoint designers recommend clearing all formatting from the table so that you can concentrate on the numbers and letters and not be distracted by the colors and borders. To clear formatting, click the Clear Table command at the bottom of the Table Styles gallery (Table Design tab | Table Styles group). Then, add a table style once you have verified that all table data is correct.

Tables

The table on Slide 2 (shown earlier in Figure 3–1d) contains information about specific trees for sale, including their mature heights and sale prices. This data is listed in two columns and six rows.

To begin developing this table, you first must create an empty table and insert it into the slide. You must specify the table's **dimension**, which is the total number of rows and columns. This table will have a 2 × 5 dimension: the first number indicates the number of columns and the second specifies the number of rows. You will fill the cells with data pertaining to each tree and its maximum height. Later in this module you will add a column to show the sale price for each tree. Then you will format the table using a table style. You will also add a table row to display information about dogwood trees.

To Insert an Empty Table

The following steps create a new slide and insert an empty table with two columns and five rows into a content placeholder on the slide. **Why?** The first row will contain the column headings, and the additional rows will have information about four trees. The two columns will contain tree names and the mature heights.

1

- Click the New Slide button to add a new slide to the presentation with the Title and Content layout (Figure 3–21).

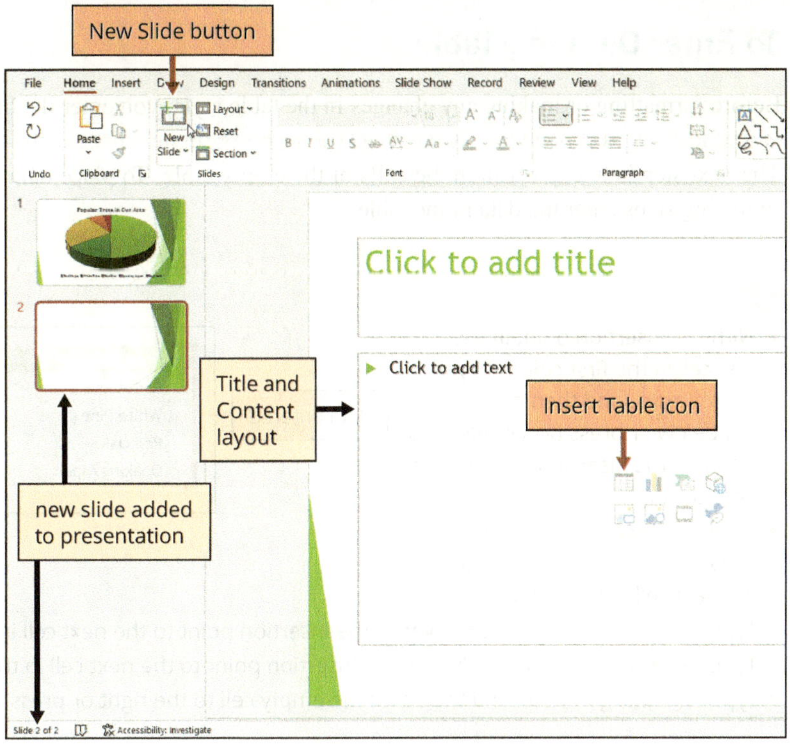

Figure 3–21

2

- Click the Insert Table icon in the content placeholder to display the Insert Table dialog box.
- Click the down arrow to the right of the 'Number of columns' box three times so that the number 2 appears in the box.
- Click the up arrow to the right of the 'Number of rows' box three times so that the number 5 appears in the box (Figure 3–22).

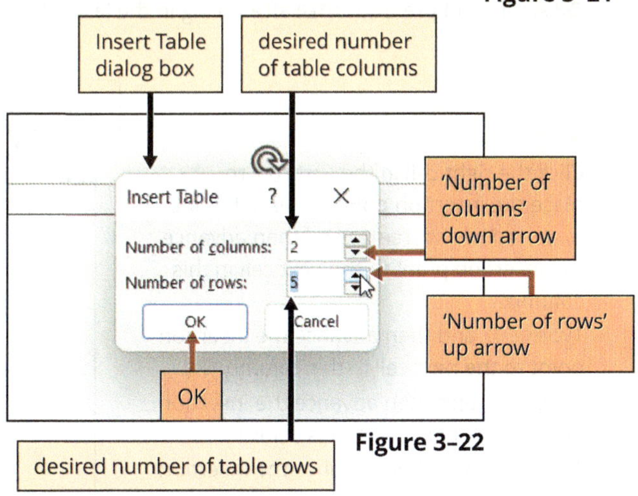

Figure 3–22

3

- Click OK (Insert Table dialog box) to insert the table into Slide 2 (Figure 3–23).

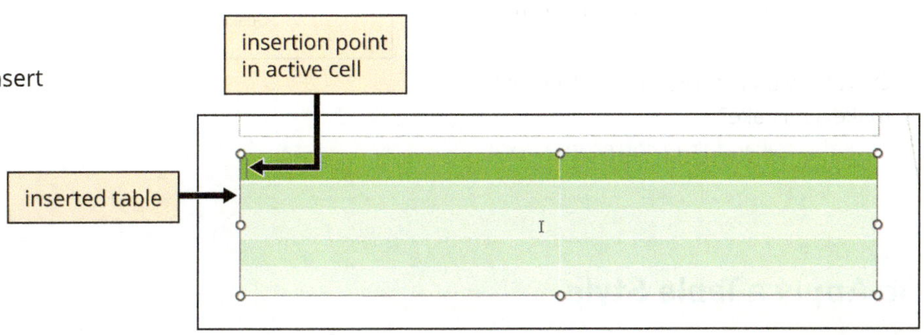

Figure 3–23

Other Ways

1. Click Table (Insert tab | Tables group), drag to select columns and rows, click or press ENTER

To Enter Data in a Table

Before formatting or making any changes in the table style, you enter the data in the table. **Why?** It is easier to see formatting and style changes applied to existing data. The second column will have the mature height for each tree listed in the first column. The next step is to enter data in the cells of the empty table. To place data in a cell, you click the cell and then type text. The following steps enter the data in the table.

1

- With the insertion point in the first cell in the first column, type **Tree Name** and then click the cell below or press DOWN ARROW to advance the insertion point to the next cell in this column.
- Type **Red Maple** and then advance the insertion point to the next cell in this column.
- Type **White Pine** and then advance the insertion point to the next cell in this column.
- Type **Red Oak** and then advance the insertion point to the next cell in this column.
- Type **Quaking Aspen** and then click the empty cell to the right or press TAB (Figure 3–24).

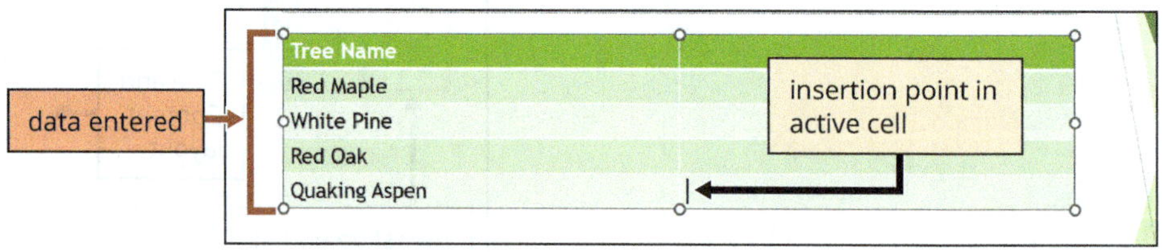

Figure 3–24

Q&A What if I pressed ENTER after filling in the last cell?

Press BACKSPACE.

2

- Click the right cell in the first row to place the insertion point in this cell. Type **Mature Height (feet)** and then advance the insertion point to the next cell in this column.
- Type **60** and then advance the insertion point to the next cell in this column.
- Type **80** and then advance the insertion point to the next cell in this column.
- Type **75** and then advance the insertion point to the next cell in this column.
- Type **50** as the cell content (Figure 3–25).

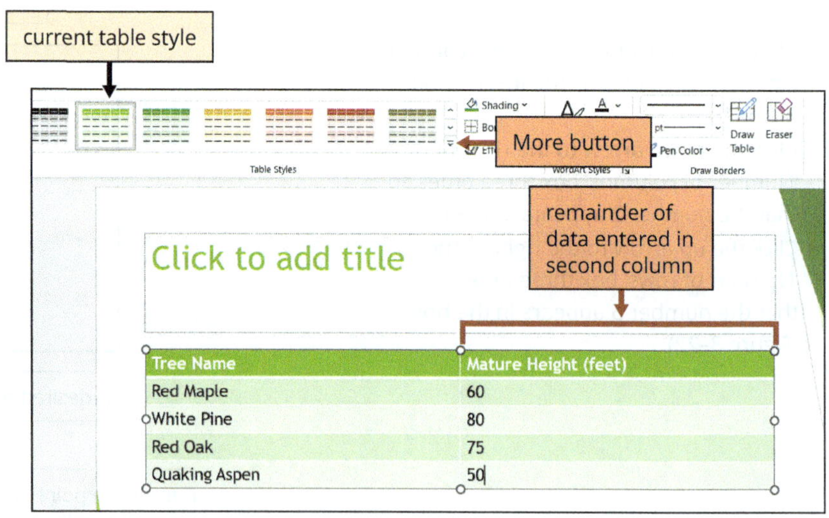

Figure 3–25

Q&A How do I correct cell contents if I make a mistake?

Click the cell and then correct the text.

To Apply a Table Style

When you inserted the table, PowerPoint automatically applied a style. Thumbnails of this style and others are displayed in the Table Styles gallery. These styles use a variety of colors and shading and are grouped in the categories of Best Match for

Document, Light, Medium, and Dark. The following steps apply a table style in the Medium area to the Slide 2 table. **Why?** The green styles in the Medium area use the colors appearing on the slide, so they coordinate nicely with the Facet theme colors in this presentation.

1

- With the insertion point in the table and the Table Design tab displayed, click the More button in the Table Styles gallery (Table Design tab | Tables Styles group) (shown in Figure 3–25) to expand the Table Styles gallery.
- Point to 'Medium Style 1 – Accent 2' in the Medium area (third style in the first Medium row) to display a live preview of that style applied to the table (Figure 3–26).

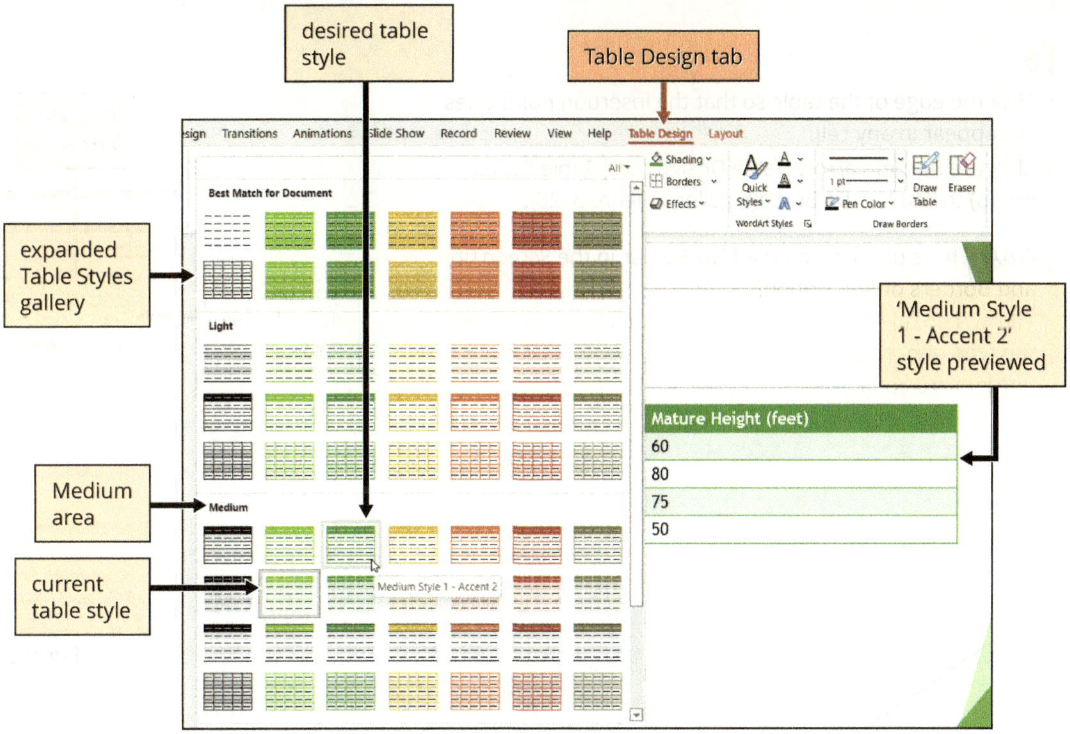

Figure 3–26

- **Experiment:** Point to various styles in the Table Styles gallery and watch the colors and format change on the table.

2

- Click 'Medium Style 1 – Accent 2' in the Table Styles gallery to apply the selected style to the table (Figure 3–27).

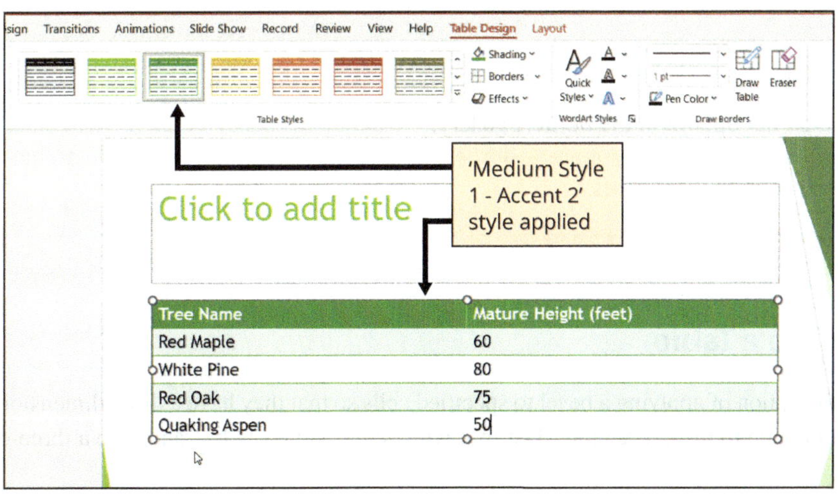

Figure 3–27

Q&A Can I resize the columns and rows or the entire table?

Yes. To resize columns or rows, drag a **column boundary** (the border to the right of a column) or the **row boundary** (the border at the bottom of a row) until the column or row is the desired width or height. To resize the entire table, drag a **table sizing handle**, the small circle that appears when you point to any corner of a table.

To Add Borders to a Table

The Slide 2 table does not have borders around the entire table or between the cells. The following steps add borders to the entire table. **Why?** These details will give the chart some dimension and add to its visual appeal.

1

- Click the edge of the table so that the insertion point does not appear in any cell.
- Click the Borders arrow (Table Design tab | Table Styles group) to display the Borders gallery (Figure 3–28).

Q&A Why is the button called No Border in the ScreenTip and Borders on the ribbon?
The ScreenTip name for the button will change based on the type of border, if any, present in the table. Currently, no borders are applied.

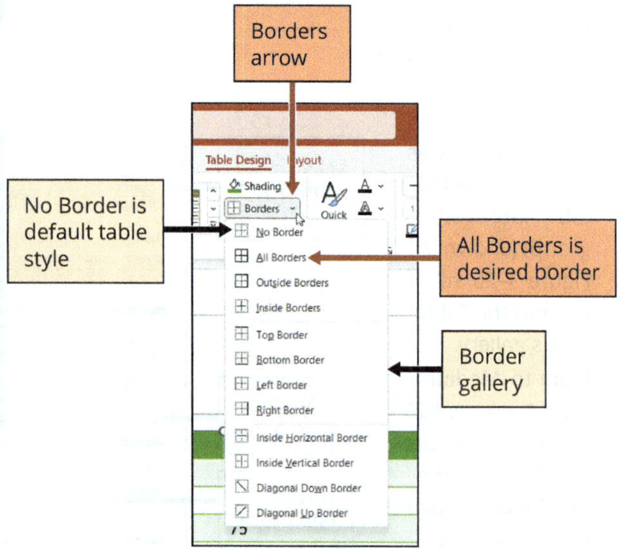

Figure 3–28

2

- Click All Borders in the Borders gallery to add borders around the entire table and to each table cell (Figure 3–29).

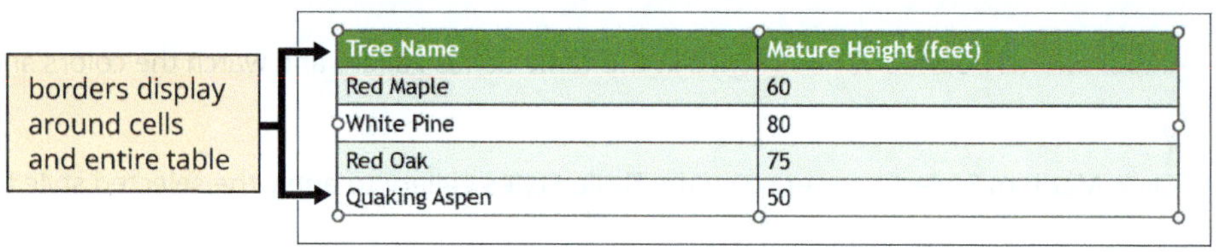

Figure 3–29

Q&A Why is the border color black?
PowerPoint's default border color is black. This color is displayed on the Pen Color button (Table Design tab | Draw Borders group).

Can I apply any of the border options in the Borders gallery?
Yes. You can vary the look of your table by applying borders only to the cells, around the table, to the top, bottom, left, or right edges, or a combination of these areas.

To Add an Effect to a Table

PowerPoint gives you the option of applying a bevel to specified cells so that they have a three-dimensional appearance. You also can add a shadow or reflection to the entire table. The following steps add a shadow and give a three-dimensional appearance to the entire table. **Why?** Adding an effect will enhance the table design.

1

- With the table selected, click the Effects button (Table Design tab | Table Styles group) to display the Effects menu.

Q&A What is the difference between a shadow and a reflection?
A shadow gives the appearance that light is falling on the table, which causes a shadow behind the graphic. A reflection gives the appearance that the table is shiny, so a mirror image appears below the actual graphic.

2

- Point to Shadow to display the Shadow gallery (Figure 3–30).

Q&A How do the shadows differ in the Outer, Inner, and Perspective categories?
The Outer shadows are displayed on the outside of the table, whereas the Inner shadows are displayed in the interior cells. The Perspective shadows give the illusion that a light is shining from the right or left side of the table or from above, and the table is casting a shadow.

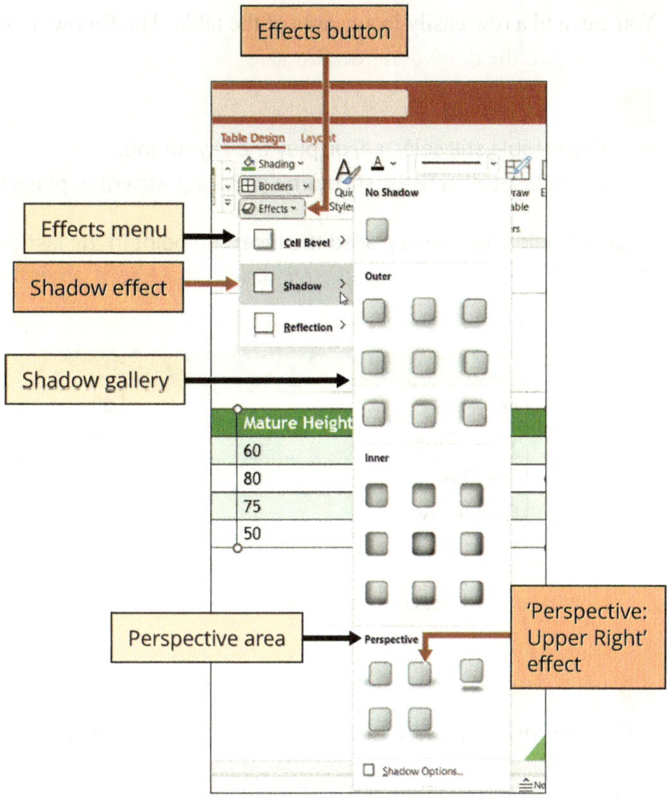

Figure 3–30

3

- Point to 'Perspective: Upper Right' in the Perspective category (second shadow in the first row) to display a live preview of this shadow (Figure 3–31).
- **Experiment:** Point to the various shadows in the Shadow gallery and watch the shadows change in the table.

4

- Click 'Perspective: Upper Right' to apply this shadow to the table.

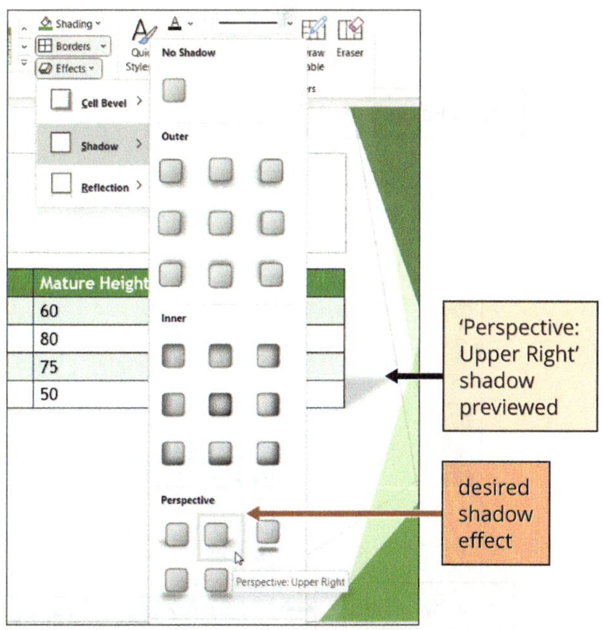

Figure 3–31

To Insert a Table Row

You can add a row easily in any area of the table. The following steps insert a row in the table. **Why?** You want to add information pertaining to the dogwood trees for sale.

1

- With the table still selected, display the Layout tab.
- Click the last cell in the first column (Quaking Aspen) to place the insertion point in this cell (Figure 3–32).

Q&A Could I also have placed the insertion point in the last cell in the second column (50)?
Yes. You are going to insert the row below these cells, so either location would work.

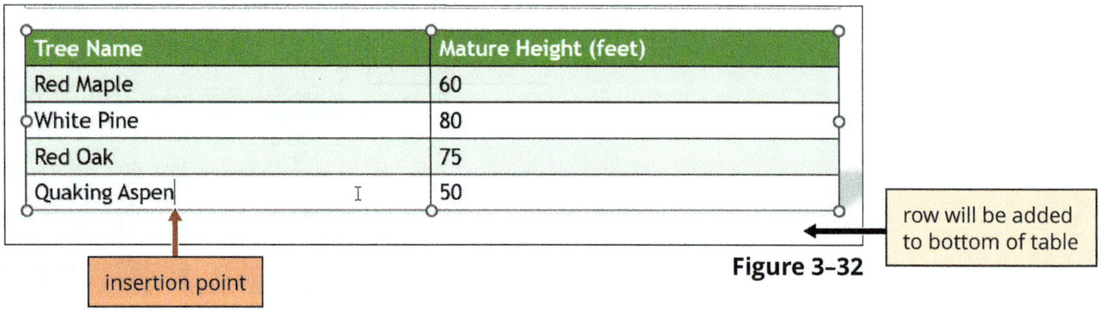

Figure 3–32

2

- Click the Insert Below button (Layout tab | Rows & Columns group) to insert a new row at the bottom of the table (Figure 3–33).

Q&A Can I insert a row anywhere in the table?
Yes. You can insert the row either below or above the cell where the insertion point is positioned.

If I am using a touch screen, how do I add rows to the table?
Press and hold the bottom-right cell, tap Insert on the shortcut menu, and then tap Insert Rows Below.

BTW
Touch Mode Differences
The Microsoft 365 and Windows interfaces may vary if you are using a touch screen. For this reason, you might notice that the function or appearance of your touch screen differs slightly from this module's presentation.

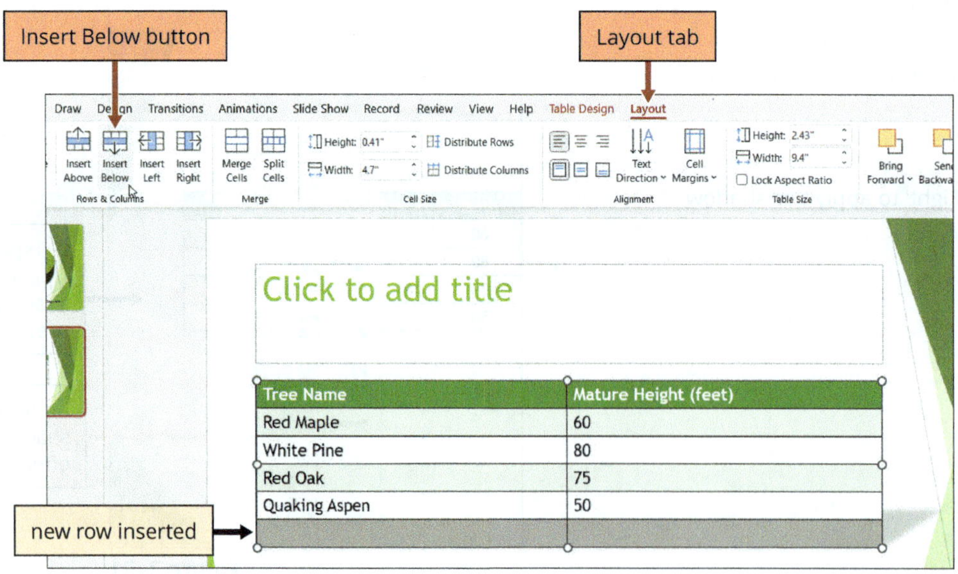

Figure 3–33

3

- Click the new cell in the Tree Name column and then type **Dogwood** in the cell.
- Type **25** in the new Mature Height column cell (Figure 3–34).

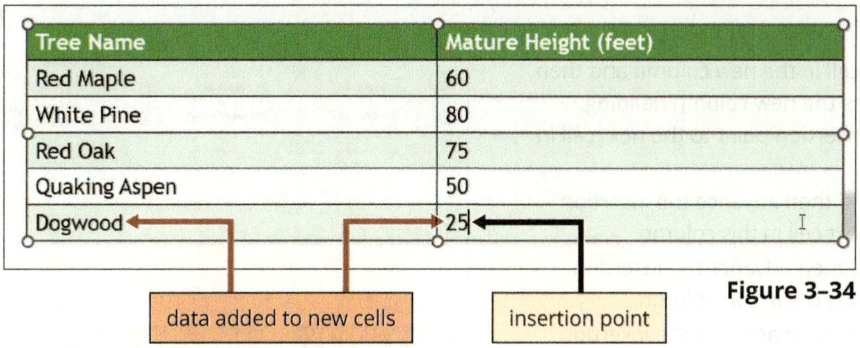

Figure 3–34

Other Ways

1. Position insertion point in bottom-right cell, press TAB

To Insert a Table Column

You add a column in a similar manner that you added a row to the table. The following steps insert a column in the table. **Why?** The right table column lists each tree's maximum height. A third column can list the selling price.

1

- With the insertion point still in the lower-right cell (25), click the Insert Right button (Layout tab | Rows & Columns group) to insert a column to the right of the Mature Height column (Figure 3–35).

Q&A Could I have placed the insertion anywhere in the Mature Height column?
Yes. You are going to insert the row to the right of these cells, so any location in the column would work.

Can I insert a column anywhere in the table?
Yes. You can insert the column to the left or the right of any cell where the insertion point is positioned.

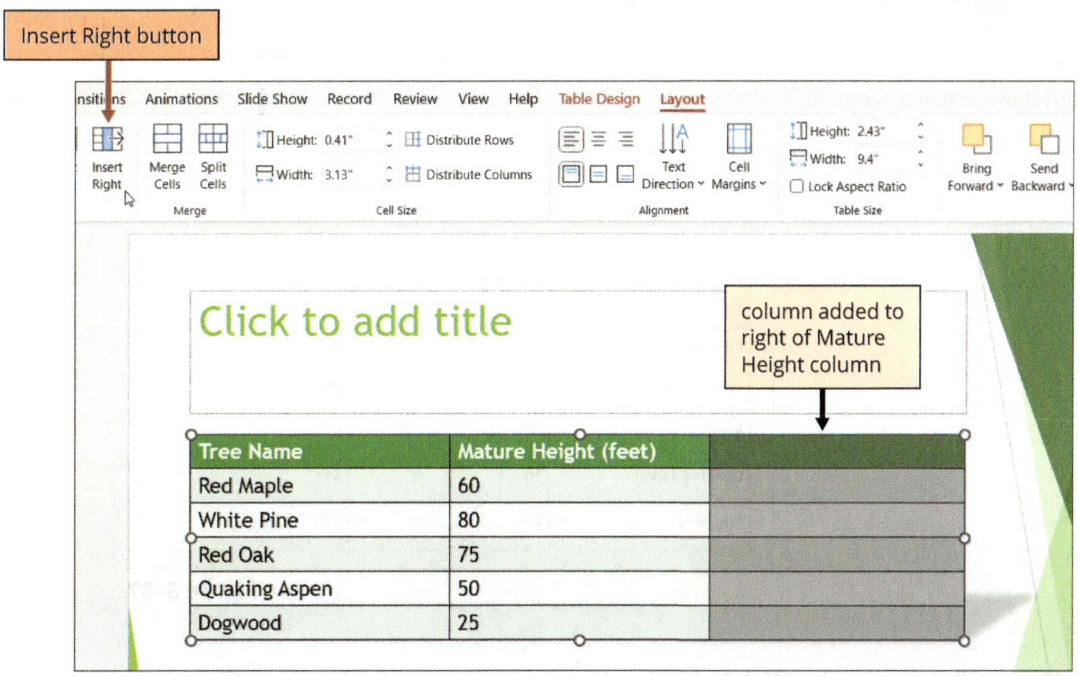

Figure 3–35

2

- Click the first cell in the new column and then type **Price** as the new column heading. Advance the insertion point to the next cell in this column.
- Type **$20** and then advance the insertion point to the next cell in this column.
- Type **$9** and then advance the insertion point to the next cell in this column.
- Type **$13** and then advance the insertion point to the next cell in this column.
- Type **$17** and then advance the insertion point to the next cell in this column.
- Type **$45** as the cell content (Figure 3–36).

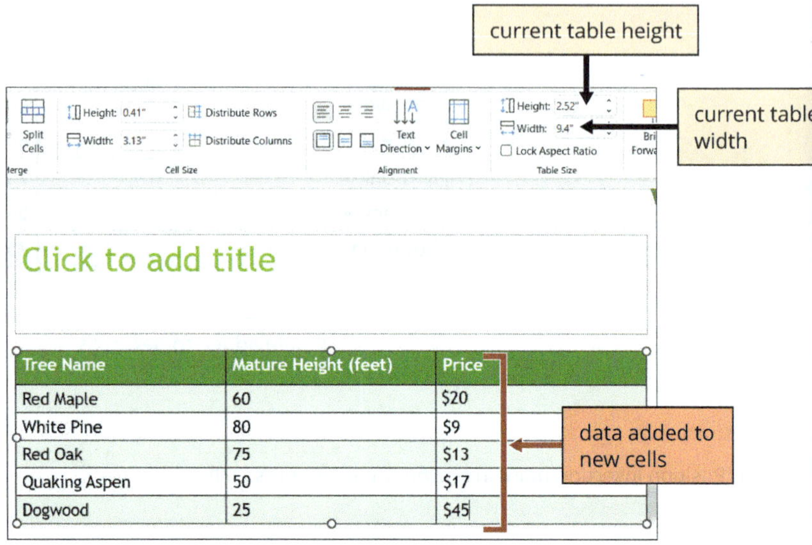

Figure 3–36

To Resize a Table

You resize a table the same way you resize a chart, a SmartArt graphic, or any other graphical object. The following steps resize the table on Slide 2. **Why?** Slide 2 has much white space below the chart. If you resize the table to fill this white space, it will be more readable.

1

- With the table still selected and the Layout tab displayed, click the Height up arrow (Layout tab | Table Size group) repeatedly until 4" is displayed in the box.
- Click the Width down arrow (Layout tab | Table Size group) repeatedly until 9" is displayed in the box (Figure 3–37).

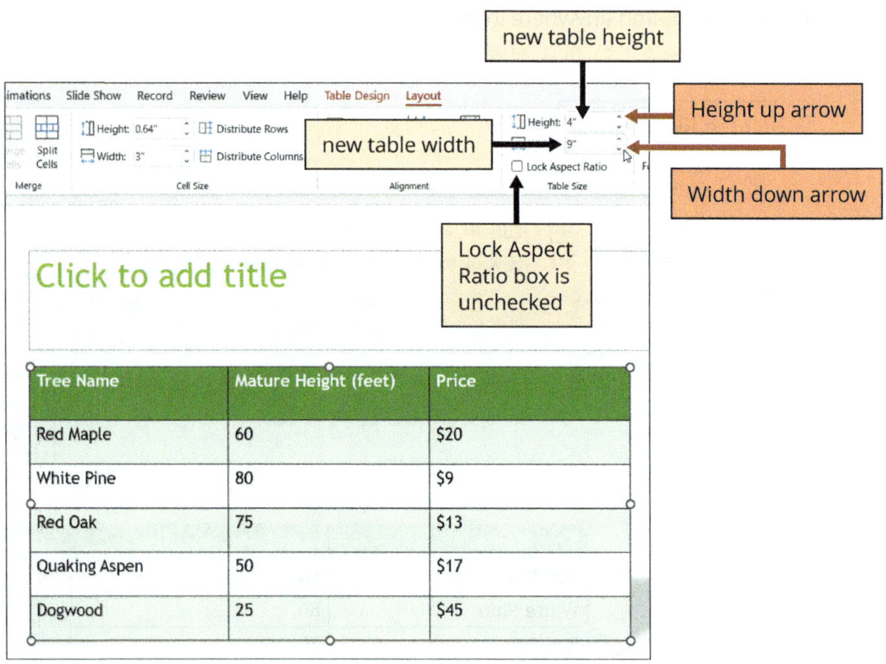

Figure 3–37

Q&A What happens when the Lock Aspect Ratio box (Layout tab | Table Size group) is checked?
The same ratio between the table height and width is maintained when the table is resized.

To Align a Table

The resized table can be positioned directly in the center of the slide. **Why?** Your slide content looks balanced when it is aligned between the left and right slide edges. The following steps align the table.

1

- With the table selected and the Layout tab displayed, click the Align button (Layout tab | Arrange group) to display the Align Objects menu (Figure 3–38).

Q&A What is the difference between the commands on the Layout tab | Arrange group and the commands on the Layout tab | Alignment group?

The items in the Arrange group align objects, such as tables, charts, and images, on the slide, while the Alignment buttons align text within an object or placeholder.

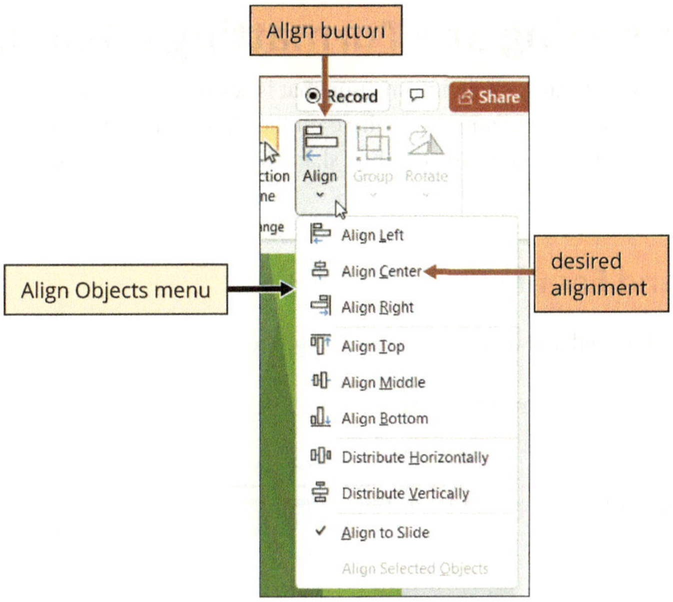

Figure 3–38

2

- Click Align Center on the Align Objects menu to position the table in the center of the slide (Figure 3–39).

Q&A Can I use the smart guides to align the table?

Yes.

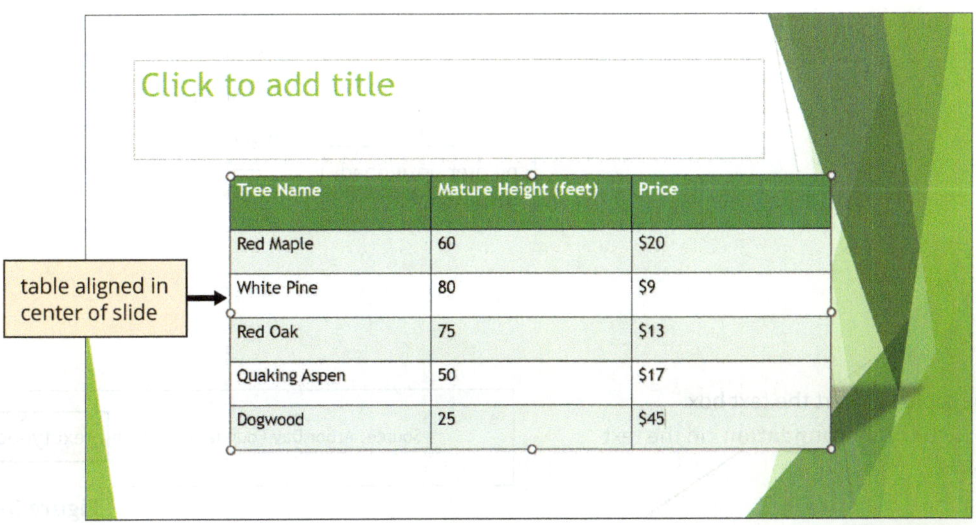

Figure 3–39

To Add a Slide Title

The slide needs a title to inform your audience about the table content. The following steps add a title to Slide 2.

1. With Slide 2 displayed, type **Trees for Sale** in the title text placeholder.
2. Change the title text font to Century Schoolbook.
3. Bold this title text, increase the font size to 54 point, and then center it in the title text placeholder.

Inserting and Formatting a Text Box

A text box can contain information that is separate from the title or content placeholders. You can place this slide element anywhere on the slide and format the letters using any style and effect. You also can change the text box shape by moving the sizing handles.

To Insert a Text Box and Format Text

The following steps insert a text box and add text. **Why?** You want to reference the source of the table data.

1

- Display the Insert tab, click the Text Box button (Insert tab | Text group), and then position the pointer below the table (Figure 3–40).

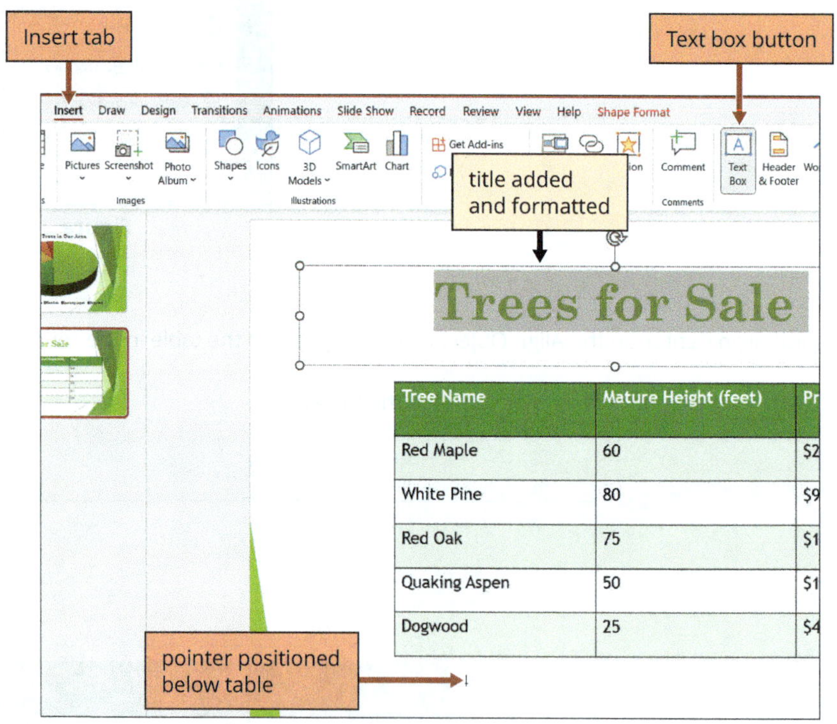

Figure 3–40

2

- Click below the table to insert the text box.
- Type **Source: Arbor Day Foundation** in the text box (Figure 3–41).

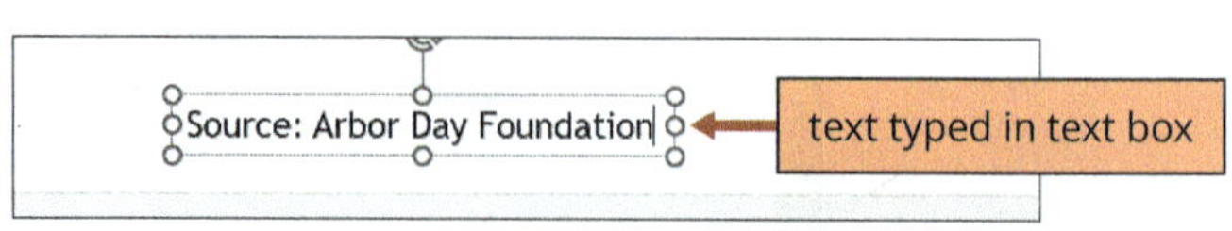

Figure 3–41

To Format Text Box Characters

The following steps format the text box characters to coordinate the font with the title text font.

1. Select the text in the text box, increase the font size to 20 point, and then change the font to Century Schoolbook.

2. Use the smart guides to align the text box, as shown in Figure 3–42.

Q&A Can I change the shape of the text box?
Yes. Drag the sizing handles to the desired dimensions.

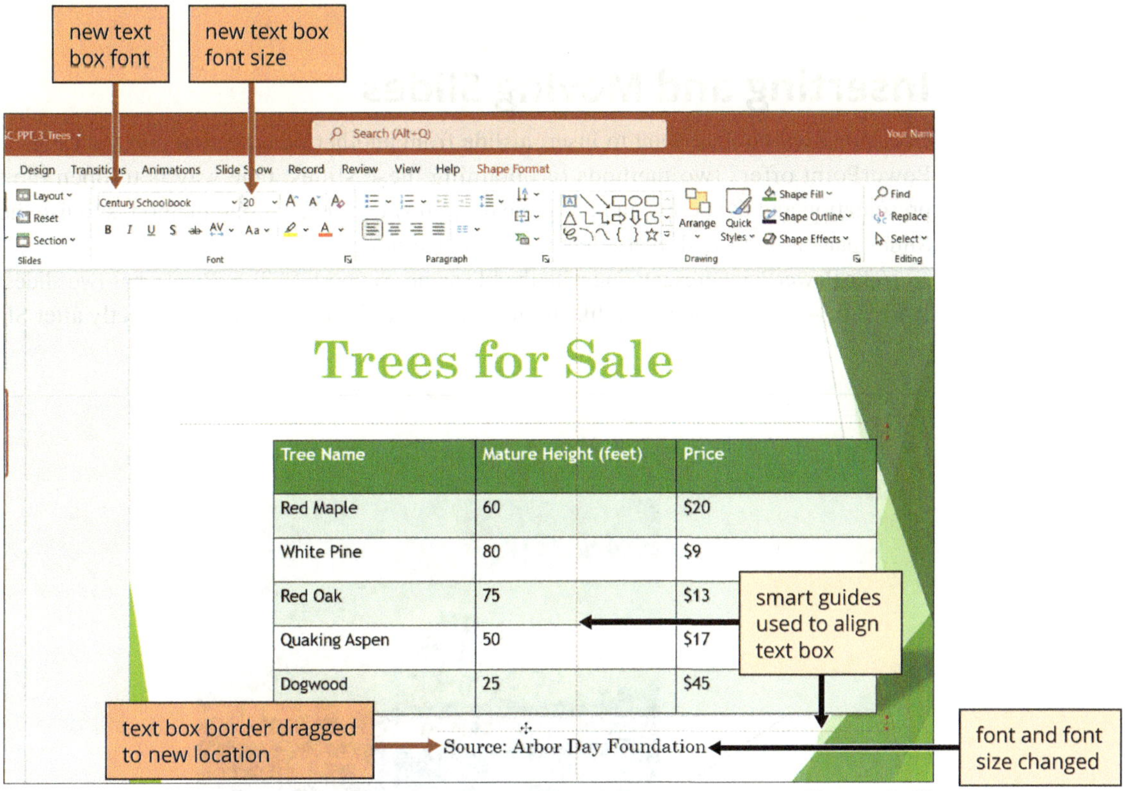

Figure 3–42

3. Click outside the text box to deselect this object.

To Apply a Preset Shape Effect

Once you have inserted a text box, you can format it in a variety of ways to draw attention to slide content. You can, for example, add a fill to change the inside color of the text box. A **fill** is a color, pattern, texture, picture, or gradient applied to the interior of a shape or slide background. You also can combine multiple individual effects to create a custom design. To apply a preset shape effect to the text box, you would perform the following steps.

1. Select the text box.
2. Display the Shape Format tab and then click the Shape Effects button (Shape Format tab | Shape Styles group) to display the Shape Effects menu.
3. Select the desired effect (Shadow, Reflection, Glow, Soft Edges, Bevel, or 3-D Rotation).

To Change Text Box Defaults

You can set the formatting of the text box you inserted as the default for all other text boxes you insert into the presentation so that the text boxes have a consistent look. To change the text box defaults, you would perform the following steps.

1. Right-click the text box outline to display the shortcut menu.
2. Click 'Set as Default Text Box' on the shortcut menu.

Break Point: If you wish to take a break, this is a good place to do so. Be sure the Trees file is saved and then you can exit PowerPoint. To resume later, start PowerPoint, open the file called SC_PPT_3_Trees, and continue following the steps from this location forward.

Inserting and Moving Slides

Occasionally you may want to insert a slide from another presentation into your presentation. PowerPoint offers two methods of obtaining these slides. One way is to open the second presentation and then copy and paste the desired slides. The second method is to use the Reuse Slides pane to view and then select the desired slides.

The PowerPoint presentation with the file name, Support_PPT_3_Reuse, has two slides, shown in Figure 3–43, that you would like to insert into your Trees presentation directly after Slide 3.

Mbll/Pixabay

Figure 3–43(a): Slide 1 (Insert and Use as Title Slide)

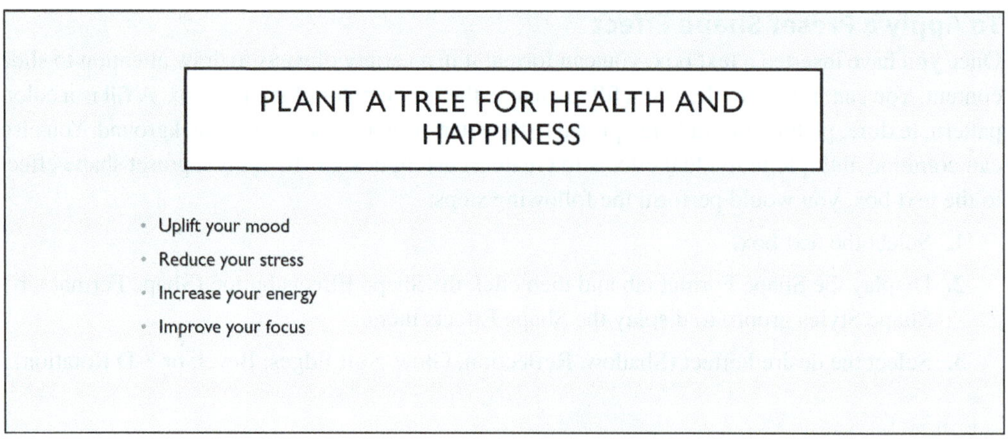

Figure 3–43(b): Slide 1 (Insert and Move to Slide 2)

To Reuse Slides from an Existing Presentation

PowerPoint converts inserted slides to the theme and styles of the current presentation, so the inserted slides will inherit the styles of the current Facet theme. The Support_PPT_3_Reuse.pptx presentation is in your Data Files. The following steps add these two slides to your presentation and specify that you want to change the design to the Facet formatting. **Why?** One slide has a picture you can change, and the second has useful information about the mental and physical health benefits that trees provide.

1

- If necessary, display the Home tab and then click the New Slide arrow (Home tab | Slides group) to display the Facet layout gallery (Figure 3–44).

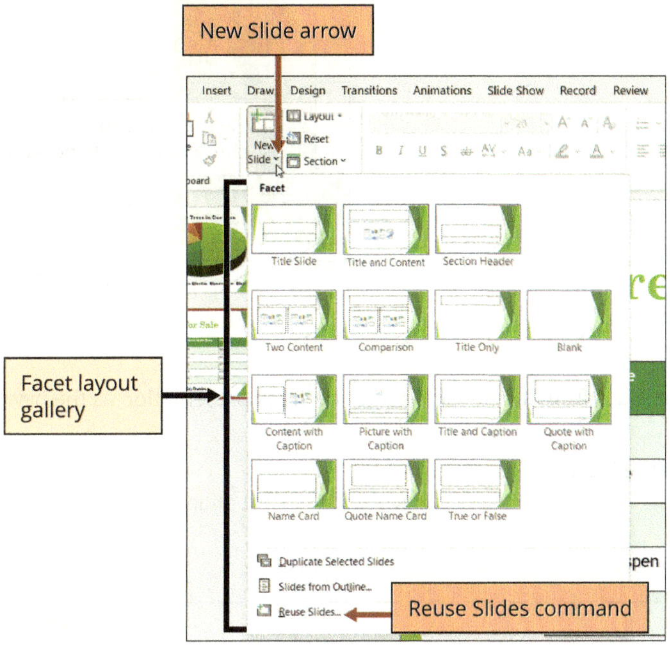

Figure 3–44

2

- Click Reuse Slides in the Facet layout gallery to display the Reuse Slides pane.
- Click the Browse button (Reuse Slides pane) to display the Browse dialog box.
- If necessary, navigate to the location of your Data Files and then click Support_PPT_3_Reuse.pptx to select the file.
- Click the Open button (Browse dialog box) to display thumbnails of the two slides in the Reuse Slides pane (Figure 3–45).

Q&A Could I have clicked the 'Open a PowerPoint File' link to display the Browse dialog box?
Yes. Either method will display the dialog box.

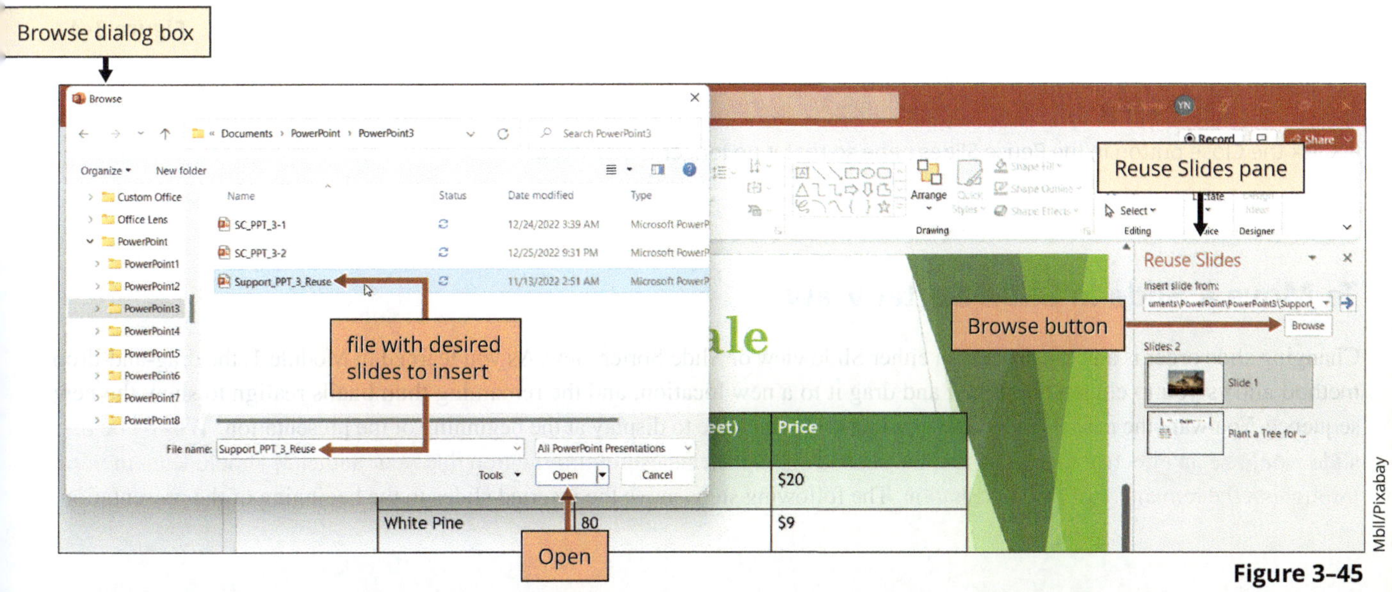

Figure 3–45

3

- Right-click either slide thumbnail to display the Reuse Slides menu (Figure 3–46).

Q&A What would happen if I click the 'Keep source formatting' check box at the bottom of the Reuse Slides pane?
PowerPoint would preserve the formatting characteristics found in the Reuse file's Mesh theme for the slides that you insert.

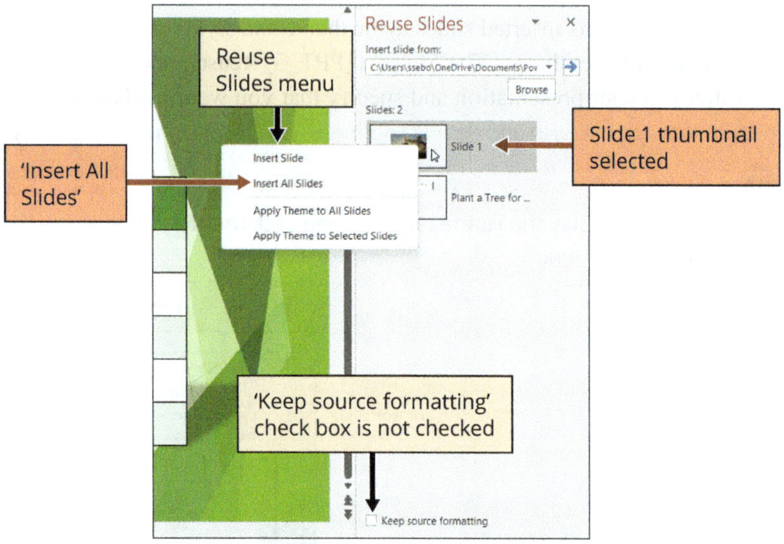

Figure 3–46

4

- Click 'Insert All Slides' to insert both slides from the Reuse file into the Trees presentation as the new slides 3 and 4 (Figure 3–47).

Q&A Can I insert only one slide in the Insert file?
Yes. Click the thumbnail of the slide you wish to insert and then click 'Insert Slide.'

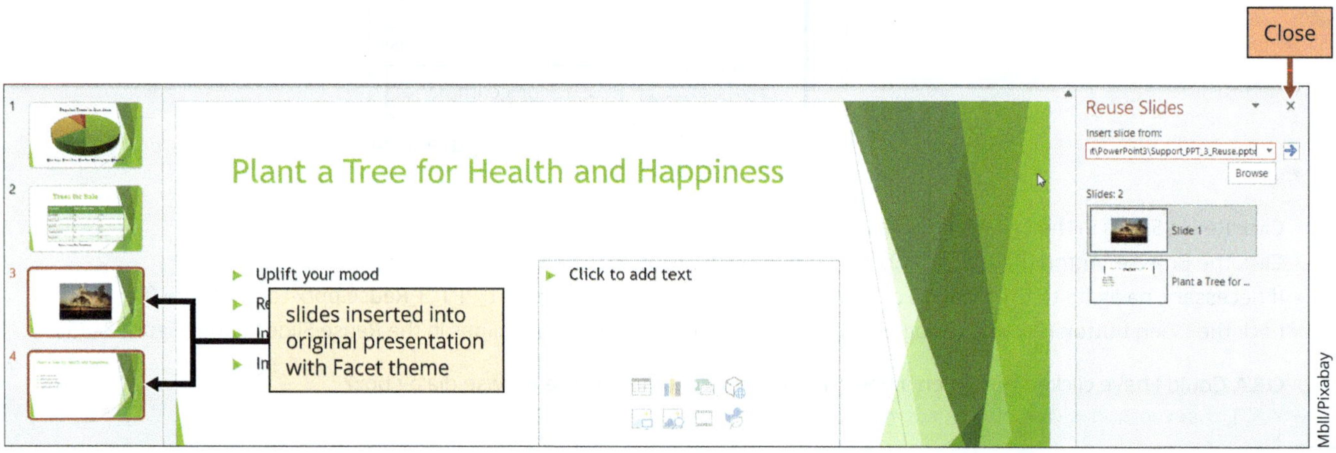

Figure 3–47

5

- Click the Close button in the Reuse Slides pane so that it no longer is displayed.

To Move a Slide in Slide Sorter View

Changing slide order is an easy process in either Slide view or Slide Sorter view. As you learned in Module 1, the drag-and-drop method allows you to click a thumbnail and drag it to a new location, and the remaining thumbnails realign to show the new sequence. You want the new slides you inserted into the Trees file to display at the beginning of the presentation. **Why?** The first slide would be an effective title slide, and the second slide presents useful information that your audience should keep in mind throughout the remainder of the presentation. The following steps move the inserted slides to the beginning of the presentation.

1

- Click the Slide Sorter view button on the right side of the status bar to display the presentation in Slide Sorter view. Click the Slide 3 thumbnail to select it (Figure 3–48).

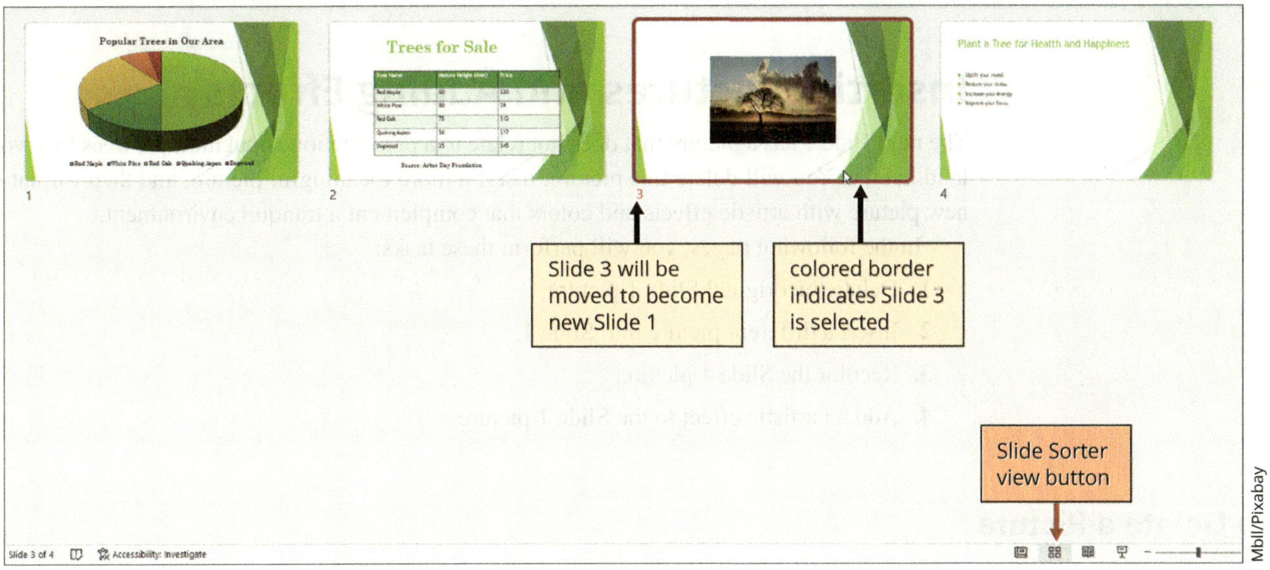

Figure 3–48

2

- Drag the Slide 3 thumbnail to the left of the current Slide 1, as shown in Figure 3–48, so that it becomes the new Slide 1 (Figure 3–49).

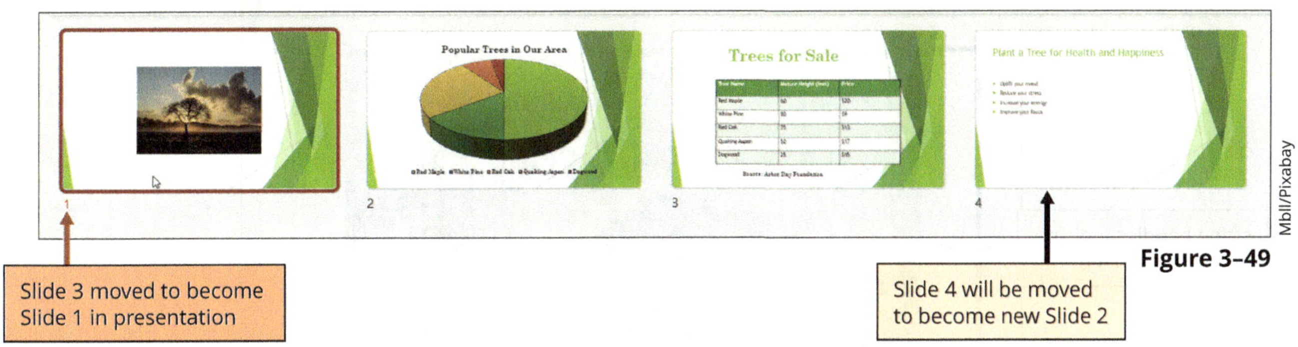

Figure 3–49

3

- Click the Slide 4 thumbnail and then drag it to the right of the new Slide 1 so that it becomes the new Slide 2 (Figure 3–50).

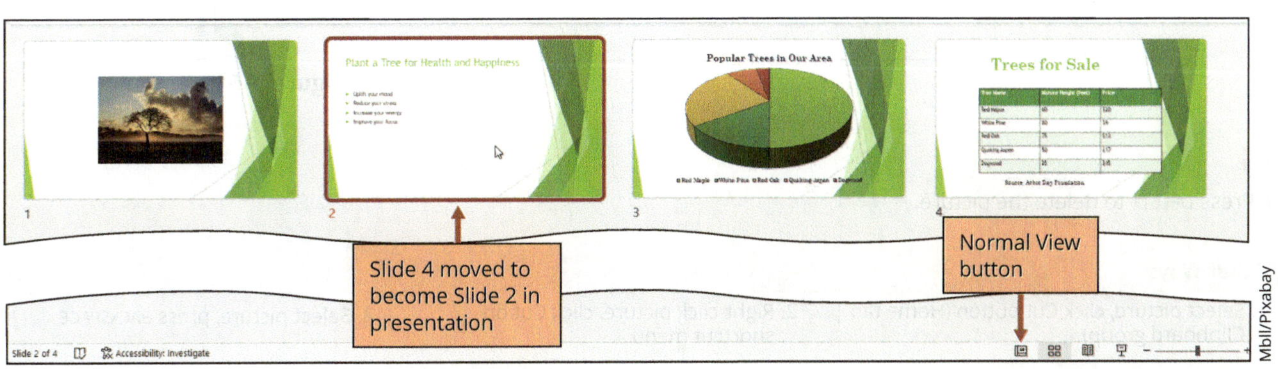

Figure 3–50

4

- Click the Normal view button to display the presentation in Normal view.

Inserting Pictures and Adding Effects

The new Slide 1 has a picture that does not relate to a presentation about multiple trees in a woodland habitat. You will delete this picture, insert a more meaningful picture, and then format this new picture with artistic effects and colors that complement a tranquil environment.

In the following pages, you will perform these tasks:

1. Delete the original Slide 1 picture.
2. Insert a different picture into Slide 1.
3. Recolor the Slide 1 picture.
4. Add an artistic effect to the Slide 1 picture.

To Delete a Picture

1

- Display Slide 1 and then click the picture to select it (Figure 3–51).

Figure 3–51

2

- Press DELETE to delete the picture.

Other Ways

1. Select picture, click Cut button (Home tab | Clipboard group)
2. Right-click picture, click Cut on shortcut menu
3. Select picture, press BACKSPACE

To Insert and Resize a Picture into a Slide without Content Placeholders

The next step in developing the title slide is to insert a different picture. The slide layout is Blank and does not have a content placeholder, so the picture will display in the center of the slide when you insert it. The picture is available in the Data Files. The following steps insert a picture into Slide 1.

1. With Slide 1 displayed, click Insert on the ribbon to display the Insert tab, click the Pictures button (Insert tab | Images group) to display the Insert Picture From menu, and then click This Device to display the Insert Picture dialog box.
2. If necessary, navigate to the picture location and then click Support_PPT_3_Landscape.jpg to select the file.
3. Click the Insert button (Insert Picture dialog box) to insert the picture into Slide 1. Close the Design Ideas pane if it opens.
4. Click the Size Dialog Box Launcher in the Picture Format | Size group and make sure the Lock aspect ratio box is unchecked in the Format Picture pane.
5. Resize the picture to an approximate height of 6.6" and width of 12". Use the smart guides to move the picture to the center of the slide, as shown in Figure 3–52.

Figure 3–52

To Crop a Picture

You can remove the unnecessary elements of the picture and crop it. **Why?** The left side of the picture contains a grove of trees, and you want to focus on this particular area. When you crop a picture, you trim the vertical or horizontal sides so that the most important area of the picture is displayed. Any picture file type except animated GIF can be cropped. The following steps crop the title slide picture.

1

- With the picture selected and the Picture Format tab displayed, click the Crop button (Picture Format tab | Size group) to display the cropping handles on the picture.
- Position the pointer over the center cropping handle on the right edge of the picture (Figure 3–53).

Q&A Why did my pointer change shape?
The pointer changed to indicate you are about to crop a picture.

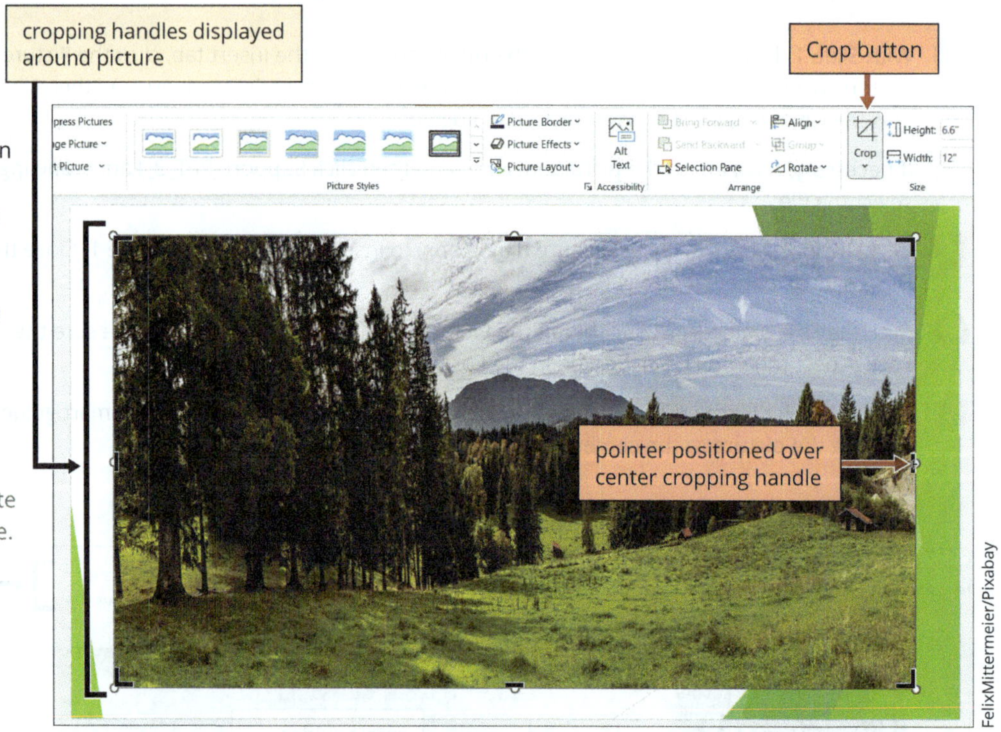

Figure 3–53

2

- Drag the center cropping handle on the right edge of the picture inward so that the right edge of the marquee is along the right edge of the grove of trees.
- Drag the center cropping handle on the bottom edge of the picture inward toward the trunk of the left tree (Figure 3–54).

Q&A Does cropping actually cut the picture's edges?
No. Although you cannot see the cropped edges, they exist until you save the file.

Can I crop a picture to exact dimensions?
Yes. Right-click the picture and then click Format Picture to open the Format Picture pane. Click the Picture icon, then Crop. Under Picture position, enter the measurements in the Width and Height boxes.

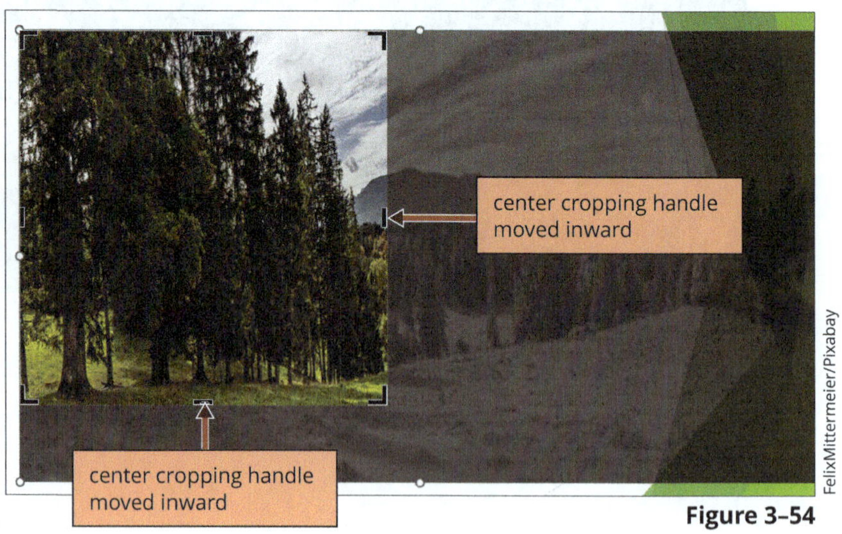

Figure 3–54

3

- Click the Crop button again to crop the edges (Figure 3–55).

Q&A Can I press ESC to crop the edges?
Yes.

Can I change the crop lines?
If you have not saved the file, you can undo your crops by clicking Undo on the Quick Access Toolbar, clicking the Reset Picture button (Picture Format tab | Adjust group), or pressing CTRL+Z. If you have saved the file, you cannot undo the crop.

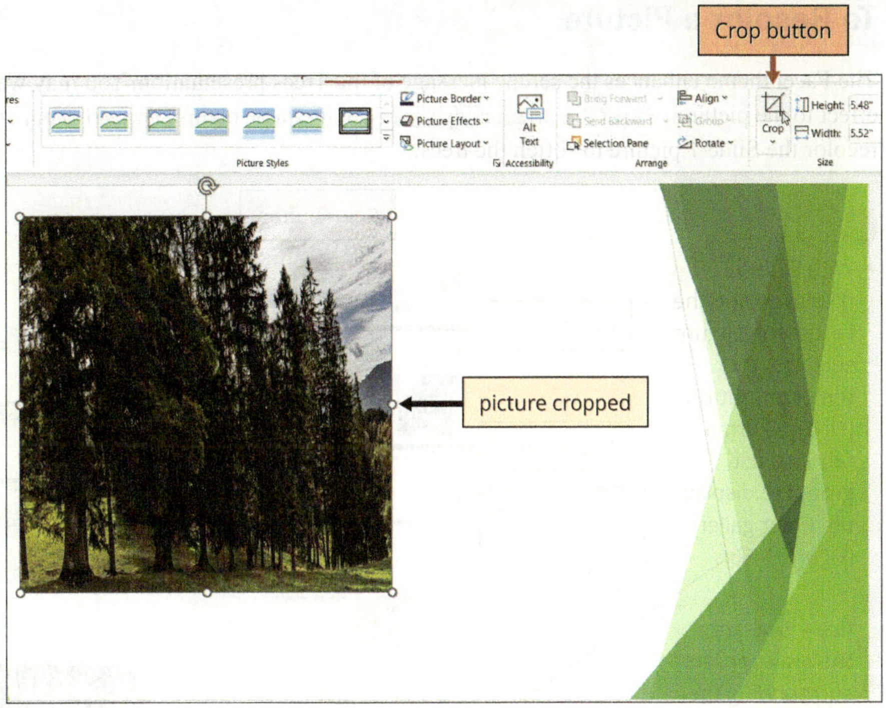

FelixMittermeier/Pixabay

Figure 3–55

Other Ways

1. Right-click picture, click Crop on Mini toolbar

To Crop a Picture to a Shape

In addition to cropping a picture, you can change the shape of a picture by cropping it to a specific shape. The picture's proportions are maintained, and it automatically is trimmed to fill the shape's geometry. To crop to a specific shape, you would perform the following steps.

1. Select the picture you want to crop.
2. Display the Picture Format tab and then click the Crop arrow (Picture Format tab | Size group) to display the Crop menu.
3. Point to 'Crop to Shape' and then click the desired shape in the Shape gallery.

BTW
Simultaneous Cropping on Two or Four Sides
To crop equally on two sides simultaneously, press CTRL while dragging the center cropping handle on either side inward. To crop all four sides equally, press CTRL while dragging a corner cropping handle inward.

Adjusting Picture Colors

PowerPoint allows you to adjust picture colors. The Color gallery has a wide variety of preset formatting combinations. The thumbnails in the gallery display the more common color saturation, color tone, and recolor adjustments. **Color saturation** changes the intensity of colors. High saturation produces vivid colors; low saturation produces gray tones. **Color tone** affects the coolness, called blue, or the warmness, called orange, of pictures. Color tones are denoted by temperature in degrees Kelvin (K), with lower numbers having coolness and higher numbers having warmness. When a digital camera does not measure the tone correctly, a **color cast** occurs, and, as a result, one color dominates the picture. **Recolor** effects convert the picture into a wide variety of hues. The more common recolor effects are **grayscale**, which changes a color picture into black, white, and shades of gray, and **sepia**, which changes picture colors into brown, gold, and yellow, reminiscent of a faded picture. You also can fine-tune the color adjustments by clicking the Picture Color Options and More Variations commands in the Color gallery.

To Recolor a Picture

The Facet theme enhances the serene message of the Trees presentation. You may want to supplement this theme by adding an effect to the picture. **Why?** An effect adds variety to the presentation and helps enhance ordinary pictures. The following steps recolor the Slide 1 picture to soften the trees.

1

- With Slide 1 displayed and the landscape picture selected, click the Color button (Picture Format tab | Adjust group) to display the Color gallery (Figure 3–56).

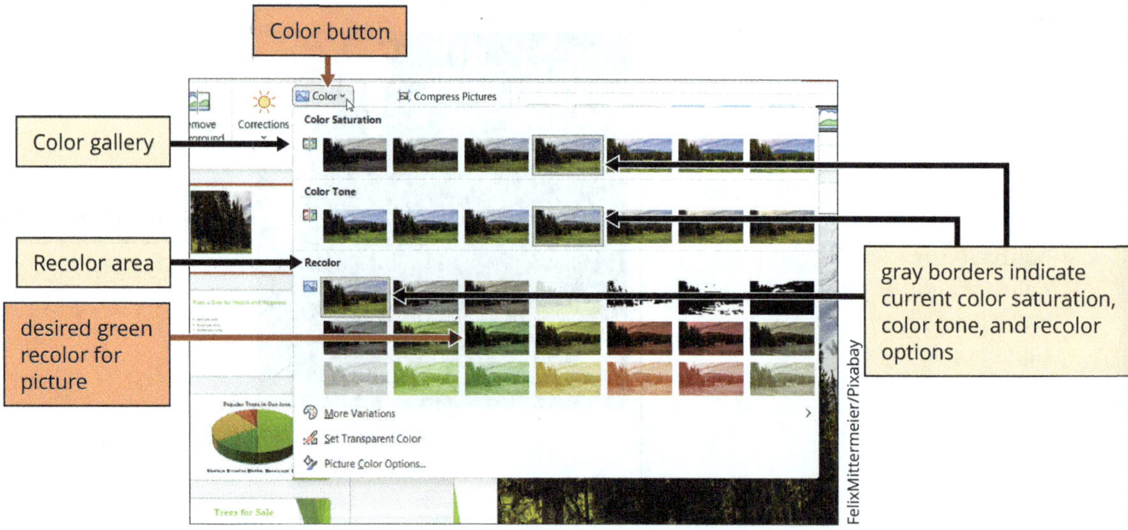

Figure 3–56

Q&A Why are the gray borders surrounding the thumbnails in the Color Saturation, Color Tone, and Recolor areas in the gallery?
The gray borders show the color saturation, tone, and recolor settings currently in effect for the image on Slide 1.

2

- Point to 'Dark Green, Accent color 2 Dark' (third thumbnail in the second Recolor row) to display a live preview of this adjustment on the picture (Figure 3–57).
- **Experiment:** Point to various thumbnails in the Recolor area and watch the colors change on the picture in Slide 1.

3

- Click 'Dark Green, Accent color 2 Dark' to apply this setting to the landscape picture.

Figure 3–57

Q&A Could I have applied this recoloring to the picture if it had been a background instead of a file inserted into the slide?
No. Artistic effects and recoloring cannot be applied to backgrounds.

Other Ways

1. Click Format Picture on shortcut menu, click Picture icon (Format Picture pane), click Picture Color, click Recolor

To Add an Artistic Effect to a Picture

Artists use a variety of techniques to create effects in their paintings. They can vary the amount of paint on their brushstroke, use fine bristles to add details, mix colors to increase or decrease intensity, and smooth their paints together to blend the colors. You, likewise, can add similar effects to your pictures using PowerPoint's built-in artistic effects. **Why?** The completed Slide 1 will have both a picture and WordArt, so applying an artistic effect to the picture will provide a contrast between the two images. The following steps add an artistic effect to the Slide 1 picture.

1

- With the landscape picture still selected, click the Artistic Effects button (Picture Format tab | Adjust group) to display the Artistic Effects gallery (Figure 3–58).

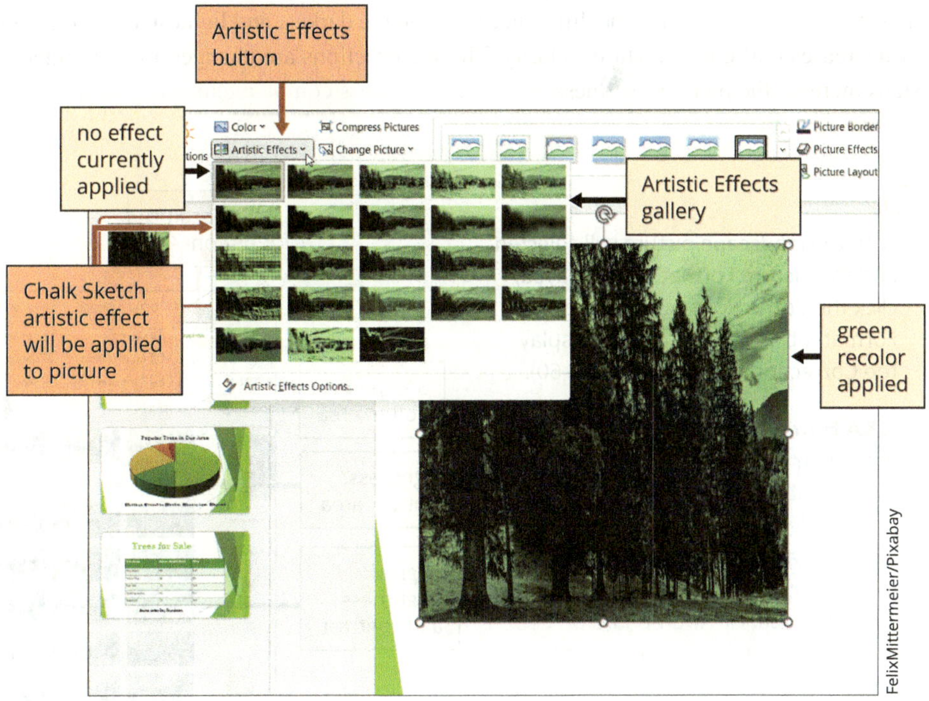

Figure 3–58

2

- Point to Chalk Sketch (first thumbnail in the second row) to display a live preview of this effect on the picture (Figure 3–59).
- **Experiment:** Point to various artistic effects and watch the hues change on the picture in Slide 1.

3

- Click Chalk Sketch to apply this artistic effect to the picture.

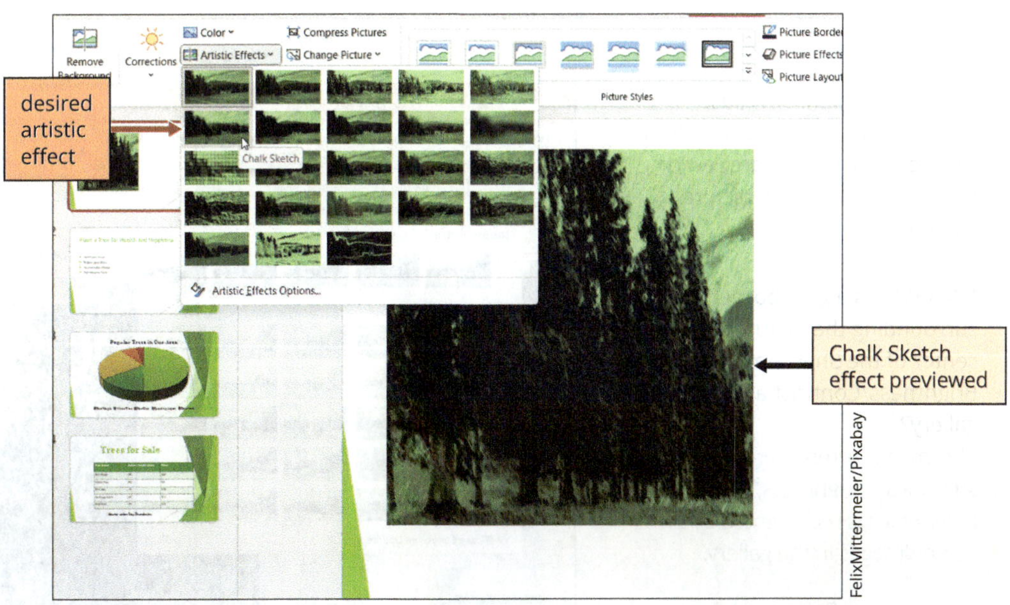

Figure 3–59

Q&A Can I adjust a picture by recoloring and applying an artistic effect?
Yes. You can apply both a color and an effect. You may prefer at times to mix these adjustments to create a unique image.

Other Ways

1. Click Format Picture on shortcut menu, click Effects icon, click Artistic Effects

To Change the Picture Softness

The Corrections tools allow you to change a picture's brightness, contrast, sharpness, and softness. A picture's color intensity can be modified by changing the brightness and contrast. **Brightness** determines the overall lightness or darkness of the entire image, whereas **contrast** is the difference between the darkest and lightest areas of the image. **Sharpness** increases (sharpens) or decreases (softens) a picture's clarity. These corrections are changed in predefined percentage increments. The following steps increase the picture's softness. **Why?** The softness complements the calm theme and allows the audience to focus on the overall message.

1

- With the landscape picture still selected and the Picture Format tab displayed, click the Corrections button (Picture Format tab | Adjust group) to display the Corrections gallery (Figure 3–60).

Q&A How are the thumbnails arranged?
The thumbnails on the left of the Sharpen/Softness area show more softness, and those on the right show more sharpness. In the Brightness/Contrast area, the thumbnails on the left are less bright than those on the right, and the thumbnails on the top have less contrast than those on the bottom.

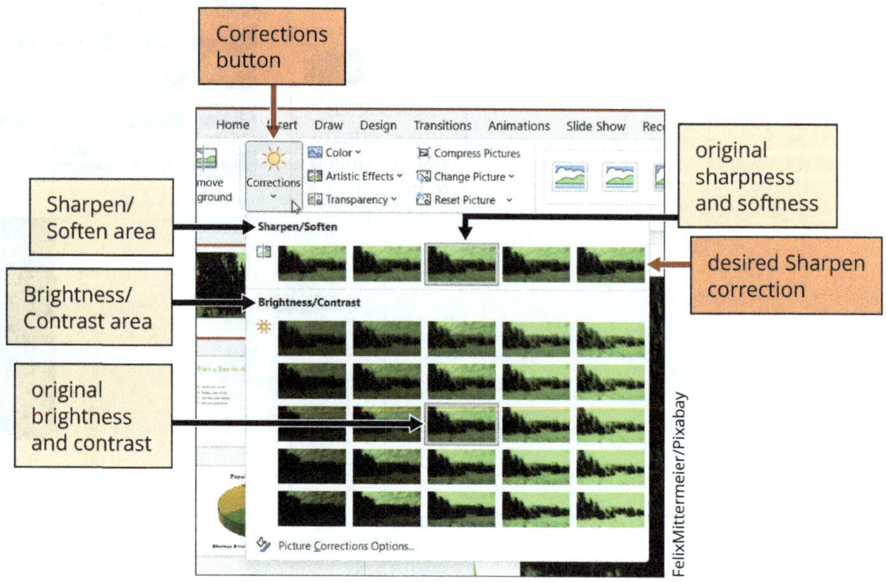

Figure 3–60

2

- Point to Sharpen: 50% (last thumbnail in the Sharpen/Soften row) to display a live preview of this correction on the picture (Figure 3–61).

Q&A Why is a gray border surrounding the pictures in the center of the Sharpen/Soften and Brightness/Contrast areas of the gallery?
The image currently has normal sharpness, brightness, and contrast (0%), which is represented by these center images in the gallery.

- **Experiment:** Point to various pictures in the Sharpen/Soften area and watch the sharpness change on the picture in Slide 1.

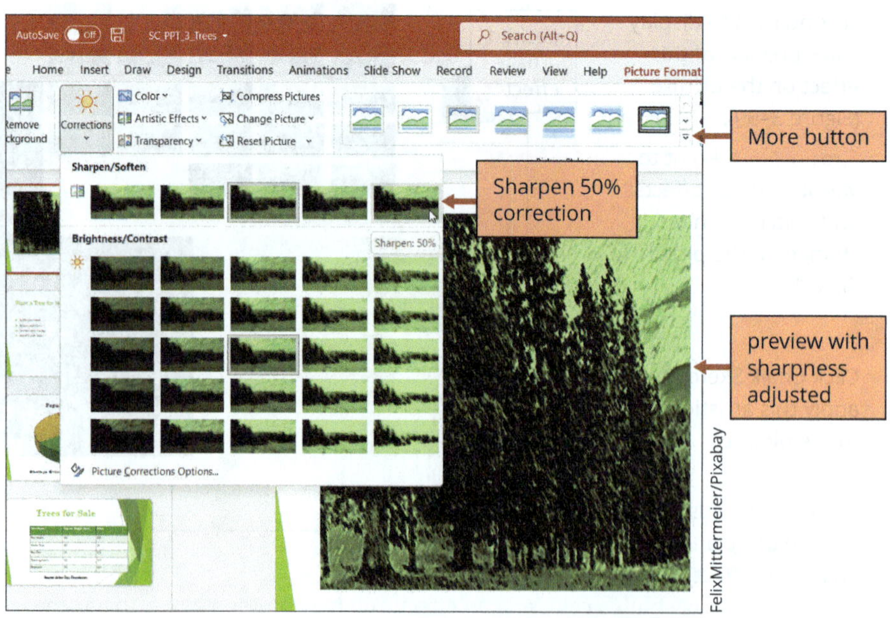

Figure 3–61

3

- Click Sharpen: 50% to apply this correction to the landscape picture.

Q&A How can I remove all effects from the picture?
Click the Reset Picture button (Picture Format tab | Adjust group).

Can I fine-tune any correction?
Yes. Click Picture Corrections Options and then move the slider for Sharpness, Brightness, or Contrast.

Other Ways

1. Click Picture Corrections Options (Corrections gallery), move Sharpness slider, or enter number in box next to slider (Format Picture pane)

To Apply a Picture Style

A **style** is a named collection of formats that can be applied to text or objects. The picture on Slide 1 emphasizes the health benefits of walking among trees, and you can increase its visual appeal by applying a picture style. **Why?** PowerPoint provides more than 25 picture styles that enable you to change a picture's look to a more visually appealing style, including a variety of shapes, angles, borders, and reflections. You want to use a style that applies a shadow to the landscape picture. The following steps apply a picture style to the Slide 1 picture.

1

- With the Slide 1 picture selected and the Picture Format tab displayed, click the More button in the Picture Styles gallery (Picture Format tab | Picture Styles group) (shown in Figure 3–61) to expand the gallery.
- Point to 'Soft Edge Oval' in the Picture Styles gallery (sixth style in the third row) to display a live preview of that style applied to the picture in the document (Figure 3–62).
- **Experiment:** Point to various picture styles in the Picture Styles gallery and watch the style of the picture change in the document window.

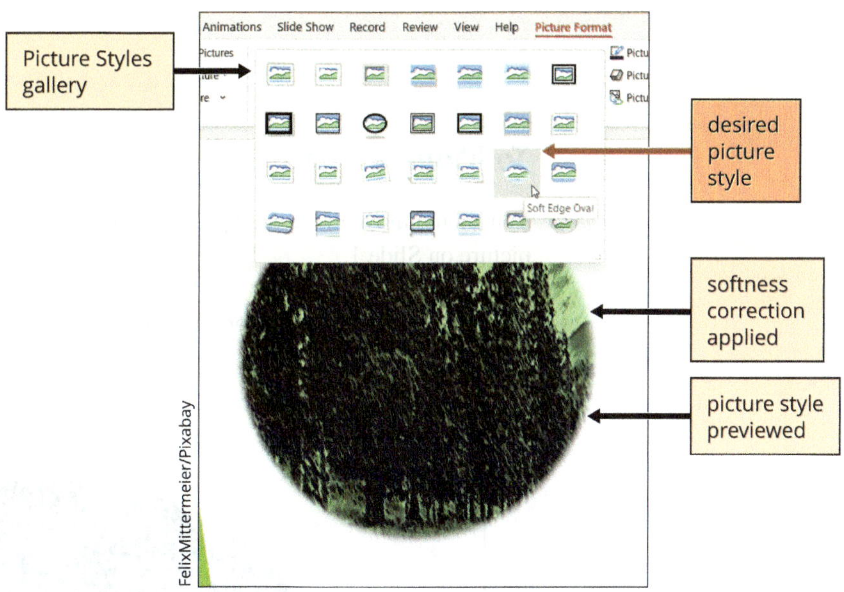

Figure 3–62

2

- Click 'Soft Edge Oval' in the Picture Styles gallery to apply the style to the selected picture.

To Size a Picture

The formatted picture is too small for Slide 1, so you need to resize it. You can resize this slide element by dragging the sizing handles or by specifying exact measurements for the height and width. The following step resizes the picture by entering an exact measurement.

1. With the picture selected and the Picture Format tab displayed, move the sizing handles so that the Height measurement is approximately 6" and the Width measurement is approximately 8.5" (Figure 3–63).

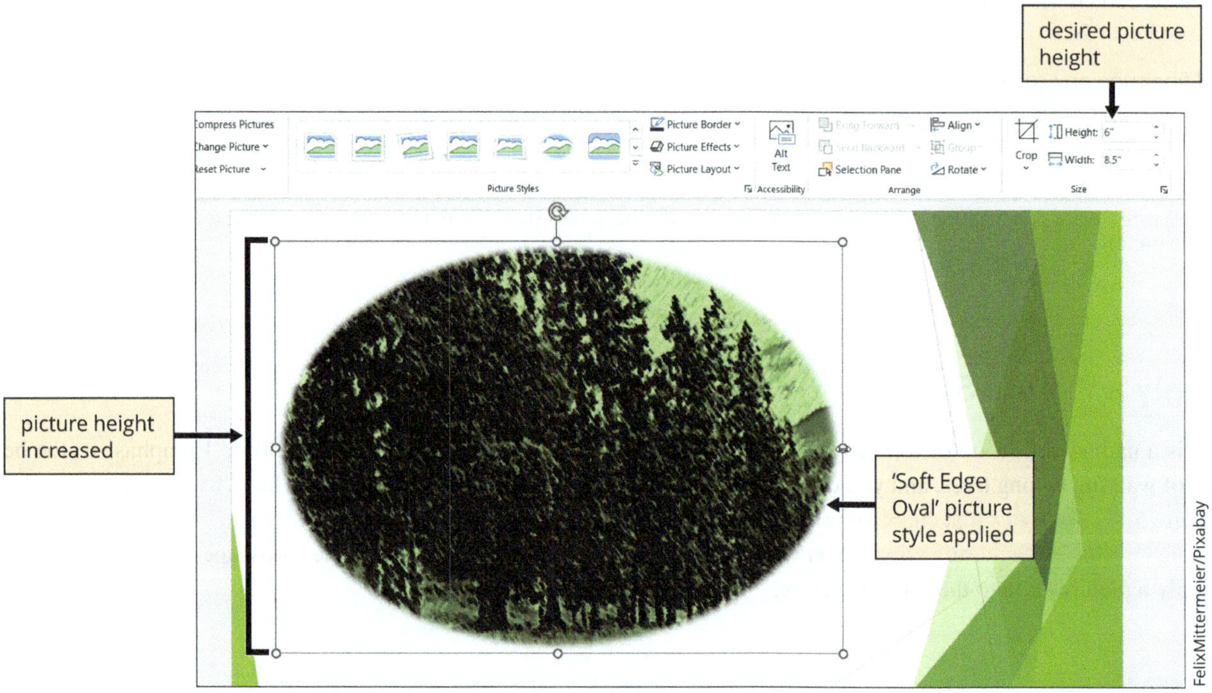

Figure 3–63

To Move a Picture

You should move the resized picture to allow space for a slide title. The following step moves the picture on Slide 1.

1. With the picture selected, use the smart guides to position the picture as shown in Figure 3–64.

Figure 3–64

To Align Pictures

You should move the picture to the top of Slide 1. **Why?** You want to add a slide title at the bottom of the slide, so you need to make room for this graphical element. The following steps align the picture at the top of the slide.

1

- With the picture selected and the Picture Format tab displayed, click the Align button (Picture Format tab | Arrange group) to display the Align Objects menu (Figure 3-65).

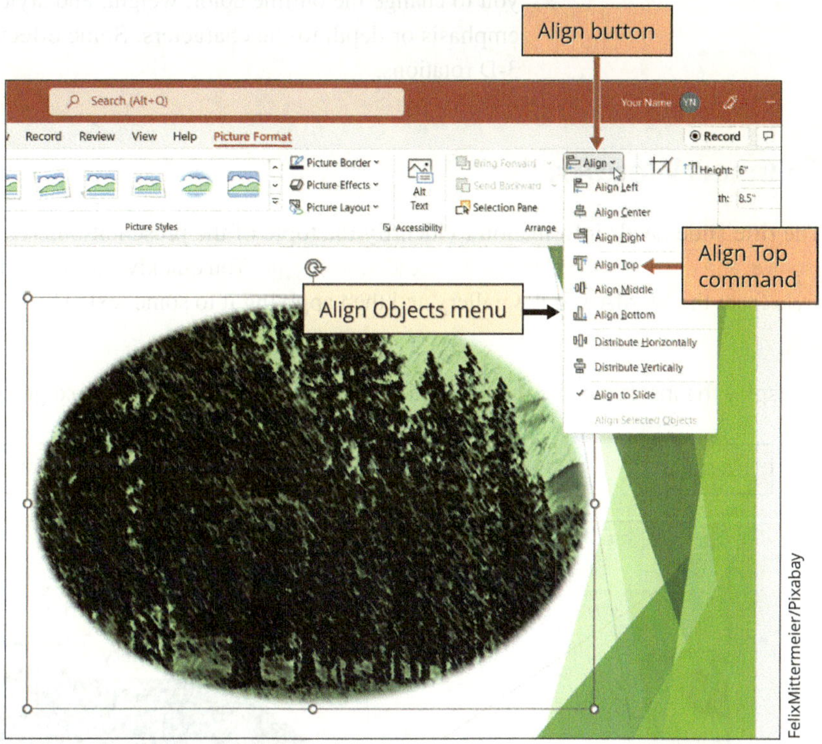

Figure 3-65

2

- Click Align Top to move the picture to the top edge of the slide (Figure 3-66).

Figure 3-66

Creating and Formatting WordArt

One method of adding appealing visual elements to a presentation is by using **WordArt**, formatted decorative text. This feature is found in other Microsoft 365 applications, including Word and Excel.

This gallery of decorative effects allows you to type new text or convert existing text to WordArt. You then can add elements such as fills, outlines, and effects.

WordArt fill in the interior of a letter can consist of a solid color, texture, picture, or gradient. The WordArt **outline** is the exterior border surrounding each letter or symbol. PowerPoint allows you to change the outline color, weight, and style. You also can add an **effect**, which helps add emphasis or depth to the characters. Some effects are shadows, reflections, glows, bevels, and 3-D rotations.

To Insert WordArt

The title slide needs information to identify the topic of the presentation. **Why?** Audience members will see the woodlands picture, and the text will reinforce the presentation topic. You quickly can add a visual element to the slide by selecting a WordArt style from the WordArt Styles gallery and then applying it to some text. The following steps insert WordArt.

1

- Display the Insert tab and then click the WordArt button (Insert tab | Text group) to display the WordArt gallery (Figure 3–67).

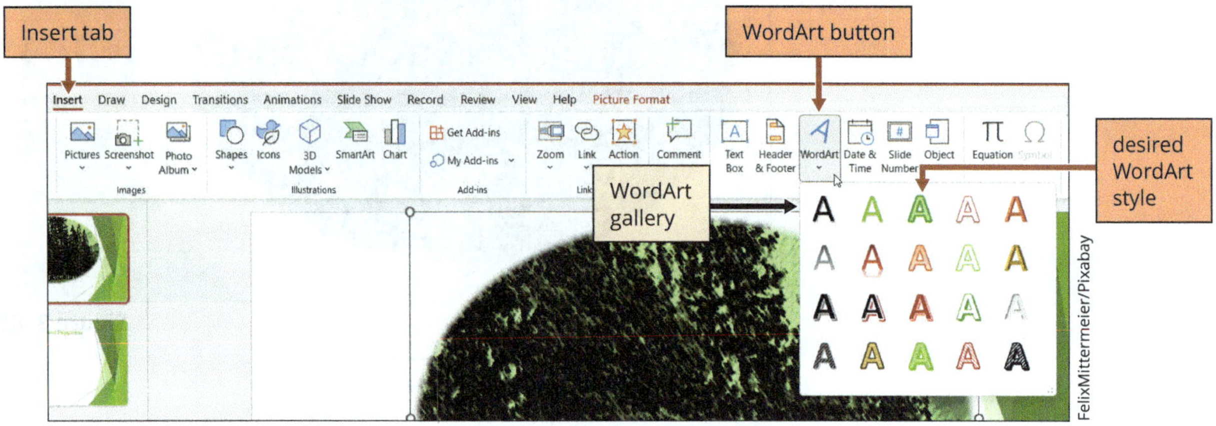

Figure 3–67

2

- Click 'Fill: Dark Green, Accent color 2; Outline: Dark Green, Accent color 2' (third style in the first row) to insert the WordArt object (Figure 3–68).

Figure 3–68

3

- Type **Wellness in the Woods** in the object as the WordArt text (Figure 3–69).

Q&A Why did the Shape Format tab appear automatically in the ribbon?
It appears when you select text to which you could add a WordArt style or other effect.

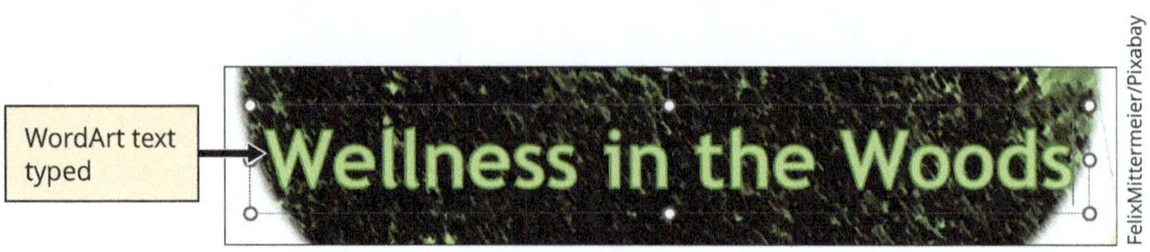

Figure 3–69

To Change the WordArt Shape

PowerPoint provides a variety of graphical shapes that add interest to WordArt text. The following steps change the Transform effect of the WordArt shape to 'Double Wave: Down-Up'. **Why?** The text provides the presentation's subject, and you want to emphasize the serene topic further by changing the WordArt shape.

1

- With the WordArt object still selected, click the Text Effects button (Shape Format tab | WordArt Styles group) to display the Text Effects menu (Figure 3–70).

Figure 3–70

2

- Point to Transform in the Text Effects menu to display the WordArt Transform gallery (Figure 3–71).

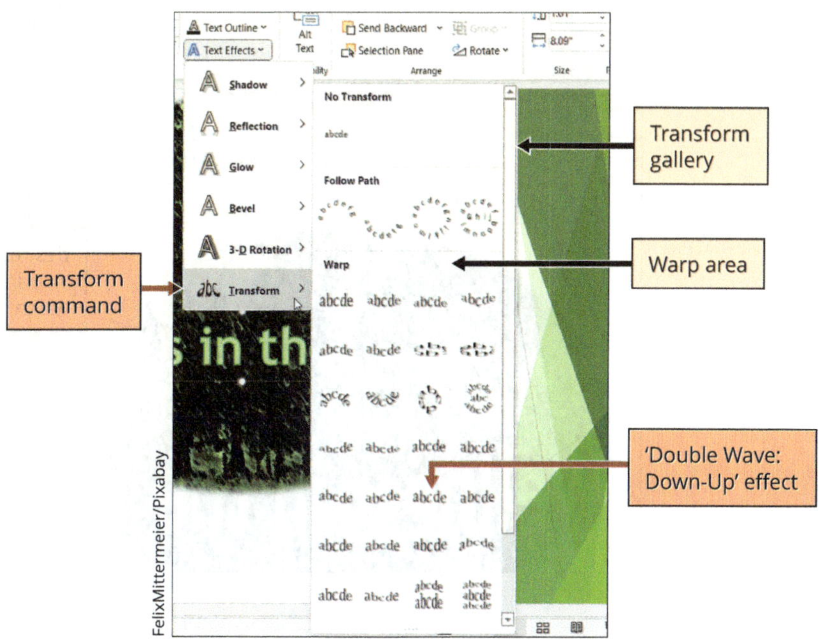

Figure 3–71

3

- Point to the 'Double Wave: Down-Up' effect in the Warp area (third effect in the fifth row in the Warp area) to display a live preview of that text effect applied to the WordArt object (Figure 3–72).
- **Experiment:** Point to various effects in the Transform gallery and watch the format of the text and borders change.

Q&A How can I see the preview of a Transform effect if the gallery overlays the WordArt letters?
Move the WordArt box to the left or right side of the slide and then repeat Steps 1 and 2.

4

- Click the 'Double Wave: Down-Up' effect to apply this text effect to the WordArt object.

Q&A Can I change the effect I applied to the WordArt?
Yes. Position the insertion point in the box and then repeat Steps 1 and 2.

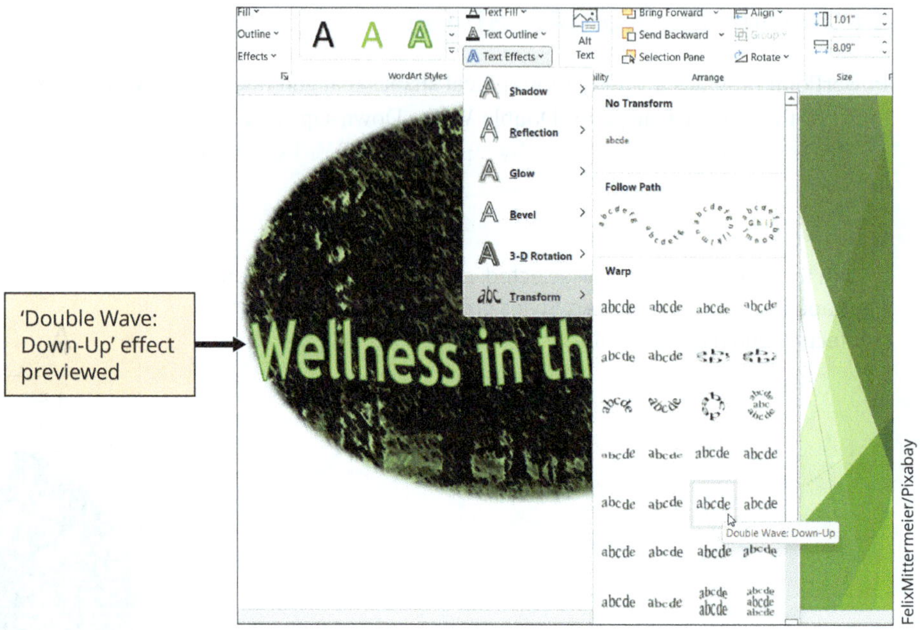

Figure 3–72

5

- Click the Shape Height box up arrow until the Height measurement is 1.5".
- Click the Shape Width box up arrow until the Width measurement is 10" (Figure 3–73).

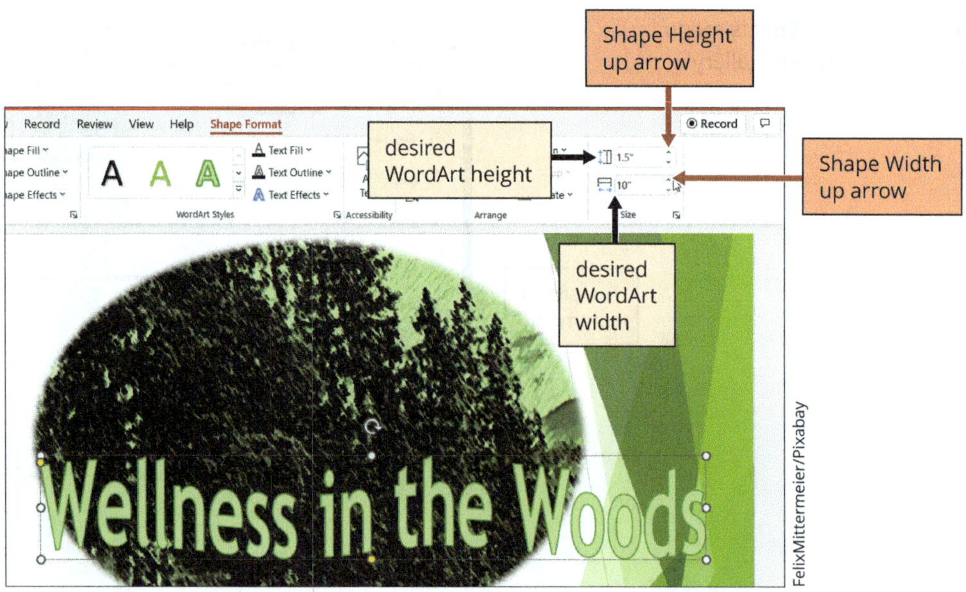

Figure 3–73

6

- Use the smart guides to position the WordArt as shown in Figure 3–74.

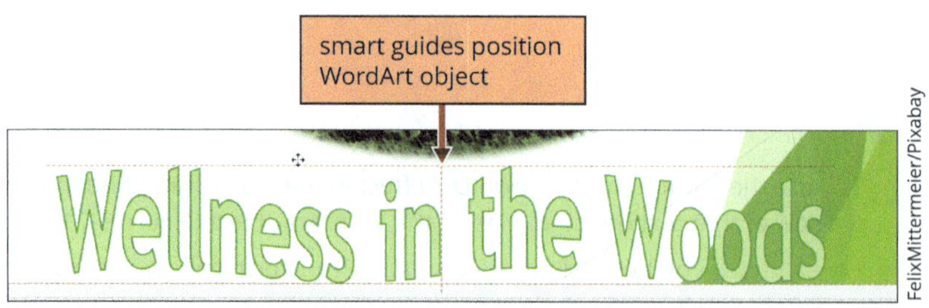

Figure 3–74

To Change the WordArt 3-D Rotation Effect

The following steps change the WordArt 3-D rotation effect. **Why?** The 3-D effect is a subtle visual element that enhances the slide feature.

1

- With the WordArt object still selected, display the Text Effects menu.
- Point to 3-D Rotation to display the 3-D Rotation gallery.
- Point to 'Perspective: Relaxed Moderately' (second rotation in the second Perspective row) to display a live preview of this effect (Figure 3–75).
- **Experiment:** Point to various rotations in the gallery and watch the WordArt change.

2

- Click 'Perspective: Relaxed Moderately' to apply this rotation to the WordArt.

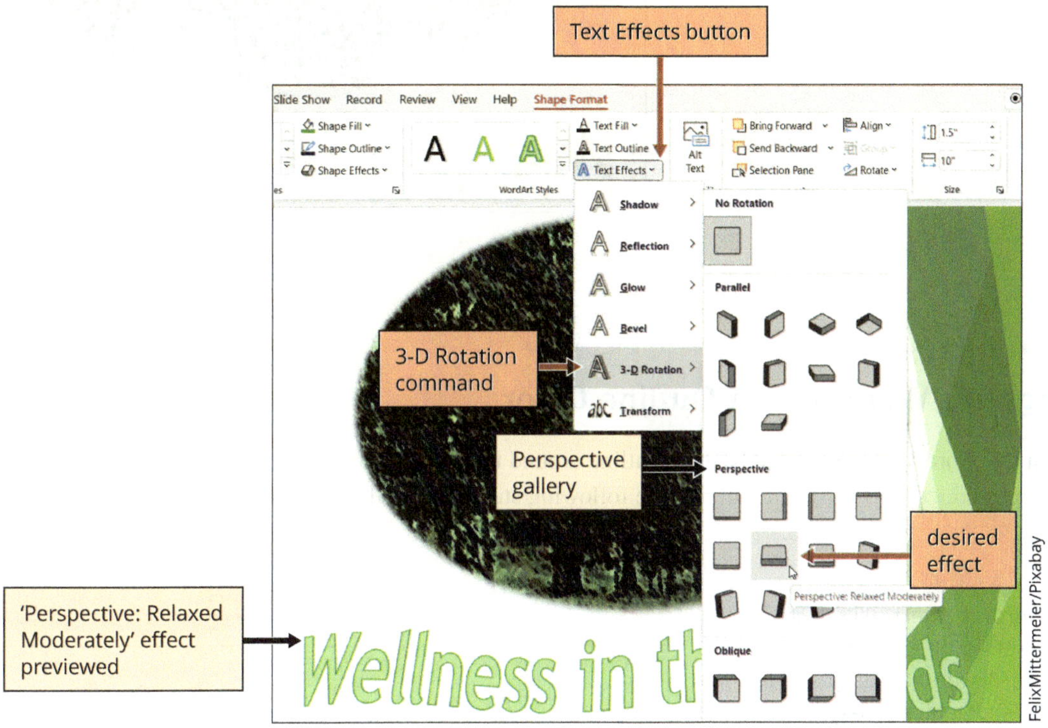

Figure 3–75

To Change the WordArt Text Fill Color

The Facet theme determines the available WordArt fill colors. You can change the default WordArt colors to give the characters a unique look. **Why?** The green fill coordinates well with the Facet background colors. The following steps change the WordArt text fill color.

1

- With the WordArt object selected, click the Text Fill arrow (Shape Format tab | WordArt Styles group) to display the Text Fill gallery.
- Point to 'Brown, Accent 6' (last color in the first Theme Colors row) to display a live preview of that color applied to the WordArt object (Figure 3–76).
- **Experiment:** Point to various colors and watch the fill color change.

2

- Click 'Brown, Accent 6' to apply this color as the fill for the WordArt object.

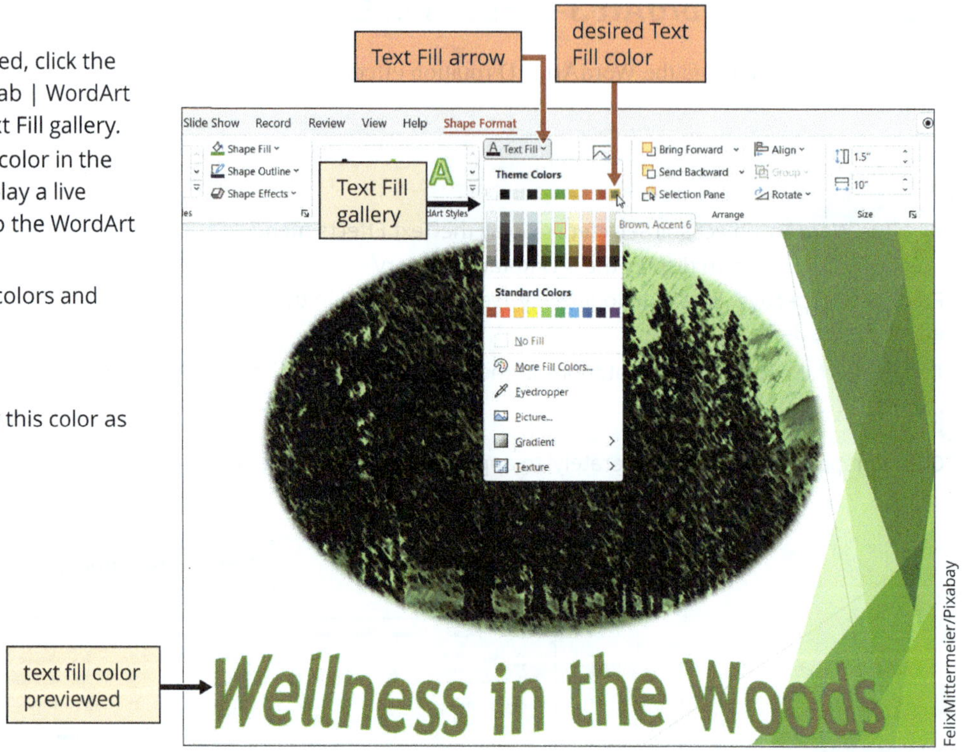

Figure 3–76

To Change the WordArt Text Outline Color

The letters in the WordArt style applied have an outline around the edges. You can change the color of the outline. **Why?** You used this color previously for the chart outline. The following steps change the WordArt outline color.

1

- With the WordArt object still selected, click the Text Outline arrow (Shape Format tab | WordArt Styles group) to display the Text Outline gallery.
- Point to Dark Blue (ninth color in the Standard Colors row) to display a live preview of that color applied to the WordArt outline (Figure 3–77).
- **Experiment:** Point to various colors and watch the outline color change.

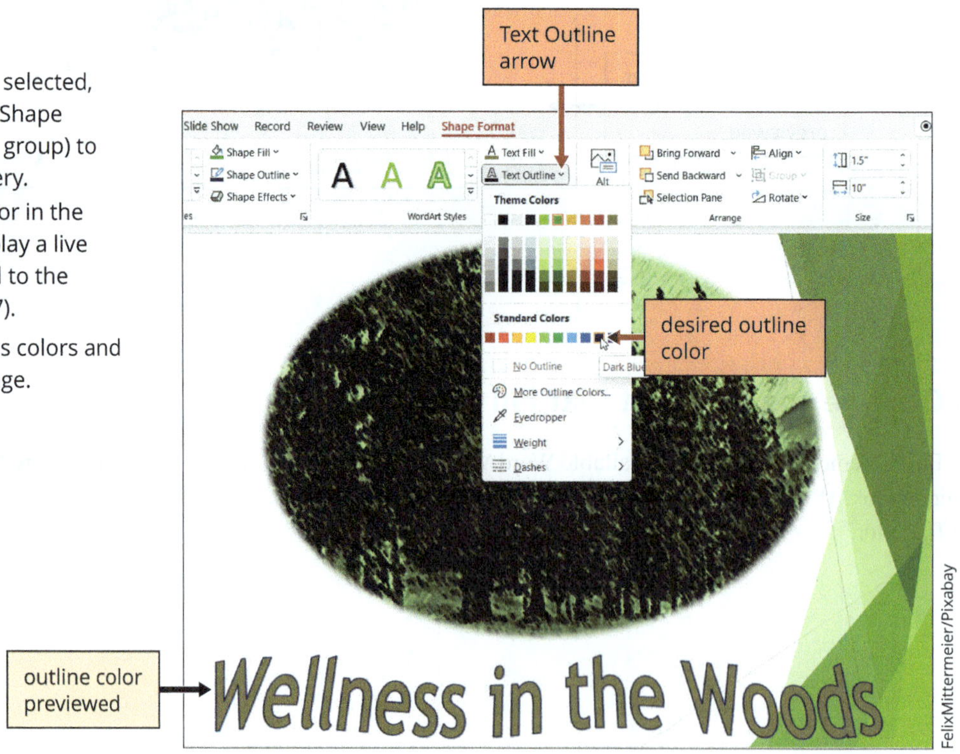

Figure 3–77

2

- Click Dark Blue to apply this color to the WordArt outline.

Q&A Can I change the outline line width?
Yes. Click the Text Outline button, point to Weight, and then click the desired line weight.

Must my text have an outline?
No. To remove the outline, click No Outline in the Text Outline gallery.

To Convert Text to WordArt

You wish to convert the title text letters on Slide 2 to WordArt. **Why?** WordArt can enhance the visual appeal of the slide. The following steps convert the title text of Slide 2 to WordArt.

1

- Display Slide 2 and then select the title text (Plant a Tree for Health and Happiness) (Figure 3–78).

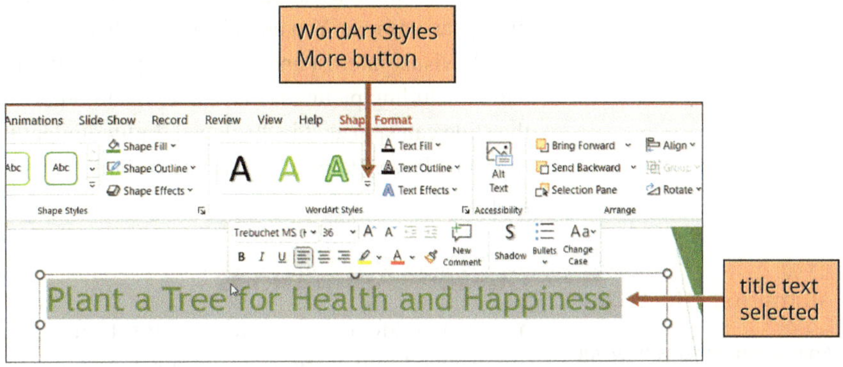

Figure 3–78

2

- If necessary, display the Shape Format tab and then click the WordArt Styles More button (Shape Format tab | WordArt Styles group) (shown in Figure 3–78) to display the WordArt Styles gallery.
- Point to 'Fill: Dark Green, Accent color 2; Outline: Dark Green, Accent color 2' (third color in the first row) to display a live preview of that style applied to the title text (Figure 3–79).
- **Experiment:** Point to various styles and watch the text change.

Figure 3–79

3

- Click 'Fill: Dark Green, Accent color 2; Outline: Dark Green, Accent color 2' to apply this style to the title text.

To Resize WordArt Proportionally

The WordArt object can be stretched, shrunk, or resized in two ways: using the sizing handles or changing the Size options on the Shape Format tab. To maintain the height and width proportions, press and hold SHIFT when dragging a sizing handle. Similarly, if you want to keep the proportions and also keep the center in the same location, press and hold both CTRL and SHIFT while dragging the sizing handle. On Slide 2, you want to resize the WordArt object proportionally. **Why?** Moving the WordArt above the bulleted list allows extra space on the slide for the video you insert later in this module. The following step resizes the WordArt proportionally.

1

- With the WordArt object still selected, press and hold SHIFT and then drag the middle sizing handle on the right side of the box inward, as shown in Figure 3–80.

Q&A Does resizing change the WordArt font size?
No. Resizing a WordArt object only resizes the box the WordArt is in. If you want to resize the WordArt characters, you would select the text and then change the font size on the Home tab of the ribbon.

Figure 3–80

Animating Slide Content

Animation includes special effects applied to text or other objects that make the object appear, disappear, or move. You already are familiar with one form of animation: transitions between slides. To add visual interest and clarity to a presentation, you can animate various parts of an individual slide, including pictures, shapes, text, and other slide elements. For example, each paragraph on the slide can spin as it is displayed. Individual letters and shapes also can spin or move in various motions. PowerPoint has a variety of built-in animations that will fade, wipe, or fly-in text and graphics.

BTW
Animation Effect Icon Colors
Animation effects allow you to control how objects enter, move on, and exit slides. Using a traffic signal analogy may help you remember the sequence of events. Green icons indicate when the animation effect starts on the slide. Yellow icons represent the object's motion; use them with caution so they do not distract from the message you are conveying to your audience. Red icons indicate when the object stops appearing on a slide.

Custom Animations

You can create a **custom animation** to meet your unique needs. Custom animation effects are grouped into categories: entrance, exit, emphasis, and motion paths. An **entrance effect**, as the name implies, determines how slide elements first appear on a slide. An **exit effect** works in the opposite manner: It determines how slide elements disappear. An **emphasis effect** modifies text and objects displayed on the screen. For example, letters may darken or increase in font size. The entrance, exit, and emphasis animations are grouped into categories: Basic, Subtle, Moderate, and Exciting. You can set the animation speed to Very Fast, Fast, Medium, Slow, or Very Slow.

Slide 2 has two elements with text: the WordArt title and the content placeholder with four bulleted paragraphs. When the slide is displayed, the audience will see the WordArt enter from the top of the slide. Then, the four paragraphs will display simultaneously. In the following steps, you will perform these tasks:

1. Apply an entrance effect to the WordArt.
2. Change the WordArt direction.
3. Change the animation start option.
4. Preview the animation sequence.
5. Modify the entrance timing.
6. Animate text paragraphs.
7. Change the animation sequence.

To Animate an Object Using an Entrance Effect

The WordArt will enter the slide from the top when you display this slide. **Why?** The graphic is positioned above the bulleted paragraphs, so you want it to enter and then move into this location. Entrance effects are colored green in the Animation gallery. The following step applies an entrance effect to the WordArt in Slide 2.

1

- With the WordArt on Slide 2 still selected, click Animations on the ribbon to display the Animations tab.
- Click the Float In animation in the Animation gallery (Animations tab | Animation group) to display a live preview of this animation and to apply this entrance animation to the WordArt object (Figure 3–81).

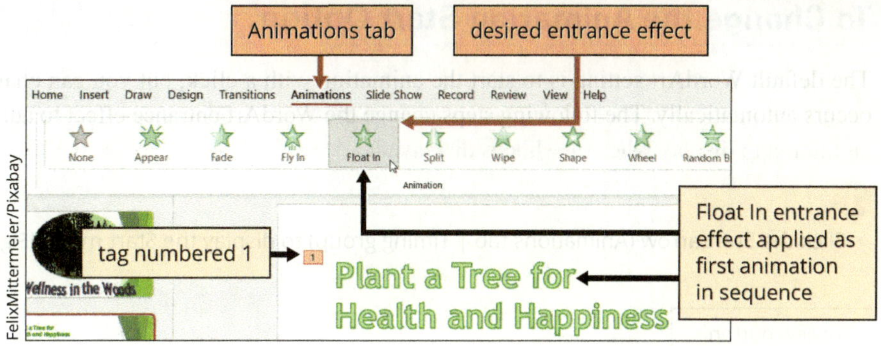

Figure 3–81

Q&A Are more entrance animations available?
Yes. Click More in the Animation gallery to see additional animations. You can select one of the entrance animations that are displayed, or you can click the 'More Entrance Effects' command to expand the selection. You can click any animation to see a preview of the effect.

Why does the number 1 appear in a box on the left side of the WordArt?
The 1 is a sequence number and indicates Float In is the first animation that will appear on the slide when you click the slide.

To Change Animation Direction

You can modify an animation's direction and specify that it enters from another side or from a corner. The following steps change the WordArt entrance animation to enter from the top. **Why?** By default, the WordArt appears on the slide by entering from the bottom edge, and you want it to enter from the top.

1

- Click the Effect Options button (Animations tab | Animation group) to display the Direction gallery (Figure 3–82).

Q&A Why does a box appear around the Float Up arrow?
Float Up is the default entrance direction applied to the animation.

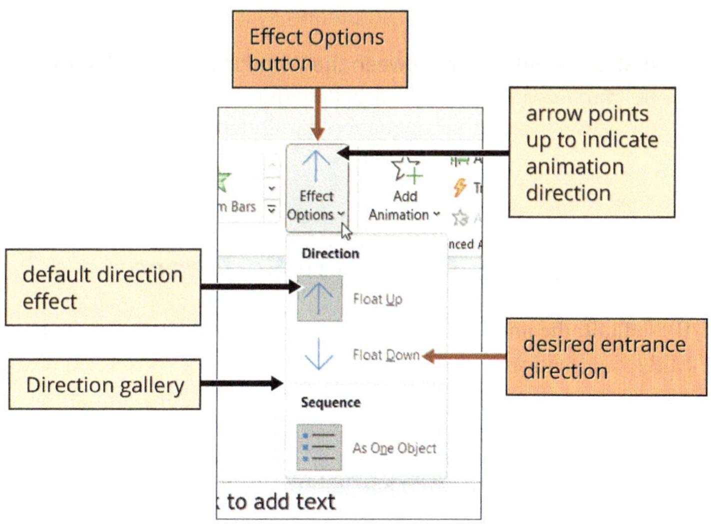

Figure 3–82

2

- Click the Float Down arrow to see a preview of this animation and apply this direction to the entrance animation (Figure 3–83).

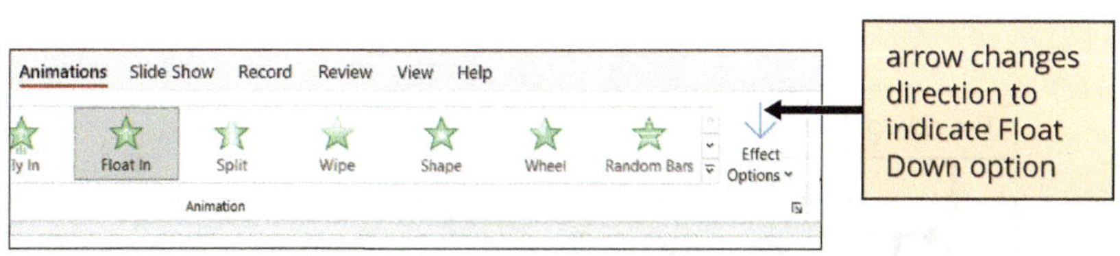

Figure 3–83

Q&A Can I change an entrance effect?
Yes. Repeat Step 1 to select another direction if several effects are available.

How can I delete an animation effect?
Click the number associated with the animation you wish to delete and then press DELETE.

To Change the Animation Start Option

The default WordArt setting is to start the animation with a click, but you can change this setting so that the entrance effect occurs automatically. The following steps change the WordArt entrance effect to automatic. **Why?** You want the slide title text animation to display when the slide is displayed.

1

- Click the Start arrow (Animations tab | Timing group) to display the Start menu (Figure 3–84).

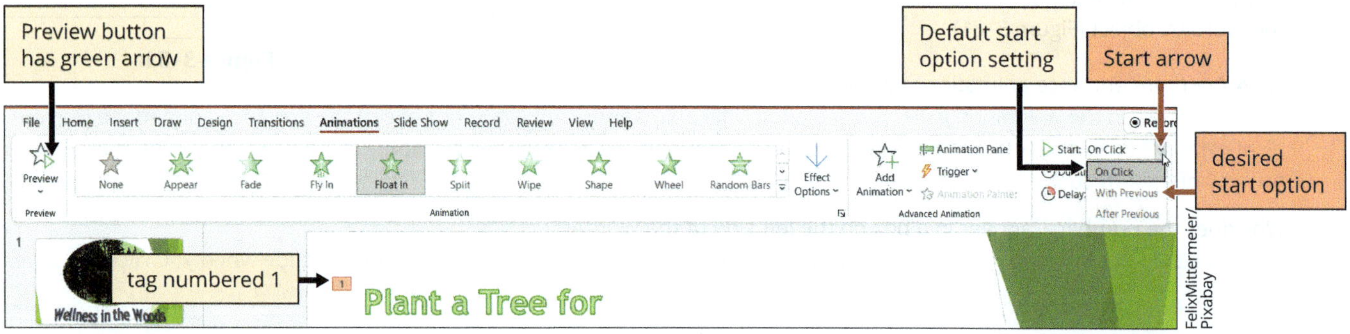

Figure 3–84

2

- Click With Previous to change the start option.

Q&A Why did the numbered tag change from 1 to 0?
The animation now occurs automatically without a click.

What is the difference between the With Previous and After Previous settings?
The With Previous setting starts the effect simultaneously with any prior animation; the After Previous setting starts the animation after a prior animation has ended.

To Preview an Animation Sequence

By default, the animations will be displayed when you run the presentation and click the slide. The following step previews the Slide 2 animation. **Why?** Although you have not completed developing the presentation, you should view the animation you have added to check for continuity and verify that the animation is displaying as you expected.

1

- Click the Preview button (Animations tab | Preview group) to view the Slide 2 animation (Figure 3–85).

Q&A Why does a red square appear in the middle of the Preview button when I click that button?
The red square indicates the animation sequence is in progress. Ordinarily, a green arrow is displayed in the button.

Figure 3–85

To Change the Animation Duration

The entrance animation effect is displayed quickly. To create a dramatic effect, you can change this setting so that the entrance effect occurs slowly during a specified number of seconds. The following step modifies the duration setting for the entrance animation. **Why?** You want the slide title text to move down from the top of the slide slowly.

1

- Click the Duration up arrow (Animations tab | Timing group) several times to increase the time from 01.00 second to 02.00 seconds (Figure 3-86).
- Click the Preview button to view the animation.

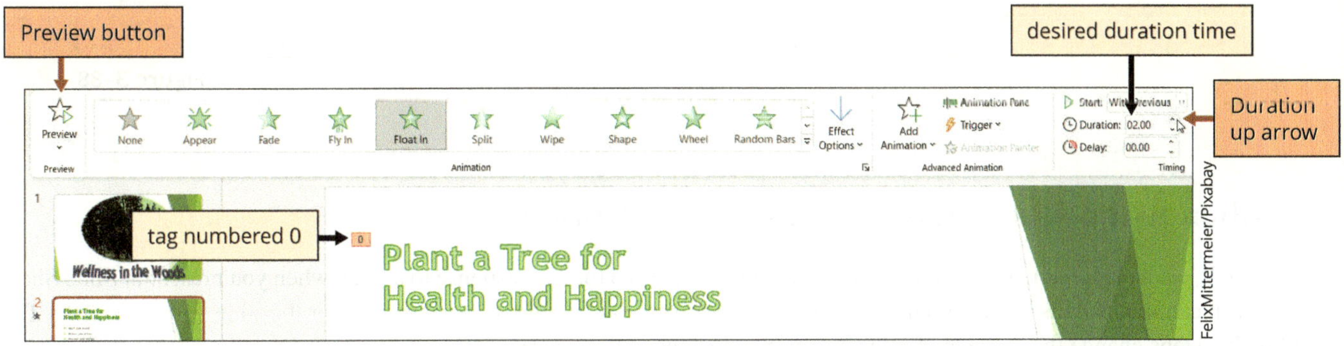

Figure 3-86

Q&A What is the difference between the duration time and the delay time?
The duration time is the length of time in which the animation occurs; the delay time is the length of time that passes before the animation begins.

Can I type the speed in the Duration box instead of clicking the arrow to adjust the speed?
Yes. Typing the numbers allows you to set precise timing.

To Animate Text

You can animate the four bulleted paragraphs in the left Slide 2 content placeholder. **Why?** For a special effect, you can display each paragraph individually during a presentation rather than have all four paragraphs appear together. The following steps animate the bulleted list paragraphs.

1

- Click any bulleted list text in the Slide 2 left content placeholder to select the placeholder (Figure 3-87).

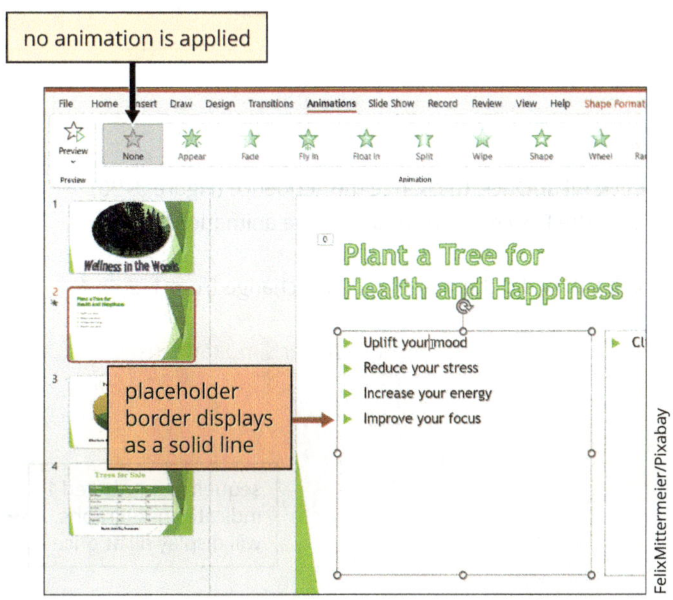

Figure 3-87

2

- Click the Fade entrance effect in the Animation gallery to add and preview this animation.
- Change the Duration time to 02.00 seconds (Figure 3–88).
- Click the Preview button to view the animations.

Figure 3–88

To Change the Animation Sequence Effect Option

By default, each paragraph in the content placeholder enters one at a time in response to a click when you present in Slide Show view. You can modify this entrance sequence setting. **Why?** You want all the paragraphs to enter the slide simultaneously. The following steps change the sequence for the paragraphs to appear all at once.

1

- Click the Effect Options button to display the Effect Options menu (Figure 3–89).

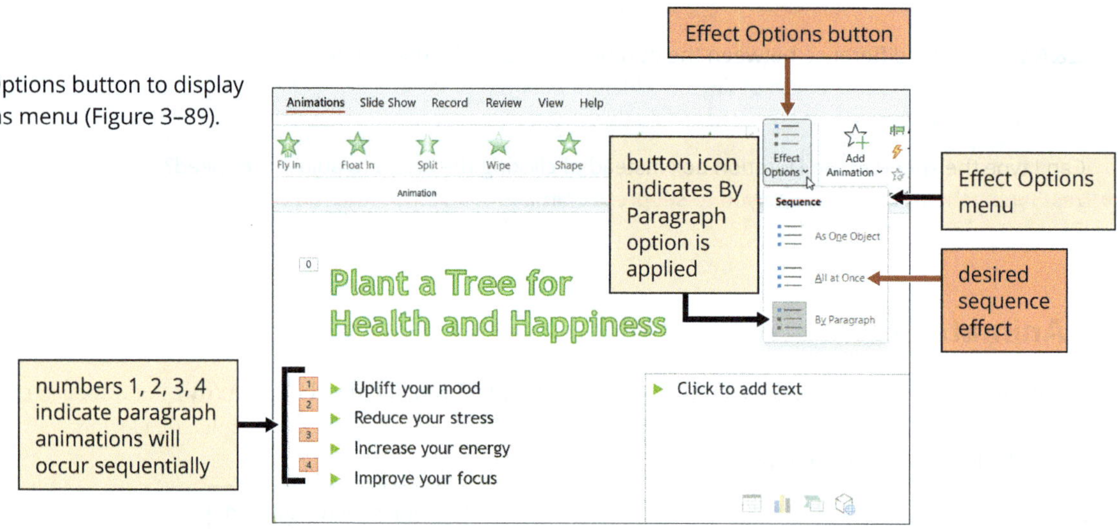

Figure 3–89

2

- Click 'All at Once' to change the sequence (Figure 3–90).
- Click the Preview button to view the animations.

Q&A Why did the numbered tags change from 1, 2, 3, 4 to 1, 1, 1, 1?

All four paragraphs now will appear simultaneously.

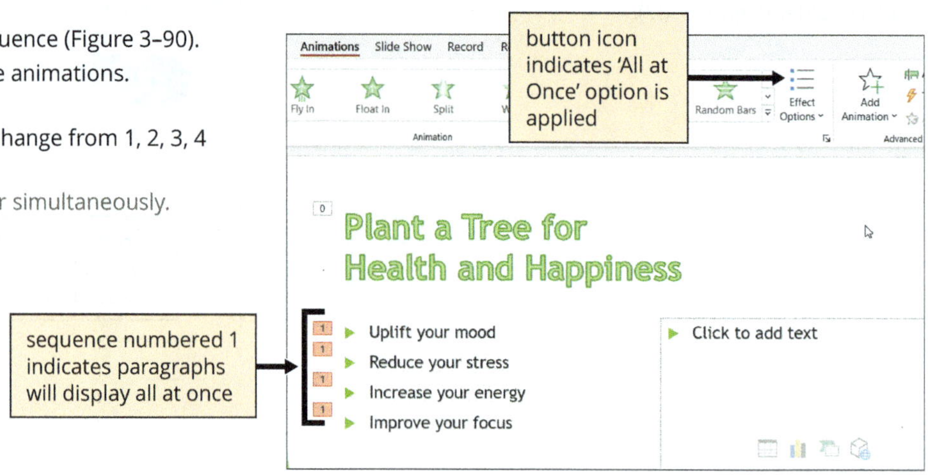

Figure 3–90

Adding Media to Slides

Media files can enrich a presentation if they are used correctly. Video files can be downloaded from the Internet or produced with a camera and editing software. Sound files also can come from the Internet, be stored on your computer, or be an audio track on other media. If you did not create the media files you use in a PowerPoint presentation, ensure you have permission to use them and give the original creators credit for their work.

Once an audio or video clip is inserted into a slide, you can specify options that affect how the file is displayed and played. For example, you can have the video play automatically when the slide is displayed, or you can click the video frame when you are ready to start the playback. You also can have the video fill the entire slide, which is referred to as **full screen**. If you decide to play the slide show automatically and have it display full screen, you can drag the video frame to the gray area off the slide so that it does not display briefly before going to full screen. You can select the 'Loop until Stopped' option to have the video repeat until you click the next slide, or you can choose not to have the video frame display on the slide until you click the slide.

If your video clip has recorded sounds, the volume controls give you the option to set how loudly this audio will play. They also allow you to mute the sound so that your audience will hear no background noise or music.

In the following steps, you will perform these tasks:

1. Insert a video file into Slide 2.
2. Resize and move the clip.
3. Change the clip contrast.
4. Play the video automatically.

BTW
Using Codecs
Video and audio content developers use a codec (compressor/decompressor) to reduce the file size of digital media. The reduced file size helps transfer files across the Internet quickly and smoothly and helps save space on storage media. Your computer can play any compressed file if the specific codec used to compress the file is available on your computer. If the codec is not installed or is not recognized, your computer attempts to download this file from the Internet. Many codec files are available to download from the Internet at no cost.

To Insert a Video File

When you run your slide show, you want to show a video clip in the Slide 2 content placeholder of trees along a path in a forest. **Why?** This clip emphasizes the tranquil experience of walking along the Nature Center's trails. PowerPoint allows you to insert this clip into your slide in the same manner that you insert a picture in a content placeholder. The following steps insert this video clip into Slide 2.

1

- With Slide 2 still displayed, click the Insert Video icon in the right content placeholder to display the Insert Video dialog box.
- Navigate to the location where your Data Files are located.
- Click Support_PPT_3_Forest.mp4 to select the file (Figure 3–91).

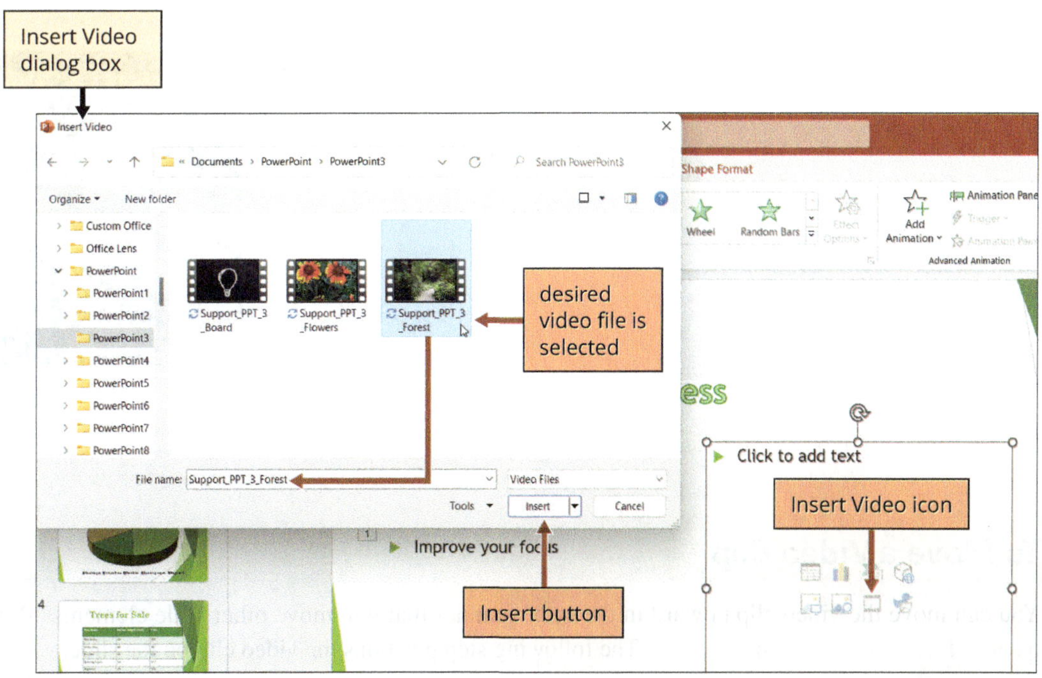

Athree23/Pixabay; MixailMixail/Pixabay; Caelan/Pixabay

Figure 3–91

2

- Click the Insert button (Insert Video dialog box) to insert the video clip into Slide 2 (Figure 3–92).
- If the Design Ideas pane opens, close it.

Q&A Can I adjust the color of a video clip?
Yes. You can correct the brightness and contrast, and you also can recolor a video clip using the same methods you learned in this module to color a picture. You will adjust the contrast and brightness later in this module.

3

- Click the Play/Pause button to review the video clip.

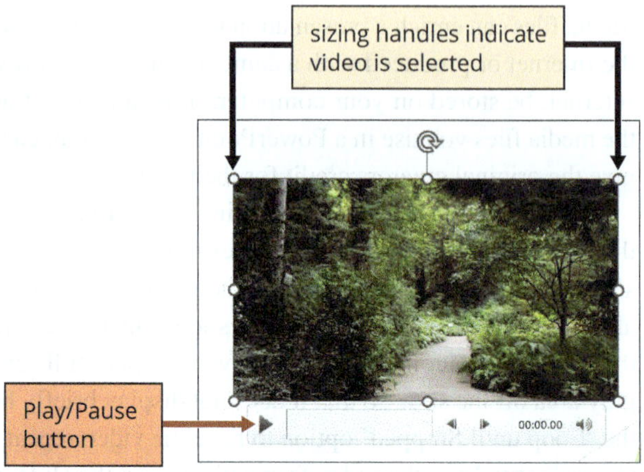

Figure 3–92

To Resize a Video Clip

You can change the dimensions of the video clip in the same manner that you adjust the size of a picture. **Why?** You have sufficient space on the slide to resize the video clip. The following step adjusts the video clip size.

1

- With the Video Format tab displayed, click the Size Dialog Box Launcher in the Video Format | Size group and make sure the Lock aspect ratio box is unchecked in the Format Video pane.
- Click the Video Height up arrow several times until the height is approximately 5".
- Click the Video Width down arrow several times until the width is approximately 7.5" (Figure 3–93).

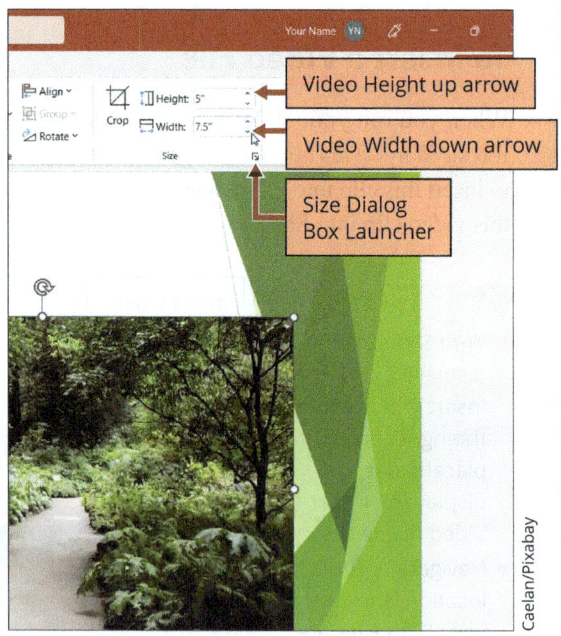

Figure 3–93

To Move a Video Clip

You can move the video clip upward in the same manner that you move other slide elements. **Why?** The video clip size is balanced with the content placeholder. The following step positions the video clip on the slide.

1 Use the smart guides to position the video clip, as shown in Figure 3–94.

Figure 3–94

To Change Video Contrast

PowerPoint provides the ability to correct a video by changing the brightness and contrast. The following steps increase the video clip brightness and contrast. **Why?** The video clip you inserted is dark, so you want to apply these corrections to help viewers see the clip clearly.

1

- With the video clip selected, click the Corrections button (Video Format tab | Adjust group) to display the Brightness/ Contrast gallery (Figure 3–95).

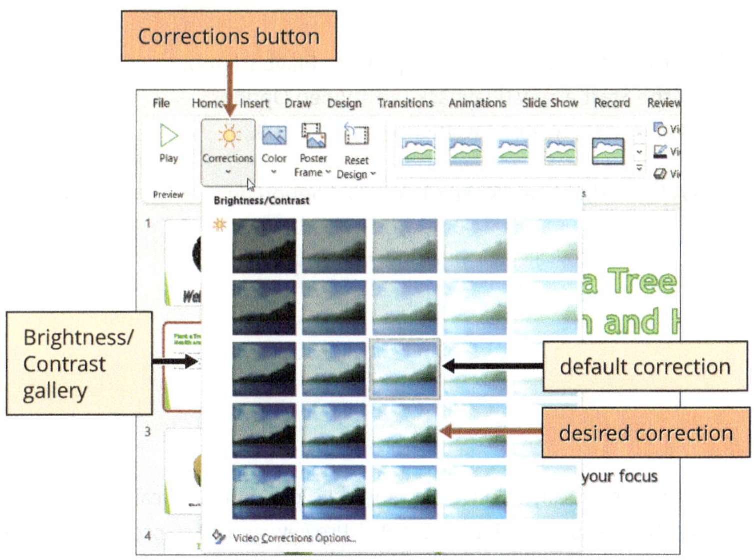

Figure 3–95

2

- Point to 'Brightness: 0% (Normal) Contrast: +20%' (third thumbnail in the fourth row) to display a preview of this correction on the clip (Figure 3–96).

Q&A Why does the gray box display in the center of the gallery?
That setting is the default brightness/contrast setting of 'Brightness: 0% (Normal) Contrast: 0% (Normal).'

- **Experiment:** Point to various pictures in the Brightness/Contrast area and watch the brightness and contrast change on the video clip.

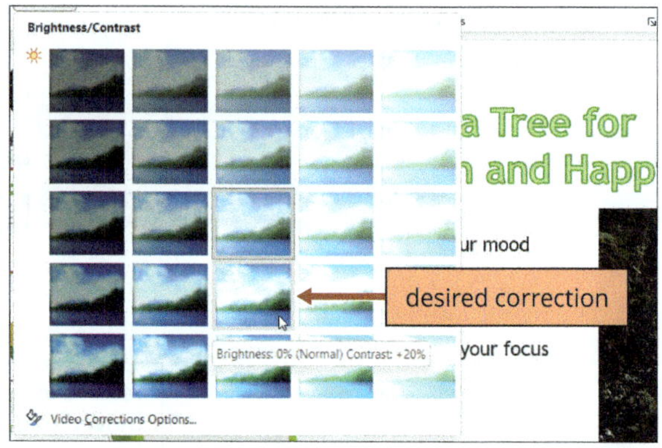

Figure 3–96

3

- Click 'Brightness: 0% (Normal) Contrast: +20%' (third thumbnail in the fourth row) to apply this correction to the video clip.

To Play a Video File Automatically

Once the video clip is inserted, you can specify that the video plays automatically when the slide is displayed. **Why?** When you are giving your presentation, you do not want to click the mouse to start the video. The following steps play the video file automatically.

1

- With the video clip selected, display the Playback tab.
- Click the Start arrow (Playback tab | Video Options group) to display the Start menu (Figure 3–97).

Q&A What does the 'When Clicked On' option do?
The video clip would begin playing when the presenter clicks the video frame during the slide show.

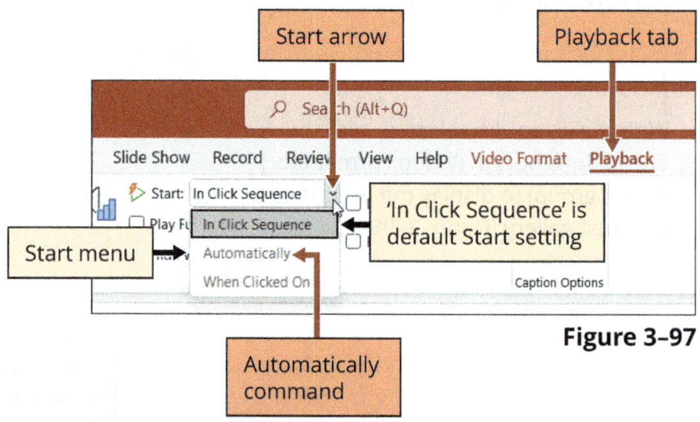

Figure 3–97

2

- Click Automatically to have the video clip play automatically when the slide is displayed.
- Click the Play button (Playback tab | Preview group) to preview the video (Figure 3–98).

Q&A Why did the Play button change to Pause when the video was playing?
The button changes to allow you to stop the preview if desired.

BTW
Restricting Permissions
You can allow PowerPoint users to see your presentation but not allow them to change the slide content, copy the slides, or print the presentation. To protect your presentation, click File on the ribbon to open Backstage view, display the Info tab, click Protect Presentation, and then click Always Open Read-Only.

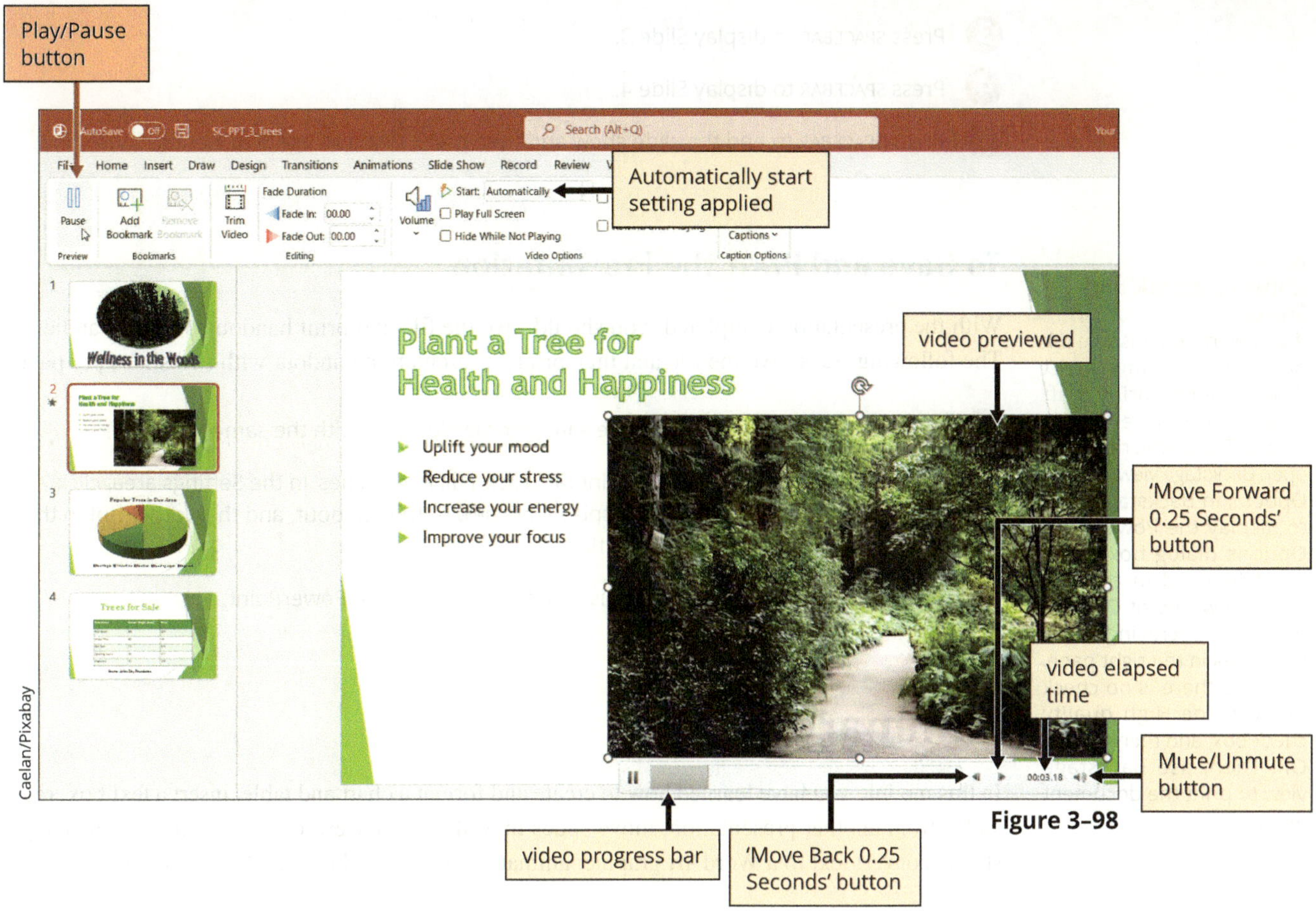

Figure 3–98

To Add a Transition between Slides

A final enhancement you will make in this presentation is to apply the Wind transition in the Exciting category to all slides and change the transition duration to 3.00. The following steps apply this transition to the presentation.

1. Apply the Wind transition in the Exciting category (Transitions tab | Transition to This Slide group) to all four slides in the presentation.
2. Change the transition duration from 02.00 to 03.00 for all slides.

To Run a Slide Show with Animations and Video

All changes are complete, so you now can view the Trees presentation. The following steps start Slide Show view.

1. Display Slide 1 and then click the Slide Show button on the status bar to begin the presentation.
2. Press SPACEBAR to display Slide 2. Watch the WordArt appear. Press SPACEBAR to view the four bulleted paragraphs and watch the video clip.

BTW

Printing Document Properties

PowerPoint does not allow you to print document properties. This feature, however, is available in Microsoft 365 Word.

BTW

Distributing a Document

Instead of printing and distributing a hard copy of PowerPoint slides, you can distribute the slides electronically. Options include sending the slides via email; posting it on cloud storage (such as OneDrive) and sharing the link with others; posting it on social media, a blog, or other website; and sharing a link associated with an online location of the slides. You also can create and share a PDF or XPS image of the slides, so that users can view the file in Acrobat Reader or XPS Viewer instead of in PowerPoint.

3. Press SPACEBAR to display Slide 3.
4. Press SPACEBAR to display Slide 4.
5. Press SPACEBAR to end the slide show and then press SPACEBAR again to exit the slide show.

BTW
Conserving Ink and Toner
If you want to conserve ink or toner, you can instruct PowerPoint to print draft quality documents by clicking File on the ribbon to open Backstage view, clicking Options in Backstage view to display the PowerPoint Options dialog box, clicking Advanced in the left pane (PowerPoint Options dialog box), scrolling to the Print area in the right pane, verifying there is no check mark in the High quality check box, and then clicking OK. Then, use Backstage view to print the document as usual.

To Save and Print the Presentation

With the presentation completed, you should save the file and print handouts for your audience. The following steps save the file and then print a presentation handout with two slides per page.

1. Save the presentation again in the same storage location with the same file name.
2. Open Backstage view, click the Print tab, click 'Full Page Slides' in the Settings area, click 2 Slides in the Handouts area to display a preview of the handout, and then click Print in the Print gallery to print the presentation.
3. sam Because the project now is complete, you can exit PowerPoint.

Summary

In this module you have learned how to create and format a chart and table, insert a text box, reuse slides from another presentation, move slides in Slide Sorter view, crop a picture and then apply styles, convert text to a WordArt graphic, animate an object and text, and insert a video.

Consider This: Plan Ahead

What decisions will you need to make when creating your next presentation?

Use these guidelines as you complete the assignments in this module and create your own slide show decks outside of this class.

1. Audiences recall visual concepts more quickly and accurately than text alone, so consider using graphics in your presentation.
   a) Decide the precise message you want to convey to your audience.
   b) Determine if a chart or table is the better method of presenting the information.
2. Choose an appropriate chart or table.
   a) Charts are excellent visuals to show relationships between groups of data, especially numbers.
   b) Tables are effective for organizing information in a grid.
   c) Decide which chart or table type best conveys the points you are attempting to make in your presentation. PowerPoint provides a wide variety of styles within each category, so determine which one is most effective in showing the relationships.
3. Obtain information for the graphic from credible sources.
   a) Text or numbers should be current and correct.
   b) Verify the sources of the information.
   c) Be certain you have typed the data correctly.
   d) Acknowledge the source of the information on the slide or during your presentation.
4. Choose an appropriate WordArt style.
   a) Determine which style best represents the concept you are attempting to present.
5. Test your visual elements.
   a) Show your slides to several friends or colleagues and ask them to interpret what they see.
   b) Have your test audience summarize the information they perceive on the tables and charts and compare their analyses to what you are attempting to convey.

Student Assignments

Apply Your Knowledge

Reinforce the skills and apply the concepts you learned in this module.

Creating and Formatting a Chart, Table, and WordArt

Note: To complete this assignment, you will be required to use the Data Files. Please contact your instructor for information about accessing the Data Files.

Instructions: Start PowerPoint. Garden club members have scheduled a variety of programs for the next year. They want to encourage community members to attend the events and have asked you to develop slides to publicize the schedule. The annual meeting in January covers budgetary concerns, including sources of revenue. Open the presentation called SC_PPT_3-1.pptx, which is located in the Data Files. You will create a chart and table, format WordArt and a picture, and insert a video to create the presentation shown in Figure 3–99.

Perform the following tasks:

1. On Slide 1 (Figure 3–99a), convert the title text, Garden Club Annual Meeting, to WordArt by applying the 'Pattern Fill: Dark Red, Accent color 1, 50%; Hard Shadow: Dark Red, Accent color 1' WordArt style (third style in the last row). Change the WordArt outline weight to 2¼ pt and the outline color to 'Olive Green, Accent 4' (eighth color in the Theme Colors row). Apply the Square transform text effect (first effect in the first Warp row). Increase the WordArt height to 4".
2. Insert the video with the file name Support_PPT_3_Flowers.mp4 in the Slide 1 content placeholder. Start the video Automatically. Unlock the aspect ratio and then increase the video height to 4.5". Use the smart guides to position the video as shown in Figure 3–99a.
3. Insert a text box under the WordArt and video and then type **Join us at the Fieldhouse on January 15** as the text box text. Change the font to Papyrus and increase the font size to 40 point. Use the smart guides to center the text box near the bottom of the slide, as shown in Figure 3–99a.

   If requested by your instructor, insert a text box on Slide 1 in the lower-right area of the slide and add the name of the first school you attended.
4. On Slide 2 (Figure 3–99b), insert two table rows and then enter the data shown in Table 3–1. Apply the 'Medium Style 2 – Accent 1' table style (second style in the second Medium row). Change the table height to 4" and the width to 9". Align the table in the center of the slide.

Table 3–1

Date	Topic
February 6	Native Plants
April 2	Woodland Flowers
June 4	Garden Walk
August 6	Beneficial Insects
October 8	Garden Design

5. Convert the title text, Upcoming Programs, to WordArt and then apply the 'Fill: Olive Green, Accent color 5; Outline: White, Background color 1; Hard Shadow: Olive Green, Accent color 5' (third style in the third row) style. Change the WordArt outline weight to 1½ pt and the outline color to Dark Red (first color in the Standard Colors row).
6. Apply the Wave: Down transform text effect (first effect in the fifth Warp row) to the title text and then decrease the width to 7.5".

Continued on next page

7. On Slide 3 (Figure 3–99c), delete the title text placeholder. Insert a Pie chart and change the layout to Doughnut (last layout in the Pie gallery). Insert the data shown in Table 3–2.

Table 3–2: Garden Club YTD Revenue

	YTD Revenue
Membership	$2,700
Donations	$2,200
Rentals	$1,100
Grants	$500

8. Increase the chart height to 7" and the width to 11.5". Increase the chart title text to 40 point and change the font to Papyrus. Increase the legend to 20 point and change the font to Papyrus. Align the chart in the middle and the center of the slide.
9. Insert the picture Support_PPT_3_Dahlias.png. Crop the picture as shown in Figure 3–99c. Make sure the Lock aspect ratio box is checked, change the height to 4", and then use the smart guides to align the picture in the center of the slide.
10. Apply the 'Center Shadow Rectangle' picture style (sixth style in the second row) to the picture and then change the color tone to 'Temperature: 11200 K' (last thumbnail).
11. Apply the Fall Over transition in the Exciting category to all slides and then change the duration to 3.00 seconds.
12. View the presentation and then save the file using the file name, **SC_PPT_3_Garden** and submit the revised presentation in the format specified by your instructor.
13. **Consider This:** In this assignment, you formatted WordArt and a picture. You also changed the table style and formatted the chart. How did these edits enhance the presentation? Does the video clip add interest to the presentation? Why or why not?

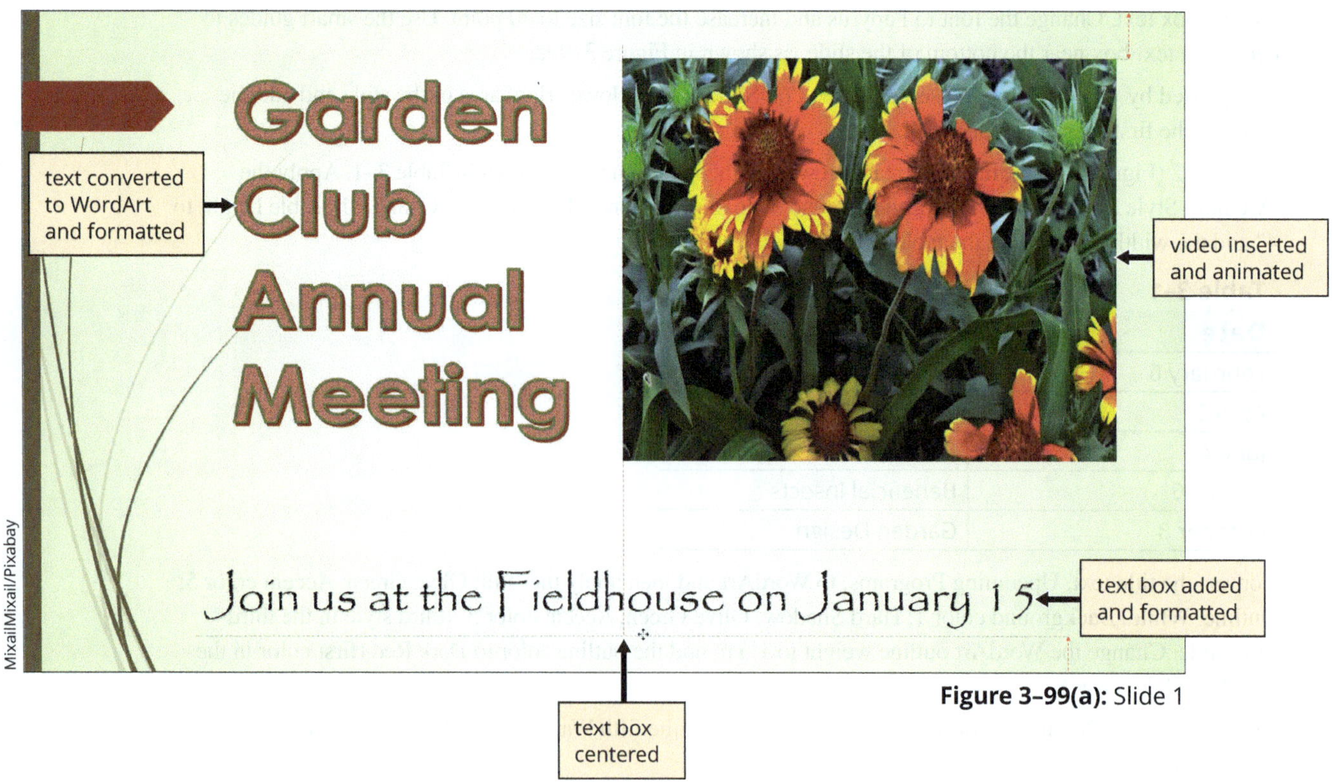

Figure 3–99(a): Slide 1

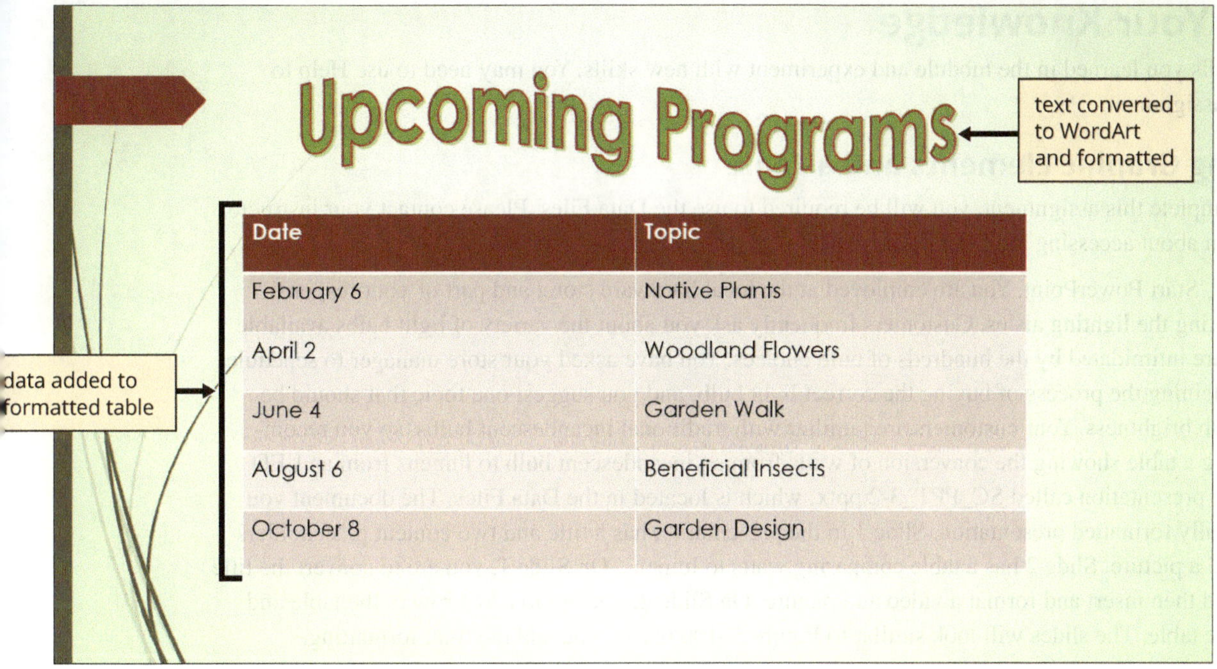

Figure 3–99(b): Slide 2

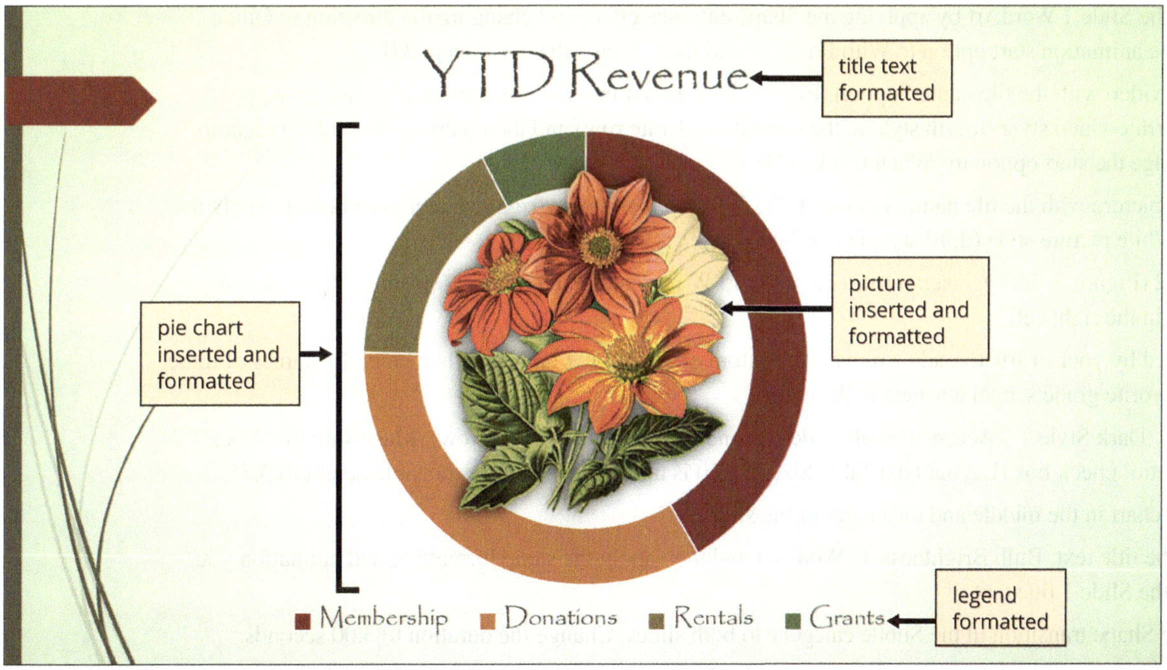

Darkmoon_Art/Pixabay

Figure 3–99(c): Slide 3

Extend Your Knowledge

Extend the skills you learned in the module and experiment with new skills. You may need to use Help to complete the assignment.

Formatting Graphic Elements and a Table

Note: To complete this assignment, you will be required to use the Data Files. Please contact your instructor for information about accessing the Data Files.

Instructions: Start PowerPoint. You are employed at the local hardware store, and part of your responsibilities is stocking the lighting aisles. Customers frequently ask you about the variety of light bulbs available because they are intimidated by the hundreds of bulb choices. You have asked your store manager to schedule a seminar explaining the process of buying the correct light bulb, and you suggest one topic that should be included is bulb brightness. Your customers are familiar with traditional incandescent bulbs, so you recommend including a table showing the conversion of watts from an incandescent bulb to lumens from an LED bulb. Open the presentation called SC_PPT_3-2.pptx, which is located in the Data Files. The document you open is a partially formatted presentation. Slide 1 in the presentation has a title and two content placeholders for a video and a picture. Slide 2 has a table comparing watts to lumens. On Slide 1, you are to convert the title to WordArt and then insert and format a video and picture. On Slide 2, you are to add a row to the table and then format the table. The slides will look similar to Figure 3–100 before you add the final formatting.

Perform the following tasks:

1. On Slide 1 (Figure 3–100a), convert the title text, Buying the Right Light Bulb, to WordArt style 'Fill: White; Outline: Gold, Accent color 1; Glow: Gold, Accent color 1' (fourth style in the second row). Change the text fill color to 'Black, Text 1' (second color in the first Theme Colors row) and then add the 'Glow: 11 point; Gold, Accent color 1' glow text effect (first variation in the third Glow Variations row). Increase the font size to 60 point.
2. Animate the Slide 1 WordArt by applying the Shape entrance effect and changing the direction to Out. Change the animation start option to With Previous and then change the duration to 3.00.
3. Insert the video with the file name Support_PPT_3_Board.mp4 into the left content placeholder. Apply the Rotated White video style (fourth style in the second Moderate row) and then increase the video height to 3.5". Change the start option to 'When Clicked On'.
4. Insert the picture with the file name Support_PPT_3_Bulbs.jpg into the right content placeholder. Apply the Rotated White picture style (third style in the third row).
5. On Slide 2 (Figure 3–100b), insert a row below the 75 W row and then type **100 W** in the left cell and **1500 lm** in the right cell.

   If requested by your instructor, add a row at the bottom of the Slide 2 table and then enter the names of three of your favorite grade school teachers in the cells.
6. Apply the 'Dark Style 1 – Accent 1' table style (second style in the first Dark row). Make sure the 'Lock Aspect Ratio' check box (Layout tab | Table Size group) is unchecked. Change the table height to 3.75".
7. Align the chart in the middle and the center of the slide.
8. Convert the title text, Bulb Brightness, to WordArt and then apply the same formatting and animation you added to the Slide 1 title text.
9. Apply the Shape transition in the Subtle category to both slides. Change the duration to 3.00 seconds.
10. View the presentation and then save the file using the file name, **SC_PPT_3_Bulb** and submit the revised presentation in the format specified by your instructor.
11. **Consider This:** You applied the same formatting and animation to the title text on both slides. You also applied the same style to the picture and video. Does this consistency help or hinder the presentation? Why? In Step 6, you chose a table style in the Dark category. Was this style effective? How did this style improve the slide and increase the audience's attention to the table content?

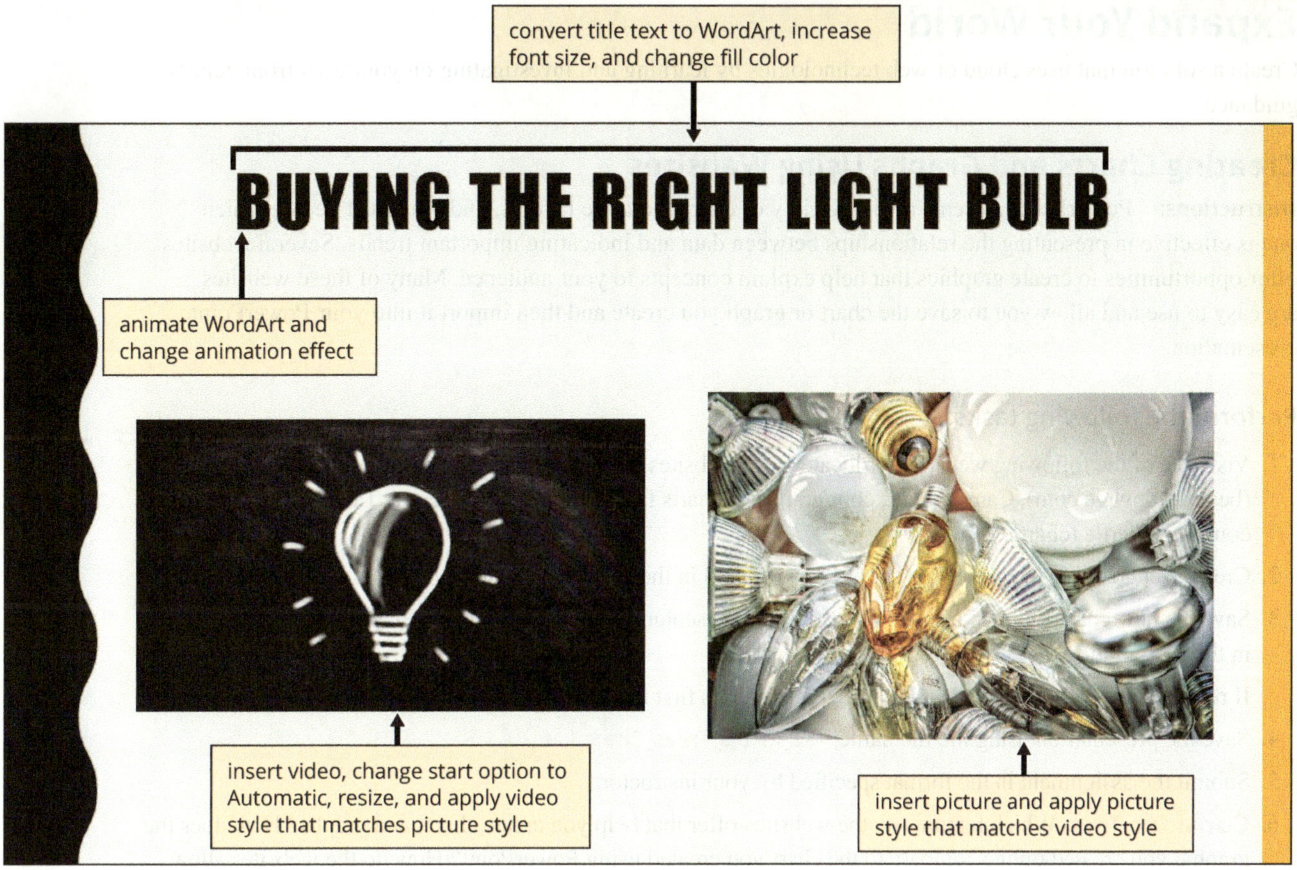

Athree23/Pixabay; Analogicus/Pixabay

Figure 3–100(a): Slide 1

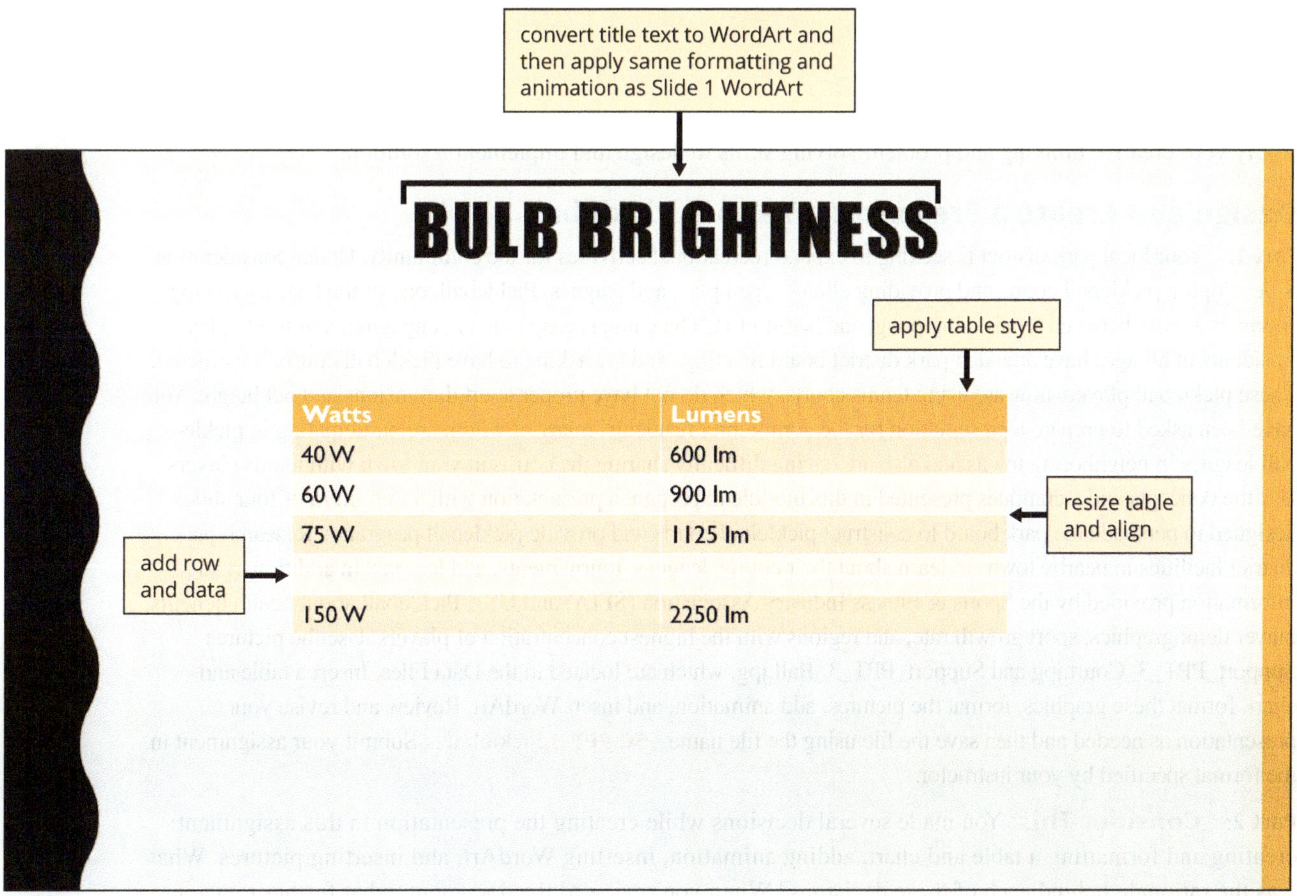

Figure 3–100(b): Slide 2

Expand Your World

Create a solution that uses cloud or web technologies by learning and investigating on your own from general guidance.

Creating Charts and Graphs Using Websites

Instructions: PowerPoint presents a wide variety of chart and table layouts, and you must decide which one is effective in presenting the relationships between data and indicating important trends. Several websites offer opportunities to create graphics that help explain concepts to your audience. Many of these websites are easy to use and allow you to save the chart or graph you create and then import it into your PowerPoint presentation.

Perform the following tasks:

1. Visit one of the following websites, or locate other websites that help you create a chart or graph: Beam (beam.venngage.com), Canva (canva.com/graphs/), Charts Builder (charts.hohli.com), Lucidchart (lucidchart.com), or Chartle (chartle.com).
2. Create a chart using the same data supplied for Slide 3 in the Trees presentation.
3. Save the new chart and then insert it into the Trees presentation as a new Slide 3. Delete the original Slide 3 in the presentation.

   If requested by your instructor, add your grandparent's first name to the chart title.
4. Save the presentation using the file name, **SC_PPT_3_Trees_Chart**.
5. Submit the assignment in the format specified by your instructor.
6. **Consider This:** Which features do the websites offer that help you create charts and graphs? How does the graphic you created online compare to the chart you created using PowerPoint? How do the websites allow you to share your graphics using social networks?

In the Lab

Apply your creative thinking and problem-solving skills to design and implement a solution.

Design and Create a Presentation about Pickleball

Part 1: Your local park district is seeking to expand recreational activities for the community. Under consideration is developing pickleball courts and providing clinics, open play, and leagues. Pickleball, one of the fastest-growing sports, is a cross between tennis, ping pong, and badminton. The game is easy to learn, engaging, and fun to play. Residents of all ages have attended park district board meetings and are asking to have pickleball courts constructed. These pickleball players now are using tennis courts, which do not have proper court dimensions and net height. You have been asked to prepare a presentation for the community residents, many of whom are participating in pickleball leagues in neighboring towns and also are having difficulty sharing the courts in your town with tennis players. Use the concepts and techniques presented in this module to prepare a presentation with a minimum of four slides designed to persuade the park board to construct pickleball courts and provide pickleball programs. Research park district facilities in nearby towns to learn about their courts, leagues, tournaments, and lessons. In addition, read information provided by the Sports & Fitness Industry Association (SFIA) and USA Pickleball about health benefits, player demographics, sport growth rate, and regions with the highest concentration of players. Use the pictures Support_PPT_3_Court.jpg and Support_PPT_3_Ball.jpg, which are located in the Data Files. Insert a table and chart, format these graphics, format the pictures, add animation, and insert WordArt. Review and revise your presentation as needed and then save the file using the file name, **SC_PPT_3_Pickleball**. Submit your assignment in the format specified by your instructor.

Part 2: **Consider This:** You made several decisions while creating the presentation in this assignment: creating and formatting a table and chart, adding animation, inserting WordArt, and inserting pictures. What was the rationale behind each of these decisions? When you reviewed the document, what further revisions did you make and why? Where would you recommend showing this slide show?

Creating a Worksheet and a Chart

Objectives

After completing this module, you will be able to:

- Start an app
- Identify the components of the Microsoft Office ribbon
- Describe the Excel worksheet
- Enter text and numbers
- Use the Sum button to sum a range of cells
- Enter a simple function
- Copy the contents of a cell to a range of cells using the fill handle
- Apply cell styles
- Format cells in a worksheet
- Create a pie chart
- Change a worksheet name and sheet tab color
- Change document properties
- Preview and print a worksheet
- Use the AutoCalculate area to display statistics
- Correct errors on a worksheet
- Use Microsoft Office Help

Introduction

Almost every organization collects vast amounts of data. Often, data is consolidated into a summary so that people in the organization better understand the meaning of the data. An Excel worksheet allows data to be summarized and charted easily. A **chart** is a graphic element that illustrates data using bars, columns, dots, lines, or other symbols to make data easier to understand. In this module, you will create a worksheet that includes a chart. The data in the worksheet and chart comprise a budget that contains quarterly estimates for each income and expense category.

Project: Catering Company Budget Worksheet and Chart

The project in this module follows proper design guidelines and uses Excel to create the worksheet and chart shown in Figure 1–1a and Figure 1–1b. The worksheet contains budget data for Clue Catering Company. Clue Catering Company has compiled a list of the projected expenses and sources of income and wants to use this information to create an easy-to-read worksheet. In addition, they would like a pie chart to show the estimated quarterly expenses by category.

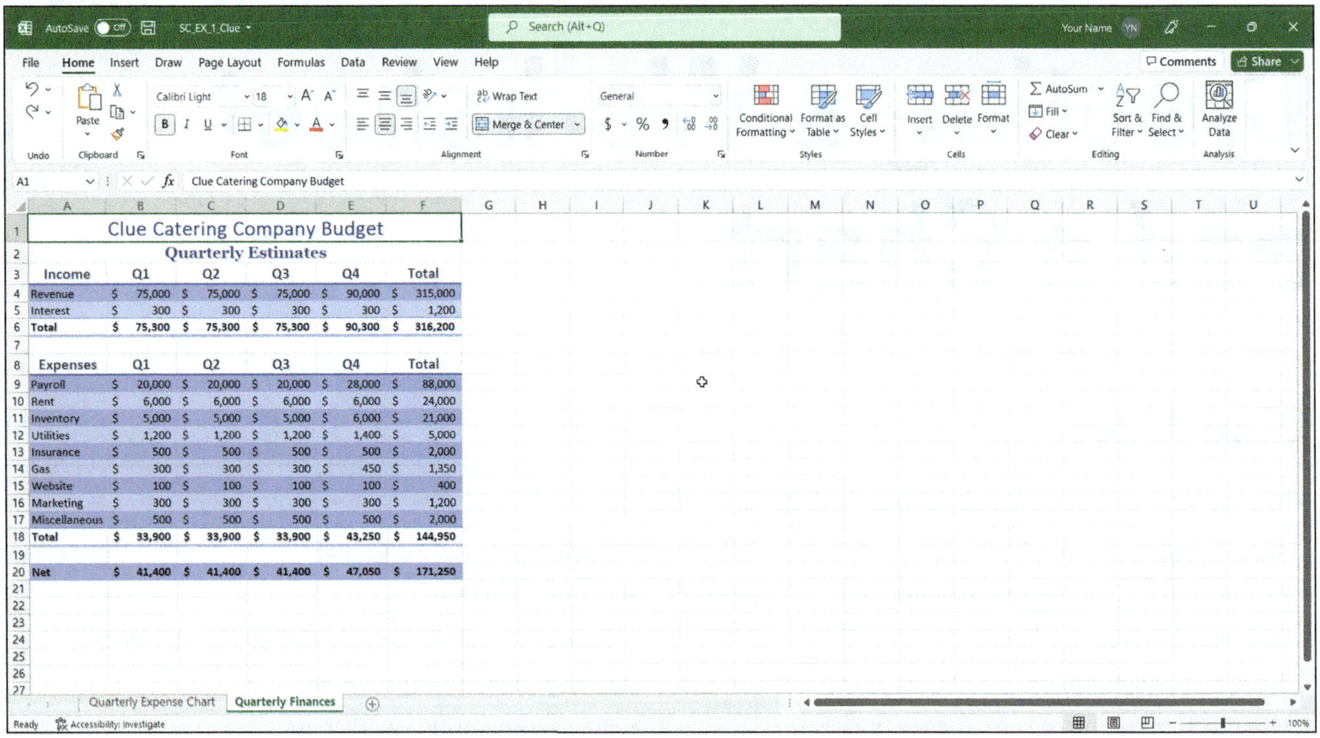

Figure 1–1(a)

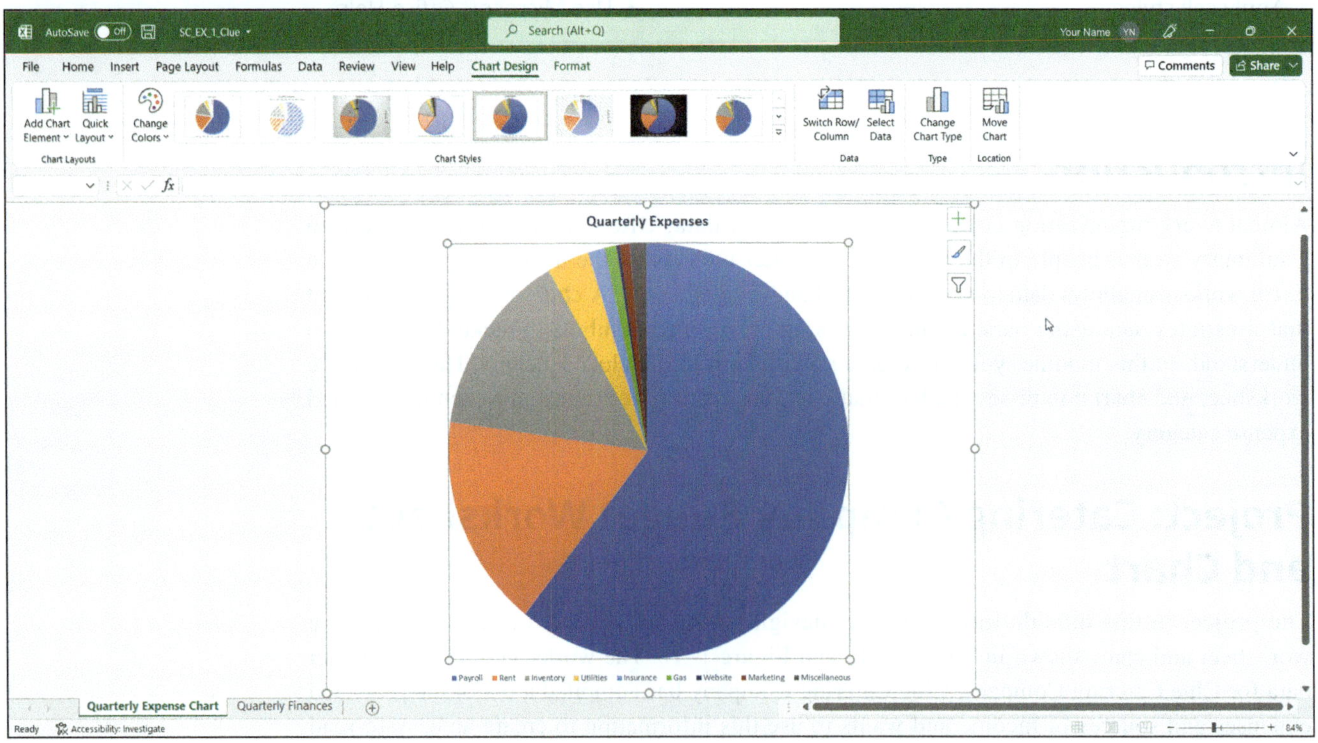

Figure 1–1(b)

The first step in creating an effective worksheet is to make sure you understand what is required. The person or persons requesting the worksheet may supply their requirements in a requirements document, or you can create one. A requirements document includes a needs statement, a source of data, a summary of calculations, and any other special requirements for the worksheet, such as charting and web support. Figure 1–2 shows the requirements document for the new workbook to be created in this module.

Worksheet Title	Clue Catering Company Budget
Need	A yearly projection of Clue Catering Company's budget
Source of data	Data supplied by Clue Catering Company includes quarterly estimates for income and expenses
Calculations	The following calculations must be made: 1. For each quarter, a total for income and expenses 2. For each budget item, a total for the item 3. For the year, total all income and expenses 4. Net income = Total income − Expenses

Figure 1–2

Consider This

Why is it important to plan a worksheet?

The key to developing a useful worksheet is careful planning. Careful planning can reduce your effort significantly and result in a worksheet that is accurate, easy to read, flexible, and useful. When analyzing a problem and designing a worksheet solution, what steps should you follow?

1. Define the problem, including need, source of data, calculations, charting, and web or special requirements.
2. Design the worksheet.
3. Enter the data and formulas.
4. Test the worksheet.

After carefully reviewing the requirements document (Figure 1–2) and making the necessary decisions, the next step is to design a solution or draw a sketch of the worksheet based on the requirements, including titles, column and row headings, the location of data values, and the pie chart, as shown in Figure 1–3. The dollar signs and commas in the sketch of the worksheet indicate formatted numeric values.

Catering Company Budget Worksheet

Income	Q1	Q4	Total
Revenue	$99,999	$99,999	$99,999
Interest			
Total	$99,999	$99,999	$99,999
Expenses	**Q1**	**Q4**	**Total**
Payroll	$99,999	$99,999	$99,999
Rent			
Inventory			
Utilities			
Insurance			
Gas			
Website			
Marketing			
Miscellaneous			
Total	$99,999	$99,999	$99,999
Net	$99,999	$99,999	$99,999

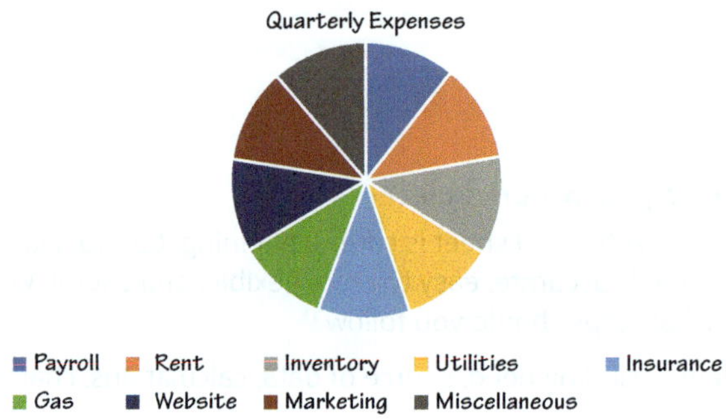

Figure 1–3

With a good understanding of the requirements document, an understanding of the necessary decisions, and a sketch of the worksheet, the next step is to use Excel to create the worksheet and chart.

Starting and Using Excel

What Is Excel?

Microsoft Excel 365 is a powerful spreadsheet app that allows users to organize data, complete calculations, make decisions, graph data, develop professional-looking reports, publish organized data to the web, and access real-time data from websites. The four major parts of Excel are as follows:

- **Workbooks and Worksheets:** A workbook is like a notebook. Inside the workbook are sheets, each of which is called a worksheet. A **worksheet** is a single sheet in a workbook file that lets you enter and manipulate data, perform calculations with data, and analyze data. Thus, a workbook is a collection of worksheets. Worksheets allow users to enter, calculate, manipulate, and analyze data, such as numbers and text. The terms "worksheet" and "spreadsheet" are interchangeable.
- **Charts:** Excel can draw a variety of charts, such as column charts and pie charts.
- **Tables:** Tables organize and store data within worksheets. For example, once a user enters data into a worksheet, an Excel table can sort the data, search for specific data, and select data that satisfies defined criteria.

- **Web Support:** Web support allows users to save Excel worksheets or parts of a worksheet in a format that a user can view in a browser, so that a user can view and manipulate the worksheet using a browser. Excel web support also provides access to real-time data, such as stock quotes, using web queries.

To Start Excel and Create a Blank Workbook

Across the bottom of the Windows desktop is the taskbar. The taskbar contains the **Start button**, a clickable button at in the lower-left corner of the Windows 11 screen that you click to open the Start menu. The **Start menu**, which appears after you click the Start button, provides access to all programs, documents, and settings on the computer. The Start menu may contain one or more folders, and these folders can be used to group related apps together. A **folder** is an electronic container that helps you organize related computer files, like a manilla folder on your desk; it can contain subfolders for organizing files into smaller groups.

The Start menu allows you to start programs, store and search for documents, customize the computer or mobile device, and sign out of a user account or shut down the computer or mobile device. A **menu** is a list of related items, including folders, programs, and commands. Each **command** on a menu performs a specific action, such as saving a file or obtaining help. **Why?** Commands are one of the principal ways you communicate with an app so you can tell it what you want it to do.

The following steps, which assume Windows is running, use the Start menu to start Excel and create a blank workbook based on a typical installation. You may need to ask your instructor how to start Excel on your computer.

1

- **sam** Click the Start button on the Windows taskbar to display the Start menu containing a list of apps installed on the computer or mobile device.
- If necessary, scroll to display Excel (Figure 1–4).

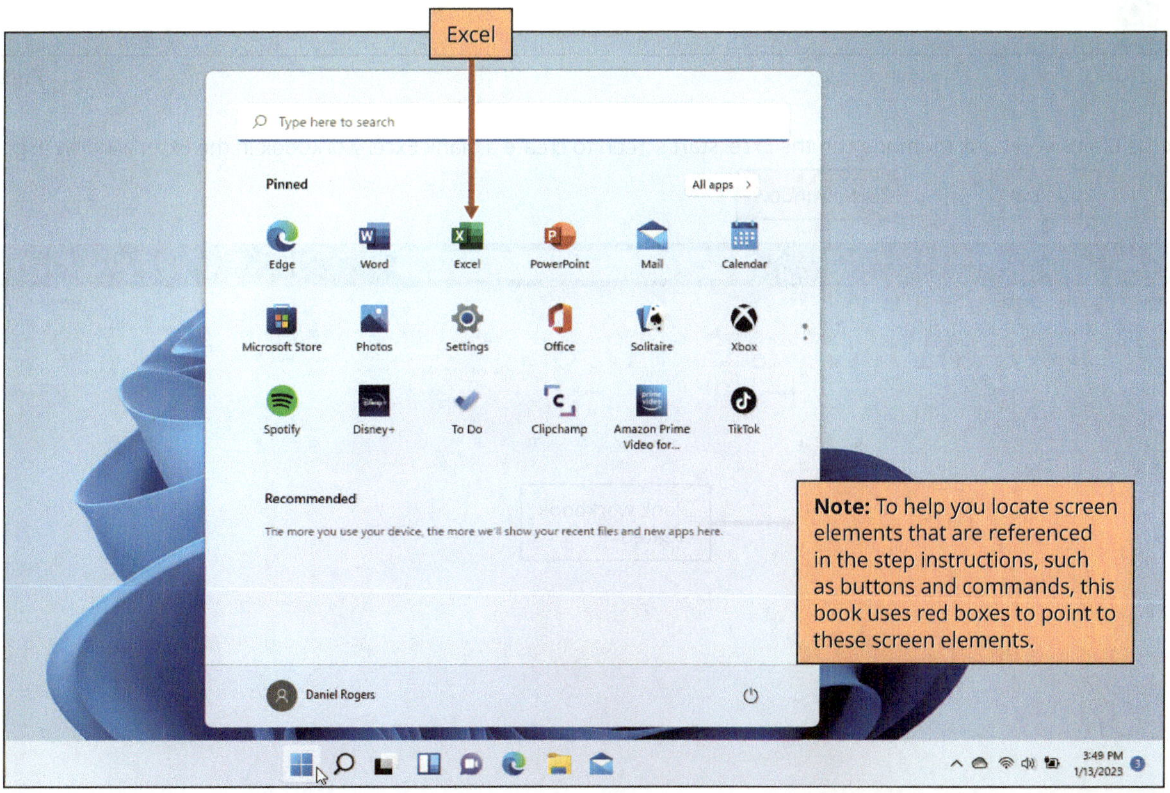

Figure 1–4

2

- Click Excel to start the app (Figure 1–5).

Q&A Why does my screen look different?
Although you will always have an option to create a blank workbook, additional thumbnails may differ based on your software version or how you use Excel.

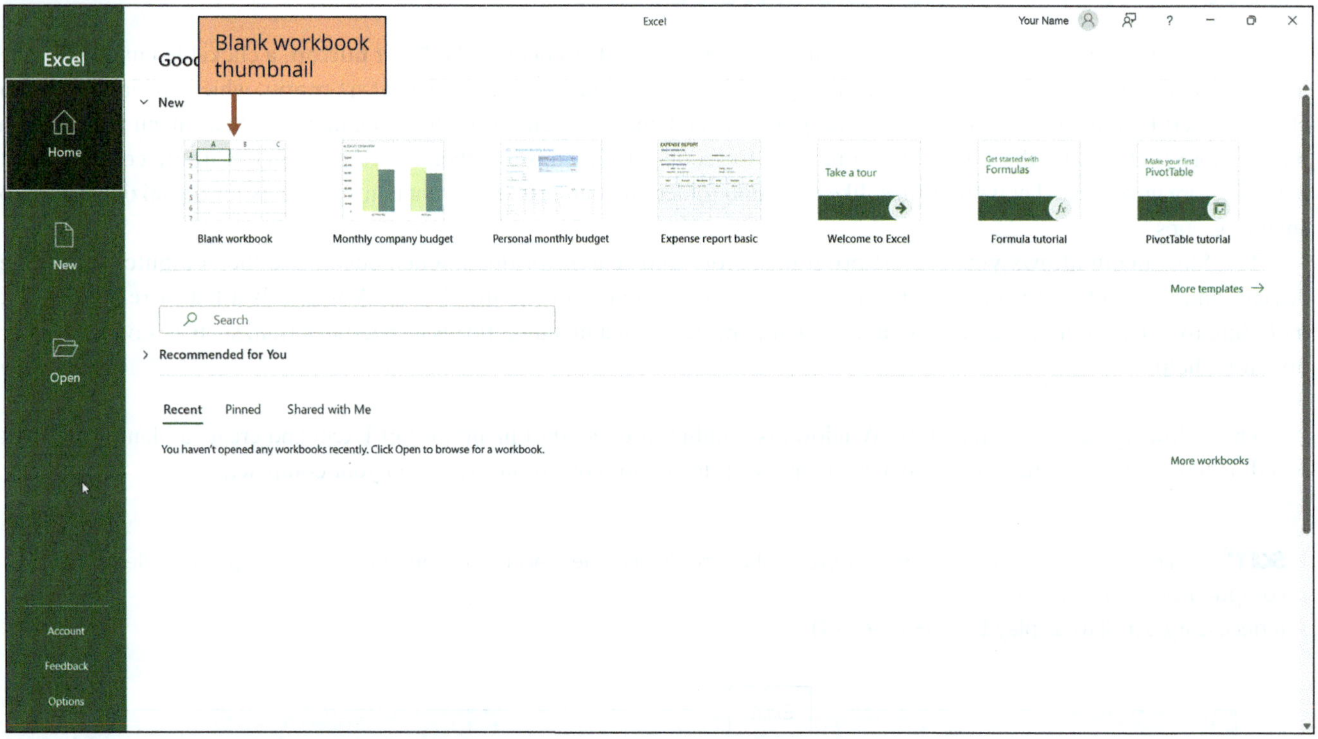

Figure 1–5

3

- Click the Blank workbook thumbnail on the Excel start screen to create a blank Excel workbook in the Excel window (Figure 1–6).

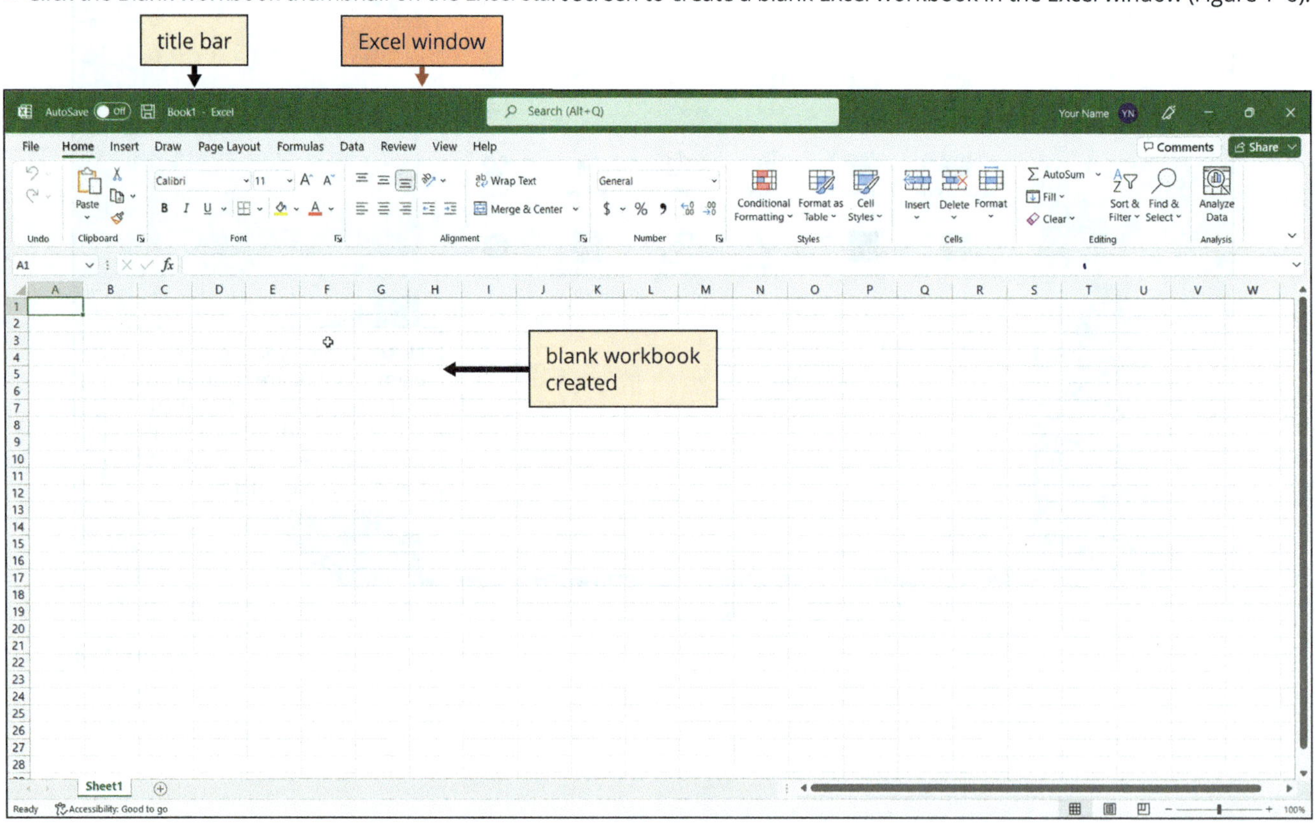

Figure 1–6

Q&A What happens when I start Excel?
Excel provides a means for you to create a blank document, as shown in Figure 1-5. After you click the Blank workbook thumbnail, the Excel window shown in Figure 1-6 opens. A **window** is a rectangular-shaped work area that displays an app or a collection of files, folders, and Windows tools. A window has a **title bar**, an area at the top of a document window or app window that displays the file name and program name.

Other Ways

1. Type app name in search box, click app name in results list
2. Double-click file created in app you want to start

The Excel Window

The Excel window consists of a variety of components to make your work more efficient and worksheets more professional. These include the worksheet window, ribbon, Search box, Quick Access Toolbar, and Microsoft Account area.

Excel opens a new workbook with one worksheet. If necessary, you can add additional worksheets. Each worksheet has a sheet name that appears on a **sheet tab**, an indicator at the bottom of the window that identifies a worksheet. For example, Sheet1 is the name of the active worksheet displayed in the blank workbook shown in Figure 1–7. You can add more sheets to the workbook by clicking the New sheet button.

Worksheet The worksheet is organized into a rectangular grid containing vertical columns and horizontal rows. A column letter in a box above the grid, also called the **column heading**, appears above each worksheet column to identify it. A row number in a box on the left side of a worksheet row, also called the **row heading**, identifies each row.

The intersection of each column and row is a cell. A **cell** is the box, formed by the intersection of a column and a row, where you enter data. Each worksheet in a workbook has 16,384 columns and 1,048,576 rows for a total of 17,179,869,184 cells. Only a small fraction of the active worksheet appears on the screen at one time.

A cell is referred to by its unique address, or **cell reference**, which is the column letter and row number location that identifies a cell within a worksheet, such as A1. To identify a cell, specify the column letter first, followed by the row number. For example, cell reference D3 refers to the cell located at the intersection of column D and row 5 (Figure 1–7).

One cell on the worksheet, designated the **active cell**, is the worksheet cell into which you are entering data, the currently selected cell in the active sheet. The active cell in Figure 1–7 is A1. The active cell is identified in three ways. First, a heavy border surrounds the cell; second, the active cell reference shows immediately above column A in the Name box; and third, the column heading A and row heading 1 are highlighted so that it is easy to see which cell is active (Figure 1–7).

The evenly spaced horizontal and/or vertical lines used in a worksheet or chart are called **gridlines**. Gridlines make a worksheet easier to read. If desired, you can turn the gridlines off so that they do not show on the worksheet. While learning Excel, gridlines help you to understand the structure of the worksheet.

The pointer appears as a block plus sign whenever it is located in a cell on the worksheet. Another common shape of the pointer is the block arrow. The pointer turns into the block arrow when you move it outside the worksheet or when you drag cell contents between rows or columns.

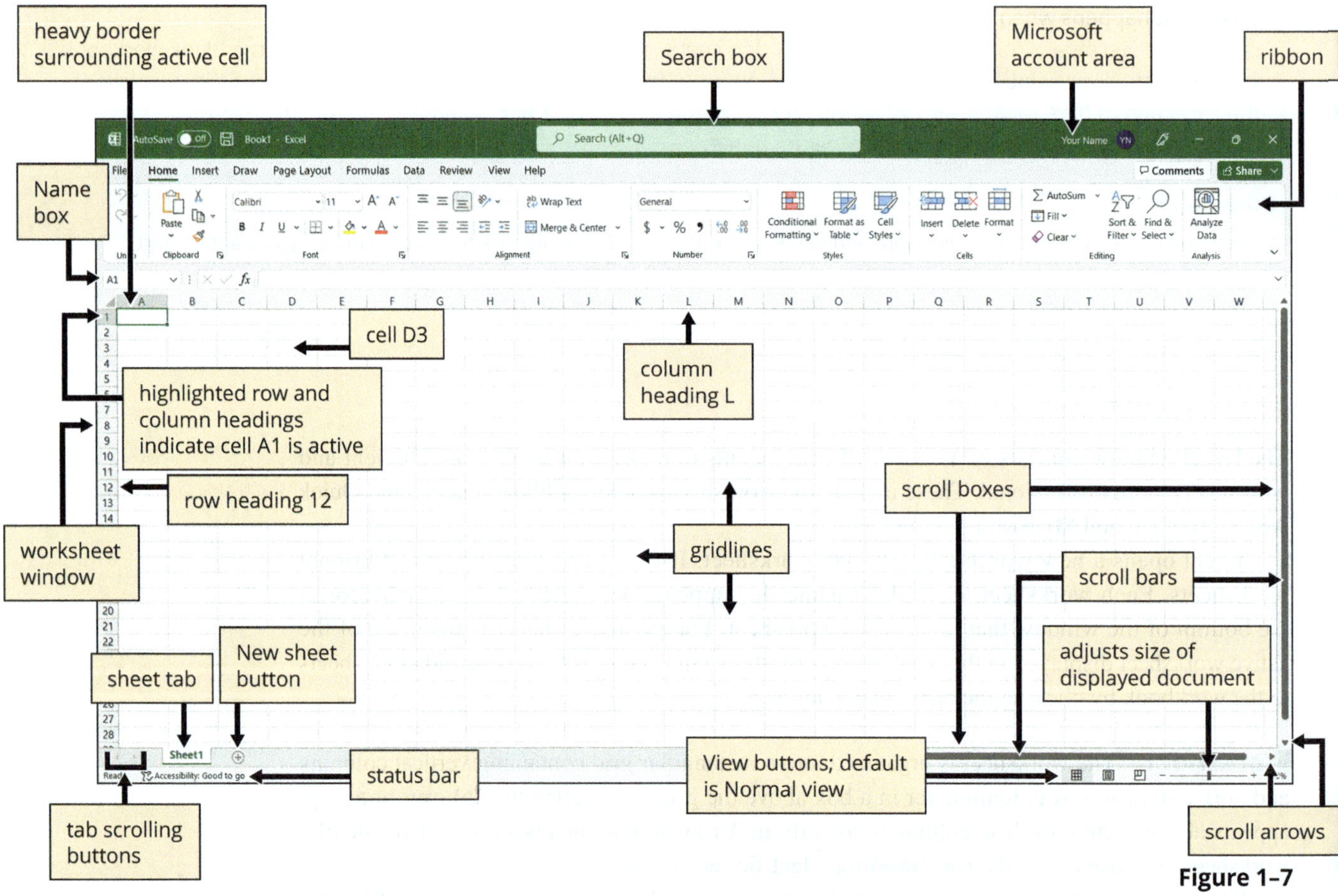

Figure 1–7

Scroll Bars **Scroll bars** on the right edge (vertical scroll bar) and bottom edge (horizontal scroll bar) of a document window let you view a document that is too large to fit on the screen at once. You use a scroll bar to display different portions of a document in the document window. On a scroll bar, the position of the scroll box reflects the location of the portion of the document that is displayed in the document window.

Status Bar The **status bar** is the gray bar at the bottom of the Excel window that shows status information about the currently open worksheet, as well as view buttons and zoom controls. As you type text or perform certain tasks, various indicators and buttons may appear on the status bar. The right side of the status bar includes buttons and controls you can use to change the view of a document and adjust the size of the displayed document.

Ribbon The **ribbon** (shown in Figure 1–7) is a horizontal strip near the top of the window that contains tabs (pages) of grouped command buttons that you click to interact with the app. Each **tab** in the ribbon contains a group of related commands and settings. Each **group** is a section of a tab on the ribbon that contains related commands (shown in Figure 1–8). When you start an Office app, such as Excel, it initially displays several main tabs, also called default or top-level tabs. All Office apps have a Home tab, which contains the more frequently used commands. When you start Excel, the ribbon displays 10 main tabs: File, Home, Insert, Draw, Page Layout, Formulas, Data, Review, View, and Help. (If you are using a desktop computer, you might not see the Draw tab.)

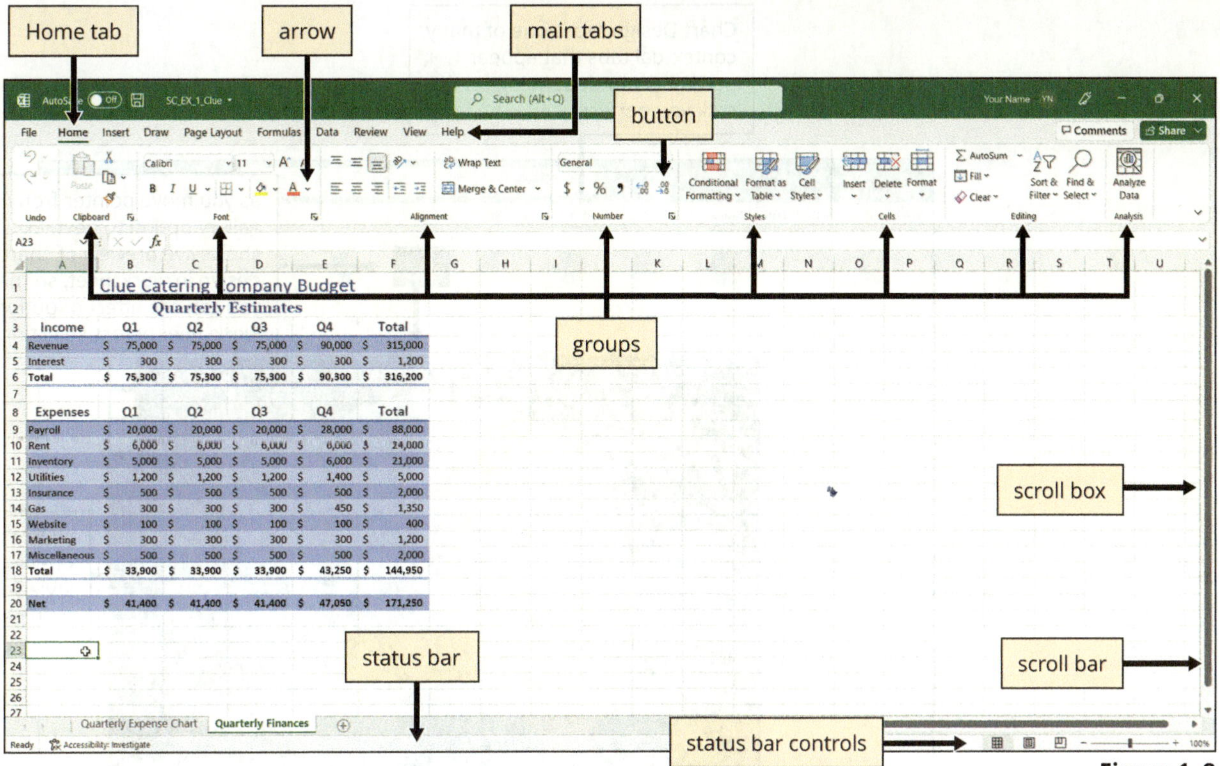

Figure 1–8

In addition to the main tabs, Excel displays other tabs, called **contextual tabs** (Figure 1–9), tabs in addition to the main tabs on the ribbon that appear only in context—that is, when particular types of objects are selected or active, such as pictures or tables, and contain commands for modifying that object. If you insert a chart in an Excel workbook, for example, the Chart Design tab and Format tab appear. When you are finished working with the chart and deselect it, the Chart Design and Format tabs disappear from the ribbon. Excel determines when contextual tabs should appear and disappear based on tasks you perform.

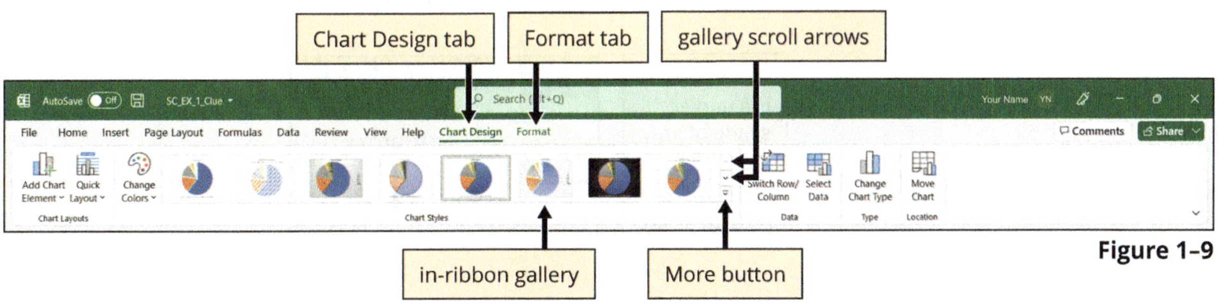

Figure 1–9

Items on the ribbon include buttons and galleries (shown in Figures 1–8 and 1–9). A **gallery** is a collection of choices, arranged in a grid or list, that you can browse through before making a selection of items such as fonts or templates. You can scroll through choices in a gallery by clicking its scroll arrows. You can also click a gallery's More button to view more gallery options on the screen at a time.

Some buttons and boxes have arrows that, when clicked, also display a gallery; others always cause a gallery to be displayed when clicked. Most galleries display a **live preview**, an Office feature that shows the results that would occur in your file, such as the effects of formatting options on a document's appearance, if you clicked the option you are pointing to (Figure 1–10). Live preview works only if you are using a mouse; if you are using a touch screen, you will not be able to view live previews.

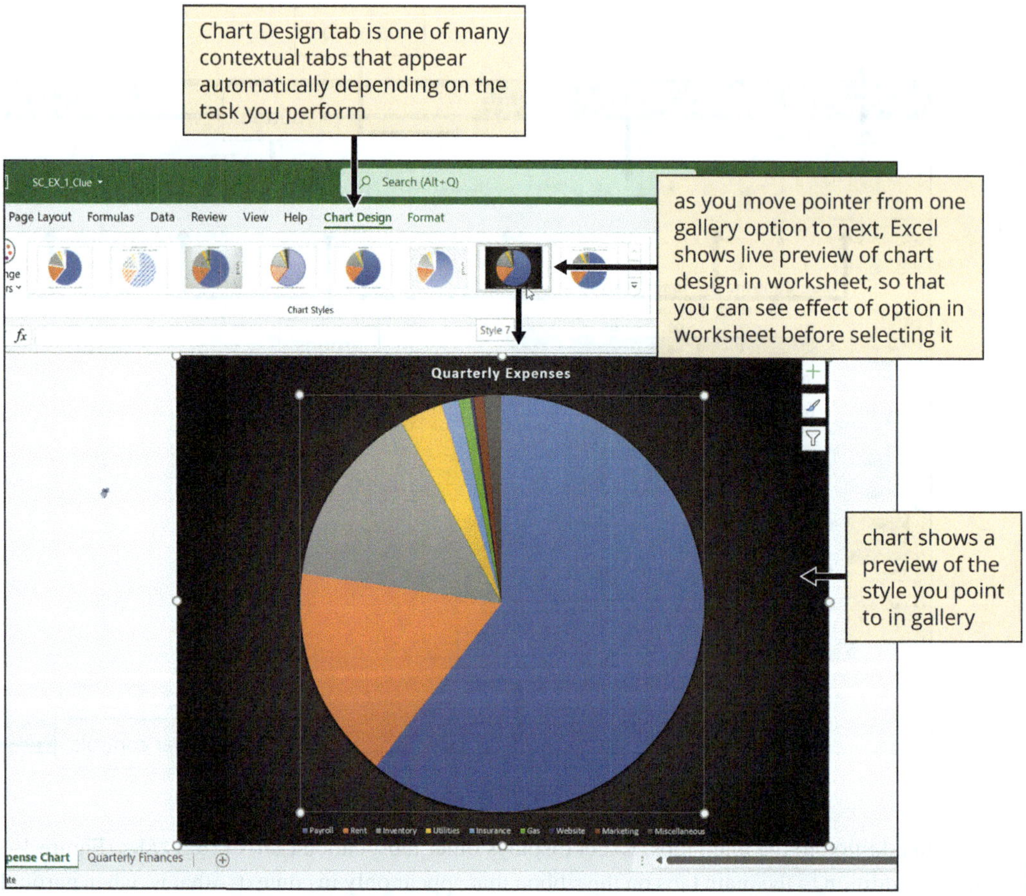

Figure 1–10

Some commands on the ribbon display an image to help you remember their function. When you point to a command on the ribbon, the button is outlined in a dark shade of gray and a ScreenTip appears on the screen. A **ScreenTip** (Figure 1–11) is a label that appears when you point to a button or object, which may include the name, purpose, or keyboard shortcut for the object. It may also include a link to associated Help topics, if any.

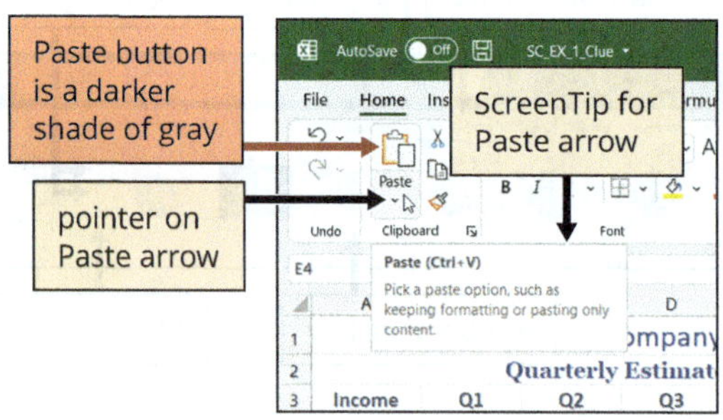

Figure 1–11

Some groups on the ribbon have a small arrow in the lower-right corner, called a **Dialog Box Launcher**, that when clicked displays a dialog box or a pane with more options for the group (Figure 1–12). When presented with a dialog box, you make selections and must close the dialog box before returning to the document. A **pane**, in contrast to a dialog box, is a section of a window, such as the navigation pane in the File Explorer window, that can remain open and visible while you work in the document.

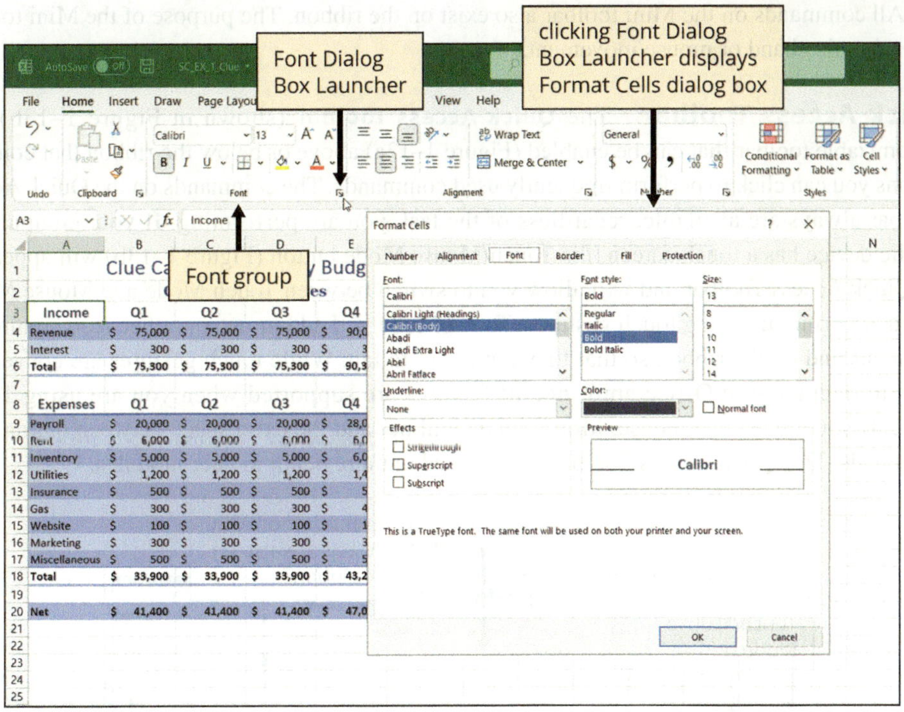

Figure 1–12

Mini Toolbar The **Mini toolbar** is a small toolbar that appears automatically next to selected text and that contains the most frequently used text formatting commands, such as bold, italic, font color, and font size (Figure 1–13b). If you do not use the Mini toolbar, it disappears from the screen. The buttons, arrows, and boxes on the Mini toolbar may vary, depending on whether you are using Touch Mode versus Mouse Mode. If you right-click an item in the document window, Excel displays both the Mini toolbar and a shortcut menu, which is discussed in a later section in this module.

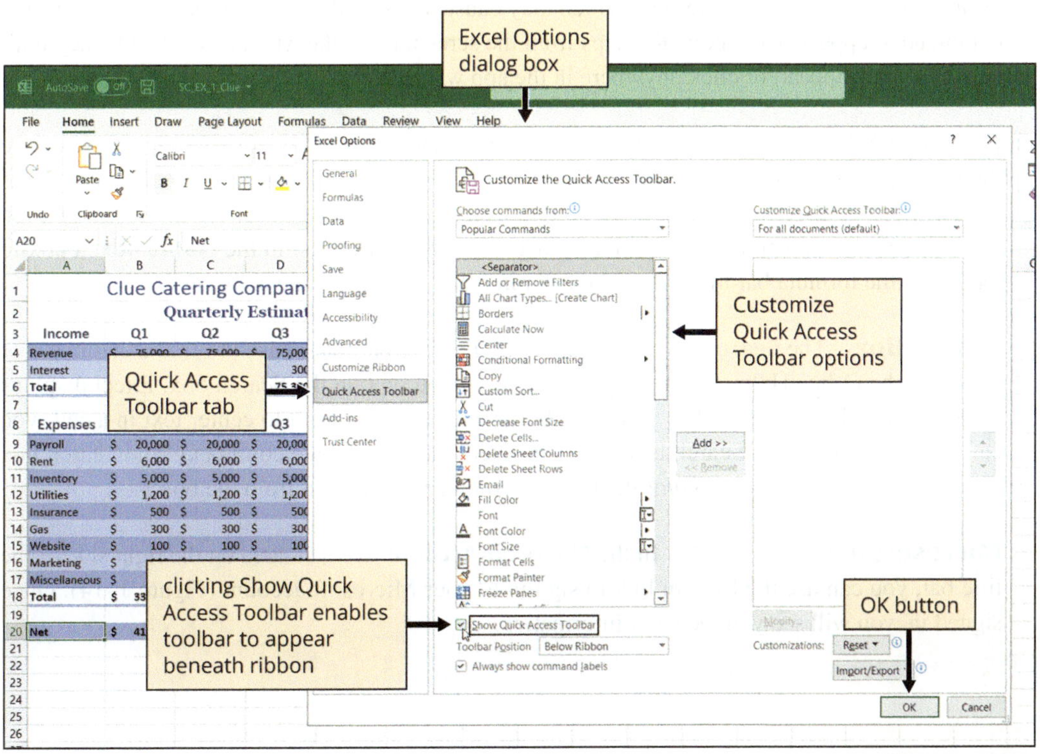

Figure 1–13(a)

All commands on the Mini toolbar also exist on the ribbon. The purpose of the Mini toolbar is to minimize hand or mouse movement.

Quick Access Toolbar The **Quick Access Toolbar** (shown in Figure 1–13b) is a customizable toolbar that can be enabled (Figure 1–13a) above or below the ribbon that contains buttons you can click to perform frequently used commands. The commands on the Quick Access Toolbar always are available, regardless of the task you are performing. If your computer or mobile device has a touch screen, the Touch/Mouse Mode button (Figure 1–13b) will appear on the Quick Access Toolbar and will allow you to switch between Touch Mode and Mouse Mode. If you are primarily using touch gestures, Touch Mode will add more space between commands on menus and on the ribbon so that they are easier to tap. While touch gestures are convenient ways to interact with Office apps, not all features are supported when you are using Touch Mode. If you are using a mouse, Mouse mode will not add the extra space between buttons and commands. The Quick Access Toolbar is discussed in more depth in later modules.

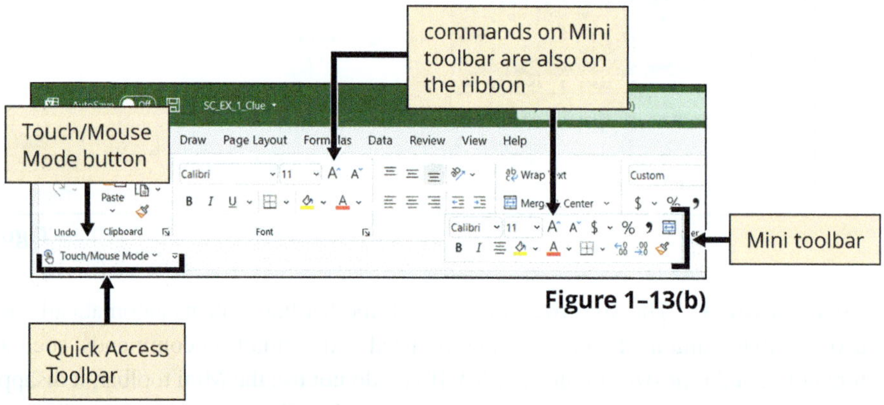

Figure 1–13(b)

KeyTips If you prefer using the keyboard instead of the mouse, you can display KeyTips for certain commands (Figure 1–14). **KeyTips** are labels that appear over each tab and command on the ribbon when the ALT key is pressed. To select a command using the keyboard, press the letter or number displayed in the KeyTip, which may cause additional KeyTips related to the selected command to appear. To remove KeyTips from the screen, press the ALT key or the ESC key until all KeyTips disappear, or click anywhere in the app window.

Formula Bar As you type, Excel displays your entry in the **formula bar**, the area above the worksheet grid where you enter or edit data in the active cell (Figure 1–14). You can make the formula bar larger by dragging the bottom of the formula bar or clicking the expand button to the right of the formula bar. Excel also displays cell information in the **Name box**, a box to the left of the formula bar that shows the cell reference or name of the active cell.

Search Box The **Search box** is a text box on the title bar that is used to find a command or to access the Office Help system (Figure 1–14). As you type in the Search box, Excel displays search results that are refined as you type. For example, if you want to center text in a cell, you can type "center" in the Search box and then select the appropriate command. The Search box also lists related commands and/or the last five commands accessed from the box.

Microsoft Account Area In the **Microsoft Account area**, an area on the right side of the title bar, you can use the Sign in link to sign in to your Microsoft account (Figure 1–14). Once signed in, you will see your account information.

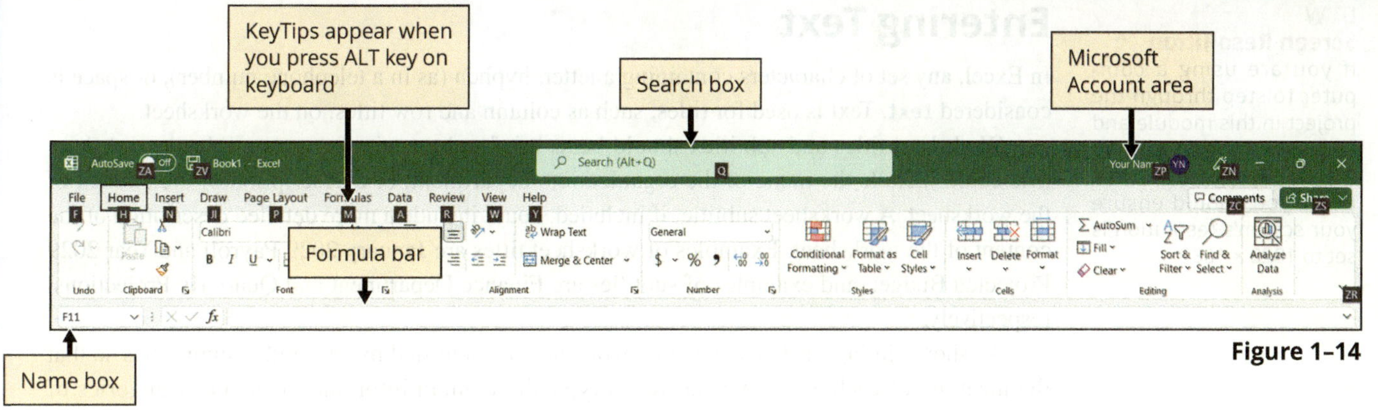

Figure 1–14

To Display a Different Tab on the Ribbon

The ribbon tab currently displayed is called the **active tab**. The following step displays the Insert tab; that is, it makes it the active tab. **Why?** When working with an Office app, you may need to switch tabs to access other options for working with a document.

1

- Click Insert on the ribbon to display the Insert tab (Figure 1–15).
- **Experiment:** Click the other tabs on the ribbon to view their contents.
- Click the View tab, click the Page Layout tab, and then click the Insert tab again.

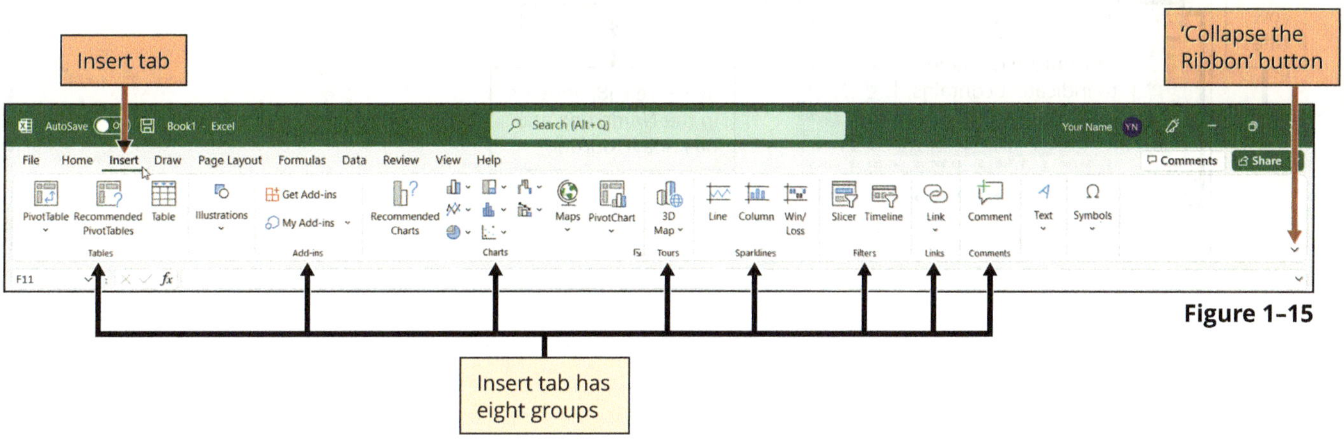

Figure 1–15

Other Ways

1. Press ALT, press letter corresponding to tab to display

Selecting a Cell

To enter data into a cell, you first must select it. The easiest way to **select** a cell (to make it active) is to use the mouse to move the block plus sign pointer to the cell and then click.

An alternative method is to use the arrow keys that are located on a standard keyboard. An arrow key selects the cell adjacent to the active cell in the direction of the arrow on the key.

You know a cell is selected, or active, when a heavy border surrounds the cell and the active cell reference appears in the Name box on the left side of the formula bar. Excel also changes the color of the active cell's column and row headings to a darker shade.

BTW
Touch Mode Differences
The Office and Windows interfaces may vary if you are using Touch Mode. For this reason, you might notice that the function or appearance of your touch screen differs slightly from this module's presentation.

BTW
Screen Resolution
If you are using a computer to step through the project in this module and you want your screens to match the figures in this book, you should ensure your screen's resolution is set to 1920 × 1080.

Entering Text

In Excel, any set of characters containing a letter, hyphen (as in a telephone number), or space is considered **text**. Text is used for titles, such as column and row titles, on the worksheet.

Worksheet titles and subtitles should be as brief and meaningful as possible. A worksheet title could include the name of the organization, department, or a description of the content of the worksheet. A worksheet subtitle, if included, could include a more detailed description of the content of the worksheet. Examples of worksheet titles are January 2029 Payroll and Year 2029 Projected Budget, and examples of subtitles are Finance Department and Quarterly Projections, respectively.

As shown in Figure 1–16, data in a worksheet is identified by row and column titles so that the meaning of each entry is clear. Rows typically contain information such as categories of data. Columns typically describe how data is grouped in the worksheet, such as by quarter or by department.

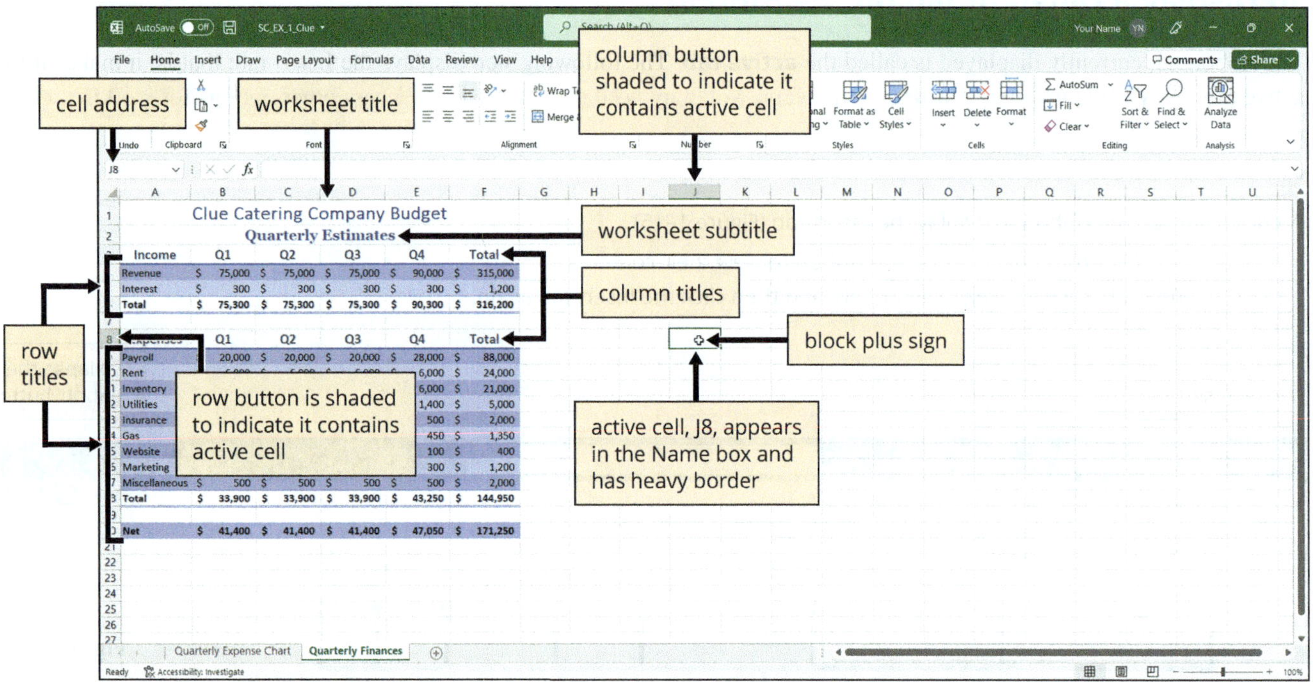

Figure 1–16

To Enter the Worksheet Titles

As shown in Figure 1–16, the worksheet title, Clue Catering Company Budget, identifies the purpose of the worksheet. The worksheet subtitle, Quarterly Estimates, identifies the type of data contained in the worksheet. **Why?** A title and subtitle help the reader to understand clearly what the worksheet contains. The following steps enter the worksheet titles in cells A1 and A2. Later in this module, the worksheet titles will be formatted so that they appear as shown in Figure 1–16.

1

- Click Home on the ribbon to display the Home tab.
- If necessary, click cell A1 to make cell A1 the active cell (Figure 1–17).

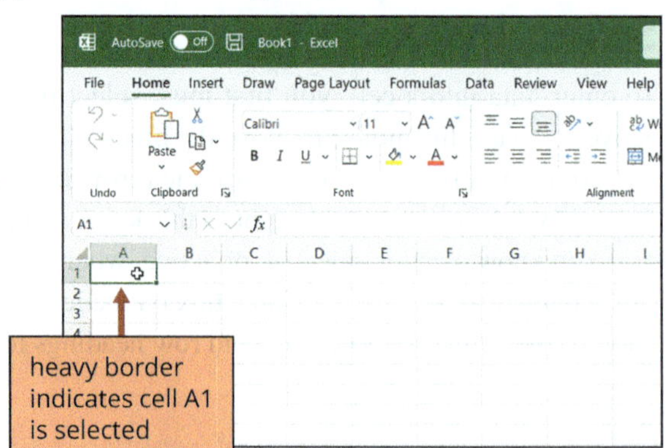

Figure 1–17

2

- Type **Clue Catering Company Budget** in cell A1 (Figure 1–18).

Q&A Why did the appearance of the formula bar change?
Excel displays the title in the formula bar and in cell A1. When you begin typing a cell entry, Excel enables two additional buttons in the formula bar: The Cancel button and the Enter button. Clicking the Enter button completes an entry. Clicking the Cancel button cancels an entry.

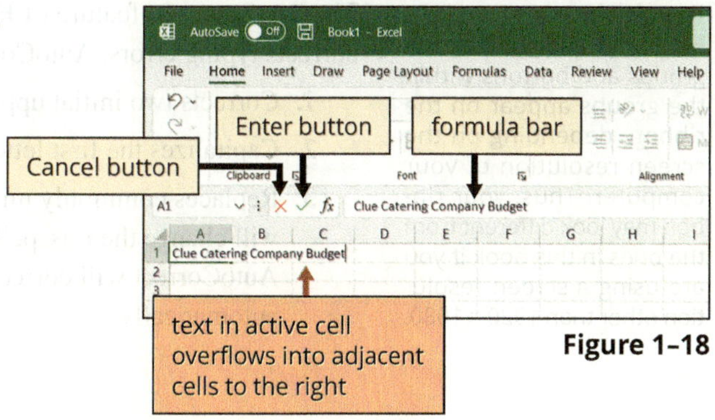

Figure 1–18

3

- Click the Enter button in the formula bar to complete the entry and enter the worksheet title (Figure 1–19).

Q&A Why does the entered text appear in three cells?
When the typed text is longer than the width of a cell, Excel displays the overflow characters in adjacent cells to the right as long as those adjacent cells contain no data. If the adjacent cells contain data, Excel hides the overflow characters. The overflow characters are visible in the formula bar whenever that cell is active.

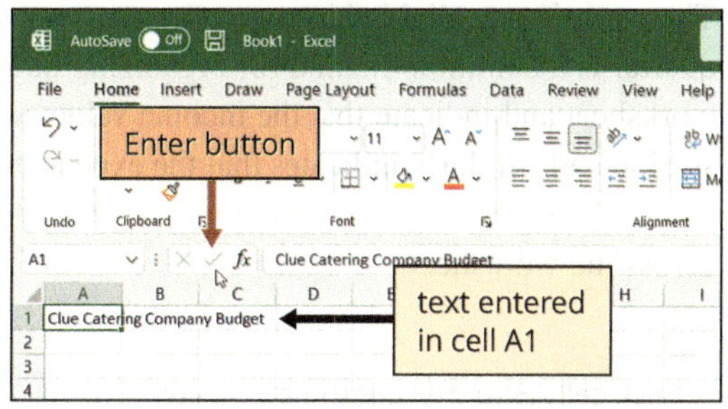

Figure 1–19

4

- Click cell A2 to select it.
- Type **Quarterly Estimates** as the cell entry.
- Click the Enter button to complete the entry and enter the worksheet subtitle (Figure 1–20).

Q&A What happens when I click the Enter button?
When you complete an entry by clicking the Enter button, the insertion point disappears and the cell in which the text is entered remains the active cell.

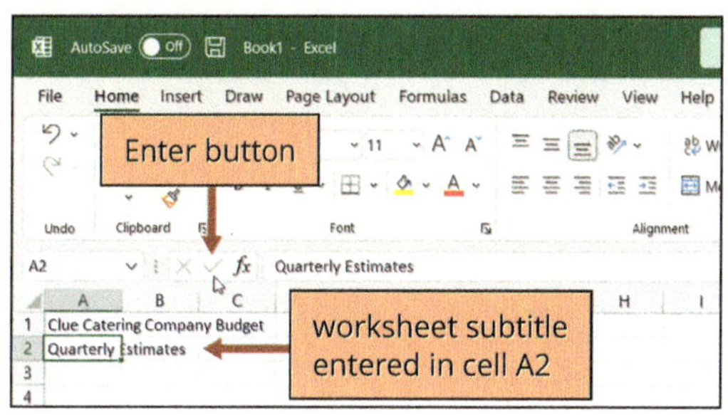

Figure 1–20

Other Ways

1. Click any cell other than active cell
2. Press ENTER
3. Press HOME, PAGE UP, PAGE DOWN, END, UP ARROW, DOWN ARROW, LEFT ARROW, or RIGHT ARROW

Consider This

Why is it difficult to read the text on my screen?

If you are having trouble reading the cell values in your spreadsheet, you can zoom in to make the cells larger. When you zoom in, fewer columns and rows display on your screen, and you might have to scroll more often. To zoom in, drag the zoom slider on the right side of the status bar, or click the plus button on the zoom slider, until you reach your desired zoom level. You also can zoom by clicking the Zoom button (View tab | Zoom group), selecting a desired zoom percentage (Zoom dialog box), and then clicking OK (Zoom dialog box).

BTW
Ribbon and Screen Resolution
Excel may change how the groups and buttons within the groups appear on the ribbon, depending on the screen resolution of your computer. Thus, your ribbon may look different from the ones in this book if you are using a screen resolution other than 1920 × 1080.

AutoCorrect

The **AutoCorrect** feature of Excel works behind the scenes, where it automatically detects and corrects typing errors. AutoCorrect makes three types of corrections for you:

1. Corrects two initial uppercase letters by changing the second letter to lowercase.
2. Capitalizes the first letter in the names of days.
3. Replaces commonly misspelled words with their correct spelling. For example, it will change the misspelled word "recieve" to "receive" when you complete the entry. AutoCorrect will correct the spelling of hundreds of commonly misspelled words automatically.

To Enter Column Titles

The worksheet is divided into two parts, income and expense, as shown in Figure 1–16. Grouping income and expense data by quarter is a common method for organizing budget data. The column titles shown in row 3 identify the income section of the worksheet and indicate that the income values will be grouped by quarter. Likewise, row 8 is clearly identified as the expense section and similarly indicates that the expense values will be estimated on a per-quarter basis. **Why?** Data entered in columns should be identified using column titles to identify what the column contains. The following steps enter the column titles across the worksheet.

1

- Click cell A3 to make it the active cell.
- Type **Income** to begin entry of a column title in the active cell (Figure 1–21).

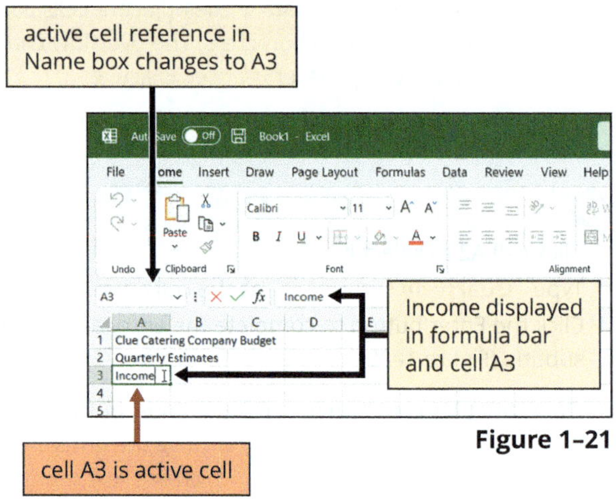

Figure 1–21

2

- Press the RIGHT ARROW key to enter the column title and make the cell to the right the active cell (Figure 1–22).

Q&A Why is the RIGHT ARROW key used to complete the entry in the cell?
Pressing an arrow key to complete an entry makes the adjacent cell in the direction of the arrow (up, down, left, or right) the next active cell. However, if your next entry is in a nonadjacent cell, you can complete your current entry by clicking the next cell in which you plan to enter data. You also can press ENTER and then click the appropriate cell for the next entry.

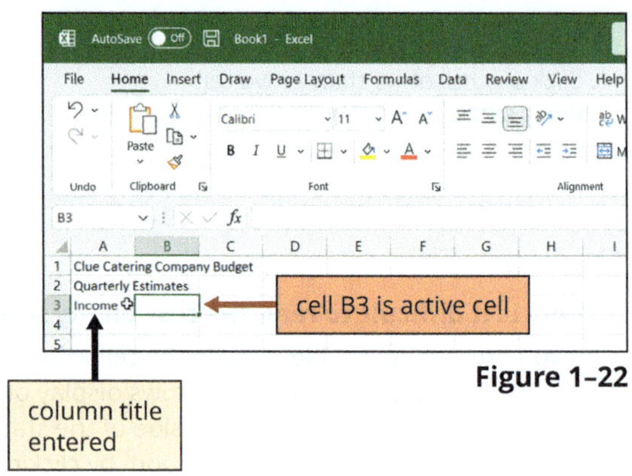

Figure 1–22

3

- Repeat Steps 1 and 2 to enter the remaining column titles; that is, enter **Q1** in cell B3, **Q2** in cell C3, **Q3** in cell D3, **Q4** in cell E3, and **Total** in cell F3 (complete the last entry in cell F3 by clicking the Enter button in the formula bar).
- Click cell A8 to select it.
- Repeat Steps 1 and 2 to enter the remaining column titles; that is, enter **Expenses** in A8, enter **Q1** in cell B8, **Q2** in cell C8, **Q3** in cell D8, **Q4** in cell E8, and **Total** in cell F8 (complete the last entry in cell F8 by clicking the Enter button in the formula bar) (Figure 1–23).

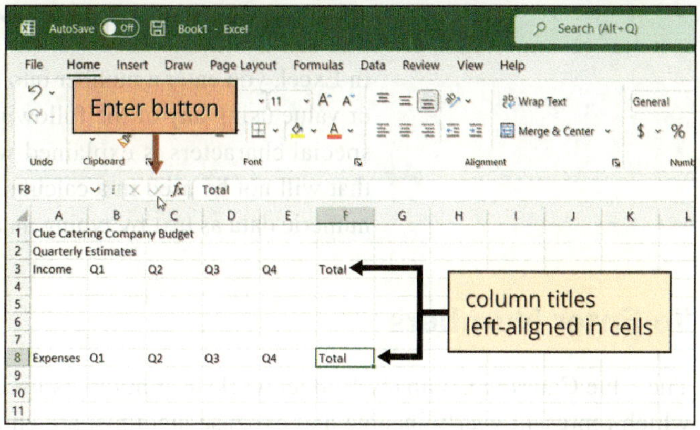

Figure 1–23

To Enter Row Titles

The next step in developing the worksheet for this project is to enter the row titles in column A. For the Clue Catering Company Budget worksheet data, the row titles contain a list of income types and expense types. Each income or expense item should be placed in its own row. **Why?** Entering one item per row allows for maximum flexibility, in case more income or expense items are added in the future. The following steps enter the row titles in the worksheet.

1

- Click cell A4 to select it.
- Type **Revenue** and then click cell A5 or press the DOWN ARROW key to enter a row title (Figure 1–24).

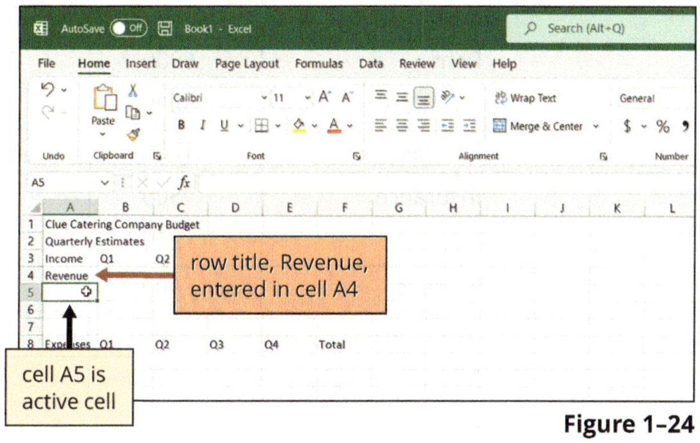

Figure 1–24

2

- Repeat Step 1 to enter the remaining row titles in column A; that is, enter **Interest** in cell A5, **Total** in cell A6, **Payroll** in cell A9, **Rent** in cell A10, **Inventory** in cell A11, **Utilities** in cell A12, **Insurance** in cell A13, **Gas** in cell A14, **Website** in cell A15, **Marketing** in cell A16, **Miscellaneous** in cell A17, **Total** in cell A18, and **Net** in cell A20 (Figure 1–25).

Q&A Why is the text left-aligned in the cells?
Excel automatically left-aligns the text in the cell. Excel treats any combination of numbers, spaces, and nonnumeric characters as text. For example, Excel would recognize the following entries as text: 401AX21, 921–231, 619 321, 883XTY. How to change the text alignment in a cell is discussed later in this module.

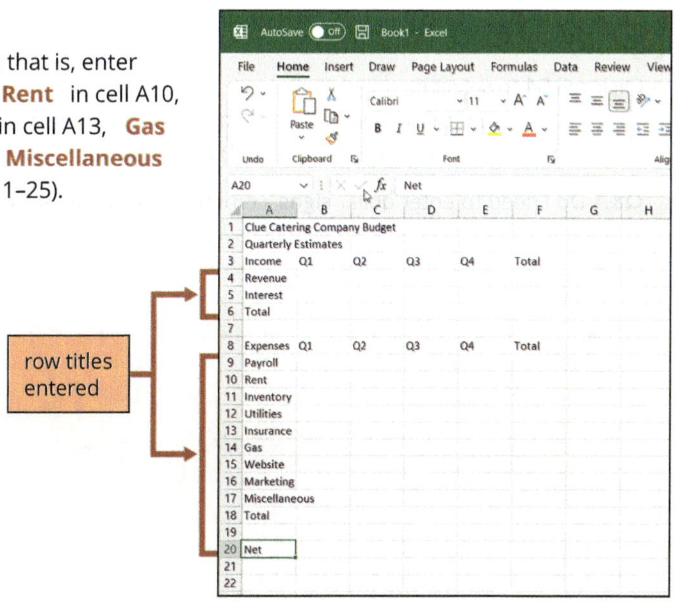

Figure 1–25

Entering Numbers

In Excel, you enter a number into a cell to represent an amount or value. A **number** is an amount or value using any of the following characters: 0 1 2 3 4 5 6 7 8 9 + – ( ) , / . $ E e. The use of special characters is explained when they are used in this book. If you are entering numbers that will not be used in a calculation, you should format those numbers as text. You can format numeric data as text by typing an apostrophe before the number(s).

To Enter Numbers

The Clue Catering Company Budget worksheet numbers used in Module 1 are summarized in Table 1–1. These numbers, which represent yearly income and expense amounts, are entered in rows 4–5 and 9–17. **Why?** One of the most powerful features of Excel is the ability to perform calculations on numeric data. Before you can perform calculations, you first must enter the data. The following steps enter the numbers in Table 1–1 one row at a time.

Table 1–1: Clue Catering Company Budget Worksheet

Income	Q1	Q2	Q3	Q4
Revenue	75000	75000	75000	90000
Interest	300	300	300	300

Expenses	Q1	Q2	Q3	Q4
Payroll	20000	20000	20000	28000
Rent	6000	6000	6000	6000
Inventory	5000	5000	5000	6000
Utilities	1200	1200	1200	1400
Insurance	500	500	500	500
Gas	300	300	300	450
Website	100	100	100	100
Marketing	300	300	300	300
Miscellaneous	500	500	500	500

1

- Click cell B4 to select it.
- Type **75000** and then press the RIGHT ARROW key to enter the data in the selected cell and make the cell to the right (cell C4) the active cell (Figure 1–26).

Q&A Do I need to enter dollar signs, commas, or trailing zeros for the amounts?
You are not required to type dollar signs, commas, or trailing zeros. When you enter a dollar value that has cents, however, you must add the decimal point and the numbers representing the cents. Later in this module, you will learn how to format numbers with dollar signs, commas, and trailing zeros to improve their appearance and readability.

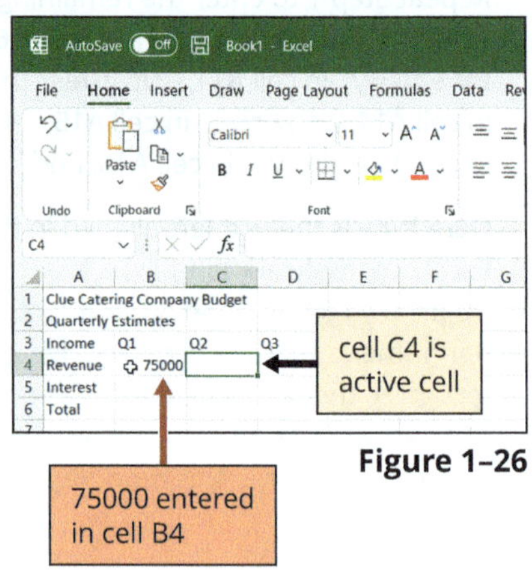

Figure 1–26

2

- Refer to Table 1-1 and enter the appropriate values in cells C4, D4, and E4 to complete the first row of numbers in the worksheet (Figure 1-27).

Q&A Why are the numbers right-aligned?
When you enter numeric data in a cell, Excel recognizes the values as numbers and automatically right-aligns the values in order to vertically align decimal and integer values.

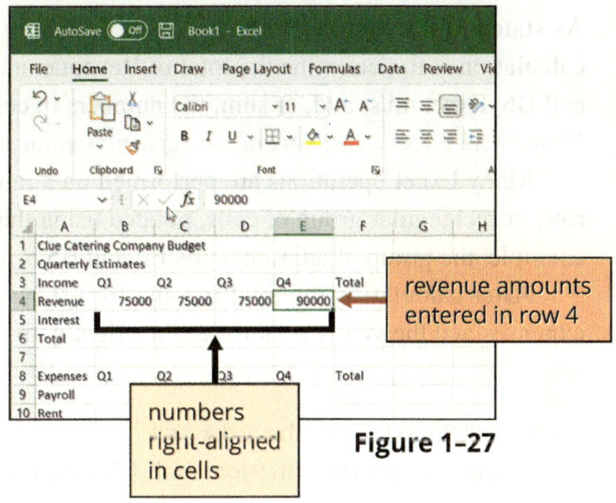

Figure 1-27

3

- Click cell B5 to select it.
- Enter the remaining numbers provided in Table 1-1 for each of the ten remaining budget items in row 5 and rows 9–17 (Figure 1-28).

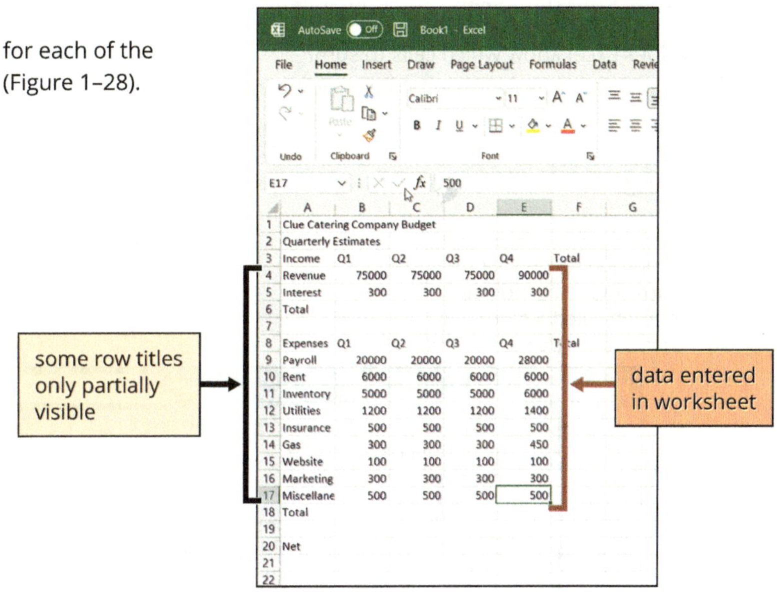

Figure 1-28

Calculating Sums and Using Formulas

The next step in creating the worksheet is to perform any necessary calculations, such as calculating the column and row totals. In Excel, you can easily perform calculations using a function. A **function** is a special, predefined formula that provides a shortcut for a commonly used calculation, for example, SUM or COUNT. When you use functions, Excel performs the calculations for you, which helps to prevent errors and allows you to work more efficiently.

To Sum a Column of Numbers

As stated in the requirements document in Figure 1–2, totals are required for each quarter and each budget item. The first calculation is to determine the total of Revenue and Interest income in the first quarter (column B). To calculate this value in cell B6, Excel must add, or sum, the numbers in cells B4 and B5. The **SUM function** adds all the numbers in a range of cells. **Why?** The Excel SUM function is an efficient means to accomplish this task.

Many Excel operations are performed on a range of cells. A **range** is a series of two or more adjacent cells in a column, row, or rectangular group of cells, notated using the cell address of its upper-left and lower-right corners, such as B5:C10. For example, the group of adjacent cells B4 and B5 is a range.

After calculating the total income for Q1, you will use the fill handle to calculate the quarterly totals for income and expenses and the yearly total for each budget item. The following steps sum the numbers in column B.

1

- Click cell B6 to make it the active cell.
- Click the AutoSum button (Home tab | Editing group) to enter a formula in the formula bar and in the active cell (Figure 1–29).

Q&A What if my screen displays the Sum menu?
If you are using a touch screen, you may not have a separate AutoSum button and AutoSum arrow. In this case, select the desired option (Sum) on the AutoSum menu.

How does Excel know which cells to sum?
Excel automatically selects what it considers to be your choice of the range to sum. When proposing the range, Excel first looks for a range of cells with numbers above the active cell and then to the left. If Excel proposes the wrong range, you can correct it by dragging through the correct range before pressing ENTER. You also can enter the correct range by typing the beginning cell reference, a colon (:), and the ending cell reference.

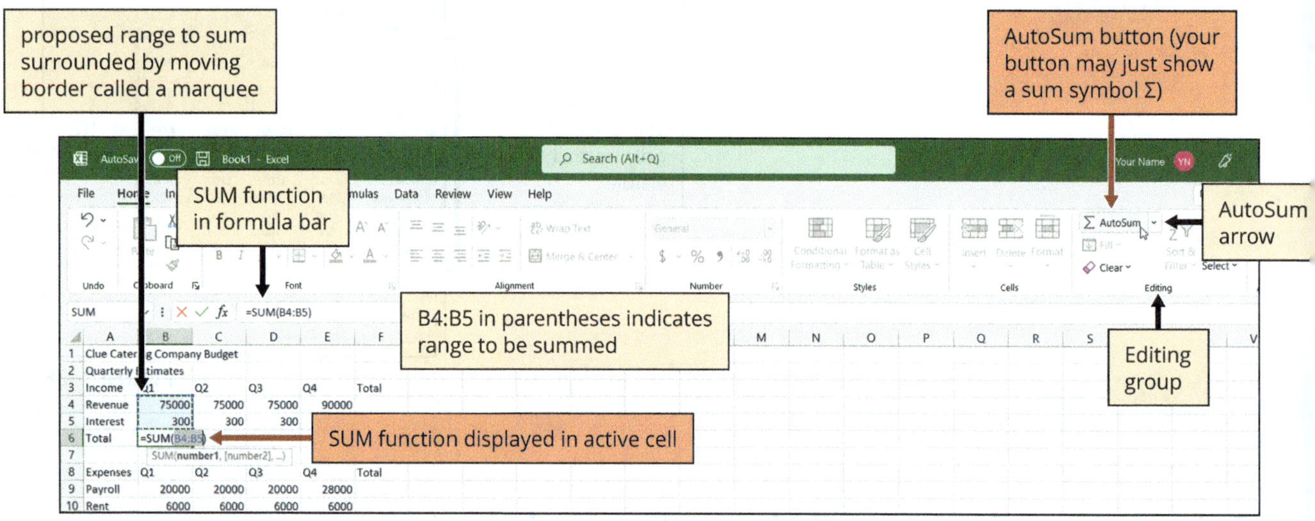

Figure 1–29

2

- Click the Enter button in the formula bar to enter the sum in the active cell.

Q&A What is the purpose of the arrow next to the AutoSum button on the ribbon?
The AutoSum arrow (shown in Figure 1–29) displays a list of functions that allow you to easily determine the average of a range of numbers, the number of items in a selected range, or the maximum or minimum value of a range.

3

- Repeat Steps 1 and 2 to enter the SUM function in cell B18 (Figure 1-30).

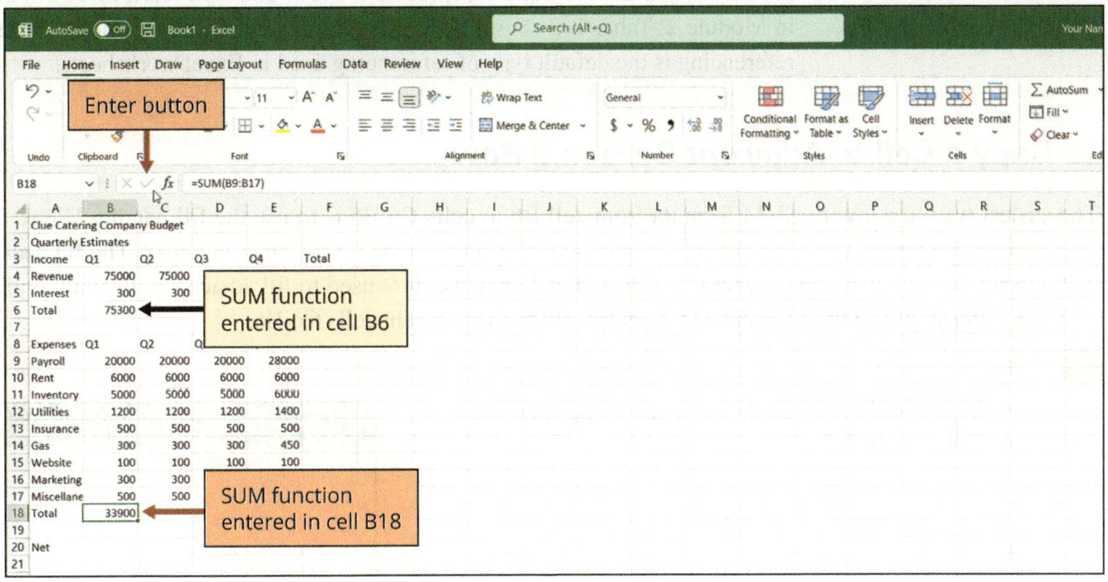

Figure 1-30

Other Ways

1. Click Insert Function button in formula bar, select SUM in Select a function list, click OK (Insert Function dialog box), click OK (Function Arguments dialog box)
2. Click AutoSum arrow (Home tab | Editing group), click More Functions in list, scroll to and then click SUM (Insert Function dialog box), click OK, select range (Function Arguments dialog box), click OK
3. Type **=s** in cell, select SUM in list, select range, click Enter button
4. Press ALT+EQUAL SIGN (=) twice

Using the Fill Handle to Copy a Cell to Adjacent Cells

You want to calculate the income totals for each quarter in cells B6:E6. Table 1–2 illustrates the similarities between the function and range used in cell B6 and the function and ranges required to sum the totals in cells C6, D6, and E6.

To calculate each total for each range across the worksheet, you could follow the same steps shown previously in Figure 1–29 and Figure 1–30. A more efficient method, however, would be to copy the SUM function from cell B6 to the range C6:E6. A range of cells you are cutting or copying is called the **source area** or **copy area**. The range of cells to which you are pasting is called the **destination area** or **paste area**.

BTW
The SUM Function
You can use the SUM function to add values in different ways. In addition to using a cell range, you can also use individual values or cell references. For instance, =SUM(B4:B5) returns the same value as =SUM(B4, B5).

Table 1–2: Sum Function Entries in Row 6

Cell	SUM Function Entries	Result
B6	=SUM(B4:B5)	Sums cells B4 and B5
C6	=SUM(C4:C5)	Sums cells C4 and C5
D6	=SUM(D4:D5)	Sums cells D4 and D5
E6	=SUM(E4:E5)	Sums cells E4 and E5

Although the SUM function entries in Table 1–2 are similar to each other, they are not exact copies. The range in each SUM function entry uses cell references that are one column to the right of the previous column. When you copy and paste a formula that includes a cell reference,

Excel uses a **relative reference**, a cell address that automatically changes to reflect the new location when the formula is copied or moved. You will learn more about relative references in Module 2. Table 1–2 shows how Excel adjusts the SUM functions entries in row 6. Relative referencing is the default type of referencing used in Excel worksheets.

To Copy a Cell to Adjacent Cells in a Row

The easiest way to copy the SUM formula from cell B6 to cells C6:E6 is to use the fill handle. **Why?** Using the fill handle copies content to adjacent cells using one action, which is more efficient than other methods. The **fill handle** is a black square that appears in the lower-right corner of a selected cell or range. It is used to fill adjacent cells with duplicate or similar data. The following steps use the fill handle to copy cell B6 to the adjacent cells C6:E6.

1

- With cell B6 active, point to the fill handle; your pointer changes to a crosshair (Figure 1–31).

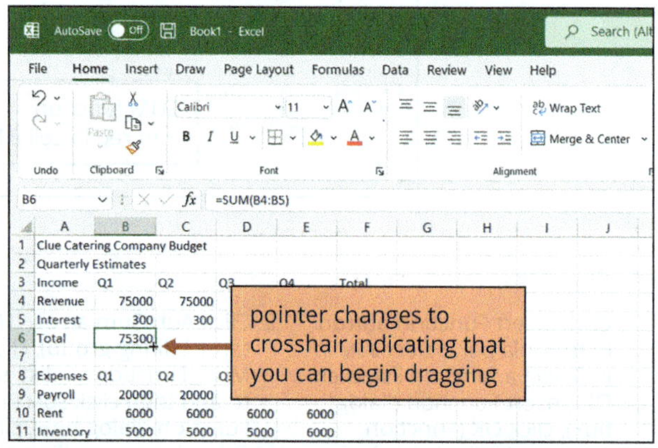

Figure 1–31

2

- Drag the fill handle to select the destination area, the range C6:E6, which will draw a heavy green border around the source area and the destination area (Figure 1–32). Do not release the mouse button.

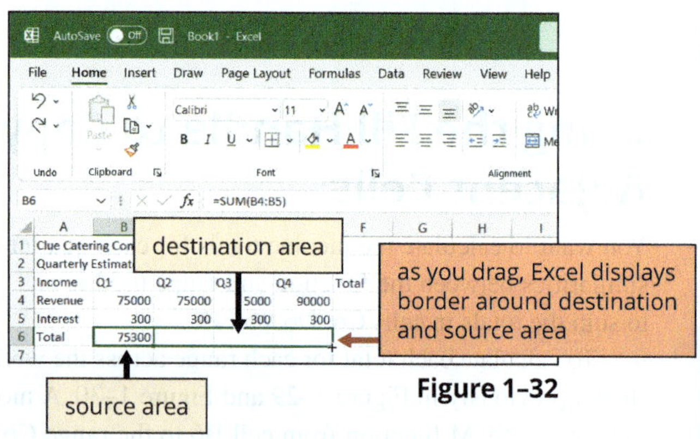

Figure 1–32

3

- Release the mouse button to copy the SUM function from the active cell to the destination area and calculate the sums (Figure 1–33).

Q&A What is the purpose of the Auto Fill Options button?
The Auto Fill Options button allows you to choose whether you want to copy the values from the source area to the destination area with the existing formatting, without the formatting, or with the formatting but without the functions.

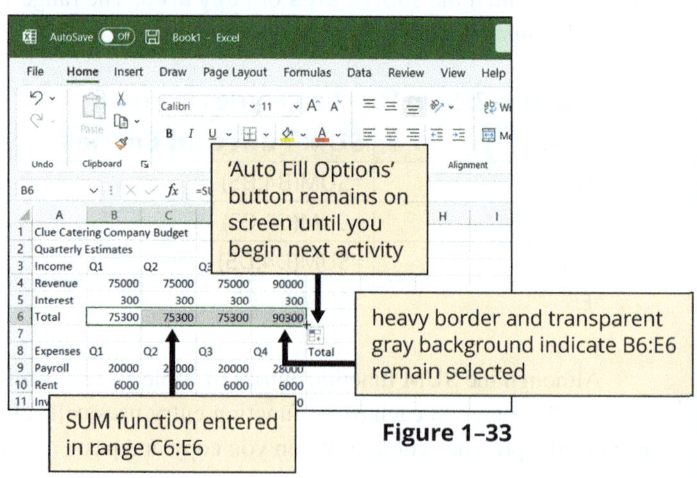

Figure 1–33

4

- Repeat Steps 1–3 to copy the SUM function from cell B18 to the range C18:E18 (Figure 1–34).

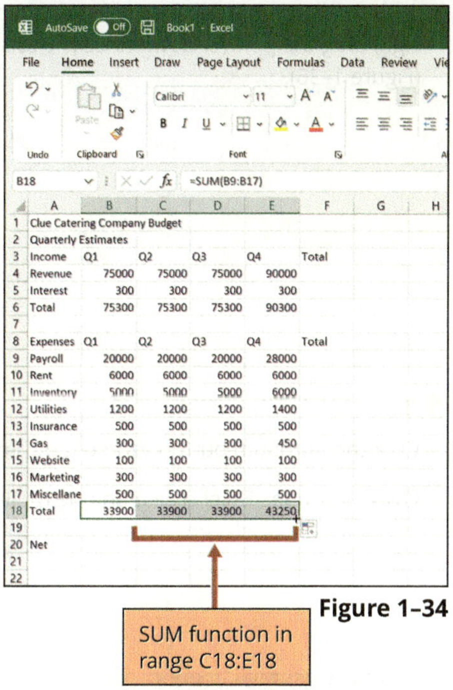

Figure 1–34

Other Ways

1. Select source area, click Copy button (Home tab | Clipboard group), select destination area, click Paste button (Home tab | Clipboard group)
2. Right-click source area, click Copy on shortcut menu, select and right-click destination area, click Paste on shortcut menu
3. Select source and destination areas, click Fill arrow (Home tab | Editing group), click Sum

To Calculate Multiple Totals at the Same Time

The next step in building the worksheet is to determine the total income, total expenses, and total for each budget item in column F. To calculate these totals, you use the SUM function similarly to how you used it to total the income and expenses for each quarter in rows 6 and 18.

In this case, however, Excel will determine totals for all of the rows at the same time. **Why?** By determining multiple totals at the same time, the number of steps to add totals is reduced. The following steps sum multiple totals at once.

1

- Click cell F4 to make it the active cell (Figure 1–35).

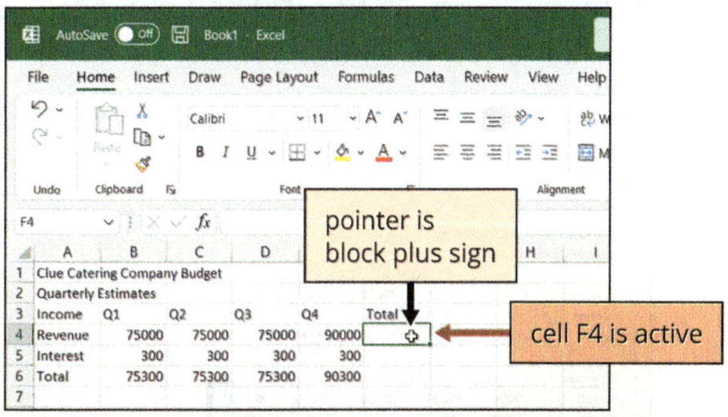

Figure 1–35

2

- With the pointer in cell F4 and in the shape of a block plus sign, drag the pointer down to cell F6 to select the range (Figure 1–36).

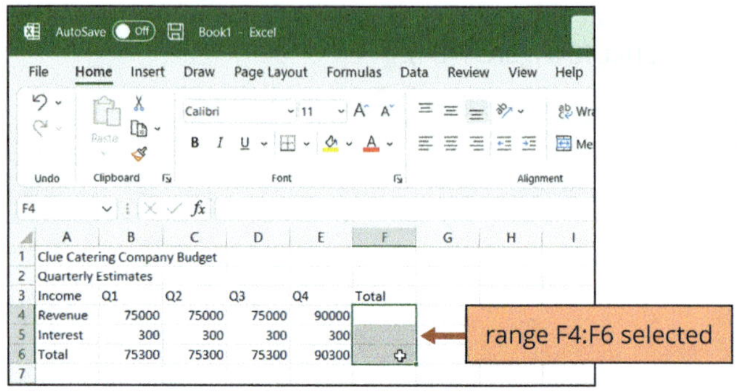

Figure 1–36

3

- Click the AutoSum button (Home tab | Editing group) to calculate the sums of all three rows (Figure 1–37).

Q&A How does Excel create unique totals for each row?

If each cell in a selected range is adjacent to a row of numbers, Excel assigns the SUM function to each cell when you click the Sum button.

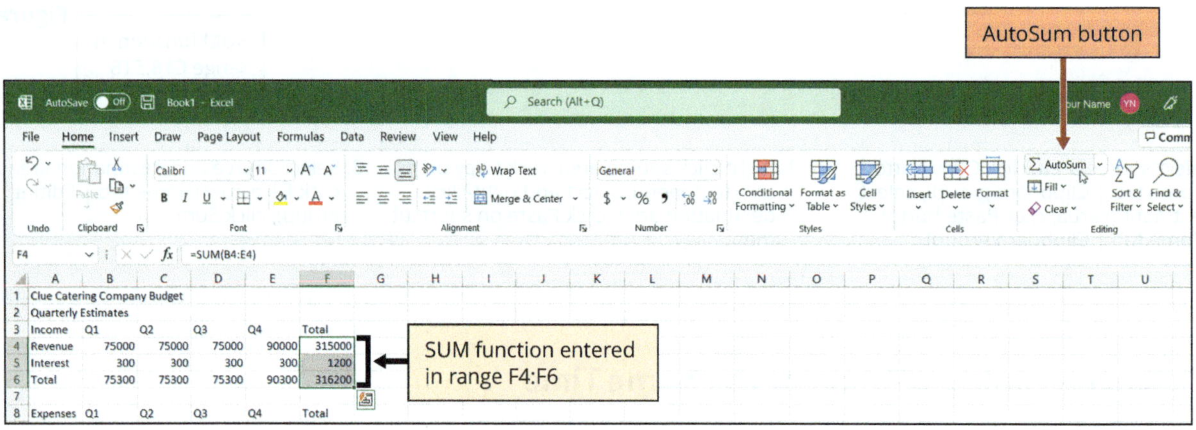

Figure 1–37

4

- Repeat Steps 1–3 to select cells F9 to F18 and calculate the sums of the corresponding rows (Figure 1–38).

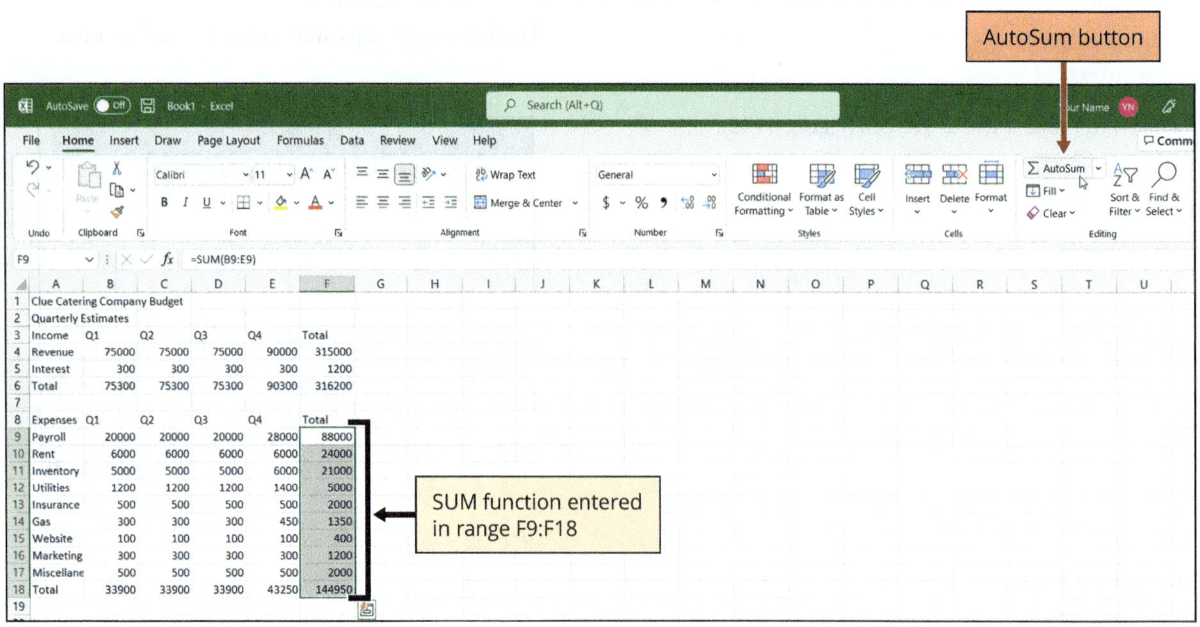

Figure 1–38

Calculating Average, Maximum, and Minimum Values

As you learned earlier in this module, the AutoSum list lets you calculate not only sums but also the average, the number of items, or the maximum or minimum value of a range. You can calculate these using three additional functions: AVERAGE, MAX, and MIN. The AVERAGE function calculates the average value in a range of cells, the MAX function calculates the maximum value in a range of cells, and the MIN function calculates the minimum value in a range of cells. Table 1–3 shows examples of each of these functions.

Table 1-3: AVERAGE, MAX, and MIN Functions

Function	Result
=AVERAGE(H1:H5)	Determines the average of the values in cells H1, H2, H3, H4, and H5
=MAX(H1:H5)	Determines the maximum value entered in cells H1, H2, H3, H4, and H5
=MIN(H1:H5)	Determines the minimum value entered in cells H1, H2, H3, H4, and H5

To Enter a Formula Using the Keyboard

The net for each quarter, which will appear in row 20, is equal to the income total in row 6 minus the expense total in row 18. The formula needed in the worksheet is noted in the requirements document as follows:

Net income (row 20) = Total income (row 6) – Total Expenses (row 18)

The following steps enter the net income formula in cell B20 using the keyboard. **Why?** Sometimes a predefined function does not fit your needs; therefore, you enter a formula of your own.

1

- Select cell B20 to deselect the selected range.
- Type **=b6-b18** in the cell. The formula is displayed in the formula bar and the current cell, and colored borders are drawn around the cells referenced in the formula (Figure 1–39).

Q&A What occurs on the worksheet as I enter the formula?
The equal sign (=) preceding b6–b18 in the formula alerts Excel that you are entering a formula or function and not text. Because the most common error when entering a formula is to reference the wrong cell, Excel highlights the cell references in the formula in color and uses the same colors to highlight the borders of the cells to help ensure that your cell references are correct. The minus sign (–) following b6 in the formula is the arithmetic operator that directs Excel to perform the subtraction operation.

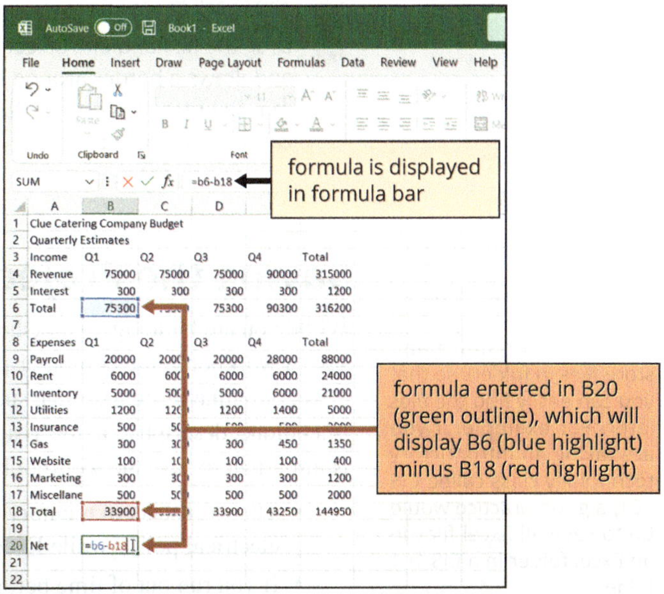

Figure 1–39

2

- Click cell C20 to complete the arithmetic operation, display the result in the worksheet, and select the cell to the right (Figure 1-40).

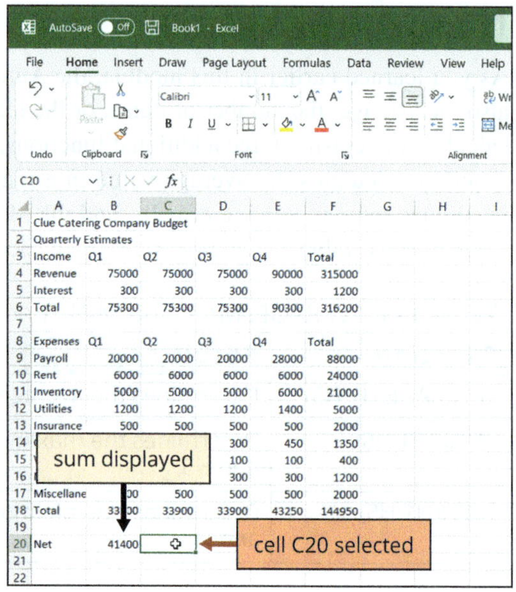

Figure 1-40

To Copy a Cell to Adjacent Cells in a Row Using the Fill Handle

The easiest way to copy the SUM formula from cell B20 to cells C20, D20, E20, and F20 is to use the fill handle. The following steps use the fill handle to copy the formula in cell B20 to the adjacent cells C20:F20.

1. Select cell B20.
2. Drag the fill handle to select the destination area, range C20:F20, which highlights and draws a border around the source area and the destination area. Release the mouse button to copy the function from the active cell to the destination area and calculate the results.

BTW
Organizing Files and Folders
You should organize and store files in folders so that you can easily find the files later. For example, if you are taking an introductory technology class called CIS 101, a good practice would be to save all Excel files in an Excel folder in a CIS 101 folder.

Saving the Project

While you are building a worksheet in a workbook, the computer stores it in memory. When you save a workbook, the computer places it on a storage medium such as a hard drive, USB flash drive, or online using a service such as OneDrive. A saved workbook is called a **file**. A **file name** is a unique, descriptive name assigned to a file when you save it; it identifies the file's contents. It is important to save the workbook frequently for the following reasons:

- The worksheet in memory will be lost if the computer is turned off or you lose electrical power while Excel is open.
- If you run out of time before completing your workbook, you may finish your worksheet at a future time without starting over.

Consider This

Where should you save the workbook?

When saving a workbook, you must decide which storage medium to use:

- If you always work on the same computer and have no need to transport your projects to a different location, then your computer's hard drive will suffice as a storage location. It is a good idea, however, to save a backup copy of your projects on a separate medium, such as an external drive, in case the file becomes corrupted or the computer's hard drive fails. The workbooks used in this book are saved to the computer's hard drive.
- If you plan to work on your workbooks in various locations or on multiple computers or mobile devices, then you should save your workbooks on a portable medium, such as a USB flash drive. Alternatively, you can save your workbooks to an online cloud storage service such as OneDrive.

To Save a Workbook

The following steps save a workbook in the Documents library on the hard drive using the file name, Clue Catering Company Budget. **Why?** You have performed many tasks while creating this project and do not want to risk losing the work completed thus far.

1

- Click File on the ribbon to open Backstage view (Figure 1–41).

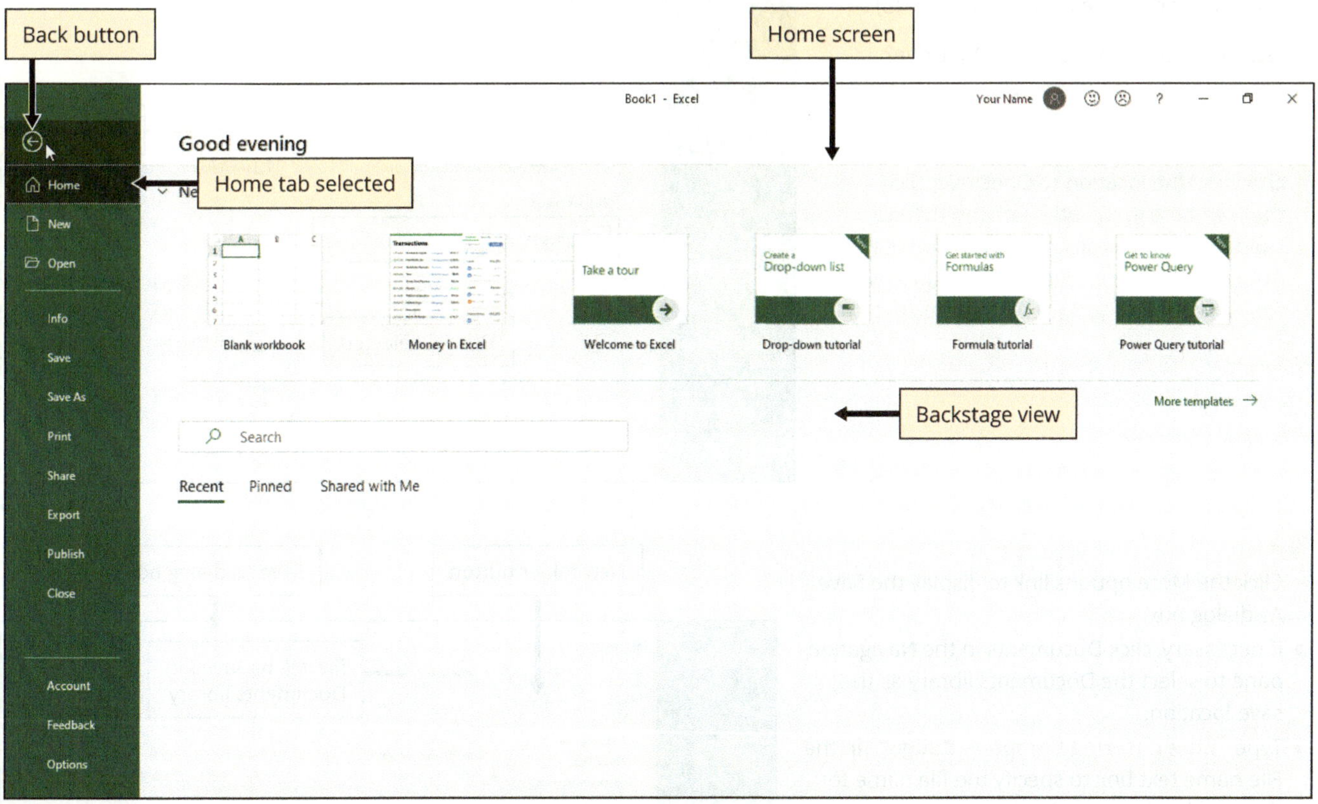

Figure 1–41

2

- Click Save As in Backstage view to display the Save As screen (Figure 1–42).

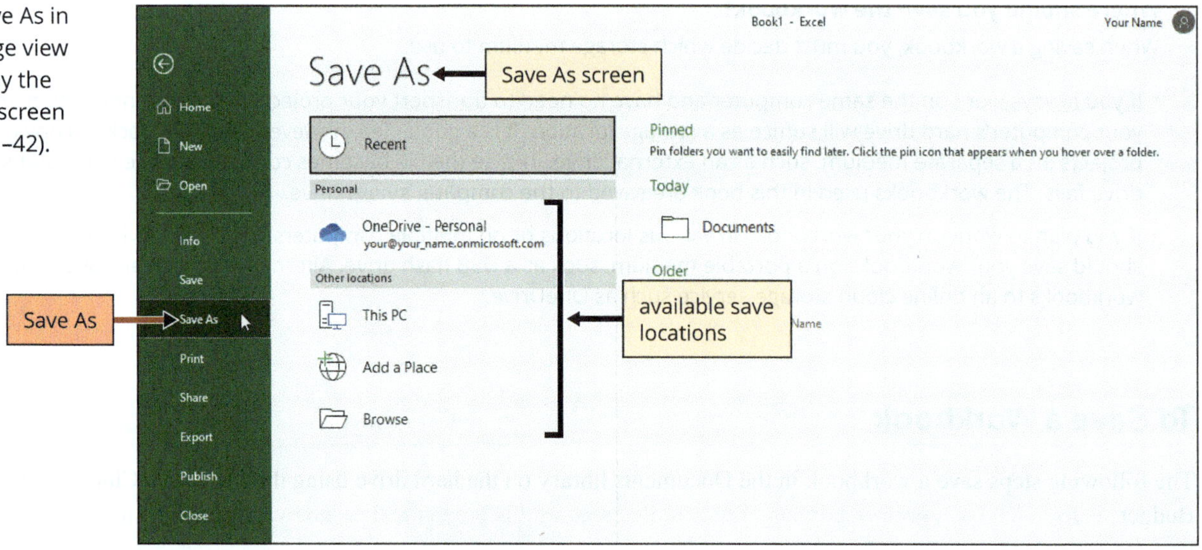

Figure 1–42

3

- Click This PC in the Other locations section to display the default save location on the computer or mobile device (Figure 1–43).

Q&A How can I save a file to OneDrive?
To save a new workbook to OneDrive, click the Save button on the Title bar. To save an existing workbook with the same name while changing the location to OneDrive, click the file name in the title bar, and then click Upload. In both cases, Excel turns on the AutoSave button on the title bar and saves the workbook as you make changes to it.

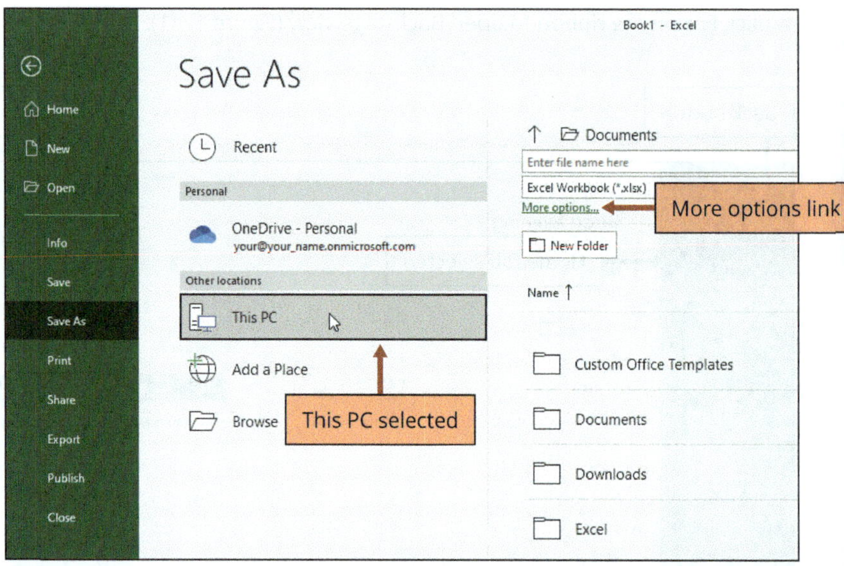

Figure 1–43

4

- Click the More options link to display the Save As dialog box.
- If necessary, click Documents in the Navigation pane to select the Documents library as the save location.
- Type **Clue Catering Company Budget** in the File name text box to specify the file name for the workbook (Figure 1–44).

Q&A Do I have to save to the Documents library?
No. You can save to any device or folder. A folder is a specific location on a storage medium. You can save to the default folder or a different folder. You also can create your own folders by clicking the New folder button shown in Figure 1–44. To save to a different location, navigate to that location in the Navigation pane instead of clicking Documents.

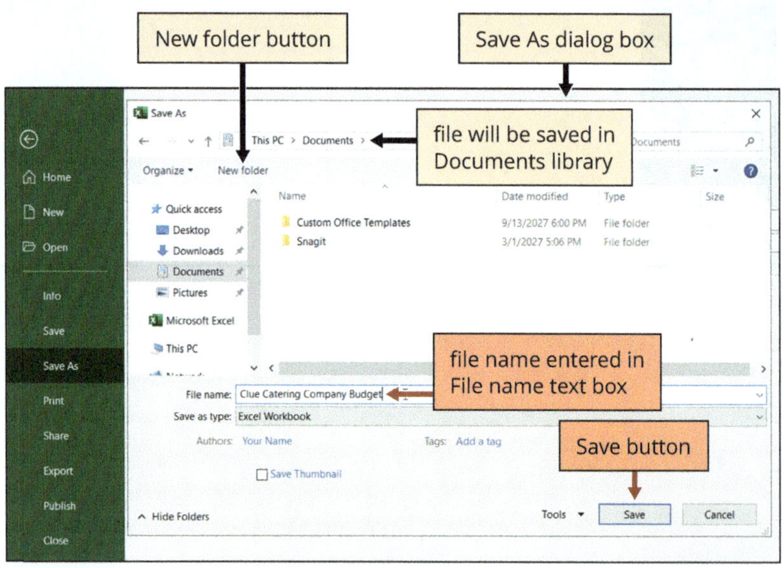

Figure 1–44

Q&A What characters can I use in a file name?
The only invalid characters are the backslash (\), slash (/), colon (:), asterisk (*), question mark (?), quotation mark ("), less than symbol (<), greater than symbol (>), and vertical bar (|).

Why is my list of files, folders, and drives arranged and named differently from those shown in the figure?
Your computer or mobile device's configuration determines how the list of files and folders is displayed and how drives are named. You can change the save location by clicking links in the Navigation pane.

5

- Click the Save button to save the workbook with the file name Clue Catering Company Budget to the default save location (Figure 1–45).

Q&A How do I know that Excel saved the workbook?
While Excel is saving your file, it briefly displays a message on the status bar indicating the amount of the file saved. When the workbook appears after saving, the new file name and the word, Saved, appear in the title bar.

Why is the AutoSave button turned off on the title bar?
If you are saving the file to a computer or mobile device, the AutoSave button on the title bar is turned off. If you are saving the file to OneDrive, the AutoSave button is turned on, allowing Excel to save the workbook as you make changes to it. If AutoSave is turned off, you will need to continue saving your changes manually.

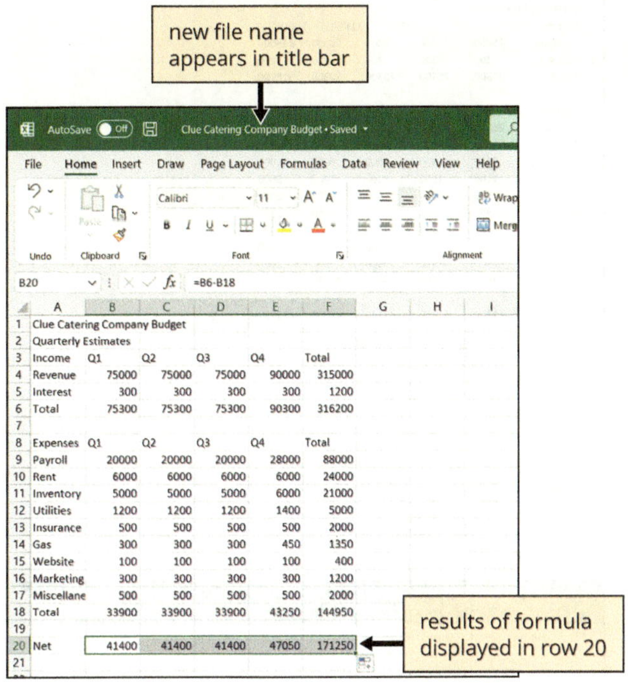

Figure 1–45

Other Ways

1. Press F12, type file name (Save As dialog box), navigate to desired save location, click Save button

Break Point: If you want to take a break, this is a good place to do so. You can exit Excel now. To resume later, start Excel, open the file called Clue Catering Company Budget, and continue following the steps from this location forward.

Formatting the Worksheet

The text, numeric entries, and functions for the worksheet now are complete. The next step is to format the worksheet. You **format** a worksheet to enhance the appearance of information by changing its font, size, color, or alignment.

Figure 1–46a shows the worksheet before formatting. Figure 1–46b shows the worksheet after formatting. As you can see from the two figures, a worksheet that is formatted not only is easier to read but also looks more professional.

Consider This

What steps should you consider when formatting a worksheet?

The key to formatting a worksheet is to consider the ways you can enhance the worksheet so that it appears professional. When formatting a worksheet, consider the following steps:

- Identify in what ways you want to emphasize various elements of the worksheet.
- Increase the font size of cells.
- Change the font color of cells.
- Center the worksheet titles, subtitles, and column headings.
- Modify column widths to best fit text in cells.
- Change the font style of cells.

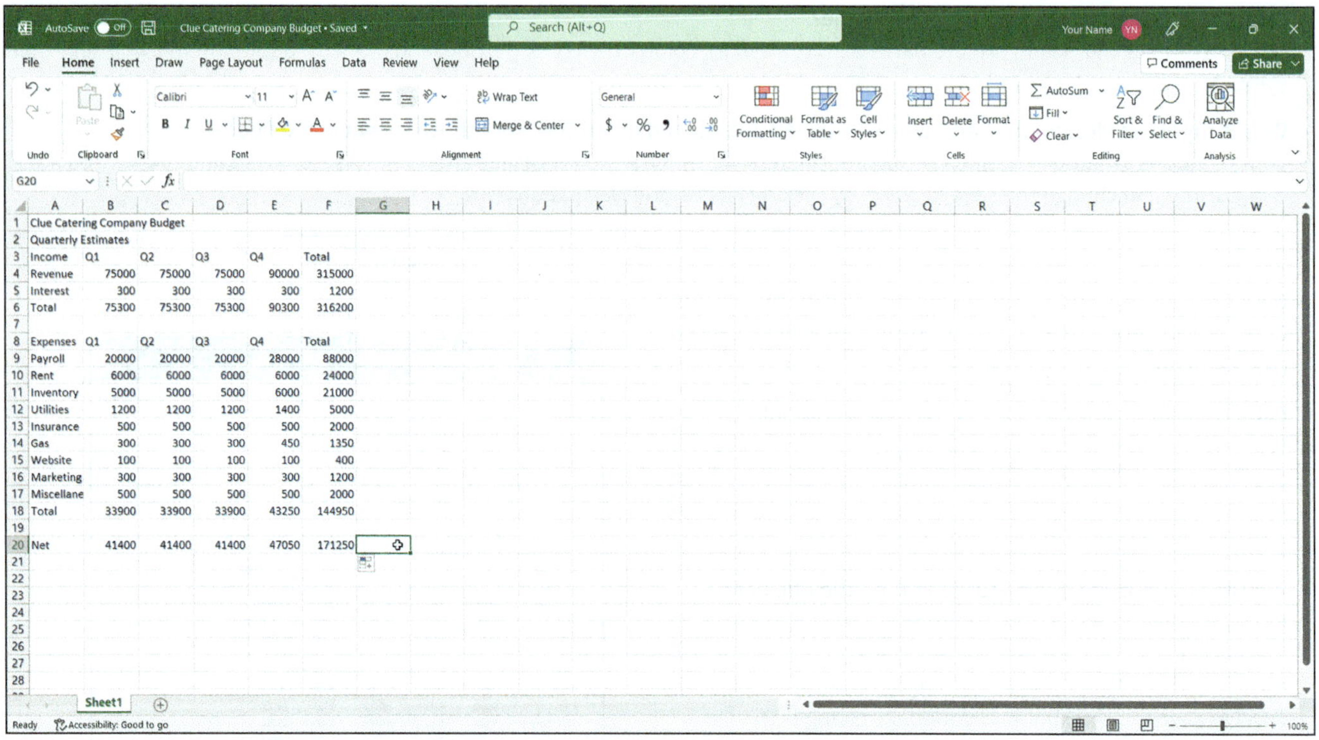

Figure 1–46(a)

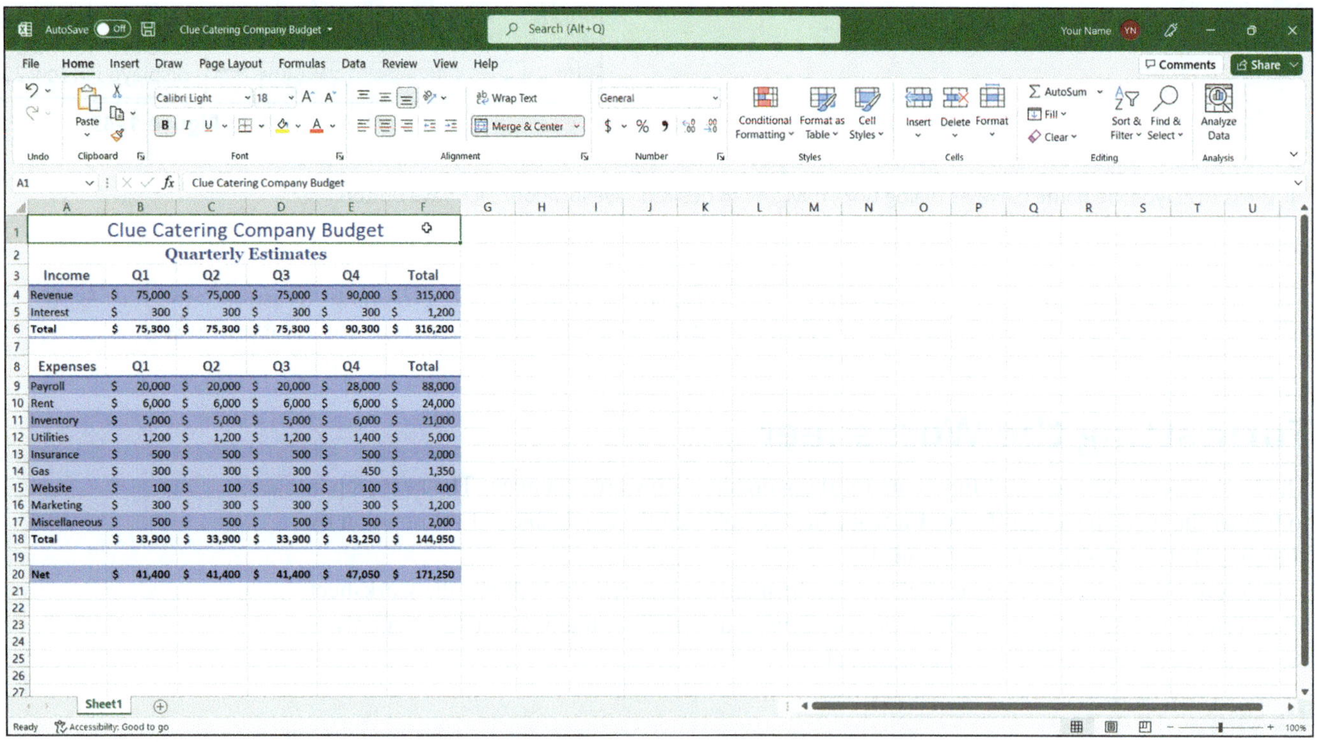

Figure 1–46(b)

To change the unformatted worksheet in Figure 1–46a so that it looks like the formatted worksheet in Figure 1–46b, the following tasks must be completed:

1. Change the font, change the font style, increase the font size, and change the font color of the worksheet titles in cells A1 and A2.
2. Center the worksheet titles in cells A1 and A2 across columns A through F.

3. Format the body of the worksheet. The body of the worksheet, range A3:G20, includes the column titles, row titles, and numbers. Formatting the body of the worksheet changes the numbers to use a dollar format, changes the styles of some rows; adds borders that emphasize portions of the worksheet; and modifies the column widths to fit the text in the columns and make the text and numbers readable.

Although the formatting procedures are explained in the order described above, you could make these format changes in any order. Modifying the column widths, however, is usually done last because other formatting changes may affect the size of data in the cells in the column.

Font Style, Size, and Color

The characters that Excel displays on the screen are a specific font, style, size, and color. The **font** defines the appearance and shape of the letters, numbers, and special characters. Examples of fonts include Calibri, Cambria, Times New Roman, Arial, and Courier. A **font style** is a format that indicates how characters are emphasized, such as bold, underline, and italic. The **font size** refers to the size of characters, measured in units called points. A **point** is a unit of measure used for font size and, in Excel, row height; one point is equal to 1/72 of an inch. Thus, a character with a **point size** of 10 is 10/72 of an inch in height. Finally, Excel has a wide variety of font colors. **Font color** refers to the color of the characters in a spreadsheet.

When Excel first starts, the default font for the entire workbook is Calibri, with a font size, font style, and font color of 11-point regular black. You can change the font characteristics in a single cell, a range of cells, the entire worksheet, or the entire workbook.

To Change a Cell Style

You can change several characteristics of a cell, such as the font, font size, and font color, all at once by assigning a predefined cell style to a cell. A **cell style** is a predesigned combination of font, font size, and font color that you can apply to a cell. **Why?** Using the predesigned styles provides a consistent appearance to common portions of your worksheets, such as worksheet titles, worksheet subtitles, column headings, and total rows. The following steps assign the Title cell style to the worksheet title in cell A1.

1

- Click cell A1 to make cell A1 the active cell.
- Click the Cell Styles button (Home tab | Styles group) to display the Cell Styles gallery (Figure 1–47).

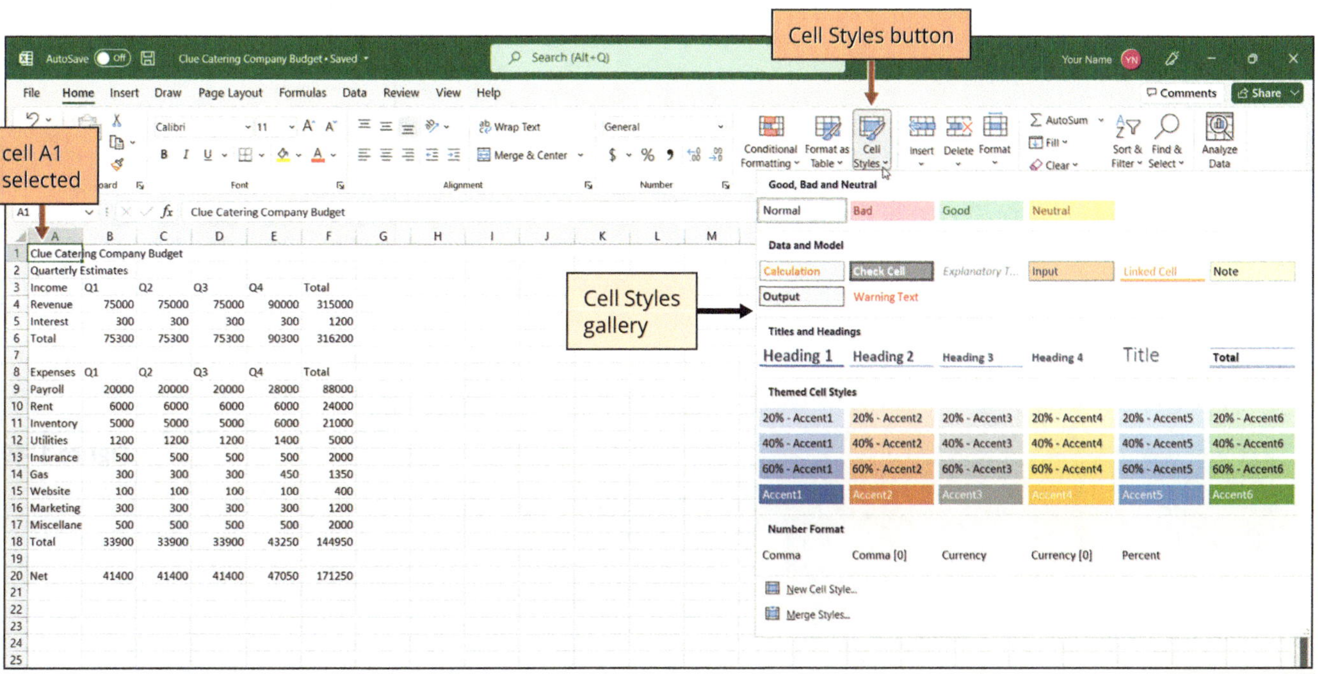

Figure 1–47

2

- Point to the Title cell style in the Titles and Headings area of the Cell Styles gallery to see a live preview of the cell style in the active cell (Figure 1–48).
- **Experiment:** If you are using a mouse, point to other cell styles in the Cell Styles gallery to see a live preview of those cell styles in cell A1.

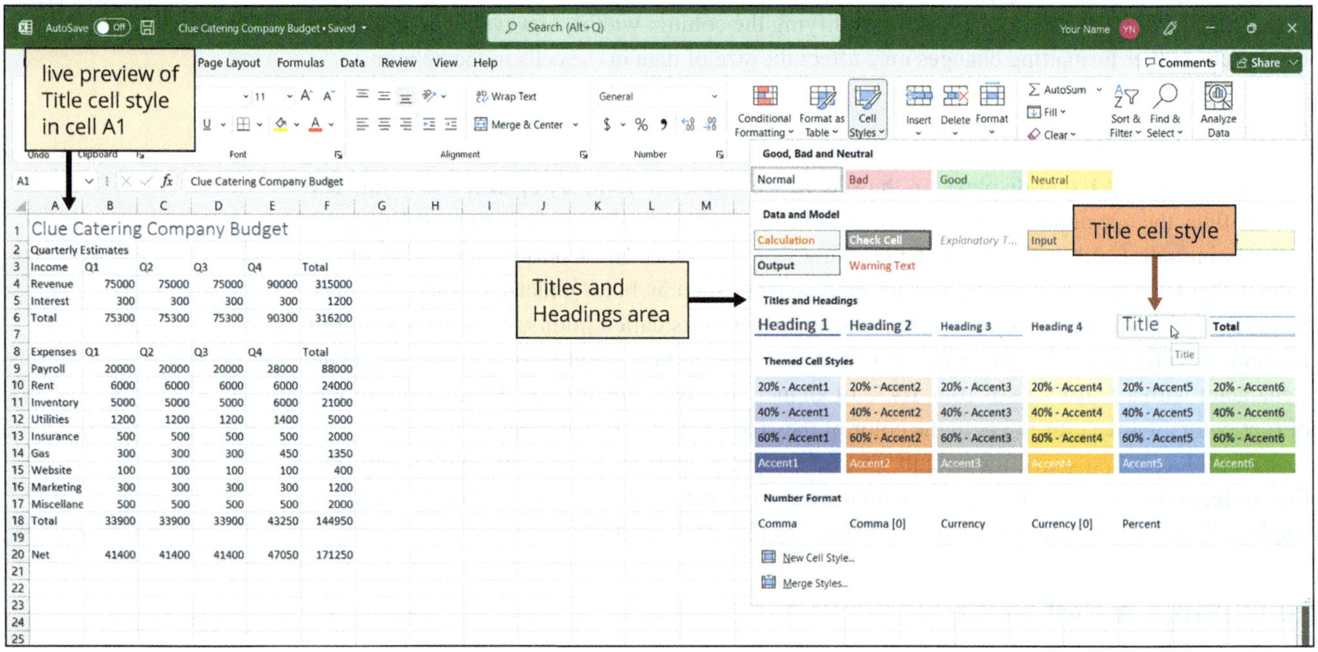

Figure 1–48

3

- Click the Title cell style to apply the cell style to the active cell (Figure 1–49).

Q&A Why do settings in the Font group on the ribbon change?
The font and font size change to reflect the font changes applied to the active cell, cell A1, as a result of applying the Title cell style.

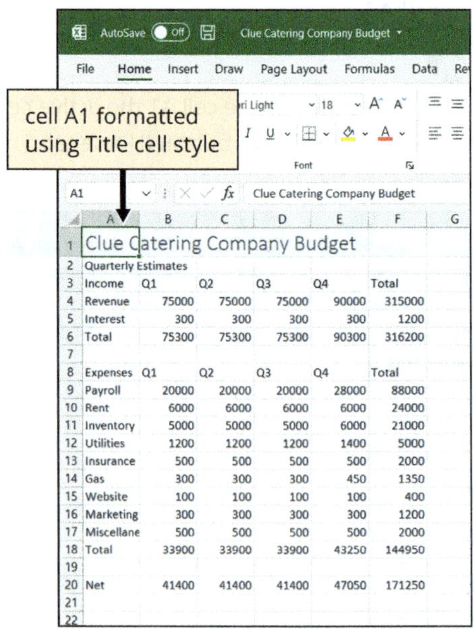

Figure 1–49

To Change the Font

Why? Different fonts are often used in a worksheet to make it more appealing to the reader and to relate or distinguish data in the worksheet. The following steps change the worksheet subtitle's font to Georgia.

1

- Click cell A2 to make it the active cell.
- Click the Font arrow (Home tab | Font group) to display the Font gallery. Scroll to Georgia.
- Point to Georgia in the Font gallery to see a live preview of the selected font in the active cell (Figure 1-50).
- **Experiment:** If you are using a mouse, point to several other fonts in the Font gallery to see a live preview of the other fonts in the selected cell.

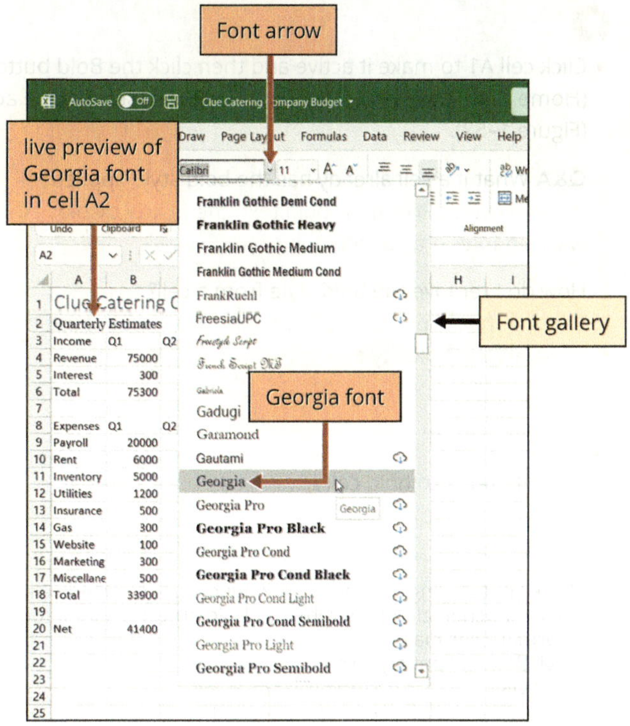

Figure 1-50

2

- Click Georgia in the Font gallery to change the font of the worksheet subtitle to Georgia (Figure 1-51).

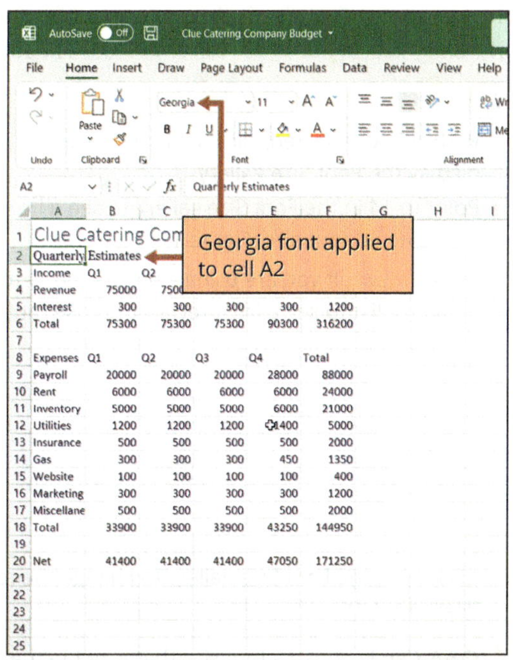

Figure 1-51

Other Ways

1. Click Font Settings Dialog Box Launcher, click Font tab (Format Cells dialog box), click desired font in Font list, click OK
2. Right-click the cell to display Mini toolbar, click Font arrow on Mini toolbar, click desired font in Font list
3. Right-click selected cell, click Format Cells on shortcut menu, click Font tab (Format Cells dialog box), click desired font in Font list, click OK

To Apply Bold Style to a Cell

Bold, or boldface, text has a darker appearance than normal text. **Why?** You apply bold style to a cell to emphasize it or make it stand out from the rest of the worksheet. The following steps apply bold style to the worksheet title and subtitle.

1

- Click cell A1 to make it active and then click the Bold button (Home tab | Font group) to change the font style of the active cell to bold (Figure 1–52).

Q&A What if a cell already has the bold style applied?
If the active cell contains bold text, then Excel displays the Bold button with a darker gray background.

How do I remove the bold style from a cell?
Clicking the Bold button (Home tab | Font group) a second time removes the bold style.

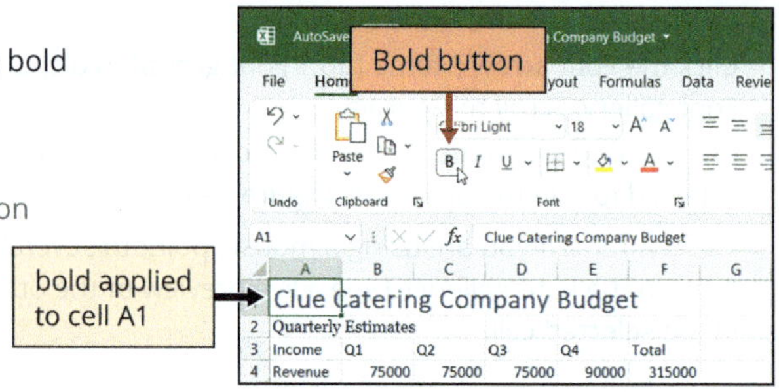

Figure 1–52

2

- Repeat Step 1 to bold cell A2.

Other Ways

1. Click Font Settings Dialog Box Launcher, click Font tab (Format Cells dialog box), click Bold in Font style list, click OK
2. Right-click selected cell, click Bold button on Mini toolbar
3. Right-click selected cell, click Format Cells on shortcut menu, click Font tab (Format Cells dialog box), click Bold in Font style list, click OK
4. Press CTRL+B

To Increase the Font Size of a Cell Entry

Increasing the font size is the next step in formatting the worksheet subtitle. **Why?** You increase the font size of a cell so that the entry stands out and is easier to read. The following steps increase the font size of the worksheet subtitle in cell A2.

1

- With cell A2 selected, click the Font Size arrow (Home tab | Font group) to display the Font Size gallery.
- Point to 14 in the Font Size gallery to see a live preview of the active cell with the selected font size (Figure 1–53).
- **Experiment:** If you are using a mouse, point to several other font sizes in the Font Size list to see a live preview of those font sizes in the selected cell.

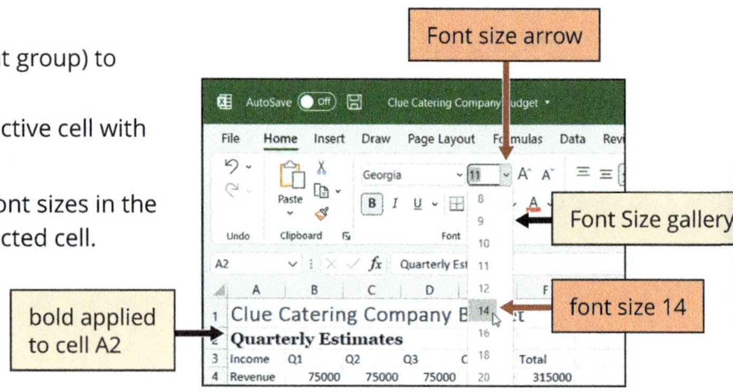

Figure 1–53

2

- Click 14 in the Font Size gallery to change the font size in the active cell (Figure 1–54).

Q&A Can I choose a font size that is not in the Font Size gallery?
Yes. To select a font size not displayed in the Font Size gallery, such as 13, click the Font Size box (Home tab | Font group), type the font size you want, and then press ENTER.

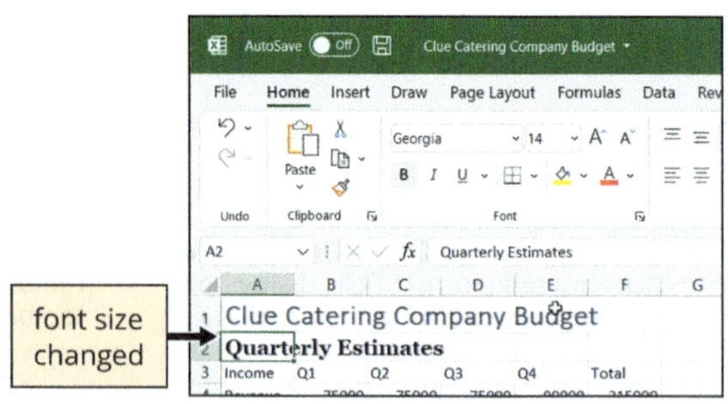

Figure 1–54

Other Ways

1. Click 'Increase Font Size' button (Home tab | Font group) or 'Decrease Font Size' button (Home tab | Font group)
2. Click Font Settings Dialog Box Launcher, click Font tab (Format Cells dialog box), click desired size in Size list, click OK
3. Right-click cell to display Mini toolbar, click Font Size arrow on Mini toolbar, click desired font size in Font Size gallery
4. Right-click selected cell, click Format Cells on shortcut menu, click Font tab (Format Cells dialog box), select font size in Size box, click OK

To Change the Font Color of a Cell Entry

The next step is to change the color of the font in cells A1 and A2 to green. **Why?** Changing the font color of cell entries can help the text stand out more. You also can change the font colors to match a company's or product's brand colors. The following steps change the font color of a cell entry.

1

- Click cell A1 and then click the Font Color arrow (Home tab | Font group) to display the Font Color gallery.
- If you are using a mouse, point to Blue, Accent 1, Darker 25% (column 5, row 5) in the Theme Colors area of the Font Color gallery to see a live preview of the font color in the active cell (Figure 1–55).
- **Experiment:** Point to several other colors in the Font Color gallery to see a live preview of other font colors in the active cell.

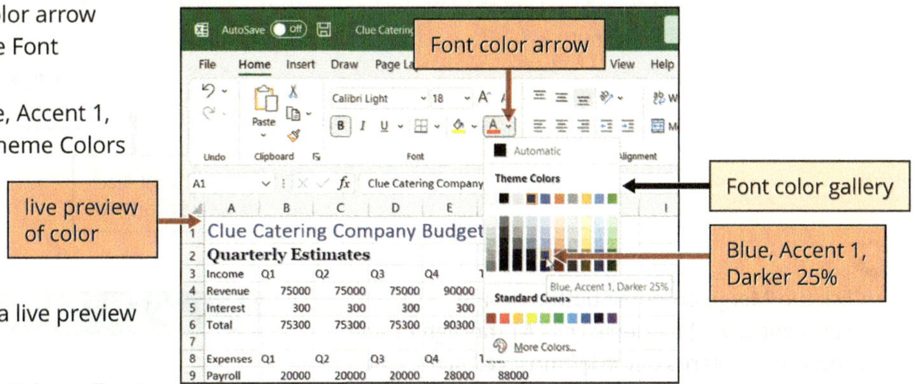

Figure 1–55

Q&A How many colors are in the Font Color gallery?
You can choose from approximately 70 different font colors in the Font Color gallery. Your Font Color gallery may have more or fewer colors, depending on the color settings of your operating system. The Theme Colors area contains colors that are included in the current workbook's theme. The Standard Colors at the bottom of the gallery remain the same regardless of the workbook theme.

2

- Click Blue, Accent 1, Darker 25% (column 5, row 5) in the Font Color gallery to change the font color of the worksheet title in the active cell (Figure 1–56).

Q&A Why does the Font Color button change after I select the new font color?
When you choose a color in the Font Color gallery, Excel changes the Font Color button (Home tab | Font group) to your chosen color. Then when you want to change the font color of another cell to the same color, you need only to select the cell and then click the Font Color button (Home tab | Font group).

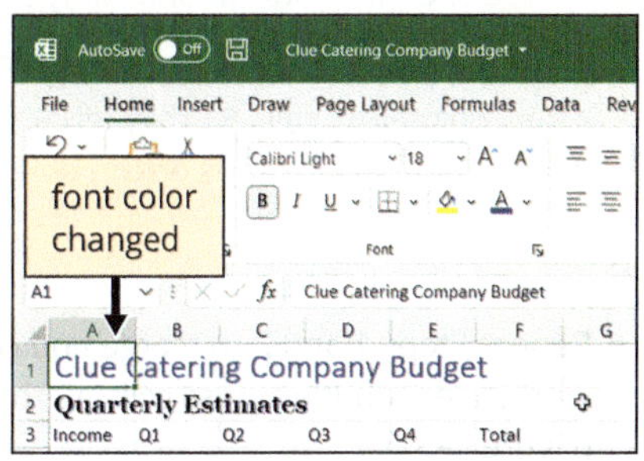

Figure 1–56

3

- Click cell A2.
- Click the Font Color button to apply Blue, Accent 1, Darker 25% (column 5, row 5) to cell A2.

Other Ways

1. Click Font Settings Dialog Box Launcher, click Font tab (Format Cells dialog box), click desired font color in Color list, click OK
2. Right-click cell to display Mini toolbar, click Font Color arrow on Mini toolbar, click desired color in Font Color gallery
3. Right-click selected cell, click Format Cells on shortcut menu, click Font tab (Format Cells dialog box), click Color arrow, click desired color, click OK

To Center Cell Entries across Columns by Merging Cells

The final step in formatting the worksheet title and subtitle is to center them across columns A through F. **Why?** Centering a title across the columns used in the body of the worksheet improves the worksheet's appearance. To do this, the six cells in the range A1:F1 are combined, or merged, into a single cell that is the width of the columns in the body of the worksheet. The six cells in the range A2:F2 are merged in a similar manner. When you **merge** cells, you combine multiple adjacent cells into one larger cell. To unmerge cells, you **split** them to display the original range of cells. The following steps center the worksheet title and subtitle across columns by merging cells.

1

- Select cell A1 and then drag to cell F1 to highlight the range to be merged and centered (Figure 1-57).

Q&A What if a cell in the range B1:F1 contains data?
For the 'Merge & Center' button (Home tab | Alignment group) to work properly, all the cells except the leftmost cell in the selected range must be empty.

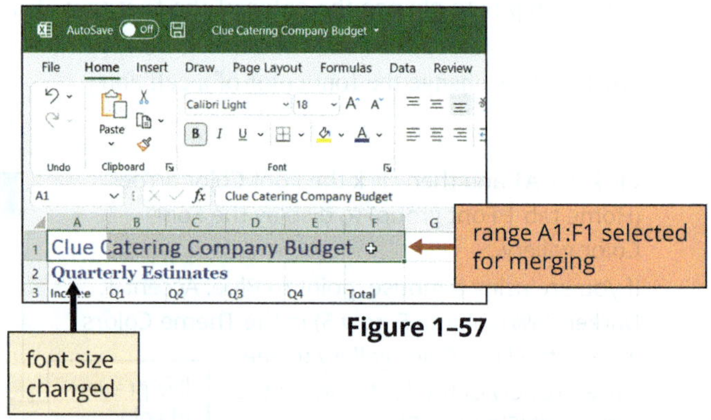

Figure 1-57

2

- Click the 'Merge & Center' button (Home tab | Alignment group) to merge cells A1 through F1 and center the contents of the leftmost cell across the selected columns (Figure 1-58).

Q&A What if my screen displays a Merge & Center menu?
If you are using a touch screen, Excel might display a Merge & Center menu. Select the desired option on the Merge & Center menu if you do not have a separate 'Merge & Center' button and 'Merge & Center' arrow.

What happened to cells B1 through F1?
After the merge, cells B1 through F1 no longer exist. The new cell A1 now extends across columns A through F.

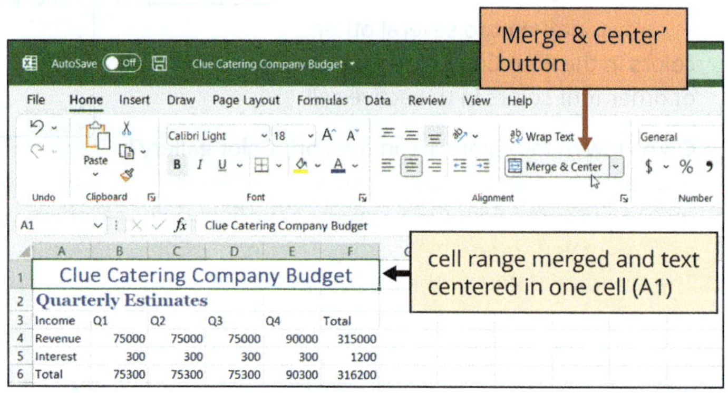

Figure 1-58

3

- Repeat Steps 1 and 2 to merge and center the worksheet subtitle across cells A2 through F2 (Figure 1-59).

Q&A Are cells B1 through F1 and B2 through F2 lost forever?
No. You can split a merged cell to redisplay the individual cells. You split a merged cell by selecting it and clicking the 'Merge & Center' button. For example, if you click the 'Merge & Center' button a second time in Step 2, it will split the merged cell A1 into cells A1, B1, C1, D1, E1, and F1, and move the title to its original location in cell A1.

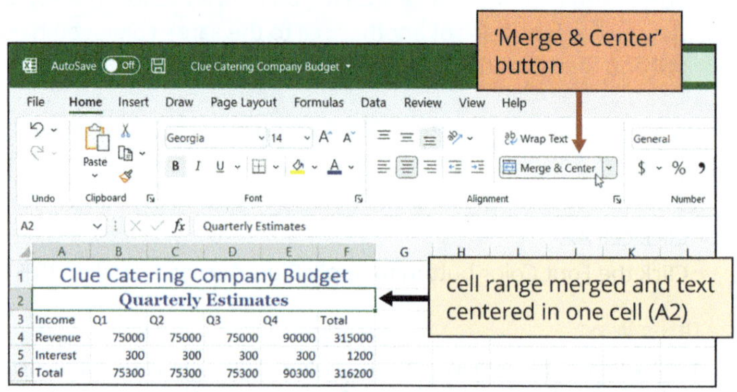

Figure 1-59

Other Ways

1. Right-click selection, click 'Merge & Center' button on Mini toolbar
2. Right-click selected cell, click Format Cells on shortcut menu, click Alignment tab (Format Cells dialog box), select 'Center Across Selection' in Horizontal list, click OK

To Format Rows Using Cell Styles

The next step to format the worksheet is to format the rows. **Why?** Row titles and the total row should be formatted so that the column titles and total row can be distinguished from the data in the body of the worksheet. Data rows can be formatted to make them easier to read as well. The following steps format the column titles and total row using cell styles in the default worksheet theme.

1

- Click cell A3 and then drag to cell F3 to select the range.
- Click the Cell Styles button (Home tab | Styles group) to display the Cell Styles gallery.
- Point to the Heading 1 cell style in the Titles and Headings area of the Cell Styles gallery to see a live preview of the cell style in the selected range (Figure 1–60).

- **Experiment:** If you are using a mouse, point to other cell styles in the Titles and Headings area of the Cell Styles gallery to see a live preview of other styles.

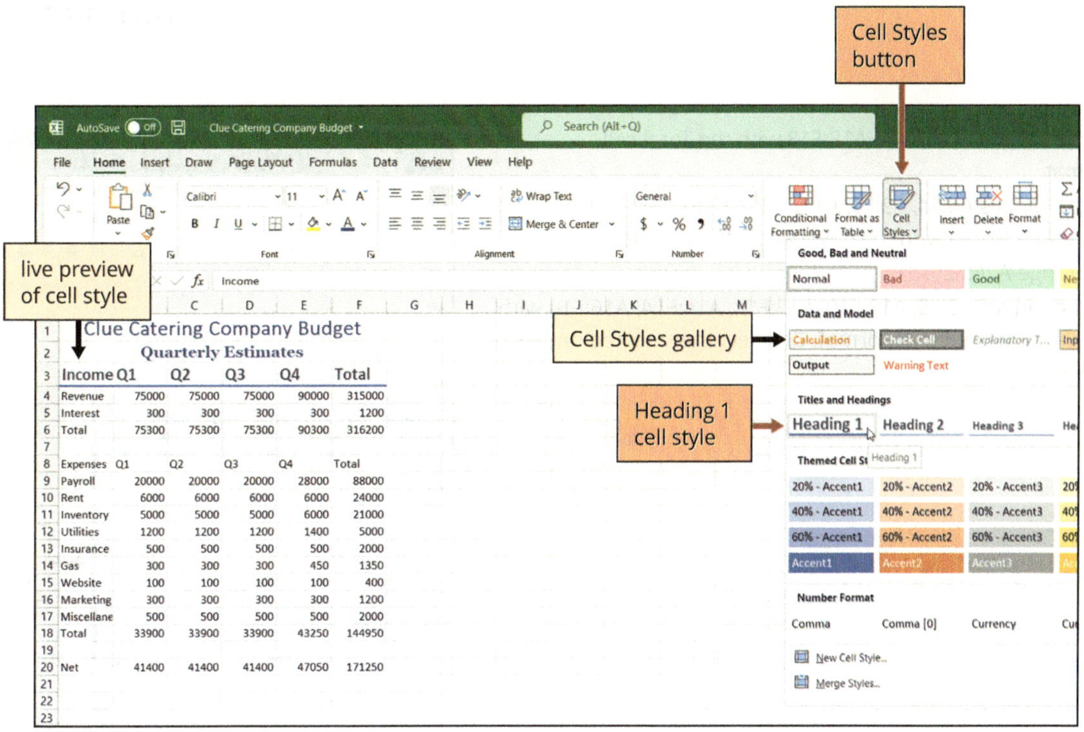

Figure 1–60

2

- Click the Heading 1 cell style to apply the cell style to the selected range.
- Click the Center button (Home tab | Alignment group) to center the column headings in the selected range.
- Click the Font Size box (Home tab | Font group), type 13, and then press ENTER to change the font size for range A3:F3 to size 13.
- Select the range A8 to F8 (Figure 1–61).

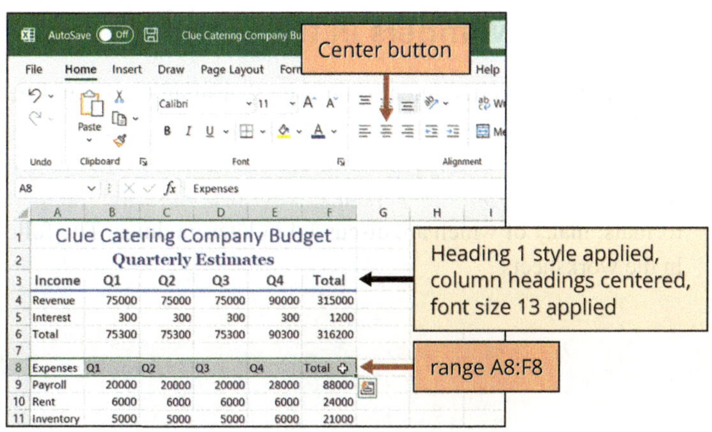

Figure 1–61

3

- Apply the Heading 1 cell style format, center the headings, and apply font size 13 (Figure 1–62).

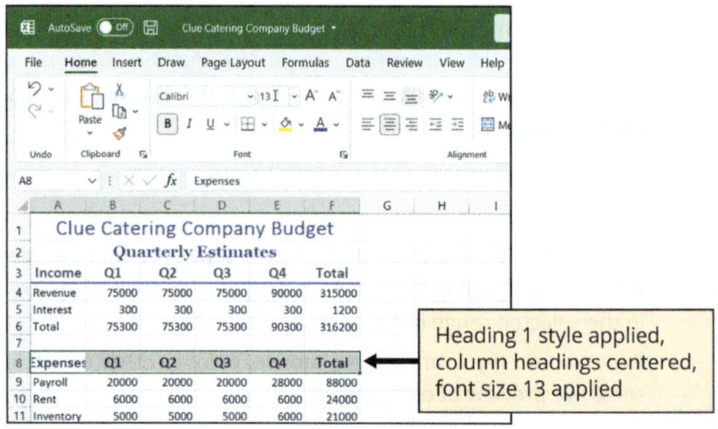

Figure 1–62

4

- Format the ranges A6:F6 and A18:F18 with the Total cell style format.
- Format the ranges A4:F4, A9:F9, A11:F11, A13:F13, A15:F15, A17:F17, and A20:F20 with the 60% - Accent1 cell style format.
- Bold the range A20:F20.
- Format the ranges A5:F5, A10:F10, A12:F12, A14:F14, A16:F16 with the 40% - Accent1 cell style format. Deselect the selected ranges (Figure 1–63).

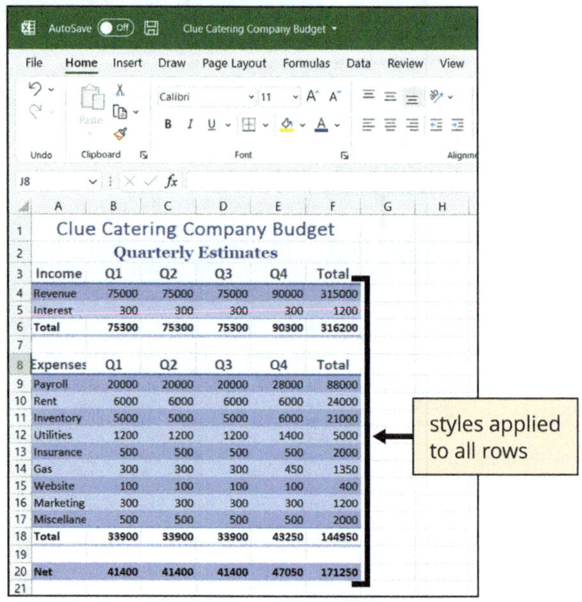

Figure 1–63

To Format Numbers in the Worksheet

The requirements document requested that numbers should be formatted with a dollar and comma format without cents displayed. **Why?** Using a dollar format makes it clear to users of the worksheet that the numbers represent dollar values with dollar signs, and applying the comma format makes larger numbers easier to read. As all the cent values will be zero, removing them from the worksheet will also make the numbers easier to read. Excel allows you to apply various number formats, many of which are discussed in later modules. The following steps use buttons on the ribbon to format the numbers in the worksheet.

1

- Select the range B4:F4.
- Click the 'Accounting Number Format' button (Home tab | Number group) to apply the accounting number format to the cells in the selected range.
- Select the range B5:F5 (Figure 1–64).

Q&A What if my screen displays an Accounting Number Format menu?
If you are using a touch screen, you may not have a separate 'Accounting Number Format' button and 'Accounting Number Format' arrow. In this case, select the desired option on the Accounting Number Format menu.

What effect does the accounting number format have on the selected cells?
The accounting number format causes numbers to be displayed with two decimal places, dollar signs, and to align vertically. Cell widths are adjusted automatically to accommodate the new formatting.

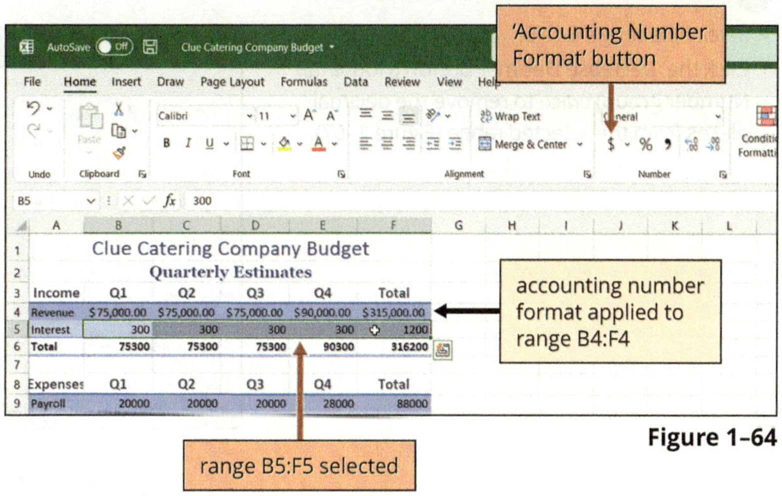

Figure 1–64

2

- Click the Comma Style button (Home tab | Number group) to apply the comma style format to the selected range.

Q&A What effect does the comma style format have on the selected cells?
The comma style format formats numbers to have two decimal places and commas as thousands separators.

- Select the range B6:F6 to make it the active range (Figure 1–65).

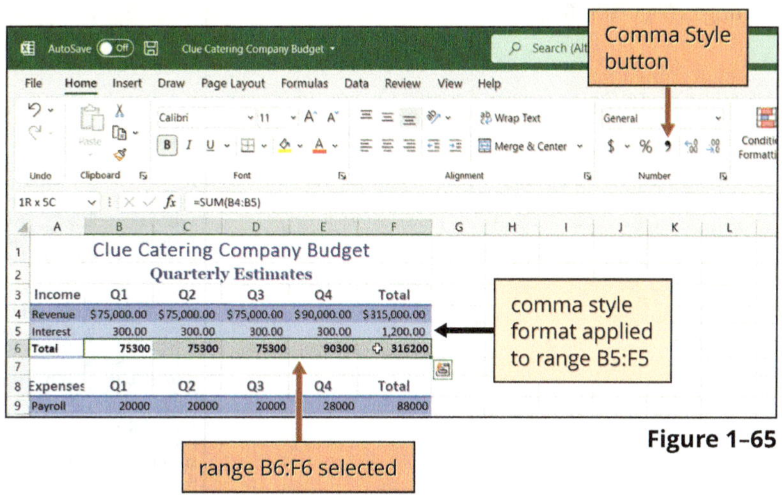

Figure 1–65

3

- Click the 'Accounting Number Format' button (Home tab | Number group) to apply the accounting number format to the cells in the selected range.

4

- Format the ranges B9:F9, B18:F18, and B20:F20 with the accounting number format.
- Format the range B10:F17 with the comma style format. Click cell A1 to deselect the selected ranges (Figure 1–66).

Q&A How do I select the range B10:F17?
Select this range the same way as you select a range of cells in a column or row; that is, click the first cell in the range (B10, in this case) and drag to the last cell in the range (F17 in this case).

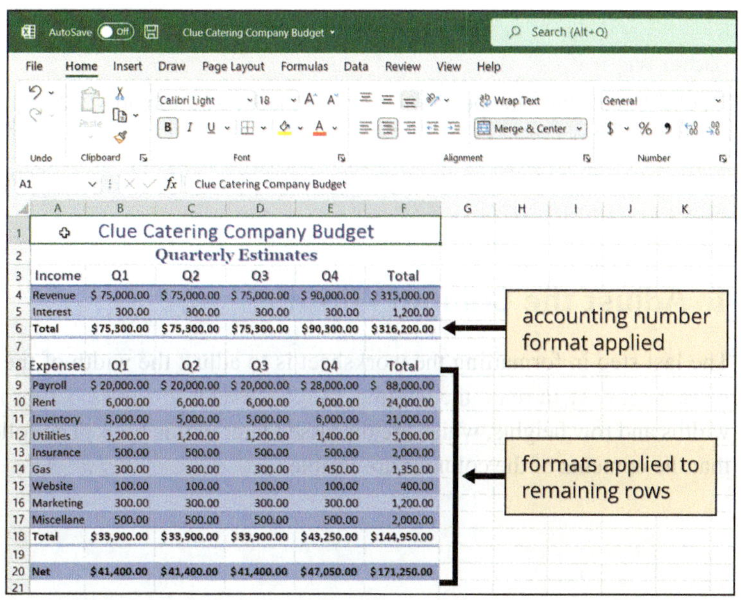

Figure 1–66

5

- Select the range B4:F6.
- Click the 'Decrease Decimal' button (Home tab | Number group) twice to remove the decimal places from the selected range (Figure 1–67).

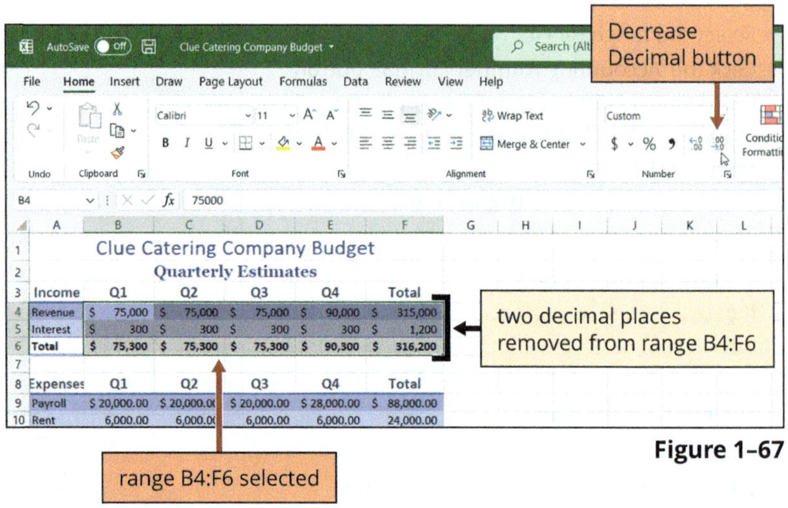

Figure 1–67

6

- Format the ranges B9:F18 and B20:F20 to remove two decimal places. Click cell A1 to deselect the ranges (Figure 1–68).

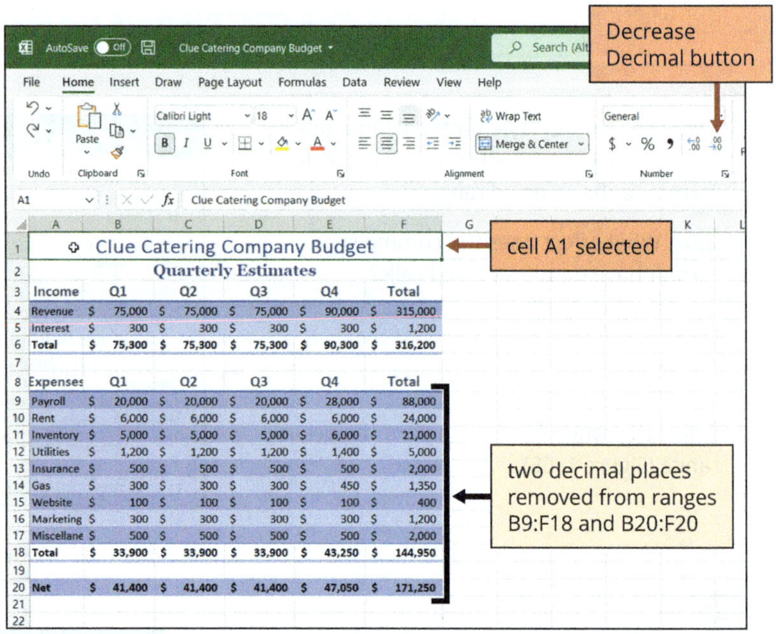

Figure 1–68

Other Ways

1. Click 'Accounting Number Format' or Comma Style button on Mini toolbar
2. Right-click selected cell, click Format Cells on shortcut menu, click Number tab (Format Cells dialog box), select Accounting in Category list or select Number and click 'Use 1000 Separator', set decimal places to 0, click OK

To Adjust the Column Width

The last step in formatting the worksheet is to adjust the width of the columns so that each title is visible. **Why?** To make a worksheet easy to read, the column widths should be adjusted appropriately. Excel offers other methods for adjusting cell widths and row heights, which are discussed later in this book. The following steps adjust the width of columns A through F so that the contents of the columns are visible.

1

- Point to the boundary on the right side of the column A heading above row 1 to change the pointer to a split double arrow (Figure 1–69).

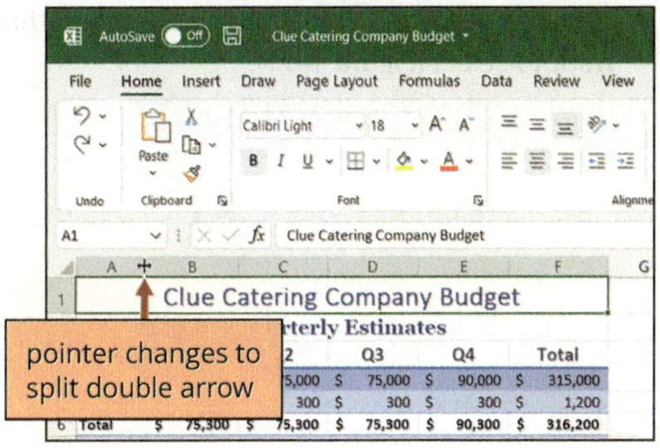

Figure 1–69

2

- Double-click the boundary to adjust the width of the column to accommodate the width of the longest item in the column (Figure 1–70).

Q&A What if all of the items in the column are already visible?
If all of the items are shorter in length than the width of the column and you double-click the column boundary, Excel will reduce the width of the column to the width of the widest entry.

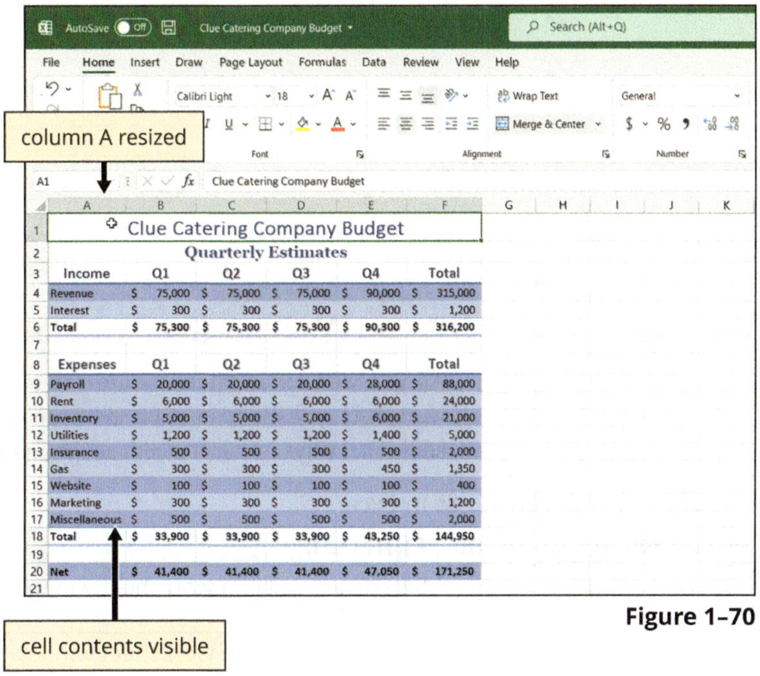

Figure 1–70

Other Ways

1. Select column heading, click Format (Home tab | Cells group), click AutoFit Column Width

To Use the Name Box to Select a Cell

The next step is to chart the quarterly expenses. To create the chart, you need to identify the range of the data you want to feature on the chart and then select it. In this case, you want to start with cell A3. Rather than clicking cell A3 to select it, you will select the cell by using the Name box, which is located to the left of the formula bar. **Why?** You might want to use the Name box to select a cell if you are working with a large worksheet and it is faster to type the cell name rather than scrolling to and clicking it. The following steps select cell A3 using the Name box.

1

- Click the Name box in the formula bar and then type **a3** as the cell you want to select (Figure 1–71).

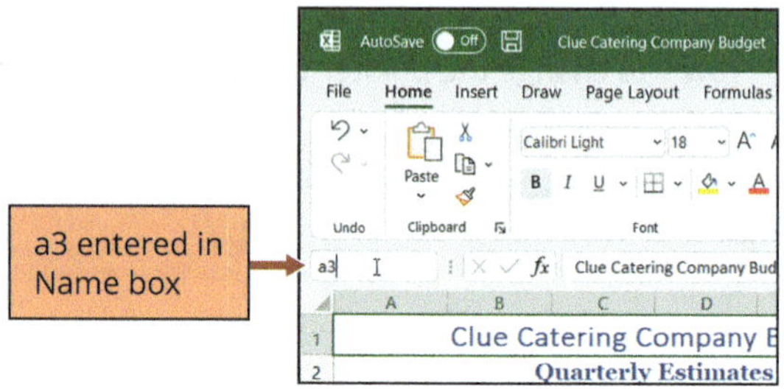

Figure 1–71

2

- Press ENTER to change the active cell in the Name box and make cell A3 the active cell (Figure 1–72).

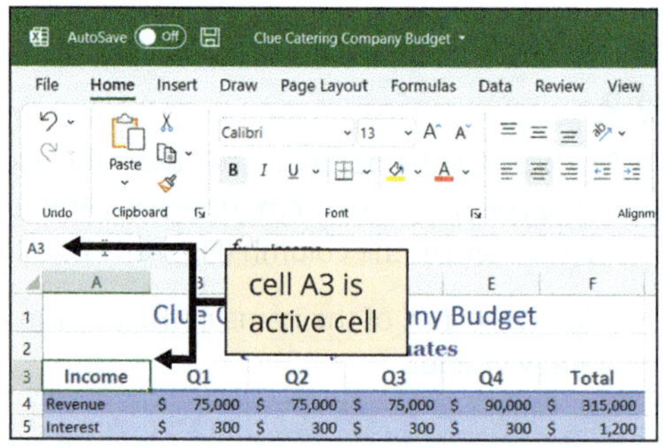

Figure 1–72

Other Ways to Select Cells

As you will see in later modules, in addition to using the Name box to select any cell in a worksheet, you also can use it to assign names to a cell or range of cells. Excel supports several additional ways to select a cell, as summarized in Table 1–4.

Table 1–4: Selecting Cells in Excel

Key, Box, or Command	Function
ALT+PAGE DOWN	Selects the cell one worksheet window to the right and moves the worksheet window accordingly.
ALT+PAGE UP	Selects the cell one worksheet window to the left and moves the worksheet window accordingly.
ARROW	Selects the adjacent cell in the direction of the arrow on the key.
CTRL+ARROW	Selects the border cell of the worksheet in combination with the arrow keys and moves the worksheet window accordingly. For example, to select the rightmost cell in the row that contains the active cell, press CTRL+RIGHT ARROW. You also can press END, release it, and then press the appropriate arrow key to accomplish the same task.
CTRL+HOME	Selects cell A1 or the cell one column and one row below and to the right of frozen titles and moves the worksheet window accordingly.
Find command on Find & Select menu (Home tab | Editing group) or SHIFT+F5	Finds and selects a cell that contains specific contents that you enter in the Find and Replace dialog box. If necessary, Excel moves the worksheet window to display the cell. You also can press CTRL+F to display the Find and Replace dialog box.
Go To command on Find & Select menu (Home tab | Editing group) or F5	Selects the cell that corresponds to the cell reference you enter in the Go To dialog box and moves the worksheet window accordingly. You also can press CTRL+G to display the Go To dialog box and its Special button to go to special worksheet elements, such as formulas.
HOME	Selects the cell at the beginning of the row that contains the active cell and moves the worksheet window accordingly.
Name box	Selects the cell in the workbook that corresponds to the cell reference you enter in the Name box.
PAGE DOWN	Selects the cell down one worksheet window from the active cell and moves the worksheet window accordingly.
PAGE UP	Selects the cell up one worksheet window from the active cell and moves the worksheet window accordingly.

Break Point: If you want to take a break, this is a good place to do so. Be sure to save the Clue Catering Company Budget file again, and then you can exit Excel. To resume later, start Excel, open the file called Clue Catering Company Budget, and continue following the steps from this location forward.

Adding a Pie Chart to the Worksheet

Excel includes 17 chart types from which you can choose, including column, line, pie, bar, area, XY (scatter), map, stock, surface, radar, treemap, sunburst, histogram, box & whisker, waterfall, funnel, and combo. The type of chart you choose depends on the type and quantity of data you have and the message or analysis you want to convey.

A column chart is a good way to compare values side by side. A line chart is often used to illustrate changes in data over time. Pie charts show the contribution of each piece of data to the whole, or total, of the data. A pie chart can go even further in comparing values across categories by showing each pie piece in comparison with the others. Area charts, like line charts, illustrate changes over time but are often used to compare more than one set of data, and the area below the lines is filled in with a different color for each set of data. An XY (scatter) chart is used much like a line chart, but each piece of data is represented by a dot and is not connected with a line. Scatter charts are typically used for viewing scientific, statistical, and engineering data. A map chart depicts data based on geographic location. A stock chart provides a number of methods commonly used in the financial industry to show fluctuations in stock market data. A surface chart compares data from three columns and/or rows in a 3-D manner. A radar chart can compare aggregate values of several sets of data in a manner that resembles a radar screen, with each set of data represented by a different color. A funnel chart illustrates values during various stages. A combo chart allows you to combine multiple types of charts.

As outlined in the requirements document in Figure 1–2, the budget worksheet should include a pie chart to graphically represent the yearly expense totals for each item in Clue Catering Company's budget. The pie chart shown in Figure 1–73 is on its own sheet in the workbook. The pie chart resides on a separate sheet, called a chart sheet. A **chart sheet** is a separate sheet in a workbook that contains only a chart, which is linked to the workbook data.

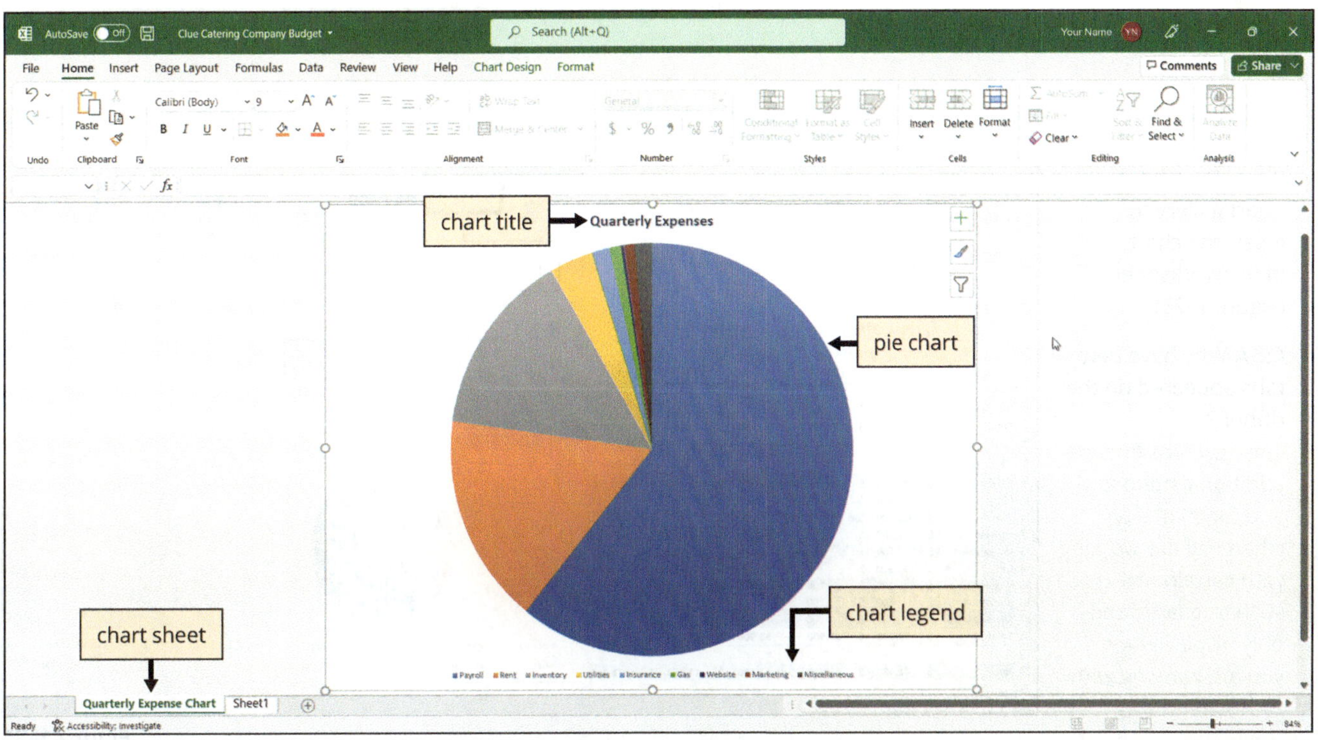

Figure 1–73

In this worksheet, the ranges you want to chart are the nonadjacent ranges A9:A17 (expense titles) and F9:F17 (yearly expense totals). The expense titles in the range A9:A17 will identify the slices of the pie chart; these entries are called category names. The range F9:F17 contains the data that determine the size of the slices in the pie; these entries are called the data series. A **data series** is a column or row in a datasheet and also the set of values represented in a chart. Because nine budget items are being charted, the pie chart contains nine slices.

To Add a Pie Chart

Why? When you want to see how each part relates to the whole, you use a pie chart. The following steps draw the pie chart. The following steps will add a pie chart to the workbook.

1

- Select the range A9:A17 to identify the range of the category names for the pie chart.
- While holding down CTRL, select the nonadjacent range F9:F17.
- Click Insert on the ribbon to display the Insert tab.
- Click the 'Insert Pie or Doughnut Chart' button (Insert tab | Charts group) to display the Insert Pie or Doughnut Chart gallery (Figure 1–74).

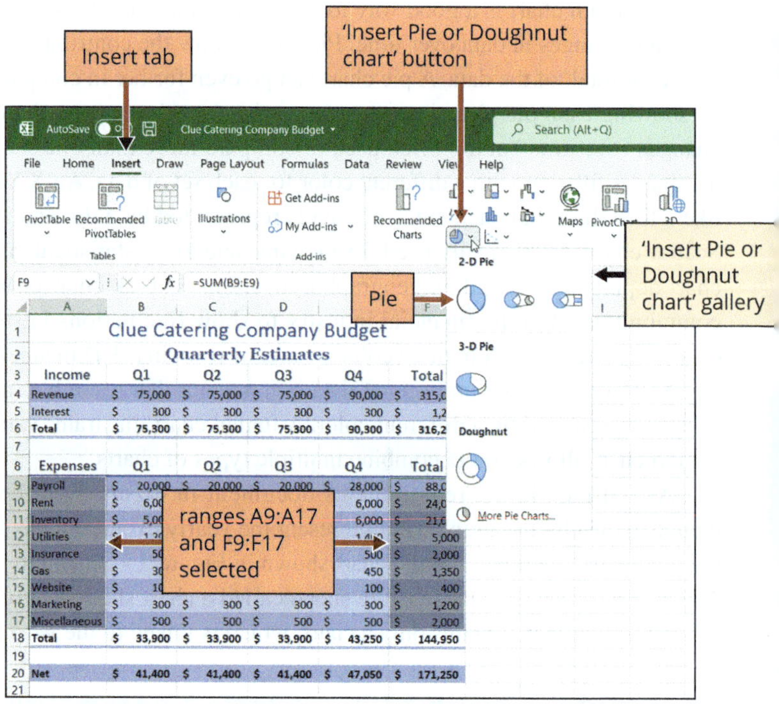

Figure 1–74

2

- Click Pie in the 2-D Pie category of the Insert Pie or Doughnut Chart gallery to insert the chart in the worksheet (Figure 1–75).

Q&A Why have new tabs appeared on the ribbon?
The new tabs provide additional options and functionality when you are working with certain objects, such as charts, and only display when you are working with those objects.

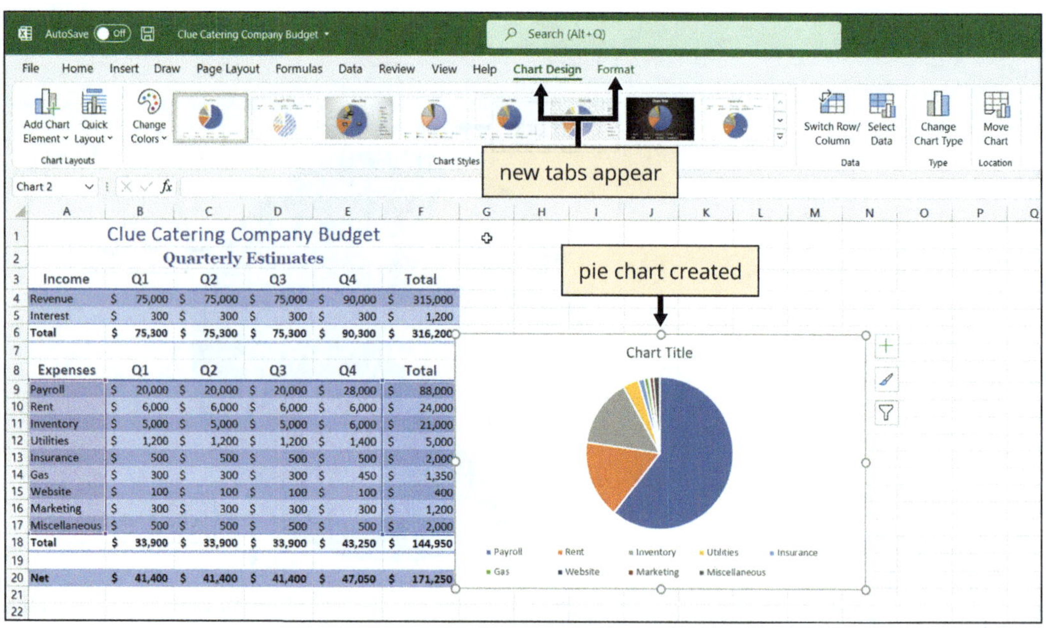

Figure 1–75

3

- Click the chart title to select it.
- Click and drag to select all the text in the chart title.
- Type **Quarterly Expenses** to specify the title.
- Click a blank area of the chart to deselect the chart title (Figure 1–76).

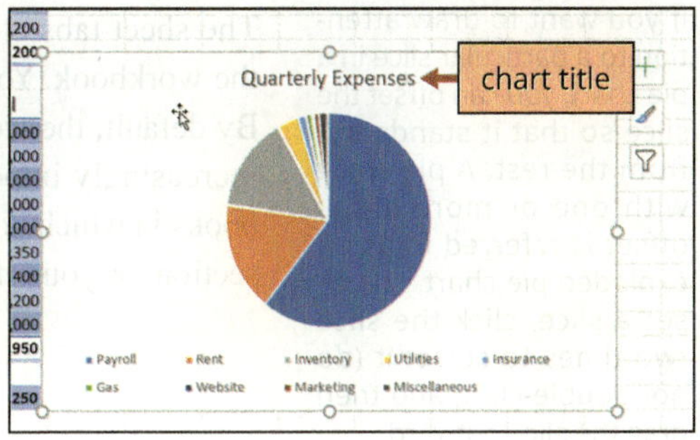

Figure 1–76

To Apply a Style to a Chart

Why? If you want to enhance the appearance of a chart, you can apply a chart style. The following steps apply Style 5 to the pie chart.

1

- Click the Chart Styles button to the right of the chart to display the Chart Styles gallery.
- Scroll in the Chart Styles gallery to display the Style 5 chart style (Figure 1–77).

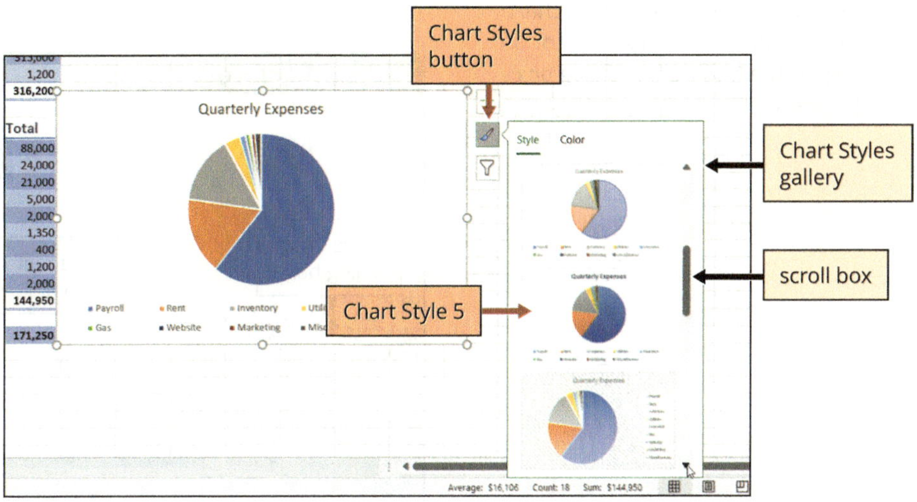

Figure 1–77

2

- Click Style 5 in the Chart Styles gallery to change the chart style to Style 5 (Figure 1–78).

3

- Click the Chart Styles button to close the Chart Styles gallery.

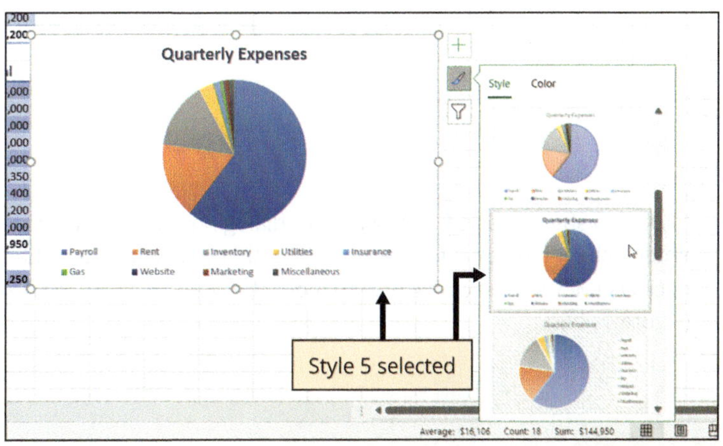

Figure 1–78

BTW
Exploding a Pie Chart
If you want to draw attention to a particular slice in a pie chart, you can offset the slice so that it stands out from the rest. A pie chart with one or more slices offset is referred to as an exploded pie chart. To offset a slice, click the slice two times to select it (do not double-click) and then drag the slice outward.

Changing the Sheet Tab Names and Colors

The sheet tabs at the bottom of the window allow you to navigate between any worksheet in the workbook. You click the sheet tab of the worksheet you want to view in the Excel window. By default, the worksheets are named Sheet1, Sheet2, and so on. The worksheet names become increasingly important as you move toward more sophisticated workbooks, especially workbooks in which you place objects such as charts on different sheets, which you will do in the next section, or you reference cells between worksheets.

To Move a Chart to a New Sheet

Why? By moving a chart to its own sheet, the size of the chart will increase, which can improve readability. The following steps move the pie chart to a chart sheet named Quarterly Expenses.

1

- Click the Move Chart button (Chart Design tab | Location group) to display the Move Chart dialog box (Figure 1–79).

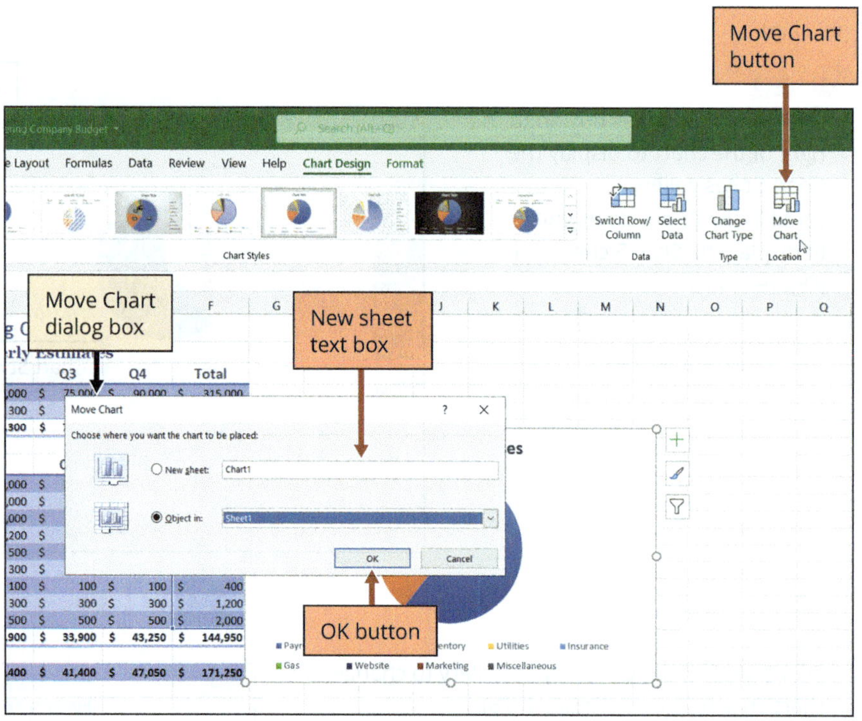

Figure 1–79

2

- Click New sheet to select it (Move Chart dialog box) and then type **Quarterly Expense Chart** in the New sheet text box to enter a sheet tab name for the worksheet that will contain the chart.
- Click OK (Move Chart dialog box) to move the chart to a new chart sheet with the sheet tab name, Quarterly Expense Chart (Figure 1–80).

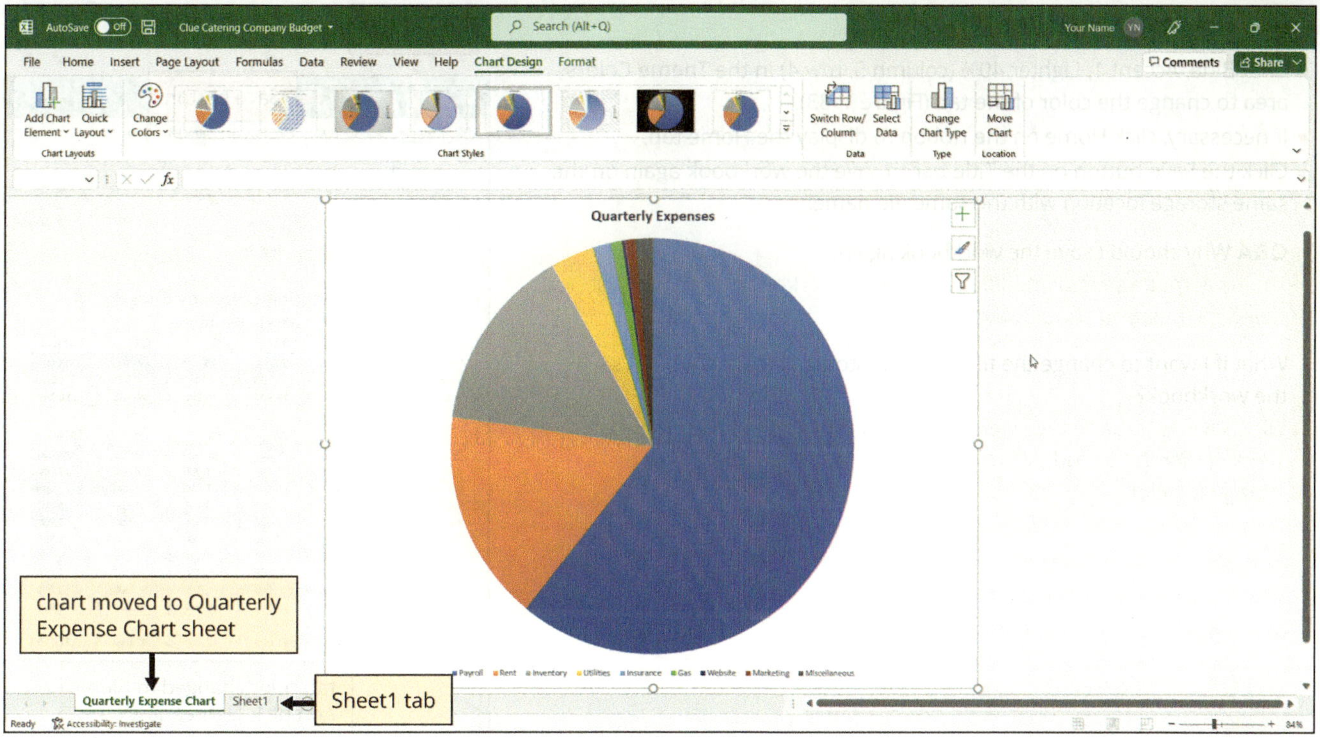

Figure 1–80

To Change the Sheet Tab Name and Color

You decide to change the name and color of the Sheet1 tab to Quarterly Finances. **Why?** Use simple, meaningful names for each sheet tab. Sheet tab names often match the worksheet title. If a worksheet includes multiple titles in multiple sections of the worksheet, use a sheet tab name that encompasses the meaning of all of the sections. Changing the tab color also can help uniquely identify a sheet. The following steps rename the sheet tab and change the tab color.

1

- Double-click the sheet tab labeled Sheet1 in the lower-left corner of the window.
- Type **Quarterly Finances** as the sheet tab name and then press ENTER to assign the new name to the sheet tab (Figure 1–81).

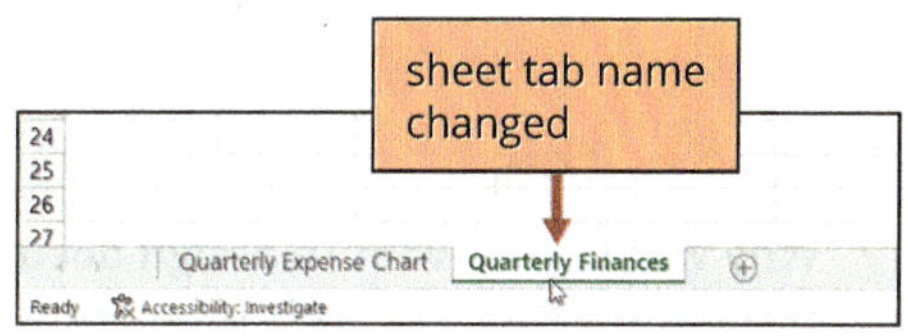

Figure 1–81

Q&A What is the maximum length for a sheet tab name?
Sheet tab names can be up to 31 characters (including spaces) in length. Longer worksheet names, however, mean that fewer sheet tabs will appear on your screen. If you have multiple worksheets with long sheet tab names, you may have to scroll through sheet tabs, making it more difficult to find a particular sheet.

2

- Right-click the sheet tab labeled Quarterly Finances, in the lower-left corner of the window, to display a shortcut menu.
- Point to Tab Color on the shortcut menu to display the Tab Color gallery (Figure 1–82).

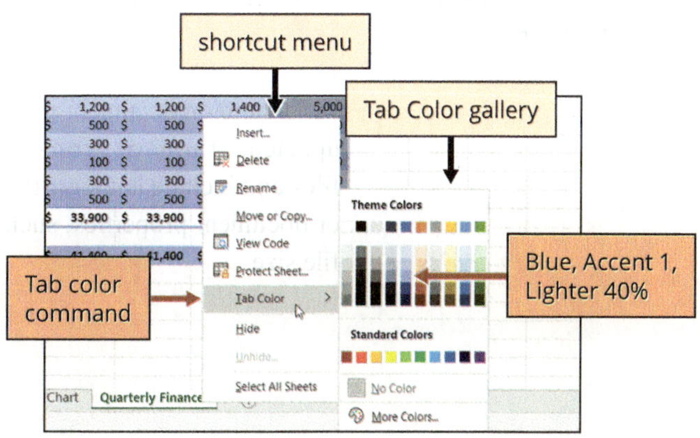

Figure 1–82

3

- Click Blue, Accent 1, Lighter 40% (column 5, row 4) in the Theme Colors area to change the color of the tab (Figure 1–83).
- If necessary, click Home on the ribbon to display the Home tab.
- Click the Save button on the Title bar to save the workbook again on the same storage location with the same file name.

Q&A Why should I save the workbook again?
You have made several modifications to the workbook since you last saved it. Thus, you should save it again.

What if I want to change the file name or storage location when I save the workbook?
Click Save As in Backstage view and follow the "To Save a Workbook" steps earlier in this module to specify a different file name and/or storage location.

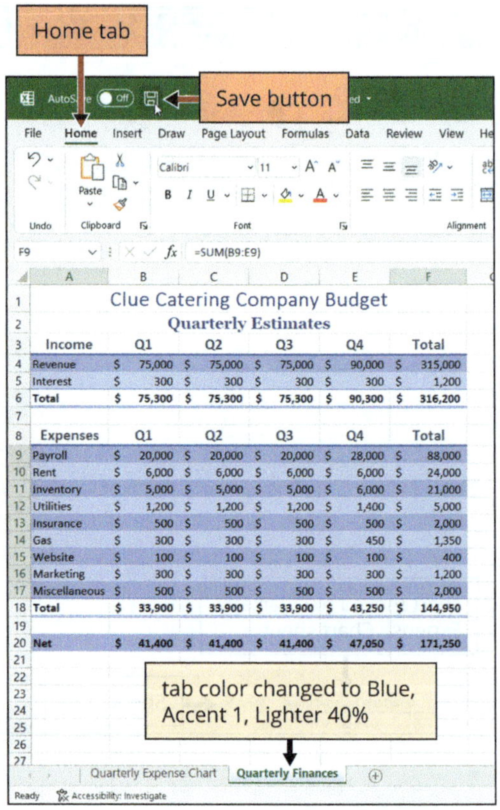

Figure 1–83

Document Properties

Excel helps you organize and identify your files by using **document properties**, which are the details about a file such as the project author, title, and subject. For example, you could use the class name or topic to describe the workbook's purpose or content in the document properties.

Consider This

Why would you want to assign document properties to a workbook?

Document properties are valuable for a variety of reasons:

- Users can save time locating a particular file because they can view a file's document properties without opening the workbook.
- By creating consistent properties for files having similar content, users can better organize their workbooks.
- Some organizations require Excel users to add document properties so that other employees can view details about these files.

Common document properties include standard properties and those that are automatically updated. **Standard properties** are document properties associated with all Microsoft Office files and include author, title, and subject. **Automatically updated properties** are file system or document properties, such as the date you create or change a file, and statistics, such as the file size.

To Change Document Properties To change document properties, you would follow these steps.

1. Click the File tab on the ribbon to open Backstage view and then click Info in Backstage view to display the Info screen. The Properties list is located in the right pane of the Info screen.
2. If the property you want to change is in the Properties list, click to the right of the property category to display a text box. (Note that not all properties are editable.) Type the desired text for the property and then click anywhere in the Info screen to enter the data or press TAB to navigate to the next property. Click the Back button in the upper-left corner of Backstage view to return to the Excel window.
3. If the property you want to change is not in the Properties list or you cannot edit it, click the Properties button to display the Properties menu, and then click Advanced Properties to display the Summary tab in the Properties dialog box. Type your desired text in the appropriate property text boxes. Click OK (Properties dialog box) to close the dialog box and then click the Back button in the upper-left corner of Backstage view to return to the workbook.

Q&A Why do some of the document properties in my Properties dialog box contain data?
Depending on where you are using Excel, your school, university, or place of employment may have customized the properties.

Printing a Worksheet

After creating a worksheet, you may want to preview and print it. A **preview** is an onscreen view of your document prior to printing, to see exactly how the printed document will look. Printing a worksheet enables you to distribute the worksheet to others in a form that can be read or viewed but not edited. It is a good practice to save a workbook before printing a worksheet, in the event you experience difficulties printing.

Consider This

What is the best method for distributing a workbook?

The traditional method of distributing a workbook uses a printer to produce a hard copy. A **hard copy** or **printout** is information that exists on paper. Hard copies can be useful for the following reasons:

- Some people prefer proofreading a hard copy of a workbook rather than viewing it on the screen to check for errors and readability.
- Hard copies can serve as a backup reference if your storage medium is lost or becomes corrupted and you need to recreate the workbook.

Instead of distributing a hard copy of a workbook, users can distribute the workbook as an electronic image that mirrors the original workbook's appearance. An electronic image of a workbook is not an editable file; it simply displays a picture of the workbook. The electronic image of the workbook can be sent as an email attachment, posted on a website, or copied to a portable storage medium such as a USB flash drive. Two popular electronic image formats, sometimes called fixed formats, are PDF by Adobe Systems and XPS by Microsoft. In Excel, you can create electronic image files through the Save As dialog box and the Export, Share, and Print options in Backstage view. Electronic images of workbooks, such as PDF and XPS, can be useful for the following reasons:

- Users can view electronic images of workbooks without the software that created the original workbook (e.g., Excel). Specifically, to view a PDF file, you use a program called Adobe Acrobat Reader, which can be downloaded free from the Adobe website. Similarly, to view an XPS file, you use a program called XPS Viewer, which is included in Windows 10 and can be downloaded and installed in Windows 11.
- Sending electronic workbooks saves paper and printer supplies. Society encourages users to contribute to **green computing**, which involves reducing the electricity consumed and environmental waste generated when using computers, mobile devices, and related technologies.

To Preview and Print a Worksheet in Landscape Orientation

With the completed workbook saved, you may want to print it. **Why?** A printed copy is sometimes necessary for a report delivered in person.

An on-screen preview of your worksheet lets you see each page of your worksheet in the current orientation. **Portrait orientation** describes a printed copy with the short (8½") edge at the top of the printout; the printed page is taller than it is wide. **Landscape orientation** describes the page orientation in which the page is wider than it is tall. The print settings allow you to change the orientation as well as the paper size, margins, and scaling. **Scaling** determines how the worksheet fits on the page. You may want to adjust scaling to ensure that your data fits on one sheet of paper. **Why?** A printed worksheet may be difficult to read if it is spread across more than one page. The following steps print one or more hard copies of the contents of the worksheet.

1

- Click File on the ribbon to open Backstage view.
- Click Print in Backstage view to display the Print screen (Figure 1–84).

Q&A How can I print multiple copies of my worksheet?
Increase the number in the Copies box on the Print screen.

What if I decide not to print the worksheet at this time?
Click the Back button in the upper-left corner of Backstage view to return to the workbook window.

Why does my Print screen look different?
Depending on the type of printer you select, your Print screen may display different options.

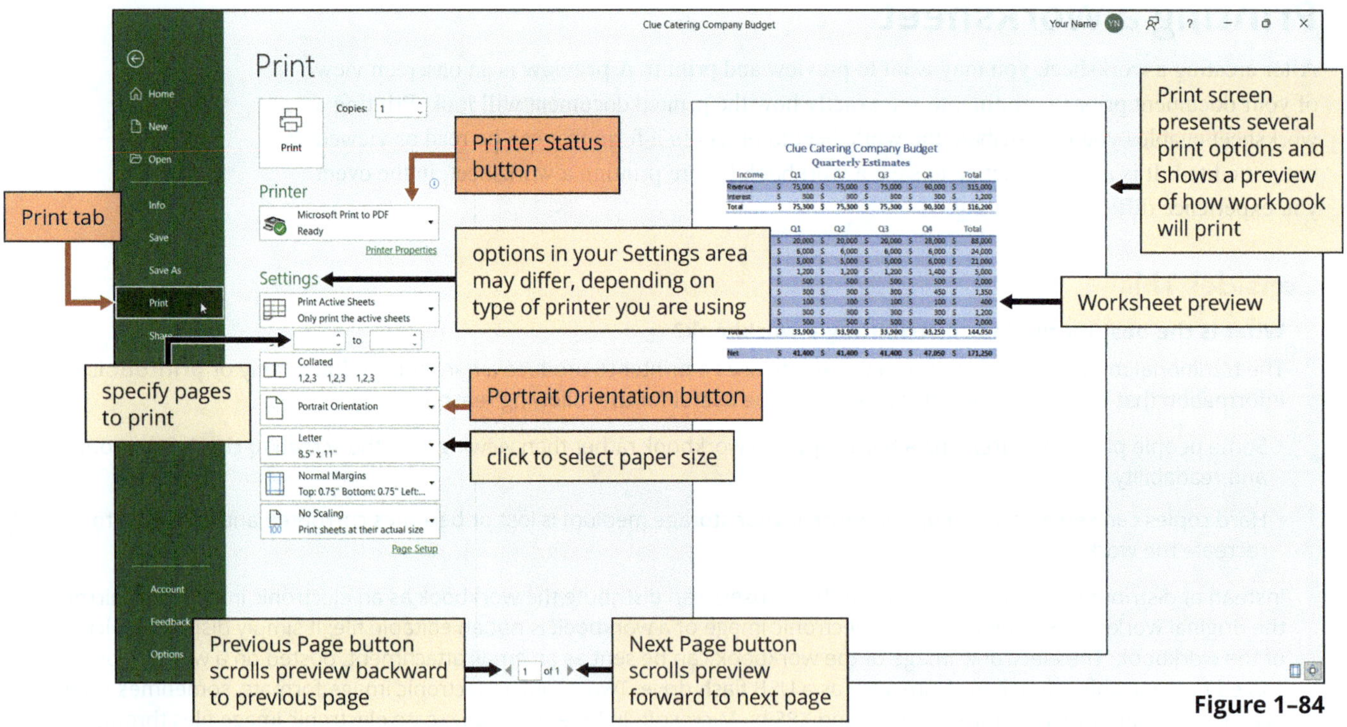

Figure 1–84

2

- Verify that the printer listed on the Printer Status button is the printer you want to use. If necessary, click the Printer Status button to display a list of available printer options and then click the desired printer to change the currently selected printer.
- If you want to print more than one copy, use the Copies up arrow to increase the number.
- If you want to change the paper size, use the paper size arrow (which currently reads Letter 8.5" × 11") to view and select a different one.

3

- Click the Portrait Orientation button in the Settings area and then select Landscape Orientation to change the orientation of the page to landscape (Figure 1–85).

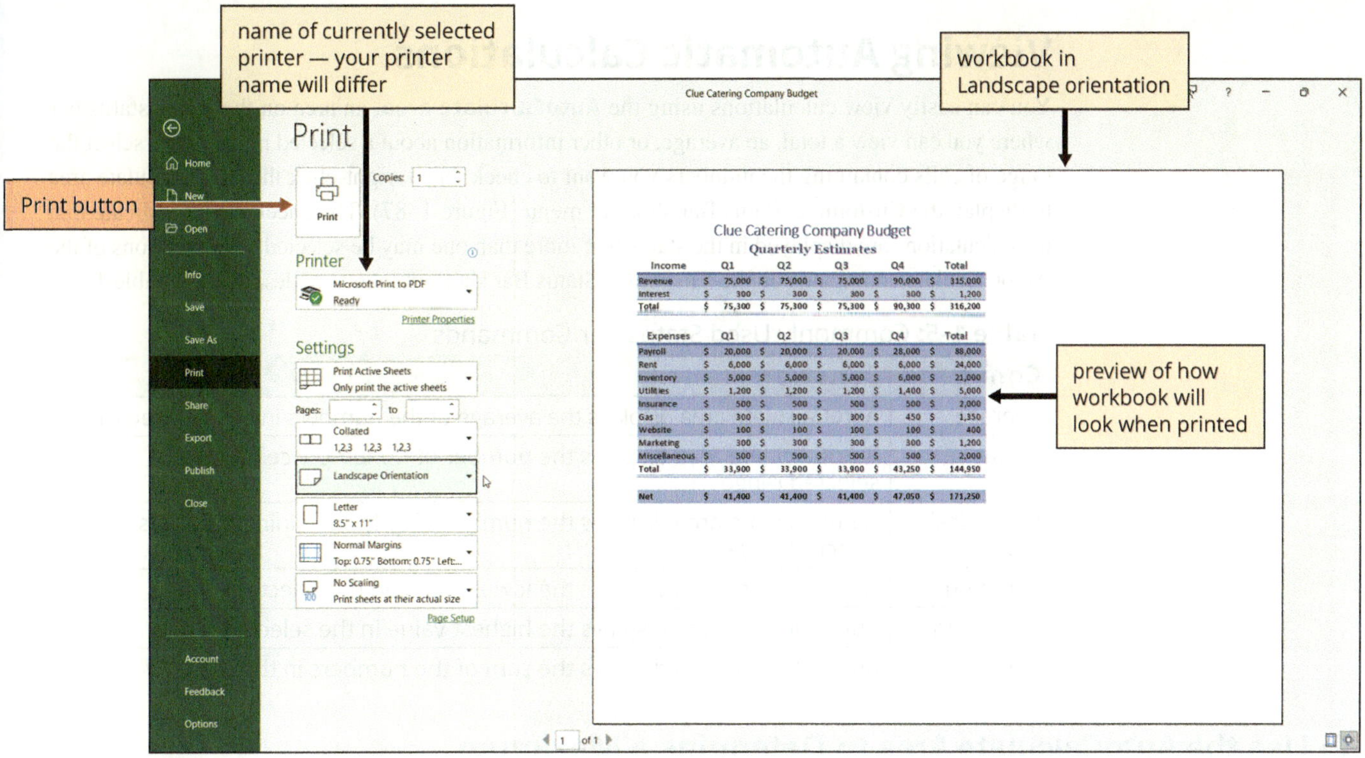

Figure 1–85

4

- Click the Print button on the Print screen to print the worksheet in landscape orientation on the currently selected printer.
- When the printer stops, retrieve the hard copy (Figure 1–86).

Q&A Do I have to wait until my worksheet is complete to print it?
No, you can print a document at any time while you are creating it.

Clue Catering Company Budget
Quarterly Estimates

Income	Q1	Q2	Q3	Q4	Total
Revenue	$ 75,000	$ 75,000	$ 75,000	$ 90,000	$ 315,000
Interest	$ 300	$ 300	$ 300	$ 300	$ 1,200
Total	**$ 75,300**	**$ 75,300**	**$ 75,300**	**$ 90,300**	**$ 316,200**

Expenses	Q1	Q2	Q3	Q4	Total
Payroll	$ 20,000	$ 20,000	$ 20,000	$ 28,000	$ 88,000
Rent	$ 6,000	$ 6,000	$ 6,000	$ 6,000	$ 24,000
Inventory	$ 5,000	$ 5,000	$ 5,000	$ 6,000	$ 21,000
Utilities	$ 1,200	$ 1,200	$ 1,200	$ 1,400	$ 5,000
Insurance	$ 500	$ 500	$ 500	$ 500	$ 2,000
Gas	$ 300	$ 300	$ 300	$ 450	$ 1,350
Website	$ 100	$ 100	$ 100	$ 100	$ 400
Marketing	$ 300	$ 300	$ 300	$ 300	$ 1,200
Miscellaneous	$ 500	$ 500	$ 500	$ 500	$ 2,000
Total	**$ 33,900**	**$ 33,900**	**$ 33,900**	**$ 43,250**	**$ 144,950**
Net	**$ 41,400**	**$ 41,400**	**$ 41,400**	**$ 47,050**	**$ 171,250**

Figure 1–86

Other Ways

1. Press CTRL+P to open the Print screen, press ENTER

Viewing Automatic Calculations

You can easily view calculations using the **AutoCalculate area**, an area on the Excel status bar where you can view a total, an average, or other information about a selected range. First, select the range of cells containing the numbers you want to check. Next, right-click the AutoCalculate area to display the Customize Status Bar shortcut menu (Figure 1–87). The check marks indicate that the calculations are displayed in the status bar; more than one may be selected. The functions of the AutoCalculate commands on the Customize Status Bar shortcut menu are described in Table 1–5.

Table 1-5: Commonly Used Status Bar Commands

Command	Function
Average	AutoCalculate area displays the average of the numbers in the selected range
Count	AutoCalculate area displays the number of nonempty cells in the selected range
Numerical Count	AutoCalculate area displays the number of cells containing numbers in the selected range
Minimum	AutoCalculate area displays the lowest value in the selected range
Maximum	AutoCalculate area displays the highest value in the selected range
Sum	AutoCalculate area displays the sum of the numbers in the selected range

To Use the AutoCalculate Area to Determine a Maximum

The following steps determine the largest quarterly total in the budget. **Why?** *Sometimes, you want a quick analysis, which can be especially helpful when your worksheet contains a lot of data.*

1

- Select the range B20:E20. Right-click the status bar to display the Customize Status Bar shortcut menu (Figure 1-87).

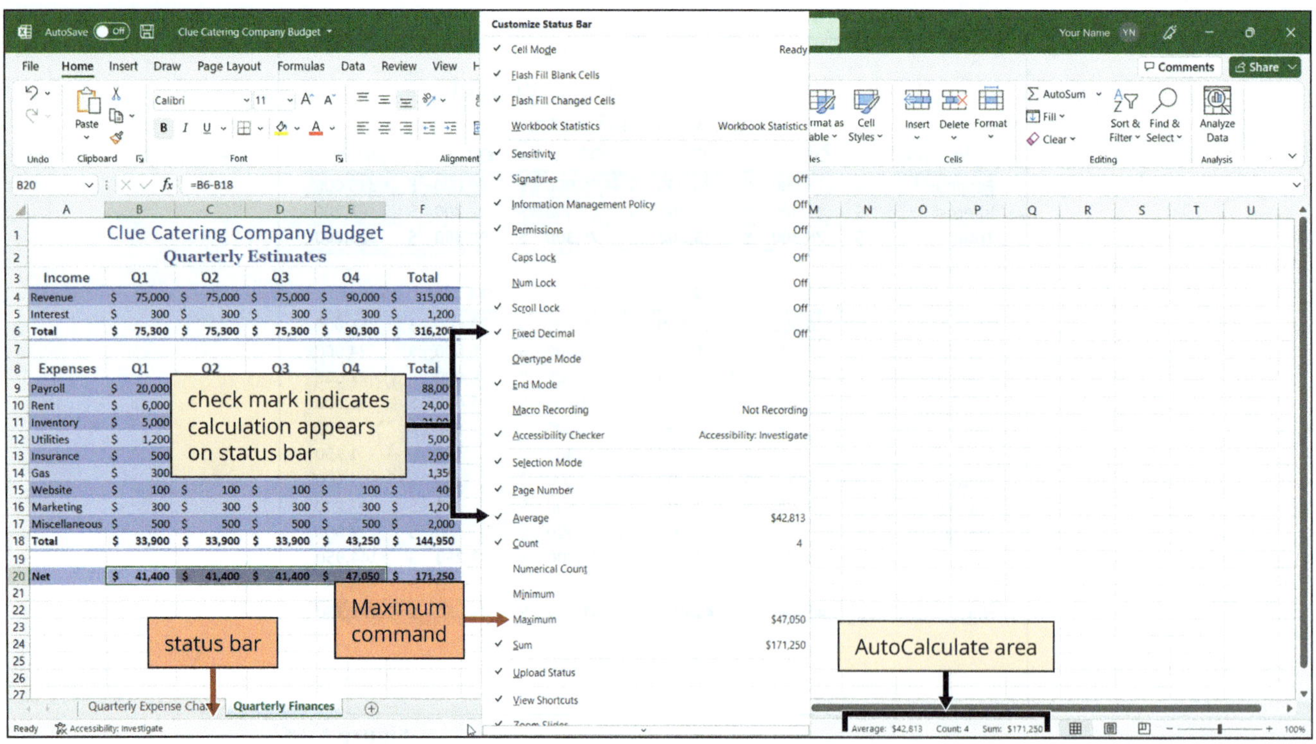

Figure 1-87

2

- Click Maximum on the shortcut menu to display the Maximum value in the range B20:E20 in the AutoCalculate area of the status bar.
- If necessary, click anywhere on the worksheet to close the shortcut menu (Figure 1-88).

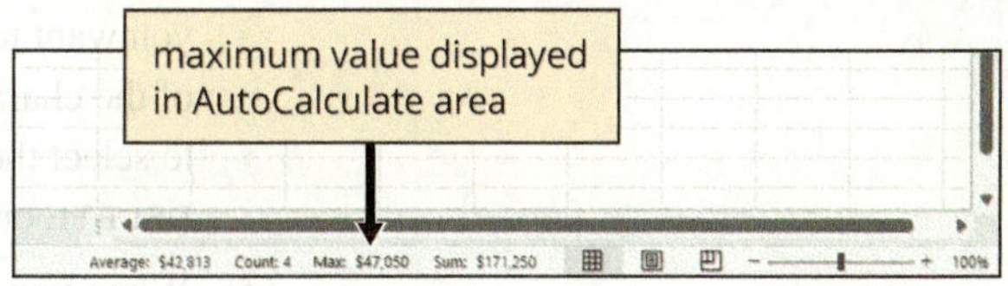

Figure 1-88

3

- Right-click the AutoCalculate area and then click Maximum on the shortcut menu to deselect it. The Maximum value will no longer appear on the status bar.
- If necessary, close the shortcut menu.

Correcting Errors

You can correct data entry errors on a worksheet using one of several methods. The method you choose will depend on the extent of the error and whether you notice it while entering the data or after you have entered the incorrect data into the cell.

Correcting Errors while Entering Data into a Cell

If you notice an error while you are entering data into a cell, press BACKSPACE to erase the incorrect character(s) and then enter the correct character(s). If the error is a major one, click the Cancel box in the formula bar or press ESC to erase the entire entry and then reenter the data.

Correcting Errors after Entering Data into a Cell

If you find an error in the worksheet after entering the data, you can correct the error in one of two ways:

1. If the entry is short, select the cell, retype the entry correctly, and then click the Enter button or press ENTER. The new entry will replace the old entry.
2. If the entry in the cell is long and the errors are minor, using Edit mode may be a better choice than retyping the cell entry. In **Edit mode**, a mode that lets you make changes to a cell's content within the cell, Excel displays the active cell entry in the formula bar and a flashing insertion point in the active cell. There you can edit the contents directly in the cell — a procedure called **in-cell editing.**

   a. Double-click the cell containing the error to switch Excel to Edit mode (Figure 1–89).

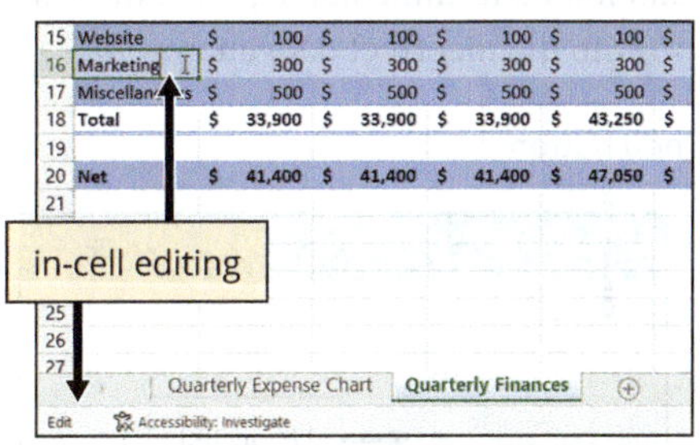

Figure 1-89

   b. Make corrections using the following in-cell editing methods.

      (1) To insert new characters between two characters, place the insertion point between the two characters and begin typing. Excel inserts the new characters to the left of the insertion point.

(2) To delete a character in the cell, move the insertion point to the left of the character you want to delete and then press DELETE, or place the insertion point to the right of the character you want to delete and then press BACKSPACE. You also can drag to select the character or adjacent characters you want to delete and then press DELETE or CTRL+X or click the Cut button (Home tab | Clipboard group).

(3) When you are finished editing an entry, click the Enter button or press ENTER.

There are two ways to enter data in Edit mode: Insert mode and Overtype mode. **Insert mode** is the default Excel mode that inserts a character and moves all characters to the right of the typed character one position to the right. You can change to Overtype mode by pressing INSERT. In **Overtype mode**, Excel replaces, or overtypes, the character to the right of the insertion point. The INSERT key toggles the keyboard between Insert mode and Overtype mode.

While in Edit mode, you may want to move the insertion point to various points in the cell, select portions of the data in the cell, or switch from inserting characters to overtyping characters. Table 1–6 summarizes the more common tasks performed during in-cell editing.

Table 1-6: Summary of In-Cell Editing Tasks

	Task	Mouse Operation	Keyboard
1	Move the insertion point to the beginning of data in a cell.	Point to the left of the first character and click.	Press HOME.
2	Move the insertion point to the end of data in a cell.	Point to the right of the last character and click.	Press END.
3	Move the insertion point anywhere in a cell.	Point to the appropriate position and click the character.	Press RIGHT ARROW or LEFT ARROW.
4	Highlight one or more adjacent characters.	Drag through adjacent characters.	Press SHIFT+RIGHT ARROW or SHIFT+LEFT ARROW.
5	Select all data in a cell.	Double-click the cell with the insertion point in the cell if the data in the cell contains no spaces.	
6	Delete selected characters.	Click the Cut button (Home tab | Clipboard group).	Press DELETE.
7	Delete characters to the left of the insertion point.		Press BACKSPACE.
8	Delete characters to the right of the insertion point.		Press DELETE.
9	Toggle between Insert and Overtype modes.		Press INSERT.

Undoing the Last Cell Entry

The Undo button on the ribbon (Figure 1–90) allows you to erase recent cell entries. Thus, if you enter incorrect data in a cell and notice it immediately, click the Undo button and Excel changes the cell entry to what it was prior to the incorrect data entry.

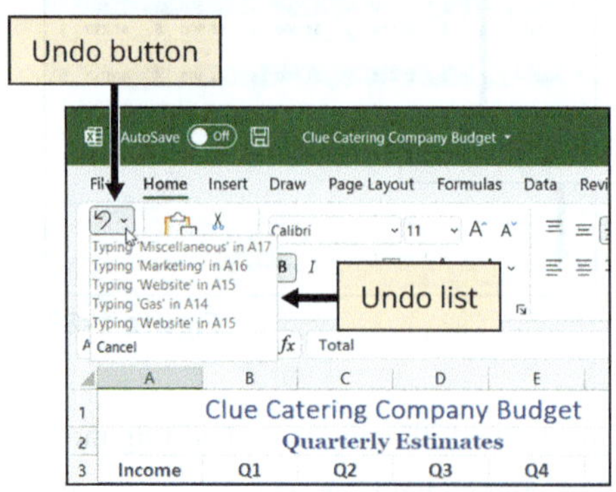

Figure 1–90

Excel remembers the last 100 actions you have completed. Thus, you can undo up to 100 previous actions by clicking the Undo arrow to display the Undo list and then clicking the action to be undone (Figure 1–90). You can drag through several actions in the Undo list to undo all of them at once. If no actions are available for Excel to undo, then the dimmed appearance of the Undo button indicates that it is unavailable.

The Redo button, next to the Undo button on the ribbon, allows you to repeat previous actions; that is, if you accidentally undo an action, you can use the Redo button to perform the action again.

Clearing a Cell or Range of Cells

If you enter data into the wrong cell or range of cells, you can erase, or clear, the data using one of the first four methods listed below. The fifth method clears the formatting from the selected cells. To clear a cell or range of cells, you would perform the following steps:

To Clear Cell Entries Using the Fill Handle To clear cell entries using the fill handle, you would follow these steps.

1. Select the cell or range of cells and then point to the fill handle so that the pointer changes to a crosshair.
2. Drag the fill handle back into the selected cell or range until a shadow covers the cell or cells you want to erase.

To Clear Cell Entries Using the Shortcut Menu To clear cell entries using the shortcut menu, you would follow these steps.

1. Select the cell or range of cells to be cleared.
2. Right-click the selection.
3. Click Clear Contents on the shortcut menu.

To Clear Cell Entries Using the Delete Key To clear cell entries using the Delete key, you would follow these steps.

1. Select the cell or range of cells to be cleared.
2. Press DELETE.

To Clear Cell Entries and Formatting Using the Clear Button To clear cell entries and formatting using the Clear button, you would follow these steps.

1. Select the cell or range of cells to be cleared.
2. Click the Clear button (Home tab | Editing group).
3. Click Clear Contents on the Clear menu, or click Clear All to clear both the cell entry and the cell formatting.

To Clear Formatting Using the Cell Styles Button To clear formatting using the Cell Styles button, you would follow these steps.

1. Select the cell or range of cells from which you want to remove the formatting.
2. Click the Cell Styles button (Home tab | Styles group) and then click Normal in the Cell Styles gallery.

As you are clearing cell entries, always remember that you should never press the SPACEBAR to clear a cell. Pressing the SPACEBAR enters a blank character. A blank character is interpreted by Excel as text and is different from an empty cell, even though the cell may appear empty.

Clearing the Entire Worksheet

If the required worksheet edits are extensive or if the requirements drastically change, you may want to clear the entire worksheet and start over. To clear the worksheet or delete an embedded chart, you would use the following steps.

To Clear the Entire Worksheet To clear the contents of an entire worksheet, you would follow these steps.

1. Click the Select All button on the worksheet. The Select All button is located above the row 1 identifier and to the left of the column A heading.

2. Click the Clear button (Home tab | Editing group) and then click Clear All on the menu to delete both the entries and formats.

The Select All button selects the entire worksheet. To clear an unsaved workbook, click the Close Window button on the workbook's title bar or click the Close button in Backstage view. Click the No button if the Microsoft Excel dialog box asks if you want to save changes. To start a new, blank workbook, click the New button in Backstage view.

Using Excel Help

Once an Office app's Help window is open, you can use several methods to navigate Help. You can search for help by using the Help pane or the Search box.

To Obtain Help Using the Search Text Box

Assume for the following example that you want to know more about functions. The following steps use the Search text box to obtain useful information about functions by entering the word, functions, as search text. **Why?** You may not know the exact help topic you are looking to find, so using keywords can help narrow your search.

1

- Click Help on the ribbon to display the Help tab (Figure 1-91).

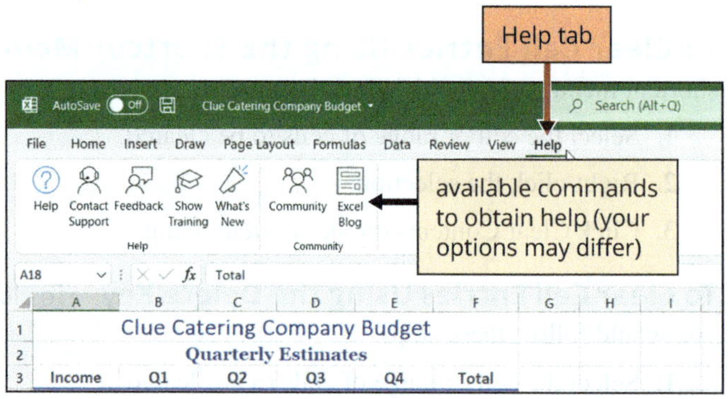

Figure 1-91

2

- Click the Help button (Help group) to display the Help pane (Figure 1-92).

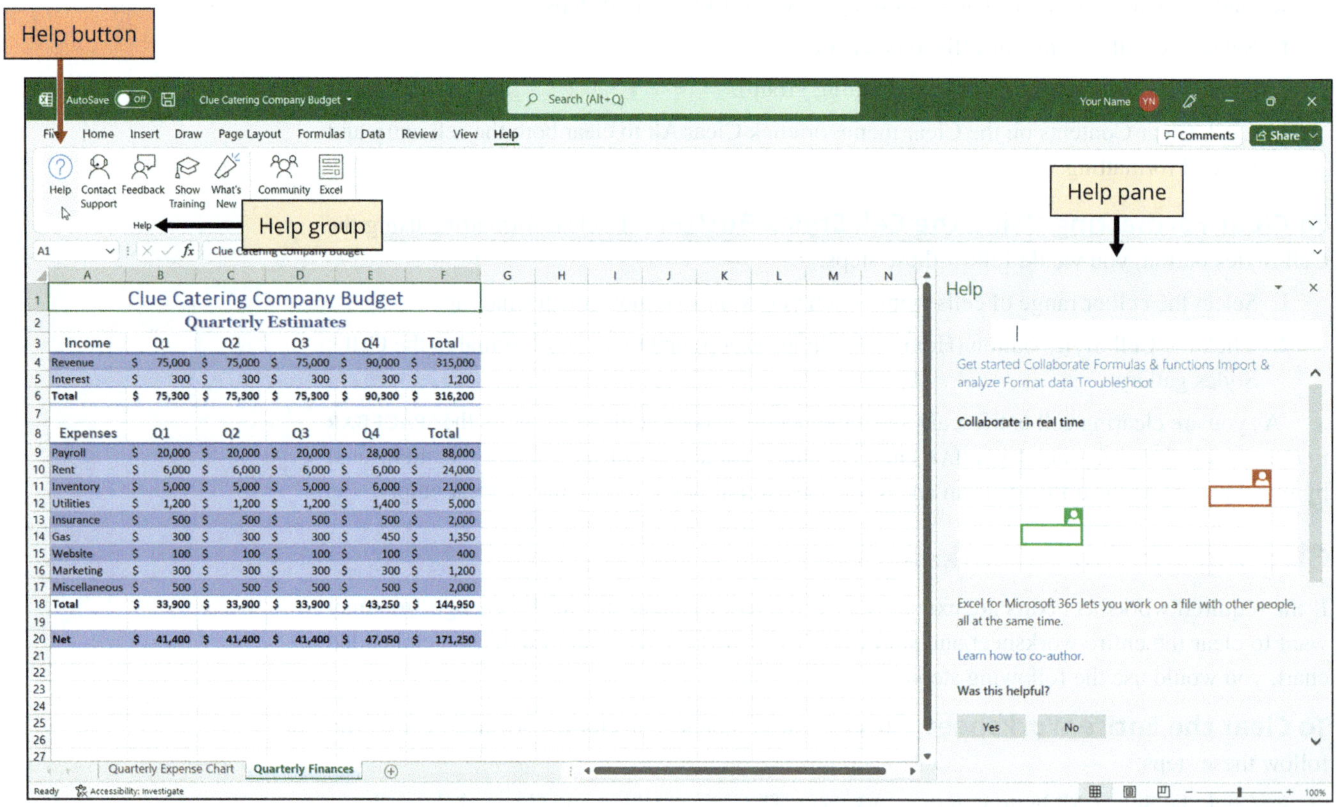

Figure 1-92

3

- Type **functions** in the Search help box at the top of the Help pane to enter the search text (Figure 1–93).

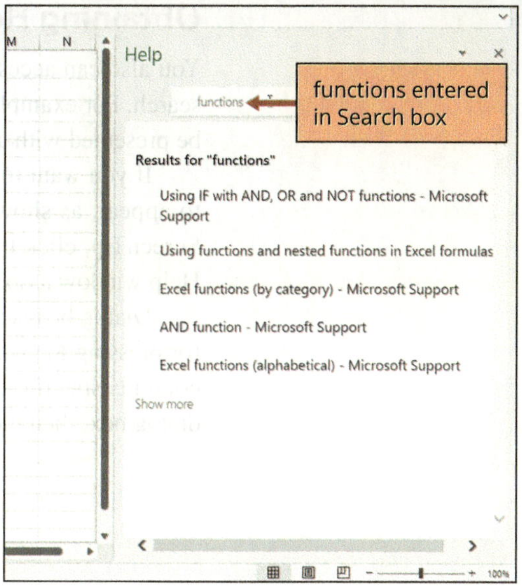

Figure 1–93

4

- Press ENTER to display the search results (Figure 1–94).

Q&A Why do my search results differ?
If you do not have an Internet connection, your results will reflect only the content of the Help files on your computer. When searching for help online, results also can change as content is added, deleted, and updated on the online Help webpages maintained by Microsoft.

Why were my search results not very helpful?
When initiating a search, be sure to check the spelling of the search text; also, keep your search specific to return the most accurate results.

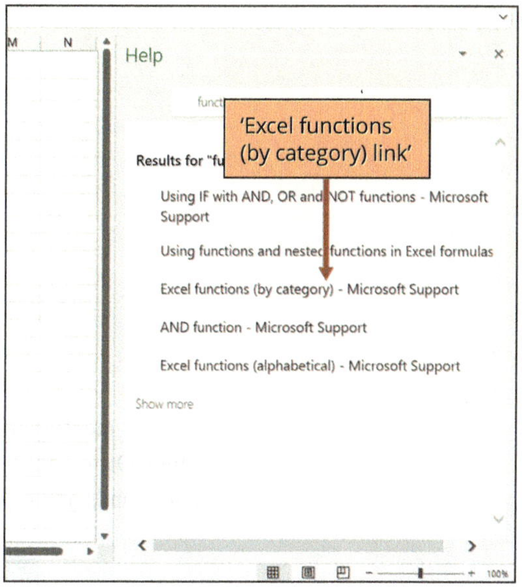

Figure 1–94

5

- Click the 'Excel functions (by category)', or similar, link to display the Help information associated with the selected topic (Figure 1–95).

6

- Click the Close button in the Help pane to close the pane.
- Click Home on the ribbon to display the Home tab.

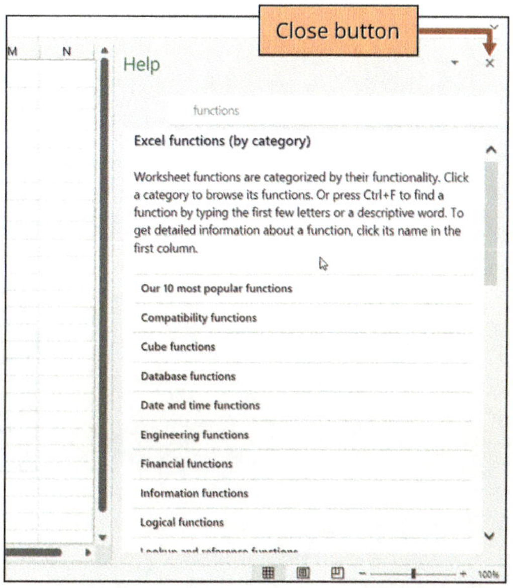

Figure 1–95

Obtaining Help while Working in an Office App

You also can access the Help functionality without first opening the Help pane and initiating a search. For example, you may be uncertain about how a particular command works, or you may be presented with a dialog box that you are not sure how to use.

If you want to learn more about a command, point to its button and wait for the ScreenTip to appear, as shown in Figure 1–96. If the Help icon and 'Tell me more' link appear in the ScreenTip, click the 'Tell me more' link (or press F1 while pointing to the button) to open the Help window associated with that command.

Dialog boxes also contain Help buttons, as shown in Figure 1–97. Clicking the Help button (or pressing F1) while the dialog box is displayed opens a Help window, which will display help contents specific to the dialog box, if available. If no help file is available for that particular dialog box, then the window will display the Help home page.

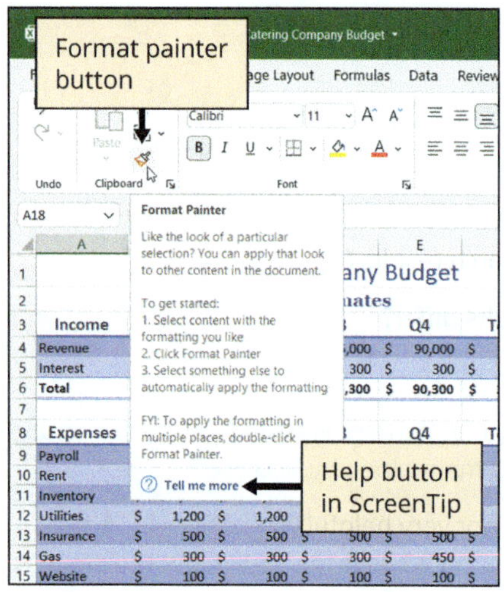

Figure 1–96

As mentioned previously, the Search box is integrated into the title bar in Excel and most other Office apps and can perform a variety of functions, including providing easy access to commands and help content as you type.

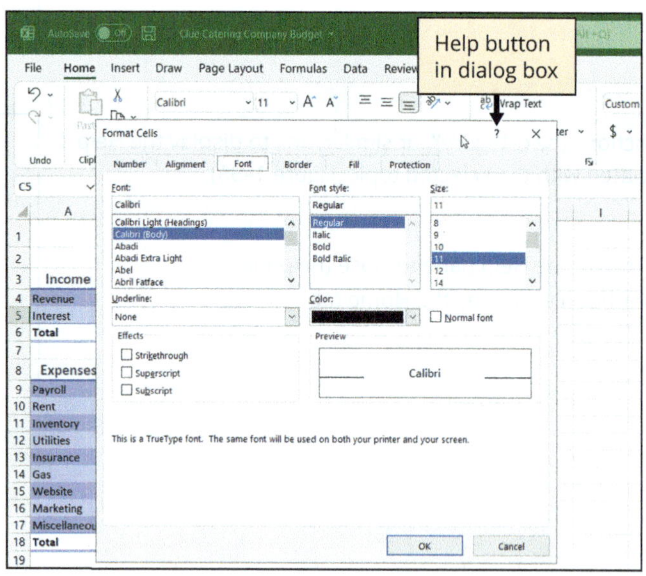

Figure 1–97

To Obtain Help Using the Search Box

If you are having trouble finding a command in Excel, you can use the Search box to search for the function you are trying to perform. As you type, the Search box will suggest commands that match the search text you are entering. **Why?** You can use the Search box to access commands quickly you otherwise may be unable to find on the ribbon. The following steps find commands related to headers and footers.

1

- Type **header and footer** in the Search box and watch the search results appear (Figure 1–98).

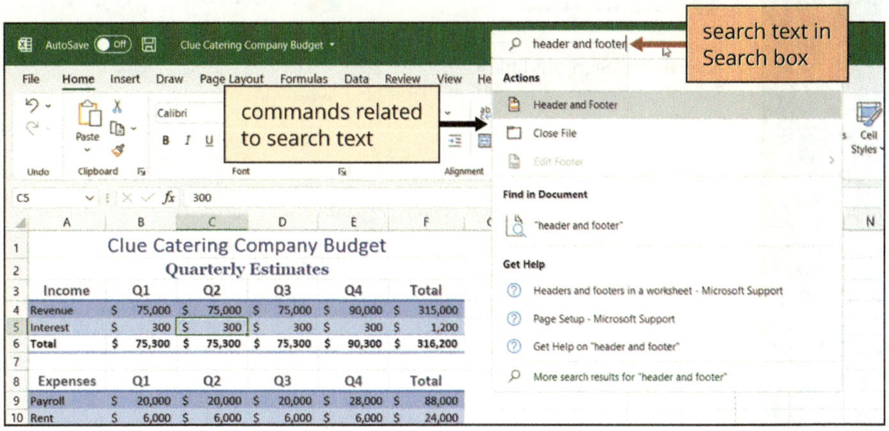

Figure 1–98

To Save a Workbook with a Different File Name

To save a copy of the existing file, you can save the file with a new file name. **Why?** You have finished working on the Clue Catering Company Budget workbook and would like to save a copy of the workbook with a new file name.

The following steps save the Clue Catering Company Budget workbook with a new file name.

1. Click File on the ribbon to open Backstage view.
2. Click Save As in Backstage view to display the Save As screen.
3. Type **SC_EX_1_Clue** in the File name text box, replacing the existing file name.
4. Click the Save button to save the workbook with the new name.

To Sign Out of a Microsoft Account

If you are using a public computer or otherwise want to sign out of your Microsoft account, you should sign out of the account from the Accounts screen in Backstage view. **Why?** For security reasons, you should sign out of your Microsoft account when you are finished using a public or shared computer. Staying signed in to your Microsoft account might enable others to access your files.

The following steps sign out of a Microsoft account and exit the Excel program. If you do not want to sign out of your Microsoft account or exit Excel, read these steps without performing them.

1. Click File on the ribbon to open Backstage view.
2. Click Account to display the Account screen (Figure 1–99).
3. Click the Sign out link, which displays the Remove Account dialog box. If a Can't remove Windows accounts dialog box appears instead of the Remove Account dialog box, click OK and skip the remaining steps.

Q&A Why does a Can't remove Windows accounts dialog box appear?

If you signed in to Windows using your Microsoft account, then you also must sign out from Windows rather than signing out from within Excel. When you are finished using Windows, be sure to sign out at that time.

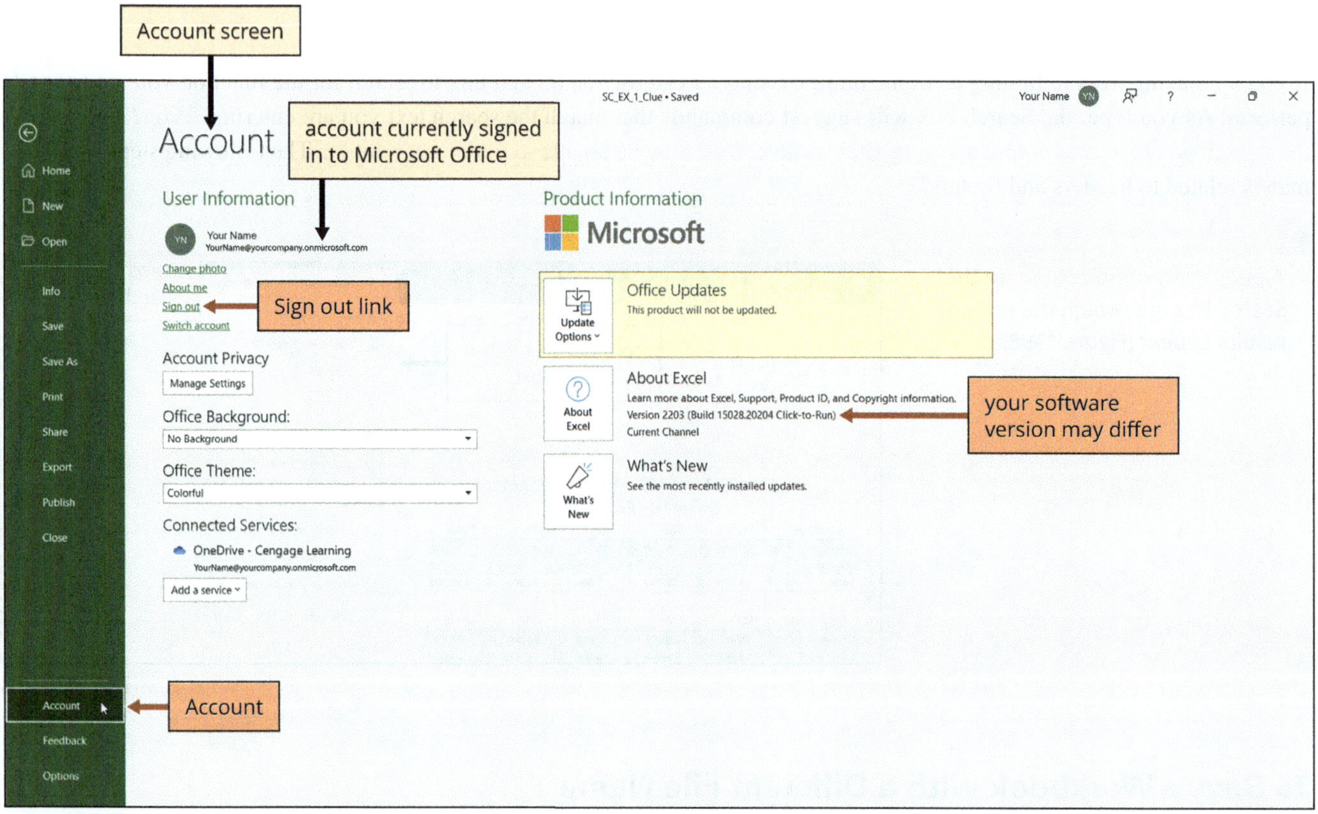

Figure 1–99

4. Click the Yes button (Remove Account dialog box) to sign out of your Microsoft account on this computer.

Q&A Should I sign out of Windows after removing my Microsoft account?
When you are finished using the computer, you should sign out of Windows for maximum security.

5. Click the Back button in the upper-left corner of Backstage view to return to the document.

6. sam Click the Close button to close the workbook and exit Microsoft Excel. If you are prompted to save changes, click Yes.

Summary

In this module, you have learned how to create a catering company budget worksheet and chart. Topics covered included starting Excel and creating a blank workbook, selecting a cell, entering text, entering numbers, calculating a sum, using the fill handle, formatting a worksheet, adding a pie chart, changing sheet tab names and colors, printing a worksheet, using the AutoCalculate area, correcting errors, and obtaining help.

Consider This: Plan Ahead

What decisions will you need to make when creating workbooks and charts in the future?

Use these guidelines as you complete the assignments in this module and create your own spreadsheets outside of this class.

1. Determine the workbook structure.
   a) Determine the data you will need for your workbook.
   b) Sketch a layout of your data and your chart.
2. Create the worksheet.
   a) Enter titles, subtitles, and headings.
   b) Enter data, functions, and formulas.
3. Format the worksheet.
   a) Format the titles, subtitles, and headings using styles.
   b) Format the totals.
   c) Format the numbers.
   d) Format the text.
   e) Adjust column widths.
4. Create the chart.
   a) Determine the type of chart to use.
   b) Determine the chart title and data.
   c) Determine the chart location
   d) Format the chart.

Student Assignments

Apply Your Knowledge

Reinforce the skills and apply the concepts you learned in this module.

Changing the Values in a Worksheet

Note: To complete this assignment, you will be required to use the Data Files. Please contact your instructor for information about accessing the Data Files.

Instructions: Start Excel. Open the workbook called SC_EX_1-1.xlsx (Figure 1–100a), which is located in the Data Files. You are a sales and marketing associate for Edgeview Real Estate and have been asked to update sales agent data for June. You are to edit data, apply formatting to the worksheet, and move the chart to a new sheet tab.

Perform the following tasks:

1. Make the changes to the worksheet described in Table 1–7. As you edit the values in the cells containing numeric data, watch the totals in row 8, the totals in column I, and the chart change.

Table 1–7: New Worksheet Data

Cell	Change Cell Contents To
A2	June Agent Sales
B6	252800
C5	32450
D7	740050
E6	89900
F5	45900
G6	197000
H5	12675

2. Change the worksheet title in cell A1 to the Title cell style and then merge and center it across columns A through I.
3. Use buttons on the Home tab to change the worksheet subtitle in cell A2 to 14-point font and then merge and center it across columns A through I. Change the font color of cell A2 to Green, Accent 6, Darker 25%.
4. Name the worksheet, Agent Sales, and apply the Green, Accent 6 color to the sheet tab.
5. Move the chart to a new sheet called Sales Chart. Change the chart title to June Sales Totals.

   If requested by your instructor, on the Agent Sales worksheet, replace Edgeview in cell A1 with your last name.
6. Save the workbook with the file name, SC_EX_1_Edgeview, and submit the revised workbook (shown in Figures 1–100b and 1–100c) in the format specified by your instructor and exit Excel.
7. **Consider This:** Besides the styles used in the worksheet, what other changes could you make to enhance the worksheet?

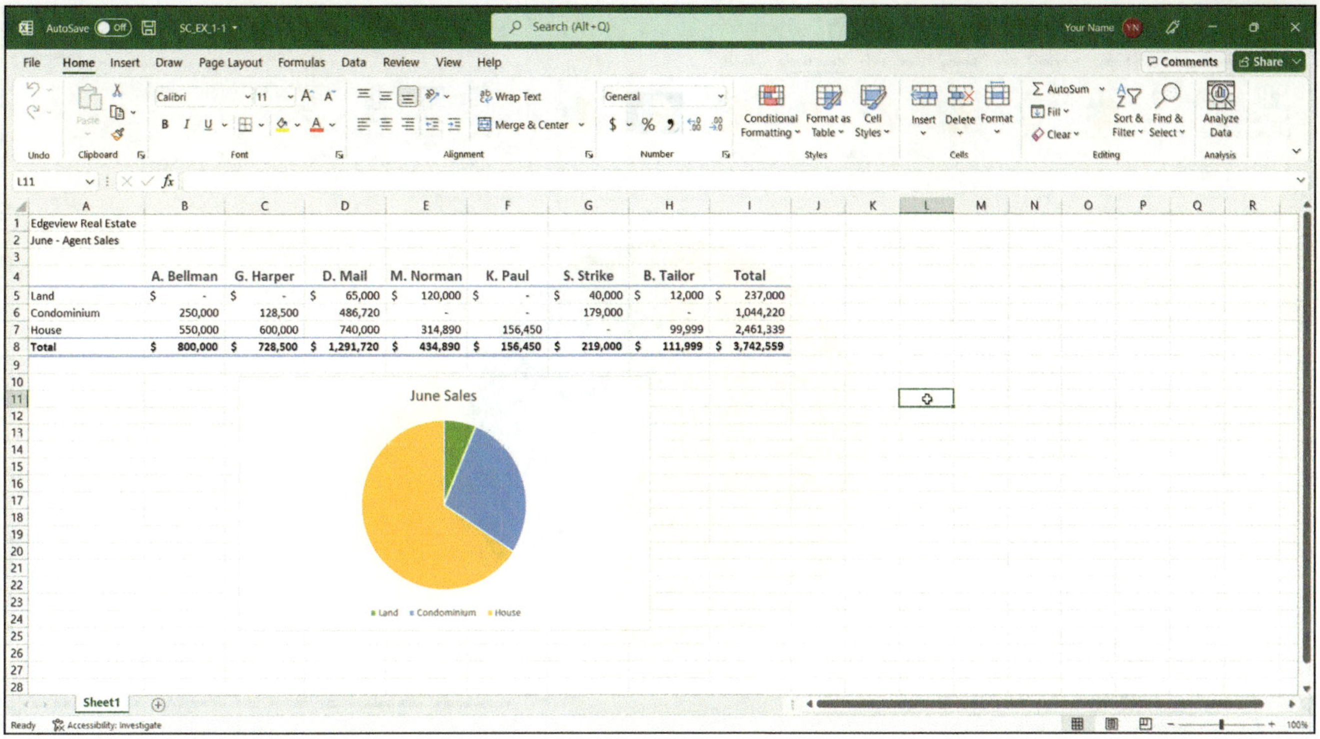

Figure 1–100(a) Worksheet before Formatting

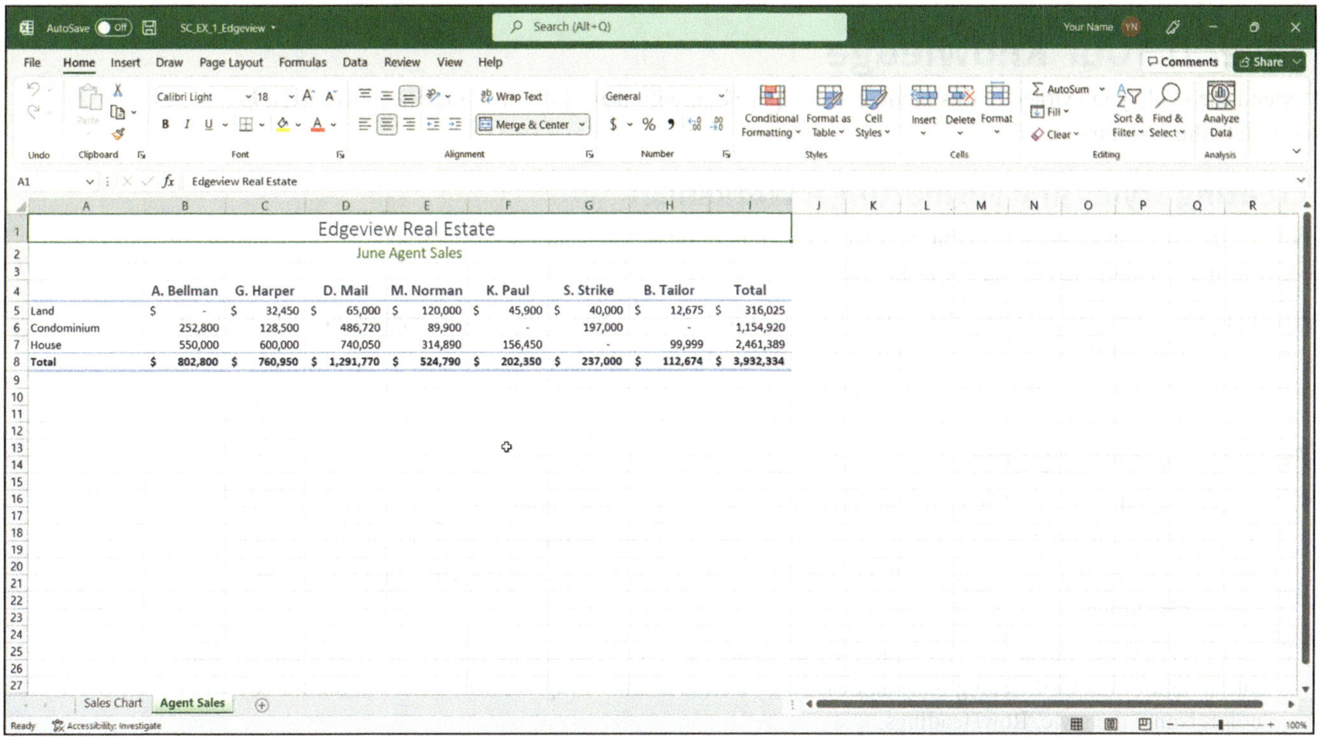

Figure 1–100(b) Worksheet after Formatting

Continued on next page

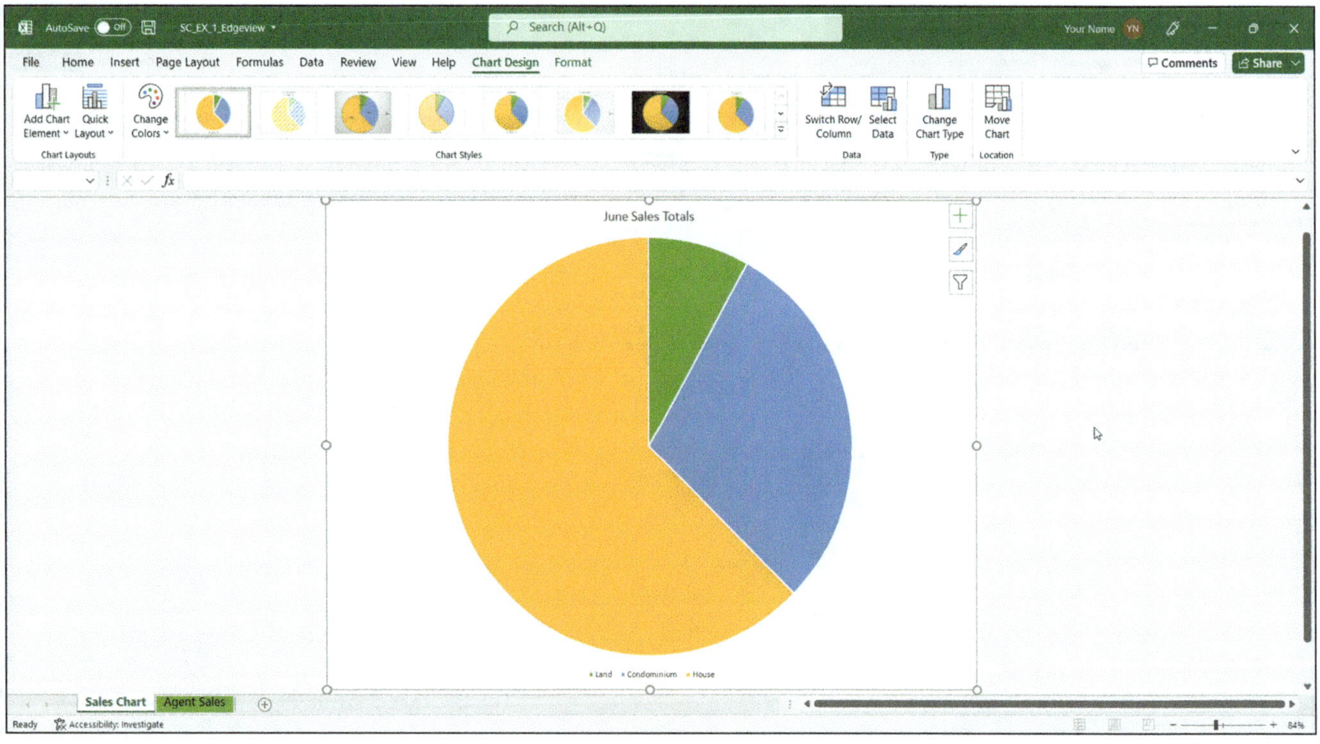

Figure 1–100(c) Pie Chart on Separate Sheet

Extend Your Knowledge

Extend the skills you learned in this module and experiment with new skills. You may need to use Help to complete the assignment.

Creating Styles and Formatting a Worksheet

Note: To complete this assignment, you will be required to use the Data Files. Please contact your instructor for information about accessing the Data Files.

Instructions: Start Excel. Open the workbook called SC_EX_1-2.xlsx, which is located in the Data Files. As a sales assistant for the Almond Tea Clothing Company, you have been asked to compare recent sales for the company's four product lines. You are to create styles and format a worksheet using them.

Perform the following tasks:

1. Select cell A4. Use the New Cell Style command in the Cell Styles gallery display the Style dialog box (Figure 1–101). Use the Format button and the Font tab in the Format Cells dialog box to create a style that uses the Green, Accent 6, Darker 25%, font color (row 5, column 10). Name the style, ColumnHeadings.
2. Select cell A5. Create a new style using the Style dialog box to create a cell fill style (**Hint:** Use the Fill tab in the Format Cells dialog box) that uses the Green, Accent 6, Lighter 40% (row 4, column 10) fill color. Name the style, RowHeadings.
3. Select cell B5. Create a new style using the Style dialog box to create a cell fill style that uses the Green, Accent 6, Lighter 80% (row 2, column 10) fill color. Name the style, TableFill.
4. Select cell range B4:I4. Apply the ColumnHeadings style to the cell range (**Hint:** Your custom styles appear in the Custom group.)
5. Select the cell range A5:A9. Apply the RowHeadings style to the cell range.
6. Select the cell range B5:I8. Apply the TableFill style to the cell range.

7. Name the sheet tab and apply a tab color of your choice.

   If requested by your instructor, change the font color of the text in cells A1 and A2 to the color of your eyes.

8. Save the workbook with the file name, SC_EX_1_Almond, and submit the revised workbook in the format specified by your instructor, and then exit Excel.

9. **Consider This:** What other styles would you create to improve the worksheet's appearance?

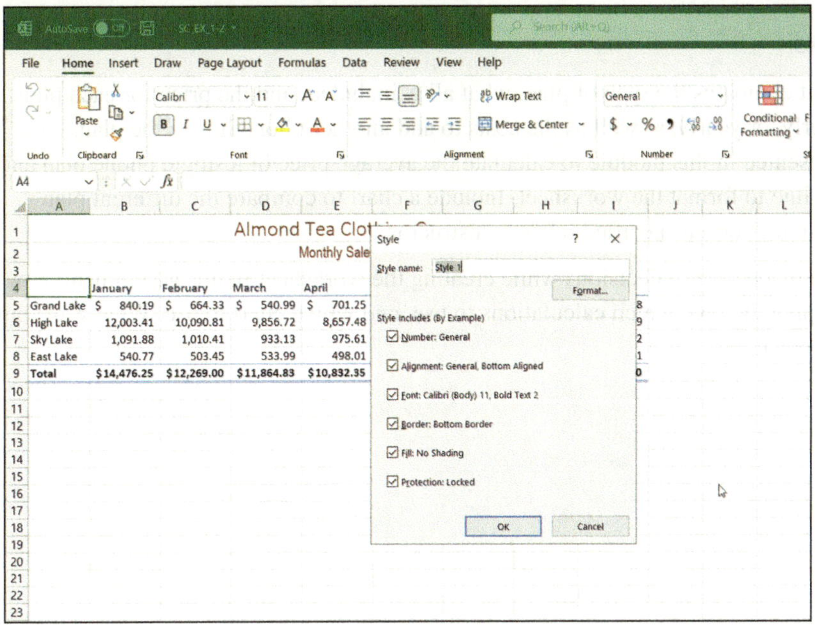

Figure 1–101

Expand Your World

Create a solution that uses cloud or web technologies by learning and investigating on your own from general guidance.

Monthly Budget

Instructions: Start Excel. You are to going to determine a monthly budget. You decide to download and use one of the Excel templates to create your worksheet.

Perform the following tasks:

1. Click New in Backstage view and then search for and click the monthly budget template of your choice that can calculate a monthly budget. This could be a personal budget, company budget, food budget, etc..

2. Enter fictitious (and realistic) information for a monthly budget, including projected and actual costs, and expenses. If the template you chose does not include a place for this information, add the information in an appropriate location. Search the web to look up realistic numbers regarding costs and expenses. Make sure to personalize your monthly budget with a title and unique numbers.

3. Save the file as SC_EX_1_MonthlyBudget, print the worksheet, and submit the assignment in the format specified by your instructor and then exit Excel.

4. **Consider This:** Which template would you use if you wanted to plan and keep track of a budget for a wedding?

In the Lab

Design and implement a solution using creative thinking and problem-solving skills.

Create a Worksheet Comparing Cell Phone Plans

Problem: You are shopping for a new cell phone plan and want to compare the prices of three different plans from different providers. You will compare plans with similar specifications, but where the plans and/or providers are different.

Perform the following tasks:

Part 1: Create a worksheet that compares the type of plan, what all is included, and the price for each plan, whether that be monthly, quarterly, or yearly, as well as the costs to add another phone line to the plan. Use the concepts and techniques presented in this module to calculate the average price of a single phone plan and average cost of adding an extra line to format the worksheet. Include a chart to compare the different plan costs. Submit your assignment in the format specified by your instructor.

Consider This: Part 2: You made several decisions while creating the worksheet in this assignment: how to organize the data, how to display the text, which calculations to use, and which chart to use. What was your rationale behind each of these decisions?

Formulas, Functions, and Formatting

Objectives

After completing this module, you will be able to:

- Use Flash Fill
- Enter formulas using the keyboard
- Enter formulas using Point mode
- Apply the MAX, MIN, and AVERAGE functions
- Verify a formula using Range Finder
- Apply a theme to a workbook
- Apply a date format to a cell or range
- Add conditional formatting to cells
- Change column width and row height
- Check the spelling on a worksheet
- Change margins and headers in Page Layout view
- Preview and print versions and sections of a worksheet

Introduction

In Module 1, you learned how to enter data, sum values, format a worksheet to make it easier to read, and draw a chart. This module continues to illustrate these topics and presents some new ones.

The new topics covered in this module include using formulas and functions to create a worksheet. Recall from Module 1 that a function is a special, predefined formula that provides a shortcut for a commonly used calculation. Other new topics include using option buttons, verifying formulas, applying a theme to a worksheet, adding borders, formatting numbers and text, using conditional formatting, changing the widths of columns and heights of rows, checking spelling, generating alternative worksheet displays and printouts, and adding page headers and footers to a worksheet. One alternative worksheet display and printout shows the formulas in the worksheet instead of the values. When you display the formulas in the worksheet, you see exactly what text, data, formulas, and functions you have entered.

Project: Worksheet with Formulas and Functions

The project in this module follows proper design guidelines and uses Excel to create the worksheet shown in Figure 2–1. Every two weeks, the owners of Atlas City Spa create a salary report by hand, where they keep track of employee service and commission data. Before paying employees, the owners must summarize the hours worked, pay rate, and commission information for each employee to ensure that the business properly compensates its employees. This report includes the following information for each employee: name, email address, service amounts, store front sales as well as gross pay and gross sales information. As the complexity of creating the salary report increases, the owners want to use Excel to make the process easier.

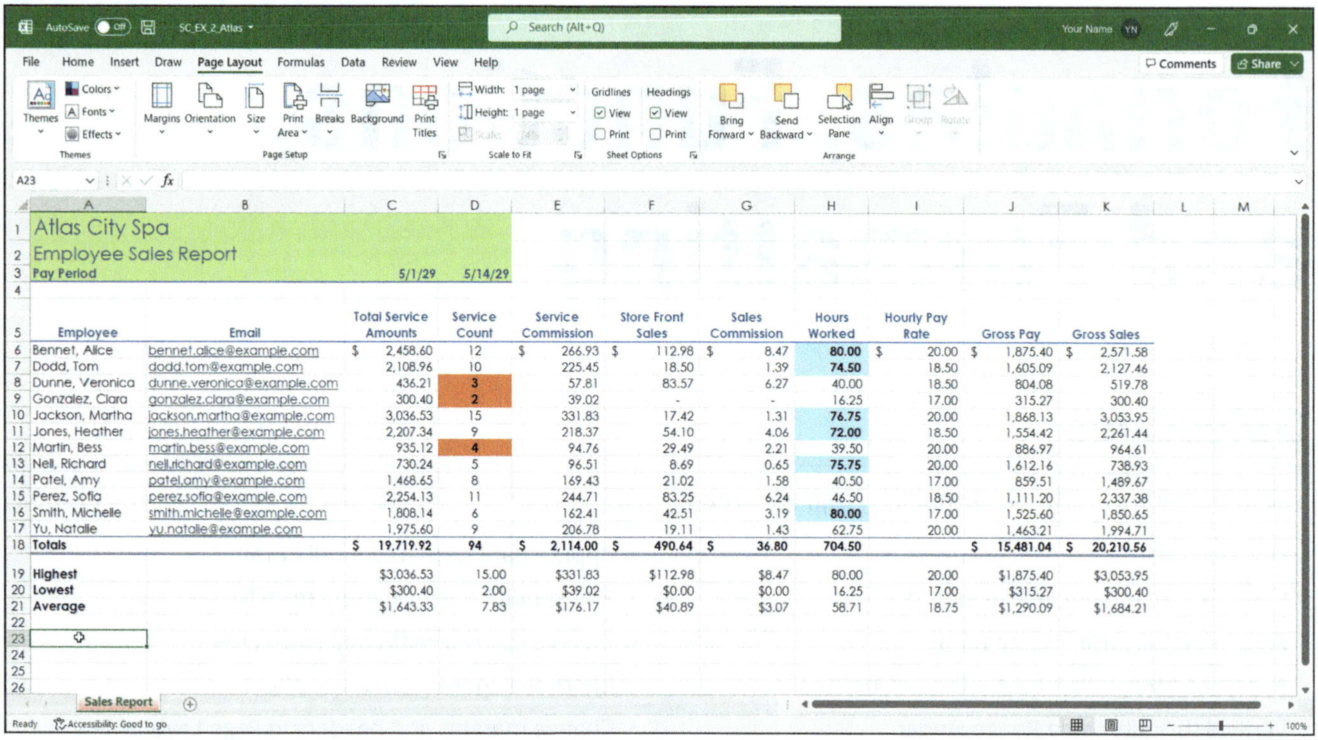

Figure 2–1

Recall that the first step in creating an effective worksheet is to make sure you understand what is required. The people who request the worksheet usually provide the requirements. The requirements document for the Atlas City Spa Employee Sales Report worksheet includes the following needs: source of data, summary of calculations, and other facts about its development (Figure 2–2).

Worksheet Title	Atlas City Spa Employee Sales Report
Needs	An easy-to-read worksheet that summarizes the company's sales report (Figure 2–3). For each employee, the worksheet is to include the employee's name, total service amount and count, service commission, store front sales, sales commission, hours worked, gross pay, and gross sales. The worksheet also should include the highest value, lowest value, and average for each category of data.
Source of Data	Supplied data includes employee names, total service amount and count, store front sales, hours worked, and hourly pay rate.
Calculations	The following calculations must be made for each of the employees: 1. Service Commission = (Total Service Amount * 0.05) + (Service Count * 12) 2. Sales Commission = Store Front Sales * 0.075 3. Gross Pay = Service Commission + Sales Commission + (Hours Worked * Hourly Pay Rate) 4. Gross Sales = Total Service Amounts + Store Front Sales 5. Compute the totals for total service amounts, service count, service commission, store front sales, sales commission, hours worked, gross pay, and gross sales. 6. Use the MAX and MIN functions to determine the highest and lowest values for total service amounts, service count, service commission, store front sales, sales commission, hours worked, hourly pay rate, gross pay, and gross sales. 7. Use the AVERAGE function to determine the average for number of total service amounts, service count, service commission, store front sales, sales commission, hours worked, hourly pay rate, gross pay, and gross sales.

Figure 2–2

In addition, using a sketch of the worksheet can help you visualize its design. The sketch for the Atlas City Spa Employee Sales Report worksheet includes a title, a subtitle, column and row headings, and the location of data values (Figure 2–3). It also uses specific characters to define the desired formatting for the worksheet, as follows:

1. The row of Xs below the leftmost column heading defines the cell entries as text, such as employee names.

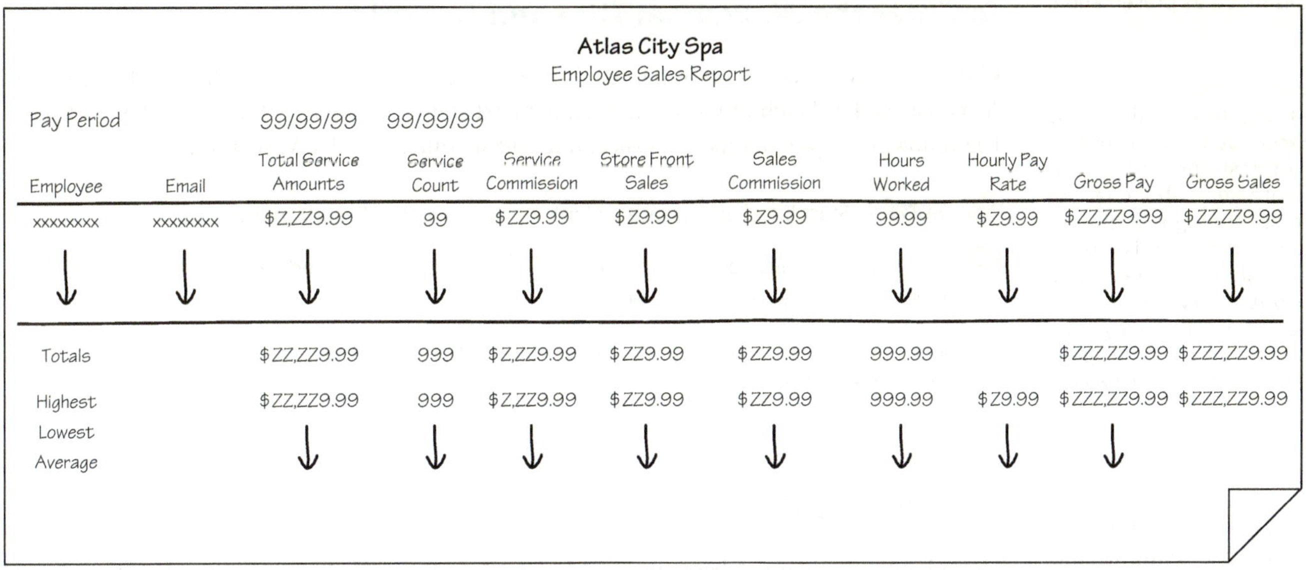

Figure 2–3

2. The rows of Zs and 9s with slashes, dollar signs, decimal points, commas, and percent signs in the remaining columns define the cell entries as numbers. The Zs indicate that the selected format should instruct Excel to suppress leading 0s. The 9s indicate that the selected format should instruct Excel to display any digits, including 0s.
3. The decimal point means that a decimal point should appear in the cell entry and indicates the number of decimal places to use.
4. The slashes in the third row identify the cell entry as a date.
5. The dollar signs that are adjacent to the Zs below the totals row signify a floating dollar sign, or one that appears next to the first significant digit.
6. The commas indicate that the selected format should instruct Excel to display a comma separator only if the number has sufficient digits (values in the thousandths) to the left of the decimal point.

Consider This

What is the function of an Excel worksheet?

The function, or purpose, of a worksheet is to provide a user with direct ways to accomplish tasks. In designing a worksheet, functional considerations should supersede visual aesthetics. Consider the following when designing your worksheet:

- Avoid the temptation to use flashy or confusing visual elements within the worksheet. This helps keep the worksheet accessible for anyone who may use or view the worksheet. You will learn more about accessibility in Module 3.
- Understand the requirements document.
- Choose the proper functions and formulas.

BTW
Touch Mode Differences
The Office and Windows interfaces may vary if you are using touch mode. For this reason, you might notice that the function or appearance of your touch screen differs slightly from this module's presentation.

Entering the Titles and Numbers into the Worksheet

The first step in creating the worksheet is to enter the titles and numbers into the worksheet. The following sets of steps enter the worksheet title and subtitle and then the sales report data shown in Table 2–1.

BTW
Excel Help
At any time while using Excel, you can find answers to questions and display information about various topics through Excel Help. Used properly, this form of assistance can increase your productivity and reduce your frustrations by minimizing the time you spend learning how to use Excel.

To Enter the Worksheet Title and Subtitle

With a good comprehension of the requirements document, an understanding of the necessary decisions, and a sketch of the worksheet, the next step is to use Excel to create the worksheet. The following steps enter the worksheet title and subtitle into cells A1 and A2.

1. Start Excel and create a blank workbook in the Excel window.
2. If necessary, select cell A1. Type **Atlas City Spa** in the selected cell and then press the DOWN ARROW key to enter the worksheet title.
3. Type **Employee Sales Report** in cell A2 and then press the DOWN ARROW key to enter the worksheet subtitle.

BTW
Screen Resolution
If you are using a computer to step through the project in this module and you want your screens to match the figures in this book, you should change your screen's resolution to 1920 × 1080.

To Enter the Column Titles

The column titles in row 5 begin in cell A5 and extend through cell K5. The employee names and the row titles begin in cell A3 and continue down to cell A21. The employee data is entered into rows 6 through 17 of the worksheet. The remainder of this section explains the steps required to enter the column titles, service and sales data, and row titles, as shown in Figure 2–4, and then to save the workbook. The following steps enter the column titles.

1. Select cell A5 selected, type **Employee** and then press the RIGHT ARROW key to enter the column heading.
2. Type **Email** in cell B5 and then press the RIGHT ARROW key.
3. Type **Total Service Amounts** in cell C5 and then press the RIGHT ARROW key.
4. Type **Service Count** in cell D5 and then press the RIGHT ARROW key.
5. Type **Service Commission** in cell E5 and then press the RIGHT ARROW key.
6. Type **Store Front Sales** in cell F5 and then press the RIGHT ARROW key.
7. Type **Sales Commission** in cell G5 and then press the RIGHT ARROW key.
8. Type **Hours Worked** in cell H5 and then press the RIGHT ARROW key.
9. Type **Hourly Pay Rate** in cell I5 and then press the RIGHT ARROW key.
10. Type **Gross Pay** in cell J5 and then press the RIGHT ARROW key.
11. Type **Gross Sales** in cell K5 and then press the RIGHT ARROW key.
12. Click cell A5 and drag across row 5 until K5 to highlight the cells.
13. Click the Wrap Text button (Home tab | Alignment group).

BTW
ALT+ENTER
If you want to control where each line ends in the cell, rather than letting Excel wrap the text based on the cell width, you must end each line with ALT+ENTER. You press ALT+ENTER in order to start a new line in a cell. The final line can be completed by clicking the Enter button, pressing ENTER, or pressing one of the arrow keys. When you see ALT+ENTER in a step, press ENTER while holding down ALT and then release both keys.

To Enter the Salary Data

Excel considers a date to be a number, and, therefore, it displays the date right aligned in the cell. The following steps enter the data for each employee.

1. Select cell A3. Type **Pay Period** then press the RIGHT ARROW key two times to enter the text and make cell C3 the active cell.
2. Type **5/1/29** and then press the RIGHT ARROW key.
3. Type **5/14/29** in cell D3 and press Enter to enter the date.
4. Select cell A6. Type **Bennet, Alice** and then press the RIGHT ARROW key twice.
5. Type **2458.60** in cell C6 and then press the RIGHT ARROW key.

   Q&A Why did 2458.60 change to 2458.6 when I pressed the RIGHT ARROW key?
   Depending on the number format applied to the cell, Excel might remove trailing zeros from a cell value.

6. Type **12** in cell D6 and then press the RIGHT ARROW key two times to enter the service count and make cell F6 the active cell.
7. Type **112.98** in cell F6 then press the RIGHT ARROW key two times to enter the store front sales and make cell H6 the active cell.
8. Type **80.00** in cell H6 and then press the RIGHT ARROW key.
9. Type **20.00** in cell I6.
10. Enter the payroll data in Table 2–1 for the eleven remaining employees in rows 7 through 17. Click the Enter button when you have finished entering the value in the last cell.

   Q&A In Step 1, why did the date change from 5/1/29 to 5/1/2029?
   When Excel recognizes a date in mm/dd/yy format, it formats the date as mm/dd/yyyy. Many professionals prefer to view dates in mm/dd/yyyy format as opposed to mm/dd/yy format to avoid confusion regarding the intended year. For example, a date displayed as 3/3/50 could imply a date of 3/3/1950 or 3/3/2050.

BTW
Two-Digit Years
When you enter a two-digit year value (xx) that is less than 30, Excel changes that value to 20xx; when you enter a value that is 30 or greater (zz), Excel changes the value to 19zz. Use four-digit years, if necessary, to ensure that Excel interprets year values the way you intend.

Table 2–1: Atlas City Spa Employee Sales Report Data

Employee	Total Service Amounts	Service Count	Store Front Sales	Hours Worked	Hourly Pay Rate
Dodd, Tom	2108.96	10	18.50	74.50	18.50
Dunne, Veronica	436.21	3	83.57	40.00	18.50
Gonzalez, Clara	300.40	2	0	16.25	17.00
Jackson, Martha	3036.53	15	17.42	76.75	20.00
Jones, Heather	2207.34	9	54.10	72.00	18.50
Martin, Bess	935.12	4	29.49	39.50	20.00
Nell, Richard	730.24	5	8.69	75.75	20.00
Patel, Amy	1468.65	8	21.02	40.50	17.00
Perez, Sofia	2254.13	11	83.25	46.50	18.50
Smith, Michelle	1808.14	6	42.51	80.00	17.00
Yu, Natalie	1975.60	9	19.11	62.75	20.00

BTW

The Ribbon and Screen Resolution

Excel may change how the groups and buttons within the groups appear on the ribbon, depending on the screen resolution of your computer. Thus, your ribbon may look different from the ones in this book if you are using a screen resolution other than 1920 × 1080.

Flash Fill

When you are entering data in a spreadsheet, occasionally Excel will recognize a pattern in the data you are entering. **Flash Fill** is an Excel feature that looks for patterns in the data and automatically fills or formats data in remaining cells based on those patterns. For example, if column A contains a list of 10 phone numbers without parentheses around the area code or dashes after the prefix, Flash Fill can help automatically create formatted phone numbers with parentheses and dashes with relative ease. To use Flash Fill, simply start entering formatted phone numbers in cells next to the unformatted numbers. After you enter a few formatted phone numbers, Flash Fill will suggest similarly formatted phone numbers for the remaining cells in the column. If you do not want to wait for Excel to offer suggestions, type one or two examples and then click the Flash Fill button (Data tab | Data Tools group). Flash Fill will autocomplete the remaining cells. If Flash Fill makes a mistake, simply click the Undo button, enter a few more examples, and try again. In addition to formatting data, Flash Fill can perform tasks such as concatenating data from multiple cells and separating data from one cell into multiple cells.

To Use Flash Fill

In the Atlas City Spa Employee Sales Report worksheet, you can use Flash Fill to generate email addresses using first and last names from another column in the worksheet. **Why?** The Flash Fill feature is a convenient way to avoid entering a lot of data manually. The following steps use Flash Fill to generate employee email addresses using the names entered in column A.

1

- Click cell B6 to select it.
- Type **bennet.alice@example.com** and then press the DOWN ARROW key to select cell B7.
- Type **dodd.tom@example.com** and Flash Fill will automatically generate the remaining email addresses in the range B8:B17 (Figure 2–4).
- Click the Enter button to enter Tom Dodd's email address in cell B7 and the similarly formatted email addresses in the range B8:B17.
- Click Data on the ribbon to select the Data tab.
- Click the Flash Fill button (Data tab | Data Tools group) to enter similarly formatted email addresses in the range B6:B12 (Figure 2–5).
- If necessary, remove any entries from cells B1 and B2.

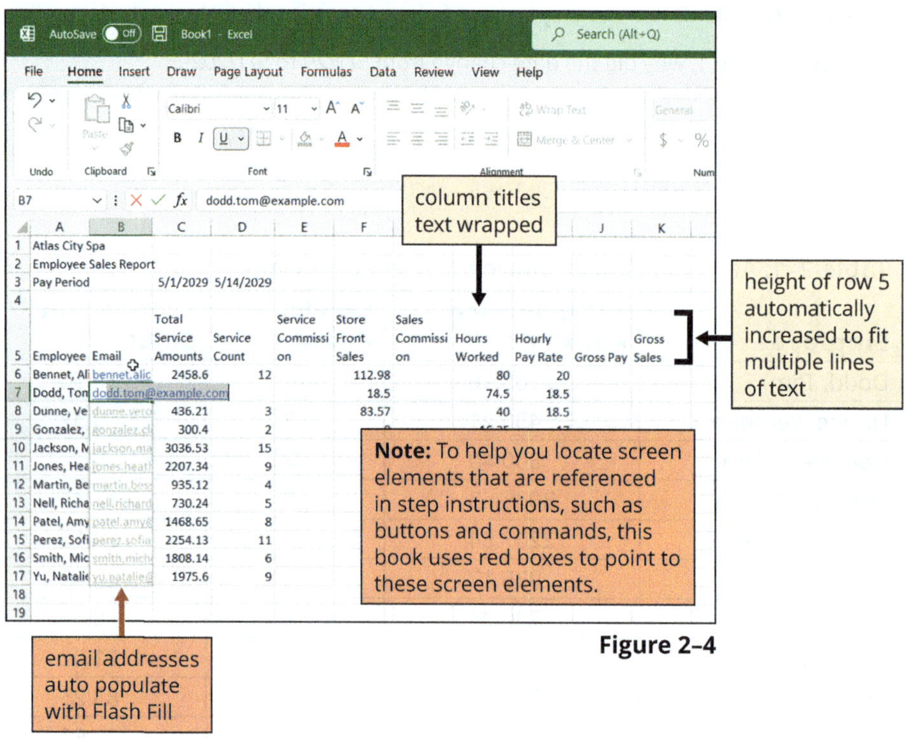

Figure 2–4

BTW

Manual Use of Flash Fill

In the case that Excel does not automatically generate a Flash Fill option, you can manually use the Flash Fill button in the ribbon.

Q&A Why was I unable to click the Flash Fill button after entering the first email address?

One entry might not have been enough for Excel to recognize a pattern. For instance, Flash Fill might have used the letter b before each last name in the email address instead of using the first initial and last name.

What would have happened if I kept typing examples without clicking the Flash Fill button?

As soon as Excel recognized a pattern, it would have displayed suggestions for the remaining cells. Pressing ENTER when the suggestions appear will populate the remaining cells.

Why did my Flash Fill not work?

Check cells for spelling errors or typos, as these can disrupt the Flash Fill process.

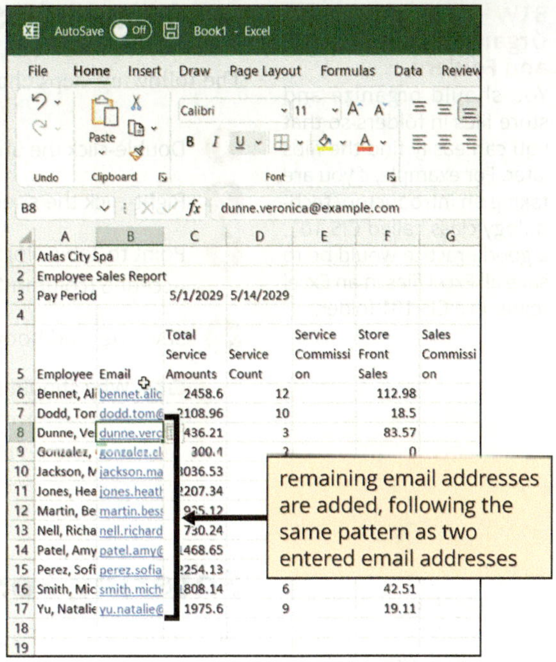

Figure 2–5

To Enter the Row Titles

The following steps add row titles for the rows that will contain the totals, highest, lowest, and average amounts.

1. Select cell A18. Type **Totals** and then press the DOWN ARROW key to enter a row header.
2. Type **Highest** in cell A19 and then press the DOWN ARROW key.
3. Type **Lowest** in cell A20 and then press the DOWN ARROW key.
4. Type **Average** in cell A21 and then press the DOWN ARROW key (Figure 2–6).

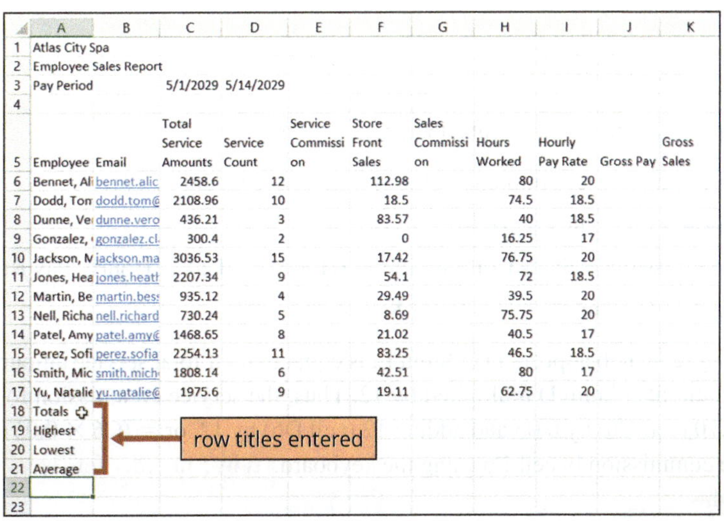

Figure 2–6

BTW
Formatting Worksheets
With early spreadsheet programs, users often skipped rows to improve the appearance of the worksheet. With Excel it is not necessary to skip rows because you can increase row heights to add white space between information.

BTW
Organizing Files and Folders
You should organize and store files in folders so that you can easily find the files later. For example, if you are taking an introductory technology class called CIS 101, a good practice would be to save all Excel files in an Excel folder in a CIS 101 folder.

To Change the Sheet Tab Name and Color

The following steps change the sheet tab name, change the tab color, and save the workbook.

1. Double-click the Sheet1 tab, enter **Sales Report** as the sheet tab name, and then press ENTER.
2. Right-click the sheet tab to display the shortcut menu.
3. Point to Tab Color on the shortcut menu to display the Tab Color gallery. Click Green, Accent 6 (column 10, row 1) in the Theme Colors area to apply the color to the sheet tab.
4. Save the workbook using SC_EX_2_Atlas as the file name.

Q&A Why should I save the workbook at this time?
You have performed many tasks while creating this workbook and do not want to risk losing work completed thus far.

BTW
Entering Numbers in a Range
An efficient way to enter data into a range of cells is to select a range and then enter the first number in the upper-left cell of the range. Excel responds by accepting the value and moving the active cell selection down one cell. When you enter the last value in the first column, Excel moves the active cell selection to the top of the next column.

Entering Formulas

One of the reasons Excel is such a valuable tool is that you can assign a formula to a cell, and Excel will calculate the result. A **formula** is a mathematical statement in a spreadsheet or table cell that calculates a value using cell references, numbers, and arithmetic operators such as +, −, *, and /. Consider, for example, what would happen if you had to multiply 112.98 by 0.075 and then manually enter the product for Sales Commission, 8.47, in cell G6. Every time the value in cell F6 changed, you would have to recalculate the product and enter the new value in cell G6. By contrast, if you enter a formula in cell G6 to multiply the values in cell F6 by 0.075, Excel recalculates the product whenever new values are entered into those cells and displays the result in cell G6.

In a spreadsheet, an error that occurs when one of the defining values in a cell is itself is called a **circular reference**. Excel warns you when you create circular references. In almost all cases, circular references are the result of an incorrect formula. A circular reference can be direct or indirect. For example, placing the formula =A1 in cell A1 results in a direct circular reference. A **direct circular reference** occurs when a formula refers to the same cell in which it is entered. An **indirect circular reference** occurs when a formula in a cell refers to another cell or cells that include a formula that refers back to the original cell.

To Enter a Formula Using the Keyboard

The formulas needed in the worksheet are noted in the requirements document as follows:

1. Service Commission (column E) = (Total Service Amounts × 0.05) + (Service Count × 12)
2. Sales Commission (column G) = Store Front Sales × 0.075
3. Gross Pay (column J) = Service Commission + Sales Commission + (Hours Worked × Hourly Pay Rate)
4. Gross Sales (column K) = Total Service Amounts + Store Front Sales

The service commission for each employee, which appears in column E, is equal to their total service amount in column C multiplied by 5 percent plus their service count in column D multiplied by 12. Thus, the service commission for Alice Bennet in cell E6 is obtained by multiplying 2,458.70 (cell C6) by 0.05 and adding 12 (cell D6) by 12, or = (C6 × 0.05) + (D6 × 12). The following steps enter the initial service commission in cell E6 using the keyboard. **Why?** In order for Excel to perform the calculations, you must first enter the formulas.

1

- With cell E6 selected, type **=(c6*0.05)+(d6*12)** in the cell to display the formula in the formula bar and the current cell and to display colored borders around the cells referenced in the formula (Figure 2–7).

Q&A What happens when I enter the formula?
The **equal sign (=)** preceding (c6*0.05)+(d6*12) alerts Excel that you are entering a formula or function—not text. Because the most common error when entering a formula is to reference the wrong cell, Excel colors the cells referenced in the formula. The colored cells help you determine whether the cell references are correct. The asterisk (*) following c6 and d6 is the arithmetic operator for multiplication.

Is there a function, similar to the SUM function, that calculates the product of two or more numbers?
Yes. The **PRODUCT function** calculates the product of two or more numbers. For example, the function, =PRODUCT(D6,E6) will calculate the product of cells D6 and E6.

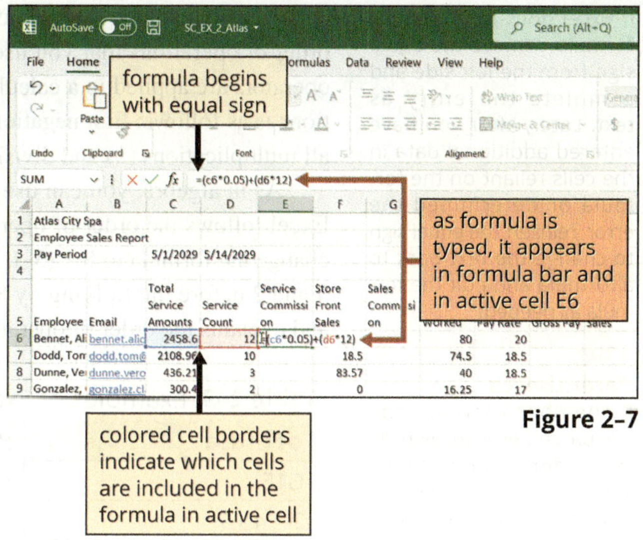

Figure 2–7

2

- Press TAB to complete the arithmetic operation indicated by the formula, display the result in the worksheet, and select the cell to the right (Figure 2–8). The number of decimal places on your screen may be different from that shown in Figure 2–8, but these values will be adjusted later in this module.

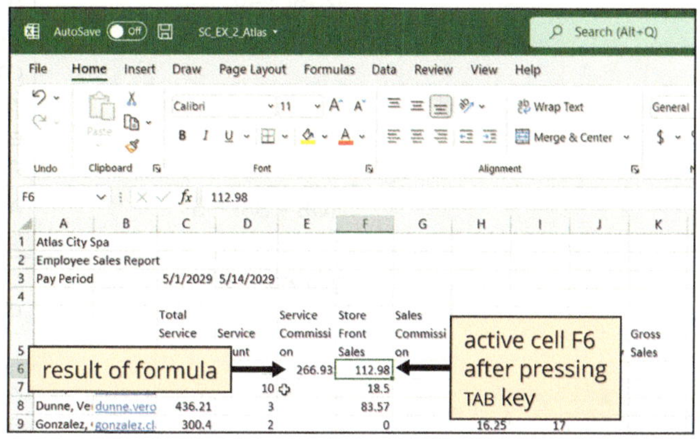

Figure 2–8

Arithmetic Operations

Excel provides powerful functions and capabilities that allow you to perform arithmetic operations easily and efficiently. Table 2–2 describes multiplication and other valid Excel arithmetic operators, listed in the order in which Excel performs them.

Table 2–2: Arithmetic Operations Listed in Order of Operations

Arithmetic Operator	Meaning	Example of Usage	Result
–	Negation	–78	Negative 78
%	Percentage	=23%	Multiplies 23 by 0.01
^	Exponentiation	=3 ^ 4	Raises 3 to the fourth power
*	Multiplication	=61.5 * C5	Multiplies the contents of cell C5 by 61.5
/	Division	=H3 / H11	Divides the contents of cell H3 by the contents of cell H11
+	Addition	=11 + 9	Adds 11 and 9
–	Subtraction	=22 – F15	Subtracts the contents of cell F15 from 22

BTW
Automatic Recalculation
Every time you enter a value into a cell in the worksheet, Excel automatically recalculates all formulas. You can change to manual recalculation by clicking the Calculation Options button (Formulas tab | Calculation group) and then clicking Manual. In manual calculation mode, pressing F9 instructs Excel to recalculate all formulas on all worksheets. Press SHIFT+F9 to recalculate the active worksheet. To recalculate all formulas in all open workbooks, press CTRL+ALT+F9.

BTW
Troubling Formulas
If Excel does not accept a formula, remove the equal sign from the left side and complete the entry as text. Later, after you have entered additional data in the cells reliant on the formula or determined the error, reinsert the equal sign to change the text back to a formula and edit the formula as needed.

BTW
Parentheses
Remember that you can use parentheses to override the order of operations. You cannot use brackets or braces in place of parentheses in arithmetic operations.

Order of Operations

When more than one arithmetic operator is involved in a formula, Excel follows the same basic order of operations that you use in algebra. The **order of operations** is the sequence in which operators are applied in a calculation. Moving from left to right in a formula, the order of operations is as follows: first negation (−), then all percentages (%), then all exponentiations (^), then all multiplications (*) and divisions (/), and, finally, all additions (+) and subtractions (−).

As in algebra, you can use parentheses to override the order of operations. For example, if Excel follows the order of operations, 8 * 3 + 2 equals 26. If you use parentheses, however, to change the formula to 8 * (3 + 2), the result is 40, because the parentheses instruct Excel to add 3 and 2 before multiplying by 8. Table 2–3 illustrates several examples of valid Excel formulas and explains the order of operations.

Table 2-3: Examples of Excel Formulas

Formula	Result
=G15	Assigns the value in cell G15 to the active cell.
=2 ^ 4 + 7	Assigns the sum of 16 + 7 (or 23) to the active cell.
=100 + D2 or =D2 +100 or =(100 + D2)	Assigns 100 plus the contents of cell D2 to the active cell.
=25% * 40	Assigns the product of 0.25 times 40 (or 10) to the active cell.
- (K15 * X45)	Assigns the negative value of the product of the values contained in cells K15 and X45 to the active cell. *Tip:* You do not need to type an equal sign before an expression that begins with a minus sign, which indicates a negation.
=(U8 - B8) * 6	Assigns the difference between the values contained in cells U8 and B8 times 6 to the active cell.
=J7 / A5 + G9 * M6 - Z2 ^ L7	Completes the following operations, from left to right: exponentiation (Z2 ^ L7), then division (J7 / A5), then multiplication (G9 * M6), then addition (J7 / A5) + (G9 * M6), and finally subtraction (J7 / A5 + G9 * M6) - (Z2 ^ L7). If cells A5 = 6, G9 = 2, J7 = 6, L7 = 4, M6 = 5, and Z2 = 2, then Excel assigns the active cell the value -5; that is, 6 / 6 + 2 * 5 - 2 ^ 4 = -5.

To Enter Formulas Using Point Mode

The sketch of the worksheet in Figure 2–3 calls for the sales commission, gross pay, and gross sales for each employee to appear in columns G, J, and K, respectively. All three of these values are calculated using formulas in row 6:

Sales Commission = 0.075 × Store Front Sales or = 0.075 * F6
Gross Pay = Service Commission + Sales Commission + (Hours Worked × Hourly Pay Rate) or = E6 + G6 + (H6 * I6)
Gross Sales = Total Service Amounts + Store Front Sales or = C6 + F6

An alternative to entering the formulas in cells G6, J6, and K6 using the keyboard is to enter the formulas using the pointer and Point mode. **Point mode** allows you to select cells for use in a formula by using the pointer or a screen tap. The following steps enter formulas using Point mode. **Why?** Using Point mode makes it easier to create formulas without worrying about typographical errors when entering cell references.

1

- With cell G6 selected, type **=0.075*** to begin the formula and then click cell F6 to add a cell reference in the formula (Figure 2–9).

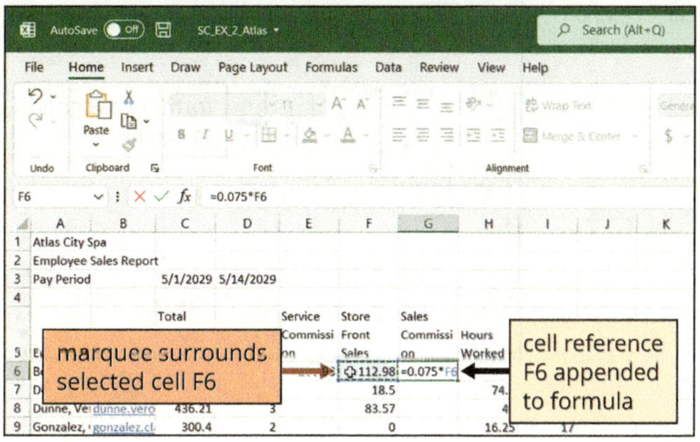

Figure 2–9

2

- Click the Enter button in the formula bar.

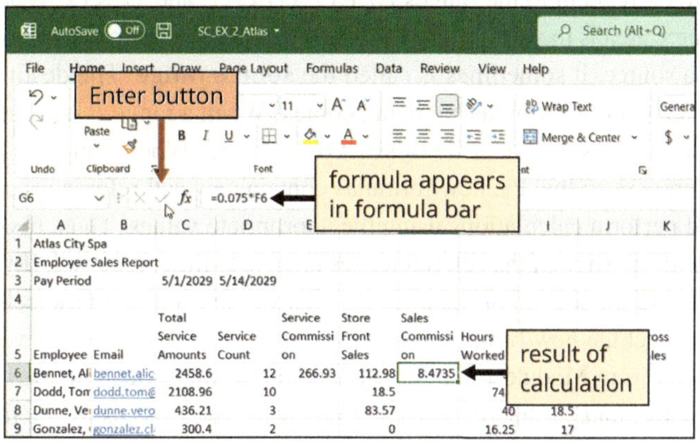

Figure 2–10

3

- Select cell J6 to prepare to enter the next formula.
- Type **=** (equal sign) and then click cell E6 to add a cell reference to the formula.
- Type **+** (plus sign) and then click cell G6 to add a cell reference to the formula.
- Type **+(** (plus sign followed by an open parenthesis) and then click cell H6 to add a cell reference to the formula.
- Type ***** (multiplication sign) and then click cell I6 to add a cell reference to the formula.
- Type **)** (closed parenthesis) and click the Enter button in the formula bar to enter the formula in cell J6 (Figure 2–11).

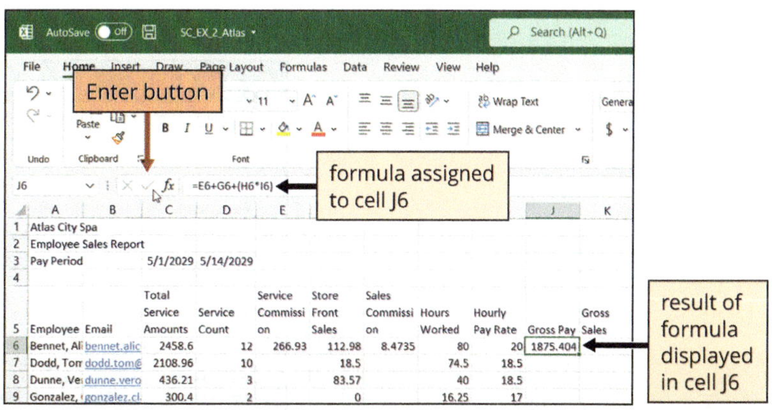

Figure 2–11

Q&A Why should I use Point mode to enter formulas?

Using Point mode to enter formulas often is faster and more accurate than using the keyboard, but only when the cell you want to select does not require you to scroll. In many instances, as in these steps, you may want to use both the keyboard and pointer when entering a formula in a cell. You can use the keyboard to begin the formula, for example, and then use the pointer to select a range of cells.

4

- Click cell K6, type = (equal sign) and then click cell C6.
- Type + (plus sign) and then click cell F6 (Figure 2–12).
- Click the Enter button.

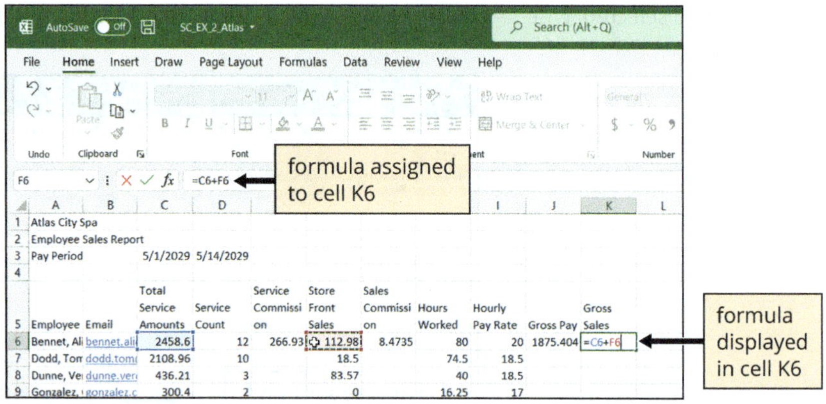

Figure 2–12

To Copy Formulas Using the Fill Handle

The four formulas for Alice Bennet in cells E6, G6, J6, and K6 now are complete. The next step is to copy them to the ranges E7:E17, G7:G17, and J7:K17. When copying formulas in Excel, the source area is the cell, or range, from which data or formulas are being copied. When a range is used as a source, it sometimes is called the **source range**. The destination area is the cell, or range, to which data or formulas are being copied. When a range is used as a destination in a data exchange, it sometimes is called the **destination range**. When you copy a formula, Excel adjusts the cell references so that the new formulas contain new cell references corresponding to the new locations and perform calculations using the appropriate values. Thus, if you copy downward, Excel adjusts the row portion of the cell references relative to the source cell. If you copy across, then Excel adjusts the column portion of the cell references to the source of the cell. Cells that automatically change to reflect the new location when the formulas are copied or moved are called **relative references**. Recall from Module 1 that the fill handle is a small square in the lower-right corner of the active cell or active range. The following steps copy the formulas using the fill handle.

1. Select the source cell or range, cell E6 in this case, point to the fill handle, then drag the fill handle down through cell E17.
2. Release the mouse button to copy the formulas to the destination range (Figure 2–13).

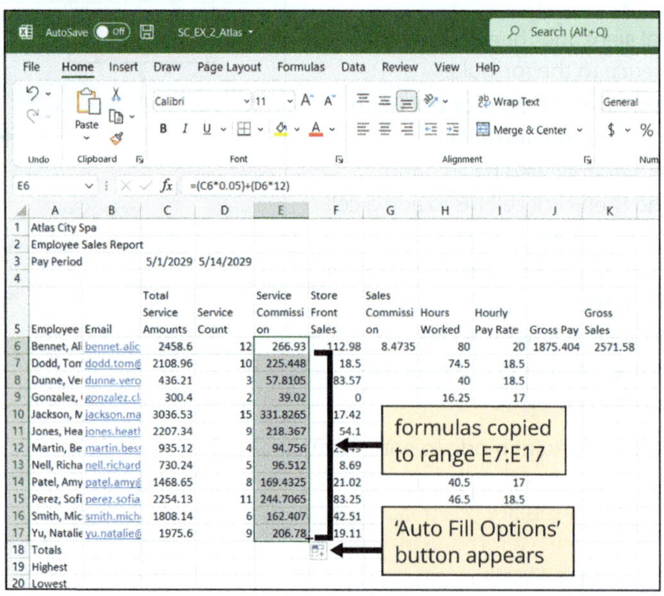

Figure 2–13

3. Select cell G6, point to the fill handle, then drag the fill handle down through cell G17. Release the mouse button to copy the formulas to the destination range.

4. Select range J6:K6, point to the fill handle, drag the fill handle down through cell K17, and then continue to hold the mouse button to select the destination range. Release the mouse button to copy the formulas to the destination range (Figure 2–14).

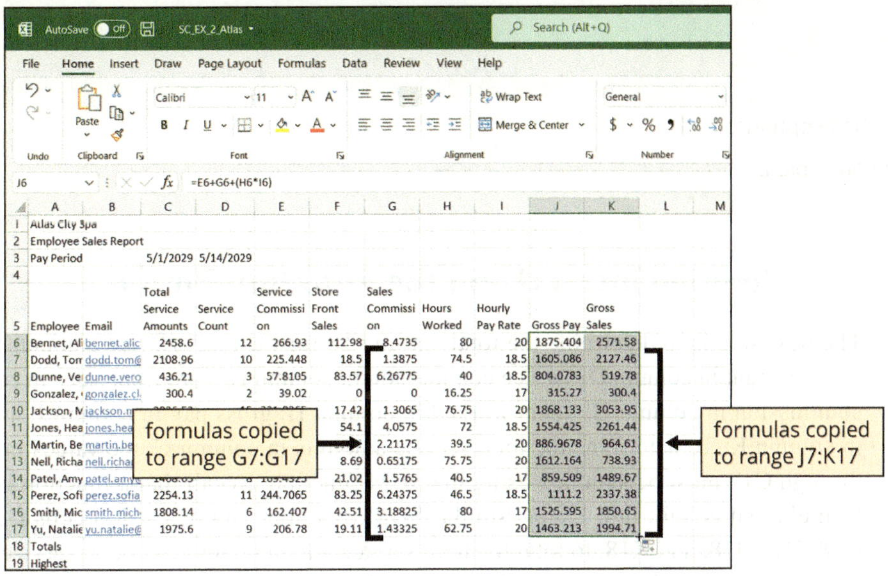

Figure 2–14

Option Buttons

Excel displays option buttons in a worksheet to indicate that you can complete an operation using automatic features such as AutoCorrect, Auto Fill, error checking, and others. For example, the 'Auto Fill Options' button shown in Figure 2–13 appears after a fill operation, such as dragging the fill handle. When an error occurs in a formula in a cell, Excel displays the Trace Error button next to the cell and identifies the cell with the error by placing a green triangle in the upper left of the cell.

Table 2–4 summarizes the option buttons available in Excel. When one of these buttons appears on your worksheet, click its arrow to produce the list of options for modifying the operation or to obtain additional information.

Table 2–4: Option Buttons in Excel

Name	Menu Function
Auto Fill Options	Provides options for how to fill cells following a fill operation, such as dragging the fill handle
AutoCorrect Options	Undoes an automatic correction, stops future automatic corrections of this type, or causes Excel to display the AutoCorrect Options dialog box
Insert Options	Lists formatting options following an insertion of cells, rows, or columns
Paste Options	Specifies how moved or pasted items should appear (for example, with original formatting, without formatting, or with different formatting)
Trace Error	Lists error-checking options following the assignment of an invalid formula to a cell

Consider This

Why is the Paste Options button important?

The Paste Options button provides powerful functionality. When performing copy and paste operations, the button allows you great freedom in specifying what it is you want to paste. You can choose from the following options:

- Paste an exact copy of what you copied, including the cell contents and formatting.
- Paste only formulas.
- Paste only formatting.
- Paste only values.
- Paste a combination of these options.
- Paste a picture of what you copied.

BTW

Selecting a Range

You can select a range using the keyboard. Press F8 and then use the arrow keys to select the desired range. After you are finished, make sure to press F8 to turn off the selection process or you will continue to select ranges.

To Determine Totals Using the AutoSum Button

The next step is to determine the totals in row 18 for the total service amounts in column C, service count in column D, service commission in column E, store front sales in column F, sales commission in column G, hours worked in column H, gross pay in column J, and gross sales in column K. To determine the total service amounts in column C, the values in the range C6 through C17 must be summed using the SUM function. Recall that a function is a prewritten formula that is built into Excel. Similar SUM functions can be used in cells D18, E18, F18, G18, H18, J18, and K18, to total the total service amounts, service count, service commission, store front sales, sales commission, hours worked, gross pay, and gross sales, respectively. The following steps determine totals in ranges C18:H18, and J18:K18.

1. Select the range to contain the sum, range C18:H18 in this case. Click the AutoSum button (Home tab | Editing group) to sum the contents of the range C6:C17 in cell C18, the contents of the range D6:D17 in cell D18, and so on.

2. Select the range to contain the sums, range J18:K18 in this case. Click the AutoSum button (Home tab | Editing group) to display totals in the selected range (Figure 2–15).

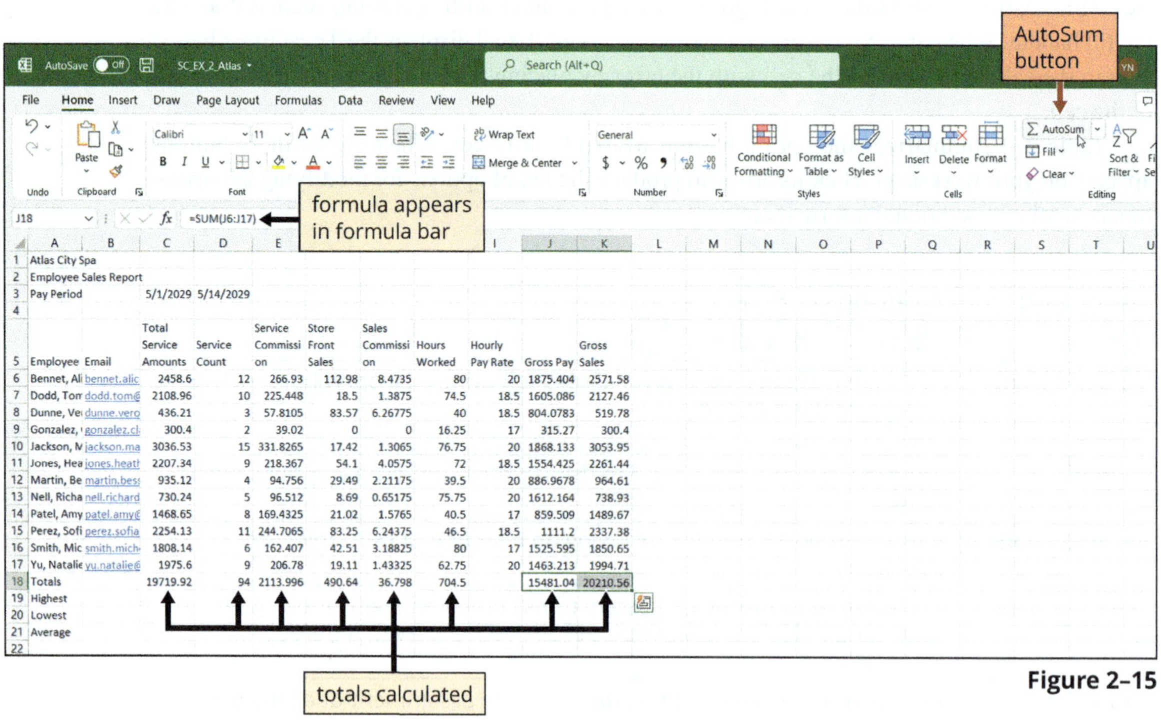

Figure 2–15

Using the AVERAGE, MAX, MIN, and Other Statistical Functions

The next step in creating the Atlas City Spa Employee Sales Report worksheet is to compute the highest value, lowest value, and average value for the total service amounts listed in the range C6:C17 using the MAX, MIN, and AVERAGE functions in the range C19:C21. Once the values are determined for column C, the entries can be copied across to the other columns. Other useful statistical functions include COUNT, which counts the number of cells in a range that contain numbers, and COUNTA, which counts the number of cells in a range that are not empty.

With Excel, you can enter functions using one of five methods: (1) keyboard, touch gesture, or pointer; (2) the Insert Function button in the formula bar; (3) the AutoSum button (Home tab | Editing group); (4) the AutoSum button (Formulas tab | Function Library group); and (5) the Name box area in the formula bar. The method you choose will depend on your typing skills and whether you can recall the function name and required arguments.

In the following sections, you will use three of these methods. You will use the Insert Function button in the formula bar method to determine the highest number of total service amounts (cell C19). You will use the AutoSum menu to determine the lowest number of total service amounts (cell C20). You will use the keyboard and pointer to determine the average number of total service amounts (cell C21).

BTW
Statistical Functions
Excel usually considers a blank cell to be equal to 0. The statistical functions, however, ignore blank cells. Excel thus calculates the average of three cells with values of 10, blank, and 8 to be 9 [(10 + 8) / 2] and not 6 [(10 + 0 + 8) / 3].

To Determine the Highest Number in a Range of Numbers Using the Insert Function Dialog Box

The next step is to select cell C19 and determine the highest (maximum) number in the range C6:C17. As you learned in Module 1, Excel includes a function called the **MAX function** that displays the highest value in a range. The following steps use the Insert Function dialog box to enter the MAX function. **Why?** Although you could enter the MAX function using the keyboard and Point mode as described previously, an alternative method to entering the function is to use the Insert Function button in the formula bar to display the Insert Function dialog box. The Insert Function dialog box is helpful if you do not remember the name of a function or need to search for a particular function by what it does.

1

- Select the cell to contain the maximum number, cell C19 in this case.
- Click the Insert Function button in the formula bar to display the Insert Function dialog box.
- Click MAX in the Select a function list (Insert Function dialog box; Figure 2–16). You may need to scroll.

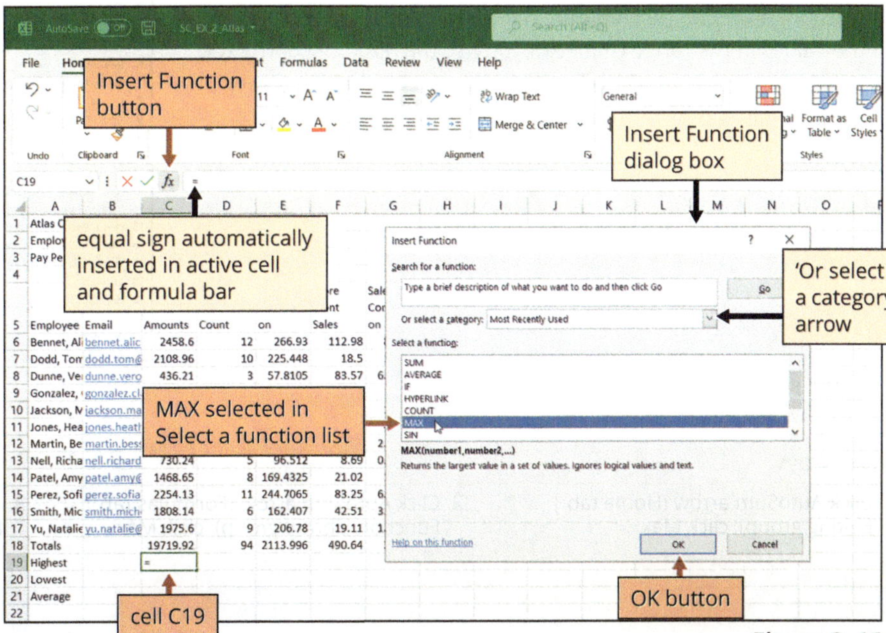

Figure 2–16

Q&A What if the MAX function is not in the Select a function list?
Click the 'Or select a category' arrow to display the list of function categories, select All, and then scroll down and select the MAX function in the Select a function list.

How can I learn about other functions?
Excel has more than 400 functions that perform nearly every type of calculation you can imagine. These functions are categorized in the Insert Function dialog box shown in Figure 2–16. To view the categories, click the 'Or select a category' arrow. The MAX function is in the Statistial category. Click the name of a function in the Select a function list to display a description of the function.

2

- Click OK (Insert Function dialog box) to display the Function Arguments dialog box.
- Replace the text in the Number1 box with the text, **c6:c17** (Function Arguments dialog box) to enter the first argument of the function (Figure 2–17).

Q&A What are the numbers that appear to the right of the Number1 box in the Function Arguments dialog box?
The numbers shown to the right of the Number1 box are the values in the selected range (or if the range is large, the first few numbers only). Excel also displays the value the MAX function will return to cell C19 in the Function Arguments dialog box, shown in Figure 2–16.

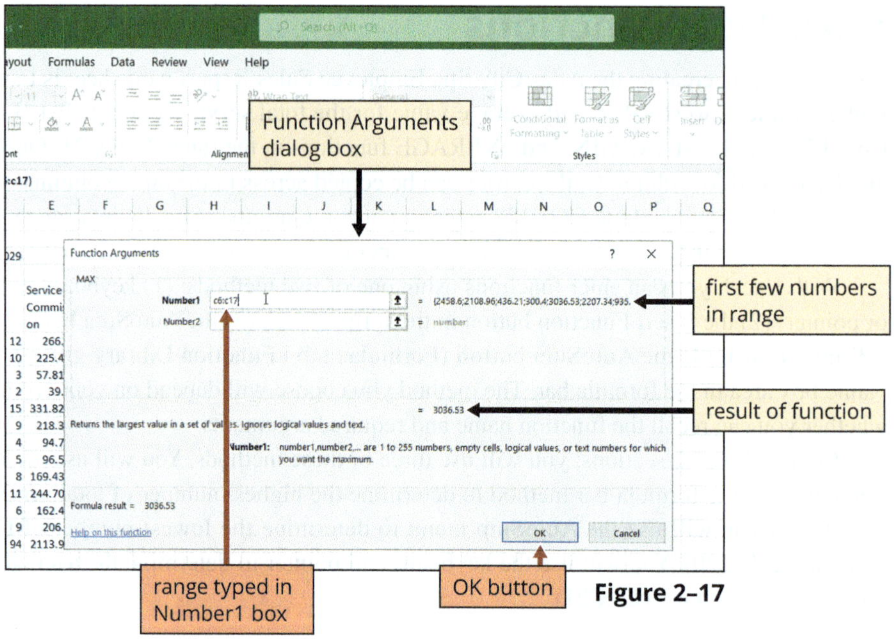

Figure 2–17

3

- Click OK (Function Arguments dialog box) to display the highest value in the chosen range in cell C19 (Figure 2–18).

Q&A Why should I not just enter the highest value that I see in the range C6:C17 in cell C19?
In this example, rather than entering the MAX function, you could examine the range C6:C17, determine that the highest total service amount is 3036.53, and manually enter the number 3036.53 as a constant in cell C19. Excel would display the number similar to how it appears in Figure 2–18. However, because C19 would then contain a constant, Excel would continue to display 3036.53 in cell C19 even if the values in the range change. If you use the MAX function, Excel will recalculate the highest value in the range each time a new value is entered in the range.

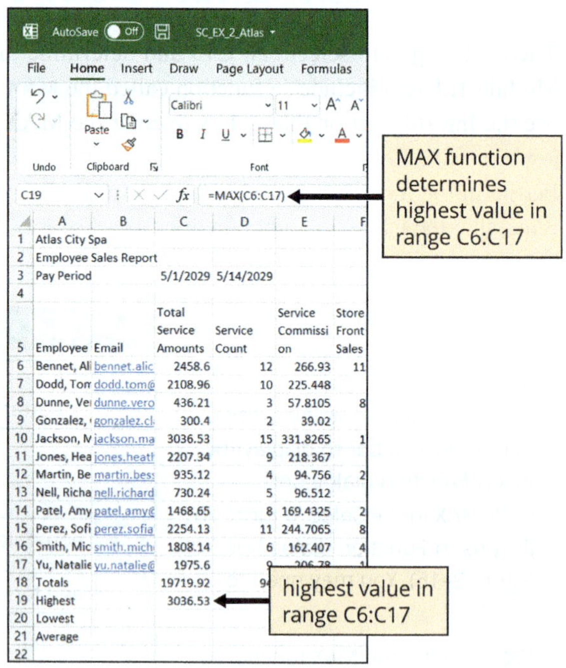

Figure 2–18

Other Ways

1. Click AutoSum arrow (Home tab | Editing group), click Max
2. Click AutoSum arrow (Formulas tab | Function Library group), click Max
3. Type **=MAX(** in cell, specify range, type **)**

To Determine the Lowest Number in a Range of Numbers Using the Sum Menu

The next step is to enter the **MIN function** in cell C20 to determine the lowest (minimum) number in the range C6:C17. Although you can enter the MIN function using the method used to enter the MAX function, the following steps illustrate an alternative method using the AutoSum button (Home tab | Editing group). **Why?** Using the AutoSum menu allows you quick access to five commonly used functions, without having to memorize their names or required arguments.

1

- Select cell C20 and then click the AutoSum arrow (Home tab | Editing group) to display the AutoSum menu (Figure 2–19).

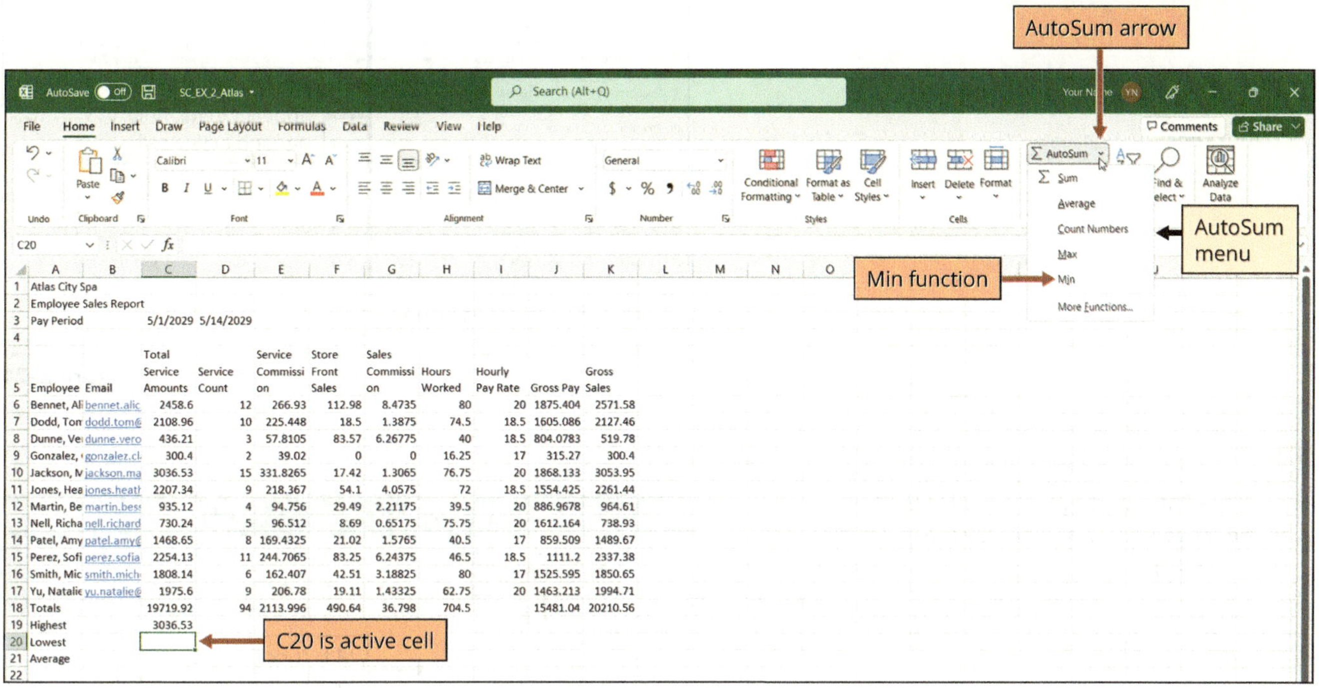

Figure 2–19

2

- Click Min to display the MIN function in the formula bar and in the active cell (Figure 2–20).

Q&A Why does Excel select the incorrect range?
The range selected by Excel is not always the right one. Excel attempts to guess which cells you want to include in the function by looking for ranges containing numeric data that are adjacent to the selected cell.

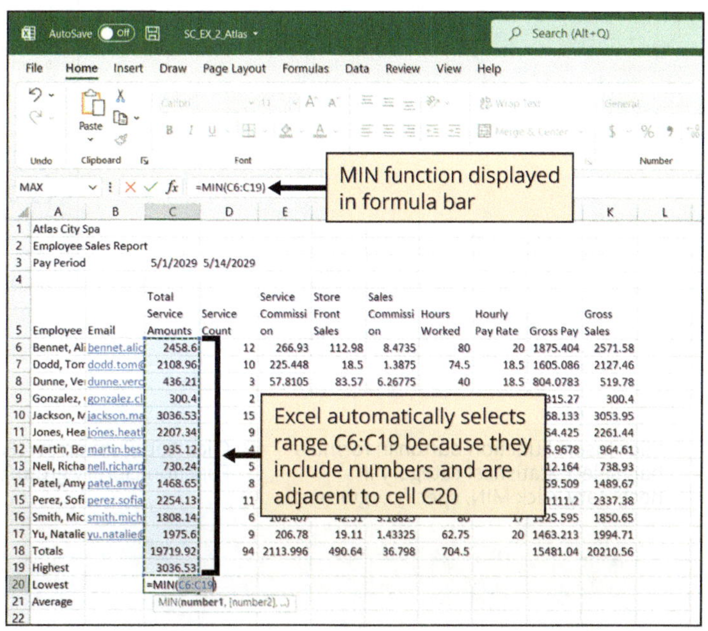

Figure 2–20

3

- Click cell C6 and then drag through cell C17 to update the function with the new range (Figure 2–21).

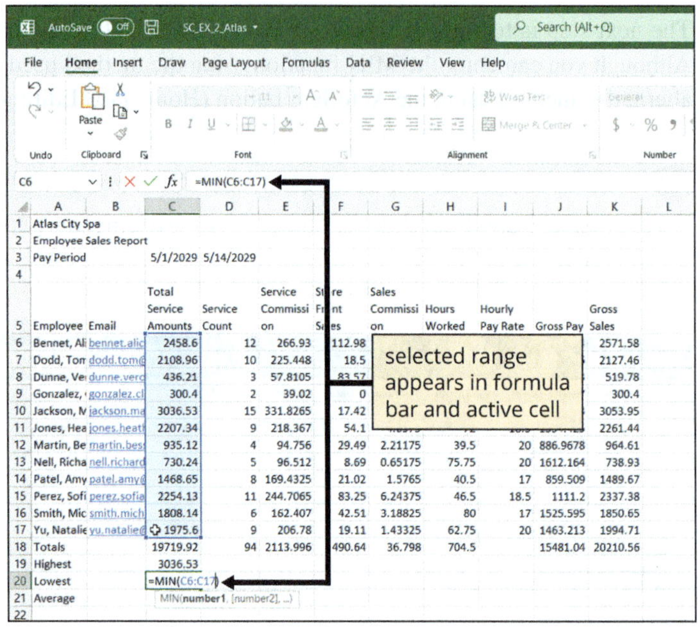

Figure 2–21

4

- Click the Enter button to determine the lowest value in the range C6:C17 and display the result in cell C20 (Figure 2–22).

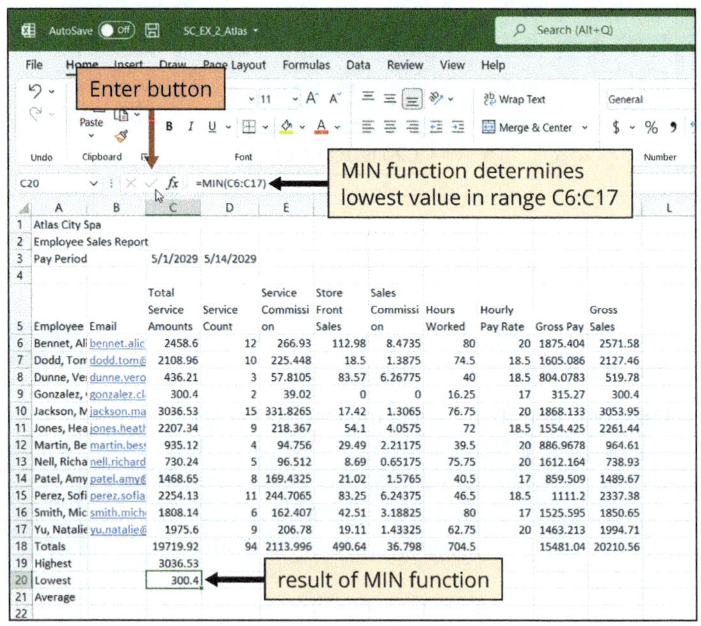

Figure 2–22

Other Ways

1. Click Insert Function button in formula bar, select Statistical category if necessary, click MIN, specify arguments
2. Click AutoSum arrow (Formulas tab | Function Library group), click Min
3. Type **=MIN(** in cell, fill in arguments, type **)**

To Determine the Average of a Range of Numbers Using the Keyboard

The **AVERAGE function** is an Excel function that calculates the average value of a collection of numbers. The following steps use the AVERAGE function to determine the average of the numbers in the range C6:C17. **Why?** The AVERAGE function calculates the average of a range of numbers.

1

- Select the cell to contain the average, cell C21 in this case.
- Type **=av** in the cell to display the Formula AutoComplete list. Press the DOWN ARROW key to highlight the AVERAGE function (Figure 2–23).

Q&A What is happening as I type?
As you type the equal sign followed by the characters in the name of a function, Excel displays the Formula AutoComplete list. This list contains those functions whose names match the letters you have typed.

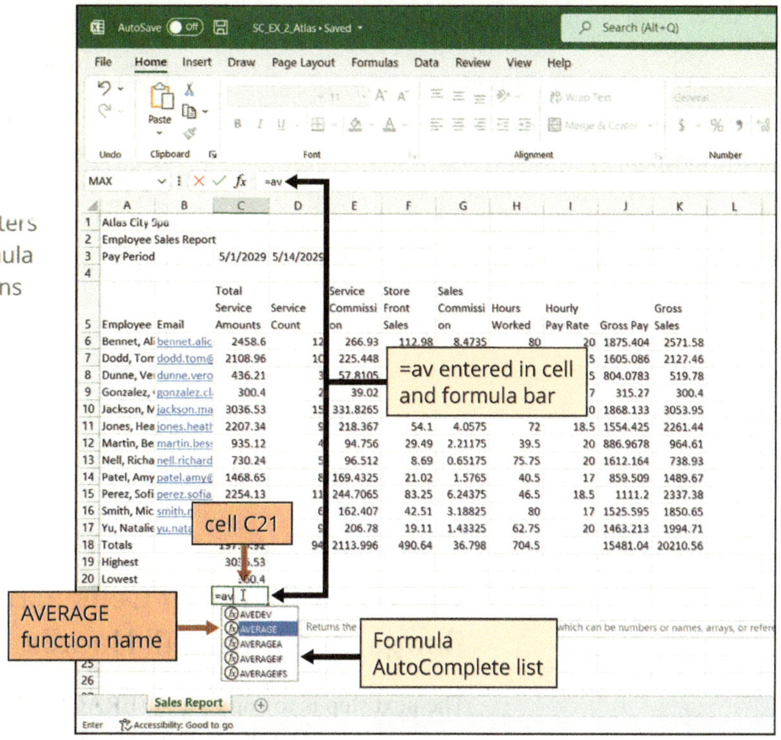

Figure 2–23

2

- Press TAB to select the function.
- Select the range to be averaged, C6:C17 in this case, to insert the range as the argument to the function (Figure 2–24).

Q&A As I drag, why does the function in cell C21 change?
When you click cell C6, Excel surrounds cell C6 with a marquee and appends C6 to the left parenthesis in the formula bar. When you begin dragging, Excel appends to the argument a colon (:) and the cell reference of the cell where the pointer is located.

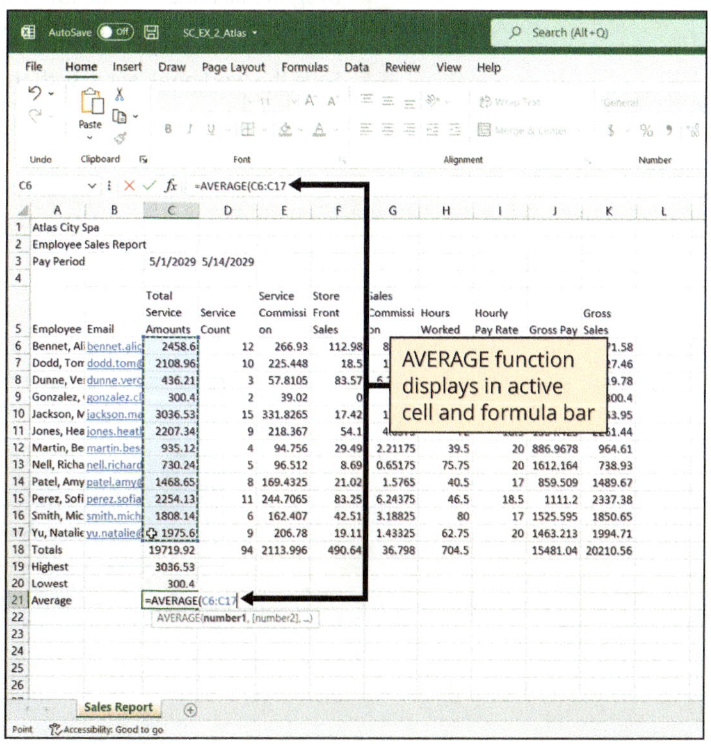

Figure 2–24

3

- Click the Enter button to compute the average of the numbers in the selected range and display the result in the selected cell (Figure 2–25).

Q&A Can I use the arrow keys to complete the entry instead?

No. While in Point mode, the arrow keys change the selected cell reference in the range you are selecting instead of completing the entry.

What is the purpose of the parentheses in the function?

Most Excel functions require that the argument (in this case, the range C6:C17) be included within parentheses following the function name. In this case, Excel appended the right parenthesis to complete the AVERAGE function when you clicked the Enter button.

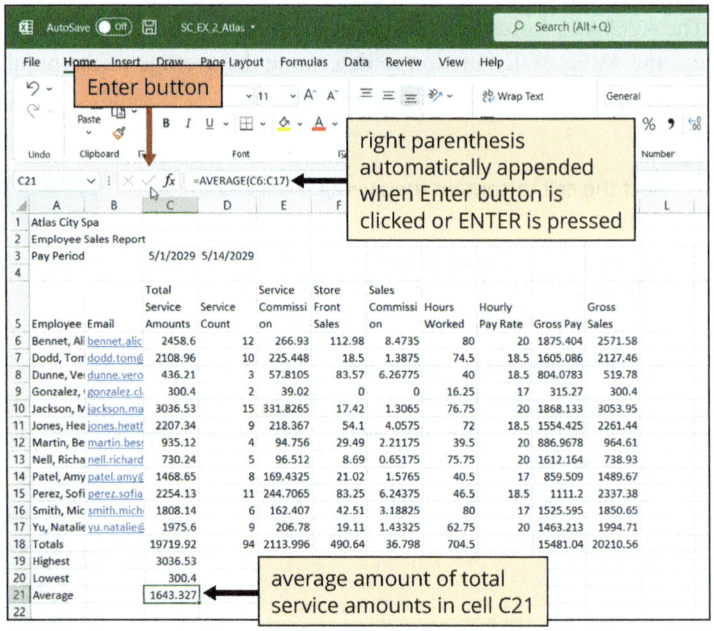

Figure 2–25

To Copy a Range of Cells across Columns to an Adjacent Range Using the Fill Handle

The next step is to copy the AVERAGE, MAX, and MIN functions in the range C19:C21 to the adjacent range D19:K21. The following steps use the fill handle to copy the functions.

1. Select the source range from which to copy the functions, in this case C19:C21.
2. Drag the fill handle in the lower-right corner of the selected range through cell K21 to copy the three functions to the selected range (Figure 2–26).
3. Save the workbook again with the same file name.

Q&A How can I be sure that the function arguments are correct for the cells in range D19:K21?

Remember that Excel adjusts the cell references in the copied functions so that each function refers to the range of numbers above it in the same column. Review the functions in rows 19 through 21 by clicking on individual cells and examining the function as it appears in the formula bar. You should see that the functions in each column reference the appropriate ranges.

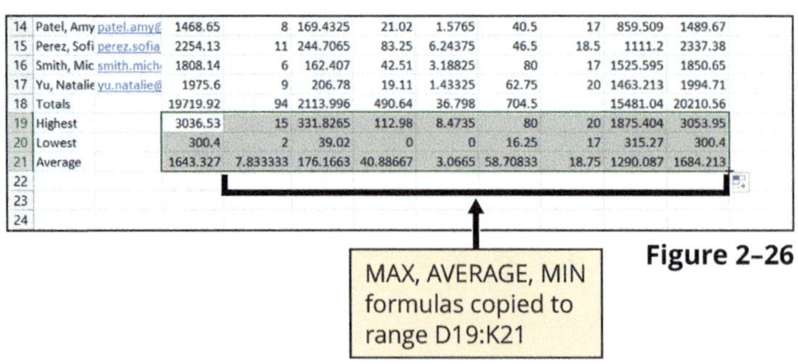

Figure 2–26

Other Ways

1. Select source area, click Copy button (Home tab | Clipboard group), select destination area, click Paste button (Home tab | Clipboard group)
2. Right-click source area, click Copy on shortcut menu; right-click destination area, click Paste icon on shortcut menu
3. Select source area and then point to border of range; while holding down CTRL, drag source area to destination area
4. Select source area, press CTRL+C, select destination area, press CTRL+V

Break Point: If you want to take a break, this is a good place to do so. You can exit Excel now. To resume later, start Excel, open the file called SC_EX_2_Atlas, and continue following the steps from this location forward.

Verifying Formulas Using Range Finder

One of the more common mistakes made with Excel is to include an incorrect cell reference in a formula. An easy way to verify that a formula references the cells you want it to reference is to use Range Finder. **Range Finder** checks which cells are referenced in the formula assigned to the active cell.

To use Range Finder to verify that a formula contains the intended cell references, double-click the cell with the formula you want to check. Excel responds by highlighting the cells referenced in the formula so that you can verify that the cell references are correct.

To Verify a Formula Using Range Finder

Why? Range Finder allows you to correct mistakes by making immediate changes to the cells referenced in a formula. The following steps use Range Finder to check the formula in cell E6.

1

- Double-click cell E6 to activate Range Finder (Figure 2–27).

2

- Press ESC to quit Range Finder and then click anywhere in the worksheet, such as cell A23, to deselect the current cell.

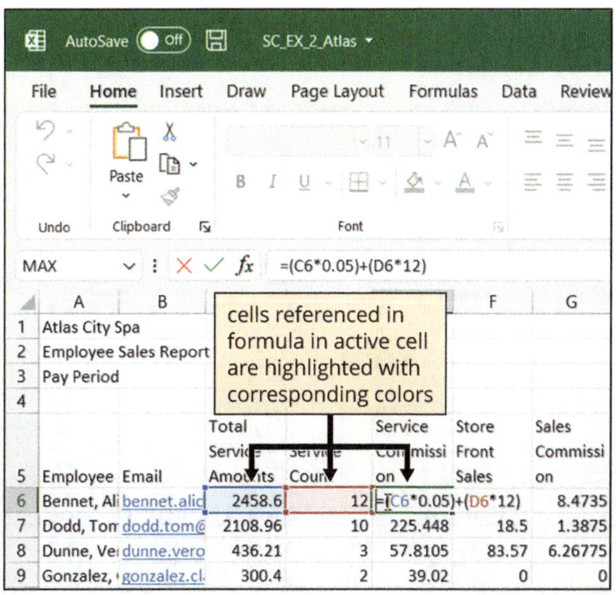

Figure 2–27

Formatting the Worksheet

Although the worksheet contains the appropriate data, formulas, and functions, the text and numbers need to be formatted to improve their appearance and readability.

In Module 1, you used cell styles to format much of the worksheet. This section describes how to change the unformatted worksheet in Figure 2–28a to the formatted worksheet in Figure 2–28b using a theme and other commands on the ribbon. A **theme** formats a worksheet by applying a collection of fonts, font styles, colors, and effects to give it a consistent appearance.

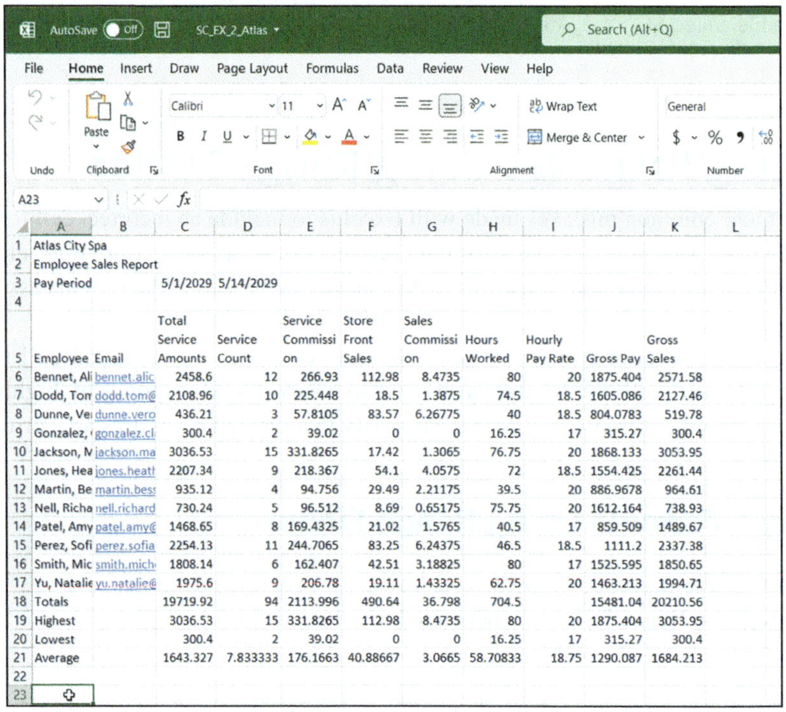

Figure 2–28(a)

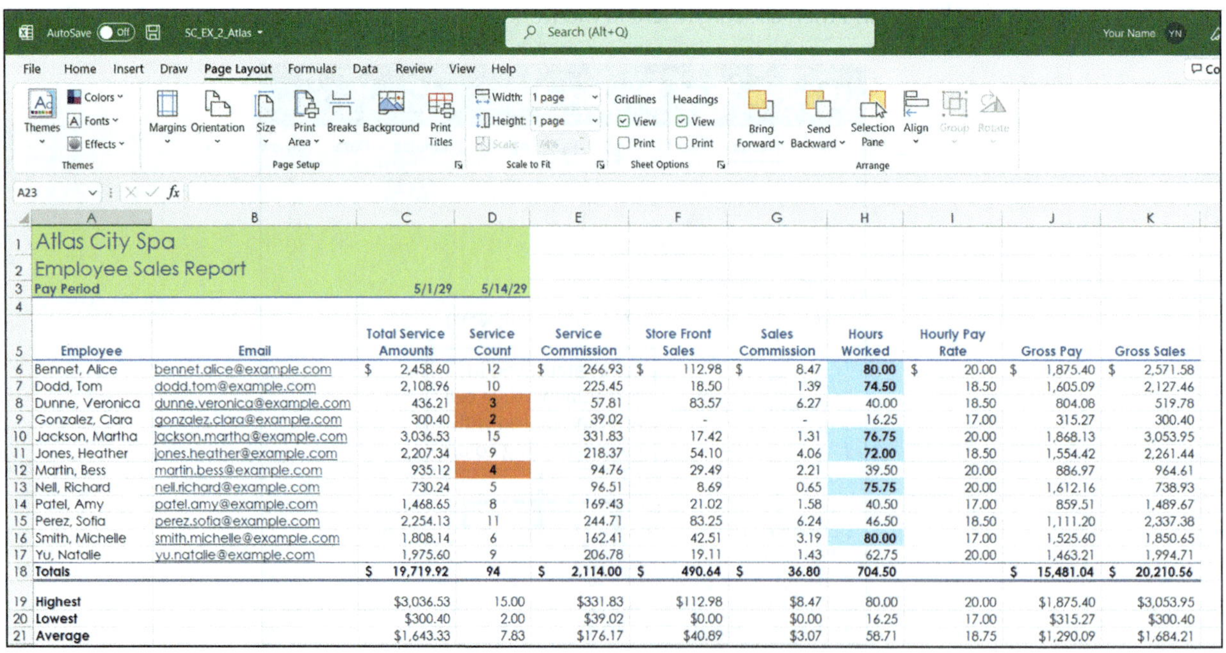

Figure 2–28(b)

To Change the Workbook Theme

Why? A company or department may choose a specific theme as their standard theme so that all of their documents have a similar appearance. Similarly, you may want to have a theme that sets your work apart from the work of others. Other Office programs, such as Word and PowerPoint, include the same themes so that all of your Microsoft Office documents can share a common look. The following steps change the workbook theme to the Gallery theme.

1

- Click Page Layout to display the Page Layout tab.
- Click the Themes button (Page Layout tab | Themes group) to display the Themes gallery (Figure 2–29).
- **Experiment:** Point to several themes in the Themes gallery to preview the themes.

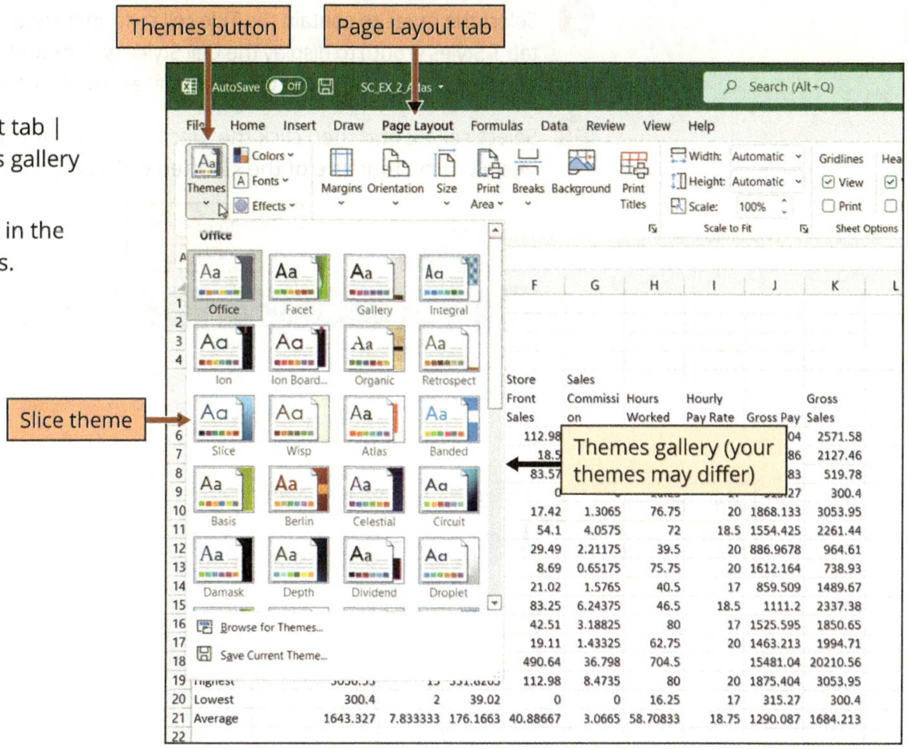

Figure 2–29

2

- Click Slice in the Themes gallery to change the workbook theme (Figure 2–30).

Q&A Why did the cells in the worksheet change? Originally, the cells in the worksheet were formatted with the default font of the default Office theme. The Slice theme has a different default font than the Office theme, so when you changed the theme, the font changed. If you had modified the font for any cells, those cells would not have changed to the default font of the Slice theme.

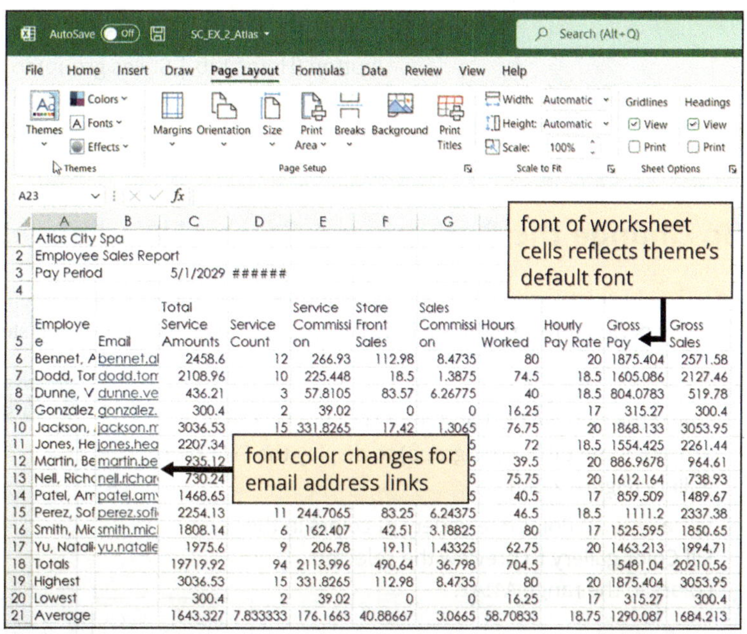

Figure 2–30

To Format the Worksheet Titles

The following steps apply the Title cells style to the worksheet titles, decrease the font of the worksheet subtitle, apply a Heading cell style to the pay period information, and add a fill color.

1. Display the Home tab.
2. Select the range to contain the Title cell style, in this case A1:A2, click the Cell Styles button (Home tab | Styles group) to display the Cell Styles gallery, and then click the Title cell style in the Titles and Headings group in the Cell Styles gallery to apply the Title cell style to the selected range.
3. Select cell A2 and then click the 'Decrease Font Size' button (Home tab | Font group) to decrease the font size of the selected cell to the next lower font size (Figure 2–31).

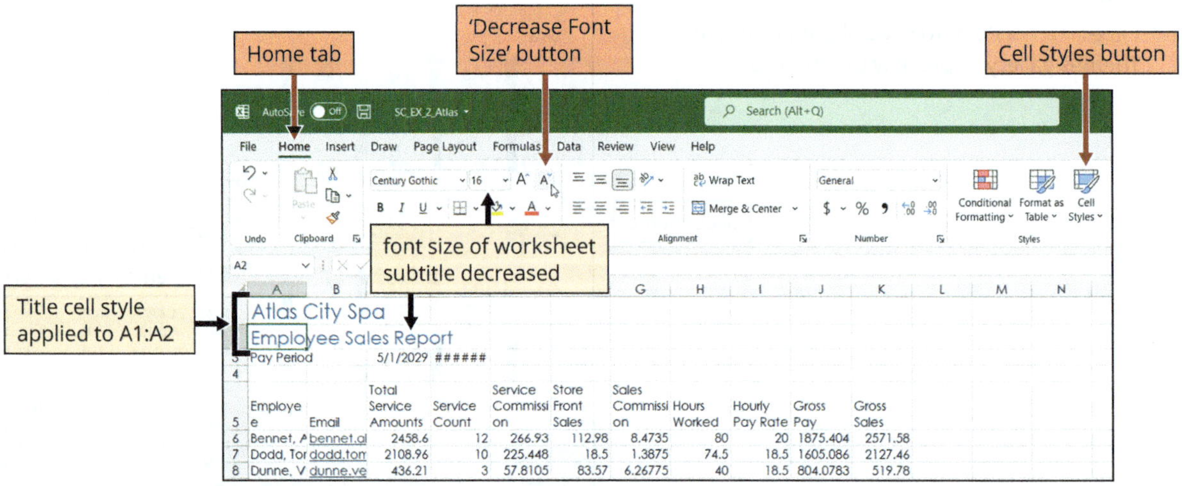

Figure 2–31

Q&A What happens when I click the 'Decrease Font Size' button?
When you click the 'Decrease Font Size' button, Excel assigns the next smaller font size in the Font Size gallery to the selected range. The 'Increase Font Size' button works in a similar manner, assigning the next larger font size in the Font Size gallery to the selected range.

4. Select the range to contain the Heading cell style, in this case A3:D3, click the Cell Styles button (Home tab | Styles group) to display the Cell Styles gallery, and then click the Heading 3 cell style in the Titles and Headings group in the Cell Styles gallery to apply the Heading 3 cell style to the selected range.

To Change the Background Color of Worksheet Header

Why? A background color can draw attention to the title of a worksheet. The final format assigned to the worksheet title, subtitle, and pay period information is a blue background color. The following steps complete the formatting of the worksheet titles.

1.
- Select the range A1:D3 and then click the Fill Color arrow (Home tab | Font group) to display the Fill Color gallery (Figure 2–32).
- **Experiment:** Point to a variety of colors in the Fill Color gallery to preview the selected colors in the range A1:A2.

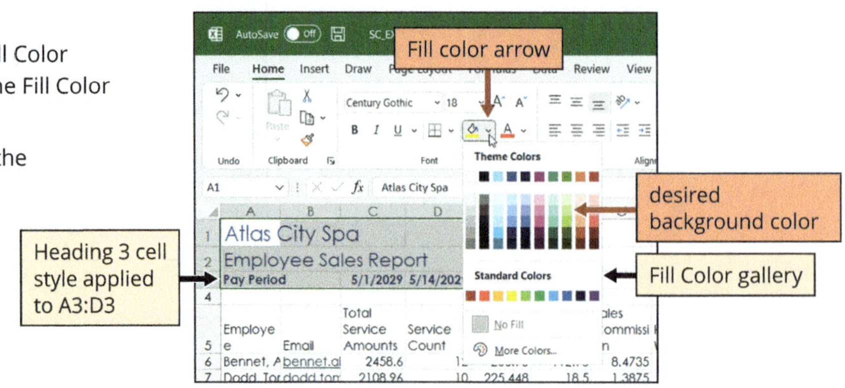

Figure 2–32

2

- Click Dark Green, Accent 4, Lighter 60 percent (column 8, row 3) in the Theme Colors area to change the background color of the range of cells.
- Click anywhere in the worksheet, such as cell A23, to deselect the current range (Figure 2–33).

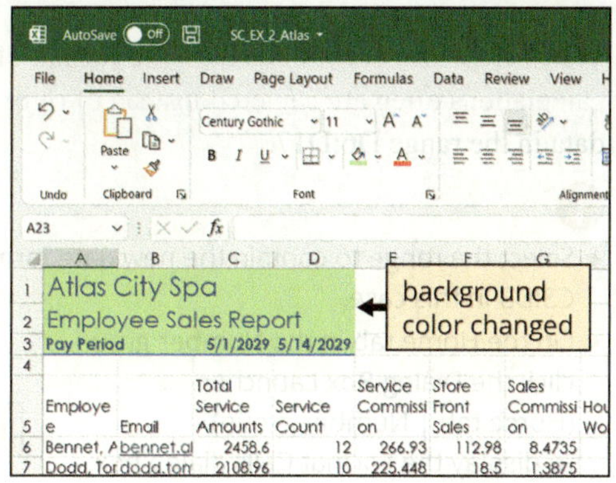

Figure 2–33

Other Ways

1. Click Font Settings Dialog Box Launcher (Home tab | Font group), click Fill tab (Format Cells dialog box), click desired fill, click OK
2. Right-click range, click Format Cells on shortcut menu, click Fill tab (Format Cells dialog box), click desired fill, click OK
3. Press CTRL+1, click Fill tab (Format Cells dialog box), click desired fill, click OK

To Apply a Cell Style to the Column Headings and Format the Total Rows

As shown in Figure 2–28b, the column titles (row 5) should have the Heading 3 cell style and the totals row (row 18) should have the Total cell style. The headings in the range A19:A21 should be bold. The following steps assign these styles and formats to row 5, row 18, and the range A19:A21.

BTW
Background Colors
The most popular background color is blue. Research shows that the color blue is used most often because this color connotes serenity, reflection, and proficiency. Use color in spreadsheets to highlight data or to format worksheet elements such as titles. In most cases, colors should not be used for numbers because it may make them less visible.

1. Select the range to be formatted, cells A5:K5 in this case.
2. Use the Cell Styles gallery to apply the Heading 3 cell style to the range A5:K5.
3. Click the Center button (Home tab | Alignment group) to center the column headings.
4. Apply the Total cell style to the range A18:K18.
5. Bold the range A19:A21 (Figure 2–34).

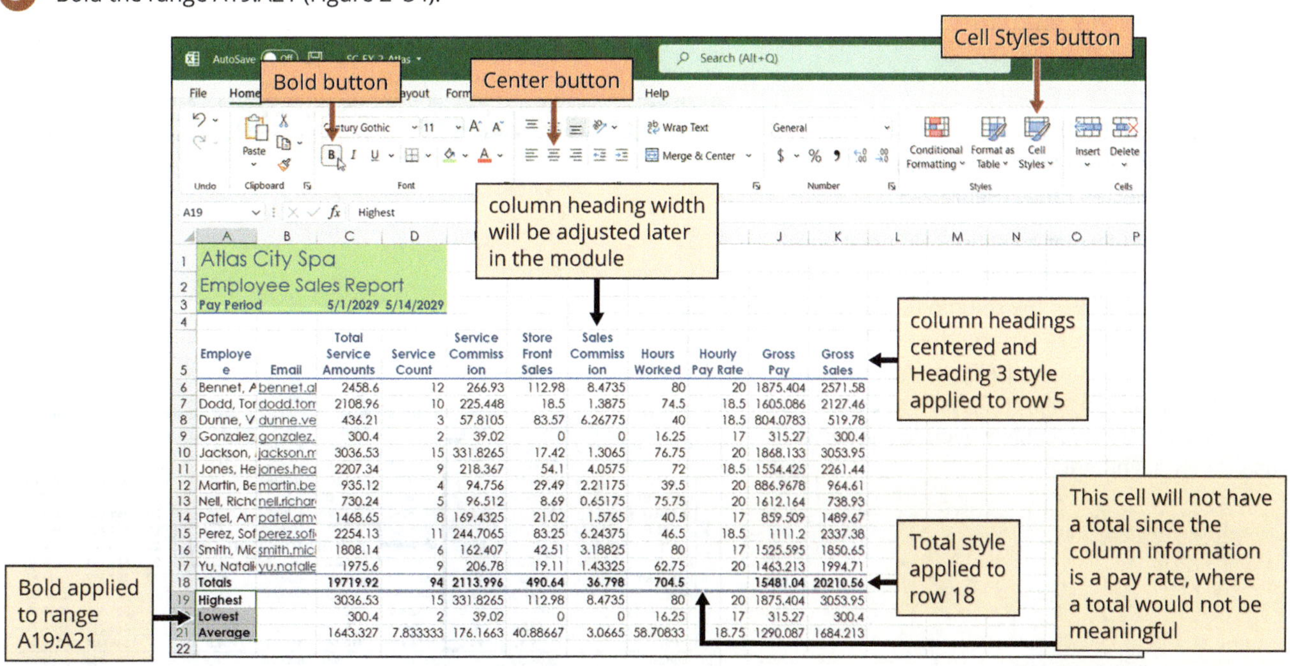

Figure 2–34

To Format Dates and Center Data in Cells

Why? You may want to change the format of the dates to better suit your needs. In addition, numbers that are not used in calculations often are centered instead of right aligned. The following steps format the dates in the range C3:D3 and center the data in the range D6:D17.

1

- Select the range to contain the new date format, cells C3:D3 in this case.
- On the Home tab in the Number group, click the Dialog Box Launcher (Home tab | Number group) to display the Format Cells dialog box.
- If necessary, click the Number tab (Format Cells dialog box), click Date in the Category list, and then click 3/14/12 in the Type list to choose the format for the selected range (Figure 2–35).
- Click OK (Format Cells dialog box) to format the dates in the current column using the selected date format style (Figure 2–36).

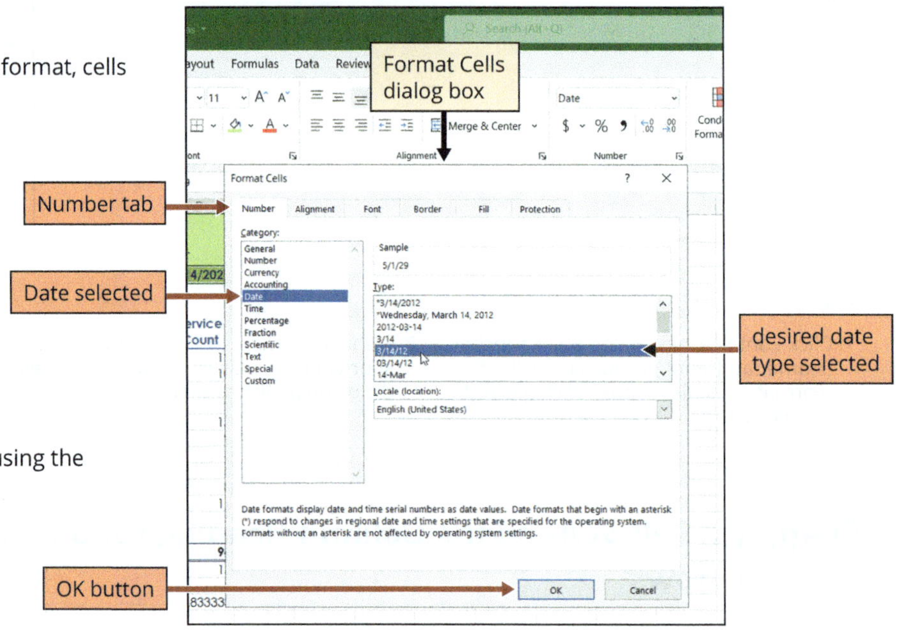

Figure 2–35

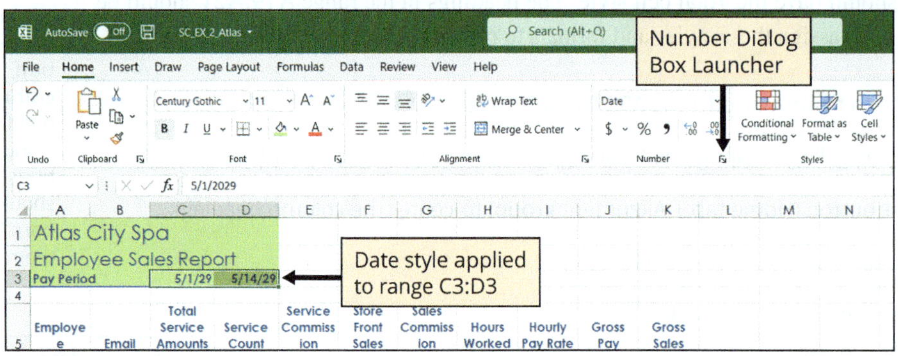

Figure 2–36

2

- Select the range D6:D18 and then click the Center button (Home tab | Alignment group) to center the data in the selected range (Figure 2–37).

Q&A How can I format an entire column at once?

Instead of selecting the range D6:D18 in Step 4, you could have clicked the column D heading immediately above cell D1, and then clicked the Center button (Home tab | Alignment group). In this case, all cells in column D down to the last cell in the worksheet would have been formatted to use center alignment.

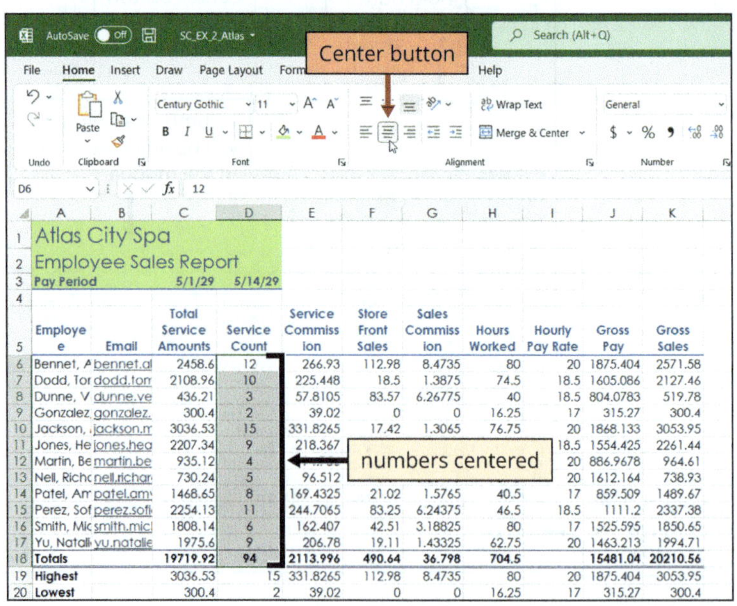

Figure 2–37

Other Ways

1. Right-click range, click Format Cells on shortcut menu, click Number tab (Format Cells dialog box), click desired number format, click OK
2. Press CTRL+1, click Number tab (Format Cells dialog box), click desired number format, click OK

To Apply an Accounting Number Format and Comma Style Format Using the Ribbon

As shown in Figure 2–28b, the worksheet is formatted to resemble an accounting report. In column C, columns E through G, and columns I though K, the numbers in the first row (row 6), the totals row (row 18), and the rows below the totals (rows 19 through 21) have dollar signs, while the remaining numbers (rows 7 through 17) in column C, columns E through G, and columns I through K do not. The following steps assign formats using the 'Accounting Number Format' button and the Comma Style button. **Why?** This gives the worksheet a more professional look.

1. Select the cell to contain the accounting number format, cell C6 in this case.
2. While holding down CTRL, select the range E6:G6, the range I6:K6, cell C18, the range E18:G18, and the range J18:K18 to select the nonadjacent ranges and cells.
3. Click the 'Accounting Number Format' button (Home tab | Number group) to apply the accounting number format with fixed dollar signs to the selected nonadjacent ranges.

Q&A What is the effect of applying the accounting number format?
The 'Accounting Number Format' button assigns a fixed dollar sign to the numbers in the ranges and rounds the figure to the nearest 100th. A fixed dollar sign is one that appears to the far left of the cell, with multiple spaces between it and the first digit in the cell.

4. Select the ranges to contain the comma style format, range C7:C17, range E7:K17, and cells H6 and H18 in this case.
5. Click the Comma Style button (Home tab | Number group) to assign the comma style format to the selected ranges.
6. Select the range D19:D21 and H19:I21 and then click the Comma Style button (Home tab | Number group) to assign the comma style format to the selected range (Figure 2–38).

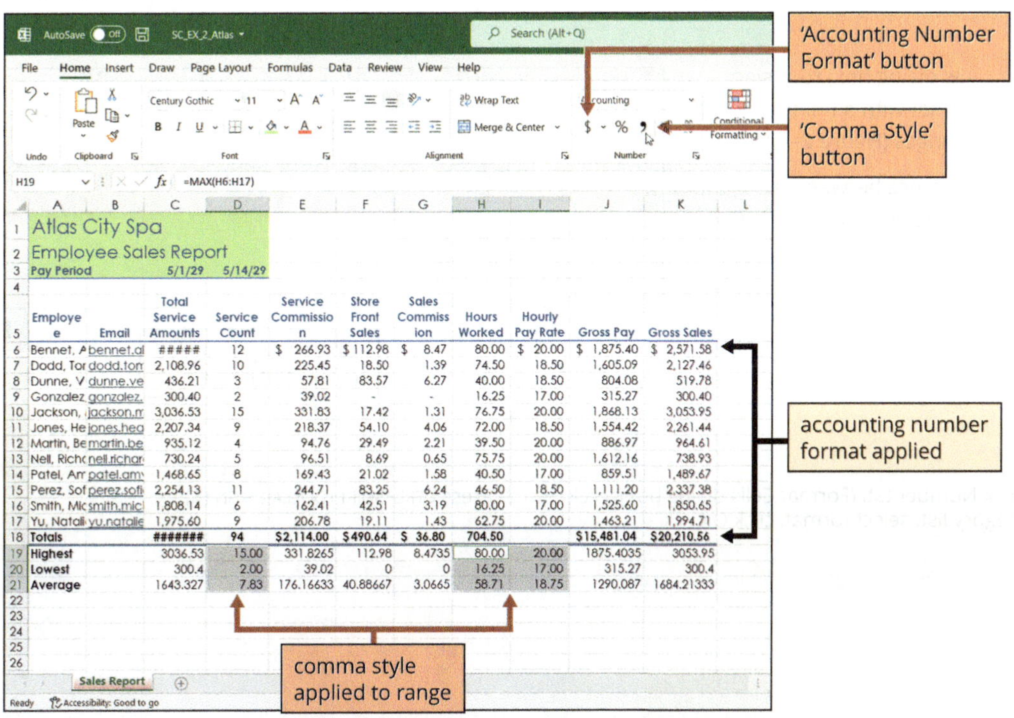

Figure 2–38

To Apply a Currency Style Format with a Floating Dollar Sign Using the Format Cells Dialog Box

Why? The Currency format places dollar signs immediately to the left of the number (known as floating dollar signs, as they change position depending on the number of digits in the cell) and displays a zero for cells that have a value of zero. The following steps use the Format Cells dialog box to apply the currency style format with a floating dollar sign to the numbers in the ranges C19:C21, E19:G21, and J19:K21.

1

- Select the ranges (C19:C21, E19:G21, and J19:K21) and then on the Home tab in the Number group, click the Dialog Box Launcher to display the Format Cells dialog box.
- If necessary, click the Number tab to display the Number sheet (Format Cells dialog box).
- Click Currency in the Category list to select the necessary number format category and then click the third style ($1,234.10) in the Negative numbers list to select the desired currency format for negative numbers (Figure 2-39).

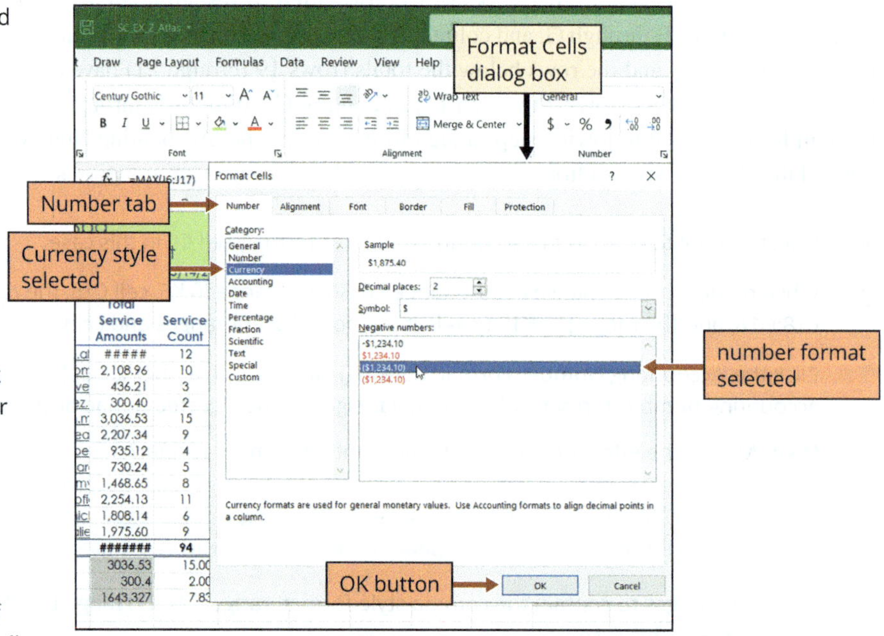

Figure 2-39

Q&A How do I decide which number format to use?
Excel offers many ways to format numbers. Once you select a number category, you can select the number of decimal places, whether to include a dollar sign (or a symbol of another currency), and how negative numbers should appear. Selecting the appropriate negative numbers format is important, because some formats add a space to the right of the number in order to align numbers in the worksheet on the decimal points and some do not.

2

- Click OK (Format Cells dialog box) to assign the currency style format with a floating dollar sign to the selected ranges (Figure 2-40).

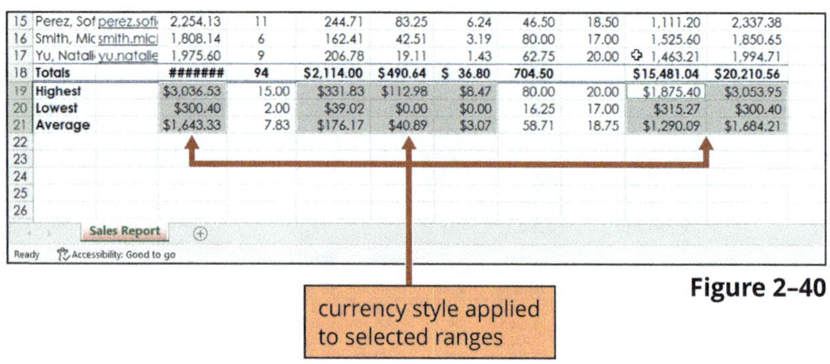

Figure 2-40

Q&A What is the difference between using the accounting number style and currency style?
When using the currency style, recall that a floating dollar sign always appears immediately to the left of the first digit. With the accounting number style, the fixed dollar sign always appears on the left side of the cell.

Other Ways

1. Press CTRL+1, click Number tab (Format Cells dialog box), click Currency in Category list, select format, click OK
2. Press CTRL+SHIFT+DOLLAR SIGN ($)

Conditional Formatting

Conditional formatting is special formatting—the font, font color, background fill, and other options—that is applied if cell values meet specified criteria. Excel offers a variety of commonly used conditional formatting rules, along with the ability to create your own custom rules and formatting. The next step is to emphasize the values less than 5 in column D and values greater than 70 in column H, by formatting them to appear bolded with an orange background and a blue background, respectively.

BTW
Conditional Formatting
You can assign any format to a cell, a range of cells, a worksheet, or an entire workbook conditionally. If the value of the cell changes and no longer meets the specified condition, Excel suppresses the conditional formatting.

To Apply Conditional Formatting

The following steps assign conditional formatting to the ranges D6:D17, and H6:H17. **Why?** After formatting, any cell with values less than 5 in column D and values greater than 70 in column H, will appear bolded with an orange background and a blue background, respectively.

1

- Select the range D6:D17.
- Click the Conditional Formatting button (Home tab | Styles group) to display the Conditional Formatting menu (Figure 2-41).

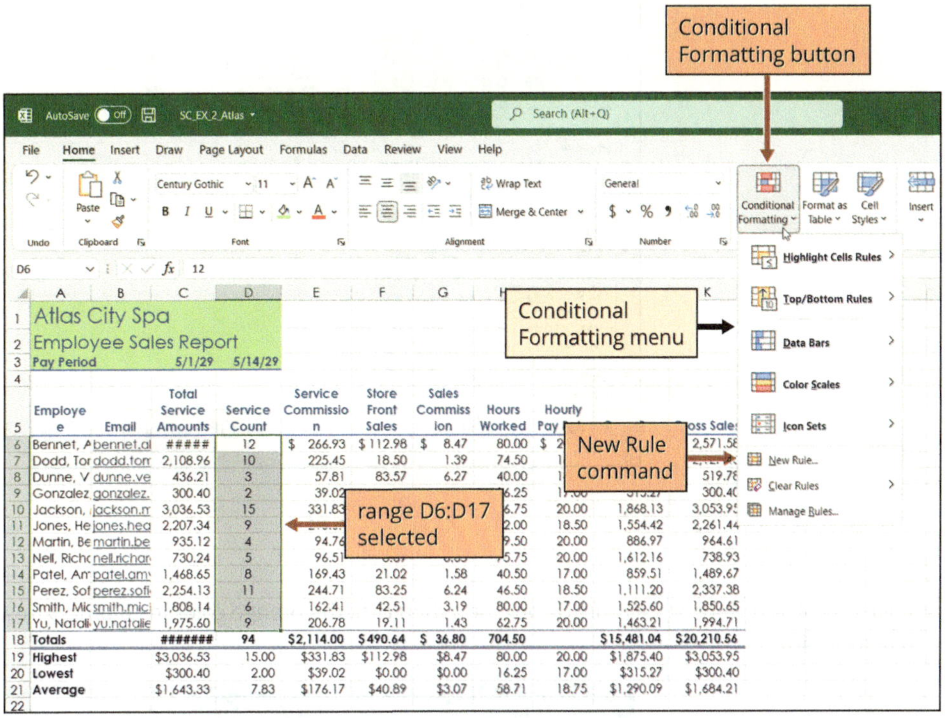

Figure 2-41

2

- Click New Rule on the Conditional Formatting menu to display the New Formatting Rule dialog box.
- Click 'Format only cells that contain' in the Select a Rule Type area (New Formatting Rule dialog box) to change the Edit the Rule Description area.
- In the Edit the Rule Description area, click the arrow in the relational operator box (second box) to display a list of relational operators, and then select less than to select the desired operator.
- Click in the rightmost box, and then type **5** to enter the value of the rule description (Figure 2-42).

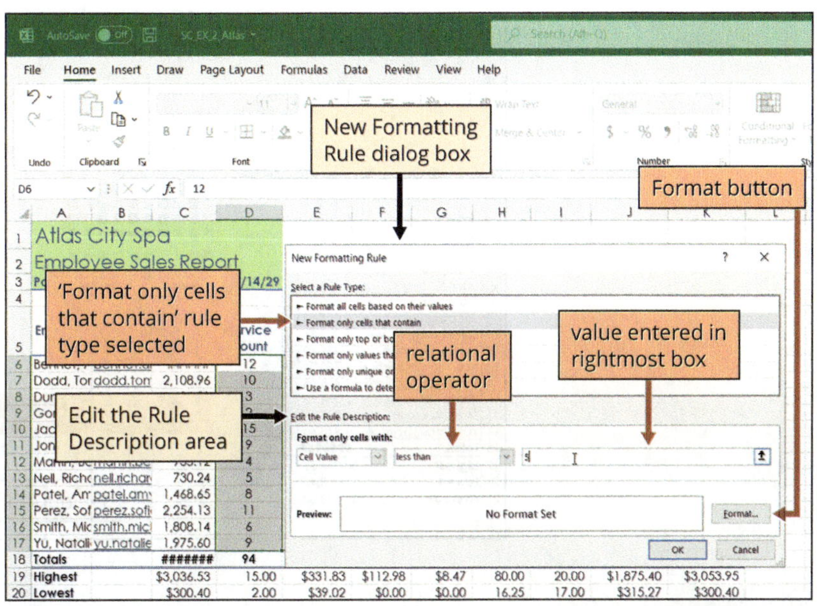

Figure 2-42

Q&A What do the changes in the Edit the Rule Description area indicate?

The Edit the Rule Description area allows you to view and edit the rules for the conditional format. In this case, the rule indicates that Excel should format only those cells with cell values less than 5.

3

- Click the Format button (New Formatting Rule dialog box) to display the Format Cells dialog box.
- If necessary, click the Font tab (Format Cells dialog box) to display the Font sheet. Click Bold in the Font Style gallery (Figure 2–43).

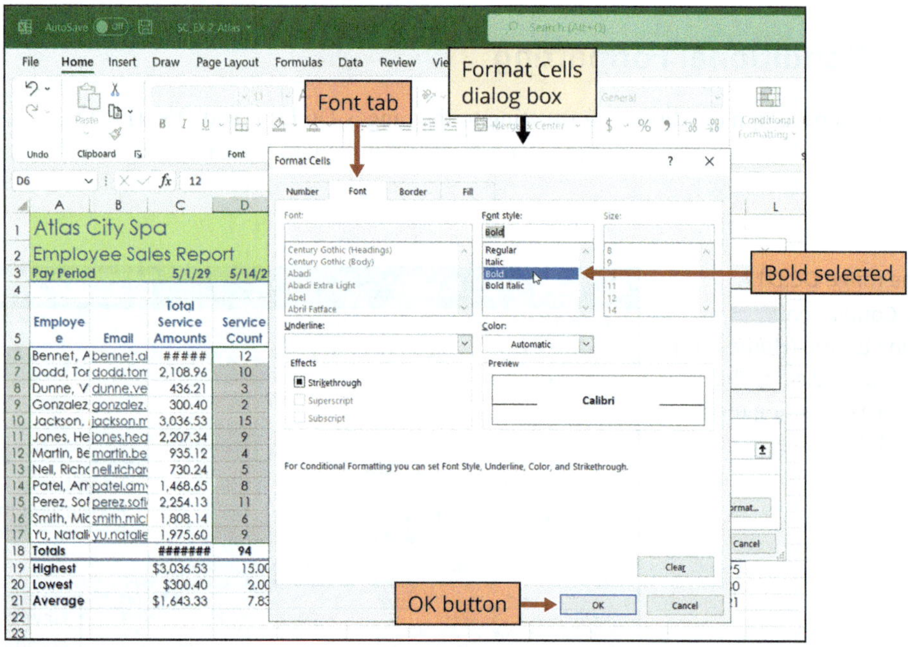

Figure 2–43

4

- Click the Fill tab (Format Cells dialog box) and then click the orange color in column 9, row 1 to select the background color (Figure 2–44).

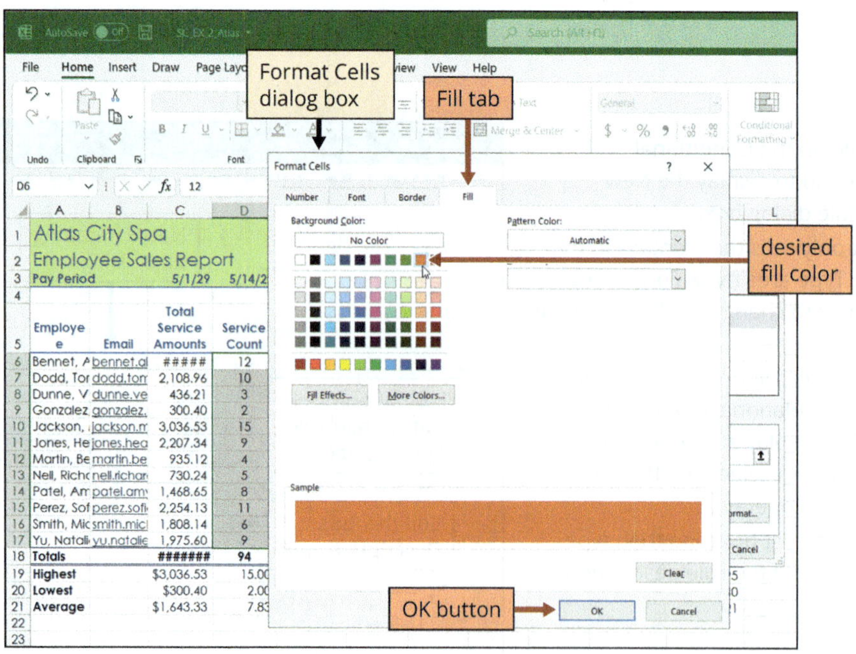

Figure 2–44

5

- Click OK (Format Cells dialog box) to close the Format Cells dialog box and display the New Formatting Rule dialog box with the desired font and background colors displayed in the Preview area (Figure 2–45).

Q&A What should I do if I make a mistake setting up a rule?
If after you have applied the conditional formatting you realize you made a mistake when creating a rule, select the cell(s) with the rule you want to edit, click the Conditional Formatting button (Home tab | Styles group), select the rule you want to edit, and then click either the Edit Rule button (to edit the selected rule) or the Delete Rule button (to delete the selected rule).

How can I delete a conditional formatting rule?
If you no longer want a conditional formatting rule applied to a cell, select the cell or cells, click the Conditional Formatting button (Home tab | Styles group), click Clear Rules, and then select Clear Rules from Selected Cells.

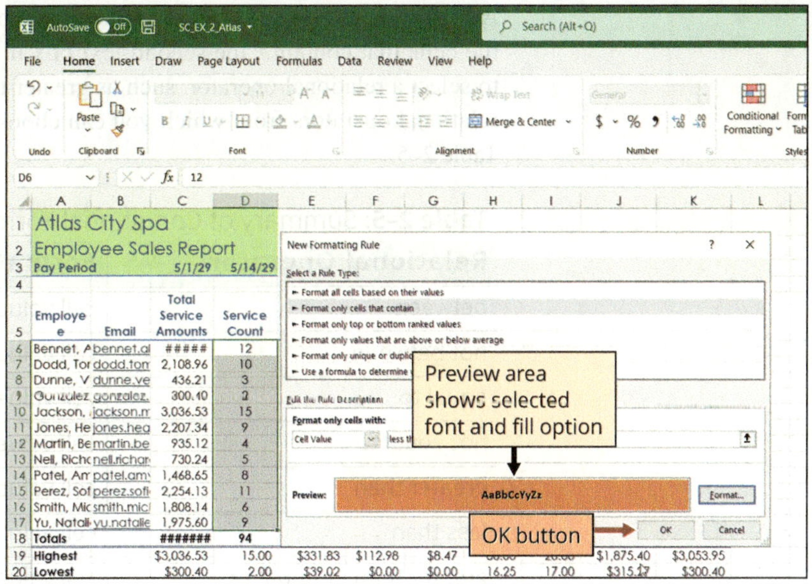

Figure 2–45

6

- Click OK (New Formatting Rule dialog box) to assign the conditional format to the selected range (as shown in Figure 2–46).

7

- Select range H6:H17.
- Click the Conditional Formatting button (Home tab | Styles group) to display the Conditional Formatting menu.
- Click New Rule on the Conditional Formatting menu to display the New Formatting Rule dialog box.
- Click 'Format only cells that contain' in the Select a Rule Type area (New Formatting Rule dialog box) to change the Edit the Rule Description area.
- In the Edit the Rule Description area, click the arrow in the relational operator box (second box) to display a list of relational operators, and then select greater than to select the desired operator.
- Click in the rightmost box, and then type **70** to enter the value of the rule description.

8

- Click the Format button (New Formatting Rule dialog box) to display the Format Cells dialog box.
- If necessary, click the Font tab (Format Cells dialog box) to display the Font sheet. Click Bold in the Font Style gallery.
- Click the Fill tab (Format Cells dialog box) and then click the blue color in column 3, row 4 to select the background color.

9

- Click OK (Format Cells dialog box) to close the Format Cells dialog box and display the New Formatting Rule dialog box with the desired font and background colors displayed in the Preview area.
- Click OK (New Formatting Rule dialog box) to assign the conditional format to the selected range.
- Click anywhere in the worksheet, such as cell A23, to deselect the current range (Figure 2–46).

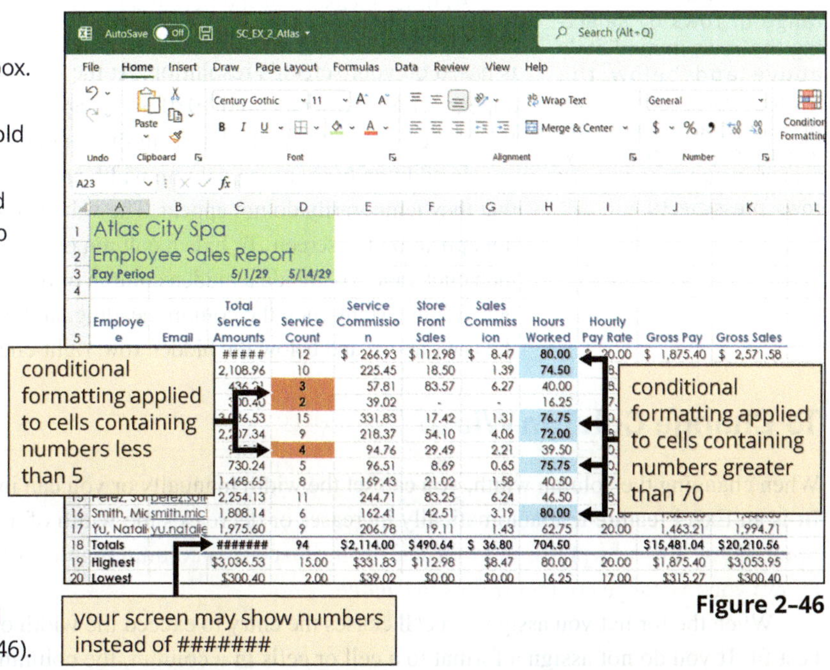

Figure 2–46

Conditional Formatting Operators

As shown in the New Formatting Rule dialog box, when the selected rule type is "Format only the cells that contain," the second text box in the Edit the Rule Description area allows you to select a relational operator, such as greater than, to use in the condition. The eight different relational operators from which you can choose for conditional formatting are summarized in Table 2–5.

Table 2-5: Summary of Conditional Formatting Relational Operators

Relational Operator	Formatting Will Be Applied If...
between	cell value is between two numbers
not between	cell value is not between two numbers
equal to	cell value is equal to a number
not equal to	cell value is not equal to a number
greater than	cell value is greater than a number
less than	cell value is less than a number
greater than or equal to	cell value is greater than or equal to a number
less than or equal to	cell value is less than or equal to a number

BTW
Hidden Rows and Columns
For some people, trying to unhide a range of columns using the mouse can be frustrating. An alternative is to use the keyboard: select the columns to the right and left of the hidden columns and then press CTRL+SHIFT+) (RIGHT PARENTHESIS). To use the keyboard to hide a range of columns, press CTRL+0 (zero). You also can use the keyboard to unhide a range of rows by selecting the rows immediately above and below the hidden rows and then pressing CTRL+SHIFT+ ((LEFT PARENTHESIS). To use the keyboard to hide a range of rows, press CTRL+9.

Changing Column Width and Row Height

You can change the width of the columns or height of the rows at any time to make the worksheet easier to read or to ensure that an entry fits properly in a cell. By default, all of the columns in a blank worksheet have a width of 8.43 characters, or 64 pixels. This value may change depending on the theme applied to the workbook. For example, when you applied the Slice theme to the workbook in this module, the default width of the columns changed to 8.1 characters. A **character** is defined as a letter, number, symbol, or punctuation mark. An average of 8.43 characters in 11-point Calibri font (the default font used by Excel) will fit in a cell. (Note that column widths may vary depending on the width of the font defined for the Normal style of your workbook.)

The default row height in a blank worksheet is 15 points (or 20 pixels), which easily fits the 11-point default font. Recall from Module 1 that a point is equal to 1/72 of an inch. Thus, 15 points is equal to about 1/5 of an inch.

Another measure of the height and width of cells is pixels. A **pixel**, which is short for picture element, is an individual point of color on a display screen or printout. The size of the dot is based on your screen's resolution. At the resolution of 1920 × 1080, for example, 1920 pixels appear across the screen and 1080 pixels appear down the screen for a total of 2,073,600 pixels. It is these 2,073,600 pixels that form the font and other items you see on the screen.

In addition to changing column width and row heights, you also can hide columns and rows so that they temporarily do not appear. The values in the columns and rows will remain, but they will not appear on the screen. To hide a column or row, right-click the column letter or row number and then click hide. To unhide a hidden column or row, select the columns to the left and right of the hidden column, right-click the column heading, and then click Unhide. To unhide a hidden row, select the rows above and below the hidden row, right-click the row numbers, and then click Unhide.

To Change Column Width

When changing the column width, you can set the width manually or you can instruct Excel to size the column to best fit. **Best fit** is an Excel feature that automatically increases or decreases the width of a column so that the widest entry will fit. **Why?** Sometimes, you may prefer more or less white space in a column than best fit provides. To change the white space, Excel allows you to change column widths manually.

When the format you assign to a cell causes the entry to exceed the width of a column, Excel changes the column width to best fit. If you do not assign a format to a cell or cells in a column, the column width will remain 8.43 characters (depending on your computer settings, your column width may differ slightly.) Recall from Module 1 that to set a column width to best fit, double-click the right boundary of the column heading above row 1. The following steps change the column widths heading above row 1. The following steps change the column widths.

1

- Select column B.
- Point to the boundary on the right side of column heading B to cause the pointer to become a split double arrow (Figure 2–47).

Q&A What if I want to make a large change to the column width?
If you want to increase or decrease column width significantly, you can right-click a column heading and then use the Column Width command on the shortcut menu to change the column's width. To use this command, however, you must select one or more entire columns.

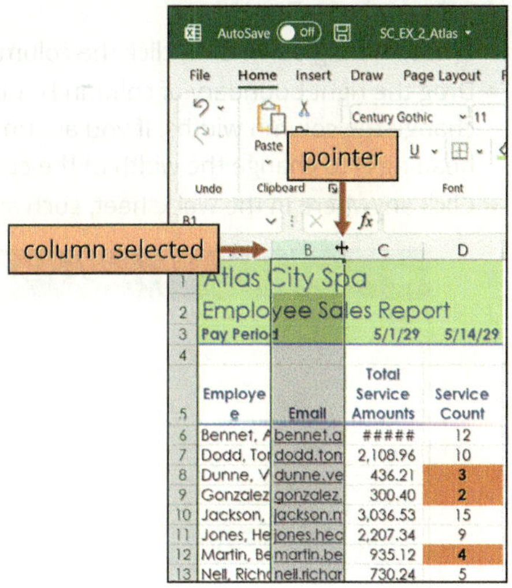

Figure 2–47

2

- Double-click the right boundary of column heading B to change the width of the selected columns to best fit.
- Point to the right boundary of the column A heading above row 1.
- When the pointer changes to a split double arrow, drag until the ScreenTip indicates Width: 16.30 (170 pixels) (Figure 2–48). (If dragging does not display the required number, use the Column Width dialog box at Home tab, Cells group, Format/Column Width)

Q&A What happens if I change the column width to zero (0)?
If you decrease the column width to 0, the column is hidden. Hiding cells is a technique you can use to hide data that might not be relevant to a particular report. To instruct Excel to display a hidden column, position the pointer to the right of the column heading boundary where the hidden column is located and then drag to the right.

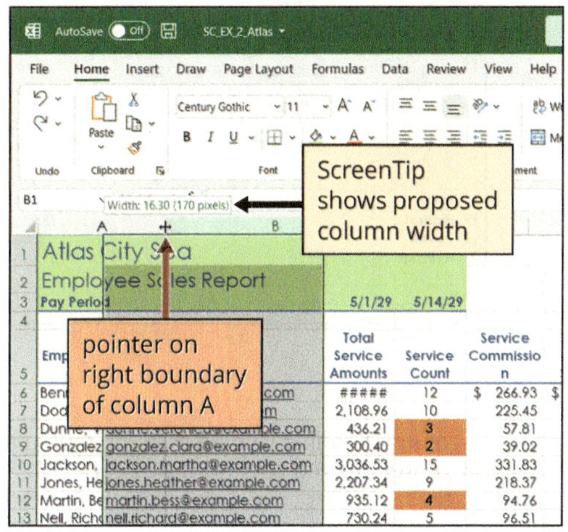

Figure 2–48

3

- Release the mouse button to change the column width.
- Select column C.
- While holding down CTRL, click and drag through column headings E, F, and G so the nonadjacent columns are selected.
- While holding down CTRL, click and drag through column headings I, J, and K so the nonadjacent columns are selected.
- Point to the boundary on the right side of the column G heading above row 1.
- Drag until the ScreenTip indicates Width: 13.30 (140 pixels). Do not release the mouse button. If you are unable to drag and reach the specified width, double-click the right boundary of column heading G to change the width of the columns to best fit (Figure 2–49).

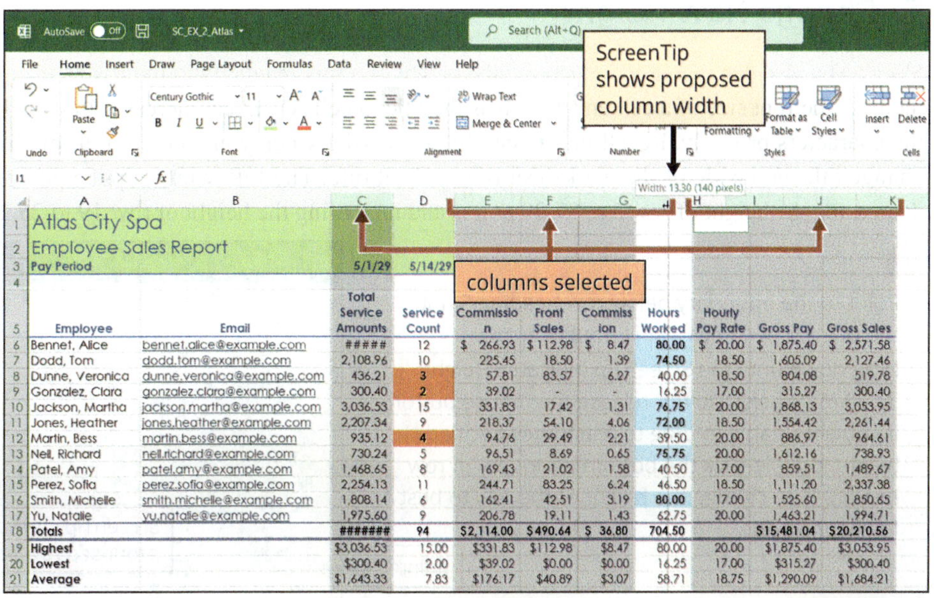

Figure 2–49

4

- Release the mouse button to change the column widths.
- Select column D.
- While holding down CTRL, click the column H heading above row 1 so that nonadjacent columns are selected.
- Drag the right boundary of column H until the ScreenTip indicates Width: 10.00 (107 pixels). Release the mouse button to. change the column widths. If you are unable to drag and reach the specified width, double-click the right boundary of column heading H to change the width of the columns to best fit.
- Click anywhere in the worksheet, such as cell A23, to deselect the columns (Figure 2–50).

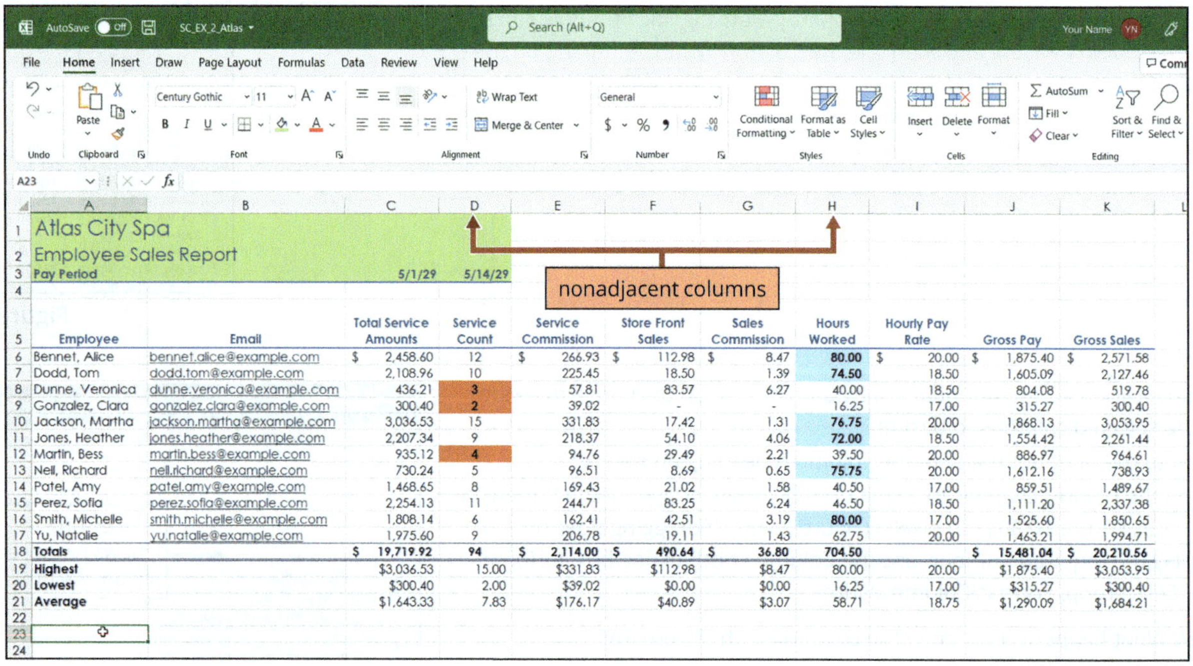

Figure 2–50

Other Ways

1. Click column heading or drag through multiple column headings, right-click selected column, click Column Width on shortcut menu, enter desired column width, click OK

To Change Row Height

Why? You also can increase or decrease the height of a row manually to improve the appearance of the worksheet. When you increase the font size of a cell entry, such as the title in cell A1, Excel increases the row height to best fit so that it can display the characters properly. Recall that Excel did this earlier when you entered multiple lines in a cell in row 5, and when you changed the cell style of the worksheet title and subtitle. The following steps improve the appearance of the worksheet by decreasing the height of row 5 to 37.20 points and increasing the height of row 19 to 25.20 points.

1

- Point to the boundary below row heading 5 until the pointer becomes a split double arrow.
- Drag down until the ScreenTip indicates Height: 37.20 (62 pixels). Do not release the mouse button. If you are unable to drag to reach the specified height, double-click the bottom boundary of row heading 5 to change the height of the row to best fit (Figure 2–51).

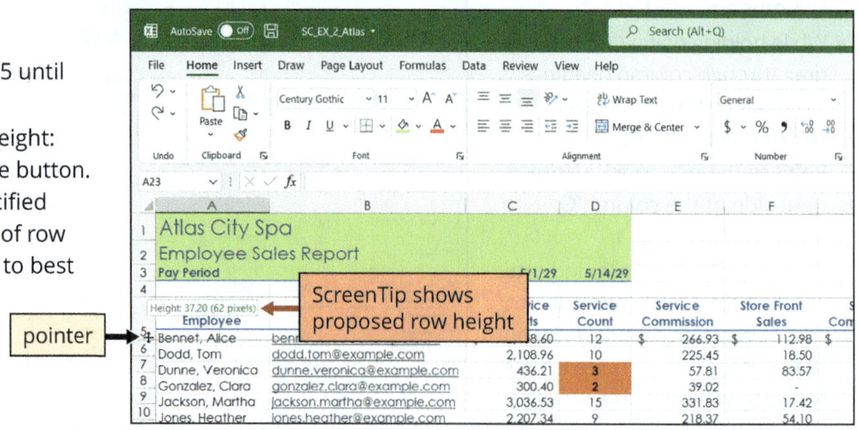

Figure 2–51

2

- Release the mouse button to change the row height.
- Point to the boundary below row heading 19 until the pointer becomes a split double arrow and then drag downward until the ScreenTip indicates Height: 24.00. Do not release the mouse button (Figure 2–52).

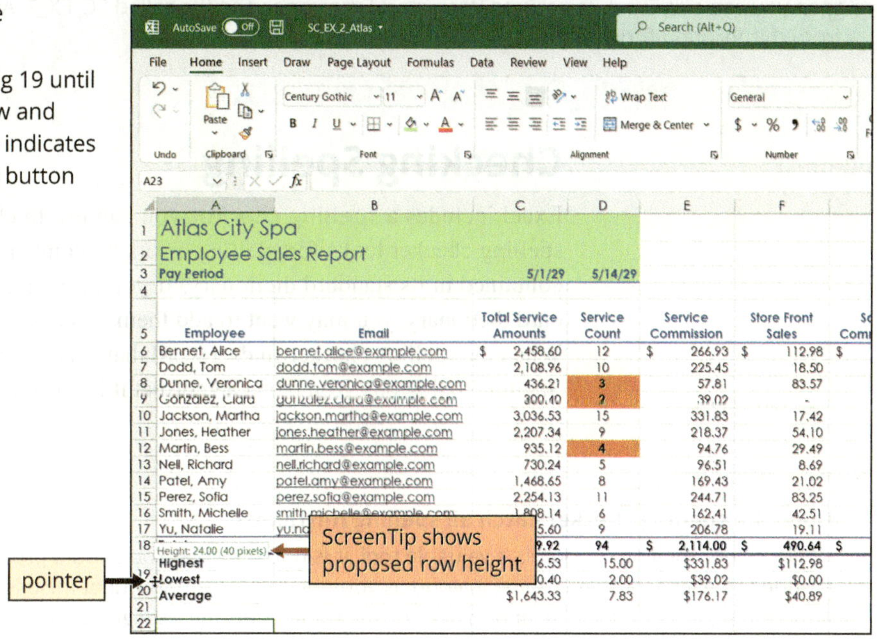

Figure 2–52

3

- Release the mouse button to change the row height.
- Click anywhere in the worksheet, such as cell A23, to deselect the current cell (Figure 2–53).

Q&A Can I hide a row?

Yes. As with column widths, when you decrease the row height to 0, the row is hidden. To instruct Excel to display a hidden row, position the pointer just below the row heading boundary where the row is hidden and then drag downward. To set a row height to best fit, double-click the bottom boundary of the row heading. You also can hide and unhide rows by right-clicking the row or column heading and selecting the option to hide or unhide the cells.

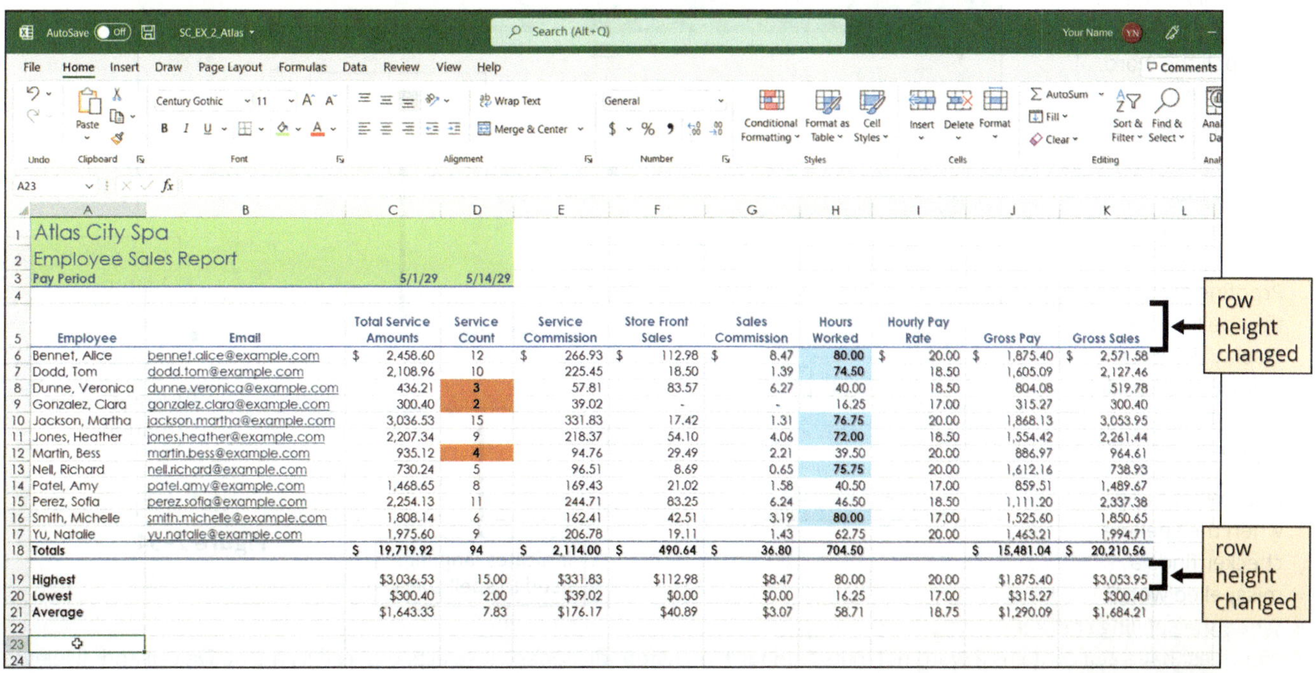

Figure 2–53

Other Ways

1. Right-click row heading or drag through multiple row headings, right-click selected heading(s), click Row Height on shortcut menu, enter desired row height, click OK

Break Point: If you want to take a break, this is a good place to do so. Be sure to save the SC_EX_2_Atlas file again and then you can exit Excel. To resume later, start Excel, open the file called SC_EX_2_Atlas, and continue following the steps from this location forward.

Checking Spelling

Excel includes a **spelling checker** you can use to check a worksheet for spelling errors. The spelling checker looks for spelling errors by comparing words on the worksheet against words contained in its standard dictionary. If you often use specialized terms that are not in the standard dictionary, you may want to add them to a custom dictionary using the Spelling dialog box. When the spelling checker finds a word that is not in either dictionary, it displays the word in the Spelling dialog box. You then can correct it if it is misspelled.

Consider This

Does the spelling checker catch all spelling mistakes?

While Excel's spelling checker is a valuable tool, it is not infallible. You should proofread your workbook carefully by pointing to each word and saying it aloud as you point to it. Be mindful of misused words such as its and it's, through and though, your and you're, and to and too. Nothing undermines a good impression more than a professional report with misspelled words.

To Check Spelling on the Worksheet

Why? Everything in a worksheet should be checked to make sure there are no spelling errors. To illustrate how Excel responds to a misspelled word, the following steps purposely misspell the word, Employee, in cell A3 as the word, Empolyee, as shown in Figure 2–54.

1

- With cell A5 selected, type **Empolyee** to misspell the word, Employee.
- Click Review on the ribbon to display the Review tab.
- Click the Spelling button (Review tab | Proofing group) to use the spelling checker to display the misspelled word in the Spelling dialog box (Figure 2–54).

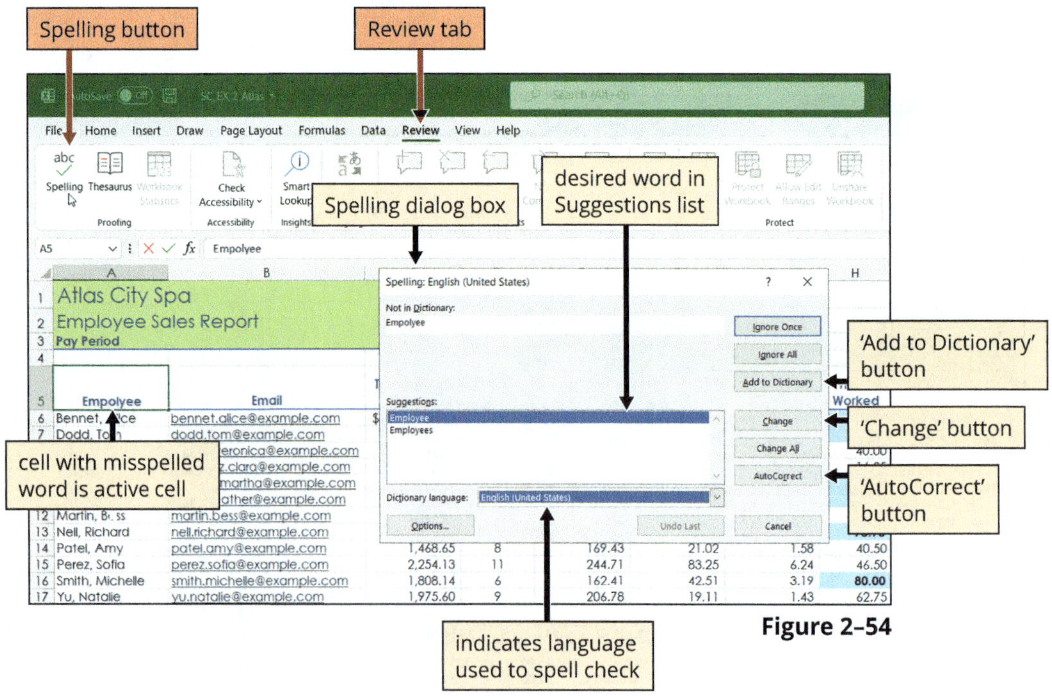

Figure 2–54

Q&A What happens when the spelling checker finds a misspelled word?

When the spelling checker identifies that a cell contains a word not in its standard or custom dictionary, it selects that cell as the active cell and displays the Spelling dialog box. The Spelling dialog box displays the word that was not found in the dictionary and offers a list of suggested corrections (Figure 2–55).

2

- Verify that the word highlighted in the Suggestions area is correct.
- Click the Change button (Spelling dialog box) to change the misspelled word to the correct word.
- A dialog box will display when the spelling checker reaches the end of the worksheet, asking if you want to continue checking at the beginning, click Yes to check the rest of the worksheet.
- If a Microsoft Excel dialog box is displayed, click OK (Figure 2–55).

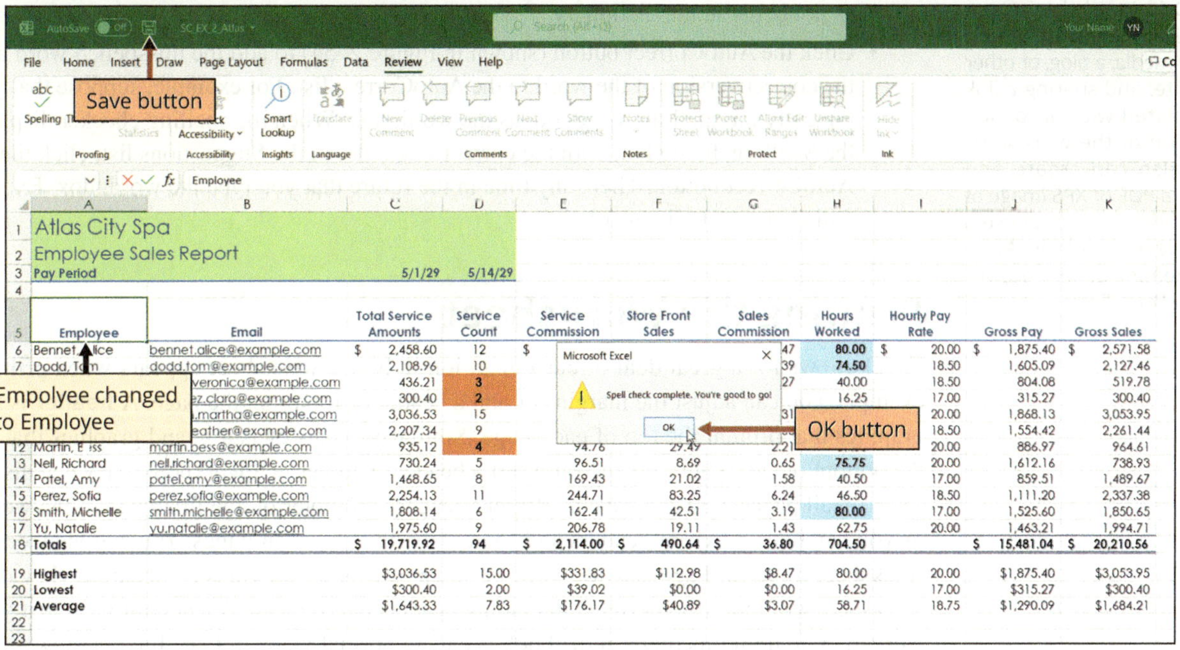

Figure 2–55

3

- Click anywhere in the worksheet, to deselect the current cell.
- Display the Home tab.
- Save the workbook again on the same storage location with the same file name.

Q&A What other actions can I take in the Spelling dialog box?

If one of the words in the Suggestions list is correct, select it and then click the Change button. If none of the suggested words are correct, type the correct word in the 'Not in Dictionary' text box and then click the Change button. To change the word throughout the worksheet, click the Change All button instead of the Change button. To skip correcting the word, click the Ignore Once button. To have Excel ignore the word for the remainder of the worksheet, click the Ignore All button.

Other Ways

1. Press F7

Additional Spelling Checker Considerations

Consider these additional guidelines when using the spelling checker:

- To check the spelling of the text in a single cell, double-click the cell to make the formula bar active and then click the Spelling button (Review tab | Proofing group).
- If you select a single cell so that the formula bar is not active and then start the spelling checker, Excel checks the remainder of the worksheet, including notes and embedded charts.
- If you select a cell other than cell A1 before you start the spelling checker, Excel displays a dialog box when the spelling checker reaches the end of the worksheet, asking if you want to continue checking at the beginning.

BTW

Error Checking

Always take the time to check the formulas of a worksheet before submitting it to your supervisor. You can check formulas by clicking the Error Checking button (Formulas tab | Formula Auditing group). You also should test the formulas by employing data that tests the limits of formulas. Experienced spreadsheet specialists spend as much time testing a workbook as they do creating it, and they do so before distributing the workbook.

BTW
Distributing a Workbook
Instead of printing and distributing a hard copy of a workbook, you can distribute the workbook electronically. Options include sending the workbook via email; posting it on cloud storage (such as OneDrive) and sharing the file with others; posting it on social media, a blog, or other website; and sharing a link associated with an online location of the workbook. You also can create and share a PDF or XPS image of the workbook, so that users can view the file in Acrobat Reader or XPS Viewer instead of in Excel.

- If you select a range of cells before starting the spelling checker, Excel checks the spelling of the words only in the selected range.
- To check the spelling of all the sheets in a workbook, right-click any sheet tab, click 'Select All Sheets' on the sheet tab shortcut menu, and then start the spelling checker.
- To add words to the dictionary, such as your last name, click the 'Add to Dictionary' button in the Spelling dialog box (shown in Figure 2–54) when Excel flags the word as not being in the dictionary.
- Click the AutoCorrect button (shown in Figure 2–54) to add the misspelled word and the correct version of the word to the AutoCorrect list. For example, suppose that you typically misspell the word, do, as the word, dox. When the spelling checker displays the Spelling dialog box with the correct word, do, in the Suggestions list, click the AutoCorrect button. Then, any time in the future that you type the word, dox, Excel will change it to the word, do.

Printing the Worksheet

Excel allows for a great deal of customization in how a worksheet appears when printed. For example, you can adjust the margins or add a header or footer on the page. A **header** is text and graphics that print at the top of each page. Similarly, a **footer** is text and graphics that print at the bottom of each page. When you insert a header or footer in a workbook, they can display the same on all pages, you can have a different header and footer on the first page of the workbook, or you can have different headers and footers on odd and even pages. You can view or edit the worksheet footer in Page Layout view. **Page Layout view** provides an accurate view of how a worksheet will look when printed, including headers and footers. The default view that you have worked in up until this point in the book is called Normal view. In Page Layout view, when you click in the header or footer area, the Header & Footer tab appears in the ribbon, where you can select display options in the Options group.

To Change the Worksheet's Margins, Header, and Orientation in Page Layout View

The following steps change to Page Layout view, narrow the margins of the worksheet, change the header of the worksheet, and set the orientation of the worksheet to landscape. **Why?** *You may want the printed worksheet to fit on one page. You can do that by reducing the page margins and changing the page orientation to fit wider printouts across a sheet of paper. You can use the header to identify the content on each page.* **Margins** are the space between the page content and the edges of the page. The current worksheet is too wide for a single page and requires landscape orientation to fit on one page in a readable manner.

1

- Click the Page Layout button on the status bar to view the worksheet in Page Layout view (Figure 2–56).

Q&A What are the features of Page Layout view?
Page Layout view shows the worksheet divided into pages. A gray background separates each page. The white areas surrounding each page indicate the print margins. The top of each page includes a Header area, and the bottom of each page includes a Footer area. Page Layout view also includes rulers at the top and left margin of the page that assist you in placing objects on the page, such as charts and pictures.

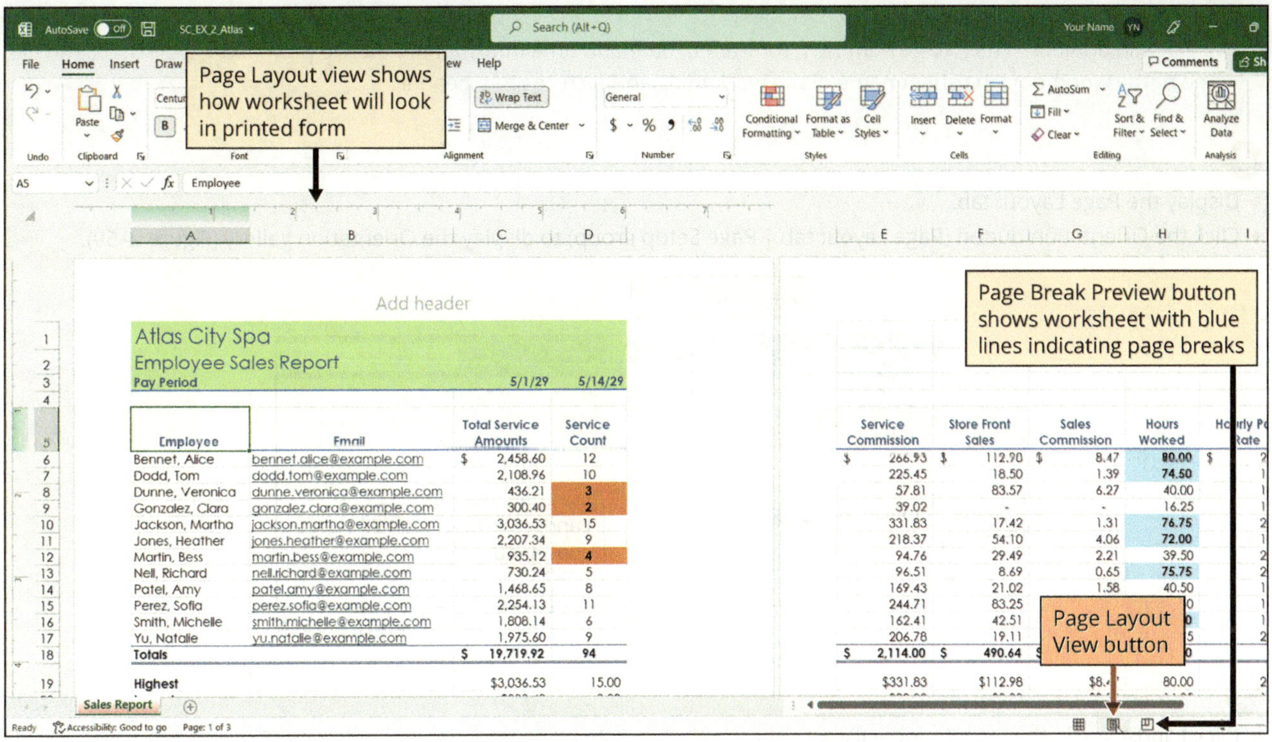

Figure 2–56

2

- Display the Page Layout tab.
- Click the Margins button (Page Layout tab | Page Setup group) to display the Margins gallery (Figure 2–57).

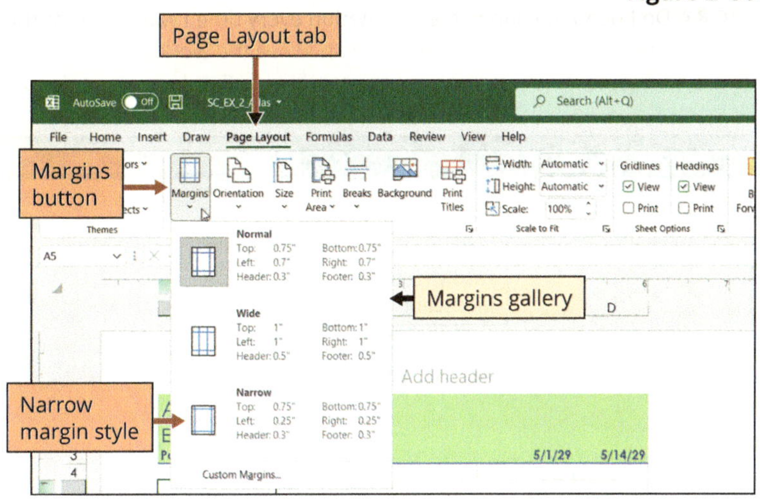

Figure 2–57

3

- Click Narrow in the Margins gallery to change the worksheet margins to the Narrow margin style.
- If necessary, scroll up to display the Header area.
- Click the center of the Header area above the worksheet title.
- Type **Santana Moore** and then press ENTER. Type **Accounting** to complete the worksheet header (Figure 2–58).
- If requested by your instructor, type your name instead of Santana Moore.
- Select cell A5 to deselect the header.

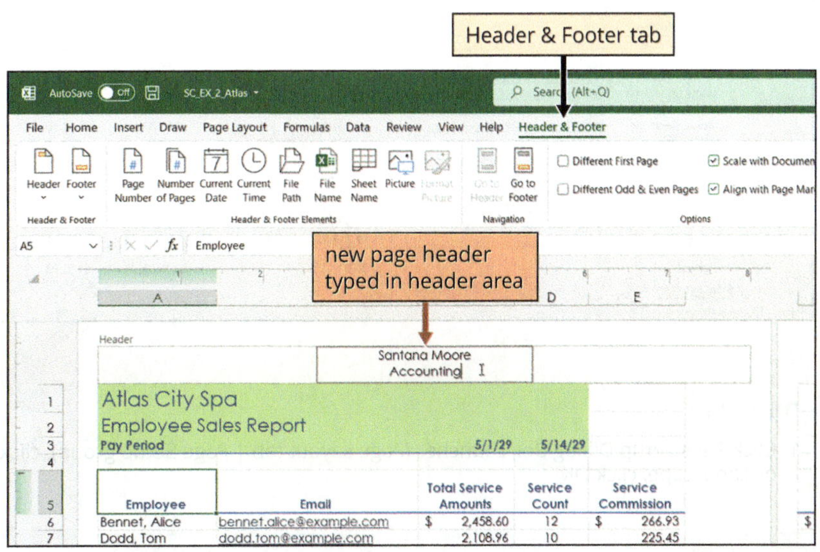

Figure 2–58

Q&A What else can I place in a header?

You can add additional text, page number information, date and time information, the file path of the workbook, the file name of the workbook, the sheet name of the workbook, and pictures to a header.

4

- Display the Page Layout tab.
- Click the Orientation button (Page Layout tab | Page Setup group) to display the Orientation gallery (Figure 2–59).

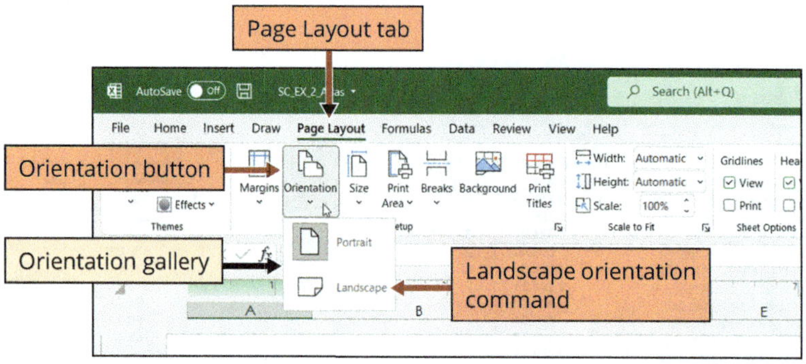

Figure 2–59

5

- Click Landscape in the Orientation gallery to change the worksheet's orientation to landscape (Figure 2–60).

Q&A Do I need to change the orientation every time I want to print the worksheet?

No. Once you change the orientation and save the workbook, Excel will save the orientation setting for that workbook until you change it. When you open a new workbook, Excel sets the orientation to portrait.

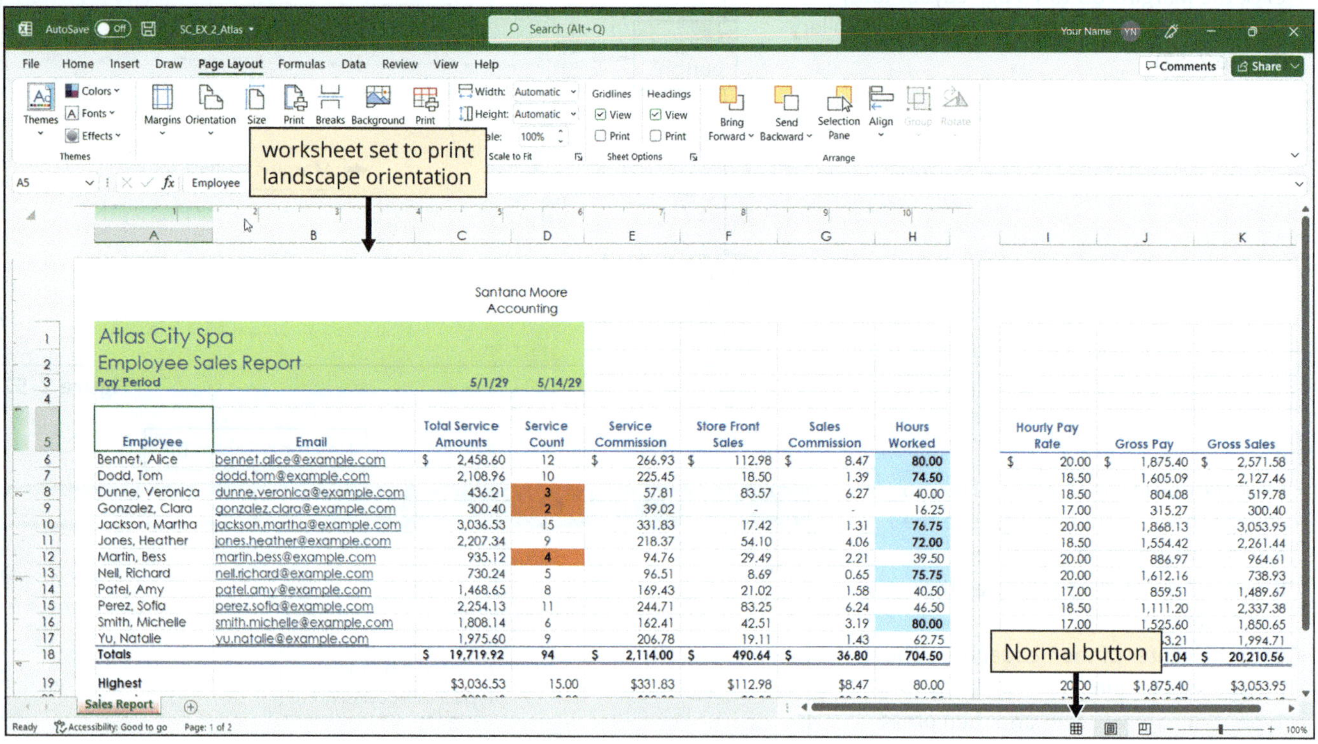

Figure 2–60

Other Ways

1. Click Page Setup Dialog Box Launcher (Page Layout tab | Page Setup group), click Page tab (Page Setup dialog box), click Portrait or Landscape, click OK

To Print a Worksheet

Excel provides multiple options for printing a worksheet. In the following sections, you first print the worksheet and then print a section of the worksheet. The following steps print the worksheet.

1. Click File on the ribbon to open Backstage view.
2. Click Print to display the Print screen.
3. If necessary, click the Printer button on the Print screen to display a list of available printer options and then click the desired printer to change the currently selected printer.
4. Click the No Scaling button and then select 'Fit Sheet on One Page' to select it.
5. Click the Print button on the Print screen to print the worksheet on one page in landscape orientation on the currently selected printer.
6. When the printer stops, retrieve the hard copy (Figure 2–61).

Santana Moore
Accounting

Atlas City Spa
Employee Sales Report
Pay Period 5/1/29 5/14/29

Employee	Email	Total Service Amounts	Service Count	Service Commission	Store Front Sales	Sales Commission	Hours Worked	Hourly Pay Rate	Gross Pay	Gross Sales
Bennet, Alice	bennet.alice@example.com	$ 2,458.60	12	$ 266.93	$ 112.98	$ 8.47	**80.00**	$ 20.00	$ 1,875.40	$ 2,571.58
Dodd, Tom	dodd.tom@example.com	2,108.96	10	225.45	18.50	1.39	**74.50**	18.50	1,605.09	2,127.46
Dunne, Veronica	dunne.veronica@example.com	436.21	**3**	57.81	83.57	6.27	40.00	18.50	804.08	519.78
Gonzalez, Clara	gonzalez.clara@example.com	300.40	**2**	39.02	-	-	16.25	17.00	315.27	300.40
Jackson, Martha	jackson.martha@example.com	3,036.53	15	331.83	17.42	1.31	**76.75**	20.00	1,868.13	3,053.95
Jones, Heather	jones.heather@example.com	2,207.34	9	218.37	54.10	4.06	**72.00**	18.50	1,554.42	2,261.44
Martin, Bess	martin.bess@example.com	935.12	**4**	94.76	29.49	2.21	39.50	20.00	886.97	964.61
Nell, Richard	nell.richard@example.com	730.24	5	96.51	8.69	0.65	**75.75**	20.00	1,612.16	738.93
Patel, Amy	patel.amy@example.com	1,468.65	8	169.43	21.02	1.58	40.50	17.00	859.51	1,489.67
Perez, Sofia	perez.sofia@example.com	2,254.13	11	244.71	83.25	6.24	46.50	18.50	1,111.20	2,337.38
Smith, Michelle	smith.michelle@example.com	1,808.14	6	162.41	42.51	3.19	**80.00**	17.00	1,525.60	1,850.65
Yu, Natalie	yu.natalie@example.com	1,975.60	9	206.78	19.11	1.43	62.75	20.00	1,463.21	1,994.71
Totals		**$ 19,719.92**	**94**	**$ 2,114.00**	**$ 490.64**	**$ 36.80**	**704.50**		**$ 15,481.04**	**$ 20,210.56**
Highest		$3,036.53	15.00	$331.83	$112.98	$8.47	80.00	20.00	$1,875.40	$3,053.95
Lowest		$300.40	2.00	$39.02	$0.00	$0.00	16.25	17.00	$315.27	$300.40
Average		$1,643.33	7.83	$176.17	$40.89	$3.07	58.71	18.75	$1,290.09	$1,684.21

Figure 2–61

To Print a Section of the Worksheet

You can print portions of the worksheet by selecting the range of cells to print and then clicking the Selection option button in the Print what area in the Print dialog box. **Why?** To save paper, you only want to print the portion of the worksheet you need, instead of printing the entire worksheet. The following steps print the range A5:E21.

1.

- Select the range to print, cells A5:E21 in this case.
- Click File on the ribbon to open Backstage view.
- Click Print to display the Print screen.
- Click 'Print Active Sheets' in the Settings area (Print screen | Print list) to display a list of options that determine what Excel should print (Figure 2–62).

2

- Click Print Selection to instruct Excel to print only the selected range and display only the selected range in the preview area.
- Click the Print button in the Print screen to print the selected range of the worksheet on the currently selected printer (Figure 2–63).
- Click the Normal button on the status bar to return to Normal view.
- Click anywhere in the worksheet, such as cell A23, to deselect the range A5:E21.

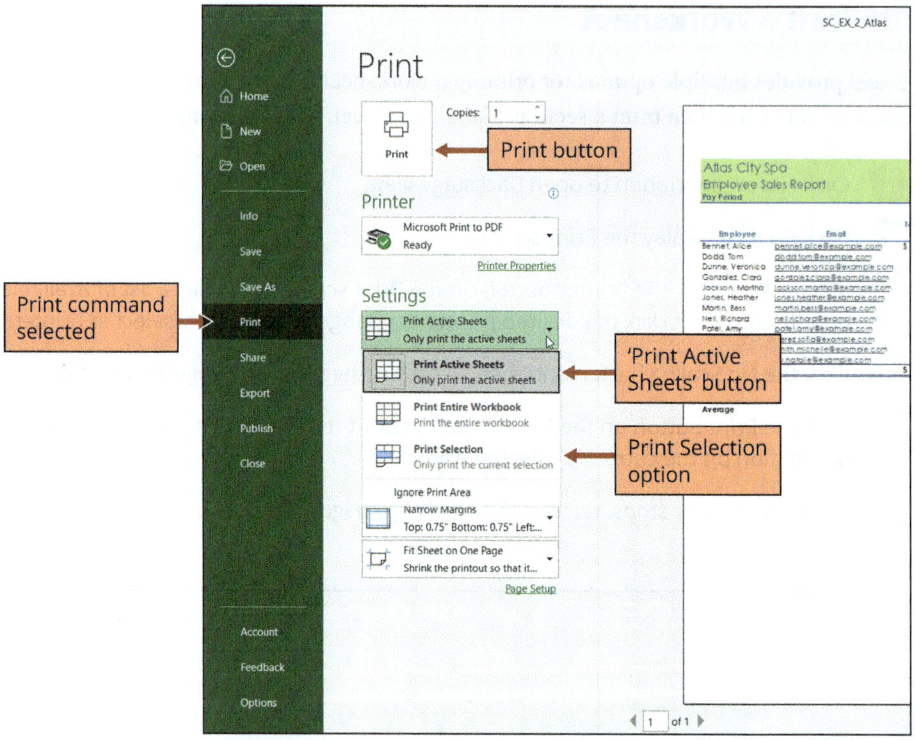

Figure 2–62

Q&A What can I print?
Excel includes three options for selecting what to print (Figure 2–62). As shown in the previous steps, the Print Selection option instructs Excel to print the selected range. The 'Print Active Sheets' option instructs Excel to print the active worksheet (the worksheet currently on the screen) or selected worksheets. Finally, the 'Print Entire Workbook' option instructs Excel to print all of the worksheets in the workbook.

Santana Moore
Accounting

Employee	Email	Total Service Amounts	Service Count	Service Commission
Bennet, Alice	bennet.alice@example.com	$ 2,458.60	12	$ 266.93
Dodd, Tom	dodd.tom@example.com	2,108.96	10	225.45
Dunne, Veronica	dunne.veronica@example.com	436.21	3	57.81
Gonzalez, Clara	gonzalez.clara@example.com	300.40	2	39.02
Jackson, Martha	jackson.martha@example.com	3,036.53	15	331.83
Jones, Heather	jones.heather@example.com	2,207.34	9	218.37
Martin, Bess	martin.bess@example.com	935.12	4	94.76
Nell, Richard	nell.richard@example.com	730.24	5	96.51
Patel, Amy	patel.amy@example.com	1,468.65	8	169.43
Perez, Sofia	perez.sofia@example.com	2,254.13	11	244.71
Smith, Michelle	smith.michelle@example.com	1,808.14	6	162.41
Yu, Natalie	yu.natalie@example.com	1,975.60	9	206.78
Totals		**$ 19,719.92**	**94**	**$ 2,114.00**
Highest		$3,036.53	15.00	$331.83
Lowest		$300.40	2.00	$39.02
Average		$1,643.33	7.83	$176.17

Figure 2–63

Other Ways

1. Select range, click Print Area button (Page Layout tab | Page Setup group), click 'Set Print Area', click File tab to open Backstage view, click Print tab, click Print button

Displaying and Printing the Formulas Version of the Worksheet

Thus far, you have been working with the values version of the worksheet, which shows the results of the formulas you have entered, rather than the actual formulas. Excel also can display and print the formulas version of the worksheet, which shows the actual formulas you have entered, rather than the resulting values.

The formulas version is useful for debugging a worksheet. **Debugging** is the process of finding and correcting errors in the worksheet. Viewing and printing the formulas version instead of the values version makes it easier to see any mistakes in the formulas.

When you change from the values version to the formulas version, Excel increases the width of the columns so that the formulas do not overflow into adjacent cells, which makes the formulas version of the worksheet significantly wider than the values version. To fit the wide printout on one page, you can use landscape orientation, which already has been selected for the workbook, and the Fit to option in the Page tab in the Page Setup dialog box.

BTW
Values versus Formulas
When completing class assignments, do not enter numbers in cells that require formulas. Most instructors will check both the values version and the formulas version of your worksheets. The formulas version verifies that you entered formulas, rather than numbers, in formula-based cells.

To Display the Formulas in the Worksheet and Fit the Printout on One Page

The following steps change the view of the worksheet from the values version to the formulas version of the worksheet and then print the formulas version on one page. **Why?** Printing the formulas in the worksheet can help you verify that your formulas are correct and that the worksheet displays the correct calculations.

1

- Press CTRL+ACCENT MARK (`) to display the worksheet with formulas.
- Click the right horizontal scroll arrow until column K appears (Figure 2–64).

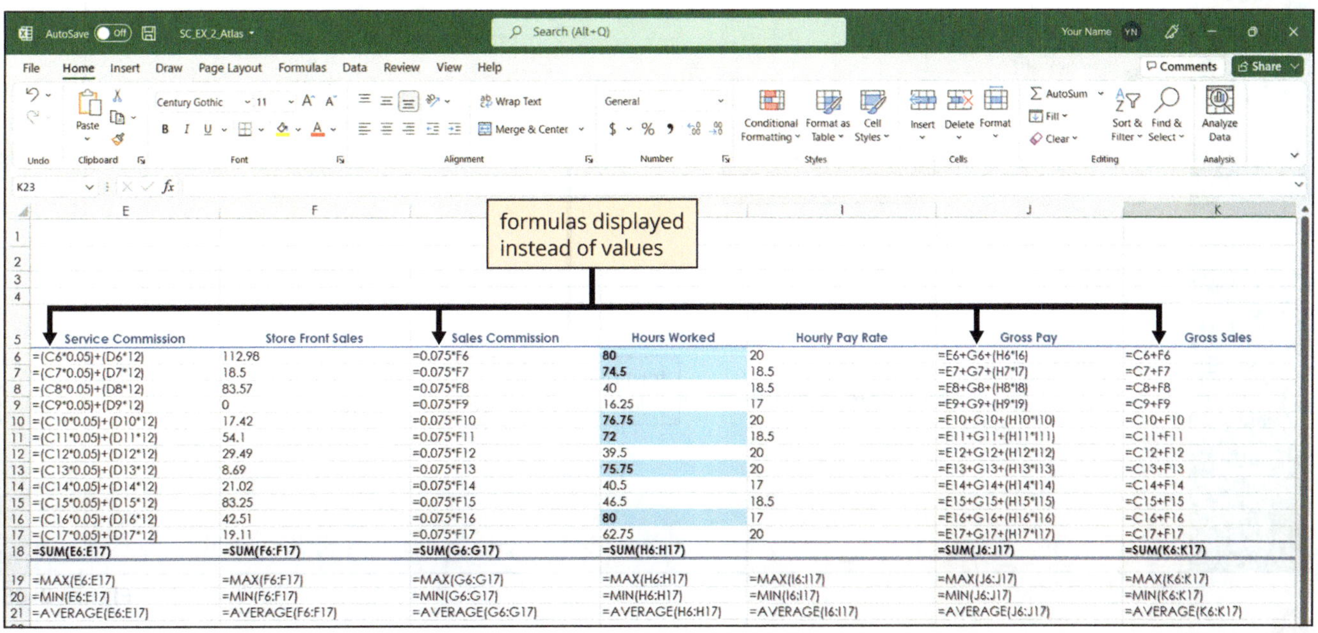

Figure 2–64

2

- Click the Page Setup Dialog Box Launcher (Page Layout tab | Page Setup group) to display the Page Setup dialog box (Figure 2–65).
- If necessary, click Landscape in the Orientation area in the Page tab to select it.
- If necessary, click the Fit to option button in the Scaling area to select it.

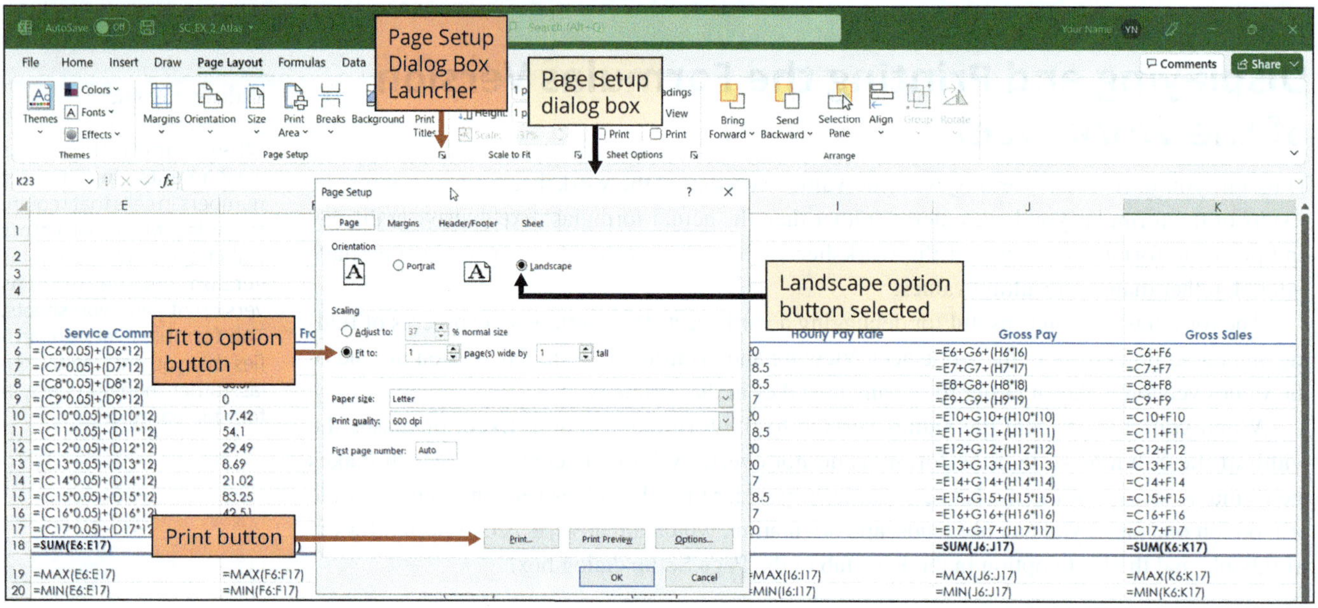

Figure 2–65

3

- Click the Print button (Page Setup dialog box) to open the Print screen in Backstage view. In Backstage view, click the Print Selection button in the Settings area of the Print gallery and then click Print Active Sheets (Figure 2–66).
- Click the Print button to print the worksheet.

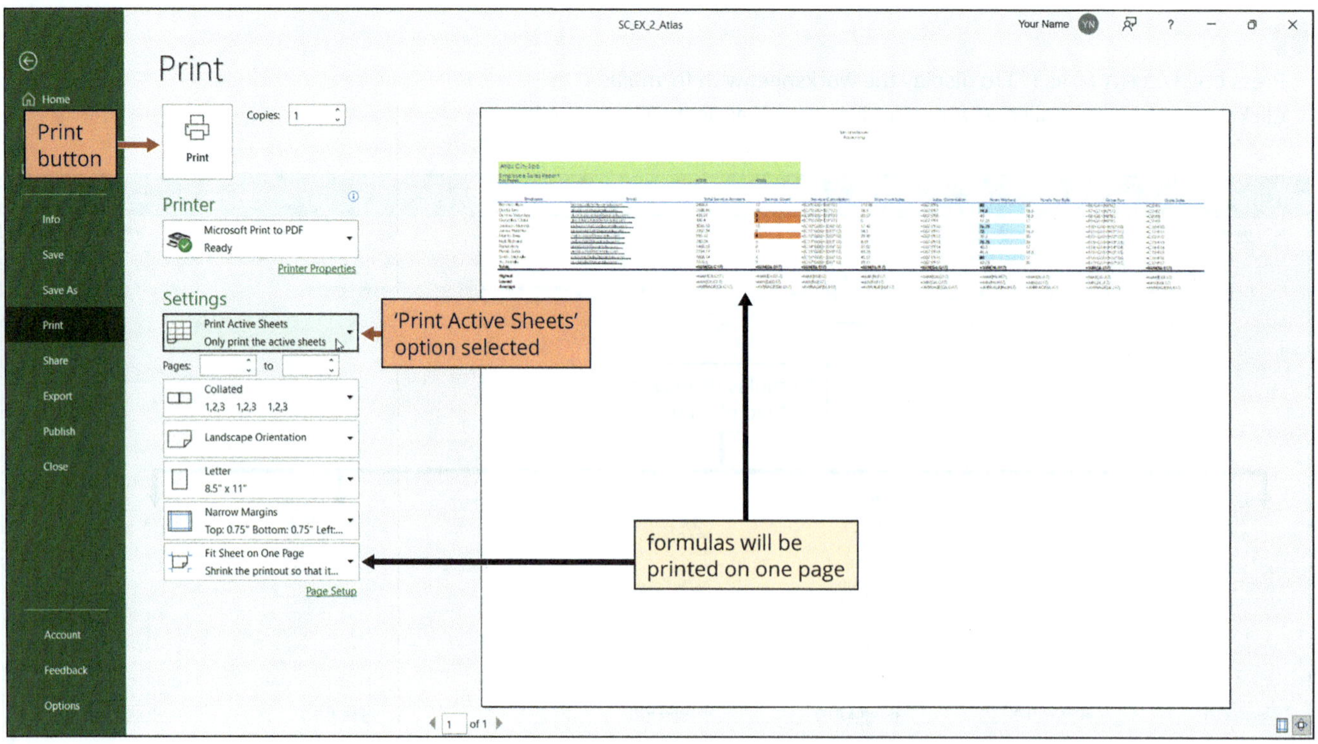

Figure 2–66

4

- After viewing and printing the formulas version, press CTRL+ACCENT MARK (`) to display the values version.
- Click the left horizontal scroll arrow until column A appears.

To Change the Print Scaling Option Back to 100 percent

Depending on your printer, you may have to change the Print Scaling option back to 100 percent after using the Fit to option. Doing so will cause the worksheet to print at the default print scaling of 100 percent. The following steps reset the Print Scaling option so that future worksheets print at 100 percent, instead of being resized to print on one page.

1. If necessary, display the Page Layout tab and then click the Page Setup Dialog Box Launcher (Page Layout tab | Page Setup group) to display the Page Setup dialog box.
2. If necessary, click the Adjust to option button in the Scaling area to select the Adjust to setting.
3. If necessary, type **100** in the Adjust to box to adjust the print scaling to 100 percent.
4. Click OK (Page Setup dialog box) to set the print scaling to normal.
5. Display the Home tab.
6. Save the workbook again on the same storage location with the same file name.
7. If desired, sign out of your Microsoft account.
8. sam Exit Excel.

Q&A What is the purpose of the Adjust to box in the Page Setup dialog box?
The Adjust to box allows you to specify the percentage of reduction or enlargement in the printout of a worksheet. The default percentage is 100 percent. When you click the Fit to option button, this percentage changes to the percentage required to fit the printout on one page.

Summary

In this module, you have learned how to enter formulas, calculate an average, find the highest and lowest numbers in a range, verify formulas using Range Finder, add borders, align text, format numbers, change column widths and row heights, and add conditional formatting to a range of numbers. In addition, you learned how to use the spelling checker to identify misspelled words in a worksheet, print a section of a worksheet, and display and print the formulas version of the worksheet using the Fit to option.

Consider This: Plan Ahead

What decisions will you need to make when creating workbooks in the future?

1. Determine the workbook structure.
   a) Determine the formulas and functions you will need for your workbook.
   b) Sketch a layout of your data and functions.
2. Create the worksheet.
   a) Enter the titles, subtitles, and headings.
   b) Enter the data, desired functions, and formulas.
3. Format the worksheet.
   a) Determine the theme for the worksheet.
   b) Format the titles, subtitles, and headings using styles.
   c) Format the totals, minimums, maximums, and averages.
   d) Format the numbers and text.
   e) Resize columns and rows.

Student Assignments

Apply Your Knowledge

Reinforce the skills and apply the concepts you learned in this module.

Cost Analysis Worksheet

Note: To complete this assignment, you will be required to use the Data Files. Please contact your instructor for information about accessing the Data Files.

Instructions: Start Excel. Open the workbook called SC_EX_2-1.xlsx, which is located in the Data Files. The workbook you open contains information about student costs for Rolling Rivers Summer Academy. You are to enter and copy formulas and functions and apply formatting to the worksheet in order to analyze the costs associated with supplies and lunches for each student, as shown in Figure 2–67.

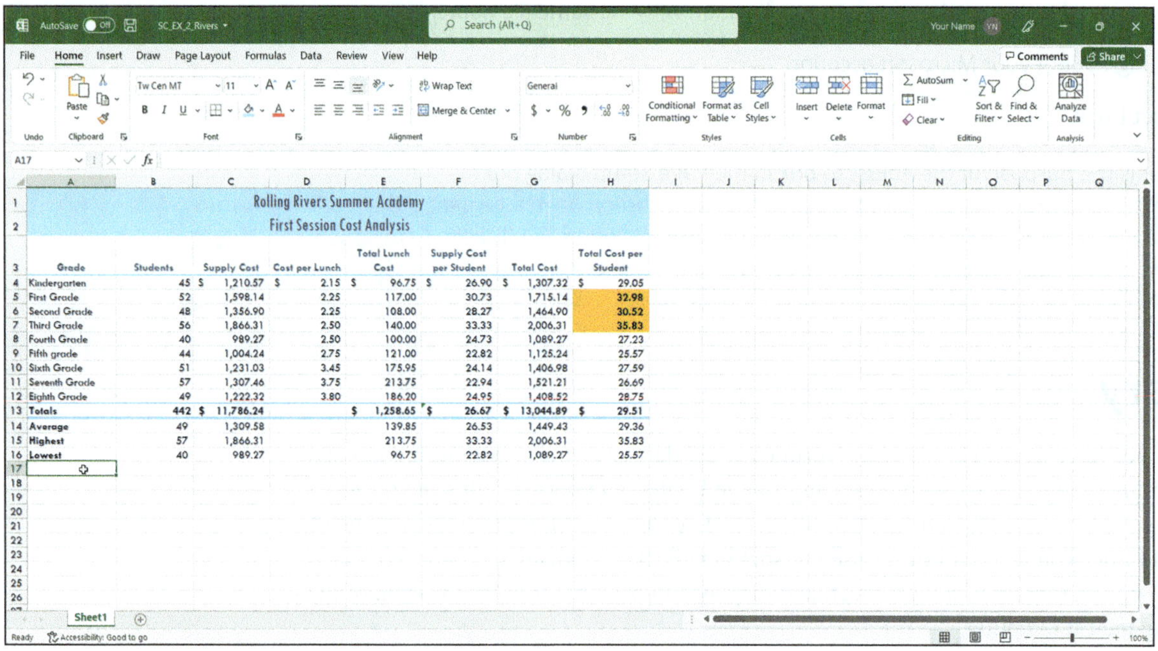

Figure 2–67

Perform the following tasks:

1. Use the following formulas in cells E4, F4, G4, and H4:

   Total Lunch Cost (cell E4) = Students * Cost per Lunch or = B4 * D4

   Supply Cost per Student (cell F4) = Supply Cost / Students or = C4 / B4

   Total Cost (cell G4) = Supply Cost + Total Lunch Cost or = C4 + E4

   Total Cost per Student (cell H4) = Total Cost / Students or = G4 / B4

   Use the fill handle to copy the four formulas in the range E4:H4 to the range E5:H12.

2. Determine totals for the students, supply cost, total lunch cost, and total cost in row 13. Copy the formula in cell F12 to F13 to assign the formula in cell F12 to F13 in the total line. Copy the formula in cell H12 to H13 to assign the formula in cell H12 to H13 in the total line. Reapply the Total cell style to cells F13 and H13.

3. In the range B14:B16, determine the average value, highest value, and lowest value, respectively, for the values in the range B4:B12. Use the fill handle to copy the three functions to the range C14:C16. Copy the functions to the range E14:H16.

4. Format the worksheet as follows:
   a. Change the workbook theme to Integral by using the Themes button (Page Layout tab | Themes group)
   b. Cell A1: change to Title cell style
   c. Cell A2: change to Title cell style and a font size of 16
   d. Cells A1:A2: Turquoise, Accent 1, Lighter 60 percent fill color
   e. Cells C4:H4, C13, E13:H13: accounting number format with two decimal places and fixed dollar signs by using the 'Accounting Number Format' button (Home tab | Number group)
   f. Cells C5:H12, C14:C16, and E14:H16: comma style format with two decimal places by using the Comma Style button (Home tab | Number group)
   g. Cells B4:B16: comma style format with no decimal places
   h. Cells H4:H12: apply conditional formatting so that cells with a value greater than 30.00 appear with an orange fill color and bold font
5. If necessary, increase the size of any columns that do not properly display data.
6. Switch to Page Layout view. Enter your name, course, and any other information, as specified by your instructor, in the header area.
7. Preview and print the worksheet in landscape orientation so that it appears on one page. Save the workbook using the file name, SC_EX_2_Rivers.
8. Use Range Finder to verify the formula in cell G12.
9. Print the range A3:E16. Press CTRL+ACCENT MARK (`) to change the display from the values version of the worksheet to the formulas version. Print the formulas version in landscape orientation on one page by using the Fit to option in the Page tab in the Page Setup dialog box. Press CTRL+ACCENT MARK (`) to change the display of the worksheet back to the values version. Close the workbook without saving it.
10. Submit the workbook in the format specified by your instructor and exit Excel.
11. **Consider This:** Besides adding a header to your document, can you think of anything else that could be added when printing the worksheet?

Extend Your Knowledge

Extend the skills you learned in this module and experiment with new skills. You may need to use Help to complete the assignment.

Creating a Vendor Tracking Worksheet for Northern Tribute Supplies

Note: To complete this assignment, you will be required to use the Data Files. Please contact your instructor for information about accessing the Data Files.

Instructions: Start Excel. Open the workbook SC_EX_2-2.xlsx, which is located in the Data Files. The workbook you open contains vendor information for Northern Tribute Supplies. You will use Flash Fill and four types of conditional formatting to cells in a worksheet.

Perform the following tasks:

1. Add vendor codes to the cells in the range D4:D14. Determine the codes by taking the first letter of the vendor's first name, the first initial of the vendor's last name, followed by the entire vendor number. For example, the account identifier for B. Brown is BB684999. Continue entering two or three account identifiers, then use Flash Fill to complete the remaining cells. Add the bottom border back to cell D14 (Figure 2–68).
2. Select the range G4:G14. In the New Formatting Rule dialog box, create a new rule using the 'Format only top or bottom ranked values' in the New Formatting Rule dialog box.
3. For the rule description, enter 20 in the Edit the Rule Description (New Formatting Rule dialog box) area, and then select the '% of the selected range' check box to select it.

Continued on next page

4. Set the rule to place an Aqua, Accent 4, Lighter 80 percent fill in the cells containing data that match the rule. Accept your settings in the dialog boxes to return to the worksheet, which should show the top 20 percent of cells in the range with a light blue fill.

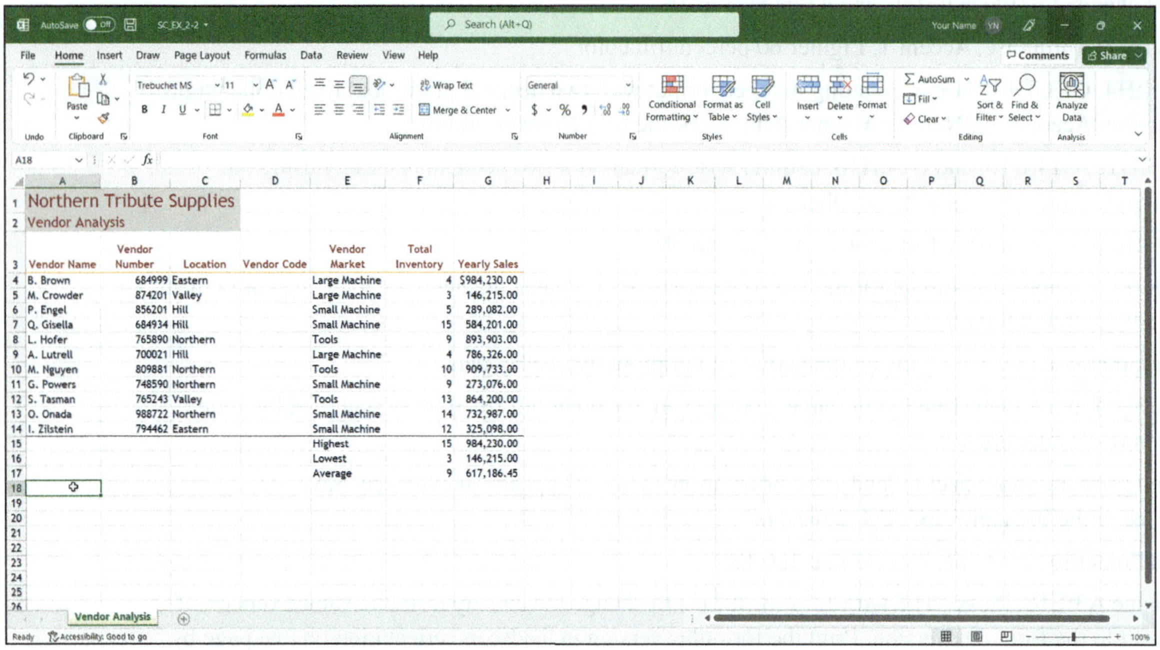

Figure 2–68

5. With range G4:G14 still selected, apply a conditional format to the range that uses a light red fill with dark red text to highlight cells with scores that are below average. **Hint:** Explore some of the preset conditional rules, such as the Top/Bottom Rules category, to assist with formatting this range of cells.
6. Select the range F4:F14, apply a conditional format to the range that uses a light orange fill to highlight cells that contain a value between 2–8.
7. Select the range E4:E14 selected, apply a conditional format to the range that uses a background color of your choice to highlight cells that contain Large Machine and another background color of your choice for cells that contain Small Machine. (**Hint:** You need to apply two separate formats, one for Large Machine and one for Small Machine.)
8. Save the file with the file name, SC_EX_2_Tribute, and submit the revised workbook in the format specified by your instructor.
9. **Consider This:** Why did you choose the background colors for the Large Machine and Small Machine vendor markets in Step 7?

Expand Your World

Create a solution that uses cloud or web technologies by learning and investigating on your own from general guidance.

Study Abroad Cost Calculator

Instructions: You are to create an estimate of the cost of studying abroad for a semester of college. You decide to create the worksheet using Excel Online so that you can share it with your friends online.

Perform the following tasks:

1. If necessary, sign in to your Microsoft account on the web and start Excel Online.
2. Create a blank workbook. In the first worksheet, use column headings for each of the proposed study abroad destinations (Paris, Barcelona, Berlin, Tokyo, and Buenos Aires). For the row headings, use your current expenses (such as rent, travel, tuition, study abroad fees, and food).
3. Enter expenses for each location based upon estimates you find by searching the web. (**Hint:** Convert to US Dollars.)
4. Calculate the total for each column. Also determine highest, lowest, and average values for each column.
5. Using the techniques taught in this module, create appropriate titles and format the worksheet accordingly.
6. Save the file with the file name, SC_EX_2_StudyAbroadExpenses, and submit the workbook in the format specified by your instructor.
7. **Consider This:** When might you want to use Excel Online instead of the Excel app installed on your computer?

In the Lab

Design and implement a solution using creative thinking and problem-solving skills.

Create a Worksheet Comparing Laptop Prices

Problem: You and your friends have decided to purchase new laptops. You would like to maximize utilization while keeping costs low.

Perform the following tasks:

Part 1: Research and find three different laptop brands. For each company find different models of laptops, from the most basic to the most advanced. Use the concepts and techniques presented in this module to create and format a worksheet showing the results of your research. Using the cost figures you find, calculate the cost per gigabyte of storage. Include totals, minimum, maximum, and average values.

Part 2: **Consider This:** You made several decisions while creating the worksheet in this assignment: how to display the data, how to format the worksheet, and which formulas to use. What was the rationale behind each of these decisions?

Working with Large Worksheets, Charting, and What-If Analysis

Objectives

After completing this module, you will be able to:

- Rotate text in a cell
- Create a series using the fill handle
- Copy, paste, insert, and delete cells
- Format numbers using format symbols
- Enter and format the system date
- Use absolute and mixed cell references in a formula
- Use the IF function to perform a logical test
- Create and format sparkline charts
- Change sparkline chart types and styles
- Use the Format Painter button to format cells
- Create a clustered column chart on a separate chart sheet
- Use chart filters to display a subset of data in a chart
- Change the chart type and style
- Reorder sheet tabs
- Change the worksheet view
- Freeze and unfreeze rows and columns
- Answer what-if questions
- Goal seek to answer what-if questions
- Research financial terms using Smart Lookup
- Use accessibility features

Introduction

This module introduces you to techniques that will enhance your ability to create worksheets and draw charts. This module also covers other methods for entering values in cells, such as allowing Excel to automatically enter and format values based on a pattern Excel perceives in the existing values. In addition, you will learn how to use absolute cell references and how to use the IF function to assign a value to a cell based on a logical test.

When you set up a worksheet, you should use cell references in formulas whenever possible, rather than constant values. The use of a cell reference allows you to change a value in multiple formulas by changing the value in a single cell. The cell references in a formula are called assumptions. **Assumptions** are cell values that you can change to determine new values for formulas. This module emphasizes the use of assumptions and shows how to use assumptions to answer what-if questions, such as what happens to the five-year gross margin if you decrease the occupancy rate assumption. Being able to analyze the effect of changing values in a worksheet is an important skill in making business decisions.

Worksheets are normally much larger than those you created in the previous modules, often extending beyond the size of the Excel window. When you cannot view the entire worksheet on the screen at once, working with a large worksheet can be frustrating. This module introduces several Excel commands that allow you to control what is displayed on the screen so that you can focus on critical parts of a large worksheet. One command allows you to freeze rows and columns so that they remain visible, even when you scroll. Another command splits the worksheet into separate panes so that you can view different parts of a worksheet on the screen at once. Another changes the magnification to allow you to see more content, albeit at a smaller size. This is useful for reviewing the general layout of content on the worksheet.

From your work in Module 1, you know how easily you can create charts in Excel. This module covers additional charting techniques that allow you to convey meaning visually, such as by using sparkline charts or clustered column charts. This module also introduces the Accessibility checker, which is a feature that flags items in a document that make it less accessible for people with disabilities.

Project: Financial Projection Worksheet with What-If Analysis and Chart

BTW
Screen Resolution
If you are using a computer to step through the project in this module and you want your screens to match the figures in this book, you should change your screen's resolution to 1920 × 1080.

The project in this module uses Excel to create the worksheet and clustered column chart shown in Figures 3–1a and 3–1b. Northern Getaway Hotel operates in Upstate New York, and has a restaurant, spa, and event space. Each year, the chief executive officer projects yearly revenues, costs of goods sold, and the gross margin for a five-year period, based on figures from the previous year. The CEO requires an easy-to-read worksheet that shows financial projections for the upcoming five years to use for procuring partial financing and for determining staffing needs. The worksheet should allow for quick analysis when projected numbers change, such as the projected occupancy rate, or the revenue of the events space. In addition, you need to create a column chart that shows the breakdown of expenses for each year in the period.

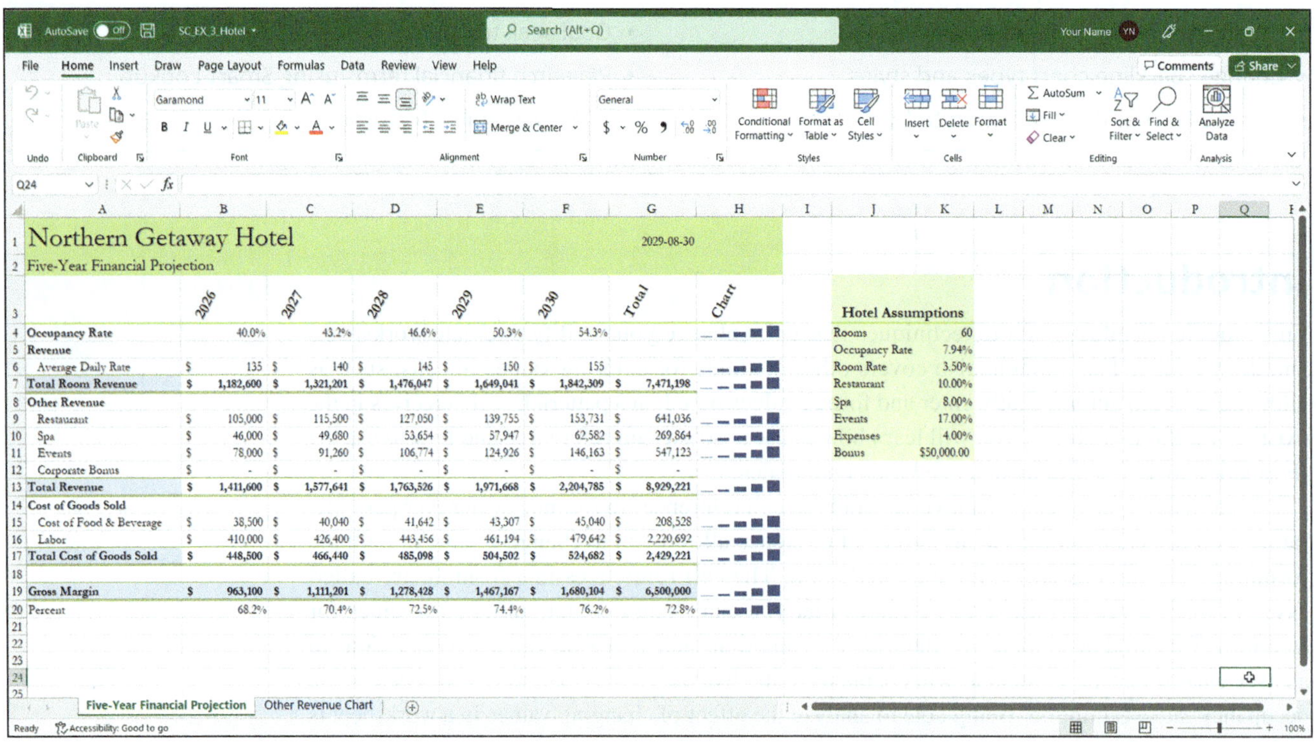

Figure 3–1(a)

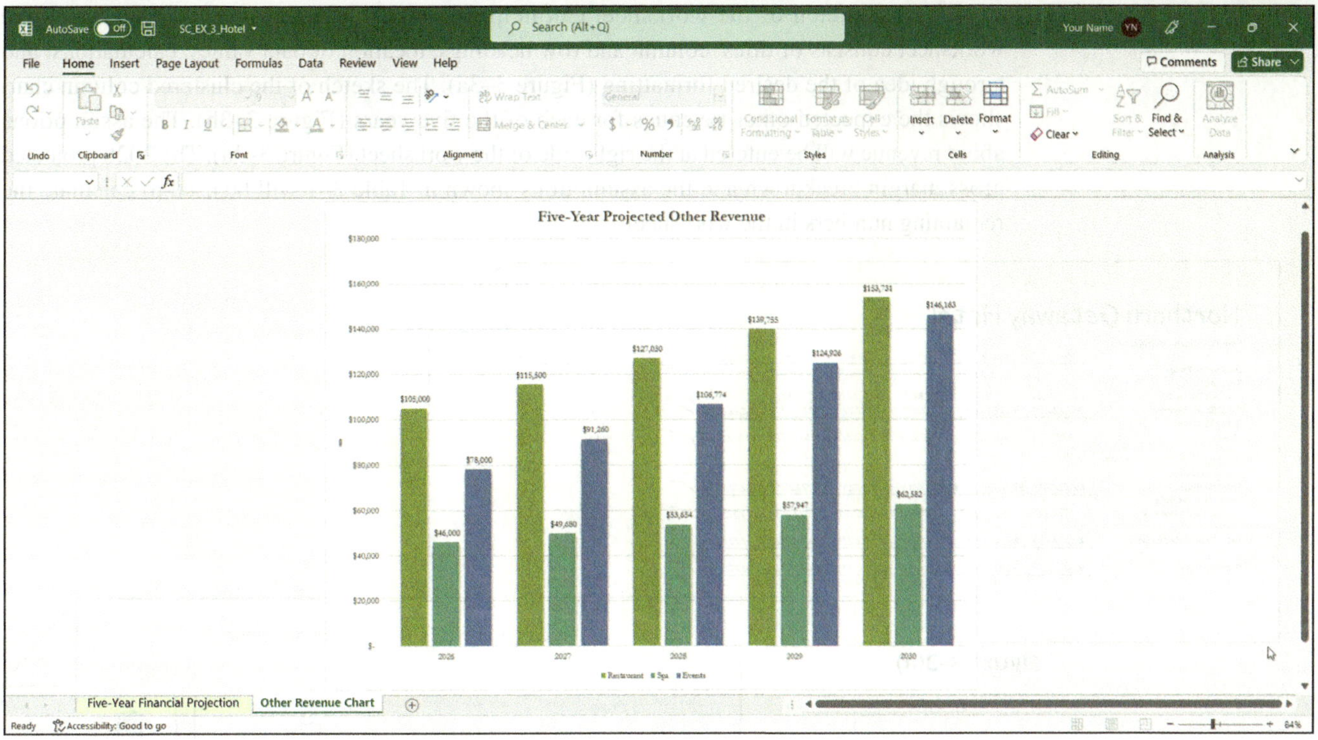

Figure 3–1(b)

The requirements document for the Northern Getaway Hotel, Five-Year Financial Projection worksheet is shown in Figure 3–2. It includes the needs, source of data, summary of calculations, and chart requirements.

BTW

Touch Mode Differences

The Office and Windows interfaces may vary if you are using Touch Mode. For this reason, you might notice that the function or appearance of your touch screen differ slightly from this module's presentation.

Worksheet Title	Northern Getaway Hotel, Five-Year Financial Projection
Needs	• A worksheet that shows Northern Getaway Hotel's projected yearly sales revenue, cost of goods sold, and gross margin for a five-year period. • A clustered column chart that shows the expected contribution of each revenue category.
Source of Data	Data supplied by the business owner includes projections of the current occupancy rate, the average daily room rate, yearly revenue and cost of goods sold based on prior year figures (see Table 3–1). Remaining numbers in the worksheet are based on formulas.
Calculations	The following calculations are needed for each year: • Occupancy Rate = Occupancy Rate * (1 + Occupancy Rate percentage) • Average Daily Rate = Average Daily Rate * (1 + Room Rate percentage) • Total Room Revenue = Rooms * Average Daily Rate * Occupancy Rate * 365 • Restaurant = Restaurant * (1 + Restaurant percentage) • Spa = Spa * (1 + Spa percentage) • Events = Events * (1 + Events percentage) • Corporate Bonus = Predetermined bonus amount if Other Revenue exceeds 20% of Total Room Revenue, otherwise Bonus = 0 • Total Revenue = Sum of all revenue • Cost of Food & Beverage = Cost of Food & Beverage * (1 + Expenses percentage) • Labor = Labor * (1 + Expenses percentage) • Total Cost of Goods Sold = Sum of all Cost of Goods Sold • Gross Margin = Total Revenue – Total Cost of Goods Sold • Percentage = Gross Margin / Total Revenue
Chart Requirements	• Show sparkline charts for revenue and each of the items noted in the calculations area above. • Show a clustered column chart that shows the contributions of each year's other revenue category to total revenue.

Figure 3–2

Using a sketch of the worksheet can help you visualize its design. The sketch of the worksheet consists of titles, column and row headings, location of data values, calculations, and a rough idea of the desired formatting (Figure 3–3a). The sketch of the clustered column chart shows the expected other revenues for each of the five years (Figure 3–3b). The assumptions about revenue will be entered at the right side of the worksheet (Figure 3–3a). The 2026 projected gross margin breakdown and the assumptions shown in Table 3–1 will be used to calculate the remaining numbers in the worksheet.

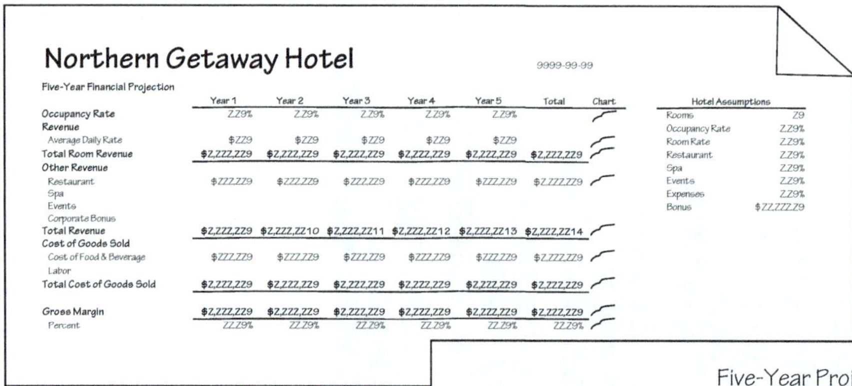

Figure 3–3(a)

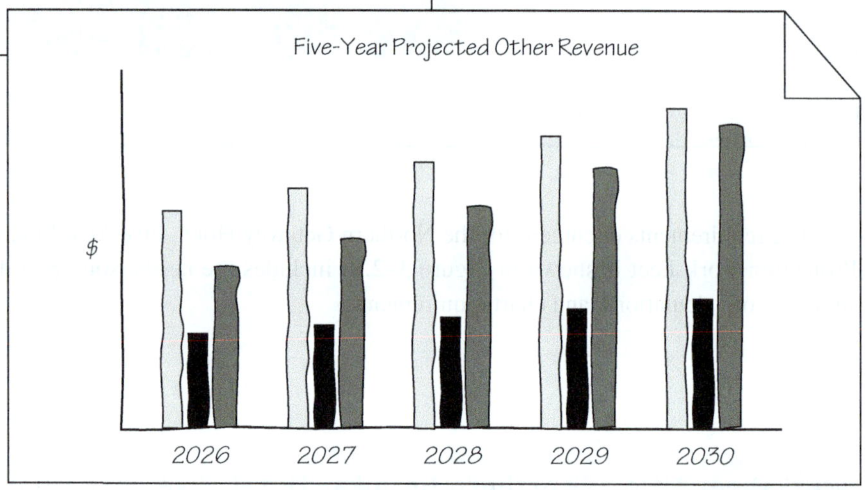

Figure 3–3(b)

Table 3–1: Northern Getaway Hotel Five-Year Financial Projections Data and Hotel Assumptions

2026 Gross Margin Breakdown	
Occupancy Rate	40%
Average Daily Rate	135
Restaurant	105,000
Spa	46,000
Events	78,000
Cost of Food & Beverage	38,500
Labor	410,000
Hotel Assumptions	
Rooms	60
Occupancy Rate	5.0%
Room Rate	3.5%
Restaurant	10.0%
Spa	8.0%
Events	15.0%
Expenses	4.0%
Bonus	50,000

With a solid understanding of the requirements document, an understanding of the necessary decisions, and a sketch of the worksheet, the next step is to use Excel to create the worksheet.

BTW
Excel Help
At any time while using Excel, you can find answers to questions and display information about various topics through Excel Help. Used properly, this form of assistance can increase your productivity and reduce your frustrations by minimizing the time you spend learning how to use Excel.

BTW
Ribbon and Screen Resolution
Excel may change how the groups and buttons within the groups appear on the ribbon, depending on the screen resolution of your computer. Thus, your ribbon may look different from the ones in this book if you are using a screen resolution other than 1920 × 1080.

To Enter the Worksheet Titles and Apply a Theme

The worksheet contains two titles, in cells A1 and A2. In Module 1 the title was centered across the worksheet, due to the smaller scale of the worksheet. With large worksheets that extend beyond the size of a window, it is best to leave titles left-aligned, as shown in the sketch of the worksheet in Figure 3–3a, so that the worksheet will print the title on the first page if the worksheet requires multiple pages. This allows the user to easily find the worksheet title when necessary. The following steps enter the worksheet titles and change the workbook theme to Organic.

1. **sam** Start Excel and create a blank workbook in the Excel window.
2. Select cell A1 if necessary and then type **Northern Getaway Hotel** as the worksheet title.
3. Select cell A2, type **Five-Year Financial Projection** as the worksheet subtitle, and then press ENTER to enter the worksheet subtitle.
4. Apply the Organic theme to the workbook.

Rotating Text and Using the Fill Handle to Create a Series

The data on the worksheet, including month names and the Hotel Assumptions section, now can be added to the worksheet.

BTW
Rotating Text in a Cell
In Excel, you use the Alignment tab in the Format Cells dialog box (shown in Figure 3–5) to position data in a cell by centering, left-aligning, or right-aligning; indenting; aligning at the top, bottom, or center; and rotating.

Consider This

What should you take into account when planning a worksheet layout?

Using Excel, you can change text and number formatting in many ways, which affects the visual impact of the worksheet. Rotated text often provides a strong visual appeal. Rotated text also allows you to fit more text into a smaller column width. When laying out a worksheet, keep in mind the content you want to emphasize and the length of the cell titles relative to the numbers below them in the worksheet.

To Rotate Text in a Cell

The design of the worksheet calls specifically for data for five years. Because there always will be only five years of data in the worksheet, place the years across the top of the worksheet as column headings rather than as row headings. Place the revenue categories in rows, as they are more numerous than the number of years. This layout allows you to easily navigate the worksheet. Ideally, a proper layout will create a worksheet that is longer than it is wide.

When you first enter text, its angle is zero degrees (0°), and it reads from left to right in a cell. Excel allows you to rotate text in a cell counterclockwise by entering a number between 1° and 90°. If you specify an exact value by entering 90 in the Degrees box in the Orientation area, the text will appear vertically and read from bottom to top in the cell. Why? Rotating text is one method of making column headings visually distinct. The following steps enter the year, 2026, in cell B3 and format cell B3 by rotating the text.

1

- If necessary, click the Home tab and then select cell B3 because this cell will include the first year in the series of years.
- Type **2026** as the cell entry and then click the Enter button.
- On the Home tab in the Alignment group, click the Dialog Box Launcher to display the Format Cells dialog box (Figure 3–4).

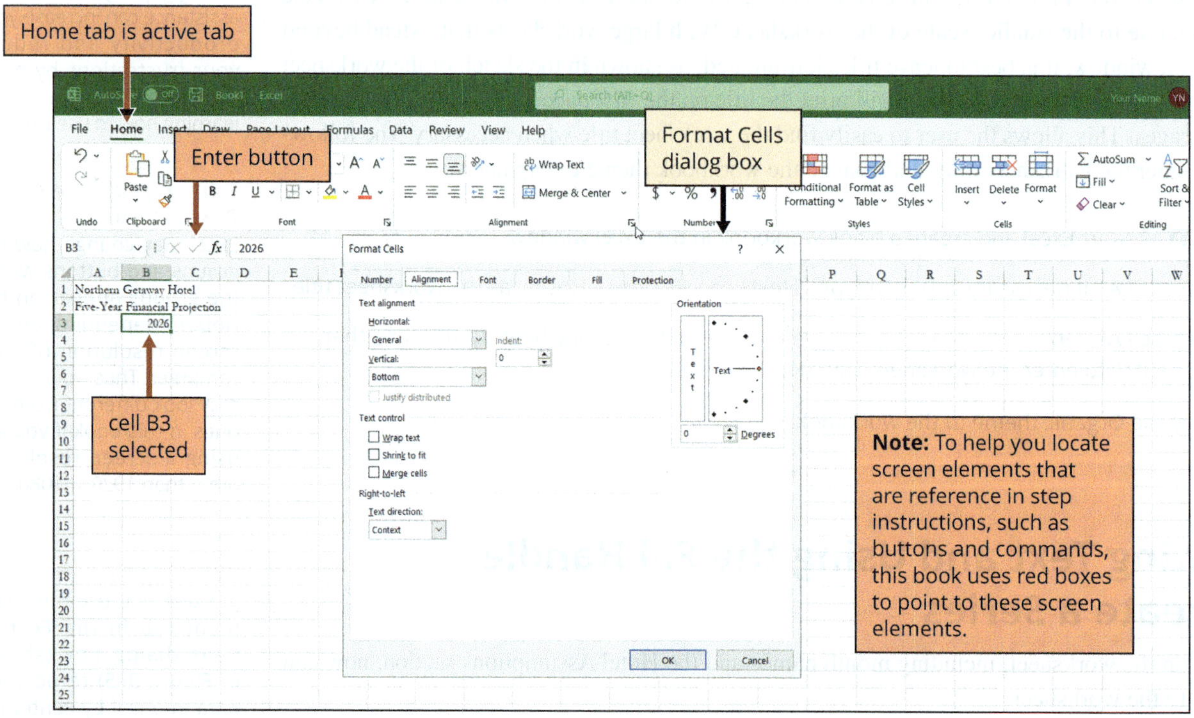

Figure 3–4

2

- Click the 60° point in the Orientation area (Format Cells dialog box) to move the indicator in the Orientation area to the 60° point and display a new orientation in the Degrees box (Figure 3–5).

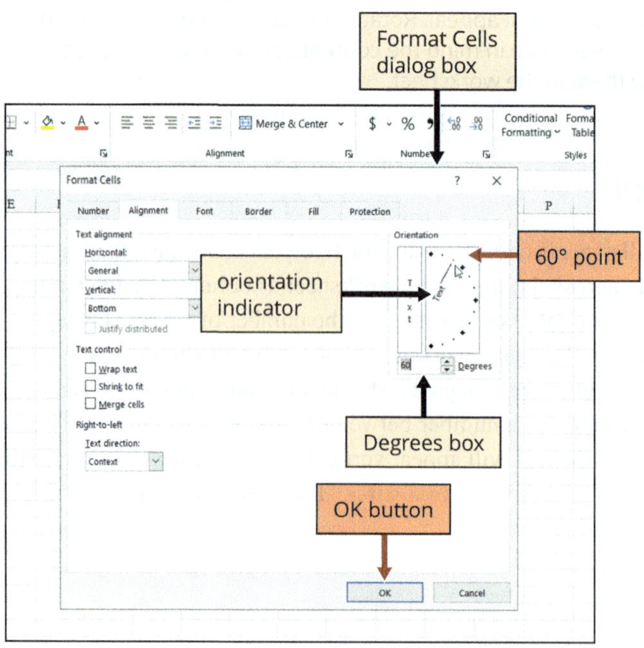

Figure 3–5

3

- Click OK (Format Cells dialog box) to rotate the text to the preset angle in the active cell and if necessary, increase the height of the current row to best fit the rotated text (Figure 3–6).

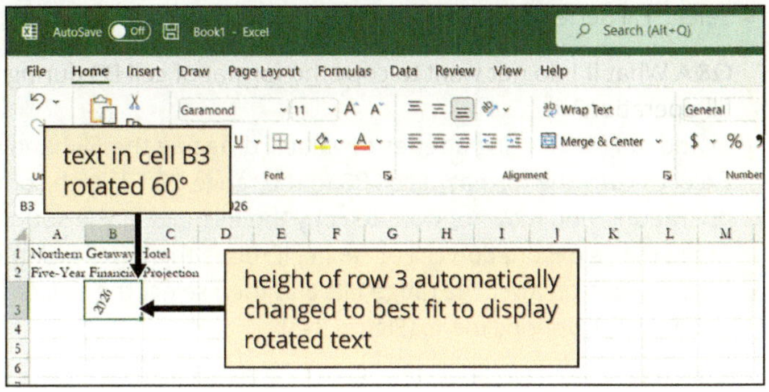

Figure 3–6

Other Ways

1. Right-click selected cell, click Format Cells on shortcut menu, click Alignment tab (Format Cells dialog box), click 60° point, click OK

To Use the Fill Handle to Create a Series of Years

Why? Once the first year in the series has been entered and formatted, you can complete the data series using the fill handle rather than typing and formatting all the entries. The following steps use the fill handle and the entry in cell B3 to create a series of years in cells C3:F3.

1

- Drag the fill handle on the lower-right corner of cell B3 to the right to select the range to fill, C3:F3 in this case. Do not release the mouse button (Figure 3–7).

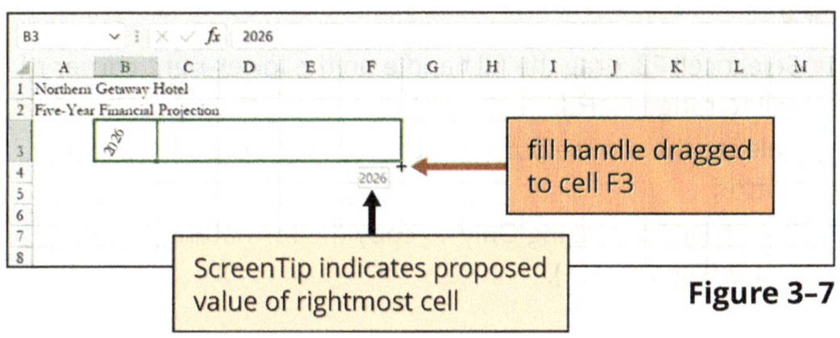

Figure 3–7

2

- Release the mouse button to create a series in the selected range and copy the format of the selected cell to the selected range.
- Click the 'Auto Fill Options' button below the lower-right corner of the fill area to display the Auto Fill Options menu (Figure 3–8).

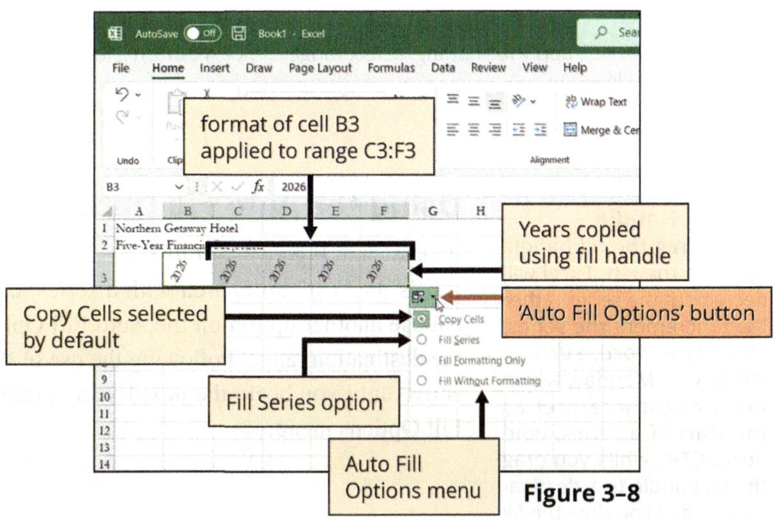

Figure 3–8

3

- Select 'Fill Series' to create a series of years (Figure 3–9).

Q&A What if I do not want to copy the format of cell B3 during the auto fill operation?
In addition to creating a series of values, dragging the fill handle instructs Excel to copy the format of cell B3 to the range C3:F3. With some fill operations, you may not want to copy the formats of the source cell or range to the destination cell or range. If this is the case, click the 'Auto Fill Options' button after the range fills and then select the desired option on the Auto Fill Options menu (Figure 3–8).

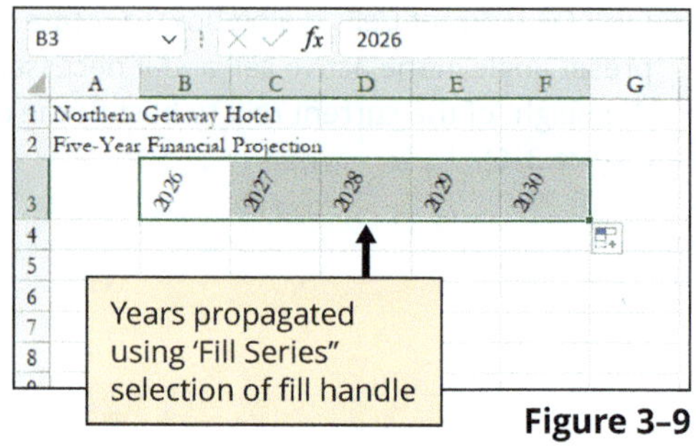

Figure 3–9

4

- Select cell G3, type **Total**, and then press the RIGHT ARROW key to enter a column heading.
- Type **Chart** in cell H3 and then press the RIGHT ARROW key (Figure 3–10).

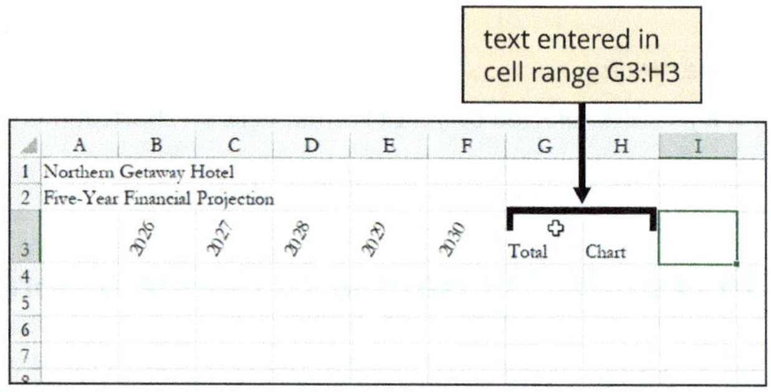

Figure 3–10

5

- Select cell F3, drag the fill handle on the lower-right corner of cell to range F3:H3.
- Release the mouse button and select the 'Auto Fill Options' button.
- Select 'Fill Formatting Only' to copy the formatting to cells F3:H3 (Figure 3–11).

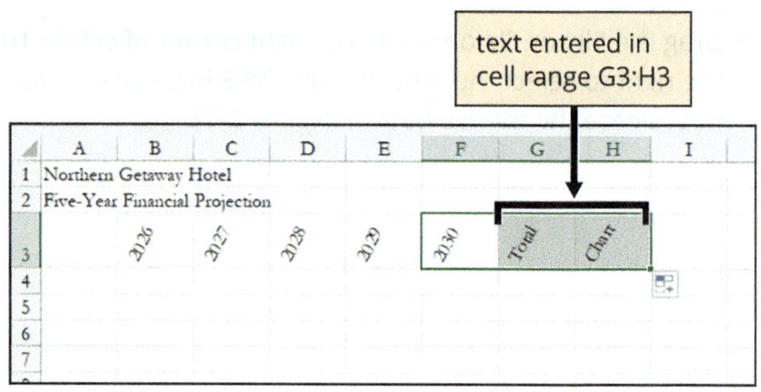

Figure 3–11

Other Ways

1. Type text in cell, apply formatting, select range, click Fill button (Home tab | Editing group), click Series, click AutoFill (Series dialog box), click OK

BTW
The Fill Handle
If you drag the fill handle up or to the left, Excel will decrement the series rather than increment the series. To copy a word, such as January or Monday, which Excel might interpret as the start of a series, hold down CTRL while you drag the fill handle to a destination area. If you drag the fill handle back into the middle of a cell, Excel erases the contents of the cell.

Using the Auto Fill Options Menu

As shown in Figure 3–8, Fill Series is a useful option that Excel uses to fill an area, which means it fills the destination area with a series, using the same formatting as the source area. If you choose another option on the Auto Fill Options menu, Excel changes the content or Format of the destination range. Following the use of the fill handle, the 'Auto Fill Options' button remains active until you begin the next Excel operation. Table 3–2 summarizes the options on the Auto Fill Options menu.

Table 3–2: Options Available on the Auto Fill Options Menu

Auto Fill Option	Description
Copy Cells	Fills destination area with contents using format of source area. Does not create a series.
Fill Series	Fills destination area with series using format of source area. This option is the default.
Fill Formatting Only	Fills destination area using format of source area. No content is copied unless fill is series.
Fill Without Formatting	Fills destination area with contents, without applying the formatting of source area.
Fill Years	Fills destination area with series of years using format of source area. Same as Fill Series and shows as an option only if source area contains a year.

BTW
Auto Fill Options Button
If you drag the fill handle and the Quick Analysis button appears instead of the Auto Fill Options button, make sure the 'Show Paste Options button when content is pasted' check box contains a check mark in the Advanced options.

You can create several different types of series using the fill handle. Table 3–3 illustrates several examples. Notice that, if you use the fill handle to create a series of nonsequential numbers 4, 7, 9, and 11, or nonsequential months, you must enter the first item in the series in one cell and the second item in the series in an adjacent cell, and then select both cells and drag the fill handle through the destination area. Excel extrapolates the series based on the previous input.

Table 3–3: Examples of Series Using the Fill Handle

Example	Contents of Cell(s) Copied Using the Fill Handle	Next Three Values of Extended Series
1	4:00	5:00, 6:00, 7:00
2	Qtr2	Qtr3, Qtr4, Qtr1
3	Quarter 1	Quarter 2, Quarter 3, Quarter 4
4	22-Jul, 22-Sep	22-Nov, 22-Jan, 22-Mar
5	2027, 2028	2029, 2030, 2031
6	1, 2	3, 4, 5
7	625, 575	525, 475, 425
8	Mon	Tue, Wed, Thu
9	Sunday, Tuesday	Thursday, Saturday, Monday
10	4th Section	5th Section, 6th Section, 7th Section
11	2205, 2208	2211, 2214, 2217

You can create your own custom fill sequences for use with the fill handle. For example, if you often type the same list of products or names in Excel, you can create a custom fill sequence. You then can type the first product or name and then use the fill handle to automatically fill in the remaining products or names. To create a custom fill sequence, display the Excel Options dialog box by clicking Options in Backstage view. Click the Advanced tab (Excel Options dialog box) and then click the 'Edit Custom Lists' button in the General section (Excel Options dialog box).

To Increase Column Widths

Why? In Module 2, you increased column widths after the values were entered into the worksheet. Sometimes, you may want to increase the column widths before you enter values and, if necessary, adjust them later. You can resize columns to exact widths using dragging, as described below. You can also resize columns to an approximate value by dragging until the cell contents are displayed in a visually pleasing way, without regard for the numbers displayed. The following steps increase the column widths to specific values.

1

- Move the pointer to the boundary between column heading A and column heading B so that the pointer changes to a split double arrow in preparation for adjusting the column widths.
- Drag the pointer to the right until the ScreenTip displays the desired column width, Width: 27.88 (228 pixels) in this case. Do not release the mouse button. If you are unable to drag and reach the specified width, get as close as you can, or double-click the right boundary of column heading A to change the width of the column to best fit (Figure 3–12).

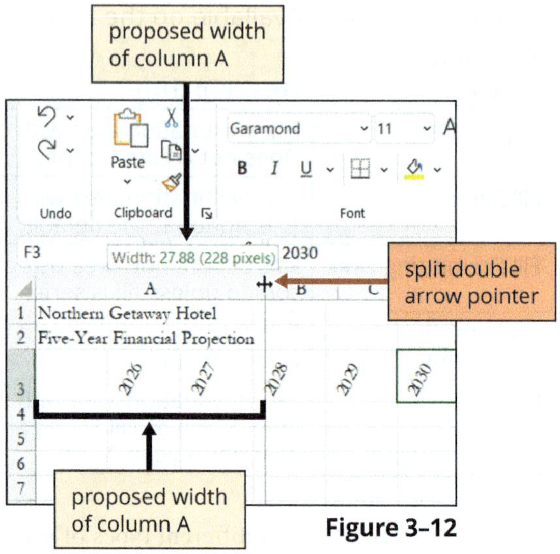

Figure 3–12

2

- Release the mouse button to change the width of the column.
- Click column heading B to select the column and then drag through column heading H to select the range in which to change the widths.
- Move the pointer to the boundary between column headings B and C in preparation for resizing column B and then drag the pointer to the right until the ScreenTip displays the desired width, Width: 15.25 (127 pixels) in this case. Do not lift your finger or release the mouse button. If you are unable to drag and reach the specified width, get as close as you can (Figure 3–13).

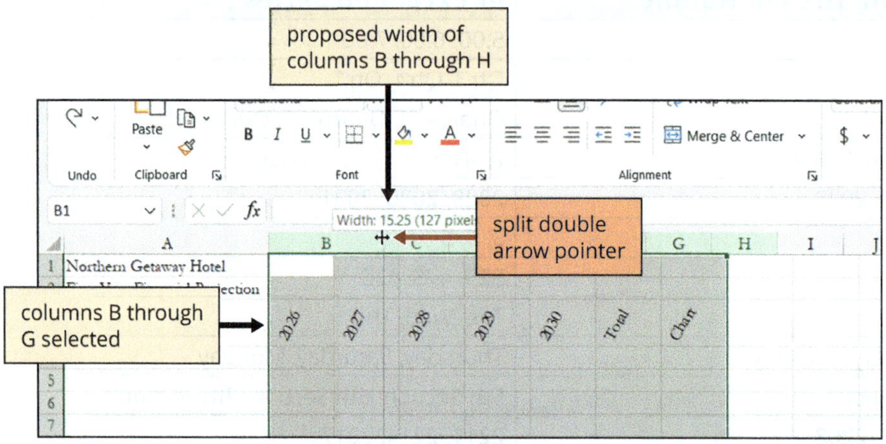

Figure 3–13

3

- Release the mouse button to change the width of the selected columns.

To Enter and Indent Row Titles

Excel allows you to indent text in cells. The following steps enter the row titles in column A and indent several of the row titles. **Why?** Indenting rows helps you create a visual hierarchy by indenting some of the row titles, like in an outline or table of contents.

1

- Enter **Occupancy Rate** in cell A4, **Revenue** in cell A5, **Average Daily Rate** in cell A6, **Total Room Revenue** in cell A7, **Other Revenue** in cell A8, **Restaurant** in cell A9, **Spa** in cell A10, **Events** in cell A11, **Corporate Bonus** in cell A12, **Total Revenue** in cell A13, **Cost of Goods Sold** in cell A14, **Cost of Food & Beverage** in cell A15, **Labor** in cell A16, **Total Cost of Goods Sold** in cell A17, **Gross Margin** in cell A19, and **Percent** in cell A20.

- Select cell A6 and then click the Increase Indent button (Home tab | Alignment group) to increase the indentation of the text in the selected cell.
- Select the range A9:A12 and then click the Increase Indent button (Home tab | Alignment group) to increase the indentation of the text in the selected range.
- Select the range A15:A16 and then click the Increase Indent button (Home tab | Alignment group) to increase the indentation of the text in the selected range (Figure 3–14).

2

- Select cell J3 to finish entering the column titles and deselect the current cell.

Q&A What happens when I click the Increase Indent button?

The Increase Indent button (Home tab | Alignment group) indents the contents of a cell two spaces to the right each time you click it. The Decrease Indent button decreases the indent by two spaces each time you click it.

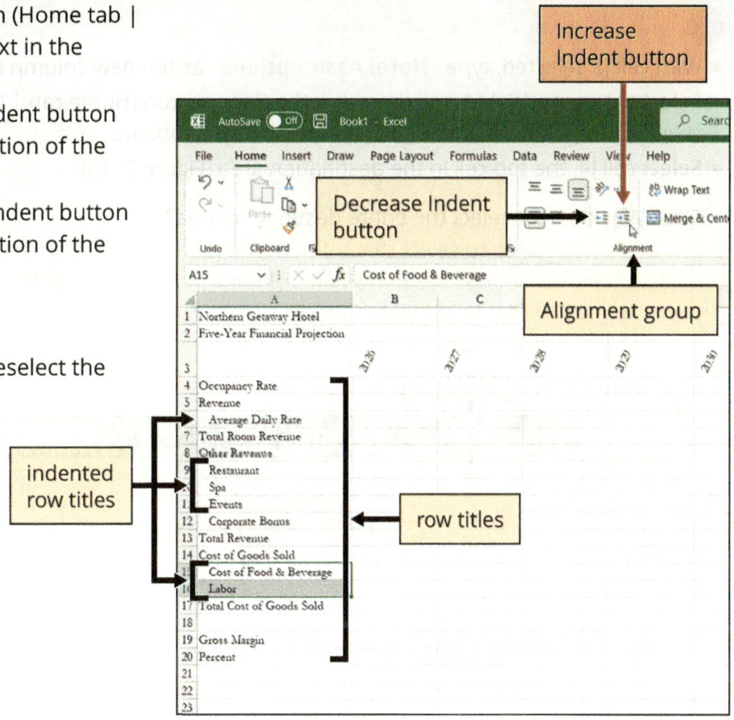

Figure 3–14

Other Ways

1. Right-click range, click Format Cells on shortcut menu, click Alignment tab (Format Cells dialog box), click Left (Indent) in Horizontal list, type number of spaces to indent in Indent box, click OK (Format Cells dialog box)

Copying a Range of Cells to a Nonadjacent Destination Area

The Hotel Assumptions section should be placed in an area of the worksheet that is accessible yet does not impair the view of the main section of the worksheet. As shown in Figure 3–3a, the Hotel Assumptions will be placed to the right of the calculations in the worksheet. This will allow the reader to see the main section of the worksheet when first opening the workbook. Additionally, as shown in Figure 3–1a, the row titles in the Other Revenue area are similar to some of row titles in the Hotel Assumptions table. Hence, some of the row titles in the Hotel Assumptions table can be created by copying the range A9:A11 to the range J7:J9. You cannot use the fill handle to copy the range because the source area (range A9:A11) is not adjacent to the destination area (range J7:J9).

A more versatile method of copying a source area is to use the Copy button and Paste button (Home tab | Clipboard group). You can use these two buttons to copy a source area to an adjacent or nonadjacent destination area.

BTW
Fitting Entries in a Cell
An alternative to increasing column widths or row heights is to shrink the characters in a cell to fit the current width of the column. To shrink to fit, on the Home tab in the Alignment group, click the Dialog Box Launcher and then place a check mark in the 'Shrink to fit' check box in the Text control area (Format Cells dialog box).

To Copy a Range of Cells to a Nonadjacent Destination Area

The Copy button copies the contents and format of the source area to the **Office Clipboard**, a temporary storage area in the computer's memory that allows you to collect text and graphics from any Office document and then paste them into almost any other type of document; the Office Clipboard can hold a maximum of 24 items. The Paste button pastes a copy of the contents of the Office Clipboard in the destination area. **Why?** Copying the range of cells rather than reentering the content ensures consistency within the worksheet. The following steps enter the Hotel Assumptions row heading and then use the Copy and Paste buttons to copy the range A9:A11 to the nonadjacent range J7:J9.

1

- With cell J3 selected, type **Hotel Assumptions** as the new column title and then click the Enter button.
- Select the range A9:A11 and then click the Copy button (Home tab | Clipboard group) to copy the values and formats of the selected range, A9:A11 in this case, to the Office Clipboard.
- Select cell J4, the top cell in the destination area (Figure 3–15).

Q&A Why do I not select the entire destination area?
You are not required to select the entire destination area (J4:J6) because Excel only needs to know the upper-left cell of the destination area. In the case of a single column range, such as J4:J6, the top cell of the destination area (cell J4) also is the upper-left cell of the destination area.

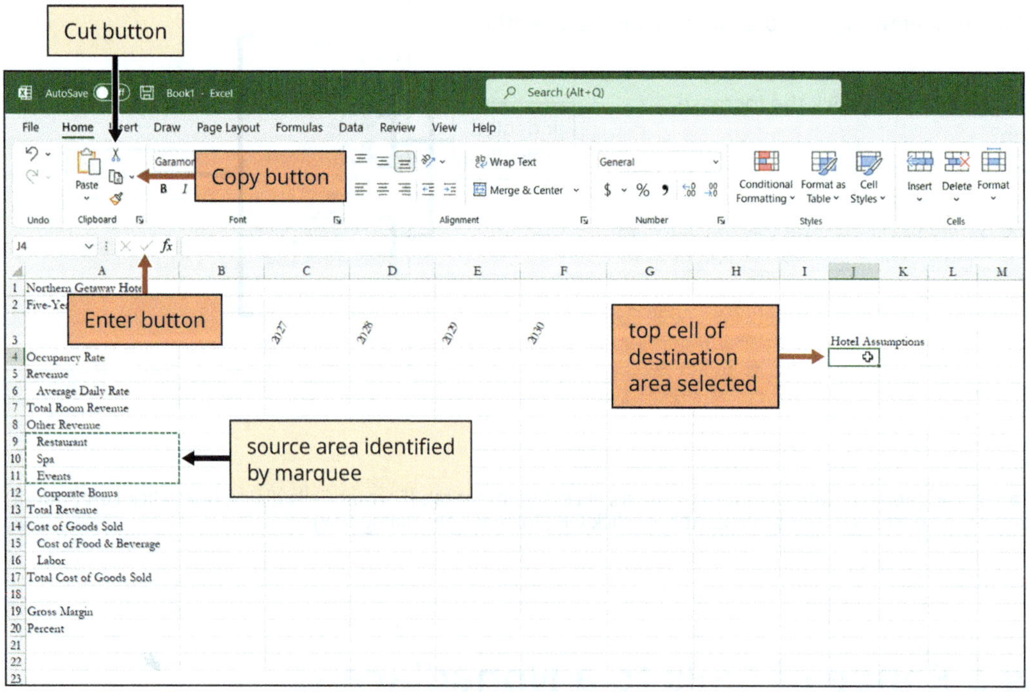

Figure 3–15

2

- Click the Paste button (Home tab | Clipboard group) to paste the values and formats of the last item placed on the Office Clipboard, range A9:A11, to the destination area, J4:J6 (Figure 3–16).

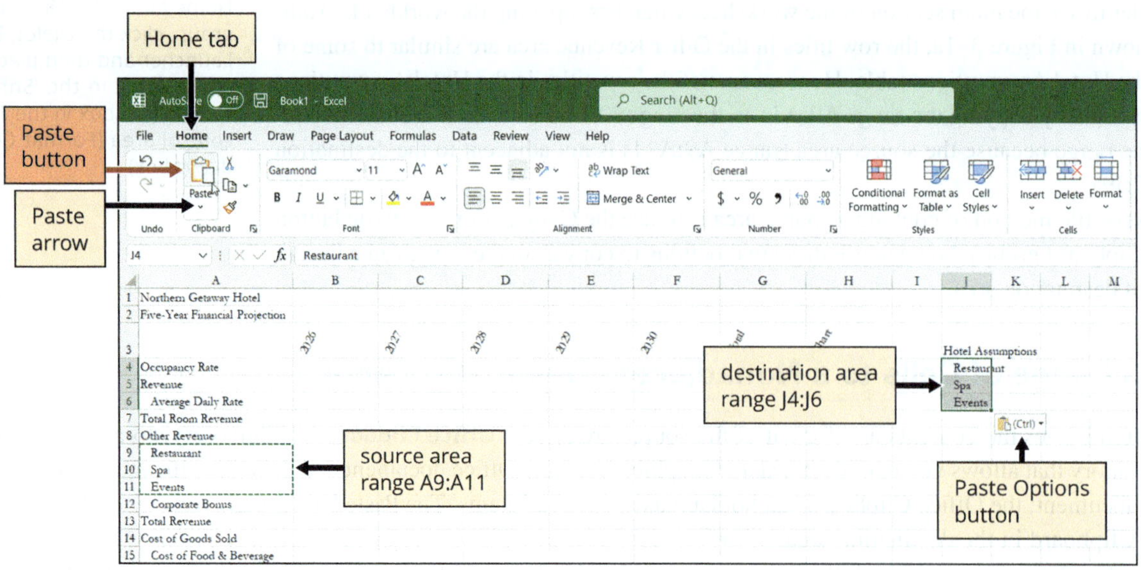

Figure 3–16

Q&A What if there was data in the destination area before I clicked the Paste button?

Any data contained in the destination area prior to the copy and paste would be lost and replaced by the pasted information. When you complete a copy/paste, the values and formats in the destination area are replaced with the values and formats of the source area. If you accidentally delete valuable data, click the Undo button on the Quick Access Toolbar or press CTRL+Z.

3

- Click the Decrease Indent button (Home tab | Alignment group) to decrease the indentation of the text in the selected cell (Figure 3–17).

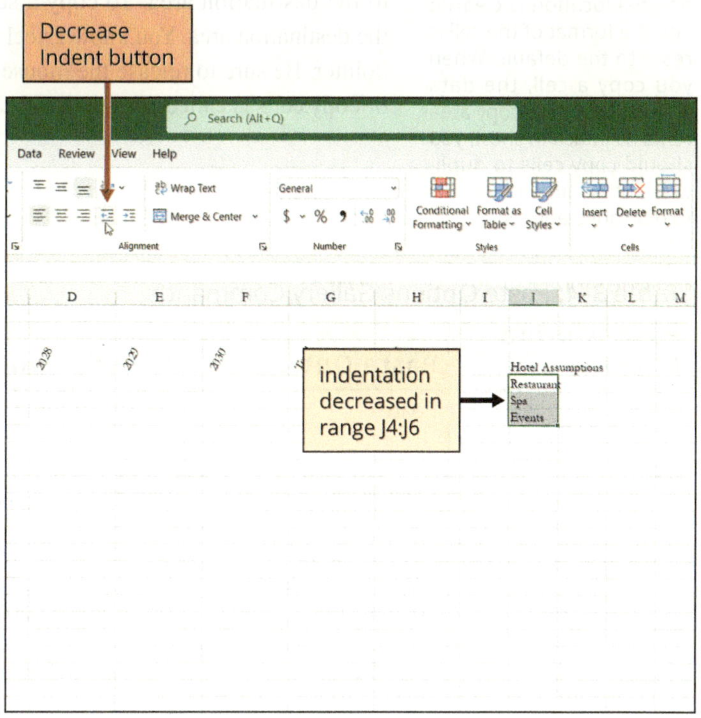

Figure 3–17

Other Ways

1. Right-click source area, click Copy on shortcut menu, right-click destination area, click Paste button on shortcut menu
2. Select source area and point to border of range; while holding down CTRL, drag source area to destination area
3. Select source area, press CTRL+C, select destination area, press CTRL+V

Using the Paste Options Menu

After you click the Paste button, Excel displays the Paste Options button below and to the right of the pasted range, as shown in Figure 3–16. If you click the Paste Options button and select an option in the Paste Options gallery, Excel modifies the most recent paste operation based on your selection. Table 3–4 summarizes the options available in the Paste Options gallery. When the Paste Options button is visible, you can use keyboard shortcuts to access the paste commands available in the Paste Options gallery. Additionally, you can use combinations of the options in the Paste Options gallery to customize your paste operation. That is, after clicking one of the options in the Paste Options gallery, you can display the gallery again to further adjust your paste operation. The Paste button (Home tab | Clipboard group) includes an arrow that, when clicked, displays the same options as the Paste Options button.

An alternative to clicking the Paste button is to press ENTER. Pressing ENTER completes the paste operation, removes the marquee from the source area, and disables the Paste button so that you cannot paste the copied source area to other destination areas. The ENTER key was not used in the previous set of steps so that the capabilities of the Paste Options button could be discussed. The Paste Options button does not appear on the screen when you use ENTER to complete the paste operation.

BTW

Copying and Pasting from Other Programs

If you need data in Excel that is stored in another program, copying and pasting likely will help you. You might need to experiment before you are successful, because Excel might attempt to copy formatting or other information that you did not intend to paste from the other program. Trying various Paste Option buttons will solve most of such problems.

BTW
Move It or Copy It
Contrary to popular belief, move and copy operations are not the same. When you move a cell, the data in the original location is cleared and the format of the cell is reset to the default. When you copy a cell, the data and format of the copy area remains intact. In short, you should copy cells to duplicate entries and move cells to rearrange entries.

Using Drag and Drop to Move or Copy Cells

You also can use the mouse to move or copy cells. First, you select the source area and point to the border of the cell or range. You know you are pointing to the border of the cell or range when the pointer changes to a four-headed arrow. To move the selected cell or cells, drag the selection to the destination area. To copy a selection, hold down CTRL while dragging the selection to the destination area. You know Excel is in Copy mode when a small plus sign appears next to the pointer. Be sure to release the mouse button before you release CTRL. Using the mouse to move or copy cells is called **drag and drop**.

Table 3-4: Paste Options Gallery Commands

Paste Option Button	Paste Option	Description
	Paste	Paste contents and format of source area. This option is the default.
	Formulas	Paste formulas from the source area, but not the contents and format.
	Formulas & Number Formatting	Paste formulas and format for numbers and formulas of source area, but not the contents.
	Keep Source Formatting	Paste contents, format, and styles of source area.
	No Borders	Paste contents and format of source area, but not any borders.
	Keep Source Column Widths	Paste contents and format of source area. Change destination column widths to source column widths.
	Transpose	Paste the contents and format of the source area, but transpose, or swap, the rows and columns.
	Values	Paste contents of source area but not the formatting for formulas.
	Values & Number Formatting	Paste contents and format of source area for numbers or formulas, but use format of destination area for text.
	Values & Source Formatting	Paste contents and formatting of source area but not the formula.
	Formatting	Paste format of source area but not the contents.
	Paste Link	Paste contents and format and link cells so that a change to the cells in source area updates the corresponding cells in destination area.
	Picture	Paste an image of the source area as a picture.
	Linked Picture	Paste an image of the source area as a picture so that a change to the cells in source area updates the picture in destination area.

Using Cut and Paste to Move Cells

Another way to move cells is to select them, click the Cut button (Home tab | Clipboard group) (Figure 3–15) to remove the cells from the worksheet and copy them to the Office Clipboard, select the destination area, and then click the Paste button (Home tab | Clipboard group) or press ENTER. The cell(s) you move using the Cut command either can contain a static value or a formula. You also can use the Cut command on the shortcut menu instead of the Cut button on the ribbon.

BTW
Cutting
When you cut a cell or range of cells using the Cut command on a shortcut menu or Cut button (Home tab | Clipboard group), Excel copies the cells to the Office Clipboard; it does not remove the cells from the source area until you paste the cells in the destination area by either clicking the Paste button (Home tab | Clipboard group) or pressing ENTER. When you complete the paste, Excel clears the cell's or range of cell's entries and their formats from the source area.

Inserting and Deleting Cells in a Worksheet

At any time while the worksheet is on the screen, you can insert cells to enter new data or delete cells to remove unwanted data. You can insert or delete individual cells; a range of cells, rows, or columns; or entire worksheets. As you insert cells into your worksheet, making the worksheet larger, it may print on multiple pages. If you want to indicate where one page should stop and the next page should start, you can insert a page break. To insert a page break, first select the cell immediately below where you want to insert the page break. Next, click the Breaks button (Page Layout tab | Page Setup group) and then click Insert Page Break. If you want to remove a page break, you should instead click the 'Remove Page Break' command. To remove all page breaks from a worksheet, click the 'Reset All Page Breaks' command.

To Insert a Cell

Why? According to the sketch of the worksheet in Figure 3–3a, three cells must be inserted in the Hotel Assumptions table, above Restaurant. The following steps insert three cells into the worksheet.

1

- Right-click cell J4, the cell below where you want to insert a cell, to display the shortcut menu (Figure 3–18).

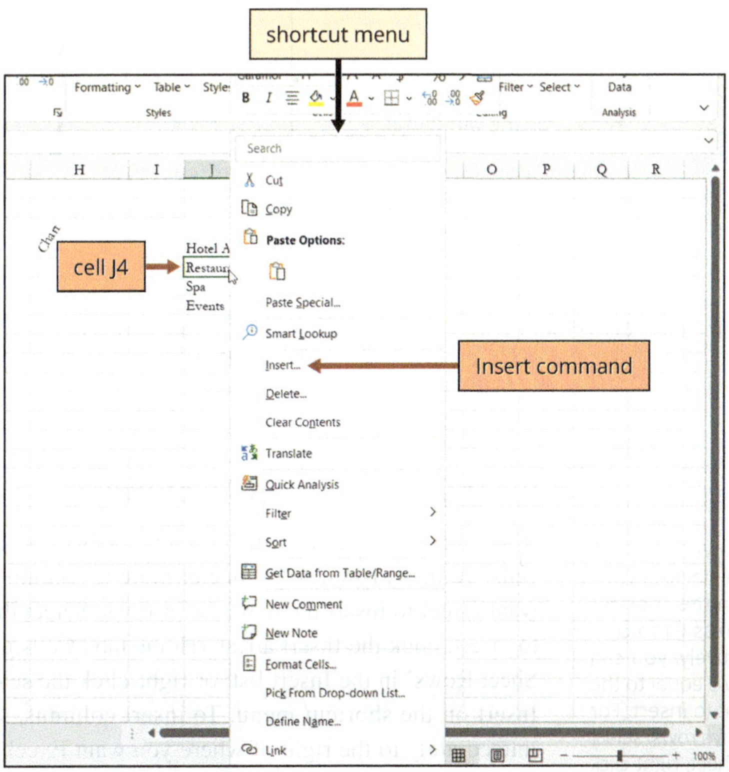

Figure 3–18

2

- Click Insert on the shortcut menu.
- Select 'Shift cells down' in the Insert dialog box (Figure 3-19).
- Click the OK button to insert a new cell in the worksheet by shifting the selected cell and all cells below it down one cell (Figure 3-20).
- Repeat this process two more times to insert two more cells above Restaurant.
- Select cell J4 if necessary and then type **Rooms,** enter **Occupancy Rate** in cell J5, enter **Room Rate** in cell J6, enter **Expenses** in cell J10, and enter **Bonus** in cell J11 to finish entering all the row titles (Figure 3-21).

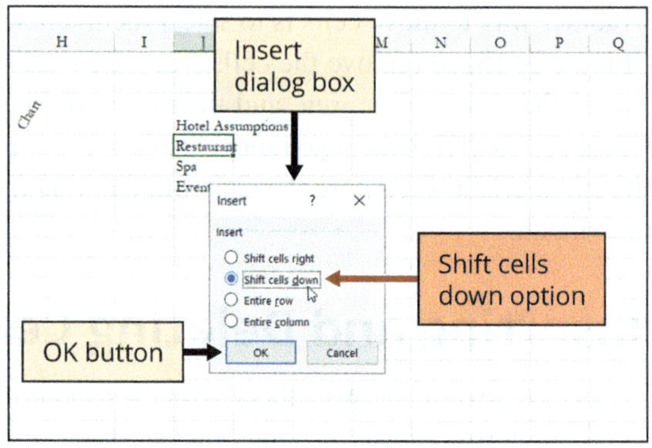

Figure 3-19

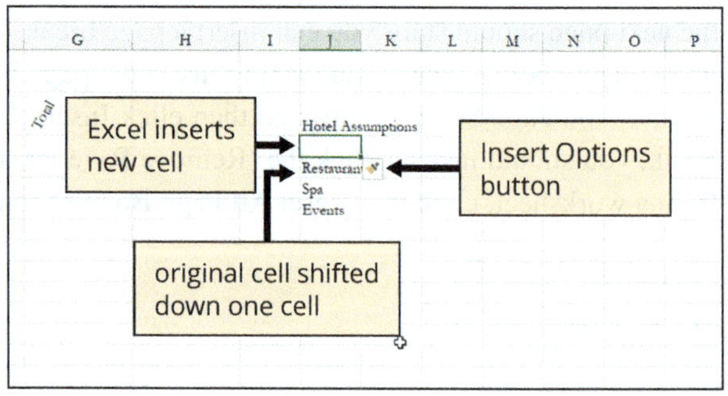

Figure 3-20

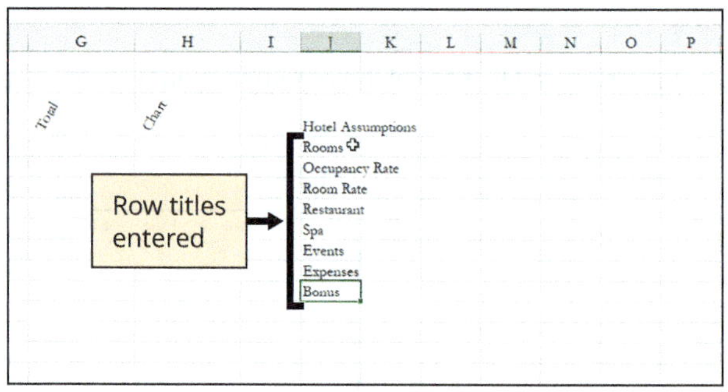

Figure 3-21

Q&A What is the resulting format of the new cell?

The new cell inherits the format of the cell in the row above it. You can change this behavior by clicking the Insert Options button that appears below the inserted cell. Following the insertion of a cell, the Insert Options button allows you to select from the following options: (1) 'Format Same As Above', (2) 'Format Same As Below', and (3) Clear Formatting. The 'Format Same As Above' option is the default. The Insert Options button remains active until you begin the next Excel operation. Excel does not display the Insert Options button if the initial cell does not contain any formatted data.

What would happen if cells in the shifted cells were included in formulas?

If the cells that shift down included cell references in formulas located in the worksheet, Excel would automatically adjust the cell references in the formulas to their new locations. Thus, in Step 2, if a formula in the worksheet referenced cell J4 before the insert, then Excel would adjust the cell reference in the formula to J7 after inserting three cells.

3

- Save the workbook using **SC_EX_3_Hotel** as the file name.

Other Ways

1. Click Insert Cells arrow (Home tab | Cells group), click 'Insert Cells...'
2. Press CTRL+SHIFT+PLUS SIGN, click Shift cells down (Insert dialog box), OK

BTW
Inserting Multiple Rows
If you want to insert multiple rows, you have two choices. You can insert a single row by using the Insert command on the shortcut menu and then repeatedly press F4 to continue inserting rows. Alternatively, you can select a number of existing rows equal to the number of rows that you want to insert. For instance, if you want to insert five rows, select five existing rows in the worksheet, right-click the selected rows, and then click Insert on the shortcut menu.

Inserting Rows and Columns

Inserting rows and columns into a worksheet is similar to the way you insert cells. To insert rows, select one or more rows immediately below of where you want Excel to insert the new row or rows. Select the number of rows you want to insert, click the Insert arrow (Home tab | Cells group), and then click 'Insert Sheet Rows' in the Insert list; or right-click the selected rows(s) and then click Insert on the shortcut menu. To insert columns, select one or more columns immediately to the right of where you want Excel to insert the new column or columns. Select the number of columns you want to insert, click the Insert arrow (Home tab | Cells group), and then click 'Insert Sheet Columns' in the Insert list; or right-click the selected column(s) and then click Insert on the shortcut menu. The Insert command on the shortcut menu requires that you select an entire row or column to insert a row or column. Following the insertion of a row or column, Excel displays the Insert Options button, which allows you to modify the insertion.

Deleting Columns and Rows

The Delete button (Home tab | Cells group) or the Delete command on the shortcut menu removes cells (including the data and formatting) from the worksheet. Deleting cells is not the same as clearing cells. The Clear Contents command, described in Module 1, clears the data from the cells, but the cells remain in the worksheet. The Delete command removes the cells from the worksheet and shifts the remaining rows up (when you delete rows) or shifts the remaining columns to the left (when you delete columns). If formulas located in other cells reference cells in the deleted row or column, Excel does not adjust these cell references. Rather, Excel displays the error message **#REF!** in those cells to indicate a cell reference error. For example, if cell A7 contains the formula =A4+A5 and you delete row 5, Excel assigns the formula =A4+#REF! to cell A6 (originally cell A7) and displays the error message, #REF!, in cell A6. Excel also displays an Error Options button when you select the cell containing the error message, #REF!, which allows you to select options to determine the nature of the problem.

BTW
Dragging Ranges
You can move and insert a selected cell or range between existing cells by holding down SHIFT while you drag the selection to the gridline where you want to insert the selected cell or range. You also can copy and insert by holding down CTRL+SHIFT while you drag the selection to the desired gridline.

BTW
Ranges and Undo
The incorrect use of copying, deleting, inserting, and moving cell ranges can make a worksheet incorrect. Carefully review the results of these actions before continuing on to the next task. If you are not sure the result of the action is correct, click the Undo button on the Quick Access Toolbar.

To Enter Numbers with Format Symbols

The next step in creating the Financial Projection worksheet is to enter the hotel assumptions values in the range K4:K11. The numbers in the table can be entered and then formatted using techniques from Modules 1 and 2, or each number can be entered with **format symbols**, which assign a format to numbers as they are entered. When a number is entered with a format symbol, Excel displays it with the assigned format. Valid format symbols include the dollar sign ($), comma (,), and percent sign (%).

If you enter a whole number, it appears without any decimal places. If you enter a number with one or more decimal places and a format symbol, Excel displays the number with two decimal places. Table 3–5 illustrates several examples of numbers entered with format symbols. The number in parentheses in column 4 indicates the number of decimal places.

BTW
Organizing Files and Folders
You should organize and store files in folders so that you easily can find the files later. For example, if you are taking an introductory technology class called CIS 101, a good practice would be to save all Excel files in an Excel folder in a CIS 101 folder.

Table 3–5: Numbers Entered with Format Symbols

Format Symbol	Typed in Formula Bar	Displays in Cell	Comparable Format
,	374,149	374,149	Comma(0)
	5,833.6	5,833.60	Comma(2)
$	$58917	$58,917	Currency(0)
	$842.51	$842.51	Currency(2)
	$63,574.9	$63,574.90	Currency(2)
%	85%	85%	Percent(0)
	12.80%	12.80%	Percent(2)
	68.2242%	68.2242%	Percent(4)

Why? In some cases, using a format symbol is the most efficient method for entering and formatting data. The following step enters the numbers in the Hotel Assumptions table with format symbols.

1

- Enter the following values, using format symbols to apply number formatting: **60** in cell K4, **5.00%** in cell K5, **3.50%** in cell K6, **10.00%** in cell K7, **8.00%** in cell K8, **15.00%** in cell K9, **4.00%** in cell K10, and **$50,000.00** in cell K11 (Figure 3–22).

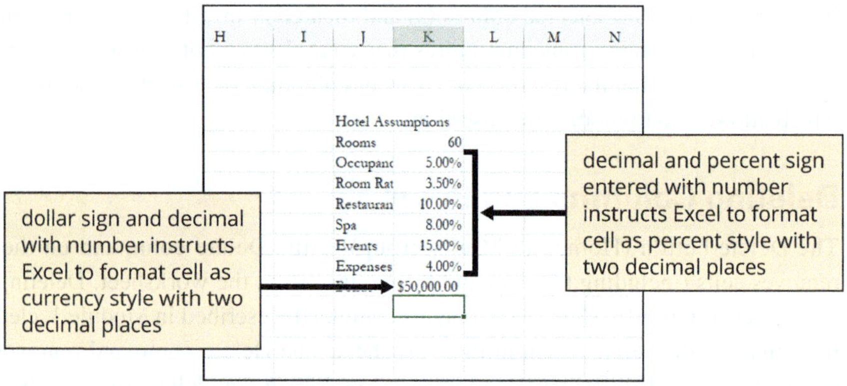

Figure 3–22

Other Ways

1. Right-click range, click Format Cells on shortcut menu, click Number tab (Format Cells dialog box), click category in Category list, select desired format, click OK
2. Press CTRL+1, click Number tab (Format Cells dialog box), click category in Category list, select desired format, click OK

To Enter the First Year of Projected Revenue and Expenses

The following steps enter the first year of projected gross margin components, listed previously in Table 3–1, in column B.

1 Enter **40%** in cell B4, **135** in cell B6, **105,000** in cell B9, **46,000** in cell B10, **78,000** in cell B11, **38,500** in cell B15, and **410,000** in cell B16 (Figure 3–23).

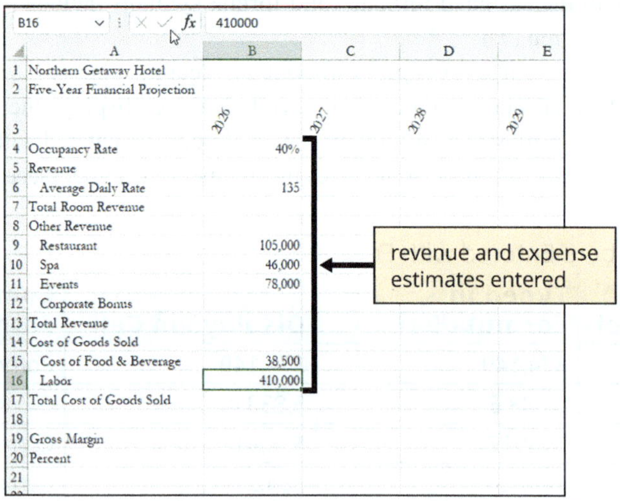

Figure 3–23

To Enter and Format the System Date

Why? The sketch of the worksheet in Figure 3–3a includes a date stamp on the right side of the heading section. A date stamp shows the date a workbook, report, or other document was created or the time period it represents. In business, a report is often meaningless without a date stamp. For example, if a printout of the worksheet in this module were distributed to the company's analysts, the date stamp could show when the five-year projections were made, as well as what time period the report represents.

A simple way to create a date stamp is to use the NOW function to enter the system date tracked by your computer in a cell in the worksheet. The NOW function is one of 24 date and time functions available in Excel. When assigned to a cell, the **NOW function** returns (displays) a number that corresponds to the system date and time beginning with December 31, 1899.

For example, January 1, 1900 equals 1, January 2, 1900 equals 2, and so on. Noon equals .5. Thus, noon on January 1, 1900 equals 1.5 and 6:00 p.m. on January 1, 1900 equals 1.75. If the computer's system date is set to the current date, then the date stamp is equivalent to the current date. The following steps enter the NOW function and then change the format.

1

- Select cell G1 and then click the Insert Function button in the formula bar to display the Insert Function dialog box.
- Click the 'Or select a category' arrow (Insert Function dialog box) and then select 'Date & Time' to populate the 'Select a function' list with date and time functions.
- Scroll down in the 'Select a function' list and then click NOW to select the required function (Figure 3–24).

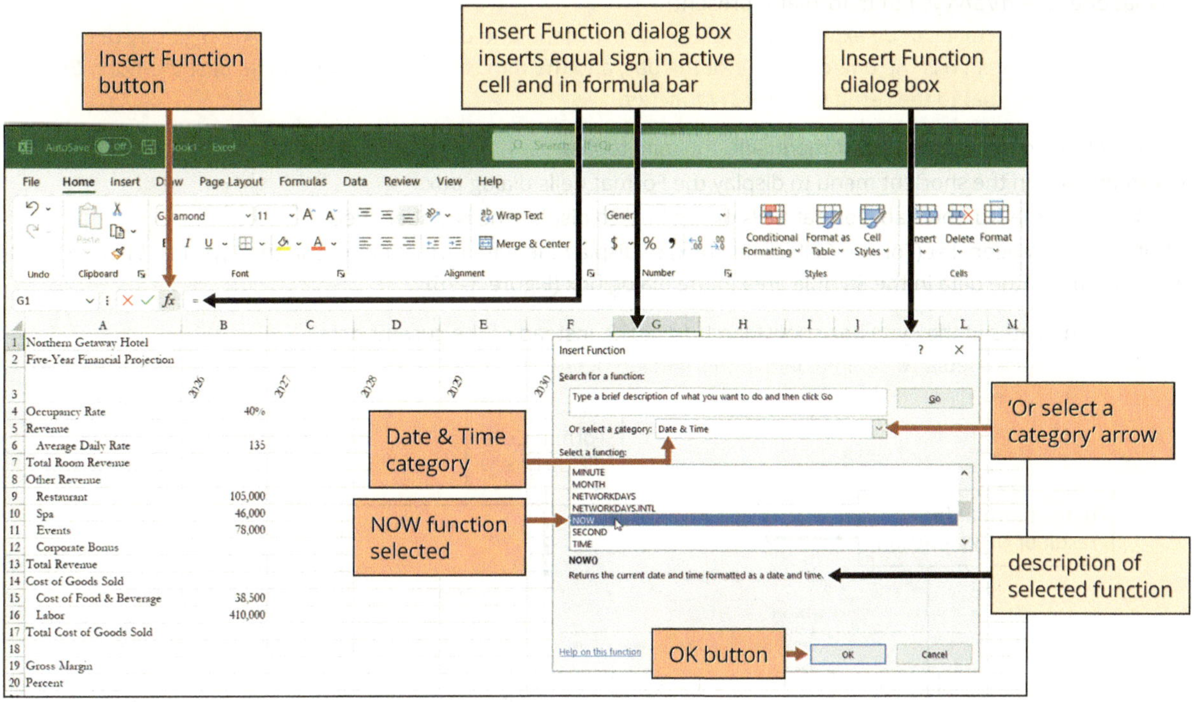

Figure 3–24

2

- Click OK (Insert Function dialog box) to close the Insert Function dialog box and display the Function Arguments dialog box (Figure 3–25).

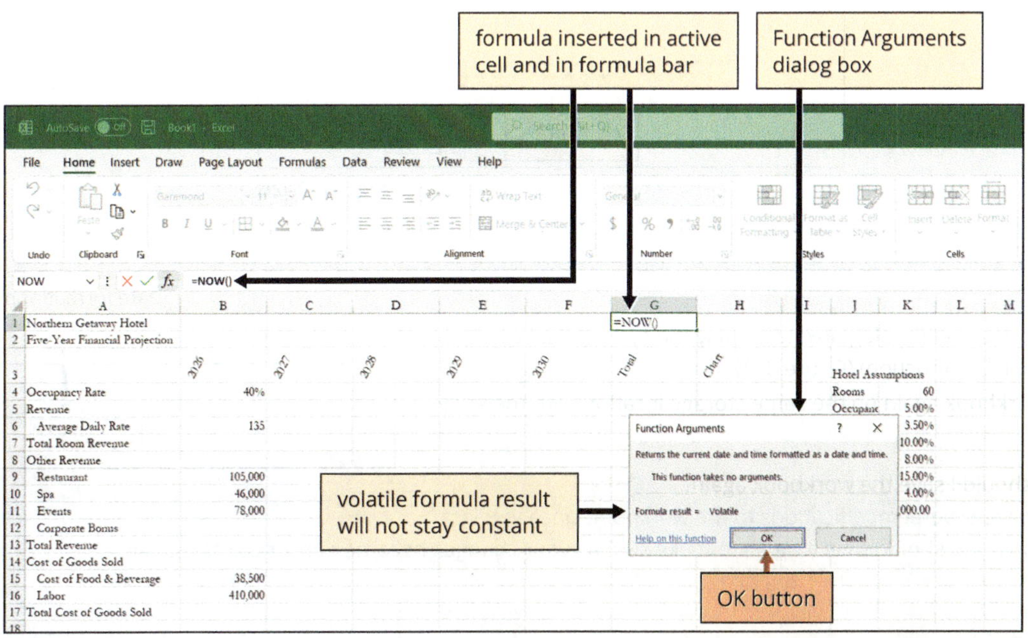

Figure 3–25

Q&A What is meant by 'Formula result = Volatile' in the Function Arguments dialog box?
The NOW function is an example of a volatile function. A **volatile function** is one where the number that the function returns is not constant but changes each time the worksheet is opened. As a result, any formula using the NOW function will have a variable result.

3

- Click OK (Function Arguments dialog box) to display the system date and time in the selected cell, using the default date and time format, which is m/d/yyyy h:mm.

Q&A What does the m/d/yyyy h:mm format represent?
The m/d/yyyy h:mm format can be explained as follows: the m is the one-digit month, d is the one-digit day of the month, yyyy is the four-digit year, h is the one-digit hour of the day, and the mm is the two-digit minutes past the hour. Excel applies this date and time format to the result of the NOW function.

- Right-click cell G1 to display a shortcut menu and the mini toolbar.
- Click Format Cells on the shortcut menu to display the Format Cells dialog box.
- If necessary, click the Number tab (Format Cells dialog box) to display the Number sheet.
- Click Date in the Category list (Format Cells dialog box) to display the date format options in the Type list. Click 2012-03-14 to display a sample of the data in the Sample area in the dialog box (Figure 3–26).

Q&A Why do the dates in the Type box show March 14, 2012, instead of the current date?
March 14, 2012, is just used as a sample date in this version of Office.

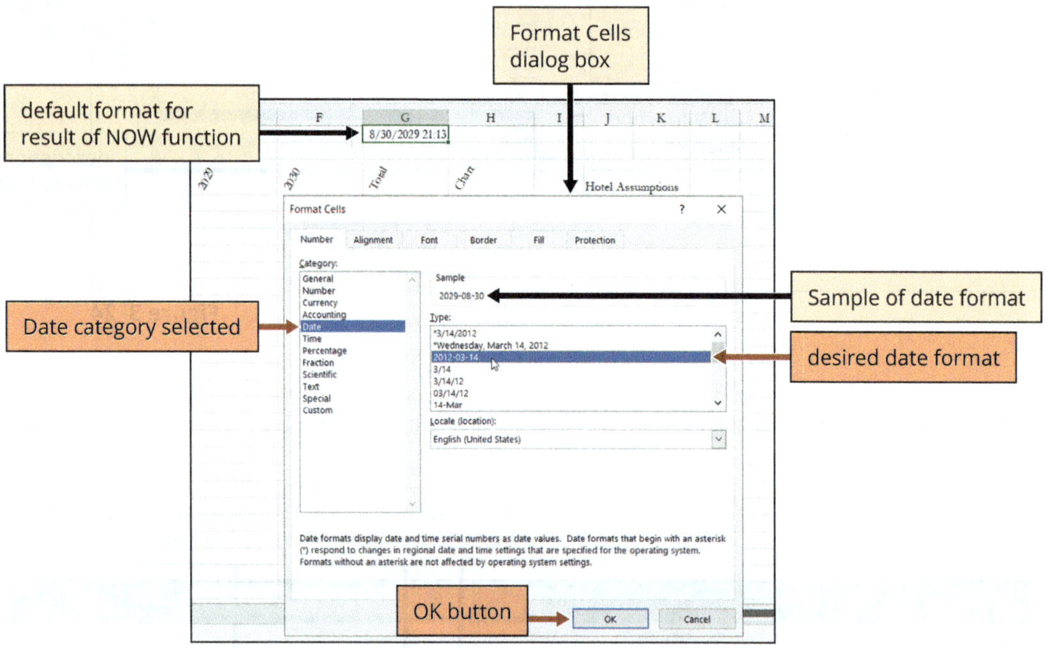

Figure 3–26

4

- Click OK (Format Cells dialog box) to display the system date (the result of the NOW function) (Figure 3–27).
- Save the workbook again on the same storage location with the same file name.

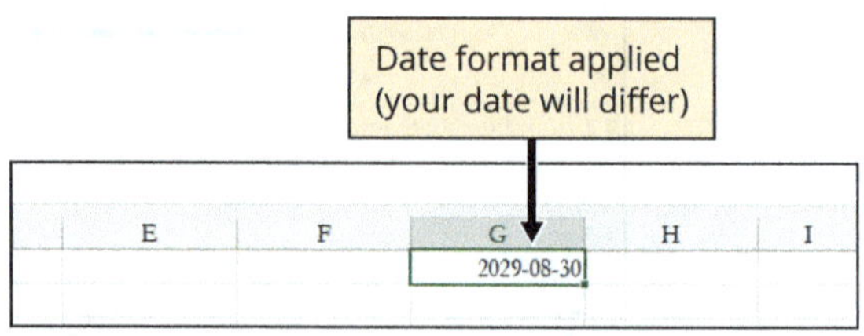

Figure 3–27

Q&A Why should I save the workbook again?
You have made several modifications to the workbook since you last saved it. Thus, you should save it again to make sure all your changes become part of the saved file.

Other Ways

1. Click 'Date & Time' button (Formulas tab | Function Library group), click NOW	2. Press CTRL+SEMICOLON (this enters the date as a static value, meaning the date will not change when the workbook is opened at a later date)	3. Press CTRL+SHIFT+# to format date as day-month-year

Consider This

When would you not want to use the system date?

Using the system date results in the date value being updated whenever the worksheet is opened. Think carefully about whether or not this is the result you want. If you want the date to reflect the current date, using the system date is appropriate. If you want to record when the worksheet was created, using a hard-coded date, a date that is entered manually, not generated by a formula, makes more sense. If both pieces of information may be important, consider two date entries in the worksheet: a fixed entry identifying the date the worksheet was created and the volatile system date.

Break Point: If you want to take a break, this is a good place to do so. You can exit Excel now. To resume later, start Excel, open the file called SC_EX_3_Hotel, and continue following the steps from this location forward.

Absolute versus Relative Addressing

The next sections describe the formulas and functions needed to complete the calculations in the worksheet.

As you learned in Modules 1 and 2, Excel modifies cell references when copying formulas. However, sometimes while copying formulas you do not want Excel to change a cell reference. To keep a cell reference constant when copying a formula or function, Excel uses a technique called absolute cell referencing. An **absolute cell reference** in a formula is a cell address that refers to a specific cell and does not change when you copy the formula and paste it in another location. To specify an absolute cell reference in a formula, enter a dollar sign ($) before any column letters or row numbers you want to keep constant in formulas you plan to copy. For example, $B$4 is an absolute cell reference, whereas B4 is a relative cell reference. Both reference the same cell. The difference becomes apparent when you copy the formula and paste it to a destination area. A formula using the absolute cell reference $B$4 instructs Excel to keep the cell reference B4 constant (absolute) in the formula as it is copied to the destination area. A formula using the relative cell reference B4 instructs Excel to adjust the cell reference as it is copied to the destination area. A **relative cell reference** is a cell address in a formula that automatically changes to reflect the new location when the formula is copied or moved. This is the default type of referencing used in Excel worksheets and is also called a relative reference. When a cell reference combines both absolute and relative cell addressing, it is called a **mixed cell reference**. A mixed cell reference includes a dollar sign before the column or the row, not before both. When planning formulas, be aware of when you might need to use absolute, relative, and mixed cell references. Table 3–6 provides some additional examples of each of these types of cell references.

Figure 3–28 illustrates how the type of cell reference used affects the results of copying a formula to a new place in a worksheet. In Figure 3–28a, cells D6:D9 contain formulas. Each formula multiplies the content of cell A2 by 2; the difference between formulas lies in how cell A2 is referenced. Cells C6:C9 identify the type of reference: absolute, relative, or mixed.

BTW

Absolute Referencing

Absolute referencing is one of the more difficult worksheet concepts to understand. One point to keep in mind is that the paste operation is the only operation affected by an absolute cell reference. An absolute cell reference instructs the paste operation to use the same cell reference as it copies a formula from one cell and pastes it to another.

Table 3–6: Examples of Absolute, Relative, and Mixed Cell References

Cell Reference	Type of Reference	Meaning
$B$4	Absolute cell reference	Both column and row references remain the same when you copy this cell, because the cell references are absolute.
B4	Relative cell reference	Both column and row references are relative. When copied to another cell, both the column and row in the cell reference are adjusted to reflect the new location.
B$4	Mixed reference	This cell reference is mixed. The column reference changes when you copy this cell to another column because it is relative. The row reference does not change because it is absolute.
$B4	Mixed reference	This cell reference is mixed. The column reference does not change because it is absolute. The row reference changes when you copy this cell reference to another row because it is relative.

Figure 3–28b shows the values that result from copying the formulas in cells D6:D9 to ranges E6:E9, F7:F10, and G11:G14. Figure 3–28c shows the formulas that result from copying the formulas. While all formulas initially multiplied the content of cell A2 by 2, the values and formulas in the destination ranges illustrate how Excel adjusts cell references according to how you reference those cells in original formulas.

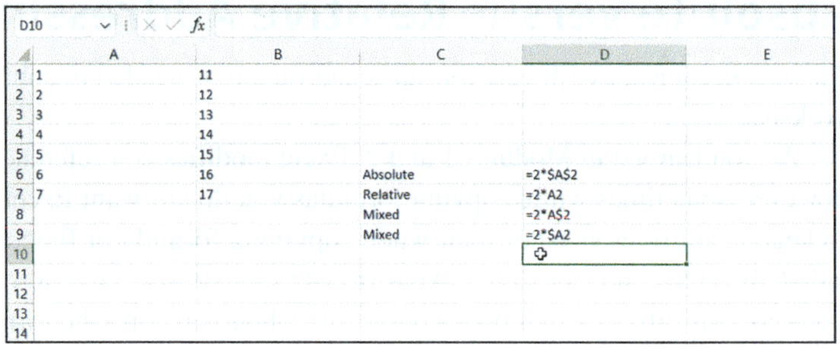

Figure 3–28(a)

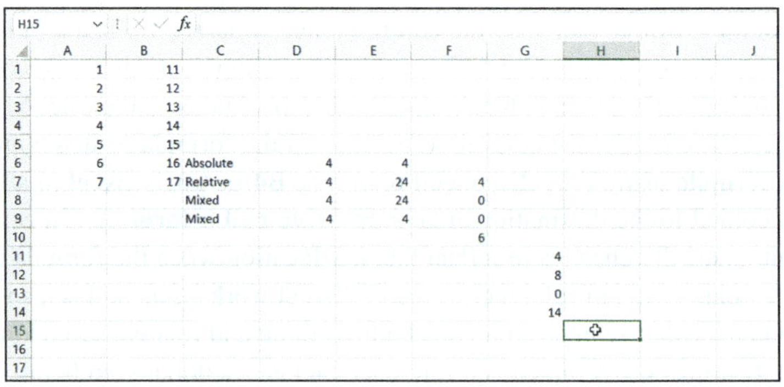

Figure 3–28(b)

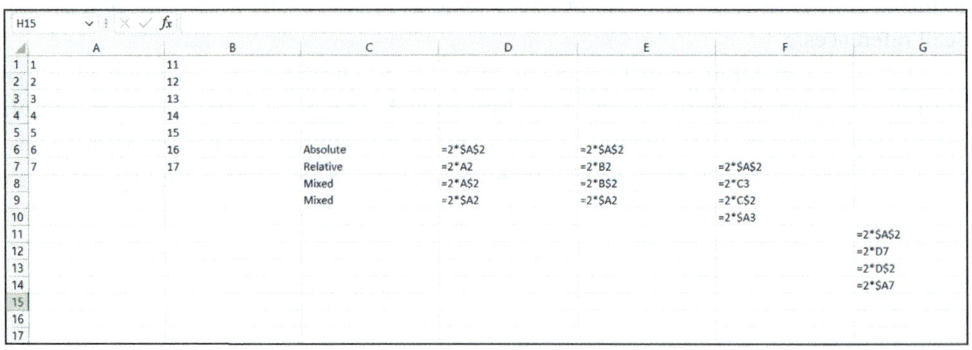

Figure 3–28(c)

In the SC_EX_3_Hotel worksheet, you need to enter formulas that calculate the following values for 2026: total room revenue (cell B7), corporate bonus (cell B12), total revenue (cell B13), total cost of goods sold (cell B17), gross margin (cell B19), and percent, which is gross margin expressed as a percentage of total revenue (cell B20). Additionally, you need to use formulas to calculate the projected yearly revenue and expenses for 2027: occupancy rate (cell C4), average daily rate (cell C6), restaurant (cell C9), spa (cell C10), events (cell C11), cost of food & beverage (cell C15), and labor (cell C16). The formulas are also based on the projected 2026 revenue and expenses in column B and the assumptions in the range J4:K11. When using assumptions to calculate projections, the formulas add 1 to the assumption percentage, which allows you to calculate a total projection, instead of a fraction of the projection.

The calculations for each column (year) are the same, Thus, the formulas for used in 2026 can be entered in column B and then copied to columns C through F. The formulas used in 2027 can be copied to columns D through F. The steps below will guide you in entering the formulas shown in Table 3–7 which determine the 2026 total rooms revenue, corporate bonus, total revenue, total cost of goods sold, and gross margin in column B, and the projected 2027 occupancy rate, total daily rate, other revenues and cost of goods sold.

Table 3–7: Formulas for Determining 2026 and 2027 Values

Cell	Row Title	Calculation	Formula
B7	Total Room Revenue	Rooms times Occupancy Rate times Average Daily Rate times 365	=K4*B4*B6*365
B12	Corporate Bonus	Bonus equals value in K11 or 0	=IF(SUM((B9:B11))>(B7*20%), K11,0)
B13	Total Revenue	Sum of Other Revenue	=B7+SUM(B9:B12)
B17	Total Cost of Goods Sold	Sum of Cost of Goods Sold	=SUM(B15:B16)
B19	Gross Margin	Total Revenue minus Total Cost of Goods Sold	=B13–B17
B20	Percent	Gross Margin divided by Total Revenue	=B19/B13
C4	Occupancy Rate	Occupancy Rate times (1 plus Occupancy Rate %)	=B4*(1+K5)
C6	Average Daily Rate	Average Daily Rate times (1 plus Room Rate %)	=B6*(1+K6)
C9	Restaurant	Restaurant times (1 plus Restaurant %)	=B9*(1+K7)
C10	Spa	Spa times (1 plus Spa %)	=B10*(1+K8)
C11	Events	Events times (1 plus Events %)	=B11*(1+K9)
C15	Cost of Food & Beverage Labor	Cost of Food & Beverage times (1 plus Expenses %)	=B15*(1+K10)
C16		Labor times (1 plus Expenses %)	=B16*(1+K10)

To Enter a Formula Containing Absolute Cell References

Why? As you enter the formulas in column B for 2026 and column C for 2027, shown in Table 3–7, in the steps below and then copy and paste them through column F (year 2030) in the worksheet, Excel will adjust the cell references for each column. After the copy/paste, the 2027 Total Room Revenue in cell C7 would be =L4*C4*C6*365. While the cell references C4 and C6 (2027 occupancy rate and average daily rate) is correct, the cell reference L4 references an empty cell. The formula for cell C10 should read =K4*C4*C6*365, rather than =L4*C4*C6*365, because K4 references the Room value in the Hotel Assumptions table. In this instance, you must use an absolute cell reference to keep the cell reference in the formula the same, or constant, when it is copied. To enter an absolute cell reference, you can type the dollar sign ($) as part of the cell reference or enter it by pressing F4 with the insertion point in or to the right of the cell reference to change it to absolute. The following steps enter the cost of goods sold formula =K4*B4*B6*365 in cell B7 using Point mode, and then change the cell reference to an absolute reference.

1

- Click cell B7 to select the cell in which to enter the first formula.
- Type = (equal sign), select cell K4, type ***b4*b6*365** to continue entering the formula, and then move the cursor in between K4 and * then press F4 to change the cell reference from a relative cell reference to an absolute cell reference (Figure 3–29).

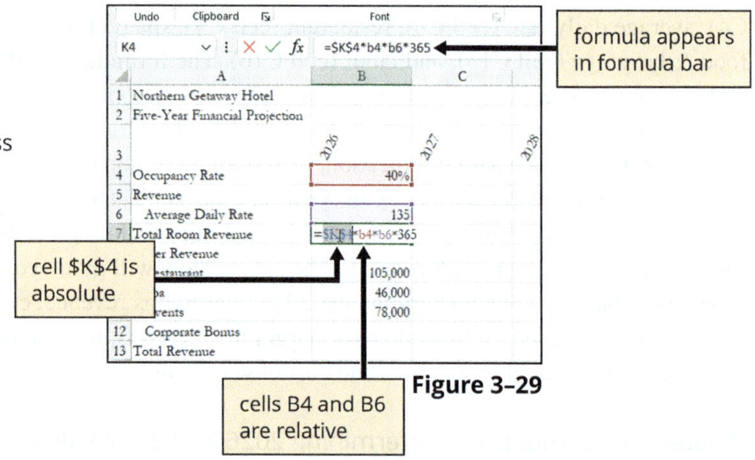

Figure 3–29

Q&A Is an absolute reference required in this formula?

No, a mixed cell reference also could have been used. The formula in cell B7 will be copied across columns, rather than down rows. So, the formula entered in cell B7 in Step 1 could have been entered as =$K4*B4*B6*365 using a mixed cell reference, rather than =$K$4*B4*B6*365, because when you copy a formula across columns, the row does not change. The key is to ensure that column K remains constant as you copy the formula across columns. To change the absolute cell reference to a mixed cell reference, continue to press F4 until you achieve the desired cell reference.

2

- Click the Enter button in the formula bar to display the result, 1182600, instead of the formula in cell B7 (Figure 3–30).

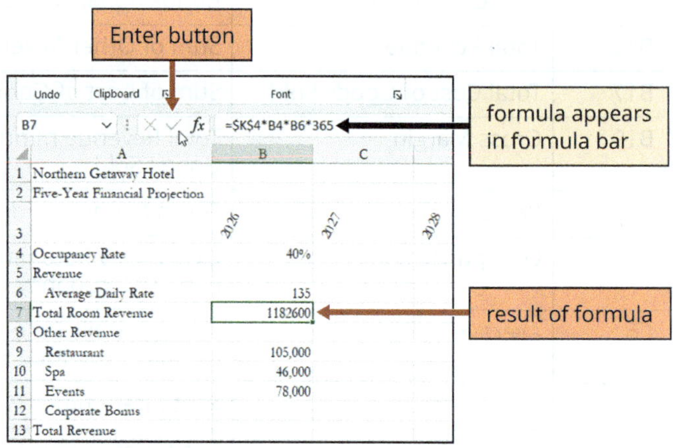

Figure 3–30

Making Decisions—The IF Function

In addition to calculations that are constant across all categories, you may need to make calculations only if a particular condition or set of conditions is met. For this project, you need to vary compensation according to how much revenue is generated in any particular year. According to the requirements document in Figure 3–2, a bonus will be paid in any year where the sum of restaurant, spa, and event revenue is greater than 20 percent of the total room revenue for bonus value. If the sum of the projected restaurant, spa, and event revenue is greater than 20 percent of the projected total room revenue in cell B7 (1,182,600), then the projected 2026 corporate bonus value in cell B12 is equal to the bonus value in cell K11 (50,000.00); otherwise, the value in cell B12 is equal to 0. One way to assign the projected 2026 bonus value in cell K12 is to manually check to see if the sum of the projected restaurant, spa, and events revenue exceeds 20 percent of the total room revenue in cell B7 and, if so, then to enter 50,000.00 in cell B12. You can use this manual process for all five years by checking the values for each year. However, using the IF function automates this process and saves time. The IF function uses a **logical test**, which is the decision-making process that determines if a particular condition is met

Because the data in the worksheet changes each time a report is prepared or the figures are adjusted, however, it is preferable to have Excel calculate the monthly bonus. To do so, cell B12 must include a function that performs the logical test, comparing the sum of the projected restaurant, spa, and event revenue with 20 percent of the projected total room revenue in cell B7, and displays 50,000.00 or 0.00 (zero). This decision-making process can be represented in diagram form, as shown in Figure 3–31.

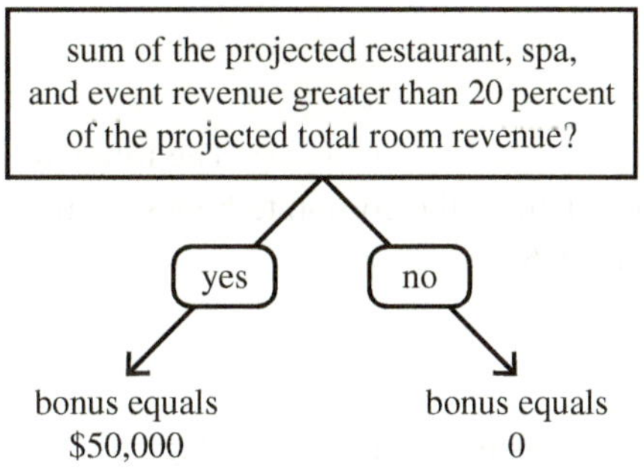

Figure 3–31

BTW

Logical Operators in IF Functions

The IF function can use logical operators, such as AND, OR, and NOT. For example, the three IF functions =IF(AND(A1>C1, B1<C2), "OK", "Not OK") and =IF(OR(K5>J5, C3<K6), "OK", "Not OK") and =IF(NOT(B10<C10), "OK", "Not OK") use logical operators. In the first example, both logical tests (A1<C1 and B1<C2) must be true for the value_if_true (OK) to be assigned to the cell. In the second example, one or the other logical tests (K5>J5, or C3<K6) must be true for the value_if_true OK to be assigned to the cell. In the third example, the logical test B10<C10 must be false for the value_if_true OK to be assigned to the cell.

In Excel, you use the **IF function** when you want to assign a value to a cell based on a logical test. For example, cell B12 can be assigned the following IF function:

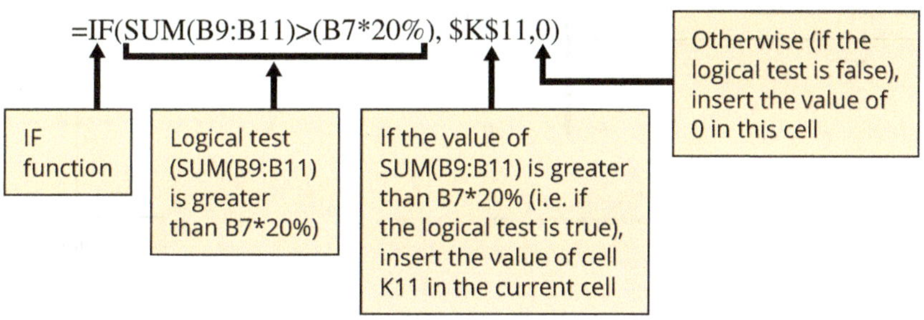

This IF function instructs Excel that if the sum of the projected restaurant, spa, and event revenue is greater than 20 percent of the projected total room revenue in cell B7 (if the logical test is true), then Excel should display the bonus value found in cell K11. If the sum of the projected restaurant, spa, and event revenue is not greater than 20 percent of the projected total room revenue (i.e., if the logical test is false) then Excel should display a 0 (zero) in cell B12.

The general form of the IF function is:

=IF(logical_test, value_if_true, value_if_false)

The argument, logical test, is made up of two expressions and a comparison operator. Each **expression** can be a cell reference, a number, text, a function, or a formula. In this example, the logical test compares the sum of projected other revenues in cell range B9:B11 with the projected total room revenue amount in cell B7, using the comparison operator greater than. Table 3–8 shows valid comparison operators, their meanings, and examples of their use in IF functions. The argument, value_if_true, is the value you want Excel to display in the cell containing the function when the logical test is true. The argument, value_if_false, is the value you want Excel to display in the cell containing the function when the logical test is false.

Table 3-8: Comparison Operators

Comparison Operator	Meaning	Example
=	Equal to	=IF(A1=A2, "True", "False")
<	Less than	=IF(A1<A2, "True", "False")
>	Greater than	=IF(A1>A2, "True", "False")
>=	Greater than or equal to	=IF(A1>=A2, "True", "False")
<=	Less than or equal to	=IF(A1<=A2, "True", "False")
<>	Not equal to	=IF(A1<>A2, "True", "False")

To Enter an IF Function

Why? Use an IF function to determine the value for a cell based on a logical test. The following steps assign the IF function =IF(SUM(B9:B11)>(B7*20%), $K$11,0) to cell B12, to calculate the corporate bonus, if any. This IF function determines whether or not the worksheet assigns a corporate bonus for 2026.

1

- Click cell B12 to select the cell for the next formula.
- Click the Insert Function button in the formula bar to display the Insert Function dialog box.
- Click the 'Or select a category' arrow (Insert Function dialog box) and then select Logical in the list to populate the 'Select a function' list with logic functions.
- Click IF in the 'Select a function' list to select the required function (Figure 3-32).

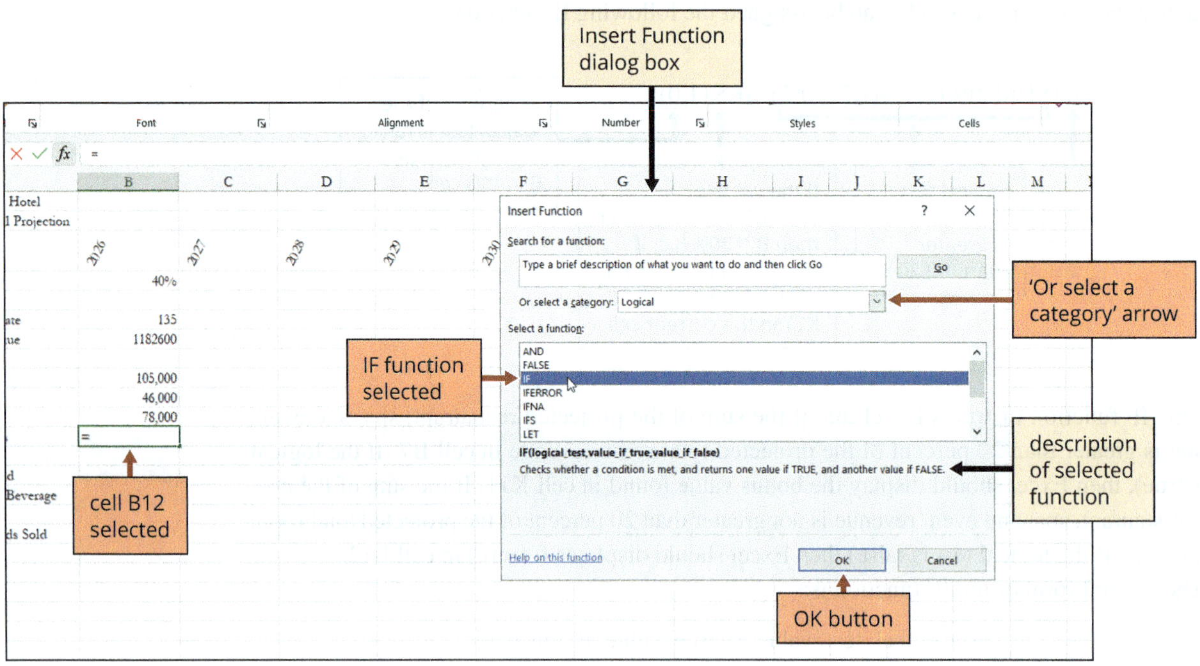

Figure 3-32

2

- Click OK (Insert Function dialog box) to display the Function Arguments dialog box.
- Type **sum(b9:b11)>(b7*20%)** in the Logical_test box to enter a logical test for the IF function.
- Type **k11** in the Value_if_true box to enter the result of the IF function if the logical test is true.
- Type **0** (zero) in the Value_if_false box to enter the result of the IF function if the logical test is false (Figure 3-33).

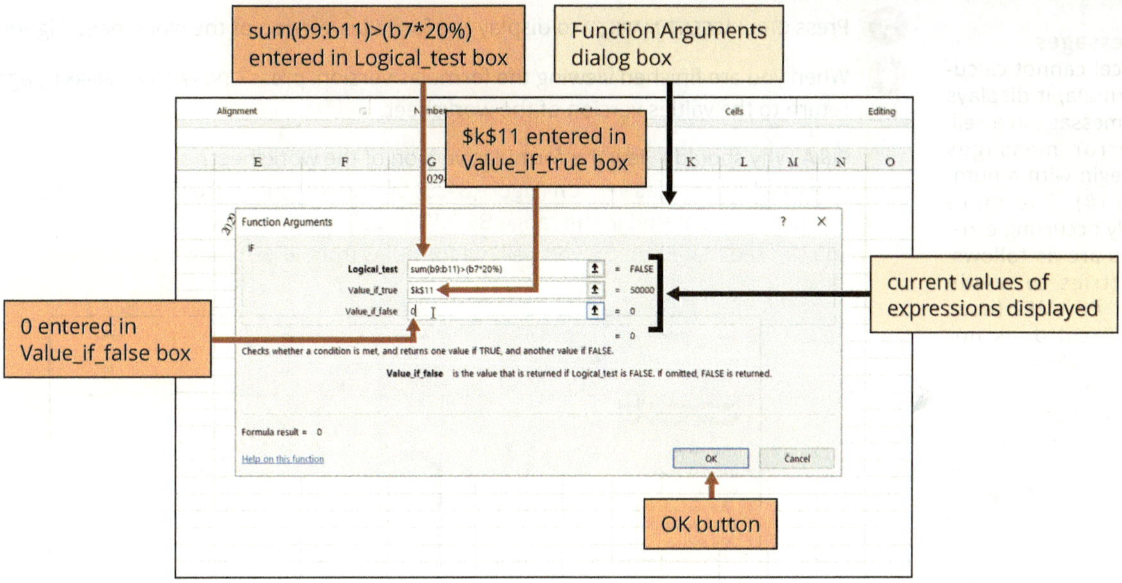

Figure 3–33

3

- Click OK (Function Arguments dialog box) to insert the IF function in the selected cell (Figure 3–34).

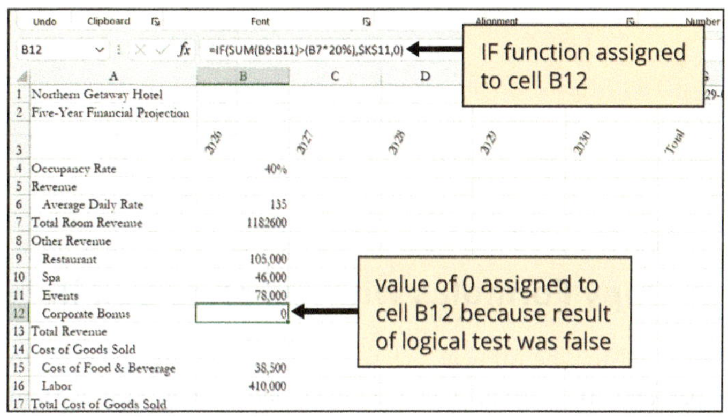

Figure 3–34

Other Ways

1. Click Logical button (Formulas tab | Function Library group), click IF

To Enter the Remaining Formulas for 2026 and 2027

The following steps enter the remaining formulas for 2026 and 2027.

1. Select cell B13. Type **=b7+sum(b9:b12)** then click the Enter button.
2. Select cell B17. Click the AutoSum button (Home tab | Editing group) twice to insert a SUM function in the selected cell.
3. Select cell B19. Type **=b13-b17** and then press the DOWN ARROW key to enter the formula in the selected cell. Type **=b19/b13** and then press the DOWN ARROW key again.
4. Select cell C4. Type **=b4*(1+k5)** and then press the DOWN ARROW key twice to enter the formula in the selected cell and navigate to cell C6. Type **=b6*(1+k6)** and then press the DOWN ARROW key three times to enter the formula in the selected cell and navigate to cell C9. Type **=b9*(1+k7)**, press the DOWN ARROW key, type **=b10*(1+k8)**, press the DOWN ARROW key, type **=b11*(1+k9)** and then press the DOWN ARROW key four times to enter the formula in the selected cell and navigate to cell C15. Type **=b15*(1+k10)**, press the DOWN ARROW key, type **=b16*(1+k10)**, and then press the DOWN ARROW key again.

BTW
Replacing a Formula with a Constant
Using the following steps, you can replace a formula with its result so that the cell value remains constant: (1) click the cell with the formula; (2) press F2 or click in the formula bar; (3) press F9 to display the value in the formula bar; and (4) press ENTER.

BTW
Error Messages
When Excel cannot calculate a formula, it displays an error message in a cell. These error messages always begin with a number sign (#). The more commonly occurring error messages are as follows: #DIV/0! (tries to divide by zero); #NAME? (uses a name Excel does not recognize); #N/A (refers to a value not available); #NULL! (specifies an invalid intersection of two areas); #NUM! (uses a number incorrectly); #REF (refers to a cell that is not valid); #VALUE! (uses an incorrect argument or operand); and ##### (refers to cells not wide enough to display entire entry).

5. Press CTRL+ACCENT MARK (`) to display the formulas version of the worksheet (Figure 3–35).

6. When you are finished viewing the formulas version, press CTRL+ACCENT MARK (`) again to return to the values version of the worksheet.

Q&A Why should I view the formulas version of the worksheet?
Viewing the formulas version (Figure 3–35) of the worksheet allows you to check the formulas you entered in the range B4:B20. Recall that formulas were entered in lowercase. You can see that Excel converts all the formulas from lowercase to uppercase.

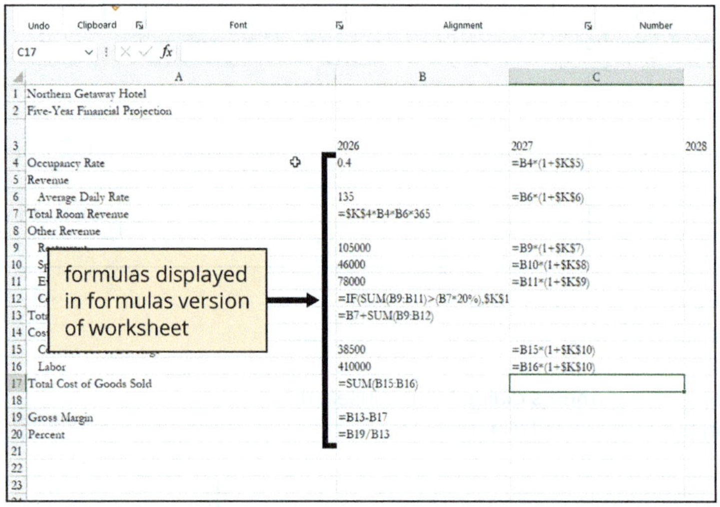

Figure 3–35

To Copy Formulas with Absolute Cell References Using the Fill Handle

Why? Using the fill handle ensures a quick, accurate copy of the formulas. The following steps use the fill handle to copy the 2026 and 2027 formulas in columns B and C to the other years in columns C through F.

1.
- Select the range C4:C16 and then point to the fill handle in the lower-right corner of the selected cell, C16 in this case, to display the crosshair pointer (Figure 3–36).

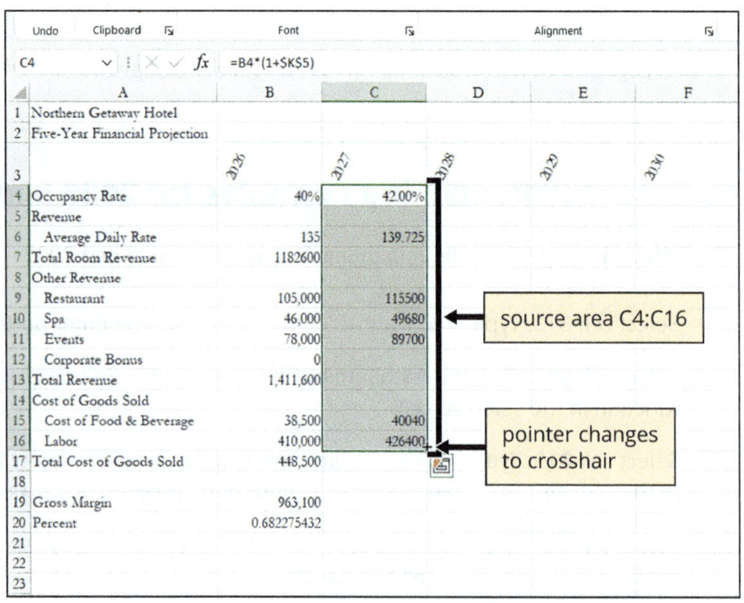

Figure 3–36

2

- Drag the fill handle to the right to copy the formulas from the source area, C4:C16 in this case, to the destination area, D4:F16 in this case, and display the calculated amounts (Figure 3–37).

Q&A What happens to the formulas after performing the fill operation?
Because the formulas in the range C4:C16 use absolute cell references, when they are copied to the range D4:F16, they still refer to the values in the Hotel Assumptions table.

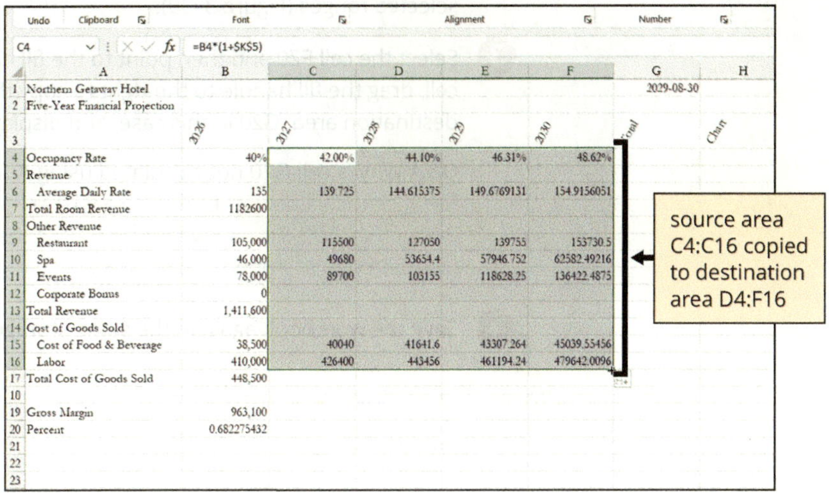

Figure 3–37

3

- Select the cell B7 and then point to the fill handle in the lower-right corner of the selected cell, drag the fill handle to the right to copy the formula from the source area to the destination area, C7:F7 in this case, and display the calculated amounts.

4

- Select the range B12:B13 and then point to the fill handle in the lower-right corner of B13, drag the fill handle to the right to copy the formulas from the source area to the destination area, C12:F13 in this case, and display the calculated amounts.

5

- Select cell B17 and then point to the fill handle in the lower-right corner of the selected cell, drag the fill handle to the right to copy the formula from the source area to the destination area, C17:F17 in this case, and display the calculated amounts.

6

- Select the range B19:B20 and then point to the fill handle in the lower-right corner of B20, drag the fill handle to the right to copy the formulas from the source area to the destination area, C19:F20 in this case, and display the calculated amounts (Figure 3–38).

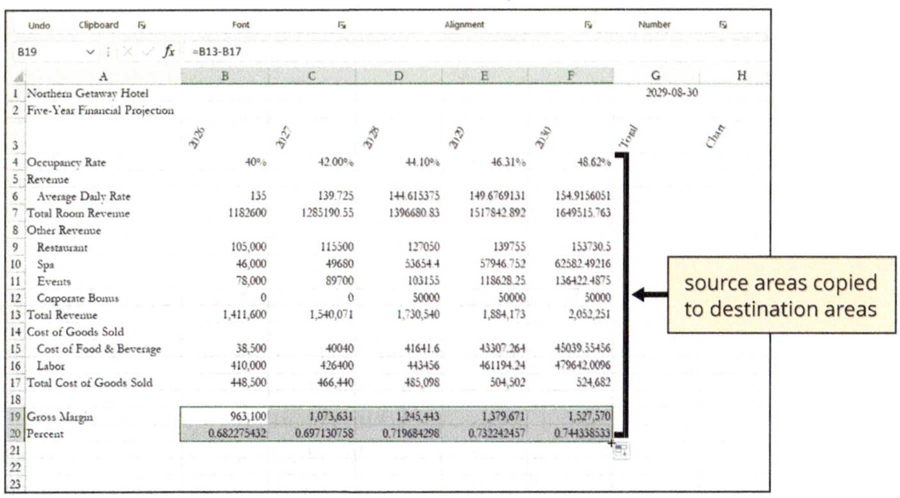

Figure 3–38

To Determine Row Totals in Nonadjacent Cells

The following steps determine the row totals in column G. To determine the row totals using the Sum button, select only the cells in column G containing numbers in adjacent cells to the left. If, for example, you select the range G7:G19, Excel will display 0s as the sum of empty rows in cells G7, G14, and G18.

1 Select the cell G7. While holding down CTRL, select the ranges G9:G13 and G15:G17, and the cell G19, as shown in Figure 3–39.

2. Click the Auto Sum button (Home tab | Editing group) to display the row totals in the selected ranges (Figure 3–39).

3. Select the cell F20 and then point to the fill handle in the lower-right corner of the selected cell, drag the fill handle to the right to copy the formula from the source area to the destination area, G20 in this case, and display the calculated amount.

   Q&A Why is cell G20 not calculated using AutoSum?
   Because the value of the cells in row 20 are showing the gross margin calculation as a percentage. We do not want to sum all of the individual percentages in row 20, rather calculate G20 as another percentage.

4. Save the workbook again in the same storage location with the same file name.

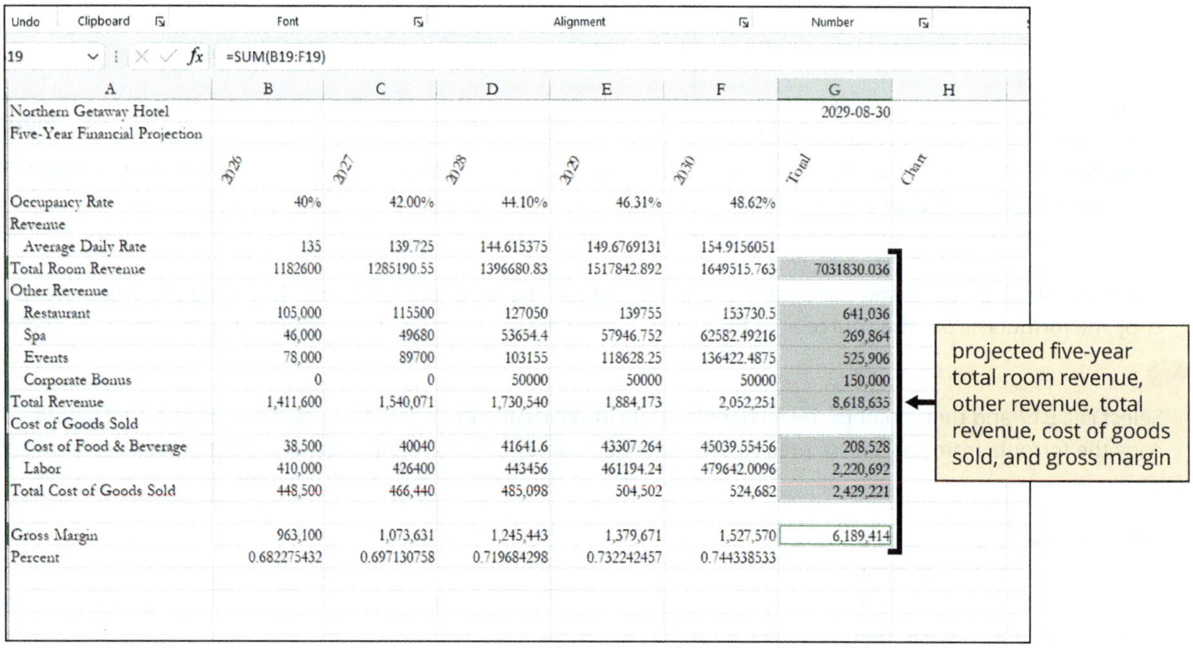

Figure 3–39

Adding and Formatting Sparkline Charts

Sometimes you may want to condense a range of data into a small chart in order to show a trend or variation in the range, and Excel's standard charts may be too large or extensive for your needs. A sparkline chart provides a simple way to show trends and variations in a range of data within a single cell. Excel includes three types of sparkline charts: line, column, and win/loss. Because sparkline charts appear in a single cell, you can use them to convey succinct, eye-catching summaries of the data they represent.

To Add a Sparkline Chart to the Worksheet

Each row of yearly data, including those containing formulas, provides useful information that can be summarized by a line sparkline chart. **Why?** A line sparkline chart is a good choice because it shows trends over the five-year period for each row of data. The following steps add a line sparkline chart to cell H4 and then use the fill handle to create line sparkline charts in the range H6:H20 to represent the yearly data shown in rows 6 through 20.

1

- Select cell H4 to prepare to insert a sparkline chart in the cell.
- Display the Insert tab and then click the Line button (Insert tab | Sparklines group) to display the Create Sparklines dialog box (Figure 3–40).

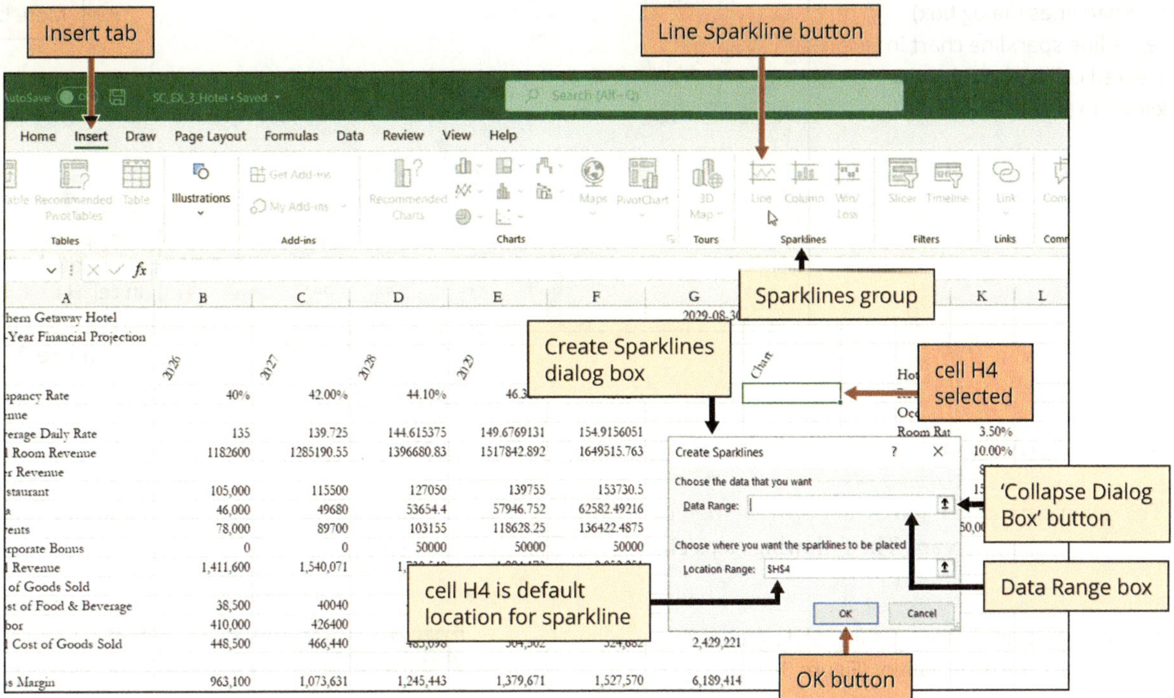

Figure 3–40

2

- Drag through the range B4:F4 to select the range. Do not release the mouse button (Figure 3–41).

Q&A What happened to the Create Sparklines dialog box?

When a dialog box includes a 'Collapse Dialog Box' button (Figure 3–40), selecting cells or a range collapses the dialog box so that only the current text box is visible. This allows you to select your desired range without the dialog box getting in the way. Once the selection is made, the dialog box expands back to its original size. You also can click the 'Collapse Dialog Box' button to make your selection and then click the 'Expand Dialog Box' button (Figure 3–41) to expand the dialog box.

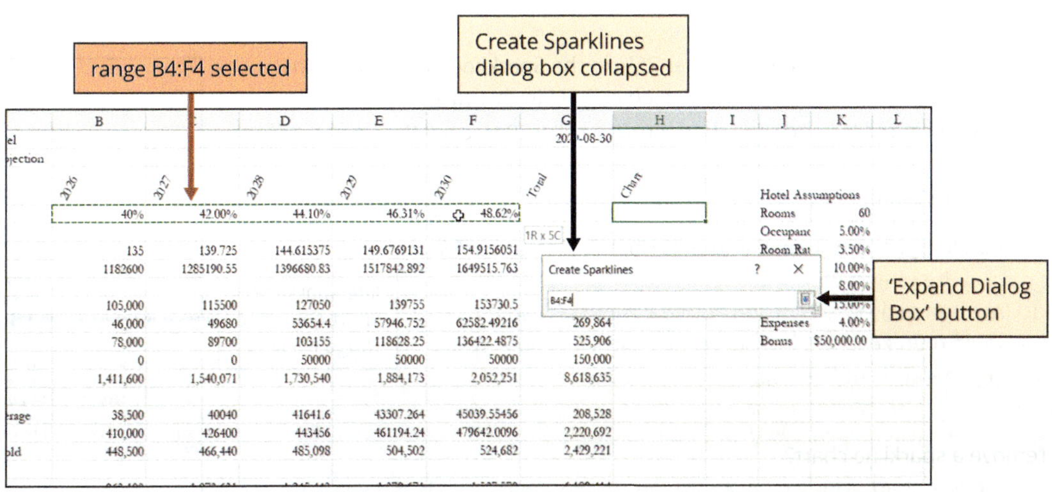

Figure 3–41

3

- Release the mouse button to insert the selected range, B4:F4 in this case, in the Data Range box.
- Click OK as shown in Figure 3–40 (Create Sparklines dialog box) to insert a line sparkline chart in the selected cell and display the Sparkline tab (Figure 3–42).

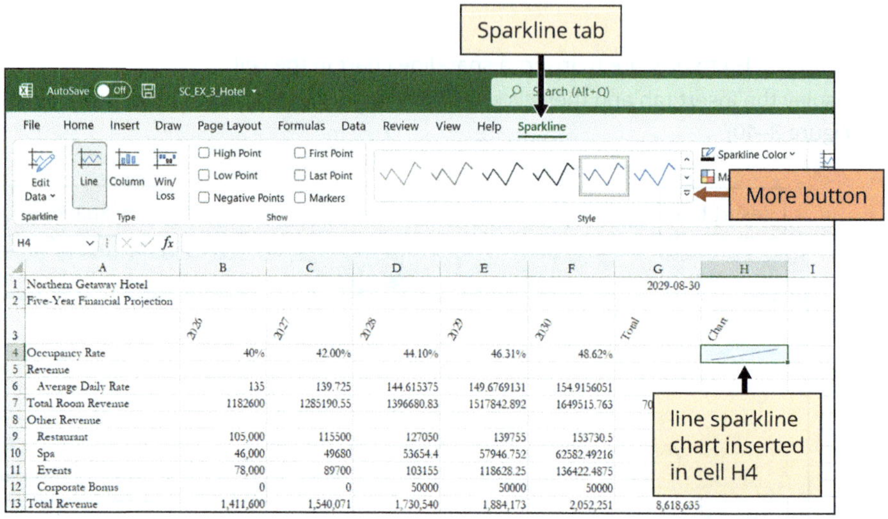

Figure 3–42

To Change the Sparkline Style and Copy the Sparkline Chart

Why? The default style option may not provide the visual impact you seek. Changing the sparkline style allows you to alter how the sparkline chart appears. The following steps change the sparkline chart style.

1

- Click the More button (Sparkline tab | Style group) to display the Sparkline Style gallery (Figure 3–43).

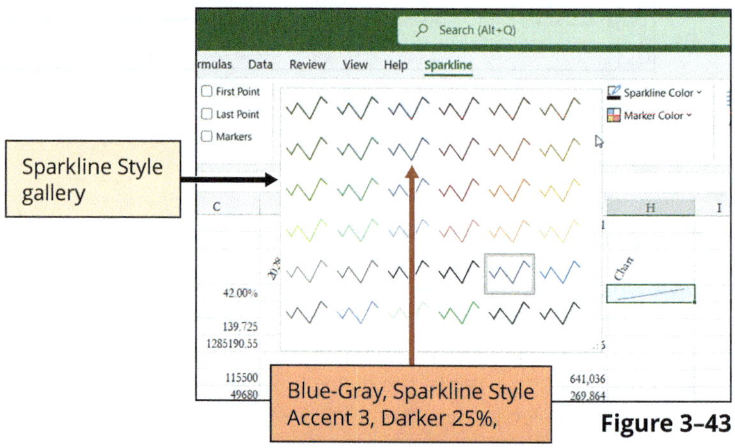

Figure 3–43

2

- Click 'Blue-Gray, Sparkline Style Accent 3, Darker 25% in the Sparkline Style gallery to apply the style to the sparkline chart in the selected cell, H4 in this case.
- Point to the fill handle in cell H4 and then drag through cell H20 to copy the line sparkline chart.
- Select cell H22 (Figure 3–44).

Q&A Why do sparkline charts not appear in cells H5, H8, H14, and H18?
There is no data in the ranges B5:H5, B8:H8, B14:H14, and B18:H18, so Excel cannot draw sparkline charts. If you added data to cells in those ranges, Excel would then generate line sparkline charts for those rows, because the drag operation defined sparkline charts for cells H5, H8, H14, and H18.

How can I remove a sparkline chart?
To remove a sparkline chart from a worksheet, you should clear it. To clear a sparkline chart, select the cell(s) containing the sparkline(s) to clear, and then click Clear (Sparkline tab | Group group).

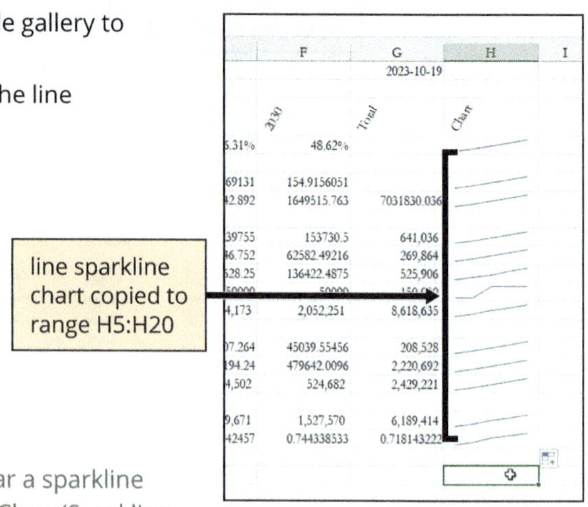

Figure 3–44

To Change the Sparkline Type

In addition to changing the sparkline chart style, you also can change the sparkline chart type. **Why?** You may decide that a different chart type will better illustrate the characteristics of your data. As shown in Figure 3–44, most of the sparkline charts look similar. Changing the sparkline chart type allows you to decide if a different chart type will better present your data to the reader. The following steps change the line sparkline charts to column sparkline charts.

1

- Select the range H4:H20 to select the sparkline charts.
- Click the Sparkline tab to make it the active tab.
- Click the Column button (Sparkline tab | Type group) to change the sparkline charts in the selected range to the column type (Figure 3–45).

2

- Select cell I22.
- Save the workbook again in the same storage location with the same file name.

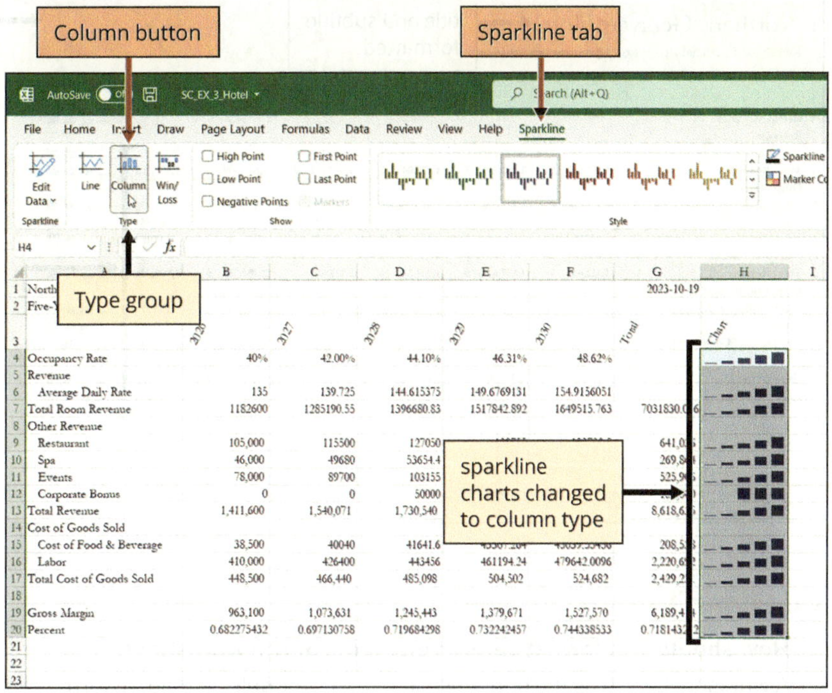

Figure 3–45

Customizing Sparkline Charts

You can customize sparkline charts using commands on the Sparkline tab. To show markers on specific values on the sparkline chart, such as the highest value, lowest value, any negative numbers, the first point, or the last point, use the corresponding check boxes in the Show group. To show markers on all line sparkline points, select the Markers check box in the Show group. You can change the color of sparklines or markers by using the Sparkline Color and Marker Color buttons in the Style group. You can group sparklines so changes apply to all sparklines in the group by using the Group command in the Group group.

Formatting the Worksheet

The worksheet created thus far shows the financial projections for the six-month period from January to June. Its appearance is uninteresting, however, even though you performed some minimal formatting earlier (formatting assumptions numbers, changing the column widths, formatting the date, and formatting the sparkline chart). This section completes the formatting of the worksheet by making the numbers easier to read and emphasizing the titles, assumptions, categories, and totals, as shown in Figure 3–46.

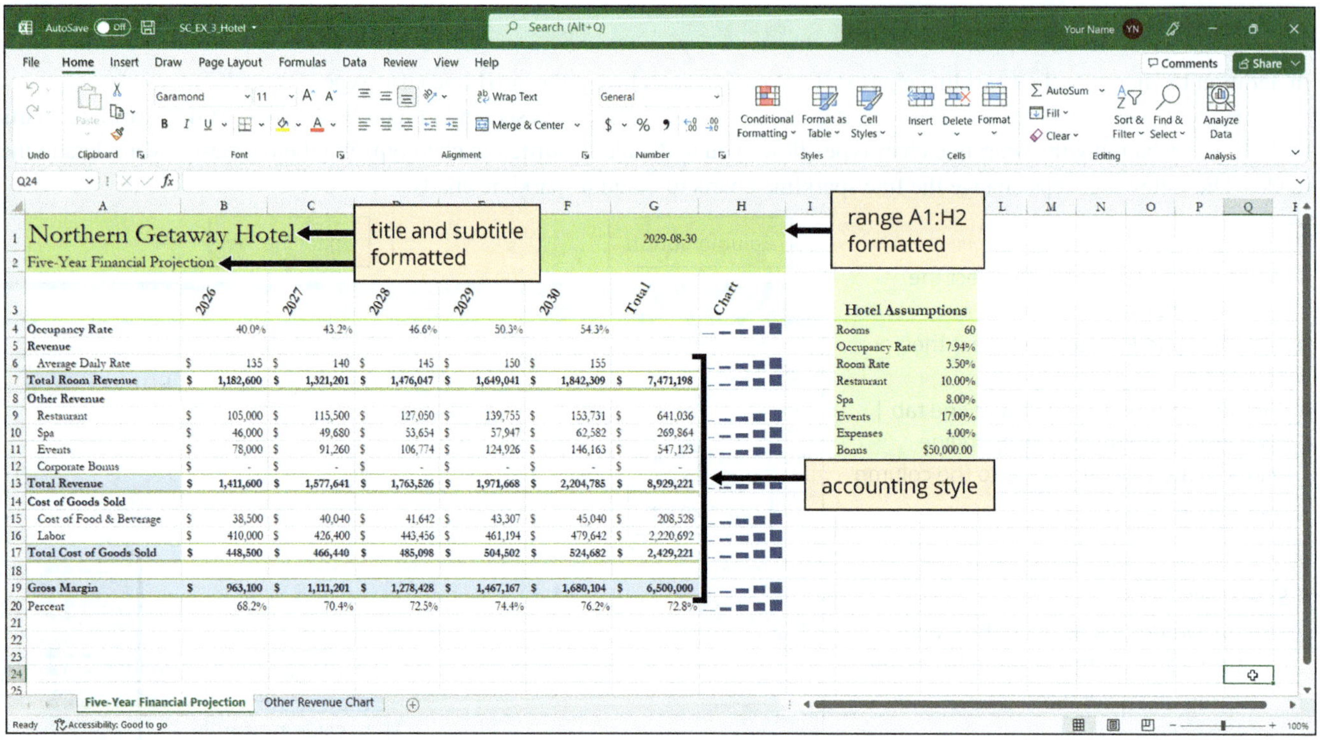

Figure 3–46

Consider This

How should you format various elements of the worksheet?

A worksheet, such as the one presented in this module, should be formatted in the following manner: (1) format the numbers; (2) format the worksheet title, column titles, row titles, and total rows; and (3) format the assumptions table. Dollar amounts should be formatted with a currency symbol. The assumptions table should be diminished in its formatting so that it does not distract from the main data and calculations in the worksheet. Assigning a smaller font size to the data in the assumptions table would visually illustrate that it is supplementary information and set it apart from other data formatted with a larger font size.

To Assign Formats to Nonadjacent Ranges

The following steps assign formats to the numbers in rows 4 through 20. **Why?** These formats increase the readability of the data.

1

- Select the range B4:F4 as the first range to format.
- While holding down CTRL, select the nonadjacent ranges B20:G20, and then release CTRL to select nonadjacent ranges.
- On the Home tab in the Number group, click the Percent Style button and then the Increase Decimal button (Figure 3–47).
- Click an empty cell to deselect the range.

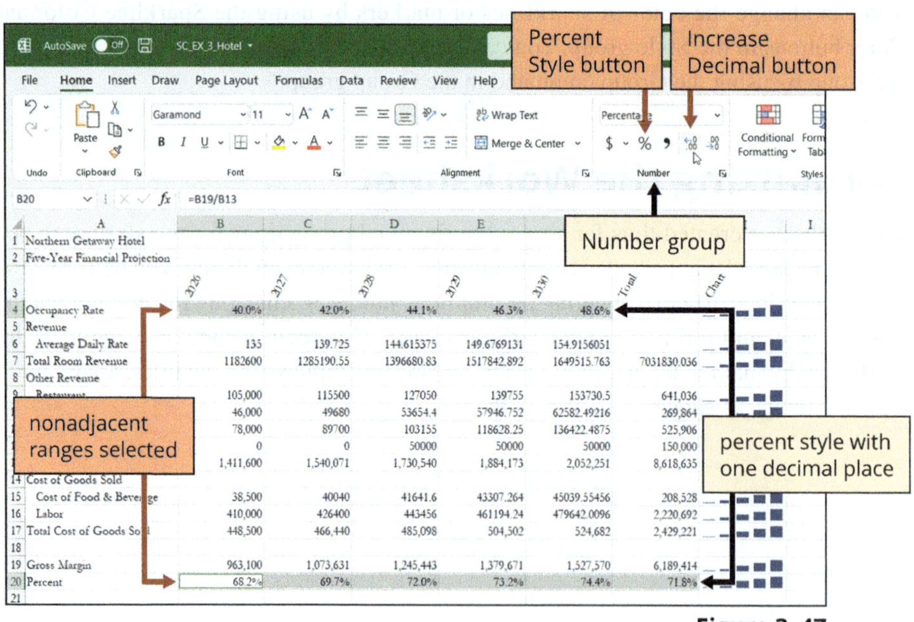

Figure 3–47

2

- Select the range B6:F7.
- While holding down CTRL, select the nonadjacent ranges B9:G13, B15:G17, B19:G19, and cell G7, and then release CTRL to select nonadjacent ranges.
- On the Home tab in the Number group, click the Accounting Style button to apply a dollar sign, click the Decrease Decimal button twice to remove the cents (Figure 3–48).

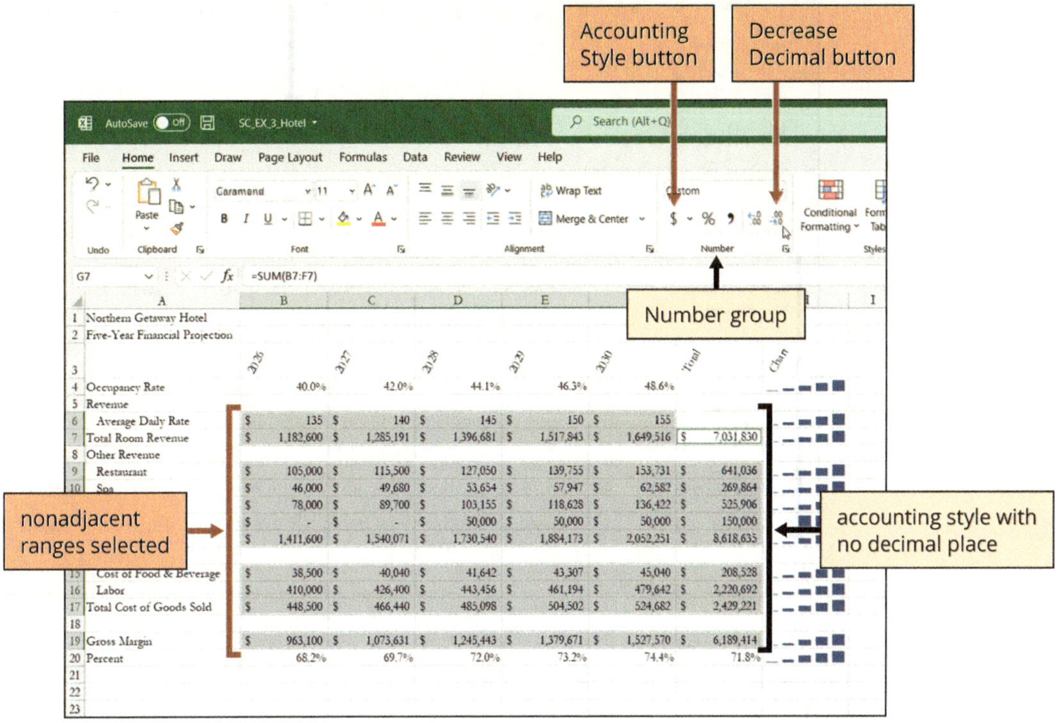

Figure 3–48

Other Ways

1. Right-click range, click Format Cells on shortcut menu, click Number tab (Format Cells dialog box), click category in Category list, select format, click OK (Format Cells dialog box)
2. Press CTRL+1, click Number tab (Format Cells dialog box), click category in Category list, select format, click OK (Format Cells dialog box)
3. Click Currency arrow (Home tab | Number group), select desired format

To Format the Worksheet Titles

The following steps emphasize the worksheet titles in cells A1 and A2 by changing the font and font size. The steps also format all of the row headers in column A with a bold font style.

1. Select cell A1 and increase the font size in cell A1 to 24 point.
2. Increase the font size in cell A2 to 14 point.
3. Apply the Bold font style to the row headers, cells A4, A5, A7, A8, A13, A14, A17, and A19.
4. Select the range A1:H2 and change the fill color to Green, Accent 1, Lighter 60% to add a background color to the selected range.
5. With A1:H2 selected, change the font color to Dark Grey, Text 2.
6. Click an empty cell to deselect the range (Figure 3–49).

BTW
Toggle Commands
Many of the commands on the ribbon, in galleries, and as shortcut keys function as toggles. For example, if you click Freeze Panes in the Freeze Panes gallery, the command changes to Unfreeze Panes the next time you view the gallery. These types of commands work like on-off switches, or toggles.

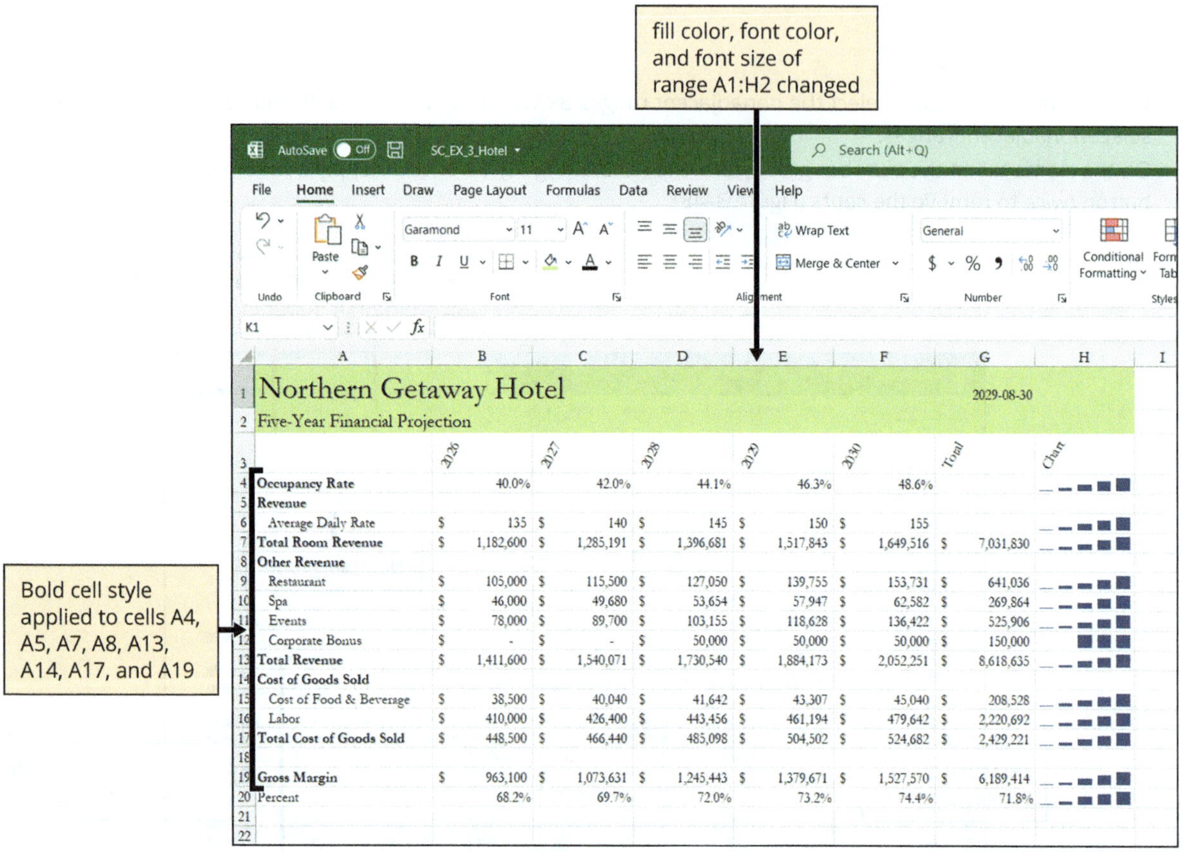

Figure 3–49

Other Ways

1. Right-click range, click Format Cells on shortcut menu, click Fill tab (Format Cells dialog box) to color background (or click Font tab to color font), click OK
2. Press CTRL+1, click Fill tab (Format Cells dialog box) to color background (or click Font tab to color font), click OK

To Assign Cell Styles to Nonadjacent Rows and Colors to a Cell

The following steps improve the appearance of the worksheet by formatting the headings in row 3 and the totals in rows 7, 13, 17, and 19. Row 19 also is formatted with a background color.

1. Select the range A3:H3 and apply the Heading 2 cell style.
2. Select the range A7:G7 and then press CTRL, making sure to hold CTRL down, select the ranges A13:G13, A17:G17, and A19:G19.
3. Apply the Total cell style to the selected nonadjacent ranges.
4. Select range A19:G19 and click the Fill Color arrow (Home tab | Font group) to apply the fill color Blue-Gray, Accent 3, Lighter 80% to the cell contents (Figure 3–50).

BTW

The Fill and Font Color Buttons

You may have noticed that the color bar at the bottom of the Fill Color and Font Color buttons (Home tab | Font group) (Figure 3–49) changes to the most recently selected color. To apply this same color to a cell background or text, select a cell and then click the Fill Color button to use the color as a background or click the Font Color button to use the color as a font color.

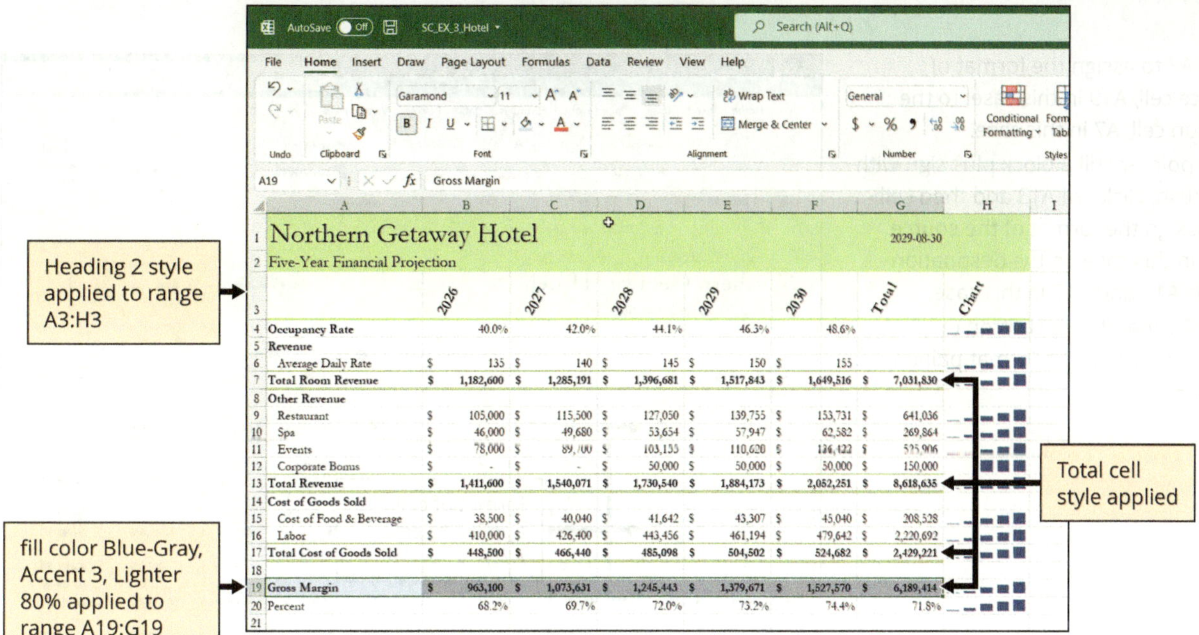

Figure 3–50

To Copy a Cell's Format Using the Format Painter Button

Why? Using the format painter, you can format a cell quickly by copying a cell's format to another cell or a range of cells. The following steps use the format painter to copy the format of cell A19 to cells A7, A13, and A17.

1

- If necessary, click cell A19 to select a source cell for the format to paint.
- Double-click the Format Painter button (Home tab | Clipboard group) and then move the pointer onto the worksheet to cause the pointer to change to a block plus sign with a paintbrush (Figure 3–51).

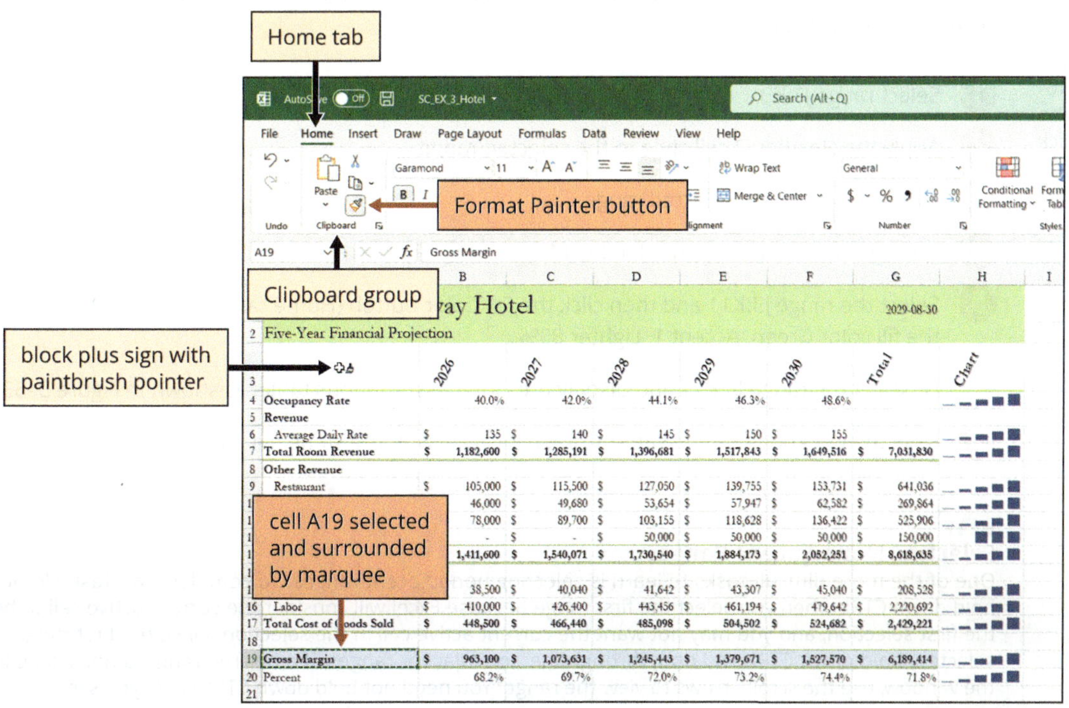

Figure 3–51

2

- Click cell A7 to assign the format of the source cell, A19 in this case, to the destination cell, A7 in this case.
- With the pointer still a block plus sign with a paintbrush, click cell A13 and then cell A17, to assign the format of the source cell, A19 in this case, to the destination cells, cells A13 and A17 in this case.
- Click the Format Painter button or press ESC to turn off the format painter (Figure 3–52).

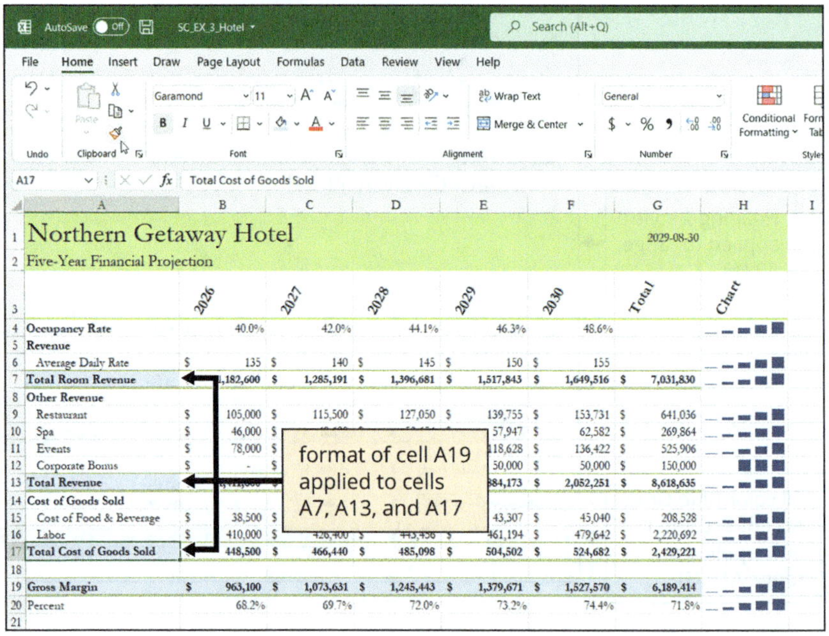

Figure 3–52

Other Ways

1. Click Copy button (Home tab | Clipboard group), select cell, click Paste arrow (Home tab | Clipboard group), click Formatting button in Paste gallery
2. Right-click cell, click Copy on shortcut menu, right-click cell, click Formatting button on shortcut menu

BTW
Painting a Format to Nonadjacent Ranges
Double-click the Format Painter button (Home tab | Clipboard group) and then drag through the nonadjacent ranges to paint the formats to the ranges. Click the Format Painter button again or press ESC to deactivate it.

To Format the What-If Assumptions Table

The following steps format the Hotel Assumptions table, the final step in improving the appearance of the worksheet.

1. Select range J3:K3.
2. Apply the Heading 2 cell style to the selected range.
3. Merge & Center the selected range.
4. Change the width of column J to best fit.
5. Select the range J3:K11 and then click the Fill Color button (Home tab | Font group) to apply the fill color Green, Accent 1, Lighter 80%
6. Deselect the range J3:K11 and display the Hotel Assumptions table, as shown in Figure 3-53.
7. Save the workbook on the same storage location with the same file name.

BTW
Selecting Nonadjacent Ranges
One of the more difficult tasks to learn is selecting nonadjacent ranges. To complete this task, do not hold down CTRL when you select the first range because Excel will consider the current active cell to be the first selection, and you may not want the current active cell in the selection. Once the first range is selected, hold down CTRL and drag through the nonadjacent ranges. If a desired range is not visible in the window, use the scroll arrows to view the range. You need not hold down CTRL while you scroll.

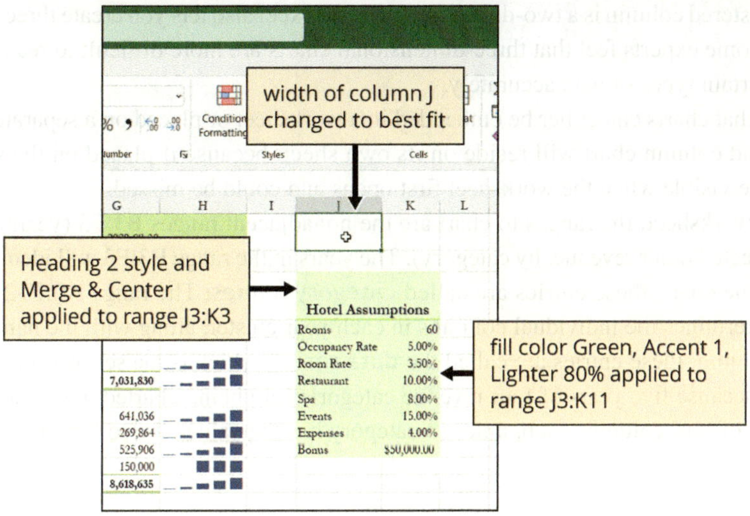

Figure 3–53

Break Point: If you want to take a break, this is a good place to do so. You can exit Excel now. To resume later, start Excel, open the file called SC_EX_3_Hotel, and continue following the steps from this location forward.

Adding a Clustered Column Chart to the Workbook

The next step in the module is to create a clustered column chart on a separate sheet in the workbook, as shown in Figure 3–54, that shows the Restaurant, Spa, and Events Revenue. Use a clustered column chart to compare values side by side, broken down by category. Each column shows the value for a particular category, by year in this case.

The clustered column chart in Figure 3–54 shows the projected other revenue amounts, by category, for each of the five years. The clustered column chart allows the user to see how the various expense categories compare with each other each month, and across months.

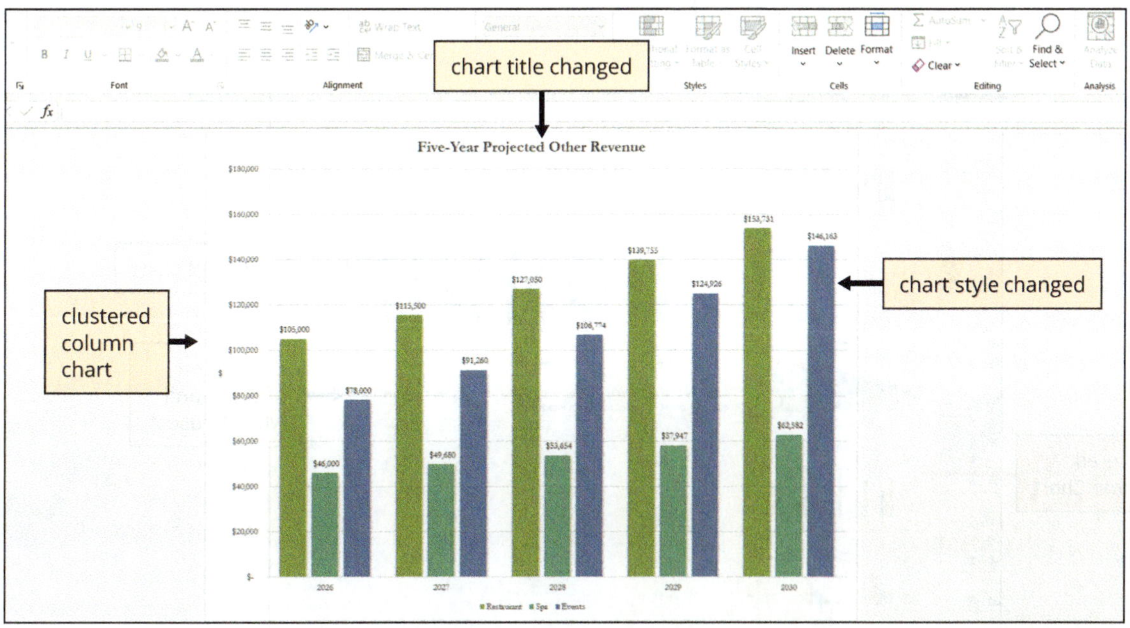

Figure 3–54

BTW
Charts
When you change a value on which a chart is dependent, Excel immediately redraws the chart based on the new value.

BTW
Chart Items
When you rest the pointer over a chart item, such as a legend, bar, or axis, Excel displays a chart tip containing the name of the item.

The clustered column is a two-dimensional chart. Excel also lets you create three-dimensional charts, but some experts feel that three-dimensional charts are more difficult to read and may not represent certain types of data accurately.

Recall that charts can either be embedded in a worksheet or placed on a separate chart sheet. The clustered column chart will reside on its own sheet, because if placed on the worksheet, it would not be visible when the worksheet first opens and could be missed.

In this worksheet, the ranges to chart are the nonadjacent ranges B3:F3 (years) and A9:F12 (yearly projected other revenue, by category). The years in the range B3:F3 will identify the major groups for the chart; these entries are called **category names**. The range A9:F12 contains the data that determines the individual columns in each year cluster, along with the names that identify each column; these entries are called the **data series**, which is the set of values represented in a chart. Because five years of four revenue categories are being charted, the chart will contain five clusters of four columns each, unless a category has the value of zero for a given year.

To Draw a Clustered Column Chart on a Separate Chart Sheet Using the Recommended Charts Feature

Why? This Excel feature evaluates the selected data and makes suggestions regarding which chart types will provide the most suitable representation. The following steps use the Recommended Charts feature to draw the clustered column chart on a separate chart sheet.

1

- Select the range A3:F3 to identify the range of the categories.
- Hold down CTRL and select the data range A9:F12.
- Display the Insert tab.
- Click the Recommended Charts button (Insert tab | Charts group) to display the Insert Chart dialog box with the Recommended Charts tab active (Figure 3–55).
- **Experiment:** Click the various recommended chart types, reading the description for each of its best use and examining the chart preview.

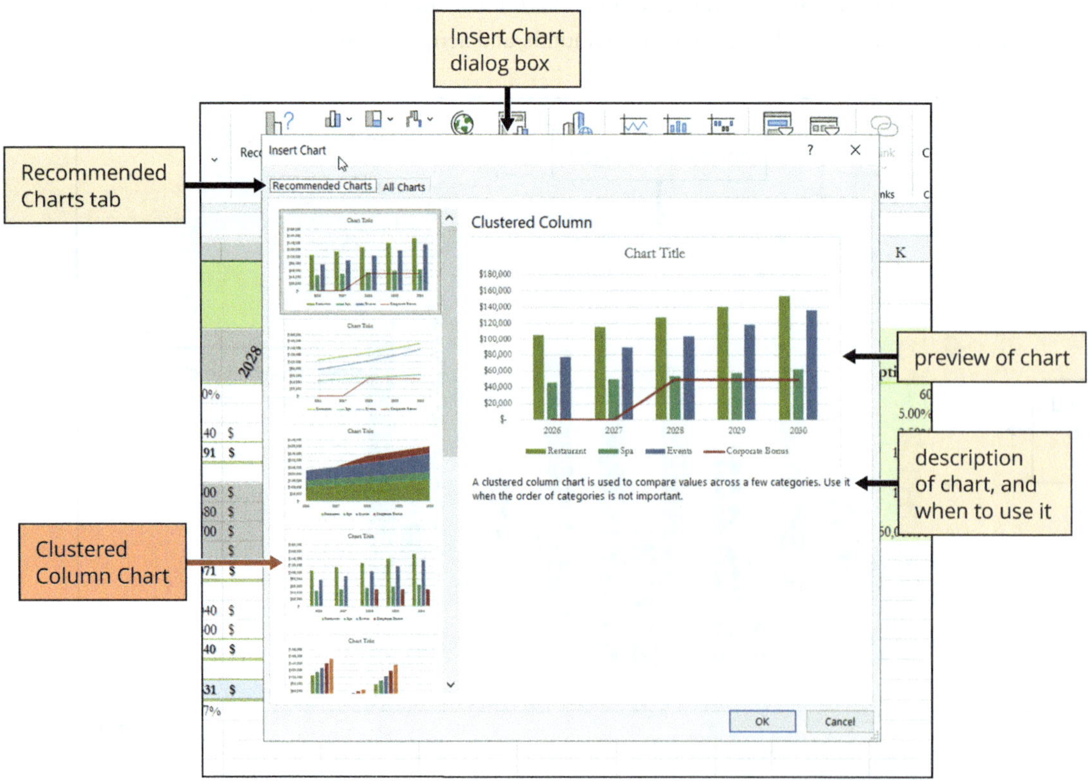

Figure 3–55

2

- Click the Clustered Column recommended chart that has all four categories displayed as columns to select it and then click OK (Insert Chart dialog box).
- After Excel draws the chart, click the Move Chart button (Chart Design tab | Location group) to display the Move Chart dialog box.
- Click the New sheet option button (Move Chart dialog box) and then type **Other Revenue Chart** in the New sheet text box to enter a sheet tab name for the chart sheet (Figure 3–56).

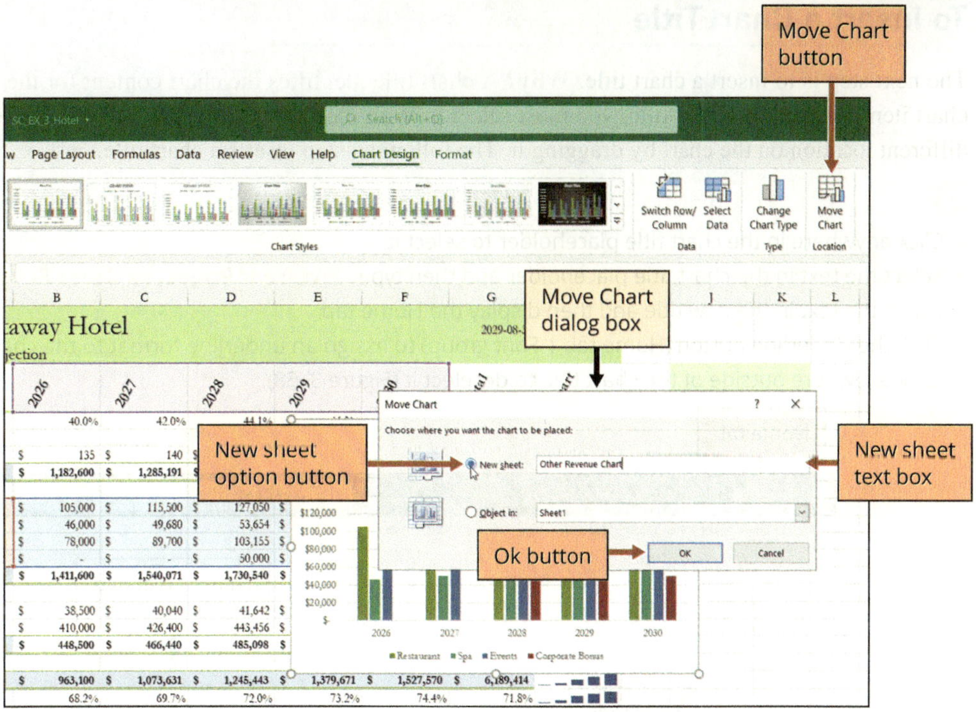

Figure 3–56

3

- Click OK (Move Chart dialog box) to move the chart to a new chart sheet with a new sheet tab name, Expense Chart Sheet (Figure 3–57).

Q&A Why do 2026 and 2027 have only three columns charted?
2026 and 2027 have a value of $0 for the Corporate Bonus category. Values of zero are not charted in a column chart, so these two years have one fewer column than the other years.

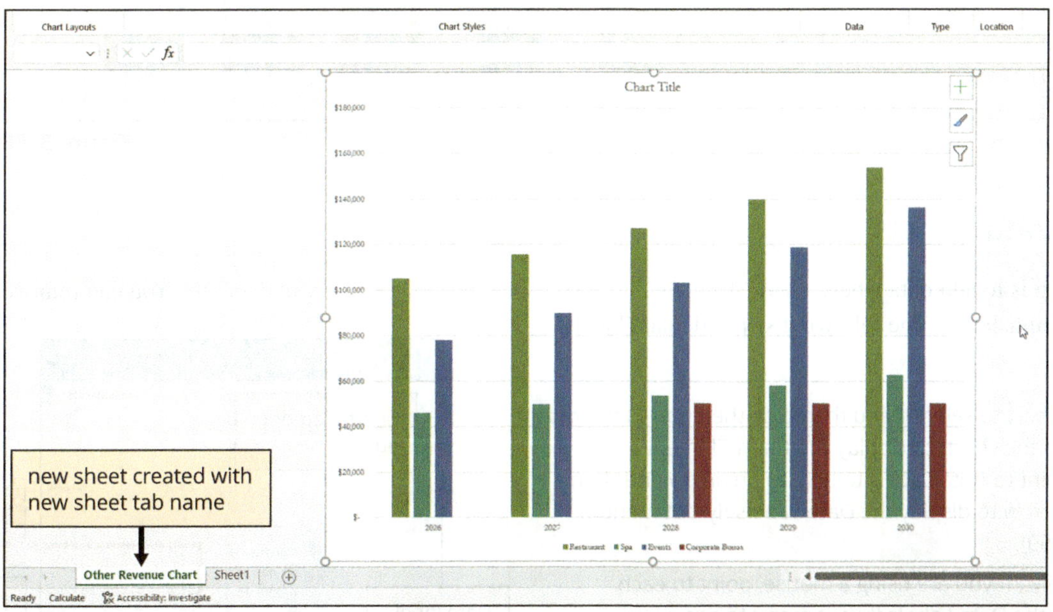

Figure 3–57

Other Ways

1. Select range to chart, press F11

To Insert a Chart Title

The next step is to insert a chart title. **Why?** A chart title identifies the chart content for the viewer. Before you can format a chart item, such as the chart title, you must select it. With the chart title or other chart element selected, you can move it to a different location on the chart by dragging it. The following step inserts a chart title.

1

- Click anywhere in the chart title placeholder to select it.
- Select the text in the chart title placeholder and then type **Five-Year Projected Other Revenue** to add a new chart title.
- Select the text in the new title and then display the Home tab.
- Click the Underline button (Home tab | Font group) to assign an underline format to the chart title.
- Click anywhere outside of the chart title to deselect it (Figure 3–58).

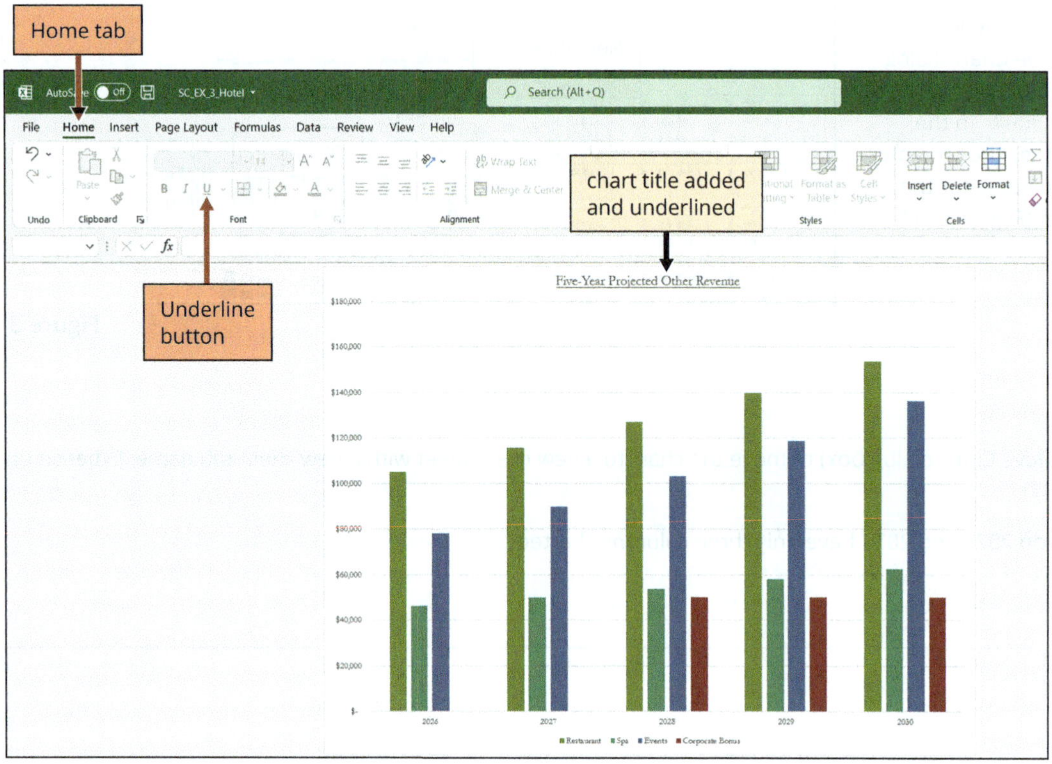

Figure 3–58

To Add Data Labels

The next step is to add data labels. **Why?** Data labels can make a chart more easily understood. You can remove them if they do not accomplish that. The following steps add data labels.

1

- Click the chart to select it and then click the Chart Elements button (on the chart) to display the Chart Elements gallery. Point to Data Labels to display an arrow and then click the arrow to display the Data Labels fly-out menu (Figure 3–59).
- **Experiment:** If you are using a mouse, point to each option on the Data Labels fly-out menu to see a live preview of the data labels.

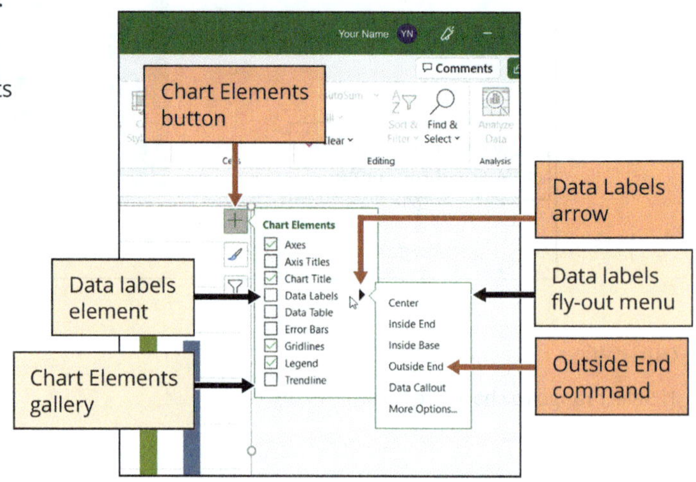

Figure 3–59

2

- Click Outside End on the Data Labels fly-out menu so that data labels are displayed outside the chart at the end of each column.
- Click the Chart Elements button to close the gallery (Figure 3–60).

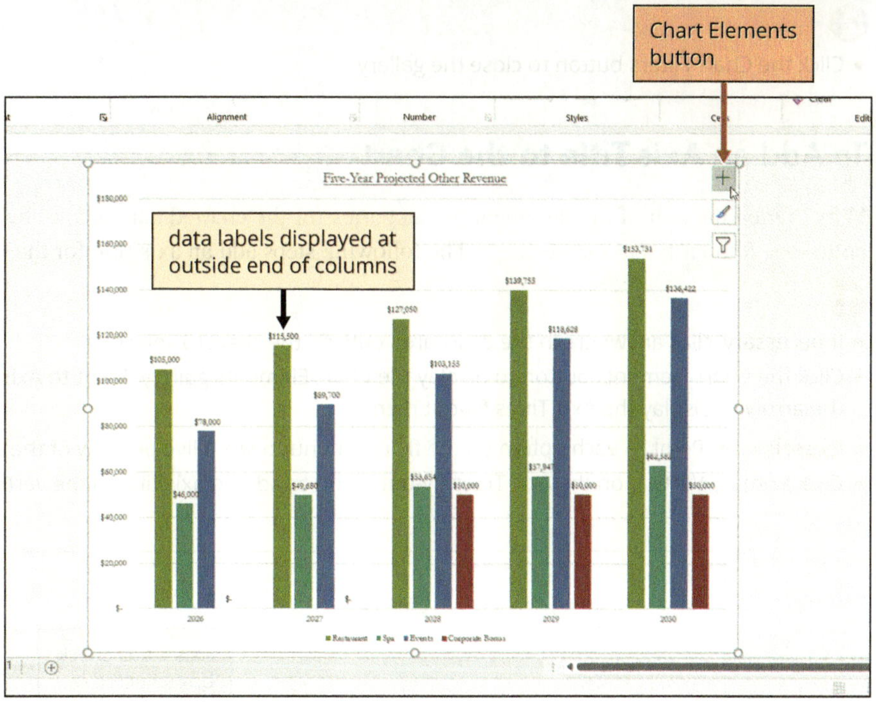

Figure 3–60

To Apply Chart Filters

Why? With some data, you may find that certain data series or categories make it difficult to examine differences and patterns between other series or categories. Excel allows you to easily filter data series and categories to allow more in-depth examinations of subsets of data. In this case, filters can be used to temporarily remove the Corporate Bonus category from the chart, to allow a comparison across the non-bonus other revenue. The following steps apply filters to the clustered column chart.

1

- Click the Chart Filters button (on the chart) to display the Chart Filters gallery.
- In the Series section, click the Corporate Bonus check box to remove the check mark and then click the Apply button to filter the series from the chart (Figure 3–61).

Q&A What happens when I remove the check marks from Corporate Bonus?
When you remove the check marks from Corporate Bonus, Excel filters the Corporate Bonus series out and redraws the chart without it.

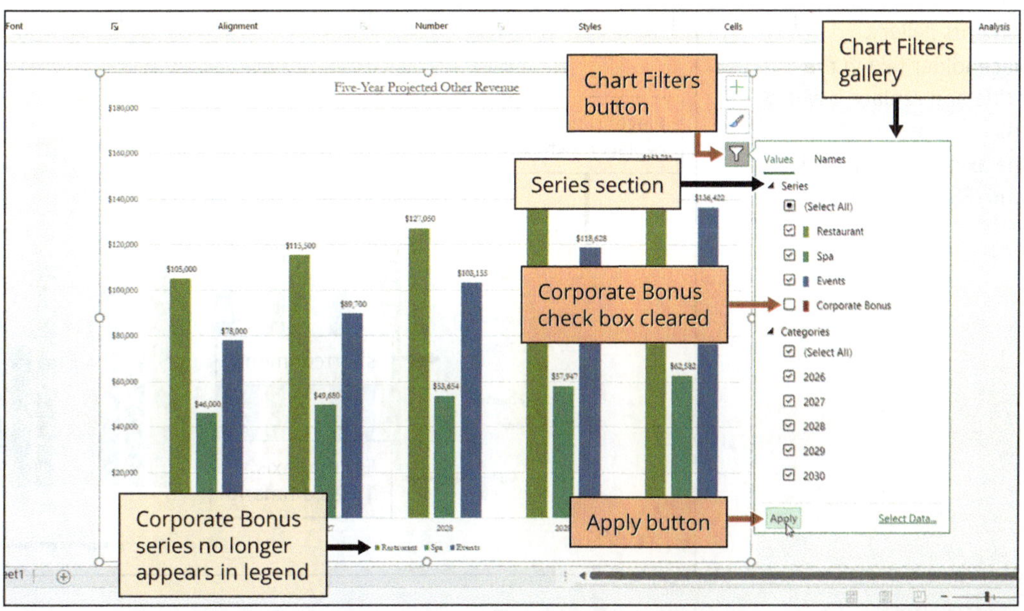

Figure 3–61

2

- Click the Chart Filters button to close the gallery.

To Add an Axis Title to the Chart

Why? Often the unit of measurement or categories for the charted data is not obvious. You can add an axis title, or titles for both axes, for clarity or completeness. The following steps add an axis title for the vertical axis.

1

- If necessary, click anywhere in the chart area outside the chart to select it.
- Click the Chart Elements button to display the Chart Elements gallery. Point to Axis Titles to display an arrow and then click the arrow to display the Axis Titles fly-out menu.
- **Experiment:** Point to each option on the fly-out menu to see a live preview of the axes' titles.
- Click Primary Vertical on the Axis Titles fly-out menu to add an axis title to the vertical axis (Figure 3–62).

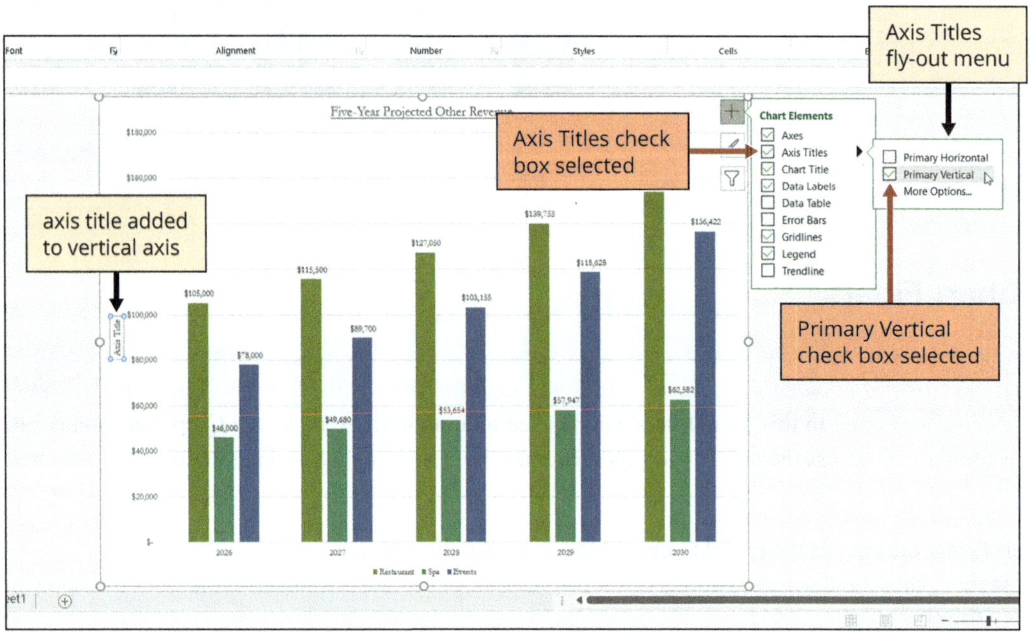

Figure 3–62

2

- Click the Chart Elements button to close the Chart Elements gallery.
- Select the placeholder text in the vertical axis title and replace it with $ (a dollar sign).
- Right-click the axis title to display a shortcut menu (Figure 3–63).

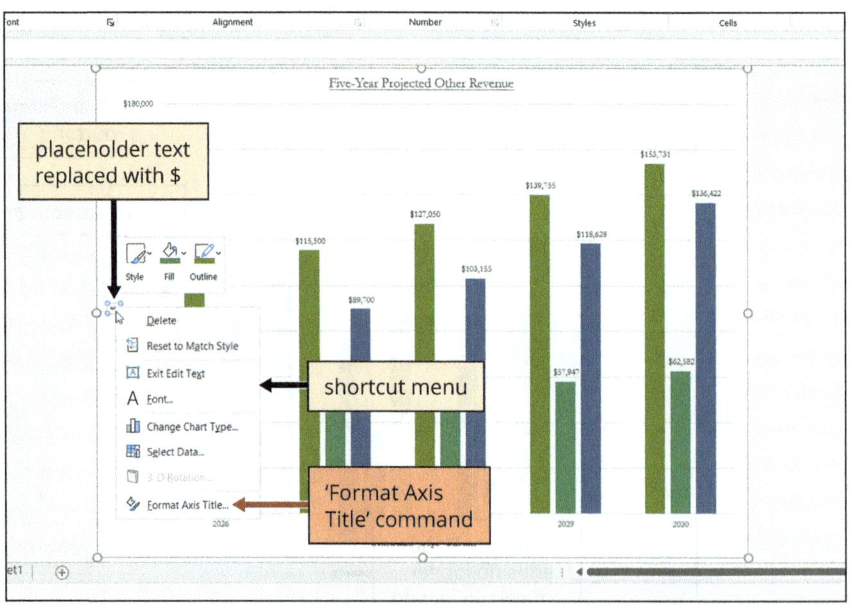

Figure 3–63

3

- Click 'Format Axis Title' on the shortcut menu to open the Format Axis Title pane.
- If necessary, click the Title Options tab, click the 'Size & Properties' button, and then, if necessary, click the Alignment arrow to expand the Alignment section.
- Click the Text direction arrow to display the Text direction list (Figure 3-64).
- Click Horizontal in the Text direction list to change the orientation of the vertical axis title.
- Click the Close button (shown in Figure 3-64) on the pane to close the Format Axis Title pane.

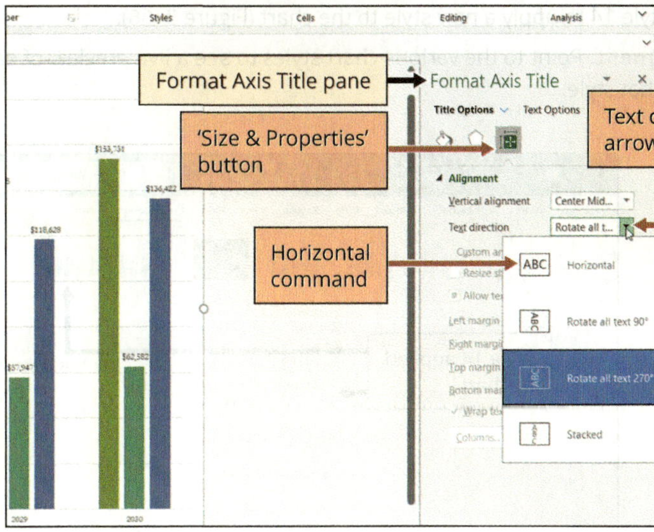

Figure 3-64

To Change the Chart Style

Why? You decide that a chart with a different look would better convey meaning to viewers. The following steps change the chart style.

1

- Display the Chart Design tab and then click the More button (Chart Design tab | Chart Styles group) to display the Chart Styles gallery (Figure 3-65).

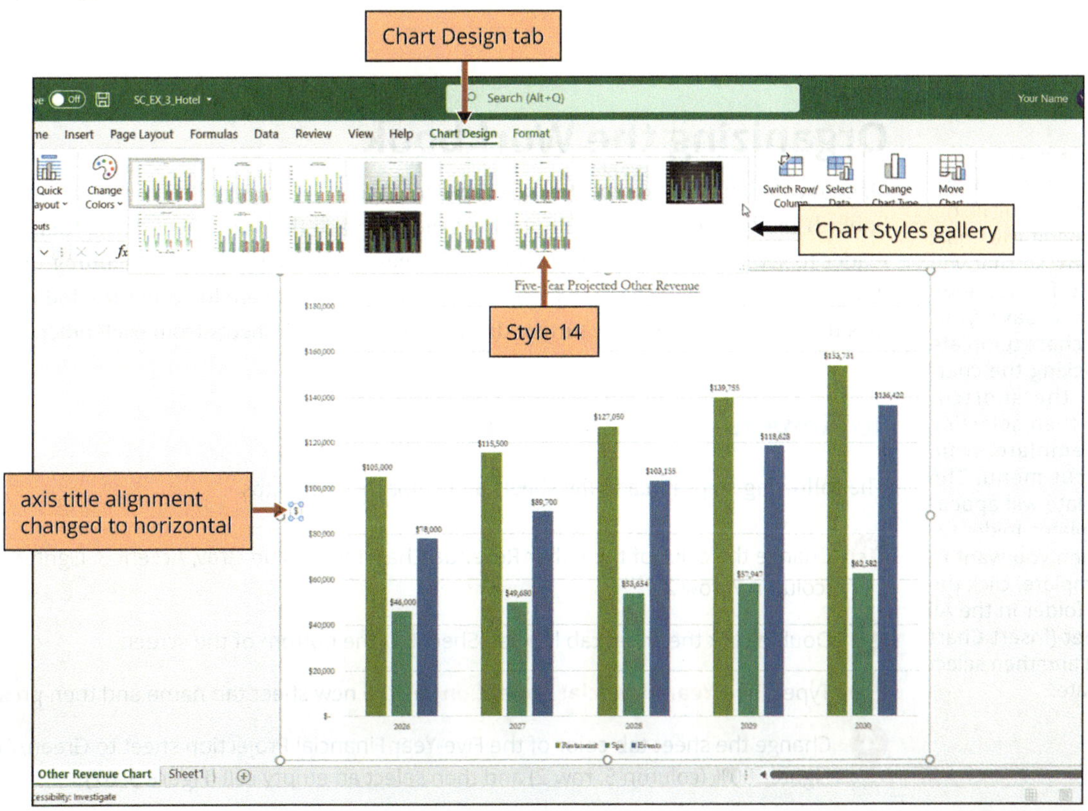

Figure 3-65

2

- Click Style 14 to apply a new style to the chart (Figure 3–66).
- **Experiment:** Point to the various chart styles to see a live preview of each one. When you have finished, click Style 14 to apply that style.

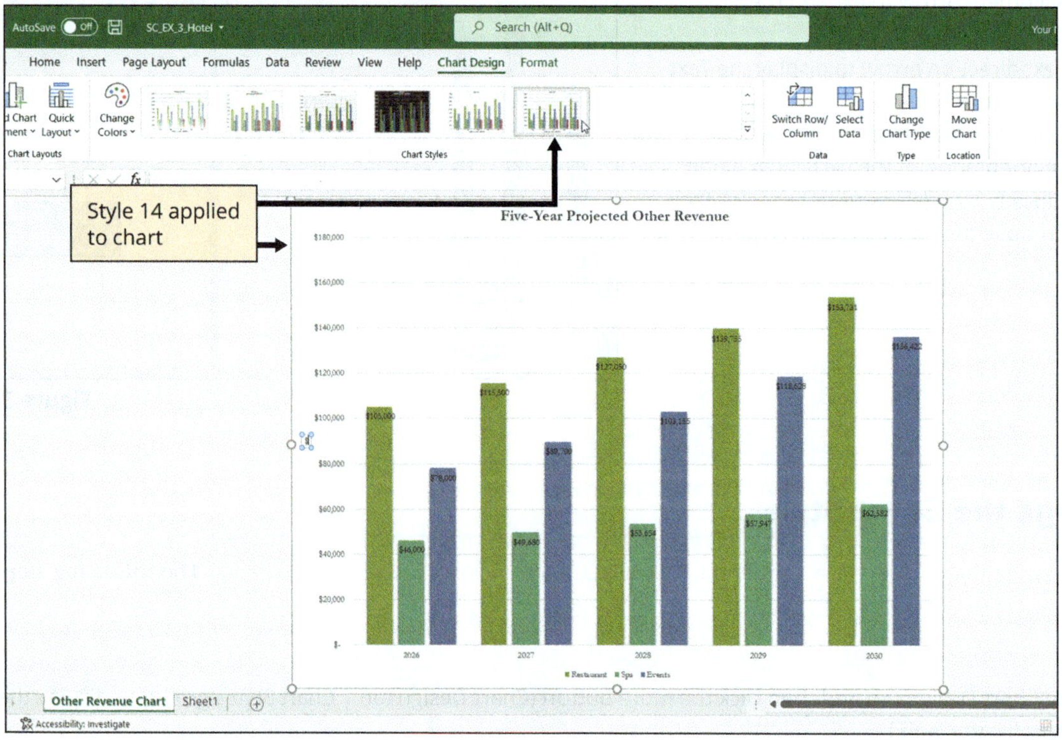

Figure 3–66

BTW
Chart Templates
Once you create and format a chart to your liking, consider saving the chart as a template so that you can use it to format additional charts. Save your chart as a chart template by right-clicking the chart to display the shortcut menu and then selecting 'Save as Template' from that shortcut menu. The chart template will appear in the Templates folder for Charts. When you want to use the template, click the Templates folder in the All Charts sheet (Insert Chart dialog box) and then select your template.

Organizing the Workbook

Once the content of the workbook is complete, you can address the organization of the workbook. If the workbook has multiple worksheets, place the worksheet on top that you want the reader to see first. Default sheet names in Excel are not descriptive. Renaming the sheets with descriptive names helps the reader find information that they are looking for. Modifying the sheet tabs through the use of color further distinguishes multiple sheets from each other.

To Rename and Color Sheet Tabs

The following steps rename the sheets and color the sheet tabs.

1. Change the color of the Other Revenue Chart tab to Blue-Gray, Accent 3. Lighter 80% (column 7, row 2).
2. Double-click the sheet tab labeled Sheet1 at the bottom of the screen.
3. Type **Five-Year Financial Projection** as the new sheet tab name and then press ENTER.
4. Change the sheet tab color of the Five-Year Financial Projection sheet to Green, Accent 1, Lighter 80% (column 5, row 2) and then select an empty cell (Figure 3–67).

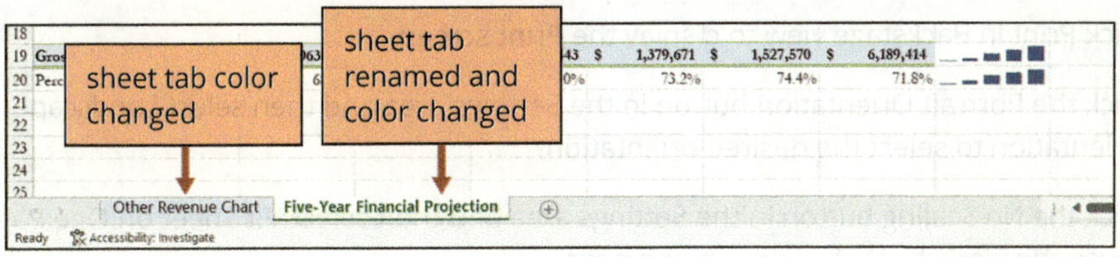

Figure 3–67

To Reorder the Sheet Tabs

Why? You want the most important worksheets to appear first in a workbook, so you need to change the order of sheets. The following step reorders the sheets so that the worksheet precedes the chart sheet in the workbook.

1

- Drag the Five-Year Financial Projection tab to the left so that it precedes the Other Revenue Chart tab to rearrange the sequence of the sheets (Figure 3–68).

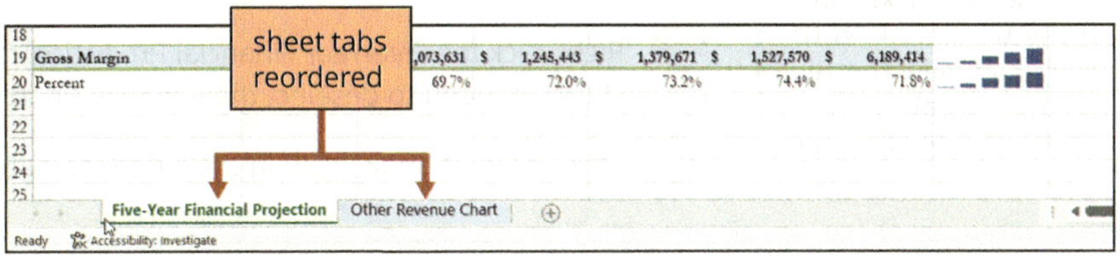

Figure 3–68

Other Ways

1. To move sheet, right-click sheet tab, click Move or Copy on shortcut menu, click OK

To Check Spelling in Multiple Sheets

By default, the spelling checker reviews spelling only in the selected sheets. It will check all the cells in the selected sheets unless you select a range of two or more cells. Before checking the spelling, the following steps select both worksheets in the workbook so that both are checked for any spelling errors.

BTW
Checking Spelling
Unless you first select a range of cells or an object before starting the spelling checker, Excel checks the entire selected worksheet, including all cell values, cell comments, embedded charts, text boxes, buttons, and headers and footers.

1. With the Five-Year Financial Projection sheet active, press CTRL+HOME to select cell A1. Hold down CTRL and click the Other Revenue Chart tab to select both sheets (continue to hold down CTRL.).
2. Display the Review tab and then click the Spelling button (Review tab | Proofing group) to check spelling in the selected sheets.
3. Correct any errors and then click OK (Spelling dialog box or Microsoft Excel dialog box) when the spelling checker is finished.

To Preview and Print the Worksheet

After checking the spelling, the next step is to preview and print the worksheets. As with spelling, Excel previews and prints only the selected sheets. In addition, because the worksheet is too wide to print in portrait orientation, the orientation must be changed to landscape. The following steps adjust the orientation and scale, preview the worksheets, and then print the worksheets.

1. If both sheets are not selected, hold down CTRL and then click the tab of the inactive sheet.
2. Click File on the ribbon to open Backstage view.

BTW
Distributing a Workbook
Instead of printing and distributing a hard copy of a workbook, you can distribute the workbook electronically. Options include sending the workbook via email; posting it on cloud storage (such as OneDrive) and sharing the file with others; posting it on social media, a blog, or other website; and sharing a link associated with an online location of the workbook. You also can create and share a PDF or XPS image of the workbook, so that users can view the file in Acrobat Reader or XPS Viewer instead of in Excel.

3. Click Print in Backstage view to display the Print screen.
4. Click the Portrait Orientation button in the Settings area and then select Landscape Orientation to select the desired orientation.
5. Click the No Scaling button in the Settings area and then select 'Fit Sheet on One Page' to cause the worksheets to print on one page.
6. Verify that the desired printer is selected. If necessary, click the printer button to display a list of available printer options and then click the desired printer to change the currently selected printer.
7. Click the Print button in the Print gallery to print the worksheet in landscape orientation on the currently selected printer.
8. When the printer stops, retrieve the printed worksheets (shown in Figure 3–69a and Figure 3–69b).
9. Right-click the Five-Year Financial Projection tab, and then click Ungroup Sheets on the shortcut menu to deselect the Expense Chart Sheet tab.
10. Save the workbook again in the same storage location with the same file name.

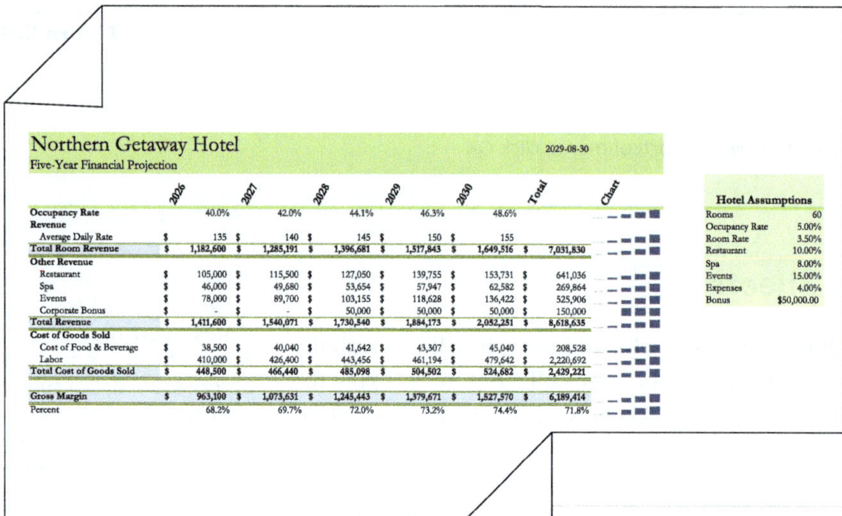
Northern Getaway Hotel 2029-08-30
Five-Year Financial Projection

	2026	2027	2028	2029	2030	Total	Chart
Occupancy Rate	40.0%	42.0%	44.1%	46.3%	48.6%		
Revenue							
Average Daily Rate	$ 135	$ 140	$ 145	$ 150	$ 155		
Total Room Revenue	$ 1,182,600	$ 1,285,191	$ 1,396,681	$ 1,517,843	$ 1,649,516	$ 7,031,830	
Other Revenue							
Restaurant	$ 105,000	$ 115,500	$ 127,050	$ 139,755	$ 153,731	$ 641,036	
Spa	$ 46,000	$ 49,680	$ 53,654	$ 57,947	$ 62,582	$ 269,864	
Events	$ 78,000	$ 89,700	$ 103,155	$ 118,628	$ 136,422	$ 525,906	
Corporate Bonus	$ -	$ -	$ 50,000	$ 50,000	$ 50,000	$ 150,000	
Total Revenue	$ 1,411,600	$ 1,540,071	$ 1,730,540	$ 1,884,173	$ 2,052,251	$ 8,618,635	
Cost of Goods Sold							
Cost of Food & Beverage	$ 38,500	$ 40,040	$ 41,642	$ 43,307	$ 45,040	$ 208,528	
Labor	$ 410,000	$ 426,400	$ 443,456	$ 461,194	$ 479,642	$ 2,220,692	
Total Cost of Goods Sold	$ 448,500	$ 466,440	$ 485,098	$ 504,502	$ 524,682	$ 2,429,221	
Gross Margin	$ 963,100	$ 1,073,631	$ 1,245,443	$ 1,379,671	$ 1,527,570	$ 6,189,414	
Percent	68.2%	69.7%	72.0%	73.2%	74.4%	71.8%	

Hotel Assumptions	
Rooms	60
Occupancy Rate	5.00%
Room Rate	3.50%
Restaurant	10.00%
Spa	8.00%
Events	15.00%
Expenses	4.00%
Bonus	$50,000.00

Figure 3–69(a)

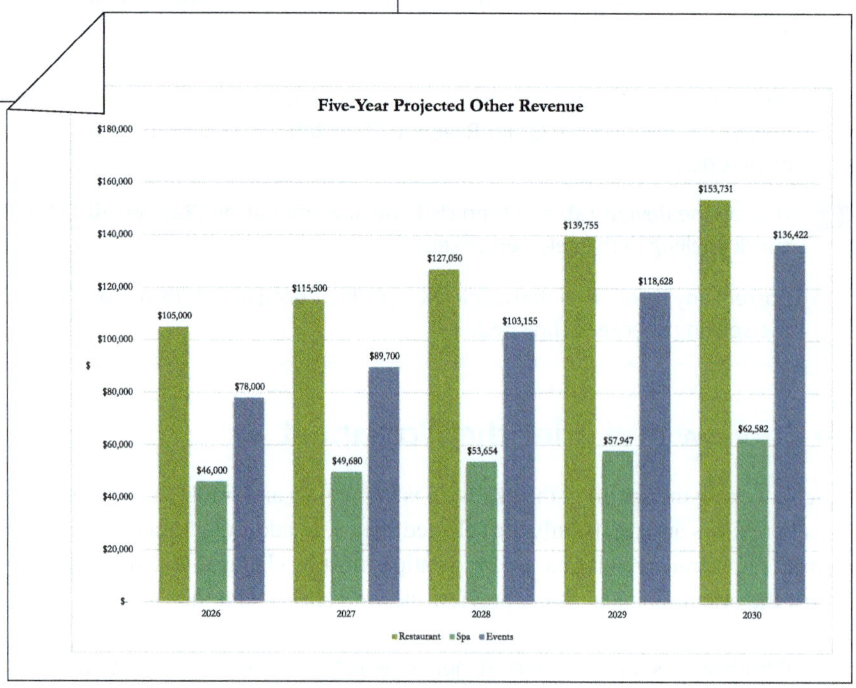

Figure 3–69(b)

Changing the View of the Worksheet

With Excel, you easily can change the view of the worksheet. For example, you can magnify or shrink the view of the worksheet on the screen. Magnifying or shrinking the view does not affect the printed worksheet. You also can view different parts of the worksheet at the same time by using panes.

To Shrink and Magnify the View of a Worksheet or Chart

You can magnify (zoom in) or shrink (zoom out) the appearance of a worksheet or chart by using the Zoom button (View tab | Zoom group). **Why?** When you magnify a worksheet, Excel enlarges the view of the characters on the screen but shows fewer columns and rows. Alternatively, when you shrink a worksheet, Excel is able to display more columns and rows. Magnifying or shrinking a worksheet affects only the view; it does not change the window size or the size of the text on the worksheet or chart or the appearance of the printed document. If you have a range of cells selected, you can click the 'Zoom to Selection' button (View tab | Zoom group) to zoom the worksheet so that the selected range fills the entire window. The following steps shrink and magnify the view of the worksheet.

1

- If cell A1 is not active, press CTRL+HOME.
- Display the View tab and then click the Zoom button (View tab | Zoom group) to display a list of magnifications in the Zoom dialog box (Figure 3–70).

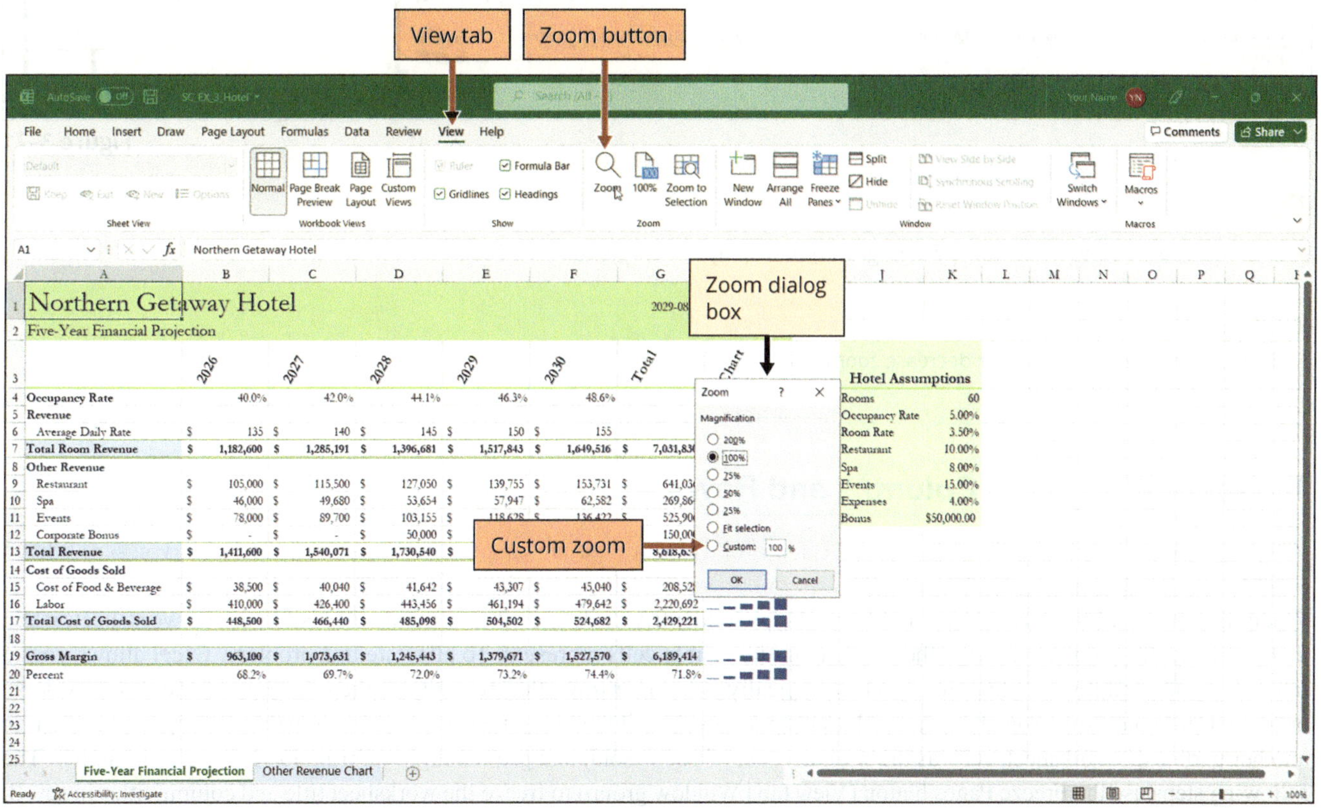

Figure 3–70

2

- Select Custom, type 115 in the percent box, and then click OK (Zoom dialog box) to magnify the display of the worksheet (Figure 3–71). The number of columns and rows appearing on your screen may differ from Figure 3–71.

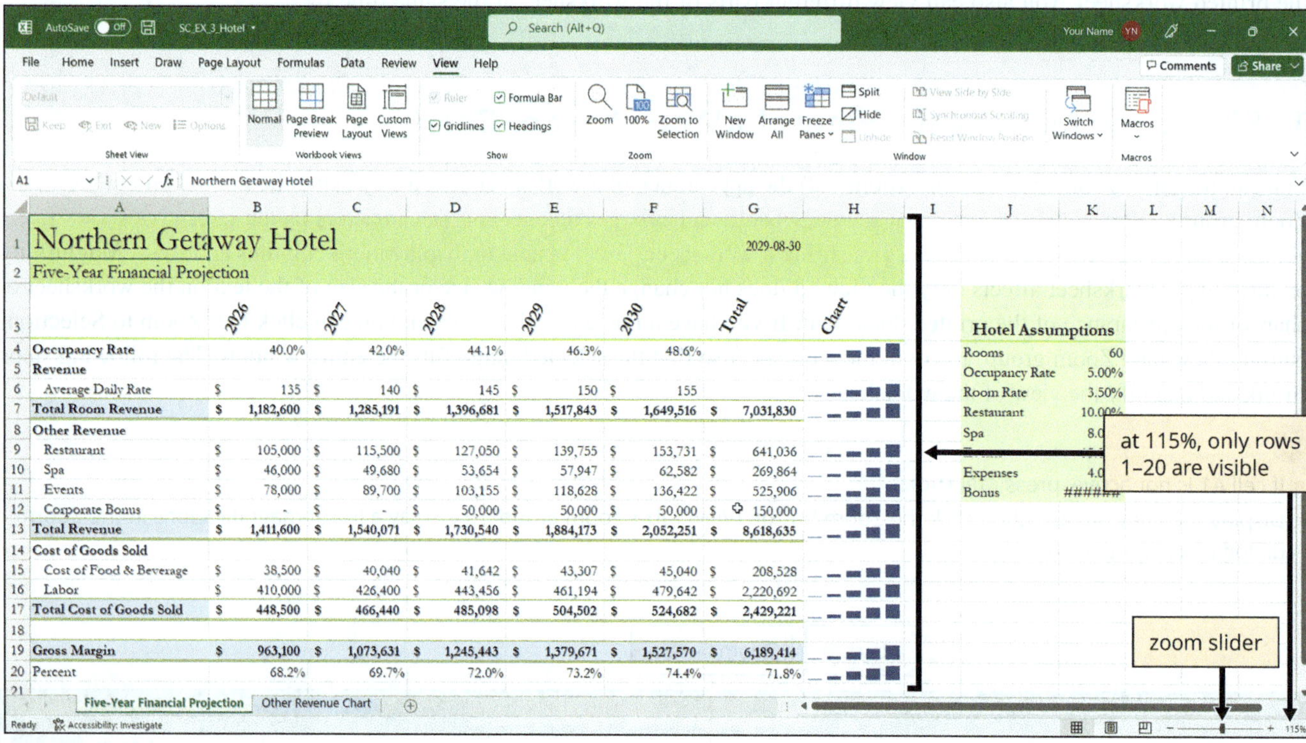

Figure 3–71

3

- Click the 100% button (View tab | Zoom group) to display the worksheet at 100%.

Other Ways

1. Drag zoom slider to increase or decrease zoom level

To Freeze Worksheet Columns and Rows

Why? Freezing worksheet columns and rows is a useful technique for viewing worksheets. Normally, when you scroll down or to the right, the column content in the top rows and the row content in the leftmost columns no longer appear on the screen. When the content of these rows and/or columns helps to identify or define other content still visible on the worksheet, it can make it difficult to remember what the numbers in the visible cells represent. To alleviate this problem, Excel allows you to freeze columns and rows, so that their content, typically column or row titles, remains on the screen, no matter how far down or to the right you scroll. You also may wish to keep numbers visible that you need to see when making changes to content in another part of the worksheet, such as the revenue, cost of goods sold, and gross margin information in rows 4 through 6. The following steps use the Freeze Panes button (View tab | Window group) to freeze the worksheet title and column titles in row 3, and the row titles in column A.

1

- Scroll the worksheet until Excel displays row 3 at the top of the worksheet window and column A as the first column on the screen.
- Select cell B4 as the cell on which to freeze panes.
- Click the Freeze Panes button (View tab | Window group) to display the Freeze Panes gallery (Figure 3–72).

Q&A Why should I ensure that row 3 is the first row visible?
Before freezing the titles, it is important to align the first row that you want frozen with the top of the worksheet. For example, if you used the Freeze Panes button in cell B4 while displaying row 1, then Excel would freeze and display the worksheet title and subtitle, leaving only a few rows of data visible in the Five-Year Financial Projection area of the worksheet. To ensure that you can view as much data as possible, always scroll to a row that maximizes the view of your important data before freezing panes.

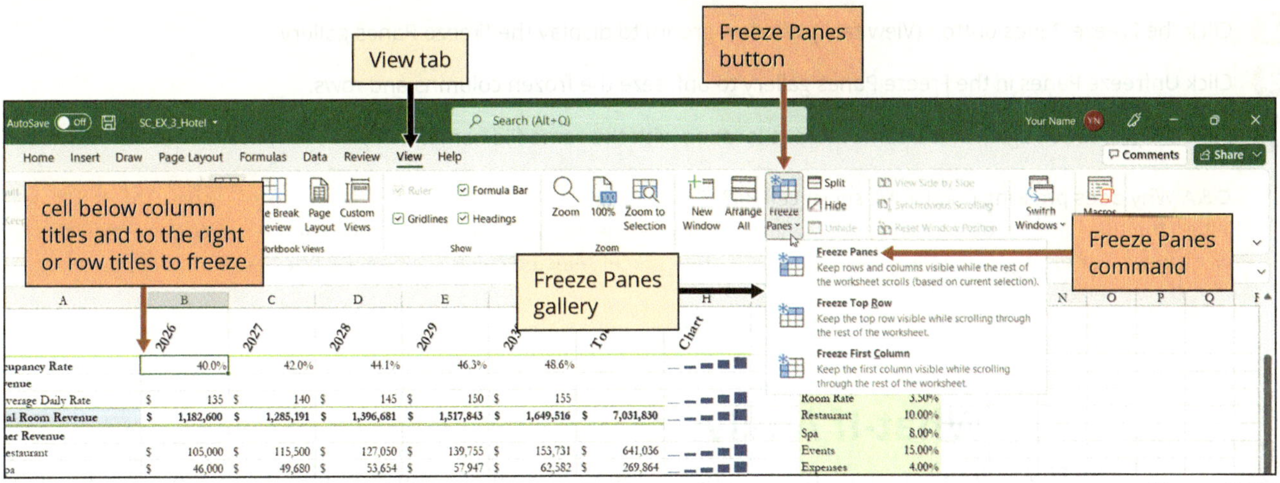

Figure 3–72

2

- Click Freeze Panes in the Freeze Panes gallery to freeze rows and columns to the left and above the selected cell, column A and row 3 in this case.
- Scroll down in the worksheet until row 8 is displayed directly below row 3 (Figure 3–73).

Q&A What happens after I click the Freeze Panes command?
Excel displays a thin, dark gray line on the right side of column A, indicating the split between the frozen row titles in column A and the rest of the worksheet. It also displays a thin, dark gray line below row 3, indicating the split between the frozen column titles in row 3 and the rest of the worksheet. Scrolling down or to the right in the worksheet will not scroll the content of row 3 or column A off the screen (Figure 3–73).

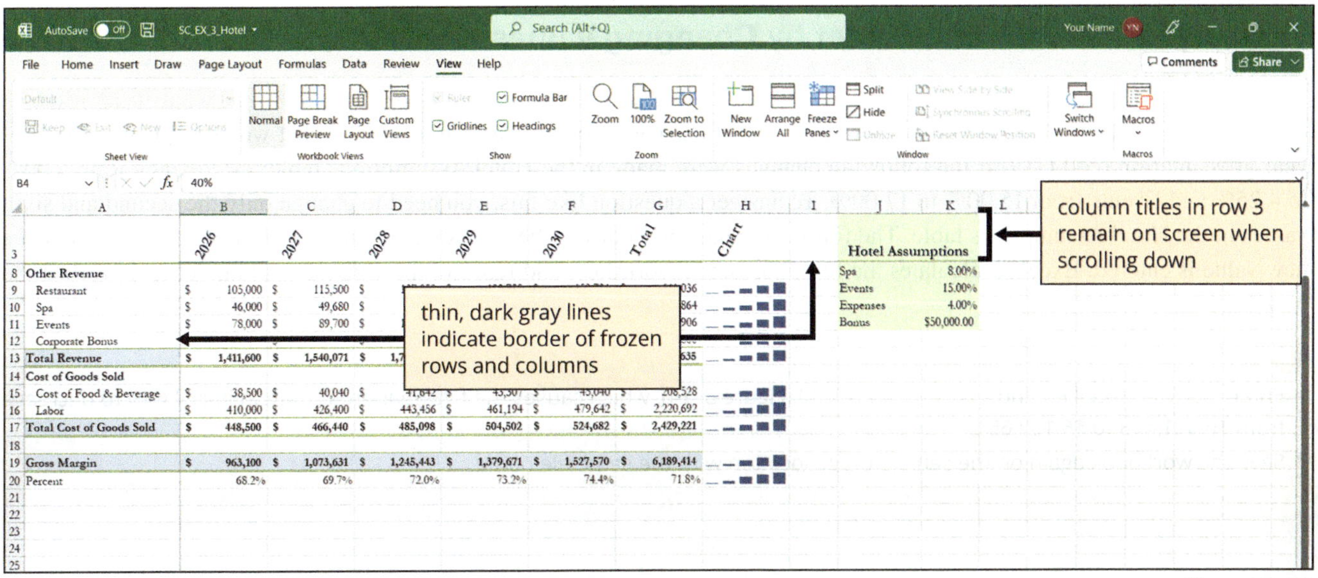

Figure 3–73

To Unfreeze the Worksheet Columns and Rows

Why? When you no longer need to view frozen columns and rows at all times, you should unfreeze them so that all columns and rows are displayed. The following steps unfreeze the titles in column A and row 3 to allow you to work with the worksheet without frozen rows and columns, or to freeze the worksheet at a different location.

1. Press CTRL+HOME to select cell B4 and view the upper-left corner of the screen.
2. Click the Freeze Panes button (View tab | Window group) to display the Freeze Panes gallery.
3. Click Unfreeze Panes in the Freeze Panes gallery to unfreeze the frozen columns and rows.
4. Save the workbook again in the same storage location with the same file name.

Q&A Why does pressing CTRL+HOME select cell B4?
When the titles are frozen and you press CTRL+HOME, Excel selects the upper-leftmost cell of the unfrozen section of the worksheet. For example, in Step 1 of the previous steps, Excel selected cell B4. When the titles are unfrozen, pressing CTRL+HOME selects cell A1.

BTW
Freezing Titles
If you want to freeze only column headings, select the appropriate cell in column A before you click the Freeze Panes button (View tab | Window group). If you want to freeze only row titles, select the appropriate cell in row 1 before you click the Freeze Panes button. To freeze both column headings and row titles, select the cell that is the intersection of the column and row titles before you click the Freeze Panes button.

What-If Analysis

The automatic recalculation feature of Excel is a powerful tool that can be used to analyze worksheet data. **What-if analysis** is a decision-making tool in which changing input values recalculate formulas, in order to predict various possible outcomes. When new data is entered, Excel not only recalculates all formulas in a worksheet but also redraws any associated charts.

In the workbook created in this module, many of the formulas are dependent on the assumptions in the range K4:K11. Thus, if you change any of the assumption values, Excel recalculates all formulas. Excel redraws the clustered column chart as well because it is based on these numbers.

To Analyze Data in a Worksheet by Changing Values

Why? The effect of changing one or more values in the Hotel Assumptions table—essentially posing what-if questions—allows you to review the results of different scenarios. In this case, you are going to examine what would happen to the five-year gross margin (cell G19) if the following changes were made in the Hotel Assumptions table: Occupancy Rate 5.00% to 4.25% and Events from 15.00% to 17.00%. To answer a question like this, you need to change only the second and sixth values in the Hotel Assumptions table. The following changes values in the worksheet to answer a what-if question. When a new value is entered, Excel recalculates the formulas in the worksheet and redraws the clustered column chart to reflect the new data.

1

- Enter **4.25%** in cell K5 and **17.00%** in cell K9 (Figure 3–74), which causes the five-year gross margin in cell G19 to decrease from $6,081,433 to $6,152,651.
- Save the workbook again on the same storage location with the same file name.

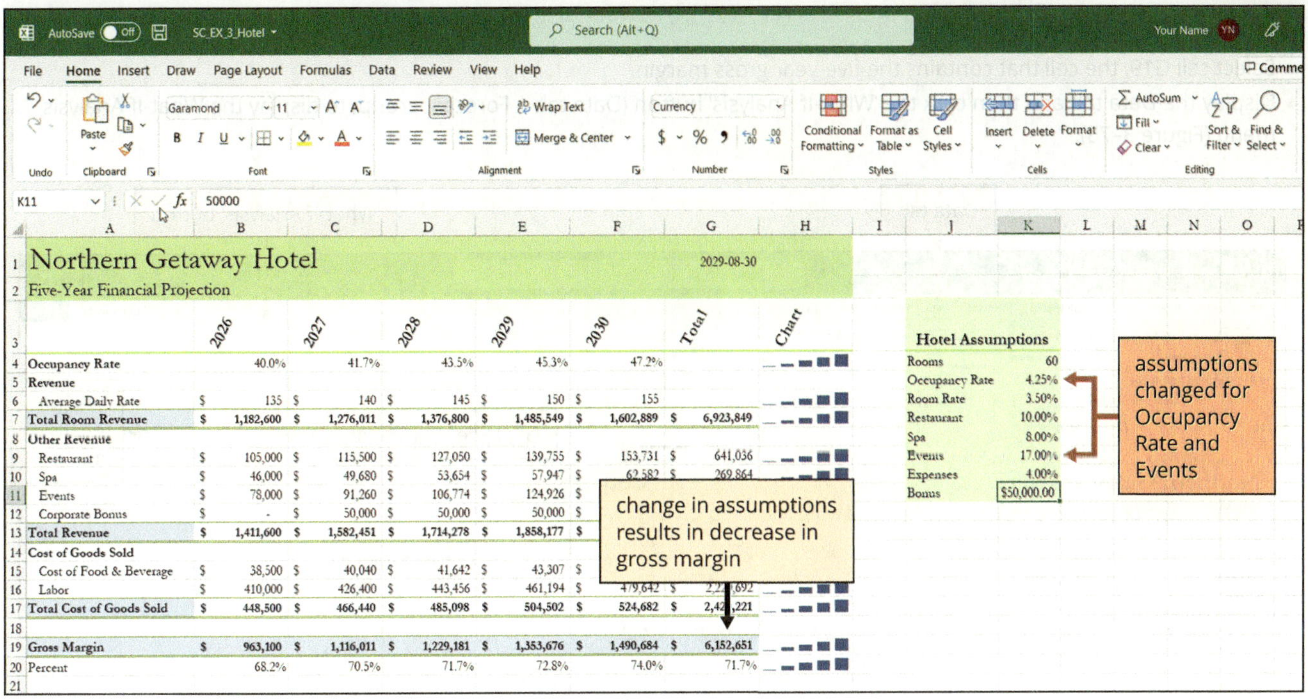

Figure 3–74

Goal Seeking

Goal seek is a problem-solving method in which you specify a solution and then find the input value that produces the answer you want. In this example, to change the five-year gross margin in cell G19 to $6,500,000.00, the Occupancy Rate percentage in cell K5 must increase by 3.69% from 4.25% to 7.94%.

You can see from this goal seeking example that the cell to change (cell K5) does not have to be referenced directly in the formula or function. For example, the five-year gross margin in cell G19 is calculated by the function =SUM(B19:F19). Cell K5 is not referenced in this function. Instead, cell K5 is referenced in the formulas in row 4, on which the total room revenue in row 7 are based. By tracing the formulas and functions, Excel can obtain the desired five-year gross margin by varying the value for the Occupancy Rate assumption.

To Goal Seek

Why? If you know the result you want a formula to produce, you can use goal seeking to determine the value of a cell on which the formula depends. The previous step, which made changes to the Hotel Assumptions table, resulted in a gross margin that approaches but does not reach $6,500,000. The following steps use the Goal Seek command (Data tab | Forecast group) to determine what Occupancy Rate (cell K5), in conjunction with the earlier changes in assumptions, will yield a five-year gross margin of $6,500,000 in cell G19, rather than the $6,152,651 calculated in the previous set of steps.

1

- Select cell G19, the cell that contains the five-year gross margin.
- Display the Data tab and then click the 'What-If Analysis' button (Data tab | Forecast group) to display the What-If Analysis menu (Figure 3–75).

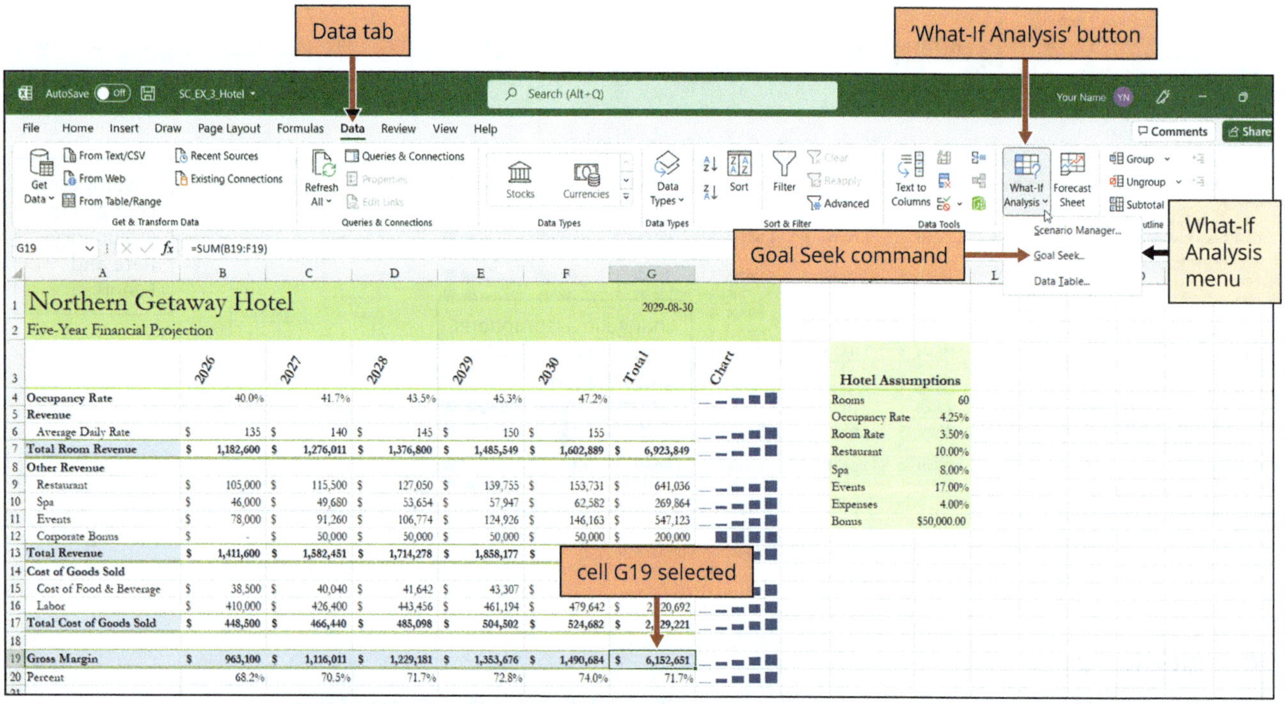

Figure 3–75

2

- Click Goal Seek to display the Goal Seek dialog box with the Set cell box set to the selected cell, G19 in this case.
- Click the To value text box, type **6,500,000** and then click the 'By changing cell' box to select it.
- Click cell K5 on the worksheet to assign the current cell, K5 in this case, to the 'By changing cell' box (Figure 3–76).

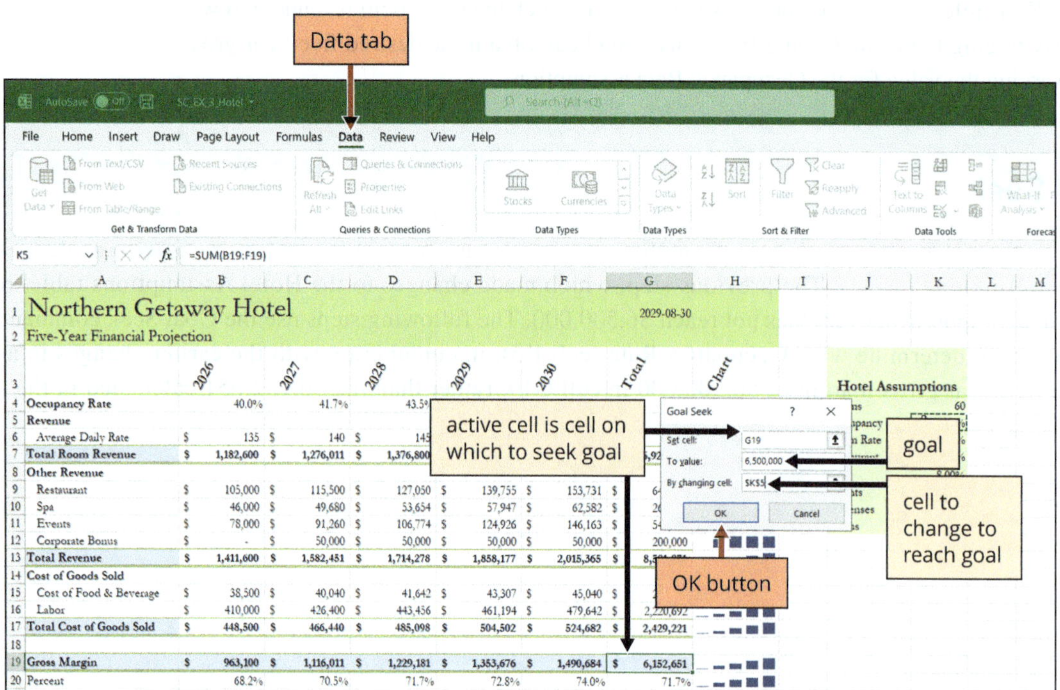

Figure 3–76

3

- Click OK (Goal Seek dialog box) to goal seek for the sought-after value in the To value text box, $6,500,000 in cell G19 in this case (Figure 3–77).

Q&A What happens when I click Cancel?
If you click the Cancel button, Excel redisplays the original values. If you click OK, Excel keeps the new values in the worksheet.

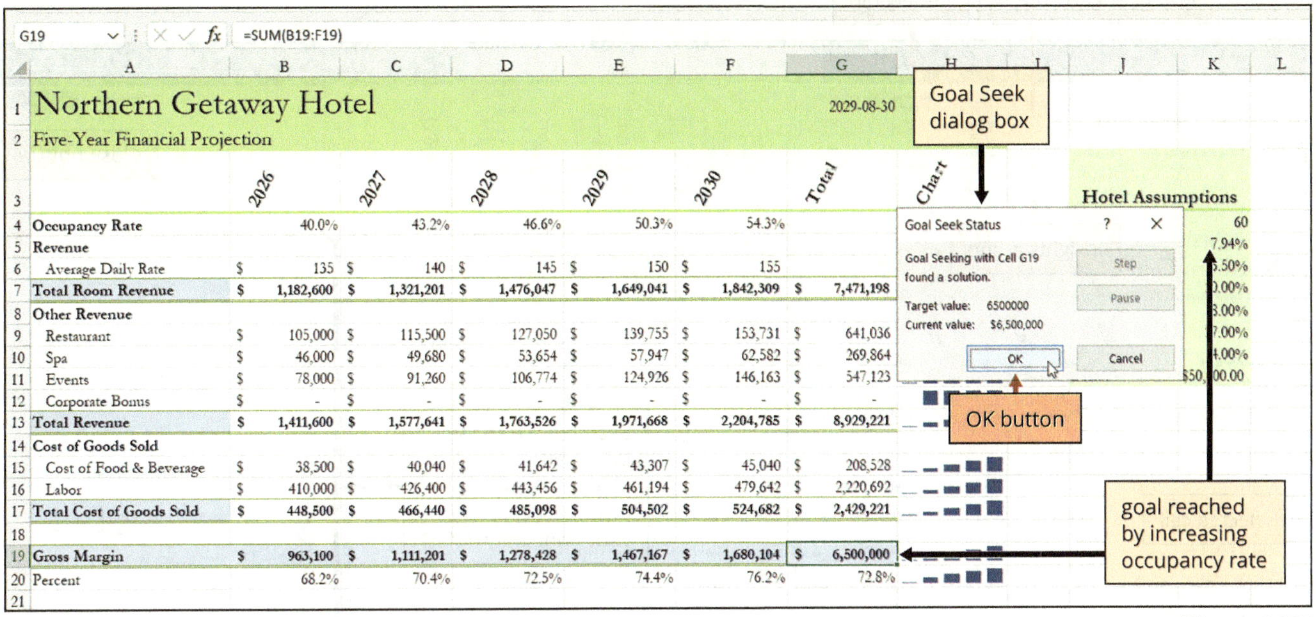

Figure 3–77

4

- Click the OK button in the Goal Seek Status dialog box to display the new values in the worksheet.

Insights

The Insights feature in Excel uses the Bing search engine and other Internet resources to help you locate more information about the content in your workbooks. One common use of this feature is to look up the definition of a word. When looking up a definition, Excel uses contextual data so that it can return the most relevant information.

To Use the Smart Lookup Insight

Smart Lookup locates useful information about text in your spreadsheet and then displays that information in the Search pane. **Why?** You want to locate additional information about the contents of your worksheet. The following steps use Smart Lookup to look up information about the text in cell A6.

1

- Select cell A19.
- Display the Review tab and then click Smart Lookup (Review tab | Insights group) to display the Search pane containing information about the text in the selected cell. If necessary, click the Turn on button to turn on intelligent services (Figure 3–78).
- Close the Smart Lookup Search pane.

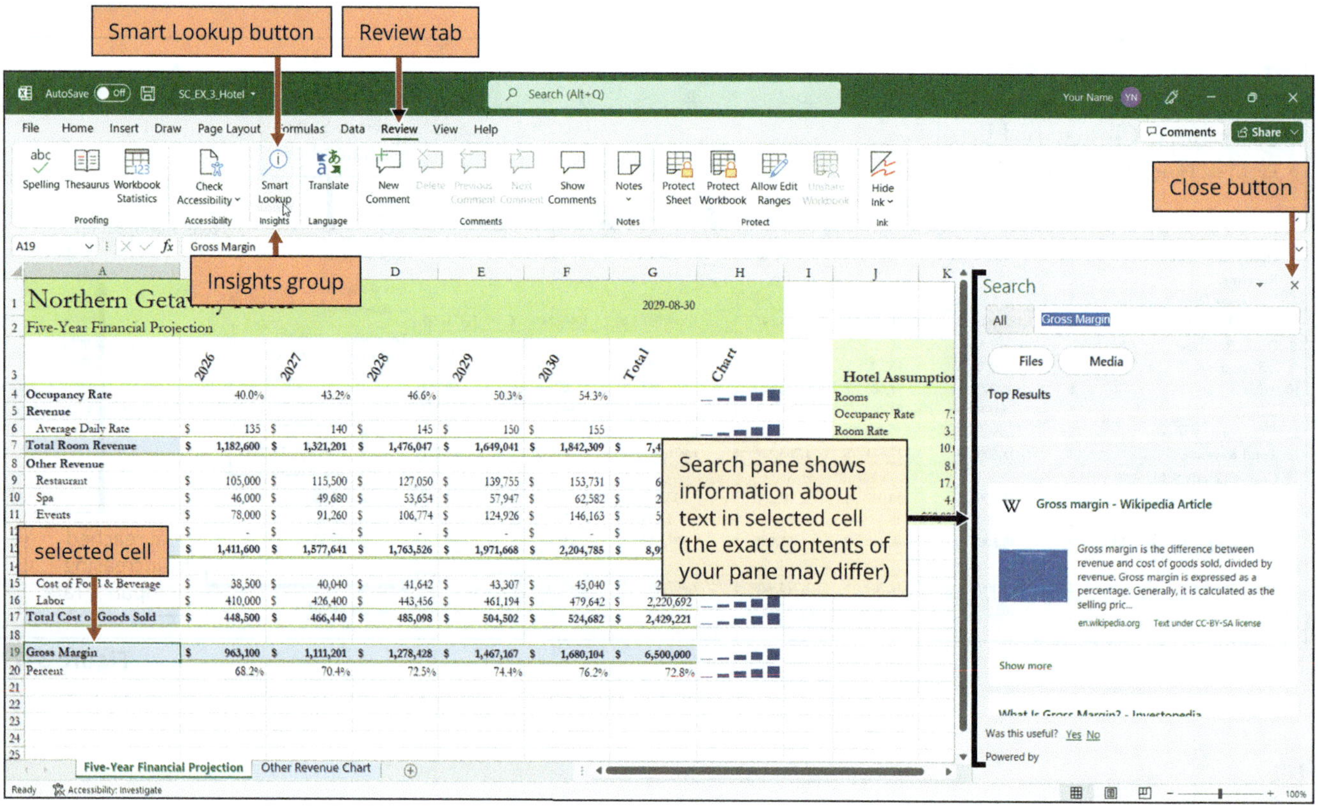

Figure 3–78

Accessibility Features

Excel provides a utility that can be used to check a workbook for potential issues related to accessibility. **Accessibility** refers to the practice of removing barriers that may prevent individuals with disabilities from interacting with data or an app. To use the Check Accessibility command, click the Accessibility Checker on the status bar at the bottom left of the worksheet or the Check Accessibility button (Review tab | Accessibility group). Excel will check your workbook for content that could prove difficult for people with disabilities to read, either alone or with adaptive tools. The resulting report (Figure 3–80 shows an example) will identify issues and offer suggestions for addressing the reported issues.

To Use the Accessibility Checker

Why? The Accessibility Checker can identify issues that could prove difficult for people with disabilities to read, either alone or with adaptive tools, such as screen readers. The following steps use the Accessibility Checker to identity and fix an accessibility issue.

1

- If necessary, click the Review tab and then click the 'Check Accessibility' button (Review tab | Accessibility group) to display the Accessibility menu (Figure 3–79).

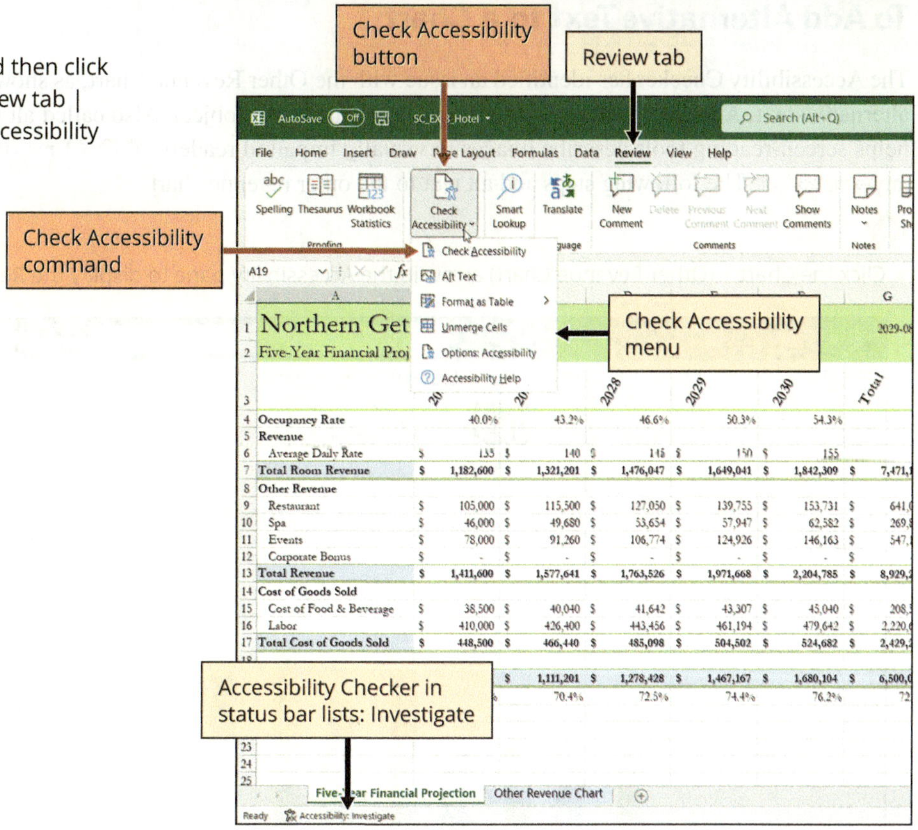

Figure 3–79

2

- Click Check Accessibility to display the Accessibility pane with a list of Errors or Warnings in the Inspection Results box.
- Click the Missing alternative text (1) expand arrow to display the object affected by the issue (Figure 3–80).

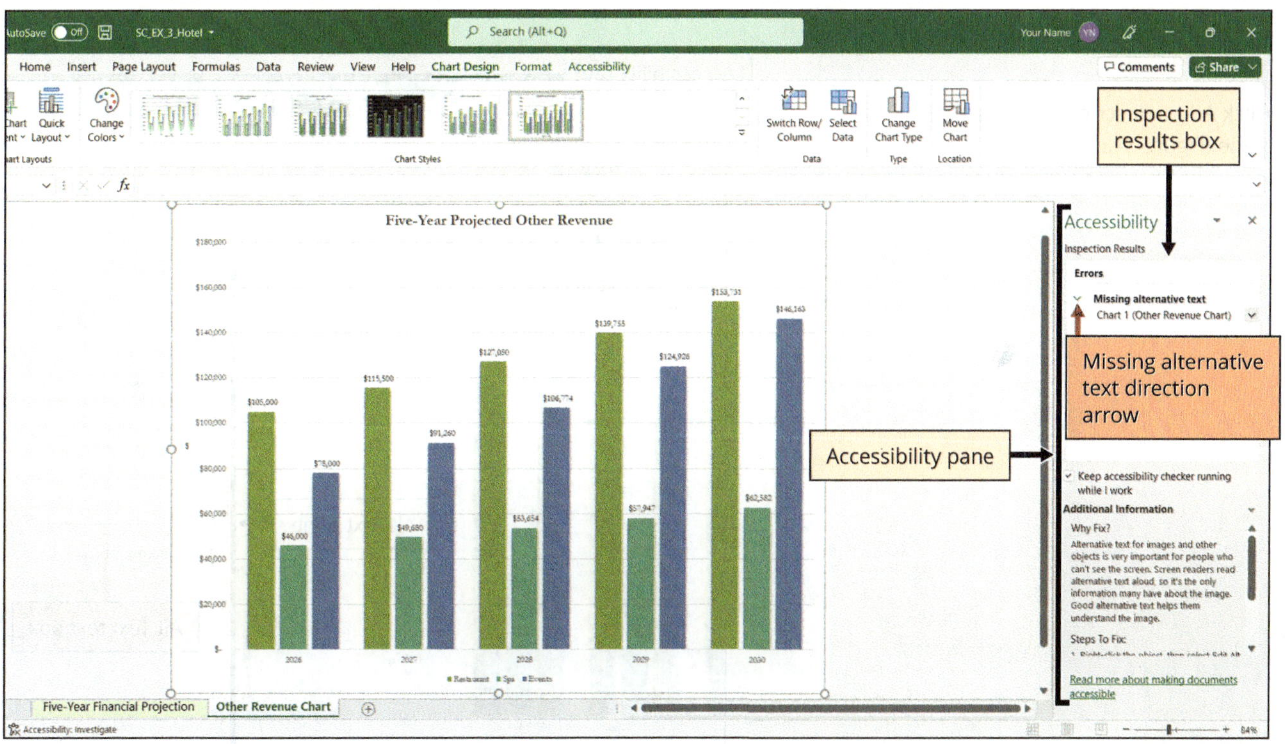

Figure 3–80

To Add Alternative Text to a Chart

The Accessibility Checker has identified an issue with the Other Revenue Chart, as shown in Figure 3–80. The chart is missing alternative text. **Alternative text** is descriptive text added to an object. Also called alt text. Adding alternative text to images helps screen-reading tools describe images to visually impaired readers. **Why?** Ensuring accessibility is a key component of any worksheet. The following steps add alt text to the other revenue chart.

1

- Click the Chart 1 (Other Revenue Chart) arrow in the Accessibility pane to display the Recommended Actions list (Figure 3–81).

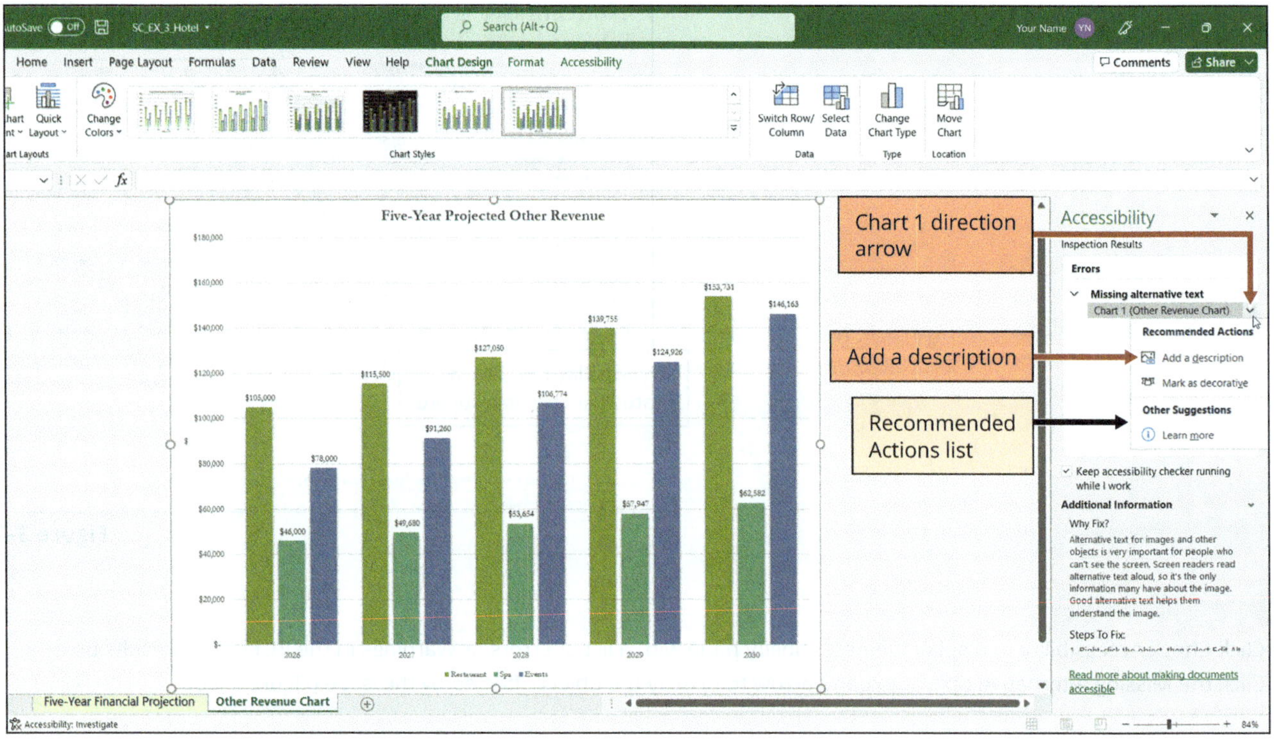

Figure 3–81

2

- Click Add a description to display the Alt Text pane (Figure 3–82).

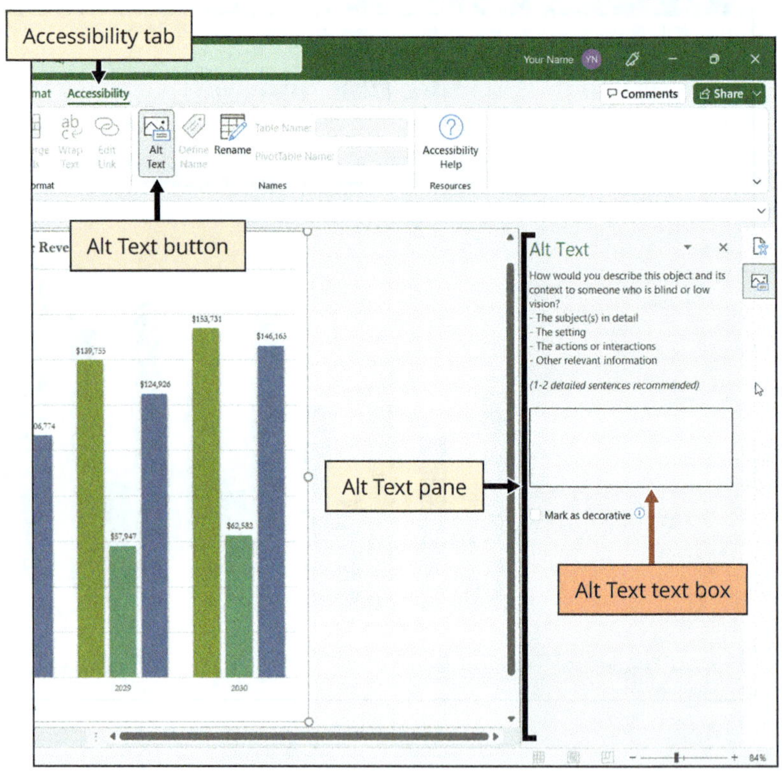

Figure 3–82

3

- Enter the following alt text description in the text box: **Clustered column chart showing an upward trend in the five-year projected other revenue categories. Restaurant, spa, and events are the categories shown in the chart.** Shown in (Figure 3–83).

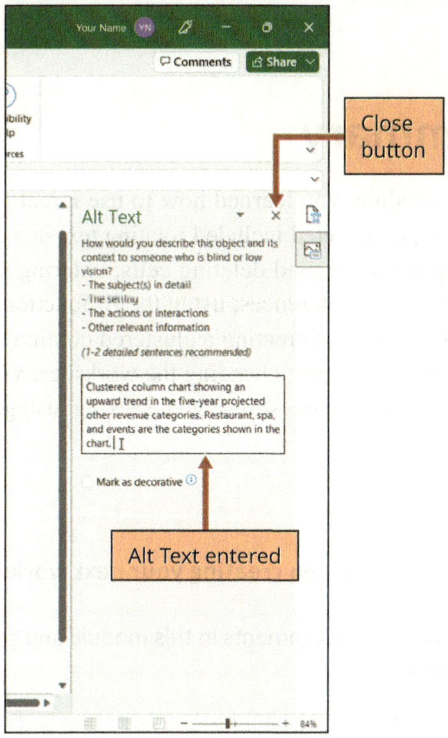

Figure 3–83

4

- Click the close button on the Alt text pane to enter the alt text and close the pane. The Accessibility pane is now updated to show no accessibility issues in the worksheet (Figure 3–84).

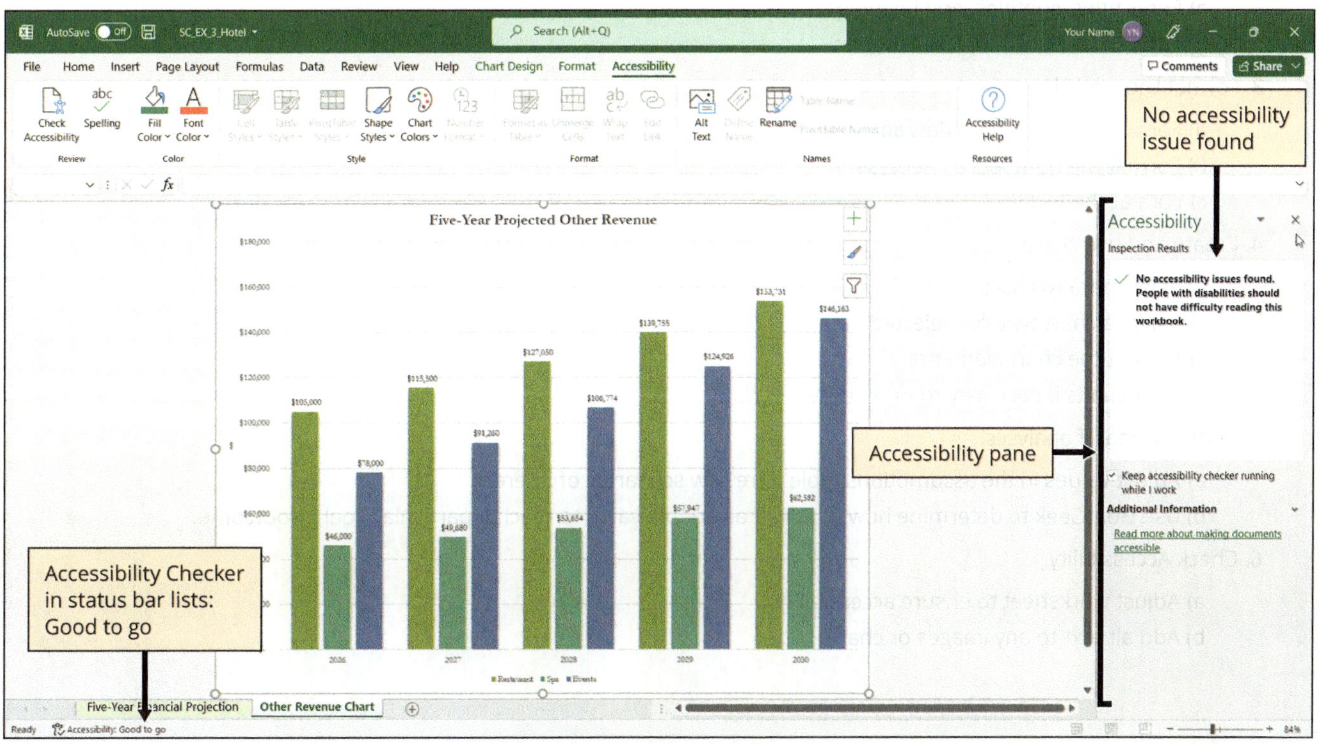

Figure 3–84

5

- sam Click the close button on the Accessibility pane to close the pane.
- Save the workbook again on the same storage location with the same file name.
- If desired, sign out of your Microsoft account.
- Exit Excel.

Summary

In this module, you learned how to use Excel to create a five-year financial projection workbook. Topics covered included rotating text in a cell; creating a series of month names; copying, pasting, inserting, and deleting cells; entering and formatting the system date; using absolute and mixed cell references; using the IF function; creating and changing sparkline charts; using the format painter; creating a clustered column chart; using chart filters; exploring chart types; reordering sheet tabs; changing the worksheet view; freezing and unfreezing rows and columns; answering what-if questions; goal seeking; using Smart Lookup; and understanding accessibility features.

Consider This: Plan Ahead

What decisions will you need to make when creating your next worksheet to evaluate and analyze data using what-if analysis?

Use these guidelines as you complete the assignments in this module and create your own worksheets for evaluating and analyzing data outside of this class.

1. Determine the workbook structure.
   a) Determine the data you will need for your worksheet.
   b) Determine the layout of your data on the worksheet.
   c) Determine the layout of the assumptions table on the worksheet.
   d) Determine the location and features of any charts.
2. Create the worksheet.
   a) Enter titles, subtitles, and headings.
   b) Enter data, functions, and formulas.
3. Format the worksheet.
   a) Format the titles, subtitles, and headings.
   b) Format the numbers as necessary.
   c) Format the text.
4. Create and use charts.
   a) Select data to chart.
   b) Select a chart type for selected data.
   c) Format the chart elements.
   d) Filter charts if necessary to view subsets of data.
5. Perform what-if analyses.
   a) Adjust values in the assumptions table to review scenarios of interest.
   b) Use Goal Seek to determine how to adjust a variable value to reach a particular goal or outcome.
6. Check Accessibility.
   a) Adjust worksheet to ensure accessibility.
   b) Add alt text to any images or charts.

Student Assignments

Apply Your Knowledge

Reinforce the skills and apply the concepts you learned in this module.

Sales Projection Worksheet

Note: To complete this assignment, you will be required to use the Data Files. Please contact your instructor for information about accessing the Data Files.

Instructions: Start Excel. Open the workbook SC_EX_3-1.xlsx, which is located in the Data Files. The workbook you open contains an incomplete twelve-month sales projection for Red Pond Lawn & Garden. To complete the sales projections, you will use the fill handle, enter formulas and functions, apply formatting, and create a chart, as shown in Figures 3–85a and 3–85b.

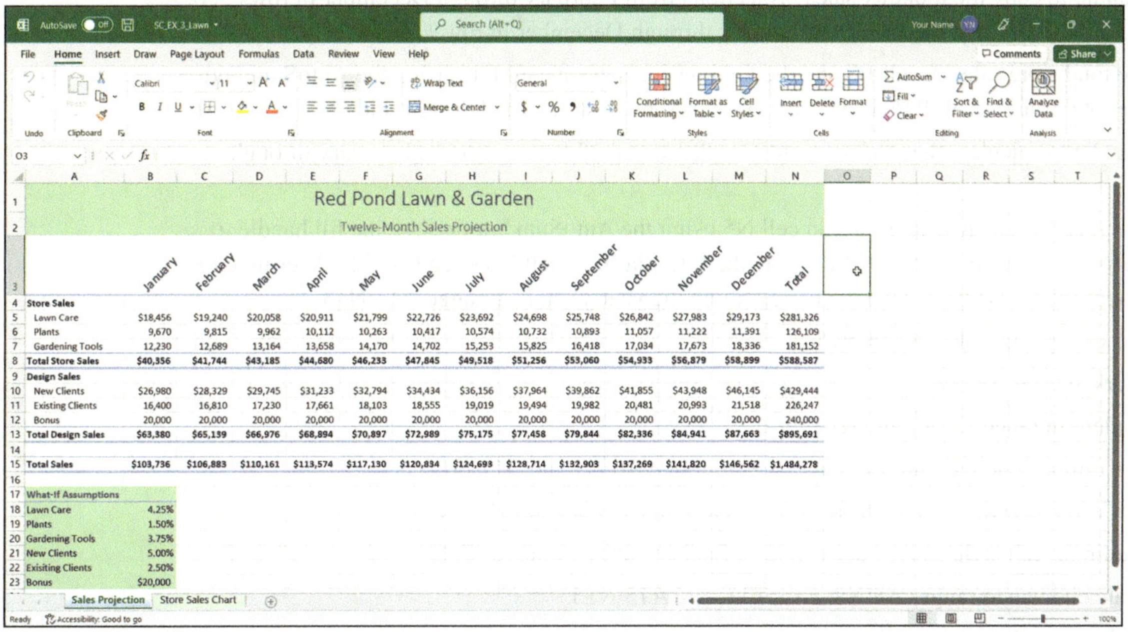

Figure 3–85(a)

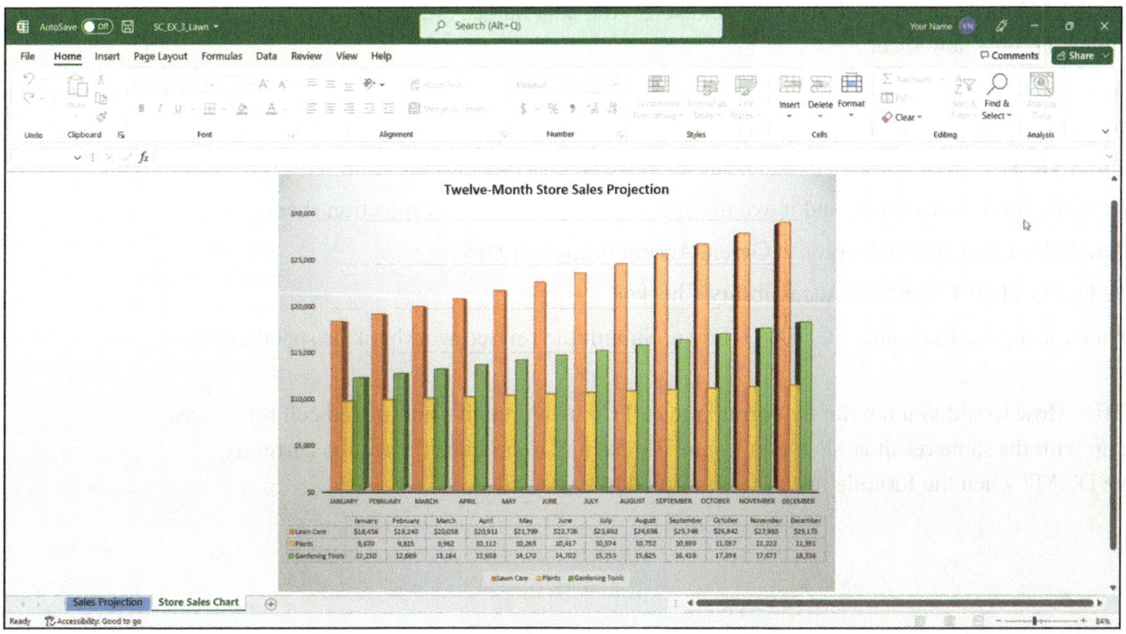

Figure 3–85(b)

Continued on next page

Perform the following tasks:

1. Use the fill handle to complete the monthly column headings in the range B3:M3. Cell N3 should read **Total**. If necessary, use the fill handle to apply the formatting from adjacent cell M3.
2. Use the following formulas in cells C5, C6, C7, C10, and C11.

   C5 = B5*(1+$B$18)

   C6 = B6*(1+$B$19)

   C7 = B7*(1+$B$20)

   C10 = B10*(1+$B$21)

   C11 = B11*(1+$B$22)
3. Write an IF function in cell B12 that assigns the value of B23 if the value of that month's New Clients sales are greater than Existing Clients sales, and a value of 0 if that is not true. Hint: Remember to use an absolute cell reference for cell B23 in the formula.
4. Use the fill handle to copy the monthly sales projections from February through December in rows 5, 6, 7, 10, and 11, and the bonus projection from January through December in row 12.
5. Determine the total store sales in cell B8 and the total design sales in cell B13 using the AutoSum button. Determine the total sales in cell B15 as the sum of total store sales and total design sales.
6. Use the fill handle to calculate the total sales in rows 8, 13, and 15 for the months February through December.
7. Determine the yearly total lawn care sales in cell N5 using the AutoSum button. Use the fill handle to determine the yearly totals in range N6:N8. Copy the formula from cell N8 to cell N10 to determine the yearly new client sales. Use the fill handle to determine the yearly totals in range N11:N13.
8. Determine the yearly total sales in cell N15.
9. Format the worksheet as follows:
   a. Increase Indent in range A5:A7 and A10:A12.
   b. Apply the Comma style with no decimal places to range B6:N7 and B11:N12.
   c. Apply the Currency style with no decimal places to range C5:N5 and C10:N10.
   d. Apply Heading 2 cell style and fill color White, Background 1 to range A3:N3.
   e. Apply Total cell style to ranges A8:N8, A13:N13, and A15:N15.
   f. Apply Bolding to cells A4 and A9.
10. Select the range A3:M3, press and hold down CTRL and select the data range A5:M7, and insert a 3-D clustered column chart on a new sheet.
11. Change the chart title to Twelve-Month Store Sales Projection.
12. Add a data table with legend keys to the chart. Change the chart colors to Colorful Palette 3 and change the chart style to Style 3.
13. Name the chart sheet, Store Sales Chart, and move the sheet to follow the Sales Projection sheet.
14. Change the Store Sales Chart sheet tab color to Green, Accent 6, Lighter 80%.
15. Add alternative text to Chart 1 using the Accessibility Checker.
16. Save the workbook using the file name, SC_EX_3_Lawn. Submit the revised workbook as specified by your instructor.
17. **Consider This:** How would you rewrite the formula in cell C7 using relative and mixed cell references only, to come up with the same result as shown in Figure 3–85a, and to produce the results currently shown in range D7:M7 when the formula in cell C7 is copied to those cells?

Extend Your Knowledge

Extend the skills you learned in this module and experiment with new skills. You may need to use Help to complete the assignment.

Using IF Functions and What-If Analysis

Note: To complete this assignment, you will be required to use the Data Files. Please contact your instructor for information about accessing the Data Files.

Instructions: Start Excel. Open the workbook SC_EX_3-2.xlsx, shown in Figure 3–86, which is located in the Data Files. The workbook you open contains student exam grades. You will determine the missing information in the workbook. You are to use the fill handle and enter functions as directed.

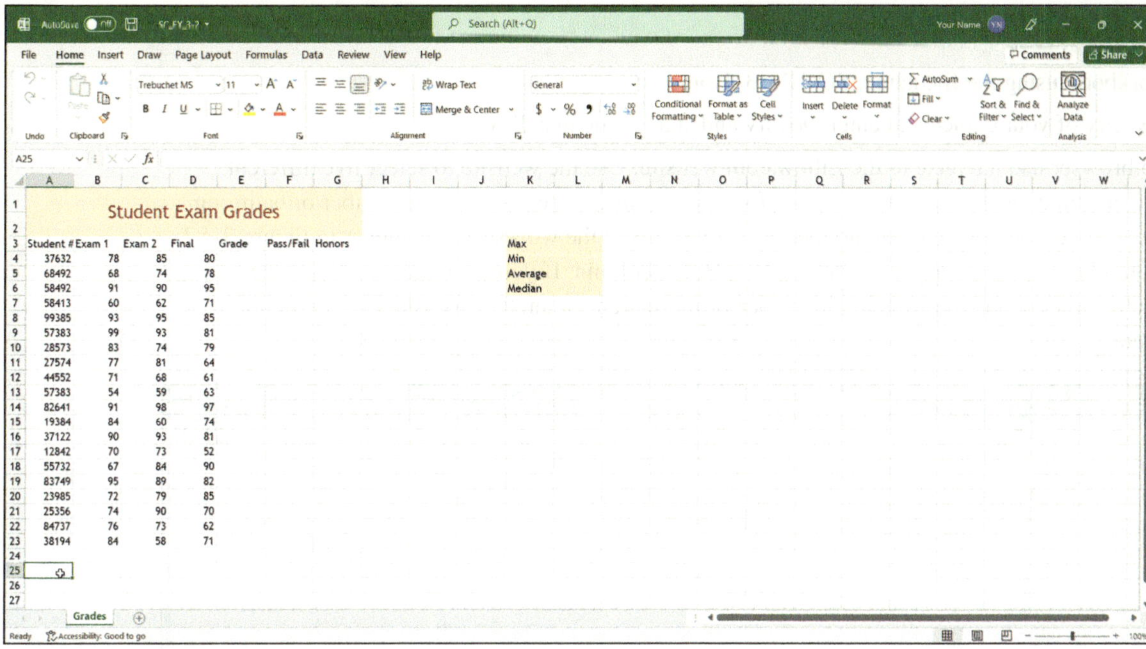

Figure 3–86

Perform the following tasks:

1. Use the following formula to determine students' grade in cell E4, where the average of the first two exams is worth 60% of the grade and the final is worth 60% of the grade.
   Grade = (AVERAGE(B4:C4)*60%)+(D4*40%)
2. Use the fill handle to copy this formula to cells E5:E23.
3. Calculate the Maximum, Minimum, Average, and Median grades in column E using functions in range L3:L6.
4. Write an IF function in cell F4 that assigns a grade of "Pass" if the grade in cell E4 is 65 or above, and a grade of "Fail" if the score in cell E4 is below 65. Copy this function to cells F5:F23.
5. Write an IF function in cell G4 that assigns a "Yes" if the student received Honors in the class for earning a grade above the average, and a "No" if the student earned a grade the same or below the average. Copy this function cells G5:G23.
6. Using Goal Seek, determine what student #57383 (row 13) would have needed to score on their final to receive a grade of 65.
7. Using Goal Seek, determine what student #28573 (row 10) would have needed to score on Exam 1 to receive a grade of 80.
8. Save the workbook using the file name, SC_EX_3_Exam. Submit the revised workbook as specified by your instructor.
9. **Consider This:** How did you decide to use any absolute or relative cell references in the IF functions you wrote?

Expand Your World

Create a solution that uses cloud or web technologies by learning and investigating on your own from general guidance.

Note: To complete this assignment, you will be required to use the Data Files. Please contact your instructor for information about accessing the Data Files.

Instructions: You are working as part of a group creating a report that includes data about home prices in your city. Your task is to complete and format the worksheet using information from the Zillow.com website, chart the data, and make the chart available to your group using OneDrive. Start Excel. Open the workbook called SC_EX_3-3.xlsx, which is located in the Data Files. This workbook contains a basic structure to represent the home data.

Perform the following tasks:

1. Save the workbook using the file name, SC_EX_3_Home.
2. Select a U.S. city of your choice and enter the city and state name in cell A3.
3. Open a web browser and navigate to the Zillow.com website. Use the website to select five different homes in the city, and record their price, square footage, number of bedrooms, and number of bathrooms for each home. Enter the information into the respective cells in the worksheet, as shown in Figure 3–87 but using your chosen city, listing the address in the Home column. If you are unable to locate the necessary data, either choose a different city or perform a search for another website containing the necessary data.

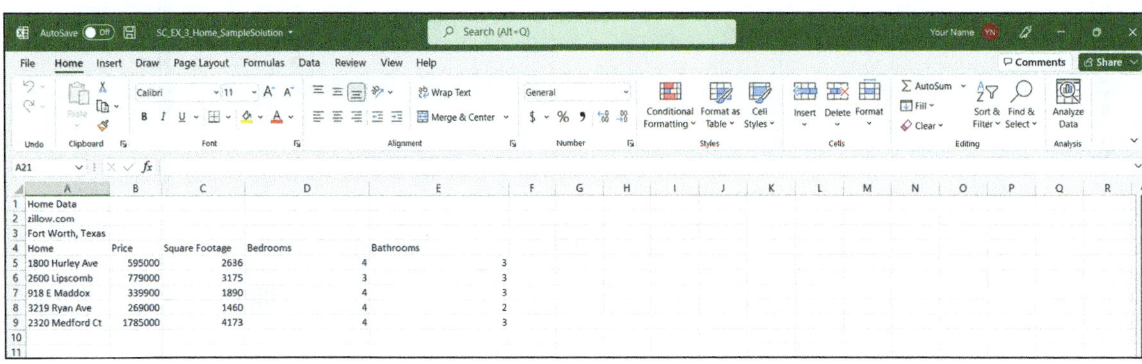

Figure 3–87

4. Format the worksheet using techniques you have learned to present the data in a visually appealing form.
5. Create two charts that present the data for each of the four categories of data. Compare the price and square footage in one chart, and compare the price, bedrooms, and bathrooms in a second chart. Decide which chart types will best present the data. (**Hint:** If you are not sure which types to use, consider selecting the data and using the Recommended Chart button to narrow down and preview suitable choices.) Place each chart on a separate sheet and format the charts to best present the data in a clear, attractive format.
6. Give each worksheet a descriptive name and color the tabs using theme colors. Reorder the sheets so that the data table appears first, followed by the charts.
7. Add alternative text for each chart.
8. If requested by your instructor, export the file to OneDrive.
9. Submit the revised workbook as specified by your instructor.
10. **Consider This:** Justify your choice of chart types in Step 5. Explain why you selected these types over other suitable choices.

In the Lab

Design and implement a solution using creative thinking and problem-solving skills.

Comparing Shipping Costs

Problem: You have started a new small business selling graphic t-shirts and sweatshirts. You will need to calculate how much to charge for shipping for your small business. You decide to research several different shipping methods and create a financial projection of the shipping cost over a year.

Part 1: Research the cost of shipping a small flat rate box and a medium flat rate box with four different shipping companies. After you find the cost of shipping each, you will use formulas to calculate the shipping cost for each company for one month, six months, and one year. You will need to have an assumption table with the number of small boxes sent each month, and the number of medium boxes sent each month. Develop a worksheet following the general layout in Table 3–9 that shows the shipping cost analysis. Add a chart showing the cost comparisons as an embedded chart.

Table 3–9: Shipping Cost Analysis

Company	Flat Rate Small Box Cost	Flat Rate Medium Box Cost	Shipping Cost 1 Month	Shipping Cost 6 Months	Shipping Cost 1 Years
Company 1			Formula A	Formula B	Formula C
Company 2			—	—	—
Company 3			—	—	—
Company 4			—	—	—
Assumptions					
Small packages per Month					
Medium packages per Month					

Part 2: **Consider This:** You made several decisions while creating the workbook for this assignment: how to lay out the data in the worksheet and which chart types to use. What was the rationale behind each of these decisions? What other costs might you want to consider when making your purchase decision?

Databases and Database Objects: An Introduction

Objectives

After completing this module, you will be able to:

- Describe the features of the Access window
- Create a database
- Create a database using a template
- Create a table using Datasheet view
- Modify properties of a table's primary key
- Display a table's structure in Design view
- Add records to a table
- Resize a table's columns in Datasheet view
- Create a table using Design view
- Import a table
- Create a query using the Simple Query Wizard
- Run a query
- Create a form
- Create a report using the Report Wizard
- Explain special database operations

Introduction

The term **database** describes a collection of data organized in a manner that allows access, retrieval, and use of that data. Microsoft 365 Access, usually referred to as simply Access, is a database management system. A **database management system** is software that allows you to use a computer to create a database; add, change, and delete data in the database; ask and answer questions concerning the data; and create forms and reports using the data.

Project: Database Creation

Clearnet Logistics is a freight brokerage company that connects carriers with freight customers. Up until now, the tracking system has been paper-based. The two partners who run Clearnet have been using a large book to record freight loads, with each page containing specific information such as pickup and dropoff locations. Each page has slots for additional stops or detailed load information, which are made in pencil to allow for changes. Clearnet wants to computerize the tracking system with an Access database. The partners are ready to expand and need to hire an office assistant and, eventually, a tracker and another broker. To facilitate team-wide communication, they need to make the tracking system easier to use and more efficient. To accomplish that goal, the company needs computer-based record keeping.

Clearnet needs to record contact, license, and insurance information about the carriers they work with. Contact names, emails, and phone numbers for arranging loads are essential pieces of information. In addition, the team must be able to contact drivers quickly. The staff needs to record each load's driver name and mobile phone number to efficiently coordinate and track loads from shippers.

Keeping accurate load information allows for timely and accurate payments to carriers and their drivers. Each load's pickup and dropoff dates, mileage, start and end points, and agreed-upon payment terms should be recorded so that information can be easily retrieved for efficient tracking and billing. Load information should include the freight customer's billing information, which is needed to collect payments. The database should also contain each carrier's payment information for bank transfers or mailing checks.

The cost to transport each load is agreed upon before booking the load and is called the rate confirmation or "rate con" for short. This information needs to be recorded up front and then billed as loads are completed. The database system must also track locations for pickup and dropoff.

By recording all its load-tracking information in Access, Clearnet will be able to keep its data current and accurate and can analyze it for trends. Using a database will also allow Clearnet to create a variety of useful reports; for example, tracking the frequency of certain load types or areas with increased levels of transportation activity. These reports are vital for planning purposes and researching leads for more loads, carriers, and drivers.

In a **relational database**, such as those maintained by Access, a database consists of a collection of tables, each of which contains information on a specific subject. Figure 1–1 shows the database for Clearnet. It consists of five tables: the Shippers table (Figure 1–1a) contains information about the customers hiring freight transportation services, the Locations table (Figure 1–1b) contains information for pickup and dropoff locations for freight loads, the Loads table (Figure 1–1c) contains information about the transportation of loads, the Truck Type table (Figure 1–1d) contains information about the type of truck needed for the various kinds of freight, and the Carriers table (Figure 1–1e) contains a listing of the transportation companies that own and operate the trucks carrying loads.

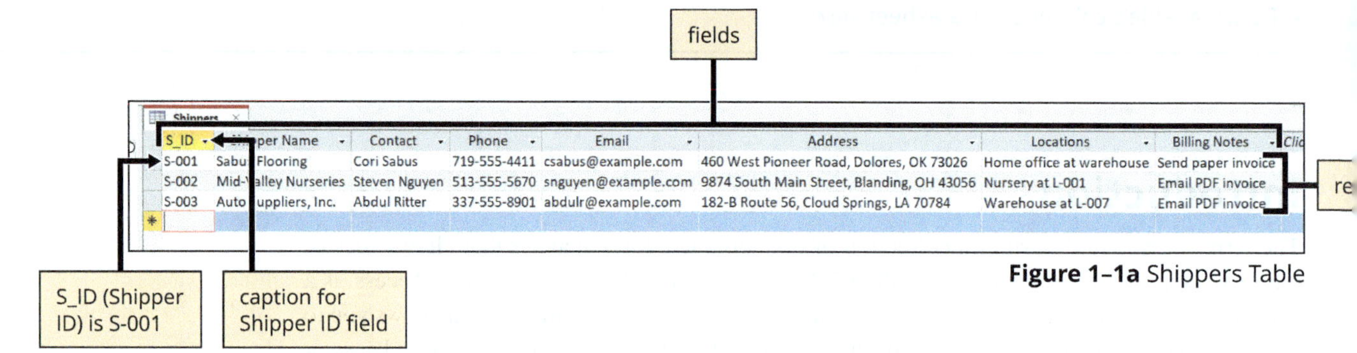

S_ID	per Name	Contact	Phone	Email	Address	Locations	Billing Notes
S-001	Sabu Flooring	Cori Sabus	719-555-4411	csabus@example.com	460 West Pioneer Road, Dolores, OK 73026	Home office at warehouse	Send paper invoice
S-002	Mid-alley Nurseries	Steven Nguyen	513-555-5670	snguyen@example.com	9874 South Main Street, Blanding, OH 43056	Nursery at L-001	Email PDF invoice
S-003	Auto uppliers, Inc.	Abdul Ritter	337-555-8901	abdulr@example.com	182-B Route 56, Cloud Springs, LA 70784	Warehouse at L-007	Email PDF invoice

Figure 1–1a Shippers Table

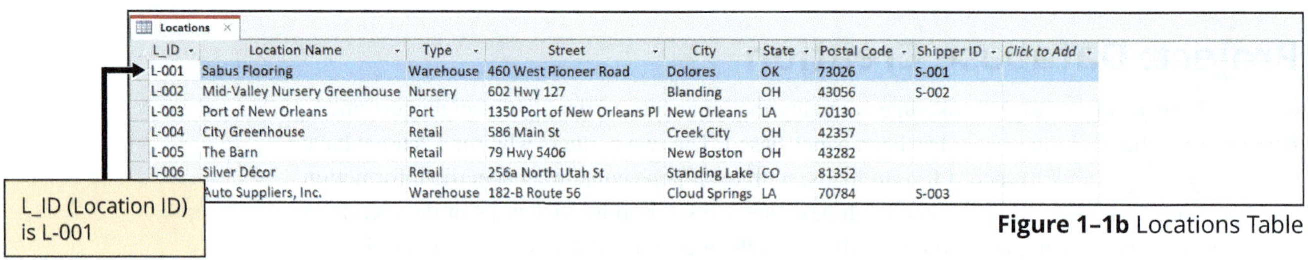

L_ID	Location Name	Type	Street	City	State	Postal Code	Shipper ID	Click to Add
L-001	Sabus Flooring	Warehouse	460 West Pioneer Road	Dolores	OK	73026	S-001	
L-002	Mid-Valley Nursery Greenhouse	Nursery	602 Hwy 127	Blanding	OH	43056	S-002	
L-003	Port of New Orleans	Port	1350 Port of New Orleans Pl	New Orleans	LA	70130		
L-004	City Greenhouse	Retail	586 Main St	Creek City	OH	42357		
L-005	The Barn	Retail	79 Hwy 5406	New Boston	OH	43282		
L-006	Silver Décor	Retail	256a North Utah St	Standing Lake	CO	81352		
	Auto Suppliers, Inc.	Warehouse	182-B Route 56	Cloud Springs	LA	70784	S-003	

Figure 1–1b Locations Table

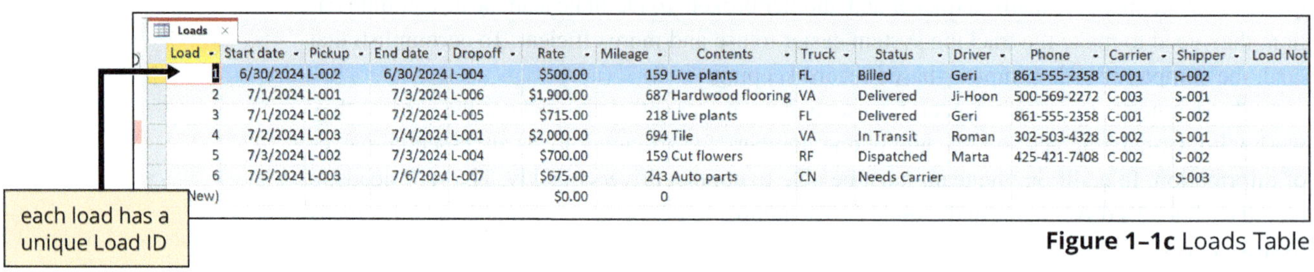

Load	Start date	Pickup	End date	Dropoff	Rate	Mileage	Contents	Truck	Status	Driver	Phone	Carrier	Shipper	Load Not
1	6/30/2024	L-002	6/30/2024	L-004	$500.00	159	Live plants	FL	Billed	Geri	861-555-2358	C-001	S-002	
2	7/1/2024	L-001	7/3/2024	L-006	$1,900.00	687	Hardwood flooring	VA	Delivered	Ji-Hoon	500-569-2272	C-003	S-001	
3	7/1/2024	L-002	7/2/2024	L-005	$715.00	218	Live plants	FL	Delivered	Geri	861-555-2358	C-001	S-002	
4	7/2/2024	L-003	7/4/2024	L-001	$2,000.00	694	Tile	VA	In Transit	Roman	302-503-4328	C-002	S-001	
5	7/3/2024	L-002	7/3/2024	L-004	$700.00	159	Cut flowers	RF	Dispatched	Marta	425-421-7408	C-002	S-002	
6	7/5/2024	L-003	7/6/2024	L-007	$675.00	243	Auto parts	CN	Needs Carrier				S-003	
New)					$0.00	0								

Figure 1–1c Loads Table

Truck Type

T_ID	Truck Type	Target Rate	Rate Notes	Click to Add
CN	Container	$2.75		
FL	Flatbed	$3.25		
HL	Heavy equipment-Long	$5.00	Distances over 500 miles	
HS	Heavy equipment-Short	$3.00	Distances under 500 miles	
PI	Premium insurance	$4.00	Premium insurance coverage for high-value loads	
RF	Reefer	$3.15	Temperature-controlled/refrigerated	
TK	Tanker	$3.00	Tanker endorsement	
VA	Dry van	$2.75	Standard trailer	
VM	Dry van-Team	$2.75	Multiple drivers	
VZ	Dry van-Hazmat	$3.15	Hazmat restrictions	
*		$0.00		

target rate for new VA (dry van) loads

Figure 1–1d Truck Type Table

Carriers

C_ID	Carrier Name	Contact	Phone	Email	Address	MC Number	USDOT	Insurance	
C-001	Williams Trucking	Marco Bailey	220-238-6682	mbailey@newmail.com	9887 Dover Rd, Searcy, AK 72210	MC01015276	1435917	Shipping Insurance, Inc.	Bank transfe
C-002	Freightliners Inc.	Teresa Gomez	435-222-4545	tgomez@newmail.com	6214 Lansing, Gainesville, UT 84511	MC00111937	2971533	Overland Insurers	Mail check t
C-003	Spotters Freight	Lata Gaspar	617-732-9888	latag@newmail.com	456 Hwy 46 S, Crestview, TN 37055	MC10011438	2297585	US Motor Group	Bank transfe
*									

Carrier ID for each carrier

Figure 1–1e Carriers Table

The rows in the tables are called **records**. A record contains information about a given person, item, or event. A row in the Shippers table, for example, contains information about a specific shipping company, such as the company's name, address, and other data.

The columns in the tables are called fields. A **field** contains a specific piece of information within a record. In the Shippers table, for example, the fourth field, Phone, contains the phone number for the main contact person at the shipping company.

The first field in the Shippers table is S_ID, which is an abbreviation for Shipper Identification. Clearnet assigns each shipper an identifying number; the Shipper ID consists of one uppercase letter followed by a three-digit number.

Each Shipper ID is unique; that is, no two shippers have the same number. Such a field is a **unique identifier**. A unique identifier, as its name suggests, is a way of uniquely identifying each record in the table. A given shipper number will appear only in a single record in the table. Only one record exists, for example, in which the Shipper ID is S-002. A unique identifier is also called a **primary key**. Thus, the Shipper ID field is the primary key for the Shippers table. This means the Shipper ID field, which has the caption S_ID, can be used to uniquely identify any record in the table. No two records can have the same value in the Shipper ID field.

The next seven fields in the Shippers table are Shipper Name, Contact, Phone, Email, Address, Locations, and Billing Notes. For example, Shipper ID S-002 is Mid-Valley Nurseries whose primary contact is Steven Nguyen. Steven can be reached at the phone number or the email address listed in the table.

Clearnet's database also contains a table called Locations. Within the Locations table, each location used for load pickup or dropoff is assigned a unique identifier called Location ID (the caption L_ID is a shortened version of this identifier). For example, Sabus Flooring's warehouse location has a Location ID of L-001. No other location has this Location ID. The location's name is indicated in the Location Name field. The location type under the Type field is recorded as Warehouse with an address in Dolores, OK. If relevant, Clearnet associates the location with the shipping company that owns it by including a field in the Locations table called Shipper ID. If the location is owned by a shipper, then the Shipper ID field in the Locations table displays a Shipper ID from the Shippers table. For instance, the L-001 warehouse is owned by a unique shipping company with the Shipper ID S-001. However, the Port of New Orleans location, which has the Location ID L-003, is not owned by a shipping company because it is used by many shippers. Therefore, it does not have information in the Shipper ID field.

BTW
Captions
You can change a field's caption, or the wording that appears as the field's name, to language that is more descriptive, shorter, or meets some other requirement.

BTW
Reserved Words
Access has several reserved words, words that have a special meaning to Access. You cannot use these reserved words as field names. For example, Name is a reserved word and could not be used on its own as a field name in the Shippers table to describe a shipping company's name. For a complete list of reserved words in Access, consult Access Help.

There are three other tables within the Clearnet database. The Loads table records each load that has been transported. Each load is assigned a Load ID, listed in the Load field. This ID is unique for each load booked through Clearnet's broker service. For example, Load ID 1 transported live plants on June 30, 2024. This load was carried on a flatbed trailer, which typically costs more than some other truck types. The target rate for flatbed freight is listed in the fourth table, Truck Type. The Truck Type table lists the types of trucks booked by Clearnet. Each truck type is assigned a unique identifier called Truck Type ID, which is a two-letter abbreviation of the truck type name. For example, Truck Type VA is a standard trailer called a dry van that does not offer any specialized equipment for transport. Therefore, this truck type costs less to hire than other truck types. Truck Type RF, which is short for reefer, provides a refrigerated truck with a controlled temperature. Because these trailers must comply with special regulations, a reefer often costs more to hire.

Finally, there is a table called Carriers that lists carriers who have hired Clearnet's brokerage service. Each carrier has a unique Carrier ID that is associated with the carrier's contact, insurance, and billing details. For example, Carrier ID C-001 is Williams Trucking, in Searcy, AK, and the primary contact is Marco Bailey. Their insurance policy is through Shipping Insurance, Inc. Payments to this carrier are made by bank transfer to their account at Liberty Bank.

Consider This

How would you find the shipper's contact information for a specific load?

Suppose a shipment of tile, Load ID 4, encounters significant delays from a hurricane, and Clearnet needs to contact the shipper to keep them informed. The broker could easily find the shipper contact's name and phone number by looking in the Loads table and then in the Shipper's table. In the Loads table, locate the affected load and read across until you come to the Shipper ID, which is S-001. Then, in the Shippers table, locate the record which has the Shipper ID S-001, and read across to find the primary contact's name and phone number.

Consider This

How would you find the pickup address for a specific load?

First, look in the Loads table to identify the specific load, and then check its Pickup location. Suppose the Load's ID is 3. Once you locate it in the table, you can read across and see that its pickup location has the ID L-002. Next, look in the Locations table for Location L-002 and find that the physical address for this location is 602 Hwy 127, Blanding, OH 43056.

Creating a Database

In Access, all the tables, reports, forms, and queries that you create are stored in a single file called a database. A database is a structure that can store information about multiple types of objects, the properties of those objects, and the relationships among the objects. The first step is to create the database that will hold your tables, reports, forms, and queries. You can start with either a blank database or a template to create a new database. If you already knew the tables and fields you wanted in your database, you would use the Blank database option in Access. If not, you can use a database template. Templates can guide you by suggesting some commonly used tables and fields in certain kinds of databases.

To Create a Database

Because you already know the tables and fields you want in the Clearnet database, you will use the Blank database option rather than a template to create the database. **Why?** The Blank database is the most efficient way to create a database for which you already know the intended data needs. The following steps create the database.

1

- Click the Windows Start button to display the Windows menu.
- Click the Access button to start Access (Figure 1–2a).

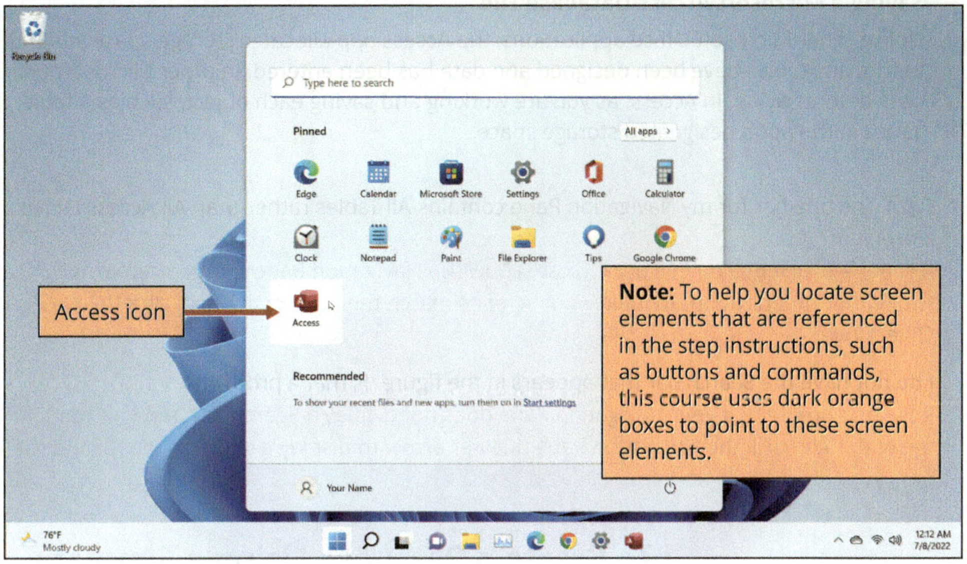

Figure 1–2a

2

- Click the Blank database button to specify the type of database to create.
- sam Type **SC_AC_01_Clearnet** in the File Name text box, and then click the Create button to create the database (Figure 1–2).

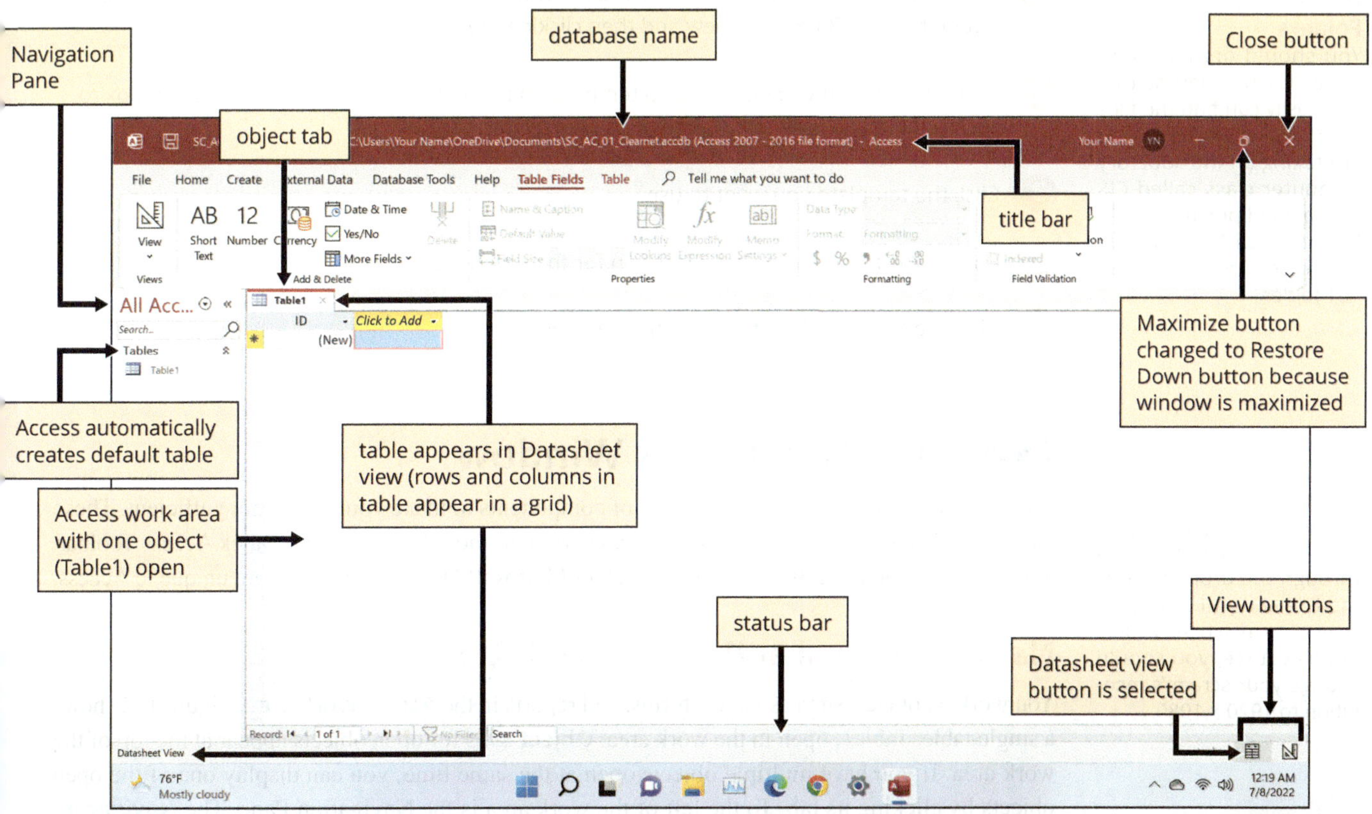

Figure 1–2

Consider This

Saving a Microsoft Access Database File

Unlike other Microsoft Office applications, the Access app allocates storage space when the database is created, even before any tables have been designed and data has been entered. In other Microsoft Office applications, you can enter data before saving. In Access, as you are working and saving each object, such as a table, the entire database is being saved in the app's designated storage space.

Q&A The title bar for my Navigation Pane contains All Tables rather than All Access Objects, as in the figure. Is that a problem?

It is not a problem. The title bar indicates how the Navigation Pane is organized. You can carry out the steps in the text with either organization. To make your screens match the ones in the text, click the Navigation Pane arrow and then click Object Type.

I do not have the Search bar that appears in the figure. Is that a problem?

It is not a problem. If your Navigation Pane does not display a Search bar and you want your screens to match the ones in the text, right-click the Navigation Pane title bar arrow to display a shortcut menu, and then click Search Bar.

To Create a Database Using a Template

Ideally, you will design your own database, create a blank database, and then create the tables you have determined that your database should contain. If you are not sure what database design you will need, you can use a template. Templates can guide you by suggesting some commonly used databases containing predesigned objects such as tables and reports. To create a database using a template, you would use the following steps.

1. If you have another database open, close it without exiting Access by clicking File on the ribbon to open Backstage view and then clicking Close.
2. Click File – New. If you do not see a template that you want, you can use the Search box to search the many online templates provided by Microsoft.
3. Click the template you want to use.
4. Enter a file name and select a location for the database.
5. Click the Create button to create the database.

BTW
Organizing Files and Folders
You should organize and store files in folders so that you easily can find the files later. For example, if you are taking an introductory computer class called CIS 101, a good practice would be to save all Access files in an Access folder within a CIS 101 folder.

Exploring the Access Window

The Access window consists of a variety of components to make your work more efficient. These include the Navigation Pane, Access work area, ribbon, shortcut menus, and Quick Access Toolbar. Some of these components are common to other Microsoft Office apps; others are unique to Access.

BTW
Access Screen Resolution
If you are using a computer or mobile device to step through the project in this module and you want your screens to match the figures in this course, you should change your screen's resolution to 1920 × 1080.

Navigation Pane and Access Work Area

You work on objects such as tables, forms, and reports in the **Access work area**. Figure 1–2 shows a single table, Table1, open in the work area. **Object tabs** for open objects appear at the top of the work area. If you have multiple objects open at the same time, you can display one of the open objects by clicking its tab. To the left of the work area is the Navigation Pane. The **Navigation Pane** contains a list of all the objects in the database. You use this pane to open an object. You can also customize the way objects are displayed in the Navigation Pane.

The **status bar**, located at the bottom of the Access window, presents information about the database object, the progress of current tasks, and the status of certain commands and keys; it also provides controls for viewing the object. As you type text or perform certain commands, various indicators might appear on the status bar. The left edge of the status bar in Figure 1–2 shows that the table object is open in **Datasheet view**. In Datasheet view, the table is represented as a collection of rows and columns called a **datasheet**. Toward the right edge are View buttons, which you can use to change the view that currently appears.

Determining Tables and Fields

Once you have created the database, you need to create the tables and fields that your database will contain. Before doing so, however, you need to make some decisions regarding the tables and fields.

Naming Tables and Fields

In creating your database, you must name tables, fields, and other objects. Before beginning the design process, you must understand the rules Access applies to table and field names. These rules are:

1. Names can be up to 64 characters in length.
2. Names can contain letters, digits, and spaces, as well as most common punctuation symbols.
3. Names cannot contain periods (.), exclamation points (!), accent graves (`), or square brackets ([ ]).
4. Each field in a table must have a unique name.

It's a good idea to follow the same naming conventions throughout all of your tables and fields so that they are easier to understand and easier to remember when you need to refer to them later. The approach to naming tables and fields used in this text is to begin all names with an uppercase letter. In multiple-word names, each word begins with an uppercase letter, and there is a space between words (for example, Owner Street Address).

Determining the Primary Key

For each table, you need to determine the primary key, the unique identifier. In many cases, you will have clear choices, such as Shipper ID or Carrier ID. If you do not have a clear choice, you can use the primary key that Access creates automatically. The default ID field is an **autonumber field**, which means that Access will assign the value 1 to the first record, 2 to the second record, and so on.

Determining Data Types for the Fields

For each field in your database, you must determine the field's **data type**, that is, the type of data that can be stored in the field. Four of the most commonly used data types in Access are:

1. **Short Text** — The field can contain any characters. A maximum number of 255 characters is allowed in a field whose data type is Short Text.
2. **Number** — The field can contain only numbers. The numbers can be either positive or negative. Fields assigned this type can be used in arithmetic operations. You usually assign fields that contain numbers but will not be used for arithmetic operations (such as postal codes) a data type of Short Text instead.
3. **Currency** — The field can contain only monetary data. The values will appear with currency symbols, such as dollar signs, commas, and decimal points, and with two digits following the decimal point. Like numeric fields, you can use currency fields in arithmetic operations. Access assigns a size to currency fields automatically.
4. **Date/Time** — The field can contain dates and/or times.

Table 1–1 shows the other data types that are available in Access.

BTW
Naming Tables
Database designers typically have their own guidelines for naming tables. Some use the singular version of the object being described while others use the prefix tbl with a table name, such as tbl_students. This course uses the singular or plural version of the object (Shippers, Carriers, Loads, Locations, and Truck Type).

BTW
Multiple-Word Names
There are several ways to handle multiple-word names. You can include the space (Shipper ID), omit the space (ShipperID), or use an underscore in place of the space (Shipper_ID). Other options include using a hyphen in place of a space and/or using the same case for all letters (SHIPPER-ID or shipper-id).

BTW
Data Types
Different database management systems have different available data types. Even data types that are essentially the same can have different names. The Currency data type in Access, for example, is referred to as Money in SQL Server.

BTW
AutoNumber Fields
AutoNumber fields also are called AutoIncrement fields. In Design view, the New Values field property allows you to increment the field sequentially (Increment) or randomly (Random). The default is Increment.

Table 1–1 Additional Data Types

Data Type	Description
Long Text	Field can store up to a gigabyte of text, although only the first 64,000 characters can be displayed.
Large Number	Field can store numeric data up to 8 bytes.
Date/Time Extended	Field can store date and time data up to 42 bytes with a longer date range and more granular fractional precision.
AutoNumber	Field can store a unique number that Access assigns to a record. Access can increment the number by 1 as each new record is added or choose random values.
Yes/No	Field can store only one of two values. The choices are Yes/No, True/False, or On/Off.
OLE Object	Field can store an OLE object, which is an image, graph, or other object linked to or embedded in the table. The object can be up to 2 GB.
Hyperlink	Field can store text that can be used as a hyperlink address to a file stored on the Internet, an intranet, a local area network (LAN), or the local computer.
Attachment	Field can contain an attached file. Images, spreadsheets, documents, charts, and other elements can be attached to this field in a record in the database. You can view and edit the attached file.
Calculated	Field is specified as a calculation based on other fields. The value is not actually stored.
Lookup Wizard	While not a data type, this option is used to define a simple or complex lookup field to draw data from another table or a value list as records are created later.

BTW
Currency Symbols
To show the symbol for the Euro (€) instead of the dollar sign, change the Format property for the field whose data type is currency. To change the default symbols for currency, change the settings in Windows.

In the Shippers table, because the Shipper ID, Shipper Name, Contact, Phone, Email, Address, Locations, and Billing Notes can all contain letters or symbols, their data types should be Short Text. The data type for Phone is Short Text instead of Number because you typically do not use phone numbers in arithmetic operations; for example, it's not common practice to add phone numbers or find an average phone number. The Shipper ID field also contains numbers, but you will not use these numbers in arithmetic operations, so its data type should be Short Text.

Similarly, in the Loads table, the data type for the Pickup, Dropoff, Contents, Truck, Status, Driver, Phone, Carrier, and Shipper fields should all be Short Text. The Pickup date and Dropoff date fields should have a data type of Date/Time. In the Truck Type table, the Target Rate contains monetary amounts, so its data type should be Currency.

For fields whose data type is Short Text, you can change the field size, that is, the maximum number of characters that can be entered in the field. If you set the field size for the Location table's State field to 2, for example, Access will not allow the user to enter more than two characters in the field. This is especially important for increasing database security and for helping ensure the data entered is correct. On the other hand, fields whose data type is Number often require you to change the field size, which is the storage space assigned to the field by Access. Table 1–2 shows the possible field sizes for Number fields.

Table 1–2 Field Sizes for Number Fields

Field Size	Description
Byte	Integer value in the range of 0 to 255
Integer	Integer value in the range of −32,768 to 32,767
Long Integer	Integer value in the range of −2,147,483,648 to 2,147,483,647
Single	Numeric values with decimal places up to 7 significant digits—requires 4 bytes of storage
Double	Numeric values with decimal places up to 15 significant digits—requires 8 bytes of storage
Replication ID	Special identifier required for replication
Decimal	Numeric values with decimal places to more accuracy than Single or Double—requires 12 bytes of storage

Consider This

What is the appropriate size for a Postal Code field?

By default, a Short Text field will allocate 255 spaces for data. However, a postal code normally would only take 9 spaces (or 10 if you include the hyphen). It is more efficient to change the Short Text field size limit to nine spaces, which accounts for the five-digit postal code followed by four numbers identifying a specific delivery route.

Creating a Table Using Datasheet View

To create a table in Access, you must define its structure. That is, you must define all the fields that make up the table and their characteristics. You must also indicate the primary key.

In Access, you can use two different views to create a table: Datasheet view and Design view. Although the main reason to use Datasheet view is to add or update records in a table, you can also use it to create a table or to later modify its structure. The other view, **Design view**, is only used to create a table or to modify the structure of a table.

As you might expect, Design view has more functionality than Datasheet view for creating a table. That is, there are certain actions that can only be performed in Design view or that are easier in Design view. One such action is choosing how new values are selected for an AutoNumber field. In this module, you will create the first table, the Shippers table, in Datasheet view. Once you have created the table in Datasheet view, you will use Design view to check (and fix as necessary) field properties such as field size and data type.

Whichever view you choose to use, before creating the table, you need to know the names and data types of the fields that will make up the table. You can also decide to enter a description for a particular field to explain important details about the field. When you select this field, this description will appear on the status bar. You might also choose to assign a **caption** to a particular field. If you assign a caption, Access will display the value you assign, rather than the field name, in datasheets and in forms. If you do not assign a caption, Access will display the field name.

BTW
Naming Files
The following characters cannot be used in a file name: question mark (?), quotation mark ("), slash (/), backslash (\ ), colon (:), asterisk (*), vertical bar (|), greater than symbol (>), and less than symbol (<).

Consider This

When would you want to use a caption?

You would use a caption whenever you wanted something other than the field name displayed. One common example is when the field name is relatively long and the data in the field is relatively short. In the Shippers table, the name of the first field is Shipper ID, but the field contains data that is only five characters long. You will change the caption for this field to S_ID, which is much shorter than Shipper ID, yet still describes the field. Doing so will enable you to greatly reduce the width of the column.

The results of these decisions for the fields in the Shippers table are shown in Table 1–3. The table also shows the data types and field sizes of the fields as well as any special properties that need to be changed. The Shipper ID short text field has a caption of S_ID, enabling the width of the Shipper ID column to be reduced in the datasheet. Other fields have captions as well to reduce redundancy in field names.

Table 1–3 Structure of Shippers Table

Field Name	Data Type	Field Size	Description and/or Caption
Shipper ID	Short Text	5	Primary Key **Description:** Unique identifier of shipping company **Caption:** S_ID
Shipper Name	Short Text	50	
Shipper Contact	Short Text	50	**Caption:** Contact
Shipper Phone	Short Text	12	**Caption:** Phone
Shipper Email	Short Text	50	**Caption:** Email
Shipper Address	Short Text	255	**Caption:** Address
Shipper Locations	Short Text	255	**Caption:** Locations
Shipper Billing Notes	Long Text		**Caption:** Billing Notes

BTW
Using Table Names in Field Names
Some database designers include a portion of a table's name in many of its field names. Field names such as Phone, Email, and Address are often used in many tables for different entities (such as listing phone numbers, email addresses, and physical addresses in both the Shippers and Carriers tables). When working with advanced database tasks, there are times when fields that all have exactly the same name but belong to different tables could be confusing to work with. Including a portion of the table's name in these field names, such as Shipper Name or Carrier Name rather than simply Name, can help minimize confusion and mistakes later.

Consider This

How do you determine the field size?

You need to determine the maximum number of characters that can be entered in the field. In some cases, the number of characters will be consistent from record to record. Field sizes of 2 for a State field and 9 for a Postal Code field are appropriate choices. In other cases, you need to determine how many characters you want to allow. In the list shown in Table 1-3, Clearnet decided that allowing 50 characters was sufficient for the name, contact, and email fields. You can change this field size later if it proves to be insufficient.

BTW

Tabbed Documents Versus Overlapping Windows

By default, Access displays database objects, such as tables, in tabbed documents instead of in overlapping windows. If your database is in overlapping windows mode, click File on the ribbon, click Options in Backstage view, click Current Database in the Access Options dialog box, and select the 'Display Document Tabs' check box and the Tabbed Documents option button. Click the OK button in the Access Options dialog box to save your changes.

To Modify the Primary Key

When you first create a database, Access automatically creates a table for you. You can immediately begin defining the fields. If, for any reason, you do not have this table or you inadvertently delete it, you can create the table by clicking Create on the ribbon and then clicking the Table button (Create tab | Tables group). In either case, you are ready to define the fields.

The following steps change the name, data type, and other properties of the first field to match the Shipper ID field in Table 1–3, which is the primary key. **Why?** Access has already created the first field as the primary key field, which it has named ID. Shipper ID is a more appropriate name.

1

- Right-click the column heading for the ID field to display a shortcut menu (Figure 1-3).

Q&A Why does my shortcut menu look different?

You may have displayed a shortcut menu for the column instead of the column heading. Be sure you right-click the column heading.

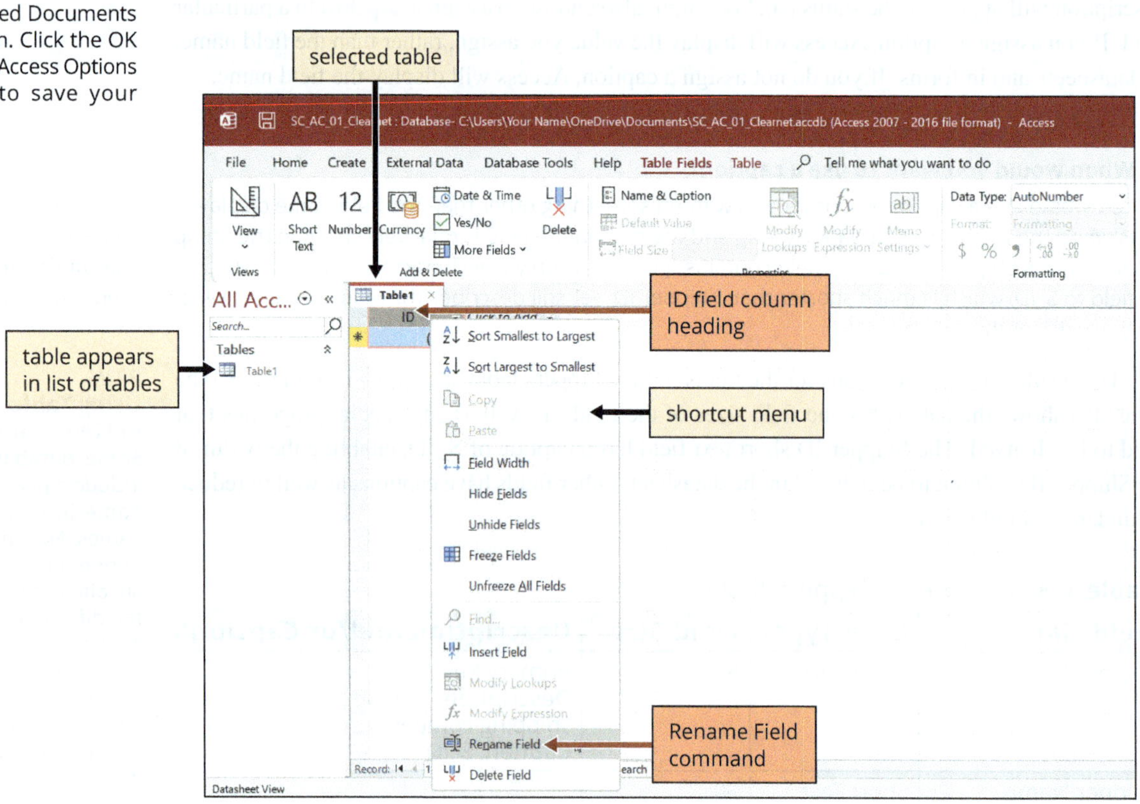

Figure 1-3

2

- Click Rename Field on the shortcut menu to highlight the current name.
- Type **Shipper ID** to assign a name to the new field.
- Click the white space immediately below the field name to complete the addition of the field (Figure 1–4).

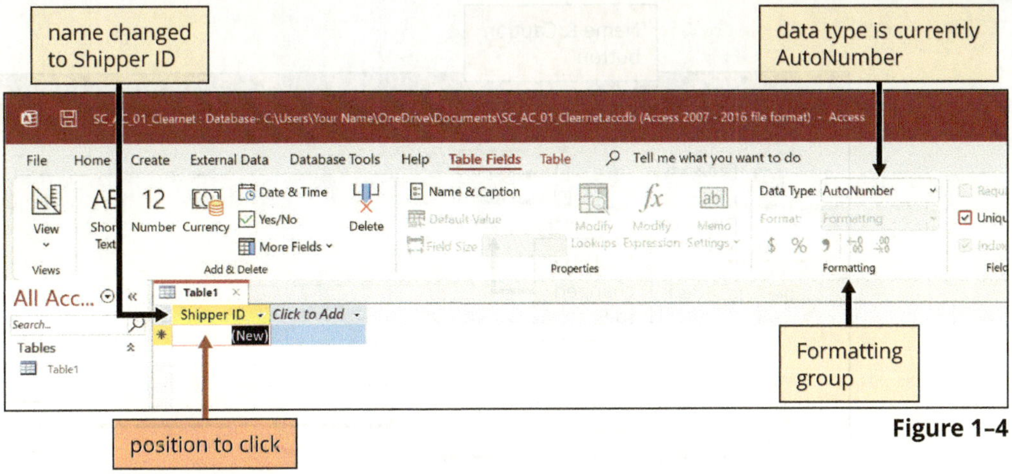

Figure 1–4

Q&A Why does the full name of the field not appear?
The default column size might not be large enough for Shipper ID, or a later field such as Shipper Billing Notes, to be displayed in its entirety. If necessary, you will address this issue in later steps.

3

- Because the data type needs to be changed from AutoNumber to Short Text, click the Data Type arrow (Table Fields tab | Formatting group) to display a menu of available data types (Figure 1–5).

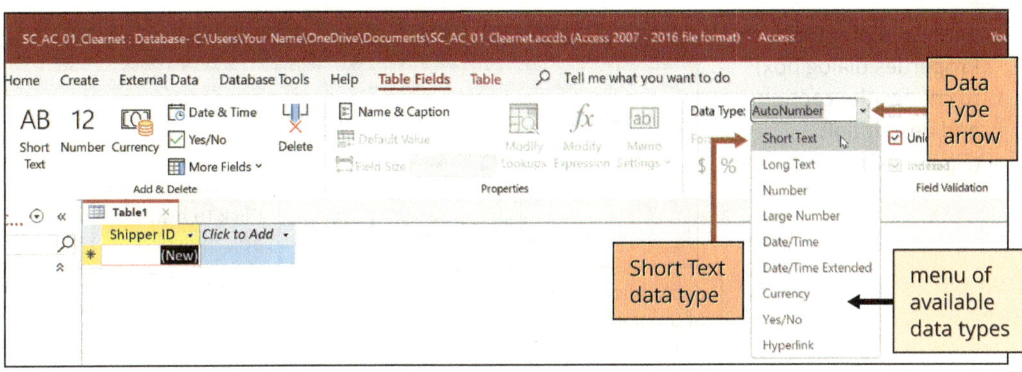

Figure 1–5

4

- Click Short Text to select the data type for the field (Figure 1–6).

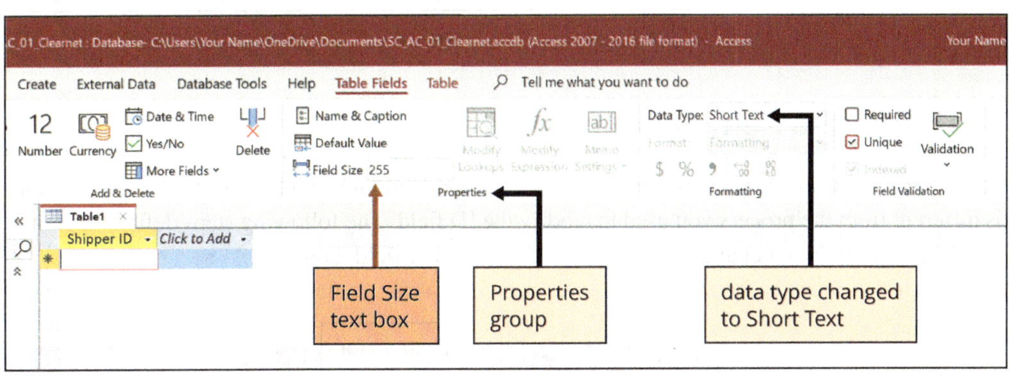

Figure 1–6

5

- Click the Field Size text box (Table Fields tab | Properties group) to select the current field size, use either DEL or BACKSPACE to erase the current field size if necessary, and then type **5** as the new field size.
- Click the Name & Caption button (Table Fields tab | Properties group) to display the Enter Field Properties dialog box.
- Click the Caption text box (Enter Field Properties dialog box), and then type **S_ID** as the caption.
- Click the Description text box, and then type **Unique identifier of shipping company** as the description (Figure 1–7).

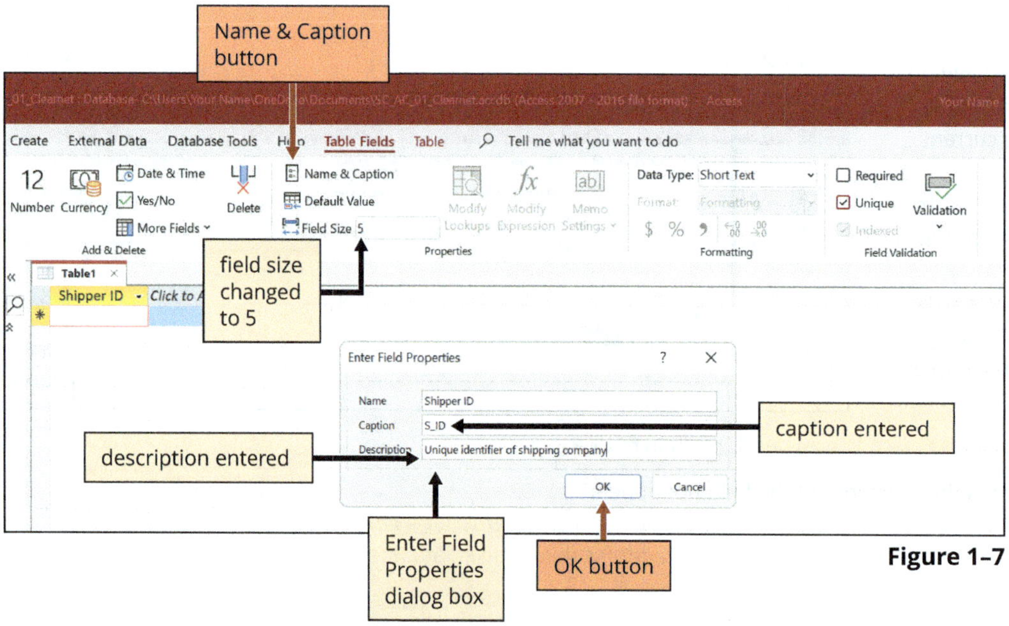

Figure 1–7

6

- Click OK (Enter Field Properties dialog box) to change the caption and description (Figure 1–8).

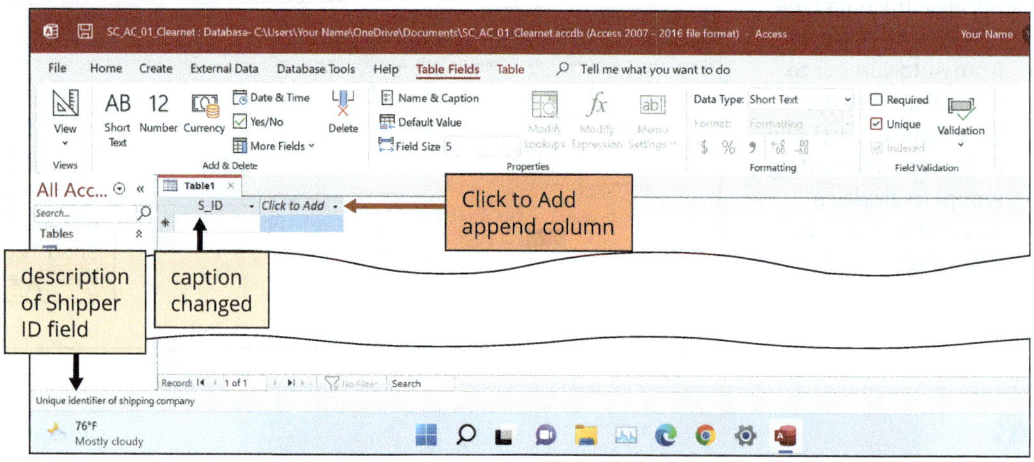

Figure 1–8

To Define the Remaining Fields in a Table

To define an additional field, you click the Click to Add column heading, select the data type, and then type the field name. This is different from the process you used to modify the ID field. The following steps define the remaining fields shown in Table 1–3.

These steps do not change the field size of the number field, however. **Why?** You can only change the field size of a number field in Design view. Later, you will use Design view to change the field size and change the format.

1

- Click the Click to Add column heading to display a menu of available data types (Figure 1–9).

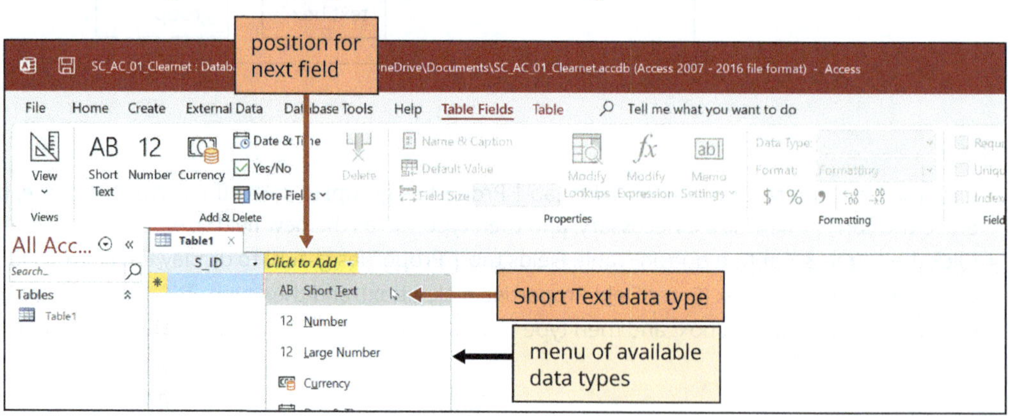

Figure 1–9

2

- Click Short Text in the menu of available data types to select the Short Text data type.
- Type **Shipper Name** to enter a field name.
- Click the blank space below the field name to complete the change of the name. Click the blank space a second time to select the field (Figure 1–10).

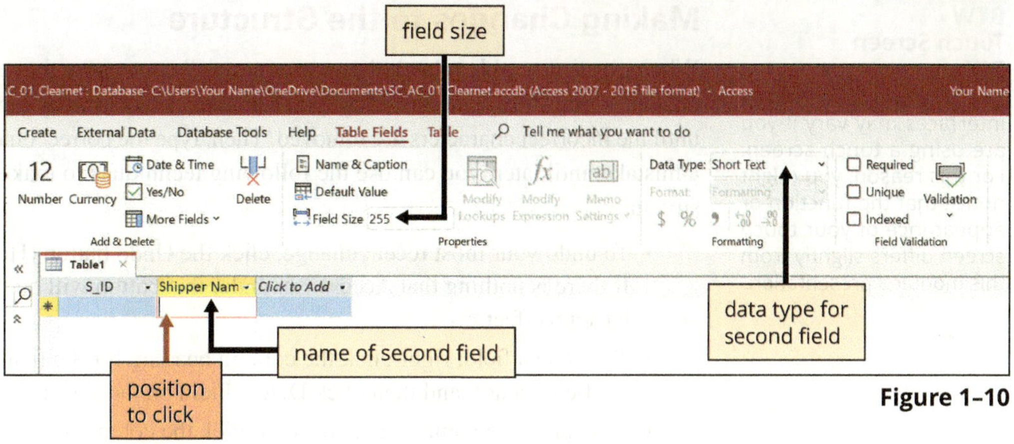

Figure 1–10

- If necessary, enlarge the field name box to display the entire name by clicking between Shipper Name and the Click to Add box. Drag the pointer, which is now a double-tipped arrow, to the right so that the entire field name of Shipper Name is visible.

Q&A After entering the field name, I realized that I selected the wrong data type. How can I correct it?
Click the Data Type arrow, and then select the correct type.

I inadvertently clicked the blank space before entering the field name. How can I correct the name?
Right-click the field name, click Rename Field on the shortcut menu, and then type the new name.

3

- Change the field size to **50** just as you changed the field size of the Shipper ID field.
- Using the same technique, add the remaining fields in the Shippers table. For the Shipper Contact, Shipper Phone, Shipper Email, Shipper Address, and Shipper Locations fields, use the Short Text data type, but change the field sizes to match Table 1–3. For the Shipper Billing Notes field, use the Long Text data type. Add Captions for the new fields as indicated in Table 1–3. Your Shippers table should look like Figure 1–11.

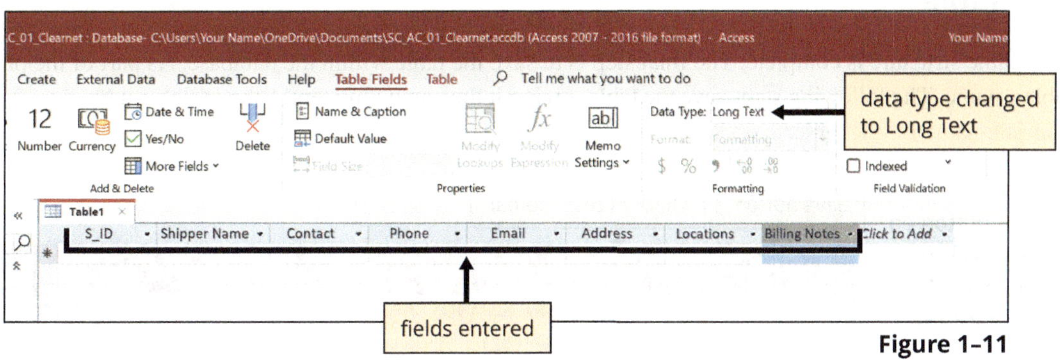

Figure 1–11

Q&A I have an extra row between the row containing the field names and the row that begins with the asterisk. What happened? Is this a problem? If so, how do I fix it?
You inadvertently added a record to the table by pressing a key. Even pressing SPACEBAR adds a record. You now have an unwanted record. To fix it, select the blank record, click the Delete button (Home tab | Records group), and then click Yes to confirm the deletion.

When I try to move on to specify another field, I get an error message indicating that the primary key cannot contain a null value. How do I correct this?
First, click the OK button to remove the error message. Next, press ESC or click the Undo button on the Home tab to undo the action. You may need to do this more than once.

BTW
Touch Screen Differences
The Office and Windows interfaces may vary if you are using a touch screen. For this reason, you might notice that the function or appearance of your touch screen differs slightly from this module's presentation.

Making Changes to the Structure

When creating a table, check the entries carefully to ensure they are correct. If you discover a mistake while still typing the entry, you can correct the error by repeatedly pressing BACKSPACE until the incorrect characters are removed. Then, type the correct characters. If you do not discover a mistake until later, you can use the following techniques to make the necessary changes to the structure:

- To undo your most recent change, click the Undo button (Home tab | Undo group). If there is nothing that Access can undo, this button will be dim, and clicking it will have no effect.
- To delete a field, right-click the column heading for the field (the position containing the field name), and then click Delete Field on the shortcut menu.
- To change the name of a field, right-click the column heading for the field, click Rename Field on the shortcut menu, and then type the desired field name.
- To insert a field as the last field, click the Click to Add column heading, click the appropriate data type on the menu of available data types, type the desired field name, and, if necessary, change the field size.
- To insert a field between existing fields, right-click the column heading for the field that will follow the new field, and then click Insert Field on the shortcut menu. Right-click the column heading for the new field, click Rename Field on the shortcut menu, and then type the desired field name.
- To move a field, click the column heading for the field to be moved to select the field, and then drag the field's black bar to the desired position.

As an alternative to these steps for correcting your table's structure, you might want to start over. To do so, click the Close button for the table, and then click the No button in the Microsoft Access dialog box. Click Create on the ribbon, and then click the Table button to create a table. You then can repeat the process you used earlier to define the fields in the table.

To Save a Table

The Shippers table structure is complete. The final step is to save the table within the database. As part of the process, you will give the table a name. The following steps save the table, giving it the name Shippers. **Why?** Clearnet has decided that Shippers is an appropriate name for the table.

1

- Click the Save button on the Quick Access Toolbar to display the Save As dialog box (Figure 1–12).

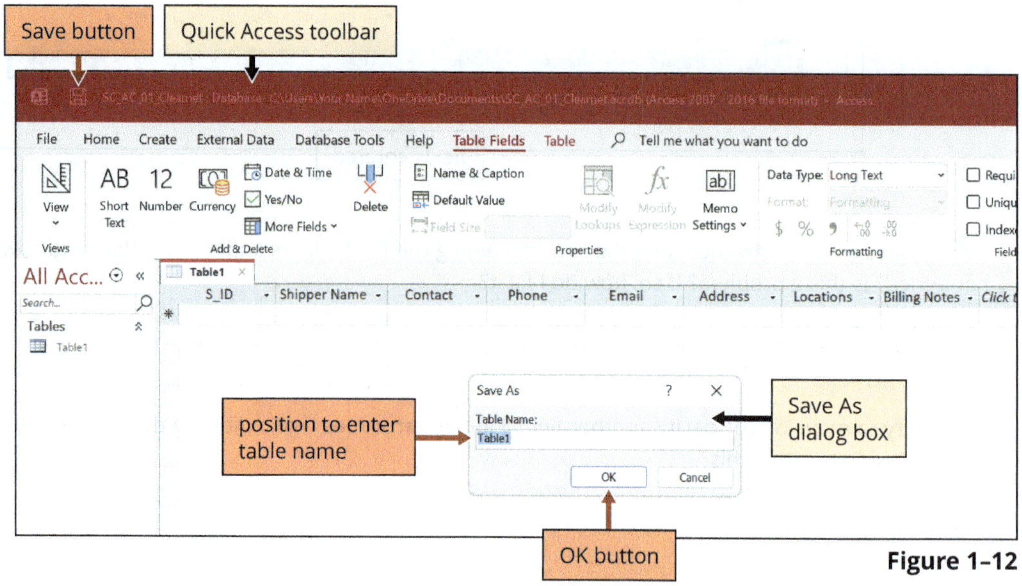

Figure 1–12

2

- Type **Shippers** to change the name assigned to the table.
- Click OK (Save As dialog box) to save the table (Figure 1–13).

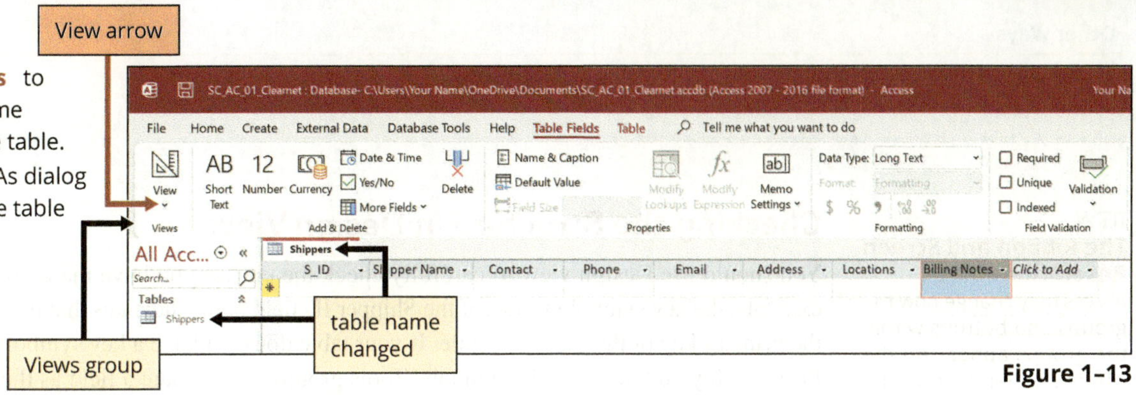

Figure 1–13

Other Ways

1. Click File on the ribbon, click Save in Backstage view to save table
2. Right-click table's tab, click Save on shortcut menu to save table
3. Press CTRL+S to save table

To View the Table in Design View

Even when creating a table in Datasheet view, Design view can be helpful. **Why?** You easily can view the fields, data types, and properties to ensure you have entered them correctly. It is also easier to determine the primary key in Design view. The following steps display the structure of the Shippers table in Design view so you can verify the design is correct.

1

- Click the View arrow (Table Fields tab | Views group) to display the View menu (Figure 1–14).

Q&A Could I just click the View button rather than the arrow?
Yes. Clicking the button is equivalent to clicking the command represented by the icon that currently appears on the button. Because the icon on the button in Figure 1–14 is for Design view, clicking the button would display the table in Design view. If you are uncertain, you can always click the arrow and select Design View from the menu.

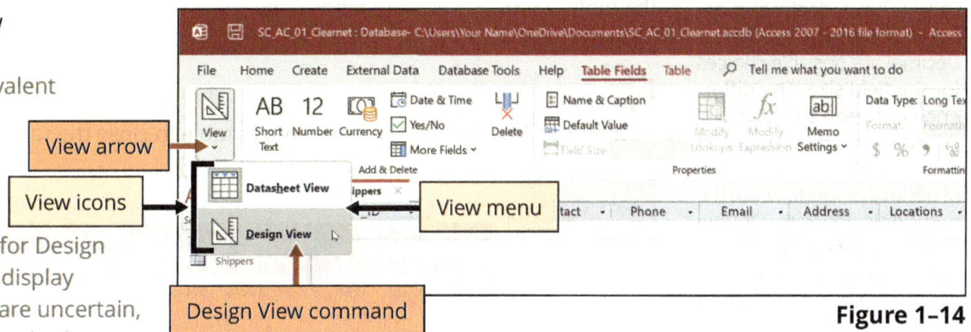

Figure 1–14

2

- Click Design View on the View menu to view the table in Design view (Figure 1–15).

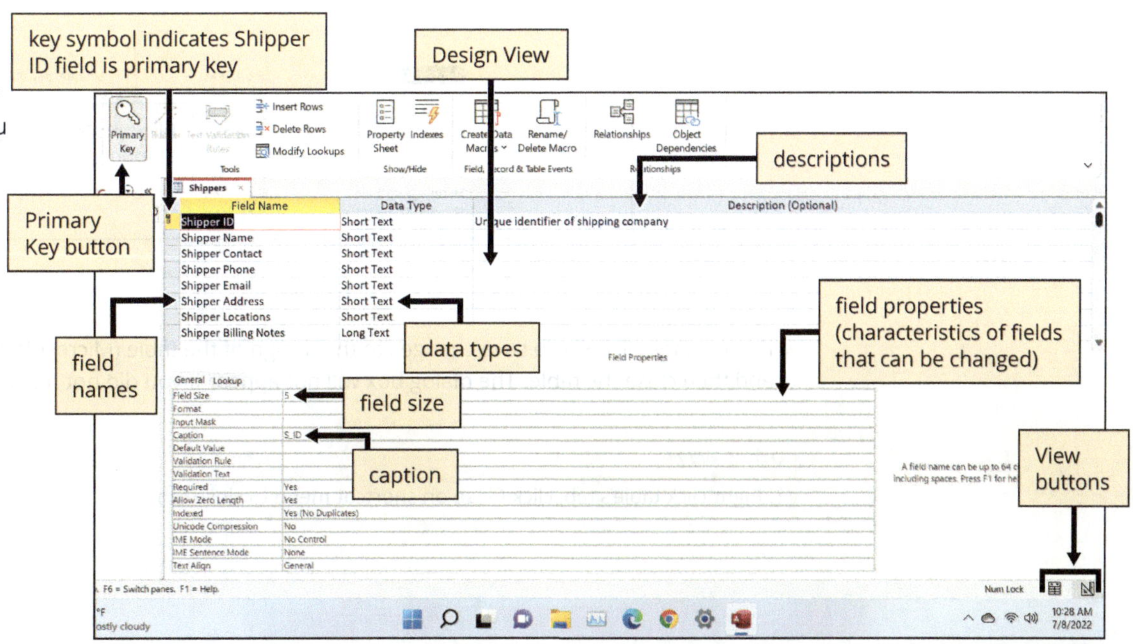

Figure 1–15

Other Ways

1. Click Design View button on status bar to view table in Design view

BTW
The Ribbon and Screen Resolution
Access may change how the groups and buttons within the groups appear on the ribbon, depending on the computer's screen resolution. Thus, your ribbon may look different from the ones in this course if you are using a screen resolution other than 1920 × 1080.

BTW
Changing a Field Size in Design View
Most field size changes can be made in either Datasheet view or Design view. However, changing the field size for Number fields can only be done in Design view. If field values have decimal places, only Single, Double, or Decimal are possible choices for the field size. The difference between these choices concerns the amount of accuracy, that is, the number of decimal places to which the number is accurate. Double is more accurate than Single, for example, but requires more storage space. If a field has only two decimal places, Single is an acceptable choice.

Checking the Structure in Design View

You should use Design view to carefully check the entries you have made. In Figure 1–15, for example, the key symbol in front of the Shipper ID field name indicates that the Shipper ID field is the primary key of the Shippers table. If your table does not have a key symbol, you can click the Primary Key button (Table Design tab | Tools group) to designate a field as the primary key. You can also check that the data type, description, field size, and caption are all correct for the first field.

For the other fields, you can see the field name, data type, and description without taking any special action. To see the field size and/or caption for a field, click the field's **row selector**, the small box to the left of the field. Clicking the row selector for the Shipper Name field, for example, displays the properties for that field in the Field Properties pane in the lower portion of the window. You then can check to see that the field size is correct. In addition, if the field has a caption, you can confirm it is correct. If you find any mistakes, you can make the necessary corrections on this screen. When you have finished, click the Save button to save your changes.

To Close the Table

Once you are sure that your entries are correct and you have saved your changes, you can close the table. **Why?** Closing database objects keeps the workspace uncluttered. The following step closes the table.

1

- Click the Close button for the Shippers table to close the table (Figure 1–16).

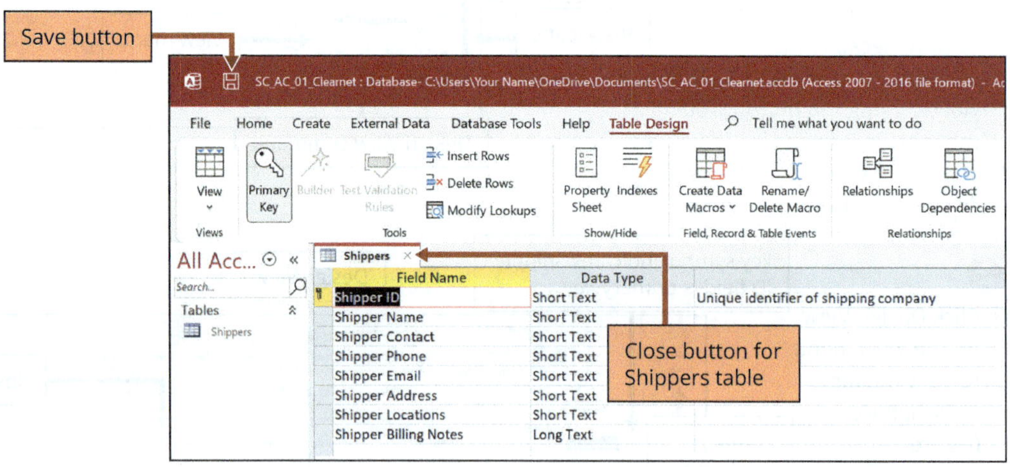

Figure 1–16

- If necessary, click Yes to save changes to the design of the table (Microsoft Access dialog box) and then close the table. The dialog box will not appear if you did not make any changes.

Other Ways

1. Right-click table's tab, click Close on shortcut menu to close table

To Add Records to a Table

Creating a table by building the structure and saving the table is the first step in the two-step process of using a table in a database. The second step is to add records to the table. To add records to a table, the table must be open. When making changes to records, you work in Datasheet view.

You often add records in phases. **Why?** You might not have enough time to add all the records in one session, or you might not have all the records currently available. The following steps open the Shippers table in Datasheet view and then add three records in the Shippers table (Figure 1–17).

S_ID	Shipper Name	Contact	Phone	Email	Address	Locations	Billing Notes
S-001	Sabus Flooring	Cori Sabus	719-555-4411	csabus@example.com	460 West Pioneer Road, Dolores, OK 73026	Home office at warehouse	Send paper invoice
S-002	Mid-Valley Nurseries	Steven Nguyen	513-555-5670	snguyen@example.com	9874 South Main Street, Blanding, OH 43056	Nursery at L-001	Email PDF invoice
S-003	Auto Suppliers, Inc.	Abdul Ritter	337-555-8901	abdulr@example.com	182-B Route 56, Cloud Springs, LA 70784	Warehouse at L-007	Email PDF invoice

Figure 1–17

1

- Right-click the Shippers table in the Navigation Pane to display the shortcut menu (Figure 1–18).

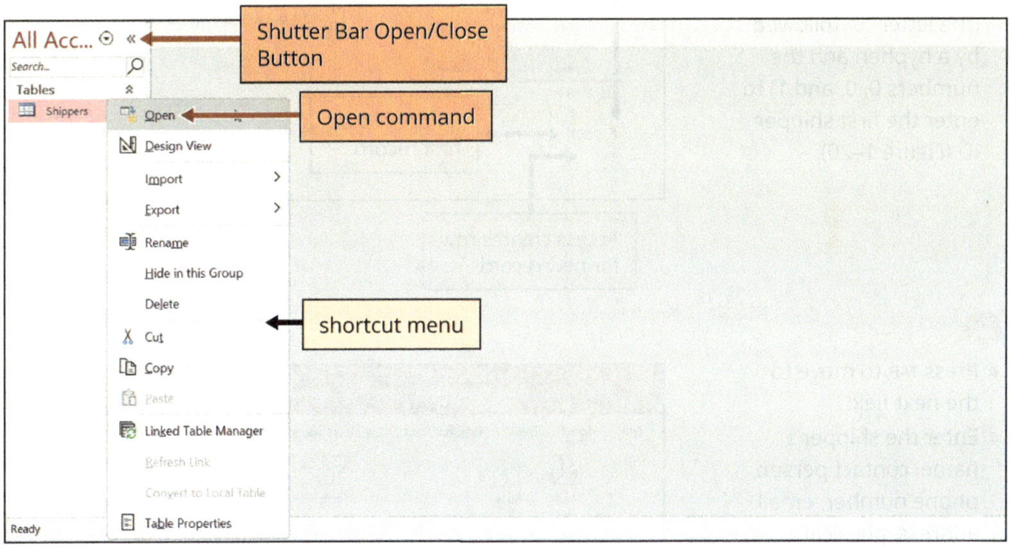

Figure 1–18

2

- Click Open on the shortcut menu to open the table in Datasheet view.
- Click the 'Shutter Bar Open/Close Button' to close the Navigation Pane (Figure 1–19).

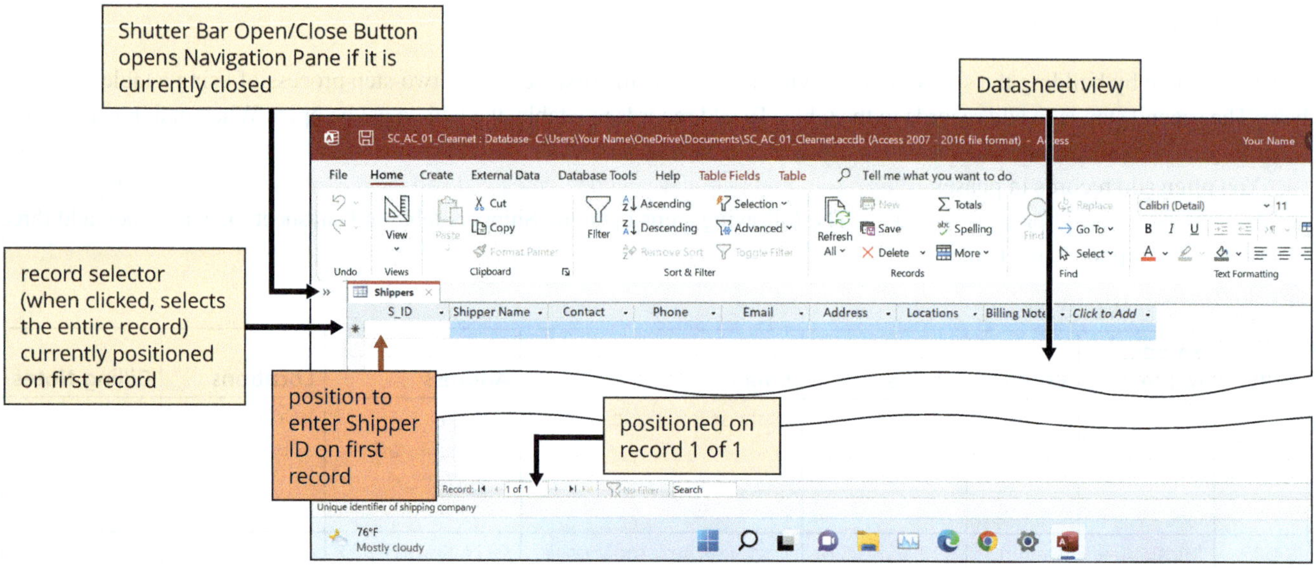

Figure 1–19

3

- Click the first row in the S_ID field if necessary to display an insertion point, and type **S-001** (the letter "S" followed by a hyphen and the numbers 0, 0, and 1) to enter the first shipper ID (Figure 1–20).

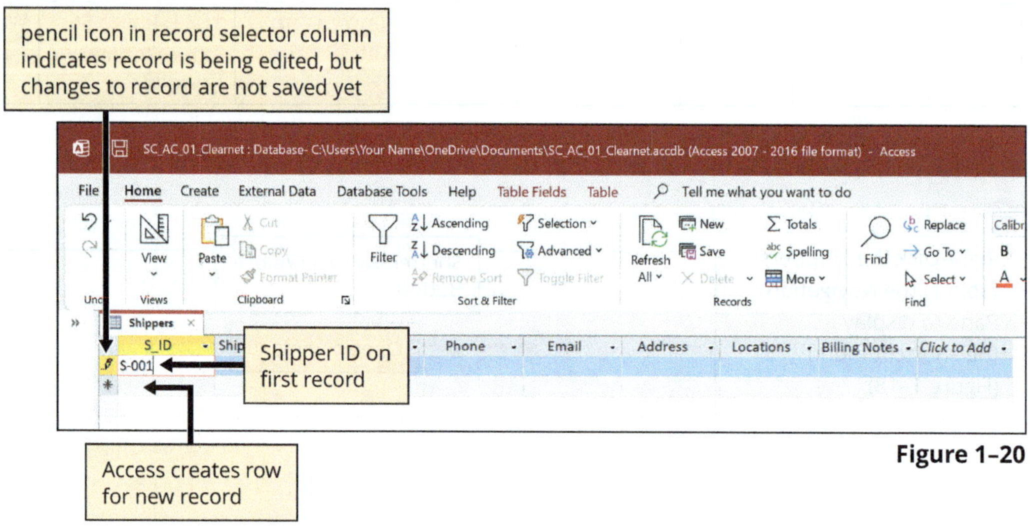

Figure 1–20

4

- Press TAB to move to the next field.
- Enter the shipper's name, contact person, phone number, email address, physical address, a list of locations, and billing notes by typing the following entries, as shown in Figure 1–21, pressing TAB after each entry: **Sabus Flooring** as the shipper's name, **Cori Sabus** as the contact person, **719-555-4411** as the contact's phone number, **csabus@example.com** as the contact's email address, **460 West Pioneer Road, Dolores, OK 73026** as the physical address, **Home office at warehouse** as the shipper's locations, and **Send paper invoice** as the billing notes.

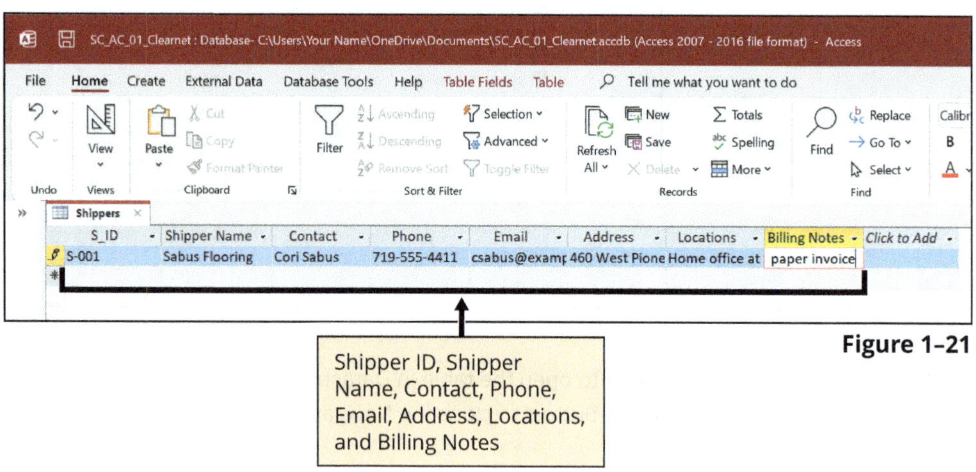

Figure 1–21

5

- Press TAB to complete the entry of the first record (Figure 1–22).

Q&A How and when do I save the record?

As soon as you have entered or modified a record and moved to another record, Access saves the original record. This is different from other applications. The rows entered in an Excel worksheet, for example, are not saved until the entire worksheet is saved.

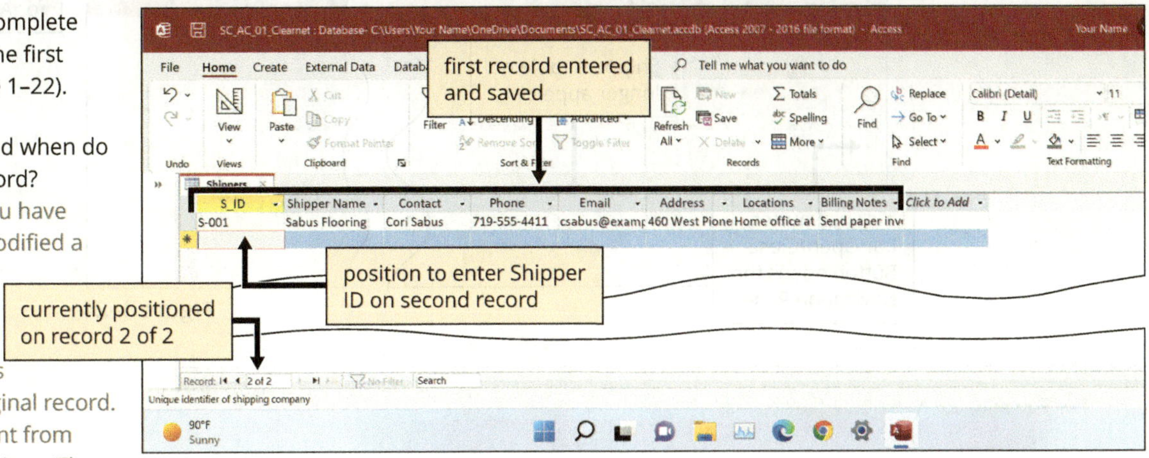

Figure 1–22

BTW

Append Row

Notice the asterisk * in the new row that is waiting for the next record to be entered. That row is called the **Append row**, the row where the next record can be added onto the table. The word append means to add onto the end of something.

6

- Use the techniques in Steps 3 through 5 to enter the data for the second and third records, referring to Figure 1–17 as needed for data to be entered (Figure 1–23).

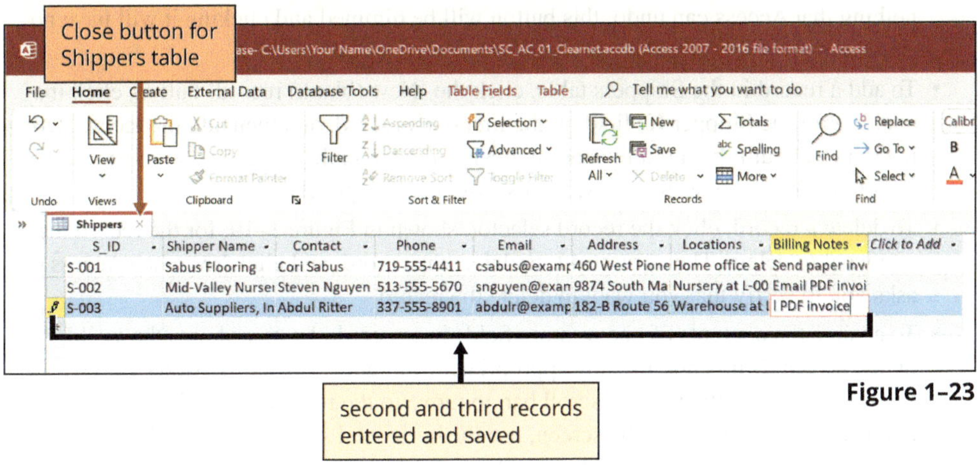

Figure 1–23

Q&A Does it matter that I entered Shipper ID S-001 after I entered Shipper ID S-002? Should the Shipper IDs be in order?

The order in which you enter the records is not important. When you close and later reopen the table, the records will be sorted in Shipper ID order, because the Shipper ID field is the primary key.

I made a mistake in entering the data. When should I fix it?

It is a good idea to fix it now, although you can fix it later as well. In any case, the following section gives you techniques you can use to make any necessary corrections. If you want to fix it now, read that section and make your corrections before proceeding to the next step.

7

- Click the Close button for the Shippers table, shown in Figure 1–23, to close the table (Figure 1–24).
- Exit Access.

Q&A Is it necessary for me to exit Access at this point?

No. The step is here for two reasons. First, you will often not be able to add all the records you need to add in one sitting. In such a case, you will add some records, and then exit Access. When you are ready to resume adding the records, you will start Access, open the table, and then continue the addition process. Second, there is a break point coming up in the module. If you want to take advantage of that break, you need to first exit Access.

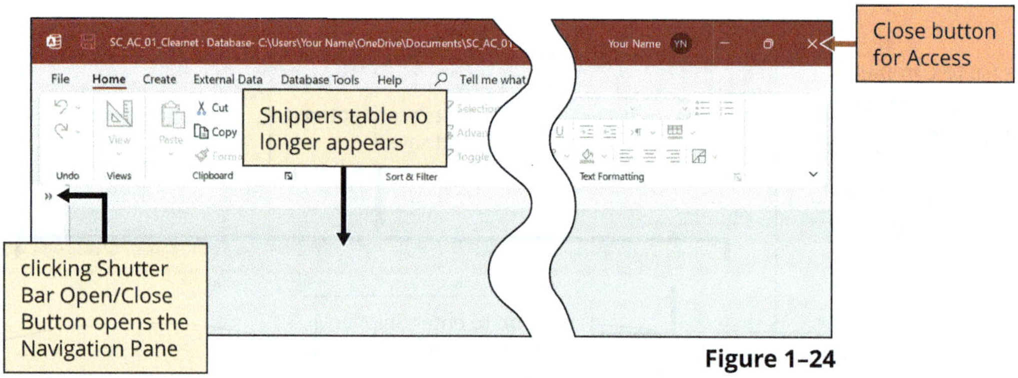

Figure 1–24

BTW
AutoCorrect Feature
The AutoCorrect feature of Access corrects common data entry errors. For example, AutoCorrect corrects two capital letters by changing the second letter to lowercase and capitalizes the first letter in the names of days. It can also correct commonly misspelled words, and you can add a custom dictionary for more assistance.

Making Changes to the Data

As you enter data in the datasheet view, check your entries carefully to ensure they are correct. If you make a mistake and discover it before you press TAB, correct it by pressing BACKSPACE until the incorrect characters are removed, and then type the correct characters. If you do not discover a mistake until later, you can use the following techniques to make the necessary corrections to the data:

- To undo your most recent change, click the Undo button on the Home tab. If there is nothing that Access can undo, this button will be dimmed and clicking it will have no effect.
- To add a record in the Shippers table, click the 'New (blank) record' button, click the position for the Shipper ID field on the first open record, and then add the record. Do not worry about it being in the correct position in the table. Access will reposition the record based on the primary key, in this case, the Shipper ID.
- To delete a record, click the record selector, shown in Figure 1–19, for the record that you want to delete. Then press DEL to delete the record, and click Yes when Access asks you to verify that you want to delete the record.
- To change the contents of one or more fields in a record, the record must be visible on the screen. If it is not, use any appropriate technique, such as UP ARROW and DOWN ARROW or the vertical scroll bar, to move to the record. If the field you want to correct is not visible on the screen, use the horizontal scroll bar along the bottom of the screen to shift all the fields until the one you want appears. If the value in the field is currently highlighted, you can simply type the new value. If you would rather edit the existing value, you must have an insertion point in the field. You can place the insertion point by clicking in the field or by pressing F2. You then can use the arrow keys, DEL, and BACKSPACE for making the correction. You can also use INS to switch between Insert and Overtype mode. When you have made the change, press TAB to move to the next field.

BTW
Spell Checking
To check the spelling in a table, Select the Home tab, Records group, Spelling.

Consider This

Duplicate Values in the Primary Key Field

When entering new records, if you inadvertently type the same value in the primary key field as another record, Access will display a dialog box saying that the changes were not successful because they would create duplicate values in the index, primary key, or relationship. To correct this problem, change the value of the primary key to a different value that has not yet been used.

If you cannot determine how to correct the data, you may find that you are "stuck" on the record, in which case Access neither allows you to move to another record nor allows you to close the table until you have made the correction. If you encounter this situation, simply press ESC. Pressing ESC will remove from the screen the record you are trying to add. You then can move to any other record, close the table, or take any other action you desire.

BTW
Other AutoCorrect Options
Using the Office AutoCorrect feature, you can create entries that will replace abbreviations with spelled-out names and phrases automatically. To specify AutoCorrect rules, click File on the ribbon to open Backstage view, click Options, and then click Proofing in the Access Options dialog box.

Break Point: If you wish to take a break, this is a good place to do so. You can exit Access now. To resume at a later time, start Access, open the database called SC_AC_01_Clearnet.accdb, and continue following the steps from this location forward.

Navigation Buttons

You will often need to update tables with new records. You can open a table that already contains data and add records using a process similar to that used to add records to an empty table. The only difference is that you place the insertion point after the last record before you enter the additional data. To position the insertion point after the last record, you can use the **Navigation buttons**, which are buttons used to move within a table, found near the lower-left corner of the screen when a table is open. It is a good habit to use the 'New (blank) record' button to select the append row. Once a table contains more records than will fit on the screen, it is easier to click the 'New (blank) record' button to move to the append row rather than scrolling to get to the row. The purpose of each Navigation button is described in Table 1–4.

BTW
Enabling Content
If the database is one that you created, or if it comes from a trusted source, you can enable the content. You should disable the content of a database if you suspect that your database might contain harmful content or damaging macros.

Table 1–4 Navigation Buttons in Datasheet View

Button	Purpose
First record	Moves to the first record in the table
Previous record	Moves to the previous record in the table
Next record	Moves to the next record in the table
Last record	Moves to the last record in the table
New (blank) record	Moves to the end of the table to a position for entering a new record in the Append row

To Resize Columns in a Datasheet

Access assigns default column sizes, which do not always provide space to display all the data in the field. In some cases, the data might appear but some of the field name is not visible. You can correct this problem by resizing the column (changing its size) in the datasheet. In some instances, you might want to reduce the size of a column. Why? Some fields, such as the S_ID field, are short enough that they do not require all the space on the screen that is allotted to them. Changing a column width changes the layout, or design, of a table. The following steps resize the columns in the Shippers table and save the changes to the layout.

1

- Start Access, unless it is already running.
- Open the database, SC_AC_01_Clearnet.accdb, from your hard drive, OneDrive, or other storage location (Figure 1–25). You created this database earlier in this module.
- If a Security Warning appears, click the Enable Content button.

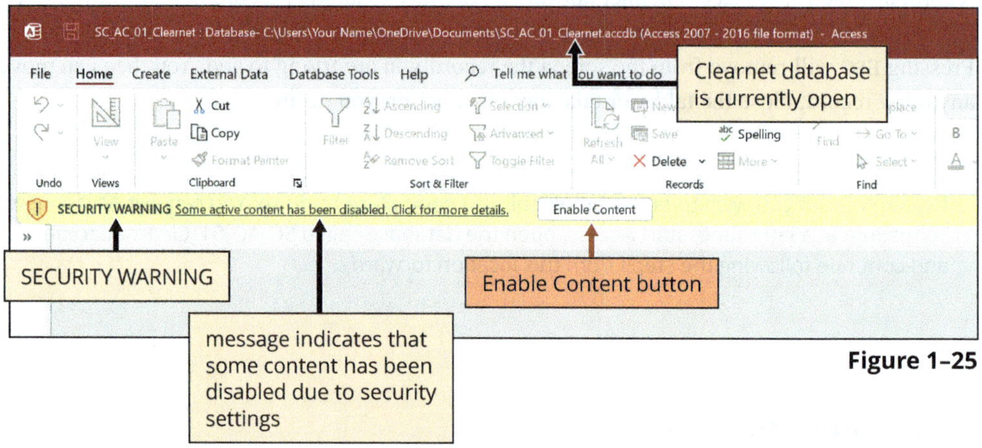

Figure 1–25

2

- If the Navigation Pane is closed, click the Shutter Bar Open/Close Button, shown in Figure 1–24, to open the Navigation Pane (Figure 1–26).

Figure 1–26

3

- Right-click the Shippers table in the Navigation Pane to display a shortcut menu.
- Click Open on the shortcut menu to open the table in Datasheet view.

Q&A Why do the records appear in a different order from how I entered them?
When you open a table, they are sorted in order based on the primary key, which may not be the order in which you entered them. In this case, the records appear in Shipper ID order.

4

- Point to the right boundary of the field selector for the Shipper Name field (Figure 1–27) so that the pointer becomes a two-headed arrow.

Q&A I am using touch and I cannot see the pointer. Is this a problem?
It is not a problem. Remember that if you are using your finger on a touch screen, you will not see the pointer.

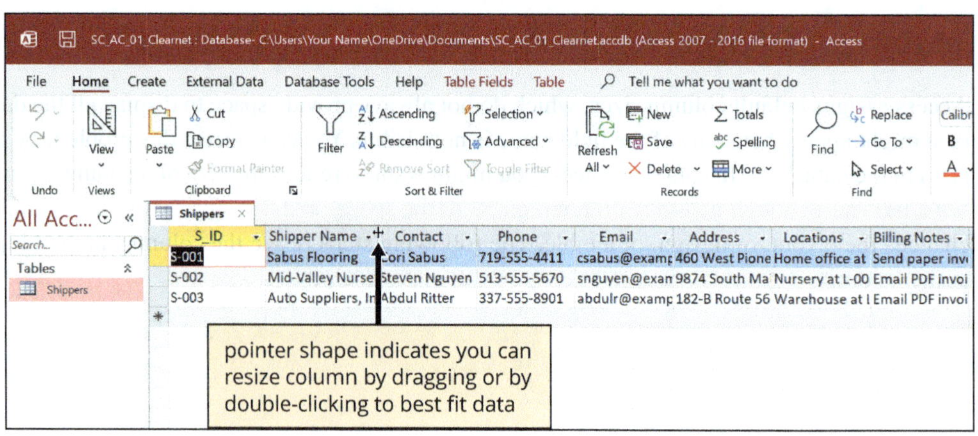

Figure 1–27

5

- Double-click the right boundary of the field selector to resize the field so that it best fits the data.
- Use the same technique to resize all the other fields to best fit the data.
- Save the changes to the layout by clicking the Save button on the Quick Access Toolbar (Figure 1–28).

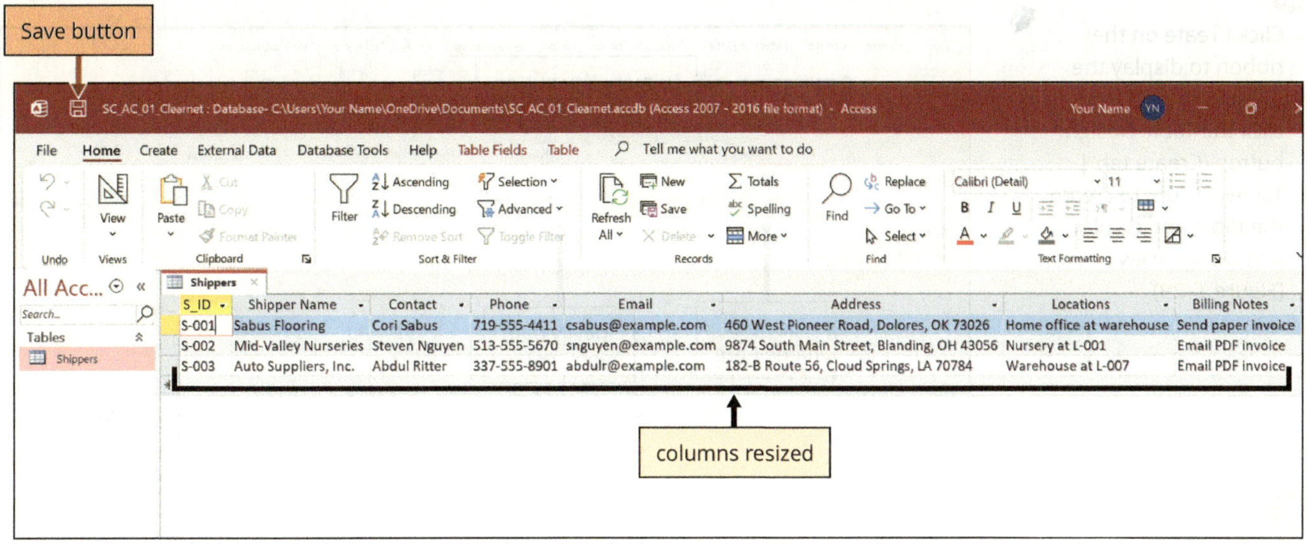

Figure 1–28

6

- Click the table's Close button (shown in Figure 1–23) to close the table.

Q&A What if I closed the table without saving the layout changes?
You would be asked if you want to save the changes.

Other Ways

1. Right-click field name, click Field Width, click Best Fit to resize field

Consider This

What is the best method for distributing database objects?

The traditional method of distributing database objects such as tables, reports, and forms uses a printer to produce a hard copy. A hard copy or printout is information that exists on a physical medium such as paper. Hard copies can be useful for the following reasons:

- Some people prefer proofreading a hard copy of a document rather than viewing it on the screen to check for errors and readability.
- Hard copies can serve as a backup reference if your storage medium is lost or becomes corrupted and you need to recreate the document. Instead of distributing a hard copy, users can distribute the document as an electronic image that mirrors the original document's appearance. The electronic image of the document can be emailed, posted on a website, or copied to a portable storage medium such as a USB flash drive. Two popular electronic image formats, sometimes called fixed formats, are PDF by Adobe Systems and XPS by Microsoft.

In Access, you can create electronic image files through the External Data tab on the ribbon. Electronic images of documents, such as PDF and XPS, can be useful for the following reasons:

- Users can view electronic images of documents without the software that created the original document (e.g., Access). Specifically, to view a PDF file, you use a program called Adobe Acrobat Reader, which can be downloaded free from Adobe's website. Similarly, to view an XPS file, you use a program called XPS Viewer, which is included in older versions of Windows and can be installed for free in newer versions of Windows.
- Sending electronic documents saves paper and printer supplies. Society encourages users to contribute to green computing, which involves reducing the electricity consumed and environmental waste generated when using computers, mobile devices, and related technologies.

To Create a Table Using Design View

The following steps use Design view to create a table. **Why?** Design view is a more efficient way to create a table than Datasheet view because you specify field name, data type, and size all in one view.

1

- Click Create on the ribbon to display the Create tab, and then click the Table Design button (Create tab | Tables group) to create the table and display it in Design view (Figure 1–29).

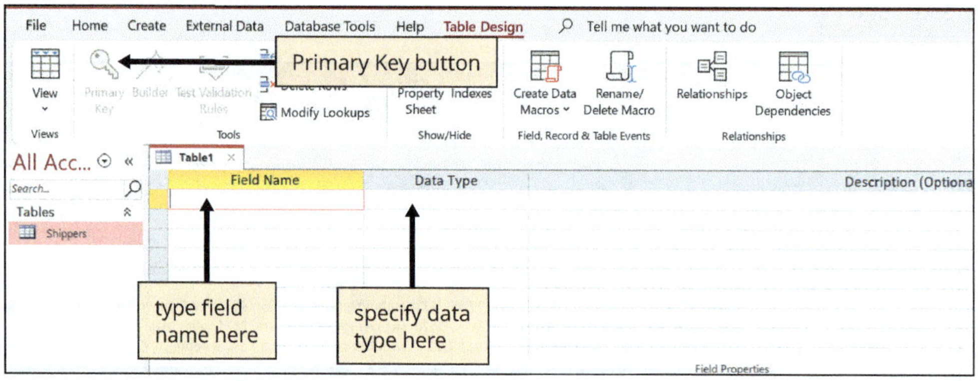

Figure 1–29

2

- Click in the empty field below Field Name if necessary to place the insertion point, and then type **Location ID** to enter the first field's name. Continue entering the data for the Locations table, as shown in Figure 1–30.

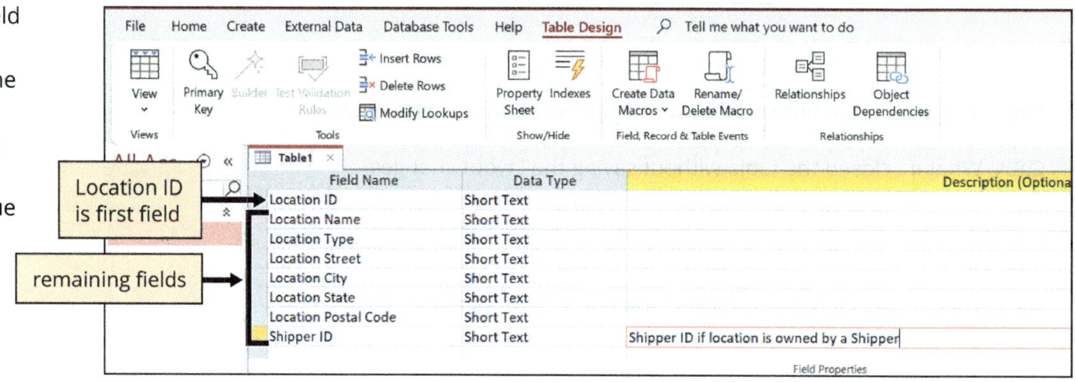

Figure 1–30

3

- Click the Location ID row selector, if necessary, and then click the Primary Key button to assign Location ID as the primary key field (Figure 1–31).

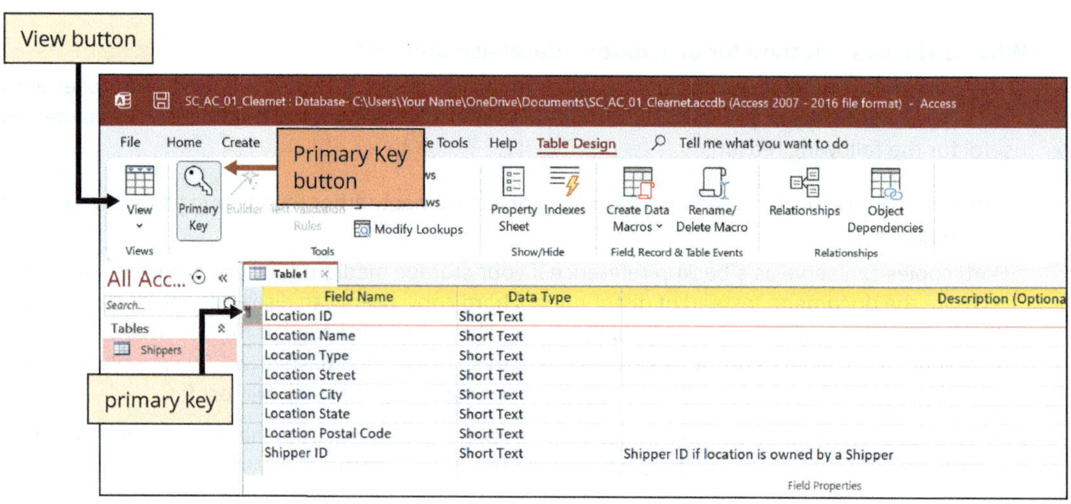

Figure 1–31

- Adjust the fields' sizes and captions as listed in Table 1–5.

Table 1–5 Structure of Locations Table

Field Name	Data Type	Field Size	Description
Location ID	Short Text	5	Primary Key **Caption:** L_ID
Location Name	Short Text	50	
Location Type	Short Text	15	**Caption:** Type
Location Street	Short Text	50	**Caption:** Street
Location City	Short Text	25	**Caption:** City
Location State	Short Text	2	**Caption:** State
Location Postal Code	Short Text	10	**Caption:** Postal Code
Shipper ID	Short Text	5	**Description:** Shipper ID if location is owned by a Shipper

- Click the Save button on the Quick Access toolbar and enter **Locations** in the text box to save the table with the name, Locations.

Q&A How do I rename a field in Design view?
In Design view, click on the end of the field you want to rename and press BACKSPACE until the name is removed. Enter the correct name.

Correcting Errors in the Structure

Whenever you create or modify a table in Design view, you should check the entries carefully to ensure they are correct. If you make a mistake and discover it before you press TAB, you can correct the error by repeatedly pressing BACKSPACE until the incorrect characters are removed. Then, type the correct characters. If you do not discover a mistake until later, you can click the entry, type the correct value, and then press ENTER. You can use the following techniques to make changes to the structure:

- If you accidentally add an extra field to the structure, select the field by clicking the row selector (the leftmost column on the row that contains the field to be deleted). Once you have selected the field, press DEL. This will remove the field from the structure.
- If you forget to include a field, select the field that will follow the one you want to add by clicking the row selector, and then press INS. The remaining fields move down one row, making room for the missing field. Make the entries for the new field in the usual manner.
- If you made the wrong field a primary key field, click the correct primary key entry for the field and then click the Primary Key button (Table Design tab | Tools group).
- To move a field, click the row selector for the field to be moved to select the field, and then drag the field to the desired position.

Click the Save button to save changes to the table's structure.

As an alternative to these steps, you might want to start over. To do so, click the Close button for the window containing the table, and then click the No button in the Microsoft Access dialog box. You then can repeat the process you used earlier to define the fields in the table.

Populating the Locations Table

Now that you have created the Locations table, you can populate the table by entering the data in Datasheet view. Populating the table means entering data into the tables.

1 Click the View button (Table Design tab | Views group) to change to Datasheet view.

2 Enter the location data, as shown in Figure 1–32.

Location							
L_ID	Location Name	Type	Street	City	State	Postal Code	Shipper ID
L-001	Sabus Flooring	Warehouse	460 West Pioneer Road	Dolores	OK	73026	S-001
L-002	Mid-Valley Nursery Greenhouse	Nursery	602 Hwy 127	Blanding	OH	43056	S-002
L-003	Port of New Orleans	Port	1350 Port of New Orleans Pl	New Orleans	LA	70130	
L-004	City Greenhouse	Retail	586 Main St	Creek City	OH	42357	
L-005	The Barn	Retail	79 Hwy 5406	New Boston	OH	43282	
L-006	Silver Décor	Retail	256a North Utah St	Standing Lake	CO	81352	
L-007	Auto Suppliers, Inc.	Warehouse	182-B Route 56	Cloud Springs	LA	70784	S-003

Figure 1–32

Q&A How do I type the accented é in the word Décor?

In the Locations table, type the non-accented word Decor. When you tab to the next field, Access will automatically replace the non-accented e with the accented é (called an e-acute).

To Close the Table

Now that you have completed and saved the Locations table, you can close it. The following step closes the table.

1 Click the Close button for the Locations table (Figure 1–33) to close the table.

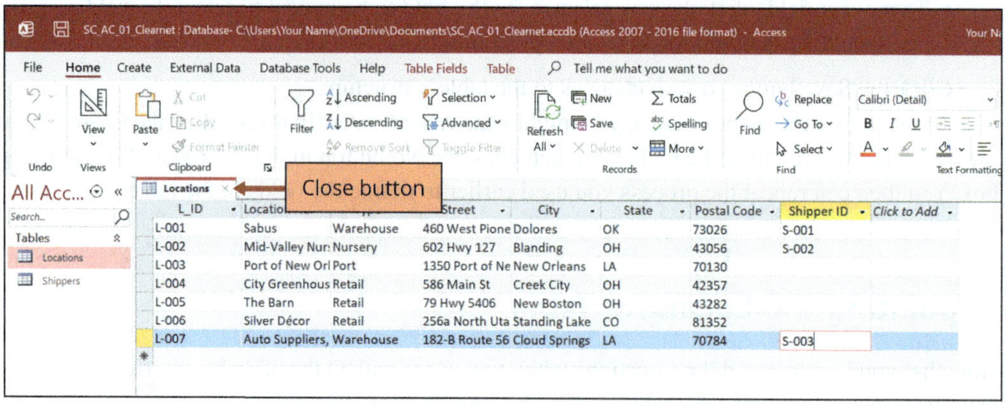

Figure 1–33

To Resize Columns in a Datasheet

You can resize the columns in the datasheet for the Locations table just as you resized the columns in the datasheet for the Shippers table. The following steps resize the columns in the Locations table to best fit the data.

1. Open the Locations table in Datasheet view.
2. Double-click the right boundary of the field selectors of each of the fields to resize the columns so that they best fit the data.
3. Save the changes to the layout by clicking the Save button on the Quick Access Toolbar.
4. Close the table.

BTW
Resizing Columns
To resize all columns in a datasheet to best fit simultaneously, select the column heading for the first column, hold down SHIFT and select the last column in the datasheet. Then, double-click the right boundary of any field selector. Click the Save button to save your changes.

Importing Additional Access Database Tables into an Existing Database

Access users frequently need to import tables that contain data into an existing database. **Why?** Organizations have data in tables that needs to be used in other databases. Importing tables ensures efficiency and accuracy. In addition to shippers and locations, Clearnet must also keep track of loads and the carriers hired to transport those loads. This information exists in another database. The following steps import three tables into the Clearnet database.

1

- Find the database file Support_AC_01_Clearnet-Extra-Tables in the Data Files and save it to the storage location specified by your instructor.
- If necessary, open your Clearnet database.
- Click External Data on the ribbon to display the External Data tab (Figure 1–34).

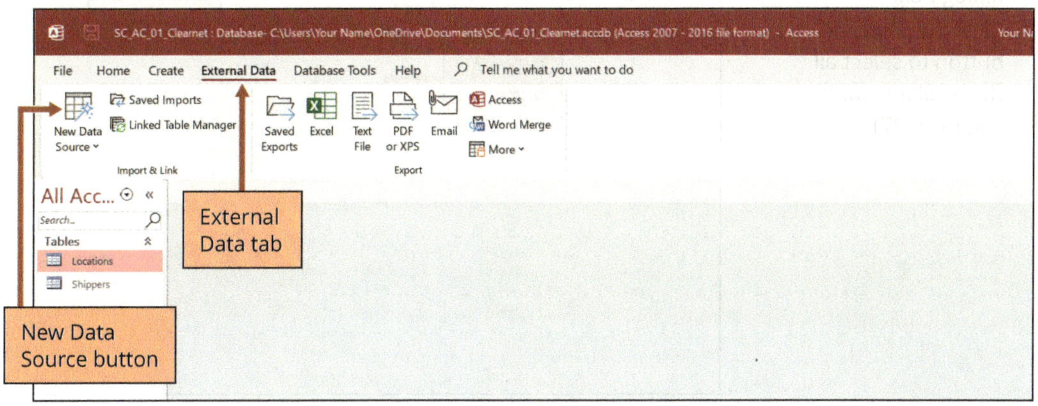

Figure 1–34

2

- Click the New Data Source button (External Data tab | Import & Link group) to open a menu.
- Point to From Database to display a menu (Figure 1–35), and then click Access to display the Get External Data – Access Database dialog box.

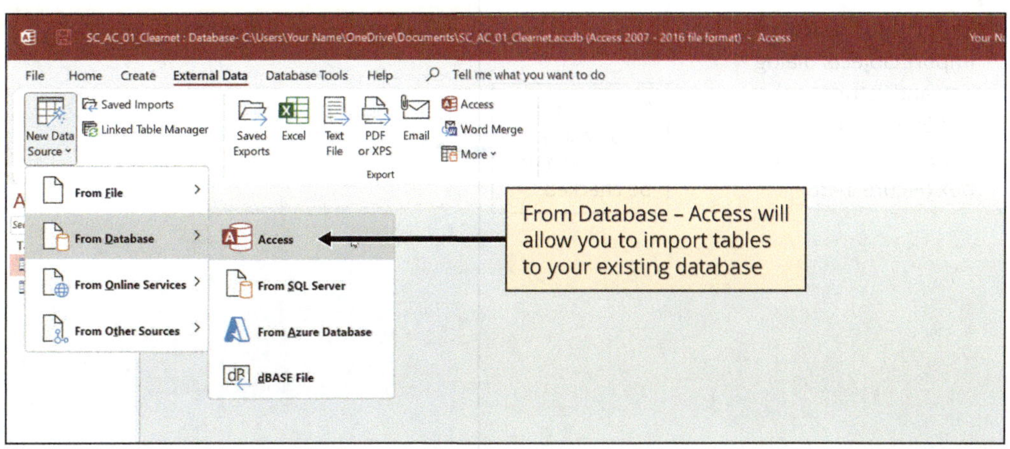

Figure 1–35

3

- Click the Browse button, navigate to the storage location for the Support_AC_01_Clearnet-Extra-Tables.accdb file, and then click Open to specify the source of the data you are importing.
- Click the 'Import tables, queries, forms, reports, macros, and modules into the current database' option button to specify how and where you want to store the data. (Figure 1–36).

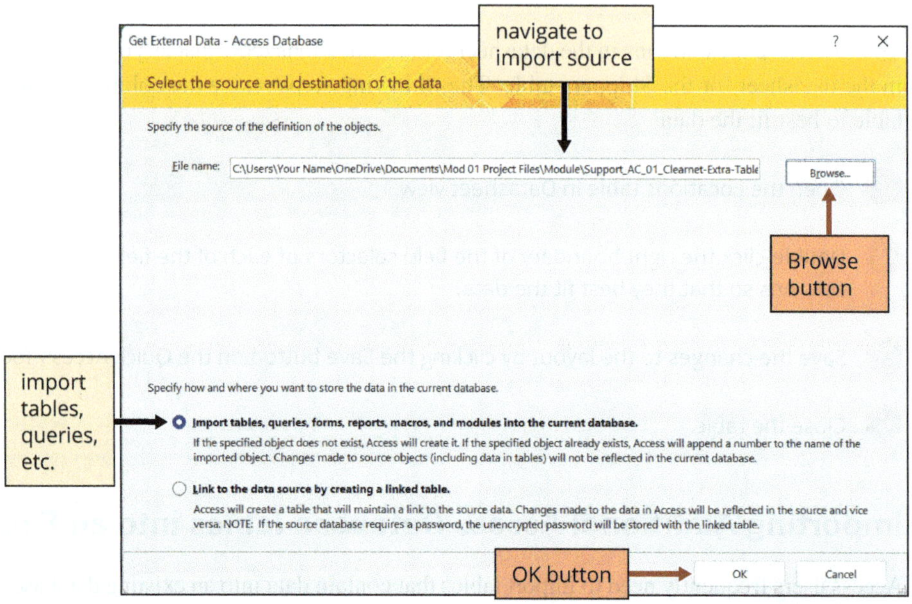

Figure 1–36

4

- Click OK to display the Import Objects dialog box.
- Click the Select All button to select all the available tables (Figure 1–37).

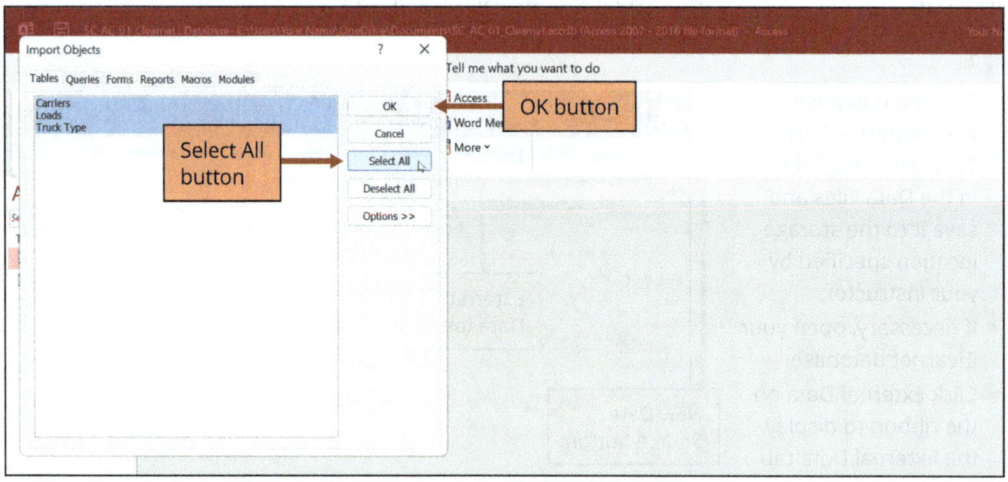

Figure 1–37

5

- Click OK to close the Import Objects dialog box and return to the Get External Data – Access Database dialog box (Figure 1–38)

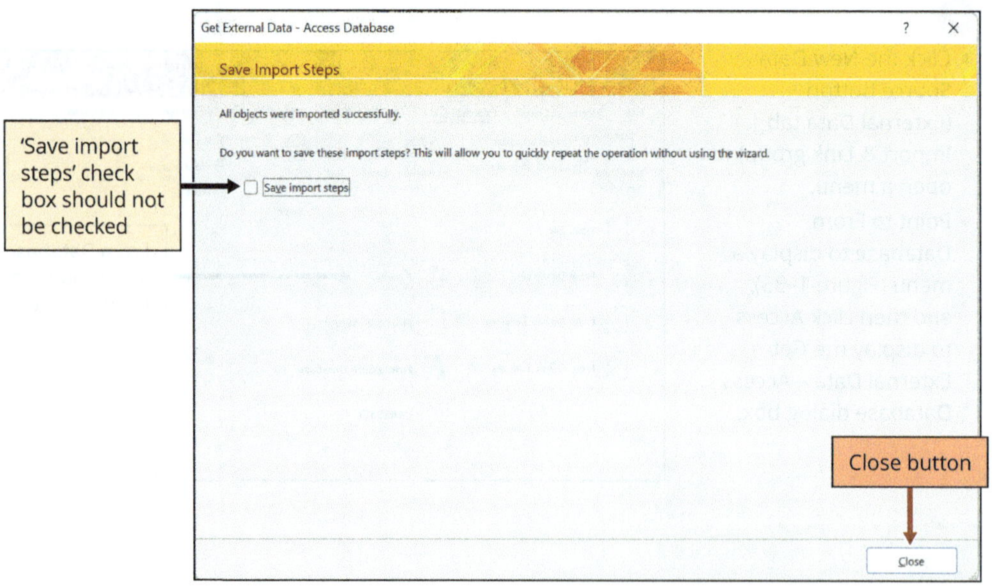

Figure 1–38

6

- Click the Close button to close the Import Objects dialog box without saving the Import steps (Figure 1–39).

Q&A Do I need to repeat this process for each table?
You have completed the import and will not repeat this import procedure in this project.

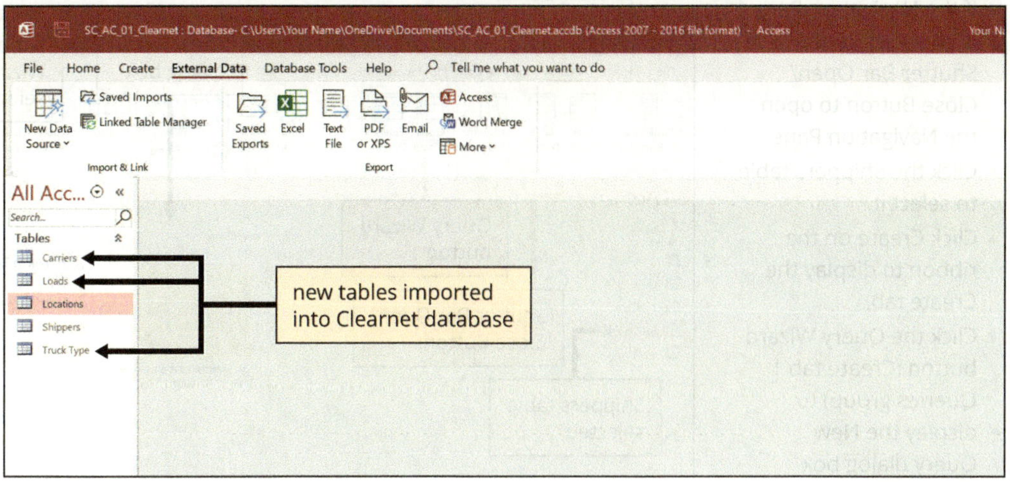

Figure 1–39

- Open the Loads table to explore its data and then close the table.

Q&A The Loads table includes a Rate field. When adding a record to the Loads table, do you need to type a dollar sign when adding data to the Rate field?
You do not need to type dollar signs or commas. In addition, because the digits to the right of the decimal point are both zeros, you do not need to type either the decimal point or the zeros.

Break Point: If you wish to take a break, this is a good place to do so. You can exit Access now. To resume at a later time, start Access, open the database called SC_AC_01_Clearnet.accdb, and continue following the steps from this location forward.

Additional Database Objects

A database contains many types of objects. Tables are the objects you use to store and manipulate data. Access supports other important types of objects as well; each object has a specific purpose that helps maximize the benefits of a database. Through queries (questions), Access makes it possible to ask complex questions concerning the data in the database and then receive instant answers. Access also allows the user to produce attractive and useful forms for viewing and updating data. Additionally, Access includes report creation tools that make it easy to produce sophisticated reports for presenting data.

BTW
Creating Queries
The Simple Query Wizard is a convenient way to create straightforward queries. It is a good method to learn about queries, although you will find that many of the queries you create require more control than the wizard provides.

Creating Queries

Queries are simply questions, the answers to which are in the database. Access contains a powerful query feature that helps you find the answers to a wide variety of questions. Once you have examined the question you want to ask to determine the fields involved in the question, you can begin creating the query. If the query involves no special sort order, restrictions, or calculations, you can use the Simple Query Wizard.

To Use the Simple Query Wizard to Create a Query

The following steps use the Simple Query Wizard to create a query that Clearnet can use to obtain a list of their shippers and create a call list for the day **Why?** The Simple Query Wizard is the quickest and easiest way to create a query. This query displays the Shipper's name, primary contact person, and their phone number and email address.

1

- If the Navigation Pane is closed, click the Shutter Bar Open/Close Button to open the Navigation Pane.
- Click the Shippers table to select it.
- Click Create on the ribbon to display the Create tab.
- Click the Query Wizard button (Create tab | Queries group) to display the New Query dialog box (Figure 1–40).

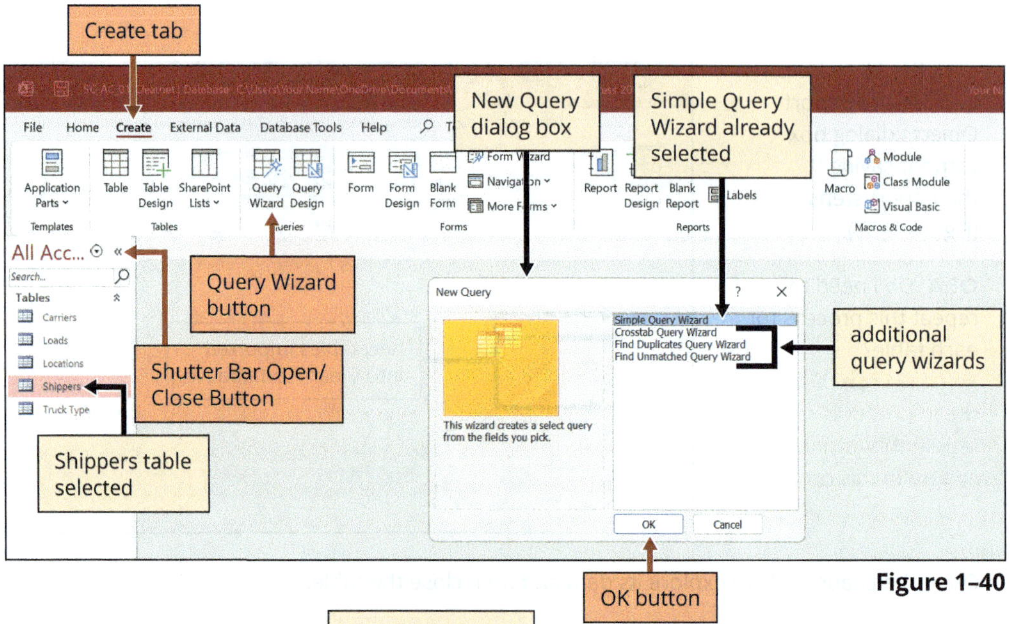

Figure 1–40

2

- Be sure Simple Query Wizard is selected, and then click OK (New Query dialog box) to display the Simple Query Wizard dialog box (Figure 1–41).

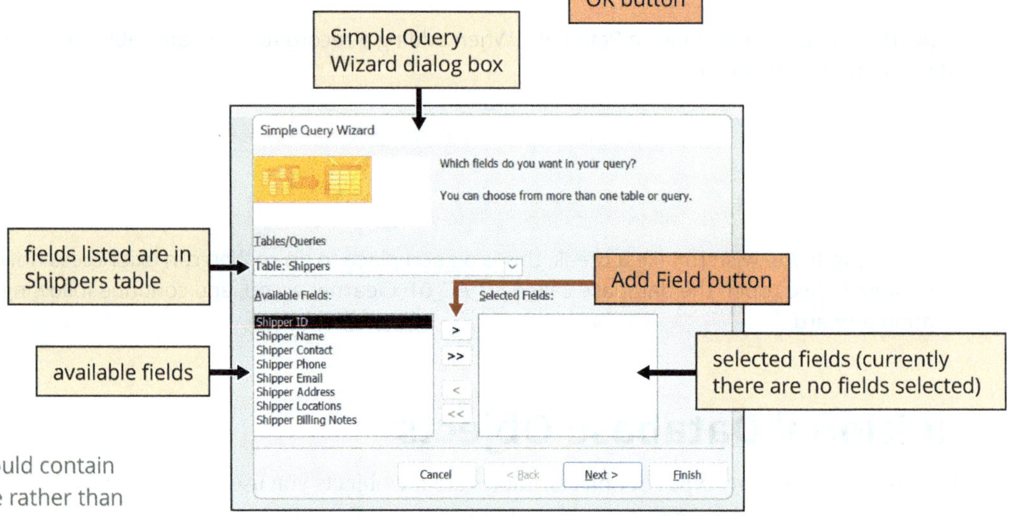

Figure 1–41

Q&A What would happen if the Carriers table were selected instead of the Shippers table?

The list of available fields would contain fields from the Carriers table rather than the Shippers table.

If the list contained Carriers table fields, how could I make it contain Shippers table fields?

Click the arrow in the Tables/Queries box, and then click the Shippers table in the list that appears.

3

- Select the Shipper Name field, and then click the Add Field button to move the field to the Selected Fields area.
- With the Shipper Contact field selected, click the Add Field button a second time to move the field to the Selected Fields area.
- Using the same technique, move the Shipper Phone and Shipper Email fields (Figure 1–42) to the query.

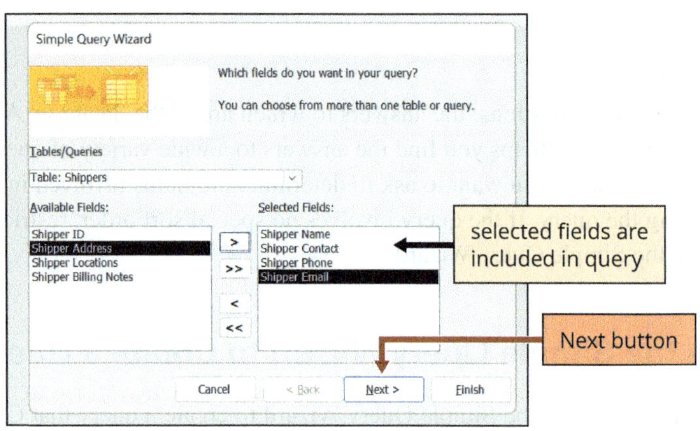

Figure 1–42

4

- Click Next to move to the next screen.
- Confirm that the title of the query is Shippers Query (Figure 1–43).

Q&A What should I do if the title is incorrect?
Click the box containing the title to produce an insertion point. Erase the current title and then type Shippers Query.

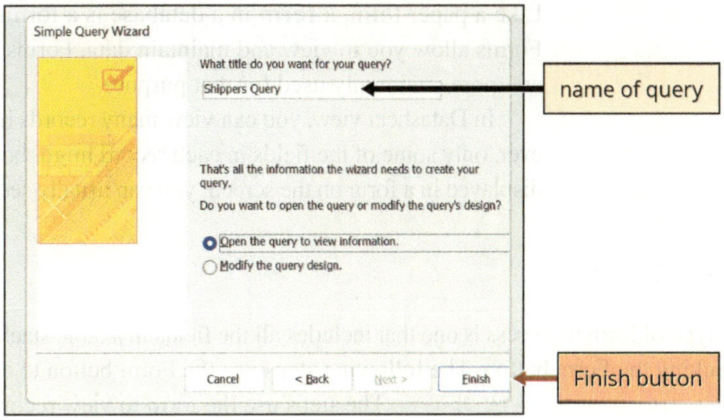

Figure 1–43

5

- Click the Finish button to create the query (Figure 1–44).
- Click the Close button for the Shippers Query to remove the query results from the screen.

Q&A If I want to use this query in the future, do I need to save the query?
Normally you would. The one exception is a query created by the wizard. The wizard automatically saves the query it creates.

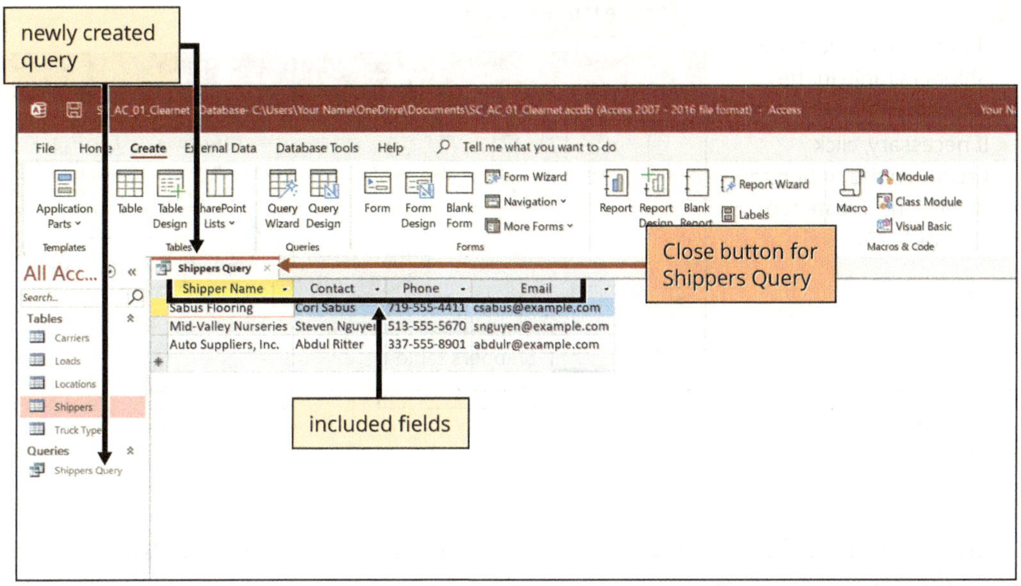

Figure 1–44

Using Queries

After you have created and saved a query, Access stores it as a database object and makes it available for use in a variety of ways:

- If you want to change the design of the query, right-click the query in the Navigation Pane and then click Design View on the shortcut menu to open the query in Design view.
- To view the results of the query from Design view, click the Run button (Query Design tab | Results group) to instruct Access to **run** the query, that is, to perform the necessary actions to produce and display the results in Datasheet view.
- To view the results of the query from the Navigation Pane, open it by right-clicking the query and clicking Open on the shortcut menu. Access automatically runs the query and displays the results in Datasheet view.

You can switch between views of a query using the View button (Home tab | Views group). Clicking the arrow in the bottom of the button produces the View button menu. You then click the desired view in the menu. The two query views you will use in this module are Datasheet view (which displays the query results) and Design view (for changing the query design). You can also click the top part of the View button; in which case, you will switch to the view identified by the icon on the button. For the most part, the icon on the button represents the view you want, so you can usually simply click the button.

Creating Forms

Like a paper form, a **form** in a database is a formatted document with fields that contain data. Forms allow you to view and maintain data. Forms can also be used to print data, though reports are more commonly used for that purpose.

In Datasheet view, you can view many records in a form at once. If there are many fields, however, only some of the fields in each record might be visible at a time. In **Form view**, where data is displayed in a form on the screen, you can usually see all the fields, but only for one record at a time.

To Create a Form

The simplest type of form in Access is one that includes all the fields in a table stacked one above the other, which can be achieved by simply clicking the Form button. The following steps use the Form button to create a form. **Why?** Using the Form button is the simplest way to create this type of form. The steps use the form to view records and then save the form.

1

- If necessary, select the Shippers table in the Navigation Pane.
- If necessary, click Create on the ribbon to display the Create tab (Figure 1–45).

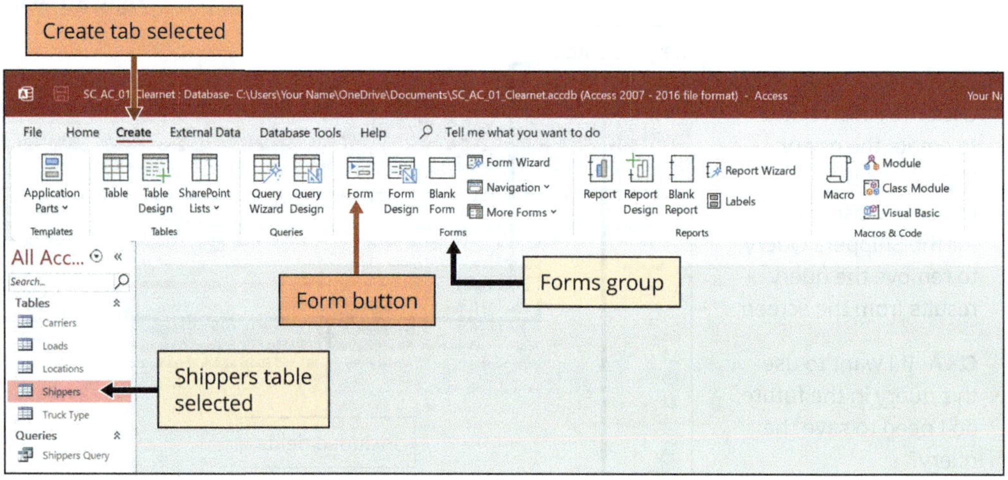

Figure 1–45

2

- Click the Form button (Create tab | Forms group) to create a simple form (Figure 1–46).

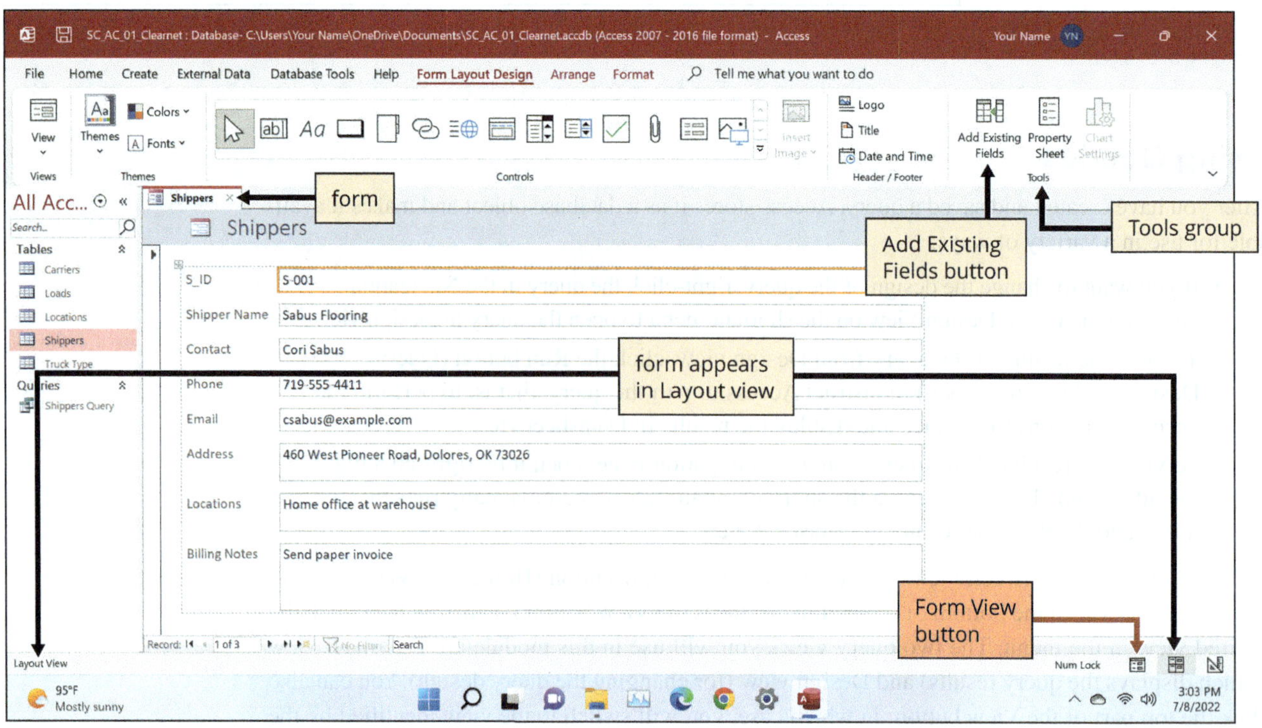

Figure 1–46

Q&A A Field list appeared on my screen. What should I do?
Click the 'Add Existing Fields' button (Form Layout Design tab | Tools group) to remove the Field list from the screen.

3

- Click the Form View button on the Access status bar to display the form in Form view rather than Layout view.

Q&A What is the difference between Layout view and Form view?
Layout view allows you to make changes to the look of the form. Form view is the view you use to examine or make changes to the data.

How can I tell which view is active?
Access identifies the current view in two ways. The left side of the status bar will list the name of the view, such as Layout view, and the current view's button will be selected on the right side of the status bar.

- Click the Next record button once to advance through the records (Figure 1–47).

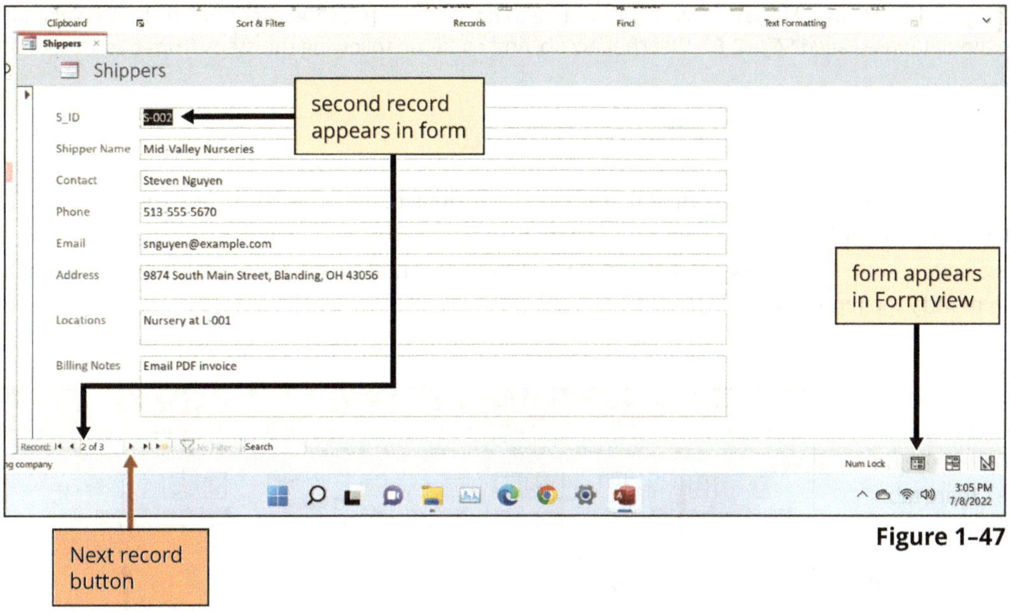

Figure 1–47

Q&A Why is the form title Shippers?
Access automatically assigns the name of the table or query used as the basis of the form or report as its title. It also automatically includes the date and time. You can change either of these later.

4

- Click the Save button on the Quick Access Toolbar to display the Save As dialog box (Figure 1–48).

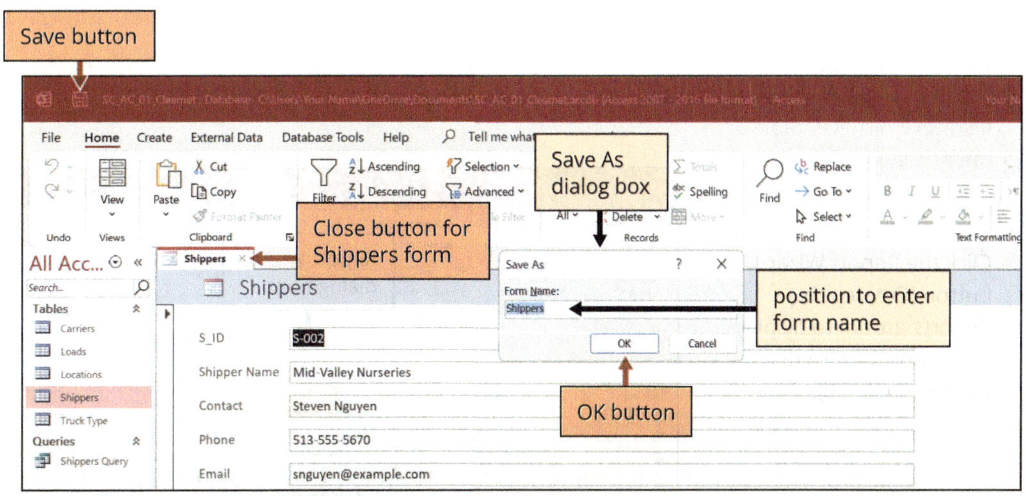

Figure 1–48

Q&A Do I have to click the Next record button before saving?
No. The only reason you were asked to click the button was so that you could experience navigation within the form.

5

- Type **Shippers Form** as the form name, and then click OK to save the form.
- Click the form's Close button to close the form.

Other Ways

1. Click View button (Home tab | Views group) to change view

Using a Form

After you have saved a form, you can use it at any time by right-clicking the form in the Navigation Pane and then clicking Open on the shortcut menu. In addition to viewing data in the form, you can also use it to enter or update data, a process that is similar to updating data using a datasheet. If you plan to use the form to enter or revise data, you must ensure you are viewing the form in Form view.

Break Point: If you wish to take a break, this is a good place to do so. You can exit Access now. To resume at a later time, start Access, open the database called SC_AC_01_Clearnet.accdb, and continue following the steps from this location forward.

To Create a Report Using the Report Wizard

A **report** in a database presents data in a format that is easily distributed, either as hard copy (printouts) or in other formats. You will use the Report Wizard to create a report for Clearnet. **Why?** Using the Report Wizard is an easy way to get started in creating professional reports. The following steps create and save an initial report containing some of the fields in the Loads table. They also modify the report title.

1

- Select the Loads table in the Navigation Pane.
- Click Create on the ribbon to display the Create tab (Figure 1–49).

Q&A Do I need to select the Loads table prior to clicking Create on the ribbon?
You do not need to select the table at that point. You do need to select a table prior to clicking the Report Wizard button, because Access will include all the fields in whichever table or query is currently selected.

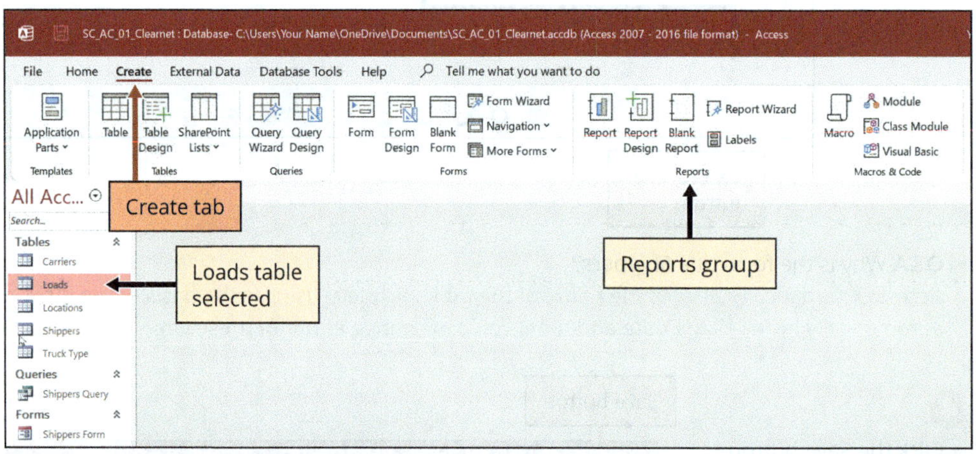

Figure 1–49

2

- Click the Report Wizard button (Create tab | Reports group) to display the Report Wizard dialog box (Figure 1–50).

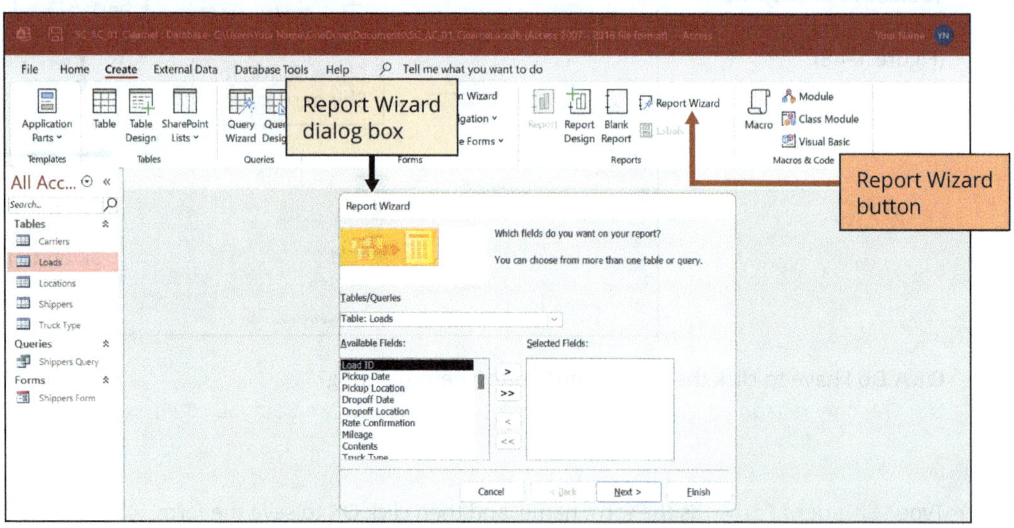

Figure 1–50

3

- In the Available Fields area, select Load ID and then click the Add Field button to add the field to the Selected Fields area.
- Click the arrow button a second time to move the Pickup Date field to the Selected Fields area.
- Move the Dropoff Date, Rate Confirmation, Truck Type, Status, and Carrier fields to the Selected Fields box (Figure 1–51).

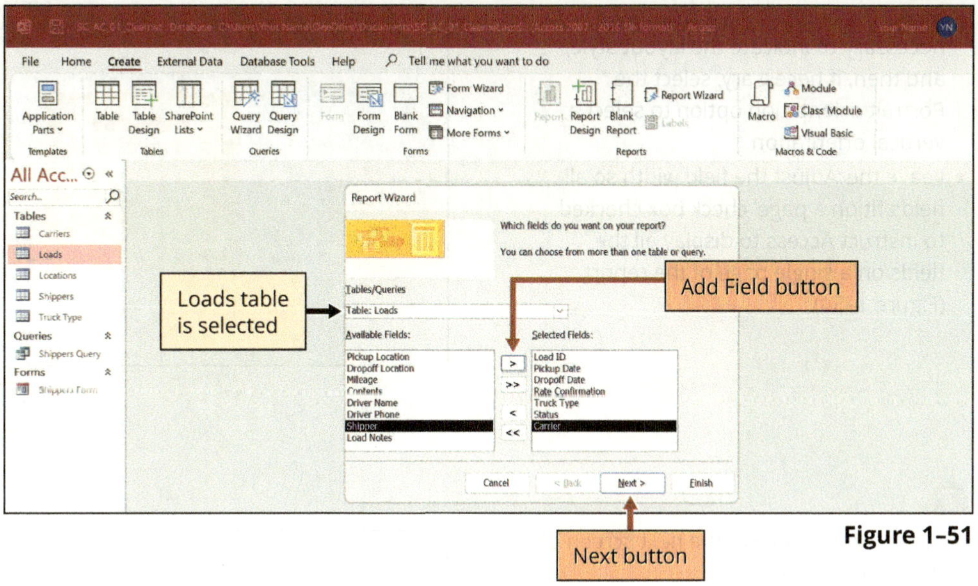

Figure 1–51

4

- Click Next, and then select Status. Click the Add Field button in the 'Do you want to add any grouping levels' area to indicate that the report will be grouped by Status (Figure 1–52).

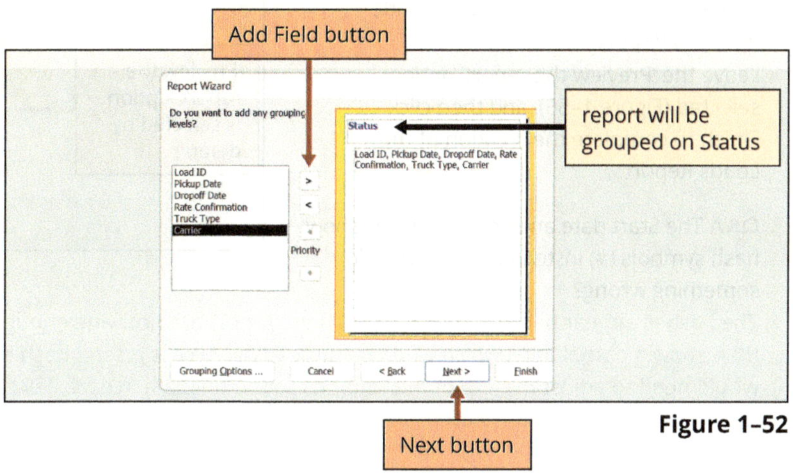

Figure 1–52

5

- Click Next to move to the next screen in the Report Wizard (Figure 1–53).

Q&A How do I correct a mistake I made in the Report Wizard?
The Report Wizard lets you click the Back button at any time to undo an action.

- Click Next again to move to the next screen without indicating a sort order or summary information for detail records.

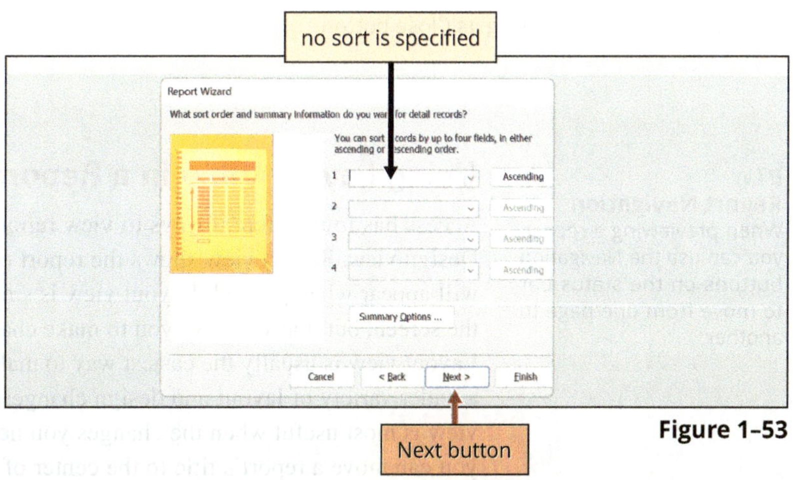

Figure 1–53

6

- Select the Stepped layout option if necessary to indicate the layout style, and then, if necessary, select the Portrait orientation option to select a vertical orientation.
- Leave the 'Adjust the field width so all fields fit on a page' check box checked to instruct Access to display all the fields on a single page of the report (Figure 1-54).

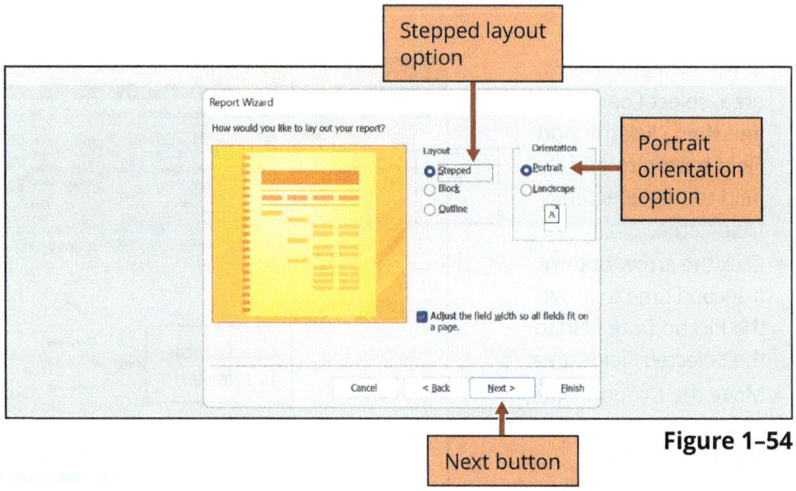

Figure 1-54

7

- Click Next to move to the next screen of the Report Wizard.
- Click to the right of the word Loads, and then type **Report** to change the title to Loads Report.
- Leave the 'Preview the report' option selected (Figure 1-55), and then click Finish to complete the creation of the Loads Report.

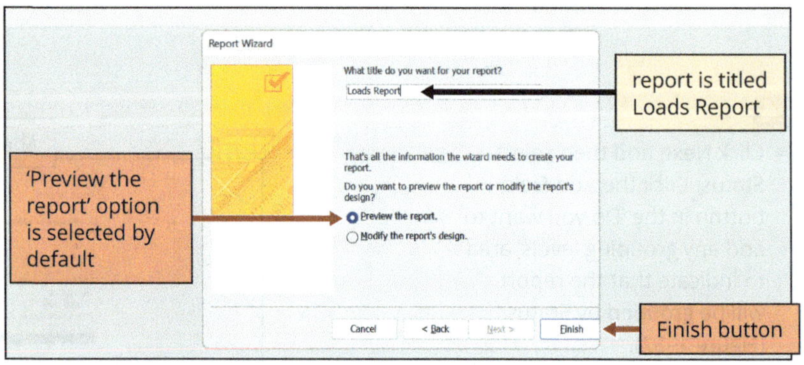

Figure 1-55

Q&A The Start date and End date fields show hash symbols (#) instead of data. Did I do something wrong?

The hashes appear because the columns in the report are not wide enough to show the entire date in each record. Rather than show a partial date, which could be misleading, Access inserts hash symbols instead. Before printing the report, you would need to adjust the size of the columns so the full date in each cell can be displayed. This skill is covered in a later module. For now, you can leave the report as is.

8

- Close the report by clicking its Close button.

BTW
Report Navigation
When previewing a report, you can use the Navigation buttons on the status bar to move from one page to another.

Using Layout View in a Report

Access has four different ways to view reports: Report view, Print Preview, Layout view, and Design view. Report view shows the report on the screen. Print Preview shows the report as it will appear when printed. Layout view is similar to Report view in that it shows the report on the screen, but it also allows you to make changes to the design and layout of the report. Using Layout view is usually the easiest way to make such changes. Design view allows you to make a wider variety of layout and design changes, but does not show you the actual report. Design view is most useful when the changes you need to make are especially complex. For example, you can move a report's title to the center of the page by dragging and dropping the label box (Figure 1-56).

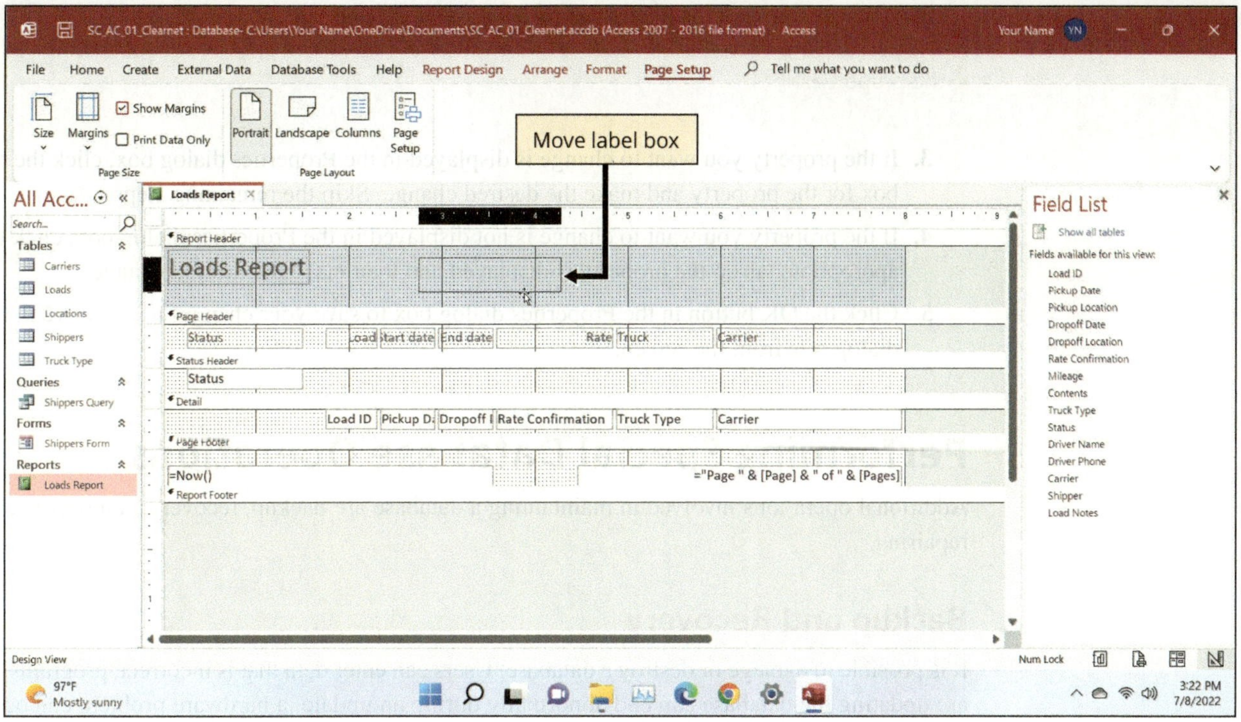

Figure 1–56

Identifying Database Properties

Access helps you organize and identify your databases by using **database properties**, which are the details about a file. Database properties, also known as **metadata**, can include such information as the project author, title, or subject. **Keywords** are words or phrases that further describe the database. For example, a class name or database topic can describe the file's purpose or content.

Five different types of database properties exist, but the more common ones used in this course are standard and automatically updated properties. **Standard properties** are associated with all Microsoft Office documents and include author, title, and subject. **Automatically updated properties** include file system properties, such as the date you create or change a file, and statistics, such as the file size.

Consider This

Why would you want to assign database properties to a database?

Database properties are valuable for a variety of reasons:

- Users can save time locating a particular file because they can view a file's database properties without opening the database.
- By creating consistent properties for files having similar content, users can better organize their databases.
- Some organizations require Access users to add database properties so that other employees can view details about these files.

To Change Database Properties

To change database properties, you would follow these steps.

1. Click File on the ribbon to open Backstage view and then, if necessary, click the Info tab in Backstage view to display the Info gallery.
2. Click the 'View and edit database properties' link in the right pane of the Info gallery to display the Clearnet Properties dialog box.

Q&A Why are some of the database properties already filled in?
The person who installed Office on your computer or network might have set or customized the properties.

3. If the property you want to change is displayed in the Properties dialog box, click the text box for the property and make the desired change. Skip the remaining steps.
4. If the property you want to change is not displayed in the Properties dialog box, click the appropriate tab so the property is displayed and then make the desired change.
5. Click the OK button in the Properties dialog box to save your changes and remove the dialog box from the screen.

Performing Special Database Operations

Additional operations involved in maintaining a database are backup, recovery, compacting, and repairing.

Backup and Recovery

It is possible to damage or destroy a database. Users can enter data that is incorrect, programs that are updating the database can end abnormally during an update, a hardware problem can occur, and so on. After any such event has occurred, the database might contain invalid data or it might be totally destroyed.

You cannot allow a situation in which data has been damaged or destroyed to go uncorrected. You must somehow return the database to a correct state. This process is called recovery; that is, you **recover** the database.

The simplest approach to recovery involves periodically making a copy of the database (called a **backup copy** or a **save copy**). This is referred to as **backing up** the database. If a problem occurs, you correct the problem by overwriting the actual database—often referred to as the **live database**—with the backup copy.

To back up the database that is currently open, you use the Back Up Database command on the Save As tab in Backstage view. In the process, Access suggests a name that is a combination of the database name and the current date. For example, if you back up the Clearnet database on October 20, 2027, Access will suggest the name, Clearnet_2027-10-20. You can change this name if you desire, although it is a good idea to use this name. Doing so will make it easy to distinguish between all the backup copies you have made to determine which is the most recent. In addition, if you discover that a critical problem occurred on October 18, 2027, you might want to go back to the most recent backup before October 18. If, for example, the database was not backed up on October 17 but was backed up on October 16, you would use Clearnet_2027-10-16.

To Back Up a Database

You would use the following steps to back up a database to a file on a hard drive, high-capacity removable disk, or other storage location.

1. Open the database to be backed up.
2. Click File on the ribbon to open Backstage view, and then click the Save As tab.
3. With Save Database As selected in the File Types area, click 'Back Up Database' in the Save Database As area, and then click the Save As button.
4. Navigate to the desired location in the Save As box. If you do not want the name Access has suggested, enter the desired name in the File name text box.
5. Click the Save button to back up the database.

Access creates a backup copy with the desired name in the desired location. Should you ever need to recover the database using this backup copy, you can simply copy it over the live version.

Compacting and Repairing a Database

As you add more data to a database, it naturally grows larger. When you delete an object (tables, queries, forms, or reports), the space previously occupied by the object does not become available for additional objects. Instead, the additional objects are given new space, that is, space that was not already allocated. To remove this empty space from the database, you must **compact** the database. The same option that compacts the database also repairs problems that might have occurred in the database.

To Compact and Repair a Database

You would use the following steps to compact and repair a database.

1. Open the database to be compacted.
2. Click File on the ribbon to open Backstage view, and then, if necessary, select the Info tab.
3. Click the 'Compact & Repair Database' button in the Info gallery to compact and repair the database.

The database now is the compacted form of the original.

Additional Operations

Additional special operations include closing a database without exiting Access and saving a database with another name. They also include deleting a table (or another object) as well as renaming an object.

When you are working in a database and you open another database from within Access, Access will automatically close the database that was previously open. Alternatively, you can open another database at the same time by opening the second database from File Explorer in Windows. Similarly, before deleting or renaming an object, you should ensure that the object has no dependent objects, that is, other objects that depend on the object you want to delete.

To Close a Database without Exiting Access

You would use the following steps to close a database without exiting Access.

1. Click File on the ribbon to open Backstage view.
2. Click Close.

To Save a Database with Another Name

To save a database with another name, you would use the following steps.

1. Click File on the ribbon to open Backstage view, and then select the Save As tab.
2. With Save Database As selected in the File Types area and Access Database selected in the Save Database As area, click the Save As button.
3. Enter a name and select a location for the new version.
4. Click the Save button.

Consider This

If you want to make a backup, could you just save the database with another name?

You could certainly do that. Using the backup procedure discussed earlier is useful because doing so automatically includes the current database name and the date in the name of the file it creates.

BTW
Access Help
At any time while using Access, you can find answers to questions and display information about various topics through Access Help. Used properly, this form of assistance can increase your productivity and reduce your frustration by minimizing the time you spend learning how to use Access.

To Delete a Table or Other Object in the Database

You would use the following steps to delete a database object.

1. Right-click the object in the Navigation Pane.
2. Click Delete on the shortcut menu.
3. Click the Yes button in the Microsoft Access dialog box.

To Rename an Object in the Database

You would use the following steps to rename a database object.

1. Right-click the object in the Navigation Pane.
2. Click Rename on the shortcut menu.
3. Type the new name and press ENTER.

To Exit Access

All the steps in this module are now complete.

1. If desired, sign out of your Microsoft account.
2. sam Exit Access.

Summary

In this module you have learned to create an Access database, create tables, add records to a database, import tables, create queries, create forms, create reports, and change database properties.

Consider This: Plan Ahead

What decisions will you need to make when creating your next database?

Use these guidelines as you complete the assignments in this module and create your own databases outside of this class.

1. Identify the information you want to record in the tables.
2. Determine the fields within those tables.
3. Determine the primary key for each table.
4. Determine the data types for the fields in the table.
5. Determine additional properties for fields.
   a. Determine if a caption is warranted.
   b. Determine if a description of the field is warranted.
   c. Determine field sizes.
   d. Determine formats.
6. Determine a storage location for the database.
7. Determine any simple queries, forms, or reports needed.

Student Assignments

Apply Your Knowledge

Reinforce the skills and apply the concepts you learned in this module.

Adding a Caption; Changing a Data Type; and Creating a Query, Form, and Report

Note: To complete this assignment, you will be required to use the Data Files. Please contact your instructor for information about accessing the Data Files.

Instructions: Start Access. Open the database, SC_AC_01-1.accdb, which is located in the Data Files folder. Enable the content. The database contains tables used to track students and counselors at City Tutoring Services. The company employs several trained and certified educational counselors to help their clients navigate their academic pursuits, from preschool through graduate school. City Tutoring has a database that keeps track of its counselors and its students. Each student is assigned to a single counselor; each counselor may be assigned many students. The database has two tables. The Students table contains data on the students who use City Tutoring. The Counselors table contains data on the educational counselors. You will add a caption; change a data type; and create a query, a form, and a report, as shown in Figure 1–57.

Perform the following tasks:

1. Save the database using the file name SC_AC_01_City-Tutoring. Enable the content.
2. Open the Counselors table in Datasheet view, and add CN # as the caption for the Counselor Number field.
3. Resize all columns to best fit the data. Save the changes to the layout of the table and close the table.
4. Open the Students table in Design view and change the data type for the Counselor Number field to Short Text. Change the field size for the field to 4 and add CN # as the caption for the Counselor Number field. Save the changes to the table and close the table.
5. Use the Simple Query Wizard to create a query for the Students table that contains the Student Number, Student Name, and Counselor Number. Use the name Students Query for the query and close the query.
6. Create a simple form for the Counselors table. Save the form and use the name Counselors for the form. Close the form.
7. Use the Report Wizard to create the report shown in Figure 1–57 for the Students table. After closing the Report Wizard, use Design View to move the report title's label box to the center of the Report Header section. Save the report as Student Counselor Report.
   If requested by your instructor, add your last name to the title of the report; that is, change the title to Student Counselor Report LastName where LastName is your actual last name. Recenter the title's label box as needed, and then re-save the report.
8. Close the report.
9. Compact and repair the database.
10. Submit the revised database (shown in Figure 1-57) in the format specified by your instructor and exit Access.
11. **Consider This:** How would you change the field name of the Street field in the Students table to Address?

Continued on next page

Student Counselor Report

Counselor Number	Student Name	Street	City
103			
	Kirk D'Elia	378 Stout Ave.	Carlton
	Heidi Croft	245 Beard St.	Kady
	Cindy Platt	178 Fletcher Rd.	Conradt
	Moss Mann	109 Fletcher Dr.	Carlton
	Carly Cohen	87 Fletcher Rd.	Conradt
120			
	Katy Cline	255 Main St.	Kady
	Irena Lam	876 Redfern Rd.	Kady
	Bob Schwartz	443 Cheddar St.	Kady

Figure 1–57

Extend Your Knowledge

Extend the skills you learned in this module and experiment with new skills. You may need to use Help to complete the assignment.

Using a Database Template to Create a Rental Properties Database

Instructions: Start Access. Access includes a variety of database templates. You can use a template to create a beginning database that can be modified to meet your specific needs. You will use a template to create a Rental Properties database. The database template includes sample tables, queries, forms, and reports. You will modify the database and create the Tenants Relationship Query shown in Figure 1–58.

Perform the following tasks:

1. Find and select the Real estate template in the template gallery.
2. Create a new database with the file name SC_AC_01_Rental-Properties.
3. Enable the content and close the Property List form.
4. If necessary, open the Navigation Pane and change the organization to Object Type.
5. Open the Tenant table in Datasheet view and delete the Attachments field in the table. The Attachments field has a paperclip as the column heading.
6. Add the field Tenant Status to the end of the table. Assign it the Short Text data type with a field size of 15.
7. Save the changes to the Tenant table and close the table.
8. Use the Simple Query Wizard to create the Tenant Status Query shown in Figure 1–58. Close the query.

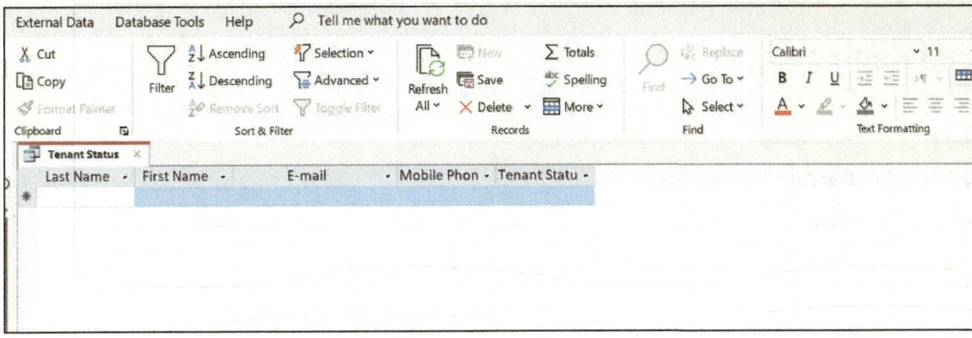

Figure 1–58

9. Open the Lease Application report in Layout view. Delete the controls containing the current date and current time in the upper-right corner of the report. Change the title of the report to Tenant Application List.
10. Save the changes to the report.
    If requested to do so by your instructor, add your first and last names to the end of the report title and save the changes to the report.
11. Submit the revised database in the format specified by your instructor.
12. a. **Consider This:** Why would you use a template instead of creating a database from scratch with just the fields you need?
    b. **Consider This:** The Attachment data type allows you to attach files to a database record. If you were using this database to keep track of tenants, what specific documents might you attach to a Tenant record?

Expand Your World

Create a solution that uses cloud or web technologies by learning and investigating on your own from general guidance.

Note: To complete this assignment, you will be required to use the Data Files. Please contact your instructor for information about accessing the Data Files.

Instructions: Start Access. Open the database called SC_AC_01-2.accdb, which is located in the Data Files folder, and enable the content. As a volunteer project, you and a few friends are creating a database for a local computer store that provides technical assistance to retirees in their homes. You want to be able to share query results and reports, so you have decided to store the items in the cloud. You are still learning Access, so you are going to create a sample query and the report shown in Figure 1–59, export the results, and save them to a cloud storage location, such as Microsoft OneDrive, Dropbox, or Google Drive.

Perform the following tasks:

1. Save the database using the filename, SC_AC_01_Solutions-IT-Support. Enable the content.
2. Use the Simple Query Wizard to create a query that includes the Client Number, First Name, Last Name, and Technician Number. Save the query as Client Query.
3. Export the Client Query as an XPS document to a cloud-based storage location of your choice. If the XPS document opens, review it and close it. You might need to activate the XPS Viewer feature in Windows to view the report. Do not save the export steps. Close the query.
4. Create the report shown in Figure 1–59. Save the report as Client Technician Report.

Continued on next page

Client Technician Report

Client Number	Last Name	First Name	Technician Number
AU10	Autley	Francis	203
BE16	Behrens	Alexa	205
DE35	Devi	Yaron	205
HE07	Heiston	Bill	203
KL12	Klingman	Cynthia	203
MA34	Marston	Libby	207
PR80	Priestly	Martin	205
SA23	Sanders	Marya	207

Figure 1–59

5. Export the Client Technician Report as a PDF document to a cloud-based storage location of your choice. You do not need to change any optimization or export settings. If the PDF opens, close it. Do not save the export steps.
   If requested to do so by your instructor, open the Technician table and change the last name and first name for Technician 203 to your last name and your first name.
6. Submit the database, query, and report files in the format specified by your instructor.
7. **Consider This:** Which cloud-based storage location did you use for this assignment and why?

In the Lab

Design and implement a solution using creative thinking and problem-solving skills.

Lab: Creating Objects for the Great Outdoors Camp Database

Note: To complete this assignment, you will be required to use the Data Files. Please contact your instructor for information about accessing the Data Files.

Problem: Great Outdoors Camp is a non-profit campground that runs several camp events each year for students ages 9 to 18. One of the administrative staff is familiar with Microsoft Access and created a database to help keep track of the various events, campers, and employees. This database tracks staff scheduling, camper enrollment, event dates, equipment storage, and cabin assignments. The database and tables have been created, but the Status field needs to be added to the Staff table. This field will identify "Seasonal" staff members, who are employed only during certain months while events are taking place. The records shown in Figure 1–60 must be added to the Staff table. Great Outdoors Camp would like to finish storing this data in a database and has asked you to help.

Perform the following tasks:

Part 1: Open the SC_AC_01-3.accdb database from the Data Files folder, and enable the content. Save the file with the name SC_AC_01_Great-Outdoors, and enable the content. Add a Status field to the Staff table. Assign an appropriate data type to hold a one-word identifier, and set the field size at 10.

Add the records shown in Figure 1–60.

Sf_ID	FullName	WorkTeam	Phone	Status
11	Otto Jensson	Instructor	7175555402	Seasonal
12	Ahmad Grady	Instructor	7175555432	Seasonal
13	Markku Twist	Instructor	7175558793	Seasonal
14	Vera Ognianov	Instructor	7175558798	Seasonal
15	Elli Rosario	Instructor	7175558789	Seasonal
16	Martyn Bell	Instructor	7175555368	Seasonal

Figure 1–60

Change the Cabins table's fields as necessary so that each is an appropriate data type and an appropriate length for the data contained in those fields. Note that you might receive a warning about validation rules; click Yes to continue. Add an appropriate caption to the CounselorName field. Save your changes.

Create a query that displays the CabinID, CounselorName, and CabinName data, and save the query using an appropriate name.

Create the report shown in Figure 1–61 for the ActivityZones table. When designing the report, remember that the caption name may differ from the field name. Save the report.

Activity Zone Assignments

Staff Name	AZ_Name	Type
Vera	Crafts	Indoor
Ahmad	Hiking	Woods
Lata	Horseback Riding	Barn
Markku	Kayaking	Lake
Maya	Survival Class	Indoor
Martyn	Swimming	Lake
Elli	Team Sports	Fields
Otto	Ziplining	Woods

Figure 1–61

If requested to do so by your instructor, change any data in the database to reflect your own personal information.

Submit the revised database in the format specified by your instructor.

Part 2: **Consider This:** The Waiver field in the Campers table is the Yes/No Data Type. Why is this appropriate?

Querying a Database

Objectives

After completing this module, you will be able to:

- Add a field to the design grid
- Use text and numeric data in criteria
- Use a wildcard in a query
- Hide a field used in a query
- Require a parameter for a query
- Use compound criteria in a query
- Sort data in query results
- Join tables in a query
- Create a report from a query
- Print a report or form
- Create a form from a query
- Export data from a query to another application
- Require a query to group or perform calculations on results
- Create crosstab queries
- Customize the Navigation Pane

Introduction

One of the primary benefits of using a database management system such as Access is having the ability to find answers to questions related to data stored in the database. When you pose a question to Access, or any other database management system, the question is called a query. A query is simply a question presented in a way that Access can process.

To find the answer to a question, you first create a corresponding query using the techniques illustrated in this module. After you have created the query, you instruct Access to run the query, that is, to perform the steps necessary to obtain the answer. Access then displays the results in Datasheet view.

In this module, you will work with a database created by a paralegal who works for the Partners Law Firm. The Partners Law Firm is owned by a group of real estate developers who also run a law firm on the side to support their main business. The paralegals are employed by the law firm, while most of the other employees work for the real estate development company. The paralegals support law firm activities, including occasional property purchases or sales, called closings, for residential and commercial properties. One of the paralegals created an Access database to help track the clients, properties, and other companies (such as mortgage companies, real estate agents, title companies, and other law firms) involved in these closings.

Project: Querying a Database

Examples of queries related to the data in the Partners database are shown in Figure 2–1. They answer questions such as which closings take place with a particular mortgage company or within a particular state. In addition to these questions, Partners paralegals also need to find information such as closing date or title company as they work, without creating a new query every time. The paralegals can use a parameter query to accomplish this task. A **parameter query** prompts you to enter a search term and then displays the results based on the search term you entered. Partners paralegals also want to summarize data in a specific way, such as by mortgage company or payoff amount, which might involve performing calculations, and they can use a crosstab query to present the data in the desired form.

In this module, you will learn how to create and use queries, including those shown in Figure 2–1.

m02q01

C_ID	Closing Date	Payoff	Payoff_MID	Loan	Purchase_MID	B_ID
C-001	4/28/2027	$246,152.28	M-001	$492,000.00	M-002	B-001
C-003	4/30/2027	$142,983.79	M-003	$325,000.00	M-002	B-003
*		$0.00		$0.00		

Figure 2–1a Closings with a Specific Mortgage Company

m02q03

Seller Name	Email	S_Agent
Riya Sumner	riyas@example.com	Laura Rosario
Alyssa Schubert	alyssa@example.com	Margary Kools
*		

Figure 2–1b Sellers Located in a Specific Area Code

m02q05

C_ID	Closing Date	B_ID
C-002	4/29/2027	B-002
C-003	4/30/2027	B-003
*		

Figure 2–1c Closings After a Specific Date

Property - State Query

P_ID	Street	City	State	Seller ID
P-001	219 Phillips St	Donahue	PA	S-001
P-002	852 Scranton Dr	Jonestown	PA	S-002
P-004	186 Alabama Hwy	Hartford	PA	S-004
P-006	87 Georgetown Rd, #2	East Barnard	PA	S-006
*				

Figure 2–1d Properties Located in a Specific State

Closings and Properties

C_ID	Closing Date	P_ID	Street	Seller ID
		P-006	87 Georgetown Rd, #2	S-006
		P-005	Route 15, Box 281	S-005
C-004	4/28/2027	P-004	186 Alabama Hwy	S-004
C-001	4/28/2027	P-001	219 Phillips St	S-001
C-002	4/29/2027	P-002	852 Scranton Dr	S-002
C-003	4/30/2027	P-003	46 Hwy 82 S	S-003
*				

Figure 2–1e Property Street Address for Each Closing Date

Creating Queries

As you learned previously, you can use queries in Access to find answers to questions about the data contained in the database. **Note:** In this module, you will save each query example. When you use a query for another task, such as to create a form or report, you will assign a specific name to a query, for example, Properties – Closings Query. In situations in which you will not use the query again, you will assign a name using a convention that includes the module number and a query number, for example, m02q01. These queries are numbered consecutively.

BTW
Select Queries
The queries you create in this module are select queries. In a select query, you retrieve data from one or more tables using criteria that you specify and display the data in a datasheet.

To Save the Partners Database with a New File Name and Add Records to the Database

With three new closings scheduled for the end of this month, the paralegals need to add records to the database prior to making queries, to ensure the queries return complete and accurate information for the month. **Why?** Databases often change over time as users add new information and adjust the structure and objects included in the database. The following steps open the Buyers, Sellers, and Properties tables and add data. Please see your instructor for information about accessing the Data Files.

1

- sam Start Access. Open the database, SC_AC_02-1.accdb, which is located in the Data Files folder. Save the file on your hard drive, OneDrive, or other storage location using the file name, **SC_AC_02_Partners**. Enable the content.
- Open the Sellers table in Datasheet view, and then click the 'Shutter Bar Open/Close Button' to close the Navigation Pane.

Q&A Is it necessary to close the Navigation Pane?
No. Closing the pane gives you more room for entering data in the table, however, so it is usually a good practice.

2

- Click the empty cell below S-003 to enter a new seller ID.
- Enter the data for seller S-004, Nadia Sutherland, as shown in Figure 2–2a.

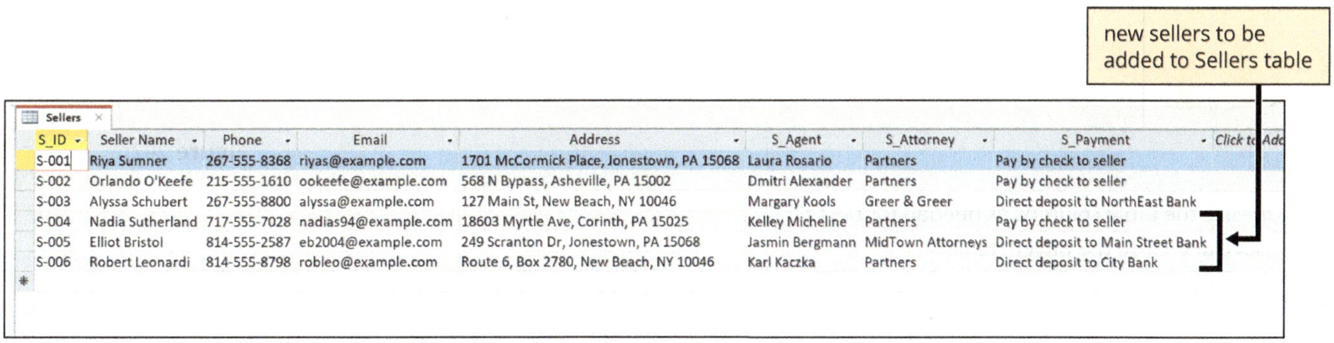

S_ID	Seller Name	Phone	Email	Address	S_Agent	S_Attorney	S_Payment
S-001	Riya Sumner	267-555-8368	riyas@example.com	1701 McCormick Place, Jonestown, PA 15068	Laura Rosario	Partners	Pay by check to seller
S-002	Orlando O'Keefe	215-555-1610	ookeefe@example.com	568 N Bypass, Asheville, PA 15002	Dmitri Alexander	Partners	Pay by check to seller
S-003	Alyssa Schubert	267-555-8800	alyssa@example.com	127 Main St, New Beach, NY 10046	Margary Kools	Greer & Greer	Direct deposit to NorthEast Bank
S-004	Nadia Sutherland	717-555-7028	nadias94@example.com	18603 Myrtle Ave, Corinth, PA 15025	Kelley Micheline	Partners	Pay by check to seller
S-005	Elliot Bristol	814-555-2587	eb2004@example.com	249 Scranton Dr, Jonestown, PA 15068	Jasmin Bergmann	MidTown Attorneys	Direct deposit to Main Street Bank
S-006	Robert Leonardi	814-555-8798	robleo@example.com	Route 6, Box 2780, New Beach, NY 10046	Karl Kaczka	Partners	Direct deposit to City Bank

Figure 2–2a

3

- Enter the data for the additional sellers shown in the figure.
- Resize the table columns as needed for best fit.
- Save and close the Sellers table.

4

- Click the Navigation Pane bar to open the Navigation Pane, open the Properties table in Datasheet view, and then close the Navigation Pane.
- The existing Property ID numbers do not conform with the company's naming convention. As you work with a database, you might find inconsistencies such as this one. It's a good habit to watch for these problems and fix them as you go. Change the Property ID numbers for the existing properties so they are consistent with Figure 2–2b.

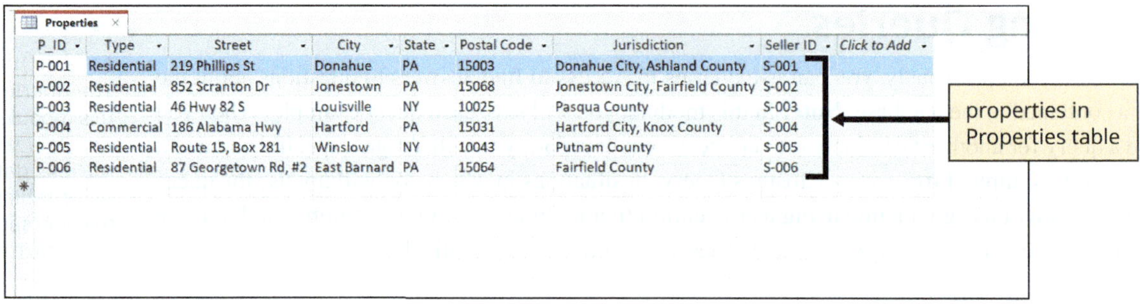

P_ID	Type	Street	City	State	Postal Code	Jurisdiction	Seller ID	Click to Add
P-001	Residential	219 Phillips St	Donahue	PA	15003	Donahue City, Ashland County	S-001	
P-002	Residential	852 Scranton Dr	Jonestown	PA	15068	Jonestown City, Fairfield County	S-002	
P-003	Residential	46 Hwy 82 S	Louisville	NY	10025	Pasqua County	S-003	
P-004	Commercial	186 Alabama Hwy	Hartford	PA	15031	Hartford City, Knox County	S-004	
P-005	Residential	Route 15, Box 281	Winslow	NY	10043	Putnam County	S-005	
P-006	Residential	87 Georgetown Rd, #2	East Barnard	PA	15064	Fairfield County	S-006	

Figure 2–2b

- Click the empty cell below P-003 to enter an ID for Property P-004 on Alabama Hwy. Enter the property's information as shown in Figure 2–2b.

5

- Enter the data for the remaining properties as shown in the figure.
- Resize the table columns as needed for best fit.
- Save and close the Properties table.

6

- Click the Navigation Pane bar to open the Navigation Pane, open the Buyers table in Datasheet view, and then close the Navigation Pane.
- Click the empty cell below B-004 to enter a new buyer's ID.
- Enter the data for Riya Sumner as shown in Figure 2–2c.

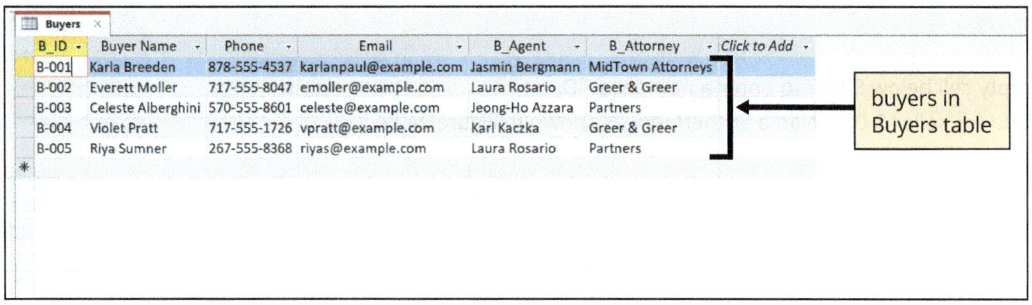

B_ID	Buyer Name	Phone	Email	B_Agent	B_Attorney	Click to Add
B-001	Karla Breeden	878-555-4537	karlanpaul@example.com	Jasmin Bergmann	MidTown Attorneys	
B-002	Everett Moller	717-555-8047	emoller@example.com	Laura Rosario	Greer & Greer	
B-003	Celeste Alberghini	570-555-8601	celeste@example.com	Jeong-Ho Azzara	Partners	
B-004	Violet Pratt	717-555-1726	vpratt@example.com	Karl Kaczka	Greer & Greer	
B-005	Riya Sumner	267-555-8368	riyas@example.com	Laura Rosario	Partners	

Figure 2–2c

- Resize the table columns as needed for best fit.
- Save and close the Buyers table.

To Create a Query in Design View

You have already used the Simple Query Wizard to create a query. Most of the time, however, you will use Design view, which is the primary option for creating queries. **Why?** Once you have created a new query in Design view, you have more options than with the wizard and can specify fields, criteria, sorting, calculations, and so on. The following steps create a new query in Design view.

1

- Click Create on the ribbon to display the Create tab (Figure 2–3).

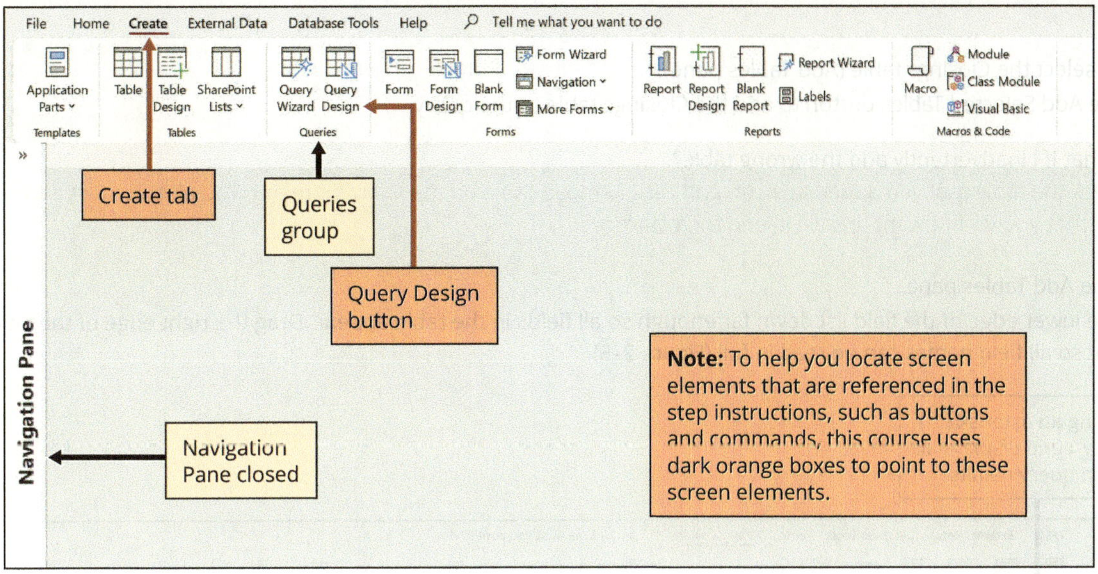

Figure 2–3

2

- Click the Query Design button (Create tab | Queries group) to create a new query (Figure 2–4).

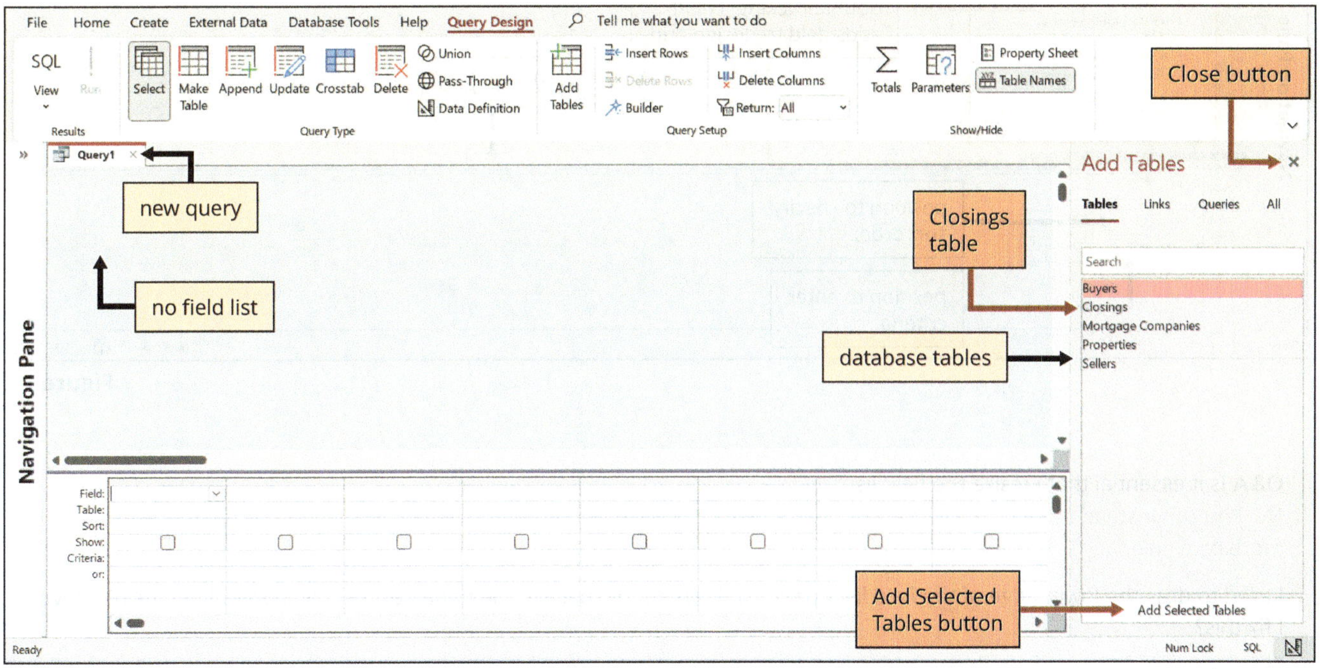

Figure 2–4

3

- Click to select the Closings table (Add Tables pane).
- Click the Add Selected Tables button to add the Closings table to the query.

Q&A What if I inadvertently add the wrong table?

Right-click the table that you added in error, and click Remove Table on the shortcut menu. You also can just close the query, indicate that you do not want to save it, and then start over.

- Close the Add Tables pane.
- Drag the lower edge of the field list down far enough so all fields in the table appear. Drag the right edge of the field list to the right so all field names can be read in full (Figure 2–5).

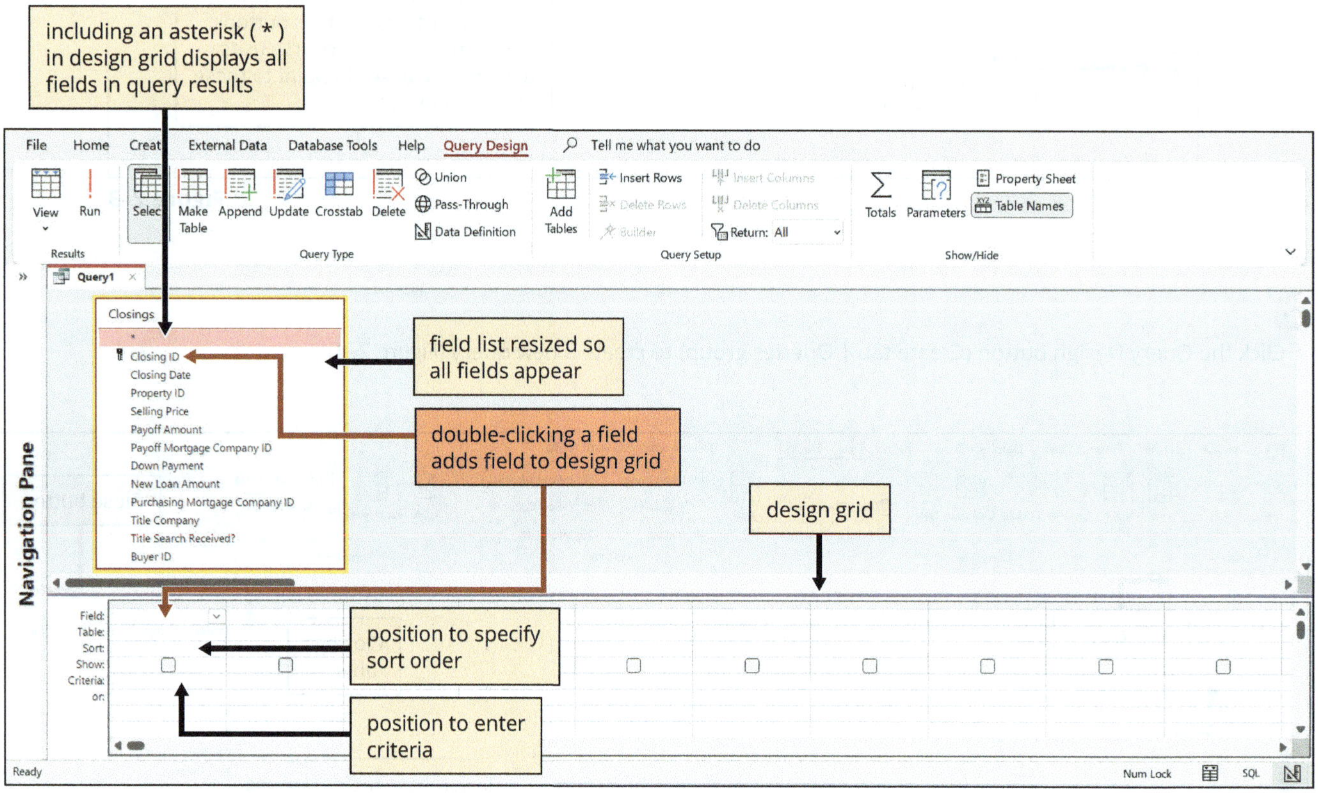

Figure 2–5

Q&A Is it essential that I resize the field list?

No. You can instead scroll through the list of fields using the scroll bar. Resizing the field list so that all fields appear is usually more convenient.

I tried to drag the lower edge of the field list down, but I ran out of space in the pane before I could see all the fields. How do I fix this?

You can resize the panes so more space is given to the field list area. Point to the thick, gray bar between the upper pane and the lower pane until you see a two-pointed arrow. Click and drag that arrow up or down to resize the panes.

Other Ways

1. Double-click table name in Add Tables pane to add it to query

To Add Fields to the Design Grid

Once you have a new query displayed in Design view, you are ready to make entries in the **design grid**, the portion of the window where you specify fields and criteria for the query. The design grid is located in the lower pane of the window. You add the fields you want included in the query to the Field row in the grid. **Why add fields to the grid?** Only the fields that appear in the design grid are included in the query results. The following steps begin creating a query that Partners Law Firm can use to obtain the closing dates, payoff information, new loan information, and information for buyers.

1

- Double-click the Closing ID field in the field list to add the field to the query's design grid.

Q&A What if I add the wrong field?
Click just above the field name in the design grid to select the column, and then press DEL to remove the field. Alternatively, you can click the arrow next to the field name and select the correct field.

2

- Double-click the Closing Date field in the field list to add the field to the query's design grid.
- Add the Payoff Amount, Payoff Mortgage Company ID, New Loan Amount, Purchasing Mortgage Company ID, and Buyer ID fields to the query's design grid (Figure 2-6).

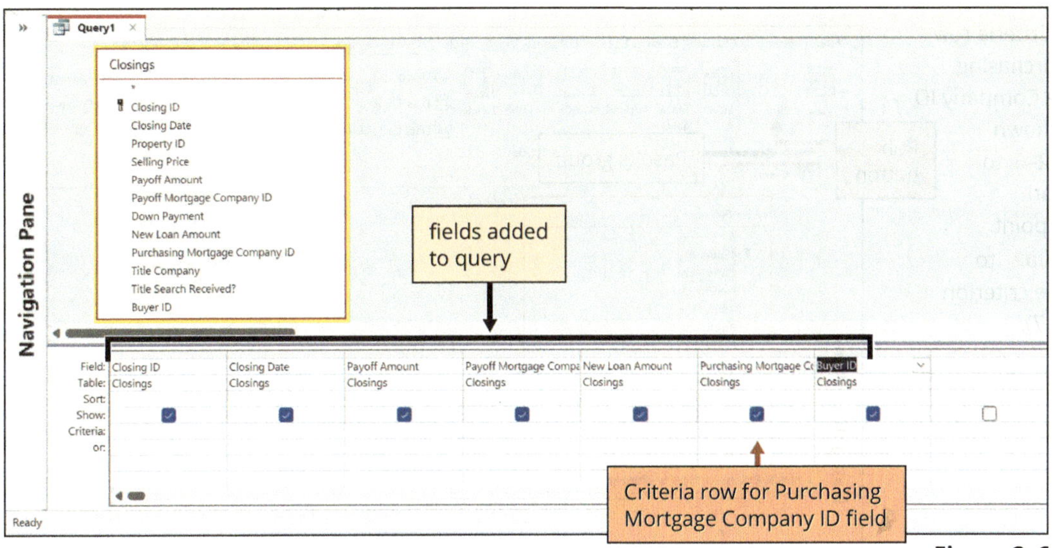

Figure 2-6

Q&A What if I want to include all fields? Do I have to add each field individually?
No. Instead of adding individual fields, you can double-click the asterisk (*) to add the asterisk to the design grid. The asterisk is a shortcut indicating all fields are to be included.

Determining Criteria

When you use queries, usually you are looking for those records that satisfy some criterion. For example, you might want to see closing dates and financial information for one of the mortgage companies. You enter criteria in the Criteria row in the design grid below the field name to which the criterion applies. For example, to find purchase closings with Cheshire Mortgage, you first must add the Purchasing Mortgage Company ID field to the design grid. For ease of typing, the mortgage companies were given ID numbers, for example, Cheshire Mortgage's ID is M-002, and Atlas Mortgage's ID is M-001. Therefore, when you enter the Mortgage ID, you will only need to type M-001 or M-002 in the Criteria row. For example, you will only need to type M-002 for Cheshire Mortgage in the Criteria row below the Purchasing Mortgage Company ID field.

BTW
Touch Screen Differences
The Office and Windows interfaces may vary if you are using a touch screen. For this reason, you might notice the function or appearance of your touch screen differs slightly from this module's presentation.

BTW
Access Screen Resolution
If you are using a computer or mobile device to step through the project in this module and you want your screens to match the figures in this course, you should change your screen's resolution to 1920 × 1080.

Running the Query

After adding the appropriate fields and defining the query's criteria, you must run the query to get the results. To view the results of the query from Design view, click the Run button to instruct Access to run the query, that is, to perform the necessary actions to produce and display the results in Datasheet view.

To Use Text Data in a Criterion

To use **text data** (data in a field whose data type is Short Text) in criteria, simply type the text in the Criteria row below the corresponding field name, just as you did previously. In Access, you typically do not need to enclose text data in quotation marks as you do in many other database management systems. **Why?** Access will enter the quotation marks automatically, so you can simply type the desired text. The following steps finish creating a query that Partners paralegals might use to obtain closing dates and financial information for closings where Cheshire Mortgage will be the buyer's new mortgage company. These steps also save the query.

1

- Click the Criteria row for the Purchasing Mortgage Company ID field, as shown in Figure 2–6, to produce an insertion point.
- Type **M-002** to specify the criterion (Figure 2–7).

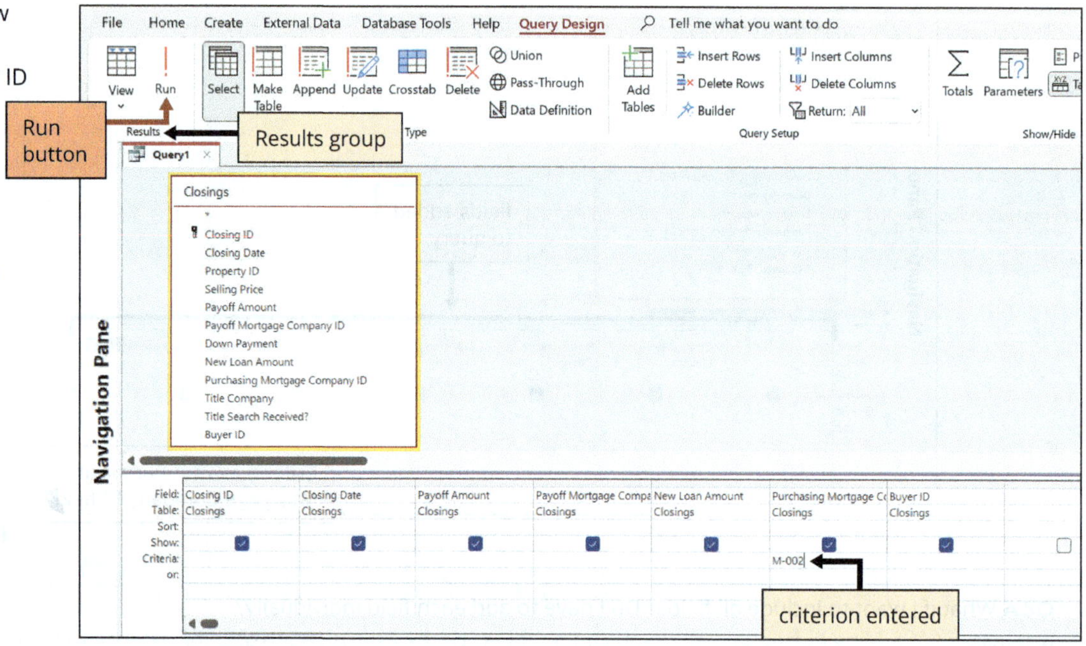

Figure 2–7

2

- Click the Run button (Query Design tab | Results group) to run the query (Figure 2–8) and display closings with new mortgages at Cheshire Mortgage.

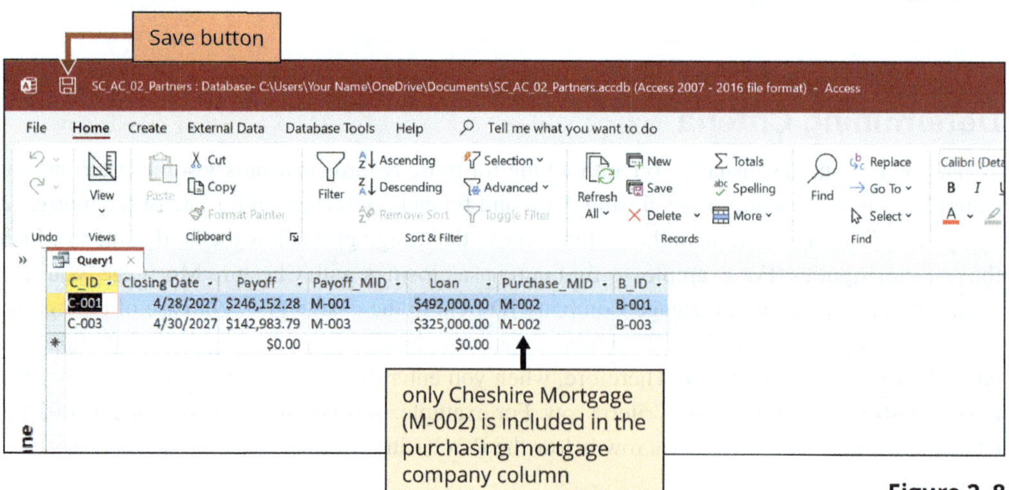

Figure 2–8

Q&A Can I also use the View button in the Results group to run the query?
Yes. You can click the View button to view the query results in Datasheet view.

My records are in a different order. Is this a problem?
No. The important thing is which records are included in the results. You will see later in this module how you can specify the order you want for situations when the order is important.

3

- Click the Save button on the Quick Access Toolbar, as shown in Figure 2–8, to display the Save As dialog box.
- Type **m02q01** as the name of the query (Figure 2–9).

Q&A Can I also save from Design view?
Yes. You can save the query when you view it in Design view just as you can save it when you view query results in Datasheet view.

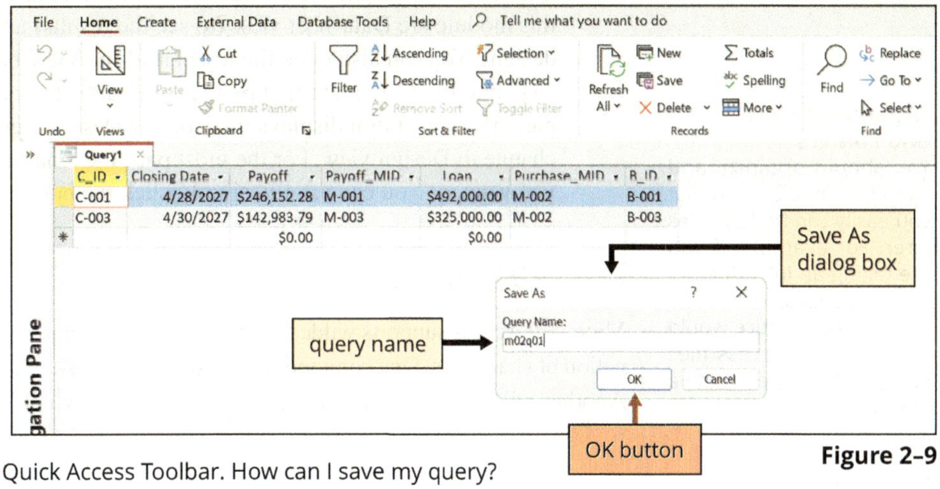

Figure 2–9

I don't see the Save button on the Quick Access Toolbar. How can I save my query?
You can either click File to enter Backstage view and click Save, or you can press CTRL+S.

4

- Click OK (Save As dialog box) to save the query (Figure 2–10), and then close the m02q01 query.

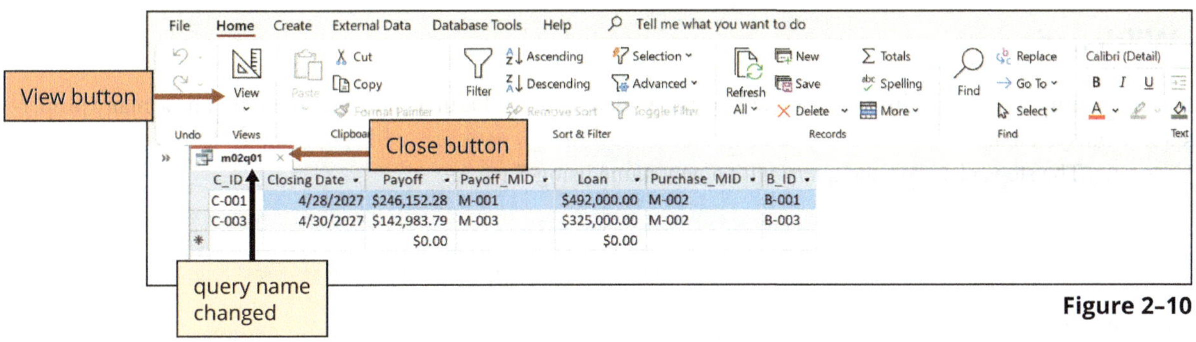

Figure 2–10

Other Ways

1. Right-click query tab, click Save on shortcut menu to save query

Using Saved Queries

After you have created and saved a query, you can use it in a variety of ways:

- To view the results of a query that is not currently open, open it by double-clicking the query in the Navigation Pane. Alternatively, you can right-click the query in the Navigation Pane and click Open on the shortcut menu.
- If you want to change the design of a query that is already open, return to Design view and make the changes.
- If you want to change the design of a query that is not currently open, right-click the query in the Navigation Pane and then click Design View on the shortcut menu to open the query in Design view.

BTW
The Ribbon and Screen Resolution
Access may change how the groups and buttons within the groups appear on the ribbon, depending on the computer or mobile device's screen resolution. Thus, your ribbon may look different from the ones in this course if you are using a screen resolution other than 1920 × 1080.

- To print the results of an open query, click File on the ribbon, click the Print tab in Backstage view, and then click Quick Print.
- To print a query without first opening it, be sure the query is selected in the Navigation Pane and click File on the ribbon, click the Print tab in Backstage view, and then click Quick Print.
- You can switch between views of a query using the View button (Home tab | Views group). Clicking the arrow at the bottom of the button produces the View button menu. You then click the desired view in the menu. The two query views you use in this module are Datasheet view (to see the results) and Design view (to change the design). You can also click the top part of the View button, in which case you will switch to the view identified by the icon on the button. In Figure 2–10, for example, the View button displays the icon for Design view, so clicking the button would change to Design view. For the most part, the icon on the button represents the view you want, so you can usually simply click the button.

BTW
Organizing Files and Folders
You should organize and store files in folders so that you easily can find the files later. For example, if you are taking an introductory computer class called CIS 101, a good practice would be to save all Access files in an Access folder inside a CIS 101 folder.

Using Wildcards

Microsoft Access supports wildcards. **Wildcards** are symbols that represent any character or combination of characters. One common wildcard, the **asterisk (*)**, represents any collection of characters. Another wildcard symbol is the **question mark (?)**, which represents any individual character.

Consider This

What does S* represent? What does T?m represent?

S* represents the letter, S, followed by any collection of characters. A search for S* might return System, So, or Superlative. T?m represents the letter, T, followed by any single character, followed by the letter, m. A search for T?m might return the names Tim or Tom.

To Use a Wildcard

The following steps modify an existing query to use the asterisk wildcard so that Partners paralegals can find how many properties are located in Pennsylvania. *Why? Because you do not know how many characters will follow the P, the asterisk wildcard symbol is appropriate.* The steps also save the query with a new name using Save As.

1

- Open the Navigation Pane, and then open the Properties Query in Design View.
- Click the Criteria row below the Property State field to produce an insertion point.
- If there were any existing data in the Criteria row, you would use DEL or BACKSPACE. Because there is no existing criteria, you can simply type the criteria.
- Type **P*** as the criterion (Figure 2–11).

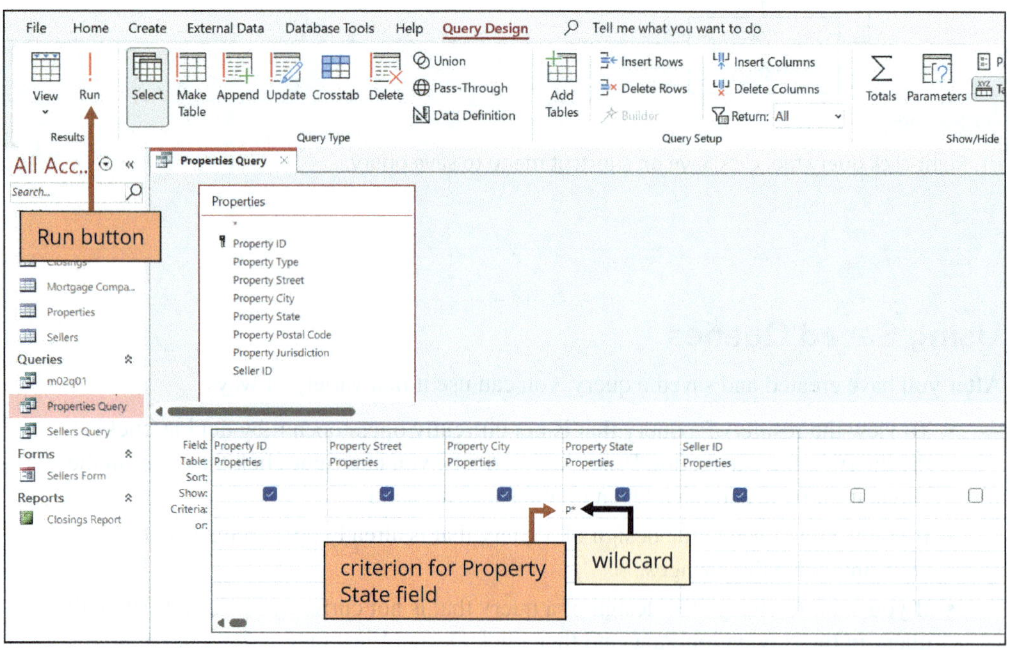

Figure 2–11

2

- Run the query by clicking the Run button (Query Design tab | Results group) (Figure 2–12).

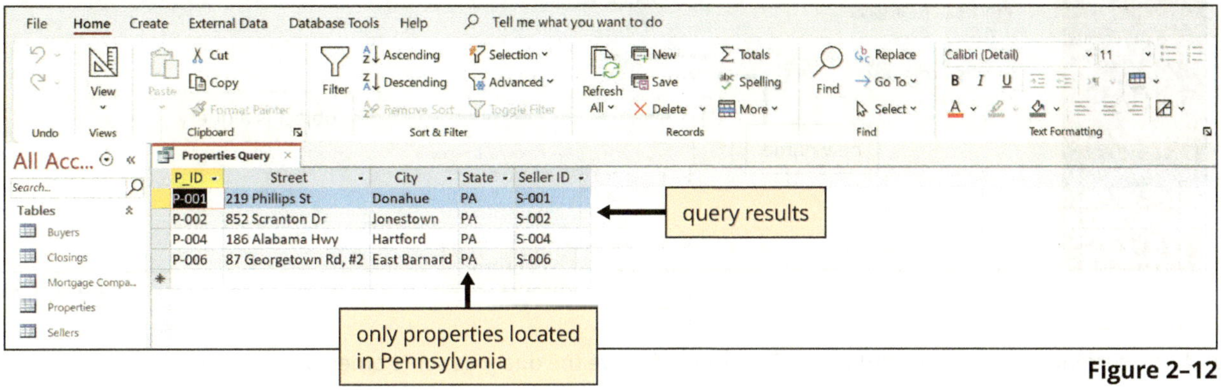

Figure 2–12

- **Experiment:** Change the letter P to lowercase in the criterion and run the query to determine whether case makes a difference when entering a wildcard.

Q&A The text I entered is now preceded by the word, Like. What happened?
Criteria that include wildcards need to be preceded by the word, Like. However, you do not have to type it; Access adds the word automatically to any criterion involving a wildcard.

3

- Click File on the ribbon to open Backstage view.
- Click the Save As tab in Backstage view to display the Save As gallery.
- Click 'Save Object As' in the File Types area (Figure 2–13).

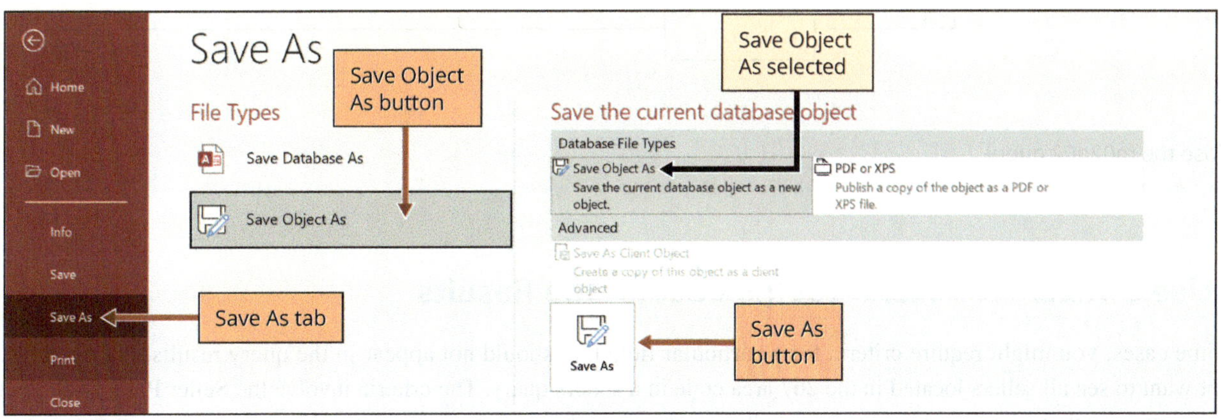

Figure 2–13

Q&A Can I just click the Save button on the Quick Access Toolbar as I did when saving the previous query?
If you clicked the Save button, you would replace the previous query with the version you just created. Because you want to save both the previous query and the new one, you need to save the new version with a different name. To do so, you must use Save Object As, which is available through Backstage view.

4

- With Save Object As selected in the File Types gallery, click the Save As button to display the Save As dialog box.
- Erase the name of the current query and type **m02q02** as the name for the saved query (Figure 2–14).

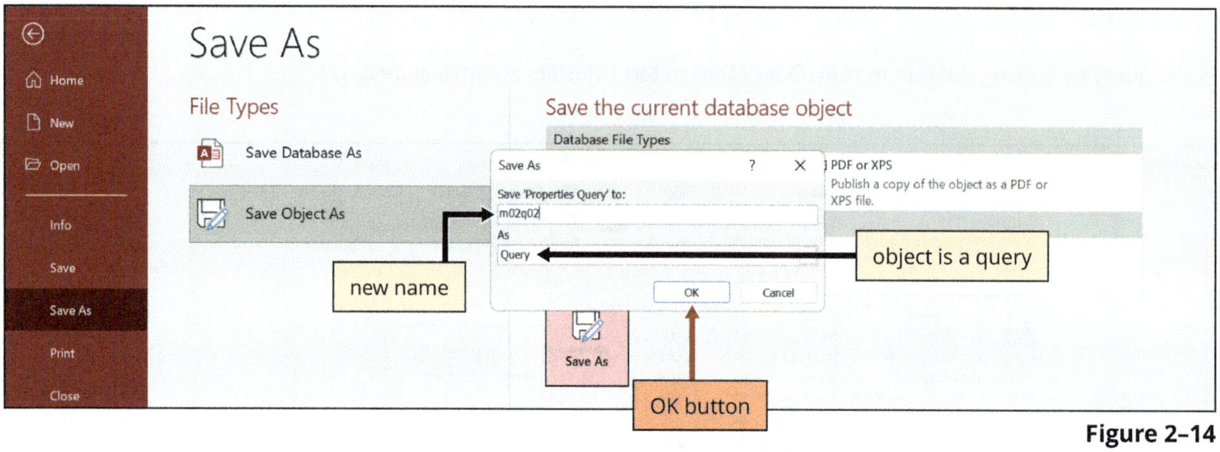

Figure 2–14

Q&A The current entry in the As text box is Query. Could I save the query as some other type of object?
Although you usually would want to save the query as another query, you can also save it as a form or report by changing the entry in the As text box. If you do, Access would create either a simple form or a simple report for the query.

5

- Click OK (Save As dialog box) to save the query with the new name and close Backstage view (Figure 2–15).

Q&A How can I tell that the query was saved with the new name?
The new name will appear on the tab.

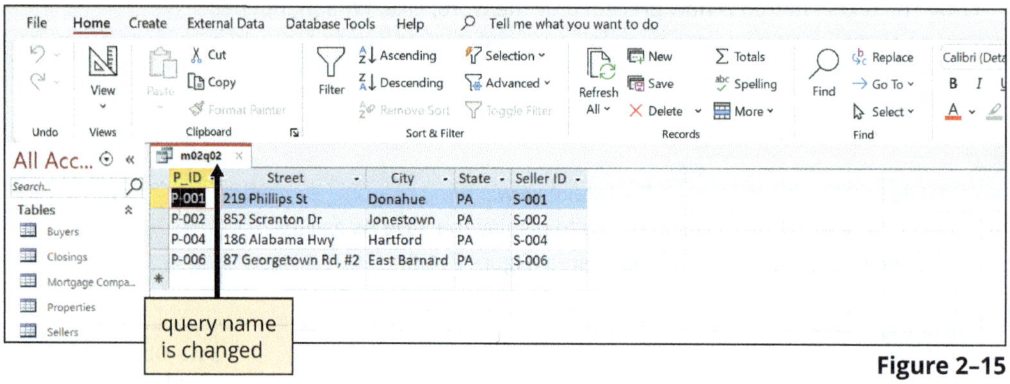

Figure 2–15

6

- Close the m02q02 query.

To Use Criteria for a Field Not Included in the Results

In some cases, you might require criteria for a particular field that should not appear in the query results. For example, you might want to see all sellers located in the 267 area code in a sellers query. The criteria involve the Seller Phone field, but you do not want to include the Phone field in the results because this information is sensitive and you do not want everyone viewing the query to see this information.

To enter a criterion for the Seller Phone field, it must be included in the design grid. Normally, it would then appear in the results. To prevent it from appearing, remove the check mark from its check box in the Show row of the grid. **Why?** A check mark in the Show check box instructs Access to show the field in the results. If you remove the check mark, you can use the field in the query without displaying it in the query results.

The following steps modify a previous query so that Partners paralegals can select only those sellers located in the 267 area code. Partners paralegals do not want the Seller Phone field to appear in the results, however. The steps also save the query with a new name.

1

- Open the Sellers Query in Design view.
- Type **267*** as the criterion for the Seller Phone field (Figure 2–16).

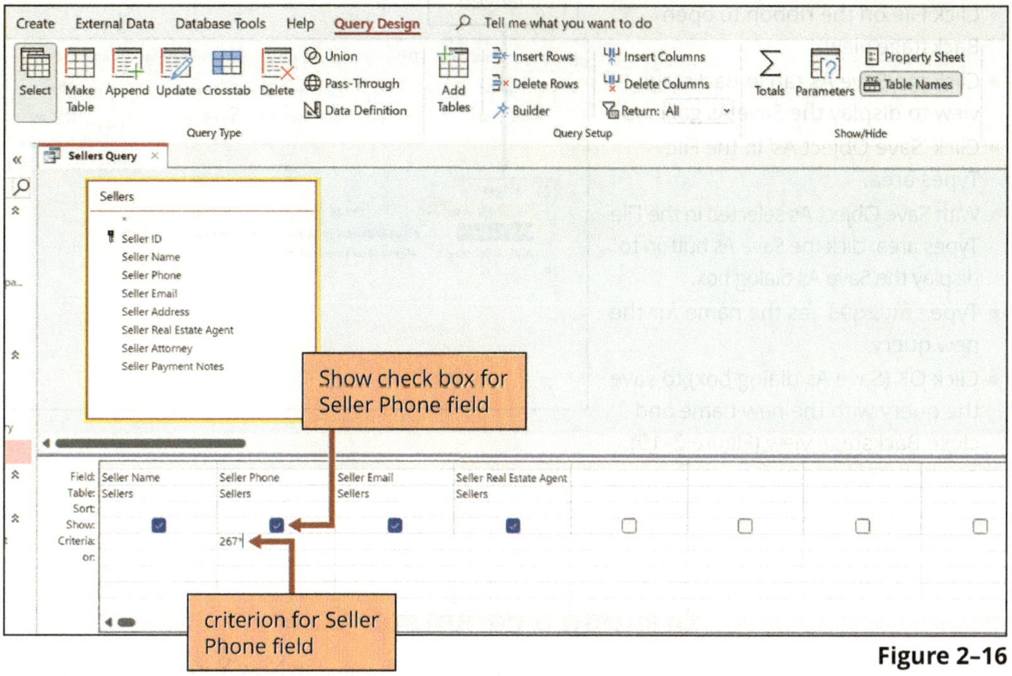

Figure 2–16

2

- Click the Show check box for the Seller Phone field to remove the check mark (Figure 2–17).

Q&A Could I have removed the check mark before entering the criterion?
Yes. The order in which you perform the two operations does not matter.

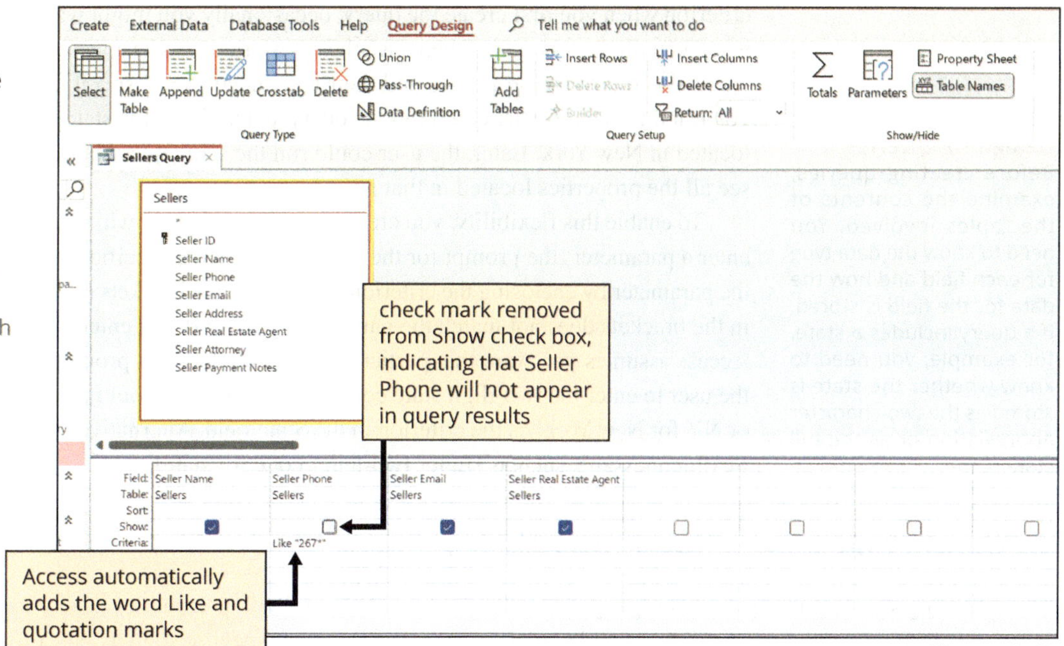

Figure 2–17

- Run the query (Figure 2–18).
- **Experiment:** Click the View button to return to Design view, enter a different area code, such as 814*, as the criterion, and run the query. Repeat this process with additional area codes, including at least one area code that is not in the database. When finished, retype the Seller Phone criteria as 267*.

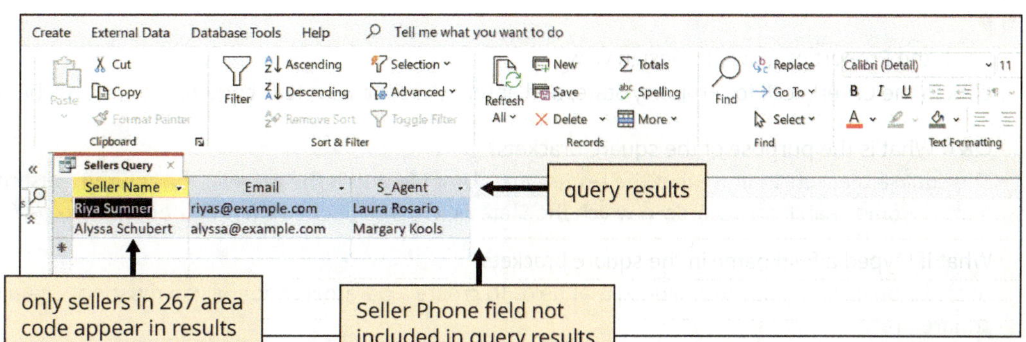

Figure 2–18

3

- Click File on the ribbon to open Backstage view.
- Click the Save As tab in Backstage view to display the Save As gallery.
- Click 'Save Object As' in the File Types area.
- With Save Object As selected in the File Types area, click the Save As button to display the Save As dialog box.
- Type **m02q03** as the name for the new query.
- Click OK (Save As dialog box) to save the query with the new name and close Backstage view (Figure 2–19).
- Close the query.

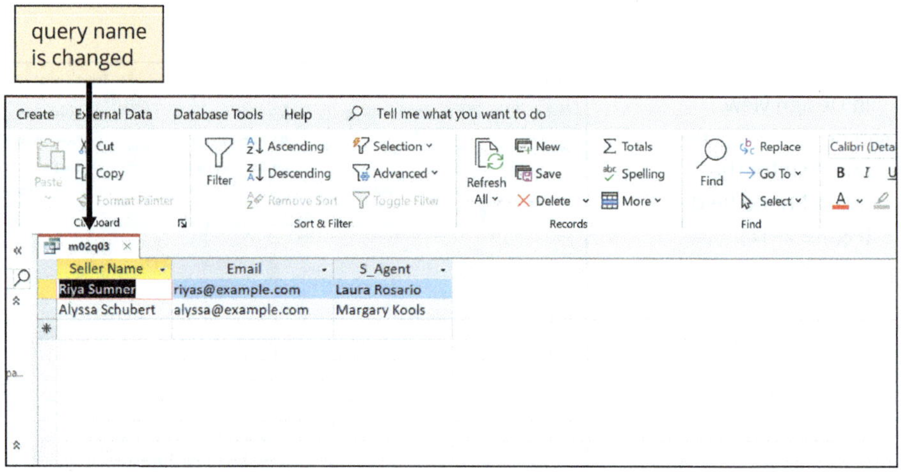

Figure 2–19

Creating a Parameter Query

If you want to find properties located in New York, you would either have to create a new query or modify the existing query by replacing P* with N* as the criterion. Rather than giving a specific criterion when you first create the query, occasionally you might want to enter part of the criterion when you run the query and then have the appropriate results appear. For example, you might want a query to return the properties and their associated states, specifying a different state each time you run the query. A user could run the query, enter NY as the state, and then see all the properties located in New York. Later, the user could run the same query but enter a different state and then see all the properties located in that state.

To enable this flexibility, you create a parameter query, which prompts the user for input. You enter a parameter (the prompt for the user) rather than a specific value as the criterion. You create the parameter by enclosing the criterion value in square brackets ([ ]). It is important that the value in the brackets does not match the name of any field. If you enter a field name in square brackets, Access assumes you want that particular field and does not prompt the user for input. To prompt the user to enter the two-digit state code as the input, you could place [Enter PA for Pennsylvania or NY for New York] as the criterion in the State field. Alternatively, you could use a shorter, more flexible message, such as [Enter two-letter code for state].

BTW
Designing Queries
Before creating queries, examine the contents of the tables involved. You need to know the data type for each field and how the data for the field is stored. If a query includes a state, for example, you need to know whether the state is stored as the two-character abbreviation or as the full state name.

To Create and View a Parameter Query

The following steps create a parameter query. **Why?** The parameter query will give paralegals at Partners Law Firm the ability to enter a different state each time they run the query rather than having a specific state as part of the criterion in the query. The steps also save the query with a new name.

1

- Open the Properties Query in Design view.
- Click in the Criteria cell for Property State, and enter **[Enter two-letter code for state]** as the new criterion (Figure 2–20).

Q&A What is the purpose of the square brackets?

The square brackets indicate that the text entered is not text that the value in the column must match. Without the brackets, Access would search for records in which the State field contains the value *Enter two-letter code for state*.

What if I typed a field name in the square brackets?

Access would simply use the value in that field. To create a parameter query, you must not use a field name in the square brackets.

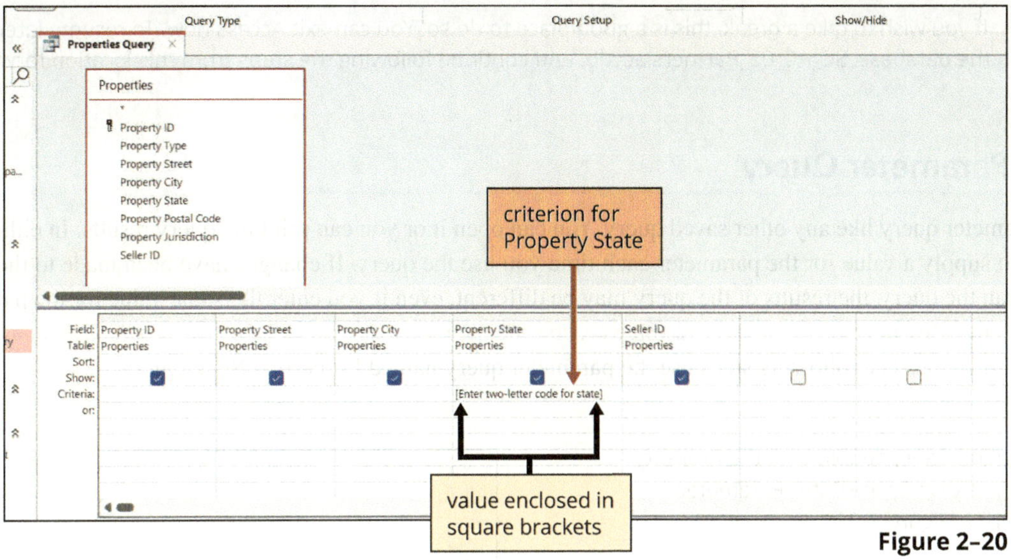

Figure 2–20

2

- Click the Run button (Query Design tab | Results group) to display the Enter Parameter Value dialog box (Figure 2–21).

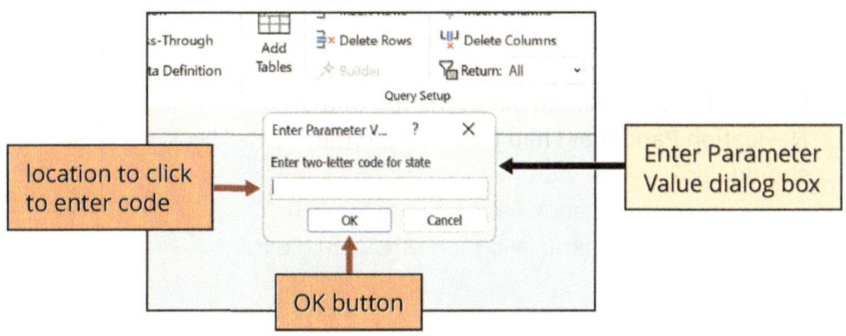

Figure 2–21

3

- Type **NY** as the parameter value in the Enter Parameter Value text box, and then click OK (Enter Parameter Value dialog box) to close the dialog box and view the query (Figure 2–22).
  - **Experiment:** Try using other characters between the square brackets. In each case, run the query. When finished, change the text between the square brackets back to Enter two-letter code for state.

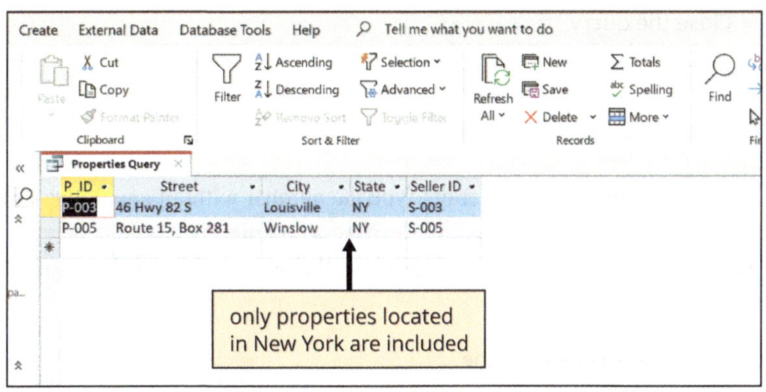

Figure 2–22

4

- Click File on the ribbon to open Backstage view.
- Click the Save As tab in Backstage view to display the Save As gallery.
- Click 'Save Object As' in the File Types area.
- With Save Object As selected in the File Types area, click the Save As button to display the Save As dialog box.
- Type **Property - State Query** as the name for the saved query.
- Click OK (Save As dialog box) to save the query with the new name.

5

- Close the Property - State Query.

Break Point: If you wish to take a break, this is a good place to do so. You can exit Access now. To resume later, start Access, open the database, SC_AC_02_Partners.accdb, and continue following the steps from this location forward.

To Use a Parameter Query

You use a parameter query like any other saved query. You can open it or you can print the query results. In either case, Access prompts you to supply a value for the parameter each time you use the query. If changes have been made to the data since the last time you ran the query, the results of the query may be different, even if you enter the same value for the parameter. **Why?** In addition to the ability to enter different field values each time the parameter query is run, the query always uses the data that is currently in the table. The following steps use the parameter query named Property – State Query.

1

- In the Navigation Pane, double-click the Property – State Query to display the Enter Parameter Value dialog box (Figure 2–23).

Q&A The title bar for my Navigation Pane contains Tables and Related Views rather than All Access Objects as it did previously. What should I do?
Click the Navigation Pane arrow, and then click 'Object Type'.

I do not have the Search bar at the top of the Navigation Pane that I had previously. What should I do?
Right-click the Navigation Pane title bar arrow to display a shortcut menu, and then click Search Bar.

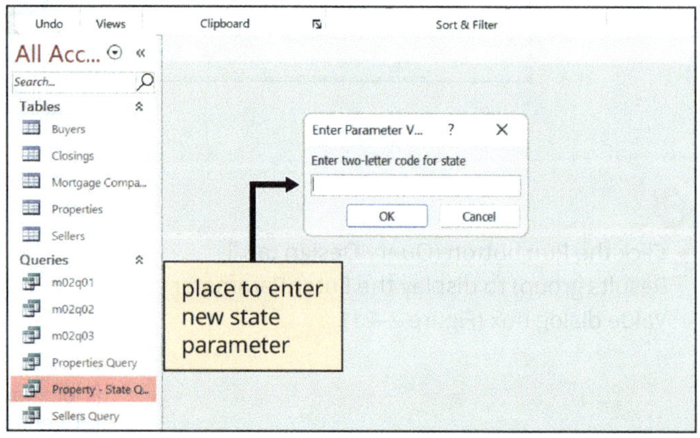

Figure 2–23

2

- Type **PA** in the Enter two-letter code for state text box, and then click OK (Enter Parameter Value dialog box) to display the results.
- Close the query.

To Use a Number in a Criterion

To enter a number in a criterion, type the number without any dollar signs or commas. **Why?** If you enter a dollar sign, Access assumes you are entering text. If you enter a comma, Access considers the criterion invalid. The following steps create a query that Partners paralegals might use to display all closings with new loans of $325,000. The steps also save the query with a new name.

1

- Close the Navigation Pane.
- Click Create on the ribbon to display the Create tab.
- Click the Query Design button (Create tab | Queries group) to create a new query.
- If necessary, click the Tables tab (Add Tables pane), and click the Closings table (Add Tables pane) to select the table.
- Click the Add Selected Tables button to add the selected table to the query.
- Close the Add Tables pane.
- Resize the field list so all fields in the list are displayed.
- In the following order, include the Closing ID, Closing Date, Purchasing Mortgage Company ID, and New Loan Amount fields in the query.

Q&A I entered the fields into the query in the wrong order. How do I fix this?
The fields will be listed in the query in the order you insert them. If you inserted fields in the wrong order, you can delete one or more fields and reinsert them in the correct order or you can move one or more fields. To move a field in the design grid, click the column selector for the field to select the field and drag it to the appropriate location.

- Type **325000** as the criterion for the New Loan Amount field (Figure 2–24).

Q&A Do I need to enter a dollar sign, comma, or decimal point?
No. Access will interpret 325000 as $325,000.00 because the data type for the New Loan Amount field is currency.

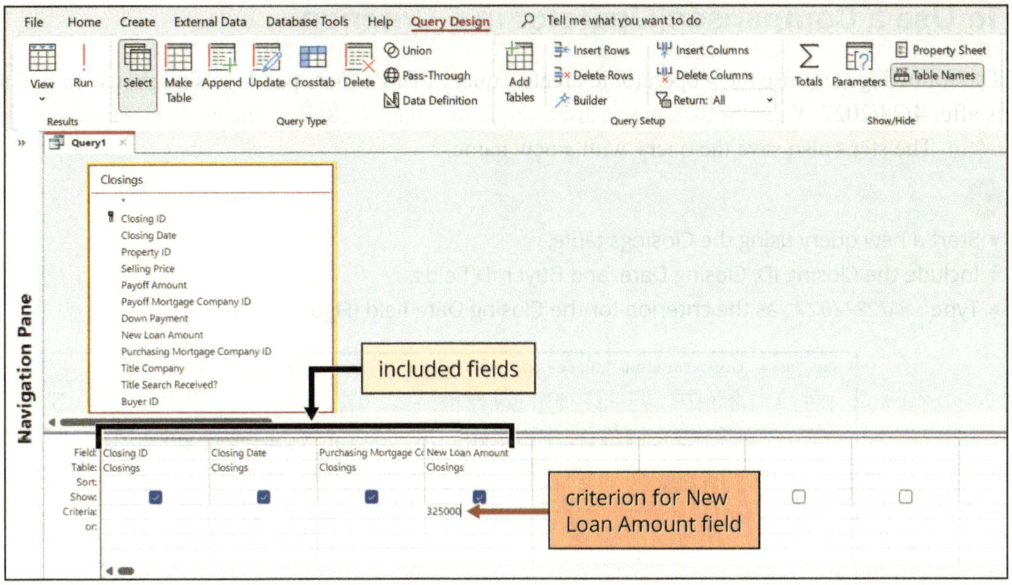

Figure 2–24

2

- Run the query (Figure 2–25).

Q&A Why did Access display the results as $325,000.00 when I only entered 325000?
Access uses the format for the field to determine how to display the result. In this case, the format indicated that Access should include the dollar sign, decimal point, and two decimal places.

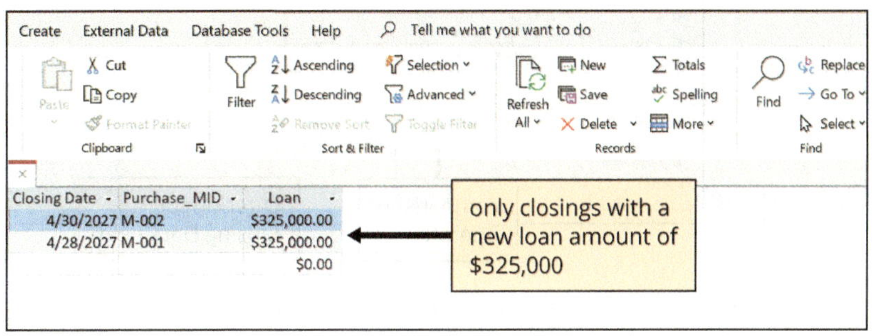

Figure 2–25

- Save the query as **m02q04**.

Q&A How do I know when to use the Save button to save a query or use Backstage view to perform a Save As?
If you are saving a new query, the simplest way is to use the Save button on the Quick Access Toolbar or press CTRL+S. If you are saving changes to a previously saved query but do not want to change the name, use the Save button. If you want to save a previously saved query with a new name, you must use Backstage view and perform a Save Object As.

- Close the query.

Comparison Operators

Unless you specify otherwise, Access assumes that the criteria you enter involves equality (exact matches). In the last query, for example, you were requesting those closings with new loan amounts of exactly $325,000. In other situations, you might want to find a range of results; for example, you could request closings whose closing date is after 4/28/2027. If you want a query to return something other than an exact match, you must enter the appropriate **comparison operator**. The comparison operators are > (greater than), < (less than), >= (greater than or equal to), <= (less than or equal to), and NOT (not equal to).

To Use a Comparison Operator in a Criterion

The following steps use the > operator to create a query that Partners paralegals might use to find all closings whose closing date is after 4/28/2027. **Why?** A date that is after, or greater than, 4/28/2027 means the date might conflict with a proposed training event. The steps also save the query with a new name.

1

- Start a new query using the Closings table.
- Include the Closing ID, Closing Date, and Buyer ID fields.
- Type **>4/28/2027** as the criterion for the Closing Date field (Figure 2–26).

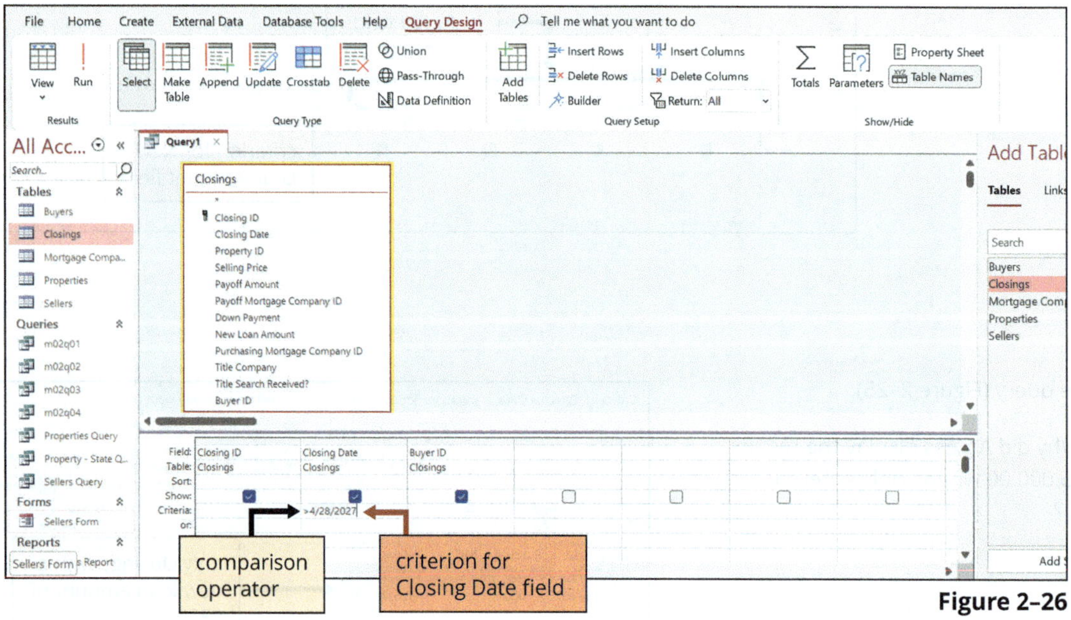

Figure 2–26

Q&A Why did I not have to type the leading zero in the Month portion of the date?
It is fine as you typed it. You also could have typed 04/28/2027. Some people often type the day or month using two digits even if the date is a single digit as the numbers 1 through 9. You also could type a leading zero for both the month and the day, such as 05/01/2027.

I noticed that Access changed >4/28/2027 to >#4/28/2027#. Why does the date now have hash signs around it?
This is the date format in Access. You usually do not have to enter the number signs because in most cases Access will insert them automatically.

2

- Run the query (Figure 2–27).
- **Experiment:** Return to Design view. Try a different criterion involving a comparison operator in the Closing Date field and run the query. When finished, return to Design view, enter the original criterion (>4/28/2027) in the Closing Date field, and run the query.

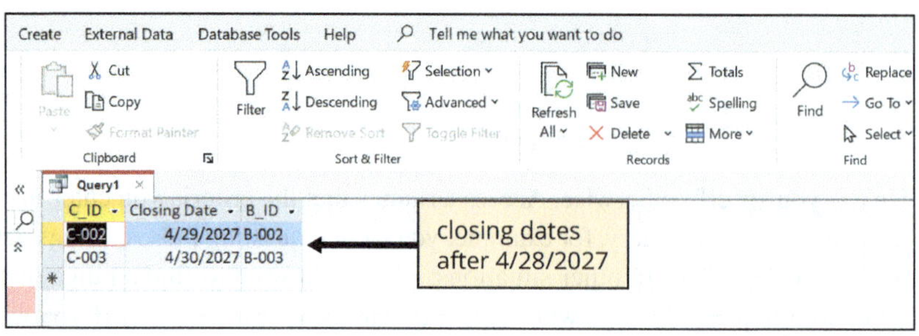

Figure 2–27

Q&A Can I use the same comparison operators with text data?
Yes. Comparison operators function the same whether you use them with number fields, currency fields, date fields, or text fields. With a text field, comparison operators use alphabetical order in making the determination.

3

- Save the query as **m02q05**.
- Close the query.

Using Compound Criteria

Often your search data must satisfy more than one criterion. This type of criterion is called a **compound criterion** and is created using the words AND or OR.

In an **AND criterion**, both individual criterion must be true in order for the compound criterion to be true. For example, an AND criterion would allow you to find closings after 4/28/2027 that are creating a new loan with the Cheshire Mortgage company.

An **OR criterion** is true if either individual criterion is true. An OR criterion would allow you to find closings after 4/28/2027 or closings that will create a loan with Cheshire Mortgage. In this case, any appointment after 4/28/2027 (regardless of mortgage company) or using Cheshire Mortgage (regardless of closing date) will be displayed.

BTW
Queries: Query-by-Example
Query-by-Example, often referred to as QBE, was a query language first proposed in the mid-1970s. In this approach, users asked questions by filling in a table on the screen. The Access approach to queries is based on Query-by-Example.

To Use a Compound Criterion Involving AND

To combine criteria with AND, place the criteria on the same row of the design grid. Why? Placing the criteria in the same row indicates that both criteria must be true in Access. It is important to note that sometimes when you view the results of a query, there are no records that meet the criterion entered. At this point, you might want to check to be certain the criterion was entered correctly. And, if the criterion is entered correctly, it becomes easier to trust the results even though you might have expected different results. The following steps use an AND criterion to enable Partners paralegals to find those closings with a closing date after 4/28/2027 and a new loan with Cheshire Mortgage. The steps also save the query.

1

- Start a new query using the Closings table.
- Include the Closing ID, Closing Date, Purchasing Mortgage Company ID, and Buyer ID fields.
- Type **>4/28/2027** as the criterion for the Closing Date field.
- Type **M-002** as the criterion for the Purchasing Mortgage Company ID field (Figure 2–28).

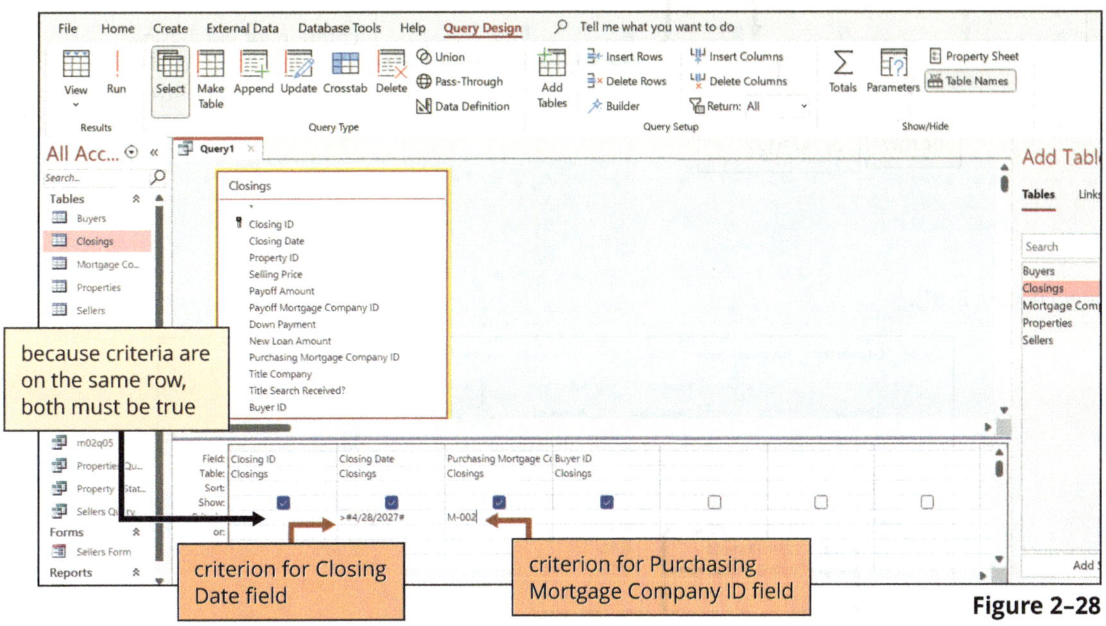

Figure 2–28

2

- Run the query (Figure 2–29) and notice that only one of the closings after 4/28/2027 will use Cheshire Mortgage.

3

- Save the query as **m02q06**. Do not close it yet.

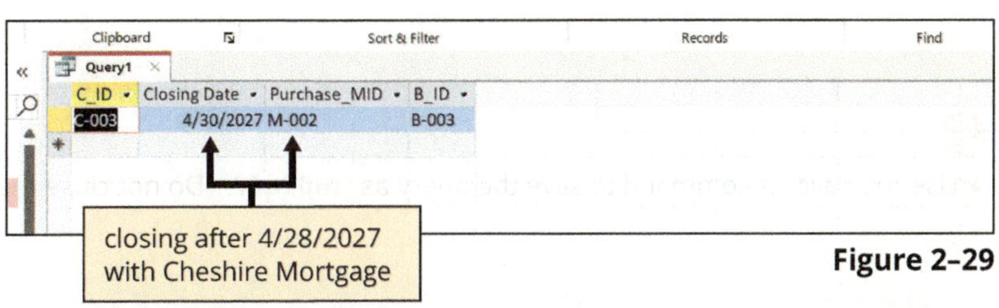

Figure 2–29

To Use a Compound Criterion Involving OR

To combine criteria with OR, each criterion must go on separate rows in the Criteria area of the grid. **Why?** Placing criteria on separate rows indicates at least one criterion must be true in Access and also shows true if both criterion are true. The following steps use an OR criterion to enable Partners paralegals to find those Closings with a Closing Date greater than 4/28/2027 or closings with new loans from Cheshire Mortgage. The steps also save the query with a new name.

1

- Return to Design view.
- In the Criteria row for the Purchasing Mortgage Company ID field, delete the existing text.
- Click the or row (the row below the Criteria row) for the Purchasing Mortgage Company ID field, and type **M-002** (Figure 2–30).

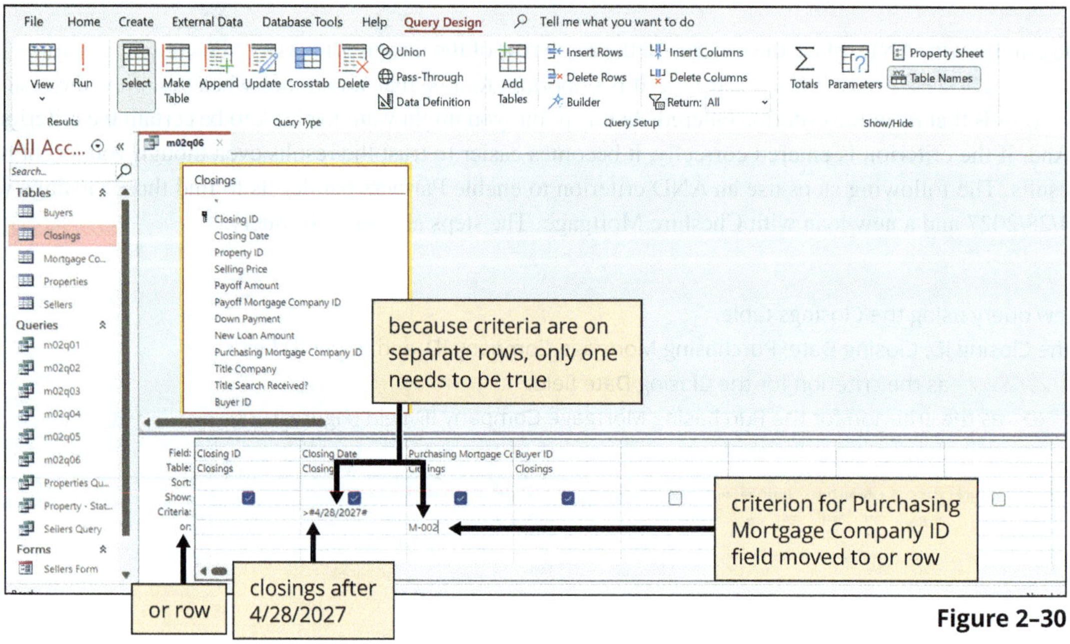

Figure 2–30

2

- Run the query (Figure 2–31).

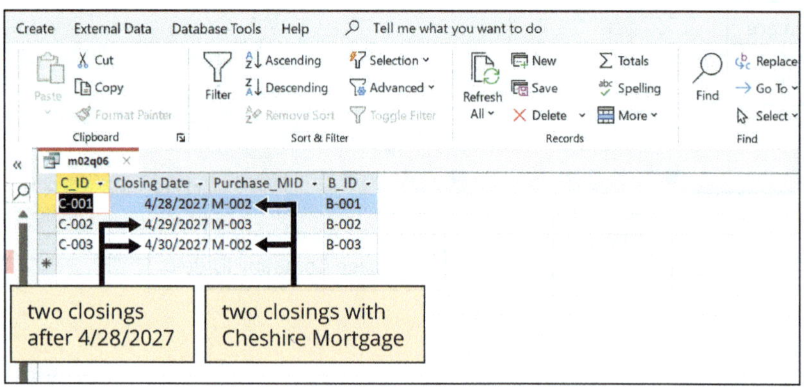

Figure 2–31

3

- Use the Save As command to save the query as **m02q07**. Do not close the query yet.

Special Criteria

You can use three special criteria in queries:

1. If you want to create a criterion involving a range of values in a single field, you can use the **AND operator**. You place the word AND between the individual conditions. For example, if you wanted to find all new loans greater than $300,000 and less than $400,000, you would enter >300000 AND <400000 as the criterion in the New Loan Amount column.
2. You can select values in a given range by using the **BETWEEN operator**. This is often an alternative to the AND operator. For example, to find all closings between 5/15/2027 and 5/31/2027, inclusive, you would enter BETWEEN 5/15/2027 AND 5/31/2027 as the criterion in the Closing Date column. This is equivalent to entering >=5/15/2027 AND <=5/31/2027.
3. You can select a list of values by using the **IN operator**. You follow the word IN with the list of values in parentheses. For example, to find the properties located in Pennsylvania (PA) or New York (NY), you would enter IN ('PA', 'NY'). Unlike when you enter a simple criterion, you must enclose text values in single quotation marks. The IN operator is like the OR operator, but it returns multiple values.

Consider This

How would you find properties located in Pennsylvania or New York without using the IN operator?

Place the text PA in the Criteria row of the State column. Place the text NY in the or row of the State column.

Sorting

In some queries, the order in which the records appear is irrelevant. All you need to be concerned about are the records that appear in the results. It does not matter which one is first or which one is last.

In other queries, however, the order can be very important. You might want to see new loan amounts arranged in ascending order (1,2,3,4,5, and so on), which is smallest to largest, or descending order (5,4,3,2,1), which is largest to smallest. Perhaps you want to see loan amounts listed by mortgage company in alphabetical order.

To order the records in a query result in a particular way, you **sort** the records. The field or fields on which the records are sorted is called the **sort key**. If you are sorting on more than one field (such as sorting by loan amount by mortgage company), the more important field (New Loan Amount) is called the **major key** (also called the **primary sort key**) and the less important field (Purchasing Mortgage Company) is called the **minor key** (also called the **secondary sort key**).

To sort in Microsoft Access, specify the sort order in the Sort row of the design grid below the field that is the sort key. If you specify more than one sort key, the sort key on the left will be the major sort key, and the one on the right will be the minor key.

BTW

Sorting Data in a Query

When sorting data in a query, the records in the underlying tables (the tables on which the query is based) are not actually rearranged. Instead, the DBMS determines the most efficient method of simply displaying the records in the requested order. The records in the underlying tables remain in their original order.

To Clear the Design Grid

Why? If the fields you want to include in the next query are different from those in the previous query, it is usually simpler to start with a clear grid, that is, one with no fields already in the design grid. You always can clear the entries in the design grid by closing the query and then starting over. A simpler approach to clearing the entries is to select all the entries and then press DEL. The following steps return to Design view and clear the design grid.

1
- If necessary, click the Design View button to display m02q07 in Design view.
- Click just above the Closing ID column heading in the grid to select the column.

Q&A I clicked above the column heading, but the column is not selected. What should I do?
You did not point to the correct location. Be sure the pointer changes into a down-pointing arrow, and then click again.

- Press and hold SHIFT and click just above the Buyer ID column heading to select all the columns (Figure 2-32).

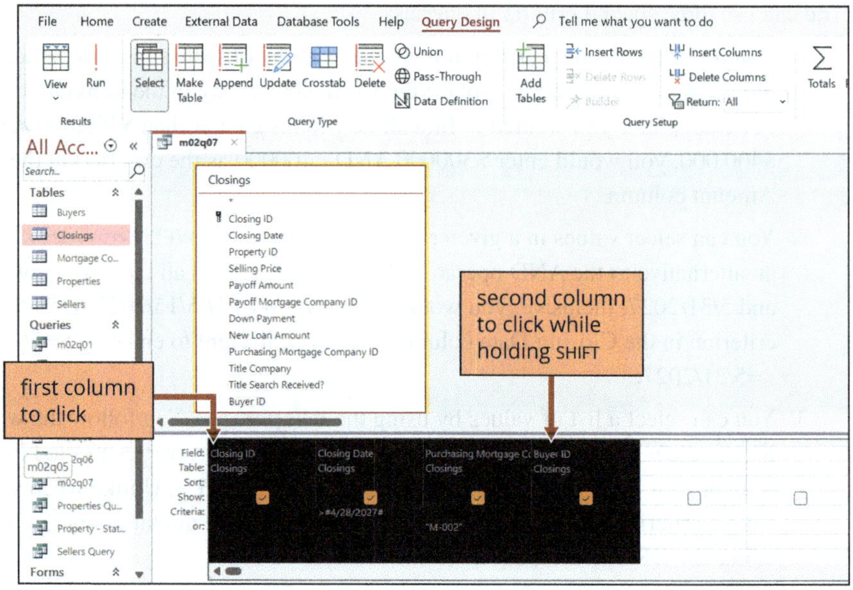

Figure 2-32

2
- Press DEL to clear the design grid.

3
- Close the query without saving these changes.

BTW
Clearing the Design Grid
You can also clear the design grid using the ribbon. To do so, click the Home tab, click the Advanced Filter Options button to display the Advanced menu (Home tab | Sort & Filter group), and then click Clear Grid on the Advanced Filter Options menu.

To Sort Data in a Query

If you determine that the query results should be sorted, you will need to specify the sort key. The following steps sort the new loan amounts in the Closings table by indicating that the New Loan Amount field is to be sorted. The steps specify Ascending sort order. **Why?** When sorting numerical data, Ascending sort order arranges the results from smallest to largest values.

1
- Create a new query in Design view based on the Closings table.
- Include the Closing ID, New Loan Amount, and Purchasing Mortgage Company ID fields in the design grid.
- Click the Sort row in the New Loan Amount field column, and then click the Sort arrow to display a menu of possible sort orders (Figure 2-33).

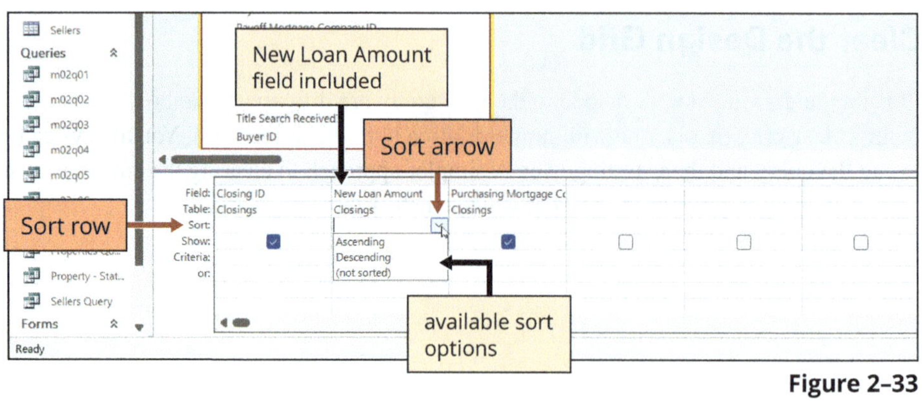

Figure 2-33

2

- Click Ascending to select the sort order (Figure 2–34).

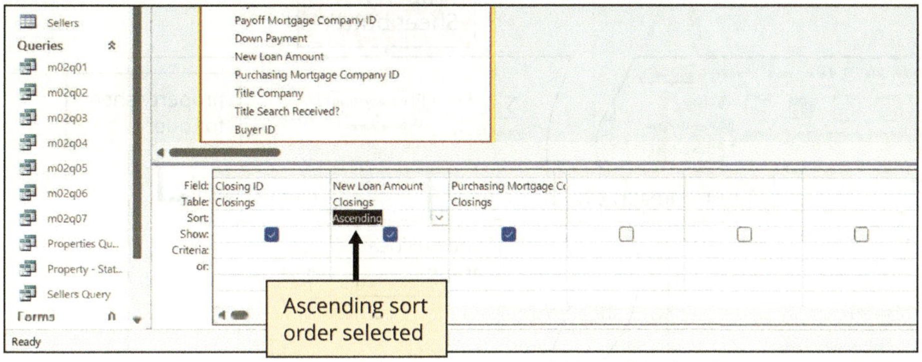

Figure 2–34

3

- Run the query (Figure 2–35) to display the loan amounts sorted in ascending order (lowest to highest).

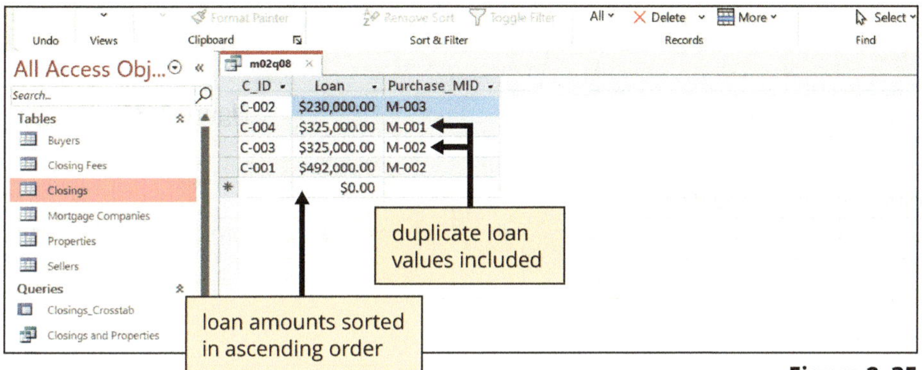

Figure 2–35

- Save the query as **m02q08**.
- **Experiment:** Return to Design view and change the sort order to Descending. Run the query. Return to Design view and change the sort order back to Ascending. Run the query.

Q&A Why do some loan amounts appear more than once?
The same loan amount is associated with multiple closings.

To Omit Duplicates

When you sort data, duplicates normally are included. In the query shown in Figure 2–35, for example, $325,000.00 appears more than once. You eliminate duplicates using the query's property sheet. A **property sheet** is a pane containing the various properties of the object. To omit duplicates, you will use the property sheet to change the Unique Values property from No to Yes.

The following steps create a query that Partners paralegals might use to obtain a sorted list of the new loan amounts in the Closings table in which each loan amount is listed only once. **Why?** Unless you wanted to know how many loan amounts are in the Closings table, the duplicates typically do not add any value. The steps also save the query with a new name.

1

- Click the Design View button to return to Design view.
- In the design grid, click just above the Closing ID field to select the field and then press DEL to remove the Closing ID field from the query.
- Similarly, delete the Purchasing Mortgage Company ID field.
- Click the second field (the empty field to the right of New Loan Amount) in the design grid to produce an insertion point.

- If necessary, click Query Design on the ribbon to display the Query Design tab.
- Click the Property Sheet button (Query Design tab | Show/Hide group) to display the property sheet (Figure 2–36).

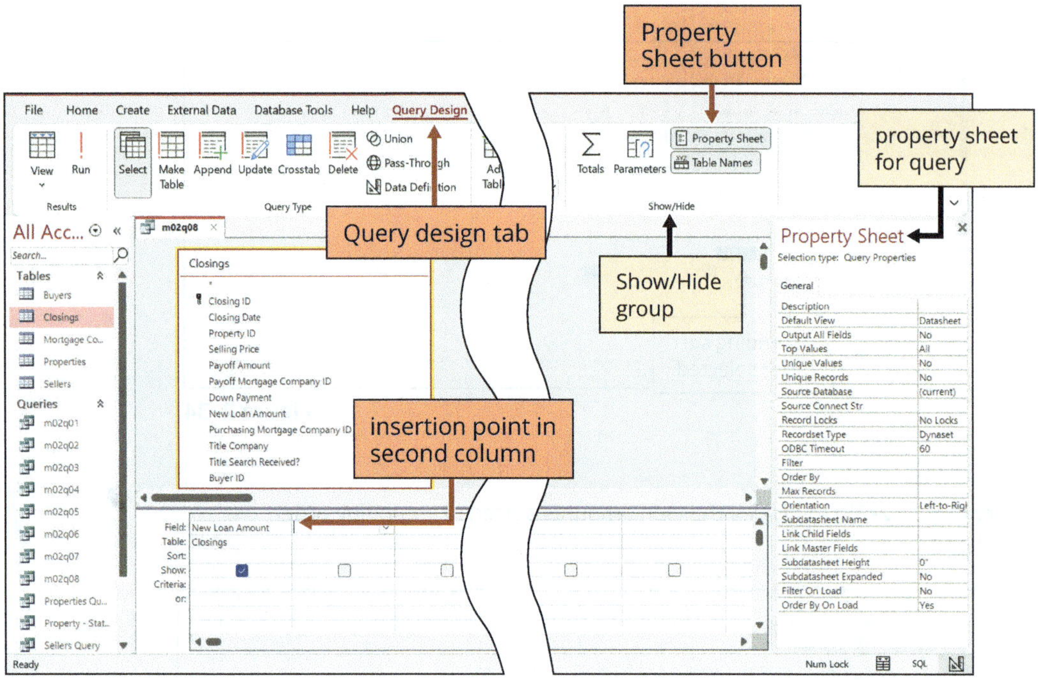

Figure 2–36

Q&A My property sheet looks different. What should I do?
If your sheet looks different, close the property sheet pane and repeat this step, making sure first to insert your insertion point in the first blank field to the right of the New Loan Amount field.

Other Ways

1. Right-click first blank field in design grid, click Properties to open Property Sheet pane

2

- Click the Unique Values property box, and then click the Unique Values arrow to display a list of available choices (Figure 2–37).

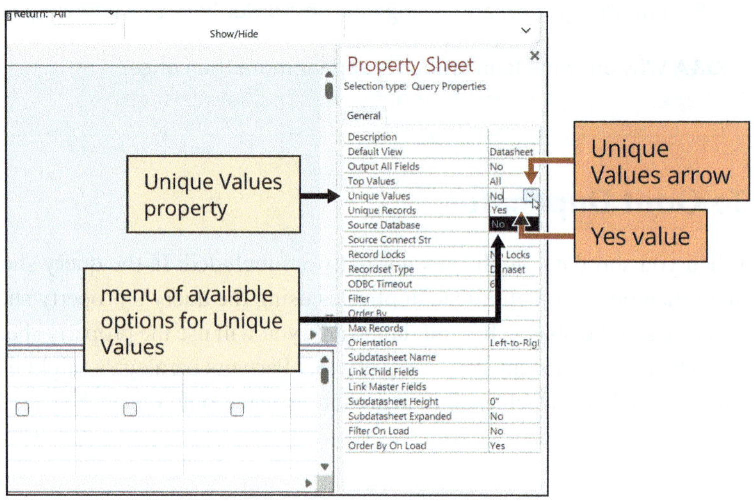

Figure 2–37

3

- Click Yes to indicate that the query will return unique values, which means that each value will appear only once in the query results.
- Close the Query Properties property sheet by clicking the Property Sheet button (Query Design tab | Show/Hide group) a second time.
- Run the query (Figure 2–38).
- Use the Save As command to save the query as **m02q09** and close the query.

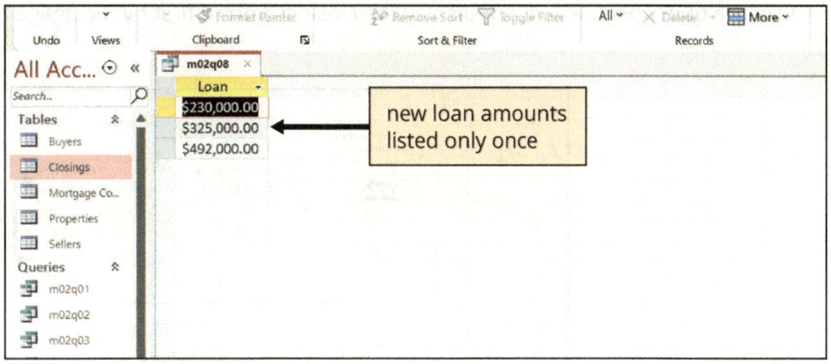

Figure 2–38

Other Ways

1. Click Close button in Property Sheet pane to close pane

To Sort on Multiple Keys

The following steps sort on multiple keys. Specifically, Partners paralegals need the data to be sorted by New Loan Amount (low to high) within Purchasing Mortgage Company ID, which means that the Purchasing Mortgage Company ID field is the major key and the New Loan Amount field is the minor key. Therefore, the steps place the Purchasing Mortgage Company ID field to the left of the New Loan Amount field. **Why?** In Access, the major key must appear to the left of the minor key. The steps also save the query.

1

- Create a new query based on the Closings table and add fields in the following order: Closing ID, Closing Date, Purchasing Mortgage Company ID, and New Loan Amount.
- Select Ascending as the sort order for both the Purchasing Mortgage Company ID field and the New Loan Amount field (Figure 2–39).

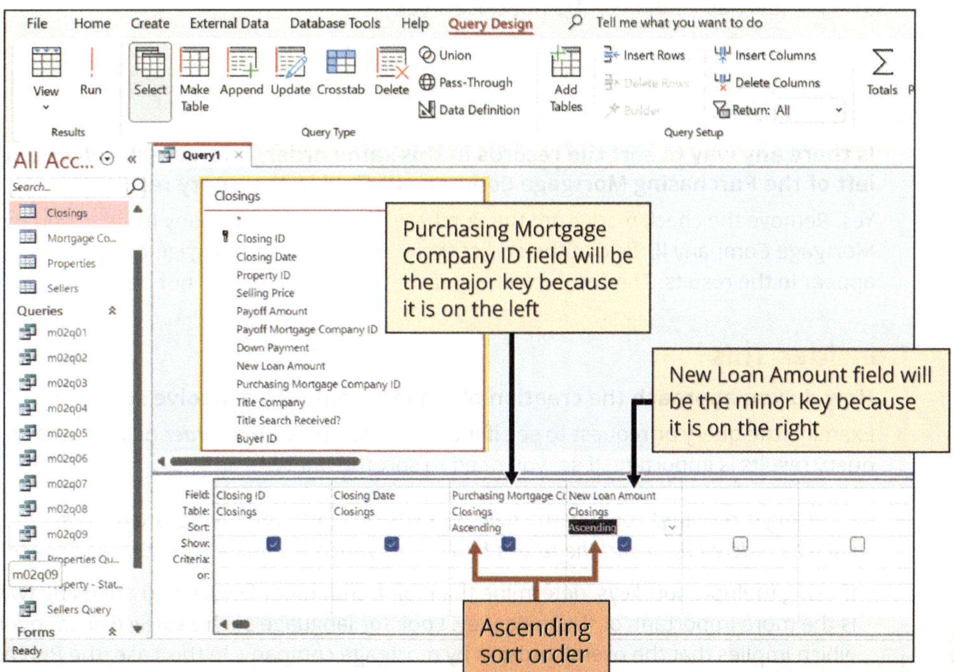

Figure 2–39

2

- Run the query (Figure 2–40) to display the closings sorted first by mortgage companies and then by new loan amount.

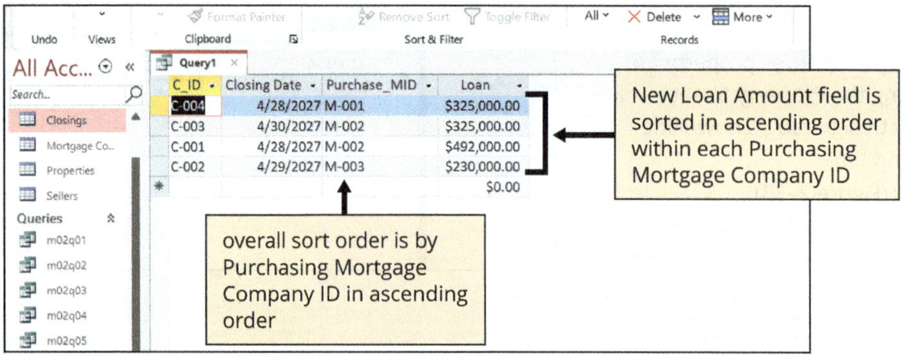

Figure 2–40

- **Experiment:** Return to Design view and try other sort combinations for the Purchasing Mortgage Company ID and New Loan Amount fields, such as Descending for the mortgage companies or Descending for the loan amounts. You might also try applying a sort order for other fields. In each case, run the query to see the effect of the changes. When finished, return the sort order to Ascending for the Purchasing Mortgage Company ID and New Loan Amount fields with no sort applied to any other field.

Q&A What if the New Loan Amount field is to the left of the Purchasing Mortgage Company ID field?
It is important to remember that the major sort key must appear to the left of the minor sort key in the design grid. If you attempted to sort by New Loan Amount within Purchasing Mortgage Company ID but placed the New Loan Amount field to the left of the Purchasing Mortgage Company ID field, your results would not accurately represent the intended sort.

3

- Save the query as **m02q10**. Do not close it yet.

Consider This

Is there any way to sort the records in this same order, but have the New Loan Amount field appear to the left of the Purchasing Mortgage Company ID field in the query results?

Yes. Remove the check mark from the Purchasing Mortgage Company ID field, and then add an additional Purchasing Mortgage Company ID field at the end of the query. The first mortgage company field will be used for sorting but will not appear in the results. The second will appear in the results but will not be involved in the sorting process.

Consider This

How do you approach the creation of a query that might involve sorting?

Examine the query or request to see if it contains words such as *order* or *sort*. Such words imply that the order of the query results is important. If so, you need to sort the query.

- If sorting is required, identify the field or fields on which the results are to be sorted. In the request, look for language such as *ordered by* or *sort the results by*, both of which would indicate that the specified field is a sort key.
- If using multiple sort keys, determine the major and minor keys. If you are using two sort keys, determine which one is the more important, or the major key. Look for language such as *view loan amounts within each mortgage company*, which implies that the overall order is by mortgage company. In this case, the Purchasing Mortgage Company ID field would be the major sort key and the New Loan Amount field would be the minor sort key.
- Determine sort order. Words such as *increasing*, *ascending*, or *low to high* imply Ascending order. Words such as *decreasing*, *descending*, or *high to low* imply Descending order. Sorting in *alphabetical order* implies Ascending order. If there were no words to imply a particular order, you would typically use Ascending.
- Examine the query or request to see if there are any special restrictions. One common restriction is to exclude duplicates. Another common restriction is to list only a certain number of records, such as the first five records.

To Create a Top-Values Query

Rather than show all the results of a query, you might want to show only a specified number of records or a percentage of records. **Why?** You might not need to see all the records, just enough to get a general idea of the results. Creating a **top-values query** allows you to restrict the number of records that appear. When you sort records, you can limit results to those records with the highest (descending sort) or lowest (ascending sort) values. To do so, first create a query that sorts the data in the desired order. Next, use the Return box on the Query Design tab to change the number of records to be included from All to the desired number or percentage.

The following steps create a query for Partners paralegals that shows only the first two records that were included in the results of the previous query. The steps also save the resulting query with a new name.

1

- Return to Design view.
- If necessary, click Query Design on the ribbon to display the Query Design tab.
- Click the Return arrow (Query Design tab | Query Setup group) to display the Return menu (Figure 2–41).

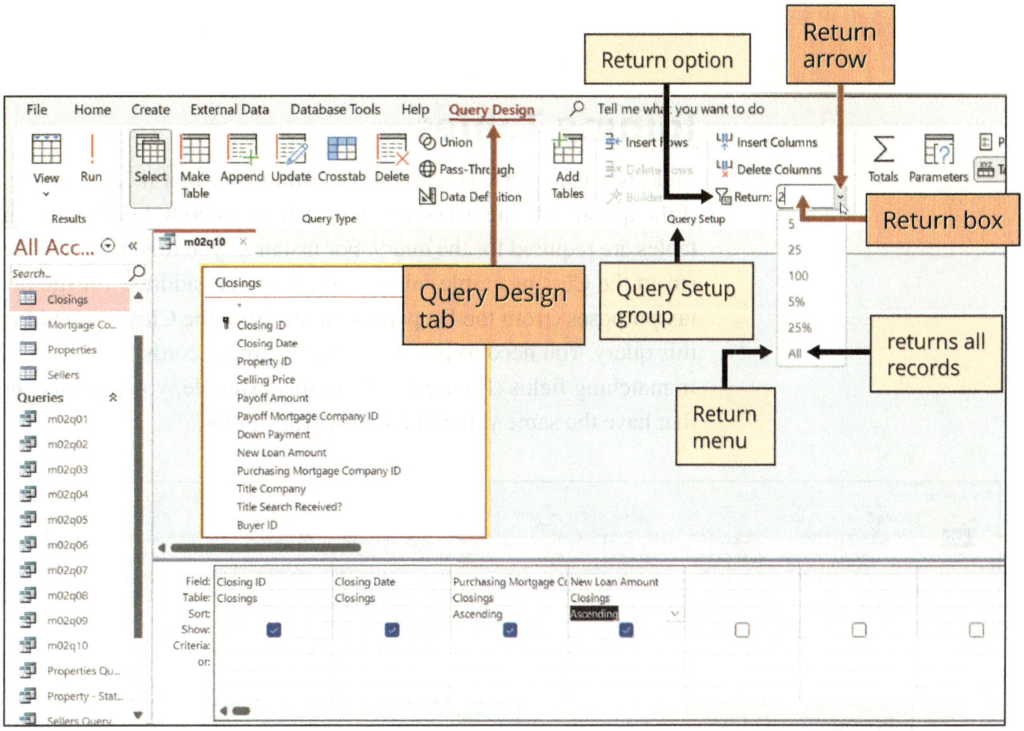

Figure 2–41

2

- Type **2** in the Return box. Access might suggest 25; delete the 5 and ensure only 2 is listed to specify that the query results should contain the first two rows.

Q&A Why does Access suggest 25 records instead of 2?
Many databases contain hundreds of records, and so requesting the top 25 records would be more useful than just the top two records. When learning how to use Access, it's easier to work with fewer records.

- Run the query (Figure 2–42) to display only the first two records.

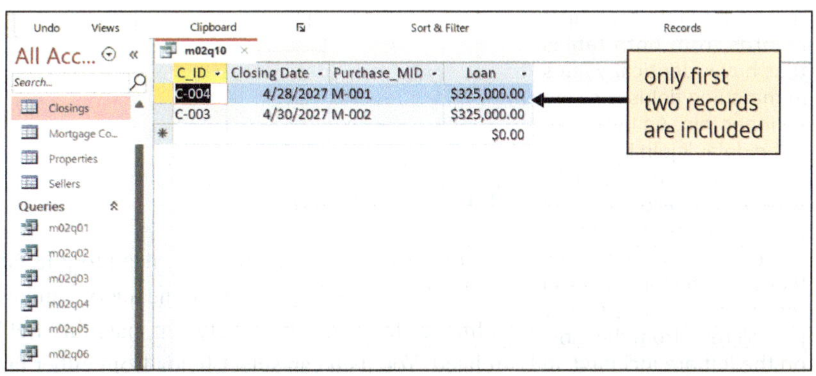

Figure 2–42

3

- Use the Save As command to save the query as **m02q11**.
- Close the query.

Q&A Do I need to close the query before creating my next query?

Not necessarily. When you use a top-values query, however, it is important to change the value in the Return box back to All. If you do not change the Return value back to All, the previous value will remain in effect for later queries created from this one. Consequently, you might not get all the records you should in the next query. A good practice whenever you use a top-values query is to close the query as soon as you are done. That way, you will begin your next query from scratch, which ensures that the value is reset to All.

Joining Tables

In designing a query, you need to determine whether more than one table is required. For example, if the question being asked involves data from both the Closings and Properties tables, then both tables are required for the query. For instance, you might want a query that shows the closing dates (from the Closings table) along with the street address for the property and the jurisdiction for tax purposes (from the Properties table). Both the Closings and Properties tables are required for this query. You need to **join** the tables to find records in the two tables that have identical values in matching fields (Figure 2–43). In this example, you need to find records in the Closings table that have the same value in the Properties fields.

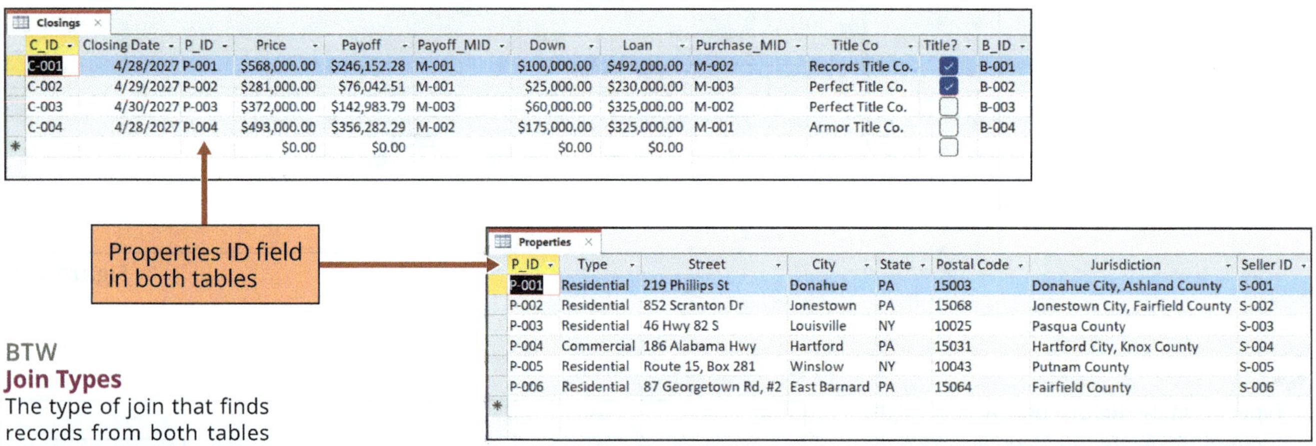

C_ID	Closing Date	P_ID	Price	Payoff	Payoff_MID	Down	Loan	Purchase_MID	Title Co	Title?	B_ID
C-001	4/28/2027	P-001	$568,000.00	$246,152.28	M-001	$100,000.00	$492,000.00	M-002	Records Title Co.	☑	B-001
C-002	4/29/2027	P-002	$281,000.00	$76,042.51	M-001	$25,000.00	$230,000.00	M-003	Perfect Title Co.	☑	B-002
C-003	4/30/2027	P-003	$372,000.00	$142,983.79	M-003	$60,000.00	$325,000.00	M-002	Perfect Title Co.	☐	B-003
C-004	4/28/2027	P-004	$493,000.00	$356,282.29	M-002	$175,000.00	$325,000.00	M-001	Armor Title Co.	☐	B-004
*			$0.00	$0.00		$0.00	$0.00			☐	

P_ID	Type	Street	City	State	Postal Code	Jurisdiction	Seller ID
P-001	Residential	219 Phillips St	Donahue	PA	15003	Donahue City, Ashland County	S-001
P-002	Residential	852 Scranton Dr	Jonestown	PA	15068	Jonestown City, Fairfield County	S-002
P-003	Residential	46 Hwy 82 S	Louisville	NY	10025	Pasqua County	S-003
P-004	Commercial	186 Alabama Hwy	Hartford	PA	15031	Hartford City, Knox County	S-004
P-005	Residential	Route 15, Box 281	Winslow	NY	10043	Putnam County	S-005
P-006	Residential	87 Georgetown Rd, #2	East Barnard	PA	15064	Fairfield County	S-006
*							

Figure 2–43

BTW

Join Types

The type of join that finds records from both tables that have identical values in matching fields is called an inner join. An inner join is the default join in Access. Outer joins are used to show all the records in one table as well as the common records; that is, the records that share the same value in the join field. In a left outer join, all rows from the table on the left are included. In a right outer join, all rows from the table on the right are included.

To Join Tables

If you have determined that you need to join tables in a query, you first will bring field lists for both tables to the upper pane of the query window while working in Design view. Access will draw a line, called a **join line**, between matching fields in the two tables, indicating that the tables are related. You then can select fields from either table. Access joins the tables automatically.

The first step is to create a new query and add the Closings table to the query. Then, add the Properties table to the query. A join line should appear, connecting the Property ID fields in the two field lists. **Why might the join line not appear?** If the names of the matching fields differ from one table to the other, Access will not insert the line. You can insert it manually, however, by clicking one of the two matching fields and dragging the pointer to the other matching field.

The following steps create a query to display information from both the Closings table and the Properties table.

1

- Create a new query using the Closings table.
- Double-click the Properties table (Add Tables pane) to add a field list for the Properties table (Figure 2–44).

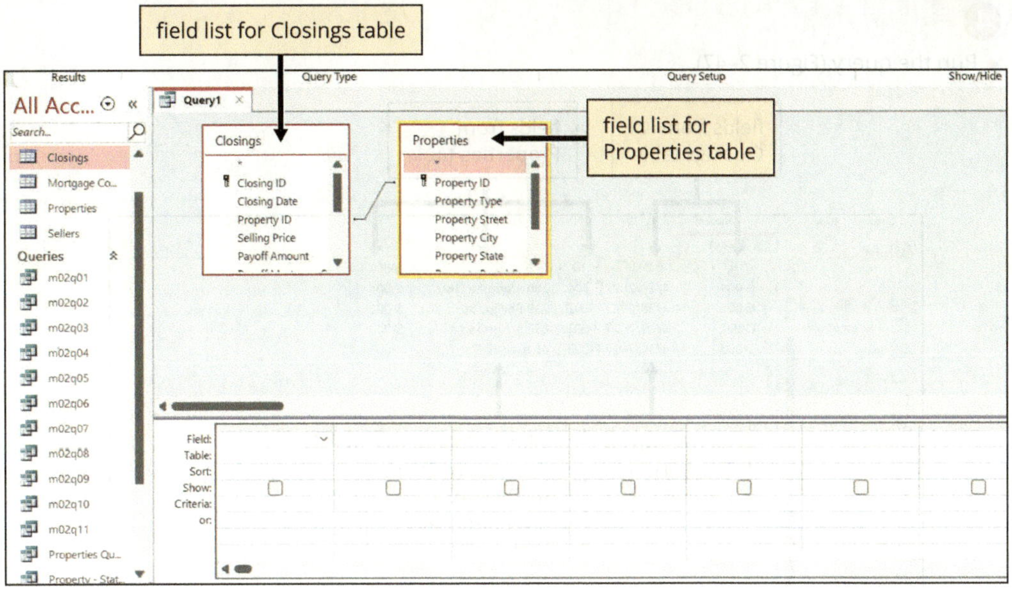

Figure 2–44

2

- Close the Add Tables pane.
- Expand the size of the two field lists so all the fields in the Closings and Properties tables appear (Figure 2–45).

Q&A I did not get a join line. What should I do?
Ensure that the names of the matching fields are the same, the data types are the same, and the matching field is the primary key in one of the two tables. If all these factors are true and you still do not have a join line, you can produce one by pointing to a matching field and dragging to the other matching field.

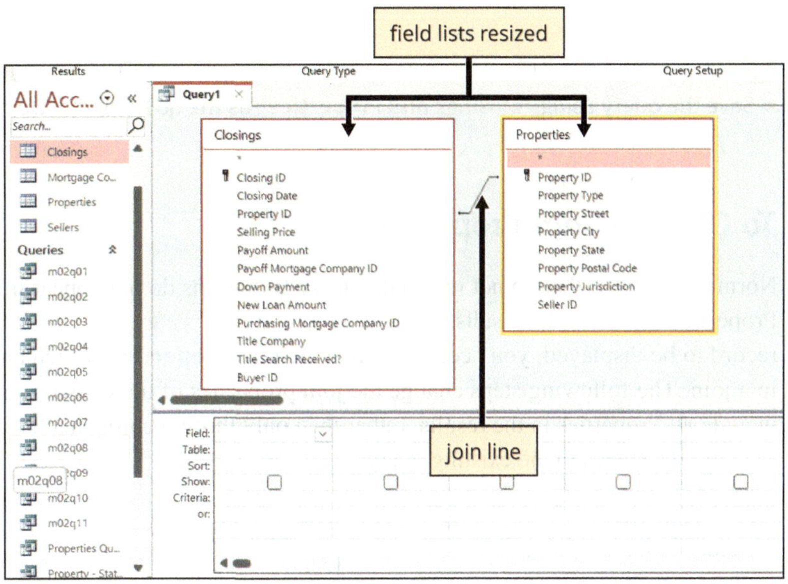

Figure 2–45

3

- In the design grid, add the Closing ID and Closing Date fields from the Closings Table, and then the Property ID, Property Street, and Seller ID fields from the Properties Table.
- Select Ascending as the sort order for both the Closing Date field and the Property Street field (Figure 2–46).

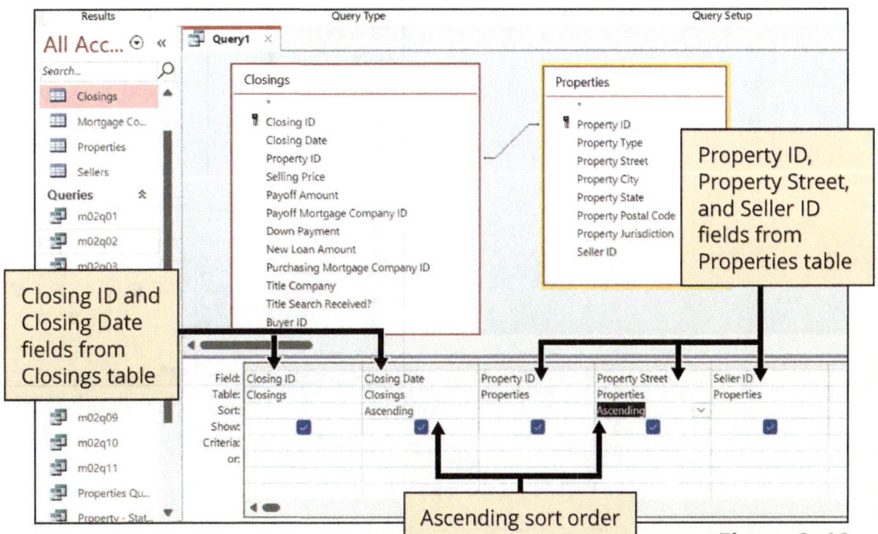

Figure 2–46

4

- Run the query (Figure 2–47).

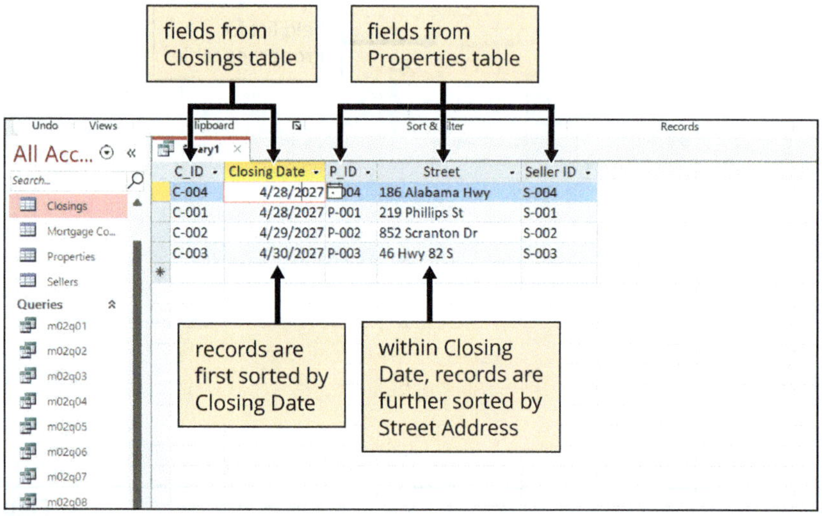

Figure 2–47

BTW

Join Line

If you do not get a join line automatically, there might be a problem with one of your table designs. Open each table in Design view, and make sure that the data types are the same for the matching field in both tables and that one of the matching fields is the primary key in a table. If not, correct these errors and create the query again.

5

- Save the query using **Closings and Properties** as the query name. Do not close it yet.

To Change Join Properties

Normally, records that do not match the query conditions do not appear in the results of a join query. For example, not all the Properties appear in the results. **Why?** Not all properties currently have a closing date associated with them. To cause such a record to be displayed, you need to change the **join properties**, which are the properties that indicate which records appear in a join. The following steps change the join properties of the Closings and Properties query so that Partners paralegals can include all Properties in the results, rather than only those records that have closing dates associated with them. The steps also save these changes to the existing query.

1

- Return to Design view.
- Right-click the join line to produce a shortcut menu (Figure 2–48).

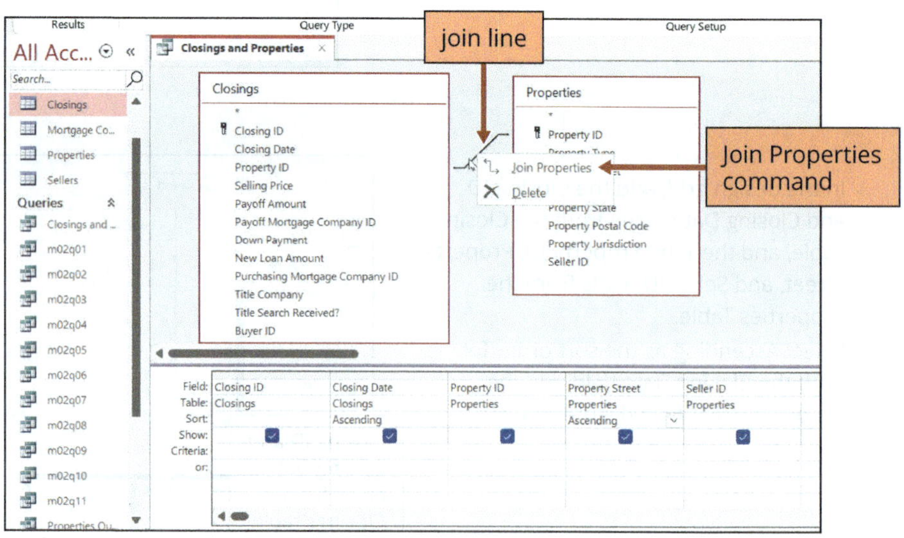

Figure 2–48

2

- Click Join Properties on the shortcut menu to display the Join Properties dialog box (Figure 2–49).

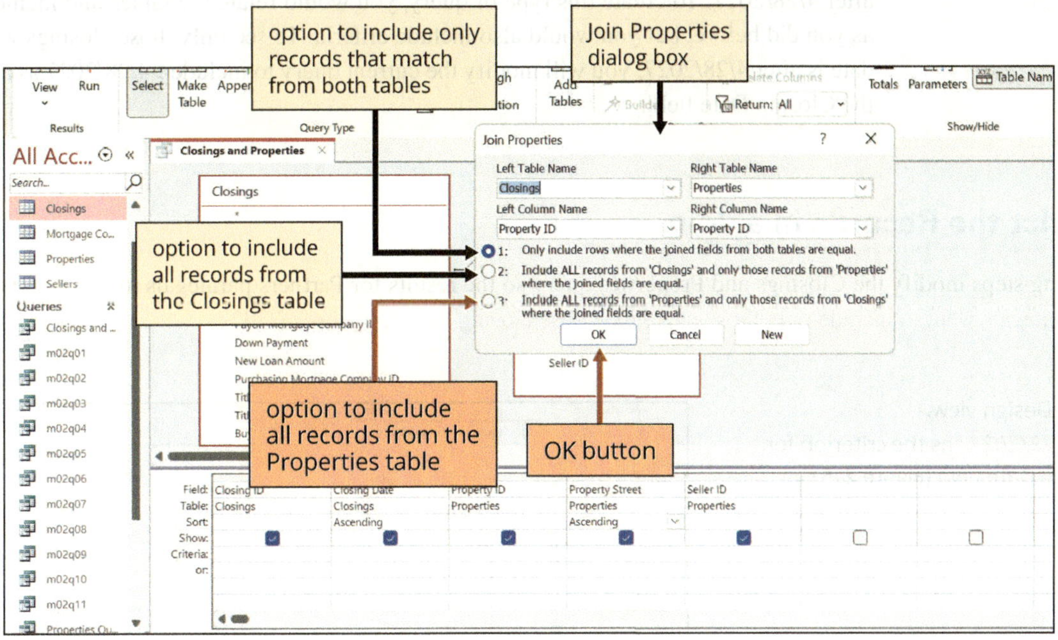

Figure 2–49

Q&A I do not see Join Properties on my shortcut menu. What should I do?
If Join Properties does not appear on your shortcut menu, you did not point to the appropriate portion of the join line. You will need to point to the middle portion and right-click again.

3

- Click option 3 (Join Properties dialog box) to include all records from the Properties table regardless of whether they match any closing dates.
- Click OK (Join Properties dialog box) to modify the join properties and close the Join Properties dialog box.
- Run the query (Figure 2–50).
- **Experiment:** Return to Design view, change the Join properties, and select option 2. Run the query to see the effect of this option. When done, return to Design view, change the Join properties, and once again select option 3.

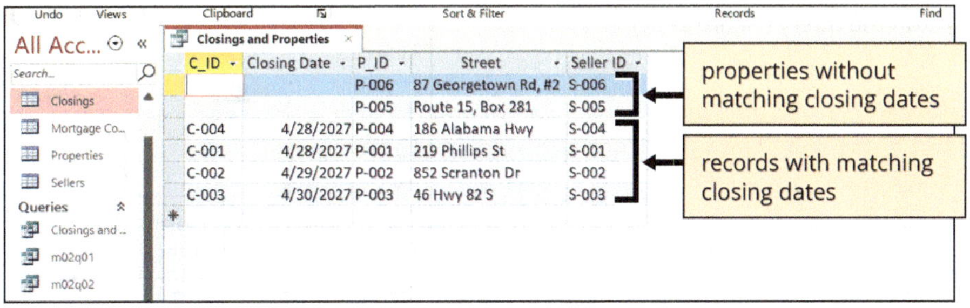

Figure 2–50

4

- Save the changes to the query.

Q&A I see a dialog box that asks if I want to save the query. What should I do?
Click OK to save the query.

Adding Criteria to a Join Query

Sometimes you will want to join tables, but you will not want to include all possible records. For example, the Partners paralegals need a query showing only those closings whose closing date is after 4/28/2027. To create this type of query, you would relate the tables and include fields just as you did before, but you would also include criteria. To see only those closings whose closing date is after 4/28/2027, you will modify the current query to include >4/28/2027 as a criterion for the Closing Date field.

To Restrict the Records in a Join

The following steps modify the Closings and Properties query so the results for Partners paralegals include a criterion. **Why?** Partners paralegals want to include only those closings whose closing date is after 4/28/2027.

1

- Return to Design view.
- Type **>4/28/2027** as the criterion for the Closing Date field (Figure 2–51).

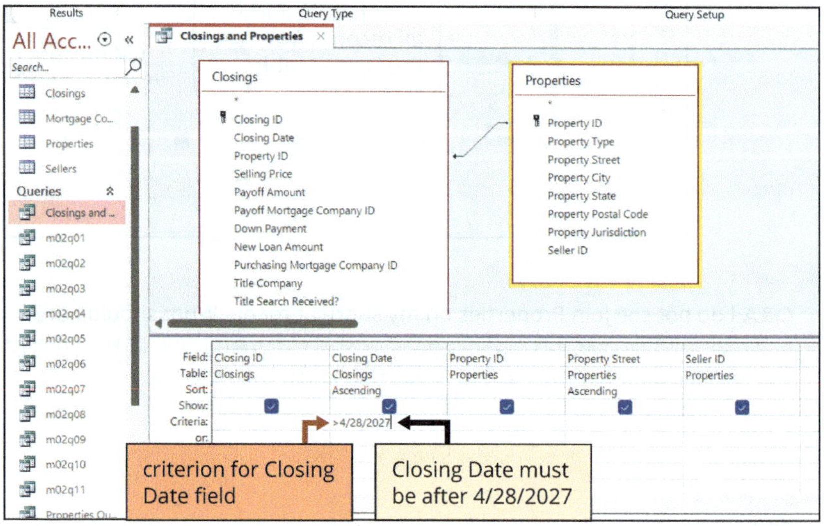

Figure 2–51

2

- Run the query (Figure 2–52).

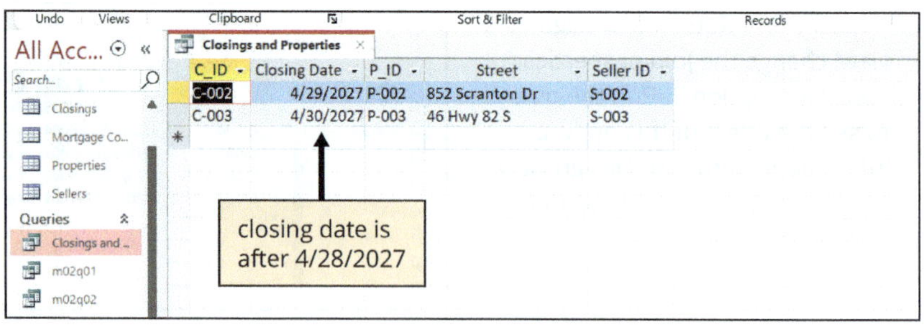

Figure 2–52

3

- Close the query.
- When asked if you want to save your changes, click No.

Q&A What would happen if I saved the changes?

The next time you used this query, you would only see closings whose closing date is after 4/28/2027.

To Create a Report from a Query

You can use queries in the creation of reports. The report in Figure 2–51 involves data from more than one table. The Closing ID and Closing Date fields are in the Closings table. The Property Type, Property Street, and Seller ID fields are from the Properties table. The Property ID field is in both tables. **Why?** The easiest way to create such a report is to base it on a query that joins the two tables. The following steps use the Report Wizard and the Closings and Properties query to create the report shown in Figure 2–53.

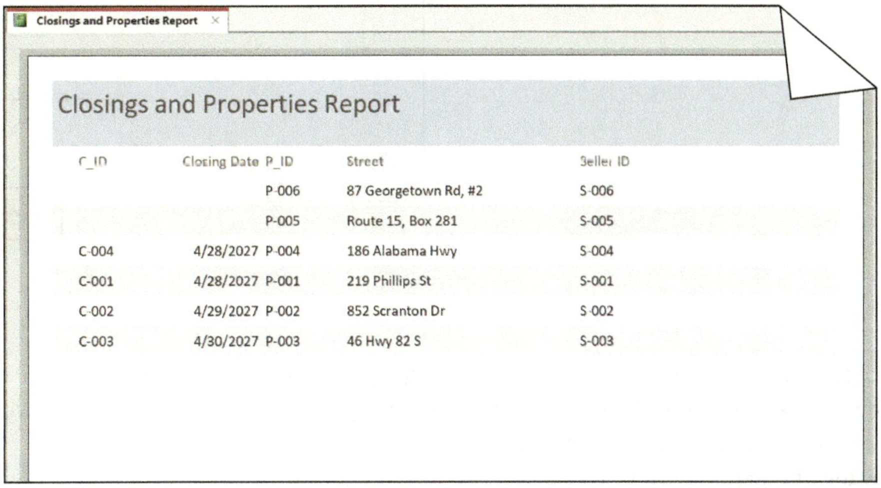

Figure 2–53

1

- Select the Closings and Properties query in the Navigation Pane.
- Click Create on the ribbon to display the Create tab.
- Click the Report Wizard button (Create tab | Reports group) to display the Report Wizard dialog box (Figure 2–54).

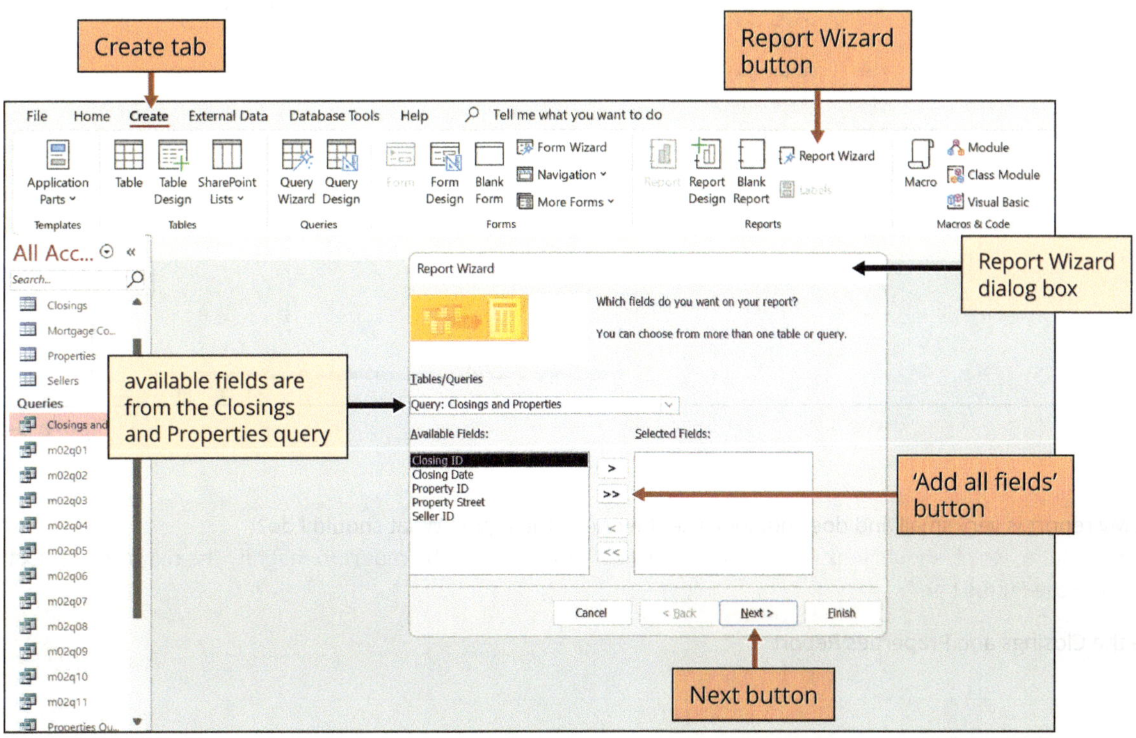

Figure 2–54

2

- Click the 'Add All Fields' button (Report Wizard dialog box) to add all the fields from the Closings and Properties query.
- Click Next to display the next Report Wizard screen (Figure 2–55).

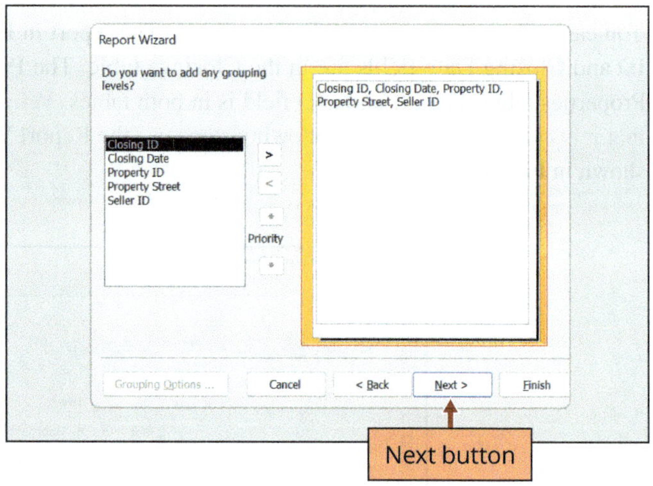

Figure 2–55

3

- Because you will not specify any grouping, click Next again to display the next Report Wizard screen.
- Because you already specified the sort order in the query, click Next again to display the next Report Wizard screen.
- Make sure Tabular is selected for Layout and Portrait is selected for Orientation.
- Click Next to display the next Report Wizard screen.
- Enter **Report** at the end of the Closings and Properties title so that Closings and Properties Report appears as the complete title.
- Click the Finish button to produce the report (Figure 2–56).

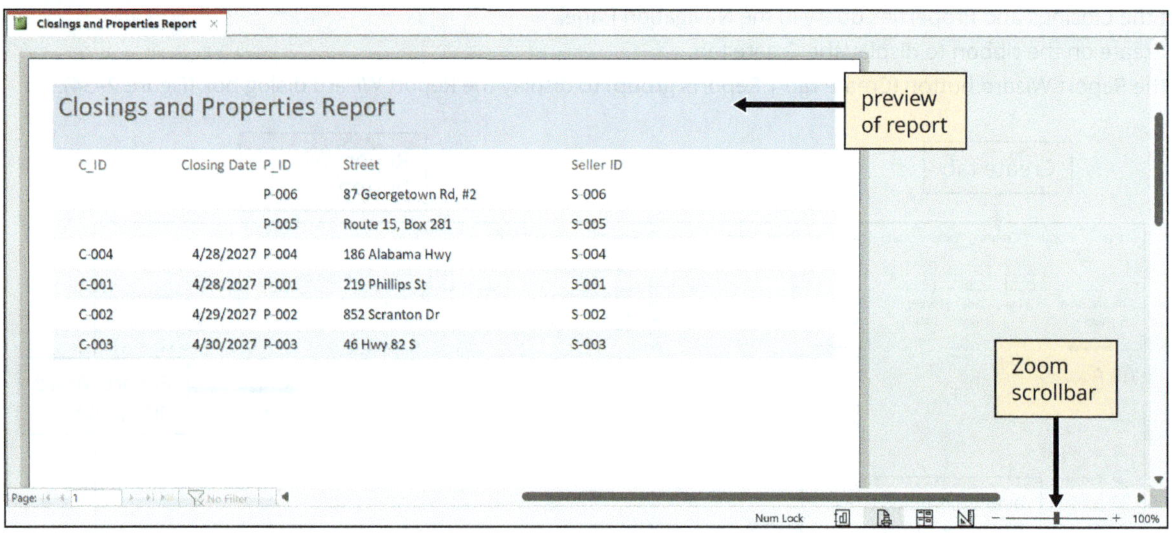

Figure 2–56

Q&A My report is very small and does not look like the one in the figure. What should I do?
Click the pointer, which should look like a magnifying glass, anywhere in the report to magnify the report or adjust the Zoom scrollbar in the Status bar.

- Close the Closings and Properties Report.

To Print a Report

Often, users will need to distribute database information in a printed format. **Why?** Partners would like to share the Closings and Properties Report with executives who prefer a hard copy. The following steps print a hard copy of the report.

1

- In the Navigation Pane, click the Closings and Properties Report to select it.
- Click File on the ribbon to open Backstage view.

2

- Click the Print tab in Backstage view to display the Print gallery.

3

- Click Print Preview to see a preview of the report before printing it and to make other changes, such as page size and page layout.
- If required by your instructor, click the Print button (Print Preview tab | Print group) to print the report. Otherwise, click Close Print Preview (Print Preview tab | Close Preview group), and then close the Closings and Properties report.

Consider This

How would you approach the creation of a query that might involve multiple tables?

- Examine the request to see if all the fields involved in the request are in one table. If the fields are in two (or more) tables, you need to join the tables.
- If joining is required, identify within the two tables the matching fields that have identical values. Look for the same column name in the two tables or for column names that are similar.
- Determine whether sorting is required. Queries that join tables often are used as the basis for a report. If this is the case, it may be necessary to sort the results. For example, the Closings and Properties Report is based on a query that joins the Closings and Properties tables. The query is sorted by Closing Date and Property Street.
- Examine the request to see if there are any special restrictions. For example, the user may only want closings scheduled after 4/28/2027.
- Examine the request to see if you only want records from both tables that have identical values in matching fields. If you want to see records in one of the tables that do not have identical values in the other table, then you need to change the join properties.

Creating a Form for a Query

You have already learned how to create a form for a table. You can also create a form for a query. Recall that a form in a database is a formatted document with fields that contain data. Forms allow you to view and maintain data. Note that changing data using a form based on a query changes the data in the underlying table.

To Create a Form for a Query

The following steps create a form, then save the form. **Why?** The form will be available for future use in viewing and maintaining the data in the query.

1

- Select the Closings and Properties query in the Navigation Pane.
- Click Create on the ribbon to display the Create tab (Figure 2–57).

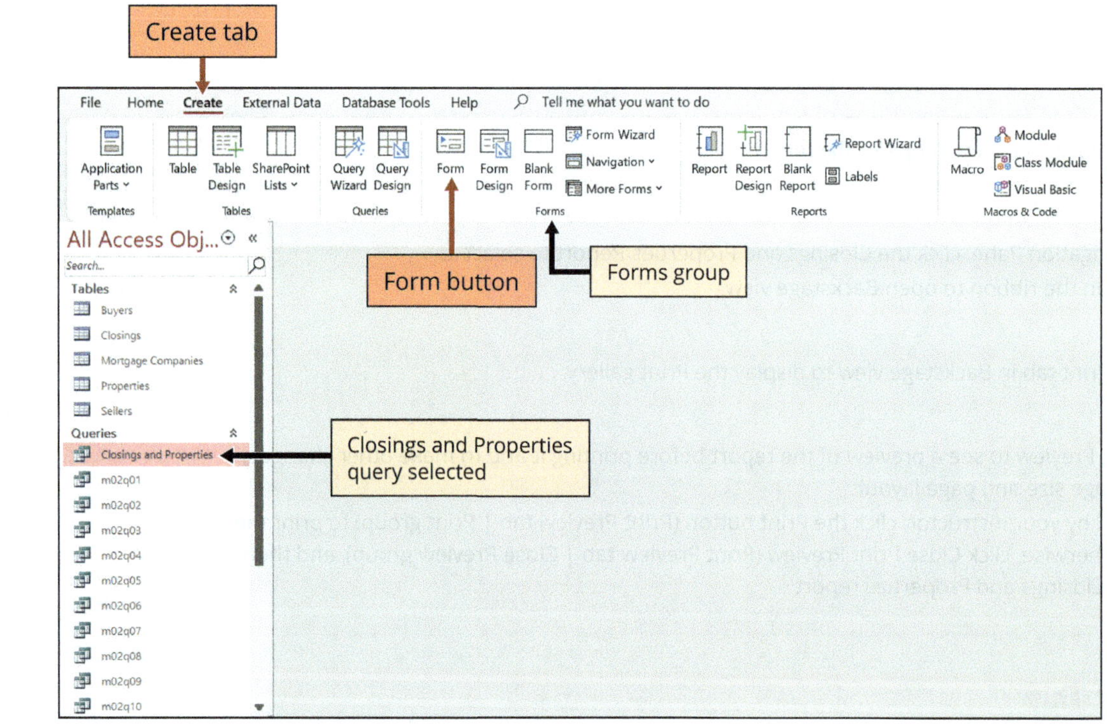

Figure 2–57

2

- Click the Form button (Create tab | Forms group) to create a simple form (Figure 2–58).

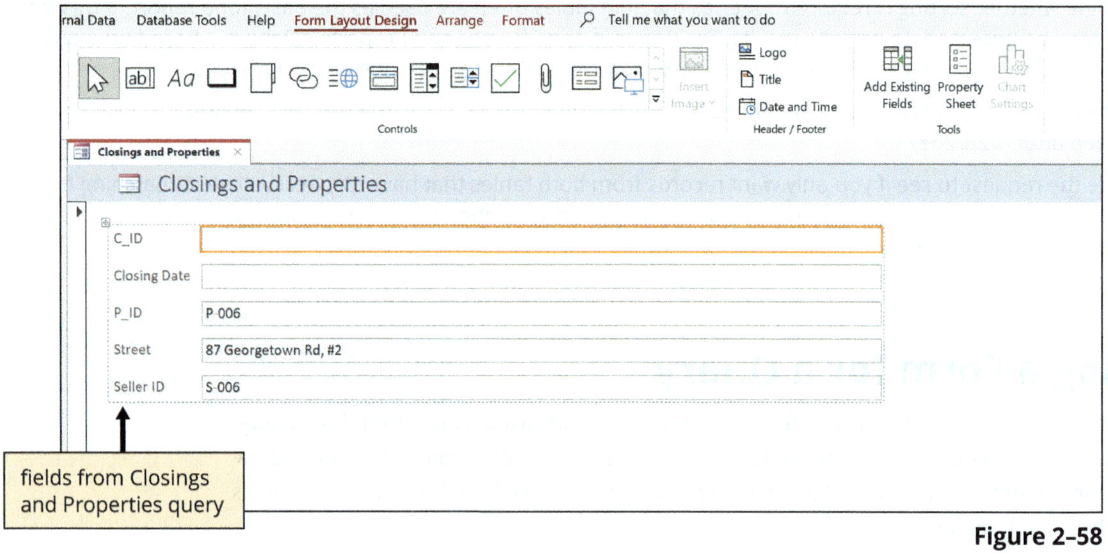

Figure 2–58

Q&A I see a field list pane also. What should I do?
Click Close for the Field List pane.

3

- Click the Save button on the Quick Access Toolbar to display the Save As dialog box.
- Enter **Form** at the end of the Closings and Properties name so that Closings and Properties Form appears as the complete name.
- Click OK to save the form.
- Close the form.

Using a Form

After you have saved a form, you can use it at any time by double-clicking the form in the Navigation Pane. If you plan to use the form to enter or edit data, you must ensure you are viewing the form in Form view.

Break Point: If you wish to take a break, this is a good place to do so. You can exit Access now. To resume later, start Access, open the database called SC_AC_02_Partners.accdb, and continue following the steps from this location forward.

Exporting Data from Access to Other Applications

You can **export**, or copy, tables or queries from an Access database so that another application (for example, Excel or Word) can use the data. The application that will receive the data determines the export process to be used. You can export to text files in a variety of formats. For applications to which you cannot directly export data, you often can export an appropriately formatted text file that the other application can import. Figure 2–59 shows the workbook produced by exporting the Closings and Properties query to Excel. The columns in the workbook have been resized to best fit the data.

BTW
Exporting Data
You frequently need to export data so that it can be used in other applications and by other users in an organization. For example, the Accounting department might require financial data in an Excel format to perform certain financial functions. Legal might require a list of buyer or seller names and property addresses in Word or rich text format (RTF) for filing documents at the appropriate courthouse.

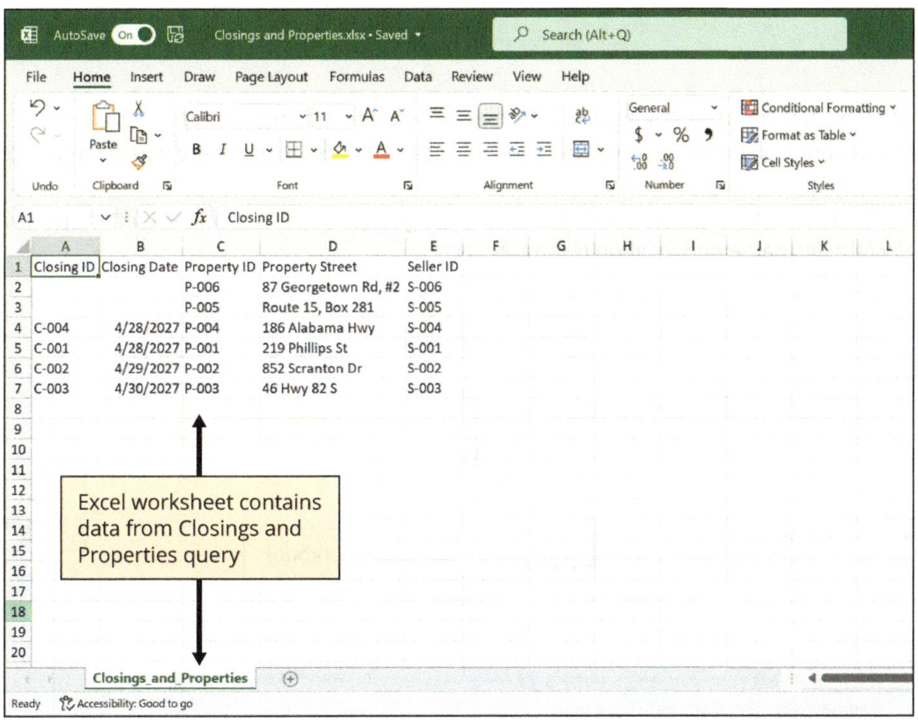

Figure 2–59

To Export Data to Excel

For Partners paralegals to make the Closings and Properties query available to Excel users, they need to export the data. To export data to Excel, select the table or query to be exported and then click the Excel button in the Export group on the External Data tab. The following steps export the Closings and Properties query to Excel and save the export steps. **Why save the export steps?** By saving the export steps, you could easily repeat the export process whenever you like without going through all the steps. You can then use the saved steps to export data in the future by clicking the Saved Exports button (External Data tab | Export group) and then selecting the steps you saved.

1

- If necessary, click the Closings and Properties query in the Navigation Pane to select it.
- Click External Data on the ribbon to display the External Data tab (Figure 2–60).

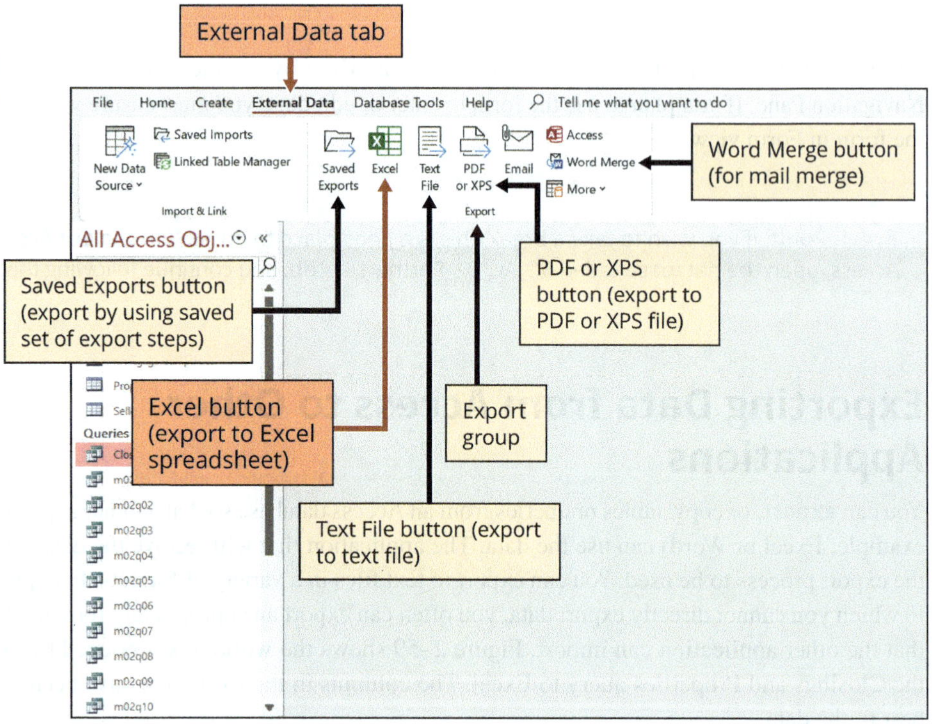

Figure 2–60

2

- Click the Excel button (External Data tab | Export group) to display the Export – Excel Spreadsheet dialog box.
- Click the Browse button (Export – Excel Spreadsheet dialog box), and then navigate to the location where you want to export the query (your hard drive, OneDrive, or other storage location).
- Confirm that the file format is Excel Workbook (*.xlsx), and the file name is Closings and Properties, and then click the Save button (File Save dialog box) to select the file name and location (Figure 2–61).

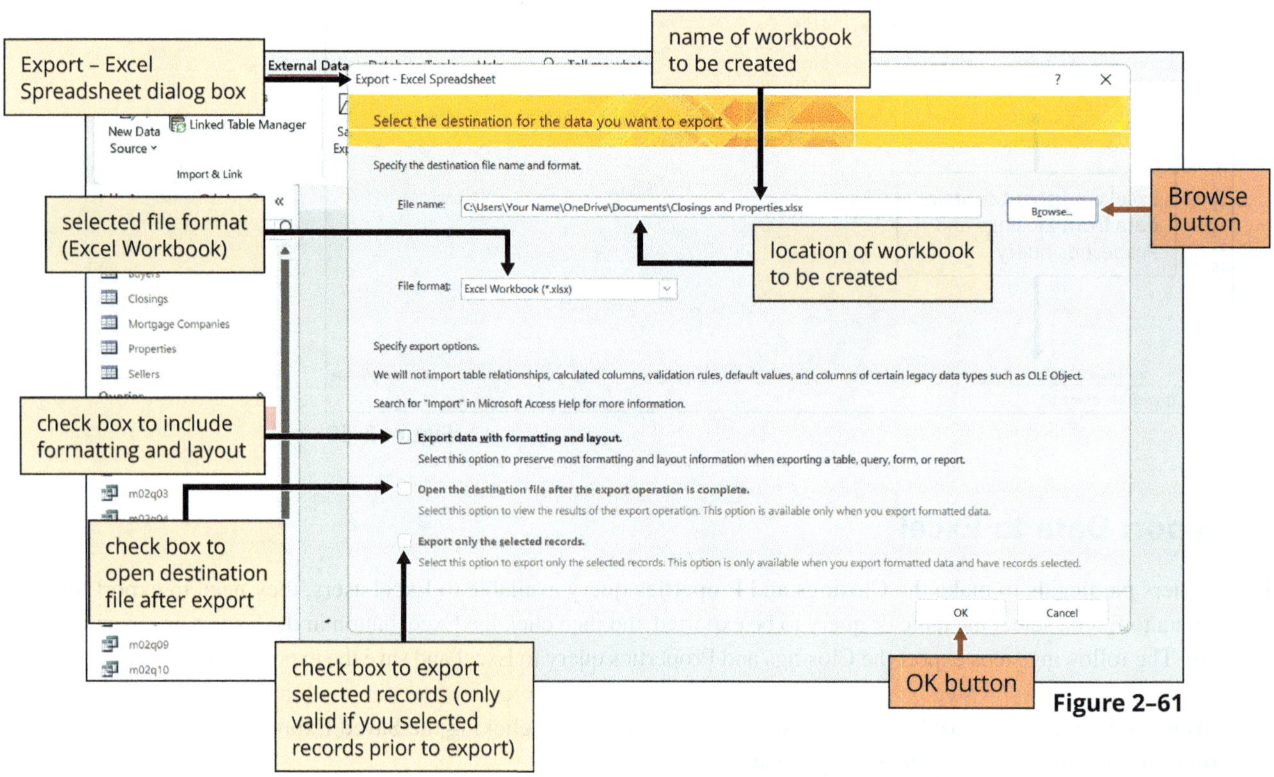

Figure 2–61

Q&A Did I need to browse?
No. You could type the appropriate file path location.

Could I change the name of the file?
You could change it. Simply replace the current file name with the one you want.

What if the file I want to export already exists?
Access will indicate that the file already exists and ask if you want to replace it. If you click Yes, the file you export will replace the old file. If you click No, you must either change the name of the export file, change its location, or cancel the process.

3

- Click OK (Export – Excel Spreadsheet dialog box) to export the data (Figure 2–62).

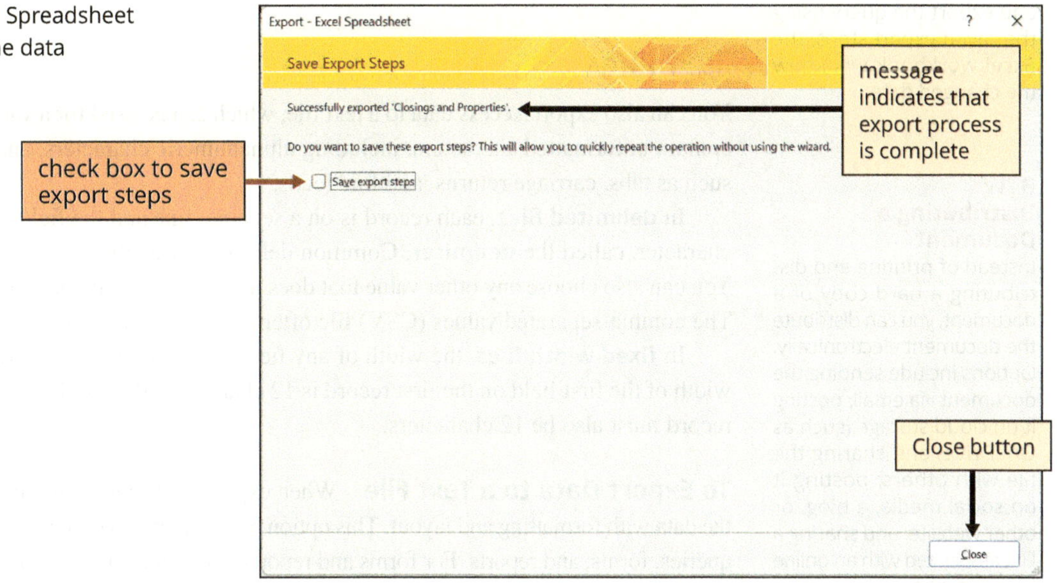

Figure 2–62

4

- Click the 'Save export steps' check box (Export – Excel Spreadsheet dialog box) and then click the Save Export button that appears (Figure 2–63).

Q&A How could I reuse the export steps?
You can use these steps to export data in the future by clicking the Saved Exports button (External Data tab | Export group) and then selecting the steps you saved.

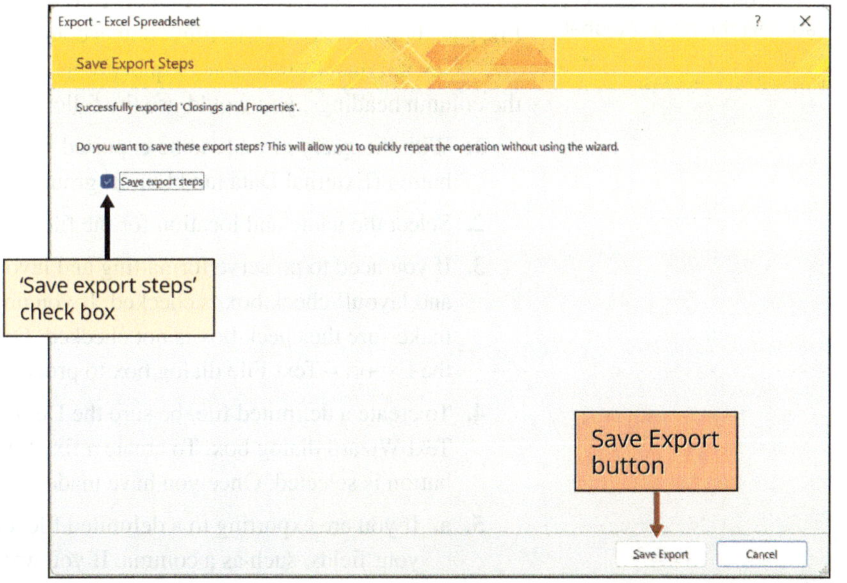

Figure 2–63

Other Ways

1. Right-click database object in Navigation Pane, point to Export, choose export format to export object

BTW
Saving Export Steps
Because query results are based on the data in the underlying tables, a change to an underlying table would result in a new query result. For example, if the closing date for a property changed from 4/28/2027 to 4/30/2027, the change would be made in the Closings table. If you run the Closings and Properties query again and export the query using the saved export steps, the Excel workbook will show the changed date.

BTW
Distributing a Document
Instead of printing and distributing a hard copy of a document, you can distribute the document electronically. Options include sending the document via email; posting it on cloud storage (such as OneDrive) and sharing the file with others; posting it on social media, a blog, or other website; and sharing a link associated with an online location of the document. You also can create and share a PDF or XPS image of the document, so that users can view the file in Acrobat Adobe Reader or XPS Viewer instead of in Access.

To Export Data to Word It is not possible to export data from Access to the standard Word format. It is possible, however, to export the data as an RTF file, which Word can open. To export data from a query or table to an RTF file, you would use the following steps.

1. With the query or table to be exported selected in the Navigation Pane, click the More button (External Data tab | Export group) and then click Word on the More menu to display the Export – RTF File dialog box.
2. Navigate to the location in which to save the file and assign a file name.
3. Click the Save button, and then click OK to export the data.
4. Save the export steps if you want, or simply click Close in the Export – RTF File dialog box to close the dialog box without saving the export steps.

Text Files

You can also export Access data to a text file, which can be used for a variety of purposes. Text files contain unformatted characters, including alphanumeric characters, and some special characters, such as tabs, carriage returns, and line feeds.

In **delimited files**, each record is on a separate line and the fields are separated by a special character, called the **delimiter**. Common delimiters are tabs, semicolons, commas, and spaces. You can also choose any other value that does not appear within the field contents as the delimiter. The comma-separated values (CSV) file often used in Excel is an example of a delimited file.

In **fixed-width files**, the width of any field is the same on every record. For example, if the width of the first field on the first record is 12 characters, the width of the first field on every other record must also be 12 characters.

To Export Data to a Text File When exporting data to a text file, you can choose to export the data with formatting and layout. This option preserves much of the formatting and layout in tables, queries, forms, and reports. For forms and reports, this is the only option for exporting to a text file.

If you do not need to preserve the formatting, you can choose either delimited or fixed-width as the format for the exported file. The most common option, especially if formatting is not an issue, is delimited. You can choose the delimiter. You can also choose whether to include field names on the first row. In many cases, delimiting with a comma and including the field names is a good choice.

To export data from a table or query to a comma-delimited file in which the first row contains the column headings, you would use the following steps.

1. With the query or table to be exported selected in the Navigation Pane, click the Text File button (External Data tab | Export group) to display the Export – Text File dialog box.
2. Select the name and location for the file to be created.
3. If you need to preserve formatting and layout, be sure the 'Export data with formatting and layout' check box is checked. If you do not need to preserve formatting and layout, make sure the check box is not checked. Once you have made your selection, click OK in the Export – Text File dialog box to proceed to the Export Text Wizard.
4. To create a delimited file, be sure the Delimited option button is selected in the Export Text Wizard dialog box. To create a fixed-width file, be sure the Fixed Width option button is selected. Once you have made your selection, click the Next button.
5. a. If you are exporting to a delimited file, choose the delimiter that you want to separate your fields, such as a comma. If you want to include field names on the first row, click the 'Include Field Names on First Row' check box. If you want to select a text qualifier, select it in the Text Qualifier list. When you have made your selections, click the Next button.
   b. If you are exporting to a fixed-width file, review the position of the vertical lines that separate your fields. If any lines are not positioned correctly, follow the directions on the screen to reposition them. When you have finished, click the Next button.

6. Click the Finish button to export the data.
7. Save the export steps if you want, or simply click Close in the Export – Text File dialog box to close the dialog box without saving the export steps.

To Import a Table

Partners Law Firm requires additional data to be able to run some of its required queries. As you learned previously, you can import data from external sources. The following steps import the Closing Fees table from the Partners Extra Tables database.

1

- Open the database, Support_AC_02_Partners-Extra-Tables.accdb, which is located in the Data Files folder. Enable the content. View the Closing Fees table to see what information is included. Close the Closing Fees table, and close the Extra Tables database.

2

- In the Partners database, click the 'New Data Source button' (External Data tab | Import & Link group).
- Click From Database in the New Data Source menu, and then click Access to display the Get External Data - Access Database dialog box.

3

- Click the Browse button and navigate to your storage location for the file, Support_AC_02_Partners-Extra-Tables.accdb.
- Select Support_AC_02_Partners-Extra-Tables.accdb, and then click the Open button to select this database as the data source.

4

- If necessary, click the 'Import tables, queries, forms, reports, macros, and modules into the current database' option to indicate how and where to store the data in the current database.
- Click OK to display the Import Objects dialog box.

5

- If necessary, click the Tables tab (Import Objects dialog box).
- Select the Closing Fees table to indicate the object to import, and then click OK to import the table.

6

- Close the Get External Data - Access Database dialog box without saving the import steps.
- Confirm the Closing Fees table is now listed as a table object in the Navigation Pane.

Calculations

If a special calculation is required for a query, you need to determine whether the calculation is an **individual record calculation** (for example, adding the values in two fields for one record) or a **group calculation** (for example, finding the total of the values in a particular field on all the records).

Partners paralegals might want to know the total real estate commissions assigned in the Closing Fees table (for the buying and selling agents) for each closing. This would seem to pose a problem because the table does not include a field for total cost. You can calculate it, however, because the total amount is equal to the sum of both listed commissions. A field that can be computed from other fields is called a **calculated field** or a **computed field** and is not usually included in the table. Including it introduces the possibility for errors in the table. If the value in the field does not happen to match the results of the calculation, the data is inconsistent. A calculated field is an individual record calculation because each calculation only involves fields in a single record.

Partners paralegals might also want to calculate the average attorney fees for all closings. This type of calculation is called a group calculation because each calculation involves groups of records. A group calculation can apply to all records from the source table or to only a subset of records.

To Use a Calculated Field in a Query

If you need a calculated field in a query, you enter a name (also called an alias) for the calculated field, a colon, and then the calculation in one of the columns in the Field row of the query's design grid. Any fields included in the expression must be enclosed in square brackets ([ ]). For example, for the total amount, you will type Total Cost:[Quantity]*[Cost] as the expression.

You can use addition (+), subtraction (-), multiplication (*), or division (/) in calculations. If you have multiple calculations in an expression, you can include parentheses to indicate which calculations should be done first.

You can type the expression directly into the Field row in Design view. The preferred method, however, is to select the column in the Field row and then use the Zoom command on its shortcut menu. When Access displays the Zoom dialog box, you can enter the expression. **Why use the Zoom command?** You will not be able to see the entire entry in the Field row, because the space available is not large enough.

The following steps create a query that Partners paralegals will be able to use to obtain total real estate commissions for each closing, by adding the selling agent's commission and the buying agent's commission, which is a calculated field.

1

- Create a query using the Closing Fees table.
- Add the Settlement Sheet ID, Closing ID, Selling Agent Commission, and Buying Agent Commission fields to the query.
- Right-click the Field row in the first empty column in the design grid to display a shortcut menu (Figure 2-64).

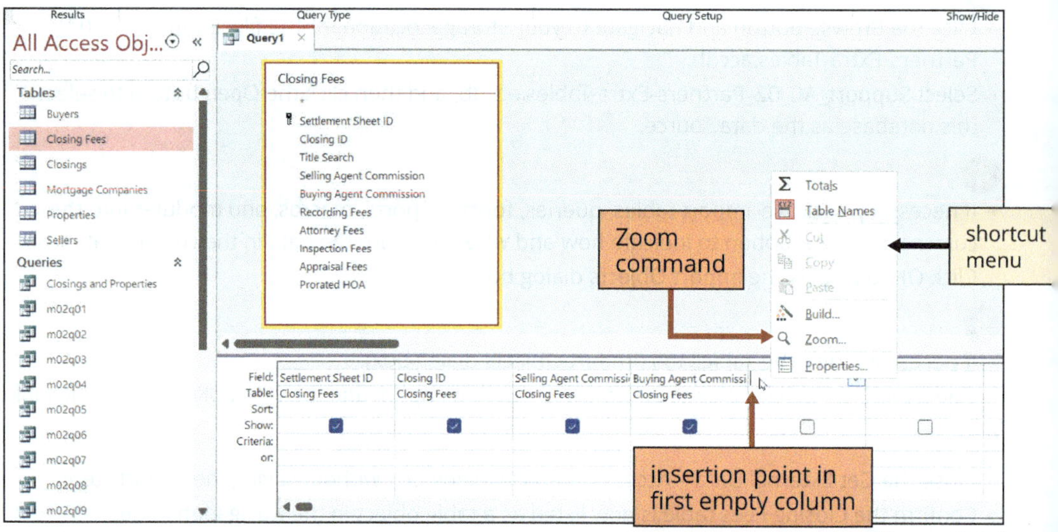

Figure 2-64

2

- Click Zoom on the shortcut menu to display the Zoom dialog box.
- Type **Total Commission:[Selling Agent Commission]+[Buying Agent Commission]** in the Zoom dialog box (Figure 2-65) to enter the expression.

Q&A Do I always need to put square brackets around field names?
If the field name does not contain spaces, square brackets are technically not required. It is a good practice, however, to get in the habit of using the brackets in field calculations.

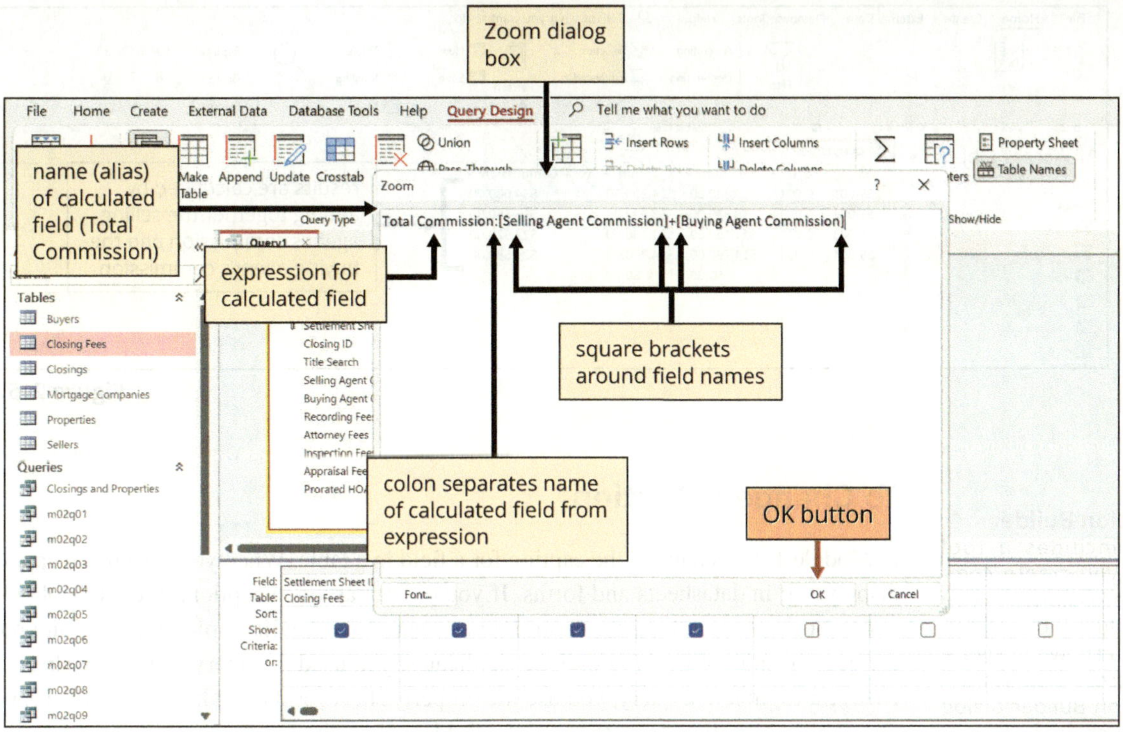

Figure 2–65

Other Ways

1. Press SHIFT+F2 to display Zoom dialog box

3

- Click OK (Zoom dialog box) to complete the expression and close the dialog box.
- Resize the Total Commission column to see all the content (Figure 2–66).

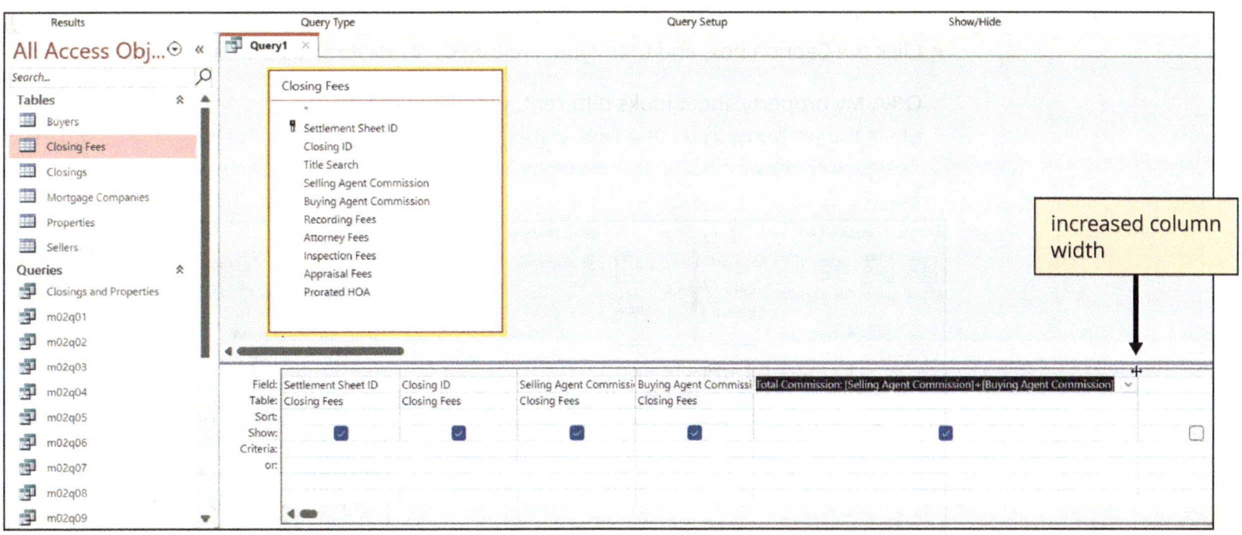

Figure 2–66

- Run the query to see the calculated results for the new Total Commission field.
- Resize all columns for best fit (Figure 2–67).
- **Experiment:** Return to Design view and try other expressions. In at least one case, omit the Total Commission and the colon. In at least one case, intentionally misspell a field name. In each case, run the query to see the effect of your changes. When finished, re-enter the original expression.

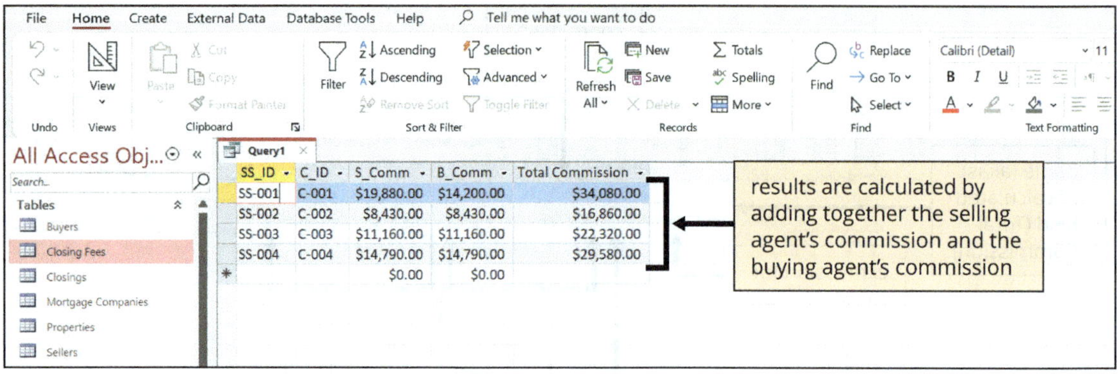

Figure 2-67

BTW
Expression Builder
Access includes a tool to help you create complex expressions. If you click Build on the shortcut menu shown in Figure 2-64, Access displays the Expression Builder dialog box, which includes an expression box, operator buttons, and expression elements. You can type parts of the expression directly and paste operator buttons and expression elements into the box. You also can use functions in expressions.

To Change a Caption

In Module 1, you changed the caption for a field in a table. When you assigned a caption, Access displayed it in datasheets and forms. If you did not assign a caption, Access displayed the field name. You can also change a caption in a query. Access will display the caption you assign in the query results. When you omitted duplicates, you used the query's property sheet. When you change a caption in a query, you use the property sheet for the field. In the field's property sheet, you can change other properties for the field, such as the format and number of decimal places. The following steps change the caption of each commission field to better identify which agent is being paid. **Why?** These changes give more descriptive, yet very readable, column headings for the fields. The steps also save the query with a new name.

1

- Return to Design view.
- If necessary, click Query Design on the ribbon to display the Query Design tab.
- Click the Selling Agent Commission field in the design grid, and then click the Property Sheet button (Query Design tab | Show/Hide group) to display the properties for the Selling Agent Commission field.
- Click the Caption box, and then type **Selling Commission** as the caption (Figure 2-68).

Q&A My property sheet looks different. What should I do?
Close the property sheet and repeat this step, making sure to select the correct field in the design grid before clicking the Property Sheet button.

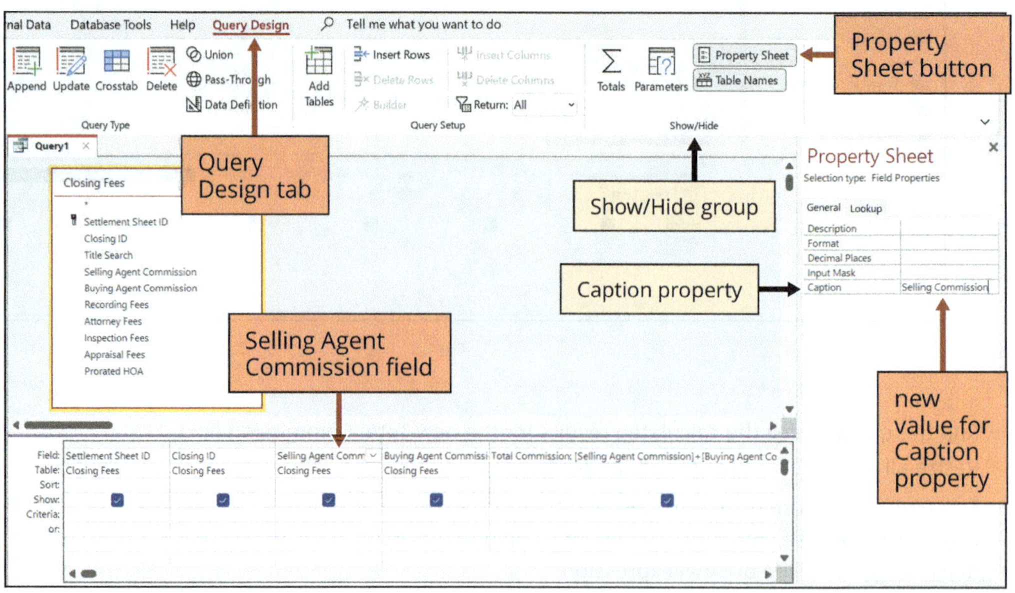

Figure 2-68

2

- Click the Buying Agent Commission field in the design grid to view its properties in the Property Sheet.
- Click the Caption box, and then type **Buying Commission** as the caption.
- Close the Property Sheet by clicking the Property Sheet button a second time.
- Run the query.
- Resize the query columns for best fit (Figure 2-69).

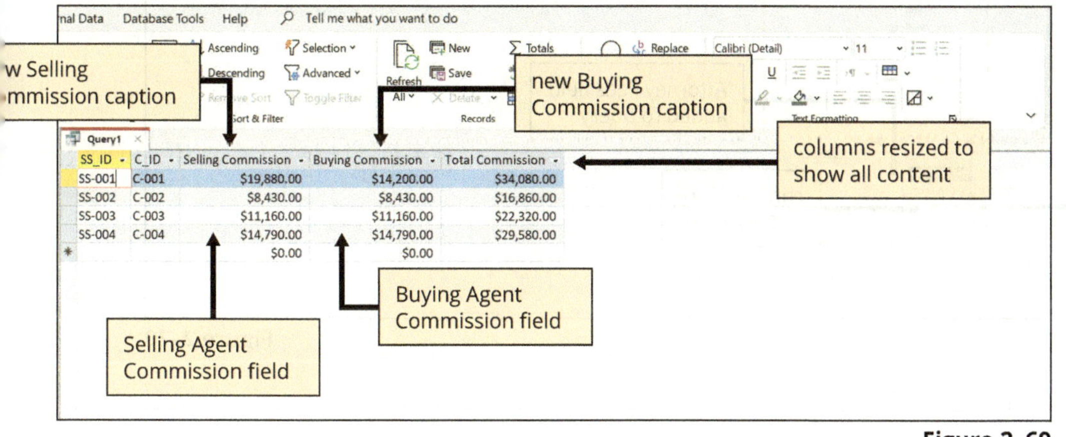

Figure 2-69

3

- Save the query as **m02q13**.
- Close the query.

Other Ways

1. Right-click field in design grid, click Properties to open Property Sheet pane

To Calculate Statistics

For group calculations, Microsoft Access supports several built-in statistics: COUNT (count of the number of records), SUM (total), AVG (average), MAX (largest value), MIN (smallest value), STDEV (standard deviation), VAR (variance), FIRST (first value), and LAST (last value). These statistics are called aggregate functions. An **aggregate function** is a function that performs some mathematical function against a group of records. To use an aggregate function in a query, you include it in the Total row in the design grid. In order to do so, you must first include the Total row by clicking the Totals button on the Design tab. **Why?** The Total row usually does not appear in the grid. Statistical calculations are performed regularly in Access queries by some, but not all learners. So, the process for these calculations requires extra steps.

The following steps create a new query for the Closing Fees table. The steps include the Total row in the design grid, and then calculate the average cost for all attorney fees.

1

- Create a new query using the Closing Fees table.
- Click the Totals button (Query Design tab | Show/Hide group) to include the Total row in the design grid.
- Add the Attorney Fees field to the query (Figure 2-70).

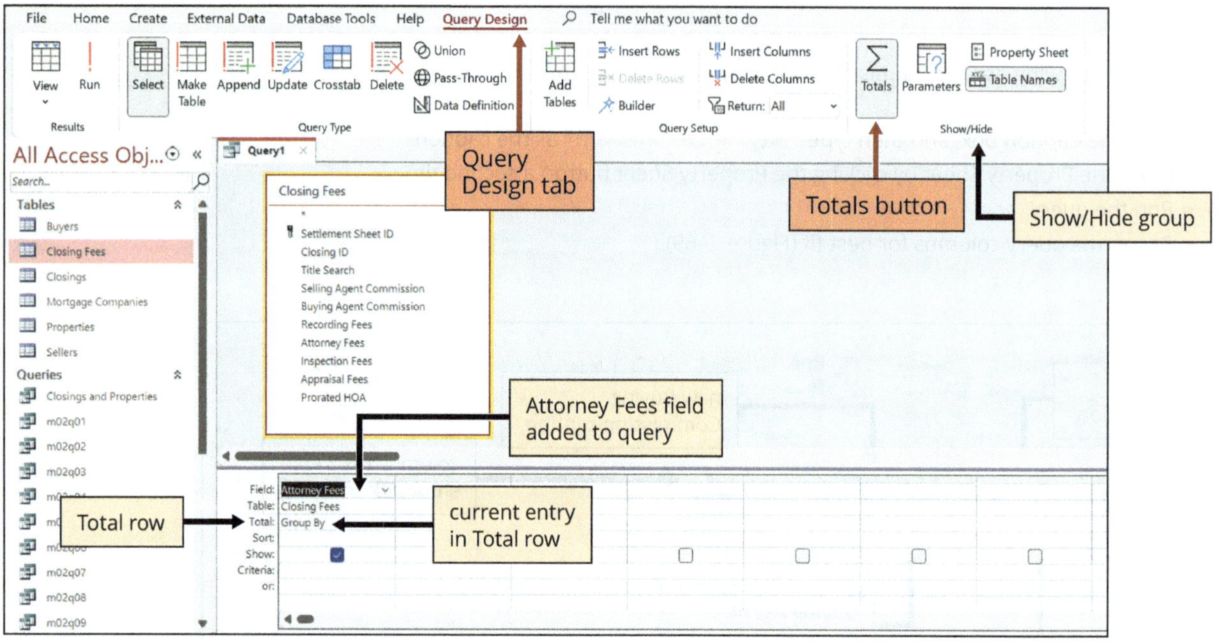

Figure 2–70

2

- Click the Total row in the Attorney Fees column to display the Total arrow.
- Click the Total arrow to display the Total list (Figure 2–71).

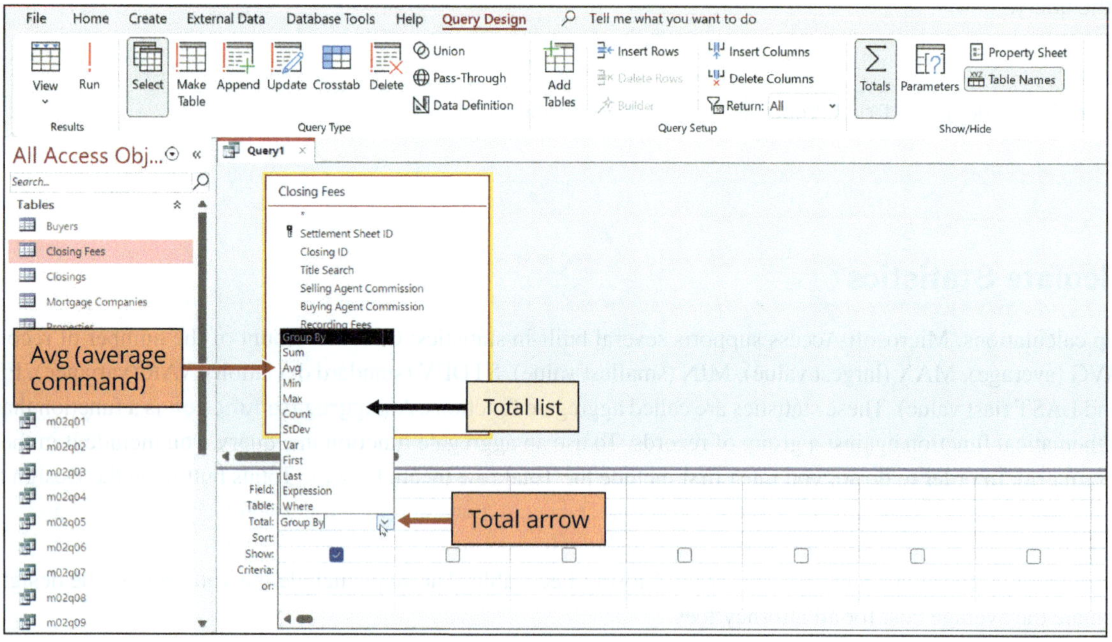

Figure 2–71

3

- Click Avg to select the calculation that Access is to perform (Figure 2–72).
- Run the query (Figure 2–73).
- **Experiment:** Return to Design view and try other aggregate functions. In each case, run the query to see the effect of your selection. When finished, select Avg once again.

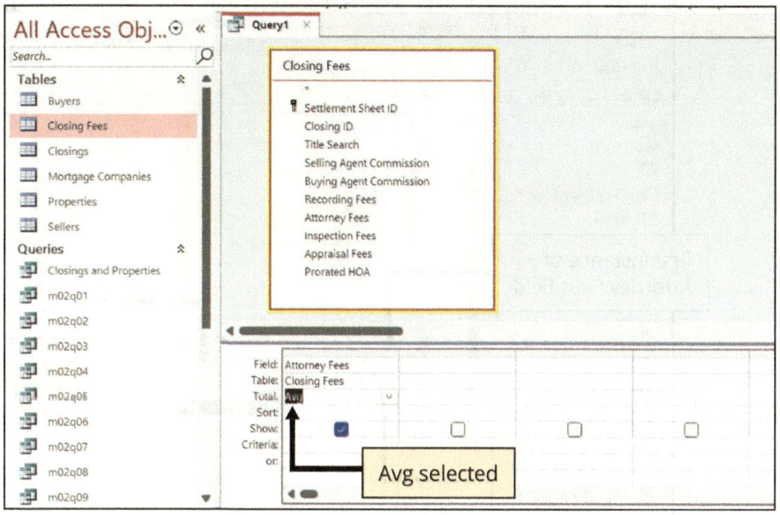

Figure 2–72

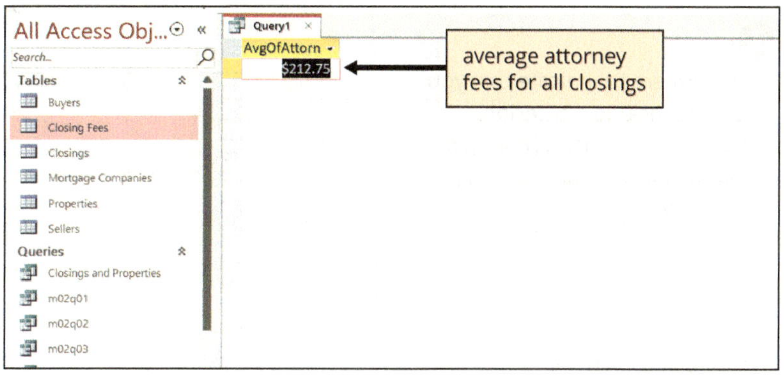

Figure 2–73

To Use Criteria in Calculating Statistics

Sometimes calculating statistics for all the records in the table is appropriate. In other cases, however, you will need to calculate the statistics for only those records that satisfy certain criteria. Notice in the previous query that the average is skewed lower than it should be because one of the clients is a family member and is paying a lower-than-normal fee. **Why?** Including a criterion that only includes records where the attorney fee is more than $200 will yield a more accurate result. To enter a criterion in a field, first you select Where as the entry in the Total row for the field, and then enter the criterion in the Criteria row. Access uses the word, Where, to indicate that you will enter a criterion. The following steps use this technique to calculate the average attorney fees where the fee is more than $200. The steps also save the query.

1

- Return to Design view.
- Include the Attorney Fees field again, this time in the second column in the design grid. The Attorney Fees field will be listed twice in the design grid.
- Click the Total row in the second Attorney Fees column.
- Click the Total arrow in the second Attorney Fees column to display the Total list (Figure 2–74).

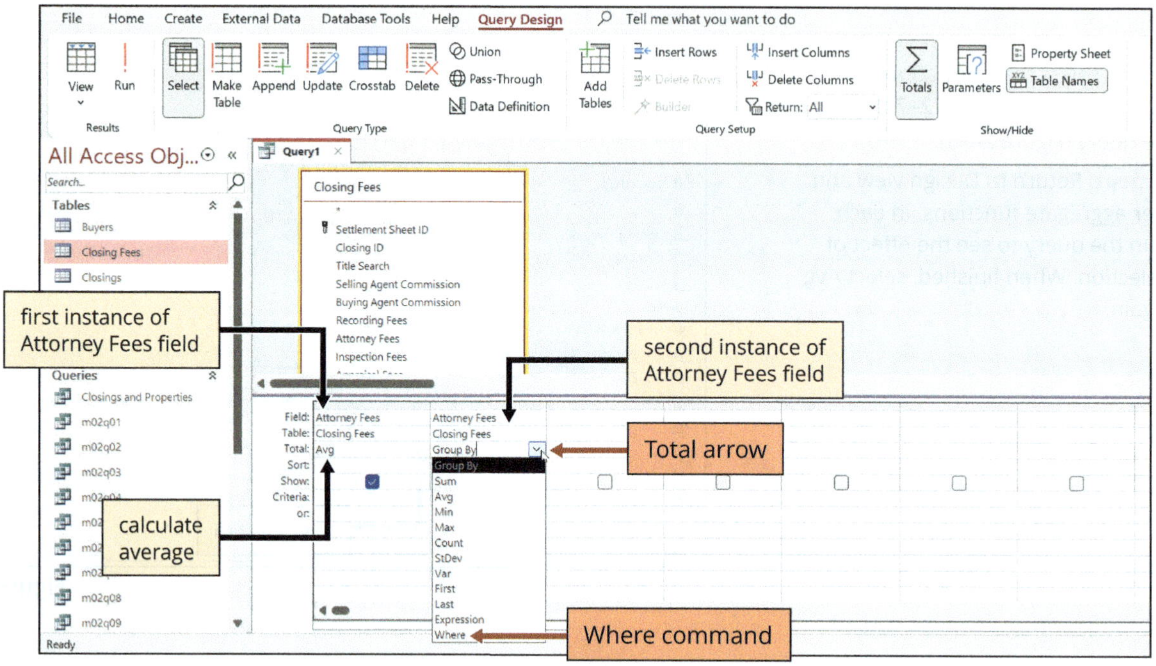

Figure 2–74

2

- Click Where to indicate that you want to include a criterion.
- Type **>200** as the criterion for the second Attorney Fees field (Figure 2–75).

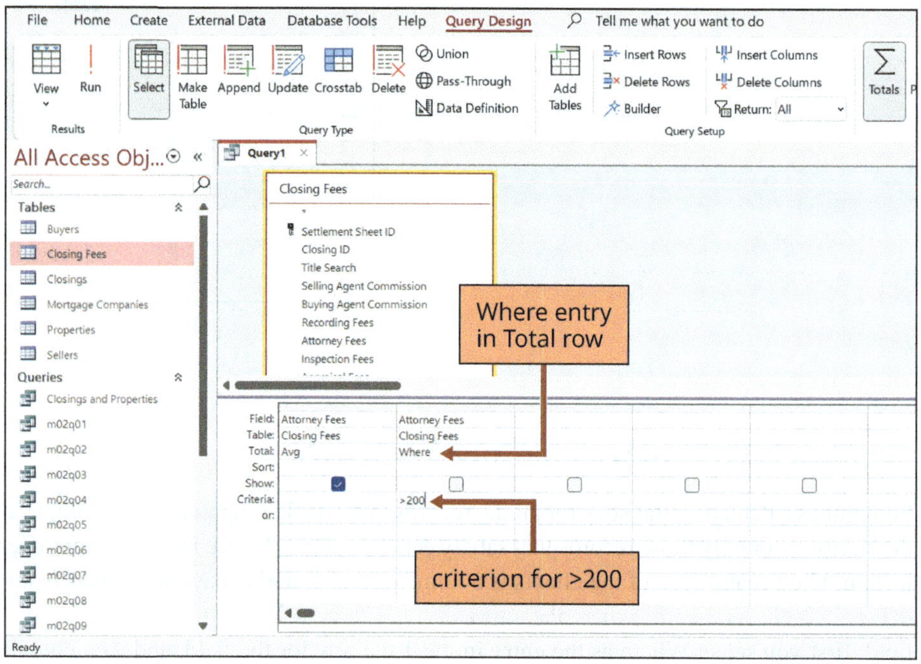

Figure 2–75

BTW

Criterion for Where

Access treats the criterion for the Where object just as it would for any criterion in a field. For example, you could also use a wildcard rather than spelling out the entire criterion, such as Part* for Partners Law Firm. Access recognizes and utilizes the wildcard to find the desired result.

3

- Run the query (Figure 2–76) to display the average attorney fees where the fee is more than $200.

4

- Save the query as **m02q14**.
- Close the query.

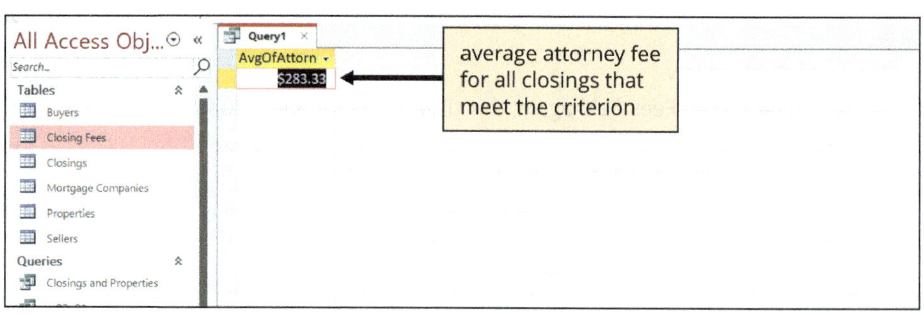

Figure 2–76

To Use Grouping

Statistics are often used in combination with grouping; that is, statistics are calculated for groups of records. For example, Partners paralegals could calculate the average new loan amount for each mortgage company, which would require the average for the mortgage company specified in the criteria. **Grouping** means creating groups of records that share some common characteristic. In grouping new loans by mortgage company, for example, the new loans with Atlas Mortgage would form one group, the new loans with Cheshire Mortgage would form a second group, and the new loans with County Mortgage would form a third group. The calculations are then made for each group. To indicate grouping in Access, select Group By as the entry in the Total row for the field to be used for grouping. Even though the entry indicates Group By, the mortgage companies will appear individually. **Why?** Access needs to know the field that you want to review the averages on, and it indicates this by the text Group By. Group By does not mean that it will group together all the mortgage companies, it just refers to looking at that particular group.

The following steps create a query that calculates the average new loan amount with each mortgage company involved in closings with Partners Law Firm. The steps also save the query.

1

- Create a query using the Closings table.
- Add the New Loan Amount and Purchasing Mortgage Company ID fields to the query.
- Click the Totals button (Query Design tab | Show/Hide group) to include the Total row in the design grid.
- Select Avg as the calculation in the Total row for the New Loan Amount field (Figure 2–77).

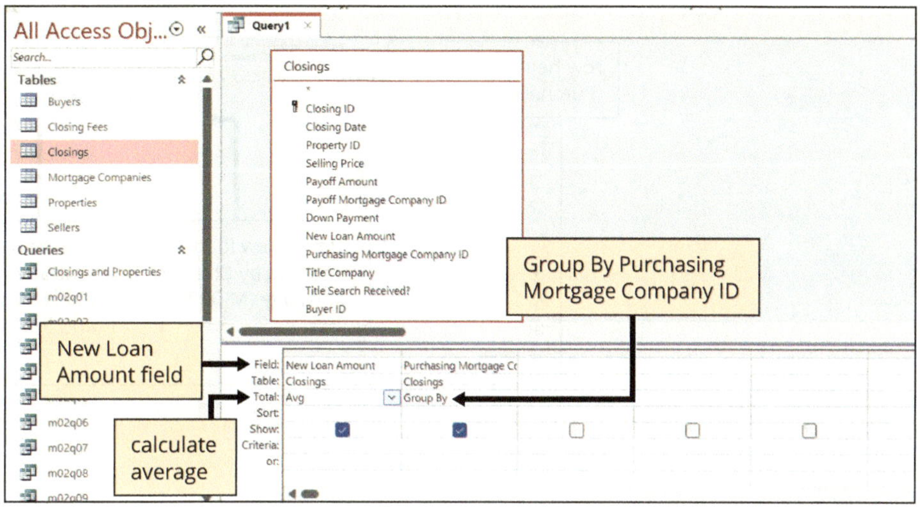

Figure 2–77

Q&A Why was it not necessary to change the entry in the Total row for the Purchasing Mortgage Company ID field?
Group By, which is the initial entry in the Total row when you add a field, is correct. Thus, you did not need to change the entry.

2

- Run the query (Figure 2–78).

3

- Save the query as **m02q15**.
- Close the query.

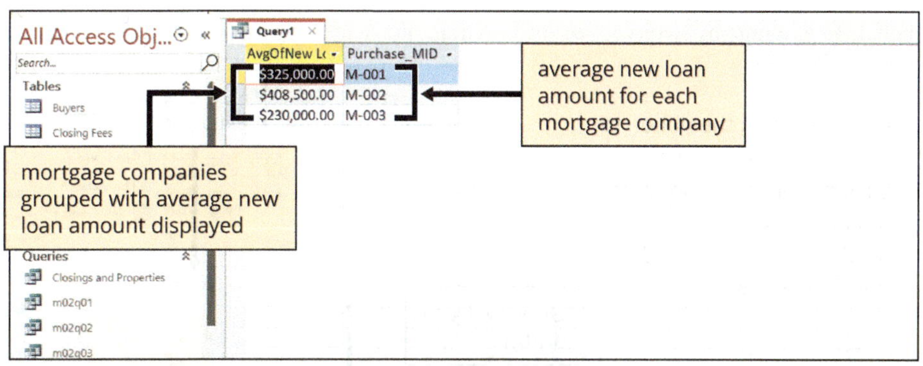

Figure 2–78

Crosstab Queries

A **crosstab query**, or simply, crosstab, calculates a statistic (for example, sum, average, or count) for data that is grouped by two different types of information. One of the types will appear down the side of the resulting datasheet, and the other will appear across the top. Crosstab queries are useful for summarizing data by category or group.

For example, if a query must summarize the sum of new loan amounts grouped by both mortgage company and title company, you could have mortgage company IDs as the row headings—that is, down the side. You could have title companies as the column headings—that is, across the top. The entries within the datasheet represent the total of new loan amounts. Figure 2–79 shows a crosstab in which the total of new loan amounts is grouped by both mortgage company ID and title company, with mortgage company IDs down the left side and title company names across the top. For example, the entry in the row labeled M-002 and in the column labeled Perfect Title represents the total of the new loan amounts by all closings using Perfect Title and Cheshire Mortgage (M-002).

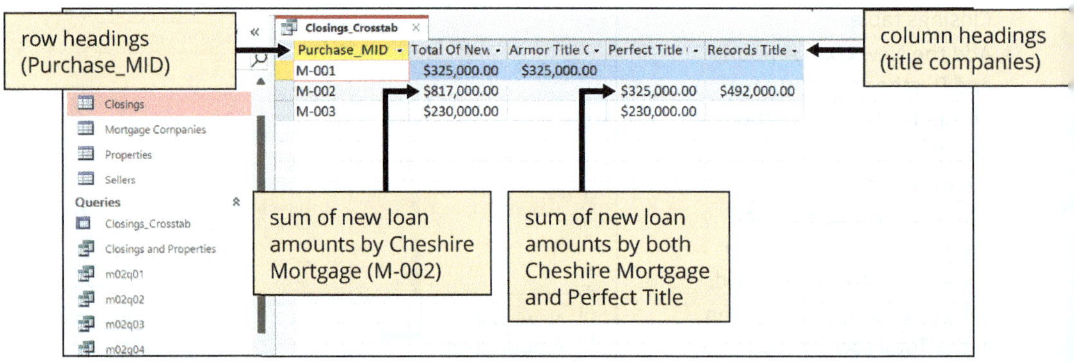

Figure 2–79

Consider This

How do you know when to use a crosstab query?

If data is to be grouped by two different types of information, you can use a crosstab query. You will need to identify the two types of information. One of the types will form the row headings and the other will form the column headings in the query results.

To Create a Crosstab Query

The following steps use the Crosstab Query Wizard to create a crosstab query. **Why?** Partners paralegals want to group data on new loan amounts by two types of information: mortgage company ID and title company.

1

- Click Create on the ribbon to display the Create tab.
- Click the Query Wizard button (Create tab | Queries group) to display the New Query dialog box (Figure 2–80).

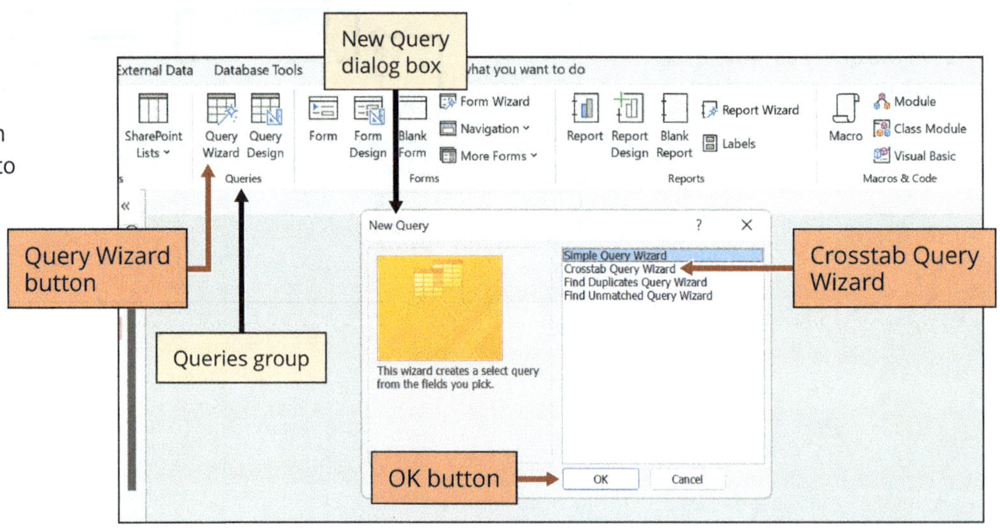

Figure 2–80

2

- Click Crosstab Query Wizard (New Query dialog box).
- Click OK to display the Crosstab Query Wizard dialog box (Figure 2–81).

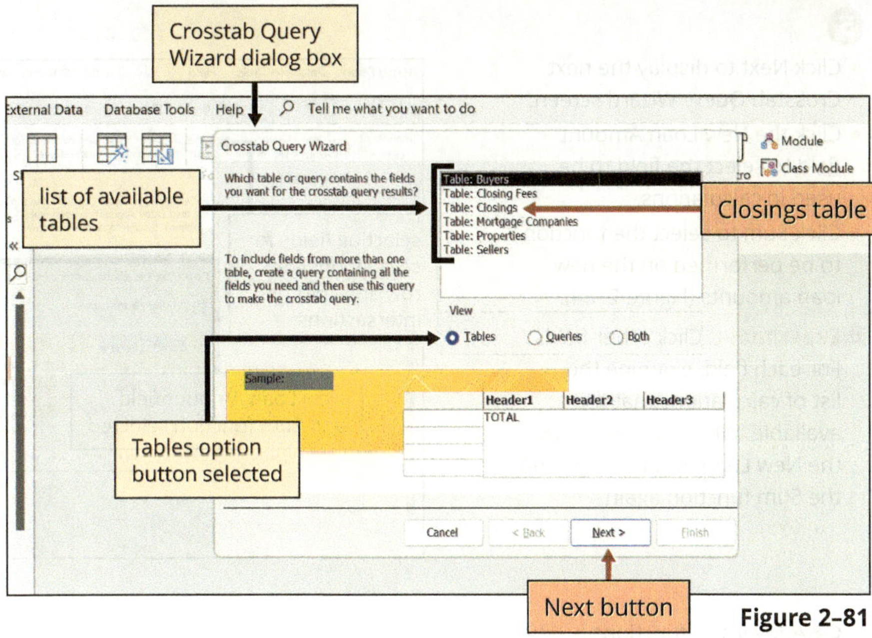

Figure 2–81

3

- With the Tables option button selected, click Table: Closings to select the Closings table, and then click the Next button to display the next Crosstab Query Wizard screen.
- Click the Purchasing Mortgage Company ID field, and then click the Add Field button to select the Purchasing Mortgage Company ID field for row headings (Figure 2–82).

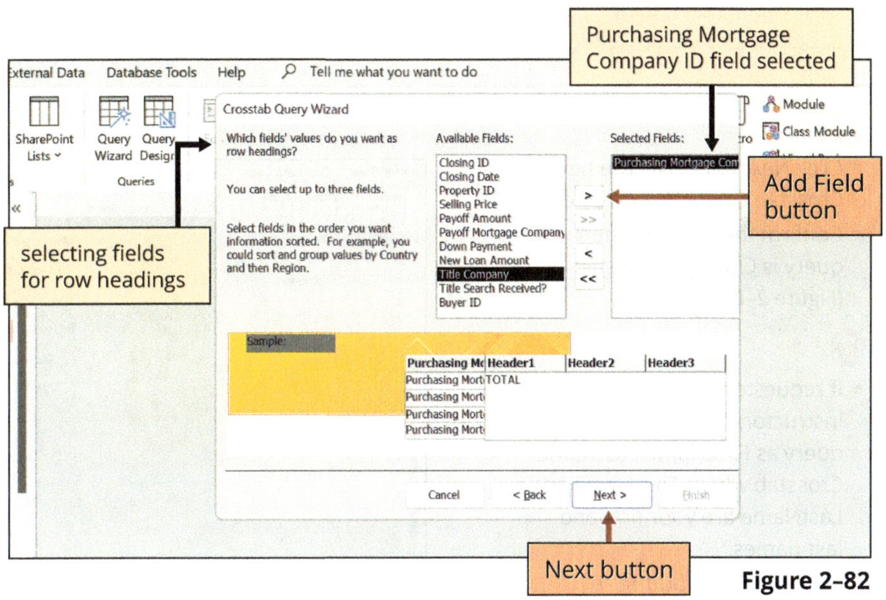

Figure 2–82

4

- Click the Next button to display the next Crosstab Query Wizard screen.
- Click the Title Company field to select the field for column headings (Figure 2–83).

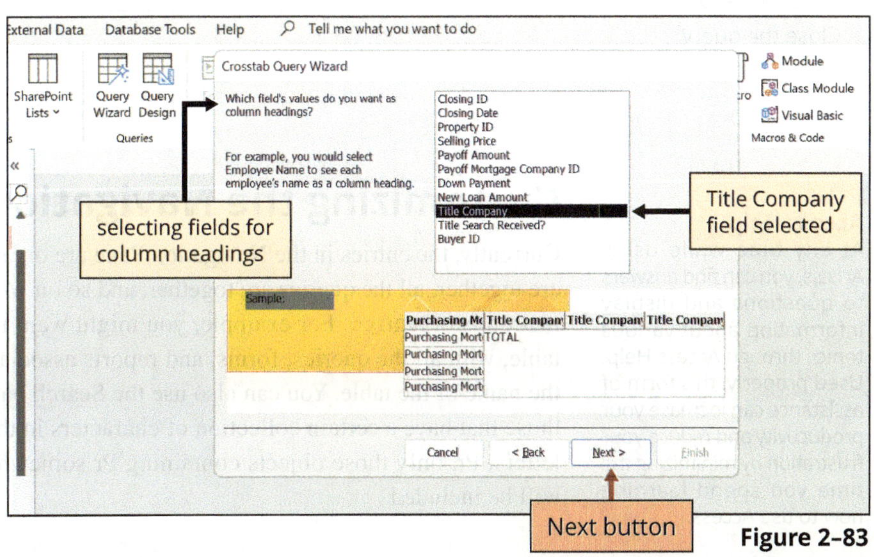

Figure 2–83

5

- Click Next to display the next Crosstab Query Wizard screen.
- Click the New Loan Amount field to select the field to be used in calculations.
- Click Sum to select the function to be performed on the new loan amounts (Figure 2–84).
- **Experiment:** Click other fields. For each field, examine the list of calculations that are available. When finished, click the New Loan Amount field and the Sum function again.

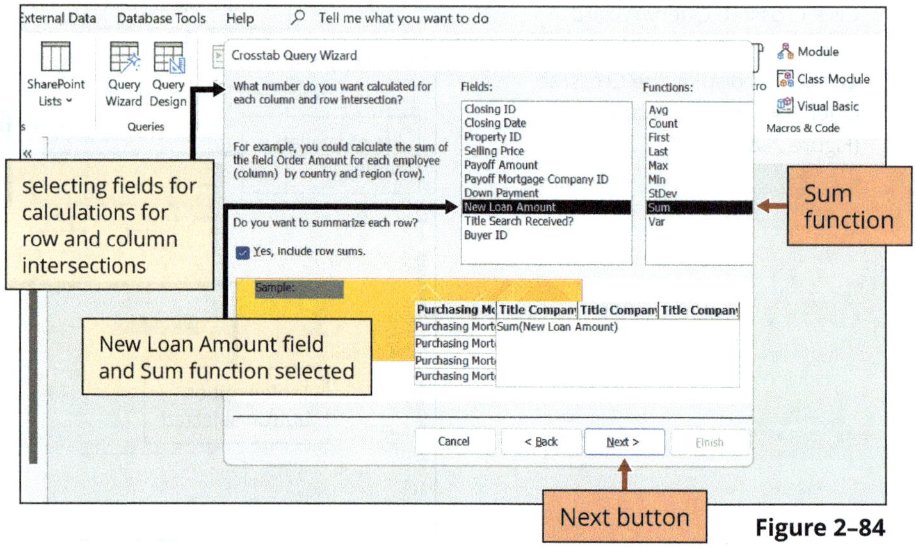

Figure 2–84

Q&A My list of functions is different. What did I do wrong?
Either you clicked the wrong field, or the New Loan Amount field has the wrong data type. For example, if you mistakenly assigned it the Short Text data type, you would not see Sum in the list of available calculations.

6

- Click Next to display the next Crosstab Query Wizard screen.
- Confirm the name of the query is Closings_Crosstab (Figure 2–85).

7

- If requested to do so by your instructor, name the crosstab query as FirstName LastName Crosstab where FirstName and LastName are your first and last names.
- Click the Finish button to produce the crosstab shown in Figure 2–79.
- Close the query.

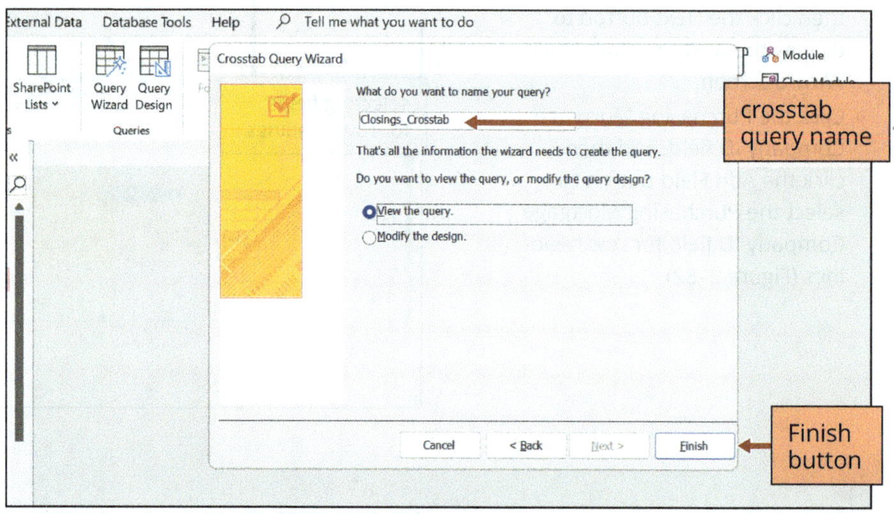

Figure 2–85

BTW
Access Help
At any time while using Access, you can find answers to questions and display information about various topics through Access Help. Used properly, this form of assistance can increase your productivity and reduce your frustration by minimizing the time you spend learning how to use Access.

Customizing the Navigation Pane

Currently, the entries in the Navigation Pane are organized by object type. That is, all the tables are together, all the queries are together, and so on. You might want to change the way the information is organized. For example, you might want to have the Navigation Pane organized by table, with all the queries, forms, and reports associated with a particular table appearing after the name of the table. You can also use the Search bar to restrict the objects that appear to only those that have a certain collection of characters in their name. For example, if you entered the letters, Pr, only those objects containing Pr somewhere within the name (such as Properties) will be included.

To Customize the Navigation Pane

The following steps change the organization of the Navigation Pane. They also use the Search bar to restrict the objects that appear. **Why?** Using the Search bar, you can reduce the number of objects that appear in the Navigation Pane and just show the ones in which you are interested.

1

- If necessary, click the 'Shutter Bar Open/Close Button' to open the Navigation Pane.
- Click the Navigation Pane arrow to display the Navigation Pane menu and then click 'Tables and Related Views' to organize the Navigation Pane by table rather than by object type (Figure 2–86).

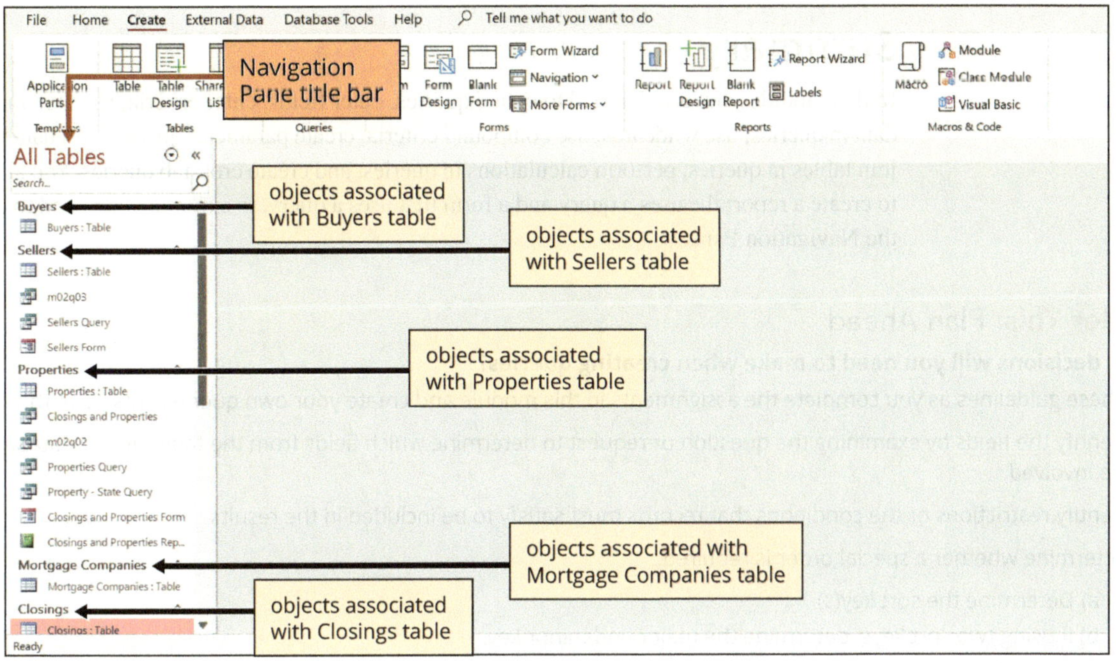

Figure 2–86

2

- Click the Navigation Pane arrow to display the Navigation Pane menu.
- Click Object Type to once again organize the Navigation Pane by object type.
- **Experiment:** Select different Navigate To Category options to see the effect of the option. With each option you select, select different Filter By Group options to see the effect of the filtering. When you have finished experimenting, select 'Object Type' for the Navigate To Category option and 'All Access Objects' for the Filter By Group option.
- If the Search bar does not appear, right-click the Navigation Pane and click Search Bar on the shortcut menu.
- Click in the Search box to produce an insertion point.
- Type **pr** as the search string to restrict the objects displayed to only those containing the desired string (Figure 2–87).

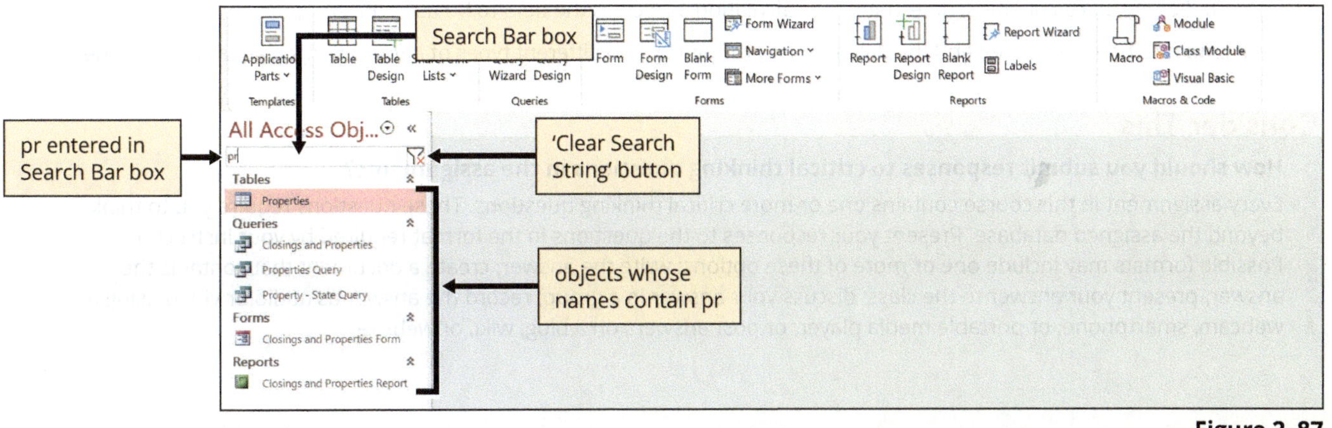

Figure 2–87

3

- Click the 'Clear Search String' button to remove the search string and redisplay all objects.

Q&A Did I have to click the button to redisplay all objects? Could I simply have erased the current string to achieve the same result?
You did not have to click the button. You could have used DEL or BACKSPACE to erase the current search string.

- If desired, sign out of your Microsoft account.
- sam Exit Access.

Summary

In this module you have learned to create queries, enter fields, enter criteria, use text and numeric data in queries, use wildcards, use compound criteria, create parameter queries, sort data in queries, join tables in queries, perform calculations in queries, and create crosstab queries. You also learned to create a report the uses a query and a form that uses a query, to export a query, and to customize the Navigation Pane.

Consider This: Plan Ahead

What decisions will you need to make when creating queries?

Use these guidelines as you complete the assignments in this module and create your own queries outside of this class.

1. Identify the fields by examining the question or request to determine which fields from the tables in the database are involved.
2. Identify restrictions or the conditions that records must satisfy to be included in the results.
3. Determine whether a special order is required.
   a) Determine the sort key(s).
   b) If using two sort keys, determine the major and minor key.
   c) Determine sort order. If there are no words to imply a particular order, you would typically use Ascending sort order.
   d) Determine restrictions, such as excluding duplicates.
4. Determine whether more than one table is required.
   a) Determine which tables to include.
   b) Determine the matching fields.
   c) Determine whether sorting is required.
   d) Determine restrictions.
   e) Determine join properties.
5. Determine whether calculations are required.
   a) For individual record calculations, determine the calculation and a name for the calculated field.
   b) For group calculations, determine the calculation as well as the field to be used for grouping.
6. If data is to be summarized and the data is to be grouped by two different types of information, create a crosstab query.

Consider This

How should you submit responses to critical thinking questions in the assignments?

Every assignment in this course contains one or more critical thinking questions. These questions require you to think beyond the assigned database. Present your responses to the questions in the format required by your instructor. Possible formats may include one or more of these options: write the answer; create a document that contains the answer; present your answer to the class; discuss your answer in a group; record the answer as audio or video using a webcam, smartphone, or portable media player; or post answers on a blog, wiki, or website.

Student Assignments

Apply Your Knowledge

Reinforce the skills and apply the concepts you learned in this module.

Using Wildcards in a Query, Creating a Parameter Query, Joining Tables, and Creating a Report

Note: To complete this assignment, you will be required to use the Data Files. Please contact your instructor for information about accessing the Data Files.

Instructions: Start Access. Open the database, SC_AC_02-2.accdb, which is located in the Data Files folder. Enable the content. The database was created by the new project manager at Build It Construction. Before she was hired, the owners kept a "mental list" of which subcontractor was hired for each construction project. When the new project manager started work, she realized this was inefficient and allowed for many mistakes, miscommunications, and delayed projects. She created a small database with a table for job sites, a table for subcontractors, and a query to produce a checklist she can use to track communications throughout each work week. The project manager has exported some payment information from another system. She needs you to add this data to her database. You will import the Accounting table, create some queries with this information, and create a report.

Perform the following tasks:

1. Save the database using the file name, SC_AC_02-Construction. Enable the content.
2. Import the Accounting table from the Support_AC_02_Construction-Extra-Tables.accdb database. Do not save the import steps.
3. Create a query using the Accounting table and add the SC # (stands for Subcontractor Number), Subcontractor Name, Amount Paid, and JS # (stands for Job Site Number) fields to the design grid. Sort the records in descending order by Amount Paid. Add a criterion for the JS # field that allows the user to enter a different job site number each time the query is run. Run the query and enter 112 as the job site number to test the query. Save the query as Apply 2 Step 3 Query. Close the query.
4. Create another query for the Accounting table and add the SC #, Subcontractor Name, and Current Due fields to the design grid. Add a criterion to find all subcontractors whose current due amount is less than $500. Run the query and then save it as Apply 2 Step 4 Query. Close the query.
5. Create a query that joins the Job Sites and Subcontractors tables. Add the Job Site Number, Owner, and City fields from the Job Sites table and the Subcontractor Number and Subcontractor Name fields from the Subcontractors table to the design grid. Sort the records in ascending order by Subcontractor Number and Job Site Number. Run the query and save it as Job Site-Subcontractor Query. **Note:** If any error messages appear, check the field types of the fields in the query tables and make changes as necessary. Close the query.
6. Create the report shown in Figure 2–88. The report uses the Job Site-Subcontractor Query.

   If requested to do so by your instructor, rename the Job Site-Subcontractor Report in the Navigation Pane as LastName-Subcontractor Report where LastName is your last name.
7. Submit the revised database, including all objects shown in the Navigation Pane in Figure 2–88, in the format specified by your instructor.

Continued on next page

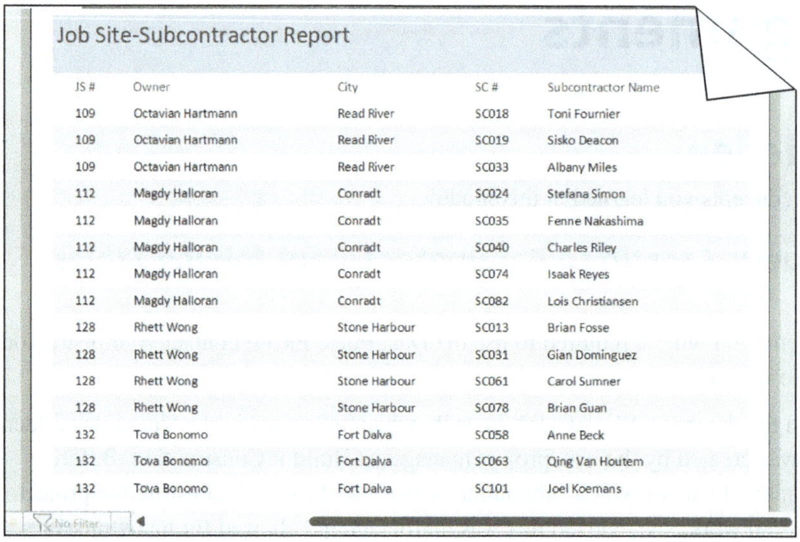

Job Site-Subcontractor Report

JS #	Owner	City	SC #	Subcontractor Name
109	Octavian Hartmann	Read River	SC018	Toni Fournier
109	Octavian Hartmann	Read River	SC019	Sisko Deacon
109	Octavian Hartmann	Read River	SC033	Albany Miles
112	Magdy Halloran	Conradt	SC024	Stefana Simon
112	Magdy Halloran	Conradt	SC035	Fenne Nakashima
112	Magdy Halloran	Conradt	SC040	Charles Riley
112	Magdy Halloran	Conradt	SC074	Isaak Reyes
112	Magdy Halloran	Conradt	SC082	Lois Christiansen
128	Rhett Wong	Stone Harbour	SC013	Brian Fosse
128	Rhett Wong	Stone Harbour	SC031	Gian Dominguez
128	Rhett Wong	Stone Harbour	SC061	Carol Sumner
128	Rhett Wong	Stone Harbour	SC078	Brian Guan
132	Tova Bonomo	Fort Dalva	SC058	Anne Beck
132	Tova Bonomo	Fort Dalva	SC063	Qing Van Houtem
132	Tova Bonomo	Fort Dalva	SC101	Joel Koemans

Figure 2–88

8. **Consider This:** What criteria would you enter in a query using the Mobile Phone field if you wanted to find all subcontractors whose phone numbers begin with the area code 405?

Extend Your Knowledge

Extend the skills you learned in this module and experiment with new skills. You may need to use Help to complete the assignment.

Creating Queries Using Criteria and Exporting a Query

Note: To complete this assignment, you will be required to use the Data Files. Please contact your instructor for information about accessing the Data Files.

Instructions: Start Access. Open the database, SC_AC_02-3.accdb, which is located in the Data Files folder, and enable the content. The Asset Management database provides a lending library database structure for lending out equipment to employees in various departments. You will enter some initial data, create a query, enter data in a form, and export a report.

Perform the following tasks:

1. Save the database using the file name, SC_AC_02_IT-Assets. Enable the content.
2. Enter the asset information shown in Figure 2–89 into the Assets List that appears when the database is opened.

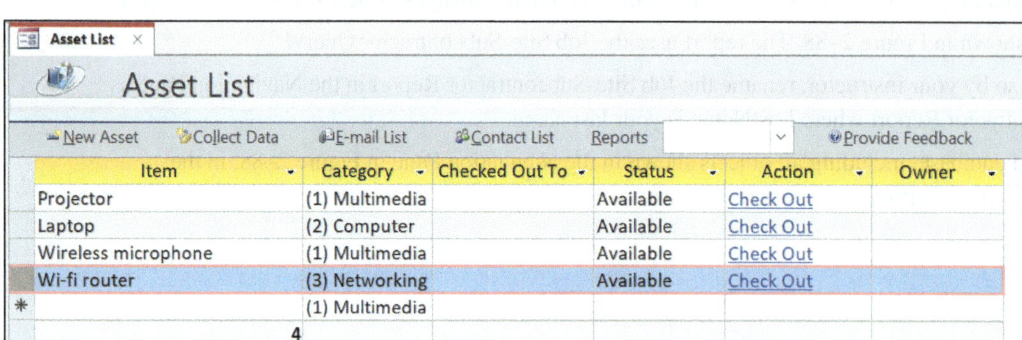

Item	Category	Checked Out To	Status	Action	Owner
Projector	(1) Multimedia		Available	Check Out	
Laptop	(2) Computer		Available	Check Out	
Wireless microphone	(1) Multimedia		Available	Check Out	
Wi-fi router	(3) Networking		Available	Check Out	
	(1) Multimedia				
4					

Figure 2–89

3. Enter the contact information shown in Figure 2–90 into the Contacts table.

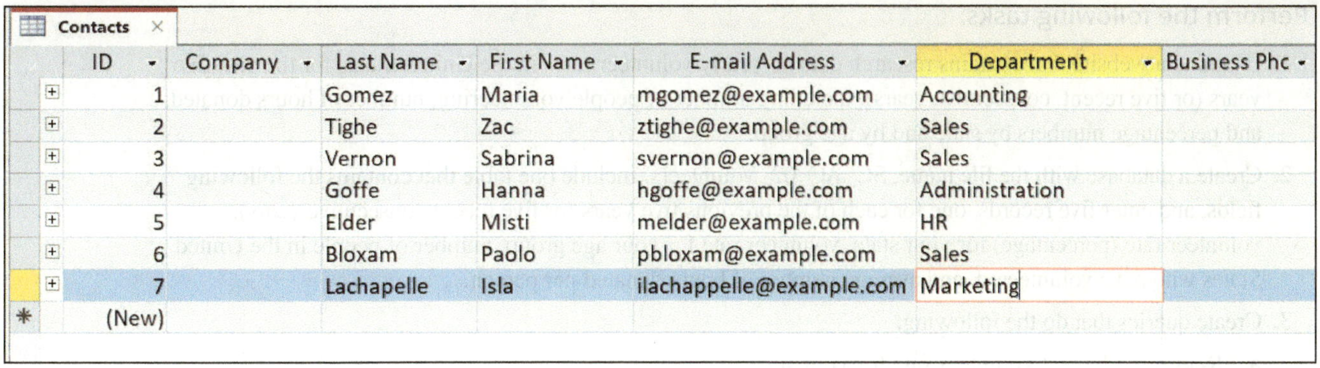

ID	Company	Last Name	First Name	E-mail Address	Department	Business Phc
1		Gomez	Maria	mgomez@example.com	Accounting	
2		Tighe	Zac	ztighe@example.com	Sales	
3		Vernon	Sabrina	svernon@example.com	Sales	
4		Goffe	Hanna	hgoffe@example.com	Administration	
5		Elder	Misti	melder@example.com	HR	
6		Bloxam	Paolo	pbloxam@example.com	Sales	
7		Lachapelle	Isla	ilachappelle@example.com	Marketing	
(New)						

Figure 2–90

4. Create a query to find all Assets in the "(1) Multimedia" category. Include the ID, Item, and Category fields. Save the query as Extend 2 Step 4 Query.
5. Enter information for Tyron Black into the Contact Details form, as shown in Figure 2–91.

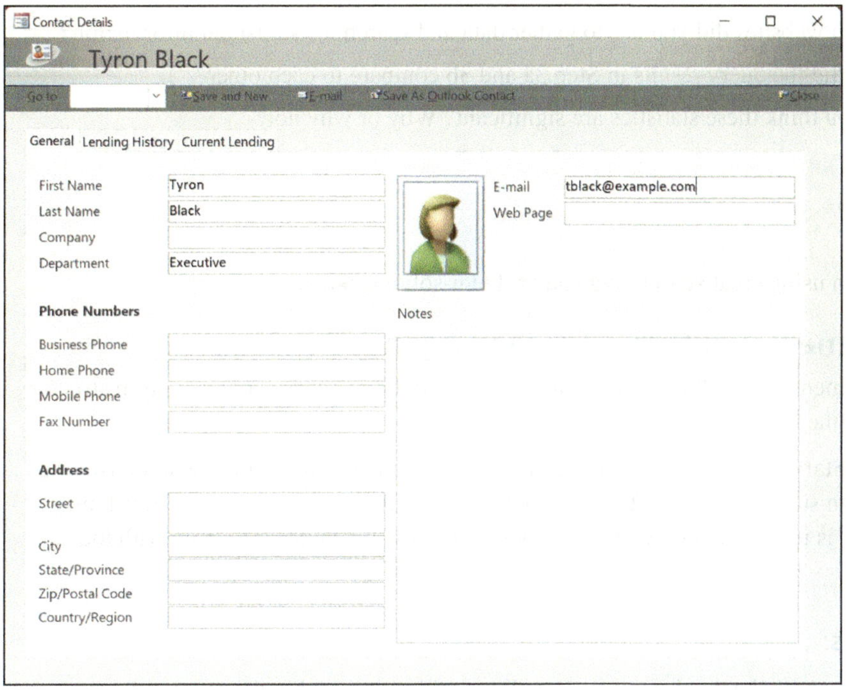

Figure 2–91

6. Open the All Assets report and delete the date and time from the upper-right corner of the report.
7. Export the report as a Word file named All Assets List and save the export steps.
8. Submit the database and the exported RTF file in the format specified by your instructor.
9. **Consider This:** How would you alter the query in Step 4 so it shows assets that are *not* in the Multimedia category?

Expand Your World

Create a solution, which uses cloud and web technologies, by learning and investigating on your own from general guidance.

Instructions: Start Access. You are taking a sociology course and the instructor would like you to gather some statistics and query the statistics on the rates of volunteer hours donated by various groups of people.

Continued on next page

Perform the following tasks:

1. Examine a website that contains research data on yearly volunteer rates in the United States for the past five years (or five recent, consecutive years), including number of people volunteering, number of hours donated, and percentage numbers by state and by age group.
2. Create a database with the file name, SC_AC_02_Volunteers. Include one table that contains the following fields, and enter five records, one for each of the previous five years (or five recent consecutive years): volunteer rate (percentage) for your state, volunteer rate for your age group, number of people in the United States who have volunteered, and average number of hours donated per person.
3. Create queries that do the following:
   a. Return the largest volunteer rate for your state.
   b. Return the largest volunteer rate for your age group.
   c. Calculate the difference between the largest volunteer rate in your state and the lowest volunteer rate in your state over the past five years.
4. Submit the database in the format specified by your instructor.
5. Use an Internet search engine to find three volunteer opportunities in your community.
6. a. **Consider This:** Which websites did you use to gather data and search for statistical information?
   b. **Consider This:** How did the query results in Step 3a and 3b compare to each other?
   c. **Consider This:** Do you think these statistics are significant? Why or why not?

In the Lab

Design and implement a solution using creative thinking and problem-solving skills.

Lab: Querying the Homegrown Nurse Staffing Agency Database

Note: To complete this assignment, you will be required to use the Data Files. Please contact your instructor for information about accessing the Data Files.

Problem: Homegrown Nurse Staffing Agency was founded by a team of three travel nurses who transitioned to building and running their own staffing agency. They've recently started using Access to track travel nurses and their assignments. Your task is to experiment with some queries to show the tables are set up with the needed information.

Perform the following tasks:

Part 1: Open the SC_AC_02-4.accdb database from the Data Files folder, and enable the content. Save the file with the name SC_AC_02_Travel-Nurses, and enable the content. Use the concepts and techniques presented in this module to create queries for the following.

a) Create a new query called Assignments - Facilities Query that joins the Assignments and Facilities tables and shows travelers assigned to each facility. In the query, include Assignment ID and Facility ID from the Assignments table, Facility Name and Facility Type from the Facilities table, and then Traveler ID from the Assignments table. Sort in Ascending order by Facility ID.

b) Create a new query that finds the Traveler ID, Name, License, and Availability for travelers with an SD license only. Name the query SD Travelers Query.

c) Create a new query that finds all apartment-style housing. Include the Housing ID and Location ID fields without showing the Housing Type in the query results, and name the query Apartments Query.

d) Find all assignments that include housing reimbursement. Include the Assignment ID, Facility ID, Traveler ID, and Reimbursements fields. The result should appear as shown in Figure 2–92. Name the query Assignments with Housing Query.

Assignments with Housing Query

A_ID	Facility	Traveler	Reimbursements
A-001	F-001	T-001	Housing, update license
A-002	F-005	T-002	Housing, travel
A-005	F-004	T-007	Housing
A-006	F-003	T-005	Housing+meals
A-007	F-002	T-010	Housing+meals, travel
A-010	F-004	T-013	Housing+meals, travel
A-011	F-006		Housing

Figure 2-92

Submit your database in the format specified by your instructor.

Part 2: Consider This: You made several decisions while creating the queries in this assignment. What was the rationale behind your decisions? How would you modify the query in Part 1.d to include assignments with travel reimbursement? How would you further modify the query to sort the query results by highest bill rates without showing bill rate information in the results?

Maintaining a Database

Objectives

After completing this module, you will be able to:

- Create a split form
- Add records using a form
- Search for a record
- Delete a record
- Filter records in a table
- Add a lookup, multivalued, or calculated field to a table
- Use an action query to add, change, or delete records
- Specify validation rules, default values, and formats
- Use a lookup field
- Include a Total row in a datasheet
- Format a datasheet
- Include a multivalued field in query results
- Create a relationship between tables
- Use a subdatasheet
- Explain how to handle data inconsistency

Introduction

Once you have created a database and loaded it with data, you must maintain it. **Database maintenance** means modifying the data to keep it up to date by adding new records, changing the data for existing records, and deleting records. Updating can include mass updates or mass deletions (i.e., updates to, or deletions of, many records at the same time).

Database maintenance can also involve the need to **restructure** the database periodically. Restructuring can include adding new fields to a table, changing the characteristics of existing fields, and removing existing fields. Restructuring also includes the creation of validation rules and referential integrity. Validation rules ensure the validity of the data in the database, whereas referential integrity ensures the validity of the relationships between entities. Maintaining a database can also include filtering records. This process ensures only the records that satisfy some criterion appear when viewing and updating the data in a table. Changing the appearance of a datasheet is also a maintenance activity.

BTW
Organizing Files and Folders
You should organize and store files in folders so that you easily can find the files later. For example, if you are taking an introductory computer class called CIS 101, a good practice would be to save all Access files in an Access folder in a CIS 101 folder.

Project: Maintaining a Database

Clearnet Logistics faces the task of keeping its database up to date. As the company takes on new shippers and carriers, it will need to add new records, make changes to existing records, and delete records. Clearnet is also planning to hire a third shipping agent, and the owners believe they can track loads and payments better by changing the structure of the database to categorize the loads according to which agent arranges each load. The company will do this first by adding an Agent field to the Loads table. Further, Clearnet would like to adjust its database to handle multiple pickup or dropoff locations for a single load. Because loads might involve more than one pickup or dropoff location, the pickup and dropoff fields will each be a multivalued field, which is a field that can store multiple values or entries. Along with these changes, Clearnet wants to change the appearance of a datasheet when displaying data.

Clearnet also would like the ability to make mass updates, that is, to update or delete many records in a single operation. It wants rules that limit users to entering only valid, or appropriate, data into the database. Clearnet also wants to ensure that the database cannot contain a load that is not associated with a specific shipper.

Figure 3–1 summarizes some of the various types of activities involved in maintaining the Clearnet database.

Figure 3–1

BTW
The Ribbon and Screen Resolution
Access may change how the groups and buttons within the groups appear on the ribbon, depending on the computer or mobile device's screen resolution. Thus, your ribbon may look different from the ones in this course if you are using a screen resolution other than 1920 x 1080.

Updating Records

Keeping the data in a database current requires updating records in three ways: adding new records, changing the data in existing records, and deleting existing records. You can add records to a database using Datasheet view, and as you add records, the records appear on the screen in a datasheet. The data looks like a table. When you need to add additional records, you can use the same techniques.

You can use a simple form to view records. You can also use a **split form**, which is a form that allows you to simultaneously view both the simple form and Datasheet views of the data. You can use either portion of a split form to add or update records. To add new records, change existing records, or delete records, you use the same techniques you used in Datasheet view.

To Save the Clearnet Database with a New File Name and Create a Split Form

The following steps create a split form. **Why?** With a split form, you have the advantage of seeing a single record in a form while simultaneously viewing several records in a datasheet.

1

- sam Start Access. Open the database, SC_AC_03-1.accdb, which is located in the Data Files folder. Save the file on your hard disk, OneDrive, or other storage location using the file name, **SC_AC_03_Clearnet**. Enable the content.
- Open the Navigation Pane if it is currently closed.
- If necessary, click the Loads table in the Navigation Pane to select it.

- Click Create on the ribbon to display the Create tab.
- Click the More Forms button (Create tab | Forms group) to display the More Forms menu (Figure 3–2).

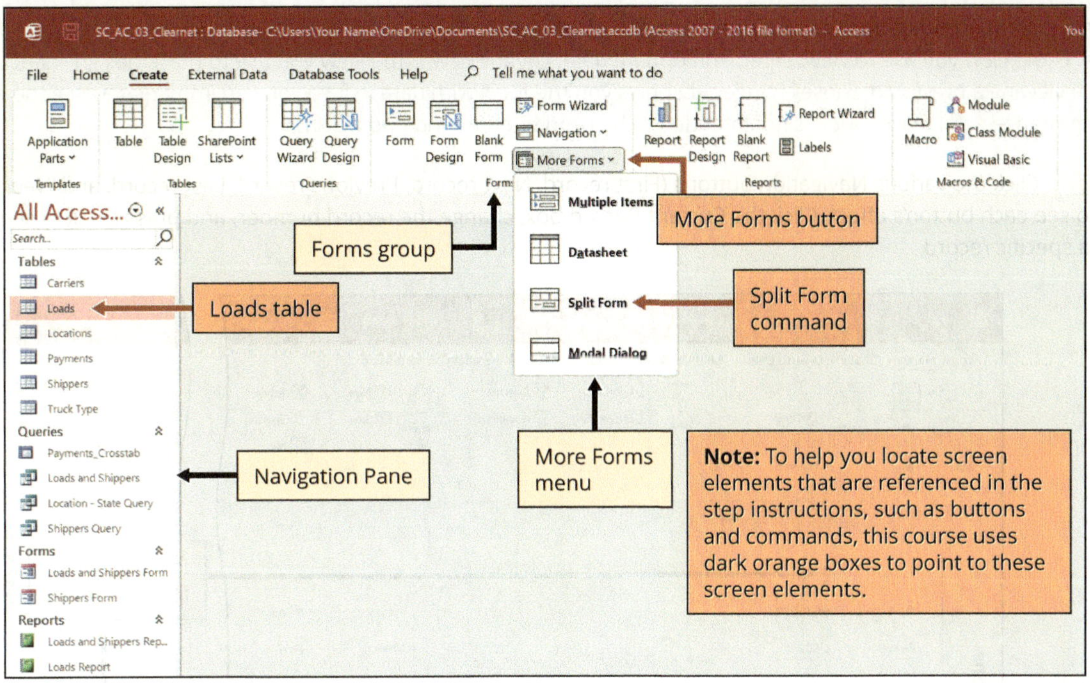

Figure 3–2

2

- Click Split Form to create a split form based on the Loads table.
- Close the Navigation Pane (Figure 3–3).

Q&A Is the form automatically saved?

No. You will take specific actions later to save the form.

A field list pane appeared when I created the form. What should I do?

Click the 'Add Existing Fields' button (Form Layout Design tab | Tools group) to close the field list.

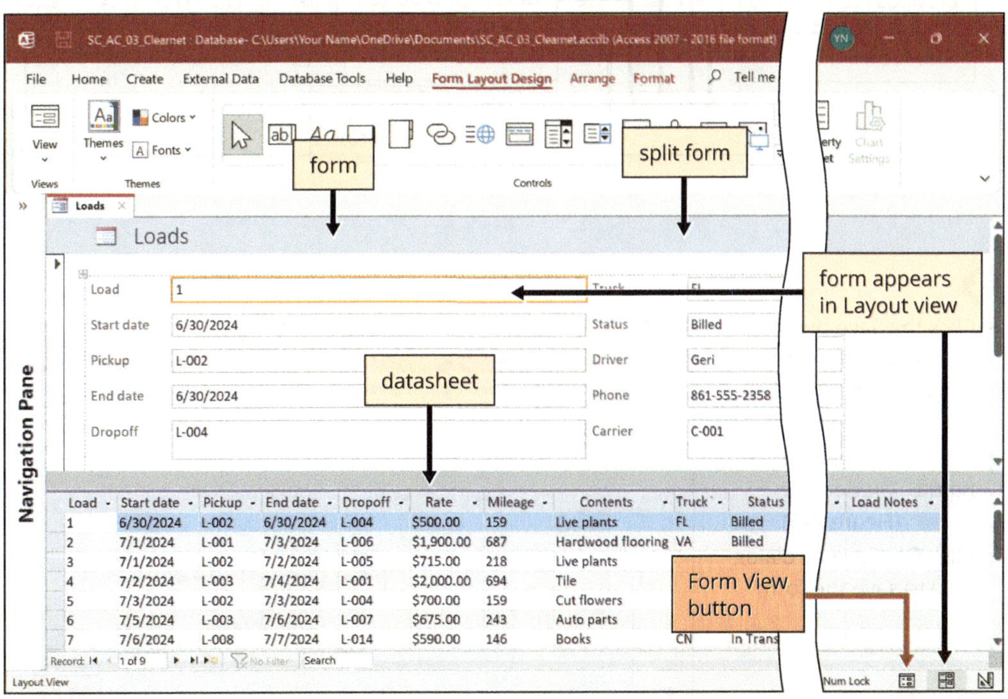

Figure 3–3

3

- Click the Form View button on the Access status bar to display the form in Form view rather than Layout view (Figure 3–4).

Q&A What is the difference between Form view and Layout view?
Form view is the view you use to view, enter, and update data. Layout view is the view you use to make design changes to the form while viewing a preview of those changes. It shows you the form with data in it so you can immediately see the effects of any design changes you make, but it is not intended to be used to enter and update data.

- **Experiment:** Click the various Navigation buttons (First record, Next record, Previous record, Last record, and 'New (blank) record') to see each button's effect. Click the Current Record box, change the record number, and press ENTER to see how to move to a specific record.

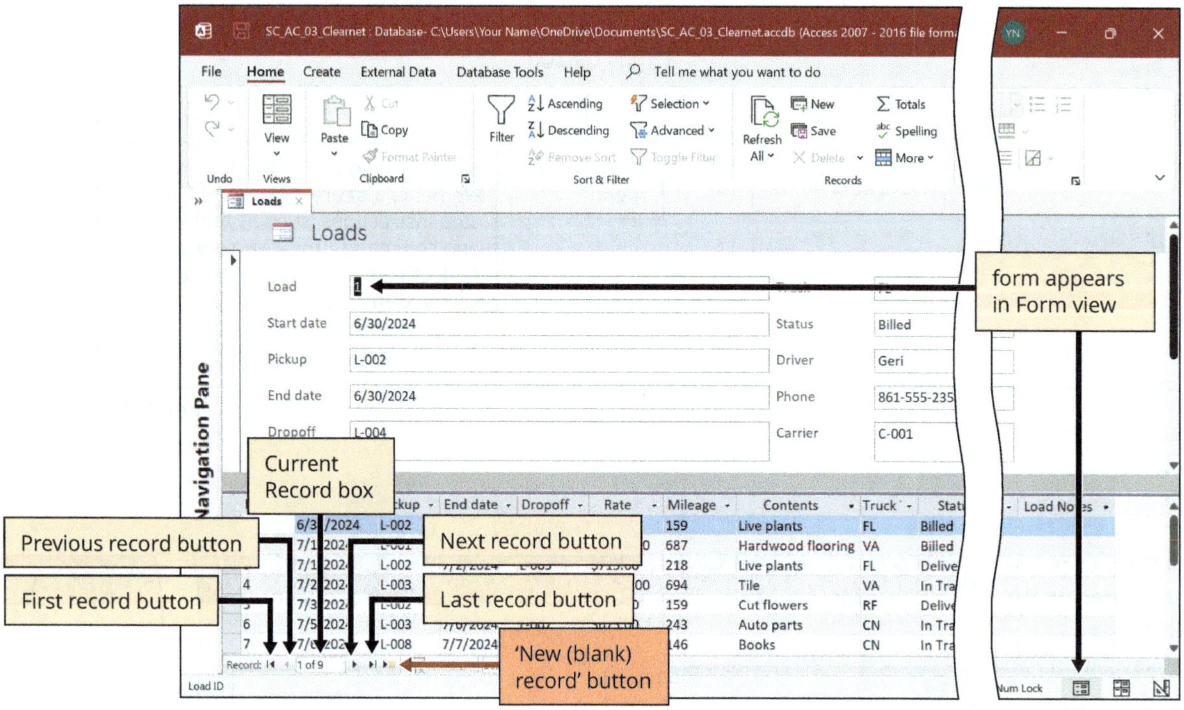

Figure 3–4

4

- Click the Save button on the Quick Access Toolbar to display the Save As dialog box.
- Save the form with the name **Loads Split Form** (Figure 3–5).
- Click OK (Save As dialog box) to save the form.

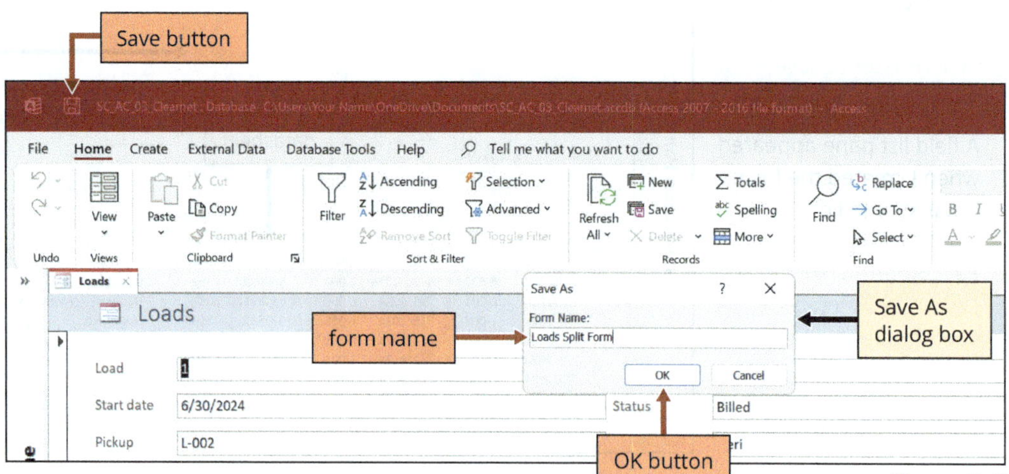

Figure 3–5

Other Ways

1. Right-click form's tab, click Form View on shortcut menu to change view

To Use a Form to Add Records

Once a form or split form is open in Form view, you can add records using the same techniques you used to add records in Datasheet view. In a split form, the changes you make on the form are automatically made on the datasheet. You do not need to take any special action. The following steps use the split form that you just created to add records. **Why?** With a split form, as you add a record, you can immediately see the effect of the addition on the datasheet.

1

- Click the 'New (blank) record' button on the Navigation bar to enter a new record, and then type the data for the new record, as shown in Figure 3-6, keeping in mind that the ID field is an autonumber and will appear automatically when typing in a new record. Press TAB after typing the data in each field. Note that pressing tab after typing the data for the final field (Load Notes) will complete the entry of the record.
- Click the Save button on the Quick Access Toolbar to save the form.
- Close the form.

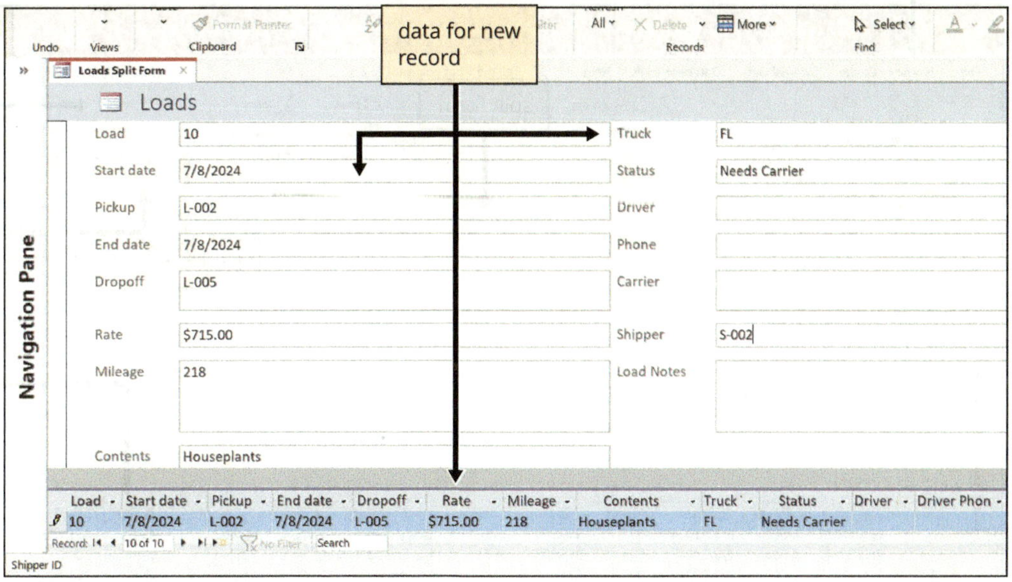

Figure 3-6

Other Ways

1. Click New button (Home tab | Records group) to create new record
2. Press CTRL+PLUS SIGN (+) to create new record

To Search for a Record

In a database environment, **searching** means looking for records that satisfy some criterion. Looking for a load driven by Roman is an example of searching. Running a query is another way of searching. In a query, Access must locate those records that satisfy one or more criteria.

You can perform a search in Form view or Datasheet view without creating a query. The following steps search for Roman's loads. **Why?** You want to locate the record quickly so you can update this load's status.

1

- Open the Navigation Pane.
- Right-click Loads Split Form to display a shortcut menu, and then click Open on the shortcut menu to open the form in Form view.
- Click the Driver field in the datasheet portion of the split form.

Q&A I see both Layout view and Design view in the shortcut menu, but no option for Form view. Which command gives me Form view?

The Open command opens the form in Form view.

- Close the Navigation Pane (Figure 3–7).

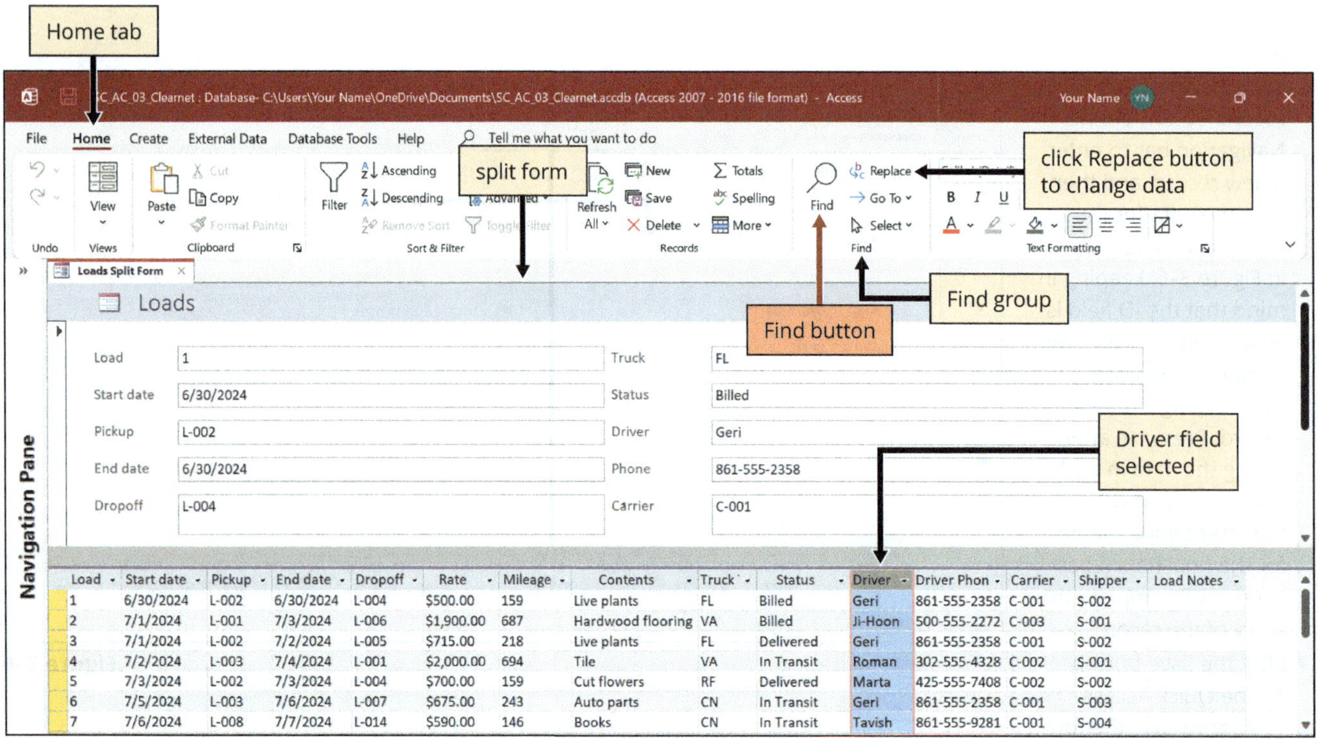

Figure 3–7

2

- Click the Find button (Home tab | Find group) to display the Find and Replace dialog box.
- Type **Roman** in the Find What text box (Find and Replace dialog box), and then click the Find Next button to find Roman's in-transit load and display the record in the form (Figure 3–8).

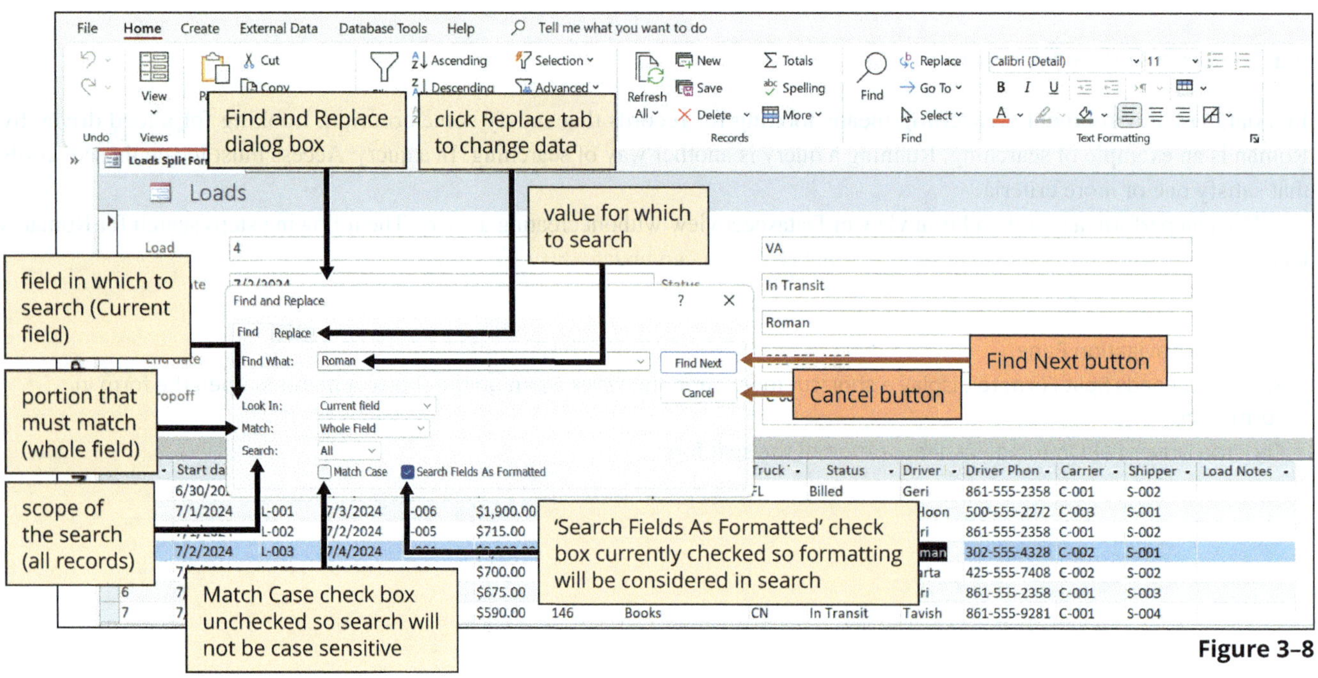

Figure 3–8

Q&A My search didn't find any records. How can I fix this?

By default, the search parameters are configured to only look in the current field, not all fields. Make sure you select the Driver field in either portion of the split form before doing the search. Also confirm your search term is typed correctly.

Why does the button in the dialog box read Find Next, rather than simply Find?

In some cases, after locating a record that satisfies a criterion, you might need to find the next record that satisfies the same criterion. For example, you might want to find the next load that is scheduled after the driver's current load is delivered; or, if the first load was already delivered, you might then want to find that driver's load that is still in transit. To do so, click the Find Next button. You will not need to retype the value each time.

3

- Click Cancel (Find and Replace dialog box) to remove the dialog box from the screen.

Q&A Can I find records using this method in both Datasheet view and Form view?

Yes. You use the same process to find (and replace) records whether you are viewing the data with a split form, in Datasheet view, or in Form view.

Other Ways

1. Press CTRL+F to search for text

Consider This

Can you replace one value with another using the Find and Replace dialog box?

Yes. Either click the Replace button (Home tab | Find group) or click the Replace tab in the Find and Replace dialog box. You then can enter both the value to find and the new value.

To Update the Contents of a Record

The following step uses Form view to change a load's status. **Why?** Roman has successfully delivered his load. After locating the record to be changed, select the field to be changed by clicking the field. You can also press TAB repeatedly until the desired field is selected. Then make the appropriate changes. (Clicking the field automatically produces an insertion point. If you use TAB, you will need to press F2 to produce an insertion point.)

1

- Click in the Status field in the form portion of the split form for Load 4 immediately to the right of the In Transit text.
- Backspace and replace In Transit with **Delivered**.
- Press TAB to complete the change and move to the next field (Figure 3–9).

Q&A Could I have changed the contents of the field in the datasheet portion of the split form?

Yes. You first need to ensure the record to be changed appears in the datasheet. You then can change the value just as in the form.

Do I need to save my change?

No. Once you move to another record or close this form, the change to the name is saved automatically.

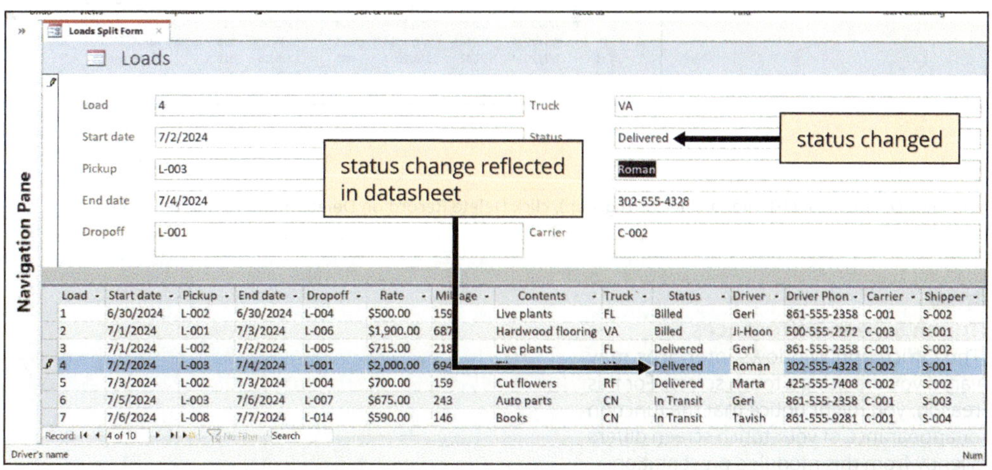

Figure 3–9

To Delete a Record

When records are no longer needed, you should delete them (remove them) from the table. The following steps delete Load 8, which was to deliver raw milk to a food processing factory. **Why?** The farm's refrigeration unit for this load failed, ruining the milk, so the record can be deleted.

1

- With the Loads Split Form still open, click the record selector in the datasheet portion of the form for Load 8, coming from pickup location L-011 on 7/7/2024 to select the record (Figure 3–10).

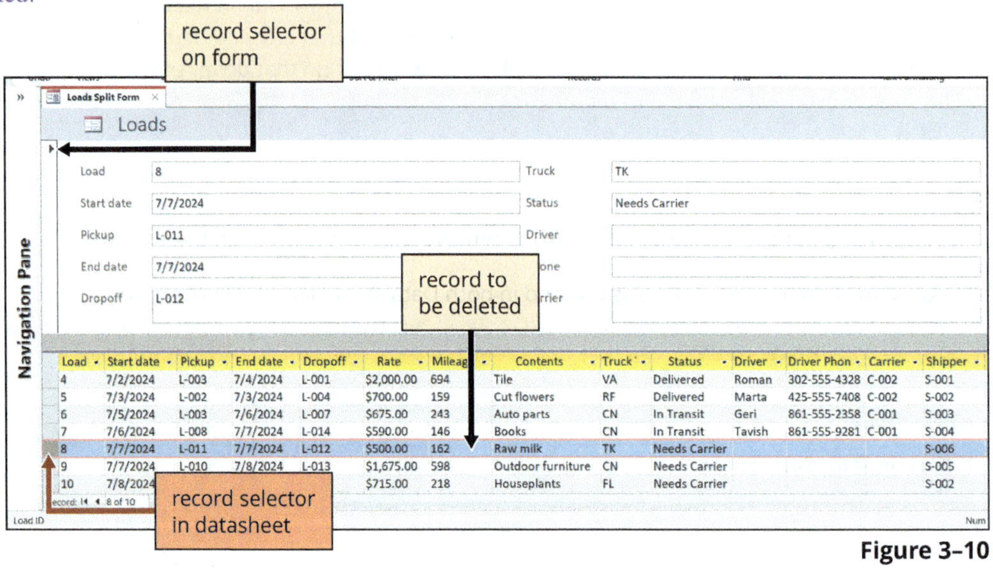

Figure 3–10

Q&A This technique works in the datasheet portion. How do I select the record in the form portion?
With the desired record appearing in the form, click the record selector (the triangle in front of the record) to select the entire record.

What do I do if the record I want to delete does not appear on the screen?
First search for the record you want to delete using the Find and Replace dialog box.

2

- Press DEL to delete the record (Figure 3–11).

3

- Click Yes to complete the deletion.
- Save and close the Loads Split Form.

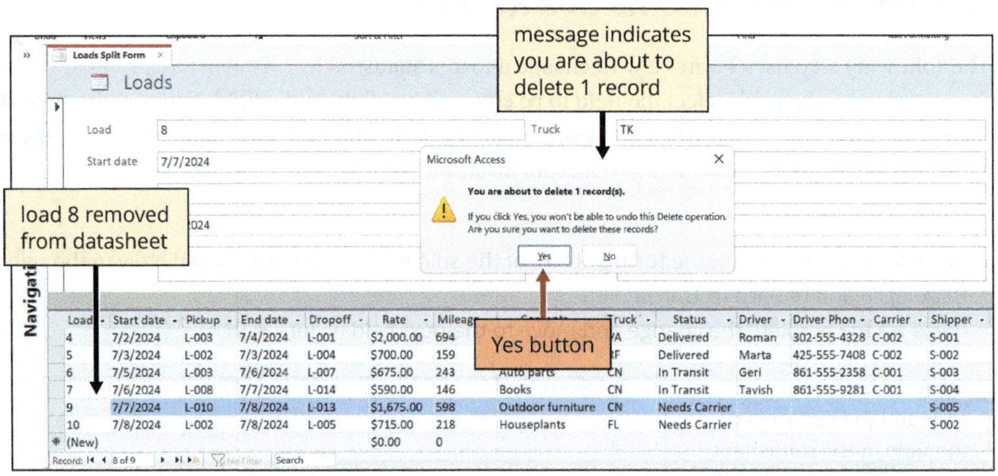

Figure 3–11

Other Ways

1. Click Delete arrow (Home tab | Records group), click Delete Record on Delete menu to delete record

BTW
Touch Screen Differences
The Office and Windows interfaces may vary if you are using a touch screen. For this reason, you might notice that the function or appearance of your touch screen differs slightly from this module's presentation.

Filtering Records

You can use the Find button in either Datasheet view or Form view to locate a record quickly that satisfies some criterion (for example, the ID 2). However, using these approaches show all records, not just the record or records that satisfy the criterion. To have only the record or records that satisfy the criterion appear, use a **filter**. Four types of filters are available: Filter By Selection, Common Filters, Filter By Form, and Advanced Filter/Sort. You can use a filter in either Datasheet view or Form view.

BTW
Using the Find Button
You can use the Find button (Home tab | Find group) to search for records in datasheets, forms, query results, and reports.

To Use Filter By Selection

To use Filter By Selection, you give Access an example of the data you want by selecting the data within the table. You then choose the option you want on the Selection menu. The following steps use Filter By Selection in Datasheet view to display only the records for loads in transit. *Why? Filter By Selection is appropriate for displaying these records and is the simplest type of filter.*

1

- Open the Navigation Pane.
- Open the Loads table in Datasheet view, and then close the Navigation Pane.
- Click the Status field on Load 6 (the sixth record) to specify In Transit as the desired status for the filter (Figure 3–12).

Q&A Could I have selected the Status field on another record where the status is also In Transit to select the same status?
Yes. It does not matter which record you select, as long as the status is In Transit.

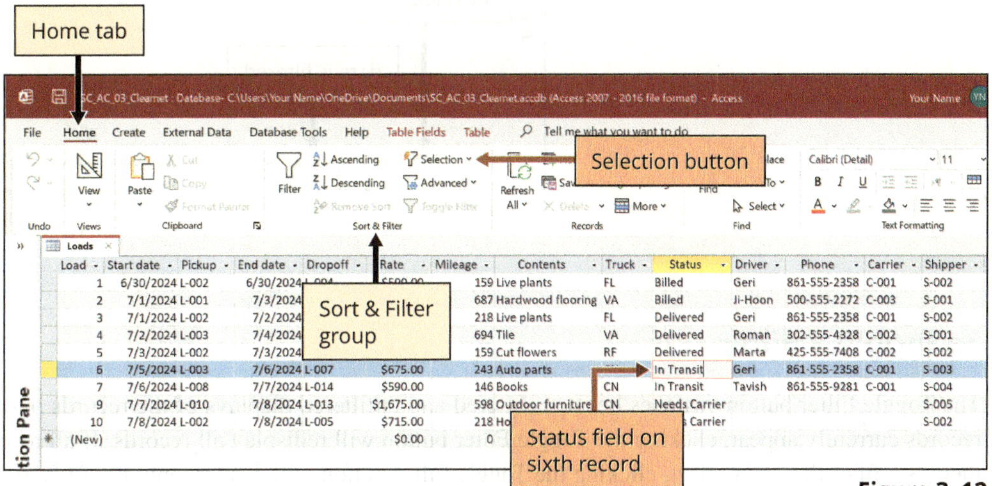

Figure 3–12

2

- Click the Selection button (Home tab | Sort & Filter group) to display the Selection menu (Figure 3–13).

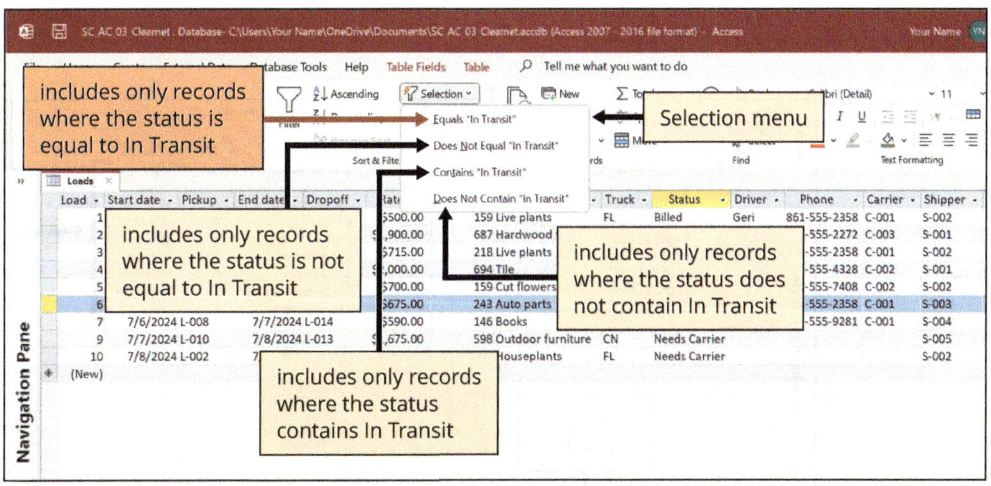

Figure 3–13

3

- Click 'Equals "In Transit"' to select only those loads whose status is In Transit (Figure 3–14).

Q&A Can I also filter in Form view?

Yes. Filtering works the same whether you are viewing the data with a split form, in Datasheet view, or in Form view.

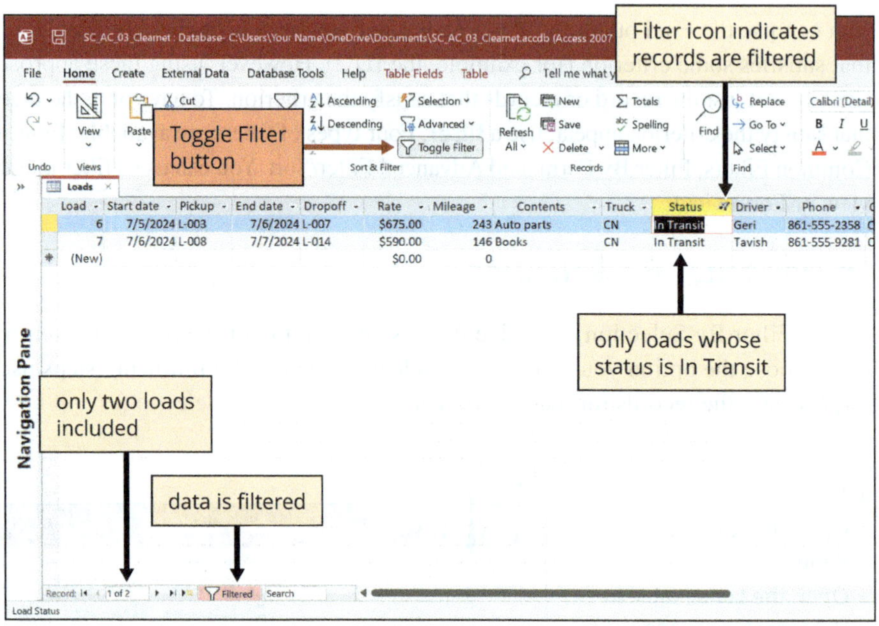

Figure 3–14

To Toggle a Filter

The Toggle Filter button switches between filtered and unfiltered displays of the records in the table. That is, if only filtered records currently appear, clicking the Toggle Filter button will redisplay all records. If all records are currently displayed and there is a filter that is in effect, clicking the Toggle Filter button will display only the filtered records. If no filter is active, the Toggle Filter button will be dimmed, so clicking it would have no effect.

The following step toggles the filter. **Why?** Clearnet wants to once again view all the records.

1

- Click the Toggle Filter button (Home tab | Sort & Filter group) to toggle the filter and redisplay all records (Figure 3–15).

Q&A Does this action clear the filter?

No. The filter is still in place. If you click the Toggle Filter button a second time, you will again see only the filtered records using the previously configured filter.

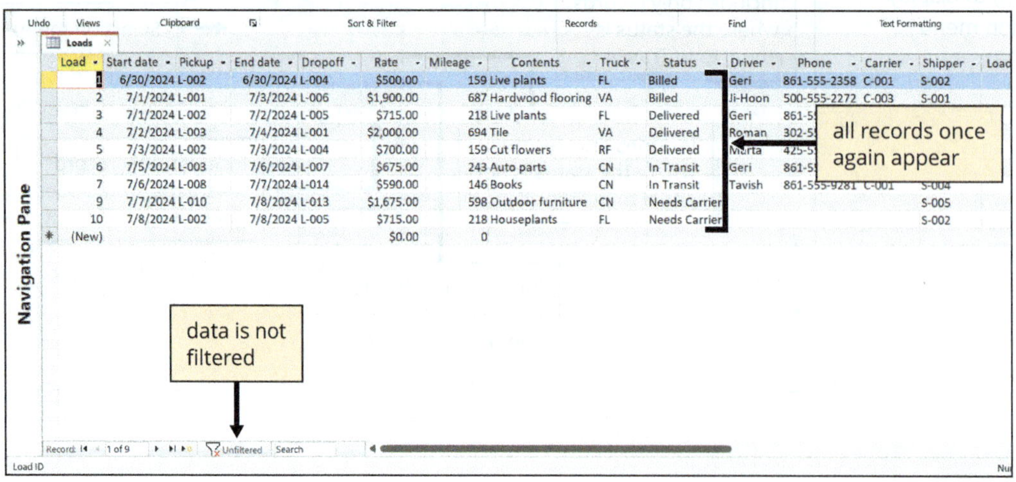

Figure 3–15

To Clear a Filter

Once you have finished using a filter, you can clear (remove) the filter. After doing so, you no longer will be able to use the filter by clicking the Toggle Filter button. The following steps clear the filter.

BTW
Access Screen Resolution
If you are using a computer or mobile device to step through the project in this module and you want your screens to match the figures in this course, you should change your screen's resolution to 1920 x 1080.

1. Click the Advanced button (Home tab | Sort & Filter group) to display the Advanced menu (Figure 3–16).

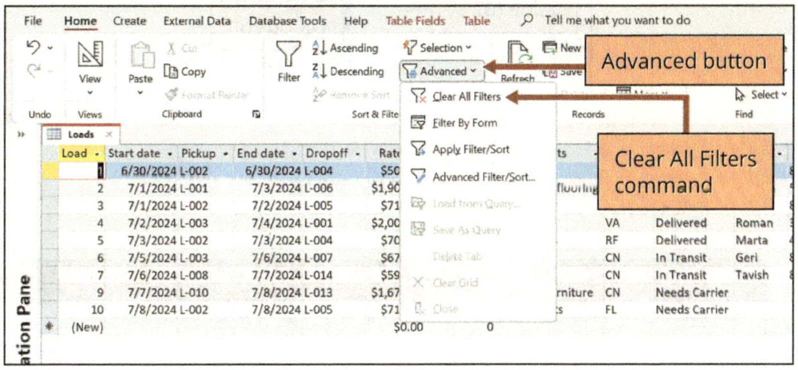

Figure 3–16

2. Click Clear All Filters on the Advanced menu. Leave the Loads table open for now.

To Use a Common Filter

Suppose you have determined you want to look at locations whose city begins with the letter B. In this case, Filter By Selection would not be appropriate. None of the options within Filter By Selection would support this type of criterion. You can filter individual fields by clicking the arrow to the right of the field name and using one of the **common filters** that are available for the field. **Why?** Access includes a collection of filters that perform common filtering tasks; you can modify a common filter by customizing it for the specific field. The following steps customize a common filter to include only those locations whose city begins with B.

1.
- Open the Navigation Pane.
- Open the Locations table in Datasheet view, and then close the Navigation Pane.
- Click the City arrow to display the common filter menu.
- Point to the Text Filters command to display the custom text filters (Figure 3–17).

Q&A If I wanted certain cities included, could I use the check boxes?
Yes. Be sure the cities you want are the only ones checked.

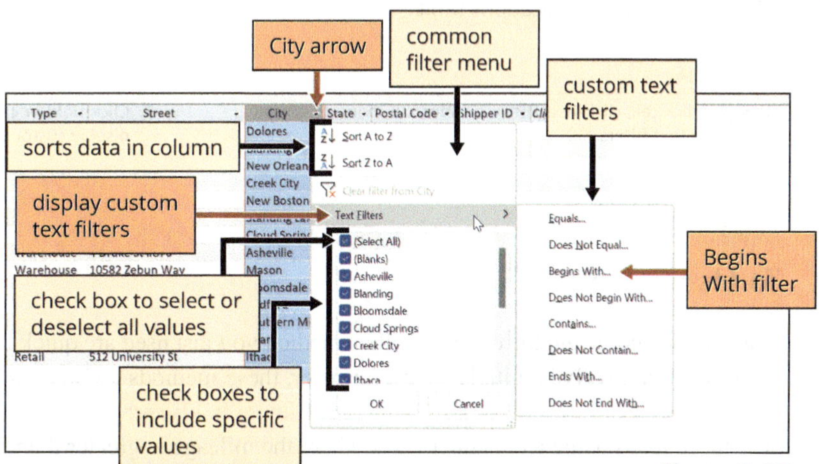

Figure 3–17

2

- Click Begins With to display the Custom Filter dialog box.
- Type **B** as the City begins with value (Figure 3–18).

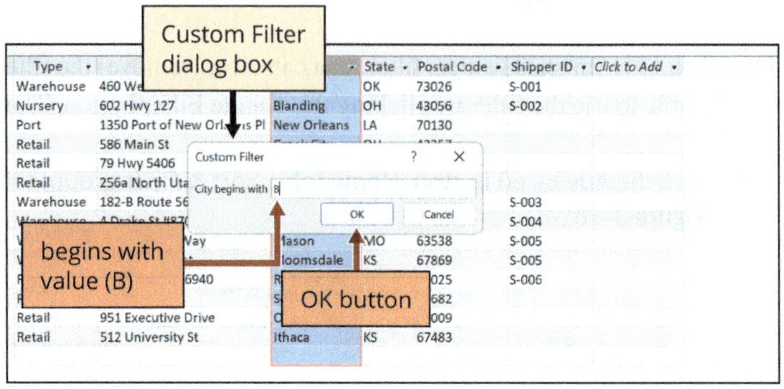

Figure 3–18

3

- Click the OK button to filter the records (Figure 3–19).
- **Experiment:** Try other options in the common filter menu to see their effects. When done, once again select those accounts whose city begins with B.

Q&A Can I use the same technique in Form view?
In Form view, you would need to click the field and then click the Filter button to display the Common Filter menu. The rest of the process is the same.

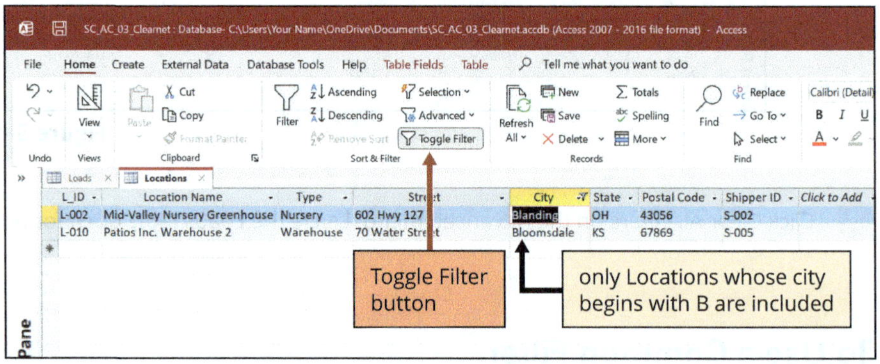

Figure 3–19

4

- Click the Toggle Filter button (Home tab | Sort & Filter group) to toggle the filter and redisplay all records.
- Save and close the Locations table.

Other Ways

1. Right-click cell, click Text Filters on shortcut menu to display custom text filters
2. Click field or cell, click Filter button (Home tab | Sort & Filter group) to display custom text filters

To Use Filter By Form

Filter By Selection and the common filters method you just used are quick and easy ways to filter by the value in a single field. For filters that involve multiple fields, however, these methods are not appropriate, so you would use Filter By Form. **Why?** Filter By Form allows you to filter based on multiple fields and criteria. For example, Filter By Form would allow you to find only those loads using a container truck where the mileage is greater than 500 miles. The following steps use Filter By Form to restrict the records that appear.

1

- With the Loads table tab active, click the Advanced button (Home tab | Sort & Filter group) to display the Advanced menu (Figure 3–20).

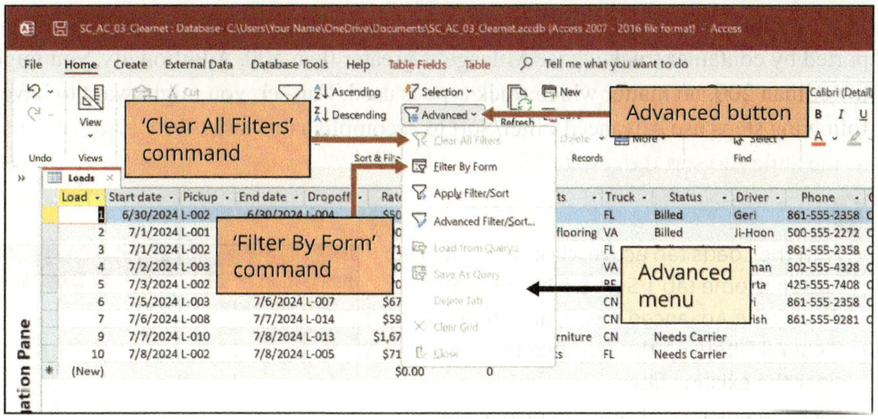

Figure 3–20

2

- If necessary, clear the existing filter by clicking Clear All Filters on the Advanced menu. Then click the Advanced button again to display the Advanced menu a second time.
- Click Filter By Form on the Advanced menu.
- Click the blank row below the Mileage field, and then type **>500** to display loads with a mileage more than 500 miles.
- Click the blank row in the Truck field, click the arrow that appears, and then choose 'CN' from the menu to enter a criterion for the Truck field (Figure 3–21).

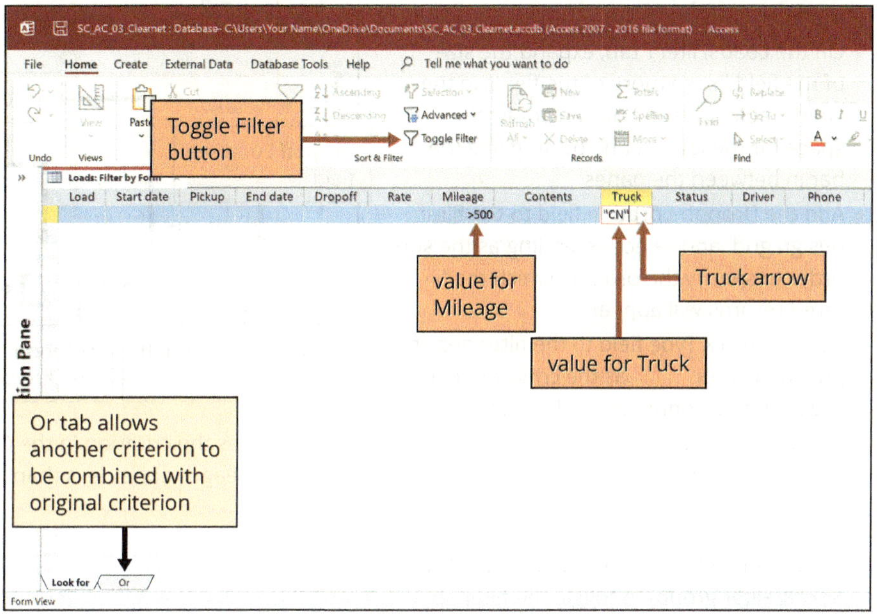

Figure 3–21

Q&A Could I have clicked the arrow in the Mileage field and then made a selection, rather than typing a criterion?

No. Because your criterion involves something other than equality, you need to type the criterion rather than selecting from a list.

Is there any difference in the process if I am viewing a table in Form view rather than in Datasheet view?

In Form view, you will make your entries in a form rather than a datasheet. Otherwise, the process is the same.

3

- Click the Toggle Filter button (Home tab | Sort & Filter group) to apply the filter (Figure 3–22).
- **Experiment:** Select Filter By Form again and enter different criteria. In each case, toggle the filter to see the effect of your selection. When done, once again select those loads whose truck type is CN and whose mileage is >500.

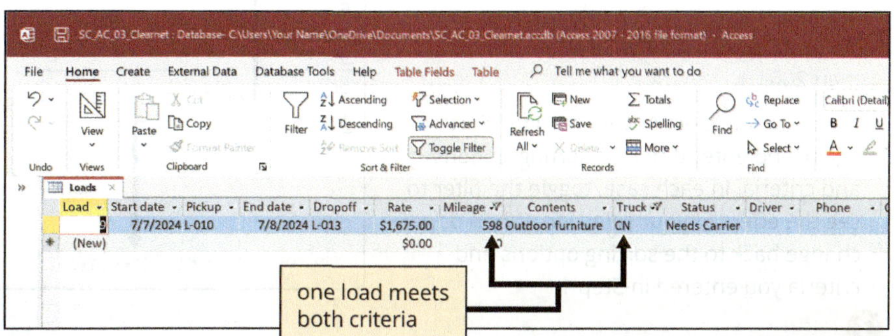

Figure 3–22

Other Ways

1. Click the Advanced button (Home tab | Sort & Filter group), click Apply Filter/Sort on Advanced menu to see filter results

To Use Advanced Filter/Sort

In some cases, your criteria will be too complex even for Filter By Form. You might decide you want to include any load transported by container truck whose Mileage is greater than 500. Additionally, you might want to include any load with a mileage lower than 200, no matter which truck type is used. Further, you might want to have the results sorted by dropoff location. The following steps use Advanced Filter/Sort to accomplish this task. **Why?** Advanced Filter/Sort supports complex criteria as well as the ability to sort the results.

1

- With the Loads tab active, click the Advanced button (Home tab | Sort & Filter group) to display the Advanced menu, and then click Clear All Filters on the Advanced menu to clear the existing filter.
- Click the Advanced button to display the Advanced menu a second time.
- Click Advanced Filter/Sort on the Advanced menu.
- On the LoadsFilter1 tab, expand the size of the field list so more of the fields in the Loads table appear. You can adjust the space for the lower pane by dragging the bar in between the panes.
- Add the Dropoff Location field to the filter design grid, and select Ascending as the sort order to specify the order in which the filtered records will appear.
- Add the Truck Type field to the filter design grid, and enter **CN** as the criterion to limit the search to container truck types.

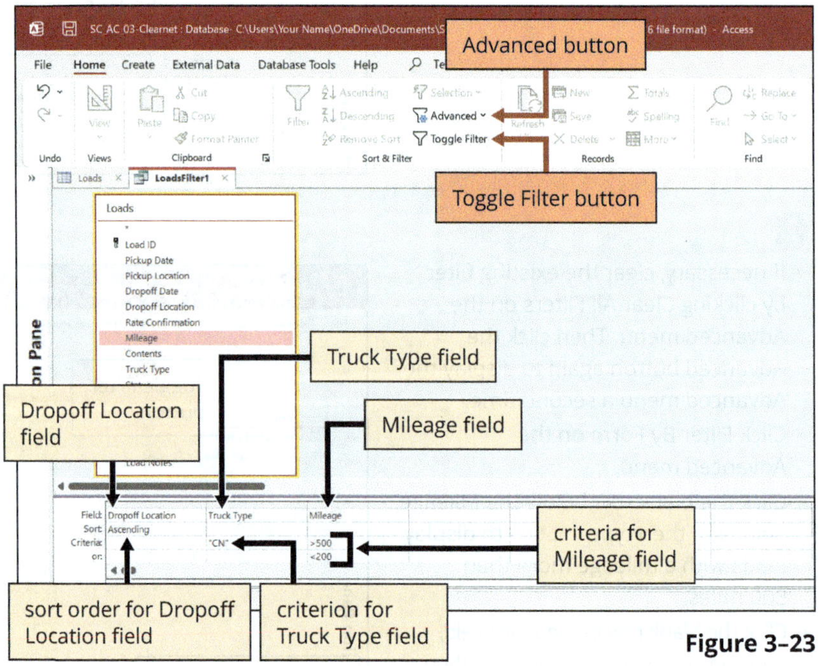

Figure 3–23

- Add the Mileage field to the filter design grid. Enter **>500** as the criterion in the Criteria row and **<200** as the criterion in the or row (Figure 3–23) to limit the search to loads with mileages either less than 200 or greater than 500.

2

- Click the Toggle Filter button (Home tab | Sort & Filter group) to toggle the filter so that only records that satisfy the criteria will appear (Figure 3–24).

Q&A Why are these particular records included in the filter results?

Record 9 is included because the Truck Type is CN for container *and* the mileage is greater than 500. The other records are included because their mileages are less than 200.

- **Experiment:** Select Advanced Filter/Sort again, and enter different sorting options and criteria. In each case, toggle the filter to see the effect of your selection. When done, change back to the sorting options and criteria you entered in Step 1.

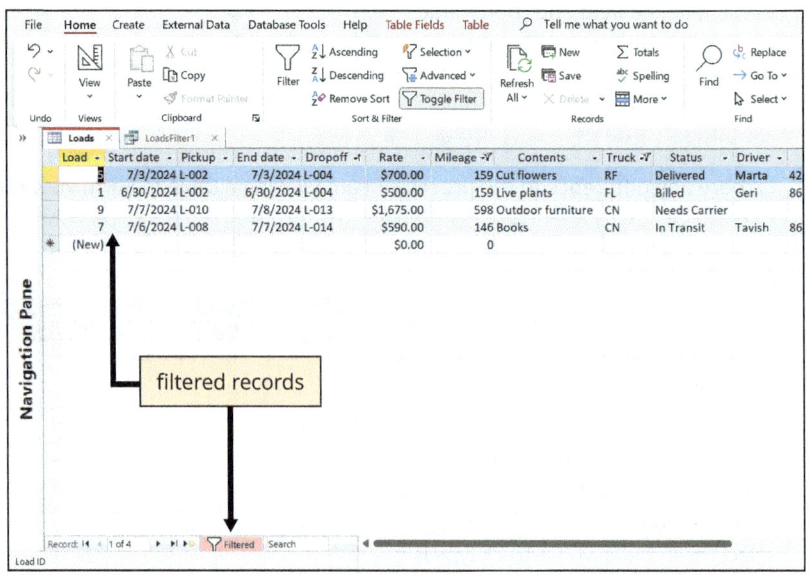

Figure 3–24

3

- Close the Loads table. When asked if you want to save your changes, click the No button.

Q&A Shouldn't I have cleared all filters before closing the table?

If you are closing a table and not saving the changes, it is not necessary to clear the filter. No filter will be active when you next open the table.

Filters and Queries

Now that you are familiar with how filters work, you might notice similarities between filters and queries. Both objects are used to locate data that meets specific criteria. Filters and queries are related in three ways.

1. You can apply a filter to the results of a query just as you can apply a filter to a table.
2. Once you create a filter using Advanced Filter/Sort, you can save the filter settings as a query by using the Save as Query command on the Advanced menu.
3. You can restore filter settings that you previously saved in a query by using the Load from Query command on the Advanced menu.

BTW
Using Wildcards in Filters
Both the question mark (?) and the asterisk (*) wildcards can be used in filters created using Advanced Filter/Sort.

Consider This

How do you determine whether to use a query or a filter?

The following guidelines apply to this decision.

- If you think that you will frequently want to display records that satisfy this exact criterion, you should consider creating a query whose results contain only the records that satisfy the criterion. To display those records in the future, simply open the query.
- If you are viewing data in a datasheet or form and decide you want to restrict the records to be included, it is easier to create a filter than a query. You can create and use the filter while you are viewing the data.
- If you have created a filter that you would like to be able to use again, you can save the filter as a query.

Consider This

Once you have decided to use a filter, how do you determine which type of filter to use?

- If your criterion for filtering is that the value in a particular field matches or does not match a certain specific value, you can use Filter By Selection.
- If your criterion only involves a single field but is more complex (for example, the criterion specifies that the value in the field begins with a certain collection of letters), you can use a common filter.
- If your criterion involves more than one field, use Filter By Form.
- If your criteria involve more than a single And or Or statement, or if your filter involves sorting, you will probably find it simpler to use Advanced Filter/Sort.

Break Point: If you wish to take a break, this is a good place to do so. You can quit Access now. To resume at a later time, start Access, open the database called SC_AC_03_Clearnet.accdb, and continue following the steps from this location forward.

Changing the Database Structure

When you initially create a database, you define its **structure**; that is, you assign names and data types to all the fields. In many cases, the structure you first define will not continue to be appropriate as you use the database.

Perhaps a field currently in the table is no longer necessary. If no one ever uses a particular field, it is not needed in the table. Because it is occupying space and serving no useful purpose, you should remove it from the table. You would also need to delete the field from any forms, reports, or queries that include it.

More commonly, an organization will find that it needs to add data that was not anticipated at the time the database was first designed. The organization's own requirements may have changed. In addition, outside regulations that the organization must satisfy may change as well. Either case requires the addition of fields to an existing table.

Datasheet and Design View

Although you can make some changes to the database structure in Datasheet view, it is usually easier and better to make these changes in Design view. The following steps compare your options within each view for various tasks. You will often think you can complete a structure change in Datasheet view but then find the one change necessitates other changes. And then these other changes can only be made in Design view. Therefore, it's a good idea to develop the habit of using Design view for database structure changes.

BTW
Changing Data Types
It is possible to change the data type for a field that already contains data. Before doing so, you should consider the effect on other database objects, such as forms, queries, and reports. For example, you could convert a Short Text field to a Long Text field if you find that you do not have enough space to store the data that you need. You also could convert a Number field to a Currency field or vice versa.

Note that you cannot change a field's data type to AutoNumber once data has been added anywhere in the table.

To Change a Field's Data Type, Properties, and Primary Key

A field in one of your tables might need a change of its data type and properties; for example, a data type might have been set that prevents users from including the field in calculations. To make a change to the data type and properties of a field, you would use the following steps.

1. Open the table in Design view.
2. Next to the field name, click the box under Data Type.
3. Choose the correct data type from the menu.
4. A description of the field may be added under the Description column.
5. If necessary, change the field size in the Field Properties General tab in the lower pane.
6. To change the key field, select the new key field by clicking in the gray box to the left of the field name. On the ribbon, click Primary Key (Table Design tab | Tools group).
7. When you close the table, you will be prompted to save the changes. Select Yes.

To Change a Field's Properties in Datasheet View

Alternatively, some of these changes may be done in Datasheet view. To use Datasheet view to change a field's name, caption, or data type, you would use the following steps.

1. Open the table in Datasheet view.
2. Select the desired field and click the Table Fields tab.
3. Click Name & Caption (Table Fields tab | Properties group), and set a caption and description for the field.
4. In the Formatting group, you can set a data type.

To Delete a Field in Design View

If a field in one of your tables is no longer needed, you should delete the field. For example, it might not serve a useful purpose, or it might have been included by mistake. To delete a field, you would use the following steps.

1. Open the table in Design view.
2. Click the row selector for the field to be deleted.
3. Press DEL.
4. When Access displays the dialog box requesting confirmation that you want to delete the field, click Yes.

To Delete a Field in Datasheet View

1. In Datasheet view, right-click the field and then click Delete Field.

To Move a Field in Design View

If you decide you would rather have a field in one of your tables in a different position in the table, you can move it. To move a field, you would use the following steps.

1. Open the table in Design view.
2. Click the row selector for the field to be moved.

3. Drag the field to the desired position.
4. Release the mouse button to place the field in the new position.

To Move a Field in Datasheet View

If you are working in Datasheet view and want to move a field, you would use the following steps.

1. In Datasheet view, select the field to be moved.
2. Drag the field to the desired position.
3. Release the mouse button to place the field in the new position.

To Change a Number Field Size in Design View

Most field size changes can be made in either Datasheet view or Design view. However, changing the field size for Number fields, such as the Mileage field, is best done in Design view to access the full list of options. This is because number fields can carry qualitatively different types of data. Consider that the values in the Mileage field do not need any decimal places and will never exceed a few thousand miles for loads in North America. Integer, Long Integer, or Single field sizes could all meet these requirements. One difference between these options concerns the amount of storage space required. For example, the Integer field size requires 2 bytes of storage space per record per field. Long Integer, in contrast, requires 4 bytes of storage space per entry, as does Single. Double can store up to 15 significant digits but requires 8 bytes of storage space per entry.

Another difference between these field sizes is the degree of accuracy if decimal places are needed, that is, the number of decimal places to which the number is accurate. For example, Double is more accurate than Single by allowing more decimal places (15 significant digits versus 7 significant digits); however, Double requires more storage space.

Because the mileage values in this table are not tracked to any decimal places, Integer is the best choice, providing sufficient digits while minimizing required storage space in the database. The following steps change the field size of the Mileage field to Integer, the format to Fixed, and the number of decimal places to 0, along with extending those changes to any form or report that uses this field. **Why change the format and number of decimal places?** Changing the format and number ensures that each value will appear with no decimal places.

1

- Open the Navigation Pane, open the Loads table in Design view, and then close the Navigation Pane.
- If necessary, click the vertical scroll bar to display the Mileage field, and then click the row selector for the Mileage field to select the field (Figure 3–25).

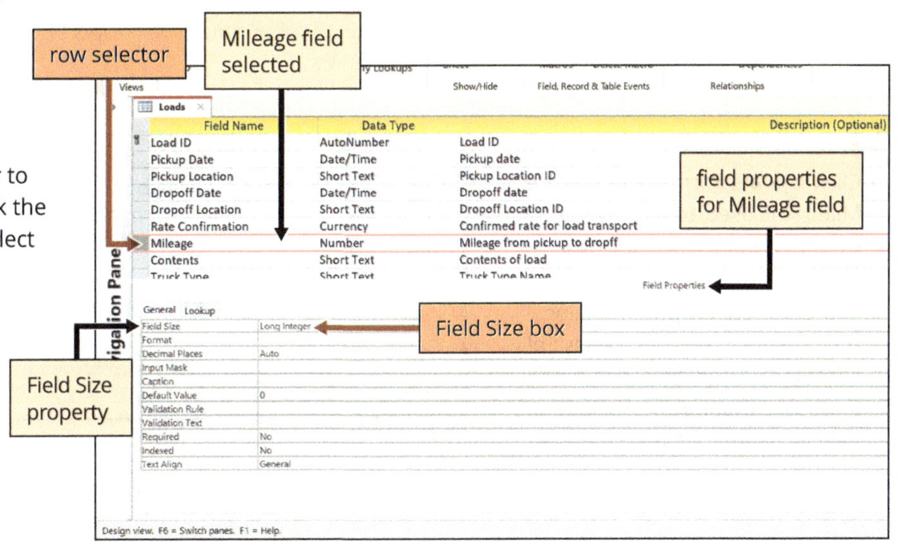

Figure 3–25

2

- Click the Field Size box to display the Field Size arrow.
- Click the Field Size arrow to display the Field Size menu (Figure 3–26).

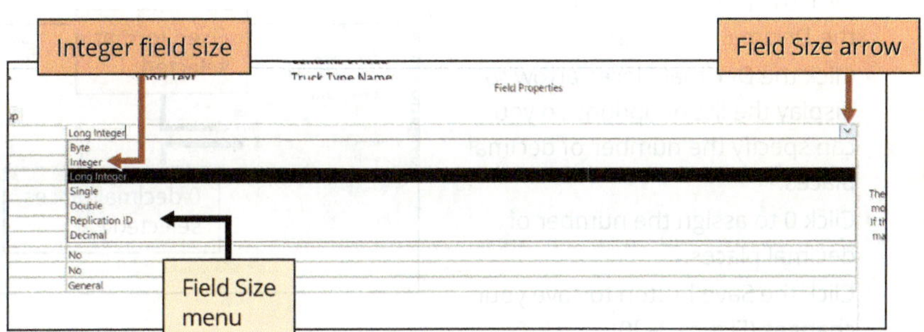

Figure 3–26

Q&A What would happen if I left the field size set to Long Integer?

If the field size is Long Integer, Single, Double, or Decimal, the database will set aside much more space for that field than is needed. For example, using Long Integer, a value of 100 would be stored as 0000000100, using ten digits. With Integer, a value of 100 is stored as 00100, using only five digits.

3

- Click Integer to select the smaller field size.
- Click the Format box to display the Format arrow.
- Click the Format arrow to display the Format menu (Figure 3–27).

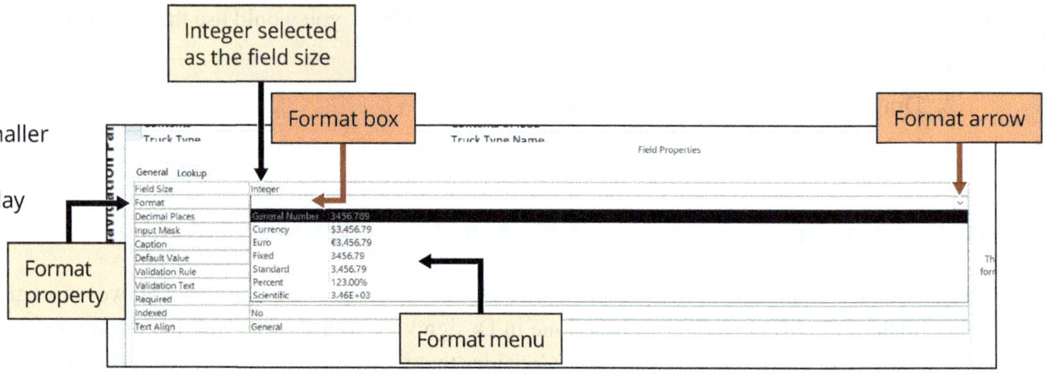

Figure 3–27

4

- Click Fixed to select fixed as the format.
- Click the 'Property Update Options' button to display the options for updating the property of this field to any form or report that uses this field (Figure 3–28).

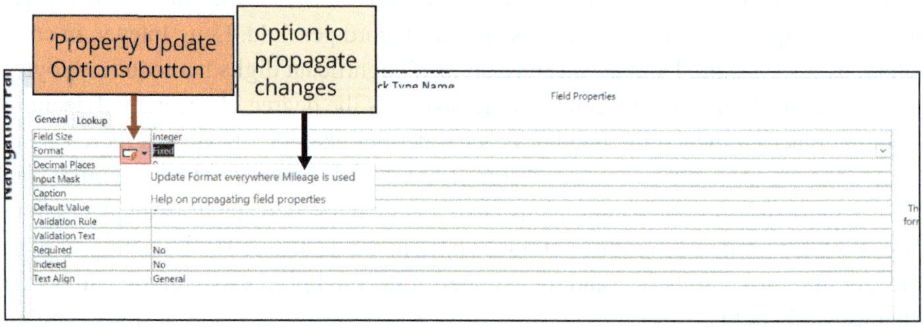

Figure 3–28

Q&A Why did the 'Property Update Options' button appear?

You changed the number of digits used to store the number data. The 'Property Update Options' button offers a quick way of making the same change everywhere Mileage appears.

5

- Click 'Update Format everywhere Mileage is used' to display the Update Properties dialog box (Figure 3–29).
- In the Update Properties dialog box, ensure that Form: Loads Split Form is selected, and then click Yes to update that form to include the new field size for the Mileage field.

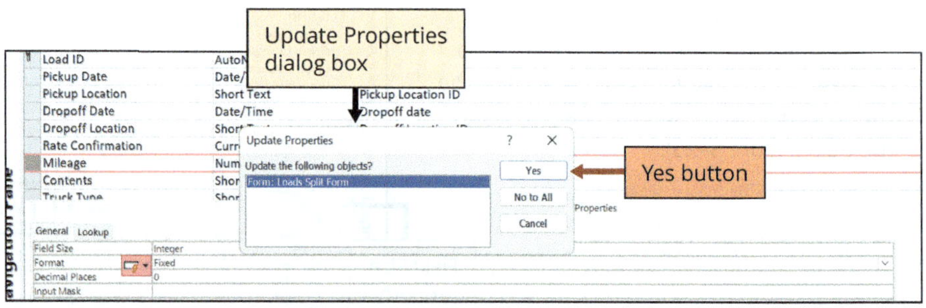

Figure 3–29

6

- Click the Decimal Places box to display the Decimal Places arrow.
- Click the Decimal Places arrow to display the list of options so you can specify the number of decimal places.
- Click 0 to assign the number of decimal places.
- Click the Save button to save your changes (Figure 3–30).

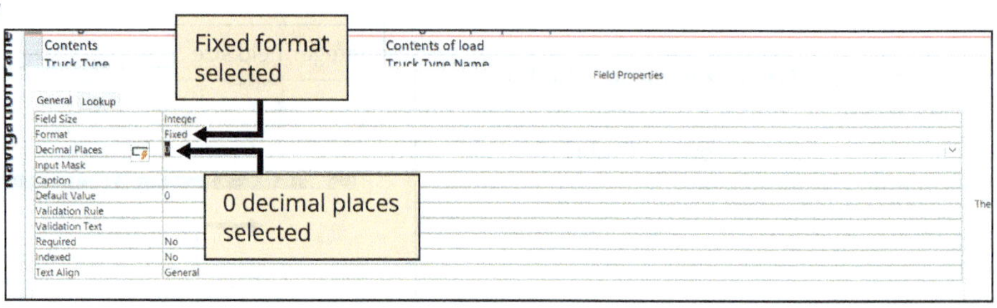

Figure 3–30

To Change the Format of a Number Field in Datasheet View

Although the field size of number formatted fields cannot be changed in Datasheet view, the format of a number field can be changed in Datasheet view. The number format can be General Number, Currency, Euro, Fixed, Standard, Percent, or Scientific. To change the format of a number field in the datasheet, you would use the following steps.

1. Open the table in Datasheet view.
2. Select the field that you want to change.
3. Click the Format arrow (Table Fields tab | Formatting group) to display the Format menu, and then select the desired number format.

To Add a New Field

Clearnet has recently hired a new agent. The owners realized their database needs to track which agent arranges each load so they can properly assign commissions. You can add fields to a table in a database. The following step adds the Agent field to the Loads table immediately after the Load Notes field. **Why?** Clearnet has decided that it can track agents with an additional field, Agent, in the Loads table. The possible values for Agent are Emery, Ariel, or Becka.

1

- With the Loads table still open in Design view, click the Field Name column in the blank row below the Load Notes field to produce an insertion point.
- Type **Agent** as the field name and then press TAB to move to the data type space.

To Create a Lookup Field

A **lookup field** allows the user to select from a list of values when updating the contents of the field. The following steps make the Agent field a lookup field. **Why?** The Agent field has only three possible values, making lookup field an appropriate data type for this field.

1

- Click the Data Type arrow to display the menu of available data types (Figure 3–31).

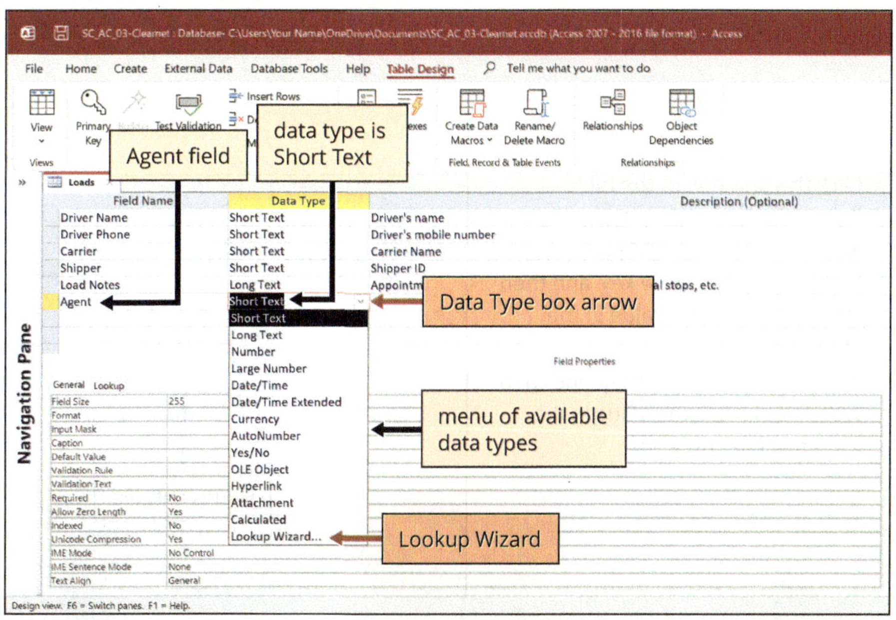

Figure 3–31

2

- Click Lookup Wizard, and then click the 'I will type in the values that I want.' option button (Lookup Wizard dialog box) to indicate that you will list the values (Figure 3–32).

Q&A When would I use the other option button?

You would use the other option button if the items to be entered in this field were found in another table or query.

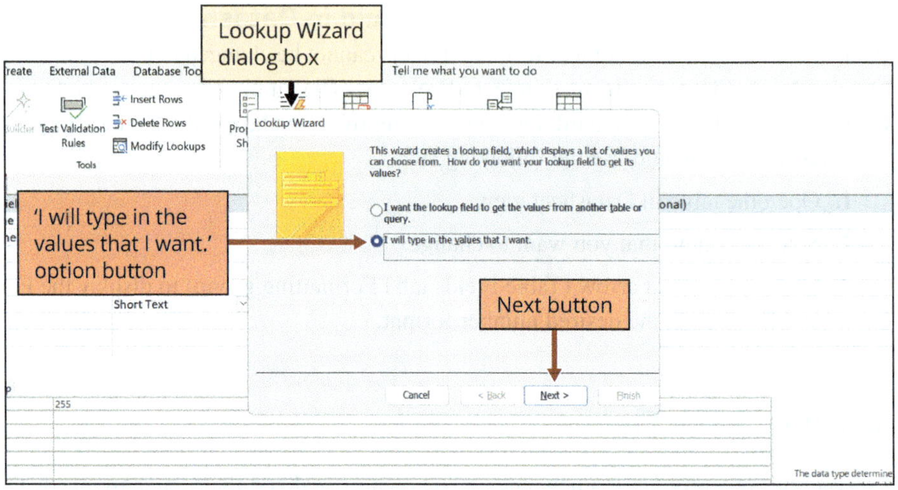

Figure 3–32

3

- Click the Next button to display the next Lookup Wizard screen (Figure 3–33).

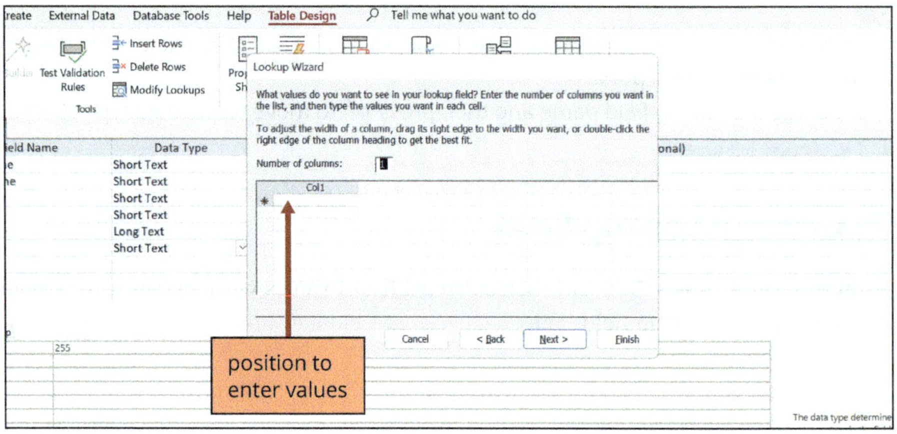

Figure 3–33

4

- Click the first row of the table (below Col1), and then type **Emery** as the value in the first row.
- Press the DOWN ARROW key, and then type **Ariel** as the value in the second row.
- Press the DOWN ARROW key, and then type **Becka** as the value in the third row (Figure 3–34).

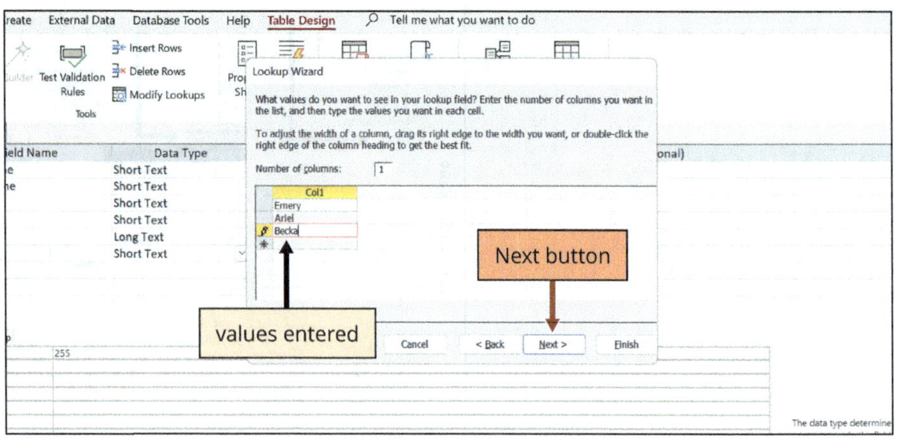

Figure 3–34

5

- Click the Next button to display the next Lookup Wizard screen.
- Ensure Agent is entered as the label for the lookup field and that the Allow Multiple Values check box is NOT checked (Figure 3–35).

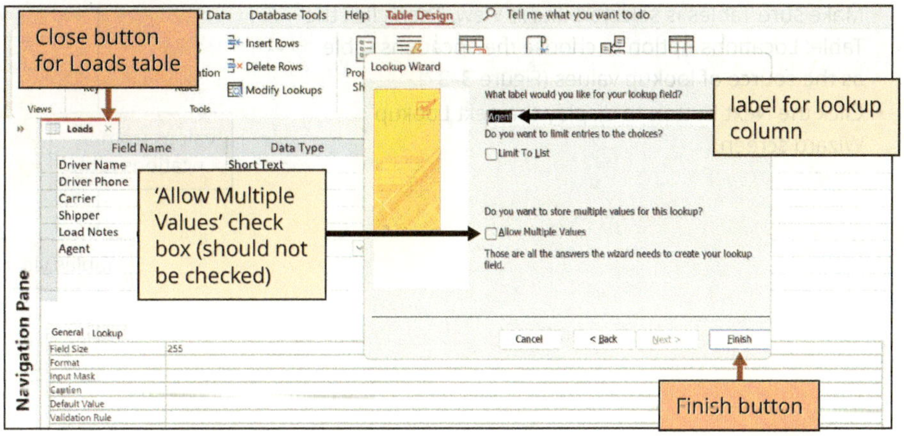

Figure 3–35

Q&A What is the purpose of the Limit To List check box?
With a lookup field, users can select from the list of values, in which case they can only select items in the list. They can also type their entry, in which case they are not necessarily limited to items in the list. If you check the Limit To List check box, users will be limited to items in the list, even if they type their entry. You will accomplish this same restriction later in this module with a validation rule, so you do not need to check this box.

6

- Click Finish to complete the definition of the lookup field.
- Save and close the table.

Q&A Why does the data type for the Agent field still show Short Text?
The data type is still Short Text because the values entered in the wizard were entered as text.

Why did I not change the field size for the Agent field?
You could have changed the field size to something like 10 or 15, but it is not necessary. When you create a lookup field and indicate specific values for the field, you automatically restrict the field size.

To Add a Multivalued Field

Normally, fields contain only a single value. In Access, it is possible to have **multivalued fields**, that is, fields that can contain more than one value. Clearnet wants to use such a field to store load pickup and dropoff locations. Occasionally, a shipper needs a truck to pick up items at two different locations or deliver to multiple locations. Allowing multiple locations for pickup or dropoff will provide more flexibility in record-keeping that will more accurately represent the reality of a truck's trip. Additionally, Clearnet would like to pull these available values from the Location ID field in the Locations table. This way, the Lookup field list in the Loads table will not need to be manually updated as new locations are added to the database.

BTW
Multivalued Fields
Do not use multivalued fields if you eventually plan to move your data to another relational database management system, such as SQL Server. SQL Server and other relational DBMSs do not support multivalued fields.

Creating a multivalued field uses the same process as creating a lookup field, with the exception that you check the Allow Multiple Values check box. In this case, you will also have the lookup field get values from another table instead of typing the available values. The following steps change two Short Text fields to multivalued fields that get possible values from another table.

1

- Open the Loads table in Design view.

2

- Click the Data Type arrow to display the menu of available data types for the Pickup Location field, and then click Lookup Wizard in the menu of available data types to start the Lookup Wizard.
- Make sure the 'I want the lookup field to get the values from another table or query.' option button is selected (Figure 3–36).
- Click the Next button to display the next Lookup Wizard screen.

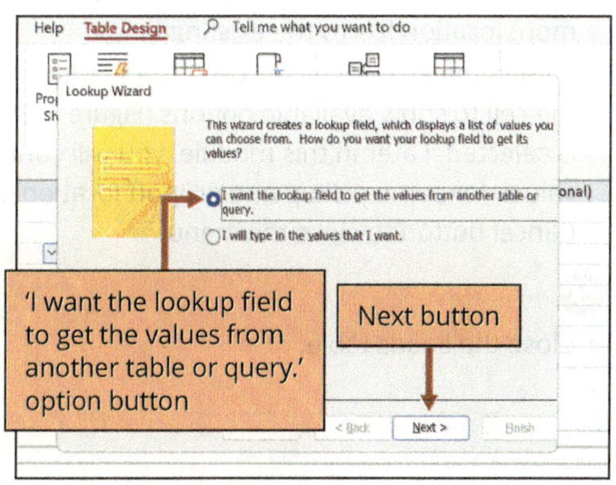

Figure 3–36

3

- Make sure Tables is selected under View. Then click the Table: Locations option to choose the Locations table as the source of lookup values (Figure 3-37).
- Click the Next button to display the next Lookup Wizard screen.

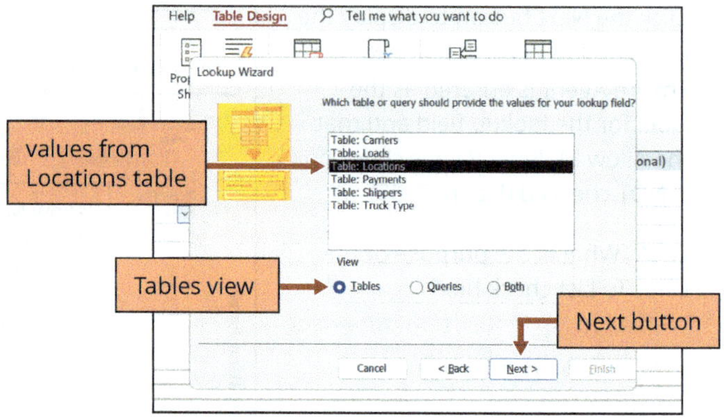

Figure 3-37

4

- Make sure Location ID is selected under Available Fields, and then click the Select Field button (Figure 3-38).
- Click the Next button to display the next Lookup Wizard screen.

5

- You will not configure a sort order for lookup values, so click the Next button to display the next Lookup Wizard screen.
- You will not change the column width, so click the Next button to display the next Lookup Wizard screen.

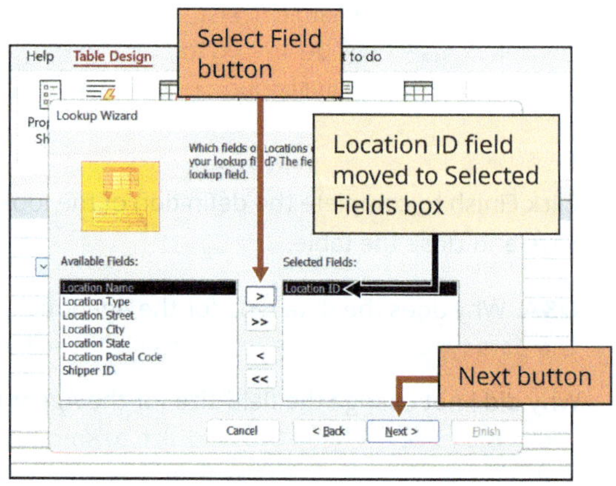

Figure 3-38

6

- Ensure that Pickup Location is entered as the label for the lookup field.
- Click the Allow Multiple Values check box to allow the user to enter multiple values.
- Click the Finish button to complete the definition of the Lookup Wizard field.
- You will see a warning to confirm you want to make the change because you will not be able to undo the change once saved. Click the Yes button.
- You will see a warning saying you must save the table to create the relationship between the tables for the lookup field. Click the Yes button.

7

- Repeat Steps 2 through 6 for the Dropoff Location field in the Loads table, ensuring that the label for this field is Dropoff Location.

8

- Switch to Datasheet view. The Pickup and Dropoff fields contain the same data they had before. However, you now can also add more location IDs to the existing fields.
- Click in the Pickup cell for Load 1, and then click the arrow for the cell to show available options (Figure 3-39). Currently, L-002 is selected. Later in this module, you will configure multiple values for some pickup and dropoff locations. For now, click the Cancel button to close the menu.

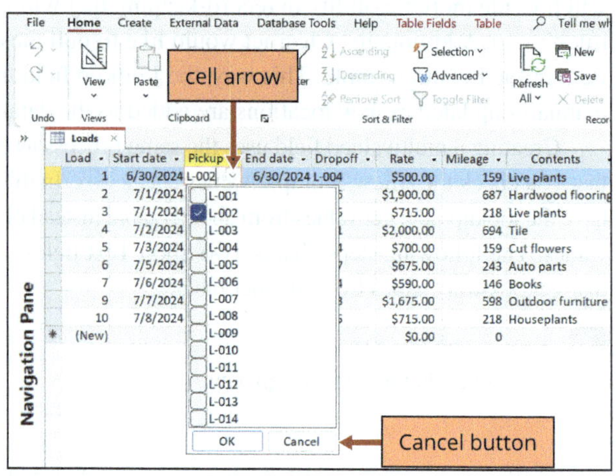

Figure 3-39

9

- Close the Loads table.

To Modify Single Valued or Multivalued Lookup Fields

At some point, you might want to change the list of choices in a lookup field. If you needed to modify a single value or multivalued lookup field, you would use the following steps.

1. Open the table in Design view and select the field to be modified.
2. Click the Lookup tab in the Field Properties pane.
3. Change the list in the Row Source property to the desired list of values.

To Add a Calculated Field

As you learned in Module 2, a field that can be computed from other fields is called a calculated field or a computed field. You can create a calculated field in a query. In Access 2019 and later versions, it is also possible to include a calculated field in a table. Users will not be able to update this field. **Why?** Access will automatically perform the necessary calculation and display the correct value whenever you display or use this field in any way. The following steps add to the Payments table a field that calculates the remainder of the payment due to the Carrier after the Agent Commission and Brokerage Fees are removed.

1

- Open the Payments table in Design view.
- Right-click the row selector for the Carrier Payment Status field (Figure 3–40), and then click Insert Rows on the shortcut menu to insert a blank row above the selected field.
- Type **Carrier Payment** as the field name, and then press TAB.
- Click the Data Type arrow to display the menu of available data types (Figure 3–41).

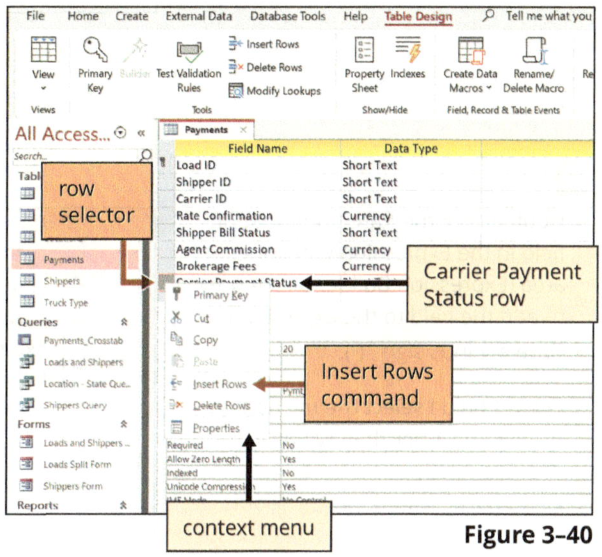

Figure 3–40

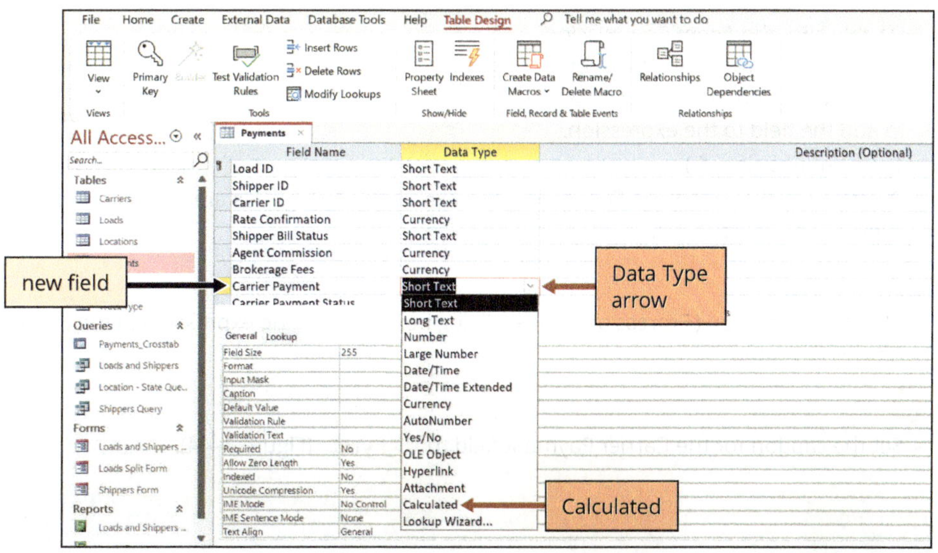

Figure 3–41

2

- Click Calculated to select the Calculated data type and display the Expression Builder dialog box (Figure 3–42).

Q&A I do not have the list of fields in the Expression Categories area. What should I do?

Click Payments in the Expression Elements area.

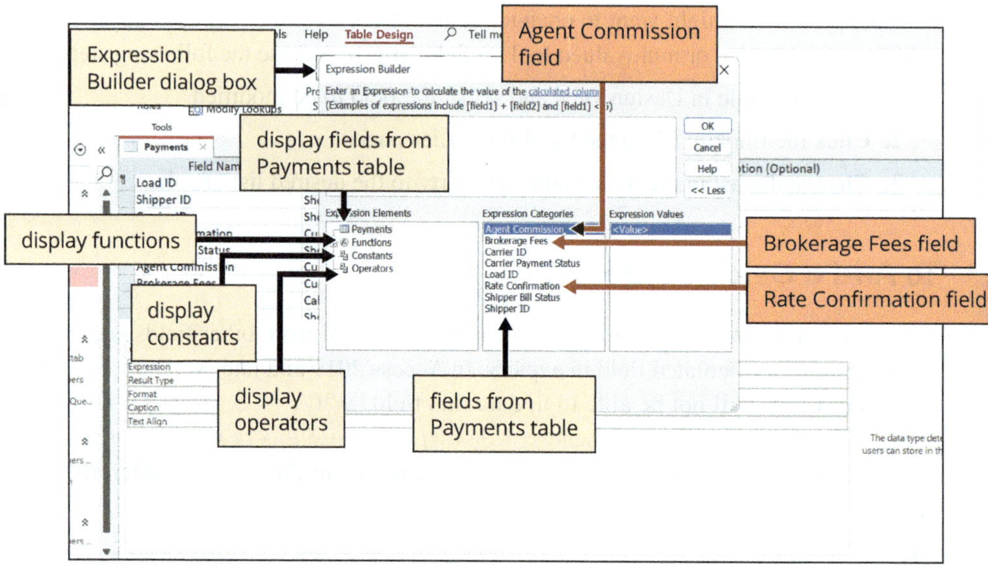

Figure 3–42

3

- Double-click the Rate Confirmation field in the Expression Categories area (Expression Builder dialog box) to add the field to the expression.
- Type a minus sign (-).

Q&A Could I select the minus sign from a list rather than typing it?

Yes. Click Operators in the Expression Elements area to display available operators, and then double-click the minus sign.

- Double-click the Agent Commission field in the Expression Categories area (Expression Builder dialog box) to add the field to the expression.
- Type a minus sign (-).
- Double-click the Brokerage Fees field in the Expression Categories area (Expression Builder dialog box) to add the field to the expression (Figure 3–43).

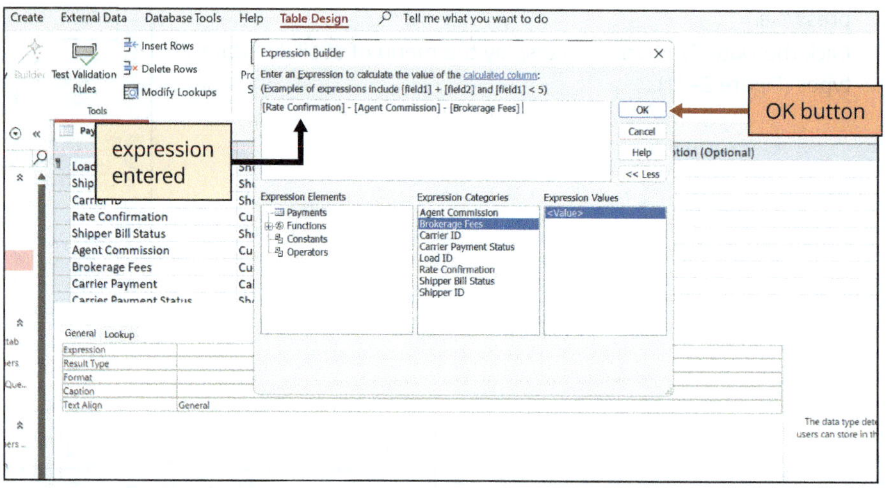

Figure 3–43

4

- Click the OK button (Expression Builder dialog box) to enter the expression in the Expression property of the Carrier Payment.

5

- Set the caption for the Carrier Payment field to **C_Pymt** (Figure 3–44).

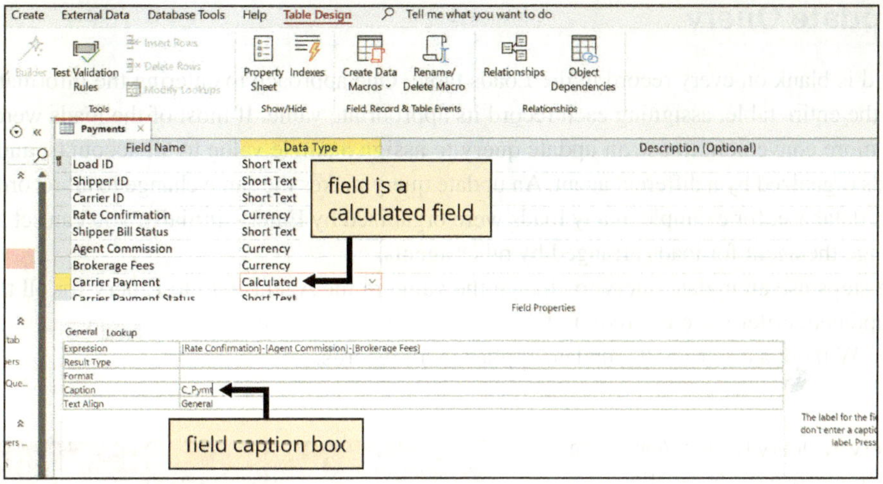

Figure 3–44

6

- Click the Save button on the Quick Access Toolbar to save the changes.
- Switch to Datasheet view to see the calculated amounts. Adjust the C_Pymt column size to the best fit.
- Save and close the table.

Q&A Could I have typed the expression in the Expression Builder dialog box rather than selecting the fields from a list?
Yes. You can use whichever technique you find more convenient.

Earlier, when I entered a calculated field in a query, I typed the expression in the Zoom dialog box. Could I have used the Expression Builder then instead?
Yes. To do so, you would click Build rather than Zoom on the shortcut menu.

Could I make a calculated field in the Datasheet view of a table?
Yes. To do so, open the table in Datasheet view, click the Click to Add arrow in the rightmost blank field space, select Calculated Field, and then indicate the type of data you want in that calculated field. Access displays the Expression Builder, where you can complete the calculated field.

Can I modify the calculated field in Design view?
Yes. In Design view, select the calculated field. In the Field Properties pane, click the General tab, if necessary, and click to the right of the Expression for the calculated field. Click the small box with three dots to open the Expression Builder dialog box.

Mass Changes

In some cases, rather than making individual changes to records, you will want to make mass changes. That is, you will want to add, change, or delete many records in a single operation. You can do this with action queries. Unlike select queries, which simply present data in specific ways, an **action query** adds, deletes, or changes data in a table. An **update query** allows you to make the same change to all records satisfying some criterion. If you omit the criterion, you will make the same changes to all records in the table. A **delete query** allows you to delete all the records satisfying some criterion. You can add the results of a query to an existing table by using an **append query**. You also can add the query results to a new table by using a **make-table query**.

BTW
Database Backup
If you are making mass changes to a database, be sure to back up the database prior to doing the updates.

To Use an Update Query

The new Agent field is blank on every record in the Loads table. One approach to entering the information for the field would be to step through the entire table, assigning each record its appropriate value. If most of the loads were arranged by the same agent, it would be more convenient to use an update query to assign a single value to all accounts, and then update the agent name for those loads organized by a different agent. An update query makes the same change to all records satisfying a criterion.

In the Clearnet database, for example, many loads were organized by Emery. Initially, you can set all the values to Emery. Later, you can change the agent for loads arranged by other agents.

The following steps use an update query to change the value in the Agent field to Emery for all the records. Because all records are to be updated, criteria are not required. **Why?** If a criterion is used, the update only applies to those records that satisfy the criterion. Without a criterion, the update applies to all records.

1

- Create a new query in Query Design View using the Loads table, and then close the Navigation Pane and the Add Tables pane. Resize the fields list as desired.
- Click the Update button (Query Design tab | Query Type group) to specify an update query.
- Double-click the Agent field to add the field to the query design grid.
- Click the Update To row in the first column of the design grid, and then type **Emery** as the new value (Figure 3-45).

Q&A If I change my mind and do not want an update query, how can I change the query back to a select query?
Click the Select button (Query Design tab | Query Type group).

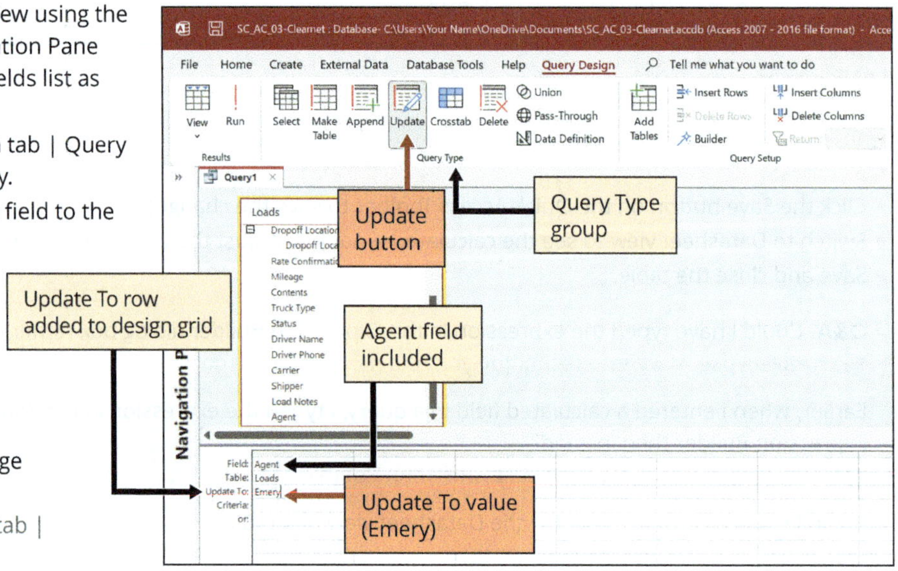

Figure 3-45

2

- Click the Run button (Query Design tab | Results group) to run the query and update the records (Figure 3-46).

Q&A The dialog box did not appear on my screen when I ran the query. What happened?
If the dialog box did not appear, it means that you did not click the Enable Content button when you first opened the database. Close the database, open it again, and enable the content. Then, create and run the query again.

- Click the Yes button to make the changes. Leave the query open for now.
- Open the Navigation Pane, and open the Loads table in Datasheet view to confirm all the updates were made correctly. Then close the Loads table.

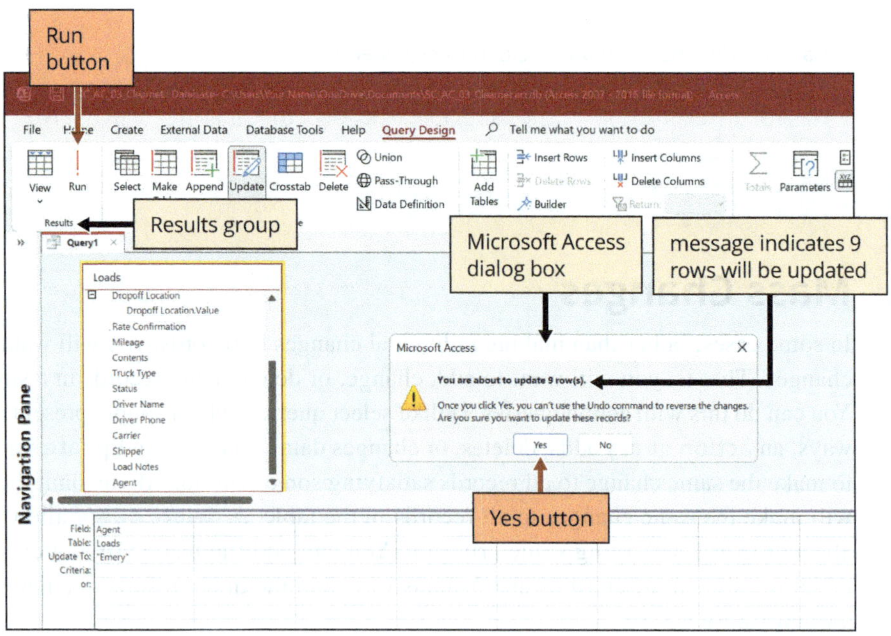

Figure 3-46

- **Experiment:** Create an update query to change the account type to MC. Enter a criterion to restrict the records to be updated, such as loads for Shipper S-001, and then run the query. Open the table to view your changes. When finished, create and run an update query to change the agent name to Emery on all records.
- Close the query. Because you do not need to use this update query again, do not save the query.

Other Ways

1. Right-click any open area in upper pane, click the Query Type arrow on shortcut menu, click Update Query on Query Type submenu to choose Update query type

To Use a Delete Query

In some cases, you might need to delete several records at a time. If, for example, Clearnet no longer dealt with loads being delivered to locations in Colorado (CO), the locations with this value in the State field could be deleted from the Clearnet database. Instead of deleting these accounts individually, which could be very time-consuming in a large database, you can delete them in one operation by using a delete query, which is a query that deletes all the records satisfying the criteria entered in the query. To create a delete query, you would use the following steps.

1. Create a query for the table containing the records to be deleted.
2. In Design view, indicate the fields and criteria that will specify the records to delete.
3. Click the Delete button (Query Design tab | Query Type group).
4. Click the Run button (Query Design tab | Results group) to run the query.
5. When Access indicates the number of records to be deleted, click the Yes button.

BTW
Viewing Records before Updating
You can view records affected by an update query before running the query. To do so, use the Select button to convert the query to a select query, add any additional fields that would help you identify the records, and then view the results. Make any necessary corrections to the query in Design view. When you are satisfied, use the Update button to once again convert the query to an update query.

To Use an Append Query

An append query adds a group of records from one table, called the Source table, to the end of another table, called the Destination table. For example, suppose that Clearnet acquires some new shippers; these new shippers are accompanied by a related database. To avoid entering all this information manually, you can append it to the Shippers table in the Clearnet database using the append query. To create an append query, you would use the following steps.

1. Create a select query for the Source table.
2. In Design view, indicate the fields to include, and then enter any necessary criteria.
3. View the select query results to be sure you have specified the correct data, and then return to Design view.
4. Click the Append button (Query Design tab | Query Type group).
5. When Access displays the Append dialog box, specify the name of the Destination table and its location. The Destination table might be in the same database or in a different one. When you're ready, click the OK button (Append dialog box).
6. Run the query by clicking the Run button (Query Design tab | Results group).
7. When Access indicates the number of records to be appended, click the OK button.

BTW
Delete Queries
If you do not specify any criteria in a delete query, Access will delete all the records in the table.

To Use a Make-Table Query

In some cases, you might want to create a new table that contains only records from an existing table. If so, use a make-table query to add the records to a new table. To create a make-table query, you would use the following steps.

1. Create a select query for the Source table.
2. In Design view, indicate the fields to include, and then enter any necessary criteria.
3. View the query results to be sure you have specified the correct data, and then return to Design view.
4. Click the Make Table button (Query Design tab | Query Type group).

BTW
Archive Tables
You can use a make-table query to create an archive table. An archive table is a table that contains data that is no longer used in operations but that might still be needed by the organization.

5. When Access displays the Make Table dialog box, specify the name of the Destination table and its location. The Destination table might be in the same database or in a different one. When you're ready, click the OK button (Make Table dialog box).
6. Run the query by clicking the Run button (Query Design tab | Results group).
7. When Access indicates the number of records to be inserted, click the OK button.

Break Point: If you wish to take a break, this is a good place to do so. You can quit Access now. To resume at a later time, start Access, open the database called SC_AC_03_Clearnet.accdb, and continue following the steps from this location forward.

BTW
Using the BETWEEN Operator in Validation Rules
You can use the BETWEEN operator to specify a range of values. For example, to specify that entries in the Mileage field must be between 0 and 3,000, type BETWEEN 0 and 3000 as the rule.

Validation Rules

You now have created, loaded, queried, and updated a database. Nothing you have done so far, however, restricts users to entering only valid data, that is, data that follows the rules established for data in the database. An example of such a rule would be that agents can only be Emery, Ariel, or Becka. To ensure the entry of valid data, you create **validation rules**, or rules that a user must follow when entering the data. When the database contains validation rules, Access prevents users from entering data that does not follow the rules. You can also specify **validation text**, which is the message that appears if a user attempts to violate the validation rule.

Validation rules can indicate a **required field**, a field in which the user *must* enter data; failing to enter data into a required field generates an error. Validation rules can also restrict a user's entry to a certain **range of values**; for example, the values in the Mileage field must be between 0 and 3,000; including a practical limit like this for the data in that field helps prevent errors in data entry. Alternatively, rules can specify a **default value**, that is, a value that Access will display on the screen in a particular field before the user begins adding a record. To make data entry of account numbers more convenient for the user, you can also have lowercase letters appear automatically as uppercase letters. Finally, validation rules can specify a collection of acceptable values.

BTW
Using Wildcards in Validation Rules
You can include wildcards in validation rules. For example, if you enter the expression, like T?, in the validation rule for the State field, the only valid entries for the field will be TN or TX. However, erroneous data also could be entered, such as TE or TA.

To Change a Field Size

The Field Size property for text fields represents the maximum number of characters a user can enter in the field. For example, the default field size for the Postal Code field in the Locations table was 255, but a user would never enter a postal code that long. Currently, the field is set to be 10 characters, which allows for a 5-digit postal code, a hyphen, and four route digits in that field. Occasionally, you will find that the field size that seemed appropriate when you first created a table is no longer appropriate. In the Locations table, the Postal Code field needs to be adjusted to fit 20 characters, in case there is a foreign postal code that is longer than the postal code plus four. To allow this longer postal code in the table, you need to change the field size for the Location Postal Code field. The following steps change the field size for the Location Postal Code field from 10 to 20.

1

- Open the Locations table in Design view and close the Navigation Pane.
- Select the Location Postal Code field by clicking its row selector.
- Click the Field Size property to select it, delete the current entry (10), and then type **20** as the new field size.

2

- Save and close the table.

To Specify a Required Field

To specify that a field is to be required, change the value for the Required property from No to Yes. The following step specifies that the Agent field in the Loads table is a required field. **Why?** Users will not be able to leave the Agent field blank when entering or editing records.

1

- Open the Navigation Pane, open the Loads table in Design view, and then close the Navigation Pane.
- Scroll down and select the Agent field by clicking its row selector.
- Click the Required property box in the Field Properties pane, and then click the arrow that appears.
- Click Yes in the list to make Agent a required field (Figure 3–47).

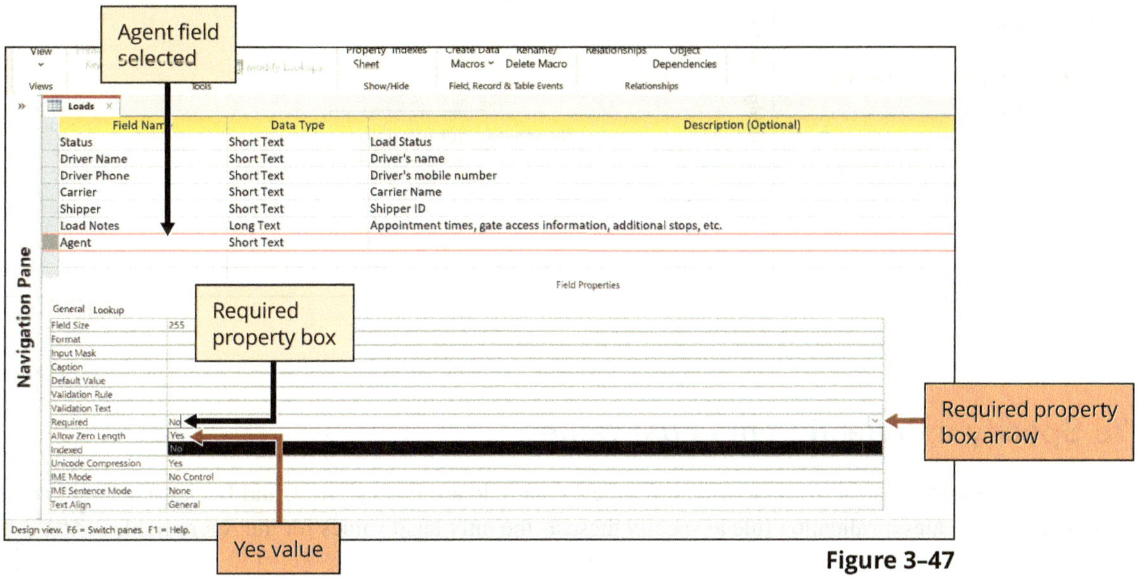

Figure 3–47

To Specify a Range

The following step specifies that entries in the Mileage field must be greater than 0 and less than 3,001. To indicate this range, the criterion specifies that the Mileage amount must be both > 0 (greater than 0) and <= 3000 (less than or equal to 3,000). **Why?** Combining these two criteria with the word, and, is logically equivalent to being between 0 and 3,001.

1

- Select the Mileage field by clicking its row selector, click the Validation Rule property box to produce an insertion point, and then type **>0 and <=3000** as the rule.
- Click the Validation Text property box to produce an insertion point, and then type **Must be greater than 0 and at most 3,000** as the text (Figure 3–48).

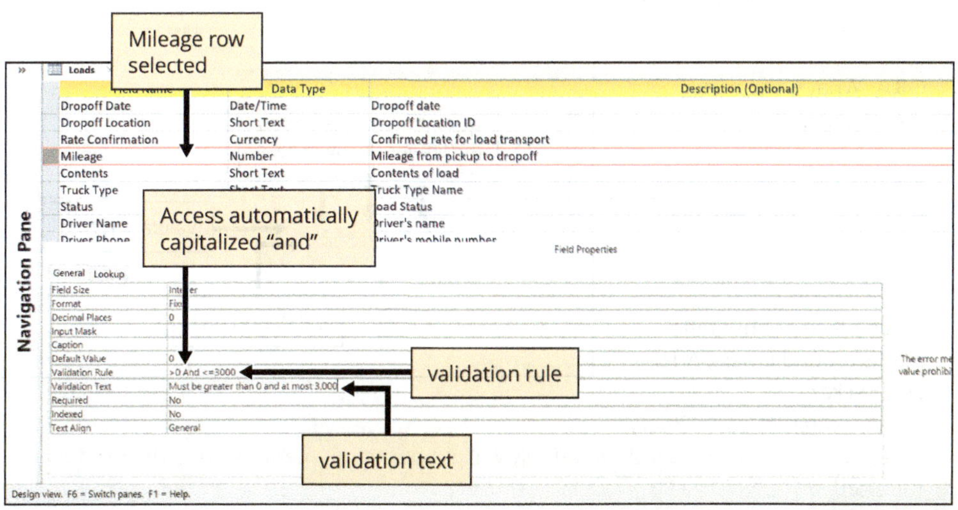

Figure 3–48

Q&A What is the effect of this change?

Users will now be prohibited from entering a Mileage amount that is either less than or equal to 0 or greater than 3,000 when they add records or change the value in the Mileage field.

To Specify a Default Value

To specify a default value, enter the value in the Default Value property box. The following step specifies Emery as the default value for the Agent field. **Why?** Emery is currently the only full-time agent, and so arranges the majority of loads. By making Emery's name the default value, if a user does not enter an Agent, the agent value will be Emery.

1

- Select the Agent field, click the Default Value property box to produce an insertion point, and then type **=Emery** as the value (Figure 3–49).

Q&A Do I need to type the equal (=) sign?
No. You could enter just Emery as the default value.

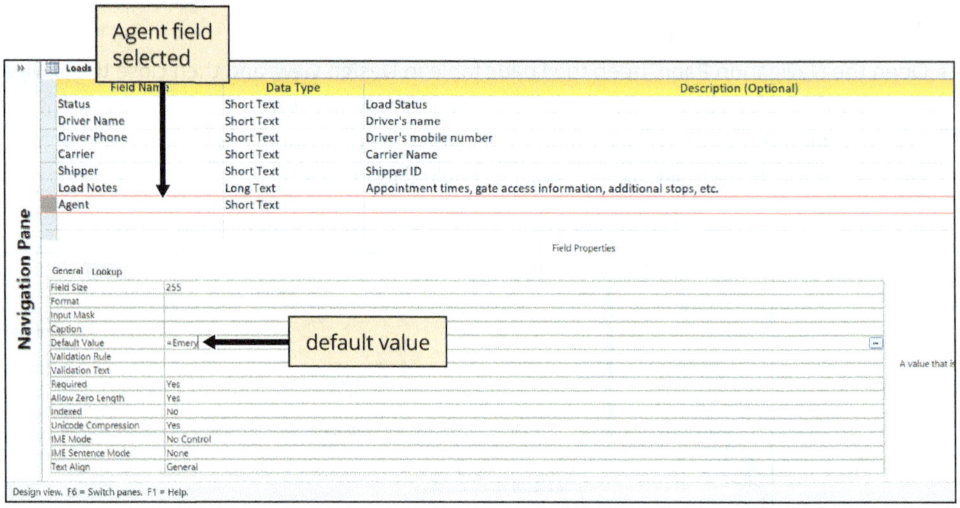

Figure 3–49

To Specify a Collection of Legal Values

The only **legal values**, or **allowable values**, for the Agent field are Emery, Ariel, and Becka. The following step creates a validation rule to specify these as the only legal values for the Agent field. **Why?** The validation rule prohibits users from entering any other value in the Agent field.

BTW
Database Design: Validation
In most organizations, decisions about what is valid and what is invalid data are made during the requirements-gathering process and the database design process.

1

- With the Agent field selected, click the Validation Rule property box to produce an insertion point and then type **=Emery or =Ariel or =Becka** as the validation rule.
- Click the Validation Text property box, and then type **Must be Emery, Ariel, or Becka** as the validation text (Figure 3–50).

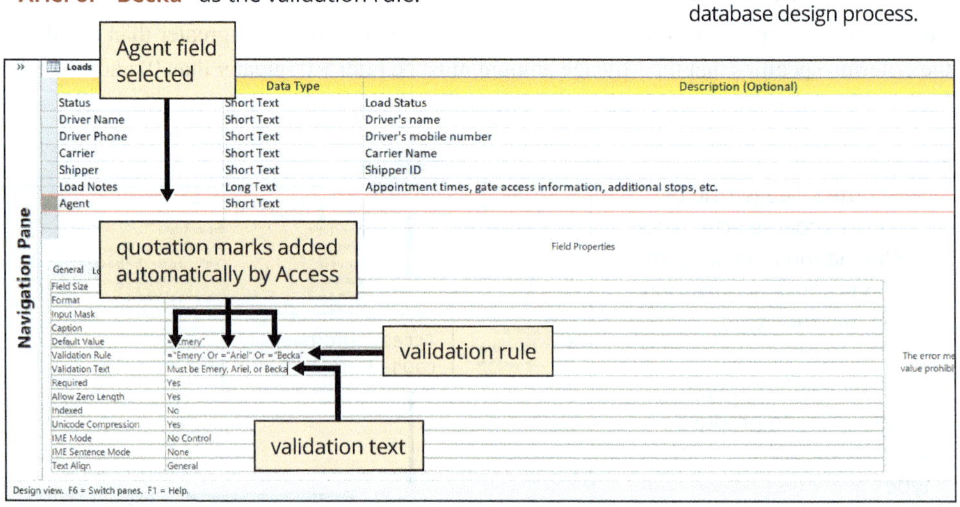

Figure 3–50

Q&A What is the effect of this change?
Users will now only be allowed to enter Emery, Ariel, or Becka in the Agent field when they add records or make changes to this field.

Do I have to put quotation marks around Emery, Ariel, and Becka?
No, you can just type =Emery or =Ariel or =Becka. Access automatically will put quotation marks around the product types and capitalize both instances of the word, or.

To Save the Validation Rules, Default Values, and Formats

The following steps save the validation rules, default values, and formats.

1

- Click the Save button on the Quick Access Toolbar to save the changes (Figure 3–51).

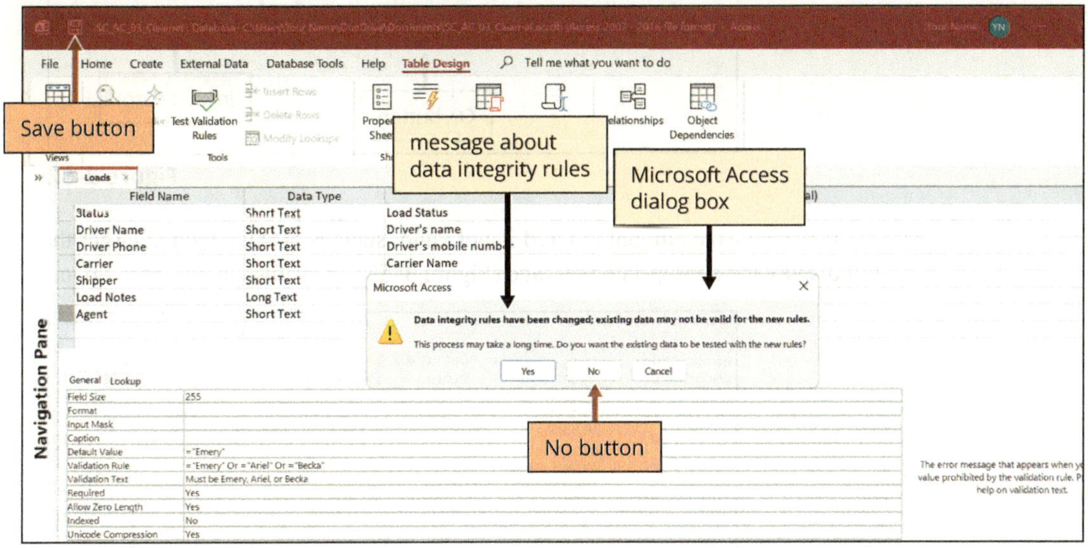

Figure 3–51

2

- If a Microsoft Access dialog box appears, click No to save the changes without testing current data.

Q&A When would you want to test current data?
If you have any doubts about the validity of the current data, you should be sure to test the data before saving changes.

3

- Close the Loads table.

Q&A Can I set validation rules, validation text, and properties in Datasheet view?
Yes, in Datasheet view, select the field and display the Table Fields tab. Click the Default Value button (Table Fields tab | Properties group) to open the Expression Builder. In the Properties group, you can also modify lookups. In the Field Validation group, you can set validation.

Updating a Table That Contains Validation Rules

Now that the Clearnet database contains validation rules, Access restricts the user to entering data that is valid and is formatted correctly. If a user enters a number that is out of the required range, for example, or enters a value that is not one of the permitted choices, Access displays an error message in the form of a dialog box. The user cannot update the database until the error is corrected.

If the Agent name entered is not valid, such as Kirsten, which is not one of the three names you specified, Access will display the text message you specified (Figure 3–52) and prevent the data from being entered into the database.

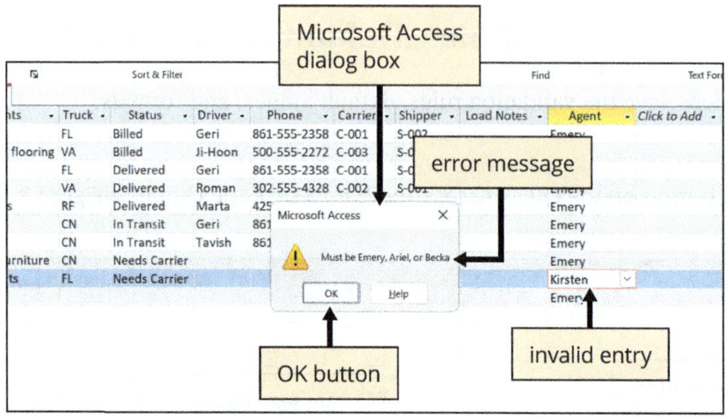

Figure 3–52

If the Mileage amount entered is not valid, such as 5000, which is larger than 3000, Access will display the appropriate message (Figure 3–53) and refuse to accept the data.

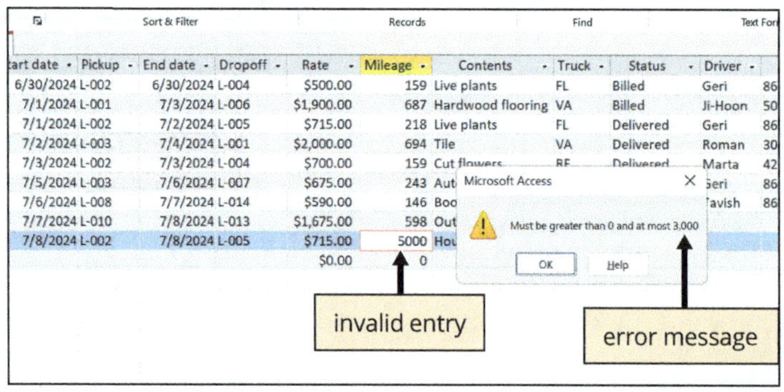

Figure 3–53

If a required field contains no data, Access indicates this by displaying an error message as soon as you attempt to leave the record (Figure 3–54). The field must contain a valid entry before Access will move to a different record, even if you did not specify validation text.

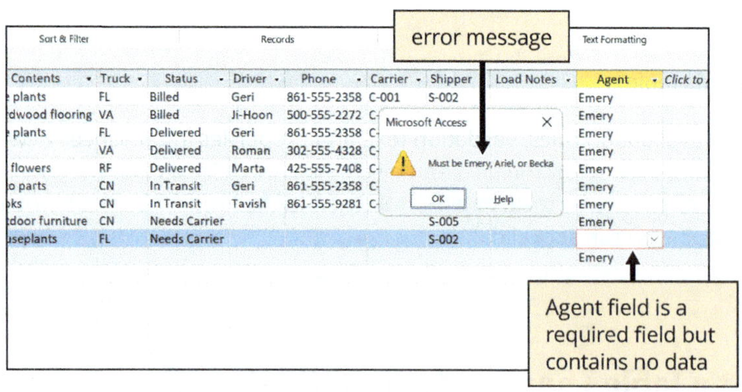

Figure 3–54

Consider This

When entering invalid data into a field with a validation rule, is it possible that you could not enter the data correctly? What would cause this? If it happens, what should you do?

If you cannot remember the validation rule you created or if you created the rule incorrectly, you might not be able to enter the data. In such a case, you will be unable to leave the field or close the table because you have entered data into a field that violates the validation rule.

If this happens, first try again to type an acceptable entry. If this does not work, repeatedly press BACKSPACE to erase the contents of the field, and then try to leave the field. If you are unsuccessful using this procedure, press ESC until the record is removed from the screen. The record will not be added to the database.

Should the need arise to take this drastic action, you probably have a faulty validation rule. Use the techniques of the previous sections to correct the existing validation rules for the field.

Making Additional Changes to the Database

Now that you have changed the structure and created validation rules, there are additional changes to be made to the database. You will use both the lookup and multivalued lookup fields to change the contents of the fields. You will also update both the form and the report to reflect the changes in the table.

To Use a Lookup Field

Earlier, in the Loads table, you changed all the entries in the Agent field to Emery. You have created a rule to ensure that only legitimate values (Emery, Ariel, or Becka) can be entered in the field. You also made Agent a lookup field. **Why?** You can make changes to a lookup field for individual records by simply clicking the field to be changed, clicking the arrow that appears in the field, and then selecting the desired value from the list. The following steps change the incorrect Agent values to the correct values.

1

- Open the Navigation Pane, open the Loads table in Datasheet view, and then close the Navigation Pane.
- Click in the Agent field on the third record (ID 3) to display an arrow.
- Click the arrow to display the drop-down list of available choices for the Agent field (Figure 3–55).

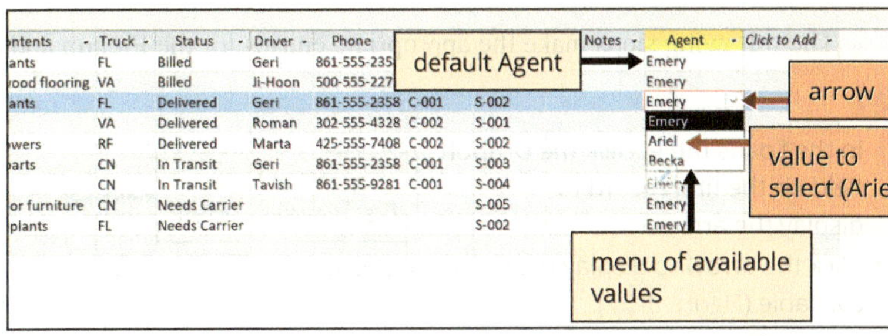

Figure 3–55

Q&A I got the drop-down list as soon as I clicked. I did not need to click the arrow. What happened?
If you click in the position where the arrow would appear, you will get the drop-down list. If you click anywhere else, you would need to click the arrow.

2

- Click Ariel to change the value.

Q&A Could I type the value instead of selecting it from the list?
Yes. Once you have either deleted the previous value or selected the entire previous value, you can begin typing. You do not have to type the full entry. When you begin with the letter, A, for example, Access will automatically suggest the full name.

3

- In a similar fashion, change the values on Loads 5 and 6 to Ariel, and change the value on Load 9 to Becka. Make sure the Agent field values match those shown in Figure 3–56.

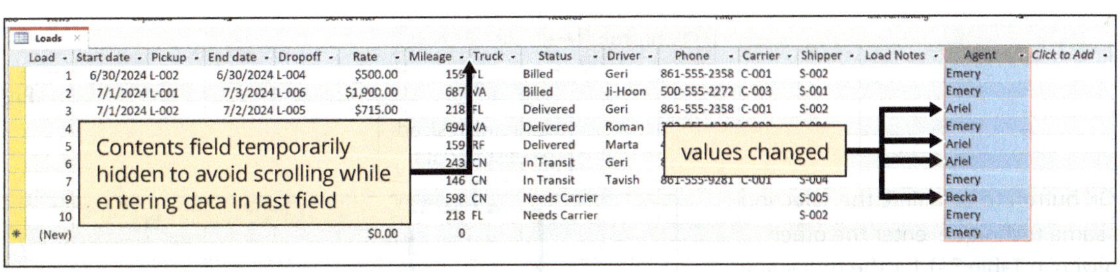

Figure 3–56

Q&A It's awkward scrolling back and forth on the table to choose the correct Load ID, and then choose the correct value in the Agent column. Is there a way to see both these columns at once?
Yes. You can temporarily hide some of the unneeded columns, and then unhide them when you're finished. To hide a column, right-click the column header (such as Contents) and click Hide Fields. When you're finished entering data, unhide all hidden fields by right-clicking any visible column header and selecting the check box for each hidden field (Unhide Columns dialog box), and then click Close.

To Use a Multivalued Lookup Field

Using a multivalued lookup field is similar to using a regular lookup field. The difference is that when you display the list, the entries are all preceded by check boxes. **Why?** Having the check boxes allows you to make multiple selections. You check all the entries that you want. Table 3–1 shows the appropriate entries for the loads with more than one pickup or dropoff location. As indicated in the table, only a few loads include multiple pickup or dropoff locations.

Table 3–1 Multivalued Pickup and Dropoff Locations

Load ID	Pickup Locations	Dropoff Locations
2	L-001	L-005, L-006
3	L-002	L-004, L-005
9	L-009, L-010	L-013

The following steps make the appropriate entries for the Pickup and Dropoff fields in the Loads table.

1

- In the Loads table, click the Dropoff field on the first record to display the arrow.
- Click the arrow to display the list of Locations available (Figure 3–57).

Q&A What if there were too many locations to fit?

Access would automatically include a scroll bar that you could use to scroll through all the choices.

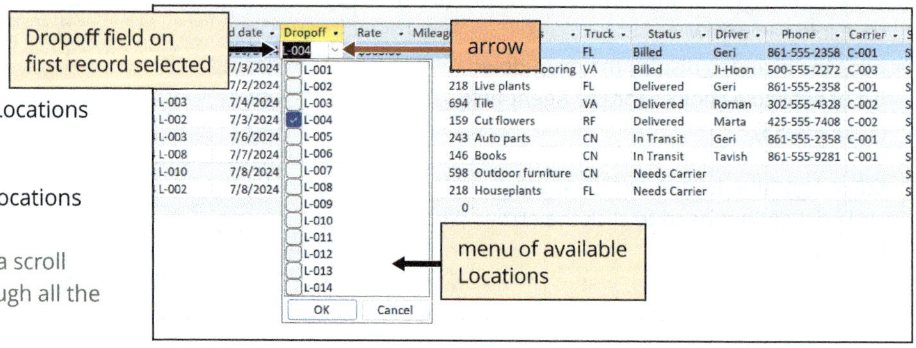

Figure 3–57

2

- Click the L-005 check box to select the additional dropoff location for the second load; Location L-004 has already been selected (Figure 3–58).

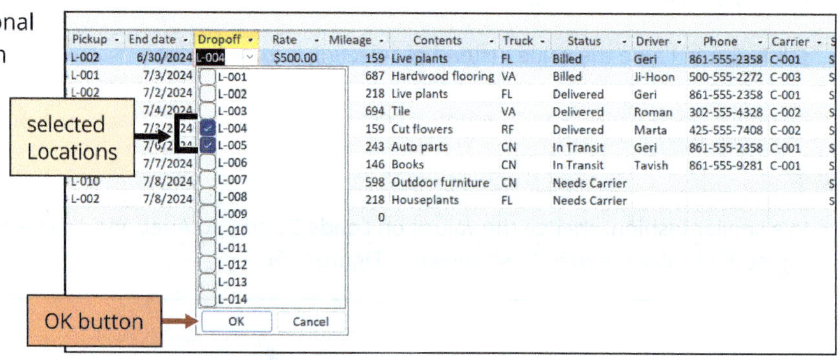

Figure 3–58

3

- Click the OK button to complete the selection.
- Using the same technique, enter the other locations given in Table 3–1 for the remaining accounts.
- Double-click the right boundary of the field selector for the Pickup field to resize the column so that it best fits the data. Repeat for the Dropoff field (Figure 3–59).

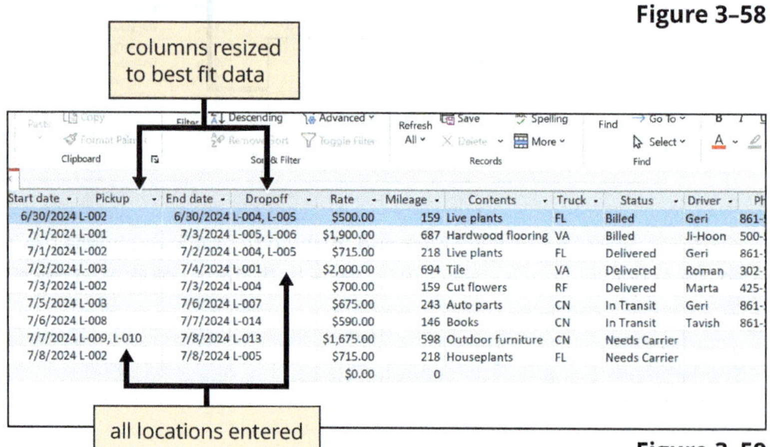

Figure 3–59

4

- Save the changes to the layout and close the Loads table.

Q&A What if I closed the table without saving the layout changes?
You would be asked if you want to save the changes.

Changing the Appearance of a Datasheet

You can change the appearance of a datasheet in a variety of ways. You can include totals in the datasheet. You can also change the appearance of gridlines or the text colors and font.

To Include Totals in a Datasheet

The following steps first include an extra row, called the Total row, in the datasheet for the Payments table. Note that this is not a calculated field. **Why?** It is possible to include totals and other statistics at the bottom of a datasheet in the Total row. The steps then display the total amount of money collected for all loads.

1

- Open the Navigation Pane, open the Payments table in Datasheet view, and then close the Navigation Pane.
- Click the Totals button (Home tab | Records group) to include the Total row in the datasheet. Note that a blank row for the next new record will remain above the Total row.
- Click the Total row in the RateCon column to display an arrow.
- Click the arrow to display a menu of available calculations (Figure 3–60).

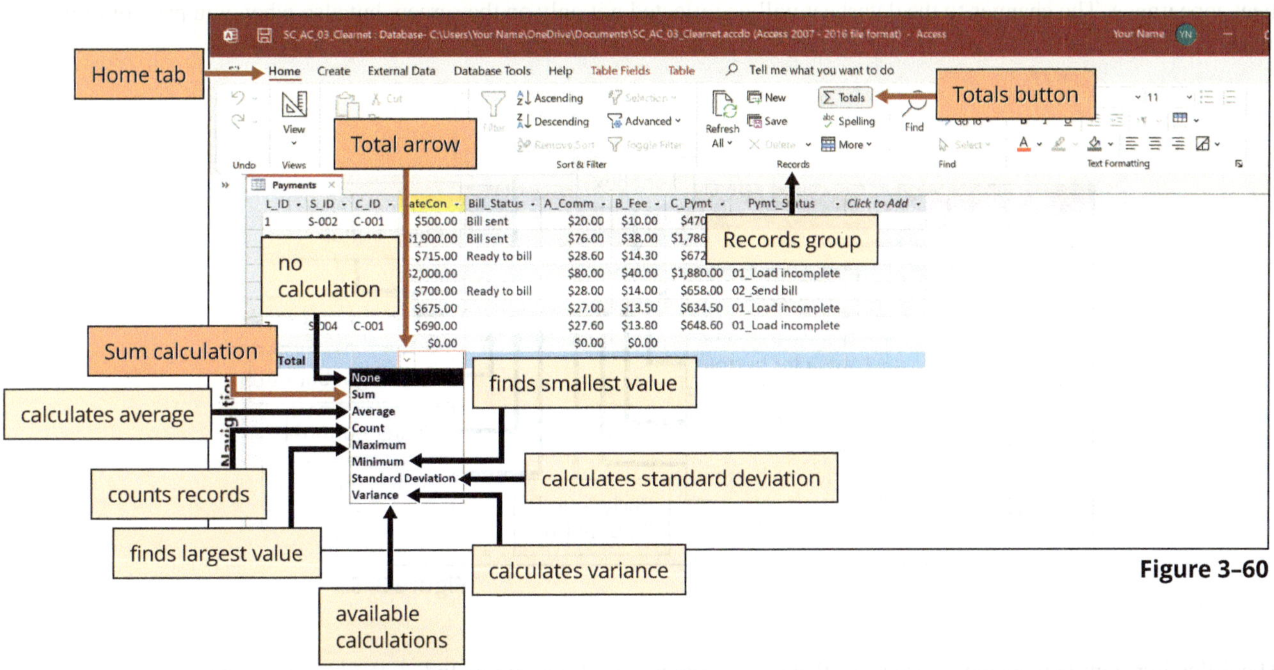

Figure 3–60

Q&A Can I also create a totals row in a query?
Yes, you can create a totals row in the Datasheet view of a query just like you did in the Datasheet view of the table.

Will I always get the same list?
No. You will only get the items that are applicable to the type of data in the column. You cannot calculate the sum of text data, for example.

2

- Click Sum to calculate the total of the RateCon amounts.
- Resize the RateCon column to best fit the total amount (Figure 3-61), if necessary.
- **Experiment:** Experiment with other statistics for the RateCon column and for other columns. When finished, once again select Sum for the RateCon column and clear any other statistics in other columns on the Total row.

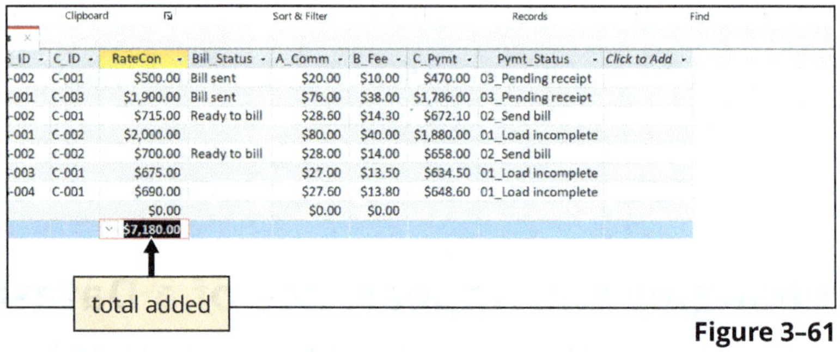

Figure 3-61

To Remove Totals from a Datasheet

If you no longer want the totals to appear as part of the datasheet, you can remove the Total row. The following step removes the Total row.

1

- Click the Totals button (Home tab | Records group), which is shown in Figure 3-60, to remove the Total row from the datasheet.

To Change Gridlines in a Datasheet

Figure 3–62 shows the various buttons, located in the Text Formatting group on the Home tab, that are available to change the datasheet appearance. The changes to the datasheet will be reflected not only on the screen, but also when you print or preview the datasheet.

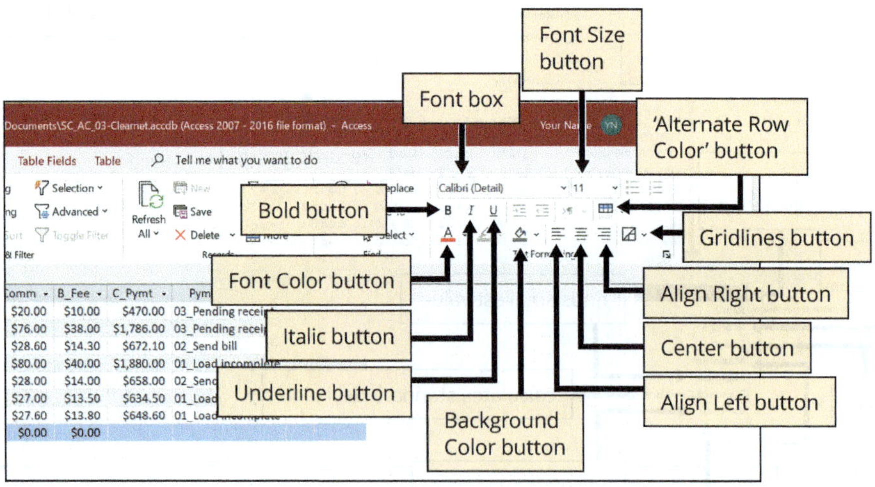

Figure 3-62

The following steps change the datasheet so that only horizontal gridlines are included. **Why?** You might prefer the appearance of the datasheet with only horizontal gridlines.

1

- With the Payments table open in Datasheet view, click the datasheet selector, which is the box in the upper-left corner of the datasheet, to select the entire datasheet (Figure 3-63).

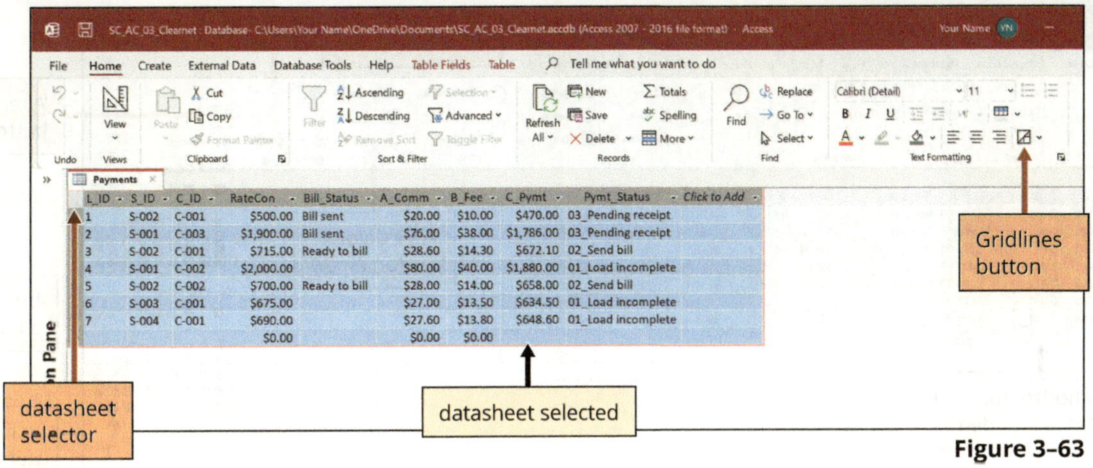

Figure 3–63

2

- Click the Gridlines button (Home tab | Text Formatting group) to display the Gridlines gallery (Figure 3–64).

Q&A Does it matter whether I click the button or the arrow?

In this case, it does not matter. Either action will display the gallery.

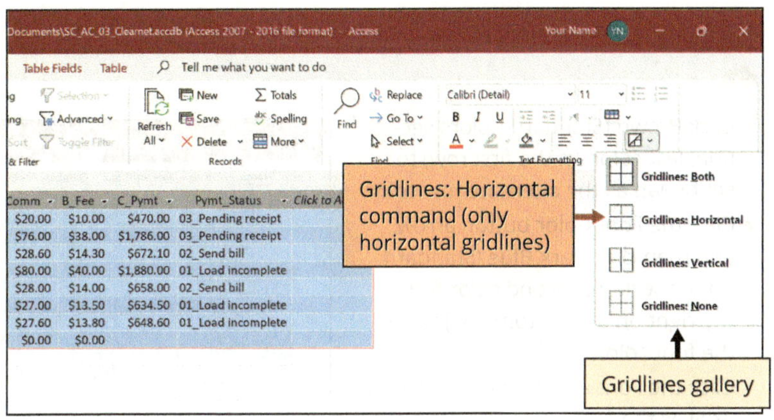

Figure 3–64

3

- Click Gridlines: Horizontal in the Gridlines gallery to include only horizontal gridlines.
- **Experiment:** Experiment with other gridline options. When finished, once again select horizontal gridlines.

To Change the Colors and Font in a Datasheet

You can also modify the appearance of the datasheet by changing the colors and the font. The following steps change the Alternate Fill color, a color that appears on every other row in the datasheet. **Why?** Having rows appear in alternate colors is an attractive way to visually separate the rows. The steps also change the font color, the font, and the font size.

1

- With the datasheet for the Payments table selected, click the Alternate Row Color button arrow (Home tab | Text Formatting group) to display the color palette (Figure 3–65).

Q&A Does it matter whether I click the button or the arrow?

Yes. Clicking the arrow produces a color palette. Clicking the button applies the currently selected color. When in doubt, you should click the arrow.

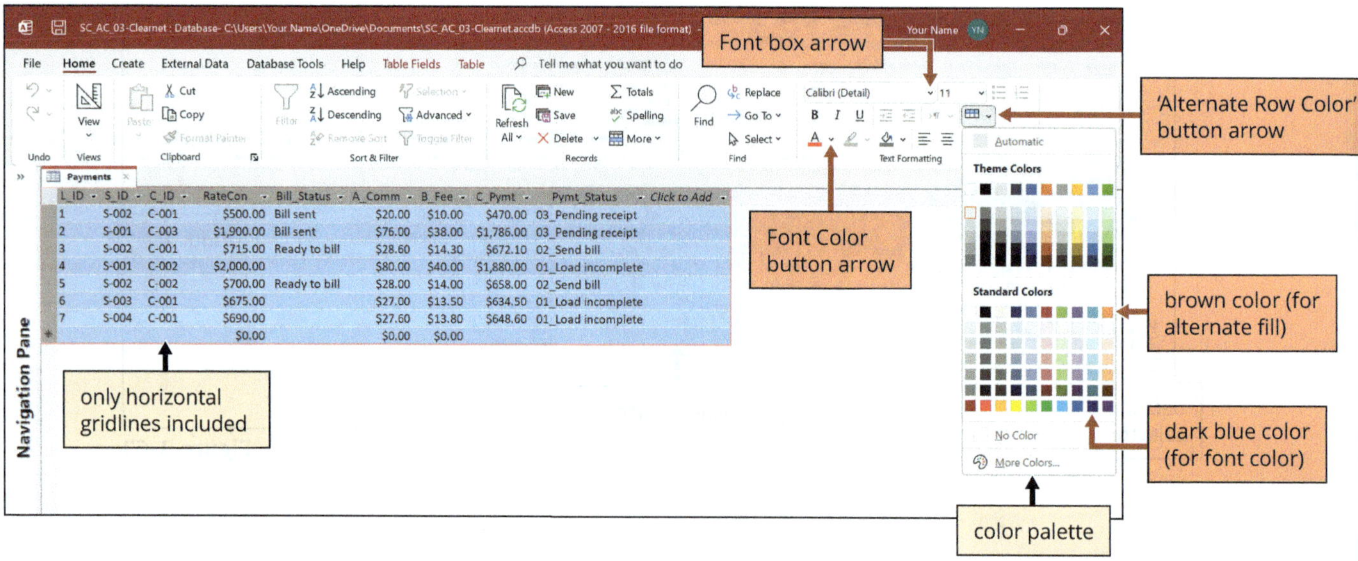

Figure 3–65

2

- Click Brown (Standard Colors section, last color on the first row) to set brown as the alternate row color.
- Click the Font Color button arrow, and then click Dark Blue (Standard Colors section, second color from the right on the bottom row) to set the font color.
- Click the Font arrow, and then select Arial as the font. (If Arial is not available, select any font of your choice.)
- Click the Font Size arrow and select 10 as the font size (Figure 3–66).

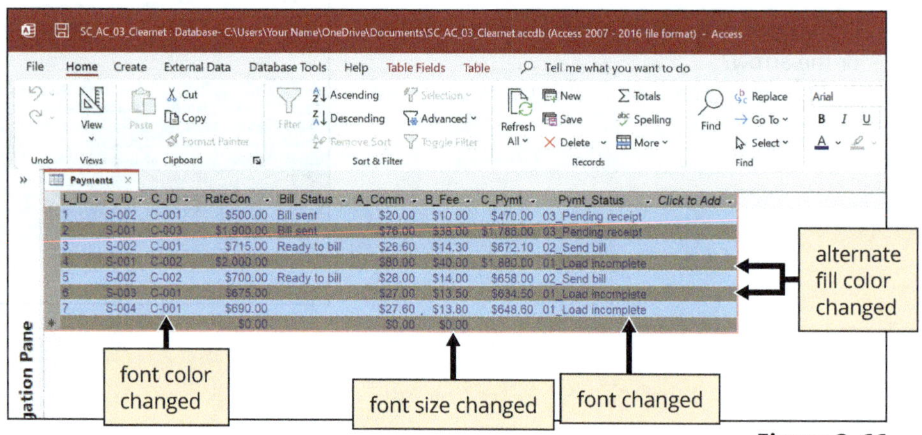

Figure 3–66

Q&A Does the order in which I make these selections make a difference?

No. You could have made these selections in any order.

- **Experiment:** Experiment with other colors, fonts, and font sizes. When finished, return to the options selected in these steps.

BTW

Microsoft Office Color Palettes

Microsoft Office color palettes are often divided into two main sections: Theme Colors and Standard Colors. In Access, the listed theme colors are based on the selected theme for the active object. The colors in the first row of theme colors each have a name, such as Blue or Gold, and a statement of their intended use, such as Background 1, Text 1, or Accent 2. You can see this name if you are using a mouse and hover your cursor over each color. For most devices, a screen tip will appear showing the color's name.

The colors in the rows immediately below the first row offer shades of these theme colors. The first row of shades is the lightest with the colors labeled by percentage of intensity, such as Lighter 80% or Darker 5%. Each row going lower gets darker and is named progressively according to the change of shading, such as Lighter 60%, Lighter 40%, and so on.

The standard colors are common to all themes but might vary according to color palette, screen resolution, Office version, etc. Screen resolution might also affect the location of the standard colors within the color palette. Standard colors also have names, such as Medium Gray or Dark Blue.

Most of the lower rows in the Standard Colors section are numbered according to shade, such as Medium Gray 1, Medium Gray 2, and so on. The bottom row provides colors that are more widely consistent across color palettes, use cases, and applications. These colors also have names, such as Dark Red and Dark Blue. Note that a color on one row with the same name as a color on another row is not necessarily the same color, such as the two Dark Blue colors in the Standard Colors section. When needing to choose a color from a color palette, read the instructions carefully and check figures when provided to help you select the correct color.

Using the Datasheet Formatting Dialog Box

As an alternative to using the individual buttons, you can click the Datasheet Formatting dialog box launcher, which is the arrow at the lower-right corner of the Text Formatting group, to display the Datasheet Formatting dialog box (Figure 3–67). You can use the various options within the dialog box to make changes to the datasheet format. Once you are finished, click the OK button to apply your changes.

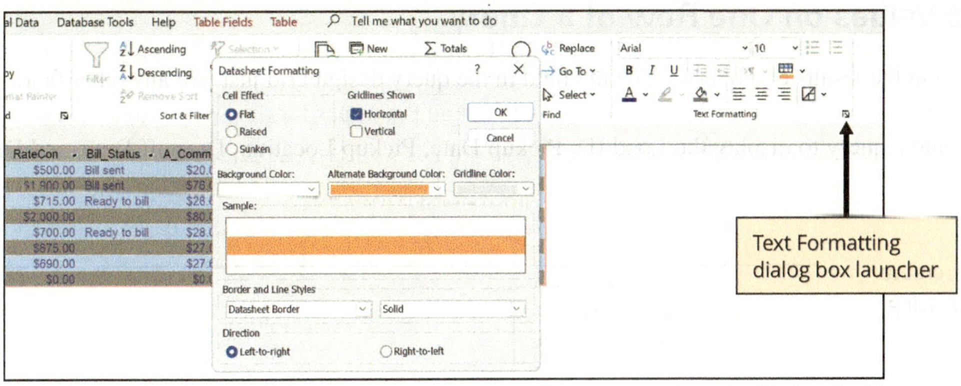

Figure 3–67

Q&A Can I also format my datasheet in other ways?
There are many other formatting options for your table in Datasheet view. You can select all the records as shown in Figure 3–63 by clicking the datasheet selector. Then you can bold, underline, or italicize your font (Home tab | Text Formatting group). Additionally, you can set the background color and align the data.

To Close the Datasheet without Saving the Format Changes

The following step closes the datasheet without saving the changes to the format. Because the changes are not saved, the next time you open the Account Manager table in Datasheet view it will appear in the original format. If you had saved the changes, the changes would be reflected in its appearance.

1

- Close the Payments table.
- Click the No button in the Microsoft Access dialog box when asked if you want to save your changes.

Q&A I like some of the formatting changes made to this table. Why are these changes not being saved?
When using formatting elements in tables, it's best practice to use the same or similar formatting for all tables in the database. Spending the time needed to make that many formatting changes in this project is not necessary.

Consider This

What kind of decisions should I make in determining whether to change the format of a datasheet?

- You'll need to ask yourself a series of questions to help determine which format changes are needed. For example, consider the following questions.
- Would totals or other calculations be useful in the datasheet? If so, include the Total row and select the appropriate computations.
- Would another gridline style make the datasheet more useful? If so, change to the desired gridlines.
- Would alternating colors in the rows make them easier to read? If so, change the alternate fill color.
- Would a different font and/or font color make the text stand out better? If so, change the font color and/or the font.
- Is the font size appropriate? Can you see enough data at one time on the screen and yet have the data be readable? If not, change the font size to an appropriate value.
- Is the column spacing appropriate? Are some columns wider than they need to be? Do some columns not display all the data? Change the column sizes as necessary.

As a general guideline, once you have decided on a particular look for a datasheet, all datasheets in the database should have the same look, unless there is a compelling reason for a datasheet to differ.

Multivalued Fields in Queries

You can use multivalued fields in queries in the same way you use other fields in queries. You can choose to display the multiple values either on a single row or on multiple rows in the query results.

To Include Multiple Values on One Row of a Query

To include a multivalued field in the results of a query, place the field in the query design grid just like any other field. **Why?** When you treat the multivalued field like any other field, the results will list all the values for the multivalued field on a single row. The following steps create a query to display the Load ID, Pickup Date, Pickup Location, Dropoff Date, and Dropoff Location for the Loads table.

1

- Open the Navigation Pane, create a query for the Loads table using Design view, and then close the Navigation Pane and Add Tables pane.
- Include the Load ID, Pickup Date, Pickup Location, Dropoff Date, and Dropoff Location fields in the query (Figure 3–68).

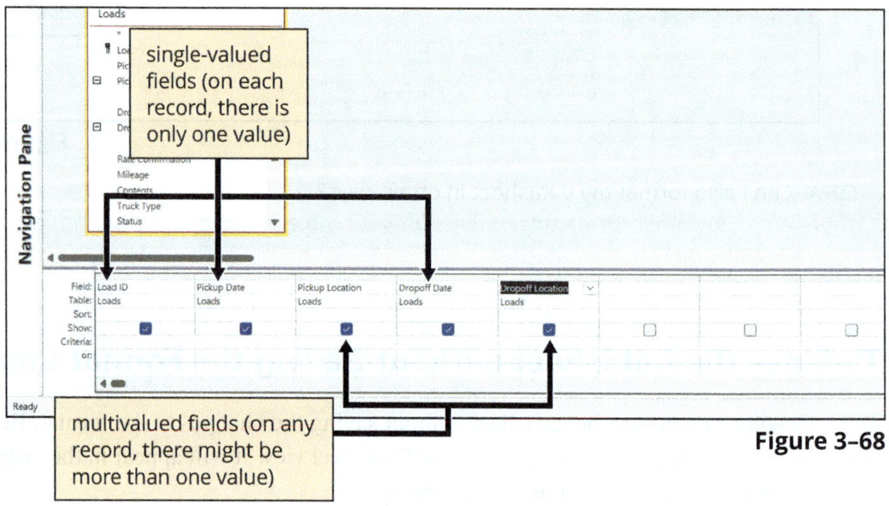

Figure 3–68

2

- Run the query and view the results (Figure 3–69).

Q&A Can I include criteria for a multivalued field?
Yes. You can include criteria for a multivalued field.

- Save the query as **m03q01**. Leave it open for now.

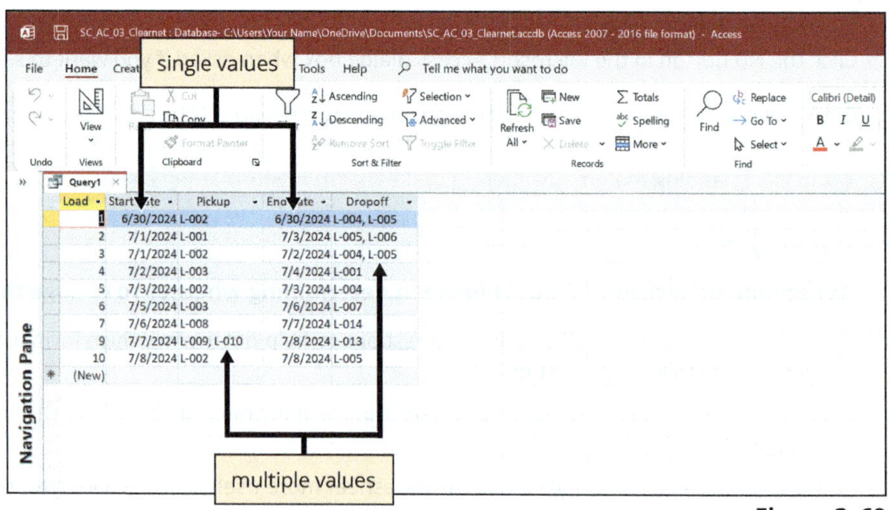

Figure 3–69

To Include Multiple Values on Multiple Rows of a Query

You might want to see the multiple pickup or dropoff locations for a load on separate rows rather than on a single row. **Why?** Each row in the results will focus on one specific location. To do so, you need to use the Value property of the Pickup and Dropoff fields by following the name of each field with a period and then the word, Value. The following steps use the Value property to display each location on a separate row.

1

- In the query, switch back to Design view and ensure that the Load ID, Pickup Date, Pickup Location, Dropoff Date, and Dropoff Location fields are included in the design grid.
- In the design grid, click the Pickup Location field name to produce an insertion point, press END to move the insertion point to the end of the field name, and then type a period (**.**).

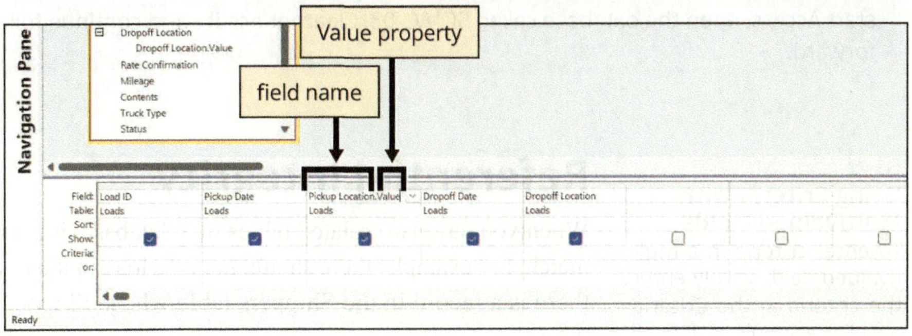

Figure 3–70

- If the word, Value, does not automatically appear after the period, type the word **Value** after the period following the word, Location, to use the Value property (Figure 3–70). You might need to press END again to see if the word, Value, was automatically inserted, or resize the column.

Q&A I do not see the word, Value. Did I do something wrong?
No. There is not enough room to display the entire name. If you want to see it without using the navigation buttons on your keyboard, you can point to the right boundary of the column selector and then either drag or double-click to resize the column.

I see Pickup Location.Value as a field in the Loads table's field list. Could I have deleted the Pickup Location field from the design grid and added the Pickup Location.Value field?
Yes. Either approach is fine.

2

- In the design grid, click the Dropoff Location field to produce an insertion point, press END to move the insertion point to the end of the field name, and then type a period (**.**).
- If the word, Value, does not automatically appear after the period, type the word **Value** after the period following the word, Location, to use the Value property. You might need to press END again to see if the word, Value, was automatically inserted.

3

- Run the query and view the results, resizing the Loads.Pickup Location.Value field and the Loads.Dropoff Location.Value field to display the entire heading for each column (Figure 3–71).

Q&A Can I now include criteria for the multivalued field?
Yes. You could enter a criterion just like in any other query.

Could I sort the rows by Start date or End date?
Yes. Select Ascending as the sort order just as you have done in other queries.

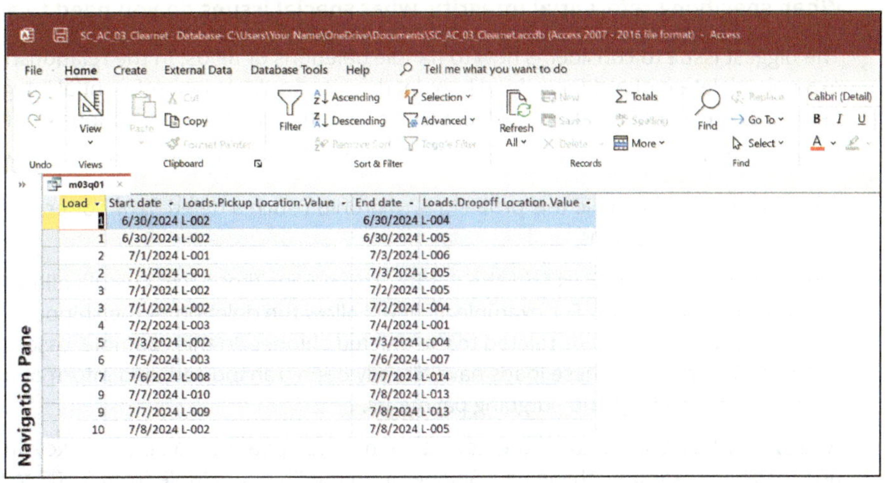

Figure 3–71

4

- Use the Save Object As operation to save the query as a new object in the database named **m03q02**.
- Close the query.

Break Point: If you wish to take a break, this is a good place to do so. You can quit Access now. To resume at a later time, start Access, open the database called SC_AC_03_Clearnet.accdb, and continue following the steps from this location forward.

BTW
Using Criteria with Multivalued Fields
To enter criteria in a multivalued field, simply enter the criteria in the Criteria row. For example, to find all loads being delivered to location L-005 in the Loads table, enter L-005 in the Criteria row under Dropoff Location.

Referential Integrity

When you have two related tables in a database, it is essential that the data in the common fields match. For example, there should not be a load in the Loads table whose shipper ID is S-002 unless there is a record in the Shippers table whose Shipper ID is S-002. This restriction is enforced through **referential integrity**, which is the property that ensures the value in a foreign key must match that of another table's primary key.

A **foreign key** is a field in one table whose values are required to match the *primary key* of another table. In the Loads table, the Shipper ID field is a foreign key that must match the primary key of the Shippers table; that is, the Shipper ID for any load must exist as a Shipper ID currently in the Shippers table. A load whose Shipper ID is L-009, for example, should not be stored in the Loads table because no such shipper currently exists in the Shippers table.

In Access, to specify referential integrity, you must explicitly define a relationship between the tables by using the Relationships button. As part of the process of defining the relationship, you indicate that Access is to enforce referential integrity. Access then prohibits any updates to the database that would violate referential integrity.

The type of relationship between two tables specified by the Relationships command is referred to as a **one-to-many relationship**. This means that *one* record in the first table is related to, or matches, *many* records in the second table, but each record in the second table is related to only *one* record in the first. In the Clearnet database, for example, a one-to-many relationship exists between the Shippers table and the Loads table. *One* shipper is associated with *many* loads, but each load is associated with only one shipper. In general, the table containing the foreign key will be the *many* part of the relationship.

Consider This

When specifying referential integrity, what special issues do you need to address?

The biggest issue to consider is how to handle deletions of fields. In the relationship between shippers and loads, for example, deletion of a shipper for whom loads exist would violate referential integrity. Specifically, if Shipper S-002 is deleted in the Shippers table, Load ID 1 would no longer relate to any shipper in the Shippers table.

You can handle this issue in one of two ways. For each relationship, you need to decide which of these approaches is appropriate.

- The normal way to avoid this problem is to prohibit such a deletion. If no records can be deleted in either table, the problem never happens.
- The other option is to **cascade the delete**. This means that Access would allow the deletion but then delete all related records in other tables. For example, it would allow the deletion of the shipper from the Shippers table but then automatically delete any loads related to the deleted shipper. In this example, cascading the delete would not be appropriate because many of these loads have already been transported, and information from those loads must be kept for processing incoming and outgoing payments.

A second critical issue is to decide how to handle the update of the primary key. In the relationship between shippers and loads, for example, changing a Shipper ID in the Shippers table from S-002 to S-009 would cause a problem because some records in the Loads table are related to Shipper ID S-002. These loads no longer would relate to any shipper.

You can handle this issue in one of two ways. For each relationship, you need to decide which of these approaches is appropriate.

- The normal way to avoid this problem is to prohibit this type of update. If primary key fields can't be changed, relationships remain intact across tables.
- The other option is to **cascade the update**. This means to allow the change, but make the corresponding change in the foreign key on all related records. In the relationship between shippers and loads, for example, Access would allow the update but then automatically make the corresponding change for any load where the Shipper ID is S-002. It would change the Shipper ID for those loads to S-009.

To Specify Referential Integrity

The following steps use the Relationships button on the Database Tools tab to specify referential integrity by explicitly indicating a relationship between the Shippers and Loads tables. The steps also ensure that updates will cascade, but that deletes will not. **Why?** This combination of configurations allows sufficient flexibility for updating records as information changes, while not allowing deletions of records in the Shippers table. By indicating a relationship between tables, and specifying that updates will cascade, it will be possible to change the Shipper ID for a shipper, and the same change will automatically be made for all loads related to that shipper. By not specifying that deletes will cascade, it will not be possible to delete any shipper who has loads in the database.

1

- Click Database Tools on the ribbon to display the Database Tools tab. (Figure 3–72).

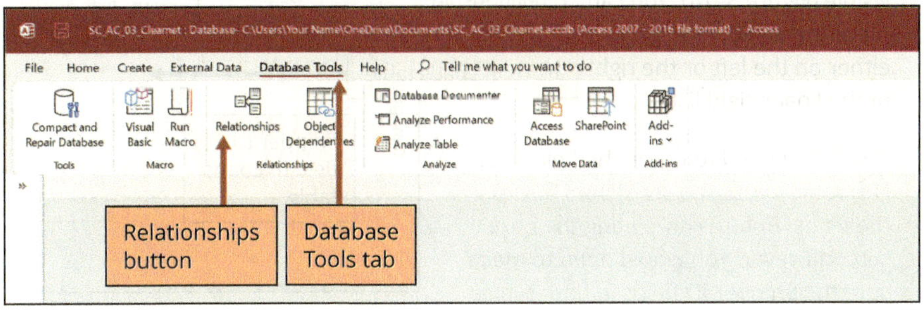

Figure 3–72

2

- Click the Relationships button (Database Tools tab | Relationships group) to open the Relationships window and display the Add Tables pane. If the Add Tables pane does not open automatically, click the Add Tables button (Relationships Design tab | Relationships group). If necessary, click the Tables tab (Add Tables pane) to see the list of tables (Figure 3–73).

Q&A The field lists in the Relationships area are spread out, and I can't see all the field lists at one time. How can I fix this?
Drag the field list boxes as desired to position the boxes in a way you can see all the lists at one time. However, keep the boxes in the same order from left to right. Resize the field list boxes as desired so you can see all the fields listed within each box.

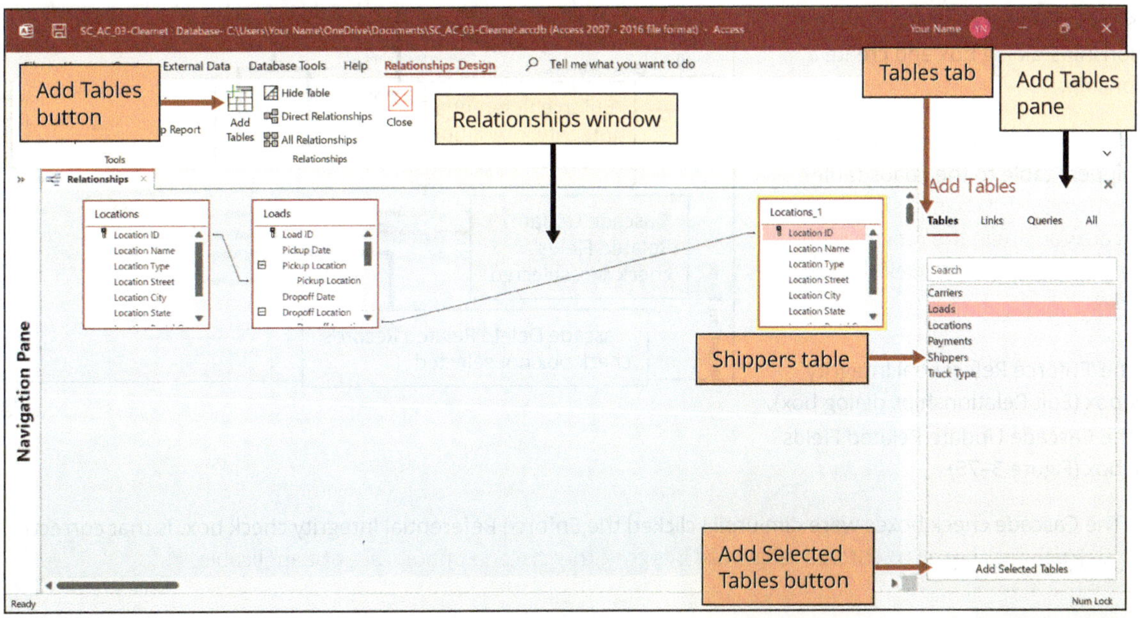

Figure 3–73

3

- Click the Shippers table (Add Tables pane), and then click the Add Selected Tables button to add a field list for the Shippers table to the Relationships window.
- Close the Add Tables pane.
- Reposition and resize the field lists in the Relationships window so all fields are visible (Figure 3–74). You can place the Shippers field list either on the left or the right of the Loads field list.

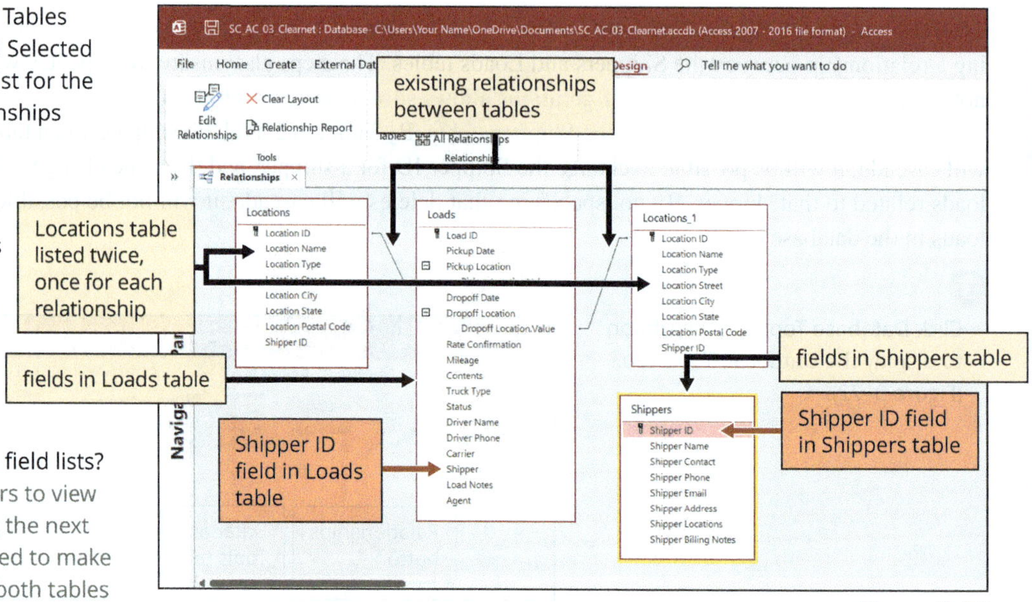

Figure 3–74

Q&A Do I need to resize the field lists?
No. You can use the scroll bars to view the fields. Before completing the next step, however, you would need to make sure the Shipper ID fields in both tables appear on the screen. Note that, in the Loads table, the Shipper ID field is called Shipper.

The Shipper ID field in the Loads table only says Shipper, not Shipper ID. Is that a problem?
No. When the Loads table was created, the Shipper ID field was given a shortened name, which was sufficient to identify its purpose in the context of the Loads table. So long as the data types match and the field contains the correct data, you can still create the relationship.

4

- Drag the Shipper ID field in the Shippers table field list to the Shipper field in the Loads table field list to display the Edit Relationships dialog box and create a relationship.

Q&A Do I actually move the field from the Shippers table to the Loads table?
No. The pointer will change shape to indicate you are in the process of dragging, but the field itself does not move.

- Click the 'Enforce Referential Integrity' check box (Edit Relationships dialog box).
- Click the Cascade Update Related Fields check box (Figure 3–75).

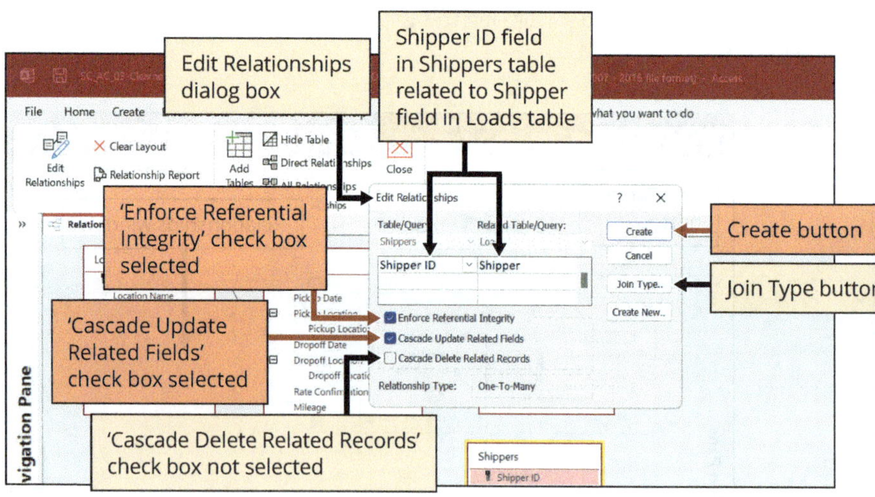

Figure 3–75

Q&A The Cascade check boxes were dim until I clicked the Enforce Referential Integrity check box. Is that correct?
Yes. Until you have chosen to enforce referential integrity, the cascade options are not applicable.

5

- Click the Create button (Edit Relationships dialog box) to complete the creation of the relationship (Figure 3–76).

Q&A What is the symbol at the lower end of the join line?
It is the mathematical symbol for infinity. It is used here to denote the "many" end of the relationship.

Can I print a copy of the relationship?
Yes. Click the Relationship Report button (Relationships Design tab | Tools group) to produce a report of the relationship. You can print the report. You can also save it as a report in the database for future use. If you do not want to save it, close the report after you have printed it and do not save the changes.

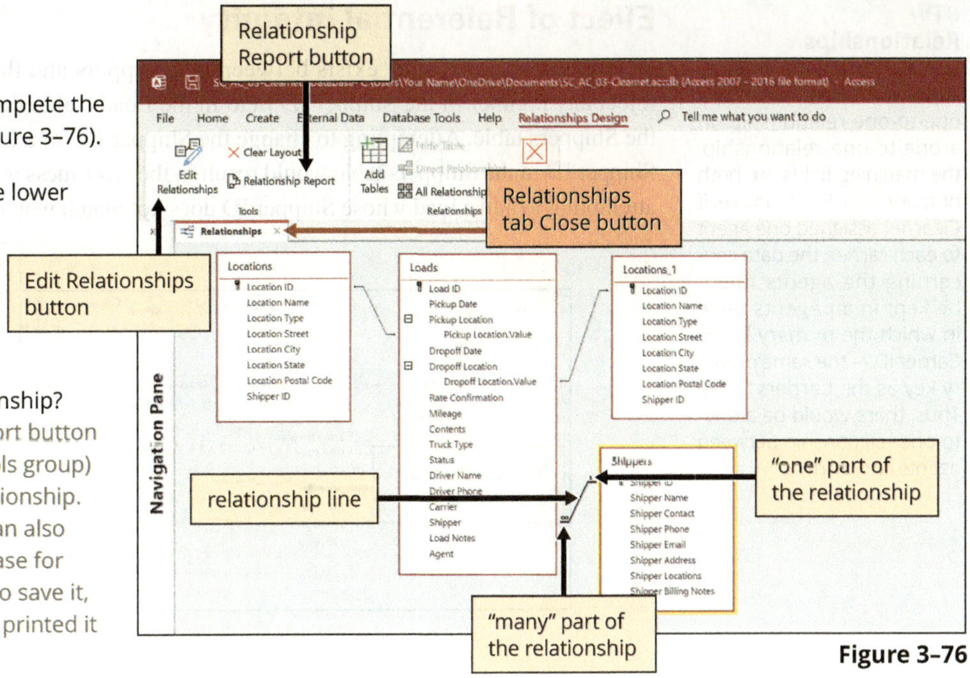

Figure 3–76

6

- Click the Save button on the Quick Access Toolbar to save the relationship you created.
- Click the Close button on the Relationships tab (the X next to the tab name) to close the Relationships window.

Q&A What is the purpose of saving the relationship?
The relationship ensures that the data has referential integrity.

Can I later modify the relationship if I want to change it in some way?
Yes. Click Database Tools on the ribbon to display the Database Tools tab, and then click the Relationships button (Database Tools tab | Relationships group) to open the Relationships window. To add another table, click the Add Tables button on the Relationships Design tab. To remove a table, click the Hide Table button. To edit a relationship, select the relationship and click the Edit Relationships button.

BTW
Exporting a Relationship Report
You also can export a relationship report. To export a report as a PDF or XPS file, right-click the report in the Navigation Pane, click Export on the shortcut menu, and then click PDF or XPS as the file type.

Consider This

Can I change the join type as I can in queries?

Yes. Click the Join Type button in the Edit Relationships dialog box. Click option button 1 to create an INNER join, that is, a join in which only records with matching values in the join fields appear in the result. Click option button 2 to create a LEFT join, that is, a join that includes all records from the left-hand table, but only records from the right-hand table that have matching values in the join fields. Click option button 3 to create a RIGHT join, that is, a join that includes all records from the right-hand table, but only records from the left-hand table that have matching values in the join fields.

Other Ways

1. Click Close button on Relationships Design tab to close Relationships window

BTW
Relationships
You also can use the Relationships window to specify a one-to-one relationship. In a one-to-one relationship, the matching fields are both primary keys. For example, if Clearnet assigned one agent to each carrier, the data concerning the agents might be kept in an Agents table in which the primary key is Carrier ID — the same primary key as the Carriers table. Thus, there would be a one-to-one relationship between agents and carriers.

Effect of Referential Integrity

Referential integrity now exists between the Shippers and the Loads tables. Access now will reject any number in the Shipper ID field in the Loads table that does not match a Shipper ID in the Shippers table. Attempting to change the Shipper ID for a load to one that does not match any Shipper ID in the Shippers table would result in the error message shown in Figure 3–77. Similarly, attempting to add a load whose Shipper ID does not match would produce the same error message.

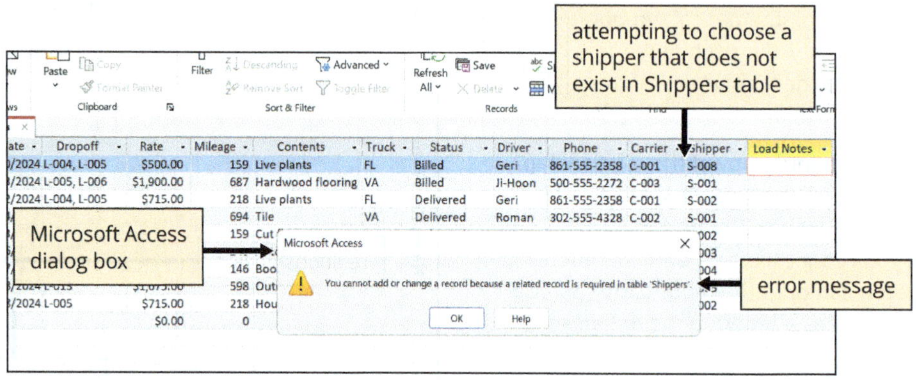

Figure 3–77

Access also will reject the deletion of a Shipper ID for whom related loads exist. Attempting to delete Shipper ID S-002 from the Shippers table, for example, would result in the message shown in Figure 3–78.

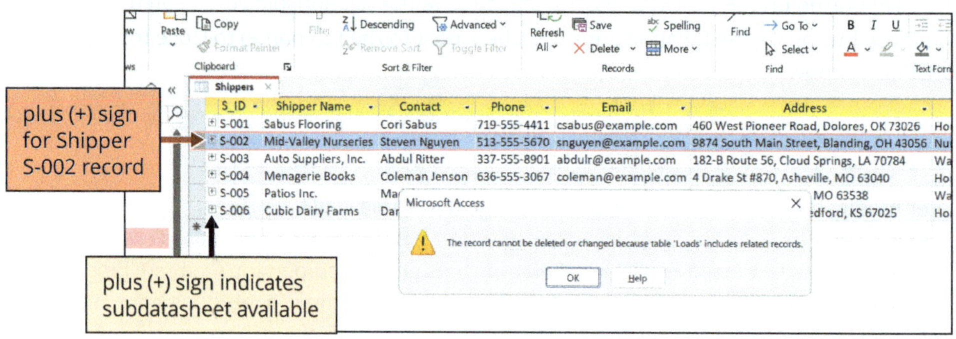

Figure 3–78

Access would, however, allow the change of a Shipper ID in the Shippers table. It would then automatically make the corresponding change to the Shipper ID for all the loads related to that shipper. For example, if you changed a Shipper ID in the Shippers table from S-002 to S-009, the Shipper ID S-009 would appear in the Shipper ID field for loads whose Shipper ID had been S-002.

To Use a Subdatasheet

One consequence of the tables being explicitly related is that a shipper's loads can appear below the Shipper ID in a **subdatasheet**. Because the two tables are joined by a common field, the data for the loads belonging to the shipper can be embedded within that particular shipper's record. **Why is a subdatasheet useful?** A subdatasheet is useful when you want to review or edit data in joined or related tables. The availability of such a subdatasheet is indicated by a plus sign that appears in front of the rows in the Shippers table. The following steps display the subdatasheet for Shipper S-002.

1

- Open the Navigation Pane, open the Shippers table in Datasheet view, and then close the Navigation Pane.

2

- Click the plus sign in front of the row for Shipper ID S-002 to display the subdatasheet (Figure 3–79).

Q&A How do I hide the subdatasheet when I no longer want it to appear?
When you clicked the plus sign, it changed to a minus sign. Click the minus sign to collapse the subdatasheet.

- **Experiment:** Display subdatasheets for other owners. Display more than one subdatasheet at a time. Remove the subdatasheets from the screen.

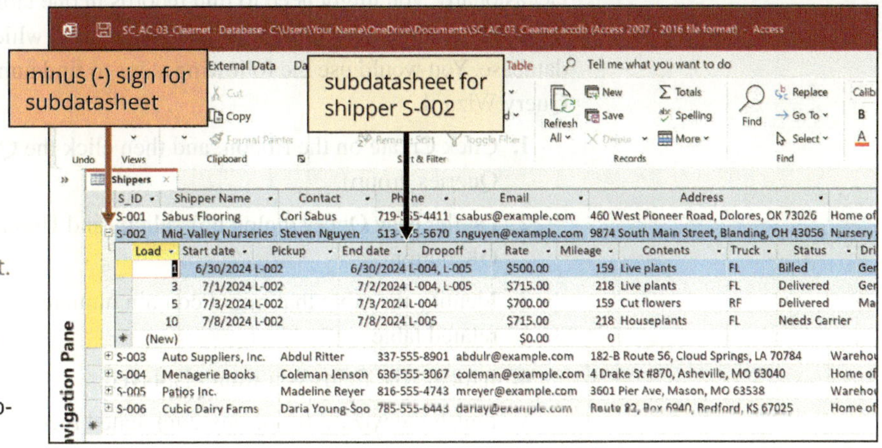

Figure 3–79

Q&A How do I remove a subdatasheet?
Open the table. With the subdatasheet closed, click the More button (Home tab | Records Group) to display a menu. Select Subdatasheet, Remove.

3

If requested by your instructor, replace the city and state for Shipper ID S-001 with your city and state.
- Close the Shippers table.
- Click the No button (Microsoft Access dialog box) when asked if you want to save your changes.

Handling Data Inconsistency

In many organizations, databases evolve and change over time. One department might create a database for its own internal use. Employees in another department might decide they need their own database containing much of the same information. For example, the Purchasing department of an organization might create a database of products that it buys, and the Receiving department might create a database of products that it receives. Each department is keeping track of the same products. When the organization eventually merges the databases, they might discover inconsistencies and duplication. The Find Duplicates Query Wizard and the Find Unmatched Query Wizard can assist in clearing the resulting database of duplication and errors.

To Find Duplicate Records

One reason to include a primary key for a table is to eliminate duplicate records. A possibility still exists, however, that duplicate records can get into your database. You would use the following steps to find duplicate records using the Find Duplicates Query Wizard.

1. Click Create on the ribbon, and then click the Query Wizard button (Create tab | Queries group).
2. On the New Query dialog box, click Find Duplicates Query Wizard and then click the OK button.
3. Identify the table and field or fields that might contain duplicate information.
4. Indicate any other fields you want displayed.
5. Finish the wizard to see any duplicate records.

To Find Unmatched Records

Occasionally, you might need to find records in one table that have no matching records in another table. For example, you might want to determine which shippers currently have no loads in the database. You would use the following steps to find unmatched records using the Find Unmatched Query Wizard.

1. Click Create on the ribbon, and then click the Query Wizard button (Create tab | Queries group).
2. On the New Query dialog box, click Find Unmatched Query Wizard and then click the OK button.
3. Identify the table that might contain unmatched records, and then identify the related table.
4. Indicate the fields you want displayed.
5. Finish the wizard to see any unmatched records.

Sorting Records

Normally, Access sequences the records in the Shippers table by Shipper ID when listing them because the Shipper ID field is the table's primary key. You can change this order, if desired.

To Use the Ascending Button to Sort Records

To change the order in which records appear, use the Ascending or Descending buttons. Either button reorders the records based on the field in which the insertion point is located. The following steps sort the records by Shipper Name in alphabetical order using the Ascending button. **Why?** Using the Ascending button is the quickest and easiest way to order records.

1

- Open the Navigation Pane, open the Shippers table in Datasheet view, and then close the Navigation Pane.
- Click the Shipper Name field on the first record to select the field (Figure 3–80).

Q&A Did I have to click the field on the first record?
No. Any other record would have worked as well.

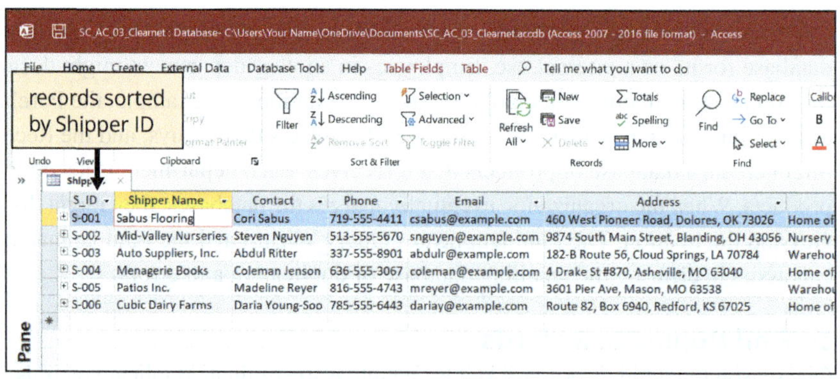

Figure 3–80

2

- Click the Ascending button (Home tab | Sort & Filter group) to sort the records by Shipper Name (Figure 3–81).

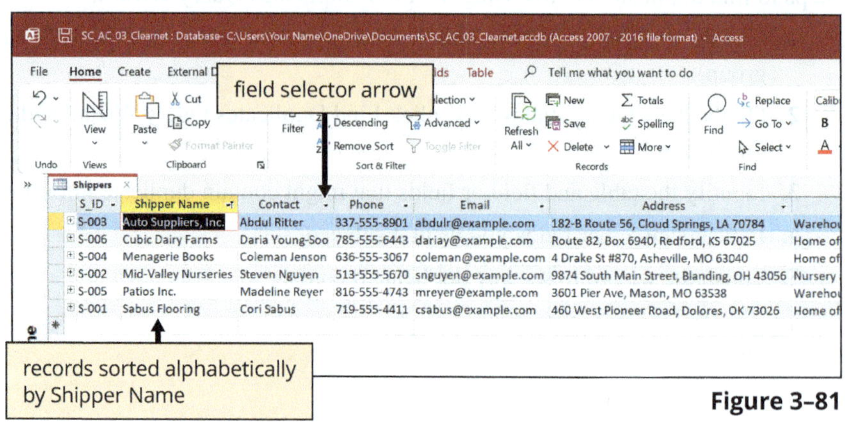

Figure 3–81

3

- Close the Shippers table.
- Click the No button (Microsoft Access dialog box) when asked if you want to save your changes.

Q&A What would happen if I saved the changes?
The next time you open the table, the records will be sorted by Shipper Name.

- If desired, sign out of your Microsoft account.
- **sam** Exit Access.

Other Ways

1. Right-click field name, click Sort A to Z (for ascending) or Sort Z to A (for descending) to sort records
2. Click field selector arrow, click Sort A to Z or Sort Z to A to sort records

To Use the Ascending Button to Sort Records on Multiple Fields

Just as you are able to sort the answer to a query on multiple fields, you can also sort the data that appears in a datasheet on multiple fields. To do so, the major and minor keys must be next to each other in the datasheet with the major key on the left. If this is not the case, you can drag the columns into the correct position. Instead of dragging, however, usually it will be easier to use a query that has the data sorted in the desired order.

To sort on a combination of fields where the major key is just to the left of the minor key, you would use the following steps.

1. Click the field selector at the top of the major key column to select the entire column.
2. Hold down SHIFT and then click the field selector for the minor key column to select both columns.
3. Click the Ascending button to sort the records.

BTW
Modifying Table Properties
You can change the properties of a table by opening the table in Design view and then clicking the Property Sheet button (Table Design tab | Show/Hide group). This opens the Property Sheet pane on the right side of the screen. To display the records in a table in an order other than primary key (the default sort order), use the Order By property. For example, to display the Payments table automatically in Carrier ID order, change the Order By property setting to Payments.Carrier ID in the property box, close the property sheet, and save the change to the table design. When you open the Payments table in Datasheet view, the records will be sorted in Carrier ID order.

Summary

In this module you have learned how to create a split form, use a form to add records to a table, search for records, delete records, filter records, change the database structure, create and use lookup fields, create and use multivalued fields, create calculated fields, make mass changes, create validation rules, change the appearance of a datasheet, specify referential integrity, and use subdatasheets.

BTW
Access Help
At any time while using Access, you can find answers to questions and display information about various topics through Access Help. Used properly, this form of assistance can increase your productivity and reduce your frustrations by minimizing the time you spend learning how to use Access.

Consider This: Plan Ahead

What decisions will you need to make when maintaining your own databases?

Use these guidelines as you complete the assignments in this module and maintain your own databases outside of this class.

1. Determine when it is necessary to add, change, or delete records in a database.
2. Determine whether you should filter records.
    a) If your criterion for filtering is that the value in a particular field matches or does not match a certain specific value, use Filter By Selection.
    b) If your criterion only involves a single field but is more complex, use a common filter.
    c) If your criterion involves more than one field, use Filter By Form.
    d) If your criterion involves more than a single And or Or, or if it involves sorting, use Advanced Filter/Sort.
3. Determine whether additional fields are necessary or whether existing fields should be deleted.
4. Determine whether validation rules, default values, and formats are necessary.
    a) Can you improve the accuracy of the data entry process by enforcing data validation?
    b) What values are allowed for a particular field?
    c) Are there some fields in which one particular value is used more than another?
    d) Should some fields be required for each record?
    e) Are there some fields for which special formats would be appropriate?
5. Determine whether changes to the format of a datasheet are desirable.
    a) Would totals or other calculations be useful in the datasheet?
    b) Would different gridlines make the datasheet easier to read?
    c) Would alternating colors in the rows make them easier to read?
    d) Would a different font and/or font color make the text stand out better?
    e) Is the font size appropriate?
    f) Is the column spacing appropriate?
6. Identify related tables to implement relationships between the tables.
    a) Is there a one-to-many relationship between the tables?
    b) If so, which table is the one table?
    c) Which table is the many table?
7. When specifying referential integrity, address deletion and update policies.
    a) Decide how to handle deletions. Should deletion be prohibited or should the delete cascade?
    b) Decide how to handle the update of the primary key. Should the update be prohibited or should the update cascade?

Consider This

How should you submit solutions to critical thinking questions in the assignments?

Every assignment in this course contains one or more critical thinking questions. These questions require you to think beyond the assigned database. Present your responses to the questions in the format required by your instructor. Possible formats may include one or more of these options: write the answer; create a document that contains the answer; present your answer to the class; discuss your answer in a group; record the answer as audio or video using a webcam, smartphone, or portable media player; or post answers on a blog, wiki, or website.

Student Assignments

Apply Your Knowledge

Reinforce the skills and apply the concepts you learned in this module.

Adding Lookup Fields, Specifying Validation Rules, Updating Records, Updating Reports, and Creating Relationships

Note: To complete this assignment, you will be required to use the Data Files. Please contact your instructor for information about accessing the Data Files.

Instructions: Start Access. Open the database, SC_AC_03-2.accdb, which is located in the Data Files folder. Enable the content.

Perform the following tasks:

1. Save the database using the file name, SC_AC_03_City-Tutoring. Enable the content.
2. Open the Students table in Design view.
3. Add a single-valued Lookup field called Student Type to the Students table. The field should be inserted after the Counselor Number field. The field will contain data on the type of student. The student types are GR (meaning grade school), HS (meaning high school), HE (meaning higher education), and AE (meaning adult education). Save the changes to the Students table.
4. Create the following validation rules for the Students table.
   a. Specify the legal values GR, HS, HE, and AE for the Student Type field. Enter **Must be GR, HS, HE, or AE** as the validation text.
   b. Make the Student Name field a required field.
5. Save the changes and close the table. You do not need to test the current data.
6. Create an update query for the Students table. Change all the entries in the Student Type field to GR. Run the query and save it as Student Type Update Query, and then close the query.
7. Update the following records in the Students table, and then close the table:
   a. Change the student type for students BB35, CC25, CP03, and YD45 to HS.
   b. Change the student type for students MM01 and PS67 to AE.
8. Create a split form for the Students table. Save the form as Students Split Form.
9. Open the Students Split Form in Form view, find student HN23, and change the student's name from Henry Niemer to Henry Neimer. Close the form.
10. Establish referential integrity between the Counselors table (the one table) and the Students table (the many table). Display the Add tables pane if necessary and add the appropriate tables. Cascade the update but not the delete. Save the relationship and close the Relationships tab.
    If requested to do so by your instructor, rename the Students Split Form as Split Form for First Name Last Name, where First Name Last Name is your name.
11. Submit the revised database in the format specified by your instructor.
12. **Consider This:** The values in the Student Type field are currently in the order GR, HS, HE, and AE. How would you reorder the values to GR, HS, AE, and HE in the Student Type list?

Extend Your Knowledge

Extend the skills you learned in this module and experiment with new skills. You may need to use Help to complete the assignment.

Creating Action Queries, Changing Table Properties, and Adding Totals to a Datasheet

Note: To complete this assignment, you will be required to use the Data Files. Please contact your instructor for information about accessing the Data Files.

Instructions: Start Access. Open the database, SC_AC_03-3.accdb, which is located in the Data Files folder. A physical therapy clinic in Lebanon, Arizona, is being sold to another clinic in a nearby town. The office staff need to do some database maintenance by finding duplicate records and finding unmatched records.

Perform the following tasks:

1. Save the database using the file name, SC_AC_03_Physical-Therapy. Enable the content.
2. Create a make-table query to create the Potential Clients table in the Physical Therapists database shown in Figure 3–82. Run the query and save it as Make Table Query.

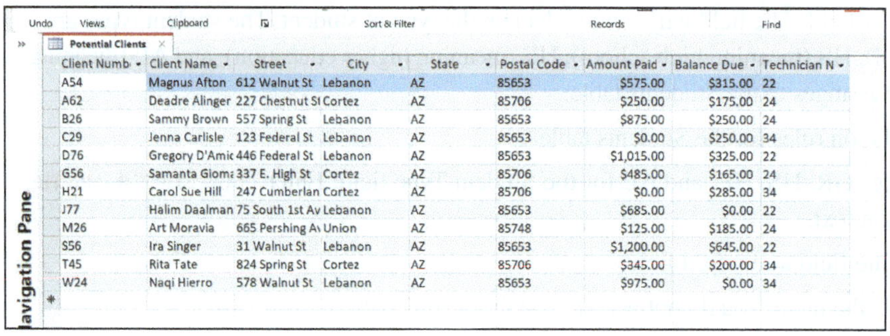

Client Numb	Client Name	Street	City	State	Postal Code	Amount Paid	Balance Due	Technician N
A54	Magnus Afton	612 Walnut St	Lebanon	AZ	85653	$575.00	$315.00	22
A62	Deadre Alinger	227 Chestnut St	Cortez	AZ	85706	$250.00	$175.00	24
B26	Sammy Brown	557 Spring St	Lebanon	AZ	85653	$875.00	$250.00	24
C29	Jenna Carlisle	123 Federal St	Lebanon	AZ	85653	$0.00	$250.00	34
D76	Gregory D'Amic	446 Federal St	Lebanon	AZ	85653	$1,015.00	$325.00	22
G56	Samanta Giom:	337 E. High St	Cortez	AZ	85706	$485.00	$165.00	24
H21	Carol Sue Hill	247 Cumberlan	Cortez	AZ	85706	$0.00	$285.00	34
J77	Halim Daalman	75 South 1st Av	Lebanon	AZ	85653	$685.00	$0.00	22
M26	Art Moravia	665 Pershing Av	Union	AZ	85748	$125.00	$185.00	24
S56	Ira Singer	31 Walnut St	Lebanon	AZ	85653	$1,200.00	$645.00	22
T45	Rita Tate	824 Spring St	Cortez	AZ	85706	$345.00	$200.00	34
W24	Naqi Hierro	578 Walnut St	Lebanon	AZ	85653	$975.00	$0.00	34

Figure 3–82

3. Open the Potential Clients table and select the datasheet. Change the font to Arial with a font size of 10. Resize the columns to best fit the data. Save the changes to the table and close the table.
4. Open the Technician table and add the Totals row to the table. Calculate the average hourly rate and the sum of Earnings YTD. Save the changes to the table layout and close the table.
5. Use the Find Duplicates Query Wizard to find duplicate information in the City field of the Client table. Include the Client Name in the query. Save the query as City Duplicates Query and close the query.
6. Use the Find Unmatched Query Wizard to find all records in the Technician table that do not match records in the Client table. Technician Number is the common field in both tables. Include the Technician Number, Last Name, and First Name in the query. Save the query as Technician Unmatched Query and close the query.
   If requested to do so by your instructor, change the client name in the Client table for client number S56 to First Name Last Name, where First Name Last Name is your name. If your name is longer than the space allowed, simply enter as much as you can.
7. Submit the revised database in the format specified by your instructor.
8. **Consider This:** What differences, if any, are there between the Client table and the Potential Clients table you created with the make-table query?

Expand Your World

Create a solution, which uses cloud and web technologies, by learning and investigating on your own from general guidance.

Note: To complete this assignment, you will be required to use the Data Files. Please contact your instructor for information about accessing the Data Files.

Instructions: Start Access. Open the database, SC_AC_03-4.accdb, which is located in the Data Files folder, and enable the content. Solutions IT Support wants to ensure that all Clients are matched with Technicians. The database needs a relationship created to ensure this matching. Your boss wants a copy of the report of this relationship.

Perform the following tasks:

1. Save the database using the file name, SC_AC_03_Solutions-IT-Support. Enable the content.
2. Create a relationship between the Client table and the Technician table using an appropriate field for this task. Enforce referential integrity and Cascade Update Related Fields.
3. Create a relationship report for the relationship and save the report as First Name Last Name Relationship Report where First Name Last Name is your name.
4. Export the report as a PDF file to a cloud-based storage location of your choice. Do not save the export steps. Close the report and the Relationships tab.
5. Research the web to find how diagrams depict a one-to-many relationship for a relational database. (**Hint:** Use your favorite search engine and enter keywords such as ERD diagram, entity-relationship diagram, or one-to-many relationship.)
6. Create your own graphic using a drawing tool, such as app.diagrams.net. Your diagram should illustrate the one-to-many relationship between the Client table and the Technician table. Export the image as a .png or .jpg file.
7. Submit the revised database, the PDF report, and the relationship diagram in the format specified by your instructor.
8. a. **Consider This:** Which cloud-based storage location did you use?

   b. **Consider This:** How did you locate your diagram samples?

   c. **Consider This:** Which app did you use to create your diagram?

In the Lab

Design and implement a solution using creative thinking and problem-solving skills.

Lab: Maintaining the Great Outdoors Database

Note: To complete this assignment, you will be required to use the Data Files. Please contact your instructor for information about accessing the Data Files.

Problem: Great Outdoors Camp needs to make some updates to their database to track Camper payments and remove campers who haven't made a payment before a certain date. Additionally, campground counselors want to organize some backup plans for when one of them needs to cover for another. One of the staff has also asked you to add some validation rules to ensure required information is included when campers or counselors are entered into the database.

Continued on next page

Perform the following tasks:

Part 1: Open the SC_AC_03-5.accdb database from the Data Files folder. Save the file with the name SC_AC_03_Great-Outdoors, and enable the content. Use the concepts and techniques presented in this module to modify the database according to the following requirements:

1. Import the Camper Payments table from the Support_AC_03_Great-Outdoors-Extra-Tables.accdb database. Do not save the import steps.
2. The accountant in charge of camper payments has asked for a calculated field that will add the amount campers have paid plus their balance due to determine their total fees (paid fees + unpaid fees = total fees), which will help with budgeting for the season. Create this calculated field in the appropriate table.
3. Create rules for the Counselors table that require information in the Counselor FirstName and LastName fields for every record. You do not need to test the data.
4. Using Filter By Form, delete all the records where any camper's amount paid is zero and the balance due is greater than zero. Save and close the table.
5. Camp staff have decided they need to know who can oversee which activities in case any instructors are out sick. They would like an additional multivalued lookup field, Activities, added to the Staff table. These activities will include items from the ActivityZones table in addition to alternative activities that are not usually scheduled but can be used when needed. As you create the field, refer to Table 3–2, which lists the Activities to be added to the list of lookup values.

Table 3–2 Activity Abbreviations and Descriptions

Abbreviations	Names
CRFT	Crafts
HKG	Hiking
HRSB	Horseback Riding
KYK	Kayaking
SRVL	Survival Class
SWM	Swimming
ZPLN	Ziplining
PING	Ping-Pong
SOC	Soccer
TGFB	Tag Football

6. Change the Activities field size to 50.
7. Add the data shown in Table 3–3 to the Staff table for the Activities field. Resize the field to best fit.

Table 3–3

Staff ID	First Name	Last Name	Activities
14	Vera	Ognianov	CRFT, PING
12	Ahmad	Grady	HKG
3	Lata	Gaspar	HRSB
13	Markku	Twist	KYK, SWM
2	Maya	Dillard	SRVL, CRFT
16	Martyn	Bell	SWM, KYK
11	Otto	Jensson	ZPLN
15	Elli	Rosario	SOC, TGFB

8. In the Counselors table, find the record for Co_ID 78978, and change the Co_ID to 78797.
If requested to do so by your instructor, in the Campers table, change the last name for Camper ID 34872 to your last name. If your last name is longer than 15 characters, simply enter as much as you can.

9. In the Enrollments table, change the Camper ID field to Short Text with a field size of 20.

10. a. Establish referential integrity between the Campers table (the one table) and the Enrollments table (the many table). Cascade the update but not the delete.

    b. **Consider This:** Why do you think you get an error message?

    c. Fix the problem, and then create the relationship.

Submit the revised database in the format specified by your instructor.

Part 2: **Consider This:** The Activities field currently has 10 values. If Great Outdoors Campground picked up another sport, such as fishing, how would you add FSH to the Activities field list? You added a calculated field in the Camper Payments table. Do the results of the calculated field actually exist in the database? Are there any issues that you need to consider when you create a calculated field?

Index

Note: **Bold** page numbers refer to pages where key terms are defined.

B

D

E

F

G

H

N

O

P

Q

T

X

Y

Z

ISBN-13: 978-0357881521
90000
9 780357 881521